5th International Joint Conference on Natural Language Processing 2011

(IJCNLP 2011)

Chiang Mai, Thailand
8-13 November 2011

Volume 1 of 2

ISBN: 978-1-62276-505-8

Printed from e-media with permission by:

Curran Associates, Inc.
57 Morehouse Lane
Red Hook, NY 12571

Some format issues inherent in the e-media version may also appear in this print version.

Printed by Curran Associates, Inc. (2013)

Association for Computational Linguistics
209 N. Eighth Street
Stroudsburg, Pennsylvania 18360

Phone: 1-570-476-8006
Fax: 1-570-476-0860

acl@aclweb.org

Additional copies of this publication are available from:

Curran Associates, Inc.
57 Morehouse Lane
Red Hook, NY 12571 USA
Phone: 845-758-0400
Fax: 845-758-2634
Email: curran@proceedings.com
Web: www.proceedings.com

IJCNLP 2011

Proceedings of the Fifth International Joint Conference on Natural Language Processing

November 8 – 13, 2011
Chiang Mai, Thailand

We wish to thank our sponsors

Gold Sponsors

www.google.com

www.baidu.com

The Office of Naval Research (ONR)

The Asian Office of Aerospace Research and Development (AOARD)

Department of Systems Engineering and Engineering Managment, The Chinese University of Hong Kong

Silver Sponsors

Microsoft Corporation

Bronze Sponsors

Chinese and Oriental Languages Information Processing Society (COLIPS)

Supporter

Thailand Convention and Exhibition Bureau (TCEB)

We wish to thank our sponsors

Organizers

Asian Federation of Natural Language Processing (AFNLP)

National Electronics and Computer Technology Center (NECTEC), Thailand

Sirindhorn International Institute of Technology (SIIT), Thailand

Rajamangala University of Technology Lanna (RMUTL), Thailand

Organizers

Maejo University, Thailand

Chiang Mai University (CMU), Thailand

FOREWORD

IJCNLP2011, where Anna(s) meet the king(s) for sharing knowledge in natural language

IJCNLP2011 is held in Chiang Mai. It is a historic city situated in the northern part of Thailand. Organizing the conference in this part of Asia made us think of the classic movie "The King and I" (1956), where King Mongkut of Siam invited Anna Leonowens an Anglo-Indian school teacher to Siam to teach his family English. Similar to the movie, IJCNLP2011 brings together scientists and practitioners from the East and West in pursuit of the knowledge of natural language processing (NLP).

Virach, Hitoshi and I compiled this passage collaboratively online using our own iPads. Despite us being physically apart, in Thailand, Japan and Hong Kong respectively, our collaborative editorial work went smoothly with virtually no distance. The increasing popularity of smart handheld devices, such as iPhones and iPads has practically made the world flat. The hurdles and boundaries between people have effectively been lifted enabling friends and relatives over the globe to keep in close contact with each other. We use email, blog, facebook and twitter regularly and ubiquitously for communications. Non-traditional they may be, the languages for communication over these channels are natural as they are used by the netizens (human) for information exchange. Processing of these natural languages is inevitably unconventional and the task is challenging, which requires much innovation. For this reason, NLP is a key research area both in the industry and in universities worldwide. Therefore, it is not surprising that we have received over 500 submissions from different countries around the world in this year's IJCNLP. This number is in fact the largest in the history of the conference series.

Organizing a conference of the scale of IJCNLP2011 (with over 300 participants) is never easy. We worked closely as a team in the past ten months. It is really not easy for us to express our gratitude to any one individual. The names of the hard working conference officers, the track chairs, the workshop chairs, the tutors as well as the reviewers are enlisted in the proceedings. We owe everyone a billion. Without their hard work IJCNLP2011 would never have reached this stage. So please help me praise and thank them when you meet them in the conference.

Chiang Mai is a cultural city full of history and traditions, with many famous attractions such as its melodious colloquial language, Lanna style of clothing, mellow taste of food, etc. During the conference period, we will experience the "Loi Krathong Festival" where people float krathong (floating basket) on a river to pay respect to the spirit of the waters. IJCNLP2011 in November Chiang Mai is unique. It coincides with the unforgettable Lanna Festival. Locally known as "Yi Peng", the festival will bring to you a memorable cultural experience. You will witness a multitude of Lanna-style sky lanterns (khom loi, literally "floating lanterns") gently rising in the air. These lanterns resemble large flocks of giant fluorescent jellyfish gracefully floating by through the sky. Honestly, these attractions are just too good to be missed.

Dear friends and colleagues of the world NLP communities, honorable guests of Chiang Mai, we are glad to see you in IJCNLP2011. We hope you find the technical program useful to your research and can discover something insightful at the end. And before closing, as one often said "seeing is believing", we urge you to spare some time after the conference to explore and to enjoy the city.

Ka Poon Kap (thank you)

Kam-Fai Wong, General Chair, The Chinese University of Hong Kong (CUHK), China

Virach Sornlertlamvanich, Organization Co-Chair, National Electronics and Computer Technology Center (NECTEC), Thailand

Hitoshi Isahara, Organization Co-Chair, Toyohashi University of Technology, Japan

November 7, 2011

PREFACE

As the flagship conference of the Asian Federation of Natural Language Processing (AFNLP), IJCNLP has now rapidly grown into a renowned international event. IJCNLP 2011 covers a broad spectrum of technical areas related to natural language processing. The conference includes full papers, short papers, demonstrations, a student research workshop, as well as pre- and post-conference tutorials and workshops.

This year, we received a record 478 valid paper submissions, which is well beyond our initial expectations. This represents an increasing interest of research on NLP and the growing reputation of IJCNLP as an international event. The 478 submissions include 385 full-paper submissions and 93 short-paper submissions from more than 40 countries. Specifically, approximately 61% of the papers are from 16 countries and areas in Asia Pacific, 22% from 16 countries in Europe, 14% from the United States and Canada; we also have 2% of the papers from the Middle East and Africa, and 1% from South America.

We would like to thank all the authors for submitting papers to IJCNLP 2011. The significant increase in the number of submissions and the wide range of demographic areas represent a rapid growth of our field. We would also like to thank the 22 area chairs and 474 program committee members for writing over 1400 reviews and meta-reviews and for paving the way for the final paper selection. Of all 478 submissions, a total of 176 papers were accepted, representing a healthy 36% acceptance rate. The accepted papers are comprised of 149 full papers (8+ pages), of which 107 are presented orally and 42 as posters, and 27 short papers (4+ pages) where 25 are presented orally and 2 as posters. We are extremely grateful to the area chairs and program committee members for all their hard work, without which the preparation of this program would not be possible.

We are delighted to have invited three strategic keynote speakers addressing different application aspects of NLP for the Web in IJCNLP2011. Mathew Lease will talk about "crowdsourcing", which is a trendy and effective means to perform a task that requires hundreds/thousands of people, such as corpus tagging. Wai Lam will present the latest techniques for information extraction, which is essential for today's Internet business. And last but not the least, Mengqiu Wang, Vice President of Baidu, the largest Internet search company in China, will share with us the recent trends in search and social network technologies and how NLP techniques can be applied to improve performance in the real world. These speeches will surely be informative and enlightening to the audience leading to many innovative research ideas. We are excited about it and are looking forward to them. Best paper awards will be announced in the last session of the conference as well.

We thank General Chair Kam-Fai Wong, the Local Arrangements Committee headed by Virach Sornlertlamvanich and Hitoshi Isahara, and the AFNLP Conference Coordination Committee chaired by Yuji Matsumoto, for their help and advice. Thanks to Min Zhang and Sudeshria Sarkar, the Publication Co-Chairs for putting the proceedings together, and all the other committee chairs for their work.

We hope that you enjoy the conference!

Haifeng Wang, Baidu

David Yarowsky, Johns Hopkins University

November 7, 2011

Honorary Conference Chair

Chaiyong Eurviriyanukul, Rajamangala University of Technology Lanna, Thailand
Chongrak Polprasert, Sirindhorn International Institute of Technology, Thailand
Thaweesak Koanantakool, NSTDA, Thailand

General Chair

Kam-Fai Wong, The Chinese University of Hong Kong, China

Program Co-Chairs:

Haifeng Wang, Baidu, China
David Yarowsky, John Hopkins University, USA

Organisation Co-Chairs:

Virach Sornlertlamvanich, NECTEC, Thailand
Hitoshi Isahara, Toyohashi University of Technology, Japan

Workshop Co-Chairs:

Sivaji Bandyopadhyay, Jadavpur University, India
Jong Park, KAIST, Korea
Noriko Kando, NII, Japan

Tutorial Co-Chairs:

Kentaro Inui, Tohoku University, Japan
Wei Gao, The Chinese University of Hong Kong, China
Dawei Song, Robert Gordon University, UK

Demonstration Co-Chairs:

Ken Church, Johns Hopkins University, USA
Yunqing Xia, Tsinghua University, China

Publication Co-Chairs:

Min Zhang, I2R, Singapore
Sudeshna Sarkar, IIT Kharagpur, India

Finance Co-Chairs:

Vilas Wuwongse, AIT, Thailand
Gary Lee, POSTECH, Korea

Sponsorship Co-Chairs:

Asanee Kawtrakul, Kasetsart University, Thailand
Methinee Sirikrai, NECTEC, Thailand
Hiromi Nakaiwa, NTT, Japan

Publicity Committee:

Steven Bird, University of Melbourne, Australia
Le Sun, CIPS, China
Kevin Knight, USC, USA
Nicoletta Calzolari, Istituto di Linguistica Computazionale del CNR, Italy
Thanaruk Theeramunkong, SIIT, Thailand

Webmasters:

Swit Phuvipadawat, Tokyo Institute of Technology, Japan
Wirat Chinnan, SIIT, Thailand

Area Chairs:

Discourse, Dialogue and Pragmatics
David Schlangen, The University of Potsdam, Germany

Generation /Summarization
Xiaojun Wan, Peking University, China

Information Extraction
Wenjie Li, The Hong Kong Polytechnic University, Hong Kong

Information Retrieval
Gareth Jones, Dublin City University, Ireland

Language Resource
Eneko Agirre, University of the Basque Country, Spain

Machine Translation
David Chiang, USC-ISI, USA
Min Zhang, Institute for Infocomm Research, Singapore
Hua Wu, Baidu, China

Phonology/morphology, POS tagging and chunking, Word Segmentation
Richard Sproat, Oregon Health & Science University, USA
Gary Lee, Pohang University of Science and Technology, Korea

Question Answering
Jun Zhao, Institute of Automation, Chinese Academy of Sciences, China

Semantics
Pushpak Bhattacharyya, Indian Institute of Technology, India
Hinrich Schuetze, University of Stuttgart, Germany

Sentiment Analysis, Opinion Mining and Text Classification
Rafael Banchs, Institute for Infocomm Research, Singapore
Theresa Wilson, Johns Hopkins University, USA

Spoken Language Processing
Chung-Hsien Wu, National Cheng Kung University, Taiwan

Statistical and ML Methods
Miles Osborne, The University of Edinburgh, UK
David Smith, University of Massachusetts Amherst, USA

Syntax and Parsing
Stephen Clark, University of Cambridge, UK
Yusuke Miyao, National Institute of Informatics, Japan

Text Mining and NLP Applications
Juanzi Li, Tsinghua University, China
Patrick Pantel, Microsoft Research, USA

Reviewers

Ahmed Abbasi, Omri Abend, Akiko Aizawa, Ahmet Aker, Enrique Alfonseca, DAUD ALI, Ben Allison, Robin Aly, Alina Andreevskaia, Masayuki Asahara, Ai Azuma

Jing Bai, Alexandra Balahur, Timothy Baldwin, Kalika Bali, Carmen Banea, Srinivas Bangalore, Mohit Bansal, Marco Bbaroni, Roberto Basili, Timo Baumann, Emily Bender, Shane Bergsma, Pushpak Bhattacharyya, Dan Bikel, Wang Bin, Lexi Birch, Michael Bloodgood, Phil Blunsom, Nate Bodenstab, Ester Boldrini, Gemma Boleda, Danushka Bollegala, Luc Boruta, Stefan Bott, Chris Brew, Sam Brody, Julian Brooke, Paul Buitelaar, Miriam Butt

Aoife Cahill, Li Cai, Yi Cai, Nicoletta Calzolari, Jaime Carbonell, Marine Carpuat, John Carroll, Paula Carvalho, Suleyman Cetintas, Debasri Chakrabarti, Nate Chambers, Niladri Chatterjee, Wanxiang Che, Berlin Chen, Boxing Chen, Chia-Ping Chen, Hsin-Hsi Chen, Wenliang Chen, Ying Chen, Yufeng Chen, Pu-Jen Cheng, Colin Cherry, Jackie Chi KiCheung, Key-Sun Choi, Monojit Choudhury, Christos Christodoulopoulos, Kenneth Church, Alex Clark, Shay Cohen, Trevor Cohn, Gao Cong, Marta R. Costa-jussa, Paul Crook, Montse Cuadros, Ronan Cummins

Robert Damper, Kareem Darwish, Dipanjan Das, Niladri Dash, Adrià de Gispert, Daniel de Kok, Eric De La Clergerie, Stijn De Saeger, Steve DeNeefe, Pascal Denis, Ann Devitt, Arantza Diaz de Ilarraza, Anne Diekema, Markus Dreyer, Rebecca Dridan, Jinhua Du, Xiangyu Duan, Amit Dubey, Kevin Duh, Chris Dyer, Michal Dziemianko

Jacob Eisenstein, Michael Elhadad, Micha Elsner, Martin Emms

Angela Fahrni, Hui Fang, Yi Fang, Li Fangtao, Christiane Fellbaum, Raquel Fernandez, Colum Foley, Jennifer Foster, Timothy Fowler, Stella Frank, Guohong Fu, Atsushi Fujii, Kotaro Funakoshi, Hagen Fürstenau

Matthias Galle, Michael Gamon, Michaela Geierhos, Eugenie Giesbrecht, Alastair Gill, Roxana Girju, Bruno Golenia, Carlos Gomez-Rodriguez, Zhengxian Gong, Matt Gormley, Amit Goyal, João Graça, Jens Grivolla, Iryna Gurevych

Stephanie Haas, Barry Haddow, Eva Hajicova, David Hall, Keith Hall, Xianpei Han, Kazuo Hara, Donna Harman, Kazi Hasan, Chikara Hashimoto, Koiti Hasida, Eva Hasler, Samer Hassan, Claudia Hauff, Xiaodong He, Yulan He, Zhongjun He, Carlos Henriquez, Tsutomu Hirao, Hieu Hoang, Tracy Holloway King, Matthew Honnibal, Mark Hopkins, Meishan Hu, Chien-Lin Huang, Fei Huang, Minlie Huang, Ruizhang Huang, Xiaojiang Huang, Xuanjing Huang, Yun Huang, Zhongqiang Huang

Francisco Iacobelli, Diana Inkpen, Aminul Islam, Ruben Izquierdo

Heng Ji, Sittichai Jiampojamarn, Hongfei Jiang, Wenbin Jiang, Xing Jiang, Cai Jie, Rong Jin, Richard Johansson, Hanmin Jung

Sarvnaz Karimi, Daisuke Kawahara, Jun'ichi Kazama, Liadh Kelly, Maxim Khalilov, Mitesh Khapra, Adam Kilgarriff, Byeongchang Kim, Irwin King, Alistair Knott, Philipp Koehn, Rob Koeling, Oskar Kohonen, Mamoru Komachi, Grzegorz Kondrak, Fang Kong, Valia Kordoni, Lili Kotlerman, Zornitsa Kozareva, Wessel Kraaij, Parton Kristen, Lun-Wei Ku, Sudip Kumar Naskar, June-Jei Kuo, Kow Kuroda, Sadao KUROHASH, Kui-Lam Kwok, Han Kyoung-Soo

Sobha Lalitha Devi, Wai Lam, Joel Lang, Jun Lang, Matt Lease, Cheongjae Lee, Jung-Tae Lee, Sungjin Lee, Tan Lee, Russell Lee-goldman, Alessandro Lenci, Johannes Leveling, Abby Levenberg, Gina-Anne Levow, Baoli Li, Daifeng Li, Haizhou Li, linlin li, Mu Li, Qing Li, Shoushan Li, Sujian Li, Yunyao Li, Shasha Liao, Yuan-Fu Liao, Chin-Yew Lin, Pierre Lison, Ken Litkowski, Marina Litvak, Bing Liu, Fei Liu, Feifan Liu, Kang Liu, Pengyuan Liu, Qun Liu, Shui Liu, Xiaohua Liu, Yang Liu (UT Dallas), Yang Liu (ICT CAS), Yi Liu, Ying Liu, Yiqun Liu, Zhanyi Liu, Hector Llorens, Elena Lloret, Wai-Kit Lo, QIU Long, Adam Lopez, Yajuan Lu

Bin Ma, Yanjun Ma, Walid Magdy, OKUMURA Manabu, Suresh Manandhar, Maria Antonia Marti, David Martinez, Andre Martins, Yuji Matsumoto, Yutaka Matsuo, Takuya Matsuzaki, Mike Maxwell, Jonathan May, Diana McCarthy, David McClosky, Ryan McDonald, Paul McNamee, Beata Megyesi, Donald Metzler, Haitao Mi, Lukas Michelbacher, Dipti Mishra Sharma, Mandar Mitra, Daichi Mochihashi, Saif Mohammed, Behrang Mohit, Karo Moilanen, Christian Monson, Paul Morarescu, Jin'ichi Murakami, Sung Hyon Myaeng

Seung-Hoon Na, Masaaki Nagata, Mikio Nakano, Preslav Nakov, Jason Naradowsky, Vivi Nastase, Roberto Navigli, Mark-Jan Nederhof, Ani Nenkova, Vincent Ng, Truc-Vien T. Nguyen, Eric Nichols, Tadashi Nomoto, Scott Nowson, Andreas Nuernberger, Pierre Nugues

Diarmuid O Seaghdha, Brendan O'Connor, Neil O'Hare, Stephan Oepen, Kemal Oflazer, Kemal Oflazer, Alice Oh, Naoaki Okazaki, Constantin Orasan, Arantxa Otegi, Myle Ott, Jahna Otterbacher, You Ouyang

Alexandre Patry, Soma Paul, Adam Pease, Ted Peders, Wei Peng, Gerald Penn, Sasa Petrovic, Christian Pietsch, Juan Pino, Matt Post, John Prager, Daniel Preotiuc, Matthew Purver

Vahed Qazvinian, Guang Qiu, Chris Quirk

Altaf Rahman, Ganesh Ramakrishnan, Karthik Raman, AnanthakrishnRamanathan, Sujith Ravi, Bunescu Razvan, Jonathon Read, Marta Recasens, Jeremy Reffin, Roi Reichart, Jason Riesa, Verena Rieser, Arndt Riester, Stefan Riezler, German Rigau, Laura Rimell, Carlos Rodriguez, Kepa Rodriguez, Robert Ross, Michael Roth, Sasha Rush

Kenji Sagae, Benoît Sagot, Agnes Sandor, Anoop Sarkar, Sudeshna Sarkar, Ryohei Sasano, Roser Sauri, Helmut Schmid, Satoshi Sekine, Arulmozi Selvaraj, Pavel Serdyukov, Gao Sheng, Masashi Shimbo, Darla Shockley, Luo Si, Khalil Sima'an, Ben Snyder, Ruihua Song, Young-In Song, Sebastian Spiegler, Valentin Spitkovsky, Caroline Sporleder, Manfred Stede, Mark Steedman, Mark Stevenson, Nicola Stokes, Veselin Stoyanov, Michael Strube, Jian Su, Keh-Yih Su, Zhifang Sui, Aixin Sun, Jun Sun, Weiwei Sun, Mihai Surdeanu

Oscar Tackstrom, Hiroya Takamura, Jianhua Tao, Joel Tetreault, Stefan Thater, Jörg Tiedemann, Ivan Titov, Takenobu Tokunaga, Kentaro Torisawa, Lamia Tounsi, Kristina Toutanova, Roy Tromble, Reut Tsarfaty, Yuen-Hsien Tseng, Hajime Tsukada

Christina Unger, Takehito Utsuro

Antal van den Bosch, Gertjan van Noord, Vasudeva Varma, Silvia Vazquez, Tony Veale, Olga Vechtomova, Sriram Venkatapathy, Yannick Versley, Jesus Vilares, Sami Virpioja, Andreas Vlachos, Piek Vossen

Stephen Wan, Bin Wang, Bo Wang, Dingding Wang, Hsin-Min Wang, Ting Wang, Wei Wang, Zhichun Wang, Taro Watanabe, Yotaro Watanabe, Bonnie Webber, Furu Wei, Richard Wicentowski, Shuly Wintner, Kristian Woodsend, Gang Wu, Zhiyong Wu

Yunqing Xia, Tong Xiao, Xin Xin, Deyi Xiong, Qiu Xipeng, Jun Xu, Ruifeng Xu

Christopher Yang, Grace Yang, Muyun Yang, Yuhang Yang, Zi Yang, Benajiba Yassine, Mark Yatskar, Patrick Ye, Jui-Feng Yeh, Ainur Yessenalina, Scott Wen-tauYih, Bei Yu, Hong Yu

Taras Zagibalov, Benat Zapirain, Alessandra Zarcone, Duo Zhang, Hao Zhang, Jiajun Zhang, Jing Zhang, Lanbo Zhang, Lei Zhang, Min Zhang, Qi Zhang, Yi Zhang (UCSC), Yi Zhang (DFKI), Yue

Zhang, Shiqi Zhao, Tiejun Zhao, Haitao Zheng, Zhi Zhong, Bowen Zhou, Dong Zhou, GuoDong Zhou, Qiang Zhou, Yu Zhou, Muhua Zhu, Xiaodan Zhu, Chengqing Zong

Table of Contents

Part A: Full Papers

Part B: Short Papers

Conference Program

November 9

(9:00-9:20) Welcome

(9:20-10:20) Keynote – Mengqiu Wang (Baidu)

(10:20 - 10:50) Coffee Break

(10:50-12:05) Text Mining I

Analyzing the Dynamics of Research by Extracting Key Aspects of Scientific Papers
Sonal Gupta and Christopher Manning

Dependency-directed Tree Kernel-based Protein-Protein Interaction Extraction from Biomedical Literature
Longhua Qian and Guodong Zhou

Learning Logical Structures of Paragraphs in Legal Articles
Ngo Xuan Bach, Nguyen Le Minh, Tran Thi Oanh and Akira Shimazu

(10:50-12:05) Machine Translation I

Extracting Pre-ordering Rules from Predicate-Argument Structures
Xianchao Wu, Katsuhito Sudoh, Kevin Duh, Hajime Tsukada and Masaaki Nagata

Context-Sensitive Syntactic Source-Reordering by Statistical Transduction
Maxim Khalilov and Khalil Sima'an

Discriminative Phrase-based Lexicalized Reordering Models using Weighted Reordering Graphs
Wang Ling, João Graça, David Martins de Matos, Isabel Trancoso and Alan W Black

November 9 (continued)

(10:50-12:05) Machine Learning I

Active Learning Strategies for Support Vector Machines, Application to Temporal Relation Classification
Seyed Abolghasem Mirroshandel, Gholamreza Ghassem-Sani and Alexis Nasr

A Fast Accurate Two-stage Training Algorithm for L1-regularized CRFs with Heuristic Line Search Strategy
Jinlong Zhou, Xipeng Qiu and Xuanjing Huang

Automatic Topic Model Adaptation for Sentiment Analysis in Structured Domains
Geoffrey Levine and Gerald DeJong

(10:50-12:05) Discourse / Dialog I

Multi-modal Reference Resolution in Situated Dialogue by Integrating Linguistic and Extra-Linguistic Clues
Ryu Iida, Masaaki Yasuhara and Takenobu Tokunaga

Single and multi-objective optimization for feature selection in anaphora resolution
Sriparna Saha, Asif Ekbal, Olga Uryupina and Massimo Poesio

A Unified Event Coreference Resolution by Integrating Multiple Resolvers
Bin Chen, Jian Su, Sinno Jialin Pan and Chew Lim Tan

(12:05-13:30) Lunch

(13:30-15:10) Machine Translation II

Handling verb phrase morphology in highly inflected Indian languages for Machine Translation
Ankur Gandhe, Rashmi Gangadharaiah, Karthik Visweswariah and Ananthakrishnan Ramanathan

Japanese Pronunciation Prediction as Phrasal Statistical Machine Translation
Jun Hatori and Hisami Suzuki

Comparing Two Techniques for Learning Transliteration Models Using a Parallel Corpus
Hassan Sajjad, Nadir Durrani, Helmut Schmid and Alexander Fraser

A Semantic-Specific Model for Chinese Named Entity Translation
Yufeng Chen and Chengqing Zong

November 9 (continued)

(13:30-15:10) Text Mining II

Mining Revision Log of Language Learning SNS for Automated Japanese Error Correction of Second Language Learners
Tomoya Mizumoto, Mamoru Komachi, Masaaki Nagata and Yuji Matsumoto

Modality Specific Meta Features for Authorship Attribution in Web Forum Posts
Thamar Solorio, Sangita Pillay, Sindhu Raghavan and Manuel Montes-Gomez

Keyphrase Extraction from Online News Using Binary Integer Programming
Zhuoye Ding, Qi Zhang and Xuanjing Huang

Improving Related Entity Finding via Incorporating Homepages and Recognizing Fine-grained Entities
Youzheng Wu, Chiori Hori, Hisashi Kawai and Hideki Kashioka

(13:30-15:10) Semantics I

Enhancing Active Learning for Semantic Role Labeling via Compressed Dependency Trees
Chenhua Chen, Alexis Palmer and Caroline Sporleder

Semantic Role Labeling Without Treebanks?
Stephen Boxwell, Chris Brew, Jason Baldridge, Dennis Mehay and Sujith Ravi

Japanese Predicate Argument Structure Analysis Exploiting Argument Position and Type
Yuta Hayashibe, Mamoru Komachi and Yuji Matsumoto

An Empirical Study on Compositionality in Compound Nouns
Siva Reddy, Diana McCarthy and Suresh Manandhar

November 9 (continued)

(13:30-15:10) Syntax I

Feature-Rich Log-Linear Lexical Model for Latent Variable PCFG Grammars
Zhongqiang Huang and Mary Harper

Improving Dependency Parsing with Fined-Grained Features
Guangyou Zhou, Li Cai, Kang Liu and Jun Zhao

Natural Language Programming Using Class Sequential Rules
Cohan Sujay Carlos

Treeblazing: Using External Treebanks to Filter Parse Forests for Parse Selection and Treebanking
Andrew MacKinlay, Rebecca Dridan, Dan Flickinger, Stephan Oepen and Timothy Baldwin

(15:10-15:30) Coffee Break

(15:30-17:10) Text Mining / Information Extraction

Cross-Language Entity Linking
Paul McNamee, James Mayfield, Dawn Lawrie, Douglas Oard and David Doermann

Generating Chinese Named Entity Data from a Parallel Corpus
Ruiji Fu, Bing Qin and Ting Liu

Learning the Latent Topics for Question Retrieval in Community QA
Li Cai, Guangyou Zhou, Kang Liu and Jun Zhao

Identifying Event Descriptions using Co-training with Online News Summaries
William Yang Wang, Kapil Thadani and Kathleen McKeown

November 9 (continued)

(15:30-17:10) Phonology / Morphology I

Automatic Labeling of Voiced Consonants for Morphological Analysis of Modern Japanese Literature
Teruaki Oka, Mamoru Komachi, Toshinobu Ogiso and Yuji Matsumoto

S^3 - Statistical Sandhi Splitting
Abhiram Natarajan and Eugene Charniak

Improving Chinese Word Segmentation and POS Tagging with Semi-supervised Methods Using Large Auto-Analyzed Data
Yiou Wang, Jun'ichi Kazama, Yoshimasa Tsuruoka, Wenliang Chen, Yujie Zhang and Kentaro Torisawa

CODACT: Towards Identifying Orthographic Variants in Dialectal Arabic
Pradeep Dasigi and Mona Diab

(15:30-17:10) Sentiment I

Enhancing the HL-SOT Approach to Sentiment Analysis via a Localized Feature Selection Framework
Wei and Jon Atle Gulla

Fine-Grained Sentiment Analysis with Structural Features
Cäcilia Zirn, Mathias Niepert, Heiner Stuckenschmidt and Michael Strube

Predicting Opinion Dependency Relations for Opinion Analysis
Lun-Wei Ku, Ting-Hao Huang and Hsin-Hsi Chen

Detecting and Blocking False Sentiment Propagation
Hye-Jin Min and Jong C. Park

November 9 (continued)

November 10

November 10 (continued)

(10:30 - 12:10) Syntax II

Grammar Induction from Text Using Small Syntactic Prototypes
Prachya Boonkwan and Mark Steedman

Transferring Syntactic Relations from English to Hindi Using Alignments on Local Word Groups
Aswarth Dara, Prashanth Mannem, Hemanth Sagar Bayyarapu and Avinesh PVS

Generative Modeling of Coordination by Factoring Parallelism and Selectional Preferences
Daisuke Kawahara and Sadao Kurohashi

Syntactic Parsing for Ranking-Based Coreference Resolution
Altaf Rahman and Vincent Ng

(10:30 - 12:10) Generation / Summarization

TriS: A Statistical Sentence Simplifier with Log-linear Models and Margin-based Discriminative Training
Nguyen Bach, Qin Gao, Stephan Vogel and Alex Waibel

Social Summarization via Automatically Discovered Social Context
Po Hu, Cheng Sun, Longfei Wu, Donghong Ji and Chong Teng

Simultaneous Clustering and Noise Detection for Theme-based Summarization
Xiaoyan Cai, Renxian Zhang, Dehong Gao and Wenjie Li

Extractive Summarization Method for Contact Center Dialogues based on Call Logs
Akihiro Tamura, Kai Ishikawa, Masahiro Saikou and Masaaki Tsuchida

November 10 (continued)

(10:30 - 12;10) Spoken Language Processing

Indexing Spoken Documents with Hierarchical Semantic Structures: Semantic Tree-to-string Alignment Models
Xiaodan Zhu, Colin Cherry and Gerald Penn

Structured and Extended Named Entity Evaluation in Automatic Speech Transcriptions
Olivier Galibert, Sophie Rosset, Cyril Grouin, Pierre Zweigenbaum and Ludovic Quintard

Normalising Audio Transcriptions for Unwritten Languages
Adel Foda and Steven Bird

Similarity Based Language Model Construction for Voice Activated Open-Domain Question Answering
Istvan Varga, Kiyonori Ohtake, Kentaro Torisawa, Stijn De Saeger, Teruhisa Misu, Shigeki Matsuda and Jun'ichi Kazama

(12:10-13:55) Lunch

(13:55-15:10) Machine Learning III

The application of chordal graphs to inferring phylogenetic trees of languages
Jessica Enright and Grzegorz Kondrak

Cross-domain Feature Selection for Language Identification
Marco Lui and Timothy Baldwin

A Wikipedia-LDA Model for Entity Linking with Batch Size Changing Instance Selection
Wei Zhang, Jian Su and Chew-Lim Tan

November 10 (continued)

(13:55-15:10) Information Retrieval II

Discovering Latent Concepts and Exploiting Ontological Features for Semantic Text Search
Vuong M. Ngo and Tru H. Cao

CLGVSM: Adapting Generalized Vector Space Model to Cross-lingual Document Clustering
Guoyu Tang, Yunqing Xia, Min Zhang, Haizhou Li and Fang Zheng

Thread Cleaning and Merging for Microblog Topic Detection
Jianfeng Zhang, Yunqing Xia, Bin Ma, Jianmin Yao and Yu Hong

(13:55-15:10) Dialog/Discourse II

Training a BN-based user model for dialogue simulation with missing data
Stéphane Rossignol, Olivier Pietquin and Michel Ianotto

Automatic identification of general and specific sentences by leveraging discourse annotations
Annie Louis and Ani Nenkova

An Evaluation of Alternative Strategies for Implementing Dialogue Policies Using Statistical Classification and Hand-Authored Rules
David DeVault, Anton Leuski and Kenji Sagae

(13:55-15:10) Sentiment II

A POS-based Ensemble Model for Cross-domain Sentiment Classification
Rui Xia and Chengqing Zong

Ensemble-style Self-training on Citation Classification
Cailing Dong and Ulrich Schäfer

Back to the Roots of Genres: Text Classification by Language Function
Henning Wachsmuth and Kathrin Bujna

November 10 (continued)

(15:10-15:30) Coffee Break

(15:30-17:10) Machine Translation III

Transductive Minimum Error Rate Training for Statistical Machine Translation
Yinggong Zhao, Shujie Liu, Yangsheng Ji, Jiajun Chen and Guodong Zhou

Distributed Minimum Error Rate Training of SMT using Particle Swarm Optimization
Jun Suzuki, Kevin Duh and Masaaki Nagata

Going Beyond Word Cooccurrences in Global Lexical Selection for Statistical Machine Translation using a Multilayer Perceptron
Alexandre Patry and Philippe Langlais

System Combination Using Discriminative Cross-Adaptation
Jacob Devlin, Antti-Veikko Rosti, Sankaranarayanan Ananthakrishnan and Spyros Matsoukas

(15:30-17:10) Semantics II

Word Sense Disambiguation by Combining Labeled Data Expansion and Semi-Supervised Learning Method
Sanae Fujita and Akinori Fujino

Combining ConceptNet and WordNet for Word Sense Disambiguation
Junpeng Chen and Juan Liu

It Takes Two to Tango: A Bilingual Unsupervised Approach for Estimating Sense Distributions using Expectation Maximization
Mitesh M Khapra, Salil Joshi and Pushpak Bhattacharyya

Dynamic and Static Prototype Vectors for Semantic Composition
Siva Reddy, Ioannis Klapaftis, Diana McCarthy and Suresh Manandhar

November 10 (continued)

(15:30-17:10) Information Extraction

Using Prediction from Sentential Scope to Build a Pseudo Co-Testing Learner for Event Extraction
Shasha Liao and Ralph Grishman

Text Segmentation and Graph-based Method for Template Filling in Information Extraction
Ludovic Jean-Louis, Romaric Besançon and Olivier Ferret

Joint Distant and Direct Supervision for Relation Extraction
Truc-Vien T. Nguyen and Alessandro Moschitti

A Cross-lingual Annotation Projection-based Self-supervision Approach for Open Information Extraction
Seokhwan Kim, Minwoo Jeong, Jonghoon Lee and Gary Geunbae Lee

(15:30-17:10) Syntax III

Exploring Difficulties in Parsing Imperatives and Questions
Tadayoshi Hara, Takuya Matsuzaki, Yusuke Miyao and Jun'ichi Tsujii

A Discriminative Approach to Japanese Zero Anaphora Resolution with Large-scale Lexicalized Case Frames
Ryohei Sasano and Sadao Kurohashi

An Empirical Comparison of Unknown Word Prediction Methods
Kostadin Cholakov, Gertjan van Noord, Valia Kordoni and Yi Zhang

Training Dependency Parsers from Partially Annotated Corpora
Daniel Flannery, Yusuke Miayo, Graham Neubig and Shinsuke Mori

(19:00-21:00) Banquet

November 11

(9:00-10:00) Keynote – Wai Lam (Chinese University of Hong Kong)

(10:00-10:30) Coffee Break

(10:30-12:10) Machine Translation / Machine Learning (short papers)

Reducing Asymmetry between language-pairs to Improve Alignment and Translation Quality
Rashmi Gangadharaiah

Clause-Based Reordering Constraints to Improve Statistical Machine Translation
Ananthakrishnan Ramanathan, Pushpak Bhattacharyya, Karthik Visweswariah, Kushal Ladha and Ankur Gandhe

Generalized Minimum Bayes Risk System Combination
Kevin Duh, Katsuhito Sudoh, Xianchao Wu, Hajime Tsukada and Masaaki Nagata

Enhancing scarce-resource language translation through pivot combinations
Marta R. Costa-jussà, Carlos Henríquez and Rafael E. Banchs

A Baseline System for Chinese Near-Synonym Choice
Liang-Chih Yu, Wei-Nan Chien and Shih-Ting Chen

Cluster Labelling based on Concepts in a Machine-Readable Dictionary
Fumiyo Fukumoto and Yoshimi Suzuki

(10:30-12:10) Semantics (short papers)

Text Patterns and Compression Models for Semantic Class Learning
Chung-Yao Chuang, Yi-Hsun Lee and Wen-Lian Hsu

Potts Model on the Case Fillers for Word Sense Disambiguation
Hiroya Takamura and Manabu Okumura

Improving Word Sense Induction by Exploiting Semantic Relevance
Zhenzhong Zhang and Le Sun

Predicting Word Clipping with Latent Semantic Analysis
Julian Brooke, Tong Wang and Graeme Hirst

(10:30-12:10) Text Mining / Question Answering (short papers)

Domain Independent Model for Product Attribute Extraction from User Reviews using Wikipedia
Sudheer Kovelamudi, Sethu Ramalingam, Arpit Sood and Vasudeva Varma

Finding Problem Solving Threads in Online Forum
Zhonghua Qu and Yang Liu

Compiling Learner Corpus Data of Linguistic Output and Language Processing in Speaking, Listening, Writing, and Reading
Katsunori Kotani, Takehiko Yoshimi, Hiroaki Nanjo and Hitoshi Isahara

Mining the Sentiment Expectation of Nouns Using Bootstrapping Method
Miaomiao Wen and Yunfang Wu

An Analysis of Questions in a Q&A Site Resubmitted Based on Indications of Unclear Points of Original Questions
Masahiro Kojima, Yasuhiko Watanabe and Yoshihiro Okada

Diversifying Information Needs in Results of Question Retrieval
Yaoyun Zhang, Xiaolong Wang, Xuan Wang, Ruifeng Xu, Jun Xu and ShiXi Fan

November 11 (continued)

(10:30-12:10) Other NLP topics (short papers)

Beyond Normalization: Pragmatics of Word Form in Text Messages
Tyler Baldwin and Joyce Chai

Chinese Discourse Relation Recognition
Hen-Hsen Huang and Hsin-Hsi Chen

Improving Chinese POS Tagging with Dependency Parsing
Zhenghua Li, Wanxiang Che and Ting Liu

Exploring self training for Hindi dependency parsing
Rahul Goutam and Bharat Ram Ambati

Reduction of Search Space to Annotate Monolingual Corpora
Prajol Shrestha, Christine Jacquin and Beatrice Daille

Toward a Parallel Corpus of Spoken Cantonese and Written Chinese
John Lee

(12:00-13:30) Lunch

(13:30-15:35) Machine Translation IV

A Breadth-First Representation for Tree Matching in Large Scale Forest-Based Translation
Sumukh Ghodke, Steven Bird and Rui Zhang

Bayesian Subtree Alignment Model based on Dependency Trees
Toshiaki Nakazawa and Sadao Kurohashi

Enriching SMT Training Data via Paraphrasing
Wei He, Shiqi Zhao, Haifeng Wang and Ting Liu

Translation Quality Indicators for Pivot-based Statistical MT
Michael Paul and Eiichiro Sumita

Source Error-Projection for Sample Selection in Phrase-Based SMT for Resource-Poor Languages
Sankaranarayanan Ananthakrishnan, Shiv Vitaladevuni, Rohit Prasad and Prem Natarajan

November 11 (continued)

November 11 (continued)

(13:30-15:35) Question Answering

Identification of relations between answers with global constraints for Community-based Question Answering services
Hikaru Yokono, Takaaki Hasegawa, Genichiro Kikui and Manabu Okumura

Automatically Generating Questions from Queries for Community-based Question Answering
Shiqi Zhao, Haifeng Wang, Chao Li, Ting Liu and Yi Guan

Question classification based on an extended class sequential rule model
Zijing Hui, Juan Liu and Lumei Ouyang

K2Q: Generating Natural Language Questions from Keywords with User Refinements
Zhicheng Zheng, Xiance Si, Edward Chang and Xiaoyan Zhu

Answering Complex Questions via Exploiting Social Q&A Collection
Youzheng Wu, Chiori Hori, Hisashi Kawai and Hideki Kashioka

(15:35-16:05) Coffee Break

(16:05-17:15) Best paper session (2 plenary papers announced during this session)

(17:15-17:25) Presentation of Future Conferences (including ACL/IJCNLP 2012)

(17:25-17:35) Closing Ceremony

November 9

(18:00-21:00) Poster Session

Text Mining

Safety Information Mining — What can NLP do in a disaster—
Graham Neubig, Yuichiroh Matsubayashi, Masato Hagiwara and Koji Murakami

A Character-Level Machine Translation Approach for Normalization of SMS Abbreviations
Deana Pennell and Yang Liu

Using Text Reviews for Product Entity Completion
Mrinmaya Sachan, Tanveer Faruquie, L. V. Subramaniam and Mukesh Mohania

Mining bilingual topic hierarchies from unaligned text
Sumit Negi

Efficient Near-Duplicate Detection for Q&A Forum
Yan Wu, Qi Zhang and Xuanjing Huang

Information Extraction

A Graph-based Method for Entity Linking
Yuhang Guo, Wanxiang Che, Ting Liu and Sheng Li

Harvesting Related Entities with a Search Engine
Shuqi Sun, Shiqi Zhao, Muyun Yang, Haifeng Wang and Sheng Li

Acquiring Strongly-related Events using Predicate-argument Co-occurring Statistics and Case Frames
Tomohide Shibata and Sadao Kurohashi

November 9 (continued)

Semantics

Sentiment

Phonology/Morphology

Analyzing the Dynamics of Research by Extracting Key Aspects of Scientific Papers

Sonal Gupta
Department of Computer Science
Stanford University
sonal@cs.stanford.edu

Christopher D. Manning
Department of Computer Science
Stanford University
manning@cs.stanford.edu

Abstract

We present a method for characterizing a research work in terms of its focus, domain of application, and techniques used. We show how tracing these aspects over time provides a novel measure of the influence of research communities on each other. We extract these characteristics by matching semantic extraction patterns, learned using bootstrapping, to the dependency trees of sentences in an article's abstract. We combine this information with pre-calculated article-to-community assignments to study the influence of a community on others in terms of techniques borrowed and the 'maturing' of some communities to solve other problems. As a case study, we show how the computational linguistics community and its sub-fields have changed over the years with respect to their foci, methods used, and domain problems. For instance, we show that part-of-speech tagging and parsing have increasingly been adopted as tools for solving problems in other domains. We also observe that speech recognition and probability theory have had the most seminal influence.

1 Introduction

The evolution of ideas and the dynamics of a research community can be studied using the scientific articles published by the community. For instance, we may be interested in how methods spread from one community to another, or the evolution of a topic from a focus of research to a problem-solving tool. We might want to find the balance between technique-driven and domain-driven research within a field. Establishing such a rich insight of the development and progress of scientific research requires an understanding of more than just the "topics" of discussion or citation links between articles, which have been used in the previous work to study trend and impact of articles. As an example, to determine whether technique-driven researchers have greater or lesser impact, we need to be able to identify styles of work. To achieve this level of detail and to be able to connect together how methods and ideas are being pursued, it is essential to move beyond bag-of-words topical models. This requires an understanding of sentence and argument structure, and is therefore a form of information extraction.

To study the application *domains*, the *techniques* used to approach the domain problems, and the *focus* of scientific articles in a community, we propose to extract the following concepts from the articles

> FOCUS: an article's main contribution
> TECHNIQUE: a method or a tool used in an article, for example, expectation maximization and conditional random fields
> DOMAIN: an article's application domain, such as speech recognition and classification of documents.

For example, if an article concentrates on regularization in support vector machines and shows improvement in parsing accuracy, then its FOCUS and TECHNIQUE are regularization and support vector machines, and its DOMAIN is parsing. In contrast, an article that focuses on lexical features to improve parsing accuracy and uses support vector machines to train the model has FOCUS as lexical features and parsing, the TECHNIQUE being lexical features and support vector machines, and its DOMAIN still is parsing.[1] In this case, even though TECHNIQUEs and DOMAIN of both papers

[1] A community vs. a DOMAIN: a community can be as broad as computer science or statistics, whereas a DOMAIN is a specific application such as Chinese word segmentation.

are very similar, the FOCUS phrases distinguish them from each other. Note that a DOMAIN of one article can be a TECHNIQUE of another, and vice-versa. For example, an article that shows improvements in named entity recognition (NER) has DOMAIN as NER, however, an article that uses named entities as an intermediary tool to extract relations has NER as one of its TECHNIQUEs.

Our work uses information extraction patterns to extract the above three category phrases from articles. The phrases are extracted by matching semantic patterns in dependency trees of sentences. The input to the extraction system are some seed patterns (see Table 1 for examples) and it learns more patterns using a bootstrapping approach. Using a bag-of-words based approach, such as topic models, for this problem is not straightforward; true to their name, topic models generally only identify the topic or area of a paper (such as 'parsing' or 'speech recognition'), and neither provide nor label different cross-cutting aspects like techniques used or the application domain of the paper.

As a case study, we examine the articles published in the computational linguistics community. We study the influence of the community's sub-fields, such as parsing and machine translation, using the FOCUS, TECHNIQUE, and DOMAIN phrases extracted from the articles. We use the document collection from the ACL Anthology dataset[2] (Bird et al., 2008; Radev et al., 2009), since it has full text of papers available. To get the the sub-fields of the community, we use latent Dirichlet allocation (Blei et al., 2003) to find topics and label them by hand.[3] However, our general approach can be used to study any case of the influence of academic communities, including looking more broadly at the influence of statistics or economics across the social sciences.

We study how communities influence each other in terms of techniques that are reused, and show how some communities 'mature' so that the results they produce get adopted as tools for solving other problems. For example, the products of the part-of-speech tagging (POS) community have been adopted by many other communities that use POS tagging as an intermediary step, which is also confirmed in our results.

We also show the timeline of influence of communities. For example, our results show that formal computational semantics and unification-based grammars had a lot of influence in the late 1980s. The speech recognition and probability theory fields showed an upward trend of influence in the mid-1990s, and even though it has decreased in recent years, they still have a lot of influence on recent papers mainly due to techniques like expectation maximization and hidden Markov models. Therefore, our results show that overall they have been the most influential fields in the last two decades. Probability theory, unlike speech recognition, is traditionally not a separate sub-field of computational linguistics, but it is an important topic since many papers use and work on probabilistic approaches. We also show that the study of influence is different from studying popularity or hotness of communities, such as in (Griffiths and Steyvers, 2004; Hall et al., 2008), which is based on the expected number of papers published in the community in a given year.

Contributions We introduce a new categorization of key aspects of scientific articles, which is (1) FOCUS: main contribution, (2) TECHNIQUE: method or tool used, and (3) DOMAIN: application domain. We extract the aspects by matching semantic patterns to dependency trees and learn the patterns using bootstrapping. We propose a new definition of influence of a research community in terms of its key aspects adopted as techniques by the other communities. We present a case study on the computational linguistics community using the the three aspects extracted from its articles, both for verifying the results of our system, and for showing novel results for the dynamics and the overall influence of computational linguistics sub-fields. We introduce a dataset of abstracts labeled with the three categories.[4]

2 Related Work

While there is some connection to keyphrase selection in text summarization (Radev et al., 2002), extracting FOCUS, TECHNIQUE and DOMAIN phrases is fundamentally a form of information extraction, and there has been a wide variety of prior work in this area. Some work, including the seminal (Hearst, 1992), identified patterns (IS-A relations) using hand-written rules, while other work has learned patterns over dependency graphs (Bunescu and Mooney, 2005). This work builds

[2] http://www.aclweb.org/anthology

[3] In this paper, we use the terms communities, sub-communities and sub-fields interchangeably.

[4] The dataset is available at http://cs.stanford.edu/people/sonal/fta for the research community.

on previous successful use of bootstrapping learning techniques in NLP (Yarowsky, 1995; Collins and Singer, 1999; Riloff and Jones, 1999); in its use of dependency patterns it is perhaps especially close to (Yangarber et al., 2000).

Topic models have been used to study popularity of communities (Griffiths and Steyvers, 2004), the history of ideas (Hall et al., 2008), and scholarly impact of papers (Gerrish and Blei, 2010). However, topic models do not extract detailed information from text as we do. Still, we use topic-to-word distributions from topic models as a way of describing sub-fields.

Demner-Fushman and Lin (2007) used hand written knowledge extractors to extract information, such as population and intervention, in their clinical question-answering system to improve ranking of relevant abstracts. Our categorization of key aspects is applicable for broader range of communities, and we learn the patterns by bootstrapping. Li et al. (2010) used semantic metadata to create a semantic digital library for chemistry and identified experimental paragraphs using keywords features. Xu et al. (2006) and Ruch et al. (2007) proposed systems, in clinical-trials and biomedical domain, respectively, to classify *sentences* of abstracts corresponding to categories such as introduction, purpose, method, results and conclusion to improve article retrieval by using either structured abstracts,[5] or hand-labeled sentences. Some summarization systems also use machine learning approaches to find 'key sentences'. The systems built in these papers are complimentary to ours since one can find relevant paragraphs or sentences and then extract the key aspects from them. Note that a sentence can have multiple phrases corresponding to our three categories, and thus classification of sentences will not be enough.

3 Approach

In this section, we explain how to extract phrases for each of the three categories (FOCUS, TECHNIQUE and DOMAIN) and how to compute the influence of communities.

3.1 Pattern Matching and Learning

From an article's abstract and title, we use the dependency trees of sentences and a set of semantic extraction patterns to extract phrases in each of

[5]Structure abstracts, which are used by some journals, have multiple sections such as PURPOSE and METHOD.

FOCUS	present $\rightarrow$ (direct object) work $\rightarrow$ (preposition_on) propose $\rightarrow$ (direct object)
TECHNIQUE	using $\rightarrow$ (direct object) apply $\rightarrow$ (direct object) extend $\rightarrow$ (direct object)
DOMAIN	system $\rightarrow$ (preposition_for) task $\rightarrow$ (preposition_of) framework $\rightarrow$ (preposition_for)

Table 1: Some examples of semantic extraction patterns that extract information from dependency trees of sentences. A pattern is of the form $T \rightarrow (d)$, where T is the trigger word and d is the dependency that the trigger word's node has with its successor.

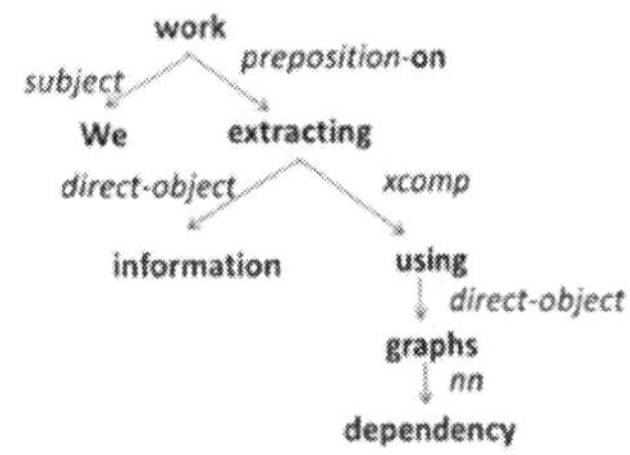

Figure 1: The dependency graph for '*We work on extracting information using dependency graphs*'. Our semantic patterns (shown in Table 1) will extract '*extracting information using dependency graphs*' as FOCUS, and '*dependency graphs*' as TECHNIQUE.

FOCUS, TECHNIQUE and DOMAIN categories. A dependency tree of a sentence is a parse tree that gives dependencies (such as direct-object, subject) between words in the sentence. Figure 1 shows the dependency graph for the sentence 'We work on extracting information using dependency graphs.' Each semantic pattern is of the form $T \rightarrow d$, where T is a trigger word (such as 'use', 'present') and d is a dependency (such as 'direct-object'). We start with a few handwritten patterns (some shown in Table 1) and learn more patterns automatically using a bootstrapping approach. We run an iterative algorithm that extracts phrases using semantic patterns and then learns new patterns from the extracted phrases. The details of each step are described below.

Extracting Phrases from Patterns A dependency tree matches a pattern $T \rightarrow (d)$, if (1) it contains T, and (2) the trigger word's node has a successor (dependent or granddependent upto 4 levels) whose dependency with its parent is d. In the rest of the paper, we call the subtree headed by the successor as the matched phrase-tree. We extract the phrase corresponding to the matched phrase-tree and label it with the pattern's category. For example, the dependency tree in Figure 1 matches the FOCUS pattern [*work* $\rightarrow$ *(preposition_on)*] and the TECHNIQUE pattern [*using* $\rightarrow$ *(direct-object)*]. Thus, the system labels the phrase corresponding to the phrase-tree headed by 'extracting', which is 'extracting information using dependency graphs', with the category FOCUS, and similarly labels the phrase 'dependency graphs' as TECHNIQUE.

We have special rules for paper titles since authors usually include the main contribution of the paper in the title. We label the whole title as FOCUS if we are not able to extract a FOCUS phrase using the patterns. For titles from which we can extract a TECHNIQUE phrase, we label rest of the words (except for the trigger words) with DOMAIN. For example, for title 'Studying the history of ideas using topic models', our system extracts 'topic models' as TECHNIQUE using the pattern [*using* → *(direct-object)*], and then labels 'Studying the history of ideas' as DOMAIN.

Learning Patterns from Phrases After extracting phrases with patterns, we want to be able to construct and learn new patterns. For each sentence whose dependency tree has a subtree corresponding to one of the extracted phrases, we construct a pattern $T \rightarrow (d)$ by considering the ancestor (parent or grandparent) of the subtree as the trigger word T, and the dependency between the head of the subtree and its parent as the dependency d. The weighting of newly constructed patterns is done as follows. For a set of phrases (P) that extract a pattern (q), the weight of the pattern q for the category FOCUS is $\sum_{p \in P} \frac{1}{z_p} count(p \in \text{FOCUS})$, where z_p is the total frequency of the phrase p. Similarly, we get weights of the pattern for the other two categories. Note that we do not need smoothing since the phrase-category ratios are aggregated over all the phrases from which the pattern is constructed. After weighting all the patterns that have not been selected in the previous iterations, we select the top k patterns in each category (k=2 in our experiments). Table 3 shows some patterns learned through the iterative method.

3.2 Communities and their Influence

We define communities as fields or sub-fields that one wishes to study. To study communities using the articles published, we need to know which communities each article belongs to. The article-to-community assignment can be computed in several ways, such as by manual assignment, using metadata, or by text categorization of papers. In our case study, we use the topics formed by applying latent Dirichlet allocation (Blei et al., 2003) to the text of the papers by considering each topic as one community. In recent years, topic modeling has been widely used to get 'concepts' from text; it has the advantage of producing soft, probabilistic article-to-community assignment scores in an unsupervised manner. We combine these soft assignment scores with the phrases extracted in the previous section to score a phrase for each community and each category as follows. The score of a phrase p, which is extracted from an article a, for a community c and the category TECHNIQUE is calculated as

$$tScore(c, p, a) = \frac{1}{z_p} count(p \in \text{TECHNIQUE} \mid a) P(c \mid a, \theta) \quad (1)$$

where the function $P(c \mid a, \theta)$ gives the probability of a community (i.e., a topic) for the article a given the topic modeling parameters θ. The normalization constant for the phrase, z_p, is the frequency of the phrase in all the abstracts.

We define influence such that communities receive higher scores if they use techniques earlier than other communities do or produce tools that are used to solve other problems. For example, since *hidden Markov model* introduced by the speech recognition community and *part-of-speech tagging* tools built by the part-of-speech community have been widely used as techniques in other communities, these communities should receive higher scores than the nascent or not-so-widely-used ones. Thus, we define influence of a community based on the number of times its FOCUS, TECHNIQUE or DOMAIN phrases have been used as a TECHNIQUE in other communities. To calculate the overall influence of one community on another, we first need to calculate influence because of individual articles in the community, which is calculated as follows. The influence of community c_1 on another community c_2 because of a phrase p extracted from an article a_1 is

$$tInfl(c_1, c_2, p, a_1) = allScore(c_1, p, a_1) \sum_{\substack{a_2 \in D \\ y_{a_2} > y_{a_1}}} tScore(c_2, p, a_2) C(a_2, a_1) \quad (2)$$

where the function $allScore(c, p, a)$ is computed the same way as in Eq. 1, but by using $count(p \in \text{ALL} \mid a)$, where ALL means the union of phrases extracted in all three categories. The variable D is the set of all articles, and y_{a_2} means year of publication of the article a_2. The summation term computes the influence of the phrase p extracted from the article a_1 on all the articles from the community c_2 published at a later date. The function $C(a_2, a_1)$ is a weighting function based on citations, whose value is 1 if a_2 cites a_1, and λ otherwise. If λ is 0, the system calculates influence based on just citations, which can be noisy and incomplete. In our experiments, we used λ as 0.5 since we want to study the influence even when an article does not explicitly cite another article. The technique-influence score of community c_1 on community c_2 in year y is computed by summing up the previous equation for all phrases (P) and for all articles in D. It is computed as

$$tInfl(c_1, c_2, y) = \sum_{p \in P} \sum_{\substack{a \in D \\ y_{a_1} = y}} tInfl(c_1, c_2, p, a) \quad (3)$$

Straightforwardly, the overall influence of community c_1 on the community c_2 and on all other communities is calculated as

$$tInfl(c_1, c_2) = \sum_y tInfl(c_1, c_2, y) \quad (4)$$

$$tInfl(c_1) = \sum_{c_2 \neq c_1} tInfl(c_1, c_2) \quad (5)$$

Next, we present a case study over the sub-fields of computational linguistics using the influence scores described above.

4 Experimental Setup

Dataset We studied the computational linguistics community from 1965 to 2009 using titles and abstracts of 15,016 articles from the ACL Anthology Network and the ACL Anthology Reference corpus (Bird et al., 2008; Radev et al., 2009). We found 52 pairs of abstracts that had more than 80% of words in common with each other, and thus while calculating the influence scores, we ignored the influence of earlier-published paper on the later-published paper in the pairs. We used the Stanford Parser (Marneffe et al., 2006) to generate dependency trees of sentences. For testing, we hand labeled 474 abstracts with the three categories to measure the precision and recall scores. For each abstract and each category, we compared the unique non-stop-words extracted from our algorithm to the hand labeled dataset. We calculated precision, recall measures for each abstract and averaged them to get the results for the dataset.

When extracting phrases from the matched phrase trees, we ignored tokens with part-of-speech tags as pronoun, number, determiner, punctuation or symbol, and removed all subtrees in the matched phrase trees that had either relative-clause-modifier or clausal-complement dependency with their parents since, even though we want full phrases, including these sub-trees introduced extraneous phrases and clauses. We also added phrases from the subtrees of the matched phrase trees to the set of extracted phrases.

We used 13 seed patterns for FOCUS, 7 for TECHNIQUE and 15 for DOMAIN. When constructing a new pattern, we ignored the ancestors that were not a noun or a verb since most trigger words are a noun or a verb (such as *use*, *constraints*). We also ignored conjunction, relative-clause-modifier, dependent (most generic dependency), quantifier-modifier, and abbreviation dependencies[6] since they either are too generic or introduced extraneous phrases and clauses.

Learning new patterns did not help in improving the FOCUS category phrases when tested over a hand labeled test set. It got relatively high scores when using just the seed patterns and the titles, and hence learning new patterns reduced the precision without any significant improvement in recall. Thus, we learned new patterns only for the TECHNIQUE and DOMAIN categories. We ran 50 iterations for both categories, which was chosen as a reasonable trade-off between pattern precision and recall based on some earlier pilot experiments. After extracting all the phrases, we removed common phrases that are frequently used in scientific articles, such as 'this technique' and 'the presence of', using a stop words list of 3,000 phrases. The list was created by taking the top most occurring 1 to 3 grams from 100,000 random articles with an abstract in the ISI web of knowledge database[7]. We ignored phrases that were either one character or more than 15 words long. In a step towards finding canonical names, we automatically detected abbreviations and their expanded forms from the full text of papers by searching for text between two parentheses, and considered the phrase before the parentheses as the expanded form (similar to (Schwartz and Hearst, 2003)). We got a high precision list by picking the top most occurring pairs of abbreviations and their expanded forms and created groups of phrases by merging all the phrases that use same abbreviation. We then changed all the phrases in the extracted phrases dataset to their canonical names.

[6] see (Marneffe et al., 2006) for details of dependencies
[7] www.isiknowledge.com

Paper Title	FOCUS	TECHNIQUE	DOMAIN
Studying the history of ideas using topic models	studying the history of ideas using topic	latent dirichlet allocation; topic; topic; unsupervised topic; historical trends; that all three conferences are converging in the topics	studying the history of ideas; topic; model of the diversity of ideas , topic entropy; probabilistic
A Bayesian Hybrid Method For Context-Sensitive Spelling Correction.	new hybrid method , based on bayesian classifiers; bayesian hybrid method for context-sensitive spelling correction	decision lists; bayesian; bayesian classifiers; ambiguous; part-of-speech tags; methods using decision lists; single strongest piece of evidence; spelling	context-sensitive spelling correction; for context-sensitive spelling correction; spelling

Table 2: Extracted phrases for some papers. The word 'model' is missing from the end of some phrases as it was removed during post-processing.

We also removed 'model', 'approach', 'method', 'algorithm', 'based', 'style' words and their variants when they occurred at the end of a phrase.

Baseline To compare against a non-information-extraction based baseline, we extracted all noun phrases, along with phrases from the sub-trees of the noun phrase trees, from the abstracts and labeled them with all the three categories. In addition, we labeled the titles (and their sub-trees) with the category FOCUS. We then scored the phrases with a tf-idf inspired measure, which was the ratio of the frequency of the phrase in the abstract and the sum of the total frequency of the individual words, and removed phrases that had the tf-idf measure less than 0.001 (best out of many experiments). We call this approach as 'Baseline tf-idf NPs'.[8]

To get communities in the computational linguistics literature, we considered the topics generated using the same ACL Anthology dataset by Bethard and Jurafsky (2010) as communities. They ran latent Dirichlet allocation on the full text of the papers to get 100 topics. We hand labeled the topics and used 72 of them in our study; the rest of them were about common words. When calculating the scores in Eq. 1, we considered the value of $P(c \mid a, \theta)$ to be 0 if it was less than 0.1.

5 Results and Discussion

Extraction

The total numbers of phrases extracted were 25,525 for FOCUS, 24,430 for TECHNIQUE, and 33,203 for DOMAIN. The total numbers of phrases after including the phrases extracted from subtrees of the matched phrase trees were 64,041, 38,220 and 46,771, respectively. Examples of phrases extracted from some papers are shown in Table 2.

[8]As discussed in Section 1, using an unsupervised or weakly-supervised bag-of-words based approach is not straightforward for identifying FOCUS, TECHNIQUE and DOMAIN of an article, and hence we do not compare against one.

TECHNIQUE	DOMAIN
model → (nn)	improve → (direct-object)
rules → (nn)	used → (preposition_for)
extracting → (direct-object)	evaluation → (nn)
identify → (direct-object)	parsing → (nn)
constraints → (amod)	domain → (nn)
based → (preposition_on)	applied → (preposition_to)

Table 3: Examples of patterns learned using the iterative extraction algorithm. The dependency 'nn' is the noun compound modifier dependency.

Approach	F_1	Precision	Recall
FOCUS			
Baseline tf-idf NPs	35.60	24.36	66.07
Seed Patterns	**55.29**	**44.67**	**72.54**
Inter-Annotator Agreement	53.33	50.80	56.14
TECHNIQUE			
Baseline tf-idf NPs	26.65	17.87	**52.41**
Seed Patterns	20.09	23.46	21.72
Iteration 50	**36.86**	**30.46**	46.68
Inter-Annotator Agreement	72.02	66.81	78.11
DOMAIN			
Baseline tf-idf NPs	30.13	19.90	**62.03**
Seed Patterns	25.27	**30.55**	26.29
Iteration 50	**37.29**	27.60	57.50
Inter-Annotator Agreement	72.31	75.58	69.32

Table 4: The precision, recall, and F_1 scores of each category for the different approaches. Note that the inter-annotator agreement is calculated on a smaller set.

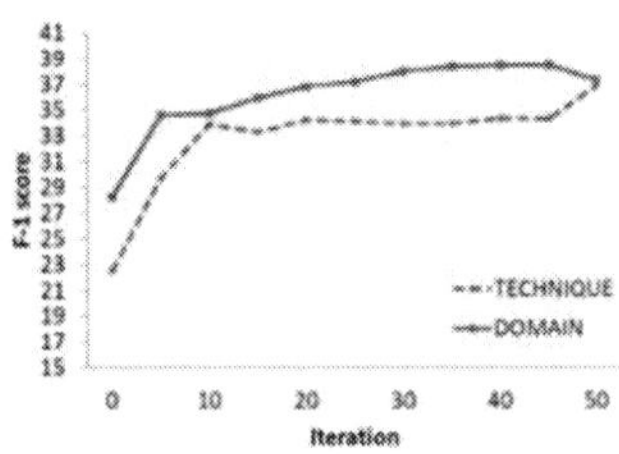

Figure 2: The F_1 scores for TECHNIQUE and DOMAIN categories after every five iterations. For reasons explained in the text, we do not learn new patterns for FOCUS.

Table 4 compares precision, recall, and micro-averaged F_1 scores for the three categories when we use: (1) only the seed patterns, (2) the combined set of learned and seed patterns, (3) the baseline, and (4) the inter-annotator agreement. We calculated inter-annotator agreement for 30 abstracts, where each abstract was labeled by 2 annotators,[9] and the precision-recall scores were calculated by randomly choosing one annotation as gold and another as predicted for each article. We

[9]The first author annotated 30 abstracts and two doctoral candidates in computational linguistics annotated 15 each.

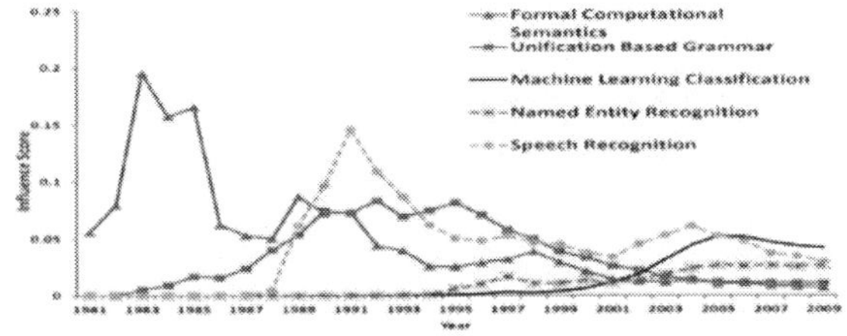

(a) The influence of communities in each year.

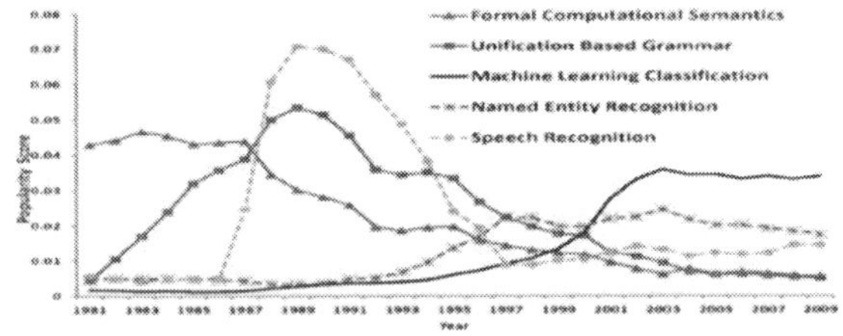

(b) Popularity of communities in each year.

Figure 3: The first figure shows influence scores of communities in each year. The second figure shows the popularity of each community in each year (see (Hall et al., 2008)), which is measured by summing up the article-to-topic scores for the articles published in that year. The scores are smoothed with weighted scores of 2 previous and 2 next years, and L1-normalized for each year. The scores are lower for all communities in late 2000s since the probability mass is more evenly distributed among many communities.

can see in the table that both precision and recall scores increase for TECHNIQUE because of the learned patterns, though for DOMAIN, precision decreases but recall increases. The recall scores for the baseline are higher as expected but the precision is very low. Three possible reasons explain the mistakes made by our system: (1) authors sometimes use generic phrases to describe their system, which were not annotated with any of the three categories in the test set but were extracted by the system (such as 'simple method', 'faster model', 'new approach'); (2) the dependency trees of some sentences were wrong; and (3) some of the patterns learned for TECHNIQUE and DOMAIN were low-precision but high-recall. Figure 2 shows the F_1 scores for TECHNIQUE and DOMAIN after every 5 iterations.

Influence

Table 5 shows the most influential communities overall (computed using Eq. 5) and their respective influential phrases that have been widely adopted as techniques by other communities. We can see that speech recognition is the most influential community because of the techniques like hidden Markov models and other stochastic methods it introduced in the computational linguistics literature, which shows that its long-term seeding influence is still present despite the limited recent

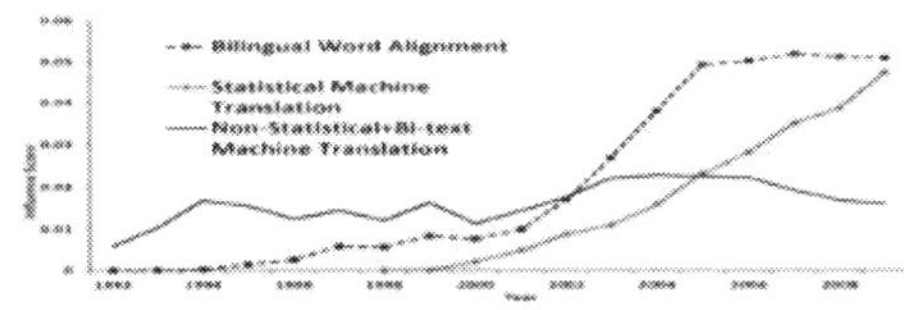

(a) The influence of communities in each year.

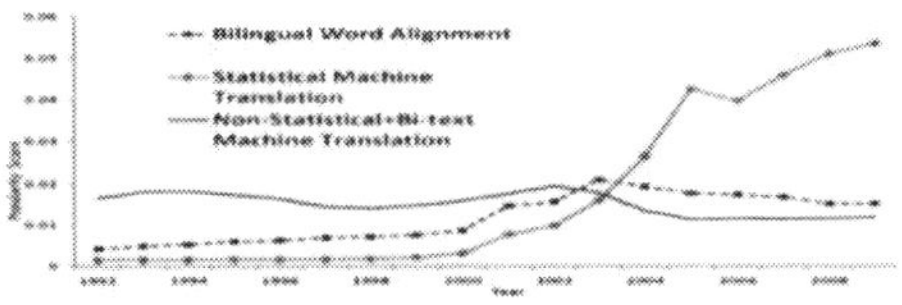

(b) Popularity of communities in a each year.

Figure 4: Comparing machine translation related communities in the same way as in Figure 3. The statistical machine translation community, which is a topic from the topic model, is more phrase-based.

popularity. Probability theory also gets a high score since many papers in the last decade have used stochastic methods. The communities part-of-speech tagging and parsing get high scores because they adopted some techniques that are used in other communities, and because other communities use part-of-speech tagging and parsing in the intermediary steps for solving other problems.

Figure 3(a) shows the change in a community's influence over time, and Figure 3(b) shows the change in its popularity. The popularity of a community is the sum of article-to-topic scores for the community topic and for all articles published in a given year.[10] The scores in both figures are normalized such that the total score for all communities in a year sum to one. Compare the relative scores of communities in Figure 3(a) with the relative scores in Figure 3(b). We can see influence of a community is different from the popularity of a community in a given year. As mentioned before, we observe that although influence score for speech recognition has declined in recent years, it still has a lot of influence, though the popularity of the community in recent years is very low. Machine learning classification has been both popular and influential in recent years. Named entity recognition's popularity has decreased since 2003, though its influence has either increased or remained same. Figure 4 compares the machine translation communities in the same way as we compare other communities in Figure 3. We can see that statistical machine translation (more phrase-based) community's popularity has steeply increased in the last 5 years, however, its influ-

[10]See (Hall et al., 2008) for more analysis. Note that this analysis uses just bag-of-words based topic models.

Community	Most Influential Phrases	Score
Speech Recognition (recognition, acoustic, error, speaker, rate, adaptation, recognizer, vocabulary, phone)	expectation maximization; hidden markov; language; contextually; segment; context independent phone; snn hidden markov; n gram back off language; multiple reference speakers; cepstral; phoneme; least squares; speech recognition; intra; hi gram; bu; word dependent; tree structured; statistical decision trees	1.35
Probability Theory (probability, probabilities, distribution, probabilistic, estimation, estimate, entropy, statistical, likelihood, parameters)	hidden markov; maximum entropy; language; expectation maximization; merging; expectation maximization hidden markov; natural language; variable memory markov; standard hidden markov; part of speech; inside outside; segmentation only; minimum description length principle; continuous density hidden markov; part of speech information; forward backward	1.31
Bilingual Word Alignment (alignment, alignments, aligned, pairs, align, pair, statistical, parallel, source, target, links, brown, ibm, null)	hidden markov; expectation maximization; maximum entropy; spectral clustering; statistical alignment; conditional random fields , a discriminative; statistical word alignment; string to tree; state of the art statistical machine translation system; single word; synchronous context free grammar; inversion transduction grammar; ensemble; novel reordering	1.2
POS Tagging (tag, tagging, pos, tags, tagger, part-of-speech, tagged, unknown, accuracy, part, taggers, brill, corpora, tagset)	maximum entropy; machine learning; expectation maximization hidden markov; part of speech information; decision tree; hidden markov; transformation based error driven learning; entropy; part of speech tagging; part of speech; variable memory markov; viterbi; second stage classifiers; document; wide coverage lexicon; using inductive logic programming	1.13
Machine Learning Classification (classification, classifier, examples, classifiers, kernel, class, svm, accuracy, decision, methods, labeled, vector, instances)	support vector machines; ensemble; machine learning; gaussian mixture; expectation maximization; flat; weak classifiers; statistical machine learning; lexicalized tree adjoining grammar based features; natural language processing; standard text categorization collection; pca; semisupervised learning; standard hidden markov; supervised learning	1.12
Statistical Parsing (parse, treebank, trees, parses, penn, collins, parsers, charniak, accuracy, wsj, head, statistical, constituent, constituents)	propbank; expectation maximization; supervised machine learning; maximumentropy classifier; ensemble; lexicalized tree adjoining grammar based features; neural network; generative probability; incomplete constituents; part of speech tagging; treebank; penn; 50 best parses; lexical functional grammar; maximum entropy; full comlex resource	0.92
Statistical Machine Translation (More-Phrase-Based) (bleu, statistical, source, target, phrases, smt, reordering, translations, phrase-based)	maximum entropy; hidden markov; expectation maximization; language; linguistically structured; ihmm; cross language information retrieval; ter; factored language; billion word; hierarchical phrases; string to tree; state of the art statistical machine translation system; statistical alignment; ist inversion transduction grammar; bleu as a metric; statistical machine translation	0.82

Table 5: The top most influential communities, along with the top most words that describe the communities obtained by the topic model, and the corresponding most influential phrases that have been widely used as techniques. The third column is the score of the community computed by Eq. 5.

Community	Communities that have influenced most (descending order)
Named Entity Recognition	Chunking/Memory Based Models; Discriminative Sequence Models; POS Tagging; Machine Learning Classification; Coherence Relations; Biomedical NER; Bilingual Word Alignment
Statistical Parsing	Probability Theory; POS Tagging; Discriminative Sequence Models; Speech Recognition; Parsing; Syntactic Theory; Clustering+DistributionalSimilarity; Chunking/Memory Based Models
Word Sense Disambiguation	Clustering + DistributionalSimilarity; Machine Learning Classification; Dictionary Lexicons; Collocations/Compounds; Syntax; Speech Recognition; Probability Theory

Table 6: The community in the first column has been influenced the most by the communities in the second column. The scores are calculated using Eq. 4

ence has increased at a slower rate. On the other hand, the influence of bilingual word alignment (the most influential community in 2009) has increased during the same period, mainly because of its influence on statistical machine translation. The influence of non-statistical machine translation has been decreasing recently, though slower than its popularity. Table 6 shows the communities that have the most influence on a given community (the list is in descending order of scores by Eq. 4).

6 Future Directions

We are working towards incorporating the date of publication of the articles to learn better patterns to increase precision and recall of the system. We are also exploring ways to use our system for studying citation and co-authorship networks. We plan to study the dynamics and impact of broader communities like biology, statistics and the social sciences. The approach can also be used to study innovation in interdisciplinary research, since we can track if interdisciplinary research results in applying old techniques from one community to solve problems in other community, or if it results in the evolution of better suited techniques.

7 Conclusions

This paper presents a framework for extracting detailed information from scientific articles, such as main contributions, tools and techniques used, and domain problems addressed, by matching semantic extraction patterns in dependency trees. We start with a few hand written seed patterns and learn new patterns using a bootstrapping approach. We use this rich information extracted from articles to study the dynamics of research communities and to define a new way of measuring influence of one research community on another. We present a case study on the computational linguistics community, where we find the *influence* of its sub-fields and observed that speech recognition and probability theory have had the most seminal influence.

References

Steven Bethard and Dan Jurafsky. 2010. Who should I cite: learning literature search models from citation behavior. In *Proceedings of the Conference on Information and Knowledge Management*.

Steven Bird, Robert Dale, Bonnie J. Dorr, Bryan Gibson, Mark T. Joseph, Min yen Kan, Dongwon Lee, Brett Powley, Dragomir R. Radev, and Yee Fan Tan. 2008. The ACL anthology reference corpus: A reference dataset for bibliographic research in computational linguistics. In *Proceedings of the Conference on Language Resources and Evaluation*.

David M. Blei, Andrew Y. Ng, and Michael I. Jordan. 2003. Latent Dirichlet allocation. *Journal of Machine Learning Research*.

Razvan C. Bunescu and Raymond J. Mooney. 2005. A shortest path dependency kernel for relation extraction. In *Proceedings of the Human Language Technology Conference and Conference on Empirical Methods in Natural Language Processing*.

Michael Collins and Yoram Singer. 1999. Unsupervised models for named entity classification. In *Proceedings of the Joint SIGDAT Conference on Empirical Methods in Natural Language Processing and Very Large Corpora*.

Dina Demner-Fushman and Jimmy Lin. 2007. Answering clinical questions with knowledge-based and statistical techniques. *Computational Linguistics*.

Sean M. Gerrish and David M. Blei. 2010. A language-based approach to measuring scholarly impact. In *Proceedings of the International Conference on Machine Learning*.

T. L. Griffiths and M. Steyvers. 2004. Finding scientific topics. *Proceedings of the National Academy of Sciences*.

David Hall, Daniel Jurafsky, and Christopher D. Manning. 2008. Studying the history of ideas using topic models. In *Proceedings of the Conference on Empirical Methods in Natural Language Processing*.

Marti A. Hearst. 1992. Automatic acquisition of hyponyms from large text corpora. In *Proceedings of the Conference on Computational linguistics*.

Na Li, Leilei Zhu, Prasenjit Mitra, Karl Mueller, Eric Poweleit, and C. Lee Giles. 2010. OreChem ChemXSeer: a semantic digital library for chemistry. In *Proceedings of the Joint Conference on Digital libraries*.

Marie-Catherine De Marneffe, Bill MacCartney, and Christopher D. Manning. 2006. Generating typed dependency parses from phrase structure parses. In *Proceedings of the Conference on Language Resources and Evaluation*.

Dragomir R. Radev, Eduard Hovy, and Kathleen McKeown. 2002. Introduction to the special issue on summarization. *Computational Linguistics*.

Dragomir R. Radev, Pradeep Muthukrishnan, and Vahed Qazvinian. 2009. The acl anthology network corpus. In *Proceedings of the 2009 Workshop on Text and Citation Analysis for Scholarly Digital Libraries*.

Ellen Riloff and Rosie Jones. 1999. Learning dictionaries for information extraction by multi-level bootstrapping. In *Proceedings of the National Conference on Artificial Intelligence (AAAI)*.

Patrick Ruch, Clia Boyer, Christine Chichester, Imad Tbahriti, Antoine Geissbhler, Paul Fabry, Julien Gobeill, Violaine Pillet, Dietrich Rebholz-Schuhmann, Christian Lovis, and Anne-Lise Veuthey. 2007. Using argumentation to extract key sentences from biomedical abstracts. *International Journal of Medical Informatics*.

Ariel S. Schwartz and Marti A. Hearst. 2003. A simple algorithm for identifying abbreviation definitions in biomedical text.

Rong Xu, Kaustubh Supekar, Yang Huang, Amar Das, and Alan Garber. 2006. Combining text classification and hidden markov modeling techniques for categorizing sentences in randomized clinical trial abstracts. *Proceedings of the Association of Moving Image Archivists Annual Symposium*.

Roman Yangarber, Ralph Grishman, Pasi Tapanainen, and Silja Huttunen. 2000. Unsupervised discovery of scenario-level patterns for information extraction. In *Proceedings of the Conference on Applied Natural Language Processing*.

David Yarowsky. 1995. Unsupervised word sense disambiguation rivaling supervised methods. In *Proceedings of the Association for Computational Linguistics*.

Dependency-directed Tree Kernel-based Protein-Protein Interaction Extraction from Biomedical Literature

Longhua Qian **Guodong Zhou**
Natural Language Processing Lab
School of Computer Science and Technology, Soochow University
1 Shizi Street, Suzhou, China 215006
{qianlonghua,gdzhou}@suda.edu.cn

Abstract

Structured information plays a critical role in many NLP tasks, such as semantic relation extraction between named entities and semantic role labeling. This paper proposes a principled way to automatically generate constituent structure representation for tree kernel-based protein-protein interaction (PPI) extraction. The main idea behind our approach is that the critical portion in a constituent parse tree for PPI extraction can be automatically determined by the shortest dependency path between the two involved proteins, while other portion can be regarded as noise and ignored safely. Evaluation on multiple PPI corpora shows that our dependency-directed tree kernel-based method achieves promising results. This justifies the effectiveness of tree kernel-based methods for PPI extraction, in particular the advantage of dependency-directed constituent structure representation.

1 Introduction

Since determining protein interaction partners is crucial to understand both the functional role of individual proteins and the organization of the entire biological process, there is a significant interest in protein-protein interaction (PPI) extraction. However, manual collection of relevant PPI information from thousands of biomedical research papers published every day (e.g. MEDLINE) is so time-consuming and labor-demanding that automatic extraction approaches with the help of NLP techniques become necessary.

In principle, PPI extraction is much like the semantic relation extraction subtask (so called Relation Detection and Classification, RDC) defined by the ACE project (ACE, 2002-2007) in the newswire domain. Therefore, various kinds of machine learning methods have been borrowed from the newswire domain to the biomedical domain: feature-based methods (Mitsumori et al., 2006; Giuliano et al., 2006; Sætre et al., 2007; Liu et al., 2010) and kernel-based methods (Bunescu et al., 2005a; Erkan et al., 2007; Airola et al., 2008; Kim et al., 2010).

Early studies on PPI extraction employ feature-based methods. However, the feature-based methods often fail to effectively capture the structured information, which is essential to identify the relationship between two proteins in a constituent or dependency-based syntactic representation.

With the wide adoption of kernel-based methods to many NLP tasks, particularly for semantic relation extraction and semantic role labeling, various kernels such as subsequence kernels (Bunescu et al., 2005a) and tree kernels (Li et al., 2008) have been applied to PPI extraction. On one hand, dependency-based kernels, such as edit distance kernels (Erkan et al. 2007), graph kernels (Airola et al., 2008) and subsequence kernels (Kim et al., 2010), show some promising results for PPI extraction. This suggests that dependency information plays a critical role in PPI extraction, much like semantic relation extraction in the newswire narratives (Culotta and Sorensen, 2004; Bunescu et al., 2005b). On the other hand, while tree kernels based on constituent parse trees achieve great success in semantic relation extraction (Zhang et al., 2006; Zhou et al., 2007a; Qian et al., 2008) and semantic role labeling (Moschitti, 2004; Zhang et al., 2008) from the newswire narratives, they haven't been fully explored for PPI extraction in the biomedical domain. Considering the similarity between the task of PPI extraction from the biomedical domain and that of relation extraction from the newswire domain, one question naturally arises: "How can kernel-based

PPI extraction benefit from the constituent parse tree structure?"

To address this question, this paper presents a principled way to automatically generate a precise and concise constituent parse tree representation for kernel-based methods, motivated by the success of employing dependency information in PPI extraction. This is done by taking advantage of the shortest dependency path between two involved proteins in the dependency parse tree structure of a sentence. Specifically, only the words appearing on the shortest dependency path and their associated constituents in the constituent parse tree are considered as necessary and thus kept as the essential part of the constituent parse tree. In this paper, we refer to it as SDP-CPT (Shortest Dependency Path-directed Constituent Parse Tree). Experimental results on several major PPI corpora show the effectiveness of dependency-directed constituent structure representation and its preference over other state-of-the-art structure representations.

The rest of this paper is organized as follows. First, related work in PPI extraction is overviewed in Section 2. Then, Section 3 elaborates our shortest dependency path-directed constituent parse tree structure. Section 4 reports the experimental results on major PPI corpora. Finally we conclude our work in Section 5.

2 Related Work

Due to space limitation, this section only gives an overview on kernel-based methods on PPI extraction in the biomedical domain as well as semantic relation extraction in the newswire domain. For details about feature-based methods, please refer to related studies in the biomedical domain (Mitsumori et al., 2006; Giuliano et al., 2006; Liu et al., 2010) and those in the newswire domain (Zhao et al., 2005; Zhou et al. 2005, 2007b), respectively.

PPI extraction in biomedical domain

Representative kernel-based methods on PPI extraction take advantage of lexical or dependency information.

Bunescu et al. (2005a) adopt a generalized substring kernel over a mixture of words and word classes to extract protein interactions from biomedical corpora and semantic relations from newswire corpora. Particularly, they achieve the F1-score of 54.2 in extracting protein interactions from the AIMed corpus. Erkan et al. (2007) first define two similarity functions based on cosine similarity and edit distance among dependency paths between two entities, and then incorporate them in semi-supervised learning for PPI extraction using SVM and KNN classifiers. Sætre et al. (2007) use a tree kernel over dependency structures from two parsers and achieve the F1-score of 52.0 for PPI extraction from the AIMed corpus. Airola et al. (2008) introduce an all-dependency-paths graph kernel to capture complex dependency relationships between words and attain a significant performance boost at the expense of computational complexity. They achieve the F1-score of 56.4 in PPI extraction from the AIMed corpus. Kim et al. (2010) adopt a walk-weighted subsequence kernel based on shortest dependency paths to explore various substructures such as e-walks, partial match, and non-contiguous paths. They achieve the F1-score of 56.7 on the AIMed corpus.

Semantic relation extraction in newswire domain

In the literature, various kernels-based methods (Zelenko et al., 2003; Culotta and Sorensen, 2004; Bunescu et al., 2005b; Zhang et al., 2006; Zhou et al., 2007a; Qian et al., 2008) have been widely used in semantic relation extraction in the newswire domain. In particular, Zhang et al. (2006), Zhou et al. (2007a) and Qian et al. (2008) adopt convolution tree kernels (Collins and Duffy, 2001) over constituent parse trees and show great success with comparable or even better performance than feature-based ones, motivated by the pioneer work of Moschitti et al. (2004; 2008) on semantic role labeling.

While convolution kernels (Haussler et al., 1999) can effectively capture structured information in discrete objects, the key problem for tree kernel-based methods lies largely in how to appropriately represent structured syntactic information inherent in relation instances. Zhang et al. (2006) discover that the Shortest Path-enclosed Tree (SPT) achieves the best performance among five tree setups. Zhou et al. (2007a) further extend it to Context-Sensitive Shortest Path-enclosed Tree (CS-SPT), which includes necessary predicate-linked path information. Qian et al. (2008) propose to automatically determine the appropriate part of a constituent parse tree by considering constituent dependencies on each node along the shortest path between two entity mentions and discarding irrelevant nodes. However, their adopted constituent dependency rules are manually constructed and thus difficult to adapt to other domains and languages.

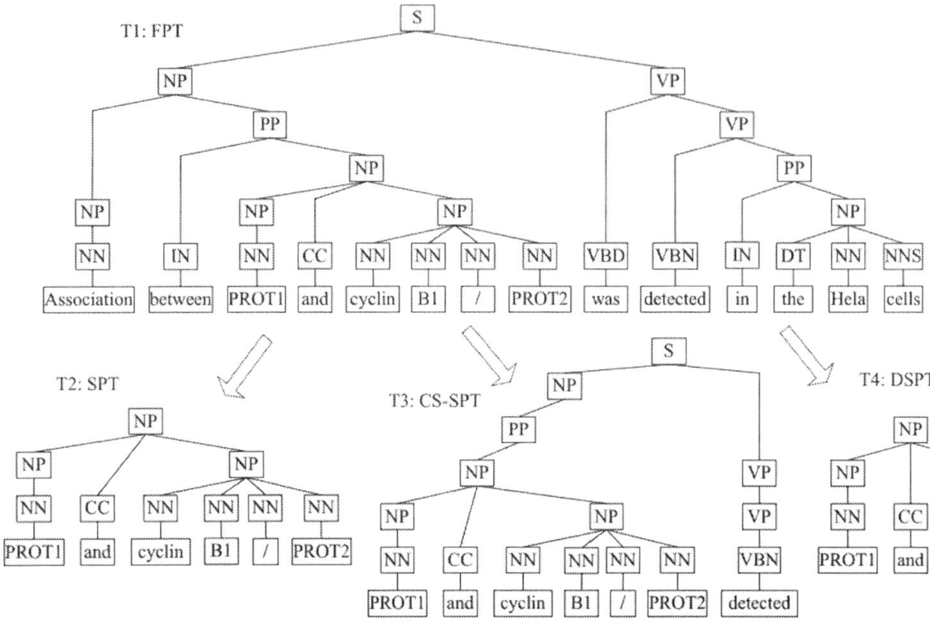

Figure 1. Different tree setups for a PPI instance between PROT1 and PROT2 from sentence "Association between PROT1 and cyclin B1 / PROT2 was detected in the HeLa cells." in the AIMed corpus

In this paper, we make use of the shortest dependency path in the dependency tree to refine the constituent parse tree. Specifically, all the words which appear on the shortest dependency path, together with their associated constituents, are kept in the constituent parse tree, while other constituents are removed, forming a Shortest Dependency Path-directed Constituent Parse Tree (SDP-CPT).

3 Constituent Structure Representation

This section first illustrates the limitations of commonly-used constituent parse tree setups, then emphasizes the importance of shortest dependency path in representing the constituent parse tree, and finally presents the shortest dependency path-directed constituent parse tree (SDP-CPT).

3.1 Limitations of Current Tree Setups

It is widely acknowledged that the key problem for the success of tree kernel-based semantic relation extraction is how to represent the constituent parse tree in a precise and concise manner. Zhang et al. (2006) explore five kinds of tree setups and find that the Shortest Path-enclosed Tree (SPT) achieves the best performance. However, unlike the locality of semantic relations in the newswire domain (Zhou et al., 2005), most of PPI instances in the biomedical domain spans a relatively long distance, leading to more complexity and diversity (Bunescu et al., 2005c; Airola et al., 2008). Therefore, it is not surprising that previous tree kernels over constituent parse trees have not yet achieved promising results for PPI extraction just as they do in the news domain. Miyao et al. (2008) conduct a comprehensive comparison of different syntactic representations for PPI extraction and find that the phrase structure tree in the form of the constituent parse tree (called PTB in their paper) performs significantly worse than the other representations. Tikk et al. (2010) extensively compares different kernel-based methods on PPI extraction and show that the tree kernel over the constituent parse tree only achieves the F1-score of 34.6 on the AIMed corpus. Actually, our preliminary experiment on PPI extraction via the convolution tree kernel over SPT only achieves the F1-score of about 47 on the AIMed corpus. Such poor performance can be justified to a certain extent via a typical instance as illustrated in Figure 1, where the interaction between PROT1 and PROT2 (their actual names have been replaced) can be only determined by the overall constituent structure of the sentence. Obviously, SPT will fail to identify this interaction instance since SPT ignores the constituents outside the shortest path (Figure 1: T_2: SPT).

For the Context-Sensitive SPT (CS-SPT), as proposed in Zhou et al. (2007a), which extends necessary predicate-linked path information outside SPT, some critical information is still missing while there exists some noisy information. For the instance as shown in Figure 1 (T_3: CS-SPT), although the word "detected" and its associated constituents are added, the more important portion of "association between" and their associated constituents are still missing while the noisy words "cyclin B1 / " still remaining.

In order to overcome the shortcomings in SPT and CS-SPT, Qian et al. (2008) propose a dynamic syntactic parse tree (DSPT) by exploiting constituent dependencies to refine the constituent parse tree. Specifically, they manually devise five categories of constituent dependencies, motivated by various kinds of lexical dependencies. When refining each node along the shortest path in the constituent parse tree, these constituent dependencies are used to determine how to remove or reduce futile constituents, eventually leading to a more precise and concise parse tree structure. However, this tree structure still suffers from the following three shortcomings:

1) It disregards the constituents beyond the lowest common ancestor to the tree root, similar to CS-SPT as proposed in Zhou et al. (2007a). This may be largely due to the locality of semantic relations as defined in the ACE RDC corpus, which Zhou et al (2007a) and Qian et al. (2008) tackle.
2) The rules adopted to tackle constituent dependencies are manually constructed and thus may not be easily adapted to other domains and languages. For example, while the constituent dependencies related to noun phrases are effective in the newswire domain (e.g. the ACE RDC corpus), this may not be true for PPI extraction in the biomedical literature.
3) The constituent dependencies have been divided into only five categories. Such division may be too coarse to reflect the substantial difference between various kinds of dependencies (considering there are 55 kinds of minor-typed dependencies for the Stanford Dependency representation).

In this paper, we attempt to address these problems by considering the shortest dependency path in the dependency parse tree for reshaping the constituent parse tree in a principled way in the context of PPI extraction from the biomedical literature.

3.2 Shortest Dependency Path

Lexical dependencies can indicate both local and long-range relationships among words occurring in the same sentence. Such dependency relationships offer a condensed representation of the information necessary to assess the relationship between two proteins or entities. In order to capture the necessary information inherent in the depedency parse tree for extracting PPI instances, various kernels based on dependency paths, such as edit distance kernel (Erkan et al., 2007), all-dependency-path graph kernel (Airola et al., 2008), and walk-weighted subsequence kernels (Kim et al., 2010) have been proposed. Likewise for semantic relation extraction in the newswire domain, the kernels on dependency trees (Culotta and Sorensen, 2004) and the shortest dependency path (Bunescu et al., 2005b) have been proposed. One common characteristic to these kernels is that they all contain the shortest dependency path and usually assign more weights to them than to other ones, similar to the graph kernel proposed by Airola et al. (2008). This indicates the importance of the shortest dependency path over other paths in the dependency path tree or the dependency graph.

Currently, there are two established dependency representations available, viz. CoNLL scheme (adopted by CoNLL'2007 and CoNLL'2008 Shared tasks) (Nivre et al., 2007; Surdeanu et al., 2008) and Standford scheme (adopted by Stanford parser) (de Marneffe et al., 2006). These two schemes differ significantly in the representation of passive construction, position of auxiliary and modal verb, or coordination. It is generally acknowledged that the Stanford scheme is closer to the targeted semantic representation from the perspective of relation extraction (Buyko and Hahn, 2010). Particularly, among the four styles of Stanford representations, "collapsed dependency" can much simplify patterns in relation extraction since dependencies involving preposition, conjunct as well as referent of relative clause are effectively collapsed to reflect direct dependencies between content words. Therefore, the collapsed variant of Stanford scheme is adopted in this paper to refine the constituent parse tree as described in the next subsection.

3.3 SDP-CPT: Shortest Dependency Path-directed Constituent Parse Tree

Considering the importance of dependency path in PPI extraction and the effectiveness of employing dependency information to refine the constituent parse tree for tree kernel-based semantic relation extraction in the newswire domain, it is a natural idea to automatically generate the proper constituent parse tree with the help of the shortest dependency path. Specifically, we can reshape the constituent parse tree by making use of the shortest dependency path between two proteins. Figure 2 describes the procedure to generate the Shortest Dependency Path-directed Constituent Parse Tree (SDP-CPT).

Note that Step 3(a) in Figure 2 is necessary since a dependency tuple of the type "prep_*xx*(*governor*, *dependent*)" implies a relationship between the preposition *xx* and the *dependent*, which is important to PPI. For Step 3(b), when a word on which the two proteins are directly or indirectly dependent is discovered, it is natural to add this path for maintaining the integrality of SDP-CPT.

Input: a sentence and two proteins in it
Output: an SDP-CPT
Steps:

1) Given the input sentence, generate the constituent parse tree using a constituent parser, and various dependency tuples using a dependency parser.
2) Given the two proteins, extract the shortest constituent path (SCP, i.e. the shortest path-enclosed tree) from the constituent parse tree and construct the shortest dependency path (SDP) from the dependency tuples.
3) For each word along the SDP, add the corresponding leaf word node and its upper constituents to the SCP. Particularly,
   a) when the dependency type is "prep_*xx*", such as "prep_of", the preposition *xx* and its associated constituent are also added;
   b) when the word to be added is outside the SCP, a new path from the current lowest common ancestor to one of the added words' ancestors is also added.
4) Merge any two consecutive NP/VP nodes along the paths into a single one.

Figure 2. Procedure for generating SDP-CPT

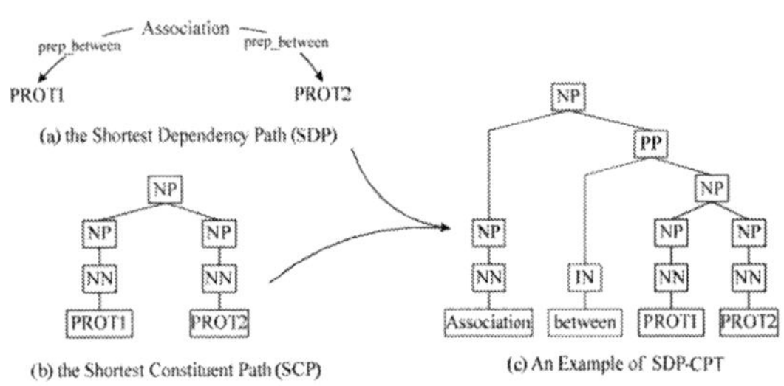

Figure 3. Generation of an example of SDP-CPT

In order to demonstrate the process of generating a SDP-CPT, we take the sentence and the two proteins shown in Figure 1 as an example. Figure 3 illustrates the detailed generation process. First, the shortest dependency path (SDP) and the shortest constituent path (SCP) are generated as depicted in Figure 3(a) and 3(b) respectively. Then, every word in the SDP is added into the SCP together with its associated constituents. In this case, since the two protein names in the SDP share a common ancestor "Association", the word "Association" together with its constituent ancestors are added into the SCP and a new path "NP→PP→NP" is created as rendered by the dashed lines. Finally, since the dependency type between "PROT1" and "Association" is *prep_between*, the preposition word "between" and its constituent ancestors are added into the SCP as rendered by the dotted lines. Since no further post-processing is necessary in this example, SDP-CPT is eventually formed. Compared to other tree setups in Figure 1, namely SPT, CS-SPT and DSPT, obviously SDP-CPT is much more concise and precise for this PPI instance.

4 Experimentation

This section systematically evaluates the performance of our shortest dependency path-directed constituent parse tree (SDP-SPT) on PPI extraction across several major PPI corpora.

4.1 Data Sets and Preprocessing

In order to fairly compare our work with other PPI extraction systems, we use five PPI corpora, i.e., AIMed (Bunescu et al., 2005a), BioInfer (Pyysalo et al., 2007), HPRD50 (Fundel et al., 2007), IEPA (Ding et al., 2002) and LLL (Nédellec, 2005). Particularly, most of the evaluation is done on the widely-used AIMed corpus, which contains 177 Medline abstracts with PPI instances, and 48 abstracts without any PPI instances. Totally, there are 4,084 protein references and around 1,000 annotated protein-protein interactions in this data set.

In this paper, a potential PPI instance is generated for any pair of two proteins in a sentence That is, if a sentence contains n proteins, $\binom{n}{2}$ protein pairs are generated. In particular, all the self-interactions (59 instances) are removed and all the PPI instances with nested protein names are retained (154 instances), as adopted in most literature. Eventually, 1000 positive instances and 4834 negative instances are generated. Besides, for a potential PPI instance, the two involved proteins are replaced by PROT1 and PROT2 respectively in order to blind the learner for fair comparison with other work. Finally, all the sentences in these corpora are parsed using the Stanford Parser[1] to generate both the con-

---
[1] http://nlp.stanford.edu/software/lex-parser.shtml

stituent parse trees and their corresponding dependency tuples.

4.2 Classifier and Evaluation Metrics

In our experimentation, we select Support Vector Machines (SVM) as the classifier since SVM represents the state-of-the-art in the machine learning research community. In particular, we use the SVM^{light} (Joachims, 1998) with the convolution tree kernel function SVM^{light}–TK (Moschitti, 2004)[2] to compute the similarity between two constituent parse trees.

Evaluation is done using 10-fold document-level cross-validation, each of which contains 90% of documents as the training data and 10% as the test data. Particularly, for the AIMed corpus we apply the exactly same 10-fold split as widely used in a series of relevant studies (e.g., Bunescu et al., 2005a; Giuliano et al., 2006). Following conventions, the parameters C for SVM is set to the ratio of negative instances to positive ones in respective corpora, and λ for the convolution tree kernel is set to default 0.4. Furthermore, the OAOD (One Answer per Occurrence in the Document) strategy is adopted, which means that the correct interaction must be extracted for each occurrence. This guarantees the maximal use of the available data, and more importantly, allows fair comparison with relevant work. All the experiments are evaluated using commonly-used Precision (P), Recall (R) and harmonic F1-score (F1). As an alternative to F1-score, the AUC (*area under the receiver operating characteristics curve*) score is proved to be invariant to the class distribution of the test dataset. Therefore, we also provide the AUC score of our system for referrence as by Airola et al. (2008).

4.3 Experimental Results

Comparison of different lengths of dependency paths on the AIMed corpus

Table 1 reports the performance of PPI extraction on the AIMed corpus corresponding to different lengths of the dependency paths using all kinds of dependency types. Here, two partial dependency paths on SDP, starting from each of the two proteins respectively, are utilized to generate the tree representation. The length of these two paths is shown in the 1st column. The words corresponding to the nodes on these two paths together with these words' associated constituents in the parse tree are added to SCP. For example, the length of 0 (L0) means that not a single word or constituent will be added to SCP, while the length of 1 (L1) means that the words corresponding to the parents of two proteins on SDP and these words' associated constituents in the parse tree are added to SCP. Meanwhile, the performance of the SPT setup is also listed as the baseline for comparison.

Length	P (%)	R (%)	F1	AUC
SPT	57.0	40.7	47.1	79.9
SCP+L0 (SCP)	45.0	19.5	26.5	67.9
SCP+L1	59.7	45.8	51.4	80.2
SCP+L2	59.2	51.7	55.0	82.3
SCP+L3	58.0	51.9	54.6	82.2
SCP+L4	59.3	54.0	56.2	82.6
SDP-CPT	59.6	54.3	56.7	82.7

Table 1. Performance comparison of PPI extraction on the AIMed corpus with different lengths of dependency paths using all kinds of dependency types

This table shows that the constituent parse tree directed by the shortest dependency path (SDP-CPT) achieves the best performance of 59.6/54.3/56.7/82.7 in P/R/F1/AUC, significantly outperforming SPT by 9.6 units in F1 and 2.8 units in AUC largely due to the substantial increase in recall. This indicates that SDP-CPT can remove much noise in SPT while adding some useful information. It also shows

- The performance of the SCP corresponding to the length of 0 is lowest, since they contain no information derived from the shortest dependency path.
- With the increase of the length of dependency paths, more and more useful information derived from SDP is included in the constituent parse tree and the performance reaches the highest for SDP-CPT (all the words corresponding to all the nodes on the SDP and their associated constituents are added).

In summary, the above results suggest that SDP-CPT can achieve the best performance. Therefore, all the subsequent experiments adopt the SDP-CPT setup unless specified.

Contribution of different kinds of dependencies on the AIMed corpus

Table 2 compares the contribution of various kinds of dependencies in SDP-CPT on the AIMed corpus. All the typed dependency relations are grouped into 4 major classes, namely *Modifier*, *Argument*, *Conjunction* and *Others*. For every major type, minor dependency types, if

[2] http://ai-nlp.info.uniroma2.it/moschitti/

any exists, are further ordered by their potential importance. The percentage of occurring frequency with which each minor type is employed when generating the SDP-CPT with respect to the total number of dependency tuples is listed in Column 2. Particularly, the tree setup without using any dependency type, which corresponds to that with the length of 0 (SCP) in Table 1, is displayed at the top row. Furthermore, the dependency types are added in two different ways:

- Individual: the dependency types are added individually with their performance scores shown inside the parentheses;
- Accumulative: the dependency types are incrementally added one by one with their performance scores shown outside the parentheses. The "+" sign before the type means that its addition can boost the performance in F1-score or AUC score and thus will be passed down to the next iteration.

Typed Dependency	%	P(%)	R(%)	F1	AUC
SCP+L0	-	45.0	19.5	26.5	67.9
Argument					
+subj	10	52.5 (52.6)	33.2 (33.2)	40.4 (40.4)	72.7 (72.7)
+obj	31	56.2 (53.8)	46.2 (42.4)	50.4 (47.0)	76.6 (76.6)
+arg-others	2	56.1 (48.8)	47.0 (14.6)	50.9 (21.3)	76.5 (68.6)
Modifier					
+nn	10	58.1 (54.9)	53.4 (38.5)	55.1 (44.6)	81.4 (77.5)
+prep	20	58.2 (53.4)	55.2 (39.2)	56.6 (44.8)	83.1 (76.2)
+mod-others	5	**59.1** (46.8)	**57.6** (15.7)	**58.1** (22.3)	**83.3** (67.3)
Conjunction	12	58.9 (48.9)	55.0 (23.5)	56.7 (30.5)	82.8 (69.8)
Others	10	58.4 (47.5)	53.8 (14.8)	55.8 (20.4)	83.0 (69.5)

Table 2. Contribution of different typed dependencies on the AIMed corpus with the SDP-CPT setup in the accumulative mode (outside parentheses) and in the individual mode (inside parentheses)

Table 2 shows that with the addition of all *Argument* types and all *Modifier* types, the SDP-CPT attains the best performance of 59.1/57.6/58.1/83.3 in P/R/F1/AUC as shown in bold fonts, outperforming the SDP-CPT with all dependency types added (59.6/54.3/56.7/82.7 in P/R/F1/AUC). Particularly, it shows

- The dependency types of *subj, obj, prep* and *nn* yield substantial performance improvement both in the accumulative mode and in the individual mode;
- The dependency types of *Conjunction* and *Others* harm the performance in the accumulative mode, though *Conjunction* improves the performance in the individual mode;
- It is interesting to note that while the dependency types of *arg-others* and *mod-others* harm the performance in the individual mode, they slightly improve the performance in the accumulative mode.

Since the governors of *subj* and *obj* types are verbs, those of the *prep* type are nouns and prepositions, and those of the *nn* type are nouns, the above results are consistent with our observation that some verbs like "bind" or "interact", some prepositions like "with" or "of", and some nouns like "interaction" or "expression", on which two proteins are directly or indirectly dependent, are particularly important for PPI extraction. Henceforth, in the following experiments all the *Argument* and *Modifier* types are included while the *Conjunction* and *Others* types are excluded.

Tree setups	AIMed	BioInfer	HPRD 50	IEPA	LLL
Ratio of POS/NEG	1000/ 4834	2534/ 7119	163/ 270	335/ 482	164/ 166
MCT	31.8 (78.0)	53.8 (76.7)	48.0 (73.4)	62.3 (78.6)	77.1 (73.4)
SPT (baseline)	47.1 (79.9)	54.2 (73.7)	61.3 (81.6)	66.6 (82.2)	79.4 (86.1)
CS-SPT	46.5 (80.2)	54.5 (74.5)	63.6 (79.9)	66.8 (81.0)	80.1 (86.0)
DSPT	50.0 (77.8)	58.3 (78.5)	66.0 (80.3)	68.6 (80.9)	77.3 (79.3)
SDP-CPT	**58.1** (83.3)	**62.4** (83.6)	**68.8** (83.4)	**69.8** (82.0)	**84.6** (89.2)

Table 3. Comparison of F1-score(outside parentheses) and AUC(inside parentheses) between SDP-CPT and different tree setups across major PPI corpora

Comparison of different constituent parse tree structures across major PPI corpora

Table 3 compares the performance of F1-score (outside parenthesis) and AUC (inside parentheses) between SDP-CPT and the previously-used tree setups across major PPI corpora. Particularly, SPT is used as a baseline and for comparison we re-implement two other effective tree setups for semantic relation extraction in the newswire domain, i.e. CS-SPT (Zhou et al., 2007a) and DSPT (Qian et al., 2008). Significance tests are conducted between each of them and the baseline.

Additionally, the numbers of positive and negative instances in each corpus are reported in the 1st row and the performance scores of MCT (Minimum Complete Tree, the complete sub-tree rooted by the lowest common ancestor of the two proteins under consideration) are also listed in the 2nd row for reference. The table shows

- Among all tree setups SDP-CPT performs best and significantly outperforms SPT consistently on most PPI corpora.
- CS-SPT slightly outperforms SPT on most corpora while DSPT performs divergently on different corpora. The reason that DSPT performs excellently in the newswire domain (Qian et al., 2008) but not so much for PPI extraction may be that the heuristic rules they use to prune the constituent trees are more suitable for the newswire domain, thus limiting their capability of domain adaptation.

In summary, the above results suggest the superiority and generality of our SDP-CPT on various kinds of PPI corpora from the biomedical literature.

PPI extraction systems	P(%)	R(%)	F1
Our SDP-CPT kernel	59.1	57.6	**58.1**
Dependency path: Kim et al. (2010)	61.4	53.3	56.7
Dependency graph: Airola et al. (2008)	52.9	**61.8**	56.4
Word subsequence: Bunescu et al. (2005a)	**65.0**	46.4	54.2
Constituent parse tree: Tikk et al. (2010)	39.2	31.9	34.6
BOW+Dependency path: Sætre et al. (2007)	**64.3**	44.1	52.0
BOW+Constituent parse tree: Miyao et al. (2008)	50.9	56.1	53.0
Global+Local context: Giuliano et al. (2006)	60.9	57.2	59.0
Dependency+Predicate Argument Structure: Miyao et al. (2008)	54.9	**65.5**	59.5
BOW+Shortest Path+Depencency graph: Miwa et al. (2009)	-	-	**64.2**

Table 4. Performance comparison of kernel-based PPI extraction systems on the AIMed corpus

Comparison of kernel-based PPI extraction systems on the AIMed corpus

Table 4 compares our kernel-based system with other state-of-the-art kernel-based ones on the AIMed corpus using the exactly same 10-fold data splitting. It shows that our individual kernel-based system performs better than all the other individual kernel-based systems on the AIMed corpus. Particularly, our SDP-CPT kernel significantly outperforms the Partial Tree kernel over constituent parse trees (Tikk et al., 2010). It even significantly outperforms the composite kernel combining BOW and constituent parse trees (Miyao et al., 2008). Although our individual kernel performs worse than the composite kernels as adopted by Miyao et al. (2008) and Miwa et al. (2009), the strength of our kernel-based system lies in the simplicity of our shortest dependency path-directed constituent parse tree.

5 Conclusion and Future Work

This paper presents a principled way to automatically generate the constituent parse tree for PPI extraction by making use of the shortest dependency path between two proteins. Although previous research indicates the difficulty of employing constituent parse tree information for PPI extraction due to the relatively long distance between two proteins, our detailed analysis and evaluation indicate that the constituent parse tree can achieve promising results for PPI extraction. Moreover, our dependency-directed constituent parse tree structure provides a general way to automatically determine the constituent parse tree for a wide class of related learning tasks, such as semantic relation extraction, semantic role labeling and even coreference resolution.

For future work, we would like to apply our approach to other NLP tasks. Meanwhile, we will investigate the effect of constituent parse information on dependency-based relational learning in better exploring the synergy between dependency and constituent-based syntactic information.

Acknowledgement

This research is supported by Projects 60873150, 60970056, and 90920004 under the National Natural Science Foundation of China, and the Project BK2010219 under the Provincial Natural Science Foundation of Jiangsu, China.

References

ACE. 2002-2007. The Automatic Content Extraction (ACE) Projects. 2007. http//www.ldc.upenn.edu/ Projects/ACE/.

Airola A., Pyysalo S., Björne J., Pahikkala T., Ginter F. and Salakoski T. 2008. All-paths graph kernel for protein-protein interaction extraction with evaluation of cross corpus learning. *BMC Bioinformatics*.

Bunescu R. and Mooney R. 2005a. Subsequence kernels for relation extraction. In *Proceedings of NIPS'05*: 171–178. December 2005.

Bunescu R. and Mooney R.. 2005b. A shortest path dependency kernel for relation extraction. In *Proceedings of EMNIP'05*: 724–731. Vancover, B.C.

Bunescu R., Ge R., Kate R., Marcotte E., Mooney R., Ramani A. and Wong Y. 2005c. Comparative Experiments on learning information extractors for Proteins and their interactions. *Journal of Artificial Intelligence in Medicine*, 33(2): 139–155.

Buyko E. and Hahn U. 2010. Evaluating the impact of alternative dependency graph encodings on solving event extraction tasks. In *Proceedings of EMNLP'2010*: 982-992.

Collins M. and Duffy N. 2001. Convolution Kernels for Natural Language. *NIPS 2001*: 625-632.

Culotta A. and Sorensen J. 2004. Dependency Tree Kernels for Relation Extraction. In *Proceedings of ACL'04*. July 2004. Barcelona, Spain.

de Marneffe M.-C., MacCartney B. and Manning C. D. 2006. Generating typed dependency parses from phrase structure parses. In *LREC 2006*.

Ding J., Berleant D., Nettleton D. and Wurtele E. 2002. Mining medline: abstracts, sentences, or phrases? *Pacific Symposium on Biocomputing*, pages 326–337.

Erkan G., Ozgur A. and Radev D.R. 2007. Semi-Supervised Classification for Extracting Protein Interaction Sentences using Dependency Parsing, In *Proceedings of EMNLP-CoNLL'07*: 228–237. June, 2007, Prague, Czech.

Fundel K., Kuffner R. and Zimmer R. 2007. Relex—relation extraction using dependency parse trees. *Bioinformatics*, 23(3):365–371.

Giuliano C., Lavelli A. and Romano L. 2006. Exploiting Shallow Linguistic Information for Relation Extraction from Biomedical Literature. In *Proceedings of EACL'06*: 401–408. April, 2006, Trento, Italy.

Haussler D. 1999. Convolution Kernels on Discrete Structures. *Technical Report UCS-CRL-99-10*, University of California, Santa Cruz.

Joachims T. 1998. Text Categorization with Support Vector Machine: learning with many relevant features. *In Proceedings of European Conference on Machine Learning(ECML'1998)*: 137-142.

Kim S., Yoon J., Yang J. and Park S. 2010. Walk-weighted subsequence kernels for protein-protein interaction extraction. *Journal of BMC Bioinformatics*, 2010, 11:107.

Li J., Zhang Z., Li X. and Chen H. 2008. Kernel-Based Learning for Biomedical Relation extraction. *Journal of the American Society for Information Science and Technology*, 59(5):756–769.

Liu B., Qian L.H., Wang H.L. and Zhou G.D. 2010. Dependency-Driven Feature-based Learning for Extracting Protein-Protein Interactions from Biomedical Text. In *Proceedings of COLING'2010*: 757-765 (Poster).

Mitsumori T., Murata M., Fukuda Y., Doi K. and Doi H. 2006. Extracting protein-protein interaction information from biomedical text with SVM. *IEICE Transactions on Information and Systems*, E89-D (8): 2464–2466.

Miwa M., Sætre R., Miyao Y. and Tsujii J. 2009. A Rich Feature Vector for Protein-Protein Interaction Extraction from Multiple Corpora. In *Proceedings of EMNLP'09*: 121–130. August 2-7, 2009, Singapore.

Miyao Y., Sætre R., Sagae K., Matsuzaki T. and Tsujii J. 2008. Task-oriented evaluation of syntactic parsers and their representations. In *Proceedings of the 45th Meeting of the Association for Computational Linguistics (ACL'08: HLT)*: 46-54.

Moschitti A. 2004. A Study on Convolution Kernels for Shallow Semantic Parsing. In *Proceedings of ACL'2004*. July 21-26, 2004. Barcelona, Spain.

Moschitti A., Pighin D. and Basili R. 2008. Tree Kernels for Semantic Role Labeling, Special Issue on Semantic Role Labeling, *Computational Linguistics*. 34(2): 194-224.

Nédellec C. 2005. Learning language in logic-genic interaction extraction challenge. In *Proceedings of the LLL'05 Workshop*.

Nivre J., Hall J., Kubler S., McDonald R., Nilsson J., Riedel S. and Yuret D. 2007. The CoNLL 2007 Shared Task on Dependency Parsing. *EMNLP-CoNLL 2007*: 915–932.

Pyysalo S., Ginter F., Heimonen J., Björne J., Boberg J., Jarvinen J. and Salakoski T. 2007. Biolnfer: A corpus for information extraction in the biomedical domain. *BMC Bioinformatics*, 8:50.

Qian L.H., Zhou G.D., Zhu Q.M. and Qian P.D. 2008. Exploiting constituent dependencies for tree kernel-based semantic relation extraction. *COLING-2008*: 697-704. Manchester, UK.

Surdeanu M., Johansson R., Meyers A., Màrquez L., and Nivre J. 2008. The CoNLL-2008 Shared Task on joint parsing of syntactic and semantic dependencies. *CoNLL'2008*.

Sætre R., Sagae K. and Tsujii J. 2007. Syntactic features for protein-protein interaction extraction. In *Proceedings of LBM'07*, (319): 6.1–6.14.

Tikk D., Thomas P., Palaga P., Hakenberg J. and Leser U. 2010. A Comprehensive Benchmark of Kernel Methods to Extract Protein–Protein Interactions from Literature. *PLoS Computational Biology*, 6(7).

Zelenko D., Aone C. and Richardella A.. 2003. Kernel Methods for Relation Extraction. *Journal of Machine Learning Research*, (2): 1083-1106.

Zhang M., Zhang J., Su J. and Zhou G.D. 2006. A Composite Kernel to Extract Relations between Entities with both Flat and Structured Features. *ACL/COLING-2006*: 825-832. Sydney, Australia.

Zhang M., Che W.X., Zhou G.D., Aw A.T., Tan C.L., Liu T. and Li S. 2008. Semantic Role Labeling using a Grammar-driven Convolution Tree Kernel. *IEEE Transaction on Audio, Speech and Language Processing*. 2008, 16(7): 1315-1329.

Zhao S.B. and Grishman R. 2005. Extracting relations with integrated information using kernel methods. *ACL-2005*: 419-426.

Zhou G.D., Su J., Zhang J. and Zhang M. 2005. Exploring various knowledge in relation extraction. In *Proceedings of ACL'2005*: 427-434. 25-30 June 2005, Ann Arbor, Michigan, USA

Zhou G.D., Zhang M., Ji D.H. and Zhu Q.M. 2007a. Tree Kernel-based Relation Extraction with Context-Sensitive Structured Parse Tree Information. *EMNLP/CoNLL-2007*: 728-736.

Zhou G.D. and Zhang M. 2007b. Extracting relation information from text documents by exploring various types of knowledge. *Information Processing and Management*. 43(2007): 969-982.

Learning Logical Structures of Paragraphs in Legal Articles

Ngo Xuan Bach, Nguyen Le Minh, Tran Thi Oanh, Akira Shimazu
School of Information Science,
Japan Advanced Institute of Science and Technology,
1-1 Asahidai, Nomi, Ishikawa, 923-1292, Japan
{bachnx,nguyenml,oanhtt,shimazu}@jaist.ac.jp

Abstract

This paper presents a new task, learning logical structures of paragraphs in legal articles, which is studied in research on Legal Engineering (Katayama, 2007). The goals of this task are recognizing logical parts of law sentences in a paragraph, and then grouping related logical parts into some logical structures of formulas, which describe logical relations between logical parts. We present a two-phase framework to learn logical structures of paragraphs in legal articles. In the first phase, we model the problem of recognizing logical parts in law sentences as a multi-layer sequence learning problem, and present a CRF-based model to recognize them. In the second phase, we propose a graph-based method to group logical parts into logical structures. We consider the problem of finding a subset of complete sub-graphs in a weighted-edge complete graph, where each node corresponds to a logical part, and a complete sub-graph corresponds to a logical structure. We also present an integer linear programming formulation for this optimization problem. Our models achieve 74.37% in recognizing logical parts, 79.59% in recognizing logical structures, and 55.73% in the whole task on the Japanese National Pension Law corpus.

1 Introduction

Legal Engineering (Katayama, 2007) is a new research field which aims to achieve a trustworthy electronic society. Legal Engineering regards that laws are a kind of software for our society. Specifically, laws such as pension law are specifications for information systems such as pension systems. To achieve a trustworthy society, laws need to be verified about their consistency and contradiction.

Legal texts have some specific characteristics that make them different from other kinds of documents. One of the most important characteristics is that legal texts usually have some specific structures at both sentence and paragraph levels. At the sentence level, a law sentence can roughly be divided into two logical parts: *requisite part* and *effectuation part* (Bach, 2011a; Bach et al., 2011b; Tanaka eta al., 1993). At the paragraph level, a paragraph usually contains a main sentence[1] and one or more subordinate sentences (Takano et al., 2010).

Analyzing logical structures of legal texts is an important task in Legal Engineering. The outputs of this task will be beneficial to people in understanding legal texts. They can easily understand 1) what does a law sentence say? 2) what cases in which the law sentence can be applied? and 3) what subjects are related to the provision described in the law sentence? This task is the preliminary step, which supports other tasks in legal text processing (translating legal articles into logical and formal representations, legal text summarization, legal text translation, question answering in legal domains, etc) and serves legal text verification, an important goal of Legal Engineering.

There have been some studies analyzing logical structures of legal texts. (Bach et al., 2011b) presents the RRE task[2], which recognizes the logical structure of law sentences. (Bach et al., 2010) describes an investigation on contributions of words to the RRE task. (Kimura et al., 2009) focuses on dealing with legal sentences including itemized and referential expressions. These works, however, only analyze logical structures of legal texts at the sentence level. At the paragraph

[1] Usually, the first sentence is the main sentence.

[2] The task of Recognition of Requisite part and Effectuation part in law sentences.

level, (Takano et al., 2010) classifies a legal paragraph into one of six predefined categories: A, B, C, D, E, and F. Among six types, Type A, B, and C correspond to cases in which the main sentence is the first sentence, and subordinate sentences are other sentences. In paragraphs of Type D, E, and F, the main sentence is the first or the second sentence, and a subordinate sentence is an embedded sentence in parentheses within the main sentence.

In this paper, we present a task of learning logical structures of legal articles at the paragraph level. We propose a two-phase framework to complete the task. We also describe experimental results on real legal data.

Our main contributions can be summarized in the following points:

- Introducing a new task to legal text processing, *learning logical structures of paragraphs in legal articles*.
- Presenting an annotated corpus for the task, the *Japanese National Pension Law corpus*.
- Proposing a two-phase framework and providing solutions to solve the task.
- Evaluating our framework on the real annotated corpus.

The rest of this paper is organized as follows. Section 2 describes our task and its two sub-tasks: *recognition of logical parts* and *recognition of logical structures*. In Section 3, we present our framework and proposed solutions. Experimental results on real legal articles are described in Section 4. Finally, Section 5 gives some conclusions.

2 Formulation

Learning logical structures of paragraphs in legal articles is the task of recognition of *logical structures* between *logical parts* in law sentences. A logical structure is usually formed from a pair of a *requisite part* and an *effectuation part*. These two parts are built from other kinds of logical parts such as *topic parts*, *antecedent parts*, *consequent parts*, and so on (Bach, 2011a; Bach et al., 2011b)[3]. Usually, consequent parts describes a law provision, antecedent parts describes cases in which the law provision can be applied, and topic

[3]We only recognize logical structures (a set of related logical parts). The task of translating legal articles into logical and formal representations is not covered in this paper.

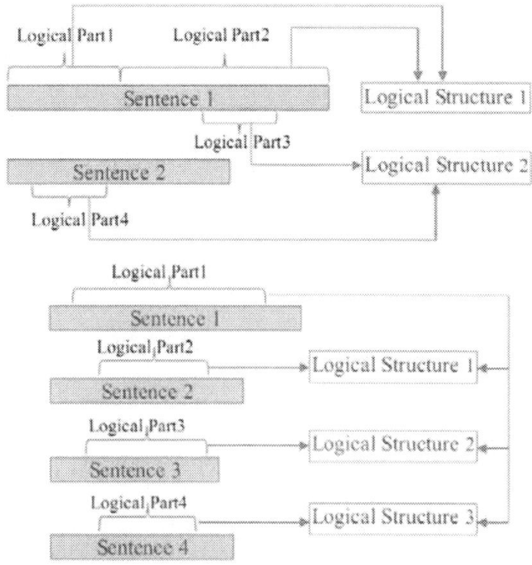

Figure 1: Two cases of inputs and outputs of the task.

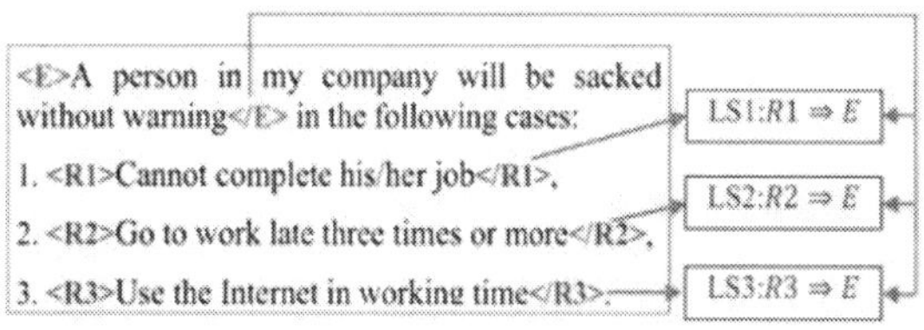

Figure 2: An example in natural language (E means *Effectuation part*, R means *Requisite part*, and LS means *Logical Structure*).

parts describe subjects which are related to the law provision. In this paper, a logical structure can be defined as a set of some related logical parts.

Figure 1 shows two cases of the inputs and outputs of the task. In the first case, the input is a paragraph of two sentences, and the outputs are four logical parts, which are grouped into two logical structures. In the second case, the input is a paragraph consisting of four sentences, and the outputs are four logical parts, which are grouped into three logical structures. An example in natural language[4] is presented in Figure 2.

2.1 Sub-Task 1: Recognition of Logical Parts

Let s be a law sentence in the law sentence space S, then s can be represented by a sequence of words $s = [w_1 w_2 \ldots w_n]$. A legal paragraph x in the legal paragraph space X is a sequence of law sentences $x = [s_1 s_2 \ldots s_l]$, where $s_i \in S, \forall i = 1, 2, \ldots, l$. For each paragraph x, we denote a log-

[4]Because law sentences are very long and complicated, we use toy sentences to illustrate the task.

ical part p by a quad-tuple $p = (b, e, k, c)$ where b, e, and k are three integers which indicate *position of the beginning word, position of the end word*, and *sentence position* of p, and c is a logical part category in the set of predefined categories C. Formally, the set P of all possible logical parts defined in a paragraph x can be described as follows:

$P = \{(b, e, k, c) | 1 \leq k \leq l, 1 \leq b \leq e \leq len(k), c \in C\}$.

In the above definition, l is the number of sentences in the paragraph x, and $len(k)$ is the length of the kth sentence.

In this sub-task, we want to recognize some *non-overlapping* (but possibly *embedded*) logical parts in an input paragraph. A solution for this task is a subset $y \subseteq P$ which does not violate the *overlapping* relationship. We say that two logical parts p_1 and p_2 are *overlapping* if and only if they are in the same sentence ($k_1 = k_2$) and $b_1 < b_2 \leq e_1 < e_2$ or $b_2 < b_1 \leq e_2 < e_1$. We denote the *overlapping* relationship by $\sim$. We also say that p_1 is *embedded* in p_2 if and only if they are in the same sentence ($k_1 = k_2$) and $b_2 \leq b_1 \leq e_1 \leq e_2$, and denote the *embedded* relationship by $\prec$. Formally, the solution space can be described as follows: $Y = \{y \subseteq P | \forall u, v \in y, u \not\sim v\}$. The learning problem in this sub-task is to learn a function $R : X \rightarrow Y$ from a set of m training samples $\{(x^i, y^i) | x^i \in X, y^i \in Y, \forall i = 1, 2, \ldots, m\}$.

In our task, we consider the following types of logical parts:

1. An antecedent part is denoted by A
2. A consequent part is denoted by C
3. A topic part which depends on the antecedent part is denoted by T_1
4. A topic part which depends on the consequent part is denoted by T_2
5. A topic part which depends on both the antecedent part and the consequent part is denoted by T_3
6. The left part of an equivalent statement is denoted by EL
7. The right part of an equivalent statement is denoted by ER
8. An object part, whose meaning is defined differently in different cases, is denoted by Ob
9. An original replacement part, which will be replaced by other replacement parts (denoted by $RepR$) in specific cases, is denoted by $RepO$.

Compared with previous works (Bach et al., 2011b), we introduce three new kinds of logical parts: Ob, $RepO$, and $RepR$.

2.2 Sub-Task 2: Recognition of Logical Structures

In the second sub-task, the goal is to recognize a set of logical structures given a set of logical parts.

Let $G =< V, E >$ be a complete undirected graph with the vertex set V and the edge set E. A real value function f is defined on E as follows:

$f : E \rightarrow R, e \in E \mapsto f(e) \in R$.

In this sub-task, each vertex of the graph corresponds to a logical part, and a complete sub-graph corresponds to a logical structure. The value on an edge connecting two vertices expresses the degree that the two vertices belong to one logical structure. The positive (negative) value means that two vertices are likely (not likely) to belong to one logical structure.

Let G_s be a complete sub-graph of G, then $v(G_s)$ and $e(G_s)$ are the set of vertices and the set of edges of G_s, respectively. We define the total value of a sub-graph as follows:

$f(G_s) = f(e(G_s)) = \sum_{e \in e(G_s)} f(e)$.

Let Ω be the set of all complete sub-graphs of G. The problem becomes determining a subset $\Psi \subseteq \Omega$ that satisfies the following constraints:

1. $\forall g \in \Psi, |v(g)| \geq 2$,
2. $\cup_{g \in \Psi} v(g) = V$,
3. $\forall g_1, g_2 \in \Psi | v(g_1) \subseteq v(g_2) \Rightarrow v(g_1) = v(g_2)$,
4. $\forall g \in \Psi, \cup_{h \in \Psi, h \neq g} v(h) \neq V$, and
5. $\sum_{g \in \Psi} f(g) \rightarrow$ maximize.

Constraint 1), *minimal constraint*, says that each logical structure must contain at least two logical parts. There is the case that a logical structure contains only a consequent part. Due to the characteristics of Japanese law sentences, however, our corpus does not contain such cases. A logical structure which contains a consequent part will also contain a topic part or an antecedent part or both of them. So a logical structure contains at least two logical parts. Constraint 2), *complete constraint*, says that each logical part must belong to at least one logical structure. Constraint 3), *maximal constraint*, says that we cannot have two different logical structures such that the set of logical parts in one logical structure contains the set of logical parts in the other logical structure. Constraint 4), *significant constraint*, says that if we remove any logical structure from the solution, Constraint 2) will be violated. Although Constraint 3) is guaranteed by Constraint 4), we introduce it because of its importance.

3 Proposed Solutions

3.1 Multi-layer Sequence Learning for Logical Part Recognition

This sub-section presents our model for recognizing logical parts. We consider the recognition problem as a multi-layer sequence learning problem. First, we give some related notions.

Let s be a law sentence, and P be the set of logical parts of s, $P = \{p_1, p_2, \ldots, p_m\}$. $Layer^1(s)$ (outer most layer) is defined as a set of logical parts in P, which are not embedded in any other part. $Layer^i(s)$ is defined as a set of logical parts in $P \backslash \cup_{k=1}^{i-1} Layer^k(s)$, which are not embedded in any other part in $P \backslash \cup_{k=1}^{i-1} Layer^k(s)$. Formally, we have:

$Layer^1(s) = \{p | p \in P, p \not\prec q, \forall q \in P, q \neq p\}$.

$Layer^i(s) = \{p | p \in Q^i, p \not\prec q, \forall q \in Q^i, q \neq p\}$, where

$Q^i = P \backslash \cup_{k=1}^{i-1} Layer^k(s)$

Figure 3 illustrates a law sentence with four logical parts in three layers: Part 1 and Part 2 in $Layer^1$, Part 3 in $Layer^2$, and Part 4 in $Layer^3$.

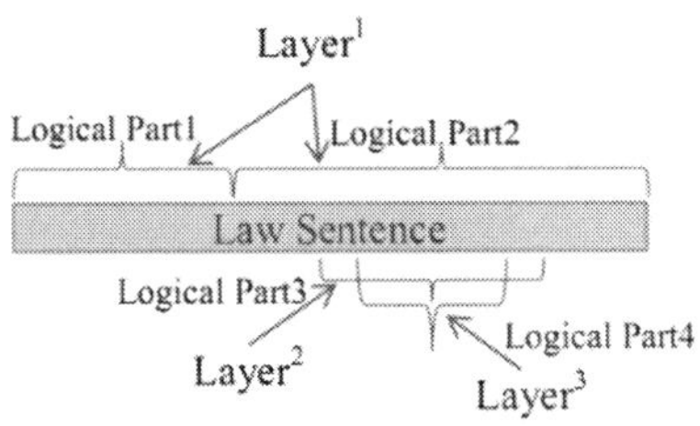

Figure 3: A law sentence with logical parts in three layers.

Input Sentence	w_1	w_2	...	w_{k-1}	w_k	w_{k+1}	w_{k+2}	...	w_{n-1}	w_n
$Layer^1$	Topic Part 2 (T_2)					Consequence Part (C)				
$Layer^2$							Left Side Part (EL)			
Labels in $Layer^1$	I-T_2	I-T_2	...	I-T_2	E-T_2	I-C	I-C	...	I-C	E-C
Labels in $Layer^2$						O	I-EL	...	E-EL	O

Figure 4: An example of labeling in the multi-layer model.

Let K be the number of layers in a law sentence s, our model will recognize logical parts in K steps. In the kth step we recognize logical parts in $Layer^k$. In each layer, we model the recognition problem as a sequence labeling task in which each word is an element. Logical parts in $Layer^{i-1}$ will be used as input sequence in the ith step (in the first step, we use original sentence as input).

Figure 4 gives an example of labeling for an input sentence. The sentence consists of three logical parts in two layers. In our model, we use IOE tag setting: the last element of a part is tagged with E, the other elements of a part are tagged with I, and an element not included in any part is tagged with O.

Let K^* be the maximum number of layers in all law sentences in training data. We learn K^* models, in which the kth model is learned from logical parts in the $Layer^k$ of training data, using Conditional random fields (Lafferty et al., 2001; Kudo, CRF toolkit). In the testing phase, we first apply the first model to the input law sentence, and then apply the ith model to the predicted logical parts in $Layer^{i-1}$.

3.2 ILP for Recognizing Logical Structures

Suppose that G' is a sub-graph of G such that G' contains all the vertices of G and the degree of each vertex in G' is greater than zero, then the set of all the maximal complete sub-graphs (or cliques) of G' will satisfy all the *minimal*, *complete*, *maximal*, and *significant* constraints. We also note that, a set of cliques that satisfies all these four constraints will form a sub-graph that has two properties like properties of G'.

Let Λ be the set of all such sub-graphs G' of G, the sub-task now consists of two steps:

1. Finding $G' = argmax_{G' \in \Lambda} f(G')$, and
2. Finding all cliques of G'.

Each clique found in the second step will correspond to a logical structure.

Recently, some researches have shown that integer linear programming (ILP) formulations is an effective way to solve many NLP problems such as semantic role labeling (Punyakanok, 2004), coreference resolution (Denis and Baldridge, 2007), summarization (Clarke and Lapata, 2008), dependency parsing (Martins et al., 2009), and so on. The advantage of ILP formulations is that we can incorporate non-local features or global constraints easily, which are difficult in traditional algorithms. Although solving an ILP is NP-hard in general, some fast algorithms and available tools[5]

[5] We used *lp-solve* from http://lpsolve.sourceforge.net/

make it a practical solution for many NLP problems (Martins et al., 2009).

In this work, we exploit ILP to solve the first step. Let N be the number of vertices of G, we introduce a set of integer variables $\{x_{ij}\}_{1 \leq i < j \leq N}$. The values of $\{x_{ij}\}$ are set as follows. If $(i, j) \in e(G')$ then $x_{ij} = 1$, otherwise $x_{ij} = 0$. ILP formulations for the first step can be described as follows:

//- - - - - - - - Objective function - - - - - - - -//

$$Maximize: \sum_{1 \leq i < j \leq N} f(i,j) * x_{ij} \quad (1)$$

//- - - - - - - - - - Constraints - - - - - - - - - -//

$$Integer: \{x_{ij}\}_{1 \leq i < j \leq N}. \quad (2)$$

$$0 \leq x_{ij} \leq 1, (1 \leq i < j \leq N). \quad (3)$$

$$\sum_{i=1}^{j-1} x_{ij} + \sum_{k=j+1}^{N} x_{jk} \geq 1, (1 \leq j \leq N). \quad (4)$$

The last constraint guarantees that there is at least one edge connecting to each vertex in G'.

The second step, finding all cliques of an undirected graph, is a famous problem in graph theory. Many algorithms have been proposed to solve this problem efficiently. In this work, we exploit the Bron-Kerbosch algorithm, a backtracking algorithm. The main idea of the Bron-Kerbosch algorithm is using a branch-and-bound technique to stop searching on branches that cannot lead to a clique (Bron and Kerbosch, 1973).

The remaining problem is how to define the value function f. Our solution is that, first we learn a binary classifier C using maximum entropy model. This classifier takes a pair of logical parts as the input, and outputs $+1$ if two logical parts belong to one logical structure, otherwise it will output -1. Then, we define the value function f for two logical parts as follows:

$f(p_1, p_2) = Prob(C(p_1, p_2) = +1) - 0.5.$

Function f will receive a value from -0.5 to $+0.5$, and it equals to zero in the case that the classifier assigns the same probability to $+1$ and -1.

4 Experiments

4.1 Corpus

We have built a corpus, Japanese National Pension Law (JNPL) corpus, which consists of 83 legal articles[6] of Japanese national pension law. The architecture of JNPL is shown in Figure 5. The law

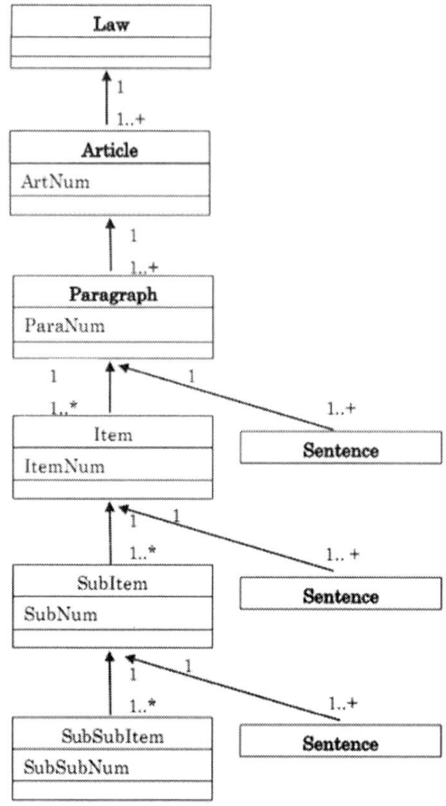

Figure 5: The architecture of JNPL.

consists of articles, articles consist of paragraphs, and paragraphs contain sentences. A sentence may belong to items, sub-items, or sub-sub-items of a paragraph.

Figure 6 illustrates the relationship between a law sentence and logical parts. A law sentence may contain some logical parts, and a logical part may be embedded in another one.

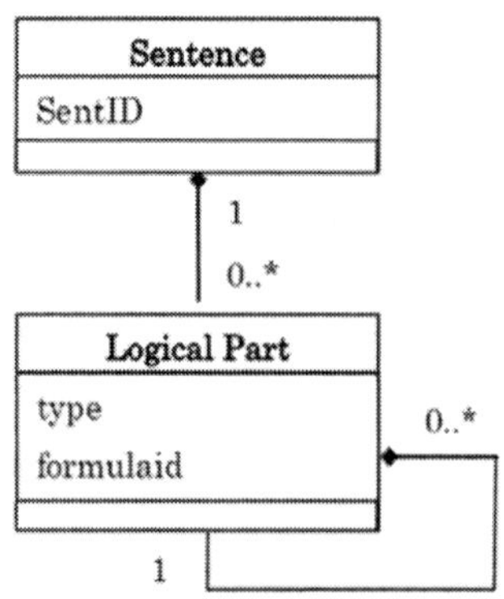

Figure 6: Relationship between a sentence and logical parts.

In our corpus, a logical part is annotated with information about its *type* (kind of part) and *formula-id* (logical parts with the same id will be-

[6]Because building corpus is an expensive and time-consuming task, we only annotate a part of JNPL.

```
<Sentence sentID="1">
<Part type="T2" formula-id="1">
    政府は、
</Part>
<Part type="C" formula-id="1">
    政令の定めるところにより，
    <Part type="C" formula-id="2">
        市町村
    </Part>
   (<Part type="A" formula-id="2">
        特別区
    </Part>
    を含む。以下同じ。)に対し、市町村長がこの法律又はこの法
    律に基づく政令の規定によって行う事務の処理に必要な費用を
    交付する。
</Part>
</Sentence>
```

Figure 7: An annotated sentence in the JNPL corpus. The sentence contains two logical structures with four logical parts.

long to one logical structure). An example of annotated sentence in the JNPL corpus is shown in Figure 7.

We employed two people in a data-making company, who analyzed and annotated our corpus. The corpus consists of 83 legal articles, which contain 119 paragraphs with 426 sentences. On average, each paragraph consists of 3.6 sentences. The total number of logical parts is 807, and the number of logical structures is 351. On average, each paragraph consists of 6.8 logical parts and 3 logical structures.

Table 1 shows some statistics on the number of logical parts of each type. Main types of parts are $A(35.4\%)$, $C(30.7\%)$, $T_2(14.1\%)$, $ER(7.1\%)$, and $EL(6.8\%)$. Five main types of parts make up more than 94% of all types.

4.2 Evaluation Methods

We divided the JNLP corpus into 10 sets, and conducted 10-fold cross-validation tests. For the first sub-task, we evaluated the performance of our system by precision, recall, and F_1 scores as follows:

$$precision = \frac{|correct\ parts|}{|predicted\ parts|},\ recall = \frac{|correct\ parts|}{|actual\ parts|},$$
$$F_1 = \frac{2*precision*recall}{precision+recall}.$$

For the second sub-task, we used MUC precision, recall, and F_1 scores as described in (Vilain et al., 1995). We summarize them here for clarity.

Let $P_1, P_2, \ldots, P_n$ be n predicted logical structures, and $G_1, G_2, \ldots, G_m$ be the correct answers or gold logical structures. To calculate recall, for each gold logical structure $G_i (i = 1, 2, \ldots, m)$, let $k(G_i)$ be the smallest number such that there exist $k(G_i)$ predicted structures $P_1^i, P_2^i, \ldots, P_{k(G_i)}^i$ which satisfy $G_i \subseteq \cup_{j=1}^{k(G_i)} P_j^i$:

$$recall = \frac{\sum_{i=1}^{m}(|G_i|-k(G_i))}{\sum_{i=1}^{m}(|G_i|-1)}.$$

To calculate precision, we switch the roles of predicted structures and gold structures. Finally, F_1 score is computed in a similar manner as in the first sub-task.

4.3 Experiments on Sub-Task 1

4.3.1 Baseline: Filter-Ranking Perceptron Algorithm

We chose the Filter-Ranking (FR) Perceptron algorithm proposed by (Carreras and Marquez, 2005; Carreras et al., 2002) as our baseline model because of its effectiveness on phrase recognition problems, especially on problems that accept the *embedded* relationship[7]. We use FR-perceptron algorithm to recognize logical parts in law sentences one by one in an input paragraph.

For *beginning/end* predictors, we got features of words, POS tags, and Bunsetsu[8] tags in a window size 2. Moreover, with *beginning* predictor, we used a feature for checking whether this position is the beginning of the sentence or not. Similarly, with *end* predictor, we use a feature for checking whether this position is the end of the sentence or not.

With each logical part candidate, we extract following kinds of features:

1. Length of the part
2. Internal structure: this feature is the concatenation of the top logical parts, punctuation marks, parenthesis, and quotes inside the candidate. An example about internal structure may be $(A+, +C+.)$ (plus is used to concatenate items)
3. Word (POS) uni-gram, word (POS) bi-gram, and word (POS) tri-gram.

4.3.2 Experimental Results

In our experiments, we focus on paragraphs in Type A, B, and C defined in (Takano et al., 2010). In these types, the first sentence is the main sentence, which usually contains more logical parts than other sentences. The other sentences often have a few logical parts, and in most cases these logical parts only appear in one layer. The first

[7]We re-implement the FR-perceptron algorithm by ourself.

[8]In Japanese, a Bunsetsu is an unit of sentence which is similar to a chunk in English.

Table 1: Statistics on logical parts of the JNPL corpus

Logical Part	C	A	T_1	T_2	T_3	EL	ER	Ob	RepO	RepR
Number	248	286	0	114	12	55	57	9	12	14

Table 2: Experimental results for Sub-task 1 on the JNLP corpus(W:Word; P: POS tag; B: Bunsetsu tag)

Model	Prec(%)	Recall(%)	F_1(%)
Baseline	**79.70**	52.54	63.33
W	79.18	69.27	73.89
W+P	77.62	68.77	72.93
W+B	79.63	**69.76**	**74.37**
W+P+B	77.89	69.39	73.39

Table 3: Experimental results in more details

Logical Part	Prec(%)	Recall(%)	F_1(%)
C	**83.41**	**75.00**	**78.98**
EL	76.74	60.00	67.35
ER	41.94	22.81	29.55
Ob	0.00	0.00	0.00
A	**80.42**	**80.42**	**80.42**
RepO	100	16.67	28.57
RepR	100	28.57	44.44
T_2	**83.64**	**80.70**	**82.14**
T_3	60.00	25.00	35.29
Overall	**79.63**	**69.76**	**74.37**

sentences usually contain logical parts in two layers.

We divided sentences into two groups. The first group consists of the first sentences in paragraphs, and the second group consists of other sentences. We set the number of layers k to 2 for sentences in the first group, and to 1 for sentences in the second group. To learn sequence labeling models, we used CRFs (Lafferty et al., 2001; Kudo, CRF toolkit).

Experimental results on the JNPL corpus are described in Table 2. We conducted experiments with four feature sets: words; words and POS tags; words and Bunsetsu tags; and words, POS tags, and Bunsetsu tags. To extract features from source sentences, we used the CaboCha tool (Kudo, Cabocha), a Japanese morphological and syntactic analyzer. The best model (word and Bunsetsu tag features) achieved 74.37% in F_1 score. It improves 11.04% in F_1 score (30.11% in error rate) compared with the baseline model.

Table 3 shows experimental results of our best model in more detail. Our model got good results on most main parts: C(78.98%), A(80.42%), and T_2(82.14%). The model got low results on the other types of parts. It is understandable because three types of logical parts C, A, and T_2 make up more than 80%, while six other types only make up 20% of all types.

4.4 Experiments on Sub-Task 2

4.4.1 Baseline: a Heuristic Algorithm

Our baseline is a heuristic algorithm to solve this sub-task on graphs. This is an approximate algorithm which satisfies *minimal*, *complete*, *maximal*, and *significant* constraints. The main idea of our algorithm is picking up as many positive edges as possible, and as few negative edges as possible. We consider two cases: 1) There is no positive value edge on the input graph; and 2) There are some positive value edges on the input graph.

In the first case, because all the edges have negative values, we build logical structures with as few logical parts as possible. In this case, each logical structure contains exactly two logical parts. So we gradually choose two nodes in the graph with the maximum value on the edge connecting them. An example of the first case is illustrated in Figure 8. The maximum value on an edge is -0.1, so the first logical structure will contain node 1 and node 3. The second logical structure contains node 2 and node 4[9].

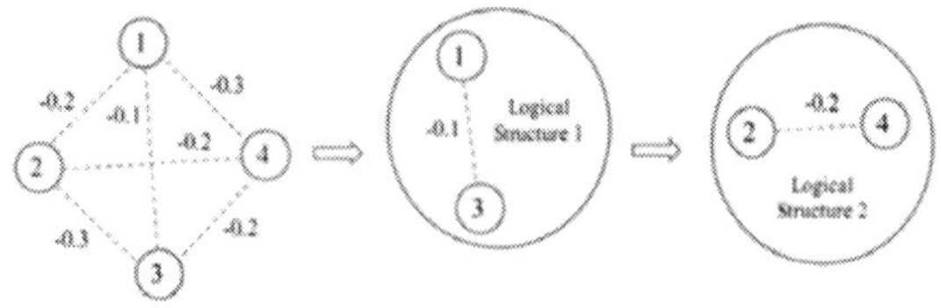

Figure 8: An example of the first case.

In the second case, we first consider the sub-graph which only contains non-negative value edges. In this sub-graph, we repeatedly build logical structures with as many logical parts as possi-

[9]If the number of nodes is odd, the final logical structure will consist of the final node and another node, so that the edge connecting them has the maximal value.

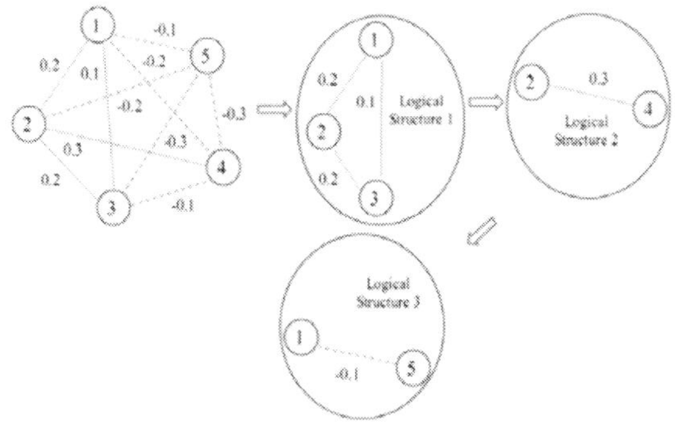

Figure 9: An example of the second case.

Table 4: Experiments on Sub-task 2

	Gold Input Setting		
Model	Prec(%)	Recall(%)	F_1(%)
Heuristic	**81.24**	71.19	75.89
ILP	76.56	**82.87**	**79.59**
	End-to-End Setting		
Model	Prec(%)	Recall(%)	F_1(%)
Heuristic	54.88	47.84	51.12
ILP	**57.51**	**54.06**	**55.73**

ble. After building successfully a logical structure, we remove all the nodes and the edges according to it on the graph. When have no positive edge, we will build logical structures with exactly two logical parts.

An example of the second case is illustrated in Figure 9. First, we consider the sub-graph with positive edges. This sub-graph consists of five nodes $\{1, 2, 3, 4, 5\}$ and four edges $\{(1, 2), (1, 3), (2, 3), (2, 4)\}$. First, we have a logical structure with three nodes $\{1, 2, 3\}$. We remove these nodes and the positive edges connecting to these nodes. We have two nodes $\{4, 5\}$ with no positive edges. Now we build logical structures with exactly two nodes. We consider node 4. Among edges connecting to node 4, the edge $(2, 4)$ has maximal value. So we have the second logical structure with two nodes $\{2, 4\}$. Next, we consider node 5, and we have the third logical structure with two nodes $\{1, 5\}$.

4.4.2 Experimental Results

In our experiments, to learn a maximum entropy binary classification we used the implementation of Tsuruoka (Tsuruoka, MEM). With a pair of logical parts, we extracted the following features (and combinations of them):

- Categories of two parts.
- Layers of two parts.
- The positions of the sentences that contain two parts (the first sentence or not).
- Categories of other parts in the input paragraph.

We conducted experiments on this sub-task in two settings. In the first setting, we used annotated logical parts (gold inputs) as the inputs to the system. The purpose of this experiment is to evaluate the performance of the graph-based method on Sub-task 2. In the second setting, predicted logical parts (end-to-end) outputted by the Sub-task 1 were used as the inputs to the system. The purpose of this experiment is to evaluate the performance of our framework on the whole task.

In the second setting, end-to-end setting, because input logical parts may differ from the correct logical parts, we need to modify the MUC scores. Let $P_1, P_2, \ldots, P_n$ be n predicted logical structures, and $G_1, G_2, \ldots, G_m$ be the gold logical structures. For each gold logical structure $G_i (i = 1, 2, \ldots, m)$, let D_i be the set of logical parts in G_i which are not included in the set of input logical parts. $D_i = \{p \in G_i | p \notin \cup_{j=1}^{n} P_j\}$. Let $k(G_i)$ be the smallest number such that there exist $k(G_i)$ predicted structures $P_1^i, P_2^i, \ldots, P_{k(G_i)}^i$ which satisfy $G_i \subseteq (\cup_{j=1}^{k(G_i)} P_j^i) \cup D_i$.

$recall = \frac{\sum_{i=1}^{m}(|G_i|-|D_i|-k(G_i))}{\sum_{i=1}^{m}(|G_i|-1)}$.

To calculate the precision, we switch the roles of predicted structures and gold structures.

Table 4 shows experimental results on the second sub-task. The ILP model outperformed the baseline model in both settings. It improved 3.70% in the F_1 score (15.35% in error rate) in the gold-input setting, and 4.61% in the F_1 score (9.43% in error rate) in the end-to-end setting compared with the baseline model (heuristic algorithm).

5 Conclusion

We have introduced the task of learning logical structures of paragraphs in legal articles, a new task which has been studied in research on Legal Engineering. We presented the Japanese National Pension Law corpus, an annotated corpus of real legal articles for the task. We also described a two-phase framework with multi-layer sequence learning model and ILP formulation to complete the task. Our results provide a baseline for further researches on this interesting task.

In the future, we will continue to improve this task. On the other hand, we also investigate the task of translating legal articles into logical and formal representations.

Acknowledgments

This work was partly supported by the 21st Century COE program 'Verifiable and Evolvable e-Society', Grant-in-Aid for Scientific Research, Education and Research Center for Trustworthy e-Society, and JAIST Overseas Training Program for 3D Program Students.

We would like to give special thanks to Kenji Takano and Yoshiko Oyama, who analyzed law sentences and built the corpus, and the reviewers, who gave us valuable comments.

References

N.X. Bach. 2011a. A Study on Recognition of Requisite Part and Effectuation Part in Law Sentences. *Master Thesis*, School of Information Science, Japan Advanced Institute of Science and Technology.

N.X. Bach, N.L. Minh, A. Shimazu. 2011b. RRE Task: The Task of Recognition of Requisite Part and Effectuation Part in Law Sentences. In *International Journal of Computer Processing Of Languages (IJCPOL)*, Volume 23, Number 2.

N.X. Bach, N.L. Minh, A. Shimazu. 2010. Exploring Contributions of Words to Recognition of Requisite Part and Effectuation Part in Law Sentences. In *Proceedings of JURISIN*, pp. 121-132.

C. Bron and J. Kerbosch. 1973. Algorithm 457: Finding All Cliques of an Undirected Graph. In *Communications of the ACM, Volume 16, Issue 9*, pp. 575-577.

X. Carreras and L. Marquez. 2005. Filtering-Ranking Perceptron Learning for Partial Parsing. In *Machine Learning*, Volume 60, Issue 1-3, pp. 41-71.

X. Carreras, L. Marquez, V. Punyakanok, D. Roth. 2002. Learning and Inference for Clause Identification. In *Proceedings of ECML*, pp. 35-47.

J. Clarke and M. Lapata. 2008. Global Inference for Sentence Compression: An Integer Linear Programming Approach. In *Journal of Artificial Intelligence Research (JAIR)*, Volume 31, pp. 399-429.

P. Denis and J. Baldridge. 2007. Joint Determination of Anaphoricity and Coreference Resolution Using Integer Programming. In *Proceedings of HLT-NAACL*, pp. 236-243.

T. Katayama. 2007. Legal Engineering - An Engineering Approach to Laws in e-Society Age. In *Proceedings of JURISIN.*

Y. Kimura, M. Nakamura, A. Shimazu. Treatment of Legal Sentences Including Itemized and Referential Expressions - Towards Translation into Logical Forms. *New Frontiers in Artificial Intelligence*, volume 5447 of LNAI, pp.242-253.

T. Kudo. Yet Another Japanese Dependency Structure Analyzer. *http://chasen.org/taku/software/cabocha/.*

T. Kudo. CRF++: Yet Another CRF toolkit. *http://crfpp.sourceforge.net/.*

J. Lafferty, A. McCallum, F. Pereira. 2001. Conditional Random Fields: Probabilistic Models for Segmenting and Labeling Sequence Data. In *Proceedings of ICML*, pp.282-289.

A.F.T. Martins, N.A. Smith, E.P. Xing. 2009. Concise Integer Linear Programming Formulations for Dependency Parsing. In *Proceedings of ACL*, pp.342-350.

M. Nakamura, S. Nobuoka, A. Shimazu. 2007. Towards Translation of Legal Sentences into Logical Forms. In *Proceedings of JURISIN.*

V. Punyakanok, D. Roth, W. Yih, D. Zimak. 2004. Semantic Role Labeling Via Integer Linear Programming Inference. In *Proceedings of COLING*, pp. 1346-1352.

K. Takano, M. Nakamura, Y. Oyama, A. Shimazu. 2010. Semantic Analysis of Paragraphs Consisting of Multiple Sentences - Towards Development of a Logical Formulation System. In *Proceedings of JURIX*, pp. 117-126.

K. Tanaka, I. Kawazoe, H. Narita. 1993 Standard Structure of Legal Provisions - for the Legal Knowledge Processing by Natural Language - (in Japanese). In *IPSJ Research Report on Natural Language Processing*, pp. 79-86.

Y. Tsuruoka. A simple C++ library for maximum entropy classification. *http://www-tsujii.is.s.u-tokyo.ac.jp/ tsuruoka/maxent/.*

M. Vilain, J. Burger, J. Aberdeen, D. Connolly, L. Hirschman. 1995. A Model-Theoretic Coreference Scoring Scheme. In *Proceedings of MUC-6*, pp. 45-52.

Extracting Pre-ordering Rules from Predicate-Argument Structures

Xianchao Wu, Katsuhito Sudoh, Kevin Duh, Hajime Tsukada, Masaaki Nagata
NTT Communication Science Laboratories, NTT Corporation
2-4 Hikaridai Seika-cho, Soraku-gun Kyoto 619-0237 Japan
{wu.xianchao,sudoh.katsuhito,kevin.duh,tsukada.hajime,nagata.masaaki}@lab.ntt.co.jp

Abstract

Word ordering remains as an essential problem for translating between languages with substantial structural differences, such as SOV and SVO languages. In this paper, we propose to automatically extract pre-ordering rules from predicate-argument structures. A pre-ordering rule records the relative position mapping of *a predicate word* and its *argument phrases* from the source language side to the target language side. We propose 1) a linear-time algorithm to extract the pre-ordering rules from word-aligned HPSG-tree-to-string pairs and 2) a bottom-up algorithm to apply the extracted rules to HPSG trees to yield target language style source sentences. Experimental results are reported for large-scale English-to-Japanese translation, showing significant improvements of BLEU score compared with the baseline SMT systems.

1 Introduction

Statistical machine translation (SMT) suffers from an essential problem for translating between languages with substantial structural differences, such as between English which is a subject-verb-object (SVO) language and Japanese which is a typical subject-object-verb (SOV) language.

Numerous approaches have been consequently proposed to tackle this word-order problem, such as lexicalized reordering methods, syntax-based models, and pre-ordering ways. First, in order to overcome the shortages of traditional distance based distortion models (Brown et al., 1993; Koehn et al., 2007), phrase dependent lexicalized reordering models were proposed by several researchers (Tillman, 2004; Kumar and Byrne, 2005). Lexicalized reordering models learn local orientations (monotone or reordering) with probabilities for each bilingual phrase from the training data. For example, by taking lexical information as features, a maximum entropy phrase reordering model was proposed by Xiong et al. (2006).

Second, syntax-based models attempt to solve the word ordering problem by employing syntactic structures. For example, linguistically syntax-based approaches (Galley et al., 2004; Liu et al., 2006) first parse source and/or target sentences and then learn reordering templates from the subtree fragments of the parse trees. In contrast, hierarchical phrase based translation (Chiang, 2005) is a formally syntax-based approach which can automatically extract hierarchical ordering rules from aligned string-string pairs without using additional parsers. These approaches have been proved to be both algorithmically appealing and empirically successful.

However, most of current syntax-based SMT systems use IBM models (Brown et al., 1993) and hidden Markov model (HMM) (Vogel et al., 1996) to generate word alignments. These models have a penalty parameter associated with long distance jumps, and tend to misalign words which move far from the window sizes of their expected positions (Xu et al., 2009; Genzel, 2010).

The third type tackles the word-order problem in pre-ordering ways. Through the usage of a sequence of pre-ordering rules, the word order of an original source sentence is (approximately) changed into the word order of the target sentence. Here, the pre-ordering rules can be manually or automatically extracted. For manual extraction of pre-ordering rules, linguistic background and expertise are required for predetermined language pairs, such as for German-English (Collins et al., 2005), Chinese-to-English (Wang et al., 2007), Japanese-to-English (Katz-Brown and Collins, 2007), and English-to-SOV languages (Xu et al., 2009).

Specially, for English-to-Japanese translation, Isozaki et al. (2010b) proposed to move syntactic or semantic heads to the end of corresponding phrases or clauses so that to yield head finalized English (HFE) sentences which follow the word order of Japanese. The head information of an English sentence is detected by a head-driven phrase structure grammar (HPSG) parser, Enju[1] (Miyao and Tsujii, 2008). In addition, transformation rules were manually written for appending particle seed words, refining POS tags to be used before parsing, and deleting English determiners. Due to the usage of the same parser, we take this HFE approach as one of our baseline systems.

The goal in this paper, however, is to learn pre-ordering rules from parallel data in an *automatic* way. Under this motivation, pre-ordering rules can be extracted in a language-independent manner. A number of researches follow this automatic way. For example, in (Xia and McCord, 2004), a variety of heuristic rules were applied to bilingual parse trees to extract pre-ordering rules for French-English translation. Rottmann and Vogen (2007) learned reordering rules based on sequences of part-of-speech (POS) tags, instead of parse trees. Dependency trees were used by Genzel (2010) to extract source-side reordering rules for translating languages from SVO to SOV, etc..

The novel idea expressed in this paper is that, predicate-argument structures (PASs) are introduced to extract fine-grained pre-ordering rules. PASs have the following merits for describing reordering phenomena:

- predicate words and argument phrases respectively record reordering phenomena in a *lexicalized level* and an *abstract level*;
- PASs provide a *fine-grained classification* of the reordering phenomena since they include factored representations of syntactic features of the predicate words and their argument phrases.

The idea of using PASs for pre-ordering follows (Komachi et al., 2006). Several reordering operations were manually designed by Komachi et al. (2006) to pre-ordering Japanese sentences into SVO-style English sentences. For comparison, our proposal 1) makes use of not only PASs but also the source syntactic tree structures for pre-ordering rule matching, 2) extracts pre-ordering rules in an automatic way, and 3) use factored representations of syntactic features to refine the pre-ordering rules.

Following (Wu et al., 2010a; Isozaki et al., 2010b), we use the HPSG parser Enju to generate the PASs of English sentences. HPSG (Pollard and Sag, 1994) is a lexicalist grammar framework. In HPSG, linguistic entities such as words and phrases are represented by a data structure called a *sign*. A sign gives a factored representation of the syntactic features of a word/phrase, as well as a representation of their *semantic content* which corresponds to PASs.

In order to record the relative positions among a predicate word and its argument phrases, we propose a linear-time algorithm to extract pre-ordering rules from word-aligned HPSG-tree-to-string pairs[2]. The syntactic features included in signs and the types of PASs enable us to extract fine-grained pre-ordering rules and thus make it easier to select appropriate rules for given source HPSG trees. We further propose a bottom-up algorithm to apply the extracted rules to HPSG trees to pre-order source sentences. Using the pre-ordered source sentences, we retrain word alignments again.

The remaining of this paper is organized as follows. In the next section, we describe the algorithms guided by using a real example for extracting and applying PAS-based pre-ordering rules. Then, we design experiments on large-scale English-to-Japanese translation to testify our proposal. Employing Moses (Koehn et al., 2007), we show that our proposal can significantly improve BLEU scores of 2.47$\sim$3.15 points compared with using the original English sentences. We finally conclude this paper by summarizing our proposal and the experiment results.

2 Pre-ordering Rule Extraction and Application

2.1 An example

Figure 1 shows a word-aligned HPSG-tree-to-string pair for English-to-Japanese translation. PASs among lexical nodes and their argument nodes in this HPSG tree are described by arrows in thick-lines. For simplicity, we only draw the identifiers for the signs of the nodes in the HPSG tree. Note that the identifiers that start with 'c'

[1] http://www-tsujii.is.s.u-tokyo.ac.jp/enju/index.html

[2] These word alignments are gained by running GIZA++ (Och and Ney, 2003) on the original parallel sentences.

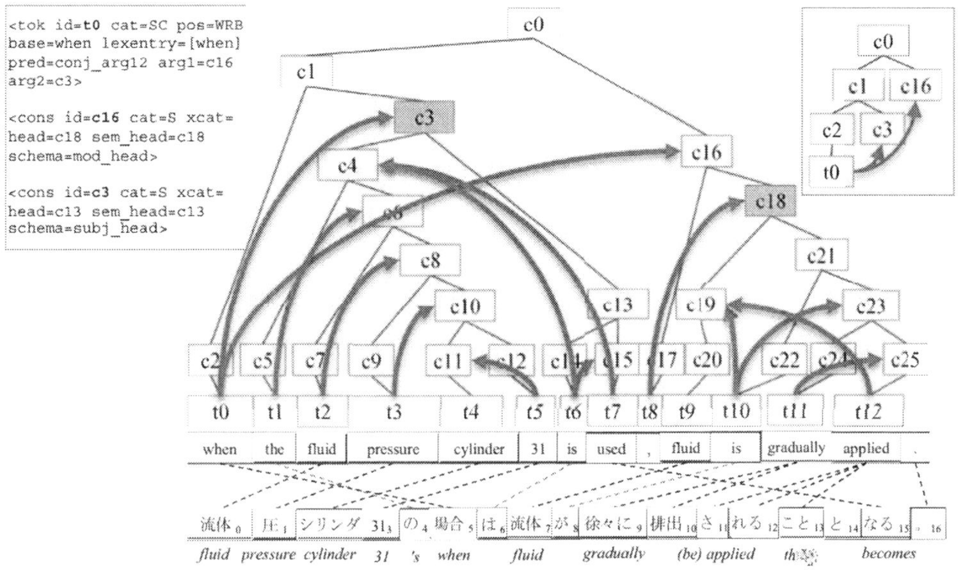

Figure 1: Illustration of a word-aligned HPSG-tree-to-string pair for English-to-Japanese translation.

denote non-terminal nodes (e.g., c0, c1), and the identifiers that start with 't' denote terminal nodes (e.g., t0, t2). In a complete HPSG tree (Wu et al., 2010b), factored syntactic features listed in Table 1 are included in the terminal and non-terminal signs. These features are used by us to sub-categorize pre-ordering rules. As an example of the XML output of Enju, the signs of "when" (t0) and its arguments c16, c3 are shown in the top-left corner of Figure 1.

2.2 Data structures

We define the following data structures for both extracting and applying pre-ordering rules. First, a PAS-based pre-ordering rule is defined to be a four-tuple <*pw*, *args*, srcOrder, trgOrder>. Here, *pw* is the predicate word, *args* are the argument nodes of *pw*, and srcOrder and trgOrder respectively record the relative positions among *pw* and *args* in the source and target language sides.

Then, we suppose an HPSG tree/subtree object contains the following methods:

- localize(): localize syntactic/semantic heads;
- computeSrcSpans(): topologically compute the source span of each node;
- computeSpans(A): topologically compute the source and target spans of each node (Galley et al., 2004). A is the word alignment;
- getArgs(*pw*): return the argument nodes of *pw*;

Name	Description	Examples
WORD	surface word form	"when"
BASE	base word form	"when"
POS	part-of-speech	WRB ("when")
LE	lexical entry	[when] ("when")
PRED	type of predicate argument structure	conj_arg12 ("when")
CAT	syntactic category	SC ("when")
TENSE	tense of a verb (past, present, untensed)	present ("used")
ASPECT	aspect of a verb (none, prefect, progressive, prefect-progressive)	none ("used")
VOICE	voice of a verb (passive, active)	passive ("used")
AUX	auxiliary verb or not (minus, modal, have, be, do, to, copular)	minus ("used")
CAT	syntactic category	S (c16), S (c3)
XCAT	extended category	
HEAD	syntactic head	R (c16), R(c3)
SEM_HEAD	semantic head	R (c16), R (c3)
SCHEMA	schema rule	mod_head (c16)

Table 1: Templates of atomic features included in the predicate node (top size) and its argument nodes (bottom side).

- MCT(*pw*, *args*): return the minimum cover tree (Wu et al., 2010a) of *pw* and *args*.

To implement the localize() method, we use the approach described in (Wu et al., 2010a). That is, we replace the pointer values of HEAD and SEM_HEAD features in non-terminal nodes with three labels: "S" for single daughter, "L" for the left-hand-side daughter, and "R" for the right-hand-side daughter. For example, for node c16 in Figure 1, its HEAD and SEM_HEAD will change from c18 to "R".

We use the concept of *minimum covering trees* (MCT) defined in (Wu et al., 2010b) to guide the pre-ordering process. A MCT is a subtree of the original HPSG tree that takes a predicate node and its argument nodes as (new) leaf nodes. For example, as shown in the top-right corner of Figure 1, the MCT of "when" (t0) and its argument nodes c3, c16 is "c0(c1(c2(t0)c3)c16)".

Finally, the attributes in the nodes of an HPSG tree include: 1) pred: the PAS of a leaf node, 2) srcSpan: the index set of the source words that current node covers, 3) trgSpan: the index set of the target words that srcSpan aligned to, and 4) srcPhrase that stores the pre-ordered source phrase covered by current node.

2.3 Rule extraction algorithm

We express the idea for extracting PAS-based pre-ordering rules by using the first word "when" of the English sentence in Figure 1. Given the PAS information of "when" (t0) in the English side, we need to determine the target-side-order among t0 and its two arguments c16, c3. To achieve this, we compute the target spans of these three nodes by using current word alignment and then sort their target spans. Through referring to the word alignment shown in Figure 1, we can collect the target spans which are {5}, {4,0,1,2,3,6,15}, and {7,8,9,10,11,12,13} respectively for t0, c3, and c16. However, we cannot sort these three spans since there are overlapping between the first two spans[3]. In order to solve this problem, we sort the spans in a heuristic way. Note that in c3's target span, five indices are smaller than 5 yet only two indices are larger than 5. Thus, we take {4,0,1,2,3,6,15} to be *dominantly smaller* than {5}. Now, we can determine the pre-order rule guided by the PAS of t0 to be "t0 c3 c16 → c3 t0 c16" and formally to be "$t0_0$ $c3_1$ $c16_2$ → 1 0 2". Generally, we use the following heuristic rules to sort two spans, named span A and span B:

- if more than half of numbers in A is bigger than the maximum number in B, or if more than half of numbers in B is smaller than the minimum number in A, then B < A;

[3]In this example, the overlapping is caused by the wrong/ambiguous alignments between "used" and "naru$_{15}$", and between "is" and "ha$_6$".

Algorithm 1 Pre-ordering Rule Extraction

Input: HPSG tree T_E of an English sentence E, word alignment A

Output: a pre-ordering rule set $\mathcal{R}$

1: T_E.localize()
2: T_E.computeSpans(A)
3: **for** each leaf node t of T_E **do**
4:   **if** t.pred is opened and t.trgSpan != NULL **then**
5:     Node[] *args* ← T_E.getArgs(t)
6:     **if** all nodes in *args* are aligned **then**
7:       int[] srcOrder ← SORTSPANS(t.srcSpan, srcSpans of *args*)
8:       int[] trgOrder ← SORTSPANS(t.trgSpan, trgSpans of *args*)
9:       $\mathcal{R}$.add(< t, *args*, srcOrder, trgOrder>)
10:     **end if**
11:   **end if**
12: **end for**

- if more than half of numbers in B is bigger than the maximum number in A, or if more than half of numbers in A is smaller than the minimum number in B, then A < B.

In case of a tie (e.g., A={3,4,7,8}, B={5,6}), we keep the original order of A and B in the source-side sentence without any reordering.

Algorithm 1 sketches the pre-ordering rule extraction algorithm guided by PASs. The algorithm collect pre-ordering rules through a traversal of the leaf nodes in an HPSG tree. A non-terminal node will not be accessed unless it is an argument of some predicate node(s). Thus, this algorithm runs in a time that is approximately *linear* to the number of leaf nodes in the tree, i.e., the number of words in the source sentence.

We define that a terminal node's PAS is *opened* if at least one of its arguments is neither empty nor unknown. We will not extract a pre-ordering rule if the terminal node is unaligned or any of its argument node is unaligned. These constraints are reflected by Line 4 and 6 in Algorithm 1. After heuristically sorting the source/target spans of a predicate node and its argument nodes, we finally extract a pre-ordering rule.

Table 2 summarizes the PAS-based pre-ordering rules extracted from the example shown in Figure 1. Application of these pre-ordering rules to the original English sentence yields the following Japanese style sentence:

- `the fluid pressure cylinder 31 is used when, fluid is gradually applied.`

2.4 Applying pre-ordering rules

Word	PRED	Pre-ordering Rule
when	conj_arg12	when c3 c16 → c3 when c16
the	det_arg1	the c6 → the c6
fluid	adj_arg1	fluid c8 → fluid c8
pressure	noun_arg1	pressure c10 → pressure c10
cylinder	noun_arg0	-
31	adj_arg1	c11 31 → c11 31
is	aux_arg12	c4 is c15 → c4 is c15
used	verb_arg12	c4 used → c4 used
,	punct_arg1	, c18 → , c18
fluid	noun_arg0	-
is	aux_arg12	c19 is c23 → c19 is c23
gradually	adj_arg1	gradually c25 → gradually c25
applied	verb_arg12	c19 applied → c19 applied

Table 2: PAS-based pre-ordering rules extracted from the example shown in Figure 1. We use real words instead of predicate nodes here for intuitive understanding.

Algorithm 2 Pre-ordering Rule Application

Input: HPSG tree T_E of an English sentence $E[]$, rule set $\mathcal{R}$
Output: srcPhrase in the root node of T_E

```
1: T_E.localize()
2: T_E.computeSrcSpans()
3: mct_rule ← {}
4: for each leaf node t of T_E do
5:     Node[] args ← T_E.getArgs(t)
6:     int[] srcOrder ← SORTSPANS(t.srcSpan, srcSpans of args)
7:     Rule r ←RULEMATCH(R, < t, args, srcOrder>)
8:     if r != NULL then
9:         mct ← T_E.MCT(t, args)
10:        mct_rule.add(<mct, r >)
11:    end if
12: end for
13: for each mct in mct_rule in a bottom-up order do
14:    Rule r ← mct_rule.get(mct)
15:    mct.root().srcPhrase ← '' ▷ root() returns root node
16:    for i from 0 to r.trgOrder.length-1 do
17:        mct.root().srcPhrase += ' ' + mct.leaves()[r.trgOrder[i]].srcPhrase
18:    end for
19: end for
20: for each node n in T_E in a topological order do
21:    if n is a terminal node then
22:        n.srcPhrase ← E[n.srcSpan[0]]
23:    else if n.srcPhrase = NULL then
24:        n.srcPhrase ← CONNECT(n.children().srcPhrase)
25:    end if
26: end for
```

Algorithm 2 sketches the algorithm for applying pre-ordering rules to a given HPSG tree T_E. The algorithm contains three parts: rule matching (Lines 4-12), bottom-up rule applying (Lines 13-19), and sentence collecting (Lines 20-26). We first retrieve available pre-ordering rules from rule set $\mathcal{R}$ by a left-to-right traversal of the leaf nodes of T_E. For each leaf node, we select one pre-ordering rule with the highest frequency. Our experiments testified that this greedy rule selection strategy worked quite well. We selected 93% of the top frequent rule without facing a tie.

The terminal node t, the argument nodes of t, and their source-side ordering are taken as the key for rule matching. Available rules will be assigned to the MCT of t. Then, we apply the available rules to the root nodes of each MCT through a bottom-up traversal of T_E. A competitive problem is that, a non-terminal node can be shared by several MCTs. For example, node c3 and c18 (gray color) in Figure 1 are respectively shared by two MCTs (t6 and t7, t10 and t12). In order to avoid duplicated reordering of these nodes, we first pick the pre-ordering rule in which there are no "gaps" among the predicate words and argument phrases. For example, there is a gap (t6) between t7 and its argument node c4. We then pick a rule by frequency if there are still more than one rule available. Finally, after applying all available rules, we collect the pre-ordered source sentence from the root node of the HPSG tree.

3 Experiments

3.1 Setup

We test our proposal by translating from English to Japanese. We use the NTCIR-9 English-Japanese patent corpus[4] as our experiment set. Since the reference set of the official test set has not been released yet, we instead split the original development set averagely into two parts, named dev.a and dev.b. In our experiments, we first take dev.a as our development set for minimum-error rate tuning (Och, 2003) and then report the final translation accuracies on dev.b. For direct comparison with other systems in the future, we use the configuration of the official baseline system[5]:

- Moses[6] (Koehn et al., 2007): revision = "3717" as the baseline decoder. Note that we also train Moses using HFE sentences (Isozaki et al., 2010b) and the English sentences pre-ordered by PASs;
- GIZA++: giza-pp-v1.0.3[7] (Och and Ney, 2003) for first training word alignment using the original English sentences for pre-ordering rule extraction, and then for retrain-

[4]http://ntcir.nii.ac.jp/PatentMT/
[5]http://ntcir.nii.ac.jp/PatentMT/baselineSystems
[6]http://www.statmt.org/moses/
[7]http://giza-pp.googlecode.com/files/giza-pp-v1.0.3.tar.gz

	Train	Dev.a	Dev.b
# of sent.	2,032,679	1,000	1,000
# of En words	48,322,058	31,890	31,935
Enju suc. rate	99.3%	98.9%	98.7%
parse time (sec./sent.)	0.30	0.38	0.48
# of Jp words	53,865,629	37,066	35,921

Table 3: Statistics of the experiment sets.

# of args	Train	Dev.a	Dev.b
0	22.9%	22.4%	22.3%
1	47.0%	47.0%	47.5%
2	29.5%	29.8%	29.4%
3	0.6%	0.8%	0.8%
4	0.0%	0.0%	0.0%

Table 4: Statistics of the number of arguments of the predicate words in the experiment sets.

ing word alignments using the pre-ordered English sentences;

- SRILM[8] (Stolcke, 2002): version 1.5.12 for training a 5-gram language model using the target sentences in the total training set;
- Additional scripts[9]: for preprocessing English sentences and cleaning up too long (# of words > 40) parallel sentences;
- Japanese word segmentation: Mecab v0.98[10] with the dictionary of mecab-ipadic-2.7.0-20070801.tar.gz[11].

The statistics of the filtered training set, dev.a, and dev.b are shown in Table 3. The success parsing rate ranges from 98.7% to 99.3% by using Enju2.3.1. The averaged parsing time for each English sentence ranges from 0.30 to 0.48 seconds.

3.2 Statistics of PASs and PAS-based pre-ordering rules

Figure 2 shows the number (natural log) of the 40 types of the PASs that appeared in the HPSG trees of the three experiment sets. Top five types of opened PASs include adj_arg1, det_arg1, prep_arg12, noun_arg1, and verb_arg12. By comparing the distributions of the number of PASs in the three sets, we can see that the distributions approximately share the same tendency. Thus, the pre-ordering rules learned from the PASs in the training set can be expected to be properly applied in dev.a and dev.b.

Besides, the statistics of the number of arguments for the predicate words is shown in Table 4. From this table, we find that the ratio of the number of arguments in the three sets are approximately similar. In particular, nearly half of the predicate words have one argument. The number of predicate words that contain two arguments occurs around 30.0% of all the predicate words. Also, we can not extract pre-ordering rules from around 23.0% of the predicate words since they do not contain any arguments. Finally, less than 1% of predicate words contain three arguments and we only find one four-argument example of verb_arg1234 in the training set.

	Number	Ratio
Parse success	45,617,387	94.4%
Opened	35,004,893	76.7%
Aligned	33,966,923	97.0%
Contiguous	30,256,858	89.1%

Table 5: Statistics of predicate words in the training set for rule extraction.

Now, in Table 5, we show the statistics of predicate words in the training set for pre-ordering rule extraction. Of the 48.3 million English words in the training set, there are 45.6 million words (94.4%) that are included in the HPSG trees that were successfully generated. Then, in the PASs of these 45.6 million words, there are 35.0 million words whose PASs are opened. We also list the number (34.0 million) of aligned predicate words, since we only extract pre-ordering rules from predicate words that are aligned to some target word(s) in Algorithm 1. Finally, there are 89.1% of aligned predicate words that are aligned to contiguous target words.

In order to investigate the sub-categorization effectiveness of the syntactic features included in the pre-ordering rules, we pick four subsets of the total feature set (Table 1). These feature subsets, named from PAS-a to PAS-d, are listed in Table 6. Through the comparison of these four feature subsets, we also attempt to investigate the data-sparseness problem of available pre-ordering rules cased by the factored features.

PAS-a includes all the syntactic features listed in Table 1. In PAS-b, we only keep three features for the predicate word and one feature for the argu-

[8] http://www.speech.sri.com/projects/srilm/

[9] http://homepages.inf.ed.ac.uk/jschroe1/how-to/scripts.tgz

[10] http://sourceforge.net/projects/mecab/files/

[11] http://sourceforge.net/projects/mecab/files/mecab-ipadic/

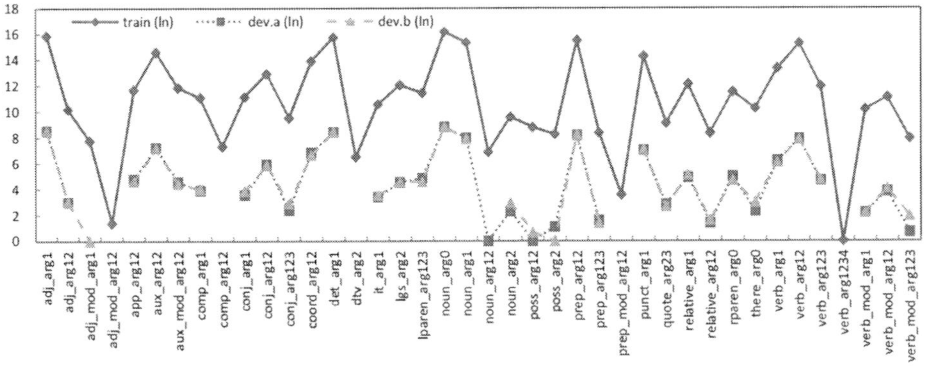

Figure 2: Number (natural log) of the types of the PASs that appeared in the experiment sets.

Feature	PAS-a	PAS-b	PAS-c	PAS-d
WORD	√	√	√	√
BASE	√			
POS	√			
LE	√			
PRED	√	√	√	√
CAT	√	√		
TENSE	√			
ASPECT	√			
VOICE	√			
AUX	√			
CAT	√	√	√	
XCAT	√			
HEAD	√			
SEM_HEAD	√			
SCHEMA	√			
# rules	469,014	203,184	200,968	148,047
# reorder	179,062	63,378	62,694	37,104
reorder ratio	38.2%	31.2%	31.2%	25.1%
avg. # train	12.0	12.1	12.1	12.1
avg. # dev.a	16.2	16.4	16.4	16.5
avg. # dev.b	16.2	16.4	16.4	16.5

Table 6: Feature subsets used in pre-ordering rules and statistics of the extraction and application of the pre-ordering rules under these feature subsets.

ment nodes. We further remove one feature (CAT) of the predicate word in PAS-c. In the fourth subset PAS-d, we only use two features WORD and PRED in the predicate word for sub-categorizing pre-ordering rules. Thus, PAS-d is only related to PASs (which can be generated by any kinds of parser) since it does not include additional features generated by the typical HPSG parser.

As the number of syntactic features decreases, more rules can be unified together. Thus, the number of pre-ordering rules and reordering rules, as shown in Table 6, also decreases. The number of reordering rules occurs from 25.1% (PAS-d) to 38.2% (PAS-a) in the pre-ordering rules. For each English sentence in the training set, there are averagely 12 *reordering* rules (instead of monotonic

Source sent.	BLEU	RIBES
Original sentences	0.2773	0.6619
PAS-a reordered	**0.3088**	**0.7406**
PAS-b reordered	0.3054	0.7334
PAS-c reordered	0.3063	0.7336
PAS-d reordered	0.3020	0.7265

Table 7: Translation accuracies by using the original English sentences or the pre-ordered English sentences under four types of pre-ordering rules.

pre-ordering rules) available under either of the four feature subsets. For each English sentence in dev.a and dev.b, the number of available *reordering* rules is averagely 16. Around 99.1%, 99.0%, and 98.6% English sentences were respectively reordered in the training set, dev.a set, and dev.b set.

3.3 Results

Table 7 shows the final translation accuracies under BLEU score (Papineni et al., 2002) and RIBES[12], i.e., the software implementation of Normalized Kendall's τ as proposed by (Isozaki et al., 2010a) to automatically evaluate the translation between distant language pairs based on rank correlation coefficients and significantly penalizes word order mistakes. Making use of our pre-ordered English sentences significantly ($p < 0.01$) improved BLEU scores from 2.47 (PAS-d) to 3.15 (PAS-a) points. The effectiveness of our proposal for tackling word-ordering problem can also be proved by comparing the scores of RIBES.

In addition, the accuracies change slightly among using the four types of pre-ordering rules. Among PAS-a, PAS-b, and PAS-c, we did significant test and could not differ them under $p < 0.01$ or $p < 0.05$. The only significant difference

[12]Code available at http://www.kecl.ntt.co.jp/icl/lirg/ribes

Source sent.	BLEU	RIBES	Same	PAS
HFE	0.3134	0.7370	-	-
HFE+PAS-a	0.3278	0.7379	11.0%	34.7%
HFE+PAS-b	**0.3302**	**0.7397**	12.3%	32.8%
HFE+PAS-c	0.3300	0.7380	10.8%	35.0%
HFE+PAS-d	0.3256	0.7337	11.5%	32.8%

Table 8: Translation accuracies by combining HFE and PAS based pre-ordering approach.

($p < 0.05$) appeared between PAS-a and PAS-d. Thus, we argue that the factored syntactic features such as WORD, PRED, and CAT are more essential for sub-categorizing pre-ordering rules than the remaining syntactic features.

As former mentioned, we also take the language-dependent HFE approach (Isozaki et al., 2010b) as another baseline. Note that word alignment was retrained using head-finalized English sentences and Japanese sentences in this HFE approach. Through comparing the HFE results listed in Table 8, we observe that the results are comparable between PAS-a and HFE: HFE is slightly better under BLEU score and PAS-a is slightly better under RIBES score.

Since similar HPSG parser (Enju) yet different linguistic information (syntactic head information vs. PASs) are used in HFE approach and our proposal. A straightforward question is whether we can combine these approaches together. Under this motivation, we select a better pre-ordered English sentence generated by the HFE method and our PAS-based method. Following (Genzel, 2010), we use *crossing score* as the metric for sentence selection. Crossing score is the number of crossing alignment links for a given aligned sentence pair. For monotonic alignments without reordering, crossing score is zero. During selection, we found that nearly 10% of the pre-ordered English sentences yielded by head-finalization and PAS-based methods were similar. In addition, among the different sentences, around 30% of PAS-based pre-ordering sentences were selected. Since we can not compute crossing score in the development/test sets, we instead take both kinds of pre-ordered English sentences as inputs and pick one output with a higher translation score.

The translation result based on this reselection approach is shown in Table 8. Compared with HFE approach, the reselection approach significantly ($p < 0.01$) improved BLEU scores of from 1.22 (PAS-d) to 1.68 (PAS-b) points. These interesting results reflect that syntactic head information and PASs describe the linguistic information of an English sentence in different aspects. Furthermore, compared with the single head-finalization rule, the automatically extracted pre-ordering rules kept the variety of word-ordering by dynamically inferring the word order of target sentences and thus enlarged the reordering space.

Source sent.	Averaged τ	$\tau \geq 0.8$
English	0.407	0.106
HFE	0.708	0.487
PAS-a	0.571	0.291
HFE+PAS-a	**0.809**	**0.643**

Table 9: Comparison of Kendall's τ.

3.4 Alignment comparison

In order to investigate how closely the pre-ordered English sentences follow target language word order, we measured Kendall's τ (Kendall, 1948), a rank correlation coefficient, as shown in Table 9. We exactly follow Isozaki et al. (2010b) to compute Kendall's τ. From Table 9, we can see that the quality of word alignments approximately reflects the final BLEU scores listed in Table 7 and 8.

4 Conclusion

We have proposed a pre-ordering approach by making use of predicate argument structures. The pre-ordering rules record the relative source-target position mapping among predicate words and their argument phrases. We first proposed an algorithm for automatically extracting these lexical pre-ordering rules from aligned HPSG-tree-to-string pairs. Then, we apply these pre-ordering rules to HPSG trees to yield pre-ordered source sentences that follow the word order of target sentences. Finally, we do word alignment again by using the pre-ordered source sentences together with the original target sentences.

Employing Moses (Koehn et al., 2007), our proposal significantly improved 2.47~3.15 BLEU points compared with using the original English sentences. Combining with the HFE approach (Isozaki et al., 2010b), our approach significantly and impressively improved 5.29 points of BLEU score from 0.2773 to 0.3302. We finally argue that our proposal is not difficult to be implemented and can be easily applied to translate English into other languages.

References

Peter F. Brown, Vincent J. Della Pietra, Stephen A. Della Pietra, and Robert L. Mercer. 1993. The mathematics of statistical machine translation: parameter estimation. *Computational Linguistics*, 19(2):263–311.

David Chiang. 2005. A hierarchical phrase-based model for statistical machine translation. In *Proc.of ACL*, pages 263–270.

Michael Collins, Philipp Koehn, and Ivona Kucerova. 2005. Clause restructuring for statistical machine translation. In *Proc.of ACL*, pages 531–540.

Michel Galley, Mark Hopkins, Kevin Knight, and Daniel Marcu. 2004. What's in a translation rule? In *Proc.of HLT-NAACL*.

Dmitriy Genzel. 2010. Automatically learning source-side reordering rules for large scale machine translation. In *Proc.of COLING*, pages 376–384.

Hideki Isozaki, Tsutomu Hirao, Kevin Duh, Katsuhito Sudoh, and Hajime Tsukada. 2010a. Automatic evaluation of translation quality for distant language pairs. In *Proc.of EMNLP*, pages 944–952.

Hideki Isozaki, Katsuhito Sudoh, Hajime Tsukada, and Kevin Duh. 2010b. Head finalization: A simple reordering rule for sov languages. In *Proc.of WMT-MetricsMATR*, pages 244–251.

Jason Katz-Brown and Michael Collins. 2007. Syntactic reordering in preprocessing for japanese-english translation: Mit system description for ntcir-7 patent translation task. In *Proc.of NTCIR-7 Workshop Meeting*, pages 409–414.

Maurice Kendall. 1948. *Rank Correlation Methods*. Charles Griffin.

Philipp Koehn, Hieu Hoang, Alexandra Birch, Chris Callison-Burch, Marcello Federico, Nicola Bertoldi, Brooke Cowan, Wade Shen, Christine Moran, Richard Zens, Chris Dyer, Ondřej Bojar, Alexandra Constantin, and Evan Herbst. 2007. Moses: Open source toolkit for statistical machine translation. In *the ACL 2007 Demo-Poster*, pages 177–180.

Mamoru Komachi, Masaaki Nagata, and Yuji Matsumoto. 2006. Phrase reordering for statistical machine translation based on predicate-argument structure. In *Proc.of IWSLT*, pages 77–82.

Shankar Kumar and William Byrne. 2005. Local phrase reordering models for statistical machine translation. In *Proc.of HLT-EMNLP*, pages 161–168.

Yang Liu, Qun Liu, and Shouxun Lin. 2006. Tree-to-string alignment templates for statistical machine transaltion. In *Proc.of COLING-ACL*, pages 609–616, Sydney, Australia.

Yusuke Miyao and Jun'ichi Tsujii. 2008. Feature forest models for probabilistic hpsg parsing. *Computational Lingustics*, 34(1):35–80.

Franz Josef Och and Hermann Ney. 2003. A systematic comparison of various statistical alignment models. *Computational Linguistics*, 29(1):19–51.

Franz Josef Och. 2003. Minimum error rate training in statistical machine translation. In *Proc.of ACL*, pages 160–167.

Kishore Papineni, Salim Roukos, Todd Ward, and Wei-Jing Zhu. 2002. Bleu: a method for automatic evaluation of machine translation. In *Proc.of ACL*, pages 311–318.

Carl Pollard and Ivan A. Sag. 1994. *Head-Driven Phrase Structure Grammar*. University of Chicago Press.

Kay Rottmann and Stephan Vogel. 2007. Word reordering in statistical machine translation with a pos-based distortion model. In *Proc.of TMI*, pages 171–180, Skovde, Sweden.

Andreas Stolcke. 2002. Srilm-an extensible language modeling toolkit. In *Proc.of ICSLP*, pages 901–904.

Christoph Tillman. 2004. A unigram orientation model for statistical machine translation. In Daniel Marcu Susan Dumais and Salim Roukos, editors, *HLT-NAACL 2004*, pages 101–104.

Stephan Vogel, Hermann Ney, and Christoph Tillmann. 1996. Hmm-based word alignment in statistical translation. In *COLING*, pages 836–841.

Chao Wang, Michael Collins, and Philipp Koehn. 2007. Chinese syntactic reordering for statistical machine translation. In *Proc.of EMNLP-CoNLL*, pages 737–745.

Xianchao Wu, Takuya Matsuzaki, and Jun'ichi Tsujii. 2010a. Fine-grained tree-to-string translation rule extraction. In *Proc.of the 48th ACL*, pages 325–334.

Xianchao Wu, Takuya Matsuzaki, and Jun'ichi Tsujii. 2010b. Improve syntax-based translation using deep syntactic structures. *Machine Translation (Special Issue : Pushing the frontiers of SMT)*, 24(2):141–157.

Fei Xia and Michael McCord. 2004. Improving a statistical mt system with automatically learned rewrite patterns. In *Proc.of COLING*, pages 508–514.

Deyi Xiong, Qun Liu, and Shouxun Lin. 2006. Maximum entropy based phrase reordering model for statistical machine translation. In *Proc.of COLING-ACL*, pages 521–528.

Peng Xu, Jaeho Kang, Michael Ringgaard, and Franz Och. 2009. Using a dependency parser to improve smt for subject-object-verb languages. In *Proc.of HLT-NAACL*, pages 245–253.

Context-Sensitive Syntactic Source-Reordering by Statistical Transduction

Maxim Khalilov[†] and **Khalil Sima'an**
Institute for Logic, Language and Computation
University of Amsterdam
P.O. Box 94242
1090 GE Amsterdam, The Netherlands
{m.khalilov,k.simaan}@uva.nl

Abstract

How well can a phrase translation model perform if we permute the source words to fit target word order as perfectly as word alignment might allow? And how well would it perform if we limit the allowed permutations to ITG-like tree-transduction operations on the source parse tree? First we contribute oracle results showing great potential for performance improvement by source-reordering, ranging from 1.5 to 4 BLEU points depending on language pair. Although less outspoken, the potential of tree-based source-reordering is also significant. Our second contribution is a source reordering model that works with two kinds of tree transductions: the one permutes the order of sibling subtrees under a node, and the other first deletes layers in the parse tree in order to exploit sibling permutation at the remaining levels.The statistical parameters of the model we introduce concern individual tree transductions *conditioned on contextual features* of the tree resulting from all preceding transductions. Experiments in translating from English to Spanish/Dutch/Chinese show significant improvements of respectively 0.6/1.2/2.0 BLEU points.

1 Motivation

Word order differences between languages are a major challenge in Machine Translation (MT). Phrase-based Statistical Machine Translation (PBSMT) (Och and Ney, 2004; Zens et al., 2002; Koehn et al., 2003) deals with word order differences in two subcomponents of a translation model. Firstly, using the local word reordering implicitly encoded in phrase pairs. Secondly, using an explicit reordering model which may reorder target phrases relative to their source sides, e.g., as a monotone phrase sequence generation process with the possibility of swapping neighboring phrases (Tillman, 2004).

Arguably, local phrase reordering models cannot account for long-range reordering phenomena, e.g., (Chiang, 2005; Chiang, 2007). Hierarchical models of phrase reordering employ synchronous grammars or tree transducers, e.g., (Wu and Wong, 1998; Chiang, 2005). These models explore a more varied range of reordering phenomena, e.g., defined by at most inverting the order of sibling subtrees under each node in binary source/target trees (akin to ITG (Wu and Wong, 1998)).

Undoubtedly, the word order of source and target sentences is intertwined with the lexical choices on both side. Statistically speaking, however, one may first select a target word order given the source only, and then choose target words given the selected target word order and source words. One application of this idea is known as source reordering (or -permutation), e.g., (Collins et al., 2005; Xia and McCord, 2004; Wang et al., 2007; Li et al., 2007; Khalilov and Sima'an, 2010). Briefly, the words of the source string s are reordered to minimize word order differences with the target string t, leading to the source permuted string $\acute{s}$. Presumably, a standard PBSMT system trained to translate from $\acute{s}$ to t should have an easier task than translating directly from s to t. The source reordering part, s to $\acute{s}$,

[†]Currently, the first author is employed by TAUS B.V., Amsterdam (The Netherlands).

can be realized in various ways and may manipulate morpho-syntactic parse trees of s, e.g., (Collins et al., 2005; Xia and McCord, 2004; Li et al., 2007).

It may seem that source reordering should provide only limited improvement over the standard PBSMT approach. The literature reports mixed performance improvements for different language pairs, e.g., (Collins et al., 2005; Xia and McCord, 2004; Wang et al., 2007; Li et al., 2007; Khalilov and Sima'an, 2010). But what is the *potential improvement* of source reordering? We contribute experiments measuring oracle performance improvement for English to Dutch/Spanish/Chinese translations. Beside string-driven oracles, we report results using ITG-like transductions over a single syntactic parse tree of s. Our results confirm that reordering a single syntactic tree could be insufficient (e.g., (Huang et al., 2009)), yet they show substantial potential.

Our second contribution is a novel source reordering model that manipulates the source parse tree with two kinds of tree transduction operators: the one permutes the order of sibling subtrees under a node, and the other first abolishes layers in the parse tree in order to exploit sibling permutation at the remaining levels. The latter is the opposite of parse binarization using Expectation-Maximization (Huang et al., 2009). We use Maximum-Entropy training (Berger et al., 1996) to learn a sequence of tree transductions, each conditioned on contextual features *in tree resulting from outcome of the preceding transduction.* The conditioning on the outcome of preceding transductions is a departure from earlier approaches at learning independent source permutation steps, e.g., (Tromble and Eisner, 2009; Visweswariah et al., 2010).

The aim for the rest of this paper is firstly, to quantify the potential performance improvement of a standard PBSMT system if preceded by source reordering and secondly, to show that statistical Markov approach to tree transduction, where the probability of each transduction step is conditioned on the outcome of preceding steps, can improve the quality of PBSMT output significantly.

2 Source-Reordering: Framework

We start out from a word-aligned parallel corpus, consisting of triples $\langle s, a, t\rangle$, a source s, target t and word alignment a. Source reordering assumes that a permutation of s, called $\grave{s}$, is first generated with a model $P_r(\grave{s} \mid s)$ followed by a phrase translation model $P_t(t \mid \grave{s})$. The desired permutation $\grave{s}$ is one that has minimum word order divergence from t, i.e., when word-aligned again with t would have least number of crossing alignments.

Practically, the original parallel corpus $\{\langle s, a, t\rangle\}$ is split to two parallel corpora: (1) a source-to-permutation parallel corpus (consisting of $\langle s, a, \grave{s}\rangle$) and (2) a permutation-to-target parallel corpus (consisting of $\langle g\grave{s}, \grave{a}, t\rangle$), where $g\grave{s}$ is the output of a source reordering model (guessing at $\grave{s}$), and $\grave{a}$ results from automatically word aligning $\langle g\grave{s}, t\rangle$. The latter parallel corpus is used for training a phrase-based translation system $P_t(t \mid g\grave{s})$, while the former corpus is used for training a source reordering model $P_r(\grave{s} \mid s)$. The problem of permuting the

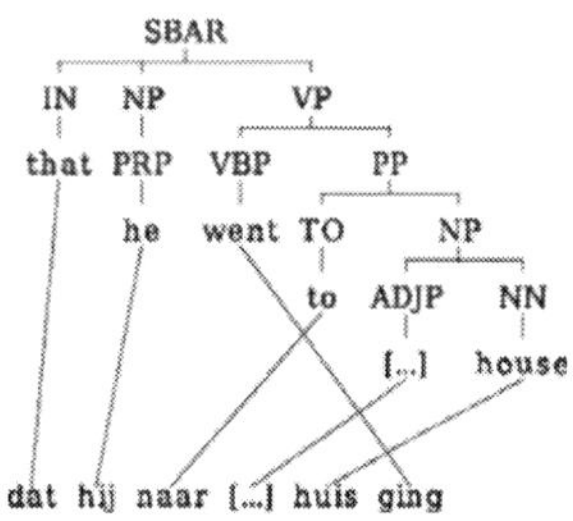

Figure 1: Example crossing alignments and long-distance reordering using a source parse tree.

source string to unfold the crossing alignments is computationally intractable (see (Tromble and Eisner, 2009)). However, various constraints can be made on unfolding the crossing alignments in a. A common approach is to assume a binary parse tree for the source string, and define a set of eligible permutations by binary ITG transductions. This defines permutations resulting from at most inverting pairs of children under nodes of the source tree. Figure 1 exhibits a long-range reordering of the verb in English-to-Dutch translation: inverting the order of the children of the VP node would unfold the crossing alignment. However, crossing alignments represented as non-constituents cannot be resolved. This difficulty can be circumvented by employing multiple alternative parse trees, by applying heuristic transforms (e.g., binarization) to the tree to fit the alignments (Wang et al., June 2010), or by defining new local transductions, on top child permutation (ITG) as we do next.

3 Existing work on source permutation

Source reordering has been shown useful for PBSMT for a wide variety of language pairs with high mutual word order disparity (Collins et al., 2005; Popovic' and Ney, 2006; Zwarts and Dras, 2007; Xia and McCord, 2004). In Costa-jussà and Fonollosa (2006) statistical word classes as well as POS tags are used as patterns for reordering the input sentences and producing a new bilingual pair.

A rather popular class of source reordering algorithms involves syntactic information and aims at minimizing the need for reordering during translation by permuting the source sentence (Collins et al., 2005; Wang et al., 2007; Khalilov and Sima'an, 2010; Li et al., 2007). Some systems perform source permutation using a set of handcrafted rules (Collins et al., 2005; Wang et al., 2007; Ramanathan et al., 2008), others make use of automatically learned reordering patterns extracted from the plain training data, the corresponding parse or dependency trees and the alignment matrix (Visweswariah et al., 2010).

Inspiring this work, source reordering as a pre-translation step is viewed as a word permutation learning problem in Tromble and Eisner (2009) and Li et al. (2007). The space of permutations is approached efficiently using a binary ITG-like synchronous context-free grammar put on the parallel data. Similarly, a local ITG-based tree transducer with contextual conditioning is used in Khalilov and Sima'an (2010) and Li et al. (2007), and preliminary experiments on a single language pair show improved performance.

Particularly, the model in (Li et al., 2007) is explicitly aimed at long-distance reorderings (English-Chinese), prunes the alignment matrix gradually to fit the source syntactic parse and employs Maximum-Entropy modeling to choose the optimal local ITG-like permutation step of sister subtrees but interleaves that step with a translation step. The model which we present in Section 2 differs substantially from (Li et al., 2007) and other earlier work because it (1) incorporates other kinds of tree transduction operations than those promoted by ITG, and (2) works with the unmodified alignment matrix but learns reorderings only from those alignments that are consistent with the tree, thereby avoiding the effects of heuristics for pruning alignments to fit the tree-structure, e.g., (Li et al., 2007).

In this paper we take the idea of learning source permutation one step further along a few dimensions. We show the utility of other kinds of tree transduction operations, besides those promoted by ITG, stress the importance of using a wide range of conditioning context features during learning, and report oracle and test results on *three* language pairs.

The majority of existing work reports encouraging performance improvements by source reordering. Next we aim at quantifying the potential improvement by oracle source reordering at the string level, if all permutations were to be allowed, and at the source syntactic tree level, by limiting the permutations with two kinds of local transductions.

4 Oracle source reordering results

Source reordering for PBSMT assumes that permuting the source words to minimize the order differences with the target sentence could improve translation performance. However, the question "how much?" is rarely asked. Here, we attempt answering this question with a set of oracle systems[1], in which we perform unfolding operations on the crossing links in alignment a (estimated between corpora s and t) that leads to a more monotone alignment $\grave{a}$ (between $\grave{s}$, which is a permutation of s, and t). We introduce a set of tree-based constraints that control the unfolding of alignment crossings. We measure the impact of (un)folded alignment crossings on the performance of the PBSMT system (see Table 1).

Oracle String. This method scans the alignment a from left-to-right and unfolds all the crossing links between bilingual phrases (*Oracle string*). Figure 2 shows an example of word reordering done on the string level. NULL aligned words do not move from their positions.

Oracle parse tree with permute siblings. The oracle system unfolds an alignment crossing if and

[1]All the source permutation methods presented in this Section are based on automatic alignments, which inevitably contain wrong links. In the future we plan to involve manual alignments to the computation of oracle permutation

only if the source side of the alignment crossing is covered by the same node in the syntactic source tree, and the alignment pair subject to crossing can be unfolded by permuting the order of the sibling nodes. NULL aligned words do not prevent unfolding crossings because we include them with the adjacent words that are involved in the crossings. We call this configuration *Oracle tree*.

Figure 1 shows an example. According to the *Oracle tree* constraint, the word "went" can be placed in the end of the sentence since the replacement can be done as a swapping of "VBP" and "PP" categories. The same happens for the word "reflect" swapping with "S" constituent in Figure 1, but not for the chunks "the positions" and "not properly": this crossing cannot be resolved under the tree constraint since they are not dominated by sibling syntactic categories.

Oracle tree with delete descendants, permute siblings. This oracle implements an additional mechanism of tree modification to increase the number of reordering permutations in comparison with *Oracle tree* algorithm. Here we allow for an additional tree transduction operation that deletes intervening layers before applying sibling permutation. This is illustrated in Figure 3. The word "must" can not be moved to the beginning of the sentence in Figure 3a by *Oracle tree*. Instead, this is done in two steps. Firstly, the VP dominating the words "must" and "apply" is deleted under the current node S, the transformed tree is shown in Figure 3b. Subsequently, the siblings under S in the resulting tree are permuted, "must" is reordered across the whole clause and placed to the first position (see Figure 3c). We call this system *Oracle mod*.
Figure 4 shows an example in which crossing alignment links cannot be unfolded without deleting 4 intervening layers.

Oracle results Table 1 contrasts the oracle results with the performance shown by standard PBSMT systems. The experimental setup is detailed in Section 6. We consider the following baseline configurations: *PBSMT* - Moses-based PBSMT with distance-based reordering model; *PBSMT+MSD* - Moses-based PBSMT with distance-based reordering model and MSD and *Moses-chart* - hierarchical Moses-chart-based PBSMT.

Depending on number of parse tree levels allowed to be deleted, we consider three *Oracle mod* systems: with two (*2lt*), three (*3lt*) and five (*5lt*) levels of descendants allowed to be deleted for a more flat parse tree structure before sibling permutation.

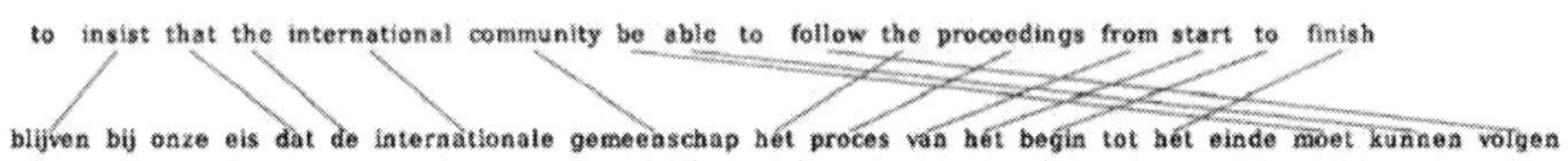

(a) Original bilingual phrase.

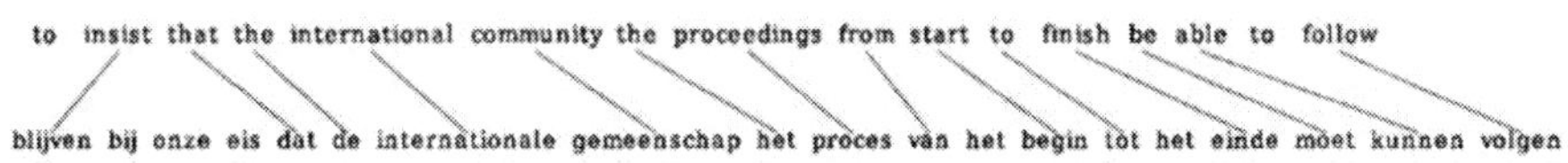

(b) Reordered bilingual phrase.

Figure 2: Example of *Oracle string* unfolding.

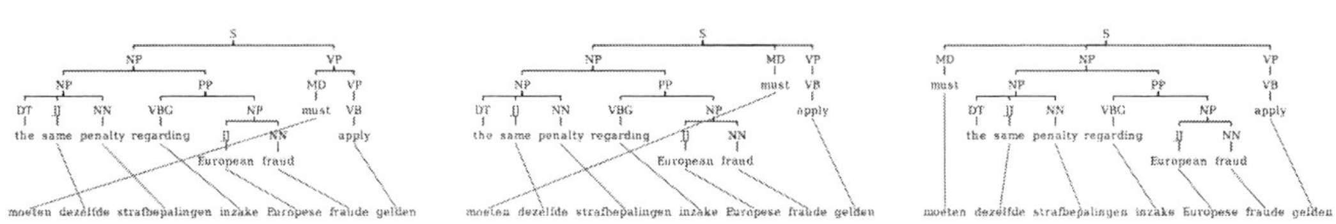

(a) Original parse tree. (b) Parse tree with deleted VP category. (c) Reordered parse tree.

Figure 3: Example of text monotonization with tree transformation.

The impact of corpus monotonization on translation system performance is measured using the final point of weight optimization on the development set (*Dev BLEU*), as well as on the test set (*Test BLEU/NIST*).

The major conclusion that can be drawn from the oracle results is that the source reordering defined in terms of parse tree transduction can potentially lead to increased translation quality (up to 1.2 BLEU points for English-Dutch, 0.5 for English-Spanish and 1.7 for English-Chinese). At the same time, a huge gap between performance shown by *Oracle string* and tree oracle systems (≈2.2 BLEU points for English-Dutch, ≈1.3 for English-Spanish and ≈2.5 for English-Chinese) shows that there are many crossing alignments which cannot be unfolded with simple, local transductions over a single source-side syntactic tree.

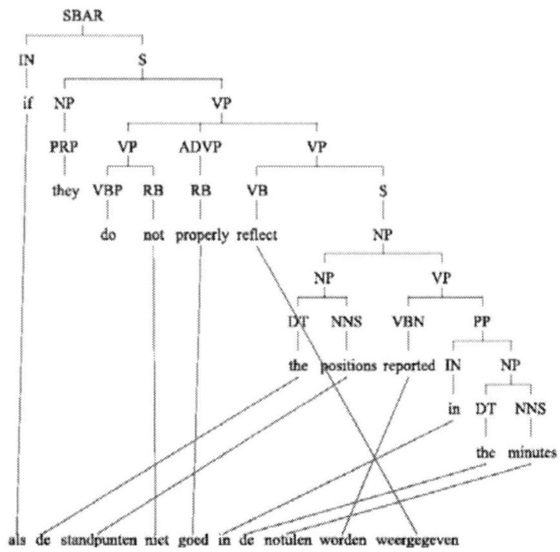

Figure 4: Example of unfoldable alignment crossings.

5 Conditional Tree-Transductions

Our model aims at learning from the source permuted parallel corpus (containing tuples $\langle s, a, \grave{s} \rangle$) a probabilistic optimization $(\arg\max_{\pi(s)} P_r(\pi(s) \mid s, \tau_s))$, where τ_s is the source parse and $\pi(s)$ is some eligible permutation of s. We view the permutations leading from s to $\grave{s}$ as a sequence of local tree transductions $\tau_{\grave{s}_0} \to \ldots \to \tau_{\grave{s}_n}$, where $\grave{s}_0 = s$ and $\grave{s}_n = \grave{s}$, and each transduction $\tau_{\grave{s}_{i-1}} \to \tau_{\grave{s}_i}$ is defined using any of two kinds of local tree transduction operations used in Section 4 or alternatively NOP (No Operation).

The sequence $\tau_{\grave{s}_0} \to \ldots \to \tau_{\grave{s}_n}$ is obtained by taking the next node in a top-down tree traversal, then statistically selecting the most likely of three transduction operations and applying the selected operation to the current node. If the current tree is $\tau_{\grave{s}_{i-1}}$, and the current node has address x, is syntactically labeled N_x, directly dominates α_x (the ordered sequence of node labels under x), we approximate the conditional probability $P(\tau_{\grave{s}_i} \mid \tau_{\grave{s}_{i-1}})$ with the transduction operation it employs:

- Permute the children of x in $\tau_{\grave{s}_{i-1}}$ with probability

$$\approx P(\pi(\alpha_x) \mid N_x \to \alpha_x, C_x) \quad (1)$$

where $\pi(\alpha_x)$ is a permutation of α_x (the ordered sequence of node labels under x) and C_x is a local tree context of node x in tree $\tau_{\grave{s}'_{i-1}}$.

- Select a child of x to delete, pull its children up directly under x, effectively changing α_x to some α_x^d, and then permute the children of the latter.

$$\approx P(\alpha_x \leadsto \alpha_x^d, \pi(\alpha_x) \mid N_x \to \alpha_x, C_x) \quad (2)$$

where $(\alpha_x \leadsto \alpha_x^d$ symbolizes the result of deleting a subtree under a child of x. This operation applies also to subtrees of depth $n \in \{1, 2, 3, 5\}$ under x, i.e., a child is depth 1, a child with its children is depth 2 and so on.

Obviously, the number of possible permutations of α_x is factorial in the length of α_x. Fortunately, the source permuted training data exhibits only a fraction of possible permutations even for longer α_x sequences. Furthermore, by conditioning the probability on local context C_x, the number of permutations is limited to a handful set.

Theoretically, we could define the probability of the sequence of local tree transductions $\tau_{\grave{s}_0} \to \ldots \to \tau_{\grave{s}_n}$ as

$$P(\tau_{\grave{s}_0} \to \ldots \to \tau_{\grave{s}_n}) = \prod_{i=1}^{n} P(\tau_{\grave{s}_i} \mid \tau_{\grave{s}_{i-1}}) \quad (3)$$

System	EnNl			EnEs			EnZh		
	Dev	Test		Dev	Test		Dev	Test	
	BLEU	BLEU	NIST	BLEU	BLEU	NIST	BLEU	BLEU	NIST
Baselines									
PBSMT	23.88	24.04	6.29	32.31	31.70	7.48	18.71	22.21	5.28
PBSMT+MSD	24.07	24.04	6.28	32.45	31.85	7.47	18.99	21.18	5.30
Moses-chart	23.94	24.93	6.39	30.58	31.80	7.41	19.93	23.90	5.41
Oracle results									
Oracle tree	24.70	24.80	6.32	32.76	32.21	7.51	20.23	23.44	5.35
Oracle string	26.28	27.02	6.50	34.09	33.52	7.60	23.01	26.08	5.52
Oracle mod+2lt	25.05	25.04	6.36	32.24	32.18	7.51	20.64	23.75	5.37
Oracle mod+3lt	25.11	25.27	6.37	32.22	32.34	7.52	20.71	23.59	5.37
Oracle mod+5lt	25.07	25.23	6.37	32.51	32.37	7.55	20.93	23.93	5.39

Table 1: Summary of oracle results.

However, unlike earlier work (e.g., (Tromble and Eisner, 2009)), we cannot afford to do so because every local transduction conditions on context C_x of an intermediate tree, which quickly risks becoming intractable (even when we use packed forests). Furthermore, the problem of calculating the most likely permutation under such a model is made difficult by the fact that different transduction sequences may lead to the same permutation, which demands summing over these sequences (another intractable summation). Earlier work has avoided conditioning context, effectively assuming that the each intermediate permutation is independent from the preceding ones.

Instead, we take a pragmatic approach and greedily select at every intermediate point $\tau_{\acute{s}_{i-1}} \rightarrow \tau_{\acute{s}_i}$ the single most likely local transduction that can be applied to a node in the current intermediate tree $\tau_{\acute{s}_{i-1}}$ using an interpolation of the terms in Equations 1 and 2 with probability ratios of the language model $\acute{s}$ as follows:

$$P(TRANS_i|\, N_x \rightarrow \alpha_x, C_x) \times \frac{P_{lm}(\acute{s}_{i-1})}{P_{lm}(\acute{s}_i)}$$

where $TRANS_i$ is any of the two transduction operations or NOP, and P_{lm} is a language model trained on the $\acute{s}$ side of the corpus $\{\langle s, a, \acute{s}\rangle\}$. The rationale behind this log-linear interpolation is that our source permutation approach aims at finding the optimal permutation $\acute{s}$ of s that can serve as input for a subsequent translation model. Hence, we aim at tree transductions that are syntactically motivated that also lead to improved string permutation. In this sense, the tree transduction definitions can be seen as an efficient and syntactically informed way to define the space of possible permutations.

Estimates. We estimate the string probabilities $P_{lm}(.)$ using 3-gram language models trained on the $\acute{s}$ side of the source permuted parallel corpus $\{\langle s, a, \acute{s}\rangle\}$. We estimate the conditional probability $P_r(TRANS \mid N_x \rightarrow \alpha_x, C_x)$ using a Maximum-Entropy framework, where feature functions are defined to capture the permutation as a class, the node label N_x and its head POS tag, the child sequence α_x together with the corresponding sequence of head POS tags and other features corresponding to different contextual information.

Features in use. We used a set of 15 features to capture reordering permutations from the syntactic and linguistic perspectives: *Local tree topology:* sub-tree instances that include parent node and the ordered sequence of child node labels (1); *Dependency features:* features that determine the POS tag of the head word of the current node (2), together with the sequence of POS tags of the head words of its child nodes (3) and the POS tag of the head word of the parent (4) and grandparent nodes (5); *Syntactic features:* apart from the whole path from the current node to the tree root node (6), we used three binary features from this class describe: (7) whether the parent node is a child of the node annotated with the same syntactic category, (8) whether the parent node is a descendant of the node annotated with the same syntactic category, and (9) if the current subtree is embedded into a "*S-SBAR*" sub-tree[2]; *POS lexical features:* bi- and tri-grams of POS tags of the left- and right-hand side neighboring words (10-13); *Counters:* a number of words covered by a given constituent (14) and a number of children of the given node (15).

6 Translation and reordering experiments

Data. In our experiments we used English-Dutch and English-Spanish European Parliament data and an extraction from the English-Chinese Hong Kong Parallel Corpus. All the sets were provided with one reference translation. Basic statistics of the training data can be found in Table 2, development datasets contained 0.5K, 1.9K and 0.5K lines and test datasets contained 1K, 1.9K and 0.5K for Dutch, Spanish and English, respectively.

Experimental setup. Word alignment was found using GIZA++[3] (Och, 2003), supported by mkcls[4] (Och, 1999) tool. The PBSMT systems we consider in this study is based on Moses toolkit (Koehn et al., 2007). We followed the guidelines provided on the Moses web page[5].

Two phrase reordering methods are widely used in phrase-based systems. A distance-based reordering model providing the decoder with a cost linear to the distance between words that are being reordered. This model constitutes the default for the Moses system. And, a lexicalized block-oriented data-driven reordering model (Tillman, 2004) considers three orientations: monotone (M), swap (S), and discontinuous (D), while the reordering probabilities are conditioned on the lexical context of each phrase pair.

All language models were trained with SRI LM toolkit (Stolcke, 2002). Language models for Dutch, Spanish and Chinese use 5-grams, while the idealized English ($\hat{s}$) is modeled using 3-grams.

We use Stanford parser[6] (Klein and Manning, 2003) as a source-side parsing engine. The parser was trained on the WSJ Penn treebank provided with 14 syntactic categories and 48 POS tags. The evaluation conditions were case-sensitive and included punctuation marks. For Maximum Entropy modeling we used the maxent toolkit[7].

Translation scores. Table 3 shows the results of automatic evaluation using BLEU (Papineni et al., 2002) and NIST (Doddington, 2002) metrics.

MERrd configuration corresponds to the PBSMT system with the source side of the parallel corpus reordered using our Maximum Entropy model, but the transduction operations are limited to permutation of the children only. *MERrd+xlt* configuration refers to the set of systems which, beside child permutation, includes a deletion operation with the maximum number of tree layers that can be deleted set to x. All reordered systems include a MSD model as a supporting reordering mechanism.

BLEU scores measured on the test data, which are statistically significant from the best PBSMT results are marked with bold. The statistical significance calculations have been done for a 95% confidence interval and 1000 resamples, following the guidelines in Koehn (2004).

Analysis. Our results show that source-reordering is beneficial for the language pairs with high mutual word order disparity. In contrast to English-Dutch and English-Chinese translation tasks, the statistical significance test reveals that all but the *MERrd+5lt* English-Spanish PBSMT systems with rearranged input are not different from the translation quality delivered by Moses. This disappointing result for the English-to-Spanish translation task may be explained by the fact that many reordering differences are resolved by standard reordering models (distance-based and MSD).

Table 3 shows the results of automatic translation quality evaluation. A gap between the maximum reachable performance shown by tree transduction systems and the translation quality delivered

[2]The latter feature intends to model the divergence in word order in relative clauses between Dutch and English which is illustrated in Figure 1.

[3]code.google.com/p/giza-pp/

[4]http://www.fjoch.com/mkcls.html

[5]http://www.statmt.org/moses/

[6]http://nlp.stanford.edu/software/lex-parser.shtml

[7]http://homepages.inf.ed.ac.uk/lzhang10/maxent_toolkit.html

Parameter	Dutch	English	Spanish	English	Chinese	English
Training corpus						
Sentences	1.2 M	1.2 M	1.4 M	1.4 M	1.5 M	1.5 M
Words	32.9 M	33.0 M	40.1 M	38.54 M	35.35 M	35.00 M
Vocabulary	228 K	104 K	168 K	119 K	136 K	245 K
Average sentence length	27.20	27.28	28.80	27.67	24.06	23.83

Table 2: Statistics of the training, development and test corpora.

by our model is 0.05-0.29 BLEU points for English-Dutch, 0.01-0.09 for English-Spanish and 0.27-0.76 for English-Chinese. These numbers demonstrate that there are some potentially usable regularities not captured by our current conditional tree-transduction model.

7 Conclusions and future work

We present a source reordering system for PBSMT, in which the reordering decisions are conditioned on features from the source parse tree. Our system allows for two operations over the parse tree: permuting the order of sibling nodes and deleting child nodes in order to make the tree flatter and exploit sibling permutations at the remaining layers.

Our contribution can be summarized as follows: (1) we report detailed results of maximum potential performance that can be achieved with source reordering under different constraints, (2) we define a source-reordering process through an efficient sequence of greedy, context-conditioned transduction operations over the source parse trees.

The method was tested on three different translation tasks. The results show that our approach is more effective for language pairs with significant difference in word order. Another important observation is that our model demonstrate translation quality comparable with the one delivered by SMT systems based on hierarchical phrases.

The introduced reordering algorithm and the results obtained present many opportunities for future work. We plan to perform a detailed analysis of the structure of the extracted phrases to find out the particular cases where the improvement comes from. We also propose to discover other possible transduction operations to better explore the reordering space.

8 Acknowledgements

This work is supported by The Netherlands Organization for Scientific Research (NWO) under VIDI grant (nr. 639.022.604).

System	EnNl			EnEs			EnZh		
	Dev	Test		Dev	Test		Dev	Test	
	BLEU	BLEU	NIST	BLEU	BLEU	NIST	BLEU	BLEU	NIST
Baselines									
PBSMT	23.88	24.04	6.29	32.31	31.70	7.48	18.71	22.21	5.28
PBSMT+MSD	24.07	24.04	6.28	32.45	31.85	7.47	18.99	21.18	5.30
Moses-chart	23.94	24.93	6.39	30.58	31.80	7.41	19.93	23.90	5.41
Reordering systems									
MERrd	24.64	**24.72**	6.33	31.97	32.19	7.52	19.82	**23.17**	5.33
MERrd+2lt	24.61	**24.99**	6.35	31.70	32.11	7.50	20.02	23.01	5.33
MERrd+3lt	24.82	**24.98**	6.34	31.65	32.25	7.52	20.21	**23.14**	5.34
MERrd+5lt	24.78	**25.12**	6.37	31.99	**32.38**	7.52	20.29	**23.17**	5.35

Table 3: Experimental results.

References

A. Berger, S. Della Pietra, and V. Della Pietra. 1996. A maximum entropy approach to natural language processing. *Computational Linguistics*, 1(22):39–72.

D. Chiang. 2005. A hierarchical phrase-based model for statistical machine translation. In *Proceedings of ACL'05*, pages 263–270, Ann Arbor, MI, USA.

D. Chiang. 2007. Hierarchical phrase-based translation. *Computational Linguistics*, 2(33):201–228.

M. Collins, P. Koehn, and I. Kučerová. 2005. Clause restructuring for statistical machine translation. In *Proceedings of ACL'05*, pages 531–540, Ann Arbor, MI, USA.

M. R. Costa-jussà and J. A. R. Fonollosa. 2006. Statistical machine reordering. In *Proceedings of HLT/EMNLP'06*, pages 70–76, New York, NY, USA.

G. Doddington. 2002. Automatic evaluation of machine translation quality using n-grams co-occurrence statistics. In *Proceedings of HLT'02*, pages 128–132, San Diego, CA, USA.

L. Huang, H. Zhang, D. Gildea, and K. Knight. 2009. Binarization of synchronous context-free grammars. *Computational Linguistics*, 35(4):559–595.

M. Khalilov and K. Sima'an. 2010. A discriminative syntactic model for source permutation via tree transduction. In *Proceedings of SSST-4 workshop at COLING'10*, pages 92–100, Beijing, China.

D. Klein and C. Manning. 2003. Accurate unlexicalized parsing. In *Proceedings of ACL'03*, pages 423–430, Sapporo, Japan.

Ph. Koehn, F. Och, and D. Marcu. 2003. Statistical phrase-based machine translation. In *Proceedings of the HLT-NAACL'03*, pages 48–54, Edmonton, Canada.

Ph. Koehn, H. Hoang, A. Birch, C. Callison-Burch, M. Federico, N. Bertoldi, B. Cowan, W. Shen, C. Moran, R. Zens, C. Dyer, O. Bojar, A. Constantin, and E. Herbst. 2007. Moses: open-source toolkit for statistical machine translation. In *Proceedings of ACL'07*, pages 177–180, Prague, Czech Republic.

Ph. Koehn. 2004. Statistical significance tests for machine translation evaluation. In *Proceedings of EMNLP'04*, pages 388–395, Barcelona, Spain.

C. Li, L. Minghui, D. Zhang, M. Li, M. Zhou, and Y. Guan. 2007. A probabilistic approach to syntax-based reordering for statistical machine translation. In *Proceedings of ACL'07*, pages 720–727, Prague, Czech Republic.

F. Och and H. Ney. 2004. The alignment template approach to statistical machine translation. *Computational Linguistics*, 30(4):417–449.

F. Och. 1999. An efficient method for determining bilingual word classes. In *Proceedings of ACL'99*, pages 71–76, Maryland, MD, USA.

F. Och. 2003. Minimum error rate training in statistical machine translation. In *Proceedings of ACL'03*, pages 160–167, Sapporo, Japan.

K. Papineni, S. Roukos, T. Ward, and W. Zhu. 2002. Bleu: a method for automatic evaluation of machine translation. In *Proceedings of ACL'02*, pages 311–318, Philadelphia, PA, USA.

M. Popovic' and H. Ney. 2006. POS-based word reorderings for statistical machine translation. In *Proceedings of LREC'06*, pages 1278–1283, Genoa, Italy, May.

A. Ramanathan, P. Bhattacharyya, J. Hegde, R.M. Shah, and M. Sasikumar. 2008. Simple syntactic and morphological processing can help english-hindi statistical machine translation. In *In Proceedings of IJCNLP'08*, Hyderabad, India.

A. Stolcke. 2002. SRILM: an extensible language modeling toolkit. In *Proceedings of SLP'02*, pages 901–904.

C. Tillman. 2004. A unigram orientation model for statistical machine translation. In *Proceedings of HLT-NAACL'04*, pages 101–104, Boston, MA, USA.

R. Tromble and J. Eisner. 2009. Learning linear ordering problems for better translation. In *Proceedings of EMNLP'09*, pages 1007–1016, Singapore.

K. Visweswariah, J. Navratil, J. Sorensen, V. Chenthamarakshan, and N. Kambhatla. 2010. Syntax based reordering with automatically derived rules for improved statistical machine translation. In *Proceeding of COLING'10*, pages 1119–1127, Beijing, China.

C. Wang, M. Collins, and Ph. Koehn. 2007. Chinese syntactic reordering for statistical machine translation. In *Proceedings of EMNLP-CoNLL'07*, pages 737–745, Prague, Czech Republic.

W. Wang, J. May, K. Knight, and D. Marcu. June 2010. Re-structuring, re-labeling, and re-aligning for syntax-based machine translation. *Computational Linguistics*, 36:247–277.

D. Wu and H. Wong. 1998. Machine translation wih a stochastic grammatical channel. In *Proceedings of ACL-COLING'98*, pages 1408–1415, Columbus, OH, USA.

F. Xia and M. McCord. 2004. Improving a statistical MT system with automatically learned rewrite patterns. In *Proceedings of COLING'04*, pages 508–514, Geneva, Switzerland.

R. Zens, F. Och, and H. Ney. 2002. Phrase-based statistical machine translation. In *Proceedings of KI: Advances in Artificial Intelligence*, pages 18–32.

S. Zwarts and M. Dras. 2007. Syntax-based word reordering in phrase-based statistical machine translation: Why does it work? In *Proceedings of the MT Summit XI*, Copenhagen, Denmark.

Discriminative Phrase-based Lexicalized Reordering Models using Weighted Reordering Graphs

Wang Ling, João Graça, David Martins de Matos, Isabel Trancoso, Alan Black
L[2]F Spoken Systems Lab, INESC-ID, Lisboa, Portugal
Language Technologies Institute, Carnegie Mellon University, Pittsburgh, PA, USA
{wang.ling,joao.graca,isabel.trancoso,david.matos}@inesc-id.pt
awb@cs.cmu.edu

Abstract

Lexicalized reordering models play a central role in phrase-based statistical machine translation systems. Starting from the distance-based reordering model, improvements have been made by considering adjacent words in word-based models, adjacent phrases pairs in phrase-based models, and finally, all phrases pairs in a sentence pair in the reordering graphs. However, reordering graphs treat all phrase pairs equally and fail to weight the relationships between phrase pairs. In this work, we propose an extension to the reordering models, named weighted reordering models, that allows discriminative behavior to be defined in the estimation of the reordering model orientations. We apply our extension using the weighted alignment matrices to weight phrase pairs, based on the consistency of their alignments, and define a distance metric to weight relationships between phrase pairs, based on their distance in the sentence. Experiments on the IWSLT 2010 evaluation dataset for for the Chinese-English language pair yields an improvement of 0.38 (2%) and 0.94 (3.7%) BLEU points over the state-of-the-art work's results using weighted alignment matrices.

1 Introduction

Reordering in Machine Translation (MT) is the task of word-order redistribution of translated words. An early reordering paradigm uses a simple distance based reordering model, which penalizes words that diverge from their original position after being translated (Koehn et al., 2003). This works moderately well for language pairs where reordering distances are small, but performs poorly for language pairs such as Chinese-English, where the opposite occurs. One of many approaches to implement improved reordering models is to use the lexical information during the phrase extraction algorithm to predict reordering orientations, using word-aligned bilingual sentences. However, the fact that spurious word alignments might occur leads to the use of alternative representations for word alignments that allow multiple alignment hypotheses, rather than the 1-best alignment (Venugopal et al., 2009; Mi et al., 2008; Christopher Dyer et al., 2008). More recently, a more efficient representation of multiple alignments was proposed in (Liu et al., 2009) named weighted alignment matrices, which represents the alignment probability distribution over the words of each parallel sentence. The method for building a word-based lexicalized reordering model using these matrices is proposed in (Ling et al., 2011). However, phrase-based reordering models have been shown to perform better than word-based models for several language pairs (Tillmann, 2004; Su et al., 2010; Galley and Manning, 2008), such as Chinese-English and Arabic-English.

In this work, we propose an extension to the phrase-based lexicalized model approach using reordering graphs presented in (Su et al., 2010), which allows phrase pairs to be weighted differently, rather than uniformly as in the original proposal. Then, we will present a phrase-based approach to estimate the orientations of the reordering model from the weighted alignment matrices using this extension.

2 Lexicalized Reordering models

In this section we will present the lexicalized reordering models approaches that are relevant for this work.

2.1 Word-based Reordering

The lexicalized reordering model is possibly the most used lexicalized reordering model and it calculates, as features, the reordering orientation for the previous and the next word, for each phrase pair. In the word-based reordering model (Axelrod et al., 2005), during the phrase extraction, given a source sentence S and a target sentence T, the alignment set A, where a_i^j is an alignment from i to j, the phrase pair with words in positions between i and j in S, S_i^j, and n and m in T, T_n^m, can be classified with one of three orientations with respect to the previous word. The orientation is

- Monotonous - if only the previous word in the source is aligned with the previous word in the target, or, more formally, if $a_{i-1}^{n-1} \in A \wedge a_{j+1}^{n-1} \notin A$.
- Swap - if only the next word in the source is aligned with the previous word in the target, or more formally, if $a_{j+1}^{n-1} \in A \wedge a_{i-1}^{n-1} \notin A$.
- Discontinuous - if neither of the above are true, which means, $(a_{i-1}^{n-1} \in A \wedge a_{j+1}^{n-1} \in A) \vee (a_{i-1}^{n-1} \notin A \wedge a_{j+1}^{n-1} \notin A)$.

The orientations with respect to the next word are given analogously. The reordering model is generated by grouping the phrase pairs that are equal, and calculating the probabilities of the grouped phrase pair being associated each orientation type and direction, based on the orientations for each direction that are extracted. Formally, the probability of the phrase pair p having a monotonous orientation is given by:

$$P(p, mono) = \frac{C(p, mono)}{C(p, mono) + C(p, swap) + C(p, disc)} \quad (1)$$

Where $C(p, o)$ is the number of times a phrase is extracted with the orientation o in that group of phrase pairs.

2.2 Word-based Reordering using alignment matrices

The work in (Ling et al., 2011) adapts the word-based reordering model to extract the reordering orientations from the weighted alignment matrices. This is done by changing the $C(p, o)$ from a count function over a given set of phrase pairs P to a weighted sum given by:

$$C(p, o) = \sum_{p \in P} Sc(p) P_c(p, o) \quad (2)$$

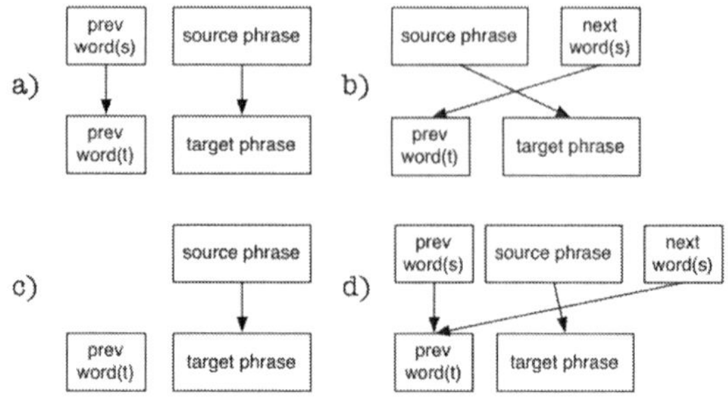

Figure 1: Enumeration of possible reordering cases with respect to the previous word. Case a) is classified as monotonous, case b) is classified as swap and cases c) and d) are classified as discontinuous.

The score $Sc(p)$ of a phrase pair p is given by the algorithm described in (Liu et al., 2009), which is based on its alignments. This score is higher if the alignment points in the phrase pair have high probabilities, and if the alignment is consistent. Thus, if a phrase pair has better quality, its orientation is given more weight than phrase pairs with worse quality. Rather than classifying each phrase pair with either monotonous (M), swap (S) or discontinuous (D), a probability distribution for the orientations is calculated. Thus, for the previous word, given a weighted alignment matrix W, the phrase pair between the indexes i and j in S, S_i^j, and n and m in T, T_n^m, the probability values for each orientation are given by:

- $P_c(p, M) = W_{i-1}^{n-1}(1 - W_{j+1}^{n-1})$
- $P_c(p, S) = W_{j+1}^{n-1}(1 - W_{i-1}^{n-1})$
- $P_c(p, D) = W_{i-1}^{n-1} W_{j+1}^{n-1} + (1 - W_{i-1}^{n-1})(1 - W_{j+1}^{n-1})$

2.3 Phrase-based Reordering

The problem with the word-based lexicalized reordering model is that it is assumed that the adjacent words are translated by themselves, which is not always true in phrase-based SMT. The reordering model presented in (Tillmann, 2004) uses adjacent phrases to generate the phrase orientations. In this model, the previous orientation of a phrase pair p:

- Monotonous if there is a phrase pair with the source S_x^{i-1} that ends at $i-1$ and starts at any x, that is aligned to the target phrase T_y^{n-1}, that ends at $n-1$ and starts at any y. In another words, if there is an adjacent phrase pair that occurs before p, both in the source and in the target sentences.

- Swap if there is a phrase pair with the source S_{j+1}^{x} that starts at $j+1$ and ends at any x, that is aligned to the target phrase T_{y}^{n-1}, that ends at $n-1$ and starts at any y. In another words, if there is an adjacent phrase pair that occurs before p in the target sentence and after p in the source sentence.

- Discontinuous - if neither of the above are true.

The work presented in (Tillmann, 2004) only considers phrases that are smaller than a fixed size, since the possible phrases for each bilingual sentence are generated and kept in memory making the time and memory needed to store and lookup all possible phrases grows rapidly as the size grows. The work in (Galley and Manning, 2008) implements a shift-reduce parsing algorithm that updates the previously extracted phrase pair orientations when a new phrase pair is extracted, which allows arbitrary sized phrase pairs to be considered.

2.4 Phrase Reordering using Reordering Graphs

The phrase based model considers the existence of a single adjacent phrase, which is not ideal, since many possible adjacent phrases exist for each extracted phrase pair, which can generate different orientations. In work done in (Su et al., 2010) the orientation is computed by considering all possible reorderings of phrase pairs that are extracted in the sentence pair. Once again $C(p, o)$ is given by the weighted count:

$$C(p, o) = \sum_{p \in Ph} P_c(p, o) \qquad (3)$$

Where $P_c(p, o)$ is extracted by structuring the extracted phrase pairs into a reordering graph. This graph is created for each sentence pair, using extractable phrase pairs as nodes and connecting adjacent phrase pairs in the target side with an edge. Each edge is associated with a reordering orientation, dependent on the source side of the connected phrase pairs. If these are not adjacent in the source side, the edge is given a discontinuous orientation, otherwise, the edge is given a monotonous or swap orientation depending on whether they are in the same order or not in the source side, respectively.

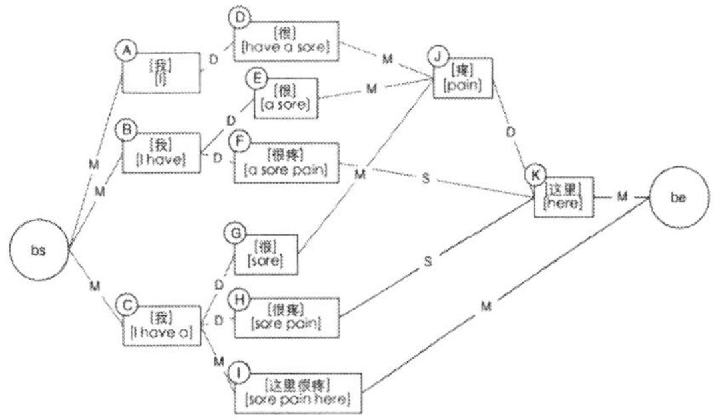

Figure 2: Reordering Graph for the sentence pair with source "我这里很疼 (wo zhe li hen teng)" and target 'I have a sore pain here". Each extracted phrase pair is denoted as a rectangle, with the source and target phrases inside. Each phrase pair is also labeled for reference. The edges are labeled with its orientation (the colors are only for easier visualization).

Furthermore, phrase pairs with no adjacent phrase pairs are linked to the nearest phrase pair. These arcs are also given a discontinuous orientation.

A start node bs is added and is linked to all phrase pairs at the start of the target sentence , and a end node be, which is linked by all phrase pairs that end the target sentence.

For the previous orientation weight, the probability $P_c(p, o)$ of the phrase pair p having a given orientation o, considering the set $Prev(o)$, with all phrase pairs that are linked to p that would lead to a orientation o, is given by:

$$P_c(p, o) = \sum_{p' \in Prev(o)} \frac{\alpha(p')\beta(p)}{\beta(bs)} \qquad (4)$$

In this equation, $\alpha(p')$ is the number of paths to the p' node from the first phrase, $\beta(p)$ is the number of paths from p to the last phrase and $\beta(bs)$ results in the number of possible paths. We can see from this equation that $\alpha(p') \times \beta(p)$ results in the number of paths containing the arc from p' to p, thus not only multiple adjacent phrase pairs are considered, but these are also weighted by the number of possible translation segmentations that would use that phrase pair.

An example of a reordering graph is illustrated in figure 2. We can see in that for the phrase pair "这里 (zhe li)"→"here", instead of simply giving the swap orientation due to the adjacent phrase pair "很疼 (hen teng)"→"sore pain", it also considers the case where "疼 (teng)" is translated by itself to "pain", in which case the orientation would be discontinuous. In this case, the weight is evenly distributed between the 2 orientations since there are 2 paths that contain an edge with each orientation.

3 Phrase-based reordering using Weighted Reordering Graphs

We see in the example given in section 2.4 that the phrase pair "这里 (zhe li)"→"here" is given an equal weight to the swap and discontinuous orientations. However, if we translate "疼 (teng)" by itself, we would have to translate "很 (hen)" without "疼 (teng)". The translation for "很 (hen)" by itself to "sore" is not very probable, since "很 (hen)" without context is generally translated to "very", "much" or "quite". Thus, it is more probable during decoding that the segmentation "很疼 (hen teng)" is used. Although the phrase-based reordering model presented in section 2.3 gives a better reordering estimate in this case, in cases where there is an equal probability of both segmentations the graph-based approach would be better. Hence, we argument that by treating phrase pairs discriminatively, we can improve reordering orientations estimate in both cases. In this work, we propose an extension to the reordering graphs to allow the definition of discriminative behavior during training. We will start by describing our model for the Weighted Reordering Graph and then we proceed into the definition of the algorithm to extract the word orientations from the Weighted Reordering Matrices.

3.1 Weighted Reordering Graph Model

We define a weighted reordering graph for a given sentence pair S as $G_S = (V, E, W_v, W_e)$, where V is the set of all vertices, which are phrase pairs $p_1, p_2, ..., p_n$, and E is the set of all edges and we denote a edge from p_1 to p_2 as $e(p_1, p_2)$. W_v and W_e are functions that map each element in V and E to a weight.

We define a path $PH(bs, p_1, p_2, be)$ as a path starting in bs and through p_1, then p_2 and ending in be. The weight of a path $PH(p_1, p_2, ..., p_{k-1}, p_k)$ is given by the product of the weights of its phrase pairs $W_v(p_1)W_v(p_2)...W_v(p_{k-1}), W_v(p_k)$ and the weights of the edges connecting the phrases in the path $e(p_1, p_2)...e(p_{k-1}, p_k)$. If both weight functions W_v and W_e are set to return 1 we define the same behavior as a reordering graph described in section 2.4, since all paths will have the weight of 1.

Following equation 4, we define the probability of a given orientation, $P_c(p, o)$, for a weighted reordering graph as:

$$P_c(p, o) = \sum_{p' \in Prev(o)} \frac{\alpha_w(p')W_e(e(p', p))\beta_w(p)}{\beta_w(bs)} \quad (5)$$

Where $\alpha_w(p')$ is the sum of weights of paths from bs to p' and $\beta_w(p)$ is the sum of the weights of the paths from p to be. It is also crucial to consider the weight of the edge $e(p', p)$, since it is not weighted in neither $\alpha_w(p')$ nor $\beta_w(p)$. This is not present in equation 4 since all edges are weighted as 1.

The functions α_w and β_w can be defined as:

$$\alpha_w(p) = W_v(p) \sum_{p' \in Prev(p)} \alpha_w(p')W_e(e(p', p)) \quad (6)$$

$$\beta_w(p) = W_v(p) \sum_{p' \in Next(p)} \beta_w(p')W_e(e(p', p)) \quad (7)$$

Where $Prev(p)$ and $Next(p)$ are sets of all phrase pairs that are linked to and linked from p, respectively. We also initiate $\alpha_w(bs) = 1$ and $\beta_w(be) = 1$. These two values can be initialized with any value, as this will not affect the normalized result from equation 5.

The pre-computation of α_w and β_w can be performed using an approach similar to the forward-backward algorithm and calculating the forward probabilities for α_w and backward probabilities for β_w, with time complexity in the order $O(N^2T)$, where N is the number of different phrase pairs and T is the length of sequences. To compute α_w, we need to take into account that the vertices/phrase pairs can be ordered topologically in an array so that a vertice in the index i does not have edges pointing to any vertice at any index at or before $i - 1$. This can be done by ordering the phrase pairs by the ending position of the target phrase n, starting with bs, since we know that the phrase pairs ending at n can only have links to phrase pairs ending at least at $n + 1$, according to the definition of an edge in a reordering graph.

The algorithm for computing β_w can be done analogously, by starting from be and sorting according to the target phrase's starting position.

3.2 Choosing W_v and W_e

In this work, we use the information given by the Weighted Alignment Matrices to define $W_v(p)$. We set $W_v(p)$ using the phrase pair scoring algorithm presented in (Liu et al., 2009), which calculates the weight of a phrase pair based on its alignment points. This weight can be seen as the

Algorithm 1 Compute α_w

Require: sorted phrase pairs P
  $\alpha_w(P) = \{0, ..., 0\}$
  for p in P **do**
    if $p = bs$ **then**
      $\alpha_w(bs) := W_v(bs)$
    end if
    for p' in followingNodes(p) **do**
      $w = W_e(e(p, p'))W_v(p')$
      $\alpha_w(p') := \alpha_w(p') + w\alpha_w(p)$
    end for
  end for
  return extractedPhrasePairs

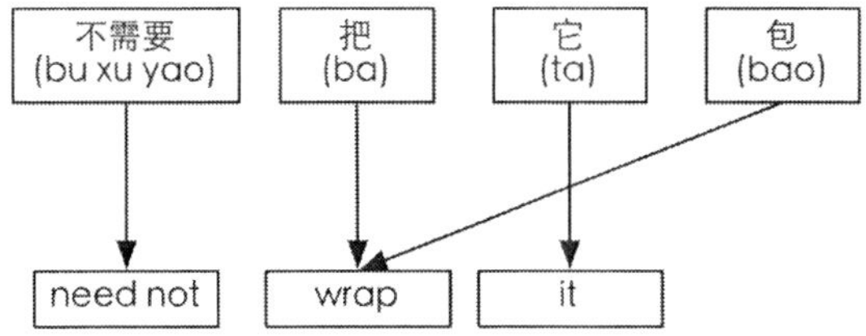

Figure 3: Illustration of a case where no adjacent phrase pairs exits for a phrase pair. In this case, the phrase pair "不需要 (bu xu yao)"→"need not" and the phrase pair "它 (ta)"→"it" are linked by an edge even though they are not adjacent.

probability of that phrase pair being extractable according to the heuristic proposed in (Koehn et al., 2003).

We also set $W_e(e(p^a, p^b))$ to a distance function between the phrases p^a and p^b in the target, to better cope with the situation where there are no adjacent phrase pairs to a phrase pair and an edge is added to the closest adjacent phrase. An example of such a case instance is displayed in figure 3. In this case, the phrase ending with the target word "wrap" can not be extracted, since it is aligned with "把 (ba)" and "包 (bao)". Thus, consistent phrase pairs that can be extracted must at least contain these 2 words to have "wrap" in the target. Another situation where this might also happen is the case where a phrase is not extracted due to size constraints. In both cases the reordering orientation of the edge is always discontinuous since the target phrases are not adjacent. We find that the reordering orientations that originates from these edges are not very precise. In the first case, the next orientation for the phrase pair "不需要 (bu xu yao)"→"need not" would be divided between monotonous from the edge to the phrase pair "把它包 (ba ta bao)"→"wrap it" and discontinuous from the edge to the phrase pair from "它 (ta)" to "it". However, in an actual translation the only way to translate this sentence correctly would be to treat "把它包 (ba ta bao)" as a segment, which favors the monotonous orientation. Furthermore, even if we could translate "把 (ba)" and "包 (bao)" to "wrap", the orientation would still be monotonous. In the second case, an edge between phrase pairs p^a and p^b that is created because a phrase pair p^c between p^a and p^b was not extracted due to size constraints, would mean that there is a missing edge from p^a to p^c and another from p^b to p^c, and no edge from p^a to p^b. Thus, the orientation of this edge is likely to be spurious, and should be given a lower weight.

This cannot be done by setting this weight to 0 (removing the arc), since it will render all paths that contain that edge to 0. For instance, if we set the maximum phrase pair size to 7 and the first 8 words of the source and target are aligned in a way that no smaller translation units can be extracted, there would be an edge from bs to the 9th word. Therefore, if we set the weight of the edge to 0, any path we take would have 0 weight, rendering the whole sentence pair useless. Hence, we define the W_e function as:

$$W_e(e(p, p')) = \frac{1}{(1+\lambda)^d} \quad (8)$$

Where d is the distance between p and p' defined by the number of words in the target sentence between p and p', and λ is a positive value defining the penalty as d increases. In this work, we empirically set $\lambda = 0.5$, and leave the optimization of this parameter as future work.

3.3 Reordering Model Comparison

In order to illustrate the performance of the different reordering models, we consider two training sentences taken from the IWSLT 2010 DIALOG task. The weighted alignment matrices for these sentences are illustrated in tables 1 and 2. For simplicity in terms of illustration, we assume that algorithms that do not use the alignment matrices, consider all non-zero cells as alignment points. The probability distribution for different previous orientations of each reordering model for the phrase pair "这里 (zhe li)→here" from sentence 1 and the phrase pair "今天 (jin tian)→today" from sentence 2 are calculated in tables 3 and 4, respectively.

Sentence 1	I	have	a	sore	pain	here
我 (wo)	0.90					
这里 (zhe li)						0.75
很 (hen)				0.50		
疼 (teng)					0.80	

Table 1: Weighted alignment matrix for a training sentence pair from DIALOG training corpus from IWSLT 2010.

Sentence 2	Are	there	any	baseball	games	today
今天 (jin tian)						1
有 (you)		0.60	0.90			
棒球 (bang qiu)				1		
比赛 (bi sai)					0.65	
吗 (ma)						

Table 2: Weighted alignment matrix for a training sentence pair from DIALOG training corpus from IWSLT 2010.

We can see that the word-based reordering models classify the word orientation as discontinuous, since the previous word in the target is not aligned to adjacent words in the source. This leads to inaccurate orientations for the first phrase pair, since the words "很 (hen)" and "疼 (teng)" have a high probability of being translated together. In the second phrase pair, it gives a good approximation of the correct orientation, since "棒球 (bang qiu)" and "比赛 (bi sai)" are good translations even when translated without "有 (you)".

The opposite occurs with the phrase-based reordering model, since it considers the source phrase segmentation "很疼 (hen teng)" and "有棒球比赛 (you bang qiu bi sai)", respectively. Thus, the estimation of the orientation is better for the former and worse for the latter phrase pair.

Using the reordering graph, orientations are estimated for different adjacent phrase pairs. In the first phrase pair, both cases where the source phrase "很疼 (hen teng)" and "疼 (teng)" are used as translation units are taken into account, and the same happens with the second phrase pair. As it was already referred in section 3, the problem with this estimation is that it fails to consider that "疼 (teng)" is more likely to be translated with "很 (hen)", otherwise the translation of "很 (hen)" is less likely to be accurate.

这里 (zhe li)→here	Mono	Swap	Disc
Word-based	0	0	1
Weighted-Word-based	0	0	1
Phrase-based	0	1	0
Graph-based	0	0.333	0.333
Weighted-graph-based	0	0.271	0.180

Table 3: Previous orientation probabilities for different lexicalized reordering models for the phrase pair "这里 (zhe li)"→"here", taken from sentence 1.

今天 (jin tian)→today	Mono	Swap	Disc
Word-based	0	0	1
Weighted-Word-based	0	0	1
Phrase-based	0	1	0
Graph-based	0	0.166	0.500
Weighted-graph-based	0	0.187	0.416

Table 4: Previous orientation probabilities for different lexicalized reordering models for the phrase pair "今天 (jin tian)"→"today", taken from sentence 2.

Finally, by using weighted-reordering-graph, using phrase scores calculated from weighted alignment matrices, paths in the graph that contain phrase pairs that are better aligned are given more weight.

4 Experiments

We implemented both word-based and phrase-based lexicalized reordering models described above, and compared the translation results with our algorithm.

4.1 Corpus

Our experiments were performed over two datasets, the BTEC and the DIALOG parallel corpora from the latest IWSLT evaluation in 2010 (Paul et al., 2010). The experiments performed with the BTEC corpus used the French-English subset, while the ones perfomed with the DIALOG corpus used the Chinese-English subset. The training corpora contains about 19K and 30K sentences, respectively.

The development corpus for the BTEC task was the CSTAR03 test set composed by 506 sentences, and the test set was the IWSLT04 test set composed by 500 sentences and 16 references. As for the DIALOG task, we performed 2 tests, one using the evaluation datasets from IWSLT evaluation in 2006 (IWSLT06) and in 2008 (IWSLT08). The development from the IWSLT06 evaluation is composed by 489 sentences, and the test set was composed by 500 sentences and 7 references. The development from IWSLT08 evaluation is composed by 245 sentences, and the test set was composed by 506 sentences and 7 references.

4.2 Setup

We use two setups for the different corpora that are used. Word-based (word-based), phrase-based (phrase-based), and phrase-based using reordering graphs (graph-based) reordering models are generally used with the regular phrase extraction algorithm, with alignment constraints defined in (Koehn et al., 2003). Thus, we compare our method with the methods above in this environment. The weighted word-based reordering model (weighted word-based) described in section 2.2 was tested using the phrase extraction algorithm described in (Liu et al., 2009), where phrase pairs are filtered out based on their scores, which are calculated from their alignment probabilities. So, we also test our algorithm under these conditions. In our work, we set the threshold for filtering out phrase pairs to 0.1, which was the threshold used in (Ling et al., 2011). We also test separately our implementation of W_v (graph-based W_v), which weights phrase pairs according to their scores, and W_e (graph-based W_e), a penalty based on the distance between phrase pairs. Then, we test both approaches combined (graph-based W_vW_e).

The word alignments and the weighted alignment matrices are generated using the Geppetto toolkit[1], using a regular HMM-based word alignment model (V. Graça et al., 2010), without restraints. The optimum alignment is found using posterior decoding, and the weighted alignment matrices are obtained from the same alignment posteriors.

The optimization of the translation model weights was done using MERT tuning. Each experiment was run three times, and the final scores are calculated as the average of the three runs in order to stabilize the results. The results were evaluated using BLEU-4 and METEOR, and computed with 16 references.

4.3 Results

Tables 5, 6 and 7 show the scores using the different reordering models. Consistent improvements

[1]http://code.google.com/p/geppetto/

BTEC	BLEU	METEOR
regular phrase extraction		
word-based	**57.97**	**63.82**
phrase-based	57.56	63.57
graph-based	57.53	63.63
graph-based W_v	57.30	63.42
graph-based W_e	57.47	63.49
graph-based W_vW_e	57.66	63.63
weighted phrase extraction		
weighted word-based	**62.01**	**66.31**
graph-based W_v	61.10	65.75
graph-based W_vW_e	61.75	66.19

Table 5: Results for the BTEC task.

IWSLT06 DIALOG	BLEU	METEOR
regular phrase extraction		
word-based	14.88	36.61
phrase-based	15.32	36.90
graph-based	15.28	37.14
graph-based W_v	15.65	37.40
graph-based W_e	15.39	37.09
graph-based W_vW_e	**15.81**	**37.66**
weighted phrase extraction		
weighted word-based	17.58	40.33
graph-based W_v	17.84	40.53
graph-based W_vW_e	**17.96**	**40.90**

Table 6: Results for the DIALOG task using the test set from IWSLT06.

IWSLT08 DIALOG	BLEU	METEOR
regular phrase extraction		
word-based	23.30	40.39
phrase-based	23.42	40.27
graph-based	23.52	40.37
graph-based W_v	23.97	**40.74**
graph-based W_e	23.67	40.70
graph-based W_vW_e	**24.13**	40.69
weighted phrase extraction		
weighted word-based	24.53	44.59
graph-based W_v	25.34	**45.38**
graph-based W_vW_e	**25.47**	44.62

Table 7: Results for the DIALOG task using the test set from IWSLT08.

in the DIALOG corpus scores over state-of-the-art reordering models when using the weighted reordering graphs. We can see that both W_v and W_e generate improved results, and their combination generally performs better than both when used individually. The METEOR score is not always higher using our algorithm, but we believe this roots from the fact that the MERT tuning was set to optimize the BLEU score.

For the BTEC corpus, we observe that phrase-based models do not perform as well, although the difference in BLEU is only 0.26 (0.4%) in the weighted case with respect to the weighted word-based model. We believe that this is because a large percentage of translation units that are used during decoding is one-to-one, as it was reported in (Ling et al., 2010). It is highly likely that this roots from the fact that the training set is small, so the probability of finding large sequences of strings in the training set that matches the ones in the test set is rather low. In this case the word-based reordering models yield better reordering estimates, since considering longer training phrase-pairs that will not even be present in the test set will only degenerate the orientation probabilities. This suggests for future work that adding prior knowledge about the probability of a phrase-pair given its size could improve the translation quality. In the extreme case, we can give more weight to phrase pairs with the source that is present in the test set, for estimating the orientations, generating a reordering model that is specific for each test set.

5 Conclusions

In this work, we presented the current state of the art in improving the lexicalized model orientation estimates. The basic word based lexicalized reordering model uses neighboring words to perform the orientation estimates. However, since words are not always translated by themselves, these estimates can be improved by considering neighboring phrases rather than words. Another way to improve the phrase based reordering model is to consider multiple adjacent phrases, which can be done using a reordering graph. Finally, another improvement can be made by addressing the limitations of the lexicalized reordering models extracted from a single alignment, and generate the orientation estimates using weighted alignment matrices.

We extend the reordering graph model to allow the discriminative treatment of different paths. Using scores extracted from weighted alignment matrices to weight phrase pairs and a distance penalty function to penalize paths with phrase pairs that are not adjacent, improvements of 0.38 (2%) and 0.94 (3.4%) in BLEU over the state of the art algorithms using weighted alignment matrices for the Chinese-English language pair can be achieved.

As future work, we will experiment with different types of phrase pair and edge scorers and extending the weighted reordering graphs to allow multiple scorers to be combined and optimized. Additionally, we will evaluate the impact of our algorithm in larger corpora, since we believe that using a larger training corpora will result in bigger improvements over the word-based approaches, since longer sequences of words in the test set will be found in the training set, resulting in longer translation units.

The code used in this work is currently integrated with the Geppetto toolkit[2] , and it will be made available in the next version for public use.

6 Acknowledgements

This work was partially supported by FCT (INESC-ID multiannual funding) through the PIDDAC Program funds, and also through projects CMU-PT/HuMach/0039/2008 and CMU-PT/0005/2007.

The PhD thesis of Wang Ling is supported by FCT grant SFRH/BD/51157/2010.

The authors also wish to thank the anonymous reviewers for many helpful comments.

References

Amittai Axelrod, Ra Birch Mayne, Chris Callison-burch, Miles Osborne, and David Talbot. 2005. Edinburgh system description for the 2005 iwslt speech translation evaluation. In *In Proc. International Workshop on Spoken Language Translation (IWSLT.*

Christopher Dyer, Smaranda Muresan, and Philip Resnik. 2008. Generalizing Word Lattice Translation. Technical Report LAMP-TR-149, University of Maryland, College Park, February.

Michel Galley and Christopher D. Manning. 2008. A simple and effective hierarchical phrase reordering model. In *In Proceedings of EMNLP 2008.*

[2]http://code.google.com/p/geppetto/

Philipp Koehn, Franz Josef Och, and Daniel Marcu. 2003. Statistical phrase-based translation. In *Proceedings of the 2003 Conference of the North American Chapter of the Association for Computational Linguistics on Human Language Technology - Volume 1*, NAACL '03, pages 48–54, Morristown, NJ, USA. Association for Computational Linguistics.

Wang Ling, Tiago Luís, João Graça, Luísa Coheur, and Isabel Trancoso. 2010. Towards a general and extensible phrase-extraction algorithm. In *IWSLT '10: International Workshop on Spoken Language Translation*, pages 313–320, Paris, France.

Wang Ling, Tiago Luís, João Graça, Luísa Coheur, and Isabel Trancoso. 2011. Reordering modeling using weighted alignment matrices. In *Proceedings of ACL-2011: HLT*, Portland, Oregon, June. Association for Computational Linguistics.

Yang Liu, Tian Xia, Xinyan Xiao, and Qun Liu. 2009. Weighted alignment matrices for statistical machine translation. In *Proceedings of the 2009 Conference on Empirical Methods in Natural Language Processing: Volume 2 - Volume 2*, EMNLP '09, pages 1017–1026, Morristown, NJ, USA. Association for Computational Linguistics.

Haitao Mi, Liang Huang, and Qun Liu. 2008. Forest-based translation. In *Proceedings of ACL-08: HLT*, pages 192–199, Columbus, Ohio, June. Association for Computational Linguistics.

Michael Paul, Marcello Federico, and Sebastian Stüker. 2010. Overview of the iwslt 2010 evaluation campaign. In *IWSLT '10: International Workshop on Spoken Language Translation*, pages 3–27.

Jinsong Su, Yang Liu, Yajuan Lü, Haitao Mi, and Qun Liu. 2010. Learning lexicalized reordering models from reordering graphs. In *Proceedings of the ACL 2010 Conference Short Papers*, ACLShort '10, pages 12–16, Stroudsburg, PA, USA. Association for Computational Linguistics.

Christoph Tillmann. 2004. A unigram orientation model for statistical machine translation. In *Proceedings of HLT-NAACL 2004: Short Papers*, HLT-NAACL-Short '04, pages 101–104, Stroudsburg, PA, USA. Association for Computational Linguistics.

João V. Graça, Kuzman Ganchev, and Ben Taskar. 2010. Learning Tractable Word Alignment Models with Complex Constraints. *Comput. Linguist.*, 36:481–504.

Ashish Venugopal, Andreas Zollmann, Noah A. Smith, and Stephan Vogel. 2009. Wider pipelines: N-best alignments and parses in MT training.

Active Learning Strategies for Support Vector Machines, Application to Temporal Relation Classification

Seyed Abolghasem Mirroshandel[⋆,†] **Gholamreza Ghassem-Sani**[⋆] **Alexis Nasr**[†]
[⋆]Computer Engineering Department, Sharif university of Technology, Tehran, Iran
[†]Laboratoire d'Informatique Fondamentale de Marseille- CNRS - UMR 6166
Université Aix-Marseille, Marseille, France
(ghasem.mirroshandel@lif.univ-mrs.fr, sani@sharif.edu, alexis.nasr@lif.univ-mrs.fr)

Abstract

Temporal relations between events is a valuable source of information which can be used in a large number of natural language processing applications such as question answering, summarization, and information extraction. Supervised temporal relation classification requires large corpora which are difficult, time consuming, and expensive to produce. Active learning strategies are well-suited to reduce this effort by efficiently selecting the most informative samples for labeling. This paper presents novel active learning strategies based on support vector machines (SVM) for temporal relation classification. A large number of empirical comparisons of different active learning algorithms and various kernel functions in SVM shows that proposed active learning strategies are effective for the given task.

1 Introduction

The identification of temporal relations between events, in texts, is a valuable information for many natural language processing (NLP) tasks, such as summarization, question answering, and information extraction. In question answering, one expects the system to answer questions such as "when an event occurred", or "what is the chronological order of some desired events". In text summarization, especially in the multi-document type, knowing the order of events is important for correctly merging related information.

Most existing algorithms for temporal relation learning are supervised, they rely on manual annotations of corpora. Producing such annotated corpora has shown to be a time consuming, hard, and expensive task (Mani et al., 2006). In this paper we explore active learning techniques as a way to control and speed up the annotation process.

In the active learning framework, the learner has control over choosing the instances that will constitute the training set. A typical active learning algorithm begins with a small number of annotated data, and selects one or more informative instances from a large set of unlabeled instances, named the pool. The chosen instance(s) are then labeled and added to other annotated data, and the model is updated with this new information. These steps are repeated until at least one termination condition is satisfied.

While there have been numerous applications of active learning to NLP researches (Settles and Craven, 2008; Xu et al., 2007), it has not been applied, to our knowledge, to temporal relation classification.

This paper presents a novel active learning strategy for SVM-based classification algorithm. The proposed algorithm considers three measures: *uncertainty*, *representativeness*, and *diversity* to select the instances that will be annotated. The method we propose is generic, it could be applied to any SVM based classification problem. Temporal relation classification has been selected, in this paper, for illustration purpose. Our experiments show that state-of-the-art results can be reproduced with a significantly smaller part of training data.

The remainder of this paper is organized as follows: Section 2 is about temporal relation classification and its related work. Section 3 describes some of existing active learning methods. Our proposed method will be presented in Section 4. Section 5 briefly presents the characteristics of the corpora that we have used. Section 6 demonstrates the evaluation of the proposed algorithm. Finally, Section 7 concludes the paper and presents some possible future work.

2 Temporal Relation Classification with SVM

For a given ordered pair (x_1, x_2), where x_1 and x_2 are time expressions or events, a temporal information processing system identifies the type of relation that temporally links x_1 to x_2. For example in "If all the debt is converted $(event_1)$ to common, Automatic Data will issue $(event_2)$ about 3.6 million shares; last Monday $(time_1)$, the company had $(event_3)$ nearly 73 million shares outstanding.", taken from document *wsj_0541* of TimeBank (Pustejovsky et al., 2003), there are two temporal relations between pairs $(event_1, event_2)$ and $(time_1, event_3)$. The task of a temporal relation extraction system is to automatically tag these pairs with relations *BEFORE* and *INCLUDES*, respectively.

Several researchers have focused on temporal relation learning (Chklovski and Pantel, 2005; Lapata and Lascarides, 2006; Bethard et al., 2007; Chambers et al., 2007; Bethard and Martin, 2008; Mirroshandel and Ghassem-Sani, 2010; Puscasu, 2007) among which SVM has shown good performances. In this section, we describe two of the most successful SVM-based methods.

Inderjeet Mani was the first to propose an SVM-based temporal relation classification model which is based on a linear kernel (Mani et al., 2006). His system (referred to as (k_{Mani})) uses five temporal attributes that have been tagged in the standard corpora (Pustejovsky et al., 2003) plus the string of words that constitute the events, as well as their part of part of speech tags.

The other successful SVM-based temporal classification method uses a polynomial convolution tree kernel, named argument ancestor path distance kernel (AAPD), and outperforms Mani's method (Mirroshandel et al., 2010). In this model, the algorithm adds event-event syntactic properties to the simple event features described above. In order to use syntactic properties, a convolution tree kernel is applied to the parse trees of sentences containing event pairs. Through this process, useful syntactic features can be gathered for classification by SVM. The two kernels are then polynomially combined.

3 Active Learning

Supervised methods usually need a large number of annotated samples in the training phase. In most applications including temporal relation classification, the preparation of such samples is a hard, time consuming, and expensive task (Mani et al., 2006). On the other hand, all these annotated samples may not be useful, because some samples contain little (or even no) new information. Active learning algorithms overcome this problem by adding only the most informative instances labeled by an oracle (e.g., a human expert) to the learning model. Three scenarios have been proposed for the selection of instances: 1) membership query synthesis, 2) stream-based selective sampling, and 3) pool-based sampling (Settles, 2010).

In membership query synthesis, the model itself generates some instances rather than using real-world unlabeled instances (Angluin, 2004).

In stream-based selective sampling, instances are presented in a stream and the learner decides, based on its specific control measure, whether or not to query its label (Atlas et al., 1990; Cohn et al., 1994).

In pool based sampling, which is the scenario that we have chosen), a large number of unlabeled instances are collected to form the *pool* $\mathcal{U}$. The algorithm begins with a small number of labeled data $\mathcal{L}$, and then chooses one or more informative instances from $\mathcal{U}$. The chosen instance(s) are labeled and added to $\mathcal{L}$. A new model is then learned and the process iterated (Lewis and Gale, 1994).

3.1 Sample Selection Strategies

In all active learning strategies, the informativeness of each unlabeled instance is evaluated by the learner, and the most informative instance(s) are labeled. Different informativeness measures have been proposed: 1) uncertainty sampling, 2) query by committee, 3) expected model change, 4) expected error reduction, 5) variance reduction, and 6) density weighted methods (Settles, 2010).

Uncertainty sampling is the simplest and the most commonly used selection strategy. In this strategy, instances for which the prediction of the label is the most uncertain are selected by the learner (Lewis and Gale, 1994).

In query by committee, there is a committee of models trained on the current labeled data $\mathcal{L}$ based on different hypotheses. For each unlabeled instance, committee models vote for their label. The most informative instance is one with the largest disagreement on the votes (Seung et al., 1992). In the expected model change, the most informative instance is the one which causes the most change to the model (Settles et al., 2008). In expected error reduction, the learner selects instances which reduce expected error of model as much as possible (Roy and McCallum, 2001). In density weighted methods, selected instances must be both uncertain and representative in order to decrease the effect of outliers which may cause some problems especially in uncertainty sampling and query by committee strategies (Settles and Craven, 2008).

4 Proposed Algorithm

In this section, we present an active learning method based on SVM. There have been other efforts in using active learning in combination with SVM (Brinker, 2003; Xu et al., 2007), our contribution is the design of new uncertainty measures used for sample selection. In addition, the way representativeness and diversity measures are computed and combined are novel.

The algorithm is pool-based. At each iteration, k ($k \geq 1$) instances are selected from a pool $\mathcal{U}$. To select the more informative instance(s), three measures are used: *uncertainty*, *representativeness* and *diversity*. In the next subsections, we begin with an overview of multi-class classification with SVM, then introduce our three measures and describe the active learning algorithm.

4.1 Multi-class classification

In SVM binary classification, positive and negative instances are linearly partitioned by a hyper-plane (with maximum marginal distance to instances) in the original or a higher dimensional feature space. In order to classify a new instance x, its distance to the hyper-plane is computed and x is assigned to the class that corresponds to the sign of the computed distance. The distance between instance x and hyper-plane H, supported by the support vectors $x_1 \dots x_l$, is computed as follows (Han and Kamber, 2006):

$$d(x, H) = \sum_{k=1}^{l} y_k \alpha_k x_k x^T + b_0 \quad (1)$$

where y_k is the class label of support vector x_k; α_k and b_0 are numeric parameters that are determined automatically.

For multi-class classification with m classes, in one-versus-one case, a set $\mathcal{H}$ of $\frac{m(m-1)}{2}$ hyper-planes, one for every class pair is defined. The hyper-plane that separates class i and j will be noted $H_{i,j}$. We note $\mathcal{H}_i \subset \mathcal{H}$ the set of the $m-1$ hyper-planes that separate class i from the others.

In order to classify a new instance x, its distance to each hyper-plane $H_{i,j}$ is computed and x is assigned to class i or j. At the end of this process, for every instance x, every class i has accumulated a certain number of votes, noted $V_i(x)$ (number of time a classifier has attributed the class i to instance x). The final class of x, noted $C(x)$ will be the one that has accumulated the highest number of votes.

$$C(x) = \arg\max_{1 \leq i \leq m} V_i(x) \quad (2)$$

4.2 Uncertainty

Uncertainty is one of the most important measures of informativeness of an instance. If the learner is uncertain about an instance, that shows that the learning model is not able to deal with the instance properly. As a result, knowing the correct label of this uncertain instance will improve the quality of learning model.

In the process described in subsection 4.1, there are two places where uncertainty can be measured. In the first case, a decision is taken based on the difference of two distances. The smaller the difference, the less reliable the decision is. In the second case, a decision is taken based on the result of a vote. If the outcome of the vote does not show a clear majority, the decision will be less reliable.

Four measures of uncertainty are presented below, the first and second are based on distances while the third and fourth are based on the result of the vote procedure.

4.2.1 Nearest to One Hyper-Plane (NOH)

Uncertainty of an instance x is defined here as the distance to its closest class separating hyper-planes.

$$\varphi(x) = \min_{H \in \mathcal{H}_{C(x)}} |d(x, H)| \tag{3}$$

4.2.2 Nearest to All Hyper-Planes (NAH)

NAH defines the uncertainty of instance x as the sum of its distances to all its class separating hyper-planes.

$$\varphi(x) = \sum_{H \in \mathcal{H}_{C(x)}} |d(x, H)| \tag{4}$$

4.2.3 Least Votes Margin (LVM)

LVM estimates the uncertainty of an instance by the difference between the two highest votes for this instance.

$$\varphi(x) = V_i(x) - V_j(x) \tag{5}$$

where i is the class that has collected the highest number of votes and j the class that has collected the second higher number of votes.

4.2.4 Votes Entropy (VE)

VE is based on the entropy of the distribution of the vote outcome:

$$\varphi(x) = - \sum_{1 \leq i \leq m} P(V_i(x)) \log P(V_i(x)) \tag{6}$$

where $P(V_i(x))$ is simply estimated as its relative frequency $V_i(x)/m$.

4.3 Representativeness

Representativeness is another important measure for choosing samples in active learning. In figure 1, sample 1 is the nearest instance to decision boundary, it is therefore the instance that will be selected using uncertainty criterion. But it should be clear that this sample is not appropriate for selection, annotation, and addition to the training data, because it is in fact an outlier and non representative instance.

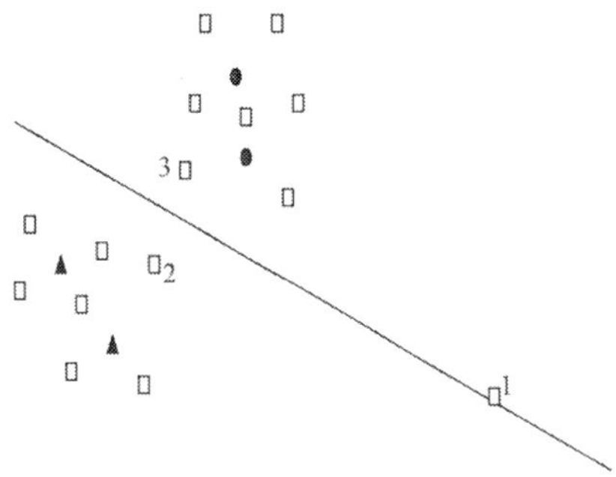

Figure 1: The weakness of uncertainty measure for dealing with outliers. Circles and triangles represent labeled instances while squares represent unlabeled instances.

This simple example shows that uncertainty measure alone is not suited to fight against outliers and noisy samples. In order to prevent the learner to select such instances, a representativeness measure ψ is used. It simply computes the average distance between an instance and all other instances in the pool:

$$\psi(x) = \frac{1}{N} \sum_{x' \in \mathcal{U}} \left| dist(x, x') \right| \tag{7}$$

where N is the number of instances in the pool, and $dist$ is the distance between two samples which can be computed by simply applying a kernel function on them:

$$dist(x_i, x_j) = kernel(x_i, x_j) \tag{8}$$

As it is shown in equation 7, the samples which are more similar to other samples of the pool will be considered to be more representative.

In order to take into account representativeness in the active learning algorithm, the distance between every sample pairs of the pool must be computed. This computation is a costly process, but these distances can be computed only once for the whole active learning algorithm. Algorithm 1 describes how representativeness and uncertainty measures have been combined.

4.4 Diversity

Diversity is the third measure that is used for instance selection. Instances that are both unreliable and representative may be very close to each other

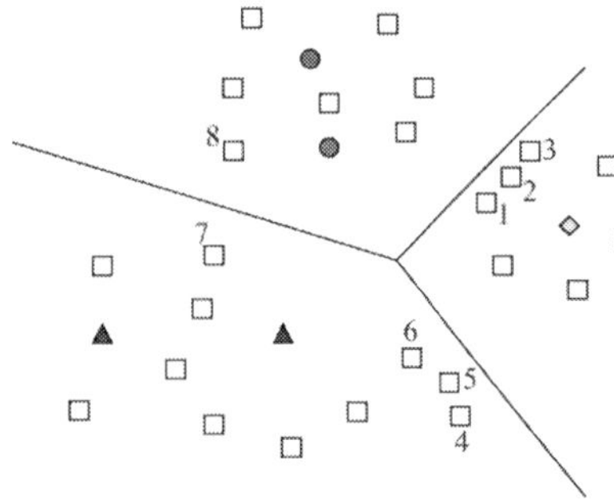

Figure 2: The necessity of applying diversity measure to select samples from the whole problem space.

and it might be interesting, in order to better cover the problem space, to select instances that are different from each other. This is done by taking diversity into account.

Figure 2 illustrates the effect of considering the diversity measure on a simple problem. In this problem, the learner chooses 4 instances for each iteration. Based on uncertainty and representativeness measures, samples 1, 2, 3, and 5 should be selected. However, 1, 2 and 3 are very similar, and only one of such samples may be enough for learning. Besides, selecting 7 and 8 will lead to a better covering of the problem space.

In our algorithm, diversity is taken into account after uncertainty and representativeness were. First, B_I instances are chosen, based on uncertainty and representativeness. A distance matrix is then constructed, based on the distance measure of equation 8. The B_I instances are then grouped into B_F ($B_F < B_I$) clusters, using hierarchical clustering and the centroid of each cluster is selected for labeling. This process is explained in algorithm 1.

4.5 Proposed Algorithm

The pseudo-code of our active learning algorithm is shown in Algorithm 1. This algorithm first trains the model based on the initial labeled data, and applies a combination of uncertainty and representativeness measures to select B_I samples from the pool. Then hierarchical clustering is applied to the extracted samples to select B_F most diverse samples. Chosen samples are then labeled and added to the training labeled set. This process is iterated until

Algorithm 1 THE PROPOSED ACTIVE LEARNING

α: Uncertainty coefficient
$\mathcal{L}$: Labeled set
$\mathcal{U}$: Unlabeled pool
$\varphi(x)$: Uncertainty measure
$\psi(x)$: Representativeness measure
B_I: Initial query batch size
B_F: Final query batch size

while termination condition is not satisfied **do**
  $\theta = train(\mathcal{L})$; $\mathcal{T}_I = \emptyset$;
  for $i = 1$ to B_I **do**
    // Find most uncertain and representative instance
    $\hat{x} = \arg\max_{x \in \mathcal{U}}[\alpha\varphi(x) + (1-\alpha)\psi(x)]$;
    $\mathcal{T}_I = \mathcal{T}_I \cup \{\hat{x}\}$;
  end for
  Apply Hierarchical clustering on $\mathcal{T}_I$ to extract set $\mathcal{T}_F$ of B_F diverse samples;
  $\mathcal{U} = \mathcal{U} - \mathcal{T}_F$;
  $\mathcal{L} = \mathcal{L} \cup \mathcal{T}_F$;
end while

at least one termination condition is satisfied. In our experiments, the algorithm stops when all instances of the pool were selected and labeled.

Our algorithm may seem much more costly than the original SVM algorithm. However, it is easy to show, similar to (Brinker, 2003), that it only multiply by a coefficient of N/B_F (N is the final number of labeled instances) the total computational complexity of original SVM.

5 Corpus Description

Two standard corpora were used for our expriments: TimeBank (v. 1.2)(Pustejovsky et al., 2003) and Opinion (`www.timeml.org`). TimeBank is composed of 183 newswire documents and 64 077 words, and Opinion comprises 73 documents with 38 709 words. These two datasets have been annotated with TimeML (Pustejovsky et al., 2004). There are 14 temporal relation types (*SIMULTANEOUS, IDENTITY, BEFORE, AFTER, IBEFORE, IAFTER, INCLUDES, IS_INCLUDED, DURING, DURING_INV, BEGINS, BEGUN_BY, ENDS, ENDED_BY*) in the TLink class of TimeML. Similar to (Mani et al., 2006; Chambers et al., 2007), we used a normalized version of these 14 temporal relation types, which contains only the following six temporal relations:

SIMULTANEOUS ENDS BEGINS
BEFORE IBEFORE INCLUDES

In order to convert 14 relations into 6, the inverse relations were omitted (e.g., *BEFORE* and *AFTER*), and *IDENTITY* and *SIMULTAENOUS*, as well as *IS_INCLUDED* and *DURING* were collapsed, respectively.

Relation Type	OTC
IBEFORE	131
BEGINS	160
ENDS	208
SIMULTANEOUS	1528
INCLUDES	950
BEFORE	3170
TOTAL	6147

Table 1: The normalized TLink class distribution in OTC.

In our experiments, as in several previous work, we merged the two datasets to generate a single corpus called OTC. Table 1 shows the normalized TLink class distribution (only for Event-Event relations) for OTC corpora.

6 Experimental Results

The algorithm described above was evaluated on OTC corpus with our four uncertainty measures with and without representativeness and diversity. We used random instance selection (i.e., passive learning) as the baseline strategy.

Several kernels can be used for such experiments. As explained in section 2, we decided to use the kernel proposed in (Mani et al., 2006), which we will refer to as Mani's kernel, and the Argument Ancestor Path Distance (AAPD) polynomial kernel proposed in (Mirroshandel et al., 2010). AAPD polynomial is the state of the art pattern-based algorithm, which exclusively combines gold standard features of events and grammatical structures of sentences.

All evaluations are based on a 5-fold cross validation. The original corpora was randomly partitioned into 5 parts, out of which, a single part was retained for testing the model, and the remaining 4 parts were used for the training and applying our instance selection strategies. This process was then repeated 5 times (the folds), with each of the 5 parts being used exactly once as the test data. To perform the experiments, we started from initial labeled set with 100 randomly selected samples, and in each iteration, 25 samples were selected, labeled, and added to the previously labeled set.

6.1 Uncertainty Measure Alone

Figures 3 and 4 show the result of applying our four uncertainty measures for "instance selection" in OTC, using Mani's (Figure 3) and AAPD kernels (Figure 4).

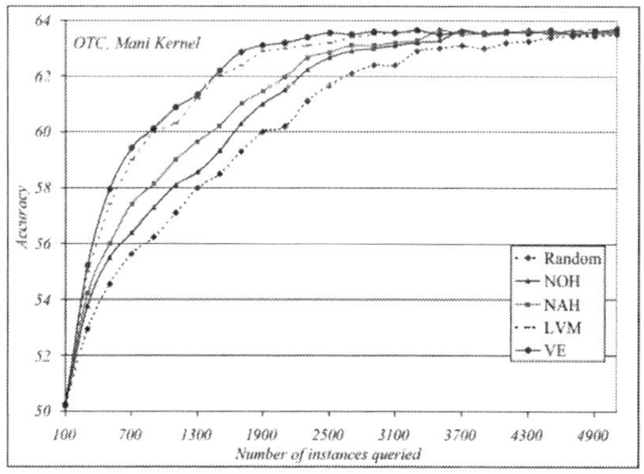

Figure 3: Learning curves for different uncertainty instance selection strategies applied to OTC using Mani's kernel.

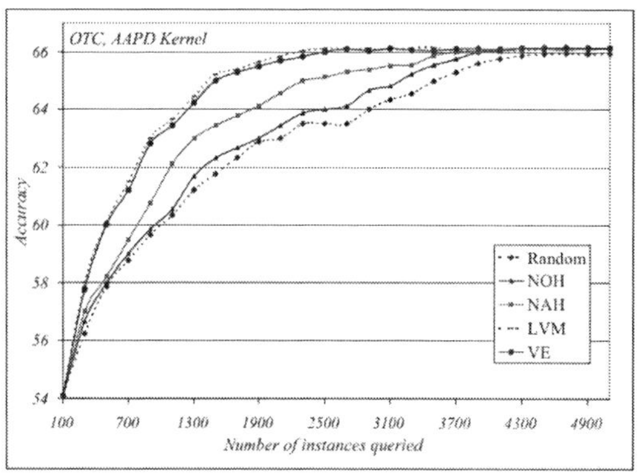

Figure 4: Learning curves for different uncertainty instance selection strategies applied to OTC using AAPD kernel.

The figures show that all proposed uncertainty instance selection strategies are effective and lead to learning curves that are above the baseline. Vote based measures have outperformed distance based ones. Among the two distance based measures, NAH led to better results than NOH, showing that averaging (aggregation) over the distances to the different separating hyperplanes is more robust than taking into account only the distance to the closest one.

The two vote based methods led to very close results, which seems to indicate that the system usually hesitates between two classes (and not more) when trying to classify an instance.

6.2 Combining Uncertainty and Representativeness Measures

Representativeness has been introduced in order to fight against outliers. Such outliers have two different origins. The first one is data sparseness: some temporal relation events are poorly represented in the data. Eliminating such instances will degrade the results on the corresponding class but will introduce less noise in the data. The second origin of outliers is the difficulty of problem, even for human annotators (Pustejovsky et al., 2003). This causes some mistakes in annotation and generates some outliers.

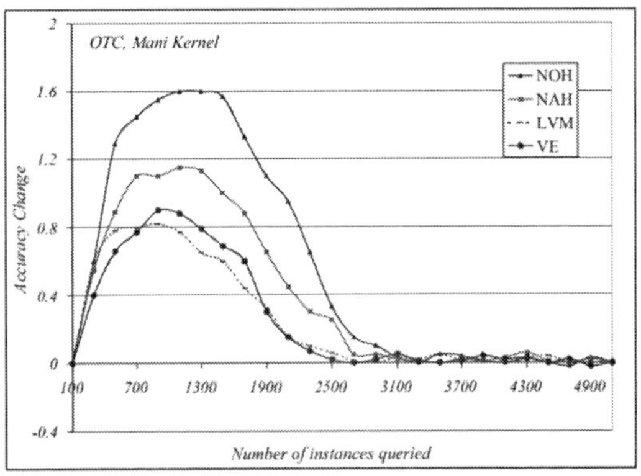

Figure 5: Accuracy improvement when adding representativeness measure to the uncertainty instance selection in Mani's kernel.

In the second series of experiments, we combined a representativeness measure with different uncertainty instance selection strategies to tackle outliers' side effects. In our different experiments, the best value for uncertainty coefficient (α) was 0.65. Figure 5 (resp. 6) shows the accuracy improvement when adding representativeness to uncertainty with Mani's (resp. AAPD) kernel. We have chosen to

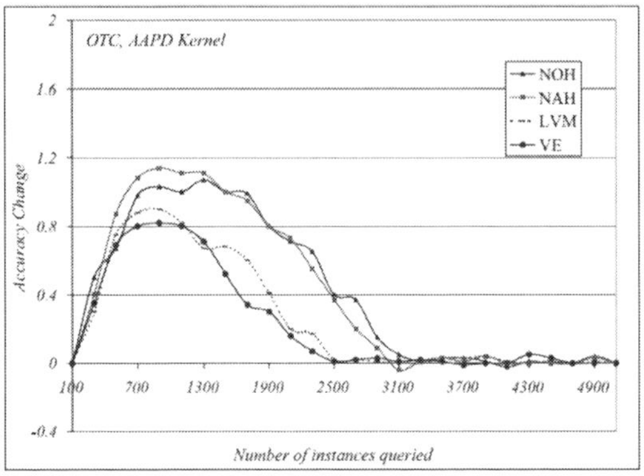

Figure 6: Accuracy improvement when adding representativeness measure to the uncertainty instance selection in AAPD kernel.

represent just the improvement rather than the learning accuracy, because the learning curves were not easy to compare.

The results show that distance based measures are more sensitive to outliers than vote based ones. Figures 5 and 6 also show that the representativeness measure has less impact on AAPD kernel than it has on Mani's kernel. This is because AAPD kernel is more resistant to outliers than Mani's kernel.

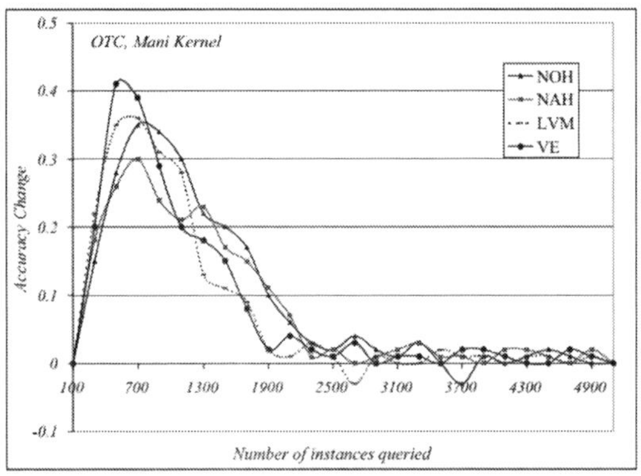

Figure 7: Accuracy improvement when adding diversity in the instance selection with Mani's kernel.

6.3 Combining Uncertainty, Representativeness and Diversity

In the last series of experiments, diversity was added to the instance selection procedure. In each iteration, first 80 instances of the pool were selected by combination of uncertainty and representativeness mea-

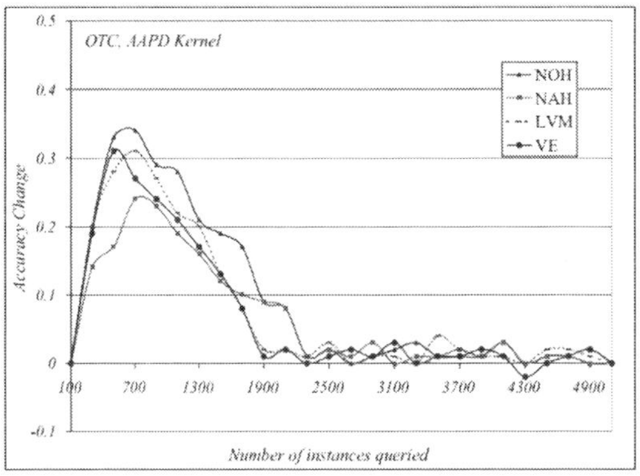

Figure 8: Accuracy improvement when adding diversity in the instance selection with AAPD kernel.

sures. Next, a hierarchical clustering method was used to select the final 25 instances. The accuracy improvement, as it is shown in Figures 7 and 8, is moderate.

The reasons why introducing diversity did not have a greater impact on the results is not clear. That may be due to the way diversity was introduced in our model. It could also come from the distribution of the data: if instances that are both unreliable and representative are not close to each other, selecting instances that are different from each other for better coverage of the problem space is not an issue. More work has to be done to investigate that point.

The final learning curves, when uncertainty, representativeness, and diversity were all considered, are shown in figures 9 and 10. As shown, vote-based uncertainty measures still obtain better results than distance based measures.

7 Conclusion

In this paper, we have addressed the problem of active learning based on support vector machines for temporal relation classification. Three different kind of measures have been used for selecting the most informative instances: uncertainty, representativeness and diversity. The results showed that the three measures improved the learning curve although diversity had a moderate effect.

Future work will focus on three points, the first one is trying other sample selection strategies, as query by committee, the second will focus on combining the two families of uncertainty measures that we have proposed: distance based and vote based. The third one is about diversity. As mentioned above, we do not know if this phenomenon is not well handeled by the model or if it is not an issue for the problem at hand.

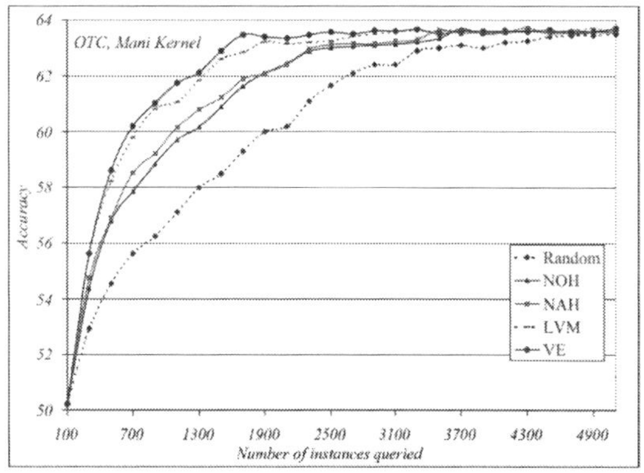

Figure 9: Learning curves for combined uncertainty, representative and diversity measures with Mani's kernel.

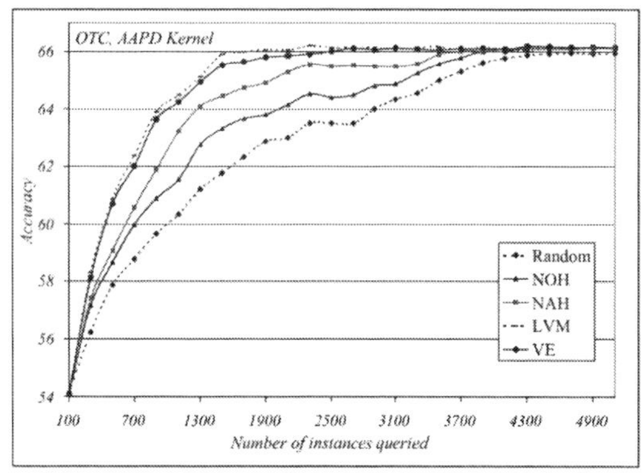

Figure 10: Learning curves for combined uncertainty, representative and diversity measures with AAPD kernel.

Acknowledgement

This work has been funded by the French Agence Nationale pour la Recherche, through the project SEQUOIA (ANR-08-EMER-013).

References

D. Angluin. 2004. Queries revisited. *Theoretical Computer Science*, 313(2):175–194.

L. Atlas, D. Cohn, R. Ladner, MA El-Sharkawi, and II Marks. 1990. Training connectionist networks with queries and selective sampling. In *Advances in neural information processing systems 2*, pages 566–573. Morgan Kaufmann Publishers Inc.

S. Bethard and J.H. Martin. 2008. Learning semantic links from a corpus of parallel temporal and causal relations. In *Proceedings of the 46th Annual Meeting of the Association for Computational Linguistics on Human Language Technologies: Short Papers*, pages 177–180. Association for Computational Linguistics.

S. Bethard, J.H. Martin, and S. Klingenstein. 2007. Finding temporal structure in text: Machine learning of syntactic temporal relations. *International Journal of Semantic Computing*, 1(4).

K. Brinker. 2003. Incorporating diversity in active learning with support vector machines. In *MACHINE LEARNING-INTERNATIONAL WORKSHOP THEN CONFERENCE-*, volume 20, pages 59–66.

N. Chambers, S. Wang, and D. Jurafsky. 2007. Classifying temporal relations between events. In *Proceedings of the 45th Annual Meeting of the ACL on Interactive Poster and Demonstration Sessions*, pages 173–176. Association for Computational Linguistics.

T. Chklovski and P. Pantel. 2005. Global path-based refinement of noisy graphs applied to verb semantics. *Natural Language Processing–IJCNLP 2005*, pages 792–803.

D. Cohn, L. Atlas, and R. Ladner. 1994. Improving generalization with active learning. *Machine Learning*, 15(2):201–221.

J. Han and M. Kamber. 2006. *Data mining: concepts and techniques*. Morgan Kaufmann.

M. Lapata and A. Lascarides. 2006. Learning sentence-internal temporal relations. *Journal of Artificial Intelligence Research*, 27(1):85–117.

D.D. Lewis and W.A. Gale. 1994. A sequential algorithm for training text classifiers. In *Proceedings of the 17th annual international ACM SIGIR conference on Research and development in information retrieval*, pages 3–12. Springer-Verlag New York, Inc.

I. Mani, M. Verhagen, B. Wellner, C.M. Lee, and J. Pustejovsky. 2006. Machine learning of temporal relations. In *Proceedings of the 21st International Conference on Computational Linguistics and the 44th annual meeting of the Association for Computational Linguistics*, pages 753–760. Association for Computational Linguistics.

S.A. Mirroshandel and G. Ghassem-Sani. 2010. Temporal Relations Learning with a Bootstrapped Cross-document Classifier. In *Proceeding of the 2010 conference on ECAI 2010: 19th European Conference on Artificial Intelligence*, pages 829–834. IOS Press.

S.A. Mirroshandel, G. Ghassem-Sani, and M. Khayyamian. 2010. Using Syntactic-Based Kernels for Classifying Temporal Relations. *Journal of Computer Science and Technology*, 26(1):68–80.

G. Puscasu. 2007. Wvali: Temporal relation identification by syntactico-semantic analysis. In *Proceedings of the 4th International Workshop on SemEval*, pages 484–487.

J. Pustejovsky, P. Hanks, R. Sauri, A. See, R. Gaizauskas, A. Setzer, D. Radev, B. Sundheim, D. Day, L. Ferro, et al. 2003. The timebank corpus. In *Corpus Linguistics*, volume 2003, page 40.

J. Pustejovsky, B. Ingria, R. Sauri, J. Castano, J. Littman, R. Gaizauskas, A. Setzer, G. Katz, and I. Mani. 2004. The specification language TimeML. *The Language of Time: A Reader. Oxford University Press, Oxford.*

N. Roy and A. McCallum. 2001. Toward optimal active learning through sampling estimation of error reduction. In *MACHINE LEARNING-INTERNATIONAL WORKSHOP THEN CONFERENCE-*, pages 441–448. Citeseer.

B. Settles and M. Craven. 2008. An analysis of active learning strategies for sequence labeling tasks. In *Proceedings of the Conference on Empirical Methods in Natural Language Processing*, pages 1070–1079. Association for Computational Linguistics.

B. Settles, M. Craven, and S. Ray. 2008. Multiple-instance active learning. In *In Advances in Neural Information Processing Systems (NIPS*. Citeseer.

Burr Settles. 2010. Active Learning Literature Survey. Technical Report Technical Report 1648, University of Wisconsin-Madison.

H.S. Seung, M. Opper, and H. Sompolinsky. 1992. Query by committee. In *Proceedings of the fifth annual workshop on Computational learning theory*, pages 287–294. ACM.

Z. Xu, R. Akella, and Y. Zhang. 2007. Incorporating diversity and density in active learning for relevance feedback. *Advances in Information Retrieval*, pages 246–257.

A Fast Accurate Two-stage Training Algorithm for L1-regularized CRFs with Heuristic Line Search Strategy

Jinlong Zhou
Fudan University
Shanghai, China
abc9703@gmail.com

Xipeng Qiu
Fudan University
Shanghai, China
xpqiu@fudan.edu.cn

Xuanjing Huang
Fudan University
Shanghai, China
xjhuang@fudan.edu.cn

Abstract

Sparse learning framework, which is very popular in the field of nature language processing recently due to the advantages of efficiency and generalizability, can be applied to Conditional Random Fields (CRFs) with L1 regularization method. Stochastic gradient descent (SGD) method has been used in training L1-regularized CRFs, because it often requires much less training time than the batch training algorithm like quasi-Newton method in practice. Nevertheless, SGD method sometimes fails to converge to the optimum, and it can be very sensitive to the learning rate parameter settings. We present a two-stage training algorithm which guarantees the convergence, and use heuristic line search strategy to make the first stage of SGD training process more robust and stable. Experimental evaluations on Chinese word segmentation and name entity recognition tasks demonstrate that our method can produce more accurate and compact model with less training time for L1 regularization.

1 Introduction

Conditional Random Fields (CRFs) (Lafferty et al., 2001; Sutton and McCallum, 2006) are one of the most widely-used machine learning approach in the field of nature language processing, for their ability to handle large feature sets and structural dependency between output labels. The applications of CRFs cover a wide range of tasks such as part-of-speech (POS) tagging (Lafferty et al., 2001), semantic role labeling (Toutannova et al., 2005) and syntactic parsing (Finkel et al., 2008). CRFs outperform other models like Maximum Entropy Markov models (McCallum et al., 2000), because they overcome the problem of "label bias". Moreover, CRFs can output the probabilistic of labeling result for further use as pipeline or reranking.

For all types of CRFs, the maximum-likelihood method can be applied for parameter estimation, which means training the model is done by maximizing the log-likelihood on the training data. To avoid overfitting the likelihood is often penalized with the regularization term. There were two common regularization methods named L1 and L2 regularization. L1 regularization, also called Laplace prior, penalizes the weight vector with its L1-norm. L2 regularization, also called Gaussian prior, uses L2-form. Based on the work of Gao et al. (2007), there is no significant difference between these two regularization methods in terms of accuracy. But L1 regularization has a major advantage that L1-regularized training can produce models, of which the feature weights can be very sparse, then the size of the model will be much smaller than that produced by L2 regularization. Compact models are more interpretable, generalizable and manageable, require less resources like memory and storage. It is very meaningful especially for the rapid development of mobile application nowadays, which suffer the scarcity of resources. In many NLP tasks, the feature sets can reach the magnitude of several million.

Besides, L1 regularization method can implicitly perform the feature selection, and provide the result for further process such as iterative approach (Vail et al., 2007; Peng and McCallum, 2004). This task requires that we need to train the model as accurate as possible, as to converge to the optimum. The feature selection can be regarded as reliable and unbiased after such a process.

Quasi-Newtion method was successfully and efficiently used in L1-regularized model by Andrew and Gao (2007). They presented an algorithm called Orthant-Wise Limited-memory Quasi-Newton (OWL-QN), which is based on L-

BFGS algorithm (Liu and Nocedal, 1989) and achieve better convergence than the method introduced by Kazama and Tsujii (2003).

Stochastic gradient descent (SGD) methods are another kind of L1-regularized training methods. It is a very attractive framework for it often requires much less training time than the batch training algorithm in practice. Tsuruoka et al. (2009) presented a variant of SGD that can efficiently produce compact models with L1 regularization. The main idea is to keep track of the total penalty and the penalty each weight has applied, so that the penalization smooth away the noisy gradient.

Although SGD method with cumulative penalty is very efficient, it sometimes fails to converge to the optimum, because the training process is usually terminated at a certain number of iterations without explicit stop criteria as in quasi-Newton method. Another problem is that the training result of SGD method is very sensitive to the parameter settings of learning rate, therefore we have to tune the values of parameters for different tasks, which is not efficient in practice.

In this paper, we present a two-stage L1-regularized training algorithm to solve these two problems. In the first stage, we use the SGD method to get a relative good solution quickly. In the second stage, we use the OWL-QN method to improve the model which has been dealt with the SGD method. By this means we can fast get the accurate model. The learning rate scheduling in the first stage is done by heuristic line search, which makes the process more robust and stable.

Our experiments are conducted on two tasks, Chinese word segmentation and name entity recognition. We show that our method can produce more accurate and compact model with less training time for L1 regularization. We also verify that the result of SGD training method will be more robust when using the heuristic line search strategy.

The rest of the paper is organized as follows. Section 2 introduces the basics of CRFs. Section 3 describe the two-stage algorithm for L1-regularized models. Experimental results are shown in Section 4. We conclude the work in Section 5.

2 Conditional Random Fields

In this section, we briefly describe the basics of conditional random fields (CRFs) (Lafferty et al., 2001; Sutton and McCallum, 2006) and introduce the definition of some concepts and parameters.

2.1 Linear-chain CRFs

CRFs defines the conditional probabilistic distribution over possible output sequences $\mathbf{y}$ for observation $\mathbf{x}$ as following:

$$p(\mathbf{y}|\mathbf{x}) = \frac{1}{Z(\mathbf{x})} \exp\left\{\sum_{k=1}^{K} \lambda_k F_k(\mathbf{x},\mathbf{y})\right\}, \quad (1)$$

where $F_k(\mathbf{x},\mathbf{y})$is equal to $\sum_{t=1}^{T} f_k(\mathbf{x}, y_{t-1}, y_t, t)$. $\{f_k\}$ is a set of feature function and λ_k is the weight of the feature, and $Z(\mathbf{x})$ is the normalization factor defined by

$$Z(\mathbf{x}) = \sum_{\mathbf{y}} \exp\left\{\sum_{k=1}^{K} \lambda_k F_k(\mathbf{x},\mathbf{y})\right\}. \quad (2)$$

The feature function can be divided into unigram features and bigram features, here we simply rewrite $f_k(\mathbf{x}, y_t, t)$ as $f_k(\mathbf{x}, y_{t-1}, y_t, t)$ for convenient.

2.2 Training

The maximum-likelihood method is a commonly used way applied for parameter estimation, which means we train the model by minimize the negated conditional log-likelihood $L(\lambda)$ on the training data:

$$\begin{aligned} L(\lambda) &= -\sum_{(\mathbf{x},\mathbf{y})} \log p(\mathbf{x},\mathbf{y}) \quad (3) \\ &= \sum_{(\mathbf{x},\mathbf{y})} \left\{\log Z(\mathbf{x}) - \sum_{k=1}^{K} \lambda_k F_k(\mathbf{x},\mathbf{y})\right\}. \end{aligned}$$

To avoid overfitting, the likelihood is often penalized with the regularization term, which we will talk about in the later sections.

The partial derivative of $L(\lambda)$ by the feature weights λ_k are given by

$$\begin{aligned} \frac{\partial}{\partial \lambda_k} L &= \sum_{(\mathbf{x},\mathbf{y})} \sum_{t=1}^{T} E_{p(\mathbf{y}|\mathbf{x})} f_k(\mathbf{x}, y_{t-1}, y_t, t) \\ &\quad - \sum_{(\mathbf{x},\mathbf{y})} \sum_{t=1}^{T} f_k(\mathbf{x}, y_{t-1}, y_t, t) \quad (4) \end{aligned}$$

where $E_{p(\mathbf{y}|\mathbf{x})}$ denotes the conditional expectation under the model distribution:

$$\begin{aligned} &E_{p(\mathbf{y}|\mathbf{x})} f_k(\mathbf{x}, y_{t-1}, y_t, t) = \\ &\sum_{(y',y)} f_k(\mathbf{x}, y', y, t) P(y_{t-1} = y', y_t = y|\mathbf{x}) \quad (5) \end{aligned}$$

Computing the conditional expectation directly is impractical for the large number of possible tag sequences, which is exponential in the length of the observation. Thus, a dynamic programming approach known as the Forward-Backward algorithm originally described for Hidden Markov models (Rabiner, 1989), is applied in a slightly modified form. For the forward recursions, we have

$$\alpha_0(\perp) = 1$$
$$\alpha_{t+1}(y) = \sum_{y'} \alpha_t(y') \exp\left\{\sum_{k=1}^{K} \lambda_k f_k(\mathbf{x}, y', y, t)\right\}$$

and for the backward recursion, we have

$$\beta_{T+1}(\top) = 1$$
$$\beta_t(y') = \sum_{y} \beta_{t+1}(y) \exp\left\{\sum_{k=1}^{K} \lambda_k f_k(\mathbf{x}, y', y, t)\right\}$$

for $0 \leq t \leq T$ and $y \in Y$, where $\perp$ and $\top$ are defined as special states for the begin and end of the sequence. Then the normalization factor is computed by

$$Z(\mathbf{x}) = \beta_0(\perp), \tag{6}$$

and the conditional probabilities $P(y_{t-1} = y', y_t = y|\mathbf{x})$ are given by

$$\alpha_t(y') \exp\left\{\sum_{k=1}^{K} \lambda_k f_k(\mathbf{x}, y', y, t)\right\} \beta_{t+1}(y)/Z(\mathbf{x})$$

3 L1 Regularization in CRFs

3.1 Regularization

The logarithmic loss function $L(\lambda)$ defined by (3) is usually penalized with an additional regularization term, which prevents the model from overfitting the training data. There are two common regularization methods named L1 and L2 regularization, in the case of L1 regularization, the term is defined as:

$$R(\lambda) = C \sum_{k} |\lambda_k|, \tag{7}$$

where C is the regularization parameter that controls the trade-off between fitting exactly the observations and the L1-norm of the weight vector. This value is usually tuned by cross-validation or using the heldout data.

Now we can redefine the objective loss function as

$$L(\lambda) + R(\lambda). \tag{8}$$

3.2 Orthant-Wise Limited-memory Quasi-Newton

It is not easy to use some common numerical optimization strategies such as limited memory BFGS (Liu and Nocedal, 1989) directly with L1 regularization, because the regularization term is not differentiable when the weight is zero.

A very efficient strategy called Orthant-Wise Limited-memory Quasi-Newton (OWL-QN) method is introduced in (Andrew and Gao, 2007). This algorithm is motivated by the observation that the L1 regularization term is differentiable when restricted to a set of points in which each coordinate never changes sign (called its "orthant"). Furthermore it is a linear function of its argument, which means the second-order behavior of the regularized objective function on a given orthant is determined by the log-likelihood component alone. Only a few steps of the standard L-BFGS algorithm have been changed in the OWL-QN method, and these differences are listed below:

1. The "pseudo-gradient" is used in place of the gradient.
2. The resulting search direction is constrained to match the sign pattern of the negated pseudo-gradient.
3. Each parameter is projected back onto the initial orthant of the previous value during the line search.

Andrew and Gao (2007) proved that OWL-QN method is guaranteed to converge to a globally optimal result.

3.3 Stochastic Gradient Descent

Stochastic gradient approaches use a small batch of the observations to get a crude approximation of the gradient of the objective function given by (3). The small batch size makes us possible to update the parameters more frequently than the origin gradient descent and speed up the convergence. Only considering the log-likelihood term, the updates have the following form

$$\hat{\lambda}_k^j = \lambda_k^j + \eta_j \left.\frac{\partial L(\lambda)}{\partial \lambda_k}\right|_{\lambda=\lambda^j} \tag{9}$$

where j is the iteration counter and η_j is the learning rate. It should be noted that the partial derivative we presented here is not the true gradient but the crude approximation from small randomly-selected subset of the training samples. In (Tsuruoka et al., 2009), a variant of SGD that can efficiently train L1-regularized CRFs was presented. The main idea can be concluded as follows:

1. Only update the weights of the features that are used in the current observation, called "lazy update".

2. "Clip" the parameter value when it crosses zero.

3. Keep track of the cumulated penalty that the weights of features should been received if the fluctuationless gradient were used, and use this value to the update.

Let z_j be the total L1-penalty that each weight should been received, it is simply accumulated as:

$$z_j = \frac{C}{N}\sum_{t=1}^{j} \eta_t. \quad (10)$$

Then the process of regularization can be formalized as follows

$$\lambda_k^{j+1} = \begin{cases} \max(0, \hat{\lambda}_k^j - (z_j + q_k^{j-1}) & \hat{\lambda}_k^j > 0 \\ \min(0, \hat{\lambda}_k^j + (z_j - q_k^{j-1}) & \hat{\lambda}_k^j < 0 \end{cases}$$

where q_k^j is the total L1-penalty that λ_k has actually received:

$$q_k^j = \sum_{t=1}^{j} (\lambda_k^{t+1} - \hat{\lambda}_k^t). \quad (11)$$

Tsuruoka et al. (2009) demonstrated that this algorithm can be much more quickly than the OWL-QN method and yield a comparable performance, while the value of objective function and the number of active features are not as good as OWL-QN. The reason is that we usually terminated the training process at a certain number of iterations, because there are no explicit stop criteria for SGD.

Another issue is that the scheduling of learning rates can be very tricky. Tsuruoka et al. (2009) suggest that exponential decay is a good choice in practice compared with the method used in (Collins et al., 2008). This kind of scheduling of learning rates have the following form:

$$\eta_j = \eta_0 \alpha^{j/N}, \quad (12)$$

where η_0 and α are both constant. We name η_0 the initiation learning rate parameter and α the descent learning rate parameter. These learning rate parameters have a great influence on the result of SGD training, and they need to be tuned for different tasks, which is not very efficient in practice.

3.4 Two-stage L1-regularized Training

Based on what we have mentioned above, we know that the SGD method sometimes fails to converge to the global optimal solution, for it does not have the explicit stop criteria as in the quasi-Newton method. Although the scheduling of learning rate found in (Collins et al., 2008):

$$\eta_j = \frac{\eta_0}{1 + j/N} \quad (13)$$

guarantees ultimate convergence theoretically. Its actual convergence speed is poor in practice (Darken and Moody,1990). We have to take quite a number of iterations if we need the result close enough to the best solution. This contradicts to the main motivation we use SGD method for parameter estimation that can speed up the training process.

On the other hand, based on the work of Andrew and Gao (2007), we know that OWL-QN method guarantees the convergence. And we can test the relative change in the objective function value averaged over the several previous iterations for stop criteria.

Tsuruoka et al. (2009) demonstrated that SGD method converges much faster than OWL-QN method especially in the first few iterations. This fact motivates us to use a two-stage training strategy. In the first stage, we use the SGD method to quickly get a relative good solution. In the second stage, we use the OWL-QN method to improve the model which has been dealt with the SGD method.

This method can be also driven from an alternative view. In the theory of convex optimization (Boyd and Vandenberghe, 2004), the asymptotic convergence rate of Newton's method is quadratic if we start at a point close enough to the global optimum.[1] In fact, the iterations in Newton's method can fall into two stages. The second stage, which occurs once the searching point is quite close to the optimum solution, is called "quadratically convergent stage". The first stage is usually referred as the "damped Newton phase", because the algorithm may choose a step size that is different from the exact Newton step to satisfy the backtracking

[1] Quasi-Newton method shares many properties with Newton's method, though its convergence rate is generally superlinear but not quadratic.

condition.[2] The quadratically convergent stage is also called the "pure Newton phase" since the full Newton step is always chosen in these iterations . This fact demonstrates that if we can find a solution close to the global optimum, it will not only increase the average convergence rates, but also reduce the time consuming needed for backtracking line search. This is what we achieved by the first stage of SGD training method.

3.5 Heuristic Line Search

Another problem of SGD method is the troublesome learning rate parameters tuning, and these parameters have a significant influence on the result of SGD training. No matter which way to set the learning rate, if it is fixed without taking the actual effect of the current training sample update into consideration, it may be too large or too small for some situation. In order to get a more robust and stable method for learning rate scheduling, we present a heuristic line search strategy inspired by the implementation of CRFsgd (Bottou, 2007) for learning rate calibration.

For the purpose of convenience, we define the objective function for a single sample as

$$l(\lambda, \mathbf{x}) = -\log p(\mathbf{x}, \mathbf{y}) + \frac{C}{N} \sum_{\lambda_k \in \mathbf{X}} |\lambda_k|. \quad (14)$$

Notice here we only use these active features in the current sample as the L1 regularization term, for we only update these associate parameters in a lazy fashion.

Now we try to find the learning rate that decrease the value of this objective function as much as possible without consuming too much search time. We simply use a heuristic line search strategy as follows: (1) We use the learning rate calculated by Eq.12 as initiation and get the initial value of Eq.14. (2) Then we go on to increase the learning rate until the maximum number of trials for search is reached or the value of Eq.14 is worse than the initial value, we just decrease the learning rate from the initiation if the latter situation happens. (3) At last we just use the learning rate that yields the best result of Eq.14 during the search. For the calculation of Eq.14 only needs the weights of the features that are used in the current sample, so it will still be very efficient. The whole algorithm in pseudo-code was showed in Algorithm 1.

[2]To ensure the objective function decrease a certain value and guarantee the convergence.

Algorithm 1 SGD heuristic line search

```
for k = 0 to MaxIterations
  Select sample j
  bestr ← LearningRate(k)
  UpdateWeights (j,bestr)

procedure LearningRate(k)
  r(0) ← initialed by Eq.12
  init_obj ← initialed by Eq.14
  for i = 0 to MaxTrialTime
    UpdateWeights(j,r(i))
    obj(i) ← Eq.14
    Recover weights before update
    if obj(i) is worse than init_obj then
      label flag
    if flag status is changed then
      r(i + 1) ← r(0) * decay
    else
      if flag is not set then
        r(i + 1) ← r(i)/decay
      else
        r(i + 1) ← r(i) * decay
  bestr = argmin_{r(i)} obj(i)
  return bestr.
```

It should be noted that we need not set a large number for maximum trial time, because it will generally take a lot of search time and may not yield a good result but arrives at the local optimum, for we only optimize the objective value of a single training sample. Here we set the value to 3 empirically. The changing rate for line search can be any positive number that smaller than 1, it is set to 0.5 as mostly accepted.

4 Experiments

We evaluate the effectiveness and performance of our training algorithm using two NLP tasks that includes Chinese words segmentation and name entity recognition, which are very typical problems in the field of NLP.

To show the improvement of our algorithm, we compare it with the OWL-QN algorithm and SGD algorithm on the same data sets. For the purpose of run-times comparison, we implemented all the algorithm in a quite similar way, especially in feature extraction and gradient computation. For example, we compute the forward/backward scores in logarithm domain instead of scaling

Table 1: Feature templates for Chinese word segmentation task.

(1) $c_{i-1}y_i$, c_iy_i, $c_{i+1}y_i$
(2) $c_{i-1}c_iy_i$, $c_ic_{i+1}y_i$, $c_{i-1}c_{i+1}y_i$
(3) $y_{i-1}y_i$

method, though the latter method was claimed faster (Lavergne et al., 2010). All experiments were performed on a server with Xeon 2.66GHz.

4.1 Chinese Word Segmentation

The first set of experiments used the Chinese word segmentation corpus from the Second International SIGHAN Bakeoff data sets (Emerson, 2005), provided by Peking University. The training data consists of 19,054 sentences, 1,109,947 Chinese words, 1,826,448 Chinese characters and the testing data consists of 1,944 sentences, 104,372 Chinese words, 172,733 Chinese characters. We separated 1,000 sentences from the training data and use them as the heldout data. The test data was only used for the final accuracy report.

The feature templates we used in this experiment were listed in Table 1, where c_i denotes the ith Chinese character in an instance, y_i denotes the ith label in the instance. Based on the work of Huang and Zhao (2007), it was shown that 6 label representation is a better choice in practice. Compare with the origin 2 label representation or 4 label representation, it can represent richer label information. We did not use any extra knowledge such as Chinese and Arabic numbers.

For OWL-QN method and SGD method, we followed the experiment settings in (Tsuruoka et al., 2009). The meta-parameters for OWL-QN method were the same with the default settings of the optimizer developed by Andrew and Gao (2007), the convergence tolerance was 1e-4; the L-BFGS memory parameter was 10. The regularization parameter C was tuned in the way that it maximized the log-likelihood of the heldout data when using the OWL-QN algorithm. We also used this value as the regularization parameter in the SGD method. The learning rate parameters for SGD were tuned in the way that they maximized the value of the objective function in 30 passes. We first set the initiation learning rate parameter (η_0) by testing 1.0, 0.5, 0.2, and 0.1, then we set the descent learning rate parameter (α) by testing 0.9, 0.85, and 0.8 with the fixed initiation learning

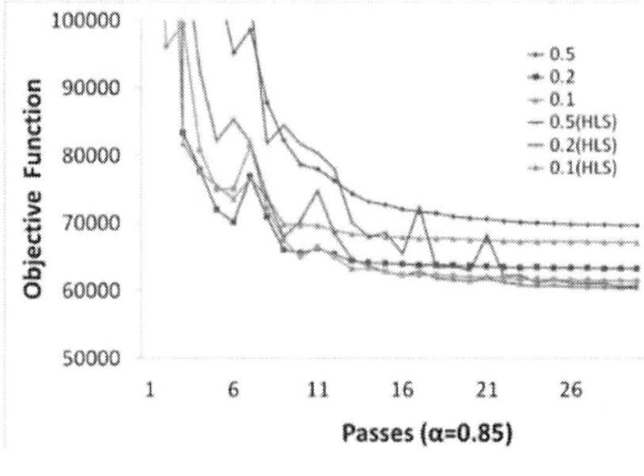

Figure 1: Bakeoff 2005 Chinese word segmentation task: Objective function with fixed α.

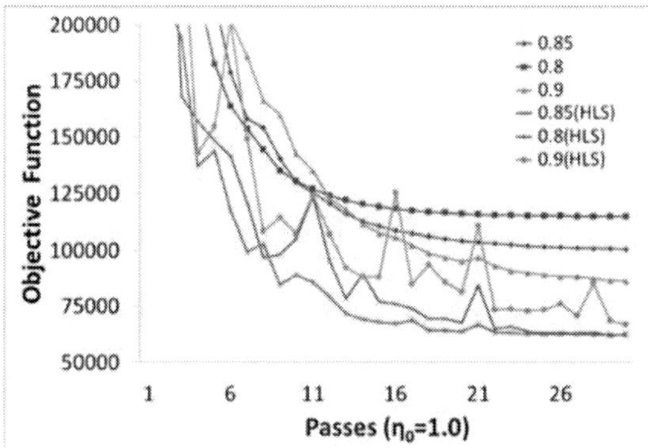

Figure 2: Bakeoff 2005 Chinese word segmentation task: Objective function with fixed η_0.

rate parameter.

For our method, we first measured the progress of the SGD algorithm with heuristic line search we presented against the origin SGD method. We use the same parameters settings with the former method including both regularization parameter and learning rate parameters. The number of passes performed over the training data was also set to 30. Then we compare the results of both methods during the training process of the model with the same parameters, and they were shown in Figure 1 and Figure 2.

Figure 1 shows how the value of the objective function changed as the training proceeded with the same descent learning rate parameter ($\alpha = 0.85$), the figure contains six curves representing the results of SGD method with heuristic line search and the origin SGD method with different initiation learning rate parameter settings (η_0). "HLS" stands for the heuristic line search strategy. The results shows SGD method with heuristic line search shows better convergence and more robust

Table 2: Bakeoff 2005 Chinese word segmentation task. Accuracy of the model on the testdata.

	$L + R$	# Features	F score
OWL-QN	56451.8	114,942	94.81
SGD	61398.6	232,585	94.92
Ours	56481.9	117,374	94.78

Table 3: Bakeoff 2005 Chinese word segmentation task. Training time of the model on the testdata.

	Passes	Time
OWL-QN	141	2h59min
SGD	30	58min
Ours	5 + 88	2h06min

result than the origin SGD method when using the same learning rate parameter settings. Figure 2 shows the results with different settings of learning rate parameters (fixed $\eta_0 = 1$), and it demonstrates the same trend as Figure 1.

Then we trained the models with the training data and evaluated the accuracy of the Chinese word segmenter on the test data. The number of passes performed over the training data in SGD was also set to 30. In our method, we set the SGD iteration times to 5. It is worth noting that we didn't spend much time in tuning the value of this parameter. Based on a cursory view of the training process, we found that it converge to a relative "good" result after the first 5 iteration. We used this value throughout all the experiments. Because we would take the OWL-QN method to guarantee the final convergence, and the SGD method with heuristic line search strategy is insensitive to the learning rate parameters, this value would not have a significant influence on the performance.

The results are shown in Table 2 and Table 3. In Table 2, the second column shows the final value of the objective function. The third column shows the number of active features in the final resulting model. The fourth column shows the F score of the Chinese word segment results, which is the harmonic mean of precision P (percentage of output Chinese words that exactly match the golden standard Chinese words) and recall R (percentage of golden standard Chinese words that returned by our system). In Table 3, the second column shows the number of passes performed in the training, in our method, this value includes the the number of

Table 4: Feature templates for name entity recognition task.

(1) $c_{i-2}y_i$, $c_{i-1}y_i$, c_iy_i, $c_{i+1}y_i$, $c_{i+2}y_i$
(2) $c_{i-1}c_iy_i$, $c_ic_{i+1}y_i$
(3) $y_{i-1}y_i$

passes both in the first stage of SGD and the second stage of OWL-QN process. The third column shows the training time.

In the terms of accuracy, there was no significant difference between all the models, the origin SGD method yield the slightly better result, probably due to the model has larger features sets. This doesn't contradict to our original purpose, for we have got a substantial improved result in both the final value of the objective function and the number of active features compared with the origin SGD method, and to the same level as OWL-QN method. Notice the origin feature sets are over 6 millon, L1 regularization methods produced the models which are compact indeed. The official best result in the closed test achieved an F score of 95.00, and our result is quite close to that, ranked 4th of 23 official runs.

On the other hand, our method took about 30% less than the OWL-QN method in the training time. Our method only needs 88 passes over the whole training data in the second stage for convergence compared with 141 in the OWL-QN method, which shows a significant improvement in training time consuming, for we have used the first stage of SGD method to get a nearly optimal and stable result beforehand.

4.2 Name Entity Recognition

The second set of experiments used the name entity recognition corpus from the Fourth International SIGHAN Bakeoff data sets (Jin and Chen, 2008), provided by Microsoft Research Asia. The training data consists of 23,182 sentences, 1,089,050 Chinese characters and the testing data consists of 4,636 sentences, 219,197 Chinese characters. We separated 1,000 sentences from the training data and use them as the heldout data. The training data is annotated with the "IOB" tags representing name entities including person, location and organization.

The feature templates we used in this experiment were listed in Table 4. Notice we did not change the label representation made by the origin

Table 5: Fourth SIGHAN Bakeoff name entity recognition task. Training time of the model on the testdata.

	$L+R$	Passes	Time
OWL-QN	11247.1	219	5h26min
SGD	13993.3	30	1h08min
Ours	11245.5	5 + 122	3h10min

Table 6: Fourth SIGHAN Bakeoff name entity recognition task. Accuracy of the model on the testdata.

	# Feat.	LOC	ORG	PER
OWL-QN	34,579	89.94	82.61	90.65
SGD	113,005	89.39	82.75	90.78
Ours	36,709	90.05	82.25	90.49

training data for convenient. Again a richer label representation may yield a better performance.

The other experiment settings are the same with the experiment on Chinese word segmentation. The comparison results are shown in Table 5, Figure 3 and Figure 4. The trend in the results is the same as that of the Chinese word segmentation task. SGD method with heuristic line search strategy produced more stable and robust result than the origin SGD method. Although there will have fluctuations sometimes (in Figure 4), the line search strategy shows the ability to find an appreciate step size in that case. Again our method converged to a much better solution against SGD in both the final value of the objective function and number of active features, and took about 40% less training time than OWL-QN.

The accuracy of the results is shown in Table 6, there was no significant difference between all the models as well. The F score of organization name entity recognition was worse than the results in person and location name entity, for organization name entities in Chinese often have a relative long distance dependency, which is not easy to be captured by our local feature templates in the Chinese character level.

5 Conclusion

We have presented a two-stage algorithm that can efficiently train L1-regularized CRFs. Experiments on two NLP tasks demonstrated that our method is effective and efficient by utilizing both

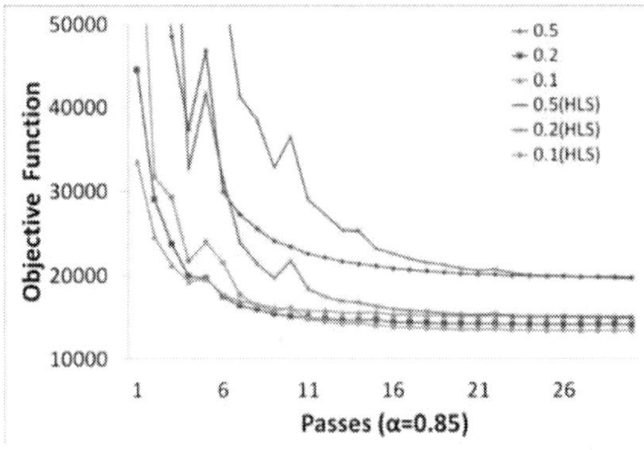

Figure 3: Fourth SIGHAN Bakeoff name entity recognition task: Objective function with fixed α.

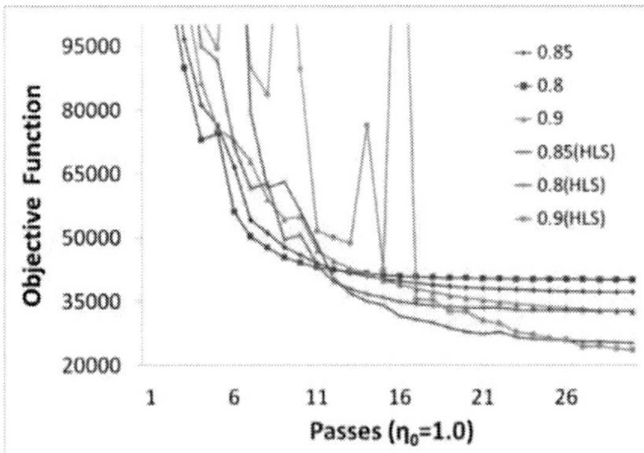

Figure 4: Fourth SIGHAN Bakeoff name entity recognition task: Objective function with fixed η_0.

the advantages of SGD and OWL-QN.

In the future, we intend to study how to use the results of the first stage of SGD learning to estimate the Hessian information, which can be provided for the second stage of quasi-Newton method to enhance the effectiveness of training. Borders et al. (2009) looked into this problem in a similar way. It is also worthwhile to investigate whether other adaptive learning rate scheduling algorithms can result in fast training with our method, as in (Vishwanathan et al., 2006; Huang et al., 2007).

Acknowledgments

The author wishes to thank the anonymous reviewer for their helpful suggestions. This work was (partially) funded by NSFC (No. 61003091 and No. 61073069) and Shanghai Committee of Science and Technology (No. 10511500703)

References

Galen Andrew and Jianfeng Gao. 2007. Scalable training of l1-regularized log-linear models. In *Proceedings of the International Conference on Machine Learning*, pages 33–40. Corvalis, Oregon, USA.

Antoine Bordes, Léon Bottou, and Patrick Gallinari. 2009. SGD-QN: Careful quasi-Newton stochastic gradient descent. In *The Journal of Machine Learning Research*, 10: 1737–1754.

Léon Bottou. 2007. Stochastic gradient descent (sgd) implementation. http://leon.bottou.org/projects/sgd.

Stephen Boyed and Lieven Vandenberghe. 2004. *Convex Optimiaztion*. Cambridge University Press.

Michael Collins, Amir Globerson, Terry Koo, Xavier Carreras, and Peter L. Bartlett. 2008. Exponentiated gradient algorithms for conditional random fields and max-margin markov networks. In *The Journal of Machine Learning Research*, 9: 1775–1822.

Christian Darken and John Moody. 1990. Note on learning rate schedules for stochastic optimization. In *Proceedings of Advances in Neural Information Processing Systems 3*, pages 832–838. Colorado, USA.

Tom Emerson. 2005. The second international Chinese word segmentation bakeoff. In *Proceedings of Fourth SIGHAN Workshop on Chinese Language Processing*. Korea.

Jenny Rose Finkel, Alex Kleeman, and Christopher D.Manning. 2008. Efficient, feature-based, conditional random field parsing. In *Proceedings of the Annual Meeting of the Association for Computational Linguistics*, pages 959–967. Columbus, Ohio, USA.

Jianfeng Gao, Galen Andrew, Mark Johnson, and Kristina Toutanova. 2007. A comparative study of parameter estimation methods for statistical natural language processing. In *Proceedings of the Annual Meeting of the Association for Computational Linguistics*, pages 824–831. Prague, Czech republic.

Changning Huang and Hai Zhao. 2007. Chinese word segmentation: A decade review. In *Journal of Chinese Information Processing*, 21(3): 8–19.

Han-Shen Huang, Yu-Ming Chang, and Chun-Nan Hsu. 2007. Training conditional random fields by periodic step size adaptation for large-scale text mining. In *Proceedings of the IEEE International Conference on Data Mining*, pages 511–516. Omaha, Nebraska, USA.

Guangjin Jin and Xiao Chen. 2008. The fourth international Chinese language processing bakeoff: Chinese word segmentation, named entity recognition and Chinese pos tagging. In *Proceedings of Sixth SIGHAN Workshop on Chinese Language Processing*. India.

Junichi Kazama and Junichi Tsujii. 2003. Evaluation and extension of maximum entropy models with inequality constraints. In *Proceedings of the Conference on Empirical Methods in Natural Language Processing*, pages 137–144.

John Lafferty, Andrew McCallum, and Fernando Pereira. 2001. Conditional random fields: probabilistic models for segmenting and labeling sequence data. In *Proceedings of the International Conference on Machine Learning*, pages 282–289. Prague, Czech republic.

Thomas Lavergne, Olivier,Cappé, and François Yvon. 2010. Practical very large scale CRFs. In *Proceedings the Annual Meeting of the Association for Computational Linguistics*, pages 504–513. Uppsala, Sweden.

Dong C. Liu and Jorge Nocedal. 1989. On the limited memory BFGS method for large scale optimization. *Mathematical Programming*, 45: 503–528.

Andrew Mccallum, Dayne Freitag, and Fernando Pereira. 2000. Maximum Entropy Markov Models for Information Extraction and Segmentation. In *Proceedings of the International Conference on Machine Learning*, pages 591–598. California, USA.

Naoaki Okazaki. 2007. CRFsuite: A fast implementation of conditional random fields (CRFs). http://www.chokkan.org/software/crfsuite/.

Fuchun Peng, and Andrew McCallum. 2004. Accurate Information Extraction from Research Papers using Conditional Random Fields. In *Proceedings of the North American Chapter of the Association for Computational Linguistics*, pages 329–336. Massachusetts, USA.

Lawrence Rabiner. 1989. A Tutorial on Hidden Markov Models and Selected Applications in Speech Recognition. In *Proceedings of the IEEE*, 77(2): 257–286.

Charles Sutton and Andrew McCallum. 2006. An introduction to conditional random fields for relational learning. *Introduction to Statistical Relational Learning*. The MIT Press.

Kristina Toutanova, Aria Haghighi, and Christopher Manning. 2005. Joint learning improves semantic role labeling. In *Proceedings of the Annual Meeting of the Association for Computational Linguistics*, pages 589–596. Michigan, USA.

Yoshimasa Tsuruoka, Junichi Tsujii, and Sophia Ananiadou. 2009. Stochastic gradient descent training for l1-regularized log-linear models with cumulative penalty. In *Proceedings the Annual Meeting of the Association for Computational Linguistics*, pages 477–485. Suntec, Singapore.

Douglas Vail, John Lafferty, and Manuela Veloso. 2007. Feature Selection in Conditional Random Fields for Activity Recognition. In *Proceedings of the IEEE/RSJ International Conference on Intelligent Robots and Systems*, pages 3379–3384. California, USA.

S. V. N. Vishwanathan, Nicol N. Schraudolph, Mark W. Schmidt, and Kevin P. Murphy. 2006. Accelerated training of conditional random fields with stochastic gradient methods. In *Proceedings of the International Conference on Machine learning*, pages 969–976. Pittsburgh, Pennsylvania, USA.

Automatic Topic Model Adaptation for Sentiment Analysis in Structured Domains

Geoffrey Levine and **Gerald DeJong**
University of Illinois at Urbana-Champaign
Urbana, IL
levine@illinois.edu and mrebl@illinois.edu

Abstract

We present a novel topic modeling approach to sentiment analysis for documents organized into hierarchical categories. In our approach, positive, negative, and subject matter topics are learned and used to infer document labels. A Markov chain Monte Carlo model procedure adapts the number and structure of topics based on a minimum description length objective function. We apply our approach to Yelp.com business reviews and Amazon.com book reviews and demonstrate that 1) the model adaptation procedure selects a high quality model from the space of alternatives, and 2) the resulting model performs well relative to state of the art regression and topic modeling approaches.

1 Introduction

Selecting an appropriate model is an important part of any machine learning endeavor. The model must be chosen in a manner so as to balance two objectives: 1) Be sufficiently rich to capture the relevant patterns in the data, and 2) Be simple enough to avoid spurious patterns in the training data (overfitting). In natural language processing tasks, there are often many modeling choices to be made regarding what feature granularities and interactions to consider. It is important to make these decisions in a manner such that the resulting model strikes a balance between these two somewhat contradictory objectives.

In order to appropriately make these choices, we must consider not only the task involved but also the training data available. With copious data we can reliably calibrate complex models, but with limited data complex models risk overfitting. Many general model selection techniques exist in which each candidate model is fit to the training data and scored with respect to a particular criterion. While these approaches allow us to compare a small number of models in order to select the most appropriate, they require calibrating each model's parameters to the training data. However, when there are many modeling choices to be made and thus a large space of alternative models, fitting all of them to the training data is computationally prohibitive.

In this paper, we present a novel topic modeling approach for structured sentiment analysis domains and an automatic model adaptation approach that takes advantage of categorical metadata. This model adaptation approach resolves the structure of the metadata with the significant patterns in the training data to determine the number and range of latent topics.

We demonstrate our approach on Yelp.com business reviews as well as Amazon.com book reviews. We show that our model adaptation approach selects an appropriate model given a particular amount of training data, and the resulting model is high quality relative to alternative regression and topic modeling approaches.

2 Background

Sentiment analysis, in which the opinion of the author is estimated from a document, has recently grown in popularity. Many works have explored unigram models (Pang and Lee, 2005; Snyder and Barzilay, 2007). Higher-order n-gram models are explored in (Pang and Lee, 2008; Baccianella et al., 2009). In order to combat the high dimensional feature space that accompanies such models, models restricting features based on part of speech patterns (Baccianella et al., 2009) or opinion templates (root, modifiers, negation words) (Qu et al., 2010) have been introduced.

Topic models are generative models in which the words in a document are assumed to be associated with one of a number of abstract "topics." Latent Dirichlet allocation (Blei et al., 2003) is a popular topic model in which the topic distribution per document is assumed to have a Dirichlet prior. In supervised LDA (Blei and McAuliffe, 2007), the distribution of document topics is used to produce a document label. (Zhao et al., 2010; Titov and McDonald, 2008b; Titov and McDonald, 2008a) focus on topic modeling based approaches to aspect-based sentiment summarization, identifying product features and the opinion associated with each.

Model selection is the act of using data to choose a statistical model from a set of candidates. Often, this task is performed by fitting each candidate model to the training data and using a criterion to score the models and select one. Popular criteria include the Akaike information criterion (AIC) (Akaike, 1974), the Bayesian information criterion (BIC) (Schwarz, 1978), and the minimum description length principle (MDL) (Rissanen, 1978; Grunwald, 2007). Structural Risk Minimization (Vapnik, 1995) defines a general framework in which a nested hierarchy of hypotheses can be defined based on prior knowledge of the domain, such that a hypothesis balancing goodness of fit with simplicity can be identified. The work presented in this paper is closely related to the model adaptation procedure presented in (Levine et al., 2010), in which a hill-climbing approach is used to explore a large space of generative models.

3 Topic Modeling for Sentiment Analysis in Structured Domains

Our approach takes advantage of hierarchical categorical metadata. Formally, this hierarchy forms a tree structure, which we refer to as $\mathcal{C}$ (See Figure 1). Individual nodes in the tree are called *categories*, for which we use notation c. A *categorization*, $\mathbf{c}$, is a set of categories, $\mathbf{c} = \{c_{d,1}, c_{d,2}, ...\}$. $\mathbf{c}$ can be thought of as metadata about a product/service being reviewed. For example, with regard to a book review, $\mathbf{c}$ could equal {"Fiction", "Fiction\Drama", "Fiction\Drama\Romance", ... }. $\mathbf{c}$ must be well formed. That is, if a node $c \in \mathcal{C}$ appears in categorization $\mathbf{c}$, all ancestors of c (in the tree $\mathcal{C}$) must also appear in $\mathbf{c}$. $\mathbf{c}$ can contain multiple distantly related categories. For example, a particular book could belong to both "Fiction\Poetry" and "Children\Humor."

Documents, or examples, are denoted d = $\langle \mathbf{x_d}, \mathbf{c_d}, y_d \rangle$. $\mathbf{x_d} = [w_{d,1}, w_{d,2}, ..., w_{d,|\mathbf{x_d}|}]$ is a vector of *words*. Each word is an element from the *vocabulary*, $V = \{w_1, w_2, ..., w_{|V|}\}$. $\mathbf{c_d}$ is the document's categorization. y_d is a numeric *rating* from a discrete space ({1,2,3,4,5} for our domains). The rating is an overall score given by the document's author to the product or service being reviewed.

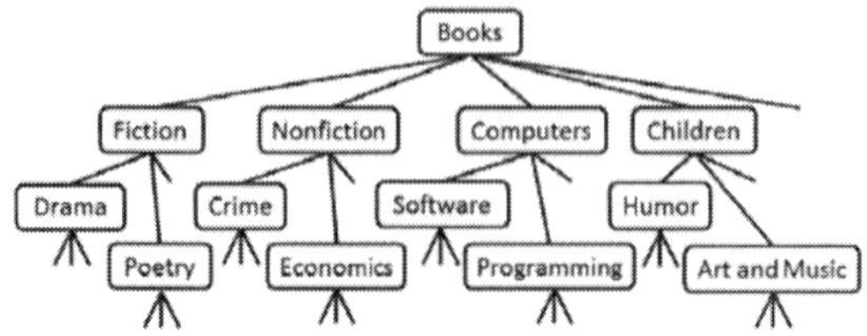

Figure 1: A subtree of the category tree, $\mathcal{C}$, corresponding to the Amazon Books domain.

We are given a collection of documents, $\mathcal{D}$, and our goal is to learn a function $f(\langle \mathbf{x}, \mathbf{c} \rangle)$ to predict rating $\hat{y}$ from an *unlabeled document* so as to minimize the expected loss over the unknown distribution of documents:

$$E\left(\text{loss}(y, f(\langle \mathbf{x}, \mathbf{c} \rangle))\right) \qquad (1)$$

We use the squared error loss function.

3.1 Model Structure

We will start by presenting our generative document topic model. In this model, each review is composed of a mixture of topics, and each topic is associated with a distribution over words. We use $t \in T$ to denote a topic, and P_t to denote t's word distribution. Within a document, each word is assumed to be generated from a particular topic, although which topic is unobservable. In many topic model approaches, such as latent Dirichlet allocation (Blei et al., 2003), topics are learned in an unsupervised or weekly supervised fashion (as is the case with supervised LDA).

In our model, we assume each document is generated according to a rigid topic distribution (more similar to labeled LDA (Ramage et al., 2011)). Each document is a mixture of three topics: 1) a *positive* topic (+), in which the reviewer is speaking favorably about the product/service, 2) a *negative* topic (-), in which the reviewer is speaking unfavorably, and 3) a *subject* topic (s_i) corresponding to general text about the content/features of the product.

The proportion of positive words to negative words is a function of the rating score. Subject topics reflect the language used when discussing a particular product or group of products, and do not directly influence a document's rating. Still, learning these topics appropriately is crucial to the performance of the model. When a word is indicative of either the positive or negative topic, it is important to account for its probability in the subject topic. For example, the word "good" may be less indicative of a book review's rating if the review discusses a book about ethics. Furthermore, if subject topics are not learned appropriately, words related to the subject matter of products/services with a disproportionate number of positive training reviews would be attributed to the positive word topic. This will lead to poor performance on unseen data. On the other hand, if these words are correctly attributed to the subject topic, then the high ratings will appropriately be attributed to the unconditional positive words appearing in the reviews.

What constitutes a subject worthy of having its own topic? For books, should we only make broad distinctions such as fiction vs. non-fiction? Should we learn a unique subject topic for each book? Should we use something in between these two extremes? In answering these questions, we need to balance goodness of fit to the training data with model simplicity. There is no optimal answer, it is a function both of the domain (in that we need to make the most "significant" distinctions), and the amount of training data available to calibrate our model (more training data allows us to reliably learn the additional parameters introduced by making additional distinctions).

There exists a many-to-one relationship between documents and subject topics. The mapping from document to subject topic is a function of the document's categorization, $s_i = g(\mathbf{c_d})$, $s_i \in T$. We call the function g the *topic mapping function*. The range of g is the set of subject topics, $\{s_1, s_2, ..., s_N\} \subset T$. In Sections 3.1.1 and 3.1.2 we assume that g is fixed. In Section 3.2, we consider exploring the space of alternative topic mapping functions.

We assume that in expectation, a fixed but unknown fraction, α of each document is composed of the subject topic. The remainder of the review is composed of the positive and negative topics, and the positive/negative ratio is related to the document's rating. Let y_{min} and y_{max} represent the minimum and maximum scores in the rating scale. For document d with score y_d the expected fractional breakdown into topics is as follows:

$$\begin{aligned} \texttt{Positive:} \quad f_+(y_d) &= (1-\alpha)\frac{y_d - y_{min}}{y_{max} - y_{min}} \\ \texttt{Negative:} \quad f_-(y_d) &= (1-\alpha)\frac{y_{max} - y_d}{y_{max} - y_{min}} \\ \texttt{Subject:} \quad f_s(y_d) &= \alpha \end{aligned} \tag{2}$$

In total, a model M is composed of the topic mapping function, the value α, and the word distributions associated with each topic. $M = (g, \alpha, P_+, P_-, P_{s_1}, P_{s_2}, ..., P_{s_N})$.

3.1.1 Training

Expectation maximization (Hastie et al., 2001) can be used to train our topic model. The procedure works by iteratively updating 1) the assignment of words in each document to latent topics (Expectation Step), and 2) the word distributions associated with each topic (Maximization Step). EM proceeds as follows:

Expectation Step

Each word is assigned an expected topic distribution. For word i in document d:

$$\begin{aligned} q_{d,i}(+) &= \frac{f_+(y_d)P_+(w_{d,i})}{Z_{d,i}} \\ q_{d,i}(-) &= \frac{f_-(y_d)P_-(w_{d,i})}{Z_{d,i}} \\ q_{d,i}(g(\mathbf{c_d})) &= \frac{f_s(y_d)P_{g(\mathbf{c_d})}(w_{d,i})}{Z_{d,i}} \\ Z_{d,i} &= \sum_{t \in \{+,-,g(\mathbf{c_d})\}} f_t(y_d)P_t(w_{d,i}) \end{aligned} \tag{3}$$

Maximization Step

Topic word distributions are updated so as to maximize the likelihood of the training data. For each topic t:

$$P_t(w) = \frac{\sum_{d \in \mathcal{D}} \sum_{i=1}^{|\mathbf{x_d}|} \mathbf{I}_w(w_{d,i}) q_{d,i}(t)}{\sum_{d \in \mathcal{D}} \sum_{i=1}^{|\mathbf{x_d}|} q_{d,i}(t)} \tag{4}$$

where

$$\mathbf{I}_w(w_{d,i}) = \begin{cases} 1 & \text{if } w_{d,i} = w \\ 0 & \text{otherwise} \end{cases} \tag{5}$$

3.1.2 Inference

Given the trained topic models we use Bayes' theorem to compute the probability that an unlabeled document $\langle \mathbf{x_d}, \mathbf{c_d} \rangle$ is associated with a particular rating. Let $T_d = \{+, -, g(\mathbf{c_d})\}$:

$$P(y|\mathbf{x_d}, \mathbf{c_d}) = \frac{P(y)P(\mathbf{x_d}, \mathbf{c_d}|y)}{P(\mathbf{x_d}, \mathbf{c_d})}$$
$$= \frac{P(y)\prod_{i=1}^{|\mathbf{x_d}|}\left(\sum_{t\in T_d} f_t(y)P_t(w_{d,i})\right)}{\sum_{y'} P(y')\prod_{i=1}^{|\mathbf{x_d}|}\left(\sum_{t\in T_d} f_t(y)P_t(w_{d,i})\right)} \quad (6)$$

For evaluation purposes, we output the expected value of y and compute the squared error to the true value.

3.2 Model Adaptation

In this section we introduce a Markov chain Monte Carlo approach to selecting a topic mapping function g. Here, we stochastically explore the space of topic mapping functions, driven by the minimum description length principle and estimates of the effect of modifications to g. This approach resists local minima and efficiently finds a high quality topic mapping function.

3.2.1 Minimum Description Length Objective

Our goal is to find a model that balances fit to the training data with simplicity, and concentrates its flexibility where most useful to capture relevant patterns in the domain. We accomplish this by utilizing a two part minimum description length objective function. The objective is the sum of 1) the description length (in bits) required to encode the model and 2) the description length of the data given the model.

$$\mathrm{L}(M, \mathcal{D}) = \mathrm{L}(M) + \mathrm{L}(\mathcal{D}|M) \quad (7)$$

where $\mathrm{L}(M)$ is a function of the number of model parameters ($\approx$ the product of the number of topics and the vocabulary size) and $\mathrm{L}(\mathcal{D}|M)$ is the negative log likelihood of the data given the model. Thus the goal is to jointly minimize the complexity of the model and maximize the likelihood of the data given the model, and the objective can be rewritten as:

$$\mathrm{L}(M, \mathcal{D}) = \beta(N+2)|V| + -log\left(l(\mathcal{D}|M)\right) \quad (8)$$

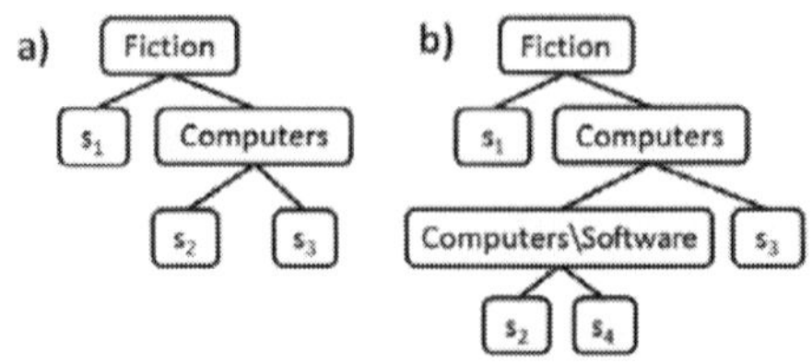

Figure 2: Two possible partitioning trees for the Amazon.com Books category tree (Figure 1). Tree b) is formed by splitting s_2 in a) based on membership in the "Computer\Software" category.

where β is a complexity penalty constant, which is selected via cross-validation.

3.2.2 Topic Mapping Functions

The topic mapping function g maps from categorization $\mathbf{c}$ to a subject topic $s_i \in T$. We select a particular g from the space of *binary partitioning trees*, G. In a binary partitioning tree, each internal node references a category c, and each leaf node references a subject topic s_i. See Figure 2. Starting at the root, a categorization, $\mathbf{c}$ is recursively assigned by each internal node to 1) the left subtree if the referenced category c is in $\mathbf{c}$, and 2) the right subtree otherwise, until a leaf (with associated subject topic) is reached. For example, within the book review domain, a node may reference the category "Computers." In this case, computer books are recursively assigned a subject topic by the left subtree, and all others by the right subtree. We allow only well formed partitioning trees: Any node in g that references a category c with parent category $parent(c) \in \mathcal{C}$ must have an ancestor that references $parent(c)$. For example, we do not allow a node in g to reference "Computers\Software", unless we have already conditioned on the "Computers" category. This constraint guarantees that we partition the space of categorizations into coherent regions (we would never assign "Computer\Hardware" and "Fiction" books to the same subject topic while assigning "Computer\Software" to a different topic).

3.2.3 Adjacent Model Estimation

In order to guide the search through G, we consider 2 types of modification operations: We can 1) Split a leaf based on category $c \in \mathcal{C}$, splitting one partition into two, adding an additional subject topic to the model, or 2) Merge two leaves with the same parent, combining two partitions into one, removing a subject topic from the model.

Given a particular g, there are a finite number of possible merge and split operations to the leaves. Key to our search is the fact that we can estimate the change to the description length objective that each possible modification will cause, using the latent topic distributions assigned to each topic during expectation maximization. Consider merging two subject topics s_i and s_j:

$$\widehat{\Delta L} = -\beta|V| - \sum_{t\in\{s_i,s_j\}} \sum_{w\in V} \#_t(w) log \frac{P_{m_{i,j}}(w)}{P_t(w)} \tag{9}$$

where

$$\#_t(w) = \sum_{d\in\mathcal{D}} \sum_{i=1}^{|\mathbf{x_d}|} \mathbf{I}_w(w_{d,i}) q_{d,i}(t)$$

$$P_{m_{i,j}}(w) = \frac{\sum_{t\in\{s_i,s_j\}} \#_t(w)}{\sum_{t\in\{s_i,s_j\}} \sum_{d\in(D)} \sum_{i=1}^{|\mathbf{x_d}|} q_{d,i}(t)} \tag{10}$$

Now consider splitting subject topic s_i based on category c:

$$\widehat{\Delta L} = \beta|V| - \sum_{t\in\{s_{i,c},s_{i,!c}\}} \sum_{w\in V} \#_t(w) log \frac{P_t(w)}{P_{s_i}(w)} \tag{11}$$

where

$$\#_{s_{i,c}}(w) = \sum_{\substack{d=(\mathbf{x},\mathbf{c},y)\in\mathcal{D} \\ s.t. c\in\mathbf{c}}} \sum_{i=1}^{|\mathbf{x_d}|} \mathbf{I}_w(w_{d,i}) q_{d,i}(s_i)$$

$$P_{s_{i,c}}(w) = \frac{\#_{s_{i,c}}(w)}{\sum_{\substack{d=(\mathbf{x},\mathbf{c},y)\in\mathcal{D} \\ s.t. c\in\mathbf{c}}} \sum_{i=1}^{|\mathbf{x_d}|} q_{d,i}(s_i)}$$

$$\#_{s_{i,!c}}(w) = \sum_{\substack{d=(\mathbf{x},\mathbf{c},y)\in\mathcal{D} \\ s.t. c\notin\mathbf{c}}} \sum_{i=1}^{|\mathbf{x_d}|} \mathbf{I}_w(w_{d,i}) q_{d,i}(s_i)$$

$$P_{s_{i,!c}}(w) = \frac{\#_{s_{i,!c}}(w)}{\sum_{\substack{d=(\mathbf{x},\mathbf{c},y)\in\mathcal{D} \\ s.t. c\notin\mathbf{c}}} \sum_{i=1}^{|\mathbf{x_d}|} q_{d,i}(s_i)} \tag{12}$$

These estimates are upper bounds on the change to the description length objective function. Incorporating these changes (and the associated word distributions) and then retraining the model with expectation maximization may further reduce the objective. These bounds serve as a guide to estimate the objective for models that have *not* been fit to the training data, which will drive our search through G for the optimal topic mapping function.

3.2.4 MCMC exploration

Markov chain Monte Carlo (Gilks et al., 1996) stochastically steps through the space of alternative topic mapping functions. At each iteration of MCMC, the topic model with the current topic mapping function is fit to the training data and the objective change associated with all possible merges and splits is estimated. We then construct a proposal distribution for alternative models that can be reached with these operations. Limiting the proposal distribution to these candidate models, as in (Titov and Klementiev, 2011) and (Singh et al., 2011) induces a decomposable, feasible computation. A model is sampled from this distribution and adopted if certain criteria on its fitness are met.

MCMC will converge to a probability distribution over models. By making better models (those with a lower objective) more probable, the MCMC chain will be driven towards higher quality models. We use an exponential distribution over models:

$$P(M) = \frac{e^{-L(M,\mathcal{D})}}{Z_P} \tag{13}$$

with normalization factor Z_P.

The proposal distribution, Q assigns some probability to all candidate models that can be reached by a single merge or split to each of the leaves in the current partitioning tree. In Q, splits and merges to leaves without a common parent are independent by construction. Now, consider a particular leaf, l, that has the following possible splits, $S = \{c_1, c_2, ..., c_l\}$, and cannot be merged with another leaf. For example, in Figure 2a, the leaf corresponding to s_1 meets this condition as it cannot be merged to another leaf and has possible splits {"Fiction\Drama", "Fiction\Poetry", "Nonfiction", "Computers", "Children", ... }. Let M_l represent the subset of models where l is not split, and M_{l,c_i} represent the subset of candidate models where l has been split with respect to category c_i.

$$Q(M_l) = \frac{e^{-\tau L(M,\mathcal{D})}}{Z_l}$$

$$Q(M_{l,c_i}) = \frac{e^{-\tau \hat{L}(M_{l,c_i},\mathcal{D})}}{|S|Z_l}$$

$$Z_l = \left(e^{-\tau L(M,\mathcal{D})} + \sum_{c\in S} \frac{1}{|S|} e^{-\hat{L}(M_{l,c},\mathcal{D})}\right) \tag{14}$$

$0 < \tau \leq 1$ controls a balance between having the proposal distribution completely influenced by the estimated objectives vs. a uniform proposal distribution.

For all pairs of leaves that share a common parent, we entertain a merge operation. In Figure 2a the leaves corresponding to s_2 and s_3 meet this criteria. Suppose two leaves, l and l' have possible splits $S = \{c_1, c_2, ..., c_l\}$ and $S' = \{c'_1, c'_2, ..., c'_{l'}\}$ respectively. In addition to the one merged alternative, there are $w = (|S|+1)(|S'|+1)$ alternatives that involve only splits to the two leaves. Let $M_{l,l'}$ represent the subset of candidate models where l and l' are merged

$$Q(M_{l,l'}) = \frac{w^{-\frac{1}{2}} e^{-\tau \widehat{L}(M_{l,l'}, \mathcal{D})}}{w^{-\frac{1}{2}} e^{-\tau \widehat{L}(M_{l,l'}, \mathcal{D})} + (Z_l)(Z_{l'})} \qquad (15)$$

The factor of $w^{-\frac{1}{2}}$ accounts for the difference between the number of neighbors that the models with l and l' merged vs. split have. If the two leaves are not merged, then the conditional probability for each of the $(|S|+1)(|S'|+1)$ remaining structural alternatives is computed in Equation 14.

A new topic mapping function g' is sampled from Q and fit to the training data via the expectation maximization presented in Section 3.1.1. If a random value sampled uniformly from $\mathcal{U}[0, 1)$ is less than

$$\frac{P(M_{g'})Q(g|g')}{P(M_g)Q(g'|g)} \qquad (16)$$

then g' is accepted as the new topic mapping function g^{t+1}. This guarantees that the Markov chain will converge to the distribution P as $t \to \infty$. Because the ratio $P(M_{g'})/P(M_g)$ appears in Equation 16, the normalization factor Z_P in Equation 13 cancels out and does not need to be computed.

4 Empirical Evaluation

We perform a set of experiments to demonstrate the following:

1) Given the topic model structure outlined in Section 3.1, the model adaptation procedure in section 3.2 selects a high performing topic mapping function while only evaluating a small fraction of the total number of funtions.

2) The topic model resulting from model adaptation is high quality relative to alternative state-of-the-art approaches.

4.1 Data

We demonstrate our approach to two structured sentiment analysis datasets. First, we gathered a collection of approximately 8,000 Yelp.com business reviews from the greater New York area. For this data, businesses are assigned into categories and subcategories based on the Yelp.com business hierarchy. There are 22 primary categories {Arts and Entertainment, Education, Financial Services, Restaurants,...}, each with 6 to 100 subcategories (restaurants have the most subcategories, {Japanese, Barbeque, Cafe, Fast Food, Burgers, Ultra High Enc, Formal, Full Bar,...}). Businesses can be assigned to multiple categories and subcategories within the hierarchy.

Second, we utilize 20,000 Amazon.com book reviews, extracted from the data set first presented in (Qu et al., 2010). Categorical distinctions in these domains are related to the Amazon.com product hierarchy. A small portion of the product hierarchy appears in Figure 1. Books can be assigned to multiple distantly related categories. For example, the book *Six Wives of Henry VIII* belongs to "History\Europe\England\Tudor and Stuart," "Biographies and Memoirs\Specific Groups\Women" and three other categories

For each domain, we have at most one review corresponding to any particular business/book. This allows for a broad coverage of the space of categorizations.

4.2 Results and Discussion

To compensate for extreme variations in the training data we apply two smoothing steps. First, we found that for longer reviews, the assumption that each word is drawn independently from the document's topics is too strong, and so for reviews with more than 35 words, we scale the term counts such that the total is 35. Second, because of the large size of the vocabulary, after training, some rare words have zero or near zero probability in some of the topics. When these words are observed during inference, they have a very strong effect on the document's expected rating. We found that smoothing the subject topics with the overall word distribution across topics stabilizes the predicted ratings and improves performance. The amount of smoothing could be optimized to maximize the likelihood of the test data, but we found that performance varied little for a wide range of values and so we choose a 1 to 1 smoothing.

From each dataset, we sample a subset of size 1000 for cross validation parameter tuning and use the remaining examples for experimentation.

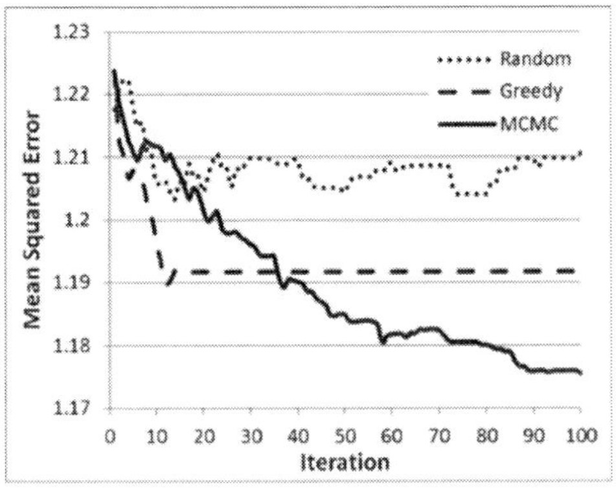

Figure 3: Learning curves for three model sampling approaches on Yelp.com test data with 500 training examples (averaged over 20 trials).

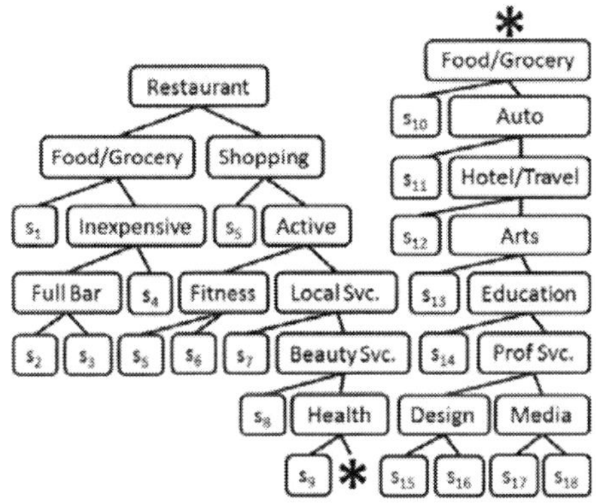

Figure 4: A representative partitioning tree learned from 500 training examples on the Yelp.com data.

The validation data is used to learn the values of α, the subject topic fraction, and β, the complexity penalty. We found that setting τ, the MCMC smoothing factor, equal to .1 worked well across our datasets. For each trial, then, disjoint training and test sets are sampled from the remaining data.

First, we apply our Markov chain Monte Carlo model adaptation procedure along with greedy and random alternatives to demonstrate the necessity of a directed and stochastic approach. In the greedy approach, at each iteration we estimate the objective for all candidate models that can be reached with a single split/merge to each subject topic and adopt the model with the minimum estimate. For the random approach, at each iteration we start with the simplest topic mapping function (mapping all categorizations to one subject topic), and uniformly at random add distinctions until the model has the same number of subject topics as the optimal model found by the MCMC approach. We choose this instead of sampling at random from all possible topic mapping functions as the vast majority of such functions have nearly as many subject topics as training examples. For each approach, at iteration i, we chart the test mean squared error for the best (lowest objective) model observed during training in iterations 1 to i.

Figure 3 charts the per iteration mean squared error on the Yelp test data for the three model adaptation approaches. The greedy approach initially makes the fastest progress, but it is susceptible to local minima, and it levels off before being overtaken by the MCMC approach. As the random approach does not leverage the data in determining what distinctions to make, it fails to make progress at the rate of the other approaches. Its poor performance is indicative of the importance of having an efficient directed model adaptation approach, as high performing models are few and far between, even if we limit our search to models of the appropriate complexity level (number of subject topics). Figure 4 shows a representative partitioning tree learned from the Yelp.com dataset.

Next we compare our approach to alternative regression and topic modeling approaches. In order to implement regression, we 1) Form a vector of unigram (and optionally bigram) occurrences normalized to length 1 (which we found to work better than unnormalized or frequency vectors), and 2) Form a vector corresponding to categorical membership with one element for each node in category tree $\mathcal{C}$. For each example, we set each element in the vector to value γ if the example belongs to the corresponding category, and 0 otherwise. The feature vector is the concatenation of these two vectors. We tested three regression approaches: ridge regression, lasso, and ϵ-support vector regression with a quadratic kernel (Chang and Lin, 2001). In each case, the cross validation dataset is used to tune the value of γ and the regularization parameter (for ridge regression and lasso) or ϵ and the cost parameter (for ϵSVR). We found that in all cases, lasso and ϵSVR were ouperformed by ridge regression, and so omit their results.

For the supervised latent Dirichlet allocation approach, as the space of labels is numeric and discrete, we can treat the task either as a regression problem (Blei and McAuliffe, 2007), or as a multiclass classification problem (Wang et al., 2009).

	Yelp.com Data					Amazon.com Data				
	Training Examples					Training Examples				
	500	1000	2000	4000	6000	500	1000	2000	4000	6000
TMSD, MCMC	**1.207**	**1.062**	**.983**	**.915**	**.870**	**1.243**	**1.161**	**1.090**	**1.019**	**.981**
TMSD, Simple	1.252	1.108	1.017	.951	.893	1.300	1.256	1.158	1.075	1.027
TMSD, Complex	1.284	1.123	—	—	—	1.281	1.198	—	—	—
RR, Uni	1.319	1.182	1.103	1.020	.949	1.337	1.265	1.145	1.081	1.033
RR, Uni/Bi	1.285	1.164	1.059	.971	.903	1.310	1.237	1.119	1.041	1.001
SLDA	1.664	1.649	1.606	1.556	1.479	1.621	1.632	1.607	1.581	1.555

Figure 5: Mean Squared Error for 1) the presented topic model for structured domains (TMSD) using MCMC Model Adaptation (MCMC), the simplest topic mapping function (Simple), or the most complex topic mapping function (Complex), 2) ridge regression (RR) with unigrams (Uni) or unigrams and bigrams (Uni/Bi), and 3) multiclass supervised latent Dirichlet allocation (SLDA). Results are averaged over 10 trials, each with 1000 test examples. The MCMC approach significantly outperforms all other approaches for each training set size (Yelp.com: $p < .01$, Amazon.com: $p < .05$).

We used an open source implementation of each approach, (Chang, 2010) and (Wang, 2009), and found that utilizing the multiclass approach and predicting the expected rating based on the posterior likelihood of each class outperformed the regression approach, so we present these results. The cross validation data is used to learn the number of latent topics and Dirichlet distribution parameter.

For the Markov chain Monte Carlo approach, in order to hasten learning for this comparison, starting from the simplest topic mapping function, we perform a greedy model adaptation until reaching an estimated local minimum, and then apply 50 additional iterations of MCMC model adaptation.

Figure 5 shows the average mean squared error for each approach for various amounts of training data. Our topic model with model adaptation has lower error than each of the alternatives. Paired t-tests reveal that the differences are statistically significant in all cases ($p < .01$ for all Yelp.com and $p < .05$ for all Amazon.com tests). Using MCMC model adaptation also outperforms using either the simplest topic mapping function or the most complex mapping function (which maps each distinct training categorization to a different subject topic).

Ridge regression with unigrams uses the same word and categorical representations as our approach. However, it is unable to entertain the non-linear relationships between document categorizations and words and is outperformed in all cases. Bigrams improve the performance of ridge regression, especially for larger amounts of training data. This suggests that accounting for word ordering could potentially improve the performance of our topic model as well. sLDA is unable to take advantage of the categorical information during topic construction, and with the limited training data available, its performance is marginally better than guessing the mean label (MSE: 1.675 for Yelp.com data and 1.660 for Amazon.com data).

5 Conclusion

We present an approach to sentiment analysis for structured domains. In our approach, positive, negative, and subject topics are learned and used to infer document labels. Partitioning tree based topic mapping functions define the number and structure of subject topics. A Markov chain Monte Carlo model adaptation procedure explores the space of topic mapping functions based on a minimum description length objective. We demonstrate the approach on two sentiment analysis domains and show that the model adaptation procedure efficiently finds a high performance model that leverages the categorical structure of the documents to outperform other regression and topic modeling approaches.

Acknowledgment

This material is based upon work supported by the Office of Naval Research under Award No. ONR Grant N00014-09-1-0693. Any opinions, findings, and conclusions or recommendations expressed in this publication are those of the authors and do not necessarily reflect the views of the Office of Naval Research.

References

H. Akaike. 1974. A new look at the statistical model identification. *IEEE Transactions on Automatic Control*, 19(6):716–723.

S. Baccianella, A. Esuli, and F. Sebastiani. 2009. Muli-facet rating of product reviews. In *The 31st European Conference on Information Retrieval Research*, pages 461–472.

D. Blei and J. McAuliffe. 2007. Supervised topic models. In *Neural Information Processing Systems*.

D. Blei, A. Ng, and M. Jordan. 2003. Latent dirichlet allocation. *Journal of Machine Learning Research*, 3:993–1022.

Chih-Chung Chang and Chih-Jen Lin, 2001. *LIBSVM: A Library for Support Vector Machines*. Software available at `http://www.csie.ntu.edu.tw/~cjlin/libsvm`.

J. Chang. 2010. Lda: Collapsed gibbs sampling methods for topic models. online.

W. Gilks, S. Richardson, and D. Spiegelhalter. 1996. *Markov Chain Monte Carlo in Practice*. Chapman and Hall.

P. Grunwald. 2007. *The Minimum Description Length Principle*. The MIT Press, Cambridge, Mass.

T. Hastie, R. Tibshirani, and J. Friedman. 2001. *The Elements of Statistical Learning*. Springer, New York, NY.

G. Levine, G. DeJong, L. Wang, R. Samdani, S. Vembu, and D. Roth. 2010. Automatic model adaptation for complex structured domains. In *The European Conference on Machine Learning and Principles and Practice of Knowledge Discovery in Databases*, pages 243–258.

B. Pang and L. Lee. 2005. Seeing stars: Exploiting class relationships for sentiment categorization with respect to rating scales. In *The 43rd Annual Meeting of the Association for Computational Linguistics: Human Language Technologies*, page 124.

B. Pang and L. Lee. 2008. Opinion mining and sentiment analysis. *Foundations and Trends in Information Retrieval*, 2(1–2):1–135.

L. Qu, G. Ifrim, and G. Weikum. 2010. The bag-of-opinions method for review rating prediction from sparse text patterms. In *The International Conference on Computational Linguistics*, pages 913–921.

D. Ramage, D. Hall, R. Nallapati, and C. Manning. 2011. Labeled lda: A supervised topic model for credit attribution in multi-labeled corpora. In *The Conference on Empirical Methods in Natural Language Processing*.

J. Rissanen. 1978. Modeling by shortest data description. *Automatica*, 14:445–471.

G. E. Schwarz. 1978. Estimating the dimension of a model. *Annals of Statistics*, 6(2):461–464.

S. Singh, A. Subramanya, F. Pereira, and A. McCallum. 2011. Large-scale cross-document coreference using distributed inference and hierarchical models. In *The 49th Annual Meeting of the Association for Computational Linguistics: Human Language Technologies*.

B. Snyder and R. Barzilay. 2007. Multiple aspect ranking using the good grief algorithm. In *The 8th Annual Conference of the North American Chapter of the Association for Computational Linguistics: Human Language Technologies*, pages 300–307.

I. Titov and A. Klementiev. 2011. A bayesian model for unsupervised semantic parsing. In *The 49th Annual Meeting of the Association for Computational Linguistics*.

I. Titov and R. McDonald. 2008a. A joint model of text and aspect ratings for sentiment summarization. In *The 46th Annual Meeting of the Association for Computational Linguistics: Human Language Technologies*, pages 308–316.

I. Titov and R. McDonald. 2008b. Modeling online reviews with multi-grain topic models. In *The Seventeenth International Conference on World Wide Web*, pages 111–120.

V. Vapnik. 1995. *The Nature of Statistical Learning Theory*. Springer-Verlag.

C. Wang, D. Blei, and L. Fei-Fei. 2009. Simultaneous image classification and annotation. In *IEEE Conference on Computer Vision and Pattern Recognition*.

C. Wang. 2009. Supervised latent dirichlet allocation for classification. online.

W. Zhao, J. Jiang, H. Yan, and X. Li. 2010. Jointly modeling aspects and opinions with a maxent-lda hybrid. In *The Conference on Empirical Methods in Natural Language Processing*, pages 56–65.

Multi-modal Reference Resolution in Situated Dialogue by Integrating Linguistic and Extra-Linguistic Clues

Ryu Iida, Masaaki Yasuhara, Takenobu Tokunaga
Department of Computer Science,
Tokyo Institute of Technology
W8-73, 2-12-1 Ohokayama Meguro Tokyo, 152-8552 Japan
{ryu-i,yasuhara,take}@cl.cs.titech.ac.jp

Abstract

This paper focuses on examining the effect of extra-linguistic information, such as eye gaze, integrated with linguistic information on multi-modal reference resolution. In our evaluation, we employ eye gaze information together with other linguistic factors in machine learning, while in prior work such as Kelleher (2006) and Prasov and Chai (2008) the incorporation of eye gaze and linguistic clues was heuristically realised. Conducting our empirical evaluation using a data set extended the REX-J corpus (Spanger et al., 2010) including eye gaze information, we examine which types of clues are useful on these three data sets, which consist largely of pronouns, non-pronouns and both respectively. Our results demonstrate that a dynamically moving visible indicator within the computer display (e.g. a mouse cursor) contributes to reference resolution for pronouns, while eye gaze information is more useful for the resolution of non-pronouns.

1 Introduction

The task of reference resolution has received much attention because it is important for applications that require interpreting text. In recent work on reference resolution within a text, several machine learning-based approaches have been proposed (McCarthy and Lehnert, 1995; Ge et al., 1998; Soon et al., 2001; Ng and Cardie, 2002; Iida et al., 2003; Yang et al., 2003; Denis and Baldridge, 2008), each of which mainly exploits linguistic clues motivated by the Centering Theory (Grosz et al., 1995) to model the discourse salience of all candidate antecedents. For instance, Yang et al. (2003) and Iida et al. (2003) presented machine learning-based reference resolution models where a pairwise comparison of candidate antecedents, in line with the basic idea of the Centering Theory, leads to the selection of the candidate with the highest salience for a given context. Denis and Baldridge (2008) extended the model by integrating the set of pairwise comparisons into ranking candidates to directly learn which clues of antecedents are useful.

Through the empirical evaluations using the data sets provided by the Message Understanding Conference (MUC)[1] and the Automatic Content Extraction (ACE)[2], which consist of newspaper articles and transcripts of broadcasts, linguistically motivated approaches have achieved better performance than state-of-the-art rule-based reference resolution systems (e.g. Soon et al. (2001) and Ng and Cardie (2002)).

In contrast to this research paradigm (i.e. research focusing on only the linguistic aspect of reference), research in the area of multi-modal interfaces has focused on referring expressions used in multi-modal conversations, in other words, identifying referents of referring expressions in a static scene or a situated world (e.g. objects depicted in a computer display), taking extra-linguistic clues into account (Byron, 2005; Prasov and Chai, 2008; Prasov and Chai, 2010; Schütte et al., 2010, etc.). For instance, Kelleher and van Genabith (2004) used the centrality and size of a object in the display to determine its visual salience. Prasov and Chai (2008) and Prasov and Chai (2010) exploited eye fixations to detect users' focus of attention in terms of visual prominence; their research has been motivated by work in the cognitive sciences (Tanenhaus et al., 1995; Tanenhaus et al., 2000; Hanna et al., 2003; Hanna and Tanenhaus, 2004; Hanna and Brennan, 2007; Metzing and Brennan, 2003; Ferreira and Tanenhaus, 2007; Brown-Schmidt et al., 2002).

[1] www-nlpir.nist.gov/related projects/muc/
[2] www.itl.nist.gov/iad/mig/tests/ace/

These previous studies have shown how promising using eye gaze information for multi-modal reference resolution can be. However, they rely on heuristic techniques for determining visual salience. Hence, there is still room for improvement by introducing eye gaze information in a more systematic and principled manner[3]. This paper, therefore, focuses on a multi-modal reference resolution model that integrates eye gaze and linguistic information by using a machine learning technique. Adapting a ranking-based anaphora resolution model, such as was proposed by Denis and Baldridge (2008), we integrate extra-linguistic information with other linguistic factors for more accurate reference resolution. With the above as a suitable background, this paper focuses on the issue of how to effectively combine linguistic and extra-linguistic factors for multi-modal reference resolution, taking collaborative task dialogues in Japanese as our target data set.

This paper is organised as follows. We first explain related work and our stance on multi-modal reference resolution in Section 2; we then present which multi-modal task we chose and how we merge eye gaze information into the predefined multi-modal task in Section 3. Section 4 introduces what types of information are used in the experiments shown in Section 5. We finally conclude this paper and discuss future directions in Section 6.

2 Related work

Within the field of computational linguistics, researchers have focused on developing computational models of reference resolution, taking into account various linguistic factors, such as grammatical, semantic and discourse clues mainly acquired from the relationship between an anaphor and any candidate antecedents (Mitkov, 2002; Lappin and Leass, 1994; Brennan et al., 1987; Strube and Hahn, 1996, etc.). Research trends for reference resolution have shifted from handcrafted rule-based approaches to corpus-based approaches due to the growing success of machine learning algorithms (e.g. Support Vector Machines (Vapnik, 1998)). For instance, an approach to coreference resolution proposed by Soon et al. (2001), in which the problem of reference resolution is decomposed into a set of binary classification problems of whether a pair of markables (e.g. NP) are anaphoric or not, achieved performance comparable to the state-of-the-art rule-based system, even though they used only a limited number of simple features. Researchers' concerns in this area cover a broad range of research topics from modeling the coreferential transitivity of a set of markables, to integrating discourse salience motivated by the Centering Theory (Grosz et al., 1995). This research area has continued to produce novel reference resolution models over the years, but the target of reference resolution is limited to only written texts or transcripts of speech.

In contrast to the above research area, researchers in the multi-modal community also have paid attention to reference resolution because it is also a crucial task for realising interaction between humans and computers. In this area, the evaluation is typically conducted in the situation where a set of objects (i.e. candidate referents) are depicted within a computer display. For instance, Stoia et al. (2008) designed an experiment where two participants controlled an avatar in a virtual world for exploring hidden treasures. In this case, the task of reference resolution is to identify an object shown on the computer display as referred to by a referring expression used by the participants during dialogue. The task becomes more complicated than typical coreference resolution for written texts because a referent is considered as either *anaphoric* (i.e. it has already appeared in the previous discourse history) or *exophoric*, (i.e. the reference resolution system needs to search for the referent from the set of objects shown in a computer display).

In order to capture the characteristics of exophoric cases, extra-linguistic information acquired from participants' eye gaze data and the visual prominence of each object are also exploited together with linguistic information. A series of research by Kelleher and his colleagues (Kelleher and van Genabith, 2004; Kelleher et al., 2005; Kelleher, 2006; Schütte et al., 2010) tackled the problem of modeling visual salience of objects in situated dialogue. In their algorithm, the visual salience of each object is estimated based on its centrality within the scene and its size; their hy-

[3]Frampton et al. (2009) employed the incorporation of linguistic and visual features on reference resolution of multi-party dialogues. However, their target was limited to only the expression *you* in dialogues, while our focus is to investigate the use of the expressions bridging between a dialogue and the real world (e.g. expressions referring to puzzle pieces on a computer display).

pothesis was that the salience is higher if a object is larger and is placed nearer the centre of the computer display. In Kelleher (2006)'s approach to reference resolution, linguistic clues such as ranking rules of candidate referents based on the Centering Theory (Grosz et al., 1995) were introduced in addition to using visual salience, but the integration of both clues was done in a heuristic way.

In addition to the visual salience assessed from the characteristics of objects in the world, eye gaze has received much attention as a clue for reference resolution. Prasov and Chai (2008), for example, employed eye gaze on the task of identifying a referent in the situation where objects are placed in a static scene. The time span after a speaker most recently fixates on an object is incorporated into their reference resolution model as well as the information of how recently the object was referred to by a referring expression. Although the results of their evaluation demonstrated that eye gaze significantly contributes to increasing performance, there is still room for improvement by adapting machine learning techniques, because in their work the linguistic and visual attention information was heuristically integrated.

In contrast, our previous work (Iida et al., 2010) employed a machine learning technique to identify the most likely candidate referent, taking into account linguistic features together with cues capturing visual salience found within the situated dialogues contained in the REX-J corpus (Spanger et al., 2010). We reported that extra-linguistic information contributes to improving performance (especially, in pronominal reference). However, in Iida et al. (2010) eye gaze information was not considered, even though in the area of cognitive science researchers have demonstrated that a speaker's eye fixations are strong clues for identifying a referent of a referring expression (Tanenhaus et al., 1995; Tanenhaus et al., 2000; Hanna et al., 2003; Hanna and Tanenhaus, 2004; Hanna and Brennan, 2007; Metzing and Brennan, 2003; Ferreira and Tanenhaus, 2007; Brown-Schmidt et al., 2002). Against this background, we investigate the effect of linguistic and extra-linguistic information including eye gaze on multi-modal reference resolution, extending Iida et al. (2010)'s reference resolution model.

3 Collecting eye gaze data in situated dialogues

In our evaluation of automatic reference resolution, we focus on investigating the interaction between linguistic and extra-linguistic clues including eye fixations on multi-modal reference resolution. Therefore, corpora where participants frequently utter both anaphoric and exophoric referring expressions are preferable for our evaluation.

In recent multi-modal problem settings for data collection, researchers have been concerned with more realistic situations, such as dynamically changing scenes rendered in a 3D virtual world (e.g. (Byron, 2005)). However, if we use data collected from such a scenario, referring expressions will be relatively skewed to exophoric cases because of frequently occurring scene updates. On the other hand, if we adopt the data collected using a static scene, we will have a disadvantage in that the change of visual salience of objects is not observed because the centrality and size of each object is fixed through dialogues.

For these reasons, we adopt the same task setting as introduced in the REX-J corpus (Spanger et al., 2010), which consists of collaborative work (solving Tangram puzzles) by two participants; the setting of this corpus is more suitable for our purposes because of the frequent occurrence of both anaphoric and exophoric referring expressions.

For collecting data, we recruited 18 Japanese graduate students, and split them into 9 pairs[4]. All pairs knew each other previously and were of the same gender and approximately the same age. Each pair was instructed to solve four different Tangram puzzles. The goal of the puzzle is to construct a given shape by arranging seven pieces (of different simple shapes) as shown in Figure 1. The precise positions of every piece and every action that the participants make are recorded by the Tangram simulator in which the pieces on the computer display can be moved, rotated and flipped with simple mouse operations. The piece position and the mouse actions were recorded at intervals of 1/65 msec. The simulator displays two areas: a goal shape area (the left side of Figure 1) and a working area (the right side of Figure 1) where pieces are shown and can be manipulated.

A different role was assigned to each participant

[4]Note that the first pair was used to adjust the settings of our data collection, so 4 dialogues collected from that pair were not included in the evaluation data set used in Section 5.

	time	OP-UT	SV-UT	OP-REX	SV-REX	ERR-OP	ERR-SV
total	4:22:20	2,382	4,613	239 / 270	434 / 1,192	–	–
average	9:43	88.2	170.9	8.85 / 10.0	16.1 / 44.1	14.0%	13.9%
SD	3:32	69.8	86.8	10.2 / 11.3	15.9 / 24.4	9.9	10.4

OP-UT (SV-UT) stands for the number of utterances of operators (solvers). The right side of OP-REX (SV-REX) is the frequency of referring expressions uttered by the operators (solvers), whereas the left side stands for the frequency of pronominal expressions uttered by the operators (solvers). ERR-OP (ERR-SV) is the error rate of measuring the operators' (solvers') eye gaze. SD means the standard derivation.

Table 1: Referring expressions in the extended REX-J corpus

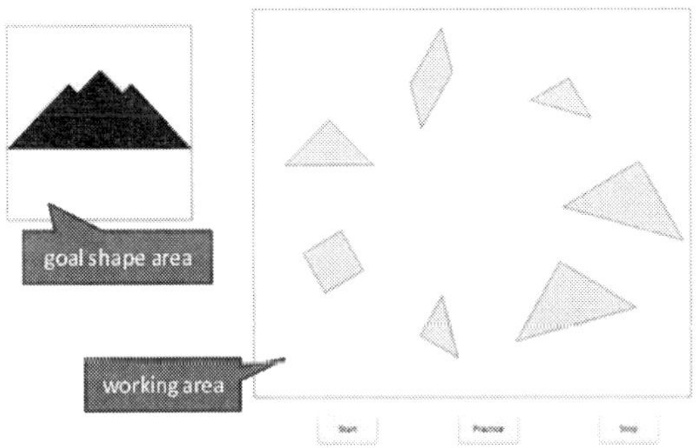

Figure 1: Screenshot of the Tangram simulator

of a pair: a *solver* and an *operator*. Given a certain goal shape, the solver thinks of the necessary arrangement of the pieces and gives instructions to the operator for how to move them. The operator manipulates the pieces with the mouse according to the solver's instructions. During this interaction, frequent uttering of referring expressions is needed to distinguish between the different puzzle pieces. This collaboration is achieved by placing a set of participants side by side, each with their own display showing the work area and the mouse cursor begin manipulated by the operator in real time, and a shield screen set between them to prevent the operator from seeing the goal shape, which is visible only on the solver's screen, and to further restrict their interaction to only speech. We put no constraint on the contents of their dialogues.

In addition to the attributes considered in the original REX-J corpus, we also collected eye gaze data synchronized with speech by using the Tobii T60 Eye Tracker, sampling at 60 Hz for recording users' eye gaze with 0.5 degrees in accuracy. Because the tracking results acquired from Tobii contain tracking errors, 5 dialogues in which the tracking results contain more than 40% errors were removed from the data set used in our evaluation.

Annotating referring expressions and their referents were conducted in the same manner as Spanger et al. (2010), i.e. annotation was conducted using a multimedia annotation tool, ELAN[5]; an annotator manually detects a referring expression and then selects its referent out of the possible puzzle pieces shown on the computer display. Note that only Tangram pieces were tagged as referents of referring expressions, therefore the expressions referring to abstract entities such as an action and event were not annotated. In the corpus multiple pieces were annotated as a single referent, but such referents were excluded in our evaluation because of their infrequent occurrence. Table 1 summarises the statistics of our new version of the REX-J corpus, consisting of 27 dialogues.

4 Multi-modal reference resolution

4.1 Base models

To investigate the impact of extra-linguistic information on reference resolution, we conducted an empirical evaluation in which a reference resolution model chooses a referent (i.e. a piece) for a given referring expression from the set of pieces on the computer display.

As a basis of our reference resolution model, we adopt an existing model for reference resolution. Recently, machine learning-based approaches to reference resolution (Soon et al., 2001; Ng and Cardie, 2002, etc.) focus on identifying anaphoric relations in texts, and have achieved better performance than hand-crafted rule-based approaches. These models for reference resolution take into account linguistic factors, such as relative salience of candidate antecedents, which have been discussed mainly in Centering Theory (Grosz et al., 1995) by ranking candidate antecedents appearing in the preceding discourse (Iida et al., 2003; Yang et al., 2003; Denis and Baldridge, 2008). In order to take advantage of existing models, we adopt the ranking-based approach as a basis for our reference resolution model. More precisely, we em-

[5]www.lat-mpi.eu/tools/elan/

eye gaze features		
GZ1:	[0,1]	the frequency of fixating P in the time period $[t - T, t]$, normalised by the frequency of the total fixations during the period.
GZ2:	[0,1]	the length of a fixation on P in the time period $[t - T, t]$, nomalised by T.
GZ3:	[0,1]	the length of a fixation on P in the time period $[t - T, t]$, nomalised by the total length of fixation.
GZ4:	[0,1]	the frequency of fixating P in the time period uttering a referring expression, normalised by the frequency of the total fixations during the period.
GZ5:	[0,1]	the length of a fixation on P in the time period uttering a referring expression, nominalised by T.
GZ6:	[0,1]	the length of a fixation on P in the time period uttering a referring expression, nominalised by the total length of fixation.
GZ7:	yes,no	whether the frequency of fixating P in the time period $[t - T, t]$ is most frequent.
GZ8:	yes,no	whether the frequency of fixating P in the time period $[t - T, t]$ is more than 1.
GZ9:	yes,no	whether the fixation time of P in the time period $[t - T, t]$ is longest out of all pieces.
GZ10:	yes,no	whether there exists the fixation time of P in the time period $[t - T, t]$.
GZ11:	yes,no	whether the frequency of fixating P in the time period uttering a referring expression is most frequent.
GZ12:	yes,no	whether the frequency of fixating P in the time period uttering a referring expression is more than 1.
GZ13:	yes,no	whether the fixation time of P in the time period uttering a referring expression is longest out of all pieces.
GZ14:	yes,no	whether there exists the fixation time of P in the time period uttering a referring expression.

t is the onset time of a referring expression. P denotes a piece, T is a fixed time window (1500ms).

Table 2: Eye gaze features

ploy Denis and Baldridge (2008)'s ranking-based model because they demonstrated their model outperformed the model based on simple pairwise ranking (e.g. Yang et al. (2003)).

In Denis and Baldridge (2008)'s ranking-based model, the most likely candidate antecedent is decided by simultaneously ranking all candidate antecedents. To induce a ranker used in the ranking process, we adopt the Ranking SVM algorithm (Joachims, 2002)[6], which learns a weight vector to rank candidates for a given partial ranking of each referent, while the original work by Denis and Baldridge (2008) uses Maximum Entropy to create their ranking-based model. Each training instance is created from the set of all referents for each referring expression. To define the partial ranking of referents, we simply rank referents of a given referring expression as first place and any other referents as second place.

4.2 Eye gaze features

As we mentioned in Section 2, a speaker's eye gaze contributes to disambiguating referents appearing in the speaker's utterances because the speaker tends to see the target object before it is referred to by a referring expression (Spivey et al., 2002). Several aspects must be considered in order to integrate a speaker's eye gaze data. First, because the eye gaze data includes saccades, the inhibition factor of perceptual sensitivity, we extract only eye fixations as discussed in Richardson et al. (2007). For separating saccades and eye fixations, we employ Dispersion-threshold identification (Salvucci and Anderson, 2001), detecting fixations by using the concentration of eye gaze based on the fact the fixations are relatively slower than saccades. Second, because of the errors in measuring eye gaze by the eye tracker, the fixation data needs to be interpolated by the surrounding data. More specifically, if the error interval is less than 100 msec and the difference of the centers of two fixations is smaller then 16 pixels, these fixations are concatenated according to the work by Richardson et al. (2007).

The clues exploited in this paper are based on the fact that the direction of eye gaze directly reflects the focus of attention (Richardson et al., 2007; Just and Carpenter, 1976) , i.e. when one utters a referring expression, he potentially focuses on the object involved by fixating his eyes on it. Therefore, we use the eye fixations as clues for identifying the pieces focused on using the following criteria: the nearest piece to the eye fixation point is more likely a target of focus over all other pieces. To reflect this, we introduce the feature set shown in Table 2. We henceforth call these features the *eye gaze features*. Note that the parameter T is set to 1,500 ms based on the previous work done by Prasov and Chai (2010).

5 Empirical Evaluation

In order to investigate the effect of extra-linguistic information with or without linguistic factors, we conducted empirical evaluations using the updated version of the REX-J corpus explained in

[6]www.cs.cornell.edu/People/tj/svm_light/svm_rank.html

(a) **Linguistic features**		
L1 :	yes, no	whether P is referred to by the most recent referring expression.
L2 :	yes, no	whether the time distance to the last mention of P is less than or equal to 10 sec.
L3 :	yes, no	whether the time distance to the last mention of P is more than 10 sec and less than or equal to 20 sec.
L4 :	yes, no	whether the time distance to the last mention of P is more than 20 sec.
L5 :	yes, no	whether P has never been referred to by any mentions in the preceding utterances.
L6 :	yes, no, N/A	whether the attributes of P are compatible with the attributes of R.
L7 :	yes, no	whether R is followed by the case marker '*o* (accusative)'.
L8 :	yes, no	whether R is followed by the case marker '*ni* (dative)'.
L9 :	yes, no	whether R is a pronoun and the most recent reference to P is not a pronoun.
L10 :	yes, no	whether R is not a pronoun and was most recently referred to by a pronoun.
(b) **Task specific features**		
T1 :	yes, no	whether the mouse cursor was over P at the beginning of uttering R.
T2 :	yes, no	whether P is the last piece that the mouse cursor was over when feature T1 is 'no'.
T3 :	yes, no	whether the time distance is less than or equal to 10 sec after the mouse cursor was over P.
T4 :	yes, no	whether the time distance is more than 10 sec and less than or equal to 20 sec after the mouse cursor was over P.
T5 :	yes, no	whether the time distance is more than 20 sec after the mouse cursor was over P.
T6 :	yes, no	whether the mouse cursor was never over P in the preceding utterances.
T7 :	yes, no	whether P is being manipulated at the beginning of uttering R.
T8 :	yes, no	whether P is the most recently manipulated piece when feature T7 is 'no'.
T9 :	yes, no	whether the time distance is less than or equal to 10 sec after P was most recently manipulated.
T10 .	yes, no	whether the time distance is more than 10 sec and less than or equal to 20 sec after P was most recently manipulated
T11 :	yes, no	whether the time distance is more than 20 sec after P was most recently manipulated.
T12 :	yes, no	whether P has never been manipulated.

P stands for a piece of the Tangram puzzle (i.e. a candidate referent of a referring expression) and R stands for the target referring expression.

Table 3: Feature set

Section 3.

5.1 Experimental settings

We employed two models as baselines: a model using only discourse history features, and one using only eye gaze features.

Because the task setting is the same as the evaluation conducted in Iida et al. (2010), we employ the same feature set, consisting of linguistically motivated features, and also features which capture the task specific extra-linguistic information of each object. We call these two kinds of features the *linguistic features* and *task specific features*, respectively. The details of these features are summarised in Table 3.

As reported in Iida et al. (2010), the referential behaviour of pronouns is completely different from non-pronouns. For this reason, we separately create two reference resolution models; one called the *pronoun model*, which identifies a referent of a given pronoun, and another called the *non-pronoun model*, which is for all other expressions. During the training phase, we use only training instances whose referring expressions are pronouns for creating the pronoun model, and all other training instances for the non-pronoun model. We group these two models together, selecting which one to use based on the referring expression. In other words, the pronoun model is selected if a referring expression is a pronoun, and the non-pronoun model otherwise. We will hereafter refer to the selectional model which alternatively picks between the pronoun and non-pronoun models as the *separated model*.

We also train a third model using all training instances without distinguishing between pronouns and non-pronouns. This model we will refer to as the *combined model*.

model	pronoun	non-pronoun
Ling	56.0	65.4
Gaze	56.7	48.0
TaskSp	**79.2**	21.1
Ling+Gaze	66.5	75.7
Ling+TaskSp	79.0	67.1
TaskSp+Gaze	78.0	48.4
Ling+TaskSp+Gaze	78.7	**76.0**

Ling, TaskSp and Gaze stand for the models using the linguistic, task specific and eye gaze features respectively.

Table 4: results in the separated model (accuracy)

5.2 Results

Table 4 shows the accuracy results of our empirical evaluation separately evaluating pronouns and non-pronouns. In reference resolution of pronouns

model	combined	separated
Ling	62.7	61.8
Gaze	51.1	51.2
TaskSp	43.7	42.8
Ling+Gaze	69.9	72.3
Ling+TaskSp	69.9	71.5
TaskSp+Gaze	55.2	59.5
Ling+TaskSp+Gaze	**72.5**	**77.0**

Table 5: Overall results (accuracy)

	pronoun model		non-pronoun model	
rank	feature	weight	feature	weight
1	T1	0.4744	L6	0.6149
2	T3	0.2684	GZ10	0.1566
3	L1	0.2298	GZ9	0.1566
4	T7	0.1929	GZ7	0.1255
5	T9	0.1605	GZ11	0.1225
6	GZ10	0.1547	GZ14	0.1134
7	GZ9	0.1547	GZ13	0.1134
8	L6	0.1442	GZ12	0.1026
9	GZ7	0.1267	L2	0.1014
10	L2	0.1164	GZ1	0.0750

Table 6: 10 highest weights of the features in each model

the results show that the model using only the linguistic features (Ling) achieved performance comparable to the one using only the eye gaze features (Gaze). Moreover, the model using only the task specific features (TaskSp) obtained performance significantly better than the others. This is because a mouse cursor is the only shared visual stimulus between the operator and solver. Therefore, it becomes the most important clue for pronouns, while the eye fixations of a speaker are not necessarily shared between them.

In contrast to pronouns, the non-pronoun model using only the linguistic features (Ling) outperforms the one using either eye gaze features or the task specific features (Gaze and TaskSp). This may be because one linguistic feature (L6) works more effectively than the other features. As shown later (see Table 6), in non-pronoun cases, the feature L6, which is the binary value indicating the compatibility of the attributes between two referring expressions, has the highest feature weight, leading to the best performance out of all three models (Ling, Gaze and TaskSp).

In addition, combining the linguistic and eye gaze features (Ling+Gaze) on non-pronoun reference resolution contributes to increasing performance. This means that these two features work in a complementary manner when a referring expression cannot be judged on a superficial level whether it refers to a discourse referent or a visually focused referent. From these results, we can see that the clues from utterances of participants are also essential for precise reference resolution, while the previous work focusing on eye fixations tends to concentrate on modeling only eye gaze information.

The accuracy results in Table 5 show the performance of the combined and separated models for different settings of feature selection. Table 5 shows that the two models achieved almost the same performance when the linguistic, eye gaze and task specific features are individually used. However, it also shows that the separated model outperforms the combined model when more than two feature types are utilised. This indicates that separating the models with regard to the type of referring expression does make sense even when we employ eye fixations as a clue for recognising referent objects. It also shows that both the combined and separated models obtained the best performance for each model using all the features. In other words, the three types of features work in a complementary manner on multi-modal reference resolution.

We next investigated the significance of each feature for the pronoun and non-pronoun models. We calculate the weight of a feature f shown in Table 6 according to the following formula.

$$\text{weight}(f) = \sum_{x \in SVs} w_x z_x(f) \qquad (1)$$

where *SVs* is a set of the support vectors in a ranker induced by the Ranking SVM algorithm, w_x is the weight of the support vector x, $z_x(f)$ is the function that returns 1 if f occurs in x, respectively.

Table 6 shows the top 10 features with the highest weights of each model. It demonstrates that in the pronoun model the task specific features have the highest weight, while in the non-pronoun model these features are less significant. As shown in Table 4, pronouns are strongly related to the situation where the mouse cursor is over a piece, which is consistent with the results reported in Iida et al. (2010).

In contrast, the highest features in the non-pronoun model are occupied by the eye gaze features, except for L6. This indicates that in the situation where a speaker mentions pieces realised as non-pronouns, the eye fixations become a good clue for identifying the current focus of the speaker, while the task specific features such as the location of the mouse cursor are less significant. In addition, Table 6 also shows that the discourse feature L6 obtains the highest significance. This means that exploiting the linguistic factors together with eye fixations is essential for more accurate reference resolution.

6 Conclusion

In this paper we focused on investigating the impact of eye fixations on reference resolution compared to using other extra-linguistic information. We conducted an empirical evaluation using referring expressions appearing in collaborative work dialogues from the extended REX-J corpus, synchronised with eye gaze information. We demonstrated that the referents of pronouns are relatively easily identified, as they rely on the visual salience such as is indicated by moving the mouse cursor, and that non-pronouns are strongly related to eye fixations on its referent. In addition, our results also show that combining linguistic, eye gaze and other extra-linguistic factors contribute to increasing the overall performance of identifying all referring expressions.

There are several future directions for making the multi-modal reference resolution more accurate and robust. First, we need to introduce more task dependent information reflecting the characteristics of each multi-modal task. In the Tangram puzzle task, for example, once a piece becomes part of a partially constructed shape, the piece tends to be less salient because a solver typically gives an instruction to move a scattered piece to a partially constructed shape. We expect that introducing such task specific clues into the reference resolution model as features will contribute to improving performance.

Second, in our evaluation we adopted collaborative work dialogues where two participants solve Tangram puzzles. Since all objects (i.e. puzzle pieces) have nearly the same size, this results in explicitly rejecting the factor that a relatively larger object occupying the computer display has higher prominence over smaller objects, which has been considered by Byron (2005). In order to take such a factor into account, we need further data collection and then to incorporate additional factors into the current reference resolution model.

A third possible direction for future work is to examine the relation between linguistic and intentional structures, which are discussed in Grosz and Sidner (1986). In our problem setting, when a solver instructs an operator how to construct a goal shape, a series of utterances by the solver reflects the solver's intentions. As we already mentioned above, objects which a solver wants an operator to manipulate tend to draw a solver's attention, while the other objects (especially, the objects representing the partially constructed shape) are considered less salient. Exploiting the importance of the speaker's intentions also needs to be considered in future work.

References

S. E. Brennan, M. W. Friedman, and C. Pollard. 1987. A centering approach to pronouns. In *Proceedings of the 25th Annual Meeting of the Association for Computational Linguistics (ACL)*, pages 155 162.

S. Brown-Schmidt, E. Campana, and M. K. Tanenhaus. 2002. Reference resolution in the wild: On-line circumscription of referential domains in a natural, interactive, problem-solving task. In *Proceedings of the 24th annual meeting of the Cognitive Science Society*, pages 148–153.

D. K. Byron. 2005. Utilizing visual attention for crossmodal coreference interpretation. In *In Proceedings of Fifth International and Interdisciplinary Conference on Modeling and Using Context*, pages 83–96.

P. Denis and J. Baldridge. 2008. Specialized models and ranking for coreference resolution. In *Proceedings of the 2008 Conference on Empirical Methods in Natural Language Processing*, pages 660–669.

F. Ferreira and M. K. Tanenhaus. 2007. Introduction to the special issue on language–vision interactions. *Journal of Memory and Language*, 57:455–459.

M. Frampton, R. Fernández, P. Ehlen, M. Christoudias, T. Darrell, and S. Peters. 2009. Who is "you"? combining linguistic and gaze features to resolve second-person references in dialogue. In *Proceedings of the 12th Conference of the European Chapter of the ACL (EACL 2009)*, pages 273–281.

N. Ge, J. Hale, and E. Charniak. 1998. A statistical approach to anaphora resolution. In *Proceedings of the 6th Workshop on Very Large Corpora*, pages 161–170.

Barbara J. Grosz and Candace L. Sidner. 1986. Attention, intentions, and the structure of discourse. *Computational Linguistics*, 12(3):175–204.

B. J. Grosz, A. K. Joshi, and S. Weinstein. 1995. Centering: A framework for modeling the local coherence of discourse. *Computational Linguistics*, 21(2):203–226.

J. E. Hanna and S. E. Brennan. 2007. Speakers' eye gaze disambiguates referring expressions early during face-to-face conversation. *Journal of Memory and Language*, 57.

J. E. Hanna and M. K. Tanenhaus. 2004. Pragmatic effects on reference resolution in a collaborative task: evidence from eye movements. *Cognitive Science*, 28:105–115.

J. E. Hanna, M. K. Tanenhaus, and J. C. Trueswell. 2003. The effects of common ground and perspective on domains of referential interpretation. *Journal of Memory and Language*, 49(1):43–61.

R. Iida, K. Inui, H. Takamura, and Y. Matsumoto. 2003. Incorporating contextual cues in trainable models for coreference resolution. In *Proceedings of the 10th EACL Workshop on The Computational Treatment of Anaphora*, pages 23–30.

R. Iida, S. Kobayashi, and T. Tokunaga. 2010. Incorporating extra-linguistic information into reference resolution in collaborative task dialogue. In *Proceeding of the 48st Annual Meeting of the Association for Computational Linguistics (ACL)*, pages 1259–1267.

T. Joachims. 2002. Optimizing search engines using clickthrough data. In *Proceedings of the ACM Conference on Knowledge Discovery and Data Mining (KDD)*, pages 133–142.

M. Just and P. A. Carpenter. 1976. Eye fixations and cognitive processes. *Cognitive Psychology*, 8:441–480.

J. Kelleher and J. van Genabith. 2004. Visual salience and reference resolution in simulated 3-d environments. *Artificial Intelligence Review*, 21(3):253–267.

J. Kelleher, F. Costello, and J. van Genabith. 2005. Dynamically structuring updating and interrelating representations of visual and linguistic discourse. *Artificial Intelligence*, 167:62–102.

J. D. Kelleher. 2006. Attention driven reference resolution in multimodal contexts. *Artificial Intelligence Review*, 25:21–35.

S. Lappin and H. J. Leass. 1994. An algorithm for pronominal anaphora resolution. *Computational Linguistics*, 20(4):535–561.

J. F. McCarthy and W. G. Lehnert. 1995. Using decision trees for coreference resolution. In *Proceedings of the 14th International Joint Conference on Artificial Intelligence*, pages 1050–1055.

C. Metzing and S. E. Brennan. 2003. When conceptual pacts are broken: Partner-specific effects on the comprehension of referring expressions. *Journal of Memory and Language*, 49:201–213.

R. Mitkov. 2002. *Anaphora Resolution*. Studies in Language and Linguistics. Pearson Education.

V. Ng and C. Cardie. 2002. Improving machine learning approaches to coreference resolution. In *Proceedings of the 40th Annual Meeting of the Association for Computational Linguistics (ACL)*, pages 104–111.

Z. Prasov and J. Y. Chai. 2008. What's in a gaze? the role off eye-gaze in reference resolution in multimodal conversational interface. In *In Proceedings of the 13th international conference on Intelligent user interfaces*, pages 20–29.

Z. Prasov and J. Y. Chai. 2010. Fusing eye gaze with speech recognition hypotheses to resolve exophoric references in situated dialogue. In *Proceedings of the 2010 Conference on Empirical Methods in Natural Language Processing*, pages 471–481.

D. C. Richardson, R. Dale, and M. J. Spivey. 2007. Eye movements in language and cognition: A brief introduction, methods in cognitive linguistics. In M. Gonzalez-Marquez, I. Mittelberg, S. Coulson, and M. J. Spivey, editors, *Methods in Cognitive Linguistics*, pages 323–344. John Benjamins.

D. D. Salvucci and J. R. Anderson. 2001. Automated eye-movement protocol analysis. *Human-Computer Interaction*, 16:39–86.

N. Schütte, J. D. Kelleher, and B. Mac Namee. 2010. Visual salience and reference resolution in situated dialogues: A corpus-based evaluation. In *In Proceedings of the AAAI Symposium on Dialog with Robots, Arlington, Virginia, USA. 11th - 13th Nov 2010.*

W. M. Soon, H. T. Ng, and D. C. Y. Lim. 2001. A machine learning approach to coreference resolution of noun phrases. *Computational Linguistics*, 27(4):521–544.

P. Spanger, M. Yasuhara, R. Iida, T. Tokunaga, A. Terai, and N. Kuriyama. 2010. REX-J: Japanese referring expression corpus of situated dialogs. *Language Resources & Evaluation*.

M. J. Spivey, M. K. Tanenhaus, K. M. Eberhard, and J. C. Sedivy. 2002. Eye movements and spoken language comprehension: Effects of visual context on syntactic ambiguity resolution. *Cognitive Psychology*, 45(4):447–481.

L. Stoia, D. M. Shockley, D. K. Byron, and E. Fosler-Lussier. 2008. Scare: A situated corpus with annotated referring expressions. In *Proceedings of the Sixth International Conference on Language Resources and Evaluation (LREC 2008)*.

M. Strube and U. Hahn. 1996. Functional centering. In *Proceeding of the 34st Annual Meeting of the Association for Computational Linguistics (ACL)*, pages 270–277.

M. K. Tanenhaus, M. J. Spivey-Knowlton, K. M. Eberhard, and J. C. Sedivy. 1995. Integration of visual and linguistic information in spoken language comprehension. *Science*, 268(5217):1632–1634.

M. K. Tanenhaus, J. S. Magnuson, D. Dahan, and C. Chambers. 2000. Eye movements and lexical access in spoken-language comprehension: Evaluating a linking hypothesis between fixations and linguistic processing. *Journal of Psycholinguistic Research*, 29(6):557–580.

V. N. Vapnik. 1998. *Statistical Learning Theory*. Adaptive and Learning Systems for Signal Processing Communications, and control. John Wiley & Sons.

X. Yang, G. Zhou, J. Su, and C. L. Tan. 2003. Coreference resolution using competition learning approach. In *Proceedings of the 41st Annual Meeting of the Association for Computational Linguistics (ACL)*, pages 176–183.

Single and Multi-objective Optimization for Feature Selection in Anaphora Resolution

Sriparna Saha [1] **Asif Ekbal** [1] **Olga Uryupina** [2] **Massimo Poesio** [3,2]
[1] Department of Computer Science and Engineering, IIT Patna, India,
{sriparna,asif}@iitp.ac.in
[2] University of Trento, Center for Mind/Brain Sciences, uryupina@unitn.it
[3] University of Essex, Language and Computation Group, poesio@essex.ac.uk

Abstract

There is no generally accepted metric for measuring the performance of anaphora resolution systems, and the existing metrics—MUC, B^3, CEAF, Blanc, among others—tend to reward significantly different behaviors. Systems optimized according to one metric tend to perform poorly with respect to other ones, making it very difficult to compare anaphora resolution systems, as clearly shown by the results of the SEMEVAL 2010 Multilingual Coreference task. One solution would be to find a single completely satisfactory metric, but it's not clear whether this is possible and at any rate it is not going to happen any time soon. An alternative is to optimize models according to multiple metrics simultaneously. In this paper, we show, first of all, that this is possible to develop such models using Multi-objective Optimization (MOO) techniques based on Genetic Algorithms. Secondly, we show that optimizing according to multiple metrics simultaneously may result in better results with respect to each individual metric than optimizing according to that metric only.

1 Introduction

In anaphora resolution,[1] as in other HLT tasks, optimization to a metric is essential to achieve good performance (Hoste, 2005; Uryupina, 2010). However, many evaluation metrics have been proposed for anaphora resolution, each capturing what seems to be a key intuition about the task: from MUC (Vilain et al., 1995) to B^3 (Bagga and Baldwin, 1998), from the ACE metric (Doddington et al., 2004) to CEAF (Luo, 2005) to BLANC (Recasens and Hovy, 2011). And unlike in other areas of HLT, none has really taken over. This would not matter so much if those metrics were to reward the same systems; but in fact, as dramatically demonstrated by the results of the Coreference Task at SEMEVAL 2010 (Recasens et al., 2010), the opposite is true—almost every system could come on top depending on which metric was chosen.

It seems unlikely that the field will converge on a single metric any time soon. Given that many of the proposed metrics do capture what would seem to be plausible intuitions, it would seem desirable to develop methods to optimize systems according to more than one metric at once—in particular, according to at least one metric of what we might call the 'link-based' cluster of metrics (e.g., MUC) and at least one of what we will call the 'entity-based' cluster (e.g., CEAF).

As it happens, techniques for doing just that have been developed in the area of Genetic Algorithms: so-called **multi-objective optimization** (MOO) (Deb, 2001) techniques. In this paper, we will show how these techniques can be used to optimize anaphora resolution models (we focused for the time being on feature selection) by looking for a solution in the space defined by a multiplicity of metrics (we used MUC and CEAF (in two variants) as the optimization functions). Perhaps the most interesting result of this work is the finding that by working in such a multi-metric space it is possible to find solutions that are better with respect to an individual metric than when trying to optimize for that metric alone—which arguably suggests that indeed both families of metrics capture some fundamental intuition about anaphora, and taking into account both intuitions we avoid local optima.

The structure of the paper is as follows. We first review the literature on using genetic algorithms for both single function and multi function opti-

[1] We use the term 'anaphora resolution' to refer to the task perhaps most commonly referred to as 'coreference resolution,' which many including us find a misnomer. For the purposes of the present paper the two terms could be seen as interchangeable.

mization. Next, we discuss the particular method of multi-objective optimization we used in this paper, Non-Dominated Sorting Genetic Algorithm II (Deb et al., 2002). After that we discuss how the method was used, and present our results. We then compare our work with other approaches to optimization for anaphora found in the literature.

2 Background: Optimizing for Anaphora Resolution

A great number of statistical approaches to anaphora resolution have been proposed in the past ten years. These approaches differ with respect to their underlying models (e.g., mention pair model (Soon et al., 2001) vs. tournament model (Iida et al., 2003; Yang et al., 2005), vs. entity-model (Luo et al., 2004)), machine learners (e.g., decision trees vs. maximum entropy vs. SVMs vs. TiMBL) and their parameters, and with respect to feature sets used. There have been, however, only few attempts at explicit optimization of these aspects, and in those few cases, optimization tends to be done by hand.

An early step in this direction was the work by Ng and Cardie (2002), who developed a rich feature set including 53 features, but reported no significant improvement over their baseline when all these features were used with the MUC6 and MUC7 corpora. They then proceeded to manually select a subset of features that did yield better results for the MUC-6/7 datasets. A much larger scale and very systematic effort of manual feature selection over the same dataset was carried out by Uryupina (2007), who evaluated over 600 features.

The first systematic attempt at automatic optimization of anaphora resolution we are aware of was carried out by Hoste (2005), who investigated the possibility of using genetic algorithms for automatic optimization of both feature selection and of learning parameters, also considering two different machine learners, TiMBL and Ripper. Her results suggest that such techniques yield improvements on the MUC-6/7 datasets. Recasens and Hovy (2009) carried out an investigation of feature selection for Spanish using the ANCORA corpus.

These approaches focused on a single metric only; the one proposal simultaneously to consider multiple metrics, Zhao and Ng (2010) still optimized for each metric individually.

The effect of optimization on anaphora resolution was dramatically demonstrated by Uryupina's contribution to SEMEVAL 2010 Multilingual Coreference Task (Uryupina, 2010). Uryupina directly optimizes two parameters of her system: the choice of a model (mention-pair vs. ILP with various constraints) and the definition of mention types for training separate classifiers. The optimization is done on the development data in a brute-force fashion, in order to maximize the performance according to a pre-defined metric (MUC, CEAF or BLANC). The results on the SEMEVAL-10 dataset clearly show that existing metrics of coreference rely on different intuitions and therefore a system, optimized for a particular metric, might show inferior results for the other ones. For example, the reported BLANC difference between the runs optimized for BLANC and CEAF is around 10 percentage points.

This highlights the importance of the multi-objective optimization (MOO) for coreference, that suggests a family of systems, showing reliable performance according to all the desired metrics. A form of MOO was applied to coreference by Munson et al. (2005). Their general conclusion was negative, stating that "ensemble selection seems too unreliable for use in NLP", but they did see some improvements for coreference.

3 Optimization with Genetic Algorithms

In this section, we review optimization techniques using genetic algorithms (GAs) (Goldberg, 1989). We first discuss single objective optimization, that can optimize according to a single objective function, and then multi-objective optimization (MOO), that can optimize more than one objective function, in particular, a popular MOO technique named Non-dominated Sorting Genetic Algorithm (NSGA)-II (Deb et al., 2002).

3.1 Genetic Algorithms

Genetic algorithms (GAs) (Goldberg, 1989) are randomized search and optimization techniques guided by the principles of evolution and natural genetics. In GAs the parameters of the search space are encoded in the form of strings (called *chromosomes*). A collection of such strings is called a *population*. Initially, a random population is created, which represents different points in the search space. An *objective* or *fitness* function is associated with each string that represents the degree of *goodness* of the string. Based on the principle of survival of the fittest, a few of the strings are selected and each is assigned a number of copies that go into the mating pool. Biologically inspired operators like *crossover* and *mutation* are applied on these strings to yield a new generation of strings. The processes of selection, crossover and mutation continues for a fixed number of generations or till a termination condition is satisfied.

3.2 Multi-objective Optimization

Multi-objective optimization (MOO) can be formally stated as follows (Deb, 2001). Find the vectors $\overline{x}^* = [x_1^*, x_2^*, \ldots, x_n^*]^T$ of decision variables that simultaneously optimize the M objective values

$$\{f_1(\overline{x}), f_2(\overline{x}), \ldots, f_M(\overline{x})\}$$

while satisfying the constraints, if any.

An important concept in MOO is that of **domination**. In the context of a maximization problem, a solution $\overline{x_i}$ is said to dominate $\overline{x_j}$ if $\forall k \in 1, 2, \ldots, M$, $f_k(\overline{x_i}) \geq f_k(\overline{x_j})$ and $\exists k \in 1, 2, \ldots, M$, such that $f_k(\overline{x_i}) > f_k(\overline{x_j})$.

Among a set of solutions P, the nondominated set of solutions P' are those that are not dominated by any member of the set P. The nondominated set of the entire search space S is called the **globally Pareto-optimal set**. In general, a MOO algorithm usually admits a set of solutions not dominated by any solution encountered by it.

3.3 Nondominated Sorting Genetic Algorithm-II (NSGA-II)

Genetic algorithms (GAs) are known to be more effective than classical methods such as weighted metrics, goal programming (Deb, 2001), for solving MOO primarily because of their population-based nature. A particularly popular GA of this type is NSGA-II (Deb et al., 2002).

In NSGA-II, initially a random parent population P_0 is created and the population is sorted based on the *partial order* defined by the non-domination relation. This results in a sequence of nondominated **fronts**. Each solution is assigned a fitness value which is equal to its non-domination level in the partial order. A child population Q_0 of size N is then created from the parent population P_0 by using binary tournament selection, recombination, and mutation operators. In general, in the tth iteration, a combined population $R_t = P_t + Q_t$ is formed. The size of R_t is $2N$, as the size of both P_t and Q_t is N. All the solutions of R_t are sorted according to non-domination. If the total number of solutions belonging to the best nondominated set F_1 is smaller than N, then F_1 is totally included in $P_{(t+1)}$. The remaining members of the population $P_{(t+1)}$ are chosen from the subsequent nondominated fronts in the order of their ranking. To choose exactly N solutions, the solutions of the last included front are sorted using the crowded comparison operator (Deb et al., 2002) and the best among them (i.e., those with lower crowding distance) are selected to fill in the available slots in $P_{(t+1)}$. The new population $P_{(t+1)}$ is then used for selection, crossover and mutation to create a population $Q_{(t+1)}$ of size N.

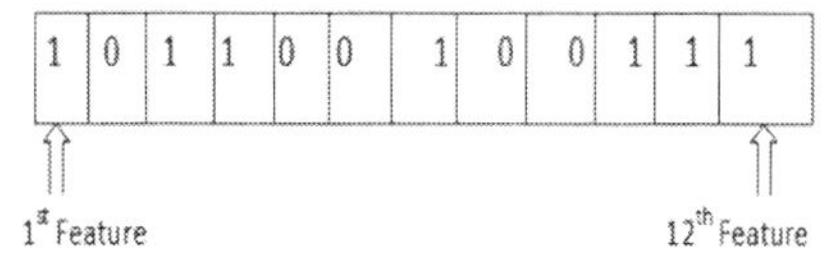

Figure 1: Chromosome representation for GA based feature selection

4 Two Algorithms for Feature Selection in Anaphora Resolution

Below we discuss how single and multi-objective optimization techniques can be used feature selection in the anaphora resolution task.

4.1 Chromosome Representation and Population Initialization

If the total number of features is F, then the length of the chromosome is F. As an example, the encoding of a particular chromosome is represented in Figure 1. Here $F = 12$ (i.e., total 12 different features are available). The chromosome represents the use of 7 features for constructing a classifier (first, third, fourth, seventh, tenth, eleventh and twelfth features). The entries of each chromosome are randomly initialized to either 0 or 1. Here, if the ith position of a chromosome is 0 then it represents that i^{th} feature does not participate in constructing the classifier. Else if it is 1 then the ith feature participates in constructing the classifier.

4.2 Fitness Computation

For fitness computation, the following procedure is executed:

1. Suppose there are N number of features present in a particular chromosome (i.e., there are total N number of 1's in that chromosome).

2. Construct the coreference resolution system (i.e., BART) with only these N features.

3. This coreference system is evaluated on the development data. The recall, precision and F-measure values of three metrics are calculated.

In case of single objective optimization (SOO), the objective function corresponding to a particular chromosome is the F-measure value of a single metric. This objective function is optimized using the search capability of GA. For MOO, the objective functions corresponding to a particular chromosome are F_{MUC} (for the MUC metric), F_{ϕ_3} (for CEAF using the ϕ_3 entity alignment function (Luo, 2005)) and F_{ϕ_4} (for CEAF using the ϕ_4 entity alignment function). These three objective functions are simultaneously optimized using the search capability of NSGA-II.

4.3 Genetic Operators

In case of SOO, a single point crossover operation is used with a user defined crossover probability, μ_c. A mutation operator is applied to each entry of the chromosome with a mutation probability, μ_m, where the entry is randomly replaced by either 0 or 1. In this approach, the processes of fitness computation, selection, crossover, and mutation are executed for a maximum number of generations. The best string seen up to the last generation provides the solution to the above feature selection problem. Elitism has been implemented at each generation by preserving the best string seen upto that generation in a location outside the population. Thus on termination, this location contains the best feature combination.

We use crowded binary tournament selection as in NSGA-II, followed by conventional crossover and mutation for the MOO based feature selection. The most characteristic part of NSGA-II is its elitism operation, where the non-dominated solutions (Deb, 2001) among the parent and child populations are propagated to the next generation. The near-Pareto-optimal strings of the last generation provide the different solutions to the feature selection problem.

5 Methods

5.1 The BART System

For our experiments, we use BART (Versley et al., 2008), a modular toolkit for anaphora resolution that supports state-of-the-art statistical approaches to the task and enables efficient feature engineering. BART implements different models of anaphora resolution (mention-pair and entity-mention; best-first vs. ranking), has interfaces to different machine learners (MaxEnt, SVM, decision trees) and provides a large set of linguistically motivated features, along with the possibility to design new ones. It is thus ideally suited for experimenting with optimization and feature selection.

In this study, we specifically focus on feature selection.[2] The complete list of features currently implemented in BART is listed in Table 1; all were considered in the present experiments. We used a simple mention-pair model without ranking as in (Soon et al., 2001). In the mention-pair model, anaphora resolution is recast as a binary classification problem. Each classification instance consists of two mentions, i.e. an anaphor M_j and its potential antecedent M_i $(i < j)$. Instances are modeled as feature vectors (cf. Table 1) and are handed over to a binary classifier that decides, whether the anaphor and its candidate antecedent are mentions of the same entity or not. All the feature values are computed automatically.

We train a maximum entropy classifier and follow the approach of (Soon et al., 2001) to partition mentions into coreference sets given the classifier's decisions.

5.2 The Data Sets

We evaluated our approach on the ACE-02 dataset, which is divided in three subsets: bnews, npaper, and nwire. We provide results for both gold (hand-annotated) versions of the datasets (gbnews, gnpaper, gnwire) and system mentions extracted with CARAFE[3] (cbnews, cnpaper, cnwire).

Table 2 compares the performance level obtained using all the features in Table 1 with that of a loose re-implementation of the system proposed by Soon et al. (2001), commonly used as baseline and relying only on very shallow information. Our reimplementation of the Soon et al. model uses only a subset of features: those marked with an asterisk in Table 1. We also provide in Table 2 typical state-of-the-art figures on the ACE-02 dataset, as presented in an overview by Poon and Domin-

[2] The choice of the best model and the best machine learner, along with its parameters, is the main direction of our future work.

[3] `http://sourceforge.net/projects/carafe`

Table 1: Features used by BART: each feature describes a pair of mentions $\{M_i, M_j\}$, $i < j$, where M_i is a candidate antecedent and M_j is a candidate anaphor

Mention types and subtypes	
MentionType*	relevant types of M_i and M_j, as identified in Soon et al.
MentionType_Ante_Salient	M_i is demonstrative; M_i is an NE
MentionType_Ante_Extra	M_i is a pronoun
MentionType_Ana	M_j is a definite, demonstrative or indefinite NP, or pronoun of a specific type
MentionType2	relevant types of M_i and M_j, as identified in Soon et al.
MentionType_Salience	combination of $MentionType$ and $MentionType\_Ana$
FirstSecondPerson	M_i is a pronoun of the 1st/second person, same for M_j
PronounLeftRight	4 possible values for $<M_i$ is a pronoun$>$ $*$ $<M_j$ is a pronoun$>$
PronounWordForm	lemma for M_i if it's a pronoun; same for M_j
SemClassValue	semantic class of M_i, and M_j and the pair
BothLocation	both M_i and M_j are locations or geo-political
Agreement	
GenderAgree*	M_i and M_j agree in gender
NumberAgree*	M_i and M_j agree in number
AnimacyAgree*	M_i and M_j agree in animacy
Aliasing	
Alias*	heuristical NE-matching
BetterNames	heuristical matching for personal names
Syntax	
Appositive*	M_i and M_j are in an apposition
Appositive2	M_i and M_j are adjacent
Coordination	M_i is a coordination; same for M_j
HeadPartOfSpeech	POS of M_i's head; same for M_j and the pair
SynPos	depth of M_i's node in the parse tree
Attributes	M_i and M_j have incompatible premodifiers
Relations	M_i and M_j have incompatible postmodifiers
Matching	
StringMatch*	M_i and M_j have the same surface form after stripping off the determiners
NonPro_StringMatch	both M_i and M_j are non-pronominal and $Stringmatch(M_i, M_j) == 1$
Pro_StringMatch	both M_i and M_j are pronominal and $Stringmatch(M_i, M_j) == 1$
NE_StringMatch	both M_i and M_j are NE and $Stringmatch(M_i, M_j) == 1$
HeadMatch	M_i and M_j have the same head
MinSame	M_i and M_j have the same minimal span
LeftRightMatch	M_j is a prefix or suffix substring of M_i or vice versa
StringMatchExtra	extra string-macthing for bare plurals
StringKernel	approximate matching
Salience	
First_Mention	M_i is the first mention in its sentence
CorefChain	Size of the coreference chain suggested for M_i so far (with a threshold)
NonProSalience	for non-pronominal M_i, number of preceding mentions with the same head lemma
Web	
Wiki	M_i and M_j have the same wikipedia entry
Yago	M_i and M_j are linked in Yago via `means` or `typeof` relation
WebPatterns	specific contexts for co-reference extracted from the web
Proximity	
DistanceMarkable	distance in mentions between M_i and M_j
DistanceSentenceInt*	distance in sentences between M_i and M_j
DistanceSentence	log-distance in sentences between M_i and M_j
DistanceSentence2	log-distance in sentences between M_i and M_j, different formula
DistDiscrete	distance in sentences between M_i and M_j discretized into $\{0,1,>=2\}$
Miscellaneous	
Speech	M_i is in quoted speech; same for M_j and the pair

Table 2: Baseline performance on the ACE-02 dataset

	gold mentions								
	gbnews			gnpaper			gnwire		
	F_{MUC}	F_{ϕ_3}	F_{ϕ_4}	F_{MUC}	F_{ϕ_3}	F_{ϕ_4}	F_{MUC}	F_{ϕ_3}	F_{ϕ_4}
following Soon et al. (2001)	71.6	67.2	69.6	67.8	62.6	67.5	66.7	67.9	69.7
All features (Table 1)	75.8	70.6	74.4	72.5	64.7	67.0	71.2	70.3	72.2
state-of-the-art	65-69	-	-	70-72	-	-	54-67	-	-
	system mentions								
	cbnews			cnpaper			cnwire		
	F_{MUC}	F_{ϕ_3}	F_{ϕ_4}	F_{MUC}	F_{ϕ_3}	F_{ϕ_4}	F_{MUC}	F_{ϕ_3}	F_{ϕ_4}
following Soon et al. (2001)	61.3	56.7	55.9	63.3	57.6	54.0	60.8	58.2	57.0
All features (Table 1)	62.3	57.9	57.5	65.5	55.9	52.7	60.6	56.8	55.6

Table 3: Feature vectors identified via single-objective optimization.

DataSet	Metric opt.	Features Selected	F_{MUC}	F_{ϕ_3}	F_{ϕ_4}
gbnews	MUC	00100110110111100111111000111001001111111010	76.8	71.5	74.5
	ϕ_3,ϕ_4	10011000111010110000101101010011011011000001	76.7	$71.8^{\dagger}$	$74.9^{\dagger}$
gnpaper	MUC	10000001001111110101011101110000101010100111	74.6	67.1	$70.1^{\dagger}$
	ϕ_3	10101001100100110100100000010100010001101100	72.2	67.6	69.1
	ϕ_4	11101001100100110100111000100101110010001100	71.4	65.2	70.3
gnwire	MUC	10111011011111110010101010011010011011001011	$74.0^{\dagger}$	$70.3^{\dagger}$	$73.1^{\dagger}$
	ϕ_3	11011011100001000011110110101110111110001101	71.4	72.3	73.6
	ϕ_4	11101001100100110100111000100101110010001100	71.7	72.1	74.4
cbnews	MUC,ϕ_3	11111001100101000011011100101101101111001100	64.6	59.7	58.4
	ϕ_4	11111001100001000011110100101111101110001101	63.6	59.6	58.8
cnpaper	MUC,ϕ_3	010001001001010110010000010111100101100001000	66.5	$59.7^{\dagger}$	$54.7^{\dagger}$
	ϕ_4	10100101101011100011111110010100100010010011	66.2	59.1	$55.6^{\dagger}$
cnwire	MUC	00101111101110101001100000010101001011001001	63.8	60.0	58.1
	ϕ_3,ϕ_4	00011000101110100010000010011000100110000100	63.4	61.2	58.4

gos (2008). The results clearly show that although even larger sets of features have been proposed (Uryupina, 2007; Bengtson and Roth, 2008), the set of features already included in BART is sufficient to achieve results well above the state of the art on the dataset we used.

The results in Table 2 also confirm the intuition that, contrary to what is suggested by some of the early papers (Soon et al., 2001; Ng and Cardie, 2002) working on smaller datasets, linguistic factors do play a crucial role in anaphora resolution and therefore rich feature sets may lead to performance improvements once larger datasets are considered (a similar result was also obtained by Bengtson and Roth (2008)). Such improvements, however, come at high costs, as both using larger datasets and larger sets of features learning a model becomes slower and requires much more memory.

This suggests that automatic feature selection may be essential not just to improve performance but also to be able to train a model—i.e., that an efficient coreference resolution system should combine rich linguistic feature sets with automatic feature selection mechanisms.

5.3 Genetic Algorithm Parameter Setting

We set the following parameter values for both single (i.e., GA) and MOO (i.e., NSGA-II): population size=20, number of generations=30, probability of mutation $\mu_m = 0.2$ and probability of crossover $\mu_c = 0.9$. Both approaches are executed on development data to determine the optimal feature vector(s). Final results are reported on the test data. It is to be noted that GA is a stochastic approach and outputs different results for trials with different seeds and initial populations. Initial seeds and population are chosen randomly. Thus for each data set we executed the proposed single and multi objective based approaches 3 times. Finally, we report the maximum values of these 3 runs.

6 Results

6.1 Single Objective Optimization

Single objective GA based feature selection was executed on the six data sets to determine the appropriate set of features. For each data set three sets of experiments were carried out by optimizing the F-measure values of the three different evaluation metrics. The binary-valued feature vectors identified by the single objective GA based feature selection technique for the six data sets and the corresponding F-measure values are shown in Table 3. The order of the features in the vector corresponds to their order in Table 1; the values of 0's and 1's represent the absence and presence of the corresponding features. Significant improvements over the classifier based on all the features are indicated with † (sign test, $p < 0.05$).

These results show that for all the datasets, the proposed single objective GA-based feature selection technique performs better than the baseline approach of using all features. Moreover, the results show that the technique based on SOO (i.e., conventional GA-based method) with different objective functions provides different evaluation figures. Thus, it is meaningful to optimize each objective function separately.

It is also evident from Table 3 that the optimal feature set obtained by optimizing a single objective function may not be optimal with respect to another objective function. Thus, it is not possible to come up with common patterns in the set of optimal features. For example, in case of *gbnews*, the F-measure value of the first metric, i.e. of MUC corresponding to the optimal feature vector optimizing second metric, i.e. ϕ_3 is 76.7. This is obviously less than the evaluation figure obtained by optimizing the first metric.

6.2 Multi-objective Optimization

Thereafter we apply our proposed MOO based feature selection technique on the six data sets. The MOO approach provides a set of non-dominated solutions on the final Pareto optimal front. All the solutions are equally important from the algorithmic point of view. In Table 4, we show the final solutions obtained by the MOO based approach for all the data sets. Significant improvements over the classifier based on all the features are indicated with † (sign test, $p < 0.05$).

The results in Table 4 indicate that the MOO based technique achieves higher performance than the single objective GA based approach. For the *gbnews* data set, MOO achieves 0.6, 0.3 and 0.8 F-measure points increments for three metrics over the single objective GA based technique. For the *gnpaper* data set, there are increments of 2.5 F-measure points on second metric and 1.0 F-measure point on third metric over the corresponding single objective GA based technique. Similarly, for all other datasets the MOO based approach attains superior performance over the SOO-based approach.

7 Comparison with Related Work

As discussed in Section 2 most work on optimization in anaphora resolution relies on manual optimization; the one significant exception is the work of Hoste (2005).

There are two major differences between the approach of Hoste (2005) and that followed in our study. First, the scope of (Hoste, 2005) is restricted to *single-objective* optimization. As we saw above, this might provide unstable solutions, that are too tailored to a particular scoring metric. Second, the feature set of Hoste (2005) is relatively small and therefore does not provide an efficient test-bed for a feature selection approach. Not surprising, parameter optimization shows a more consistent effect on the overall performance than feature selection in (Hoste, 2005)'s experiments.

8 Discussion and Conclusions

In this paper we showed that it may not be necessary to choose one among the existing metrics for anaphora resolution—in fact, that developing systems attempting to optimize according to a combination of them may lead to better results.

In subsequent work, we plan to expand the optimization technique to consider also learning parameters optimization, classifier selection, and learning model selection.

Table 4: Feature vectors identified by the MOO based approach.

DataSet	Features	F_{MUC}	F_{ϕ_3}	F_{ϕ_4}
gbnews	0001111011011111001110110101111110111001O101	77.20	71.50	75.70
	0011010011011111001010110101111110011001O101	77.20	72.00	75.50†
	0011111011111111001110110101111110011001O101	77.00	72.10	75.10
	001110101101111100111011010111111001100001O0	77.30	71.50	74.40
	001111001001111100101011010111111011000101O1	77.40	71.30	74.70†
gnpaper	0100101110101011011111100001001010101100001O	73.90	70.10†	71.10†
	1000000100111111010101110111000010101010011 1	74.60	67.10	70.10
	010010101010101101111110001101101010110000 10	73.80	70.10	71.30
	110111111000111100111100111101101001110000 10	74.30	67.90	70.00
	110010101010111001111110001100101010110000 10	74.10	69.30	70.70
	100111101010111100111100001101111010110000 10	74.40	67.20	69.60
	110011101010111001111110101111101000110000 10	74.40	67.50	69.10
	100011101010111001111110001101111010111000 10	74.50†	66.90	69.40
	010011101010101101111110100111001000110000 10	74.20	68.80	70.90
gnwire	10101100111011100110101001011011100110000100	74.90†	72.30†	73.80
	10101100101011100110101011101010100110000100	73.80	73.10†	74.70
	10101100101011100100101001011011100010000100	74.80†	73.40†	74.00†
	10001100111011100110101011101010100110000100	74.30†	72.80†	74.60†
	10001100101011100110101001011011100010000100	74.80†	73.30†	74.10
cbnews	01011010011111001111100110011110001110001011	64.80†	60.30	59.10†
	00111010111111001111100100011010000110011011	65.10	60.60	58.90
cnpaper	10011010110111110001111000110110001111001000	67.40	60.00†	55.00
	11011000110011110000110000111110001011111010	66.40	58.20†	56.10†
	00011111110010010001011110110111000011001001	66.20	59.60	55.20†
	10011011010011110001110010110110000011011000	66.60	58.30†	55.90†
	11011000110011110010110000111110101011111010	66.70	59.40†	55.70†
cnwire	11110000111011010111101100011111100110000100	63.90	60.90	58.50
	11011100111011010111101100010111101110000100	64.30	61.40	58.10
	01011100101011110000101000100110001111100010	63.70	60.70	59.20
	01011110101010110001101000100111001111100010	63.00	61.00	58.70
	01011111101011110001101111100110000111100010	64.50	60.20	58.40
	11011100101011110000100000100110001111100010	63.80	60.30	58.90
	01001101101011110000101000100110001111100010	63.90	60.60	58.80

References

Amit Bagga and Breck Baldwin. 1998. Algorithms for scoring coreference chains. In *Proc. of the LREC workshop on Linguistic Coreference*, pages 563–566, Granada.

Eric Bengtson and Dan Roth. 2008. Understanding the value of features for coreference resolution. In *Proc. of EMNLP*.

Kalyanmoy Deb, Amrit Pratap, Sameer Agarwal, and T. Meyarivan. 2002. A fast and elitist multiobjective genetic algorithm: NSGA-II. *IEEE Transactions on Evolutionary Computation*, 6(2):181–197.

Kalyanmoy Deb. 2001. *Multi-objective Optimization Using Evolutionary Algorithms*. John Wiley and Sons, Ltd, England.

George Doddington, Alexis Mitchell, Mark Przybocki, Lance Ramshaw, Stephanie Strassell, and Ralph Weischedel. 2004. The automatic content extraction (ACE) program–tasks, data, and evaluation. In *Proc. of LREC*.

David E. Goldberg. 1989. *Genetic Algorithms in Search, Optimization and Machine Learning*. Addison-Wesley, New York.

Veronique Hoste. 2005. *Optimization Issues in Machine Learning of Coreference Resolution*. Ph.D. thesis, Antwerp University.

Ryu Iida, Kentaro Inui, Hiroya Takamura, and Yuji Matsumoto. 2003. Incorporating contextual cues in trainable models for coreference resolution. In *Proc. EACL Workshop on the Computational Treatment of Anaphora*.

Xiaoqiang Luo, Abe Ittycheriah, Hongyan Jing, Nanda Kambhatla, and Salim Roukos. 2004. A mention-synchronous coreference resolution algorithm based on the Bell Tree. In *Proc. of ACL 2004*, pages 136–143.

Xiaoqiang Luo. 2005. On coreference resolution performance metrics. In *Proc. NAACL / EMNLP*, Vancouver.

Art Munson, Claire Cardie, and Rich Caruana. 2005. Optimizing to arbitrary NLP metrics using ensemble selection. In *Proceedings of HLT/EMNLP*, pages 539–546.

Vincent Ng and Claire Cardie. 2002. Improving machine learning approaches to coreference resolution. In *Proceedings of the 40th Annual Meeting on Association for C omputational Linguistics*, pages 104–111.

Hoifung Poon and Pedro Domingos. 2008. Joint unsupervised coreference resolution with Markov logic. In *Proceedings of the Conference on Empirical Methods in Natural Language Processing*.

Marta Recasens and Eduard Hovy. 2009. A deeper look into features for coreference resolution. In S. Lalitha Devi, A. Branco, and R. Mitkov, editors, *Anaphora Processing and Applications (DAARC 2009*, number 5847 in LNAI, pages 29–42, Berlin / Heidelberg. Springer-Verlag.

Marta Recasens and Eduard Hovy. 2011. Blanc: Implementing the rand index for coreference evaluation. *Natural Language Engineering*.

Marta Recasens, Lluis Màrquez, Emili Sapena, M. Antònia Martí, Mariona Taulé, Véronique Hoste, Massimo Poesio, and Yannick Versley. 2010. Semeval-2010 task 1: Coreference resolution in multiple languages. In *Proc. SEMEVAL 2010*, Uppsala.

Wee Meng Soon, Hwee Tou Ng, and Daniel Chung Yong Lim. 2001. A machine learning approach to coreference resolution of noun phrases. *Computational Linguistic*, 27(4):521–544.

Olga Uryupina. 2007. *Knowledge Acquisition for Coreference Resolution*. Ph.D. thesis, University of the Saarland.

Olga Uryupina. 2010. Corry: a system for coreference resolution. In *Proceedings of the 5th International Workshop on Semantic Eval uation (SemEval'10)*.

Yannick Versley, Simone Paolo Ponzetto, Massimo Poesio, Vladimir Eidelman, Alan Jern, Jason Smith, Xiaofeng Yang, and Alessandro Moschitti. 2008. BART: a modular toolkit for coreference resolution. In *Proceedings of the 46th Annual Meeting of the Association for Computational Linguistics on Human Language Technologies*, pages 9–12.

Marc Vilain, John Burger, John Aberdeen, Dennis Connolly, and Lynette Hirschman. 1995. A model-theoretic coreference scoring scheme. In *Proc. of the Sixth Message Understanding Conference*, pages 45–52.

Xiaofeng Yang, Jian Su, and Chew Lim Tan. 2005. A twin-candidate model of coreference resolution with non-anaphor identification capability. In *Proc. of IJCNLP*, pages 719–730.

Shanheng Zhao and Hwee Tou Ng. 2010. Maximum metric score training for coreference resolution. In *Proceeding of COLING-2010*.

A Unified Event Coreference Resolution by Integrating Multiple Resolvers

Bin Chen[1], Jian Su[2], Sinno Jialin Pan[3] and Chew Lim Tan[4]

[1,2,3]Institute for Infocomm Research, Singapore [4]National University of Singapore

[1]bchen, [2]sujian, [3]jspan@i2r.a-star.edu.sg [4]tancl@comp.nus.edu.sg

Abstract

Event coreference is an important and complicated task in cascaded event template extraction and other natural language processing tasks. Despite its importance, it was merely discussed in previous studies. In this paper, we present a globally optimized coreference resolution system dedicated to various sophisticated event coreference phenomena. Seven resolvers for both event and object coreference cases are utilized, which include three new resolvers for event coreference resolution. Three enhancements are further proposed at both mention pair detection and chain formation levels. First, the object coreference resolvers are used to effectively reduce the false positive cases for event coreference. Second, A revised instance selection scheme is proposed to improve link level mention-pair model performances. Last but not least, an efficient and globally optimized graph partitioning model is employed for coreference chain formation using spectral partitioning which allows the incorporation of pronoun coreference information. The three techniques contribute to a significant improvement of 8.54% in B^3 F-score for event coreference resolution on OntoNotes 2.0 corpus.

1 Introduction

Coreference resolution, the task of resolving and linking different mentions of the same object/event in a text, is important for an intelligent text processing system. The resolved coreferent mentions form a coreference chain representing a particular object/event. Following the natural order in the texts, any two consecutive mentions in a coreference chain form an anaphoric pair with the latter mention referring back to the prior one. The latter mention is called the anaphor while the prior one is named as the antecedent.

Most of previous works on coreference resolution such as (Soon et al, 2001; Yang et al, 2006), aimed at object coreference which both the anaphor and its antecedent are mentions of the same real world object such as person, location and organization. In contrast, an event coreference as defined in (Asher, 1993) is an anaphoric reference to an event, fact, and proposition which is representative of eventuality and abstract entities. In the following example:

> *"Israel has **[fired]** missiles on the offices of the Palestinian Authority.*
> ***[It]** has caused 7 deaths with many injuries...*
> *Israel helicopter gunships **[fired]** across the Gaza Strip for more than two hours.*
> ***[The attack]** in Gaza has been said to cause more violence in Gaza and West Bank and terminate the current round of mid-East peace talk in an unexpected way."*

The four mentions here, ***[fired]***, ***[it]***, ***[fired]*** and ***[the attack]*** are referring to the same event (an Israel attack in Gaza Strip on Palestinian Authority). The pronouns noun phrases and action verbs are taken as the representation of events which is also in line with OntoNotes 2.0 practices.

Event coreference resolution is an important task in natural language processing (NLP) research. According to our corpus study, 68.05% of articles in OntoNotes 2.0 corpus contain at least one event chain while 15.52% of all coreference chains are event chains. In addition to the significant proportion, event coreference resolution allows event extraction system to acquire necessary details. Considering the previous example, resolving the event chain ***[fired]-[it]-[fired]-[the attack]*** will provide us all necessary details about the "*air strike*" event mentioned in different sentences. Such details includes "Israel/Israel helicopter gunships" as the actuator, "offices of Palestinian Authority" as the target, "7 deaths and many injuries" as the consequence, "Gaza Strip" as the location and "more than two hours" as the duration. Without a successful event coreference resolution such separated pieces of information cannot be assembled properly.

On the other hand, event coreference resolution incurs more difficulties comparing to the traditional object coreference from two aspects. In a semantic view, an object (such as a person, location and etc.) is uniquely defined by its name (e.g. Barrack Obama) while an event requires its role[1] information to distinguish it from other events. For example, "the crash yesterday" – "crash in 1968" shares the same event head phrase "crash", but they are distinguished by the time arguments. In a syntactic view, object coreferences only involve mentions from noun category while event coreference involves mentions from different categories. The syntactic differences will cause the tradition coreference features crippled or malfunctioned as reported by (Chen et al, 2010a;b) for Verb-Pronoun/Verb-NP resolution. In addition to their findings, we further find that even the event NP-Pronoun/NP-NP resolution requires more sophisticated feature engineering than the traditional ones. For example, previous semantic compatibility features only focus on measuring the compatibility between object such as "person", "location" and etc. Event cases are generally falls in the "other" category which provides us no useful information in distinguishing different events. These extra syntactic and semantic difficulties make event coreference resolution a more complicated task comparing to object coreferences.

In this paper, we address the various different event coreference phenomena with seven distinct mention-pair resolvers designed with sophisticated features. We then propose three enhancements to boost up performance at both mention pair detection and chain formation level. First, for the mention-pair resolvers, we have proposed the technique to utilize competitive classifiers' results to further boost mention-pair resolvers' performances. Second, a revised instance selection strategy is proposed to avoid mention-pair resolvers from being misguided by locally preferred instances used previously. Last, on top of coreferent pairs identified by the mention-pair resolvers, we have incorporated the spectral partitioning approach to form the coreference chains in a globally optimized way. Especially, we proposed a technique to enhance the chain level performance by incorporating the pronoun information which the previous attempts did not utilized.

The rest of this paper will be organized in the following way. The next section (section 2) will introduce related works. A review on coreference resolution framework and its weaknesses is presented in section 3. After that we will move on to our proposed model to overcome the weaknesses in section 4. Section 5 will present the experiment results with discussions. Last section will wrap up with a conclusion and future research directions.

2 Previous Work

Although event coreference resolution is an important task, it has not attracted much attention. There is only a limited number of previous works related to this task.

In (Asher, 1993) chapter 6, a method to resolve references to abstract entities using discourse representation theory is discussed. However, no computational system was proposed.

Besides linguistic studies, there are only a few previous works attempting to tackle subproblems of the event coreference resolution. (Byron, 2002; Müller, 2007; Chen et al, 2010a) attempted event pronoun resolution. (Chen et al, 2010b) attempted resolving noun phrases to verb mentions. All these works only focused on identifying pairs of coreferent event mentions in their targeted phenomena. The ultimate goal, which is extracting event chain, is lack of attention.

(Pradhan, et al, 2007) applied a conventional co-reference resolution system to OntoNotes1.0 corpus using the same set of features for object coreference resolution. However, there is no specific performance reported on event coreference. As (Chen et al, 2010b) pointed out, the conventional features do not function properly on event coreference problem. Thus, a thorough investigation on event coreference phenomena is required for a better understanding of the problem.

3 Resolution Framework

Before we introduce our proposed system to event coreference, we would like to revisit the two-step resolution framework to understand some of its weaknesses. Most of previous coreference resolution system employs a two-steps approach as in (Soon et al, 2001; Nicolae & Nicolae, 2006) and many others. The first step identifies all the pairs of coreferent mentions. The second step forms coreference chains using the coreferent pairs identified from the first step.

[1] Event roles refer to the arguments of the event such as actuator, patient, time, location and etc.

Although a handful of single-step frameworks were proposed recently such as (Cai & Strube, 2010), two-step framework is still widely in use because it has been well-studied. Conceptually, the two-step framework adopts a divide-and-conquer strategy which in turn, allows us to focus on different sub-problems at different stages. The mention-pair detection step allows us to employ many features associated with strong linguistic intuitions which have been proven useful in the previous linguistic study. The chain formation step allows us to leverage on efficient and robust graph partitioning algorithms such spectral partitioning used in this paper. Practically, the two-step framework is also more mature for practical uses and has been implemented as a number of standard coreference resolution toolkits widely available such as RECONCILE in (Stoyanov et al, 2010) and BART in (Versley et al, 2008). Performance-wise, two-step approaches also show comparable performance to single step approaches on some benchmark datasets[2].

In this paper, we are exploiting a brand new type of coreference phenomenon with merely previous attempts. Therefore, we employed the much matured two-step framework with innovative extensions to accommodate complicated event coreference phenomena. Such a divide-and-conquer strategy will provide us more insight for further advancements as well.

3.1 Mention-Pair Resolution Models

Most of mention-pair models adopt the well-known machine learning framework for object coreference as proposed in (Soon et al, 2001).

Instances Generation

In this learning framework, a training/testing instance has the form of *fv(cand$_i$, ana)*, where *ana* is the anaphor and *cand$_i$* is the ith candidate of the given anaphor. During training, we employed the widely used instance selection strategy described in (Ng & Cardie, 2002). In brief, only the closest antecedent of a given anaphor is used as positive instance while only candidates in between the anaphor and its closest antecedent are used as negative instances. During testing, an instance is generated in a similar manner with an additional constraint that the candidate must be within n sentences from the anaphor.

An obvious weakness of such an instance selection strategy is the representation power of the selected instances. Ideally, the selected instances should represent the coreferent status between any two mentions. However this strategy turns the selected set into a local preference representation. The positive instance is the closest preferred mention while the negatives are local non-preferable ones. Such an instance set may help in locally choosing a preferable candidate. But it may be harmful if we want to use the classifier's results in a global approach such as graph partitioning. In the section 4, we will propose a revised instance selection strategy to overcome such a weakness.

SVM with Tree-Kernel

In such a learning framework, many well-known learning models can be applied to the coreference resolution task. In this paper, support vector machine (SVM) is employed for its robust performance in high dimensional space.

In addition to the traditional SVM, we incorporate the syntactic structures through a convolution tree kernel. Tree kernel is used to capture the implicitly structural knowledge embedded in the syntax tree. Effectiveness of various structures was investigated in (Yang et al, 2006; Chen et al, 2010a;b). Based on their findings, we choose minimum-expansion for this paper. In brief, it contains only the path in the parse tree connecting an anaphor and its antecedent. The convolution tree kernel and traditional flat kernel are combined to form a composite kernel.

3.2 Coreference Chain Formation

After the coreferent mention pairs are identified, coreference chains are formed based on those coreferent pairs. There are two major ways to form coreference chains in the literature, best-link heuristic and graph partitioning.

Best-Link Heuristics Approach

The best-link heuristic selects the candidate with highest confidence for each anaphor and forms a "best-link" between them. After that, it simply joins all the mentions connected by "best-links" into the same coreference chain. The best-link heuristic approach is widely used as in (Soon et al, 2001; Yang et al, 2006) because of its simplicity and reasonably good performance.

---

[2] (Stoyanov et al, 2010) reported RECONCILE(two-steps) achieving 74.25% B^3 f-score on ACE 2005. (Haghighi & Klein, 2010) using single-step approach reported 75.10% B^3 f-score on the same dataset with same train/test-splitting. According to our experiences, such a 0.95% difference is not statistically significant. Other single-step works as (Rahman & Ng, 2009) and (Poon & Domingo, 2008) reported clearly lower B^3 f-score than RECONCILE using same datasets but different train/test-splitting.

The major critics of best-link heuristic fall on its lack of global consideration when forming the coreference chains. The mentions are only joined through locally selected "best-links". Thus the chain consistency is not enforced. Remedies to such a critic are proposed such as best-cut in the next subsection and our proposed method.

Graph Partitioning Approach

Graph partitioning approaches are proposed by various researchers to form coreference chains with global consideration. Here we take Best-Cut proposed in (Nicolae & Nicolae, 2006) as a representative of graph partitioning approaches. Best-Cut is a variant from the well-known minimum-cut algorithm. A graph is formed using all the mentions as vertices. An edge is added between two mentions if a positive output from the mention-pair model. Then the set of edges are iteratively cut to form the coreference chains.

According to (Nicolae & Nicolae, 2006), best-cut does not utilize coreferent pairs involving pronouns. However, event coreference chains contain a significant proportion of pronouns (18.8% of event coreference mentions in the OntoNotes2.0 corpus). Leaving them untouched is obviously not a preferable choice. In the next section, we will propose an alternative chain formation method to incorporate coreferent pronouns into the graph partitioning to accommodate its intensive occurrences in event chains.

4 Our Proposed Model

Our proposed resolution framework follows a similar system flow as the two-step framework which is illustrated in figure 1 for an overview of our resolution system. A brief discussion on various types of event coreference is given in the first subsection 4.1. Each type corresponds to a distinct mention-pair resolver. New features are proposed to capture 3 newly encountered phenomena. After that, we proposed two techniques to improve the mention-pair performance, namely a revised instance selection strategy and utilizing competing classifiers' results. At chain formation step, we also proposed the alternative method, spectral graph partitioning to utilizing pronoun coreferent information.

4.1 Seven Distinct Mention-Pair Models

As we mentioned, one major difficulty of event coreference lies in the gap between different syntactic types of mentions (e.g. nouns, verbs and pronouns). As discussed in (Chen et al, 2010a;b), different syntactic types of coreferent mentions behave differently which requires different features to resolve them. Following this insight, we have built five distinct resolution models for event coreferences involving noun phrases (NP), pronouns and verbs. They are Verb-Pronoun, Verb-NP, Verb-Verb, NP-NP and NP-Pronoun

Figure 1: System Overview

resolver. Conventionally, pronouns can only appear as anaphor but not antecedent. Therefore we do not train Pronoun-Pronoun resolvers.

In addition to the syntactic difference, we find event NPs have different behaviors from the object NPs. Event NPs require the event roles to distinguish it from other events while the object NPs are quite self-explaining. The conventional features such as string-matching and head-matching will not work properly when handling cases like "confliction in Mid-East" vs. "confliction in Afghanistan". In our approach, a sophisticated argument matching feature is proposed to capture such information. The arguments information is extracted automatically from the pre-modifiers and propositional phrase attachments.

Similarly, conventional features try to match mentions into semantic categories like person, location and etc. Then it evaluates the semantic-matching features to pair-up mentions from the same semantic type. However, event NPs exhibit a very different hierarchy in WordNet from the object NPs. A dedicated event hierarchy matching feature is proposed to match event of the same type. With respect to the differences between object NPs and Event NPs, we train two distinct models to handle object NP-NP and event NP-NP resolution separately with distinct features. Similarly, we train separate resolvers with distinct features for event/object NP-Pronoun. In total we have seven distinct mention-pair resolvers for different syntactic and semantic types of mentions. Five of them focus on event coreference while the other two aim at object coreference. Object coreference results are used to enhance event coreference performance by rule out in appropriate anaphors. All the features we incorporated are tabulated below.

Features	Detail	Used In
Distance	Sentence Distance, Word Distance, Phrase Distance and etc.	All
String-Matching	Full-Match, Partial-Match, Head-Match, Contained-In, Similarity Measures and etc.	eNN oNN VV
Argument-Matching	Event arguments from pre-modifiers and PP-attachments	VN VV eNN
Contexts-Matching	Non-stop-words near the anaphor and antecedent	eNN VN
NP Type	Definite / Indefinite / Proper Name	oNN eNN VN NP
Verb Type	Predicative / Model / Passive / Common	VN VP VV
Pronoun Type	Possessive/Reflexive/Common	oNP VP NP
NE-Semantic	Named entity semantic type	oNN
WN-Event-Semantic	WordNet semantic types of event	eNN eNP
WN-Object-Semantic	WordNet semantic types of object	oNN oNP
Grammatical Roles	Subject/Object in main/sub clauses	All
Synonymic Relation	If anaphor and antecedent share synonym list	eNN VV VN
Morphological Relation	If anaphor and antecedent are morphological	VN
Structural Information	Minimum-Expansion	Except o/eNN

Table 1: Feature List (e:Event; o:object; N:NP; P:Pronoun; V:Verb)

Besides the new features we proposed above (e.g. Event-Semantic and Argument-Matching), the other features we used in the seven mention pair resolvers are employed from a number of previous works such as (Soon et al, 2001; Yang et al, 2008) for object coreference feature, (Chen et al, 2010a;b) for features involving verbs.

Utilizing Competing Classifiers' Results

For the same mention, different mention-pair resolvers will resolve it to different antecedents. Some of these resolution results contradict each other. In the following example:

> *"USA Today reports **{some evidence}** that has been uncovered shows Bin Laden financed **[the attack]** and assigned one of his top assistants to supervise **[it]**."*

For the anaphor ***[it]***, event NP-Pronoun resolver may pick ***[the attack]*** as antecedent while object NP-Pronoun resolver may pick ***{some evidence}*** as antecedent. Instead of choosing one as the final resolution result from these contradicting outputs, we feed the object resolver results into the event resolvers as a feature and re-train the event resolvers. The idea behind is to provide the learning models with a confidence on how likely the anaphor refers to an object.

Revised Training Instances Selection Strategy

As we mentioned previously, the traditional training instance selection strategy as in (Ng & Cardie, 2002) has a significant weakness. The original purpose of mention pair resolvers is to identify any two coreferent mentions (not restricted to the closest one). By using the previous training instance selection strategy, the selected training instances actually represent a sample space of locally closest preferable mention vs. locally non-preferable mentions. In most of previous works, it shows a reasonably good performance when using with "best-link" chain formation technique. Our investigation shows it actually misguided the graph partitioning methods. Therefore, we propose a revised training instance selection strategy which reflects the true sample space of the original coreferent/non-coreferent status between mentions. In brief, our revised strategy exhaustively selects all the coreferent mention-pairs as positive instances and non-coreferent pairs as negative instances regardless of their closeness to the anaphor. Considering the following example,

> *"...linking **{Saudi terrorist Osama Bin Laden}** to **[the bombing]**. **{USA Today}** reports **{some evidence}** that has been uncovered shows **{Bin Laden}** financed **[the attack]** and assigned one of his **{top assistants}** to supervise **[it]**."*

The traditional instance selection scheme will only select ***[the attack]–[it]*** as positive instance and ***{top assistants}–[it]*** as negative instance. Our revised instance selection scheme will select an additional positive instance ***[the bombing]–[it]*** and additional negative instance as ***{Bin Laden}–[it]***, ***{USA Today}–[it]*** and other curly brackets NP mentions. Thus the full sample space is represented using our training instances selection strategy.

4.2 Spectral Graph Partitioning

After deriving the potential coreferent mention pairs, we further use spectral graph partitioning as described in (Ng et al, 2002) to form the globally optimized coreference chains. As we mentioned previously, traditional chain formation technique suffers from a local decision (as in best-link approaches) or failure to incorporate pronoun information (as in best-cut approaches). Spectral graph partitioning shows its advantages over previous approaches. Spectral graph partitioning (aka. Spectral clustering) has made its success in a number of fields such as image segmentation in (Shi & Malik, 2000) and gene expression clustering in (Shamir & Sharan, 2002).

Compared to the "traditional algorithms" such as k-means or minimum-cut, spectral clustering has many fundamental advantages. Results obtained by spectral clustering often outperform the traditional approaches, spectral clustering is very simple to implement and can be solved efficiently by standard linear algebra methods. More attractively, according to (Luxburg, 2006), spectral clustering does not intrinsically suffer from local optima problem. In this paper, the similarity graph is formed in similar way as in (Nicolae & Nicolae, 2006) using SVM confidence[3] outputs.

Utilizing Pronoun Information

Besides the simplicity and efficiency of spectral graph partitioning, one particular reason to employ spectral partitioning is that the previous best-cut approach failed to incorporate pronoun information in their similarity graph. It may not be an issue in object coreference scenario as pronouns are only a relatively small proportion (9.78% of object mentions in OntoNotes). However, in event cases, pronouns contribute 18.8% of the event mentions. As we further demonstrated in our corpus study, event chains are relatively more sparse and shorter than object chains. Removing pronouns from the similarity graph will break a significant proportion of the event chains. Thus we propose this spectral graph partitioning approach to overcome this weakness from the previous models.

Instead of re-implementing the minimum-cut algorithm, we apply the spectral partitioning to a similarity graph without pronoun information. This setting is based on two considerations. Firstly, spectral partitioning is theoretically equivalent to minimum-cut partitioning which means they can handle the same problem set. Secondly, by using the same model, we can eliminate any empirical difference in these two partitioning algorithms and show the true contribution from incorporating pronoun information.

[3] Confidence is computed from kernel outputs using sigmoid function.

5 Experiment Settings and Results

In this section, we present various sets of experiment results to verify the effectiveness of our proposed methods individually and collectively.

5.1 Corpus Study

The corpus we used is OntoNotes2.0 which contains 300K of English news wire data from Wall Street Journal and 200K of English broadcasting news from various sources including (ABC, CNN and etc.). OntoNotes2.0 provides gold annotation for parsing, named entity, and coreference. The distribution of event coreference is tabulated below.

	# of Articles	# of Chains	# of Mentions
Event	1033	2693	7314
Object	1511	14655	54753
Total	1518	17348	62067

Table 2: Event Coreference Distribution in OntoNotes2.0

The distribution of event chains is quite sparse. In average, an article contains only 2.6 event chains comparing to 9.7 object chains. Furthermore, event chains are generally shorter than object chains. Each event chain contains 2.72 mentions comparing to 3.74 in the object chains.

5.2 Performance Metrics & Experiment Settings

In this work, we employ two performance metrics for evaluation purposes. At mention-pair level, we used the standard pair-wise precision/recall/f-score to evaluate the seven mention-pair resolvers. At coreference chain level, we use B-Cube (B^3) measure as proposed in (Bagga & Baldwin, 1998). B^3 provides an overall evaluation of coreference chains instead of coreferent links. Thus it is widely used in previous works.

For each experiment conducted, we use the following data splitting. 400 articles are reserved to train the object NP-Pronoun and NP-NP resolvers. (400 news articles are sufficient for object coreference training, comparing with other data sets used for both training and testing such as 519 articles in ACE-02, 60 articles in MUC-6 and 50 articles in MUC-7.) Among the remaining 1118 articles, we random selected 894 (80%) for training the 5 event resolvers while the other 224 articles are used for testing.

In order to separate the propagated errors from preprocessing procedures such as parsing and NE tagging, we used OntoNotes 2.0 gold annotation for Parsing and Named Entities only. Coreferent mentions are generated by our system instead of using the gold annotations.

In order to test the significance in performance differences, we perform paired t-test at 5% level of significance. We conduct the experiments 20 times through a random sampling method to perform meaningful statistical significance test.

5.3 Experiment Results

In this section, we will present the experiment results to verify each of the improvements we proposed in previous sections.

Mention-Pair Models Performances

The first set of experiment results presented here is the seven mention-pair resolvers using all conventional settings without any proposed methods.

The Verb-Verb resolver performance is particularly low due to lack of training instances where only 48 positive instances available from the corpus. Our Mention-pair models are not directly comparable with (Chen et al, 2010a;b) which used gold annotation for object coreference information while we resolve such coreferent pairs using our trained resolvers. There are also a number of differences in the preprocessing stage which makes the direct comparison impractical.

Mention-Pair Score	Precision	Recall	F-Score
Event Resolvers			
Verb-Pronoun	32.34	68.32	43.90
Verb-NP	54.22	68.56	60.55
Verb-Verb	22.47	83.33	35.40
NP-Pronoun	46.62	70.47	56.12
NP-NP	48.83	60.08	53.88
Object Resolvers			
NP-NP	58.89	66.04	62.26
NP-Pronoun	61.37	84.33	71.04
Event Chain B^3	**Precision**	**Recall**	**F-Score**
BL	26.67	68.09	38.33

Table 3: Mention-Pair Performance in %

The coreference chains formed using spectral partitioning without any proposed improvements yields a B^3 f-score of 38.33% which serves as our initial baseline (BL) for further comparisons.

Utilizing Competing Classifiers' Results

Since object resolver results are in general better than event resolver, we propose to utilize competing object classifiers' results to improve event resolvers' performance. The experiment results are tabulated below. The "BL+CC" row presents the performance when utilized competing classifiers' results into the baseline system.

Mention-Pair	Precision	Recall	F-Score
Event Verb-Pronoun Resolver			
w/o object info	32.34	68.32	43.90
with object info	45.09	64.73	53.00
Event Verb-NP Resolver			
w/o object info	54.22	68.56	60.55
with object info	56.67	67.61	61.66
Event NP-Pronoun Resolver			
w/o object info	46.62	70.47	56.12
with object info	57.83	69.15	62.99
Event NP-NP Resolver			
w/o object info	48.83	60.08	53.88
with object info	51.35	59.20	55.00
Event Chain B^3	**Precision**	**Recall**	**F-Score**
BL	26.67	68.09	38.33
BL + CC	32.33	67.08	43.61

Table 4: Performance in % using competing classifiers' results

By incorporating the object coreference information, we manage to improve the event coreference resolution significantly, more than 9% F-score for Verb-Pronoun resolver and about 7% F-score for event NP-Pronoun resolver. Object coreference information improves pronoun resolution more than NP resolution. This is mainly because pronouns contain much less information than NP. Such additional information will helps greatly in preventing object pronouns to be resolved by event resolvers mistakenly. Although object coreference is incorporated at mention-pair level, we still measures its contribution to B^3 score at chain level. It improves the B^3 f-score from 38.33% to 43.61% which is a 5.28% improvement. This observation also shows the importance of collective decision of multiple classifiers.

Revised Instance Selection

The second technique we proposed is a revised training instances selection strategy. Table 5 shows improvement using revised instance selection strategy. We refer the traditional instance selection strategy as "BL+CC" and our proposed instance selection strategy as "BL+CC+RIS" (Revised Instance Selection). At mention-pair level we take event NP-Pronoun resolver for demonstration. Similar behaviors are observed in all the mention-pair models. In order to demonstrate power of revised instance selection scheme, we evaluate the mention-pair results in two different ways. The best-candidate evaluation follows the traditional mention pair evaluation. It firstly groups mention-pair predictions by anaphor. Then an anaphor is correctly resolved as long as the candidate-anaphora pair with highest resolver's score is the true antecedent-anaphor pair. The correct/wrong of other candidates' resolution outputs are not counted at all. The coreferent link evaluation counts each candidate-anaphor pair resolution separately. Intuitively, best-candidate evaluation measures how good a resolver can rank the candidates while the coreferent link evaluation measures the how good a resolver identifies coreferent pairs.

An interesting phenomenon here is the performance evaluation using the best candidate actually drops 3.26% in f-measure when employing the revised instance selection scheme. But when we look at the coreferent link results, the revised instance selection scheme improves the performance by 2.84% f-measure. As a result, our revised instance selection scheme trains better classifier with higher coreferent link prediction results. Since this coreferent link information is further used in the final chain formation step. Our revised scheme contributes an improvement on the final event chain formation by 2.02% F-Score in B^3 measure.

Mention-Pair Score	Precision	Recall	F-Score
Event NP-Pronoun using **Best Candidate** Evaluation			
BL+CC	57.83	69.15	62.99
BL+CC+RIS	52.05	67.11	58.63
Event NP-Pronoun using **Coreferent Link** Evaluation			
BL+CC	39.96	64.03	49.21
BL+CC+RIS	43.33	65.47	52.15
Event Chain B^3	**Precision**	**Recall**	**F-Score**
BL+CC	32.33	67.08	43.61
BL+CC+RIS	35.21	64.74	45.63[4]

Table 5: Performance in % using revised instance selection

This observation shows that the traditional mention-pair model should be revised to maximize the coreferent link performance instead of the traditional best-candidate performance. Because the coreferent link performance is more influential to the final chain formation process using graph partitioning approach.

Spectral Partitioning Utilizing Pronoun Information

The third improvement we proposed is the spectral partitioning with pronoun information. The performance improvement is demonstrated in table 6. In order to separate the contribution from incorporating pronouns and revising instance selection, we conducted the experiment using traditional training instance selection.

B^3 Performance	Precision	Recall	F-Score
BL	26.67	68.09	38.33
BL+CC	32.33	67.08	43.61
BL+CC+Pron	34.14	69.65	45.82[5]
BL+CC+RIS+Pron	35.27	70.02	46.91

Table 6: Performance in % using pronoun information

By incorporating the coreferent pronoun information, the performance is significantly improved by 2.19% in f-measure. By further incorporating the revised instance selection scheme, we achieve B^3-Precision/Recall/F-Score as 35.27 / 70.02 / 46.91% respectively which is an 8.54% F-score improvement from the initial resolution system. 46.91% F-score is the highest performance we achieved in this event coreference resolution work.

6 Conclusion and Future Works

This paper presents a unified event coreference resolution system by integrating multiple mention-pair classifiers including 3 new mention-pair resolvers. Furthermore, we proposed three techniques to enhance the resolution performance. First, we utilize the competing classifiers' results to enhance mention-pair model. Then we propose the revised training instance selection scheme to provide better coreferent link information to graph partitioning model. Lastly, we employ spectral partitioning method with pronoun information to improve chain formation performance. All the three techniques contribute to a significant improvement of 8.54% over the initial 38.33% in B^3 F-score. In future, we plan to incorporate more semantic knowledge for mention-pair models such as semantic roles and word senses. For chain formation, we plan to incorporate domain knowledge to enforce chain consistency.

[4] The B^3-F-Score difference between RIS and Baseline is statistically significant using paired t-test at 5% level of significance

[5] The B^3-F-Score difference between Baseline and Baseline+Pronoun is statistically significant using paired t-test at 5% level of significance

References

Asher,N. 1993. *Reference to Abstract Objects in Discourse.* Kluwer Academic Publisher.

Bagga,A. & Baldwin,B. 1998. Algorithms for scoring coreference chains. *In Proceedings of the Linguistic Coreference Workshop at Conference on Language Resources and Evaluation (LREC-1998).*

Byron,D. 2002. Resolving Pronominal Reference to Abstract Entities, In *Proceedings of the 40th Annual Meeting of the Association for Computational Linguistics (ACL)*, USA.

Cai,J. & Strube,M. 2010. End-to-End Coreference Resolution via Hypergraph Partitioning. In *Proceedings of the International Conference on Computational Linguistics (COLING),* China,

Chen,B.; Su,J. & Tan,C.L. 2010a. A Twin-Candidate Based Approach for Event Pronoun Resolution using Composite Kernel. In *Proceedings of the International Conference on Computational Linguistics (COLING),* China,

Chen,B.; Su,J. & Tan,C.L. 2010b. Resolving Noun Phrases to their Verbal Mentions. In *Proceeding of conference on Empirical Methods in Natural Language Processing (EMNLP)*, USA.

Hovy,E.; Marcus,M.; Palmer,M.; Ramshaw,L. & Weischedel,R. 2006. OntoNotes: The 90% Solution. In *Proceedings of the Human Language Technology Conference of the NAACL*, USA

Luxburg,U. 2006. A tutorial on spectral clustering. *In (MPITechnical Reports No. 149).* Tubingen: Max Planck Institute for Biological Cybernetic

Müller,C. 2007. Resolving it, this, and that in unrestricted multi-party dialog. *In Proceedings of ACL-2007*, Czech Republic.

Ng,A.; Jordan,M. & Weiss,Y. 2002. On spectral clustering: analysis and an algorithm. *In Advances in Neural Information Processing Systems* 14 (pp. 849 – 856). MIT Press

Ng,V. & Cardie,C. 2002. Combining sample selection and error-driven pruning for machine learning of coreference rules. In *Proceedings of conference on Empirical Methods in Natural Language Processing (EMNLP)*, USA.

Nicolae,C & Nicolae,G. 2006. BESTCUT: A Graph Algorithm for Coreference Resolution. In *Proceedings of conference on Empirical Methods in Natural Language Processing (EMNLP)*, Austrilia.

Poon,H. & Domingos.P. 2008. Joint Unsupervised Coreference Resolution with Markov Logic. In *Proceedings of the Conference on Empirical Methods in Natural Language Processing (EMNLP), 2008.*

Pradhan,S.; Ramshaw,L.; Weischedel,R.; MacBride,J. & Micciulla,L. 2007. Unrestricted Coreference: Identifying Entities and Events in OntoNotes. In *Proceedings of the IEEE International Conference on Semantic Computing (ICSC)*, USA.

Shamir,R.; and Sharan,R. 2002. Algorithmic approaches to clustering gene expression data. *Current Topics in Computational Molecular Biology*, 269–300.

Shi,J. & Malik,J. 2000. Normalized cuts and image segmentation. *IEEE Transactions on Pattern Analysis and Machine Intelligence(PAMI).*

Sidner,C.L. 1983. Focusing in the comprehension of definite anaphora. In *Computational Models of Discourse.* MIT Press.

Soon,W.; Ng,H. & Lim, D. 2001. A machine learning approach to coreference resolution of noun phrases. *Computational Linguistics*, 27(4):521– 544.

Stoyanov,V.; Cardie,C.; Gilbert,N.; Riloff,E.; Buttler,D. & Hysom,D. 2010 Coreference Resolution with Reconcile. In *Proceedings of the Conference of the 48th Annual Meeting of the Association for Computational Linguistics (ACL 2010)*

Versley,Y.; Ponzetto,S.P.; Poesio,M.; Eidelman,V.; Jern,A.; Smith,J.; Yang,X. & Moschitti,A. 2008. BART: A Modular Toolkit for Coreference Resolution. In *Proceedings of the 6th International Conference on Language Resources and Evaluation (LREC 2008).*

Yang,X.; Su,J. & Tan,C.L. 2006. Kernel-Based Pronoun Resolution with Structured Syntactic Knowledge. *In Proceedings of the Conference of the 46th Annual Meeting of the Association for Computational Linguistics.* Australia.

Yang,X.; Su,J. & Tan,C.L. 2008. A Twin-Candidates Model for Learning-Based Coreference Resolution. In *Computational Linguistics*, 34(3):327-356.

Handling verb phrase morphology in highly inflected Indian languages for Machine Translation

Ankur Gandhe, Rashmi Gangadharaiah, Karthik Visweswariah, and Ananthakrishnan Ramanathan
IBM Research, India
{ankugand, rashgang, v-karthik, aramana2}@in.ibm.com

Abstract

The phrase based systems for machine translation are limited by the phrases that they see during the training. For highly inflected languages, it is uncommon to see all the forms of a word in the parallel corpora used during training. This problem is amplified for verbs in highly inflected languages where the correct form of the word depends on factors like gender, number and tense aspect. We propose a solution to augment the phrase table with all possible forms of a verb for improving the overall accuracy of the MT system. Our system makes use of simple stemmers and easily available monolingual data to generate new phrase table entries that cover the different variations seen for a verb. We report significant gains in BLEU for English to Hindi translation.

1 Introduction

Data driven approaches have become widely popular as they use little or no language specific knowledge. The main drawback of these approaches is the need for large amounts of data. (Koehn et al., 2003) have shown that the quality of the translations produced by data driven approaches mainly depends on the amount of parallel data available for the language-pair under consideration. Creation of a large bilingual corpus is expensive and time consuming if high quality manual translations are required. Hence, building MT systems for language-pairs with limited amounts of data is a big challenge.

Approaches have been suggested in the past to mine the world-wide-web to automatically obtain large amounts of parallel data. For example, news articles in two different languages describing the same event can be sentence-aligned to obtain a parallel corpus. Although this approach has shown improvements, this cannot be extended to languages that have little or no data on the world wide web.

The situation gets worse for languages that are rich in morphology. Clearly large amounts of parallel data are required to observe all variations of a word. Popovic and Ney (2004) applied transformations to verbs to reduce the number of out-of-vocabulary words and showed improvements in translation quality when morphemes were considered.

Yang and Kirchhoff (2006) used a back off model in a Phrase-based SMT system which translated word forms in the source language by hierarchical morphological abstractions. Unknown words in the test data were stemmed and phrase-table entries were modified such that words sharing the same root were replaced by their stems. Freeman et al. (2006) and Habash (2008) find in-vocabulary words for OOV words that could be morphological variants of the OOV words. Phrases in the phrase table containing these invocabulary words are then replaced by OOV words to create new entries. Vilar et al. (2007) used a letter-based MT system that treated the source and target sentences as a string of letters for translating unknown words.

All the above approaches handled OOV issues that arise when the source language is morphologically rich. Generation of the target sentence when the target language is morphologically rich from a source language that is not rich in morphology is non-trivial as the source language does not contain all the information for inflecting the target words. Minkov et. al (2007) predicted inflected forms of a sequence of word stems on languages that are morphologically rich using syntactic and rich morphological sources. This inflection generation model was then applied in MT by (Toutanova et al., 2008) while translating English into morphologically complex languages and showed improvement in translation quality. Their methods require a syntactic analyzer and a very rich morphological analyzer which may not be available for many rare or low-density languages. Also, their feature set includes bilingual features that require expensive and difficult to get bilingual corpora. We rely more on monolingual data and a small amount of parallel data. In cases of multi word compound words (explained in section 1.1) , since inflections on the light verb might change with change in the root verb compounding with it, we need to predict these verbs together and not as separate words.

In this paper, we consider Indian languages which are considered as low density languages as they do not have rich knowledge sources such as parsers or complex morphological analyzers. These languages also suffer from data sparsity and hence form ideal languages for the analysis of our proposed method. We also consider only various forms of verbs and do not consider other words such as noun phrases and adjectives affected by inflections.

1.1 Background on Indian Languages

India has fifteen official languages which originated from the Indo-Iranian branch of the Indo-European language family, the non-Indo-European Dravidian family, Austro-Asiatic, Tai-Kadai and the Sino-Tibetan language families (Microsoft Encarta Online Encyclopedia, 1997). The languages that stem from the Dravidian family, are - Tamil, Kannada, Malayalam and Telugu, spoken in the South Indian states. Languages in North India, such as Hindi, Urdu, Punjabi, Gujarati, Bengali, Marathi, Kashmir, Sindhi, Konkani, Rajasthani, Assamese and Oriya, stem from Sanskrit and Pali.

Indian languages are verb final i.e., verbs are placed at the end of the sentences. Verbs in these languages are inflected to contain information about gender (masculine and feminine), tense, aspect and number of the subject (singular or plural). A few examples showing inflections on the verbs in Hindi are shown below:

वो(he) साफ कर रहा (cleaning) है (is)
[vo saapha kara rahaa hai.n]
वो(she) साफ कर रही (cleaning) है (is)
[vo saapha kara rahI hai.n]
वो (she) साफ (clean) करेगी (will)
[vo saapha karegI]

These languages also contain compound verbs (multi-word compound representing a single verb). They contain a light verb which receives inflections and another component that can be a noun or a verb responsible for conveying the meaning. For example, in Hindi, most commonly used light verbs are "karna" (to make), "lena" (to take), "hona" (to happen) and "dena" (to give).

2 Motivation

When translating from a morphologically poor language such as English to any of the Indian languages, finding the right translation along with the inflections on the verbs becomes difficult, especially when the amount of bilingual data available is scarce. We try to use the pattern behavior of verbs to tackle this problem. Table 1 gives an example of hindi verbs classified according to their light verbs. Hindi side is transliterated for the sake of clarity. It shows how the verb phrase of one compound verb (clean) can generate verb phrase for words in the same group (help and forgive) just by replacing the corresponding source and target root words. The suffixes (shown in bold) are separated from the word to show how the actual process takes place. This paper tries to automatically group the different kinds of verbs occurring in the language based on their light verbs and generates the variation for all the verbs in one group by looking at the variations of any one member.

Karna	Lena	Dena
saaph (clean)	sokh (absorb)	saaza (punish)
maaph (forgive)	bhaag (participate)	jawab (answer)
madad (help)	goad (adopt)	anumati (allow)

he will be *clean* **ing** -> vo *saaph* kar **egaa**
he will be *forgive* **ing** -> vo *maaph* kar **egaa**
he will be *help* **ing** -> vo *madad* kar **egaa**

Table 1: Example of verbs belonging to different groups based on their light verb

The novel concept of this paper is generation of verb phrases on the source side and their translations using a) source and target monolingual data, b) simple morphological segmentation on source and target side and c) Small amount of manual translations or d) Word alignments of parallel corpora. We have described two methods of generating these verb phrase translations in the following sections.

3 Manual Generation

The idea here is to get the manual translations of source and target verb pairs which could capture the entire range of variations seen in the source and the target verb phrases. These translations can then be used to generate the variations for rest of the verb pairs. The entire flow of the method is shown in Figure 1.

3.1 Verb Phrase Chunking

Given a language pair (e,f), we extract all verb phrases that occur in the source monolingual data using a verb phrase chunker. Part of speech (POS) tags can be used to extract verb phrases for languages having a good POS tagger. In our experiments for English-Hindi language pair, POS tags were used for English verb phrase chunking. Modals in English were included as a part of the verb phrase since their counterparts in Hindi appear as verbs. For Hindi, the verb phrase chunker was trained on a small set of 6000 sentences, where the reference markings were obtained by projecting the verb phrases from English. The 6000 sentences were hand aligned with the corresponding English sentences, hence helping with the accuracy of the projected verb phrases. On this data, we built a CRF based chunker (Lafferty et al., 2001) using word and POS tag features.

3.2 Verb Classing

Using a segmenter, the root verb is separated from its inflected suffix for all the extracted verb phrases. These extracted verb phrases are then clustered based on the root verb so that all the variations of a root verb '<verb>' are grouped together into one cluster. As an example, a part of the verb cluster for 'play' is shown below. Note that all possible variations of each verb (both source and target side) are under one cluster.

play
was play +ing
should have play +ed
ought be played
would have been play +ed
is play +ed
cannot be play +ed
is being play +ed

The different variations within each verb cluster are normalized by replacing the root verb by a normalization tag '<verb>' so that similar root verb clusters now contain exactly the same variations and can be aggregated together easily. These clusters are put in N different 'verb classes' so that all verbs occurring with the same variations are under a single class and those with different variations are put in separate classes. For instance, since 'play' and 'help' have the same variations, they would belong to the same class. Choosing any one member of the class will cover all the variations of that class and by choosing one member from each of the N classes, all possible variations of all verbs in a given language are covered.

Class	Verb Class	No of words
AH	No Auxiliary	854
BH	'karna' as Auxiliary	1772
CH	'dena' as Auxiliary	212
DH	'lena' as Auxiliary	90
EH	'hona' as Auxiliary	242
	Rest	309

Table 2: Count of verbs belonging to different classes in Hindi

For English, we used morphA, (Minnen et al., 2000) an open source stemming package, to get the root form of the head verb in the extracted English verb phrases. It was observed that all the root verb clusters had the same variations of verb phrases and hence all belonged to the same class. Thus, from the source (English) side, only one verb could be picked up to cover all the variations, which could be then replicated for all the others verbs. We call that class 'AE'.

In Hindi, as explained in section 1.1, many verbs occur as compound verbs where a noun followed by a light verbs is considered as a verb and hence we also included these for our clustering and classification. The extracted verb phrases were segmented using a stemmer similar to one in (Ramanathan et al., 2003). After clustering the verb phrases based on their root verbs into groups and classing them based on the different variations, the main classes depended on the a) whether the verb has a light verb or not and b) the type of light verb attached. Table 2 shows the different classes found along with the number of verbs within each class.

There were more classes with a different auxiliary verb but we neglected them since the frequency of verbs in those classes was insignificant. 'lena' and 'dena' verb forms take the same variations (differing only in one character), we could easily generate one from another. Overall, only 3 classes were used for manual translation on the Hindi side(AH,BH and CH). Note that we allow a verb to belong to more than one class, suggesting that a word can be used in more than just one way depending on the context.

3.3 Root verb translation pairs

Given a parallel corpus, it is possible to extract source root verb to target root verb translation. Since a parallel corpus will contain the inflected form of a verb, it is necessary to stem them to their root form before calculating the word translation probabilities. Hence, given a parallel corpus, sentences are machine aligned by a maxent model as described in (Ittycheriah and Roukos, 2005) and then the verbs on both the source and target side are stemmed to the respective root forms using a suitable stemmer. Given the list of possible source verbs and target words from the previous clustering step, the forward and reverse translation probabilities for these verbs is calculated from the alignments using by relative frequency:

$$P(f_i/e_j) = count(f_i, e_j)/\sum_f count(f, e_j) \quad (1)$$

$$P(e_i/f_j) = count(e_i, f_j)/\sum_e count(e, f_j) \quad (2)$$

Using these forward and reverse probability, a mapping file that maps the source root verb to the corresponding target root verb(s) is created by empirically combining the two probabilities.

$$P_{tot}(e_i/f_j) = 0.5 * P(e_i/f_j) + 0.5 * P(f_j/e_i) \quad (3)$$

We allow one source verb mapping to multiple target verb, since the meaning can change due to context in the test sentence. TopM translations of source word are selected for translations, provided $P_{tot} > P_{thresh}$. We empirically found the P_{thresh} = 0.2 and M=4 to work reasonably well. Two or more worded root verb, such as phrasal verbs 'take off', 'figure out', were not considered while creating the mapping since the meaning is often different that the individual words and the generation of verb phrases from these root verbs is more tricky. Such constructions, where one word verb may translate to multiple words, occurred for only 3% of the verbs in the test data and hence could be ignored without any significant loss in improvement.

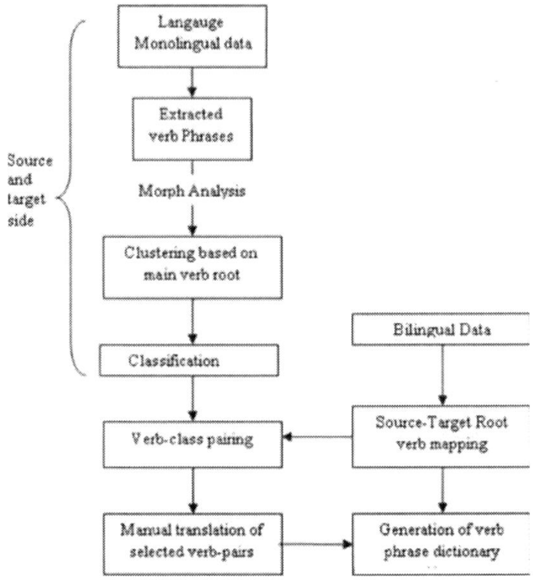

Figure 1: Steps involved in manual generation of verb phrases

3.4 Generation of Verb Phrase Dictionary

Given the root verb mapping and the classes to which these source and target root verb belong to, we create a 'source class' to 'target class' mapping, or a 'verb-pair class', by replacing the root verbs with their corresponding verb classes. This causes each of the verb pair to fall under some particular verb-pair class. If there are n classes in the source side and m on the target side, the maximum number of verb-pair classes are

N = m*n

By picking any one root verb pair from each of these verb-pair classes, we can cover all the possible variations of verb phrase translation pairs. These pairs can then be given for human translation, by creating all possible variations of either the source side or target side and asking humans to translate to the other.

Templates for each of the N verb-pair class are created from the manually translated data by segmenting the verb phrase pairs on both sides and replacing the root verb by the '<verb>' tag. An example of such translation pair for English-Hindi is shown

was <verb> +ing == <verb> raha tha [Class AH-AE]
was <verb> +ing == <verb> kar raha tha [Class BH-AE]

Picking root verb pairs from each verb-pair class and replacing the <verb< tag with corresponding verbs, these templates are used to create new verb phrases which may not be present in the parallel data to a large extent. A reverse morphological tool or joiner is used to recombine the segmented verb phrases and create a verb phrase dictionary.

In our paper, English had one class and Hindi had 3. Thus, only 3 Hindi-English verb pairs needed to be translated, one from each of the verb-pair classes AH-AE, BH-AE, and CH-AE. We created different variations of the English verbs, since it had only one class and could be easily generated using manually built rules. Grammar rules contain number (singular/plural), tense and aspect agreement between different auxiliary forms (for example: was, is, were, can, might, could not, wouldn't, etc) and verbs (for example: answer, punishing, cleaned, etc.). A unique Hindi-English verb pair is picked from each of the verb-pair classes obtained earlier and their English verbs are used in generating the English verb forms. For example, "saaf" belonged to the "karna" cluster, so its English translation, "clean" is used for creating verb forms. Gender information is also added to the Verb forms which will be required for the Hindi counterparts. About $\approx$ 970 verb forms were generated for each of the 3 verbs. Examples of a few Verb forms are given below:

[he] will clean
[we] will clean
[I(he)] will clean
[he] may not have been cleaning
[she] could have been cleaning
[we] may have been cleaning
[I(she)] may have cleaned

'Not' is included as a part of the extracted verb phrases since it is the most common adverb that occurs within the verb phrases. Other adverbs such as 'now', 'also' have not been dealt with in this paper. These variations, along with the mapping of the English-Hindi root verb was given to the annotators for translation. The subject information within '[]' helps the annotators to decide on the number and gender inflections on the target (Hindi) side. These are removed before using in the machine translation system. The reverse morphology of the generated verb phrases is done using MorphG (Minnen et al., 2000) for English and a simple suffix joiner for hindi.

4 Automatic generation

Although manual translation is a clean and effective way of generating these verb phrases, a human is still required in the loop to complete the setup. Instead, both side monolingual data can be employed to extract all the variations for each root verb, parallel corpus can be used to get the source-verb to root-verb pairs, and finally a model can be learnt to align the source verb phrase to target verb phrase using the verb alignments from the hand alignments and machine alignments.

4.1 Verb pairs

Using the technique described in section 3.3, a source to target root verb mapping are obtained.

4.2 Clustering

Clustering of verb phrases on source and target side is done as explained in section 3.2 so that each cluster contains different variations of the same root verb form. The phrases within each cluster are segmented on both sides using the techniques described section 3.2 and are generalized by replacing the root verb in the segmented verb phrase by a '<verb>' tag as this will help while aligning the source verb phrase to its corresponding target verb phrase.

4.3 Verb Phrase Translations

In order to learn a verb phrase alignment model, we need good quality verb phrase alignments from the parallel corpora. We concentrate on hand aligned data and accurate machine alignments. Machine aligned verb phrases that occurred less than three times were treated as inaccurate. The source side verb phrases are extracted using the scheme similar to one in section 3.1, and by looking at the target words they align to, verb phrase alignments are obtained. The aligned verb phrases are segmented on both the target and the source side using the strategy described in section 3.2 and then normalized by replacing the head word for both the source side verb phrase and the target side verb phrase by a '<verb>' tag. The '<verb>' tagged verb phrases act as templates for verb alignments. Since all the root forms of verb will not occur in the extracted verb alignments, it's necessary to normalize them to be able to learn a general model. This way, if the translation of a particular source verb phrase variation is known, its generalized form can be used to get the translation of a different root verb for the same variation. This is similar to our claim in section 3.4 that translation of one root verb can generate translations for all other verbs belonging to the same class.

A simple word alignment model is used to learn the word translation probabilities. Please note that the suffixes of the verbs are also treated as words since they contain important information about tense, gender and number. We used GIZA++ model 4 to learn P(V_{si}/V_{tj}), which is the probability of the ith source word/segment aligning to the jth target word/segment.

4.4 Automatic Alignment and Generation

From the root-verb pairs obtained in section 4.1, each verb pair is picked and the best translation for a source verb phrase in source-side verb cluster is searched for in the target verb cluster. If a cluster for the source or target verb does not exist, that pair is ignored. Both the source and the target verb clusters contain the generalized verb phrase of the form '... aux_{-1} <verb> aux_1 aux_2.. '. First, a perfect match of a source phrase and target verb phrase is searched in the hand aligned and machine aligned verb phrase pairs. If found, that phrase pair is treated as a valid verb phrase pair. If no perfect match is found, word alignment probabilities obtained in previous section are use to get the source to target verb phrase alignments. Any verb phrase alignment pair with score lower than a threshold score of 0.5 is ignored.

After obtaining all the valid verb phrase pairs, the tag <verb> is replaced by their corresponding root verbs and as in section 3.4 and the suffixes are joined to the root verb to get the automatically generated verb phrase dictionary which can be used in the MT system.

5 Experiments

In this section, we report our experimental results on English - Hindi language pair. We first report on the coverage ratio, which gives an estimate of number of exact verb phrases covered by the baseline system and our method. In addition, we also report on English to Hindi Machine translation results for phrase based systems.

5.1 Discovery of new data

The data used for clustering and classification on source and target side, the parallel corpora and the test set details are shown in table 3.

Data	No of Sentences
English Monolingual	6 million
Hindi Monolingual	1.4 million
Test set 1	4000
Test set 2	715
Training Data	280k

Table 3: Data used for experiments

The Hindi monolingual data was used to collect 4320 Hindi verb clusters belonging to 3 different classes (section 3.2) and the English monolingual yielded 4872 clusters. Many of these clusters were false positives due to the bad quality of verb phrase chunker but were eliminated in the subsequent steps. The parallel data was aligned using a maxent model (Ittycheriah and Roukos, 2005) and gave us 2944 verb-pairs.

For manual generation method, 3 verb pairs were given to annotators for translation, with about 972 different English verb forms in each. The generated dictionary from the manual translations had 2.7 million verb phrases. The automatic method aligned the corresponding clusters of the 2944 verb-pairs and produced about 300k new verb phrases. The considerably lesser size of the automatically created verb phrase dictionary compared to the manual dictionary can be attributed to the fact that the manual dictionary contains variations that are not seen in our monolingual data.

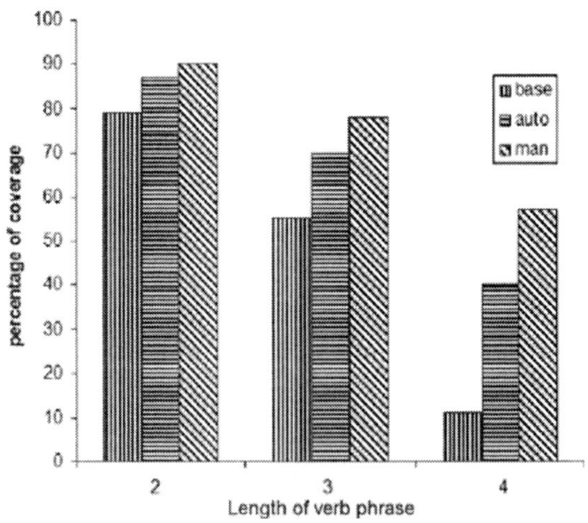

Figure 2: Coverage percentage for different settings

We claim that the manually and automatically

created verb phrase dictionaries add new data to the system and have a higher chance of finding a matching source verb phrase in a given corpus than our phrase based system. We verify this claim by extracting verb phrases from two test sets and searching for them in:

1. Baseline Phrase table
2. Base+Manual generated Dictionary
3. Base+Auto generated Dictionary

Figure 2 shows the ratio of the number of verbs phrases found in the three cases to the total number of verbs searched. We call this as coverage ratio. The verb phrases are divided based on their lengths. The plot clearly shows that the coverage increases considerably by the addition of these generated verb phrases which may or may not be seen in the training data, especially as the length of the verb phrase increases. Verb phrases of length 1 are not shown since the coverage was almost same for the 3 settings.

5.2 Machine translation Results

Table 3 shows the training data and the two test sets used for evaluation. The bilingual parallel data is split into training data and Test set 1. Test set 2 is a generic test set. All the data (training and test) used is predominately contains news. We report are results on BLEU (Papineni et al., 2002).

The verb phrase pairs were generated as explained in manual generation section and then added to the baseline system as a part of corpus(Base+manVPcorp). To emphasis on the improvement from generated verb phrases, an experiment where only the human translated verb phrases are added to the baseline corpus was also conducted(Base+humanVPcorp).

Table 4 shows the results on Moses - a state of the art phrase based system, and on a phrase based system (PBMT) similar to (Tillman et al., 2006) on test sets 1 and 2. Both systems were trained on 280k parallel sentences. On the in-domain data, we had an improvement of 4.8 BLEU points for Moses and 0.9 for PBMT. On the more generic test set, Moses gave a BLEU score improvement of 1.1 whereas the PBMT performance was comparable. One reason for this difference in the BLEU score jumps is the better alignments in the PBMT system, aligned by a maxent model as described in (Ittycheriah and Roukos, 2005). The PBMT system thus has a higher chances of having a good verb phrase in the baseline system than Moses and hence on adding generated verb phrases, we would see a lesser gain. Since the PBMT system had comparable results on the in-domain data with Moses and performed better on the out of domain (more generic) test set, the remaining experiments have been conducted with the PBMT system.

	Moses		**PBMT**	
	Set 1	Set2	Set 1	Set2
Baseline	13.5	08.6	13.4	**16.1**
Base+humanVPcorp	14.1	08.6	14.0	16.1
Base+manVPcorp	**18.3**	**9.7**	**14.3**	16.0

Table 4: BLEU score on test set 1 and 2 for different settings on moses and PBMT

Adding the generated phrases as a parallel corpus can alter the translation probabilities of individual words and sub-phrases. This is one of the reasons for no improvement in the bleu score of the PBMT system when the generated verb phrases are added as corpus. A better method would be to add the verb phrases directly to the phrase table. We added the manual dictionary to the PBMT system and the results are tabulated in table 5.

	Set 1	**Set2**
Baseline	13.4	16.1
Base+humanVP-PT	14.0	16.1
base+manVP-PT	**14.9**	**16.5**
base+autoVP-PT	14.8	16.3

Table 5: BLEU score for PBMT system after adding verb phrases directly to Phrase Table (PT)

Adding the verb phrases directly to the system keeps the rest of the phrases and their scores intact. Only phrases with matching source side phrase need to be re-normalized to adjust the translation probabilities. This would mean that the probability of only the verb phrases we add to the baseline phrase table would be affected while the rest of the translation model would be the same. Table 5 shows that addition of manually generated data to the phrase table(Base+manVP-PT), gives a good improvement of 1.5 points on the in-domain data and 0.4 on the out of domain data. A significant improvement of 1.4 BLEU points is seen even when the automatically generated verb phrases are added (Base+autoVP-PT), which was not seen when these were added as a corpus to the system.

Figure 3 shows the variation of BLEU score

with change in the corpus size. We should expect that the gain be higher in the case of low corpus size. However, note that the verb-pair list used to generate the verb phrases also changes with the change in corpus size, since decreasing the corpus size would decrease the quality of the overall alignments and the number of verbs seen. Thus, while the verb-pair list using 160k sentences had a total of 2499 verb pairs, the 20k corpus produced only 1347 verb pairs. So, for a smaller corpus size, the number of new verb phrases added to the table would also be lesser. This explains the rather constant gain in BLEU score throughout the graph.

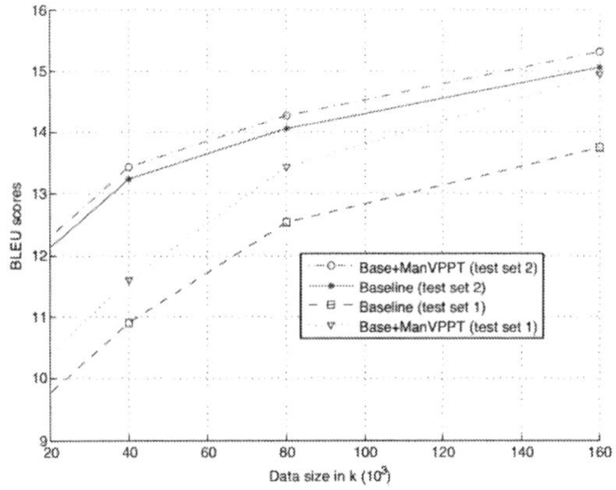

Figure 3: Change in BLEU for different corpus sizes

6 Conclusion and Future Work

We showed an improvement of up to 1.5 bleu points on the in domain data set and an improvement of 0.4 bleu on the generic test set. However, there are still some errors in respect to the morphology of the verb phrases, which the Language Model is unable to tackle. These are primarily the long range dependencies which includes determining the gender and number of the subject or object to get the appropriate inflection. Having a dynamic feature based system, which does not require rich morphological resources, and predicts the suffixes and inflections would be able to solve this problem. Also, when a verb has more than one meaning, the contextual information is not captured efficiently in the current method and often produces a more literal translation than the the reference.

Apart from adding the verb phrases to the phrase table, filtering of poor verb phrase pairs from the original phrase table is another approach to consider. The two methods together can give a higher boost to the translation than just one of them. A more language independent method of extraction of verb phrases also needs to be constructed, which does not require building language dependent stemmers and verb phrase chunkers.

References

Einat Minkov, Kristina Toutanova and Hisami Suzuki. 2007. *Generating Complex Morphology for Machine Translation,* in Proc. 45th Annual Meeting of the Association for Computational Linguistics, 2007, pp. 128-135.

Kristina Toutanova, Hisami Suzuki and Achim Ruopp 2008. *Applying Morphology Generation Models to Machine Translation,* in Proc. 46th Annual Meeting of the Association for Computational Linguistics, 2008.

D. Vilar, J. Peter, H. Ney, and L. F. Informatik 2007. *Can we translate letters?,* In Proceedings of Association Computational Linguistics Workshop on SMT, pages 33-39, 2007.

A. T. Freeman, S. L. Condon, and C. M. Ackerman 2006. *Cross linguistic name matching in english and arabic: a "one to many mapping" extension of the levenshtein edit distance algorithm.* , In Proceedings of the main conference on Human Language Technology, Conference of the North American Chapter of the Association of Computational Linguistics.

N Habash 2008. *Four techniques for online handling of out-of-vocabulary words in arabic-english statistical machine translation* , In Proceedings of Association for Computational Linguistics-08.

M. Popovic and H. Ney 2004. *Towards the use of word stems and suffixes for statistical machine translation,* In Proceedings of The International Conference on Language Resources and Evaluation.

M. Yang and K. Kirchhoff 2006 *Phrase-based backoff models for machine translation of highly inflected languages,* In Proceedings of the European Chapter of the ACL, pages 41-48, 2006.

Philipp Koehn, Franz Josef Och, Daniel Marcu. 2003. *Statistical Phrase-Based Translation,* In Proceedings of HLT-NAACL 2003.

Eleftherios Avramidis, Philipp Koehn 2008. *Enriching Morphologically Poor Languagesfor Statistical Machine Translation* , In Proceedings of ACL-08, HLT.

Ananthakrishnan Ramanathan and Durgesh Rao 2003. *A Lightweight Stemmer for Hindi 2003,* Workshop on Computational Linguistics for South-Asian Languages, EACL.

Ananthakrishnan Ramanathan, Pushpak Bhattacharyya, Jayprasad Hegde, Ritesh M. Shah., Sasikumar M 2007 *Simple Syntactic and Morphological Processing Can Help English-Hindi Statistical Machine Translation*, In Proceedings of International Joint Conference on Natural Language Processing,2007.

Christoph Tillman 2006 *Efficient Dynamic Programming Search Algorithms for Phrase-based SMT*, In Proceedings of the Workshop CHPSLP at HLT'06.

Minnen, G., J. Carroll and D. Pearce 2000 *Robust, applied morphological generation*, In Proceedings of the 1st International Natural Language Generation Conference, Mitzpe Ramon, Israel pp 201-208.

Abraham Ittycheriah and Salim Roukos 2005. *A maximum entropy word aligner for arabic-english machine translation*, In Proceedings of HLT/EMNLP, HLT-05, pages 89-96, Stroudsburg, PA, USA. Association for Computational Linguistics.

John Lafferty, Andrew McCallum, and Fernando Pereira 2002. *Conditional random fields: Probabilistic models for segmenting and labeling sequence data* , in Proc. International Conference on Machine Learning (ICML), 2001.

Papineni, K., Roukos, S., Ward, T., and Zhu, W. J. 2002. *BLEU: a method for automatic evaluation of machine translation* , in Proc. ACL-2002: 40th Annual meeting of the Association for Computational Linguistics pp. 311 - 318.

Japanese Pronunciation Prediction as Phrasal Statistical Machine Translation

Jun Hatori[1] **Hisami Suzuki**[2]
[1]Department of Computer Science, University of Tokyo
7-3-1 Hongo, Bunkyo, Tokyo 113-0033, Japan
[2]Microsoft Research / One Microsoft Way, Redmond, WA 98052, USA
hatori@is.s.u-tokyo.ac.jp hisamis@microsoft.com

Abstract

This paper addresses the problem of predicting the pronunciation of Japanese text. The difficulty of this task lies in the high degree of ambiguity in the pronunciation of Japanese characters and words. Previous approaches have either considered the task as a word-level classification problem based on a dictionary, which does not fare well in handling out-of-vocabulary (OOV) words; or solely focused on the pronunciation prediction of OOV words without considering the contextual disambiguation of word pronunciations in text. In this paper, we propose a unified approach within the framework of phrasal statistical machine translation (SMT) that combines the strengths of the dictionary-based and substring-based approaches. Our approach is novel in that we combine word- and character-based pronunciations from a dictionary within an SMT framework: the former captures the idiosyncratic properties of word pronunciation, while the latter provides the flexibility to predict the pronunciation of OOV words. We show that based on an extensive evaluation on various test sets, our model significantly outperforms the previous state-of-the-art systems, achieving around 90% accuracy in most domains.

1 Introduction

This paper[1] explores the problem of assigning pronunciation to Japanese text, which consists of a mixture of ideographic and phonetic characters. The task is naturally important for the text-to-speech application (Schroeter et al., 2002), and has been researched in that context as letter-to-phoneme conversion, which converts an orthographic character sequence into phonemes. In addition to speech applications, the task is also crucial for those languages such as Chinese and Japanese, where users generally type in the pronunciations of words, which are then converted into the desired character string via the software application called input methods (e.g. Gao et al. (2002a); Gao et al. (2002b)).

Predicting the pronunciation of Japanese text is particularly challenging because the word and character pronunciations are highly ambiguous. Japanese orthography employs four sets of characters: *hiragana* and *katakana* (called generally as *kana*), which are syllabary systems and thus phonemic; *kanji*, which is ideographic and consists of several thousand characters; and Roman alphabet. Out of these, kanji characters typically have multiple possible pronunciations[2]; especially those in frequent use tend to have many — between 5 and 10, sometimes as many as 20. This yields an exponential number of pronunciation possibilities when multiple kanji characters are combined in a word. Also, the pronunciation of a word is frequently idiosyncratic.

This idiosyncratic property of the word pronunciation naturally motivates us to take a dictionary-based approach. Traditionally, most approaches to Japanese pronunciation prediction have regarded the problem as a word pronunciation disambiguation task. Since there are no white spaces between words in Japanese text, these approaches first segment an input sentence/phrase into words, and then select a word-level pronunciation among those defined in a dictionary (Nagano et al., 2006; Neubig and Mori, 2010). For example, given a word "人気", these methods try to select the most appropriate pronunciation out of the three dictionary entries: *ninki* (popularity), *hitoke* (sign of life) and *jinki* (people's atmosphere), depending on the context. However, in these approaches, seg-

[1]This work was conducted during the first author's internship at Microsoft Research.

[2]In UniDic (Den et al., 2007), the average number of pronunciations per kanji character is 2.3.

mentation errors tend to result in the failure of the following step of pronunciation prediction. Moreover, since the dictionary-based approach is inapplicable to those words that are not in the dictionary, there needs to be a separate mechanism for handling out-of-vocabulary (OOV) words.

Nonetheless, the problem of OOV words has received little attention to date. Traditional systems either bypass this problem completely and assign no pronunciation to OOV words, as Mecab (Kudo et al., 2004), a Japanese morphological analyzer, does; or use a simple model to cover them (e.g. Neubig and Mori (2010) uses a noisy-channel model with a character bigram language model). Our previous work (Hatori and Suzuki, 2011) explicitly addresses the problem of predicting the pronunciation of OOV words, but focuses solely on predicting the pronunciation of nouns that are found in Wikipedia in isolation, and does not address the contextual disambiguation of pronunciation at the sentence level.

In this paper, we propose a unified approach based on the framework of phrasal statistical machine translation (SMT), addressing the whole sentence pronunciation assignment while integrating the OOV pronunciation prediction as part of the whole task. The novelty of our approach lies in using word and single-character pronunciations from a dictionary within the SMT framework: the former captures the idiosyncratic properties of word pronunciation, while the latter provides the flexibility to predict the pronunciation of OOV words based on the sequence of pronunciations at the substring level.

In addressing the pronunciation disambiguation problem within the framework of phrasal SMT, we extend the use of composed operations, which were applied in a limited manner in Hatori and Suzuki (2011). Within our dictionary-based model, the composed operations are able to incorporate the composition of dictionary words (i.e. phrases) as well as substrings of the character sequence (i.e. (partial) words). In this sense, our approach is more like a standard monotone phrasal SMT, rather than the substring-based string transduction. We also propose to use the joint n-gram model as a feature function, which has been proven to be effective in the letter-to-phoneme conversion task (Bisani and Ney, 2008; Jiampojamarn et al., 2010). In the context of our current task, this feature not only incorporates smoothed contextual information for the purpose of pronunciation disambiguation, but also captures the dependency between single-kanji pronunciations, which is effective for predicting the pronunciation of OOV words.

We collected an extensive evaluation set for the task, including newswire articles, search query logs, person names, and Wikipedia-derived instances. Using these test sets, we show that our model significantly outperforms the previous state-of-the-art systems, achieving around 90% accuracy in most test domains, which is the best known result on the task of Japanese pronunciation prediction to date. We also give a detailed analysis of the comparison of the proposed model with an SVM-based model, KyTea (Neubig and Mori, 2010), through which we hope to shed light on the remaining issues in solving this task.

2 Background

2.1 Pronunciation Prediction: Task Setting

We define the task of pronunciation prediction as converting a string of orthographic characters representing a sentence (or a word or phrase) into a sequence of hiragana, which corresponds to how the string is pronounced. For example, given a Japanese sentence "東京都美術館の狩野探幽展に行った。" ("I went to the Exhibition of Tanyu Kano at the Tokyo Metropolitan Art Museum."), the system is expected to output a sequence of hiragana, "とうきょうとびじゅつかんのかのうたんゆうてんにいった。", pronounced as *tookyoo to bijutsukan no kanoo tanyuu ten ni itta*. The task involves two sub-problems: (a) contextual disambiguation of a word pronunciation, e.g., 行った can be pronounced either as いった *itta* "went" or おこなった *okonatta* "did" depending on the context; (b) pronunciation prediction of OOV words, e.g., in the above example, 狩野探幽展 ("the Exhibition of Tanyu Kano") is not likely to be in the dictionary, so the pronunciation must be reasonably guessed based on the possible pronunciations of individual characters.

2.2 Related Work

Our research on pronunciation prediction is inspired by previous research on string transduction. The most directly relevant is the work on letter-to-phoneme conversion. Previous approaches to this task include joint n-gram models (e.g., Bisani and Ney (2002); Chen (2003); Bisani and Ney (2008)) and discriminatively trained substring-based models (e.g., Jiampojamarn et al. (2007); Jiampojamarn et al. (2008)). This task is typically evaluated at the word level, and therefore does not include contextual disambiguation.

Similar techniques to the letter-to-phoneme task

have also been widely applied to the transliteration task (Knight and Graehl (1998)). The most relevant to the current task include an approach based on substring operations in the SMT framework (e.g., Sherif and Kondrak (2007), Cherry and Suzuki (2009)), and those that use joint n-gram estimation method for the task of transliteration (e.g., Li et al. (2004); Jiampojamarn et al. (2010)). However, similarly to the letter-to-phoneme task, the contextual disambiguation of the words has not received much attention.

The task of Japanese pronunciation prediction itself has been a topic of investigation. Sumita and Sugaya (2006) proposed a method to use the web for assigning word pronunciation, but their focus is limited to the pronunciation disambiguation of known proper nouns. Kurata et al. (2007) and Sasada et al. (2009) discuss the methods of disambiguating new word pronunciation candidates using speech data. Nagano et al. (2006) and Mori et al. (2010b) investigated the use of the joint n-gram estimation to this task.

More recently, Neubig and Mori (2010) proposed a classifier-based system called KyTea, which is one of the current state-of-the-art systems for the task of Japanese pronunciation prediction. As we use this system as one of our baseline systems, we describe this work in some detail here. KyTea exploits an SVM-based two-step approach, which performs a word segmentation step, followed by a pronunciation disambiguation step for each word segment. In the pronunciation prediction step, if the word in question exists in the dictionary, KyTea uses character and character-type n-grams within a window as features for the SVM classifier. For OOV words, a simple OOV model based on a noisy channel model with a character bigram language model is used. While KyTea uses the discriminative indicator features, our model instead uses character/joint n-gram language models and composed operations (to be explained in Section 3.3.2) to capture the context for the purpose of pronunciation disambiguation. The use of the indicator features essentially requires probabilistic optimization of a large number of weights, making the training less scalable than our model, which only requires frequencies of operations and phrases in the training data.

In our previous work (Hatori and Suzuki, 2011), we addressed the pronunciation prediction of Japanese words in a semi-supervised, substring-based framework, using word-pronunciation pairs automatically extracted from Wikipedia. Though we obtained more than 70% accuracy on Wikipedia data, the model is quite specific to handling the noun phrases in Wikipedia, and it is not clear if the approach can handle the pronunciation assignment of a general text, which includes the pronunciation prediction and disambiguation of the words of all types at the sentence level. Since our current work is an extension of this approach, we also adopt our previous work as one of our baseline models in Section 4.4.

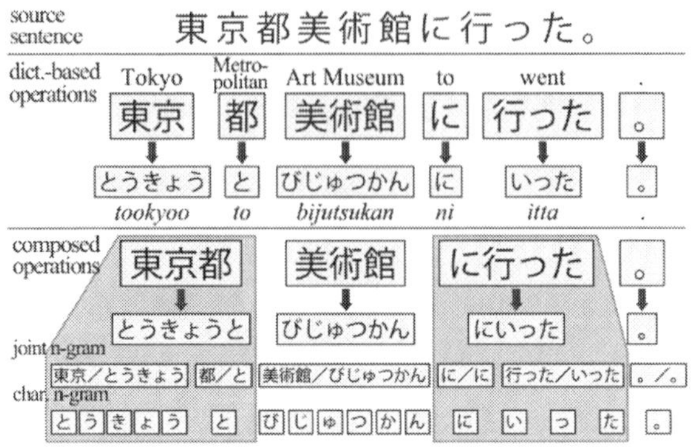

Figure 1: Overview of the model.

3 Pronunciation Prediction Model

This section describes our phrasal SMT-based approach to pronunciation prediction, which is an extension of our previous work (Hatori and Suzuki, 2011). We assume that the task of translating a Japanese orthography string to a hiragana string is basically monotone and without insertion or deletion. The overview of our model is given in Figure 1. The components of the model will be explained below.

3.1 Training and Decoding

As is widely used in SMT research (Och, 2003), we adopt a discriminative learning framework that uses component generative models as real-valued features (Cherry and Suzuki, 2009). Given the source sequence s and the target character sequence t, we define real-valued features over s and t, $f_i(s,t)$ for $i \in \{1,\ldots,n\}$. The score of a sequence pair $\langle s,t\rangle$ is given by the inner product of the weight vector $\boldsymbol{\lambda} = (\lambda_1,\ldots,\lambda_n)$ and the feature vector $\mathbf{f}(s,t)$.

For the training of model parameters, we use the averaged perceptron (Collins and Roark, 2004): given a training corpus of transduction derivations, each of which describes a word/substring operation sequence converting s into t, the perceptron iteratively updates the weight vector every time it encounters an instance for which the model outputs a wrong sequence. For decoding, we use a

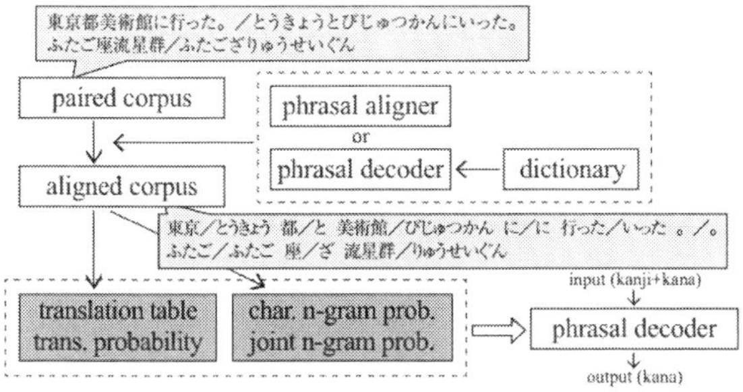

Figure 2: Overview of the training.

stack decoder (Zens and Ney, 2004).

3.2 Features

For our baseline model features, we first use those from Hatori and Suzuki (2011): the bidirectional translation probabilities, $P(t|s)$ and $P(s|t)$, the target character n-gram probability, $P(t)$, the target character count, and the phrase count. In addition, we incorporate the joint n-gram probability, $P(s,t)$, as a feature (described in Section 3.2.1). The estimation of the translation and joint/character n-gram probabilities requires a set of training corpus with source and target alignment at the word/substring level. Once these probabilities have been estimated by using the frequency of (the sequences of) operations in the training set, we only need a small tuning set to adjust the feature weights of the model. This makes online training and domain adaptation easy, and makes our model more scalable compared to fully discriminative systems with indicator features, such as KyTea.

3.2.1 Joint n-gram Language Model Feature

Motivated by the success in the transliteration task (Jiampojamarn et al., 2010), we incorporate the joint n-gram language model into our SMT-based framework. The joint n-gram sequence is the sequence of operations used in the transduction: for example, when a paired sentence "床屋に行く／とこやにいく" is decomposed into three operations "床屋→とこや, に→に, 行く→いく", the corresponding joint n-gram sequence is "⟨ 床屋, とこや ⟩ ⟨ に, に ⟩ ⟨ 行く, いく ⟩". The effectiveness of this feature is confirmed in our experiments in Section 5.2.

3.3 Translation Table

The corpora we use are a collection of pairs of a Japanese sentence and its hiragana sequence, as described as "paired corpus" in Figure 2. These are just like bilingual corpora if we regard the hiragana sequence as monotonically translated from Japanese text. Since the original corpora do not have any word segmentation or word/substring alignments, we first need to obtain them to construct the translation table for the decoder. In previous work, KyTea used a corpus that is manually aligned using words as a unit of alignment, while Hatori and Suzuki (2011) used an unsupervised substring-based alignment. The former is not scalable easily, while the latter cannot take advantage of existing dictionaries. In this work, we use a novel application of dictionary-based phrasal decoder in order to create an aligned corpus, which allows us to use dictionary information while learning substring-based alignments for handling OOV pronunciation prediction.

3.3.1 Dictionary-based model

In the dictionary-based model we propose, alignments are obtained using a phrasal decoder which is based on a dictionary. This essentially treats the dictionary entries as the minimal unit of substring operations, instead of using single-kanji pronunciations estimated from training corpora as in the case of the substring-based model (Hatori and Suzuki, 2011). We first build a simple dictionary-based decoder with only two features: the forward translation probability and the phrase count; and then use it to decode a paired corpus to obtain the alignments between the source and target strings. In this process, instances including any operation that is not defined in the dictionary are discarded; this is a major difference with the substring-based model of Hatori and Suzuki (2011), which uses all instances of training data.

Since Japanese dictionaries typically include single-kanji entries as well as word entries[3], dictionary-based substring operations actually consist of both single-kanji (that is not a word per se) and word pronunciations. This is why our dictionary-based model is still able to handle OOV words. We show in Section 5 that the benefit of removing noisy training samples by this process outweighs the risk of discarding infrequent or non-standard pronunciations that do not exist in the dictionary.

3.3.2 Composed operations

Our previous work (Hatori and Suzuki, 2011) exploits composed operations in order to include local contextual information in the substring-based model. Given a paired corpus, they use an aligner to obtain single-character alignments, which maps

[3]This is because each kanji character is a morpheme representing a meaning, and is worth an entry in dictionaries.

one kanji to one or more kana characters, which are then composed into larger operations. This procedure makes it possible to obtain longer alignments with limited memory, rather than using the source phrase length larger than one. In the current work, we extend the use of composed operations so that they work properly with the joint n-gram estimation.

The composed operations are beneficial for capturing contextual information. For example, the phrase "行った" can be pronounced in two ways: *itta* "went" and *okonatta* "did", which cannot be distinguished without any context. However, if this phrase is preceded by a hiragana particle に *ni* "to", we can assume that the correct pronunciation is most likely *itta*, because the pronunciation *ni okonatta* is unusual (行った *okonatta* is seldom preceded by に *ni*). The composed operations are also useful in capturing the pronunciation of compound nouns: for example, due to the phonological process called *rendaku* (sequential voicing) (Vance, 1987), 食器-棚 "plate rack" is pronounced as *shokki-dana*, while the components of this word are individually pronounced as *shokki* ("plate") and *tana* ("rack"). By considering the compositions of operations, we can capture the pronunciation in the context of a compound word. Our phrasal decoder considers all (i.e. composed and non-composed) operations during the decoding, but longer (composed) operations are generally preferred when available because the phrase count feature usually receives a negative weight.

However, the simultaneous use of these operations of different size may cause a problem when the joint n-gram estimation is applied: because composed operations include multiple non-composed operations, they break the independence assumption of n-gram occurrences in the language model. For example, given a parallel phrase "展覧会に行った／てんらんかいにいった" (went to an exhibition), which is decomposed into "展覧会／てんらんかい, に／に, 行った／いった" by dictionary-based alignments, the joint n-gram language model expects that the occurrence of "に／に" (non-composed operation) is independent of that of "に-行った／に-いった" (composed operation), but this is not the case. To avoid this, we let the model retain the original operations even after they are composed. As shown in Figure 1, even after the two operations "に→に" and "行った→いった" are merged into a composed operation "に-行った→に-いった", the joint n-gram probability is still estimated based on the original (non-composed) operations. For efficiency purposes, we only retain the decomposition of the first appearance of each composed operation even if multiple different decompositions are possible.

4 Experiments

4.1 Dictionary

In the dictionary-based framework, we need a dictionary based on which we obtain the alignments. We use a combination of three dictionaries: UniDic (Den et al., 2007), Iwanami Dictionary, and an in-house dictionary that was available to us of unknown origin. UniDic is a dictionary resource available for research purposes, which is updated on a regular basis and includes 625k word forms as of the version 1.3.12 release (July 2009). Iwanami Dictionary consists of 107k words, which expands into 325k surface forms after considering *okurigana* (verb inflectional ending) variants. The in-house dictionary consists of a total of 226k words and single-kanji pronunciations. After removing duplicates, the combined dictionary consists of 770k entries. Note that these dictionaries are also used as part of training data.

4.2 Training and Test Data

As described in Section 3, we need word/substring-aligned parallel corpora to train the models. We used three different sources of training data in our experiments. First, following Hatori and Suzuki (2011), we used Wikipedia: following the heuristics described in the paper, we extracted about 460k noisy word-pronunciation pairs from Japanese Wikipedia articles as of January 24, 2010. Of these pairs, we set aside 3k instances for use in development and evaluation, and used the rest for training (referred to as "Wiki-Train"). Secondly, since word-pronunciation pairs extracted from Wikipedia are noisy[4] and mostly consist of noun phrases, we also used a newspaper corpus, which is comprised of 1.4m sentence pairs, referred to as "News-Train". Finally, for the comparison with KyTea, we use a publicly available corpus, the Balanced Corpus of Contemporary Written Japanese (Maekawa (2008)). Specifically, we use the 2009 Core Data of this corpus, which consists of 37k sentences annotated with pronunciations (referred to as "BCCWJ").

Our test data consist of six datasets from various domains. Table 1 shows the statistics of these corpora, with the OOV rate estimated using KyTea[5]

[4]We have found that roughly 10% of these instances are invalid word-pronunciation pairs.

[5]We ran KyTea 0.13 with the built-in default model. For

Test set	#Instance	Avg. len.	OOV rate
News-1 (N1)	867	51.8	0.3%
News-2 (N2)	739	44.9	0.3%
Query-1 (Q1)	1,049	3.8	3.5%
Query-2 (Q2)	3,078	5.7	12.7%
Name (PN)	9,170	3.0	23.4%
Wiki (WP)	2,000	4.1	13.7%

Table 1: Statistics of test sets, where "Avg. len." is the average length of an instance in the number of characters.

- **News-1**(N1) and **News-2**(N2): collections of newswire articles available as Microsoft Research IME Corpus (Suzuki and Gao, 2005). These articles are from different newspapers from the news corpus we used in training. In preparing these test sets, instances including Arabic and kanji numerals (0,1,⋯,9, 〇, 一,⋯, 九), or Roman alphabets are excluded[6].
- **Query-1**(Q1) and **Query-2**(Q2): query logs from a search engine (source undisclosed for blind reviewing). These sets consist of various instances ranging from general noun phrases to relatively new proper nouns.
- **Name**(PN): a collection of difficult-to-pronounce words, mostly consisting of person names.
- **Wiki**(WP): manually-cleaned word-pronunciation pairs from Wikipedia, which consists mostly of proper nouns including names of people and locations as well as terms that are difficult to pronounce.

For the tuning of the weights of the model, we used 200 held-out instances for each test domain, except that the development set of Query-1 is also used for the tuning for Query-2, and the set of Wiki is used for the tuning for Name.

4.3 Experimental settings

We use our original implementation of the phrasal aligner and decoder, which is also used as our implementation of the substring-based model of Hatori and Suzuki (2011). An ITG-based aligner with EM algorithm (Zhang et al., 2008) is used with monotonic setting; we set the source (kanji) and target (kana) phrase length limits to 1 and 4, and prohibit alignments to a null symbol in either source or target side. The decoder runs with the beam size of 20. The maximum number of composed operations is 4 for the substring-based model of Hatori and Suzuki (2011), and 3 for the proposed dictionary-based model. In the substring-based model, character 5-gram and joint 4-gram language models with Kneser-Ney smoothing and the BoS (beginning-of-string) and EoS (end-of-string) symbols are used; in the dictionary-based model, character 5-gram and joint 3-gram models with the same settings are used. We did not use the infrequent operation cutoff. All of these parameters and settings are set based on the preliminary experiments. As the evaluation measure, we use instance-level accuracy, which is calculated based on the percentage of the outputs that exactly match the gold standard: instances correspond to sentences in News-1/2, and to words or phrases in all other test domains. The statistical significance of the results is given using McNemar's test.

4.4 Baseline Models

We describe three baseline models that we use as reference in our experiment.

- **Mecab**: *Mecab* version 0.98[7], which is the state-of-the-art morphological analyzer for Japanese that also outputs pronunciations of words (Kudo et al., 2004), with the off-the-shelf IPA Dictionary containing 392k word entries provided at the author's page.
- **KyTea**: *KyTea* version 0.13[8], which is described in Section 2.2. In our comparison experiment, we run KyTea version 0.13 both as is (using their pre-trained model), and as trained by us to allow the comparison of the framework using the same publicly available training data.
- **HS11**: *HS11* is our reimplementation of the substring-based model by Hatori and Suzuki (2011), which was shown to outperform the substring-based joint trigram model on a Wikipedia test set.

5 Results and Discussion

5.1 Main Results

Table 2 shows the performance of the proposed model along with various baseline models. The first two lines are the result of the off-the-shelf, pre-trained systems. Mecab achieves around or above 80% accuracy on five out of six test sets, although the result on Wiki is below 60% because

News-1/2, the OOV rate in the table is the OOV word rate based on the KyTea's output. For the other test sets, the figures show the rate of the instances (words or phrases) that contain any OOV word, again based on the KyTea's output

[6]This is because there exist different standards in how to pronounce them. For example, the literal pronunciation is preferred for text-to-speech applications, whereas just outputting numerals as such suits better for the training of Japanese input methods.

[7]http://mecab.sourceforge.net/

[8]http://www.phontron.com/kytea/

Model	N1	N2	Q1	Q2	PN	WP
Mecab	78.8	79.7	88.0	79.8	79.8	55.9
KyTea	83.6	85.9	92.9	85.6	52.9	62.9
HS11	23.3	31.8	87.7	73.3	83.9	64.5
HS11+	37.6	31.8	93.3	82.7	90.5	**72.9**
Proposed	**89.7**	**88.6**	**95.5**	**87.8**	**92.9**	70.2

Table 2: Instance-level accuracy (in %) of pronunciation prediction models. The upper two models use the off-the-shelf models; the lower three models are trained using the same resources: Wiki-Train, News-Train, and the combined dictionary.

the system does not have a mechanism to handle OOV words. The second row shows the result of KyTea using the off-the-shelf "full SVM model"[9], which is trained on several resources including BCCWJ and UniDic. It generally does better than Mecab, but the accuracies on the high OOV rate domains (i.e. Name and Wiki) are still quite low.

The bottom three models are all trained with the same resources: Wiki-Train and News-Train with all the three dictionaries. "HS11" is the substring-based model proposed by Hatori and Suzuki (2011), while "HS11+" is the model enhanced with two additional features: the joint n-gram feature (as described in Section 3.2), and the dictionary feature, whose value is the total length (in souce characters) of words matching any dictionary entry.[10] By comparing these two models, the effectiveness of these features over the model "HS11" is quite clear. However, the accuracy is below 40% on newswire test sets, where each instance is a full sentence. We assume that this is because the substring-based model cannot capture the contextual information that is broad enough, and also is easily affected by noise in the training data. Our proposed model, corresponding to the last line in the table, overcomes this problem and achives the best accuracy in all but one test domain (Wiki), showing the effectiveness and robustness of the dictionary-based approach. We lags behind "HS11+" on Wiki, probably because the dictionary-based model discards many operations that are uncommon, but are still useful for the pronunciation of OOV words in Wikipedia.

Table 3 shows the direct comparison between KyTea and the proposed model trained[11] with exactly the same datasets: BCCWJ, Wiki-Train, and UniDic, all of which are from publicly available resources. Whereas "KyTea (w/noise)" uses all the instances for training, "KyTea (wo/noise)" uses only the instances that are filtered using dictionary-based operations[12]. Note that this cleaning process is also a novel contribution of our work. As is observed from Table 3, this cleaning process resulted in a large improvement in accuracy, with the exception of the Name and Wiki sets. After inspecting the errors manually, we have found that this is because the UniDic-based operations do not include many single-kanji pronunciations that are commonly used in person's names, such as "美 *mi*" and "人 *to*". However, this problems seems negligible when a larger dictionary including common pronunciations for person's names is available. In the comparison in Table 2, where the models use a combination of three dictionaries, the dictionary-based model "Proposed" performs better than the substring-based model "HS11+" even on the Name set.

Model	N1	N2	Q1	Q2	PN	WP
KyTea (w/noise)	68.5	65.3	88.0	79.5	**67.9**	**65.8**
KyTea (wo/noise)	**75.3**	**75.5**	91.5	83.4	61.7	64.1
Proposed	73.8	75.4	**92.8**†	**84.9**†	62.8	64.3

Table 3: Instance-level accuracy (in %) of the models trained on Wiki-Train and BCCWJ with UniDic. "$\dagger$" denotes a statistically-significant ($p < 0.01$) difference between "KyTea (wo/noise)" and "Proposed".

Overall, the proposed model outperforms "KyTea (wo/noise)" in four out of six test sets, and the differences in the remaining two sets (News-1/2) are not statistically significant. Considering also that the training data is relatively small in this comparison experiment[13], we can conclude that our model has at least a comparable performance to KyTea for the task of pronunciation disambiguation, while achieving a superior performance on the task of pronunciation prediction for OOV words. A manual analysis of the results also showed that our model indeed has an advantage in outputting phonetically natural pronunciation sequences, partially resolving problems related to *on/kun*[14] and *rendaku*, as in 契約-切れ *keiyaku-*

[9]We could not train KyTea with the same dataset as the proposed model uses due to memory limitation.

[10]The dictionary is also used as the training data.

[11]Our training of KyTea is performed as follows: we first train a segmentation model for KyTea using BCCWJ and UniDic, and use this model to segment the substring-aligned Wiki-Train instances to obtain a corpus with consistent segmentation, which is then used to train the final model.

[12]27.6% of the instances in Wiki-Train is filtered out. This percentage is larger than the noise rate of 10% in this corpus, which Hatori and Suzuki (2011) reported, because the sole use of UniDic does not cover many single-kanji pronunciations, as mentioned later in this paragraph.

[13]Since the translation probabilities in our model are based on unregularized frequency, our model is less powerful with small training data, while it is more scalable.

[14]Pronunciations of kanji are classified into *on* and *kun* pronunciations (corresponding to their origin, Chinese and

Model	N1	N2	Q1	Q2	PN	WP
Proposed (D)	89.7	88.6	95.5	87.8	92.9	70.2
- wo/joint n-gram	-5.5	-3.3	-1.5	-3.8	-4.4	-4.2
- wo/composed op.	-3.9	-4.0	-2.6	-1.2	-1.8	-2.9

Table 4: Feature ablation results for the dictionary-based model trained with Wiki-Train, News-Train and the combined dictionary. All the losses in accuracy were statistically significant ($p < 0.01$).

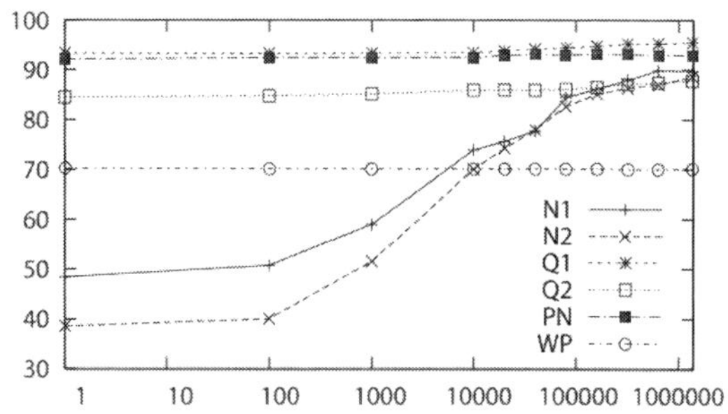

Figure 3: Performance (accuracy in %) of the proposed model with respect to the log of the number of additional training sentences from News-Train.

gire (individually pronounced as *keiyaku* and *kire*; "contract expiration"). Although KyTea wrongly output *keiyaku-kire* to this instance, the proposed model was able to output the correct pronunciation by learning that the pronunciation of 切れ tends to be *gire* after the pronunciation *ku*, from other instances such as 句-切れ *ku-gire* (segments in haiku). On the other hand, KyTea is better at capturing generalized context by using a character-type feature, resolving instances such as "ブランド-米" (katakana + *mai*; "brand rice"), while the proposed model wrongly output the most frequent pronunciation *bei* for 米.

5.2 Feature Ablation Experiments

Table 4 shows the results of the feature ablation experiment of the proposed model. As we mentioned in Section 3.2.1, the advantage of the joint n-gram language model is twofold: incorporating smoothed context into word pronunciation disambiguation (which is the dominant problem in News-1/2), as well as incorporating single-kanji pronunciation dependencies into pronunciation prediction for OOV words (considered to be common in Name and Wiki). The improvement observed in these domains suggests that the joint n-gram probability successfully captured these two aspects. The use of composed operations showed large improvement particularly on News-1/2, proving its utility for the pronunciation disambiguation aspect of this task.

5.3 Data Ablation Experiments

Figure 3 shows the performance of the proposed model with respect to the number of News-Train sentences used for training. In this experiment, the model is first trained only with Wiki-Train; then, sentences from News-Train are incrementally added. This can be seen as a process for adapting a word-based model to a fully sentential, disambiguation-capable model. As expected, the accuracy is consistently improved in the news domain as more sentences are added, while the accuracy remains almost unchanged in the rest of the domains, without showing any negative effect by the additional out-of-domain training data. These results suggest that our model is robust and can adapt to new domains with a simple addition of training data.

6 Conclusion

We have presented a unified approach to the task of Japanese pronunciation prediction. Based on the framework of phrasal SMT, our model seamlessly and robustly integrates the task of word pronunciation disambiguation and pronunciation prediction for OOV words. Its basic components are trained in an unsupervised manner, and work in the presence of noise in training data. The model also has potential to adapt to a new domain when additional training data is available. We have performed an extensive evaluation on various test sets, and showed that our model achieves the new state-of-the-art accuracy on the task of Japanese pronunciation prediction.

Looking into the future, we would like to see if the proposed model is effective in a general task of transliteration within a sentential context, which is conceivable as an application of phonetic input (e.g., inputting Arabic using Roman text and converting it automatically into Arabic scripts). On the task of Japanese pronunciation prediction, we are also interested in incorporating class-based features, such as character type information and on/kun dependencies, by using both existing resources and clustering methods.

Acknowledgement

We are grateful to Graham Neubig for providing us with detailed information on KyTea, and to anonymous reviewers for useful comments.

Japanese), each of which tends to be used consecutively.

References

Maximilian Bisani and Hermann Ney. 2002. Investigations on joint-multigram models for grapheme-to-phoneme conversion. In *Proceedings of the International Conference on Spoken Language Processing*.

Maximilian Bisani and Hermann Ney. 2008. Joint-sequence models for grapheme-to-phoneme conversion. *Speech Communication*, 50:434–451.

Stanley F. Chen. 2003. Conditional and joint models for grapheme-to-phoneme conversion. In *Proceedings of the European Conference on Speech Communication and Technology*.

Colin Cherry and Hisami Suzuki. 2009. Discriminative substring decoding for transliteration. In *EMNLP*.

Michael Collins and Brian Roark. 2004. Incremental parsing with the perceptron algorithm. In *ACL*.

Yasuharu Den, Toshinobu Ogiso, Hideki Ogura, Atsushi Yamada, Nobuaki Minematsu, Kiyotaka Uchimoto, and Hanae Koiso. 2007. The development of an electronic dictionary for morphological analysis and its application to Japanese corpus linguistics (in Japanese). *Japanese linguistics*, 22:101–122.

Jianfeng Gao, Mingjing Li, Joshua T. Goodman, and Kai-Fu Lee. 2002a. Toward a unified approach to statistical language modeling for chinese. *ACM Transactions on Asian Language Information Processing*, 1:3–33.

Jianfeng Gao, Hisami Suzuki, and Yang Wen. 2002b. Exploiting headword dependency and predictive clustering for language modeling. In *EMNLP*.

Jun Hatori and Hisami Suzuki. 2011. Predicting word pronunciation in Japanese. In *CICLing 2011, Lecture Notes in Computer Science (6609)*, pages 477–492. Springer.

Sittichai Jiampojamarn, Grzegorz Kondrak, and Tarek Sherif. 2007. Applying many-to-many alignments and hidden markov models to letter-to-phoneme conversion. In *HLT-NAACL*.

Sittichai Jiampojamarn, Colin Cherry, and Grzegorz Kondrak. 2008. Joint processing and discriminative training for letter-to-phoneme conversion. In *ACL*.

Sittichai Jiampojamarn, Colin Cherry, and Grzegorz Kondrak. 2010. Integrating joint n-gram features into a discriminative training framework. In *NAACL*.

Kevin Knight and Jonathan Graehl. 1998. Machine transliteration. *Computational Linguistics*, 24.

Taku Kudo, Kaoru Yamamoto, and Yuji Matsumoto. 2004. Appliying conditional random fields to Japanese morphological analysis. In *EMNLP*.

Gakuto Kurata, Shinsuke Mori, Nobuyasu Itoh, and Masafumi Nishimura. 2007. Unsupervised lexicon acquisition from speech and text. In *Proceedings of ICASSP-2007*.

Haizhou Li, Min Zhang, and Jian Su. 2004. A joint source-channel model for machine transliteration. In *ACL*.

Kikuo Maekawa. 2008. Compilation of the KOTONOHA-BCCWJ corpus (in Japanese). *Nihongo no kenkyu (Studies in Japanese)*, 4:82–95.

Shinsuke Mori, Tetsuro Sasada, and Graham Neubig. 2010b. Language model estimation from a stochastically tagged corpus (in Japanese). *Technical Report, SIG, Information Processing Society of Japan*.

Tohru Nagano, Shinsuke Mori, and Masafumi Nishimura. 2006. An n-gram-based approach to phoneme and accent estimation for tts (in Japanese). *Transactions of Information Processing Society of Japan*, 47:1793–1801.

Graham Neubig and Shinsuke Mori. 2010. Word-based partial annotation for efficient corpus construction. In *Proceedings of the Seventh International Conference on Language Resources and Evaluation (LREC 2010)*.

Franz Josef Och. 2003. Minimum error rate training for statistical machine translation. In *ACL*.

Tetsuro Sasada, Shinsuke Mori, and Tatsuya Kawahara. 2009. Domain adaptation of statistical kana–kanji conversion system by automatic acquisition of contextual information with unknown words (in Japanese). In *Proceedings of the 15th Annual Meeting of the Association for Natural Language Processing*.

Juergen Schroeter, Alistair Conkie, Ann Syrdal, Mark Beutnagel, Matthias Jilka, Volker Strom, Yeon-Jun Kim, Hong-Goo Kang, and David Kapilow. 2002. A perspective on the next challenges for TTS research. In *Proceedings of the IEEE 2002 Workshop on Speech Synthesis*.

Tarek Sherif and Grzegorz Kondrak. 2007. Substring-based transliteration. In *ACL*.

Eiichiro Sumita and Fumiaki Sugaya. 2006. Word pronunciation disambiguation using the web. In *NAACL*.

Hisami Suzuki and Jianfeng Gao. 2005. Microsoft Research IME Corpus. MSR Technical Report No. 2005-168.

Timothy J. Vance. 1987. *An Introduction to Japanese Phonology*. State University of New York Press.

Richard Zens and Hermann Ney. 2004. Improvements in phrase-based statistical machine translation. In *HLT-NAACL*.

Hao Zhang, Chris Quirk, Robert C. Moore, and Daniel Gildea. 2008. Bayesian learning of non-compositional phrases with synchronous parsing. In *ACL*.

Comparing Two Techniques for Learning Transliteration Models Using a Parallel Corpus

Hassan Sajjad **Nadir Durrani** **Helmut Schmid** **Alexander Fraser**
Institute for Natural Language Processing
University of Stuttgart
{sajjad,durrani,schmid,fraser}@ims.uni-stuttgart.de

Abstract

We compare the use of an unsupervised transliteration mining method and a rule-based method to automatically extract lists of transliteration word pairs from a parallel corpus of Hindi/Urdu. We build joint source channel models on the automatically aligned orthographic transliteration units of the automatically extracted lists of transliteration pairs resulting in two transliteration systems. We compare our systems with three transliteration systems available on the web, and show that our systems have better performance. We perform an extensive analysis of the results of using both methods and show evidence that the unsupervised transliteration mining method is superior for applications requiring high recall transliteration lists, while the rule-based method is useful for obtaining high precision lists.

1 Introduction

Urdu and Hindi are closely related languages which have a similar phonological, semantic and syntactic structure. Hindi is derived from Sanskrit and Urdu is a mixture of Persian, Arabic, Turkish and Sanskrit. Both share closed class vocabulary which they inherit from Sanskrit. They differ however in the open class vocabulary and in the writing script used. Hindi is written in Devanagari script and borrows most of the open class vocabulary from Sanskrit. Urdu is written in Perso-Arabic script and borrows most of the open class vocabulary from Persian, Arabic, Turkish and Sanskrit. Both languages have lived together for centuries and now share a large part of their vocabulary with each other. In an initial study on a small parallel corpus, we found that both languages share approximately 82% (tokens) and 62% (types) of the vocabulary. Transliterating overlapping words will help to bridge the scripting gap between Hindi and Urdu. The remaining words must be converted into the other language with a bilingual dictionary which is beyond the scope of this work.

In this paper, the term *transliteration pair* refers to a word pair where the words are transliterations of each other and the term *transliteration unit* refers to a character pair where the characters are transliterations of each other. We are interested in building joint source channel models for transliteration. Because we do not have a list of transliteration pairs to use as training data in building such a transliteration model, we use two methods to extract the list of transliteration pairs from a parallel corpus of Hindi/Urdu. The first method uses the transliteration mining algorithm of Sajjad et al. (2011) to automatically extract transliteration pairs. This approach does not use any language specific knowledge. The second method uses handcrafted transliteration rules specific to the mapping between Hindi and Urdu to extract transliteration pairs. We automatically align the two lists of extracted transliteration pairs at the character level and learn two transliteration models. We compare the results with three other transliteration systems. Both of our transliteration systems perform better than the other systems.

The 1-best output of the transliteration system built on the list extracted using the rule-based method is better than the 1-best output of the system built on the automatically extracted list. The rule-based extraction method is focused on obtaining a high precision list as compared to the automatic method which obtains a higher recall list. The 10-best and 20-best output of the transliteration system built on the automatically extracted list is better than the N-best outputs of the system built on the list extracted using the rule-based method. The wide coverage of transliteration units in the automatically extracted list helps the transliteration system to produce difficult transliterations which are hard to learn using the rule-based list.

The transliteration task between Hindi and Urdu is non-trivial. The missing short vowels in the writing of Urdu and a missing short vowel in the writing of Hindi are a particular problem, and we identify other areas of difficulty. We provide a detailed error analysis to account for the complexities in Hindi to Urdu transliteration motivated by linguistic phenomena.

The paper is organized as follows. Previous work on transliteration is summarized in Section 2. The two methods used to extract lists of transliteration pairs are described in Section 3. The joint probability model for transliteration is explained in Section 4. The evaluation and the results in comparison with three other transliteration systems are presented in Section 5. A detailed discussion and error analysis is presented in Section 6. Section 7 concludes.

2 Previous Work

Transliteration can be done with phoneme-based or grapheme-based models. Knight and Graehl (1998), Stalls and Knight (1998), Al-Onaizan and Knight (2002) and Pervouchine et al. (2009) use the phoneme-based approach for transliteration. Kashani et al. (2007) and Al-Onaizan and Knight (2002) use a grapheme-based model to transliterate from Arabic into English. Al-Onaizan and Knight (2002) compare a grapheme-based approach, a phoneme-based approach and a linear combination of both for transliteration. They build a conditional probability model. The grapheme-based model performs better than the phoneme-based model and the hybrid model. This motivates our use of grapheme-based models.

In this paper, we use a grapheme-based approach for transliteration from Hindi to Urdu. The phoneme-based approach would involve the conversion of Hindi and Urdu text into a phonemic representation which is not a trivial task as the short vowel 'a' is not written in Hindi text and no short vowels are written in Urdu text. The difficulty of this additional step would be likely to lead to additional errors.

Malik et al. (2008) and Malik et al. (2009) work on transliteration from Hindi to Urdu and Urdu to Hindi respectively. They use the rules of SAMPA (Speech Assessment Methods Phonetic Alphabets) and X-SAMPA[1] to develop a phoneme-based mapping scheme between Urdu and Hindi (J C. Wells, 1995).

Hindi	SAMPA	Urdu			
ज़	z	ز	ض	ظ	ذ
स	s	س	ص	ث	
ह	h	ہ	ھ	ح	
त	t_d	ت	ط		

Table 1: Ambiguous Hindi characters (characters which can transliterate to many different Urdu characters)

Malik et al. (2008) reported an accuracy of 97.9% for transliterating Hindi to Urdu. However, this number is not comparable to ours. Some Hindi characters can be ambiguously transliterated to several Urdu characters (see Table 1). Malik et al. (2008) do not deal with these ambiguous characters and count any occurrence of an ambiguous character as a correct transliteration in all scenarios. We discuss this further in Section 6.

In the previous work, a transliteration system is built on transliteration units learned either automatically from a list of transliteration pairs (Li et al., 2004), (Pervouchine et al., 2009) or using a heuristic-based method (Ekbal et al., 2006). We do not have a list of transliteration pairs for the training of our Hindi to Urdu transliteration system. Therefore we use two methods to extract transliteration pairs from parallel data of Hindi/Urdu. In the first approach, we use the transliteration mining algorithm proposed by Sajjad et al. (2011) to extract transliteration pairs. This method does not use any language dependent information. In the second approach, we use a rule-based method to extract transliteration pairs. Both processes are imperfect, meaning that there is noise in the extracted list of transliteration pairs. We build a joint source channel model as described by Li et al. (2004) and Ekbal et al. (2006) on the extracted list of transliteration pairs. The following sections describe the two mining approaches and the model in detail.

3 Extraction of Transliteration Pairs

We automatically word-align the parallel corpus and extract a word list, later referred to as *"list of word pairs"* (see Section 5, for details on training data). We use two methods to extract transliteration pairs from the list of word pairs. In the first

[1]SAMPA and XSAMPA are used to represent the IPA symbols using 7-bit printable ASCII characters.

approach, we automatically extract transliteration pairs using the transliteration mining algorithm as proposed in Sajjad et al. (2011). We align the transliteration pairs at character level using a character aligner. In the second approach, we use an edit distance metric and handcrafted equivalence rules to extract transliteration pairs from a parallel corpus. We align the list of transliteration pairs at character level using the edit distance metric. The transliteration system is then trained on these character aligned transliteration pairs which is described in Section 5. The following subsections describe the extraction methods in detail.

3.1 Automatic Extraction of Transliteration Pairs

In this section, we review the transliteration mining approach described by Sajjad et al. (2011) to automatically extract the transliteration pairs from the list of word pairs. The approach consists of two algorithms, Algorithm 1, which performs an iterative filtering of the word pair list, and Algorithm 2, which determines when Algorithm 1 should be stopped. The details of this process follow.

Algorithm 1 is based on an iterative process. In each iteration, it first builds a joint transliteration model using g2p (grapheme-to-phoneme converter (Bisani and Ney, 2008)) on the current list of word pairs. It then filters out 5% of the word pairs which are least likely to be transliterations according to their normalized joint probability, resulting in a reduced word pair list, after which the next iteration begins. In each iteration the word pair list is reduced by 5%.

Algorithm 2 is used to select the optimal stopping iteration for Algorithm 1. Algorithm 2 is an extension of Algorithm 1. It divides the original list of word pairs into two halves which are used as training and held-out data. The division is done using a special splitting method which keeps the morphologically related word pairs from the list of word pairs either in the training data or in the held-out data. It builds a joint sequence model on the training data (approximately half of the list of word pairs) and filters out those 5% word pairs which are least likely to be transliteration pairs. Then it builds a transliteration system using the Moses toolkit (Koehn et al., 2003) on the filtered data and tests it on the source side of the held-out data. It repeats this process for 100 iterations. The iteration which best predicts the held-out data is selected as the stopping iteration for the transliteration mining algorithm.

We first ran Algorithm 2 on the list of word pairs for 100 iterations. It returned the 45th iteration as the best stopping iteration for Algorithm 1. Then we ran Algorithm 1 for 45 iterations and obtained a list of 2245 transliteration pairs. Due to data sparsity, there were two Hindi characters which were missing in the extracted list of transliteration pairs. We could either add complete word examples or just transliteration units of the missing Hindi characters to the list of transliteration pairs. Adding examples will provide context information which may bias the results of the evaluation. Thus we added only the two missing 1-to-1 transliteration units to the list of transliteration pairs.

We align the list of transliteration pairs at the character level using a character aligner[2]. The aligner uses the Forward-Backward algorithm to learn the character alignments between the transliteration pairs. It allows only 0 or 1 character on either side of the transliteration unit. So, a source character can align either to a target character or to $\emptyset$ and a target character can align either to a source character or to $\emptyset$. We get three kinds of alignments of Hindi characters to Urdu characters i.e. $\emptyset \rightarrow 1$, $1 \rightarrow \emptyset$ and $1 \rightarrow 1$. We modify the $\emptyset \rightarrow 1$ alignments by merging the Urdu character with the left neighboring aligned pair. If it is the left-most character, then it is merged with the right neighboring aligned character pair. Table 2 shows the alignment of Hindi characters with Urdu characters before and after the merging of unaligned Urdu characters.

a)	Hindi	$\emptyset$	b	c	$\emptyset$	e	f
	Urdu	A	X	C	D	$\emptyset$	F
b)	Hindi		b	c		e	f
	Urdu		AX	CD		$\emptyset$	F

Table 2: Hindi-Urdu alignment pairs for transliteration where a) shows initial alignment with NULL alignments and b) shows final alignments after merging of NULL alignments

3.2 Rule-based Extraction of Transliteration Pairs

As an alternative to automatic extraction of transliteration pairs, we use our own knowledge

[2] We were unable to get character alignments from g2p. We use a separate character aligner to align the list of transliteration pairs at the character level.

of the Hindi and Urdu scripts to make the initial transliteration units. The rules are further extended by looking into available Hindi-Urdu transliteration systems and other resources (Gupta, 2004; Malik et al., 2008; Jawaid and Ahmed, 2009). Table 3 shows some examples of equivalence rules. Each transliteration unit is assigned a cost. A Hindi character which is always mapped to the same Urdu character is assigned zero cost. In some cases, a Hindi character, say H_1, can be mapped to several different Urdu characters, say U_1, U_2 and U_3. We assign an equal cost of 0.3 to all three mappings H_1 to U_1, H_1 to U_2 and H_1 to U_3 as shown in the last three rows of Table 3.

Hindi character	SAMPA	Urdu character	Cost
ब	b	ب	0
ल	l	ل	0
ज़	z	ض	0.3
ज़	z	ظ	0.3
ज़	z	ذ	0.3

Table 3: Hindi-Urdu handcrafted equivalence rules

The edit distance metric allows insert, delete and replace operations. The handcrafted rules define the cost of replace operations as shown in Table 3. Each insert and delete operation costs 0.6, except for the deletion of Hindi diacritics where the cost is 0.

If two identical characters occur next to each other in an Urdu word then either only one character is written with a shadda sign ّ after it or both characters are written next to each other. The shadda sign is treated as a diacritic by most Urdu writers and is thus frequently omitted in Urdu text. We deleted all shadda characters in a preprocessing step in order to obtain a consistent representation. Hindi, on the other hand, uses a special joining symbol between two characters to write conjuncts. If the joining symbol is used between two identical characters then it will be transliterated with a shadda in Urdu. Assume the joining symbol is "z" and L is a character in Hindi.

The occurrence L"z"L in Hindi will be transliterated as L ّ in Urdu. In the handcrafted rules, we add separate entries mapping Hindi L"z"L to Urdu L.

Urdu and Hindi differ in their word definition for some particular categories. For example, in Hindi the case marker is always attached to the pronoun, whereas in Urdu, the case marker can be written either as a separate token after the pronoun or can be attached to the pronoun. The edit distance metric was modified to avoid penalizing spaces in Urdu text.

The raw list of word pairs contains translations (that are not transliterations), transliterations and alignment errors. We apply the edit distance metric to the list of word pairs and extract the list of transliteration pairs. We optimized the costs on a held-out set. We filter out word pairs with a cost of more than 0.6 thus allowing only one deletion/insertion or at most three ambiguous replacements in the Hindi-Urdu pairs (Table 3). If we decrease the filtering threshold or increase the replacement cost, the number of types extracted reduces significantly. We obtained 1695 types in the list of transliteration pairs. Due to data sparsity, there were about 5 Hindi characters which were not covered in the list of transliteration pairs. We added transliteration units for the missing Hindi characters to the list of transliteration pairs.

We align the list of word pairs at the character level using the same handcrafted equivalence rules and the edit distance algorithm. We get three kinds of alignments of Hindi characters to Urdu characters i.e. $\emptyset \rightarrow 1$, $1 \rightarrow \emptyset$ and $1 \rightarrow N$. The character alignments produced using the edit distance metric differ from those produced using the character aligner (Section 3.1). The character aligner allows only one character on the source and the target side. The edit distance metric allows a Hindi character to align to more than one Urdu character. We postprocess the alignment $\emptyset \rightarrow 1$ as described in Section 3.1.

4 Transliteration Model

The character-based translation probability $p_{char}(H, U)$ is defined as follows:

$$p_{char}(H, U) = \sum_{a_1^n \in align(H,U)} p(a_1^n) \quad (1)$$

$$= \sum_{a_1^n \in align(H,U)} \prod_{i=1}^{n} p(a_i | a_{i-k}^{i-1}) \quad (2)$$

where a_i is an aligned pair consisting of the i-th Hindi character h_i and a sequence of 0 or more Urdu characters. Usually a Hindi character is aligned with one Urdu character, but some

Hindi characters map to zero or two Urdu characters. The short vowels except the short vowel 'a' are always written in Hindi while in Urdu short vowels are usually not written. Hence, Hindi short vowels should be aligned to zero Urdu characters. $align(H, U)$ is the set of all possible alignments between the characters of U and H.

During transliteration we need to maximize $P(H, U)$ over all possible sequences U but we can not efficiently compute the sum over all possible different alignment pairs in equation 1. Therefore we resort to the Viterbi approximation and extract the most probable alignment.

The parameter k in equation 2 indicates the amount of context used (e.g. if $k = 2$, we use a trigram model on character pairs). A good value of k for our transliteration system is 4. Table 5 (Section 5) shows the variation of results on different values of k.

The SRILM-Toolkit (Stolcke, 2002) was applied in the implementation. Add-one smoothing was used for unigrams and Kneser-Ney smoothing was used for order > 1.

5 Evaluation Setup

5.1 Training and Test Data

We use a Hindi-Urdu parallel corpus taken from the EMILLE corpus[3]. In both Urdu and Hindi, there are cases where one character can be represented either as one Unicode character or as a combination of two Unicode characters. These characters are normalized to have only one representation. In Urdu, short vowels are represented with diacritics which are usually missing in written text. In order to keep the corpus consistent, all diacritics were removed from the Urdu corpus.

A Hindi news corpus of 5000 tokens (1330 types) was randomly selected from BBC News. The tokens that can be transliterated into Urdu were manually extracted and a test corpus of 819 transliteration pairs was obtained.

5.2 Word Alignment

We automatically generate two word alignments using GIZA++ (Och and Ney, 2003), and refine them using the grow-diag-final-and heuristic (Koehn et al., 2003). We extracted a total of 107323 alignment pairs from the sentence aligned parallel corpus of 7007 sentences. The M-N and N-1 alignment pairs were ignored as they are unlikely to be transliterations. Most of the 1-N alignment pairs are cases where the Urdu part of the alignment actually consist of two (or three) words which are sometimes written without a space because of lack of standard writing convention in Urdu. For example جا سکتے (can go ; d_ZA s@kt_de) is alternatively written as جاسکتے (can go ; d_ZAs@kt_de) , i.e., without a space before the "s" sound. These are always written as a single token in Hindi. We drop 1-N alignments with gaps, but keep alignments with contiguous words. We refer to the word-aligned corpus generated from 1-1 and 1-N alignments as "list of word pairs" later on.

5.3 Baselines

5.3.1 Phrase-based MT

Our first baseline is a phrase-based machine translation system (PSMT) for transliteration built using the Moses toolkit. We use the default settings but the distortion limit is set to zero (no reordering). Minimum error rate training (MERT) is used to optimize the parameters. The list of transliteration pairs is divided into 90% training and 10% development data (used for MERT).

5.3.2 External Transliterators

We also compare our systems with three Hindi-Urdu transliteration systems, HUMT[4] , CRULP[5] and Malerkotla[6] (MAL), available on the internet. HUMT is based on finite state transducers. It implements a phoneme-based mapping scheme between Hindi and Urdu. The HUMT system is described in Section 2 (Malik et al., 2008). CRULP is a rule-based transliterator which uses a direct orthographic mapping between Hindi and Urdu. Little information is available on the method of the Malerkotla transliterator. If there are two legal transliterations of a Hindi word, it transliterates it to the most frequent Urdu word. We suspect that Malerkotla may use a bilingual word list to override the basic transliteration scheme.

5.4 Experiments

Phrase-based MT: We first build a PSMT system on the list of word pairs. Due to the amount of noise in the training data, it shows 45.9% accuracy. The low score of the PSMT system supports our

[3]http://www.emille.lancs.ac.uk/

[4]http://www.puran.info/HUMT/HUMT.aspx

[5]http://www.crulp.org/software/langproc/h2utransliterator.html

[6]http://www.malerkotla.org/Transh2u.aspx

No filtering	Automatic	Rule-based
45.9%	70.3%	72.7%

Table 4: Results of Phrase-based MT

work of extracting the transliteration pairs from the list of word pairs to build a transliteration system.

The PSMT is then trained on the transliteration pairs extracted using the automatic method and the rule-based method. The purpose of this experiment is to compare the quality of the extracted lists by building an identical model on them. The PSMT shows best accuracy on the transliteration pairs extracted using the rule-based method (Table 4). The rule-based extraction method is based on high precision and thus extracted fewer transliteration pairs than the the automatic method. The list extracted using the automatic method contains close transliterations as well, which are word pairs which only differ by one or two characters from correct transliterations. The close transliteration pairs help to learn transliteration information but also add noise to the system.

Our systems: We build two versions of our system, using the list of transliteration pairs extracted in Section 3.1 (AUTO) and using the list of transliteration pairs extracted in Section 3.2 (RULE). We use a context size of $k = 4$ (see eq. 2) for our systems. The results of our transliteration system RULE with different context sizes are shown in Table 5. The accuracy of the transliteration system is stable at context sizes greater than three.

1	2	3	4	5
64.5%	76.3%	80.7%	81.6%	81.6%

Table 5: Accuracies of RULE for different context sizes

AUTO shows an accuracy of 76% on the test data of 819 types as shown in Table 6. It could not learn certain language specific phenomena due to data sparsity. The system had problems to learn the mapping of a Hindi character to an Urdu conjunct. The system could not learn the shadda cases (see Section 3.2). There are 18 types (2% of the test data) with shadda phenomena. AUTO correctly transliterates only 28% of these types. This might be due to the character aligner which can not capture the information where a Hindi character can be aligned to more than one Urdu character and vice versa. The other factor is the preprocessing step where we delete diacritics and the character joiner from the Hindi word aligned corpus.

AUTO	RULE	MAL	CRULP	HUMT
76%	81.6%	73.4%	69.8%	69.5%

Table 6: Accuracies of the joint model built on lists from AUTO and RULE, compared with the three baseline transliterators

The rule-based system (RULE) shows the best results of 81.6%. It obtains 100% accuracy in transliterating the shadda cases. Due to the inclusion of transliteration units in the training data (Section 3.2), it contains at least one entry of every transliteration unit in its training corpus.

Results of other transliteration systems: We test three other transliterators (HUMT, CRULP and MAL) on the test corpus of 819 types. The results are shown in Table 6. The HUMT system performs worst with an accuracy of 69.5%. The HUMT system does not handle ambiguous characters as mentioned in Section 2. It maps each ambiguous Hindi character to the most frequent matching Urdu character without taking into account the transliteration context. CRULP has difficulty in disambiguating Hindi characters which map to several different Urdu characters. Table 11 shows some examples of such transliteration units. The ambiguous Hindi characters (Table 1) can not be predicted correctly on the basis of the neighboring characters but these Hindi characters (Table 11) can be predicted correctly by looking at the context. MAL mostly performs well on ambiguous Hindi characters. The results of MAL are discussed in detail in the next section.

6 Discussion & Error Analysis

In this section, we discuss the errors made by the transliteration systems by dividing the test data into different subclasses. The transliteration between Hindi and Urdu is strongly motivated by the language of origin and script of the word to be transliterated.

Proper nouns: The test corpus contains a large number of words borrowed from other languages which are differently transliterated to Hindi and to Urdu. Words borrowed from Arabic contain ambiguous characters which make the transliteration task more challenging. Proper nouns form 19% of the test corpus. In a second set of experiments, we evaluated only on the proper nouns from the test corpus. All five transliterators perform poorly in transliterating proper nouns as shown in Table 7.

AUTO	RULE	MAL	CRULP	HUMT
59.1%	65.6%	56.5%	56.5%	57.1%

Table 7: Accuracies of AUTO, RULE and three baseline transliterators on proper nouns

Most of the proper nouns were names borrowed from English and other languages. We observed that there is sometimes a difference between the pronunciation of borrowed words in Hindi and Urdu. Consider the English name "Donald": the character "a" in "Donald" is transliterated using a long vowel into Hindi as डोनाल्ड (donAld) and using a short vowel into Urdu as ڈونلڈ (don@ld). There are some foreign words which are directly transliterated in Hindi and borrowed from another language in Urdu. Consider the word "America" which is transliterated as अमेरिका (@"mErIk@) in Hindi but borrowed from Arabic as امریکہ (A@mrikA) in Urdu. Table 7 shows the results of our transliterators in comparison with other transliterators.

Ambiguous characters: The ambiguous characters frequently occur in Hindi text and are found in 52% of the types in the test corpus. There are four ambiguous characters as shown in Table 1. For each such character, we extract the tokens containing this character from the test corpus. There were 15%, 19%, 13% and 3.8% occurrences of words with ह (h), स (s), त (t_d) and ज़ (z) respectively. Table 8 shows the results of the three baseline transliterators on these four cases.

	MAL	CRULP	HUMT
ह (h)	74.4%	60.8%	60%
स (s)	69.8%	62.9%	66%
त (t_d)	76.4%	66%	66%
ज़ (z)	32.3%	41.9%	3.2%

Table 8: Results of the baseline transliteration systems on words containing ambiguous characters

Malerkotla shows poor results on words containing ज़ (z). These words form only 3.8% types of the test corpus and thus do not substantially affect the overall accuracy achieved by Malerkotla. Table 9 shows the results of Malerkotla and our transliteration systems. RULE performs best on all cases of ambiguous characters.

Sometimes, the use of several ambiguous characters in a string leads to two legal Urdu words as shown in Table 10. The disambiguation between two legal Urdu words requires word context.

Ambiguous transliteration units: There are some characters in Hindi that may map to different Urdu characters depending on the context. Table 11 shows some examples. In the first column, the Hindi characters may map to any of the three Urdu characters in the same row. Sometimes, there is no phonological difference between the Urdu characters but conventionally they are written in one way or the other.

	AUTO	RULE	MAL
ह (h)	69.6%	78.4%	74.4%
स (s)	69.8%	74.8%	69.8%
त (t_d)	77.4%	79.3%	76.4%
ज़ (z)	64.5%	74.2%	32.3%

Table 9: Results of Malerkotla and our transliteration systems on words containing ambiguous characters

Hindi	SAMPA	Urdu-1	Urdu-2
बाज़	bAz	بعض Some	باز Eagle
असरार	A@srAr	اصرار Insist	اسرار Israr
सहरा	s@hrA	صحرا Desert	سہرا Credit

Table 10: Highly ambiguous words in Urdu that have the same sound but that are written with different characters and represent different meanings

Hindi	SAMPA	Urdu		
ा	A	ا	ه	ع
आ	A	ا	آ	ع
ऊ	AU	ا	او	و

Table 11: Some ambiguous transliteration units

Pronunciation differences between Hindi and Urdu speakers: Different pronunciations of Hindi and Urdu speakers also cause confusion for the transliteration systems. For example, the English word "bazaar" is written in Hindi as बाजार (bAd_ZAr) and in Urdu as بازار (bAzAr). The transliteration system has to disambiguate by mapping the character representing "d_Z" in Hindi to either the "d_Z" sound or the "z" sound in Urdu. Table 12 shows some of these examples.

N-best analysis of RULE and AUTO: The transliterators show poor performance on words containing ambiguous characters. In the 20-best output, we find the correct solution for many words with ambiguous characters as shown in Table 13. However, if a word contains two ambigu-

Hindi	Urdu
बाजार (bAd_ZAr)	بازار (bAzAr)
फोल (fol)	پھول (p_hul)
श्रीलंका (SIril@nkA)	سری لنکا (sIril@nkA)

Table 12: Pronunciation differences between Hindi and Urdu

ous characters, it was difficult for the transliterator to transliterate it correctly. We hope that the tokens with ambiguous characters can be correctly transliterated using context by a statistical machine translation system. The unknown transliterations in the 20-best output will get lower scores from the language model as compared to known words. If two words in the 20-best output are known, the language model helps to choose the right output based on the word context.

The 10-best and 20-best results of AUTO are competitive with RULE[7]. The automatically extracted list obtains high recall and thus contains close transliterations which RULE's list does not contain. Close transliterations are word pairs which only differ by one or two characters from correct transliterations. The close transliteration pairs are useful for the transliteration system as they provide information about transliteration units and help avoid the problem of data sparseness. However, the transliteration system also learns noise from them and might not produce correct 1-best output. Table 14 shows two examples which are correctly transliterated by AUTO but are wrongly transliterated by RULE in the 10-best output. These examples are difficult to transliterate as most of the characters are ambiguous and have more than one possible transliteration. The system built on AUTO is able to transliterate them correctly as it contains more instances of infrequent ambiguous characters. For the incorporation of a transliteration model in a machine translation system, AUTO would be a better option as it is language independent and has better 10-best and 20-best scores.

7 Conclusion

We have implemented a joint source channel model to transliterate Hindi words into Urdu words. We have used two approaches to extract transliteration pairs from a parallel corpus of Hindi/Urdu – an unsupervised transliteration mining method and a method based on handcrafted rules. We then built models on the automatically aligned orthographic transliteration units of the extracted Hindi/Urdu transliteration pairs. Our best transliteration system achieved an accuracy of 81.6% which is 8% better than the best of three other systems. The 10-best and 20-best results of our transliteration system built on the automatically extracted transliteration pairs showed that it is suitable for integration with machine translation which will allow the use of translation context to choose the best transliteration (Hermjakob et al., 2008; Durrani et al., 2010).

[7] We also aligned AUTO with the edit-distance based aligner to verify that alignments differences were not important. The results dropped a little less than 1-point for 1-best, 10-best and 20-best, which is still better than RULE for 10-best and 20-best, so the differences in alignment did not unduly influence the results.

	AUTO	RULE
1-Best	76%	81.6%
10-Best	93.8%	91.5%
20-Best	95.1%	92.3%

Table 13: Comparison of 1-Best, 10-Best and 20-Best outputs of our transliteration systems

Hindi	Urdu	SAMPA
अफ्रीका	افریقہ	AfrIcA
आउट	آؤٹ	OUT

Table 14: In the 10-best output, these examples are correctly transliterated by AUTO but are wrongly transliterated by RULE

Acknowledgments

The authors wish to thank the anonymous reviewers for their comments. Hassan Sajjad and Nadir Durrani were funded by the Higher Education Commission (HEC) of Pakistan. Helmut Schmid was supported by Deutsche Forschungsgemeinschaft grant SFB 732. Alexander Fraser was funded by Deutsche Forschungsgemeinschaft grant Models of Morphosyntax for Statistical Machine Translation. This work was supported in part by the IST Programme of the European Community, under the PASCAL2 Network of Excellence, IST-2007-216886. This publication only reflects the authors' views.

References

Yaser Al-Onaizan and Kevin Knight. 2002. Machine transliteration of names in Arabic text. In *ACL Workshop on Computational Approaches to Semitic Languages*, Morristown, NJ, USA.

Maximilian Bisani and Hermann Ney. 2008. Joint-sequence models for grapheme-to-phoneme conversion. *Speech Communication*, 50(5).

Nadir Durrani, Hassan Sajjad, Alexander Fraser, and Helmut Schmid. 2010. Hindi-to-Urdu machine translation through transliteration. In *Proceedings of the 48th Annual Conference of the Association for Computational Linguistics*.

Asif Ekbal, Sudip Kumar Naskar, and Sivaji Bandyopadhyay. 2006. A modified joint source-channel model for transliteration. In *Proceedings of the COLING/ACL poster sessions*, pages 191–198, Sydney, Australia. Association for Computational Linguistics.

Swati Gupta. 2004. Aligning Hindi and Urdu bilingual corpora for robust projection. Masters project dissertation, Department of Computer Science, University of Sheffield.

Ulf Hermjakob, Kevin Knight, and Hal Daumé III. 2008. Name translation in statistical machine translation - learning when to transliterate. In *Proceedings of ACL-08: HLT*, pages 389–397, Columbus, Ohio. Association for Computational Linguistics.

J C. Wells. 1995. Computer-coding the IPA: a proposed extension of SAMPA. University College, London.

Bushra Jawaid and Tafseer Ahmed. 2009. Hindi to Urdu conversion: beyond simple transliteration. In *Conference on Language and Technology 2009*, Lahore, Pakistan.

Mehdi M. Kashani, Fred Popowich, and Anoop Sarkar. 2007. Automatic transliteration of proper nouns from Arabic to English. In *Second Workshop on Computational Approaches to Arabic Script-based Languages*, Stanford University, USA.

Kevin Knight and Jonathan Graehl. 1998. Machine transliteration. *Computational Linguistics*, 24(4):599–612.

Philipp Koehn, Franz J. Och, and Daniel Marcu. 2003. Statistical phrase-based translation. In *Proceedings of the Human Language Technology and North American Association for Computational Linguistics Conference*, pages 127–133, Edmonton, Canada.

Haizhou Li, Zhang Min, and Su Jian. 2004. A joint source-channel model for machine transliteration. In *ACL '04: Proceedings of the 42nd Annual Meeting on Association for Computational Linguistics*, pages 159–166, Barcelona, Spain. Association for Computational Linguistics.

M G Abbas Malik, Christian Boitet, and Pushpak Bhattacharyya. 2008. Hindi Urdu machine transliteration using finite-state transducers. In *Proceedings of the 22nd International Conference on Computational Linguistics*, Manchester, UK.

M G Abbas Malik, Laurent Besacier, Christian Boitet, and Pushpak Bhattacharyya. 2009. A hybrid model for Urdu Hindi transliteration. In *Proceedings of the 2009 Named Entities Workshop, ACL-IJCNLP*, Suntec, Singapore.

Franz J. Och and Hermann Ney. 2003. A systematic comparison of various statistical alignment models. *Computational Linguistics*, 29(1):19–51.

Vladimir Pervouchine, Haizhou Li, and Bo Lin. 2009. Transliteration alignment. In *Proceedings of the 47th Annual Meeting of the Association for Computational Linguistics and the 4th IJCNLP of the AFNLP*, Suntec, Singapore.

Hassan Sajjad, Alexander Fraser, and Helmut Schmid. 2011. An algorithm for unsupervised transliteration mining with an application to word alignment. In *Proceedings of the 49th Annual Conference of the Association for Computational Linguistics*, Portland, USA.

Bonnie G. Stalls and Kevin Knight. 1998. Translating names and technical terms in Arabic text. In *Proceedings of the COLING/ACL Workshop on Computational Approches to Semitic Languages*.

Andreas Stolcke. 2002. SRILM - an extensible language modeling toolkit. In *Intl. Conf. Spoken Language Processing*, Denver, Colorado.

A Semantic-Specific Model for Chinese Named Entity Translation

Yufeng Chen and **Chengqing Zong**
National Laboratory of Pattern Recognition
Institute of Automation, Chinese Academy of Sciences
Beijing, China, 100190
{chenyf,cqzong}@nlpr.ia.ac.cn

Abstract

We observe that (1) it is difficult to combine transliteration and meaning translation when transforming named entities (NE); and (2) there are different translation variations in NE translation, due to different semantic information. From this basis, we propose a novel semantic-specific NE translation model, which automatically incorporates the global context from corpus in order to capture substantial semantic information. The presented approach is inspired by example-based translation and realized by log-linear models, integrating monolingual context similarity model, bilingual context similarity model, and mixed language model. The experiments show that the semantic-specific model has substantially and consistently outperformed the baselines and related NE translation systems.

1 Introduction

Named entity (NE) translation, which transforms a name entity from source language to target language, plays a very important role in translingual language processing tasks, such as machine translation and cross-lingual information retrieval.

Generally, NE translation[1] includes transliteration and meaning translation. Recently, many researches have been devoted to NE transliteration (most person names) or NE meaning translation (organization names) individually. However, there are still two main challenges in statistical Chinese-English (*C2E*) NE translation.

(1) The combination of transliteration and meaning translation. Either transliteration or meaning translation is only a subtask of NE translation. There has been less work devoted to the combination of transliteration and meaning translation for translating NEs.

(2) The selection of NE translation variations. Segments in different NEs could be translated differently due to NEs' origins and enrich language phenomenon (Huang et al., 2005). As shown in Table 1, the same Chinese character "金" is translated into different English variations (highlighted in aligned parts).

Transliteration variations
金炳华 —— **Jin** Binghua
金成勋 —— **Kim** Sung-Hoon
何塞 华金 布伦纳 —— Jose Joa**quin** Brunner
若阿金·希潘德 —— Joa**quim** Chipande
马丁路德金 —— Martin Luther **King**
金丸信 —— **Kane**maru Shin
米斯金 —— Mis**kine**
麦金托什 —— Aaron M**cin**tosh
文森特·伯金 —— Vincent Bur**gen**
埃尔金·杰拉辛 —— Er**gin** Celasin
阿利亚夫金 —— Alyav**din**
卡列伊金 —— Kalei**kin**
……
Meaning translation variations
阿斯特基金 —— Astor **Fund**
北京冶金学院 —— Beijing Institute of **Metallurgy**
……

Table 1. *C2E* Translation variations of a character "金" in different instances

Furthermore, we randomly extract 100 Chinese characters from the person names of LDC2005T34 corpus, and find out all the characters have more than one translation variations. And each character has about average 7.8 translation variations. Also, (Li et al., 2004) have indicated that there is much confusion in *C2E* transliteration and Chinese NEs have much lower perplexity than English NEs.

According to the above two problems, we find that a crucial problem of *C2E* NE translation is selecting a correct syllable/word at each step,

[1] NE translation referred to in this paper denotes bilingual NE transformation (either transliteration or meaning translation), and meaning translation is proposed as distinct from transliteration.

unlike traditional Statistical machine translation (SMT), which mainly focuses on (word, phrase or syntax) alignment and reordering. The selection in NE translation is much related to its *semantic information*, including NE types, origins, collocations of included Chinese characters, and position-sensitive etc. We want the translation model could automatically learn the semantic information. However, this semantic information for translation is various and difficult to classify.

Given an input "卡科夫金(Kakov**kin**)", how to identify the translation of "金"? Only selecting high probable translation across the training set is not reliable in this case. After simply comparing "卡科夫金" with the instances in Table 1, we find that the input is much relevant to "卡列伊金(**kin**)", since both of them include "金" at the end position, and their contexts are much related (they share a common Chinese character usage mainly due to the same origin (Russia), such as "卡", "列", and "夫" etc., according to clues supplied by global context). If we only considers the left/right context of "金", "卡科夫金" would have been related to "阿利亚夫金(**din**)" wrongly. From this view, this strongly suggests using a global context as the knowledge base for the final translation decision.

Therefore, we propose a semantic-specific NE translation model, which makes use of those related instances in the training data (defined as *global context*), to capture semantic information. The main idea is: for each input Chinese NE segment, it is assumed that its correct translation exists somewhere in the instances of the training set. What we need to do is to find out the correct answers based on semantic clues. It is achieved by selecting relevant instances, of which the semantic information is much relevant with the input. In other word, we choose those relevant instances from corpus to imitate translation. Here, semantic information is not directly learned, but is used as a bridge to measure the relevance or similarity between the input and those instances.

The proposed semantic-specific model has two advantages. Firstly, traditional translation approaches only exploit a general model to transform a source name into the target name with the same rules or distributions. Whereas our model could capture the transformation differences by measuring semantic similarity among different instances (global context). Secondly, we do not need define exact semantic labels for translation, such as various origins or NE types.

2 Framework

Formally, given a source (Chinese) name $C = c_1,...,c_k,...c_K$, which consists of K Chinese segments, we want to find its target (English) translation $E = e_1,...e_k,...e_K$ of the highest probability. Here, it is assumed that an NE is literally translated, without insertion or deletion during the transformation. Within a probabilistic framework, a translation system produces the optimum target name, E^*, which yields the highest posterior probability given the source Chinese name.

$$E^* = \arg\max_{E \in \Phi_E} P(E \mid C) \quad (1)$$

where Φ_E is the set of all possible translations for the Chinese name. In order to incorporate enrich language phenomenon of NEs (i.e. origins or other semantic information that affect NE translation) for capturing more exact translation, $P(E \mid C)$ is rewritten as:

$$\begin{aligned} P(E \mid C) &= \sum_S P(E,S \mid C) \\ &\cong \max_S P(E,S \mid C) \end{aligned} \quad (2)$$

where S is the semantic-specific information for C and E. Inspired by example-based machine translation model (Nagao, 1984; Sato and Nagao, 1990), we assume that certain mappings in the training set are identical with the transformation of the input NE. Thus we materialize the semantic information as a set of *C2E* mappings coming from the training set $S = s_1^K = s_1,...,s_k,...s_K$. A mapping s_k is defined as a segment[2] pair $[sc_k, se_k]$, where sc_k is similar to the input NE segment c_k on the source side, while se_k is the corresponding transformation of sc_k on the target side. Such as [金, Jin], [金, din], or [基金, Fund]. Therefore,

$S = [sc_k, se_k]_1^K = \{[sc_1, se_1],...,[sc_k, se_k],...,[sc_K, se_K]\}$.

For example, given an input NE "日本松山芭蕾舞团 (Japanese Matsuyama Ballet Troupe)", one of its mapping sets would be {[日本, Japanese],[松山, Matsuyama],[芭蕾舞团, Ballet Troupe]}, or {[日本, Japanese],[松, Matsu], [山, yama],[芭蕾, Ballet], [舞团, Troupe]} and so on. Therefore, the semantic-specific translation model incorporates semantic information by finding out the most likely mappings coming

[2] The source side of one mapping could be a character, a word or several words. The target side of one mapping could be several syllables or words. Therefore one mapping is defined as a segment pair.

from the training set to capture the semantic structure. If the mappings are known, the translation is achieved. Thus the semantic-specific model is further derived as:

$$\begin{aligned} & P(E,S \mid C) \\ & = P(E,[sc_k,se_k]_1^K \mid C) = P(E,sc_1^K,se_1^K \mid C) \\ & = P(sc_1^K \mid C) \times P(E,se_1^K \mid sc_1^K,C) \\ & = P(sc_1^K \mid C) \times P(se_1^K \mid sc_1^K,C) \times P(E \mid se_1^K,sc_1^K,C) \\ & \cong P(sc_1^K \mid C) \times P(se_1^K \mid sc_1^K,C) \times P(E) \end{aligned} \quad (3)$$

where $P(sc_1^K \mid C)$ is the probability to segment the input C into several source parts sc_1^K. And $P(se_1^K \mid sc_1^K, C)$ is used to assign preference to target segments se_1^K across global context given the input and the source segments sc_1^K. Finally, $P(E)$ is the probability to connect the target segments as the final translation E .Therefore, in our semantic-specific model, the traditional NE translation problem is transferred as searching the most probable (higher semantic similarity) mappings from the training data and then constructing the final translation.

In the proposed model (Eq (3)), those features are equally weighted. However, they should be weighted differently according to their contributions. Considering the advantages of the maximum entropy model (Berger et al., 1996) to integrate different kinds of features, we use this framework to model the probability $P(E,S \mid C)$. Suppose that we have a set of M feature functions $h_m(C,E,S)$, $m=1,...M$. For each feature function, there exists a model parameter λ_m, $m=1,...M$ .The decision rule is used to choose the most probable target NE (Och and Ney, 2002):

$$(\hat{E},\hat{S}) = \arg\max_{E,S} \left\{ \sum_{m=1}^{M} \lambda_m h_m(C,E,S) \right\} \quad (4)$$

Here, the feature functions $h_1^M(C,E,S)$ are modeled by the probabilities of $P(sc_1^K \mid C)$, $P(se_1^K \mid sc_1^K, C)$, and $P(E)$ respectively. Next, we discuss these three features in detail.

3 Feature Functions

3.1 Monolingual Similarity Model

The First feature $P(sc_1^K \mid C)$ segments the source into several related segments assumed independence.

$$h_1(C,E,S) = P(sc_1^K \mid c_1^K) \approx \prod_{k=1}^{K} P(sc_k \mid c_k) \quad (5)$$

The probability $P(sc_k \mid c_k)$ describes the relationship of sc_k and the source NE segment c_k. Since sc_k and c_k are on the same language side, $P(sc_k \mid c_k)$ can be commonly measured by the frequency of sc_k . However, this measurement usually produces short and high frequent segments, which is not really suitable for NE translation with multiple variations.

To better estimate the distribution $P(sc_k \mid c_k)$, this paper proposes a much more generic model called monolingual similarity model, which captures phonetic characteristics and corpus statistics, and also removes the bias of choosing shorter segment.

$$\begin{aligned} & P(sc_k \mid c_k) \\ & \cong sim_l(sc_k,c_k) \times tf(sc_k) \times idf(sc_k) \times \log(|sc_k|+1) \end{aligned} \quad (6)$$

Here we first adopt a local similarity function $sim_l(sc_k,c_k)$ to measure the relationship of the input Chinese segment c_k and a possible Chinese segment sc_k . It is measured on literal level (shallow level based on Chinese character and phonetic similarity).

$$sim_l(sc_k,c_k) = \begin{cases} 1.0, & \text{if } sc_k = c_k \\ \frac{1}{I}\sum_{i=1}^{I} P(e_i \mid sc_k) \times P(e_i \mid c_k), & \text{otherwise} \end{cases} \quad (7)$$

If all the characters of the two segments are identical ($sc_k = c_k$), their similarity is assigned as a high score 1.0. However, many phonetically similar segments are usually translated into a same syllable, such as "肯" and "坎" could align to a same syllable "cam". So we use NE alignment result to evaluate the phonetic similarity of two segments by $\frac{1}{I}\sum_{i=1}^{I} P(e_i \mid sc_k) \times P(e_i \mid c_k)$, where e_i denotes the same syllables they aligned in the training set.

On the other hand, a global concept, which is borrowed from tf×idf scheme in information retrieval (Chen et al., 2003), is used in Eq (7). Term frequency (tf) of a Chinese segment $tf(sc_k)$ denotes the number of occurrences of sc_k. Document frequency (df) of sc_k is the number of English segments that sc_k is translated to. And $idf(sc_k)$ is formulated as $\log(N / df(sc_k))$. Here, it is assumed there are totally N English segments according to $C2E$ NE alignment result.

Therefore, Eq (7) prefers Chinese segments that occur frequently, but rarely have different English transformations. Besides, since a longer segment has less disambiguation of its translation variations, we also favor longer Chinese segments, so that the length of a Chinese segment, i.e., $|sc_k|$, is also considered.

3.2 Bilingual Similarity Model

The second feature is formulated as follows:

$$h_2(C,E,S)=P(se_1^K \mid sc_1^K,c_1^K)\approx\prod_{k=1}^{K}P(se_k \mid sc_k,c_k) \quad (8)$$

The probability $P(se_k \mid sc_k,c_k)$ identifies the target segment se_k, of which the semantic information is consistent with the input c_k. This distribution estimates the bilingual similarity of se_k and c_k, thus is formulated as follows:

$$P(se_k \mid sc_k,c_k) \cong \sum_{sc_k\in KNN} sim_s(sc_k,c_k)y(sc_k,se_k) \quad (9)$$

Here, we borrow the idea of KNN (K Nearest Neighbor) algorithm. Translation variations for each c_k could be seen as different categories. To classify c_k into a correct translation, we could find the instance sc_k in the training set that is most semantically similar to c_k, and then assign the translation (category) se_k of this nearest neighbor to c_k. Since there would be $K(K>1)$ nearest neighbors for c_k, we generalize the nearest neighbor to K nearest instances of c_k. If the translation of sc_k in the instance is se_k, $y(sc_k,se_k)=1$, otherwise $y(sc_k,se_k)=0$.

On the other hand, $sim_s(sc_k,c_k)$ measures the semantic consistency between sc_k and c_k, which ensures the two have the same translation. Note that $sim_s(sc_k,c_k)$ is different from $sim_l(sc_k,c_k)$, which only measures the literal similarity based on characters or syllables as shown in Eq (7). Because it is difficult to measure the semantic similarity of two segments directly, we quantify their similarity in terms of their specific contexts. The context of c_k is the input NE C, while the context of sc_k is an instance SC that includes sc_k in the training set. For example: given an input NE "日本松山芭蕾舞团" that acts as a context, we want to find the translation of a segment "松", the segment "松" in the training data have different global contexts, such as "斯文松 (Sven**sson**)", "亚松森 (A**sun**cion)", and "赤松广隆 (Aka**matsu** Hirotaka)" and so on.

To address this problem, we adopt a vector space model that describes the context of c_k and sc_k. Some notions are defined here. A term set $T=\{t_{-n},...,t_{-1},t_1,...,t_n\}$ is an orderly character set of the context of c_k, where $[-n,n]$ is a Character-based n-range context window for c_k. This term set not only represents the character set of the context, but also presents the position information of the context. The similar action is applied to SC (the context of sc_k). Therefore, the context of c_k (the input Chinese NE) and each instance that includes sc_k would be transformed into vectors. For example, given a segment "松" in the input NE "日本松山芭蕾舞团", its term vector is {/s, 日，本，山，芭，蕾} when $n=3$, "/s" denotes the start position. While "松" in the instance "赤松广隆", its vector is {/, /s, 赤, 广, 隆, /e}, where "/" denotes a valid character and "/e" represents the end position.

We don't use Boolean weighting or tf/idf conceptions as traditional information retrieval (IR) to calculate the terms' weight, due to the sparse data problem. The mutual information is adopted to calculate the weight of t, which expresses the relevance between the context of c_k and the context of sc_k.

$$t_{weigh}=MI(t_C,t_{SC})=\log\frac{p(t_C,t_{SC})}{p(t_C)\times p(t_{SC})} \quad (10)$$

After transferring the contexts into general vectors, the similarity of two vectors is measured by computing the cosine value of the angle between them. This measure, called cosine-similarity measure, has been widely used in information retrieval tasks (Baeza-Yates and Ribeiro-Neto, 1999), and is thus utilized here.

$$sim_s(sc_k,c_k)=\frac{V_C\bullet V_{SC}}{\|V_C\|\times\|V_{SC}\|} \quad (11)$$

The numerator is the inner product of two vectors. The denominator is product of the length of V_C and the length of V_{SC}. If an instance SC (including the segment sc_k) is much related to the input NE C (including the segment c_k), this case suggests that the semantic similarity between c_k and sc_k is much high. In other words, the two probably have the same translation se_k. Here sc_k

acts as a bridge to realize the transformation from c_k to se_k.

3.3 Mixed Language Model

The probability $P(E)$ in Eq (3) encodes the popularity distribution of an English NE E, i.e. English language model. As mentioned above, there are two transformation styles for NEs: transliteration and meaning translation. Hence the glue rules for the final result are different. Transliteration is syllable-connecting without space on the English side, such as "Matsu (松)" and "yama (山)" are connected as "Matsuyama (松山)", its language model can be defined as a syllable-based n-gram model $P_{LM}(E_{tl}) = \prod_{k=1}^{K} \prod_{j=1}^{J} P(e_{k,j} \mid e_{k,j-n+1}^{k,j-1})$ (suppose there are j letters in the k segment). In contrast, the output of meaning translation is chained word by word with spaces, for example, "Wuyi (武夷)" and "Mountain (山)" are connected as "Wuyi Mountain", of which the language model is presented as a general word-based n-gram model $P_{LM}(E_{ts}) = \prod_{k=1}^{K} P(e_k \mid e_{k-n+1}^{k-1})$. For some NEs (most organization names), transliteration and meaning translation coexist. Hence we denote E_{tl} as the included transliteration part, while E_{ts} as the meaning-translation part. Intuitively, the whole language model is estimated as follows.

$$h_3(C,E,S) = P(E) = P_{LM}(E_{tl}) \times P_{LM}(E_{ts}) \quad (12)$$

Moreover, the language models $P_{LM}(E_{tl})$ and $P_{LM}(E_{ts})$ could be further normalized for removing the bias induced by different word/syllable lengths.

4 Training and Search

Without Chinese word segmentation, we have to calculate every possible mapping to determine the most probable one in a large corpus, which will make the search space significantly huge. Therefore, we only measure those instances that including at least one character of the input NE. And the candidates, of which the feature values are below a threshold, are discarded.

4.1 ME Parameter Training

The weighting coefficients for the three features in Eq (3) can be learned from the development set via Maximum Entropy (ME) training.

One way to get the associated weighting coefficients for those log-probability-factors adopted in the model is to regard each of them as real-valued features, and then use ME framework to find their corresponding lambda values, which are just the weighting coefficients that we look for. Following (Och et al. 2002; Liu et al. 2005), we use the GIS (Generalized Iterative Scaling) algorithm (Darroch and Ratcliff, 1972) to train the model parameters $\lambda_1,...\lambda_M$ of the log-linear models according to Eq (4). In practice, YASMET[3] package is adopted here to train the model parameters $\lambda_1,...\lambda_M$. In our case, $M = 3$.

4.2 Search

We use a greedy search algorithm to search the translation with highest probability in the space of all possible mappings. A state in this space is a partial mapping. A transition is defined as the addition of a single mapping to the current state. Our start state is the empty translation result, where there is no selected mapping. A terminal state is a state in which no more mappings can be added to increase the probability of the current alignment. Our task is to find the terminal state with the highest probability.

We can compute *gain*, a heuristic function, to figure out a probability when adding a new mapping, which is defined as follows:

$$gain(S,s_k) = \frac{\exp[\sum_{m=1}^{M} \lambda_m h_m(C,E,S \cup s_k)]}{\exp[\sum_{m=1}^{M} \lambda_m h_m(C,E,S)]} \quad (13)$$

where $S \cup s_k$ means a single mapping s_k is added to S. Since we have assumed that NE is literally translated in our model, there is a restriction: no overlap is allowed between the mapping s_k and the mapping set S.

The greedy search algorithm for general log-linear models is formally described as follows:

Input: C **and aligned training set**
Output: E, S

1. Start with $S = \phi$;
2. Do for each s_k and $s_k \cap S = \varnothing$:
   Compute $gain(S,s_k)$;
3. Terminate if $\forall s_k, gain(S,s_k) \le 1$ or sc_1^K covers all segments in C;
4. Add s_k with the maximal $gain(S,s_k)$ to S;
5. Go to 2.

---

[3] http://www.fjoch.com/YASMET.html

The above search algorithm generates the final translation result by adding one mapping for each time.

5 Experiments

The training-set, testing-set, and development-set all come from Chinese-English Named Entity List v1.0 (LDC2005T34). The training-set consists of 218,172 proofread bilingual entries: 73,052 person name pairs, 76,460 location name pairs and 68,660 organization name pairs. Besides, 300 person names, 300 organization names, and 300 names of various NE types (including person names, location names and organization names) are used as three testing-sets respectively. Development-set includes 500 randomly selected name pairs of various NE types. There is no overlap between the training set, the development set and the open test sets.

Note that in the training set, the included transliterated parts and the meaning translated parts, which have been manually labeled, are trained separately. 218,172 NE pairs are split into 185,339 transliterated pairs (*TL-training set*) and 62,453 meaning translated pairs (*TS-training set*) (since transliteration and meaning translation would occur in one NE pair, so 185,339+62.453>218,172).

In the TL-training set, the Chinese name of an NE pair is transformed into a character-based sequence and its aligned English name is split into syllables, of which the split rules are described in (Jiang et al., 2007). Afterwards, GIZA++[4] tool is invoked to align characters to syllables. On the other hand, for TS-training set, the Chinese part of an NE is also treated as a character-based sequence, while the English part is regarded as a word-based sequence. The alignment between Chinese characters and English words are achieved by GIZA++ toolkit as well.

We use the recall of top-N hypotheses (Yang et al, 2008) as the evaluation metrics, and also adopt the Mean Reciprocal Rank (MRR) metric (Kantor and Voorhees, 2000), a measure that is commonly used in information retrieval, assuming there is precisely one correct answer. Each NE translation generates at most top-50 hypotheses for each input when computing MRR.

First, we will show the experimental results when setting different parameters for the semantic similarity model, which is done on the development set with equal feature weightings. We set different ranges of the context window (the parameter n) to find which range could get the best performance. Figure 1 illustrates the effect of the range parameter n for the final translation result (by MRR metric). From Figure 1, we could find that when n=3, the proposed model gets the best performance (MRR value=0.498). Therefore, n=3 is chosen for further study.

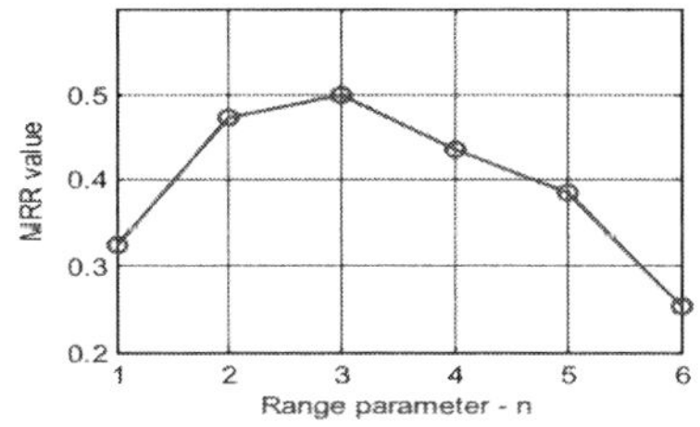

Figure 1. Effects of different context ranges (n) on translation results (by MRR metric)

Because the proposed three features cannot be used separately, we do not compare their individual effectiveness. Those normalized weighting coefficients (i.e., normalized lambda-values) obtained from YASMET package is 0.248, 0.565 and 0.187 (we all use 3-gram in the mixed language model). It is not surprising to find that λ_2 (corresponding to the bilingual similarity feature) receives the highest value. This clearly indicates that the bilingual similarity model plays a critical role in our semantic-specific translation model.

5.1 Semantic-Specific Model Vs. Baselines

We adopt a traditional statistical translation model (a phrase-based machine translation model, Moses[5] decoder) to process transliteration, meaning translation, and their combination as three baselines respectively. All of the baselines generate Top-50 candidates for each input. Table 2 shows their different settings comparing the proposed semantic-specific (SS) model.

Setting	SS-model	Baseline I	Baseline II	Baseline III
Input	Un-segmented	Character-based	Word-based	Character-based
Training data	TL-training set + TS-training set	TL-training set	TS-training set	TL-training set + TS-training set
Language model	Mix of syllable-based and word-based	Syllable-based	Word-based	Word-based

Table 2. The experiment configurations of baselines

[4] http://www.fjoch.com/GIZA++.html

[5] http://www.statmt.org/moses/

Note that baseline III combines transliteration and meaning translation only by training TL training set and TS training set individually, and then directly integrating generated syllable-based alignment and word-based alignment into a whole translation table.

Firstly, Table 3 compares the semantic-specific model (*SS-model*) with three baselines for the translation of person names. From Table 3, we find that the proposed model raises the recall of top-50 6.2% over Baseline I. It proves that our proposed model is effective for the transliteration of person names, and outperforms the traditional transliteration model. Baseline II can not output result due to its used TS-training set is out of the range of transliterating. It is interesting that the performance of baseline III even deteriorates after combing TS and TL training sets. One explanation might be that the language model of baseline III is only trained on word level, so that there is a severe data sparse problem.

Metric	SS-model	Baseline I	Baseline II	Baseline III
Top1	25.6%	17.7%	0%	14.2%
Top10	44.9%	28.2%	0%	23.7%
Top50	62.5%	56.3%	0%	39.8%
MRR	0.348	0.229		0.197

Table 3. Semantic-specific model vs. baselines for person names' translation

Metric	SS-model	Baseline I	Baseline II	Baseline III
Top1	34.4%	0%	26.5%	30.8%
Top10	38.7%	0%	29.8%	36.4%
Top50	46.9%	0%	35.2%	40.2%
MRR	0.381		0.297	0.336

Table 4. Semantic-specific model vs. baselines for organization names' translation

Secondly, the comparison between SS-model and three baselines for translating organization names are shown in Table 4. Baseline III outperforms baseline II for combining both TL-training set and TS-training set. Also SS-model has substantially raised the Top-N recall and MRR value over the baselines. Intuitively, we might expect that SS model could play a greater advantage on translating organization names, because organization names usually combine transliteration and meaning translation. However, comparing Table 3 with Table 4, the performance gaps between SS-model and baselines for organization names is smaller than that for person names. After checking those errors, this phenomenon is probably due to the word reordering problem, which usually occurs in the translation of organization names, but has not been considered by SS-model. Further study would be required for this problem.

Thirdly, we measure the overall effect of SS-model in Table 5. Evidently, the proposed SS-model yields significantly better results than the three baselines at all aspects. It is not surprising to find that the proposed SS-model is effective in translating various NEs of different NE types.

Metric	SS-model	Baseline I	Baseline II	Baseline III
Top1	30.7%	9.5%	11.8%	22.4%
Top10	36.2%	14.2%	16.7%	30.8%
Top50	55.3%	23.5%	32.8%	42.3%
MRR	0.337	0.139	0.142	0.256

Table 5. Semantic-specific model vs. baselines for various names' translation

5.2 Semantic-Specific Model Vs. Joint Transliteration Model

Actually, the proposed semantic-specific model captures semantic information by incorporating the global context information in the corpus, which is similar to the joint transliteration model proposed by (Li et al., 2004). However, the joint model only utilized the local context of the input (joint n-gram model of transliteration pairs) $P(E|C)=\prod_{k=1}^{K} P(<e,c>_k|<e,c>_{k-n+1}^{k-1})$, whereas our model measures the similarity of the global context amongst corpus. Table 6 gives the comparison of the joint model and SS-model for person names' transliteration. Here previous used training-set I and 300 person names are adopted for training and testing here. Also we use 3-gram in both of the two models. As shown in Table 6, even though the performance gap of Top1 (+0.8%) is not much obvious, the performance gap gets larger when the top-N hypotheses increase. This evidently proves the superiority of the proposed model on selecting the correct translation variation from global context.

System	Top1	Top10	Top50	MRR
Joint model	24.8%	40.2%	54.2%	0.319
SS-model	25.6 % (+0.8%)	43.9% (+3.7%)	61.4% (+7.2%)	0.348

Table 6. Semantic-specific model vs. joint model for person names' translation

5.3 Semantic-Specific Model Vs. Origin-Based Model

To further validate the capability of our proposed model, we measure its sensitivity to NE origin information. Thus we compare it with a well-known semantic transliteration model (Li et al., 2007), which only deals with transliteration. Li's semantic transliteration model, called *origin-based model* here, firstly identifies the NE's origin O by $O = \arg\max_O P(O \mid C)$, and then uses its corresponding trained model, which is trained on instances all from origin O. The training and decoding process also use the Moses decoder.

In this experiment, we adopt training-set II, which includes 7,021 person names from USA, Japan and Korea (International *whoswho* corpus in LDC2005T34). And then we randomly select 100 person names from USA, Japan and Korea respectively (also in *whoswho* corpus) as our test data. Also, there is no overlap between the training set II and those test data. Here, baseline I is also the transliteration model, but trained on training set II, and we use the MRR criterion as well.

Test data	Baseline I	SS-model	Origin-based model
Origin=USA	0.289	0.417	0.335
Origin=Japan	0.257	0.473	0.489
Origin=Korea	0.213	0.406	0.368

Table 7. Semantic-specific model vs. origin-based model for person names' translation

Considering Table 7, though there is a slight drop comparing our model with origin-based model for the Japanese person names, the translation improvements on the person names of the other two origins show the superiority of our semantic-specific translation model. Actually, there would be much more origins to classify. For instance, there are more than 100 origins in *whoswho* data; it is tedious to train a large number of models in practice. And the origin labeled data for person names is hard to acquire. By using semantic-specific model, we could directly cluster instances of similar origin, and generate final translation result for origin consistency. The experiments prove that the SS-model is effective on capturing NE origin information to assist NE translation, and it could further accommodate more different semantic information.

6 Related Work

There are two strategies for NE translation. One is to extract NE translation pairs from the Web or from parallel/comparable corpora. This is essentially the same as constructing NE-pair dictionary (lee et al., 2006; Jiang et al., 2009), which is usually not a real-time translation model and is limited by the coverage of the used corpus and the Web resource.

The other is to directly translate an NE phonetically or according to its meaning. For transliteration, several transliteration approaches have been applied to various language pairs (Knight and Graehl, 1998; Tsuji 2002; Li et al. 2004; Oh and Choi, 2005; Pervouchine et al., 2009; Durrani et al., 2010). In contrast, for NE meaning translation, (Zhang et al., 2005; Chen and Zong, 2008; Yang et al., 2009) have proposed different statistical translation models only for organization names.

So far, semantic transliteration has been proposed for learning language origin and gender information of person names (Li et al., 2007). However, semantic information is various for NE translation. It is complicated to define different semantic types, and is tedious to train a large number of models used for different semantic information. Moreover, a semantically labeled training corpus is hard to acquire. Hence this paper does not directly learn NE semantic information, but measures the semantic similarity between the input and global context to capture exact NE translation.

7 Conclusion

In this paper, we present a novel semantic-specific model which could adaptively learn semantic information via instance-based similarity measurement from global context. Accordingly, this model combines transliteration and meaning translation, and automatically selects most probable translation candidates on the basis of the NE semantic-specific information. In summary, our experiments show that the semantic-specific model is much more effective than the traditional statistical model for named entity translation, which achieves a remarkable 31.6% relative improvement in MRR (Table 5). Furthermore, the proposed model yields a comparable result with the joint transliteration model (also using context) and the origin-based model, which shows its advantage on capturing semantic information from global context, such as origin information.

It is expected that the proposed semantic-specific translation model could be further applied to other language pairs, as no language dependent linguistic feature (or knowledge) is adopted in the model/algorithm used.

Acknowledgments

The research work has been funded by the Natural Science Foundation of China under Grant No. 6097 5053 and 61003160 and also supported by the External Cooperation Program of the Chinese Academy of Sciences. The authors also extend sincere thanks to Prof. Keh-Yih Su for his keen in-sights and suggestions on our work.

References

R. Baeza-Yates and B. RiBeiro-Neto. 1999. Modern Information Retrieval. *ISBN 0-201-39829-X.*

Adam L. Berger, Stephen A. Della Pietra and Vincent J. Della Pietra. 1996. A Maximum Entropy Approach to Natural Language Processing. *Computational Linguistics*, 22(1):39-72, March.

Hsin-His Chen, Changhua Yang and Ying Lin. 2003. Learning Formulation and Transformation Rules for Multilingual Named Entities. In *Proceedings of ACL 2003 Workshop on Multilingual and Mixed-language Named Entity Recognition*, pages 1-8.

Yufeng Chen, Chengqing Zong. 2008. A Structure-based Model for Chinese Organization Name Translation. *ACM Transactions on Asian Language Information Processing*, 7(1): 1-30, February 2008.

J. N. Darroch and D. Ratcliff. 1972. Generalized iterative scaling for log-linear models. *Annuals of Mathematical Statistics*, 43: 1470-1480.

Nadir Durrani, Hassan Sajjad, Alexander Fraser, and Helmut Schmid. 2010. Hindi-to-Urdu Machine Translation Through Transliteration. In *Proceedings of the 48th Annual Meeting of the Association for Computational Linguistics*, pages 465–474.

Fei Huang. 2005. Cluster-Specific Name Transliteration. In *Proceedings of the HLT-EMNLP 2005*, Vancouver, BC, Canada.

Long Jiang, Ming Zhou, Lee-Feng Chien, and Cheng Niu. 2007. Named Entity Translation with Web Mining and Transliteration. In *Proceedings of IJ-CAI-2007.*

Long Jiang, Shiquan Yang, Ming Zhou, Xiaohua Liu, and Qingsheng Zhu. 2009. Mining Bilingual Data from the Web with Adaptively Learnt Patterns. In *Proc. of ACL-2009 and the 4th IJCNLP of the AFNLP*, pages 870-878.

Paul B. Kantor and Ellen M. Voorhees, 2000, The TREC-5 Confusion Track: Comparing Retrieval Methods for Scanned Text. *Informational Retrieval*, 2, pp. 165-176.

Kevin Knight and Jonathan Graehl. 1998. Machine Transliteration. *Computational Linguistics*, 24(4).

Chun-Jen Lee, Jason S. Chang and Jyh-Shing R. Jang. 2006. Alignment of Bilingual Named Entities in Parallel Corpora Using Statistical Models and Multiple Knowledge Sources. *ACM Transactions on Asian Language Information Processing (TALIP)*, 5(2): 121-145.

Haizhou Li, Min Zhang and Jian Su. 2004. A Joint Source Channel Model for Machine Transliteration. In *Proceedings of 42nd ACL*, pages 159-166.

Haizhou Li, Khe Chai Sim, Jin-shea Kuo, and Minghui Dong. 2007. Semantic Transliteration of Personal Names, In *Proceedings of 45th ACL*, pages 120-127.

Yang Liu, Qun Liu and Shouxun Lin. Log-linear Models for Word Alignment. 2005. In *Proceedings of the 43rd Annual meeting of the ACL*, pages 459-466.

M. Nagao. 1984. A Framework of a Mechanical Translation between Japanese and English by Analogy Principle, In *Artificial and Human Intelligence*, pages 173-180. NATO publications.

Franz Josef Och and Hermann Ney. 2002. Discriminative Training and Maximum Entropy Models for Statistical Machine Translation. In *Proceedings of the 40th Annual Meeting of the ACL*, pages 295-302.

J.-H. Oh and Choi, K.-S. 2005. An ensemble of grapheme and phoneme for machine transliteration. In *Proceedings of IJCNLP*, pages 450–461.

Vladimir Pervouchine, Haizhou Li and Bo Lin. 2009. Transliteration Alignment. In *Proceedings of ACL-09*, pages 136-144.

S. Sato and M. Nagao. 1990. Toward Memory-Based Translation. In *Proceedings of COLING 1990*, Vol.3. pages 247-252.

K. Tsuji. 2002. Automatic extraction of translational Japanese-KATAKANA and English word pairs from bilingual corpora. *Int. J. Comput. Process Oriental Lang.* 15(3): 261-279.

Fan Yang, Jun Zhao, Bo Zou, Kang Liu, Feifan Liu. 2008. Chinese-English Backward Transliteration Assisted with Mining Monolingual Web Pages, In *Proceeding of the 46th Annual Meeting of the Association for Computational Linguistics*, pages 541-549, Columbus, OH.

Fan Yang, Jun Zhao, Kang Liu. 2009. A Chinese-English Organization Name Translation System Using Heuristic Web Mining and Asymmetric Alignment. In *Proceedings of the 47th Annual Meeting of the ACL*, Singapore. August 2 -7.

Min Zhang, Haizhou Li, Jian Su, and Hendra Setiawan. 2005. A Phrase-Based Context-Dependent Joint Probability Model for Named Entity Translation. *IJCNLP 2005*, pages 600-611.

Mining Revision Log of Language Learning SNS for Automated Japanese Error Correction of Second Language Learners

Tomoya Mizumoto
NAIST, Japan
tomoya-m@is.nasit.jp

Mamoru Komachi
NAIST, Japan
komachi@is.naist.jp

Masaaki Nagata
NTT, Japan
nagata.masaaki@lab.ntt.co.jp

Yuji Matsumoto
NAIST, Japan
matsu@is.naist.jp

Abstract

We present an attempt to extract a large-scale Japanese learners' corpus from the revision log of a language learning SNS. This corpus is easy to obtain in large-scale, covers a wide variety of topics and styles, and can be a great source of knowledge for both language learners and instructors. We also demonstrate that the extracted learners' corpus of Japanese as a second language can be used as training data for learners' error correction using an SMT approach. We evaluate different granularities of tokenization to alleviate the problem of word segmentation errors caused by erroneous input from language learners. Experimental results show that the character-wise model outperforms the word-wise model.

1 Introduction

The number of Japanese language learners around the world has increased more than 30-fold in the past three decades. The Japan Foundation reports that more than 3.65 million people in 133 countries and regions are studying Japanese in 2009 [1]. However, there are only 50,000 Japanese language teachers overseas, and thus it is in high demand to find good instructors for writers of Japanese as a Second Language (JSL).

Recently, natural language processing research has begun to pay attention to second language learning (Rozovskaya and Roth, 2011; Park and Levy, 2011; Liu et al., 2011; Oyama and Matsumoto, 2010; Xue and Hwa, 2010). However, most previous research for second language learning deals with restricted types of learners' errors. For example, research for JSL learners' errors mainly focus on Japanese case particles (Oyama and Matsumoto, 2010; Imaeda et al., 2003; Nampo et al., 2007; Suzuki and Toutanova, 2006), however they focus only on case particles whereas we attempt to correct all types of errors.

However, real JSL learners' writing contains not only errors of Japanese case particles but also various other errors including spelling and collocation errors. For instance, a Japanese language learner who speaks Chinese may write:

何で日本語はこんなに難しい<u>な</u>の？
(Why does Japanese are so difficult?)

which has a grammatical error of inserting 'な' due to literal translation from Chinese. Park and Levy (2011) proposed an EM-based unsupervised approach to perform whole sentence grammar correction, but the types of errors must be predetermined to learn the parameters for their noisy channel model. It requires expert knowledge of L2 teaching, which is often hard to obtain.

One promising approach for correcting unrestricted errors of JSL learners is Brockett et al. (2006)'s automated error correction method using statistical machine translation (SMT). The advantage of their method is that it does not require expert knowledge. Instead, it learns a correction model from sentence-aligned corrected learners' corpora. However, it is not easy to acquire large-scale learners' corpora. In fact, Brockett et al. (2006) used regular expressions to automatically create erroneous corpora from native corpora.

To solve the knowledge acquisition bottleneck, we propose a method of mining revision logs to create a large-scale learners' corpus. The corpus is compiled from error revision logs from a language learning social network service (SNS), which covers a wide variety of topics and styles. The main advantage of using revision logs is three-fold: (1) it benefits from the wisdom of crowds, (2) it can be obtained in large-scale, and (3) it is a great source

[1] http://www.jpf.go.jp/e/japanese/survey/result/index.html

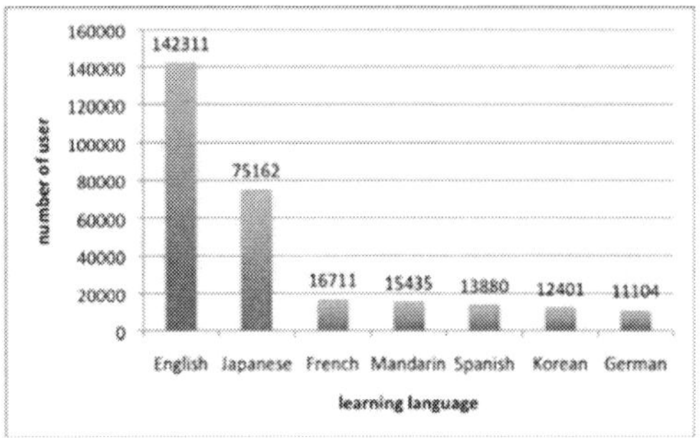

Figure 1: Number of users for each learning language in Lang-8

of knowledge not only for learners but also for language teachers. In this paper, we show that the method using SMT techniques with a large-scale learners' corpus can correct JSL learners' error with reasonable accuracy.

The rest of this paper is organized as follows. Section 2 describes the JSL corpus created from revision logs of a language learning SNS. Section 3 explains an SMT-based approach to JSL error correction. In section 4, we report the experimental results of SMT-based JSL error correction using large-scale real corpus. In section 5, we conduct error analysis and discuss issues of the proposed method. Section 6 concludes this work and presents future direction.

2 A Large Scale Japanese Language Learners' Corpus from Revision Logs

Recent growth of the web has opened the possibility of using the internet to break the barriers of space and time. Specifically, social network service (SNS) has begun to receive a lot of attention recently. There are a number of SNS sites that help language learners across the world, including smart.fm, Livemocha and Lang-8, to name a few. We will look briefly at each SNS below.

First, smart.fm [2] (formerly iKnow!) is a SNS-based language learning service that helps learners practice language learning. Smart.fm provides a tailored curriculum for each user to memorize learning content through simple exercises.

Second, Livemocha [3] is also a language learning SNS that offers course of grammar instructions, reading comprehension exercises and practice for both writing and speaking. Users can submit a free composition on a subject and receive feedbacks from other users of the native language. However, they are not able to write about arbitrary topics.

Third, Lang-8 is a "Multi-lingual language learning and language exchange Social Networking Service" [4] , which has over 200,000 registered members at the moment. As soon as the learners write a passage, mostly a part of a diary, in a language they are learning, native speakers of the language correct it for them. The learners in turn are encouraged to correct other members' composition errors according to their first language (L1). Hence, the SNS is called "language exchange". It supports 77 languages, facilitating multilingual communication.

2.1 Japanese Language Learners' Corpora

One of the most famous learners' corpus is Teramura Error Data [5]. The corpus was mainly collected in 1986 from Japanse compositions written by foreign students, mostly from Asian countries. The corpus consists of several styles including free composition, cloze (gap filling) test, and pattern composition. Unlike this data, JSL learners in Lang-8 encompass the whole world. Also, Lang-8 offers a wide variety of free compositions of the learner's choice, and the size of the data is orders of magnitude (448MB without all the tags) larger than Teramura's data (420KB, 4,601 sentences written by 339 students). Also, although Teramura Error Data is annotated with error types, the correct words or strings are not often provided, which makes it difficult to use it for automatic correction of learners' errors.

Ohso [6] created a database of Japanese compositions by JSL learners. It is annotated with error types with correct forms to allow error analysis. However, similar to Teramura Error Data, the corpus does not cover many topics because it was collected at only four institutions. In addition, it is limited in size (756 files, average file size is 2KB).

The corpus most related to ours is the JSL learners parallel database of Japanese writings and their translation of learners' L1 [7] created by National Institute for Japanese Language and Linguistics. It collects 1,500 JSL learners' writings and their

[2] `http://smart.fm/`

[3] `http://www.livemocha.com/`

[4] `http://lang-8.com/`

[5] `http://www.lang.nagoya-u.ac.jp/tonoike/teramura.html`

[6] `https://kaken.nii.ac.jp/ja/p/08558020/1998/6/en`

[7] `http://jpforlife.jp/taiyakudb.html`

self-translations. There are around 250 writings corrected with error types by several Japanese language teachers. The advantage of this corpus is that some of the texts are annotated by professional language teachers and can be used as a source of error correction. However, again, the size of this corpus is limited since it is hard to obtain annotations from language teachers. Our approach differs from them in that we employ the wisdom of crowds of native speakers, not necessarily language teachers, to compile a large-scale learners' corpus.

2.2 Features of Lang-8 Data

We created a large-scale language learners' corpus from error revision log of Lang-8. Figure 1 shows that approximately 75,000 users are learning Japanese [8]. Table 1 shows the top seven languages in the corpus. There are 925,588 sentences of JSL learners [9]. Out of 925,588 sentences, 763,971 (93.4%) sentences are corrected by human annotators. A sentence written by JSL learners might have two or more revision sentences in Lang-8 by different voluntary reviewers [10]. Therefore, the total number of corrected sentences amounts to 1,288,934. In other words, one sentence gets corrected approximately 1.69 times on average.

There are several distinguishing features of the data obtained from Lang-8. First, since Lang-8 is a language learning SNS, we can obtain pairs of learner's sentence and corrected sentence. Using this data, it is possible to collect the learner's errors. We will describe how to build a learners' corpus from revision logs later in this section.

Second, Lang-8 data may have more than one correction for the same sentence. We could exploit this feature to acquire paraphrases in a similar way to (Barzilay and McKeown, 2001). Table 2 shows an example of multiple correction. Two annotators correct the same learner's sentence. In this example, one can infer that "なりの表現で (in one's own expressions)" and "なりに (in one's own way)" are paraphrases of each other.

Third, we could obtain multi-lingual parallel sentences. Figure 2 shows examples of parallel

Figure 2: Parallel sentence in Lang-8

sentences in Lang-8. In this example, the JSL learner writes two Japanese sentences and their translation for each sentence to tell what he or she wants to say. Although the sentences written in the learning language may contain errors and mistakes, we can align the English translation to the corrected Japanese sentence. The parallel corpus created from the revision log of SNS would be a remarkable source of colloquial expressions ideal for translating consumer generated media such as blogs and SNS.

Fourth, annotators of Lang-8 sometimes add in-line comments to the corrected sentences. It is often written in parentheses to indicate that the string is a comment, but not always. Depending on the first language of the language learner, annotators put comments in either the learning language or the learner's L1. This can be a great source of extracting useful information for language learning, since the comment itself explains pitfalls that the language learners often come across.

2.3 Extracting corrected sentence from HTML

All the error revisions are made through a web-based editing interface that allows annotators to delete, insert or change any character sequence of the learner's text by any sequence. Table 3 illustrates an example of the HTML generated from Lang-8's revision editor. The tag `<span class="sline">` shows that the characters within the tags should be removed. The color tags `<span class="red">` and `<span class="f_blue">` are used somewhat arbitrarily by annotators. In general, they indicate correct strings. In the example, the annotator used delete line and red color to point out and correct the first error, and blue color to indicate inserted characters.

From this observation, we apply simple

[8] We counted learning language in user profile. Some learners register two or more learning languages.

[9] We counted learning language written for each journal because learners may write in different languages.

[10] The correction of a new review might be affected by the previous corrections by others.

Table 1: Number of sentences for each language in Lang-8

Language	English	Japanese	Mandarin	Korean	Spanish	French	German
Number of sentences	1,069,549	925,588	136,203	93,955	51,829	58,918	37,886

Table 2: An illustraive example of multiple correction

Sentence written by a JSL learner	三人はそれぞれ自分 の方式で 感情を表 れ ます。
Sentence corrected by an annotator1	三人はそれぞれ自分 なりの表現で 感情を表 し ます。 (Each of three expresses their feelings in their own expressions.)
Sentence corrected by an annotator2	三人はそれぞれ自分 なりに 感情を表 し ます。 (Each of three expresses their feelings in their own way.)

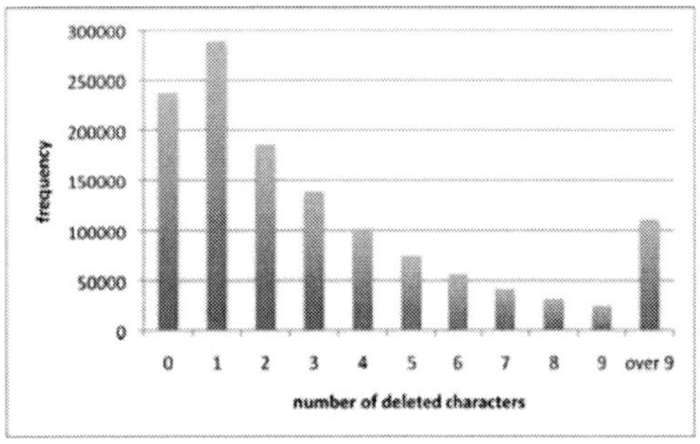

Figure 3: Summary of number of deletion

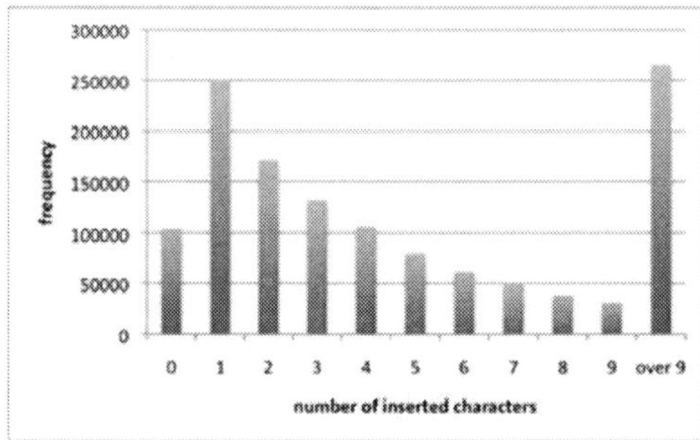

Figure 4: Summary of number of insertion

heuristics to extract corrected sentences from Lang-8. First, we remove all the `<span class="sline">` tags and characters within them. Then, we discard other tags, retaining the characters surrounded by the tags. After this rule, we obtain the corrected sentence shown in the bottom row in Table 4.

2.4 Data Statistic and Filtering by Edit Distance

In an actual correction, it is expected that annotators do not completely rewrite the original sentence and most character strings remain the same as the original sentence. Thus, we investigated the quantitative distribution of Lang-8 data by breaking down the sentences according to the edit distance between the original and corrected sentences (number of deletion / number of insertion of characters in revision log).

Figures 3 and 4 summarize the numbers of deleted and inserted characters. These figures reveal that both distributions of deletion and insertion are comparable. On the other hand, they differ in the absolute frequency of deletion and insertion. For example, the number of cases with no deletion is considerably more than the number with no insertion. Also, the frequency of sentences with more than nine insertions is higher than that for deletions. This reflects the fact that there are many sentences with comments (insertions) and that people tend not to remove too many characters to keep the information of the original sentence written by the learner.

From observations of the created corpus, a correction can be divided into two types: (1) a correction by insertion, deletion, or substitution of strings, (2) a correction with a comment. Table 4 shows examples of correction from Lang-8. The first example is a sentence written by JSL learners containing an error, and is corrected by inserting a character. In the second example the learner's sentence is correct; in addition the annotator writes a comment [11]. Besides, there exist "corrected" sentences to which only the word "GOOD" is appended at the end. In this case, original sentence is not modified at all by the annotator. The inserted comment merely informs the learner that there is no mistake in the learner's writing.

To handle these comments, we conduct the following three pre-processing steps: (1) if the corrected sentence contains only "GOOD" or "OK", we do not include it in the corpus, (2) if edit dis-

[11] Some annotator erase a learner's original sentence and rewrite it to "OK".

Table 3: Extracting corrected sentence from HTML

Sentence written by a JSL learner	去年は参加してなかった、見るだけ。 (I was not participating last year, just watching.)
Corrected sentence with tags	去 年 は 参 加<span class="sline">し て な かった</span><span class="red">せ ず に</span>、見るだけ<span class="f_blue">だった</span>。
Seen on the browser	去年は参加~~してなかった~~せずに、見るだけだった。
Corrected sentence	去年は参加せずに、見るだけだった。 (I did not participate but watched last year.)

Table 4: Examples of correction in Lang-8

Sentence written by a JSL learner	ビデオゲームをやました (Video games Yamashita.)
Sentence corrected by an annotator	ビデオゲームをやりました (I played video games.)
Sentence written by a JSL learner	銭湯に行った。 (I went to a public bath.)
Sentence corrected by an annotator (with comment)	銭湯に行った。 いつ行ったかがある方がいい (I went to a public bath. It is better to say when you went.)

tance between the learner's sentence and corrected sentence is 5, we simply drop the sentence for the corpus, and (3) if the corrected sentence ends with "GOOD" or "OK", we remove it and retain the sentence pair. As a result, we obtained a corpus of 849,894 corrected and aligned sentence pairs by JSL learners.

Another notable issue is that annotators may not correct all the errors in a sentence. Table 5 shows an example of JSL learner's sentence for confusing case markers of "が" (NOM) and "は" (TOP). In this example, "は" and "が" should be corrected to "が" and "は", respectively. However, the annotator left the second case markers "は" unchanged. Because the number of these cases seems low, we regard it as safe to ignore this issue for creating the corpus.

3 Error Correction Using SMT

In this study, we attempt to solve the problem of JSL learners' error correction using the SMT technique. The well-known SMT formulation using the noisy channel model (Brown et al., 1993) is:

$$\hat{e} = \arg\max_{e} P(e|f) = \arg\max_{e} P(e)P(f|e) \quad (1)$$

where e represents target sentences and f represents source sentences. $P(e)$ is the probability of the language model (LM) and $P(f|e)$ is the probability of the translation model (TM). TM is learned from sentence-aligned parallel corpus while LM is learned from target language corpus.

To adapt SMT to error correction, f can be regarded as the sentences written by Japanese learners, whereas e represents the manually-corrected Japanese sentences. TM can be learned from the sentence-aligned learners' corpus. LM can be learned from a monolingual corpus of the language to be learned. Once we obtain a manually-corrected corpus of language learners, it is possible to translate erroneous sentences into correct sentences using SMT.

The use of SMT for spelling and grammar correction has the following three advantages. (1) It does not require expert knowledge. (2) It is straightforward to apply SMT tools to this task. (3) Error correction using SMT can benefit from the improvement of SMT method.

Related work on error correction using phrase-based SMT includes research on English and Japanese (Brockett et al., 2006; Suzuki and Toutanova, 2006). Brockett et al. (2006) proposed to correct mass noun errors using SMT and used 45,000 sentences as training sets randomly extracted from automatically created 346,000 sentences. Our work differs from them in that we (1) do not restrict ourselves to a specific error type such as mass noun; and (2) exploit a large-scale real world data set. Suzuki and Toutanova (2006) proposed a machine learning-based method to pre-

Table 5: Problem of correction in Lang-8

Sentence written by a JSL learner	この4つが僕は少年のころに発売されて (As for me, these four were sold when I was a kid.)
Sentence corrected by an annotator	この4つは僕は少年のころに発売されて (As for these four, I was sold when I was a kid.)
Corrt sentence	この4つは僕が少年のころに発売されて (As for these four, they were sold when I was a kid.)

dict Japanese case particles using a monolingual corpus in the context of SMT.

3.1 Statistical Error Correction with Different Granularity of Tokenization

When translating a sentence from Japanese to another language with SMT, one usually performs word segmentation as a pre-processing step. However, JSL learners' sentences contain a lot of errors and hiragana (phonetic characters), which are hard to tokenize by traditional morphological analyzer trained on newswire text. Suppose we want to tokenize into words the following real sentence written by a JSL learner:

でもじょずじゃりません

The correct counterpart would be:

でもじょうずじゃありません
(But I am not good at it.)

The corrected sentence has "う" and "あ" inserted [12]. These sentences written by a learner and corrected by a native speaker are tokenized as follows by MeCab [13], which is one of the most popular Japanese Morphological Analyzer:

でも　じ　ょずじゃりません
(but (fragment) (garbled word))

でも　じょうず　じゃ　あり　ません
(but good at be not)

These examples illustrate the difficulty of correcting JSL learners' sentence using word-wise SMT.

To alleviate this problem, we propose to build a character-wise segmented corpus with phrase-based SMT. Character-wise model is not affected by word segmentation errors, thus it is expected to be more robust for the task of correcting JSL errors. For the above-mentioned two example sentences, we split sentences into characters rather than words:

This enables the phrase-based SMT to learn the alignment between "じょず" and "じょうず", resulting in a more robust model to correct JSL errors than word-wise model.

4 Experiments on JSL Learner's Error Correction with SMT

We carried out an experiment to see (1) the effect of granularity of tokenization as described in Section 3.1; (2) the effect of corpus size; (3) the difference of L1 model. We used Moses 2.1 [14] as a decoder and GIZA++ 1.0.5 [15] as an alignment tool. We used Japanese morphological analyzer MeCab 0.97 with UniDic 1.3.12 [16] for word segmentation.

We created a word-wise model as baseline. Hereafter, we refer to this as W and also constructed model with entries from UniDic for better alignment, denoted as W+Dic. We used word trigram as LM for W and W+Dic. We built two character-wise models: character 3-gram and 5-gram represented as C3 and C5, respectively. We also conducted minimum error rate training (MERT) (Och, 2003) in all experiments [17].

4.1 Experimental Data

All the data was created from 849,894 Japanese sentences extracted from revision logs of Lang-8 crawled in December 2010. To see the difference of errors stemming from L1, we carried out an experiment with two L1s: English and Mandarin. ALL extracts training data from the entire corpus for the translation model. There are 320,655 Japanese sentences whose L1 is English

[12] It is hard for JSL learners of certain L1 to distinguish Japanese short and long vowels.

[13] `http://mecab.sourceforge.net/`

[14] `http://www.statmt.org/moses/`

[15] `http://www-i6.informatik.rwth-aachen.de/Colleagues/och/software/GIZA++.html`

[16] `http://www.tokuteicorpus.jp/dist/`

[17] We performed minimum error rate training to maximize BLEU (5-gram).

and 186,807 Japanese sentences whose L1 is Mandarin. For each L1 JSL corpus, we split the corpus into two parts: 500 sentences for testing and development, and the rest for training.

We shuffled the training data to prepare the corpus for learning LM and TM. We manually re-annotated 500 sentences to make gold-standard data and used 200 sentences for testing, and 300 sentences for development.

4.2 Evaluation Metrics

As evaluation metrics, we use automatic evaluation criteria. To be precise, we used recall (R) and precision (P) based on longest common subsequence (LCS) (Mori et al., 1999; Aho, 1990) and character-based BLEU (Papineni et al., 2002).

Park and Levy (2011) adopted character-based BLEU for automatic assessment of ESL errors. We followed their use of BLEU in the error correction task of JSL learners. Since we perform minimum error rate training using BLEU we can directly compare each model's performance.

Recall and precision based on LCS are defined as follows:

$$Recall = \frac{N_{LCS}}{N_{SYSTEM}}, \quad Precision = \frac{N_{LCS}}{N_{CORRECT}}$$

where N_{LCS}, N_{SYSTEM}, and $N_{CORRECT}$ denote the number of character containing longest common subsequences of system results and corrected answers, the number of character containing system results, and the number of character containing corrected answer, respectively. Also, F-measure is the harmonic average between R and P. To illustrate recall and precision based on LCS, let us consider the following example:

CORRECT: 私 は 学生 です
(I am a student)

SYSTEM: 私 わ[18]学生
(I ring student)

LCS consists of three characters "私 学 生", and $N_{LCS} = 3$. Number of characters in the corrected sentence is six and that in the system is four, so $N_{CORRECT} = 6$ and $N_{SYSTEM} = 4$. Thus, $Recall = 3/4$ and $Precision = 3/6$.

4.3 Experimental Results

Comparison of granularity of tokenization Table 6 illustrates the performance with different methods (Training Corpus: L1 = ALL; Test Corpus: L1 = English; TM: 0.3M sentences; LM: 1M sentence). The character-wise models outperform the word-wise model in both recall and precision. C5 achieved the best precision, F and BLEU, while C3 obtained the best recall.

Table 6: Comparison of the performance (recall, precision, F, BLEU) of error correction for each system with different granularity of tokenization (TM: 0.3M sentences, LM: 1M sentence)

	W	W+Dic	C3	C5
R	0.9043	0.9083	**0.9089**	0.9083
P	0.9175	0.9210	0.9234	**0.9243**
F	0.9109	0.9146	0.9161	**0.9162**
B	0.8072	0.8101	0.8163	**0.8181**

Effects of corpus size We varied the size of TM while fixing the size of LM to 1M sentences to see the effect of corpus size on the performance. Figure 5 shows the performance (BLEU) with different TM size (Training Corpus: L1 = ALL; Test Corpus: L1 = English). The larger the size of the TM, the higher the BLEU. This confirms that the large scale JSL learner's corpus extracted from Lang-8 is a great source of learning learners' errors. Although TM trained on 0.85M sentences exhibits lower performance than TM trained on 0.3M sentences, the difference is not statistically significant.

Comparison of L1 of the training model Table 7 shows result for each L1 trained translation model [19].

Basically, performance was better when TM was trained with the same L1 as the test set. In the case where L1 of test data is English, the model trained from ALL is comparable to L1 English. This is because the model trained from ALL includes many sentence written by learners whose L1 is English.

5 Discussion

As we discussed in Section 2, the extracted corpus still contains comments in the corrected sentences. However, it does not greatly affect the performance of the JSL learner's error correction, demonstrating that we were able to build a large-scale JSL learners' corpus from revision logs. Moreover, we have checked all the output of

[18] The pronunciation of "わ" is the same as "は".

[19] Note that LM was trained from the whole training corpus. We did not change L1 for LM.

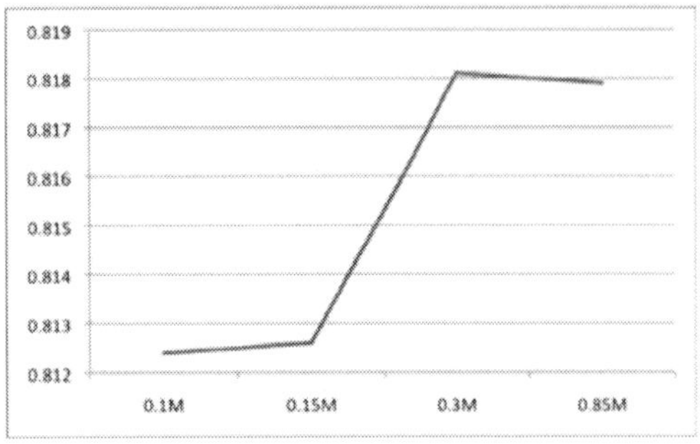

Figure 5: Comparison of the performance (BLEU) of error correction for different size of TM (fixing the size of LM to 1M sentence)

our SMT-based error correction system, but none of the errors of the system derive from the annotators' comments.

Here are some examples illustrating the difference of the scale of the training corpus.. We compared translation models TM trained on 0.1M sentences and 0.3M sentences in Figure 5. Note that the model trained on 0.1M sentences gave the worst result, wheares model trained on 0.3M sentences achieved the best. All the models were trained on 1M sentence for LM. Both models corrected the examples below:

Original: またどもう ありがとう
(Thanks, Matadomou (OOV))

Correct: またどうも ありがとう
(Thank you again)

Also, both of them corrected a case marker error frequently found in JSL learners' writing as in:

Original：TRUTHわ美しいです
(TRUTH wa beautiful)

Correct：TRUTHは美しいです
(TRUTH is beatiful)

On the other hand, the model trained on 0.3M sentences corrected the following example:

Original: 学生なるたら学校に行ける
(the learner made an error in conjugation form.)

Correct: 学生なったら学校に行ける
(Becoming a student, I can go to school.)

0.1M: 学生なるため学校に行ける
(I can go to school to be student)

0.3M: 学生なったら学校に行ける
(Becoming a student, I go to a school)

Table 7: Comparison of the performance (recall, precision, F, BLEU) of error correction trained on different first language (L1). (TM: 0.18M sentences, LM: 1M sentences)

			L1 of test data	
			English	Mandarin
L1 of training data	English	R	0.9079	0.9339
		P	0.9241	0.9387
		F	0.9159	0.9363
		B	**0.8148**	0.8573
	Mandarin	R	0.9063	0.9357
		P	0.9169	0.9388
		F	0.9116	0.9373
		B	0.8083	**0.8589**
	ALL	R	0.9099	0.9349
		P	0.9183	0.9367
		F	0.9141	0.9358
		B	0.8121	0.8553

This example also illustrates the fact that there remains uncorrected errors (missing "ni" case marker after "学生" *student*) as we discussed in Section 2.4.

Another remaining issue is evaluation metric. We have used character-based BLEU, recall and precision based on the longest common subsequence. These methods have the advantage of allowing automatic system evaluation, but they do not reflect the importance of the errors that language learners make. There is still much room for improvement in the evaluation metric for error correction of language learners.

6 Conclusions

We proposed to extract a large-scale learners' corpus from the revision log of a language learning SNS. This corpus is easy to obtain in a large-scale, covers a wide variety of topics and styles, and can be a great source of knowledge for both language learners and instructors. We adopted phrase-based SMT approaches to alleviate the problem of erroneous input from language learners. Experimental results show that the character-wise model outperforms the word-wise model. We plan to apply factored language and translation models incorporating the POS information of the words on the target side, while learners' input is processed by a character-wise model.

Acknowledgements

We would like to thank Hiromi Oyama, Seiji Kasahara and Joseph Irwin for their useful comments on this study. Special thanks to Yangyang Xi for maintaining Lang-8.

References

Alfred V. Aho. 1990. Algorithms for Finding Patterns in Strings. In J. van Leeuwen, editor, *Handbook of Theoretical Computer Science: Volume A: Algorithms and Complexity*, pages 255–300. Elsevier, Amsterdam.

Regina Barzilay and Kathleen R. McKeown. 2001. Extracting Paraphrases from a Parallel Corpus. In *Proceedings of ACL*, pages 50–57.

Chris Brockett, William B. Dolan, and Michael Gamon. 2006. Correcting ESL Errors Using Phrasal SMT Techniques. In *Proceedings of COLING-ACL*, pages 249–256.

Peter F. Brown, Stephen A. Della Pietra, Vincent J. Della Pietra, and Robert L. Mercer. 1993. The Mathematics of Statistical Machine Translation: Parameter Estimation. *Computational Linguistics*, 19(2):266–311.

Koji Imaeda, Atsuo Kawai, Yuji Ishikawa, Ryo Nagata, and Fumito Masui. 2003. Error Detection and Correction of Case particles in Japanese Learner's Composition (in japanese). In *Proceedings of the Information Processing Society of Japan SIG*, pages 39–46.

Xiaohua Liu, Bo Han, and Min Zhou. 2011. Correcting Verb Selection Errors for ESL with the Perceptron. In *Proceedings of the 12th international conference on Computational linguistics and intelligent text processing - Volume Part II*, CICLing'11, pages 411–423, Berlin, Heidelberg. Springer-Verlag.

Shinsuke Mori, Masatoshi Tsuchiya, Osamu Yamako, and Makoto Nagao. 1999. Kana-Kanji Conversion by a Stochastic Model (in japanese). *Transaction of Information Processing Society of Japan*, 40(7):2946–2953.

Ryota Nampo, Hokuto Ototake, and Kenji Araki. 2007. Automatic Error Detection and Correction of Japanese Particles Using Features within Bunsetsu (in japanese). In *Proceedings of the Information Processing Society of Japan SIG*, pages 107–112.

Franz Josef Och. 2003. Minimum Error Rate Training in Statistical Machine Translation. In *Proceedings of ACL*, pages 160–167.

Hiromi Oyama and Yuji Matsumoto. 2010. Automatic Error Detection Method for Japanese Case Particles in Japanese Language Learners. In *Corpus, ICT, and Language Education*, pages 235–245.

Kishore Papineni, Salim Roukos, Todd Ward, and Wei-Jing Zhu. 2002. BLEU: A Method for Automatic Evaluation of Machine Translation. In *Proceedings of ACL*, pages 311–318.

Y. Albert Park and Roger Levy. 2011. Automated Whole Sentence Grammar Correction Using a Noisy Channel Model. In *Proceedings of ACL*, pages 934–944.

Alla Rozovskaya and Dan Roth. 2011. Algorithm Selection and Model Adaptation for ESL Correction Tasks. In *Proceedings of ACL*, pages 924–933.

Hisami Suzuki and Kristina Toutanova. 2006. Learning to Predict Case Markers in Japanese. In *Proceedings of ACL*, pages 1049–1056.

Huichao Xue and Rebecca Hwa. 2010. Syntax-Driven Machine Translation as a Model of ESL Revision. In *Proceedings of COLING*, pages 1373–1381.

Modality Specific Meta Features for Authorship Attribution in Web Forum Posts

Thamar Solorio and **Sangita Pillay**
The University of Alabama at Birmingham
1300 University Boulevard
Birmingham, AL 35294, USA
{solorio,rsangita}@cis.uab.edu

Sindhu Raghavan
The University of Texas at Austin
1 University Station C0500
Austin, TX 78712, USA
sindhu@cis.uab.edu

Manuel Montes y Gómez
The University of Alabama at Birmingham
1300 University Boulevard
Birmingham, AL 35294, USA
National Institute of Astrophysics, Optics, and Electronics
Luis Enrique Erro No. 1
Tonantzintla, Puebla, Mexico
mmontesg@ccc.inaoep.mx

Abstract

This paper presents a new method for Authorship Attribution (AA) on online forum posts. The idea behind the method is to generate meta features that capture modality specific similarity relations among texts from different authors. Each modality represents a particular linguistic dimension (syntactic, lexical, stylistic). To evaluate this approach we measure prediction accuracy on data from an online forum with up to 100 candidate authors. We also compare our results with a state of the art approach that has shown to perform well across different genres. We have found the meta features to be especially helpful in the online forum domain, where the documents are very short, showing this to be a very promising direction for AA on a realistic web forum scenario.

1 Introduction

Authorship attribution (AA) refers to the task of analyzing a document to identify the potential author who wrote the text. Earlier work on this problem involved gathering statistics about the frequency of words with specific length, together with other stylistic characteristics extracted from written samples that were in most cases an entire book or volume (Mendenhall, 1887; Mosteller and Wallace, 1964). Current approaches to AA relay on casting this problem as a text classification task, where instead of aiming to do a thematic classification of documents the goal is to have the models learn the distinguishable characteristics in the written work of authors. The focus of analysis on more recent work has also shifted from book-length pieces to documents with length ranging from a couple of blocks (Hirst and Feiguina, 2007) to samples with at most 140 characters (Layton et al., 2010).

AA can help settle disputes over the original creators of a given piece of text. But other practical applications include using AA for building a prosecution case against an online abuser. This is an important application, especially when we consider the raising trends in cyber-bullying and other electronic forms of teen violence[1].

Achieving good accuracy in AA on spontaneous online data is, however, far more challenging than the typical scenario for AA. One of the major complicating factors involves the limited amount of training data. In the typical scenario, we may have an entire document (several pages long), or even an entire book, while in the case of online data from social media we will have very short texts that are a couple of sentences long. Another challenge related to online data from social media is the number of potential authors that the model will need to learn. Consider aiming to do AA for data of online web forums, which is the goal in our work. In this case the potential author of a given post is one out of the thousands of registered users in that forum. In contrast, the majority of the text classification problems have a small number of classes. Lastly, we have to consider the problems with processing spontaneous written

[1] http://cyberbullying.us/index.php

language, and in particular, from informal interactions of web forum posts. The fact that the written fragments are informal is not by itself a complicating factor. We can argue that because they are informal they allow the writer to express more freely and thus they may contain more revealing information. But if we are to use syntactic analyzers to extract features for our learning model, as previous work in AA has done, then these informal and spontaneous samples can cause the analyzers to break, or output very noisy information.

This paper presents a new approach for AA on web forum data that generates informative meta features that can help discriminate the posts from different authors. The meta features in our work are derived from clustering of the feature vectors. However, different from distributional clustering and related approaches such as (Baker and McCallum, 1998; Slonim and Tishby, 2001; Dhillon et al., 2003), we do not cluster the features, but the instances in an unsupervised fashion. The goal of the meta features is to encode high level relations of similarities among posts from different authors, and not to reduce the feature set or find semantically related features as in the work listed above. Moreover, another difference and contribution of our work is the idea of generating modality specific meta features. This modality specific framework allows to reach higher AA accuracy on short texts than that achieved by the standard approach using only first level features and competitive state of the art approaches.

The question we aim to answer here is whether generating these metafeatures, which contribute to the computational cost, are indeed helpful in the scenario of AA on web forum posts. Our experiments are done on a much smaller scale than that of the real scenario, with data sets of up to 100 authors and in a closed-class setting. However, they represent the best results reported so far under similar conditions and thus they show promise to scale up. The results we present show that the modality specific meta features are indeed helpful for short online data, and outperform accuracy of previous work.

The next section reviews related work on AA. Then in Section 3 we discuss our approach to generating meta features from clustering the instances using different "views" of the posts. A discussion of the first level features is presented in Section 4. Section 5 presents the data sets used in our experiments. The evaluation of our approach is outlined in Section 6, where we also discuss our baseline system and results. The last section summarizes our findings and outlines our research goals for the immediate future.

2 Related Work

Authorship Attribution (AA) and related author analysis tasks, such as plagiarism detection and author profiling, have received a lot of attention recently, but most of the evaluation sets have a small number of authors. Here we highlight previous work that involves a large number of authors (at least 50) and refer the reader to the survey by (Stamatatos, 2009).

Luyckx and Daelemans studied the impact on accuracy of the number of potential authors and the size of the training data per author (Luyckx and Daelemans, 2010). They measured classification accuracy of a memory-based learner on three datasets with up to 145 candidate authors for one of them. The features used in their experiments include lexical features, such as word and lemma n-grams, type/token ratio, and readability measures; the syntactic features include Parts-of-Speech (POS), grammatical relations, chunk n-grams, and tokens with POS attached. They also used character n-grams, features that have been found to work well for AA (Peng et al., 2004; Plakias and Stamatatos, 2008). As expected, accuracy reported for 145 authors ($\tilde{1}2\%$) was considerably lower than that achieved when the number of authors was smaller. An important characteristic of Luyckx and Daelemans work is that the 145 author set has only one document per author. In the experimental setup they partitioned each document into 10 fragments and used 9 of these fragments for training their model while testing on the remaining one. We believe that training a model on pieces of the same document used for testing is not exactly the task of AA, at least not in a realistic scenario. However, we recognize that the limited training data is an important constraint.

(Layton et al., 2010) shows results from using the Source Code Authorship Profile (SCAP) method on Twitter data where the microblogs are restricted to a maximum of 140 characters. The SCAP method, as developed by (Frantzeskou et al., 2007), determines authorship by measuring the overlap in character n-grams from the text document to the concatenated documents of each author. On a set with 50 authors, the SCAP method reached an accuracy of 55%, although when the `@username` was included in the text their accuracy increased to little over 70%. As the authors suggest, expecting to have this `@username` information from an author that wants to remain anonymous is not realistic.

Koppel *et al.* (2011) present a study of AA using blog data crawled from `blogger.com`. The approach used by them is based on computing cosine similarity from vectors of character 4-grams, and the number of candidate authors is by far the largest reported in the literature: for some experiments they trained on 10,000 authors and tested on 1,000. Precision and Recall in this setting were reported at 87.9% and 28.2%, respectively. However, we should also note that in these experiments text was also fragmented into snippets, and similar to what Luyckx and Daelemans did, the similarity model uses fragments of the same source text to predict authorship. In our opinion, the task resembles more a data provenance problem than an AA one. Moreover, because the blog data used in this work was not controlled for topic, and given that they used character 4-grams as features in a similarity based approach, we speculate that in the Koppel *et al.* setting there is more risk to bias the task from AA to a semantic or topic categorization and the only way to disentangle the two is by controlling for topic variation.

In another interesting recent work on AA, Probabilistic Context-Free Grammars (PCFGs) were proposed for AA (Raghavan et al., 2010). The number of authors in the evaluation data sets was rather small (3 to 6) but it included different domains, such as poetry, football, business, travel, and cricket, and all the data was harvested from the Internet. Raghavan et al. trained a PCFG for each author independently and authorship on the test data was assigned by taking the highest likelihood score from these grammars. To overcome the data sparseness problem, they mixed treebanked data from the Wall Street Journal (WSJ). They also enriched this mostly syntactic models with lexical information by combining the output with a bag-of-words Maximum Entropy classifier and a word-based n-gram language model. In their case, the combined model performed better than the baseline and the other machine learning approaches for most of the datasets. What is very interesting from this previous work is the fact that the same inexpensive PCFG-based approach worked reasonably well on all the data sets tested. In our experiments we evaluate this approach on the web forum data and the results show this to be a competitive method, even though the number of potential authors increased by a large margin and the documents are shorter than those used in (Raghavan et al., 2010).

3 Modality Specific Meta Features for Authorship Attribution

The standard formulation of text classification considers having a set of labeled examples, l, where each document is represented by a feature vector $\mathbf{x} \in R^n$ and their corresponding labels y, where $y_i \in \{0,1\}$ in a binary classification. The feature vectors and their true class values are then input to a learning algorithm that will then build a model to predict the class of new instances. In contrast, we extract a set of smaller feature vectors that are then the basis for generating meta features, or more concretely, meta feature vectors.

Our approach starts with the extraction of first-level features to generate a feature vector representation for each instance. However, in our framework instead of having a single feature vector for $\mathbf{x}$, we generate m smaller vectors that contain complementary types of features, or views, describing the instances. We call these different views multimodal because they represent different characteristics of the text. More formally, an instance $\mathbf{x}$ is now represented as $\{\mathbf{x}_1, \mathbf{x}_2, ..., \mathbf{x}_m\}$ where each $\mathbf{x}_i$ is a vector with $|\mathbf{x}_i|$ features in modality i. Note that $\textbf{union}(\mathbf{x}_1, \mathbf{x}_2, ..., \mathbf{x}_m) = \mathbf{x}$ and $\textbf{intersection}(\mathbf{x}_1, \mathbf{x}_2, ..., \mathbf{x}_m) = \emptyset$ since we are only generating sub vectors (or complementary views) from the original feature set.

The generation of meta features uses these m different vectors to produce m clustering solutions for the training data with k clusters each. That means that we end up with different arrangements of the training instances into clusters, one arrangement per modality. Note that since clustering is performed per modality, k may be different in each clustering solution. From each cluster c_k in each of the m clustering solutions, we compute a centroid by averaging all the feature vectors in that cluster.

$$\textbf{centroid}_{m_i} = \frac{1}{\mid c_{m_i} \mid} \sum_{x_j \in c_{m_i}} \mathbf{x}_j \qquad (1)$$

where i above ranges from 1 to k, the number of clusters. We then measure the *similarity* of each instance to these centroids using the cosine function. These $m \times k$ similarity values are then used as the meta features, x', and we compute them for training and testing instances. Thus, as a result of this step each instance $\mathbf{x}$ is now represented by m tuples of vectors, the first level feature vectors $\langle \mathbf{x}_{i_1}, ..., \mathbf{x}_{i_{|x_i|}} \rangle$ and the newly generated meta feature vectors $\langle \mathbf{x'}_{i_1}, ..., \mathbf{x'}_{i_k} \rangle$ for each modality i.

In our problem of AA, we consider four types of first level features: stylistic features, lexical features, syntactic features, and perplexity values from character 3-gram language models. That is, in these experiments $m = 4$. Therefore, in our problem we have $x = \{\mathbf{x}_{sty}, \mathbf{x}_{lex}, \mathbf{x}_{ppl}, \mathbf{x}_{syn}\}$, where $\mathbf{x}_{sty}$ refers to the feature vector containing only stylistic features, $\mathbf{x}_{lex}$ is the vector for lexical features, $\mathbf{x}_{ppl}$ is the feature vector for perplexity values, and lastly, $\mathbf{x}_{syn}$ is the vector of syntactic features. Section 4 describes the features we are using in more detail.

To summarize, our MSMF approach is different from previous machine learning approaches to AA in that it has an intermediate step where we generate meta features from clustering the training instances per modality. Thus, all the vectors $\mathbf{x}_{sty}$ in the training data are input to a k-means clustering algorithm. Similarly, the set of vectors $\mathbf{x}_{lex}$, $\mathbf{x}_{ppl}$, and $\mathbf{x}_{syn}$ are clustered separately.

We are proposing to generate new meta features from clustering the data that can better represent posts from each author, but more important, the relation, i.e. closeness, to posts from other authors. It should be noted that no class information is used during clustering as the idea is to uncover regularities across the posts from authors on individual modalities as a result of the clustering. New in this work as well is the idea of a multimodal clustering, where each feature modality is clustered separately. Our assumption is that generating clusters by looking at feature sets separately will allow contrasting authors' characteristics in a subdimensional space without the risk of blurring differences, or similarities, across authors that can occur when clustering the entire feature vector at once. For instance, one author may have a similar style on the use of emoticons to a subset of authors while sharing similar syntactic characteristics to a very different subset of authors. This information, we hope, will be captured by the metafeatures, and will yield higher classification accuracy than the first level features by themselves.

4 First Level Features

The previous section motivated and described the use of the meta features. This section describes the first level features, where by first level features we refer to features computed directly from the documents.

Table 1 shows a list of the features used arranged by modality. For the *stylistic* modality we crafted a list of features tuned for written interactions in social networks. Thus, we use percentages of non-alphanumeric characters that are commonly used in emoticons. We also include percentages of capitalized words, use of quotations, and use of signature, that we believe allow writers more freedom to express their unique writing style. The *lexical* modality is the standard bag of words representation used in text classification that has also been commonly used in previous AA work (Argamon and Levitan, 2005; Zhao and Zobel, 2005). In the modality noted as *perplexity* in Table 1 we use perplexity values as computed by character 3-gram language models. We use the training data to train one language model per author and each model generates a perplexity, or cross entropy, value per instance. For training the language models and computing perplexity values we used the SRI-LM toolkit (Stolcke, 2002). Frequencies of character n-grams have also been successfully used to build author profiles (Keselj et al., 2003). However, to the best of our knowledge, this is the first work exploiting character-based language models for AA, although, Raghavan *et al.*'s work on PCFGs is closely related to this. Lastly, in the *syntactic* modality we have unigrams, bigrams, and trigrams of POS tags, and typed dependency relations extracted using the Stanford parser (Marneffe et al., 2006), that have been used before in AA.

5 Data Sets

To test our approach we downloaded posts from the Chronicle of Higher Education (CHE). Because our focus is on evaluating the use of metafeatures for the problem of AA in web forum posts, we need to control potential confounding characteristics in the data. Therefore, for our evaluation we downloaded posts from a single topic and generated 5 data sets with a different number

Modality	Features
Stylistic	Total number of words
	Average number of words per sentence
	Binary feature indicating use of quotations
	Binary feature indicating use of signature
	Percentage of all caps words
	Percentage of non-alphanumeric characters
	Percentage of sentence initial words with first letter capitalized
	Percentage of digits
	Number of new lines in the text
	Average number of punctuations (!?.;:,) per sentence
	Percentage of contractions (won't, can't)
	Percentage of two or more consecutive non-alphanumeric characters
Lexical	Bag of words (freq. of unigrams)
Perplexity	Perplexity values from character 3-grams
Syntactic	Part-of-Speech (POS) tags
	Dependency relations
	Chunks (unigram freq.)

Table 1: Feature breakdown by modality

of authors each. Table 2 shows some statistics on these data sets.

Because the forum is related to higher education it is expected that users of this forum will be more conscious about their writing and grammar. This is one of the reasons why we decided to start working on this data as a first cut on the problem of AA on online forums. However, it is still a spontaneous and informal setting. Table 3 shows some excerpts from the forum that show this to be a middle ground between carefully edited and written text and typical social media samples.

"OH MY GOD. ARE YOU THE STUPIDEST MAN... WAIT STUPIDEST PERSON ON THE FACE OF THIS EARTH?
"We've been married for xx years and you STILL can't figure it out? Look, here's a quarter. Why don't you call someone and see if they will help you PULL YOUR HEAD OUT OF YOUR A$$."

Table 3: Excerpts from the CHE forums

Our datasets are available to the research community by contacting the authors[2].

6 Empirical Evaluation

For all our experiments we chose a fixed partition of training and testing for all collections. We randomly divided each data set into 80% training and 20% testing. We are presenting results of using Support Vector Machines (SVMs) (Schölkopf and Smola, 2002) as the underlying learner as implemented in WEKA (Witten and Frank, 2005). We report classification accuracy as the evaluation metric.

6.1 Baseline Experiments for AA

The first set of experiments we present are aimed at establishing a good baseline for our approach. Following the baselines presented in previous work, we measure prediction performance for AA on the CHE collection using a bag-of-words approach.

Authors	Baseline
5	51.30
10	44.59
20	36.58
50	29.20
100	27.95

Table 4: Baseline accuracy using SVMs and bag of words for the CHE data set

The results are shown in Table 4. The baselines chosen are strong. Especially for the data set with 100 authors, where SVMs reached an accuracy of close to 30%, much higher than a simple majority predictor (1/100), but also considerably higher than that reported for datasets with a similar number of authors (Luyckx and Daelemans, 2010). As expected, accuracy drops as the number of potential authors increases, with the 100 authors data set posing the greatest challenge for the classifier.

6.2 First Level Features (FLF) for AA

Before we evaluate the meta features approach we want to assess the value of the first level features for this problem. The features described in Section

[2]Because the CHE data set exceeds the 10MB limit we were unable to upload it as supplementary material.

Dataset	Authors	Total Number of Posts	Avg Number of Posts per Author	Avg Number of Words per Author
1	5	2,889	577.8	39,664
2	10	5,579	557.9	40,953
3	20	9,779	488.95	35,838
4	50	15,543	310.86	21,502
5	100	16,171	161.71	11,322

Table 2: Summary of the CHE data set

4 were tailored to the web forum domain, therefore we expect them to be valuable for learning to discriminate the writeprint of each author. We used SVMs as the underlying algorithm. The results are shown in Table 5. In all cases the FLF outperformed the baseline results.

Authors	FLF Accuracy
5	69.21
10	70.81
20	67.06
50	60.12
100	57.78

Table 5: Results using First Level Features (FLF) and SVMs for the CHE data set

These results are higher than what has been reported on AA for a similar number of authors. The FLF have shown to be competitive and in some cases the improvement in accuracy over the baseline reaches 100%. In most cases accuracy decreased with a larger number of potential authors, although, for the data set with 10 authors accuracy was a little bit higher than with 5 authors. Moreover, the drop in accuracy is not as pronounced as in the baseline system, suggesting that BOWs are not sufficient to solve this task and that a combination of features, such as those included in our FLF are more appropriate for this problem.

6.3 Using Modality Specific Meta Features (MSMF)

After establishing the baseline performance in our data set, and the performance of using only FLF, we want to evaluate the idea of generating meta features that are modality specific. As described in Section 3, we cluster each of the four types of feature vectors in the training data set separately. Because we use a k-means clustering algorithm, implemented in CLUTO, the first step is to choose the number of clusters. Determining the optimal number of clusters is challenging and beyond the scope of this exploratory work. But it is still an important parameter in our solution since the value of k determines the number of meta features generated per modality. The role of these meta features is to extract relations among the posts of different authors on a given modality. A reasonable assumption is then to set k as a function of the number of authors. We experimented setting k =number of authors $\times n$, with values of $n = 1, 3, 5, 10, 15$. For example, for the data set with 5 authors we experimented with values of $k = 5, 15, 25, 50, 75$.

Authors	K	MSMF	FLF	MSMF+FLF
5	1×5	45.04	69.21	73.39
	3×5	50.95		74.6
	5×5	53.91		74.08
	10×5	62.60		75.47
	15×5	65.04		**76.17**
10	1×10	37.47	70.81	77.38
	3×10	47.29		75.85
	5×10	50.09		76.3
	10×10	61.16		**77.38**
	15×10	59.54		76.84
20	1×20	35.35	67.06	70.81
	3×20	40.03		71.22
	5×20	43.78		71.37
	10×20	48.40		**71.42**
	15×20	49.58		70.96
50	1×50	32.77	60.12	63.20
	3×50	37.66		62.75
	5×50	39.83		63.72
	10×50	43.50		**63.79**
	15×50	44.53		63.33
100	1×100	33.15	57.78	60.41
	3×100	40.11		60.95
	5×100	42.02		61.17
	10×100	42.52		**62.10**
	15×100	43.34		59.54

Table 6: Accuracy results for AA on the CHE collection when using modality specific metafeatures (MSMF), first level features (FLF) and the combination of both (MSMF+FLF)

Table 6 summarizes our results showing accuracy values. For comparison purposes we include in this table results from using only first level features (FLF), only modality specific meta features (MSMF), and the combination of both (MSMF+FLF). The results show several consistent trends across all 5 data sets. First, meta features by themselves are always outperformed by the first level features. This is not surprising since the meta features aggregate posts from different authors depending on similarity and thus predicting authorship only on these features does not work as well as the standard approach of using first level features. However, these meta features do outperform the bag of words baseline results (compare column MSMF in Table 6 with results shown in Table 4), underscoring the fact that the CHE data set is harder than the typical text classification task where the lexical features by themselves can solve the problem with very high accuracy. Moreover, the combination of first level features and meta features (MSMF+FLF) consistently achieves higher accuracy than any of the other two alternatives, this is the second trend and the most relevant to our work. These results show that the modality specific meta features are important and yield improvements of up to 10% in accuracy over the standard approach of using only FLF, and of more than 100% in accuracy over a strong bag of words baseline. Third, with respect to the value of k, the results show that for all values chosen, the MSMF outperforms the baseline results, and that using the combined set of features (MSMF+FLF) will yield a higher accuracy than that of using only the first level features. However, it does seem that higher values of k result in higher accuracy, suggesting that trying to find more clusters, and therefore finer-grained clusters in the data is resulting in the extraction of more meaningful relations among the posts of different authors. The results also show that the best k overall was $k = 10\times$ number of authors. For larger k values only the data set with 5 authors reached better results. Overall, it is interesting to see as well that both types of features yield classifiers that are less affected by the larger number of authors, as the drop in accuracy seems to be less pronounced than in the baseline system (see Table 4).

Our previous results show that the meta features contribute to a better prediction of authorship. But what about the multi modal framework? In order to assess if generating modality specific meta features is helpful we performed additional experiments where all instances are represented by a single vector that concatenates all modality feature vectors. The rest of the meta features approach remains unchanged, the vectors are clustered using k-means clustering and we generate metafeatures for each instance. The results are shown in Table 7 and for all cases we chose k = number of authors$\times$10. The results under AMMF are the meta features generated without separate processing per modality, AMMF+FLF shows results of combining first level features with "all modalities together" meta features. As we speculated, there is a considerable gain in accuracy from the independent processing per modality. The gain in accuracy of MSMF over AMMF ranges from 73% to ~250%. This gain possibly comes from the ability to aggregate feature vectors that semantically represent the same type of information, which can be difficult to maintain when all modalities are grouped together. Both approaches improve accuracy when they are combined with FLF, but again the combination using modality specific meta features (MSMF+FLF) yields the best results. However, the gain in accuracy observed when going from AMMF+FLF (Column 4 in Table 7) to MSMF+FLF (Column 5 in Table 7) is not as large as that observed when going from using only AMMF (Column 2 in Table 7) to MSMF (Column 3 in Table 7). This is expected since both approaches share the same set of FLF, which we know are by themselves very powerful. Further experiments and analysis are needed to better characterize the advantages of the MSMF approach. We plan to leave this for future work.

6.4 Benchmark Comparisons

To explore further the intuition that our approach is a good alternative for AA on web forum data we performed additional experiments where we evaluated the PCFG-based approaches in (Raghavan et al., 2010). In their experiments they have three systems: one is the standard PCFG approach, noted as PCFG in Table 8, the second version uses treebanked data from the WSJ mixed with the original CHE data. This interpolated version is called PCFG-I in that table. We followed the same approach of training the parser on the first 10 sections of the WSJ. For the interpolation, we added Section 20 of the WSJ and replicated the original author's data twice. The third version, noted as PCFG-E, is the combination of the PCFG with the bag-of-words MaxEnt model, and an n-gram language model. The results in Table 8 show that the best accuracy in the CHE collection is achieved by our method in all four data sets. For comparison purposes we also included here the baseline results

Authors	AMMF	MSMF(% gain)	AMMF+FLF	MSMF+FLF(% gain)
5	36.00	62.60 (73%)	71.47	**75.47**(5%)
10	19.63	61.16 (211%)	70.99	**77.38**(9%)
20	19.63	48.40 (146%)	69.06	**71.42**(3%)
50	12.44	43.50 (249%)	61.65	**63.79**(3%)
100	15.07	42.52 (182%)	59.16	**62.10**(4%)

Table 7: Accuracy comparison on CHE data set between generating modality specific meta features (MSMF) and meta features with all modalities together (AMMF), and the combination of each with first level features (FLF).

Approach	5 Authors	10 Authors	50 Authors	100 Authors
SVM	51.3	44.59	29.20	27.95
PCFG	62.95	58.46	31.41	29.77
PCFG-I	64.17	61.26	46.02	44.43
PCFG-E	64.00	55.85	36.11	34.72
Our Approach	**75.47**	**77.38**	**63.79**	**62.10**

Table 8: Benchmark comparison of AA accuracy on the CHE collection

shown in Table 4. The baseline results are consistently outperformed by all of the PCFG-based approaches, showing yet again PCFGs to be robust to different genres but more important, to scale up well to a larger number of authors. However, the results were considerably lower than those of our method. These results support our hypothesis that the modality specific meta features are appropriate for online forum data where the documents are short, the number of potential authors is larger, the stylistic features are more discriminative, and there are less restrictions with respect to standards of writing. Another interesting finding from these experiments is the fact that the PCFG-I method always reached higher accuracies than the ensemble in the CHE collection. In Raghavan *et al.*'s collection, the ensemble (PCFG-E) was the most accurate model. We believe this difference is because of the fact that the CHE collection is single topic, having a more semantically uniform collection prevented the lexical-based components, such as bag of words and n-gram language models, used in the ensemble to boost accuracy.

7 Concluding Remarks

Following recommendations from previous work in AA, we have gathered a single topic evaluation data set of web forum posts with up to 100 candidate authors. The main contribution of this work is the use of modality specific meta features generated by an unsupervised approach. Previous work has used distributional clustering to aggregate features that share the same relation with the class (Baker and McCallum, 1998; Slonim and Tishby, 2001; Dhillon et al., 2003). Our proposed framework is different, we generate meta features from similarity metrics between centroids from an unsupervised clustering of instances and the instances themselves. The additional cost in clustering instances shows to be valuable for AA as we can gain up to 100% improvements in accuracy over strong baselines. Further analysis of results also showed that treating each modality separately to generate the meta features is also important and can yield gains of close to 10% in accuracy over the standard approach of using only first level features. To the best of our knowledge, this is by far the best result reported for AA in a task having up to 100 authors. The framework is general enough that it can be extended to other classification problems where instances can be represented using different modalities.

The experimental evaluation presented here shows that a relatively inexpensive approach based on PCFGs can scale up to a larger number of authors, even if the documents are only a couple of sentences long. However, this syntactically driven approach is outperformed by our proposed modality specific meta features framework.

The results are very promising although we recognize that this is not yet a real world scenario for web forum data, so we are currently gathering data sets with a larger number of authors. We also want to evaluate this work on different data sets to analyze the robustness and suitability of this method. Lastly, we want to study the effect of having more than one topic in the data set as in the work of (Schein et al., 2010).

Acknowledgements

This work was partially supported by a UAB faculty development grant to the first author. It was also supported in part by the CONACYT-Mexico (project no. 134186) and by the European Commission as part of the WIQ-EI project (project no. 269180) within the FP7 People Programme.

References

S. Argamon and S. Levitan. 2005. Measuring the usefulness of function words for authorship attribution. In *Proceedings of the Conference of the Association for Computers and the Humanities and the Association for Literary and Linguistic Computing*.

L. Douglas Baker and Andrew McCallum. 1998. Distributional clustering of words for text classification. In *SIGIR 98: Proceedings of the 21st Annual International ACM SIGIR*, pages 96–103, Melbourne, Australia, August. ACM.

Inderjit S. Dhillon, Subramanyam Mallela, and Rahul Kumar. 2003. A divisive information-theoretic feature clsutering algorithm for text classification. *Journal of Machine Learning Research*, 3:1265–1287.

G. Frantzeskou, E. Stamatatos, S. Gritzalis, and C. E. Chaski. 2007. Identifying authorship by byte-level n-grams: The source code author profile (SCAP). *Journal of Digital Evidence*, 6(1).

Graeme Hirst and Ol'ga Feiguina. 2007. Bigrams of syntactic labels for authorship discrimination. *Literary and Linguistic Computing*, 22(4):405–417, October.

V. Keselj, F. Peng, N. Cercone, and C. Thomas. 2003. N-gram based author profiles for authorship attribution. In *Proceedings of the Pacific Association for Computational Linguistics*, pages 255–264.

Moshe Koppel, Jonathan Schler, and Shlomo Argamon. 2011. Authorship attribution in the wild. *Language Resources and Evaluation*, 45:83–94.

Robert Layton, Paul Watters, and Richard Dazeley. 2010. Authorship attribution for twitter in 140 characters or less. In *Second Cybercrime and Trustworthy Computing Workshop, CTC 2010*, pages 1–8, Ballart, VIC, Australia, July.

Kim Luyckx and Walter Daelemans. 2010. The effect of author set size and data size in authorship attribution. *Literary and Linguistic Computing*, pages 1–21, August.

M.C. De Marneffe, Bill Maccartney, and Christopher D. Manning. 2006. Generating typed dependency parses from phrase structure parses. In *LREC 2006*.

T.C. Mendenhall. 1887. The characterstic curves of composition. *Science*, IX:237–249.

F. Mosteller and D. L. Wallace. 1964. *Inference and Disputed Authorship: The Federalist*. Addison-Wesley.

F. Peng, D. Shuurmans, and S. Wang. 2004. Augmenting naive Bayes classifiers with statistical language models. *Information Retrieval Journal*, 7(1):317–345.

S. Plakias and E. Stamatatos. 2008. Tensor space models for authorship attribution. In *Proceedings of the 5th Hellenic Conference on Artificial Intelligence: Theories, Models and Applications*, volume 5138 of *LNCS*, pages 239–249, Syros, Greece.

Sindhu Raghavan, Adriana Kovashka, and Raymond Mooney. 2010. Authorship attribution using probabilistic context-free grammars. In *Proceedings of the ACL 2010 Conference Short Papers*, pages 38–42, Uppsala, Sweden, July. Association for Computational Linguistics.

Andrew I. Schein, Johnnie F. Caver, Randale J. Honaker, and Craig H. Martell. 2010. Author attribution evaluation with novel topic cross-validation. In *The 2010 International Conference on Knowledge Discovery and Information Retrieval*, Valencia, Spain, October.

Bernhard Schölkopf and Alexander J. Smola. 2002. *Learning with Kernels: Support Vector Machines, Regularization, Optimization and Beyond*. MIT Press.

Noam Slonim and Naftali Tishby. 2001. The power of word clusters for text classification. In *23rd European Colloquium on Information Retrieval Research (ECIR)*.

Efstathios Stamatatos. 2009. A survey on modern authorship attribution methods. *Journal of the American Society for Information Science and Technology*, 60(3):538–556.

Andreas Stolcke. 2002. SRILM - an extensible language modeling toolkit. pages 901–904.

Ian H. Witten and Eibe Frank. 2005. *Data Mining: Practical Machine Learning Tools and Techniques*. Morgan Kauffmann, 2nd edition.

Y. Zhao and J. Zobel. 2005. Effective and scalable authorship attribution using function words. In *Proceedings of 2nd Asian Information Retrieval Symposium*, volume 3689 of *LNCS*, pages 174–189, Jeju Island, Korea.

Keyphrase Extraction from Online News Using Binary Integer Programming

Zhuoye Ding, Qi Zhang, Xuanjing Huang
Fudan University
School of Computer Science
{09110240024,qz,xjhuang}@fudan.edu.cn

Abstract

In recent years, keyphrase extraction has received great attention, and been successfully employed by various applications. Keyphrases extracted from news articles can be used to concisely represent main contents of news events. Keyphrases can help users to speed up browsing and find the desired contents more quickly. In this paper, we first present several criteria of high-quality news keyphrases. After that, in order to integrate those criteria into the keyphrase extraction task, we propose a novel formulation which converts the task to a binary integer programming problem. The formulation cannot only encode the prior knowledge as constraints, but also learn constraints from data. We evaluate the proposed approach on a manually labeled corpus. Experimental results demonstrate that our approach achieves better performances compared with the state-of-the-art methods.

1 Introduction

Keyphrase extraction is a long studied topic in natural language processing. A keyphrase, which consists a word or a group of words, is defined as a precise and concise expression of one or more documents. It has been widely used in various applications such as summarization, clustering, categorizing, browsing, and so on. In recent years, keyphrase extraction has received much attention (Witten et al., 1999; Zha, 2002; Hulth, 2003; Tomokiyo and Hurst, 2003; Chen et al., 2005; Medelyan et al., 2009; Liu et al., 2009).

Keyphrases are usually manually chosen by authors, for scientific publications, magazine articles, books, et al. Due to the expensive and time consuming effort of manually assigning keyphrase, web pages and online news rarely contain keyphrases. It should be useful to automatically extract keyphrases from online news to represent their main contents. There are already a number of studies which focus on extracting keyphrases from scientific publications or single news article (Frank et al., 1999; Turney, 2000; Wan and Xiao, 2008; Jiang et al., 2009). We also notice that, currently, many websites provide the service which group related news together to facilitate users' browsing. In this paper, we focus on extracting keyphrases from a group of news articles which describe the same news event by different publishers.

Previous studies on keyphrase extraction can be roughly categorized into two groups: supervised and unsupervised. Unsupervised approaches usually select a set of candidates and use different ranking methods to select the candidates with the highest scores as keyphrases. Most of ranking methods are based on the information extracted from the document, such as TF·IDF, position, syntactic relation with other words, and so on. Supervised methods convert the task into a binary classification problem, which categorizes phrases as keyphrases or non-keyphrases. Similar as other tasks applied by supervised methods, a large amount of domain dependent training data is required. When the domain is changed, the labeled corpus should also be changed. And corpus labeling is a time-consuming and tedious task.

Most of the current methods focus on judging the importance of each phrase, and individually extract phrases with the highest scores. After analyzing the human assigned keyphrases, we observe that the keyphrases of news should satisfy the following properties:

1. **Relevance**. The keyphrases should be semantically relevant to the news theme. The most important ones should be selected as keyphrases.

2. **Coverage**. The keyphrases should be indicative of the whole news event. The extracted keyphrases should cover most of the aspects of the news event.

3. **Coherence**. The keyphrases should be semantically related to each other, and logically consistent and holding together as a harmonious whole.

4. **Conciseness**. The keyphrases should not contain keyphrases with redundant information.

In order to automatically select keyphrases which can satisfy the above properties, in this paper, we propose a novel formulation which converts keyphrase extraction to a binary integer programming problem (BIP) (Alevras and Padberg, 2001). An objective function and a number of constraints which high-quality keyphrases should satisfy are specified. BIP, which is the special case of integer programming and a well-studied optimization framework, is used to efficiently search the entire space to extract keyphrases. The formulation provides a flexible framework for integrating different criteria as objective functions or constraints.

The major contributions of this work can be summarized as follows: 1) We propose a novel formulation of keyphrase extraction as a binary integer programming problem; 2) Several criteria which high-quality keyphrases should satisfy are converted to the objective function and a set of constraints in order to fit the formulation; 3) Keyphrases are extracted as a set with consideration of their relationships; 4) Experimental results on the dataset consisting of 150 groups of news articles with human annotated keyphrases demonstrate that the proposed method performs better than the state-of-the-art algorithms.

The rest of this paper is organized as follows: Section 2 reviews some related studies. We propose our approach in Section 3. In Section 4, the experimental results are shown and discussed. Finally, we conclude this paper in Section 5.

2 Related Work

As mentioned in the previous section, most of current studies on keyphrase extraction can be roughly divided into two categories: supervised and unsupervised approaches.

Unsupervised approaches usually select general sets of candidates and use a ranking step to select the most important candidates. For example, Mihalcea and Tarau proposed a graph-based approach called TextRank, where the graph nodes are tokens and the edges reflect cooccurrence relations between tokens in the document (Mihalcea and Tarau, 2004). Wan and Xiao expanded TextRank by using a small number of topic-related documents to provide more knowledge, which improved results compared with standard TextRank and a tf.idf baseline (Wan and Xiao, 2008). Tomokiyo and Hurst used pointwise KL-divergence between language models derived from the documents and a reference corpus (Tomokiyo and Hurst, 2003). Matsuo and Ishizuka presented a statistical keyphrases extraction approach that did not make use of a reference corpus, but was based on cooccurrences of terms in a single document (Y.Matsuo and M.Ishizuka, 2004). In this paper the proposed BIP based method can combine those unsupervised methods as assignment value in the objective function. TF·IDF and locality information are used in our approach.

Supervised approaches use a corpus of training data to learn a keyphrase extraction model that is able to classify candidates as keyphrases or non-keyphrases. A well known supervised system is KEA that uses all n-grams of a certain length as candidates, and ranks them based on a Naive Bayes classifier using tf.idf and position as its features (Frank et al., 1999). Then Medelyan and Witten presented the improved KEA++ that selected candidates with reference to a controlled vocabulary from a thesaurus or Wikipedia (Medelyan and Witten, 2006). "Extractor" was another supervised system that used stems and stemmed n-grams as candidates (Turney, 2000). Its features are tuned using a genetic algorithm. Turney introduced a feature set based on statistical word association to ensure that the returned keyphrases set is coherent (Turney, 2003). Experimental results showed that coherence features can significantly improve the performance and they were not domain-specific. Nguyen and Kan presented a keyphrase extraction algorithm for scientific publications and introduced novel features towards scientific publications such as section information and certain morphological phenomena often found in scientific papers (T.D.Nguyen and Kan., 2007).

Since integer linear programming (Alevras and Padberg, 2001) can be used to incorporate both local features and non-local features, which are difficult to handle with traditional algorithms, it has received much attention in various NLP problems in recent years. Roth and Yih (2005) extended CRF models by applying inference procedure based on ILP to naturally and efficiently support general constraint structures. They applied their model on semantic role labeling (SRL) task. Martin et al. (2009) formulated the problem of nonprojective dependency parsing as a polynomial-sized integer linear program. Woodsend and Lapata (2010) presented a joint content selection and compression model for single-document summarization using an integer linear programming formulation.

3 Keyphrase Extraction Using BIP

The objective of keyphrase extraction is to select the most informative group of phrases, which are relevant to the news event and subject to constraints including the number of phrases, topic/aspect coverage, and coherence. Since these constraints are global, and cannot be adequately satisfied by optimizing each of them individually, our approach uses the BIP formulation, a well-studied optimization framework, which can be efficiently solved using standard optimization tools, to extract keyphrases.

Integer Linear Programming (ILP) denotes a set of constraint optimization problems which have a linear objective function, subject to linear equality and linear inequality constraints, and require the objective variables to be integers. ILP can be expressed in canonical form:

$$\begin{aligned} \text{maximize} \quad & c^T x \\ \text{subject to} \quad & Ax \leq b \\ & Gx = d \\ & x \in \mathbf{Z}^n \end{aligned} \tag{1}$$

Binary Integer Programming (BIP) is the special case of ILP where variables are either 0 or 1.

In this paper, we treat the keyphrase extraction task as a two class labeling problem. Given a group of documents D, for each word $w \in D$, we decide to select this word as a keyphrase (assign label "1" to the word), or non-keyphrase (assign label "0"). We use a vector of binary variables $x = (x_1, x_2, ..., x_n)$ over word $w_i \in D$, to indicate whether the corresponding word should be selected or not. With the objective variables x and word $w_i \in D$, $c = (c_1, c_2, ..., c_n)$ is defined as the assignment value. The variable c_i gives the expected value of labeling w_i as a keyphrase. The basic extraction model is shown in Eq.(2). Our goal is to find the optimal point of weights x^* satisfying the constraints.

$$\begin{aligned} \text{maximize} \quad & c^T x \\ \text{subject to} \quad & 0 \leq x_i \leq 1 \\ & x \in \mathbf{Z}^n \end{aligned} \tag{2}$$

3.1 Objective Function

With the BIP formulation, objective function $c^T x = \sum_k c_k x_k$ denotes the expected informative scores over all the words of a solution x. Maximizing the expected scores biases the words with highest c_i values as keyphrases. Various features can be considered as the values c. In this work, we use two basic features TF·IDF and locality. They have also been widely used in existing keyphrase extraction methods. The objective function is given in the Eq.(3).

$$\begin{aligned} c^T x, \; c_i = \; & \alpha \cdot \frac{\sum_{d \in D} TF{\cdot}IDF(w_i, d)}{|D|} \\ & + \beta \cdot \mu_i + \gamma \cdot \nu_i \end{aligned} \tag{3}$$

Three parameters α,β, and γ are used to tradeoff among the different parts, $|D|$ is the number of documents in this news group. The latter section provides detailed description of this equation.

3.1.1 TF·IDF

TF·IDF compares the frequency of a phrase in a particular document with that in general corpus. The TF·IDF for word w_i is computed as:

$$TF{\cdot}IDF(w_i, d) = \frac{\text{freq}(w_i, d)}{|d|} \cdot \log_2 \frac{N}{df(w_i)}, \text{ where}$$

freq(w_i, d) is the number of times w_i occurs in d; $df(w_i)$ is the number of documents containing w_i in the global corpus; N is the size of the global corpus; $|d|$ is the length of the document of d..

In this paper, we use the average TF·IDF over all the news articles belonging to the same group. TF·IDF has also been used as features by almost all the keyphrase extraction algorithms.

3.1.2 Locality

The first occurrence position of the candidate phrase is an important feature for keyphrase extraction. It has also been used by many existing methods (Witten et al., 1999; Zha, 2002; Liu et al., 2009). In this paper, we also incorporate the information as parts of objective function.

For the words in the title of news articles, we define a bonus μ for their informative scores. It is the second component in the Eq.(3). The μ_i is defined as follows:

$$\mu_i = \begin{cases} \mu, & w_i \in T \\ 0, & \text{otherwise} \end{cases}$$

, where T represents the set of all the title words.

Similarly, we define ν for those words which occur in the first sentences. It is the third component of the objective function. The ν_i is defined as follows:

$$\nu_i = \begin{cases} \nu, & w_i \in FS \\ 0, & \text{otherwise} \end{cases}$$

,where FS represents the set of words which occur in the first sentences.

3.2 Constraints

One limitation of existing keyphrase extraction methods is that they usually separately make judgment of individual phrase instead of considering the qualities of the set of phrases as a whole. In this section, we define several constraints converted from the coverage and coherence criteria, and the number of extracted phrases.

3.2.1 Coverage

From both observations we make, and the properties proposed by Liu et al.(2009), we believe that high-quality keyphrases should cover the whole document or group of documents well. For example, if we have a document describing "Toyota recalls Prius" from various aspects of "reason", "scope", "influence" and so on., the extracted keyphrases should cover as many aspects as possible.

In order to satisfy this criterion, topic model is used to estimate words distribution over topics. In this paper, we use latent Dirichlet allocation (LDA) (Blei et al., 2003) to do it[1]. LDA is a three-level hierarchical Bayesian model, in which each word is modeled as a finite mixture over an underlying set of topics. Each topic is, in turn, modeled as an infinite mixture over an underlying set of topic probabilities.

[1]We use MALLET 2.0.6 in the experiments

From LDA model, we can get $p(w|z)$, which represents aspect distributions over words. It indicates which words are important to an aspect. We use matrix G to represent $p(w|z)$. The vector g_i denote the distribution over words of aspect i. The projection $g_i^T x$ gives us the aspect coverage of topic i under current solution x. We want the coverage of every aspect to exceed the same threshold ζ. The constraint can be expressed as follows:

$$G^T x \succeq \zeta$$

3.2.2 Coherence

According to the properties which high-quality keyphrases should satisfy, the keyphrases should be semantically related and coherent. Turney (2003) also mentioned this issue and pointed out that incoherent keyphrases might highly impact the quality and user experience.

An intuitive method for measuring word relations is based on word cooccurrence relations within the document. It indicates that word pairs with high cooccurrence frequency should be selected together. For instance, the words "economy", "unemployment", and "loan" are likely to cooccur in documents about "financial crisis". And we are aiming to extract them together to ensure coherence property. In this paper, we use mutual information (MI) to measure the word's coherence. MI is a measure of association which quantifies the discrepancy between the dependent joint distribution and the independent individual distributions.

For each word pair $< w_i, w_j >$, whose mutual information $I(w_i, w_j)$ is bigger than a pre-defined threshold ξ, we add the following constraint:

$$x_i - x_j = 0$$

It encodes the fact that keyphrases pairs with high cooccurrence frequency should be selected together.

3.2.3 Number of Extracted Phrases

According to the limitations of space or other constraints given by applications, the number of extracted phrases should also be constrained. Since we use a vector of binary variables $x = (x_1, x_2, ..., x_n)$ over words $w_i \in D$, the constraint can be represented as follows:

$$\sum_{i=1}^{n} x_i \leq K$$

,where K is the pre-defined threshold.

3.3 BIP Problem

Putting the objective function and all the constraints together, we obtain the BIP program to extract keyphrases as follows:

$$\begin{aligned} \text{maximize} \quad & c^T x \\ \text{subject to} \quad & G^T x \succeq \zeta \\ & x_i - x_j = 0\ ,\ \text{ if } I(w_i, w_j) \geq \xi \\ & \sum_{i=1}^{n} x_i \leq K \\ & x_i \in \{0, 1\}\ ,\ i = 1 \cdots n \end{aligned} \quad (4)$$

Binary integer programming is a popular optimization technique and many effective solvers have been developed. In this paper we use CPLEX solver, which is part of AIMMS[2] system, to estimate the optimal solution from the Eq.(4).

4 Experiments

In this section, we perform evaluations of the proposed method. The data sets we used in the experiments are described in the first part. After that, experimental results are given and detailedly described in the following sections.

4.1 Dataset and Evaluation Metric

There are almost no publicly available datasets with manually annotated gold standard keyphrases for news, due to the high expense of labor and time for manual annotation. In this experiment, we randomly selected 150 groups of online news articles from Goolge News. Three annotators participated in the annotation task. They were asked to manually assign keyphrases for each group of news. The keyphrases which at least two annotators have agreed on are selected as the "Golden" ones. Statistics on the dataset are shown in Table 1. The corpus data is divided into development set and test set. The development set, which contains 50 groups of news, is used to tune the parameters. The other 100 groups of news are used as test set.

We regard an extracted keyphrase as "correct" if it matches one of the ground truth. We measure the performance by Precision (the percentage of correct extracted keyphrases out of all the extracted ones), Recall (the percentage of correct extracted keyphrases out of the ground truth) and F-Measure (the harmonic mean of the precision and recall).

Description	value
# News articles	1103
# Words	345K
# News articles per group	7.35
# Labeled keyphrases per group	5.83

Table 1: Statistics on the dataset

4.2 Comparisons with Other Methods

Since the dataset used in this paper is manually labeled by ourselves, we implement three baseline methods on the same dataset for comparison.

BL-1: The titles of news articles provide a reasonable summary or keyphrase sequence. So baseline 1 is performed based on the titles of news articles. We sort the phrases in multi-news titles according to the TF·IDF scores and select top-k as keyphrases. We assign K to 6 after tuning the parameter.

BL-2: Many existing methods converted the keyphrase extraction as a classification problem. In this paper, we used SVM[3] as baseline 2. The features include TF·IDF, "First occurrence", and "Is in title or not". Those feature sets are similar to our objective function. We divided the dataset into five subsets and conducted a 5-fold cross-validation.

BL-3: We re-implemented the ranking approach proposed by Jiang et al. (2009) as baseline 3. This method employed Ranking SVM (Joachims, 2006), the learning to rank method, to perform keyphrase extraction. Feature sets are the same as the feature sets used in the BL-2. We also conducted a 5-fold cross-validation.

We used the following default values for the parameters of our method: $\alpha = 0.4$, $\beta = 0.3$, $\gamma = 0.3$, $\mu = 0.1$, $\nu = 0.05$, $\zeta = 0.005$, $\xi = 16.5$, and $K = 6$. The meaning of these parameters are described in the previous section. And how to learning the optimal values will be discussed in section 4.4. The test set is used in this experiment. Since the average number of manual-

[2] http://www.aimms.com/

[3] SVM^{light} is used in our experiments, which can be downloaded from http://www.cs.cornell.edu/People/tj/svm_light.

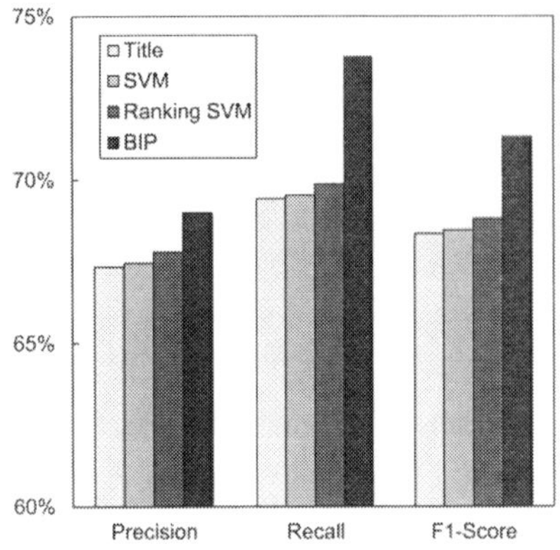

Figure 1: Comparison results of Title, SVM, Ranking SVM and our BIP-based methods .

labeled keyphrases is six, we selected the top 6 ones as keyphrases in all three baseline methods.

Figure 1 shows the performance comparison of BIP-based method with baselines. From the figure, we have the following observations. Firstly, BIP-based method consistantly outperforms all baselines under all evaluation metrics – Precision, Recall, and F1-Score. This indicates the robustness and effectiveness of our method. Furthermore, compared with the supervised methods, BIP-based method does not need any labeled corpus. Secondly, Ranking SVM performs slightly better than SVM. This is congruence with the previous conclusion given by Jiang et al. (2009). However, the improvement of BL-3 over BL-2 is not significant. We also observe that the performances of BL-1 are quite good. The precision, recall, and F1-score achieved by it are comparable with results of SVM and Ranking SVM.

4.3 Contribution of Constraints and Objective Function

To determine the contribution of different components of objective function and individual constraints, we omit components and constraints one by one to identify its contribution to the performance. Table 2 shows the results on development set. The first row represents the performance of the BIP-based method with all constraints and objective function with all three components. The parameters are default ones listed in the previous section.

The contribution of different components in the objective function is shown from the second row to fourth row. From the results we can observe that, TF·IDF is the most important feature in the objective function. Without the feature of TF·IDF, the evaluation metrics drop sharply from 72.68% to 59.82%. The candidate occurs in the title is also an important feature. It is consistent with the observations given by the results of BL-1. It gives about 17.27% relative improvement over the performance without it. Compared with the two features, the occurrence in the first sentence gives less contribution. The improvement given by it is not significant.

The fifth row shows the results without the coverage constraint. From the result, we observe that the coverage constraint is effective, which can give more than 4.2% relative improvement. The contribution of coherence constraint is shown in the end of the table. Althoug its contribution is less than that of coverage constraint, an outlier keyphrase may highly impact the user experience. Coherence constraint is important to improve user experience.

Table 2: Contribution of different components of objective function (TFIDF, InTitle, InFirstSenetence) and two constraints (Coverage and Coherence) under Precision, Recall, and F1-Score.

	Pre.	**Rec.**	**F.**
All	**71.45%**	**73.96%**	**72.68%**
All - TF·IDF	58.86%	60.82%	59.82%
All - InTitle	60.96%	62.77%	61.85%
All - InFirstSentence	71.00%	73.20%	72.08%
All - Coverage	68.56%	70.68%	69.60%
All - Coherence	70.67%	72.85%	71.74%

4.4 Varying Parameters

As we mentioned in the previous section, there are eight parameters which should be adjusted in our method. One may concern the problem of parameters tuning. In order to answer this question, in this section, we explore the impact of different parameters on our approach's performance in the development set. Except the parameter under investigation, the other parameters are set to the default values which are listed in the Section 4.2.

4.4.1 Number of Keyphrases K

Figure 2 presents the performance varying the number of keyphrases, which ranges from 1 to 10. K is one of the most important arguments leading to the trade-off between precision and recall. Larger K increases recall but decreases precision. From this figure, we observe that the best

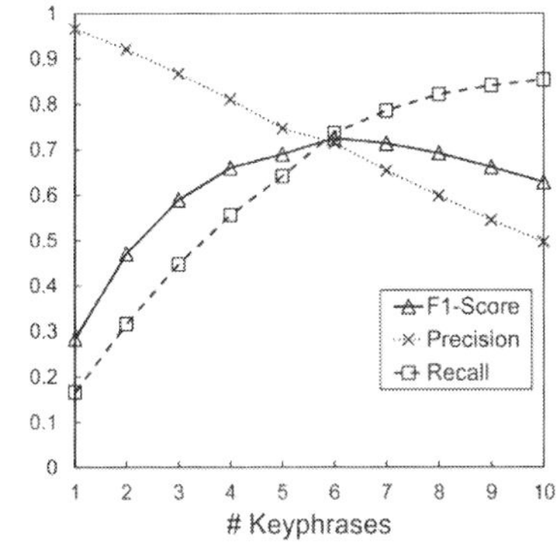

Figure 2: Results of varying the number of extracted keyphrases using the proposed BIP-based extraction method.

result is achieved at the point $K = 6$, which is similar to the average number of manually selected keyphrases. We also observe that the F1-Score drops quickly when K is bigger than 7. The main reason is that only a small number of phrases which should be selected are ranked after the top 10.

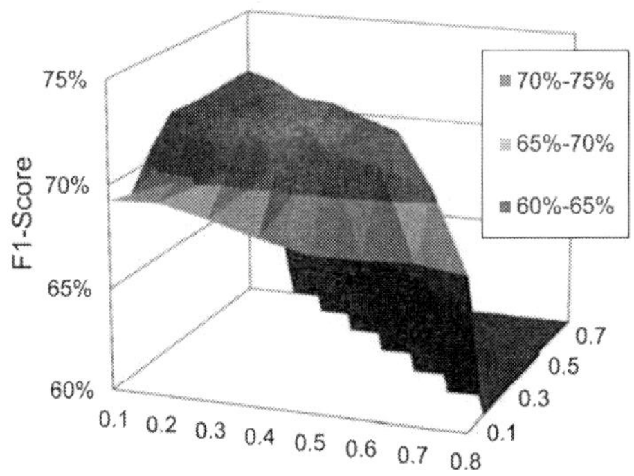

Figure 3: Results of varying the parameters α, β, γ in the objective function.

4.4.2 α, β, γ in the Objective Function

In the objective function, there are three parameters α,β, and γ , which are used to trade off among TF·IDF and two locality features. Figure 3 gives the F1-Score surface varying α and β. Since $\alpha + \beta + \gamma$ equals to 1, α and β are used as x-axis and y-axis in the figure. We have found that the surfaces are almost concave around a number of areas. Therefore, a simple hill-climbing search can be used to optimize F1-Score. Since the surface is almost concave, the global maximum can be easily achieved though a few initial seeds. For example, the optimal parameters for this experiment are $\alpha = 0.4$, $\beta = 0.3$. The γ can be calculated through function $1 - \alpha - \beta$.

Table 3: Influence of the Coverage threshold ζ

ζ	Pre.	Rec.	F.
0.001	69.44%	71.59%	70.50%
0.002	70.33%	72.50%	71.40%
0.003	71.22%	73.43%	72.31%
0.004	71.00%	73.20%	72.08%
0.005	**71.45%**	**73.65%**	**72.53%**
0.006	71.33%	73.54%	72.42%
0.007	71.22%	73.43%	72.31%
0.008	71.11%	73.31%	72.19%
0.009	70.67%	72.85%	71.74%

4.4.3 Coverage threshold ζ

Coverage threshold ζ represents the property that the extracted keyphrases should cover most of the important aspects of a news event. We want the aspect coverage for all topics to exceed the threshold. Table 3 shows the results when ζ ranges from 0.001 to 0.009. All of them perform better than the result without coverage constraint, and the best result is achieved at $\zeta = 0.005$. From the results, we observe that the coverage threshold ζ can also be easily selected. From 0.005 to 0.008, the changes of F1-score are not significant. When the coverage threshold is above 0.02, in order to get the solution of the ILP program, the impact of objective function would be limited. We think that it is the main reason of why best result is achieved at a small value threshold.

4.4.4 Coherence threshold ξ

Finally, we explore the inference of ξ, which is used to represent the word coherence. When the threshold is below 12, there would be too many coherence constraints. More than 30.05% word pairs can satisfy the threshold. Under this condition, no solution can be estimated in some cases. When the threshold is above 32, there are rarely word pairs satisfying the threshold. In other words, there would be no coherence constraints. In table 4 we show the influence of ξ, which ranges from 15 to 18. Similar to the results of coverage threshold, a large range of ξ's value can achieve satisfactory result. $\xi = 16.5$ achieves the best result 72.53%.

Table 4: Influence of the Coherence threshold ξ

ξ	Pre.	Rec.	F.
15.0	68.00%	70.10%	69.04%
15.5	69.89%	72.05%	70.95%
16.0	70.78%	72.97%	71.85%
16.5	**71.45%**	**73.65%**	**72.53%**
17.0	71.22%	73.43%	72.30%
17.5	71.00%	73.20%	72.08%
18.0	71.00%	73.20%	72.08%

4.5 Extracting Example

Table 5 shows examples of extracted keyphrases by different methods from a group of news articles about "Master Kong applies for TDR listing in Taiwan". Top 6 extracted keyphrases for each method are shown in the table, and the correct ones are marked with "(+)". From table 5, we observe that keyphrases extracted through BIP-based method are relevant, coherent, with good coverage. Without the coverage constraint, "Taiwan Depositary Receipt" and it's abbreviation "TDR" are both selected. And, the topic coverage cannot be well satisfied through the top keyphrases. For SVM and Ranking SVM, they separately consider each word, some of the high frequency words are selected as keyphrases, such as "billion", and "issue". However, those words are not meaningful.

Table 5: Example of extracted keyphrases by SVM, Ranking SVM and BIP-based method*.

BIP
Masker Kong(+), Ting Hsin International Group(+), Taiwan Depositary Receipt(+), instant noodle, Taiwan Stock Exchange(+), NT$30 billion
BIP without Coverage constraint
Masker Kong(+), Taiwan Depositary Receipt(+), TDR, lunch, Taiwan Stock Exchange(+), Taiwan
BIP without Coherence constraint
Masker Kong(+), Taiwan Depositary Receipt(+), Taiwanese-invested food producer(+), IPO, issue, Taiwan Stock Exchange(+)
SVM
Taiwan Depositary Receipt(+), Masker Kong(+), China market, TDR, Hong Kong Exchanges, billion
Ranking SVM
Masker Kong(+), China market, TDR, Taiwan Depositary Receipt(+), issue, Taiwan

*The keyphrases are translated from Chinese.

5 Conclusions

In this paper, we have presented a novel keyphrase extraction approach. It adapts the integer linear programming methods to the keyphrase extraction problem by casting features and criteria as objective function and constraints.

By integrating TF·IDF and two locality features as objective function, and the coverage and coherence properties as constraints, the proposed ILP-based unsupervised approach achieves better performance than the state-of-the-art supervised approaches, SVM and Ranking SVM. Contributions of constraints and different components of the object function are experimental evaluated. In the objective function, the TF·IDF is the most important feature. Locality features can further improve the performance. Results also demonstrate that both the coverage and coherence constraints are useful to keyphrase extraction task. We also detail the impact of parameters used in our approach. Through experimental results, we demonstrate that the parameters are not sensitive. The value of them can be easily estimated using simple hill-climbing search methods.

Acknowledgments

The author wishes to thank the anonymous reviewers for their helpful comments. This work was partially funded by 973 Program (2010CB327906), National Natural Science Foundation of China (61003092, 61073069), Shanghai Science and Technology Development Funds(10dz1500104), Doctoral Fund of Ministry of Education of China (200802460066), Shanghai Leading Academic Discipline Project (B114), and Key Projects in the National Science & Technology Pillar Program(2009BAH40B04).

References

Dimitris Alevras and Manfred W. Padberg. 2001. *Linear Optimization and Extensions: Problems and Solutions*. Springer.

David M. Blei, Andrew Y. Ng, and Michael I. Jordan. 2003. Latent dirichlet allocation. *J. Mach. Learn. Res.*, 3:993–1022, March.

Mo Chen, Jian-Tao Sun, Hua-Jun Zeng, and Kwok-Yan Lam. 2005. A practical system of keyphrase extraction for web pages. In *Proceedings of the 14th ACM international conference on Information and knowledge management*, CIKM '05, pages 277–278, New York, NY, USA. ACM.

Eibe Frank, Gordon W. Paynter, Ian H. Witten, Carl Gutwin, and Craig G. Nevill-Manning. 1999. Domain-specific keyphrase extraction. In *Proceedings of the 16th international joint conference on Artificial intelligence - Volume 2*, pages 668–673, San Francisco, CA, USA. Morgan Kaufmann Publishers Inc.

Anette Hulth. 2003. Improved automatic keyword extraction given more linguistic knowledge. In *Proceedings of the 2003 conference on Empirical methods in natural language processing - Volume 10*, pages 216–223, Morristown, NJ, USA. Association for Computational Linguistics.

Xin Jiang, Yunhua Hu, and Hang Li. 2009. A ranking approach to keyphrase extraction. In *Proceedings of the 32nd international ACM SIGIR conference on Research and development in information retrieval*, SIGIR '09, pages 756–757, New York, NY, USA. ACM.

Thorsten Joachims. 2006. Training linear svms in linear time. In *Proceedings of the 12th ACM SIGKDD international conference on Knowledge discovery and data mining*, KDD '06, pages 217–226, New York, NY, USA. ACM.

Zhiyuan Liu, Peng Li, Yabin Zheng, and Maosong Sun. 2009. Clustering to find exemplar terms for keyphrase extraction. In *Proceedings of the 2009 Conference on Empirical Methods in Natural Language Processing: Volume 1 - Volume 1*, EMNLP '09, pages 257–266, Morristown, NJ, USA. Association for Computational Linguistics.

André F. T. Martins, Noah A. Smith, and Eric P. Xing. 2009. Concise integer linear programming formulations for dependency parsing. In *Proceedings of the Joint Conference of the 47th Annual Meeting of the ACL and the 4th International Joint Conference on Natural Language Processing of the AFNLP: Volume 1 - Volume 1*, ACL-IJCNLP '09, pages 342–350, Morristown, NJ, USA. Association for Computational Linguistics.

Olena Medelyan and Ian H. Witten. 2006. Thesaurus based automatic keyphrase indexing. In *Proceedings of the 6th ACM/IEEE-CS joint conference on Digital libraries*, JCDL '06, pages 296–297, New York, NY, USA. ACM.

Olena Medelyan, Eibe Frank, and Ian H. Witten. 2009. Human-competitive tagging using automatic keyphrase extraction. In *Proceedings of the 2009 Conference on Empirical Methods in Natural Language Processing: Volume 3 - Volume 3*, EMNLP '09, pages 1318–1327, Morristown, NJ, USA. Association for Computational Linguistics.

Rada Mihalcea and Paul Tarau. 2004. Textrank: Bringing order into texts. In Dekang Lin and Dekai Wu, editors, *Proceedings of EMNLP 2004*, pages 404–411, Barcelona, Spain, July. Association for Computational Linguistics.

Dan Roth and Wen-tau Yih. 2005. Integer linear programming inference for conditional random fields. In *Proceedings of the 22nd international conference on Machine learning*, ICML '05, pages 736–743, New York, NY, USA. ACM.

T.D.Nguyen and M.-Y. Kan. 2007. Keyphrase extraction in scientific publications. In *Proceedings of International Conference on Asian Digital Libraries*.

Takashi Tomokiyo and Matthew Hurst. 2003. A language model approach to keyphrase extraction. In *Proceedings of the ACL 2003 workshop on Multiword expressions: analysis, acquisition and treatment - Volume 18*, pages 33–40, Morristown, NJ, USA. Association for Computational Linguistics.

Peter D. Turney. 2000. Learning algorithms for keyphrase extraction. volume 2, pages 303–336, Hingham, MA, USA, May. Kluwer Academic Publishers.

Peter D. Turney. 2003. Coherent keyphrase extraction via web mining. In *Proceedings of the 18th international joint conference on Artificial intelligence*, pages 434–439, San Francisco, CA, USA. Morgan Kaufmann Publishers Inc.

Xiaojun Wan and Jianguo Xiao. 2008. Single document keyphrase extraction using neighborhood knowledge. In *Proceedings of the 23rd national conference on Artificial intelligence - Volume 2*, pages 855–860. AAAI Press.

Ian H. Witten, Gordon W. Paynter, Eibe Frank, Carl Gutwin, and Craig G. Nevill-Manning. 1999. Kea: practical automatic keyphrase extraction. In *Proceedings of the fourth ACM conference on Digital libraries*, DL '99, pages 254–255, New York, NY, USA. ACM.

Kristian Woodsend and Mirella Lapata. 2010. Automatic generation of story highlights. In *Proceedings of the 48th Annual Meeting of the Association for Computational Linguistics*, ACL '10, pages 565–574, Morristown, NJ, USA. Association for Computational Linguistics.

Y.Matsuo and M.Ishizuka. 2004. Keyword extraction from a single document using word co-occurrence statistical information. In *International Journal on Artificial Intelligence Tools*.

Hongyuan Zha. 2002. Generic summarization and keyphrase extraction using mutual reinforcement principle and sentence clustering. In *Proceedings of the 25th annual international ACM SIGIR conference on Research and development in information retrieval*, SIGIR '02, pages 113–120, New York, NY, USA. ACM.

Improving Related Entity Finding via Incorporating Homepages and Recognizing Fine-grained Entities

Youzheng Wu Chiori Hori Hisashi Kawai Hideki Kashioka
Spoken Language Communication Group,MASTAR Project
National Institute of Information and Communications Technology (NiCT)
2-2-2 Hikaridai, Keihanna Science City, Kyoto 619-0288, Japan
{youzheng.wu, chiori.hori, hisashi.kawai, hideki.kashioka}@nict.go.jp

Abstract

This paper describes experiments on the TREC entity track that studies retrieval of homepages representing entities relevant to a query. Many studies have focused on extracting entities that match the given coarse-grained types such as organizations, persons, locations by using a named entity recognizer, and employing language model techniques to calculate similarities between query and supporting snippets of entities from which entities are extracted to rank the entities. This paper proposes three improvements over baseline, i.e., 1) incorporating homepages of entities to supplement supporting snippets, 2) recognizing fine-grained named entities to filter out or negatively reward extracted entities that do not match the specified fine-grained types of entities such as a university, airline, author, and 3) adopting a dependency tree-based similarity method to improve language model techniques. Our experiments demonstrate that the proposed approaches can significantly improve performance, for instance, the absolute improvements of nDCG@R and P@1 scores are 8.4%, and 27.5%.

1 Introduction

Many user information needs would be better answered by presenting a ranked list of entities directly, instead of just a list of relevant documents. Based on this assumption, increasing attention has been devoted to related entity finding tasks that aimed at finding documents representing entities of a correct type that are relevant to a query. The TREC expert finding track (Nick, 2005), for example, focused on creating an ordered list of experts who have skills and experiments on a given topic. The INEX entity ranking task (Vries, 2007) studied at ranking Wikipedia entities given a query, in which target entity types are shifted from a single type of entity (person) to any Wikipedia category. The TREC related entity finding (REF) track (Balog, 2010) started in 2009, is defined as: Given an input entity, by its name and homepage, the type of the target entity[1], as well as the nature of their relation, described in free text, find related entities that are of a target type, standing in the required relation to the input entity. The REF task is also similar to a combination of the TREC list QA (Voorhees, 2003) and homepage finding (Hawking, 2001) tasks. In short, all these entity finding tasks generally aim at performing entity-oriented search tasks on the Web. This paper is concerned with the TREC REF track. Figure 1 shows an example of this.

```
<query>
<num>7</num>
<entity_name>Boeing 747</entity_name>
<entity_URL>clueweb09-en0005-75-02292</entity_URL>
<target_entity>organization</target_entity>
<narrative>Airlines that currently use Boeing 747 planes.</narrative>
</query>
```

Figure 1: Test query in TREC 2009 entity track.

The key challenge in the REF task involves entity ranking, that is, estimating the likelihood of the extracted entities being answer entities for a given query. Many related studies (Bron, 2010; Fang, 2010) have employed language model techniques to estimate the likelihoods of the extracted entities being answer entities via calculating similarities between query and supporting documents/snippets of entities. This technique may fail in cases where supporting documents/snippets of entities do not support their being answer entities.

[1]TREC 2010 limits the track's scope to searches for instances of the organizations, people, locations and product entity types.

To improve the above approach, this paper first argues that candidate entities' homepages are important supplements to supporting snippets and should be effectively exploited. Homepage information is, however, ignored by many TREC participants' systems. Second, much of the work to date only extracts coarse-grained types of entities (such as people, organizations, locations and products specified in *target_entity* field as shown in Figure 1) by using entity repositories such as YAGO (Suchanek, 2007) or named entity recognizers (Ratinov, 2009), and then rank them. However, some queries specify fine-grained types of target entities in *narrative* fields, such as airlines in Figure 1. In these cases, fine-grained entity recognition is necessary and helpful for improving performance, which can recognize fine-grained named entities such as airlines, publishers, drivers, or newspapers. Third, a dependency tree-based similarity approach is implemented to substitute language model techniques, which proved superior to the latter.

The contributions of this paper include 1) incorporating homepages of entities, and 2) recognizing fine-grained types of entities for improving entity ranking. Furthermore, we propose an unsupervised method of generating training examples for fine-grained entity recognition and exploit multiple-contexts of entities as classification features. In related studies, only single-contexts of entities are employed. The experimental results in terms of the TREC 2010 entity track test data set demonstrate that the nDCG@R improvements of our three proposals, i.e., dependency-tree similarity, incorporating homepage and recognizing fine-grained named entity components, are 2.3%, 4.1%, and 2.1%, respectively. Compared with baseline, the accumulative improvements of our REF system in terms of nDCG@R, P@1 and P@5 scores are 8.4%, 27.5%, and 12.0%, respectively.

2 Related Work

The TREC REF task is highly related to a combination of the TREC list QA and homepage finding, INEX entity ranking, and TREC expert search tasks. The TREC list QA task (2001-2007) (Voorhees, 2003) required systems to assemble an unordered list of answer strings to factoid questions such as *Who are six actors who have played Tevye in "Fiddler on the Roof"?* The underlying information need is of a more informational nature. However, the REF task is situated in explorative search tasks. Moreover, the list QA task also does not require returning to the homepage for each answer string. In recent years, retrieval-based (Yang, 2003), pattern-based (Ravichandran, 2002), deep NLP-based (Moldovan, 2002; Harabagiu, 2003), and supervised/unsupervised machine learning based approaches (Ittycheriah, 2002; Wu, 2007) have been proposed. The TREC homepage finding task (2001-2003) assumes that incoming queries (like "IJCNLP 2011") are attempts to navigate to the homepage of a particular web site (`http://www.ijcnlp2011.org/`).

The TREC expert search task (2005-2008) (Nick, 2005) focused on creating an ordered list of experts who have skills and experiments on a specific topic with enterprise data. Most of the proposed approaches generally fall into two categories: generative language models and discriminative models. For example, Balog (2006) proposed profile-centric (directly models the knowledge of an expert from associated documents) and document-centric (locates documents on the topic and then finds the associated experts) generative language models (LMs). Cao (2005) proposed a two-stage language model consisting of a document relevance and co-occurrence model. There are many other generative probabilistic models such as (Fang, 2007; Serdyukov, 2008). Fang (2010) proposed a principled relevance-based discriminative model that integrates a variety of document evidence and document candidate association features for improving expert searching.

The INEX entity ranking task (2007-2010) (Vries, 2007) studies ranking of Wikipedia entities to a query topic. Apart from estimating similarities between Wikipedia pages and the given query topic, many systems (Pehcevski, 2008) have exploited Wikipedia link structure and Wikipedia categories, for instance, estimating overlap between the set of categories associated with target Wikipedia pages and the categories specified in a given query topic.

The TREC REF task (2009-2010) (Balog, 2010) aims at entity-oriented search on the Web. The most typical system is a cascade of the following components. (1) Document Retriever retrieves top relevant documents to a given query from the given Clueweb09 collection with 503 million English pages. (2) Entity Extractor extracts candidate entities that match the given target types from the

	Types of Anwers	Source of Answers	Entity Extraction	Main Models used
List QA	Noun phrase	Newspaper texts	Needed	IR-based, NLP-based, and machine learning-based models
Expert Search	Person only	W3C corpus	No	IR-based model
INEX Entity	Any Wikipedia category	Wikipedia data	No	IR-based model with Wikipedia category and link
TREC REF	Location, person, organization, and product	Clueweb09, a snapshot of the Web	Needed	IR-based model due to the task is originally situated in a search problem

Table 1: Comparison of entity ranking tasks. W3C corpus is a simulation of enterprise data crawled from public W3C (*.w3.org) sites in June 2004.

top relevant documents by using entity repositories such as Wikipedia, or using named entity recognizers. (3) Entity Ranker estimates the probabilities of the extracted entities being answer entities by using supporting documents and/or snippets in which entities and queries co-occur. A number of language modeling techniques borrowed from expert search systems were employed (Bron, 2010; Fang, 2010; Li, 2010). (4) Homepage Finder assigns primary homepages for the top ranked entity names by using entity names as queries, or homepage identifiers.

Table 1 compares these tasks from four aspects.

3 Our System

We can see that TREC entity ranking task is very complicated, and each component is an independent research topic in the fields of NLP and IR. This paper cannot cover all of them, and only focuses on Entity Ranker component, that is, given a query Q, and a list of extracted entities $E = \{e_i|i = 1, 2, ...n\}$ associated with their homepages $H = \{h_{e_i}|i = 1, 2, ..., n\}$, how to effectively rank these entities.

The other three components are beyond the scope of this paper. For better understanding of the REF system, we simply introduce them. Our Document Retriever first employs Yahoo! BOSS API[2] to search relevant pages from the Web and then map them to documents in Clueweb09. Since one lesson from TREC 2009 is that commercial search engines such as Yahoo! are generally superior in locating relevant documents for the search engine, we used the Indri tool for building. In Entity Extractor, an NER tool developed at UIUC (Ratinov, 2009)[3] is employed. In particular, phrases/words tagged with PER, ORG, LOC and MISC tags are extracted when the target entities are people, organizations, locations, and products, respectively. For Homepage Finder, the DBpedia homepage data[4] is used to train a binary classifier and features are similar to (Upstill, 2003). It is noted that we reverse the sequence of the Entity Ranker and Homepage Finder to enable incorporating homepage for ranking (introduced in section 3.3), that is, we first assign homepage for each entity, and then rank them.

3.1 Baseline

In the context of expert search, the task is to find out what is the probability of a candidate person being an expert to a query. The REF system can be simply regarded as the task of estimating $p(e_i|Q)$, the probability of an entity e_i being answer entity given a query Q. Therefore, approaches proposed in expert search can be used for entity finding. In TREC expert search, document model (referred as Model 2) (Balog, 2006) turned out to be one of the most prominent and effective models for estimating $p(e_i|Q)$. Model 2 is also used as our baseline, which can be expressed by,

$$p(e_i|Q) \propto \sum_{j=1}^{n} p(Q|es_{ij}) * p(e_i|es_{ij}, Q) \quad (1)$$

In (1) es_{ij} stands for the j-th supporting snippet from which entity e_i is extracted, n is the number of supporting snippets, $p(Q|es_{ij})$ denotes the relevance between query and supporting snippet, and can be relatively easy to determine using a language model (the KL-divergence language model used in this paper), $p(e_i|es_{ij}, Q)$ denotes the co-occurrence of the query and entity in the snippet. Because unique characteristics of the W3C corpus used in expert search, meta-based co-occurrence

[2]http://developer.yahoo.com/

[3]http://l2r.cs.uiuc.edu/~cogcomp

[4]http://dbpedia.org/About

model is commonly used. In entity ranking task, the KL-divergence language model is adopted to calculate $p(e_i|es_{ij}, Q)$. Model 2 can be further improved in the context of REF task as follows.

3.2 Improvement 1: Dependency Tree-based Similarity

To improve unigram KL-divergence language model that can not capture relations between query words, this paper adopts a dependency tree-based similarity algorithm to calculate $p(Q|es_{ij})$, which can be expressed by,

$$p(Q|es_{ij}) \propto \frac{DP_Q \cap DP_{es_{ij}}}{\sqrt{|DP_Q| \times |DP_{es_{ij}}|}} \quad (2)$$

where DP_Q and $DP_{es_{ij}}$ stand for a set of sub-trees generated from dependency trees of query Q and text snippet es_{ij}, respectively. Dependency trees are obtained by parsing Q and es_{ij} using Lin's dependency parser, Minipar[5], and the subtree is defined as any node up to its two descendants and extracted with the Freqt toolkit[6].

3.3 Improvement 2: Incorporating Homepage

The goal of the REF task is to return homepages representing entities to a query, and homepages sometimes contain valuable information for ranking. Therefore, it is easy and necessary to incorporate homepages of entities in ranking. As input in entity finding, we receive a query Q, a list of candidate entities $E = \{e_i|i = 1, 2, ..., n\}$ associated with their homepages $H = \{h_{e_i}|i = 1, 2, ..., n\}$. The Entity Ranker can be reformulated to estimate a conditional probability $p(e_i, h_{e_i}|Q)$. The top k entities with their homepages are deemed the most probable answer entities.

By assuming entity e_i is independent of its homepage h_{e_i}, we obtain,

$$p(e_i, h_{e_i}|Q) = p(e_i|Q) \times p(h_{e_i}|Q) \quad (3)$$

where $p(e_i|Q)$ stands for the probability of entity e_i being an answer given query Q, and can be calculated using Equation (1) and (2), $p(h_{e_i}|Q)$ stands for the probability of homepage h_{e_i} being an answer given query Q.

By applying the Bayes' Theorem and assuming that $p(h_{e_i})$ is uniform for all homepages h_{e_i}, we obtain,

$$p(h_{e_i}|Q) = \frac{p(Q|h_{e_i}) \times p(h_{e_i})}{p(Q)} \propto p(Q|h_{e_i}) \quad (4)$$

In some cases, homepages such as that of racecar driver Michael Schumacher (`http://www.michael-schumacher.de/`) do not contain any valuable information but intend to greet visitors and provide information about the site or its owner. Thus, we retrieve text snippets hs_{e_i} from a homepage site using query Q to build a back-off model for $p(h_{e_i}|Q)$ built from the homepage (the opening or main page of the homepage site). Finally, we can obtain,

$$p(Q|h_{e_i})' = \alpha \times p(Q|h_{e_i}) + \beta \times p(Q|hs_{e_i}) \quad (5)$$

where $\alpha + \beta = 1$, $p(Q|h_{e_i})$ and $p(Q|hs_{e_i})$ are estimated using the KL-divergence language model.

In short, conditional probability $p(e_i, h_{e_i}|Q)$ of the likelihood of entity e_i with its homepage h_{e_i} being answer is calculated by using Equation (3), (5), (1) and (2).

3.4 Improvement 3: Fine-grained Entity Recognition

As mentioned, entities are extracted by using NER tool. There exist two problems. First, the NER tool can only identify coarse-grained types of entities such as organizations or locations. However, users' queries sometimes specify fine-grained types of named entities such as airlines, universities, or actresses. Second, many incorrect entities are extracted. The main reason lies in: the NER tool is trained on newspapers, but we use it to tag web data. Therefore, it is necessary to filter out or negatively reward entities that do not match the fine-grained entity types if specified in queries. For example, this step can hopefully remove or negatively reward the extracted entities that are not airlines for the TREC 2009 test query shown in Figure 1.

Many semi-supervised methods have been proposed to recognize fine-grained types of entities. For example, Hearst (1992) used lexical patterns such as "X, such as Y". Fleischman (2002) employed a supervised learning method that considered the local context surrounding the entity as well as global semantic information. Etzioni (2005) started with a set of "*predicates*" and bootstrapped the extraction process from high-precision generic patterns. Oh (2009) exploited

[5] `http://webdocs.cs.ualberta.ca/~lindek`
[6] `http://chasen.org/~taku/software`

Wikipedia structure information and textual context to determine fine-grained types of Wikipedia entities. Generally, these methods mainly exploit the single-context of an entity as classification feature, which may result in errors in cases in which the relation between entity and its fine-grained type is not explicitly expressed.

Our proposal differs: 1) we utilize multiple contexts in which entities and their fine-grained types co-occur, 2) multiple contexts obtained by querying the Web with entities and their fine-grained types are helpful to disambiguate entities, 3) a dependency pattern-based approach is proposed for fine-grained classification of named entities. More specifically, our goal is to assign a class label ("yes" or "no") for each ⟨entity, fine-grained type⟩ pair. A "yes" means the entity belongs to the corresponding fine-grained type. Otherwise, it does not. The details are as follows.

3.4.1 Step-1: Preparation of Training Examples

A certain number of ⟨entity e, its fine-grained type fgt, multi-contexts they co-occur mc⟩ training triples are needed to build a classifier of fine-grained entities. The key challenge here is to prepare positive and negative $\langle e, fgt \rangle$ pairs.

A Wikipedia article usually starts with a definition sentence like "*Continental Airlines is an American airline based and headquartered in Continental Center I in downtown Houston, Texas.*" We find that it is practicable to automatically extract entity ("Continental Airlines" in this example) and its fine-grained type ("airline") from such well-formed sentences. To extract the pairs from these definition sentences, we first use Minipar to parse all Wikipedia definition sentences and then extract the pairs using heuristic rules such as *(be (Wikipedia-entity) (fine-grained-type))*. In this example, ⟨Continental Airlines, airline⟩ is extracted. Finally, 41,495 pairs are generated. These pairs will be used as positive instances. In order to construct negative training pairs, we first adopt the NER tool to recognize named entities in the Wikipedia definition sentences, and then pair the fine-grained type and the identified entities, except for the Wikipedia entity, as negative examples. For example, ⟨Continental Center I, airline⟩, ⟨Houston, airline⟩, and ⟨Texas, airline⟩ pairs are generated. Finally, 122,686 negative pairs are collected from Wikipedia.

Multi-context mc can be easily obtained by querying a search engine with the entity and its type and merging the first k snippets returned. Formally, $mc = \bigcup_{j=1}^{k} s_j$, where s_j denotes the j-th snippet. For ambiguous entities such as "Michael Collins", it is hard to recognize their fine-grained types with fewer frequencies from multiple contexts obtained by querying the Web with entities only. Multiple contexts learned with entities and their fine-grained types can partially solve this problem.

3.4.2 Step-2: Building Classifier

In order to handle long distance relations between words, dependency patterns are extracted as features for classification. First, textual contexts of $\langle e, fgt, mc \rangle$ triples are parsed using Lin's Minipar. Then, the shortest dependency paths between e and fgt are extracted as dependency patterns. Figure 2 shows two examples. To reduce the dimensionality of the feature space, we calculate the precision of each dependency pattern by using the equation, $precison = Cnt_p/(Cnt_p + Cnt_n)$, where, Cnt_p and Cnt_n denote total numbers of patterns occurring in positive and negative triples, respectively. We sort the extracted dependency patterns in deceasing order of precision and empirically select the top 500 patterns as classification features.

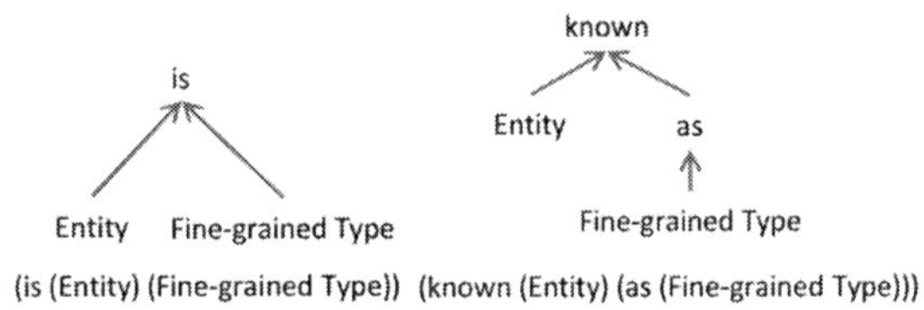

Figure 2: Examples of dependency patterns.

For the classifier, we employ multivariate classification SVMs that can directly optimize a large class of performance measures such as F_1-Score, prec@k and rec@k (the precision and recall of a classifier that predicts exactly $k = 100$ examples to be positive) (Joachims, 2005). For our experiment we held out 500 pairs from each of the positive and negative instances for testing. The remainder are used for training. Table 2 reports the results on the testing data. These results are quite promising. The classifier optimizing F_1-Score is finally used in our REF system.

3.4.3 Step-3: Using Classifier

To use the classifier in the REF system, we recognize fine-grained type fgt_Q of the target entity

	Rec@k	Prec@k	F1-score
Precision	80.8	89.3	86.4
Recall	97.4	83.6	91.6
F-measure	88.3	86.4	88.9

Table 2: Fine-grained named entity classifiers optimizing different measures.

from the *narrative* field of query Q according to the predefined heuristic rules such as the head of the first non-stop noun phrase being fine-grained. For exmaple, *gallery* in "*What art galleries are located in Bethesda, Maryland?*" is identified as fine-grained type.

For each entity e_i extracted via the Entity Extractor, the following steps are performed. (1) obtain textual contexts by querying the Yahoo! search engine with entity e_i and the identified fine-grained type fgt_Q, and merging the Yahoo! snippets returned. (2) parse contexts using Lin's Minipar and extract dependency patterns between e_i and fgt_Q. (3) employ the classifier to determine whether the entity e_i belongs to the fine-grained type fgt_Q, and remove or negatively reward the entities that are not fine-grained type identified from the query.

4 Experiments

Our experiments are conducted in the context of the TREC 2010 REF task. Relevance judgements in the TREC were performed in two stages. In phase one, all participant systems were pooled to a depth of the 20. The submitted homepages were judged on a three-point relevance scale: (2) primary homepage devoted to and in control of the entity, (1) relevant homepage devoted to the entity, but is not in control of the entity, and (0) non-relevant homepage that only mentions the entity but is not about the entity. Note that the Wikipedia page of a given entity is regarded as non-relevant by definition in TREC 2010. In phase two, homepages belonging to the same entity are grouped together. The test set used in the TREC 2010 entity track contains 50 test queries. In the official evaluation, only 47 test queries are used because no answers to the other three queries are found. Among 47 test queries, 31 are for organization, 7 for location, 8 for person, and 1 for product name. The average number of answered homepages per topic is 14 (Balog, 2010).

The TREC metrics are based on the homepages only because the ultimate goal of the REF system is to find the homepages of the entities. The main metric is nDCG@R; that is, the normalized discounted cumulative gain at rank R (the number of primary and relevant homepages for that topic) where a record with a primary gets a gain of 3, and a record with a relevant gets a gain of 1. We also report P@N, that is, the fraction of primary homepages in the first N ranks. Experimental results are computed using the *eval-entity.pl* script released by TREC.

4.1 Overall Performance

Table 3 reports the results of the four runs. Best_T and Median_T denote the best and median scores among all TREC 2010 participants' systems, respectively. Perfect_O means the manual ranking system, which can indicate the performance ceiling that our Entity Ranker can achieve. Our_{comb} denotes the proposed system that negatively reward all entities not belonging to the fine-grained entity type by simply putting them at the end of the ranking list.

	nDCG@R	P@1	P@5	P@10
Our_{comb}	.1865	.3404	.20	.1596
Perfect_O	.3564	.8298	.5872	.3787
Median_T	.12	-	-	-
Best_T	.38	-	-	-

Table 3: Comparison of four runs.

The results demonstrate that: i) Our_{comb} significantly improves the median performance of the TREC participant systems from 12% to 18.65% in terms of nDCG@R. However, Perfect_O (the performance ceiling) is much high than our automatic system, Our_{comb}. This means that there is still much room for improving the entity ranking component. ii) Figure 3 shows the performance of each target type. Product-type queries achieve a worse score due to poor product (PRO) name recognition of the NER tool. The best P@1 score is obtained for organization (ORG) type queries. The nDCG@R score for the person (PER) type is, however, better than that for ORG-type queries. This is because the average number of answer homepages for the ORG-type (29.5) is significantly larger that that of the PER-type (10.5), and the recall for ORG type queries is relatively poor. iii) The Best_T (Yang, 2010)

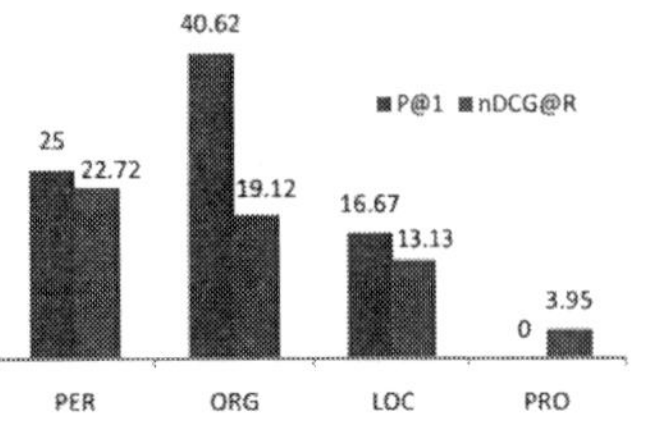

Figure 3: Results per topic type.

is even better than our Perfect$_O$. This indicates that the recall of our entity extraction is unsatisfactory. Note that this paper is mainly concerned with entity ranking, and entity extraction is not the scope of this paper. Yet the proposed methods can be incorporated into Best$_T$ and it can be expected to further improve its performance. Because Best$_T$ only use co-occurrence information between entities in ranking. For better understanding, Table 4 analyzes the recalls of the answer entities in the Document Retriever and Entity Extractor modules. #que represents the number of queries in which at least one answer entity is contained. #ent represents the number of answer entities of all test queries contained. This table indicates that the recall of the Entity Extractor is only 37% ($= 266/715$).

	Golden Answers [a]	Document Retriever [b]	Entity Extractor [c]
#que	47	45	40
#ent	715	384	266

[a] Golden answers are proved by TREC 2010 http://trec.nist.gov/data/entity10.html
[b] No answer entities are retrieved for queries 34 and 44.
[c] No answer entities are extracted for queries 28, 36, 37, 65, and 66.

Table 4: Recalls of answer entities.

The following sections mainly analyze the impacts of the dependency tree-based similarity, incorporating homepage and the fine-grained entity recognition to the REF system; thus, we exclude the queries for which no answer entities are extracted in the Entity Extractor, and the following experiments are based on 40 queries of the TREC 2010 test set.

4.2 Impact of Homepage and Fine-grained Entity Recognition

Table 5 shows the contributions of the dependency tree-based similarity (DTBS), incorporating homepage information (HP), and fine-grained named entity recognition (FG-NER). The baseline is Model 2 discussed in section 3.1. Significance tests are conducted. †: significantly better than the system without this component at the $p = 0.05$ level using two-sided t-tests; $^\flat$: significantly better at the 0.01 level.

	nDCG@R	P@1	P@5	P@10
Baseline	.1336	.125	.115	.1075
+DTBS	.1562†	.25†	.135	.1225
+HP	.1969$^\flat$	.20	.20$^\flat$	.175$^\flat$
+FG-NER	.2181†	.40$^\flat$	.235	.1875

Table 5: Contribution of each component.

The experimental results indicate that: i) the DTBS method can greatly improve Baseline, e.g., the nDCG@R and P@1 scores are significantly improved by 16.9% and 100.0%, respectively. We expect this because the DTBS method considers the relation between words. ii) homepage (HP) can positively impact the REF system in terms of nDCG@R, P@5, and P@10 metrics, which, however, leads to a lower P@1 score. When a non-homepage but one highly-related to the query is assigned as the homepage of an incorrect entity, incorporating homepage information will cause a negative influence. iii) the FG-NER can greatly improve the P@1 score from 20.0% to 40.0% and the P@10 score by 7.1% (not significant). This indicates that the FG-NER on TREC answer entities has nice precision and but poor recall. Table 2, however, shows that our FG-NER can achieve promising precision and recall. It is hard for TREC non-famous entities to retrieve snippets from the Web that conform to the dependency patterns extracted from snippets of Wikipedia entities, which results in poor performance.

In short, it is effective to use a dependency tree-based similarity, homepage information, and fine-grained named entity recognition in the REF system. Figure 4 shows the nDCG@R scores of Our$_{comb}$ and Baseline for each of the 40 queries.

4.3 Evaluation on Entity Names

The experiments above are based on homepages only in which correct entities with wrong homepages are not rewarded. This section discusses the performance based on named entities in which failures of finding homepage are ignored. In calculating nDCG@R, each answer entity gains 1 and a

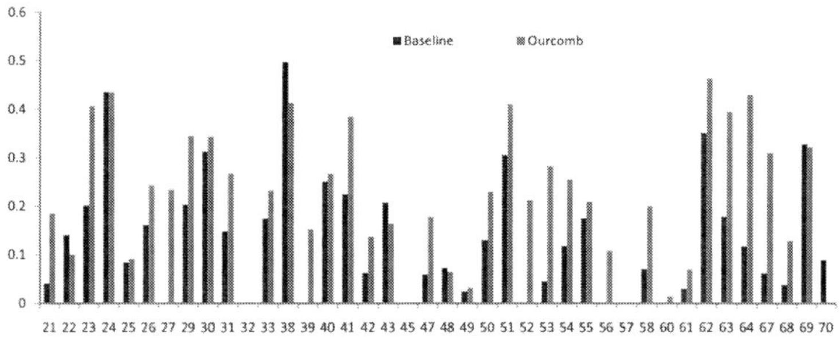

Figure 4: nDCG@R score for each test query.

non-relevant entity gains 0. Figure 5 shows the performance. This figure indicates that the improvements from each proposed component are more significant when errors from homepage finding are ignored. For example, the absolute enhancements of the FG-NER in terms of P@1 and nDCG@R scores are 22.5%, and 3.1%, respectively. This experiment indicates that the Homepage Finder component needs to be improved.

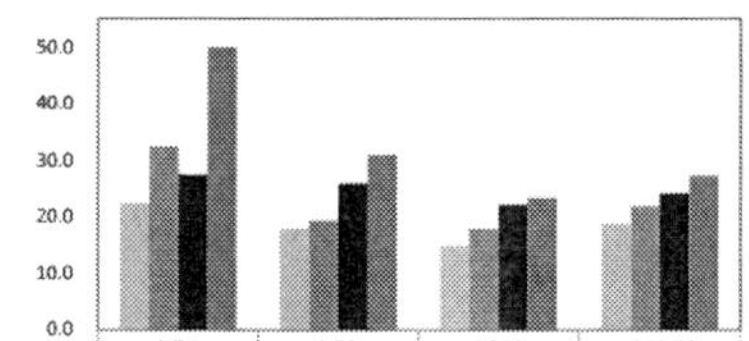

	P@1	P@5	P@10	nDCG@R
Baseline	22.5	18.0	15.0	18.9
+ DTBS	32.5	19.5	18.0	22.0
+ p(Q|hei)	27.5	26.0	22.3	24.3
Ourcomb	50.0	31.0	23.5	27.4

Figure 5: Metrics based on named entities.

5 Conclusion

This paper focused on developing a model for retrieving homepages of entities relevant to a query from a huge collection, and proposed three algorithms for improvements: a dependency tree-based similarity method, incorporating homepages of entities to supplement text snippets that the entities are from, and fine-grained classification of named entities. The comparison experiments on the TREC 2010 test data set showed that the proposed algorithms can significantly improve the system; e.g., the cumulative improvements of the nDCG@R, P@1, and P@5 scores over the Baseline reach 8.4%, 27.5%, and 12.0%, respectively. Moreover, our approaches can also be used in other tasks such as factoid QA. For example, in the TREC 2007 QA test set, about 50% questions (except for questions which answers are numeric and time expresses) contain fine-grained types of answers. Thus, our fine-grained entity recognition module can be expected to lead to improvements in QA systems.

In the future, we will work toward entity extraction and fine-grained named entity recognition. Table and list-based entity extraction may be essential due to the considerable number of answer entities scattered in tables, lists, and other structured forms. For example, answer entities to TREC 2010 query 29 (Find companies that are included in the Dow Jones industrial average.) are contained in a table at `http://www.1728.com/dowjone2.htm`. Li (2010) summarized the statistics of the TREC 2010 test queries in which answer entities are expressed in tables and lists. This means the NER tool trained by the newspaper corpus might fail at identifying the entities from tables and lists, and we have a great deal of work to do in order to correctly identify them. For fine-grained named entity recognition, more studies are needed on identifying fine-grained types of non-famous entities. For example, it is hard to determine whether "Rosenberg Gallery" is a gallery from the snippets relevant to the query "Rosenberg Gallery, gallery".

References

Abdessamad Echihabi and Daniel Marcu. 2003. A Noisy-Channel Approach to Question Answering. In *Proc. of ACL 2003*, Japan.

Abraham Ittycheriah, and Salim Roukos. 2002. IBM's Statistical Question Answering System-TREC 11. In *Proc. of TREC 2002*.

Arjen P. de Vries, Anne-Marie Vercoustre, James A. Thom, et al. 2007. Overview of the INEX 2007 Entity Ranking Track. In *Proc. of INEX 2007*.

Claudio Giuliano. 2009. Fine-Grained Classification of Named Entities Exploiting Latent Semantic Kernels. In *Proc. of CoNLL 2009*, pp. 201-209.

Dan Moldovan, Sanda Harabagiu, Roxana Girju, et al. 2002. LCC Tools for Question Answering. In *Proc. of TREC 2002*.

David Hawking, and Nick Craswell. 2001. Overview of the TREC 2001 Web Track. In *Proc. of TREC 2001*.

Deepak Ravichandran, and Eduard Hovy. 2002. Learning Surface Text Patterns for a Question Answering System. In *Proc. of ACL 2002*.

Ellen M. Voorhees. 2003. Overview of the TREC 2003 Question Answering Track. In *Proc. of TREC 2003*, pp.54-68, USA.

Fabian M. Suchanek, Gjergji Kasneci, and Gerhard Weikum. 2007. YAGO: A Core of Semantic Knowledge Unifying WordNet and Wikipedia. In *Proc. of WWW 2007*, pp.697-706.

Hui Fang and ChengXiang Zhai. 2007. Probabilistic Models for Expert Finding. In *Proc. of ECIR 2007*, pp.418-430.

Hui Yang, and Tat-Seng Chua. 2003. QUALIFIER: Question Answering by Lexical Fabric and External Resources. In *Proc. of EACL 2003*, pp.363-370.

John Lafferty and Chengxiang Zhai. 2001. Document Language Models, Query Models, and Risk Minimization for Information Retrieval. In *Proc. of SIGIR-2001*.

Jong-Hoon Oh, Kiyotaka Uchimoto, and Kentaro Torisawa. 2009. Bilingual Co-Training for Monolingual Hyponymy-Relation Acquisition. In *Proc. of ACL 2010*, pp.432-440.

Jovan Pehcevski, Anne-Marie Vercoustre, and James Thom. 2008. Exploiting Locality of Wikipedia Links in Entity Ranking. In *Proc. of ECIR 2008*.

Krisztian Balog, Leif Azzopardi, and Maarten de Rijke. 2006. Formal Models for Expert Finding in Enterprise Corpora. In *Proc. of SIGIR 2006*, pp.43-50.

Krisztian Balog, Leif Azzopardi, and Maarten de Rijke. 2010. Overview of TREC 2010 Entity Track. In *Proc. of TREC 2010*.

Lev Ratinov and Dan Roth. 2009. Design Challenges and Misconceptions in Named Entity Recognition. In *Proc. of CoNLL 2009*.

Marc Bron, Krisztian Balog, and Maarten de Rijke. 2010. Ranking Related Entities: Components and Analysis. In *Proc. of CIKM 2010*.

Marc Bron, Jiyin He, Katja Hofmann, et al. 2010. The University of Amsterdam at TREC 2010 Session, Entity, and Relevance Feedback. In *Proc. of TREC 2010*.

Marti A. Hearst. 1992. Automatic Acquisition of Hyponyms from Large Text Corpora. In *Proc. of COLING-92*, pp.539-545.

Michael Fleischman and Eduard Hovy. 2002. Fine Grained Classification of Named Entities. In *Proc. of COLING-2002*.

Nick Craswell, Arjen P. de Vries, and Ian Soboroff. 2005. Overview of the TREC-2005 Enterprise Track. In *Proc. of TREC 2005*, pp.1-7.

Oren Etzioni, Michael Cafarella, Doug Downey, et al. 2005. Unsupervised Named-Entity Extraction from the Web: An Experimental Study. *Artificial Intelligence*, Volume 165 Issue 1.

Pavel Serdyukov, Henning Rode, and Djoerd Hiemstra. 2008. Modeling multi-step relevance propagation for expert finding. In *Proc. of CIKM 2008*.

Qi Li and Daqing He. 2010. Searching for Entities: When Retrieval Meets Extraction. In *Proc. of TREC 2010*.

Qing Yang, Peng Jiang, Chunxia Zhang, and et al. 2010. Reconstruct Logical Hierarchical Sitemap for Related Entity Finding. In *Proc. of TREC 2010*.

Rianne Kaptein, Pavel Serdyukov, Arjen de Vries, and Jaap Kamps. 2010. Entity Ranking using Wikipedia as a Pivot. In *Proc. of CIKM 2010*.

Sanda M. Harabagiu, Steven J. Maiorano and Marius A. Pasca. 2003. Open-Domain Textual Question Answering Techniques. In *Natural Language Engineering* 9 (3): 1-38.

Thorsten Joachims. 2005. A Support Vector Method for Multivariate Performance Measures. In *Proc. of ICML 2005*.

Trystan Upstill. 2003. Query-Independent Evidence in Home Page Finding. In *ACM Transactions on Information Systems*, Vol21, No3, pp.286-313.

Yi Fang, Luo Si, and Aditya P. Mathur. 2010. Discriminative Models of Integrating Document Evidence and Document-Candidate Associations for Expert Search. In *Proc. of SIGIR 2010*, pp.683-690.

Yi Fang, Luo Si, Zhengtao Yu, et al. 2010. Purdue at TREC 2010 Entity Track: A Probabilistic Framework for Matching Types Between Candidate and Target Entities. In *Proc. of TREC 2010*.

Youzheng Wu, Ruiqiang Zhang, Xinhui Hu, Hideki Kashioka. 2007. Learning Unsupervised SVM Classifier for Answer Selection in Web Question Answering. In *Proc. of EMNLP-CoNLL 2007*.

Youzheng Wu and Hideki Kashioka. 2009. NiCT at TREC 2009: Employing Three Models for Entity Ranking Track. In *Proc. of TREC 2009*.

Yunbo Cao, Jingjing Liu, Shenghua Bao, and Hang Li. 2005. Research on expert search at enterprise track of TREC 2005. In *Proc. of TREC 2005*.

Yutaka Sasaki. 2005. Question Answering as Question-Biased Term Extraction: A New Approach toward Multilingual QA. In *Proc. of ACL 2005*.

Enhancing Active Learning for Semantic Role Labeling via Compressed Dependency Trees

Chenhua Chen, Alexis Palmer, and Caroline Sporleder
Computational Linguistics and Phonetics
Saarland University, Saarbrücken, Germany
ch.chenua@googlemail.com, {apalmer, csporled}@coli.uni-sb.de

Abstract

This paper explores new approaches to active learning (AL) for semantic role labeling (SRL), focusing in particular on combining typical informativity-based sampling strategies with a novel measure of representativeness based on compressed dependency trees (CDTs). In essence, the compressed representation encodes the target predicate and the key dependents of the verb complex in the sentence. We first present our method for producing CDTs from the output of an existing dependency parser. The compressed trees are used as features for training a supervised SRL system. Second, we present a study of AL for SRL. We investigate a number of different sample selection strategies, and the best results are achieved by incorporating CDTs for example selection based on both informativity and representativeness. We show that our approach can reduce by up to 50% the amount of training data needed to attain a given level of performance.

1 Introduction

The focus of this paper is active learning for semantic role labeling, a little-studied intersection of two rather substantial bodies of work.

One aim of active learning (AL) is to reduce the number of labeled training instances required to reach a given performance level using supervised machine learning techniques. This is accomplished by allowing the learner to guide the selection of examples to be annotated and added to the training set; at each iteration the learner queries for the example (or set of examples) that will be most informative to its present state. AL is an attractive idea for natural language processing (NLP) because of its potential to dramatically reduce the need for expensive expert annotation, and it has been successfully applied in various areas of natural language processing (Tang et al., 2002; Settles and Craven, 2008), including named entity recognition (Shen et al., 2004),text classification (Yang et al., 2009), image retrieval (Zhou, 2006), part-of-speech tagging (Ringger et al., 2007), morpheme glossing (Baldridge and Palmer, 2009), and syntactic parsing (Hwa, 2004; Osborne and Baldridge, 2004).

The problems of scarce annotated data and the expense of annotating new data are at least as relevant for semantic role labeling (SRL) as for the above-mentioned areas of NLP. Existing work on automatic SRL usually explores supervised machine learning approaches to mark the semantic roles of predicates automatically by training classifiers using large annotated corpora.[1] Although such approaches can achieve reasonably good performance, annotating a large corpus is still expensive and time consuming. Moreover, the performance of trained classifiers may degrade remarkably when they are applied to out-of-domain data (Johansson and Nugues, 2008a). There is very little work on AL for SRL (e.g. Roth and Small (2006)), although much interesting work has been done with semi-supervised and unsupervised approaches to the problem (Grenager and Manning, 2006; Fürstenau and Lapata, 2009; Lang and Lapata, 2010; Titov and Klementiev, 2011, among others).

In this paper we explore the use of compressed dependency trees (CDTs) as features for supervised semantic role labeling and, most importantly, as a way of measuring how representative an individual instance is of the input data. We then incorporate representativeness as part of the metric used for sample selection in active learning. The

[1] For recent work on SRL, see, among others: (Das et al., 2010; Hajič et al., 2009; Surdeanu et al., 2008; Carreras and Màrquez, 2005; Baker et al., 2007).

compressed dependency trees encode the target predicate and the key dependents of the verb complex in a sentence. As illustrated in Section 3, the structural relationships defined by the compressed dependency trees well encapsulate key features used in automatic SRL.

For a more complete picture of the potential for AL with respect to SRL, we investigate a set of strategies designed to select the most **informative** training examples. We further develop a more effective approach to select training examples concerning both their informativity and **representativeness**. We use the compressed dependency trees to measure the similarity of two sentences, and select the training examples with a higher priority which are more informative and representative among the unlabeled sentences in the pool. The experimental results show that our approaches can reduce up to 50% of training examples compared to traditional supervised learning solutions.

We begin with a brief description of the semantic role labeling task and our supervised learning model. Section 3 presents our method for compressing dependency tree representations, followed by the active learning model, including definitions of all sampling strategies investigated in this work (Section 4). Experiments and results are presented and discussed in Section 5 and Section 6. We end with related work (Section 7) and brief conclusions.

2 Semantic Role Labeling

Parsing the semantic argument structure of a sentence involves identification and disambiguation of target predicates as well as identification and labeling of their arguments. Because our focus is on the active learning more so than on the semantic role labeling itself, we address only the argument labeling stage of the process, assuming that predicates and argument spans alike have already been identified and correctly labeled.

Broadly speaking, there are two different styles of semantic parsing and semantic role labeling (SRL): those based on FrameNet-style analysis (Ruppenhofer et al., 2006) and those using PropBank-style analysis (Palmer et al., 2005). This work takes the PropBank approach, which considers only verbal predicates and is strongly tied to syntactic structure. In (1), for example, the two arguments of the predicate *idolize* are labeled as *Arg0* and *Arg1*.

(1) [John]$_{Arg0}$ idolizes [his sister]$_{Arg1}$.

In this text, we refer to each argument to be labeled, together with its target predicate, as an **instance**; the sentence in (1) contains two instances.

2.1 Supervised Learning Model

The aim of the current work is not to surpass state-of-the-art performance on semantic role labeling. Therefore, although state-of-the-art semantic role labelers are freely available, we chose to implement our own labeler in order to have more control over the underlying machinery. This allows straightforward access to the predicted probability of outputs, which is crucial for the informativity-based selection strategies in Section 4. In addition, compressed dependency trees (Section 3) serve as features for our labeler as well as guiding sample selection in the active learning experiments.

In our study, we applied an L1-regularized[2] logistic regression model (Lee et al., 2006) for labeling instances, using the liblinear package (Lin et al., 2007) to build one classifier per label. There are 6 core and 13 non-core argument labels in PropBank annotations. Thus our SRL system is a suite of binary classifiers, and we then use the one-versus-all method (Duda et al., 2001) to assign labels to each instance.

2.2 Data and Features

We used the version of PropBank provided for the CoNLL-2008 SRL shared task (Surdeanu et al., 2008). A test set of 500 randomly selected sentences was constructed at the outset of the project; this was used only for evaluation of both supervised and active learning models. In all AL experiments, we simulate the oracle by hiding and then uncovering gold-standard labels.

The CoNLL-2008 data set includes both gold-standard dependency parses and automatic dependency parses from the Malt parser (Nivre and Hall, 2005). We use a combination of features taken directly from the gold-standard parses,[3] features derived from the Malt parses, and features from the output of the Stanford dependency parser (de

[2]Note that logistic regression is used together with a regularized term to avoid the overfitting problem by penalizing the complexity of the trained model. Generally, the regularized term is defined as a function of the learned parameters over the weights. The L1 regularization, also called lasso penalty, is used to penalize both large and small weights.

[3]In ongoing work, we replace gold-standard parses with more realistic automatic parses.

Table 1: Three feature groups: CoNLL basic, CoNLL derived, and from additional parser

FEATURE TYPE	EXPLANATION/EXAMPLE
Part of Speech	JJR, JJS, LS, CD, etc.
Head word	Head words of predicate and argument
isNEG	Instance includes NOT or NEVER
Argument position	Before or after predicate
Argument chunk position	Beginning or end of corresponding chunk
Lemma of argument	Lemma of argument whose dependency role is PRD or DIR
Lemma context	Two words before and after argument
Cue words	DIR ('up', 'toward', 'forward', 'along') REC ('self' as suffix) PRD ('as', 'as if') CAU ('because', 'why', 'as a result of')
Voice of predicate	Active or passive
Dependency relation of predicate and argument	LOC, TMP, etc. 1) Sbj*, obj* are defined as: Sbj* ← Obj_Passive Sbj* ← LGS_passive Sbj* ← Active_vt_sbj Obj* ← Sbj_Passive Obj* ← Sbj_VI (intransitive verb) Obj* ← Obj_Active
Predicate Properties	VT = 1; transitive VI = 2; intransitive TO_IM=3; begins with 'to' V_ Adj = 4; verb followed by adjective words (e.g. 'sounds good', 'looks pretty') PV = 5; phrasal verb (e.g. 'pick up')
Verb Complex	e.g. "has not been set" in figure 1
Acomp	adjectival complement
Advmod	adverbial modifier
Infmod	infinitival modifier
Rcmod	relative clause modifier
Rel	relative (word introducing an rcmod)
Xsbj	controlling subject
Iobj	indirect object
Advcl	adverbial clause modifier
Prep_to,Prep_in, Prep_for, Prep_with	Prepositional phrases with 'to', 'in', 'for', 'with'

Marneffe et al., 2006). To apply the logistic regression model, the features are represented in a binary fashion. The features are described in Table 1, in three groups separated by double lines. The derived features, including a heuristically-identified verb complex and altered dependency labels, are described in more detail in Section 3.

We use cross-validation on the training data to select for each individual classifier the subset of features most relevant for that label. In feature selection, features are ranked based on their Fisher score calculated using the training data set (as in Duda et al. (2001)).

3 Dependency Tree Compression

Given a sentence, the task of dependency parsing is to identify the head word and its corresponding dependents and to classify their functional relationships according to a set of dependency relations (e.g., subject, modifier). Thus, a dependency tree of a sentence encodes the dependency relation between the head words and their dependents. It has been reported that SRL can benefit from phrase-structure and dependency-based syntactic parsing (Hacioglu, 2004; Johansson and Nugues,

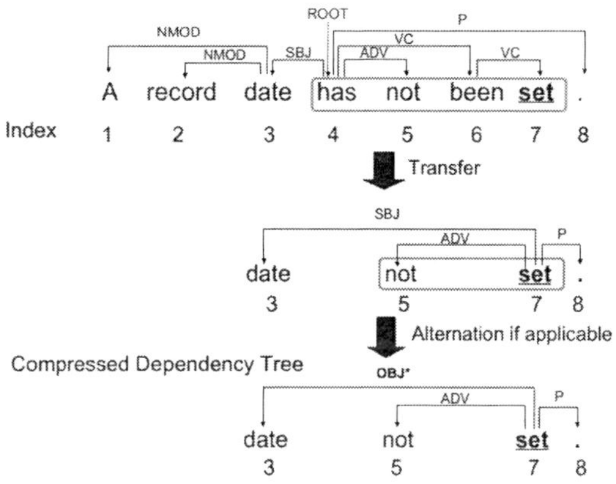

Figure 1: Producing compressed dependency tree

2008b; Pradhan et al., 2005). At the same time, much of the structural and relational information represented in a dependency tree is not relevant for the SRL task.

We use a **compressed dependency tree** (CDT) to encode just the relationships between a target predicate and the key dependents of the verb complex. The new tree is always rooted in the target predicate, which often means resetting the root from an auxiliary or other finite main verb. We generate the CDT from the output of an existing dependency parser through the process described in a simplified form below, using the example sentence in Fig. 1.

1. Fix target predicate (e.g. *set*) as root of CDT.
2. Identify the verb chain to which the target predicate belongs; this group of tokens will now be treated as the **verb complex**. The verb chain is produced by collecting elements connected by relevant dependency relations (VC, IM, CONJ), stopping when a ROOT node, a subordinate clause (SUB), or a verbal OBJ node is encountered.
3. Collect direct dependents of each word in the new verb complex; set these as dependents of the target predicate in the CDT, transferring the dependency relation to the target predicate. (e.g. *date* is a dependent of *have*).
4. Negation, modal verbs, and other main verbs in the verb complex also become dependents of the root predicate in the CDT. In some cases of 'new' dependency relations introduced by the tree compression process, we use output from the Stanford parser to complement the dependency relations found in the gold-standard data.

5. Heuristically determine voice of clause and alter some CDT dependency labels(e.g. SBJ_PASSIVE becomes OBJ*); these are the asterisk-marked relations in Table. 1.

For example, in (2):

(2) At the same time, the government did not want to appear to favor GM by allowing a minority stake that might preclude a full bid by Ford.

the verb complex is {*did, n't, want, appear, favor*}. The subject phrase *the government*, originally a dependent of *did*, becomes a dependent of the new three-verb predicate {*want, appear, favor*}; the negation word *n't* is a dependent of the target predicate *want*.

4 Active Learning

This section provides some background on the active learning process, as well as detailing the various sampling strategies we investigate.

4.1 The basic model

In this study we apply a standard active learning model (Settles, 2010; Lewis and Gale, 1994) to the task of semantic role labeling. Algorithm 1 illustrates this model as we use it.[4]

Algorithm 1 Active learning for SRL.

```
1: Randomly select initial seed of labeled instances;
2: Add initial seed to the training data;
3: Apply logistic regression model to train system of classifiers, one for each label;
4: while number of instances in training data is less than X do
5:     Randomly select pool of Y unlabeled sentences;
6:     Select a sentence or sentences from the unlabeled pool according to a given selection strategy;
7:     Ask oracle to label the selected unlabeled sentence;
8:     Add instances from selected sentence to training data;
9:     Re-train system using the updated training data;
10:    Use system to label test data, record accuracy;
11: end while
```

Much recent work in AL has to do with Step 6 of Algorithm 1, designing and refining selection strategies. The main selection criterion used to date has been **informativity**, measuring how much a training example can help to reduce the uncertainty of a statistical model. A less-frequently considered criterion, especially in AL for NLP, is **representativeness**, or how well a training example represents the overall input patterns of the unlabeled data.

While some results from AL are robust across different datasets and even different tasks, it is clear that there is no single approach to AL that is suitable for all situations (Tomanek and Olsson, 2009). Because there is very little previous work on AL for the task of semantic role labeling, we do not assume previous solutions but rather investigate a number of different strategies.

4.2 Informativity

Informativity is exploited in our approaches in terms of uncertainty, which is measured based on how confidently the system labels instances and, by extension, sentences. The lower the confidence on labeling a particular sentence, the more uncertainty is assigned to the sentence. At each iteration, then, we select from the unlabeled pool the single sentence with the greatest uncertainty. We compare 4 different scoring functions for measuring the system's certainty (CER) regarding an unlabeled sentence. These are presented below as INF1-INF4.

Let s represent an unlabeled sentence with instances $i = 1$ to n. Given a set of binary classifiers, one each for labels $y = 1$ to m, let $p_{i,y}$ be the probability of i being labeled as y. Finally, P is a pool of unlabeled sentences. At each iteration, we select the single $s \in P$ with the lowest value for CER.

RAND: Random selection. Random selection (randomly select an unlabeled sentence $s \in P$) serves as a strong baseline in active learning.

INF1: Average uncertainty. After labeling each instance in a sentence with the most-likely predicted label, we calculate uncertainty for the sentence as the average of the classifiers' confidence in assigning the predicted labels. Let $Top(i) = p_{i,y_k}$, where $\forall h \neq k, p_{i,y_k} > p_{i,y_h}$; $CER(s) = (\sum_{j=1}^{n} Top(i_j))/n$.

INF2: Average uncertainty variance. Our second informativity-based strategy evaluates the uncertainty of the labeling for an instance using the variance of the confidence for each instance. A smaller variance implies that it is more difficult for the system to differentiate between possible label assignments for the instance. We then calculate sentence uncertainty as the average variance for

[4] Recall that each sentence contains one or more instances.

all instances. Let $AVG(i) = (\sum_{k=1}^{m} p_{i,y_k})/m$, $VAR(i) = \sum_{k=1}^{m}(p_{i,y_k} - AVG(i))^2/(m-1)$; $CER(s) = \sum_{j=1}^{n} VAR(i_j)/n$.

INF3: Average top-2 Margin. The intuition behind this approach is that the top 2 most confident labels are likely to be more informative than other labels. Therefore, we only select the two most likely labels to calculate uncertainty.[5] Let $Margin(i) = p_{i,y_{k_1}} - p_{i,y_{k_2}}$, where $p_{i,y_{k_1}} > p_{i,y_{k_2}} \wedge \forall h \neq k_1, k_2, p_{i,y_{k_2}} > p_{i,k_h}$; $CER(s) = (\sum_{j=1}^{n} Margin(i_j))/n$.

INF4: Most top-2 Margin Instances. Finally, we further extend the approach of INF3 by selecting the sentence which has the greatest number of instances with a small margin between the top 2 labels (which means that the sentence is more uncertain than other sentences). Let Q be a set of instances with the top-2 margin less than a small threshold (i.e., $Margin(i) \leq 0.1$). $CER(s)$ is defined as the inverse of the number of instances of s that are in Q (i.e. $1/\#$ *qualifying instances*). Ties are resolved by random selection.

4.3 Representativeness

A disadvantage of selecting examples based only on informativity is the tendency of the learner to query outliers (Settles, 2010). It has therefore been proposed (Dredze and Crammer, 2008; Settles and Craven, 2008) to temper such selection strategies with a notion of relevance or representativeness. Ours is the first work to use such a combined strategy for SRL. We measure the representativeness of unlabeled sentences based on sentence similarity, taking two different approaches: cosine similarity, and a measure based on CDTs.

COS: Cosine Similarity. Given two sentences s and s', let $i_1, i_2, \ldots, i_m$, and $i'_1, i'_2, \ldots, i'_n$ be their instances, respectively. The similarity of the two sentences, denoted as $similarity(s, s')$, is defined as $\sum_{j=1}^{m}\sum_{k=1}^{n} sim(i_j, i'_k)$, where $sim(i_j, i'_k)$ is the similarity between the instances i_j and i'_k, defined as the cosine of the two feature vectors.[6] For purposes of comparison, we use the same formulation of COS as Settles and Craven (2008).

[5] Note that in the binary classification case, INF3 is equivalent to INF1.

[6] Features are extracted from CDTs rather than full sentences, reducing to some extent the appearance of noisy information (e.g. stop words). Whether this can be further reduced by a modified implementation of COS is a question for future work.

Given a pool P of unlabeled sentences, for every unlabeled sentence $s \in P$, the representativeness of the sentence, denoted as $rep(s)$, is measured as the sum of the similarity between the sentence and all the other sentences in the pool, that is, $rep(s) = \sum sim(s, s')$, where $s' \in P \wedge s' \neq s$.

COS evaluates the similarity of two sentences based on the cosine of their instances. This may not be accurate enough because the instances include more information than the relationships between the target predicate and the key dependents of the verb complex in the sentence. Therefore, we exploit the compressed dependency trees as a metric to evaluate the similarity between two sentences, as illustrated below:

CDT: Compressed Dependency Trees. For target predicate p, let (p, r_i, a_i) be the edges of the CDT rooted in p, where a_i is an argument and r_i is the dependency relationship between p and a_i. We call two edges similar if **all** of p, r, and a meet their respective similarity criteria. Two predicates are considered to be similar if they have the same value for the PREDICATE PROPERTIES feature as defined in Table 1 (e.g. both are transitive verbs). Two relations are considered to be similar if they have the same dependency relation label (e.g. SBJ, TMP, MOD, etc.). Finally, two arguments are considered to be similar if they share the same coarse-grained part-of-speech tag.

Given a pool P of unlabeled sentences, for every unlabeled sentence $s \in P$, the representativeness of the sentence, denoted as $rep(s)$, is defined as $n_{similar}$, representing the number of edges in the pool that are similar to the edges of the CDT for s. Intuitively, the larger the number of similar CDT edges in the unlabeled pool, the more representative the sentence is overall of the input data.

4.4 Combining Informativity and Representativeness

The final step in our model is to define a selection strategy that incorporates *both* selection criteria. We define the priority of selecting a sentence as $priority(s) = \alpha \times rep(s) - (1-\alpha) \times CER(s)$. Given a pool P, we select the single $s \in P$ with the highest value for $priority(s)$. This approach is very similar to the information density (ID) approach of Settles and Craven (2008); the key difference is in the balance between the two criteria. Ours is a linear combination; ID instead multiplies informativity by a weighted measure of rep-

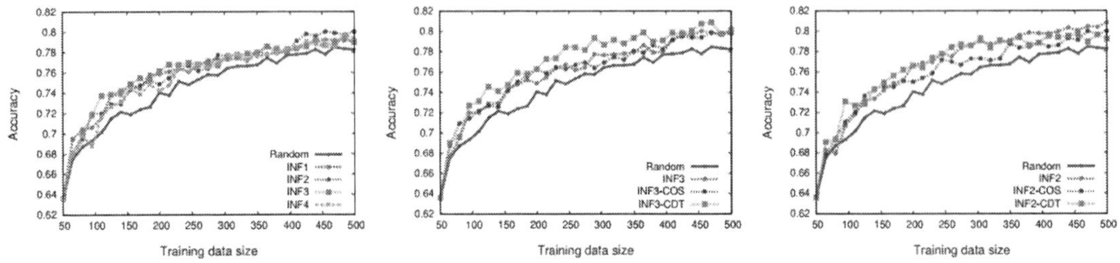

(a) Informativity-only strategies (b) INF3 with COS & CDT (c) INF2 with COS &CDT

Figure 2: Combining informativity and representativeness.

resentativeness.

5 Experimental Setup

To evaluate our approach to AL for SRL, we investigate three different questions. First, which informativity strategy is most appropriate for the task? Second, which representativeness measure works best? And third, how shall we weight the trade-off between the two selection criteria?

All of our active learning experiments share some characteristics. First, we randomly select a seed of 50 instances from the labeled training data. The seed set, as well as the test data, are kept consistent across all experimental conditions. In each iteration of the training-selection cycle (see Algorithm 1), a new unlabeled pool (n=500) is selected, and from that pool a single example is labeled by the oracle and added to the training set. We stop once 500 examples have been labeled.

To evaluate the effectiveness of each strategy, we tested the classifier in each interaction, and measured the accuracy of the predicted labels. The accuracy measure is defined as the number of correct labelings divided by the total number of labelings in the test data. Results are presented as the average over 20 runs.

To investigate the influence of representativeness, we run the same experiment with all cross-combinations of {INF1,INF2,INF3,INF4} and {COS,CDT}. For weighting the two criteria, we use both information density (ID) as defined in Settles and Craven (2008) and our *priority* metric (Section 4.4) with α set at 0.3, 0.5, and 0.7.

6 Results and Discussion

In this section, we analyze and discuss the experimental results. The gains achieved by AL can be measured in a number of different ways; first, we plot number of labeled training examples against system accuracy (Figure 2 and Figure 3). The figures presented here stop at 500 training examples, with averaged accuracies in the range of 80%. For comparison, the fully-supervised system when trained on *20000* instances performed at 89.71%. Second, we calculate the percent reduction in error of each strategy compared to the random selection baseline (Table 2), following Melville and Mooney (2004). Because most gains from AL happen early in the learning curve, we consider performance at two different points.

6.1 Informativity-based Strategies

Fig. 2a shows the expected result that the four informativity-based strategies outperform the random selection baseline. INF3 performs best early in the learning curve, but is overtaken by INF2 at the end of our curve. To reach the accuracy achieved by the four informativity strategies at the halfway point (250 training instances), RAND needs 100-150 additional instances.

6.2 Informativity plus Representativeness

Fig. 2b shows the result of combining the informativity (INF3) and representativeness (both COS and CDT). As illustrated in Section 6.1, INF3 outperforms the other informativity-based strategies. However, we see that Fig. 2b shows combining CDT with INF3 achieves a better performance than using INF3 only ($\alpha = 0.3$); representativeness improves performance, outperforming RAND by approximately 250 training instances. For INF3, COS is a less effective measure of representativeness. This may be because the feature vectors for the training instances share too much information, including stop words and a large number of 0-valued features, to make them easily differentiated. As a result, the most representative sentence selected using COS may not reflect the real simi-

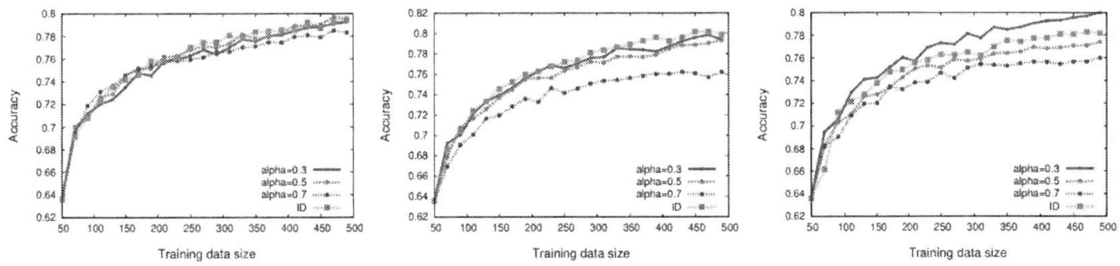

(a) INF3 with COS (b) INF3 with CDT (c) INF2 with CDT

Figure 3: Trade-off between informativity and representativeness.

larity of the sentences. In CDT, we choose only the structural relation between the predicate and its arguments to measure the similarity between sentences. As a result, the sentences selected using CDT are more representative than that of using COS, as confirmed by the result in Fig. 2b.

We also applied the solution of combining informativity and representativeness (4.3) to other informativity-based strategies. However, the advantage the combined solution for other strategies is less obvious than for INF3. For example, Fig. 2c shows the result of combining INF2 ($\alpha = 0.3$) with both COS and CDT. The result shows that the combined solution with CDT performs slightly better than using INF2 only when the number of training instances is less than 200. However, when the number of instances is larger than 350, the solution of using INF2 only achieves a higher accuracy than the combined solution. This may be due to a conflict between the two selection criteria. In any event, there is clearly a trade-off between informativity and representativeness, and results are influenced by the details of the manner of combining the two.

The results of other INF/REP combinations are presented in Table 2, in terms of their reduction in error compared to random selection.

6.3 Weighting the two criteria

Finally, we set α with different values (i.e., 0.3, 0.5 and 0.7) to investigate how the trade-off between informativity and representativeness may affect the SRL performance. We also compare our solution to the information density solution proposed by *et al.* (Settles and Craven, 2008) (denoted as ID) multiplies the informativity and representativeness instead of summing them. Here we display only the results of INF2 and INF4 combining with CDT in Fig. 3. Other combinations share a similar pattern with these results and their error reduction percentage can be found in Table. 2. Fig. 3a and Fig. 3b compare the two representativity measures for INF3, as the best overall result was achieved by INF3 in combination with CDT. We see that parameter tuning seems to be more influential for the CDT measure than for the COS measure.

Fig. 3c shows how parameter tuning affects INF2; $\alpha = 0.3$ has a higher accuracy than that of 0.5 and 0.7. We can observe that when $\alpha = 0.3$, our solution (INF2) has a better performance than that of ID. However, regarding the combination of INF4 and CDT, ID performs better (no graph; see 2. Note that the INF4 selects the sentences which has greatest number of instances with a small margin. Then representativeness of the sentences within the margin was calculated. In other word, the combination was done step by step not in parallel as the other combination. Therefore, the combination of INF4 and CDT accounts for informativity prior to representativeness; this may be why ID is more successful.

In general, the balance and trade-offs between the two criteria deserve further investigation.

7 Related Work

Much research efforts have been devoted to statistical machine learning methodologies for SRL (Bjkelund et al., 2009; Gildea and Jurafsky, 2002; Shi et al., 2009; Johansson and Nugues, 2008a; Lang and Lapata, 2010; Pradhan et al., 2008; Fürstenau and Lapata, 2009; Titov and Klementiev, 2011, among others). For example, Johansson *et al.* (Johansson and Nugues, 2008a) applied logistic regression with L2 norm to dependency-based SRL. Similarly, we also use logistic regression to train the classifier with a probabilistic explanation. However, we use L1 normed

Table 2: Percentage error reduction over RAND(200 / 500 examples)

	NOREP	COS	CDT	COS-ID	CDT-ID
INF1	6.56 / 5.18	3.68 / -0.86	2.60 / -0.74	7.43 / 6.45	6.44 / 6.60
INF2	5.12 / 8.31	5.51 / 5.37	7.74 / 8.19	7.21 / 5.67	3.49 / 2.24
INF3	5.07 / 5.54	6.13 / 5.52	8.15 / 9.54	5.94 / 5.72	5.65 / 7.18
INF4	7.37 / 5.79	1.41 / 2.01	-0.01 / -5.08	2.29 / 2.85	3.31 / 3.29

logistic regression due to its desirable property that can result in few nonzero feature weights. This allows us to select the most important features from an otherwise very large feature set.

Roth *et al.* (Roth and Small, 2006) proposed a margin based active learning framework for structured output and experiment on SRL task. They defined structured output by constraining the relations among class labels, e.g., one predicate only has one of the labels. The classification problem is defined via constraints among output labels. The most uncertain instances are selected to satisfy predefined constraints. Rather than a structured relation between output labels, our work exploits the structure of the sentences themselves via compressed dependency trees.

In the area of sentence similarity measurement, most current work focuses on semantic similarity (Haghighi et al., 2005; Tang et al., 2002; Shen and Lapata, 2007). We define similarity between sentences in terms of the nodes and edges in the dependency tree instead of semantic/lexical similarity of the sentences. We are interested in the structure of a sentence and how it is constructed due to the need of SRL tasks. Wang and Neumann (2007) use a similar sort of compressed dependency tree comprised of keywords and collapsed dependency relations to calculate the semantic similarity of sentences for the textual entailment task. Under their approach, dependency relations themselves are collapsed; we keep the specific dependency relations and collapse the trees, aiming for structural rather than semantic similarity.

In addition, Filippova *et al.* (Filippova and Strube, 2008) proposed to compress a sentence using dependency trees and take the importance of words as weight. They found compressed dependency tree can better ensure the grammaticality of the sentences to preserve the same lexical meaning as much as possible. In our work, we are more interested in the explicit dependency relation of predicate-argument pairs. Our goal is to apply compressed dependency tree to extract explicit relation between predicate and argument as precise as possible for SRL purpose. Therefore, we construct the compressed tree by identifying predicate-argument units and then re-linking them if there exist dependency relation among them. Consequently, most of the nodes in our compressed tree are predicates and arguments.

8 Conclusions

This paper investigates the use of active learning for semantic role labeling. To improve the learning accuracy and reduce the size of training set, compressed dependency trees are exploited as features. Strategies to select informative unlabeled sentences are proposed. Moreover, the compressed dependency trees are also utilized as a criterion to measure the representativeness of unlabeled sentences. A solution to select unlabeled sentences combining both informativeness and representativeness is developed. The experimental results show that our solution can save up to 50% on a small training data set compared to the supervised learning solution.

Possibilities for future work include exploring the use of constraints on label outputs, implementation of entropy-based informativity metrics, and perhaps combining COS andCDT for measuring representativeness. Another potentially promising direction is to employ multi-kernel based methods as a structure-oriented similarity measurement.

Acknowledgments

Our thanks to the anonymous reviewers for their valuable commentary and suggestions, and to Ivan Titov for invaluable, insightful discussions and feedback. This research has been funded by the German Research Foundation (DFG) under the MMCI Cluster of Excellence.

References

C. Baker, M. Ellsworth, K. Erk. 2007. SemEval-2007 task 19: Frame semantic structure extraction. In *Proc. of SemEval-2007*.

J. Baldridge, A. Palmer. 2009. How well does active learning actually work? time-based evaluation of cost-reduction strategies for language documentation. In *Proc. of EMNLP 2009*.

A. Bjkelund, L. Hafdell, P. Nugues, 2009. *Multilingual Semantic Role Labeling*, 43–48. 2009.

X. Carreras, L. Màrquez. 2005. Introduction to the CoNLL-2005 shared task: Semantic role labeling. In *Proc. of CoNLL-2005*.

D. Das, N. Schneider, D. Chen, N. A. Smith. 2010. Probabilistic frame-semantic parsing. In *Proc. of NAACL-HLT 2010*.

M.-C. de Marneffe, B. MacCartney, C. D. Manning. 2006. Generating typed dependency parses from phrase structure parses. In *Proc. of LREC 2006*.

M. Dredze, K. Crammer. 2008. Active learning with confidence. In *Proc. of ACL 2008*.

R. Duda, P. Hart, D. Stork. 2001. *Pattern classification*, volume 2. Wiley.

K. Filippova, M. Strube. 2008. Dependency tree based sentence compression. In *Proc. of INLG 2008*.

H. Fürstenau, M. Lapata. 2009. Semi-supervised semantic role labeling. In *Proc. of EACL 2009*.

D. Gildea, D. Jurafsky. 2002. Automatic labeling of semantic roles. *Computational Linguistics*, 28.

T. Grenager, C. Manning. 2006. Unsupervised discovery of a statistical verb lexicon. In *Proc. of EMNLP 2006*.

K. Hacioglu. 2004. Semantic role labeling using dependency trees. In *Proc. of COLING 2004*.

A. D. Haghighi, A. Y. Ng, C. D. Manning. 2005. Robust textual inference via graph matching. In *Proc. of HLT 2005*.

J. Hajič, M. Ciaramita, R. Johansson, D. Kawahara, M. A. Martí, L. Màrquez, A. Meyers, J. Nivre, S. Padó, J. Štěpánek, P. Straňák, M. Surdeanu, N. Xue, Y. Zhang. 2009. The CoNLL 2009 shared task: Syntactic and semantic dependencies in multiple languages. In *Proceedings of CoNLL 2009*.

R. Hwa. 2004. Sample selection for statistical parsing. *Computational Linguistics*, 30(3):253–276.

R. Johansson, P. Nugues. 2008a. Dependency-based semantic role labeling of propbank. In *Proc. of EMNLP 2008*.

R. Johansson, P. Nugues. 2008b. The effect of syntactic representation on semantic role labeling. In *Proc. of COLING 2008*.

J. Lang, M. Lapata. 2010. Unsupervised induction of semantic roles. In *Proc. of HLT 2010*.

S. Lee, H. Lee, P. Abbeel, A. Ng. 2006. Efficient L1 regularized logistic regression. In *Proc. of the Ntl. Conf. on AI*, volume 21.

D. D. Lewis, W. A. Gale. 1994. A sequential algorithm for training text classifiers. In *Proc. of SIGIR 1994*.

C.-J. Lin, R. C. Weng, S. S. Keerthi. 2007. Trust region newton methods for large-scale logistic regression. In *Proc. of ICML 2007*.

P. Melville, R. J. Mooney. 2004. Diverse ensembles for active learning. In *Proc. of ICML 2004*.

J. Nivre, J. Hall. 2005. Maltparser: A language-independent system for data-driven dependency parsing. In *Proc. of the TLT 2005*.

M. Osborne, J. Baldridge. 2004. Ensemble-based active learning for parse selection. In *Proc. of HLT-NAACL 2004*.

M. Palmer, D. Gildea, P. Kingsbury. 2005. The Proposition Bank: An Annotated Corpus of Semantic Roles. *Computational Linguistics*, 31(1):71–105.

S. Pradhan, W. Ward, K. Hacioglu, J. H. Martin, D. Jurafsky. 2005. Semantic role labeling using different syntactic views. In *Proc. of ACL 2005*.

S. S. Pradhan, W. Ward, J. H. Martin. 2008. Towards robust semantic role labeling. *Computational Linguistics*, 34:289–310.

E. Ringger, P. McClanahan, R. Haertel, G. Busby, M. Carmen, J. Carroll, D. Lonsdale. 2007. Active learning for part-of-speech tagging: Accelerating corpus annotation. In *Proc. of the Linguistic Annotation Workshop*.

D. Roth, K. Small. 2006. Active learning with perception for structured output. In *ICML Workshop on Learning in Structured Output Spaces*.

J. Ruppenhofer, M. Ellsworth, M. R. L. Petruck, C. R. Johnson, J. Scheffczyk. 2006. FrameNet II: Extended Theory and Practice.

B. Settles, M. Craven. 2008. An analysis of active learning strategies for sequence labeling tasks. In *Proc. of EMNLP 2008*.

B. Settles. 2010. Active learning literature survey. Technical Report Computer Sciences Technical Report 1648, University of Wisconsin-Madison, 2010.

D. Shen, M. Lapata. 2007. Using semantic roles to improve question answering. In *Proc. of EMNLP-2007*.

D. Shen, J. Zhang, J. Su, G. Zhou, C.-L. Tan. 2004. Multi-criteria-based active learning for named entity recognition. In *Proc. of ACL 2004*.

H. Shi, G. Zhou, P. Qian, X. Li. 2009. Semantic role labeling based on dependency tree with multi-features. In *Proc. of IJCBS 2009*.

M. Surdeanu, R. Johansson, A. Meyers, L. Màrquez, J. Nivre. 2008. The CoNLL 2008 shared task on joint parsing of syntactic and semantic dependencies. In *Proc. of CoNLL 2008*.

M. Tang, X. Luo, S. Roukos. 2002. Active learning for statistical natural language parsing. In *Proc. of ACL 2002*.

I. Titov, A. Klementiev. 2011. A bayesian model for unsupervised semantic parsing. In *Proc. of ACL 2011*.

K. Tomanek, F. Olsson. 2009. A Web Survey on the Use of Active learning to support annotation of text data. In *Proc. of AL-NLP workshop, NAACL HLT 2009*.

R. Wang, G. Neumann. 2007. Recognizing textual entailment using sentence similarity based on dependency tree skeletons. In *Proc. of RTE 2007*.

B. Yang, J.-T. Sun, T. Wang, Z. Chen. 2009. Effective multi-label active learning for text classification. In *Proc. of KDD 2009*.

Z.-H. Zhou. 2006. Learning with unlabeled data and its application to image retrieval. In *Proc. of PRICAI 2006*.

Semantic Role Labeling Without Treebanks?

Stephen A. Boxwell[1], **Chris Brew**[2], **Jason Baldridge**[3], **Dennis Mehay**[1], and **Sujith Ravi**[4]

[1]The Ohio State University, {boxwell,mehay}@ling.ohio-state.edu
[2]The Educational Testing Service, cbrew@ets.org
[3]The University of Texas at Austin, jbaldrid@mail.utexas.edu
[4]ISI, sravi@isi.edu

Abstract

We describe a method for training a semantic role labeler for CCG in the absence of gold-standard syntax derivations. Traditionally, semantic role labeling is performed by placing human-annotated semantic roles on gold-standard syntactic parses, identifying patterns in the syntax-semantics relationship, and then predicting roles on novel syntactic analyses. The gold standard syntactic training data can be eliminated from the process by extracting training instances from semantic roles projected onto a packed parse chart. This process can be used to rapidly develop NLP tools for resource-poor languages of interest.

1 Introduction

Semantic role labeling is the process of generating sets of semantic roles from syntactic analyses. The process of training a semantic role labeler, however, is costly in resources. First, it requires gold-standard semantic role data, like Propbank (Palmer et al., 2005). Secondly, it requires a detailed syntactic annotation of the same resource. We are fortunate to have the reasonably-sized Penn Treebank (Marcus et al., 1993) and adaptations for formalisms like Tree Adjoining Grammar (Chen and Shanker, 2004) and Combinatory Categorial Grammar (Hockenmaier and Steedman, 2007) alongside the Propbank data, but for other languages, such resources are unlikely to be available. There has been work in generating semantic role labelers using gold-standard trees in the absence of semantic training data (Fürstenau and Lapata, 2009; Lang and Lapata, 2010). But what if we had semantic training data, but no syntactic training data? If we could develop and train a semantic role labeler without syntactic training data, we could greatly reduce the cost and development time of NLP tools for languages of interest.

One option is to use some automatic means to generate a treebank – instead of creating a corpus of syntax trees by hand, we could use an automatic parser. This, however, leads to a chicken-and-egg problem – we would need a high-quality parse model to choose a single-best analysis for each training sentence, and a parse model needs syntactic training data. No automatic parser can currently generate high quality single-best parses in the absence of a parse model. But a parser can, given word tags and combinatory rules, generate a parse forest – a very large collection of possible analyses – and say little or nothing about their relative merit.

In this paper, we extract SRL features from the entire parse forest, effectively training on every possible parse in the training set simultaneously. This can be done efficiently by representing the parse chart as a hypergraph, enabling us to iterate over every constituent in the parse forest without enumerating every individual parse (which would be computationally infeasible). This, combined with the parsing advantages afforded by Combinatory Categorial Grammar (CCG), enables us to train a semantic role labeler without gold-standard trees.

2 Combinatory Categorial Grammar

Combinatory Categorial Grammar (Steedman, 2000) is a grammar formalism that describes words in terms of their combinatory potential. For example, determiners belong to the category NP/N, or "the category of words that become noun phrases when combined with a noun to the right". The rightmost category indicates the argument that the category is seeking, the leftmost category indicates the result of combining this category with its argument, and the slash indicates the direction of combination. Categories can be nested within each other: a transitive verb like *devoured* belongs to the category (S\NP)/NP, or "the category that would become a sentence if it could combine with a noun phrase to the right and another noun phrase to the left". The process of automatically assigning CCG categories to words is called "supertagging", and CCG categories are sometimes informally referred to as "supertags". An example of how categories combine to make sentences is shown in Figure 1.

CCG has many capabilities that go beyond that of a typical context-free grammar. First, it has a sophisticated internal system of managing syntactic heads and dependencies[1]. These dependencies are used to great effect in CCG-based semantic role labeling systems (Gildea and Hockenmaier, 2003; Boxwell et al., 2009), as they do not suffer the same data-sparsity effects encountered with treepath features in CFG-based SRL systems. Secondly, CCG permits these dependencies to be passed through intermediary categories in grammatical structures like relative clauses. In Figure 2, *the steak* is still in the object relation to *devoured*, even though the verb is inside a relative clause. Finally and most importantly, *these dependencies are represented directly on the CCG categories themselves*. This is crucial for the prediction of semantic roles inside a packed parse chart – because the dependency is formed when the two heads combine, it is available to be used as a local feature by the semantic role labeler. This property of CCG and its impact on packed-chart SRL is described extensively in Boxwell et al. (2010). This ability to predict dependencies (and semantic roles) at parse time figures heavily into the process described here.

3 Brutus: A CCG Based Semantic Role Labeler

The Brutus Semantic Role Labeler (Boxwell et al., 2009)[2] is a semantic role labeling system for CCG.

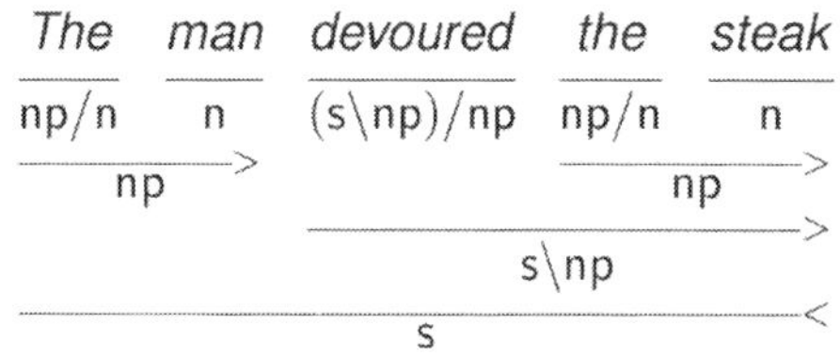

Figure 1: A simple CCG derivation.

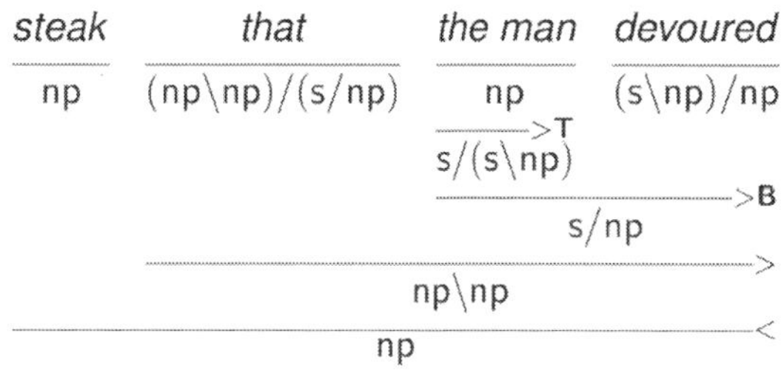

Figure 2: An example of CCG's treatment of relative clauses. The syntactic dependency between *devoured* and *steak* is the same as it was in figure 1.

It is trained using CCGbank and a version of Propbank that has been aligned to the CCGbank in order to account for discrepancies in terminal indexation (Honnibal and Curran, 2007; Boxwell and White, 2008). The system is organized in a two-stage pipeline of maximum entropy models[3], following the organization of a previous CFG-style approach (Punyakanok et al., 2008). The first stage is the identification stage, where, for each predicate in the sentence, each word is tagged as either a role or a nonrole (figure 3). The second stage is the classification stage, where the roles are sorted into ARG0, ARG1, and so on (figure 4). The identification model and the classification model share the same features, but they are trained and run separately.

For the results presented here, we use a version of Brutus that has been stripped down to only use local features so as to enable us to perform SRL at parse time. Recall from section 1 that we wish to extract training features not from a complete parse tree, but from a packed parse chart. For this reason, global features (those that are inaccessible to a single edge in the parse chart) cannot be used. After removing all global features from the seman-

[1] A complete explanation of CCG predicate-argument dependencies can be found in the CCGbank user manual (Hockenmaier and Steedman, 2005)

[2] Found at `http://www.ling.ohio-state.edu/~boxwell/software/brutus.html`

[3] We use the Zhang Le maxent toolkit, available at `http://homepages.inf.ed.ac.uk/s0450736/maxent_toolkit.html`, using the BFGS training method, trained to 500 iterations with gaussian priors of 1 and 5, for the identification and classification steps, respectively.

tic role labeler, the local features that remain are as follows:

- **Words.** A three-word window surrounding the candidate word.
- **Predicate.** The predicate whose semantic roles the system is looking for.
- **Predicate Category.** The CCG category of the predicate.
- **Result Category Detail.** This indicates the feature on the result category of the predicate. Possible values include DCL (for declarative sentences), PSS (for passive sentences), NG (for present-progressive phrases like "running the race"), etc. These are read trivially off of the verbal category.
- **Syntactic Dependency.** As with a previous approach in CCG semantic role labeling (Gildea and Hockenmaier, 2003), this feature shows the exact nature of the syntactic dependency between the predicate and the word we are considering, if any such dependency exists. This feature is represented by the category of the predicate, the argument slot that this word fits into, and whether or not the predicate is the head of the resultant category, represented with a left or right arrow.
- **Before / After.** A binary indicator feature indicating whether the candidate word is before or after the predicate.

4 Parsing Without Syntactic Training Data

In order to test the performance of our semantic role labeler, we will need automatically generated parses to run the SRL models over. Even though we are able to train SRL models in the absence of syntactic training data, we still need test parses on which to predict roles. So why not use the fast, accurate CCG parser (Clark and Curran, 2004b) used with previous CCG-based SRL systems? It makes sense to use the highest quality parses available. But recall that the reason for this roundabout way of training the semantic role labeler is to enable us to generate SRL models *without syntactic training data*. If we use an off-the-shelf syntactic parser that was trained on gold-standard training data, we introduce a source of additional training

Combinator	Penalty
Function Application	0
Function Composition	1
Crossing Composition	1
Type Raising	1
Null Coordination	2
Full Coordination	0
Substitution	∞

Table 1: The complete sub-baseline model, which requires no syntactic training data. The substitution combinator is used to model parasitic gaps in English, which are so rare that we make the pragmatic decision to disallow substitution entirely.

data that we wish to exclude. But how will we generate reasonably accurate parses without a trained parse model? Even a simple MLE-style approach requires training data.
To satisfy this need, we develop a very simple parse model that penalizes any non-normal-form rule applications, effectively relying on the CCG supertags to identify likely grammatical relations. Specifically, combinators like function composition and type raising are penalized by a fixed amount, while function application is allowed to pass without penalty. The candidate analysis with the lowest penalty is chosen as the single-best – in case of a tie, the most right-branching analysis is chosen. The complete parse model is shown in table 1.

5 Experiment 1: Generating Traditional Identification and Classification Models from the Chart

In the first experiment, we use a parser to create a set of parse forests from the training set. The individual parses are not enumerated – we extract features from every possible syntactic derivation simultaneously by iterating over every edge in the packed chart. Local syntactic features are accessible, as are the gold-standard semantic roles from Propbank. The identifier and classifier models are then trained from these features, instead of from features obtained from gold-standard syntactic derivations. We will call this two-part SRL model the CHART model. We compare this model to the more traditional GOLD model, which uses the same features but is generated from gold standard trees. We test the system using both gold-standard parse trees and single-best auto-

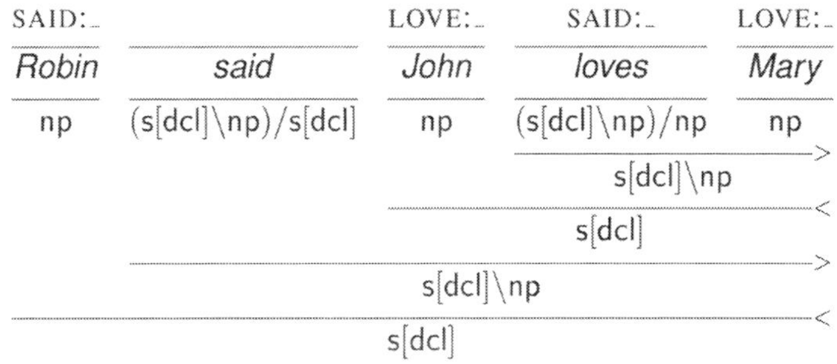

Figure 3: In the first stage of the semantic role labeling process, candidate semantic roles are chosen by the identifier model. We have not yet decided which role (ARG0, ARG1, etc) each word plays, only that there is a role there.

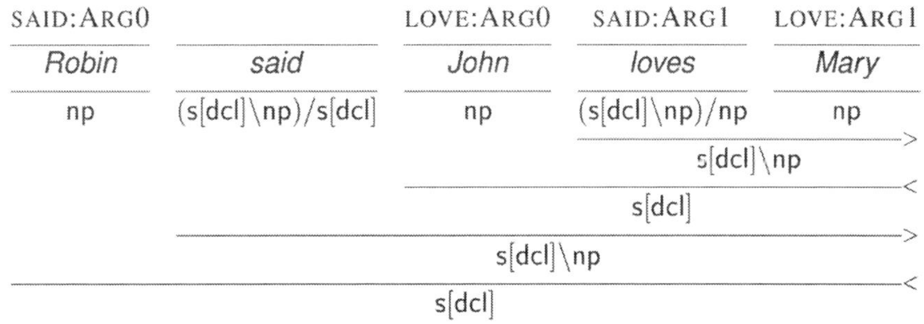

Figure 4: In the second stage of the semantic role labeling process, the classifier model sorts the roles into ARG0, ARG1, etc.

matically generated parse trees (generated from gold-standard supertags by the parser from section 4). Interestingly, SRL performance drops only slightly between gold standard test parses and automatically generated parses when using the chart-based SRL model. Table 2 shows the results for the development set, and table 3 shows the results for the test set.

	Gold Parse			Auto Parse		
Train	P	R	F	P	R	F
GOLD	89.7	84.8	87.2	85.8	80.0	82.8
CHART	84.6	70.4	76.9	83.0	67.7	74.6

Table 3: SRL performance on the test set (section 23) using the same models as table 2.

	Gold Parse			Auto Parse		
Train	P	R	F	P	R	F
GOLD	88.4	85.7	87.0	84.8	80.4	82.5
CHART	83.5	70.8	76.6	83.0	69.4	75.6

Table 2: SRL performance on gold-standard parses and automatic parses from the development set (section 00). The models are defined in section 5.

Manual inspection of the results reveals that the CHART model frequently fails to identify modifier roles, contributing to the very low recall score. This was traced to a consistent weakening of the adjunct dependency feature, resulting largely from the ambiguous attachment of auxiliary verbs. Consider a simple sentence *Jon will visit tomorrow*. Syntactically, there are two possible attachments for *tomorrow*. It can be attached low, to *visit* (figure 5), or it can be attached high, to *will visit* (figure 6). The former will result in a dependency between *visit* and *tomorrow*, while the latter will result in a dependency between *will* and *tomorrow*. Now, imagine training over this sentence's chart. For both analyses, we notice that a role should be placed on *tomorrow*. In one case, there is a dependency between *visit* and *tomorrow*, and in one case there is not. Our simple parsing model does not necessarily do a good job of discriminating in favor of the analysis that we want, so the SRL components may see both options with nearly equal weight. Empirically, the identification model learns that the dependency feature is not a good predictor of modifier roles. This is in-

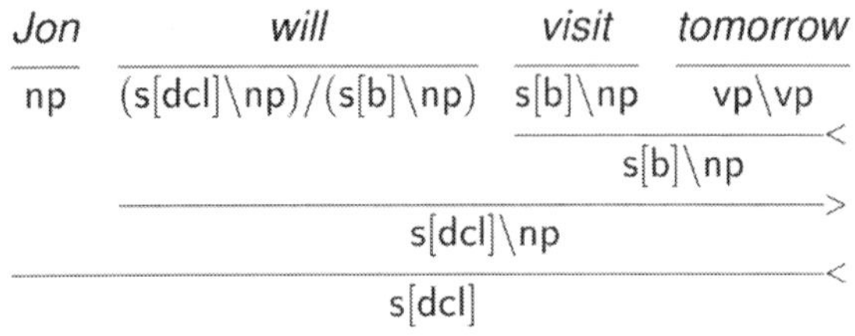

Figure 5: The correct analysis for *Jon will visit tomorrow*. In this case, there is a syntactic dependency between *tomorrow* and *visit*. Note that vp is an abbreviation for s\np.

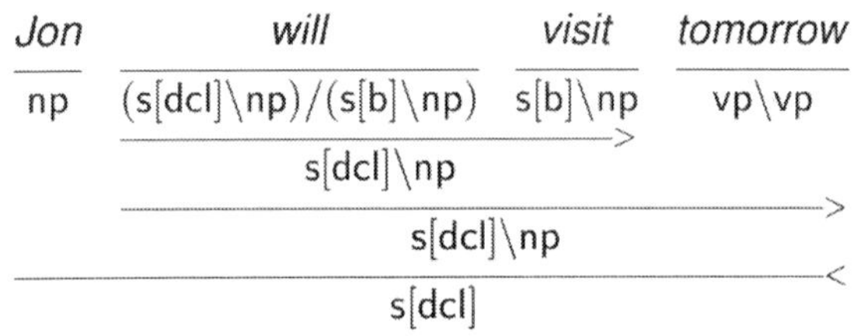

Figure 6: An erroneous analysis for *Jon will visit tomorrow*. There is no syntactic dependency between *tomorrow* and *visit*.

correct – in fact, the presence of a syntactic dependency between a predicate and a target word is almost always a dead giveaway to the presence of a semantic role. In our effort to downplay the role of syntax we may have set up a situation in which a sophisticated machine-learning based argument identifier does exactly the wrong thing. It could be that a less sophisticated argument identifier will be better suited to the task that our system requires.

6 Experiment 2: Improving Argument Identification with a Simpler Model

The CHART identification model performs poorly because it does not recognize syntactic dependencies as good predictors of semantic roles. Suppose that instead of using that identification model, we used a simple heuristic: if there is a syntactic dependency between a word and the predicate, then label that word with a semantic role – otherwise, do not. This simple identification "model" requires no training – it simply relies on the pattern that semantic role bearing units tend to be joined to their predicates by syntactic dependencies. We will refer to this as the chart-dependency model, or C-DEP. In addition to this model, we propose another model that similarly identifies roles with dependencies, but enumerates certain exceptional dependencies that do not predict semantic roles (like those originating from auxiliary verbs like *to* and *has*) according to the Propbank guidelines. We will refer to this as the improved chart-dependency model, or C-DEP+[4]. In both cases, the classification model is identical to that of the CHART model.

Tables 4 and 5 show the effect of using the two chart-dependency identification models compared to the GOLD and CHART models from section 5. Performance using the C-DEP and C-DEP+ models greatly improves on the disappointing recall of the CHART model, while retaining the favorable property of eschewing gold-standard syntactic training data. Instead of systematically weakening the most predictive identification feature available, the simple identification models use *only* that feature. This results in a major improvement in recall at the cost of an acceptable drop in precision.

	Gold Parse			Auto Parse		
Train	P	R	F	P	R	F
GOLD	88.4	85.7	87.0	84.8	80.4	82.5
CHART	83.5	70.8	76.6	83.0	69.4	75.6
C-DEP	**75.9**	**83.0**	**79.3**	**72.5**	**78.1**	**75.1**
C-DEP+	**81.6**	**82.8**	**82.2**	**77.9**	**77.8**	**77.9**

Table 4: SRL performance on the development set (section 00) using the four models. The GOLD and CHART models are defined in section 5. The C-DEP and C-DEP+ models are defined in section 6.

	Gold Parse			Auto Parse		
Train	P	R	F	P	R	F
GOLD	89.7	84.8	87.2	85.8	80.0	82.8
CHART	84.6	70.4	76.9	83.0	67.7	74.6
C-DEP	**76.7**	**83.2**	**79.8**	**73.0**	**77.7**	**75.2**
C-DEP+	**82.8**	**82.9**	**82.8**	**78.7**	**77.4**	**78.1**

Table 5: SRL performance on the test set (section 23), using the same models as in table 4.

[4] The C-DEP+ model ignores all dependencies originating from the following categories: (s[to]\np)/(s[b]\np), (s[dcl]\np)/(s[pt]\np), (s[dcl]\np)/(s[pss]\np), (s[b]\np)/(s[pss]\np), and (s[dcl]\np)/(s[ng]\np).

7 Experiment 3: Generating an SRL Model Without Gold-Standard Supertags

In the experiments described in sections 5 and 6, we used four different training methods to generate semantic role labeling models, which are then tested on gold standard syntactic parses and parses that were automatically generated from gold-standard supertags. But much of the challenge of parsing in CCG comes down to the choice of supertags – choosing the correct supertag for a preposition, for example, makes the difference between attaching the prepositional phrase high or low. But surely using gold-standard supertags gives us an unfair advantage; in real-world applications, these supertags would have to be predicted. We could use an off-the-shelf CCG supertagger (Clark and Curran, 2004a), but this would open us to the same chicken-and-egg problem already encountered with automatic parsers – the C&C supertagger is trained on gold-standard syntactic data. Doing without a supertagger and using every possible supertag in a tag dictionary is computationally infeasible; most words have at least two or three possible tags; the most ambiguous word has 133 supertags (*as*). Therefore, we have no choice but to investigate ways to get supertags that do not rely on gold-standard syntactic annotation.

We use a weakly supervised approach to supertagging that augments an HMM with an oracle CCG tag dictionary and a set of broad grammar-informed constraints (Baldridge, 2008; Ravi et al., 2010). The tag dictionary provides only a simple mapping from word to supertag – it does not use any kind of cutoff, nor does it give a prior probability on individual supertags. Using an HMM that has been initialized with grammar-based transition probabilities, combined with a two-stage integer programming strategy, this approach can achieve single-best accuracy of 64.3% on ambiguous supertags. These supertags are then used to generate parse forests, which are used to train the CHART, C-DEP, and C-DEP+ models. Notice that, although most of the tag sequences do not produce spanning analyses, we can still produce a packed chart and generate SRL training features.

We also train a secondary discriminative supertagger using the induced tags that are the output of the tag-dictionary-based HMM supertagger for the training set, and use this supertagger with the parser from section 4 to generate single-best parses to test the SRL models on. It is necessary to train a secondary supertagger over the induced tags because the induced tags by themseleves are unlikely to produce a spanning analysis. The induced supertags from the HMM are only given for the most probable sequence from the HMM; using the beta-best tag predictions of the secondary supertagger produces acceptable coverage. This supertagger is a simple Maxent tagger conditioned on a 5-word window surrounding the target word and trained using a gaussian prior of 5. SRL performance over automatic parses generated with these predicted supertags is not as strong as with gold standard supertags, but is reasonable considering the absence of syntactic training data. Results for the development set are shown in table 6, and results for the test set are shown in table 7.

	Gold Supertags Auto Parse			Auto Supertags Auto Parse		
Train	P	R	F	P	R	F
CHART	83.0	69.4	75.6	64.1	60.0	61.9
C-DEP	72.5	78.1	75.1	65.5	60.5	62.9
C-DEP+	77.9	77.8	77.9	68.8	60.2	64.2

Table 6: SRL performance on the development set (section 00) comparing automatic parses generated using gold-standard supertags and automatically induced supertags.

	Gold Supertags Auto Parse			Auto Supertags Auto Parse		
Train	P	R	F	P	R	F
CHART	83.0	67.7	74.6	63.8	61.7	62.7
C-DEP	73.0	77.7	75.2	66.8	61.1	63.8
C-DEP+	78.7	77.4	78.1	70.0	60.7	65.0

Table 7: SRL performance on the test set (section 23), using the same models as table 7.

Manual inspection of the induced supertag data reveals some unusual predictions of supertags. For example, it is difficult to think of a valid category for the determiner *the* besides NP/N. The word *the* almost always has the category NP/N in CCGbank. CCGbank does assign other categories for *the*, though most, if not all, of them are errors. Table 8 shows the token frequencies of select categories for *the* from the training set of CCGbank. Even though there are 46 possible categories in all, only one of them is really worth considering (18 of the categories appear only once). The automatic method for inducing supertags from the tag dictionary, however, frequently predicts categories for *the* that are extremely rare in the English CCGbank. This is because the tag dictionary is generated with no cutoff and provides no prior probability across tags – each tag in the dictionary is given equal consideration by the Markov Model, which ranks them according to how well they interact with their neighbors.

For this reason, we revisit our earlier decision to generate a tag dictionary with no cutoff. Instead, we generate a tag dictionary of categories that make up at least 10% of the word tokens. For example, suppose the word *direct* appears in the corpus 100 times. For a category to be listed for the word *direct* in the tag dictionary, it must appear as the category for *direct* no fewer than 10 times. This can effectively eliminate a large number of very rare categories that overwhelm the HMM. It also more closely simulates a hand-written tag dictionary for closed-class words, or a tag dictionary that was generated automatically from a traditional part-of-speech dictionary. Using a tag dictionary with a 10% cutoff greatly improves performance on semantc role labeling, coming to within 7% accuracy of using gold-standard supertags. The results for the development set are shown in table 9, and the results for the test set are shown in table 10.

Category	Frequency
NP/N	47255
N/N	99
((S\NP)\(S\NP))/NP	78
⋮	⋮
(S/S)/(S/S)	1
(S[adj]\NP)/N	1
(N\N)/N	1

Table 8: The frequencies of select categories for *the* from sections 02-21 of the CCGbank (there are 46 in all). Some categories, like NP/N, are extremely common, whereas others, like (N\N)/N, appear only once.

We have shown that simple and easy syntactic processing is still beneficial for SRL.

	Gold Supertags Auto Parse			Auto Supertags Auto Parse		
Train	P	R	F	P	R	F
CHART	83.0	69.4	75.6	67.5	66.3	66.9
C-DEP	72.5	78.1	75.1	69.3	69.5	69.4
C-DEP+	77.9	77.8	77.9	74.0	69.2	71.5

Table 9: SRL performance on the development set (section 00) using cutoff of 10% on tag dictionary.

	Gold Supertags Auto Parse			Auto Supertags Auto Parse		
Train	P	R	F	P	R	F
CHART	83.0	67.7	74.6	67.8	65.7	66.7
C-DEP	73.0	77.7	75.2	70.1	68.4	69.2
C-DEP+	78.7	77.4	78.1	75.2	68.2	71.5

Table 10: SRL performance on the test set (section 23) using cutoff of 10% on tag dictionary and the same models as table 9.

For completeness, we briefly explore another option, even simpler than this: we trained SRL models that relied on no syntactic features at all. Specifically, we included the word, predicate, and before/after features (described in detail in section 3). Unsurprisingly, the performance was unacceptably low (P=.73, R-.31, F=.44), most of that coming from successful identification of the predicate itself. This method makes the identifier exceptionally timid, and on the rare occasion that a word *is* identified as a role-bearing unit, it is often assigned roles corresponding to every predicate in the sentence. We conclude that it is necessary to include syntactic features, but that these can be rough and ready.

8 Conclusions and Future Work

In the three experiments presented, we demonstrated that an effective SRL model can be trained without a corpus of parse trees. This can be achieved by using a simple baseline parser to generate a parse forest for a large amount of unannotated newspaper text, then extracting training instances from all possible syntactic analyses simultaneously. This approach is most effective when we have some syntactic knowledge of the sentence in the form of supertags, but is still effective when only a tagging dictionary is available.

In the future, we hope to expand this work into

other languages. Armed only with a Propbank-like corpus of semantic roles and a tag dictionary, we can train a surprisingly effective semantic role lableler. To this end, we hope to further investigate issues surrounding the generation of supertags – particularly, minimally supervised approaches to generating CCG tag dictionaries. Recall that performance actually improved when very rare categories were excluded from the tag dictionary; one option to achieve similar results is to annotate by hand, say, the 200 most common words (almost certainly syntactically interesting closed class words), then using these to guide the generation of a comprehensive tag dictionary, or perhaps by bootstrapping from traditional part-of-speech tags. It would also be beneficial to investigate alternate methods of inducing tags from the tag dictionary that produce n-best tag predictions, as this would improve coverage over the training set.

Another avenue of future research could be the generation of semantic predictions without committing single-best test sentences. Recall that in order to test the semantic role labeler, we needed to generate parse trees for the target sentences. Because we assume that gold-standard syntactic training data is not available, we use a sub-baseline model that requires no training data. But is it really necessary to choose a single best parse at all? Because the version of Brutus used here can extract features from inside the chart, it can also predict semantic roles at parse time (Boxwell et al., 2010). We could therefore predict all possible roles in the chart and explore ways of identifying likely rolesets, using a mechanism for the enforcement of global constraints, such as the integer linear programming solution of Punyakanok et al (2008).

References

J. Baldridge. 2008. Weakly supervised supertagging with grammar-informed initialization. In *Proceedings of the 22nd International Conference on Computational Linguistics-Volume 1*, pages 57–64. Association for Computational Linguistics.

Stephen A. Boxwell and Michael White. 2008. Projecting Propbank Roles onto the CCGbank. In *Proceedings of the Sixth International Language Resources and Evaluation Conference (LREC-08)*, Marrakech, Morocco.

Stephen A. Boxwell, Dennis N. Mehay, and Chris Brew. 2009. Brutus: A semantic role labeling system incorporating CCG, CFG, and Dependency features. In *Proc. ACL-09*.

Stephen A Boxwell, Dennis N Mehay, and Chris Brew. 2010. What a parser can learn from a semantic role labeler and vice versa. In *Proceedings of the 2010 Conference on Empirical Methods in Natural Language Processing*, pages 736–744, Cambridge, MA, October. Association for Computational Linguistics.

J. Chen and V. Shanker. 2004. Automated extraction of TAGs from the Penn Treebank. *New developments in parsing technology*, pages 73–89.

S. Clark and J.R. Curran. 2004a. The importance of supertagging for wide-coverage CCG parsing. In *Proceedings of COLING*, volume 4, pages 282–288.

Stephen Clark and James R. Curran. 2004b. Parsing the WSJ using CCG and Log-Linear Models. In *Proc. ACL-04*.

H. Fürstenau and M. Lapata. 2009. Semi-supervised semantic role labeling. In *Proceedings of the 12th Conference of the European Chapter of the Association for Computational Linguistics*, pages 220–228. Association for Computational Linguistics.

Daniel Gildea and Julia Hockenmaier. 2003. Identifying semantic roles using Combinatory Categorial Grammar. In *Proc. EMNLP-03*.

J. Hockenmaier and M. Steedman. 2005. CCGbank manual. Technical report, MS-CIS-05-09, University of Pennsylvania.

Julia Hockenmaier and Mark Steedman. 2007. CCGbank: A Corpus of CCG Derivations and Dependency Structures Extracted from the Penn Treebank. *Computational Linguistics*, 33(3):355–396.

M. Honnibal and J.R. Curran. 2007. Improving the complement/adjunct distinction in CCGbank. In *Proceedings of the 10th Conference of the Pacific Association for Computational Linguistics (PACLING-07)*, pages 210–217. Citeseer.

J. Lang and M. Lapata. 2010. Unsupervised induction of semantic roles. In *Human Language Technologies: The 2010 Annual Conference of the North American Chapter of the Association for Computational Linguistics*, pages 939–947. Association for Computational Linguistics.

M. P. Marcus, B. Santorini, and M. A. Marcinkiewicz. 1993. Building a Large Annotated Corpus of English: The Penn Treebank. *Computational Linguistics*, 19(2):313–330.

Martha Palmer, Daniel Gildea, and Paul Kingsbury. 2005. The Proposition Bank: An Annotated Corpus of Semantic Roles. *Computational Linguistics*, 31(1):71–106.

Vasin Punyakanok, Dan Roth, and Wen tau Yih. 2008. The Importance of Syntactic Parsing and Inference in Semantic Role Labeling. *Computational Linguistics*, 34(2):257–287.

S. Ravi, J. Baldridge, and K. Knight. 2010. Minimized models and grammar-informed initialization for supertagging with highly ambiguous lexicons. In *Proceedings of the 48th Annual Meeting of the Association for Computational Linguistics*, pages 495–503. Association for Computational Linguistics.

Mark Steedman. 2000. *The Syntactic Process*. MIT Press.

Japanese Predicate Argument Structure Analysis Exploiting Argument Position and Type

Yuta Hayashibe **Mamoru Komachi** **Yuji Matsumoto**
Graduate School of Information Science
Nara Institute of Science and Technology
8916-5, Takayama, Ikoma Nara 630-0192, Japan
{ yuta-h, komachi, matsu }@is.naist.jp

Abstract

We propose an approach to Japanese predicate argument structure analysis exploiting *argument position* and *type*. In particular, we propose the following two methods. First, in order to use information in the sentences in preceding context of the predicate more effectively, we propose an improved similarity measure between argument positions which is more robust than a previous co-reference-based measure. Second, we propose a flexible selection-and-classification approach which accounts for the minor types of arguments. Experimental results show that our proposed method achieves state-of-the-art accuracy for Japanese predicate argument structure analysis.

1 Introduction

The goal of predicate-argument structure analysis is to extract semantic relations such as "who did what to whom" that hold between a predicate and its arguments constituting a semantic unit of a sentence. It is an important step in many Natural Language Processing applications such as machine translation, summarization and information extraction.

Arguments are classified into three categories according to their positions relative to the predicates: intra-sentential arguments (those that have direct syntactic dependency with the predicates), zero intra-sentential arguments (those appearing as zero-pronouns but have their antecedents in the same sentence), and inter-sentential arguments (those appearing as zero-pronouns and their antecedents are not in the same sentence). We call them *INTRA_D, INTRA_Z*, and *INTER* respectively. Furthermore, we call these categories the *argument types*. While the analysis of INTRA_D is comparatively easy, INTRA_Z and INTER are more difficult. We consider that there are two reasons for this.

The first reason is the poverty of features for argument identification compared to INTRA_D. While for INTRA_D we have important clues such as the function word or directly dependency relation, we don't for INTRA_Z and INTER.

The second reason is the limited amount of training examples. For example, in a Japanese newswire corpus, INTRA_Z and INTER account for 30.5% and 12.4% of all the nominative (ga) cases, and 13.1% and 0.2% of all of the accusative (wo) cases (Iida et al., 2007).

In this paper, in order to solve these problems we propose the following two methods exploiting *argument position* and type.

First, we propose an improved similarity measure between argument positions of two predicates that take semantically similar arguments. For example, someone possibly arrested can also surrender him/herself, that is, objects of "arrest" and subjects of "surrender (oneself)" are occupied by semantically similar nouns. Gerber and Chai (2010) proposed analysis of English nominal predicates with this similarity to take discourse context into account. However, the similarity measure they used has drawbacks: it requires a co-reference resolver and a large number of documents. We improve their similarity measure alleviating these drawbacks by using argument position. We detail previous work on capturing discourse context in Section 2, and our proposal in Section 3.1.

Second, we propose a selection-and-classification approach. In this approach, in order to compensate for the relative infrequency of examples of INTRA_Z and INTER, we select a candidate argument for each argument type independently. After selecting candidates, we use classifiers to choose the correct argument type. This allows us to flexibly design features for each step and we can use pairwise features between the candidate arguments. We detail this in Section 3.2.

The experimental results demonstrated that our proposed method achieved the state-of-the-art of Japanese predicate argument structure analysis.

2 Related Work Capturing Discourse Context

2.1 Salient Reference List

Iida et al. (2003) used Salient Reference List (Nariyama, 2002) based on Centering Theory (Grosz et al., 1995), which explains the structure of discourse and the transition of topics in order to capture discourse context. The list has the following four ordered slots.

TOPIC (marked by *wa*-particle)
> SUBJECT (*ga*)
> INDIRECT OBJECT (*ni*)
> DIRECT OBJECT (*wo*),

We check whether each candidate corresponds to any slots from the beginning of a document. If the candidate corresponds to a slot, we (over)write the slot with the candidate. We repeat this until we reach the predicate to analyze. We use the ranks of candidates in the list as a feature.

2.2 Argument Frequency

Iida et al. (2003) used a feature (*CHAIN LENGTH*) that stands for how often each candidate is used as an argument of predicates in preceding context. Imamura et al. (2009) used a similar binary feature (*USED*) that shows if each candidate is ever used as an argument of predicates or not. However, they did not investigate the effect of these features explicitly in their systems. Therefore we also investigate these in this paper.

2.3 Similarity between an Argument Position and a co-Reference Chain

In the study of implicit arguments[1] for English nominal predicates, Gerber and Chai (2010) used similarity features between an argument position and a co-reference chain, inspired by Chambers and Jurafsky (2008), who proposed unsupervised learning of narrative event chains using pointwise mutual information (PMI) between syntactic positions. This method stands on the assumption that similar argument positions tend to have the arguments which belong to a common co-reference chain. For instance, co-referring arguments at such argument positions like $\langle plead, ARG_0\rangle$, $\langle admit, ARG_0\rangle$, $\langle convict, ARG_1\rangle$, tend to take semantically similar nouns as the argument positions like $\langle sentence, ARG_1\rangle$, $\langle parole, ARG_1\rangle$.

They first automatically label a subset of the Gigaword corpus (Graff, 2003) with verbal and nominal semantic role labeling. They then identify co-references between arguments using a co-reference resolver. They compute PMI as follows.

Suppose the resulting data has N co-referential pairs of argument positions and M of these pairs comprising $E_a = \langle P_a, A_a\rangle$, $E_b = \langle P_b, A_b\rangle$, and $E_c = \langle P_c, A_c\rangle$. P_a, P_b, and P_c are predicates, and A_a, A_b, and A_c are labels such as ARG_0 or ARG_1.

$$pmi(E_a, E_b) = \log \frac{G(E_a, E_b)}{G(E_a, *)G(E_b, *)}$$

$$G(E_a, E_b) = \frac{M}{N}$$

With this similarity between argument positions, they defined scores between an argument position and a co-reference chain.

3 Predicate Argument Structure Analysis Exploiting Argument Position and Type

3.1 Similarity between Argument Positions using Distribution Similarity

Suppose we want to identify the argument of **自首した** (surrendered) in Example (1). The argument is an antecedent of zero-pronoun ϕ of the predicate.

(1) 警察 (police) は (*wa*-particle) 花子 (hanako) を (*wo*-particle) 逮捕した (arrested).
Police arrested Hanako.

私 (I) は (ϕ が) **自首した** (had surrendered) と (that) 聞いた (heard).
I heard that ϕ *had surrendered*.

With Salient Reference List for "自首する (surrendered)", the rank of "警察 (police)" is higher than that of "花子 (Hanako)" and it is noisy information for analysis. We also cannot distinguish them with argument frequency information, because frequencies of both "花子 (Hanako)" and "警察 (police)" are 1.

Though it is reasonable to use the similarity between an argument position and a co-reference

[1] In short, this is equivalent to INTER.

1599	が 自首する (surrender)	5651	が 逮捕する (arrest)	82112	を 逮捕する (arrest)
136	-者 person	702	署員 PS staff	15285	人 person
117	犯人 criminal	698	警察 police	8484	-者 person
96	彼 he	376	警察官 police officer	5563	男 man
68	人 person	368	-署 police station	2804	-名 name
63	男 man	230	県警 prefectural police	1188	犯人 criminal
36	-犯 crime	177	-員 -staff	1185	男性 male
30	少年 boy	153	府警 prefectural police	763	-ら -s
26	高校生 high-scool student	137	当局 authorities	671	おまえ you

Table 1: Argument distributions of each argument position (Sorted by frequency)

chain, the similarity measure described in Section 2.3 has two problems.

One is the strong dependency on the accuracy of co-reference resolver system. In fact, the accuracy of Japanese co-reference resolvers is not accurate enough to create co-reference chains in good quality.[2] The other problem is the problem that it needs a lot of documents, because the method does not use any non co-referring nouns.

To avoid using an unreliable co-reference resolver, we can suppose the same noun lemmas without pronouns in the same document are co-references. Pekar (2006) called the noun lemmas *anchors* and they supposed the similarity measure between syntactic positions. For example, there are two anchors: "Mary" and "house" in the sentences "Mary bought a house. The house belongs to Mary." They extract two groups: { buy(obj:X), belong(subj:X) } and {buy(subj:X), belong(to:X). } Nevertheless, this method also requires many documents because noun lemmas without anchors are not used for the calculation.

In this paper, we propose a more robust similarity measure between argument positions which does not depend on unreliable co-reference annotations by the resolver.

Table 1 shows the list of nouns that have direct dependency arcs in syntactic dependency structures along with case markers が (nominative case), を (accusative case) and に (dative case) extracted from the *WEB* corpus described in Section 4. According to Table 1, the distributions of nouns of "自首する (surrender)" following が and "逮捕する (arrest)" following を look alike. We can expect that an arrested person is more likely to be a person who has surrendered than an arrestee. We define a novel similarity of two argument positions

[2]We implemented the method proposed by Iida et al. (2005a), and the F-measure was 66%.

		E_1	E_2	E_3
E_1	が 自首する (nominative case of *surrender*)	0	0.5409	0.2431
E_2	が 逮捕する (nominative case of *arrest*)	0.5409	0	0.5139
E_3	を 逮捕する (accusative case of *arrest*)	0.2431	0.5139	0

Table 2: An example of similarities between argument positions calculated with *WEB* corpus.

encoding such information as Jensen-Shannon divergence between argument distributions of argument positions. A sample of the calculated similarities is shown in Table 2. This table illustrates the most similar argument positions are the nominative (が) case of "自首する (surrender)" (E_1) and the accusative (を) case of "逮捕する (arrest)" (E_3). We will use these values as features of predicate-argument analysis in the experiments.

3.2 Selection-and-Classification Approach Considering Argument Type

In previous work, argument analysis was performed with common features regardless its argument type. However, these methods have difficulty in distinguishing the marginal cases where two candidates have different argument types because of the difference of quantity by argument types. Thus we propose the *selection-and-classification approach* for Japanese predicate argument structure analysis. This approach consists of two steps: the *selection* step and the *classification* step.

This approach is inspired by two models. The first is the selection-and-classification model (Iida et al., 2005b) for noun phrase anaphora resolution. The model first selects a likely antecedent of the target (possibly) anaphoric expression. Second, the model classifies the target anaphoric ex-

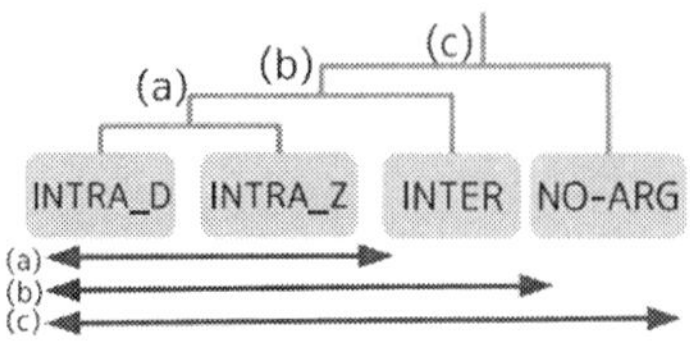

Figure 1: Argument selection in the 'Classification' step from three most likely argument candidates

	Label	Arguments to make features
a	INTRA_D	⟨*INTRA_D*, INTRA_Z⟩
	INTRA_Z	⟨INTRA_D, *INTRA_Z*⟩
b	INTRA	⟨*INTRA_D*, INTER⟩, ⟨*INTRA_Z*, INTER⟩
	INTER	⟨{INTRA_D or INTRA_Z }, *INTER*⟩
c	HAVE-ARG	⟨{INTRA_D or INTRA_Z or INTER}⟩
	NO-ARG	⟨*INTRA_D*⟩, ⟨*INTRA_Z*⟩, ⟨*INTER*⟩

Table 3: Examples made for training. *Italic texts* in (b) and (c) refer most likely argument which (a) and (b) selected respectively. Non-italic texts refer to the correct argument.

pression either true anaphoric or not with the most likely antecedent. They took this approach since there are almost no clues for a Japanese noun phrase to determine anaphoric or not by looking only at the noun phrase.

Similarly, in our approach, after selecting the most likely candidate of the argument, we classify it into either of INTRA_D, INTRA_Z, INTER or no argument.

The second is the *tournament model* (Iida et al., 2003) for zero-anaphora resolution. For all the candidate antecedents (virtually all noun phrases appearing in preceding context), the model repeats two-class classification: which candidate in the pair of candidates is likely to be the antecedent for the zero-anaphora. The advantage of the tournament model is that the model can use pairwise features of candidates. Similarly, in the classification step of our approach we select an argument comparing most likely candidates of arguments of each argument type.

A Method of Argument Analysis

Selection: At the first step, we select three most likely arguments of INTRA_D, INTRA_Z, and INTER for each predicate using any argument identification model. We may use different features for models of different argument types.

Classification: At the second step, we determine which INTRA_D, INTRA_Z, and INTER is the correct argument or if there is no explicit argument appearing in the context. This step is composed

Gold Scope	Example made for training
NO-ARG	(c)NO-ARG
INTER	(b)INTER, (c)HAVE-ARG
INTRA_Z	(a)INTRA_Z, (b)INTRA, (c)HAVE-ARG
INTRA_D	(a)INTRA_D, (b)INTRA, (c)HAVE-ARG

Table 4: Examples made for training with human-annotated data. Generated examples depend on the argument type.

of three binary classification models illustrated in Figure 1.

(a) Judge which of INTRA_D or INTRA_Z is more likely to be an argument of the predicate.
(b) Judge which of INTER or the candidate selected at (a) is more likely to be an argument of the predicate.
(c) Judge whether the candidate selected at (b) qualifies as an argument of the predicate or not.

We show the example of analysis of ϕ in Example (1). We first select argument candidates of INTRA_D, INTRA_Z, and INTER. Suppose the most likely argument of INTRA_D is not selected and "私 (I)" and "花子 (Hanako)" are selected as ones of INTRA_Z and INTER respectively in the 'selection' step. Because INTRA_D is not selected, the classifier selects INTRA_Z at (a). Suppose INTER is selected at (b) comparing "私" selected at (a) and "花子". Finally, "花子" is selected as the argument by the classifier of (c).

Furthermore, though we tried different orders for 'Classification' step in the preliminary experiment, this order was the best.

Training Method of Classifiers for the 'Classification' Step

We train each binary classifier in the order of (a), (b), and (c). We create training examples of classifiers with two argument candidates and a predicate as shown in Tables 3 and 4. The following arguments are used for training:

(a) the correct argument and the most likely argument selected at the 'Selection' step
(b) the correct argument and the most likely argument selected by (a) at the 'Classification' step
(c) the correct argument and the most likely argument selected by (b) in the 'Classification' step

For instance, ϕ in Example (1) is "花子 (Hanako)" whose argument type is INTER. Hence

CHAIN_LENGTH	A frequency of being arguments in previous sentences (Iida et al., 2003)
USED	Whether being arguments in former sentences or not (Imamura et al., 2009)
SIM_COREF	Scores between an argument position and co-reference chain calculated with the similarity which Gerber and Chai (2010) used (described in Section 2.3)
SIM_CS	Scores between an argument position and co-reference chain calculated with our proposed similarity

Table 5: Discourse context features used in the experiment

we generate two training examples: One is an example of (b) with the label INTER, "花子", and the most likely argument selected by (a) at 'Classification' step. The other one is an example of (c) with the label HAVE-ARG and "花子".

4 Evaluation Setting of Predicate Argument Structure Analysis Exploiting Argument Position and Type

We evaluate our proposed selection-and-classification approach by comparing it with other models and the discourse context features shown in Table 5 by adding them to the baseline features at Japanese predicate argument structure analysis of nominative case.

In the experiment, systems refer only nouns in co-reference chains which are intra-sentential arguments. In addition, we used human annotated data of co-reference and predicate-argument structure to make discourse context features. For SIM_COREF and SIM_CS, we used maximum, minimum and average scores of similarities.

4.1 Dataset for Similarity Calculation

We used two datasets for the calculation of similarities: the Newspapers (NEWS) and the Web texts (WEB).

NEWS: We used about 21,000,000 sentences in Mainichi newspapers published from 1991 to 2003 (excluded 1995). We part-of-speech tagged the data with MeCab 0.98[3] and dependency structure parsed with CaboCha 0.60pre4[4]. Both taggers used the NAIST Japanese Dictionary 0.6.3[5]. We extracted 27,282,277 pairs of a predicate and an argument.[6]

We also extracted 111,173,873,092 co-reference chains to calculate SIM_COREF with the anaphora resolver which is our re-implementation of (Iida et al., 2005a). These chains include 2,280,417,516,455 nouns. We used 173,778,624 pairs of a predicate and an argument with the case maker が(ga), を(wo) and に(ni).

WEB: We used about 500,000,000 sentences which Kawahara and Kurohashi (2006) collected from the web. They are part-of-speech tagged with JUMAN[7] and dependency structure parsed with KNP[8]. We extracted 1,101,472,855 pairs of a predicate and an argument.[9]

4.2 Training and Evaluation Dataset

We used NAIST Text Corpus 1.4β (Iida et al., 2007) for training and evaluation. It is based on Kyoto Text Corpus 3.0[10] and annotated with predicate-argument structure, event noun structure, and co-reference of nouns about 40,000 sentences of Japanese newspaper text. We excluded 11 articles due to annotation error.

We conducted five-fold cross-validation. In the experiments, base phrases and dependency relations are acquired from the Kyoto Text Corpus 3.0 in the same way of related work.

4.3 A Model in the 'Selection' Step

In order to identify the most likely argument candidate of each INTRA_D, INTRA_Z, and INTER, we used the tournament model. We emphasize that our proposed approach can use any argument identification model to identify the most likely candidate of an argument.

4.4 Baseline Features and Classifier

As baseline features, we employed features proposed by Iida et al. (2005a, 2007a) and Imamura et al. (2009) in addition to a novel one 'PRED DEP POS' shown in Table 6.

We used Support Vector Machine (Cortes and Vapnik, 1995) for each classification model with

[3] http://mecab.sourceforge.net/

[4] http://chasen.org/~taku/software/cabocha/

[5] http://sourceforge.jp/projects/naist-jdic/

[6] Unique total are; Verb: 31,012, Noun: 327,174, Pair: 7,071,627

[7] http://nlp.kuee.kyoto-u.ac.jp/nl-resource/juman.html

[8] http://nlp.kuee.kyoto-u.ac.jp/nl-resource/knp.html

[9] Unique total are; Verb:about 801 million, Noun: about 288 million, Pair: 15,994 million

[10] http://nlp.kuee.kyoto-u.ac.jp/nl-resource/corpus.html

Type	Name	Description (NP and PRED refer a noun phrase and a predicate.)
Lexical	HEAD BF	Head word of NP and PRED.
Grammatical	PRED IN MATRIX	1 if PRED exists in the matrix clause; otherwise 0.
	PRED IN EMBEDDED	1 if PRED exists in the relative clause; otherwise 0.
	PRED VOICE	1 if PRED contains auxiliaries such as '(ra)reru'; otherwise 0.
	PRED AUX	1 if PRED contains auxiliaries such as '(sa)seru', 'hosii', 'morau'
	PRED ALT	0 if PRED VOICE and PRED AUX are 1; otherwise 1.
	POS	Part-of-speech of NP.
	DEFINITE	1 if NP contains the article corresponding to DEFINITE 'the', such as 'sore' or 'sono'; otherwise 0.
	DEMONSTRATIVE	1 if NP contains the article corresponding to DEMONSTRATIVE 'that' or 'this', such as 'kono', 'ano'; otherwise 0.
	PARTICLE	Particle followed by NP.
	PARTICLE IF PRED VOICE	PARTICLE followed by NP if PRED VOICE is 1.
Semantic	NE	Named entity of NP: PERSON, ORGANIZATION, LOCATION, ARTIFACT, DATE, TIME, MONEY, PERCENT or N/A.
	PRONOUN TYPE	Pronoun type of NP. (e.g. 'kare (he)': PERSON, 'koko (here)': LOCATION, 'sore (this)': OTHERS)
	SELECT REST	1 if NP satisfies selectional restrictions in Nihongo Goi Taikei (Japanese Lexicon) (Ikehara et al., 1997); otherwise 0.
	NCV NPS PMI	PMI score of [⟨Noun, Case⟩,⟨Predicate⟩] calculated from the WEB corpus.
Positional	DIST NP PRED	Distance between NP and PRED.
	DIST NPS	Distance between NP and NP.
	BEGINNING	1 if NP is located in the beginning of sentence; otherwise 0.
	END	1 if NP is located in the end of sentence; otherwise 0.
	PRED NP	1 if PRED proceeds NP; otherwise 0.
	NP PRED	1 if NP precedes PRED; otherwise 0.
	DEP PRED	1 if NP depends on PRED; otherwise 0.
	DEP NP	1 if PRED depends on NP; otherwise 0.
	PRED DEP POS	Part-of-speech of head word depended by PRED.
	IN QUOTE	1 if NP exists in the quoted text; otherwise 0.
	PATH	Dependency relation between PRED and NP.
Context	SRL RANK	A rank of NP in Salient Reference List.
	GA REF	1 if the phrase which contains noun and 'ga' depend on NP with 'nagara', 'te', 'shi', 'tsutsu', 'tameni', 'tari', ϕ; otherwise 0.

Table 6: Baseline features of classifiers in the 'Selection' step and the 'Classification' step.

a linear kernel. We used the implementation of LIBLINEAR 1.7[11] with its default parameters.

4.5 Targets for Comparison of Predicate Argument Analysis Model

We evaluate our selection-and-classification approach by comparing our baseline model with two previous approaches TA and IM.

TA: Taira et al. (2008) used decision lists where features were sorted by their weights learned from Support Vector Machine. They simultaneously solved the argument of event nouns in the same lists.

IM: Imamura et al. (2009) used discriminative models based on maximum entropy. They added the special noun phrase NULL, which expresses that the predicate does not have any argument.

Because previous work use different features and machine learning methods and experiment on different setting from ours, we also compare with a baseline model BL in order to analyze the effect of dividing a model considering argument type.

BL: This model has a single step in 'classification' step. In other words, 'selection' step in this model selects the most likely argument from all noun phrases preceding the predicate.

5 Discussion

Table 7 presents the result of the experiments. According to the bottom row in Table 7, we achieved the state-of-the-art of Japanese predicate argument structure analysis by combining all discourse context features (+A+B+C+D+E).

We investigate our result from five different standpoints.

5.1 Effect of the Selection-and-Classification Approach

We analyze the effect of our proposed selection-and-classification approach by comparing the first row of Table 7. SC is superior to BL in all types. This shows that dividing a model considering argument type improves the performance.

[11]http://www.csie.ntu.edu.tw/~cjlin/liblinear/

Section		INTRA_D			INTRA_Z			INTER		
		P	R	F_1	P	R	F_1	P	R	F_1
5.1	BL : Our baseline	84.06	50.74	63.24	27.02	56.13	36.46	16.44	13.70	14.89
	SC : Our proposed method	80.71	85.35	82.96	47.57	45.74	46.64	23.79	15.93	19.07
5.2	TA : Taira et al. 2008	-	-	75.53	-	-	30.15	-	-	23.45
	IM : Imamura et al. 2009	85.2	88.8	87.0	58.8	43.4	50.0	47.5	7.6	13.1
5.3, 5.4	SC+A (CHAIN_LENGTH)	85.39	88.79	87.05	51.64	52.22	51.93	25.31	18.63	21.44
	SC+B (USED)	85.59	88.44	86.99	54.40	53.32	53.86	**26.09**	21.27	**23.43**
	SC+C (SIM_COREF_NEWS)	86.82	88.90	87.85	54.07	52.89	53.47	25.83	20.08	22.58
	SC+D (SIM_CS_NEWS)	**88.42**	**91.10**	**89.74**	59.05	58.12	58.58	24.81	19.91	22.08
	SC+E (SIM_CS_WEB)	87.00	90.44	88.69	**64.76**	**60.27**	**62.43**	25.63	**21.32**	23.27
5.4	SC+D+E	89.70	91.55	90.62	65.08	61.37	63.17	24.86	21.57	23.08
5.5	ALL (SC+A+B+C+E+D)	89.93	91.70	90.81	67.39	62.18	64.68	25.86	22.93	24.30
	ALL-A	90.44	91.34	90.89	68.12	61.95	64.89	25.72	23.77	24.69
	ALL-B	90.48	91.48	90.98	66.83	62.06	64.35	**25.48**	22.71	24.01
	ALL-C	89.30	91.65	90.46	65.19	61.92	63.50	25.71	**22.22**	**23.83**
	ALL-D	**87.65**	**90.48**	**89.04**	66.14	61.21	63.57	26.03	22.85	24.32
	ALL-E	89.66	90.73	90.19	**62.47**	**59.04**	**60.71**	25.56	22.49	23.92

Table 7: Comparison of predicate argument structure analysis of nominative case: P, R, and F_1 indicate Precision, Recall, and F-measure($\beta = 1$), respectively.

5.2 Comparison between previous work

By comparing SC and TA, and SC+USED and IM[12], the result of our proposed method is competitive or superior to others. Additionally, recall is higher in any type; therefore we consider there is still much room for improvement by replacing the argument identification model in the selectional step with other models.

5.3 Effect of Similarity Metrics

On comparing +A (CHAIN_LENGTH), +B (USED), and +C (SIM_COREF_NEWS) or +D (SIM_CS_NEWS) in Table 7, similarity-based features are superior or competitive to frequency-based feature.

(2) 婚姻は毎年一万—四万組も増え、 ...
The number of marriages increases 10,000 to 40,000 couples annually ...

... **流行して** ...の引き金となったインフルエンザが、
The flu that *has been going around* and triggered ...,

For instance, the argument of "流行し (be going around)" in Example (2) is "インフルエンザ (flu)" of INTER and is not an argument of previous arguments. Though the topic changes between two sentences, A and B cannot take it into account this and output "婚姻 (Marriages)" which is an argument of "増え (increase)" because the frequency-based feature is active. In contrast, C and D handle this because the similarity between the nominative case of "増え" and "流行し" is low.

On comparing +C (SIM_COREF_NEWS) and +D (SIM_CS_NEWS) in Table 7, our proposed similarity metrics work better than the co-reference-based metrics in INTRA_D or INTRA_Z by a large margin. This result shows the robustness of our metrics compared to the co-reference based similarity between argument positions.

5.4 Effect of In and Out-of-domain Data

On comparing +D (SIM_CS_NEWS) and +E (SIM_CS_WEB) in Table 7 respectively, the similarity measure using the newswire texts works better for INTRA_D and one using the web texts works better for INTRA_Z and INTER.

Additionally, the result of +D+E shows that combining proposed similarities calculated from different sources work complementary.

5.5 Ablation Features

Removing features one by one from ALL (Adding all of A to E), we inquire about features which have strong effect on ALL. Table 7 shows that the F-measures of INTRA_D and INTRA_Z fall by a large margin, by removing D and E respectively. Though the F-measure of INTER degrades by removing C, it makes little difference to other argument types. This shows it is our proposed similarity that mainly contributes to the improvement of the F-measure of the overall system.

6 Error Analysis

We analyze errors where our proposed similarity does not work well.

[12]We compare SC+USED and IM, because IM used the USED feature.

6.1 Copula

In NAIST Text Corpus, the copula "だ"(In English, "be") is annotated as a predicate.

(3) マンション価格が ... 下がってきた ...。
The price of apartments is going down.

... (φが) 前年は五・八倍であった
φ of last year *was* 5.8 times higher than that of this year.

However, the behavior of copula is different from other predicates, thus it is difficult to resolve them with the same model. To solve this problem, the model of copula should be separated.

6.2 Light Verb Construction

In this experiment, we regarded the predicate of "する (do) + noun" such as "逮捕する (do arrest)" as a single predicate. On the other hand, we regarded the predicate of "する (do) + particle + noun" such as "まかせにする" in Example (4) as "する (do)."

(4) (φが) 分権を国 <u>まかせ (relegation)</u> に(ni) する *(do)* のではなく、...
φ should not relegate promotion of decentralization ...

However, verbs like "do" in such examples do not play central roles, whereas the noun such as "まかせ (relegation)" carries the main meaning of the event. This phenomenon is called "light verb construction" (Miyamoto, 1999).

"まかせ" is the nominalized form of the verb "まかせる (relegate)." Thus we need to calculate similarity with "まかせる" instead of "する". When the predicate is a light verb, we have to use the original verb to calculate the similarity.

6.3 Predicate Sense Ambiguity

A predicate may have several senses and hence have several argument distributions. For example, "詰める" has two senses at least: to pack and to bring to a conclusion. "詰める" in Example (5) means the latter.

(5) (φが) 数字を早急に**詰める**必要性を強調した。
They emphasized that φ should be brought to an conclusion as soon as possible.

The distributions of arguments of such ambiguous verbs tend to have a mixture of several distributions of arguments. Therefore this makes it hard to calculate the similarity of an argument position and a co-reference chain. Additionally, it is even more difficult when the predicate is more essential verb such as "持つ (have)" and "取る (take)." This suggests the close relationship between the word sense disambiguation and the predicate argument structure analysis. In fact, Meza-Ruiz and Riedel (2009) showed that the joint model for semantic role labeling and word sense disambiguation performs better than a pipeline system.

Since NAIST Text Corpus is not annotated with verb senses, we are annotating the sense of verbs to allow similar analysis.

7 Conclusion

We improved Japanese predicate argument structure analysis exploiting *argument position* and *type*. In particular, we proposed two methods: the improved similarity measure between argument positions and the selection-and-classification approach considering argument type.

Experimental results show that our proposed method achieved state-of-the art accuracy for the Japanese predicate argument structure analysis. Proposed similarity between argument positions exploiting case maker is more robust than previous co-reference-based method that makes use of an unreliable automatic co-reference resolver. Furthermore, we proposed flexible approach which accounts for the minor types of arguments.

Future work includes four topics: (1) to distinguish copula from other predicates; (2) to combine internal argument to take semantic argument into consideration if the verb is in light verb construction; (3) to perform word sense disambiguation before calculating similarity; (4) to conduct experiments not only on nominative case but also on other cases .

Acknowledgments

We thank Daisuke Kawahara and Sadao Kurohashi for providing the web texts and Joseph Irwin for his comments on the earlier draft.

References

Nathanael Chambers and Dan Jurafsky. 2008. Unsupervised Learning of Narrative Event Chains. In

Proceedings of Annual Meeting of the Association for Computational Linguistics-08 with the Human Language Technology Conference, pages 789–797.

Corinna Cortes and Vladimir Vapnik. 1995. Support-Vector Networks. *Machine learning*.

Matthew Gerber and Joyce Y. Chai. 2010. Beyond NomBank: A Study of Implicit Arguments for Nominal Predicates. In *Proceedings of the 48th Annual Meeting of the Association for Computational Linguistics*, pages 1583–1592. Association for Computational Linguistics.

David Graff. 2003. *English Gigaword*. Linguistic Data Consortium.

Barbara J. Grosz, Aravind K. Joshi, and Scott Weinstein. 1995. Centering: A Framework for Modeling the Local Coherence of Discourse. *Computational Linguistics*, 21(2):203–225.

Ryu Iida, Kentaro Inui, Hiroya Takamura, and Yuji Matsumoto. 2003. Incorporating Contextual Cues in Trainable Models for Coreference Resolution. In *Proceedings of the 10th EACL Workshop on the Computational Treatment of Anaphora*, pages 23–30.

Ryu Iida, Kentaro Inui, and Yuji Matsumoto. 2005a. Anaphora Resolution by Antecedent Identification Followed by Anaphoricity Determination. *ACM Transactions on Asian Language Information Processing*, 4(4):417–434.

Ryu Iida, Kentaro Inui, and Yuji Matsumoto. 2005b. On the Issue of Combining Anaphoricity Determination and Antecedent Identification in Anaphora Resolution. In *International Conference on Natural Language Processing and Knowledge Engineering*, pages 244–249.

Ryu Iida, Mamoru Komachi, Kentaro Inui, and Yuji Matsumoto. 2007. Annotating a Japanese Text Corpus with Predicate-Argument and Coreference Relations. In *Proceedings of the Linguistic Annotation Workshop*, pages 132–139. Association for Computational Linguistics.

Satoru Ikehara, Masahiro Miyazaki, Satoshi Shirai, Akio Yokoo, Hiromi Nakaiwa, and Kentaro Ogura. 1997. *Nihongo Goi Taikei :A Japanese Lexicon*. Iwanami Shoten.

Kenji Imamura, Kuniko Saito, and Tomoko Izumi. 2009. Discriminative Approach to Predicate-Argument Structure Analysis with Zero-Anaphora Resolution. In *Proceedings of the Joint conference of the 47th Annual Meeting of the Association for Computational Linguistics and the 4th International Joint Conference on Natural Language Processing of the Asian Federation of Natural Language Processing*, pages 85–88.

Daisuke Kawahara and Sadao Kurohashi. 2006. Case Frame Compilation from the Web using High-Performance Computing. In *Proceedings of the 5th International Conference on Language Resources and Evaluation*, pages 1344–1347.

Ivan Meza-Ruiz and Sebastian Riedel. 2009. Jointly identifying predicates, arguments and senses using markov logic. In *Proceedings of Human Language Technologies: The 2009 Annual Conference of the North American Chapter of the Association for Computational Linguistics*, pages 155–163.

Tadao Miyamoto. 1999. *The Light Verb Construction in Japanese: the role of the verbal noun*. John Benjamins Publishing Company.

Sigeko Nariyama. 2002. Grammar for Ellipsis Resolution in Japanese. In *Proceedings of the 9th International Conference on Theoretical and Methodological Issues in Machine Translation*, pages 135–145.

Viktor Pekar. 2006. Acquisition of Verb Entailment from Text. In *Proceedings of the main conference on Human Language Technology Conference of the North American Chapter of the Association of Computational Linguistics*, pages 49–56. Association for Computational Linguistics.

Hirotoshi Taira, Sanae Fujita, and Masaaki Nagata. 2008. A Japanese Predicate Argument Structure Analysis Using Decision Lists. In *Proceedings of the Conference on Empirical Methods in Natural Language Processing*, pages 523–532.

An Empirical Study on Compositionality in Compound Nouns

Siva Reddy
University of York, UK
siva@cs.york.ac.uk

Diana McCarthy
Lexical Computing Ltd, UK
diana@dianamccarthy.co.uk

Suresh Manandhar
University of York, UK
suresh@cs.york.ac.uk

Abstract

A multiword is compositional if its meaning can be expressed in terms of the meaning of its constituents. In this paper, we collect and analyse the compositionality judgments for a range of compound nouns using Mechanical Turk. Unlike existing compositionality datasets, our dataset has judgments on the contribution of constituent words as well as judgments for the phrase as a whole. We use this dataset to study the relation between the judgments at constituent level to that for the whole phrase. We then evaluate two different types of distributional models for compositionality detection – constituent based models and composition function based models. Both the models show competitive performance though the composition function based models perform slightly better. In both types, additive models perform better than their multiplicative counterparts.

1 Introduction

Compositionality is a language phenomenon where the meaning of an expression can be expressed in terms of the meaning of its constituents. Multiword expressions (Sag et al., 2002, MWEs) are known to display a continuum of compositionality (McCarthy et al., 2003) where some of them are compositional e.g. "swimming pool", some are non-compositional e.g. "cloud nine", and some in between e.g. "zebra crossing".

The past decade has seen interest in developing computational methods for compositionality in MWEs (Lin, 1999; Schone and Jurafsky, 2001; Baldwin et al., 2003; Bannard et al., 2003; McCarthy et al., 2003; Venkatapathy and Joshi, 2005; Katz and Giesbrecht, 2006; Sporleder and Li, 2009). Recent developments in vector-based semantic composition functions (Mitchell and Lapata, 2008; Widdows, 2008) have also been applied to compositionality detection (Giesbrecht, 2009).

While the existing methods of compositionality detection use constituent word level semantics to compose the semantics of the phrase, the evaluation datasets are not particularly suitable to study the contribution of each constituent word to the semantics of the phrase. Existing datasets (McCarthy et al., 2003; Venkatapathy and Joshi, 2005; Katz and Giesbrecht, 2006; Biemann and Giesbrecht, 2011) only have the compositionality judgment of the whole expression without constituent word level judgment, or they have judgments on the constituents without judgments on the whole (Bannard et al., 2003). Our dataset allows us to examine the relationship between the two rather than assume the nature of it.

In this paper we collect judgments of the contribution of constituent nouns within noun-noun compounds (section 2) alongside judgments of compositionality of the compound. We study the relation between the contribution of the parts with the compositionality of the whole (section 3). We propose various constituent based models (section 4.3) which are intuitive and related to existing models of compositionality detection (section 4.1) and we evaluate these models in comparison to composition function based models. All the models discussed in this paper are built using a distributional word-space model approach (Sahlgren, 2006).

2 Compositionality in Compound Nouns

In this section, we describe the experimental setup for the collecting compositionality judgments of English compound nouns. All the existing datasets focused either on verb-particle, verb-noun or adjective-noun phrases. Instead, we focus on *compound nouns* for which resources are relatively scarce. In this paper, we only deal with compound nouns made up of two words separated by space.

2.1 Annotation setup

In the literature (Nunberg et al., 1994; Baldwin et al., 2003; Fazly et al., 2009), compositionality is discussed in many terms including simple decomposable, semantically analyzable, idiosyncratically decomposable and non-decomposable. For practical NLP purposes, Bannard et al. (2003) adopt a straightforward definition of a compound being compositional if *"the overall semantics of the multi-word expression (here compound) can be composed from the simplex semantics of its parts, as described (explicitly or implicitly) in a finite lexicon"*. We adopt this definition and pose compositionality as a literality issue. *A compound is compositional if its meaning can be understood from the literal (simplex) meaning of its parts.* Similar views of compositionality as literality are found in (Lin, 1999; Katz and Giesbrecht, 2006). In the past there have been arguments in favor/disfavor of compositionality as literality approach (e.g. see (Gibbs, 1989; Titone and Connine, 1999)). The idea of viewing compositionality as literality is also motivated from the shared task organized by Biemann and Giesbrecht (2011). From here on, we use the terms compositionality and literality interchangeably.

We ask humans to score the compositionality of a phrase by asking them *how literal the phrase is*. Since we wish to see in our data the extent that the phrase is compositional, and to what extent that depends on the contribution in meaning of its parts, we also ask them *how literal the use of a component word is within the given phrase*.

For each compound noun, we create three separate tasks – one for each constituent's literality and one for the phrase compositionality. The motivation behind using three separate tasks is to make the scoring mechanism for each task independent of the other tasks. This enables us to study the actual relation between the constituents and the compound scores without any bias to any particular annotator's way of arriving at the scores of the compound w.r.t. the constituents.

There are many factors to consider in eliciting compositionality judgments, such as ambiguity of the expression and individual variation of annotator in background knowledge. To control for this, we ask subjects if they can interpret the meaning of a compound noun from *only* the meaning of the component nouns where we also provide contextual information. All the possible definitions of a compound noun are chosen from WordNet (Fellbaum, 1998), Wiktionary or defined by ourselves if some of the definitions are absent. Five examples of each compound noun are randomly chosen from the ukWaC (Ferraresi et al., 2008) corpus and the same set of examples are displayed to all the annotators. The annotators select the definition of the compound noun which occurs most frequently in the examples and then score the compound for literality based on the most frequent definition.

We have two reasons for making the annotators read the examples, choose the most frequent definition and base literality judgments on the most frequent definition. The first reason is to provide a context to the decisions and reduce the impact of ambiguity. The second is that distributional models are greatly influenced by frequency and since we aim to work with distributional models for compositionality detection we base our findings on the most frequent sense of the compound noun. In this work we consider the compositionality of the noun-noun compound type without token based disambiguation which we leave for future work.

2.2 Compound noun dataset

We could not find any compound noun datasets publicly available which are marked for compositionality judgments. Korkontzelos and Manandhar (2009) prepared a related dataset for compound nouns but compositionality scores were absent and their set contains only 38 compounds. There are datasets for verb-particle (McCarthy et al., 2003), verb-noun judgments (Biemann and Giesbrecht, 2011; Venkatapathy and Joshi, 2005) and adjective-noun (Biemann and Giesbrecht, 2011). Not only are these not the focus of our work, but also we wanted datasets with each constituent word's literality score. Bannard et al. (2003) obtained judgments on whether a verb-particle construction implies the verb or the particle or both. The judgments were binary and not on a scale and there was no judgment of compositionality of the whole construction. Ours is the first attempt to provide a dataset which have both scalar compositionality judgments of the phrase as well as the literality score for each component word.

We aimed for a dataset which would include compound nouns where: 1) both the component words are used literally, 2) the first word is used literally but not the second, 3) the second word is used literally but not the first and 4) both the words are used non-literally. Such a dataset would provide stronger evidence to study the relation between the constituents of the compound noun and its compositionality behaviour.

We used the following heuristics based on WordNet to classify compound nouns into 4 above classes.

1. Each of the component word exists either in the hypernymy hierarchy of the compound noun or in the definition(s) of the compound noun. e.g. *swimming pool* because *swimming* exists in the WordNet definition of *swimming pool* and *pool* exists in the hypernymy hierarchy of *swimming pool*
2. Only the first word exists either in the hypernymy hierarchy or in the definition(s) of the compound and not the second word. e.g. *night owl*
3. Only the second word exists either in the hypernymy hierarchy or in the definition(s) of the compound and not the first word. e.g. *zebra crossing*
4. Neither of the words exist either in hypernymy hierarchy or in the definition(s) of the compound noun. e.g. *smoking gun*

The intuition behind the heuristics is that if a component word is used literally in a compound, it would probably be used in the definition of the compound or may appear in the synset hierarchy of the compound. We changed the constraints, for example decreasing/increasing the depth of the hypernymy hierarchy, and for each class we randomly picked 30 potential candidates by rough manual verification. There were fewer instances in the classes 2 and 4. In order to populate these classes, we selected additional compound nouns from Wiktionary by manually inspecting if they can fall in either class.

These heuristics were only used for obtaining our sample, they were *not* used for categorizing the compound nouns in our study. The compound nouns in all these temporary classes are merged and 90 compound words are selected which have at least 50 instances in the ukWaC corpus. These 90 compound words are chosen for the dataset.

2.3 Annotators

Snow et al. (2008) used Amazon mechanical turk (AMT) for annotating language processing tasks. They found that although an individual turker (annotator) performance was lower compared to an expert, as the number of turkers increases, the quality of the annotated data surpassed expert level quality. We used 30 turkers for annotating each single task and then retained the judgments with sufficient consensus as described in section 2.4.

For each compound noun, 3 types of tasks are created as described above: a judgment on how literal the phrase is and a judgment on how literal each noun is within the compound. For 90 compound nouns, 270 independent tasks are therefore created. Each of these tasks is assigned to 30 annotators. A task is assigned randomly to an annotator by AMT so each annotator may work on only some of the tasks for a given compound.

2.4 Quality of the annotations

Recent studies[1] shows that AMT data is prone to spammers and outliers. We dealt with them in three ways. **a).** We designed a qualification test[2] which provides an annotator with basic training about literality, and they can participate in the annotation task only if they pass the test. **b).** Once all the annotations (90 phrases * 3 tasks/phrase * 30 annotations/task = 8100 annotations) are completed, we calculated the average Spearman correlation score (ρ) of every annotator by correlating their annotation values with every other annotator and taking the average. We discarded the work of annotators whose ρ is negative and accepted all the work of annotators whose ρ is greater than 0.6. **c).** For the other annotators, we accepted their annotation for a task only if their annotation judgment is within the range of ± 1.5 from the task's mean. Table 1 displays AMT statistics. Overall, each annotator on average worked on 53 tasks randomly selected from the set of 270 tasks. This lowers the chance of bias in the data because of any particular annotator.

Spearman correlation scores ρ provide an estimate of annotator agreement. To know the difficulty level of the three types of tasks described in section 2, ρ for each task type is also displayed in

[1] A study on AMT spammers `http://bit.ly/elIPil`

[2] The qualification test details are provided with the dataset. Please refer to footnote 3.

No. of turkers participated	260	
No. of them qualified	151	
Turkers with $\rho <= 0$	21	
Turkers with $\rho >= 0.6$	81	
No. of annotations rejected	383	
Avg. submit time (sec) per task	30.4	
	highest ρ	avg. ρ
ρ for phrase compositionality	0.741	0.522
ρ for first word's literality	0.758	0.570
ρ for second word's literality	0.812	0.616
ρ for over all three task types	0.788	0.589

Table 1: Amazon Mechanical Turk statistics

Function f	ρ	R^2
ADD	0.966	0.937
MULT	0.965	0.904
COMB	0.971	0.955
WORD1	0.767	0.609
WORD2	0.720	0.508

Table 3: Correlations between functions and phrase compositionality scores

table 1. It is evident that annotators agree more at word level than phrase level annotations.

For each compound, we also studied the distribution of scores around the mean by observing the standard deviation σ. All the compound nouns along with their mean and standard deviations are shown in table 2.

Ideally, if all the annotators agree on a judgment for a given compound or a component word, the deviation should be low. Among the 90 compounds, 15 of them are found to have a deviation $> \pm 1.5$. We used this threshold to signify annotator disagreement. The reason for disagreement could be due to the ambiguity of the compound e.g. *silver screen, brass ring* or due to the subjective differences of opinion between the annotators.

Overall, the inter annotator agreement (ρ) is high and the standard deviation of most tasks is low (except for a few exceptions). So we are confident that the dataset can be used as a reliable gold-standard with which we conduct experiments. The dataset is publicly available for download[3].

[3]Annotation guidelines, Mechanical Turk hits, qualification test, annotators demographic and educational background, and final annotations are downloadable from `http://sivareddy.in/downloads` or `http://www.dianamccarthy.co.uk/downloads.html`

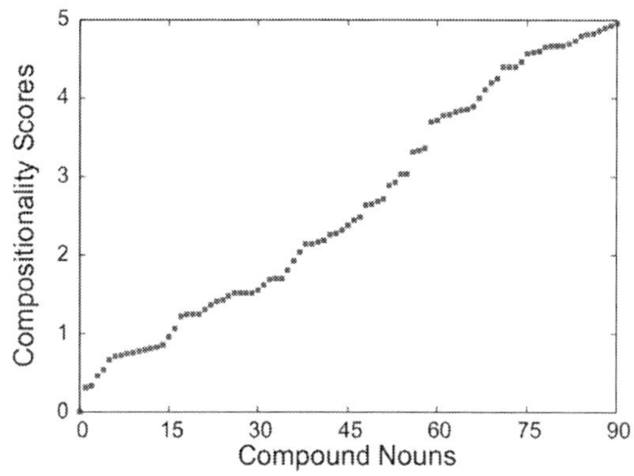

Figure 1: Mean values of phrase-level compositionality scores

3 Analyzing the Human Judgments

By analyzing the mean values of the phrase level annotations, we found that compounds displayed a varied level of compositionality. For some compounds annotators confirm that they can interpret the meaning of a compound from its component words and for some they do not. For others they grade in-between. Figure 1 displays the mean values of compositionality scores of all compounds. Compounds are arranged along the X-axis in increasing order of their score. The graph displays a *continuum of compositionality* (McCarthy et al., 2003). We note that our sample of compounds was selected to exhibit a range of compositionality.

3.1 Relation between the constituents and the phrase compositionality judgments

The dataset allows us to study the relation between constituent word level contributions to the phrase level compositionality scores.

Let $w1$ and $w2$ be the constituent words of the compound $w3$. Let $s1$, $s2$ and $s3$ be the mean literality scores of $w1$, $w2$ and $w3$ respectively. Using a 3-fold cross validation on the annotated data, we tried various function fittings f over the judgments $s1$, $s2$ and $s3$.

- ADD: $a.s1 + b.s2 = s3$
- MULT: $a.s1.s2 = s3$
- COMB: $a.s1 + b.s2 + c.s1.s2 = s3$
- WORD1: $a.s1 = s3$
- WORD2: $a.s2 = s3$

where a, b and c are coefficients.

We performed 3-fold cross validation to evaluate the above functions (two training samples and

Compound	Word1	Word2	Phrase	Compound	Word1	Word2	Phrase
climate change	4.90±0.30	4.83±0.38	4.97±0.18	engine room	4.86±0.34	5.00±0.00	4.93±0.25
graduate student	4.70±0.46	5.00±0.00	4.90±0.30	swimming pool	4.80±0.40	4.90±0.30	4.87±0.34
speed limit	4.93±0.25	4.83±0.38	4.83±0.46	research project	4.90±0.30	4.53±0.96	4.82±0.38
application form	4.77±0.42	4.86±0.34	4.80±0.48	bank account	4.87±0.34	4.83±0.46	4.73±0.44
parking lot	4.83±0.37	4.77±0.50	4.70±0.64	credit card	4.67±0.54	4.90±0.30	4.67±0.70
ground floor	4.66±0.66	4.70±0.78	4.67±0.60	mailing list	4.67±0.54	4.93±0.25	4.67±0.47
call centre	4.73±0.44	4.41±0.72	4.66±0.66	video game	4.50±0.72	5.00±0.00	4.60±0.61
human being	4.86±0.34	4.33±1.14	4.59±0.72	interest rate	4.34±0.99	4.69±0.53	4.57±0.90
radio station	4.66±0.96	4.34±0.80	4.47±0.72	health insurance	4.53±0.88	4.83±0.58	4.40±1.17
law firm	4.72±0.52	3.89±1.50	4.40±0.76	public service	4.67±0.65	4.77±0.62	4.40±0.76
end user	3.87±1.12	4.87±0.34	4.25±0.87	car park	4.90±0.40	4.00±1.10	4.20±1.05
role model	3.55±1.22	4.00±1.03	4.11±1.07	head teacher	2.93±1.51	4.52±1.07	4.00±1.16
fashion plate	4.41±1.07	3.31±2.07	3.90±1.42	balance sheet	3.82±0.89	3.90±0.96	3.86±1.01
china clay	2.00±1.84	4.62±1.00	3.85±1.27	game plan	2.82±1.96	4.86±0.34	3.83±1.23
brick wall	3.16±2.20	3.53±1.86	3.79±1.75	web site	2.68±1.69	3.93±1.18	3.79±1.21
brass ring	3.73±1.95	3.87±1.98	3.72±1.84	case study	3.66±1.12	4.67±0.47	3.70±0.97
polo shirt	1.73±1.41	5.00±0.00	3.37±1.38	rush hour	3.11±1.37	2.86±1.36	3.33±1.27
search engine	4.62±0.96	2.25±1.70	3.32±1.16	cocktail dress	1.40±1.08	5.00±0.00	3.04±1.22
face value	1.39±1.11	4.64±0.81	3.04±0.88	chain reaction	2.41±1.16	4.52±0.72	2.93±1.14
cheat sheet	2.30±1.59	4.00±0.83	2.89±1.11	blame game	4.61±0.67	2.00±1.28	2.72±0.92
fine line	3.17±1.34	2.03±1.52	2.69±1.21	front runner	3.97±0.96	1.29±1.10	2.66±1.32
grandfather clock	0.43±0.78	5.00±0.00	2.64±1.32	lotus position	1.11±1.17	4.78±0.42	2.48±1.22
spelling bee	4.81±0.77	0.52±1.04	2.45±1.25	silver screen	1.41±1.57	3.23±1.45	2.38±1.63
smoking jacket	1.04±0.82	4.90±0.30	2.32±1.29	spinning jenny	4.67±0.54	0.41±0.77	2.28±1.08
number crunching	4.48±0.77	0.97±1.13	2.26±1.00	guilt trip	4.71±0.59	0.86±0.94	2.19±1.16
memory lane	4.75±0.51	0.71±0.80	2.17±1.04	crash course	0.96±0.94	4.23±0.92	2.14±1.27
rock bottom	0.74±0.89	3.80±1.08	2.14±1.19	think tank	3.96±1.06	0.47±0.62	2.04±1.13
night owl	4.47±0.88	0.50±0.82	1.93±1.27	panda car	0.50±0.56	4.66±1.15	1.81±1.07
diamond wedding	1.07±1.29	3.41±1.34	1.70±1.05	firing line	1.61±1.65	1.89±1.50	1.70±1.72
pecking order	0.78±0.92	3.89±1.40	1.69±0.88	lip service	2.03±1.25	1.75±1.40	1.62±1.06
cash cow	4.22±1.07	0.37±0.73	1.56±1.10	graveyard shift	0.38±0.61	4.50±0.72	1.52±1.17
sacred cow	1.93±1.65	0.96±1.72	1.52±1.52	silver spoon	1.59±1.47	1.44±1.77	1.52±1.45
flea market	0.38±0.81	4.71±0.84	1.52±1.13	eye candy	3.83±1.05	0.71±0.75	1.48±1.10
rocket science	0.64±0.97	1.55±1.40	1.43±1.35	couch potato	3.27±1.48	0.34±0.66	1.41±1.03
kangaroo court	0.17±0.37	4.43±1.02	1.37±1.05	snail mail	0.60±0.80	4.59±1.10	1.31±1.02
crocodile tears	0.19±0.47	3.79±1.05	1.25±1.09	cutting edge	0.88±1.19	1.73±1.63	1.25±1.18
zebra crossing	0.76±0.62	4.61±0.86	1.25±1.02	acid test	0.71±1.10	3.90±1.24	1.22±1.26
shrinking violet	2.28±1.44	0.23±0.56	1.07±1.01	sitting duck	1.48±1.48	0.41±0.67	0.96±1.04
rat race	0.25±0.51	2.04±1.32	0.86±0.99	swan song	0.38±0.61	1.11±1.14	0.83±0.91
gold mine	1.38±1.42	0.70±0.81	0.81±0.82	rat run	0.41±0.62	2.33±1.40	0.79±0.66
nest egg	0.79±0.98	0.50±0.87	0.78±0.87	agony aunt	1.86±1.22	0.43±0.56	0.76±0.86
snake oil	0.37±0.55	0.81±1.25	0.75±1.12	monkey business	0.67±1.01	1.85±1.30	0.72±0.69
smoking gun	0.71±0.75	1.00±0.94	0.71±0.84	silver bullet	0.52±1.00	0.55±1.10	0.67±1.15
melting pot	1.00±1.15	0.48±0.63	0.54±0.63	ivory tower	0.38±1.03	0.54±0.68	0.46±0.68
cloud nine	0.47±0.62	0.23±0.42	0.33±0.54	gravy train	0.30±0.46	0.45±0.77	0.31±0.59

Table 2: Compounds with their constituent and phrase level mean±deviation scores

one testing sample at each iteration). The coefficients of the functions are estimated using least-square linear regression technique over the training samples. The average Spearman correlation scores (ρ) over testing samples are displayed in table 3. The goodness of fit R^2 values when trained over the whole data are also displayed in table 3.

Results (both ρ and R^2) clearly show that a relation exists between the constituent literality scores and the phrase compositionality. Existing compositionality approaches on noun-noun compounds such as (Baldwin et al., 2003; Korkontzelos and Manandhar, 2009) use the semantics of only *one* of the constituent words (generally the head word) to determine the compositionality of the phrase. But the goodness of fit R^2 values show that the functions ADD, COMB and MULT which intuitively make use of *both* the constituent scores fit the data better than functions using only one of the constituents. Furthermore, COMB and ADD suggest that additive models are preferable to multiplicative. In this data, the first constituent word plays a slightly more important role than the second in determining compositionality.

Overall, this study suggests that *it is possible to estimate the phrase level compositionality scores given the constituent word level literality scores*. This motivates us to present constituent based models (section 4.3) for compositionality score estimation of a compound. We begin the next section on computational models with a discussion of related work.

4 Computational Models

4.1 Related work

Most methods in compositionality detection can be classified into two types - those which make use of lexical fixedness and syntactic properties of the MWEs, and those which make use of the semantic similarities between the constituents and the MWE.

Non compositional MWEs are known to have lexical fixedness in which the component words have high statistical association. Some of the methods which exploit this feature are (Lin, 1999; Pedersen, 2011). This property does not hold always because institutionalized MWEs (Sag et al., 2002) are known to have high association even though they are compositional, especially in the case of compound nouns. Another property of non-compositional MWEs is that they show syntactic rigidness which do not allow internal modifiers or morphological variations of the components, or variations that break typical selectional preferences. Methods like (Cook et al., 2007; McCarthy et al., 2007; Fazly et al., 2009) exploit this property. This holds mostly for verbal idioms but not for compound nouns since the variations of any compound noun are highly limited.

Other methods like (Baldwin et al., 2003; Sporleder and Li, 2009) are based on semantic similarities between the constituents and the MWE. Baldwin et al. (2003) use only the information of the semantic similarity between one of the constituents and the compound to determine the compositionality. Sporleder and Li (2009) determine the compositionality of verbal phrases in a given context (token-based disambiguation) based on the lexical chain similarities of the constituents and the context of the MWE. Bannard et al. (2003) and McCarthy et al. (2003) study the compositionality in verb particles and they found that methods based on the similarity between simplex parts (constituents) and the phrases are useful to study semantics of the phrases. These findings motivated our constituent based models along with the findings in section 3.1.

In addition to the constituent based models (section 4.3), there are composition function based vector models (Mitchell and Lapata, 2008; Widdows, 2008) which make use of the semantics of the constituents in a different manner. These models are described in section 4.4 and are evaluated in comparison with the constituent-based models.

The vector space model used in all our experiments is described as follows.

4.2 Vector space model of meaning

Our vector space model is also called a word space model (Sahlgren, 2006, WSM) since we represent a word's meaning in a dimensional space. In the WSM, a word meaning is represented in terms of its Co-occurrences observed in a large corpora where the co-occurrences are stored in a vector format. The lemmatised context words around the target word in a window of size 100 are treated as the co-occurrences. The top 10000 frequent content words in the ukWaC (along with their part-of-speech category) are used for the feature co-occurrences i.e. the dimensionality of the WSM. To measure similarity between two vectors, cosine similarity (sim) is used. Following Mitchell and Lapata (2008), the context words in the vector are set to the ratio of probability of the context word given the target word to the overall probability of the context word[4].

4.3 Constituent based models

Given a compound word $w3$ with the constituents $w1$ and $w2$, constituent based models determine the compositionality score $s3$ of the compound by first determining the literality scores $s1$ and $s2$ of $w1$ and $w2$ respectively (section 4.3.1) and then using one of the functions f (described in section 3.1), the compositionality score $s3$ is estimated using $s3 = f(s1, s2)$ (section 4.3.2).

4.3.1 Literality scores of the constituents

If a constituent word is used literally in a given compound it is highly likely that the compound and the constituent share common co-occurrences. For example, the compound *swimming pool* has the co-occurrences *water*, *fun* and *indoor* which are also commonly found with the constituents *swimming* and *pool*.

We define the literality of a word in a given compound as the similarity between the compound and the constituent co-occurrence vectors i.e. if the number of common co-occurrences are

[4]This is similar to pointwise mutual information without logarithm

numerous then the constituent is more likely to be meant literally in the compound.

Let $v1$, $v2$ and $v3$ be the co-occurrence vectors of $w1$, $w2$ and $w3$. The literality scores $s1$ and $s2$ of $w1$ and $w2$ in the compound $w3$ are defined as

$$s1 = sim(v1, v3)$$
$$s2 = sim(v2, v3)$$

where sim is the cosine similarity between the vectors.

4.3.2 Compositionality of the compound

Given the literality scores $s1$ and $s2$ of the constituents, we can now compute the compositionality score $s3$ of the compound $w3$ using any of the functions f defined in section 3.1.

$$s3 = f(s1, s2)$$

4.4 Composition function based models

In these models (Schone and Jurafsky, 2001; Katz and Giesbrecht, 2006; Giesbrecht, 2009) of compositionality detection, firstly a vector for the compound is composed from its constituents using a compositionality function $\oplus$. Then the similarity between the composed vector and true co-occurrence vector of the compound is measured to determine the compositionality: the higher the similarity, the higher the compositionality of the compound. Guevara (2011) observed that additive models performed well for building composition vectors of phrases from their parts whereas Mitchell and Lapata (2008) found in favor of multiplicative models. We experiment using both the compositionality functions simple addition[5] and simple multiplication, which are the most widely used composition functions, known for their simplicity and good performance.

Vector $\mathbf{v1} \oplus \mathbf{v2}$ for a compound w_3 is composed from its constituent word vectors $\mathbf{v1}$ and $\mathbf{v2}$ using the vector addition $a\mathbf{v1} + b\mathbf{v2}$ and simple multiplication $\mathbf{v1v2}$ where the ith element of $\mathbf{v1} \oplus \mathbf{v2}$ is defined as

$$(a\mathbf{v1} + b\mathbf{v2})_i = a.\mathrm{v1}_i + b.\mathrm{v2}_i$$
$$(\mathbf{v1v2})_i = \mathrm{v1}_i.\mathrm{v2}_i$$

[5]Please note that simple additive model (Mitchell and Lapata, 2008) is different from the additive model described in (Guevara, 2011). In (Mitchell and Lapata, 2008) the coefficients are real numbers whereas in (Guevara, 2011) they are matrices.

	first constituent	second constituent
s1	0.616	–
s2	–	0.707

Table 4: Constituent level correlations

The compositionality score of the compound is then measured using $s3 = sim(\mathbf{v1} \oplus \mathbf{v2}, \mathbf{v3})$ where $\mathbf{v3}$ is the co-occurrence vector of the compound built from the corpus. For more details of these models please refer to (Mitchell and Lapata, 2008; Giesbrecht, 2009).

4.5 Evaluation

We evaluated all the models on the dataset developed in section 2. Since our dataset has constituent level contributions along with phrase compositionality judgments, we evaluated the constituent based models against both the literality scores of the constituents (section 4.3.1) and the phrase level judgments (section 4.3.2). The composition function models are evaluated only on phrase level scores following (McCarthy et al., 2003; Venkatapathy and Joshi, 2005; Biemann and Giesbrecht, 2011): higher correlation scores indicate better compositionality predictions.

Constituent based models evaluation

Spearman's ρ correlations of s1 and s2 with the human constituent level judgments are shown in table 4. We observed that the predictions for the second constituent are more accurate than those for the first constituent. Perhaps these constitute an easier set of nouns for modelling but we need to investigate this further.

For the phrase compositionality evaluation we did a 3-fold cross validation. The parameters of the functions f (section 4.3.2) are predicted by least square linear regression over the training samples and optimum values are selected. The average Spearman correlation scores of phrase compositionality scores with human judgements on the testing samples are displayed in table 5. The goodness of fit R^2 values when trained over the whole dataset are also displayed.

It is clear that models ADD and COMB which use both the constituents are better predictors of phrase compositionality compared to the single word based predictors WORD1 and WORD2. Both ADD and COMB are competitive in terms of both the correlations (accuracy) and goodness of

Model	ρ	R^2
Constituent Based Models		
ADD	0.686	0.613
MULT	0.670	0.428
COMB	0.682	0.615
WORD1	0.669	0.548
WORD2	0.515	0.410
Compositionality Function Based Models		
$a\mathbf{v1} + b\mathbf{v2}$	0.714	0.620
v1v2	0.650	0.501
RAND	0.002	0.000

Table 5: Phrase level correlations of compositionality scores

fit values. The model MULT shows good correlation but the goodness of fit is lower. First constituent (model WORD1 i.e. $sim(\mathbf{v1}, \mathbf{v3})$) was found to be a better predictor of phrase compositionality than the second (WORD2) following the behaviour of the mechanical turkers as in table 3.

Composition function based models evaluation

These models are evaluated for phrase compositionality scores. As with the constituent based models, for estimating the model parameters a and b of the composition function based models, we did a 3-fold cross validation. The best results of additive model on the training samples are found at a=0.60 and b=0.40. Average Spearman correlation scores of both addition and multiplication models over the testing samples are displayed in table 5. The goodness of fit R^2 values when trained over the whole dataset are also displayed.

Vector addition has a clear upper hand over multiplication in terms of both accuracy and goodness of fit for phrase compositionality prediction.

Winner

For phrase compositionality prediction (table 5), both constituent based and compositionality function based models are found to be competitive, though compositionality function based models perform slightly better. The reason could be because while constituent based models use contextual information of each constituent *independently*, composition function models make use of collective evidence from the contexts of both the constituents *simultaneously*. In the public evaluations of compositionality detection (Biemann and Giesbrecht, 2011), our system (Reddy et al., 2011) which uses the notion of contexts salient to both the constituents achieved better performance than the system which uses only one of the constituent's contexts.

All the results when compared with random baseline (RAND in table 5), which assigns a random compositionality score to a compound, are highly significant.

5 Conclusions

In this paper we examined the compositionality judgments of noun compounds and also the literality judgments of their constituent words. Our study reveals that both the constituent words play a major role in deciding the compositionality of the phrase. We showed that the functions which predict the compositionality using both the constituent literality scores have high correlations with compositionality judgments. Based on this evidence we proposed constituent based models for compositionality detection. We compared constituent based models with compositionality function based models. The additive compositionality functions were slightly superior to the best performing constituent models (again additive) but performance is comparable and we plan to examine more sophisticated constituent models in the future.

All the 8100 annotations collected in this work are released publicly. We hope the dataset can reveal more insights into the compositionality in terms of the contribution from the constituents. Future directions of this work include token based disambiguation of phrases and designing more sophisticated constituent based models. Extending this study on other kinds of phrases such as adjective-noun, verb particle, verb-noun phrases may throw more light into our understanding of compositionality.

Acknowledgements

This work is supported by the European Commission via the EU FP7 INDECT project, Grant No.218086, Research area: SEC-2007-1.2-01 Intelligent Urban Environment Observation System.

References

Timothy Baldwin, Colin Bannard, Takaaki Tanaka, and Dominic Widdows. 2003. An empirical model of multiword expression decomposability. In *Proceedings of the ACL 2003 workshop on Multiword expressions: analysis, acquisition and treatment*, MWE '03.

Colin Bannard, Timothy Baldwin, and Alex Lascarides. 2003. A statistical approach to the semantics of verb-particles. In *Proceedings of the ACL 2003 workshop on Multiword expressions: analysis, acquisition and treatment*, MWE '03.

Chris Biemann and Eugenie Giesbrecht. 2011. Distributional Semantics and Compositionality 2011: Shared Task Description and Results. In *Proceedings of DISCo-2011 in conjunction with ACL 2011*.

Paul Cook, Afsaneh Fazly, and Suzanne Stevenson. 2007. Pulling their weight: exploiting syntactic forms for the automatic identification of idiomatic expressions in context. In *Proceedings of the Workshop on a Broader Perspective on Multiword Expressions*, MWE '07.

Afsaneh Fazly, Paul Cook, and Suzanne Stevenson. 2009. Unsupervised type and token identification of idiomatic expressions. *Computional. Linguististics.*, 35:61–103, March.

Christiane Fellbaum, editor. 1998. *WordNet: An Electronic Lexical Database*. The MIT Press.

A. Ferraresi, E. Zanchetta, M. Baroni, and S. Bernardini. 2008. Introducing and evaluating ukWaC, a very large web-derived corpus of English. In *Proceedings of the WAC4 Workshop at LREC 2008*.

Raymond W. Gibbs. 1989. Understanding and Literal Meaning. *Cognitive Science*, 13(2):243–251.

Eugenie Giesbrecht. 2009. In Search of Semantic Compositionality in Vector Spaces. In *Proceedings of the 17th International Conference on Conceptual Structures: Conceptual Structures: Leveraging Semantic Technologies*, ICCS '09.

Emiliano Raul Guevara. 2011. Computing Semantic Compositionality in Distributional Semantics. In *Proceedings of the Ninth International Conference on Computational Semantics*, IWCS '2011.

Graham Katz and Eugenie Giesbrecht. 2006. Automatic identification of non-compositional multiword expressions using latent semantic analysis. In *Proceedings of the Workshop on Multiword Expressions: Identifying and Exploiting Underlying Properties*, MWE '06.

Ioannis Korkontzelos and Suresh Manandhar. 2009. Detecting compositionality in multi-word expressions. In *Proceedings of the ACL-IJCNLP 2009 Conference Short Papers*.

Dekang Lin. 1999. Automatic identification of noncompositional phrases. In *Proceedings of the ACL 1999*.

Diana McCarthy, Bill Keller, and John Carroll. 2003. Detecting a continuum of compositionality in phrasal verbs. In *Proceedings of the ACL 2003 workshop on Multiword expressions: analysis, acquisition and treatment*, MWE '03.

Diana McCarthy, Sriram Venkatapathy, and Aravind K. Joshi. 2007. Detecting Compositionality of Verb-Object Combinations using Selectional Preferences. In *Proceedings of EMNLP-CoNLL 2007*.

Jeff Mitchell and Mirella Lapata. 2008. Vector-based Models of Semantic Composition. In *Proceedings of ACL-08: HLT*, pages 236–244, Columbus, Ohio.

Geoffrey Nunberg, Thomas Wasow, and Ivan A. Sag. 1994. Idioms. *Language*, 70(3):491–539.

Ted Pedersen. 2011. Identifying Collocations to Measure Compositionality : Shared Task System Description . In *Proceedings of DISCo-2011 in conjunction with ACL 2011*.

Siva Reddy, Diana McCarthy, Suresh Manandhar, and Spandana Gella. 2011. Exemplar-Based Word-Space Model for Compositionality Detection: Shared Task System Description. In *Proceedings of the ACL Workshop on Distributional Semantics and Compositionality*.

Ivan A. Sag, Timothy Baldwin, Francis Bond, Ann A. Copestake, and Dan Flickinger. 2002. Multiword Expressions: A Pain in the Neck for NLP. In *Proceedings of the CICLing 2002*.

Magnus Sahlgren. 2006. *The Word-Space Model: Using distributional analysis to represent syntagmatic and paradigmatic relations between words in high-dimensional vector spaces*. Ph.D. thesis, Stockholm University.

Patrick Schone and Daniel Jurafsky. 2001. Is Knowledge-Free Induction of Multiword Unit Dictionary Headwords a Solved Problem? In *Proceedings of EMNLP 2001*.

Rion Snow, Brendan O'Connor, Daniel Jurafsky, and Andrew Y. Ng. 2008. Cheap and fast—but is it good?: evaluating non-expert annotations for natural language tasks. In *Proceedings of EMNLP 2008*.

Caroline Sporleder and Linlin Li. 2009. Unsupervised recognition of literal and non-literal use of idiomatic expressions. In *Proceedings of the EACL 2009*.

Debra A. Titone and Cynthia M. Connine. 1999. On the compositional and noncompositional nature of idiomatic expressions. *Journal of Pragmatics*, 31(12):1655 – 1674. Literal and Figurative Language.

Sriram Venkatapathy and Aravind K. Joshi. 2005. Measuring the relative compositionality of verb-noun (V-N) collocations by integrating features. In *Proceedings of the HLT-EMNLP 2005*.

Dominic Widdows. 2008. Semantic Vector Products: Some Initial Investigations. In *Second AAAI Symposium on Quantum Interaction, Oxford*, March.

Feature-Rich Log-Linear Lexical Model for Latent Variable PCFG Grammars

Zhongqiang Huang and **Mary Harper**
Department of Computer Science
University of Maryland, College Park
{zqhuang,mharper}@umd.edu

Abstract

Context-free grammars with latent annotations (PCFG-LA) have been found to be effective for parsing many languages; however, currently their lexical model may be subject to over-fitting and requires language engineering to handle out-of-vocabulary (OOV) words. Inspired by previous studies that have incorporated rich features into generative models, we propose to use a feature-rich log-linear lexical model to train PCFG-LA grammars that are more robust to rare and OOV words. The proposed lexical model has three advantages: over-fitting is alleviated via regularization, OOV words are modeled using rich features, and lexical features are exploited for grammar induction. Our approach results in significantly more accurate PCFG-LA grammars that are flexible to train for different languages (with test F scores of 90.5, 85.0, and 81.9 on WSJ, CTB6, and ATB, respectively).

1 Introduction

The latent variable approach of (Matsuzaki et al., 2005; Petrov et al., 2006) is capable of learning high accuracy context-free grammars directly from a raw treebank, and has achieved state-of-the-art parsing accuracies on multiple languages, outperforming many other parsers that are engineered for performance in a particular language (Petrov, 2009; Green and Manning, 2010). However, the lexical model of PCFG-LA grammars (responsible for emitting words from latent POS tags) is not designed to effectively handle OOV words universally. In fact, hand-crafted rules designed for English OOV words were used in the multi-language study of (Petrov, 2009) for non-English languages, leaving room for further improvement for each of the languages studied.

Huang and Harper (2009) and Attia et al. (2010) studied the impact of rare and OOV word handling for parsing with PCFG-LA grammars, especially for non-English languages. They both found that language-specific handling of OOV words significantly improves parsing performance. However, hand tailoring of the language-specific module with expert knowledge may produce suboptimal results, and would not be applicable to new languages. Petrov and Klein (2008) presented a discriminatively trained PCFG-LA model that makes use of rich morphological features for handling OOV words and obtained improved performance on some languages; however, this method was considerably less accurate than its strong generative counterpart on English WSJ.

Berg-Kirkpatrick et al. (2010) demonstrated that each generation step of a generative process can be modeled as a locally normalized log-linear model so that rich features can be incorporated for learning unsupervised models, e.g., POS induction. Inspired by their work, we propose a log-linear lexical model for generative PCFG-LA grammars. It maintains the advantages of generative models, while providing a principled way to: 1) alleviate over-fitting via regularization, 2) handle OOV words using rich features, and 3) exploit lexical features for grammar induction. The proposed approach produces significant improvements for all of the three studied languages.

The rest of the paper is structured as follows. We first review PCFG-LA grammars and issues related to the lexical model in Section 2, and then describe the proposed log-linear lexical model and the training methods in Sections 3 and 4, respectively. Experiments are presented in Section 5. Section 6 concludes this paper.

2 PCFG-LA Grammar

PCFG grammars with latent annotations (Matsuzaki et al., 2005; Petrov et al., 2006) augment the observed parse trees in the treebank with a latent variable at each tree node. Each latent variable effectively refines an observed category t into a set of latent subcategories $\{t_x | x = 1, \cdots, |t|\}$, where $|t|$ denotes the number of latent tags split from t. Each syntactic category in the original tree in Figure 1(a) is split into multiple latent subcategories, and that parse tree is decomposed into many derivation trees whose non-terminals are latent categories; Figure 1(b) depicts one such derivation tree, where each grammar rule expands a latent non-terminal category into a sequence of latent non-terminals and/or terminal words, e.g., VP-4→VBD-5 NP-6.

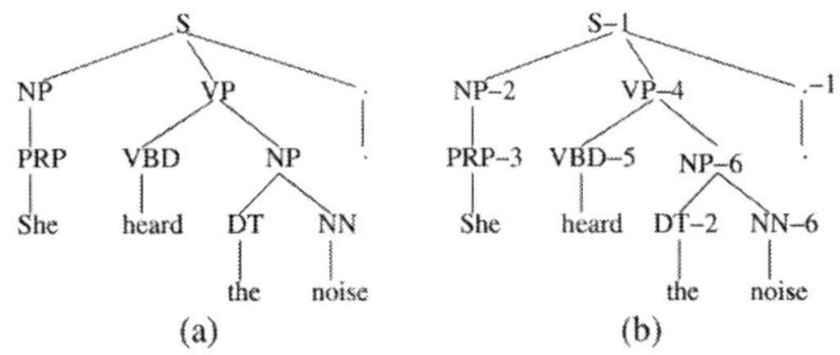

Figure 1: (a) treebank tree (b) derivation tree

The objective of PCFG-LA training is to induce a grammar with latent variables that maximizes the probability of the training trees. Given a PCFG-LA grammar with model parameter θ, $\mathcal{R}$ denotes the set of grammar rules, $\mathcal{D}(T)$ the set of derivation trees for parse tree T, and $\mathcal{R}(T)$ and $\mathcal{R}(D)$ the sets of rules comprising T and D, respectively. The probability of T under the grammar is computed as:

$$\mathrm{P}_\theta(T) = \sum_{D \in \mathcal{D}(T)} \mathrm{P}_\theta(D) = \sum_{D \in \mathcal{D}(T)} \prod_{r \in \mathcal{R}(D)} \mathrm{P}_\theta(r)$$

An EM-algorithm is used to optimize θ based on the training likelihood. The E-step computes the expected count e_r of rule r over the training set $\mathcal{T}$ under the current model parameter θ':

$$e_r \leftarrow \sum_{T \in \mathcal{T}} \sum_{r' \in \mathcal{R}(T)} \delta(r', r) \mathrm{P}_{\theta'}(r' | T) \qquad (1)$$

where $\delta(\cdot, \cdot)$ is an indicator function that returns 1 if the two operands are identical and 0 otherwise, and $\mathrm{P}_{\theta'}(r'|T)$ is the posterior probability of having (latent) rule r' in parse tree T. The M-step aims to maximize the intermediate objective:

$$l(\theta) = \sum_{r \in \mathcal{R}} e_r \log \mathrm{P}_\theta(r) \qquad (2)$$

which results in the following update formula for lexical rule probability $\theta_{t_x \to w} = \mathrm{P}_\theta(w|t_x)$:

$$\mathrm{P}_\theta(w|t_x) = \frac{e_{t_x,w}}{\sum_{w'} e_{t_x,w'}} \qquad (3)$$

where $e_{t_x,w}$ denotes the expected count of lexical rule $r{=}t_x{\to}w$. The phrasal rule probabilities are updated similarly.

In order to allocate the grammar complexity to where it is most needed, Petrov et al. (2006) developed a simple split-and-merge procedure. In every split-merge (SM) round, each latent category is first split into two, and the model is re-estimated using several rounds of EM iterations. A likelihood criterion is then used to merge back the least useful splits. The result is that categories, such as NP and VB, that occur frequently in different syntactic environments, are split more heavily than categories such as UH (interjection). This approach also creates a hierarchy of latent categories that enables efficient coarse-to-fine parsing (Petrov and Klein, 2007).

We next discuss two important issues related to the lexical model of PCFG-LA grammars: over-fitting and OOV word handling.

2.1 Over-fitting

As the number of latent annotations increases, a PCFG-LA grammar has an increasing power to fit the training data through EM training, leading to over-fitting. In order to counteract this behavior, Petrov et al. (2006) introduced a linear smoothing method to smooth lexical emission probabilities:

$$\bar{\mathrm{P}} = \frac{1}{|t|} \sum_x \mathrm{P}_\theta(w|t_x)$$
$$\mathrm{P}_\theta(w|t_x) \leftarrow \epsilon \bar{\mathrm{P}} + (1-\epsilon) \mathrm{P}_\theta(w|t_x)$$

A similar smoothing method was used for phrasal rules.

While the above method has been found to be effective, Huang and Harper (2009) observed that rare words suffer more from over-fitting than frequent words and suggested tying rare words together when estimating their emission probabilities. Using their approach, all words with a frequency less than a threshold τ are mapped to symbol *rare*[1], and their emission probability $\mathrm{P}_\theta(w|t_x)$ is set in proportion to their co-occurrences with the surface POS tag:

$$\mathrm{P}_\theta(w|t_x) = \frac{c_{t,w}}{\sum_{w': c_{\cdot,w'} < \tau} c_{t,w'}} \mathrm{P}_\theta(\mathit{rare}|t_x)$$

[1] τ is tuned on the development set.

where $c_{\cdot,w}$ and $c_{t,w}$ are the observed counts of words and word/tag pairs, respectively, and $\mathrm{P}_\theta(rare|t_x)$ is a free parameter estimated by the EM algorithm. This constraint greatly reduces the number of free parameters and was found to significantly improve parsing accuracies.

2.2 OOV Handling

Since the lexical model can only generate words observed in the training data, a separate module is needed to handle OOV words that can appear in novel test sentences. A simple approach might be to estimate the emission probability of an OOV word w based on how likely it is that t_x generates a rare word in the training data:

$$\mathrm{P}_\theta(w|t_x) = \mathrm{P}_\theta(rare|t_x)$$

We call this type of approach the *simple* method[2].

A better approach would exploit the word formation process for the language being modeled. As with other generative English parsers, the PCFG-LA parser implementation of (Petrov et al., 2006) classifies OOV words into a set of OOV signatures based on the presence of features such as capital letters, digits, dashes, as well as a list of indicative suffixes (e.g., *-ing*, *-ion*, *-er*), and estimates the emission probability of an OOV word w given a latent tag t_x as:

$$\mathrm{P}_\theta(w|t_x) \propto \mathrm{P}_\theta(s|t_x)$$

where s is the OOV signature for w and $\mathrm{P}_\theta(s|t_x)$ is computed by $e_{t_x,s}/e_{t_x,\cdot}$.

While this approach performs well for English, the same OOV word handling module would not be adequate for other languages since they have different word formation processes, which should be exploited for better disambiguation of OOV words. For example, Huang and Harper (2009) improved Chinese parsing performance by estimating the emission probability of an OOV word using the geometric average of the emission probabilities of all of the characters ch_k in the word:

$$\mathrm{P}_\theta(w|t_x) = \sqrt[n]{\prod_{ch_k \in w, \mathrm{P}_\theta(ch_k|t_x) \neq 0} \mathrm{P}_\theta(ch_k|t_x)}$$

where $n = |\{ch_k \in w | \mathrm{P}_\theta(ch_k|t_x) \neq 0\}|$. As will be shown later in Section 5, handling Arabic OOV words in a similar way to Chinese produces improved parsing performance on Arabic[3]; however, the aforementioned language dependent OOV handling approaches are most likely suboptimal and designing a method for a new language could be nontrivial. We call this type of approach the *heuristic* method.

Researchers have exploited discriminative parsing models (Finkel et al., 2008; Petrov and Klein, 2008) to utilize naturally occurring overlapping features, including features for OOV handling. The discriminative version of the PCFG-LA grammar (Petrov and Klein, 2008) was found to be more accurate than its generative counterpart on some languages, partially due to its use of regularization and multi-scale grammars to alleviate data sparsity and rich features to improve OOV word handling. However, such a model is much slower to train and considerably less accurate on English WSJ than its strong generative counterpart. Hence, we will investigate a locally normalized log-linear lexical model to take advantage of rich features within the generative learning framework.

3 Log-Linear Lexical Model for PCFG-LA grammars

Instead of treating each $\mathrm{P}_\theta(w|t_x)$ as a free parameter of a multinomial distribution as in a standard PCFG-LA grammar, we first model the conditional probability of latent tag t_x given the surface POS tag t and word w using a log-linear model:

$$\mathrm{P}_\phi(t_x|t,w) = \frac{\exp\langle\phi, \mathbf{f}(t_x,w)\rangle}{\sum_{x'} \exp\langle\phi, \mathbf{f}(t_{x'},w)\rangle} \quad (4)$$

where $\mathbf{f}(t_x, w)$ represents the feature vector extracted from the pair (t_x, w), ϕ is the feature weight vector, and the denominator sums over all latent tags for POS tag t. This model is applicable to both known and OOV words as long as there are active features; otherwise, a uniform latent tag distribution would be assumed. We call this the *latent lexical model* as it deals with the distribution of latent tags.

The conditional probability of t_x given word w can then be expressed as:

$$\mathrm{P}_\theta(t_x|w) = \mathrm{P}_\theta(t_x,t|w) = \mathrm{P}_\phi(t_x|t,w)\mathrm{P}(t|w)$$

and finally the word emission probability given a latent tag can be computed via Bayes' rule:

$$\mathrm{P}_\theta(w|t_x) = \frac{\mathrm{P}_\phi(t_x|t,w)\mathrm{P}(t|w)\mathrm{P}(w)}{\sum_{w'} \mathrm{P}_\phi(t_x|t,w')\mathrm{P}(t|w')\mathrm{P}(w')} \quad (5)$$

[2] This method is used in the simple lexicon of the Berkeley parser.

[3] We use prefixes and suffixes up to three characters for handling Arabic OOV words.

This new lexical model is composed of the latent lexical model $P_\phi(t_x|t, w)$ and two other parts: $P(t|w)$ and $P(w)$, which are computed differently for known and OOV words.

For words observed in the training data, both $P(t|w)$ are $P(w)$ are computed using the maximum-likelihood estimation (based on the observed training trees) so that $P_\theta(w|t_x)$ forms a proper distribution of observed words during grammar induction.

For OOV words, we use a log-linear *OOV model* to estimate the POS tag distribution:

$$P_\gamma(t|w) = \frac{\exp\langle\gamma, \mathbf{g}(t, w)\rangle}{\sum_{t'} \exp\langle\gamma, \mathbf{g}(t', w)\rangle} \quad (6)$$

where $\mathbf{g}(t, w)$ represents the feature vector extracted from the pair (t, w), γ is the feature weight vector, and the denominator sums over all POS tags with active features. The *simple* approach in Subsection 2.2 is used when no feature is active. $P(w)$ is approximated by one over the number of training tokens. It should be noted that $P_\gamma(t|w)$ may use different features than $P_\phi(t_x|t, w)$.

Compared with modeling $P_\theta(w|t_x)$ directly as a multinomial distribution, the new lexical model separates $P(t|w)$ from $P_\phi(t_x|t, w)$, offering three important advantages:

- The parameter ϕ of the latent lexical model $P_\phi(t_x|t, w)$ can be smoothed through regularization to address data sparsity.
- Rich features can be utilized in the OOV model $P_\gamma(t|w)$ to estimate POS tag distributions of OOV words for a variety of languages. This is important when working on new languages.
- Rich features can be utilized in the latent lexical model $P_\phi(t_x|t, w)$ to guide the induction of latent POS tags.

The reader should note that Berg-Kirkpatrick et al. (2010) modeled $P_\theta(w|t_x)$ directly using a log-linear model:

$$P_\phi(w|t_x) = \frac{\exp\langle\phi, \mathbf{f}(t_x, w)\rangle}{\sum_{w'} \exp\langle\phi, \mathbf{f}(t_x, w')\rangle}$$

This would be problematic for our parsing model because it would not be trained to estimate the probability of OOV words given a latent tag. For parsing, we must model OOV words that can appear in previously unseen sentences. One might compute the numerator for an OOV word based on its features and divide it by a denominator approximated using the words in the training data, but such an estimate is inaccurate and results in poor performance in our preliminary experiments.

We also choose not to model $P_\theta(t_x|w)$ directly using a log-linear model:

$$P_\phi(t_x|w) = \frac{\exp\langle\phi, \mathbf{f}(t_x, w)\rangle}{\sum_{t'} \sum_{x'} \exp\langle\phi, \mathbf{f}(t'_{x'}, w)\rangle}$$

and compute $P_\theta(w|t_x)$ via Bayes' rule. Such a model cannot guarantee that the probability $P_\theta(t|w)$ computed by $\sum_x P_\theta(t_x|w)$ is equal to the maximum likelihood estimate, which is a reasonable constraint.

4 Model Training

The parameter θ for our parser model consists of ϕ for the log-linear latent lexical model, γ for the log-linear OOV model, and ψ for the phrasal rule expansion probabilities. The other parameters (e.g., $P(t|w)$ and $P(w)$ for known words and $P(rare|t_x)$) can be computed based on observable or fractional counts once θ is determined.

γ of the OOV model is independent of the latent categories, and we simply use a gradient-based optimization approach to maximize the following objective:

$$l'(\gamma) = \sum_{t,w} c_{t,w} \log P_\gamma(t|w) - \kappa' ||\gamma||^2$$

where $c_{t,w}$ is the count of the pair (t, w) in the training data, and κ' is the regularization weight.

For parameters ψ and ϕ, we follow the split-merge training procedure in (Petrov et al., 2006) to induce latent categories. Given a set of latent categories, the goal is to find θ that maximizes the regularized training likelihood:

$$L(\theta) = \sum_{T \in \mathcal{T}} \log P_\theta(T) - \kappa ||\phi||^2 \quad (7)$$

where $\kappa||\phi||^2$ is the regularization term[4] for the feature weights of the latent lexical model.

The two optimization approaches described in (Berg-Kirkpatrick et al., 2010) can be extended naturally to our problem. One approach is EM-based with an E-step identical to Equation 1 in

[4]Both κ' and κ are tuned on the development set. We could also use L1 regularization and leave it to future work.

Section 2. The objective of the M-step becomes:

$$l(\theta) = \sum_{w \to t_x \in \mathcal{R}_l} e_{t_x,w} \log \mathrm{P}_\phi(w|t_x) - \kappa||\phi||^2 + \sum_{r \in \mathcal{R}_p} e_r \log \mathrm{P}_\psi(r)$$

where we separate the set of rules $\mathcal{R}$ into lexical rules $\mathcal{R}_l$ and phrasal rules $\mathcal{R}_p$. The phrasal rule parameter ψ is updated as before by normalizing the expected rule counts and is smoothed in the same way as in (Petrov et al., 2006). The intermediate objective function $l(\phi)$ related to ϕ, i.e.,

$$l(\phi) = \sum_{w \to t_x \in \mathcal{R}_l} e_{t_x,w} \log \mathrm{P}_\phi(w|t_x) - \kappa||\phi||^2$$

can be optimized by a gradient descent optimization algorithm (we use LBFGS (Liu and Nocedal, 1989)). Its gradient has the following form:

$$\nabla l(\phi) = \sum_{w \to t_x \in \mathcal{R}_l} e^*_{t_x,w} \Delta_{t_x,w}(\phi) - 2\kappa \cdot \phi$$

$$\Delta_{t_x,w}(\phi) = \mathbf{f}(t_x, w) - \sum_{x'} \mathrm{P}_\phi(t_{x'}|w,t)\mathbf{f}(t_{x'}, w)$$

where $e^*_{t_x,w} = e_{t_x,w} - e_{t_x,\cdot}\mathrm{P}_\phi(w|t_x)$.

It can be shown that $l(\phi)$ is not a concave function with respect to ϕ, but this created no problems in our experiments. It should be noted that if we set the regularization weight κ to 0, the maximum of $l(\phi)$ is achieved when $\mathrm{P}_\phi(w|t_x)$ is set to $e_{t_x,w}/e_{t_x,\cdot}$, which is identical to the update formula in Equation 3, and would thus be unable to use rich features. This is less of an issue when regularization takes effect as it favors common discriminative features to reduce the penalty term.

The second approach, which was found to outperform the EM-based approach in (Berg-Kirkpatrick et al., 2010), optimizes on the regularized log-likelihood (Equation 7) directly by updating both ψ and ϕ using a gradient descent approach. In order to convert this to an unconstrained optimization problem[5], we set each phrasal rule expansion probability ψ_i as the output of a log-linear model, i.e., $\psi_i = \exp(\psi'_i)/Z$ with Z being the normalization factor, and treat ψ' as the parameter for the phrasal rules to be optimized. The gradient of $L(\theta)$ with respect to ϕ turns out to be the same as in the first approach (Salakhutdinov et al., 2003). The gradient of $L(\theta)$ with respect to ψ' can be derived similarly. We omit the details here due to space limitations.

In the original EM-based training approach (Petrov et al., 2006), many of the rule expansion probabilities become very small and are pruned to dramatically reduce the grammar size. The phrasal rule probabilities computed from the log-linear model with parameter ψ' are not usually low enough to be pruned, due to the fact that a large decrease in ψ'_i results in a much smaller change in ψ_i when ψ_i is already relatively small. In order to address this problem, we combine the two optimization approaches together: first run rounds of EM-based optimization to initialize the grammar parameters and prune many of the useless phrasal rules, and then switch to the direct gradient descent optimization approach. This combined approach outperforms the standalone EM-based approach in our study and is used in the experiments reported in this paper.

5 Experiments

In this section, we will show the effect of rare word smoothing and OOV handling on the accuracy of the standard PCFG-LA grammars, and investigate how the proposed feature-rich lexical model addresses these problems. In what follows, we first describe the experimental data and then the results of the standard PCFG-LA grammars. We then describe the features and results of the PCFG-LA grammars with log-linear lexical models, and present some analyses. Finally, additional features are discussed and the final test results are compared with the literature.

5.1 Data & Setup

We experiment with three languages: English, Chinese, and Arabic. For English, we used the WSJ Penn Treebank (Marcus et al., 1999) and the commonly used data splits (Charniak, 2000). For Chinese, we used the Penn Chinese Treebank 6.0 (CTB6) (Xue et al., 2005) and the preparation steps and data splits in (Huang and Harper, 2009). For Arabic, we used the Penn Arabic Treebank (ATB) (Maamouri et al., 2009) and the preparation steps[6] and data splits in (Green and Manning, 2010; Chiang et al., 2006). Table 1 provides gross statistics for each treebank. As we can see, CTB6 and ATB both have a higher OOV rate than WSJ,

[5]The elements of ψ are constrained to form proper probability distributions.

[6]Except that clitic marks were removed, which results in about 0.3 degradation in F score (p.c.).

and hence have greater need for effective OOV handling.

	Statistics	Train	Dev	Test
	#sents	39832	1700	2416
English	#tokens	950.0k	40.1k	56.7k
(WSJ)	%oov_types	-	12.8%	13.2%
	%oov_tokens	-	2.8%	2.5%
	#sents	24416	1904	1975
Chinese	#tokens	678.8k	51.2k	52.9k
(CTB6)	%oov_types	-	20.6%	20.9%
	%oov_tokens	-	5.0%	5.3%
	#sents	18818	2318	2313
Arabic	#tokens	597.9k	70.7k	70.1k
(ATB)	%oov_types	-	15.6%	16.7%
	%oov_tokens	-	3.2%	3.4%

Table 1: Gross Statistics of the treebanks.

Due to the variability (caused by random initialization) among the grammars (Petrov, 2010), we train 10 grammars with different seeds in each experiment and report their average F score on the development set. The best grammar selected using the development set is used for evaluation on the test set.

5.2 Standard PCFG-LA Grammars

We first study the effect of rare word smoothing and OOV handling on the standard PCFG-LA grammars using our reimplementation of the Berkeley parser. The *no+simple* row in Table 2 represents the baseline, for which the grammars are trained without rare word smoothing described in Subsection 2.1 and OOV words are handled by the simple method described in Subsection 2.2. Each language-dependent heuristic-based OOV word handling method improves parsing accuracies, and the rare word smoothing method provides even greater improvement across the languages. Their combination results in further improvement. This confirms that both over-fitting and OOV words are issues to consider for training accurate PCFG-LA grammars.

Rare Word Smoothing	OOV	WSJ	CTB6	ATB
no	simple	89.86	82.52	79.12
no	heuristic	90.07	82.98	79.44
yes	simple	90.53	83.25	80.30
yes	heuristic	90.69	83.73	80.64

Table 2: The effect of rare word smoothing and OOV handling on parsing F scores evaluated on the respective development set.

5.3 Log-Linear Lexical Model

Here we investigate a core set of features that have proven effective for POS tagging to demonstrate the effectiveness of our model and its robustness across languages, and leave it to future work to include additional features as discussed in Subsection 5.5. Table 3 lists the templates we used to extract predicates on words. For the log-linear OOV model, we use the *full* feature set, i.e., (t, pred) pairs extracted using all of the predicates. For the log-linear latent lexical model, we experiment with two feature sets: 1) the *wid* feature set containing only (t_x, wid) pairs, which are the same as those used in the standard PCFG-LA grammars, 2) the *full* feature set using all of the predicates.

Predicate	Explanation
$\delta(w = \cdot)$	word identity (wid)
$\delta(\text{hasDigit}(w) = \cdot)$	contains a digit?
$\delta(\text{hasHyphen}(w) = \cdot)$	contains a hyphen?
$\delta(\text{initCap}(w) = \cdot)$	first letter capitalized?
$\delta(\text{prefix}_k(w) = \cdot)$	prefix of length $k \leq 3$
$\delta(\text{suffix}_k(w) = \cdot)$	suffix of length $k \leq 3$

Table 3: Predicate templates on word w.

We first evaluate the effectiveness of regularization and the log-linear OOV model by training the latent lexical model using the *wid* feature set with regularization and examining different OOV handling methods. As shown in Table 4, the *wid+simple* and *wid+heuristic* approaches[7] produce results comparable to the corresponding PCFG-LA grammars trained with rare word smoothing and respective OOV handling. This shows that regularizing the latent lexical model alleviates data sparsity, however, we will illustrate in Subsection 5.4 that this is achieved in a different way than rare word smoothing.

The log-linear OOV model using the *full* feature set results in improved parsing performance over all languages, with the most improvement seen on Arabic (0.71 F), followed by Chinese (0.28 F), confirming that the log-linear OOV model is more accurate than the heuristic approach, and can be flexibly used for different languages. The improvement on English is marginal possibly because the signature-based OOV features are sufficiently accurate for handling English unknown

[7] Training the latent lexical model using the *wid* feature set and handling OOV words using the *simple* or *heuristic* approach.

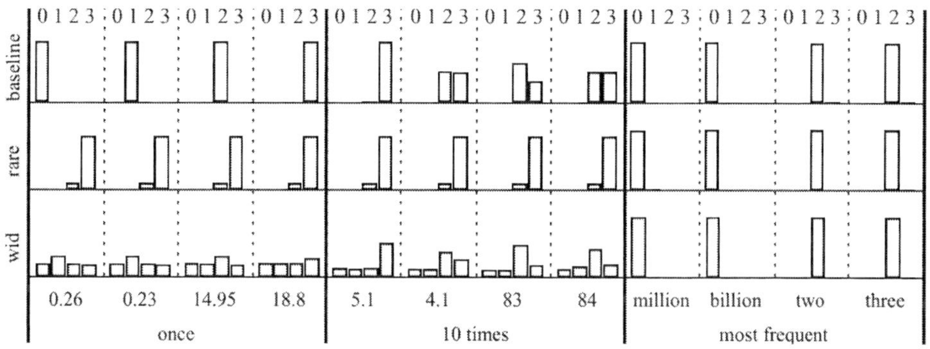

Figure 2: The conditional distribution $P(t_x|t, w)$ of latent tags for selected cardinal numbers (e.g., 0.26, million) that appear only once, 10 times, or frequently for standard PCFG-LA grammars trained with (labeled rare) or without (labeled baseline) rare word smoothing and for PCFG-LA grammars with regularized feature-rich lexical model using the *wid* feature set (labeled wid). The distribution is represented by the four bars separated by dotted vertical lines, and each bar represents the conditional probability of a latent tag.

words after years of expert crafting.

We next investigate the effect of training the latent lexical model using the *full* feature set. Compared with the *wid+full* model, the *full+full* model improves 0.38 F on Arabic and 0.27 F on Chinese, despite the fact that the additional features are very simple, mostly prefixes and suffixes of words. The improvement on English is again marginal possibly because the features do not provide such insights on fine-grained syntactic subcategories (e.g., suffix *-ed* is indicative of past tense verbs, but not their sub-categories). Admittedly, many of the features are noisy, but as we will show in Subsection 5.4, some of the features can guide the learning of the latent categories to reflect the similarity between syntactically similar words of the same POS type.

Compared with the baseline (*no+simple* in Table 2), the feature-rich *full+full* model significantly improves parsing F scores by 1.03, 1.66, and 2.67 absolute on English, Chinese, and Arabic, respectively.

Latent Lexical	OOV	WSJ	CTB6	ATB
wid	simple	90.54	83.18	80.32
wid	heuristic	90.71	83.63	80.70
wid	full	90.81	83.91	81.41
full	full	90.89	84.18	81.79

Table 4: The effect of features (wid vs. full) for training the latent lexical model and the OOV handling methods (simple, heuristic, or the log-linear model using the full feature set) on parsing performance (F score) on the development set.

5.4 Analysis

We examine in Figure 2 the effect of regularization and rare word smoothing on the learned rules by looking at the distribution $P(t_x|t, w)$ for PCFG-LA grammars trained in different ways[8]. For standard PCFG-LA grammars trained without rare word smoothing (labeled baseline), rare words have sparse distributions of latent tags, which are determined solely based on limited contexts and are thus not reliable. The rare word smoothing approach (labeled rare) collapses all rare words into a single token so that $P(t_x|t, w) = P(t_x|t, \mathit{rare})$ is identical for any rare word w. This constraint greatly reduces data sparsity; however, treating all rare words as one token could eliminate too much lexical information (e.g., the distribution of latent tags is the same for all rare cardinal numbers no matter whether they appear only once or 10 times). Regularization of the log-linear latent lexical model (labeled wid) favors a uniform distribution (zero penalty when all feature weights are zero). There is not much evidence to skew the distribution from uniform for rare words. However, when more evidence is available, the distribution becomes smoothly skewed to reflect the different syntactic preferences of the individual words, and it can eventually become as spiky as in the other approaches given sufficient evidence.

In order to provide some insights into why parsing accuracies are improved for Arabic and Chinese by using the *full* feature set when training the latent lexical model, we look at the country names

[8]For standard PCFG-LA grammars, $P(t_x|t, w)$ is simply computed by $e_{t_x,w}/e_{t,w}$; whereas, for the feature-rich lexical model, $P(t_x|t, w)$ is computed from the latent lexical model.

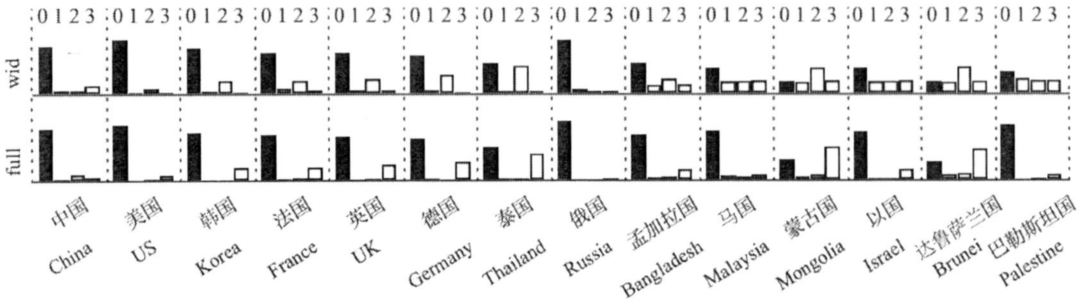

Figure 3: The conditional distribution $P(t_x|t, w)$ of latent tags for selected country names (proper nouns) listed in order of decreasing frequency from the Chinese treebank (English translations are provided under Chinese names), after training using the *wid* and the *full* feature set, respectively. The distribution is represented by the four bars separated by dotted vertical lines, and each bar represents the conditional probability of a latent tag. The preferred latent tag for country names is highlighted in black.

that end with the character 国 (country) in the Chinese treebank. These names appear in similar contexts and would be expected to favor certain latent tag or tags; however, when training using the *wid* feature set, this is only true for the frequent names as shown in Figure 3. For the rare names, there is not much evidence to divert the distribution away from uniform. When training with the *full* feature set, the suffix1=国 predicate is active for all of those country names and has a large feature weight associated with the preferred latent tag. As a result, the distribution of latent tags for the rare names is skewed more toward the preferred latent tag due to strong evidence from that suffix feature.

5.5 Other Features

Our model supports any local features that can be extracted from the pair (t_x, w), including the language-dependent features studied in (Attia et al., 2010). In addition, features related to word semantics (e.g., using WordNet (Fellbaum, 1998)) or word clusters (e.g., using unsupervised clustering (Brown et al., 1992; Koo et al., 2008; Goyal and Daume, 2011)) might also be beneficial for modeling $P_\phi(t_x|t, w)$ and/or $P_\gamma(t|w)$. Features extracted from (t, w) could also be helpful for providing some smoothing effect across the latent tags. Moreover, it might be beneficial to perform feature selection prior to training. We leave this to future work.

5.6 Final Results

Table 5 compares the final test results of our best grammars (the *full+full* approach) with the literature[9]. Our PCFG-LA grammars with a feature-rich lexical model significantly outperform the standard PCFG-LA grammars of (Petrov and Klein, 2007) for all of the three languages, especially on Chinese (+1.6 F) and Arabic (+2.2 F).

TB	Parser	LP	LR	F
WSJ	Charniak (2000)	89.9	89.5	89.7
	Petrov and Klein (2007)	90.2	90.1	90.1
	Petrov and Klein (2008)	-	-	89.4
	Huang and Harper (2009)	90.4	89.9	90.1
	This Paper	**90.8**	**90.3**	**90.5**
CTB6	Charniak (2000)	80.5	79.5	80.0
	Petrov and Klein (2007)	84.0	82.9	83.4
	Huang and Harper (2009)	85.1	83.2	84.1
	This Paper	**85.9**	**84.2**	**85.0**
ATB	Petrov and Klein (2007)	80.5	78.9	79.7
	This Paper	**82.7**	**81.2**	**81.9**

Table 5: Final test set accuracies.

6 Conclusions

We have presented a feature-rich lexical model for PCFG-LA grammars to: 1) alleviate over-fitting via regularization, 2) handle OOV words using rich features, and 3) exploit lexical features for grammar induction. Experiments show that the proposed approach allows us to train more effective PCFG-LA grammars for more accurate and robust parsing of three different languages. It is expected that even more accurate parsers can be produced by using this approach together with self-training (Huang and Harper, 2009) and/or product models (Petrov, 2010; Huang et al., 2010).

Acknowledgments

This research was supported in part by NSF IIS-0703859. We would like to thank Spence Green for providing the processed Arabic Treebank data and lots of insightful suggestions.

[9]All of the parsers from the referenced papers are trained and evaluated using the data splits in our experiments.

References

Mohammed Attia, Jennifer Foster, Deirdre Hogan, Joseph Le Roux, Lamia Tounsi, and Josef van Genabith. 2010. Handling unknown words in statistical latent-variable parsing models for Arabic, English and French. In *Proceedings of the North American Chapter of the Association for Computational Linguistics conference*.

Taylor Berg-Kirkpatrick, Alexandre Bouchard-Côté, John DeNero, and Dan Klein. 2010. Painless unsupervised learning with features. In *Proceedings of the Conference of the North American Chapter of the Association for Computational Linguistics on Human Language Technology*.

Peter F. Brown, Vincent J. Della Pietra, Peter V. deSouza, Jenifer C. Lai, and Robert L. Mercer. 1992. Class-based n-gram models of natural language. *Computational Linguistics*.

Eugene Charniak. 2000. A maximum-entropy-inspired parser. In *Proceedings of the Annual Meeting of the Association for Computational Linguistics*.

David Chiang, Mona Diab, Nizar Habash, Owen Rambow, and Safiullah Shareef. 2006. Parsing Arabic dialects. In *Conference of the European Chapter of the Association for Computational Linguistics*.

Christiane Fellbaum. 1998. *WordNet: An Electronic Lexical Database*. The MIT Press.

Jenny Rose Finkel, Alex Kleeman, and Christopher D. Manning. 2008. Efficient, feature-based, conditional random field parsing. In *Proceedings of the Annual Meeting of the Association for Computational Linguistics*.

Amit Goyal and Hal Daume. 2011. Approximate scalable bounded space sketch for large data NLP. In *Proceedings of the Conference on Empirical Methods in Natural Language Processing*.

Spence Green and Christopher D. Manning. 2010. Better Arabic parsing: Baselines, evaluations, and analysis. In *Proceedings of the International Conference on Computational Linguistics*.

Zhongqiang Huang and Mary Harper. 2009. Self-training PCFG grammars with latent annotations across languages. In *Proceedings of the Conference on Empirical Methods in Natural Language Processing*.

Zhongqiang Huang, Mary Harper, and Slav Petrov. 2010. Self-training with products of latent variable. In *Proceedings of the Conference on Empirical Methods in Natural Language Processing*.

Terry Koo, Xavier Carrera, and Michael Collins. 2008. Simple semi-supervised dependency parsing. In *Proceedings of the Annual Meeting of the Association for Computational Linguistics*.

Dong C. Liu and Jorge Nocedal. 1989. On the limited memory BFGS method for large scale optimization. *Mathematical Programming*.

Mohamed Maamouri, Ann Bies, Sondos Krouna, Fatma Gaddeche, and Basma Bouziri. 2009. Penn Arabic treebank guidelines. Technical report, Linguistic Data Consortium, University of Pennsylvania.

Mitchell P. Marcus, Beatrice Santorini, Mary Ann Marcinkiewicz, and Ann Taylor, 1999. *Treebank-3*. Linguistic Data Consortium, Philadelphia.

Takuya Matsuzaki, Yusuke Miyao, and Jun'ichi Tsujii. 2005. Probabilistic CFG with latent annotations. In *Proceedings of the Annual Meeting of the Association for Computational Linguistics*.

Slav Petrov and Dan Klein. 2007. Improved inference for unlexicalized parsing. In *Proceedings of the Conference of the North American Chapter of the Association for Computational Linguistics on Human Language Technology*.

Slav Petrov and Dan Klein. 2008. Sparse multi-scale grammars for discriminative latent variable parsing. In *Proceedings of the Conference on Empirical Methods in Natural Language Processing*.

Slav Petrov, Leon Barrett, Romain Thibaux, and Dan Klein. 2006. Learning accurate, compact, and interpretable tree annotation. In *Proceedings of the Annual Meeting of the Association for Computational Linguistics*.

Slav Petrov. 2009. *Coarse-to-fine natural language processing*. Ph.D. thesis, University of California at Bekeley.

Slav Petrov. 2010. Products of random latent variable grammars. In *Proceedings of the Conference of the North American Chapter of the Association for Computational Linguistics on Human Language Technology*.

Ruslan Salakhutdinov, Sam Roweis, and Zoubin Ghahramani. 2003. Optimization with EM and expectation-conjugate-gradient. In *Proceedings of the International Conference on Machine Learning*.

Nianwen Xue, Fei Xia, Fu-dong Chiou, and Marta Palmer. 2005. The Penn Chinese Treebank: Phrase structure annotation of a large corpus. *Natural Language Engineering*.

Improving Dependency Parsing with Fined-Grained Features

Guangyou Zhou, Li Cai, Kang Liu, and Jun Zhao
National Laboratory of Pattern Recognition
Institute of Automation, Chinese Academy of Sciences
95 Zhongguancun East Road, Beijing 100190, China
{gyzhou,lcai,kliu,jzhao}@nlpr.ia.ac.cn

Abstract

In this paper, we present a simple and effective fine-grained feature generation scheme for dependency parsing. We focus on the problem of grammar representation, introducing fine-grained features by splitting various POS tags to different degrees using HowNet hierarchical semantic knowledge. To prevent the oversplitting, we adopt a threshold-constrained bottom-up strategy to merge the derived subcategories. We conduct the experiments on the Penn Chinese Treebank. The results show that, with the fine-grained features, we can improve the dependency parsing accuracies by 0.52% (absolute) for the unlabeled first-order parser, and in the case of second-order parser, we can improve the dependency parsing accuracies by 0.61% (absolute).

1 Introduction

In natural language parsing, part-of-speech (POS) information is seen as crucial to resolving ambiguous relationships, yet POS tags are usually too general to encapsulate a word's syntactic behavior. It is therefore attractive to consider intermediate entities which exist at a finer level than the POS tags, and the relationship between specific words and their syntactic contexts may be best modeled.

In this paper, we introduce the fine-grained features by splitting various POS tags to different degrees. First, we split the POS tags of each word in the Treebank using HowNet hypernym-hyponymy hierarchical semantic knowledge (Dong and Dong, 2000). Then we adopt a threshold-constrained bottom-up strategy to merge the semantic-related subcategories which are plagued by the oversplitting problems. Finally, we use the generated sub-categories to construct a new fine-grained feature mapping for a discriminative learner. We are thus relying on the ability of discriminative learning methods to identify and exploit informative features.

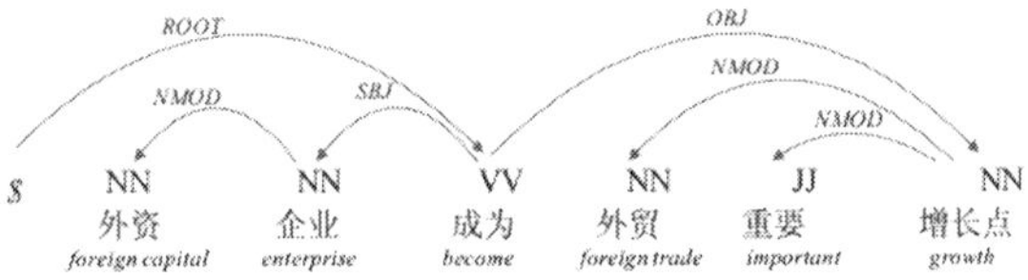

Figure 1: An example of a labeled dependency tree. The tree contains a special token "$" which is always the root of the tree. Each arc is directed from head to modifier and has a label describing the function of the attachment.

To demonstrate the effectiveness of our approach, we conduct the dependency parsing experiments on the Penn Chinese Treebank (CTB) (Xue et al., 2005). The results show that, with the fine-grained features, we can obtain mildly significant improvements both for first-order and second-order parsing (e.g., the absolute improvements are 0.52% and 0.61%, respectively) (see Section 6).

The remainder of this paper is organized as follows. Section 2 introduces the Motivation. Section 3 gives background on dependency parsing and HowNet hierarchical semantic knowledge. Section 4 describes the fine-grained feature generation scheme. Section 5 presents fine-grained features. Experimental evaluation and results are reported in Section 6. Section 7 discusses related work. Finally, in Section 8 we draw conclusion.

2 Motivation

In dependency parsing, we attempt to build head-modifier (or head-dependent) relations between words in a sentence. A simple example is shown in Figure 1, where NN, VV, and JJ are POS tags.

Currently, a variety of statistical methods have

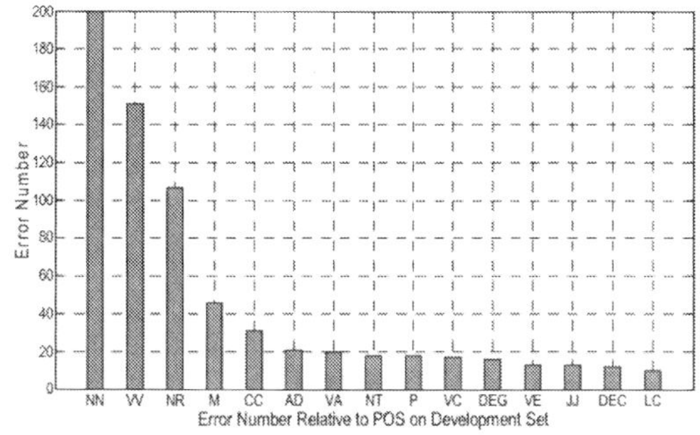

Figure 2: The number of the most frequent errors relative to POS types on development set for first-order parsing.

been developed for dependency parsing, such as **graph-based** (McDonald et al., 2005; McDonald and Pereira, 2006), **transition-based** (Yamada and Matsumoto, 2003; Hall et al., 2006), or **hybrid methods** (Nivre and McDonald, 2008; Martins et al., 2008; Zhang and Clark, 2008). These methods mainly rely on the POS information as important features, but the POS tags are usually too general to encapsulate a word's syntactic behavior, especially for Chinese dependency parsing on CTB (e.g., it assumes that all the words with the POS tag NN share the same syntactic behavior). In the limit, each word may well have its own unique syntactic behavior (Petrov and Klein, 2006). However, in practice, given limited data, the relationships between the specific words and their context dependencies may be best modeled at a level finer than the POS tags but coarser than the words themselves. Take the sentence in Figure 1 for example, although the words 外资(foreign capital) and 增长点(growth) have the same POS tag NN, they should have different context dependencies in dependency parsing tree. In HowNet, the two words are defined with different hypernyms. The word 外资(foreign capital) is defined as a kind of objective things, while the word 增长点(growth) is defined as an event role feature. Intuitively, the different senses can represent their different syntactic behavior, and we attempt to split the POS tags to different degrees based on hierarchical semantic knowledge.

Figure 2 shows the number of the most frequent errors relative to POS types on the development set for the first-order parsing. From the figure, it is seen that the main errors are nominal and verbal categories. Therefore, we may suspect that whether the complex and frequent categories like NN and VV should be split heavily while barely split rare or simple ones. Our experiments demonstrate that this strategy can be quite effective in Chinese dependency parsing task (see Table 2 in Section 4 for empirical results).

3 Background

3.1 Dependency Parsing

In dependency parsing, we attempt to build head-modifier (or head-dependent) relations between words in a sentence. The discriminative parser we used in this paper is based on the *part-factored* model and features of the MSTParser (McDonald et al., 2005; McDonald and Pereira, 2006; Carreras, 2007). The parsing model can be defined as a conditional distribution $p(y|\mathbf{x};\mathbf{w})$ over each projective parse tree y for a particular sentence $\mathbf{x}$, parameterized by a vector $\mathbf{w}$. The probability of a parse tree is

$$p(y|\mathbf{x};\mathbf{w}) = \frac{1}{Z(\mathbf{x};\mathbf{w})}\exp\Big\{\sum_{\rho\in y}\mathbf{w}\cdot\mathbf{\Phi}(\mathbf{x},\rho)\Big\} \quad (1)$$

where $Z(\mathbf{x};\mathbf{w})$ is the partition function and $\mathbf{\Phi}$ are *part-factored* feature functions that include *head-modifier* parts, *sibling* parts and *grandchild* parts. Given the training set $\{(\mathbf{x}_i, y_i)\}_{i=1}^{N}$, parameter estimation for log-linear models generally resolve around optimization of a regularized conditional log-likelihood objective $\mathbf{w}^* = \arg\min_{\mathbf{w}} L(\mathbf{w})$ where

$$L(\mathbf{w}) = -C\sum_{i=1}^{N}\log p(y_i|\mathbf{x}_i;\mathbf{w}) + \frac{1}{2}||\mathbf{w}||^2 \quad (2)$$

The parameter $C > 0$ is a constant dictating the level of regularization in the model. Since objective function $L(\mathbf{w})$ is smooth and convex, which is convenient for standard gradient-based optimization techniques. In this paper we use the dual exponentiated gradient (EG)[1] descent, which is a particularly effective optimization algorithm for log-linear models (Collins et al., 2008).

3.2 HowNet Semantic Knowledge

HowNet is a bilingual general knowledge-base describing relations between concepts and relations between the attributes of concepts in Chinese and their English equivalents (Gan and Wong, 2000).

HowNet constructs a hierarchical structure of its knowledge base from hypernym-hyponymy

[1] http://groups.csail.mit.edu/nlp/egstra/

relations. The unit of meaning is called sememe that can not be further decomposed, which can be represented in Chinese and their English equivalents, such as the sememe **fund**|资金. The explicated relations of HowNet include hypernym-hyponymy, synonymy, metonymy, antonymy, part-whole, attribute-host, material-product, dynamic role and concept co-occurrence, and so on. In this paper, we only consider the hypernym-hyponymy relations at different levels of granularities. Since a word may have different senses, and therefore different definitions in HowNet, we just use the first definition as the semantic-related tag of the word. Take the concept 外资(foreign capital) for example, its definition and the hypernym-hyponymy relations are listed below from speciality to generality, which we call the hierarchical semantic information in this paper.

Definition:

DEF = {fund|资金:modifier= {foreign|外国}}

Hierarchy:

fund|资金→wealth|钱财→artifact|人工物→inanimate|无生物→physical|物质→thing|万物→entity|实体

In the definition, HowNet decomposes the concept into sememes 'fund|资金', 'wealth|钱财', 'artifact|人工物', 'inanimate|无生物', 'physical|物质', 'thing|万物', 'entity|实体'. The sememe appearing in the first position of Definition ('fund|资金') is the categorical attribute, which names the hypernym of the concept 外资(foreign capital). Those sememes appearing in other positions (e.g., 'foreign|外国') are additional attributes, which give more specific information to the concept.

It is clear that the word 外资(foreign capital) has hypernyms from the most special hypernym fund|资金 to the most general hypernym entity|实体 in a hierarchical way.

HowNet contains very limited words, so there are many words which cannot be found in HowNet. In this paper, we extend HowNet with Chinese Knowledge base "TongYiCiLin" (abbreviation: CiLin) (Mei et al., 1983), which represents 77,343 words in a dendrogram (or tree).

CiLin is organized as a hierarchical tree structure, each node represents a semantic category. To balance the words coverage, we extract semantic categories at level 3, which covers 1,400 subcategories.

HowNet and CiLin have different ontologies and representations of semantic categories (Xiong et al., 2005), we combine the two dictionaries: given a word w, if we cannot find in HowNet, but found in CiLin, we try to replace w with a synonym s in the synset defined by CiLin. If the synonym s can be found in HowNet, the corresponding semantic-related tag in HowNet will be assigned to w.

4 Fine-Grained Feature Generation

4.1 Splitting the POS Tags

In this subsection, we split the original POS tags to different degrees based on HowNet hierarchical semantic knowledge. The challenge is how to deal with the problem of polysemous words. Since each word may have multiple senses, and therefore different definitions in HowNet. Following Xiong et al. (2005) and Lin et al. (2009), we just use the first sense to determine the sense of each token instance of a target word (e.g., all token instances of a given word are tagged with the sense that occurs most frequently in HowNet).

As mentioned in Section 3.2, the semantic information of each word can be represented as hierarchical hypernym-hyponymy relations. In this paper, we attempt to establish the mapping from top to down and split the words into different subcategories based on hypernym-hyponymy relations defined in HowNet. For easy explanation of the splitting process, we take the words with POS tag NN for example; the fine-grained feature generation is shown in Figure 3. The left part of the figure is the word subcategories, which is split based on HowNet hierarchy. As shown by the dashed line from left to right, we generate each subcategory with the hierarchical semantic-related tag, such as NN-event, NN-entity, NN-thing, NN-time and so on. If the hypernym node has no hyponym, the corresponding subcategory will stop splitting (e.g., at the level 3 in figure 3, "fruit" is the most speciality hypernym of the corresponding words "banana" and "apple" in HowNet hierarchy, which cannot be further decomposed). The details of HowNet hierarchy were presented in Dong and Dong (2000).

As shown in Figure 3, the original relationships between the words and their syntactic contexts are modeled by the POS tag NN, after hierarchically split, the relationships can be best modeled at the

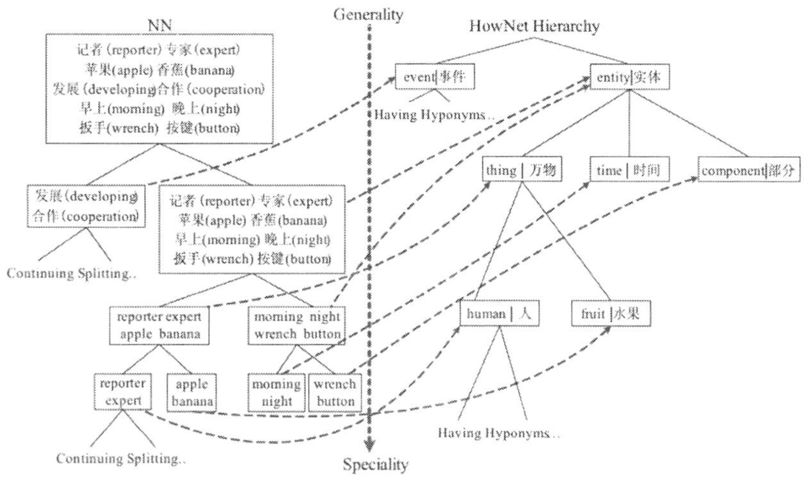

Figure 3: Fine-grained feature generation for words with POS tag NN. The left part is word subcategory and the right part is HowNet hierarchy from generality to speciality.

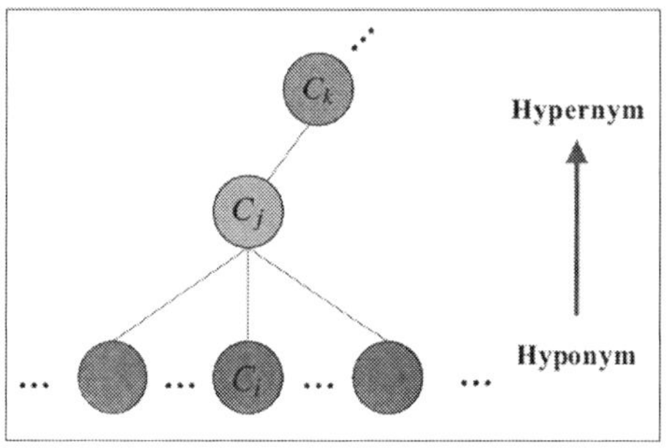

Figure 4: The merging procedure based on hypernym-hyponymy relations from bottom-up.

different levels of the fine-grained subcategories. By this observation, the fine-grained feature generation is just a hierarchical clustering of words themselves with the fine-grained semantic-related tags. Unlike the previous work, such as word cluster technique (Koo et al., 2008), data-driven split manner (Matsuzaki et al., 2005; Petrov and Klein, 2006), our approach does not exploit unlabeled data, and the splitting is based on hierarchical semantic knowledge instead of maximizing posterior probability, which is much simpler than their methods.

4.2 Merging Based on Threshold Constraint

Intuitively, creating more subcategories can increase parsing accuracy. On the other hand, oversplitting can be a serious problem, the details were presented in Klein and Manning (2003). To prevent oversplitting, we merge the subcategories based on the threshold constraint. After the splitting, each subcategory contains a group of words which share the same semantic-related tag. Then we measure the size of each subcategory to determine whether the subcategory should be further merged. For easy explanation, we show an example in Figure 4, where each node C_i denotes a subcategory, C_j is the nearest hypernym subcategory of C_i , C_k is the nearest hypernym subcategory of C_j , and so on. Assuming that $f(C_i)$, $f(C_j)$ and $f(C_j)$ denote the number of the words contained in the subcategory C_i , C_j and C_k respectively, f is the threshold. We judge C_i should be further merged into C_j if $f(C_i) < f$, and update the number of the words contained in C_j using the following formula:

$$f^{update}(C_j) = \begin{cases} f(C_i) + f(C_j) & \text{if } f(C_i) < f \\ f(C_j) & \text{other} \end{cases} \quad (3)$$

where $f^{update}(C_j)$ is the number of the words contained in the updated subcategory C_j . In this way, we repeatedly merge each subcategory from bottom-up through the hypernym ladders according to the formula (3). Finally, we generate appropriate granularity of the fine-grained subcategories by splitting and merging approach.

In our approach, each POS tag is divided into several subcategories. The subcategories of some POS tags with the words are shown in Table 1. The categories compose of the original POS tags and the subcategories derived from HowNet. For example, NN is split into NN-InstitutePlace, NN-aValue, and so on. The subcategories' number of each POS tag is shown in Table 2. Nominal categories are the most heavily split. For ex-

NN		VV	
NN-InstitutePlace	企业(enterprise) 公司(company)	VV-event	猜到(guess) 预见(foresee)
NN-aValue	经济(economy)国际(international)	VV-aValue	小心(care) 可以(can)
NN-organization	国家(country) 政府(government)	VV-SelfMoveInDirection	进行(conduct) 扩散(spread)
NN-event	发展(developing)合作(cooperation)	VV-change	增长(increase) 涨价(deform)
NN-human	记者(reporter) 专家(expert)	VV-attribute	简称(abbreviation) 库容(storage capacity)
NN-affairs	贸易(trading) 金融(financial)	VV-entity	经历(experience) 考虑(consider)
NN-mental	情绪(mood) 感受(feelings)	VV-AlterRelation	围困(siege) 脱离(separate)
NN-entity	后者(latter) 机会(opportunity)	VV-AlterPossession	借用(borrow) 购进(buy)
NN-artifact	棉花(cotton) 维生素(vitamin)	VV-AlterPhysical	建造(build) 制成(make)
...	...	...	...
AD		**JJ**	
AD-aValue	以后(after) 唯有(only)	JJ-aValue	共同(together) 特别(special)
AD-event	还(also) 不管(no matter)	JJ-event	继续(continue) 相对(relatively)
...	...	...	...

Table 1: The two words with their English translations in the subcategories of some POS tags.

NN	24	VC	2	MSP	1
VV	17	VE	1	OD	1
NR	5	ON	1	DEV	1
JJ	8	P	4	BA	1
CC	7	NT	3	LJ	1
DEG	1	CS	3	LB	1
M	5	AD	5	DER	1
VA	4	SB	1	SP	1
LC	1	CD	1	IJ	1
PN	1	DEC	1	ETC	1
DT	1	AS	1	PU	1

Table 2: The number of subcategories generated by our hierarchical semantic knowledge based split-merge procedure.

ample, common noun (NN) category is divided into the maximum number of subcategories (24). One subcategory consists primarily of objective things, whose typical semantic knowledge is an entity. Another subcategory is defined as an attribute, and so on. These kinds of semantic-related subcategories are typical, and give a division similar to the distributional clustering results like those of Schuetze (1998). The proper noun (NR) category is split into the 5 subcategories, including entity, institute-Places, attribute, aValue, and so on, which are defined in HowNet. The temporal noun (NT) category is also split into 3 subcategories.

Verbal categories are also heavily split. Verbal subcategories sometimes reflect syntactic selectional preferences, and sometimes reflect other aspects of verbal syntax (Petrov and Klein, 2006). For example, the common verb (VV) category is divided into the number of 17 subcategories based on hierarchical split-merge procedure. The predictive adjective (VA) category is also split into 4 subcategories.

Functional categories generally have fewer splits shown in Table 2. Intuitively, those categories are known to be strongly correlated with syntactic behavior. For example, determiner (DT), interjection (IJ), onomatopoeia (ON), and so on.

5 Feature Design

Key to the success of our approach is the use of HowNet hierarchical semantic knowledge to generate the fine-grained features to assist the dependency parsers. The feature sets we used in this paper are similar to other feature sets in the literature (McDonald et al., 2005; McDonald and Pereira, 2006; Carreras, 2007), so we will not attempt to give an exhaustive description of the features in this Section. Rather, we describe our fine-grained features at a high level and concentrate on our motivations. In the experiments, our employed two different feature sets: a baseline feature set which draws upon "normal" information sources such as word forms and POS, and a fine-grained feature set that also information derived from the HowNet hierarchical semantic knowledge.

Our first-order baseline feature set is similar to the feature set of McDonald et al. (2005) and McDonald and Pereira (2006). The second-order baseline features are the same as those of Carreras (2007) and include indicators for triples of POS tags for sibling interactions and grandparent interactions, as well as additional bigram features based on pairs of words involved these higher order interactions.

The first- and second-order fine-grained features are complementary with the baseline features. We generate the fine-grained features by mimicking the word-to-tag and tag-to-tag interactions between the head and modifier of a dependency. Also, We include indicators for triples of fine-grained subcategory tags for sibling and grandparent interactions. Examples of these features are provided in Table 3.

Till now, we have demonstrated our fine-grained generation scheme using HowNet hierarchical semantic knowledge. With the derived subcategories, we can construct a new fine-grained

Baseline	Fine-grained
ht, mt	hf, mf
hw, mw	hw, mf
hw, ht, mt	hf, mw
hw, ht, mw, mt	hw, hf, mf
ht, mt, gt	hw, hf, mw, mf
ht, mt, st	hf, mf, gf
ht, mt, gt, st	hf, mf, sf
...	hf, mf, gf
gt, ht, mt, st	...
	gf, hf, mf, sf

Table 3: Baseline (left) and fine-grained (right) feature templates. Abbreviation: ht=head POS, hw= head word, hf=fine-grained POS of head, mf=fineg-grained POS of modifier. st, gt, sf, gf= likewise for sibling and grandchild.

feature mapping for a discriminative learner, similar to (Koo et al., 2008). We are relying on the ability of discriminative learning methods to identify and exploit informative features.

6 Experiments

In order to evaluate the effectiveness of the proposed approach, we conducted dependency parsing experiments in Chinese. The experiments were performed on the Penn Chinese Treebank (CTB) version 5.0 (Xue et al., 2005), using a set of head-selection rules (Zhang and Clark, 2008) to convert the phrase structure syntax of the Treebank to a dependency tree representation, dependency labels were obtained via the "Malt" hard-coded setting.[2] We split the data into training set (files 1-270 and files 400-931), development set (files 301-325) and test set (files 271-300). The development and test set were used gold-standard segmentation and POS tags in CTB.

We measured the parser quality by the unlabeled attachment score (UAS), e.g., the percentage of tokens (excluding all punctuation tokens) with the correct HEAD. And we also evaluated on complete dependency analysis (CM).

6.1 Splitting Experiments

In this subsection, we conduct the experiments only using the splitting operator. The results are shown in Table 4, where Ord1/Ord2 refers to a first-/second-order parsers (McDonald et al., 2005; McDonald and Pereira, 2006; Carreras, 2007) with baseline features. Ord1f/Ord2f refers to a first-/second-order parsers with baseline+fine-grained features, and the im-

[2] http://w3.msi.vxu.se/ nivre/research/MaltXML.html

Models	UAS	CM
Ord1	86.57	42.24
Ord1f	86.72 (+0.15)	42.81
Ord2	88.27	46.84
Ord2f	88.51 (+0.24)	47.99

Table 4: Dependency parsing results on the test set only using the splitting operator.

provements by the fine-grained features over the baseline features are shown in parentheses. There are some clear trends in the results.

First, the performance increases with the order of the parser: the first-order model (Ord1) has the lowest performance, adding sibling and grandparent interactions (Ord2) yield better performance. Similar observations regarding the effect of model order have also been made by Carreras (2007) and Koo et al. (2008).

Second, note that the parsers using the fine-grained features outperform the baseline, regardless of model order. Moreover, the benefits of the fine-grained features can improve the performance with the increasing of the model order. For example, increasing the model order from Ord1 to Ord1f results in a relative reduction in error of roughly 1.12%, while introducing fine-grained features from Ord2 to Ord2f yields an additional relative error reduction of roughly 2.05%.

6.2 Merging Experiments

To prevent oversplitting, we merge the subcategories based on the threshold constraint. For parameter f in equation (3), different POS tags (e.g., NN, VV, JJ, ON, $\cdots$) need different values. We do the experiments on the development set to determine the best value among 10, 20, 50, 100, 200, 300, $\cdots$, 1,000 in terms of UAS for each POS tag. The number of the subcategories are shown in Table 2 (in Section 4). Our experiments corresponding to the best parameter values are evaluated on the test set of CTB 5.0.

Table 5 shows the results. The performances can be further increased after using the merging operator. Such a fact validates the effectiveness of merging operator. Overall, for the first-order parser, we find that there is an absolute improvement of 0.52 points (UAS) by adding fine-grained features. For the second-order parser, we get an absolute improvement of 0.61 points (UAS) by including fine-grained features. The improvements of parsing with fine-grained features are mildly significant using the Z-test of Collins et al. (2005).

Models	UAS	CM
Ord1	86.57	42.24
Ord1f	**87.09**	43.39
improvement	+0.52	-
significant level	$p < 0.08$	-
Ord2	88.27	46.84
Ord2f	**88.88**	48.85
improvement	+0.61	-
significant level	$p < 0.05$	-

Table 5: Dependency parsing results on the test set after using the merging operator.

Systems	≤40 words (UAS)	Full (UAS)
Wang et al. (2007)	86.6	-
Yu at al. (2008)	-	87.26
Zhao et al. (2009)	88.9	87.0
Chen et al. (2009)	**92.34**	**89.91**
Ours	90.86	88.88

Table 6: Dependency parsing results on this data set for our second-order model and the previous work.

Systems	UAS
Duan et al. (2007)	84.38
Zhang and Clark (2008)	**86.21**
Huang and Sagae (2010)	85.20
Ours	85.45

Table 7: Comparison of our final results with other best-performing systems on this data set.

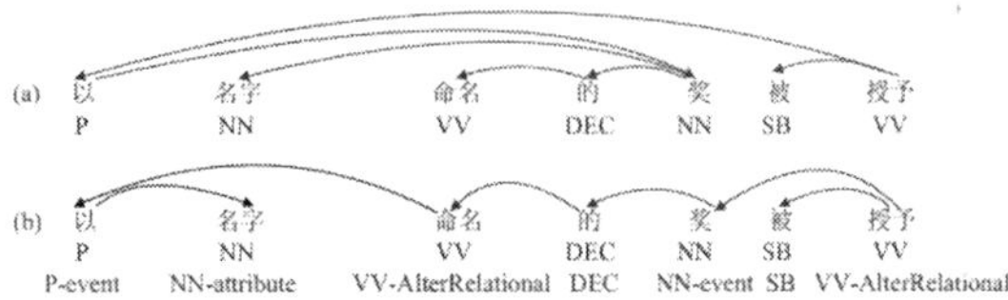

Figure 5: Dependency trees of an example sentence "以(with) 名字(name) 命名(named) 的(of) 奖(prize) 被(by) 授予(award)" as its English translation "··· prize named by ··· name is awarded ···". (a) Dependency tree produced by the baseline model; (b) Dependency tree produced by the proposed approach.

6.3 Comparison with Previous Work

To put our results in perspective, we also compare our second-order system with other best systems: Wang et al. (2007), Yu at al. (2008), Zhao et al. (2009) and Chen et al. (2009), respectively. The results are shown in Table 6, our approach outperforms the first three systems. Chen et al. (2009) reports a very high performance using subtree features from auto-parsed data. In our systems, our do not use such knowledge.

Some researchers conducted experiments on CTB with a different data split: files 1-815 and files 1001-1136 for training, files 816-885 and files 1137-1147 for test, files 886-931 and 1148-1151 for development. The development and test sets were also performed using the gold-standard assigned POS tags. We report the experimental results as well as the performance of previous work on this data set shown in Table 7. Our results are better than most previous work, although Zhang and Clark (2008) achieved an even higher accuracy (86.21) by combining both graph-based and transition-based parsing into a single system for training and decoding. Moreover, their technique is orthogonal to ours, and we suspect that integrating the fine-grained features into the combined parsers might get an even better performance.

6.4 Discussion

Our purpose in this paper is to incorporate the fine-grained features to assist the dependency parsing. Figure 5 shows an example of dependency trees produced by the baseline parser and our proposed approach.

In Figure 5(a), the baseline parser incorrectly assigned 奖/NN (prize) as the modifier of 以/P (with) and the head of 以/P was also incorrectly recognized as 授予/VV (award). The reason may be that the POS features (**P→NN** and **VV→P**) are too general to model the syntactic dependencies. However, after introducing the fine-grained features **P-event→NN-attribute** and **VV-AlterRelational→P-event**, 名字/NN (name) was selected as modifier of 以/P (with) and the head of 以/P (with) was correctly recognized (Figure 5(b)).

Besides, there exist a large number of neighborhood ambiguities in Chinese dependency parsing, such as "NN NN NN", "JJ NN NN", "AD VV VV", "JJ NN CC NN" and so on they have possible parsing trees as shown in Figure 6. For those ambiguities, our approach can provide the fine-grained features as additional information for the parser. For example, we have the following case in the data set: "外商NN(foreign tradesman)/投资NN(investment) /企业NN(enterprise)/". We can provide additional information about the relations of "外商**NN-human**(foreign tradesman)/ 企业**NN-InstitutePlace**(enterprise)" and "外商**NN-human**(foreign tradesman)/投资**NN-event**(investment)", which can be used to help the parser make the correct decision. Our approach

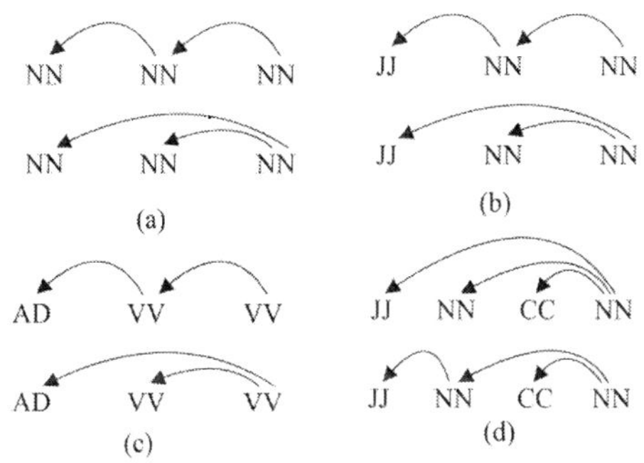

Figure 6: Neighborhood ambiguities in Chinese dependency parsing.

can also help the longer dependencies, such as "JJ NN NN NN" and "NN NN NN NN". For "JJ NN1 CC NN2" ambiguity, we can provide the additional information about the relations of JJ/NN1 and JJ/NN2. In this case, the dependency parser can correctly differentiate the ambiguity.

Our proposed approach is only a preliminary work. Despite the success, there are still some problems which should be extensively discussed in the future work.

(1) In this paper we split the POS tags by using the gold-standard POS tags of CTB. However, in many real application problems, the sentences to be parsed are often from the plain text and the POS tagging is an inevitable phase before dependency parsing. But the split of POS tags will bring great difficulty to the POS tagging phase. Whether the increase the parsing performance will cover the decrease of the POS tagging, this is a very appealing and challenging task in practice. We will leave it for future research.

(2) To deal with the problem of polysemous words, we just use the first definitions in HowNet. A natural avenue for further research would be the development of word sense disambiguation (WSD) technology to solve this problem.

7 Related Work

In this paper, we have focused on developing new representations for POS information. The idea of exploiting different granularities of information for dependency parsing has previously been investigated.

Liu et al. (2007) subdivided verbs according to their grammatical functions and integrated the information of verb subclasses into the dependency parsing model. They regarded the verb subdividing process as a classification task. In contrast, we split the POS tags based on HowNet hierarchical semantic knowledge and relax the subdivision to be all types of POS tags, which is much simpler than the classification-based method.

Koo et al. (2008) introduced lexical intermediaries at a coarser level than words themselves via a cluster method. Our approach is similar to theirs in that we used the fine-grained feature generation scheme based on HowNet hierarchical semantic knowledge, and the fine-grained features can be viewed as being a kind of "back-off" version of the baseline features. However, we focus on the problem of POS representation instead of lexical representation.

Recently, there are some studies focusing on parsing task using semantic knowledge. Agirre et al. (2008) used word sense information to improve English parsing and PP attachment. Xiong et al. (2005) and Lin et al. (2009) extracted hypernym features from HowNet semantic knowledge and integrated the features into a generative model for Chinese constituent parsing. As with their work, we also use semantic knowledge for parsing. However, our gold is to employ HowNet hierarchical semantic knowledge to generate fine-grained features to dependency parsing, rather than to PCFGs, requiring a substantially different model formulation. Besides, Bansal and Klein (2011) and Zhou et al. (2011) exploited web-scale semantic information for parsing.

8 Conclusion

In this paper, we focus on the problem of grammar representation, introducing fine-grained features by splitting various POS tags to different degrees using HowNet hierarchical semantic knowledge. To prevent the oversplitting, we adopt a threshold-constrained bottom-up strategy to merge the derived subcategories. The results show that, with the fine-grained features, we can improve the dependency parsing accuracies by 0.52% (absolute) for the unlabeled first-order parser, and in the case of second-order parser, we can improve the dependency parsing accuracies by 0.61% (absolute).

Acknowledgments

This work was supported by the National Natural Science Foundation of China (No. 60875041 and No. 61070106). We thank the anonymous reviewers for their insightful comments.

References

E. Agirre, T. Baldwin, and D. Martinez. 2008. Improving parsing and PP-attachment performance with sense information. In *Proceedings of ACL-08: HLT*, pages 317-325.

M. Bansal and D. Klein. 2011. Web-Scale Features for Full-Scale Parsing. In *Proceedings of ACL-HLT*, pages 693-702.

X. Carreras. 2007. Experiments with a higher-order projective dependency parser. In *Proceedings of EMNLP-CoNLL*, pages 957-961.

W. Chen, D. Kawahara, K. Uchimoto, and Torisawa. 2009. Improving dependency parsing with subtrees from auto-parsed data. In *Proceedings of EMNLP*, pages 570-579.

M. Collins, A. Globerson, T. Koo, X. Carreras, and P. L. Bartlett. 2008. Exponentiated gradient algorithm for conditional random fields and max-margin markov networks. *Journal of Machine Learning Research*, pages 1775–1822.

M. Collins, P. Koehn, and I. Kucerova. 2005. Clause restructuring for statistical machine translation. In *Proceedings of ACL*, pages 531-540.

Z. Dong and Q. Dong. 2000. HowNet Chinese-English conceptual database. *Technical report online software database, released at ACL*, http://www.keenage.com.

X. Duan, J. Zhao, and B. Xu. 2007. Probabilistic Models for action-based Chinese dependency parsing. In *Proceedings of ECML/PKDD*.

K. W. Gan and P. W. Wong. 2000. Annotating information structures in Chinese texts using HowNet. In *Proceedings of ACL*.

J. Hall, J. Nivre, and J. Nilsson. 2006. Discriminative classifier for deterministic dependency parsing. In *Proceedings of ACL*, pages 316-323.

L. Huang and K. Sagae. 2010. Dynamic Programming for Linear-Time Incremental Parsing. In *Proceedings of ACL*, pages 1077-1086.

D. Klein and C. Manning. 2003. Accurate unlexicalized parsing. In *Proceedings of ACL*, pages 423-430.

T. Koo, X. Carreras, and M. Collins. 2008. Simple semi-supervised dependency parsing. In *Proceedings of ACL-08: HLT*, pages 595-603.

X. Lin, Y. Fan, M. Zhang, X. Wu, H. Chi. 2009. Refining grammars for parsing with hierarchical semantic knowledge. In *Proceedings of EMNLP*, pages 1298-1307.

T. Liu, J. Ma, H. Zhang, and S. Li. 2007. Subdivided verbs to improve syntactic parsing. *Journal of electronics*, 24(3).

T. Matsuzaki, Y. Miyao, and J. Tsujii. 2005. Probabilistic CFG with latent annotation. In *Proceedings of ACL*, pages 75-82.

A. F. T. Martins, D. Das, N. A. Smith, and E. P. Xing. 2008. Stacking dependency parsers. In *Proceedings of EMNLP*, pages 157-166.

R. McDonald and F. Pereira. 2006. Online learning of approximate dependency parsing algorithms. In *Proceedings of EACL*, pages 81-88.

R. McDonald, K. Crammer, and F. Pereira. 2005. Online large-margin training of dependency parsers. In *Proceedings of ACL*, pages 91-98.

J. Mei, Y. Zhu, Y. Gao, and H. Yin. 1983. TongYiCiLin. *Shanghai Lexicographical Publishing House.*.

J. Nivre and R. McDonld. 2008. Integrating graph-based and transition-based dependency parsing. In *Proceedings of ACL-08: HLT*, pages 950-958.

S. Petrov and D. Klein. 2006. Learning accurate, compact, and interpretable tree annotation. In *Proceedings of COLING-ACL*, pages 433-440.

H. Schuetze. 1998. Automatic word sense discrimination. *Computational Linguistics*, 24(1): 97-124.

Q. I. Wang, D. Lin, and D. Schuurmans. 2007. Simple training of dependency parsers via structured boosting. In *Proceedings of IJCAI*, pages 1756-1762.

D. Xiong, S. Li, Q. Liu, S. Lin, and Y. Qian. 2005. Parsing the Penn Chinese Treebank with semantic knowledge. In *Proceedings of IJCNLP*.

N. Xue, F. Xia, F.-D. Chiou, and M. Palmer. 2005. The Penn Chinese Treebank: Phrase structure annotation of a large corpus. *Natural Language Engineering*, 10(4):1-30.

Yamada and Matsumoto. 2003. Statistical dependency analysis with support vector machines. In *Proceedings of IWPT*, pages 195-206.

K. Yu, D. Kawahara, and S. Kurohashi. 2008. Chinese dependency parsing with large scale automatically constructed case structures. In *Proceedings of COLING*, pages 1049-1056.

Y. Zhang and S. Clark. 2008. A tale of two parsers: investigating and combining graph-based and transition-based dependency parsing using beam-search. In *Proceedings of EMNLP*, pages 562-571.

H. Zhao, Y. Song, C. Kit and G. Zhou. 2009. Cross language dependency parsing using a bilingual lexicon. In *Proceedings of ACL*, pages 55-63.

G. Zhou, J. Zhao, K. Liu and L. Cai. 2011. Exploiting web-derived selectional preference to imporve statistical dependency parsing. In *Proceedings of ACL-HLT*, pages 1556-1665.

Natural Language Programming Using Class Sequential Rules

Cohan Sujay Carlos
Aiaioo Labs
Bangalore, India
cohan@aiaioo.com

Abstract

This paper presents a system for Natural Language Programming using Class Sequential Rules (CSR). The system recognizes a number of procedural primitives and operators. The domain of the system is presently limited to the world of numbers and operations on numbers. We evaluate the effectiveness of CSRs at the task of Natural Language Programming using an annotated corpus of programming instructions in natural language, achieving a precision and recall of 85% and 64% respectively. We also compare the performance of a system trained on annotated data with that of a system using handcrafted rules.

1 Introduction

Since the early days of computing, there have been those who have longed for a programming system wherein the use of a formal symbolism for programming was not strictly necessary. Though high level languages greatly improve the ease of programming, it might be easier for a user to be allowed to communicate with an application in a natural language rather than a formal language with a specialized syntax. Moreover, a significant fraction of the population of the world is not conversant in the English language or remains unfamiliar with the Roman alphabet, and for them, a system for programming in their native tongues would be of great benefit. It is also easy to foresee a future where speech recognition systems are so accurate and robust that users might seek to provide instructions by means of speech to their computers. Thus there seems to be a need for algorithms capable of accepting commands and programming instructions in unconstrained human languages.

Type	Arity	Example
if	2 or 3	If x is 2, say "Hi"
unless	2	Exit unless x is 2
while	2	While $x \leq 2 \ldots$
until	2	Till x is 2 add 1 to x
continuation	1	Also, increment y
assignment	2	Let x be 1
imperatives	0 to ∞	Display x
questions	1	What is y?
y/n questions	1	Is x equal to 2?

Table 1: Types of Procedural Primitives.

We present a Natural Language Programming system capable of accepting programming commands in a natural language, executing them and returning any requested results to the user. It is limited to the domain of real numbers and can be used to write programs to compute the values of various functions of real numbers, or to generate different number series. The system can recognize nine broad categories of procedural primitives, some of which are conditionals, loops, assignments and function calls (imperatives). The complete list of types of procedural primitives with their arity and examples of usage can be found in Table 1.

We also present and evaluate a novel approach for processing user instructions. Instead of the traditional programming language approach of using a parser to produce a parse tree starting from modules or blocks of programming instructions, we first break up the programming instructions into sentences. We then use a short text classifier to first classify each resulting sentence into one of the categories of primitives listed above. Then we perform entity extraction to obtain as many contiguous and non-overlapping word subsequences as the arity of the primitive recognized, and then repeat the process with each of the word subsequences. Our system is capable of learning to recognize programming instructions belonging to the categories described above from an annotated corpus. It can also use manually crafted rules for the recognition of commands from sentences in a natural language.

The output of the above process is a semantic parse of the program. The semantic parses of consecutive sentences are joined into blocks if continuations are indicated. For example, if the first line is "If x is 3, display x." and the second line is "Also, increment x.", the first line is semantically parsed into "x = 3 =>print(x)." and the second line is parsed to "also(++x)." Then the two lines are combined to get "x = 3 =>print(x) && ++x." The semantic parse is also an interlingua representation that can be stored, used to perform an automatic translation of the program from one language to another, or executed to obtain the output.

Mihalcea et al (2006) distinguish the two complementary programming tasks of *description* and *proceduralization*. The present paper deals with proceduralization, the process of constructing procedures out of steps, blocks, conditionals and loops. Of the procedural primitives listed in Table 1, the first two are *conditional* statement primitives; the next two are *loop* primitives; the fifth is used to construct *blocks* of statements by agglutination; the remainder are primitives for *steps*.

Imperatives tend to be function calls or commands that result in an action or change. Examples of imperatives include calls to "display the value of x" and "Go to the step marked 'Subroutine 1'."

Wh-questions and yes/no questions have the effect of displaying the value of a variable, literal or expression. Yes/no questions are distinguished from wh-questions because their argument is constrained to be a boolean expression whereas wh-questions can refer to non-boolean variables, literals and expressions.

The set of expressions supported by the system is listed in Table 2. It will be observed that many commonly used mathematical operations like exponentiation and logarithms are not included in the list. The list does however include the arithmetic and relational operators that have their own keywords in the C, C++ and Java programming languages. At present, only two of the logical operators, namely *or* and *and*, are supported.

The rest of this paper is organized as follows:

Expression	Arity
addition	2
subtraction	2
multiplication	2
division	2
modulus	2
divisible	2
equality	2
inequality	2
less than	2
less than or equal to	2
greater than	2
greater than or equal to	2
conjunction	2
disjunction	2
negation	1

Table 2: Expressions.

Section 2 presents related work on the topic of natural language programming. The annotated corpus used to evaluate the system and the annotation guidelines for the same are presented in Section 3. Section 4 describes the entity recognition algorithms in some detail. The entity recognition systems are evaluated in Section 5 on the annotated corpus, and the novel approach of training a natural language programming system from annotated text is compared with the approach of using manually crafted rules. The conclusions and future directions are presented in Section 6.

2 Related Work

Attempts to develop natural language programming systems have been made in the past, and a working prototype called "NLC" was described by Ballard and Biermann (1979). NLC was capable of accepting English commands in the imperative mood. It did not accept declaratives and interrogatives. Each input was required to begin with an imperative verb. However, NLC was capable of dealing with pronominal references, like the ones in the command "Put the average of the first four entries in that row into its last entry" and with procedure definitions and loops, though not with conditionals. A sample NLC program from Ballard and Biermann (1979) is provided in Table 3. An example of a looping instruction in NLC is the last line of the sample program that instructs the computer to repeat the preceding steps over other rows of the matrix under consideration. Biermann et

"Choose a row in the matrix" "Divide its last entry by 3" "Repeat for the other rows"

Table 3: Sample NLC Program.

Take the array [3, 5, 7, 4, 6, 2, 1]. Count from one up to the size of the array: Go over the array from the beginning to the end minus the counter: If the current element is bigger than the following element then exchange the current element with the following element. Print "After: " and print the array.

Table 4: Sample Pegasus Program.

Write a program to generate 1000 numbers between 0 and 99 inclusive. You should count how many times each number is generated and write these counts out to the screen.

Table 5: Programming Assignment.

al (1983) also described attempts to provide commands to the NLC system using the Nippon Electric DP-200 Connected Speech Recognizer.

Knoell and Mezini (2006) described a programming language called Pegasus that lets users program using plain German or English statements. Pegasus uses a handcrafted phrase structure grammar to parse English or German language commands and convert them into an intermediate representation. The intermediate representation is turned into a Java program using a dictionary of code snippets or translated into a different language. Knoell and Mezini (2006) did not perform an evaluation of the system on a corpus of natural language programming commands. A sample program written in the Pegasus language (see Table 4) was provided in the paper to show what a Pegasus program to sort an array of numbers would look like.

Objections to Natural Language Programming have been recorded, most notably by Dijkstra (1978) in an article titled 'On the Foolishness of "Natural Language Programming"'. Knoell and Mezini (2006) on the other hand opine that a system capable of dealing with both, formal symbolism and natural text, might be better than one that only understands either.

A system for generating program skeletons from the text of programming assignments like the one shown in Table 5 was described by Mihalcea et al (2006). The system did not attempt to generate an executable program.

Pane and Myers (2000) studied how non-programmers would describe solutions to problems arising within a Pacman game, and from their study, Pane and Myers (2001) proposed several principles of usability for developing a programming system for children. Lieberman and Liu (2006) examine mixed-initiative dialog as a way of more precisely ascertaining user intention with respect to programming commands, again in the context of the Pacman game.

The present work is also related to the area of natural language understanding. Shapiro (2001) describes a system that understands user statements about their beliefs about the world. This is in essense a form of descriptive programming, similar to that described in Lieberman and Liu (2005) who explore the possibility of using natural language descriptions as a representation for programs, and describe a system called "Metafor" capable of generating Python scaffolding (referred to as the visualization code) from them, though not fully specified programs.

There has been, to our knowledge, no prior attempt to measure the performance of a natural language programming system using a corpus of annotated programming statements in a natural language. There has also not been, to our knowledge, any prior attempt to use entity recognition on natural language commands to generate fully specified programs. We also believe that this is the first attempt to learn patterns of language for programming from an annotated corpus.

3 Data Set

At the time of writing, there was no corpus available for evaluating the performance of a system for procedural programming in a natural language. Therefore, a corpus was developed[1] consisting of sentences in the English language, which the contributors of the sentences perceived to be commands that ought to invoke the programming primitives listed in Table 1 or specify the expressions listed in Table 2.

[1]The annotated corpus can be downloaded from the URL http://www.aiaioo.com/corpora/vaklipi2011.

Order	Survey Question
1	How would you say "x = 2" in English?
2	How would you say "x != 2" in English?
4	How would you say "$x \leq 2$" ?
6	How would you say "$x \geq 2$" ?
9	How would you say "x multiplied by 2" ?
10	How would you say "x / 2" ?

Table 6: Survey Questions.

The sentences were collected by setting up an online survey on a website, sending out requests over social networks and using email. All the questions were presented to the user at the same time, and the instructions at the top said:

> Please type into the box under each of the following, one way of saying the same thing in English and click on the Submit link below it. You can repeatedly enter different phrases if you can think of many ways of saying the same thing. For example, to communicate the idea of $x = y$, you might say x and y are equal or assign the value y to x.

The survey consisted of a total of thirty questions, and took approximately thirty minutes to complete. All users were presented with the same set of questions and in the same order. The answers provided by previous users were not made available to subsequent survey takers.

A total of 3,517 sentences[2] was collected over a period of one month.

The annotation procedure involved recategorizing the submissions according to the procedural primitive or expression they most closely matched and marking the entity spans according to the following annotation rules:

- **Conditional primitives:** A complex sentence specifying a condition for performing an action is a conditional statement. It is classified as an *if conditional statement* if it is conditional upon a **positive** outcome of the conditioning expression and the action to be taken does not undeniably suggest repeatedly checking the conditioning expression as a precondition for performing the action. It is classified as an *unless conditional statement* if it is conditional upon a **negative** outcome of the conditioning expression.

- **Loop primitives:** A complex sentence specifying a condition that is repeatedly evaluated for performing an action until it is satisfied or denied is a loop statement. It is classified as a *while loop statement* if it is conditional upon a **positive** outcome of the conditioning expression. It is classified as an *until loop statement* if it is conditional upon a **negative** outcome of the conditioning expression.

- **Operations with side effects:** Requests to add a value to a variable or to subtract a value from a variable are considered increment and decrement operations if the value of the variable would normally be considered to have changed at the end of the operation. For example, "Add 2 to x" would be considered an increment operation, whereas "Add x to 2" would not. The latter would be considered an addition operation and not an increment operation since it does not suggest a change in the value of x whereas the former does.

- **Operations without side effects:** Sentences in the indicative mood, informative clauses and phrases are classified as operations that do not have side effects, if they are not expected to alter the value of a variable. For example, "x added to 5" and "x by 5" have no side effects.

- **Relational Operations:** The classification of relational operations like *less than* depends on the order in which the parameters are supplied. So, "x is less than 2" and "x is not greater than or equal to 2" are both valid ways of representing "$x < 2$", but not "2 is greater than x". The last example is classified as a *greater than* operator.

From the counts for the categories *if conditional statement* (95 before annotation and 118 after cleaup) and the *unless conditional statement* (64 before and 15 after) it appears to be the case that people strongly prefer using an *if conditional statement* to an *unless conditional statement*. Thus the number of test sentences in each of the categories is not balanced.

[2]The number 3,517 included blank sentences and names as well. When these were removed, we were left with about 3,100 sentences of which we annotated 3,000.

4 System Description

As the system is intended for use as a multilingual teaching tool for students of computer programming, especially for those who do not possess a knowledge of English or the Roman alphabet, it was thought desirable to use a method of processing natural language programming instructions that would permit the rules for processing instructions to be learnt from annotated text in a number of possibly very different human languages.

One approach that seemed very promising was Class Sequential Rules (CSR) as described by Hu and Liu (2006). CSRs have been shown to outperform existing methods at the task of associating opinions with product features (Liu et al, 2006). Moreover, CSRs can also be easily created by hand since they are a subset of cascading grammar rules such as those described by the Common Pattern Specification Language (CPSL) (Appelt, 1996), which incidentally was developed as a language for specifying finite-state grammars for the purpose of information extraction. It was intuitively felt that a less powerful formalism might not only suffice for the task of processing programming commands, but also prove learnable from an annotated corpus.

4.1 Class Sequential Rules

A Class Sequential Rule consists of a sequence of ordered tokens, that we indicate by the symbols $i_1 \ldots i_n$, for example, $I = < i_1 i_2 i_3 >$. A CSR matches a sentence only when each token in the CSR's token sequence matches a word token in the text under evaluation, in the right order. The CSR I will match a sentence s if and only if, in the sentence, there is a token s_3 that matches i_3, and this token follows a token s_2 that matches i_2. This second token must in turn follow a token s_1 that matches i_1. For example, I will match the sequence $< i_1 x_3 i_2 x_4 i_3 x_5 >$ but not $< i_2 i_3 >$ or $< i_3 i_2 i_1 >$. CSRs like I can be used for classification as follows: a number of mutually exclusive CSRs are assigned to each class and used in conjunction with a priority or ordering scheme to resolve conflicts when CSRs from different classes match the input.

CSRs can also have class labels $c_1 \ldots c_n$ in their sequences. A class label can match zero or more tokens in the sentence. The tokens that class labels match represent entites in the sentences when

Sequences
$< c_2 keab >$
$< dc_2 kb >$

Table 7: Sequence database.

Length	Sequences
1	$< c_2 >$
2	$< c_2 k >$
3	$< c_2 kb >$

Table 8: Extracted sequences with support 2.

CSRs are used for entity extraction. For example, the CSR $J =< i_1 c_4 i_2 c_5 i_3 >$ will match the sentence $< i_1 x_3 x_4 i_2 i_3 >$. The two class labels in J, namely c_4 and c_5 will at the same time match the sub-sequence $< x_3 x_4 >$ and the empty sequence $<>$ respectively. As you can see, the actual matching is performed by the sequence tokens $i_1 \ldots i_n$. The class labels pick up the tokens in between.

If two class labels follow one another in quick succession (are not separated by a token in the sequence), for example $< i_1 c_2 c_3 i_4 >$, the extents of their spans are not well defined. The tokens that class labels match can be thought of as entities. Thus, in addition to classification, CSRs can be said to be capable of performing entity extraction.

The task of understanding a programming command given in natural language can be broken down into the two sub-tasks that CSRs perform: a) classifying the command into one of several categories of commands; and b) extracting the arguments for further processing. Both tasks can be performed by CSRs in a single step.

The algorithm for mining CSRs used in the present work is described in more detail in Hu and Liu (2006). Using the algorithm, it is possible to mine sequences with a given minimum *support*. For instance, given two sequences such as those shown in Table 7, and a minimum required support of 2, it is possible to extract all the patterns of length 1, 2 and 3 indicated in Table 8. CSRs are only a special case of sequential patterns. With CSRs, the sequential patterns mined are text tokens. Some algorithms for sequential pattern mining have been studied in Agrawal and Srikant (1995).

Other pattern exraction concepts closely related to CSRs include the surface patterns described by

Sequences
Also { $x = 2$ }.
Also, { $x = 2$ }.
Also { if $x = 3$, ++x }.

Table 9: Three annotated sentences that demonstrate the inadequacy of CSRs for natural language programming.

Order	CSRs
1	Also , EXPRESSION .
2	Also EXPRESSION .

Table 10: Class Sequential Rules for the entity spans in Table 9.

Ravichandran and Hovy (2002), Hearst (1992), Snow et al (2005) and Lin and Pantel (2001).

In the course of developing a hand-crafted set of rules for natural language programming using CSRs, it was observed that the discriminative power of CSRs did not always suffice. For example, it was observed that CSRs could not accurately identify the entity spans in the three sentences listed in Table 9.

The reason is that the two rules in Table 10 are needed to match the spans in the first two sentences and these are ordered to fire one behind the other as shown in the table. Now, however, the first rule "Also , EXPRESSION ." incorrectly picks out the single entity span in the third sentence owing to the comma in the middle of the sentence, and there is no way to rectify the problem using a different number of CSRs or changing the ordering.

Thus, a family of rules with more discriminative power was needed. We attempted to extend the concept of CSRs to give them more discriminative power, as described in the next subsection.

4.2 Extended Class Sequential Rules

The extension that solved the problem described in the preceding section was that of allowing each token in the CSR to be an n-gram. The rules presented in Table 11 contain a special term "NONE" which indicates an n-gram constraint as follows:

Order	Extended CSRs
1	Also NONE , EXPRESSION .
2	Also EXPRESSION .

Table 11: Two CSRs of the extended variety.

- When the term "NONE" appears between two tokens, the tokens they match in a sentence must be consecutive tokens. This is equivalent to making tokens on either side of "NONE" part of an n-gram. In the example in Table 11, the first rule can only match sentences where a comma immediately follows the word "Also."

- The term "NONE" can also appear at the beginning of an extended CSR to indicate that the following token must appear at the beginning of the matched sentence.

- Similarly, it can appear at the end of an extended CSR to indicate that the preceding token can only appear as the last token of a matched sentence.

The set of rules in Table 11 will be seen to be able to match all three sentences' spans correctly.

4.3 Rule Selection and Ordering

The two parameters used to evaluate the suitability of a rule are *support* (the percentage the sentences belonging to a category that it correctly identifies as belonging to that category) and *confidence* (the percentage of matches of the rule that were right), which are analogous to precision and recall. Only those rules were selected whose support and confidence values on the training data both exceeded minimum thresholds. The selected rules were ordered as follows:

- Rules whose accuracy of span matching exceeded the threshold were placed first.

- Rules whose accuracy of span matching fell below the threshold followed.

- Within the two categories described above, longer rules went ahead of shorter rules.

4.4 Intermediate Representation

The intermediate representation is a programming language that mimics the ambiguities of the language used in mathematics. The intermediate representation differs from a conventional programming language like Python in the following ways:

- Terms which tend to be ambiguous in natural language remain so in the intermediate representation. For example, the 'assignment operator' doubles as the 'equal to operator'

Let x be 3. y is 9. What is x times y? While x is less than y, print x and then increment x.

Table 12: Sample commands in our system.

in many natural languages. This overloading poses no problem since the right form can be resolved from context.

- The intermediate representation also attempts to capture the logical operator priority of Indian languages. In many Indian languages, it is not possible to set *or*-phrases as subphrases of *and*-phrases. So, we have chosen a priority order for operations in the intermediate representation that naturally maintains the restriction.

A program written in the present system would look like that in Table 12.

5 Evaluation and Results

The natural language programming system was evaluated against the annotated corpus described in Section 3. The manual rules used in the evaluation were developed and fixed prior to the start of corpus collection to avoid the introduction of biases through any knowledge of the corpus to be tested on.

5.1 Categories

The categories that were used in testing were equality, inequality, less than, greater than, less than or equal to, greater than or equal to, addition, subtraction, multiplication, division, increment, decrement, if, while, unless, until, print, conjunctive, disjunctive, divisible and continuation.

The categories in the corpus that were left out of the evaluation were as follows:

- Three categories were left out because of the lack of manually crafted rules for those categories.
- Of the three categories recognized as the print command by the manual rules, only one was retained for the experiment.
- Two of the omitted categories were merely synomyms for boolean constants 'true' and 'false.'

Category	Cnt	Precision	Recall	F1
equality	298	79.0 ± 06	66.5 ± 19	71.9 ± 10
inequality	165	90.6 ± 14	78.6 ± 06	84.3 ± 09
less than	151	66.8 ± 10	88.4 ± 07	76.8 ± 08
$\leq$	137	99.1 ± 02	75 ± 13	86.0 ± 07
more than	158	76.6 ± 08	83.1 ± 06	79.6 ± 02
$\geq$	132	92.9 ± 05	80.8 ± 13	86.5 ± 09
addition	140	97.9 ± 04	61.2 ± 10	77.2 ± 06
subtract	113	92.5 ± 15	71.0 ± 06	80.8 ± 06
multiply	144	98.8 ± 02	64.1 ± 12	79.4 ± 08
division	143	89.8 ± 10	69.8 ± 08	79.2 ± 09
increment	136	92.5 ± 08	57.3 ± 08	72.8 ± 08
decrement	131	96.9 ± 06	23.5 ± 15	46.7 ± 15
if	118	84.2 ± 05	96.0 ± 08	89.8 ± 04
while	61	92.1 ± 02	88.0 ± 12	89.8 ± 11
unless	15	100 ± 00	60.7 ± 15	77.6 ± 09
until	86	98.8 ± 02	85.8 ± 15	91.9 ± 08
print	82	92.3 ± 06	33.9 ± 14	55.1 ± 09
and	68	52.8 ± 11	82.8 ± 14	66.1 ± 12
or	67	92.1 ± 08	37.8 ± 04	58.8 ± 03
divisible	66	92.7 ± 08	71.1 ± 18	80.7 ± 10
continue	48	78.3 ± 23	22.1 ± 11	40.0 ± 05

Table 13: Evaluation of CSR-EX.

- The modulus operator was left out of the evaluation because the manual rules treated the operator as 'modulus' whereas the question used in the survey used to develop the corpus had suggested that the operator was the 'absolute value' operator.

5.2 Experiments

The 3,000 sentences in the annotated corpus belong to 29 distinct categories of which 21 are used for evaluating the system. Support and confidence values of 0.0001 and 0.70[3] respectively were used during training (for rule discovery).

Since we performed 3-fold cross validation, three sets of experiments were conducted for each of the following settings, for a total of 9 experiments in all:

- Conventional CSRs (CSR-BL)
- Extended CSRs (CSR-EX)
- Manually crafted rules (CSR-Man)

[3]These values were manually chosen keeping in mind the small size of the corpus. The support threshold was chosen to be low enough to not affect rule selection. The confidence threshold was kept low enough to permit single failures (incorrect matches) from time to time.

Setting	Prec.	Recall	F1
CSR-Man	89.2 ± 3.7	64.8 ± 6.2	73.0 ± 4
CSR-BL	85.7 ± 4.5	65.3 ± 5.9	73.1 ± 4
CSR-EX	88.4 ± 3.4	66.5 ± 5.6	74.8 ± 3

Table 14: Categorization Evaluation.

Metric	CSR-Man	CSR-BL	CSR-EX
PSCS	52.4 ± 9.1	50.2 ± 8.4	49.7 ± 8.6

Table 15: Entity Span Matching Evaluation.

In all experiments, the Precision, Recall and F1 Score (the harmonic mean of Precision and Recall) were measured for each of the categories, as well as the overall accuracy of categorization. The Precision, Recall and F1 scores for the CSR-EX algorithm are presented in Table 13. In the second column of the table is listed the number of sentences used in the test. This value in some cases drops to as low as fifteen sentences. The confidence intervals are rather high, making it difficult to draw comparisons between algorithms based on this data. The average of these scores for all categories is reported in Table 14.

The accuracy of entity span boundary detection is measured as follows: A recall-based score for correct span detection is computed by dividing the number of sentences with perfectly identified spans by the number of sentences in the category. This score is reported as the PSCS (percentage of sentences with correct spans). This score is similar to but not quite the same as the PCS (percentage of correct scopes) metric used in Councill et al (2010).

The PSCS scores for the three algorithms are reported in Table 15. We observe from the results that for the corpus the evaluation was performed on, there is no significant difference between the algorithms evaluated.

The overall accuracy scores presented in Table 16 again reveal no significant differences between CSR-Man, CSR-BL and CSR-EX in their behaviour with respect to the data-set.

Metric	CSR-Man	CSR-BL	CSR-EX
Acc.	64.3 ± 7	64.4 ± 6	66.0 ± 4

Table 16: Accuracies.

6 Conclusions and Future Work

This paper presents a system for Natural Language Programming capable of recognizing a number of categories of procedural programming instructions in a natural language. The system uses Class Sequential Rules to convert a natural language representation of a program into an intermediate representation that can be executed. The system is capable of using manually crafted rules or rules learnt from an annotated corpus.

Since no corpus was available for evaluation of a system for Natural Language Programming, a corpus consisting of 3,000 sentences in twenty-nine categories (of which only twenty-one were used), was collected over the internet, cleaned, re-categorized, annotated with entity spans and made publicly available.

Since the existing formalism of Class Sequential Rules (CSR-BL) was not powerful enough to tease certain sets of sentences apart into the right categories, an extension to Class Sequential Rules was proposed (CSR-EX) and implemented.

Finally, the system was evaluated by three-fold cross validation using the corpus. Three settings of the system were tested: a) a setting where it used extended CSR-EX rules manually crafted before the collection of the corpus; b) a setting where it used CSR-BL rules learnt from the annotated corpus; and c) a setting where it used CSR-EX rules learnt from the annotated corpus. Precisions of around 85% and recalls of approximately 64% were measured with confidence intervals as large as 7%. The large confidence intervals make it impossible to establish if one of the approaches works better than the others with the present corpus and the present set of categories.

Future research could include an evaluation on a larger corpus, on more languages and on the system's ability to adapt to new domains. It would also be interesting to examine system accuracies with an increased number of categories covering more operations and functions. It might also be of interest to build a corpus of complete programs rather than individual sentences, to capture more variations in language.

Acknowledgments

We are very grateful to all the volunteers who contributed to the corpus and to Govind Sharma, Kartik Asooja, Dr. Pushpak Bhattacharyya and the reviewers for helpful suggestions and references.

References

Rakesh Agrawal and Ramakrishnan Srikant. 1995. *Mining Sequential Patterns*. In *Proceedings of the Eleventh International Conference on Data Engineering IEEE Computer Society Washington, DC, USA. 1995.*

Douglas E. Appelt. 1996. *The Common Pattern Specification Language*. In *Proceedings of a workshop on held at Baltimore, Maryland. 1996*, 23–30.

Bruce W. Ballard, Alan W. Biermann. 1979. *Programming in Natural Language: "NLC" as a prototype. Proceedings of the 1979 annual conference. 1979*, 228–237.

Alan W. Biermann, R. Rodman, Bruce W. Ballard, T. Betancourt, G. Bilbro, H. Deas, L. Fineman, P. Fink, K. Gilbert, D. Gregory, F. Heidlage. 1983. *Interactive natural language problem solving: a pragmatic approach*. In *ANLC '83, Proceedings of the first conference on Applied Natural Language Processing, 1983.*

Isaac G. Councill , Ryan McDonald , Leonid Velikovich. 2010. *Whats Great and Whats Not: Learning to Classify the Scope of Negation for Improved Sentiment Analysis*. In *Proceedings of the Workshop on Negation and Speculation in Natural Language Processing (NeSp-NLP 2010). 2010.*

Edsger W. Dijkstra. 1978. *On the foolishness of "Natural Language Programming"*. In *Program Construction. 1978*, 51–53.

Marti A. Hearst. 1992. *Automatic Acquisition of Hyponyms from Large Text Corpora*. In *Proceedings of the 14th conference on Computational Linguistics - Volume 2. 1992.*

Minqing Hu and Bing Liu. 2006. *Opinion Feature Extraction Using Class Sequential Rules. AAAI Spring Symposium on Computational Approaches to Analyzing Weblogs, Palo Alto, USA, March 2006.*

Roman Knoell and Mira Mezini. 2006. *Pegasus First Steps Toward a Naturalistic Programming Language*. In *Companion to the 21st ACM SIGPLAN symposium on Object-oriented programming systems, languages, and applications. 2006*, 542–559.

Henry Lieberman and Hugo Liu. 2005. *Metafor: Visualizing stories as code*. In *10th International Conference on Intelligent User Interfaces. 2005.*

Henry Lieberman and Hugo Liu. 2006. *Feasibility studies for programming in natural language. Lieberman, Paterno, Wulf (Eds.): End-User Development (Human-Computer Interaction Series Vol. 9), Springer, 2006*, 459–474.

Dekang Lin and Patrick Pantel. 2001. *Discovery of inference rules for question-answering*. In *Journal Natural Language Engineering archive Volume 7 Issue 4, Cambridge University Press New York, NY, USA. December 2001.*

Bing Liu, Minqing Hu and Junsheng Cheng. 2005. *Opinion Observer: Analyzing and Comparing Opinions on the Web*. In *Proceedings of the 14th International World Wide Web conference (WWW-2005), Chiba, Japan. 2005.*

Rada Mihalcea and Hugo Liu and Henry Lieberman. 2006. *NLP (Natural Language Processing) for NLP (Natural Language Programming)*. In *Proceedings of CICLing. 2006*, 319–330.

John F. Pane and Brad A. Myers. 2000. *The Influence of the Psychology of Programming on a Language Design: Project Status Report*. In *Proceedings of the 12th Annual Meeting of the Psychology of Programmers Interest Group, A. F. Blackwell and E. Bilotta, Eds. Corigliano Calabro, Italy: Edizioni Memoria, April 10-13 2000*, 193–205.

John F. Pane, Chotirat Ann Ratanamahatana and Brad A. Myers. 2001. *Studying the language and structure in non-programmers' solutions to programming problems*. In *International Journal of Human-Computer Studies Volume 54, Issue 2, February 2001*, 237–264.

Deepak Ravichandran and Eduard Hovy. 2002. *Learning Surface Text Patterns for a Question Answering System*. In *Proceedings of the 40th Annual Meeting of the Association for Computational Linguistics, 2002.*

Stuart C. Shapiro. 1989. *The CASSIE Projects: An Approach to Natural Language Competence. EPIA, 1989*, 362–380.

Rion Snow, Daniel Jurafsky, Andrew Y. Ng. 2005. *Learning Syntactic Patterns for Automatic Hypernym Discovery*. In *Advances in Neural Information Processing Systems 17. 2005*, 1297–1304.

Treeblazing: Using External Treebanks to Filter Parse Forests for Parse Selection and Treebanking

Andrew MacKinlay[◇♡], **Rebecca Dridan**[◇♡], **Dan Flickinger**[♣], **Stephan Oepen**[♠] **and Timothy Baldwin**[◇♡]

[◇] Dept of Computer Science and Software Engineering, University of Melbourne, Australia

[♡] NICTA Victoria Research Laboratories, University of Melbourne, Australia

[♣] Center for Study of Language and Information, Stanford University, USA

[♠] Department of Informatics, Universitetet i Oslo, Norway

amack@csse.unimelb.edu.au, rdridan@csse.unimelb.edu.au, danf@stanford.edu, oe@ifi.uio.no, tb@ldwin.net

Abstract

We describe "treeblazing", a method of using annotations from the GENIA treebank to constrain a parse forest from an HPSG parser. Combining this with self-training, we show significant dependency score improvements in a task of adaptation to the biomedical domain, reducing error rate by 9% compared to out-of-domain gold data and 6% compared to self-training. We also demonstrate improvements in treebanking efficiency, requiring 25% fewer decisions, and 17% less annotation time.

1 Introduction

Computational linguistic research is driven by the development of reference resources for specific tasks and languages. The advent of services such as Amazon's Mechanical Turk has driven down the cost of annotation considerably, assuming a given task can be broken down into piecemeal units which are intuitive and manageable for non-experts. This is not an option, however, for fine-grained tasks which require an expert understanding of a theory or domain, such as syntactic treebanking or discourse annotation.

Two main approaches have been adopted to efficiently create new resources: (1) domain adaptation, where a trained model from one domain is stochastically adapted to a new domain, using unlabelled data from the new domain (Daumé III and Marcu, 2006); and (2) annotation projection, where the labels in a pre-existing resource are semi-automatically translated into an independent formalism, e.g. in translating the PTB into the CCG formalism (Hockenmaier and Steedman, 2002). This paper looks at both of these approaches: domain adaptation from unannotated data in the form of self-training combined with resource translation over the GENIA treebank (Yuka et al., 2005), in the context of training an HPSG parse selection model for biomedical text, and using the GENIA treebank annotations and retrained parse selection model to accelerate treebanking.

Our contributions are: (1) we propose a series of methods for transferring annotation from a traditional phrase structure treebank to constrain the parse forest of a precision grammar; (2) we show that this constrained forest can be used to domain-adapt a parse selection model; (3) we demonstrate improvements in treebanking performance using the constrained forest; and (4) we develop a small-scale HPSG treebank for the biomedical domain.

2 Related Work

Domain adaptation is an active research area, triggered by the observation that parsers trained on one domain show decreased performance when used in other domains (Gildea, 2001). Much domain-adaptation work involves some small amount of in-domain data to tune a model, but McClosky et al. (2006) showed "self-training" using unannotated in-domain data could achieve significant improvements in parser accuracy.

In parsing-related research that has used annotated data, but in an incompatible format, we see two main use cases. The first uses an existing treebank to create a treebank for some completely different linguistic framework, generally to induce a grammar in that framework. Xia (1999) presents work on transforming Penn Treebank (PTB) trees into Lexicalized Tree Adjoining Grammar (LTAG) structures. The work of Hockenmaier and Steedman (2002) is roughly parallel, but targets Combinatory Categorial Grammar (CCG). The techniques include binarisation, adding an extra level of NP structure, and remapping node labels to CCG categories. An analog in the framework of Head-driven Phrase Structure Grammar (HPSG) is described by Miyao et al. (2004).

The second use case is to use the incompatible annotations to select the correct tree from the output of a compatible parser. Sometimes, a function over the original annotations produces a score of the new analysis candidates, and a single best analysis is selected (Wang et al., 1994; Niu et al., 2009). In other work, the original annotations do not uniquely disambiguate the parse forest, but the partial annotations can still be used. Riezler et al. (2002) used PTB annotations to partially disambiguate a parse forest built using a grammar in the Lexical-Functional Grammar (LFG) framework (Butt et al., 2002), and then built a model using the partially-disambiguated forest. Another use of partially disambiguated forests is described by Tanaka et al. (2005), who manually created a Japanese treebank (Bond et al., 2004) by selecting the best parses from the candidate parses offered as candidates from JaCy, an HPSG grammar of Japanese. The annotators reject or affirm *discriminants* to select the best tree, as is described in more detail in §3.1. Their data was already human-annotated with POS tags, which they used to constrain the parse forest, requiring on average 19.5% fewer decisions and 15% less time per tree.

Tanaka et al. (2005) used only POS tags. Our work can be viewed as a syntactic extension of this. We investigate strategies for adapting the English Resource Grammar (ERG: Flickinger (2000)) to the biomedical domain using information contained in the GENIA treebank (GTB), a corpus of 1,999 abstracts from PubMed in the domain of human blood cells and transcription factors, annotated according to a slightly simplified version of the PTB II annotation guidelines.

3 Setup

We explore two branches of experimentation using a common core of tools, resources and methods. This section describes the necessary details of our treebanking process, the test data we use, and some peculiarities of parsing biomedical data that affected our experiments.

3.1 Treebanking

All our experiments are based on the Redwoods treebanking methodology (Oepen et al., 2004), where the treebank is constructed by selecting from a parse forest of candidate trees licensed by the grammar. All experiments reported in this paper make use of the ERG. We first parse an input, and then select the (up to) 500 top-ranked parse trees according to a parse selection model. This set of parse trees is then presented to the human treebanker in the form of *discriminants* (Carter, 1997; Oepen et al., 2004). The discriminants used here correspond to instantiations of the 200 lexical and syntactic rules of the ERG, as well as the lexical entries themselves, but only those that correspond to ambiguity in the parse forest and can thus discriminate between candidate parse trees.

During treebanking, the annotator confirms or rejects some subset of discriminants, and at each stage, the Redwoods machinery performs inference to automatically reject those discriminants that are incompatible with the current set of manually-selected and inferred discriminants. This means that each manual decision can directly or indirectly rule out a large number of trees, and the number of decisions required is on average proportional to the logarithm of the number of parses (Tanaka et al., 2005).

Treebanking gives us a large number of rejected trees, along with the single correct gold tree, which can be used to build a discriminative parse selection model, in our case using TADM (Malouf, 2002). This is applied to parsing unseen data, and also for the next iteration of treebanking.

3.2 Data: a new biomedical HPSG treebank

In order to evaluate the impact of the proposed method on parser accuracy over biomedical text, we require a gold-standard treebank in the target domain. We use a subset of the data used in the GTB, created by first removing those abstracts (approximately half) that overlap with the GENIA event corpus (GEC: Kim et al. (2008)), to hold out for future work. From this filtered set, our test corpus comes from the 993 sentences of the first 118 abstracts (PubMed IDs 1279685 to 2077396).

Our treebankers both have detailed knowledge of the ERG, but no domain-specific biomedical expertise. As a proxy for this, they used the original GTB syntactic annotations when a tie-breaker was needed for ambiguities such as PP-attachment or co-ordination. The annotators were instructed to only refer to GTB trees when the ambiguity was not resolvable on linguistic grounds. The first 200 sentences of the corpus were double-annotated in each round of treebanking (agreement figures for unseen data are shown in §6.3)

The first round of annotation of a 500-sentence subset of the corpus served to determine a suitable parser configuration and calibrate between annotators using the 200-sentence overlap. From this, we developed a set of annotation guidelines, which will be made available with the corpus. One key domain-specific guideline related to the treatment of noun compounds, which are never disambiguated in the flat GTB structure. In the biomedical domain, noun compounds are generally left-bracketed – 83% of three-word compounds according to Nakov and Hearst (2005) – so we stipulated that noun compounds should be left-bracketed and adjectives attached high in cases of doubt, as a tie-breaking strategy.

We also used this first-iteration treebank to build a domain-tuned parse-selection model (duplicating the data 10 times and combining it with a larger out-of-domain corpus, using the DUPLIC method of MacKinlay et al. (2011) to provide improvements for sparse in-domain data). The external corpus was the WeScience corpus (Ytrestøl et al., 2009), a selection of Wikipedia articles on NLP. We improved the parser's handling of named entities, as described in §3.3, and then reparsed the treebank with the new parsing configuration and parse selection model, giving 866 parseable sentences. After updating the treebank according to the new guidelines using this new parse forest, and checking inter-annotator agreement on the overlap, we annotated the remaining sentences. All accuracy figures we report are over the data set of 669 trees complete at the time of experimentation.

3.3 Biomedical parsing setup

We parsed sentences using the ERG with the PET parser (Callmeier, 2000), which uses POS tags to constrain unknown words. Following Velldal et al. (2010), we primarily use the biomedically trained GENIA tagger (Tsuruoka et al., 2005), but defer to TnT (Brants, 2000) for tagging nominal elements, because it makes a useful distinction between common and proper nouns.

Biomedical text poses a unique set of challenges, mostly relating to named entities, such as proteins, DNA and cell lines. To address this, we used the GENIA tagger as a named-entity (NE) recogniser, treating named entities as atomic lexical items. However, the NE tagging is often overzealous and discards internal structure, misleading the parser. To overcome this, we supply multi-token NEs as both a single atomic NE token and the individual words, thus giving PET a lattice as input. The increased parse coverage and better parse quality made this a worthwhile strategy, with the downside of increased ambiguity, making parse selection more difficult.

4 Blazing

In §2, we reviewed work that uses linguistic information from superficially incompatible formalisms for treebanking or parse selection. Our experiments here use syntactic information from the GTB to partially disambiguate the parse forest produced by the ERG. We do this by disallowing certain candidate ERG trees on the basis of GTB-derived information, and we follow Tanaka et al. (2005) in denoting this process "blazing".[1]

As detailed below, we can use this partially disambiguated forest: (1) to train parse selection models; and (2) to reduce treebanking effort, abstractly similarly to Tanaka et al. (2005). The goal is not to apply all constraints from the GTB to the ERG parse trees; rather, we want to apply the *minimal* amount of constraints possible, while still sufficiently restricting the parse forest for our target application. We call the set of trees remaining after blazing *silver* trees, to represent the fact that they are not gold standard, but are generally of better quality than the discarded analyses.

For an iteration of blazing, we parse each GTB sentence, obtaining the top-500 trees according to the parse selection model. Each discriminant (as discussed in §3.1) which corresponds to a meaningful difference between the candidate trees (derivations) is supplied to the blazing module.

A given discriminant can be ruled out, ignored or asserted to be true, but we never make use of the latter, since we can just rule out incompatible discriminants, which are easier to identify. This process happens with all discriminants for a sentence simultaneously, so it is possible to rule out all parse trees. This may indicate that none of the candidate parses are desirable, or that the imperfect blazing process is not completely successful.

The blazing module is given the GTB XML source for the tree, and a set of discriminants, each of which includes the name of the rule or lexical

[1] Which is a term in forestry: marking trees for removal.

entry, as well as the corresponding character span in the source tree. It applies some pre-configured transformations to the GTB tree, and examines each discriminant for whether it should be ruled out, by comparing to the corresponding GTB constituents overlapping with the supplied character span. Primarily, these decisions depend on whether a discriminant is a *crossing-bracket discriminant*, i.e. corresponds to phrase structures in the ERG derivation trees which would have crossing brackets with any overlapping constituents (ignoring punctuation). As discussed below, in some configurations we can also use the rule name or lexical type to rule out particular discriminants.

5 Parse Selection

Our first set of experiments was designed to evaluate the impact of blazing on parse selection, specifically in a domain-adaptation scenario. As mentioned in §3.1, parse selection is the process of selecting the top *n* parses, using a discriminative statistical model trained using the correct and incorrect trees from the treebanking process. However, as discussed in §2, statistical models are highly sensitive to differences in domain, and ideally, one would domain-tune off in-domain treebank data. Self-training (e.g. McClosky et al. (2006)) bypasses this need for in-domain annotations, by parsing the new domain with an out-of-domain model, treating the top-ranked parse as gold, and training a new model accordingly. In this work, we extend that idea by using blazing to transfer annotations from the GTB, hopefully filtering out incorrect trees in the process, and arrive at better-quality top-ranked parses.

5.1 Blazing configurations

Blazing depends on the fact that the ERG and the GTB both have a theoretical linguistic underpinning, and so we expect they would share many assumptions about phrase structure, particularly for phenomena such as PP-attachment and co-ordination. However there are also disparities, even between the unlabelled bracketing of the GTB and ERG trees.

One pervasive difference is the attachment of specifiers and pre- and post-modifiers to NPs. The GTB attaches pre-modifiers and specifiers as low as possible, before attaching post-modifying PPs at a higher level, while the ERG makes the opposite decision and disallows this order of attachment. The other important difference is phrase branching – the GTB allows arbitrarily many children per node, while the ERG allows at most two. We show a sample NP exemplifying the differences in Figure 1.

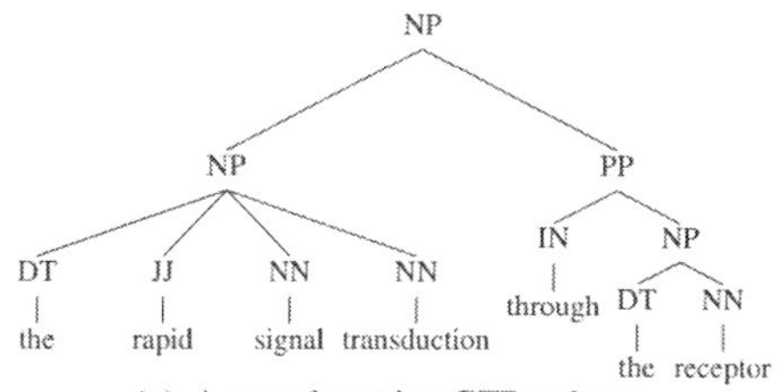

(a) A sample native GTB subtree

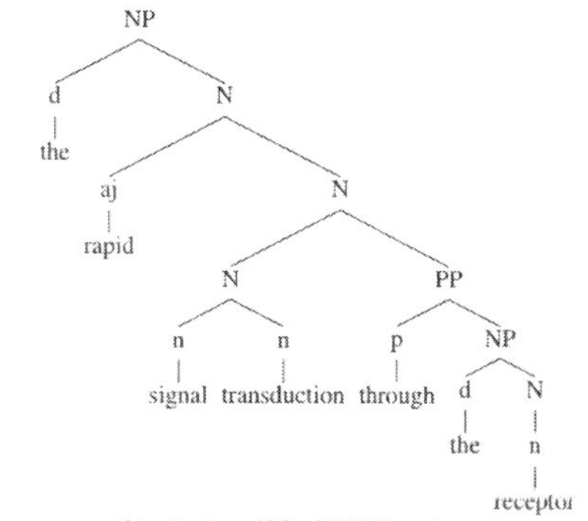

(b) A simplified ERG subtree

Figure 1: Sample trees

One strategy for handling this is to make as few assumptions as possible while avoiding spurious conflicts. Denoted **IEP** (*ignore equal parent*), it involves ignoring GTB nodes with the same label as the parent when looking for crossing-bracket constituents. From the GTB tree in Figure 1, the blazing module would ignore the boundaries of the second-level NP when looking for crossing-bracket discriminants. This ensures that we never rule out the corresponding good subtree shown in the figure in favour of some invalid bracketing from the ERG that by chance has no conflicts with the GTB tree; meanwhile the PP would still be considered. Note that for a flat NP with no post-modifiers, no changes are necessary as the external boundaries still correspond with the edges of the top-level NP in the ERG, and the extra internal boundaries in the ERG have no effect since they cannot cause any crossing brackets.

Alternatively, to avoid discarding possibly valid syntactic information, we can attempt to account for the systematic differences by mapping the GTB as closely as possible to the structures we would expect in the ERG before looking for crossing-bracket discriminants. Firstly, the phrases are binarised in a similar way to much previous work (Miyao et al., 2004; Hockenmaier and Steedman, 2002). We heuristically determine the head of each phrase using a simple category match between the phrase category and the POS, then recursively split multiple-branched nodes. This binarisation applies to all phrasal categories, not just NPs. We then systematically alter the attachment positions of determiners and pre-nominal modifiers, forcing them to attach as high as possible, but preserving the binary branching. As a lightweight but imperfect attempt to avoid creating invalid structures for appositions and conjunctions, this NP rearrangement is abandoned if any tokens are parentheses, commas or conjunctions. The transformation is labelled **RP** (*raise premods*).

5.2 Experimental Configuration

We create a parse forest by parsing 10747 sentences from a GTB subset not overlapping with the test corpus, using the WeScience model to determine the top 500 parses. The best-performing method we found to create parse selection models from this parse forest was to apply the blazing configurations to determine the *silver* trees, and then select the top-ranked parse from that set, according to the WeScience model. We call this top parse our *pseudo-gold* analysis. Remaining silver trees are ignored, while incorrect trees are used as negative data as usual. To show how much effect blazing has, we also used two other methods to select the pseudo-gold parse: random selection from that same top 500, to give us a baseline, and 'plain' self-training using the top-ranked parse without the blazing-based filtering, in each case using other trees from the forest as negative data. We then trained parse selection models using the gold standard out-of-domain (WeScience) data plus the in-domain pseudo-gold analyses from each configuration, and evaluated by parsing our test corpus.

5.3 Evaluation

We use two different styles of evaluation metric. In keeping with previous work using the ERG, we report exact match figures, denoted Acc_N, representing the percentage of sentences for which the exact gold tree was in the top *N* parses. Here, as in Zhang et al. (2007), we use Acc_1 and Acc_{10}. However, exact match can be very blunt for the fine-grained ERG analyses, giving no indication of how 'right' or 'wrong' the top analysis is. To supplement Acc_N, we use Elementary Dependency Match (EDM: Dridan and Oepen (2011)). This is based on triples extracted from the semantic output of the parser, providing a more granular measure of the quality of the analyses. We use the EDM_{NA} configuration that is arguably the most compatible with other dependency-based parser evaluation, although we make no claims of direct comparability.

Config	Gold Added	Acc A_1 / A_{10}	EDM_{NA} P / R / F
(WeSc only)	WeSc	12.3 / 39.2	82.4 / 79.2 / 80.7
Random	WeSc	6.1 / 20.0	70.7 / 70.2 / 70.5
Self-train	WeSc	12.9 / 39.2	82.4 / 80.3 / 81.3 *
IEP + S-T	WeSc	12.9 / 39.2	83.5 / 80.9 / 82.2 *** ††
RP + S-T	WeSc	13.3 / 40.1	83.8 / 81.2 / 82.5 *** †††

Table 1: Results over the test corpus. "WeSc only" shows parsing using a pure WeScience model. Other configurations used models trained from the same training sentence parse forest, setting a pseudo-gold tree either randomly, self-trained (best from a WeScience model), or blazing (highest-ranked of the silver trees, other silver trees discarded). The gold WeScience data is also used for training. Significance figures are against "WeSc only", (*: $p < 0.05$; ***:$p < 0.001$), and "Self-train", (††: $p < 0.01$; †††: $p < 0.001$)

5.4 Results

We present our results in Table 1, including the best-performing blazing configurations, the self-training results and the weak baseline trained on a random tree from the same GTB parse forest as used in blazing.

We also show the parsing accuracy results obtained using only out-of-domain data, designated "WeSc only", as a strong baseline. We see some evidence that self-training can be a useful domain-adaptation strategy, giving a weakly significant F-score improvement over using WeScience only. This echoes previously mentioned work, although has not been evaluated for this parser or grammar before. More importantly, our blazing strategy yields strongly significant F-score improvements over both the strong baseline out-of-domain model and the standard self-training.

5.5 Discussion

There is strong evidence that these blazing methods can help create a parse selection model to give

	IEP	RP
Discrims/Sent	144.2	144.2
Rejected/Sent	40.8	42.8
Unblazed Sents	3.9%	3.4%
Overblazed Sents	14.2%	15.3%
Usably Blazed Sents	81.9%	81.3%
Trees/Sent (overall)	423.3	423.3
Silver Trees/Sent (blazed)	98.4	88.5
Silver Trees/Sent (usable)	120.1	108.8

Table 2: Blazing Statistics, over all 10747 parseable training sentences. The first block shows discriminants available per sentence, and how many were rejected by the blazing (removing ≥ 1 tree). The second block shows percentage of unblazed sentences (no discriminants rejected), overblazed sentences (all trees removed) and usably-blazed sentences (≥ 1 removed and ≥ 1 silver tree remaining). The third block shows how many parses were produced initially, the average number of trees remaining over blazed sentences (inc. overblazed with 0 trees) and the average number remaining over usably blazed.

a significant boost in dependency score without needing additional human annotation. The exact match results are inconclusive – the best improvement is not significant, although the granular EDM metric may provide a better reflection of performance for downstream applications in any case.

In our initial investigations, a range of configurations failed to provide improvements over the baseline. If we don't augment the training data with human-annotated WeScience data, the performance drops. Also, if we don't use the self-training/blazing combination as described but instead treated all silver trees as pseudo-gold (i.e treat all remaining post-blazing parse trees as if they were manually marked as good), the model performs poorly. Table 2 provides some explanation for this. Over sentences which provide usable discriminative training data (at least one incorrect and one silver tree), on average more than 100 silver trees remain, so it is failing to disambiguate sufficiently between the ERG analyses. This is probably due to an imperfect transfer process and shallower, less precise GTB analyses.

6 Reducing treebanking labour

Blazing is designed to reduce the size of the parse forest, so it seems natural to evaluate its impact on the treebanking process, and whether we can reduce the amount of time and number of decisions required to enable more efficient treebanking.

6.1 Mapping between treebanks

In addition to the transformation strategies mentioned in §5.1, we used a number of additional strategies (most of which we had already tried initially, for parse selection, but rejected). One rule concerns the internals of noun compounds, which are flat in the GTB; we may wish to add some structure to them. As discussed in §3.2, biomedical noun compounds are predominantly left-bracketed, and left-bracketing was also our tie-breaking policy for annotating the test set. In the **BNC** strategy (*bracket noun compounds*), we added bracketing to noun compounds to have noun sequences maximally left bracketed, and adjectives attaching as high as possible. This makes assumptions which are not explicitly licensed by the data (and arguably overfits to our data set), so this transformation is only applied where no useful distinctions are made by less restrictive approaches.

We also use a mapping strategy which does not make changes to the tree structure but which use the POS labels to rule out trees, denoted **MP** for *map POS*. It uses the prefixes of the lexical types – e.g. a simple transitive verb would have the lexical type *v_np_le*, where the prefix 'v' indicates 'verb'. We used a mapping constructed by manual inspection of a correspondence matrix between the POS tags produced by TnT (Brants, 2000) and the lexical type prefixes from the gold-standard ERG parse of the same sentences over a WeScience subset. This gave us the matching ERG type prefixes for 20 PTB/GTB POS tags, which are mostly what we would expect for the open classes – e.g. *VB** verb tags map to the 'v' prefix.

During mapping, given a pairing of a GENIA tree and a set of ERG discriminants, for each POS tag or inner node in the GENIA tree, we find all lexical discriminants with the same character span. If there are multiple discriminants with different matching labels, and there is at least one allowed and one disallowed by the mapping, then we reject all disallowed discriminants. This is less sophisticated than the mapping technique of Tanaka et al. (2005) for various reasons.

6.2 Selecting a blazing strategy

There are a range of blazing strategies and combinations thereof, with varying levels of validity and restrictiveness. Ideally, during treebanking we would start with a more restrictive blazing strat-

		Standard		Blazed	
Ann 1	Decisions	6.25	7	3.51	4
	Time (sec)	150	144	113	107
Ann 2	Decisions	6.42	7	4.68	4
	Time (sec)	105	101	96	80

Table 3: Number of decisions and treebanking time (mean then median) using the fallback blazing configuration (80 sentences for each column)

	Ann. 1			
	Std	Blz		
Agreed Sentences	42.5	45.0	Std	Ann. 2
Agreed, excl rej	32.4	33.3		
Rejection F-score	80.0	82.4		
Constituent F-score	88.7	87.6		
Agreed Sentences	42.5	57.5	Blz	
Agreed, excl rej	39.5	45.2		
Rejection F-score	44.4	78.3		
Constituent F-score	86.2	84.8		

Table 4: Agreement figures for different combinations of blazed and unblazed overlap between annotators 1 and 2, with 40 sentences per cell. 'Agreed' is the percentage of those with an identical tree selected, or all trees rejected; 'excl rej' ignores sentences rejected by either annotator. 'Constituent F-score' (also excludes rejections) is the harmonic mean of the labelled per-constituent precision. 'Rejection F-score' is the harmonic mean of the precision of rejection decisions.

egy, and dynamically fall back to a less restrictive strategy, but this capability is not yet present in the Redwoods machinery. Our approach is based on the number of decisions being logarithmic in the number of trees. If we can get roughly 40 silver trees, the remaining treebanking is very tractable and fast, only requiring a few decisions chosen from a handful of remaining discriminants. However further restriction below this saves relatively little time, and increases the chance of the blazing removing the correct tree, which we wish to avoid (the machinery does not allow the treebanker to 'undo' either manual or blazed decisions, except by clearing and restarting).

The parse forest for treebanking was created by having a list of candidate blazing strategies using various combinations of **IEP** (least restrictive), **RP**, **BNC** and **MP** – with the combination **RP +BNC +MP** as the most restrictive. For each sentence, we select the least restrictive strategy which still gives us fewer remaining trees than a threshold of 40. If no strategies do so, we use the strategy which gives us the fewest trees for the given sentence. Using another subset of the GENIA treebank containing 864 parseable sentences, 48% of sentences came below the threshold of 40, while 36% were above and 16% were not disambiguated at all. Most sentences (41%) used the least restrictive configuration using **IEP** alone.

6.3 Blazed Treebanking Results

For this strategy to be useful for treebanking, it should be both more efficient, in terms of fewer decisions and less annotation time, and valid, in terms of not introducing a bias when compared to conventional unblazed treebanking. To evaluate these questions, we selected 160 sentences at random from the previously described parse forest of 864 sentences. These sentences were divided randomly into four equal-sized groups: blazed for both annotators, standard for both annotators, and two groups blazed for one annotator only, so we could compare data about timing and decisions between the standard and blazed sentences for each annotator, and inter-annotator agreement for each possible combination of blazed and standard treebanking. The divisions took no account of whether we were able to usably blaze the sentences, reflecting the real-world scenario, so some sentences in the blazed configuration had no restrictions applied. The items were presented to the annotators so they could not tell whether the other annotator was treebanking in standard or blazed configuration, to prevent subconscious biases affecting inter-annotator agreement. The experiments were conducted after both annotators had already familiarised themselves with the treebanking environment as well as the characteristics of the domain and the annotation guidelines.

Annotators worked in a distraction-free environment so we could get accurate timing figures. The treebanking machinery records how many decisions were made as well as annotation time, both important factors in annotation efficiency. The results for efficiency are shown in Table 3 where we see a 43% reduction in the mean decisions required for annotator 1, and 27% reduction for annotator 2. Annotator 1 also shows substantial 25% reduction in mean annotation time, but the time decrease for annotator 2 is only 8%. In 30% of successfully-blazed sentences, the annotators cleared all blazed decisions, suggesting it is sometimes too zealous.

For agreement, we show results for the strictest

possible criterion of exact tree match. For a less blunt metric that still roughly reflects agreement, we also follow Tanaka et al. (2005) in reporting the (micro-averaged) harmonic mean of precision across labelled constituents indexed by character span, where constituents selected by both annotators are treated as gold (inaccurately denoted 'F-score' for brevity). Annotators should also agree on rejected trees, where no parses are valid. In Table 4, we show exact match agreement accuracy (identical trees and matching rejections both count as correct), as well as the same figure ignoring sentences rejected by either, and the harmonic mean of precision of both labelled constituents and tree rejections. The figures are similar between cells, with notable exceptions being higher exact match when both annotators had blazed forests, and a surprising dip in the rejection "F-score" in the bottom left cell. The latter is partially because the rejection scores are based on small numbers of trees (5–10, the union of the sets of rejected trees), so are sensitive to small numbers of disagreements. In this particular case, of 7 trees rejected by either annotator, 2 were rejected by both.

6.4 Blazed Treebanking Discussion

The reductions in mean numbers of decisions strongly support the efficacy of this technique, although the discrepancies between the annotators suggest that the different treebanking techniques may be more or less amenable to speed-up using these tools. The timing figures are somewhat more equivocal, although still a substantial 25% for annotator 1. This is partially to be expected, since some of the treebanking will be taken up with unavoidable tasks such as evaluating whether the final tree is acceptable that blazing cannot avoid. However, the 8% reduction in mean annotation time for annotator 2 is still fairly modest. This could be affected by annotator 2's more extensive treebanking experience leading to a lower baseline time, with less room for improvement, but as we still see a 21% reduction in median parsing time this could be due to a few outlier sentences inflating the mean for the blazed configuration.

For agreement, we are primarily concerned here with whether blazing here introduces a bias that is distinguishable from what we see when annotators are working under standard non-blazed conditions – which may be manifested in decreased agreement between configurations where only one annotator has blazed data, and when both have non-blazed data. Thus the fact that we see quite similar agreement figures between the half-blazed and standard configurations is very encouraging (apart from the low F-score for rejections in one cell). This small amount of data suggests that any changes in the resultant trees introduced by blazing are hard to distinguish from the inevitable "background noise". Given this, the fact that we see a noticeably higher exact match score when both annotators have blazed sentences suggests we may be justified in using blazing to improve inter-annotator agreement, although the lower constituent score may indicate we have insufficient data to reach that conclusion.

7 Conclusion and Future Work

We have presented a procedure for blazing – using annotations from an external phrase structure treebank to constrain the parse forest produced by a precision HPSG grammar. Our work used the GENIA treebank and the ERG as the target grammar, although it would in principle be applicable to any similar phrase structure treebank and other grammars or even frameworks. The GENIA trees were mapped onto corresponding ERG parse forests and used to exclude incompatible trees. In conjunction with self-training, we used this to create a parse selection model for the ERG adapted to the biomedical domain. We also used it as a pre-filter to the treebanking process to improve treebanking efficiency, and created an HPSG treebank of biomedical text.

For future work, we would investigate whether this training data can be useful to augment a small in-domain human-annotated treebank, and whether the methods do indeed generalise to other corpora and grammars.

Acknowledgements

We thank Phil Blunsom and Jonathon Read for their helpful advice. NICTA is funded by the Australian Government as represented by the Department of Broadband, Communications and the Digital Economy and the Australian Research Council through the ICT Centre of Excellence program. The first author's conference travel is funded by a Google Travel Award. Large-scale experimentation was in part made possible though access to the TITAN HPC facilities at the University of Oslo.

References

Francis Bond, Sanae Fujita, Chikara Hashimoto, Kaname Kasahara, Shigeko Nariyama, Eric Nichols, Akira Ohtani, Takaaki Tanaka, and Shigeaki Amano. 2004. The Hinoki treebank: A treebank for text understanding. In *In Proc. of the First IJCNLP, Lecture Notes in Computer Science*, pages 554–559. Springer Verlag.

Thorsten Brants. 2000. TnT – a statistical part-of-speech tagger. In *Proceedings of the Sixth Conference on Applied Natural Language Processing*, pages 224–231, Seattle, Washington, USA, April. Association for Computational Linguistics.

Miriam Butt, Helge Dyvik, Tracy Holloway King, Hiroshi Masuichi, and Christian Rohrer. 2002. The parallel grammar project. In *Proceedings of COLING-2002 Workshop on Grammar Engineering and Evaluation*, pages 1–7.

Ulrich Callmeier. 2000. PET – a platform for experimentation with efficient HPSG processing techniques. *Nat. Lang. Eng.*, 6(1):99–107.

David Carter. 1997. The TreeBanker. A tool for supervised training of parsed corpora. In *Proceedings of the Workshop on Computational Environments for Grammar Development and Linguistic Engineering*, pages 9–15, Madrid, Spain.

Hal Daumé III and Daniel Marcu. 2006. Domain adaptation for statistical classifiers. *Journal of Artificial Intelligence Research*, 26(1):101–126.

Rebecca Dridan and Stephan Oepen. 2011. Parser evaluation using elementary dependency matching (to appear). In *Proceedings of the 12th International Conference on Parsing Technologies*.

Dan Flickinger. 2000. On building a more efficient grammar by exploiting types. *Natural Language Engineering*, 6 (1):15–28.

Daniel Gildea. 2001. Corpus variation and parser performance. In *Proceedings of EMNLP 2001*, pages 167–202, Pittsburgh, USA.

Julia Hockenmaier and Mark Steedman. 2002. Acquiring compact lexicalized grammars from a cleaner treebank. In *Proceedings of Third International Conference on Language Resources and Evaluation*, Las Palmas.

Jin-Dong Kim, Tomoko Ohta, and Jun'ichi Tsujii. 2008. Corpus annotation for mining biomedical events from literature. *BMC Bioinformatics*, 9:10.

Andrew MacKinlay, Rebecca Dridan, Dan Flickinger, and Timothy Baldwin. 2011. Cross-domain effects on parse selection for precision grammars (to appear). *Research on Language and Computation*.

R. Malouf. 2002. A comparison of algorithms for maximum entropy parameter estimation. In *Proceedings of the Sixth Conference on Natural Language Learning (CoNLL-2002)*, pages 49–55.

David McClosky, Eugene Charniak, and Mark Johnson. 2006. Reranking and self-training for parser adaptation. In *Proceedings of the COLING/ACL 2006*, pages 337–344, Sydney, Australia.

Yusuke Miyao, Takashi Ninomiya, and Jun'ichi Tsujii. 2004. Corpus-oriented grammar development for acquiring a head-driven phrase structure grammar from the penn treebank. In *Proceedings of IJCNLP-04*.

Preslav Nakov and Marti Hearst. 2005. Search engine statistics beyond the n-gram: application to noun compound bracketing. In *Proceedings of the Ninth Conference on Computational Natural Language Learning*, CONLL '05, pages 17–24, Stroudsburg, PA, USA. Association for Computational Linguistics.

Zheng-Yu Niu, Haifeng Wang, and Hua Wu. 2009. Exploiting heterogeneous treebanks for parsing. In *Proceedings of the Joint Conference of the 47th Annual Meeting of the ACL and the 4th International Joint Conference on Natural Language Processing of the AFNLP*, pages 46–54, Suntec, Singapore, August. Association for Computational Linguistics.

S. Oepen, D. Flickinger, K. Toutanova, and C.D. Manning. 2004. LinGO Redwoods: A Rich and Dynamic Treebank for HPSG. *Research on Language & Computation*, 2(4):575–596.

Stefan Riezler, Tracy H. King, Ronald M. Kaplan, Richard Crouch, John T. Maxwell, III, and Mark Johnson. 2002. Parsing the wall street journal using a lexical-functional grammar and discriminative estimation techniques. In *Proceedings of the 40th Annual Meeting on Association for Computational Linguistics*, ACL '02, pages 271–278, Stroudsburg, PA, USA. Association for Computational Linguistics.

Takaaki Tanaka, Francis Bond, Stephan Oepen, and Sanae Fujita. 2005. High precision treebanking—blazing useful trees using POS information. In *Proceedings of the 43rd Annual Meeting of the Association for Computational Linguistics (ACL'05)*, pages 330–337, Ann Arbor, Michigan, June. Association for Computational Linguistics.

Yoshimasa Tsuruoka, Yuka Tateishi, Jin-Dong Kim, Tomoko Ohta, John McNaught, Sophia Ananiadou, and Jun'ichi Tsujii. 2005. Developing a robust part-of-speech tagger for biomedical text. *Advances in Informatics*, pages 382–392.

Erik Velldal, Lilja Øvrelid, and Stephan Oepen. 2010. Resolving speculation: MaxEnt cue classification and dependency-based scope rules. In *Proceedings of the Fourteenth Conference on Computational Natural Language Learning*, pages 48–55, Uppsala, Sweden, July. Association for Computational Linguistics.

Jong-Nae Wang, Jing-Shin Chang, and Keh-Yih Su. 1994. An automatic treebank conversion algorithm for corpus sharing. In *Proceedings of the 32nd Annual Meeting of the Association for Computational Linguistics*, pages 248–254, Las Cruces, New Mexico, USA, June. Association for Computational Linguistics.

F. Xia. 1999. Extracting tree adjoining grammars from bracketed corpora. In *Proceedings of the 5th Natural Language Processing Pacific Rim Symposium (NLPRS-99)*, pages 398–403.

Gisle Ytrestøl, Dan Flickinger, and Stephan Oepen. 2009. Extracting and annotating Wikipedia sub-domains – towards a new eScience community resource. In *Proceedings of the Seventh International Workshop on Treebanks and Linguistic Theories*, Groeningen, The Netherlands, January.

Tateisi Yuka, Akane Yakushiji, Tomoko Ohta, and Jun'ichi Tsujii. 2005. Syntax annotation for the GENIA corpus. In *Proceedings of the IJCNLP 2005*, pages 222–227, Jeju Island, Korea.

Yi Zhang, Stephan Oepen, and John Carroll. 2007. Efficiency in unification-based N-best parsing. In *Proceedings of IWPT 2007*, pages 48–59, Prague, Czech Republic.

Cross-Language Entity Linking

Paul McNamee and **James Mayfield**
HLTCOE & Applied Physics Laboratory
Johns Hopkins University
{paul.mcnamee,james.mayfield}@jhuapl.edu

Dawn Lawrie
Loyola University Maryland
lawrie@cs.loyola.edu

Douglas W. Oard
iSchool & UMIACS
University of Maryland, College Park
oard@umd.edu

David Doermann
UMIACS
University of Maryland, College Park
doermann@umiacs.umd.edu

Abstract

There has been substantial recent interest in aligning mentions of named entities in unstructured texts to knowledge base descriptors, a task commonly called *entity linking*. This technology is crucial for applications in knowledge discovery and text data mining. This paper presents experiments in the new problem of *cross-language entity linking*, where documents and named entities are in a different language than that used for the content of the reference knowledge base. We have created a new test collection to evaluate cross-language entity linking performance in twenty-one languages. We present experiments that examine issues such as: the importance of transliteration; the utility of cross-language information retrieval; and, the potential benefit of multilingual named entity recognition. Our best model achieves performance which is 94% of a strong monolingual baseline.

1 Introduction

Entity Linking involves aligning a textual mention of a named entity to the entry in a knowledge base (KB) that represents the mentioned entity, if it is present. The problem has two main complicating features: entities can be referred to using multiple name variants (*e.g.*, aliases or misspellings); and several entities can share the same name (*e.g.*, many people are named María Sánchez). Applications of entity linking include linking patient health records from separate hospitalizations, maintaining personal credit files, preventing identity crimes, and supporting law enforcement.

Starting in 2009 the NIST Text Analysis Conference (TAC) began conducting evaluations of technologies for knowledge base population (KBP). Systems addressing the entity linking subtask take as input a name string from a document and produce as output the knowledge base node, if any, corresponding to the mentioned entity. This capability is vital for knowledge discovery; without it, extracted information cannot be properly inserted in the correct KB node. We follow the TAC-KBP problem formulation and use its reference knowledge base, which was derived from a 2008 snapshot of English Wikipedia. In the present work our focus is on person entities. We seek to develop and evaluate technologies for matching foreign language names to the appropriate knowledge base descriptor (or *kbid*) in the English KB.

To support this research we created what we believe to be the first cross-language entity linking test collection. Our dataset includes twenty-one languages in addition to English, and covers five writing systems. Compared to the problem of monolingual (English) entity linking, a solution to the cross-language variant requires both a method to match foreign names to their English equivalents, and a way to compare contextual features from the non-English source document with contextual information about known entities stored in the KB. Figure 1 illustrates the process.

The rest of this paper is structured as follows. In Section 2 we discuss related work in entity linking and cross-language name matching. In Section 3 we present our approach to monolingual entity linking and describe the adaptations that are required to address the cross-language problem. Section 4 discusses the TAC-KBP evaluation and the construction of our test collection. Sections 5 and 6 present experiments exploring the effects of transliteration and cross-language content matching on the problem. Section 7 summarizes the main contributions of this work.

Figure 1: Linking an Arabic query referring to Tony Blair to a Wikipedia-derived KB using name matching and context matching features.

```
⟨entity wiki_title="Tony_Blair" type="PER" id="E0481157" name="Tony Blair"⟩
⟨facts class="Infobox Prime Minister"⟩
⟨fact name="honorific-prefix"⟩The Right Honourable⟨/fact⟩
⟨fact name="name"⟩Tony Blair⟨/fact⟩
⟨fact name="order"⟩Prime Minister of the United Kingdom⟨/fact⟩
⟨fact name="monarch"⟩⟨link entity_id="E0699345"⟩Elizabeth II⟨/link⟩⟨/fact⟩
⟨fact name="predecessor"⟩⟨link entity_id="E0614790"⟩John Major⟨/link⟩⟨/fact⟩
⟨fact name="successor"⟩⟨link entity_id="E0455080"⟩Gordon Brown⟨/link⟩⟨/fact⟩
⟨fact name="birth_date"⟩6 May 1953 (1953-05-06) (age56)⟨/fact⟩
⟨fact name="spouse"⟩⟨link entity_id="E0629105"⟩Cherie Booth⟨/link⟩⟨/fact⟩
⟨fact name="children"⟩Euan, Nicholas, Kathryn, Leo⟨/fact⟩
⟨fact name="alma_mater"⟩⟨link⟩St John's College, Oxford⟨/link⟩⟨/fact⟩
⟨fact name="profession"⟩⟨link entity_id="E0701822"⟩Lawyer⟨/link⟩⟨/fact⟩
⟨/facts⟩
⟨wiki_text⟩⟨![CDATA[Tony Blair
Anthony Charles Lynton "Tony" Blair (born 6 May 1953) is a British politician who was
Prime Minister of the United Kingdom from 2 May 1997 to 27 June 2007. He was Leader
of the Labour Party from 1994 to 2007 and the Member of Parliament for Sedgefield from
1983 to 2007...
```

Figure 2: Excerpt from the KB entry for Tony Blair (E0481157). From LDC2009E58.

2 Related Work

Three types of named entity resolution are found in the literature: *identity resolution,* which matches structured or semi-structured entity descriptions, such as database records; *coreference resolution,* which clusters textual entity descriptions; and *entity linking,* which matches a textual description to a structured or semi-structured description. All three types of resolution have significant literature on monolingual processing; cross-language matching is less well studied.

Identity resolution and its closely related cousin *record linkage* grew out of the database community, which needs to determine when two database records represent the same entity. When matching records are found, identity resolution merges the two records, while record linkage simply notes the correspondence. Brizan and Tansel (2006) present a short overview of work in these fields. Typical approaches combine algorithmic matching of individual column values with hand-coded heuristics to combine the column scores and threshold the result.

Coreference resolution operates over text, determining when two entity mentions refer to the same entity. Approaches to within-document coreference resolution typically exploit syntactic, grammatical and discourse-level features, information that is not available when trying to resolve references across documents. Ng (2010) presents a comprehensive review of recent approaches to within-document coreference resolution. In contrast, cross-document coreference resolution typically assumes that within-document references have been resolved, and tries to place all such mention chains that refer to the same entity into a single cluster that represents that entity. Because the kinds of document-specific features that guide within-document coreference resolution are missing, research in cross-document coreference resolution tends to be more directly applicable to entity linking (which also lacks those features). The Web People Search Evaluation Workshop (Artiles et al., 2010) has been one of the recent drivers of research in cross-document coreference resolution, defining a clustering task that groups Web pages for multiple people bearing the same name.

Entity linking is a hybrid of the preceding two types of named entity resolution, matching a textual entity mention to a set of structured entity representations (usually called the *knowledge base*). Ji and Grishman (2011) present a good overview of the state of the art in monolingual entity linking, as practiced in the TAC evaluation. TAC data sets use a subset of Wikipedia entities for the knowledge base, manually curated query names, and ground truth identified by human assessors without pooling. Wikipedia has been another significant source of training and test data. Adafre and de Rijke (2005) explore automatically adding links between Wikipedia pages (albeit without focusing specifically on named entities). Bunescu and Pasca (2006) trained an SVM to predict whether a query entity matches a Wikipedia page by using hyperlinks within Wikipedia itself as the source of training and test data. Cucerzan (2007) studied identifying entity mentions in text and mapping them to Wikipedia articles. Mihalcea and Csomai (2007) and Milne and Witten (2008) each attempt to identify and properly induce hyperlinks for informative terms in Wikipedia articles (again without specific focus on named entities). Cross-language entity linking has not yet been widely explored. TAC[1] and NTCIR.[2] have both for the first time announced plans for shared tasks for cross-language entity linking. Steinberger and Pouliquen (2007) describe a system that uses multilingual named entity recognition and cross-language name matching to automatically analyze tens of thousands of news stories daily; however, they do not conduct a formal evaluation of their name merging algorithm.

Contributing to each of these three kinds of named entity resolution are two essential underlying technologies: name matching and context matching. In name matching we ask the question, "Do two different strings represent the same name?" For example, we might like to know whether "Gadhafi" and "Khadafy" are two spellings of the same name. When used as a feature for machine learning, we ask the related question, "How similar are two name strings?"

Cross-language name matching is closely related to name transliteration. Indeed, transliterating a name to the language of the knowledge base, then performing monolingual name matching in that language, is a reasonable approach to cross-language name matching. Name transliteration has an extensive literature; Karimi *et al.* (2011) present a comprehensive survey of the topic.

Name matching does not demand transliteration though; transliteration is a generative process, and name matching requires only that a known name pair be given a score representing the degree of match. Snae (2007) presents a survey of popular name matching algorithms from the record linkage perspective. Monolingually, Levenshtein distance (1966) and its variants are used for basic string matching in many contexts. Cross-language approaches typically combine cross-language mappings of some sort with edit distance metrics. For example, Mani *et al.* (2008) demonstrate a machine learning approach to the problem.

The second crucial underlying technology is context matching. Monolingually, context matching can match on many contextual attributes, including words, entities, topics, or graph structures. Context matching in the translingual setting is closely related to cross-language information retrieval (CLIR); both tasks attempt to estimate the degree of similarity between texts written in different languages. Kishida (2005) presents an overview of the key methods in CLIR.

[1] http://nlp.cs.qc.cuny.edu/kbp/2011/

[2] http://ntcir.nii.ac.jp/CrossLink/

3 Cross-Language Entity Linking

Our approach to entity linking breaks the problem down into two main parts: *candidate identification* and *candidate ranking*. Candidate identification quickly identifies a small set of KB nodes that with high probability contain the correct answer, if it is present. Candidate ranking then considers each candidate in greater detail, producing a ranked list. We give a description of each of these steps in this section; complete details of our English entity linking approach, including descriptions of all of the features used and performance on the TAC-KBP datasets can be found in (McNamee, 2010).

3.1 Candidate Identification

As a KB may contain a large number of entries, we prefer to avoid brute force comparisons between the query and all KB entities. To identify the entries that might reasonably correspond to the input named entity, we rely on a set of fast name matching techniques. We have found that it is possible to achieve high recall without resorting to contextual features. We create indexes for the names in the KB to support fast lookup of potential matches. The specific techniques that we use include:

- Exact match of query and candidate names
- Known alias or nickname lookup
- Number of character 4-grams in common between query and candidate
- Sum of IDF-weighted words in common between query and candidate[3]

In tests on the TAC-KBP 2009 test collection, this approach achieved 97.1% recall. For only 2.9% of the queries, the proper KB referent for the query was not one of the candidates. These cases were particularly challenging because they involved ambiguous organization names or obscure personal nicknames. Our methods are similar to methods used in the database community, sometimes known as *blocking* (Whang et al., 2009) or *canopies* (McCallum et al., 2000).

[3] Inverse document frequency weights enable us to effectively match, for example, Q: Mary Elizabeth Surratt and KB: Mary Surratt, since *Surratt* is a highly discriminating term even though *Mary* is not.

Chinese	306165	Czech	6101
German	34101	Finnish	5639
French	23834	Swedish	5526
Arabic	19347	Danish	2648
Bulgarian	17383	Turkish	2581
Spanish	14406	Macedonian	2469
Italian	12093	Romanian	1981
Dutch	10853	Croatian	1527
Serbian	10020	Urdu	987
Greek	9590	Albanian	257
Portuguese	6335		

Table 1: Number of training pairs for transliterating to English from each language.

To perform cross-language candidate identification, we transliterate[4] the query name to English, then apply our monolingual English heuristics. We used the multilingual transliteration system and training data developed by Irvine *et al.* (2010) in their experiments in orthographic transliteration. The number of training name/transliteration pairs varied by language and is given in Table 1. The source for most of this training data is Wikipedia, which contains links between article pages in multiple languages.

3.2 Candidate Ranking

The second phase in our approach is to score each viable candidate using supervised machine learning, and to select the highest scoring one as output. Each entity linking query is represented by a feature vector $\mathbf{x}$, where $\mathbf{x} \in \mathbb{R}^{\mathbf{k}}$, and each candidate y is a member of $\mathbb{Y}$, the set of entities in the knowledge base. Individual feature functions, $f_i(\mathbf{x}, y)$, are based on intrinsic properties of the query $\mathbf{x}$, intrinsic properties of a specific KB candidate y, and most commonly, on comparisons between the query and candidate. For each query our goal is to select a single KB entity y or choose NIL if the mentioned entity is not represented in the KB.

Thus, we desire that the correct knowledge base entity y' for a query $\mathbf{x}$ receives a higher score than any other knowledge base entities $y \in \mathbb{Y}, y \neq y'$. We chose a soft maximum margin approach to learning and used the ranking Support Vector Machine approach described by Joachims (2002) and implemented in the SVM^{rank} tool. We selected a linear kernel for training speed, and set the slack parameter C to be 0.01 times the number of training examples.

In our system absence from the knowledge base is treated as a distinct ranked candidate, the so-called NIL candidate. NIL prediction is integrated into the process by including features that are indicative of no other candidate being correct. Considering absence as a ranked candidate eliminates the need to select a threshold below which NIL will be returned.

The classes of feature functions we use include:

- Name matching features between the query name (Q_{name}) and KB candidate (KB_{name})
- Text comparisons between the query document (Q_{doc}) and the text associated with the KB candidate
- Relation features, chiefly evidence from relations in the KB being evidenced in the Q_{doc}
- Co-occurring entities, detected by running named entity recognition (NER) on the Q_{doc} and finding matching names in the candidate's KB entry
- Features pertaining to the entity type of the KB candidate
- Indications that no candidate is correct and that NIL is therefore the appropriate response

3.2.1 Name matching

A variety of string similarity features are incorporated to account for misspellings, name variants, or partially specified names when trying to match the query name and KB entry. Christen (2006) discusses a variety of name matching features, several of which we adopt. One of the most useful is the Dice score over sets of character bigrams.

3.2.2 Cross-language name equivalence

In all of our cross-language experiments we added name matching features designed to directly calculate the likelihood that a given non-English name is equivalent to a given English name. The model is based on projections of character n-grams across languages (McNamee, 2008).

3.2.3 Contextual Similarity

We measure monolingual document similarity between Q_{doc} and the KB text (KB_{doc}) in two ways: using cosine similarity with TF/IDF weighting; and using the Dice coefficient over bags of words. IDF values are approximated using counts from the Google 5-gram dataset following the method of Klein and Nelson (2008). We also used features such as whether the query string occurs in the KB_{doc} and the KB_{name} occurs in the Q_{doc}.

[4] We use *transliteration* in a broad sense, to include situations where word translation rather than character transliteration is warranted.

To match contexts when the query document and KB are in different languages we treat cross-language context linking as a CLIR problem in which the query is created from the words in the vicinity of mentions of the query name. We adopt Probabilistic Structured Queries (PSQ) (Darwish and Oard, 2003), the key idea of which is to treat alternate translations of a query term as synonyms and to weight the contributions of each "synonym" using a statistical translation model. We index the Wikipedia articles in our test collection using a publicly available IR tool (Indri), learn isolated word translation probabilities from a parallel text using the Berkeley aligner[5] and Joshua,[6] and implement PSQ using Indri's *#wsyn* operator. Based on initial tests on training data, we use a contextual window size of $\pm$ 40 terms to the left and right of the query name mention as the source language query. In Roman alphabet languages, untranslated terms are retained in a character-normalized form.

3.2.4 Relation Features

As can be seen in Figure 2, the KB contains a set of attributes and relations associated with each entity (*e.g.,* age, employer, spouses, etc.). While one could run a relation extractor over the query document and look for relational equivalences, or contradictions, we chose a more straightforward approach: we simply treat the words from all facts as a surrogate "document" and calculate document similarity with the query document.

3.2.5 Named Entity Features

We applied the named entity tagger by Ratinov and Roth (2009) to query documents and created features from the tagger output, including: the percentage of NEs present in KB_{doc}; the percentage of words from all NEs that are present in KB_{doc}; and, the number of co-occurring NEs from Q_{doc} that are present in KB_{doc}. Except for an experiment described in Section 6.1, these features are only used in our monolingual English runs.

3.2.6 Entity Type Features

In English experiments the type of the query entity is determined from the NER output for the query document. Since the reference knowledge base provides a class (*e.g.,* scientist) and a type (*e.g.,* PER) for most entities, we can check whether the type of the KB entity is consistent with the query. This helps discourage selection of eponymous entries named after famous people (*e.g.,* the *USS Abraham Lincoln (CVN-72)*, a nuclear-powered aircraft carrier named after the 16th US president).

3.2.7 NIL Features

Some features can indicate whether it is likely or unlikely that there is a matching KB entry for a query. For example, if many candidates have strong name matches, it is reasonable to believe that one of them is correct. Conversely, if no candidate has high textual similarity with the query, or overlap between KB facts and the query document text, it becomes more plausible to believe that the entity is missing from the KB.

4 Building a Test Collection for Entity Linking in Twenty-One Languages

The TAC-KBP entity linking test collections from 2009 and 2010 include the following resources: (a) a large collection of English documents; (b) approximately 7,000 queries comprising English name mentions from those documents; (c) a reference knowledge base with over 818K entries; and (d) a set of annotations that identify the appropriate KB entry for each query, or absence (McNamee and Dang, 2009; Ji et al., 2010). The KB was created by processing a 2008 dump of English Wikipedia; each entry includes structured attributes obtained from Wikipedia's infoboxes in addition to the unstructured article text. A sample KB entry is shown in Figure 2. We use the TAC KB in all of our experiments.

Since the TAC-KBP queries and documents are only available in English, these data are not directly usable for cross-language entity linking. One approach would be to manually translate the TAC documents and queries into each desired language. This would be prohibitively expensive. Instead, we use parallel document collections and crowdsourcing to generate ground truth in other languages. A fundamental insight on which our work is based is that if we build an entity linking test collection using the English half of a parallel text collection, we can make use of readily available annotators and tools developed specifically for English, then project the English results onto the other language. Thus, we apply English NER to find person names in text (Ratinov and Roth, 2009), our English entity linking system to identify candidate entity IDs, and English annotators on Amazon's Mechanical Turk to select the correct

[5]http://code.google.com/p/berkeleyaligner/

[6]http://sourceforge.net/projects/joshua/

Language	Collection	Queries	Non-NIL
Albanian (sq)	SETimes	4,190	2,274
Arabic (ar)	LDC2004T18	2,829	661
Bulgarian (bg)	SETimes	3,737	2,068
Chinese (zh)	LDC2005T10	1,958	956
Croatian (hr)	SETimes	4,139	2,257
Czech (cs)	ProjSynd	1,044	722
Danish (da)	Europarl	2,105	1,096
Dutch (nl)	Europarl	2,131	1,087
Finnish (fi)	Europarl	2,038	1,049
French (fr)	ProjSynd	885	657
German (de)	ProjSynd	1,086	769
Greek (el)	SETimes	3,890	2,129
Italian (it)	Europarl	2,135	1,087
Macedonian (mk)	SETimes	3,573	1,956
Portuguese (pt)	Europarl	2,119	1,096
Romanian (ro)	SETimes	4,355	2,368
Serbian (sr)	SETimes	3,943	2,156
Spanish (es)	ProjSynd	1,028	743
Swedish (sv)	Europarl	2,153	1,107
Turkish (tr)	SETimes	3,991	2,169
Urdu (ur)	LDC2006E110	1,828	1,093
Total		55,157	29,500

Table 2: Language coverage in our collection.

kbid for each name. Finally, we use standard statistical word alignment techniques implemented in the Berkeley Word Aligner (Haghighi et al., 2009) to map from English name mentions to the corresponding names in the non-English documents.

The six parallel collections we used came from the LDC and online sources. Together, these collections contain 196,717 non-English documents in five different scripts and twenty-one different languages. The final size of the query sets by language is shown in Table 2. We partitioned these queries and their associated documents into three sets per language: 60% for training, 20% for development, and 20% for test. In other work we give additional details about the creation of our test collection (Mayfield et al., 2011).

5 Experimental Results

5.1 English Baselines

Since all of our documents are from parallel corpora, every query is available in English and at least one other language. To serve as a point of comparison, we ran our monolingual entity linking system using the English version of the queries. We also determined performance of a baseline that predicts a *kbid* if its entity's name is a unique, exact match for the English query string, and NIL otherwise.

To compare approaches we calculate the percentage of time that the top-ranked prediction from a system is correct, which we call Precision-at-rank-one (P@1).[7] For the exact match baseline (*Exact*), the mean P@1 accuracy across all query sets is 0.897; on the TAC-KBP 2010 person queries, this baseline achieves a score of 0.832, which is lower most likely because of the intentional efforts at TAC to artificially increase query name ambiguity. Results for both English baselines are included in Table 3.

5.2 Cross-Language Name Matching

Table 3 also reports cross-language experiments in twenty languages where cross-language name matching is used to project the non-English query name into English (*NameMatch*), but the document remains untranslated. If the correct transliteration is known from our transliteration training data, we perform table lookup; otherwise the 1-best transliteration produced by our model is used.

Name matching alone produces serviceable performance. Averaged over all languages, performance on all queries is 93% of the monolingual English baseline. Losses tend to be small in the languages that use a Latin alphabet.

To investigate how errors in automated transliteration affect the system, we also conducted an experiment where the human-produced translations of the entity name were obtained from the English side of the parallel data. In Table 4 we report how this condition (*PerfectTrans*) performs relative to the monolingual baseline. Perfect name translation reduces the error rate dramatically, and performance of 99.2% of monolingual is obtained.

5.3 Name Matching and Context Matching

Table 3 also reports the use of both name matching and context matching using CLIR (+Context). Over all queries, performance rises from 92.9% to 93.9% of the English baseline. Bigger gains are evident on non-NIL queries. In fact, the pan-language average hides the fact that much larger gains are observed for non-NILs in Arabic, Czech, Macedonian, Serbian, and Turkish. We checked whether these gains are significant compared to NameMatch using the sign test; values indicating significant gains ($p < 0.05$) are emboldened.

5.4 Learning Rate

Our approach depends on having a quantity of labelled data on which to train a classifier. To investigate the effect that the number of training ex-

[7] At TAC this metric is called micro-averaged accuracy.

	All Queries					Non-NIL Queries				
		English		Cross-Language			English		Cross-Language	
Set	N	Mono	Exact	NameMatch	+Context	N	Mono	Exact	NameMatch	+Context
ar	577	0.948	0.886 (93%)	0.901 (95%)	**0.926 (98%)**	136	0.838	0.552 (66%)	0.706 (84%)	**0.787 (94%)**
bg	770	0.982	0.918 (94%)	0.892 (91%)	0.892 (91%)	430	0.972	0.854 (88%)	0.821 (84%)	0.833 (86%)
cs	203	0.931	0.764 (82%)	0.828 (89%)	**0.862 (93%)**	136	0.985	0.669 (68%)	0.772 (78%)	**0.838 (85%)**
da	428	0.988	0.963 (97%)	0.965 (98%)	0.963 (97%)	225	0.982	0.933 (95%)	0.938 (95%)	0.933 (95%)
de	217	0.931	0.756 (81%)	0.871 (94%)	0.876 (94%)	154	0.987	0.675 (68%)	0.857 (87%)	0.877 (89%)
el	776	0.979	0.928 (95%)	0.833 (85%)	**0.851 (87%)**	423	0.972	0.868 (89%)	0.714 (73%)	**0.745 (77%)**
es	208	0.909	0.760 (84%)	0.889 (98%)	0.894 (98%)	149	0.960	0.685 (71%)	0.873 (91%)	**0.899 (94%)**
fi	425	0.986	0.965 (98%)	0.927 (94%)	0.941 (95%)	220	0.982	0.936 (95%)	0.868 (88%)	**0.900 (92%)**
fr	186	0.930	0.742 (80%)	0.909 (98%)	0.876 (94%)	135	0.978	0.659 (67%)	0.904 (92%)	0.911 (93%)
hr	846	0.980	0.924 (94%)	0.930 (95%)	0.920 (94%)	470	0.972	0.864 (89%)	0.889 (91%)	0.866 (89%)
it	443	0.984	0.966 (98%)	0.907 (92%)	0.914 (93%)	227	0.978	0.938 (96%)	0.833 (85%)	0.859 (88%)
mk	720	0.978	0.932 (95%)	0.822 (84%)	**0.850 (87%)**	391	0.967	0.875 (90%)	0.706 (73%)	**0.749 (78%)**
nl	441	0.984	0.964 (98%)	0.955 (97%)	0.955 (97%)	224	0.978	0.933 (95%)	0.924 (95%)	0.933 (95%)
pt	443	0.987	0.964 (98%)	0.982 (100%)	0.977 (99%)	230	0.978	0.935 (96%)	0.974 (100%)	0.961 (98%)
ro	878	0.976	0.924 (95%)	0.961 (98%)	0.961 (98%)	480	0.967	0.860 (89%)	0.935 (97%)	0.933 (97%)
sq	849	0.972	0.927 (95%)	0.889 (92%)	**0.913 (94%)**	465	0.955	0.867 (91%)	0.809 (85%)	**0.860 (90%)**
sr	799	0.976	0.920 (94%)	0.804 (82%)	**0.840 (86%)**	447	0.966	0.857 (89%)	0.653 (68%)	**0.743 (77%)**
sv	448	0.987	0.964 (98%)	0.958 (97%)	0.960 (97%)	231	0.978	0.935 (96%)	0.935 (96%)	0.944 (96%)
tr	804	0.980	0.923 (94%)	0.954 (97%)	0.968 (99%)	440	0.973	0.859 (88%)	0.925 (95%)	**0.953 (98%)**
ur	363	0.973	0.862 (89%)	0.810 (83%)	**0.840 (86%)**	215	0.967	0.772 (80%)	0.707 (73%)	**0.763 (79%)**
$\bar{x}$	541	0.968	0.897 (93%)	0.899 (93%)	0.909 (94%)	291	0.967	0.826 (85%)	0.837 (87%)	0.864 (89%)

Table 3: P@1 for a variety of experimental conditions. The left half of the table presents aggregate results for all queries; on the right performance is given for just non-NIL queries. Percentages are with respect to the monolingual English condition.

Set	Mono	NM	PerfectTrans		English NEs	
	P@1	P@1	P@1	% Mono	P@1	% Mono
ar	0.948	0.901	**0.941**	99.3%	0.901	95.1%
bg	0.982	0.892	**0.986**	100.4%	**0.855**[8]	87.0%
cs	0.931	0.828	0.882	94.7%	**0.897**	96.3%
da	0.988	0.965	**0.986**	99.8%	0.972	98.4%
de	0.931	0.871	0.899	96.5%	0.917	98.5%
el	0.979	0.833	**0.978**	99.9%	**0.872**	89.1%
es	0.909	0.889	0.914	100.5%	0.861	94.7%
fi	0.986	0.927	**0.988**	100.2%	**0.955**	96.9%
fr	0.930	0.909	0.909	97.7%	0.914	98.3%
hr	0.980	0.930	**0.972**	99.2%	**0.963**	98.3%
it	0.984	0.907	**0.987**	100.2%	**0.930**	94.5%
mk	0.978	0.822	**0.976**	99.9%	**0.881**	90.1%
nl	0.984	0.955	**0.982**	99.8%	0.964	97.9%
pt	0.987	0.982	0.987	100.0%	0.977	99.1%
ro	0.976	0.961	**0.976**	100.0%	0.960	98.4%
sq	0.972	0.889	**0.976**	100.5%	**0.933**	96.0%
sr	0.976	0.804	**0.974**	99.7%	**0.977**	100.1%
sv	0.987	0.958	**0.984**	99.8%	**0.975**	98.9%
tr	0.980	0.954	**0.984**	100.4%	0.963	98.2%
ur	0.973	0.810	**0.931**	95.7%	**0.876**	90.1%
$\bar{x}$	0.968	0.899	0.961	99.2%	0.927	95.8%

Table 4: Cross-language effectiveness (P@1) over all queries with optimal (a) transliteration and (b) named entity recognition. Simply having access to perfect transliterations achieves 99% of monolingual performance, on average. Providing lists of named entities mentioned in the document, in English, also improves performance. Bold values indicate statistically significant gains compared to the NameMatch (NM) run.

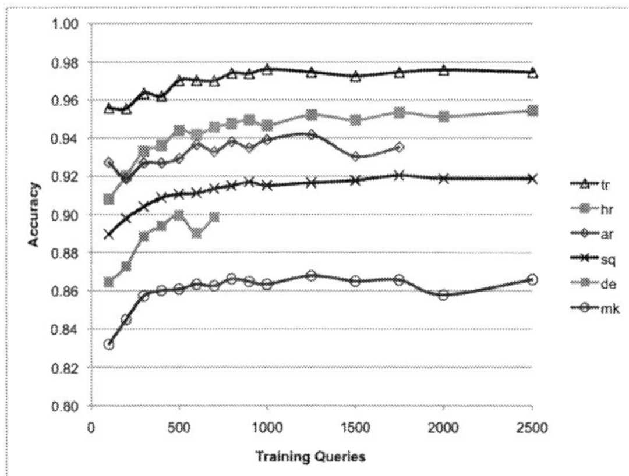

Figure 3: Classifier accuracy and training set size.

emplars has on classifier accuracy we built classifiers using fixed numbers of training queries. Figure 3 shows these results for selected languages. Each curve was produced by generating a random permutation of the training data, selecting the first k queries, and averaging the results over five trials. Note that the total amount of available training data differs by language. In all cases, accuracy rises quickly for the first 500 queries, and little improvement is observed after 1000 examples.

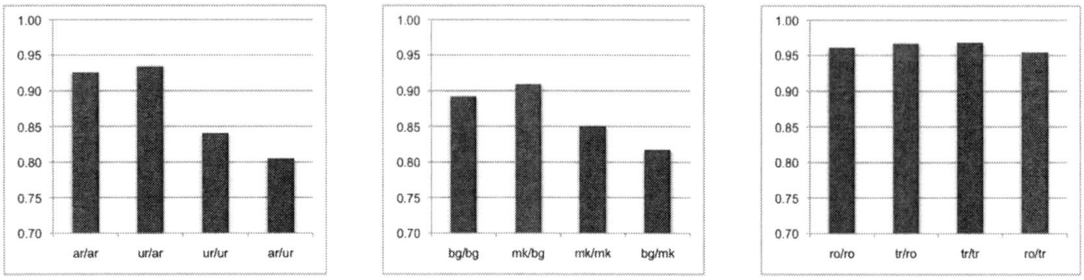

Figure 4: Training with annotations from another language using the same writing system. A label of xx/yy indicates that feature weights were trained using labelled data from language xx and then applied to queries on language yy.

6 Additional Experiments

6.1 Multilingual NER and Transliteration

We believe that the entities in a document that co-occur with a target entity are important clues for disambiguating entities. However, while we had ready access to named entity recognizers in English, we did not have NER capability in all of the languages of our collection. We would like to know how useful multilingual NER could be. To simulate this using our test collection, where all documents are from parallel texts with an English translation, we conducted an experiment that used the English documents only to recognize English named entities that co-occur with the query string; in every other respect, the untranslated foreign document was used by the system. The English NER may make errors, but we use it to simulate the performance of excellent non-English NER coupled with perfect entity translation.

Table 4 shows that co-occurring entities are a very helpful feature. Compared to name matching alone, average P@1 rises from 89.9% to 92.7%.

6.2 Cross-Language Training

Although we have demonstrated an efficient method for building a test collection for cross-language entity linking, it may still be difficult to obtain training data and tools for some less-resourced languages. Our process and feature set is largely language-independent, and we would like to know how feasible it is to make predictions without any language-specific training data by exploiting entity linking annotations from a related language. We examined pairs of languages using the same script – Arabic/Urdu, Bulgarian/Macedonian, and Romanian/Turkish – and trained classifiers using labeled data for the other language. Figure 4 shows that performance is not dramatically different when using annotations from a language sharing a common alphabet. This suggests that it is plausible to build a cross-language entity linking system without manually-produced annotations for a particular language.

7 Conclusions

In this paper we introduced a new problem, cross-language entity linking, and we described an approach to this problem that uses statistical transliteration and cross-language information retrieval. Using a newly-developed test collection for this task,[9] we demonstrated the success of the approach in twenty languages. Our best model using both name and context matching achieves average performance across twenty languages which is 94% of a strong monolingual English baseline, with individual languages ranging from 86% to 99%. Additionally, we characterized the number of training exemplars needed, demonstrated the feasibility of off-language training, and illustrated performance gains that are possible if combined multilingual NER/transliteration is available.

Acknowledgments

We are grateful to Chris Callison-Burch and Ann Irvine for their support with machine translation and orthographic transliteration, and to Tan Xu and Mohammad S. Raunak for their help in data curation. Support for one of authors was provided in part by NSF grant CCF 0916081.

[8]The English NEs run was significantly *worse* vs. NameMatch in Bulgarian (bg).

[9]The test collection is available at `http://web.jhu.edu/HLTCOE/datasets.html`.

References

Sisay Fissaha Adafre and Maarten de Rijke. 2005. Discovering missing links in Wikipedia. In *LinkKDD '05: Proceedings of the 3rd international workshop on Link discovery*, pages 90–97. ACM.

Javier Artiles, Andrew Borthwick, Julio Gonzalo, Satoshi Sekine, and Enrique Amigo. 2010. Overview of the web people search clustering and attribute extraction tasks. In *CLEF Third WEPS Evaluation Workshop*.

David Guy Brizan and Abdullah Uz Tansel. 2006. A survey of entity resolution and record linkage methodologies. *Communications of the IIMA*, 6(3):41–50.

Razvan C. Bunescu and Marius Pasca. 2006. Using encyclopedic knowledge for named entity disambiguation. In *European Chapter of the Assocation for Computational Linguistics (EACL)*.

Peter Christen. 2006. A comparison of personal name matching: Techniques and practical issues. Technical Report TR-CS-06-02, Australian National University.

Silviu Cucerzan. 2007. Large-scale named entity disambiguation based on Wikipedia data. In *Empirical Methods in Natural Language Processing*.

Kareem Darwish and Douglas W. Oard. 2003. Probabilistic structured query methods. In *ACM SIGIR*, pages 338–344. ACM.

Aria Haghighi, John Blitzer, John DeNero, and Dan Klein. 2009. Better word alignments with supervised ITG models. In *Proceedings of the Joint Conference of the 47th Annual Meeting of the ACL and the 4th International Joint Conference on Natural Language Processing*, pages 923–931. ACL.

Ann Irvine, Chris Callison-Burch, and Alexandre Klementiev. 2010. Transliterating from all languages. In *AMTA*.

Heng Ji and Ralph Grishman. 2011. Knowledge base population: Successful approaches and challenges. In *Association for Computational Linguistics*.

Heng Ji, Ralph Grishman, Hoa Trang Dang, Kira Griffitt, and Joe Ellis. 2010. Overview of the TAC 2010 Knowledge Base Population track. In *Text Analysis Conference (TAC)*.

Thorsten Joachims. 2002. Optimizing search engines using clickthrough data. In *Knowledge Discovery and Data Mining (KDD)*.

Sarvnaz Karimi, Falk Scholer, and Andrew Turpin. 2011. Machine transliteration survey. *ACM Computing Surveys*, 43(4):1–57.

Kazuaki Kishida. 2005. Technical issues of cross-language information retrieval: a review. *Information Processing and Management*, 41(3):433 – 455. Cross-Language Information Retrieval.

Martin Klein and Michael L. Nelson. 2008. A comparison of techniques for estimating IDF values to generate lexical signatures for the web. In *WIDM '08*, pages 39–46. ACM.

Vladimir I. Levenshtein. 1966. Binary codes capable of correcting deletions, insertions and reversals. *Soviet Physics–Doklady*, 10(8):707–710.

Inderjeet Mani, Alex Yeh, and Sherri Condon. 2008. Learning to match names across languages. In *MMIES '08*, pages 2–9. ACL.

James Mayfield, Dawn Lawrie, Paul McNamee, and Douglas W. Oard. 2011. Building a cross-language entity linking collection in twenty-one languages. In *Cross-Language Evaluation Forum (CLEF)*.

Andrew McCallum, Kamal Nigam, and Lyle Ungar. 2000. Efficient clustering of high-dimensional data sets with application to reference matching. In *Knowledge Discovery and Data Mining (KDD)*.

Paul McNamee and Hoa Trang Dang. 2009. Overview of the TAC 2009 Knowledge Base Population track. In *Text Analysis Conference (TAC)*.

Paul McNamee. 2008. *Textual Representations for Corpus-Based Bilingual Retrieval*. Ph.D. thesis, University of Maryland Baltimore County, Baltimore, MD.

Paul McNamee. 2010. HLTCOE efforts in entity linking at TAC KBP 2010. In *Text Analysis Conference (TAC)*, Gaithersburg, Maryland, November.

Rada Mihalcea and Andras Csomai. 2007. Wikify!: linking documents to encyclopedic knowledge. In *CIKM*, pages 233–242.

David N. Milne and Ian H. Witten. 2008. Learning to link with wikipedia. In *CIKM*, pages 509–518.

Vincent Ng. 2010. Supervised noun phrase coreference research: The first fifteen years. In *Proceedings of the 48th Annual Meeting of the Association for Computational Linguistics*, pages 1396–1411.

Lev Ratinov and Dan Roth. 2009. Design challenges and misconceptions in named entity recognition. In *Proceedings of the Thirteenth Conference on Computational Natural Language Learning (CoNLL-2009)*, pages 147–155, Boulder, Colorado, June. Association for Computational Linguistics.

Chakkrit Snae. 2007. A comparison and analysis of name matching algorithms. *Proceedings of World Academy of Science, Engineering and Technology*, 21:252–257, January.

Ralf Steinberger and Bruno Pouliquen. 2007. Cross-lingual named entity recognition. *Linguisticae Investigationes*, 30(1):135–162, January.

Steven Euijong Whang, David Menestrina, Georgia Koutrika, Martin Theobald, and Hector Garcia-Molina. 2009. Entity resolution with iterative blocking. In *SIGMOD 2009*, pages 219–232. ACM.

Generating Chinese Named Entity Data from a Parallel Corpus

Ruiji Fu, Bing Qin, Ting Liu*
Research Center for Social Computing and Information Retrieval
MOE-Microsoft Key Laboratory of Natural Language Processing and Speech
School of Computer Science and Technology
Harbin Institute of Technology, Harbin, China
{rjfu,bqin,tliu}@ir.hit.edu.cn

Abstract

Annotating Named Entity Recognition (NER) training corpora is a costly process but necessary for supervised NER systems. This paper presents an approach to generate large-scale Chinese NER training data from an English-Chinese discourse level aligned parallel corpus. Difficulty of NER is different among languages due to their unique features. For example, the performance of English NER systems is usually higher than the Chinese ones on average. In our method, we first employ a high performance NER system on one side of a bilingual corpus. And then, we project the NE labels to the other side according to the word level alignment. At last, we select high-quality labeled sentences using different strategies and generate an NER training corpus. In our experiments, we generate a Chinese NER corpus with 167,100 sentences through an English-Chinese parallel corpus. The system trained on the automatically generated corpus attains a comparable result with the one trained on the manually-annotated corpus. Further experiments show that the NER performance is significantly improved on two different evaluation sets by using the generated training data as an additional corpus to the manually-labeled data.

1 Introduction

Named Entity Recognition (NER) is the task of identifying and classifying the names of persons, locations, organizations and other named entities in text, which plays an important role in many Natural Language Processing (NLP) applications such as information extraction, information retrieval, machine translation, and so on.

Supervised machine learning systems have proved successful for NER (Zhou and Su, 2002; Chieu and Ng, 2002; Takeuchi and Collier, 2002; Settles, 2004). They usually need manually-annotated high performance textual corpora. These corpora are considered as gold standards for training statistical models. However, corpora manually-annotating is so costly and time-consuming that the existing corpora are limited in both scale and scope for Chinese NER.

More seriously, the domain overfitting problem even worsens the corpora-shortage problem. Supervised NER approaches can often achieve high accuracy when a large annotated training set similar to the test data is available (Zhou and Su, 2002; Florian et al., 2003; Klein et al., 2003; Finkel et al., 2005). Unfortunately, if the test data has some difference from the training data, these approaches tend to not perform well. For instance, Ciaramita and Altun (2005) reported that the F1-score of a named entity recognizer trained on CoNLL 2003 Reuters corpus dropped from 90.8% (when tested on a similar Reuters set) to 64.3% (when tested on a Wall Street Journal set). A similar phenomenon of performance degradation in Chinese NER will be presented later in this paper (see Table 3).

Therefore, we try to solve the problems for Chinese mentioned above by automatically constructing large scale and scope training corpora.

Chinese NER is more difficult than English NER because of the lack of capitalization and the uncertainty in word segmentation. Our motivation is to collect large-scale training data and improve Chinese NER with the help of an exist-

* Correspondence author: tliu@ir.hit.edu.cn

ing high performance English NER system and a bilingual corpus.

In this paper, we employ a high performance NER system on the English side of a bilingual corpus. And then, the NE labels are projected to the Chinese side according to the word level alignment. At last, we select high-quality labeled sentences using different strategies and generate an NER training corpus.

In our experiments, statistical models are trained on the generated corpora, and compared with the model trained on a manually annotated corpus. The results show that our corpus is comparable to the manually-labeled corpus. Furthermore, the model trained on the combined corpus (generated and manually-labeled corpora) obtains an F1-score of 67.89% on 863-Evaluation corpus and 73.20% on OntoNotes corpus, which significantly outperforms the one trained on the manually-labeled corpus.

The contributions of this paper are as follows.

First, we present a method to generate large-scale Chinese NER training data from a bilingual corpus automatically. Our method trades off manual effort to annotate named entities in documents for effort to identify pairs of parallel documents, which is easier than NE manual annotation. For example, large scale of parallel documents can be extracted from the web automatically (Resnik and Smith, 2003; Zhang et al., 2006).

Second, we propose some strategies to select high-quality training data, which are very effective and important as the experiments show.

And third, we prove that our generated training data can be used as an additional corpus to improve the NER performance.

This paper is organized as follows. Section 2 discusses the related work. Section 3 describes our approach in detail. Section 4 presents and discusses the results of our experiments. Finally, we present our conclusions and future work in section 5.

2 Related Work

In this section, we introduce some previous work about NER training data generation.

The most closed related work to our approach is Yarowsky et al. (2001). They used word alignment on parallel corpora to induce several text analysis tools from English to other languages for which such resources are scarce. An NE tagger was transferred from English to French and achieved good classification accuracy. However, Chinese NER is more difficult than French and word alignment between Chinese and English is also more complex because of the tremendous difference between the two languages.

Huang and Vogel (2002) presented an integrated approach to extract an NE translation dictionary from an English-Chinese parallel corpus while improving the monolingual NE annotation quality for both languages. They started with low-quality NE tagging for both languages and improved the annotation result using alignment information. But they did not filter the annotated data and evaluate its impact for NER as training data.

Besides, some other resources have been used to generate NE tagged corpus.

An et al. (2003) and Whitelaw et al. (2008) used seed sets of entities and search engines to collect NER training data from the web. However, constructing of a high-quality seed list is also a time-consuming work.

Richman and Schone (2008) and Nothman et al. (2008) used similar methods to create NE training data. They transformed Wikipedia's links into named entity annotations by classifying the target articles into common entity types. But the article classification seeds also had to be hand-labeled in advance.

In the biomedical domain, Vlachos and Gasperin (2006) automatically created training material for the task of gene name recognition from the broader raw corpus using existing domain resources.

In our work, we generate a large scale Chinese NER training data from a bilingual corpus without any NE seed lists and filter it by using effective strategies. And we prove that it can improve the performance of Chinese NER as additional training data.

3 Our Approach

In this section we describe our approach of generating NER training data from a parallel corpus. The framework of our system consists of four components as shown in Figure 1.

- **Alignment:** Sentence alignment and word alignment is performed on a discourse-level aligned bilingual corpus.
- **English NER:** We identify NEs on the English side of the parallel corpus, making use of an existing high performance English NER system.
- **NE Candidates Generation:** Based on the result of the word alignment, we

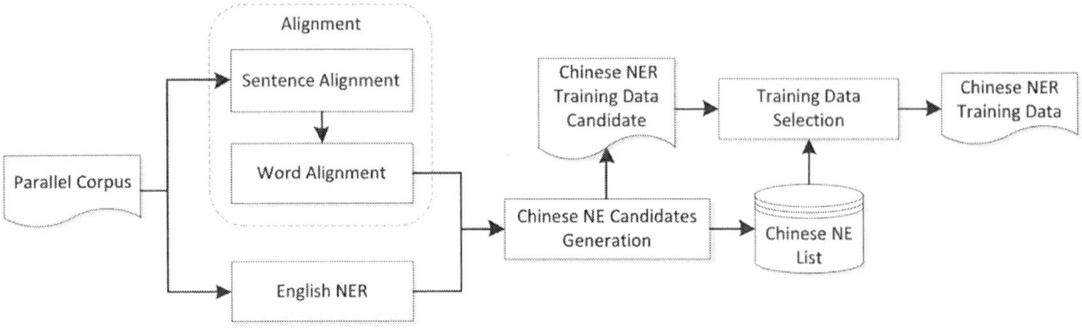

Figure 1. System Framework

project the English NE labels to the Chinese side and generate training data candidates. At the same time, we extract a Chinese NE list, which can be used as a dictionary resource.

- **Training Data Selection:** According to the different filtering strategies, we select high-quality labeled sentences from the candidates to form Chinese NER training data.

3.1 Alignment and Automatic English NER

First, we perform sentence level alignment by using Champollion toolkit[1].

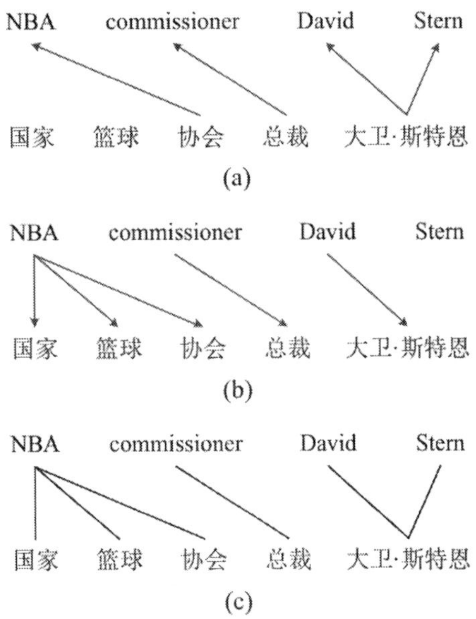

Figure 2. (a) Word Alignment from Chinese to English. (b) Word Alignment from English to Chinese. (c) The Merged Result of Both Directions. In (a), *国家* and *篮球* are aligned to NULL, the same to *Stern* in (b).

[1] http://champollion.sourceforge.net/

And then, GIZA++ toolkit[2] is used for word alignment. This toolkit can generate one-to-many word alignments in a certain direction (Chinese to English or English to Chinese). However, we need many-to-many alignments. Hence, we need GIZA++ to run on the bilingual corpus in both directions and merge the results, as shown in Figure 2.

English NER is easier than Chinese because of the capitalization information and the needlessness of word segmentation. So the performance of English NER systems is usually higher than the Chinese ones on average. Hence a widely used open-source NER system, Stanford Named Entity Recognizer[3] is employed to label NEs on the English side of the parallel corpus. The system is based on linear chain Conditional Random Field (CRF) (J.Lafferty et al., 2001) sequence models and can recognize three kinds of named entities (PERSON, LOCATION and ORGANIZATION).

To evaluate the robustness of Stanford NER system, we manually labeled 1000 English sentences from our bilingual corpus as a test set where the system achieves an F1-score of 89.32%. It is close to the result of 87.94%[4] on CoNLL 2003 NER test set.

3.2 Chinese NE Candidates Generation

After the English NER, we map the English NE labels to the Chinese side to discover Chinese NEs candidates, according to the result of word alignment.

We consider all related alignment pairs of every word within an English NE. For example, in Figure 3, the index of the organization name *NBA* is 1 and the related word alignment pairs

[2] http://www-i6.informatik.rwth-aachen.de/Colleagues/och/software/GIZA++.html
[3] http://nlp.stanford.edu/software/CRF-NER.shtml
[4] http://nlp.stanford.edu/projects/project-ner.shtml

Figure 3. An Example of Chinese NE Candidates Generation

include 1-1, 1-2 and 1-3. Therefore, we can find the boundaries (from 1 to 3) of the corresponding Chinese translation *国家 篮球 协会*. There are also some English words connecting with NULL at Chinese side. We ignore these word alignment pairs.

According to the alignment, we project the NE labels from English to Chinese and generate the named entity candidates on the Chinese side.

3.3 Training Data Selection

However, the generated NER training data candidates are noisy because of the errors in English NER or word alignment. In this section, we present the strategies of selecting training data.

3.3.1 Filtering Based on Rules

As the common definition, a named entity is a continuous string, whether it is in English or in Chinese. So we assume that every named entity alignment pair is a closed alignment pair of two continuous strings, as shown in Figure 4 (a).

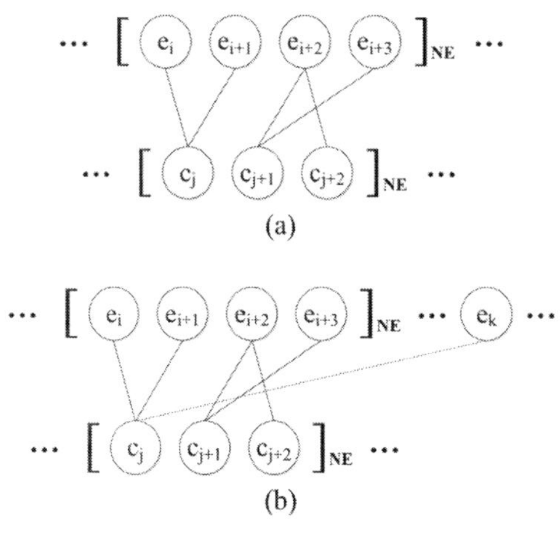

Figure 4. (a) An eligible case; (b) An ineligible case. In (b), the word alignment pair e_k - c_j is against the rule, while $k > i+3$ or $k < i$.

Based on this assumption, we make two alternative rules to filter the training data candidates. One is a soft filtering rule to retain training instances as many as possible. Another is a hard filtering rule to guarantee the quality of the generated corpus. These two rules are shown as follows:

- **Rule 1 (the soft rule):** Label a Chinese NE candidate as a non-NE, if a word within it has an alignment pair with an English word out of the corresponding English NE, such as Figure 4 (b).
- **Rule 2 (the hard rule):** Discard the whole sentence where there is a case satisfying Rule 1.

Rule 1 prefers to keep training instances as many as possible. But it may make some NEs be labeled as non-NE mistakingly on the Chinese side for incorrect word alignments, which are the noises in the generated training data. Rule 2 prefers to guarantee the quality of the generated data but may make useful training instances be discarded and the data scale shrinking.

Based on the rules, we can filter lots of ill conditioned named entity candidates, such as overlapped entities, nested entities and so on.

3.3.2 Filtering Based on Scores

Although many ill conditioned candidates are filtered out by the rules, the remaining data is still noisy because of the incorrect labeling of the English NER and the incorrect NE alignment. In fact, the accuracy of NE alignment is only affected by the boundary alignment of English and Chinese NEs. In other words, we do not care about how to align within or without the NEs. Hence, we score Chinese named entity candidates by formula 1.

$$score(N_c) = \varphi(N_e) \prod_{w \in B(N_c)} \left(\frac{1}{|A(w)|} \sum_{(e,w) \in A(w)} p(\langle e, w \rangle) \right) \quad (1)$$

Here, $\varphi(N_e)$ denotes the confidence of the English named entity N_e, which is derived from Stanford NER system. $B(N_c)$ denotes the boundaries of the Chinese named entity N_c, which are actually the left-most and the right-most word within N_c. e denotes an English word, and w denotes a Chinese word. $A(w)$ denotes all related alignment pairs of word w in current Chinese named entity N_c. $p(\langle e,w\rangle)$ denotes the probability of alignment $\langle e,w\rangle$, which is obtained from GIZA++.

As mentioned in section 3.1, Stanford NER is based on CRF. The inference of CRF is that given an observable sequence $\vec{x}$, we want to find the most likely set of labels $\vec{y}$ for $\vec{x}$. The probability of $\vec{y}$ given $\vec{x}$ is calculated as follows (J.Lafferty et al., 2001):

$$p(\vec{y}|\vec{x}) = \frac{1}{Z(\vec{x})}\prod_{j=1}^{n}\psi_j(\vec{x},\vec{y}) \quad (2)$$

$$Z(\vec{x}) = \sum_{\vec{y}'}\prod_{j=1}^{n}\psi_j(\vec{x},\vec{y}') \quad (3)$$

$$\psi_j(\vec{x},\vec{y}) = exp\left(\sum_{i=1}^{m}\lambda_i f_i(y_{j-1},y_j,\vec{x},j)\right) \quad (4)$$

In formulae 2, 3 and 4, j denotes the index of the jth word in sequence $\vec{x}$. n denotes the length of $\vec{x}$. m denotes the number of the features.

Now the substring $x_k x_{k+1} \cdots x_{k+l}$ in $\vec{x}$ is labeled as an NE N_e. The label sequence of N_e is $y_k^* y_{k+1}^* \cdots y_{k+l}^*$ which is denoted as $\vec{y}_{N_e}^*$. We compute the marginal probability $\varphi(N_e)$ as follows:

$$\varphi(N_e) = \frac{Z(N_e,\vec{x})}{Z(\vec{x})} \quad (5)$$

$$Z(N_e,\vec{x}) = \sum_{\vec{y}' : y'_{k...k+l} = \vec{y}_{N_e}^*}\prod_{j=1}^{n}\psi_j(\vec{x},\vec{y}') \quad (6)$$

The factor $\varphi(N_e)$ of every English NE is used to measure the confidence of NER. We apply the forward-backward algorithm to compute them.

For $p(\langle e,w\rangle)$, we use the probabilities of alignment pairs which are computed by GIZA++. GIZA++ outputs the probability $p(t|s)$ of translating source word s as target word t. There are two kinds of probabilities of alignment in two directions. Since our alignment is bidirectional, we merge the probabilities in two directions to come up with formula 7.

$$p(\langle e,w\rangle) = max\{p(e|w), p(w|e)\} \quad (7)$$

Particularly we set $p(t|s)$ zero while the translation pair "s → t" does not exist in the translation table given by GIZA++.

We set experiential thresholds for every category to filter the Chinese NE candidates.

3.3.3 Recalling by a Chinese NE List

During the time of filtering the NE candidates, we can also extract the high-quality candidates as an NE list. We calculate the frequencies and the average scores of the candidates. We set thresholds of frequency and average score for every kind of NE candidate, and select the candidates with the highest frequency and score to compose a list. Table 1 shows some samples of the list.

An NE may be found correctly in some sentences where word alignment is easy, while the same one may be missed in others. Hence we use the extracted NE list to recall the missed NEs in the result of the former two steps.

NEs	Label	Average Score	Freq.
北京 (Beijing)	LOC	0.637	4615
克林顿 (Clinton)	PER	0.853	969
联合国 (UN)	ORG	0.471	436
台湾海峡 (Taiwan Strait)	LOC	0.244	82

Table 1. Samples of the Chinese NE List

4 Experiments

We carried out experiments to investigate the quality and practical applicability of our NER training corpora generated from the bilingual corpus.

4.1 Data Set

We selected the LDC2003E14 multilanguage corpus and several bilingual parallel corpora[5] as the source corpus to generate NER training data. LDC2003E14 was derived from news of Foreign Broadcast Information Service (FBIS). We used the English-Chinese parallel news composed of 11,645 document pairs. The other bilingual parallel corpora contain 11,750 sentence pairs in all.

A manually annotated Chinese NER gold-standard data from People's Daily corpus was prepared as the contrasting data. The corpus was annotated with 7 tags: person, location, organization, date, time, number and miscellany. For the evaluation, the last 4 tags were removed. The corpus, composed of 47,426 sentences, was di-

[5] Six Chinese-English sentence-aligned corpora were used as extra data, including LDC2002T01, LDC2003E04, E07, E08, T17 and LDC2004T07.

vided into two parts: 37,426 for training and 10,000 for evaluation.

We also use other two corpora for the evaluation. One is the Chinese NER evaluation corpus from the National High Technology Development 863 Program of China in 2004. The other is OntoNotes Release 2.0 corpus. The tags except person, location and organization were removed in the 863-Evaluation corpus. The OntoNotes corpus was annotated with 18 fine-grained tags: 11 for named entities and 7 for numerical and time terms. We reduced the tags *NORP* and *LOCATION* into location, *FACILITY*, *GPE* and *ORGANIZATION* into organization, and *PERSON* into person. After this preprocessing, 14,547 NEs remained in the 863-Evaluation corpus and 13,658 NEs remained in the OntoNotes corpus. See Table 2 for a summary of the corpora used.

Corpus	# of sentences	
	TRAIN	TEST
People's Daily	37,426	10,000
863-Evaluation	---	3,923
OntoNotes	---	6,904

Table 2. Corpora Used for Evaluation

In addition, we manually labeled 1,000 sentences randomly extracted from FBIS corpus for the direct evaluation about the quality of our generated corpus.

4.2 The Baseline System

We trained a Maximum Entropy Markov Model (MEMM) on People's Daily training set as our baseline. State-of-the-art features (Wu et al., 2005) are used, which contain word features, POS features, position features, and labeled NE tag features. The model was evaluated on the People's Daily test set, 863-Evaluation corpus and OntoNotes corpus. The result is shown in Table 3.

	P	R	F1
People's Daily	90.77%	88.90%	89.82%
863-Evaluation	74.55%	59.13%	65.87%
OntoNotes	78.32%	64.28%	70.56%

Table 3. Evaluation Result of the Baseline System

From the evaluation result, we can see that the F1-score drops from 89.82% on People's Daily corpus to 65.87% on 863-Evaluation corpus and to 70.56% on OntoNotes corpus. It's similar to the report of Ciaramita and Altun (2005). The reason for this problem is that the model is overfitted to the training data and fails to fit the test data with different distribution. To ease the problem, we attempt to improve the coverage of the model by generating large scale and scope training corpora.

4.3 The Quality of the Generated Data

We evaluated the training data generated by using different strategies on the 1000 manually annotated sentences.

	Size	P	R	F1
Rule1 only	1,000	76.16%	48.56%	59.30%
Rule1+Score	1,000	76.36%	48.49%	59.32%
Rule1+List	1,000	73.99%	67.71%	70.71%
Rule1+Score + List	1,000	74.28%	67.65%	70.81%
Rule2 only	661	78.61%	74.76%	76.64%
Rule2+Score	661	**78.77%**	74.76%	76.72%
Rule2+List	661	78.06%	86.44%	82.04%
Rule2+Score +List	661	78.19%	**86.44%**	**82.11%**

Table 4. The Quality of Generated Corpora

Comparing the upper and lower parts of Table 4, we get a larger corpus based on Rule 1, but the recall rate is low. Rule 2 requires removing whole sentences with ineligible cases, so that we can get a higher quality but smaller corpus. The result is reasonable. If an ineligible case as shown in Figure 4 (b) occurs in a pair of English and Chinese sentences, it is possible that a named entity is labeled in the English sentence, but is not mapped to the correct Chinese string due to the errors of word alignment. For example, if *National Basketball Association* is recognized as an organization name in an English sentence, it is very possible that the translated organization name *国家篮球协会* exists in the Chinese sentence. But if *National Basketball Association* is not aligned to *国家篮球协会*, the Chinese NE will be missed. We should remove the whole sentences from the corpus, or they will be noises in the training data. The results show that Rule 2 outperforms Rule 1. In the remainder of our experiment, we use Rule 2 instead of Rule 1.

The strategy filtering candidates by scores can help to improve the precision. But the improvement of F1-score is marginal, because some correct training instances may be filtered out, which makes the recall rate decrease.

Training data	863-Evaluation corpus			OntoNotes corpus		
	P	R	F1	P	R	F1
People's Daily (PD)	74.55%	59.13%	65.87%	78.32%	64.28%	70.56%
Rule2 only	72.94%	41.73%	53.09%	77.79%	46.90%	58.52%
Rule2+Score	73.66%	41.53%	53.11%	78.42%	46.72%	58.56%
Rule2+List	72.64%	58.08%	64.55%	76.84%	61.80%	68.50%
Rule2+Score+List	73.04%	58.12%	64.73%	76.90%	61.82%	68.54%
Rule2+Score+List+PD	**75.95%**	**61.38%**	**67.89%**	**80.35%**	**67.22%**	**73.20%**

Table 5. Test Results for the Generated Training Data

We extract a Chinese NE list containing 824 NEs with the highest frequency and scores from the corpus. Based on the NE list, we can recall many NEs missed by other strategies with only a little expense of precision. The recall rates are substantially improved from 48.56% to 67.71% based on Rule 1 and from 74.76% to 86.44% based on Rule 2.

Here, we chose the best-performing thresholds of the strategies in our experiments. The results show that our strategies are effective for improve the quality of the training data.

As mentioned in section 3.1, the F1-score of Stanford NER on our parallel corpus is 89.32%. The best F1-score of the generated training data in Table 4 is 82.11%. Thus, we roughly infer that about 8.07% (= 1 - 82.11% / 89.32%) correct NE information is lost in the process of the Chinese NER training data generation.

4.4 Comparison between the Manually-labeled Data and the Generated Data

We trained MEMMs on the generated corpora using the same features as the baseline. As shown in Table 5, we get a basic result by using Rule 2. On 863-Evaluation corpus for example, we get a marginal raise (0.72%) of precision but a drop (0.20%) of recall by using Rule 2 and Score strategy, and get a substantial raise (16.35%) of recall with a drop (0.30%) of the precision by using Rule 2 and List strategy. The situation is similar on OntoNotes corpus. The results are consistent with the quality of the training data shown in Table 4. And it is reasonable that better training data leads to higher NER performance. The model trained on our corpus generated by using all of the strategies gets a comparable result with the baseline system.

We also use the generated corpus as additional training data to the gold-standard data. The last row in Table 5 shows that this approach leads to an improvement of the NER performance. We also perform a paired significance test[6], which shows that the improvement is significant.

Our generated corpus contains 167,100 sentences, which are much more than sentences in the baseline corpus. Furthermore, it is generated without any manual annotation. The size could be limitless as long as there are plenty of parallel corpora available.

4.5 The Effect of the Generated Data Size

Figure 5 illustrates the effect of varying the size of the generated training data set. Increased training data tends to improve performance until the size reaches about 67k sentences for 863-Evaluation corpus and 33k for OntoNotes corpus. But after that, improvements are marginal.

We believe that there are two reasons causing this result. On the one hand, the noises increase when more training data is used. And the training data gets a balance between the noises and the correct training instances when the size reaches a certain point. On the other hand, a subset of the training data can represent the whole data, especially for the data from a simplex source. So we should collect data from a wider range of sources.

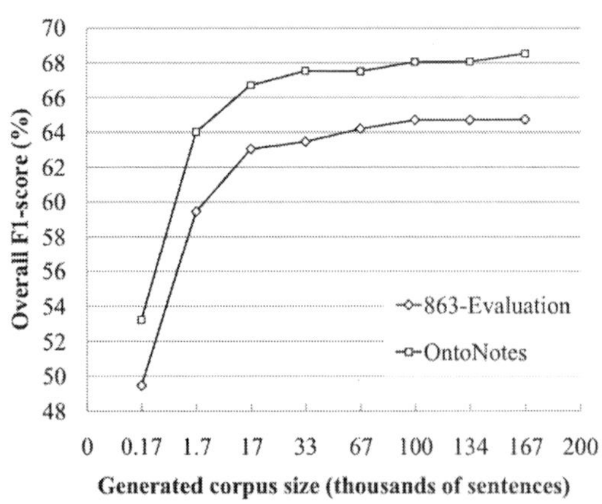

Figure 5. The Effect of Varying the Generated Corpus Size

[6] We used Zhang's significance tester (Zhang et al., 2004).

Training data	863-Evaluation corpus			OntoNotes corpus		
	PER	LOC	ORG	PER	LOC	ORG
People's Daily (PD)	59.91%	74.97%	35.61%	72.96%	76.89%	47.72%
Rule2+Score+List	62.68%	72.36%	28.81%	66.36%	76.43%	44.78%
Rule2+Score+List+PD	**66.15%**	**75.00%**	**36.22%**	**75.24%**	**78.31%**	**55.10%**

Table 6. Test Results for Each NE Category

4.6 The Performance of Each NE Category

To analyze overall error, our per-class F1-score is shown in Table 6. Training on the combined corpus could improve the performance of each NE category. The improvements are substantial in all categories except LOC on 863-Evaluation.

In general, the results of ORG entities are lower than the results of PER and LOC. The possible reason may be that ORG names are more complex than PER and LOC names. They usually consist of more words, which may result in more word alignment errors and then lead to more training instances filtered out. Fewer training instances might lead to a poorer performance. In addition, English ORG entity recognition is also more difficulty, which also results in more noises among the ORG name training instances.

5 Conclusion and Future Work

To solve the data-shortage and domain overfitting problems, we attempt to enlarge the Chinese NE training data automatically.

In this paper, we present a method of generating NER training data automatically from a bilingual parallel corpus. We employ an existing high-performance English NER system to recognized NEs at the English side, and then project the labels to the Chinese side according to the word alignment. To guarantee the quality of the training data, we propose effective filtering strategies. The results show that our training data is comparable with the manually-labeled data and can improve the performance of NER as an additional corpus.

Besides, the training data could be expanded easily as long as there are plenty of parallel corpora available. And identifying pairs of parallel documents is much easier than NE training data annotation. Generating training data from parallel corpora thus provides an alternative way of collecting data required for Chinese NER. Our method can be easily adapted to other languages.

In the future, we will try to improve the entity alignment and propose other better filtering strategies. Moreover, we will try to make use of more parallel corpora from a wider range of sources, because more parallel corpora may improve the accuracy of word alignment and widen the coverage of the generated NE corpus.

Acknowledgments

This work was supported by National Natural Science Foundation of China (NSFC) via grant 60975055 and 61073126. Special thanks to Wanxiang Che, Yanyan Zhao, Fikadu Gemechu, Yuhang Guo, Zhenghua Li, Meishan Zhang and the anonymous reviewers for insightful comments and suggestions.

References

Joohui An, Seungwoo Lee, and Gary Geunbae Lee. 2003. Automatic acquisition of named entity tagged corpus from world wide web. In *Proceedings of the 41st Annual Meeting of the Association for Computational Linguistics (ACL)*, pages 165-168.

Hai Leong Chieu and Hwee Tou Ng. 2002. Named Entity Recognition: A Maximum Entropy Approach Using Global Information. In *Proceedings of the 19th International Conference on Computational Linguistics (COLING)*, pages 190-196.

Massimiliano Ciaramita and Yasemin Altun. 2005. Named-entity recognition in novel domains with external lexical knowledge. In *Workshop on Advances in Structured Learning for Text and Speech Processing (NIPS-2005)*.

Jenny Finkel, Shipra Dingare, Christopher D. Manning, Malvina Nissim, Beatrice Alex, and Claire Grover. 2005. Exploring the boundaries: Gene and protein identification in biomedical text. *BMC Bioinformatics, 6(Suppl 1):S5*.

Radu Florian, Abe Ittycheriah, Hongyan Jing, and Tong Zhang. 2003. Named entity recognition through classifier combination. In *Proceedings of the 7th Conference on Natural Language Learning (CoNLL)*, pages 168-171.

Fei Huang and Stephan Vogel. 2002. Improved Named Entity Translation and Bilingual Named Entity Extraction. In *Proceedings of the 4th IEEE International Conference on Multimodal Interface*, pages 253-258. Pittsburgh, PA, October.

Dan Klein, Joseph Smarr, Huy Nguyen, and Christopher D. Manning. 2003. Named entity recognition with character-level models. In *Proceedings of the 7th Conference on Natural Language Learning (CoNLL)*, pages 188-191.

John Lafferty, Andrew McCallum and Fernando Pereira. 2001. Conditional random fields: Probabilistic models for segmenting and labeling sequence data. In *International Conference on Machine Learning (ICML)*, pages 282-289.

Joel Nothman, James R. Curran, and Tara Murphy. 2008. Transforming Wikipedia into named entity training data. In *Proceedings of the Australian Language Technology Workshop*, pages 124-132, Hobart, Australia.

Philip Resnik and Noah A. Smith, 2003. The Web as a Parallel Corpus. *Computational Linguistics*, v.29 n.3, pages 349-380,

Alexander E. Richman and Patrick Schone. 2008. Mining wiki resources for multilingual named entity recognition. In *Proceedings of the 46th Annual Meeting of the Association for Computational Linguistics: Human Language Technologies*, pages 1-9, Columbus, Ohio, USA.

Burr Settles. 2004. Biomedical Named Entity Recognition Using Conditional Random Fields and Rich Feature Sets. In *Proceedings of COLING 2004, the International Joint Workshop on Natural Language Processing in Biomedicine and its Applications (NLPBA)*, Geneva, Switzerland.

Koichi Takeuchi and Nigel Collier. 2002. Use of Support Vector Machines in Extended Named Entity Recognition. In *Proceedings of the 6th Conference on Natural Language Learning (CoNLL)*, pages 119-125.

Andreas Vlachos and Caroline Gasperin. 2006. Bootstrapping and evaluating named entity recognition in the biomedical domain. In *Proceedings of the Workshop on Linking Natural Language Processing and Biology: Towards Deeper Biological Literature Analysis*, pages 138-145. New York City, New York, USA.

Casey Whitelaw , Alex Kehlenbeck , Nemanja Petrovic and Lyle Ungar. 2008. Web-scale named entity recognition. In *Proceedings of the 17th ACM Conference on Information and Knowledge Management*, October 26-30, Napa Valley, California, USA.

Youzheng Wu, Jun Zhao, Bo Xu, Chinese Named Entity Recognition Model Based on Multiple Features. In *Proceedings of HLT/EMNLP 2005*, pages: 427-434, October 6-8, Vancouver, B.C., Canada.

David Yarowsky, Grace Ngai and Richard Wicentowski. 2001. Inducing multilingual text analysis tools via robust projection across aligned corpora. In *Human Language Technology Conference*, pages 109-116, San Diego, California, March.

Ying Zhang, Ke Wu, Jianfeng Gao, and Phil Vines. 2006. Automatic Acquisition of Chinese–English Parallel Corpus from the Web. In *Proceedings of ECIR-06, 28th European Conference on Information Retrieval.*

Ying Zhang, Stephan Vogel, and Alex Waibel. 2004. Interpreting BLEU/NIST scores: How much improvement do we need to have a better system? In *Proceedings of the Fourth International Conference on Language Resources and Evaluation (LREC)*, pages 2051-2054.

Guodong Zhou and Jian Su. 2002. Named entity recognition using an HMM-based chunk tagger. In *Proceedings of the 40th Annual Meeting of the Association of Comparative Linguistics (ACL)*, pages 473-480.

Learning the Latent Topics for Question Retrieval in Community QA

Li Cai, Guangyou Zhou, Kang Liu, and Jun Zhao
National Laboratory of Pattern Recognition
Institute of Automation, Chinese Academy of Sciences
95 Zhongguancun East Road, Beijing 100190, China
{lcai,gyzhou,kliu,jzhao}@nlpr.ia.ac.cn

Abstract

Community-based Question Answering (cQA) is a popular online service where users can ask and answer questions on any topics. This paper is concerned with the problem of question retrieval. Question retrieval in cQA aims to find historical questions that are semantically equivalent or relevant to the queried questions. Although the translation-based language model (Xue et al., 2008) has gained the state-of-the-art performance for question retrieval, they ignore the latent topic information in calculating the semantic similarity between questions. In this paper, we propose a topic model incorporated with the category information into the process of discovering the latent topics in the content of questions. Then we combine the semantic similarity based latent topics with the translation-based language model into a unified framework for question retrieval. Experiments are carried out on a real world cQA data set from Yahoo! Answers. The results show that our proposed method can significantly improve the question retrieval performance of translation-based language model.

1 Introduction

Over the past few years, large scale question and answer archives have become an important information resource on the Web. These include the traditional FAQ archives constructed by the experts or companies for their products and the emerging community-based online services, such as Yahoo! Answers[1] and Live QnA[2].

The major challenge for cQA retrieval is the lexical gap (or *lexical chasm*) between the queried questions and the question-answer pairs in the archives (Jeon et al., 2005; Xue et al., 2008). To solve the *lexical gap* problem, most researchers regarded the question retrieval task as a statistical machine translation problem by using IBM model 1 (Brown et al., 1993) to learn the word-to-word translation probabilities (Berger and Lafferty, 1999; Jeon et al., 2005; Xue et al., 2008; Lee et al., 2008; Bernhard and Gurevych, 2009; Cao et al., 2010). Although the translation-based language model(TRLM) has yielded the state-of-the-art performance for question retrieval, they model the word translation probabilities without taking into account the distribution of words in the whole content.

In this paper, we argue that it is beneficial to exploit the latent topic information for question retrieval. The basic idea is as follows: first we employ the topic model (e.g., LDA) to discover the latent topics in the content of questions, and calculate the semantic similarity between questions based on the latent topic information. Moreover, a distinctive feature of question-answer archives in cQA is that cQA services always organize questions into a hierarchy of categories. We propose an improved latent topic model by introducing the category information of questions. To solve the *lexical gap* problem, the translation-based language model extracts knowledge from question-answer pairs which are collected from cQA service. Latent topic model extracts knowledge from the distribution of words and categories in whole cQA archives. We assume that the two knowledge are complementary to each other, as we will show in the experiment.

In order to illustrate the above ideas clearly, we give an example of retrieving semantically equivalent or relevant to the queried questions in Figure 1. Given question $Q1$, we get a ranked list of semantically similar questions (Q_2, Q_3, Q_4, Q_5) using state-of-the-art translation-based lan-

[1] http://answers.yahoo.com
[2] http://qna.live.com

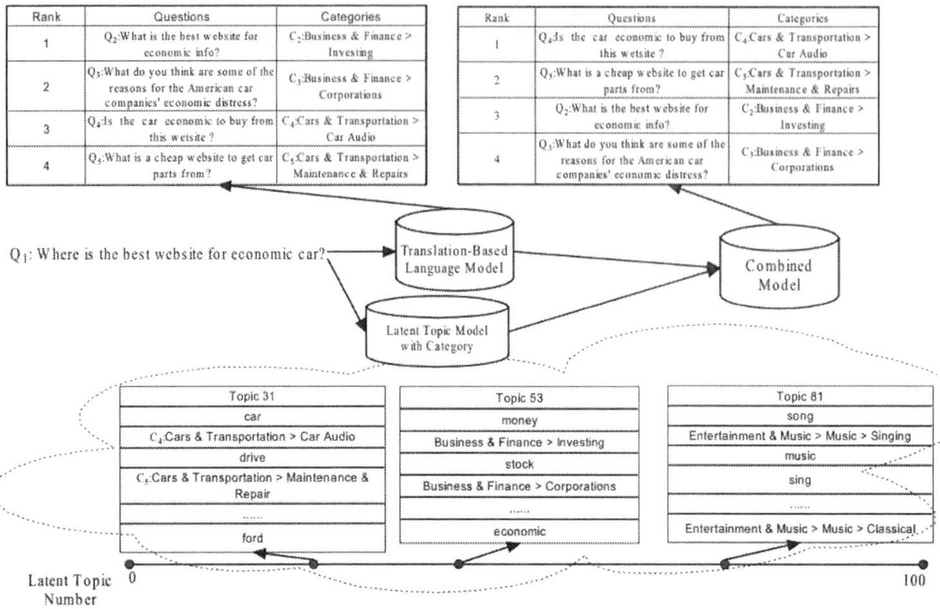

Figure 1: Illustration of our proposed approach.

guage model. All the semantically similar questions are with their corresponding categories. Our proposed latent topic model models the distribution of words, categories of the whole content. We illustrate in Figure 1 a matching of the top words and categories from a few topics. We can see that the word *car* is more related to categories "Cars & Transportation>Car Audio" and "Cars & Transportation>Maintenance & Repairs" than the word "economic" to categories "Business & Finance>Investing" and "Business & Finance>Corporations" in latent topics. Using this information from the latent topic model, we can rerank the retrieved question. Therefore, combining the translation-based language model with the latent topic model with categories, we can get the ranked list of semantically similar questions (Q_4, Q_5, Q_2, Q_3) which are better than the previous retrieval result.

Specifically, our contributions are as follows:

1. We employ the topic model to discover the latent topic information in the content of questions for cQA retrieval (in Section 4.1.)

2. We introduce the category information into the process of discovering the latent topics. (in Section and 4.2).

3. We propose to combine the semantic similarity based latent topics with the translation-based language model into a unified framework to further improve the retrieval performance (in Section 4.4).

4. Finally, we conduct the experiments on cQA data set from Yahoo! Answers for question retrieval. The results show that our proposed approach significantly outperform the state-of-the-art translation-based language model (in Section 5).

The remainder of this paper is organized as follows. Section 2 reviews the related work on community-based question retrieval. Section 3 presents the existing question retrieval models. Section 4 presents the topic model incorporated with category information for question retrieval. Section 5 presents the experimental results. Finally, we conclude and offer the further work in Section 6.

2 Related Work

Recently, the research of question retrieval has been further extended to the cQA data. Jeon et al. (2005) proposed a word-based translation model for automatically fixing the lexical gap problem. Experimental results demonstrated that translation model significantly outperformed the traditional methods (i.e., VSM, BM25, LM). Xue et al. (2008) proposed a translation-based language model for question retrieval. The results indicated that translation-based language model further improved the retrieval results and obtained the state-of-the-art performance.

Subsequent work on translation models focused on providing suitable parallel data to learn the translation probabilities. Lee et al. (2008) tried to further improve the translation probabilities based on question-answer pairs by selecting the most important terms to build compact translation models. Bernhard and Gurevych (2009) proposed to use as a parallel training data set the definitions and glosses provided for the same term by different lexical semantic resources. Cao et al. (2010) explored adding the category information into the translation model for question retrieval. Zhou et al. (2011) proposed a phrase-based translation model for question retrieval and obtained the state-of-the-art performance.

However, all the existing methods ignore the latent topics information in calculating the semantic similarity between questions. In this paper, we present a new approach to discover the latent topic of questions for improving the performance of translation-based language models for question retrieval. Moreover, we introduce the category information into the process of discovering the latent topics. To the best of our knowledge, none of the existing studies addressed question retrieval in cQA by learning the latent topics.

3 Preliminaries

3.1 Language Model

The unigram language model has been widely used for question retrieval on community-based Q&A data (Jeon et al., 2005; Xue et al., 2008; Cao et al., 2010). To avoid zero probability, we use Jelinek-Mercer smoothing (Zhai and Lafferty, 2001) due to its good performance and cheap computational cost. So the ranking function for the query likelihood language model with Jelinek-Mercer smoothing can be written as:

$$P_{LM}(q|Q) = \prod_{w \in \mathbf{q}} (1-\lambda)P_{ml}(w|Q) + \lambda P_{ml}(w|C) \quad (1)$$

$$P_{ml}(w|Q) = \frac{\#(w,Q)}{|Q|}, \; P_{ml}(w|C) = \frac{\#(w,C)}{|C|} \quad (2)$$

where q is the queried question, Q is a historical question, C is background collection, λ is smoothing parameter. $\#(t,Q)$ is the frequency of term t in Q, $|Q|$ and $|C|$ denote the length of Q and C, respectively.

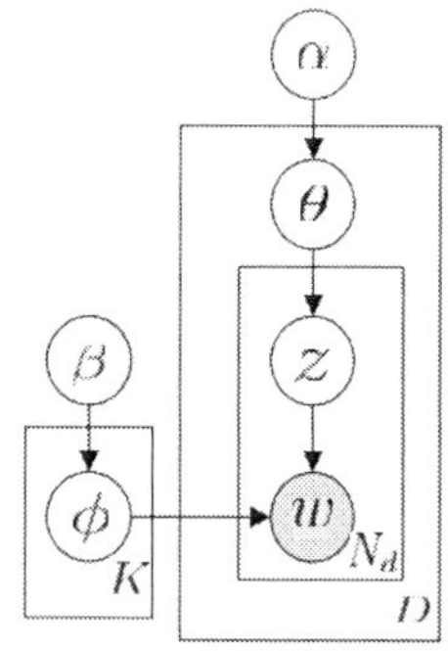

Figure 2: Latent Dirichlet Allocation.

3.2 Translation Model

Previous work (Berger et al., 2000; Jeon et al., 2005; Xue et al., 2008) consistently reported that the word-based translation models (TR) yielded better performance than the traditional methods (VSM, Okapi and LM) for question retrieval. These models exploited the word translation probabilities in a language modeling framework. According to Jeon et al. (2005) and Xue et al. (2008), the ranking function can be written as:

$$P_{TR}(q|Q) = \prod_{w \in \mathbf{q}} (1-\lambda)P_{tr}(w|Q) + \lambda P_{ml}(w|C) \quad (3)$$

$$P_{tr}(w|Q) = \sum_{t \in Q} P(w|t)P_{ml}(t|Q), \; P_{ml}(t|Q) = \frac{\#(t,Q)}{|Q|} \quad (4)$$

where $P(w|t)$ denotes the translation probability from word t to word w.

3.3 Translation-Based Language Model

Xue et al. (2008) proposed to linearly mix two different estimations by combining language model and translation model into a unified framework, called TRLM. The experiments show that this model gains better performance than both the language model and the translation model. Following Xue et al. (2008), this model can be written as:

$$P_{TRLM}(q|Q) = \prod_{w \in \mathbf{q}} (1-\lambda)P_{mx}(w|Q) + \lambda P_{ml}(w|C) \quad (5)$$

$$P_{mx}(w|Q) = \delta \sum_{t \in Q} P(w|t)P_{ml}(t|Q) + (1-\delta)P_{ml}(w|Q) \quad (6)$$

4 Topic Model Incorporated with Category Information for Question Retrieval

Previous work on question retrieval in cQA, employs different retrieval models, such as

Symbol	Description
K	the number of topics
N	the number of questions
$\|V\|$	the number of unique words
$\|C\|$	the number of unique leaf categories
N_q	the number of distinct words in question q
θ_q	multinomial distribution over topics specific to question q
ϕ_z	multinomial distribution over words specific to topic z
ψ_z	multinomial distribution over categories specific to topic z
z_{qi}	the topic of the ith word in question q
c_{qi}	the category of the ith word in question q
w_{qi}	the ith word in question q

Table 1: Meanings of the notations used in this paper

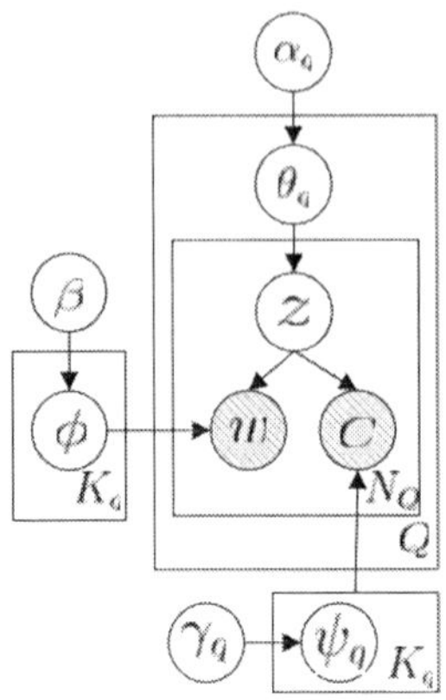

Figure 3: Topic model incorporated with category information.

VSM (Salton et al., 1975), LM (Zhai and Lafferty, 2001), TR (Jeon et al., 2005) and TRLM (Xue et al., 2008). However, all these existing models ignore the latent topics in calculating the semantic similarity between questions. In this Section, we explore the latent topic information for question retrieval.

4.1 Topic Model for Question Retrieval

Before introducing our proposed method, we first briefly describe the basic Latent Dirichlet Allocation (LDA) model (Blei et al., 2003). The notations we used in this paper are presented in Table 1, and the graphic model representations of LDA model is shown in Figure 2. LDA models the generation of document content as two independent stochastic processes by introducing latent topic space. For an arbitrary word w in document d, (1) a topic z is first sampled from the multinomial distribution θ_d, which is generated from the Dirichlet prior parameterized by α; (2) and then the word w is generated from multinomial distribution ψ_z, which is generated from the Dirichlet prior parameterized by β. The two Dirichlet priors for documents-topic distribution θ_d and topic-word distribution ψ_z reduce the probability of overfitting training documents and enhance the ability of inferring topic distribution for new documents.

In cQA, the historical questions in the archives can be considered as documents. In this paper, we employ the state-of-the-art topic model –– LDA (Blei et al., 2003) to discover the latent topics in the content of questions. We assume that a queried question q and the historical questions Q in cQA archives are represented by a distribution over topics. We obtain the topic distribution of a question by merging the topic distributions of words in question. Formally, we have

$$P_{TM}(z|q) = \frac{1}{|q|}(\lambda_1 \sum_{w \in q} P(z|w) \quad (7)$$

Then, we assume that a question Q in the archives and a queried question q have the same prior probability, so the score function between the two questions can be written as:

$$\begin{aligned} P_{TM}(q|Q) &= \sum_z P(q|z) P_{TM}(z|Q) \\ &= \sum_{z \in K} \frac{P(z|q)P(q)}{p(z)} P_{TM}(z|Q) \\ &= \frac{K}{|q|} \sum_{z \in K} P_{TM}(z|q) P_{TM}(z|Q) \quad (8) \end{aligned}$$

4.2 Topic Model Incorporated with Category Information

In cQA, the questions are organized into a hierarchy of categories. For example, the subcategory "Computer Networking" is a child category of "Computers & Internet" in Yahoo! Answers. When a user asks a question, the user chooses a category for the question and at then post the question in that category. For example, the questions in the subcategory "Computer Networking" mainly related to computer software or networking equipments.

To utilize the category information provided by cQA, we propose a topic model incorporated with category information (TMC) to discover the latent topics in the content of questions. The graphic representation of our proposed TMC model is presented in Figure 3. Inspired by the related work on topic analysis (Blei et al., 2003; Griffiths and Steyvers, 2004; Zhou et al., 2008; Wang and McCallum, 2006; Guo et al., 2008; Celikyilmaz et al., 2010; Jo and Oh, 2011), we make the following assumptions about the probabilistic structure of TMC model. First, each question is modeled as a multinomial distribution over latent topics, and each topic is modeled as a multinomial distribution over words and a multinomial distribution over categories. Second, the prior distributions for topics, words and categories follow different parameterized Dirichlet distribution, which is conjugate prior for multinomial distribution. In Figure 3, for each word w in question q, a topic z is first drawn from the multinomial distribution θ_q, and then a word is sampled from the multinomial distribution ϕ_z and a category c is also sampled from the multinomial distribution ψ_z for the word. Repeating this process N_q times, we get the words and category for a question. We obtain the whole question set by repeating the above process N times. After that, we obtain the topic distribution of a question by merging the topic distributions of words category. So equation (7) can be rewritten as:

$$P_{TMC}(z|q) = \frac{1}{1+|q|}(\lambda_2 P(z|c) + \lambda_3 \sum_{w \in q} P(z|w)) \quad (9)$$

In equation (9), the topic distribution of question category is modeled by $\lambda_2 P(z|c)$, the topic distribution of words in question is modeled by $\lambda_3 \sum_{w \in q} P(z|w)$. The relative importance of these two parts is adjusted through λ_2 and λ_3.

Introducing the category information into the process of discovering the latent topics, equation (8) can be rewritten as:

$$\begin{aligned} P_{TMC}(Q|q) &= \sum_z P(Q|z) P_{TMC}(z|q) \\ &= \sum_{z \in K} \frac{P(z|q)P(q)}{p(z)} P_{TMC}(z|Q) \\ &= \frac{K}{|q|} \sum_{z \in K} P_{TMC}(z|q) P_{TMC}(z|Q) \quad (10) \end{aligned}$$

4.3 Parameter Estimation for TMC

After introducing our proposed TMC method, we will describe how to estimate the parameter used in the model. In TMC, we introduce the new parameters, which lead to the inference not be done exactly. Expectation-Maximum (EM) algorithm is a possible choice for estimating the parameters of models with latent variables. However, EM suffers from the possibility of running into local maxima and the high computational burden. Therefore, we employ an alternative approach – Gibbs sampling (Griffiths, 2002), which is gaining popularity in recent work on latent topic analysis (Griffiths and Steyvers, 2004; Zhou et al., 2008; Wang and McCallum, 2006; Guo et al., 2008; Jo and Oh, 2011).

After training the model, we can get the following parameter estimations as:

$$\hat{\theta}_{qz} = \frac{n_{qz} + \alpha_z - 1}{\sum_{z'=1}^{K}(n_{qz'} + \alpha_{z'}) - 1}$$

$$\hat{\phi}_{zw} = \frac{n_{zw} + \beta_w - 1}{\sum_{v=1}^{|V|}(n_{zv} + \beta_v) - 1}$$

$$\hat{\psi}_{zc} = \frac{n_{zc} + \gamma_c - 1}{\sum_{c'=1}^{|C|}(n_{zc'} + \gamma_{c'}) - 1}$$

4.4 Combining the TMC with the TRLM for Question Retrieval

Since the TMC model and the translation-based language model use different strategies for question retrieval, it is interesting to explore how to combine their strength. In this section, we propose an approach to linearly combine the TMC model with the TRLM model for question retrieval. In this paper, we choose translation-based language model (TRLM) (Xue et al., 2008) as the foundation of our solution since TRLM has gained the state-of-the-art performance for question retrieval (Xue et al., 2008; Cao et al., 2010). Formally, we have

$$\begin{aligned} P_{TMC-TRLM}(q|Q) &= \mu P_{TRLM}(q|Q) \\ &+ (1-\mu) P_{TMC}(q|Q) \quad (11) \end{aligned}$$

In equation (11), the relative importance of TMC and the TRLM is adjusted through μ. When $\mu = 1$, the retrieval model is based on TMC. When $\mu = 0$, the retrieval model is based on TRLM.

5 Experiments

5.1 Data Set and Evaluation Metrics

We collect the questions from Yahoo! Answers and use the *getByCategory* function provided in Yahoo! Answers API[3] to obtain Q&A threads

[3]http://developer.yahoo.com/answers

Category	#Size	Category	# Size
Arts & Humanities	86,744	Home & Garden	35,029
Business & Finance	105,453	Beauty & Style	37,350
Cars & Transportation	145,515	Pet	54,158
Education & Reference	80,782	Travel	305,283
Entertainment & Music	152,769	Health	132,716
Family & Relationships	34,743	Sports	214,317
Politics & Government	59,787	Social Science	46,415
Pregnancy & Parenting	43,103	Ding out	46,933
Science & Mathematics	89,856	Food & Drink	45,055
Computers & Internet	90,546	News & Events	20,300
Games & Recreation	53,458	Environment	21,276
Consumer Electronics	90,553	Local Businesses	51,551
Society & Culture	94,470	Yahoo! Products	150,445

Table 2: Number of questions in each first-level category

from the Yahoo! site. More specifically, we utilize the *resolved* questions and the resulting question repository that we use for question retrieval contains 2,288,607 questions. Each resolved question consists of four parts: "question title", "question description", "question answers" and "question category". For question retrieval, we only use the "question title" part and "question category" part. It is assumed that the titles and categories of the questions already provide enough semantic information. There are 26 categories at the first level and 1,262 categories at the leaf level. Each question belongs to a unique leaf category. Table 2 shows the distribution across first-level categories of the questions in the training data set. To learn the translation probabilities, we use about one million question-answer pairs from another data set.[4]

We randomly select 252 questions for test set and another 252 questions for development set. We select the test set and development set in proportion to the number of questions and categories against the whole distribution to have a better control over a possible imbalance. To obtain the ground-truth of question retrieval, we employ the Vector Space Model (VSM) (Salton et al., 1975) to retrieve the top 20 results and obtain manual judgements. The top 20 results don't include the queried question itself. Given a returned result by VSM, an annotator is asked to label it with "relevant" or "irrelevant". If a returned result is considered semantically equivalent to the queried question, the annotator will label it as "relevant"; otherwise, the annotator will label it as "irrelevant". Two annotators are involved in the annotation process. If a conflict happens, a third person will make judgement for the final result. In the process of manually judging questions, the annotators are presented only the questions. **Metrics**: We evaluate the performance of our approach using the following metrics: **Mean Average Precision** (MAP) and **Precision@n** (P@n). MAP rewards methods that return relevant questions early and also rewards correct ranking of the results. P@n reports the fraction of the top-n questions retrieved that are relevant. We perform a significant test, i.e., a t-test with a default significant level of 0.05.

Parameter Selection: The experiments use many parameters. Following the literature, we set the smoothing parameter λ in equations (1), (3) and (5) to 0.2 (Cao et al., 2010), and the parameter δ in equation (6) to 0.8 (Xue et al., 2008; Cao et al., 2010), which controls the translation component's impact. Other parameters are tuned on the development set, as we will show in the experiments.

5.2 Topic Number Selection

In this section, we concentrate on how to select proper topic numbers to obtain our model with best performance on our test set and enough iterations in Algorithm 1 to prevent overfitting problem. Here, following (Guo et al., 2008), we use perplexity to estimate the performance of our model. We calculate the perplexity on development set, which is a sequence of tuples $(q, w, c) \in D_{dev}$:

$$\text{Perplexity}(D_{dev}) = exp\{-\frac{\sum_{(q,w,c)\in D_{dev}} \ln P(w, c|q)}{|D_{dev}|}\}$$

Here, the probability $P(w, c|q)$ is calculated according to the parameters trained from the historical question-answer pairs:

$$P(w, c|q) = \sum_{z=1}^{K} P(w|z)P(c|z)P(z|q)$$

Figure 4(a) shows the influence of iteration number of Gibbs sampling on the model generalization ability. Empirically, we set the topic number as 100 and change the iteration number in the experiments. Note that the lower perplexity value indicates better generalization ability on the hold-out testing set. From Figure 4(a), it is seen that the perplexity values decreases dramatically when the iteration times are below 200.

Figure 4(b) shows the perplexity values for different settings of topic number. From the Figure, we see that the perplexity decreases when the

[4]The Yahoo! Webscope dataset Yahoo answers comprehensive questions and answers version 1.0.2, available at http://reseach.yahoo.com/Academic_Relations.

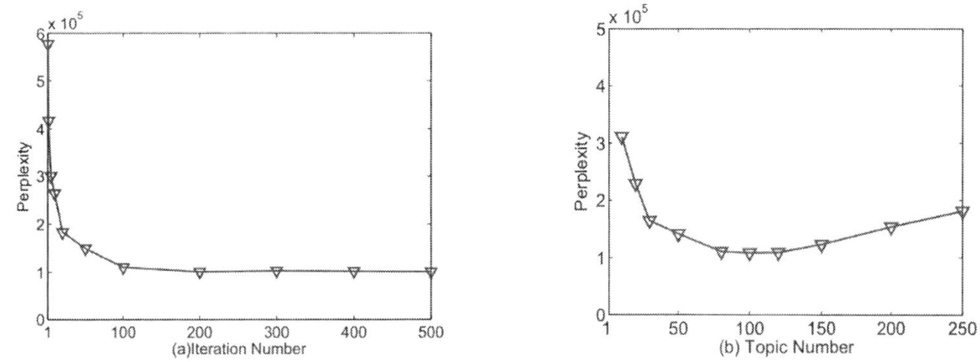

Figure 4: Perplexity on different iteration numbers(a) and topic number selection(b).

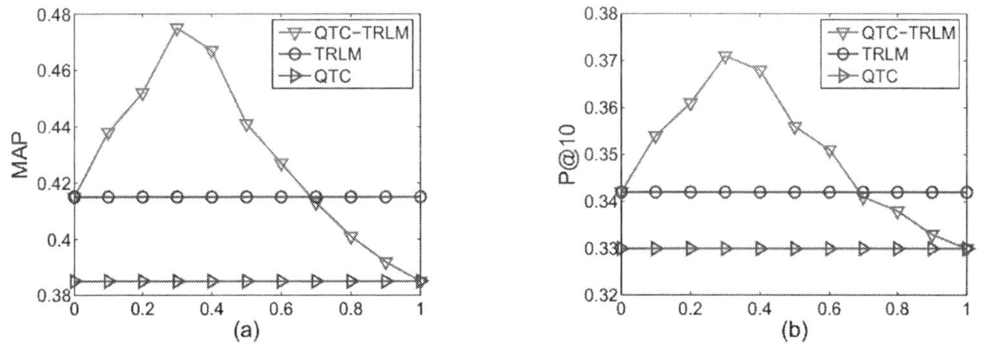

Figure 5: The relative importance of μ on the performance of TMC-TRLM.

number of topics starts to increase. However, after a certain point, the perplexity values start to increase. Based on the above experiments, we train our model using 100 topics and 200 iteration times.

5.3 The Relative Importance of Parameter μ

In equation (11), we use the parameter μ to adjust the relative importance of the TMC and the TRLM. Figure 5 illustrates the relative importance the value of μ is on the performance of question retrieval in terms of MAP and P@10, respectively. The TMC and TRLM are used for reference. The results are obtained with the 252 questions on the development set. From Figure 5, we see that for MAP and P@10, the combined model TMC-TRLM performs better than the TMC and TRLM when μ is between 0 and 0.7. In both cases, a relatively broad set for good parameter values is observed.

5.4 The Effectiveness of Our Proposed TMC Model

Table 3 shows the main results of question retrieval using the baseline methods and our proposed TMC-TRLM. In Table 3, VSM refers to the vector space model of (Salton et al., 1975); BM25 refers to the model of (Robertson et al., 1994); LM refers to the language model of (Zhai and Lafferty, 2001); TR refers to the translation model of (Jeon et al., 2005; Xue et al., 2008), TRLM refers to the translation-based language model of (Xue et al., 2008) and TRLM+CE refers to the method of (Cao et al., 2010).[5] In row 7, we show our approach and choose the best parameter $K = 100$. There are some clear trends in the results of Table 3:

#	Models	MAP	P@10
1	VSM	0.242	0.226
2	BM25	0.301	0.294
3	LM	0.352	0.327
4	TR	0.383	0.330
5	TRLM	0.415	0.342
6	TRLM+CE	0.437	0.358
7	TMC	0.385	0.331
8	**TMC-TRLM** ($K = 100$)	**0.475**	**0.371**

Table 3: Comparison with different methods for question retrieval.

[5] Here, we implement the method of (Cao et al., 2010) and use the TRLM to compute the global relevance and local relevance.

(1) The simple unigram language model (LM) performs slightly better than the classical retrieval models: VSM and BM25 (row 1 vs. row 3; row 2 vs. row 3).

(2) Translation model (TR) outperforms the LM by significant margins (row 3 vs. row 4).

(3) Translation-based language model (TRLM) significantly outperforms the translation model (TR) (row 4 vs. row 5), similar observations have been done by Xue et al. (2008).

(4) Exploiting category information of questions into the translation-based language model (TRLM) can significantly improve the question retrieval performance (row 5 vs. row 6), similar observations have been done by Cao et al. (2010).

(5) Our proposed approach TMC does not outperform the baseline methods TRLM and TRLM+CE (row 5 vs. row 7; row 6 vs. row 7). This demonstrates that the knowledge extracted from TMC is not as effective as that extracted from TRLM for question retrieval. TRLM learns the word-to-word translation probabilities from parallel corpus collected from question answer archives. However, TMC models word-category-topic distribution from the whole question answer content. The knowledge extracted from TMC is much noisier than that of TRLM. We suspect the above reason leads to the poor performance of TMC.

(6) Our proposed approach TMC-TRLM significantly outperforms the baseline methods TRLM and TRLM+CE (row 5 vs. row 8; row 6 vs. row 8). We conduct a significant test (t-test) on the improvements of our approach over TRLM and TRLM+CE. The result indicates that the improvements are statistically significant in terms of all the evaluation measures.[6] This demonstrates that the knowledge extracted from TMC is complementary to the knowledge extracted from TRLM+CE for question retrieval.

5.5 The Effectiveness of Category Information

Like the previous approaches, we treat the questions as a multinomial distribution over latent topics, and each topic is a multinomial distribution over words too. Different from previous work on topic analysis (Blei et al., 2003; Griffiths and Steyvers, 2004; Zhou et al., 2008; Wang and McCallum, 2006; Guo et al., 2008; Celikyilmaz et al., 2010; Jo and Oh, 2011), we introduce the category information of questions, which is predefined by cQA services, into the process of discovering latent topics. To see how much the category information benefit the question retrieval, we introduce a baseline method for comparison. The baseline method (denoted as TM-TRLM) is used to denote the proposed method without using the category information. Table 5 provides the comparison. From the Table, we see that the exploring category information can significantly improve the performance for question retrieval (row 1 vs. row 2).

[6] The comparisons are significant at $p < 0.05$.

#	Models	MAP	P@10
1	TM-TRLM	0.454	0.366
2	**TMC-TRLM**	**0.475**	**0.371**

Table 4: The effectiveness of category information for question retrieval.

6 Conclusions and Future Work

In this paper, we present a new approach to discover the latent topic of questions for improving the performance of translation-based language model for question retrieval. Experiments conducted on real cQA data demonstrate that our proposed approach significantly outperforms the state-of-the-art methods (TRLM and TRLM+CE).

There are some ways in which this research could be continued. First, question structure should be considered, so it is necessary to combine the proposed approach with other question retrieval methods (e.g., (Duan et al., 2008; Wang et al., 2009; Bunescu and Huang, 2010)) to further improve the performance. Second, we will try to investigate the use of the proposed approach for other kinds of data set, such as categorized questions from forum sites and FAQ sites.

Acknowledgments

This work was supported by the National Natural Science Foundation of China (No. 60875041 and No. 61070106). We thank the anonymous reviewers for their insightful comments.

References

A. Berger, R. Caruana, D. Cohn, D. Freitag, and V. Mittal. 2000. Bridging the lexical chasm: statistical approach to answer-finding. In *Proceedings of SIGIR*, pages 192-199.

A. Berger and J. Lafferty. 1999. Information retrieval as statistical translation. In *Proceedings of SIGIR*, pages 222-229.

D. Bernhard and I. Gurevych. 2009. Combining lexical semantic resources with question & answer archives for translation-based answer finding. In *Proceedings of ACL*, pages 728-736.

D. M. Blei, A. Ng, and M. Jordan. 2003. Latent dirichlet allocation. *Journal of Machine Learning Research*, 3:993-1022.

P. F. Brown, V. J. D. Pietra, S. A. D. Pietra, and R. L. Mercer. 1993. The mathematics of statistical machine translation: parameter estimation. *Computational Linguistics*, 19(2):263-311.

R. Bunescu and Y. Huang. 2010. Learing the relative usefulness of questions in community QA. In *Proceedings of EMNLP*, pages 97-107.

X. Cao, G. Cong, B. Cui, C. S. Jensen, and C. Zhang. 2009. The use of categorization information in language models for question retrieval. In *Proceedings of CIKM*.

X. Cao, G. Cong, B. Cui, and C. S. Jensen. 2010. A generalized framework of exploring category information for question retrieval in community question answer archives. In *Proceedings of WWW*.

A. Celikyilmaz, D. Hakkani-Tur, and G. Tur. 2010. LDA based similarity modeling for question answering. In *Proceedings of ACL*.

H. Duan, Y. Cao, C. Y. Lin, and Y. Yu. 2008. Searching questions by identifying questions topics and question focus. In *Proceedings of ACL*, pages 156-164.

T. Griffiths. Gibbs sampling in the generative model of latent dirichlet allocation. http://www-psych.stanford.edu/ gruffydd/cogsci02/lda.ps.

T. Griffiths and M. Steyvers. 2004. Finding scientific topics. In National Academy of Sciences.

J. Guo, S. Xu, S. Bao, and Y. Yu. 2008. Tapping on the potential of Q&A community by recommending answer providers. In *Proceedings of CIKM*.

J. Jeon, W. Bruce Croft, and J. H. Lee. 2005. Finding similar questions in large question and answer archives. In *Proceedings of CIKM*, pages 84-90.

Y. Jo and A. Oh. 2011. Aspect and sentiment unification model for online review analysis. In *Proceedings of WSDM*.

J. -T. Lee, S. -B. Kim, Y. -I. Song, and H. -C. Rim. 2008. Bridge lexical gaps between queries and questions on large online Q&A collections with compact translation models. In *Proceedings of EMNLP*, pages 410-418.

J. M. Ponte and W. B. Croft. 1998. A language modeling approach to information retrieval. In *Proceedings of SIGIR*.

S. Robertson, S. Walker, S. Jones, M. Hancock-Beaulieu, and M. Gatford. 1994. Okapi at trec-3. In *Proceedings of TREC*, pages 109-126.

G. Salton, A. Wong, and C. S. Yang. 1975. A vector space model for automatic indexing. *Communications of the ACM*, 18(11):613-620.

X. Wang and A. McCallum. 2006. Topic over time: a non-markov conditionals-time model of topical trends. In *Proceedings of SIGKDD*, pages 424-433.

K. Wang, Z. Ming, and T-S. Chua. 2009. A syntactic tree matching approach to finding similar questions in community-based qa services. In *Proceedings of SIGIR*, pages 187-194.

X. Xue, J. Jeon, and W. B. Croft. 2008. Retrieval models for question and answer archives. In *Proceedings of SIGIR*, pages 475-482.

C. Zhai and J. Lafferty. 2001. A study of smooth methods for language models applied to ad hoc information retrieval. In *Proceedings of SIGIR*, pages 334-342.

D. Zhou, J. Bian, S. Zheng, H. Zha, and C. L. Giles. 2008. Exploring social annotation for information retrieval. In *Proceedings of WWW*, pages 715-724.

G. Zhou, L. Cai, J. Zhao, and K. Liu. 2011. Phrase-based translation model for question retrieval in community question answer archives. In *Proceedings of ACL-HLT*, pages 653-662.

Identifying Event Descriptions using Co-training with Online News Summaries

William Yang Wang and **Kapil Thadani** and **Kathleen R. McKeown**
Computer Science Department
Columbia University
yww@cs.cmu.edu, {kapil, kathy}@cs.columbia.edu

Abstract

Systems that distill information about events from large corpora generally extract sentences that are relevant to a short event query. We present a novel co-training strategy for this task that employs a multi-document news summary corpus featuring 2.5 million unlabeled sentences, thus obviating the need for extensive manual annotation. Our experiments indicate that this technique significantly outperforms standard classification approaches with linear feature combination on this task. An analysis of our approach under various settings reveals how classifier and parameter choice can be used to control runtime overhead while contributing to an absolute increase of 22% in recall.

1 Introduction

Automatic identification of event descriptions is a crucial, yet difficult, problem with impact on applications such as question answering (QA), query-focused summarization (QS), and text mining (TM) systems. In such applications, a system is given a description of an event in the form of a query and the task is to identify sentences within relevant documents (retrieved by an information retrieval system) that describe the event. We define *event-relevant* sentences as those describing a unique event as specified in the query, typically occurring at a specific location, on a specific date, or with specific participants. The task is made difficult by the fact that words in the query rarely provide enough identifying information (Xu and Croft, 2000; Chirita et al., 2007) to reliably find descriptive sentences; the query may not specify all named entities and may provide other descriptive terms that are not easily matched. For example, given the query requesting a description of *"the Israeli-Palestinian peace talks"*, the sentence *"The discussions between Israelis and Palestinians follow last month's Annapolis meeting where Israeli Prime Minister and Palestinian President Mahmoud Abbas met and agreed to try to negotiate a deal before the end of 2008."* is event-relevant, whereas the sentence *"Turkey has close ties to both Israel and the Palestinians."* is not. Yet both sentences feature the named entities from the query. The term "peace talks" does not appear in the event-relevant sentence, but is implied by "negotiate".

Previous approaches have addressed this problem using supervised learning (Mani et al., 2003; Bethard and Martin, 2006; Manshadi et al., 2008), where the relation between the query and event-relevant sentences is learned. Still, gathering a large amount of training data is difficult and people often do not agree on what counts as relevant to an event description (Filatova and Hatzivassiloglou, 2003), making the process of manually labeling sentences as events both time consuming and expensive. This is supported by our own experiments with Amazon Mechanical Turk (AMT); we were only able to obtain 685 labeled event-relevant sentences on which 3 or more AMT users agreed after 16 days of posting. This is a striking contrast with use of AMT for other labeling tasks where thousands of labeled examples can be obtained in a matter of hours (Snow et al., 2008; Marge et al., 2010; Rosenthal et al., 2010).

In this paper, we present a novel semi-supervised learning method using co-training to classify sentences as salient event descriptions for a given event query. We use a small amount of manually annotated seed data, in the form of (query, sentence) pairs. Critically, we then augment this with a large amount of unlabeled news summaries, spanning nine years, from the Web. We hypothesize that the headline of each summary can be viewed as a single event query, and the corresponding summary sentences include a good number of salient event sentences that directly describe the event, as well as a small number of non-event sentences. We note that such data is abundantly available on the Web given naturally-occurring news stories as well as mature multi-document summarization systems. We use two relatively simple sets of features, one based on keywords and the other based on named entities, to train two Bayesian network classifiers on seed training data and employ co-training over the collected news summaries to incrementally augment the training set with increasingly robust labeled examples. Experimental results show a significant, absolute gain of 8% over training of the classifiers on the seed data alone.

Our primary contributions in this paper include:

- Collection of an online news summary corpus for detecting event relevance[1] that includes 166,435 summaries (2.5M sentences) generated by an online news summarizer in the period 2003-2011.
- An efficient co-training strategy for identifying event descriptions using online news summaries and compact, simple feature sets.
- An evaluation of the impact of classification techniques, experimental parameters and amount of novel Web data on the accuracy and efficiency of co-training.

In the following sections, we first present related work on event identification and then present our approach, outlining our hypothesis, the data we used, the co-training strategy and feature sets for this task. Following this, we present experimental results and conclude with a discussion of the implications and limitations of this work.

2 Related Work

The problem of identifying and understanding events in natural language text has been explored in many ways that have produced a variety of perspectives on the challenges involved. Tasks explored have included the mapping of verb-level events into aspectual classes (Siegel and McKeown, 2000), detection of specific *atomic* events (Filatova and Hatzivassiloglou, 2003), supervised event classification (Bethard and Martin, 2006) and unsupervised learning of event schemas (Chambers and Jurafsky, 2009). The notion of what constitutes an event has similarly ranged across perspectives, from general verb-level events (Siegel and McKeown, 2000; Chambers and Jurafsky, 2009) and predicate-argument pairs (Manshadi et al., 2008) to more specific news events (Spitters and Kraaij, 2002; Filatova and Hatzivassiloglou, 2003) and public health events (Fisichella et al., 2010).

Our task also adheres to a more specific definition of events: we assume that event queries refer to unique and newsworthy events such "the Beijing Olympics", rather than more general lexical-level events such as "the game". Our sentence-retrieval task aligns with the perspective of Filatova and Hatzivassiloglou (2003) who defined the notion of *atomic* events at the sentence level. They also show how event identification at this level can benefit indexing, summarization, and QA using low-level lexical features (Filatova and Hatzivassiloglou, 2004).

Many event identification tasks rely on supervised learning methods (Siegel and McKeown, 2000; Mani et al., 2003; Bethard and Martin, 2006; Manshadi et al., 2008) that can incur high annotation costs. While fully unsupervised methods (Bejan, 2008; Spitters and Kraaij, 2002) for event discovery are not encumbered by the availability of training data, they can produce event clusters or topics which are difficult to interpret. In contrast, our semi-supervised learning approach balances the pros and cons of both supervised and unsupervised approaches.

3 Our Approach

We frame the task of selecting event-relevant sentences as a binary classification problem over all sentences in the corpus. The following sections detail the data, features and techniques used.

3.1 Corpora

Seed Training Data and Test Data Annotation

Our primary corpus of news documents and queries is derived from the DARPA Global Autonomous Language Exploitation (GALE) distillation training and evaluation sets. Fifty event queries provided for the GALE task were used for our experiments (randomly divided into 30 training queries and 20 test queries), and the set of documents was restricted to those containing at least one keyword bigram from any query in the set[2]. For each query, we consider all sentences from the

[1] http://www.cs.columbia.edu/~kathy/Data/CSC.tar.gz

[2] As determined by the information-retrieval pipeline built using Lucene: `http://lucene.apache.org`

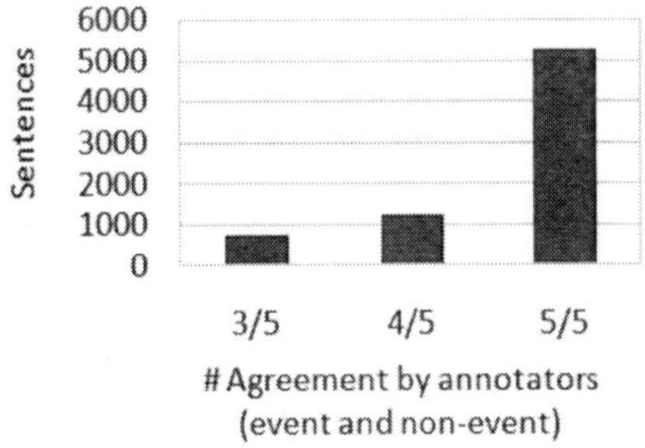

Figure 1: Number of sentences where a proportion of AMT users agreed on the classification (*event-related/unrelated*). With a binary task, 1/5 implies 4/5 agreement and 2/5 implies 3/5 agreement.

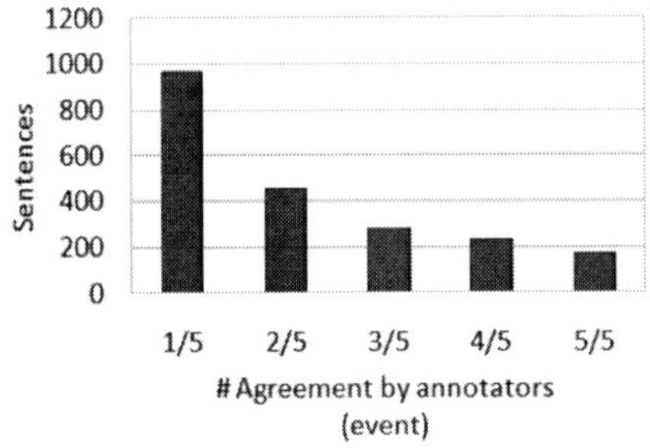

Figure 2: Number of sentences where a majority of AMT users agreed on the classification *event-related.*

top 10 retrieved documents and resort to AMT[3] to obtain sentence-level labels.

Each AMT annotation task presented AMT users with four contiguous sentences in conjunction with the query and asked them to indicate whether each of the individual sentences was relevant to the query[4]. The users could also view the entire document for context. Each task was assigned to 5 AMT users and a total of 252 unique users from the United States participated in the tasks. The full study lasted 16 days and had an overall cost of $350.

Fig. 1 shows the number of sentences (out of a total of 7161 candidates for all 50 queries) whose classification was agreed upon by a certain proportion of annotators. This result appears to suggest that annotators often agree when labeling event-relevant sentences[5]. However, these numbers are dominated by the majority class (irrelevant sentences), indicating that it is relatively easy for AMT users to agree when a sentence is not relevant. This is confirmed by Fig. 2, which displays the number of sentences that were specifically tagged as event-relevant for their respective queries. The breakdown for event-relevant sentences shows that about 30% of the sentences were identified as event-relevant by at least one AMT user and only a third of these received a majority vote for the label. This skewed distribution poses a significant challenge to the construction of a balanced training corpus for this task at low cost. Our observations are commensurate with Filatova and Hatzivassiloglou (2003) who note that event annotation is difficult for human annotators.

Unlabeled News Summary Data

Since manual creation of a large set of event-relevant sentences is difficult, we make use of a semi-supervised technique that employs a large quantity of unlabeled data to iteratively augment the small corpus described above. Unlabeled training data for our task also must comprise event queries and groups of sentences that are both related and unrelated to these events.

We experiment with automatically-generated news summaries as unlabeled training data for identifying event-related sentences. We postulate that the title of each news summary forms a single query and assume that at least some of the sentences in the summary will relate to the event mentioned in the title, while some may not. The choice of *summaries* of online news documents rather than the documents is prompted by the assumption that the distribution of query-related sentences and query-unrelated sentences is more balanced in short, informative summaries; this allows us to use the data more efficiently and avoid the sparse occurrence of event-specific sentences in online news articles.

The unlabeled dataset used in this work was retrieved from the output of an online news summarization system, Newsblaster http://newsblaster.cs.columbia.edu/, that crawls the Web for news articles, clusters them on specific topics and produces multidocument summaries for each cluster. We collected a total of 166,435 summaries containing 2.5 million sentences and covering 2,129 days in the 2003-2011 period.

As an initial experiment in augmenting the training corpus, we assumed that *all* summary sentences were relevant to the title query and trained

[3] `http://mturk.com`

[4] We also added an obviously fake sentence to detect sloppy annotators and robots.

[5] Fleiss' $\kappa = 0.417$, generally assumed to indicate moderate agreement between annotators

classifiers over a balanced corpus created by directly adding some summary data to the seed corpus. We observed the performance of these classifiers was poorer than that of classifiers trained only on the unaugmented seed corpus, suggesting that the assumption was too strong and that the summaries consist of both query-related and query-unrelated sentences. This supports the use of such a corpus in a semi-supervised setting.

3.2 Semi-Supervised Approach

The original co-training framework (Blum and Mitchell, 1998) was introduced in the context of Web page classification where one typically has access to a limited number of labeled pages but to a potentially unlimited number of unlabeled pages. Co-training involves building two independent views (classifiers), letting them automatically label the unlabeled data and incorporating this self-labeled data into the seed training set to improve system performance. Mihalcea (2004) shows that co-training is useful in word sense disamgibuation, Wan (2009) uses SVM for co-training and shows improvement for cross-lingual sentiment analysis, and recent research has established the effectiveness of co-training for a variety of NLP tasks (Yu and Kübler, 2011; Li et al., 2011; Bergsma et al., 2011). In this section, we present our co-training classifiers, as well as an algorithm that is specifically tailored to automatic event identification.

Features

Implementation of the co-training algorithm involves the design of two independent views (classifiers) for the same instance. In the original co-training algorithm for Web page classification, Blum and Mitchell (1998) use hyperlinks and bag-of-words as the approximation[6] of two distinct views of a Web page. In our approach, we choose two simple views to represent each candidate sentence for a given event query: (1) keyword features that include unigram and bigram overlaps between a candidate sentence and the event query. (2) named entity features including the number of exact entity (*Person*, *Location*, and *Organization*) matches between a candidate sentence and the query, as well as the total number of co-occurring named entity tags (regardless of the actual entity being tagged) between a candidate sentence and the query. We used the Stanford Named Entity tagger (Finkel et al., 2005) to obtain named entities features from the unlabeled data.

Note that the second view of our approach is clearly not independent of the first view, as the named entity matching is based on lexical matching. However, named entities are known as an informative source for selecting relevant sentences for a query since they serve as unique identifiers (Parton et al., 2008). Previous studies (Krogel and Scheffer, 2004) show that if the independence assumption of co-training approach is violated, the co-training approach can yield negative results. However, our results show that co-training yields improvement even though are classifiers are not independent.

The Co-training Algorithm

The motivation behind our co-training algorithm is to make use of the online summarization data for event identification, and improve recall as well as precision.The pseudo code of this algorithm is provided in Algorithm 1.

Algorithm 1 The co-training algorithm

Given:
(1) a set S of labeled seed training examples;
(2) a set U of unlabeled news summary examples;

Initialize the iteration parameter k, pool size u, and leap size v;
for $i = 1 \rightarrow k$ **do**
  Create a temporary pool by randomly choosing u examples from U;
  Use L to train a classifier C_1 using only keyword features;
  Use L to train a classifier C_2 using only named entity features;
  Run C_1 to label $u/2$ examples and select $v/2$ balanced examples;
  Run C_2 to label $u/2$ examples and select $v/2$ balanced examples;
  Add all selected examples to L;
  Return the remaining examples back to U;
end for

Earlier work (Mihalcea, 2004) indicates that by choosing only high confidence examples from the self-labeled data set, we can improve the co-training results. However, we disagree with this assumption; if low-confidence examples are re-

[6]Note that it is very difficult to prove that two views are completely independent of each other. (Du et al., 2010)

moved from training, the final co-trained classifier will have problems evaluating difficult examples in the held-out data set [7].

Our algorithm is a variation of the original co-training algorithm (Blum and Mitchell, 1998). In the original algorithm, p represents the number of self-labeled positive cases and n represents the number of self-labeled negative cases in each iteration. We now eliminate the p and n parameters, and use v to measure the *leap size*, the amount of self-labeled data added to the training set in each iteration. This is to ensure that, in each iteration, balanced selection of unlabeled examples from the two views can be added to the labeled data. We keep the unselected examples and return them to the pool U at the end of each iteration to make sure we use the unlabeled data exhaustively.

Bayesian Network Classifier

We employ a Bayesian network classification scheme for the co-training experiments described in section 4. Previous approaches to co-training have successfully used the well-known naive Bayes classification scheme (Blum and Mitchell, 1998; Mihalcea, 2004), which assumes conditional independence between features.

A Bayesian network approach is a variation on this probabilistic classification scheme that avoids making strong independence assumptions between features. Building the classifier entails an additional step for estimating the conditional dependencies between the features; this is accomplished by using search algorithms and scoring metrics[8] to learn a DAG structure representing a Bayesian network over the features. Once such structure is estimated, conditional probabilities $p(x_i|\pi_i)$ are estimated[9] where π_i represents the set of features that feature x_i is assumed to conditionally depend on. Classification of an unseen example $\mathbf{x}'$ is performed similarly to the naive Bayes approach with the estimation of $\arg\max_y p(y|\mathbf{x}')$.

[7]Under the same parameter settings, accuracy was reduced by 1% when training only with high-confidence instances (posteriors > 0.9) or low-confidence instances (posteriors < 0.75).

[8]In our experiments, we use the K2 hill-climbing search strategy to estimate network structure with the standard Bayesian scoring metric (Cooper and Herskovits, 1992).

[9]Conditional probabilities are obtained using the simple estimation strategy ($\alpha = 0.5$) as implemented in the Weka machine learning toolkit (Witten and Frank, 2000).

4 Experiments

We present four experiments to test system performance. First, we present the comparisons between our approach and other supervised/semi-supervised baselines, arbitrarily choosing settings for the number of co-training iterations k and the number of sentences added in each iteration[10]. We then test the trade-off between k and v by fixing the total amount of unlabeled data available, i.e., $k * v$ sentences[11]. In the third experiment, we test the impact of leap size v on both accuracy and efficiency by fixing k, as well as the impact of the iteration parameter k by fixing v. In the final experiment, we empirically choose the best possible v to test the influence of unlabeled data size on the recall and precision of our system. Due to the randomness in our co-training algorithm, we repeat every experiment 5 times and report the average results.

4.1 Comparing with Baseline Approaches

Table 1 shows the overall Bayesian network co-training results in comparison to various baseline systems. Previous work (Blum and Mitchell, 1998; Mihalcea, 2004; Wan, 2009) points out that naive Bayes and SVM classifiers can achieve promising results for co-training, so we use the same co-training settings ($k = 50$, $v = 500$) to compare these two classifiers with the Bayesian network classifier. Classifier 1 corresponds to the keyword matching view and Classifier 2 corresponds to the named entity view. When comparing single classifiers using either keyword matching or named entity features, SVM outperforms all other classifiers with an accuracy of 75.3%. When linearly combining all features using the seed data set, the Bayesian network yields a better result of 77.6%. The Bayesian network co-training outperforms the linear kernel SVM[12] co-training algorithm by 12.4% in accuracy, and it is also 55 times faster than SVM co-training algorithm in terms of average runtime. The co-trained result also has an absolute improvement of 8% over a Bayesian network linear combination classifier (Table 1: Combination).

Note that in all of our co-training experiments, the performance of the Bayesian network co-

[10]We use $k = 50$ iterations and $v = 500$ sentences per iteration

[11]Here we restrict $k * v = 200,000$ sentences

[12]We have also experimented with polynomial and RBF kernels, but performance was worse than the linear kernel.

Systems		Acc.	N-Prec.	N-Recall	N-F1	P-Prec.	P-Recall	P-F1
Chance		50	–	–	–	–	–	–
Classifier 1	NB	72.39	0.668	0.892	0.764	0.837	0.556	0.668
	SVM	75.29	0.747	0.764	0.756	0.759	0.741	0.750
	Bnet	75.10	0.683	**0.938**	0.790	0.901	0.564	0.694
Classifier 2	NB	70.85	0.706	0.714	0.710	0.711	0.703	0.707
	SVM	71.04	0.709	0.714	0.712	0.712	0.707	0.709
	Bnet	71.04	0.709	0.714	0.712	0.712	0.707	0.709
Combination	NB	75.48	0.777	0.714	0.744	0.736	0.795	0.764
	SVM	73.94	0.752	0.714	0.733	0.728	0.764	0.746
	Bnet	77.61	**0.815**	0.714	0.761	0.746	**0.838**	0.789
Co-training	NB	75.14	0.772	0.714	0.742	0.734	0.788	0.760
	SVM	72.97	0.737	0.714	0.725	0.723	0.745	0.734
	Bnet	**83.98**	0.780	**0.947**	**0.855**	**0.933**	0.733	**0.821**

Table 1: Comparing with baseline systems (NB: naive Bayes. SVM: linear kernel support vector machines. Bnet: Bayesian network. N-: the class of sentences unrelated to the event query P-: the class of event-related sentences). The best result in each column is indicated in boldface.

trained classifier 1 (Table 1: Co-training with $k = 50andv = 500$ improves performance substantially over the Bayesian network classifier using all features (Table 1: Combination). The performance of co-trained Classifier 2, not shown in the table[13], does not improve over the linear feature combination. The results suggest that when the keyword view is augmented with Bayesian network co-trained unlabeled data from both views, the co-training approach boosts the results, but the reverse does not hold true. These results are consistent with our previous claim (Section 3.2) that named entity features help the keyword view to identify key information in events. The above results also indicate that although the keyword view and named entity view are not independent, the Bayesian network co-training approach still produces promising results.

The strong performance of the Bayesian network classifier in these experiments is partly attributable to the fact that both classification views consist of features that are interdependent and therefore correlated to some degree, as the model assumes. The dramatic performance gains of the Bayesian network co-trained classifier when compared to Naive Bayes are therefore somewhat unsurprising; however, the poor performance of the SVM classifier was unexpected.

Although all the basic variants of classifiers using n-gram count features exhibit similar accuracy on the test corpus, we note that the Bayesian classifiers tend to select fewer high-precision event-related sentences resulting in skewed precision/recall numbers. Co-training has the effect of relaxing these models to gradually expand the set of high-precision event sentences (resulting in large gains in P-Recall and N-Precision) using the implicit information gained through new training examples classified by event features. No improvement is observed when co-training for classifiers that start out with balanced precision and recall, i.e., the SVM and all event feature classifiers. We therefore conjecture that this phenomenon of high-precision event sentence extraction is especially helpful in co-training for this task.

We aim to further analyze the effect of classifier choice in future work. For all of the following experiments in this section, we only evaluate the performance of the Bayesian network classifier.

4.2 Trade-off between Co-training Parameters

In this experiment, we evaluate the trade-off between the number of iterations and leap size in our co-training setting given a fixed amount of unlabeled data. A total number of 200,000 unlabeled summary sentences (1 year) are involved in this experiment. Fig. 3 shows the results. The horizontal axis consists of pairs of k and v. We first

[13] Table 1 only shows the best result for co-training.

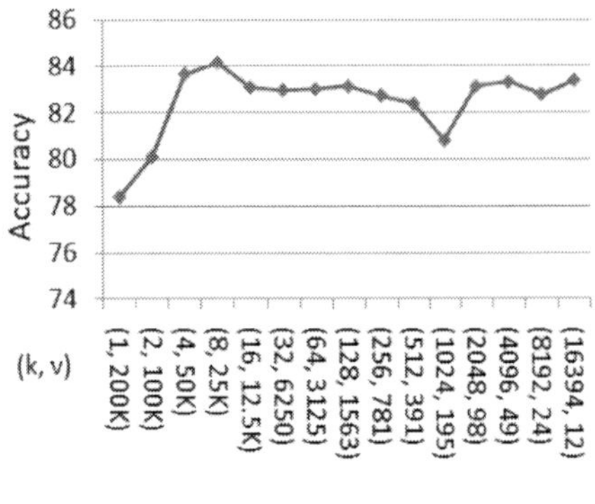

Figure 3: Trade-off between co-training parameters k and v with fixed amount of data

start with a very small ratio of k vs v ($k = 1$, $v = 200,000$), then we increase k exponentially such that $k * v$ is still equal to 200,000. We see that when $k = 8$ and $v = 25,000$, the system's performance reaches a peak accuracy of 84.2%. In addition, accuracy increases 6% from $k = 1$ to $k = 8$ which suggests that our co-training algorithm needs at least 5-10 iterations to achieve satisfactory results. We observe that there is a sudden drop when $k = 1024$ and $v = 195$; we explain this in section 4.4 and 4.3 when we test the impact of data diversity.

4.3 Influence of Leap Size

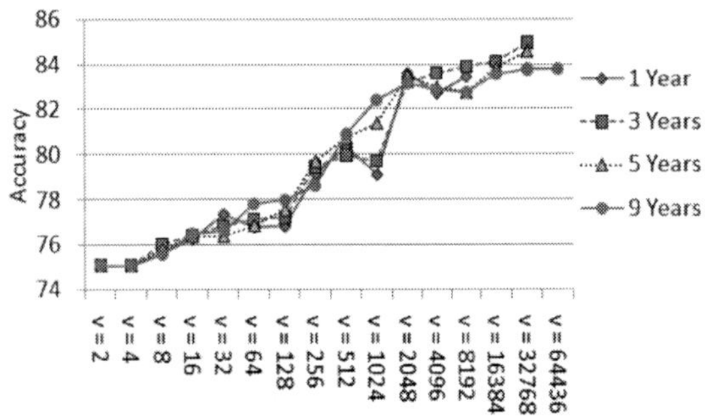

Figure 4: Performance varying leap size v with a fixed number of iterations $k = 10$

We evaluate the co-training leap size parameter v by fixing the number of iterations k to 10 and also experiment with the diversity of data by using unlabeled data drawn from different years. Fig. 4 shows that the system's performance improves significantly when using higher numbers of v. The best result is 85% accuracy when $v = 32,768$, compared to 75.1% accuracy obtained when $v = 2$. We also notice that using more diverse data from different years helps stabilize system performance and reduce the oscillation in the plot. In terms of efficiency, when using all 9 years of data, the corresponding runtime for $v = 4$ and $v = 32768$ are 15 minutes and 20 minutes, which indicates that increasing leap size is an efficient approach. Fig. 6 shows the comprehensive runtime costs from $v = 2$ to $v = 2048$. The runtime for varying v is almost a straight line, showing very little added cost as v increases.

4.4 Influence of the Iteration Parameter

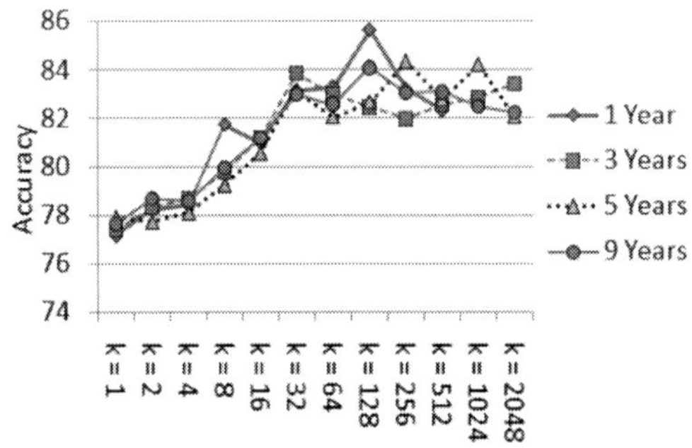

Figure 5: Performance varying the number of iterations k with fixed leap size $v = 500$

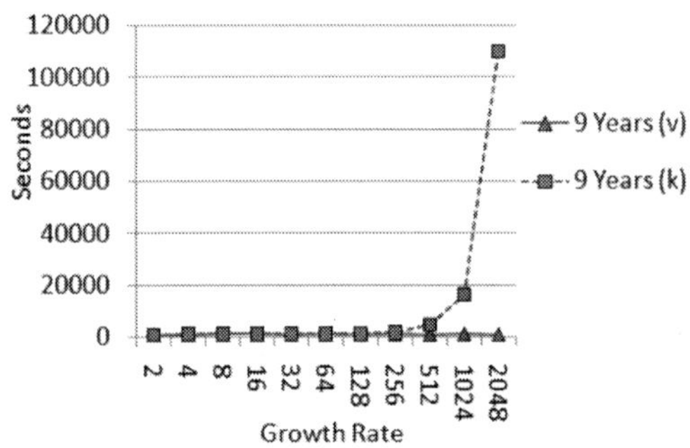

Figure 6: Average runtime costs when varying either k or v separately (and keeping the other fixed)

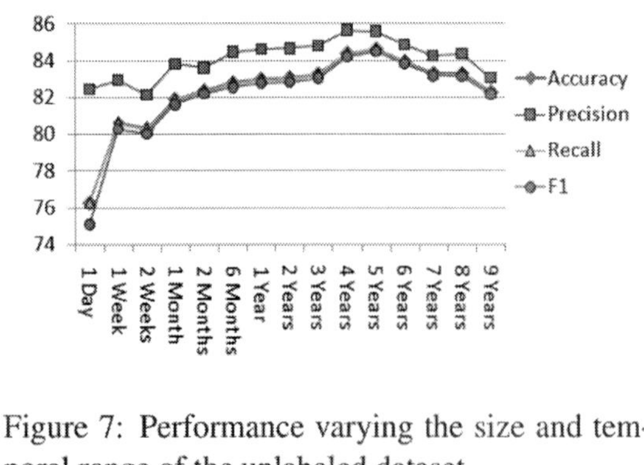

Figure 7: Performance varying the size and temporal range of the unlabeled dataset

We fix the leap size v to 500 and vary the number of iterations k to test its impact on the accuracy and efficiency of our system. We notice (Fig. 5) that when increasing the number of iterations from $k = 1$ to 32, our system performance improves significantly. After 32 iterations, the performance reaches a stable state. The best performance of 85.6% accuracy is obtained when $k = 128$; however, the cost of system runtime grows exponentially as we increase the parameter k. For example, we note that the runtimes corresponding to $k = \{256, 512, 1024, 2048\}$ are 28 minutes, 76 minutes, 270 minutes and 1829 minutes. Clearly, compared with the runtimes obtained by varying v, increasing k is not a good option. We also test impact of data diversity by using data from different years. Although using one year of data yields the best result, its overall performance is less stable than using 3, 5, or 9 years of input unlabeled data.

4.5 Influence of Size of Unlabeled Dataset

Experiments 4.3 and 4.4 show that increasing leap size v is an efficient method for introducing more data in co-training. Now, given different amounts of unlabeled news summary data from meaningful temporal time frames, we fix $k = 10$ and dynamically choose the best possible v to represent the amount of input data under consideration. Fig. 7 shows the precision and recall of the event-relevant class when co-training is performed using input unlabeled data of varying sizes (and temporal ranges). We observe that increasing the dataset size (and therefore drawing from older summaries) yields a dramatic improvement in recall accompanied by a slight decline in precision. Correspondingly, F1 generally increases when more data is added. The difference between minimum and maximum recall over the entire range is as high as 22% while precision drops by about 9%. These results suggest that introducing more unlabeled data in our co-training framework has the biggest impact on recall without sacrificing much precision.

5 Discussion

Our results show that an approach that only selects sentences with words that match the input query will not work well. As keyword matching might introduce a fair amount of noise, e.g. matched prepositional phrases that do not indicate the importance of the sentence, co-training together with a named entity based classifier can help reduce these errors. Thus when testing on unseen data, significantly better recall can be obtained via co-training. Our experiments also show that our co-training material, the nine years of news summary documents, is a reliable and effective source to augment the seed dataset, with minimum introduction of new noise or extra overhead.

The experiments show that increasing either the number of co-training iterations k or leap size v leads to improved performance; however, adding unlabeled data by increasing v adds much lower runtime overhead by avoiding repeated training iterations. The parameter trade-off experiment in section 4.2 indicates that beyond a minimum number of iterations k, unlabeled data can largely be introduced through v. This is useful in practice to maintain consistent runtime performance.

Despite the strong relative gains with co-training, the limited feature sets employed in both views (keyword and named entity) do not allow us to capture event-relevant sentences which don't share words with the event query. Although the relative gains offered by co-training are clear, we wonder if the requirement of agreement in annotation led to a corpus in which sentences that were labeled relevant tended to share keywords with the event query. Although not evident from our experiments, we nevertheless assume that query synonyms are likely occurrences in event-relevant sentences, as are sub-events which entail larger events and vice versa. Therefore, a consideration of semantic and ontological features would be a logical next step for further investigation of this task and may offer interesting new views through which co-training can be utilized.

6 Conclusion

In this paper, we aim at detecting event-relevant sentences in a news corpus given an event query. In contrast to previous work that needs expensive annotation for query-answer pairs, we use unlabeled news summaries that are readily available in large quantities online and design an efficient semi-supervised learning strategy for event identification based on co-training with Bayesian network classifiers. An analysis of different parameters in the co-training approach shows that increasing leap size is a better way to gain accuracy improvements than increase in number of iterations given efficiency costs. Our findings are applicable to question answering, summarization, and text mining domains where selection of event-relevant sentences is often critical and large-scale human annotated data is not always available.

References

Bejan, Cosmin Adrian. 2008. Unsupervised Discovery of Event Scenarios from Texts. *Proceedings of the 21st Florida Artificial Intelligence Research Society International Conference (FLAIRS'08), Applied Natural Language Processing track*, Coconut Grove, FL, USA, May 2008.

Bergsma, Shane and Yarowsky, David and Church, Kenneth. 2011. Using Large Monolingual and Bilingual Corpora to Improve Coordination Disambiguation. *ACL-HLT*.

Chambers, Nathaniel and Jurafsky, Dan. 2009. Unsupervised learning of narrative schemas and their participants. *Proceedings of the Joint Conference of the 47th Annual Meeting of the ACL and the 4th International Joint Conference on Natural Language Processing of the AFNLP: Volume 2*, Suntec, Singapore, 2009.

Chirita, Paul - Alexandru and Firan, Claudiu S. and Nejdl, Wolfgang 2007. Personalized query expansion for the web. *SIGIR '07*.

Cooper, G. and Herskovits, E.. 1992. A Bayesian method for the induction of probabilistic networks from data. *Machine Learning* , 9: 309-347, 1992.

Bethard, Steven and Martin, James H.. 2006. Identification of event mentions and their semantic class. *Proceedings of the 2006 Conference on Empirical Methods in Natural Language Processing (EMNLP)*, pages 146-154.

Blum, Avrim and Mitchell, Tom. 1998. Combining labeled and unlabeled data with co-training. *Proceedings of the eleventh annual conference on Computational learning theory*, pages 92–100.

Cortes, Corinna and Vapnik, V.. 1995. Support-Vector Networks. *Machine Learning*, 20.

Du, Jun and Ling, Charles X. and Zhou, Zhi-Hua. 2010. When Does Co-Training Work in Real Data? *IEEE TKDE*.

Filatova, Elena and Hatzivassiloglou, Vasileios. 2003. Domain-Independent Detection, Extraction, and Labeling of Atomic Events. *Proceedings of RANLP'03*, 2003.

Filatova, Elena and Hatzivassiloglou, Vasileios. 2004. Event-Based Extractive Summarization. *Text Summarization Branches Out: Proceedings of the ACL-04 Workshop*, Barcelona, Spain, July 2004.

Finkel, Jenny Rose and Grenager, Trond and Manning, Christopher. 2005. Incorporating Non-local Information into Information Extraction Systems by Gibbs Sampling. *Proceedings of the 43nd Annual Meeting of the Association for Computational Linguistics (ACL 2005)*, pages 363-370.

Fisichella, Marco and Stewart, Avaré and Denecke, Kerstin and Nejdl, Wolfgang; 2010. Unsupervised public health event detection for epidemic intelligence. *Proceedings of the 19th ACM international conference on Information and knowledge management (CIKM 2010)*, pages 1881–1884, Toronto, ON, Canada.

Krogel, Marc-A and Scheffer, Tobias. 2004. Multi-Relational Learning, Text Mining, and Semi-Supervised Learning for Functional Genomics. *Machine Learning 57*, pages 61-81.

Parton, Kristen and McKeown, Kathleen R. and Allan, James and Henestroza, Enrique.. 2008. Simultaneous Multilingual Search for Translingual Information Retrieval. *Proceedings of CIKM*.

Pustejovsky, James and Hanks, Patrick and Saur, Roser and See, Andrew and Gaizauskas, Robert and Setzer, Andrea and Radev, Dragomir and Sundheim, Beth and Day, David and Ferro, Lisa and Lazo, Marcia. 2003. The TIMEBANK Corpus. *Proc. of Corpus Linguistics*.

Li, Shoushan and Wang, Zhongqing and Zhou, Guodong and Lee, Sophia Yat Mei. 2011. Semi-supervised Learning for Imbalanced Sentiment Classification. *Proceedings of IJCAI-2011*.

Mani, Inderjeet and Schiffman, Barry and Zhang, Jianping. 2003. Inferring Temporal Ordering of Events in News. *Proceedings of the 2003 Human Language Technology Conference of the North American Chapter of the Association for Computational Linguistics (HLT-NAACL)*, 2003.

Manshadi, Mehdi and Swanson, Reid and Gordon, Andrew S.. 2008. Learning a Probabilistic Model of Event Sequences From Internet Weblog Stories. *Proceedings of the 21st Florida Artificial Intelligence Research Society International Conference (FLAIRS'08), Applied Natural Language Processing track*, 2008.

Marge, Matthew and Banerjee, Satanjeev and Rudnicky, Alexander I. 2010. Using the Amazon Mechanical Turk for Transcription of Spoken Language. *Proceedings of ICASSP*, 2010.

Siegel, Eric V. and McKeown, Kathleen R. 2000. Learning methods to combine linguistic indicators: improving aspectual classification and revealing linguistic insights. *Comput. Linguist.*, Dec. 2000.

Mihalcea, Rada. 2004. Co-training and self-training for word sense disambiguation. *Proceedings of CONLL - 04*, 2004.

Radev, Dragomir R. and Blair-Goldensohn, Sasha and Zhang, Zhu and Raghavan, Revathi Sundara. 2001. NewsInEssence: a system for domain-independent, real-time news clustering and multi-document summarization. *Proceedings of the first international conference on Human language technology research*, 2001.

Snow, Rion and O'Connor, Brendan and Jurafsky, Daniel and Ng, Andrew Y.. 2008. Cheap and fast—but is it good?: evaluating non-expert annotations for natural language tasks. *Proceedings of the Conference on Empirical Methods in Natural Language Processing*, 2008.

Rosenthal, Sara and Lipovsky, William and McKeown, Kathleen and Thadani, Kapil and Andreas, Jacob. 2010. Towards Semi-Automated Annotation for Prepositional Phrase Attachment. *LREC*, 2010.

Spitters, M. and Kraaij, W.. 2002. Unsupervised event clustering in multilingual news streams. *Proceedings of the LREC2002 Workshop on Event Modeling for Multilingual Document Linking*, pp. 4246.

Wan, Xiaojun. 2009. Co-training for cross-lingual sentiment classification. *Proceedings of the Joint Conference of the 47th Annual Meeting of the ACL and the 4th International Joint Conference on Natural Language Processing of the AFNLP*, pp. 235–243.

Witten, I.H. and Frank, E.. 2000. Data mining: Practical machine learning tools and techniques with Java implementations. *Morgan Kaufmann*, 2000.

Xu, Jinxi and Croft, W. Bruce. 1996. Query expansion using local and global document analysis. *SIGIR '96*.

Yu, Ning and Kübler, Sandra. 2011. Filling the Gap: Semi-Supervised Learning for Opinion Detection Across Domains. *Proceedings of the Fifteenth Conference on Computational Natural Language Learning*.

Automatic Labeling of Voiced Consonants for Morphological Analysis of Modern Japanese Literature

Teruaki Oka†
teruaki-o@is.naist.jp

Mamoru Komachi†
komachi@is.naist.jp

Toshinobu Ogiso‡
togiso@ninjal.jp

Yuji Matsumoto†
matsu@is.naist.jp

†Nara Institute of Science and Technology
‡National Institute for Japanese Language and Linguistics

Abstract

Since the present-day Japanese use of voiced consonant mark had established in the Meiji Era, modern Japanese literary text written in the Meiji Era often lacks compulsory voiced consonant marks. This deteriorates the performance of morphological analyzers using ordinary dictionary. In this paper, we propose an approach for automatic labeling of voiced consonant marks for modern literary Japanese. We formulate the task into a binary classification problem. Our pointwise prediction method uses as its feature set only surface information about the surrounding character strings. As a consequence, training corpus is easy to obtain and maintain because we can exploit a partially annotated corpus for learning. We compared our proposed method as a preprocessing step for morphological analysis with a dictionary-based approach, and confirmed that pointwise prediction outperforms dictionary-based approach by a large margin.

1 Introduction

Recently, corpus-based approaches have been successfully adopted in the field of Japanese Linguistics. However, the central part of the fields has been occupied by historical research that uses ancient material, on which fundamental annotations are often not yet available.

Despite the limited annotated corpora, researchers have developed several morphological analysis dictionaries for past-day Japanese. National Institute for Japanese Language and Linguistics creates Kindai-bungo UniDic,[1] a morphological analysis dictionary for modern Japanese literary text,[2] which achieves high performance on analysis for existing electronic text (e.g. Aozora-bunko, an online digital library of freely available books and work mainly from out-of-copyright materials).

However, the performance of morphological analyzers using the dictionary deteriorates if the text is not normalized, because these dictionaries often lack orthographic variations such as Okuri-gana,[3] accompanying characters following Kanji stems in Japanese written words. This is problematic because not all historical texts are manually corrected with orthography, and it is time-consuming to annotate by hand. It is one of the major issues in applying NLP tools to Japanese Linguistics because ancient materials often contain a wide variety of orthographic variations.

For example, there is an issue of voiced consonant marks. Any "Hiragana" character and "Katakana" character (called Kana character altogether) represent either consonant (k, s, t, n, h, m, y, r, w) onset with vowel (a, i, u, e, o) nucleus or only the vowel (except for nasal codas N). Furthermore, the characters alone can not represent syllables beginning with a voiced consonant (g, z, d, b) in current orthography. They are spelled with Kana and a voiced consonant mark (゛) to the upper right (see Figure 1). However, confusingly, it was not ungrammatical to put down the character without the mark to represent voiced syllable

[1] http://www2.ninjal.ac.jp/lrc/index.php?UniDic

[2] In historical linguistics, the phrase "modern Japanese" refers to the language from 1600 on to the present in a broad sense. However, most Japanese people regard the phrase to the Meiji and Taisho Era; we also use the phrase to intend the narrower sense.

[3] In Japanese Literature, both Kana (phonogramic characters) and Kanji (ideographic characters) are used together. Generally, conjugated form is ambiguous, given the preceding Kanji characters. However, the character's pronunciation can also be written using Kana characters. Thus, the pronunciation's tailing few syllables are hanged out (Okuri), using Kana (gana) characters for disambiguating the form. Although the number of Okuri-gana is fixed for each Kanji character now, it was not fixed in the Meiji Era.

ga	→	が:か (ka) + ゛	da	→	だ:た (ta) + ゛
gi	→	ぎ:き (ki) + ゛	di	→	ぢ:ち (ti) + ゛
gu	→	ぐ:く (ku) + ゛	du	→	づ:つ (tu) + ゛
ge	→	げ:け (ke) + ゛	de	→	で:て (te) + ゛
go	→	ご:こ (ko) + ゛	do	→	ど:と (to) + ゛
za	→	ざ:さ (sa) + ゛	ba	→	ば:は (ha) + ゛
zi	→	じ:し (si) + ゛	bi	→	び:ひ (hi) + ゛
zu	→	ず:す (su) + ゛	bu	→	ぶ:ふ (hu) + ゛
ze	→	ぜ:せ (se) + ゛	be	→	べ:へ (he) + ゛
zo	→	ぞ:そ (so) + ゛	bo	→	ぼ:ほ (ho) + ゛

Figure 1: Spelling syllables beginning with the voiced consonants g, z, d and b by Hiragana characters with a voiced consonant mark.

	Voiced	Voiceless
Marked	3,124	0
Ambiguous	4,032	29,332

Table 1: The contingency table of observed frequencies of characters and voiceness.

今や廣島は其名大に内外國に顯はれ苟も時事を談するものは同地の形勢如何を知らんと欲せさるはあらす

(Today, the fame of "Hiroshima" has been broadly known in and outside Japan, and if you talk about current affairs, you want to know how the place has been established.)

Figure 2: Example of sentences that includes unmarked characters. This text is an excerpt from "The tide of Hiroshima": Katsuichi Noguchi, Taiyo, No.2, p.64 (1925). Wavy-underlined characters are ambiguous character, and gray-boxed characters are unmarked character.

until the Meiji Era, because Japanese orthography dates back to the Meiji Era. Consequently, modern Japanese literary text written in the Meiji Era often lacks compulsory voiced consonant marks. The mark was used only when the author deems it necessary to disambiguate; and it was not often used if one can infer from the context that the pronunciation is voiced.

Figure 2 shows characters which lack the voiced consonant mark even though we expect it to be marked in the text. Hereafter, we call such characters as "unmarked characters." Also, we call the characters to which the voiced consonant mark can be attached as "ambiguous characters." In Table 1, we present the statistics of the voiced consonants in "Kokumin-no-tomo" corpus which we will use for our evaluation. As you can see, 12% of the ambiguous characters are actually voiced but not marked. In addition, 44% of the voiced characters have the voiced consonant mark, showing the variation of using the voiced consonant mark in the corpus.

In the modern Japanese literary text, orthographic variations are not only the unmarked. However, unmarked characters appear a lot in the text and can be annotated easily by hand. Thus, we can get natural texts for evaluation of our method at low cost (in fact, it cost only a few weeks to annotate our above-mentioned test corpus). Therefore, we decided to begin with attaching voiced consonant mark for unmarked characters as a starting point for normalizing orthographic variations.

Basically, Kindai-bungo UniDic is created for a fully annotated sentence that does not include unmarked characters, and thus if the target sentence includes unmarked character(s), the performance can degrade considerably.

There are two major approaches to handle this problem: a dictionary-based approach and a classification-based approach.

First, the dictionary-based approach creates a dictionary that has both original spellings and modified variants without the mark. For example, Kindai-bungo UniDic includes both entries "ず (zu)" and "す (zu)" for frequent words such as "ず (zu)" in auxiliary verb. This allows morphological analysis algorithms to learn the weights of both entries all together from a corpus annotated with part-of-speech tags in order to select appropriate entries during decoding.

Second, the classification-based approach employs a corpus annotated with unmarked characters to learn a classifier that labels the voiced consonant mark for unmarked characters. Unlike the dictionary-based approach, the classification-based approach does not require part-of-speech tagged nor tokenized corpora. Since it is easier for human annotators to annotate unmarked characters than word boundaries and part-of-speech tags, we can obtain a large scale annotated corpus at low cost.

Therefore, in this paper, we propose a classification-based approach to automatic labeling of voiced consonant marks as a preprocessing step for morphological analysis for modern Japanese literary language.

We formulate the task of labeling voiced consonant marks into a binary classification problem. Our method uses as its feature set only surface information about the surrounding character strings with pointwise prediction, whose training data are available at low cost. We use an online learning method for learning large spelling variation from massive datasets rapidly and accurately. Thus, we can improve its performance easily by increasing amount of training data. In addition, we perform clustering of Kanji, which is abundant in the training data, and employ class n-grams for addressing the data sparseness problem. We compared our classification-based approach with the dictionary-based approach and showed that the classification-based method outperforms the dictionary-based method, especially in an out-of-domain setting. We also conducted an experiment to demonstrate that automatic labeling of unmarked characters as a pre-processing step improves the performance of morphological analysis of historical texts without normalization by a large margin, taking advantage of large scale annotated corpus of unmarked characters.

The rest of this paper is organized as follows: In section 2 we describe related work of automatic labeling of Japanese voiced consonant marks. Section 3 details our proposed classification-based method using pointwise prediction. We then explain experimental settings and results in section 4. Section 5 concludes our work and presents future work.

2 Related Work

If we assume an unmarked character as substitution error of one voiced consonant to one voiceless consonant, the task of detecting an unmarked character can be considered as a kind of error correction. In English, we can perform error correction for the one character's error by word-based approach. However, in Japanese, we cannot simply apply word-based approach because sentences are not segmented into words.

Nagata (1998) proposed a statistical method using dynamic programming for selecting the most likely word sequences from candidate word lattice estimated from observed characters in Japanese sentence. In this method, the product of the transition probability of words is used as a word segmentation model. However, most of the historical materials that we deal with are raw text, and there exist little, if any, annotated texts with words and part-of-speech tags. Thus, a word segmentation model learned from such a limited amount of data is unreliable. Unlike Nagata's method, our classification-based method does not rely on word segmentation and can exploit low-level annotation such as voiced consonant mark, which is available quite easily.

In addition, Nagata performed clustering of characters for smoothing confusion probability among characters to narrow down correction candidates. We also perform clustering on Kanji for addressing the data sparseness problem. Though Nagata uses character's shape for clustering, we instead use neighboring characters of the Kanji character. The intuition behind this is that whether to attach voiced consonant mark is affected by surrounding contexts, like sequential voicing.

On contrary, Shinnou (1999) proposed an error detection and correction method that does not perform word segmentation. He restricts the target to Hiragana characters and uses Hiragana n-gram that is a substring of the characters. In his method, error detection is determined by the Hiragana n-gram frequency. One counts each Hiragana n-gram frequency in training corpus and judges whether the string includes error by checking if the smallest frequency among them (minimum frequency of n-gram) is larger than a threshold value. After error detection, one enumerates candidate strings and corrects the input string to the string that has the largest minimum frequency of n-gram compared to other candidates.

The reason why Shinnou restricts targets to Hiragana characters is that it narrows down candidates of error correction. He used the fact that the number of Hiragana characters is 50 at most while the total number of distinct characters is more than 6,000 in Japanese. This method works well for present-day Japanese literary texts that contain relatively long Hiragana character strings. However, modern Japanese texts contain many Kanji characters and relatively short Hiragana character strings because modern Japanese texts are similar to Kanbun-kundokubun, or the Japanese reading of a Chinese text. Therefore, Hiragana n-grams fail to model error detection well for modern Japanese texts. Moreover, error correction of unmarked characters is much simpler than error correction of all the Hiragana. Our method differs from Shinnou's method in that we focus on automatic labeling of voiced consonant marks and employ a discriminative character n-gram model using a classification-based method. Although Shinnou's generative model is not capable of using overlapping features, our classification-based approach allows flexible feature design such as including character types that may help classification on unmarked characters. In addition, Shinnou's method requires a fully annotated corpus with unmarked characters even though there is a large amount of raw text in modern literary Japanese.

3 Detecting Unmarked Character with Pointwise Prediction

We formulate the task of automatic labeling of unmarked character into a binary-classification problem. More precisely, we build a binary classifier for detecting whether the target character is unmarked or not.

In our classifier, we use only surface information about one target character and its surrounding characters, and the classifier output is either unmarked (+1) or not (-1). Since proposed method does not require a corpus annotated with word boundaries or part-of-speech tags for learning, we take advantage of a large modern a Japanese corpus, Taiyo-Corpus,[4] which is based on Japanese magazines from the Meiji Era. This corpus is not annotated with neither word boundaries nor part-of-speech tags but is manually annotated with unmarked characters.

We employed pointwise prediction which makes a single independent decision at each point: ambiguous Hiragana character or Kunoji-ten[5].[6] Therefore, our method can learn from partially annotated corpora (Neubig and Mori, 2010) including raw corpora of modern Japanese literary text, and thus it is easy to obtain training data.

Neubig et al. (2011) extend the word segmentation method proposed by Sassano (2002) to Japanese morphological analysis using pointwise prediction. In our method, we adopt the binary features from (Sassano, 2002) to this task. Unlike Sassano and Neubig et al. who use an SVM, we use an online Passive-Aggressive algorithm for exploiting large datasets while achieving high accuracy.

3.1 Features for Classification

Our approach builds a binary classifier that uses binary features indicating whether the following n-grams exist or not (shown in Figure 3).

3.1.1 Character n-grams

These features correspond to character n-grams that surround the target character. Only characters within a window of three characters are used in classification ($n \leq 3$). These n-grams are referred with relative position from the target character.

If given sentence is $c_1 c_2 \cdots c_m$ and target character is c_i, character n-grams are ($-3/c_{i-3}c_{i-2}c_{i-1}$, $-2/c_{i-2}c_{i-1}c_i$, $-1/c_{i-1}c_ic_{i+1}$, $0/c_ic_{i+1}c_{i+2}$, $1/c_{i+1}c_{i+2}c_{i+3}$, $-3/c_{i-3}c_{i-2}$, $-2/c_{i-2}c_{i-1}$, $-1/c_{i-1}c_i$, $0/c_ic_{i+1}$, $1/c_{i+1}c_{i+2}$, $2/c_{i+2}c_{i+3}$, $-3/c_{i-3}$, $-2/c_{i-2}$, $-1/c_{i-1}$, $0/c_i$, $1/c_{i+1}$, $2/c_{i+2}$, $3/c_{i+3}$).

3.1.2 Character type n-grams

These features are similar to previously mentioned character n-grams with only the modification of replacing the character itself with the character type. We deal with eleven character types, Hiragana/H, Katakana/K, Kanji/C, Odori-ji/O, Latin/L, Digit/D, dash/d, stop and comma/S, BOS ($\langle s \rangle$)/B, EOS ($\langle /s \rangle$)/E and others/o as the character types.

3.1.3 Markedness n-grams

These features are also similar to character n-grams with only the modification of replacing the character itself with 0 (voiced consonant mark cannot be attached), 1 (the mark can be attached) and 2 (it already has the mark).

3.2 Clustering on Kanji

In modern Japanese literary text, various Kanji characters were found commonly even in a sentence compared to nowadays. However, the frequency of each Kanji character varies. Learning tends to be sparse around a Kanji character that appears only several times in training corpus. For example, if "深" (deep) appeared only once in training corpus as in a word "深い" (is deep), then we will not be able to use the information "深" in a phrase "深ければ" (if it is deep) when we classify a character "は" in "深ければ."

[4] http://www2.ninjal.ac.jp/lrc/index.php?%C2%C0%CD%DB%A5%B3%A1%BC%A5%D1%A5%B9

[5] Kunoji-ten is a iteration mark, either "〳" or "〴".

[6] Katakana characters had been used for specific words like adopted words and proper nouns. Thus, we excluded Katakana characters in this paper.

target character position

↓

-3 -2 -1 0 1 2 3

⟨s⟩彼邦に讓らざるへき大雜誌を發行せんと計畫したるも、⟨/s⟩

(Though we planned to publish a big magazine that compares favorably with the one in that country,)

Character 1-gram:	-3/ら	-2/ざ -2/さ	-1/る	0/へ	1/き	2/大 2/⟨B90⟩	3/雜 3/⟨B74⟩
Character 2-gram:	-3/らざ -3/らさ	-2/ざる -2/さる	-1/るへ	0/へき	1/き大 1/き ⟨B90⟩	2/大雜 2/⟨B90⟩⟨B74⟩	
Character 3-gram:	-3/らざる -3/らさる	-2/ざるへ -2/さるへ	-1/るへき	0/へき大 0/へき ⟨B90⟩	1/き大雜 1/き ⟨B90⟩⟨B74⟩		
Character type 1-gram:	-3/H	-2/H	-1/H	0/H	1/H	2/C	3/C
Character type 2-gram:	-3/HH	-2/HH	-1/HH	0/HH	1/HC	2/CC	
Character type 3-gram:	-3/HHH	-2/HHH	-1/HHH	0/HHC	1/HCC		
Markedness 1-gram:	-3/0	-2/2 -2/1	-1/0	0/1	1/1	2/0	3/0
Markedness 2-gram:	-3/02 -3/01	-2/20 -2/10	-1/01	0/11	1/10	2/00	
Markedness 3-gram:	-3/020 -3/010	-2/201 -2/101	-1/011	0/110	1/100		

Figure 3: Feature for classification of unmarked characters.

Therefore, we carry out clustering on Kanji characters and add character class n-gramin feature sets. For example, if "深" and "寒" (cold) belong to the same class X, and "寒" appears in training corpus as in a phrase "寒ければ" (if it is cold), then features corresponding to a phrase "X けれは" (if it is X) will be learned from "寒ければ." As a result, we will be able to exploit "深" as evidence of detecting "は" in "深けれは" as unmarked character.

Clustering was performed on Kanji characters with the subsequent and the previous two characters individually based on (Pereira et al. 1993).

A Kanji character that appears left of the target character is replaced with the class of the former-clusters and that appears right is replaced with the class of the latter-clusters.

4 Experiments

We conducted two experiments for evaluating our method as follows.

4.1 Experimental Settings

We compare three approaches for automatic labeling of unmarked character as a pre-processing to morphological analysis on historical texts.

First, we built a naive generative model as baseline for labeling voiced consonant mark. This method labels voiced consonant marks that maximize the likelihood of a sentence by using a character 3-gram model. One deficiency of the baseline method is that it requires a fully annotated corpus with the marks.

Second, for the dictionary-based approach, we created a dictionary and corpus from the same training corpus used by the Kindai-bungo UniDic (U-Train) with all the marks removed. We preserved the original orthography in the field of each entry. We then trained a morphological analyzer[7] using the dictionary and corpus. Finally, we added to the dictionary entries with which we partially (or completely) replaced voiced consonant marks. This method assigns voiced consonant marks and performs morphological analysis jointly. However, it requires an annotated corpus with both the marks, word segmentation and part-of-speech tags, which are scarce to obtain.

Third, we constructed a proposed classifier from an annotated corpus with the voiced consonant marks. Our method does not need the information of word segmentation and part-of-speech. There-

[7]http://mecab.sourceforge.net/

Training corpus	positive	negative	all
U-Train	25,910	111,511	137,421
T-Train	208,097	966,308	1,174,405
K-Train	24,185	-	24,185

Table 2: Number of instances in each training corpus.

Test corpus	positive	negative	all
T-Eval	899	93,022	93,921
K-Eval	3,843	25,461	29,304

Table 3: Number of instances in each test corpus.

fore we can take advantage of Taiyo-Corpus. We use only articles written in a literary style in the corpus (398,077 sentences). We use 10% of this corpus for evaluation (T-Eval, including 33,847 sentences), and the rest for training (T-Train, including 364,230 sentences).

For evaluation, we prepared a modern Japanese magazine "Kokumin-no-Tomo" corpus (85,291 sentences). It is not annotated with word boundaries nor part-of-speech tags. From the corpus, we use four numbers for testing, No.10, 20, 30 and 36, which we had finished annotating voiced consonant mark at the time (K-Eval, including 10,587 sentences), and the rest for training (K-Train, including 74,704 sentences).

4.2 Preparing Training and Test Corpus

We extract training instances from all ambiguous characters. We regard instances with the mark as positive instances and instances without the mark as negative instances. Note that we detach voiced consonant mark from target character when extracting training instances. Although we extract test instances in a similar manner, we do not count characters originally with the mark at testing. In other words, we evaluate the accuracy only on unmarked characters present in real world setting. We show per instance breakdown of training and evaluation instances in Tables 2 and 3.

4.3 Tools

In this paper, we use an online Passive Aggressive algorithm, specifically PA-I for learning a binary classifier with (Yoshinaga et al. 2010).[8] We use a linear kernel and set the iteration number to 20. Also, we optimized the regularization parameter C by performing 10-fold cross-validation on the training corpus.

We performed clustering on Kanji with narrative sentences in training corpus. We used a clustering tool bayon[9] that implements the Repeated Bisection algorithm, which is a variant of the k-means algorithm. We use the product of probability of character bigram $P(char_1|char_{kanji})$ and trigram $P(char_2|char_{kanji}char_1)$ as distributions of two characters connecting to Kanji $P(char_1char_2|char_{kanji})$. Probabilities of character bigram and trigram are calculated by using the language modeling toolkit Palmkit.[10] We use Witten Bell smoothing. For computational efficiency, we replaced characters that are not Hiragana or Odori-ji with character type when creating the language model.

4.4 Experiment 1: intrinsic

In our first intrinsic experiment, we compared the precision, recall and F-measure of labeling voiced consonant mark with three approaches.

Table 4 presents the results of the intrinsic evaluation. The proposed method outperforms other methods in terms of precision and F-measure using the same training corpus. Moreover, by adding T-Train, the proposed method achieves the best performance in all evaluation metrics including recall. This is because our proposed method can benefit from a large-scale annotated corpus with voiced consonant marks, which is not possible for the dictionary-based method since it requires fully annotated corpus with words and part-of-speech tags. Although the baseline method can use corpora annotated with voiced consonant marks and achieves comparable performance to the proposed method regarding recall, its precision is inferior to the proposed method by a large margin. We suppose that this improvement comes from discriminative learning of the language model, which enables us to design flexible features. Generally, precisions are lower in T-Eval than in K-Eval over all methods. This is because T-Eval has relatively few positive instances and most of the instances are difficult to judge whether they are unmarked or not even for human.

In the baseline and the proposed method, performance is improved further by increasing amount of training data. By adding T-Train for U-Train, F-measure increases more than 10-points in T-Eval. We show in Figure 4 the change in recall

[8]http://www.tkl.iis.u-tokyo.ac.jp/~ynaga/opal/

[9]http://code.google.com/p/bayon/

[10]http://palmkit.sourceforge.net/

	Training corpus	Number of Kanji class(k)	Test corpus					
			T-Eval			K-Eval		
			Prec.[%]	Rec.[%]	F	Prec.[%]	Rec.[%]	F
Baseline	U	-	35.085	86.203	49.872	91.276	91.344	91.310
	U+T	-	55.248	94.702	69.784	94.141	93.651	93.895
Dictionary-based	U	-	51.525	92.102	66.082	93.473	96.513	94.969
Proposed method	U	-	58.594	83.426	68.831	95.675	94.405	95.036
		50	64.061	83.871	72.640	96.235	93.781	94.992
		100	64.098	84.205	72.788	**96.401**	94.093	95.233
		500	60.430	84.427	70.441	95.982	94.483	95.227
		1000	59.745	83.537	69.666	95.718	94.223	94.965
	U+T	-	70.943	95.328	81.347	96.120	97.996	97.049
		50	71.993	95.217	81.992	96.073	98.048	97.050
		100	72.472	94.883	82.177	96.146	98.022	**97.075**
		500	71.704	94.994	81.722	96.120	97.996	97.049
		1000	**72.727**	95.216	**82.466**	96.288	97.866	97.071
	U+T+K	-	70.723	**95.661**	81.323	95.955	98.152	97.041
		50	72.236	95.216	82.149	95.953	98.100	97.015
		100	72.054	95.217	82.032	95.977	98.074	97.014
		500	71.836	95.328	81.931	95.883	**98.179**	97.017
		1000	71.956	95.328	82.009	96.001	98.074	97.026

Table 4: Performance of intrinsic evaluation: labeling voiced consonant mark.

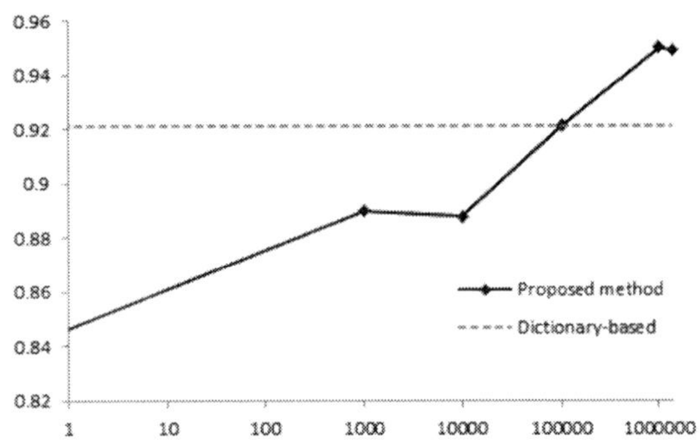

Figure 4: Improvement of recall with adding training instances.

when adding training instances from T-Train to U-Train in T-Eval (k=100). We confirmed that with just 1,000 instances added, recall increased 0.05 with the proposed method. Moreover, the proposed method's recall exceeded that of the dictionary-based approach after 100,000 instances were added. Although the F-measure was degraded by adding positive instances from K-Train, recall improved in K-Eval since positive instances add evidence for decision on voiced consonant marks. Apparently, it is effective to add instances from the same domain. However, the baseline and dictionary-based methods are not capable of using partially annotated corpora like K-Train. Our method employs pointwise prediction to make use of partially annotated corpus. Thus, we confirmed the effectiveness of using partially annotated corpora.

In addition, the proposed method shows the highest performance in k=1,000 for T-Eval and k=100 for K-Eval, respectively, when learned on T-Train and U-Train. In all settings, clustering improves precision while recall sometimes deteriorates. The performance gain is even larger when training data is scarce (See the results of U-Train). From this fact, we confirmed the effectiveness of clustering on Kanji for addressing the data sparseness problem.

Table 5 lists our features and their performance. Because the performance of detection degrades drastically when we subtract Character n-gram from All, this feature is crucial for determining unmarked characters. This is another piece of evidence that discriminative language model works quit well for this task. On the other hand, both Character type n-gram and Markedness n-gram contribute to improvement of precision. As a result, F-measure increases using those features.

We also investigated errors of the classification on our method. Although we found some errors which due to lack of training data, we found errors which are difficult to determine without discourse context, like "か"(ka) of binding particle or auxiliary verb and "が"(ga) of case-marking particle or auxiliary verb. However, these instances are difficult even for human to determine whether unmarked or not. Since the basic policy is to use the mark when there is ambiguity, the absence of the mark in an ambiguous case can be considered as evidence of non-unmarked character. Moreover,

Feature	Prec.[%]	T-Eval/K-Eval Rec.[%]	F
Character n-gram only	70.041/95.882	**95.439**/98.152	80.791/97.004
All − Character n-gram	2.521/20.000	1.001/ 0.156	1.433/0.310
All − Character Type n-gram	70.651/96.028	95.328/98.126	81.115/97.066
All − Markedness n-gram	69.764/95.884	95.217/**98.205**	80.527/97.031
All	**72.472/96.146**	94.883/98.022	**82.177/97.075**

Table 5: Performance of each feature and their combination.

our method can not refer the discourse information since we only employed local context of character n-grams. Therefore, our method excessively tend to classify characters into unmarked. On the other hand, we found instances for which both unmarked and marked form are acceptable, like "結び"(tie) and "結ひ"(tie). Note that "結び" and "結ひ" are pronounced differently as "musubi" and "yui," respectively. These instances seem to be the cause of degradation of precisions in T-Eval. For Odori-ji, it tends to fail classification because they not only depend on information of previous consonants but also on common practice such as "かえす ぐ (がえす)"(again and again).

4.5 Experiment 2: extrinsic

As a second extrinsic experiment, we investigated how effective these approaches are at improving accuracy of morphological analysis.

To create gold-standard annotation for morphological analysis, we take the result of morphological analysis for the corpus annotated with voiced consonant marks using the standard version of Kindai-bungo UniDic. Since the word and part-of-speech information are not available in Taiyo and Kokumin-no-Tomo corpus, this constitutes the upper bound of the morphological analysis performance on these data.

We evaluated the result of morphological analysis for two methods. First, we tested the dictionary-based method by performing morphological analysis using the same Kindai-bungo Unidic with additional entries that partially (or all) without voiced consonant marks as we described in section 4.1. Second, we evaluated the proposed method by pre-processing the unlabeled test corpus with the proposed method and performing morphological analysis using the standard version of Kindai-bungo Unidic. Then, we calculated the agreement rate between each method and the gold standard by counting how many sentences are identical to the gold standard. We compared each word's parts-of-speech tags and lexemes for the comparison.

	Taiyo	Kokumin-no-Tomo
Dictionary-based	91.479 [%]	88.968 [%]
Proposed method	99.016 [%]	96.647 [%]

Table 6: Performance of extrinsic evaluation: agreement rate of morphological analysis result.

Table 6 shows the results of the extrinsic evaluation. As you can see, the proposed method gives higher agreement with the gold standard in morphological analysis results than the dictionary-based approach, thanks to the large scale Taiyo corpus annotated with voiced consonant marks. In these experiments, we confirmed that pre-processing with the proposed method is effective for improving morphological analysis of unnormalized modern Japanese literary text.

5 Conclusion

In this paper, we proposed a pointwise approach to label voiced consonant marks for modern Japanese literary text. We confirmed that pointwise prediction outperforms the dictionary-based approach by a large margin. By using the proposed method as pre-processing, morphological analysis results become much closer to the gold standard than using the dictionary-based approach.

Also, we are using the method for annotating the modern Japanese literature. Thanks to the method, we are able to accelerate manual annotation with considerably small effort.

One limitation is that we only deal with unmarked characters in this work. In modern Japanese literary text, there are other orthographic variations such as Okuri-gana and Kana-usage as well. As our future work, we will work on normalizing these variations for improving accuracy of morphological analysis.

We hope this work will encourage further investigation into historical work.

References

Fernando Pereira, Naftali Tishby, and Lillian Lee. 1993. Distributional Clustering of English Words. In *Proceedings of the 31th Annual Meeting of the Association for Computational Linguistics (ACL-93)*:183-190.

George Karypis. 2003. CLUTO A Clustering Toolkit. *University of Minnesota, Department of Computer Science, Technical Report* #02-017.

Graham Neubig, Shinsuke Mori. 2010. Word-based Partial Annotation for Efficient Corpus Construction. In *Proceedings of the 7th international conference on Language Resources and Evaluation (LREC 2010)*:2723-2727.

Graham Neubig, Yosuke Nakata, Shinsuke Mori. 2011. Pointwise Predication for Robust, Adaptable Japanese Morphological Analysis. In *Proceedings of the 49th Annual Meeting of the Association for Computational Linguistics: Human Language Technologies (ACL HLT 2011)*:529-533.

Hiroyuki Shinnou. 1999. Detecting and Correction for Errors in Hiragana Sequences by a Hiragana Character N-gram. *Journal of Information Processing Society of Japan*,40(6):2690-2698.

Koby Crammer, Ofer Dekel, Joseph Keshet, Shai Shalev-Shwartz, and Yoram Singer. 2006. Online Passive-Aggressive Algorithms. *Journal of Machine Learning Research* 7:551-585.

Manabu Sassano. 2002. An Empirical Study of Active Learning with Support Vector Machines for Japanese Word Segmentation. In *Proceedings of the 40th Annual Meeting of the Association for Computational Linguistics (ACL 2002)*:505-512.

Masaaki Nagata. 1998. A Japanese OCR Error Correction Method Using Character Shape Similarity and Statistical Language Model. In *Proceedings of the 36th Annual Meeting of the Association for Computational Linguistics and 17th International Conference on Computational Linguistic (COLING-ACL '98)*:922-928.

Naoki Yoshinaga and Masaru Kitsuregawa. 2010. Kernel Slicing: Scalable Online Training with Conjunctive Features. In *Proceedings of the 23th International Conference on Computational Linguistic (COLING 2010)*:1245-1253.

S^3 - Statistical Saṃdhi Splitting

Abhiram Natarajan and Eugene Charniak
Brown Laboratory for Linguistic Information Processing
Brown University, USA
abhiram.nat@gmail.com, ec@cs.brown.edu

Abstract

The problem of Saṃdhi-Splitting is central to computational processing of Sanskrit texts. Currently the best-known algorithm for this task, given a chunk, generates all possible splits and chooses the Maximum-a-Posteriori estimate as the final answer. Our contributions to the task of Saṃdhi-Splitting are two-fold. Firstly, we improve upon the current algorithm by proposing a principled modification of the posterior probability function to achieve better results. Secondly, we propose an algorithm based on Bayesian Word-Segmentation methods. We find that the unsupervised version of our algorithm achieves a better precision than the current algorithm with the original probabilistic model. We then present a supervised version of our algorithm that outperforms all previous methods/models.

1 Introduction

Sanskrit, considered to be among the oldest languages in the world, is elaborate in its oral specifications. It possesses a set of euphonic rules called Saṃdhi[1] rules, which when applied, cause phonological changes at word or morph boundaries. These rules are enumerated in Pāṇini's Aṣṭādhyāyī, and have been devised with the aim of achieving epigrammatic brevity. There are two kinds of Saṃdhi:

1. Internal Saṃdhi: Euphonic transformation at morph boundaries; $W_1x + yW_2 \Rightarrow W_1zW_2$, where x and y are the final and initial segments of W_1 and W_2, respectively, and z respresents the smoothed phonetic transformation of x and y together
   E.g: `dīpena udvejayati` ⇒ `dīpenodvejayati`
2. External Saṃdhi: Phonetic change at word boundaries; $W_1x + W_2 \Rightarrow W_1x' + W_2$, where the final segment of the first word x changes to x'
   E.g: `utthitaḥ vidyādharaḥ` ⇒ `utthito vidyādharaḥ`

We shall refer to the process of making the euphonic transformations as *Saṃdhising* and the text formed as a result as *Saṃdhied text*. The process of undoing the euphonic transformations shall be referred to as *Analysis* or *Saṃdhi-Splitting*[2], and the text formed as a result will be referred to as *Analysed text*.

It is easy to see that the task of *Saṃdhi-Splitting* is ambiguous. For instance, any of {(ca,api), (cā,api), (ca,āpi), (cā,āpi)} could have combined to form cāpi. Contextual knowledge is necessary for perfect *analysis* of Sanskrit text (Hellwig, 2009), and current methods have not evolved enough to be able to supply context. However the field of Statistical Machine Learning, by making reasonable assumptions, allows us to provide approximations of these processes. Previous work (Beesley, 1998; Hyman, 2007) indicates that Finite State Transducers (FST) could be used to generate morphologically valid splits. Mittal (2010) considers the FST approach as well as an approach based on Optimality Theory (Prince and Smolensky, 1993), by defining a posterior probability function to choose among all morphologically valid splits of a chunk (OT1). More recently, Kumar et al. (2010) report findings using a different posterior probability function with the same Optimality Theory approach (OT2).

Firstly, we derive our own posterior probability function, which is different from OT1 and OT2.

[1] Literally means "Putting Together".

[2] We shall use these terms interchangeably.

We observe better results. Secondly, and more importantly, we present a *Saṃdhi-Splitting* technique based on the Bayesian Word-Segmentation methods presented by Goldwater et al. (2006a). These methods in turn are based on the Dirichlet process. The Dirichlet process is a continuous multivariate distribution used in nonparametric Bayesian Statistics, often as a convenient prior distribution. Gibbs sampling is used to sample from the posterior distribution of *analysed* texts given the *Saṃdhied text*.

The paper is organised as follows. In Section 2, we discuss the Optimality Theory approach in detail. In Section 3, we introduce our framework for *Saṃdhi-Splitting*. We present both the unsupervised and supervised versions of our algorithm in this section. Section 4 then provides specific details of our implementations and Section 5 contrasts the results obtained by all the methods/models considered. Section 6 concludes the paper.

2 Current Methods

The literature on *Saṃdhi-Splitting* is too huge for us to do justice. We shall stick to the best published results so far, which have been obtained by the OT method (Kumar et al., 2010; Mittal, 2010). Procedure 1 is a pseudocode representation of the OT method.

Procedure 1 : Saṃdhi-Splitting using OT

1: **for each** $chunk \in \mathcal{D}$ **do**
2: $\quad \mathbb{S} \leftarrow$ getAllPossibleSplits($chunk$)
3: $\quad \mathbb{S}' \leftarrow \{x : x \in \mathbb{S}, x$ is morphologically valid$\}$
4: $\quad l \leftarrow \arg\max_s \{\hat{P}(s) : s \in \mathbb{S}'\}$
5: $\quad$ **print** l

The procedure is quite straightforward. Each candidate chunk is recursively broken (Line 2) to generate all possible splits. Each split is passed through a morphological analyser and the splits that contain one or more invalid morphs are discarded (Line 3). Finally, the Maximum a posteriori (MAP) estimate is chosen as the answer (Line 4).

$\hat{P}(s)$ is the posterior probability function, which we derive as follows. Consider a morphologically valid split $s = < c_1, \ldots, c_m >$, where $c_1 \ldots c_m$ are its constituents, which was obtained after applying rules $r = < r_1, \ldots, r_{m-1} >$[3] on a chunk $\mathcal{C}$. We would need to find the most probable split, which is given by $\arg\max_{s \in \mathbb{S}'} P(s|\mathcal{C})$. Using the noisy channel model framework (Shannon, 1948), we get

$$\arg\max_{s \in \mathbb{S}'} P(s|\mathcal{C}) = \arg\max_{s \in \mathbb{S}'} P(\mathcal{C}|s) \times P(s) \quad (1)$$

We know that s is a result of applying r on $\mathcal{C}$ at specific points. Now, $P(\mathcal{C}|s)$ reads as the conditional probability of obtaining $\mathcal{C}$ given that r was applied at exactly those points. Clearly, this is 1. Thus the MAP estimate would be a split that maximises the probability of the prior

$$l = \arg\max_{s \in \mathbb{S}'} \hat{P}(s) \quad (2)$$

Note that we use the notation $\hat{P}$ instead of P because we can never know the true value of $P(s)$, but can only estimate it from our training set. Let us now turn our attention to $\hat{P}(s)$. We read $\hat{P}(s)$ as the probability of generating the morphs $< c_1, \ldots, c_m >$. Thus we get:

$$\hat{P}(s) = \hat{P}(c_1) \times \hat{P}(c_2 \mid c_1) \times \hat{P}(c_3 \mid c_1, c_2) \times \ldots = \prod_{j=1}^{m} \hat{P}(c_j) \quad \text{[Assuming Independence]} \quad (3)$$

Equation 3 describes a generative model in that it shows us how we can generate the morphs $< c_1, \ldots, c_m >$. Mittal (2010) defines $\hat{P}(s)$ as

$$\frac{\prod_{i=1}^{m-1}\left(\hat{P}(c_i) + \hat{P}(c_{i+1})\right) \times \hat{P}(r_i)}{m} \quad (4)$$

Kumar et al. (2010) define $\hat{P}(s)$ as

$$\frac{\left(\prod_{i=1}^{m} \hat{P}(c_i)\right) \times \left(\prod_{j=1}^{m-1} \hat{P}(r_j)\right)}{m} \quad (5)$$

In each of these models, the maximum likelihood estimators for $\hat{P}(c_i)$ and $\hat{P}(r_j)$ are used, i.e. $\hat{P}(c_i)$ is set to the relative frequency of c_i in the training set, and $\hat{P}(r_j)$ to the relative frequency of the usage of r_j in the training set.

[3] Rule r_i is applied between c_i and c_{i+1}

Note that unlike Equation 4 and Equation 5, Equation 3 does not have rule probabilities. This can be explained by keeping in mind that Equation 3 describes a generative model. If we generated morphs and knew that they had to be combined to form a chunk, the rules are uniquely determined. In Section 5, we shall compare the results obtained by using each of Equations 3, 4 and 5 on standard datasets.

3 *Saṃdhi*-Splitting based on the Dirichlet Process

Our method is similar to the two-stage modelling framework described by Goldwater et al. (2006a; 2006b). The framework has two components, a morph *generator* which generates morphs likely to be found in a lexicon, from some probability distribution, and an *adaptor* which determines how often each of these morphs occur. Section 3.1 and Section 3.2 describe the unsupervised version of our algorithm while Section 3.3 describes the supervised version.

3.1 Foundations

In the realm of the framework, a *saṃdhied* chunk $C = c_1 \ c_2 \ \ldots \ c_m$ can be viewed to be created as follows:

1. A *generator* P_s generates a super-set sequence of morphs[4]: $\mathbb{M} = M_1 \ldots M_n$ from a probability distribution P_s.

2. The *adaptor* P_γ generates a sequence of integers: $\mathbb{Z} = z_1 \ldots z_m$, each of which are identifiers of one particular item from $\mathbb{M}$. This means that $1 \leq z_i \leq n$, and $z_i = x \Rightarrow c_i = M_x$.

Once the morphs of a chunk are generated, *Saṃdhi* rules are applied between them to form C. Henceforth $TwoStage(P_\gamma, P_s)$ shall be used to denote a two-stage framework with P_γ as the adaptor and P_s as the generator. Let us move to the Chinese Restaurant Process, which we use as our *adaptor*.

[4]In the case of *Internal Saṃdhi*, we consider morph boundaries and in the case of *External Saṃdhi*, we consider word boundaries. The theoretical foundations hold good for both cases. Thus the reader must always keep in mind that the concepts presented in this section apply at word boundaries too.

3.1.1 Chinese Restaurant Process

Having studied many corpora of natural language utterances, Zipf (1932) made a famous empirical observation that word frequencies follow a power-law distribution, i.e., the frequency of a word is inversely proportional to its frequency rank. This means that the most frequent word in a corpus occurs twice as often as the second most frequent word, thrice as often as the third most frequent word, and so on. Mathematically speaking, if w_r is the r-ranked word in a corpus, then

$$f(w_r) \propto \frac{1}{r^c} \tag{6}$$

where $f(w_r)$ denotes the frequency of occurrence of w_r, and $c \approx 1$. The veracity of this law has hence been verified by a study on present-day English (Kucera and Francis, 1967).

Typically, power-law distributions are produced by stochastic processes in which outcomes accrue probability based on the probability they already have. Such processes are called preferential attachment processes. Let us turn our attention to the Chinese Restaurant Process (Aldous et al., 1985) (CRP), which is one such process. The process is best explained by specifying how to draw a sample from it. Consider a restaurant with an infinite number of tables, each with infinite capacity. Customers enter the restaurant, one at a time, and seat themselves at a table of their choice. They choose an occupied table with probability proportional to the number of people already present at the table, or an unoccupied table with probability proportional to some real-valued scalar parameter α. The first customer always sits at the first table. Then onwards, the ith customer sits at a table T_i, and T_i follows the distribution:

$$P(T_i = k \mid \text{Previous Customers}) = \begin{cases} \frac{n_k}{i-1+\alpha} & 1 \leq k \leq N_{i-1} \\ \frac{\alpha}{i-1+\alpha} & k = N_{i-1} + 1 \end{cases} \tag{7}$$

where n_k is the number of people occupying table k and N_{i-1} is total number of tables occupied by the previous $(i-1)$ customers.

When the CRP is combined with a morph *generator*, it can be used to generate a power-law distribution over morphs. Such a model can be described as $TwoStage(CRP(\alpha), P_s)$. We could view this as restaurant where each table represents a morph. Every customer is also labelled with a morph and can either sit only at tables which are labelled with the same morph, or at an unoccupied table. A customer at a table represents one occurence of the morph that is represented by the table. To get the probability distribution of the ith morph, we must sum over all the tables labelled with that morph:[5]

$$\begin{aligned}
&P(c_i = c \mid c_{-i}) \\
&\quad = P(\text{assign customer to any of the } c \text{ tables}) \\
&\qquad + P(\text{assign customer to a new table}) \\
&\quad = \frac{n_c^{c_{-i}}}{i-1+\alpha} + P_s(c) \times \frac{\alpha}{i-1+\alpha} \\
&\quad = \frac{n_c^{c_{-i}} + \alpha \times P_s(c)}{i-1+\alpha}
\end{aligned} \tag{8}$$

where $c_{-i} = c_1 \ldots c_{i-1}$ and $n_c^{c_{-i}}$ represents the number of occurrences of c in c_{-i}.

Let us examine Equation 8. It is in accordance with the principle of *preferential attachment*. This is because the probability of generating a morph that has already been generated increases as more instances of the morph are observed. Also note that the sparseness of the distribution generated increases with an increase in the value of the parameter α. This is explained by the fact that $\alpha \times P_s(c)$ is constant and it reduces w.r.t. the first summand over time. What this means is that the probability of generating a novel morph decreases (but never dissapears fully) as more data is observed.

Let us now turn our attention to the *generator*. For simplicity, we choose a unigram phoneme distribution for P_s. If a morph c_i contains the phonemes $a_1 \ldots a_d$

$$P_s(c_i) = p_{\Phi}(1 - p_{\Phi})^{d-1} \prod_{j=1}^{d} P(a_j) \tag{9}$$

where p_{Φ} is the probability of a *Saṃdhi* rule being applied at any juncture. The reasoning for the equation is quite straightforward - the *Saṃdhi* rule is not applied $(d-1)$ times, and applied at the dth phoneme. The unsupervised version of the algorithm uses an uniform distribution over phonemes.

[5]Note that two different tables may represent the same morph.

3.1.2 Dirichlet Process Model

Given a coin with an unknown bias, say p, what would be a suitable distribution that reflects our expectations about p? It would be the Beta distribution. The Dirichlet distribution is a generalisation of the Beta distribution, in that it may have more than just two dimensions. The Dirichlet process is an infinite dimensional version of the Dirichlet distribution. Each sample from a Dirichlet process returns a distribution over an infinite set of random variables.

Let us consider a Dirichlet process with its parameters as α and P_s. A sample from this process, say G, will consist of a set of all possible morphs and their corresponding probabilities. Now, we can generate each morph c_i in the corpus from the distribution G. This can be represented as follows:

$$\begin{aligned}
c_i &\sim G \\
G &\sim DP(\alpha, P_s)
\end{aligned} \tag{10}$$

Following the argument in Goldwater (2006), it is not hard to find that the model described by $TwoStage(CRP(\alpha), P_s)$ is equivalent to the model represented by Equation 10.

We must also keep in mind that, analogous to Equation 8, the probability of ith morph $c_i = c$ is given by

$$P(c_i = c \mid c_{-i}) = \frac{n_c^{c_{-i}} + \alpha \times P_s(c)}{i-1+\alpha} \tag{11}$$

where $c_{-i} = c_1 \ldots c_{i-1}$, and $n_c^{c_{-i}}$ denotes the number of occurrences of c in c_{-i}. Going ahead a little, we realise that our input corpus is a set of sentences, where each sentence contains a set of *Saṃdhied* chunks, where each chunk is in turn formed by *Saṃdhising* separate morphs. The program does not need to separate the chunks from each other, all it needs to do is to separate a chunk into its constituent morphs. Referring to Equation 3, we recall our generative model view of how a *Saṃdhied* chunk is generated. We describe the process by the following PCFG:[6]

$$\begin{aligned}
P(r_i = r_{branch} \mid r_{-i}):&\quad S \rightarrow S\ C \\
P(r_i = r_{end} \mid r_{-i}):&\quad S \rightarrow C \\
P_s(c_i = c \mid c_{-i}):&\quad C \rightarrow c
\end{aligned}$$

We shall derive an equation for $P(r_i = r_{branch} \mid r_{-i})$ in the next section.

[6]Probabilistic Context-Free Grammar

3.2 Gibbs Sampling for *Saṃdhi* Analysis

As suggested in Gilks et al. (1996), we use Gibbs Sampling to sample from the posterior distrubition of *Saṃdhi* Analyses. One iteration of the algorithm causes the program control to consider every possible splitting point in the data and form two hypotheses, say $\mathcal{H}_1$ and $\mathcal{H}_2$. These hypotheses contain the same structure, except at the point of consideration. If the point of consideration is part of a chunk c, $\mathcal{H}_2$ splits c into two individual morphs (say c_1 and c_2) while $\mathcal{H}_1$ does not. Let $\mathcal{H}^{\cap}$ denote the structure common to both $\mathcal{H}_1$ and $\mathcal{H}_2$.

Given the way Gibbs sampling works, we know that we only need the relative probabilities of $\mathcal{H}_1$ and $\mathcal{H}_2$. Also, we must recall that the order of arrival of customers in the metaphorical Chinese Restaurant does not affect seating probability, as shown by Aldous et al. (1985). This means that we could consider $\mathcal{H}^{\cap}$ to have already been generated. From Equation 11 we get

$$P\left(\mathcal{H}_1 \,|\, \mathcal{H}^{\cap}\right) = P\left(c \,|\, \mathcal{H}^{\cap}\right) = \frac{n_c^{\mathcal{H}^{\cap}} + \alpha P_s(c)}{|\mathcal{H}^{\cap}| + \alpha} \quad (12)$$

We also derive

$$\begin{aligned} &P\left(\mathcal{H}_2 \,|\, \mathcal{H}^{\cap}\right) \\ &= P\left(r_{branch} \cup c_1 \cup c_2 \,|\, \mathcal{H}^{\cap}\right) \\ &= P\left(r_{branch} \,|\, \mathcal{H}^{\cap}\right) \times \frac{n_{c_1}^{\mathcal{H}^{\cap}} + \alpha P_s(c_1)}{|\mathcal{H}^{\cap}| + \alpha} \\ &\quad \times \frac{n_{c_2}^{\mathcal{H}^{\cap}} + I(c_1 = c_2) + \alpha P_s(c_2)}{|\mathcal{H}^{\cap}| + 1 + \alpha} \end{aligned} \quad (13)$$

The extra '1' in the denominator of the third item of the product is because after c_1, we have an additional morph. Also, I is the indicator function, which is 1 when the expression inside its parathesis is true. Let us now examine $P\left(r_{branch} \,|\, \mathcal{H}^{\cap}\right)$. Clearly, each time we can choose only one among $\{r_{branch}, r_{end}\}$, so we have $P(r_{branch}) + P(r_{end}) = 1$. The number of r rules applied at the point of consideration would be $(|\mathcal{H}^{\cap}| + 1)$ - one each for the $|\mathcal{H}^{\cap}|$ morphs, and an extra one for the chunk under consideration. We apply a Beta($\frac{\rho}{2}$,$\frac{\rho}{2}$) prior to get:[7]

$$P\left(r_{branch} \,|\, \mathcal{H}^{\cap}\right) = \frac{n_{r_{branch}}^{\mathcal{H}^{\cap}} + \frac{\rho}{2}}{|\mathcal{H}^{\cap}| + 1 + \rho} \quad (14)$$

[7]Henceforth, please substitute this expression in Equation 13

The algorithm works as follows - we begin with a random *analysis* of the corpus. After that, using Equations 12 and 13, we sample every potential boundary point. An iteration is said to have completed when the sampler samples over the entire corpus. We run multiple iterations of this process, until convergence.

Simulated annealing (Aarts and Korst, 1989) is used to facilitate choosing of low probability transitions early in the algorithm, lest it gets stuck at a local maximum.

3.3 Supervised Version

As mentioned earlier, we use Gibbs Sampling to sample from the posterior distribution. Let us recall the relevant equations - Equations 12 and 13. In the supervised version of our algorithm, we use available training data (say D_{train}) to our advantage. Firstly, we define $\mathcal{H}^{\cap'} = \mathcal{H}^{\cap} \cup D_{train}$.

Also, instead of assuming a uniform distribution over phonemes, we infer phoneme probabilities from D_{train}:

$$P_s^{'}(c_i) = p_{\Phi}(1 - p_{\Phi})^{d-1} \prod_{j=1}^{d} \hat{P}(a_j) \quad (15)$$

Let Π denote the set of all phonemes found in D_{train}. Given a phoneme a_x, we set $\hat{P}(a_x)$ to be the maximum likelihood estimate:

$$\hat{P}(a_x) = \frac{n_{a_x} + \alpha_0}{n_* + \alpha_0 |\Pi|} \quad (16)$$

where n_{a_x} is the number of times a_x occurs in D_{train}, $n_* = \sum_{p \in \Pi} n_p$, and α_0 is the unigram smoothing constant.

Thus we get

$$P\left(\mathcal{H}_1 \,|\, \mathcal{H}^{\cap'}\right) = \frac{n_c^{\mathcal{H}^{\cap'}} + \alpha P_s^{'}(c)}{|\mathcal{H}^{\cap'}| + \alpha} \quad (17)$$

and

$$\begin{aligned} &P\left(\mathcal{H}_2 \,|\, \mathcal{H}^{\cap'}\right) \\ &= \frac{n_{r_{branch}}^{\mathcal{H}^{\cap'}} + \frac{\rho}{2}}{|\mathcal{H}^{\cap'}| + 1 + \rho} \times \frac{n_{c_1}^{\mathcal{H}^{\cap'}} + \alpha P_s^{'}(c_1)}{|\mathcal{H}^{\cap'}| + \alpha} \\ &\quad \times \frac{n_{c_2}^{\mathcal{H}^{\cap'}} + I(c_1 = c_2) + \alpha P_s^{'}(c_2)}{|\mathcal{H}^{\cap'}| + 1 + \alpha} \end{aligned} \quad (18)$$

The supervised version of the algorithm now works exactly the same way as the unsupervised version, except that Gibbs sampling is done using Equations 17 and 18.

4 Implementation Details

As a part of the Consortium project in India, a corpus of nearly 25000 parallel strings of *Saṃdhied* and *analysed* text has been formed (say D_1). OT trains on the 25000 string dataset and tests on a separate dataset of 2148 *Saṃdhied* Chunks (say D_2). We see that the test set used in OT only contains examples of *Internal Saṃdhi*. Thus, we merge the test set with the original 25000 string dataset ($D = D_1 \cup D_2$) and generate random samples of training data and test data. We use $\frac{3}{4}$ of the data for training (D_{train}) and $\frac{1}{4}$ for testing (D_{test}). Note that D_{test} can have instances of *Internal Saṃdhi*, *External Saṃdhi* as well as no *Saṃdhi*[8] at all. The scores we report are averaged over 5 random samples of D_{train} and D_{test} from D.

We also use the morphological analyser (Akshar Bharati, 2006) provided by the apertium group.

As for the parameters of the model, we fixed $\rho = 2$. We found that a decrease in p_Φ improved recall, but caused long words to get concatenated. At the same time higher values of p_Φ tended to cause over segmentation. It was also observed that higher α values resulted in higher lexicon recall, once again only up to a point. Although it was not possible to arrive a single best value for either α or p_Φ; we fixed them to be $p_\Phi = 0.5$ and $\alpha = 20$. The sampler is annealed with the following temperature schedule - $\frac{1}{\gamma} = 0.1$ to 1.0, in steps of 0.1.

For evaluation, standard statistical measures of Precision, Recall and F-Score were used. Precision indicates how many among the items found are correct; Recall indicates how many among the correct items are found. F-score is the harmonic mean of the Precision and the Recall.

Our implementations work with the Sanskrit Library Phonetic Basic format (SLP1). Since the morphological analyser uses the Hyderabad-Tirupati format (WX), we use the transcoding tools on the Sanskrit Library Website (Scharf and Hyman, 2010). One may refer Huet (2009) for more details about the formats.

[8]This explains why our implementations of OT achieve lower scores than what is reported in their paper. Readers must note that our implementation of OT, when trained on D_1 and tested on D_2, achieved nearly the same accuracy reported in their paper. Thus we believe our implementation of OT is accurate.

5 Results

Let OT1, OT2, OT3 denote versions of Procedure 1, using Equations 4, 5, 3 as the posterior probability functions, respectively. Precision is calculated as the percentage of correct segmentations among all the segmentations made by the algorithm. Recall is calculated as the percentage of correct segmentations made by the algorithm among all the correct segmentations that need to be made. F-Score is the harmonic mean of the Precision and Recall. Table 1 shows the scores obtained by our implementations of different versions of OT.

Method	Precision	Recall	F-Score
OT1	54.61	62.08	58.11
OT2	63.96	68.74	66.26
OT3	**70.52**	66.61	**68.51**

Table 1: Accuracies obtained by different versions of OT; OT3 outperforms OT1 and OT2 in Precision and F-Score

As we can see, using Equation 3 as the posterior probability function while obtaining the MAP estimate, we improve the previous best F-Score by nearly 3.5%. We shall now examine the results obtained by four different versions of the framework described in Section 3. Let these versions be denoted by NC1 ... NC4:

1. NC1 denotes the Two-Stage Framework in its most basic state. The algorithm possesses no linguistic knowledge whatsoever.

2. Kessler (1994) shows that each Sanskrit syllable must have only one Sonority peak. NC2 uses this knowledge to effect. The method is largely similar to NC1 except for the way in which sampling is done. We only sample when we are sure that the segments we generate do not violate Sonority Hierarchy. Refer Appendix A for more details about sonority hierarchy.

3. NC3 uses a morphological analyser. Sampling is only done when we know that the

segment we are leaving behind is morphologically valid.

4. NC4 uses a morphological analyser as well as training data. Sampling is done using Equations 17 and 18.

Method	Precision	Recall	F-Score
NC1	31.74	41.22	35.86
NC2	50.98	40.43	45.1
NC3	66.55	56.13	60.9
NC4	**76.21**	**64.84**	**70.07**

Table 2: Accuracies obtained by different versions of NC; NC4 Outperforms NC1...3, as well OT1...3 in Precision and F-Score

Results obtained by these versions are shown in Table 2. NC4 improves upon the F-Score achieved by OT2 by nearly 6%.

6 Conclusion

In this paper, we have presented an algorithm for *Saṃdhi*-Splitting which draws on expedients of Bayesian statistics. It is highly flexible in that it works even in the absence of (a) morphological analyser (b) training data. Also, one must remember that an entire corpus, as it is, can be fed to the algorithm, as opposed to OT which would require each *Saṃdhied* chunk separately. Finally, the fact that the algorithm runs in polynomial time, as opposed to OT which takes exponential time, further asserts the efficacy of the method.

References

Emile Aarts and Jan Korst. 1989. *Simulated annealing and Boltzmann machines: a stochastic approach to combinatorial optimization and neural computing*. John Wiley & Sons, Inc., New York, NY, USA.

V Sheeba Akshar Bharati, Amba P. Kulkarni. 2006. Building a wide coverage sanskrit morphological analyzer: A practical approach.

David Aldous, Illdar Ibragimov, Jean Jacod, and David Aldous. 1985. Exchangeability and related topics. In *École d'Été de Probabilités de Saint-Flour XIII - 1983*, volume 1117 of *Lecture Notes in Mathematics*, pages 1–198. Springer Berlin / Heidelberg.

Kenneth R. Beesley. 1998. Arabic morphology using only finite-state operations. In *Proceedings of the Workshop on Computational Approaches to Semitic Languages*, Semitic '98, pages 50–57. Association for Computational Linguistics.

W.R. Gilks, S. Richardson, and D.J. Spiegelhalter. 1996. *Markov chain Monte Carlo in practice*. Chapman & Hall/CRC.

Sharon Goldwater, Thomas L. Griffiths, and Mark Johnson. 2006a. Contextual dependencies in unsupervised word segmentation. In *Proceedings of the 21st International Conference on Computational Linguistics and the 44th annual meeting of the Association for Computational Linguistics*, ACL-44, pages 673–680, Stroudsburg, PA, USA. Association for Computational Linguistics.

Sharon Goldwater, Thomas L. Griffiths, and Mark Johnson. 2006b. Interpolating between types and tokens by estimating power-law generators. In *In Advances in Neural Information Processing Systems 18*, page 18.

Sharon Goldwater. 2006. *Nonparametric Bayesian models of lexical acquisition*. Ph.D. thesis, Brown University.

Oliver Hellwig. 2009. Sanskrittagger: A stochastic lexical and pos tagger for sanskrit. In *Sanskrit Computational Linguistics*, pages 266–277. Springer-Verlag, Berlin, Heidelberg.

Gérard Huet. 2009. Sanskrit computational linguistics. chapter Formal Structure of Sanskrit Text: Requirements Analysis for a Mechanical Sanskrit Processor, pages 162–199. Springer-Verlag, Berlin, Heidelberg.

Malcolm Hyman. 2007. From Paninian Sandhi to Finite State Calculus. In *First International Sanskrit Computational Linguistics Symposium*, Rocquencourt France. INRIA Paris-Rocquencourt.

Brett Kessler. 1994. Sandhi and syllables in classical sanskrit. In *The proceedings of the Twelfth West Coast Conference on Formal Linguistics*, pages 35–50, Stanford, CA, USA. CSLI Publications.

H. Kucera and W. N. Francis. 1967. *Computational analysis of present-day American English*. Brown University Press, Providence, RI.

Anil Kumar, Vipul Mittal, and Amba Kulkarni. 2010. Sanskrit compound processor. In *Sanskrit Computational Linguistics*, volume 6465 of *Lecture Notes in Computer Science*, pages 57–69. Springer Berlin / Heidelberg.

Vipul Mittal. 2010. Automatic sanskrit segmentizer using finite state transducers. In *Proceedings of the ACL 2010 Student Research Workshop*, ACLstudent '10, pages 85–90. Association for Computational Linguistics.

Alan Prince and Paul Smolensky. 1993. Optimality theory: Constraint interaction in generative grammar. Technical report, Rutgers University and University of Colorado.

Peter M. Scharf and Malcolm D. Hyman. 2010. Transcoding. `http://sanskrit1.ccv.brown.edu/tomcat/sl/TranscodeText.`

Claude E. Shannon. 1948. *A Mathematical Theory of Communication*, volume 27. Bell System Technical Journal, Champaign, IL, USA.

G. K. Zipf. 1932. *Selective Studies and the Principle of Relative Frequency in Language*. Harvard University Press.

A Sonority Hierarchy

Sonority hierarchy is as follows: Vowels > Semivowels > Nasals > Spirants > Voiced Stops > Unvoiced Stops

- Vowels = AaEOeoiIuUfFxX
- Semivowels = yvrl
- Nasals = NYRnmM
- Spirants = hSzsH
- Voiced Stops = gGjJqQdDbB
- Unvoiced Stops = kKcCwWtTpP'

A syllable is said possess a sonority violation if it has more than one sonority peak (e.g. 'rjA'). However, at the beginning of a syllable, we must rate Spirants at the same level as Unvoiced Stops (e.g. 'sTApayati' is valid).

Improving Chinese Word Segmentation and POS Tagging with Semi-supervised Methods Using Large Auto-Analyzed Data

Yiou Wang[†], **Jun'ichi Kazama**[†], **Yoshimasa Tsuruoka**[‡†],
Wenliang Chen[§†], **Yujie Zhang**[*†], **Kentaro Torisawa**[†]
[†]National Institute of Information and Communications Technology (NICT), Japan
[‡]School of Information Science, JAIST, Japan; [*]Beijing Jiaotong University, China
[§]Human Language Technology, Institute for Infocomm Research, Singapore
{wangyiou, kazama, torisawa}@nict.go.jp; tsuruoka@jaist.ac.jp
wechen@i2r.a-star.edu.sg; yjzhang@bjtu.edu.cn

Abstract

This paper presents a simple yet effective semi-supervised method to improve Chinese word segmentation and POS tagging. We introduce novel features derived from large auto-analyzed data to enhance a simple pipelined system. The auto-analyzed data are generated from unlabeled data by using a baseline system. We evaluate the usefulness of our approach in a series of experiments on Penn Chinese Treebanks and show that the new features provide substantial performance gains in all experiments. Furthermore, the results of our proposed method are superior to the best reported results in the literature.

1 Introduction

In Chinese, most language processing starts from word segmentation and part-of-speech (POS) tagging. These two steps tokenize a sequence of characters without delimiters into words and predict a syntactic label (POS tag) for each segmented word. They are considered indispensable steps for higher-level NLP tasks such as parsing and information extraction. Although the performance of Chinese word segmentation and POS tagging has been greatly improved over the past years, the task is still challenging.

To improve the accuracy of NLP systems, one of the current trends is semi-supervised learning, which utilizes large unlabeled data in supervised learning. Several studies have demonstrated that the use of unlabeled data can improve the performance of NLP tasks, such as text chunking (Ando and Zhang, 2005), POS tagging and named entity recognition (Suzuki and Isozaki, 2008), and parsing (Suzuki et al., 2009; Chen et al., 2009; Koo et al., 2008). Therefore, it is attractive to consider adopting semi-supervised learning in Chinese word segmentation and POS tagging tasks.

In this paper, we present an approach to improve the performance of both segmentation and POS tagging by incorporating large unlabeled data. We first preprocess unlabeled data with our baseline models. We then extract various items of dictionary information from the auto-analyzed data. Finally, we generate new features that incorporate the extracted information for both word segmentation and POS tagging. We also perform word clustering on the auto-segmented data and use word clusters as features in POS tagging. In addition, we introduce lexicon features by using a cross-validation technique.

The use of sub-structures from the auto-annotated data has been presented previously (Noord, 2007; Chen et al., 2008; Chen et al., 2009). Chen et al. (2009) extracted different types of subtrees from the auto-parsed data and used them as new features in standard learning methods. They showed this simple method greatly improves the accuracy of dependency parsing. The idea of combining word clusters with discriminative learning has been previously reported in the context of named entity recognition (Miller et al., 2004; Kazama and Torisawa, 2008) and dependency parsing (Koo et al., 2008). We adapt and extend these techniques to Chinese word segmentation and POS tagging, and demonstrate their effectiveness in this task.

One of our criteria in this study was to achieve high accuracy with simple and easy-to-implement techniques. To meet this, the whole system is a pipeline with a character-based CRF for word segmentation and a word-based CRF for POS tagging. The information of unlabeled data is incorporated as additional new features without changing the learning algorithm.

To demonstrate the effectiveness of our approach, we conduct segmentation and POS tagging experiments on three versions of Penn Chinese Treebank, including the newly released CTB

Word Length	1	2	3	4	5	6	7 or more
Tags	S	BE	BB_2E	BB_2B_3E	BB_2B_3ME	BB_2B_3MME	$BB_2B_3M...ME$

Table 1: Word representation with a 6-tag tagset : S, B, B_2, B_3, M, E

Type	Feature	Description
Character Unigram	c_{-1}, c_0, c_1	Previous, current and next character
Nearing Character Bigram	$(c_{-1}\ c_0), (c_0\ c_1)$	Previous (next) character and current character
Jump Character Bigram	$c_{-1}\ c_1$	Previous character and next character
Punctuation	IsPu(c_0)	Current character is punctuation
Character Type	$K(c_{-2})K(c_{-1})K(c_0)K(c_1)K(c_2)$	Types of character: date, numeral, alphabet, Chinese

Table 2: Feature templates for word segmentation

version 7.0. We show that our semi-supervised approach yields improvements for all the test collections and achieves better results than the best reported results in the literature.

2 Segmentation and POS tagging Models

We implement our approach using sequential tagging models. Following the previous work (Zhao et al., 2006; Zhao et al., 2010), we employ the linear chain CRFs (Lafferty et al., 2001) as our learning model. Specifically, we use its CRF++ (version 0.54) implementation by Taku Kudo. [1]

2.1 Baseline Segmentation Model

We employ character-based sequence labeling for word segmentation. In addition to its simplicity, the advantage of a character-based model is its robustness to the unknown word problem (Xue, 2003). In a character-based Chinese word segmentation task, a character in a given sequence is labeled by a tag that stands for its position in the word that the character belongs to. Zhao et al. (2006) reported that a 6-tag tagset shown in Table 1 is the best choice among the tagsets tested for Chinese word segmentation under the CRF framework. Therefore we also use this 6-tag tagset.

The basic types of features of our word segmentation model are listed in Table 2. These basic feature templates are based on Zhao et al. (2006; 2010) and Low et al. (2005).

2.2 Baseline POS Tagging Model

Since we employ a pipelined method, the POS tagging can be performed as a word labeling task, where the input is a sequence of segmented words. We use a CRF here as well. The feature set of our baseline POS tagger, is listed in Table 3. These are adopted from Wu et al. (2008).

[1]Available from http://crfpp.sourceforge.net/

3 Our New Features

In this section, we describe our approach of effectively integrating useful information from unlabeled (and labeled) data into the above baseline models through features. We preprocess unlabeled data with our baseline models and obtain word-segmented sentences with POS tags, and generate new features from the auto-analyzed data. Although the focus of the paper is semi-supervised learning, we also extract a lexicon from the training corpus and use it to generate features. Figure 1 shows an overview of our approach. The rest of this section describes our features in detail.

3.1 New features for Word Segmentation

3.1.1 Semi-supervised n-gram features

In this section, we describe our approach of extracting character-level n-gram lists and generating n-gram features from unlabeled data. We followed the method of Chen et al. (2009), and modified the method for word segmentation and POS tagging. First, we preprocess unlabeled data using the baseline segmenter and obtain auto-segmented data. We then extract character n-gram lists from auto-segmented sentences. Finally, we generate n-gram features for word segmentation.

By using the baseline segmenter, each character c_i in the unlabeled data is labeled with a tag t_i. In other words, the output of auto-segmentation is a sequence $\{(c_i, t_i)\}_{i=1}^{L}$. Let g be a character n-gram (e.g., uni-gram c_i, bi-gram c_ic_{i+1}, tri-gram $c_{i-1}c_ic_{i+1}$ and so on)[2], and seg be a segmentation profile for n-gram g observed at each position. The segmentation profile can be tag t_i or the combination of tags. Take a bi-gram for example, seg may be t_i or t_it_{i+1}. Then,

[2]Note that there are several alternative ways for extracting n-grams at position i, for example $c_{i-1}c_i$ for a bi-gram. In this paper, we used the way as explained here.

Feature Type	Context Position	Description
Word Unigram	w_{-2},w_{-1},w_0,w_1,w_2	Word unigram
Nearing Word Bigram	$(w_{-2}w_{-1})$,$(w_{-1}w_0)$,(w_1w_0),(w_1w_2)	Word bigram
Jump Word Bigram	(w_{-1},w_1)	Previous word and next word
First Character	$Fc(w_0)$	First character of current word
Last Character	$Lc(w_0)$	Last character of current word
Length	$Len(w_0)$	Length of current word

Table 3: Feature templates for POS tagging

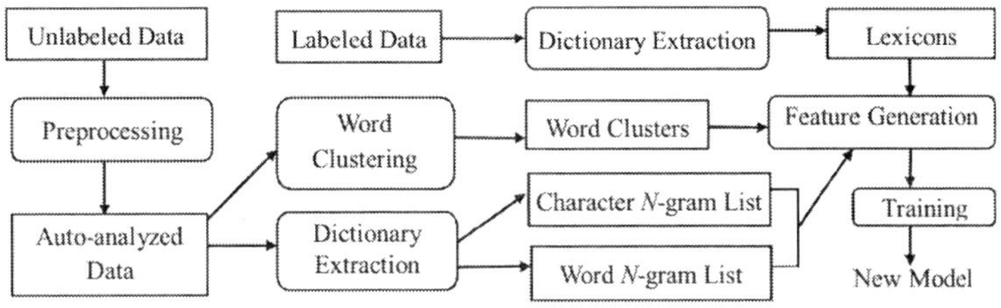

Figure 1: Overview of the proposed approach

we can extract a list of $\{(g, seg, f(g, seg))\}$ from the auto-segmented data. Here, $f(g, seg)$ is the frequency of the cases where n-gram g is segmented with the segmentation profile seg. Then, following Chen et al. (2009), we group entries in this list into three sets: high-frequency (HF), middle-frequency (MF), and low-frequency (LF). The sets are defined as follows: if (g, seg) is one of the top 5% most frequent entries, it is labeled as HF; if it is between top 5% and 20%, it is labeled as MF, otherwise it is labeled as LF. Finally the list can be transformed as a n-gram list $L_{ng} = \{(g, seg, FL(g, seg))\}$, with $FL(g, seg)$ being the frequency label determined as above.

We attempted to encode the information of the above n-gram list into a new type of features, called n-gram features. We tried several feature representations and generation methods and found that the feature derived from the bi-gram list with $seg = t_i$ was most effective.

We generate the feature for the current character c_0 as follows. We retrieve a set of entries, whose g part matches the bi-gram c_0c_1, from L_{ng}. Let this set be L_m. From an entry in L_m, we generate a feature string represented by

(a) $seg - FL(g, seg)$

Then, we concatenate the feature strings of all the entries in L_m as one n-gram feature. If there is no entry in L_m, the feature representation is "*ND*".

For example, consider that L_m is { (*幸(Xing)/福(Fu)*, *B*, *HF*), (*幸(Xing)/福(Fu)*, *B2*, *MF*), (*幸(Xing)/福(Fu)*, *E*, *LF*)} and we are processing c_kc_{k+1} = "*幸(Xing)/福(Fu)*"; consequently, the n-gram feature of c_k is represented as "*B-HF|B2-MF|E-LF*". Note that the concatenation is in lexicographic order of the feature strings for standardization.

3.1.2 Lexicon features

Although a character-based model is simple and robust to unknown words, a limitation is its inability to consider word-level information. If a sequence of characters matches a word in an existing dictionary, it may be a clue that the character sequence should be segmented as one word. Several studies showed that using a dictionary brings improvement for Chinese word segmentation (Low et al., 2005; Zhao et al., 2010). For a corpus-based word segmenter, a manually annotated corpus is essential. Thus we can easily compile a lexicon from a training corpus. We refer to the features related to this lexicon as lexicon features.

In this study, we extract a lexicon in the following way. We collect words and all possible POS tags of the words from the training corpus. For instance, for the word "交流(*JiaoLiu*)", the collected entry may be (交流(*JiaoLiu*), *NN-VV*). Here, "*NN-VV*" is a concatenation of all the observed POS tags. POS tags are in lexicographical order, as in "*NN-VV*". However, we were concerned that a lexicon compiled in this way could cause an overfitting problem and that meaningful weights for the lexicon features may not be learned. This concern was indeed confirmed by the preliminary experiments using the development set. To solve this problem, we used the following method to build and use lexicons. The method is based on the idea of cross-validation.

- Divide the training corpus into ten equal-sized sets, as in the data preparation for 10-fold cross-validation.
- For each set, we compile a lexicon using the remaining nine sets and use this lexicon to generate features for this set.
- For the development and test sets, we collect a lexicon using the entire training corpus and use it for feature generation.

Because the lexicon is extracted from other sets, the weights for this feature will not be overestimated by the learning algorithm. This kind of cross-validation-like techniques are used in studies such as Collins (2002) and Martins et al. (2008) to avoid over-fitting to the training data. Our method can be considered as its application to lexicon extraction.

Using the extracted lexicon, we generate lexicon features as follows. If a character sequence starting with character c_0 matches some words in the lexicon, we greedily choose the longest such matching word w. Letting $LEN(w)$ be the length (the number of characters) of w, we add the following feature for each character c_k in $c_0, c_1, ..., c_{LEN(w)}$:

(b) $P(c_k)$/$LEN(w)$-$POSs(w)$

Here, $P(c_k)$ is the position number (i.e., k) of the character c_k in w and $POSs(w)$ represents the POS tags of w in the lexicon. After generating these features, we increment the current position by $LEN(w)$. If there is no matching word, we proceed to the next character. That is, the forward maximum matching is used.

For example, consider that the current character sequence c_0c_1= "幸*(Xing)*/福*(Fu)*" was matched with a lexicon entry (幸福*(XingFu), JJ-NN-VA*), the feature for c_0 "幸*(Xing)*" is "*1/2-JJ-NN-VA*" and the feature for c_1 "福*(Fu)*" is "*2/2-JJ-NN-VA*".

Several feature representations have been attempted: (i) using only position information, (ii) representing the position information in a 6-tag or 4-tag tagset, or (iii) representing only one POS tag with the highest frequency. Development experiments showed that the current encoding is more effective than others in word segmentation tasks.

Note that our lexicon feature uses POS tag information for word segmentation. The fact that this feature is very effective as reported in Section 4.3 is interesting, since this can be considered as "loose" information feedback from the later process. Although we need a POS tagged corpus even for segmentation, this will not be a big problem since we usually perform POS tagging as well in many applications.

3.2 New Features for POS Tagging

We generate n-gram and lexicon features for POS tagging as well. In addition, the features that incorporate word clusters derived from a large auto-analyzed corpus (referred to as cluster features) are introduced.

3.2.1 Semi-supervised n-gram features

We preprocess auto-segmented data using the baseline POS tagger and can generate word-level n-gram lists $L_{wg} = \{w, pos, FL(w, pos)\}$. Here, w is a word n-gram and pos is the POS tagging profile of the word n-gram. Different from segmentation, features generated from the word unigram list yielded the best results.

A feature of this type for the current word w_0 is generated as follows. We retrieve a set of entries, whose w part matches the uni-gram w_0, from L_{wg}. Let this set be L_m. In the error analysis, we found that some words were associated with several odd POS tags in the uni-gram list. For instance, in addition to (研究*(YanJiu), NN, HF*) and (研究*(YanJiu), VV, HF*), (研究*(YanJiu), VA, LF*) and (研究*(YanJiu), CD, LF*) may appear as entries in the word unigram list, due to mis-tagging by the baseline POS-tagger. Therefore we further impose a restriction based on the frequency as follows: if the number of entries with a HF label $\geq$ threshold, only the entries with HF will be selected, and if the sum of entries with a HF or MF label $\geq$ threshold, the entries with either HF or MF will be selected, otherwise, all of the entries in L_m will be selected. Here the threshold is set to 2 based on the development experiments. Let these selected entries be L_s. From an entry in L_s, we generate a feature string represented by

(c) $pos - FL(w, pos)$.

Then, we concatenate the feature strings of all entries in L_s as one n-gram feature. As for the previous instance, the feature for "研究*(YanJiu)*" is encoded as "NN-HF|VV-HF".

3.2.2 Semi-supervised cluster features

Following the work of Koo et al. (2008), we produced the clusters of various levels of granularity,

Data set	CTB chapter IDs
Dev	41-80,203-233,301-325,400-409,591,613-617,643-673,1022-1035,1120-1129,2110-2159,2270-2294,2510-2569,2760-2799,3040-3109,4040-4059,4084-4085,4090,4096,4106-4108,4113-4115,4121,4128,4132,4135,4158-4162,4169,4189,4196,4236-4261,4322,4335-4336,4407-4411
Test	1-40,144-174,271-300,410-428,592,900-931,1009-1020,1036,1044,1060-1061,1072,1118-1119,1132,1141-1142,1148,2000-2010,2160-2220,2295-2330,2570-2640,2800-2845,3110-3145,4030-4039,4060-4070,4086-4087,4091,4097,4109-4112,4118-4120,4127,4133-4134,4136-4139,4163-4168,4188,4197-4235,4321,4334,4337,4400-4406

Table 4: Dev-set and test-set of CTB7 data split

	Total	Dev-$_{LDC}$	Test-$_{LDC}$	Dev	Test
NS	107,14	561	981	2,084	2,028
NM	8,420	682	917	1,618	1,646
BN	10,079	836	898	2,067	2,038
BC	12,049	0	0	2,367	2,382
NW	10,181	0	0	2,000	2,086

Table 5: Statistics of each genre of CTB7 split (Dev(Test)-$_{LDC}$ are sets of LDC split)

by using the prefixes of the Brown cluster hierarchy at various lengths [3]. After experimenting with many different feature configurations, we eventually settled on the following features:

(d) full string prefixes for w_{-1}, w_0, w_1

6-bit string prefixes for w_{-1}, w_0, w_1

The clusters are best exploited when "anchored" to words or parts of speech (Koo et al., 2008). We found it useful to make the above features in Bigram template, in CRF++ with the first character "B". With this template, a combination of the current output tag and the previous output tag (bigram) is automatically generated. In this case, the combination of the current POS tag and the previous POS tag output is automatically generated.

3.2.3 Lexicon features

We use the same lexicon extracted for word segmentation for POS tagging. We add the following feature for the current word w_0:

$(e)\ POSs(w_0)$

Here, $POSs(w_0)$ are all possible POS tags of the current word w_0 in the lexicon. We also tried to use different lexicons, as well as representing the feature with only one POS tag with the highest frequency. However, the experimental results were not better than those by using the above simple method.

[3]We used the word clustering tool, available from http://www.cs.berkeley.edu/p̃liang/software/brown-cluster-1.2.zip, to produce word clusters.

4 Experiments

We conducted word segmentation and POS tagging experiments on Penn Chinese Treebanks incorporating up to 200-million-word unlabeled data.

4.1 Data Set

To compare with previous studies, we selected the widely used CTB5 (LDC2005T01), and defined the training, development and test sets according to Kruengkrai (2009a). In order to increase the reliability of our findings, we also used CTB6 (LDC2007T36) and CTB7 (LDC2010T07), which are larger than CTB5. For CTB6, we used the same data split as recommended in the CTB6 document [4]. Because CTB7 includes data from various sources and various genres, we made a new data split according to the following criteria:

- Put the test set and the development set data described in CTB7 documents [5] into each data set.
- Put the test set and the development set data of CTB5 into each set.
- Put all double checked files into the test-set. [6]
- Keep the data of different genres and sources in balance.
- Increase the size of the development and test sets to make the evaluation more reliable. [7]

The test set and development set of the CTB7 data split used in this paper are detailed in Table 4, and we used the rest as the training set. Table 5 provides the detailed statistics of each genre: NS (Newswire), NM (News magazine), BN (Broadcast news), BC (Broadcast conversation), NW (Newsgroups weblogs). Table 6 provides the statistics of our experimental settings on the treebanks. The out-of-vocabulary (OOV) is defined as

[4]list-of-files.pdf

[5]This is the same as the CTB6 data split.

[6]In CTB7, sentences checked twice are marked, and they are expected to have higher annotation quality.

[7]CTB5 and CTB6 data splits include small development and test sets.

	# of sent. training	# of sent. dev	OOV rate (word) dev	OOV rate(word & tag) dev	# of sent. test	OOV rate (word) test	OOV rate(word & tag) test
CTB5	18,089	350	0.0811	0.0877	348	0.0347	0.0420
CTB6	23,420	2,079	0.0545	0.0635	2,796	0.0557	0.0636
CTB7	31,131	10,136	0.0549	0.0634	10,180	0.0521	0.0608

Table 6: Statistics of CTB5, CTB6 and CTB7 data splits

	CTB5			CTB6			CTB7		
method	R	P	F_1	R	P	F_1	R	P	F_1
Baseline	0.9791	0.9715	0.9753	0.9504	0.9521	0.9513	0.9503	0.9492	0.9498
+(a) n-gram	0.9830	0.9766	0.9798	0.9567	0.9568	0.9567	0.9562	0.9546	0.9554
+(b) lexicon	0.9809	0.9743	0.9776	0.9545	0.9555	0.9550	0.9548	0.9535	0.9542
+(a)+(b)	0.9845	0.9777	0.9811	0.9575	0.9583	0.9579	0.9576	0.9554	0.9565

Table 7: Results of word segmentation

POS tag method	CTB5	CTB6	CTB7
Baseline	0.9318	0.8999	0.8937
+(c) n-gram	0.9333	0.9014	0.8958
+(d) cluster	0.9350	0.9026	0.8959
+(e) lexicon	0.9346	0.9015	0.8959
+(c)+(d)+(e)	0.9359	0.9048	0.8985

Table 8: F_1 results of segmentation and POS tagging (baseline model for word segmentation)

POS tag method	CTB5	CTB6	CTB7
Baseline	0.9362	0.9061	0.8996
+(c) n-gram	0.9382	0.9078	0.9017
+(d) cluster	0.9403	0.9089	0.9020
+(e) lexicon	0.9399	0.9081	0.9019
+(c)+(d)+(e)	0.9418	0.9112	0.9046

Table 9: F_1 results of segmentation and POS tagging (our best model for word segmentation)

the words in the test set that are not in the training set (Sproat and Emerson, 2003). The development sets were used to obtain the optimal values of tunable parameters and feature configurations.

The unlabeled data for our experiments were taken from the XIN_CMN portion of Chinese Gigaword Version 2.0 (LDC2009T14), which has approximately 311 million words. Some of CTB data and Chinese Gigaword data are from the same source: Xinhua newswire between 1994 and 1998. In order to avoid overlap between the CTB data and the unlabeled data, we used only the articles published in 1991- 1993 and 1999-2004 as unlabeled data, with 204 million words.[8] Note that we only used one million words from this data for word clustering, because the clustering process is time-consuming and the amount is enough to show the impact of cluster feature.

4.2 Parameter Tuning

CRF++ has four major tunable parameters to control the training condition: a, the regularization algorithm; c, the balance between over-fitting and under-fitting; f, the cut-off threshold for the feature frequencies; and p, the number of threads. We used $a = CRF\text{-}L2$ (Gaussian regularization) and $f = 1$. We set p to 12 for all experiments to speed up the training. For the baseline segmentation model, we varied c in the range of [1.0, 5.0] and found that setting $c = 4.0$ yielded the best performance on the development set of CTB7. For our approach, we varied c in the range of [0.3, 5.0] and found that setting $c = 1.0$ yielded the best performance. For the POS tagging model, c was set to 4.0 in all of the methods . For the clustering tool, c (the number of clusters) was set to 1000.

4.3 Experimental Results

We evaluated both word segmentation (Seg) and joint word segmentation and POS tagging (Seg &Tag). We used recall (R), precision (P) and F_1 as evaluation metrics.

The experimental results of word segmentation on CTB5, CTB6 and CTB7 test sets are shown in Table 7, where (a) refers to the n-gram feature generated from the unlabeled data and (b) refers to the lexicon feature. The results show that the n-gram feature was very effective in all experiments and that the combination of (a) and (b) can provide further improvement.

The experimental results of segmentation and POS tagging on CTB5, CTB6 and CTB7 test sets are shown in Table 8 and Table 9. Table 8 shows the results when we used the baseline segmenta-

[8]This may be a too strict setting, but we wanted to test our approach in the fairest way.

	CTB5		CTB6		CTB7	
Method	Seg	Seg&Tag	Seg	Seg&Tag	Seg	Seg&Tag
Ours	0.9628	**0.9316**	**0.9619**	**0.9138**	0.9536	**0.9027**
Baseline	0.9493	0.8934	0.9564	0.9052	0.9493	0.8934
K 09b	0.9628	0.9291	0.9577	0.9063	**0.9547**	0.8989
K 09a	**0.9642**	0.9288	0.9574	0.9061	0.9533	0.8984

Table 12: F_1 Results comparison on development set

Method	Seg	Seg&Tag
Ours	**0.9811**	**0.9418**
Baseline	0.9753	0.9318
Z&C 10	0.9778	0.9367
K 09a	0.9787	0.9367
K 09b	0.9798	0.9400
Jiang 08a	0.9785	0.9341
Jiang 08b	0.9774	0.9337
N&U 07	0.9796	0.9338

Table 10: Comparison with previous studies on CTB5

	CTB6		CTB7	
Methods	Seg	Seg&Tag	Seg	Seg&Tag
Ours	**0.9579**	**0.9112**	**0.9565**	**0.9046**
Baseline	0.9513	0.8999	0.9498	0.8937
K 09a	0.9550	0.9050	0.9540	0.8986
K 09b	0.9551	0.9053	0.9546	0.8990

Table 11: Comparison with previous studies on CTB6 and CTB7

tion model and Table 9 shows the results when we used our best segmentation model (i.e., (a)+(b)). The results show that the cluster features were the most effective ones and that a combination of three types of features achieves the best performance. This suggests that these features are relatively independent in feature characteristics.

The results of our best system are compared with the previous methods in the next section.

4.4 Comparative Results

In this section, we compare our approach with the best previous approaches reported in the literature. The performance scores of previous studies are directly taken from their papers, except for N&U 07 (Nakagawa and Uchimoto, 2007), which is taken from Kruengkrai et al. (2009b). Z&C 10 refers to Zhang and Clark (2010). Two methods in Kruengkrai et al. (2009a; 2009b) are referred to as K 09a and K 09b. Jiang 08a and Jiang 08b refer to Jiang et al. (2008a; 2008b). Table 10 compares F_1 results on CTB5.0. The best score in each column is in boldface. The results of our approach are superior to those of previous studies for both Seg and Seg&Tag.

	p-value		
Models	CTB5	CTB6	CTB7
Ours vs. K 09b(Seg)	0.8054	5.0e-08	≈ 0.0
Ours vs. K 09b(Seg&Tag)	0.7060	1.6e-14	≈ 0.0
Ours vs. Base(Seg)	4.0e-06	1.8e-11	≈ 0.0
Ours vs. Base(Seg&Tag)	2.1e-06	≈ 0.0	≈ 0.0

Table 13: Results of McNemar's test.

We also conducted experiments using the system implemented by Kruengkrai for comparison on CTB6 and CTB7 with two methods (K 09a and K 09b) and the F_1 results are shown in Table 11.

For reference, the results of the development set are also shown in Table 12. Although the Seg performances of CTB5 and CTB7 are lower than K 09a and K 09b , Seg&Tag achieves the best performance on all development sets.

4.5 Statistical Significance Tests

We evaluated statistical significance using McNemar's test [9]. With McNemar' test, we compared the correctness of the labeling decisions of the two models. The null hypothesis is that the disagreements (correct vs. incorrect) are due to chance. For Seg, a word in the system output is considered correct if the word boundary is correctly identified. For Seg &Tag, a word is considered correct only when both the word boundary and its POS tag are correctly identified. Table 13 summarizes the results on test sets. These tests suggest that although the difference from K 09b for CTB5 data is not statistically significant, all other differences are clearly statistically significant ($p < 10^{-5}$).

4.6 Comparison with Self-Training

An alternative method of incorporating unlabeled data is self-training, so we also compared our results to the self-training method. Because no existing research was found concerning the self-training method on word segmentation and POS

[9] We used the version with Yates' correction, using correction factor 0.5

Sentences added	Segmentation F_1
0(Baseline)	0.9498
5k	0.9493
10k	0.9492
30k	0.9482
150k	0.9469
300k	0.9469
600k	0.9468

Table 14: Comparison with self-training (Seg)

sentences added	POS tagging F_1
0(Baseline)	0.8937
5k	0.8926
10k	0.8922
30k	0.8911
50k	0.8908

Table 15: Comparison with self-training (POS)

tagging for Chinese, we tested the simplest self-training here. We analyzed the unlabeled data with the baseline models, added the newly auto-labeled data to the training corpus, and trained a new model. Since the manually labeled data should be considered more important than the unlabeled data (McClosky et al., 2006), we also adjusted the weight of the labeled data to the integer in the range of [1,5] in experiments. The results of all the experiments were not positive – we were not able to obtain any improvement over the baseline models in either word segmentation or POS tagging. Due to space limitation, we only include the results with the labeled data weight = 1. Other weights did not change the conclusion here. Table 14 shows the F_1 results on segmentation with different sizes of the additional data on the CTB7 test set. Table 15 shows the F_1 results on segmentation and POS tagging. The segmentation by the baseline model was used for all of the POS tagging experiments here.

5 Related Work

Our approach is to incorporate large unlabeled data in Chinese word segmentation and POS tagging.

For research using large unlabeled data, Suzuki and Isozaki (2008) and Suzuki et al. (2009) proposed semi-supervised learning algorithms on giga-word-scale unlabeled data and showed performance improvement in POS tagging, syntactic chunking, and named entity recognition. Instead of using specialized semi-supervised learning algorithms, Chen et al. (2009) used features based on sub-structures in auto-parsed data and demonstrated the effectiveness of these features. Koo et al. (2008) presented the use of cluster features. The advantage of the methods by Chen et al. (2009) and Koo et al. (2008) is their simplicity and flexibility. Our research applied these techniques to word segmentation and POS tagging rather than dependency parsing.

Yu et al. (2007) proposed a character-based joint method for word segmentation and POS tagging, in which they introduced an unsupervised method for unknown word learning. However, they only learned the unknown words from the test set. Zhao and Kit (2007; 2008) proposed an approach using unsupervised segmentation criteria as features for Chinese word segmentation. However, their features were only accumulated from the training and test data. Our approach differs in that we used features generated from large unlabeled data and provided richer information, which may be unseen from the training corpus.

Kruengkrai et al. (2009a; 2009b) presented a discriminative word-character hybrid model for joint Chinese word segmentation and POS tagging and achieved the state-of-the-art accuracy for the CTB test sets. Instead of using the hybrid model, we used conceptually simpler pipelined models built with standard CRF tools. Compared with their method, our approach achieved higher performance with the help of unlabeled data.

6 Conclusion

In this paper, we presented a simple yet effective semi-supervised approach to pipelined Chinese segmentation and POS tagging. Through a series of experiments, we demonstrated that our approach provides substantial improvement over the best previously reported methods as well as the baseline methods.

References

Andr F. T.Martins, Dipanjan Das, Noah A. Smith, and Eric P. Xing 2008. *Stacking Dependency Parsers.* In Proceedings of EMNLP-2008, pages 513-521.

Canasai Kruengkrai, Kiyotaka Uchimoto, Jun'ichi Kazama, Yiou Wang, Kentaro Torisawa, and Hitoshi Isahara 2009. *An Error-Driven Word-Character Hybird Model for Joint Chinese Word Segmentation and POS Tagging.* In Proceedings of ACL-IJCNLP-2009, pages 513-521.

Canasai Kruengkrai Kiyotaka Uchimoto, Jun'ichi Kazama, Yiou Wang, Kentaro Torisawa, and Hitoshi Isahara 2009. *Joint Chinese Word Segmentation and POS Tagging Using an Error-Driven Word-Character Hybrid Model.* IEICE transactions on information and systems 92(12), pages 2298-2305.

David McClosky, Eugene Charniak, and Mark Johnson 2006. *Effective self-training for parsing.* In Proceedings of the Human Language Technology Conference of the NAACL-2006, pages 152-159.

Gertjan van Noord 2007. *Using Self-trained Ailexical Preferences to Improve Disambiguation Accuracy.* In Proceedings of IWPT-07, pages 1-10

Hai Zhao, Chang-Ning Huang, Mu Li, and Bao-Liang Lu 2006. *Effective Tag Set Selection in Chinese Word Segmentation via Conditional Random Field Modeling.* In Proceedings of the 20th Pacific Asia Conference on Language, Information and Computation.pages 87-94

Hai Zhao, Chang-Ning Huang, Mu Li, and Bao-Liang Lu 2010. *A Unified Character-Based Tagging Framework for Chinese Word Segmentation.* ACM Transactions on Asian Language Information Processing, 9(2), Article 5.

Hai Zhao and Chunyu Kit 2008. *Exploiting Unlabeled Text with Different Unsupervised Segmentation Criteria for Chinese Word Segmentation.* Research in Computing Science, Vol. 33, pages 93-104.

Hai Zhao and Chunyu Kit 2007. *Incorporating Global Information into Supervised Learning for Chinese Word Segmentation.* In Proceedings of PACLING-2007, pages 66-74.

Jin Kiat Low, Hwee Tou Ng and Wenyuan Guo 2005. *A Maximum Entropy Approach to Chinese Word Segmentation.* In Proceedings of the 4th SIGHAN Workshop on Chinese Language Processing (SIGHAN05), pages 161-164.

John Lafferty, Andrew McCallum, and JFernando Pereira 2001. *Conditional Random Fields: Probabilistic Models for Segmenting and Labeling Sequence Data.* In Proceedings of ICML01, pages 282-289.

Jun'ichi Kazama and Kentaro Torisawa 2008. *Inducing Gazetteers for Named Entity Recognition by Large-scale Clustering of Dependency Relations.* In Proceedings of ACL-2008, pages 665-673.

Jun Suzuki and Hideki Isozaki 2008. *Semi-Supervised Sequential Labeling and Segmentation using Giga-word Scale Unlabeled Data.* In Proceedings of ACL-08: HLT, pages 407-415.

Jun Suzuki, Hideki Isozaki, Xavier Carreras, and Michael Collins 2009. *An Empirical Study of Semi-supervised Structured Conditional Models for Dependency Parsing.* In Proceedings of EMNLP-2009, pages 551-560.

Kun Yu, Sadao Kurohashi, Hao Liu 2007. *Character-based Chinese Word Segmentation and Pos-tagging with Unsupervised Unknown Word Learning.* In Proceedings of NLP-2007, pages 823-826.

Michael Collins 2002. *Ranking Algorithms for Named-entity Extraction: Boosting and the Voted Perceptron.* In Proceedings of ACL-2002, pages 489-496

Nianwen Xue 2003. *Chinese Word Segmentation as Character Tagging.* Computational Linguistics and Chinese Language Processing 8(1), pages 29-48

Richard Sproat and Thomas Emerson 2003. *The First International Chinese Word Segmentation Bakeoff.* In Proceedings of the 2nd SIGHAN Workshop on Chinese Language Processing, pages, 133-143.

Rie Kubota Ando and Tong Zhang 2005. *A Framework for Learning Predictive Structures from Multiple Tasks and Unlabeled Data.* Journal of Machine Learning Research, 6, pages 1817-1853

Scott Miller, Jethran Guinness, and Alex Zamanian 2004. *Name Tagging with Word Clusters and Discriminative Training.* In Proceedings of HLT-2004, pages 337-342

Terry Koo, Xavier Carreras and Michael Collins 2008. *Simple Semi-supervised Dependency Parsing.* In Proceedings of ACL-2008, pages 595-603

Tetsuji Nakagawa and Kiyotaka Uchimoto 2007. *Hybrid Approach to Word Segmentation and Pos Tagging.* In Proceedings of ACL Demo and Poster Sessions, pages 217-220

Wenbin Jiang, Liang Huang, Qun Liu, and Yajuan Lu. 2008. *A Cascaded Linear Model for Joint Chinese Word Segmentation and Part-of-Speech Tagging.* In Proceedings of ACL-2008, pages 897-904

Wenbin Jiang, Haitao Mi and Qun Liu 2008. *Word Lattice Reranking for Chinese Word Segmentation and Part-of-Speech Tagging.* In Proceedings of COLING-2008, pages 385-392

Wenliang Chen, Daisuke Kawahara, Kiyotaka Uchimoto, Yujie Zhang, and Hitoshi Isahara 2008. *Dependency Parsing with Short Dependency Relations in Unlabeled Data.* In Proceedings of IJCNLP-2008

Wenliang Chen, Jun'ichi Kazama, Kiyotaka Uchimoto, and Kentaro Torisawa 2009. *Improving Dependency Parsing with Subtrees from auto-Parsed Data.* In Proceedings of EMNLP-2009, pages 570–579,

Yu-Chieh Wu Jie-Chi Yang and Yue-Shi Lee 2008. *Description of the NCU Chinese Word Segmentation and Part-of-Speech Tagging for SIGHAN Bakeoff 2008.* In Proceedings of the SIGHAN Workshop on Chinese Language Processing, pages 161-166.

Yue Zhang and Stephen Clark 2010. *A Fast Decoder for Joint Word Segmentation and POS-Tagging Using a Single Discriminative Model.* In Proceedings of EMNLP-2010, pages 843-852

CODACT: Towards Identifying Orthographic Variants in Dialectal Arabic

Pradeep Dasigi
Computer Science Department
Columbia University
in the City of New York
pd2359@columbia.edu

Mona Diab
Center for Computational Learning Systems
Columbia University
in the City of New York
mdiab@ccls.columbia.edu

Abstract

Dialectal Arabic (DA) is the spoken vernacular for over 300M people worldwide. DA is emerging as the form of Arabic written in online communication: chats, emails, blogs, etc. However, most existing NLP tools for Arabic are designed for processing Modern Standard Arabic, a variety that is more formal and scripted. Apart from the genre variation that is a hindrance for any language processing, even in English, DA has no orthographic standard, compared to MSA that has a standard orthography and script. Accordingly, a word may be written in many possible inconsistent spellings rendering the processing of DA very challenging. To solve this problem, such inconsistencies have to be normalized. This work is the first step towards addressing this problem, as we attempt to identify spelling variants in a given textual document. We present an unsupervised clustering approach that addresses the problem of identifying orthographic variants in DA. We employ different similarity measures that exploit string similarity and contextual semantic similarity. To our knowledge this is the first attempt at solving the problem for DA. Our approaches are tested on data in two dialects of Arabic - Egyptian and Levantine. Our system achieves the highest Entropy of 0.19 for Egyptian (corresponding to 68% cluster precision) and Levantine (corresponding to 64% cluster precision) respectively. This constitutes a significant reduction in entropy (from 0.47 for Egyptian and 0.51 for Levantine) and improvement in cluster precision (from 29% for both) from the baseline.

1 Introduction

Arabic is the native tongue of over 300M people world wide. The Arabic language exhibits a relatively unique linguistic phenomena known as diglossia (Ferguson, 1959) where two forms of the language live side by side: a standard formal form known as Modern Standard Arabic (MSA) and an informal spoken form, the vernaculars used in everyday communication referred to as Dialectal Arabic (DA). MSA is the only language of education and is used in formal settings and Broadcast news. The only written standard is in MSA using the Arabic script. Technically there are no native speakers of MSA. On the other hand, DA is the mother tongue for all native speakers of Arabic however it is not traditionally a written form of the language and it differs significantly enough from MSA on all levels of linguistic representation that results in huge inconsistencies in orthography. This was not a problem a decade ago from an NLP perspective since all the resources were in MSA. Now with the proliferation of online media and informal genres, DA is ubiquitous online. Users of DA online write in different scripts (Arabic, Romanizations interspersed with digits), they also sometimes write phonemically. Similar to other languages (not unique to DA) in these informal genres, we observe rampant speech effects such as elongations and the use of emoticons within the text which compounds the problem further for processing DA. If NLP tools want to process real Arabic as spoken by its people, they need to address DA seriously. This paper presents an initial attempt at addressing the pervasive inconsistencies in DA orthography in informal media.

We cast the problem of lack of DA orthographic standards as an identification of spelling variants problem using unsupervised clustering techniques. We evaluate our results against a gold corrected set of data in two dialects: Egyptian (EGY) and

Levantine (LEV). We focus our current efforts on identifying the orthographic variants in Arabic script though our work is extendible to the Romanizations as well. Such an identification is a necessary step for normalizing the variation which is useful for addressing the sparseness problem for DA. We contend that there are patterns in the variations that could be captured and processed. Also it is worth pointing out that this problem encompasses the spelling mistakes problem but it goes beyond it to address legitimate orthographic variants. Hence we attempt an approach that is generic enough to cover both scopes.

This paper is organized as follows: in Section 2 we show some of the variations between MSA and DA on different levels of linguistic representation; Section 3 discusses some related work; in section 4 we outline our approach and experimental conditions; in Section 5 we describe the data against which we evaluate our approach; we discuss the results and evaluation in Section 6; in Section 7 we discuss errors and performance of the system and approach proposed; finally, in Section 8 we conclude with some final remarks and a look at some future directions.

2 DA vs. MSA Phenomena

Most of the research effort, to date in creating tools and resources for Arabic has focused on MSA. In recent years we have seen a concentrated effort on making Arabic processing tools on par with English processing tools (Habash and Rambow., 2005; Diab et al., 2007; Kulick, 2010; Green and Manning., 2010). Researchers interested in handling realistic Arabic text have come to the realization that DA needs to be addressed. Applying state of the art MSA processing tools directly to DA yields very low performance proving the significant difference between the two varieties. For instance applying MSA tokenizers to DA yields a performance of 88% which is completely unacceptable as an initial processing tool performance. It is worth noting that state of the art MSA tokenization is at 99.2% (Diab et al., 2007). This low performance on DA can be explained by the genre differences (MSA tools are trained on newswire genres) but compared to English, we do not observe such a huge discrepancy between tokenizers trained on newswire when applied to informal genres. The significant drop in performance can be safely relegated to the inherent differences between the two varieties of Arabic. MSA differs from DA on the phonological, morphological, lexical, syntactic, semantic and pragmatic levels. The degree of variation depends on the specific dialect of Arabic. For instance, phonologically MSA would pronounce the word for dress as *fustAn* and spell it فستان while the same word in LEV is pronounced as *fusTAn*[1] with an emphatic T and could possibly be written phonemically in LEV as فوصطان. Morphologically, DA exhibits simpler inflectional morphology than MSA overall however cliticization is more nuanced rendering tokenization a more complex problem in DA than in MSA. For example, DA has lost all explicit marking of grammatical case and dual marking on verbal predicates. The MSA phrase *AlmwZfAn AklA*, الموظفان اكلا, meaning 'the employees_dual_nominative ate_dual', becomes *AlmwZfyn AlAtnyn AkAlw*, الموظفين الاتنين اكلو, 'the *two* employees_plural_no_case ate_plural'. Hence we note the loss of dual inflection marking and nominative case marking. On the other hand, clitization is more complex in DA as follows: EGY *mAHkytlhAlhw$*, ماحكيتلهالهوش, 'she did not recount it to him' is expressed in three words in MSA as *lm tHkyhA lh* لم تحكيها له. The lexical, syntactic, semantic and pragmatic variations abound between MSA and DA. The phonological and morphological differences lend themselves directly to the orthographic variation problem exhibited with DA. Writers of DA use a myriad of scripts to encode DA. All of which are used inconsistently even within the writings of the same author in the same post/article/blog. The most frequent scripts used are Arabic and Romanization. We note that people have use also Hebrew and Cyrillic scripts to write Arabic as well. For Arabic script we see inconsistencies in characters that exhibit regional variations such as the *qAf* sound .ق. This letter is pronounced as a glottal stop ´ in EGY and LEV but as a *g* sound in the Gulf states and *q* sound in Tunisia, in most cases. Speakers and writers pertaining to these different dialects could render it in the orthography as it appears in a word such as *he said qAl* قال as *Ál* آل [EGY], *gAl* جال [Gulf] or *qAl* قال [Tunisian]. Moreover, we observe more severe variants in the Romanized script for the same word where the writers can render the EGY as *2Al*, *AAl*,

[1] We use the Buckwalter Arabic Transliteration standard for the Romanized Arabic throughout the paper. www.qamus.org

or *qAl*. For the purposes of this paper we will focus our discussion on identifying the orthographic variants only in the Arabic script leaving the handling of orthographic variants in Romanization for future work.[2]

3 Related Work

Most of the recent work in the area of orthographic variant detection and spelling correction has been towards resolving inconsistencies in spellings of Named Entities(NE). Huang et al. (2008) use NE spelling variant detection to improve the performance of Machine Translation (MT) and Information Extraction (IE) systems. (Habash and Metsky, 2008) cluster Urdu phrases mapping to the same English phrase to automatically learn morphological variation rules. Since Urdu is a morphologically rich language, such variations result in many OOV words. They use the these rules learned, as a part of MT system to replace OOV Urdu words with in-vocabulary words online. Raghavan and Allan (2005) use the edit distance metric along with generative models trained from Automatic Speech Recognition (ASR) output to cluster queries to improve performance of Information Retrieval (IR) systems. Bhagat and Hovy (2007) attempted to generate all possible spelling variations of a person's name. One method is supervised and uses CMU speech dictionary to train a phonetic model. Another is to cluster a large set of names that are known to sound similar using Soundex (Knuth, 1973). Although some earlier work related to spelling variations (Golding and Roth, 1999) dealt with the generalized problem, most of the recent work is confined to NEs.This is because of the relevance of the problem to NLP applications such as MT, IE, IR and ASR. Accordingly we note that the problem we try to solve is more generic since the lack of orthographic standard in DA affects the spellings of all kinds of words.

4 Approach

Our goal is to identify orthographic variations in textual DA. We build a system, CODACT, that aims at identifying and eventually normalizing such DA orthographic variants. We use techniques noted in the spelling correction literature. Our approach is mainly unsupervised. We view the problem as a clustering problem where our goal is to identify if two strings are similar, and hence cluster together. To that end we explore three basic similarity measures: (a) String based Similarity as direct Levenshtein Edit Distance; (b) String based Similarity Biased Edit Distance; and (c) Contextual String Similarity. We model the strings of interest in a vector space. We build a matrix for the string types of interest. We induce the clusters from the matrix by grouping the strings in the row entries together based on the similarity of their respective vectors in the matrix. We use Cosine Similarity between vectors and we use the implementation of the CLUTO Repeated Bisection (RB) algorithm with cosine similarity being the measure of similarity between vectors. (Zhao and Karypis, 2001). CLUTO is very suitable for clustering high dimensional datasets. CLUTO's repeated bisection partition method is used for clustering. In this method, for obtaining a *k* -way clustering, *k-1* repeated bisections are made. Each partition is made to the input dataset such that the clustering criterion function is optimized.

The row entries for the matrix are referred to as the focal string types of interest. We vary the dimensions as follows: (a) for N focal words, we have the same N focal words in the matrix dimensions, yielding an NxN matrix; or (b) the dimensions are all the string types in the corpus of interest yielding an NxM matrix. The cells of the matrix are populated based on one of the different similarity measures or a combination of them after normalization. We describe the different similarity measures next.

4.1 String Based Similarity Metrics

Strings that vary from each other minimally are likely to be orthographic variants of one another. Following this intuition, strings are grouped based on their string edit distance. We explore the basic known Levenshtein Edit Distance measure as in (Levenshtein, 1966) (LEDM). Moreover we extend the LEDM to account for known phonological variations on the character level. We refer to this as the Biased Edit Distance Metric (BEDM). BEDM has the same exact formulation as LEDM as a metric however it is more relaxed in that it treats letters that are considered similar as if they are the same, i.e. they are not *substitutions* of each

[2]It is worth noting that tools such as Yamli and Maren which transliterate Romanization to Arabic script serve as in interesting platform for handling the Romanization problem that could be easily leveraged.

other. The intuition behind adding such a bias is the fact that Arabic letters may have different pronunciations depending on the context. For example, the letter ا might have a sound equivalent to the any of letters أ, آ, ؤ and ئ. This is ignored by LEDM, and they are treated as different letters therefore incurring the substitution penalty. When BEDM is applied, any two letters that have the same sound are treated as a match. For example, (1)*fstAn*, 'dress', فستان, and the possible variants (2)*fstAn*, (3)*fSTAn*, (4)*fsTAn*, and (5)*fjTAn* would have the following calculations: (1) and (2) would be a perfect match, i.e. a distance of 0 according to both LEDM and BEDM; (1) and (3) would be penalized for substituting *S, T* for *s,t* in (1), therefore a distance of 0.4 according to LEDM, however for BEDM *s* and *S* are considered similar to each other and so are *t* and *T*, then the distance of (1) and (3) is 0. Similarily for (1) and (4) according to LEDM the distance is 0.2, but for BEDM the distance is 0. For (1) and (5) the LEDM will be 0.4 and for BEDM it will be 0.2. Hence, BEDM is a more nuanced and relaxed form of LEDM. The list of similar letters is taken from scholar seeded studies of phonological variations across different DA. The list is rendered in Table 1. We refer to this list as sound change rules (SCR).[3] The SCR are not always symmetric, for example a *v* can be replaced with a *S* but not vice versa.

<table>
<tr><th>Letter</th><th>Similar Sounding Letters</th></tr>
<tr><td>A</td><td>{, <, >, ', &, }, w, y, |</td></tr>
<tr><td>'</td><td>A,{, }, <, >, |, y, &,w</td></tr>
<tr><td>}</td><td>A, y, &, ', {, <, >, |,w</td></tr>
<tr><td>&</td><td>A, y, }, ', {, <, >, |,w</td></tr>
<tr><td>|</td><td>A, y, ', {, <, >, }</td></tr>
<tr><td>{</td><td>A, y, &, ', }, <, >, |</td></tr>
<tr><td><</td><td>A, ', {, >, |, }</td></tr>
<tr><td>></td><td>A, ', {, <, |, }</td></tr>
<tr><td>t</td><td>T, v</td></tr>
<tr><td>v</td><td>s, t, S</td></tr>
<tr><td>j</td><td>q, y, $</td></tr>
<tr><td>H</td><td>h, E</td></tr>
<tr><td>d</td><td>*, D</td></tr>
<tr><td>*</td><td>d, z, Z</td></tr>
<tr><td>z</td><td>*, Z, d</td></tr>
<tr><td>s</td><td>$, S, v</td></tr>
<tr><td>$</td><td>s, v</td></tr>
<tr><td>S</td><td>s</td></tr>
<tr><td>D</td><td>Z, d, z, *</td></tr>
<tr><td>T</td><td>S, Z, t</td></tr>
<tr><td>Z</td><td>T, D, z, d, *</td></tr>
<tr><td>E</td><td>H</td></tr>
<tr><td>g</td><td>E, x</td></tr>
<tr><td>q</td><td>', A, }, k, j</td></tr>
<tr><td>k</td><td>q</td></tr>
<tr><td>h</td><td>p, A</td></tr>
<tr><td>p</td><td>h, t</td></tr>
<tr><td>w</td><td>&, A, Y</td></tr>
<tr><td>y</td><td>}, A, Y</td></tr>
<tr><td>Y</td><td>y, A</td></tr>
</table>

Table 1: Sound Change Rules for Arabic Letters as obtained from Linguistic Studies

4.2 Contextual String Similarity

We explore another relatedness measure of contextual string similarity (CSS). The intuition is that if two strings are variants of each other as they are semantically similar, they are bound to appear with similar contexts. Accordingly we model this notion via representing strings with their context co-occurrence vectors. In this framework , we represent the co-occurrence frequency of the focal string and dimensional string in all the sentences in the corpus within a window of 3 tokens. The observations are aggregated and used in the cell. If the focal string and the dimensional string never co-occur, then the cell value is set to 0. Contextual Similarity Metric (CSS) between two words is defined as a cosine similarity between their context vectors.

[3]We are aware that this list can be further refined to reflect the specific dialect under investigation. We plan to incorporate a better customized SCR depending on the variety of DA.

4.3 Experimental Conditions

We experimented with each of these measures in isolation and in combination. In the case of combination, we normalized the values of metrics. Table 2 illustrates the values contained in the cells of the constructed matrices in the different conditions.

We have two different matrix dimension sizes depending on how extensive the feature space is. The first case is NxN, meaning that the set of words corresponding to both the rows and columns of the matrix are the focal words. The second case has all the unique words in the corpus representing the columns, making it NxM. This yields 6 isolated conditions and 8 combined conditions.

Metric	Cell Values
LEDM	1.0 - Normalized Levenshtein Distance
BEDM	1.0 - Normalized Levenshtein Distance biased by phonetic similarity across letters
CSS	Co-occurrence frequencies
LEDM+BEDM	Mean of LEDM and BEDM
CSS+LEDM	Mean of LEDM and Normalized CSS (both are in range $\{0, 1\}$)
CSS+BEDM	Mean of BEDM and Normalized CSS
CSS+LEDM+BEDM	Mean of LEDM, BEDM and Normalized CSS

Table 2: Matrix Cell Values

- LEDM-NxN where the similarity measure is a LEDM and the matrix size is NxN
- BEDM-NxN where the similarity measure is a BEDM and the matrix size is NxN
- CSS-NxN where the similarity measure is a CSS and the matrix size is NxN
- LEDM-NxM where the similarity measure is a LEDM and the matrix size is NxM
- BEDM-NxM where the similarity measure is a BEDM and the matrix size is NxM
- CSS-NxM where the similarity measure is a CSS and the matrix size is NxM
- LEDM-BEDM-NxN where the similarity measure is a combination of LEDM and BEDM and the matrix size is NxN
- LEDM-CSS-NxN where the similarity measure is a combination of LEDM and CSS and the matrix size is NxN
- BEDM-CSS-NxN where the similarity measure is a combination of CSS and BEDM and the matrix size is NxN
- LEDM-BEDM-CSS-NxN where the similarity measure is a combination of LEDM, BEDM, and CSS the matrix size is NxN
- LEDM-BEDM-NxM where the similarity measure is a combination of LEDM and BEDM and the matrix size is NxM
- LEDM-CSS-NxM where the similarity measure is a combination of LEDM and CSS and the matrix size is NxM
- BEDM-CSS-NxM where the similarity measure is a combination of CSS and BEDM and the matrix size is NxM
- LEDM-BEDM-CSS-NxM where the similarity measure is a combination of LEDM, BEDM, and CSS the matrix size is NxM

5 Evaluation Data

In order to measure the performance of this approach we need data that has the variants identified. We created such data by asking native speakers of DA to normalize variants into a standard conventionalized form in Arabic script. We targeted two dialects of Arabic: Egyptian (EGY) and Levantine (LEV). For EGY we specifically focused on Cairene Egyptian. For Levantine, we had a collection of Palestinian, Jordanian, Lebanese and Syrian Dialectal data. Most of the data is considered Syrian in our LEV collection however. Both data sets for both DA are derived from the web (Diab et al., 2010). The data is part of a larger collection we refer to in this paper as COMMENTDA collection. COMMENTDA comprises 3M token strings for EGY and 3M token strings for LEV. For EGY we had 2 annotators and an adjudicator, and for LEV we had 4 annotators and an adjudicator. The annotators were instructed to identify tokens that are considered incorrect orthographically according to a specific convention that we devised known as CODA (Conventionalized Orthography for Dialectal Arabic) after being trained on CODA (Habash et al., 2011). The annotators we asked to identify three different classes of variation from the CODA convention: (a) change in spelling of a string which included dealing with speech effects such as elongations, (b) introduction of spaces or splitting a string into multiple strings, and (c) deletion of spaces or merging strings. Many corrections included simultaneously both a spelling change and a split or merge of a string as well. Table 3 gives detailed statistics of the annotated data for EGY and LEV, respectively.

Category	EGY		LEV	
	Tokens	**Types**	**Tokens**	**Types**
Inspected	39328	12703	74450	19045
Spelling Changes Only	6835	3651	5877	3519
Splits	1373	751	1013	590
Splits Only	752	288	768	169
Merges	633	440	789	598
Two String Merges	72	61	119	109
More Than Two String Merges	561	379	670	489
Merges Only	374	211	357	264
Unique Changes	7961	4150	7002	3952
All Changes Including Overlaps	9248	4720	7913	4326
Unchanged	30080	7983	66537	14719
Common Strings Across Annotators	1541	843	3271	1759
Inter-Annotator Agreements	1080 (70.08%)	576 (68.33%)	2688 (82.18%)	1489 (84.65%)

Table 3: Annotation Statistics

It is worth noting that roughly 24% of the EGY data had changes of different types on the token level corresponding to 37% of changes to the types for EGY. For LEV, only 11% of the tokens were changed corresponding to 23% of the types that were changed. This suggests that the EGY data had a lot more variability. It was actually noted that a lot of the EGY data was not consistently EGY but rather from other DA compared to LEV that was considered relatively homogeneous. The last row in the table shows the number of cases where annotators agreed with each other on the correction. It also shows their percentages to the number of common annotations as shown by the row above it.

We created the gold data clusters of variants by grouping all the strings that are mapped to the same corrected CODA form. This data consisted of 290 clusters of strings in LEV with an average of 2.6 orthographic variants per cluster, and 312 string clusters in EGY with an average of 2.5 variant per cluster. All our experiments are conducted on surface forms of the strings with no preprocessing.

6 Evaluation

In order to derive statistics to build our matrices, we use two data sets: COMMENTDA and an augmented data set (RCorpora) which is double the size of COMMENTDA for each dialect. RCorpora comprises 6M strings for EGY, and 6M strings for LEV. In the NxN matrix conditions, the size of the corpora used to derive the statistics only affects the conditions involving CSS. In the NxM conditions, the corpora sizes affect the number of matrix dimensions as well as the cell values for the CSS conditions. Application of seven metrics to four class-data size combinations gives 25 distinct runs per dialect since in NxN case, augmenting the data does not change the metrics LEDM, BEDM, and LEDM+BEDM. It has to be noted that for NxM experiments this is not the case. Table 4 gives the various statistics on the different data sizes of unique string types.

Each clustering output is compared with the gold-standard clusters using Purity and Entropy measures (Zhao and Karypis, 2001). Every word in a given cluster in the output belongs to one or more gold clusters. These gold clusters are referred to as relevant gold clusters of the given output cluster. Purity or precision of a cluster is the fraction of its words in its relevant gold clusters. Entropy gives the measure of ambiguity in the clustering output. The larger the number of word in a relevant gold cluster, the higher the entropy value. In addition to these measures, the value of recall is also calculated. This equals the fraction of words in the relevant gold clusters that are in the given cluster. Together these three measures give a complete assessment of the quality of the output clusters. As a baseline for comparison, where strings are randomly assigned to clusters assuming the gold number of clusters per dialect. Table 5 shows the results of all the experiments described.

	COMMENTDA		COMMENTDA+RCorpora (C+R)	
	EGY	LEV	EGY	LEV
NxN	729	717	729	717
NxM	205088	237598	433697	410206

Table 4: Data Size Variations in the two dimensions conditions

7 Discussion

All the systems outperform the random baseline. The best results are presented in bold in Table 5.

Phonological Bias From the results, it can be seen that of the individual metrics, BEDM consistently performs better than LEDM. This shows that introducing a phonological bias while matching letters does have a significant positive effect in identifying spelling variants. We believe that this effect will be more pronounced if the SCR are more tailored to the specific dialect under study. We note that CSS has the worst performance of the three individual metrics in all cases. This may be attributed to the level of processing of the data. The data is dealt with specifically on the surface level and Arabic being a very rich morphological language results in a very sparse distribution of forms. This can be mitigated by using even larger corpora. Typically in such studies that rely on distributional similarity an order of magnitude larger than what we employed is exploited. We relegate this to future work.

Combined Metrics Combination of LEDM and BEDM showed better precision, recall, and entropy than each of them in isolation in every case for both dialects. Although adding CSS has shows improvement in LEDM, mainly in EGY, it actually worsened the performance of BEDM. This is more evident when CSS+LEDM+BEDM is compared with LEDM+BEDM. Almost all the quality measures show that CSS metric adds noise.

NxM vs. NxN Using a bigger class of words as a feature set for vector similarity significantly improves the performance of the system. This holds for all the metrics in both the dialects.

Data Augmentation Although there are slight improvements due to increase in data, on the whole this does not seem to affect the performance of the system significantly. We only see some effect in the CSS measures which is expected.

7.1 Error analysis

Cluster type	Members
Gold	<n$' w<n$' An$A'
LEDM	w<n$ w<n$' wgnY wgnYY
BEDM	<n$' An$A' w<n$'
LEDM+BEDM	<n$' An$A' w<n$'

The example above shows a comparison between LEDM and BEDM metrics. The clusters in second and third columns are the ones nearest to the gold cluster in first column. It can be observed that An$A' is not a part of the LEDM cluster since the word has more dissimilar letters. However, BEDM captures the fact that the words are phonologically similar. The example below shows a similar pattern too. LEDM differentiates ||mdh from the other words too much to identify it to be a potential variant.

Cluster type	Members
Gold	jAmddp ||mdh jAAmdp jAmdh
LEDM	jAmddp jAAmdp jAmdh
BEDM	jAmddp ||mdh jAAmdp jAmdh
LEDM+BEDM	jAmddp ||mdh jAAmdp jAmdh

The next example illustrates the advantage of combining metrics. BEDM gives both higher precision and recall than LEDM when compared to the gold cluster. However, both of them do not have perfect precision or recall while the combined metric has both.

Cluster type	Members
Gold	btAEtY btEty
LEDM	btAEtY bnt bt
BEDM	btAEtY btEty ty
LEDM + BEDM	btAEtY btEty

A relaxed similarity metric does not necessarily result in higher clustering recall. In the next example, BEDM gives a lower recall than LEDM. However, the combined metric does better than the individual edit distance metrics in this example too.

Cluster type	Members
Gold	byqwlw byqwlh byqwlwA byqlh
LEDM	byqwlw byqwlh byqwlwA yqwlp yqwlh
BEDM	byqwlw byqwlwA
LEDM + BEDM	byqlh byqwlh byqwlw byqwlwA

Dialect	Matrix Size	Similarity Metric	Quality Metric					
			Precision		Recall		Entropy	
			C	C+R	C	C+R	C	C+R
		Baseline	29.63		34.68		0.4728	
		LEDM	44.37		50.33		0.3185	
		BEDM	58.85		63.9		0.2342	
		LEDM+BEDM	61.74		67.22		0.2084	
	NxN	CSS	25.21	23.45	31.12	34.2	0.2779	0.2575
		CSS+LEDM	45.03	44.59	50.05	49.86	0.3184	0.3207
EGY		CSS+BEDM	55.83	56.29	63.8	63.04	0.2433	0.238
		CSS+LEDM+BEDM	61.91	59.71	66.46	66.93	0.2218	0.2229
		LEDM	53.96	55.07	56.5	57.45	0.3047	0.3079
		BEDM	61.41	59.04	65.23	63.33	0.2401	0.2425
		LEDM+BEDM	**67.14**	**68.51**	**69.97**	**71.2**	**0.2006**	**0.196**
	NxM	CSS	35.94	36.06	36.57	38.09	0.4184	0.4074
		CSS+LEDM	54.54	56.71	56.69	58.3	0.3027	0.2981
		CSS+BEDM	60.63	58.79	64.28	63.9	0.2419	0.2393
		CSS+LEDM+BEDM	66.26	68.23	69.69	70.92	0.1997	0.1988
		Baseline	28.67		31.10		0.5177	
		LEDM	51.44		54.66		0.2831	
		BEDM	54.22		60.61		0.2403	
		LEDM+BEDM	63.92		64.67		0.2226	
	NxN	CSS	30.4	23.4	24.11	30.07	0.2142	0.2602
		CSS+LEDM	50.82	51.18	54.49	55	0.2883	0.2808
LEV		CSS+BEDM	54.62	56.12	62.51	60.7	0.2338	0.2459
		CSS+LEDM+BEDM	60.6	61.41	64.49	64.41	0.2156	0.2259
		LEDM	57.11	56.76	57.68	57.38	0.2728	0.2797
		BEDM	61.54	64.18	64.06	65.31	0.2305	0.2132
		LEDM+BEDM	**65.37**	**64.98**	**65.79**	**65.23**	**0.2091**	**0.205**
	NxM	CSS	45.21	37.53	27.48	34.21	0.3148	0.3992
		CSS+LEDM	57.61	55.36	57.33	57.2	0.2731	0.2745
		CSS+BEDM	59.15	63.17	62.6	65.06	0.2234	0.2113
		CSS+LEDM+BEDM	**64.17**	**64.34**	**65.36**	**65.92**	**0.2099**	**0.1998**

Table 5: Results

8 Conclusion and Future Work

We compared surface and contextual metrics for identifying spelling variants in DA. We also evaluated all the combinations of those metrics. We present an initial system CODACT. Our results hold clear cross-dialectal trends, showing that string similarity metric with a phonological bias, combined with simple edit distance as a similarity metric is better for this task than raw contextual similarity when the data is limited. The next step in this approach is to refine the co-occurrence model used in our approach. Using lemma forms instead of the surface forms can yield a potential improvement since Arabic is a morphologically rich language. Eventually we plan to develop a system that will automatically normalize orthographic variations in Dialectal Arabic to the CODA convention.

References

[Golding and Roth1999] Andrew R. Golding and Dan Roth. 1999. *A winnow-based approach to context-sensitive spelling correction* Machine Learning, 34(1-3):107–130.

[Ferguson1959] Charles A. Ferguson. 1959. *Diglossia, Word.* Journal of the Linguistic Circle of New York, Vol. 15, No. 2, August 1959, pp. 325-340

[Habash and Metsky2008] Nizar Habash and Hayden Metsky 1959. *Automatic Learning of Morphological Variations for Handling Out-of-Vocabulary Terms in Urdu-English Machine Translation.* 8th AMTA conference, Hawaii, 21-25 October 2008

[Knuth1973] Donald E. Knuth. *The Art of Computer Programming – Volume 3: Sorting and Searching* Addison- Wesley Publishing Company, 1973.

[Huang et al.2008] Fei Huang , Ahmad Emami and Imed Zitouni. *When Harry Met Harri: Cross-lingual Name Spelling Normalization.* Proceedings of the 2008 Conference on Empirical Methods in Natural Language Processing, pages 391–399.

[Hema Raghavan and James Allan2005] Hema Raghavan and James Allan. *Matching Inconsistently Spelled Names in Automatic Speech Recognizer*

Output for Information Retrieval. Proceedings of the conference on Human Language Technology and Empirical Methods in Natural Language Processing, 2005.

[Kernighan et al.1990] Mark D. Kernighan, Kenneth W. Church, and William A. Gale. 1990. *A spelling correction program based on a noisy channel model.* Proceedings of COLING-90, pages 205–210

[Diab et al.2010] Mona Diab, Nizar Habash, Owen Rambow, Mohamed Al Tantawy, Yassine Benajiba. 2010. *COLABA: Arabic Dialect Annotation and Processing.*. Proceedings of the Workshop on Semitic Language Processing, LREC, May, Malta

[Habash et al.2011] Nizar Habash, Mona Diab, Owen Rambow. 2011. *Conventional Orthography for Dialectal Arabic (CODA) V.1.0.*. Technical Report 137382, `http://academiccommons.columbia.edu/catalog/ac:137382`, Columbia University, New York, NY, USA

[Diab et al.2007] Mona Diab, Kadri Hacioglu and Daniel Jurafsky. 2007. *Automated Methods for Processing Arabic Text: From Tokenization to Base Phrase Chunking.* In Arabic Computational Morphology: Knowledge-based and Empirical Methods.

[Habash and Rambow.2005] Nizar Habash and Owen Rambow. 2005. *Arabic Tokenization, Morphological Analysis, and Part-of-Speech Tagging in One Fell Swoop.* Proceedings of the Conference of American Association for Computational Linguistics (ACL'05).

[Bhagat and Hovy.2007] Rahul Bhagat and Eduard Hovy. 2007. *Phonetic Models for Generating Spelling Variants.* Proceedings of the 20th international joint conference on Artifical intelligence.

[Green and Manning.2010] Spence Green and Christopher D. Manning. 2010. *Better Arabic Parsing: Baselines, Evaluations, and Analysis.* Proceedings of the 23rd International Conference on Computational Linguistics (Coling 2010).

[Kulick2010] Seth Kulick. 2010. *Simultaneous Tokenization and Part-of-Speech Tagging for Arabic without a Morphological Analyzer.* Proceedings of the ACL 2010 Conference Short Papers.

[Levenshtein1966] V. I. Levenshtein. 1966. *Binary codes capable of correcing deletions,insertions and reversals.* Soviet Physics Doklady, Vol. 10, p.707–710.

[Zhao and Karypis2001] Ying Zhao and George Karypis. 2004. *Empirical and Theoretical Comparisons of Selected Criterion Functions for Document Clustering.* Machine Learning, Volume 55 Issue 3, June 2004.

Enhancing the HL-SOT Approach to Sentiment Analysis via a Localized Feature Selection Framework

Wei Wei
Department of Computer and Information Science
Norwegian University of Science and Technology
wwei@idi.ntnu.no

Jon Atle Gulla
Department of Computer and Information Science
Norwegian University of Science and Technology
jag@idi.ntnu.no

Abstract

In this paper, we propose a Localized Feature Selection (LFS) framework tailored to the HL-SOT approach to sentiment analysis. Within the proposed LFS framework, each node classifier of the HL-SOT approach is able to perform classification on target texts in a locally customized index term space. Extensive empirical analysis against a human-labeled data set demonstrates that with the proposed LFS framework the classification performance of the HL-SOT approach is enhanced with computational efficiency being greatly gained. To find the best feature selection algorithm that caters to the proposed LFS framework, five classic feature selection algorithms are comparatively studied, which indicates that the TS, DF, and MI algorithms achieve generally better performances than the CHI and IG algorithms. Among the five studied algorithms, the TS algorithm is best to be employed by the proposed LFS framework.

1 Introduction

With tens and thousands of review texts being generated online, it becomes increasingly challenging for an individual to exhaustively collect and study the online reviews. Therefore, research on automatic sentiment analysis on review texts has emerged as a popular topic at the crossroads of information retrieval and computational linguistics.

Sentiment analysis on product reviews aims at extracting sentiment information from texts. It includes two tasks, i.e., labeling a target text[1] with 1) the product's attributes it mentions (attributes identification task), and 2) the corresponding sentiments mentioned therein (sentiment annotation task). Recently, Wei and Gulla proposed the HL-SOT approach (Wei and Gulla, 2010), i.e., Hierarchical Learning (HL) with Sentiment Ontology Tree (SOT), that is able to achieve the two tasks in one hierarchical classification process. In the HL-SOT approach, each target text is encoded by a vector in a globally unified d-dimensional index term space and is respectively labeled by different nodes[2] of SOT in a hierarchical manner. Although the HL-SOT approach is reported with promising classification performance on tasks of sentiment analysis, its computational efficiency, especially as d increases, becomes very low. Furthermore, as d increases it will have more chance to index noisy term into the globally unified index term space so that the classification performance of the HL-SOT approach might be depressed. Hence, we argue that if a locally customized index term space could be constructed for each node respectively, both the computational efficiency and the classification performance of the HL-SOT approach would be improved.

In this paper, we propose a Localized Feature Selection (LFS) framework tailored to the HL-SOT approach. The rationale of the proposed LFS framework draws on the following two observations. Firstly, a feature term that is relevant to a node is usually irrelevant to nodes which stay at another branch of SOT. For example, "ergonomics" might be a feature term for the node "design and usability" (see Fig. 1) but it is irrelevant to the node "image quality". Secondly, a feature ter-

[1] Each product review to be analyzed is called target text in the following of this paper.

[2] If specified otherwise in the following of this paper the term "node" refers to the classifier of the node.

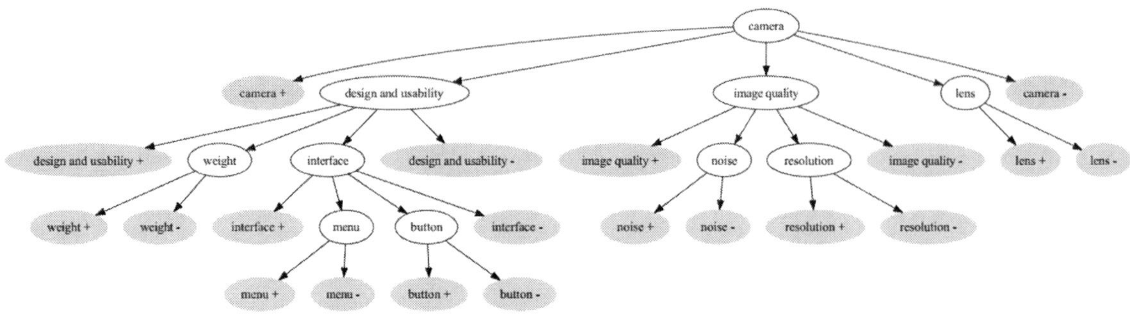

Figure 1: an example of part of a SOT for digital camera

m might become insignificant for child nodes of i even if the feature term is significant to i. For example, for a sentence commenting on a digital camera like "40D handles noise very well", terms such as "noise" and "well" are significant feature terms for the node "noise". However, the term "noise" becomes insignificant for its child nodes "noise +" and "noise -", since the hierarchical classification characteristic of the HL-SOT approach that a node only processes target texts which are labeled as true by its parent node ensures that each target text handled by the nodes "noise +" and "noise -" is already classified as related to "noise".

In the proposed LFS framework, the concept of "local hierarchy" is defined and introduced as delimitation of local scope of nodes. The localized feature selection process is conducted for each node within its local scope to generate the customized index term space for the node. The proposed LFS framework is empirically analyzed on a human-labeled data set. The experimental results show that with the proposed LFS framework the classification performance of the HL-SOT approach is enhanced and the computational efficiency is significantly improved. To test which is the best to be employed by the proposed LFS framework, we further comparatively study five classic feature selection algorithms respectively based on document frequency (DF) (Manning et al., 2008), mutual information (MI) (Manning et al., 2008; Church and Hanks, 1990), χ^2-statistic (CHI) (Manning et al., 2008), information gain (IG) (Mitchell, 1997), and term strength (TS) (Wilbur and Sirotkin, 1992). The comparatively experimental results suggest that the TS, DF, and MI algorithms achieve generally better performance than the CHI and IG algorithms. Among the five employed algorithms, the TS algorithm is the best to be employed by the proposed LFS framework. This paper makes the following contributions:

- We propose a LFS framework to enhance the classification performance and improve the computational efficiency of the HL-SOT approach;
- We conduct a comparative study on five feature selection algorithms that can be employed in the proposed LFS.

The remainder of the paper is organized as follows. In section 2, we discuss an overview of related work on sentiment analysis. In section 3, we review the HL-SOT approach proposed in (Wei and Gulla, 2010). In section 4, we present the proposed LFS framework. The empirical analysis and the results are presented in section 5. Finally, we conclude the paper and discuss the future work in section 6.

2 Related Work

Research on sentiment analysis was originally performed to extract overall sentiments from target texts. However, as shown in the experiments in (Turney, 2002), the whole sentiment of a document is not necessarily the sum of its parts. Recent work has shifted the focus from overall document sentiment to sentiment analysis based on product attributes (Hu and Liu, 2004; Popescu and Etzioni, 2005; Ding and Liu, 2007; Liu et al., 2005).

Document overall sentiment analysis is to summarize the overall sentiment in the document, which relies on two finer levels of sentiment annotation: *word-level sentiment annotation* and *phrase-level sentiment annotation*. The *word-level sentiment annotation* is to utilize the polarity annotation of words in each sentence and summarize the overall sentiment of each sentiment-bearing word to infer the overall sentiment within the text (Hatzivassiloglou and Wiebe, 2000; Andreevskaia and Bergler, 2006; Esuli and Sebastiani, 2005; Esuli and Sebastiani, 2006; Hatzivassiloglou and McKeown, 1997; Kamps et al., 2004; Devitt and Ahmad, 2007; Yu and Hatzivassiloglou, 2003). The *phrase-level sentiment annotation* focuses sentiment annotation on phrases not words with concerning that atomic units of expression is not individual words but rather appraisal groups (Whitelaw et al., 2005). In (Wilson et al., 2005), the concepts of *prior polarity* and *contextual polarity* were proposed. This paper presented a system that is able to automatically identify the *contextual polarity* for a large subset of sentiment expressions. In (Turney, 2002), an unsupervised learning algorithm was proposed to classify reviews as recommended or not recommended by averaging sentiment annotation of phrases in reviews that contain adjectives or adverbs. However, the performances of these approaches are not satisfactory for sentiment analysis on product reviews, where sentiment on each attribute of a product could be so complicated that it is unable to be expressed by overall document sentiment.

Attributes-based sentiment analysis is to analyze sentiment based on each attribute of a product. In (Hu and Liu, 2004), mining product features was proposed together with sentiment polarity annotation for each opinion sentence. In that work, sentiment analysis was performed at the product attributes level. In (Liu et al., 2005), a system with framework for analyzing and comparing consumer opinions of competing products was proposed. The system made users be able to clearly see the strengths and weaknesses of each product in the minds of consumers in terms of various product features. In (Popescu and Etzioni, 2005), Popescu and Etzioni not only analyzed polarity of opinions regarding product features but also ranked opinions based on their strength. In (Liu et al., 2007), Liu et al. proposed Sentiment-PLSA that analyzed blog entries and viewed them as a document generated by a number of hidden sentiment factors. These sentiment factors may also be factors based on product attributes. In (Lu and Zhai, 2008), Lu et al. proposed a semi-supervised topic models to solve the problem of opinion integration based on the topic of a product's attributes. The work in (Titov and McDonald, 2008) presented a multi-grain topic model for extracting the ratable attributes from product reviews. In (Lu et al., 2009), the problem of rated attributes summary was studied with a goal of generating ratings for major aspects so that a user could gain different perspectives towards a target entity. In a most recent research work (Wei and Gulla, 2010), Wei and Gulla proposed the HL-SOT approach that sufficiently utilizes the hierarchical relationships among a product attributes and solves the sentiment analysis problem in a hierarchical classification process. However, the HL-SOT approach proposed in (Wei and Gulla, 2010) uses a globally unified index term space to encode target texts for different nodes which is deemed to limit the performance of the HL-SOT approach. Therefore, the LFS framework proposed in this paper aims at overcoming the weakness of the HL-SOT approach and consequently improving its performance by generating a locally customized index term space for each node.

3 The HL-SOT Approach Review

In the HL-SOT approach (Wei and Gulla, 2010), each target text is indexed by a vector $x \in \mathcal{X}, \mathcal{X} = \mathbb{R}^d$. Weight vectors $w_i (1 \leq i \leq N)$ define linear-threshold classifiers of each node i in SOT so that the target text x is labeled true by node i if x is labeled true by i's parent node and $w_i \cdot x \geq \theta_i$. The parameters w_i and θ_i are learned from the training data set: $D = \{(r, l) | r \in \mathcal{X}, l \in \mathcal{Y}\}$, where $\mathcal{Y}$ denotes the set of label vectors. In the training process, when a new instance r_t is observed, each row vector $w_{i,t}$ is updated by a regularized least squares estimator given by:

$$w_{i,t} = (I + S_{i,Q(i,t-1)} S_{i,Q(i,t-1)}^{\top} + r_t r_t^{\top})^{-1} \times S_{i,Q(i,t-1)} (l_{i,i_1}, l_{i,i_2}, ..., l_{i,i_{Q(i,t-1)}})^{\top} \quad (1)$$

where I is a $d \times d$ identity matrix, $Q(i, t-1)$ denotes the number of times the parent of node i observes a positive label before observing the instance r_t, $S_{i,Q(i,t-1)} = [r_{i_1}, ..., r_{i_{Q(i,t-1)}}]$ is a $d \times Q(i, t-1)$ matrix whose columns are the instances $r_{i_1}, ..., r_{i_{Q(i,t-1)}}$, and $(l_{i,i_1}, l_{i,i_2}, ..., l_{i,i_{Q(i,t-1)}})^{\top}$ is a $Q(i, t-1)$-dimensional vector of the corresponding labels observed by node i. The Formula 1 restricts that the weight vector $w_{i,t}$ of the classifier i is only updated on the examples that are positive for its parent node. Then the label vector $\hat{y}_{r_t}$ is computed for the instance r_t, before the real label vector l_{r_t} is observed. Then the current threshold vector θ_t is updated by:

$$\theta_{t+1} = \theta_t + \epsilon(\hat{y}_{r_t} - l_{r_t}), \quad (2)$$

where ϵ is a small positive real number that denotes a corrective step for the current threshold vector θ_t. After the training process for each node of SOT, each target text is to be labeled by each node i parameterized by the weight vector w_i and the threshold θ_i in the hierarchical classification process.

4 The Localized Feature Selection

In this section, we propose the LFS framework to generate a locally customized index term space for each node of SOT respectively. We first discuss why localized feature selection is needed for the HL-SOT approach. Then we define the concept of local hierarchy of SOT to introduce the local feature selection scope of a node, followed by a presentation on the local hierarchy based feature selection process.

4.1 Why Localized Feature Selection for the HL-SOT

One deficiency of the HL-SOT approach is that it uses a globally unified index term space to index target texts, which cannot efficiently encode feature information required by each local individual node of SOT. When we look into the detailed classification process of each node of SOT, we observe the following two types of phenomena. Firstly, SOT organizes domain knowledge in a tree like structure. Within a particular domain knowledge represented by SOT, nodes that stay in different branches of SOT represent independent different attributes in that domain. In this way, feature terms (e.g., the term "ergonomics") that are relevant to a node (e.g., the node "design and usability") might be irrelevant to other nodes (e.g., the node "image quality") that stay at another branches of SOT; Secondly, the HL-SOT approach labels each target text in a hierarchical order which ensures that each target text that comes to be handled by a node has already been labeled as true by its parent node. Due to this characteristic, feature terms (e.g., the term "noise") that are significant to a node i (e.g., the node "noise") might become a trivial term for i's child nodes (e.g., the nodes "noise +" and "noise -"). Therefore, the purpose of the localized feature selection is to filter out irrelevant terms that are insignificant to each individual node and build a locally customized index term space for the node so that the performance of the node can be improved.

4.2 Local Feature Selection Scope for a Node

In order to select locally customized feature terms for each individual node, we need to define a suitable scope, called local feature selection scope[3], within which the feature selection process can be effectively conducted for the node. Since the HL-SOT approach is a hierarchical classification process, before we introduce the local scope for a node we first give a formal definition on local hierarchy of SOT.

Definition 1 *[Local Hierarchy] A local hierarchy Δ_u of SOT is defined to be formed by all the child nodes of u in SOT, where the node u must be a non-leaf node of the SOT.*

By the Definition 1, we say all the child nodes of u are on the same local hierarchy under u which is denoted by Δ_u. For examples, in Fig. 2 nodes "camera +", "design and usability", "image quality", "lens", "camera -" are deemed on the same local hierarchy under the node "camera" and nodes "weight +", "weight -" are deemed on the same local hierarchy under the node "weight", etc. In the hierarchical labeling process of the HL-SOT approach, after a target text is labeled as true by a node i it will go further to the local hierarchy under i and is to be labeled by all nodes on the local hierarchy Δ_i. For a target text the labeling processes of nodes on Δ_i locally can be considered as a multi-label classification process where each node is a local label. Therefore, the measurement for selecting terms as features should be calculated among nodes on the same hierarchy. Hence, the local scope for a node is defined within the local hierarchy which the node is on.

4.3 Local Hierarchy Based Feature Selection

In the proposed LFS framework, local feature selection for a node i of SOT is performed within the *local scope* of the node i. Since nodes on the same local hierarchy share the same local scope, local feature selection process for all nodes of SOT is achieved in local hierarchy based manner. Specifically, for the feature selection process on a local hierarchy Δ, let $c_1, c_2, ..., c_K$ denote the K nodes on Δ. Let D denote the training data set for the HL-SOT approach. Let D_{c_k} denote the set of instances in D that contains the label of the node $c_k (1 \leqslant k \leqslant K)$. Let D_Δ denote the training corpus for the local hierarchy Δ which is the set of

[3] In this paper, we also call it "local scope" for short.

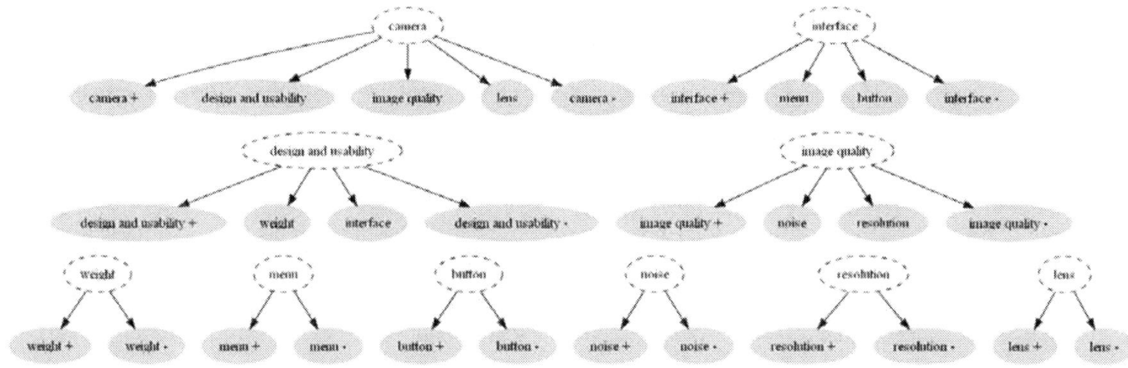

Figure 2: All local hierarchies of the example SOT: the grey nodes sharing the same parent node in dashed line are called on the same local hierarchy under the parent node

all instances in the training data set D that contain any label of nodes on the local hierarchy Δ: $D_\Delta = \bigcup_{k=1}^{K} D_{c_k}$. Let V_{c_k} denote the set of all the vocabularies that appears in D_{c_k}. Let $s_{c_k}(w)$ denote the term score that measures the suitability of w as a feature for node c_k. Let F_{c_k} denote the set of feature terms selected for c_k. Let d_{c_k} denote the number of features to be selected in F_{c_k}. A local feature selection process for nodes on the local hierarchy Δ is described in Algorithm 1.

Algorithm 1 Localized Feature Selection Algorithm

DATA INITIALIZATION:
for each node c_k on Δ **do**
  Establish D_{c_k} containing instances being labeled true by c_k;
  Establish the vocabulary set V_{c_k};
  Remove stop words from V_{c_k};
end for
Establish the training corpus: $D_\Delta = \bigcup_{k=1}^{K} D_{c_k}$;
BEGIN
for each node c_k on Δ **do**
  for each term $w \in V_{c_k}$ **do**
    with training corpus D_Δ and data instance set D_{c_k}:
    Calculate $s_{c_k}(w)$ with a specified feature selection algorithm;
  end for
  Establish feature space F_{c_k} with top d_{c_k} terms from V_{c_k};
end for
END

In the data initialization phase of the Algorithm 1, the data instance set D_{c_k} and vocabulary set V_{c_k} for each node on the local hierarchy Δ as well as the training corpus D_Δ are established. In a local feature selection process, a term score $s_{c_k}(w)$ for each term $w \in V_{c_k}$ can be calculated by a specified feature selection algorithm, taking D_Δ as the training corpus and D_{c_k} as the data instance set in the class c_k. The local feature selection process can employ any specific feature selection algorithm to calculate the term scores. After all terms in V_{c_k} are calculated, those terms with top d_{c_k} scores are selected to establish the feature space F_{c_k} for the node c_k. Since the number of terms in V_{c_k} varies from node to node, in order to produce a rational dimensionality d_{c_k} for the established feature space F_{c_k}, we introduce a feature selection rate, denoted by γ, to control d_{c_k} for each node c_k, i.e., $d_{c_k} = \ulcorner |V_{c_k}| \times \gamma \urcorner$.

After local feature selection processes for all the nods of SOT are accomplished, a locally customized index term space F_{c_k} for each node c_k is established. Each target text will be respectively indexed by a customized vector $x_{c_k} \in \mathcal{X}_{c_k} (\mathcal{X}_{c_k} = \mathbb{R}^{d_{c_k}})$ when it goes through the hierarchical classification process of the HL-SOT approach. In next section, we will present the empirical analysis on evaluating the proposed LFS framework.

5 Empirical Analysis

In this section, we conduct extensive experiments to empirically analyze the proposed LFS framework. Our experiments are intended to address the following questions: (1) can the classification performance of the HL-SOT approach be improved with the LFS framework; (2) how much computational efficiency can be gained for the HL-SOT to be implemented in the LFS framework; (3) how are the comparative performances produced by different feature selection algorithms when employed in the proposed LFS framework.

5.1 Data Set Preparation

We construct our data set based on the digital camera review data set used in the HL-SOT approach (Wei and Gulla, 2010). In total, the constructed data set contains 1500 snippets of customer reviews on digital cameras, where 35 attributes of a digital camera are mentioned in the review data. We build an ontology structure to organize the mentioned attributes and label each review text with correspondent attributes as well as sentiments, which complying the rule that if a review text is assigned with a label of a node then it is assigned with a label of the parent node. We randomly divide the labeled data set into five folds so that each fold at least contains one example instance labeled by each attribute node. To catch the statistical significance of experimental results, we perform 5 cross-fold evaluation by using four folds as training data and the other one fold as testing data. All the experimental results presented in this section are averaged over 5 runs of each experiment.

5.2 Evaluation Metrics

Since the existing HL-SOT approach is a hierarchical classification process, we use the same three classic loss functions (Wei and Gulla, 2010) for measuring classification performance. They are respectively the One-error Loss (O-Loss) function, the Symmetric Loss (S-Loss) function, and the Hierarchical Loss (H-Loss) function[4]:

- One-error loss (O-Loss) function is defined as:

$$L_O(\hat{y}, l) = \mathfrak{B}(\exists i : \hat{y}_i \neq l_i), \tag{3}$$

where $\hat{y}$ is the prediction label vector and l is the true label vector; $\mathfrak{B}(S)$ is a boolean function which is 1 if and only if the statement S is true, otherwise it is 0.

- Symmetric loss (S-Loss) function is defined as:

$$L_S(\hat{y}, l) = \sum_{i=1}^{N} \mathfrak{B}(\hat{y}_i \neq l_i), \tag{4}$$

- Hierarchical loss (H-Loss) function is defined as:

$$L_H(\hat{y}, l) = \sum_{i=1}^{N} \mathfrak{B}(\hat{y}_i \neq l_i \wedge \forall j \in \mathcal{A}(i), \hat{y}_j = l_j), \tag{5}$$

where $\mathcal{A}$ denotes a set of nodes that are ancestors of node i in SOT.

5.3 Performance Comparison

In this section, we conduct experiments to show performance improvement from the proposed LFS framework. The performance considered here include both classification performance and computational efficiency. We use the existing HL-SOT approach as a baseline. Since the HL-SOT approach used terms' document frequencies (DF) (Manning et al., 2008) algorithm to select features to build the globally unified index term space, employing the same DF feature selection algorithm we apply the proposed LFS framework on the HL-SOT approach and call the implemented method "DF-SOT". The only difference between HL-SOT and DF-SOT is the index term space for each node of SOT, i.e., in the HL-SOT all the nodes using the globally unified index term space while in the DF-SOT each node respectively using a locally customized index term space. In this way, the performance difference between the two methods will indicate the effect of the proposed LFS framework.

[4] Since the three loss functions are respectively well-defined by each formula and self-explained by their names, due to the space limitation, we do not present more explanation.

5.3.1 Comparison on Classification Performance

We conduct experiments to investigate whether the classification performance of the HL-SOT can be improved when it is implemented with the LFS framework. Fig. 3 presents the experimental results of classification accuracies between HL-SOT and DF-SOT. In the experiments, the dimensionality d of the globally unified index term space of the HL-SOT approach is set to 270, which is large enough for the HL-SOT approach to reach its best performance level. The feature selection rate γ for the locally customized index term space of the DF-SOT approach is set to 0.2 and 0.3, which brings respectively 80% and 70% vocabulary reduction. The value of the corrective step ϵ is set to varying from 0.005 to 0.05 with each step of 0.005 so that each running approach can achieve its best performance with a certain value of ϵ. From Fig. 3, we can observe that when $\gamma = 0.2$ the DF-SOT approach reaches its best performance with 0.6953 ($\epsilon = 0.02$) on O-Loss, 1.5516 ($\epsilon = 0.045$) on S-Loss, and 1.0578 ($\epsilon = 0.04$) on H-Loss, and that when $\gamma = 0.3$ the DF-SOT approach reaches its best performance with 0.6953 ($\epsilon = 0.015$) on O-Loss, 1.5531 ($\epsilon = 0.02$) on S-Loss, and 1.0547 ($\epsilon = 0.025$) on H-Loss, which outperforms the best performance of the HL-SOT approach on O-Loss 0.6984 ($\epsilon = 0.025$), on S-Loss 1.6188 ($\epsilon = 0.025$), and on H-Loss 1.0969 ($\epsilon = 0.05$). This indicates that with the proposed LFS framework, compared with the HL-SOT approach, the DF-SOT approach generally improves the classification performance.

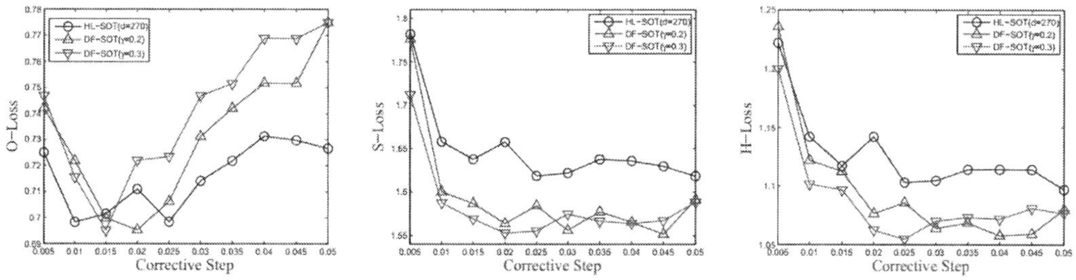

(a) O-Loss (b) S-Loss (c) H-Loss

Figure 3: Classification Performance (A Smaller Loss Value Means Better Classification Performance)

5.3.2 Comparison on Computational Efficiency

We conduct further experiments to analyze computational efficiency gained through the proposed LFS framework. All the experiments are conducted on a normal personal computer containing an Intel Pentium D CPU (2.4 GHz, Dual Core) and 4G memory. Fig. 4 summarizes the computational time consumed by experiment runs respectively for HL-SOT ($d = 270$) and DF-SOT ($\gamma = 0.2$ and $\gamma = 0.3$). From Fig. 4, we can observe that the HL-SOT approach consumes 15917695 ms to finish an experimental run, although the DF-SOT approach only takes respectively 2.29% (with $\gamma = 0.2$) and 4.91% (with $\gamma = 0.2$) of computational time as the existing HL-SOT approach consumes and achieves even better classification performance than the HL-SOT approach (see Fig.3). This confirms that much computational efficiency can be gained for the HL-SOT approach to be implemented in the LFS framework while better classification performance is ensured. Since the computational complexity of each node classifier of DF-SOT is the same as HL-SOT, the computational efficiency gained from the proposed LFS framework should be attributed to the dimension reduction of the index term space.

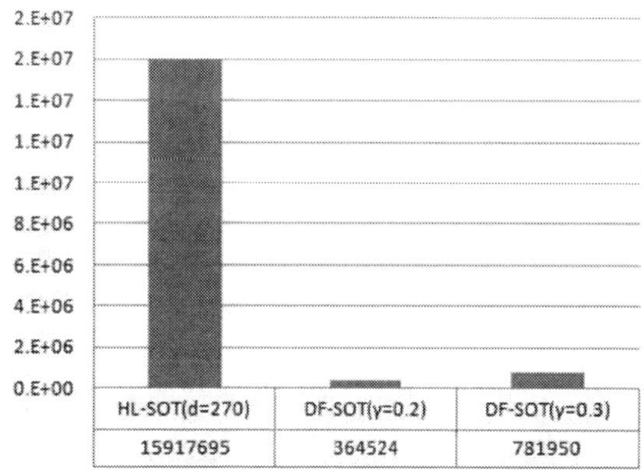

Figure 4: Time Consuming (ms)

5.4 Comparative Study on Feature Selection Algorithms

The proposed LFS framework for the HL-SOT approach can employ various feature selection algorithms to select local features for each individual node. In this section, we conduct intensive experiments to comparatively study five classic feature selection algorithms employed within the LFS framework. The five employed feature selection algorithms are respectively document frequency (DF) (Manning et al., 2008) based feature selection algorithm, mutual information (MI) (Manning et al., 2008; Church and Hanks, 1990) based feature selection algorithm, χ^2-statistic (CHI) (Manning et al., 2008) based feature selection algorithm, information gain (IG) (Mitchell, 1997) based feature selection algorithm as well as term strength (TS) (Wilbur and Sirotkin, 1992) based feature selection algorithm[5].

In the experiments, the feature selection rate γ is set to 0.2 and 0.3 respectively. The value of the corrective step ϵ varies from 0.005 to 0.05 with each step of 0.005. The experimental results are summarized in Fig. 5. From Fig. 5 it is observed that DF, MI, and TS feature selection algorithms achieve generally better performances than CHI and IG feature selection algorithms when they are employed in the proposed LFS framework. Specifically, the TS algorithm is generally the best among the five employed algorithms while the DF algorithm can also achieve as

[5]Due to the space limitation, details of the studied feature selection algorithms are not reviewed here. The mechanism of each algorithm can be read in the related references.

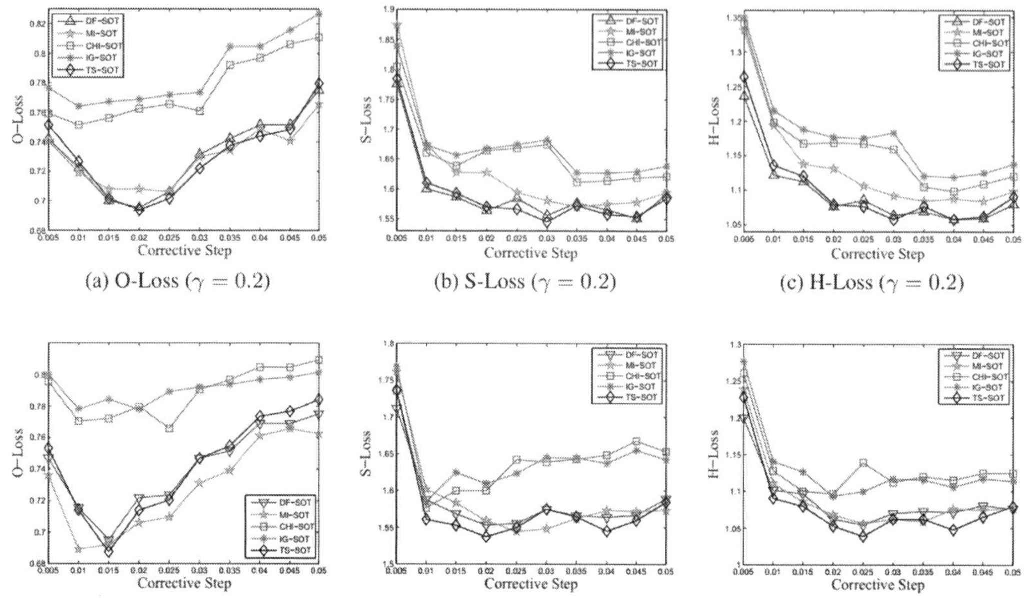

(a) O-Loss ($\gamma = 0.2$) (b) S-Loss ($\gamma = 0.2$) (c) H-Loss ($\gamma = 0.2$)

(d) O-Loss ($\gamma = 0.3$) (e) S-Loss ($\gamma = 0.3$) (f) H-Loss ($\gamma = 0.3$)

Figure 5: Comparative Performances on the Employed Feature Selection Algorithms

comparable good performance as the TS algorithm does. This is due to that both the TS and the DF algorithms favor high frequency terms and vocabularies used in customer reviews on a specific product are usually overlapping. When $\gamma = 0.3$, it can be also observed that the MI algorithm achieves as comparable good performance as the TS algorithm does. This is because, in customer reviews, although some vocabularies are rarely used they always occur as significant features in some specific categories. For example, "ergonomics" is a rare term but almost always appears in the class of "design and usability". Therefore, the MI algorithm can also achieve relatively better performance through favoring rare terms that always co-occur with specific classes.

6 Conclusions and Future Work

In this paper, we propose a LFS framework tailored to the HL-SOT approach to sentiment analysis. In the proposed LFS framework, significant feature terms of each node can be selected to construct the locally customized index term space for the node so that the classification performance and computational efficiency of the existing HL-SOT approach are improved. The effectiveness of the proposed LFS is validated against a human-labeled data set. Further comparative study on five employed feature selection algorithms within the proposed LFS framework indicates that the TS, DF, and MI algorithms achieve generally better performance than the CHI and IG algorithms. Among the five employed algorithms, the TS algorithm is the best to be employed by the proposed LFS framework.

Although the proposed LFS framework shows its effectiveness of improving on the HL-SOT approach, its improvement on the classification performance is not so obvious compared with its much improvement on computational efficiency. Due to the limited number of instances in the training data set, the classification performance still suffers from the problem that unobserved terms appear in testing cases. This problem is inherently raised by the bag-of-word model. A concept-based indexing scheme that can infer concepts of unobserved terms might alleviate the problem. We plan to investigate on this issue in the future work.

Acknowledgments

The authors would like to thank the anonymous reviewers for the helpful comments on the manuscript. This work is funded by the Research Council of Norway under the VERDIKT research programme (Project No.: 183337).

References

Alina Andreevskaia and Sabine Bergler. 2006. Mining wordnet for a fuzzy sentiment: Sentiment tag extraction from wordnet glosses. In *Proceedings of 11th Conference of the European Chapter of the Association for Computational Linguistics*.

Kenneth Ward Church and Patrick Hanks. 1990. Word association norms, mutual information, and lexicography. *Computational Linguistics*, 16(1):22–29.

Ann Devitt and Khurshid Ahmad. 2007. Sentiment polarity identification in financial news: A cohesion-based approach. In *Proceedings of 45th Annual Meeting of the Association for Computational Linguistics*.

Xiaowen Ding and Bing Liu. 2007. The utility of linguistic rules in opinion mining. In *Proceedings of the 30th Annual International ACM SIGIR Conference on Research and development in Information Retrieval*.

Andrea Esuli and Fabrizio Sebastiani. 2005. Determining the semantic orientation of terms through gloss classification. In *Proceedings of 14th ACM Conference on Information and Knowledge Management*.

Andrea Esuli and Fabrizio Sebastiani. 2006. Sentiwordnet: A publicly available lexical resource for opinion mining. In *Proceedings of 5th International Conference on Language Resources and Evaluation*.

Vasileios Hatzivassiloglou and Kathleen R. McKeown. 1997. Predicting the semantic orientation of adjectives. In *Proceedings of 35th Annual Meeting of the Association for Computational Linguistics*.

Vasileios Hatzivassiloglou and Janyce M. Wiebe. 2000. Effects of adjective orientation and gradability on sentence subjectivity. In *Proceedings of 18th International Conference on Computational Linguistics*.

Minqing Hu and Bing Liu. 2004. Mining and summarizing customer reviews. In *Proceedings of 10th ACM SIGKDD Conference on Knowledge Discovery and Data Mining*.

Jaap Kamps, Maarten Marx, R. ort. Mokken, and Maarten de Rijke. 2004. Using WordNet to measure semantic orientation of adjectives. In *Proceedings of 4th International Conference on Language Resources and Evaluation*.

Bing Liu, Minqing Hu, and Junsheng Cheng. 2005. Opinion observer: analyzing and comparing opinions on the web. In *Proceedings of 14th International World Wide Web Conference*.

Yang Liu, Xiangji Huang, Aijun An, and Xiaohui Yu. 2007. ARSA: a sentiment-aware model for predicting sales performance using blogs. In *Proceedings of the 30th Annual International ACM SIGIR Conference on Research and development in Information Retrieval*.

Yue Lu and Chengxiang Zhai. 2008. Opinion integration through semi-supervised topic modeling. In *Proceedings of 17th International World Wide Web Conference*.

Yue Lu, ChengXiang Zhai, and Neel Sundaresan. 2009. Rated aspect summarization of short comments. In *Proceedings of 18th International World Wide Web Conference*.

Christopher D. Manning, Prabhakar Raghavan, and Hinrich Schutze. 2008. *Introduction to Information Retrieval*, chapter 13, pages 271–278. Cambridge University Press.

Tom Mitchell. 1997. *Machine Learning*. McGraw-Hill.

Ana-Maria Popescu and Oren Etzioni. 2005. Extracting product features and opinions from reviews. In *Proceedings of Human Language Technology Conference and Empirical Methods in Natural Language Processing Conference*.

Ivan Titov and Ryan T. McDonald. 2008. Modeling online reviews with multi-grain topic models. In *Proceedings of 17th International World Wide Web Conference*.

Peter D. Turney. 2002. Thumbs up or thumbs down? semantic orientation applied to unsupervised classification of reviews. In *Proceedings of 40th Annual Meeting of the Association for Computational Linguistics*.

Wei Wei and Jon Atle Gulla. 2010. Sentiment learning on product reviews via sentiment ontology tree. In *Proceedings of 48th Annual Meeting of the Association for Computational Linguistics*.

Casey Whitelaw, Navendu Garg, and Shlomo Argamon. 2005. Using appraisal taxonomies for sentiment analysis. In *Proceedings of 14th ACM Conference on Information and Knowledge Management*.

J. W. Wilbur and K. Sirotkin. 1992. The automatic identification of stop words. *Journal of the American Society for Information Science*, 18:45–55.

Theresa Wilson, Janyce Wiebe, and Paul Hoffmann. 2005. Recognizing contextual polarity in phrase-level sentiment analysis. In *Proceedings of Human Language Technology Conference and Empirical Methods in Natural Language Processing Conference*.

Hong Yu and Vasileios Hatzivassiloglou. 2003. Towards answering opinion questions: Separating facts from opinions and identifying the polarity of opinion sentences. In *Proceedings of 8th Conference on Empirical Methods in Natural Language Processing*.

Fine-Grained Sentiment Analysis with Structural Features

Cäcilia Zirn† Mathias Niepert† Heiner Stuckenschmidt† Michael Strube‡

†KR & KM Research Group
University of Mannheim
Mannheim, Germany
caecilia@informatik.uni-mannheim.de

‡Heidelberg Institute for
Theoretical Studies
Heidelberg, Germany
michael.strube@h-its.org

Abstract

Sentiment analysis is the problem of determining the polarity of a text with respect to a particular topic. For most applications, however, it is not only necessary to derive the polarity of a text as a whole but also to extract negative and positive utterances on a more fine-grained level. Sentiment analysis systems working on the (sub-)sentence level, however, are difficult to develop since shorter textual segments rarely carry enough information to determine their polarity out of context. In this paper, therefore, we present a fully automatic framework for fine-grained sentiment analysis on the subsentence level combining multiple sentiment lexicons and neighborhood as well as discourse relations to overcome this problem. We use Markov logic to integrate polarity scores from different sentiment lexicons with information about relations between neighboring segments, and evaluate the approach on product reviews. The experiments show that the use of structural features improves the accuracy of polarity predictions achieving accuracy scores of up to 69%.

1 Introduction

Sentiment analysis systems have continuously improved the quality of polarity classifications of entire product reviews. For numerous real-world applications, however, classification on such a coarse level is not suitable. Even in their most enthusiastic reviews, users still tend to mention negative aspects of a particular product. Conversely, in very negative reviews there might still be mentions of several positive aspects of the product. Moreover, different opinions can even be uttered in the same sentence. Consider, for instance, the sentence "*Despite the pretty design I would never recommend it, because the sound quality is unacceptable*" which expresses both positive and negative opinions about a product. Thus, to determine both negative and positive utterances in product reviews, classification on the subsentence level is needed.

Sentiment Analysis on Subsentence Level. As basic classification unit for our fine-grained sentiment analysis system we choose discourse segments. There are various theories describing discourse, discourse segmentation and discourse relations. The most well-known theory aiming to describe some aspects of text coherence is the Rhetorical Structure Theory (RST) introduced by Mann and Thompson (1988). According to this theory, every text consists of elementary segments that are connected by relations. Segments joined by a relation form a unit, which is itself connected to other segments. This leads to a hierarchical tree structure that spans over the whole text. The example sentence given above could be divided into the three segments s_1 = *Despite the pretty design*, s_2 = *I would never recommend it* and s_3 = *because the sound quality is unacceptable*, with a CONCESSION relation[1] holding between s_1 and s_2 and a CAUSE-EXPLANATION-EVIDENCE relation holding between s_2 and s_3. As the segments form logical units, and parts of sentences bearing different polarities are contrastive and thus do not constitute a logical unit, we claim that the discourse segment level is appropriate for fine-grained sentiment analysis.

Integrating Neighborhood Relations. As discourse segments consist of only a few tokens, they

[1] Please note that in this work we do not distinguish between CONCESSION and CONTRAST relations and consider both as CONTRAST relations. In the following, we will refer to all other kind of relations as NO_CONTRAST relations.

rarely carry enough information to determine their polarity out of context. While it occurs that neighboring segments bear opposite polarities, like in the example given above, two segments following each other are mostly of the same polarity. Therefore, when determining the polarity of a discourse segment, we consider the polarity of the neighboring segments for the classification.

Leveraging Contrast Relations. Although mentioning positive and negative opinions next to each other constitutes a contrast, we cannot conclude that every contrast indicates a polarity change. We conducted a simple corpus study, focusing on the cue word *but* which is a strong indicator for contrast relations. Of all consecutive discourse segments connected by the word *but*, 40% express opposite and 60% express the same opinion. Of all the other discourse segment pairs, only 10% express differing opinions. From this experimental observation, we conclude that two neighboring segments not related by a contrast relation have a much higher probability of bearing opinions of the same polarity than segments connected by a contrast relation. In our experiments, we will investigate whether the distinction between CONTRAST and NO_CONTRAST relations will improve fine-grained sentiment analysis.

Collective classification. The challenge of fine-grained sentiment analysis is that shorter text segments pose a more difficult classification problem. There are various approaches to determining the polarity of text. One common approach is the look-up of terms in a sentiment lexicon with polarity scores. As discussed in the previous paragraphs, we claim that incorporating information about a segment's neighbors, the classification of small text segments can be improved on. Therefore, we simultaneously determine the most probable classification of all segments in a review. We use Markov logic to combine polarity scores from different sentiment lexicons with information about discourse relations between neighboring segments, and evaluate the method on product reviews.

2 Related Work

Methods for fine-grained sentiment analysis are developed by Hu and Liu (2004), Ding et al. (2008) and Popescu and Etzioni (2005). While the approaches of the former two operate on the sentence level, the system of the latter - Popescu and Etzioni (2005) - extracts opinion phrases on the subsentence level for product features. Their approaches have in common that they first extract features of a product, like the *size* of a camera or its *weight*. Then, they look for opinion words describing these features. Finally, the polarity of these terms and, thus, of the feature is determined. An even finer-grained system is presented in Kessler and Nicolov (2009). The approach aims at classifying both sentiment expressions as well as their targets using a rich set of linguistic features. However, they have not implemented the component that detects and analyses sentiment expressions, but focus on target detection.

Täckström and McDonald (2011) combine fully and partially supervised structured conditional models for a joint classification of the polarity of whole reviews and the review's sentences.

An approach based on assumptions similar to our intuition to integrate discourse relations is described in Kim and Hovy (2006) where the authors label sentences as reasons for or against purchasing a product. The system makes use of conjunctions like "and" to infer polarities and applies a specific rule to sentences including the word "but": if no polarity can be identified for the clause containing "but", the polarity of the previous phrase is taken and negated. In our system, we incorporate this information using discourse relations.

The impact of discourse relations for sentiment analysis is investigated in Asher et al. (2009). The authors conduct a manual study in which they represent opinions in text as shallow semantic feature structures. These are combined to an overall opinion using hand-written rules based on manually annotated discourse relations. An interdependent classification scenario to determine polarity as well as discourse relations is presented in Somasundaran and Wiebe (2009). In their approach, text is modeled as opinion graphs including discourse information. In Somasundaran et al. (2009) the authors try alternative machine learning scenarios with combinations of supervised and unsupervised methods for the same task. However, they do not determine discourse relations automatically but use manual annotations.

3 Statistical-Relational Representation

The basic idea of our approach is the integration of heterogeneous features such as polarity scores from sentiment lexicons and neighborhood relations between segments. We use concepts and algorithms from statistical relational learning and, in particular, Markov logic networks (Richardson and Domingos, 2006).

We briefly introduce Markov logic as a framework for combining numerical and structural features and describe how the problem of fine-grained sentiment analysis based on multiple lexicons and discourse relations can be represented in the language. Most probable polarity classifications are then derived by computing maximum a-posteriori (MAP) states in the ground Markov logic network.

3.1 Markov Logic Networks

Markov logic (Richardson and Domingos, 2006) can be as a first-order template language for log-linear models with binary variables. Log-linear models are parameterizations of undirected graphical models (Markov networks) which play an important role in the areas of reasoning under uncertainty (Koller and Friedman, 2009) and statistical relational learning (Getoor and Taskar, 2007). Please note that log-linear models are also known as maximum-entropy models in the NLP community (Manning and Schütze, 1999). The features of a log-linear model can be complex and allow the user to incorporate prior knowledge about what types of data are expected to be important for classification.

A Markov network $\mathcal{M}$ is an undirected graph whose nodes represent a set of random variables $\mathbf{X} = \{X_1, ..., X_n\}$ and whose edges model direct probabilistic interactions between adjacent nodes. More formally, a distribution P is a log-linear model over a Markov network $\mathcal{M}$ if it is associated with:

- a set of features $\{f_1(D_1), ..., f_k(D_k)\}$, where each D_i is a clique in $\mathcal{M}$ and each f_i is a function from D_i to $\mathbb{R}$,
- a set of real-valued weights $w_1, ..., w_k$, such that

$$P(\mathbf{X} = \mathbf{x}) = \frac{1}{Z} \exp\left(\sum_{i=1}^{k} w_i f_i(D_i)\right),$$

where Z is a normalization constant.

A Markov logic network is a set of pairs (F_i, w_i) where each F_i is a first-order formula and each w_i a real-valued weight associated with F_i. With a finite set of constants C it defines a log-linear model over possible worlds $\{\mathbf{x}\}$ where each variable X_j corresponds to a ground atom and feature f_i is the number of true groundings (instantiations) of F_i with respect to C in possible world $\mathbf{x}$. Possible worlds are truth assignments to all ground atoms with respect to the set of constants C. We explicitly distinguish between weighted formulas and *deterministic* formulas, that is, formulas that always have to hold.

Inference

There are two common types of inference tasks for a Markov logic network: Maximum a-posteriori inference and (conditional) probability inference. The latter computes the posterior probability distribution over a subset of the variables given an instantiation of a set of evidence variables. MAP inference, however, is concerned with finding a joint assignment to a subset of variables with maximal probability. Assume we are given a set $\mathbf{X}' \subseteq \mathbf{X}$ of instantiated variables and let $\mathbf{Y} = \mathbf{X} \setminus \mathbf{X}'$. Then, a most probable state of the ground Markov logic network is given by

$$\operatorname*{argmax}_{\mathbf{y}} \sum_{i=1}^{k} w_i f_i(D_i).$$

Parameter Learning

Given a set of first-order formulas and a set of ground atoms, we wish to find the formulas' maximum a posteriori (MAP) weights, that is, the weights that maximize the log-likelihood of the hidden variables given the evidence. There exist several learning algorithms for Markov logic such as voted perceptron, contrastive divergence, and scaled conjugate gradient (Lowd and Domingos, 2007).

We employed the voted perceptron learner for the experiments (Richardson and Domingos, 2006; Lowd and Domingos, 2007; Riedel, 2008) which performs gradient descent steps to approximately optimize the conditional log-likelihood. In a MLN, the derivative of the conditional log-likelihood with respect to a weight w_i is the difference between the number of true groundings f_i of the formula F_i in the training data and the expected number of groundings according to the model with weights $\mathbf{w}$

$$g_i = \frac{\partial}{\partial w_i} \log P(\mathbf{Y} = \mathbf{y}|\mathbf{X}' = \mathbf{x}') = f_i - E_{\mathbf{w}}[f_i].$$

The expected number of true groundings $E_{\mathbf{w}}[f_i]$ is determined by (approximately) computing a MAP state with the current weights $\mathbf{w}$. The perceptron update rule for the set of weights $\mathbf{w}$ for epoch $t+1$ is then

$$\mathbf{w}_{t+1} = \mathbf{w}_t + \eta \mathbf{g},$$

where η is the learning rate. Online learners repeat these steps updating the weight vector for a predetermined number of n epochs.

3.2 Markov Logic Formulation

Each discourse segment s is modeled with a constant symbol $c \in C$. The set C, therefore, models the discourse segments in the text under consideration and comprises the set of constants of the Markov logic network. The segments s_1, s_2, and s_3 depicted in Figure 1, for instance, would be modeled using the constant symbols c_1, c_2 and c_3. We represent the polarity of a segment using two non-observable predicates $positive$ and $negative$. Note that the state of variables modeling non-observable ground predicates is only known during weight learning. We first formulate the fact that a segment is positive or negative but cannot be $positive$ and $negative$ at the same time using the following deterministic formulas:

$$\forall x : \neg positive(x) \Rightarrow negative(x)$$
$$\forall x : negative(x) \Rightarrow \neg positive(x)$$

Furthermore, the model incorporates several numerical *a-priori* features such as the polarity scores of individual segments provided by external lexical resources. We introduce these features in the experimental section in more detail. For each of these features ℓ we wish to include in the model, we first add the following deterministic equivalence formulas

$$\forall x : positive\_source_\ell(x) \Leftrightarrow positive(x)$$
$$\forall x : negative\_source_\ell(x) \Leftrightarrow negative(x)$$

Now, in order to include a-priori polarity scores, we add the weighted formula $positive\_source_\ell(x)$ and *scale* the contribution of a *true* ground atom $positive\_source_\ell(s)$ with the a-priori polarity score of the particular segment s. This way, the parameter learning algorithm balances the contributions of the different sources according to their accuracy on the training data. The framework "Markov theBeast"[2] which we used for our experiments allows to add such real-valued features (Riedel, 2008).

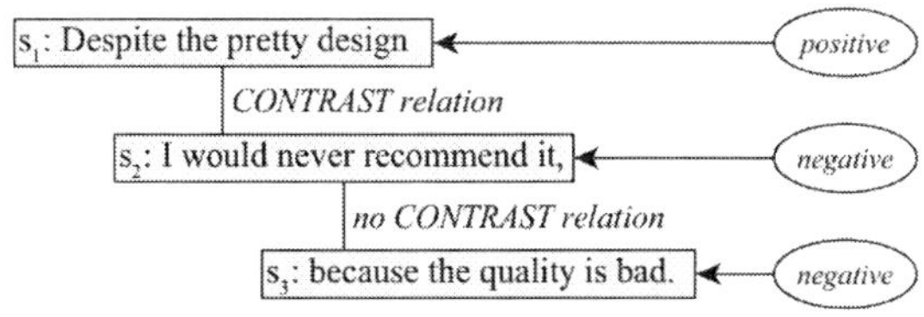

Figure 1: Sentiment polarities of and discourse relations between the segments of a sentence.

The novel contribution of the present paper, however, is the addition of *structural features*, that is, features that model specific dependencies holding between the segments of a review. We distinguish two different types of such features, namely, *neighborhood relations* and *discourse relations*.

3.2.1 Neighborhood Relations

The intuition behind *neighborhood relations* is that neighboring segments are more likely to have the same polarity. We model the fact that a segment *precedes* another segment with the observable predicate pre. Each sentence is represented as a set of ground predicates instantiated by constants modeling consecutive sentence segments. The sentence depicted in Figure 1, for instance, would be represented with the two ground atoms $pre(c_1, c_2)$ and $pre(c_2, c_3)$. The following formulas are included in the Markov logic formulation to model the dependency of preceding segments.

$$\forall x, y : pre(x, y) \wedge positive(x) \Rightarrow positive(y)$$
$$\forall x, y : pre(x, y) \wedge negative(x) \Rightarrow negative(y)$$

The weights of the above formulas (a subset of the parameters of the model) are learned during training.

3.2.2 Discourse Relations

While there are numerous types of possible discourse relations we decided to only distinguish between contrast relations ($contrast$) and all other types of relations ($nconstrast$) due to their potential impact on polarity changes between discourse segments. In principle, however, it is possible to

[2]The code can be downloaded at `http://code.google.com/p/thebeast/`

Topic	p	n	total
Cell Phones & Service	1392	1785	3177
Gourmet Food	990	616	1606
Kitchen & Housewares	1188	1405	2593
Sum	3570	3806	7376

Table 1: Amount of positive (p) and negative (n) segments.

extend the model to also incorporate additional relations. The sentence shown in Figure 1, for instance, would be represented with the two ground atoms $contrast(c_1, c_2)$ and $ncontrast(c_2, c_3)$.

In order to leverage contrast relations, we included the following formulas in the Markov logic formulation, modeling how the absence of contrast relations between segments influences their potential polarity changes.

$$\forall x, y : contrast(x, y) \wedge positive(x) \Rightarrow negative(y)$$
$$\forall x, y : contrast(x, y) \wedge negative(x) \Rightarrow positive(y)$$
$$\forall x, y : ncontrast(x, y) \wedge positive(x) \Rightarrow positive(y)$$
$$\forall x, y : ncontrast(x, y) \wedge negative(x) \Rightarrow negative(y)$$

Again, the weights of the above formulas are learned in the training phase.

The classification of a given set of segments is now equivalent to computing a maximum a-posteriori (MAP) state of the respective ground Markov logic network.

4 Experiments

In what follows, we describe the individual components of our sentiment analysis system and the data we used to experimentally evaluate it. For the evaluation, we first combine real-valued polarity scores derived from sentiment lexicons using Markov logic networks and classify all segments of a product review. We then investigate whether the addition of certain structural features improves the performance of the system.

4.1 Data

We chose a subset of the the Multi-Domain Sentiment Dataset arranged by Blitzer et al. (2007) and annotated it for our purpose. The Multi-Domain Sentiment Dataset consists of user-written product reviews downloaded from the web page `http://amazon.com`. The reviews are subdivided according to their topics. We included the three categories "Cell Phones & Service", "Gourmet Food" and "Kitchen & Housewares".

Each category consists of up to 100 reviews. A review is already classified as positive or negative according to the amount of stars the user has chosen for the product along with their review. To achieve a balanced corpus, we picked the 20 longest positive and the 20 longest negative reviews for each of the two topics, resulting in a complete amount of 120 reviews. Table 1 lists the three categories and their respective numbers of segments.

4.1.1 Gold Standard

Three independent annotators were instructed to label all passages of a review as `positive`, `negative` or `neutral`. Here, a passage is defined as a sequence of words sharing the same opinion. Each word of a review belongs to exactly one passage. The annotators were instructed to choose arbitrary passage boundaries independent of sentence or clause limits. The inter-annotator agreement among the three annotators varies from $\kappa = 0.40$ to $\kappa = 0.45$ for negative reviews, which is considered only fair agreement, and from $\kappa = 0.60$ to $\kappa = 0.84$ for positive reviews which is considered strong agreement according to Fleiss kappa (Fleiss, 1971). In our experiments, we only use the two classes `positive` and `negative`. Because of the individual segmentations, we processed the corpus word by word to determine the final polarity labels. For each word, we considered the three polarity labels the annotators had chosen for the respective passages containing the word. If one of the labels `positive` or `negative` was used in the majority, we chose this as the final label. Whenever the majority of the annotators picked `neutral` or each of the annotators chose a different label the general polarity of the entire review as given by the data set was taken as final label. This is because we estimate the user chose the star-rating according to his overall opinion on the product he is reviewing. This general opinion is expressed by the review text and, therefore, the "standard" label for the review represents the overall opinion. The numbers of positive and negative segments according to the gold standard are shown in Table 1.

The final output of our fine-grained sentiment analysis system are discourse segments labeled as positive or negative. To compare them to the gold standard, we determine the polarity labels of all tokens belonging to the segment in the gold standard and take the most-chosen label. Again, if there is the same amount of positive and negative labels, we take the overall polarity of the whole review as label.

4.2 Polarity Features

For each segment, we estimate prior positivity and negativity scores using state-of-the-art sentiment classification methods. There are two basic ways to classify polarity. One of the most common approaches is to train a classifier on labeled data that works with a bag-of-words model or uses similar features. However, named approach will have difficulties with the short text segments our system is focused on.

Another method for polarity classification is to look up terms in a pre-compiled sentiment lexicon that lists terms and their polarities. We chose the latter method for several reasons. First, lexicon-based methods do not rely on large amounts of training data. Second, lexicons can easily be exchanged or added which makes the approach more flexible. Third, the use of Markov logic allows us to combine several lexicons without additional effort. To compute the positivity and negativity score for a segment according to a lexicon, we first look up the positivity as well as the negativity of each term of the segment in this lexicon. Then, we average the positivity as well as the negativity scores. This leads to one positivity score and one negativity score per lexicon for each segment. We use a simple heuristic to consider negated polarity terms such as in *not good*. To this end, we manually compiled a list of negation terms[3]. Every time we detect such a negation indicator within a segment, we switch the positivity and the negativity scores of all terms occurring after said negation. We employ the following lexicons:

- **SentiWordNet** (SWN)
  SWN (Esuli and Sebastiani, 2006) is a lexical resource that contains positivity-scores, negativity-scores and objectivity-scores for WordNet (Fellbaum, 1998) synsets. The scores are between 0.0 and 1.0 and all three scores for a synset sum up to 1.0. For our system, we only regard positivity scores and negativity scores. We use a part-of-speech tagger and take the first word sense.

[3]We used the negation indicators *no, cannot, not, none, nothing, nowhere, neither, nor, nobody, hardly, scarcely, barely* and all negations of auxiliaries modals ending on *n't*, like *don't* or *won't*.

- **Taboada and Grieve's Turney Adjective List** (TGL)
  Taboada and Grieve (2004) created a list containing adjectives and their polarities based on a method described by Turney (2002). They first query a search engine for the adjective together with some manually chosen clearly positive adjectives, using the `near`-operator, then they do the same with a list of negative adjectives. Finally, they calculate the point-wise mutual information (Church and Hanks, 1990) between the queries.

- **Unigram Lexicon** (UL)
  There are terms whose polarity depends on the context they are used in. Consider for instance the word *large*: a *large screen* is good while a *large cell phone* is likely bad. To take domain-dependence into account, we compile a list of common positive and negative unigrams as well as punctuation marks for each of the three topics separately. Since we need 40 reviews per topic for the evaluation only the remaining reviews are used to compile the unigram lexicon. From this data, we calculate the ratio of all occurrences of a unigram in positive reviews to its occurrences in negative reviews and use this ratio as the positivity and negativity scores, respectively.

4.2.1 Discourse Parsing

We employ the discourse parser HILDA developed by duVerle and Prendinger (2009). It performs two tasks: First, it splits the review text into discourse segments which constitute the basic entities our system classifies. Second, it determines the discourse relations between segments. The actual output of HILDA is the discourse tree of a text. We convert the tree structure to a linear sequence of relations between neighboring segments. HILDA uses the set of relation labels described by Soricut and Marcu (2003) which is coarser-grained than RST and consists of 18 labels. For the experiments, we distinguished two types of relations: relations labeled as $contrast$ and all other relations. We refer to this class as $ncontrast$. We model these two relations in the Markov logic framework as described in Section 3.2.

We want to investigate whether the use of a discourse parser is improving fine-grained sentiment analysis. The discourse segments determined by

	positive			negative			
	P	R	F	P	R	F	A
majority baseline	0.00	0.00	0.00	51.60	100.00	68.07	51.60
SVM	57.05	43.06	49.08	56.44	69.47	62.28	56.66
MLN_polarity	53.21	69.58	60.31	59.90	42.62	49.80	55.67
MLN_neighborhood	66.38	72.94	**69.50**	72.02	65.34	**68.52**	**69.02**
MLN_contrast	61.39	73.47	66.89	69.48	56.65	62.41	64.79

Table 2: Results (%) for the different systems. P = precision, R = recall, F = F-measure, A = accuracy

the discourse parser constitute the basic units for our sentiment classification system. Evaluating the correctness of discourse parsing is a hard task. However, it is not of prime importance for our task that the segments are correct according to any discourse theory but that they do not include passages containing differing labels according to the gold standard. An analysis of the data shows that only 3.2% of the segments contain contradictory labels. We therefore concluded that it is appropriate to use the discourse segments as basic units for the evaluation of our system.

4.3 Experimental Setting

The goal of our system is to label discourse segments of a review as `positive` or `negative`. We employed the Markov logic network implementation "Markov theBeast"(Riedel, 2008).

We compare three different Markov logic networks. First, we only take into account the real-valued polarity features. We consider this ML formulation ("MLN_polarity") a baseline to evaluate the quality of the evidence collected from the sentiment lexicons. To compare the performance of this system to the state of the art in classification algorithms, we train a Support Vector Machine (SVM) (Platt, 1998; Keerthi et al., 2001; Hastie and Tibshirani, 1998) on the polarity features. In a second Markov logic formulation (MLN_neighborhood), we incorporate structural information about neighboring segments using the formulas described in section 3.2.1. In order to assess the impact of explicitly distinguishing between `contrast` and `ncontrast` relations, we use the Markov logic formulation described in Section 3.2.2 (MLN_contrast).

We learn the weight parameters of the Markov logic networks by running the voted perceptron online learner for 20 epochs (Riedel, 2008). We then evaluate each of the classification algorithms with 10-fold cross validation.

4.4 Results

Table 2 lists the evaluation results for the different classifiers. To determine statistical significance of the relative effectiveness of two classifiers we applied a paired t-test at a significance level of $p < 0.01$. The classifiers exclusively using polarity features have comparable accuracy values. While the SVM is showing a bias towards classifying segments as negative ML_polarity shows the opposite trend. Although the accuracy of SVM is slightly higher the relative difference of the accuracy values is not statistically significant. Including neighborhood relations increases the effectiveness relative to both non-structure based classifiers significantly. MLN_neigborhood achieves an F-measure of 69.50% for positive segments and 68.52% for negative segments with an overall accuracy of 69.02%. It also significantly outperforms the majority baseline which achieves an accuracy of 51.60%. Contrary to our hypothesis, distinguishing between `contrast` and `ncontrast` relations did *not* improve the effectiveness relative to MLN_neigborhood. MLN_contrast achieves a slightly lower accuracy than MLN_neighborhood although the difference is not statistically significant. These results suggest that the correlation of `contrast` relations and polarity changes is not significant. Furthermore, the number of contrast relations in product reviews is too small to have a significant impact. Finally, employing a discourse parser as a component of a sentiment analysis poses the problem that misclassifications might as well be caused by erroneous decisions of the component. Figure 2 depicts the accuracy values for the different classifiers on each of the ten cross-validation folds.

To the best of our knowledge, there is no sen-

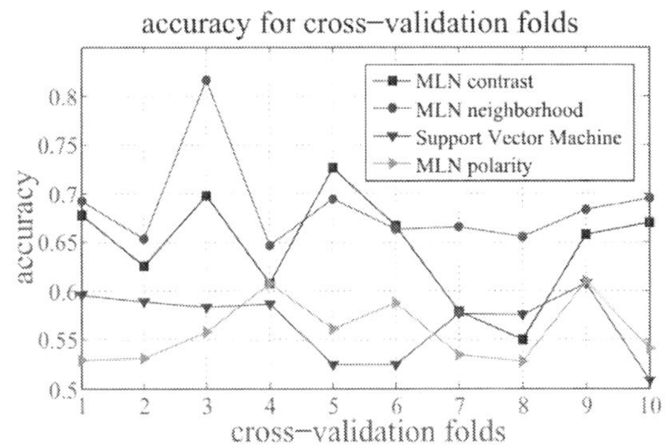

Figure 2: Accuracy values of the various algorithms for the 10 different cross-validation folds.

timent analysis system operating on the discourse segment level to which we could compare our results. However, the task is similar to that approached by Kim and Hovy (2006) whose system achieves an accuracy of 57% classifying whole sentences of reviews as positive or negative. In Täckström and McDonald (2011), the authors present a semi-supervised approach classifying sentences as positive, negative or neutral. Their approach achieves an accuracy of up to 59.1%. Considering the fact that our system is working on subsentence level we find our results promising.

5 Conclusion and Future Work

In this work, we addressed the problem of fine-grained sentiment analysis on subsentence level, achieving an accuracy of 69%. We proposed a sentiment classification method that uses Markov logic as a means to integrate polarity information from different sources and to explicitly use information about the structure of text to determine the polarity of text segments. The approach has a number of advantages. It is flexible enough to incorporate polarity scores from various sources. We used two pre-existing sentiment lexicons. To capture domain-dependent knowledge, we compiled an individual lexicon for each domain from training data. The presented approach, however, is not restricted to these sources and can include any source of polarity features. It allows for an easy combination of various existing methods into a single polarity judgement. Moreover, its major advantage is the inclusion of structural information. Again, this ability is more or less independent from a concrete method. In our work we used an existing discourse parser, however, other methods for determining the discourse structure could be used as well. Finally, the Markov logic representation can be used in a supervised and in an unsupervised setting. The experiments described in the paper are based on the supervised setting: we used a manually annotated corpus to learn weights for the formulas in the Markov logic model. In cases, where no annotated corpus is available, we could still set the weights by hand and experiment with different settings until a good setting is found.

Concerning fine-grained sentiment analysis the main result of our work is that the use of general structures found in the text systematically improves the results. As described in the paper, it turned out, however that the relation between the contrast relation and the change of polarity is not as close as we had expected. This means that the classical discourse relations are not necessarily the best choice concerning text structures to be taken into account. However, we think that focusing on cue words for discourse connectives is worth being investigated to determine features that allow us to more accurately predict such polarity changes. Further, in the work reported here, we only considered positive and negative polarity. This raises some questions concerning the treatment of segments that do not have a clear polarity. In future work, we will therefore extend our experiments to the case where segments can be classified as `positive`, `negative` or `neutral`.

Acknowledgments

We would like to thank Anette Frank for useful comments in the early phase of this work, and the annotators for annotating the product reviews.

References

Nicholas Asher, Farah Benamara, and Yannick Mathieu. 2009. Appraisal of opinion expressions in discourse. *Lingvisticae Investigations*, 31(2):279–292.

John Blitzer, Mark Dredze, and Fernando Pereira. 2007. Biographies, Bollywood, boom-boxes and blenders: Domain adaptation for sentiment classification. In *Proc. of ACL-07*, pages 440–447.

Kenneth Ward Church and Patrick Hanks. 1990. Word association norms, mutual information, and lexicography. *Computational Linguistics*, 16(1):22–29.

Xiaowen Ding, Bing Liu, and Philip S. Yu. 2008. A holistic lexicon-based approach to opinion mining. In *Proc. of WSDM-08*, pages 231–240.

David duVerle and Helmut Prendinger. 2009. A novel discourse parser based on support vector classification. In *Proc. of ACL-IJCNLP-09*, pages 665–673.

Andrea Esuli and Fabrizio Sebastiani. 2006. SentiWordNet: A publicly available lexical resource for opinion mining. In *Proc. of LREC '06*, pages 417–422.

Christiane Fellbaum, editor. 1998. *WordNet: An Electronic Lexical Database*. MIT Press, Cambridge, Mass.

Joseph L. Fleiss. 1971. Measuring nominal scale agreement among many raters. *Psychological Bulletin*, 76(5):378–382.

Lise Getoor and Ben Taskar. 2007. *Introduction to Statistical Relational Learning*. MIT Press.

Trevor Hastie and Robert Tibshirani. 1998. Classification by pairwise coupling. In Michael I. Jordan, Michael J. Kearns, and Sara A. Solla, editors, *Advances in Neural Information Processing Systems*, volume 10, pages 451–471. MIT Press.

Minqing Hu and Bing Liu. 2004. Mining and summarizing customer reviews. In *Proc. of ACM SIGKDD '04*, pages 168–177.

S.S. Keerthi, S.K. Shevade, C. Bhattacharyya, and K.R.K. Murthy. 2001. Improvements to Platt's SMO algorithm for SVM classifier design. *Neural Computation*, 13(3):637–649.

Jason S. Kessler and Nicolas Nicolov. 2009. Targeting sentiment expressions through supervised ranking of linguistic configurations. In *Proc. of ICWSM-09*, pages 90–97.

Soo-Min Kim and Eduard Hovy. 2006. Automatic identification of pro and con reasons in online reviews. In *Proc. of COLING-ACL-06 Poster Session*, pages 483–490.

Daphne Koller and Nir Friedman. 2009. *Probabilistic Graphical Models: Principles and Techniques*. MIT Press.

Daniel Lowd and Pedro Domingos. 2007. Efficient weight learning for Markov logic networks. In *Proc. of ECML/PKDD-07*, pages 200–211.

William C. Mann and Sandra A. Thompson. 1988. Rhetorical structure theory. Toward a functional theory of text organization. *Text*, 8(3):243–281.

Christopher D. Manning and Hinrich Schütze. 1999. *Foundations of statistical natural language processing*. MIT Press.

J. Platt. 1998. Fast training of support vector machines using sequential minimal optimization. In B. Schoelkopf, C. Burges, and A. Smola, editors, *Advances in Kernel Methods - Support Vector Learning*, pages 185–208. MIT Press.

Ana-Maria Popescu and Oren Etzioni. 2005. Extracting product features and opinions from reviews. In *Proc. HLT-EMNLP '05*, pages 339–346.

Matthew Richardson and Pedro Domingos. 2006. Markov logic networks. *Machine Learning*, 62(1-2):107–136.

Sebastian Riedel. 2008. Improving the accuracy and efficiency of MAP inference for Markov logic. In *Proc. of UAI-08*, pages 468–475.

Swapna Somasundaran and Janyce Wiebe. 2009. Recognizing stances in online debates. In *Proc. of ACL-IJCNLP-09*, pages 226–234.

Swapna Somasundaran, Galileo Namata, Janyce Wiebe, and Lise Getoor. 2009. Supervised and unsupervised methods in employing discourse relations for improving opinion polarity classification. In *Proc. EMNLP-09*, pages 170–179.

Radu Soricut and Daniel Marcu. 2003. Sentence level discourse parsing using syntactic and lexical information. In *Proc. of HLT-NAACL-03*, pages 149–156.

Maite Taboada and Jack Grieve. 2004. Analyzing appraisal automatically. In *Proceedings of the AAAI Spring Symposium on Exploring Attitude and Affect in Text: Theories and Applications*, Palo Alto, Cal., 22–24 March 2004, pages 158–161.

Oscar Täckström and Ryan McDonald. 2011. Semi-supervised latent variable models for sentence-level sentiment analysis. In *Proc. of ACL-11*, pages 569–574.

Peter Turney. 2002. Thumbs up or thumbs down? Semantic orientation applied to unsupervised classification of reviews. In *Proc. of ACL-02*, pages 417–424.

Predicting Opinion Dependency Relations for Opinion Analysis

Lun-Wei Ku
National Yunlin University
of Science and Technology
Douliou, Yunlin 64002, Taiwan
lwku@yuntech.edu.tw

Ting-Hao Kenneth Huang
National Taiwan University
No.1, Sec.4, Roosevelt Rd.,
Taipei, Taiwan
tinghaoh@andrew.cmu.edu

Hsin-Hsi Chen
National Taiwan University
No.1, Sec.4, Roosevelt Rd.,
Taipei, Taiwan
hhchen@ntu.edu.tw

Abstract

Syntactic structures have been good features for opinion analysis, but it is not easy to use them. To find these features by supervised learning methods, correct syntactic labels are indispensible. Two possible sources to acquire syntactic structures are parsing trees and dependency trees. For the annotation processing, parsing trees are more readable for annotators, while dependency trees are easier to use by programs. To use syntactic structures as features, this paper tried to annotate on human friendly materials and transform these annotations to the corresponding machine friendly materials. We annotated the gold answers of opinion syntactic structures on the parsing tree from Chinese Treebank, and then proposed methods to find their corresponding dependency relations on the dependency trees generated from the same sentence. With these relations, we could train a model to annotate opinion dependency relations automatically to provide an opinion dependency parser, which is language independent if language resources are incorporated. Experiment results show that the annotated syntactic structures and their corresponding dependency relations improve at least 8% of the performance of opinion analysis.

1 Introduction

Opinion analysis has drawn much attention in research communities of machine learning and natural language processing. In the early stages, words in documents were used as the main features (Pang *et al.*, 2002). Some opinion dictionaries were created for this demand (Ku *et al.*, 2007). However, researchers soon realized that word features were not sufficient for acquiring good performances, so they started to include syntactic structures and semantic information (Qiu *et al.*, 2008). Their researches showed that linguistic knowledge is helpful in determining opinions.

For various applications related to opinions, syntactic structures have become powerful tools for extracting useful clues. To find opinions in product reviews, modification relations were used to identify the product and their features (Lu *et al.*, 2009), e.g., a good *price* (feature) of this *camera* (product). To find opinion holders and targets, templates and linguistic rules were adopted (Breck *et al.*, 2007). To find more opinion words, dependency relations were utilized (Qiu *et al.*, 2011). Even when applying the basic negation rule that flips opinion polarity over, we need to find its modified word first by syntactic clues. However, we will show that syntactic relations do not directly suggest opinions.

Syntactic relations are obtained usually from all kinds of syntax trees. Parsing trees (phrase structured) and dependency trees (grammatical) are the most commonly seen ones. Parsing trees are in-order trees which keep the order of words in sentences, so they are more readable for people. Instead, nodes in dependency trees are displayed by the head-modifier relations, in which the sentence sequence probably is not remained. People could find the opinion passages if they can understand the whole sentence, i.e. from parsing trees. However, when the linguistic background is needed, it could be difficult for most people to reconstruct the whole sentence from the dependency trees in order to find the opinion passage. Therefore, if we want to find annotators to build a corpus which could be used to train an opinion relation recognizer, parsing trees are the better materials compared to dependency trees. However, compared to relations between words, complicated tree structures are more challenge to be utilized by algorithms (Doan *et al.*, 2008).

This paper focuses on extracting opinionated dependency relations from relations generated by the Stanford parser. We design an annotation mechanism on the syntactic structures on the sentence from Chinese Treebank to create an annotation environment with a lower entry barrier so that sufficient annotations can be labeled. Then these annotations are aligned to the relations in the corresponding dependency trees generated by the same parser from the same sentence as the gold standard for training the automatic annotator of the opinion dependency relations. We conduct experiments on the annotated opinion syntactic structures in parsing trees, and on the opinion dependency relations corresponding to them. The proposed process demonstrates a feasible direction toward the development of an opinion dependency parser.

2 Problem Definition

Given a set of non-collapsed dependencies parsed from a specific sentence by the Stanford dependency parser (de Marneffe and Manning, 2008; Chang *et al.*, 2009), each associated with a dependency relation between two words in this sentence, our goal is to identify which of them are with sentiment, i.e., those which reveal a part of opinions or the aroused emotions. For example, in the sentence "活动 取得 了 圆满 成功 (Activities scored le perfect success)", the Stanford dependency parser gives three relations: nmod(成功 <success>, 圆满 <perfect>), nsubj(取得 <scored>, 活动 <activities>), dobj(取得 <scored>, 成功<success>), and asp(取得 <scored>, 了<le>). The goal is to identify the former three may bear sentiment or opinions. The corresponding dependency tree is shown in Figure 1. From Figure 1 we can also see that it is not easy to read the original sentence without the linguistic background.

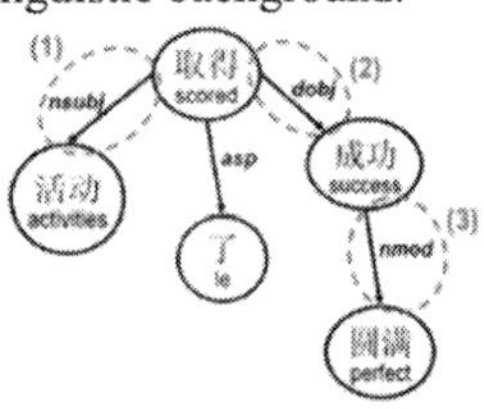

Figure 1. A sample dependency tree with three aligned opinion dependency relations.

Formally, the collection of the non-collapsed dependency relations of a sentence *S*, generated by the Stanford dependency parser, is denoted by $Rdep(S) = \{r_1, r_2, \ldots\}$, where each $r_i \in Rdep(S)$ is associate with an opinion judgment of *op(r)*.

Definition: Dependency Relation The dependency relation *r*, generated by the Stanford parser, is composed of the type of relation *rel*, the head word w_h and the modifier word w_m in the form of $rel(w_h, w_m)$. w_h and w_m are two individual words in *S*. For example, in one relation in Figure 1, *r* = nmod(成功 <success>, 圆满 <perfect>), where *rel* = nmod, w_h =成功 <success>, and w_m =圆满<perfect>. A list of *rel* is available in Stanford Parser Manual (de Marneffe and Manning, 2008; Chang *et al.*, 2009).

Definition: Opinion Judgment The opinion judgment *op(r)*, generated by the proposed system, indicates whether the corresponding dependency relation *r* is opinionated, and $op(r) \in \{true, false\}$. For example, when *r* = nmod(成功 <success>, 圆满<perfect>), *op(r)* = *true*.

Definition: Gold Opinion Judgment The gold opinion judgment, generated by mapping from manually annotated data, indicates whether the corresponding dependency relation *r* is opinionated, and $gop(r) \in \{true, false\}$.

The gold answers come from the annotations on Chinese Treebank 5.1. In a parsing tree *T* of the sentence *S*, generated by the Stanford parser, an in-ordered set of tree nodes $O = \{o_1, o_2, \ldots\}$ is used to draw a parsing tree for the annotation process, and its corresponding order, i.e., its index, is used as the node ID to record the annotations.

The way we annotate an opinion relation on a parsing tree is annotating an opinion trio (Ku *et al.*, 2009). An opinion trio *tri* = $(triID, o_{parent}, o_{left}, o_{right}, t) \in Tri$ is a structure containing a left node o_{left} and a right node o_{right} in a parsing tree, between them there is a syntactic inter-word relation $t \in Rpt$, and a nearest parent node o_{parent} of these two nodes. *Rpt* is an inter-word relation set where $Rpt \in$ {*Substantive-Modifier*, *Subjective-Predicate*, *Verb-Object*, *Verb-Complement*, *Other*}. A sample parsing tree and opinion trios within the sentence in Figure 1 are shown in Figure 2. The literal output of opinion trios are shown in

Figure 3. In the trio *tri* = (*3, NP-OBJ,* 圆满, 成功, *Substantive-Modifier*), *triID* = *3*, o_{parent} = *NP-OBJ*, o_{left} =圆满 (perfect), o_{right} =成功(success), and *t* = *Substantive-Modifier*.

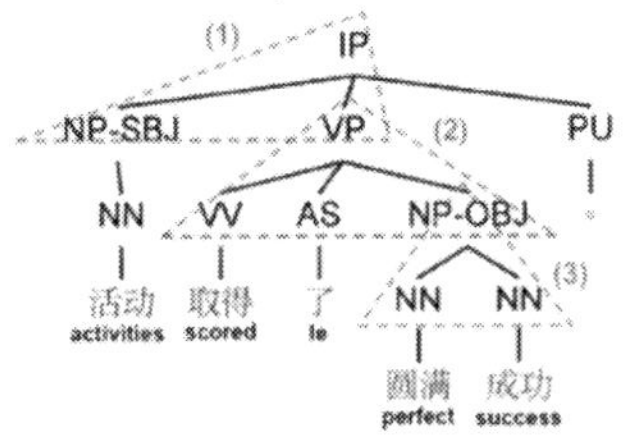

Figure 2. A sample parsing tree with trios.

1, IP, 活动, VP, Subjective-Predicate
2, VP, 取得, NP-OBJ, Verb-Object
3, NP-OBJ, 圆满, 成功, Substantive-Modifier

Figure 3. Opinion trios

Note that because the annotation of trios is on nodes of parsing trees, which appear inorderly, o_{left} will always appear before o_{right} in a sentence, and keeping this in mind will help understand the meaning of each inter-word relation *t*.

Now for the sentence *S*, we have its parsing tree *T*, the annotated opinion trios *Tri(S)* on it, and its dependency relations *Rdep(S)*. The next step is to mark the *op(r)* on *Rdep(S)* according to its corresponding *Tri(S)*. For each trio *tri*, if any descendent of its left node o_{left} and any descendent of its right node o_{right} together build a relation $r \in Rdep(S)$, the opinion judgment of *gop(r)* of the relation *r* is set to *true*. Otherwise, *gop(r)* is set to *false*. Now we have *gop(r)* for each *r* in *Rdep(S)*, our goal is to find good methods to generate *op(r)* so that it can predict *gop(r)* as precisely as possible. We propose methods to achieve this goal in Section 3.

3 Methods

As mentioned, our goal is to predict opinion dependency relations as precisely as possible. However, to use more readable materials, opinion trios are first annotated on Chinese Treebank 5.1, and then they are mapped to the corresponding dependency relations. Before the aligning process, we use the annotated trios for training to predict the opinion trios in Section 3.1. Using these predict trios for opinion analysis shall show the performance before the aligning process. After that, the aligned dependency relations, i.e., the gold opinion dependency relations are adopted for training to predict the opinion dependency relations in Section 3.2. Because the parsing tree and the dependency tree are generated by the same parser, we can always align them by the provided word ID numbers.

After prediction, the opinion dependency relations are available, and they can provide necessary information for many applications. However, we go one step further to test whether they benefit the opinion analysis. To fulfill this purpose, a basic method which uses the opinion dependency relations to extract opinionated sentences and determine their polarities is proposed in Section 3.3.

3.1 Predicting Opinion Trios

We predict the opinion trios by the sequential labeling model Conditional Random Field (*CRF*, Lafferty *et al.*, 2001). In a parsing tree, the tag of the internal node is the syntactic structure of its sub-tree, and the tag of the leaf node contains its part of speech and the content word. For each node, tags of its first four children (the first level), first four children of them (the second level), and their three children are used as features of this node. Features of its siblings (the window size is five) are considered, too.

The labels ℓ we would like the *CRF* to predict labels for each node, which are *N* or labels of the form *t-C*, where $t \in Rpt$, $C = \{L, R\}$, *L* indicates that the current node is o_{left} in some opinion trio and *R* indicates o_{right}. The label *N* indicates that the current node does not belong to any $tri \in Tri$. The cardinality of the set *Rpt* is five, so that a total of 11 labels are used in *CRF*. *CRF++*[1] is selected for experiments.

3.2 Predicting Opinion Dependency Relations

After aligning the opinion trios to the dependency relations, we will have *gop(r)* for each one of them. In the previous research, usually only some relations were selected for opinion analysis. No statistical numbers showed the connection between the dependency relations and the opinions. We believe that it is because

[1] http://crfpp.sourceforge.net/

the opinion annotation on dependency relations is more difficult than on words, sentences, or documents. However, because of this alignment, we are able to see the distribution of different dependency relations in opinion sentences and opinion segments (opinion trios). We then predict opinion dependency relations based on these distributions: the *op(r)* of the relation *r* is set to *true* when its corresponding *gop(r)* appears massively frequently to be *true* in opinion sentences. To make this method reasonable, the assumption that *there are no opinion trios in non-opinionated sentences* must hold. A similar assumption that there are no opinion segments in non-opinionated sentences was made when annotating the NTCIR MOAT corpus, too (Seki *et al.*, 2008). Under this assumption, the relation that is in most case opinionated in opinion sentences is also in most case opinionated in all sentences. We believe that this assumption holds because intuitively if there is an opinion segment in one sentence, this sentence should be opinionated.

3.3 Using Syntactic Information for Opinion Extraction

In the previous research, relations were usually extracted automatically and then were used in various applications. As these relations are available after the prediction (or alignment) and as our purpose is to provide easy to use opinion dependency relations for further applications, we simply design rules for these relations in opinion analysis to show the baseline enhancement of using them.

3.3.1 Using opinion trios

In the past, Ku *et al.* (2009) have conducted rule based experiments for opinion trios. They designed formula for trios of each $t \in Rpt$. Therefore, we adopted their rules on our augmentative experiment materials. We define the opinion scoring function *S(.)*, and its output opinion score varies with the input variables. These rules are shown by trio types as follows.

- **Substantive-Modifier Type:** o_{left} of this trio type modifies o_{right}, so that the trio's opinion weight comes from the absolute opinion score of o_{left}, while the opinion polarity is determined by the occurrence of negative o_{left} or o_{right}. If at least one of them is negative, the trio is negative, else it is positive.

$$\begin{aligned}
&\text{if } (S(o_{\text{left}}) \neq 0 \text{ and } S(o_{\text{right}}) \neq 0) \text{ then} \\
&\quad \text{if } (S(o_{\text{left}}) > 0 \text{ and } S(o_{\text{right}}) > 0) \text{ then } S(o_{\text{left}} o_{\text{right}}) = S(o_{\text{left}}) \\
&\quad \text{else } S(o_{\text{left}} o_{\text{right}}) = -1 \times |S(o_{\text{left}})| \\
&\text{else } S(o_{\text{left}} o_{\text{right}}) = S(o_{\text{left}}) + S(o_{\text{right}})
\end{aligned} \quad (1)$$

- **Subjective-Predicate Type:** o_{left} of this trio type is a subject and o_{right} is the action it performs, so that the action decides the opinion score of the trio. If the action is not an opinion or it is neutral, the subject determines the opinion score of this trio.

$$\begin{aligned}
&\text{if } (S(o_{\text{right}}) \neq 0) \text{ then } S(o_{\text{left}} o_{\text{right}}) = S(o_{\text{right}}) \\
&\text{else } S(o_{\text{left}} o_{\text{right}}) = S(o_{\text{left}})
\end{aligned} \quad (2)$$

- **Verb-Object Type:** o_{left} of this trio type acts upon o_{right}. The effect depends not only on the action but on the target. The weight is determined by the action, but the polarity is the multiplication of the signs of opinion scores of o_{left} and o_{right}.

$$\begin{aligned}
&\text{if } (S(o_{\text{left}}) \neq 0 \text{ and } S(o_{\text{right}}) \neq 0) \\
&\text{then } S(o_{\text{left}} o_{\text{right}}) = |S(o_{\text{left}})| \times SIGN(S(o_{\text{left}})) \times SIGN(S(o_{\text{right}})) \\
&\text{else } S(o_{\text{left}} o_{\text{right}}) = S(o_{\text{left}}) + S(o_{\text{right}})
\end{aligned} \quad (3)$$

- **Verb-Complement Type:** The scoring function for trios of this type is defined the same as that of a Subjective-Predicate type in Formula (2). The complement node is the deciding factor of the opinion score.

3.3.2 Using opinion dependency relations

The *usages* of opinion dependency relations were seen in several researches (Bikel and Castelli, 2008). In these researches, rules for a small number of major dependency relations were proposed in different papers but they were not listed together for a better utilization. Some rules were not ever mentioned in pervious researches. Instead, all relations are analyzed in this paper. For each relation *r* of which *gop(r)* equals *true* (when gold opinion relations are used for opinion analysis) or *op(r)* equals *true* (when predicted opinion relations are used for opinion analysis), we calculate its opinion score *ops(r)*. Let *RM(w)* be a function to return the dependency relations of word *w*'s modifiers one at a time, *n* is the total number of relations *RM(w)* returns, and *S(.)* is also the defined opinion scoring function then *ops(r)* is defined as in Formula (4).

$$ops(r) = S(rel, w_h, w_m) + \frac{1}{n}\sum ops(RM(w_m)) \quad (4)$$

That is, the opinion score of a dependency relation is an average of the aggregate scores of its descendent dependency relations. In practice, we design different rules for calculating opinion scores by the current relation type *rel* in *S(.)*. Here to simplify the problem, we adopted Formula (1) and treated w_m as o_{left} and w_h as o_{right} in it.

4 Experiments

Though there were researches which predicted opinion dependency relations, they did not predict directly from the parsing results. Instead, they predicted from documents or sentences according to the context and a large quantity of training instances were needed. They did not predict on all dependency relations either. Therefore, there is no existing dataset containing correct opinion labels on dependency relations. In this section, we describe how to generate opinionated syntactic dataset on parsing trees, and align the annotated labels to dependency trees. After that, qualitative and quantitative analyses of opinion dependency relations are provided. At the end, we discuss the evaluation results of the proposed methods.

4.1 Data Set and Preprocessing

To use the Stanford parser as our tool to generate dependency tree for experimental sentences and to avoid errors as possible, we adopted Chinese Treebank 5.1 as experiment materials. Sentences in Chinese Treebank are already segmented and part of speech tagged, and its tagging set is the same with the one Stanford parser uses. Therefore, the Stanford parser can take the data from the Chinese Treebank to generate more accurate dependency trees.

The dataset Chinese Treebank 5.1 contains 507,222 words, 824,983 Hanzi, 18,782 sentences, and 890 data files. For the opinion analysis experiments, opinionated labels, i.e., opinionated, non-opinionated, positive, neutral, negative, were annotated on all sentences in Chinese Opinion Treebank. Afterward 57,706 trios were annotated on the parsing trees of gold opinion sentences, i.e., sentences which were annotated as opinionated. Methods for generating the gold opinion sentences proposed by Ku *et al.* (2007) were adopted.

Next, the Stanford parser took all sentences in Chinese Treebank as input to generate their dependency trees. A total of 416,581 dependency relations were generated, and 284,590 of them were in opinion sentences. Then the annotated trios were aligned to their corresponding dependency relations, and because trios were only annotated on opinionated sentences, the *gop(r)* of these aligned relations were set to *true*. At the end, a total of 54,753 relations *gop(r)* were set to *true*.

	Opinion		
Polarity	Positive	Neutral	Negative
#	6,916	1,824	1,937
%	64.78	17.08	18.14
Total #	10,677		
Total %	56.84		

Table 1. Statistics of opinions.

Rpt	Number	Percentage
Substantive-Modifier	21,317	36.94
Subjective-Predicate	15,860	27.48
Verb-Object	18,010	31.21
Verb-Complement	1,208	2.09
Other	1,311	2.27
Total	57,706	100.00

Table 2. Statistics of structural trios.

Table 1 shows the distribution of the opinion and polarity labels. Table 2 shows the statistics of trios. Trios of the Substantive-Modifier and Verb-Object types are the majority in opinion sentences, while trios of the Verb-Complement type are few.

Table 3 further shows the distribution of dependency relations. It shows that previously the most adopted dependency relations for opinion analysis, e.g., *amod* (adjective modifier) or *advmod* (adverb modifier), do not certainly bear opinions or appear in opinion sentences. In Section 4.3, we will further test the performance of finding the opinionated relations with the help of the opinion word dictionary, which was also widely adopted by previous work (Feng *et al.*, 2009).

4.2 Evaluation of Opinion Trio Prediction

In this section, results of predicting opinion trios by CRF mentioned in Section 3.1 are shown. We first predicted the appearance of

o_{left} and o_{right} in trios, and then predicted the trio type $t \in Rpt$ for each trio.

The performance in Table 4 is not promising. Therefore, we consider the structure of trios, that is, o_{left} and o_{right} should appear as an ordered pair, and otherwise the label was viewed as illegal. The performance is shown in Table 5. Table 5 shows that all predicted trios were opinionated, and this tells that some opinion trios are of certain structures, but not all of them. We observed that the precisions 1.00 came from the collocations of specific words and structures, while the low recalls were from other trios which were not identified. However, these results still confirmed that we can find opinion trios by phrase structures and they may benefit in the opinion analysis process.

A	B	C	D	E (%)	F (%)	A	B	C	D	E (%)	F (%)
Dvpmod	590	501	413	84.92	82.44	Attr	3,869	2,666	140	68.91	5.25
Pass	560	399	224	71.25	56.14	Pobj	12,285	8,067	322	65.67	3.99
Dobj	32,949	24,294	13,192	73.73	54.30	clmpd	2,343	1,902	69	81.18	3.63
Npsubj	137	84	41	61.31	48.81	tcomp	2,839	1,588	53	55.94	3.34
Ba	757	575	263	75.96	45.74	Nmod	60,335	37,476	1,194	62.11	3.19
Top	2,256	1,458	661	64.63	45.34	Asp	4,176	2,889	79	69.18	2.73
Nsubj	36,902	26,102	11,058	70.73	42.36	numod	14,264	7,643	187	53.58	2.45
Neg	2,982	2,699	1,143	90.51	42.35	Clf	7,998	4,635	94	57.95	2.03
Amod	12,425	8,177	3,376	65.81	41.29	Dvpm	642	544	11	84.74	2.02
Rcmod	14,823	10,452	4,079	70.51	39.03	partmod	1,328	1,039	19	78.24	1.83
Rcomp	1,341	934	306	69.65	32.76	Det	6,021	4,083	74	67.81	1.81
Advmod	34,058	26,184	7,845	76.88	29.96	ordmod	1,220	553	10	45.33	1.81
Mmod	5,752	4,908	1,405	85.33	28.63	prnmod	770	320	5	41.56	1.56
Range	2,816	946	269	33.59	28.44	plmod	3,482	2,381	12	68.38	0.50
Assmod	12,365	9,106	1,669	73.64	18.33	Cc	7,462	5,031	17	67.42	0.34
Ccomp	40,712	31,338	4,377	76.97	13.97	Lobj	6,205	4,126	11	66.49	0.27
Vmod	866	613	79	70.79	12.89	Conj	11,414	6,967	17	61.04	0.24
Dep	17,295	8,222	887	47.54	10.79	Cpm	12,586	9,262	16	73.59	0.17
Xsubj	1,514	1,230	114	81.24	9.27	Assm	12,488	9,182	9	73.53	0.10
Comod	755	533	44	70.60	8.26	tclaus	1,583	1,140	1	72.02	0.09
Lccomp	3,102	2,063	155	66.51	7.51	Etc	1,164	663	0	56.96	0.00
Cop	625	519	37	83.04	7.13	xcomp	114	84	0	73.68	0.00
Prep	16,395	11,001	776	67.10	7.05	acomp	16	11	0	68.75	0.00

Table 3. Distributions of dependency relations and opinion dependency relations.

(A: type of dependency relations (*rel*); B: total occurrences in generated dependency trees; C: total occurrence in generated dependency trees of opinions; D: total occurrence in generated dependency trees of opinions when it bears opinions (*gop(r)* equals *true*); E: percentage that this relation appears in generated dependency trees of opinions; F: percentage that this relation appears in generated dependency trees of opinions when it bears opinions (*gop(r)* equals *true*).)

4.3 Evaluation of Opinion Dependency Relation Prediction

To predict which dependency relations are opinionated, we start with analyzing the distribution of them. Table 3 presented the distribution of dependency relations. The percentage of a relation appearing in dependency trees of opinion sentences when bearing opinions (*gop(r)* equals *true*), i.e., the value in F column, is taken as the support value. The support value indicates that in what degree this relation bears opinions. If the support value is high, it is confident to say that the relation is opinionated; otherwise, considering the content words is necessary. This idea conforms to the previous observation in Section 4.2: some of the opinions are structural, but not all of them.

According to the support value, dependency relations were divided into four categories. The Chinese opinion word dictionary *NTUSD* (Ku *et al.*, 2007) is involved to help identify opinion dependency relations when the support value is not high. The selecting criteria are listed as follows.

- **Very supportive**: with the support value above 0.8, e.g., *dvpmod*. Relations in this category are viewed as opinionated and their *gop(r)* are automatically set to *true*.
- **Supportive**: with the support value above 0.35 but lower than 0.8, e.g., *pass*, *dobj*, *npsubj*, *ba*, *top*, *nsubj*, *neg*, *amod*, *rcmod*. *RH(w)* is a function to return the word *w*'s

head in other relations of the same sentences, and *RM(w)* returns *w*'s modifier. For each $r = \{rel, w_h, w_m\}$ in this category:

$$\text{if any of } w_h, w_m, RH(w_h), RM(w_m) \text{ is in NTUSD,} \\ gop(r) = true, \\ \text{else } gop(r) = false.$$

- **Minor supportive**: with the support value above 0.2, e.g., *rcomp, advmod, mmod, range*. For each $r = \{rel, w_h, w_m\}$ in this category: $$\text{if all of } w_h, w_m, RH(w_h), RM(w_m) \text{ is in NTUSD,} \\ gop(r) = true, \\ \text{else } gop(r) = false.$$
- **Not supportive**: with the support value less than 0.2. Relations in this category are viewed as non-opinionated and their *gop(r)* are automatically set to *false*.

Experiment Settings	P	R	f-Score
Appearance: o_{left} and o_{right}	0.60	0.52	0.56
t = Substantive-Modifier	0.59	0.41	0.49
t = Subjective-Predicate	0.53	0.46	0.49
t = Verb-Object	0.62	0.65	0.64
t = Verb-Complement	0.44	0.13	0.20

Table 4. Prediction of the appearance of children nodes in trios.

Experiment Settings	P	R	f-Score
t = Substantive-Modifier	1.00	0.25	0.40
t = Subjective-Predicate	1.00	0.25	0.41
t = Verb-Object	1.00	0.39	0.56
t = Verb-Complement	1.00	0.13	0.23

Table 5. Prediction of trios.

All dependency relations			
Rel	P	R	f-Score
Nsubj	0.4507	0.7028	0.5492
Advmod	0.3675	0.6851	0.4784
Dobj	0.6097	0.8566	0.7124
Rcmod	0.4195	0.8509	0.5620
Amod	0.5031	0.7953	0.6163
Mmod	0.3289	0.7388	0.4552
Neg	0.4313	0.6404	0.5155
Range	0.3630	0.5762	0.4454
Top	0.4833	0.5461	0.5128
Rcomp	0.3371	0.5817	0.4269
Ba	0.4286	0.5817	0.4935
Dvpmod	0.8244	1.0000	0.9037
Pass	0.5819	0.7455	0.6536
Npsubj	0.5000	0.7073	0.5859
Total	**0.4713**	**0.6178**	**0.5347**
Modification dependency relations			
Total	**0.4070**	**0.2371**	**0.2997**

Table 6. Performance of predicting opinion dependency relations.

The results of two experiment settings are listed: prediction performed on all dependency relations and on only modification-related dependency relations (in the form of *lex*-mod, e.g., *amod, rcmod*, etc.) The later are the relations adopted in many previous researches. Table 6 shows the performance of predicting opinion dependency relations. It indicates that if only modification related relations were considered, the f-score dropped nearly half because more than half of the opinion dependency relations were expelled in this case. In other word, results show that predicting on all relations instead of taking only modification-related dependency relations as clues can capture more opinion relations, and hence the prediction of opinion relations is necessary.

4.4 Evaluation of Opinion Extraction Using Predicted Opinion Trios and Dependency Relations

In this section, predicted opinion trios and predicted opinion dependency relations were utilized in an opinion extraction system. In order to make use of these structural cues, opinion analysis methods proposed by Ku *et al.* (2007) were selected. Their methods calculated opinion scores of sentences from characters and words accumulatively, so syntactic cues can be added in and function jointly.

Five settings for opinion analysis were experimented:

- **C+W+N**: characters, words, and negations were used as cues for calculating opinion scores. It was the original method proposed by Ku *et al.*
- **C+W+N+goldTrio**: annotated opinion trios were utilized additionally.
- **C+W+N+Trio**: predicted opinion trios were utilized additionally.
- **C+W+N+goldDep**: opinion dependency relations aligned from the annotated trios were utilized additionally.
- **C+W+N+Dep**: predicted opinion dependency relations were utilized additionally.

The results were shown in Table 7. The performance of the opinion extraction improves 10.40% (0.7162->0.7993) when utilizing opinion trios and 8.66% (0.7162->0.7782) when utilizing opinion dependency relations. These results clearly indicate that the syntactic information benefit opinion analysis. Because of the possible information loss in the automatic alignment process, that the performance of using trios is a little better than using dependency relations matches our expectation.

Setting	f-Score
C+W+N	0.7162
C+W+N+goldTrio	0.7922
C+W+N+Trio	0.7993
C+W+N+goldDep	0.7784
C+W+N+Dep	0.7782

Table 7. Performance of using syntactic information for opinion analysis.

5 Related Work

For all we know, no previous work has annotated opinion information on all dependency relations, or mapped annotated opinionated structures to dependency relations on a large quantity of documents or sentences. Therefore, to the best of our knowledge, no statistically analysis of opinion dependency relations involving manually annotations has been conducted. Researchers designed ruled or extracted dependency relations as features for opinion analysis based on their linguistic knowledge (Qiu *et al.*, 2011).

Yet there are still several lines of related work, including (i) opinion analysis (ii) opinion corpora (iii) syntactic information. Several dozen papers have been published on the topic of opinion analysis. Two general approaches have been proposed previously. They are machine learning approaches and heuristic-rule approaches. For both approaches, syntactic structures could be utilized. For the former, they can be used as features (Abbasi *et al.*, 2008); for the later, rules can be designed according to them (Ku *et al.*, 2009). We can see from the previous work that syntactic structures can help to enhance the performance.

As to the experimental corpora, some researchers managed to generate annotated materials and gold standards under constraints. Somasundaran (2007) annotated discourse information from meeting dialogs to train a sentiment model. MPQA annotated opinions and their sources (Wiebe *et al.*, 2002). NTCIR annotated opinions, polarities, sources, and targets for its multilingual opinion analysis task (MOAT, Seki *et al.*, 2008). However, none of them were annotated on materials with syntactic structures, and it caused the lack of analysis of opinion syntactic structures.

Researchers have acquired syntactic structures (Zhou, 2008), but few of them have tried to associate syntactic structures with opinions. The most similar previous work to ours was proposed by Ku *et al.* (2009). Compared to it, the proposed process made the development of opinion dependency parser feasible. As dependency relations and the predicted opinion dependency relations are of the same form, no extra knowledge or integration is needed for the use of them.

6 Conclusions and Future Work

The proposed new process is the main contribution of this paper. It annotated opinion syntactic structures on phrase structure trees, which are more readable for annotators, and aligned these structures to grammatical structures, which facilitates their usage. Chinese Treebank was selected as the source of phrase structure trees, and dependency relations as the grammatical structures. They are both widely used in natural language processing.

Though the experiments were implemented on Chinese materials, this process is language independent. It can be applied to materials in different languages without modifications.

By predicting opinion dependency relations, we can say that a basic opinion dependency parser has been developed. Experiments have shown that the predicted opinion dependency relations are beneficial for opinion extraction. Although we still need a parser to generate syntactic structures, parsing is relatively a mature technique in natural language processing. For a comparably new research problem like opinion analysis, it is common that tools are not handy. The best of the proposed method is that it can function in a multilingual environment by incorporating a domain or language specific resources (here, NTUSD for Chinese).

Through the alignment, we made a large quantity of opinion dependency relations available. According to their distributions shown in this paper, researchers can select suitable relations to use according to their diverse needs, such as extracting evaluative features in product reviews or comments, opinions or their polarities.

References

Abbasi, A., Chen, H., and Salem, A. 2008. Sentiment analysis in multiple languages: Feature selection for opinion classification in Web forums. ACM Trans. Inf. Syst. 26, 3 (Jun. 2008), 1-34. DOI= http://doi.acm.org/10.1145/1361684.1361685

Bikel, D. M. and Castelli, V. 2008. Event Matching Using the Transitive Closure of Dependency Relations. *Proceedings of the 46th Annual Meeting on Association for Computational Linguistics*, pages 145-148.

Breck, E., Choi, Y. and Cardie, C. 2007. Identifying Expressions of Opinion in Context. *Proceedings of the 20th International Joint Conferences on Artificial Intelligence*, pages 2683-2688.

Chang, P.-C., Tseng, H., Jurafsky, D. and Manning C. D. 2009. Discriminative Reordering with Chinese Grammatical Relations Features. *Proceedings of the Third Workshop on Syntax and Structure in Statistical Translation*, pages 51-59.

Doan, H., Cao, Y., Lin, C.-Y. and Yu, Y. 2008. Searching Question by Identifying Question Topic and Question Focus. *Proceedings of the 46th Annual Meeting on Association for Computational Linguistics*, pages 156-164.

Feng, S., Wang, D., Yu, G., Yang, C. and Yang, N. 2009. Chinese Blog Clustering by Hidden Sentiment Factors. *ADMA, Vol. 5678, Springer (2009)*, pages 140-151.

Ku, L.-W. and Chen, H.-H. 2007. Mining Opinions from the Web: Beyond Relevance Retrieval. *Journal of American Society for Information Science and Technology*, Special Issue on Mining Web Resources for Enhancing Information Retrieval, 58(12), 1838-1850.

Ku, L.-W., Huang, T.-H. and Chen, H.-H. 2009. Using Morphological and Syntactic Structures for Chinese Opinion Analysis. *Proceedings of Conference on Empirical Methods in Natural Language Processing*, pages 1260-1269.

Ku, L.-W., Lo, Y.-S. and Chen H.-H. 2007. Test Collection Selection and Gold Standard Generation for a Multiply-Annotated Opinion Corpus. *Proceedings of the 45th Annual Meeting on Association for Computational Linguistics*, pages 89-92.

Lafferty, J., McCallum, A. and Pereira, F. 2001. Conditional Random Fields: Probabilistic Models for Segmenting and Labeling Sequence Data. *Proceedings of International Conference on Machine Learning*, pages 282-289.

Lu, Y., Zhai, C.X. and Sundaresan, N. 2009. Rated Aspect Summarization of Short Comments. *Proceedings of 18th International World Wide Web Conference*, pages 131-140.

de Marneffe, M.-C. and Manning, C. D. 2008. Stanford typed dependencies manual. Technichal report. http://nlp.stanford.edu/software/dependencies_manual.pdf

Pang, B., Lee, L. and Vaithyanathan, S. 2002. Thumbs up? Sentiment classification using machine learning techniques. *Proceedings of the 2002 Conference on Empirical Methods in Natural Language Processing*, pages 79-86.

Qiu, G., Wang, C., Bu, J., Liu, K. and Chen, C. 2008. Incorporate the Syntactic. Knowledge in Opinion Mining in User-generated Content. *Proceedings of NLPIX'08*.

Qiu, G., Liu, B., Bu, J. and Chen, C. 2011. Opinion Word Expansion and Target Extraction through Double Propagation. *Computational Linguistics*, March 2011, Vol. 37, No. 1: 9.27

Seki, Y., D. K. Evans, L.-W. Ku, L. Sun, H.-H. Chen and N. Kando. 2008. Overview of Multilingual Opinion Analysis Task at NTCIR-7. *Proceedings of the 7th NTCIR Workshop Meeting on Evaluation of Information Access Technologies:Information Retrieval, Question Answering, and Cross-Lingual Information Access*, pages 185-203.

Somasundaran, S., J. Ruppenhofer and J. Wiebe. 2007. Detecting arguing and sentiment in meetings. *Proceedings of the SIGdial Workshop on Discourse and Dialogue 2007*.

Wiebe, J., E. Breck, C. Buckly, C. Cardie, P. Davis, B. Fraser, D. Litman, D. Pierce, E. Riloff and T. Wilson. 2002. *NRRC summer workshop on multi-perspective question answering, final report*. ARDA NRRC Summer 2002 Workshop.

Zhou, Q. 2008. Automatic rule acquisition for Chinese intra-chunk relations. *Proceedings of International Joint Conference of Natural Language Processing (IJCNLP-2008)*.

Detecting and Blocking False Sentiment Propagation

Hye-Jin Min
CS Department, KAIST
Daejeon, Republic of Korea
hjmin@nlp.kaist.ac.kr

Jong C. Park
CS Department, KAIST
Daejeon, Republic of Korea
park@cs.kaist.ac.kr

Abstract

Sentiment detection of a given expression involves interaction with its component constituents through rules such as polarity propagation, reversal or neutralization. Such compositionality-based sentiment detection usually performs better than a vote-based bag-of-words approach. However, in some contexts, the polarity of the adjectival modifier may not always be correctly determined by such rules, especially when the adjectival modifier characterizes the noun so that its denotation becomes a particular concept or an object in customer reviews. In this paper, we examine adjectival modifiers in customer review sentences whose polarity should either be propagated (SHIFT) or not (UNSHIFT). We refine polarity propagation rules in the literature by considering both syntactic and semantic clues of the modified nouns and the verbs that take such nouns as arguments. The resulting rules are shown to work particularly well in detecting cases of 'UNSHIFT' above, improving the performance of overall sentiment detection at the clause level, especially in 'neutral' sentences. We also show that even such polarity that is not propagated is still necessary for identifying implicit sentiment of the adjacent clauses.

1 Introduction

Detecting the sentiment of a given grammatical unit such as phrase, clause or sentence has received much attention in opinion mining and sentiment analysis. While earlier work simply detected the overall polarity by computing the majority of the polarity of words within the expression, researchers are now looking more into the composition of polarity of words within the expression (Wilson et al., 2005; Moilanen and Pulman, 2007; Choi and Cardie, 2008). They have utilized either word features (e.g., 'Context Valence Shifters') or grammatical structures (e.g., 'the Principle of Compositionality'). It is shown that a machine learning approach with these features performs better than a vote-based bag-of-words approach. While the importance of salient features such as 'negation' or 'intensifier' is fully recognized, it is not yet clearly understood when the polarity of a particular word is propagated or is sacrificed.

The polarity of an adjectival modifier is often propagated to the polarity of the modified noun or noun phrases with no inherent polarity. However, sometimes the polarity is not propagated to that of the enclosing clause or sentence at all. For example, the polarity of the word 'real' is not propagated to that of the sentence "Real 501's are made of 14 oz canvas-like material." in a customer review of the pants, even though there is no salient sentiment word except for the word 'real'. Our observation shows that stopped propagation of this kind in customer reviews often appears because of the following reasons: 1) the word in question is mainly used to refer to the property or the identity of the product entity; 2) it is mainly used to describe certain processes about the author's experiences or to provide a useful guide for potential customers.

It is important to make the correct decision about the polarity propagation in particular regarding no propagation of the polarity of such an adjectival modifier, in order to detect the sentiment over customer reviews at a deeper linguistic level. For example, the word 'real' above is chosen to refer to the other comparative entity, which is regarded as a 'positive' entity, as opposed to the present one that is not 'real'. Hence, the 'positive' polarity should not be propagated to the polarity of the current reviewed product entity in the context. The benefit of this decision is that it will enhance the detection of the 'neutral' polarity of the sentences in a document. This decision can also be utilized in identifying the underlying 'negative' sentiment of the given sentence. Although it is still hard to detect the case by just looking into the sentiment of the words at the surface level, this will still work as a good clue for the detection because such a word is in contrast to the phrase 'these *Iconic Rigid* jeans' as in "These *Iconic Rigid* jeans are made of some sleazy, much lighter material", which is the sentence that follows. By considering these two sentences together, we can see that a 'negative' sentiment is conveyed. Previous work on sentiment detection from customer reviews mainly focuses on detecting sentiment of product features from the patternized sentences (Hu and Liu, 2004; Popescu and Etzioni, 2005; Titov and McDonald, 2008), so the sentences containing such implicit sentiment were not analyzed properly, despite of its importance.

In this paper, we examine adjectival modifiers in customer review sentences whose polarity should either be propagated (SHIFT) or not (UNSHIFT) when the modified noun has no inherent polarity. We refine the previous polarity propagation rules (Moilanen and Pulman, 2007) in order to enhance the performance of the propagation decision by considering both syntactic and semantic clues of the modified nouns and the verbs that take such modified nouns as arguments.

Our rules incorporating these clues into the previous rules have an important role in detecting the 'UNSHIFT' case. We found that our rules help the overall sentiment detection at the clause level especially regarding the 'neutral' cases but found also that even such polarity with no propagation is also necessary identifying the implicit sentiment of the adjacent clauses.

The rest of the paper is organized as follows. Section 2 introduces previous work analyzing the sentiment in customer reviews focusing on the detection of the polarity. Section 3 summarizes compositionality-based polarity detection in this paper. Sections 4 and 5 describe basic and refined polarity decision rules for adjectival modifiers. Section 6 analyzes our experimental results and Section 7 discusses its importance and limitation. Section 8 concludes the paper with future work.

2 Related Work

Previous work on the detection of the opinions and sentiments to a given product can be divided into three groups: graph-based method with polarity words, rule-based and machine learning-based methods focusing on sentiment detection in a compositional way. Hu and Liu (2004) identified the sentiment by counting the relevant adjectives that belong to each polarity class with a graph-based polarity lexicon. Popescu and Etzioni (2005) determined the polarity of opinion-containing phrases by identifying the polarity of the words based on relaxation labeling.

The rule-based sentiment identification methods are based on the Principle of Compositionality (Moilanen and Pulman, 2007; Neviarouskaya et al., 2009). Such methods determine the polarity of a given unit basically by composing the inherent polarity of its component lexical units or other linguistic constituents. In addition, a certain type of unit called 'valence shifters' works to contextually neutralize or intensify the polarity of the given phrase or sentence (Polanyi and Zaenen, 2004; Kennedy and Inkpen, 2006). Our work is also based on the polarity decision rules proposed by the previous work, and we modified some of them for our purpose. The benefit of rule-based approach is that it is easy to incorporate the additional rules into a rule-based framework for further detailed classification with additional categories.

Some researchers incorporated rule-based sentiment identification into machine learning techniques (Wilson et al., 2005; Choi and Cardie, 2008). Wilson and colleagues (2005) developed the classifier using AdaBoost.HM based on the idea of contextual valence shifters in order to identify contextual polarity at the phrase level. One of the features they considered is modification feature, *modifies* (parent with polarity), and *modified* (children with polarity), though they did not examine the context in which these types of feature may or may not contribute to the overall polarity. Choi and Cardie (2008) developed a machine-learning based sentiment detection method by adopting the Principle of Compositionality (Moilanen and Pulman, 2007) in order to examine whether such computational semantic-based idea can be made empirically effective. Their results show that the method incorporating compositionality performed best among all the methods. Our work is similar to their work in that we followed the idea of the Principle of Compositionality. However, our focus is on examining the characteristics of context surrounding a given adjectival modifier when its polarity is either propagated or not propagated and seeing how this propagation result affects the overall polarity of the clause.

3 Sentiment Detection based on Compositionality

Previous work on deciding the overall polarity of the given expression based on the Principle of Compositionality (Moilanen and Pulman, 2007; Neviarouskaya et al., 2009) takes into account how component lexical units are syntactically combined and develops rules to handle contextual polarity propagation, reversal, conflict or neutralization when combining the inherent polarities of the component lexical units.

We follow the polarity decision rules from previous work (Moilanen and Pulman, 2007; Shaikh et al., 2007; Neviarouskaya et al., 2009) as shown below. We apply the rules to each sentence with its dependency tree structure acquired from the Stanford parser (Klein and Manning, 2003; Marneffe et al., 2006).

- **Basic Propagation** (Moilanen and Pulman, 2007; Neviarouskaya et al., 2009): The polarity of the lexical unit at the upper level in the dependency structure of the text unit has a higher priority. If the word at the upper level has no inherent polarity, the polarity of its dependent word (at the lower level) is propagated to the polarity of the text unit.

- **OBJ/Comp domination for the case of transfer verbs** (Moilanen and Pulman, 2007): The polarity of the constituent as an object or a complement of the transfer verbs that "transmit sentiments among the arguments" (Neviarouskaya et al., 2009) is dominant when there is a polarity conflict among arguments of such verbs. (e.g., "My good old size started showing up too big or wouldn't shrink right.")

- **Reversal** (Moilanen and Pulman, 2007; Neviarouskaya et al., 2009): The negation words (e.g., 'not', 'no', 'hardly', 'reduce') reverse the polarity. We added more verb entries containing the meaning of 'reversal' from other existing review corpora.

- **Reversal for Conflict** (Both *negative* adverbs and *negative* verbs are combined from (Shaikh et al., 2007)): When two lexical units with 'negative' polarity are combined, the polarity of the unit covering both units is reversed. (e.g., "They are 501, it's hard to go wrong with these.": positive)

- **Neutralizing operators** (Condition operators (e.g., if) from Neviarouskaya et al., 2009): The polarity of the main clause or the sentence is neutralized when there are adverbial conditional clauses. We added the markers 'wh-words' or 'how' as well as the conditional marker 'if/unless'. (e.g., "How can I go wrong with the classic 501?")

4 Basic Rules for Adjectival Modifier

By following the compositionality-based polarity decision rules, the polarity of a noun or a noun phrase that has no inherent polarity is determined by its modifier's polarity. In other words, the polarity of the modifier is propagated to the upper level node in the dependency tree structure. For example, the noun phrase 'a perfect dryer' becomes to have 'positive' polarity by the result of polarity propagation. And such polarity may or may not be propagated depending on its syntactic role of the noun phrase at the clause level. If the phrase is a subject, it gets lower priority than the one that works as an object or a complement, but if the word at the upper level or the word with higher priority at the same level (i.e., object or complement) has no inherent polarity, its polarity can be propagated up to the root level by the 'Basic Propagation'. Figure 1 illustrates this case.

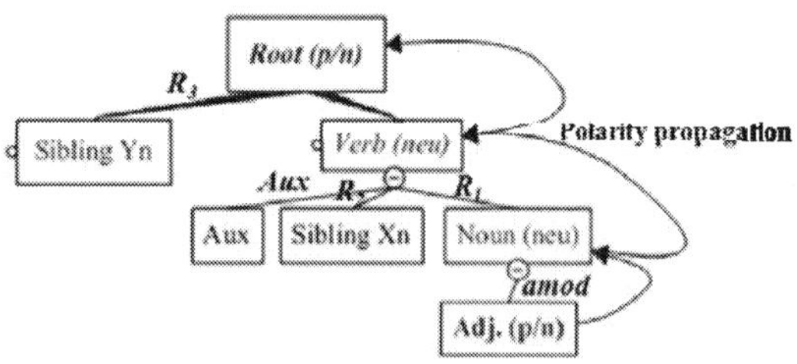

Aux = {aux, neg, intensifier, ...,}

R = {nsubj, dobj, prep, complement}

Sibling Xn: Children of the Verb with dependency relation R_2

Sibling Yn: Children of the Root with dependency relation R_3

Figure 1. Basic propagation

Nonetheless, we found that the polarity should not be propagated in some cases as shown in Example (1a).

(1) a. Real 501's are made of 14 oz canvas-like material.
b. It's a real 501's.

There is no word with inherent polarity except 'real' in (1a), so the overall polarity could be decided as 'positive' by the rules just like (1b), but it is actually closer to 'neutral' sentence. The reason is that the adjective is utilized to refer to another product entity, which is 'the original Levis 501 Jean' in this context.

Interestingly, we see that such phrases often appear in the customer reviews of a product which is a steady seller and whose quality is already well known. To detect whether the polarity of the adjectival modifier is propagated or not is crucial especially when there are no other salient polarity words except for the adjective. It is mainly used to refer to the other product entity for contrastive purposes.

In this paper, we examine the types of clues that affect the propagation of the adjectival modifier's polarity at the clause level. We also refine the previous polarity decision rules by incorporating additional clues. With the refined rules, we define our problem as follows. For a given adjectival modifier modifying a noun or a noun phrase with no inherent polarity, we label it with 'SHIFT/UNSHIFT' tags depending on the nature of propagation. If it is propagated, we label it with the 'SHIFT' tag, and if not, we do it with the 'UNSHIFT' tag.

The basic rules for labeling by considering only syntactic clues from the previous polarity decision rules are as follows.

- SHIFT: 1) if the syntactic role of the noun phrase is complement; 2) if the syntactic role of the noun phrase is object of verbs or prepositions
- UNSHIFT: 1) if the syntactic role of the noun phrase is subject (e.g., (1a)); 2) if the syntactic role of the noun phrase is object of the verb whose syntactic type is either 'gerund (*Ving*)' or 'infinitive (*to V*)'

We also regarded the case as 'UNSHIFT' where the noun phrase has lower priority than its sibling phrases in the dependency tree; for example, if there is an object with non-neutral polarity and the syntactic role of the given noun phrase is subject, the labeling is done with 'UNSHIFT'. Example (2) shows 'SHIFT' and 'UNSHIFT' for the adjectival modifier 'good' and 'great', respectively.

(2) a. It's a good buy.

b. A great shave takes a little more commitment than just breaking out a can of foam and a disposable razor.

We decided not to use machine learning techniques with the following reasons. First, our goal is not to enhance the overall performance of sentiment detection in general but to examine what kinds of additional clues are called especially for the decision of the polarity propagation of the adjectives modifying the noun with no polarity. Following Kennedy and Inkpen (2006)'s work for measuring the impact of valence shifters on sentiment classification, we believe it is not straightforward to identify major factors for the improvement with a machine learning algorithm. Second, our work focuses on relatively small cases among all the cases in the whole review sentences (See Table 5), so it is reasonable to directly apply refined rules to each case without an unnecessary training process handling other cases. We believe that the rules of this kind by taking a closer look at the focused cases could be extended regarding scalability with the help of the machine leaning techniques in the future.

5 Rule Refinement

We refined the rules with additional clues as follows because the basic rules do not work properly in some context.

5.1 Phrase-level Clues

The basic rules mainly consider the syntactic types of the noun phrase and the verb taking the noun phrase as the argument. However, the following clues at the phrase level may also affect the propagation.

- Quoted / Capital Letters (UNSHIFT)
- Types of noun in the product reviews

Example (3) shows quoted adjectival modifiers. The quotes indicate that its inherent polarity is not effective. We can see that the author of the review intentionally used them to indicate such neutralization.

(3) a. The fit on these "relaxed" jeans is just that--relaxed but not loose.

b. If you love "Happy Hippy" shower gel, this fun bath product will impress you.

Examples (4) and (5) show the polarity propagation depending on the types of modified noun by the adjectives. While the polarities in Example (4) are propagated, those in Example (5) are not propagated.

(4) a. This product also arrived in good condition and in good time. (Delivery)
b. I will never order anything from Levi again until they come back to the original levi material. (Product feature)

(5) a. They were also not much cheaper than I would have paid from a real retailer. (Location & time)
b. People with healthy, not-so-damaged, and normal hair do not need to use this stuff. (User Information)
c. All it takes for a great shave is a good safety razor, a decent brush, shaving soap and a mug. (Purpose)
d. After a quick rinse my skin looked less dull, and helped clear blotches (Process).
e. Use with Chanel loose powder and Chanel concealer for a perfectly flawless finish. (Product name)

The types of noun in Example (4) are related to explicit sentiment of the product. On the other hand, the types of noun in Example (5) are related to implicit sentiment or additional background information provided for the potential customers. In order to distinguish SHIFT cases from UNSHIFT cases resulting from such different types of noun we built a lexicon for the noun type as shown in Table 1. We collected the words belonging to each type by utilizing three different methods. We first manually collected words belonging to each noun type from the sample review texts and extended the entries by including synonyms of the seed words in WordNet (Synonyms; Miller, 1995). Some synsets of WordNet such as 'body_part'/'illness' and 'shop' are appropriate for 'User information' and 'Location'. We combined several synsets for such type (WordNet Synsets). The noun types such as 'Product name', 'Product feature', 'Purpose', and 'Process' are domain dependent, we collected the words by utilizing Point-wise Mutual Information (PMI).

Propagation	Noun Type	Method
SHIFT	Delivery	Synonyms
	Deal	
	Product feature	PMI
UNSHIFT	Time	Synonyms
	Location (shop, store)	WordNet Synsets
	User info (body part/illness)	
	Product name	PMI
	Process/Purpose	

Table 1. Types of noun

5.2 Clause-level Clues

The main reason for the second rule of the 'UNSHIFT' basic rules in Section 4 is that we assumed the given phrase/clause could be regarded as a secondary concept or topic for the main concept or topic as shown in Example (6).

(6) a. Anyone who is that determined to make the best product on the market, obviously will do whatever it takes to make it happen.
b. Getting an outstanding shave from this razor should be a cinch.

However, the given phrase/clause should be regarded as the main concept or an independent concept as shown in Example (7).

(7) a. It *seemed* to have a rich sophistication which goes with horseback riding or polo.
b. It's wonderful doing everything I need, including making my hair nice and shiny, without the heaviness.

In order to capture these differences, we refined the rules as shown in Table 2.

Infinitive (*to V*)	Gerund (*Ving*)
IF the head of the infinitive has auxiliary characteristics such as 'seem' and 'need' THEN label it with SHIFT. Otherwise, label it with 'UNSHIFT'.	IF the phrase/clause including the gerund is clausal subject THEN label it with 'UNSHIFT'. Otherwise label it with 'SHIFT'.

Table 2. Refined rules for 'UNSHIFT'

The rule for the object of prepositions should also be refined. As we mentioned in Section 5.1, the reason for mentioning some particular types of object in the review is to explain additional background information as a guide for the potential customer as well as showing the sentiment about the product. The types of noun at the phrase level cannot always solely determine the polarity propagation because such decision is still affected by the presence of other constituents in the context at the clause level. For example, by comparing (5c) with the sentence "it provides a very close, smooth shave", the polarity of 'smooth' is propagated while that of 'great' is not propagated.

To handle this case properly, we consider 'Clause-level Semantic Label' at a shallow level by taking into account both some preposition types and the noun types together that frequently appear as shown in Table 3. We named the labels by referring to 'Frame Index' from FrameNet data (Baker et al., 1998). This list of the pairs filters further 'UNSHIFT' cases from the 'SHIFT' labeled cases by the basic rules.

Semantic Label (FrameNet)	Prep. & N.Type	Ex.
Purpose (related to Shopping)	'for/with' & Purpose (Use)	(5c)
Body mark	'for/with' & User info (Body part)	(5b)
Process (related to Using)	'after' & Process	(5d)
Place (related to Shopping)	'on/from' & Time/ Location	(5a)

Table 3. Semantic Label for filtering 'UNSHIFT'

The last clue is about the sentence type. Even if the polarity of the adjectival modifier is propagated to the top node word at the clause level, the type of the sentence may block it for the overall polarity of the whole sentence. We consider three types of sentences that turn the 'SHIFT' label into the 'UNSHIFT' label as shown in Table 4.

Sentence Type	Examples
Condition	You will not be sorry *if* you are looking for the perfect brush to go with your perfect dryer (the featherweight)!
Experience (Perfect Tense & verb class)	*I have been searching* for what seems like forever for a nice cologne or perfume that is not all flowery and overpowering
Guide (Types of nominal subject)	The best *solution* for this is ... A personal *tip* I would like to suggest ...
Guide (Imperative sentence)	Make sure you shake the bottle before using for best color results (as mentioned on the packaging).

Table 4. Types of sentences for 'UNSHIFT'

As a number of previous researches also considered, we canceled the detected sentiment at the conditional clause. In addition, we considered two domain specific types of sentences, namely, *experiences sentences* and *guide sentences* as the clues for 'UNSHIFT' cases, because these types of sentences also give background information rather than explicitly mentioning the sentiment so that the polarity of the adjective tends not to be propagated. We defined *experience sentence* whose main subject is the author and which has present or past perfect tenses with purchase related verbs (e.g., buy, search, try or return). We also defined *guide sentence* that is an imperative sentence with no main subject or with the subject referring to the potential customer such as 'you' or 'people'.

The preprocessing steps before applying the rules above are as follows. First, we get the dependency relation pairs for each input sentence acquired from the Stanford parser (Klein and Manning, 2003; Marneffe et al., 2006), and constructed the dependency tree structure for tree traversal in order to process polarity propagation. Then we assigned each word to its inherent polarity (if it has one) by looking up the sentiment lexicon, 'Subjectivity Lexicon' (Riloff and Wiebe, 2003). We adapted the lexicon to product reviews by modifying the inherent polarity of 36 lexical entries (e.g., white, positive to neutral) and adding 105 additional words frequently used (e.g., small with neutral). In order to apply rules to particular types of adjective and verb such as transfer verbs or contextually polarized adjectives, we added an additional field such as 'type' into each lexical entry to show their identities (The original types of 22 entries in 'Subjective Lexicon' are modified). As for extracting clues, we utilized dependency relations for syntactic types of nouns and verbs. For semantic types of nouns and verbs, we utilized the semi-automatically constructed lexicon as mentioned in Section 5.1. In addition, in order to identify '*experience sentences*' and '*guide sentences*', we extracted tense information and noun subject by utilizing dependency parse tree.

6 Experimental Results

We performed two types of experiment in order to examine the performance of our refined polarity propagation rules and the contribution of the propagation results to the sentiment detection at the clause level.

Table 5 shows the data sets of customer reviews we used for the experiments. We first tested our rules with Set 1 (Beauty positive), a corpus utilized in (Blitzer et al., 2007) because all the reviews are classified as 'positive', so we assume that there are many adjectival modifiers with 'positive' polarity. We then performed both propagation decision and sentiment classification experiments with Set 2 (Levi's Jean), which is crawled review data from Amazon.com by ourselves. The reasons why we chose this product are as follows. First, it is a steady-selling product so that most of the reviews are regarded as positive, which makes it more important to identify negative or neutral opinions than other kinds of reviews. Hence, it is crucial to consider correct decision of propagation of the adjectival modifiers with 'positive' polarity that is mostly not propagated. Second, after the initial observation, we found that a particular expression about 'changes in quality' frequently appears in such reviews (about 20%) and the adjectival modifiers with 'positive' polarity in such expression are mostly not propagated because it would refer to other particular entities or be used to describe a certain process.

Data Sets	# for exp.	Total	%
Beauty Positive set 1	444	6,126	7.2%
Levi's Jeans set 2	147	1,655	8.8%

Table 5. Data sets

Table 6 shows the numbers of propagation rules and Table 7 shows the propagation decision results. Compared to the results by the basic rules, the performance is enhanced in general. However, we notice that the rules related to VerbType are effective on recall but not on precision for 'SHIFT'. On the other hand, as for 'UNSHIFT' the rules are effective on precision but not on recall. Rules taking into account both noun types and prepositions slightly enhance the overall performance. The overall rules that include sentence type score the best precision and recall figures, which are both effective for 'SHIFT' and 'UNSHIFT'.

Next, we apply these rules to our data set 2. Table 8 shows the propagation decision results. The accuracy for the overall test clauses is almost similar to that for set 1. While precision for 'UNSHIFT' and recall for 'SHIFT' rose, precision for 'SHIFT' and recall for 'UNSHIFT' dropped. We analyzed False Negative errors of 'UNSHIFT' cases. Most of them are unknown cases for each rule except due to parsing errors. This also led to the drop of the precision for 'SHIFT'. The strong restriction for 'UNSHIFT' also affected the result of recall for 'SHIFT'.

Table 9 shows the sentiment detection results at the clause level for set 2. The performance of 'positive' label is not much enhanced but that of 'neutral' label is enhanced. We believe that this is because if the polarity of the top node word is explicitly 'positive' because of its inherent polarity the overall polarity of the clause is obviously 'positive' regardless of the result of the polarity propagation decision. On the other hand, in the case of 'neutral' clause, the correct polarity propagation decision for 'UNSHIFT' is critical for detecting the overall polarity. This confirms that our rules have a critical role in detecting the sentiment of 'neutral' sentences.

Rules	SHIFT		UNSHIFT	
	#	∑	#	∑
Basic rules (B)	3	3	2	2
B + PhClues	0	3	4	6
B + PhClues + VerbType	2	5	2	8
B + PhClues + VerbType + SemLabel	0	5	3	11
All	0	5	3	14

Table 6. Numbers of propagation rules

Rules	SHIFT		UNSHIFT		All
	P	R	P	R	Acc.
Basic rules (B)	0.84	0.83	0.72	0.73	0.79
B + PhClues	0.84	0.83	0.72	0.74	0.80
B + PhClues + VerbType	0.83	0.89	0.79	0.70	0.82
B + PhClues + VerbType + SemLabel	0.86	0.89	0.80	0.76	0.84
All	0.90	0.88	0.80	0.84	**0.86**

Table 7. Propagation decision results (set 1)

	SHIFT		UNSHIFT		All
	P	R	P	R	Acc.
Basic Rules	0.71	0.89	0.82	0.59	0.74
Refined Rules	0.78	0.90	0.85	0.69	**0.80**

Table 8. Propagation decision results (set 2)

	Basic Rules		Refined Rules	
	P	R	P	R
Positive	0.82	0.86	0.87	0.87
Negative	0.85	0.67	0.90	0.70
Neutral	0.45	0.56	**0.51**	**0.70**
All (Acc.)	0.74		0.79	

Table 9. Sentiment detection results

By the importance of 'neutral' polarity, we conducted an error analysis on 18 False Positive cases for 'neutral' polarity as shown in Table 10.

7 Discussion

Types	Description	#
Implicit sentiment	The overall sentiment should be detected by further deep linguistic analysis.	8
Incorrect 'UNSHIFT'	The 'UNSHIFT' result is incorrect.	3
Incorrect polarity	The polarity result is incorrect due to other lexical entries	3
Parsing errors	The propagation is made incorrectly due to incorrect dependency relation.	2
Others	Comparison without 'Positive/Negative' sentiment	2

Table 10. Error distribution

We note that the reason for considering specific sentence types as addressed in this paper is that we assume that these sentences are better suited to demonstrate the need for blocking the propagation of the polarity of the given adjectival modifier.

Although we considered certain types in a limited way, we haven't fully observed what types of sentence are actually involved in propagation. In addition, we found that some sentences in the data set we considered initially as having the sentence type that blocks the propagation of polarity of the adjectival modifier do not convey 'neutral' but convey 'positive' or 'negative' polarity implicitly as shown in Example (8).

(8) a. If there is a more perfect shampoo, I haven't found it.
b. *Previously*, I *had to* visit my favorite store more than once to get my size.
c. I've had it for a year and the *elastic is* totally *stretched out* with normal wear.

The main clause in (8a) conveys 'positive' polarity implicitly even though there is no polarity-bearing word. Further processing is necessary including a proper account of negation. The phrases in (8b) and (8c) are about product entities contrastive to the currently reviewed product so that the inherently assigned polarity of 'favorite' and 'normal' is not applicable to the currently reviewed product. In order to detect the implicit intention of this kind, we should also detect the clues for contrast such as 'previously' or the relation between the phrases 'elastic' and 'be stretched out'.

Although the propagation decision for 'UNSHIFT' itself is correct, such inherent polarity of the adjectival modifier may help to identify the implicit sentiment of the adjacent clause as shown in Example (9).

(9) a. I washed them repeatedly in my very *efficient* and eco-friendly Asko washer, but the smell remained.
b. I have paid much more for *inferior* brand jeans and I can say that I won't be doing that anymore.

The implicit polarity of the underlined clause in (9a) may be both 'negative' and 'positive' depending on the context. By utilizing both the inherent polarity of 'efficient' and the role of the conjunction 'but', the conventional polarity detection rule along with conjuncts (Meena and Prabhakar, 2007) can correctly detect its polarity as 'negative'. As for (9b), by the inherent polarity 'negative' of 'inferior' and negation on the underlined clause we can detect the 'positive' polarity of the underlined clause. However, the possibility of the correctness of the detection is still chancy, and a further analysis of the underlying meaning of the clause or the sentence is called for. For example, if we label the clause containing 'inferior' in (9b) as 'action for goal achievement', we can detect the polarity of the underlined clause as 'negative' by the rule taking such label and another label related to its continuity.

8 Conclusion

In this paper, we refined the previous polarity propagation rules in order to better decide whether the polarity of the adjectival modifier should be propagated or not. We considered both phrase-level and clause-level clues by considering syntactic and semantic types of nouns and verbs. Our rules incorporating these clues into the basic rules detected the 'UNSHIFT' case particularly well. The detection results of the overall sentiment at the clause level are meaningfully enhanced as compared to those based on the previous polarity propagation rules regarding especially 'neutral' sentences. However, despite the correct decision for 'UNSHIFT', we found that such polarity of the modifiers may also help to identify the implicit sentiment without further deeper linguistic analysis.

In order to detect implicit sentiment, we will examine the clues for detecting contrast among product entities or product features for the future work. We will also classify the roles of the clause at a fine-grained level that is related to the detection of the implicit sentiment.

Acknowledgements

This work was supported in part by the National Research Foundation of Korea (NRF) grant funded by the Korea government (MEST) (No. 2011-0018262), and in part by the Intelligent Robotics Development Program, one of the 21st Century Frontier R&D Programs funded by the Ministry of Knowledge Economy of Korea. We thank the three anonymous reviewers for helpful comments and insightful suggestions.

References

Collin F. Baker, Charles J. Fillmore, and John B. Lowe. 1998. The Berkeley FrameNet Project. *In Proceedings of COLING,* Volume 1, pp. 86–90, Morristown, NJ, USA, Association for Computational Linguistics.

John Blitzer, Mark Dredze, and Fernando Pereira. 2007. Biographies, Bollywood, Boom-boxes and Blenders: Domain Adaptation for Sentiment Classification. *In Proceedings of ACL*, pp. 440-447, Prague, Association for Computational Linguistics.

Yejin Choi and Claire Cardie. 2008. Learning with Compositional Semantics as Structural Inference for Subsentential Sentiment Analysis, *In Proceedings of HLT/EMNLP*, pp. 793-801, Honolulu, Association for Computational Linguistics.

Minqing Hu and Bing Liu. 2004. Mining and summarizing customer reviews, *In Proceedings of ACM SIGKDD*, pp. 168-177, ACM Press.

Alistair Kennedy and Diana Inkpen. 2006. Sentiment Classification of Movie and Product Reviews Using Contextual Valence Shifters, *Computational Intelligence 22(2)*:110-125.

Dan Klein and Christopher D. Manning. 2003. Accurate Unlexicalized Parsing. *In Proceedings of ACL*, pp. 423-430, Sapporo, Japan, Association for Computational Linguistics.

Arun Meena and T.V. Prabhakar. 2007. Sentence Level Sentiment Analysis in the Presence of Conjuncts Using Linguistic Analysis, *In Proceedings of ECIR 2007, LNCS 4425*, pp. 573-580.

Marie-Catherine de Marneffe, Bill MacCartney and Christopher D. Manning. 2006. Generating Typed Dependency Parses from Phrase Structure Parses. *In Proceedings of LREC 2006*, pp. 449-454.

George A. Miller. 1995. WORDNET: A Lexical Database for English. *Communications of ACM* (11): pp. 39-41.

Karo Moilanen and Stephen Pulman. 2007. Sentiment Composition. *In Proceedings of RANLP-2007*, pp. 378-382, Borovets, Bulgaria.

Alena Neviarouskaya, Helmut Prendinger, and Mitsuru Ishizuka. 2009. Semantically distinct verb classes involved in sentiment analysis, *In Proceedings of IADIS International Conference Applied Computing*, pp. 27-34.

Livia Polanyi and Annie Zaenen. 2004. Contextual valence shifters, *In Working Notes of the AAAI Spring Symposium on Exploring Attitude and Affect in Text: Theories and Applications*, pp. 106-111, Menlo Park, CA, The AAAI Press.

Ana-Maria Popescu and Oren Etzioni. 2005. Extracting product features and opinions from reviews, *In Proceedings of HLT/EMNLP*, pp. 339-346, Vancouver, Association for Computational Linguistics.

Ellen Riloff and Janyce Wiebe. 2003. Learning extraction patterns for subjective expressions. *In Proceedings of EMNLP*, pp. 105-112, Sapporo, Japan, Association for Computational Linguistics.

Mostafa Al Masum Shaikh, Helmut Prendinger, and Ishizuka Mitsuru, I. 2007. Assessing sentiment of text by semantic dependency and contextual valence analysis, *In Proceedings of ACII 2007, LNCS 4738*, pp. 191-202.

Theresa Wilson, Janyce Wiebe, and Paul Hoffman. 2005. Recognizing Contextual Polarity in Phrase-Level Sentiment Analysis, *In Proceedings of HLT/EMNLP*, pp. 347-354, Vancouver, Association for Computational Linguistics.

Efficient induction of probabilistic word classes with LDA

Grzegorz Chrupała
Spoken Language Systems
Saarland University
gchrupala@lsv.uni-saarland.de

Abstract

Word classes automatically induced from distributional evidence have proved useful many NLP tasks including Named Entity Recognition, parsing and sentence retrieval. The Brown hard clustering algorithm is commonly used in this scenario. Here we propose to use Latent Dirichlet Allocation in order to induce soft, probabilistic word classes. We compare our approach against Brown in terms of efficiency. We also compare the usefulness of the induced Brown and LDA word classes for the semi-supervised learning of three NLP tasks: fine-grained Named Entity Recognition, Morphological Analysis and semantic Relation Classification. We show that using LDA for word class induction scales better with the number of classes than the Brown algorithm and the resulting classes outperform Brown on the three tasks.

1 Introduction

Word classes automatically induced from distributional evidence have proved useful in a variety of tasks, including Named Entity Recognition (Miller et al. 2004, Ratinov and Roth 2009, Chrupała and Klakow 2010, Turian et al. 2010), parsing (Koo et al. 2008, Suzuki et al. 2009, Candito and Crabbé 2009) and sentence retrieval (Momtazi and Klakow 2009).

Brown et al. (1992) introduced an algorithm which assigns word types to disjoint clusters and it remains a common choice when a simple way to automatically obtain word classes is needed. We present a word class induction method using Latent Dirichlet Allocation (Blei et al. 2003) which has attractive properties compared to Brown:

- It induces a soft, probabilistic clustering on both word types and context features.
- It runs in time linear in the number of classes.

The model maps straightforwardly to the standard document topic model, and thus has the advantage of many existing high quality implementations. We evaluate the model's usefulness on fine-grained Named Entity Recognition (NER), Morphological Analysis (MA) and semantic Relation Classification (RC) and show that

- while the word classes obtained perform better than Brown classes,
- they can be induced in a fraction of the time necessary to run the equivalent Brown model.

2 Inducing word representations

There is a variety of approaches to inducing word representations from distributional information. In this section we briefly review the research most relevant to our proposed approach.

Hard classes Brown et al. (1992) introduced an early model which induces a mapping from word types to classes. It is an agglomerative clustering algorithm which starts with K classes for the K most frequent word types and then proceeds by alternately adding the next most frequent word to the class set and merging the two classes which result in the least decrease in the mutual information between class bigrams. The result is a class hierarchy with word types at the leaves. The overall runtime of the algorithm is $O(K^2V)$ where K is the number of classes and V the number of word types. Lin and Wu (2009) use a distributed version of K-Means to assign words and phrases to hard classes, and successfully use them as features in a NER task and in query classification.

Soft classes A limitation of the Brown model is that it performs hard clustering of word types, and cannot be used to disambiguate word occurrences based on context. Hidden Markov Models have been used to induce probabilistic (soft) word classes: training an HMM on unlabeled data one obtains classes which correspond to multinomial distributions over the vocabulary (Goldwater and Griffiths 2007, Gao and Johnson 2008). Griffiths et al. (2005) propose a model factored into an HMM which generates function words and an LDA topic models which generates content words. Learning the parameters of a bigram HMM takes $O(K^2N)$ time where N is the number of word tokens in the corpus.

Other approaches Other approaches to inducing word representations do not rely on the notion of word class. Distributed word embeddings can be learned using a neural network-bases language models (Bengio et al. 2006, Collobert and Weston 2008, Mnih and Hinton 2009). Dimensionality reduction techniques such as SVD (Schütze 1995, Lamar et al. 2010) and LSA (Deerwester et al. 1990) have also been found useful for generating word representations.

3 Using word representations

Our main motivation for studying word class induction methods is to use them in a semi-supervised learning scenario, where word representations are induced from a large unlabeled corpus and subsequently used as a source of features for a supervised model. Turian et al. (2010) compare the effect of using representations based on Brown classes, the Collobert and Weston (2008) embeddings and the Mnih and Hinton (2009) embeddings in learning English syntactic chunking (CoNLL 2000) and English coarse-grained Named Entity Recognition (CoNLL 2003). For both tasks the best representation is fine-grained Brown classes (3200 and 1000 classes respectively). Combining the Brown features with distributed embeddings further improves performance on NER but not on chunking. Lin and Wu (2009) use induce word and phrase classes and report results on NER which are higher than Turian et al. (2010)'s Brown scores, but this research used 700 billion words of web text and needed a cloud computing infrastructure with 1000 CPUs to run. It is evident that the Brown clustering algorithm still provides an extremely competitive baseline nearly 20 years after it was proposed.

We thus compare the performance of the LDA word class model to the Brown model on three NLP tasks: fine grained Named Entity Recognition, Morphological Analysis, and Relation Classification. The first two tasks are difficult due to the large number of labels and high potential for ambiguity. The third task is challenging for a different reason: it involves highly abstract semantic relations, often not obviously inferable from surface lexical clues.

4 LDA model for word class induction

We propose an LDA-based model for word class induction and contrast its structure, efficiency, and performance to those exhibited by the Brown model.

4.1 Weaknesses of Brown

Here we address what we see as two related weaknesses of the Brown model. The algorithm's quadratic dependence on K makes it inconvenient to induce more than a few hundred classes: running a 1.000 class model with a 400.000 vocabulary took over 100 hours. Second, the induced clustering is hard, and the only way to model ambiguous word types is to have a separate class for each kind of ambiguity. This in turn means that we need to learn a large number of classes, which exacerbates the problem with inefficiency. Very fine-grained Brown classes are typically needed for good performance as shown by Turian et al.'s results. Our model for word class induction addresses both of the weaknesses.

4.2 LDA for word class induction

Latent Dirichlet Allocation (LDA) was initially introduced by Blei et al. (2003) in the context of topic modeling, i.e. finding coherent topics shared among subsets of a collection of documents. LDA is a generative, probabilistic hierarchical Bayesian model which induces a set of latent variables which correspond to the topics. The topics themselves are multinomial distributions over words. The graphical model is shown in plate notation in Figure 1. The generative structure of the LDA model is as follows:

$$\begin{aligned}
\phi_k &\sim \text{Dirichlet}(\beta), & k &\in [1, K] \\
\theta_d &\sim \text{Dirichlet}(\alpha), & d &\in [1, D] \\
z_{n_d} &\sim \text{Multinomial}(\theta_d), & n_d &\in [1, N_d] \\
w_{n_d} &\sim \text{Multinomial}(\phi_{z_{n_d}}), & n_d &\in [1, N_d]
\end{aligned} \quad (1)$$

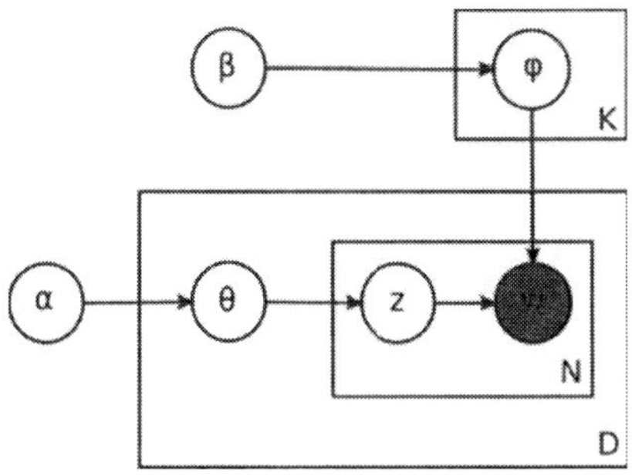

Figure 1: LDA plate diagram

The document collection is generated by drawing, for each topic k, a distribution over words ϕ_k from a Dirichlet prior with parameters β. Then for each document d we draw a multinomial distribution over topics θ_d from a Dirichlet prior parametrized by α. To generate the nth word in document d we draw the topic id z_{n_d} from the document-specific topic distribution θ_d, and then draw the word from the word distribution corresponding to the chosen topic $\phi_{z_{n_d}}$. Thus each document is a mixture of different topics, giving the model the flexibility needed to reflect the topical structures in real-world document collections. This flexibility has contributed to the popularity of LDA as a common choice in a wide range of domains beyond topic modeling. Another important reason for LDA's success is the availability of efficient and well-understood estimation methods such as Variational EM (Blei et al. 2003), and Gibbs sampling (Griffiths and Steyvers 2004). For both methods efficient, well engineered and well tested implementations are readily available. These advantages have led us to try to use a model equivalent to an LDA topic model in order to induce word classes based on distributional clues.

We associate each word type with a distribution over latent classes. Each class is in turn a distribution over contextually co-occurring features. In principle the contextual features could be arbitrary functions of the context, but to make our model use exactly the same information as the Brown model, we will restrict them to the word's immediate left and right neighbors. A direct mapping to document topic model can be seen:

Topic model	Word class induction
Document	Word type
Word	Context feature
Topic	Word class

An example "document" in our scenario, corresponding to the word type *Krzysztof* looks like the following:

Bledkowski$_R$ **Kieslowski**$_R$ **Kieslowski**$_R$ **Rutkowski**$_R$ **Sikorski**$_R$ **and**$_L$ **argues**$_L$ **argues**$_R$ **director**$_L$ **director**$_L$ **edits**$_R$ **said**$_R$

The subscript on the word indicates whether it is a left or right context feature, i.e. whether it appears to left or to the right of *Krzysztof* in the corpus.

Thus, strictly speaking our model does not generate the actual sequence of words in the corpus, but rather a collection of "documents" such as the above, or equivalently, a table listing bigram co-occurrence counts for each word type.

The generative structure of the model corresponds exactly to a standard LDA topic model in equation 1. Now K is the number of latent classes, D is the vocabulary size, and N_d is the number of left and right contexts in which word type d appears, z_{n_d} is the class of word type d in the n_d^{th} context, and f_{n_d} is the n_d^{th} context feature of word type d.

Once trained, the parameters provide two types of word representations. Each θ_d gives the latent class probability distribution given a word type. Each ϕ_k gives the feature distribution given a latent class. Thus the model provides a probabilistic representation for word types independently of their context, and also for contexts independently of the word type. This is a more powerful representation than hard word clustering: (i) soft clustering allows the modeling of ambiguity, (ii) additional source of information is available which helps determine the class of a word from its context.

Figure 2 shows an example of how the classes discovered by the model deal with ambiguity. The pie charts depict the induced class distributions for two word types *Martin* and *Cameron*. These words are ambiguous in a similar way: they are mostly used as (i) first names or (ii) family names, and (iii) additionally can appear as part of a name of a company or place. This similarity of usage is reflected in closeness of the distributions over the induced classes for those words. Thus the first class (colored red) is associated with many family names, the second (blue) with titles and first names, and the third (green) with companies and locations. This correspondence is certainly not

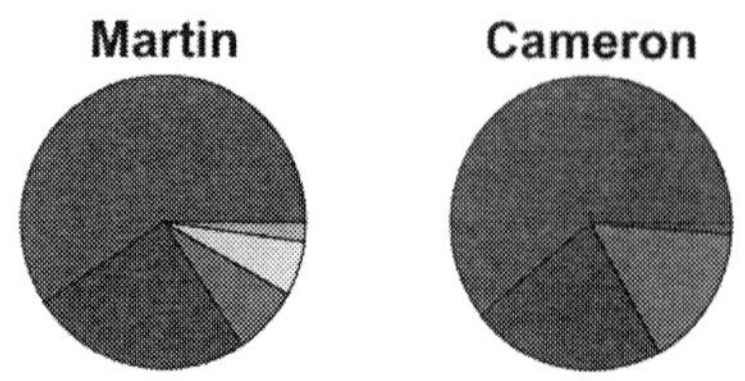

chief Gingrich Martin Newt Van Scott Roberts
Mr. Ms. John Robert President Dr. David
Street General Texas Fidelity State California

Figure 2: Class distributions for the word types *Martin* and *Cameron*. Also shown are the most common word types for the three largest.

Newt, Speaker	•	executive, operating
says, Chairman	•	Clinton, Dole, J.
Wall, West, East	•	County, AG, Journal

Figure 3: Most frequent left and right context-word features co-occurring with the three classes from Figure 2

perfect (e.g. the first class is also associated with the word *chief*) but it is suggestive that soft LDA-based clustering can successfully model and discover this type of systematic shared ambiguities.

We can use the same three classes to illustrate the second advantage of LDA word classes mentioned above: we can obtain information about the class of a particular token based on its context. Thus even for a rare word which did not appear in the corpus used for word class induction, we can still find out what word classes it is associated with just by consulting the ϕ table and retrieving the classes strongly associated with the context features. Figure 3 shows the left and right context features which co-occurred most frequently with the same three classes illustrated in Figure 2. For example the second (blue) class, which contains titles and first names, is associated with left contexts such as *says* and *Chairman* and right contexts such as *Clinton* and *Dole*.

5 Experimental evaluation

In order to evaluate the LDA word class induction model we assess two of its aspects: (i) we compare its efficiency to that of Brown clustering, and (ii) we compare the performance of the induced word classes to those obtained by Brown clustering in two difficult sequence labeling tasks and one classification task.

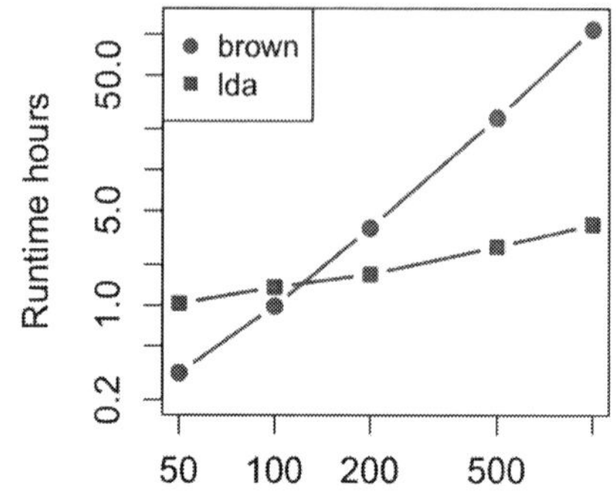

Figure 4: Brown and LDA run times

5.1 Efficiency

Two main approaches have been used to train LDA topic models: variational EM (Blei et al. 2003) and Gibbs sampling (Griffiths and Steyvers 2004). Both scale linearly with the number of topics. This property is one of the main advantages of the LDA word class induction model over HMM or Brown clustering. In this section we show that also in practice this means that LDA word classes can be induced much faster than equivalently performing Brown classes.

As training data for both models we use the North American News Text Corpus (over 60M words). For both models we only keep bigrams which occur at least 3 times. The resulting vocabulary is over 380K word types. The LDA class induction model scales as $O(KN)$ where N is the sum of all feature counts. Since we discard rare bigrams with frequencies under m, we can scale the remaining feature counts by $1/m$ and obtain an equivalent model, while reducing runtime by m times. For both models we induce 50, 100, 200, 500 and 1000 classes. For Brown we run the implementation of Liang (2005) until termination. For LDA we run 1000 iterations of a collapsed Gibbs sampler from Mallet (McCallum 2002). Figure 4 shows how the models scale with growing value of K on a log-log plot. Brown terminates in 20 minutes for K=50, but takes over 110 hours for K=1000, while LDA takes between 1 hour for K=50 and 4 hours for K=1000.

5.2 Performance

Another advantage of LDA word classes over hard clusters is the increased representational power. Ambiguity can be modeled more compactly, and there are two sources of information to draw on when deciding on the most likely class of a word in context: the word type identity, and the local context features. In this section we show that these theoretical advantages translate into performance on fine-grained Named Entity Recognition, Morphological Analysis and on semantic Relation Classification.

In each of the tasks we tried to use the Brown classes and the LDA classes in an optimal way by taking advantage of the strength of each type of representation, and also to adapt the feature sets to the specifics of the task. We followed previous work when available and ran exploratory experiments with different feature combinations on the development data. The details of the final feature sets are given in the respective sections but in general we make use of the hierarchical nature of Brown classes by using them at several levels of granularity. For LDA classes we exploit their probabilistic softness by including feature probability or rank, and include classes inferred from context words when appropriate.

5.2.1 Named entity recognition

Named-entity recognition is one of the most commonly needed NLP task. Many evaluations have focused on learning the coarse-grained CoNLL and MUC entity labels (person, organization and location). Here we evaluate on the more challenging fine-grained entities from the BBN corpus (Weischedel and Brunstein 2005). We use sections 2 to 21 as training data, section 22 for development and section 23 for final evaluation. We keep all labels appearing at least 100 times in training data. Less frequent labels we map to an existing more generic label if possible (e.g. LOCATION:LAKE_SEA_OCEAN $\mapsto$ LOCATION:OTHER), otherwise we discard them. We also discard all **description** labels which are not proper named entities. We are left with 40 labels, shown in Table 1.

We convert the labeling to the BIO format which encodes chunking information into token-level labels: each label is prefixed with B if it starts a new chunk, I if it continues the previous chunk, or O if it does not belong to a named entity chunk. Thus we end up with 81 labels after conversion.

lowercase	Map all characters to lower case
wordshape	Encodes spelling of a token by mapping sequences of upper case letters to X, lower case letters to x, digits to 0, hyphens and underlines to themselves. For example *IJCNLP-2011* maps to X-0
suffix_n	The n characters from the end of the token
$\text{rank}^n_z f(z)$	The nth class in the ranking ordered by the value of the function f
prefix_n	The first n characters from the start
z	Class id

Table 2: Meaning of feature functions

Baseline As a baseline we use a sequence-perceptron labeler (Collins 2002) with the following features: $\{w_{-2}, w_{-1}, w_0, \text{lowercase}(w_0), \text{wordshape}(w_0), \text{suffix}_1(w_0), \text{suffix}_2(w_0), \text{suffix}_3(w_0), w_1, w_2\}$. For the explanation of the feature functions see Table 2.

For inducing classes for this task we use the North American News Text Corpus described in section 5.1. When evaluating word classes we add to this feature set the Brown or LDA word class features:

Brown Class IDs encode the path in the class hierarchy, we thus use ID prefixes of different lengths to include classes at several levels of granularity. We also add feature conjunctions. The additional Brown class features are thus: $\text{prefix}_n(z(w_m))$ (for tokens at positions $m \in \{-1, 0, 1\}$, class id prefix of length n for $n \in \{4, 6, 10, 20\}$) and feature conjunctions $\{\text{prefix}_{20}(z(w_0))\} \times \{\text{lowercase}(w_0), \text{wordshape}(w_0), \text{suffix}_1(w_0), \text{suffix}_2(w_0), \text{suffix}_3(w_0)\}$. The class ID prefix sizes we adopted were shown to be effective in Ratinov and Roth (2009) and Turian et al. (2010).

LDA We rank the classes according to posterior probability and take the 3 top ranked classes given the current word d, the 1 top ranked class given the previous word w_{-1}, and 1 top ranked class given the next word w_{+1}: $\{\text{rank}^1_z P(z|d), \text{rank}^2_z P(z|d), \text{rank}^3_z P(z|d), \text{rank}^1_z P(z|w_{-1}), \text{rank}^1_z P(z|w_{+1})\}$. We add the following feature conjunctions: $\{\text{lowercase}(w_0), \text{wordshape}(w_0), \text{suffix}_1(w_0), \text{suffix}_2(w_0), \text{suffix}_3(w_0)\} \times \{\text{rank}^1_z P(z|d),$

ANIMAL CARDINAL DATE:AGE DATE:DATE DATE:DURATION DATE:OTHER DISEASE EVENT:OTHER FAC:BUILDING FAC:HIGHWAY-STREET GPE:CITY GPE:COUNTRY GPE:OTHER GPE:STATE-PROVINCE LAW LOCATION:CONTINENT LOCATION:OTHER LOCATION:REGION MONEY NORP:NATIONALITY NORP:POLITICAL ORDINAL ORGANIZATION:CORPORATION ORGANIZATION:EDUCATIONAL ORGANIZATION:GOVERNMENT ORGANIZATION:OTHER ORGANIZATION:POLITICAL PERCENT PERSON PLANT PRODUCT:OTHER PRODUCT:VEHICLE QUANTITY:1D QUANTITY:WEIGHT SUBSTANCE:CHEMICAL SUBSTANCE:DRUG SUBSTANCE:FOOD SUBSTANCE:OTHER TIME WORK-OF-ART:OTHER

Table 1: BBN named entity labels

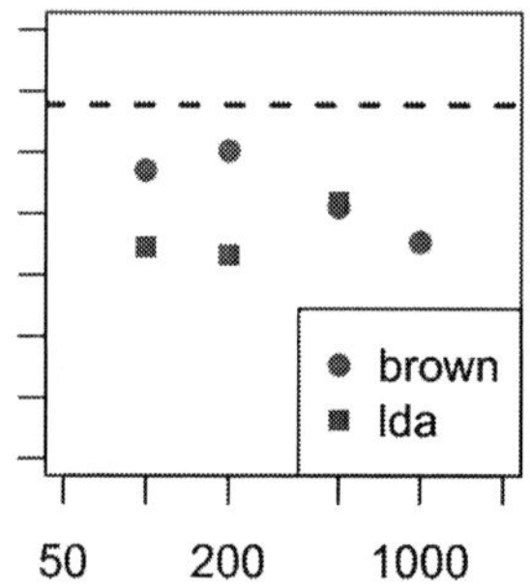

Figure 5: F1 error on NER dev. set with word classes

$\text{rank}_z^1 P(z|w_{-1}), \text{rank}_z^1 P(z|w_{+1})\}$.

Figure 5 shows the F1 error on section 22 for the baseline and for Brown and LDA classes of different granularity. A large number of classes (500 or 1000) is needed to achieve low error with Brown classes. With LDA, a lower number (100 or 200) is sufficient, and in fact the error rates are lower for LDA word class features than for Brown. The results for the test set (section 23) using Brown with 1000 classes and LDA with 200 classes are shown in the *NER* column of Table 5. We are unaware of previous published results on BBN at a comparable level of NE label granularity.

5.2.2 Morphological analysis

We next evaluate the induced word classes on a morphological analysis task. The goal is to learn to assign morpho-syntactic descriptors (MSD) (roughly speaking, fine-grained POS tags) and lemmas to tokens in sentences. The MSD tags encode all relevant inflectional features of a token such as gender, case and number for nouns or tense, aspect, person and number for verbs. A morphological tagger which performs this type of analysis is an important component for processing languages with rich inflectional morphology. Figure 6 shows example morphological annotation of

Token	Lemma	MSD	Gloss
Pero	pero	`cc`	but
cuando	cuando	`cs`	when
era	ser	`vsii3s0`	he was
niño	niño	`ncms000`	boy
le	el	`pp3csd00`	to him
gustaba	gustar	`vmii3p0`	it pleased

Figure 6: Morphosyntactic annotation of a Spanish which translates as *When he was a boy he liked it.*

a short sentence in Spanish.

As the supervised model we use the Morfette system (Chrupała et al. 2008)[1]. Morfette trains two classifiers, one for morphological tags (i.e. fine-grained POS tags) and one for lemmatization classes. The classifiers are trained separately; their output is combined during decoding. For the baseline we used the default features (see Chrupała et al. 2008) and trained the POS and lemma models for 10 and 3 iterations respectively. We added word-class features to the POS model.

Brown We use class id prefixes for the focus word: $\text{prefix}_n(z(w_0)),\ n \in \{4, 6, 10, 20\}$

LDA Morfette can use real-valued features and initial tests on this task with class distributions showed that using them directly works as well as discretizing them. We use classes for the focus token (w_0) and set probabilities below 0.15 to 0 for sparseness.

Data sets We chose two data sets for evaluation:

- Spanish Ancora corpus (Taulé et al. 2008): portion corresponding to data used by Chrupała et al. (2008), 188.803 tokens, 10.000 dev. and 10.000 test, 279 tags.

[1]Available at `http://code.google.com/p/morfette/`

CAUSE-EFFECT INSTRUMENT-AGENCY PRODUCT-PRODUCER CONTENT-CONTAINER ENTITY-ORIGIN ENTITY-DESTINATION COMPONENT-WHOLE MEMBER-COLLECTION COMMUNICATION-TOPIC

Table 3: Relation classification labels

- French Treebank (Abeillé et al. 2003), 351.873 tokens, 36.297 dev. and 37.967 test, 214 tags.

For inducing word classes we used (i) Spanish Europarl (Koehn 2005), 50M words and (ii) Est Republicain[2] 147M words.

We optimized the number of classes on the development set: for Brown the best was 500 for both languages, for LDA the best setting was 50 for Spanish and 100 for French.

Table 5 (columns *MA es* and *MA fr*) shows the joint morphological tagging-lemmatization scores on the test set. Word classes give a moderate performance boost and in both cases LDA improves more. We do not know of published results on the French data with this level of granularity. However Seddah et al. (2010) show that Morfette on French data with a reduced tagset compares well to state-of-the-art, and thus can be assumed to be a strong baseline. For Spanish, our baseline error is almost identical to the error reported by Chrupała et al. (2008) (4.98 vs 5.00): thus the word classes give 10% relative error reduction over previous results.

5.2.3 Classification of semantic relations

The last task on which we evaluate induced word classes is multi-way classification of abstract semantic relations between nominals (RC). This task appeared at the Semeval 2007 and 2010 workshops. We use the task definition and the training and testing data from 2010.

The relation inventory is shown in Table 3. For example in the sentence *The bowl was full of apples, pears and oranges* the nominal *pears* is in a CONTENT-CONTAINER relation with the nominal *bowl*.

The training set consists of sentences annotated with the relations and their directionality. The arguments (nominals) participating in the relations are marked in both the training and test examples. We used the 2010 training set of 8000 sentences

[2] http://www.cnrtl.fr/corpus/estrepublicain/

arg_1	The first argument
arg_2	The second argument
between_n	Each of the tokens between arg_1 and arg_2
before_m	Each of the 3 tokens before arg_1
after_m	Each of the 3 tokens after arg_2

Table 4: Description of features for RC

and the test set of 2717 sentences. During development, we split the training set in half, and trained on the first half, while validating on the second half. For the final evaluation we trained on all the 8000 training sentences.

We evaluated with the scoring script provided, using the official macro-averaged F1 score.

Baseline For our baseline system we used the Weka (Hall et al. 2009) implementation of the Sequential Minimal Optimization algorithm to train an SVM classifier (Platt 1999), with the default linear kernel. We treat each combination of the relation label and the direction label together as a single atomic class to be learned.

Table 4 describes the features we extracted from each sentence for the RC task.

Corpus For this task we initially used the word classes induced from The North American News Text Corpus described in section 5.1. The improvements we achieved were smaller than we expected. We suspected that the reason for this was that the training data for the RC task come from a variety of Web sources and are much less restricted in genre than the text in the NANT corpus. We thus decided to retrain word classes on the more balanced 100M-word BNC corpus (BNC Consortium 2001). As expected, the word classes from the BNC worked better. Due to time constraints, for Brown we were able to induce only up to 500 classes.

Brown With Brown classes we use class ID prefix $\text{prefix}_n(z(f))$, $n \in \{4, 6, 10, 20\}$, for each of the baseline features f listed in Table 4.

LDA For this task we use the probabilities of the classes as real-valued features, and we took classes for each of the baseline features f listed Table 4.

We optimized the number of classes on the development data (second half of training data). We found 500 classes for Brown and 100 classes for

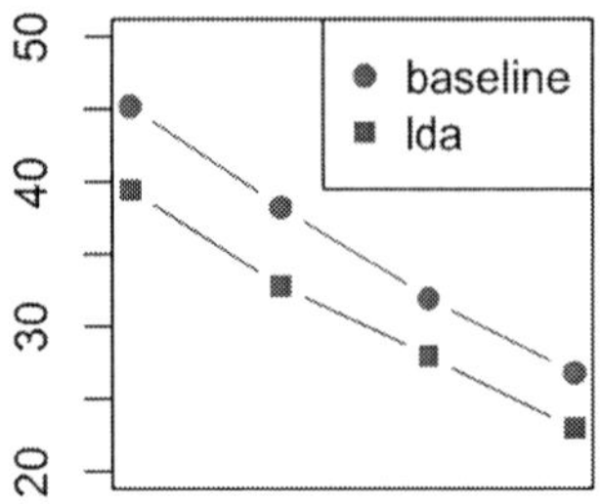

Figure 7: Relation classification error as a function of the number of training examples. The x-axis is plotted on a logarithmic scale.

LDA to give the best results, and we used these values for the final evaluation.

The impact of adding word classes can be appreciated in Figure 7, which plots the test error with and without word classes while varying the number of training examples (1000, 2000, 4000 and 8000). It can be seen that adding LDA word class features corresponds to almost doubling the amount of training data.

Table 5 (column labeled *RC*) shows the macro-averaged F1 error on test data. Similarly to the previous tasks, the improvement is larger with LDA than with Brown classes.

For comparison, during the Semeval 2010 evaluation the F1 error of the top-scoring system (Rink and Harabagiu 2010) was 17.81%; the system ranked second (Tymoshenko and Giuliano 2010) achieved 22.37%.

Both these systems used large amounts of external resources and heavy-duty linguistic processing tools. Rink and Harabagiu (2010) extracted features from dependency parses, from PropBank and FrameNet parses, from WordNet and NomLex as well as using Google n-grams and the output of TextRunner[3]. Tymoshenko and Giuliano (2010) extracted features from syntactic parses and from the massive semantic knowledge database Cyc (Lenat 1995).

In comparison, our system is extremely resource-light since our features do not rely on any manually created databases or linguistic processing tools (not even POS tags). It is thus satisfying that by automatically and efficiently inducing simple word class features we can achieve results

[3]A system for open information extraction from the Web (Yates et al. 2007).

	%Error			
Model	NER	MA es	MA fr	RC
Baseline	13.42	5.00	7.80	26.78
Brown	11.82	4.70	7.51	25.66
LDA	**11.70**	**4.50**	**7.39**	**22.97**

Table 5: Test set results on NER, MA, RC

which are close to state-of-the-art.

6 Discussion

To our knowledge LDA word class induction has not been previously used in this particular scenario. LDA variants have been proposed in other settings: Brody and Lapata (2009) use LDA to induce latent variables corresponding to word senses; Toutanova and Johnson (2007) propose an LDA-inspired model where induced word-classes are used for semi-supervised POS tagging; Dinu and Lapata (2010) use LDA-induced word-classes for measuring word similarity in context. Rather than focus on adapting LDA to a particular task, we instead induce generic word classes that can be plugged in as features in a number of NLP applications.

We show that the LDA word clustering algorithm is an attractive choice for semi-supervised learning. It is efficient to train and beats a competitive baseline provided by Brown clustering.

Acknowledgements

This work was carried out in the context of the Software-Cluster project EMERGENT (`www.software-cluster.org`). It was partially funded by the German Federal Ministry of Education and Research (BMBF) under grant number 01IC10S01O. The author assumes responsibility for the content.

References

Abeillé, A., Clément, L., and Toussenel, F. (2003). Building a treebank for French.

Bengio, Y., Schwenk, H., Senécal, J., Morin, F., and Gauvain, J. (2006). Neural Probabilistic Language Models. *Innovations in Machine Learning*, pages 137–186.

Blei, D., Ng, A., and Jordan, M. (2003). Latent dirichlet allocation. *The Journal of Machine Learning Research*, 3:993–1022.

BNC Consortium (2001). The British National Corpus, version 2 (BNC World). Distributed by Oxford University Computing Services on behalf of the BNC Consortium. `http://www.natcorp.ox.ac.uk/`.

Brody, S. and Lapata, M. (2009). Bayesian word sense induction. In *EACL 2009*.

Brown, P. F., Mercer, R. L., Della Pietra, V. J., and Lai, J. C. (1992). Class-based n-gram models of natural language. *Computational Linguistics*, 18(4):467–479.

Candito, M. and Crabbé, B. (2009). Improving generative statistical parsing with semi-supervised word clustering. In *IWPT 2009*.

Chrupała, G., Dinu, G., and Van Genabith, J. (2008). Learning morphology with Morfette. In *LREC 2008*.

Chrupała, G. and Klakow, D. (2010). A Named Entity Labeler for German: exploiting Wikipedia and distributional clusters. In *LREC 2010*.

Collins, M. (2002). Discriminative training methods for Hidden Markov Models: Theory and experiments with perceptron algorithms. In *ACL 2002*.

Collobert, R. and Weston, J. (2008). A unified architecture for natural language processing: Deep neural networks with multitask learning. In *ICML 2008*.

Deerwester, S., Dumais, S., Furnas, G., Landauer, T., and Harshman, R. (1990). Indexing by latent semantic analysis. *Journal of the American society for information science*, 41(6):391–407.

Dinu, G. and Lapata, M. (2010). Measuring distributional similarity in context. In *EMNLP 2010*.

Gao, J. and Johnson, M. (2008). A comparison of Bayesian estimators for unsupervised Hidden Markov Model POS taggers. In *EMNLP 2008*.

Goldwater, S. and Griffiths, T. (2007). A fully Bayesian approach to unsupervised part-of-speech tagging. In *ACL 2007*.

Griffiths, T. and Steyvers, M. (2004). Finding scientific topics. *PNAS*, 101(Suppl 1):5228.

Griffiths, T., Steyvers, M., Blei, D., and Tenenbaum, J. (2005). Integrating topics and syntax. In *NIPS 2005*.

Hall, M., Frank, E., Holmes, G., Pfahringer, B., Reutemann, P., and Witten, I. (2009). The weka data mining software: an update. *ACM SIGKDD Explorations Newsletter*, 11(1):10–18.

Koehn, P. (2005). Europarl: A parallel corpus for statistical machine translation. In *MT Summit 2005*.

Koo, T., Carreras, X., and Collins, M. (2008). Simple semi-supervised dependency parsing. In *ACL 2008*.

Lamar, M., Maron, Y., Johnson, M., and Bienenstock, E. (2010). SVD and clustering for unsupervised POS tagging. In *ACL 2010*.

Lenat, D. (1995). Cyc: A large-scale investment in knowledge infrastructure. *Communications of the ACM*, 38(11):33–38.

Liang, P. (2005). *Semi-supervised learning for natural language*. PhD thesis, Massachusetts Institute of Technology.

Lin, D. and Wu, X. (2009). Phrase clustering for discriminative learning. In *ACL/IJCNLP 2009*.

McCallum, A. (2002). Mallet: A machine learning for language toolkit. `http://mallet.cs.umass.edu`.

Miller, S., Guinness, J., and Zamanian, A. (2004). Name tagging with word clusters and discriminative training. In *HLT/NAACL 2004*.

Mnih, A. and Hinton, G. (2009). A scalable hierarchical distributed language model. In *NIPS 2009*.

Momtazi, S. and Klakow, D. (2009). A word clustering approach for language model-based sentence retrieval in Question Answering systems. In *CIKM 2009*.

Platt, J. (1999). Sequential minimal optimization: A fast algorithm for training support vector machines. *Advances in Kernel Methods-Support Vector Learning*, 208:98–112.

Ratinov, L. and Roth, D. (2009). Design challenges and misconceptions in named entity recognition. In *CoNLL 2009*.

Rink, B. and Harabagiu, S. (2010). Utd: Classifying semantic relations by combining lexical and semantic resources. In *SemEval 2010*, pages 256–259.

Schütze, H. (1995). Distributional part-of-speech tagging. In *ACL 1995*.

Seddah, D., Chrupała, G., Çetinoglu, Ö., van Genabith, J., and Candito, M. (2010). Lemmatization and Lexicalized Statistical Parsing of Morphologically Rich Languages: the Case of French. In *SPMRL, NAACL workshop*.

Suzuki, J., Isozaki, H., Carreras, X., and Collins, M. (2009). An empirical study of semi-supervised structured conditional models for dependency parsing. In *EMNLP 2009*.

Taulé, M., Martí, M., and Recasens, M. (2008). Ancora: Multilevel annotated corpora for Catalan and Spanish. In *LREC-2008*.

Toutanova, K. and Johnson, M. (2007). A Bayesian LDA-based model for semi-supervised part-of-speech tagging. In *NIPS 2007*.

Turian, J., Ratinov, L., and Bengio, Y. (2010). Word representations: A simple and general method for semi-supervised learning. In *ACL 2010*.

Tymoshenko, K. and Giuliano, C. (2010). Fbk-irst: Semantic relation extraction using cyc. In *SemEval 2010*.

Weischedel, R. and Brunstein, A. (2005). BBN pronoun coreference and entity type corpus. Linguistic Data Consortium.

Yates, A., Cafarella, M., Banko, M., Etzioni, O., Broadhead, M., and Soderland, S. (2007). Textrunner: Open information extraction on the web. In *NAACL-HLT 2007 Demonstration Program*.

Quality-biased Ranking of Short Texts in Microblogging Services

Minlie Huang
Dept. of Computer Science and Technology, Tsinghua University
Beijing 100084, China
aihuang@tsinghua.edu.cn

Yi Yang
School of Software
Beihang University
Beijing, China
yangyiycc@gmail.com

Xiaoyan Zhu
Dept. of Computer Science and Technology, Tsinghua University
Beijing 100084, China
zxy_dcs@tsinghua.edu.cn

Abstract

The abundance of user-generated content comes at a price: the quality of content may range from very high to very low. We propose a regression approach that incorporates various features to recommend short-text documents from Twitter, with a bias toward quality perspective. The approach is built on top of a linear regression model which includes a regularization factor inspired from the content conformity hypothesis - documents similar in content may have similar quality. We test the system on the Edinburgh Twitter corpus. Experimental results show that the regularization factor inspired from the hypothesis can improve the ranking performance and that using unlabeled data can make ranking performance better. Comparative results show that our method outperforms several baseline systems. We also make systematic feature analysis and find that content quality features are dominant in short-text ranking.

1 Introduction

More and more user-generated data are emerging on personal blogs, microblogging services (e.g. Twitter), social and e-commerce websites. However, the abundance of user-generated content comes at a price: there may be high-quality content, but also much spam content such as advertisements, self-promotion, pointless babbles, or misleading information. Therefore, assessing the quality of information has become a challenging problem for many tasks such as information retrieval, review mining (Lu et al., 2010), and question answering (Agichtein et al., 2008).

In this paper, we focus on predicting the quality of very short texts which are obtained from Twitter. Twitter is a free social networking and microblogging service that enables its users to send and read other users' updates, known as "Tweets". Each tweet has up to 140 characters in length. With more than 200 million users (March 2011), Twitter has become one of the biggest mass media to broadcast and digest information for users. It has exhibited advantages over traditional news agencies in the success of reporting news more timely, for instance, in reporting the Chilean earthquake of 2010 (Mendoza et al., 2010). A comparative study (Teevan et al., 2011) shows that queries issued to Twitter tend to seek more temporally relevant information than those to general web search engines.

Due to the massive information broadcasted on Twitter, there are a huge amount of searches every day and Twitter has become an important source for seeking information. However, according to the Pear Analytics (2009) report on 2000 sample tweets, 40.5% of the tweets are pointless babbles, 37.5% are conversational tweets, and only 3.6% are news (which are most valuable for users who seek news information). Therefore, when a user issues a query, recommending tweets of good quality has become extremely important to satisfy the user's information need: how can we retrieve trustworthy and informative posts to users?

However, we must note that Twitter is a social networking service that *encourages* various content such as news reports, personal updates, babbles, conversations, etc. In this sense, we can not say which content has better quality without considering the value to the writer or reader. For instance, for a reader, the tweets from his friends or who he follows may be more desirable than those from others, whatever the quality is. In this paper, we have a special focus on finding tweets on news topics when we construct the evaluation datasets.

We propose a method of incorporating various features for quality-biased tweet recommendation in response to a query. The major contributions of this paper are as follows:

- We propose an approach for quality-biased ranking of short documents. Quality-biased is referred to the fact that we explore various features that may indicate quality. We also present a complete feature analysis to show which features are most important for this problem.
- We propose a content conformity hypothesis, and then formulate it into a regularization factor on top of a regression model. The performance of the system with such a factor is boosted.
- It is feasible to plug unlabeled data into our approach and leveraging unlabeled data can enhance the performance. This characteristics is appealing for information retrieval tasks since only a few labeled data are available in such tasks.

The rest of the paper is organized as follows: in Section 2 we survey related work. We then formulate our problem in Section 3 and present the hypothesis in Section 4. Various features are presented in Section 5. The dataset and experiment results are presented in Section 6 and Section 7, respectively. We summarize this work in Section 8.

2 Related Work

2.1 Quality Prediction

Quality prediction has been a very important problem in many tasks. In review mining, quality prediction has two lines of research: one line is to detect spam reviews (Jindal and Liu, 2008) or spam reviewers (Lim et al., 2010), which is helpful to exclude misleading information; the other is to identify high-quality reviews, on which we will focus in this survey. Various factors and contexts have been studied to produce reliable and consistent quality prediction. Danescu-Niculescu-Mizil et al. (2009) studied several factors on helpfulness voting of Amazon product reviews. Ghose and Ipeirotis (2010) studied several factors on assessing review helpfulness including reviewer characteristics, reviewer history, and review readability and subjectivity. Lu et al. (2010) proposed a linear regression model with various social contexts for review quality prediction. The authors employed author consistency, trust consistency and co-citation consistency hypothesis to predict more consistently. Liu et al. (2008) studied three factors, i.e., reviewer expertise, writing style, and timeliness, and proposed a non-linear regression model with radial basis functions to predict the helpfulness of movie reviews. Kim et al. (2006) used SVM regression with various features to predict review helpfulness.

Finding high-quality content and reliable users is also very important for question answering. Agichtein et al. (2008) proposed a classification framework of estimating answer quality. They studied content-based features (e.g. the answer length) and usage-based features derived from question answering communities. Jeon et al. (2006) used nontextual features extracted from the Naver Q&A service to predict the quality of answers. Bian et al. (2009) proposed a mutual reinforcement learning framework to simultaneously predict content quality and user reputation. Shah and Pomerantz (2010) proposed 13 quality criteria for answer quality annotation and then found that contextual information such as a user's profile, can be critical in predicting the quality of answers.

However, the task we address in this paper is quite different from previous problems. First, the document to deal with is very short. Each tweet has up to 140 characters. Thus, we are going to investigate those factors that influence the quality of such short texts. Second, as mentioned, high-quality information on Twitter (e.g., news) is only a very small proportion. Thus, how to distill high quality content from majority proportions of low-quality content may be more challenging.

2.2 Novel Applications on Twitter

Twitter is of high value for both personal and commercial use. Users can post personal updates, keep tight contact with friends, and obtain timely information. Companies can broadcast latest news to and interact with customers, and collect business intelligence via opinion mining. Under this background, there has been a large body of novel applications on Twitter, including social networking mining (Kwark et al., 2010), real time search[1] , sentiment analysis[2], detecting influenza epidemics (Culotta, 2010), and even predicting politics elections (Tumasjan et al., 2010).

As Twitter has shown to report news more timely than traditional news agencies, detecting tweets of news topic has received much attention. Sakaki et al. (2010) proposed a real-time earthquake detection framework by treating each Twitter user as a sensor. Petrovic et al. (2010) addressed the problem of detecting new events from a stream of Twitter posts and adopted a method based on locality-sensitive hashing to make event detection feasible on web-scale corpora. To facilitate fine-grained information extraction on news tweets, Liu et al. (2010) presented a work on semantic role labeling for such texts. Corvey et al. (2010) proposed a work for entity detection and entity class annotation on tweets that were posted during times of mass emergency. Ritter et al. (2010) proposed a topic model to detect conversational threads among tweets.

Since a large amount of tweets are posted every day, ranking strategies is extremely important for users to find information quickly. Current ranking strategy on Twitter considers relevance to an input query, information recency (the latest tweets are preferred), and popularity (the retweet times by other users). The recency information, which is useful for real-time web search, has also been explored by Dong et al. (2010) who used fresh URLs present in tweets to rank documents in response to recency sensitive queries. Duan et al. (2010) proposed a ranking SVM approach to rank tweets with various features.

3 Problem Formulation and Methodology

Given a set of queries $Q = \{q_1, q_2, \cdots, q_n\}$, for each query q_k, we have a set of short documents $D_k = \{d_k^1, d_k^2, \cdots\}$ which are retrieved by our built-in search engine. The document set D_k is partially labeled, i.e., a small portion of documents in D_k were annotated with a category set C=$\{1, 2, 3, 4, 5\}$ where 5 means the highest quality and 1 lowest. Therefore, we denote $D_k = D_k^U \cup D_k^L$, where D_k^U indicates the unlabeled documents, and D_k^L the labeled documents. Each document in D_k is represented as a feature vector, $d_i = (x_1, x_2, \cdots, x_m)$ where m is the total number of features.

The learning task is to train a mapping function $f(\mathcal{D}) : \mathcal{D} \to \mathcal{C}$, to predict the quality label of a document given a query q. We use a linear function $f(\mathbf{d}) = \mathbf{w^T d}$ for learning and where $\mathbf{w}$ is the weight vector. Formally, we define an objective function as follows to guide the learning process:

$$\Theta(\mathbf{w}) = \frac{1}{n}\sum_{k=1}^{n} \frac{1}{\mid D_k^L \mid} \sum_{\mathbf{d_i} \in D_k^L} \ell(\mathbf{w}^T\mathbf{d_i}, \hat{y}_i) + \alpha \mathbf{w}^T\mathbf{w} \tag{1}$$

where $\ell(.,.)$ is the loss function that measures the difference between a predicted quality $f(\mathbf{d_i}) = \mathbf{w}^T\mathbf{d_i}$ and the labelled quality $\hat{y}_i$, D_k^L is the labeled documents for query q_k, $\hat{y}_i$ is the quality label for document $\mathbf{d_i}$, n is the total number of queries, and α is a regularization parameter for $\mathbf{w}$. The loss function used in this work is the square error loss, as follows:

$$\ell(\mathbf{w}^T\mathbf{d_i}, y_i) = (\mathbf{w}^T\mathbf{d_i} - \hat{y}_i)^2 \tag{2}$$

It's easy to see that this problem has a closed-form solution, as follows:

$$\widehat{\mathbf{w}} = \arg\min_{\mathbf{w}} \Theta(\mathbf{w}) = (\sum_{i=1}^{N_l} \mathbf{d_i d_i}^T + \alpha N_l \mathbf{I})^{-1} \sum_{i=1}^{N_l} \hat{y}_i \mathbf{d_i} \tag{3}$$

where $\mathbf{I}$ is an identity matrix of size m (the dimension of feature vector), and N_l is the total number of labeled documents in all the queries. As mentioned, there are a large number of documents retrieved for each query while we only sample a small number of documents for manual annotation. Thus there are much more unlabeled documents yet to be utilized.

4 Content Conformity Hypothesis

To make quality prediction more consistent and to utilize the unlabeled data, we propose the content conformity hypothesis which assumes that the quality of documents similar in content should be close to each other. This hypothesis can be formulated as a regularization factor in the objective, as follows:

$$\Theta_1(\mathbf{w}) = \Theta(\mathbf{w}) + \beta \sum_{k=1}^{n} \sum_{\substack{d_i, d_j \in D_k \\ \wedge IsSim(d_i, d_j)}} (\mathbf{w^T d_i} - \mathbf{w^T d_j})^2 \tag{4}$$

[1]http://twittertroll.com/

[2]http://twittersentiment.appspot.com/

where $IsSim(d_i, d_j)$ is a predicate asserting that two documents are similar, and β is an empirical parameter. Note that D_k is usually all labeled data but it may also include *unlabeled* documents for query q_k. In this way, we can utilize the unlabeled documents as well as the labeled ones. There are various ways to determine whether two documents of the same query are similar. One way is to use TF*IDF cosine similarity to find similar documents with a threshold, and another way is to use clustering where two documents in the same cluster are similar. We use the first means in this paper and leave the second for future work.

To obtain the closed-form solution of Eq. 4, we define an auxiliary matrix $A = (a_{ij})$ where each a_{ij} is 1 if document d_i is similar to document d_j for some query. Then, Eq. 4 can be re-written as follows:

$$\Theta_1(\mathbf{w}) = \Theta(\mathbf{w}) + \beta \sum_{i<j} a_{ij}(\mathbf{w}^{\mathbf{T}}\mathbf{d_i} - \mathbf{w}^{\mathbf{T}}\mathbf{d_j})^2 \quad (5)$$

Let $\mathbf{D} = [\mathbf{d_1}, \mathbf{d_2}, \ldots, \mathbf{d_N}]$ be an $m \times N$ matrix in which each $\mathbf{d_i}$ is a column feature vector for a document. Note that this matrix includes both labeled and unlabeled documents, and N is the total number of documents. Then the last term in Eq. 5 can be re-written as

$$\sum_{i<j} a_{ij}(\mathbf{w}^{\mathbf{T}}\mathbf{d_i} - \mathbf{w}^{\mathbf{T}}\mathbf{d_j})^2 = \mathbf{w}^{\mathbf{T}}\mathbf{D}\mathbf{\Lambda_A}\mathbf{D}^{\mathbf{T}}\mathbf{w} \quad (6)$$

where $\Lambda_A = \Delta_A - A$ and Δ_A is a diagonal matrix with $(\Delta_A)_{ii} = \sum_j a_{ij}$. By some mathematical manipulations, the problem in Eq. 6 has the following closed-form solution (Zhu and Goldberg, 2009):

$$\widehat{\mathbf{w}} = (\sum_{i=1}^{N_l} \mathbf{d_i}\mathbf{d_i}^T + \alpha N_l I + \beta N_l \mathbf{D}\mathbf{\Lambda_A}\mathbf{D}^{\mathbf{T}})^{-1} \sum_{i=1}^{N_l} \hat{y}_i \mathbf{d_i} \quad (7)$$

5 Features

We design several groups of features to indicate the quality of tweets from different perspectives. These features include: content quality, user profile and authority, sentiment polarity, query relevance, and Twitter specific features.

5.1 Content Quality

Documents with higher quality in content will be more desirable for users in search. We thus exploit several features to respect quality:

Tweet's length: longer tweet may be more informative as each tweet has been limited to up to 140 characters.

Average term similarity: each tweet d has a score of $\frac{1}{|D_i|}\sum_{d_i \in D_i} sim(d, d_i)$ where D_i is the document set for query q_i, and $sim(.,.)$ is a cosine TF*IDF similarity measure for two documents.

Ratio of unique words: in some tweets, the same word is repeated many times while there are only few unique words. Tweets with more unique words may have more information. The number of unique words is normalized by the total number of words.

Ratio of POS tags: We compute the ratio of nouns, verbs, adverbs, adjectives, etc. in a tweet. Each POS tag corresponds to one dimension in the feature vector.

5.2 User Profile and User Authority

A user with a real and complete profile may post tweets responsibly and accountably. Authoritative users (particularly celebrity users) are more probably to post high-quality tweets.

Profile integrity: we have several features for measuring this property: whether the user of a tweet has a description field, whether the description field contains a url, whether the user verifies her account via the registered email, and whether the user provides the location information.

User Activeness: the average number of tweets that the user posted per day and how many days a user has registered.

User authority: In the spirit of (Duan et al., 2010), we utilize follower score (the number of followers) , mention score (the number of times a user is referred to in tweets), popularity score to measure the authority of a user. The popularity score is obtained with the PageRank algorithm based on retweet relationship (two users have an edge in the graph if a tweet posted by one user is retweeted by another user).

5.3 Sentiment

As mentioned, Twitter has become a popular site for expressing opinions and personal sentiment towards public persons or events. Thus we believe that a tweet with clear sentiment polarity will be more favorable for users. Therefore, we adopt a sentiment lexicon (SentiWordNet) and collect the top 200 frequent emoticons from our tweet corpus to identify positive and negative sentiment words.

Positive sentiment: the ratio of positive sentiment words or emoticons in a tweet.

Negative sentiment: the ratio of negative sentiment words or emoticons.

Sensitive words: the number of sensitive words. We manually collect 458 offending or pornographic words.

The emoticon lexicon and the sensitive word lexicon will be available to public.

5.4 Twitter-Specific Features

Tweet has its own characteristics which may be used as features, such as whether a tweet contains a common url (such as http://www.google.com), whether the url is a tinyurl (Twitter has a service which shortens urls to very short url), the number of hashtags (topical terms leading by a '#') in a tweet, how many users are mentioned in the tweet (a user is mentioned if the tweet contains a term like @user_name), and how many times the tweet has been re-posted (so-called 'retweeted').

5.5 Query-specific Features

As our task is to supply quality-biased ranking of tweets for an input query, query-specific features will favor those tweets relevant to the input query.

Query term frequency: the frequency of the query term (exact matching) in a tweet.

BM25 score: the BM25 score is used to quantify the overall relevance of a tweet to the query.

Recency: the time lag (in days) between the current tweet and the earliest tweet in the collection for the query. In this case, the more recent tweets may contain latest information, which will be more desirable for users.

6 Dataset

To investigate the factors that influence the quality of short texts, we use the Edinburgh Twitter Corpus (Petrovic et al., 2010)[3] in which each tweet has up to 140 characters. The corpus contains 97 million tweets, and takes up 14 GB of disk space uncompressed. The corpus was collected through the Twitter streaming API from a period spanning November 11th 2009 until February 1st 2010. Each tweet has some meta-data: the timestamp of the tweet, an anonymized user name, the textual content, and the posting source (via web, mobile, etc.).

We collect a set of news queries using Google Trends. Intuitively, those hot queries in Google Trends will also have high possibility to be discussed on Twitter. The top 10 queries per day captured by Google Trends for the period 11th November, 2009 to 1st February, 2010 are collected. We then randomly sample 60 hot queries from these queries. And for each query, we use our own built-in search engine (based on BM25) to retrieve a set of tweets for manual annotation. To minimize the labeling cost, for each query, we sample 150-200 tweets for annotation as each query may return thousands of results, which makes the complete annotation impossible. These queries are grouped into four categories: thing (10 queries), person (15), event (30) and place (5). Table 1 shows some example queries of each type. For all these queries, there are about 9,000 unique tweets to be annotated.

[3]Though the corpus is not available now on the original website due to licensing problems, readers are encouraged to request a copy from us. We are downloading a new dateset for further evaluation.

Then, two computer science students were asked to annotate the tweets. The quality of a tweet was judged to a 5-star likert scale, according to the relevance, informativeness, readability, and politeness of the content. If the label difference of two tweets is larger than 1, the tweets were re-annotated until the quality difference is within 1.

Thing	**Person**
haiti relief effort	adam james
newegg	tiger woods mistress
flight 253	jennifer jones
groupon	john wall
Event	**Place**
obama ambulance	google headquarters
boeing 787 first flight	solomon islands
eureka earthquake	humanitarian bowl
shaq retires	college of charleston

Table 1: Sample queries for each query type.

6.1 Evaluation Metrics

We adopt information retrieval metrics to measure the performance since the task can be viewed as a ranking task (ranking document according to its quality). $nDCG$ (Järvelin and Kekäläinen., 2000) is used to evaluate the ranking performance, as follows:

$$nDCG(\Omega, k) = \frac{1}{|\Omega|} \sum_{q \in \Omega} \frac{1}{Z_q} \sum_{i=1}^{k} \frac{2^{r_i^q} - 1}{log(1+i)}$$

where Ω is the set of test queries, k indicates the top k positions in a ranked list, Z_q is a normalization factor obtained from a perfect ranking (based on the labels), and r_i^q is the relevance score (the annotated quality label) for the *i-th* document in the predicted ranking list for query q. We also evaluate the system in terms of MAP [4] where the document whose quality score is larger than 3 is viewed as relevant and otherwise irrelevant.

Note that the ranking task is approached as a regression problem, mean square error is thus adopted to measure the learning performance:

$$MSE(\mathcal{D}) = \frac{1}{|\mathcal{D}|} \sum_{d_j \in \mathcal{D}} (f(d_j) - \hat{y}_j)^2$$

where $\mathcal{D}$ is the test document collection, $f(d_j)$ is the predicted label, and $\hat{y}_j$ is the annotated label.

$nDCG$ and MSE have a significant difference in that $nDCG$ only considers the top k documents for each

[4]`http://en.wikipedia.org/wiki/Information_retrieval`

query while MSE takes into account all documents in the test collection.

7 Experiment and Evaluation

In this section, we will first assess whether the proposed hypothesis holds on our labeled data. We then evaluate whether the performance of the model with the regularization factor (as defined in Eq. 4) can be enhanced. We next compare the regression model with several baselines: BM25 model, Length Model (tweets containing more words may have better quality), ReTweet Model (tweets of higher quality may be re-posted by more users), and a Learning-to-Rank model (L2R) as used in (Duan et al., 2010)(a ranking SVM model). Finally, we investigate the influence of different feature groups on the performance. We conduct five-fold cross validation in the following experiments (3/5 partitions are for training, 1/5 are used as a validation set, and the left for test).

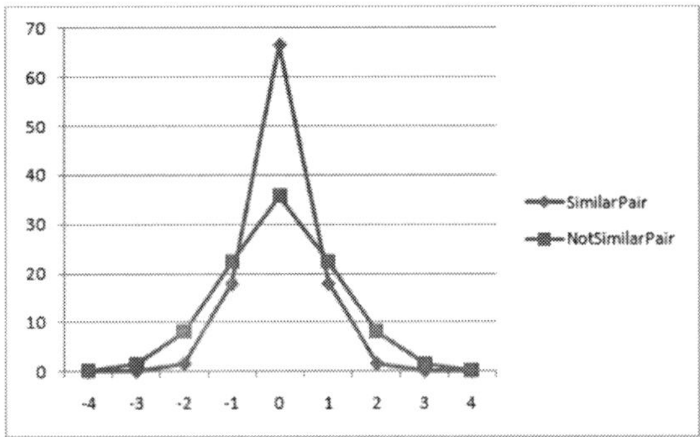

Figure 1: The hypothesis holds on the annotated dataset. y-axis is the percentage of pairs and x-axis is the quality difference between two documents in a pair.

7.1 Hypothesis Evaluation

We will evaluate whether the content conformity hypothesis holds on our manually annotated dataset. To define the similarity predicate ($IsSim$ in Eq. 4), we assume two documents are similar if their TF*IDF cosine similarity is no less than 0.6. We then compute the statistics of the quality difference of similar pairs and that of dissimilar pairs. We find that more than 53% similar pairs have exactly identical quality labels, out of all similar pairs. And more than 93% similar pairs have a quality difference within 1. For dissimilar pairs, only 35% pairs have identical quality labels. This shows that if two documents are similar, there is high probability that their quality labels are close to each other, and that if two documents are dissimilar, it's more likely that they have more divergent quality scores. These statistics are shown in Figure 1.

As shown in the figure, we can see that the hypothesis holds. Therefore, we can safely formulate the hypothesis into a regularization factor in the subsequent experiments.

7.2 Parameter Tuning

We explain here how the parameters (α, β) are chosen. In Table 2, we can see clearly that the best performance is obtained when $\alpha = 1e - 8$. In Table 3, the model that utilizes only labeled data obtains most of the best nDCG scores when $\beta = 0.001$. For the MAP metric, the scores when $\beta = 0.001$ and $\beta = 0.0001$ are very close. Unlike MSE that considers all documents in the test collection, nDCG only considers the top ranked documents, which are more desirable for parameter choosing since most users are only interested in top ranked items. In Table 4, the model that utilizes unlabeled data obtains best performance when $\beta = 0.0001$. These optimal parameters will be used in our subsequent experiments.

7.3 Influence of the Regularization Factor

In this section, we address two issues: (1) whether the regularization factor inspired by content conformity hypothesis (Eq. 4) can improve the performance; and (2) whether the performance can be improved if using unlabeled data (see D_k in Eq. 4).

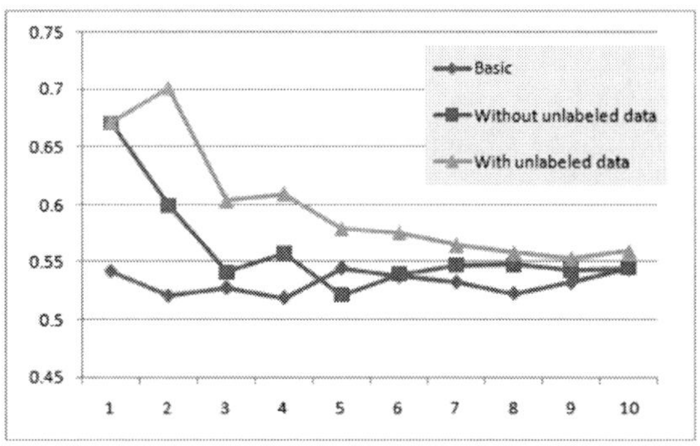

Figure 2: nDCG performance (y-axis) for top k ranks. The similarity predicate ($IsSim(a, b)$ in Eq. 4) is implemented with TF*IDF cosine similarity.

As shown in Figure 2, under the hypothesis the ranking performance is boosted compared to the basic model. As shown in Eq. 4, unlabeled data can be included in the regularization factor, thus we add the same number of unlabeled documents[5] for each query. We conduct experiments with and without such unlabeled data respectively. Adding unlabeled data can improve the ranking performance. This is appealing for most IR applications since

[5]Arbitrary number of documents may be added but we will evaluate this as future work.

α	1e-10	1e-9	1e-8	1e-7	1e-6	1e-5	0.0001	0.001	0.01
nDCG@1	0.131	0.325	**0.542**	**0.542**	**0.542**	**0.542**	**0.542**	**0.542**	**0.542**
nDCG@2	0.180	0.390	**0.521**	0.521	**0.521**	**0.521**	**0.521**	**0.521**	0.464
nDCG@3	0.209	0.377	**0.527**	**0.527**	**0.527**	**0.527**	**0.527**	0.512	0.424
nDCG@4	0.240	0.342	**0.518**	**0.518**	**0.518**	**0.518**	**0.518**	**0.518**	0.425
nDCG@5	0.235	0.350	**0.545**	0.516	0.516	0.516	0.516	0.518	0.444
nDCG@6	0.244	0.389	**0.537**	0.504	0.504	0.504	0.528	0.527	0.440
nDCG@7	0.250	0.399	**0.532**	0.528	0.528	0.528	0.530	0.523	0.432
nDCG@8	0.281	0.403	**0.522**	0.519	0.519	0.519	0.516	0.514	0.435
nDCG@9	0.291	0.411	**0.532**	0.517	0.517	0.517	0.518	0.511	0.450
nDCG@10	0.300	0.422	**0.544**	0.535	0.535	0.535	0.522	0.517	0.466
MAP	0.177	0.253	**0.390**	0.378	0.378	0.377	0.372	0.360	0.293
MSE	37.983	3.914	**1.861**	1.874	1.875	1.880	1.914	1.920	1.970

Table 2: The performance of different α parameters. The bolded cells show the optimal performance.

β	1e-10	1e-9	1e-8	1e-7	1e-6	1e-5	0.0001	0.001	0.01
nDCG@1	0.542	0.542	0.542	0.542	0.542	0.542	0.542	**0.671**	0.480
nDCG@2	0.521	0.521	0.521	0.521	0.521	0.570	0.570	**0.600**	0.472
nDCG@3	0.527	0.527	0.480	0.480	0.527	**0.596**	0.549	0.541	0.501
nDCG@4	0.520	0.518	0.481	0.481	0.518	0.543	0.515	**0.558**	0.468
nDCG@5	0.503	**0.528**	0.512	0.512	0.516	0.521	0.505	0.521	0.448
nDCG@6	0.514	0.515	0.521	0.521	0.511	0.522	0.533	**0.539**	0.468
nDCG@7	0.524	0.523	0.524	0.524	0.529	0.517	0.517	**0.547**	0.461
nDCG@8	0.515	0.525	0.514	0.514	0.527	0.521	0.519	**0.548**	0.473
nDCG@9	0.518	0.519	0.513	0.513	0.524	0.536	0.521	**0.543**	0.470
nDCG@10	0.528	0.529	0.517	0.517	0.535	0.537	**0.545**	**0.545**	0.472
MAP	0.386	0.385	0.367	0.367	0.369	0.375	**0.388**	0.387	0.264
MSE	1.863	1.862	1.893	1.893	1.859	1.845	1.763	1.315	**0.908**

Table 3: The performance of different β parameters with only labeled data (α=1e-8 according to Table 2). The bolded cells show the optimal performance.

β	1e-10	1e-9	1e-8	1e-7	1e-6	1e-5	0.0001	0.001	0.01
nDCG@1	0.542	0.542	0.542	0.542	0.542	0.542	**0.671**	0.277	0.147
nDCG@2	0.521	0.521	0.521	0.521	0.521	0.570	**0.701**	0.429	0.146
nDCG@3	0.527	0.527	0.527	0.527	0.558	0.565	**0.603**	0.438	0.168
nDCG@4	0.518	0.518	0.486	0.518	0.522	0.550	**0.610**	0.437	0.208
nDCG@5	0.519	0.516	0.488	0.545	0.548	0.527	**0.579**	0.429	0.218
nDCG@6	0.514	0.518	0.499	0.537	0.547	0.528	**0.576**	0.431	0.235
nDCG@7	0.529	0.535	0.503	0.538	0.541	0.516	**0.565**	0.453	0.256
nDCG@8	0.520	0.525	0.503	0.528	0.530	0.532	**0.558**	0.454	0.286
nDCG@9	0.513	0.518	0.520	0.521	0.535	0.534	**0.553**	0.478	0.300
nDCG@10	0.523	0.536	0.524	0.533	0.536	0.540	**0.559**	0.481	0.313
MAP	0.385	0.382	0.374	0.389	0.394	0.381	**0.427**	0.296	0.164
MSE	1.845	1.868	1.896	1.842	1.819	1.613	0.803	**0.499**	0.697

Table 4: The performance of different β parameters with unlabeled data (α=1e-8 according to Table 2). The bolded cells show the optimal performance.

most IR problems only have a small number of labeled data available.

7.4 Comparison to Baselines

To demonstrate the performance of our approach, we compare our system to three unsupervised models and one supervised model. The unsupervised models are: the BM25 model, the Length model which ranks tweets by the document length in tokens, and the RTNum model which ranks tweets by the frequency of being re-posted. The supervised model is a ranking SVM model (L2R) that was used in (Duan et al., 2010). In this experiment, the model (as indicated by "Full" in Fig. 3) is the best model presented in the preceding section.

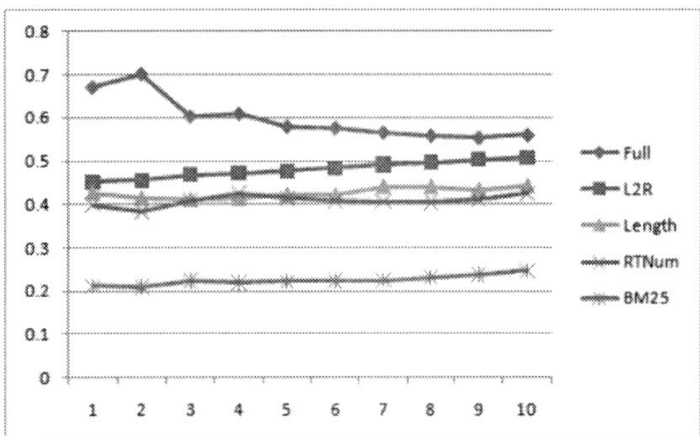

Figure 3: nDCG performance (y-axis) with different approaches. x-axis is the top k ranks. The Full model used unlabeled data with the regularization factor.

We can see that the proposed approach outperforms those unsupervised models remarkably, and it also performs better than the L2R model (Ranking SVM). Noticeably, the Length model is strong in performance, which shows the document length is a good indicator of quality. The RTNum model takes advantage of a Twitter specific property - a document of higher quality may be posted repeatedly by other users with higher probability. This is a special property for Twitter documents. Not surprisingly, the supervised methods outperform all unsupervised methods.

To further demonstrate that our approach outperforms the baselines, we list the results (in terms of $nDCG@k = 1, 5, 10$, and MAP) in Table 5 which clearly shows the advantages of our proposed approach. Note that our performance shown in Table 5 is significantly better than all the baselines (p-value<0.001 by t-test). We choose the significance level of 0.01 through the paper.

nDCG @k	Full	L2R	Length	RTNum	BM25
k=1	**0.671**	0.442	0.466	0.398	0.212
k=5	**0.579**	0.477	0.422	0.413	0.222
k=10	**0.559**	0.508	0.442	0.424	0.247
MAP	**0.427**	0.315	0.253	0.225	0.126

Table 5: Performance comparison between systems. Our results are significantly better than the baselines.

7.5 Feature Study

To investigate the influence of different features on performance, we perform a feature ablation study. As shown in Section 5, we classify features into different groups. In this experiment, we first train the basic model (as defined in Eq. 1) with all the features, and then remove one group of features each time. We also experiment with only content features to justify the effectiveness of these features.

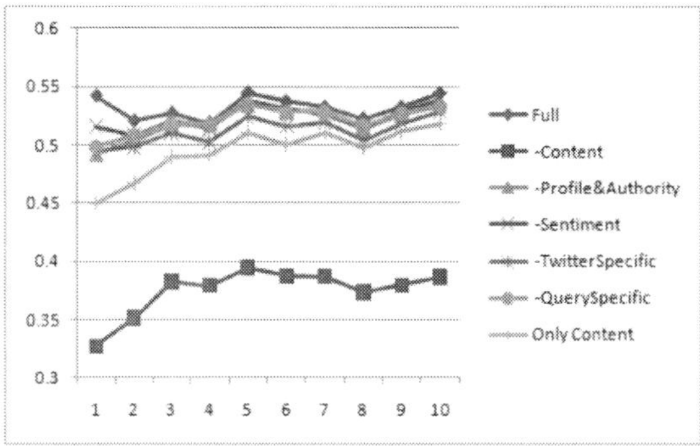

Figure 4: $nDCG@k$ performance with different feature groups. 'Full' means all the features. '-' means removing that feature group from the full feature set.

We can see that when removing content features, the performance drops substantially, which indicates that content is the most important indicator of quality. When using only content features, the performance is also fairly good (but significantly worse than the Full model, p-value<0.01 by t-test), showing that content is reliable features for this task. When removing Twitter specific features, there is a significant drop in performance (p-value<0.01). This indicates that such prior knowledge on tweets is helpful for ranking such documents. However, removing user profile and authority features does not affect the system much. Similar observation can be seen when removing sentiment features and query-specific features respectively. For query-specific features, it seems that such features play a light-weighted role. There may be two reasons for this: First, the documents are obtained from the BM25 model in our approach, thus all documents are more or less relevant to the query while our approach can be treated as a re-ranking process; Second, the document is very short, thus query-specific features may not be as important as in retrieving longer documents, more specifically, the query term frequency may not be as accurate as in longer documents.

To further investigate which specific content features are important, we conduct a further feature ablation study on content features. We find that the average term similarity (p-value<0.01), ratio of unique words (p-value=0.08), and ratio of POS tags (p-value<0.02) play more roles in performance. Not as expected, removing the length features does not lead to as a remarkable drop as removing other features (p-value=0.12). However, as shown in Figure 3, the Length model is strong in performance. This may infer that the length feature may be complemented by other content features.

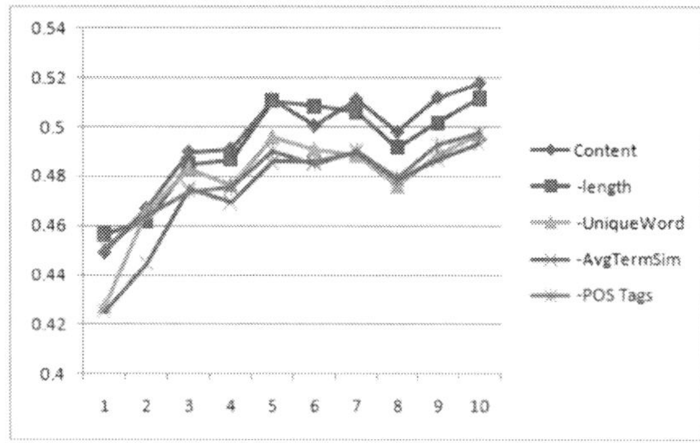

Figure 5: $nDCG@k$ performance with different content features. '-' means removing the feature group from the full content features.

Note that these experiments are performed with the basic model (Eq. 1). We also conduct similar feature studies with the regularization factor and similar observations are seen.

8 Conclusion

We presented a regression model which incorporates various features for suggesting quality-biased short-text documents. We proposed a content conformity hypothesis and formulated it into a regularization factor. The performance was boosted with such a factor. Moreover, unlabeled data can be used seamlessly in this approach, and leveraging such data leads to improvements in ranking performance. The comparative results demonstrate the effectiveness of finding high-quality tweets.

Short-text ranking is still in its infancy. There is still much work to do. For example, it is feasible to plug other hypotheses in this approach. As an instance, celebrity users may be more likely to post responsible tweets than common users. We also note that the quality of a tweet is not only determined by the text itself, but also by the external resources it points to (via a tiny URL) or it attaches (a picture or a video). Therefore, considering these factors would also be helpful in finding high-quality posts.

References

Marcelo Mendoza, Barbara Poblete, Carlos Castillo. 2010. *Twitter Under Crisis: Can we trust what we RT?*. 1st Workshop on Social Media Analytics (SOMA'10), July 25, 2010, Washington DC, USA.

Eugene Agichtein, Carlos Castillo, Debora Donato. 2008. *Finding High-Quality Content in Social Media.* WSDM'08, February 11-12, 2008, Palo Alto, California, USA. pp 183-193.

Jiang Bian, Yandong Liu, Ding Zhou, Eugene Agichtein, Hongyuan Zha. 2009. *Learning to Recognize Reliable Users and Content in Social Media with Coupled Mutual Reinforcement.* WWW 2009, April 20-24, 2009, Madrid, Spain.

Jiwoon Jeon, W. Bruce Croft, Joon Ho Lee, Soyeon Park. 2006. *A Framework to Predict the Quality of Answers with Non-Textual Features.* SIGIR'06, August 6-11, 2006, Seattle, Washington, USA

Chirag Shah, Jefferey Pomerantz. 2010. *Evaluating and Predicting Answer Quality in Community QA.* SIGIR'10, July 19-23, 2010, Geneva, Switzerland.

Takeshi Sakaki, Makoto Okazaki, Yutaka Matsuo. 2010. *Earthquake Shakes Twitter Users: Real-time Event Detection by Social Sensors.* WWW2010, April 26-30, 2010, Raleigh, North Carolina.

Haewoon Kwak, Changhyun Lee, Hosung Park, and Sue Moon. 2010. *What is Twitter, a Social Network or a News Media?* WWW 2010, April 26-30, 2010, Raleigh, North Carolina, USA.

Alan Ritter, Colin Cherry, Bill Dolan. *Unsupervised Modeling of Twitter Conversations.* 2010. Human Language Technologies: The 2010 Annual Conference of the North American Chapter of the ACL, pages 172-180.

Sasa Petrovic, Miles Osborne, Victor Lavrenko. 2010. *Streaming First Story Detection with application to Twitter.* The 2010 Annual Conference of the North American Chapter of the ACL, pages 181-189, Los Angeles, California, June 2010.

Anlei Dong, Ruiqiang Zhang, Pranam Kolari, Jing Bai, Fernando Diaz, Yi Chang, Zhaohui Zheng, Hon-gyuan Zha. 2010. *Time is of the Essence: Improving Recency Ranking Using Twitter Data.* WWW 2010, April 26-30, 2010, Raleigh, North Carolina, USA.

Aron Culotta. 2010. *Towards detecting influenza epidemics by analyzing Twitter messages.* 1st Workshop on Social Media Analytics (SOMA'10), July 25, 2010, Washington, DC, USA.

Andranik Tumasjan, Timm O. Sprenger, Philipp G. Sandner, Isabell M. Welpe. 2010. *Predicting Elections with Twitter: What 140 Characters Reveal about Political Sentiment.* Association for the Advancement of Artificial Intelligence (www.aaai.org).

Yajuan Duan, Long Jiang, Tao Qin, Ming Zhou and Heung-Yeung Shum. 2010. *An Empirical Study on Learning to Rank of Tweets.* Proceedings of the 23rd International Conference on Computational Linguistics (Coling 2010), pages 295-303, Beijing, August 2010.

Xiaohua Liu, Kuan Li, Bo Han, Ming Zhou, Long Jiang, Zhongyang Xiong and Changning Huang. 2010. *Semantic Role Labeling for News Tweets.* Proceedings of 23rd International Conference on Computational Linguistics (Coling 2010)

Pear Analytics. 2009. *Twitter Study-August 2009.*

Anindya Ghose, Panagiotis G. Ipeirotis. 2010. *Estimating the Helpfulness and Economic Impact of Product Reviews: Mining Text and Reviewer Characteristics.* (January 24, 2010), Available at SSRN: http://ssrn.com/abstract=1261751.

Yue Lu, Panayiotis Tsaparas, Alexandros Ntoulas, Livia Polanyi. 2010. *Exploiting social context for review quality prediction.* WWW 2010, April 26-30, 2010, Raleigh, North Carolina, USA.

Yang Liu, Xiangji Huang, Aijun An, Xiaohui Yu. 2008. *Modeling and Predicting the Helpfulness of Online Reviews.* 2008 Eighth IEEE International Conference on Data Mining. pp. 443-452.

Soo-Min Kim, Patrick Pantel, Tim Chklovski, Marco Pennacchiotti. 2006. *Automatically Assessing Review Helpfulness.* Proceedings of the 2006 Conference on Empirical Methods in Natural Language Processing (EMNLP 2006), pp. 423-430, Sydney, July 2006.

Nitin Jindal, Bing Liu. 2008. *Opinion Spam and Analysis.* WSDM'08, February 11-12, 2008, Palo Alto, California, USA.

Ee-Peng Lim, Viet-An Nguyen, Nitin Jindal, Bing Liu, Hady W. Lauw. 2010. *Detecting Product Review Spammers using Rating Behaviors.* CIKM'10, October 26-30, 2010, Toronto, Ontario, Canada.

William J. Corvey, Sarah Vieweg, Travis Rood, Martha Palmer. 2010. *Twitter in Mass Emergency: What NLP Techniques Can Contribute.* Proceedings of the NAACL HLT 2010 Workshop on Computational Linguistics in a World of Social Media, pages 23-24, Los Angeles, California, June 2010.

Sasa Petrovic, Miles Osborne, Victor Lavrenko. 2010. *The Edinburgh Twitter Corpus.* Proceedings of the NAACL HLT 2010 Workshop on Computational Linguistics in a World of Social Media, pages 25-26, Los Angeles, California, June 2010

Kalervo Järvelin and Jaana Kekäläinen. 1998. *Ir evaluation methods for retrieving highly relevant documents.* In SIGIR 2000: Proceedings of the 23th annual international ACM SIGIR conference on Research and development in information retrieval, pages 41-48, 2000.

Xiaojin Zhu, Andrew B. Goldberg, Ronald Brachman, Thomas Dietterich. 2009. *Introduction to Semi-Supervised Learning.* Synthesis Lectures on Artificial Intelligence and Machine Learning. Morgan & Claypool Publishers, 2009.

Jaime Teevan, Daniel Ramage, Meredith Ringel Morris. 2009. *#TwitterSearch: A Comparison of Microblog Search and Web Search.* WSDM11, February 9C12, 2011, Hong Kong, China.

Labeling Unlabeled Data using Cross-Language Guided Clustering

Sachindra Joshi
IBM Research
New Delhi, India
jsachind@in.ibm.com

Danish Contractor
IBM Research
New Delhi, India
dcontrac@in.ibm.com

Sumit Negi
IBM Research
New Delhi, India
sumitneg@in.ibm.com

Abstract

The effort required to build a classifier for a task in a *target* language can be significantly reduced by utilizing the knowledge gained during an earlier effort of model building in a *source* language for a similar task. In this paper, we investigate whether unlabeled data in the target language can be labeled given the availability of labeled data for a similar domain in the source language. We view the problem of labeling unlabeled documents in the target language as that of clustering them such that the resulting partitioning has the *best* alignment with the classes provided in the source language. We develop a cross language guided clustering (CLGC) method to achieve this. We also propose a method to discover concept mapping between languages which is utilized by CLGC to transfer supervision across languages. Our experimental results show significant gains in the accuracy of labeling documents over the baseline methods.

1 Introduction

The last few years have seen a rapid growth in the development of machine learning applications for non-English languages. This growth can be attributed to several factors such as increased Internet penetration (especially in non-English speaking countries) and wide adoption of Unicode standards that allow people to generate content in their own language.

A key guiding principal in the development of such applications for a new language (referred to as the target or resource-poor language) has been to leverage the existing models and linguistic resources available for a popular language such as English (also called source or resource-rich language). Existing literature examines two ways of utilizing this knowledge. The first way is to adapt an existing statistical model for a new target language. Examples of this is the problem of cross-lingual sentiment classification (Xiaojun Wan 2009), or in a more general setting for cross language domain adaptation for classification (Peter Prettenhofer and Benno Stein 2010). The second way is to develop linguistic resources for a target or resource-poor language by leveraging the resources available in a source or resource-rich language. An example of this is the work done for automatically transferring syntactic relations (in WordNet) from a source language (English) into a target language (Romanian) (Verginica Barbu Mititelu and Radu Ion 2005).

In this paper, we investigate another way of utilizing the knowledge gained in one language for building machine learning applications in another language. Our work focuses on generating training data (in contrast to adapting models and language resources) in the target language, given in-domain training data for the source language. The labeled data in the source language could be used to guide the grouping of unlabeled data in the target language, where each group *aligns* to a class label from the source language. We assume that the domain for both the source and target language data is similar and therefore the set of class labels across the two languages will be shared (but may not be exactly the same). As an example consider a real world scenario from a call routing application. A call routing application maps natural language utterances (typically a caller's response to an open ended question such as "how may I help you") to one of a given set of classes also called call types. Figure 1 shows examples of a few ut-

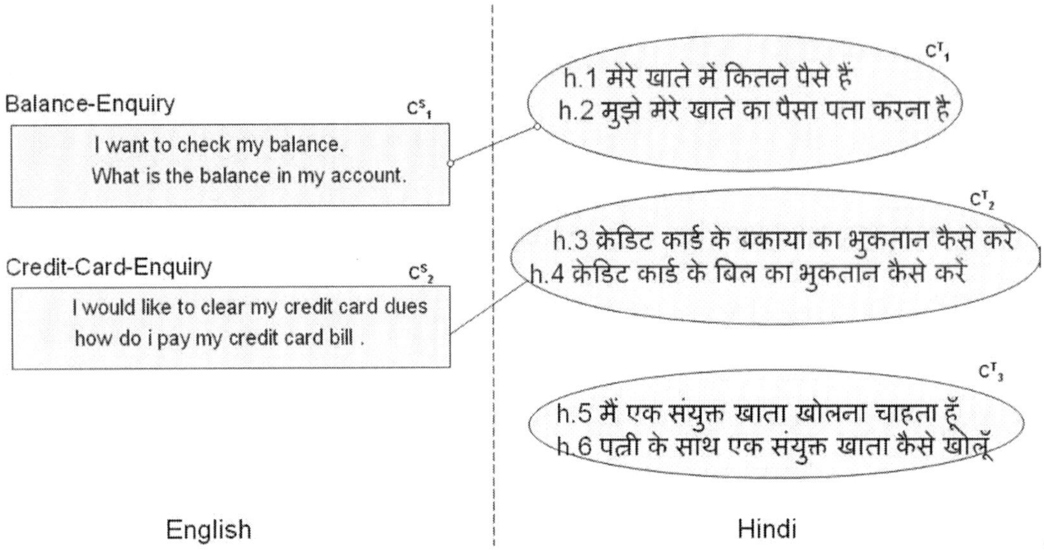

Figure 1: Utterances and class labels in source and target languages

terances (in English) along with associated class labels from the banking domain. These labeled utterances could be used as training data for building a call-routing classifier for the two class labels namely "Balance-Enquiry" and "Credit-Card-Enquiry". Let us assume that we now have utterances in a new language (in Hindi) which are unlabeled. Given that these utterances belong to the same domain, they can be labeled using the same label set as the one used for the source language. This is shown in the Figure 1 where utterances $h.1$ and $h.2$ are grouped together and labeled as "Balance-Enquiry" and utterance $h.3$ and $h.4$ is labeled as "Credit-Card-Enquiry". The labeled data can then be used to train a classifier in the target language.

To label the target language documents automatically we propose a method called cross-language guided clustering (CLGC). This method is built upon a recently proposed approach called cross guided clustering (CGC). CGC guides clustering of documents in a target domain given clusters/classes in a source domain (Bhattacharya et al. 2009). This is achieved by discovering a partitioning in the target domain that is most "similar" or "aligned" to a given partitioning in the source domain. In CLGC we view the problem of labeling unlabeled documents in the target language as that of clustering them such that the resulting partitioning has the *best* alignment with the classes provided in the source language. Since in our case the source and target data are in different languages, we extend the CGC framework to transfer supervision across different languages. We develop cross language similarity measures that use word level and concept level mappings to guide the clustering across languages. We also develop methods to discover concept level mapping between languages. Our experimental results show significant gains in the accuracy of labeling documents over the baseline methods.

One could argue that if the final goal is to classify documents in the target language, this could be achieved by either of the following approaches - (1) by adapting the source language classifier (Peter Prettenhofer and Benno Stein 2010) or (2) by translating unlabeled documents from the target language to the source language and then applying a source language classifier (Mckeown et al. 2003). We claim that our approach is more general and has several advantages over both these approaches. First, building a classifier given a training dataset is a well studied and understood problem. Several off-the-shelf machine learning tools exist that can readily be used for tasks such as feature construction, and building classifiers, provided a training dataset is available (Hall et al. 2009). Our approach can be used to generate a training dataset for the target language which enables use of existing approaches not only for building classifiers, but also for feature engineering tasks such as feature construction and feature selection. This cannot be done using either of the above mentioned approaches.

Second, a key assumption made in both these approaches is that the class labels across languages are completely shared. This may not be true in several cases as there could be categories that are specific to the target language dataset. As an example, while most of the Hindi utterances in the Figure 1 can be grouped and aligned with a class label in the source language, there exist utterances ($h.5$,$h.6$) which do not belong to any of the existing labels in the source language. Our method allows such groupings to be discovered which can then be used to build target language specific class labels. Moreover, it is worth mentioning that apart from these advantages our proposed method is more efficient than machine translation based methods as it does not require a complete machine translation system.

The specific contributions made by us in this paper are two fold. First, we introduce the problem of labeling documents in one language using the set of labeled documents in another language and show that it is not only feasible but also better than other competitor techniques. Second, we extend the CGC framework to transfer supervision across languages. For this we develop methods to discover concept level mapping between languages that is utilized to guide the clustering across languages.

The rest of the paper is organized as follows. In Section 2 we present related work. We formulate the problem in Section 3. We describe the cross-language guided clustering framework in Section 4. In Section 5, we describe the cross language similarity measure that is used in the CLGC framework. We provide the experimental results in Section 6 and conclude in Section 7.

2 Prior Work

The two research areas that are related to our work are, (1) cross lingual classification and clustering, and (2) semi-supervised clustering.

Cross Lingual Classification and Clustering: Traditional approaches to cross language text classification use linguistic resources such as bilingual dictionaries or parallel corpora to induce correspondences between two languages (Olsson 2005). Some of these methods employ latent semantic analysis (LSA) (Dumais et.al. 1997) or kernel canonical correlation analysis, CCA (Fortuna and Shawe-Taylor 2005). The major limitations of these approaches are their computational complexity and dependence on a parallel corpus. Cross-lingual clustering aims to cluster a heterogeneous (a collection of documents from different languages) document collection. Initial work done in cross-lingual document clustering employed an expensive machine translation (MT) system to fill the gap between two languages (Mckeown et al. 2003). Later work (Wu 2007) done in this area demonstrated that it was possible to achieve comparable performance to the direct MT method using simple linguistic resource such as bilingual dictionaries.

Semi-supervised clustering: Semi-supervised clustering aims to improve clustering performance by limited supervision in the form of a small set of labeled instances. Alternatively, a small set of labeled instances can be used to learn a parameterized distance function (M. Bilenko and R. J. Mooney 2003), (Klein et al. 2002). The co-clustering approach (Dhillon et al. 2003), (N. Slonim and N. Tishby 2000) clusters related dimensions simultaneously through explicitly provided relations between them, such as words and documents, or people and reviews.

The problem that we address in this paper differs significantly from the above mentioned work. Unlike others, our objective is to cluster target language documents such that the resulting clusters are most *'similar'* or best *'aligned'* to the given source language classes. This problem is an instance of semi-supervised clustering in a bilingual setting, which to the best of our best knowledge has received very little attention. Our work builds upon Cross Guided Clustering (CGC) work (Bhattacharya et al. 2009) where supervision is discovered in the form of cluster level similarities obtained from labeled instances from a different domain, having different but related labels. In our work we extend the CGC framework to transfer supervision across different languages.

3 Problem Formulation

Let $T^S = \{< d_1^S, l_1^S >, < d_2^S, l_2^S >, \ldots, < d_n^S, l_n^S >\}$ denote a training dataset in the source language S for a classification task γ. Here $d_i^S \in D^S$ denotes a document that has an associated class label $l_i^S \in L^S$ where, L^S denotes the set of class labels used in T^S. Note, that L^S induces a partitioning of D^S, where each class label l_i^S can be seen as a cluster containing documents d_i^S that have l_i^S as the class label. We are also given a set of unlabeled documents $D^T = \{d_1^T, d_2^T, \ldots, d_m^T\}$ where all the documents are from a similar domain as in T^S but are from a different language T. Our objective is to generate a training dataset using D^T

for the classification task γ. We pose this as a clustering problem over document set D^T, where the resulting clusters are *aligned* with the given classes in the source language dataset. The alignment is achieved by taking the supervision from the partitioning of D^S, which is induced by the label set L^S, to guide the clustering of document set D^T. We refer to this clustering method as *cross-language guided clustering*. In the next section, we describe cross-language guided clustering in detail.

4 Cross-Language Guided Clustering

In this section, we modify the cross guided clustering framework as described in (Bhattacharya et al. 2009) to transfer supervision across languages. Let $Dis(d_i^T, d_j^T)$ provide a distance measure between documents d_i^T and d_j^T in the target language T. A clustering method partitions the given document set into k clusters denoted by centroids $C^T = \{C_1^T, C_2^T, \ldots, C_k^T\}$ such that the total divergence $Div(C^T)$ also referred to as *target only divergence* is minimized. This is defined as follows.

$$Div^T(C^T) = \sum_{C_i^T}\sum_{d_j^T} \delta(C_i^T, d_j^T) Dis(C_i^T, d_j^T)^2 \quad (1)$$

Here $\delta(C_i^T, d_j^T)$ returns 1 if d_j^T is assigned to the centroid C_i^T else returns 0. This is a standard formulation used in the K-Means algorithm (Hall et al. 2009).

In our problem setting, we are additionally provided with a labeled dataset in the source language where the label set induces a partitioning $C^S = \{C_1^S, C_2^S, \ldots, C_l^S\}$ of D^S in the source language. Our objective is to discover partitioning of D^T such that each resulting cluster is aligned with *at most* one class label from the source language and vice-versa. This enables discovery of clusters in the target language that are aligned with the classes in the source language while simultaneously allowing for discovery of any additional concept in the target language. To do this, we require a cross-language similarity function $Sim^X(..)$ that given two documents from different languages, returns a similarity score. This is non-trivial as documents in different languages are represented in entirely separate attribute/feature space. We develop a cross-language similarity measure to achieve this in Section 5. For now, we assume that we have access to such a measure.

To find a cross-language alignment between the source partition and the target partition we construct a bipartite cross language graph G_x that has one set of vertices C^S corresponding to source centroids, and another set C^T corresponding to target centroids. An edge is added between every pair of vertices (C_i^S, C_j^T) where the weight of the edge is given by $Sim^X(C_i^S, C_j^T)$. Now finding the best cross language alignment is equivalent to finding the maximum weighted bipartite match in the graph G_x. Recall that a matching is a subset of the edges such that any vertex is spanned by at most one edge. The score of a matching is the sum of the weights of all the edges in it. In our implementation, we use the 'Hungarian method' to determine the matching (Kuhn 1955).

The matching provides an alignment between the source classes and the target clusters. We only consider those edges in the matching whose weight is more than some predefined threshold. To measure the goodness of cross-language alignment we define a cross-language divergence measure:

$$Div^X(C^S, C^T) = \sum_{C_i^S}\sum_{C_j^T} \delta^X(C_i^S, C_j^T)(1 - Sim^X(C_i^S, C_j^T))^2 |C_j^T| \quad (2)$$

Here, $\delta^X(C_i^S, C_j^T)$ returns the weight of the edge between node C_i^S and node C_j^T if these nodes are matched, else it returns 0. Here $|C_j^T|$ denotes the size of the cluster for which C_j^T is the centroid. The weighing by $|C_j^T|$ is done to make $Div^X(C^S, C^T)$ comparable to $Div(C^T)$. Now the combined divergence between the source partition and the target partition is computed by taking a weighted sum of target-only divergence and cross-language divergence.

$$Div(C^S, C^T) = \alpha * Div^T(C^T) + (1 - \alpha) * Div^X(C^S, C^T) \quad (3)$$

Here α captures the relative importance of the two divergences.

We now provide an algorithm (see Figure 2) that minimizes the objective function given in Equation 3. The algorithm starts by selecting k random data points as centroids from the target language and then executes the following two steps in each iteration. It first assigns points to their nearest centroids and then re-estimates the target centroids to minimize cross-language divergence as given in Equation 3. This is achieved by the

```
Procedure CrossLanguageGuidedClustering

  Select k centroids randomly from D^T
  % Initialize target clusters
  Iterate n times or until convergence
    Iterate m times
      Assign each d_i^T ∈ D^T to the nearest centroid
      Recompute the centroids

    % Start CLGC
    Create cross language similarity graph G_x using Sim^X
    Compute maximum bipartite graph matching over G_x
    Iterate over k target centroids in C^T
      Update centroid using the cross language update rule
      Assign each d_i^T ∈ D^T to the nearest centroid
  Return k centroids
```

Figure 2: Procedure for Cross Language Guided Clustering

following update rule that is obtained by differentiating the divergence function in Equation 3 with respect to the current target centroids.

$$C_i^T = \frac{\alpha \sum_{d_i^T \in C_i^T} d_i^T + (1-\alpha) \sum_j \delta^x(C_i^T, C_j^S)\phi(C_j^S)}{\alpha |C_i^T| + (1-\alpha)|C_i^T| \sum_j \delta^x(C_i^T, C_j^S)\phi(C_j^S)} \quad (4)$$

Here the δ^X function captures the current matching of target clusters with source classes. Intuitively, there are two factors contributing to the update rule. The first factor tries to move the current target centroid towards the center of the cluster computed using the currently assigned data points. This is similar to the standard K-means approach. The second factor that arises due to cross-language alignment tries to move the centroid towards the currently matched source class. Since the feature space used to represent source classes and target centroids are different, we use the function ϕ that projects source classes in the feature space used by the target language. We provide more details regarding the projection function and cross-language similarity in the next section.

5 Cross Language Similarity

In order to perform cross language guided clustering we need a similarity function Sim^X that given two documents d_i^S and d_j^T from source and target languages, computes a similarity score. Let V^S and V^T be the vocabularies used to represent documents in source and target language respectively. Given a word $w_i^S \in V^S$, let the function $proj(w_i^S)$ return a probability distribution $P = \{p_1, p_2, \ldots, p_{|V^T|}\}$ where p_j represents the probability of the word w_i^S being translated to the word w_j^T in target dictionary. The function $proj(..)$ has access to a statistical dictionary $\mathcal{D}_T^S$ for doing this. The dictionary could be constructed using some large general purpose parallel corpus. We now present three different methods to compute the similarity function $Sim^X(d_i^S, d_j^T)$.

Projection based Method: Let M represent a matrix of dimension $|V^S| * |V^T|$ where each ith row contains the probability distribution returned by $proj(w_i^S)$ for $1 \leq i \leq |V^S|$. Given a source document d_i^S, let $\bar{d}_i^S$ refer to its vector representation using the feature space V^S. Then the projection function $\phi(\bar{d}_i^S) = (\bar{d}_i^S)'M$ and the similarity function Sim^X can be defined as follows, where $'$ denotes transpose of a matrix:

$$Sim^X(d_i^S, d_j^T) = \phi(\bar{d}_i^S)\bar{d}_j^T = (\bar{d}_i^S)'M\bar{d}_j^T \quad (5)$$

Weighted Projection based Method: The function $proj(w_i^S)$ returns a probability distribution that captures the likelihood that w_i^S gets translated to a word w_j^T in the target dictionary. Since, this function uses a general purpose bi-lingual statistical dictionary it does not capture domain specific translations. For example, the English word "bank" may have equal probabilities for being translated as "बैंक" or "किनारा" however, given a corpus from the banking domain, it is more likely that the word "bank" translates to "बैंक". Therefore, given a source term we weigh the probability values of the target terms that it translates to, by the frequency of the target terms computed over the target corpus. We then normalize these values again to obtain a probability distribution.

Semantic Mapping based Method: There are multiple words that are synonymous to each other and can be used to represent the same meaning. For example, the word "games" and "sports" are synonymous English words and can be used to represent the same meaning as "खेल" or "गेम्स". The matrix M used in the previous methods, captures the translation probabilities at the word level. In this method we first discover the concepts in each language and then find translation probabilities at the concept level. We refer to this as semantic mapping between the two languages.

To discover the concepts, words from the source and target vocabulary are clustered into *term clusters* based on the words that occur in its *context*. For this a word-by-word co-occurrence matrix is built for the given language. The entry (i, j) in the matrix contains the number of times the word w_i and w_j occur within a fixed window of L

words in the corpus. Thus, each word is represented by a vector called "context vector" that captures words occurring in the context of the given word. We then use an off-the-shelf clustering algorithm (Hall et al. 2009) to obtain term clusters in a language. These term clusters are referred to as concepts. The Figure 3 shows examples of concepts identified in English and Hindi languages. Let $G^S = \{G_1^S, G_2^S, \ldots, G_l^S\}$ and $G^T = \{G_1^T, G_2^T, \ldots, G_m^T\}$ be the source and target concepts obtained by clustering. To find the semantic relationship across concepts from different languages, we construct a bipartite graph that has one set of vertices G^S corresponding to the source concepts, and another set G^T corresponding to the target concepts. Now for each word $w^S \in G_i^S$, we determine the set of target words T_{w^S} that it translates to along with the corresponding translation probabilities. For each word $w^T \in T_{w^S}$, we find the concept G_j^T that contains w^T and add a weight p on the edge between the vertex G_i^S and G_j^T, where p is the probability of w^S being translated to w^T. After repeating this process for all the source concepts, we normalize the edge weights such that for each G_i^S, the sum of weights corresponding to the edges connecting G_i^S and any concept in the target language equals to 1. Thus for each source concept the normalized bipartite graph contains a distribution over the target concepts. We call this normalized bipartite graph as the semantic mapping between the two languages. Note, that the normalized bipartite graph can be seen as a matrix M_{map} where the rows and columns correspond to source and target concepts respectively and the entry (i, j) denotes the probability that the ith source concept corresponds to j^{th} target concept.

Now using the matrix M_{map}, the similarity function $Sim^X(d_i^S, d_j^T)$ can be defined as follows:

$$Sim^X(d_i^S, d_j^T) = (\bar{c}_i^S)' M_{map} \bar{c}_j^T \qquad (6)$$

Here, $\bar{c}_i^S$ and $\bar{c}_j^T$ denote the concept vector representation of d_i^S and d_j^T respectively. The concept vector for a document is obtained by replacing the occurrence of each word w_i in the document by its concept.

6 Experimental Evaluation

There are three key questions for which we seek an answer through our experimental evaluation. First, whether the availability of labeled data in a source language is helpful for labeling unlabeled documents in the target language. Second,

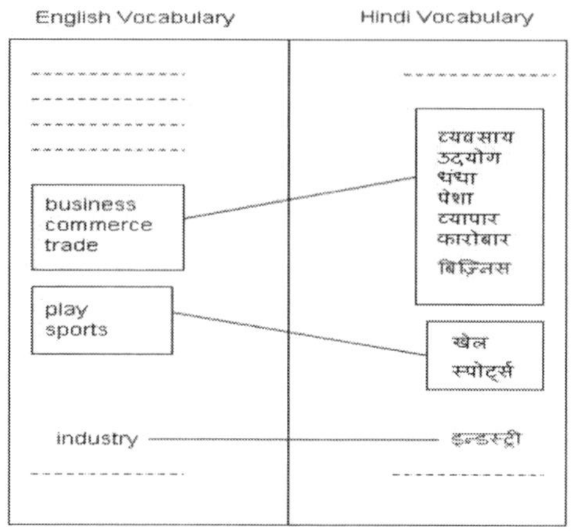

Figure 3: Vocabulary after Semantic Projection

whether discovery of concepts and concept mapping between languages improves the CLGC performance. Third, given that the target language contains exactly the same classes as the source language (which is not an assumption for CLGC), whether labeling documents using CLGC gives comparable performance to computationally more expensive method that uses a machine translation system. We next describe the dataset, baselines and evaluation metrics that we use to answer these questions.

Dataset and Resources: To evaluate the performance of our method, we constructed a dataset of news articles by crawling an English and a Hindi news site. The crawled news articles are from a four month period and belong to the following five categories, *viz*, (1) Economy and Finance - these are news reports on macro-economic events (such as cuts in interest rates, stock market and increase in taxes), (2) Healthcare and BioTech - these are business reports from the Healthcare and Biotechnology industry (mergers and acquisition, patents lawsuits , expansion etc), (3) Energy - these are news reports from the energy and utility sector, (4) sports and (5) Auto. The number of documents for each language and category are shown in Table 1. As mentioned earlier, the CLGC method does not assume that the same set of categories are present in both the languages, to verify this claim we have an additional category, viz, "Auto" in our Hindi dataset which is absent in the English dataset. Even though both English and Hindi news articles are from the same time frame these articles are not aligned.

Language	Economy	BioTech	Energy	Sports	Auto
English	1012	510	500	268	0
Hindi	412	300	350	275	153

Table 1: News Dataset used for Experimentation

	English	Hindi
Number of Unique Words	18128	14521
General Dictionary coverage	11061 (61%)	9344 (64%)
Domain Dictionary coverage	14969 (82.5%)	11767 (81%)

Table 2: Dictionary Statistics

In our experiments, we use an English-Hindi statistical dictionary which was built using the Moses toolkit (Koehn 2007). The training data for the dictionary was a collection of 150,000 English and Hindi parallel sentences sourced from a general corpus. The dictionary built using this corpus is referred to as a "general dictionary" (GD). We further collected 10,000 parallel sentences on the topics present in our news dataset. These were then used along with the earlier set of parallel sentence to learn a dictionary that contains domain specific words and their translations. We refer to this dictionary as a "domain dictionary" (DD). The statistics for these dictionaries in terms of word coverage is shown in Table 2. The objective of creating these two dictionaries is to observe the performance of CLGC when a general purpose dictionary is used in contrast to a domain specific dictionary.

Baselines: One of the objective of experimental evaluation is to see if the availability of source classes helps in clustering documents in the target language. In order to measure gains achieved by the availability of source class information, we compare the performance of CLGC against the standard k-means algorithm. We refer to this as *k-means baseline*.

Another objective of the experimental evaluation is to see whether labeling documents using CLGC gives comparable performance to computationally more expensive method that uses a machine translation system. For this we train a classifier using the English news articles referred to as source classifier. We then translate Hindi new articles into English using Google's machine translation system and then label them using the source classifier. We refer to this as *NB baseline*.

Evaluation Metric The objective of the CLGC approach is to label the unlabeled target dataset. We use the following approach for evaluating this. As the true class-labels for the target news articles are known we assign to each cluster the class-label

Dictionary	Method	F1	Purity
	K-Means	0.45	0.61
General dictionary	PB	0.49	0.63
	WPB	0.56	0.66
	SM	0.62	0.71
Domain Dictionary	PB	0.57	0.64
	WPB	0.61	0.69
	SM	0.64	0.73

Table 3: Comparison of k means with CLGC using different cross lingual similarity measures

which is the most frequent in the cluster. All articles in the cluster are now labeled with the corresponding cluster-label. Based on this labeling strategy and the available ground truth we report the accuracy/purity measure which is computed by dividing the correctly labelled documents by the total number of documents. We also evaluate clustering quality by considering the correctness of clustering decisions over all document pairs. We report the standard F1 measure over the pairwise clustering decisions. The F1 measure is the harmonic mean of precision and recall over pairwise decisions.

Experiment 1: In our first experiment, We compare the performance of k-means with the projection based method, referred to as PB, weighted projection based method referred to as WPB and semantic mapping based method, referred to as SM. For this experiment we use the English dataset as the source dataset and Hindi dataset as the target dataset with 4 and 5 categories respectively. For the semantic mapping based method, we discover concepts using the word clustering. The word clustering algorithm uses k-means algorithm. We set k to a large value (we set it to 1000) and use only the first 100 best clusters where goodness of a cluster is measured in terms of its divergence. For each word that is not covered by the first best 100 clusters, we create singleton clusters for the word. We use this procedure for both the source and target dataset. We then use the method described in Section 5 to discover concept mappings.

Since the results obtained for both the k means and all the variations of CLGC depends on the choice of initial centroids, in each experimental run all the methods are seeded with the same set of centroids. The reported results are averaged over 10 runs with random initialization. We set the value of k equal to the actual number of categories in each dataset for both k-means as well as for CLGC. The value of α in Equation 4 is set to 0.5 and value of n and m in the procedure given in the Figure 2 is kept 20 and 5 respectively.

The results are reported in Table 3. The results show that there is a significant gain that is achieved by CLGC methods over K-means. This shows that the presence of labeled data in the source language helps in the clustering of documents in the target language. We further note that the SM methods, both using "general dictionary" (GD) and "domain dictionary" (DD) outperforms all other methods in their class. This happens because words that do not get translated using the statistical dictionary, are taken into account as they become part of concept mappings that have correspondence across languages. Thus, these terms get accounted in the computation of the SM similarity measure. These terms were not being considered in the PB and WPB similarity computations. As an example the statistical dictionary did not have the translation for the word "bharti" , which is the name of a company from the telecommunication and retail sector. However the word "bharti" mapped to a concept from the source language which contained words such as "communication", "retail" and "ipo". This cluster mapped to a concept in Hindi which had words such as "सँचार", "रिटेल" and "भारती" where the first two words are translations for the words "communication" and "retail" respectively. As a result of this correspondence between the two concepts the words "bharti" and "भारती" get associated. Another key point to note is that the performance of Semantic Mapping using General Dictionary is only slightly worse than Semantic Mapping using the Domain Dictionary. This shows that the semantic mapping based method is able to achieve good performance even when it does not have access to a domain specific dictionary.

Experiment 2: In our second experiment, we compare the performance of SM method which is the best performing CLGC method with the NB baseline. We use the rainbow package (McCallum 1996) to train a naïve Bayes classifier using the English dataset. For translating Hindi documents to English, we use Google [1] translation engine. The accuracy results for this experiment are provided in Table 4.

[1] http://code.google.com/p/google-api-translate-java

Method	Accuracy
NB	0.71
SM	0.73

Table 4: Comparison of naïve Bayes with CLGC (SM using General Dictionary)

We note that the performance of SM is slightly higher than the naïve Bayes approach. We investigated the reasons behind this and found that there are a few important features that are specific to the Hindi dataset. As the naïve Bayes classifier is trained using the English dataset only, it does not have access to these features and therefore incorrectly classifies the documents that contain such features. While classification techniques such as those based on Support Vector Machines can be expected to perform better than simple NB, our aim here is only to demonstrate that in a resource poor language, where building such classifiers may not be possible (due to the lack of a good machine translation system etc), CLGC can prove to be a useful method.

7 Concluding Remarks

In this paper, we presented cross language guided clustering (CLGC) that utilizes the labeled data from a source language to label unlabeled data from a target language. CLGC tries to cluster unlabeled target language documents such that the resulting clusters are most 'similar' or best 'aligned' to the given source language classes. To achieve this alignment we defined a cross-language similarity measures that returns a similarity score between two documents in different languages. We presented and compared three cross-language similarity measure namely Projection Based, Weighted Projection Based and Semantic Mapping and demonstrate their effectiveness on real-world data-sets. Our Semantic Mapping method, which discovers concepts and their associated mapping across languages, shows the maximum gain in the accuracy of labeling documents over the baseline methods.

References

Xiaojun Wan. 2009. *Co-Training for Cross-Lingual Sentiment Classification*, Proceedings of the 47th Annual Meeting of the Association for Computational Linguistics, pages 235–243.

Peter Prettenhofer and Benno Stein. 2010. *Cross-Language Text Classification using Structural Correspondence Learning*. Proceedings of the 48th Annual Meeting of the Association for Computational Linguistics, pages 1118–1127.

Verginica Barbu Mititelu and Radu Ion. 2005. *Automatic Import of Verbal Syntactic Relations Using Parallel Corpora*. Cross-Language Knowledge Induction Workshop.

Indrajit Bhattacharya and Shantanu Godbole and Sachindra Joshi and Ashish Verma. 2009. *Cross-Guided Clustering: Transfer of Relevant Supervision across Domains for Improved Clustering*. Proceedings of the Internationl Conference on Data Mining, pages 41–50.

Mark Hall and Eibe Frank and Geoffrey Holmes and Bernhard Pfahringer and Peter Reutemann and Ian H. Witten. 2009. *The WEKA Data Mining Software: An Update*. SIGKDD Explorations, Volume 11, Issue 1.

Kathleen Mckeown and Regina Barzilay and John Chen and David Elson and David Evans and Judith Klavans and Ani Nenkova and Barry Schiffman and Sergey Sigelman. 2003. *Columbias newsblaster: New features and future directions*. In Proceedings of NAACL-HLT03.

M. Bilenko and R. J. Mooney. 2003 *Adaptive duplicate detection using learnable string similarity measures* In ACM SIGKDD International Conference on Knowledge Discovery and Data Mining, 2003.

D. Klein and S. D. Kamvar and C. Manning. 2002 *From instance level constraints to space-level constraints: Making the most of prior knowledge in data clustering* In International Conference on Machine Learning, 2002.

I. Dhillon and S. Mallela and D. S. Modha. 2003 *Information theoretic co-clustering* On ACM SIGKDD International Conference on Knowledge Discovery and Data Mining, 2003.

N. Slonim and N. Tishby. 2000 *Document clustering using word clusters via the information bottleneck method* In The Annual International ACM SIGIR Conference, 2000.

I. Bhattacharya and L. Getoor. 2007 *Collective entity resolution in relational data* ACM Transactions on Knowledge Discovery from Data, vol. 1, no. 1, pp. 1–36, March 2007.

H. W. Kuhn. 1955. *The hungarian method for the assignment problem* Naval Research Logistics Quarterly, vol. 2, pp. 83–97, 1955.

J. Scott Olsson and Douglas W. Oard and Jan Hajic. 2005. *Cross language text classification* In Proceedings of SIGIR-05, pages 645–646.

Andrew Kachites McCallum 1996. *Bow: A toolkit for statistical language modeling, text retrieval, classification and clustering.* http://www.cs.cmu.edu/ mccallum/bow.

Susan T. Dumais, Todd A. Letsche, Michael L. Littman, and Thomas K. Landauer. 1997. *Automatic cross-language retrieval using latent semantic indexing* In AAAI Symposium on Cross-Language Text and Speech Retrieval.

Blaz Fortuna and John Shawe-Taylor. 2005. *The use of machine translation tools for cross-lingual text mining.* In Proceedings of the ICML Workshop on Learning with Multiple Views.

Ke Wu and Bao-Liang Lu. 2007. *Cross-Lingual Document Clustering* . In Lecture Notes in Computer Science, Volume 4426/2007, 956–963,

Philipp Koehn, Hieu Hoang, Alexandra Birch Mayne, Christopher Callison-Burch, Marcello Federico, Nicola Bertoldi, Brooke Cowan, Wade Shen, Christine Moran, Richard Zens, Chris Dyer, Ondrej Bojar, Alexandra Constantin, Evan Herbst 2007. *Open source toolkit for statistical machine translation.* Annual Meeting of the Association for Computation Linguistics (ACL), Demonstration Session

Extracting Relation Descriptors with Conditional Random Fields

Yaliang Li[†], Jing Jiang[†], Hai Leong Chieu[‡], Kian Ming A. Chai[‡]
[†]School of Information Systems, Singapore Management University, Singapore
[‡]DSO National Laboratories, Singapore
{ylli,jingjiang}@smu.edu.sg, {chaileon,ckianmin}@dso.org.sg

Abstract

In this paper we study a novel relation extraction problem where a general relation type is defined but relation extraction involves extracting specific relation descriptors from text. This new task can be treated as a sequence labeling problem. Although linear-chain conditional random fields (CRFs) can be used to solve this problem, we modify this baseline solution in order to better fit our task. We propose two modifications to linear-chain CRFs, namely, reducing the space of possible label sequences and introducing long-range features. Both modifications are based on some special properties of our task. Using two data sets we have annotated, we evaluate our methods and find that both modifications to linear-chain CRFs can significantly improve the performance for our task.

1 Introduction

Relation extraction is the task of identifying and characterizing the semantic relations between entities in text. Depending on the application and the resources available, relation extraction has been studied in a number of different settings. When relation types are well defined and labeled relation mention instances are available, supervised learning is usually applied (Zelenko et al., 2003; Zhou et al., 2005; Bunescu and Mooney, 2005; Zhang et al., 2006). When relation types are known but little training data is available, bootstrapping has been used to iteratively expand the set of seed examples and relation patterns (Agichtein and Gravano, 2000). When no relation type is pre-defined but there is a focused corpus of interest, unsupervised relation discovery tries to cluster entity pairs in order to identify interesting relation types (Hasegawa et al., 2004; Rosenfeld and Feldman, 2006; Shinyama and Sekine, 2006). More recently, open relation extraction has also been proposed where there is no fixed domain or predefined relation type, and the goal is to identify all possible relations from an open-domain corpus (Banko and Etzioni, 2008; Wu and Weld, 2010; Hoffmann et al., 2010).

These different relation extraction settings suit different applications. In this paper, we focus on another setting where the relation types are defined at a general level but a more specific relation description is desired. For example, in the widely used ACE[1] data sets, relation types are defined at a fairly coarse granularity. Take for instance the "employment" relation, which is a major relation type defined in ACE. In ACE evaluation, extraction of this relation only involves deciding whether a person entity is employed by an organization entity. In practice, however, we often also want to find the exact job title or position this person holds at the organization if this information is mentioned in the text. Table 1 gives some examples. We refer to the segment of text that describes the specific relation between the two related entities (i.e., the two arguments) as the *relation descriptor*. This paper studies how to extract such relation descriptors given two arguments.

One may approach this task as a sequence labeling problem and apply methods such as the linear-chain conditional random fields (CRFs) (Lafferty et al., 2001). However, this solution ignores a useful property of the task: the space of possible label sequences is much smaller than that enumerated by a linear-chain CRF. There are two implications. First, the normalization constant in the linear-chain CRF is too large because it also enumerates the impossible sequences. Second, the restriction to the correct space of label sequence per-

[1]Automatic Content Extraction http://www.itl.nist.gov/iad/mig/tests/ace/

Relation	Candidate Relation Instance	Relation Descriptor
Employment (PER, ORG)	... said *ARG-1* , a vice president at *ARG-2* , which ...	a vice president
	A *ARG-2* spokesman , *ARG-1* , said the company now ...	spokesman
	At *ARG-2* , by contrast , *ARG-1* said customers spend on ...	*Nil*
Personal/Social (PER, PER)	*ARG-1* had an elder brother named *ARG-2* .	an elder brother
	ARG-1 was born at ... , as the son of *ARG-2* of Sweden ...	the son
	ARG-1 later married *ARG-2* in 1973 , ...	married
	Through his contact with *ARG-1* , *ARG-2* joined the Greek_Orthodox_Church .	*Nil*

Table 1: Some examples of candidate relation instances and their relation descriptors.

mits the use of long-range features without an exponential increase in computational cost.

We compare the performance of the baseline linear-chain CRF model and our special CRF model on two data sets that we have manually annotated. Our experimental results show that both reducing the label sequence space and introducing long-range features can significantly improve the baseline performance.

The rest of the paper is organized as follows. In Section 2 we review related work. We then formally define our task in Section 3. In Section 4 we present a baseline linear-chain CRF-based solution and our modifications to the baseline method. We discuss the annotation of our data sets and show our experimental results in Section 5. We conclude in Section 6.

2 Related Work

Most existing work on relation extraction studies binary relations between two entities. For supervised relation extraction, existing work often uses the ACE benchmark data sets for evaluation (Bunescu and Mooney, 2005; Zhou et al., 2005; Zhang et al., 2006). In this setting, a set of relation types are defined and the task is to identify pairs of entities that are related and to classify their relations into one of the pre-defined relation types. It is assumed that the relation type itself is sufficient to characterize the relation between the two related entities. However, based on our observation, some of the relation types defined in ACE such as the "employment" relation and the "personal/social" relation are very general and can be further characterized by more specific descriptions.

Recently open relation extraction has been proposed for open-domain information extraction (Banko and Etzioni, 2008). Since there are no fixed relation types, open relation extraction aims at extracting all possible relations between pairs of entities. The extracted results are (*ARG-1*, *REL*, *ARG-2*) tuples. The TextRunner system based on (Banko and Etzioni, 2008) extracts a diverse set of relations from a huge Web corpus. These extracted predicate-argument tuples are presumably the most useful to support Web search scenarios where the user is looking for specific relations. However, because of the diversity of the extracted relations and the domain independence, open relation extraction is probably not suitable for populating relational databases or knowledgebases. In contrast, the task of extracting relation descriptors as we have proposed still assumes a pre-defined general relation type, which ensures that the extracted tuples follow the same relation definition and thus can be used in applications such as populating relational databases.

In terms of models and techniques, we use standard linear-chain CRF as our baseline, which is the main method used in (Banko and Etzioni, 2008) as well as for many other information extraction problems. The major modifications we propose for our task are the reduction of the label sequence space and the incorporation of long-range features. We note that these modifications are closely related to the semi-Markov CRF models proposed by Sarawagi and Cohen (2005). In fact, the modified CRF model for our task can be considered as a special case of semi-Markov CRF where we only consider label sequences that contain at most one relation descriptor sequence.

3 Task Definition

In this section we define the task of extracting relation descriptors for a given pre-defined class of relations such as "employment." Given two named entities occurring in the same sentence, one acting as *ARG-1* and the other as *ARG-2*, we aim to extract a segment of text from the sentence that best describes a pre-defined general relation between the two entities. Formally, let $(w_1, w_2, \ldots, w_n)$

denote the sequence of tokens in a sentence, where w_p is *ARG-1* and w_q is *ARG-2* ($1 \leq p, q \leq n$, $p \neq q$). Our goal is to locate a subsequence $(w_r, \dots, w_s)$ ($1 \leq r \leq s \leq n$) that best describes the relation between *ARG-1* and *ARG-2*. If *ARG-1* and *ARG-2* are not related through the pre-defined general relation, *Nil* should be returned.

The above definition constrains *ARG-1* and *ARG-2* to single tokens. In our experiments, we will replace the original lexical strings of *ARG-1* and *ARG-2* with the generic tokens `ARG1` and `ARG2`. Examples of sentences with the named entities replaced with argument tokens are shown in the second column of Table 1.

4 Method

4.1 Representation

The relation descriptor extraction task can be treated as a sequence labeling problem. Let $\boldsymbol{x} = (x_1, x_2, \dots, x_n)$ denote the sequence of observations in a relation instance, where x_i is w_i augmented with additional information such as the POS tag of w_i, and the phrase boundary information. Each observation x_i is associated with a label $y_i \in \mathcal{Y}$ which indicates whether w_i is part of the relation descriptor. Following the commonly used BIO notation (Ramshaw and Marcus, 1995) in sequence labeling, we define $\mathcal{Y} = \{B\text{-}REL, I\text{-}REL, O\}$. Let $\boldsymbol{y} = (y_1, y_2, \dots, y_n)$ denote the sequence of labels for $\boldsymbol{x}$. Our task can be reduced to finding the best label sequence $\hat{\boldsymbol{y}}$ among all the possible label sequences for $\boldsymbol{x}$.

4.2 A Linear-Chain CRF Solution

For sequence labeling tasks in NLP, linear-chain CRFs have been rather successful. It is an undirected graphical model in which the conditional probability of a label sequence $\boldsymbol{y}$ given the observation sequence $\boldsymbol{x}$ is

$$p(\boldsymbol{y}|\boldsymbol{x}, \Lambda) = \frac{\exp\left(\sum_i \sum_k \lambda_k f_k(y_{i-1}, y_i, \boldsymbol{x})\right)}{Z(\boldsymbol{x}, \Lambda)}, \quad (1)$$

where $\Lambda = \{\lambda_k\}$ is the set of model parameters, f_k is an arbitrary feature function defined over two consecutive labels and the whole observation sequence, and

$$Z(\boldsymbol{x}, \Lambda) = \sum_{\boldsymbol{y}'} \exp\left(\sum_i \sum_k \lambda_k f_k(y'_{i-1}, y'_i, \boldsymbol{x})\right) \quad (2)$$

is the normalization constant.

Given a set of training instances $\{\boldsymbol{x}_j, \boldsymbol{y}^*_j\}$ where $\boldsymbol{y}^*_j$ is the correct label sequence for $\boldsymbol{x}_j$, we can learn the best model parameters $\hat{\Lambda}$ as follows:

$$\hat{\Lambda} = \arg\min_{\Lambda} \left(-\sum_j \log p(\boldsymbol{y}^*_j|\boldsymbol{x}_j, \Lambda) + \beta \sum_k \lambda_k^2 \right). \quad (3)$$

Here $\beta \sum_k \lambda_k^2$ is a regularization term.

4.3 Improvement over Linear-Chain CRFs

We note that while we can directly apply linear-chain CRFs to extract relation descriptors, there are some special properties of our task that allow us to modify standard linear-chain CRFs to better suit our needs.

Label sequence constraint

In linear-chain CRFs, the normalization constant Z considers all possible label sequences $\boldsymbol{y}$. For the relation descriptor extraction problem, however, we expect that there is either a single relation descriptor sequence or no such sequence. In other words, for a given relation instance, we only expect two kinds of label sequences: (1) All y_i are *O*, and (2) exactly one y_i is *B-REL* followed by zero or more consecutive *I-REL* while all other y_i are *O*. Therefore the space of label sequences should be reduced to only those that satisfy the above constraint.

One way to exploit this constraint within linear-chain CRFs is to enforce it only during testing. We can pick the label sequence that has the highest probability in the *valid* label sequence space instead of the entire label sequence space. For a candidate relation instance $\boldsymbol{x}$, let $\tilde{\mathbf{Y}}$ denote the set of valid label sequences, i.e., those that have either one or no relation descriptor sequence. We then choose the best sequence $\hat{\boldsymbol{y}}$ as follows:

$$\hat{\boldsymbol{y}} = \arg\max_{\boldsymbol{y} \in \tilde{\mathbf{Y}}} p(\boldsymbol{y}|\boldsymbol{x}, \hat{\Lambda}). \quad (4)$$

Arguably, the more principled way to exploit the constraint is to modify the probabilistic model itself. So at the training stage, we should also consider only $\tilde{\mathbf{Y}}$ by defining the normalization term $\tilde{Z}$ as follows:

$$\tilde{Z}(\boldsymbol{x}, \Lambda) = \sum_{\boldsymbol{y}' \in \tilde{\mathbf{Y}}} \exp\left(\sum_i \sum_k \lambda_k f_k(y'_{i-1}, y'_i, \boldsymbol{x})\right). \quad (5)$$

The difference between Equation (5) and Equation (2) is the set of label sequences considered. In other words, while in linear-chain CRFs the correct label sequence competes with all possible label sequences for probability mass, for our task the correct label sequence should compete with only other valid label sequences. In Section 5 we will compare these two different normalization terms and show the advantage of using Equation (5).

Adding long-range features

In linear-chain CRF models, only first-order label dependencies are considered because features are defined over two consecutive labels. Inference in linear-chain CRFs can be done efficiently using dynamic programming. More general higher-order CRF models also exist, allowing long-range features defined over more than two consecutive labels. But the computational cost of higher-order CRFs also increases exponentially with the order of dependency.

For our task, because of the constraint on the space of label sequences, we can afford to use long-range features. In our case, inference is still efficient because the number of sequences to be enumerated has been drastically reduced due to the constraint. Let $g(\boldsymbol{y}, \boldsymbol{x})$ denote a feature function defined over the entire label sequence $\boldsymbol{y}$ and the observation sequence $\boldsymbol{x}$. We can include such feature functions in our model as follows:

$$p(\boldsymbol{y}|\boldsymbol{x}, \Theta) = \frac{1}{Z(\boldsymbol{x}, \Theta)} \Bigg[\exp\Big(\sum_i \sum_k \lambda_k f_k(y_{i-1}, y_i, \boldsymbol{x}) + \sum_l \mu_l g_l(\boldsymbol{y}, \boldsymbol{x}) \Big) \Bigg], \quad (6)$$

where $\Theta = \{\{\lambda_k\}, \{\mu_l\}\}$ is the set of all model parameters. Both $\{\lambda_k\}$ and $\{\mu_l\}$ are regularized as in Equation (3). Note that although each $f(y_{i-1}, y_i, \boldsymbol{x})$ may be subsumed under a $g(\boldsymbol{y}, \boldsymbol{x})$, here we group all features that can be captured by linear-chain CRFs under f and other real long-range features under g. In Section 5 we will see that with the additional feature functions g, relation extraction performance can also be further improved.

4.4 Features

We now describe the features we use in the baseline linear-chain CRF model and our modified model.

Linear-chain features

The linear-chain features are those that can be formulated as $f(y_{i-1}, y_i, \boldsymbol{x})$, i.e., those that depend on $\boldsymbol{x}$ and two consecutive labels only. We use typical features that include tokens, POS tags and phrase boundary information coupled with label values. Let t_i denote the POS tag of w_i and p_i denote the phrase boundary tag of w_i. The phrase boundary tags also follow the BIO notation. Examples include *B-NP*, *I-VP*, etc. Table 2 shows the feature templates covering only the observations. Each feature shown in Table 2 is further combined with either the value of the current label y_i or the values of the previous and the current labels y_{i-1} and y_i to form zeroth order and first order features. For example, a zeroth order feature is "y_i is *B-REL* and w_i is `the` and w_{i+1} is `president`", and a first order feature is "y_{i-1} is *O* and y_i is *B-REL* and t_i is `N`".

Long-range features

Long-range features are those that cannot be defined based on only two consecutive labels. When defining long-range features, we treat the whole relation descriptor sequence as a single unit, denoted as `REL`. Given a label sequence $\boldsymbol{y}$ that contains a relation descriptor sequence, let $(w_r, w_{r+1}, \ldots, w_s)$ denote the relation descriptor, that is, y_r = *B-REL* and y_t = *I-REL* where $r + 1 \leq t \leq s$. The long-range features we use are categorized and summarized in Table 3. These features capture the context of the entire relation descriptor, its relation to the two arguments, and whether the boundary of the relation descriptor conforms to the phrase boundaries (since we expect that most relation descriptors consist of a single or a sequence of phrases).

5 Experiments

5.1 Data Preparation

Since the task of extracting relation descriptors is new, we are not aware of any data set that can be directly used to evaluate our methods. We therefore annotated two data sets for evaluation, one for the general "employment" relation and the other for the general "personal/social" relation.[2]

The first data set contains 150 business articles from New York Times. The articles were crawled from the NYT website between November 2009

[2] `http://www.mysmu.edu/faculty/jingjiang/data/IJCNLP2011.zip`

Description	Feature Template	Example
single token	w_{i+j} $(-2 \leq j \leq 2)$	w_{i+1} (next token) is *president*
single POS tag	t_{i+j} $(-2 \leq j \leq 2)$	t_i (current POS tag) is *DET*
single phrase tag	p_{i+j} $(-2 \leq j \leq 2)$	p_{i-1} (previous phrase boundary tag) is *I-NP*
two consecutive tokens	$w_{i+j-1}\&w_{i+j}$ $(-1 \leq j \leq 2)$	w_i is *the* and w_{i+1} is *president*
two consecutive POS tags	$t_{i+j-1}\&t_{i+j}$ $(-1 \leq j \leq 2)$	t_i is *DET* and t_{i+1} is *N*
two consecutive phrase tags	$p_{i+j-1}\&p_{i+j}$ $(-1 \leq j \leq 2)$	p_i is *B-NP* and p_{i+1} is *I-NP*

Table 2: Linear-chain feature templates. Each feature is defined with respect to a particular (current) position in the sequence. i indicates the current position and j indicates the position relative to the current position. All features are defined using observations within a window size of 5 of the current position.

Category	Feature Template Description	Example
Contextual Features	word w_{r-1} or POS tag t_{r-1} preceding relation descriptor	`, REL`
	word w_{s+1} or POS tag t_{s+1} following relation descriptor	`REL PREP`
Path-based Features	word or POS tag sequence between `ARG1` and relation descriptor	`ARG1 is REL`
	word or POS tag sequence between `ARG2` and relation descriptor	`REL PREP ARG2`
	word or POS tag sequence containing `ARG1`, `ARG2` and relation descriptor	`ARG2 's REL , ARG1`
Phrase Boundary Feature	whether relation descriptor violates phrase boundaries	1 or 0

Table 3: Long-range feature templates. r and s are the indices of the first word and the last word of the relation descriptor, respectively.

and January 2010. After sentence segmentation and tokenization, we used the Stanford NER tagger (Finkel et al., 2005) to identify PER and ORG named entities from each sentence. For named entities that contain multiple tokens we concatenated them into a single token. We then took each pair of (PER, ORG) entities that occur in the same sentence as a single candidate relation instance, where the PER entity is treated as *ARG-1* and the ORG entity is treated as *ARG-2*.

The second data set comes from a Wikipedia personal/social relation data set previously used in (Culotta et al., 2006). The original data set does not contain annotations of relation descriptors such as "sister" or "friend" between the two PER arguments. We therefore also manually annotated this data set. Similarly, we performed sentence segmentation, tokenization and NER tagging, and took each pair of (PER, PER) entities occurring in the same sentence as a candidate relation instance. Because both arguments involved in the "personal/social" relation are PER entities, we always treat the first PER entity as *ARG-1* and the second PER entity as *ARG-2*.[3]

[3]Since many personal/social relations are asymmetric, ideally we should assign *ARG-1* and *ARG-2* based on their semantic meanings rather than their positions. Here we take a simple approach.

We go through each candidate relation instance to find whether there is an explicit sequence of words describing the relation between *ARG-1* and *ARG-2*, and label the sequence of words, if any. Note that we only consider explicitly stated relation descriptors. If we cannot find such a relation descriptor, even if *ARG-1* and *ARG-2* actually have some kind of relation, we still label the instance as *Nil*. For example, in the instance "he is the son of `ARG1` and `ARG2`", although we can infer that *ARG-1* and *ARG-2* have some family relation, we regard this as a negative instance.

A relation descriptor may also contain multiple relations. For example, in the instance "`ARG1` is the CEO and president of `ARG2`", we label "the CEO and president" as the relation descriptor, which actually contains two job titles, namely, CEO and president.

Note that our annotated relation descriptors are not always nouns or noun phrases. An example is the third instance for personal/social relation in Table 1, where the relation descriptor "married" is a verb and indicates a spouse relation.

The total number of relation instances, the number of positive and negative instances as well as the number of distinct relation descriptors in each data set are summarized in Table 4.

Data Set	total	positive	negative	distinct descriptors
NYT	536	208	328	140
Wikipedia	700	122	578	70

Table 4: Number of instances in each data set. Positive instances are those that have an explicit relation descriptor. The last column shows the number of distinct relation descriptors.

5.2 Experiment Setup

We compare the following methods in our experiments:

- **LC-CRF**: This is the standard linear-chain CRF model with features described in Table 2.
- **M-CRF-1**: This is our modified linear-chain CRF model with the space of label sequences reduced but with features fixed to the same as those used in LC-CRF.
- **M-CRF-2**: This is M-CRF-1 with the addition of the contextual long-range features described in Table 3.
- **M-CRF-3**: This is M-CRF-2 with the addition of the path-based long-range features described in Table 3.
- **M-CRF-4**: This is M-CRF-3 with the addition of the phrase boundary long-range feature described in Table 3.

For the standard linear-chain CRF model, we use the package CRF++[4]. We implement our own version of the modified linear-chain CRF models.

We perform 10-fold cross validation for all our experiments. For each data set we first randomly divide it into 10 subsets. Each time we take 9 subsets for training and the remaining subset for testing. We report the average performance across the 10 runs.

Based on our preliminary experiments, we have found that using a smaller set of general POS tags instead of the Penn Treebank POS tag set could slightly improve the overall performance. We therefore only report the performance obtained using our POS tags. For example, we group *NN*, *NNP*, *NNS* and *NNPS* of the Penn Treebank set under a general tag *N*.

[4]`http://crfpp.sourceforge.net/`

We evaluate the performance using two different criteria: overlap match and exact match. Overlap match is a more relaxed criterion: if the extracted relation descriptor overlaps with the true relation descriptor (i.e., having at least one token in common), it is considered correct. Exact match is a much stricter criterion: it requires that the extracted relation descriptor be exactly the same as the true relation descriptor in order to be considered correct. Given these two criteria, we can define accuracy, precision, recall and F1 measures. Accuracy is the percentage of candidate relation instances whose label sequence is considered correct. Both positive and negative instances are counted when computing accuracy. Because our data sets are quite balanced, it is reasonable to use accuracy. Precision, recall and F1 are defined in the usual way at the relation instance level.

5.3 Method Comparison

In Table 5, we summarize the performance in terms of the various measures on the two data sets. For both the baseline linear-chain CRF model and our modified linear-chain CRF models, we have tuned the regularization parameters and show only the results using the optimal parameter values for each data set, chosen from $\beta = 10^\gamma$ for $\gamma \in [-3, -2, \ldots, 2, 3]$.

First, we can see from the table that by reducing the label sequence space, M-CRF-1 can significantly outperform the baseline LC-CRF in terms of F1 in all cases. In terms of accuracy, there is significant improvement for the NYT data set but not for the Wikipedia data set. We also notice that for both data sets the advantage of M-CRF-1 is mostly evident in the improvement of recall. This shows that a larger number of true relation descriptors are extracted when the label sequence space is reduced.

Next we see from the table that long-range features are also useful, and the improvement comes mostly from the path-based long-range features. In terms of both accuracy and F1, M-CRF-3 can significantly outperform M-CRF-1 in all settings. In this case, the improvement is a mixture of both precision and recall. This shows that by explicitly capturing the patterns between the two arguments and the relation descriptor, we can largely improve the extraction performance. On the other hand, neither the contextual long-range features nor the phrase boundary long-range features exhibit any

New York Times	Overlap Match				Exact Match			
	Accu.	Prec.	Rec.	F1	Accu.	Prec.	Rec.	F1
LC-CRF	0.8173	0.8407	0.6548	0.7303	0.8117	0.8373	0.6394	0.7186
M-CRF-1	0.8491†	0.8640	0.7202†	0.7830†	0.8454†	0.8625	0.7124†	0.7774†
M-CRF-2	0.8491	0.8627	0.7202	0.7819	0.8454	0.8617	0.7124	0.7763
M-CRF-3	**0.8659**†	**0.9000**†	**0.7364**	**0.8070**†	**0.8640**†	**0.8992**†	**0.7319**†	**0.8038**†
M-CRF-4	**0.8659**	**0.9000**	**0.7364**	**0.8070**	**0.8640**	**0.8992**	**0.7319**	**0.8038**

Wikipedia	Overlap Match				Exact Match			
	Accu.	Prec.	Rec.	F1	Accu.	Prec.	Rec.	F1
LC-CRF	0.8486	0.6513	0.3140	0.4137	0.8457	0.6489	0.2980	0.3931
M-CRF-1	0.8414	0.5648	0.4233†	0.4778†	0.8386	0.5530	0.4072†	0.4609†
M-CRF-2	0.8471	0.5859	0.4260	0.4873	0.8443	0.5741	0.4099	0.4704
M-CRF-3	0.8657†	0.6847†	**0.4488**	**0.5318**†	0.8628†	0.6823†	**0.4327**	**0.5144**†
M-CRF-4	**0.8671**	**0.6966**	0.4388	0.5278	**0.8643**	**0.6942**	0.4228	0.5105

Table 5: Comparison of different methods on the New York Times data set and Wikipedia data set. Accu., Prec., Rec. and F1 stand for accuracy, precision, recall and F1 measures, respectively. † indicates that the current value is statistically significantly better than the value in the previous row at a 0.95 level of confidence by one-tailed paired T-test.

significant impact. We hypothesize the following. For contextual long-range features, they have already been captured in the linear-chain features. For example, the long-range feature "*is REL*" is similar to the linear-chain feature "w_{i-1} = *is* & y_i = *B-R*". For the phrase boundary long-range feature, since phrase boundary tags have also been used in the linear-chain features, this feature does not provide additional information. In addition, we have found that a large percentage of relation descriptors violate phrase boundaries: 22% in the NYT data set, and 29% in the Wikipedia data set. Therefore, it seems that phrase boundary information is not important for relation descriptor extraction.

Overall, performance is much higher on the NYT data set than on the Wikipedia data set. Based on our observations during annotation, this is due to the fact that the "employment" relations expressed in the NYT data set often follow some standard patterns, whereas in Wikipedia the "personal/social" relations can be expressed in more varied ways. The lower performance achieved on the Wikipedia data set suggests that extracting relation descriptors is not an easy task even under a supervised learning setting.

Presumably relation descriptors that are not seen in the training data are harder to extract. We would therefore also like to see how well our model works on such unseen relation descriptors. We find that with 10-fold cross validation, for the NYT data set, on average our model is able to extract approximately 67% of the unseen relation descriptors in the test data using exact match criteria. For the Wikipedia data set this percentage is approximately 27%. Both numbers are lower than the overall recall values the model can achieve on the entire test data, showing that unseen relation descriptors are indeed harder to extract. However, our model is still able to pick up new relation descriptors.

5.4 The Effect of Training Data Size

In the previous experiments, we have used 90% of the data for training and the remaining 10% for testing. We now take a look at how the performance changes with different numbers of training instances. We vary the training data size from only a few instances (2, 5, and 10) to 20%, 40%, 60% and 80% of the entire data set. The results are shown in Figure 1.

As we can expect, when the number of training instances is small, the performance on both data sets is low. The figure also shows that the Wikipedia data set is the more difficult than the NYT data set. This is consistent with our observation in the previous section.

The modified linear-chain CRF model consistently outperforms the baseline linear-chain CRF model. For similar level of performance, the modified linear-chain CRF model requires less training data than the baseline linear-chain CRF model.

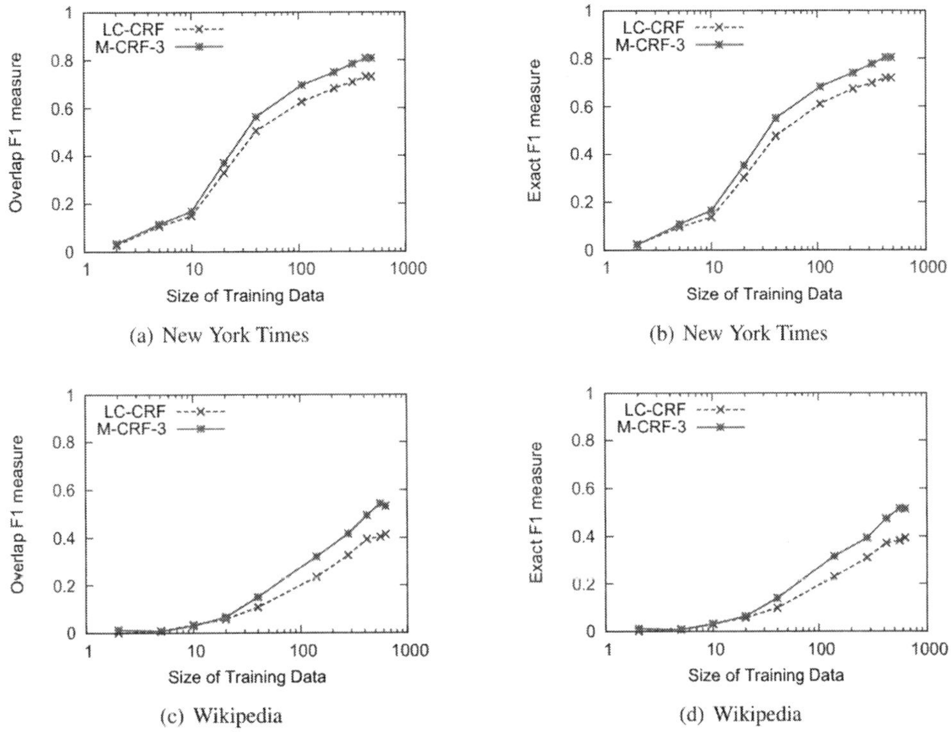

(a) New York Times

(b) New York Times

(c) Wikipedia

(d) Wikipedia

Figure 1: Performance of LC-CRF and M-CRF-3 as the training data size increases.

For example, Figure 1(b) shows that the modified linear-chain CRF model achieve 0.72 F1 with about 215 training instances, while the baseline linear-chain CRF model requires about 480 training instances for a similar F1.

6 Conclusions

In this paper, we studied relation extraction under a new setting: the relation types are defined at a general level but more specific relation descriptors are desired. Based on the special properties of this new task, we found that standard linear-chain CRF models have some potential limitations for this task. We subsequently proposed some modifications to linear-chain CRFs in order to suit our task better. We annotated two data sets to evaluate our methods. The experiments showed that by restricting the space of possible label sequences and introducing certain long-range features, the performance of the modified linear-chain CRF model can perform significantly better than standard linear-chain CRFs.

Currently our work is only based on evaluation on two data sets and on two general relations. In the future we plan to evaluate the methods on other general relations to test its robustness. We also plan to explore how this new relation extraction task can be used within other NLP or text mining applications.

Acknowledgments

This material is based on research sponsored by the Air Force Research Laboratory, under agreement number FA2386-09-1-4123. The U.S. Government is authorized to reproduce and distribute reprints for Governmental purposes notwithstanding any copyright notation thereon. The views and conclusions contained herein are those of the authors and should not be interpreted as necessarily representing the official policies or endorsements, either expressed or implied, of the Air Force Research Laboratory or the U.S. Government.

References

Eugene Agichtein and Luis Gravano. 2000. Snowball: Extracting relations from large plain-text collections. In *Proceedings of the Fifth ACM Conference on Digital Libraries*, pages 85–94, June.

Michele Banko and Oren Etzioni. 2008. The tradeoffs between open and traditional relation extraction. In *Proceedings of the 46th Annual Meeting of the Association for Computational Linguistics*, pages 28–36.

Razvan Bunescu and Raymond Mooney. 2005. A shortest path dependency kernel for relation extraction. In *Proceedings of the Human Language Technology Conference and the Conference on Empirical Methods in Natural Language Processing*, pages 724–731, October.

Aron Culotta, Andrew McCallum, and Jonathan Betz. 2006. Integrating probabilistic extraction models and data mining to discover relations and patterns in text. In *Proceedings of the Human Language Technology Conference of the North American Chapter of the Association for Computational Linguistics*, pages 296–303, June.

Jenny Rose Finkel, Trond Grenager, and Christopher D. Manning. 2005. Incorporating non-local information into information extraction systems by gibbs sampling. In *Proceedings of the 43rd Annual Meeting of the Association for Computational Linguistics*, pages 363–370, June.

Takaaki Hasegawa, Satoshi Sekine, and Ralph Grishman. 2004. Discovering relations among named entities from large corpora. In *Proceedings of the 42nd Meeting of the Association for Computational Linguistics*, pages 415–422, July.

Raphael Hoffmann, Congle Zhang, and Daniel S. Weld. 2010. Learning 5000 relational extractors. In *Proceedings of the 48th Annual Meeting of the Association for Computational Linguistics*, pages 286–295, July.

John D. Lafferty, Andrew McCallum, and Fernando C. N. Pereira. 2001. Conditional random fields: Probabilistic models for segmenting and labeling sequence data. In *Proceedings of the 18th International Conference on Machine Learning*, pages 282–289, June.

Lance A. Ramshaw and Mitchell P. Marcus. 1995. Text chunking using transformation-based learning. In *Proceedings of the Third ACL Workshop on Very Large Corpora*, pages 82–94.

Benjamin Rosenfeld and Ronen Feldman. 2006. URES : An unsupervised Web relation extraction system. In *Proceedings of the 21st International Conference on Computational Linguistics and 44th Annual Meeting of the Association for Computational Linguistics*, pages 667–674, July.

Sunita Sarawagi and William W. Cohen. 2005. Semi-Markov conditional random fields for information extraction. In *Advances in Neural Information Processing Systems 17*, pages 1185–1192.

Yusuke Shinyama and Satoshi Sekine. 2006. Preemptive information extraction using unrestricted relation discovery. In *Proceedings of the Human Language Technology Conference of the North American Chapter of the Association for Computational Linguistics*, pages 304–311, June.

Fei Wu and Daniel S. Weld. 2010. Open information extraction using Wikipedia. In *Proceedings of the 48th Annual Meeting of the Association for Computational Linguistics*, pages 118–127, July.

Dmitry Zelenko, Chinatsu Aone, and Anthony Richardella. 2003. Kernel methods for relation extraction. *Journal of Machine Learning Research*, 3:1083–1106.

Min Zhang, Jie Zhang, and Jian Su. 2006. Exploring syntactic features for relation extraction using a convolution tree kernel. In *Proceedings of the Human Language Technology Conference of the North American Chapter of the Association for Computational Linguistics*, pages 288–295, June.

GuoDong Zhou, Jian Su, Jie Zhang, and Min Zhang. 2005. Exploring various knowledge in relation extraction. In *Proceedings of the 43rd Annual Meeting of the Association for Computational Linguistics*, pages 427–434, June.

Attribute Extraction from Synthetic Web Search Queries

Marius Paşca
Google Inc.
Mountain View, California 94043
mars@google.com

Abstract

The accuracy and coverage of existing methods for extracting attributes of instances from text in general, and Web search queries in particular, are limited by two main factors: availability of input textual data to which the methods can be applied, and inherent limitations of the underlying assumptions and algorithms being used. This paper proposes a weakly-supervised approach for the acquisition of attributes of instances from input data available in the form of synthetic queries automatically generated from submitted queries. The generated queries allow for the acquisition of additional attributes, leading to extracted lists of attributes of higher quality than with comparable previous methods.

1 Introduction

Motivation: The availability of larger textual data sources has allowed research in information extraction to shift its focus towards robust methods that require little or no annotated data, operate at large scale with lower computational costs, and acquire open-domain information (Banko and Etzioni, 2008). The information is usually targeted at three levels of granularity: classes (e.g., *giant planets*), class elements or instances (e.g., *jupiter*, *uranus*, *saturn*), and relations among instances. Since these types of information would form the backbone of knowledge bases acquired automatically from text (Mooney and Bunescu, 2005), their acquisition has received increased attention over recent years.

Among other types of relations targeted by various extraction methods, attributes (e.g., *escape velocity*, *diameter* and *surface gravity*) have emerged as one of the more popular types, as they capture quantifiable properties of their respective classes (*giant planets*) and instances (*jupiter*). A variety of attribute extraction methods mine textual data sources ranging from unstructured (Tokunaga et al., 2005) or structured (Cafarella et al., 2008) text within Web documents, to human-compiled encyclopedia (Wu et al., 2008; Cui et al., 2009) and Web search query logs (Alfonseca et al., 2010), attempting to extract, for a given class or instance, a ranked list of attributes that is as comprehensive and accurate as possible. The accuracy and coverage of existing methods (Raju et al., 2008; Alfonseca et al., 2010) for extracting attributes of instances are limited by two main factors: availability of input textual data to which the methods can be applied; and inherent limitations of the underlying assumptions and algorithms being used. For example, a simple but effective method was proposed in (Paşca and Van Durme, 2007) for extracting attributes of an instance, by applying a small set of extraction patterns (e.g., *A of I*) to Web search queries (e.g., *"escape velocity of jupiter"*). If the input set of queries increased, additional candidate attributes would be extracted.

Contributions: This paper introduces a weakly-supervised approach for the acquisition of attributes of instances from query logs, by automatically expanding the set of known (organic) queries from which attributes are extracted with additional, inferred (synthetic), not-yet-submitted queries. The focus on expanding the input textual data gives a generally-applicable approach, which can be applied to existing methods for attribute acquisition from query logs, to increase coverage. In particular, the application of previously-proposed extraction patterns (Paşca and Van Durme, 2007) to the expanded set of queries allows for the acquisition of additional attributes that would otherwise not be acquired only from the set of known queries.

In order to infer new queries, known queries are aggregated into query templates (e.g., *"lyrics of ⋆ beatles"*) associated with known phrase fillers (e.g., ⋆→{*yesterday*, *hey jude*}). The known phrase fillers of each query template are then expanded into new candidate phrase fillers. In contrast to previous work on query generation (Mitkov and Ha, 2006; Heilman and Smith, 2010), new queries are generated based on query analysis alone, as opposed to individual document analysis. This has the potential advantages of scalability and robustness when applied to arbitrary, inherently-noisy queries. Among the inferred queries, the ones of higher interest to attribute extraction are those derived from a query template that fixes either a potential attribute (e.g., *"surface gravity of ⋆"*) or a potential instance (e.g., *"⋆ of jupiter"*). In experiments using a large set of anonymized search queries, the inferred queries allow for the acquisition of accurate attributes over an evaluation set of 75 instances introduced in previous work (Alfonseca et al., 2010).

Applications: Attributes are useful in information retrieval, e.g., for suggesting related queries (Bellare et al., 2007) and recommending products (Probst et al., 2007). They plan an important role in knowledge acquisition and representation (Guarino, 1992), for example as building blocks in the manual compilation of infoboxes in Wikipedia (Remy, 2002). Furthermore, the availability of a larger number of more accurate attributes allows for the development of better search interfaces geared towards structured search. Examples of such interfaces are Wolfram Alpha and Google Squared, two search tools that can take as input instances and return lists of attributes and their values.

2 Attribute Extraction

2.1 Intuitions and Scope

Intuitions: Our attribute extraction method is inspired by several intuitions. First, phrases of the same class (car models, search engines, baseball players etc.) share similar properties or attributes, enter similar relations and satisfy similar constraints. For example, car models have replacement parts, are assembled by some maker in some year, and have an estimated current value. Consequently, known queries that refer to similar phrases may overlap significantly, or even become equal once the phrases have been replaced by a common slot filled by the phrases. Thus, *"kelley blue book value of 2008 dodge charger"* and *"kelley blue book value of 2008 honda civic"* can be grouped into a shared query template *"kelley blue book of 2008 ⋆"*, whose slot ⋆ is filled by the names of car models. Second, known queries that can be grouped into a shared query template often provide a small sample of, rather than comprehensive coverage of, all phrases that would meaningfully fill the template. Therefore, new queries can be generated by filling the slots of query templates with new phrase fillers similar to known fillers. For instance, *"kelley blue book value of 2008 chrysler sebring"* can be inferred as a new candidate query if *chrysler sebring* is known to be similar to *dodge charger* and/or *honda civic*. Third, a new candidate query is meaningful if the new phrase filler is similar to the known fillers not only statically, but also in the context of the query template. This is particularly important for query templates with few, ambiguous phrase fillers. Consider the query template *"lyrics of ⋆ beatles"*, with the known fillers *come together*, *hey jude* and *yesterday*. Although phrases such as *gather together*, *earlier today* and *last friday* are highly similar to the known fillers, they are not meaningful new fillers for *"lyrics of ⋆ beatles"* and would therefore produce spurious new queries. In contrast, *lovely rita* and *here comes the sun* are similar to the known fillers both statically and in the context of the query template.

Scope: Following the above intuitions, attributes can be extracted from generated queries. In turn, generated queries are inferred by essentially replacing phrases from known queries with meaningful, similar phrases. The form (e.g., long and complex, vs. short and simple) and scope (e.g., open-domain vs. domain-specific) of known queries determine the form and scope of inferred queries. While this prevents arbitrarily complex queries from being generated, it has the advantage of homogeneity of new queries relative to known queries. Also, this should have little, if any, impact on extracted attributes, since the latter are actually extracted from queries whose form is relatively simple rather than complex. The scope of new queries is further influenced by the availability of new phrases that are similar to phrases from known queries. For example, *chrysler sebring* must be available as a phrase similar to *dodge charger* and/or *honda civic*, in order to potentially generate *"kelley blue book of 2008 chrysler sebring"* from the known queries *"kelley blue book of 2008 dodge charger"* and *"kelley blue book of 2008 honda civic"*.

2.2 Extraction from Generated Queries

Aggregation into Query Templates: The input to the method is a set of Web search queries. As described in (Paşca, 2011), the sequence of terms available in each query is split into all combinations of triples of a prefix, non-empty infix and postfix. Queries that share a common prefix and common postfix are aggregated into a query template, where the input infixes are the known phrase fillers of the template. For example, queries such as *"lyrics of yesterday beatles"* and *"lyrics of come together beatles"* are aggregated into the template *"lyrics of* $\star$ *beatles"*, where the template filler $\star$ corresponds to the set of known phrase fillers, i.e., infixes from the input queries: {*yesterday, come together*}. An input query may contribute to the creation of multiple query templates, via different infixes. For example, another template created from *"lyrics of yesterday beatles" "lyrics of yesterday toni braxton"* is *"lyrics of yesterday* $\star$*"*.

Like the subsequent stages of processing, generating all possible infixes of all input queries, especially for large input sets of queries, is a non-trivial computational challenge. However, the computation can be translated into parallelizable operations in a distributed computing framework such as Hadoop (White, 2010) or MapReduce (Dean and Ghemawat, 2004). In particular, the aggregation of queries into templates can be performed in a single MapReduce step. The mapper takes as input queries, and splits them into one or more mappings from a query template (key) to a corresponding infix, i.e., a known phrase filler (value). For each query template, the reducer simply aggregates its phrase fillers into a set.

Generation of Candidate Phrase Fillers: In order to generate new queries, the set of known phrase fillers is expanded into additional candidate phrases that may fill the query template. As a prerequisite to generating candidate phrase fillers, distributionally similar phrases (Lin and Pantel, 2002; Lin and Wu, 2009; Pantel et al., 2009) and their scores are collected in advance. The assumption is that phrases that appear in similar contexts have similar meanings. A phrase is represented as a vector of its contextual features. A feature is a token, collected from windows of three tokens centered around the occurrences of the phrase in sentences across Web documents (Lin and Wu, 2009). Alternatively, the context could be approximated via linguistic dependencies detected with noun chunking (Pantel et al., 2009) and syntactic parsing (Lin and Pantel, 2002). In the contextual vector of a phrase, the weight of a feature is the pointwise-mutual information (Lin and Wu, 2009) between the phrase P and the feature F:

$$PMI(P, F) = \log \frac{Freq(P, F) \times N}{Freq(P) \times Freq(F)} \quad (1)$$

where $Freq(P, F)$ is the frequency of the feature F occurring with the phrase P, and N is the feature vocabulary size. The distributional similarity score between two phrases P_1 and P_2 is the cosine similarity between the contextual vectors of the two phrases. Alternatively, vector similarity could be computed via the Jaccard or Dice coefficients (Pantel et al., 2009). The lists $DS(P)$ of most distributionally similar phrases of a phrase P are thus compiled offline, by ranking the similar phrases of P in decreasing order of their $DSscore$ relative to P.

The most distributionally similar (Lin and Pantel, 2002; Pantel et al., 2009) phrases, of a known phrase filler K_i from a query template T, are considered to be candidate phrase filler U of the respective query template. The score of a candidate relative to the entire set of known fillers is the average of the distributional similarity scores between the candidate and each known filler. For each template T, its candidate phrase fillers U are ranked in decreasing order of their scores. Known phrase fillers of T are discarded from the resulting list of candidate phrase fillers of T.

The generation of candidate phrase fillers translates into two MapReduce steps. The first step rearranges the mappings from a query template to a set of known phrase fillers, into mappings from a known phrase filler to a set of query templates. Concretely, the mapper takes as input mappings from a query template (key) to its set of known phrase fillers (value), as they were output after the aggregation into query templates. The mapper emits mappings from a known phrase filler (key) to a query template (value). For each phrase filler, the reducer aggregates its query templates into a set. The second MapReduce step takes this data, and joins it with distributional similarity data. The latter is available as mappings from a phrase (key) to a list of scored similar phrases (value). The mapper selects similar phrases as candidate phrase fillers for the template, as explained earlier. The output of the second step consists in mappings from a query template (key) to its set of known phrase fillers, as well as to a list of scored candidate phrase fillers (value).

Filtering of Candidate Phrase Fillers: Candidate phrase fillers generated via distributional similarities are similar to known phrases only statically. To also take the context of the query template into account, the candidates are filtered using the input queries. More precisely, the list of candidate phrases of a query template T is filtered, by retaining only known phrases of some other templates T' that are equivalent to T. Templates are deemed equivalent if they become identical after removal of stop words and other linking particles (prepositions, conjunctions etc.), term stemming and term reordering. For example, if the unfiltered candidate phrase *eleanor rigby* for the template *"lyrics of ⋆ beatles"* appears as a known phrase filler of the template *"lyrics for ⋆ by the beatles"*, then *eleanor rigby* is retained after filtering for the template *"lyrics of ⋆ beatles"*.

The filtering of candidate phrases using equivalent templates is modeled as two MapReduce steps. The first step takes as input mappings from a query template (key) to its set of known phrase fillers and list of scored candidate phrase fillers (value), as they were output after the generation of candidate phrase fillers. The mapper converts the query template into the corresponding equivalent template that contains the individual terms in lexicographic order. It emits mappings from an equivalent template (key), to a query template with its set of known phrase fillers and its list of scored candidate phrase fillers (value). For each equivalent template, the reducer simply aggregates this data. The second step takes as input mappings from an equivalent template (key) to its query templates with their sets of known phrase fillers and lists of scored candidate phrase fillers (value). For each equivalent template, the mapper iterates over its query templates. It checks which of its candidate phrase fillers occur among the known phrase fillers of the other query templates. The candidate phrase fillers that pass this test are retained as filtered phrase fillers. The mapper emits mappings from a query template (key) to its set of known phrase fillers, list of scored unfiltered phrase fillers, and list of scored filtered phrase fillers. The reducer merely emits its input, without modifications.

The relative ranking of candidate phrases from the list of inferred unfiltered phrase fillers (before filtering) is preserved in the list of inferred filtered phrase fillers (after filtering). Each filtered phrase filler inferred for a query template corresponds to a new query, generated by filling the phrase into the slot filler of the query template.

Attribute Extraction: Extraction patterns such as *"A of I"*, introduced in previous work (Paşca and Van Durme, 2007) to extract a candidate attribute A for a candidate instance I from queries, can be immediately applied to inferred queries. Thus, additional candidate attributes can be extracted from inferred queries, where the inferred queries are obtained via two types of query templates:

• query templates that specify a potential instance, and leave the attribute (e.g., A in *"A of I"*) as a phrase filler being inferred:

surface gravity of jupiter
europa of jupiter
composition of atmosphere of jupiter
father of jupiter
} "⋆ of jupiter"

Each inferred phrase filler (e.g., *core temperature, luminosity*) is collected as a candidate attribute of the phrase specified in the query template (*jupiter*). In this case, attribute extraction is equivalent to transferring an instance associated with a noisy set of attributes that are known phrase fillers of a template, to be associated with new attributes that are inferred phrase fillers of the template.

• query templates that specify a potential attribute, and leave the instance (e.g., I in *"A of I"*) as a phrase filler being inferred:

mass of positronium
mass of planets in order
mass of steel beams
mass of planet uranus
} "mass of ⋆"

For each inferred phrase filler (e.g., *cesium 137, water drop*), the phrase specified in the query template (*mass*) is collected as a candidate attribute. In this case, attribute extraction is equivalent to transferring an attribute associated with a noisy set

Phrase	Ranked List Available in Data Repository
caesium	[cesium, rubidium, strontium, barium, thallium, lanthanum, potassium, cerium, yttrium, bismuth, indium, gallium, europium, cadmium, antimony, ammonium,..]
ch3br	[ch3cl, ch4, nh3, ch 4, c2h4, ch3i, nh 3, ch3oh, c2h2, ch3f, c2h6, hcho, no2, h2s, hcn, ch30h, n2o, n20, ch3cn, hcooh, ethane, cc14, ethene, propene, hzo, c02, ch3sh, chbr3,..]
exxon valdez	[torrey canyon, amoco cadiz, sea empress, braer, 1989 exxon valdez, valdez oil, exxon valdez oil tanker, chernobyl nuclear, cosco busan, valdez oil spill, chernobyl,..]
fragile x	[fragile x, klinefelter syndrome, rett syndrome, fxtas, turner syndrome, down syndrome, friedreich ataxia, myotonic dystrophy, huntington's disease, williams syndrome, trisomy 21,..]
medal	[congressional medal of honor, navy cross, distinguished service cross, victoria cross, distinguished flying cross,air force cross, bronze star, purple heart, soldier's medal, medal honor, military cross,..]
men and women	[women and men, men and woman, males and females, men & women, young men, women, people, men, individuals, boys and girls, girls and boys, adults, sexes, females and males,..]
nerve	[ganglion, preganglionic, postganglionic, peripheral nerve, sciatic, sciatic nerve, axon, afferent, nerve root, dorsal root, ganglionic, vagus, trigeminal, median nerve,..]
yesterday	[last week, earlier today, last friday, last night, two days ago, yesturday, last thursday, earlier this week, just yesterday, last wednesday, yesteday, last monday, last month, two weeks ago,..]
whey	[protein powder, whey protein isolate, whey protein powder, soy protein, whey isolate, protein whey, casein protein, creatine, creatine monohydrate, isopure,..]

Table 1: Examples of ranked lists of similar phrases, available in the phrase similarity repository for various phrases

of instances that are known phrase fillers of a template, to be associated with new instances that are inferred phrase fillers of the template.

Regardless of whether they are specified manually or derived automatically, extraction patterns used in information extraction are imperfect (Kozareva et al., 2008). The pattern *A of I* for attribute extraction is no exception. The two types of query templates from above have known phrase fillers that are not true attributes (e.g., *europa* for the instance *jupiter*) and instances (e.g., *planets in order* for the attribute *mass*) respectively. This phenomenon is not a defect of this particular approach, but is inherited from and shared with any methods using such patterns for attribute extraction, as well as with any methods that rely on seed attributes, when the seeds are noisy rather than clean.

Attribute Ranking: As explained earlier, the score of an inferred phrase filler is computed as the average of similarity scores relative to known phrase fillers. The score is assigned to the pair of an attribute and instance extracted from the phrase filler. Attributes extracted for an instance are ranked in decreasing order of the scores.

3 Experimental Setting

Textual Data Sources: The acquisition of instance attributes relies on a random sample of around 100 million fully-anonymized queries in English submitted by Web users in 2010. Each query is accompanied by its frequency of occurrence in the query logs.

A phrase similarity repository is derived following (Pantel et al., 2009), from unstructured text available within a sample of around 200 million documents in English. The repository provides data for each of around 1 million phrases that occur as full-length queries in the input query logs. It contains ranked lists of the top 200 phrases computed to be the most distributionally similar, for each phrase. Table 1 illustrates the actual

aaa, ac compressors, acheron, acrocyanosis, adelaide cbd, african population, agua caliente casino, al hirschfeld, alessandro nesta, american fascism, american society for horticultural science, ancient babylonia, angioplasty, annapolis harbor, antarctic region, arlene martel, arrabiata sauce, artificial intelligence, bangla music, baquba, bb gun, berkshire hathaway, bicalutamide, blue jay, boulder colorado, brittle star, capsicum, carbonate, carotid arteries, chester arthur, christian songs, cloxacillin, cobol, communicable diseases, contemporary art, cortex, ct scan, digital fortress, eartha kitt, eating disorders, file sharing, final fantasy vii, forensics, habbo hotel, halogens, halophytes, ho chi minh trail, icici prudential, jane fonda, juan carlos, karlsruhe, kidney stones, lipoma, loss of appetite, lucky ali, majorca, martin frobisher, mexico city, pancho villa, phosphorus, playing cards, prednisone, right to vote, robotics, rouen, scientific revolution, self-esteem, spandex, strattera, u.s., vida guerra, visual basic, web hosting, windsurfing, wlan

Table 2: Set of 75 target instances, used in the evaluation of instance attribute extraction

ranked lists available in the repository for various phrases. The underlying similarity score between two phrases is the cosine between their vectors of context windows.

Target Instances: The performance of attribute extraction is computed over a standard set of 75 instances, previously introduced in (Alfonseca et al., 2010). As shown in Table 2, the set of instances ensures varied experimentation across multiple domains.

Experimental Runs: The experiments consist of several individual runs. Runs R_U and R_F acquire attributes from queries inferred via the first type of target query templates (e.g., *"⋆ of jupiter"*), before filtering (R_U) and after filtering (R_F). Run R_I uses queries inferred via the second type of target query templates (e.g., *"mass of ⋆"*), after filtering.

In order to compare with existing work, a previous extraction method from (Paşca and Van Durme, 2007), which uses extraction patterns, is implemented in a baseline run R_P. For consistency, the data source to the run R_P is the same set of input queries described at the beginning of the section.

Label	Value	Examples of Attributes
vital	1.0	capsicum: calorie count
		cloxacillin: side effects
		lucky ali: album songs
okay	0.5	jane fonda: musical theatre contributions
		mexico city: cathedral
		robotics: three laws
wrong	0.0	acheron: kingdom
		berkshire hathaway: tax exclusion
		contemporary art: urban institute

Table 3: Correctness labels manually assigned to attributes extracted for various instances

The per-instance ranked lists of attributes produced by the individual runs from above are concatenated in a series of combination runs. For example, run R_{FP} concatenates the attributes output by R_F and by R_P, in this order.

Evaluation Procedure: The evaluation focuses on the assessment of accuracy of the ranked list of attributes generated for each instance. To remove any undesirable bias towards higher-ranked attributes, the attributes of each list to be evaluated are sorted alphabetically into a merged list. Each attribute of the merged list is manually assigned a correctness label relative to its respective instance. In accordance with previously introduced methodology, an attribute is *vital* if it must be present in an ideal list of attributes of the instance (e.g., *side effects* for *cloxacillin*); *okay* if it provides useful but non-essential information; and *wrong* if it is incorrect (Paşca, 2007). Thus, a correctness label is manually assigned to a total of 4,833 attributes extracted for the 75 target instances.

To compute the precision score over a ranked list of attributes, the correctness labels are converted to numeric values (*vital* to 1, *okay* to 0.5 and *wrong* to 0), as shown in Table 3. Precision at some rank N in the list is measured as the sum of the correctness values of the attributes extracted up to rank N, divided by the number of those attributes.

4 Evaluation Results

Attribute Accuracy: Table 4 compares precision at various ranks, in the ranked lists of attributes

Run	Precision of Ranked Attributes				
	@1	@5	@10	@20	@50
Average (over all):					
R_P	0.61	**0.65**	**0.65**	**0.67**	**0.65**
R_I	0.61	0.62	0.60	0.61	0.60
R_U	0.45	0.37	0.33	0.31	0.30
R_F	0.64	0.58	0.57	0.55	0.51
R_{IP}	0.68	0.68	0.67	0.67	0.66
R_{IF}	0.64	0.64	0.63	0.64	0.62
R_{FP}	**0.77**	**0.69**	**0.68**	**0.65**	**0.62**
R_{FI}	**0.77**	**0.69**	**0.68**	**0.65**	**0.62**
Average (over non-empty):					
R_P	0.66	0.71	0.71	0.73	0.71
R_I	0.67	0.67	0.65	0.67	0.65
R_U	0.59	0.48	0.43	0.41	0.38
R_F	**0.83**	**0.75**	**0.74**	**0.71**	**0.66**
R_{IP}	0.69	0.69	0.67	0.68	**0.67**
R_{IF}	0.68	0.68	0.66	0.67	0.66
R_{FP}	**0.83**	**0.74**	**0.72**	**0.70**	**0.67**
R_{FI}	0.81	0.73	**0.72**	0.69	0.65

Table 4: Comparative accuracy of the ranked lists of attributes extracted in various runs, as an average over the entire set of 75 instances; and as an average over the (variable) subsets of instances for which some attributes were extracted

extracted by various runs. In the upper half of the table, average precision scores penalize instances for which no attributes are extracted. In contrast, the average scores in the lower half of the table only consider the instances for which some attributes are extracted.

The runs R_I, R_U and R_F operate directly over generated queries. One of the two types of query templates that produce attributes performs better, as illustrated by lower scores with R_F than with R_I. The difference in scores between R_U and R_F, which are about twice as high at rank 50 for the latter, illustrates the positive impact of filtering the candidate phrase fillers inferred from the query templates.

The benefit of combining the output from individual runs is illustrated by the generally higher scores given by combination runs in Table 4, relative to individual runs that they combine. Among combination runs, R_{FP} gives the highest scores at most ranks. When considering the accuracy of all runs, the highest scores over the entire evaluation set of instances are given by the combination run R_{FP}. Over subsets of instances with non-empty attribute lists, the accuracy of the individual run R_F is higher than all other individual runs, at par with the combination run R_{FP}. Table 5 shows the ranked lists of attributes extracted by R_F for a sample of instances.

Instance	[Ranked List of Inferred Attributes]
aaa	[symptoms, epidemiology, differential diagnosis, mortality, risk, surgical repair, stenting, resection, benefits, stent placement,..]
ac compressors	[manufacturer]
berkshire hathaway	[net asset value, closing price, total assets, dividend yield, par value, fair value, shares outstanding, class a shares, current price, common stock,..]
martin frobisher	[time line, routes, voyage, bibliography, explorations, ships, discoveries, travel,..]
scientific revolution	[negative effects, social impacts, social impact, theories, positive effects, accomplishments, long term effects, influences, cause and effects, scientific discoveries,..]
wlan	[limitations, risks, architectures, benefits, configurations, throughput, concepts, config, physical layer, security vulnerabilities,..]

Table 5: Examples of ranked lists of attributes extracted in run R_F from inferred filtered queries. None of these attributes are extracted for the respective instances in the baseline run R_P

5 Related Work

Previous work on attribute extraction uses a variety of types of textual data as sources for mining attributes. Taking advantage of structured and semi-structured text available within Web documents, the method introduced in (Yoshinaga and Torisawa, 2007) assembles and submits list-seeking queries to general-purpose Web search engines, and analyzes the retrieved documents to identify common structural (HTML) patterns around class labels given as input, and potential attributes. Similarly, layout (e.g., font color and size) and other HTML tags serve as clues to acquire attributes from either domain-specific documents such as those from product and auction Web sites (Wong et al., 2008) or from arbitrary documents, optionally relying on the presence of explicit itemized lists or tables (Cafarella et al., 2008). As an alternative to Web documents, articles within online encyclopedia can also be exploited as sources of structured text for attribute extraction, as illustrated by previous work using infoboxes and category labels (Suchanek et al., 2007; Nastase and Strube, 2008; Wu and Weld, 2008) associated with articles within Wikipedia.

Working with unstructured text within Web documents, the method described in (Tokunaga et al., 2005) applies manually-created lexico-syntactic patterns to document sentences in order to extract candidate attributes, given various class labels as input. The candidate attributes are ranked using several frequency statistics. If the documents are domain-specific, such as documents containing product reviews, additional heuristically-motivated filters and scoring metrics can be used to extract and rank the attributes (Raju et al., 2008). In (Bellare et al., 2007), the extraction is guided by a small set of manually-provided seed instances and attributes rather than manually-created patterns, with the purpose of generating training data and extract new pairs of instances and attributes from text.

Web search queries have also been considered as a textual data source for attribute extraction, using extraction patterns (Paşca and Van Durme, 2007) or seed attributes (Paşca, 2007) to guide the extraction, and leading to attributes of higher accuracy than those extracted with equivalent techniques from Web documents. If the input data includes query sessions in addition to sets of search queries, extracted attributes have higher quality (Paşca et al., 2010). Given an instance (e.g., *nissan gt-r*) and a numerical attribute (e.g., *width*) extracted with a method like ours, the acquisition of the corresponding values (e.g., *1.9m*) is the aim of other research endeavors (Davidov and Rappoport, 2010; Bakalov et al., 2011).

6 Conclusion

The role of Web search queries in information extraction has been previously explored. In this paper, synthetic search queries inferred from existing queries are used to acquire attributes. The queries lead to ranked lists of attributes whose accuracy is higher than with equivalent methods operating over queries. Current work investigates alternative methods for combining attributes from multiple individual runs; the expansion of the target query templates used to extract attributes; and further applications of the inferred queries, in information extraction and beyond.

References

E. Alfonseca, M. Paşca, and E. Robledo-Arnuncio. 2010. Acquisition of instance attributes via labeled and related instances. In *Proceedings of the 33rd International Conference on Research and Development in Information Retrieval (SIGIR-10)*, pages 58–65, Geneva, Switzerland.

A. Bakalov, A. Fuxman, P. Talukdar, and S. Chakrabarti. 2011. Scad: collective discovery of attribute values. In *Proceedings of the 20th World Wide Web Conference (WWW-11)*, pages 447–456, Hyderabad, India.

M. Banko and O. Etzioni. 2008. The tradeoffs between open and traditional relation extraction. In *Proceedings of the 46th Annual Meeting of the Association for Computational Linguistics (ACL-08)*, pages 28–36, Columbus, Ohio.

K. Bellare, P. Talukdar, G. Kumaran, F. Pereira, M. Liberman, A. McCallum, and M. Dredze. 2007. Lightly-supervised attribute extraction. In *Proceedings of the 21st Annual Conference on Neural Information Processing Systems (NIPS-07). Workshop on Machine Learning for Web Search*, Whistler, British Columbia.

M. Cafarella, A. Halevy, D. Wang, E. Wu, and Y. Zhang. 2008. WebTables: Exploring the power of tables on the Web. In *Proceedings of the 34th Conference on Very Large Data Bases (VLDB-08)*, pages 538–549, Auckland, New Zealand.

G. Cui, Q. Lu, W. Li, and Y. Chen. 2009. Automatic acquisition of attributes for ontology construction. In *Proceedings of the 22nd International Conference on Computer Processing of Oriental Languages*, pages 248–259, Hong Kong.

D. Davidov and A. Rappoport. 2010. Extraction and approximation of numerical attributes from the Web. In *Proceedings of the 48th Annual Meeting of the Association for Computational Linguistics (ACL-10)*, Uppsala, Sweden.

J. Dean and S. Ghemawat. 2004. MapReduce: Simplified data processing on large clusters. In *Proceedings of the 6th Symposium on Operating Systems Design and Implementation (OSDI-04)*, pages 137–150, San Francisco, California.

N. Guarino. 1992. Concepts, attributes and arbitrary relations. *Data and Knowledge Engineering*, 8:249–261.

M. Heilman and N. Smith. 2010. Good question! Statistical ranking for question generation. In *Proceedings of the 2010 Conference of the North American Association for Computational Linguistics (NAACL-HLT-10)*, pages 609–617, Los Angeles, California.

Z. Kozareva, E. Riloff, and E. Hovy. 2008. Semantic class learning from the Web with hyponym pattern linkage graphs. In *Proceedings of the 46th Annual Meeting of the Association for Computational Linguistics (ACL-08)*, pages 1048–1056, Columbus, Ohio.

D. Lin and P. Pantel. 2002. Concept discovery from text. In *Proceedings of the 19th International Conference on Computational linguistics (COLING-02)*, pages 1–7, Taipei, Taiwan.

D. Lin and X. Wu. 2009. Phrase clustering for discriminative learning. In *Proceedings of the 47th Annual Meeting of the Association for Computational Linguistics (ACL-IJCNLP-09)*, pages 1030–1038, Singapore.

R. Mitkov and L. Ha. 2006. A computer-aided environment for generating multiple-choice test items. *Natural Language Engineering*, 12(2):177–194.

R. Mooney and R. Bunescu. 2005. Mining knowledge from text using information extraction. *SIGKDD Explorations*, 7(1):3–10.

V. Nastase and M. Strube. 2008. Decoding Wikipedia categories for knowledge acquisition. In *Proceedings of the 23rd National Conference on Artificial Intelligence (AAAI-08)*, pages 1219–1224, Chicago, Illinois.

M. Paşca and B. Van Durme. 2007. What you seek is what you get: Extraction of class attributes from query logs. In *Proceedings of the 20th International Joint Conference on Artificial Intelligence (IJCAI-07)*, pages 2832–2837, Hyderabad, India.

M. Paşca, E. Alfonseca, E. Robledo-Arnuncio, R. Martin-Brualla, and K. Hall. 2010. The role of query sessions in extracting instance attributes from web search queries. In *Proceedings of the 32nd European Conference on Information Retrieval (ECIR-10)*, pages 62–74, Milton Keynes, United Kingdom.

M. Paşca. 2007. Organizing and searching the World Wide Web of facts - step two: Harnessing the wisdom of the crowds. In *Proceedings of the 16th World Wide Web Conference (WWW-07)*, pages 101–110, Banff, Canada.

M. Paşca. 2011. Asking what no one has asked before: Using phrase similarities to generate synthetic web search queries. In *Proceedings of the 20th International Conference on Information and Knowledge Management (CIKM-11)*, Glasgow, United Kingdom.

P. Pantel, E. Crestan, A. Borkovsky, A. Popescu, and V. Vyas. 2009. Web-scale distributional similarity and entity set expansion. In *Proceedings of the 2009 Conference on Empirical Methods in Natural Language Processing (EMNLP-09)*, pages 938–947, Singapore.

K. Probst, R. Ghani, M. Krema, A. Fano, and Y. Liu. 2007. Semi-supervised learning of attribute-value pairs from product descriptions. In *Proceedings of the 20th International Joint Conference on Artificial Intelligence (IJCAI-07)*, pages 2838–2843, Hyderabad, India.

S. Raju, P. Pingali, and V. Varma. 2008. An unsupervised approach to product attribute extraction. In *Proceedings of the 31st International Conference on Research and Development in Information Retrieval (SIGIR-08)*, pages 35–42, Singapore.

M. Remy. 2002. Wikipedia: The free encyclopedia. *Online Information Review*, 26(6):434.

F. Suchanek, G. Kasneci, and G. Weikum. 2007. Yago: a core of semantic knowledge unifying WordNet and Wikipedia. In *Proceedings of the 16th World Wide Web Conference (WWW-07)*, pages 697–706, Banff, Canada.

K. Tokunaga, J. Kazama, and K. Torisawa. 2005. Automatic discovery of attribute words from Web documents. In *Proceedings of the 2nd International Joint Conference on Natural Language Processing (IJCNLP-05)*, pages 106–118, Jeju Island, Korea.

Tom White. 2010. *Hadoop: the Definitive Guide*. O'Reilly Media, 2nd edition.

T. Wong, W. Lam, and T. Wong. 2008. An unsupervised framework for extracting and normalizing product attributes from multiple Web sites. In *Proceedings of the 31st International Conference on Research and Development in Information Retrieval (SIGIR-08)*, pages 35–42, Singapore.

F. Wu and D. Weld. 2008. Automatically refining the Wikipedia infobox ontology. In *Proceedings of the 17th World Wide Web Conference (WWW-08)*, pages 635–644, Beijing, China.

F. Wu, R. Hoffmann, and D. Weld. 2008. Information extraction from Wikipedia: Moving down the long tail. In *Proceedings of the 14th ACM SIGKDD Conference on Knowledge Discovery and Data Mining (KDD-08)*, pages 731–739.

N. Yoshinaga and K. Torisawa. 2007. Open-domain attribute-value acquisition from semi-structured texts. In *Proceedings of the 6th International Semantic Web Conference (ISWC-07), Workshop on Text to Knowledge: The Lexicon/Ontology Interface (OntoLex-2007)*, pages 55–66, Busan, South Korea.

Japanese Abbreviation Expansion with Query and Clickthrough Logs

Kei Uchiumi† **Mamoru Komachi**‡ **Keigo Machinaga**†

Toshiyuki Maezawa† **Toshinori Satou**† **Yoshinori Kobayashi**† *

†**Yahoo Japan Corporation**
Midtown Tower, 9-7-1 Akasaka, Minato-ku, Tokyo 107-6211, Japan
{kuchiumi,kmachina,tmaezawa,toshsato}@yahoo-corp.jp
ykobayas@google.com

‡**Nara Institute of Science and Technology**
8916-5 Takayama, Ikoma, Nara 630-0192, Japan
komachi@is.naist.jp

Abstract

A novel reranking method has been developed to refine web search queries. A label propagation algorithm was applied on a clickthrough graph, and the candidates were reranked using a query language model. Our method first enumerates query candidates with common landing pages with regard to the given query to create a clickthrough graph. Second, it calculates the likelihood of the candidates, using a language model generated from web search query logs. Finally, the candidates are sorted by the score calculated from the likelihood and label propagation. As a result, high precision and coverage were achieved in the task of Japanese abbreviation expansion, without using handcrafted training data.

1 Introduction

The query expansion technique has been widely used in recent web-search engines. Query expansion significantly improves recall in information retrieval operations. It uses a thesaurus or synonym dictionary to reformulate a query, or to correct spelling errors in search queries.

In the early days of the speller, the dictionary was manually compiled by lexicographers. However, it is time consuming to construct a broad coverage dictionary, and domain knowledge is required to achieve high quality. Moreover, the rapid growth of the web makes it even harder to maintain an up-to-date dictionary for the web.

To alleviate this problem, web-search engines often exploit web search query logs to automatically generate a thesaurus. A web search query is a query that a web user types into a web search engine to find information. It is noisy and sometimes ambiguous to detect query intent, but it is a great way to create a fresh web dictionary at low cost. Hence, the web search queries are widely used in the NLP field. For instance, Hagiwara and Suzuki (2009) used them for a query alteration task, and Sekine and Suzuki (2007) leveraged them for acquiring semantic categories.

More recently, web search clickthrough logs have been explored in the field of lexical acquisition. A web clickthrough is the process of clicking a URL and going to the page it refers. This ensures that the landing page is appropriate since the web user follows the hyperlink after checking the information displayed, such as 'title', 'URL', and 'summary' of their search. Two distinct queries landing on the same 'URL' are possibly input for the same purpose, meaning that they are likely to be related. In the NLP literature, clickthrough logs have been used to learn semantic categories (Komachi et al., 2009) and named entities (Jain and Pennacchiotti, 2010).

The main contribution of this work is two fold:

- We propose a novel method to combine web search query logs and clickthrough logs.
- To the best our knowledge, this work is the first attempt to automatically recognize full spellings given Japanese abbreviations.

This is a very first step of Japanese abbreviation expansion task using search logs.

For evaluation of query expansion method, it is desirable to use a set of queries for evaluation.

*The work of Kobayashi were performed at Yahoo Japan. Current affiliation: Google Japan, Roppongi Hills Mori Tower, 6-10-1 Roppongi, Minato-ku, Tokyo 106-6126, Japan

However, it is difficult to obtain them beforehand, because we have to check query logs to find incorrect queries and make necessary changes to define their corrections.

Therefore, in this paper, we focus on query abbreviation and evaluate our proposed approach in an abbreviation expansion task. Abbreviation expansion itself is difficult for many query expansion methods based on edit distance, because the input and output have only a few, if any, characters in common. Our clickthroughlog-based approach can expand even queries that do not share any characters at all with the abbreviated ones [1]. Since our method does not rely on any language, it is applicable to any other languages including Chinese and English.

The rest of this paper is organized as follows. Section 2 describes previous works in query expansion tasks. In Section 3, we formulate a query expansion task in a noisy channel model framework. In Section 4, we show that label propagation on a clickthrough graph can be used as a query abbreviation model and extract candidates for query correction without preparing correct candidates. Section 5 explains the query language model we use. In Section 6, we evaluate our method in an abbreviation expansion task and show its efficiency. Section 7 offers conclusions and directions for future work.

2 Related Work

Query expansion for a web-search query has to handle neologisms and slang on the web. Thus, it is labor-intensive to maintain a list of correctly spelled words for search queries. Additionally, Japanese query expansion includes several tasks, such as word segmentation, word stemming, and acronym expansion. Much of the previous work has focused on each individual task (Ahmad and Kondrak, 2005; Chen et al., 2007; Bergsma and Wang, 2007; Li et al., 2006; Peng et al., 2007; Risvik et al., 2003).

Cucerzan and Brill (2004) clarified problems of spelling correction for search queries, addressing them using a noisy channel model with a language model created from query logs. Gao et al. (2010) and Sun et al. (2010) applied a reranking method applying neural net to the search-query spelling correction candidates obtained from the Cucerzan's method. Their reranking method had the advantageous ability to incorporate clickthrough logs to a translation model learned as a ranking-feature. However, their methods are based on edit distance, and thus they did not deal with the task of synonym replacement and acronym expansion.

Wei et al. (2009) addressed synonym extraction using similarity based on Jensen-Shannon divergence of commonly clicked URL distribution between queries. Their approach is similar to our proposed method, except that they did not use a language model. Also, their method is not scalable and cannot be applied to our task using large-scale data.

Jain and Pennacchiotti (2010) proposed an unsupervised method for named entity extraction from web search query logs. They performed a clustering method using a combination of features based on query logs, web documents, and clickthrough logs. They showed that clickthrough logs give higher accuracy than query logs as a corpus.

Guo et al. (2008) proposed a unified approach for query expansion using a discriminative model. They extended feature function of CRFs (Lafferty et al., 2001) by adding ‘operation’ to the triplet variables: ‘feature’, ‘label’, and ‘operation’. ‘Operation’ represents a process for query expansion. For example, ‘operation’ can take four states (‘deletion’, ‘insertion’, ‘substitution’, and ‘transposition’) on spelling correction. However, their method needs supervised data for training and cannot deal with a word that does not occur in the corpus. In fact, they used only 10,000 queries to learn the query expansion model. Unlike their method, our approach takes advantage of an enormous amount of clickthrough logs for learning the query abbreviation model.

Query suggestion is another task that uses search logs (Mei et al., 2008; Cao et al., 2008). Query suggestion differs from our task in that it allows queries to be suggested that are different from the one that the search user types.

Furthermore, some previous works have addressed acquiring a Japanese abbreviation task. Murayama and Okumura (2008) formulated the process of generating Japanese abbreviations by noisy channel model but they did not handle abbreviation expansion. Okazaki et al. (2008) dealt with recognizing Japanese abbreviation tasks as a binary classification problem. They extracted

[1] Note that our method can be applied to query expansion as well.

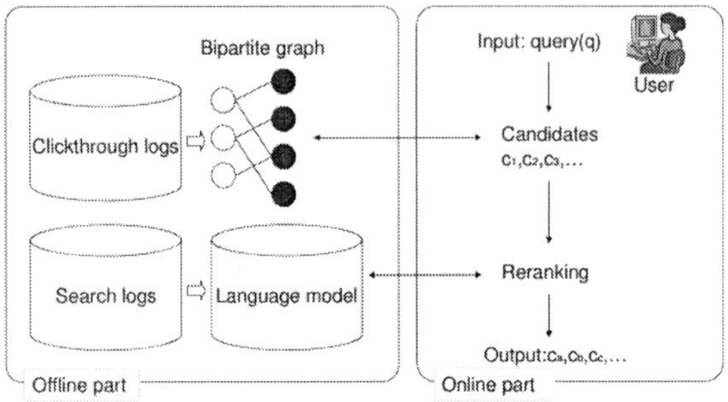

Figure 1: Combining clickthrough logs and search logs for query abbreviation expansion

pairs of words from the newspaper corpus using a heuristic and then classified them as "abbreviation" or "not-abbreviation". However, their heuristic for obtaining abbreviation candidates cannot be applied to web search queries.

3 Noisy Channel Model for Abbreviation Expansion

In this section, we explain our noisy channel based approach to query expansion. We define the query expansion problem as follows: Given a user's query q and a set of search logs L, find a correct query $c \in C$ that is most relevant to the input q. In a probabilistic framework, this can be formulated as finding the $\text{argmax}\, P(c|q)$. Applying Bayes' Rule and dropping the constant denominator, we obtain a unnormalized posterior: $\text{argmax}\, P(c)P(q|c)$(Eq.1). We now have a noisy channel model for query expansion, with two components: the source model $P(c)$ and the channel model $P(q|c)$.

$$\begin{aligned} c^* &= \underset{c}{\text{argmax}}\, P(c|q) \\ &= \underset{c}{\text{argmax}}\, \frac{P(c)P(q|c)}{P(q)} \\ &= \underset{c}{\text{argmax}}\, P(c)P(q|c) \end{aligned} \quad (1)$$

We use a language model estimated from search query logs as the source model, thus $P(c)$ represents likelihood of c as a query. As for the channel model, we use a label propagation method on a clickthrough graph as proposed by Komachi et al. (2009). Figure 1 shows the framework of our approach.

To find candidates to the input query, we construct a bipartite graph from a query and a clicked URL using the web search logs. We calculate the relatedness between the queries on this graph to select a set of candidates C. Since the label propagation is mathematically identical to the random walk with restart, probability of the label propagation can be regarded as the conditional probability $P(q|c)$. If we assume that the relatedness score represents the conditional probability of the typed query q given a candidate $c \in C$, $P(q|c)$, the c^* is calculated by $\text{argmax}\, P(c) \times P(q|c)$. As a consequence, we propose reranking in accordance with the follow equation using two probabilistic models P_{QLM} and P_{LP} and then output ranked candidates. In this paper, we will define P_{LP} interchangeably as a query abbreviation model, P_{QAM}.

$$score(q, c) = P_{QLM}(c) \times P_{QAM}(q|c) \quad (2)$$

An advantage of our proposed method is that it can correct a query by only using search logs without a manually labeled-corpora or any heuristics. Our approach is a versatile framework for query expansion and thus is not specialized for any tasks. We explain the label propagation algorithm on a clickthrough graph and the query language model below.

4 Query Abbreviation Model from Clickthrough Logs

In this section, we describe a label propagation algorithm on a clickthrough graph. It is based on a previous work by Komachi et al. (2009). The main difference between their method and ours is that we use the normalized pointwise mutual information and the 1-step approximation of a clickthrough graph.

Graph-based semi-supervised methods such as label propagation can performance well with only a few seeds and scale up to a large dataset. Figure 2 illustrates the process of label propagation using a seed term "abc".

This is a bipartite graph whose left-hand side nodes are terms and right-hand side nodes are patterns. Starting from "abc", the label propagates to other term nodes through the pattern "http://abcnews.go.com" that is strongly connected to "abc" and thus the label "abc" will be propagated to "american broadcasting corporation".

In this way, label propagation gradually propagates the label of the seed instance to neighboring

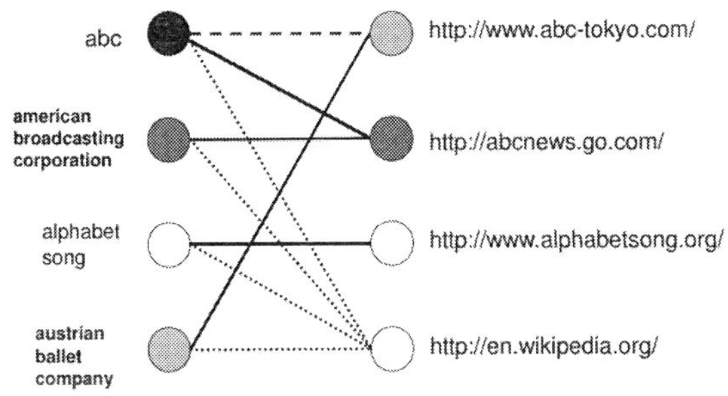

Figure 2: An illustrative example of Instance-Pattern co-occurrence graph and label propagation process.
The strength of lines indicates relatedness between each node, whereas the depth of the color of nodes represents relatedness to the seed. The darker a left-hand side node, the more likely it is similar to "abc". The darker a right-hand side node, the more likely it is the characteristic pattern of "abc".

Input :
  Seed instance vector $F(0)$
  Instance similarity matrix A
Output :
  Instance score vector $F(t)$
1: Construct the normalized Laplacian matrix
  $L = I - D^{-1/2}AD^{-1/2}$
2: Iterate
  $F(t+1) = \alpha(-L)F(t) + (1-\alpha)F(0)$
  until convergence

Figure 3: Laplacian label propagation

nodes, and optimal labels are given as the labels at which the label propagation process has converged.

However, the seed instance like that in Figure 2 possibly causes a result to be worse in a task of lexical acquisition, due to an ambiguous instance "abc", which belongs to more than one domain, e.g. "mass media" and "dance". It is expected that the label propagates to unrelated instances if we have highly frequent ambiguous nodes. This problem is called "semantic drift" and has received a lot of attention in NLP research (Komachi et al., 2008).

Komachi et al. (2008) have reported that bootstrapping algorithms like Espresso (Pantel and Pennacchiotti, 2006) can be viewed as Kleinberg's HITS algorithm (Kleinberg, 1999) and the "semantic drift" problem on the graph is the same phenomenon as "topic drift" in HITS, which converges to the eigenvector of the instance-instance similarity graph created from instance-pattern co-occurrence graph as described in the next subsection.

Our label propagation method based on Komachi et al. (2009) can be used as a relatedness measure that returns a similarity score relative to the seed instance, and thus is suitable for a query correction task.

4.1 One-step approximation of clickthrough graph

In this paper, we extract queries landing on the same URL as the one related with input query by stopping label propagation after 1-hop. These queries are possibly synonyms with the input query and thus possible to correct without semantic transformation.

Figure 3 shows the label propagation algorithm on a clickthrough graph.

Given an instance set $\mathcal{X} = \{x_1, \ldots, x_l, x_{l+1}, \ldots, x_n\}$ and a label set $\mathcal{L} = \{1, ..., c\}$, the first l instances x_i $(i < l)$ are labeled as $y_i \in \mathcal{L}$. The goal is to predict the labels of the unlabeled instances x_u $(l+1 \leq u \leq n)$.

Let $\mathcal{F}$ denote the set of $n \times c$ matrices with non-negative entries. A matrix $F = [F_1, \ldots, F_n]^T \in \mathcal{F}$ corresponds to a classification on the dataset $\mathcal{X}$ by labeling each instance x_i as a label $y_i = argmax_{j \leq c} F_{ij}$. Define F_0 as the initial F with $F_{ij} = 1$ if x_i is labeled as a label $y_i = j$ and $F_{ij} = 0$ otherwise. The (i,j)-th element of the final matrix F represents a similarity to the labeled instances. We use these similarities as $P(q|c)$ in Equation 2, where q is a seed instance, c is a labeled instance by label propagation.

The instance-instance similarity matrix A in Figure 3 is defined as $A = W^T W$ where W is an instance-pattern matrix. The (i,j)-th element of W_{ij} contains the relative frequency of occurrence of instance x_i and pattern p_j.

D is a diagonal degree matrix of A where the (i,j)-th element of D is given as $D_{ii} = \sum_j A_{ij}$. Label propagation has a parameter α $(0 \leq \alpha \leq \lambda^{-1}$, where λ is a principal eigenvalue of normalized Laplacian matrix $L)$ that controls the effect of clamping the label distribution of labeled data.

4.2 Normalized PMI

Komachi et al. (2009) suggested that the normalized frequency causes semantic drift (Jurafsky and Martin, 2009), and we confirmed this phenomenon in our preliminary experiment. They suggested using relative frequency such as pointwise mutual information (PMI) and log-likelihood ratio as countermeasure against semantic drift. Therefore, we used pointwise mutual information (PMI) shown below to handle the aforementioned semantic drift problem.

$$PMI(x,p) = ln\frac{P(x,p)}{P(x)P(p)} \tag{3}$$

PMI assigns high scores to low-frequency events. Moreover, using PMI naively makes sparse matrix W dense. Therefore, we used normalized PMI (NPMI) (Bouma, 2009) below as the relative frequency and cut off the values lower than a threshold θ ($\theta \geq 0$).

$$NPMI(x,p) = \left\{ ln\frac{P(x,p)}{P(x)P(p)} \right\} \Big/ -lnP(x,p) \tag{4}$$

$$W_{ij} = \begin{cases} NPMI(x_i, p_j) & (NPMI(x_i, p_j) > \theta) \\ 0 & (NPMI(x_i, p_j) \leq \theta) \end{cases}$$
$$,(\theta \geq 0) \tag{5}$$

NPMI prevents low-frequency events from being assigned scores that are too high by dividing by $-lnP(x,p)$ and heads off excess label propagation through them. By cutting off negative values, the range of W_{ij} can be normalized to [0,1]. Additionally, this prevents sparse matrix W from being dense and reduces the noise in the data.

5 Query Language Model

In this paper, we use a character n-gram language model to obtain the likelihood of the candidates for query expansion in Equation 2.

$$\begin{aligned} P(c) &= \prod_{i=0}^{N-1} P(x_i | x_{i-N+1}, \ldots, x_{i-1}) \\ &= \prod_{i=0}^{N-1} \frac{freq(x_{i-N+1}, \ldots, x_i)}{freq(x_{i-N+1}, \ldots, x_{i-1})} \end{aligned} \tag{6}$$

where consider c is a contiguous sequences of N characters $c = \{x_0, x_1, \ldots, x_{n-1}\}$.

In the web search, neologims appear continuously, which make it hard to compute the likelihood of queries by a word n-gram language model. Moreover, characters themselves carry essential semantic information in Chinese and Japanese. Therefore, we build a character language model for the search query logs following observations of the usefulness of character n-grams for Japanese (Asahara and Matsumoto, 2004) and Chinese (Huang and Zhao, 2006). Asahara and Matsumoto used a window of two characters to the right and to the left of the focus character, which results in using character 5-grams. We also used 5-grams for a query language model from the preliminary experiment.

6 Experiment

6.1 Test Set

We collected abbreviations of *'Acronym', 'Kanji', 'Kana'* from the Japanese version of Wikipedia, and then removed single letters and duplications. Finally, we gathered 1,916 terms and used them in our evaluation.

6.2 Construction of a Clickthrough Graph

We used queries and clicked links in Japanese clickthrough logs as instances and patterns, respectively. We tallied them in the below conditions.

1. Query and clickthrough are unique with respect to each cookie each day.
   If a user input the same query and clicked the same URL any number of times, we do not count it as occurring multiple times, i.e. we do not increase the number of clickthrough.

2. Alphanumeric characters in a query are unified to one-byte lower-case characters

3. A sequence of white space in a query is unified to single one-byte white space character

4. All the URLs included in clickthrough logs are unique, i.e., we did not generalize URLs as Tseng et al. (2009) did.

The Japanese clickthrough logs were collected from October 22 to November 9, 2009 [2] and from January 1 to 16 in Yahoo Japan web search logs.

[2] A storage device in our experimental environment became full when tallying clickthrough logs. As a result, we were not able to use clickthrough logs of some periods.

Links clicked less than 10 times were removed for efficiency reasons. Finally, we obtained 4,428,430 nodes, 16,841,683 patterns, and 16,988,516 edges.

The threshold θ of elements W_{ij} was set to 0.1 on the basis of preliminary experimental results.

The parameter α for label propagation was set to 0.0001.

6.3 Construction of Query Language Model

We used web search query logs for constructing a language model. The search query logs were collected from August 1, 2009, to January 27, 2010, in Yahoo Japan web search logs. We removed queries that occurred fewer than 10 times. Finally, we obtained 52,399,621 unique queries as a training corpus.

In this experiment, we constructed a character 5-gram language model using the query logs, all normalized by the length of the candidate's string.

6.4 Evaluation

The system output was shown to five search evaluation specialists. We evaluated all systems using *precision* and *coverage at k*. Coverage is defined as the percentage of queries for which the system returned at least one relevant query. Precision at k is the number of relevant queries amongst the top k returned. They are computed as follows:

$$precision = \frac{\text{\# of correct output at rank } k}{\text{Number of output at rank } k},$$

$$coverage = \frac{\begin{array}{c}\text{\# of queries for which the system}\\ \text{gives at least one correct output}\end{array}}{\text{Number of all input queries}} \quad (7)$$

In our experiment, the average number of candidates for each query is about 53. Therefore, we extracted 50 candidates from clickthrough logs and then reranked using three methods:

1. Ranking using abbreviation model (AM) only
2. Ranking using language model (LM) only
3. Ranking using both language model and abbreviation model.

Micro average of edit distance between input abbreviations and its correct expansions is 4.03, while the average length of queries is 3.01. These statistics show that input queries should be replaced by totally different characters and it is difficult to use edit distance for extracting correct candidates from web search logs. This is another reason clickthrough logs are essential to the query abbreviation task.

6.4.1 Judgment Guideline

We describe our guidelines to judge system outputs below. We defined four correction patterns for abbreviation expansion:

1. acronym for its English expansion
2. acronym for its Japanese orthography [4]
3. Japanese abbreviation for its Japanese orthography
4. Japanese abbreviation for its English orthography

We collected abbreviation/expansion pairs if and only if they were one of these three types: (1) named entity, (2) common expression, (3) Japanese meaning of the common expression.

Table 1 shows examples of each correction pattern along with its output type.

Ambiguous cases were discarded in the study as exceptions after discussion with experts. To calculate the agreement rate, system outputs for a hundred randomly sampled queries from test set were evaluated by two judges. The agreement rate of judgment of abbreviation/expansion pair is 47.0 percentage and Cohen's kappa measure $\kappa = 0.63$. Thus, it is considered as an upper bound of the system, and the abbreviation expansion is not considered to be a trivial task.

6.5 Experimental Results

Table 2 shows *precision at k* and coverage for three systems with k ranging from 1 to 50. Table 3 shows examples of inputs and outputs. The baseline without reranking is shown at the bottom line (k=50). The result of using only QAM in Table 2 is equivalent to the method of Komachi et al. (2009) using NPMI instead of raw frequency as elements of an instance-pattern matrix. To

[3] Underlined words are correct.

[4] Some corrections were dealt with as exceptions. For example, acronym for its Japanese *Hiragana* was treated as incorrect, but acronym for its Japanese meaning was treated as correct.

Table 1: Abbreviations and its correction

abbreviation	correct candidates（descending order of rank）	output type	correction pattern
adf	asian dub foundation	Named Entity: Organization	acronym for its expansion
ana	全日空，全日本空輸株式会社 (All Nippon Airways)	Named Entity: Organization	acronym for its Japanese orthography
ny	ニューヨーク (New York)	Named Entity: Location	acronym for its Japanese orthography
tos	テイルズオブシンフォニア (Tales of Symphonia)	Named Entity: Product	acronym for its Japanese orthography
イラレ	illustrator	Named Entity: Product	Japanese abbreviation for its English orthography
ハンスト	ハンガーストライキ (Hunger Strike)	Common expression	Japanese abbreviation for its Japanese orthograpy
阪神	阪神タイガース	Named Entity: Organization	Japanese abbreviation for its Japanese orthograpy
fyi	for your information	Common expression	acronym to its expansion

Table 2: Precision and coverage at k

k	query abbreviation model (QAM)		query language model (QLM)		QLM+QAM	
	precision	coverage	precision	coverage	precision	coverage
1	0.114	0.114	0.157	0.157	**0.161**	**0.161**
3	0.122	0.256	0.142	0.278	**0.157**	**0.321**
5	0.121	0.341	0.128	0.346	**0.142**	**0.392**
10	0.114	0.453	0.102	0.425	**0.115**	**0.465**
30	**0.087**	0.536	0.078	0.529	0.082	**0.542**
50	0.073	0.557	0.073	0.557	0.073	0.557

Table 3: Examples of input and candidates or its correction[3]

Input	Candidates
写植	写真植字，写植屋，写植機，写植 方，漫画
満鉄	満鉄調査部，南満州鉄道株式会，南満州鉄道，満鉄会，満州鉄道
はねトび	はねるのとびら，はねるのトびら，はねるの，はねるのトびら，はねるのトビラ，はねとび
vod	ビデオオンデ，ビデオ・オン・デマンド，ビデオ オンデマンド，ビデオオンデマンド
ilo	日本 ilo，ilo 協会，国際労働機関，国際労働期間，ilo 条約
pr	パブリック・リレーションズ，パブリックリレーションズ，prohoo!マ，pr 会社，プラ

Table 4: P-values of Wilcoxon's signed rank test

	QAM and QAM + QLM	QLM and QAM + QLM
p-value	0.055	$7.79e^{-10}$

our knowledge, their algorithm is the state-of-the-art algorithm in acquiring synonyms using web search logs.

The proposed ranking method using a query language model and abbreviation model learned from clickthrough logs shows the best precision and coverage within $1 \leq k \leq 10$. This is because the language and abbreviation model use different sources of information to complement each other.

The language model estimates probability of the candidate as a query, and it assigns high probability to candidates that appear frequently in query logs. Those candidates tend to co-occur with many clickthrough patterns, which results in creating generic patterns that may cause semantic drift (Komachi et al., 2009). Because we used NPMI instead of raw frequency, our label propagation method assigns high weight to instances connected to a seed instance through a few specific patterns. Consequently, low-frequency instances tend to be ranked in higher positions.

Table 4 shows the significance level between two baselines and the proposed model. We applied Wilcoxon's signed rank test to compare harmonic mean between precision and coverage of each model with k ranging from 1 to 50. The improvement of adding QAM to QLM is made statistically significant by the Wilcoxon's signed rank test at level $p < 0.00001$. Our approach outperforms the QAM without QLM although not as significant ($p < 0.06$). These mean that the ranking of our methods is similar to that of QAM. We consider the reason or this result to be that QLM introduces more information about queries under this experimental setting because the reranking process is performed after narrowing candidates down to 50 by QAM, even though we do not use QAM scores at all when evaluating QLM.

Due to time constraints and human resources for evaluation, we were unable to compare NPMI with raw frequency. There is still much room for improvement for assigning appropriate weights to edges in a clickthrough graph.

6.6 Error Analysis

We conducted error analysis of our proposed method and found that errors can be divided into three types: (1) a partial correct query, (2) a correct query but with an additional attribute word, and (3) a related but not abbreviated term.

A partial correct query The main reason for this error is that the likelihood of the partial query becomes higher than that of its correct spelling. Although we normalized the likelihood of candidates by their string length, we still fail to filter fragments of queries. We consider that this issue can be solved by modeling popularity of candidates using PageRank from web search logs. Partial correct queries do not co-occur with attribute words frequently, while correct queries co-occur with diverse attribute words. Therefore, PageRank on a query graph whose edges represent common co-occurring words between queries, will assign higher scores to correct queries than a query language model and abbreviation model.

A correct query but with an additional attribute word Examples of this error type include the combination of correct queries and commonly used attribute words in the search (e.g. "* とは"*(what does * mean?)*, "* 意味"*(* meaning)*, "* 使い方" *(how to use *)*), etc.). There were 857 queries that were classified as incorrect that co-occurred with these attribute words. The similarity of these candidates and input query tend to be higher than that of others because these attribute words frequently appear in search query logs, so the likelihood of these candidate being calculated by a language model tends to be higher too.

We consider that this issue can be solved at some level by generating a language model using the first term only, after splitting queries separated by a space in search query logs. However, attribute words are not always separated by a space, and sometimes appear as the first term in the query[5]. Another way to handle this problem is to use PageRank described earlier to decrease likelihood of candidates including attribute words.

Related but not abbreviated term A number of abbreviations coincide with other general nouns (e.g. "dog"[6]). It is hard to expand these abbreviations correctly at present. In future work, session logs and geo-location information from IP address and GPS can be used to disambiguate the intent of the query.

Besides above reasons, 280 out of 1,916 queries did not exist in clickthrough logs, resulting in our system not being able to extract the correct query. To solve this problem, we will increase clickthrough logs to improve the coverage of our corpus.

7 Conclusion

We have proposed a query expansion method using the web search query and clickthrough logs.

Our noisy channel based method uses character 5-gram of query logs as a language model and label propagation on a clickthrough graph as a channel model. In our experiment, we found that a combination of label propagation and language model outperformed other methods using either label propagation or language model in reranking of query abbreviation candidates extracted from the web search clickthrough logs.

In fact, a modified implementation of this method is currently in production use as an assistance tool for making a synonym dictionary at Yahoo Japan.

In evaluation of IR systems, Mizzaro (2008) has proposed a normalized mean average precision (NMAP) for considering difficulty of topics in data sets. However, identifying topics in our test set queries and measuring their difficulty are beyond the scope of this paper. Evaluation criteria are important for making production services.

In the future, we are going to address this task using discriminative learning as a ranking problem.

References

Farooq Ahmad and Grzegorz Kondrak. 2005. Learning a spelling error model from search query logs. In

[5]Some attributes, (e.g. "動画"*(Movie)*,"アニメ"*(Animation)*,"画像"*(Picture)*,etc.), occur often at first token in a search query, but some attributes, (e.g. "使い方", ,"意味",etc.) almost never occur at first token.

[6]DOG: Disk Original Group

Proceedings of the conference on Human Language Technology and Empirical Methods in Natural Language Processing, pages 955–962.

Masayuki Asahara and Yuji Matsumoto. 2004. Japanese unknown word identification by character-based chunking. In *Proceedings of the 20th international conference on Computational Linguistics*, pages 459–465.

Shane Bergsma and Qin Iris Wang. 2007. Learning noun phrase query segmentation. In *Proceedings of the 2007 Joint Conference on Empirical Methods in Natural Language Processing and Computational Natural Language Learning*.

Geolof Bouma. 2009. Normalized (pointwise) mutual information in collocation extraction. In *Proceedings of the Biennial GSCL Conference*, pages 31–40.

Huanhuan Cao, Daxin Jiang, Jian Pei, Qi He, Zhen Liao, Enhong Chen, and Hang Li. 2008. Context-aware query suggestion by mining click-through and session data. In *Proceeding of the 14th ACM SIGKDD international conference on Knowledge Discovery and Data Mining*, pages 875–883.

Qing Chen, Mu Li, and Ming Zhou. 2007. Improving query spelling correction using web search results. In *Proceedings of the 2007 Joint Conference on Empirical Methods in Natural Language Processing and Computational Natural Language Learning*, pages 181–189.

Silviu Cucerzan and Eric Brill. 2004. Spelling correction as an iterative process that exploits the collective knowledge of web users. In *Proceedings of the Conference on Empirical Methods in Natural Language Processing*, pages 293–300.

Jianfeng Gao, Xiaolong Li, Daniel Micol, Chris Quirk, and Xu Sun. 2010. A large scale ranker-based system for search query spelling correction. In *Proceedings of the 23rd International Conference on Computational Linguistics*, pages 358–366.

Jianfeng Guo, Gu Xu, Hang Li, and Xueqi Cheng. 2008. A unified and discriminative model for query refinement. In *Proceedings of the 31st annual international ACM SIGIR conference on Research and Development in Information Retrieval*, pages 379–386.

Masato Hagiwara and Hisami Suzuki. 2009. Japanese query alteration based on seamntic similarity. In *Proceedings of Human Language Technologies: The 2009 Annual Conference of the North American Chapter of the Association for Computational Linguistics*, pages 191–199.

Chang-Ning Huang and Hai Zhao. 2006. Which is essential for chinese word segmentation: character versus word. In *Proceedings of the 20th Pacific Asia Conference on Language, Information and Computation (PACLIC-20)*, pages 1–12.

Alpa Jain and Marco Pennacchiotti. 2010. Open entity extraction from web search query logs. In *Proceedings of the 23rd International Conference on Computational Linguistics*, pages 510–518.

Daniel Jurafsky and James H. Martin. 2009. *Speech and language processing: An introduction to natural language processing, computational linguistics, and speech recognition*. 2nd edition. Prentice Hall, Englewood Cliffs. NJ.

Jon M. Kleinberg. 1999. Authoritative sources in a hyperlinked environment. *Journal of the ACM*, 46:604–632, September.

Mamoru Komachi, Taku Kudo, Masashi Shimbo, and Yuji Matsumoto. 2008. Graph-based analysis of semantic drift in Espresso-like bootstrapping algorithms. In *Proceedings of the 2008 Conference on Empirical Methods in Natural Language Processing*, pages 1011–1020.

Mamoru Komachi, Shimpei Makimoto, Kei Uchiumi, and Manabu Sassano. 2009. Learning semantic categories from clickthrough logs. In *Proceedings of the ACL-IJCNLP 2009 Conference Short Papers*, pages 189–192.

John Lafferty, Andrew McCallum, and Fernando Pereira. 2001. Conditional random fields: Probabilistic models for segmenting and labeling sequence data. In *Proceedings of the Eighteenth International Conference on Machine Learning*, pages 282–289.

Mu Li, Yang Zhang, Muhua Zhu, and Ming Zhou. 2006. Exploring distributional similarity based models for query spelling correction. In *Proceedings of the 21st International Conference on Computational Linguistics and 44th Annual Meeting of the Association for Computational Linguistics*, pages 1025–1032.

Qiazhu Mei, Dengyong Zhou, and Kenneth Church. 2008. Query suggestion using hitting time. In *Proceeding of the 17th ACM conference on Information and Knowledge Management*, pages 469–478.

Stefano Mizzaro. 2008. The good, the bad, the difficult, and the easy: something wrong with information retrieval evaluation? In *Proceedings of the IR research, 30th European conference on Advances in information retrieval*, ECIR'08, pages 642–646, Berlin, Heidelberg. Springer-Verlag.

Norihumi Murayama and Manabu Okumura. 2008. Statistical model for Japanese abbreviations. In *Proceedings of the 10th Pacific Rim International Conference on Artificial Intelligence: Trends in Artificial Intelligence*, pages 260–272.

Naoki Okazaki, Mitsuru Ishizuka, and Jun'ichi Tsujii. 2008. A discriminative approach to Japanese abbreviation extraction. In *Proceedings of the 3rd International Joint Conference on Natural Language Processing (IJCNLP-08)*, pages 889–894.

Patric Pantel and Marco Pennacchiotti. 2006. Espresso: Leveraging generic patterns for automatically harvesting semantic relations. In *Proceedings of the 21st International Conference on Computational Linguistics and the 44th annual meeting of the ACL*, pages 113–120.

Fuchun Peng, Nawaaz Ahmed, Xin Li, and Yumao Lu. 2007. Context sensitive stemming for web search. In *Proceedings of the 30th annual international ACM SIGIR conference on Research and Development in Information Retrieval*, pages 639–646.

Knut M. Risvik, Tomasz Mikolajewski, and Peter Boros. 2003. Query segmentation for web search. In *Poster Session in The Twelfth International World Wide Web Conference*.

Satoshi Sekine and Hisami Suzuki. 2007. Acquiring ontological knowledge from query logs. In *Proceedings of the 16th international conference on World Wide Web*, pages 1223–1224.

Xu Sun, Jianfeng Gao, Daniel Micol, and Chris Quirk. 2010. Learning phrase-based spelling error models from clickthrough data. In *Proceedings of the 48th Annual Meeting of the Association for Computational Linguistics*, pages 266–274.

Huihsin Tseng, Longbin Chen, Fan Li, Ziming Zhuang, Lei Duan, and Belle Tseng. 2009. Mining search engine clickthrough log for matching N-gram features. In *Proceedings of the 14th Conference on Empirical Methods in Natural Language Processing*, pages 524–533.

Xing Wei, Fuchunk Peng, Huishin Tseng, Yumao Lu, and Benoit Dumoulin. 2009. Context sensitive synonym discovery for web search queries. In *Proceeding of the 18th ACM conference on Information and Knowledge Management*, pages 1585–1588.

Mining Parallel Documents Using Low Bandwidth and High Precision CLIR from the Heterogeneous Web

Simon Shi[1], Pascale Fung[1], Emmanuel Prochasson[2], Chi-kiu Lo[1] and Dekai Wu[1]
[1] Human Language Technology Center
Hong Kong University of Science and Technology (HKUST)
Clear Water Bay, Hong Kong
[2] Digital Butter
69 Jervois Street, Sheung Wan, Hong Kong
{eesys,pascale}@ust.hk, emmanuel@butter.com.hk,
{jackielo,dekai}@cs.ust.hk

Abstract

We propose a content-based approach to mine parallel resources from the entire web using cross lingual information retrieval (CLIR) with search query relevance score (SQRS). Our method improves mining recall by going beyond URL matching to find parallel documents from non-parallel sites. We introduce SQRS to improve the precision of mining. Our method makes use of search engines to query for target document given each source document and therefore does not require downloading target language documents in batch mode, reducing computational cost on the local machines and bandwidth consumption. We obtained a very high mining precision (88%) on the parallel documents by the pure CLIR approach. After extracting parallel sentences from the mined documents and using them to train an SMT system, we found that the SMT performance, with 29.88 BLEU score, is comparable to that obtained with high quality manually translated parallel sentences with 29.54 BLEU score, illustrating the excellent quality of the mined parallel material.

1 Introduction

Parallel resources such as bilingual lexicon and sentence translations are typically obtained from translated parallel documents. The web has now grown into an archive of trillions of URLs, heterogeneous in nature, in the last decade. There is a need to readdress the problem of how to mine parallel documents from the web.

We suggest that parallel documents can be mined with high precision from web sites that are not necessarily parallel to each other.

Parallel resources reside on a diverse range of websites which can be classified into the following categories:

Parallel websites: single website with structurally aligned bilingual pages. Typically they are websites of institutions, governments and commercial companies. (e.g. Financial Times Chinese/English, Wall Street Journal Chinese/English). Structure based methods were previously proposed to mine parallel documents from these websites:

Resnik and Smith (2003) used (1) parent pages containing links to versions of one document in different languages and (2) sibling pages contains link to translation of the current documents. They also rely on the URL and anchor text to spot language specific version of documents.

A structural alignment using DOM tree representation was proposed by Shi et al. (2006) to align parallel documents by using HTML structure. They identify the translational equivalent texts and hyperlinks between two parallel DOM trees to find parallel documents.

However, the web is a heterogeneous collection of documents that extend far beyond bilingual and comparable pages with obvious structural features, such as similar URLs or common titles. Structural features only work for bilingual websites or document pairs that are already linked by editors.

Comparable websites: websites that contain parallel content in different languages without any structural relation between document pairs. Press agencies have independent content management systems and editors for publishing news

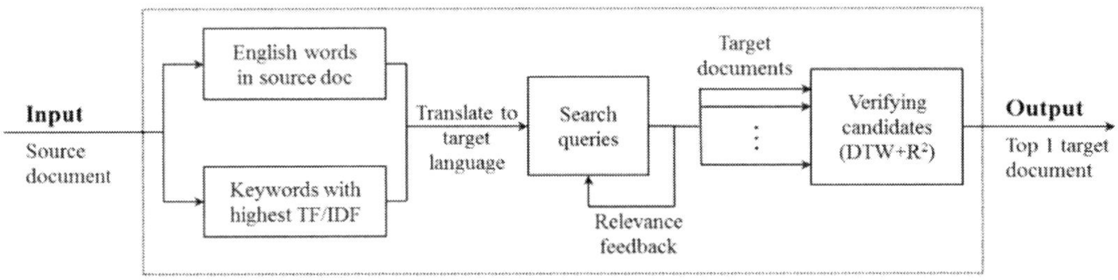

Figure 1. Parallel Document Mining using CLIR with Relevance Feedback

in different languages. (e.g. Reuters China vs. Reuters)

Quasi-comparable websites: independent websites that somewhere contain translated parallel contents. They may contain stories, documentations and books chapters in many languages on different websites. (e.g. Forbes, Fortune)

Instead of structural cues such as URLs, hyperlinks and HTML trees, content based approach are applied to find extra parallel resources from comparable and quasi-comparable websites.

Nie et al. (1999) proposed to download all source language and target language documents and then perform Cross Language Information Retrieval (Grefenstette, 1998) to extract candidate parallel documents. Munteanu and Marcu (2005, 2006) also focused on mining parallel documents from a downloaded collection of news articles, using time stamp alignment and content matching. More recently, Jiang et al. (2009) proposed an adaptive pattern-based bilingual data mining method to mine bilingual web pages for parallel phrases and terms.

Uszkoreit et al. (2010) aligned parallel documents by querying n-gram index built from translation of multilingual documents. All these approaches require a huge local achieve of both source and target documents. This can be very costly when we want to query the entire web.

Moreover, Uszkoreit et al. (2010) makes use of statistical machine translation (SMT) system to translate all documents into target language to build a query index. Due to the complexity of machine translation algorithms, it is still resource wasteful to download all target language documents, machine translate them, then select the desired candidate parallel documents.

Web content is being updated continuously. The above methods need to crawl for all documents in the target language. This is costly in terms of CPU consumption, bandwidth usage and disk storage utilization. This step can be replaced with search engine APIs by several search queries generated from source documents to save CPU and bandwidth consumption.

As most research institutions interested in mining parallel documents do not possess a large number of CPUs or storage on the scale of the world's top search companies, it is also desirable that any site can scale the mining speed and volume according to the computing resources available to them.

To this end, we propose a low bandwidth CLIR method to on the one hand complement structural matching, and on the other hand reduce the complexity of content matching.

Hong et al. (2010) proposed a mining approach on selected Chinese news article containing cue phrases. In non-oracle queries, 45% of the parallel or comparable documents were found among top search results. This is a benchmark in mining precision.

As the parallel resources mined are often times used to improve SMT systems or yield bilingual lexicons, it is desirable that the mining output is of high precision.

2 The Low Bandwidth High Precision Content Based Approach

Our proposed approach (Figure 1) primarily aims to discover parallel documents from all kinds of parallel, comparable or quasi-comparable websites on the World Wide Web. We take advantage of online search engines to find candidate documents thereby saving bandwidth, computational cost and dispenses with crawling for and storing all documents in the target language in an archive.

Content based approach queries the document in target language using keywords from documents in the source language. In our approach, queries are generated from source documents and expanded dynamically by search result quality as feedback. Neither machine translation of the full

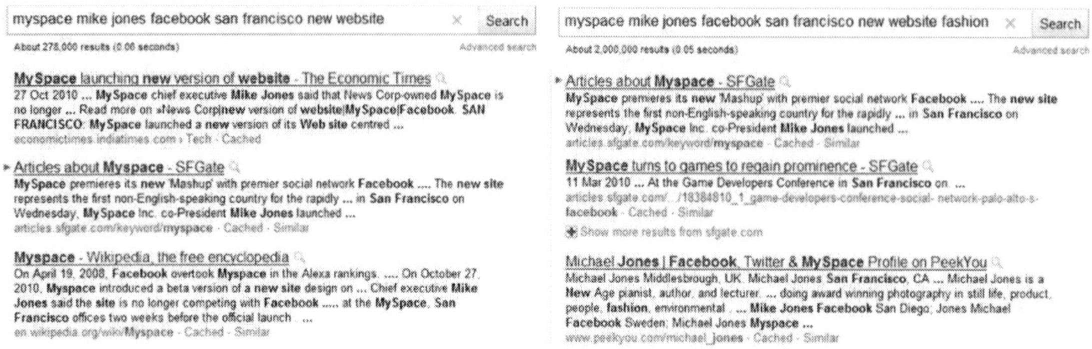

Figure 2. Search Result of Query 1 (Left) and 2 (Right) on Google.com

text no downloading of target documents is needed.

We suggest query expansion feedback score is the key in improving the precision of target documents found. If a source document is found to have no translation in the target language, the system simply returns <not-found>.

2.1 Representing Source Document

We cannot enter documents with thousands of words directly into an online search engine. We need to convert full text into keywords to perform automated queries. A keyword may exist in multiple articles. However, several keywords cam uniquely identify a document if they are grouped together as a keyword set (Jiang et al., 2009).

We then translate each keyword to target language to form the initial query.

There are several reasons why using the translated keyword set as query directly, as proposed by Hong et al. (2010), does not always yields the desired target document:

1) Keyword translation might not correspond to the actual words in the target document;
2) Certain keywords in the target document might have been removed by content editors;
3) There are errors in keyword translation or selection.

It is essential to select appropriate keywords to find the desired target document in a search engine. Two conditions that an appropriate keyword set should satisfy are: (1) they should represent the document exclusively (Jiang et al., 2009) (2) they should have unique or common translation in both languages.

We suggest that words with high TF-IDFs and English words in Chinese text are usually keywords that fulfill both conditions above.

$$K = K_T \bigcup K_E$$

K_T: set of words with high TF-IDF score

K_E: set of English words in Chinese documents

To obtain TF-IDFs that are representative of the keyword in the source document, they are trained from all source documents under the same domain name (e.g. www.ftchinese.com).

Keywords in K_E are more important because most of them are words used in the target document. However, in many cases, there are additional words in K_E so that we cannot find any document by directly searching for K_E. Our method removes keywords with the lowest TF-IDF score from K_E until a non-empty result is obtained.

2.2 Translating Source Documents with Search Query Relevance Score (SQRS)

Search engines use multiple criteria, such as keyword significance, domain popularity, date, popularity, page rank and etc., to return the most relevant documents that match the query. For mining a translated document pair, we need to somehow overcome the impact of page popularity and rank, and aim for content matching only.

Instead of ranking keywords locally and send single query, we take the above search engine criteria into account to amend queries.

To avoid adding erroneously translated keywords and further reduce the amount of undesirable documents downloaded, we introduced the *search query relevance score (SQRS),* defined in Equation 1, that describes how well the search result is and how we can refine the query. The score is determined by comparing the query with highlighted keywords in search result. Generally, a webpage has higher SQRS if the summary contains more keywords that match the query.

Commercial search engines omit some keywords when there is no document in their index containing all the keywords. In such cases, the rank of documents usually changes significantly.

The following example shows search results of two search queries (Figure 2) generated from the Chinese version of *My Space launching new version of website*[1]. "|" indicates separation of keywords.

Query 1:

myspace | mike jones | facebook | san francisco | new | website

Query 2:

myspace | mike jones | facebook | san francisco | new | website | fashion

In Query 1, the oracle (known) target document was the topmost in search result. The short summary contains every keyword we entered in the query. Rank and SQRSs are shown in Table 1.

SQRS	Search engine omitted kwd	Rank
7.742	-	1*
5.174	web(site)	3
4.951	web(site)	2
4.663	web(site)	4
4.545	web(site)	5

* Target document

Table 1. SQRS of Query 1

In Query 2, we added *fashion* which is the English translation of "新潮" (but the actual English version used *hottest*). The rank of search result changed and each summary omitted at least one keyword in the query (Table 2).

SQRS	Search engine omitted kwd(s)	Rank
6.155	fashion	5*
3.951	web(site) | fashion	1
5.867	website	3
0.871	mike | new | website | fashion	4
-2.921	mike jones | new | website | fashion	2

Table 2. SQRS of Query 2

This phenomenon suggests that the document with all keywords in Query 2 does not exist on the web. The recently added keyword *fashion* must be erroneously translated.

In many similar cases, an erroneously translated keyword can pollute the query quality and decrease the rank of target document. Parallel document mining cannot rely on the document rank of search engine. The system must have a mechanism to detect the problem when expanding the query. Otherwise, a batch of irrelevant documents will be downloaded and need to be filtered out.

We ran experiments to find target documents of 112 randomly selected source documents and compare their SQRSs. 81 or 72.3% target documents have the highest SQRS among other URLs in the search results. It implies the SQRS are an effective measure of query formation and keyword translation.

Source documents	Target documents have largest SQRSs	%
112	81	72.3

Table 3. Result quality and SQRS

Although the query may include multiple translations of a keyword in a bilingual lexicon, the SQRS ensures that there is minimum adverse effect from incorrect translations.

2.3 Query Expansion using SQRS

To improve the precision of the keyword set, we further use SQRS for relevance feedback as shown in Figure 3.

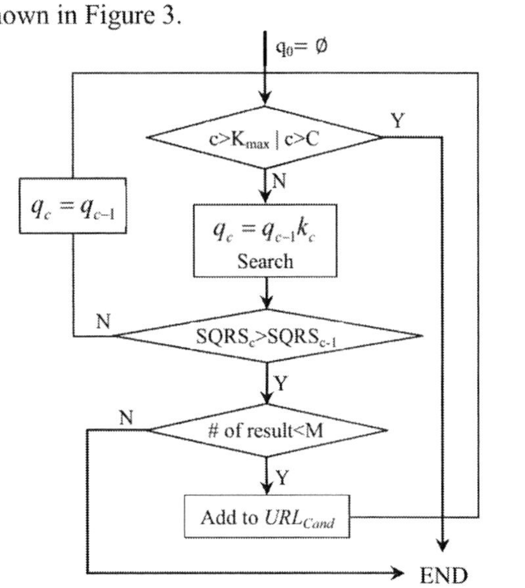

Figure 3. Flowchart of Query Expansion Algorithm

First, we rank the keywords in K_T by their TF-IDF scores. Next, the query is expanded by SQRS. When keyword w is added to current query, we compare the maximum $SQRS_c$ among top n results with the previous highest score $SQRS_p$ without w. w will be discarded from the keywords if $SQRS_c < SQRS_p$ or simply caused an

[1] Source: http://cn.reuters.com/article/CNTechNews/idCNCHINA-3233720101027 on May 10, 2011

$$Q = (k_1 k_2 ... k_C) \quad k_i = (w_{i1} w_{i2} ... w_{iJ}) \quad \Gamma K_i = \{(w_{ia} ... w_{ib}) | 0 < a < b \leq J\}$$

$$count(c,t) = \text{\# of occurrence of } c \text{ in } t, \quad \delta(c,t) = \begin{cases} 0 & \text{if } count(c,t) > 0 \\ 1 & \text{if } count(c,t) = 0 \end{cases}$$

$$SQRS(Q,T) = \sum_{c=1}^{C} \left[\sum_{s \in \Gamma K_c} [\log(count(s,T)+1)] - \delta(k_c,T) \right]$$

where Q is the query, k is keyword, w is English word and T is the short text with highlighted keywords in search result.

Equation 1. Definition of SQRS

empty search result. Otherwise, query will be expanded by adding w.

The search engine returns the total number of target documents for each query. If this number is less than a threshold M, we will add the URL of top-ranked documents to the URL_{Cand} list for verification.

To save network bandwidth, the system only considers the top K_{Max} words with the highest TF-IDF scores.

2.4 Document Verification

All candidate document pairs are subjected to a parallelness verification process before output. The system returns <not-found> if a pair failed the verification process. We propose using both dynamic time warping (DTW) and R^2 regression as in (Cheung and Fung, 2004) on every pair of the source and targets document to evaluate their parallelness.

2.4.1 Dynamic Time Warping (DTW) Score

DTW alignment is faster than machine translation (MT). We measure the word level DTW score between source document and target document with local constrain of 5 (Equation 2). Stop words are removed from the English text before DTW processing.

If the there is an entry in the bi-lexicon for a pair of i-th Chinese word and j-th English respectively, the cost of point (i,j) is 0, otherwise 1. The total cost is normalized by maximum number of steps (moves) from (0,0) to (m,n) to convert DTW score to a number between 0 and 1.

Parallel document pairs tend to have a path close to the diagonal line with high DTW score.

$$DTW(i_m, i_n) = c + \min \begin{pmatrix} DTW(i_m, i_n) & \cdots & DTW(i_m - 5, i_n) \\ \vdots & \ddots & \vdots \\ DTW(i_m, i_n - 5) & \cdots & DTW(i_m - 5, i_n - 5) \end{pmatrix}$$

Equation 2. DTW with local distance of 5

Figure 4 shows the DTW paths of a parallel document pair and a non-parallel pair. The parallel documents are aligned and the path with minimum cost is shown along the diagonal of the graph.

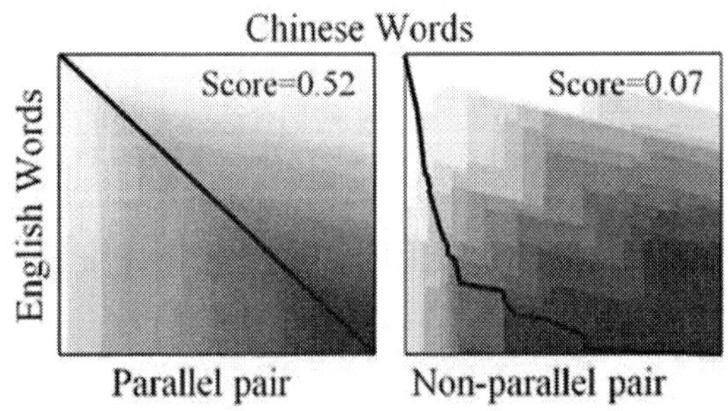

Figure 4. DTW of Parallel and Non-Parallel Pair

Table 4. is the relationship between DTW score and precision of candidate pairs. The precision of output sentences increases if the DTW score threshold is set higher.

DTW	# Pairs	# Parallel	Precision %
>0.45	122	121	99.18
>0.40	224	219	97.77
>0.35	298	288	96.64
>0.30	354	337	95.20
>0.28	389	364	93.57
>0.26	429	389	90.68
>0.25	456	403	88.38
>0.24	488	415	85.04
>0.22	545	417	76.51
>0.20	627	426	67.94

Table 4. DTW and Precision of Candidates Pairs

2.4.2 R^2 Regression

The parallel documents contain parallel sentences that may have different word orders, especially in the case of English and Chinese. The DTW score may be affected by different word order. We propose to use R^2 regression as an additional score to measure the deviation of the matching path of shared words in both documents from the diagonal. (Figure 5)

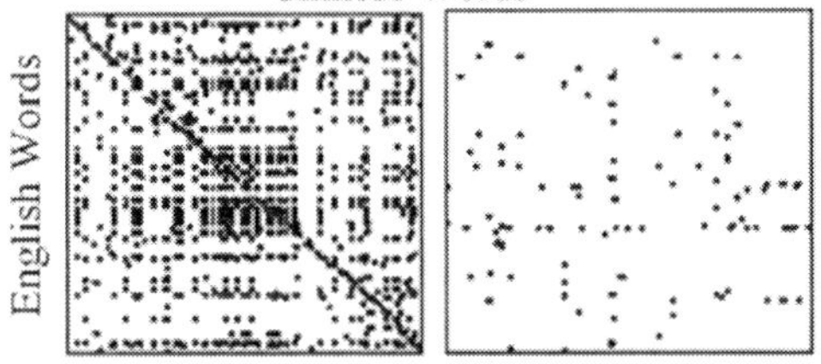

Figure 5. R^2 of Parallel and Non-Parallel Document Pairs

R^2 are normalized by the slope:

$$R^2 = R^2_{score} / Slope$$

2.4.3 Combining DTW and R^2

DTW score helps filter out non-parallel pairs and R^2 is introduced as a supplementary feature to improve the precision of extracted parallel documents.

A comparison of using these measures is shown in Table 5.

	DTW (>0.22)	R^2 (1.0E-5,1)	DTW+R^2
# Pairs	545	534	481
# Parallel	417	403	399
Precision %	76.51	75.47	82.95

Table 5. Mining Precision of DTW and R^2

2.4.4 Structural Features

The final step of verification uses structural features of the document pair candidates:

- **Language:** mined document should be in the target language
- **Absolute size:** mined documents should not have too small/large in file length
- **Size difference:** source and target documents must have similar size
- **Document type:** both documents must be content page in a website

2.5 Find One Get More

Since search engines rank target documents by various criteria, such as the popularity-based page rank, some legitimate bilingual website documents might not be found by our proposed content based method, content based approach using search engines. We propose to supplement our approach with URL matching patterns if the content based method has found several pairs of source and target documents under the same hostname.

Source	# Chinese Docs
ftchinese.com	11,009
cn.wsj.com	3,327
cn.reuters.com	8,570
forbeschina.com	6,281
fortunechina.com	593
Total	**29,780**

Table 6. Source Documents for Pure CLIR Approach

We examine the pairs found by the content based method and look for any parallel pairs coming from the same hostname or whether a pattern can be generalized from these URLs.

We apply this URL pattern to all Chinese pages under this domain.

All pairs found by both methods are subjected to pass the verification process in Section 2.4.

3 Experimental Setup

We evaluate our approach on two sets of experiments.

3.1 Baseline

As a baseline of the content base method, we directly use English words in the original Chinese document as keyword. Then, we add keywords ranked by TF-IDF to query the target document but not perform SQRS to expand query.

Finally, SQRS is used to refine each keyword to get better results.

We use both Google and Bing Search APIs to search the keyword sets. Results from different search engines are merged together by URLs. For each query, we consider eight URLs which is the default number of search engine APIs.

We generalize URL patterns (if any) from document pairs when we find some document pairs by content based method on parallel websites. By *Find One Get More*, we extract more parallel webpages that follow those URL patterns.

3.2 Parallel Document Extraction Accuracy

Source (Chinese) documents in our experiments are news from the following 5 agencies:

Parallel (bilingual) websites:

(1) Financial Times Chinese (ftchinese.com)
(2) Wall Street Journal Chinese (cn.wsj.com)

Parallel website contain both Chinese and English document under the same host and can be aligned with URL matching.

Comparable/quasi-comparable websites:

(3) Reuters China (cn.reuters.com)
(4) Forbes China (forbeschina.com)
(5) Fortune China (fortunechina.com)

Documents on quasi-comparable or comparable websites may have target documents on either the corresponding agencies' global site (e.g. cn.reuters.com and www.reuters.com) or somewhere else. Parallel documents from such websites cannot be found by URL matching.

We applied our content based approach to the above sites to find target documents and evaluate the mining precision.

The percentage of parallel documents that we can successfully find is highly dependent on the type of documents and search engine index. Calculating recall, on the other hand, is only possible for sites we already knew. For comparable or quasi-comparable sites, it is not possible to have the oracle target documents for evaluation because:

1) Some source documents may not have translation in the target language
2) Target language pages may not be indexed by search engines
3) Manual evaluation of all documents for recall calculation is not feasible

In the verification process, we discard the document pairs if:

- DTW score>0.25 (88% precision)
- R^2 score>1.0E-5
- Article size is too small
- Size of source and target too different
- URL is root (/) under hostname
- Text in wrong language

We manually evaluate the effectiveness of our method on randomly selected document pairs. Only parallel document pairs are considered as *correct*.

3.3 Parallel Sentence Extraction

In order to obtain a sentence alignment for pairs of document, we first need to extract the proper content of each page and remove the header and footers that are of little interest and are unlikely to be parallel anyway.

We first segment the documents in sentences and filter out improper ones, such as English sentence containing Chinese characters, or Chinese sentence containing roman characters only. We then use DTW again to find a continuous path in the documents and extract the longest one. The header and footer will generally not align and will be discarded; only the chunk of true alignable content will be preserved.

Using this method, we manage to find the beginning and the end of source and target content and extract it. Then discard pairs of document whose number of extracted sentences are too different. Sentence alignment is performed on the remaining documents using the Champollion ToolKit (Ma, 2006), which is already trained for Chinese-English document pairs.

Finally, we filter all the sentences using a simple word overlap score. Sentences whose lengths are too different or whose word overlap score is too low are discarded, to ensure a high precision at the end.

4 Experimental Results

4.1 Comparison of different methods

	Src doc	Doc pairs	Sent.	Improvement
i	1000	153	2483	Baseline
ii	1000	217	2907	+17.08%
iii	1000	243	3068	+23.56%

i. Direct Search of K_E
ii. Top ranked keywords without SQRS
iii. With SQRS

Table 7. Comparison of different methods

We directly search all English keywords in Chinese documents and found 153 target documents (baseline). Then we search translation of top ranked TF-IDF keywords (ii). With SQRS further improved 23.56% of output sentences comparing to baseline (Table 7). The precision in the three experiments are the same.

4.2 Parallel Document Extraction Accuracy

Among the 29,680 Chinese documents retrieved from the five news agencies, we obtained 7,253 parallel document pairs with 88% precision by content based approach alone.

In many such cases, parallel document pairs are on different websites and be found neither by URL matching nor by content-based methods that use times stamps for matching.

4.3 Find One Get More

With the *Find One Get More* approach, we increase the output of parallel documents from parallel websites. Table 8 shows that using URL matching can improve the output quantity a lot, compensating for the missing target documents with low page ranks.

Source	# of Doc	CLIR	CLIR+URL
FTChinese	11,009	2,968	9,066
WSJ	3,327	1,002	3,120
Reuters	8,570	1,911	1,911
Forbos	6,281	1,166	1,166
Fortune	593	206	206
Total	**29,780**	**7,253**	**15,469**

Table 8. Output Document Pairs of 4.2 & 4.3

For parallel bilingual websites, the pure content based method can find about 1/3 of the target documents compared to the CLIR+URL method. It shows that, however, our query expansion with relevance feedback approach has higher recall than the 18% produced by the local ranked keywords in Hong et al. (2010).

4.4 Parallel Sentence Extraction for SMT

Among the 15,469 Chinese-English document pairs, we extracted 225,374 parallel sentence pairs with mining precision of over 97% based on human evaluation on randomly selected sentence pairs . We evaluate the quality of those sentences for training machine translation with the Moses SMT engine. We compare the BLEU score obtained with a 4,097,357 sentence pairs corpus, manually aligned (baseline) and the BLEU score obtained with the same corpus, replacing 225,374 sentence pairs by the ones we extracted (CLIR). Results are presented in Table 9, they are evaluated on the NIST MT06 evaluation set.

	BLEU
Baseline	29.54
CLIR	29.88

Table 9. BLEU score obtained for SMT

These results show that our set of sentences, together with a larger parallel corpus, yield results similar to the one obtained with manually aligned sentences only.

The extracted sentences have been processed for rare word translation extraction. (Prochasson and Fung, 2011)

4.5 System Performance and Scalability

We carried out our mining experiments on workstation with 8 states of arts CPU cores. The average time taken for each source document is 30 seconds which is only bottle-necked by the usage limitation of search engine APIs.

As the TF/IDF scores are pre-trained only from the source documents, and our CLIR approach mines target document for each source document individually. Our system can be easily scaled to run in parallel on multiple servers.

5 Conclusion

In this paper, we have proposed a content based CLIR approach to search any part of the Web to find parallel documents without the limitation of URL-matched bilingual web sites. Our method transforms an input source document into a target language query set, then it makes use of search engine APIs, and a proposed query relevance feedback mechanism, and finds the target language document if it exists on the web. We propose a search query relevance score (SQRS) that checks for precision of the query keywords we use to represent the source document. Our proposed method does not require machine translation, nor does it require downloading all documents in the target language into an archive for document matching, thereby saving computational resources.

The query expansion and relevance feedback by SQRS which measures translation correctness ensures high precision in the target document found. Using a verification process, the web documents are further filtered by dynamic time warping and regression scores.

Experimental results show an 88% mining precision on the parallel documents extracted from parallel, comparable and quasi-comparable web sites.

Another experiment on extracting bilingual sentences from the mined documents shows that the sentence extraction adds another layer of verification which further improves the precision from 88% to 97%.

SMT experiments on using our mined parallel sentences, together with a larger baseline training set, to train an SMT system show comparable performances from using our data to that of using manually aligned bilingual sentences. Our system is scalable to run on multiple servers simultaneously and is linear in time to the number of input source documents. It can also be run continuously to discover and mine for newly added web documents that were not there previously. It is also extendable to mine for parallel documents in multiple target languages at the same time.

Acknowledgement

This project is partially funded by a subcontract from BBN, under the DARPA GALE project.

Reference

Sadaf Abdul-Rauf and Holger Schwenk. 2009. On the use of comparable corpora to improve SMT performance. In *Proceedings of the 12th Conference of the European Chapter of the Association for Computational Linguistics (EACL'06)*, pages 16–23.

Susumu Akamine, Yoshikiyo Kato, Daisuke Kawahara, Keiji Shinzato, Kentaro Inui, Sadao Kurohashi, and Yutaka Kidawara. 2009. Development of a large-scale web crawler and search engine infrastructure. In *Proceedings of the 3rd international Universal Communication Symposium(IUCS'09)*, pages 126–131.

Gregory Grefenstette. 1998. *Cross-Language Information Retrieval.* Kluwer Academic.

Gumwon Hong, Chi-Ho Li, Ming Zhou, and Hae-Chang Rim. 2010. An empirical study on web mining of parallel data. In *Proceedings of the 23rd International Conference on Computational Linguistics (Coling 2010)*, pages 474–482, Beijing, China, August. Coling 2010 Organizing Committee.

Rüdiger Gleim, Alexander Mehler, and Matthias Dehmer. 2006. Web corpus mining by instance of wikipedia. In *WAC '06: Proceedings of the 2nd International Workshop on Web as Corpus*, pages 67–74, Morristown, NJ, USA. Association for Computational Linguistics.

Xin Jiang, Yunhua Hu, and Hang Li. 2009. A ranking approach to keyphrase extraction. In *Proceedings of the 32nd international ACM SIGIR conference on Research and development in information retrieval*, SIGIR'09, pages 756–757, New York, NY, USA. ACM.

Xiaoyi Ma. 2006. Champollion: A robust parallel text sentence aligner. In *Proceedings of LREC-2006.*

Dragos Stefan Munteanu and Daniel Marcu. 2005. Improving machine translation performance by exploiting non-parallel corpora. *Computational Linguistics*, 31:477–504, December.

Dragos Stefan Munteanu and Daniel Marcu. 2006. Extracting parallel sub-sentential fragments from nonparallel corpora. In *Proceedings of the 21st International Conference on Computational Linguistics and the 44th annual meeting of the Association for Computational Linguistics*, ACL-44, pages 81–88, Morristown, NJ, USA. Association for Computational Linguistics.

Nie, Michel Simard, Pierre Isabelle, Richard Dur, and Universit De Montral. 1999. Cross-language information retrieval based on parallel texts and automatic mining of parallel texts from the web. In *Proceedings of the 22nd Annual International ACM SIGIR Conference on Research and Development in Information Retrieval*, pages 74–81.

Jiang Chen and Jian-Yun Nie. 2000. Parallel web text mining for cross-language information retrieval. In *Recherche d'Informations Assistée par Ordinateur (RIAO)*, pages 62–77.

Philip Resnik and Noah A. Smith. 2003. The web as a parallel corpus. *Computational Linguistics,* 29:349–380, September.

Lei Shi, Cheng Niu, Ming Zhou, and Jianfeng Gao. 2006. A dom tree alignment model for mining parallel data from the web. In *Proceedings of the 21st International Conference on Computational Linguistics and the 44th annual meeting of the Association for Computational Linguistics*, ACL-44, pages 489–496, Morristown, NJ, USA. Association for Computational Linguistics.

Jakob Uszkoreit, Jay Ponte, Ashok Popat, and Moshe Dubiner. 2010. Large Scale Parallel Document Mining for Machine Translation. In *Proceedings of the 23rd International Conference on Computational Linguistics (Coling 2010)*, pages 1101–1109, Beijing, China, August. Coling 2010 Organizing Committee.

Cheung Chi Shun and Pascale Fung. 2004. Unsupervised Learning of a Spontaneous and Colloquial Speech Lexicon in Chinese. In *International Journal of Speech Technology*, Vol. 7, No. 2, pp 173-178, Apr 2004.

Marine Carpuat, Pascale Fung, and Grace Ngai. 2006. Aligning word senses using bilingual corpora. *ACM Transactions on Asian Language and Information Processing*, 5(2):89–120.

Pascale Fung, Emmanuel Prochasson, and Simon Shi. 2010. Trillions of comparable documents, In *LREC Workshop on Building and Using Comparable Corpora*, Malta, May 2010.

Emmanuel Prochasson and Pascale Fung. 2011. Rare word translation extraction from aligned comparable documents. *The 49th Annual Meeting of the Association for Computational Linguistics (ACL'11)*, Portland, USA.

Crawling Back and Forth: Using Back and Out Links to Locate Bilingual Sites

Luciano Barbosa
AT&T Labs – Research
180 Park Ave
Florham Park, NJ 07932
lbarbosa@research.att.com

Srinivas Bangalore
AT&T Labs – Research
180 Park Ave
Florham Park, NJ 07932
srini@research.att.com

Vivek Kumar Sridhar Rangarajan
AT&T Labs – Research
180 Park Ave
Florham Park, NJ 07932
vkumar@research.att.com

Abstract

This paper presents a novel crawling strategy to locate bilingual sites. It does so by focusing on the Web graph neighborhood of these sites and exploring the patterns of the links in this region to guide its visitation policy. A sub-task in the problem of bilingual site discovery is the job of detecting bilingual sites, i.e., given a Web site, verify whether it is bilingual or not. We perform this task by combining supervised learning and language identification. Experimental results demonstrate that our crawler outperforms previous crawling approaches and produces a high-quality collection of bilingual sites, which we evaluate in the context of machine translation in the tourism and hospitality domain. The parallel text obtained using our novel crawling strategy results in a relative improvement of 22% in BLEU score (English-to-Spanish) over an out-of-domain seed translation model trained on the European parliamentary proceedings.

1 Introduction

Parallel texts are translations of the same text in different languages. Parallel text acquisition from the Web has received increased attention in the recent years, especially for machine translation (Melamed, 2001) and cross-language information retrieval (Grossman and Frieder, 2004). For many years, the European Parliament proceedings (Koehn, 2005a) and official documents of countries with multiple languages were the only widely available parallel texts. Although these are high-quality corpora, they have some limitations: (1) they tend to be domain specific (e.g., government related texts); (2) they are available in only a few languages; and (3) sometimes they are not free or there is some restriction for using them. On the other hand, Web data is free and comprises data from different languages and domains.

Previous research in the area of parallel Web data acquisition has mainly focused on the problems of document pair identification (Jiang et al., 2009; Uszkoreit et al., 2010; Munteanu and Marcu, 2005; Resnik and Smith, 2003; Melamed, 2001) and sentence alignment. Typically, document pairs are located by issuing queries to a search engine (Resnik and Smith, 2003; Hong et al., 2010). The sentences in the matched documents are then aligned using standard dynamic programming techniques. In this work, we model the problem of obtaining parallel text in two subtasks. First, locate the sites that contain bilingual data (bilingual sites). Here we assume that parallel texts are present in the same site (Chen and Nie, 2000). Second, extract parallel texts within these sites. While the latter problem of extracting of parallel text from bilingual Web sites has received a lot of attention, the former problem of automatically locating high quality parallel Web pages is still an open problem.

In this paper, we propose a crawling strategy (Olston and Najork, 2010) to discover bilingual sites on the Web. Previous work on focused crawlers (Chakrabarti et al., 1999; Diligenti et al., 2000) has been used to locate different kinds of Web sources such as Web pages in a topic (Chakrabarti et al., 2002), geographic information (Ahlers and Boll, 2009) and Web forms (Barbosa and Freire, 2007) by following outlinks. In contrast to these approaches, we explore the idea of using not only forward links but also backlinks. *Backlinks* of a page p are the links that point to p and *outlinks (forward links)* are the links that p points to. The reason for that is a single backlink page sometimes refers to many related pages, a phenomenon known as co-citation. Kumar et al. (Kumar et al., 1999) showed that co-

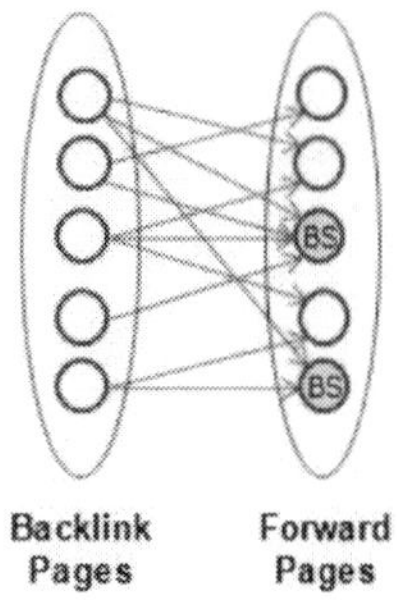

Figure 1: Bipartite graph representing the graph neighborhood visited by the crawler. Backlink pages point to pages in bilingual sites (BS) and other pages (forward pages).

citation is a common feature of Web communities and, as a result of that, Web communities are characterized by directed bipartite subgraphs. Based on that, we implemented our crawling strategy by restricting the crawler's search for bilingual sites in the bipartite graph composed by backlink pages (BPs) of the bilingual sites that were already discovered by the crawler, and pages pointed by BPs. This scheme is illustrated in Figure 1. Our assumption, therefore, is that the Web region represented by this bipartite graph is rich in bilingual sites since backlink pages typically point to multiple bilingual sites (co-citation). Finally, to focus on the most promising regions in this graph, the crawler explores the patterns in the links to guide its visitation policy.

A sub-task in the problem of bilingual site discovery is the job of detecting bilingual sites, i.e., given a Web site, verify whether it is bilingual or not. A simple approach to this task is to search the entire Web site for parallel text. However, this is computationally expensive since Web sites might contain hundreds/thousands of pages. We propose a low-cost strategy that visits very few pages in the Web site to make its prediction regarding the presence of bilingual text. Given a Web site's page, we use supervised learning to identify links on the page that are good candidates to point to parallel text within the site. Subsequently, our strategy verifies whether the pages pointed by the candidate links are in fact in the languages of interest.

The main contributions of this paper can be summarized as follows:

- A new focused crawling strategy that explores the concept of co-citation by restricting the search for targeted sources (bilingual sites in this paper) in the bipartite graph composed by the backlink pages of the targeted sources already discovered by the crawler, and the forward links pointed to by the backlink pages. The crawler uses link classifiers specialized in each set of the URLs of the pages (backward and forward pages) of the bipartite graph to focus on the most promising regions in this graph;
- A high-precision and efficient approach to detecting bilingual sites based on supervised learning and language identification.

The remainder of the paper is organized as follows. In Section 2, we present our approach to locating and detecting a bilingual site. We present experimental results in Section 3 and demonstrate the efficacy of our approach in the context of machine translation in Section 4. We review related work in Section 5 and conclude in Section 6.

2 Bilingual Site Crawler

A naive approach to collect parallel text would be to check for every pair of pages on the Web. However, this is computationally prohibitive given the scale of the Web. To make the search for parallel text more feasible, previous approaches made the assumption that parallel texts mainly occur within Web sites (Chen and Nie, 2000). Thus, the search for parallel text can be comprised of two steps. First, locate bilingual sites, and then, extract the parallel text from them. While previous approaches (Resnik and Smith, 2003; Zhang et al., 2006) have mainly focused on the latter problem of extracting sentence aligned parallel text from web, we are interested in the former problem of locating such sites.

The architecture of our crawler is presented in Figure 2. The crawler downloads a page, p and sends it to the bilingual site detector (BS Detector). If the BS Detector predicts that the site represented by p contains parallel text (see Section 2.1), the Backlink Crawler collects the backlinks of p, i.e., links that point to p, by using a search engine backlink API. The Backlink Classifier predicts the relevance of these links (see Section 2.3), and adds them to the queue that represent these links in the Frontier (backlink queue). The most promising backlink is then sent by the Frontier Scheduler to the Crawler, which downloads its content. Next, the Page Parser extracts the forward links of the backlink page and adds the most promising forward links (as identified by Forward-Link

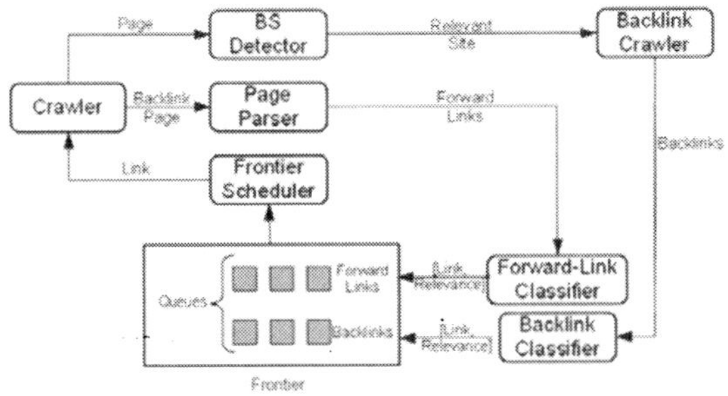

Figure 2: Architecture of our crawling strategy to locate bilingual sites.

Classifier) to the forward-link queue. The Frontier Scheduler then decides the next link to be sent to the crawler. We present the core elements of the crawler in the sections below.

2.1 Bilingual Site Detection

The performance of the bilingual site detection is essential to obtain a high-quality collection of bilingual sites. Zhang et al. (Zhang et al., 2006) perform this task by extracting the anchor text and image alt text from pages in the Web sites and match them with a pre-defined list of strings in the languages of interest. If the Web site contains at least two matched links in the different languages then it is considered as bilingual. The approach suffers from the drawback of low recall since bilingual sites that contain patterns outside the list may be missed. Another approach (Ma and Liberman, 1999) verifies the presence of bilingual text at pages of the top 3 or 4 levels of the Web site by using a language identifier. This approach can be very expensive as one might need to download a considerable portion of the Web site to make a decision.

Our solution to detecting parallel sites has some similarities with these previous approaches but tries to address their main limitations. First, instead of using a pre-defined list of patterns to detect bilingual sites, we use supervised learning to predict if a given page has links to parallel data (Link Predictor). Second, to avoid downloading a great portion of the Web site, the BS Detector only verifies whether the pages whose URLs are considered relevant by the Link Predictor are in different languages.

Link-Based Prediction. The role of the Link Predictor is to identify links that point to parallel text in a Web site. Our assumption is that pages of bilingual sites contain some common link patterns. For instance, pages in English might have a link to its version in Spanish, containing words such as "espanol" and "castellano" in its anchor, URL, etc. However, there are cases whereby the link does not provide any visible textual information to the user. Instead, only an image (usually a country flag) might represent the link. In these cases, textual information in the fields of the img html tag (e.g. alt and src) might be helpful. In order to be able to handle different types of patterns in the links, the Link Predictor uses features in 5 different contexts: tokens in the URL, anchor, around, image alt and image src. For this paper, we built the training data from non-bilingual and bilingual sites in English/Spanish. It was compiled by manually labeling 560 URLs (236 relevant and 324 non-relevant). We use probabilistic SVM (Platt, 1999) as the learning algorithm to create the Link Predictor. Probabilistic SVM is a suitable choice for this classification as it performs well on text data, and we are also interested in the class likelihood of the instances.

In essence, the Link Predictor works as a low-cost filter, its cost is associated with the link classifications which is very low. It also considerably prunes the search space for subsequent steps that are typically more expensive computationally.

Language Identification. In the second step of the bilingual site detection, the BS Detector verifies if the pages whose links were considered relevant by the Link Predictor are in the languages of interest. The motivation behind the use of language identification for our problem is, since we are interested in bilingual text, only looking at individual links of these sites might not suffice. In addition to identify the language of the pages of candidate links identified by the Link Predictor, language identification is also performed on the page that contains such links, i.e., the page that was provided as input to the BS Detector. This handles cases in which a page in a given language only contains a link to its translation in other language but not links to both versions. The language identification is then performed in all pages of that candidate list and if different pages are in the language of interest, the site is considered as bilingual. To detect the language of a given page, we use the textcat (Cavnar and Trenkle, 1994) Language Identifier.

Even though there is some cost in downloading the pages to perform this step, we show later in this section that it is only necessary to download

Min. Likelihood	Link Predictor Rec.	Prec.	F-Meas.	BS Detector Rec.	Prec.	F-Meas.	Cost (Downloads per site)
0	1	0.5	0.66	0.86	0.73	0.79	29.1
0.1	0.97	0.55	0.7	0.75	0.84	0.79	6.5
0.2	0.94	0.61	0.8	0.74	0.89	0.8	4.5
0.3	0.88	0.68	0.76	0.71	0.93	0.8	3.6
0.4	0.85	0.72	0.78	0.7	0.93	0.8	3.1
0.5	0.84	0.75	0.79	0.67	0.95	0.78	2.8
0.6	0.84	0.75	0.79	0.67	0.95	0.78	2.6
0.7	0.83	0.76	0.79	0.67	0.95	0.78	2.4
0.8	0.81	0.78	0.79	0.67	0.95	0.78	2.2
0.9	0.77	0.8	0.78	0.66	0.97	0.78	2

Table 1: Results obtained by the BS Detector (Link Predictor + language identification) and the Link Predictor only.

on average 2 to 3 pages per site, since the Link Predictor prunes the search space considerably.

Evaluation. To measure the quality of the BS Detector, we manually labeled 200 Web sites (100 positive and 100 negative) from the dmoz directory in topics related to Spanish speaking countries. A site was considered as relevant if it contained at least a pair of parallel pages. Our approach is similar to that employed by (Resnik and Smith, 2003) to label parallel text.

Since the Link Predictor outputs the likelihood of a relevant link, we varied the minimum likelihood for a link be considered as relevant. For each value, we measured its quality (precision, recall and F-measure), as well as its cost (number of downloaded pages per site in the language identification step). Table 1 presents the results for the BS Detector and the Link Predictor (first step of the BS Detector). When the minimum likelihood is 0, the language identification process checks all the links in the given pages for pairs of languages, i.e., the Link Predictor considers all the links as relevant. In this scenario, an average of 29 pages per Web site were downloaded and the recall of the BS Detector was 0.86. This implies that the language identifier was not able to detect pairs of languages in 16% of the relevant sites. As expected, the minimum likelihood is directly proportional to the precision and inversely proportional to the recall. It is interesting to note that between 0.5 and 0.8, these values do not change for the BS Detector besides the decreasing of cost. The Link Predictor shows a similar behavior. Another important observation to glean is that adding the language detection on top of the Link Predictor improves the overall precision of the bilingual site detection. For instance, when the minimum likelihood is set to 0.5, the Link Predictor's precision is 0.75 whereas that of the BS Detector is 0.95. The high precision of the BS Detector is very important to build a high-quality set of bilingual sites.

2.2 Crawling Policy

In this section, we focus our attention to our solution to locating bilingual sites on the Web. Previous work (Ma and Liberman, 1999) tries to perform this task by restricting the crawler in a top-level internet domain where it is supposed to contain a high concentration of these sites. For instance, Ma and Liberman (Ma and Liberman, 1999) focused the crawler in .de domain since they were interested in German/English language pairs. In this work, we do not restrict the crawler to any particular internet domain or topic. Our objective is to allow the crawler to perform a broad search while avoiding visits to unproductive Web regions.

We implemented this strategy by imposing the constraint that the crawler stays in the Web neighborhood graph of the bilingual sites that were previously discovered by the crawler. More specifically, the crawler explores the neighborhood graph defined by the bipartite graph composed by the backlink pages (BPs) of bilingual sites and the pages pointed by BPs (forward pages), see Figure 1. As we mentioned before, this strategy is based on the findings that Web communities are characterized by directed bipartite subgraphs (Kumar et al., 1999). Thus, our assumption is that the Web region comprised by this bipartite graph is rich in bilingual sites as backlink pages typically point to multiple bilingual sites. Finally, as we are looking for Web sites and not for single Web pages, the crawler only considers out-of-site links, i.e., it excludes from the bipartite graph links to internal pages of the sites.

The steps of our algorithm are shown in Algorithm 1. Initially, the user provides a set of seed URLs that are added to the frontier. The crawler then starts to download the links in the frontier. If the BS Detector identifies a page in a bilingual site, the backlinks to this page are collected and added back to the frontier. Backlink information can be retrieved through the "link:"

Algorithm 1 Crawling Policy

```
Input: seeds, BS_Detector
  {seeds : seeds provided by the user, BS_Detector: the Bilingual Site Detector.}
frontier = ∅
  {Create the empty frontier.}
frontier.addLinks(seeds)
  {Add the seeds to the frontier.}
repeat
  link = frontier.next()
    {Retrieve from the frontier the next link to be visited.}
  page = download(link)
    {Download the content of the page.}
  if BS_Detector.isRelevant(page) then
    backlinks = collectBacklins(page)
      {Collect the backlinks to the given page provided by a search engine API.}
    frontier.addLinks(backlinks)
      {Add the backlinks to the frontier.}
  end if
  if link.isBacklink() then
    outlinks = extractOutlinks(page)
      {Extract the outlinks of a backlink page.}
    frontier.addLinks(outlinks)
      {Add the outlinks to the frontier.}
  end if
until frontier.isEmpty()
```

API provided by search engines such as Google and Yahoo! (Bharat et al., 1998). In the next step, pages represented by the backlinks (backlink pages) are downloaded, their outlinks are extracted and added to the frontier. Notice that only the outlinks from the backlink pages are added to the frontier. The crawler does not explore outlinks of forward pages (forward pages are pages pointed by backlink pages, see Figure 1).

2.3 Forward-Link and Backlink Classifiers

Retaining the crawler in the graph neighborhood of bilingual sites (the bipartite graph) is our first attempt towards an effective search for such sites. However, there may be many links in the graph that do not lead to relevant sites. In order to identify promising URLs in the two different page sets of the bipartite graph, we employ supervised learning. For each set (backlink and forward sets), the crawler builds a classifier that outputs the relevance of a given link in that particular set. Relevant links in the forward pages' set represent URLs of bilingual sites, i.e., links that give immediate benefit, whereas relevant links in the backlink pages' set are URLs of backlink pages that contain outlinks to bilingual sites (delayed benefit).

Previous approaches for focused crawling (Chakrabarti et al., 2002; Rennie and McCallum, 1999; Barbosa and Freire, 2007) also use patterns on links to prioritize them. But instead of using link classifiers specialized in different link layers, they build a single classifier. The advantage of having multiple classifiers is that it decomposes a complex problem into simpler subproblems in which each classifier is dedicated to a subset of more homogeneous hypothesis (Gangaputra and Geman, 2006). Diligenti et al. (Diligenti et al., 2000) also proposed the use of multiple classifiers to guide the crawler. But instead of looking at link patterns, they use the content of the pages.

In summary, the Forward-Link Classifier predicts the most promising links for the forward pages, whereas the Backlink Classifier identifies the most promising links for the backlink pages. Both classifiers use as features the neighborhood of links. The link neighborhood is composed by four contextual categories: URL (without the host), host, anchor, and text around the link. Since the number of extracted features tends to be large (and most of them have very low frequency), we remove stop-words and stem the remaining words. Note that features are associated with a context. For example, if the word "hotel" appears both in the URL and anchor text of a link, it is added as a feature in both contexts. It is important to note that words in the host context have an important role, since many parallel corpus sites are in a country's internet domain, e.g., es, de, etc. In fact, as we mentioned before, some previous approaches (Ma and Liberman, 1999) restrict the crawl within these domains to collect parallel data. But instead of pre-defining a set of domains, the crawler in our work automatically identifies the most important ones during its crawling process.

As one can expect, the two classifiers perform a different role. For the Backlink Classifier, features such as "link" and "directory" in the URL obtained have high frequency in the training data. These words usually occur in the URL of pages that point to many different sites, e.g., http://www.rentaccomspain.com/links.asp. The Forward-Link Classifier is more focused on topics. Words such as "hotel", "air", "art" and "language" were some of the frequent features used by it.

The two classifiers are automatically created during the crawling process. Initially, the crawler starts with no link prioritization. After a specified number of crawled pages, a learning iteration is performed by collecting the link neighborhood of the links that point to relevant and non-relevant pages in each set. The result of this process is used as training data for the Backlink and Forward-Link classifiers. Similar to previous focused crawling approaches (Chakrabarti et al., 2002; Barbosa and Freire, 2007), we use Naive Bayes algorithm for this purpose. As a final step, the relevance of the links in the frontier are updated based on the new classifiers.

3 Crawling Experiments

In this section, we assess our crawling strategy to locate bilingual sites and compare it with other crawling approaches.

3.1 Experimental Setup

Crawling Strategies. We executed the following crawling strategies to locate bilingual sites:

- Forward Crawler (FC): The forward crawler randomly follows the forward links without any restriction;

- Focused Crawler (FocC): although our strategy does not restrict its search to a particular domain, we set up a focused crawler (Chakrabarti et al., 2002) in the travel domain for comparison. The focused crawler is composed by a page classifier that restricts the crawl to pages in the travel domain and a link classifier that guides the crawler's link visitation to avoid unproductive Web regions (see (Chakrabarti et al., 2002) for more details);

- Out-of-site Back/Forward Crawler (OBFC): The out-of-site back/forward crawler uses the crawling strategy proposed in this paper without any prioritization to the links;

- Classifier-Based Out-of-site Back/Forward Crawler (COBFC): The classifier-based out-of-site back/forward is the OBFC along with the Backlink and Forward-link classifiers to prioritize the links in the frontier. Both classifiers are created after crawling 20,000 pages.

We set up the crawlers to locate bilingual sites in English and Spanish. Each configuration collected 100,000 pages and 1,000 links were provided as seeds. These were randomly selected from the URLs available on the Open Directory Project[1] related to Spanish speaking countries.

[1]http://www.dmoz.org/

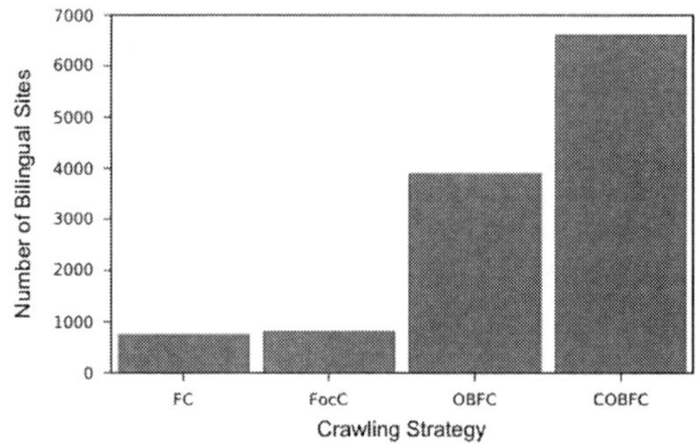

Figure 3: Total of bilingual sites collected by the crawling strategies in a crawl of 100,000 pages.

Effectiveness measure. The performance of the crawling strategies was measured by the total number of bilingual sites collected after the bilingual site detection during the crawl. The minimum likelihood used by BS Detector to consider a link as relevant was 0.8 since we are interested in obtain a high-quality collection of bilingual sites (see Section 2.1).

3.2 Assessing the Bilingual Site Crawler

In Figure 3, we present the total of bilingual sites collected by each crawling configuration after collecting 100,000 pages. Our crawling strategy, COBFC, collected the greatest number of bilingual sites (6598 sites). This result empirically confirms that our approach of restricting the crawler to the neighborhood of bilingual sites by using back and forward links, along with classifiers that prioritize these links is in fact effective for locating bilingual sites.

The comparison between the top two strategies, namely, COBFC (6598 bilingual sites) and OBFC (3894 bilingual sites) shows that: (1) the Backlink and Forward-link classifiers used to prioritize the links in the frontier improve the crawler's performance; and (2) even with no link prioritization, our strategy of restricting the search to the bipartite graph of backlink and forward pages is able to obtain good results. We can conclude from these numbers that bilingual sites are close to each other when one considers their backlinks. As we mentioned previously, this can be attributed to the fact that backlinks are typically hubs to bilingual sites.

From the experimental results, it is clear that our crawling is effective for locating bilingual sites on the Web. The main limitation, however, is that it relies on an external component (search engine) to provide backlinks. In the experiments presented in this work, the use of a search engine slowed down the crawling execution since we did not want to submit many requests to the search engine and consequently have the backlink requests halted.

A final note regarding our crawling strategy is that even though we do not restrict it to any particular topic, as the crawling process evolves, it automatically focuses on topics where there is a higher concentration of parallel data, as travel, translator sites, etc. This is different from conventional approaches that explicitly constrain the crawl based on topics.

4 Machine Translation Experiments

In this section, we exploit the parallel text obtained through our crawling strategy as augmented data in machine translation. We use a phrase-based statistical machine translation system (Koehn et al., 2007) in all the experiments.

4.1 Experimental Setup

Web data. We focus on English and Spanish as the bilingual pair of languages. We used the crawling strategy presented in the previous section to obtain a set of 20186 bilingual sites. The parallel text from these sites was mined using the technique presented in (Rangarajan et al., 2011). A total of initial 4.84M bilingual sentence pairs were obtained from this process. We used length-based and word-based filters as well as a language model to filter these initial sentence pairs. After cleanup, a total of 2,039,272 bilingual sentence pairs was obtained from the crawling data.

Development and Test Data. In order to obtain a representative reference development and test set, we manually created bilingual sentences in the hospitality and tourism domain. A bilingual speaker was given instructions to create dialogs in a variety of travel scenarios such as *making a hotel reservation, booking a taxi, checking into a hotel, calling front desk and reporting problems*, etc. A total of 49 scenarios were created that resulted in 1019 sentences, 472 of which was used for development and 547 for testing. The dialogs were created in English and then translated to Spanish. The development and test sets are not very large, mainly because creating high quality bilingual data for a particular domain is expensive. We have given due consideration to create a test set that is highly similar to the domain of operation. We are working on evaluating the performance of the crawled data on different domains as part of future work (as we translate more data through human annotations).

MT Models. We performed machine translation experiments in both directions, English-Spanish and Spanish-English. Europarl data is the only source of parallel data (English/Spanish) that we have access to, and hence it serves as the data for our baseline translation model. Although the model can be considered to be out-of-domain with respect to our test domain, its language style is more similar to our test set (spoken dialogs) in comparison with the Web data. The Europarl data comprised 1.48M bilingual sentence pairs.

The Web data translation model was trained on the sentences resulting from the Web crawler. We also used a combination of the two models that we call as combined model. The combined model uses both the phrase tables during decoding. The reordering table was also concatenated from the two models.

4.2 Results

Table 2 presents the translation performance in terms of various metrics such as BLEU (Papineni et al., 2002), METEOR (Lavie and Denkowski, 2010) and Translation Edit Rate (TER) (Snover et al., 2006). The language model was a 5 gram language model optimized on the development set based on perplexity and the translation weights of the log-linear model were learned using Minimum Error Rate Training.

While the out-of-domain model trained using Europarl data achieves a BLEU score of 20.65 on the test set (tourism and hospitality domain) for English-Spanish, the model constructed by augmenting the web crawling data to europarl data achieves a relative improvement of 22%. Similar improvements hold for Spanish-English translation. The METEOR scores reported in Table 2 were computed only for exact match (synonyms and stemmed matches were not considered). For all three objective metrics, we achieve significant improvements in translation performance. The results demonstrate the efficacy of our bilingual crawling approach for harvesting parallel text for machine translation. The bilingual crawler can be initialized with a different policy based on the test domain of interest and hence our scheme is generalizable.

Regarding the results of Europarl versus Web data alone, the reason for the lower translation

Model	Training data	English-Spanish			Spanish-English		
		BLEU	METEOR	TER	BLEU	METEOR	TER
Baseline	Europarl	20.65	16.76	71.52	25.26	41.09	64.76
	Web	16.94	14.81	79.28	23.48	39.65	66.11
	Combined	23.00	17.90	68.86	28.86	44.18	61.24

Table 2: Automatic evaluation metric scores for translation models from out-of-domain data, Web data and combined models.

quality of the web crawled data on the test set considered in the experiments is mainly due to the style of the test set. Even though the domain of the crawler is travel and hospitality, the sentences in the test set are more conversational and better matched with Europarl in terms of BLEU metric. On the other hand, the METEOR metric that accounts for the overlapping unigrams is much closer for Europarl and Web data, i.e., the vocabulary coverage is comparable.

5 Related Work

There are basically two main types of approaches to locate parallel corpora: query-based (Resnik and Smith, 2003; Resnik, 1998; Chen and Nie, 2000; Tomás et al., 2005) and crawling-based (Ma and Liberman, 1999; Chen et al., 2004).

Query-based approaches typically try to explore common patterns that occur in this kind of data by using them as search queries. For instance, STRAND (Resnik and Smith, 2003; Resnik, 1998) tries to locate candidate parallel pages by issuing queries like: (anchor:"english" OR anchor:"anglais") AND (anchor:"french" OR anchor:"francais"). Chen and Nie (Chen and Nie, 2000) used a similar principle to obtain two sets of candidate sites by issuing queries as anchor:"english version" to a search engine, and then taking the union. More recently, Hong et al. (Hong et al., 2010) proposed a method that discovers document pairs by first selecting the top words in a source language document, translating these words and issuing them as a query to a search engine. The main limitation of these previous approaches is that they only rely on the search engine results to obtain the parallel pages. And, since search engines restrict the total number of results per query and the number of requests, there is a limitation in terms of the total number of sites that can be collected. This is confirmed by the numbers presented in their experimental evaluation. For instance, Chen and Nie (Chen and Nie, 2000) reported a total of only 185 candidate sites for English-Chinese corpora.

With respect to crawling-based approaches for locating parallel text, there is not much prior work in this area. In fact, most of the research in this area is focused more on the problem of identifying the text pairs (Munteanu and Marcu, 2005; Zhang et al., 2006; Uszkoreit et al., 2010) than actually locating them. They typically use simple strategies to locate parallel text without exploring the Web link structure. For example, Ma and Liberman (Ma and Liberman, 1999) try to achieve this goal by simply restricting the crawler within in a particular internet domain whereby there might be a good chance of finding this kind of data.

6 Conclusions

This paper presents a novel focused crawling strategy to locate bilingual sites. It keeps its search in the bipartite graph composed by the backlink pages of bilingual sites (already discovered by the crawler) and the pages pointed by them. To focus on the most promising regions in this graph, the crawler explores the patterns presented in its links to guide its visitation policy. Another novelty proposed in this paper is our low-cost and high-precision strategy to detect a bilingual site. It performs this task in two steps. First, it relies on common patterns found in the internal links of these sites to compose a classifier that identifies link pages as entry points to parallel data in these sites. Second, it verifies whether these pages are in fact in the languages of interest. Our experiments showed that our crawling strategy is more effective in finding bilingual sites than the baseline approaches and that our bilingual site detection has high-precision while being efficient. We also demonstrated the efficacy of our crawling approach by performing machine translation experiments using the parallel text obtained from the bilingual sites identified by the crawler.

An interesting venue to pursue in a future work is to verify whether the crawling strategy proposed in this paper also works in other types of domains where regular focused crawling may have issues in finding the targeted Web sources.

References

D. Ahlers and S. Boll. 2009. Adaptive geospatially focused crawling. In *Proceeding of the 18th ACM conference on Information and knowledge management*, pages 445–454.

L. Barbosa and J. Freire. 2007. An adaptive crawler for locating hidden-web entry points. In *WWW*, pages 441–450.

K. Bharat, A. Broder, M. Henzinger, P. Kumar, and S. Venkatasubramanian. 1998. The connectivity server: Fast access to linkage information on the web. *Computer Networks and ISDN Systems*, 30(1-7):469–477.

W.B. Cavnar and J.M. Trenkle. 1994. N-gram-based text categorization. pages 161–175.

S. Chakrabarti, M. Berg, and B. Dom. 1999. Focused crawling: A new approach to topic-specific web resource discovery. *Computer Networks*, 31(11-16):1623–1640.

S. Chakrabarti, K. Punera, and M. Subramanyam. 2002. Accelerated focused crawling through online relevance feed back. In *WWW*, pages 148–159.

J. Chen and J.Y. Nie. 2000. Parallel web text mining for cross-language IR. In *RIAO*, volume 1, pages 62–78.

J. Chen, R. Chau, and C.H. Yeh. 2004. Discovering parallel text from the World Wide Web. In *workshop on Australasian information security, Data Mining and Web Intelligence, and Software Internationalisation*, pages 161–165.

M. Diligenti, F. Coetzee, S. Lawrence, C. Lee Giles, and M. Gori. 2000. Focused Crawling Using Context Graphs. In *VLDB*, pages 527–534.

S. Gangaputra and D. Geman. 2006. A design principle for coarse-to-fine classification. In *Computer Vision and Pattern Recognition*, volume 2, pages 1877–1884.

D.A. Grossman and O. Frieder. 2004. *Information retrieval: Algorithms and heuristics*. Kluwer Academic Pub.

G. Hong, C. Li, M. Zhou, and H. Rim. 2010. An empirical study on web mining of parallel data. In *Proceedings of the 23rd International Conference on Computational Linguistics*, COLING '10, pages 474–482, Stroudsburg, PA, USA. Association for Computational Linguistics.

L. Jiang, S. Yang, M. Zhou, X. Liu, and Q. Zhu. 2009. Mining bilingual data from the web with adaptively learnt patterns. In *Proceedings of the Joint Conference of the 47th Annual Meeting of the ACL*, pages 870–878.

P. Koehn, H. Hoang, A. Birch, C. Callison-Burch, M. Federico, N. Bertoldi, B. Cowan, W. Shen, C. Moran, R. Zens, C. Dyer, O. Bojar, A. Constantin, and E. Herbst. 2007. Moses: open source toolkit for statistical machine translation. In *Proceedings of ACL*, pages 177–180.

P. Koehn. 2005a. Europarl: A parallel corpus for statistical machine translation. In *MT summit*, volume 5.

P. Koehn. 2005b. Europarl: A parallel corpus for statistical machine translation. In *MT Summit*.

R. Kumar, P. Raghavan, S. Rajagopalan, and A. Tomkins. 1999. Trawling the Web for emerging cyber-communities. *Computer networks*, 31(11-16):1481–1493.

A. Lavie and M. Denkowski. 2010. The METEOR metric for automatic evaluation of machine translation. *Machine Translation*.

X. Ma and M. Liberman. 1999. Bits: A method for bilingual text search over the web. In *Machine Translation Summit VII*.

I.D. Melamed. 2001. *Empirical methods for exploiting parallel texts*. MIT Press.

D. S. Munteanu and D. Marcu. 2005. Improving machine translation performance by exploiting non-parallel corpora. *Comput. Linguist.*, 31:477–504, December.

C. Olston and M. Najork. 2010. Web Crawling. *Information Retrieval*, 4(3):175–246.

K. Papineni, S. Roukos, T. Ward, and W.-J. Zhu. 2002. BLEU: a method for automatic evaluation of machine translation. In *Proceedings of ACL*.

J. C. Platt. 1999. Probabilistic outputs for support vector machines and comparisons to regularized likelihood methods. pages 61–74.

V. K. S. Rangarajan, L. Barbosa, and S. Bangalore. 2011. A Scalable Approach for Building a Parallel Corpus from the Web. In *Proceedings of 12th Annual Conference of the International Speech Communication Association*.

J. Rennie and A. McCallum. 1999. Using Reinforcement Learning to Spider the Web Efficiently. In *ICML*, pages 335–343.

P. Resnik and N.A. Smith. 2003. The web as a parallel corpus. *Computational Linguistics*, 29(3):349–380.

P. Resnik. 1998. Parallel strands: A preliminary investigation into mining the web for bilingual text. *Machine Translation and the Information Soup*, pages 72–82.

Matthew Snover, Bonnie Dorr, Richard Schwartz, Linnea Micciulla, and John Makhoul. 2006. A study of translation edit rate with targeted human annotation. In *Proceedings of AMTA*.

J. Tomás, E. Sánchez-Villamil, L. Lloret, and F. Casacuberta. 2005. WebMining: An unsupervised parallel corpora web retrieval system. In *Proceedings from the Corpus Linguistics Conference*.

J. Uszkoreit, J. M. Ponte, A. C. Popat, and M. Dubiner. 2010. Large scale parallel document mining for machine translation. In *Proceedings of the 23rd International Conference on Computational Linguistics*, COLING '10, pages 1101–1109, Stroudsburg, PA, USA. Association for Computational Linguistics.

Y. Zhang, K. Wu, J. Gao, and P. Vines. 2006. Automatic Acquisition of Chinese–English Parallel Corpus from the Web. *Advances in Information Retrieval*, pages 420–431.

Grammar Induction from Text Using Small Syntactic Prototypes

Prachya Boonkwan[†,‡]
p.boonkwan@sms.ed.ac.uk
prachya.boonkwan@nectec.or.th

Mark Steedman[†]
steedman@inf.ed.ac.uk

† School of Informatics
University of Edinburgh
10 Crichton Street
Edinburgh EH8 9AB, UK

‡ National Electronics
and Computer Technology Center
112 Phaholyothin Road
Pathumthani 12120, Thailand

Abstract

We present an efficient technique to incorporate a small number of cross-linguistic parameter settings defining default word orders to otherwise unsupervised grammar induction. A syntactic prototype, represented by the integrated model between Categorial Grammar and dependency structure, generated from the language parameters, is used to prune the search space. We also propose heuristics which prefer less complex syntactic categories to more complex ones in parse decoding. The system reduces errors generated by the state-of-the-art baselines for WSJ10 (1% error reduction of F1 score for the model trained on Sections 2–22 and tested on Section 23), Chinese10 (26% error reduction of F1), German10 (9% error reduction of F1), and Japanese10 (8% error reduction of F1), and is not significantly different from the baseline for Czech10.

1 Introduction

Unsupervised grammar induction has gained general interest for several decades, offering the possibility of building practical syntactic parsers by reducing the labor of constructing a treebank from scratch. One approach is to exploit the Inside/Outside Algorithm (Baker, 1979; Carroll and Charniak, 1992), a variation of EM algorithm for PCFG, to estimate the parameters of the parser's language models. More recent advances in this approach are the constituent-context model (CCM) (Klein and Manning, 2001; Klein and Manning, 2002), dependency model with valence (DMV) based on Collin's head dependency model (1999), and the CCM+DMV mixture (Klein and Manning, 2004; Klein, 2005). Several search techniques and models have been added to CCM+DMV for dealing with local optima and data sparsity (Smith, 2006; Cohen et al., 2008; Headden III et al., 2009). Spitkovsky et al. (2010) proposed a training strategy where the model fully trained on shorter sentences and roughly trained on longer sentences tend to outperform the model fully trained on the entire dataset. Recently, Gillenwater et al. (2010) proposed the use of posterior regularization in EM in which the posterior distribution of parent-child POS tags are regulated to an expected distribution.

However, purely unsupervised learning still does not perform well because the parameter estimation can be misled by unexpected frequent cooccurrence. A common example of it is the collocation of a verb (VBZ) and a determiner (DT) in a verb phrase. This collocation results in incorrect trees such as ((VBZ DT) NN).

To avoid this problem, the use of syntactic prototypes has been proposed. Instead of enumerating every possibility, syntactic structures are cautiously constructed regarding some syntactic constraints. Haghighi and Klein (2006) proposed the use of bracketing rules extracted from WSJ10 in CCM and considerably improved accuracy. Druck et al. (2009) used dependency formation rules handcrafted by linguists to improve the accuracy of DMV. Snyder et al. (2009) do semi-supervised grammar induction from bilingual text with the help of a supervised parser on one side and word alignment. However, bilingual corpora are not available for many language pairs. Naseem et al. (2010) proposed the use of cross-linguistic knowledge represented as a set of allowable head-dependent pairs. However, this method still requires provision of language-specific rules to boost accuracy. If language-specific rules are necessary to achieve accuracy, we need more efficient ways to encode this knowledge.

This paper proposes a method for inducing language-specific word order regularities capturing cross-linguistically frequent constructions to constrain unsupervised grammar induction. We use the notion of syntactic prototype, a set of grammar rules automatically generated for such constructions. Categorial Dependency Grammar (CDG), which combines rules of constituency and dependency, is used to represent syntactic prototypes. We also propose a novel category penalty score for use in decoding, which defines the most probable parse according to a preference for less complex categories.

The paper is organized as follows. §2 details the method of encoding linguistic prior knowledge as a syntactic prototype. §3 explains an overview of our approach. §4 shows experiment results and discusses the errors. We conclude in §5.

2 Syntactic Prototypes

A *syntactic prototype* is a set of grammar rules representing default language parameters (such as word order for the most cross-linguistically frequent linguistic constructions, following Naseem et al. (2010)'s notion of cross-linguistic knowledge. This section shows how CDG rules are derived from a set of word order constraints.

2.1 Categorial Dependency Grammar

Categorial Dependency Grammar (CDG) is an extension of pure Categorial Grammar (CG) (Ajdukiewicz, 1935; Bar-Hillel, 1953) used for defining language-specific prototypes to be discovered. Its syntactic derivations define constituency and dependency in parallel. In CG, each constituent is assigned one or more syntactic categories, defined as an atomic category or a function category. For example, the proper name 'John' is assigned the atomic category np. If X and Y are categories of either kind, then X/Y and $X\backslash Y$ are function categories that map constituents of type Y respectively on the right and on the left into those of type X. For example, the intransitive verb 'walks' is assigned the function $S\backslash NP$.

We extended CG construct dependency structure alongside the syntactic derivation by encoding the direction of dependency in slashes. Using the head-outward notation for dependency of (Collins, 1999), the slash is subscripted $<$ ($>$) if the corresponding dependency is to be linked from the head on the right to its dependent on the left (the head on the left to its dependent on the right). For example, an English adjective (e.g. 'big') can be assigned the category $np/_{>}np$, while a transitive verb can be assigned $s\backslash_{>}np/_{<}np$. CDG differs from PF-CCG (Koller and Kuhlmann, 2009) in that dependency direction is specified independently from the order of function and argument, while theirs is determined by slash directionality. For them such an adjective has the implicit category $np/_{>}np$ and acts as the head of the noun phrase. The derivation rules for context-free CDG are listed below:

$$\begin{array}{llcl} X/_{<}Y : d_1 & Y : d_2 & \Rightarrow & X : h(d_1) \rightarrow h(d_2) \\ X/_{>}Y : d_1 & Y : d_2 & \Rightarrow & X : h(d_1) \leftarrow h(d_2) \\ Y : d_1 & X\backslash_{<}Y : d_2 & \Rightarrow & X : h(d_1) \rightarrow h(d_2) \\ Y : d_1 & X\backslash_{>}Y : d_2 & \Rightarrow & X : h(d_1) \leftarrow h(d_2) \end{array} \quad (1)$$

where the notations $h(d_1) \rightarrow h(d_2)$ and $h(d_1) \leftarrow h(d_2)$ mean a dependency linking from the head of the dependency structure d_1 to the head of d_2, and that linking from the head of d_2 to the head of d_1, respectively. Let us denote a constituent type with $C : w$, where C is a syntactic category and w is the head word of the constituent.

Given the CDG in (2), we obtain the syntactic derivation of the string 'John eats delicious sandwiches' in Figure 1.

$$\begin{array}{rcl} \text{John, sandwiches} & \vdash & np \\ \text{delicious} & \vdash & np/_{>}np \\ \text{eats} & \vdash & s\backslash_{>}np/_{<}np \end{array} \quad (2)$$

Figure 1(a) shows dependency-driven derivation, in which the heads of constituents are propagated. Figure 1(b) reflects the formation of the dependency structure corresponding to the dependency-driven derivation.

The attraction of using CDG for grammar induction is the integration of the constituent model and the dependency model. As shown in figure 1, the syntactic derivation defines the dependency structure, because we can directly construct a dependency structure from any head-driven syntactic derivations using the annotated directions. CDG can boost the accuracy of grammar induction by modeling rules of both constituent formation and dependency. However, the search space would become impossibly large if we had to enumerate all possible syntactic categories, including all possible arguments and dependency direction. This danger can be avoided by using small amounts of hand-crafted prior linguistic knowledge.

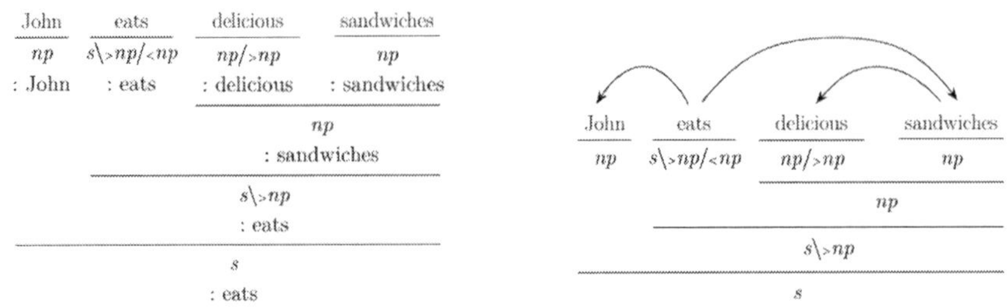

(a) Dependency-driven derivation.

(b) Equivalent dependency structure.

Figure 1: Syntactic derivation of 'John ate delicious sandwiches' based on CDG. Each constituent type is denoted by $C : w$, where C is a syntactic category and w is the head word, such as $s\backslash_{>}np/_{<}np$: eats.

However, a simple parametric syntactic prototype will give rise to parsing failures when faced with parametrically exceptional items, which occur in most if not all languages. We allow for such exceptions to be accommodated by defining an additional wildcard category $\star$ which combines with any syntactic category to yield the wildcard itself, according to the following additional combinatory rules:

$$\begin{aligned} \star : d_1 \quad X : d_2 \quad &\Rightarrow \quad \{\star : h(d_1) \leftarrow h(d_2), \\ &\qquad \star : h(d_1) \rightarrow h(d_2)\} \\ X : d_1 \quad \star : d_2 \quad &\Rightarrow \quad \{\star : h(d_1) \leftarrow h(d_2), \\ &\qquad \star : h(d_1) \rightarrow h(d_2)\} \end{aligned} \tag{3}$$

The wildcard is assigned to unknown words and large irreducible constituents so as to allow complete parses of otherwise unparsable sentences. As shown in (3), each wildcard derivation generates two possible dependency structures; i.e. d_1 and d_2 can be the head of a phrase. The wildcard will be revisited in §3.1.

2.2 Language Parameterization

We generate the CDG for each language automatically from language parameters. To facilitate this process, we have devised a questionnaire consisting of 30 questions concerning word orders for constructions that occur in most languages. Sorted by their importance, the questions can be grouped into the following categories:

1. The orders of subject, verb, direct object, and optional indirect object (1 question)
2. The argument orders of subject- and object-control verbs (2 questions)
3. The orders of adjectives, adverbs, and auxiliary verbs (4 questions)
4. The use of cardinal numbers and noun classifiers (2 questions)
5. The argument orders of adpositions, nominal modifiers, adverbials, possessive markers, relative pronouns, and subordinate conjunctions. (7 questions)
6. The orders of gerunds, infinitive markers, nominalizers, and sentential modifiers (6 questions)
7. The orders of particles, the existence of a copula, the usages of gerunds, the order of negative markers, the use of dative shifts, and the omission of discourse-given subject and object (8 questions)

These language parameters are used to automatically generate a CDG representing a syntactic prototype including language-specific types of cross-linguistically frequent categories[1] will be generated. For example, if a language has the word order SVIO, the syntactic category $s\backslash_{>}np$, $s\backslash_{>}np/_{<}np$, and $s\backslash_{>}np/_{<}np/_{<}np$ are generated and assigned by default to intransitive, transitive, and ditransitive verbs, respectively. Each slash in all syntactic categories is assigned with dependency directions according to Collins (1999)'s head percolation heuristics. All questions are optional; i.e. if any of the questions are left blank, all possible categories for that question will be generated.

Once the cross-linguistic category classes are generated, we then map them to the POS tags in a particular corpus. This part is an engineering task where the mapping should be best fitted to the

[1]E.g. intransitive verb, transitive verb, ditransitive verb, subject- and object-control verb, adjective, adverb, preposition, relative pronoun, gerund, copula, subordinate conjunction, noun classifier, infinitive marker, cardinal number, etc.

corpus. However, we will show in the experiment section that the preparation process for syntactic prototypes is quantifiable and reasonable in comparison to the improvement in accuracy attained.

3 Grammar Induction

3.1 Structure Enumeration

The first step in grammar induction is to enumerate all possible parses for each sentence. We use a table mapping from POS tags to language-specific categories to define the lexicon, and build a parse chart for each sentence with CKY Algorithm. A packed chart is used for both speed and space compactness. We apply a right-branching preference to eliminate spurious ambiguity caused by coordination and nominal compounding. In the event of a sentence yielding no parse using that lexicon, we assign the wildcard category '$\star$' to all unknown words and maximal irreducible constituents, and reparse the sentence.

3.2 Parsing Model

We extend the probabilistic context-free grammar with role-emission probabilities, defined as the product of the probability of each daughter category performing as a head or a dependent in a derivation. This model was motivated by Collins (1999)'s head-outward dependency model and Hockenmaier (2003)'s generative model for parsing CCG. Given a CDG G, we define the probability of a tree t having the constituent type $C : w$ by:

$$P(t|s,G) = \frac{1}{Z} \prod_{\substack{C:w\rightarrow\alpha \\ \in R(t)-L(t)}} \pi_{\text{exp}}(\alpha|C:w,G) \times \pi_{\text{head}}(H:w|G) \times \pi_{\text{dep}}(D:w'|G) \times \prod_{C:w\in N(t)} \pi_{\text{HE}}(w|C,G)^{\#_t(C:w)} \quad (4)$$

where Z is a normalization constant and each production α contains $H : w$ and $D : w'$, and $H : w$ and $D : w'$ are the head and the dependent, respectively. There are four types of parameters as follows.

1. $\pi_{\text{exp}}(\alpha|C : w, G)$: probability of the type $C : w$ generating a production α.

2. $\pi_{\text{head}}(C : w|G)$: probability of the type $C : w$ performing as a head.

$$\pi_{\text{head}}(C:w|G) = \frac{\sum_{C:w'} \#(C:w' \rightarrow \alpha_{\text{head}}^{C:w})}{\sum_{C':w'} \#(C':w' \rightarrow \alpha^{C:w})} \quad (5)$$

3. $\pi_{\text{dep}}(C : w|G)$: probability of the type $C : w$ performing as a dependent.

$$\pi_{\text{dep}}(C:w|G) = \frac{\sum_{C':w'} \#(C':w' \rightarrow \alpha_{\text{dep}}^{C:w})}{\sum_{C':w'} \#(C':w' \rightarrow \alpha^{C:w})} \quad (6)$$

4. $\pi_{\text{HE}}(w|C, G)$: probability of a category C generating the head w.

$$\pi_{\text{HE}}(w|C,G) = \frac{\sum_{t\in Q} \#_t(C:w)}{\sum_{t\in Q}\sum_{w'} \#_t(C:w')} \quad (7)$$

where $\alpha^{C:w}$ is a production that contains $C : w$, and $\alpha_{\text{head}}^{C:w}$ and $\alpha_{\text{dep}}^{C:w}$ have $C : w$ as the head and the dependent, respectively. $\#_t(C : w)$ is the frequency count of the category $C : w$ in the tree t. $N(t)$ is the set of all nonterminal nodes.

3.3 Parameter Estimation

Learning is achieved using the Variational Bayesian EM Algorithm (VB-EM) (Attias, 2000; Ghahramani and Beal, 2000) to estimate the parameters $\pi_{\text{exp}}, \pi_{\text{head}}, \pi_{\text{dep}}$, and π_{HE}. We followed the approach of Kurihara and Sato (2006) for training PCFGs with the VB-EM. This approach places Dirichlet priors over the multinomial grammar rule distributions. We set the Dirichlet hyperparameters to 1.0 for all rules containing the wildcard category and 5.0 for all others. In all other regards, we followed Kurihara and Sato (2006). The VB-EM algorithm iterates two processes of expectation calculation and parameter maximization. It is favored for the present purpose because it is less data-overfitting than the standard Inside/Outside Algorithm regarding its free-energy criteria for model selection. We calculate expected counts using Dynamic Programming (Baker, 1979; Lari and Young, 1990).

To further avoid the data over-fitting issue, we smoothed the probability of each substructure with the additive smoothing technique (Lidstone, 1920; Johnson, 1932; Jeffreys, 1948). An approximated parameter $\hat{\pi}(\tau)$ is calculated by

$$\hat{\pi}(\tau) = \frac{\pi(\tau)+\epsilon}{1+\epsilon} \quad (8)$$

where ϵ is a small constant value. In our experiments, we chose $\epsilon = 10^{-25}$.

3.4 Decoding with Category Penalty

By using prototypical syntactic categories in derivation, the system can be misled by complex categories. A parse containing more complex categories is preferred to one containing less complex categories, because both simple and complex syntactic categories have the same chance of occurrence in parse enumeration. When learning the parameters, rules containing complex categories tend to have relatively excessive probability, as opposed to the Zipfian distribution of syntactic categories in which less complex categories are more frequently found in CCGbank. We therefore introduce a *category penalty* score.

The category penalty score is motivated by the observation that, in practical use of language, simpler categories tend to be used more frequently than the more complex ones. The penalty score $v(c)$ of the category c is defined as follows:

$$v(c) \quad = \quad k^{S(c)} \tag{9}$$

where $S(c)$ is the count of all forward and backward slashes in c and k is the penalty constant.

We weight each tree by the product of the penalty scores of the syntactic category on each node; i.e.

$$P(t|s,G) \quad = \quad \begin{cases} v(A) \cdot \pi(A \rightarrow w) & \text{lexicon} \\ v(A) \cdot \pi(A \rightarrow \alpha) & \text{branching} \\ \cdot \prod_{i=1}^{|\alpha|} P(t_i|s,G) & \end{cases} \tag{10}$$

We use Viterbi decoding to find the most probable parse from a packed chart.

4 Experiments and Discussion

4.1 Datasets and Accuracy Metrics

In order to evaluate the method in comparison to the state of the art, we chose WSJ10, the standard collection of trees from WSJ part of PTB (Marcus et al., 1993) whose sentence length does not exceed ten words after taking out punctuation marks and empty elements. In stead of surface forms, we used a set of POS sequences taken from all WSJ10's trees to avoid the data sparsity issue. We converted the Penn Treebank into dependency structures with Collins (1999)'s head percolation heuristics. Following the literature, we trained the system with sections 2–22 and evaluated the resultant model on section 23.

For multilingual experiments, we made use of dependency corpora from the 2006 CoNLL X Shared Task (Buchholz and Marsi, 2006). Shown in Table 1, Chinese (Keh-Liann and Hsieh, 2004),

Table 1: Sizes and granularity of POS of multilingual corpora

Languages	Sentences	POS Tags
WSJ10	7,422	36
Chinese10	52,424	28
Czech10	27,375	1,149
German10	13,473	51
Japanese10	12,884	77

Czech (Bohomovà et al., 2001), German (Brants et al., 2002), and Japanese (Kawata and Bartels, 2000) were chosen for the sake of language typology variety. We also chose sentences whose length does not exceed ten words after taking out punctuation marks. As a free-word-ordered, inflectional language, the Czech dataset was particularly prepared by augmenting the POS tags with inflectional information, resulting in significantly much more granularity. However, Czech's syntactic prototype does not make use of such syntactic information to restrain the search space.

We measured the capability of our system by two metrics: directed dependency accuracy, and undirected dependency accuracy (Klein, 2005). For directed dependency accuracy, we count a directed dependency of a word pair to be correct if it exists in the gold standard. For undirected dependency accuracy, we neglect the direction of the dependency. All accuracy numbers are reported in terms of precision, recall, and F1 scores.

4.2 Construction of Syntactic Prototypes

In order to construct syntactic prototypes for each language, we conduct an interview with a non-linguist native speaker. We ask him/her each question in the questionnaire mentioned in §2.2 by giving them a sample sentence and letting them build up the corresponding sentence in their language. We then ask questions to elicit word alignment and analyze the answers. Normally it takes up to two hours per previously unseen language to complete the questionnaire.

We then study the manual of the treebank's POS tags and mapped each to one or more language-specific category classes. Normally this process takes around four to six hours to thoroughly scrutinize the usage of each POS tag and assign them to appropriate classes. It therefore takes six to ten hours to build a syntactic prototype for each language.

4.3 Results

This section presents results of English and multilingual experiments using syntactic prototypes as a guide to grammar induction.

4.3.1 Experiments on English

Table 2 shows experiment results of English grammar induction on WSJ10. In the beginning, we compared the produced trees against the gold standard produced from Collins's parser. We trained the system with Sections 2–22 of WSJ10 and tested it on Section 23. In decoding, we set the category penalty constant to 10^{-15}. The F1 score outperforms the baseline set by (Naseem et al., 2010). To exhibit the stability of the approach, we also ran ten-fold cross validation on English; i.e. we divided WSJ10 into ten parts and, for each fold, we chose nine parts for as a training set and the other one as a test set. We attained higher F1 score, as expected for cross-validation, which effectively tests on the development set.

4.3.2 Effects of Numbers of Constraints and Category Penalties

Figure 2 shows the effects of numbers of constraints towards directed and undirected F1 scores. We varied the number of constraints in English syntactic prototypes. The category class 4 (the usages of cardinal numbers and noun classifiers) was neglected, because we can treat cardinal numbers as adjectives or nouns and there are no true noun classifiers in English. Therefore there are 28 constraints in total for English. We again trained on Sections 2–22 of WSJ10 and tested on Section 23. In decoding, we set the category penalty constant to 10^{-15}. We then evaluated the accuracy against the gold standard produced by Collins's parser.

As we increased the number of constraints in syntactic prototypes, we found that both directed and undirected F1 scores increase and start to saturate after the first 20 rules. In keeping with the Zipfian distribution, the first 20 rules cover frequent linguistic phenomena. When we pruned the search space with linguistic constraints, the directed accuracy starts to approach the undirected accuracy. We also note that errors generated by the system reflect the same attachment ambiguity errors as supervised parsing.

Figure 3 shows the effects of category penalty constants on accuracy. We again trained on Sections 2–22 of WSJ10 and tested on Section 23. We then evaluated the accuracy against the gold standard produced by Collins's parser. We notice that both accuracy scores saturate at the penalty constant of 10^{-15} and slightly decay afterwards.

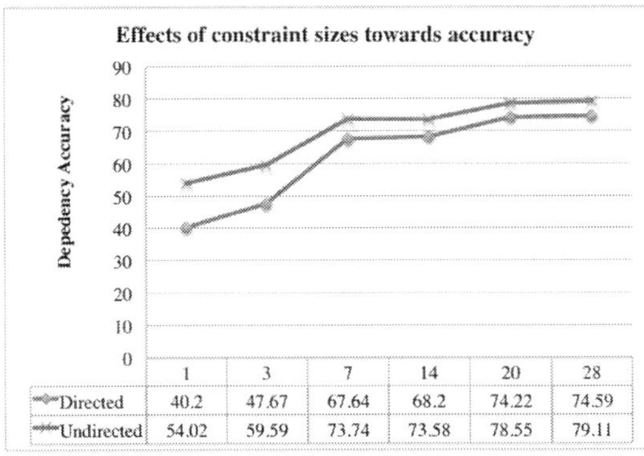

	1	3	7	14	20	28
Directed	40.2	47.67	67.64	68.2	74.22	74.59
Undirected	54.02	59.59	73.74	73.58	78.55	79.11

Figure 2: Effects of numbers of constraints on the directed and undirected dependency accuracy. The category penalty constant is fixed at 10^{-15}.

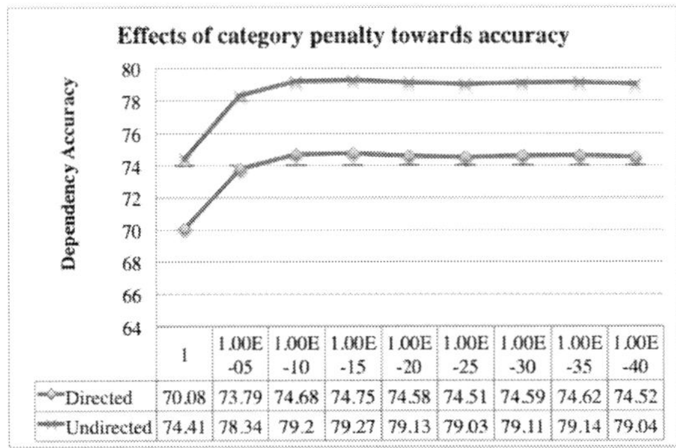

	1	1.00E-05	1.00E-10	1.00E-15	1.00E-20	1.00E-25	1.00E-30	1.00E-35	1.00E-40
Directed	70.08	73.79	74.68	74.75	74.58	74.51	74.59	74.62	74.52
Undirected	74.41	78.34	79.2	79.27	79.13	79.03	79.11	79.14	79.04

Figure 3: Effects of category penalty on the directed and undirected dependency accuracy.

4.3.3 Multilingual Experiments

We also conducted multilingual experiments on Chinese, Czech, German, and Japanese to show the stability of the approach. We ran ten-fold cross validation on each language and calculated the average F1 scores. Our baseline systems are as follows: (Naseem et al., 2010) for English, (Snyder et al., 2009) for Chinese, and (Gillenwater et al., 2010) for Czech, German, and Japanese. In Table 3, our system significantly outperforms almost all the baselines, except in the Czech experiment. We believe that the under-performance of our system on Czech is caused by the data sparsity issue. Designed based on rather fixed word ordered languages, the syntactic prototype needs to generate almost all possible syntactic categories to capture Czech's free word orderedness. Although its POS

Table 2: Undirected and directed dependency accuracy of grammar induction on English Penn Treebank. The baseline for English is (Naseem et al., 2010).

	Undirected			Directed			Baseline
	Precision	Recall	F1	Precision	Recall	F1	Directed F1
WSJ10 (Sect. 23)	79.24	79.29	79.27	74.72	74.77	**74.75**	73.80
WSJ10 (10X)	79.59	79.65	79.62	75.44	75.50	75.47	—

tags are grouped to easily map to cross-linguistic category classes, each class still contains a lot of syntactic categories. Because we do not use inflectional information in restraining the search space, the data sparsity becomes significant in Czech and therefore deteriorates the accuracy.

4.4 Error Analysis

We counted erroneous dependency pairs generated in the English experiment (10X) in §4.3.1, and we classified errors into two types: over-generation and under-generation. From Table 4, we can notice that the majority of errors are caused by adverbial and prepositional attachment (e.g. RB > VB, CD < IN, and NN < IN), and NP structural ambiguity (e.g. NN > NNP, DT > NN, and NNP > NNP).[2] These errors are common in supervised parsing. There is also under-generation of adverbial preposition phrases. We believe that the category penalty score accounts for this issue, resulting in the NP-modifying preposition (such as $np\backslash_{<}np/_{>}np$) being preferred to the adverbial one (such as $s\backslash_{>}np\backslash_{<}(s\backslash_{>}np)/_{<}np$).

5 Conclusion

We have demonstrated an efficient approach to grammar induction using linguistic prior knowledge encoded as a prototype or lexical schema. This prior knowledge was used to capture frequent linguistic phenomena. To integrate the strength of constituent and dependency models, Categorial Dependency Grammar was used as the backbone formalism. We also proposed a category penalty score preferring less complex categories, based on the observation of the Zipfian distribution of category types in CCGbank.

Syntactic prototypes can capture the most frequent constructions and improve accuracy on almost all of the selected languages. We found that dependency accuracy correlates with the Zipfian distribution as the number of constraints increases, as the increase in accuracy saturates after the first 20 rules. Error analysis suggests that the main sources of error are in adverbial and prepositional attachment, and NP structural ambiguity, which are also problematic for supervised parsing.

[2]Similar to the dependency directions in §2.1, the notations < and > are pointers to the syntactic head of the phrase. For example, DT > NN means that NN is the head and DT is its dependent.

Table 4: Top-10 over-generation and under-generation in the English experiment (10X) when compared against Collins's gold standard

Over-generation		Under-generation	
Errors	Counts	Errors	Counts
RB > VB	402	VBD < IN	364
CD < IN	200	DT > NN	331
NN < IN	197	VBD < TO	283
RB > VBN	188	VBD < RB	275
NN < TO	181	VBZ < RB	244
NNP > CD	180	IN < NN	219
MD > VB	166	JJ > NN	203
NNS < IN	149	MD < RB	194
NNP > NN	145	MD < VB	185
NN > NNP	141	NNP > NNP	179

Future work remains as follows. First, we are looking forward to improving the capability of our syntactic prototype to also handle free word ordered languages by generating syntactic categories with more flexible combination and restraining the search space with inflectional information. Second, we plan to experiment on grammar induction from untagged words by decomposing the model into tagging and parsing subproblems (Ganchev et al., 2009; Rush et al., 2010; Auli and Lopez, 2011). Third and finally, we will experiment on longer sentences to show the scalability of our approach in dealing with larger data.

Acknowledgement

We would like to thank Tom Kwiatkowski, Michael Auli, Christos Christodoulopoulos, Alexandra Birch, Mark Granroth-Wilding, and

Table 3: Undirected and directed dependency accuracy of grammar induction for English, Chinese, Czech, German, and Japanese. Our baseline systems are as follows: †(Naseem et al., 2010) for English, ‡(Snyder et al., 2009) for Chinese, and *(Gillenwater et al., 2010) for Czech, German, and Japanese.

	Undirected			**Directed**			**Baseline**
	Precision	**Recall**	**F1**	**Precision**	**Recall**	**F1**	**directed F1**
WSJ10 (10X)	79.59	79.65	79.62	75.44	75.50	**75.47**	73.80†
Chinese10 (10X)	68.80	68.88	68.84	62.21	62.29	**62.25**	35.77‡
Czech10 (10X)	59.04	61.94	60.46	53.27	55.88	54.54	**54.70***
German10 (10X)	65.13	65.20	65.17	56.68	56.74	**56.71**	47.40*
Japanese10 (10X)	75.65	78.97	77.27	67.11	70.05	**68.55**	60.80*

Emily Thomforde (University of Edinburgh), Adam Lopez (Johns Hopkins University), and Michael Collins (Columbia University) for useful comments and discussion related to this work, and the three anonymous reviewers for their useful feedback. This research was funded by the Royal Thai Government Scholarship to Prachya Boonkwan and EU ERC Advanced Fellowship 249520 GRAMPLUS to Mark Steedman.

References

Kazimierz Ajdukiewicz. 1935. Die Syntaktische Konnexität. *Polish Logic*, pages 207–231.

Hagai Attias. 2000. A variational Bayesian framework for graphical models. In *Advances in Neural Information Processing Systems (NIPS 2000)*.

Michael Auli and Adam Lopez. 2011. A comparison of loopy belief propagation and dual decomposition for integrated CCG supertagging and parsing. In *Proceedings of ACL-2011*, June.

J. K. Baker. 1979. Trainable grammars for speech recognition. In D. H. Klatt and J. J. Wolf, editors, *Speech Communication Papers for the 97th Meeting of the Acoustical Society of America*, pages 547–550.

Yehoshua Bar-Hillel. 1953. A Quasi-Arithmetical Notation for Syntactic Description. *Language*, 29:47–58.

A. Bohomovà, J. Hajic, E. Hajicova, and B. Hladka. 2001. The Prague dependency treebank: Three-level annotation scenario. In Anne Abeillé, editor, *Treebanks: Building and Using Syntactically Annotated Corpora*.

T. Brants, S. Dipper, S. Hansen, W. Lezius, and G. Smith. 2002. The TIGER Treebank. In *Proceedings Workshop on Treebanks and Linguistic Theories*.

Sabine Buchholz and Erwin Marsi. 2006. CoNLL-X shared task on multilingual dependency parsing. In *Proceedings of CoNLL-2006*, pages 149–164.

Glenn Carroll and Eugene Charniak. 1992. Two experiments on learning probabilistic depedency grammars from corpora. In C. Weir, S. Abney, R. Grishman, and R. Weischedel, editors, *Working Notes of the Workshop Statistically-Based NLP Techniques*, pages 1–13. AAAI Press, Menlo Park, CA.

Shay B. Cohen, Kevin Gimpel, and Noah A. Smith. 2008. Logistic normal priors for unsupervised probabilistic grammar induction. In *Advances in Neural Information Processing Systems 21*.

Michael Collins. 1999. *Head-Driven Statistical Models for Natural Language Parsing*. Ph.D. thesis, University of Pennsylvania.

Gregory Druck, Gideon Mann, and Andrew McCallum. 2009. Semi-supervised learning of dependency parsers using generalized expectation criteria. In *Proceedings of 47th Annual Meeting of the Association of Computational Linguistics and the 4th IJCNLP of the AFNLP*, pages 360–368, Suntec, Singapore, August.

Kuzman Ganchev, Joao Graca, Jennifer Gillenwater, and Ben Taskar. 2009. Posterior regularization for structured latent variable models. Technical Report MS-CIS-09-16, University of Pennsylvania Department of Computer and Information Science.

Zoubin Ghahramani and Matthew J. Beal. 2000. Variational inference for Bayesian mixtures of factor analyses. In *Advances in Neural Information Processing Systems (NIPS 2000)*.

Jennifer Gillenwater, Kuzman Ganchez, Joao Graça, Fernando Pereira, and Ben Taskar. 2010. Sparsity in dependency grammar induction. In *Proceedings of ACL-2010 Short Papers*, pages 194–199.

Aria Haghighi and Dan Klein. 2006. Prototype-driven grammar induction. In *Proceedings of 44th Annual Meeting of the Association for Computational Linguistics*, pages 881–888.

William P. Headden III, Mark Johnson, and David McClosky. 2009. Improving unsupervised dependency parsing with richer contexts and smoothing. In *Proceedings of the Conference of the North American Chapter of the Association for Computational Linguistics*, Boulder, Colorado, June.

Julia Hockenmaier. 2003. Parsing with generative models of predicate-argument structure. In *Proceedings of the 41st Annual Meeting of the Association for Computational Linguistics*, pages 359–366, Sapporo, Japan.

H. Jeffreys. 1948. *Theory of Probability*. Clarendon Press, Oxford, second edition.

W. E. Johnson. 1932. Probability: deductive and inductive problems. *Mind*, 41:421–423.

Y. Kawata and J. Bartels. 2000. Stylebook for the Japanese Treebank in VERBMOBIL. Technical report, Eberhard-Karls-Universität Tübingen.

Chen Keh-Liann and Yu-Ming Hsieh. 2004. Chinese treebanks and grammar extraction. In *Proceedings of IJCNLP-2004*, pages 560–565.

Dan Klein and Christopher D. Manning. 2001. Natural language grammar induction using a constituent-context model. In T. G. Dietterich, S. Becker, and Z. Ghahramani, editors, *Advances in Neural Information Processing Systems (NIPS 2001)*, volume 1, pages 35–42. MIT Press.

Dan Klein and Christopher D. Manning. 2002. A generative constituent-context model for improved grammar induction. In *Proceedings of the 40th Associations for Computational Linguistics*, pages 128–135.

Dan Klein and Christopher D. Manning. 2004. Corpus-based induction of syntactic structure: Models of dependency and constituency. In *Proceedings of the 42nd Annual Meeting of the Association for Computational Linguistics*.

Dan Klein. 2005. *The Unsupervised Learning of Natural Language Structure*. Ph.D. thesis, Stanford University, March.

Alexander Koller and Marco Kuhlmann. 2009. Dependency trees and the strong generative capacity of ccg. In *Proceedings of the 12th Conference of the European Chapter of the Association for Computational Linguistics*, pages 460–468, April.

Kenichi Kurihara and Taisuke Sato. 2006. Variational Bayesian grammar induction for natural language. In *International Colloquium on Grammatical Inference*, pages 84–96.

K. Lari and S. J. Young. 1990. The estimation of stochastic context-free grammars using the inside-outside algorithm. *Computer Speech and Language*, 4:35–56.

G. J. Lidstone. 1920. Note on the general case of the Bayes-Laplace formula for inductive or *a posteriori* probabilities. *Transactions of the Faculty of Actuaries*, 8:182–192.

Mitchell P. Marcus, Beatrice Santorini, and Mary A. Marcinkiewicz. 1993. Building a large annotated corpus of English: The Penn Treebank. *Computational Linguistics*, 19:313–330.

Tahira Naseem, Harr Chen, Regina Barzilay, and Mark Johnson. 2010. Using universal linguistic knowledge to guide grammar induction. In *Proceedings of EMNLP-2010*.

Alexander M. Rush, David Sontag, Michael Collins, and Tommi Jaakkola. 2010. On dual decomposition and linear programming relaxations for natural language processing. In *Proceedings of EMNLP-2010*.

Noah A. Smith. 2006. *Novel Estimation Methods for Unsupervised Discovery of Latent Structure in Natural Language Text*. Ph.D. thesis, Department of Computer Science, John Hopkins University.

Benjamin Snyder, Tahira Naseem, and Regina Barzilay. 2009. Unsupervised multilingual grammar induction. In *Proceedings of the Joint Conference of the 47th ACL and the 4th IJCNLP*.

Valentin I. Spitkovsky, Hiyan Alshawi, and Daniel Jurafsky. 2010. From baby steps to leapfrog: How "less is more" in unsupervised dependency parsing. In *Proceedings of NAACL-HLT 2010*.

Transferring Syntactic Relations from English to Hindi Using Alignments on Local Word Groups

Aswarth Dara, Prashanth Mannem, Hemanth Sagar Bayyarapu and Avinesh PVS
Language Technologies Research Center
International Institute of Information Technology
Hyderabad, AP, India - 500032
{abhilash.d,prashanth,hemanth.sagar,avinesh}@research.iiit.ac.in

Abstract

Various works have used word alignments in parallel corpora to transfer information like POS tags, syntactic trees and word senses from source to target sentences. In this paper, we work on the problem of projecting syntactic relations from English to morphologically rich Hindi parallel text. We show the effectiveness of Local Word Groups (LWGs) in simplifying alignments as well as in transferring syntactic dependencies by building an alignment model with LWGs as base units and training a dependency parser on the relations projected using these LWGs. The LWG alignment model using GIZA++ scores decreases the Alignment Error Rate by 1.16 points when compared to the best GIZA++ model trained on lemmas. We also show that a dependency parser trained on the syntactic relations projected using LWGs obtained statistical significant improvements over the relations projected using lemmas by a margin of 3.49%.

1 Introduction

Data driven dependency parsers rely on the availability of large amounts of annotated data and building them is a time consuming, labour intensive and expensive task. Recent efforts in treebank creation have looked at the concept of *annotation projection* from a resource-rich language to a resource-poor one in a parallel corpus (Yarowsky et al., 2001). The central idea is to transfer the relevant information from source to target text given the analysis on the source side and word-alignments in a parallel corpora. A projected dependency treebank is created by projecting source parse from an automatic parser on to a target sentence using word alignments between the source and target sentences (Hwa et al., 2005; Jiang and Liu, 2009; Spreyer and Kuhn, 2009; Spreyer et al., 2010).

Difficulties in transferring syntactic relations from the source to target sentences arise mainly due to (i) errors in the source parse, (ii) errors in word alignments and (iii) differences in the dependency annotation schemes of the two languages (Ganchev et al., 2009). The third one can be handled by systematically identifying the differences in the annotation schemes and applying relevant transformations (Hwa et al., 2005).

In this work, we minimize the scope of errors in (i) and (ii) and the effect they have on projection task by proposing a novel technique for projecting syntactic dependencies using alignments between local word groups instead of word forms. The aim is to make the projection task simpler by transferring the relations in source LWGs to the corresponding target LWGs first and then get the alignments and projections on the head words of these LWGs. We show how LWGs can effectively be used to handle the inflectional variations in Hindi and thereby improve the word alignment accuracy between English and Hindi. We also show that the projection of syntactic relations becomes easier and more effective when dealing with LWGs rather than word-forms. We present the experiments and report the improvements in results obtained by using LWGs in alignment accuracy and parsing accuracy for English-Hindi language pair. The approach described in the paper is not specific to the English-Hindi language pair and can be extended to other language pairs involving at least one morphologically rich language.

The rest of the paper is organized as follows: Section 2 gives the related work and section 3 introduces the concept of LWGs. Section 4 presents the alignment models used in this work and section 5 describes the dependency projection algorithm. Section 6 lists the experiments conducted and reports the results. Section 7 ends the paper with the concluding remarks and gives the scope of future work in this direction.

2 Related Work

Earlier works in projecting dependencies using word alignments have mainly concentrated on aligning word forms, projecting dependencies based on the aligned words and then improving the projections using post-projection transformations.

(Hwa et al., 2005) project the syntactic dependencies from one language to another using the notion of *direct correspondence*. If the syntactic tree is not fully connected, they used post-projection transformations to make it complete and reported significant improvements due to it. (Ganchev et al., 2009) used open source posterior alignment toolkit PostCAT (Graca et al., 2009) for word alignments to project the syntactic dependencies in a way similar to (Hwa et al., 2005). They use some soft-constriants for word alignments to prevent false transfer of information and also experiment with the projections by varying post-projection transformation rules.

For dependency projection, (Spreyer and Kuhn, 2009) also start with the notion of *direct correspondence* with additional constraints involving (i) only the bi-directional alignment links (alignment links marked from both source to target language and target to source language) and (ii) the completeness of the projected tree. This ensures the reduction of errors in the data. It is further extended to consider the uni-directional alignments based on the partial analyses built from the confident bi-directional links. They report no significant increase in accuracy with the above extension because of the increase in noise. To reduce this drawback and make use of non-fully connected trees, they stick to the use of bi-directional alignment links in conjunction with a fixed number of fragmented analyses in a sentence.

(Jiang and Liu, 2009) refer to an alignment matrix and a dynamic programming algorithm to search for a completed projected tree. To reduce the impact of word alignment errors, (Jiang and Liu, 2010) consider compact representation of multiple GIZA++ (Och and Ney, 2000) alignment results. For each pair of words in a target sentence, they calculate the score of an edge depending on the alignment scores and source parses information. During parsing, they treat each syntactic tree as a set of dependency edges without relying on the complete tree.

The above approaches either pick most confident alignments links for dependency projection or pick the alignments as it is and then reduce the noise in the data using post-projection transformation rules. In this work, we focus on reducing both alignment and dependency projection complexity using LWGs. The relations within LWGs are deterministically marked irrespective of the alignments and by using only the head word of each LWG during alignment we alleviate data sparseness arising due to the the presence of inflectional variations in Hindi.

3 Local Word Groups

We define *local word groups* as minimal contiguous sequence of words in a sentence with a fixed word order and deterministic (trivially predictable) syntactic structure among them. For example, `will be given` is a verb group with the syntactic structure `will`→`be`→`given` which can be determined deterministically given the POS tags. Each LWG has a head word which is the syntactic head of the group of words (`will` in the example). LWG is similar to chunk except that LWGs are always minimal and refer to the fixed order property of the components. The advantage of using LWGs over chunks is the accuracy of identifying LWGs is higher than the accuracy of identifying chunk boundaries in source and target language. Also, the dependency relations within a chunk are non-deterministic in few cases (if we consider noun chunks). Moreover they can be computed with minimum computational effort.

The advantages LWGs provide during word alignment and transfer of syntactic information from source language to target language are:

1. It transform certain kinds of many-to-one, one-to-many and many-to-many alignments between word forms as one-to-one alignments between the LWGs thereby reducing data sparsity during alignment.

2. Since the internal structure of a LWG is fixed, we can confidently mark the syntactic relations within a LWG leaving out scope for errors arising out of word alignment and source dependency parses.

3. Number of syntactic relations to be projected reduced from number of words in a sentence

to number of LWGs thereby reducing the scope of errors in projection.

In Figure 1(a), *administratively* is aligned to *prashaansanika roopa se*. Once these alignments are obtained, in order to get the dependency relations roopa→prashaansanika and roopa→se correct from the projection of dependencies, the source dependency parse should be correct and the word alignment to all the three target words should be correct. The word alignment complexity further increases in the case of aligning *does come* to *aathaa hai* correctly considering the presence of inflectional variations in Hindi. Unless all the four alignments are correct, the dependency projection will not be correct. The complexity is further increased due to the non-availability of large bilingual corpus. In such cases, LWGs play an important role in reducing the complexity as well as in reducing the scope of errors to certain extent. We consider three kinds

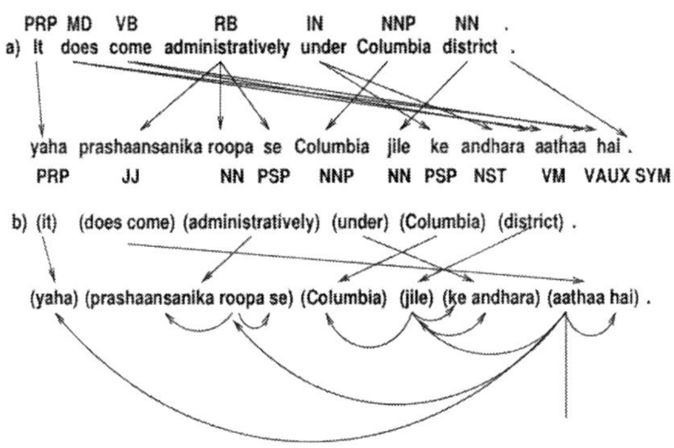

Figure 1: Alignments without and with LWGs

of LWGs verb groups (VG), preposition (postposition in case of Hindi) groups (PG) and adverb groups (ADVG). Noun groups are not considered since the internal syntactic structure is non-trivial to predict. For instance, in the example in figure 1(a), finding the syntactic structure for the words in the noun group Columbia←district is non-deterministic (non-trivial) given the POS tags. VM and VAUX are the two POS tags used to denote main verb and auxiliary verb in Hindi. Any occurrence of the pattern VM VAUX* is considered a verb LWG eg. (kara rahaa hai [*doing*], karna chahtaa hu [*want to do*]). Any continuous sequence of auxiliary verbs and a main verb is taken as a LWG in English for eg. *are going*, *did not go*. Postpositions in Hindi are also grouped into LWG. This is done to make alignments easy between prepositions in English and multi-word postpositions in Hindi such as ke saatha [*with*], ke baahara [*outside*] etc. Adverbs in English often end up as roopa se [*+ly*] morpheme in Hindi. Combining the adjective/noun with roopa se into a LWG helps the alignment model. Similarly few other cases where forming LWGs help in making alignments easy were identified and are marked as LWGs.

In Figure 1, (aathaa hai [*does come*]) is a verb group, ke andhara [*under*], are post-positions and (prashaansanika roopa se [*administratively*]) is an adverb group. The syntactic relations aathaa→hai, roopa→prashaansanika and roopa→se are marked directly irrespective of the word alignments.

Table 1 lists the corpus stats of word forms and LWGs. Apart from the advantages of LWGs listed above in this section, the reduction in the sentence length also helps improve the alignment accuracy.

Metric	English	Hindi
No. of Words	224K	251K
Avg. sentence length with words	19.29	21.61
No. of LWGs	191K	226K
Avg sentence length with LWGs	16.45	19.49

Table 1: Statistics of the entire corpus used with respect to words and LWGs.

4 Word Alignment

4.1 Scoring Function

We use a slight variant of competitive linking algorithm (CL) described in (Melamed, 2000) as scoring function and is discussed below in section 4.2. We also generate mappings between source and target language word classes from a small bilingual corpus containing hand-aligned gold alignments and manually annotated word class information. For each source word class, the mappings are stored by decreasing order of target word class co-occurrences (Wcmap).

4.2 LWG model

Instead of computing scores between source and target word forms in a two-dimensional array as in (Melamed, 2000), we compute scores between source LWGs and target LWGs. For each source LWG, the candidate LWGs are restricted to the ones whose content word's POS tag are in the mapping list of source LWG content word's POS. The alignment pair with the maximum score is chosen, the corresponding row and column are deleted for further processing. The process is repeated until it finishes. The differences here when compared to competitive linking algorithm (Melamed, 2000) are that we use LWGs instead of words and restricting the possible candidate LWGs by taking word class information into account. We refer to this model as CL-LWG in the rest of the paper.

Once the one-to-one alignments between source and target LWGs are computed, the word to word alignments have to be recovered from them in a postprocessing step. This is done by assigning alignments between all the words in a target LWG to all the words in the source LWG and vice versa. This postprocessing step makes the final set contain contain one-to-many, many-to-one and many-to-many alignments.

4.3 Case of Left Out *Units*

In the model described above, there is a possibility of source or target *units* being left out without any alignments. This is because the model only does one-to-one mapping and the number of *units* in the source and target sentence could be different. The left out *units* need not be a case of NULL alignments (such as determiners). The alignments for the left out *units* are assigned by using a greedy best first alignment strategy.

4.4 Weighted Model

The CL-LWG alignment model can be further extended to use alignment scores from GIZA++ model apart from the scoring function described in Section 4.1. A weighted score of the score from the scoring function and GIZA++ can be used to decode the model. Let s1 be the score of the scoring function described above and s2 be the score obtained from GIZA++ then the weighted score S is defined as

$$S = \lambda * s1 + (1 - \lambda) * s2; \qquad (1)$$

whereas λ is varied from 0 to 1 and the best value of λ is chosen by tuning it on the development dataset.

5 Dependency Projection

Once the alignments are obtained, projection of dependencies from source to target sentences is undertaken. The input is a set of alignments between source and target language and the source dependency parse with the projected dependency parse of the target sentence as the output. Parses for English have been obtained using first order MST parser (McDonald et al., 2005) trained on 2-21 sections of Penn Treebank (Marcus et al., 1993).

5.1 Annotation Scheme Differences

When projecting relations from source to target text, the annotation scheme of source treebank is carried over to the target side. This projected target dependency treebank may not be consistent with the annotation scheme of the target language. The annotation scheme differences need to be handled to make the projected parses consistent for dependency parse evaluation. This also ensures that the projected treebank could be used for bootstrapping parsers (Steedman et al., 2003; Reichart and Rappoport, 2007).

Some of the major differences in the English and Hindi annotation schemes are

1. Head of a Verb Phrase (VP) is the main verb in Hindi whereas the head of a VP in an English sentence is the auxiliary verb.

2. Head of a Prepositional Phrase (PP) in Hindi is noun whereas it is the preposition in English.

3. In Hindi, conjunct is the head in case of both noun and verb co-ordination whereas in English it is not.

There are two possible ways of addressing this issue. The first one is to apply tranformations before dependency projection (pre-projection) i.e., to the source parse and the second one involves applying tranformations to the target parse once the dependency projection is made (post-projection). This assures that the projected treebank is consistent with the annotation scheme of the target language. It does not make any difference while choosing whether to apply pre-projection or post-projection. In our case, we choose to apply pre-projection i.e., to the source dependency parse just for our convenience. Appropriate pre-projection transformations shown in Figure 2 have been applied to the source parse to reflect the target language annotation scheme described in (Begum et al., 2008).

Figure 2(a) presents the tranformations applied in case of finite verbs (*going*) i.e., switch the dependencies between the current parent (*has*) and finite verb (*going*) then make the rest of them as dependents to the finite verb. In case of PP chunk, switch the dependencies of noun (*complaint*) and preposition (*on*) i.e., make parent of noun as parent of preposition and make the preposition (*on*) as dependent to the noun (*complaint*) as shown in Figure 2(b). In case of noun co-ordination shown in Figure 2(c), switch the dependencies between the rightmost conjunct (*officials*) and co-ordination word (*and*). Then the remaining words (*investors*, *managers* and ,) are made as dependents to the co-ordinated word (*and*). Same co-ordination transformations shown in Figure 2(d) are applied in case of verb co-ordination except that the switching of dependencies take place between the left most finite verb (*makes*) and co-ordination word (*and*) whereas it is rightmost conjunct in case of noun co-ordination (*officials*).

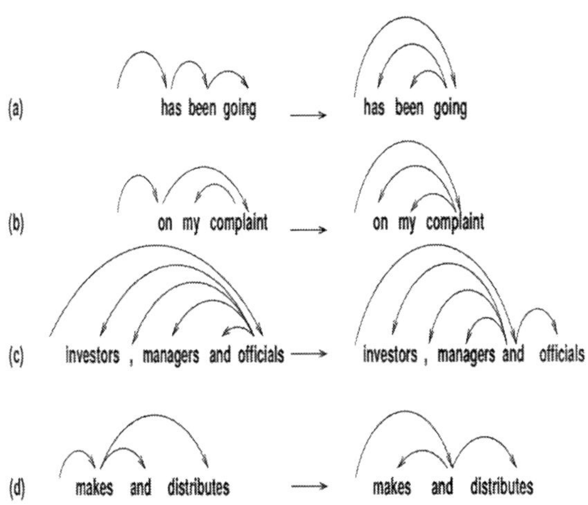

Figure 2: Transformations applied to the source parse.

5.2 Projection Algorithm

Let S(s_1,s_2,..,s_m), T(t_1,t_2,..,t_n) be the source and target language sentences of length m and n. For each dependency relation (s_i, s_j) where s_i is the head of s_j, the projection is done depending on the type of alignment s_i and s_j have with the words in the target sentence. The one-many, many-one and many-many alignments are transformed into one-one alignments by making the syntactic head word of the "many" words in the alignment as "one" representative word and the rest as the dependents of the head word.

1. If s_i is aligned to t_k (*one-one* alignment) and s_j is aligned to t_l (*one-one* alignment) then mark the dependency relation (t_k, t_l).

2. If s_i is aligned to t_a,...,tk (*one-many* alignment)and s_j is aligned to t_l (*one-one* alignment) then pick the head word t_h from t_a,...,tk target words and make the remaining as dependents to the head word and mark the dependency relation as (t_h, t_l).

3. if s_a,...,si are aligned to t_k (*many-one* alignment) and s_j is aligned to t_l then pick the head word s_h from s_a,...,si source words and repeat step 1.

4. The *many-many* alignments are also converted to *one-one* by first performing the *one-many* transformation in step 2 and then the transformation for *many-one* in step 3.

If there are any unaligned words in the target sentence then they are left as unconnected words in the projected target dependency tree. The head word from a list of words in the above transformations is obtained using word class information.

6 Experiments

Our experiments have been carried out on English-Hindi parallel text from EMILLE corpus. EMILLE is a 63 million word electronic corpus of South Asian languages, especially those spoken as minority languages in UK (Xiao et al., 2004). The dataset has 3341 training sentences and 90 manually aligned test sentences (with 1121 English words and 1323 Hindi words). It is a small corpus compared to corpora available for other language pairs.

We evaluate the word alignments as well as the projected target relations to measure the effectiveness of LWGs in alignment as well as in projection process. For evaluating the quality of projected target relations, a parser is trained on the dependency edges obtained using projections on alignments between LWGs and those obtained using projections on just word/lemma alignments.

6.1 Word Alignment Evaluation

The alignments are compared with those obtained by GIZA++ (Och and Ney, 2000) and PostCat (Graca et al., 2009). We train two GIZA++ models for comparison with our model. The first model is trained with the word forms from the above dataset and second one with the lemmas (roots) of the words. For each of these models, the best among the grow-diag, grow-diag-final and grow-diag-final-and (gdfa) modes have been taken for comparison. Two models are trained using PostCAT, same as with GIZA++, one with the word forms and the other with the lemmas of the words. For each of these models, the best among the baseline, agreement and substochastic modes have been taken for comparison. The alignment models are evaluated using the standard alignment evaluation metrics precision, recall, F score and Alignment Error Rate (AER) as described in (Hua et al., 2005).

Id	Models	P	R	AER
WF-PC	PostCAT	59.49	46.73	47.65
WF-GZ	GIZA++	47.30	**52.55**	50.2
WF-LWG	CL-LWG	**60.94**	47.1	**46.88**

Table 2: Evaluation Results with Word Forms as *Units*. WF denotes word forms, PC is PostCAT, GZ is GIZA++ and LWG is our model.

Table 2 presents the Precision (P), Recall (R) and AER (1-F) for all the models. All the models in the table use the word forms given in the parallel sentences and do not consider the lemmas. Our LWG model (*WF-LWG*) performs better than the GIZA++ model (*WF-GZ*) and PostCAT model (*WF-PC*) by a margin of 3.32 and 1.23 points respectively . This shows that the LWGs are more effective than word forms when it comes to English-Hindi parallel data.

Since Hindi is a morphologically rich language and the bilingual corpus we use is small, data sparsity becomes a major problem for word alignment. This can be alleviated to some extent by learning from lemmas instead of the word forms themselves.

Id	Models	P	R	AER
LM-PC	PostCAT	51.07	42.25	53.75
LM-GZ	GIZA++	**62.14**	**49.78**	**44.72**
LM-LWG	CL-LWG	60.15	48.58	46.24

Table 3: Evaluation Results with Root Words as *Units*. LM denotes lemmas (roots) of the words.

Table 3 lists the performance of the PostCAT, GIZA++ and LWG model when trained with lemmas. In case of LWGs, the lemmas of the head words are used. GIZA++ trained on lemmas (*LM-GZ*) has a significant reduction in AER when compared to the one trained on word forms (*WF-GZ*). This is expected due to the above mentioned reason of Hindi being morphologically rich and lemmas reducing data sparseness. The lemmatized LWG model (*LM-LWG*) under performs when compared to GIZA++ trained on lemmas (*LM-GZ*) even though in the case of training on word forms, *WF-LWG* out performed *WF-GZ*. This is because LWGs with word forms reduce the problem of data sparseness when compared to just word forms being used in GIZA++ model *WF-GZ* but the gains in lemmatized model is not that significant to beat the gains achieved in lemmatized GIZA++ model. Moreover, the scoring function of GIZA++ is more sophisticated than the one we use.

To get the combined effects of using LWGs and GIZA++'s scoring function, two models using weighted scores of scores from LWG model and GIZA++ model for word forms (*WF-LWG-WGT*) and lemmas (*LM-LWG-WGT*) were built.

Id	Models	P	R	AER
WF-LWG-WGT	WM	61.86	47.94	45.98
LM-LWG-WGT	WM	**62.85**	51.21	**43.56**

Table 4: Evaluation Results for Weighted Models (WMs)

Table 4 lists the evaluation scores for the weighted models. The combined models beat the respective best word form and lemma models (i.e., *WF-LWG* and *LM-GZ*) by 0.9 and 1.16 respectively. The best alignment accuracy was achieved by the combined model trained on lemmas.

Experiments were conducted by combining words in each LWG using underscores and also by using only head word of each LWG as input to GIZA++. Using a post-processing step, the word alignments were recovered from the resulting alignments. The alignment accuracies decreased significantly using this approach.

6.2 Evaluation of projected parses

Projections from English dependency trees using alignments produced by various models described above have been obtained and trained separately. We used a modified version of bidirectional parser (Shen and Joshi, 2008) described in (Mannem and Dara, 2011) to train the projected dependencies. The parsers evaluation was done on manually an-

Alignment	Word forms (WF)			Lemmas (LM)		
	EMILLE	*EILMT*	*BOTH*	*EMILLE*	*EILMT*	*BOTH*
PC	72.76	72.31	74.26	72.15	72.23	72.48
GZ	74.93	77.71	77.17	75.87	77.33	77.08
LWG-WGT	**78.06**	**79.50**	**79.79**	**78.76**	**80.52**	**80.57**

Table 5: Parsing accuracy corresponding to the parsers trained on projections from alignment models when evaluated with gold POS tags. The six respective parsers are referred by prefixing WF- and LM- to the three alignment models (PC, GZ and LWG-WGT).

Alignment	Word forms (WF)			Lemmas (LM)		
	EMILLE	*EILMT*	*BOTH*	*EMILLE*	*EILMT*	*BOTH*
PC	61.06	61.60	62.50	61.98	61.90	61.51
GZ	63.40	65.85	65.71	64.51	65.50	65.50
LWG-WGT	**66.86**	**67.88**	**68.37**	**67.50**	**68.22**	**68.75**

Table 6: Parsing accuracy corresponding to the parsers trained on projections from alignment models when evaluated with automatic POS tags. The six respective parsers are referred by prefixing WF- and LM- to the three alignment models (PC, GZ and LWG-WGT).

notated test data with gold POS tags released as part of ICON-2010 NLP Tools Contest (ICON, 2010). We also presented the results on the manually annotated test data with the automatic POS tags.

We use an additional English-Hindi parallel corpus containing 8169 sentences developed as part of a consortium project (Venkatapathy, 2008) [1]. This dataset wasn't used for evaluating word alignments due to the lack of manually annotated alignments. This sentence aligned corpus was developed to aid building translation systems for the tourism domain and doesn't have any human annotated word alignments. The corpus is a collection of articles about various tourist and pilgrimage places. It has a high occurrence of proper nouns as a result of this. The corpus is also noisy with typographical errors, mismatched sentences and unfaithful translations.

The parser is trained on the projected data extracted using alignments from all the three different alignment models using word forms and LWGs. Table 5 gives the Unlabeled Attached Score (UAS) of the parser on the test data. The parsers corresponding to *WF-LWG-WGT* and *LM-LWG-WGT* alignments obtained siginificant improvements of 2.62 points and 3.49 points in parsing accuracy over the ones using GIZA++ alignments on words and lemmas when both the datasets are used for training. The results obtained are statistically significant (McNemar's and $p < 0.05$). The parser trained on the projected data obtained using *LM-LWG-WGT* alignments achieved an improvement of over 0.78 points over the one trained using *WF-LWG-WGT* alignments and it is expected.

Table 6 gives the parsing accuracies on test data with automatic POS tags. The parsing accuracy corresponding to *LM-LWG-WGT* alignment model has dropped from 80.57 to 68.75 due to the difference in usage of POS tags. For all the datasets, the parser trained on the projected data obtained using word alignments from the weighted models (*WF-LWG-WGT, LM-LWG-WGT*) performed the best and the results are statistically significant (McNemar's and $p < 0.05$) over the models using alignments from GIZA++ and PostCAT in terms of both word forms and lemmas. (Ambati et al., 2010) achieved an accuracy of 85.5% UAS by training on Hyderabad Dependency Treebank (Bhatt et al., 2009) and evaluating with automatic POS tags. This would be an upper-bound for approaches like ours which do not use any annotated data to build the parser.

The Hindi dependency treebank has chunks marked for every sentence and the dependencies are marked between chunk head words. Following the tradition in Hindi dependency parsing, we

[1]The original training and test sets in this corpus contained 11,300 and 500 sentences respectively. But, both the datasets had a large number of sentence repetitions. The sizes reported in this paper are after removing all duplicate sentences. http://ltrc.iiit.ac.in/icon2008/nlptools.php

evaluate and compare the two parsing models on their inter-chunk and intra-chunk dependencies. A total of 6454 dependency relations are present in the test data out of which 3401 are intra-chunk dependencies and the rest 3053 are inter-chunk dependencies. The models which achieved best accuracy (*LM-LWG-WGT*, *WF-GZ* and *WF-PC*) are taken into comparison when both the datasets are used for training.

Table 7 gives the accuracies w.r.t few POS tags achieved by various parsing models tested with gold POS tags in the test data. These POS tags are the most frequent tags of chunk head words and the accuracies denote the inter-chunk accuracies of the models. The analysis on intra-chunk dependencies hasn't been shown since there isn't much difference in the accuracies between the two parsing models. This is because, though *WF-PC* and *WF-GZ* don't use any LWGs, the intra-chunk relations are corrected and are made similar to those produced using *LM-LWG-WGT* by using transformation rules during projection as described in section 3. As seen in Table 7 for inter-chunk dependencies, *LM-LWG-WGT* alignment based parsing model performs better than the model using *WF-GZ* and *WF-PC* alignments for most POS tags (except CC tag) when compared to *WF-GZ*. This is because of better alignments achieved by *LM-LWG-WGT* using LWGs over *WF-GZ*, *WF-PC* and thereby better dependency projections to learn from.

POS	Total	WF-PC	WF-GZ	LM-LWG-WGT
NN	1257	57.28	58.15	**66.35**
VM	710	33.10	44.65	**55.91**
NNP	444	38.29	45.27	**50.00**
CC	213	39.90	**52.58**	46.95
PRP	209	35.41	47.85	**51.67**
JJ	129	72.10	74.42	**88.37**
RB	33	24.24	45.45	**51.51**

Table 7: Parsing Accuracies on inter-chunk dependencies when both the datasets are combined. Total represent the total number of inter-chunk dependencies with each POS tag occurred in the test data. Third, fourth and fifth columns represent the percentage of correct inter-chunk dependencies for each POS tag obtained using the respective alignment models.

7 Conclusions and Future Work

In this work, we presented a novel approach for syntactic transfer of relations from source to target sentences by using alignments between LWGs instead of word forms. We also showed the effectiveness of LWGs while handling one-to-many, many-to-one and many-to-many alignments during both word alignment and dependency projection. The LWG weighted alignment model decreased the AER by 1.16 points over GIZA++ trained on lemmas and a bidirectional dependency parser trained on the syntactic relations projected using LWGs outperforms the relations projected using lemmas by a statistically significant margin of 3.49 points. We also presented evaluation of parsers in terms of inter chunk and intra chunk dependencies. Extending this work to other resource-poor Indian language pairs will be the starting point of our future work.

References

Bharat Ram Ambati, Samar Husain, Sambhav Jain, Dipti Misra Sharma, and Rajeev Sangal. 2010. Two methods to incorporate local morphosyntactic features in hindi dependency parsing. In *Proceedings of the NAACL HLT 2010 First Workshop on Statistical Parsing of Morphologically-Rich Languages*, SPMRL '10, pages 22–30, Stroudsburg, PA, USA. Association for Computational Linguistics.

R. Begum, S. Husain, A. Dhwaj, D. Sharma, L. Bai, and R. Sangal. 2008. Dependency annotation scheme for indian languages. In *In Proceedings of The Third International Joint Conference on Natural Language Processing (IJCNLP)*, Hyderabad, India.

Rajesh Bhatt, Bhuvana Narasimhan, Martha Palmer, Owen Rambow, Dipti Misra Sharma, and Fei Xia. 2009. A multi-representational and multi-layered treebank for hindi/urdu. In *Proceedings of the Third Linguistic Annotation Workshop*, ACL-IJCNLP '09, pages 186–189, Stroudsburg, PA, USA. Association for Computational Linguistics.

Kuzman Ganchev, Jennifer Gillenwater, and Ben Taskar. 2009. Dependency grammar induction via bitext projection constraints. In *ACL '09: Proceedings of the Joint Conference of the 47th Annual Meeting of the ACL and the 4th International Joint Conference on Natural Language Processing of the AFNLP: Volume 1*, pages 369–377, Morristown, NJ, USA. Association for Computational Linguistics.

J Graca, K Ganchev, and B Taskar. 2009. Postcat - posterior constrained alignment toolkit. In *In The Third Machine Translation Marathon*.

Wu Hua, Wang Haifeng, and Liu Zhanyi. 2005. Alignment model adaptation for domain-specific word alignment. In *ACL '05: Proceedings of the 43rd Annual Meeting on Association for Computational Linguistics*, pages 467–474, Morristown, NJ, USA. Association for Computational Linguistics.

Rebecca Hwa, Philip Resnik, Amy Weinberg, Clara Cabezas, and Okan Kolak. 2005. Bootstrapping parsers via syntactic projection across parallel texts. *Nat. Lang. Eng.*, 11:311–325, September.

ICON. 2010. Nlp tools contest 2010.

Wenbin Jiang and Qun Liu. 2009. Automatic adaptation of annotation standards for dependency parsing: using projected treebank as source corpus. In *Proceedings of the 11th International Conference on Parsing Technologies*, IWPT '09, pages 25–28, Stroudsburg, PA, USA. Association for Computational Linguistics.

Wenbin Jiang and Qun Liu. 2010. Dependency parsing and projection based on word-pair classification. In *Proceedings of the 48th Annual Meeting of the Association for Computational Linguistics*, ACL '10, pages 12–20, Morristown, NJ, USA. Association for Computational Linguistics.

Prashanth Mannem and Aswarth Dara. 2011. Partial parsing from bitext projections. In *Proceedings of the 49th Annual Meeting of the Association for Computational Linguistics: Human Language Technologies*, pages 1597–1606, Portland, Oregon, USA, June. Association for Computational Linguistics.

M. Marcus, B. Santorini, and M. Marcinkiewicz. 1993. Building a large annotated corpus of English: the Penn Treebank. 19(2):313–330.

R. McDonald, K. Crammer, and F. Pereira. 2005. Online large-margin training of dependency parsers. In *Proceedings of the Annual Meeting of the Association for Computational Linguistics (ACL)*.

I. Dan Melamed. 2000. Models of translational equivalence among words. *Comput. Linguist.*, 26:221–249, June.

Franz Josef Och and Hermann Ney. 2000. A comparison of alignment models for statistical machine translation. In *COLING '00: Proceedings of the 18th conference on Computational linguistics*, pages 1086–1090, Morristown, NJ, USA. Association for Computational Linguistics.

Roi Reichart and Ari Rappoport. 2007. Self-training for enhancement and domain adaptation of statistical parsers trained on small datasets. In *ACL'07*, pages 616–623.

Libin Shen and Aravind Joshi. 2008. LTAG dependency parsing with bidirectional incremental construction. In *Proceedings of the 2008 Conference on Empirical Methods in Natural Language Processing*, pages 495–504, Honolulu, Hawaii, October. Association for Computational Linguistics.

Kathrin Spreyer and Jonas Kuhn. 2009. Data-driven dependency parsing of new languages using incomplete and noisy training data. In *Proceedings of the Thirteenth Conference on Computational Natural Language Learning*, CoNLL '09, pages 12–20, Stroudsburg, PA, USA. Association for Computational Linguistics.

Kathrin Spreyer, Lilja Øvrelid, and Jonas Kuhn. 2010. Training parsers on partial trees: A cross-language comparison. In ELRA, editor, *Proceedings of the 7th International Conference on Language Resources and Evaluation (LREC'10)*.

Mark Steedman, Miles Osborne, Anoop Sarkar, Stephen Clark, Rebecca Hwa, Julia Hockenmaier, Paul Ruhlen, Steven Baker, and Jeremiah Crim. 2003. Bootstrapping statistical parsers from small datasets. In *Proceedings of the tenth conference on European chapter of the Association for Computational Linguistics - Volume 1*, EACL '03, pages 331–338, Stroudsburg, PA, USA. Association for Computational Linguistics.

Sriram Venkatapathy. 2008. Nlp tools contest 2008: Summary.

Zhonghua Xiao, Tony Mcenery, Paul Baker, and Andrew Hardie. 2004. Developing asian language corpora: standards and practice. In *In Proceedings of the Fourth Workshop on Asian Language Resources*.

David Yarowsky, Grace Ngai, and Richard Wicentowski. 2001. Inducing multilingual text analysis tools via robust projection across aligned corpora. In *Proceedings of the first international conference on Human language technology research*, HLT '01, pages 1–8, Stroudsburg, PA, USA. Association for Computational Linguistics.

Generative Modeling of Coordination by Factoring Parallelism and Selectional Preferences

Daisuke Kawahara and **Sadao Kurohashi**
Graduate School of Informatics, Kyoto University
Yoshida-Honmachi, Sakyo-ku, Kyoto, 606-8501, Japan
{dk, kuro}@i.kyoto-u.ac.jp

Abstract

We present a unified generative model of coordination that considers parallelism of conjuncts and selectional preferences. Parallelism of conjuncts, which frequently characterizes coordinate structures, is modeled as a synchronized generation process in the generative parser. Selectional preferences learned from a large web corpus provide an important clue for resolving the ambiguities of coordinate structures. Our experiments of Japanese dependency parsing indicate the effectiveness of our approach, particularly in the domains of newspapers and patents.

1 Introduction

Coordinate structures are a potential source of syntactic ambiguity in natural language. Although many methods have been proposed to resolve the ambiguities of coordinate structures, coordination disambiguation still remains a difficult problem for state-of-the-art parsers. Previous studies on coordination disambiguation used two kinds of clues:

- parallelism of conjuncts, and
- selectional preferences.

Syntactic, lexical and semantic parallelism of conjuncts is frequently observed in coordinate structures. For example, Dubey et al. (2005) empirically confirmed syntactic parallelism in coordinate structures. This clue was modeled by string matching, part-of-speech matching, number agreement, semantic similarities, and so forth (Agarwal and Boggess, 1992; Kurohashi and Nagao, 1994; Resnik, 1999; Chantree et al., 2005; Buyko and Hahn, 2008). For instance, consider the following example:

(1) eat Caesar salad and Italian pasta

We can observe lexical or semantic parallelism between *salad* and *pasta*, which can be automatically detected via a thesaurus or distributional similarity. In addition, syntactic parallelism can be observed; each conjunct has a modifier *Caesar* and *Italian*, respectively. These types of parallelism contribute to identifying the coordinate structure that conjoins *Caesar salad* and *Italian pasta*.

The other clue is selectional preferences, such as *eat* in the above example. Since *eat* is likely to have *salad* and *pasta* as its objects, it is plausible that *salad* and *pasta* are coordinated. Such selectional preferences of predicates are thought to support the construction of coordinate structures, and were used in Japanese dependency parsing by Kawahara and Kurohashi (2008). Selectional preferences of nouns (noun-noun modifications) were used by Resnik (1999), Nakov and Hearst (2005) and Kawahara and Kurohashi (2008). For example, let us see the following examples:

(2) a. mail and securities fraud

b. corn and peanut butter

In (2a), the coordination of *mail* and *securities* is guided by the estimation that *mail fraud* is a salient compound nominal phrase. In (2b), on the contrary, the coordinate structure that conjoins *corn* and *peanut butter* is led because *corn butter* is not a familiar concept.

Each clue has been empirically proven to be effective for coordination disambiguation. However, a unified approach that combines both clues has not been explored comprehensively. In this paper, we propose a unified framework for coordination disambiguation by incorporating both the clues into a generative parser. To capture syntactic parallelism of conjuncts, we formulate the generative process of pre-modifiers of conjuncts in a synchronized manner. In the above example, the generation process of *Caesar* from *salad* is synchronized with that of *Italian* from *pasta*. An interpretation of an unbalanced coordinate structure without synchronization (e.g., "Caesar salad and Italian") is penalized. Lexical parallelism, which is a tendency that some words, such as *salad* and *pasta*, are likely to be coordinated, is also modeled within the generative model.

In this paper, we focus on the Japanese language. A synchronization-based model of coordination disambiguation is integrated into a fully-lexicalized Japanese generative parser (Kawahara and Kurohashi, 2008). For the selectional preferences, we use case frames and statistics of noun-noun modifications that are automatically extracted from large raw corpora. Our method can resolve coordinate structures with parallelism on the basis of the synchronized generative model, and can also handle unlike coordinate structures using selectional preferences.

The remainder of this paper is organized as follows. Section 2 summarizes previous work related mainly to parsing models with coordination disambiguation. Section 3 briefly overviews the Japanese language and coordination ambiguity in Japanese. Section 4 illustrates our idea and describes our model in detail. Section 5 is devoted to our experiments. Finally, section 6 gives the conclusions.

2 Related Work

Resnik (1999) and van Noord (2007) incorporated parallelism and selectional preferences into coordination disambiguation or parsing. Resnik (1999) integrated semantic similarities and noun-noun modifications into voting or decision trees to disambiguate the scope ambiguities of nominal compounds "n1 and n2 n3." He did not integrate this method into parsing, but applied it to an independent task. Van Noord (2007) proposed a MaxEnt model of Dutch parsing that incorporated selectional preferences learned from a large corpus. He used various features in the MaxEnt model including some features that capture parallelism. This indirect treatment of parallelism is different from our generative model that explicitly factors parallelism.

Several other studies have considered parallelism in parsing models. Charniak and Johnson (2005) incorporated some features of syntactic parallelism in coordinate structures into their MaxEnt reranking parser. Kübler et al. (2009) used a reranking parser with automatically detected scope possibilities to improve German parsing. As for a generative parser, Dubey et al. (2006) proposed an unlexicalized PCFG parser that modified PCFG probabilities to condition the existence of a coordinate structure. Hogan (2007) proposed a generative lexicalized parser that considered the symmetry of part-of-speech tags and phrase categories of conjuncts, which is more shallow information than our synchronization model. She also used cooccurrence statistics of conjunct heads, which are similar to our modeling of lexical parallelism, but her model did not use selectional preferences.

Kurohashi and Nagao (1994) proposed a rule-based method of Japanese dependency parsing that included coordination disambiguation. Their method first detects coordinate structures in a sentence using dynamic programming, and then determines the dependency structure of the sentence under the constraints of the detected coordinate structures. Shimbo and Hara (2007) and Hara et al. (2009) considered many features for coordination disambiguation and automatically optimized their weights, which were heuristically determined in Kurohashi and Nagao (1994), by using a discriminative learning model.

3 Japanese Grammar and Coordinate Structure

3.1 Japanese Grammar

Let us first briefly introduce Japanese grammar. The structure of a Japanese sentence can be described well by the dependency relation between *bunsetsu*s. A *bunsetsu* is a basic unit of dependency, consisting of one or more content words and the following zero or more function words. A *bunsetsu* corresponds to a base phrase in English and *eojeol* in Korean. The Japanese language is head-final, that is, a *bunsetsu* depends on another *bunsetsu* to its right (but not necessarily the adjacent *bunsetsu*).

For example, consider the following sentence:[1]

[1] In this paper, we use the following abbreviations: NOM (nominative), ACC (accusative), DAT (dative), ALL (alla-

(3) *ane-to gakkou-ni itta*
sister-CMI school-ALL went

(went to school with (my) sister)

This sentence consists of three *bunsetsus*. The final *bunsetsu*, *itta*, is a predicate, and the other *bunsetsus*, *ane-to* and *gakkou-ni*, are its arguments. Their endings, *to* and *ni*, are postpositions that function as case markers.

3.2 Coordinate Structure in Japanese

Coordinate structures in Japanese are roughly classified into two types. The first type is the nominal coordinate structure.

(4) *nagai enpitsu-**to** keshigomu-wo katta*
long pencil-CNJ eraser-ACC bought

(bought a long pencil and an eraser)

The other type is the predicative coordinate structure, in which two or more predicates form a coordinate structure.

(5) *kanojo-to kekkon-**shi** ie-wo katta*
she-CMI married-CNJ house-ACC bought

(married her and bought a house)

For both of these types, we can detect the possibility of a coordinate structure by looking for a *coordination key bunsetsu* that contains *to*, *-shi*, comma and so forth. That is to say, the left and right sides of a coordination key bunsetsu constitute possible pre- and post-conjuncts, and the key bunsetsu is located at the end of the pre-conjunct.

For the evaluation of our method, which is described in section 5, we use analyzed corpora that are annotated on the basis of the annotation criteria of the Kyoto University Text Corpus (Kurohashi and Nagao, 1998).[2] Under this annotation criteria, the last *bunsetsu* in a pre-conjunct depends on the last *bunsetsu* in a post-conjunct, as shown in the dependency trees of Figure 1.

4 Our Method

4.1 Idea

Consider, for example, the following sentence.

tive), GEN (genitive), CMI (comitative), CNJ (conjunction) and TOP (topic marker).

[2]http://nlp.ist.i.kyoto-u.ac.jp/EN/index.php?Kyoto%20 University%20Text%20Corpus

(6) *houou-no kenkou-**to** tibet-no heiwa-wo*
pope-GEN health-CNJ tibet-GEN peace-ACC

inotta
prayed

(prayed (for) health of pope and peace of Tibet)

In this sentence, the coordination key "*to*" is a coordinate conjunction.[3] The coordinate structure in example (6) has four possible scopes. Among these, two structures are illustrated in Figure 1. In this figure, our parser generates the constituent words according to the arrows.

First, let us describe the effect of selectional preferences and lexical parallelism. In (a), two coordinated arguments, *kenkou* (health) and *heiwa* (peace), are generated from the verb *inotta* (prayed), and are eligible as accusative words of the verb *inotta* (prayed). *Kenkou* (health) is also generated from its coordinated head *heiwa* (peace). This generation is plausible because people often say this coordinated pair. In (b), the heads of conjuncts, *kenkou* (health) and *tibet*, are generated from the noun *heiwa* (peace). This is not appropriate because we are not referring to the nominal compound "*kenkou-no heiwa*" (peace of health). *Kenkou* (health) is also generated from its coordinated head *tibet*, but this generation has a low probability because this coordination is meaningless and rare.

These judgments are determined based on selectional preferences of predicates including nouns and lexical parallelism. As resources for considering these factors, we use automatically compiled case frames, and cooccurrences of noun-noun modifications and coordinated nouns.

Second, syntactic parallelism of conjuncts is also effective for coordination disambiguation. In (a), after the conjunct heads, *kenkou* (health) and *heiwa* (peace), are generated, the modifier in the pre-conjunct, *houou* (pope), is generated. In this generation, the generative probability of a genitive case from *kenkou* (health), $P(A(\text{GEN}) = \text{Y}|health)$, is considered. Note that $A(CASE)$=$\{\text{Y}, \text{N}\}$ is a binary function that returns Y if a case slot $CASE$ is filled with an ar-

[3]Note that the coordination key "*to*" can be used as a coordinate conjunction and also as a comitative case marker. The tasks of coordination disambiguation include the detection of coordinate conjunctions as well as the identification of coordination scopes. Both of these tasks are simultaneously carried out in our method.

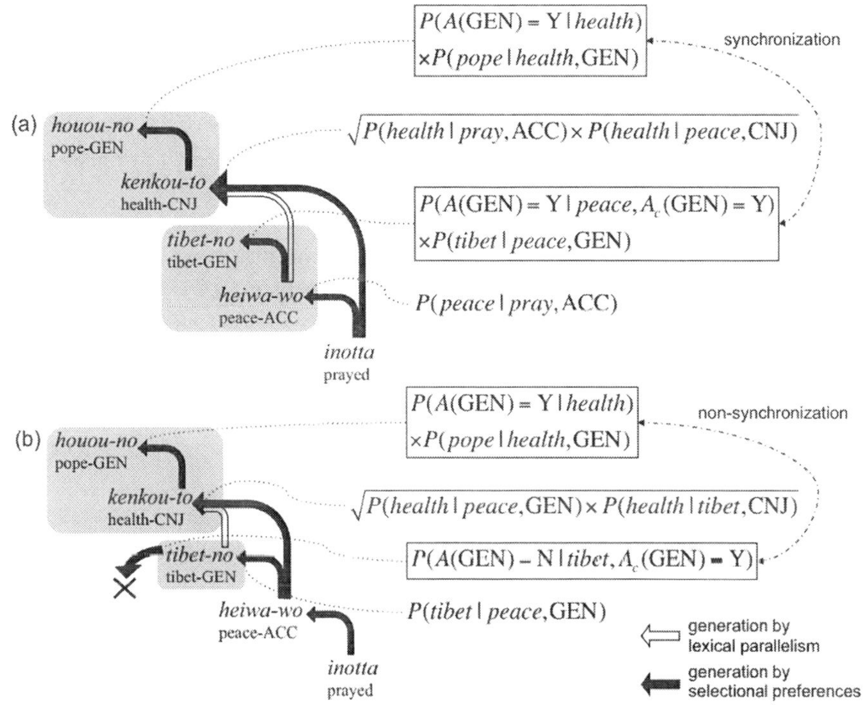

Figure 1: Two possible dependency and coordinate structures with some generative probabilities. The rounded rectangles represent conjuncts of coordinate structures.

gument; otherwise, it returns N. Subsequently, the modifier in the post-conjunct, *tibet*, is generated. This generation includes the synchronous generation of a genitive case from *heiwa* (peace) with the probability $P(A(\text{GEN}){=}\text{Y}|peace,\, A_c(\text{GEN}){=}\text{Y})$, which is conditioned on the previously generated genitive case of the pre-conjunct. Since syntactic parallelism is preferred in coordinate structures, this probability has a larger value than other probabilities $P(A(\text{GEN}){=}\text{Y}|peace)$ without coordination and $P(A(\text{GEN}){=}\text{Y}|peace,\, A_c(\text{GEN}){=}\text{N})$ without synchronization.

In (b), $P(A(\text{GEN}{=}\text{N})|tibet,\, A_c(\text{GEN}){=}\text{Y})$ means that nothing is generated from *tibet*, whereas the head of the pre-conjunct has a genitive case. This probability has a small value because of non-synchronization (unbalanced coordinate structure).

4.2 Resources

As the resources of selectional preferences to support coordinate structures, we use automatically constructed case frames and cooccurrences of noun-noun modifications. As a parser for extracting these resources, we use the Japanese dependency parser, KNP,[4] which is also used as a base model in the following sections.

	CS	examples
yaku (1) (bake)	*ga*	I:18, person:15, craftsman:10, ···
	wo	bread:2484, meat:1521, cake:1283, ···
	de	oven:1630, frying pan:1311, ···
yaku (2) (have difficulty)	*ga*	teacher:3, government:3, person:3, ···
	wo	fingers:2950
	ni	attack:18, action:15, son:15, ···
yaku (3) (burn)	*ga*	maker:1, distributor:1
	wo	data:178, file:107, copy:9, ···
	ni	R:1583, CD:664, CDR:3, ···
⋮	⋮	⋮

Table 1: Acquired case frames of *yaku*. "CS" indicates case slots, such as *ga* (NOM), *wo* (ACC), *ni* (DAT) and *de* (LOC). Example words are expressed only in English due to space limitation. The number following each word denotes its frequency.

4.2.1 Automatically Constructed Case Frames

We employ automatically constructed case frames (Kawahara and Kurohashi, 2006). This section outlines the method for constructing the case frames.

A large corpus is automatically parsed, and case

[4]http://nlp.ist.i.kyoto-u.ac.jp/EN/index.php?KNP

frames are constructed from predicate-argument examples in the resulting parses. The problems of automatic case frame construction are syntactic and semantic ambiguities. That is to say, the parsing results inevitably contain errors, and verb senses are intrinsically ambiguous. To cope with these problems, case frames are gradually constructed from reliable predicate-argument examples.

First, predicate-argument examples that have no syntactic ambiguity are extracted, and they are disambiguated by a pair consisting of a verb and its closest case component. Such pairs are explicitly expressed on the surface of text, and are thought to play an important role in sentence meanings. For instance, examples are distinguished not by verbs (e.g., *yaku* (bake/broil/have difficulty)), but by pairs (e.g., *pan-wo yaku* (bake bread), *niku-wo yaku* (broil meat), and *te-wo yaku* (have difficulty)). Predicate-argument examples are aggregated in this way, and yield basic case frames.

Thereafter, the basic case frames are clustered to merge similar case frames. For example, since *pan-wo yaku* (bake bread) and *niku-wo yaku* (broil meat) are similar, they are clustered. The similarity is measured by using a distributional thesaurus based on the study described in Lin (1998).

By using this gradual procedure, we constructed case frames from a web corpus. The case frames were obtained from approximately 1.6 billion sentences extracted from the web. They consisted of 43,000 predicates, and the average number of case frames for a verb was 22.2. In Table 1, some examples of the resulting case frames of the verb *yaku* are listed.

4.2.2 Cooccurrences of Noun-noun Modifications

Adnominal nouns have selectional preferences to nouns, and thus this characteristic is useful for coordination disambiguation. We collect dependency relations between nouns, which have the form of "N_1-*no* N_2" (N_2 of N_1), from automatic parses of a large corpus. We performed this extraction using the web corpus of 1.6 billion sentences, and obtained 55.5 million unique dependency relations. We keep a cooccurrence frequency for each relation.

4.2.3 Cooccurrences of Coordinated Nouns

Some nouns are likely to be coordinated. We use this characteristic as lexical parallelism. We collect cooccurrences of coordinated nouns from automatic parses of a large corpus. We extracted 54.1 million unique noun pairs from the web corpus of 1.6 billion sentences.

4.3 Our Model

We employ the probabilistic generative model of dependency and case structure analysis (Kawahara and Kurohashi, 2008) as a base model. This base model resolves coordination ambiguities only on the basis of selectional preferences of predicates and nouns on which conjuncts depend. To capture syntactic parallelism, we integrate the synchronized generation process into the base model. Lexical parallelism is also factored within the generation of pre-conjuncts of coordinate structures.

Our model assigns a probability to each possible dependency structure, T, and case structure, L, of the input sentence, S, and outputs the dependency and case structure that have the highest probability. In other words, the model selects the dependency structure T_{best} and the case structure L_{best} that maximize the probability $P(T, L|S)$ or its equivalent, $P(T, L, S)$, as follows:

$$\begin{aligned}(T_{best}, L_{best}) &= \text{argmax}_{(T,L)} P(T, L|S) \\ &= \text{argmax}_{(T,L)} \frac{P(T, L, S)}{P(S)} \\ &= \text{argmax}_{(T,L)} P(T, L, S). \quad (1)\end{aligned}$$

The last equation follows from the fact that $P(S)$ is constant.

In the model, a clause (or predicate-argument structure) is considered as a generation unit and the input sentence is generated from the root of the sentence. The probability $P(T, L, S)$ is defined as the product of the probabilities of generating clauses C_i as follows:

$$P(T, L, S) = \prod_{C_i \in S} P(C_i|C_h), \quad (2)$$

where C_h is the modifying clause of C_i. Since the Japanese language is head final, the main clause at the end of a sentence does not have a modifying head; we account for this by assuming C_h = EOS (End Of Sentence).

The probability $P(C_i|C_h)$ is defined in a manner similar to that in Kawahara and Kurohashi (2008). This probability is calculated as the product of generative probabilities of a case frame, its case slots and governed argument nouns. The differences between the probability in the above study and that in our study are the generative probability of case slots and the generative probability of argument nouns. We describe these two probabilities in the following sections.

4.3.1 Generative Probability of Case Slot

In the base model, the generative probability of case slots is defined as follows:

$$P(A(s_j)=\{\mathrm{Y},\mathrm{N}\}|CF_l), \quad (3)$$

where CF_l is a case frame; s_j is a case slot of the case frame CF_l; and $A(s_j)$ is a binary function that returns Y if a case slot s_j is filled with an argument; otherwise, N.

In our model, if the target predicate or noun does not constitute a coordinate structure, we use the probability (3) for the case slot generation. If the target predicate or noun constitutes a coordinate structure and has a pre-conjunct, we use the following modified probability that depends on whether the same case slot of a pre-conjunct is filled.

$$P(A(s_j)=\{\mathrm{Y},\mathrm{N}\}|CF_l, A_c(s_j)=\{\mathrm{Y},\mathrm{N}\}), \quad (4)$$

where $A_c(s_j)$ represents the situation of the same case slot of the pre-conjunct.

In practice, to avoid the data sparseness problem, we interpolate this probability, which is conditioned on case frames, with the probability conditioned on predicates in the same manner as in Collins (1999).

4.3.2 Generative Probability of Argument Nouns

In the base model, the generative probability of argument nouns in a clause is defined as the product of the generative probability of an argument noun $P_{n_{jk}}$:

$$\prod_{s_j:A(s_j)=Y} \prod_{n_{jk}\in N_{s_j}} P_{n_{jk}}, \quad (5)$$

where N_{s_j} is a set of nouns including a noun filled in the case slot s_j and its coordinated nouns. The generative probability of an argument noun is given as follows:

$$P_{n_{jk}} = P(n_{jk}|CF_l, s_j). \quad (6)$$

In our model, the direct argument noun filled in the case slot s_j is generated with the above probability. The coordinated nouns, which have no direct dependency relation to the predicate, are generated with the following probability:

$$P'_{n_{jk}} = \sqrt{P(n_{jk}|CF_l, s_j) \times P(n_{jk}|n_{jh}, \mathrm{CNJ})}, \quad (7)$$

	# of sents.	# of coord.	# of words in coord.
newspaper	1,000	630	14.7
patent	1,000	1,264	14.8
web	759	453	11.4

Table 2: Statistics of three test sets: the number of sentences, the number of coordinate structures and the average number of words that constitute a coordinate structure. Since a sentence can contain more than one coordinate structure, the number of coordinate structures in the patent set is larger than the number of sentences.

where n_{jh} is a head of n_{jk}, which constitutes a coordinate structure (designated as CNJ) with n_{jh}.

For instance, in Figure 1, the probability of generating *kenkou* (health) and *heiwa* (peace) from the verb *inoru* (pray) is written as follows:[5] [6]

$$P(\text{peace}|CF_{pray}, \mathrm{ACC})\times$$
$$\sqrt{P(\text{health}|CF_{pray}, \mathrm{ACC}) \times P(\text{health}|\text{peace}, \mathrm{CNJ})}.$$

This probability is estimated on the basis of the cooccurrence data of coordinated nouns described in section 4.2.3.

4.4 Practical Issue

The proposed model considers all the possible dependency structures including coordination ambiguities. To reduce this high computational cost, we introduced the CKY framework to the search (Eisner, 1996).

5 Experiments

5.1 Experimental Settings

We evaluated the dependency structures that were output by our proposed model. The necessary lexical resources for this parser, which include case frames, statistics of noun-noun modifications and coordinated nouns, and lexical parameters of our model, were acquired from automatic parses of 1.6 billion Japanese sentences crawled from the web (Kawahara and Kurohashi, 2006).

[5] In the probabilities in Figure 1, "pray" is used instead of "CF_{pray}" for simplicity.

[6] This probability can be intuitively understood from the approximation: $P(\text{peace, health}|\text{pray}) = P(\text{peace}|\text{pray}) \times \sqrt{P(\text{health}|\text{pray, peace})^2} \approx P(\text{peace}|\text{pray}) \times \sqrt{P(\text{health}|\text{pray}) \times P(\text{health}|\text{peace})}$.

		pref (baseline)	pref+parallelism	improve
newspaper	all	7,356/8,248 (89.2%)	7,398/8,248 (89.7%)	0.5%**
	coordination key	1,226/1,592 (77.0%)	1,251/1,592 (78.6%)	1.6%**
	coordination scope	2,291/2,631 (87.1%)	2,320/2,631 (88.2%)	1.1%**
patent	all	9,758/11,318 (86.2%)	9,852/11,318 (87.0%)	0.8%**
	coordination key	1,839/2,528 (72.7%)	1,887/2,528 (74.6%)	1.9%**
	coordination scope	3,776/4,573 (82.6%)	3,839/4,573 (83.9%)	1.3%**
web	all	4,563/5,114 (89.2%)	4,584/5,114 (89.6%)	0.4%**
	coordination key	893/1,125 (79.4%)	906/1,125 (80.5%)	1.1%*
	coordination scope	1,242/1,462 (85.0%)	1,257/1,462 (86.0%)	1.0%*

Table 3: Dependency accuracies of "pref" (baseline) and "pref+parallelism" (proposed) in the domains of newspapers, patents and web. ** and * represent statistically significant with $p < 0.01$ and with $p < 0.05$, respectively.

The parameters related to unlexical types were calculated from a training part of the Kyoto University Text Corpus. The Kyoto University Text Corpus is syntactically annotated in dependency formalism, and consists of 40K Japanese newspaper sentences. The training part is the remaining part excluding the test 1,000 sentences that are described below.

To evaluate the effectiveness of our model, our experiments were conducted using three test sets: newspaper set, patent set and web set. Table 2 lists some statistics of these test sets. As the newspaper set, we randomly extracted 1,000 sentences from the Kyoto University Text Corpus. The patent set consists of 1,000 sentences drawn from 2004's patent filings of the domain of "*Microbe/Ferment*." The web set consists of 759 sentences from the web, which are not included in the raw corpus of 1.6 billion sentences. This web set is the same as the test set used in previous studies. All the test sets follow the annotation criteria of the Kyoto University Text Corpus. As the input of our experiments, all the test sets were automatically segmented and tagged using the JUMAN morphological analyzer.[7]

We used the probabilistic generative model of dependency and case structure analysis (Kawahara and Kurohashi, 2008) as a baseline system for the purpose of comparison. This parser resolves coordination ambiguities based only on selectional preferences. We use the above-mentioned case frames in the baseline parser, which also requires automatically constructed case frames.

[7]http://nlp.ist.i.kyoto-u.ac.jp/EN/index.php?JUMAN

5.2 Evaluation

We evaluated the dependency structures analyzed by the proposed model and the baseline model. The dependency structures obtained were evaluated with regard to unlabeled dependency accuracy — the proportion of correct dependencies out of all dependencies.

Table 3 lists the dependency accuracies. In this table, "pref" represents the baseline model, which is the probabilistic parser of dependency and case structure with only selectional preferences, and "pref+parallelism" represents our proposed model. "all" represents the overall dependency accuracies. The proposed model significantly outperformed the baseline system in all the sets (McNemar's test; $p < 0.01$).

In Table 3, the dependency accuracies are further classified into *coordination key* and *coordination scope*. Coordination key means the dependency accuracy of coordination key *bunsetsus*, which possibly lead coordinate structures. Coordination scope means the dependency accuracy of *bunsetsus* inside coordinate structures of the manual annotation.

5.3 Discussions

In the newspaper and patent sets, in particular, the accuracies of both coordination key and coordination scope were improved by 1.1% to 1.9%. These improvements were conduced by the consideration of syntactic and lexical parallelism. In the web set, the accuracies of coordination related dependencies were less improved than those of the newspaper and patent sets.

Figure 2 shows improved analyses; here, the dotted lines represent the analysis performed using the baseline "pref," and the solid lines rep-

(a)	*seikentantousyatoshite-no*	*chikara-to*	*syusyo-no*	*ninki*	*ryomen-ga*	*aru-ga*	...
	person in political power-GEN	competence-CNJ	prime minister-GEN	popularity	both-NOM	have	

(have the competence as the person in political power and the popularity of the prime minister, ...)

(b)	*Yokozuna-toshite*	*hatsu-no*	*honbasyo-wo*	*mukae,*	*kousutato-wo*	*kiritai*	*Takanohana.*
	sumo champion-as	first-GEN	tournament-ACC	confront	good start-ACC	want to make	Takanohana

(Takanohana who confronts a regular tournament and wants to make a good start as a sumo champion, ...)

(c)	*kodoseicho-ga*	*tsuzuki,*	*keizai-ga*	*kanetsu,*	*bukkajoshoritsu-wa*	*saiaku-ninatta*
	high growth-NOM	continue	economy-NOM	overheat	percentage change in prices-TOP	become worst

(high growth continues, economy is overheated, and percentage change in prices becomes the worst)

Figure 2: Improved examples. The dotted lines represent the results of "pref," and the solid lines, which are correct dependencies, represent the analysis of "pref+parallelism." The underlined *bunsetsus* represent coordination key *bunsetsus*.

resent the analysis performed using the proposed method, "pref+parallelism." These sentences are incorrectly analyzed by the baseline but correctly analyzed by the proposed method. For example, in sentence (a), the head of *seikentantousyatoshite-no* (person in political power-GEN) was correctly judged as *chikara-to* (competence-CNJ). This is because the two genitive (GEN) *bunsetsus* were synchronously generated to prefer syntactic parallelism.

The proposed model did not largely outperform the baseline in the web set. One of the reasons of this result was due to weak parallelism in the web set. We found that coordinate structures in the newspaper and patent sets tend to have greater syntactic parallelism than those in the web set. The average number of words that constitute a coordinate structure in the newspaper set was 14.7 and that in the patent set was 14.8, whereas that in the web set was 11.4, as shown in Table 2. Therefore, it was hard to show substantial improvement by considering such weak parallelism of coordinate structures in the web set.

In order to compare our results with a discriminative dependency parser, we input the patent set and the web set into an SVM-based Japanese dependency parser, CaboCha (Kudo and Matsumoto, 2002),[8] which was trained using the Kyoto University Text Corpus.[9] Its dependency accuracies were 86.3% (9,770/11,320) for the patent set and 88.7% (4,534/5,114) for the web set, which are lower than those of our proposed model. This low performance can be attributed to the lack of sufficient consideration of both parallelism and selectional preferences, as mentioned in Sassano (2004). Another cause of the low performance is the out-of-domain training corpus. This SVM-based parser was trained on a newspaper corpus, while the test sets were obtained from patent filings and the web because tagged corpora of these domains that are large enough to train a supervised parser are not available. In other words, our proposed model achieved a good performance on the patent set without using in-domain corpora.

6 Conclusion

In this paper, we have proposed a unified generative model of coordination that simultaneously considers parallelism and selectional preferences. Syntactic parallelism is modeled by the synchronized generation process of pre-modifiers of conjuncts, and lexical parallelism was factored within the generation of pre-conjuncts. Selectional preferences are acquired from large raw corpora as case frames and statistics of noun-noun modifications. The experimental results indicate the effectiveness of our model, particularly in the domains of newspapers and patents. The acquired case frames can be obtained from a non-profit organization and our analysis system will be freely available at our web site. Our future research involves incorporating ellipsis resolution to develop an integrated model for syntactic, case, and ellipsis analyses.

[8] http://chasen.org/~taku/software/cabocha/

[9] We did not input the newspaper set into CaboCha, because it is included in the training corpus used in CaboCha.

References

Rajeev Agarwal and Lois Boggess. 1992. A simple but useful approach to conjunct identification. In *Proceedings of ACL1992*, pages 15–21.

Ekaterina Buyko and Udo Hahn. 2008. Are morphosyntactic features more predictive for the resolution of noun phrase coordination ambiguity than lexicosemantic similarity scores? In *Proceedings of COLING2008*, pages 89–96.

Francis Chantree, Adam Kilgarriff, Anne de Roeck, and Alistair Wills. 2005. Disambiguating coordinations using word distribution information. In *Proceedings of RANLP2005*.

Eugene Charniak and Mark Johnson. 2005. Coarse-to-fine n-best parsing and maxent discriminative reranking. In *Proceedings of ACL2005*, pages 173–180.

Michael Collins. 1999. *Head-Driven Statistical Models for Natural Language Parsing*. Ph.D. thesis, University of Pennsylvania.

Amit Dubey, Patrick Sturt, and Frank Keller. 2005. Parallelism in coordination as an instance of syntactic priming: Evidence from corpus-based modeling. In *Proceedings of Human Language Technology Conference and Conference on Empirical Methods in Natural Language Processing*, pages 827–834.

Amit Dubey, Frank Keller, and Patrick Sturt. 2006. Integrating syntactic priming into an incremental probabilistic parser, with an application to psycholinguistic modeling. In *Proceedings of COLING-ACL2006*, pages 417–424.

Jason M. Eisner. 1996. Three new probabilistic models for dependency parsing: An exploration. In *Proceedings of COLING-96*, pages 340–345.

Kazuo Hara, Masashi Shimbo, Hideharu Okuma, and Yuji Matsumoto. 2009. Coordinate structure analysis with global structural constraints and alignment-based local features. In *Proceedings of ACL-IJCNLP2009*, pages 967–975.

Deirdre Hogan. 2007. Coordinate noun phrase disambiguation in a generative parsing model. In *Proceedings of ACL2007*, pages 680–687.

Daisuke Kawahara and Sadao Kurohashi. 2006. Case frame compilation from the web using high-performance computing. In *Proceedings of LREC2006*.

Daisuke Kawahara and Sadao Kurohashi. 2008. Coordination disambiguation without any similarities. In *Proceedings of COLING2008*, pages 425–432.

Sandra Kübler, Erhard Hinrichs, Wolfgang Maier, and Eva Klett. 2009. Parsing coordinations. In *Proceedings of EACL2009*, pages 406–414.

Taku Kudo and Yuji Matsumoto. 2002. Japanese dependency analysis using cascaded chunking. In *Proceedings of CoNLL2002*, pages 29–35.

Sadao Kurohashi and Makoto Nagao. 1994. A syntactic analysis method of long Japanese sentences based on the detection of conjunctive structures. *Computational Linguistics*, 20(4):507–534.

Sadao Kurohashi and Makoto Nagao. 1998. Building a Japanese parsed corpus while improving the parsing system. In *Proceedings of LREC1998*, pages 719–724.

Dekang Lin. 1998. Automatic retrieval and clustering of similar words. In *Proceedings of COLING-ACL98*, pages 768–774.

Preslav Nakov and Marti Hearst. 2005. Using the web as an implicit training set: Application to structural ambiguity resolution. In *Proceedings of HLT-EMNLP2005*, pages 835–842.

Philip Resnik. 1999. Semantic similarity in a taxonomy: An information-based measure and its application to problems of ambiguity in natural language. *Journal of Artificial Intelligence Research*, 11:95–130.

Manabu Sassano. 2004. Linear-time dependency analysis for Japanese. In *Proceedings of COLING2004*, pages 8–14.

Masashi Shimbo and Kazuo Hara. 2007. A discriminative learning model for coordinate conjunctions. In *Proceedings of EMNLP-CoNLL2007*, pages 610–619.

Gertjan van Noord. 2007. Using self-trained bilexical preferences to improve disambiguation accuracy. In *Proceedings of IWPT2007*, pages 1–10.

Syntactic Parsing for Ranking-Based Coreference Resolution

Altaf Rahman and **Vincent Ng**
Human Language Technology Research Institute
University of Texas at Dallas
Richardson, TX 75083-0688
{altaf,vince}@hlt.utdallas.edu

Abstract

Recent research efforts have led to the development of a state-of-the-art supervised coreference model, the cluster-ranking model. However, it is not clear whether the features that have been shown to be useful when employed in traditional coreference models will fare similarly when used in combination with this new model. Rather than merely re-evaluate them using the cluster-ranking model, we examine two interesting types of features derived from syntactic parses, tree-based features and path-based features, and discuss the challenges involved in employing them in the cluster-ranking model. Results on a set of Switchboard dialogues show their effectiveness in improving the cluster-ranking model: using them to augment a baseline coreference feature set yields a 8.6–11.7% reduction in relative error.

1 Introduction

Coreference resolution is the task of determining which noun phrases (NPs) in a text or dialogue refer to the same real-world entity. According to Webber (1979), coreference resolution can be decomposed into two complementary subtasks: "(1) identifying what a text potentially makes available for anaphoric reference and (2) constraining the candidate set of a given anaphoric expression down to one possible choice". These two subtasks are commonly known as *anaphoricity determination* and *anaphora resolution*, both of which have recently been tackled using machine learning techniques. More specifically, anaphoricity determination is typically tackled by training an *anaphoricity classifier*, which determines whether an NP is anaphoric or not (e.g., Poesio et al. (2004), Zhou and Kong (2009)). If so, the NP is passed to the second component, the resolution system, which identifies an antecedent for the NP. This resolver is typically implemented by training a *mention-pair* (MP) model, which is a binary classifier that determines whether a pair of NPs are co-referring or not (e.g., Soon et al. (2001), Ng and Cardie (2002b)).

While this architecture is popularly adopted by coreference researchers and was implemented even within recently developed coreference resolvers (e.g., Bengtson and Roth (2008), Stoyanov et al. (2009)), neither the architecture itself nor its aforementioned implementation is satisfactory for at least two reasons. First, in this pipeline architecture, anaphoricity determination is performed prior to coreference resolution, so errors in anaphoricity determination can propagate to the downstream coreference component and adversely affect its performance (Ng and Cardie, 2002a). Second, the MP coreference model is fundamentally weak in that (1) the information extracted from two NPs may not be sufficient for making an informed coreference decision and (2) since the model is trained to compare the NP to be resolved (henceforth the *active NP*) against a candidate antecedent, it only determines how good the candidate is relative to the active NP, not how good the candidate is relative to other candidates.

In light of the aforementioned problems, researchers have proposed a number of solutions:

- To address the *error propagation* problem, researchers have proposed *joint inference* (Denis and Baldridge, 2007) and *joint learning* (Rahman and Ng, 2009) for anaphoricity determination and coreference resolution.
- To address the *expressiveness* problem resulting from making a coreference decision based on only two NPs, researchers have proposed the *entity-mention* model, where coreference decisions are made by determining whether an NP belongs to a preceding coreference *cluster* (e.g., Luo et al. (2004), Yang

et al. (2008)).

- To address the failure to directly compare candidate antecedents and determine the best one, researchers have proposed the *mention-ranking* model, which imposes a ranking on the candidate antecedents and therefore captures the competition among them (e.g., Denis and Baldridge (2008), Iida et al. (2009)).

Recent research efforts have led to the development of a state-of-the-art supervised coreference model that can address *all* of the aforementioned problems, namely the *joint cluster-ranking* (CR) model (Rahman and Ng, 2009). However, other than its superior empirical performance to competing coreference models (such as the MP model), little is known about the joint CR model. In particular, most of the linguistic features for coreference resolution were developed and evaluated in the context of the MP model, and thus it is not clear whether these features would fare similarly when used in combination with the joint CR model.

Motivated by this observation, our goal in this paper is to examine the value of features derived from syntactic parses for the joint CR model. Note that parse-based features have been investigated extensively for the MP model. For example, they have been used to implement Binding Constraints (e.g., Luo and Zitouni (2005)) and encode syntactic salience (e.g., Haghighi and Klein (2009)). Rather than re-evaluate them for the CR model, we investigate two types of parse-based features that we believe are particularly interesting.

First, we employ parse trees directly as *structured* features for the joint CR model. The main advantage of employing tree-based structured features is simplicity: we no longer need to design heuristics to extract the desired features (e.g., salience, Binding Constraints) from the parse trees, as designing heuristics can be time-consuming and sometimes difficult for certain tasks. Note, however, that previous attempts have employed structured features to train an MP model for anaphora resolution (Yang et al., 2006; Versley et al., 2008) and an anaphoricity classifier in the aforementioned pipeline architecture (Zhou and Kong, 2009). In both cases, the structured features are combined with their non-structured (i.e., *flat*) counterparts via a composite kernel and used to train a classification model. What is interesting for us to investigate in this paper, however, is the question of how to combine flat and structured features in a *ranking* model that employs *joint* learning. With the increasingly important role structured features and ranking models play in natural language learning, we believe that a method for combining flat and structured features for training a ranker would be of particular interest to natural language processing (NLP) researchers.[1]

Second, motivated in part by lexical semantics research (Lin and Pantel, 2001), we investigate *path-based* features, which encode the contextual relationship between an active NP and a candidate antecedent as the shortest path between the corresponding nodes in the parse tree. As with other NLP tasks, the effectiveness of a given type of features for coreference resolution depends in part on how the linguistic information it intends to capture is represented. We seek to investigate the extent to which a joint CR model can benefit from this path-based representation of context.

Unlike the vast majority of English coreference resolvers, which were evaluated using the MUC and ACE corpora, our resolver was evaluated on a set of Switchboard dialogues. To our knowledge, we are among the first to report results for the full coreference task on this dataset. As a result, our work contributes to the establishment of a baseline using a state-of-the-art supervised coreference model against which future work can be compared. Our experimental results indicate that while both the tree-based and path-based features improve coreference performance when applied to a Baseline feature set in isolation, the best performance is achieved when they are applied in combination. In particular, these two types of features yield an improvement of 2.2–3.7% in F-measure over the Baseline joint CR model, which corresponds to a 8.6–11.7% reduction in relative error.

The rest of the paper is organized as follows. Section 2 discusses our implementation of the joint CR model. Section 3 describes tree-based and path-based features and how they can be integrated into the CR model. We present evaluation results in Section 4 and conclude in Section 5.

2 The Baseline Coreference Model

This section describes the Baseline CR model. Since the CR model is a natural extension of the

[1] The dual form of Collins and Duffy's (2002) ranking algorithm can also combine flat and structured features. Note that their algorithm employs online learning, whereas ours employs batch learning in a maximum-margin fashion.

MP model, in order to understand the CR model, it helps to first understand the MP model.

2.1 The Mention-Pair Model

As noted before, the MP model is a classifier that determines whether two NPs are co-referring or not. Each instance $i(\text{NP}_j, \text{NP}_k)$ corresponds to two NPs, NP_j and NP_k, and is represented by 39 features (see Table 1 of Rahman and Ng (2009) for a description of these features). Linguistically, these features can be divided into four groups: string-matching, grammatical, semantic, and positional. However, they can also be categorized based on whether they are *relational* or *non-relational*: relational features capture the relationship between NP_j and NP_k, whereas non-relational features capture the linguistic properties of one of them.

We follow Soon et al.'s (2001) method for creating training instances. Specifically, we create (1) a positive instance for each anaphoric NP NP_k and its closest antecedent NP_j; and (2) a negative instance for NP_k paired with each of the intervening NPs, $\text{NP}_{j+1}, \text{NP}_{j+2}, \ldots, \text{NP}_{k-1}$. The classification associated with a training instance is either positive or negative, depending on whether the two NPs are coreferent. To train the MP model, we use the SVM learner from SVM^{light} (Joachims, 1999).[2]

After training, the classifier is used to identify an antecedent for an NP in a test text. Each NP, NP_k, is compared in turn to each preceding NP, NP_j, from right to left, and NP_j is selected as its antecedent if the pair is classified as coreferent. The process ends as soon as an antecedent is found for NP_k or the beginning of the text is reached.

2.2 The Cluster-Ranking Model

The CR model addresses two weaknesses of the MP model, one concerning expressiveness and the other concerning its failure to compare candidate antecedents directly and capture the competition among them. It does so by combining the strengths of the entity-mention model and the mention-ranking model. As discussed before, the mention-ranking model addresses the failure to compare candidate antecedents by training a ranker to impose a ranking on the candidate antecedents for an active NP. On the other hand, the entity-mention model addresses the expressiveness problem by determining whether an active NP belongs to a preceding, possibly partially-formed, coreference cluster. Its increased expressiveness stems from its ability to employ *cluster-level* features (i.e., features that are defined over any subset of NPs in a preceding cluster). Combining the entity-mention model and the mention-ranking model yields the CR model, which ranks the preceding clusters for an active NP so that the highest-ranked preceding cluster is the one to which the active NP should be linked.

Since the CR model ranks preceding clusters, a training instance $i(c_j, \text{NP}_k)$ represents a preceding cluster c_j and an anaphoric NP NP_k. Each instance consists of two types of features: (1) features that are computed based solely on NP_k, and (2) cluster-level features, which describe the relationship between c_j and NP_k. Motivated in part by Culotta et al. (2007), we create cluster-level features from the *relational* features in our 39-feature set using four logical predicates: NONE, MOST-FALSE, MOST-TRUE, and ALL. Specifically, for each relational feature X, we first convert X into an equivalent set of binary-valued features if it is multi-valued. Then, for each resulting binary-valued feature X_b, we create four binary-valued cluster-level features: (1) NONE-X_b is true when X_b is false between NP_k and each NP in c_j; (2) MOST-FALSE-X_b is true when X_b is true between NP_k and less than half (but at least one) of the NPs in c_j; (3) MOST-TRUE-X_b is true when X_b is true between NP_k and at least half (but not all) of the NPs in c_j; and (4) ALL-X_b is true when X_b is true between NP_k and each NP in c_j.

We follow Rahman and Ng's (2009) method for creating training instances. Specifically, for each NP, NP_k, we create a training instance between NP_k and *each* preceding cluster c_j using the features described above. Since we are training a model for jointly learning anaphoricity determination and coreference resolution, we need to provide the ranker with the option to start a new cluster by creating an additional training instance that contains features that solely describe NP_k. The rank value of a training instance $i(c_j, \text{NP}_k)$ created for NP_k is the rank of c_j among the competing clusters. If NP_k is anaphoric, the rank of $i(c_j, \text{NP}_k)$ is HIGH if NP_k belongs to c_j, and LOW otherwise. However, if NP_k is non-anaphoric, the rank of $i(c_j, \text{NP}_k)$ is LOW unless c_j corresponds to the NULL cluster, in which case its rank is HIGH. Given these training instances, we can train a ranker using SVM^{light}'s

[2]For this and subsequent uses of the SVM learner in our experiments, we set all parameters to their default values.

ranker-learning algorithm.

After training, the cluster ranker processes the NPs in a test text in a left-to-right manner. For each active NP, NP_k, we create test instances for it by pairing it with each of its preceding clusters. To allow for the possibility that NP_k is non-anaphoric, we create an additional test instance containing features that solely describe the active NP (as during training). All these test instances are then presented to the ranker. If the additional test instance is assigned the highest rank value by the ranker, then NP_k is classified as non-anaphoric and will not be resolved. Otherwise, NP_k is linked to the cluster that has the highest rank.

3 Tree-Based and Path-Based Features

In this section, we describe the tree-based and path-based features in detail and show how they can be exploited by the joint CR model.

3.1 Path-Based Features

As mentioned before, a path-based feature encodes the contextual relationship between an active NP and a candidate antecedent as the shortest path between the corresponding nodes in the parse tree. More formally, a *path* between an active NP, NP_k, and a candidate antecedent, NP_j, in a parse tree is defined as the shortest sequence of nodes in the tree that need to be traversed in order to reach NP_j from NP_k, and is represented as a sequence of non-terminal symbols, $s_1 s_2 \ldots s_m$, where s_i ($1 \leq i \leq m$) is the non-terminal symbol associated with the ith node being traversed in the path, with s_1 and s_m being the non-terminal symbol associated with the nodes spanning NP_k and NP_j, respectively. Given this representation, a path captures the shallow syntactic context in which two NPs appear.

There is a caveat, however. If the active NP and a candidate antecedent appear in different sentences, there will be no path between them. To enable the application of path-based features to these NPs, we create an additional "root" node with a random label (e.g., R) that connects the root nodes of the two trees containing these NPs. This allows a path to be established even if the two NPs appear in different sentences.

Now, to employ these paths for coreference resolution, two questions need to be answered. First, which paths should be used? In our implementation, we collect from each training text a path between each NP and each of its preceding NPs. This yields approximately 512K paths. For efficiency reasons, we reduce the number of paths being considered by removing those paths that occur less than seven times in the training set. After this filtering process, only approximately 22K paths remain. Each resulting path is represented as a binary-valued feature for coreference resolution.

Second, how can we compute the value of a path-based feature? If we were to train an MP model, its value is 1 if the path between the two NPs under consideration is the same as the path represented by the feature. Otherwise, its value is 0. Since we are training a joint CR model, where each instance corresponds to an NP, NP_k, and a preceding cluster, c_j, rather than two NPs, we compute its feature value as follows: its value is 1 if the path between NP_k and one of the NPs in c_j is the same as the path represented by the feature; otherwise, its value is 0.

We hypothesize that by capturing shallow syntactic context, path-based features can improve the performance of a coreference system. The reason is that through these features, a learner can potentially learn to distinguish between *good* paths (i.e., paths that are likely to connect coreferent NPs) and *bad* paths (i.e., paths that are likely to connect non-coreferent NPs), thus improving the resulting model's ability to identify the correct antecedent or preceding cluster for an active NP.

3.2 Tree-Based Features

Not only can parse trees be exploited to identify coreference relations via the extraction of paths, but they can be used to determine the anaphoricity of an NP. Specifically, we aim to identify *non-anaphoric* NPs by employing parse trees as structured features. While previous work has employed parse trees as structured features (Zhou and Kong, 2009), it does so in a pipeline architecture where anaphoricity determination is performed prior to coreference resolution. In contrast, we are faced with the challenge of integrating tree-based structured features with flat features in a model that involves both *joint learning* and *ranking*.

To understand how this can be done, recall that in the joint CR model, joint learning for anaphoricity determination and coreference resolution is achieved by introducing an additional training instance, $i(\text{NULL}, \text{NP}_k)$, which is formed between an active NP, NP_k, and a NULL preceding cluster, effectively providing NP_k with an option to start a new cluster. Since we aim to use tree-based features to identify non-anaphoric NPs, we augment the set of features for $\boldsymbol{i}(\text{NULL}, \text{NP}_k)$, which currently contains the flat features derived from NP_k, with these (structured) tree-based features.

Of course, having an SVM learner learn a ranking model from both the flat and tree-based features requires more than just adding the tree-based features to the feature set. In particular, we need to implement the three steps below.

Step 1: Specifying the Parse Substructure

While we want to use a parse tree directly as a feature, we do *not* want to use the *entire* tree as a feature. The reason is that a complex tree may make it difficult for the SVM learner to make generalizations: the more complex the tree is, the less likely it is to find similar trees in other instances.

To strike a better balance between having a rich representation of context and improving the learner's ability to generalize, we extract a substructure from a parse tree and use it as the value of the structured feature of an instance. This substructure was previously shown to be useful when used as a structured feature for training a classifier for determining the information status of an NP (Rahman and Ng, 2011). Given an instance $\boldsymbol{i}(\text{NULL}, \text{NP}_k)$, we extract the substructure from the parse tree containing NP_k as follows. Let $n(\text{NP}_k)$ be the root of the subtree that spans all and only the words in NP_k, and let $Parent(n(\text{NP}_k))$ be its immediate parent node. We (1) take the subtree rooted at $Parent(n(\text{NP}_k))$, (2) replace each leaf node in this subtree with a node labeled X, (3) replace the child nodes of $n(\text{NP}_k)$ with a leaf node labeled Y, and (4) use the subtree rooted at $Parent(n(\text{NP}_k))$ as the structured feature for $\boldsymbol{i}(\text{NULL}, \text{NP}_k)$. Figure 1 illustrates this substructure extraction procedure via an example.

Intuitively, the first three steps aim to provide generalizations by simplifying the tree. For example, step (1) allows us to focus on using a small window surrounding NP_k as its context. Steps (2) and (3) help generalization by ignoring the words within NP_k and its context. Note that using two labels, X and Y, helps distinguish the active NP from its context within this substructure. Also note that we simply use one node (Y) to represent the active NP, since NP-internal information (e.g., gender) has been captured by the flat features.

While this parse substructure ignores the words in NP_k, these unigrams could be useful for determining its anaphoricity, as a learner may learn from coreference-annotated data that "it" only has a moderate probability of being anaphoric, and that "the contrary" from the phrase "on the contrary" is never anaphoric. As a result, we augment the set of flat features in $\boldsymbol{i}(\text{NULL}, \text{NP}_k)$ with the unigrams extracted from NP_k.

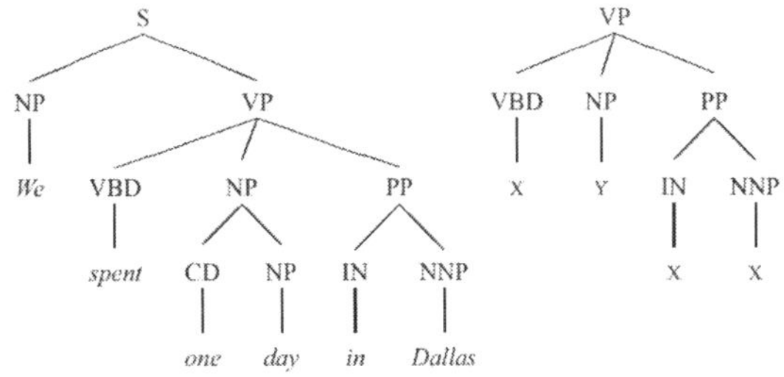

Figure 1: A parse tree (left) and the parse substructure extracted for the NP "one day" (right).

Step 2: Recasting Ranking as Classification

Existing implementations of SVMs, such as SVM^{light}-TK (Moschitti, 2004), allow us to combine flat and (structured) tree-based features to train a classifier by designing appropriate kernels. Hence, if we were to train an SVM classifier, all we need to do is to design a kernel. However, we are given a ranking problem, and it is not immediately clear how an SVM can learn a ranking model in the presence of tree-based features.

Our approach to this problem is to reduce the given ranking problem to an equivalent classification problem. Once we have a classification problem, all we need to do is to design a kernel for training a classifier, as mentioned above. To reduce a ranking problem to an equivalent classification problem, we need to convert the training set for the joint CR model to an equivalent training set that can be used to train a classifier.

Before describing the conversion process, let us first recall how the training set for a joint CR model is created. Given a training text D, we create from D a set of training instances T for a joint CR model by taking the union of $T_1, T_2, \ldots, T_n$, where T_k ($1 \leq k \leq n$) is the set of training instances generated from NP_k in D. If NP_k has $|C|$ preceding clusters, T_k will contain exactly $|C|+1$ training instances, since one training instance is generated from NP_k and each of its $|C|$ preceding clusters, and one training instance is formed between NP_k and the NULL antecedent. Each instance is associated with a rank value, which is either HIGH or LOW. Given T, the SVM ranker-learning algorithm aims to learn how to rank preceding clusters for an active NP by learning how to rank the instances within each T_k.

As noted before, to facilitate learning a ranker from both flat and tree-based features, we reformulate the given ranking problem as a set of pairwise ranking problems. The reason is that a pairwise ranking problem is essentially a *binary classification* problem, since pairwise ranking merely involves ranking two objects. Not surprisingly, this reformulation requires that we convert T into an equivalent training set T', which consists of pairwise ranking problems and can therefore be used to train a classifier (i.e., a pairwise ranker). Below we describe how to convert T to T'.

For each T_k in T, we create a training instance $inst$ for T' from each pair of training instances in T_k that have different rank values. For example, if $\boldsymbol{i}(c_i, \text{NP}_k)$ and $\boldsymbol{i}(c_j, \text{NP}_k)$ in T_k have ranks r_1 and r_2 respectively where $r_1 \neq r_2$, we create a training instance for T' whose feature vector is obtained by subtracting $\boldsymbol{i}(c_j, \text{NP}_k)$ from $\boldsymbol{i}(c_i, \text{NP}_k)$. If both feature vectors contain only flat features, the subtraction is straightforward, since each flat feature is real-valued. However, if one of the feature vectors has a tree-based feature[3] (which happens when c_i or c_j is NULL), we handle the flat features and the tree-based feature separately. Specifically, we first perform subtraction for the flat features as described above, and then append the tree-based feature to the feature set of $inst$. If $r_1 > r_2$, the class value of $inst$ is 1; otherwise, it is -1.

In sum, each T_k in T constitutes a ranking problem, and we described how to convert this ranking problem into a set of pairwise ranking problems in T'. As noted before, a pairwise ranking problem is a binary classification problem. Hence, the resulting training set, T', can be used to train a (binary) SVM classifier that minimizes the number of violations of pairwise rankings in T'.

Step 3: Designing the Composite Kernel

To train an SVM classifier on T', we need to define a kernel function for computing the similarity between a pair of instances. If both instances contain only flat features, we simply employ a normalized linear kernel, which computes similarity as the cosine of their feature vectors. However, if one or both of them has a tree-based feature, a linear kernel is not directly applicable. In this case, we need to (1) compute the similarity of their flat features and the similarity of their tree-based features separately, and then (2) employ a composite kernel, K_c, to combine the two similarity values. Specifically, we define K_c as follows:

$$K_c(F_1, F_2) = K_1(F_1, F_2) + \alpha K_2(F_1, F_2),$$

where F_1 and F_2 are the full set of features (containing both flat and structured features) that represent the two instances under consideration. K_1 is a linear kernel, which operates on the flat features. K_2 is a convolution tree kernel (Collins and Duffy, 2001), which operates on the tree-based features. Specifically, K_2 computes the similarity of two parse trees by efficiently enumerating the number of common substructures in them. To prevent the kernel value returned by K_c from being consistently dominated by one of the component kernels (i.e., K_1 and K_2), we normalize the kernel values returned by K_1 and K_2 so that they fall between 0 and 1. α is as a weight parameter that allows the two kernel values to be combined linearly, providing the flexibility to vary the relative importance of the component kernels. We will determine α empirically on the development set.

3.3 Applying the Pairwise Ranker

So far, we have described a method for training a (pairwise) ranker when the feature set contains both flat and tree-based features, which involves converting training set T to training set T'. A natural question, then, is: do we have to similarly perform this conversion on the test set so that the pairwise ranker can be applied to it?

It turns out that the answer is no. Given a set of test instances T_k to be ranked, all we need to do is to apply the pairwise ranker to each instance in T_k. The ranker produces one real value for each instance. According to the values provided by the ranker, these test instances can be ranked: the most positive value corresponds to the highest rank.

It may not be immediately clear why it makes sense to apply the pairwise ranker in the aforementioned manner to rank the test instances. Space limitations preclude a rigorous mathematical explanation. Here, we will provide a sketch of the explanation. Recall that each instance in T' was created by subtracting the feature vectors of two instances. In addition, when SVM^{light} was applied to train the pairwise ranker on T', it attempted to minimize the number of violations of

[3]Note that at most one of these two feature vectors has a tree-based feature. The reason is that exactly one of the instances in T_k has a tree-based feature, namely the one corresponding to the NULL cluster.

pairwise rankings. To do so, SVM^{light} needs to position the hyperplane so that an instance with a higher rank in T is assigned a more positive value by the hyperplane than one with a lower rank in T. Consequently, we can apply the pairwise ranker to each test instance to be ranked, and use the value returned by the ranker for each instance to impose a ranking on the test instances.

4 Evaluation

In this section, we examine the effectiveness of the tree-based and path-based features in improving the joint CR model.

4.1 Experimental Setup

Corpus. We employ in our evaluation a dataset comprising 147 coreference-annotated Switchboard dialogues, which contain a total of 68,992 NPs.[4] We partition the dialogues into a training set (117 dialogues) and a test set (30 dialogues). We extract the NPs and the parse trees directly from the gold-standard annotations, but the coreference features are computed entirely automatically.

Scoring programs. We employ two commonly-used coreference scoring programs, B^3 (Bagga and Baldwin, 1998) and ϕ_3-CEAF (Luo, 2005), both of which report results in terms of recall (R), precision (P), and F-measure (F).

4.2 Results and Discussion

The baseline mention-pair model. We employ as our first baseline the MP model, which is trained using the procedure described in Section 2.1. Given that our goal is to examine the effectiveness of the tree-based and path-based features for the joint CR model, one may wonder why the results of the MP model are relevant to our investigation. Recall from the introduction that we chose to improve the joint CR model with the two types of features derived from syntactic parses because the joint CR model has been shown to achieve state-of-the-art performance on the ACE corpus. To ensure that the joint CR model also outperforms the MP model on our Switchboard corpus (and is therefore the strongest baseline we can use), we show the results of the MP model in row 1 of Table 1. As we can see, it achieves F-measure scores of 69.1 (B^3) and 62.8 (CEAF).[5]

The baseline joint cluster-ranking model. Our second baseline is the joint CR model, which is trained using the method described in Section 2.2. In particular, this baseline model does not employ any tree-based or path-based features. Results are shown in row 2 of Table 1. In comparison to the MP model in row 1, we can see that B^3 F-measure rises from 69.1 to 74.5 and CEAF F-measure rises from 62.8 and 68.5. These results are consistent with our hypothesis that the joint CR model is indeed a stronger baseline than the MP model.

Incorporating path-based features. Next, we incorporate the path-based features into the Baseline joint CR model. Results are shown in row 3 of Table 1. In comparison to the results of the Baseline joint CR model in row 2, we can see that adding the path-based features into the feature set improves the joint CR model according to both scorers. In particular, B^3 and CEAF F-measure scores rise by 1.3% and 2.1%, respectively, suggesting the usefulness of the path-based features.

In addition to the R, P and F columns, Table 1 has two columns labeled "% err. red.", which show the error reduction of a system relative to the Baseline joint CR model. Here, we compute the error of a system by subtracting its F-measure score from the perfect F-measure (i.e., 100). With the addition of path-based features, we can see that relative error is reduced by 5.1 and 6.7 according to B^3 and CEAF, respectively.

Incorporating tree-based features. Next, we incorporate the tree-based features into the Baseline joint CR model. Recall that from a tree, we extract both flat features (i.e., unigrams) and structured features (i.e., parse substructures), so both types of features are used to augment the Baseline feature set. Because both types of features are involved, we need to tune α in the composite kernel. To ensure a fair comparison among different systems, we do *not* employ additional labeled data for tuning α. Rather, we use 75% of the available training data for training the joint CR model and reserve the remaining 25% for parameter tuning.

Results are shown in row 4 of Table 1. In comparison to the results of the Baseline joint CR model in row 2, we can see that adding the trees and the unigrams into the feature set improves the joint CR model according to both scorers. In particular, B^3 and CEAF F-measure scores rise by 1.0% and 1.9%, respectively.

[4]This dataset is released by the LDC as part of the NXT corpus (Calhoun et al., 2010).

[5]Since gold-standard NPs are used in our coreference experiments, CEAF recall, precision, and F-measure will all be the same. See Luo (2005) for details.

		B^3				CEAF			
	System	R	P	F	% err. red.	R	P	F	% err. red.
1	Baseline MP model	78.1	61.6	69.1	—	62.8	62.8	62.8	—
2	Baseline CR model	71.1	78.2	74.5	—	68.5	68.5	68.5	—
3	CR + paths	76.4	75.2	75.8	(5.10)	70.6	70.6	70.6	(6.67)
4	CR + unigrams + trees	75.1	76.0	75.5	(3.92)	70.4	70.4	70.4	(6.03)
5	CR + paths + unigrams + trees	76.6	76.8	**76.7**	(8.63)	72.2	72.2	**72.2**	(11.74)
6	CR + paths + unigrams	76.3	75.4	75.8	(5.10)	71.5	71.5	71.5	(9.52)
7	CR + paths + pipeline architecture	76.9	75.2	76.0	(5.88)	71.4	71.4	71.4	(9.21)

Table 1: Coreference results on the test set obtained using B^3 and CEAF.

Incorporating tree- and path-based features. Next, we incorporate both tree-based (i.e., unigrams and parse substructures) and path-based features into the Baseline joint CR model. As in the previous experiment, we reserve 25% of the available training data for tuning α. Results are shown in row 5 of Table 1. In comparison to the results of the Baseline joint CR model in row 2, we can see that adding both types of features improves F-measure by 2.2% (B^3) and 3.7% (CEAF), which is equivalent to a relative error reduction of 8.6% (B^3) and 11.7% (CEAF).

In comparison to the results in rows 3 and 4, we can see that better results can be obtained by applying the two types of features in combination than in isolation to the Baseline joint CR model. This suggests that although both types of features are derived from parse trees, they provide complementary information for the CR model.

Understanding the value of parse substructures. So far, we have always applied the unigrams and the parse substructures in combination in our experiments. To better understand the value of the parse substructures, we perform an ablation experiment in which we repeat the previous experiment *without* using the parse substructures.

Results are shown in row 6 of Table 1. In comparison to the results in row 5, we can see that F-measure drops by 0.9% (B^3) and 0.7% (CEAF). Since the difference in results between the two rows can be attributed entirely to the presence/absence of the parse substructures, the drop in F-measure suggests that the parse substructures are indeed useful features for the joint CR model.

Pipeline vs. joint modeling. One challenge we addressed here involves enabling the integration of structured and flat features in a ranker that performs joint learning. A natural question is: is this joint learning architecture indeed better than the traditional pipeline architecture in which anaphoricity determination is performed prior to coreference resolution? To answer this question, we show in row 7 of Table 1 the results obtained using the pipeline architecture, where (1) an anaphoricity classifier is trained with all the features used to represent an instance involving the NULL antecedent in the joint CR model in row 5 and (2) the joint CR model is trained using the Baseline and path-based features. This setup would therefore allow us to determine whether the joint architecture or the pipeline architecture can better exploit the structured features. In comparison to the results in row 5, we see that F-measure drops by 0.6–0.8%. These results suggest that joint learning is indeed better than pipeline learning in terms of exploiting structured features.

5 Conclusions

We have examined the effectiveness of tree-based and path-based features in improving a state-of-the-art supervised coreference model, the cluster-ranking model. Results on 147 Switchboard dialogues, show that both types of features are effective at improving the performance of the cluster-ranking model. In particular, when they are applied in combination, we see a reduction in relative error by 8.6–11.7%. One challenge that we addressed during the course of this investigation involves enabling flat and structured features to be employed simultaneously in a ranking model that employs joint learning. With the increasingly important role structured features and ranking models play in natural language learning, we believe that our method for combining flat and structured features for training a ranker would appeal to researchers working in different areas of NLP.

Acknowledgments

We thank the three anonymous reviewers for their invaluable comments on an earlier draft of the paper. This work was supported in part by NSF Grants IIS-0812261 and IIS-1147644.

References

Amit Bagga and Breck Baldwin. 1998. Algorithms for scoring coreference chains. In *Proceedings of the LREC Workshop on Linguistic Coreference*, pages 563–566.

Eric Bengtson and Dan Roth. 2008. Understanding the values of features for coreference resolution. In *Proceedings of EMNLP*, pages 294–303.

Sasha Calhoun, Jean Carletta, Jason Brenier, Neil Mayo, Dan Jurafsky, Mark Steedman, and David Beaver. 2010. The NXT-format Switchboard corpus: A rich resource for investigating the syntax, semantics, pragmatics and prosody of dialogue. *Language Resources and Evaluation*, 44(4):387–419.

Michael Collins and Nigel Duffy. 2001. Convolution kernels for natural language. In *Advances in NIPS*, pages 489–496.

Michael Collins and Nigel Duffy. 2002. New ranking algorithms for parsing and tagging: Kernels over discrete structures, and the voted perceptron. In *Proceedings of the ACL*, pages 263–270.

Aron Culotta, Michael Wick, and Andrew McCallum. 2007. First-order probabilistic models for coreference resolution. In *Proceedings of NAACL/HLT*, pages 81–88.

Pascal Denis and Jason Baldridge. 2007. Global, joint determination of anaphoricity and coreference resolution using integer programming. In *Proceedings of NAACL/HLT*, pages 236–243.

Pascal Denis and Jason Baldridge. 2008. Specialized models and ranking for coreference resolution. In *Proceedings of EMNLP*, pages 660–669.

Aria Haghighi and Dan Klein. 2009. Simple coreference resolution with rich syntactic and semantic features. In *Proceedings of EMNLP*, pages 1152–1161.

Ryu Iida, Kentaro Inui, and Yuji Matsumoto. 2009. Capturing salience with a trainable cache model for zero-anaphora resolution. In *Proceedings of ACL-IJCNLP*, pages 647–655.

Thorsten Joachims. 1999. Making large-scale SVM learning practical. In Bernhard Scholkopf and Alexander Smola, editors, *Advances in Kernel Methods - Support Vector Learning*, pages 44–56. MIT Press.

Dekang Lin and Patrick Pantel. 2001. DIRT: Discovery of inference rules from text. In *Proceedings of KDD*, pages 323–328.

Xiaoqiang Luo and Imed Zitouni. 2005. Multi-lingual coreference resolution with syntactic features. In *Proceedings of HLT/EMNLP*, pages 660–667.

Xiaoqiang Luo, Abe Ittycheriah, Hongyan Jing, Nanda Kambhatla, and Salim Roukos. 2004. A mention-synchronous coreference resolution algorithm based on the Bell tree. In *Proceedings of the ACL*, pages 135–142.

Xiaoqiang Luo. 2005. On coreference resolution performance metrics. In *Proceedings of HLT/EMNLP*, pages 25–32.

Alessandro Moschitti. 2004. A study on convolution kernels for shallow statistic parsing. In *Proceedings of the ACL*, pages 335–342.

Vincent Ng and Claire Cardie. 2002a. Identifying anaphoric and non-anaphoric noun phrases to improve coreference resolution. In *Proceedings of COLING*, pages 730–736.

Vincent Ng and Claire Cardie. 2002b. Improving machine learning approaches to coreference resolution. In *Proceedings of the ACL*, pages 104–111.

Massimo Poesio, Olga Uryupina, Renata Vieira, Mijail Alexandrov-Kabadjov, and Rodrigo Goulart. 2004. Discourse-new detectors for definite description resolution: A survey and a preliminary proposal. In *Proeedings of the ACL Workshop on Reference Resolution*.

Altaf Rahman and Vincent Ng. 2009. Supervised models for coreference resolution. In *Proceedings of EMNLP*, pages 968–977.

Altaf Rahman and Vincent Ng. 2011. Learning the information status of noun phrases in spoken dialogues. In *Proceedings of EMNLP*, pages 1069–1080.

Wee Meng Soon, Hwee Tou Ng, and Daniel Chung Yong Lim. 2001. A machine learning approach to coreference resolution of noun phrases. *Computational Linguistics*, 27(4):521–544.

Veselin Stoyanov, Nathan Gilbert, Claire Cardie, and Ellen Riloff. 2009. Conundrums in noun phrase coreference resolution: Making sense of the state-of-the-art. In *Proceedings of ACL-IJCNLP*, pages 656-664.

Yannick Versley, Alessandro Moschitti, Massimo Poesio, and Xiaofeng Yang. 2008. Coreference systems based on kernels methods. In *Proceedings of COLING*, pages 961–968.

Bonnie Lynn Webber. 1979. *A Formal Approach to Discourse Anaphora*. Garland Publishing, Inc.

Xiaofeng Yang, Jian Su, and Chew Lim Tan. 2006. Kernel based pronoun resolution with structured syntactic knowledge. In *Proceedings of COLING-ACL*, pages 41–48.

Xiaofeng Yang, Jian Su, Jun Lang, Chew Lim Tan, and Sheng Li. 2008. An entity-mention model for coreference resolution with inductive logic programming. In *Proceedings of the ACL*, pages 843–851.

GuoDong Zhou and Fang Kong. 2009. Global learning of noun phrase anaphoricity in coreference resolution via label propagation. In *Proceedings of EMNLP*, pages 978–986.

TriS: A Statistical Sentence Simplifier with Log-linear Models and Margin-based Discriminative Training

Nguyen Bach, Qin Gao, Stephan Vogel and **Alex Waibel**
Language Technologies Institute
Carnegie Mellon University
5000 Forbes Avenue, Pittsburgh PA, 15213
{nbach, qing, stephan.vogel, ahw}@cs.cmu.edu

Abstract

We propose a statistical sentence simplification system with log-linear models. In contrast to state-of-the-art methods that drive sentence simplification process by hand-written linguistic rules, our method used a margin-based discriminative learning algorithm operates on a feature set. The feature set is defined on statistics of surface form as well as syntactic and dependency structures of the sentences. A stack decoding algorithm is used which allows us to efficiently generate and search simplification hypotheses. Experimental results show that the simplified text produced by the proposed system reduces 1.7 Flesch-Kincaid grade level when compared with the original text. We will show that a comparison of a state-of-the-art rule-based system (Heilman and Smith, 2010) to the proposed system demonstrates an improvement of 0.2, 0.6, and 4.5 points in ROUGE-2, ROUGE-4, and $AveF_{10}$, respectively.

1 Introduction

Complicated sentences impose difficulties on reading comprehension. For instance, a person in 5th grade can comprehend a comic book easily but will struggle to understand New York Times articles which require at least 12th grade average reading level (Flesch, 1981). Complicated sentences also challenge natural language processing applications including, but not limited to, text summarization, question answering, information extraction, and machine translation (Chandrasekar et al., 1996). An example of this is syntactic parsing in which long and complicated sentences will generate a large number of hypotheses and usually fail in disambiguating the attachments. Therefore, it is desirable to pre-process complicated sentences and generate simpler counter parts. There are direct applications of sentence simplification. Dalemans et al. (2004) applied sentence simplification so that the automatically generated closed caption can fit into limited display area. The Facilita system generates accessible content from Brazilian Portuguese web pages for low literacy readers using both summarization and simplification technologies (Watanabe et al., 2009).

This paper tackles sentence-level factual simplification (SLFS). The objective of SLFS is twofold. First, SLFS will process the syntactically complicated sentences. Second, while preserving the content meaning, SLFS outputs a sequence of simple sentences. SLFS is an instance of the broader spectrum of text-to-text generation problems, which includes summarization, sentence compression, paraphrasing, and sentence fusion. Comparing to sentence compression, sentence simplification requires the conversion to be lossless in sense of semantics. It is also different from paraphrasing in that it generates multiple sentences instead of one sentence with different constructions.

There are certain specific characteristics that complicate a sentence, which include length, syntactic structure, syntactic and lexical ambiguity, and an abundance of complex words. As suggested by its objective, sentence simplification outputs "simple sentences". Intuitively, a simple sentence is easy to read and understand, and arguably easily processed by computers. A more fine-tuned definition on a simple sentence is suggested in Klebanov et al. (2004), and is termed Easy Access Sentences (EAS). EAS in English is defined as 1) EAS is a grammatical sentence; 2) EAS has one finite verb; 3) EAS does not make any claims that were not present, explicitly or implicitly; 4) An EAS should contain as many named entities as possible.

While the last two requirements are difficult to quantify, the first two provide a practical guideline for sentence simplification. In this paper, we treat the sentence simplification process as a process of statistical machine translation. Given the input of a syntactically complicated sentence, we translate it into a set of EAS that preserves as much information as possible from the original sentence. We develop the algorithm that can generate a set of EAS from the original sentence and a model to incorporate features that indicate the merit of the simplified candidates. The model is discriminatively trained on a data set of manually simplified sentences.

We briefly review related work in the area of text-to-text generation in Section 2. The proposed model for statistical sentence simplification is presented in Section 3. In Section 4 we introduce the decoding algorithm. Section 5 and 6 describe the discriminative training method we use and the feature functions. Experiments and analysis are present in Section 7, followed by the conclusion in Section 8.

2 Related Work

Given the problematic nature of text-to-text generation that takes a sentence or a document as the input and optimizes the output toward a certain objective, we briefly review state-of-art approaches of text-to-text generation methods.

Early approaches in summarization focus on extraction methods which try to isolate and then summarize the most significant sentences or paragraphs of the text. However, this has been found to be insufficient because it usually generates incoherent summaries. Barzilay and McKeown (2005) proposed sentence fusion for multi-document summarization, which produces a sentence that conveys common information of multiple sentences based upon dependency tree structures and lexical similarity.

Sentence compression generates a summary of a single sentence with minimal information loss, which can also be treated as sentence-level summarization. This approach applies word deletion, in which non informative words will be removed from the original sentence. A variety of models were developed based on this perspective, ranging from generative models (Knight and Marcu, 2002; Turner and Charniak, 2005) to discriminative models (McDonald, 2006) and Integer Linear Programming (Clarke, 2008). Another line of research treats sentence compression as machine translation, in which tree-based translation models have been developed (Galley and McKeown, 2007; Cohn and Lapata, 2008; Zhu et al., 2010). Recently, Woodsend and Lapata (2011) proposed a framework to combine tree-based simplification with ILP.

In contrast to sentence compression, sentence simplification generates multiple sentences from one input sentence and tries to preserve the meaning of the original sentence. The major objective is to transform sentences in complicated structures to a set of easy-to-read sentences, which will be easier for human to comprehend, and hopefully easier for computers to deal with.

Numerous attempts have been made to tackle the sentence simplification problem. One line of research has explored simplification with linguistic rules. Jonnalagadda (2006) developed a rule-based system that take into account the discourse information. This method is applied on simplification of biomedical text (Jonnalagadda et al., 2009) and protein-protein information extraction (Jonnalagadda and Gonzalez, 2010). Chandrasekar and Srinivas (1997) automatically induced simplification rules based on dependency trees. Additionally, Klebanov et al. (2004) develop a set of rules that generate a set of EAS from syntactically complicated sentences. Heilman and Smith (2010) proposed an algorithm for extracting simplified declarative sentences from syntactically complex sentences.

The rule-based systems performs well on English. However, in order to develop a more generic framework for other languages, a statistical framework is preferable. In this work, we follow this direction to treat the whole process as a statistical machine translation task with an online large-margin learning framework. The method is generalizable to other languages given labeled data. To ensure the information is preserved, we build a table of EAS for each object, and use stack decoding to search for the optimal combination of EAS. A feature vector is assigned to each combination and we use an end-to-end discriminative training framework to tune the parameters given a set of training data. Our method is different from Klebanov et al. (2004) in the way that we applied statistical model to rank the generated sentences. And the difference between our method and Heilman and Smith (2010) is that we integrate linguistic rules into the decoding process as soft constraints in order to explore a much larger search space.

3 Statistical Sentence Simplification with Log-linear Models

Assume that we are given an English sentence e, which is to be simplified into a set $\mathcal{S}$ of k simple sentences $\{s_1, ..., s_i, ..., s_k\}$. Among all possible simplified sets, we will select the set with the highest probability $\hat{\mathcal{S}}(e) = \arg\max_{\forall \mathcal{S}} Pr(\mathcal{S}|e)$. As the true probability distribution of $Pr(\mathcal{S}|e)$ is unknown, we have to approximate $Pr(\mathcal{S}|e)$ by developing a log-linear model $p(\mathcal{S}|e)$. In contrast to noisy-channel models (Knight and Marcu, 2002; Turner and Charniak, 2005) we directly compute simplification probability by a conditional exponential model as follow:

$$p(\mathcal{S}|e) = \frac{exp[\sum_{m=1}^{M} w_m f_m(\mathcal{S}, e)]}{\sum_{\mathcal{S}'} exp[\sum_{m=1}^{M} w_m f_m(\mathcal{S}', e)]} \quad (1)$$

where $f_m(\mathcal{S}, e), m = 1, ..., M$ are feature functions on each sentence; there exists a model parameter w_m are feature weights to be learned.

In this framework, we need to solve decoding, learning, and modeling problems. The *decoding problem*, also known as the search problem, is denoted by the arg max operation which finds the optimal $\mathcal{S}$ that maximize model probabilities. The *learning problem* amounts to obtaining suitable parameter values w_1^M subject to a loss function on training samples. Finally, the *modeling problem* amounts to developing suitable feature functions that capture the relevant properties of the sentence simplification task. Our sentence simplification model can be viewed as English-to-English log-linear translation models. The defining characteristic that makes the problem difficult is that we need to translate from one syntactically complicated sentence to k simple sentences, and k is not predetermined.

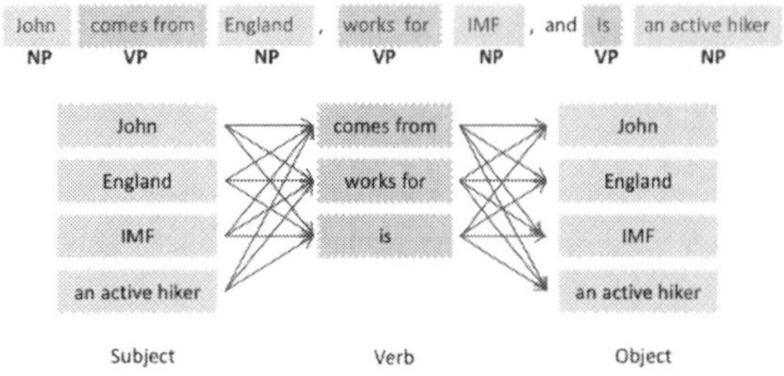

Figure 1: Constructing simple sentences

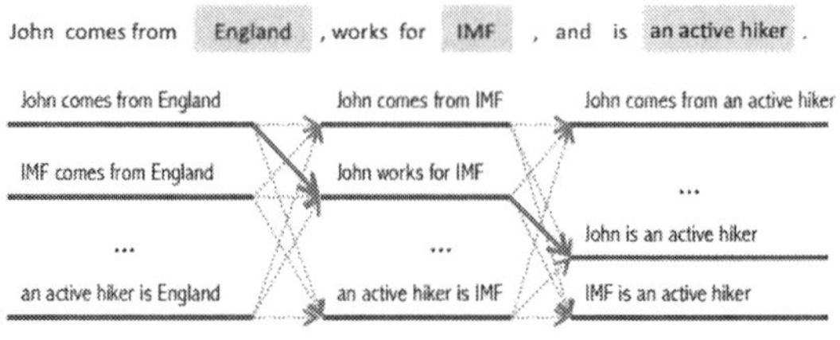

Figure 2: Left-right decoding by objects

4 Decoding

This section presents a solution to the *decoding problem*. The solution is based on a stack decoding algorithm that finds the best $\mathcal{S}$ given an English sentence e. Our decoding algorithm is inspired by the decoding algorithms in speech recognition and machine translation (Jelinek, 1998; Koehn et al., 2007). For example, with a sentence e *"John comes from England, works for IMF, and is an active hiker"*, the stack decoding algorithm tries to find $\mathcal{S}$, which is a set of three sentences: *"John comes from England"*, *"John works for IMF"* and *"John is an active hiker"*. Note that $\mathcal{S}$ is a set of k simple sentences $\mathcal{S} = \{s_1, ..., s_i, ..., s_k\}$. We can assume the items s_i are drawn from a finite set $\mathbb{S}$ of grammatical sentences that can be derived from e. Therefore, the first step is to construct the set $\mathbb{S}$.

4.1 Constructing simple sentences

We define a simple English sentence as a sentence with SVO structure, which has one subject, one verb and one object. Our definition is similar to the definition of EAS, mentioned in section 1. However, we only focus on the SVO structure and other constraints are relaxed. We assume both subjects (S) and objects (O) are noun phrases (NP) in the parse tree. For a given English sentence e, we extract a list S_{NP} of NPs and a list S_V of verbs. S_{NP} has an additional empty NP in order to handle intransitive verbs. A straightforward way to construct simple sentences is to enumerate all possible sentences based on S_{NP} and S_V. That results in $|S_{NP}|^2|S_V|$ simple sentences.

Figure 1 illustrates the constructions for *"John comes from England, works for IMF, and is an active hiker"*. The system extracts a noun phrase list S_{NP} $\{$*John, England, IMF, an active hiker*$\}$ and a verb list S_V $\{$*comes from, works for, is*$\}$. Our model constructs simple sentences such as *"John comes from England"*, *"John comes from IMF"* and *"John comes from an active hiker"*. The total number of simple sentences, $|\mathbb{S}|$, is 48.

4.2 Decoding algorithm

Given a list of simple sentences $\mathbb{S}$, the decoder's objective is to construct and find the best simplification candidate $\mathcal{S} \subset \mathbb{S}$. We call $\mathcal{S}$ a *hypothesis* in the context of the decoder. The rationale behind our left-right stack decoding algorithm is to construct a hypothesis that covers all noun phrases and verb phrases of the original sentence.

The decoding task is to find the optimal solution over all possible combinations of simple sentences, given the feature values and learned feature weights. Depending on the number of simple sentences per hypothesis, the search space grows exponentially. Since each simple sentence contains an object, we can group the candidate sentences by the object noun phrase. As a result, it is not necessary to evaluate all combinations; we can look at one object at a time from left to right. Figure 2 demonstrates the idea of decoding via objects. We have three objects *"England"*, *"IMF"* and *"an active hiker"*. The algorithm first finds potential simple sentences which have *"England"* as object. After finishing "England", the algorithm expands to *"IMF"* and *"an active hiker"*. In this example the optimal path is the path with bold arrows.

Algorithm 1 : K-Best Stack Decoding

```
1: Initialize an empty hypothesis list HypList
2: Initialize HYPS is a stack of 1-simple-sentence hypotheses
3: for i = 0 to |S_V| do
4:    Initialize stack expand_h
5:    while HYPS is not empty do
6:       pop h from HYPS
7:       expand_h ← Expand-Hypothesis(h)
8:    end while
9:    expand_h ← Prune-Hypothesis(expand_h, stack-size)
10:   HYPS ← expand_h
11:   Store hypotheses of expand_d into HypList
12: end for
13: SortedHypList ← Sort-Hypothesis(HypList)
14: Return K-best hypotheses in SortedHypList
```

Algorithm 1 is a version of stack decoding for sentence simplification. The decoding process advances by extending a state that is equivalent to a stack of hypotheses. Line 1 and 2 initialize *HYPS* stack and *HypList*. A *HYPS* stack maintains a current search state, meanwhile *HypList* stores potential hypotheses after each state. *HYPS* is initialized with hypotheses containing one simple sentence. Line 3 starts a loop over states. The number of maximum states is equal to the size of S_V plus one. Lines 4-8 represent the hypothesis expansion.

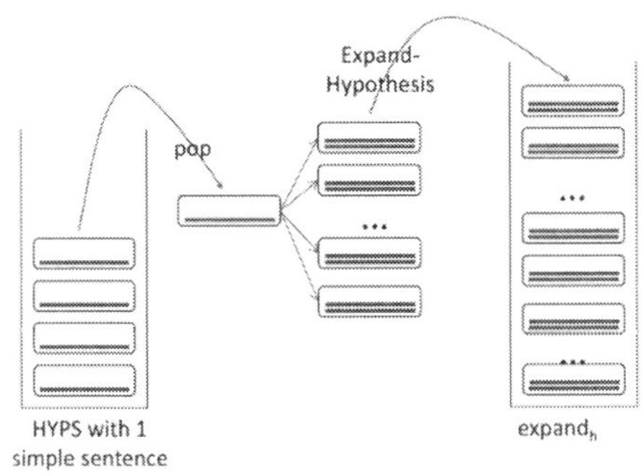

(a) Pop and Expand

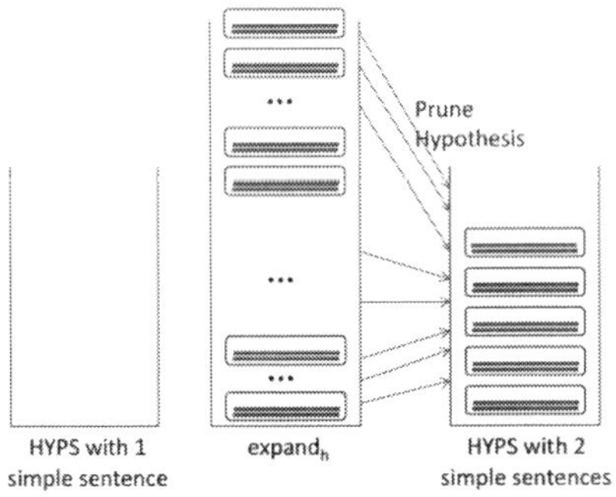

(b) Hypothesis pruning

Figure 3: A visualization for stack decoding

Figure 3a illustrates the pop-expand process of *HYPS* stack with 1-simple-sentence hypotheses. The expansion in this situation expands to a 2-simple-sentence hypotheses-stack $expand_h$. The size of $expand_h$ will exponentially increase according to the size of S_V and S_{NP}. Therefore, we prefer to maintain $expand_h$ within a limit number (*stack-size*) of hypotheses. Line 9 helps the decoder to control the size of $expand_h$ by applying different pruning strategies: word coverage, model score or both. Figure 3b illustrates the pruning process on $expand_h$ with 2-simple-sentence hypotheses. Line 10 replaces the current state with a new state of the expanded hypotheses. Before moving to a new state, *HypList* is used to preserve potential hypotheses of the current state. Line 13 sorts hypotheses in *HypList* according to their model scores and a K-best list is returned in line 14.

5 Learning

Since defining a log-linear sentence simplification model and decoding algorithm has been completed, this section describes a discriminative learning algorithm for the *learning problem*. We learn optimized weight vector w by using the Margin Infused Relaxed Algorithm or MIRA (Crammer and Singer, 2003), which is an online learner closely related to both the support vector machine and perceptron learning framework. In general, weights are updated at each step time i according to:

$$\begin{aligned} & w_{i+1} = \arg\min_{w_{i+1}} \|w_{i+1} - w_i\| \\ \text{s.t.} \quad & score(\mathcal{S}, e) \geq score(\mathcal{S}', e) + L(\mathcal{S}, \mathcal{S}') \end{aligned} \tag{2}$$

where $L(\mathcal{S}, \mathcal{S}')$ is a measure of the loss of using $\mathcal{S}'$ instead of the simplification reference $\mathcal{S}$; $score()$ is a cost function of e and $\mathcal{S}$ and in this case is the decoder score.

Algorithm 2 : MIRA training for Sentence Simplifier

training set $\tau = \{f_t, e_t\}_{t=1}^{T}$ has T original English sentences with the feature vector f_t of e_t.
ε is the simplification reference set.
m-oracle set $O = \{\}$.
The current weight vector w^i.

1: i=0
2: **for** $j = 1$ to Q **do**
3:   **for** $t = 1$ to T **do**
4:     $H \leftarrow$ get_K_Best($\mathcal{S}_t$; w^i)
5:     $O \leftarrow$ get_m_Oracle(H ; ε_t)
6:     $\gamma = \sum_{o=1}^{m} \sum_{h=1}^{K} \alpha(e_o, e_h; \varepsilon_t)(f_{e_o} - f_{e_h})$
7:     $w^{i+1} = w^i + \gamma$
8:     $i = i + 1$
9:   **end for**
10: **end for**
11: Return $\frac{\sum_{i=1}^{Q*T} w^i}{Q*T}$

Algorithm 2 is a version of MIRA for training the weights of our sentence simplification model. On each iteration, MIRA considers a single instance from the training set $(\mathcal{S}_t, e_t)$ and updates the weights so that the score of the correct simplification ε_t is greater than the score of all other simplifications by a margin proportional to their loss. However, given a sentence there are an exponential amount of possible simplification candidates. Therefore, the optimizer has to deal with an exponentially large number of constraints. To tackle this, we only consider K-best hypotheses and choose m-oracle hypotheses to support the weight update decision. This idea is similar to the way MIRA has been used in dependency parsing and machine translation (McDonald et al., 2005; Liang et al., 2006; Watanabe et al., 2007).

On each update, MIRA attempts to keep the new weight vector as close as possible to the old weight vector. Subject to margin constraints keep the score of the correct output above the score of the guessed output by updating an amount given by the loss of the incorrect output. In line 6, α can be interpreted as an update step size; when α is a large number we want to update our weights aggressively, otherwise weights are updated conservatively. α is computed as follow:

$$\alpha = \max(0, \delta)$$
$$\delta = \min \left\{ C, \frac{L(e_o, e_h; \varepsilon_t) - [score(e_o) - score(e_h)]}{||S_{e_o} - f_{e_h}||_2^2} \right\} \quad (3)$$

where C is a positive constant used to cap the maximum possible value of α; $score()$ is the decoder score; and $L(e_o, e_h; \varepsilon_t)$ is the loss function.

$L(e_o, e_h; \varepsilon_t)$ measures the difference between oracle e_o and hypothesis e_h according to the gold reference ε_t. L is crucial to guide the optimizer to learn optimized weights. We defined $L(e_o, e_h; \varepsilon_t)$ as follow

$$L(e_o, e_h; \varepsilon_t) = AveF_N(e_o, \varepsilon_t) - AveF_N(e_h, \varepsilon_t) \quad (4)$$

where $AveF_N(e_o, \varepsilon_t)$ and $AveF_N(e_h, \varepsilon_t)$ is the average n-gram (n=[2:N]) cooccurrence F-score of (e_o, ε_t) and (e_h, ε_t), respectively. In this case, we optimize the weights directly against the $AveF_N$ metric over the training data. $AveF_N$ can be substituted by other evaluation metrics such as the ROUGE family metric (Lin, 2004). Similar to the perceptron method, the actual weight vector during decoding is averaged across the number of iterations and training instances; and it is computed in line 11.

6 Modeling

We now turn to the *modeling problem*. Our fundamental question is: given the model in Equation 1 with M feature functions, what linguistic features can be leveraged to capture semantic information of the original sentence? We address the question in this section by describing features that cover different levels of linguistic structures. Our model incorporates 177 features based on information from the original English sentence e which contains chunks, syntactic and dependency parse trees (Ramshaw and Marcus, 1995; Marneffe et al., 2006).

6.1 Simple sentence level features

A simplification hypothesis s contains k simple sentences. Therefore, it is crucial that our model chooses reasonable simple sentences to form a hypothesis. For each simple sentence s_i we incorporated the following feature functions:

Word Count These features count the number word in subject (S), verb (V) and object (O), also counting the number of proper nouns in S and the number of proper nouns in O.

Distance between NPs and Verbs These features focus on the number of NPs and VPs in between S, V and O. This feature group includes the number of NPs between S and V, the number of NPs between V and O, the number of VPs between S and V, the number of VPs between V and O.

Dependency Structures It is possible that the decoder constructs semantically incorrect simple sentences, in which S, V, and O do not have any semantic connection. One way to possibly reduce this kind of mistake is analyze the dependency chain between S, V, and O on the original dependency tree of e. Our dependency structure features include the minimum and maximum distances of (S:O), (S:V), and (V:O).

Syntactic Structures Another source of information is the syntactic parse tree of e, which can be used to extract syntactic features. The sentence-like boundary feature considers the path from S to O along the syntactic parse tree to see whether it crosses the sentence-like boundary (e.g. relative clauses). For example in the original sentence "*John comes from England and works for IMF which stands for International Monetary Funds*", the simple sentence "*IMF stands for International Monetary Funds*" has sentence-like boundary feature is triggered since the path from "*IMF*" to "*International Monetary Funds*" on the syntactic tree of the original sentence contains an SBAR node.

Another feature is the PP attachment feature. This checks if the O contains a prepositional phrase attachment or not. Moreover, the single pronoun feature will check if S and O are single pronoun or not. The last feature is VO common ancestor, which looks at the syntactic tree to see whether or not V and O share the same VP tag as a common ancestor.

6.2 Interactive simple sentence features

A collection of grammatically sound simplified sentences does not necessarily make a good hypothesis Dropping words, unnecessary repetition, or even wrong order can make the hypothesis unreadable. Therefore, our model needs to be equipped with features that are capable to measure the interactiveness across simple sentences and are also able to represent s in the best possible manner. We incorporated the following features into our model:

Sentence Count This group of features consider the number of sentences in the hypothesis. It consists of an integral feature of sentence count $sc_i = |S|$, and a group of binary features $scb_k = \delta(|S|) = k$ where $k \in [1, 6]$ is the number of sentence.

NP and Verb Coverage The decoder's objective is to improve the chance of generating hypotheses that cover all NP and verbs of the original sentence e. These features count the number of NPs and verbs that have been covered by the hypothesis, by the 1st and 2nd simple sentences. Similarly, these features also count the number of missing NPs and verbs.

S and O cross sentences These features count how many times S of the 1st simple sentence is repeated as S of the 2nd simple sentence in a hypothesis. They also count the number of times O of the 1st sentence is the S of 2nd sentence.

Readability This group of features computes statistics related to readability. It includes Flesch, Gunning-Fog, SMOG, Flesch-Kincaid, automatic readability index, and average all scores (Flesch, 1948; Gunning, 1968; McLaughlin, 1969; Kincaid et al.,

1975). Also, we compute the edit-distance of hypothesis against the original sentence, and the average word per simple sentence.

Typed Dependency At simple sentence level we examine dependency chains of S, V and O, while at the hypothesis level we analyze the typed dependency between words. Our model has 46 typed dependencies which are represented by the 92 count features for the 1st and 2nd simple sentence.

7 Experiments and Analysis

7.1 Data

To enable the study of sentence simplification with our statistical models, we search for *parallel* corpora, in which the sources are original English sentences and the target is its simplification reference. For example, the source is *"Lu is married to Lian Hsiang , who is also a vajra master , and is referred as Grand Madam Lu "*. The simplification reference contains 3 simple sentences which are *"Lu is married to Lian Hsiang"*; *"Lian Hsiang is also a vajra master"*; *"Lu is referred as Grand Madam Lu"*. To the best of our knowledge, there is no such publicly available corpora under these conditions[1].

Our first attempt is to collect data automatically from original English and Simple English Wikipedia, based on the suggestions of Napoles and Dredze (2010). However, we found that the collected corpus is unsuitable for our model. For example, consider the original sentence *"Hawking was the Lucasian Professor of Mathematics at the University of Cambridge for thirty years, taking up the post in 1979 and retiring on 1 October 2009"*. The Simple Wikipedia reads *"Hawking was a professor of mathematics at the University of Cambridge (a position that Isaac Newton once had)"* and *"He retired on October 1st 2009"*. The problems with this are that *"(a position that Isaac Newton once had)"* did not appear in the original text, and the pronoun *"He"* requires our model to perform anaphora resolution which is out of scope of this work.

We finally decided to collect a set of sentences for which we obtained one manual simplification per sentence. The corpus contains 854 sentences, among which 25% sentences are from the New York Times and 75% sentences are from Wikipedia. The average sentence length is 30.5 words. We reserved 100 sentences for the unseen test set and the rest is for the development set and training data. The annotators were given instructions that explained the task and defined sentence simplification with the aid of examples. They were encouraged not to introduce new words and try to simplify by restructuring the original sentence. They were asked to simplify while preserving all important information and ensuring the simplification sentences remained grammatically correct[2]. Some examples from our corpus are given below:

Original: *"His name literally means Peach Taro ; as Taro is a common Japanese boy 's name , it is often translated as Peach Boy ."*
Simplification: *"His name literally means Peach Taro"* ; *"Taro is a common Japanese boy 's name"* ; *"Taro is often translated as Peach Boy"*

Original: *"These rankings are likely to change thanks to one player , Nokia , which has seen its market share shrink in the United States ."*
Simplification: *"These rankings are likely to change thanks to one player , Nokia"* ; *"Nokia has seen its market share shrink in the United States"*

7.2 Evaluation methods

Evaluating sentence simplification is a difficult problem. One possible way to overcome this is to use readability tests. There have been readability tests such as Flesch, Gunning-Fog, SMOG, Flesch-Kincaid, etc. (Flesch, 1948; Gunning, 1968; McLaughlin, 1969; Kincaid et al., 1975). In this work, we will use Flesch-Kincaid grade level which can be interpret as the number of years of education generally required to understand a text.

Furthermore, automatic evaluation of summaries has also been explored recently. The work of Lin (2004) on the ROUGE family metric is perhaps the best known study of automatic summarization evaluation. Other methods have been proposed such as Pyramid (Nenkova et al., 2007). Recently, Aluisio et al. (2010) proposed readability assessment for sentence simplification.

Our models are optimized toward $AveF_{10}$, which is the average F-score of n-gram concurrence between hypothesis and reference in which n is from 2 to 10. Besides $AveF_{10}$, we will report automatic evaluation scores on the unseen test set in Flesch-Kincaid grade level, ROUGE-2 and ROUGE-4. When we evaluate on a test set, a score will be reported as the average score per sentence.

7.3 Model behaviors

How well does our system learn from the labeled corpus? To answer this question we investigate the interactions of model and decoder hyper parameters over the training data. We performed controlled experiments on *stack-size*, K-best, C, and m-oracle parameters. For each parameter, all other model and decoder values are fixed, and the only change is with the parameter's value of interest. Figure 4 illustrates these experiments with parameters over the training data during 15 MIRA training iterations with $AveF_{10}$ metric. The weight vector w is initialized randomly.

[1] We are aware of data sets from (Cohn and Lapata, 2008; Zhu et al., 2010), however, they are more suitable in sentence compression task than in our task.

[2] Our corpus will be made publicly available for other researchers.

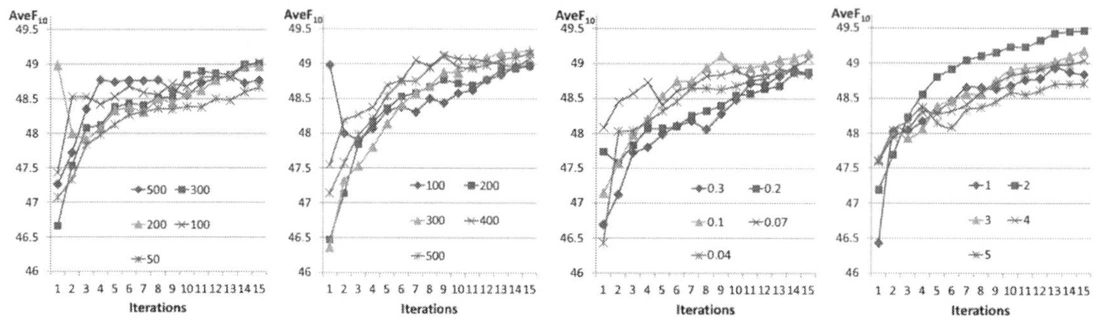

(a) *stack-size* (b) K-best (c) Constant C (d) m-oracle

Figure 4: Performance of the sentence simplifier on training data over 15 iterations when optimized toward $AveF_{10}$ metric and under various conditions.

In Figure 4a, we experimented with 5 different values from 100 to 500 hypotheses per stack. The expected outcome is when we use a larger *stack-size* the decoder may has more chance to find better hypotheses. However, a larger *stack-size* will obviously cost more memory and run time is slower. Therefore, we want to find a *stack-size* that compromises conditions. These experiments show that with a *stack-size* of 200, our model performed reasonably well in comparison with 300 and 500. A *stack-size* of 100 is no better than 200, while a *stack-size* of 50 is much worse than 200.

In Figure 4b, we experimented with 5 different values of K-best list with K from 100 to 500. We observed a K-best list of 300 hypotheses seems to perform well compare to other values. In terms of stability, the curve of 300-best list appears less fluctuation than other curves over 15 iterations.

C is the hyper-parameter which is used in Equation 3 for weight updating in MIRA. Figure 4c shows experiments with different constant C. If C is a large number, it means our model prefers an aggressive weight updating scheme, otherwise, our model updates weights conservatively. When C is 0.3 or 0.2 the performance is worse than 0.1 or 0.07 and 0.04.

The last controlled experiments are shown in Figure 4d, in which we test different values of m ranging from 1 to 5. These experiments show that using 2 oracle hypotheses consistently leads to better performances in comparison with other values.

7.4 Performance on the unseen test set

After exploring different model configurations we trained the final model with *stack-size* = 200; K-best = 300; C = 0.04; and m-oracle = 2. $AveF_{10}$ score of the final system on the training set is 50.69 which is about one $AveF_{10}$ point better than any system in Figure 4. We use the final system to evaluate on the unseen test set. Also, we compare our system with the rule-based system (henceforth H&S) proposed by Heilman and Smith (2010).[3,4]

Original	Reference	H&S	Our system
9.6	8.2	8.3	7.9

Table 1: Flesch-Kincaid grade level of original, reference, H&S, and our proposed simplification on the unseen test set.

System	$AveF_{10}$	ROUGE-2	ROUGE-4
H&S	51.0	82.2	72.3
Our system	55.5	82.4	72.9

Table 2: Results on the unseen test set with $AveF_{10}$, ROUGE-2 and ROUGE-4 scores. Our system outperforms the rule-based system proposed by Heilman and Smith (2010).

We first compare our system with H&S in the Flesch-Kincaid grade level, which indicates comprehension difficulty when reading an English text. The higher the number the more difficult the text. Table 1 shows the original text requires a reader of grade level 9 or 10. Both H&S and us provided simplification candidates, which are easier to read compared to the original text. Our model generated simpler hypotheses than the reference, while H&S outputs were slightly more difficult to read than the reference.

Next, we compare our system with H&S in ngram-based metrics such as $AveF_{10}$, ROUGE-2 and ROUGE-4 as shown in Table 2. Our results are better than H&S by 0.2 and 0.6 point in ROUGE-2 and ROUGE-4, respectively. More interestingly, our system outperformed H&S by 4.5 points in $AveF_{10}$,

[3] We thank Michael Heilman for providing us his code.

[4] We could not reach the authors of (Zhu et al., 2010) in order to obtain outputs. Kristian Woodsend kindly provided us **partial outputs** of (Woodsend and Lapata, 2011), therefore we did not include their outputs in this section.

	Positive examples
O	In 2011 , IBM gained worldwide attention for its artificial intelligence program Watson , which was exhibited on Jeopardy against game show champions Ken Jennings and Brad Rutter .
S	Watson was exhibited on Jeopardy against game show champions Ken Jennings and Brad Rutter . In 2011 , IBM gained worldwide attention for its artificial intelligence program Watson .
R	In 2011 , IBM gained worldwide attention for its artificial intelligence program Watson . Watson was exhibited on Jeopardy against game show champions Ken Jennings and Brad Rutter .
O	He told Radiozurnal that he was halting the campaign for Christmas and would restart it in the new year .
S	He told Radiozurnal . He was halting the campaign for Christmas . He would restart it in the new year .
R	He told Radiozurnal . He was halting the campaign for Christmas . He would restart it in the new year .
	Negative examples
O	He drives a 10-year-old Opel Corsa , but lives in a pleasant town house in the sleepy capital, Maseru, with wireless Internet and a housekeeper who comes twice a week .
S	He drives a 10-year-old Opel Corsa . He lives in a pleasant town house in the sleepy capital, Maseru, with wireless Internet and a housekeeper who .
R	He drives a 10-year-old Opel Corsa . He lives in a pleasant town house in the sleepy capital, Maseru, with wireless Internet and a housekeeper . a housekeeper comes twice a week .
O	An elderly Georgian woman was scavenging for copper to sell as scrap when she accidentally sliced through an underground cable and cut off Internet services to all of neighbouring Armenia , it emerged on Wednesday .
S	An elderly Georgian woman was scavenging for copper to sell . scrap cut off Internet services to all of neighbouring Armenia .
R	An elderly Georgian woman was scavenging for copper to sell as scrap . she accidentally sliced through an underground cable . she cut off Internet services to all of neighbouring Armenia . it emerged on Wednesday .

Table 3: We show the original sentence (O), our simplification (S), and simplification reference (R). Positive examples are cases when our simplifications closely match with the reference. Meanwhile, negative examples show cases when our model can not produce good simplifications.

which is a metric considering both precision and recall up to 10-gram. Over 100 sentences of the unseen test set, H&S outperforms us in 43 sentences, but is worse than our system in 51 sentences.

Table 3 shows examples of our system on the unseen test set. We present examples in cases where the proposed model works well and does not work well.

7.5 Discussions

This work shares the same line of research with (Klebanov et al., 2004; Heilman and Smith, 2010) in which we all focus on sentence-level factual simplification. However, a major focus of our work is on log-linear models which offer a new perspective for sentence simplification on decoding, training, and modeling problems. To contrast, consider rule-based systems (Klebanov et al., 2004; Daelemans et al., 2004; Siddharthan, 2006; Heilman and Smith, 2010), in which sentence simplification processes are driven by hand-written linguistic rules. The linguistic rules represent prior information about how each word and phrase can be restructured. In our model, each linguistic rule is encoded as a feature function and we allow the model to learn the optimized feature weights based on the nature of training data.

A potential issue is the proposed model might be susceptible to the sparseness issue. We alleviated this issue by using structure level and count feature functions which are lexically independent.

There are some limitations in this work. First, the proposed model does not introduce new words which may lead to generate grammatically incorrect simple sentences. Second, we focus on structure simplification and not on lexical simplification. Finally, the proposed model does not deal with anaphora resolution, which means our model can generate repeatedly noun phrases repeatedly in multiple simple sentences.

8 Conclusions

In this paper we proposed a novel method for sentence simplification based on log-linear models. Our major contributions are the stack decoding algorithm, the discriminative training algorithm, and the 177 feature functions within the model. We have presented insight the analyses of our model in controlled settings to show the impact of different model hyper parameters. We demonstrated that the proposed model outperforms a state-of-the-art rule-based system on ROUGE-2, ROUGE-4, and $AveF_{10}$ by 0.2, 0.6, and 4.5 points, respectively.

Another way to improve our model is feature engineering, which can be applied in future work. To address the data sparsity issue, we plan to use crowdsourcing such as Amazon Mechanical Turk to collect more training data. We plan to incorporate an n-gram LM to improve the grammaticality of hypotheses.

Acknowledgments

We would like to thank Colin Cherry for fruitful discussions and anonymous reviewers for helpful comments. We also thank Julianne Mentzer for proofreading the final version of the paper.

References

Sandra Aluisio, Lucia Specia, Caroline Gasperin, and Carolina Scarton. 2010. Readability assessment for text simplification. In *Proceedings of the NAACL HLT 2010 Fifth Workshop on Innovative Use of NLP for Building Educational Applications*, pages 1–9. Association for Computational Linguistics.

Regina Barzilay and Kathleen R. McKeown. 2005. Sentence fusion for multidocument news summarization. *Computational Linguistics*, 31, September.

Raman Chandrasekar and Bangalore Srinivas. 1997. Automatic induction of rules for text simplification. *Knowledge Based Systems*, 10(3):183–190.

Raman Chandrasekar, Doran Christine, and Bangalore Srinivas. 1996. Motivations and methods for text simplification. In *Proceedings of 16th International Conference on Computational Linguistics*, pages 1041–1044. Association for Computational Linguistics.

James Clarke. 2008. *Global Inference for Sentence Compression: An Integer Linear Programming Approach*. Ph.D. thesis, University of Edinburgh.

Trevor Cohn and Mirella Lapata. 2008. Sentence compression beyond word deletion. In *Proceedings of the 22nd International Conference on Computational Linguistics (Coling 2008)*, pages 137–144, Manchester, UK. August. Coling 2008 Organizing Committee.

Koby Crammer and Yoram Singer. 2003. Ultraconservative online algorithms for multiclass problems. *Journal of Machine Learning Research*, 3:951–991.

Walter Daelemans, Anja Höthker, and Erik Tjong Kim Sang. 2004. Automatic sentence simplification for subtitling in Dutch and English. In *Proceedings of the 4th International Conference on Language Resources and Evaluation (LREC-04)*, pages 1045–1048.

Rudolf Flesch. 1948. A new readability yardstick. *Journal of Applied Psychology*, 32:221–233.

Rudolf Flesch. 1981. *How to write plain English*. Barnes & Noble.

Michel Galley and Kathleen McKeown. 2007. Lexicalized Markov grammars for sentence compression. In *Proceedings of Human Language Technologies 2007: The Conference of the North American Chapter of the Association for Computational Linguistics*, pages 180–187, Rochester, New York, April. Association for Computational Linguistics.

Robert Gunning. 1968. *The technique of clear writing*. McGraw-Hill New York, NY.

Michael Heilman and Noah Smith. 2010. Extracting simplified statements for factual question generation. In *Proceedings of the 3rd Workshop on Question Generation*.

Frederick Jelinek. 1998. *Statistical Methods for Speech Recognition*. The MIT Press.

Siddhartha Jonnalagadda and Graciela Gonzalez. 2010. Sentence simplification aids protein-protein interaction extraction. *CoRR*.

Siddhartha Jonnalagadda, Luis Tari, Jörg Hakenberg, Chitta Baral, and Graciela Gonzalez. 2009. Towards effective sentence simplification for automatic processing of biomedical text. In *Proceedings of Human Language Technologies: The 2009 Annual Conference of the North American Chapter of the Association for Computational Linguistics, Companion Volume: Short Papers*, pages 177–180, Boulder, Colorado, June. Association for Computational Linguistics.

Siddhartha Jonnalagadda. 2006. Syntactic simplication and text cohesion. Technical report, University of Cambridge.

Peter Kincaid, Robert Fishburne, Richard Rogers, and Brad Chissom. 1975. Derivation of new readability formulas (Automated Readability Index, Fog Count and Flesch Reading Ease Formula) for Navy enlisted personnel (Research Branch Report 8-75). *Memphis, TN: Naval Air Station*.

Beata Klebanov, Kevin Knight, and Daniel Marcu. 2004. Text simplification for information seeking applications. In *On the Move to Meaningful Internet Systems, Lecture Notes in Computer Science*, volume 3290, pages 735–747. Morristown, NJ, USA. Springer-Verlag.

Kevin Knight and Daniel Marcu. 2002. Summarization beyond sentence extraction: A probabilistic approach to sentence compression. *Artificial Intelligence*, 139(1):91 – 107.

Philipp Koehn, Hieu Hoang, Alexandra Birch, Chris Callison-Burch, Marcello Federico, Nicola Bertoldi, Brooke Cowan, Wade Shen, Christine Moran, Richard Zens, Chris Dyer, Ondrej Bojar, Alexandra Constantin, and Evan Herbst. 2007. Moses: Open source toolkit for statistical machine translation. In *Proceedings of ACL'07*, pages 177–180, Prague, Czech Republic, June.

Percy Liang, Alexandre Bouchard-Côté, Dan Klein, and Ben Taskar. 2006. An end-to-end discriminative approach to machine translation. In *Proceedings of ACL'06*, pages 761–768, Sydney, Australia. Association for Computational Linguistics.

Chin-Yew Lin. 2004. ROUGE: A package for automatic evaluation of summaries. In Stan Szpakowicz Marie-Francine Moens, editor, *Text Summarization Branches Out: Proceedings of the ACL-04 Workshop*, pages 74–81, Barcelona, Spain, July. Association for Computational Linguistics.

Marie-Catherine Marneffe, Bill MacCartney, and Christopher Manning. 2006. Generating typed dependency parses from phrase structure parses. In *Proceedings of LREC'06*, Genoa, Italy.

Ryan McDonald, Koby Crammer, and Fernando Pereira. 2005. Online large-margin training of dependency parsers. In *Proceedings of the 43rd Annual Meeting on Association for Computational Linguistics*, ACL '05, pages 91–98. Association for Computational Linguistics.

Ryan McDonald. 2006. Discriminative sentence compression with soft syntactic evidence. In *Proceedings 11th Conference of the European Chapter of the Association for Computational Linguistics*, pages 297–304.

Hary McLaughlin. 1969. SMOG grading: A new readability formula. *Journal of Reading*, 12(8):639–646.

Courtney Napoles and Mark Dredze. 2010. Learning simple wikipedia: A cogitation in ascertaining abecedarian language. In *Proceedings of the NAACL HLT 2010 Workshop on Computational Linguistics and Writing: Writing Processes and Authoring Aids*, pages 42–50, Los Angeles, CA, USA, June. Association for Computational Linguistics.

Ani Nenkova, Rebecca Passonneau, and Kathleen McKeown. 2007. The pyramid method: Incorporating human content selection variation in summarization evaluation. *ACM Transactions on Speech and Language Processing*, 4, May.

Lance Ramshaw and Mitchell Marcus. 1995. Text chunking using transformation-based learning. In *Proceedings of the Third ACL Workshop on Very Large Corpora*, MIT, June.

Advaith Siddharthan. 2006. Syntactic simplification and text cohesion. *Research on Language and Computation*, 4(1):77–109, June.

Jenine Turner and Eugene Charniak. 2005. Supervised and unsupervised learning for sentence compression. In *Proceedings of the 43rd Annual Meeting on Association for Computational Linguistics*, ACL '05, pages 290–297. Association for Computational Linguistics.

Taro Watanabe, Jun Suzuki, Hajime Tsukada, and Hideki Isozaki. 2007. Online large-margin training for statistical machine translation. In *Proceedings of the EMNLP-CoNLL*, pages 764–773, Prague, Czech Republic, June. Association for Computational Linguistics.

W.M. Watanabe, A.C. Junior, V.R. Uzêda, R.P.M. Fortes, T.A.S. Pardo, and S.M. Aluísio. 2009. Facilita: reading assistance for low-literacy readers. In *Proceedings of the 27th ACM International Conference on Design of communication*, pages 29–36. ACM.

Kristian Woodsend and Mirella Lapata. 2011. Learning to simplify sentences with quasi-synchronous grammar and integer programming. In *Proceedings of the 2011 Conference on Empirical Methods in Natural Language Processing*, pages 409–420, Edinburgh, Scotland, UK., July. Association for Computational Linguistics.

Zhemin Zhu, Delphine Bernhard, and Iryna Gurevych. 2010. A monolingual tree-based translation model for sentence simplification. In *Proceedings of The 23rd International Conference on Computational Linguistics*, pages 1353–1361, Beijing, China, Aug.

Social Summarization via Automatically Discovered Social Context

Po Hu[1 2], Cheng Sun[1], Longfei Wu[1], Donghong Ji[1] and Chong Teng[1]
[1]Computer School, Wuhan University, China
[2]Department of Computer Science, Huazhong Normal University, China
phu@mail.ccnu.edu.cn, gensun.cc@gmail.com,
lonfee88@gmail.com, donghong_ji2000@yahoo.com.cn,
tchong616@126.com

Abstract

Heavy research has been done in recent years on tasks of traditional summarization. However, social context, which is critical in building high-quality social summarizer for web documents, is usually neglected. To address this issue, we propose a novel summarization approach based on social context. In this approach, social summarization is implemented by first employing the tripartite clustering algorithm to simultaneously discover document context and user context for a specified document. Then sentence relationships intra and inter documents plus intended user communities are taken into account to evaluate the significance of each sentence in different context views. Finally, a few sentences with highest overall scores are selected to form the summary. Experimental results demonstrate the effectiveness of the proposed approach and show the superior performance over several baselines.

1 Introduction

Now, an increasing number of Web 2.0 applications (e.g. Del.icio.us, CiteULike, LinkedIn) are allowing users to play more active roles such as annotating online documents with free-form tags, submitting opinions on the items they are interested in, or participating in social networks, etc.

Despite their focus on different resources, all of them have the common purpose of helping users organize, retrieve and share knowledge. The rich information offered by these systems provides additional clues for collaboratively summarizing online documents in a social context. However, most existing methods generate a summary based only on the information within each document or its neighboring documents, while the social context is usually ignored. This is an important issue that has not been extensively investigated in the summarization's literature.

In this study, different user's social tagging history and their tagged documents are employed and a novel social summarization approach is proposed by considering both document context and user context in the sentence evaluation process. The intuition is that if an appropriate social context is available, then integration of social context knowledge into the existing sentence evaluation process will improve the performance of traditional summarization methods.

The proposed approach takes into account both the mutual influences between documents and the impact from different user communities, which consists of the following phases.

Firstly, the tripartite clustering algorithm is adopted to discover document context and user context by clustering documents, users and tags simultaneously, which is based on the inherent structure of the three kinds of objects. In the clustering result, each document cluster is regarded as a context for each document in the cluster and all the user clusters are regarded as user communities with diverse information preferences.

Secondly, the context-sensitive ranking algorithm is applied for evaluating the significance of each sentence in different context views respectively.

Thirdly, a few significant sentences with highest overall scores are extracted from the specified document to generate the summary.

The main contribution of this paper is summarized as follows:

1) We examine an important factor called social context for document summarization.

2) We propose a novel social summarization approach by incorporating both document context and user context in the sentence evaluation process.

3) We conduct experiments to validate the effectiveness of the proposed approach on the

dataset sampled from del.icio.us and investigate how the parameters influence the summarization performance.

The paper is organized as follows: Section 2 introduces related work. Section 3 describes the details of the proposed social summarization approach. Section 4 presents experimental results and analysis. Lastly we conclude our paper in Section 5.

2 Related Work

Document summarization aims to automatically create a concise representation of a given document that delivers the main content of it. To date, a variety of methods have been developed, which can be roughly divided into two types: extractive approach and abstractive approach.

The former directly assigns each sentence a significance score and extracts a few sentences of highest scores from the original document, which depends on the combination of implicit or explicit statistical or linguistic features, while the latter usually makes use of advanced natural language understanding or generation technique to fuse, compress or reformulate information. In this paper, we focus on the extractive approach.

Much work has been done on extractive summarization including classification-based methods (Conroy and O'leary, 2001), regression-based methods (You et al., 2011), NMF-based methods (Lee et al., 2009), MMR-based methods (Carbonell and Goldstein, 1998), clustering-based methods (Nomoto and Matsumoto, 2001), etc. Recently, graph-based ranking methods are becoming more and more popular. LexRank (Erkan and Radev, 2004), TextRank (Mihalcea and Tarau, 2004), mutual reinforcement based ranking (Zha, 2002), and manifold ranking (Wan et al., 2007) are such methods using algorithms similar to PageRank and HITS to compute sentence's significance.

When summarizing a specified document, most methods employ only the information contained in the document while ignore its context. One exception is the collaborative approach proposed by Wan and Yang (2007), which improves news document summarization by use of the content from neighboring documents. This motivates us to further consider how social context knowledge might be incorporated in the sentence evaluation process to improve the performance of traditional summarization systems.

To date, much work on summarization tends to focus on a specific type of document, such as news articles (McKeown and Radev, 1995), academic papers (Qazvinian and Radev, 2010) or medical records (Afantenos et al., 2005). With the rapid growth of documents over the Internet, a large number of web documents need to be summarized. However, the content contained in a web document is observed to be sparser and noisier, and it is difficult for the traditional summarization methods that only focus on the local content of a document to capture the true meaning of web documents in a richer context environment. So it is more reasonable to summarize the web document by taking advantage of its social context (i.e. document context and user context).

Relevant work on web document summarization includes harnessing the search engine's click-through data to guide summarization (Sun et al., 2005), producing summaries by using query-result selection pairs according to their relative importance (Boydell and Smyth, 2007), etc.

The work described in this paper is concerned with producing an extractive summary for a Web document. Different from existing summarization methods that use document content or document context alone, the novelty of our approach stems from the integration of an important factor (i.e. social context) for sentence evaluation. We focus on how the richer information from social context can be utilized to improve the summarization performance, which is an interesting issue that needs to be carefully investigated.

3 The Proposed Social Summarization Approach

3.1 Overview

The main idea of the proposed summarization approach is to incorporate an important factor into sentence evaluation process by discovering social context knowledge from online bookmarking services and utilizing the discovered knowledge to collaboratively evaluate each sentence's significance.

Given a document to be summarized, the approach first clusters three types of objects (i.e. documents, users, and tags) simultaneously in a unified framework so that social context can be identified automatically. The identified document context is a cluster of documents, which are topically close to the specified document and are tagged by like-minded users. The identified user contexts include multiple user clusters with each representing a unique user community with different information preference. The discovered social context knowledge is deemed beneficial to evaluating sentences' significance from diverse views since they can provide richer external knowledge and more complementary clues to help rank sentences comprehensively.

Then the context-sensitive ranking algorithm is adopted to score all the sentences in the document context that the specified document belongs to by differentiating inter-sentence relationships in document context view and considering the impact of different user communities in user context view.

Finally, each sentence's overall significance is computed by fusing their scores from different views and a few sentences with highest overall scores are extracted from the specified document to generate the final summary.

3.2 Social Context Discovery

Social context discovery aims to find not only a set of neighboring documents similar to the specified document but also a group of intended user communities with different information preferences. Figure 1 shows an example of the social context for document d.

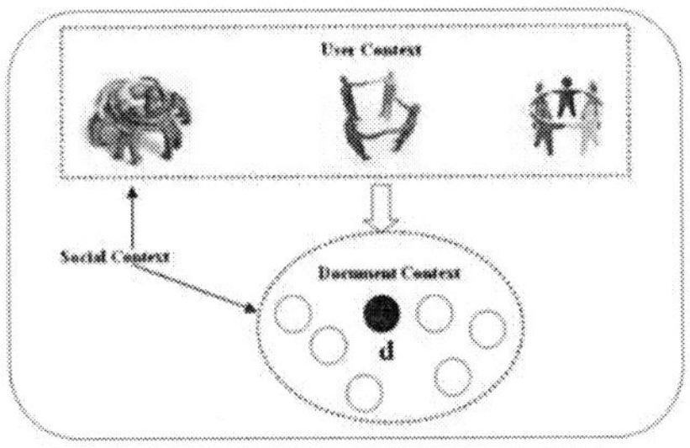

Figure 1. An Example of the Social Context for Document d.

A major characteristic of the social context knowledge acquired from bookmarking services is the tripartite relationships formed through users' social tagging behaviors, which can be illustrated through the example shown in Figure 2.

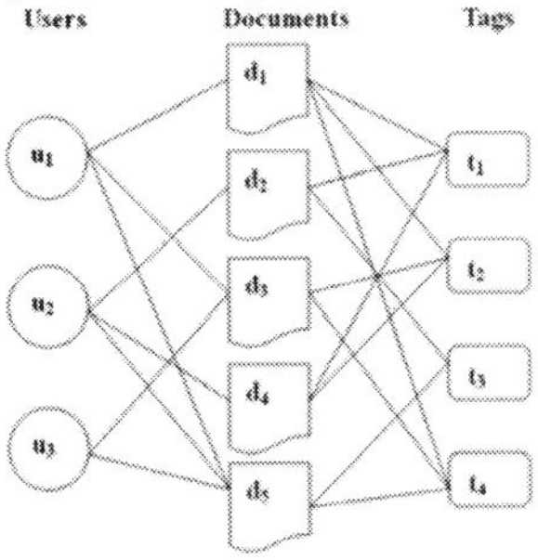

Figure 2. An Example of Tripartite Relationships among Users, Documents, and Tags.

In Figure 2, whenever a user annotates a document with a tag, a ternary relationship is built among the three kinds of objects. The tripartite nature among documents, users, and tags provides valuable information for discovering the topic-related documents, the intended user communities, and the semantics of tags. Besides, in the del.icio.us bookmarking service, it can be observed that topic-related documents are usually annotated with semantically-related tags by like-minded users with common interests, so in this study, the tripartite clustering algorithm (Lu et al., 2009) is employed to cluster documents, users, and tags simultaneously based on the inherent structure of the three kinds of objects to automatically discover the social context for a specific document.

The tripartite relationships among documents, users, and tags can be formally represented by a graph denoted as: $G=(D, U, T, E_{UD}, E_{UT}, E_{DT})$, where D, U, and T are the sets of documents, users and tags respectively, and E_{UD}, E_{UT}, and E_{DT} denote the relationships between user-document, user-tag, and document-tag respectively.

In the tripartite graph, each kind of object can be represented by a combined vector. For example, a document is naturally related to the users who have tagged it and the tags which have been used to tag it, so a document d_i can be represented by a combined vector D_i consisting of two components with one denoting user link vector and the other denoting tag link vector. i.e. $D_i=(D_i^{(U)}, D_i^{(T)})$, $D_i^{(U)}=(y_{ih}^{(U)} \mid h=1,2,\ldots,|U|)$, $D_i^{(T)}=(y_{ij}^{(T)} \mid j=1,2,\ldots,|T|)$, where $y_{ih}^{(U)}$ denotes the times that d_i is annotated by user u_h, $|U|$ denotes the total number of users, $y_{ij}^{(T)}$ denotes the times that d_i has been annotated with tag t_j, and $|T|$ denotes the total number of tags. Likewise, user and tag can be represented in the similar way.

Assuming $C_m(D)$ represent a document cluster, we can calculate the value of the centroid vector at user dimension by formula (1).

$$Centroid_{mu}^{(U)} = \frac{\sum_{d_i \in C_m^{(D)}, u_h \in C_l^{(U)}} y_{ih}^{(U)}}{|C_m^{(D)}| * |C_l^{(U)}|}, (u_u \in C_l^{(U)}) \quad (1)$$

where $C_l^{(U)}$ is a user cluster which user u_u belongs to, u_h is any user in $C_l^{(U)}$, and d_i is any document in $C_m^{(D)}$. It can be seen that the value of a document cluster's centroid at user dimension does not only depends on the links from u_u to all the cluster's documents, but also relies on the links from other users belonging to the same cluster as u_u to the cluster's documents. Likewise, the value of the centroid vector at tag dimension can be calculated in the similar way and the similarity value between a document d_i and the centroid of a document cluster $C_m^{(D)}$ can be calculated as follows,

$$Similarity(d_i, Centroid_m^{(D)}) = \alpha * Simlarity(D_i^{(U)}, Centorid_m^{(U)}) + (1-\alpha) * Simlarity(D_i^{(T)}, Centroid_m^{(T)}) \quad (2)$$

where $Simlarity(D_i^{(U)}, Centorid_m^{(U)})$ denotes the similarity between d_i and the centroid of $C_m^{(D)}$ based on the user link vector, $Simlarity(D_i^{(T)}, Centroid_m^{(T)})$ denotes the similarity of them based on the tag link vector, and α is a weighting adjusting parameter usually set to 0.5.

In this study, social context can be discovered by the tripartite clustering algorithm described in Table 1 (Lu et al., 2009).

Algorithm: Tripartite clustering based social context discovery
Input: The tripartite graph G=(D, U, T, E_{UD}, E_{UT}, E_{DT}) encoding the relationships among documents, users, and tags, the predefined number of document clusters N_{dc}, the predefined number of user clusters N_{uc}, and the predefined number of tag clusters N_{tc}. **Output:** The social context, which includes not only the document context but also the user context. 1: Assign each document (user or tag) to a random document cluster (user cluster or tag cluster); 2: **Repeat:** 3: **For** each type of objects **do** 4: Compute the centroid of each cluster based on the link features of its cluster members and the cluster structures of other two types of objects from last iteration; 5: **For** each document (user or tag) **do** 6: Compute the similarity between the object and the centroid of each document (user or tag) cluster; 7: Reassign the current object to the closest cluster based on the similarity. 8: **End For** 9: **End For** 10: **Until** the assignments no longer change.

Table 1. Tripartite Clustering Based Social Context Discovery

After that, we can discover all the document clusters. Each document cluster is regarded as a document context for any document in the cluster. At the same time, all user communities with varied information preferences can be also found. Since the 'true' numbers of document clusters, user cluster, and tag clusters are hard to predict, in this study we simply set them to the square root of the total number of documents, users, and tags respectively.

The potential benefit of adopting the tripartite clustering algorithm for social context discovery is that it can incorporate the social tagging information in a unified framework and all social context information can be simultaneously obtained by making use of the interactions among the cluster structures of different types of objects.

3.3 Social Context Based Summarization

In this study, for summarizing a single document, all the documents in its document context are firstly segmented into sentences and each sentence is evaluated in document context view and user context view respectively. Then the two scores are fused to evaluate the overall significance of a sentence. Lastly, a few sentences with highest overall scores are extracted from the specified document to generate the summary.

Sentence Scoring in Document Context View

The document-context-sensitive ranking algorithm is applied on the document context of the specified document for scoring sentences collaboratively (Wan, 2008).

In document context view, inter-sentence relationships are described by sentence affinity graph G_s with each vertex s_i representing a sentence and each edge e_{ij} representing the relationship between sentence s_i and s_j ($i \neq j$) whose weight is the similarity between the pair of sentences. G_s can be encoded by either the matrix M_{intra} or the matrix M_{inter} with each entry corresponding to the edge's weight of G_s's sub-graph G_{intra} and G_{inter}, which describe either the within-document relationships or the cross-document relationships among sentences. Then M_{intra} and M_{inter} are normalized to $\widetilde{M}_{intra}$ and $\widetilde{M}_{inter}$ by making the sum of each row equal to 1.

The document-context-sensitive score of sentence s_i is denoted as $DCScore(s_i)$ that can be computed as follows:

$$DCScore(s_i) = \lambda * DCScore_{intra}(s_i) + (1-\lambda) * DCScore_{inter}(s_i) \quad (3)$$

$$DCScore_{intra}(s_i) = \delta * \sum_{all\ j \neq i} DCScore_{intra}(s_j) * (\widetilde{M}_{intra})_{j,i} + \frac{(1-\delta)}{n} \quad (4)$$

$$DCScore_{inter}(s_i) = \delta * \sum_{all\ j \neq i} DCScore_{inter}(s_j) * (\widetilde{M}_{inter})_{j,i} + \frac{(1-\delta)}{n} \quad (5)$$

where n is the number of sentences in the document context, s_j is any other sentence linked with s_i, $DCScore_{intra}$ and $DCScore_{inter}$ are the sentence scores by considering either the within-document relationship or the cross-document relationship. δ is a damping factor usually set to 0.85 as in PageRank and λ is a weight adjusting parameter specifying the relative contribution to the score from the within-document relationship and the cross-document relationship. Since the previous research (Wan, 2008) has demonstrated that the use of cross-document relationships between sentences can much improve the performance of summarization, in this study λ is set to 0.4 to enhance the contribution from cross-document relationship.

Sentence Scoring in User Context View

Since the discovered user contexts represent different user communities, when evaluating the sentence's significance within the specified document, we should take into account the recommendation from diverse user communities. However, how to evaluate the recommendation strength becomes a difficult problem. In this paper, we propose a relevance measurement to evaluate it by computing the affinity between the document context of the specified document and the profile of each user community. The reason of using the document context instead of the document is that the expanded document context includes richer information than the single document, which can be used to match the community profile better.

In delicious, the documents annotated by a user can reflect the user's information preference to certain extent. Therefore, for a user community and two documents x and y, if the number of users in the community who annotate document x is greater than that of users who annotate document y, we may assume that the community is more interested in the content of document x than that of document y. Based on this assumption, we model the user community profile by choosing a certain number of representative documents that have been annotated by the most of users in this community. In this study, twenty percent of documents have been selected.

For scoring sentence in the user context view, each user context UC_k is firstly transformed into a pseudo-query q_k that is represented by the centroid vector of all the sentences in the user community profile. The affinity graph G_{uk} is constructed in which the vertexes include all the sentences in the specified document's context and the kth pseudo-query associated with the kth user context, and the edges encode both the relationships among the sentences and the relationship between the kth pseudo-query and the sentences. Here q_k can be processed in the same way as other sentences.

The user-context-sensitive score $UCScore_k(s_i)$ for sentence s_i in the kth user context view can be deduced from those of other sentences linked with it and the kth user context, which can be computed by the query-sensitive ranking algorithm as follows:

$$UCScore_k(s_i) = \beta * \sum_{all\ j \neq i} UCScore_k(s_j) * (\widetilde{M}_{uk})_{j,i} + (1-\beta) * Rel(s_i, q_k) \quad (6)$$

where $\widetilde{M}_{uk}$ is the normalized affinity matrix of G_{uk}, $Rel(s_i, q_k)$ denotes the Cosine relevance of the sentence s_i to the pseudo-query q_k, and β is a damping factor usually set to 0.85. The user-context-sensitive score for sentence s_i in the rest of user contexts can be deduced in the same way.

The final score of sentence s_i assigned in the user context view can be denoted as $UCScore(s_i)$, which is calculated by the combination of all scores from different user contexts.

$$UCScore(s_i) = \frac{\sum_{k=1}^{N_{uc}} RS(UC_k, DC_{s_i}) * UCScore_k(s_i)}{\sum_{k=1}^{N_{uc}} RS(UC_k, DC_{s_i})} \quad (7)$$

where N_{uc} is the number of user contexts, $RS(UC_k, DC_{s_i})$ denotes the recommendation strength of the user context UC_k to the document context DC_{s_i} of sentence s_i.

Summary Generation

In order to evaluate the overall score of each sentence s_i in the social context view, we fuse both document-context-sensitive score $DCScore(s_i)$ and user-context-sensitive score $UCScore(s_i)$ in a unified way as follows:

$$Score(s_i) = \eta * UCScore(s_i) + (1-\eta) * DCScore(s_i) \quad (8)$$

where $\eta \in [0,1]$ is a weight adjusting parameter, specifying the relative contribution to the overall scores from user context view and document context view. If η=1, only the user context's impact is considered and the score of sentence s_i equals to $UCScore(s_i)$; if η=0, only the document context's impact is considered and the score of sentence s_i equals to $DCScore(s_i)$; and if η=0.5, the two context view's impacts are considered equally.

Finally, a few sentences with highest overall scores and least redundancy are chosen into the summary according to the summary length limit.

4 Experiments

4.1 Experimental Setup

Because there is no existing benchmark dataset for social summarization, we construct a real-world dataset to evaluate the proposed method by downloading 200 bookmarked CNN news web documents from del.icio.us website on diverse topics (e.g. financial crisis, accidents and natural disasters, health, sports, etc). The "Story

Highlights" texts are extracted from each CNN news document to form the gold-standard (model) summary, which contains about 50-100 words.

The detailed statistical result of the dataset is shown in Table 2.

Summary of the Dataset	
Number of documents	200
Number of users	1194
Number of tags	2186

Table 2. The Statistical Result of the Dataset

Both intrinsic and extrinsic methods are proposed for summarization evaluation. In this paper, we employ the intrinsic method to evaluate the proposed summarization approach and all the baselines.

To date, various intrinsic evaluation methods such as ROUGE (Lin and Eduard, 2003) and Pyramid (Nenkova and Passonneau, 2004) have been proposed. In the study, The ROUGE-1.5.5 toolkit is adopted because it was officially adopted by DUC (Now TAC) for automatic summarization evaluation and has been shown to correlate with human evaluations well. ROUGE metrics measure a summary's content quality by counting overlapping units such as n-gram, word sequences, and word pairs between the automatically generated summary and the gold-standard summaries. Formally, ROUGE-N is an n-gram recall based measurement between a candidate summary and a set of reference summaries, which is computed as follows (Lin and Eduard, 2003):

$$ROUGE-N=\frac{\sum_{S\in\{reference\ summaries\}}\sum_{gram_n\in S}Count_{match}(gram_n)}{\sum_{S\in\{reference\ summaries\}}\sum_{gram_n\in S}Count(gram_n)} \quad (9)$$

where n stands for the length of the n-gram, $gram_n$, and $Count_{match}(gram_n)$ is the maximum number of n-grams co-occurring in a candidate summary and a set of reference summaries.

A few recall-oriented ROUGE metrics have been employed such as ROUGE-1 (unigram based metric), ROUGE-2 (bigram based metric), and ROUGE-SU4 (skip bigram and unigram based metric with maximum skip distance 4), etc. We report the metric scores of ROUGE-1, ROUGE-2 and ROUGE-SU4 at the confidence level of 95% in the following experiments.

4.2 Experimental Results

As a preprocessing step, in the following experiments, all the documents were segmented into sentences, stop-words were removed and the remaining words were stemmed by the Porter Stemmer. All the sentences were represented as the term vectors according to TF*ISF scheme. The process of redundancy removing and the setup of the corresponding parameters of the following baselines are also the same as that of the proposed approach.

For comparison, given a document and its document context discovered by the tripartite clustering algorithm, we implement the following methods as the baselines and each method generates a summary for each document in accordance to the length of the corresponding model summary. Since the good performance of the tripartite clustering algorithm adopted in this paper has been validated in the previous study (Lu et al., 2009), which shows that it can be applied to cluster different types of objects simultaneously and significantly outperforms the content-based K-means algorithm. In this study, we don't compare it again with the K-means algorithm in the discovery of document context.

Baseline 1 (RANDSum): RANDSum selects sentences randomly from the specified document to generate a summary.

Baseline 2 (DCISum): DCISum is a document-context-independent method which computes the significance score of a sentence based only on the within-document relationships while ignoring the document context. In this study, it is realized according to formula (4).

Baseline 3 (DCDSum): DCDSum is a document-context-dependent method which computes the significance score of a sentence based on both the cross-document relationships and the within-document relationships. In this study, it is realized according to formula (3).

Note that all the above baseline methods depend either on the internal information of the specified document or the external information of the document context, yet the user context information is entirely neglected. The proposed social context based approach ***(abbr.* SCSum)** considers not only document context but also user context in a unified framework.

We show the summarization evaluation results of different approaches in Tables 3.

Method	ROUGE-1	ROUGE-2	ROUGE-SU4
RANDSum	0.25532	0.02174	0.05634
DCISum	0.33961	0.05576	0.09039
DCDSum	0.34273	0.05522	0.09113
SCSum	**0.35880**	**0.07130**	**0.11417**

Table 3. The Summarization Evaluation Results of Different Approaches

In Table 3, the best result of our approach is achieved when the weight adjusting parameter η specifying the relative contribution from user context and document context is set to 0.4.

Seen from Table 3, our proposed approach SCSum using the discovered social context knowledge achieves the best performance on all ROUGE metrics comparable to that of the baseline approaches (i.e. RANDSum, DCISum, and DCDSum), which demonstrates that both document context and user context are very important for improving the performance of document summarization if richer context information is available for a specific document.

We also observe that the DCDSum that uses the document context information performs better than the DCISum, and RANDSum that use only the local information within the specified document. It shows the expanded document context from like-minded users can benefit the sentence's evaluation process by proving more external document information related to the specified document.

To discover how the relative contribution from user context and document context influences the summarization performance, we set the weight adjusting parameter η from 0.2 to 0.9, and Figure 3 shows the ROUGE-1 evaluation results of the proposed approach with different η value.

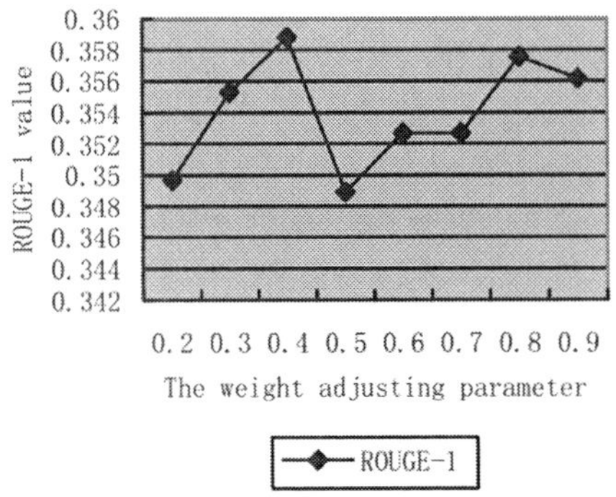

Figure 3. The ROUGE-1 evaluation results of the proposed approach with different η value

Seen from Figure 3, it is clear that the summarization performance on ROUGE-1 first increases with η, when η is larger than 0.4, the performance tends to decrease. It shows that considering appropriate user context knowledge is critical for improving summarization performance.

The reason underlying the above observations that the proposed social context summarization approach can improve the performance of document summarization is that there are many different documents on the Internet to discuss the same topic from various perspectives, and the discovered appropriate social context would guarantee that the influences through the different documents and different user communities are reliable.

5 Conclusion and Future Work

This paper examines an important factor called social context and proposes a novel social summarization approach for incorporating both document context and user context for collaborative generation of summaries. Experimental results on the dataset sampled from del.icio.us demonstrate the effectiveness of our method and show the superior performance over several baselines.

In future work, it would be interesting to investigate the performance of the approach on larger data sets with richer social annotation information. Besides, we will explore the optimization-based estimation strategy to automatically determine the parameters of our approach in an adaptive way. We also plan to make use of more implicit or explicit user feedback information, meta-content information, and hyperlink information to acquire richer social context knowledge to improve the summarization performance.

Acknowledgments

This work was supported by the National Natural Science Foundation of China (No. 90820005 and No. 61070082), and the Post-70s Scholars Academic Development Program of Wuhan University.

References

Ani Nenkova and Rebecca J. Passonneau. 2004. *Evaluating content selection in summarization: the pyramid method. Proceedings of the 2004 Human Language Technology Conference of the North American Chapter of the Association for Computational Linguistics (HLT-NAACL '04)*, 145-152.

Caimei Lu, Xin Chen, and Park E. K.. 2009. *Exploit the tripartite network of social tagging for web clustering. Proceeding of the 18th ACM conference on Information and knowledge management (CIKM '09)*, 1545-1548.

Chin-Yew Lin and Hovy Eduard. 2003. *Automatic evaluation of summaries using n-gram co-occurrence statistics. Proceedings of the 2003*

Conference of the North American Chapter of the Association for Computational Linguistics on Human Language Technology (NAACL '03).

Gunes Erkan and Dragomir R. Radev. 2004. *LexPageRank: prestige in multi-document text summarization. Proceedings of the Conference on Empirical Methods in Natural Language Processing (EMNLP' 04).*

Hongyuan Zha. 2002. *Generic summarization and keyphrase extraction using mutual reinforcement principle and sentence clustering. Proceedings of the 25th annual international ACM SIGIR conference on Research and development in information retrieval (SIGIR '02),* 113-120.

Jaime G. Carbonell, Jade Goldstein. 1998. *The use of MMR, diversity-based reranking for reordering documents and producing summaries. Proceedings of the 21st annual international ACM SIGIR conference on Research and development in information retrieval (SIGIR '98),* 335-336.

Jiantao Sun, Dou Shen, Huajun Zeng, Qiang Yang, Yuchang Lu, and Zheng Chen. 2005. *Web-page summarization using clickthrough data. Proceedings of the 28th annual international ACM SIGIR conference on Research and development in information retrieval (SIGIR '05)* , 194–201.

John M. Conroy and Dianne P. O'leary. 2001. *Text summarization via hidden Markov models. Proceedings of the 24th annual international ACM SIGIR conference on Research and development in information retrieval (SIGIR '01),* 406-407.

Ju-Hong Lee, Sun Park, Chan-Min Ahn, and Daeho Kim. 2009. *Automatic generic document summarization based on non-negative matrix factorization. Information Processing & Management,* 45(1): 20-34.

Kathleen McKeown and Dragomir R. Radev. 1995. *Generating summaries of multiple news articles. Proceedings of the 18th annual international ACM SIGIR conference on Research and development in information retrieval (SIGIR '95),* 74–82.

Oisin Boydell and Barry Smyth. 2007. *From social bookmarking to social summarization: An experiment in community-based summary generation. Proceedings of the 12th international conference on Intelligent user interfaces (IUI '07),* 42–51.

Ouyanga You, Wenjie Li, Sujian Li, and Qin Lu. 2011. *Applying regression models to query-focused multi-document summarization. Information Processing & Management,*47(2): 227-237.

Rada Mihalcea, Paul Tarau. 2004. *TextRank: bringing order into texts. Proceedings of the Conference on Empirical Methods in Natural Language Processing (EMNLP' 04).*

Stergos Afantenos, Vangelis Karkaletsis, and Panagiotis Stamatopoulos. 2005. *Summarization from medical documents: a survey. Artificial Intelligence in Medicine,* 33(2): 157–177.

Tadashi Nomoto and Yuji Matsumoto. 2001. *A new approach to unsupervised text summarization. Proceedings of the 24th annual international ACM SIGIR conference on Research and development in information retrieval (SIGIR '01),* 26-34.

Vahed Qazvinian and Dragomir R. Radev. 2010. *Identifying non-explicit citing sentences for citation-based summarization. Proceedings of the 48th Annual Meeting of the Association for Computational Linguistics (ACL'10),* 555-564.

Xiaojun Wan. 2008. *Using only cross-document relationships for both generic and topic-focused multi-document summarizations. Information Retrieval,* 11(1): 25-49.

Xiaojun Wan and Jianwu Yang. 2007. *CollabSum: Exploiting multiple document clustering for collaborative single document summarizations. Proceedings of the 30th annual international ACM SIGIR conference on Research and development in information retrieval (SIGIR '07),* 143-150.

Xiaojun Wan, Jianwu Yang, and Jianguo Xiao. 2007. *Manifold-ranking based topic-focused multi-document summarization. Proceedings of the 20th international joint conference on Artifical intelligence (IJCAI'07),* 2903–2908.

Xiaojun Wan and Jianwu Yang. 2007. *Single document summarization with document expansion. Proceedings of the 22nd national conference on Artificial intelligence (AAAI'07),* 931-936.

Simultaneous Clustering and Noise Detection for Theme-based Summarization

[1,2]Xiaoyan Cai, [2]Renxian Zhang, [2]Dehong Gao, [2]Wenjie Li

[1]College of Information Engineering, Northwest A&F University
xiaoyanc@mail.nwpu.edu.cn

[2]Department of Computing, The Hong Kong Polytechnic University
{csxcai,csrzhang,csdgao,cswjli}@comp.polyu.edu.hk

Abstract

Multi-document summarization aims to produce a concise summary that contains salient information from a set of source documents. Since documents often cover a number of topical themes with each theme represented by a cluster of highly related sentences, sentence clustering plays a pivotal role in theme-based summarization. Moreover, noting that real-world datasets always contain noises which inevitably degrade the clustering performance, we incorporate noise detection with spectral clustering to generate ordinary sentence clusters and one noise sentence cluster. We are also interested in making the theme-based summaries biased towards a user's query. The effectiveness of the proposed approaches is demonstrated by both the cluster quality analysis and the summarization evaluation conducted on the DUC generic and query-oriented summarization datasets.

1 Introduction

The exponential growth in the volume of documents available on the Internet brings the problem of finding out whether a single document can meet a user's complex information need. In order to solve this problem, multi-document summarization, which reduces the size of documents while preserves their important semantic content is highly demanded. Most of the summarization work done till date follow the sentence extraction framework, which ranks sentences according to various pre-specified criteria and selects the most salient sentences from the original documents to form summaries.

In addition to sentence salience, the other fundamental issues that must be concerned in summarization are information redundancy and information diversity (Radev et al., 2002). When the given documents are all supposed to be about the same topic, they are very likely to repeat some important information in different documents or in different places of the same document. Therefore, effectively recognizing the sentences with the same or very similar content is necessary for reducing redundancy and covering more diverse informative content in a summary. This is normally achieved by clustering highly related sentences into topical themes. Summaries can then be produced, e.g., by extracting the representative sentence(s) from each theme cluster. Thus, good sentence clusters are the guarantee of good summaries in theme-based summarization.

It is also important to stress that the noise sentences are clearly observed in the DUC datasets, i.e., the benchmark datasets for use by the summarization community (Wei et al., 2009). Take the DUC2005 d301i document set, which talks about 'International Organized Crime', as an example. The sentence like 'This well-educated, well-spoken, cosmopolitan businessman is laughing all the way.' absolutely goes too far off the point, and it is considered as a noise sentence in the context of our study. The existence of noises will inevitably degrade the clustering performance. Noise detection for summarization which has been ignored previously is emphasized in this work. Our strategy is to detect the noises by mapping the textual objects (either sentences or words) to a new representation space where the features are more discriminative. Then all the identified noises are thrown into a single cluster called noise cluster and the summaries are generated from the other regular clusters alone.

Topical themes and noises are the inherent characteristics of documents. Without doubt, effective recognition of them provides a good basis for theme-based summarization. However, summaries generated in such a way are not guaranteed to cater to the user's information need and therefore may not always be in line with his/her expectations. For example, if a user asks to "identify and describe types of organized crime that crosses borders or involves more than one country", the cases of international drug trafficking and international smuggling are definitely more relevant than the origin and the means of organized crime or the government's precautions, even though all of them are extractable main themes in the documents. That is why query-oriented summarization which requires concise information corresponding to a specific query has drawn much attention in recent years. Its challenge to theme-based summarization is how to better make use of the query information to guide the necessary clustering and ranking processes. We explore three approaches to incorporate the query information in theme-based summarization, including query-driven cluster ranking, query-embedding similarity measure and semi-supervised clustering.

The main contributions of this paper are three-fold. (1) Noisy detection is incorporated into clustering for theme-based generic summarization. (2) Three approaches are explored to incorporate the query information into query-oriented theme-based summarization. (3) Thorough experimental studies are conducted to verify the effectiveness and robustness of the proposed frameworks and approaches.

The rest of the paper is organized as follows. Section 2 reviews the related work. Section 3 explains the noise detection enhanced sentence clustering approach. Section 4 then addresses the other necessary issues in generic and query-oriented theme-based summarization. Section 5 presents experiments and evaluation results. Section 6 concludes the paper.

2 Related Work

Depending on the purpose and the target user, summarization can be either generic or query-oriented. While a generic summary reflects the author's point of view with respect to the most important information in the documents, a query-oriented summary presents the information in the documents that is most responsive to a given query.

Normally, sentence ranking is the issue of most concern in summarization (either generic or query-oriented). With the advancement of information technologies and the explosion of information on the Internet, clustering has become increasingly important in text mining and knowledge discovery. Recently it has been successfully applied in theme-based (a.k.a. clustering-based) summarization.

In terms of the roles of clustering in summarization, one could take the advantage of the clustering results to select the representative sentences in order to generate diverse summaries. The typical examples of such use are C-RR and C-LexRank proposed by Qazvinian and Radev (Qazvinian and Radev, 2008), which selected the important citation sentences from the sentence clusters generated by a hierarchical agglomeration algorithm. Alternatively, the clustering results could be used to improve or refine the sentence ranking results. Most of the clustering-based summarization approaches are of this nature. For example, Wan and Yang (Wan and Yang, 2008) presented a cluster-based conditional Markov random walk model and a cluster-based HITS model to incorporate the cluster-level information into the process of sentence ranking. Wang et al. (Wang et al., 2008a) also proposed a language model to cluster and summarize documents simultaneously using non-negative factorization. In addition, Wang et al. (Wang et al., 2008b) applied symmetric matrix factorization to generating sentence clusters. Each sentence's score is based on the linear combination of two elements. One is the average similarity score between a sentence and all the other sentences in the same cluster. The other is the similarity between the sentence and the given query. Notice that this is the only work we could find that explored clustering for query-oriented summarization.

Another important problem that we'd like to emphasize here is the existence of noisy data in any real-world dataset. To the best of our knowledge, no related work in summarization has attempted to solve this problem. In this paper, we try to address this issue by borrowing ideas from the noise detection research in the data mining literature. Existing noise detection approaches fall into two main types. One considered the data points whose distances to all cluster centers exceeded a certain threshold as noises after clustering (Dave, 1999). This type of approaches mainly focused on reducing the influence of noises on the regular clusters, but not exactly on identifying and removing noises. In this sense, the clusters output were still the noisy clusters. The other type managed to obtain one or more regular clusters and a single noise cluster that contained all noises simultaneously during clustering (Li et al., 2007). Therefore, this type of approaches was able to provide noise-free clusters. The approach we are interested in this work is of the second type.

3 Spectral Clustering with Noise Detection

Compared to the traditional clustering algorithms such as K-means and agglomerative clustering, the new clustering algorithms that emerged over the last few years such as spectral clustering have demonstrated excellent performance on some challenging tasks (Ding and Zha, 2011). The spectral clustering has many fundamental advantages. For example, it is able to obtain global optimal solution and adapt to sample spaces with any shape (Ng, Jordan and Weiss, 2001; Bach and Jordan, 2004; Yu and Shi, 2003). The algorithm is also very simple to implement. It can be solved efficiently by standard linear algebra methods (Luxburg, 2007) and can be applied on a dataset of high dimensions in the feature space and data space (Dhillon et al., 2004). Taking into account these advantages, we choose to use spectral clustering in this study.

Without exception, spectral clustering is also sensitive to noises like all the other clustering algorithms. The main reason leading to its failure on the noisy dataset is that the block structure of the affinity matrix is destroyed by noises (Li et al., 2007). A possible solution is to reshape the noisy dataset so that the block structure of the new affinity matrix can be recovered. In this paper, we incorporate noise detection with spectral clustering by mapping the text data points from their original feature space into a new feature space such that a noise cluster formed by all the noisy data points can be separated from the other regular clusters. Basically, noise detection enhanced spectral clustering involves normalized graph Laplacian construction, data re-representation and spectral embedding.

3.1 Normalized Graph Laplacian Construction

Let *G*=(*S*, *A*) be an undirected weighted graph. $S=\{s_1,s_2,\cdots,s_n\}$ is the set of nodes corresponding to the text points represented as the *m*-dimensional feature vectors, *m* is the total number of the words and *n* is the total number of the sentences in a given document collection. $A=[a_{ij}]_{n\times n}$ is a symmetric matrix where a_{ij} is the weight of the edge connecting the two nodes s_i and s_j in G ($i,j=1,2,\ldots,n$), and it is measured by the cosine similarity between the s_i and s_j vectors. The graph Laplacian L of G is defined as $L=I-A$, where I is the identity matrix, and the normalized graph Laplacian $\overline{L}$ of G is defined as

$$\overline{L}=D^{-1/2}LD^{-1/2}=I-D^{-1/2}AD^{-1/2} \quad (1)$$

where $D=[d_{ij}]_{n\times n}$ is a diagonal matrix with $d_{ii}=\sum_j a_{ij}$. A is called the affinity matrix and $\overline{A}=D^{-1/2}AD^{-1/2}$ the normalized affinity matrix.

3.2 Data Re-Representation

In order to achieve relatively compact sentence clusters and meanwhile separate the noises from them, we map the sentence nodes $\{s_i,s_2,\cdots,s_n\}$ to $\{p_1,p_2,\ldots,p_n\}$ in a new feature space with dimension equal to *n*. It is expected that the block structure of the new affinity matrix built on this new graph can be recovered. Now let's consider the following regularization framework

$$\Omega(P)=\|P-I\|_F^2+\alpha\cdot\mathrm{tr}(P^T K_r^{-1}P) \quad (2)$$

where $\|\cdot\|_F$ denotes the Frobenious norm of a matrix, $\mathrm{tr}(\cdot)$ denotes the trace of a matrix, α is a positive regularization parameter controlling the trade-off between the two terms. K_r is a graph kernel (e.g., $K_r=\overline{L}^{-1}$). K_r^{-1} is the inverse of K_r if it is non-singular or is the pseudo-inverse of K_r if it is singular. $P=[p_1,p_2,\ldots,p_n]_{n\times n}{}^T$ is the new representation of the sentence set we would like to have after mapping. The optimal P can be obtained by minimizing $\Omega(P)$, i.e., $P^*=\arg\max_P \Omega(P)$. It is easy to see that the Equation (2) is strictly convex, so we could use the derivative of Equation (2) with respect to P to get the minimum of $\Omega(P)$, i.e.,

$$P^*=(I+\alpha K_r^{-1})^{-1} \quad (3)$$

Then the new representation of s_i is p_i^* (i.e. $P^*(i,\cdot)^T$, the *i*-th row vector of P^*).

3.3 Spectral Embedding

Given $P^*=\{p_1^*,p_2^*,\cdots,p_n^*\}$, i.e., the optimal representation of $S=\{s_i,s_2,\cdots,s_n\}$ in the new feature space, we can construct a new normalized sentence graph Laplacian $\tilde{L}$. Let $\lambda_1 \le \lambda_2 \le \ldots \le \lambda_n$ be the eigenvalues of $\tilde{L}$ with the corresponding eigenvectors $v_1, v_2, \ldots, v_n$. Assume the cluster number k is known, let $V = [v_1, v_2, \ldots, v_k]_{n \times k}$. We normalize each row of V to unit length, resulting in a new matrix $\overline{V}$. The resultant row vectors correspond to the original sentence points and K-means clustering is performed on them. Then s_i is assigned to the cluster l $(1 \le l \le k)$ if and only if the i-th row vector in $\overline{V}$ (i.e., $\overline{V}(i,\cdot)$) is assigned to cluster l.

For each generated cluster, we compute the average distance between the sentence points in it and the origin. The cluster with the smallest average distance is taken as the noise cluster. The other clusters are considered as the regular clusters.

3.4 Cluster Number Estimation

Recall that spectral clustering requires a predefined cluster number k. To avoid exhaustive search for a proper cluster number for each document set, we employ the automatic cluster number estimation approach introduced in (Li et al., 2007) to predict the number of the expected clusters. Given the new normalized sentence graph Laplacian matrix $\tilde{L}$ and its eigenvalues $\lambda_1 \le \lambda_2 \le \ldots \le \lambda_n$, the optimal number of clusters k^* is defined as

$$k^* = \arg\max_k \{\lambda_{k+1}(\tilde{L}) - \lambda_k(\tilde{L})\} \quad (4)$$

where $\lambda_i(\tilde{L})$ is the i-th smallest eigenvalue of $\tilde{L}$.

4 Theme-based Summarization

4.1 Generic Theme-based Summarization

Once the sentence clusters are obtained, the summary sentences are then extracted from the original documents according to the ranks of the ordinary clusters they belong to and their ranks within the assigned clusters.

The ranking score of each regular sentence cluster is formulated as:

$$\gamma(C_{S_i}) = \frac{Score(C_{S_i})}{\sum_{i=1}^{K} Score(C_{S_i})} \quad (5)$$

$$Score(C_{S_i}) = \frac{\sum_{j=1}^{m} C_{S_i}(j) \cdot S(j)}{\sqrt{\sum_{j=1}^{m} (C_{S_i}(j))^2} \cdot \sqrt{\sum_{j=1}^{m} (S(j))^2}} \quad (6)$$

where $Score(C_{S_i})$ indicates the cosine similarity between an regular sentence cluster C_{S_i} and the whole document set S for generic summarization. K is the total number of the ordinary sentence clusters identified; m is the number of the words in the whole document set. $\gamma(C_{S_i})$ is the normalized value of $Score(C_{S_i})$, where $\gamma(C_{S_i}) \in [0,1]$ and $\sum_{k=1}^{K} \gamma(C_{S_i}) = 1$.

Within each regular sentence cluster, any reasonable ranking algorithm, can be applied to rank the sentences. In view of the successful application of PageRank-like algorithms in sentence ranking, LexRank (Qazvinian and Radev, 2008) is adopted in our work. Considering sentence position also provides important information for generic summarization, we multiply a weight to the rank score of each sentence. The weight of a sentence in a document is $1/n$, where n is the total number of the sentences in the document. This is a normal practice in generic summarization, which follows the hypothesis that the first sentence in a document is the most important and the importance decreases as the sentence gets further away from the beginning. The summaries are then generated by choosing the most salient sentence from the most salient regular cluster to the least salient regular cluster, then the second most salient sentences from the regular clusters in descending order of rank, and so on.

4.2 Query-Oriented Theme-based Summarization

For query-oriented summarization, the query's influence can be reflected in any process of ranking or clustering. Considering the focus of this study is the application of clustering in summarization, we explore three query-based approaches that center on the ranking process or the result of clustering.

4.2.1 Query-Driven Cluster Ranking

The process of it is similar to the generic theme-based summarization, except that the $Score(C_{S_i})$ is formulated as

$$Score(C_i) = \frac{\sum_{j=1}^{m} C_{S_i}(j) \cdot Q(j)}{\sqrt{\sum_{j=1}^{m} (C_{S_i}(j))^2} \cdot \sqrt{\sum_{j=1}^{m} (Q(j))^2}} \quad (7)$$

which indicates the cosine similarity between a sentence cluster and a given query Q. Moreover, the sentence position information can not be considered in query-oriented summarization.

As the query's influence is only reflected in the process of ranking in this approach, we argue that the query's influence can be not only reflected in the process of ranking, but also reflected in the process of clustering. We explore two query-based approaches that center on the result of clustering.

4.2.2 Query-Embedding Similarity Measure

Sentence clustering requires the affinity matrix that is built upon the cosine similarity between the two sentences. On top of query-driven cluster ranking, we further consider the query-driven sentence clustering by defining a new query-embedding similarity measure that biases inter-sentence relationships towards pairs of sentences possessing the same concepts expressed in the query.

The idea is intuitive. The m-dimensional sentence vector $s_i = (s_{i1}, s_{i2}, \ldots, s_{im})$ is mapped onto the l-dimensional query vector $Q = (q_1, q_2, \ldots, q_l)^T$ (l is the number of query terms). As the number of the words contained in query is much smaller than the number of the words contained in the document collection, to avoid problems resulting from exact word match, we propose to use the synsets in WordNet to map the sentence vector onto the query vector. Given a sentence s_i, for each q_t ($1 \le t \le l$), the weights of s_{ij} ($1 \le j \le m$) that are in the same synset as q_t are accumulated and contribute to be the weight of q_t. Consequently, the cosine similarity between the two sentences can be defined in the query vector space. We call it the query-embedding similarity.

4.2.3 Query-Supervised Clustering

Clustering is typically unsupervised. In the case that some limited prior knowledge is available, one can use the knowledge to "guide" the clustering process. This is called semi-supervised clustering. Inspired by this idea, we make use of the query information to supervise sentence clustering. It is expected that the sentences that correspond to certain aspects of the query will be grouped together forming the query-relevant clusters and the query-non-relevant sentences will be grouped together while the other noisy sentences fall into the noise cluster.

For this purpose, we adopt semi-supervised spectral clustering with pairwise constraints proposed by (Kamvar, Klein and Manning, 2003). We regard each query sentence as a seed for a query-relevant cluster and a sentence from the document collection which does not contain any word in the query sentences is selected to be a seed of the noise cluster. Then from the remaining sentences in the document collection, the one that has the highest cosine similarity to a seed is selected to construct a must-link constraint with that seed. Once a sentence is selected for a cluster, it cannot be assigned to the other clusters any more. Thus it can be naturally used to construct the cannot-link constraints with the other seeds.

As the query sentences are involved in clustering with this approach, the affinity matrix becomes $A = (a_{ij})_{(n+r)\times(n+r)}$, where r is the number of the sentences in the given query. Normally a_{ij} is defined as the cosine similarity between the two sentences s_i and s_j. Specially, $a_{ij} = 1$ is assigned to each pair of must-link constraint, indicating that the corresponding two sentences have to be in the same cluster. Similarly, $a_{ij} = 0$ is assigned to each pair of cannot-link constraint, indicating that the corresponding two sentences must not be in the same cluster. Then spectral clustering is applied based on this constrain-affinity matrix. We generate summaries from those clusters containing the query sentence(s). Other clusters are assumed to be either the query-non-relevant cluster(s) or the noise cluster.

4.3 Redundancy Control in Summary Generation

Since the number of documents to be summarized can be very large, information redundancy can be quite serious in the generated summaries. Redundancy control is necessary. We apply a simple yet effective way to choose summary sentences. Each time, we compare the current candidate sentence to the sentences already included in the summary. Only the sentence that is not too similar to any sentence already in the summary (i.e., the cosine similarity between them is lower than a threshold) is selected into the summary. The iteration is repeated until the length of sentences in the summary reaches the length limitation. In our experiment, the threshold is set to 0.9.

5 Experiments and Evaluation

We conduct a series of experiments on the DUC2004 generic summarization dataset and the DUC2007 query-based summarization dataset. According to task definitions, systems are required to produce a concise summary for each document set (without or with a given query description) and the length of summaries is limited to 665 bytes in DUC 2004 and 250 words in DUC2007.

A well-recognized automatic evaluation toolkit ROUGE (Lin and Hovy, 2003) is used for evaluation. We report two common ROUGE scores in this paper, namely ROUGE-1 and ROUGE-2, which base on the Uni-gram match and the Bi-gram match, respectively. Documents and queries are pre-processed by segmenting sentences and splitting words. Stop words are removed and the remaining words are stemmed using Porter stemmer.

5.1 Summarization Evaluation

To evaluate the performance of the noise detection enhanced spectral clustering approach, we compare the ROUGE scores of it with the ROUGE scores of the LexRank approach for generic summarization and query-oriented LexRank approach, which is a direct extension of LexRank in our clustering and ranking frameworks. That is, the sentence clusters are generated by the traditional spectral clustering algorithm first and then the sentences within each cluster are ranked with LexRank. With this approach, the cluster ranking and the summarization generation processes are exactly the same way as in our approaches. For LexRank and query-oriented LexRank approaches, we obtain the cluster number based on the normalized sentence graph Laplacian directly.

We choose $K_r = \overline{L}^{-1}$ and set α to 1000 for noise detection. Table 1 and Table 2 below illustrate the ROUGE results on the DUC2004 and DUC2007 datasets.

DUC2004	ROUGE-1	ROUGE-2
Noise Detection Enhanced	0.36325	0.07847
LexRank	0.36294	0.07351

Table 1. ROUGE Evaluation of Two approaches on DUC2004

DUC2007	ROUGE-1	ROUGE-2
Query-Driven Cluster Ranking	0.39351	0.09223
Query-Oriented LexRank	0.37589	0.07858

Table 2. ROUGE Evaluation of Two approaches on DUC2007

It is delighted to see that the noise detection enhanced clustering approaches consistently outperform the clustering approaches without noise detection in the both datasets. This demonstrates that removing noises can indeed benefit producing better sentence clusters that in turn can further enhance the performance of summarization.

5.2 Analysis of Cluster Quality

Our original intention to utilize noise detection enhanced spectral clustering is to hope to generate more accurate sentence clusters results by eliminating the negative impact of noises. In order to examine the quality of the generated sentence clusters, we define the following measure

$$quan = \sum_{k=1}^{K} \left(\frac{\min_{s_i \in C_k} sim(s_i, CC_{S_k})}{\sum_{l=1, l \neq k}^{K} \min_{s_i \in C_{S_l}, s_j \in C_{S_l}} sim(s_i, s_j)} \right) \quad (8)$$

where $\min_{s_i \in C_k} sim(s_i, CC_{S_k})$ denotes the distance between the cluster center and the border sentence in a cluster that is the farthest away from the center. The larger it is, the more compact the cluster is. $CC_{S_k} = \sum_{s_i \in C_{S_k}} s_i \Big/ |C_{S_k}|$ where $|C_{S_k}|$ is the size of C_{S_k}. $\min_{s_i \in C_{S_l}, s_j \in C_{S_l}} sim(s_i, s_j)$, on the other hand, denotes the distance between the most distant pair of sentences, one from each cluster. The smaller it is, the more separated the two clusters are. The distance is measured by cosine similarity. As a whole, the larger *quan* means the better cluster quality.

Table 3 and Table 4 below indeed clearly indicate the improved cluster qualities by removing noises and/or by making better use of the relationships among sentences and words. The ranges of the sentence clusters are also provided for reference.

DUC2004	*Quan*	*Cluster no.*
Noise Detection Enhanced	5.26	2-6
LexRank	4.73	2-7

Table 3. Cluster Quality Evaluation on DUC2004

DUC2007	*Quan*	*Cluster no.*
Query-Driven Cluster Ranking	4.79	3-6
Query-Oriented LexRank	4.18	3-7

Table 4. Cluster Quality Evaluation on DUC2007

5.3 Example of Effective on Noise Detection

Besides the quantitative evaluation, we also select the DUC2004 D30006 document set and DUC2007 D0702A document set to illustrate the advantages of enhancement with noise detection in generic and query-oriented summarization, respectively. The former document set contains 10 documents about 'Labor Dispute in National

Basketball Association', while the latter one contains 25 documents about 'Art and music in public schools' and the corresponding query is to 'Describe the state of teaching art and music in public schools around the word, indicate problems, progress and failures'.

Three relevant topical themes, including 'Employers' attitude', 'Employees' attitude' and 'Game Canceling' are mentioned in DUC2004 D30006 human summaries, 'Music and art education in the world', 'The problems of music and art education' and 'the progress and failure in the music and art education' are mentioned in DUC2007 D0702A, respectively.

For illustration, we compare the summaries generated by noise detection enhanced spectral clustering/query-driven cluster ranking and LexRank/query-oriented LexRank without noise detection. In order to provide better coherence of the generated summary, we group the sentences in the same cluster together in a paragraph and order them according to their ranking scores in that cluster.

If Feerick finds in favor of the owners, the reality of not being paid may spur the players to reach an agreement more quickly. In return for the concessions, the players want an increase in the minimum salary currently $ 272,500. **(Cluster 1: Employees' attitude)**
Larry Bird, in the Indiana countryside or inside Boston Garden, was a luminous exception to the governing rule. The proposal is similar to the luxury tax proposed by the union in 1995 during negotiations, but it would not be nearly as liberal. **(Cluster 2: Topic non-relevant)**
The National Basketball Association, embroiled in a labor dispute with its players, Tuesday canceled the first two weeks of the 1998 - 99season.**(Cluster 3: Game canceling)**

Table 5. System generated summary of DUC2004 D30006 using LexRank

But neither the players nor the owners are counting on the ruling by the arbitrator, John Feerick, to speed up negotiations, especially if Feerick finds in favor of the players, an award that could approach $800 million in salaries. **(Cluster 1: Employers' attitude)**
Next week, it will consider canceling the first-ever regular season games in league history. The NBA has already canceled the first two weeks of the regular season because of the labor dispute. **(Cluster 2: Game canceling)**
In return for the concessions, the players want an increase in the minimum salary currently $272,500 and creation of an average salary exception. More than 220 National Basketball Association players with guaranteed contracts will find out **(Cluster 3: Employees' attitude)**

Table 6. System generated summary of DUC2004 D30006 using noise enhanced spectral clustering

Yet many schools have overflowing classes, outdated textbooks, insufficient supplies and cuts in arts and sports. This is Inner City Arts, a nonprofit arts school that is both an enlightened model for arts education and a design landmark where education is embellished by architectural example. The Bingham Academy, in its third year, offers a five-week program for five disciplines: creative writing, dance, instrumental and vocal music, theater and visual arts. Given the national obsession with high-stakes tests, they reasoned, it made sense to promote art and music classes as a way to boost test scores. **(Cluster 1: The progress and failure in the music and art education)**
The design is also an object lesson in construction. Results of the study were released. In a variety of ways. Flamenco, for example, ties into social studies and language arts lessons on the history and culture of Spain. Test scores are rising. People want schools to teach conflict resolution by negotiation, not violence. Standardized tests have improved many American schools. And classical music in Cuba could, from this point of view, use a little rescuing. The last argument may be in trouble. **(Cluster 2: Topic non-relevant sentences)**
The requirements include four years of English; three years of math; two years of social science; two years of lab science, two years of foreign language; one year of visual or performing arts and one year of electives. Centralizing information about the arts is another matter. By some estimates, only 25 percent of American schools offer music programs as a basic part of the curriculum. Arts exchanges are only part of the business. **(Cluster 3: The problems of music and art education)**

Table 7. System generated summary of DUC2007 D0702A using query-oriented LexRank

Most had participated in Carnegie Hall's Linkup music education program, and it showed. The Roundabout Theater sends teaching artists to 40 classrooms in the city for 10 visits each. Artists from Lotus Music and Dance Studios in Chelsea work intensively with six schools across the city, including Public School 156, teaching students about the music and dance of different cultures. Delaine Easton, the State Superintendent of Public Instruction, has called for the restoration of arts education in California public schools. All arts curriculum was eliminated from the public schools. **(Cluster 1: The progress and failure in the music and art education)**
Given the national obsession with high-stakes tests, they reasoned, it made sense to promote art and music classes as a way to boost test scores. By some estimates, only 25 percent of American schools offer music programs as a basic part of the curriculum. The more prestigious University of California schools consider only the top one-eighth of the state's high school seniors, while California State University, dubbed the people's university, takes the top one-third. **(Cluster 2: The problems of music and art education)**
The rhythm, harmony and melodies of the music all create different perceptions and sensations within different regions of the brain. Areas of research will include new digital techniques for music, dance, storytelling and the visual arts. The theory that classical music makes the brain work better and they have some high-profile allies. To schedule this extra drill, students must drop an elective, like fine arts or gym. **(Cluster 3: The problems of music and art education, Benefit from the education)**

Table 8. System generated summary of DUC2007 D0702A using query-driven spectral cluster rankings

It is not difficult to conclude that the generated summaries using noise detection looks more informative than without using noise detection. We interpret the sentences of cluster 2 in Table 5 and the sentence of cluster 2 in Table 7 as the noise sentences, considering they are not relevant to any main topical theme in the corresponding document set. Such kind of sentence is not observed in Table 6 and Table 8.

5.4 Comparison of Different Approaches to Integrating the Query Information

Different from generic summarization, the query information plays an important role in query-oriented summarization. In order to examine which way is more effective to integrate the query's influence into the clustering or ranking process, we further compare the query-based cluster-ranking and clustering approaches as introduced in Section 4.2. Meanwhile, we also implement the query-sensitive similarity measure introduced in (Tombros and Rijsbergen, 2001) for comparison, which calculates the similarity between s_i and s_j as

$$Sim(s_i, s_j) = \frac{\sum_{b=1}^{m} s_{ib} \cdot s_{jb}}{\sqrt{\sum_{b=1}^{m} s_{ib}^2 \cdot \sum_{b=1}^{m} s_{jb}^2}} \cdot \frac{\sum_{b=1}^{\max(l_m, l_Q)} c_b \cdot q_b}{\sqrt{\sum_{b=1}^{l_m} c_b^2 \cdot \sum_{b=1}^{l_Q} q_b^2}} \quad (9)$$

where l_Q is the query length of the query Q, l_m is the number of common words between s_i and s_j.

Table 9 below illustrates the ROUGE results on the DUC2007 dataset.

	ROUGE-1	ROUGE-2
Query-Driven Cluster Ranking	0.39351	0.09223
Query-Sensitive Similarity	0.39644	0.09537
Query-Embedding Similarity	0.39803	0.09698
Query-Supervised Clustering	0.40118	0.10125

Table 9. ROUGE Evaluation of Query-based Noise Detection Enhanced Approaches on DUC2007

We can observe from the above table that the query-embedding similarity approach and the query-supervised clustering approach clearly outperform the query-driven cluster ranking approaches. These results are expected. While the query-driven approach makes use of the query information in cluster ranking only, the other three approaches integrate the query information in both clustering and cluster ranking.

Beyond this, as a whole, the query-supervised clustering approach performs better than the query-embedding similarity approach. It can be interpreted if we look at the cluster generated. The query-supervised clustering approach is able to generate three types of clusters, i.e., query-relevant clusters, query-irrelevant clusters and a noise cluster and the summaries are generated merely from the query-relevant clusters. So the summaries generated are truly both query-relevant and theme-focused. In contrast, the query-embedding similarity approach can only differentiate the regular clusters from the noise cluster. Though the summaries are influenced by the query in some extent, the sentences in the generated regular clusters are not guaranteed to be relevant to the query.

It is also shown that the proposed query-embedding similarity measure has the advantage over the existing query-sensitive similarity measure, which simply multiplied the sentences-query similarity with the sentence-sentence similarity and thus the role of query is not as explicit as in query-embedding similarity.

To summarize, we believe that the high performance benefits from (1) Detecting and Removing Noise during Clustering i.e. removing noise sentences to enhance the clustering results and thus consequently improve the summarization performance; and (2) Guiding Sentence Clustering with Query for Query-oriented summarization, i.e., using the query information as the prior knowledge to supervise sentence clustering.

6 Conclusion

In conclusion, we propose noise detection enhanced spectral clustering to generate sentence clusters in this study. Moreover, we test the influence of query information for summarization generation. The experimental results on the DUC summarization datasets demonstrate the effectiveness and the robustness of the proposed approach. In particular the contribution of noise detection and the query information in the clustering process are clearly observed. In the future, we will add contextual information to sentences to further enhance the sentence clustering performance.

Acknowledgement

The work described in this paper was supported by an internal grant from the Hong Kong Polytechnic University (G-YH53) and UGC grant (PolyU 5230/08E).

References

Radev, D.R., Hovy, E., and Mckeown, K. 2002. *Introduction to the Special Issue on Summarization.* Computational Linguistics, 28: 399-408.

Wei F.R., Li W.J., Lu Q. and He Y.X. 2009. *Applying Two-Level Mutual Reinforcement Ranking in Query-Oriented Multi-Document Summarization.* Journal of the American Society for Information Science and Technology, 60(10):2119-2131.

Qazvinian V. and Radev D. R. 2008. *Scientific paper summarization using citation summary networks.* In Proceedings of 22nd COLING, pp.689-696.

Wan X. and Yang J. 2008. *Multi-Document Summarization Using Cluster-Based Link Analysis.* In Proceedings of 31st SIGIR, pp.299-306.

Wang D.D., Zhu S.H., Li T., Chi Y., Gong Y.H. 2008a. *Integrting Clustering and Multi-Document Summarization to Improve Document Understanding.* In Proceedings of 17th CIKM, pp.1435-1436.

Wang D.D., Li T., Zhu S.H., Ding Chris. 2008b. *Multi-Document Summarization via Sentence-Level Semantic Analysis and Symmetric Matrix Factorization.* In Proceedings of 31st SIGIR, pp.307-314.

Dave RN. 1999. *Characterization and Detection of Noise in Clustering.* Pattern Recognist Lettter 12(11): pp.657-664.

Li Z.G., Liu J.Z., Chen S.F. and Tang X.O. 2007. *Noise Robust Spectral Clustering.* 11th ICCV, pp. 421-427.

Ding,C. and Zha H.Y. 2011. *Spectral Clustering, Ordering and Ranking.* Statistical Learning with Matrix Factorizations. 1st Edition.

Ng A.Y., Jordan M.I., Weiss Y. 2001. *On Spectral Clustering. Analysis and An Algorithm.* Advances in Neural Information Processing Systems 14: pp.849-856.

Bach F.R. and Jordan M.I. 2004. *Learning Spectral Clustering.* Advances in Neural Information Processing Systems 16, 1830-1847.

Yu S. X. and Shi J. 2003. *Multiclass Spectral Clustering.* 9th ICCV: pp.11-17.

Luxburg. U. 2007. *A Tutorial on Spectral Clustering.* Statistics and Computing. 17 (4): pp.395-416.

Dhillon I.S., Guan Y.Q. and Kulis B. 2004. *Kernel-K-means, Spectral Clustering and Normalzied Cuts.* 10th KDD, pp.551-556.

Lin, C. Y. and Hovy, E. 2003. *Automatic Evaluation of Summaries Using N-gram Co-occurrence Statistics.* HLT-NAACL2003, 71-78.

Tombros A. and Rijsbergen C.J. 2001. *Query-Sensitive Similarity Measures for the Calculation of Interdocument Relationships.* 10th CIKM, pp.17-24.

S.D.Kamvar, D.Klein, and C.D.Manning. 2003. *Spectral learning.* 18th IJCAI, pp.561-566.

Extractive Summarization Method for Contact Center Dialogues based on Call Logs

Akihiro Tamura[1*], Kai Ishikawa[2], Masahiro Saikou[2], and Masaaki Tsuchida[2]

[1]Multilingual Translation Laboratory, MASTAR Project,
National Institute of Information and Communications Technology, Kyoto, Japan

[2] Information and Media Processing Laboratories, NEC Corporation, Nara, Japan

akihiro.tamura@nict.go.jp, k-ishikawa@dq.jp.nec.com, m-saikou@ax.jp.nec.com , m-tsuchida@cq.jp.nec.com

Abstract

This paper proposes a novel extractive summarization method for speech dialogues between agents and customers in contact centers. The proposed method does not require any extra cost for applying the method such as preparing rules or creating training data. Conventional methods such as the tf*idf method, which gives importance to characteristic words in an input text, can miss the essential points for contact center work. Our proposed method evaluates the importance of each utterance from the standpoint of call agents who report calls for managing or analyzing calls. Specifically, the proposed method includes information frequently reported by call agents in summaries using past call logs commonly recorded in the contact center. Evaluation using real data (call dialogues and call logs) shows that the proposed method can extract essential points in terms of contact center work and outperforms the conventional method.

1 Introduction

In recent years, the role of contact centers has become more important in many companies. This is because each contact center is a main channel for individual customers to directly access a company and the voice of the customers can be used to improve the quality of the company's products and services.

Many contact centers have two problems of

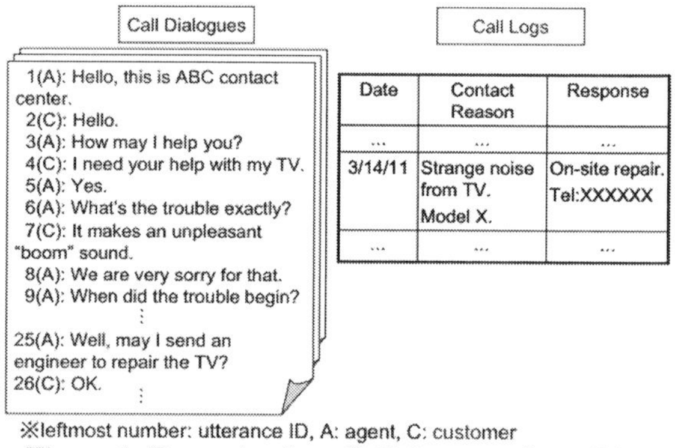

Figure 1: Example of a call dialogue and a call log

human cost. The first one is that agents spend much time documenting logs. Logs are usually generated by agents based on their memories or handwritten memos after a call. Such logs are used for reporting, managing, and analyzing their calls. Figure 1 shows an example of a call dialogue and its corresponding call log (We simply refer to these as a dialogue and a log hereafter).

The other cost is that managers also spend much time understanding the details of calls. This is because managers must listen to speech data or browse dialogue texts generated by automatic speech recognition (ASR), which are lengthy and include many uninformative parts.

Accordingly, automatic summarization of dialogues is required as an effective solution to the above problems. For the first problem, the summary can be an alternative to the logs or draft for agents. Byrd et al. (2008) have shown that automatic summarization helps to reduce the time for documenting calls. For the second one, the summary can help to reduce the time spent listening to the speech data or browsing the dialogue texts.

In previous works (Zechner, 1996; Edmundson, 2004; Orasan et al., 2004; Murray et al., 2007; Higashinaka et al., 2010), the methods summarize an input text without considering the

[*]This work was done when the author was at NEC Corporation.

requirements for contact center work such as reporting, managing, and analyzing calls. Some other works (Hirao et al., 2002; Iwasaki et al., 2005; Murray et al., 2005; Shen et al., 2007; Byrd et al., 2008; Fujii et al., 2008) can generate summaries satisfying such requirements. However, these methods generally require manual work of creating rules or training data.

In this paper, we propose a novel method that can summarize dialogues satisfying the requirements for contact center work without incurring the cost of manual works. The proposed method preferentially extracts sentences (or utterances) consisting of phrases described in logs of past calls. Such logs have been recorded through daily operation and are readily available in most contact centers. Moreover, we propose a method that bridges the gaps between the expressions in dialogues and logs to improve performance.

The main contributions of this paper are as follows.

1. We propose a method that preferentially extracts sentences consisting of phrases frequently written in logs of past calls. In our experiment using real data, we confirm that the proposed method outperforms the conventional methods (tf $*$ idf method and ridf method), baseline methods without considering the requirements for contact center work.
2. We propose a method that extracts sentences based on association strength with contents of the past logs so as to bridge gaps between the expressions in dialogues and logs, and confirm experimentally its effectiveness in summarization to improve performance.

This paper is organized as follows. In Section 2, we explain previous works and their problems. In Section 3, we propose our method. In Section 4, we describe the experiment using real contact center data. In Section 5, we discuss the experimental results. In Section 6, we summarize this paper.

2 Related Work

We describe conventional summarization methods for contact center dialogues and their problems. To reduce the burden of agents, Iwasaki et al. (2005) have proposed a method that generates a log of the input dialogue automatically. The method selects important sentences using different approaches according to sentence type (e.g. "contact reason", "response"), where the tf $*$ idf method or lead method is used. However, the method requires training data to identify the sentence type of each sentence. Hence, it takes effort to prepare the training data.

Byrd et al. (2008) built a system, Contact-Center Agent Buddies, which generates a candidate log from dialogues, and demonstrated its effectiveness in an actual contact center environment. The system normalizes the dialogue text generated by ASR, calculates the importance of each normalized sentence using a number of heuristic rules, and then extracts important sentences. However, some of the heuristic rules depend on the individual contact center (e.g. rules for annotating *cues* typically found in questions by agents). Hence, it takes effort to create rules for each contact center.

On the other hand, there are methods that do not require preparing training data or creating rules. Higashinaka et al. (2010) have proposed an extractive summarization method for contact center dialogues categorized into multiple domains (e.g. finance, mail order, PC support). The method extracts utterances that are characteristic of the input dialogue domain in relation to other domains using a particular type of hidden Markov model. However, the method cannot be applied to contact centers that do not deal with multiple domains. Additionally, the method seems to have difficulty extracting important information occurring in any domain (e.g., "a customer urgently requests support").

Other notable methods are the lead method proposed by Edmundson (1969) and the tf $*$ idf method proposed by Zechner (1996). The lead method extracts sentences from the top in order under the assumption that the important points are described first. However, important parts such as the customer's requirements and agent's responses can be located anywhere because the customer's requirements are identified through conversation interactions, which differ according to customers. Therefore, the lead method is not suitable for summarizing contact center dialogues.

The tf $*$ idf method uses word frequencies. First, the method calculates the following weight for each word w in the input text:

$$\mathrm{tf} * \mathrm{idf}(\mathrm{w}) = \mathrm{tf}(\mathrm{w}) \times \log\left(\mathrm{N_{all}}/\mathrm{N}(\mathrm{w})\right),$$

where $\mathrm{tf}(\mathrm{w})$ is the frequency of w in the input, $\mathrm{N_{all}}$ is the total number of texts, and $\mathrm{N}(\mathrm{w})$ is the number of texts containing w. Next, the method calculates the average of the weights for words in each sentence as importance of the sentence. Finally, the method extracts sentences in the order of the importance from the highest. The method extracts utterances including characteristic words that are frequent in the input text and infrequent in other texts. However, there are essential words for contact center work, although the words are frequent in other texts (e.g. words in frequent customer requests). The method does not include the words in summaries. Moreover, there are uninformative sentences including characteristic words such as the customer's speaking habits (e.g. "kind of" being frequently used by the customer). The method can extract these uninformative sentences.

Orasan et al. (2004) and Murray et al. (2007) experimentally showed that ridf(w) defined as the following function is most effective for summarizing texts in several term weighting functions including the $\mathrm{tf} * \mathrm{idf}(\mathrm{w})$.

$$\mathrm{ridf}(\mathrm{w}) = \log(\mathrm{N}_{\mathrm{all}}/\mathrm{N}(\mathrm{w})) - \log(1 - \mathrm{p}(0; \lambda_{\mathrm{w}})),$$

where $\mathrm{N}_{\mathrm{all}}$ and $\mathrm{N}(\mathrm{w})$ have the same definitions as those in the $\mathrm{tf} * \mathrm{idf}(\mathrm{w})$, and p is the Poisson distribution with parameter λ_{w}, the average number of occurrence of w per text, and $1 - \mathrm{p}(0; \lambda_{\mathrm{w}})$ is the probability of w appearing in a text at least once. However, the method using the ridf(w) also cannot generate summaries from the viewpoint of contact center work.

3 Proposed Method

We propose a novel summarization method for contact center dialogues without the problems described in Section 2. In this work, we assume that essential information for contact center work should be frequently written in past logs. First, the proposed method calculates the likelihood of being reported by agents for each utterance using past logs recorded in the contact center. Hereafter, we refer to the likelihood as *report score*. Next, the proposed method extracts utterances in the order of the report score from the highest and then outputs the extracted utterances in the order of appearance in the input dialogue as its summary.

The proposed method does not require any extra cost for applying the method because the method exploits past logs automatically accumulated in the contact center through daily operation. Additionally, the proposed method includes the essential points in terms of contact center work in summaries because the logs are described to report, manage, and analyze the contacts. Note that there is no corresponding log of an input dialogue when the method summarizes the dialogue.

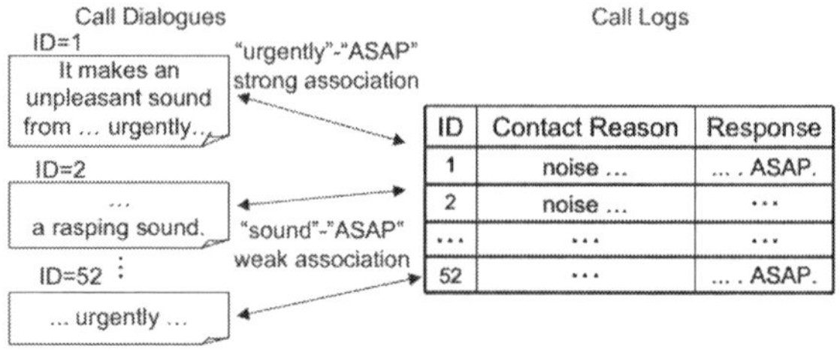

Figure 2: Association strength between words

The rest of this section is organized as follows. In Section 3.1, we first describe a method that simply calculates the report score based on frequency in past logs, and explain the problem with the simple method. In Section 3.2, we propose a method that calculates the report score based on past pairs of a dialogue and its corresponding log so as to handle the problem with the simple method.

3.1 Call Log Frequency Method (LF Method)

The LF method regards high frequency words in past logs as important, and then extracts utterances that have the high frequency words. The LF method proceeds as follows.

Step 1. $\mathrm{R\_Score}(\mathrm{w})$, the report score of a word w, for each word in an input dialogue is calculated by the following equation (1). Here, equation (1) is the document frequency of the word w, where a set of documents is a set of past logs (Call Log Frequency; LF).

$$\mathrm{R\_Score}(\mathrm{w}) = \mathrm{L}(\mathrm{w})/\mathrm{L}_{\mathrm{all}} \cdots (1).$$

Let L(w) be the number of past logs containing the word w, and let $\mathrm{L}_{\mathrm{all}}$ be the total number of past logs.

Step 2. $\mathrm{R\_Score}(\mathrm{U})$, the report score of an utterance U, for each utterance in the input dialogue is calculated as the average[1] of the report scores of the words in the utterance U as follows:

$$\mathrm{R\_Score}(\mathrm{U}) = \frac{\sum_{\mathrm{w} \in \mathrm{W}(\mathrm{U})} \mathrm{R\_Score}(\mathrm{w})}{|\mathrm{W}(\mathrm{U})|} \cdots (2).$$

Let W(U) be a set of all words in an utterance U.

Step 3. Top-K utterances in the order of the report score from the highest are extracted.

3.1.1 Problem with LF Method

In logs, concise expressions, abbreviations, and specialized terminology tend to be frequently used because the logs are generated so as to report to managers or persons involved. On the

[1] We regard sentences that express content compactly as important to summarization. Hence, we do not use the total but the average.

other hand, an agent usually uses multiple expressions in a dialogue according to the situation or customer's level of understanding. Therefore, there is a gap between the expressions in the dialogue and in its corresponding log even though those are the same in meaning.

In Figure 1, "an unpleasant 'boom' sound" in the dialogue is concisely described as "strange noise" in its corresponding log, and in Figure 2, "urgently" in a dialogue is described with the abbreviation "ASAP" in the log. However, the LF method cannot handle the differences between the expressions in dialogues and logs. Concretely, the LF method cannot select important information that is not described with the same expression in the logs.[2] Consider Figure 1, for example; the LF method cannot regard as important the words not appearing in the log such as "unpleasant", "boom" and "sound". Therefore, the LF method may not include ID 7, which is important for contact center work, in the summary.

3.2 Proposed Method

In Section 3.2.1, we propose a method that can handle the problem described in Section 3.1.1. In Section 3.2.2, we introduce a component that removes frequent utterances from the summary to improve performance of our method.

3.2.1 Association Strength Method (AS Method)

To handle differences between the expressions in dialogues and logs, we have based our proposed method on the following assumption: association strength (AS) between each occurrence of two words in past pairs of a dialogue and its corresponding log indicates semantic similarity between the two words.

Consider, for example, Figure 2. "Urgently" in dialogues and "ASAP" in logs have the same meaning. When "urgently" appears in a dialogue, "ASAP" also appears in its corresponding log (ID=1,52). Moreover, when "urgently" does not appear in a dialogue, "ASAP" also does not appear in its corresponding log (ID=2). In short, Figure 2 shows that association strength between "urgently" and "ASAP" is strong. On the other hand, "sound" and "ASAP" have different meanings. Figure 2 shows that the association strength between "sound" and "ASAP" is weak.

[2] Not only the LF method but any supervised methods using logs as training data have the same problem.

Under the above assumption, we propose the AS method, which estimates semantic similarity between a word w in dialogues and a word v in logs as $\mathrm{AS}(w, v)$, the association strength between each occurrence of w and v. $\mathrm{AS}(w, v)$ is calculated by association measures such as mutual information, chi-square value, and z-value.

We calculate the likelihood that a word w in a dialogue is reported in past logs as a word v, by the following expression (3). The expression is the product of $\mathrm{AS}(w, v)$, the semantic similarity between w and v, and the likelihood that the word v is reported in past logs.

$$\mathrm{AS}(w, v) \cdot L(v)/L_{\mathrm{all}} \cdots (3).$$

$L(v)$ and L_{all} in the expression (3) have the same definitions as $L(w)$ and L_{all} in equation (1) respectively.

Some of the words in dialogues have multiple synonymous expressions in logs. For example, "noise" in dialogues can sometimes be described as "noise" and other times as "sound" in logs. Additionally, the meaning of a word in a dialogue is often expressed with multiple words in its corresponding log. For example, the meaning of "boom" in the dialogue in Figure 1 is expressed with "strange noise" in its log. To deal with the above paraphrases, we expand expression (3). Specifically, the likelihood that the meaning of a word w in a dialogue is reported in past logs as a set of words V is calculated as the sum of expression (3) for each word v in V as follows:

$$\sum_{v \in V} \mathrm{AS}(w, v) \cdot L(v)/L_{\mathrm{all}} \cdots (4).$$

In conclusion, $\mathrm{R\_Score}(w)$, the report score of a word w, is estimated by expression (4), where V is the set of all words in past logs. Here, the amount of calculation is enormous. Therefore, we limit V in expression (4) to N words in order of $\mathrm{AS}(w, v)$ from the highest. We denote the set of such N words for a word w by $V_N(w)$. The AS method estimates $\mathrm{R\_Score}(w)$ by the following equation (5).

$$R_{\mathrm{Score}(w)} = \sum_{v \in V_N(w)} \mathrm{AS}(w, v) \cdot \frac{L(v)}{L_{\mathrm{all}}} \cdots (5).$$

Here, association strength between unrelated words should be close to zero, and the number of association words for one word is limited. Accordingly, equation (5) is not sensitive to larger N, and we assume that the AS method is effective with little or no tuning of N. We examine this point in Section 4. Hereafter, the AS method performs steps 2 and 3 in Section 3.1 in sequence.

Table 1: Performance of ASR

Speaker	Agent	Customer
P.C. (%)	91.5	89.9
W.A. (%)	87.7	84.8

Table 2: Test data

Data type	SR	MT	Log
Avg. number of utterances	175	111	-
Avg. number of characters	1,207	1,320	166

3.2.2 Removal of Frequent Utterances (RFU)

Contact center dialogues include many uninformative utterances that do not have important contents such as back-channel feedback (e.g. "Yes", "Well"), set phrases (e.g. "This is XX contact center."), and greetings (e.g. "Hello", "Good morning"). These uninformative utterances must not be included in a summary. We aim to improve performance of our method by directly detecting these uninformative utterances.

We assume that such uninformative utterances frequently occur in any dialogue. Hence, the proposed method calculates the occurrence rate for each utterance U defined as "the number of dialogues containing utterance U / total number of dialogues", and then identifies the utterances whose occurrence rates are higher than threshold θ as uninformative utterances. Finally, the proposed method removes the identified utterances from a summary.

4 Experiment

In this section, we describe the experiments using dialogues and logs in a real Japanese contact center and show their results, where we examine the following effects of our proposal.

- By preferentially including information frequently reported in past logs, the performance of automatic text summarizers for contact center works can be improved.
- Association strength between two words enables our method to handle differences between the expressions in dialogues and logs, and improves performance.
- RFU improves performance of our method.

4.1 Experimental Settings

4.1.1 Experimental data

We collected 4,596 call speech data and their corresponding logs in a real Japanese contact center, and generated the following two types of texts from the call speech data. We used the texts as dialogue data in the experiments.

1. Speech Recognition Text (SR):

The texts were generated by ASR from the read speech data. Table 1 shows the accuracy of ASR. In Table 1, P.C. is percent correct calculated by (T-S-D)/T, and W.A. is word accuracy calculated by (T-S-D-I)/T. Let T be the total number of words, S be the number of substitutions, I be the number of insertions, and D be the number of deletions.

2. Manual Transcription Text (MT):

The texts were transcribed manually from the speech data and divided manually into utterances.

4.1.2 Test Data

We used 40 pairs of dialogue data and their corresponding logs as test data, which were selected randomly from a total of 4,596 data. The average length of the dialogue data and the logs are shown in Table 2, which shows that the log corresponds to 12.6% (=166/1,320) of compressed text of the call speech data.

We used the following two types of summaries with different compression rates as the references in the experiments so as to examine the effectiveness for various types of contact center work such as reporting, managing, and analyzing contacts. The references were manually generated from the MT of the test data. Note that logs themselves are not suitable for references because there are differences between the expressions in dialogues and logs.

1. Indicative Summary:

We generated summaries with a 30% compression rate by manually extracting utterances on the assumption that these are used as alternatives to the logs or drafts for agents, and for managers to grasp the gist of calls at a glance. Here, the compression rate is defined as "number of characters in a summary / number of characters in a dialogue data". Note that we set the compression rate to 30%, which is higher than that of the logs (12.6%), because the expressions in dialogues tend to be lengthy compared to those in logs.

2. Informative Summary:

We generated summaries that are sufficient to obtain all contents by manually extracting utterances without thinking of compression rate on the assumption that these are used for managers to grasp the details of calls, and as cleansed texts for analysis of calls such as information retrieval and text mining. The average compression rate is 65.2%.

Table 3: Experiments with different N in equation (5)

N	1	2	4	8	16
F-measure	0.526	0.528	0.527	0.529	0.519
ROUGE-1	0.565	0.572	0.571	0.576	0.567
ROUGE-2	0.567	0.574	0.578	0.584	0.575
N	32	64	128	LF Method	
F-measure	0.504	0.497	0.494	0.478	
ROUGE-1	0.563	0.549	0.546	0.527	
ROUGE-2	0.568	0.550	0.548	0.543	

4.1.3 Competing Methods

We evaluate the following five methods in the experiments. For MT, each method judges each utterance manually detected as to whether it is necessary for the summary or not, and for SR, each method judges each utterance detected by the ASR engine.

1. tf $*$ idf method and ridf method:

   The methods are described in Section 2. Using a total of 4,556 dialogue data, the tf $*$ idf method calculated the tf $*$ idf score for each word and the ridf method calculated the ridf score.

2. LF method:

   The method is described in Section 3.1. In calculating the report score for each word, the method used a total of 4,556 logs.

3. AS method:

   The method is described in Section 3.2.1. Note that the method does not introduce RFU. In calculating the report score for each word, the method used a total of 4,556 pairs of the dialogue data and its corresponding logs, and used z-value as the association measure. We used various numbers as N in equation (5) to investigate the dependency of N on the performance of the AS method.

4. AS with RFU method:

   The method introduces RFU into the AS method. The settings in the AS method are the same as the above. In RFU, we used 0.5 as a threshold, which was determined by the preliminary experiment. Additionally, RFU calculated the occurrence rate using a total of 4,556 dialogue data. Here, RFU regards an utterance as the bag of content-word bigrams so as to relieve differences of the expressions between utterances (e.g. "This is XX speaking." and "This is XX."). RFU calculates the average of the occurrence rate of the bigrams in the utterance as the occurrence rate of the utterance.

4.1.4 Evaluation Measure

We used the following evaluation measures.

1. Sentence recall, precision, and F-measure:

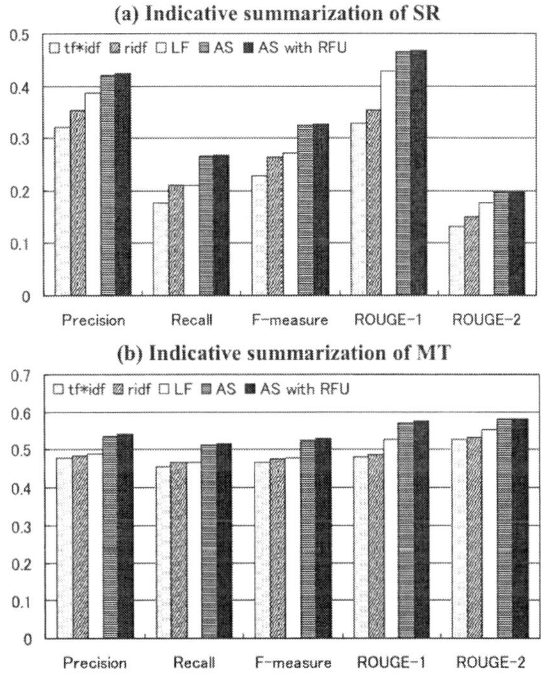

Fig 3: Result of indicative summarization

Sentence recall is the number of sentences correctly extracted by a method over the number of sentences in the reference. Sentence precision is the number of sentences correctly extracted over the number of sentences extracted by the method. F-measure is defined as follows;

$$2 \times \text{Recall} \times \text{Precision}/(\text{Recall} + \text{Precision}).$$

When SR is summarized, estimated sentence (or utterance) boundaries based on ASR results do not always agree with those in the references. In this paper, extraction of a sentence in the SR is considered as extraction of one or multiple sentences in the reference with an overlap of 50% or more words as in Hirohata et al. (2005).

2. ROUGE_N (Lin et al., 2003):

   ROUGE_N is an N-gram recall between reference (R) and the summary generated by a method (C), which indicates similarity between them. ROUGE_N is calculated as follows:

$$\text{ROUGE}_\text{N}(\text{C},\text{R}) = \frac{\text{C}_\text{m}(\text{N-gram})(\text{C},\text{R})}{\text{C}(\text{N-gram} \in \text{R})},$$

where $\text{C}_\text{m}(\text{N-gram})(\text{C},\text{R})$ is the number of co-occurrences of N-gram in C and R, and $\text{C}(\text{N-gram} \in \text{R})$ is the number of N-grams in R. In our experiments, 1-grams (ROUGE-1) and 2-grams (ROUGE-2) are used, where the words are only content words.

4.2 Experimental Results

First, we investigated the dependency of the number of association strength in estimating the

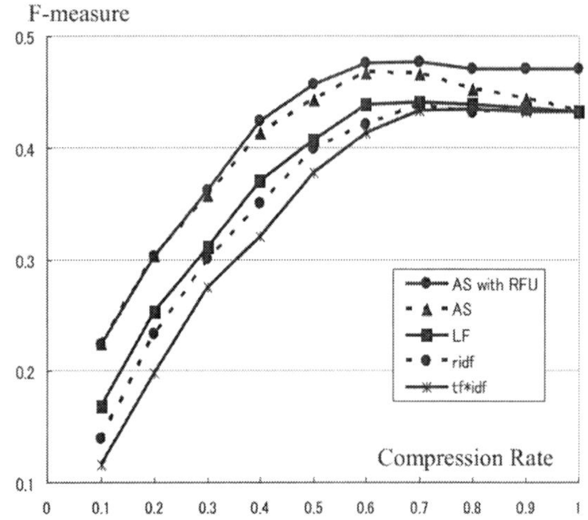

Fig 4: F-measure of informative summarization

report score (N in equation (5)) on the performance of the AS method. Table 3 shows the performance of indicative summarization with different N for MT. Table 3 shows that there is not much difference between N=64 and N=128. The result indicates that the number of related words for one word is limited and association strength between unrelated words is close to zero. Accordingly, the performance of the AS method is not sensitive to larger N. Table 3 also shows that the performance with N = 8 is best. Hereafter, let N be 8 with regard to the AS method.

Next, we examined the performance of indicative summarization for each competing method. Specifically, we summarized the dialogues in the test data by each method at a 30% compression rate, and then evaluated their results. Figure 3 shows the results. Moreover, we examined the performance of informative summarization for each competing method. Unfortunately, we cannot get the compression rate suitable for the informative summarization in each competing method. In the examination, we summarized the dialogues in the test data by each method, where the compression rate was changed from 0.1 to 1.0 at 0.1 intervals, and then evaluated their results. Figure 4 shows the F-measure for SR. Other evaluation measures and the results for MT are omitted in this paper because the results indicate a similar tendency to Figure 4, and the conclusions in this paper do not change.

Figures 3 and 4 show that the LF method, the AS method, and the AS with RFU method outperform the tf $*$ idf method and the ridf method. The results show that preferentially selecting information frequently reported in past logs is effective for summarizing dialogues from the viewpoint of contact center work regardless of compression rate.

Figures 3 and 4 also show that the AS method outperforms the LF method, and Table 3 shows that the performance of the AS method with N = 128 is better than that of the LF method. These results show that using association strength between two words in the past pairs of a dialogue and its corresponding log improves the performance of our method. This means the association measure helps to handle differences between the expressions in dialogues and logs. We discuss the point in Section 5.1 in detail. Additionally, Table 3 shows that the AS method is effective with little or no tuning of N.

Figure 4 shows that the AS with RFU method outperforms the AS method when the compression rate is high. The result shows that RFU is effective for summarization with a high compression rate. However, Figures 3 and 4 also show that when compression rate is low, there is not much difference between performance of the AS method and that of the AS with RFU method. We discuss this point in Section 5.2 in detail.

5 Discussion

5.1 Effectiveness of Association Strength between Two Words

We discuss whether the assumption described in Section 3.2.1, that the association strength between two words indicates semantic similarity, is correct or not. We examined relationships of the 500 pairs of two words with strong association in the experimental data. The result is that 67.8% are synonymous, 15.2% are *related*, and 17% are *unrelated*. Here, *related* is when the two words are associated with one another including is-a relations and part-of relations (e.g. "freeze" and "break", "ATM" and "cash"). *Unrelated* is when the two words are irrelevant to one another. The result shows that accuracy of identifying two words with the same meaning using the word pairs with high association strength is 67.8%.

Table 3 shows that the performance with N = 8 is best although the number of synonymous expressions for one word is supposed to be smaller than 8. We suppose that *related* helps to find utterances reported in the logs and 83% (total of *synonymous* and *related*) strong association is an efficient clue for summarization.

Most *unrelated* words belong to different types of information (e.g. "CUSTOMER X" and "MODEL Y", which should be respectively described in the "customer's name" and "contact

Table 4: Rate of eliminated utterances by RFU

Data Type	Compression Rate	Rate of eliminated utterances by RFU
SR	30%	1.9% (23/1,213)
	50%	2.4% (51/2,098)
	65%	9.3% (269/2,879)
	80%	35.9% (1,500/4,182)
MT	30%	0.6% (4/715)
	50%	2.3% (27/1,168)
	65%	8.0% (129/1,617)
	80%	53.8% (1,239/2,305)

reason" parts of the logs). By calculating the association measure of two words in corresponding parts of a dialogue and its log after topic segmentation of the dialogue, we can further improve our method.

5.2 Effectiveness of RFU

We examined whether the frequent utterances identified by RFU in the test set are unnecessary for the summaries (uninformative) or not. In a total of 6,985 utterances in SR, 2,102 utterances (161 varieties) are identified by RFU, and 99.4% (=2,090/2,102) are uninformative. In a total of 4,436 utterances in MT, 1,985 utterances (156 varieties) are identified by RFU, and 99.7% (=1,979/1,985) are uninformative. The results show that RFU can eliminate uninformative utterances from the summaries with high accuracy.

Additionally, we examined the rate of eliminated utterances by introducing RFU into the AS method, which is the number of frequent utterances in the summary generated by the AS method over the total number of utterances in the summary. Table 4 shows the result. Table 4 shows that there are few frequent utterances in the summary generated by the AS method when the compression rate is low. In other words, the result indicates that the AS method (without RFU) can eliminate uninformative frequent utterances when generating an indicative summary or informative summary with a low compression rate. As a result, there is not much difference between the performance of the AS method and that of the AS with RFU method in Figures 3 and 4 with a low compression rate.

On the other hand, Table 4 shows that there are a lot of frequent utterances in the summary generated by the AS method when the compression rate is high. The results indicate that when the compression rate is high, it is difficult to judge whether an utterance is important or not using only the report score based on the association strength. This is because the input dialogue can include detailed information not described in the logs, and also subjects not occurring in past calls. In the above situation, suitable utterances can be included in a summary by eliminating frequent utterances preferentially. As a result, the AS with RFU method enables maintaining the quality of summarization with a high compression rate.

5.3 Robustness to ASR errors

Figure 3 shows that performance on summarization of SR is lower than that of MT in every method. This is because the words that should be ideally included in the summary are missing in SR due to substitutions or deletions in ASR.

To examine the robustness to ASR errors, we calculated the reduction rate[3] of F-measure by comparing the performance to SR with that to MT. As a result, the reduction rate of the AS method is 37.9% and the rate of the LF method is 43.1%. The result shows that the AS method is more robust to ASR errors than the LF method.

6 Conclusions

We proposed a novel method that can summarize contact center dialogues satisfying the requirements for contact center work without any extra cost for applying the method. We proposed the idea of preferentially selecting information frequently reported in past logs so as to include the essential information for contact center work in summaries. Moreover, we proposed a method that extracts utterances based on association strength between each sentence and the past logs so as to bridge the gaps between the expressions in logs and dialogues.

In the evaluation using real data, experimental results showed that our proposed method outperforms the conventional methods (the tf $*$ idf method and the ridf method), and association strength between two words improves the performance of automatic text summarizers for contact center works. Additionally, we improved our method by removing frequent utterances from the summaries.

We are planning to prove the effectiveness of our proposed method for actual contact center work according to the cost reduction effect in the call log documentation process.

[3] (F-measure to MT – F-measure to SR) / F-measure to MT

Reference

Roy J. Byrd, Mary S. Neff, Wilfried Teiken, Youngja Park, Keh-Shin F. Cheng, Stephen C. Gates, and Karthik Visweswariah. 2008. Semi-Automated Logging of Contact Center Telephone Calls. In *Proceedings of the 17th ACM International Conference on Information and Knowledge Management*, pages 133-142.

Harold P. Edmundson. New Methods in Automatic Extracting. 1969. Journal of ACM, pages 264-285.

Yasuhisa Fujii, Kazumasa Yamamoto, Norihide Kitaoka, and Seiichi Nakagawa. 2008. Class Lecture Summarization Taking into Account Consecutiveness of Important Sentences. In *Proceedings of the 9th Annual Conference of the International Speech Communication Association*, pages 2438-2441.

Ryuichiro Higashinaka, Yasuhiro Minami, Hitoshi Nishikawa, Kohji Dohsaka, Toyomi Meguro, Satoshi Takahashi, and Genichiro Kikui. 2010. Learning to Model Domain-Specific Utterance Sequences for Extractive Summarization of Contact Center Dialogues. In *Proceedings of the 23rd International Conference on Computational Linguistics*, pages 400-408.

Tsutomu Hirao, Hideki Isozaki, Eisaku Maeda, and Yuji Matsumoto. 2002. Extracting Important Sentences with Support Vector Machines. In *Proceedings of the 19th International Conference on Computational Linguistics*, pages 342-348.

Makoto Hirohata, Yousuke Shinnaka, Koji Iwano, and Sadaoki Furui. 2005. Sentence Extraction-Based Presentation Summarization Techniques and Evaluation Metrics. In *Proceedings of the 30th International Conference on Acoustics, Speech, and Signal Processing*, pages 1065-1068.

Reijirou Iwasaki and Kenji Araki. 2005. Important Sentence Extraction Method for Automatic Generation of Business Days Report for Conversation Data of Call Center. In *Proceedings of 19th the Annual Conference of The Japanese Society for Artificial Intelligence*, 1E1-102. [in Japanese].

Chin-Yew Lin and Eduard Hovy. 2003. Automatic Evaluation of Summaries Using N-gram Co-occurrence Statistics, In *Proceedings of the 4th Meeting of the North American Chapter of the Association for Computational Linguistics and Human Language Technology*, pages 71-78.

Gabriel Murray, Steve Renals, and Jean Carletta. 2005. Extractive Summarization of Meeting Recordings. In *Proceedings of the 9th European Conference on Speech Communication and Technology*, pages 593-596.

Gabriel Murray and Steve Renals. 2007. Term-Weighting for Summarization of Multi-Party Spoken Dialogues. In A. Popescu-Belis, S. Renals, and H. Bourlard, editors, *Machine Learning for Multimodal Interaction IV, volume 4892 of Lecture Notes in Computer Science*, pages 155-166.

Constantin Orasan, Viktor Pekar, and Laura Hasler. 2004. A comparison of summarisation methods based on term specificity estimation . In *Proceedings of the 4th international conference on Language Resources and Evaluation*, pages 1037-1040.

Dou Shen, Jian-Tao Sun, Hua Li, Qiang Yang, and Zhen Chen. 2007. Document Summarization using Conditional Random Fields. In *Proceedings of the 20th International Joint Conference on Artificial Intelligence*, pages 2862-2867.

Klaus Zechner. 1996. Fast Generation of Abstracts from General Domain Text Corpora by Extracting Relevant Sentences. In *Proceedings of the 16th International Conference on Computational Linguistics*, pages 986-989.

Indexing Spoken Documents with Hierarchical Semantic Structures: Semantic Tree-to-string Alignment Models

Xiaodan Zhu & Colin Cherry
Institute for Information Technology
National Research Council Canada
{Xiaodan.Zhu,Colin.Cherry}@nrc-cnrc.gc.ca

Gerald Penn
Department of Computer Science
University of Toronto
gpenn@cs.toronto.edu

Abstract

This paper addresses a semantic tree-to-string alignment problem: indexing spoken documents with known hierarchical semantic structures, with the goal to help index and access such archives. We propose and study a number of alignment models of different modeling capabilities and time complexities to provide a comprehensive understanding of these unsupervised models and hence the problem itself.

1 Introduction

The inherent difficulties in efficiently accessing spoken documents raise the need for ways to better organize such archives. Such a need parallels with the consistently increasing demand for and availability of audio content on web pages and other digital media, which, in turn, should come as no surprise, with speech being one of the most basic, most natural forms of human communication.

When intended to be read, written documents are almost always presented as more than uninterrupted text strings; e.g., indicative structures such as section/subsection headings and tables-of-contents are standard constituents created manually to help readers, whereas structures of this kind are rarely aligned with spoken documents, which has raised little concern—in most time of history, speech has not been ready for *navigation*, until very recently, when recording, delivering, and even automatic transcription were possible.

Navigating audio documents is often inherently much more difficult than browsing text. An obvious solution, in relying on human beings' ability of reading text, is to conduct a speech-to-text conversion through ASR, which in turn raises a new set of problems to be considered. First, the convenience and efficiency of reading transcripts are affected by errors produced in transcription channels, though if the goal is only to browse the most salient parts, recognition errors in excerpts can be reduced by considering ASR confidence (Xie and Liu, 2010; Hori and Furui, 2003; Zechner and Waibel, 2000) and the quality of excerpts can be improved from various perspectives (Zhang et al., 2010; Xie and Liu, 2010; Zhu et al., 2009; Murray, 2008; Zhu and Penn, 2006; Maskey and Hirschberg, 2005). Even if transcription quality were not a problem, browsing lengthy transcripts is not straightforward, since, as mentioned above, indicative browsing structures are barely manually created for and aligned with spoken documents. Ideally, such semantic structures should be inferred directly from the spoken documents themselves, but this is known to be difficult even for written texts, which are often more linguistically well-formed and less noisy than automatically transcribed text. This paper studies a less ambitious problem: we align an already-existing hierarchical browsing structure, e.g., the electronic slides of lecture recordings, with the sequential transcripts of the corresponding spoken documents, with the aim to help index and access such archives. Specifically, we study a number of semantic tree-to-string alignment models with different modeling capabilities and time complexities in order to obtain a comprehensive understanding of these models and hence the indexing task itself.

Semantic Structures of Spoken Documents Much previous work, similar to its written-text counterpart, has attempted to find certain *flat* structures of spoken documents such as topic and slide boundaries (Malioutov et al., 2007; Zhu et al., 2008), which, however, involve no hierarchical structures of a spoken document, thought as will be shown in this paper, topic-segmentation models can be considered in our alignment task. Research has also resorted to other multimedia channels, e.g., video (Fan et al., 2006), to detect slide transitions. This type of approaches, however, are unlikely to recover semantic structures more detailed than slide boundaries.

Zhu et al. (2010) investigate the problem of aligning electronic slides with lecture transcripts by first sequentializing bullet trees on slides with a pre-order walk before conducting alignment, through which the problem is reduced to a string-to-string alignment problem and conventional methods such as DTW (dynamic time warping) based alignment can then be directly applicable. A pre-order walk of bullet tree on slides is actually a natural choice, since speakers of presentations often follow such an order to develop their talks, i.e., they discuss a parent bullet first and then each of its children in sequence. However, although some remedies may be taken (Zhu et al., 2010), sequentializing the hierarchies before alignment, in principle, enforces a full linearity/monotonicity between transcripts and slide trees, which violates some basic properties of the problem that we will discuss. More recently, the work of (Zhu, 2011) proposes a graph-partitioning based model (revisited in Section 4) and shows that the model outperforms a bullet-sequentializing model.

With this previous work available, several important questions, however, are still open in obtaining a comprehensive understanding of the semantic tree-to-string alignment task. First of all, a basic question is associated with different ways of exploiting the semantic trees when performing alignment, which, as will be studied comprehensively in this paper, results in models of different modeling capabilities and time complexities. Second, all the models discussed above consider only similarities between bullets and transcribed utterances, while similarities among utterances, which directly underline a cohesion model, are generally ignored. We will show in this paper that the state-of-the-art topic-segmentation model (Malioutov and Barzilay, 2006) can be inherently incorporated into the graph-partitioning-based alignment models. Third, the different alignment objectives, e.g., that of the graph-partitioning models versus that of basic DTW-based models, are entangled together with different ways of exploiting the bullet tree structures in (Zhu, 2011). In this paper, we discuss two more quadratic-time models to bridge the gap.

Specifically, this paper studies nine different models, with the aim to provide a comprehensive understanding of the questions discussed above. In the remainder of the paper, we will first review the related work (Section 2) and more formally describe our problem (Section 3). Then we revisit the graph-partitioning alignment model (Section 4), before present all the alignment models we will study (Section 5). We describe our experiment set-up in Section 7 and results in Section 8, and draw our conclusions in Section 9.

2 Related Work

Alignment of parallel texts In general, research on finding correspondences between parallel texts pervades both spoken and written language processing, e.g., in training statistical machine translation models, identifying relationship between human-written summaries and their original texts (Jing, 2002), force-aligning speech and transcripts in ASR, and grounding text with database facts (Snyder and Barzilay, 2007; Chen and Mooney, 2008; Liang et al., 2009). Our problem here, however, is distinguished in several major aspects, which need to be considered in our modeling. First, it involves segmentation—alignment is conducted together with the decision of the corresponding segment boundaries on transcripts; in other words, we are not finally concerned with the specific utterances that a bullet is aligned to, but the region of utterances. In such a sense, graph partitioning seems intuitively to be more relevant than models optimizing a full-alignment score. Second, unlike a string-to-string alignment task, the problem involves hierarchical tree structures. This allows for different ways of combining tree traversal with the alignment process, as will be studied in detail in this paper. Third, the hierarchical structures as well as the texts on them are fixed and unique to each document (here a lecture) and knowledge is little generalizable across different documents. We accordingly keep our solution in an unsupervised framework. Fourth, the length of transcripts and that of the hierarchies are very imbalanced, and the former can be as long as tens of thousands of utterances or hundreds of thousands of words, which requires a careful consideration of a model's time complexity.

Building Tables-of-contents on Written Text Learning semantic structures of written text has been studied in a number of specific tasks, which include, but not limited to, those finding semantic representations for individual sentences and those constructing hierarchical structures among sentences or larger text blocks. A notable effort of the latter kind, for example, is the work of (Branavan et al., 2007), which aims at the ultimate goal of building tables-of-contents for written texts, though the problem was restricted to generating titles for each text span by assuming the availability of the structures of tables-of-contents and their alignments with text spans. Our work here can be thought of as an inverse problem, in which a specific type of semantic hierarchical structures are known, and we need to establish their correspondence with the spoken documents.

Rhetoric Analysis In general, analyzing discourse structures can provide thematic skeletons (often represented as trees) of a document as well as relationship between the nodes in the trees. Examples include the widely known discourse parsing work of (Marcu, 2000). However, when the task involves the understanding of high-level discourse, it becomes more challenging than finding local discourse conveyed on small spans of text; e.g., the latter is more likely to benefit from the presence of discourse markers. Specifically for spoken documents, speech recognition errors, absence of formality and thematic boundaries, and less linguistically well-formedness of the spoken language, will further impair the conditions on which an reliable discourse-analysis algorithm is often built. In this paper, we study a less ambitious but naturally occurring problem.

3 Problem

We are given a speech sequence $U = u_1, u_2, ..., u_N$, where u_i is an utterance, and the corresponding hierarchical structure, which, in our work here, is a sequence of lecture slides containing a set of slide titles and bullets, $B = \{b_1, b_2, ..., b_M\}$, organized in a tree structure $T(\Re, \aleph, \Psi)$, where $\Re$ is the root of the tree that concatenates all slides of a lecture; i.e., each slide is a child of the root $\Re$ and each slide's bullets form a subtree. In the rest of this paper, the word *bullet* means both the title of a slide (if any) and any bullet in it. $\aleph$ is the set of nodes of the tree (both terminal and non-terminals, excluding the root $\Re$), each corresponding to a bullet b_m in the slides. Ψ is the edge set. With the definitions, our task is herein to find the triple (b_i, u_j, u_k), denoting that a bullet b_i is mapped to a region of lecture transcripts that starts from the jth utterance u_j and ends at the kth, inclusively. Constrained by the tree structure, the transcript region corresponding to an ancestor bullet contains those corresponding to its descendants; i.e., if a bullet b_i is the ancestor of another bullet b_n in the tree, the acquired boundary triples (b_i, u_{j_1}, u_{k_1}) and (b_n, u_{j_2}, u_{k_2}) should satisfy $j_1 \leq j_2$ and $k_1 \geq k_2$.

4 Graph-partitioning Models: A Revisit

To facilitate our discussion later in this paper, we briefly revisit the graph-partitioning alignment model proposed in (Zhu, 2011), which, inspired by (Malioutov and Barzilay, 2006; Shi and Malik, 2000), extended a graph-partitioning model to find the correspondence between the bullets on electronic slides and transcribed utterances.

Consider a general, simple two-set partitioning case, in which a boundary is placed on a graph $G = (V, E)$ to separate its vertices V into two sets, A and B, with all the edges between these two sets being removed. The objective, as we have mentioned above, is to minimize the following normalized-cut score:

$$Ncut(A, B) = \frac{cut(A, B)}{assoc(A, V)} + \frac{cut(A, B)}{assoc(B, V)} \quad (1)$$

In equation (1), $cut(A, B)$ is the total weight of the edges being cut, i.e., those connecting A with B, while $assoc(A, V)$ and $assoc(B, V)$ are the total weights of the edges that connect A with all vertices V, and B with V, respectively. In general, minimizing such a normalized-cut score has been shown to be NP-complete. In our problem, however, the solution is constrained by the linearity of segmentation on transcripts, similar to that in topic segmentation (Malioutov and Barzilay, 2006). In such a situation, a polynomial-time algorithm exists (Zhu, 2011).

Consider a set of sibling bullets, $b_1, ..., b_m$, that appear on the same level of a bullet tree and share the same parent b_p. For the time being, we assume the corresponding region of transcripts has already been identified for b_p, say $u_1, ..., u_n$. We connect each bullet in $b_1, ..., b_m$ with utterances in $u_1, ..., u_n$ by their similarity, which results in a bipartite graph. Our task here is to place $m - 1$ boundaries onto the bipartite graph to partition the graph into m bipartite graphs and obtain triples, e.g., (b_i, u_j, u_k), to align b_i to $u_j, ..., u_k$, where $b_i \in \{b_1, ..., b_m\}$ and $u_j, u_k \in \{u_1, ..., u_n\}$ and $j <= k$. Since we have all descendant bullets to help the partitioning, when constructing the bipartite graph, we actually include also all descendant bullets of each bullet b_i, but ignoring their orders within each b_i. We find optimal normalized cuts in a dynamic-programming process with the following recurrence relation:

$$C[i,k] = \min_{j \le k}\{C[i-1,j] + D[i,j+1,k]\} \quad (2)$$

In equation (2), $C[i,k]$ is the optimal/minimal normalized-cut value of aligning the first i sibling bullets, $b_1, ..., b_i$, with the first k utterances, $u_1, ..., u_k$. It is computed by updating $C[i-1,j]$ with $D[i,j+1,k]$, for all possible j s.t. $j \le k$, where $D[i,j+1,k]$ is a normalized-cut score for the triple (b_i, u_{j+1}, u_k) and is defined as follows:

$$D[i,j+1,k] = \frac{cut(A_{i,j+1,k}, V \setminus A_{i,j+1,k})}{assoc(A_{i,j+1,k}, V)} \quad (3)$$

where $A_{i,j+1,k}$ is the vertex set that contains the bullet b_i (including its descendant bullets, if any, as discussed above) and the utterances $u_{j+1}, ..., u_k$; $V \setminus A_{i,j+1,k}$ is its complement set.

Different from the topic segmentation problem (Malioutov and Barzilay, 2006), the graph-partitioning alignment model needs to remember the normalized-cut values between any region $u_j, ..., u_k$ and any bullet b_i in our task, which requires to use the additional subscript i in $A_{i,j+1,k}$, while in topic segmentation, the computation of both $cut(.)$ and $assoc(.)$ is only dependant on the left boundary j and right boundary k. Also, the similarity matrix here is not symmetric as in topic segmentation, but m by n, where m is the number of bullets, while n is the number of utterances.

As far as time complexity is concerned, the graph-partitioning models discussed above are quadratic with regards to N, i.e., $O(MN^2)$, where $M \ll N$; M and N denoting the number of bullets and utterances, respectively, with the loop kernel computing and filling $D[i,j,k]$ in equation 3, which is a $M \times N \times N$ matrix. Zhu (2011) applied the algorithm deterministically in traversing a bullet tree top-down: starting from the root, the normalized-cut algorithm finds the corresponding regions of transcripts for all the direct children of the root, fixes the regions, and repeats this process recursively to partition lower-level bullets. This whole algorithm is still quadratic $O(MN^2)$ but outperforms a bullet-sequentializing baseline.

5 Alignment Models

Now, we discuss the models that we will study further in this paper to address the problems rise earlier in the introduction section.

5.1 The $O(MN^4)$ Models

As discussed, Zhu (2011) proposed a graph-partitioning alignment model and applied it in a deterministic way along with a top-down traversal of bullet trees. Though such models could be very competitive in performance, an important question, however, is with regard to the performance of models that can optimize a global score rather than local ones on each set of sibling bullets, which requires a study of models with more modeling capability (containing the deterministic hierarchical models as a special case) and with higher time complexities.

Naively, searching all possible partitions to optimizing a global score needs to consider an exponential space in terms of the number of transcribed utterances, while applying dynamic programming similar to those used in syntactic parsing would keep the solution to be polynomial. In this section, we introduce such alignment models; or in another viewpoint, we formulate the alignment task in a parsing-like setting. A dynamic programming approach, e.g., that used in a conventional CYK parser, can be adapted to solve this problem, in which one can replace the splitter moving in each text span in the classic CYK with the quadratic bipartite-graph partitioning model discussed above. However, in our task here, the trees, unlike in a general parsing task, are given and fixed, meaning that the cells of a parsing table can be filled in a fixed order, i.e., a post order, so that the search speed can be improved by some constant.

Figure 1 shows an algorithm, in which we insert the bipartite graph partitioning model that works on sibling bullets (as discussed in Section 4) into a parsing search process (line (12)). We call this model **PrsCut**. Note that there are more than one way to conducting such a search, but they should yield the same results once the objective function, e.g., the normalized-cut score here, is the same.

Specifically, the *Main* function in Figure 1 takes as input an $M \times N$ similarity matrix, where, same as before, M and N denote the number of bullets and transcribed utterances in a lecture, respectively. The $Main$ function first computes the

```
Main
Input: simMat, an MxN similarity matrix
       root, the root of a bullet tree
Output: boundPos, bullets' boundaries on transcripts
1: cutCostTab = Cal_CutCostTab(simMat);
2: Build_Parsing_Tab(root, cutCostTab, prsTab);
3: boundPos = Decoding(root, prsTab);
```

```
Build_Parsing_Tab(curNd, cutCostTab, prsTab)
Input:  curNd, current node/bullet in concern
        cutCostTab, an MxNxN normalized-cut cost table
Output: prsTab, an MxNxN parsing table
4: If current node curNd is a leaf then
5:    prsTab[curNd,:,:] = cutCostTab[curNd,:,:];
6: else
7:    for each child c' of curNd do
8:       Build_Parsing_Tab(c', cutCostTab, prsTab);
9:    end for
10:   for i = 1...N do
11:      for j = i...N do
12:         bestScr = Bigraph_Alignment(curNd, prsTab, i, j);
13:         prsTab[curNd,i,j] = cutCostTab[curNd,i,j]+w*bestScr;
14:      end for
15:   end for
16: end if
```

Figure 1: An algorithm of optimizing a global normalized-cut score.

$cutCostTab$, which saves the $D[i, j+1, k]$ values defined by equation (3). Then the parsing table $prsTab$ is built with a post-order traversal algorithm *Build-Parsing-Tab*, followed by a decoding process that finds the optimal partitioning tree. As sketched in Figure 1, the *Build-Parsing-Tab* algorithm builds a 3-dimensional table $prsTab$, each cell saving a value that linearly combines the corresponding $cutCostTab$ value of the current node/bullet $curNd$ and the optimal partitioning score $bestScr$ value calculated on its descendent, if any (see line (13)); or if the current node $curNd$ is a leaf itself, its $bestScr$ score is zero; in such case, the $prsTab$ value is initialized with the $cutCostTab$ value (line (5)). The recursive algorithm traverse the bullet tree in a post-order walk, which, as discussed above, utilizes the given, fixed bullet tree structures to fill the parsing table $prsTab$. The weight w in line (13) is set in a held-out data and note that if w is set to be 0, the model degrades to be the deterministic hierarchical model discussed in (Zhu, 2011) and referred to as $HieCut$ below in Section 5.2, since in this case the $prsTab$ is same as $costCustTab$. As far as time complexity is concerned, the whole algorithm is $O(MN^4)$, shown by the nested *for*-loops of line (10)-(15) that contain the $O(MN^2)$ bigraph-partitioning alignment in line (12). Similarly, we can insert a standard DTW-based alignment model into the line (12) here, which we call the **PrsBase** model. Note that the real algorithm is a little more complicated; e.g., we need to allow a parent bullet to have a different starting position than its first child, same as in (Zhu, 2011).

5.2 The $O(MN^2)$ models

Sequential Alignment Models As discussed earlier, in a simplified situation, our problem here can be formulated as a sequential alignment problem, based on a fairly reasonable assumption (Zhu et al., 2010): a speaker follows a pre-order walk of a bullet tree to develop the talk, i.e., discussing a parent bullet first, followed by each of its children in sequence. Accordingly, the models first sequentialize bullet trees with a pre-order walk before conducting alignment, through which the problem is reduced to a string-to-string alignment problem and conventional methods such as DTW-like alignment can then be applicable. Such a pre-order walk has also been assumed by (Branavan et al., 2007) to reduce the search space in their table-of-contents generation task, a problem in which a tree hierarchy has already been aligned with a span of written text, while the title of each node on the tree needs to be generated.

With this formulation, we first included here the baseline model in (Zhu et al., 2010), which applies a typical DTW-based alignment. We refer to the model as **SeqBase**. In addition, we applied the graph-partitioning based models discussed in (Zhu, 2011) to align the sequentialized bullets and the corresponding transcribed utterances, and we call this model **SeqCut**. The motivation of studying $SeqCut$ is to further understand the benefit of graph-partitioning based models. For example, it allows us to disentangle the benefit of the deterministic graph-partitioning models in (Zhu, 2011): whether the benefit is due to the modeling advantage of the proposed partitioning objective or its avoiding sequentializing bullet trees.

In principle, sequentializing bullet trees before alignment enforces a full linearity/monotonicity between transcripts and these bullet trees, which, though based on a reasonable assumption and is fairly effective (as will be shown in our comprehensive comparison later), misses some basic properties of the problem. For example, the generative process of lecture speech, with regards to a hierarchical structure (here, bullet trees), is characterized in general by a speaker's producing detailed content for each bullet when discussing it, during which sub-bullets, if any, are talked about recursively. By the nature of the problem, words in a bullet could be repeated multiple times, even when the speaker traverses to talk about the descendant bullets in the depth of the sub-trees. That is, the content of a bullet could be mentioned not only before its children but also very likely when the speaker traverses to talk descendant bullets, if any, which violate the pre-order-walk assumption.

Though with shortcomings, an important benefit of formulating the task as a sequential-alignment problem is its computational efficiency: solutions can be acquired in quadratic time. This is of particular importance for this task, considering that the length of a document, such as a lecture or a book, is often long enough to make less efficient algorithms practically intractable. A natural question to be ask is therefore whether we can, in principle, model the problem better, but still keep the time complexity quadratic, i.e., $O(MN^2)$.

Deterministic Hierarchical Models Deterministically deciding bullets' boundaries on transcribed utterances when traversing the bullet tree can keep the solution within a quadratic time complexity and avoid a sequentialization of bullet trees beforehand. For example, in (Zhu, 2011), the graph-partitioning alignment model, as discussed above, is applied in such a deterministic way; the model recursively traverses a bullet tree by first determining transcript boundaries of the direct children of the root, fixing the boundaries found, and then determining boundaries for the descendant bullets recursively[1]. We refer to this model as $HieCut$ in this paper. Note that though working deterministically, this models utilize the similarities associated with all descendant bullets of the current sibling bullets under concern, to find the optimal boundaries between these siblings. In addition, we include a standard DTW-based alignment model in such a deterministic-decision process, called the **HieBase** model in the remainder of this paper.

One major benefit of the deterministic hierarchical alignment models is their time complexity: still quadratic, same as the sequential alignment model discussed above, though models like $HieCut$ can achieve a very competitive performance, which we will discuss in detail later. Also, the deterministic hierarchical models need less memories than the corresponding $O(MN^4)$ models and even the sequential models. For example, the memory needed by $HieCut$ is proportional to the maximal number of sibling bullets in a tree, not the total number of bullets.

6 The Topic-segmentation Model

Up to now, we have discussed a variety of alignment models with different model capabilities and time complexities, which, however, consider only similarities between bullets and utterances. Cohesion in text or speech, by itself, often evidenced by the change of lexical distribution (Hearst, 1997), can also indicate topic or subtopic transitions, even among subtle subtopics (Malioutov and Barzilay, 2006). In our problem here, when a lecturer discusses a bullet, the words used are likely to be different from those used in another bullet, suggesting that the spoken documents themselves, when ignoring the alignment model above for the time being, could potentially indicate the semantic boundaries that we are interested in here. Particularly, the cohesion conveyed by the repetition of the words that appear in transcripts but not in slides could be additionally helpful; this is very likely to happen considering the significant imbalance of text lengths between bullets and transcripts, from which the alignment models by themselves may suffer.

$$C[i,k] = \min_{j\leq k}\{C[i-1,j] + \lambda_1 D[i,j+1,k] + (1-\lambda_1)S[j+1,k]\} \quad (4)$$

where,

$$S[j+1,k] = \frac{cut(A_{j+1,k}, V \setminus A_{j+1,k})}{assoc(A_{j+1,k}, V)} \quad (5)$$

In fact, a state-of-the-art topic-segmentation model (Malioutov and Barzilay, 2006) (also called a cohesion model in this paper) can be naturally incorporated into the graph-partitioning alignment models that we have discussed. That is, we can augment the $SeqCut$, $HieCut$, and $PrsCut$ models with the cohesion models to form three new models **SeqCutTpc**, **HieCutTpc**, and **PrsCutTpc**, respectively. To achieve this, we modify equation (2) to equation (4), where $S[j+1,k]$ is calculated as in (Malioutov and Barzilay,

[1]A pre-order walk can be used here (not for sequentializing bullet trees though); other top-down transversing methods are also applicable, e.g., a breadth-first search, once a parent bullet is visited before its children.

2006), which denotes the normalized partition cost of the segment from utterance u_{j+1} to u_k, inclusively. For complexity, since the cohesion model is $O(MN^2)$, linearly combining it would not increase the time complexities of the corresponding polynomial alignment models, which are at least $O(MN^2)$ by themselves.

7 Experiment Set-up

Corpus Our experiment uses a corpus of four 50-minute university lectures taught by the same instructor, which contain 119 slides composed of 921 bullets. The automatic transcripts of the speech contain approximately 30,000 word tokens, roughly equal to a 120-page double-spaced essay in length. The lecturer's voice was recorded with a head-mounted microphone with a 16kHz sampling rate and 16-bit samples, while students' comments and questions were not recorded. The speech is split into utterances by pauses longer than 200ms, resulting in around 4000 utterances. The slides and automatic transcripts of one lecture were used as the development set. In practice, each lecture is divided into three roughly equally-long pieces in all our experiments discussed below, for pragmatic computational consideration of calculating the $O(MN^4)$ models quickly enough.

Building the Graphs The transcripts were generated with the SONIC toolkit (Pellom, 2001), with the models trained as suggested by (Munteanu et al., 2007), in which one language model was trained on SWITCHBOARD and the other used also corpus obtained from the Web through searching the words on slides. Both bullets and automatic transcripts were stemmed with the Porter stemmer and stopwords were removed. The similarities between bullets and utterances and those between utterances were calculated with different distance metrics, i.e., cosine, exponential cosine (Malioutov and Barzilay, 2006) for topic segmentation, and a normalized word-overlapping score used in summarization (Radev et al., 2004), from which we chose the one (regular cosine) that optimizes our baseline. Our graph-partitioning models then used exactly the same setting. The lexical weighting is same as in (Malioutov et al., 2007), for which we split each lecture into M chunks, the number of bullets. Finally, we obtained a M-by-N bullet-utterance similarity matrix and a N-by-N utterance-utterance matrix to optimize the alignment model and topic-segmentation model, respectively, while M and N, as already mentioned, denote the number of bullets and utterances of a lecture, respectively.

Evaluation Metric The metric used in our evaluation is straightforward—automatically acquired boundaries on transcripts for each slide bullet are compared against the corresponding gold-standard boundaries to calculate offsets measured in number of words, counted after stopwords having been removed, which are then averaged over all boundaries to evaluate model performance. Though one may consider that different bullets may be of different importance, in this paper we do not use any heuristics to judge this and we treat all bullets equally in our evaluation. Note that topic segmentation research often uses metrics such as P_k and *WindowDiff* (Malioutov and Barzilay, 2006; Beeferman et al., 1999; Pevsner and Hearst, 2002). Our problem here, as an alignment problem, has an exact 1-to-1 correspondence between a gold and automatic boundary, in which we can directly measure the exact offset of each boundary.

8 Experimental Results

Alignment Models Table 1 presents the experimental results obtained on the automatic transcripts generated by the ASR models discussed above, with WERs of 0.43 and 0.48, respectively, which are typical for lectures and conference presentations in realistic and less controlled situations (Leeuwis et al., 2003; Hsu and Glass, 2006; Munteanu et al., 2007).

The results show that among the four quadratic models, i.e., the first four models in the table, $HieCut$ achieves the best performance. The results also suggest that the improvement of $HieCut$ over $SeqBase$ comes from two aspects. First, the normalized-cut objective used in the graph-partitioning based model seems to outperform that used in the baseline, indicated by the better performance of $SeqCut$ over $SeqBase$, since both take as input the same, sequentialized bullet sequence and the corresponding transcribed utterances. The DTW-based objective used in $SeqBase$ corresponds to finding the optimal path that maximizes the similarity score between the bullet sequence and the transcripts. Second, the better performance of $HieCut$ and $SeqCut$ shows that $HieCut$ further benefits from avoiding sequentializing the bullet trees. However, this two aspects of benefit do not come independently, since the former (performance of an alignment objective) can significantly affect the latter (whether a model can benefit from avoiding sequentializing bullets). This is evident in the inferior performance of $HieBase$. Manual analysis of its errors shows that $HieBase$ is less accurate than $HieCut$ on higher-level bullets and the errors in turn severely impair the decisions made on lower-level bullets in the deterministic decision process: the errors propagate severely in such a deterministic process.

Models	WER=0.43	WER=0.48
SeqBase	15.19	18.44
SeqCut	12.87	16.16
HieBase	21.06	24.25
HieCut	12.13	15.95
PrsBase	15.05	18.18
PrsCut	12.05	15.20

Table 1: The performances of different alignment models.

A closer examination of errors made by $HieBase$ suggests that in a DTW-based alignment, a large subtree is likely to be aligned to a region larger than it should be, particularly for higher-level bullets (e.g., slides), where the subtree sizes vary more, e.g., some slides containing much textual content and others containing little. It seems that $HieCut$ could counteract this effect with its capability of normalizing partition sizes (see the denominators in both equation (1) and (3)). The usefulness of the normalization has also been discussed in other tasks such as image segmentation (Shi and Malik, 2000). Compared with those of $HieBase$, segments in the $SeqBase$ model are smaller (all non-leaf bullets do not include its descendants after being sequentialized) and the pre-order walk constrains the alignment range of bullets, which often avoid errors of long offsets. Again, the $HieCut$ model is quadratic in time, it uses less memories than the $O(MN^4)$ models and even the $SeqCut$ model, and it achieves a very competitive overall performance.

The results in Table 1 also shows that the ($O(MN^4)$) models, which conduct a more thorough search, improve the performance in all situations.

Effect of Topic-segmentation Models The effect of the topic-segmentation model is presented in Table 2. To facilitate reading, we also copy here the relevant results from Table 1. The results show that incorporating text cohesion additionally reduces the errors consistently for all models, though the specific improvement varies.

Models	WER=0.43	WER=0.48
SeqCut	12.87	16.16
SeqCutTpc	12.77	15.14
HieCut	12.13	15.95
HieCutTpc	11.82	15.28
PrsCut	12.05	15.20
PrsCutTpc	11.34	14.62

Table 2: The effect of topic-segmentation models.

9 Conclusions

In addressing the semantic tree-to-string alignment problem described, this paper proposes and studies a number of models with different modeling capabilities and time complexities. Experimental results show that among the quadratic alignment models ($O(MN^2)$), $HieCut$ consistently achieves the best performance, while the $O(MN^4)$ models that optimize a global objective score further improve the performance, though such models are, pragmatically, much more computationally expensive. This paper also relates alignment models with topic-segmentation models by showing that a state-of-the-art topic-segmentation models can be inherently incorporated into the graph-partitioning based alignment models. The experimental results show the benefit of considering such cohesion knowledge.

References

D. Beeferman, A. Berger, and J. Lafferty. 1999. Statistical models for text segmentation. *Machine Learning*, 34(1-3):177–210.

S. Branavan, Deshpande P., and Barzilay R. 2007. Generating a table-of-contents: A hierarchical discriminative approach. In *Proc. of Annual Meeting of the Association for Computational Linguistics*.

D.L. Chen and R.J. Mooney. 2008. Learning to sportscast: A test of grounded language acquisition. In *Proc. of International Conference on Machine Learning*.

Q. Fan, K. Barnard, A. Amir, A. Efrat, and M. Lin. 2006. Matching slides to presentation videos using sift and scene background. In *Proc. of ACM International Workshop on Multimedia Information Retrieval*, pages 239–248.

M. Hearst. 1997. Texttiling: Segmenting text into multi-paragraph subtopic passages. *Computational Linguistics*, 23(1):33–64.

C. Hori and S. Furui. 2003. A new approach to automatic speech summarization. *IEEE Transactions on Multimedia*, 5(3):368–378.

B. Hsu and J. Glass. 2006. Style and topic language model adaptation using hmm-lda. In *Proc. of Conference on Empirical Methods in Natural Language Processing*.

H. Jing. 2002. Using hidden markov modeling to decompose human-written summaries. *Computational Linguistics*, 28(4):527–543.

E. Leeuwis, M. Federico, and M. Cettolo. 2003. Language modeling and transcription of the ted corpus lectures. In *Proc. of IEEE International Conference on Acoustics, Speech and Signal Processing*.

P. Liang, M. Jordan, and D. Klein. 2009. Learning semantic correspondences with less supervision. In *Proc. of Annual Meeting of the Association for Computational Linguistics*.

I. Malioutov and R. Barzilay. 2006. Minimum cut model for spoken lecture segmentation. In *Proc. of International Conference on Computational Linguistics and Annual Meeting of the Association for Computational Linguistics*.

I. Malioutov, A. Park, R. Barzilay, and J. Glass. 2007. Making sense of sound: Unsupervised topic segmentation over acoustic input. In *Proc. of Annual Meeting of the Association for Computational Linguistics*, pages 504–511.

D. Marcu. 2000. The theory and practice of discourse parsing and summarization. The MIT Press.

S. Maskey and J. Hirschberg. 2005. Comparing lexial, acoustic/prosodic, discourse and structural features for speech summarization. In *Proc. of European Conference on Speech Communication and Technology*, pages 621–624.

C. Munteanu, G. Penn, and R. Baecker. 2007. Web-based language modelling for automatic lecture transcription. In *Proc. of Annual Conference of the International Speech Communication Association*.

G. Murray. 2008. *Using Speech-Specific Characteristics for Automatic Speech Summarization*. Ph.D. thesis, University of Edinburgh.

B. L. Pellom. 2001. Sonic: The university of colorado continuous speech recognizer. *Tech. Rep. TR-CSLR-2001-01, University of Colorado*.

L. Pevsner and M. Hearst. 2002. A critique and improvement of an evaluation metric for text segmentation. *Computational Linguistics*, 28:19–36.

D. Radev, H. Jing, M. Stys, and D. Tam. 2004. Centroid-based summarization of multiple documents. *Information Processing and Management*, 40:919–938.

J. Shi and J. Malik. 2000. Normalized cuts and image segmentation. *IEEE Trans. Pattern Anal. Mach. Intell.*, 22.

B. Snyder and R. Barzilay. 2007. Database-text alignment via structured multilabel classification. In *Proc. of International Joint Conference on Artificial Intelligence*.

S. Xie and Y. Liu. 2010. Using confusion networks for speech summarization. In *Proc. of International Conference on Human Language Technology and Annual Meeting of North American Chapter of the Association for Computational Linguistics*.

K. Zechner and A. Waibel. 2000. Minimizing word error rate in textual summaries of spoken language. In *Proc. of Applied Natural Language Processing Conference and Meeting of the North American Chapter of the Association for Computational Linguistics*, pages 186–193.

J. Zhang, H. Chan, and P. Fung. 2010. Extractive speech summarization using shallow rhetorical structure modeling. *IEEE Transactions on Audio, Speech and Language Processing*, 18:1147–1157.

X. Zhu and G. Penn. 2006. Summarization of spontaneous conversations. In *Proc. of International Conference on Spoken Language Processing*, pages 1531–1534.

X. Zhu, X. He, C. Munteanu, and G. Penn. 2008. Using latent dirichlet allocation to incorporate domain knowledge for topic transition detection. In *Proc. of Annual Conference of the International Speech Communication Association*.

X. Zhu, G. Penn, and F. Rudzicz. 2009. Summarizing multiple spoken documents: Finding evidence from untranscribed audio. In *Proc. of Annual Meeting of the Association for Computational Linguistics*.

X. Zhu, C. Cherry, and G. Penn. 2010. Imposing hierarchical browsing structures onto spoken documents. In *Proc. of International Conference on Computational Linguistics*.

X. Zhu. 2011. A normalized-cut model for aligning hierarchical browsing structures with spoken documents. In *Proc. of the Fifteenth Conference on Computational Natural Language Learning (to appear)*.

Structured and Extended Named Entity Evaluation in Automatic Speech Transcriptions

Olivier Galibert[1] **Sophie Rosset**[2] **Cyril Grouin**[2]
Pierre Zweigenbaum[2] **Ludovic Quintard**[1]
[1]LNE, Trappes, France [2] LIMSI–CNRS, Orsay, France
first.last@lne.fr first.last@limsi.fr

Abstract

The evaluation of named entity recognition (NER) methods is an active field of research. This includes the recognition of named entities in speech transcripts. Evaluating NER systems on automatic speech recognition (ASR) output whereas human reference annotation was prepared on clean manual transcripts raises difficult alignment issues. These issues are emphasized when named entities are structured, as is the case in the Quaero NER challenge organized in 2010. This paper describes the structured named entity definition used in this challenge and presents a method to transfer reference annotations to ASR output. This method was used in the Quaero 2010 evaluation of extended named entity annotation on speech transcripts, whose results are given in the paper.

1 Introduction

Named Entity Detection has been studied since the MUC conferences in 1987. The notion has been extended to deal with mono- or multi-word expressions that belong to a potentially interesting class for an application. Given a set of entity definitions and a natural language corpus, systems try to extract and categorize all the relevant occurring entities. These entities can be used to feed further systems such as Information Retrieval, Question-Answering, Distillation, Terminology studies, etc.

Traditional Named Entity Recognition (NER) is a task where proper nouns and numerical expressions are extracted from documents and classified into categories (person, location, organization, date, etc.). As shown by Voorhees and Harman (2000), it is a key technology of Information Extraction (IE) and Open-Domain Question Answering. NER is also used as a fundamental component in a variety of language processing applications such as text clustering, topic detection, and summarization.

While significant progress has been reported on the NER task, most of these approaches have generally focused on clean textual data such as Sang and Meulder (2003). In the mean time, Kubala et al. (1998), Palmer et al. (1999), Turmo et al. (2009) and many others have focused on speech data. Named Entity detection evaluation over French spoken data has been proposed within the Ester II project, as described by Galliano et al. (2009).

Within the framework of the *Quaero* project,we proposed an extended named entity definition with compositional and hierarchical structure. This extension raises new issues and challenges in NER evaluation. First, as we shall explain below in more detail, the usual evaluation methods cannot compute the Slot Error Rate (SER) metric when named entities are compositional and recursive. Second, following Burger et al. (1998) and Hirschman et al. (1999), we consider that the evaluation of named entity recognition on noisy text output by automatic speech recognition (ASR) systems should take as reference the named entities found in the human annotation of a human-transcribed text: what *should have been there* in the ASR output. This requires to project the clean reference to the noisy text, which is made all the more difficult because of the compositional and hierarchical structure of the named entities.

The remainder of the paper is structured as follows. We first present the extended named entities in Section 2, then the evaluation protocol in Section 3 with specific metrics adapted to the structure of the evaluated objects and data. Section 4 illustrates their use in a challenge and discusses system results in this challenge. Finally in Section 5 we conclude and draw perspectives for further work.

2 Extended Named Entities

In this section, we present our extension to named entities, starting with related work (Section 2.1) and specifying their scope (Section 2.2). Our entities are hierarchical (Section 2.3) and compositional (Section 2.4). Section 2.5 provides a discussion of the issues they raise in the evaluation of named entity recognition from speech transcripts.

2.1 Named Entity Types

Named Entity recognition was initially defined as recognizing proper names (Coates-Stephens, 1992). Since MUC-6 (Grishman and Sundheim, 1996), named entities are proper names categorized into three major classes: persons, locations and organizations. Proposals have been made to sub-divide these entities into finer-grained classes. For example, politicians for the person class by Fleischman and Hovy (2002) or cities for the location class by Fleischman (2001) as well as Lee and Lee (2005).

The CONLL conference added a miscellaneous type which includes proper names outside the previous classes. Some classes are sometimes added, e.g. product by Bick (2004). Some numerical types are also often described and used in the literature: date, time, and amounts (money and percents in most cases).

Specific entities have been proposed and handled for some tasks, e.g. language and shape by Rosset et al. (2007), or email address and phone number (Maynard et al., 2001). In specific domains, entities such as gene, protein, DNA etc. are also addressed (Ohta, 2002) and campaigns are organized for gene/protein detection (Kim et al., 2004; Galibert et al., 2010)). More recently larger extensions have been proposed: Sekine (2004) defined a complete hierarchy of named entities containing about 200 types.

2.2 Scope

Named Entities often include four major groups: name, quantity, date and duration. The overall task in which we frame information extraction is the extraction of entities and relations to build a fact base from news sources. We thus decided to start from the traditional named entities used in information extraction from newspaper corpora. We then included named entities extensions proposed by Sekine (2004) for products and Galliano et al. (2009) for functions, and we extended the definition of named entities to some expressions which are not composed of proper names (e.g., phrases built around substantives).

In this work, we decided to extend the coverage of the named entities rather than sub-dividing the existing classes as it has been done in previous work. As we aimed to build a fact database from news data, we chose to support new kinds of entities (time, function, etc.) in order to extract a maximum of information from the corpus we processed. Compared to existing named entity structuration, our approach is more general than the extensions that have been done for specific domains, and is simpler than the complete hierarchy defined by Sekine (2004). This structure allows us to cover a large amount of named entities with a basic categorization so as to be quickly suitable for all further annotation work. The extended named entities we defined are both hierarchical and compositional (Grouin et al., 2011). This hierarchical and compositional nature of the extended named entities imply a specific method when evaluating system outputs (see Section 3).

2.3 Hierarchy

We used two kinds of elements: types and components. The types with their subtypes categorize a named entity. While types and subtypes were used previously, we consider that structuring the contents of an entity (its components) is important too. Components categorize the elements inside a named entity.

Types and subtypes refer to the general category of a named entity. They give general information about the annotated expression. The taxonomy is composed of 7 types and 32 sub-types:

- Person: *pers.ind* (invidual person), *pers.coll* (collectivity of persons);
- Location: administrative (*loc.adm.town, loc.adm.reg, loc.adm.nat, loc.adm.sup*) and physical (*loc.phys.geo, loc.phys.hydro, loc.phys.astro*);
- Organization: *org.ent* (services), *org.adm* (administration);
- Amount: quantity (with unit or general object), duration;
- Time: date *time.date.abs* (absolute date: "November 8, 2011"), *time.date.rel* (date relative to the discourse: "yesterday"), and hour

time.hour.abs (absolute hour), *time.hour.rel* (hour relative to the discourse);

- Production: *prod.object* (manufactury object), *prod.art* (artistic products), *prod.media* (media products), *prod.fin* (financial products), *prod.soft* (software), *prod.award*, *prod.serv* (transportation route), *prod.doctr* (doctrine), *prod.rule* (law);
- Functions: *func.ind* (individual function), *func.coll* (collectivity of functions).

Types and subtypes constitute the first level of annotation. They refer to a general segmentation of the world into major categories. Within these categories, we defined a second level of annotation we call *components*.

Components can be considered as clues that help the annotator (human or system) to produce an annotation: either to determine the named entity type (e.g. a first name is a clue for the *pers.ind* named entity subtype), or to set the named entity boundaries (e.g. a given token is a clue for the named entity, and is within its scope, while the next token is not a clue and is outside its scope). Components are second-level elements, and can never be used outside the scope of a type or subtype element.

An entity is thus composed of components that are of two kinds: transverse components that can fit each type of entity, and specific components only used for a reduce set of components:

1. Transverse components
   - *name* (the entity name),
   - *kind* (hypernym of the entity),
   - *qualifier* (a qualifying adjective),
   - *demonym* (inhabitant or ethnic group name),
   - *val* (a number),
   - *unit* (a unit),
   - *object* (an object),
   - *range-mark* (a range between two values).
2. Specific components
   - *name.last, name.first, name.middle, title* for "pers.ind" (Figure 1),
   - *address.number, po-box, zip-code, other-address-component* for "loc.add.phys",
   - and *week, day, month, year, century, millenium, reference-era, time-modifier* for "time.date" (Figure 3).

2.4 Composition

During the Ester II evaluation campaign, there was an attempt to use compositionality in named entities for two categories (persons and functions) where a person entity could contain a function entity.[1] Nevertheless, the evaluation did not take into account this inclusion and only focused on the encompassing annotation.[2]

In the present work, we also considered the compositional nature of those extended named entities. Entities can be compositional for three reasons:

1. a type contains a component: the *pers.ind* type is composed of several components such as *name.first* and *name.last* (Figure 1);

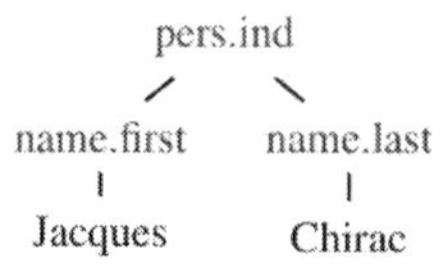

Figure 1: Basic type and component inclusion.

2. a type includes another type, used as a component. Cases of inclusion can be found in the *function* type (Figure 2), where type *func.ind*, which spans the whole expression, includes type *org.adm*, which spans the single word *Budget*:

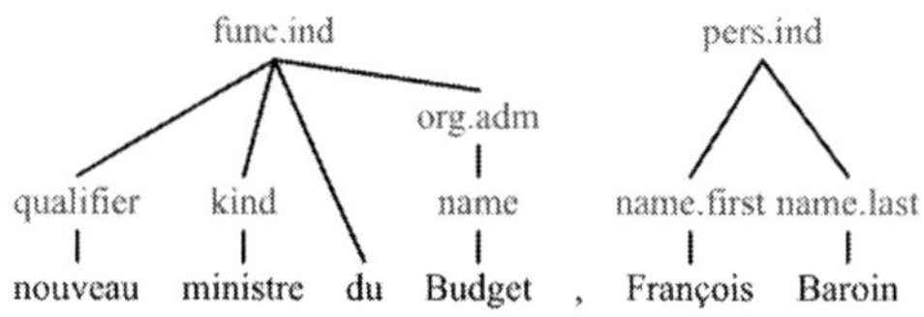

Figure 2: Multi-level annotation of entity types (red tags) and components (blue tags): *new minister of budget , François Baroin.*

[1]Example of compositionality in Ester II campaign: <pers.hum> <func.pol> *président* </func.pol> <pers.hum> *Chirac* </pers.hum> </pers.hum>

[2]Final annotation: <pers.hum> *président Chirac* </pers.hum>

3. in cases of metonymy (a term is substituted for another one in a relation of contiguity) and antonomasia (a proper name is used as a substantive and vice versa), where a type of entity is used to refer to another entity type (Figure 3). The type to which the entity intrinsically belongs is annotated. This entity is over-annotated with the type to which the expression belongs in the considered context:

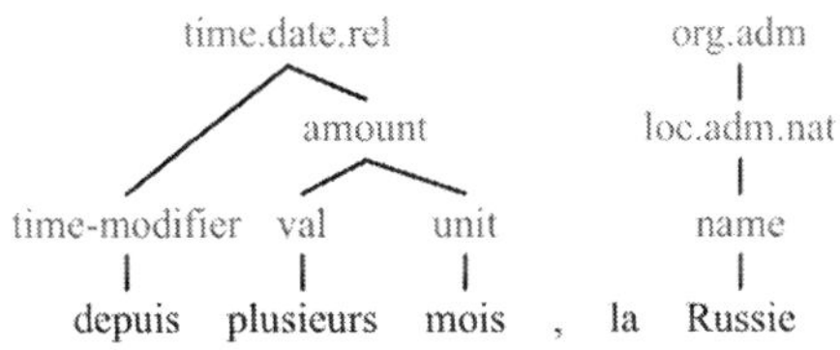

Figure 3: Annotation with types (red tags) and components (blue tags) including metonymy: *since several months , Russia...*

2.5 Discussion

Due to its non-flat structure, the representation of compositionality in extended named entities is richer than that used so far in spoken language understanding, compared with Bonneau-Maynard et al. (2006) and Mori et al. (2008); due to its extended definition, it is also richer than that used in named entity detection, in contrast with Galliano et al. (2009) or Nadeau and Sekine (2007). This calls for novel ways to evaluate named entity detection systems.

A consequence of the representation's richer structure is an increased complexity in the evaluation methodology. The 1:1 comparisons applied to traditional, flat named entities must give way to the mapping-based approaches we will present in the next section.

Moreover, when working on speech, evaluating the results of systems applied to automatic speech transcriptions is central to real-world use cases. This leads us to the issue of evaluating named entity detection systems applied to noisy inputs (produced by automatic speech recognition systems) using references built on clean data (manual transcriptions). The reference projection approach we propose will be described in the second half of the next section.

3 Evaluation methodology

We now come to the issues raised by the evaluation of automatically annotated extended named entities in speech transcripts. We first lay out the basic evaluation metrics (Section 3.1), then address the issues raised by compositionality (Section 3.2) and by ASR output errors (Section 3.3).

3.1 Metrics

The metrics used in Named Entity extraction evaluation are precision (P), recall (R), and their weighted mean F-measure (F) (van Rijsbergen, 1979). They are easy to use, since they only require to determine whether a hypothesized entity element is correct or not.

Let Ref = total number of elements in the reference, Hyp = total number of elements in the hypothesis, and C = number of correct elements in the hypothesis. Precision is defined as the observed probability for a hypothesized element to be correct:

$$P = \frac{C}{Hyp}$$

In the same way, recall is the observed probability for a reference element to have been found:

$$R = \frac{C}{Ref}$$

F-measure is the weighted harmonic mean of P and R, generally balanced with $\beta = 1$:

$$F = \frac{(1+\beta^2)RP}{\beta^2 P + R}$$

The main issue in these metrics lies in their binary decision process: either an entity element is correct, or it is not, whereas we generally want finer control.

Errors in named entities are in fact bidimensional: their span or their type can be incorrect. It is interesting to count only "half an error" if one of the two is correct. Within each category, some errors can be considered as less severe than others (e.g., presence of a determiner in span errors, entity types with fuzzy boundaries in the annotation guide).

A popular alternative is to proceed with an *error enumeration* approach, such as the Slot Error Rate (SER) defined by Makhoul et al. (1999): collect the individual errors, sum a cost for each one and divide the total by the number of elements in the reference (the slots). In our case, we went for a simple weighting scheme where insertions (I), deletions (D) and elements with errors both in span and in type (S_{ST}) cost 1, while elements with errors only in either span (S_S) or type (S_T) cost 0.5. Span or type errors are substitutions (S_S, S_T, and S_{ST}).

We chose our final score as:

$$\text{SER} = \frac{D + I + S_{ST} + 0.5 \times (S_S + S_T)}{Ref}$$

Dividing by Ref normalizes the result, allowing us to compare results more easily across different files. This value is traditionally expressed as a percentage.

3.2 Evaluation on manual transcriptions

For simple annotation guides with no compositionality, enumerating all errors is easy: a word can only be associated with at most one entity in the reference, and likewise in the hypothesis, so entities can be directly compared when they have common words without any ambiguity.

In our case, the annotation compositionality makes things harder. Entity elements (entities or components) can be nested, and words are usually associated to at least two elements: one entity and one component, and sometimes more. The enumeration phase needs to establish explicitly which hypothesis element should be compared with each reference element.

Building on methodologies used in speech diarization evaluation (Diarization Error Rate), we defined a *mapping* as a set of 1–1 associations between reference and hypothesis elements. Each element from one side can be associated to at most one from the other side, and a number of elements can remain unassociated on both sides. From a given mapping, an error list can be built, where associated elements result in either correct matches or substitutions, and unassociated elements result in insertions and deletions. Hence given a mapping, a score can be computed. The final score of a system is then defined as the minimal error rate attainable over all possible mappings.

Enumerating all possible mappings is unthinkable. Since the score is additive, and restricting the acceptable associations to elements with at least one common word, it becomes possible to apply a dynamic programming approach. We thus use a variant of the Viterbi algorithm where "time" is the word stream, "probability" the score and "hidden state" the associations.

The text is split into a series of segments cut where reference or hypothesis entities start or end. An empty association hypothesis is first created, then segments are handled in the text order.

Two phases are applied for each segment: the first one, *opening*, expands the association hypothesis set by combining each one with every possible association choice for each of the entities beginning at the segment start. Two constraints are applied at this level: an entity can only have zero or one association, and associations must not cross one another (i.e. parent-descendant links between entities must not be inverted when projected through the association set).

Once all hypotheses are built, the *closure* phase follows where ending entities are taken into account. The post-segment state of each association hypothesis is computed, including its score, and for every set of equivalent hypotheses in a dynamic programming sense, only the best score is kept.

Two association hypotheses are considered equivalent if, for every entity present in both closing and following segments, the specific hypothesized associations are identical. We underline that where no entity is present in the text (reference or hypothesis), only one association hypothesis is left. The same happens at the end of the text where the remaining association is the optimal one.

3.3 Generalization to automatic transcriptions

The main issue when evaluating a Named Entity extraction system over Automatic Speech Recognition (ASR) systems output is: what must be evaluated first? We can either evaluate *what is there* (the system annotation) or *what should have been there*.

A system should not be penalized for missing things that have been lost earlier in the pipeline, or extracting entities that were not actually said but are present in ASR output. This leads us to an evaluation methodology equivalent to that of manual transcriptions.

The ASR output is just considered as a distinct, independent document, to be annotated by humans and by systems, and the results are compared. The human annotation part becomes way more difficult. It is quite hard to annotate documents in which parts make no sense, where adjudication discussions can become endless. More significantly for an application, ASR is a step in the document handling pipeline where the end user is only interested in the final result.

We thus decided to evaluate system performance compared to *what should have been there*, expecting the systems to find the entities present in the manual transcriptions whatever the quality of the ASR output. There is room thus for developers to try methodologies to cope with ASR errors using a higher-level understanding of annotations.

Reference projection. To evaluate system output from noisy text with a reference built from a clean text, we followed Burger et al. (1998) and Hirschman et al. (1999) who proposed to *project* the clean reference on the noisy text in order to build a new reference. That new reference then allows us to apply the clean text methodology.

This projection method consists in finding new positions for the frontiers through either a dynamic programming alignment (standard sclite-type ASR evaluation alignment) or a phone-level dynamic programming alignment using canonical phonetizations. They noticed the result was too strict frontier-wise and required reducing the weight of frontier errors to obtain significant results.

In Question Answering from speech transcripts evaluation, Moreau et al. (2010) required that QA systems extract answers to natural language questions from ASR outputs of broadcast news shows. The inherent application was to replay the sound segment containing the answer, with a time interval as an answer; it tolerated a time interval around the boundaries. The results were satisfactory.

We thus decided to project the clean reference on the noisy text following five steps:

1. Build a forced alignment of the reference text to the speech signal;

2. Extract the start and end times from the reference annotations using the alignment;

3. Select a tolerance time interval;

4. Find the ASR word frontiers within the tolerance intervals placed around the frontiers of reference entity elements;

5. Build a *fuzzy* reference when multiple frontiers are possible.

A fuzzy reference means that each reference element can have multiple frontiers, which is equivalent to having multiple references, and choosing the one that gives the best score for the system. The number of possible references is way too large and the enumeration has to be done locally and coupled with the Viterbi alignment to reduce the search space to tolerable limits.

Apart from the alignment algorithm, the main difficulty is that a structurally correct reference post-projection does not always exist. Indeed, the ASR system may not output words where an entity element is supposed to be, or may merge small words into a larger one, preventing from fitting all reference elements to the available words. Such colliding elements have to be handled and we decided when encountered to remove one arbitrarily. They are rare enough for that decision to have a minor impact on the scores.

A more satisfactory method would be to merge the colliding elements into one when possible, creating reference elements with multiple acceptable types. Figure 4 illustrates the results of building a fuzzy reference.

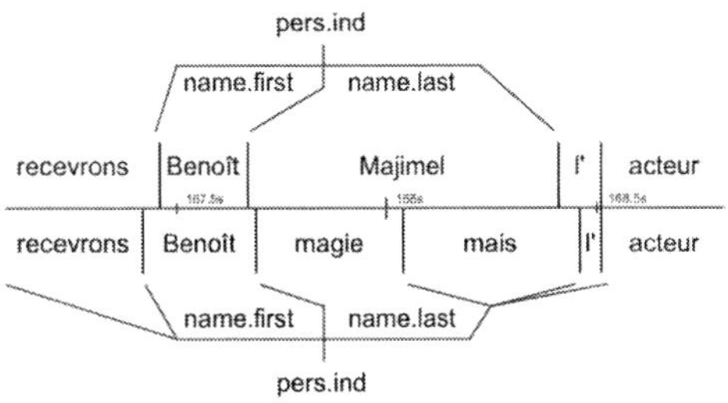

Figure 4: Example of a fuzzy reference built by temporal alignment of clean reference and noisy transcript

The top part of the figure shows the manual reference (clean reference), with a *pers.ind* entity "Benoït Magimel" which is decomposed into two components *name.first* "Benoït" and *name.last* "Magimel". In the middle, the temporal line shows the results of the forced alignment of these words on the audio signal.

In the lower part of the figure is the ASR result, "recevrons Benoït magie mais l' acteur", with its own temporal positions as given by the ASR system itself. Accepting any frontier within an interval then gives us the final fuzzy reference at the bottom, where the *name.first* component and the associated *pers.ind* can either start before "recevrons" or just after, the *name.first—name.last* transition still happens after "Benoït", and the *name.last* and complete entity can stop either after "magie", "mais" or "l'".

In our case, all systems gave the same hypothesis with "Benoït" as both *pers.ind* and *name.first*, which gave them one correct (the *name.first*), one bad frontier (the *pers.ind*) and one miss (the *name.last*). A more advanced system could have used "Benoït" as a trigger to search for "Magimel", and other last names associated with that specific first name, in a phonetic representation of the following words, or in the signal itself. Then, it may have output "magie mais" or "magie mais l'" as the last name. It is interesting to note that either hypothesis would have ended with a perfect score for the system. That example shows how the fuzzy projection methodology opens the door to the evaluation of more advanced systems that try to use higher-level knowledge to see through the ASR system errors.

An interesting and useful side effect of the mapping methodology we used is that the chosen mapping is human-readable. One can check what associations were chosen and in the ASR case what frontiers were selected among the possible ones. This is useful for both error analysis and convincing oneself of the quality of the evaluation measure. It also makes it possible to merge all of the systems outputs in an evaluation and collate the errors in order to help correct the references more efficiently where needed.

4 Quaero evaluation results

As an illustration of the use of the extended named entities and of the evaluation methods introduced above, we present here an evaluation of extended named entity recognition from speech transcripts, which we organized in the context of the project Quaero. The task consisted in extracting and categorizing a large number of named entities in transcriptions of broadcast spoken data in French. Three teams participated, each with one NER system.

The training data were those of the Ester II evaluation campaign: 188 shows from various sources have been manually transcribed and annotated given this new definition of extended named entities (Table 1, Training). The test data were composed of test and development data from the Quaero 2010 ASR evaluation (Table 1, Test) (Lamel, 2010). Several test data versions were provided:

- a manual transcription prepared by a human expert,
- three different ASR outputs (ASR1, ASR2, ASR3) with a word error rate (WER) ranging from 20.96% to 27.44% (Table 1, last three rows), and
- an improved version of the ASR1 output, where punctuation and capitalization have been automatically added (ASR1+).

The training data consisted of Broadcast News data (BN) while the test data included Broadcast News data and more varied data including talk shows and debates (Broadcast Conversations, BC; see Table 1, last two columns). One of the objectives of this work was to measure the robustness of the NER systems against different types of data and unknown types of data.

Inf. \ Data	Training	Test	Test BN	Test BC
# shows	188	18	8	10
# lines	43289	5637	1704	3933
# distinct words	39639	10139	5591	6836
# words	1251586	97871	32951	64920
# types	113885	5523	2762	2761
# distinct types	41	32	28	29
# compon.	146405	8902	4541	4361
# distinct compon.	29	22	22	21
WER ASR1	-	20.96%	16.32%	23.34%
WER ASR2	-	21.56%	18.77%	22.99%
WER ASR3	-	27.44%	24.06%	29.18%

Table 1: Data description.

Table 2 shows the results of the three participating NER systems, with a breakdown into broadcast news and broadcast conversations.

On the manual transcriptions, values of slot error rate (SER) ranged from 33.3% to 48.9% for the NER systems on the whole data. Similarly to the ASR systems, NER systems obtained better SER (from 29.7% to 42.7%) on broadcast news than on broadcast conversations (37% to 55.3%).

	Whole data				
	Man.	ASR1	ASR1+	ASR2	ASR3
P1	48.9%	71.4%	71.1%	68.3%	75.2%
P2	33.3%	61.1%	66.3%	59.3%	63.2%
P3	41.0%	72.2%	68.7%	70.7%	72.9%
	Broadcast News data				
P1	42.7%	55.3%	52.7%	58.5%	61.4%
P2	29.7%	48.5%	53.8%	52.2%	53.5%
P3	39.1%	55.6%	54.5%	60.3%	61.8%
	Broadcast Conversations data				
P1	55.3%	87.9%	89.9%	78.3%	89.2%
P2	37.0%	73.9%	79.0%	66.6%	73.0%
P3	43.0%	89.3%	83.3%	81.2%	84.1%

Table 2: SER results for the overall data, broadcast news data and broadcast conversations data. The ASR1+ column is a version of the ASR1 with automatically added punctuation and capitalization.

Obviously, the SER worsened when dealing with ASR outputs, which are all true case (*i.e.*, upper and lower case are those expected in normal text). The loss ranged from 19.4% (P1 on ASR2 with a 21.56% WER) to 33% (P2 on ASR1+ with 20.96% WER). It is interesting to note that the ASR1+ system, which is ASR1 with automatically added punctuation and capitalization at the beginning of sentences, hindered system P2.

Another interesting point is that the ASR2 output with a higher WER than the ASR1 system on the whole data allowed better performance for entity detection than the ASR1 output.

5 Conclusion and perspectives

In this paper, we presented a representation of structured named entities, and methods to evaluate the recognition of such structured named entities. We contributed a mapping between reference and hypothesis elements which allows us to enumerate errors and compute the value of the slot error rate. We also provided a projection of extended named entities from a clean reference to noisy texts produced by automatic speech transcription systems, which allows us to compute the slot error rate against what was actually said rather than against what was recognized by the ASR systems.

These extended named entities and evaluation algorithms have been used in the Quaero Named Entities on Spoken Data evaluation. Evaluation results are consistent with expectations, which is a first test of the validity of the method. Indeed, further work is planned to study more closely and more systematically the obtained alignments.

Compared to the recognition of standard named entities, this new task is harder for systems, but this new structuring will be useful to make information extraction more precise. Moreover, the evaluation methodology we proposed is very flexible and should be usable for other tasks such as syntactic analysis on spoken data. An interesting and useful side-effect of this mapping methodology is its human readability. This makes it easier to check the chosen associations, as well as the selected frontiers in the ASR case.

This work is useful for both error analysis and convincing oneself of the evaluation measure quality. It also makes it possible to merge all systems outputs in an evaluation and collate the errors to help correct the reference more efficiently where needed.

Due to the scarcity of annotated corpora in named entities, we plan to provide both guidelines and annotated corpora for free to the scientific community.

Acknowledgments

This work was partly realized as part of the Quaero Programme, funded by OSEO, French State agency for innovation and by the French ANR ETAPE project.

References

Eckhard Bick. 2004. A named entity recognizer for Danish. In *Proc. of LREC*, Lisbon, Portugal.

Hélène Bonneau-Maynard, Christelle Ayache, Frédéric Bechet, Alexandre Denis, Anne Kuhn, Fabrice Lefèvre, Djamel Mostefa, Mathieu Quignard, Sophie Rosset, Christophe Servan, and Joanne Villaneau. 2006. Results of the French Evalda-Media evaluation campaign for literal understanding. In *Proc. of LREC*, pages 2054–2059, Genoa, May.

John D. Burger, David Palmer, and Lynette Hirschman. 1998. Named entity scoring for speech input. In *Proc. of COLING*, pages 201–205.

Sam Coates-Stephens. 1992. The analysis and acquisition of proper names for the understanding of free text. *Computers and the Humanities*, 26:441–456.

Michael Fleischman and Eduard Hovy. 2002. Fine grained classification of named entities. In *Proc. of COLING*, pages 1–7. Association for Computational Linguistics.

Michael Fleischman. 2001. Automated subcategorization of named entities. In *Proc. of the ACL 2001 Student Research Workshop*, pages 25–30.

Olivier Galibert, Ludovic Quintard, Sophie Rosset, Pierre Zweigenbaum, Claire Nédellec, Sophie Aubin, Laurent Gillard, Jean-Pierre Raysz, Delphine Pois, Xavier Tannier, Louise Deléger, and Dominique Laurent. 2010. Named and specific entity detection in varied data: The Quaero named entity baseline evaluation. In Nicoletta Calzolari, Khalid Choukri, Bente Maegaard, Joseph Mariani, Jan Odijk, Stelios Piperidis, Mike Rosner, and Daniel Tapias, editors, *Proc. of LREC*, Valletta, Malta, may. European Language Resources Association (ELRA).

Sylvain Galliano, Guillaume Gravier, and Laura Chaubard. 2009. The ESTER 2 evaluation campaign for the rich transcription of French radio broadcasts. In *Proc. of InterSpeech*.

Ralph Grishman and Beth Sundheim. 1996. Message Understanding Conference - 6: A brief history. In *Proc. of COLING*, pages 466–471, Copenhagen, Denmark, August.

Cyril Grouin, Sophie Rosset, Pierre Zweigenbaum, Karën Fort, Olivier Galibert, and Ludovic Quintard. 2011. Proposal for an extension of traditional named entities: From guidelines to evaluation, an overview. In *Proc. of the Fifth Linguistic Annotation Workshop (LAW-V)*, Portland, OR, june. Association for Computational Linguistics.

Lynette Hirschman, John Burger, David Palmer, and Patricia Robinson. 1999. Evaluating content extraction from audio sources. In *ECSA, ETRW Workshop: Accessing Infomation in Spoken Audio*. University Press.

Jin-Dong Kim, Tomoko Ohta, Yoshimasa Tsuruoka, and Yuka Tateisi and. Nigel Collier. 2004. Introduction to the Bio-Entity task at JNLPBA. In *BioCreative Challenge Evaluation Workshop*, Granada, Spain.

Francis Kubala, Richard Schwartz, Rebecca Stone, and Ralph Weischede. 1998. Named entity extraction from speech. In *Proc. of the DARPA Broadcast News Transcription and Understanding Workshop*.

Lori Lamel. 2010. Quaero Program - CTC Project - Progress Report on Task 5.1: Speech to Text. Technical Report CD.CTC.5.6, Quaero Program.

Seungwoo Lee and Gary Geunbae Lee. 2005. Heuristic methods for reducing errors of geographic named entities learned by bootstrapping. In *Proc. of IJCNLP*, pages 658–669.

John Makhoul, Francis Kubala, Richard Schwartz, and Ralph Weischedel. 1999. Performance measures for information extraction. In *Proc. of DARPA Broadcast News Workshop*, pages 249–252.

Diana Maynard, Valentin Tablan, Cristian Ursu, Hamish Cunningham, and Yorick Wilks. 2001. Named entity recognition from diverse text types. In *Proc. RANLP*, Tzigov Chark.

Nicolas Moreau, Olivier Hamon, Djamel Mostefa, Sophie Rosset, Olivier Galibert, Lori Lamel, Jordi Turmo, Pere R. Comas, Paolo Rosso, Davide Buscaldi, and Khalid Choukri. 2010. Evaluation protocol and tools for question-answering on speech transcripts. In Nicoletta Calzolari (Conference Chair), Khalid Choukri, Bente Maegaard, Joseph Mariani, Jan Odijk, Stelios Piperidis, Mike Rosner, and Daniel Tapias, editors, *Proc. of LREC*, Valletta, Malta, may. European Language Resources Association (ELRA).

Renato De Mori, Frédéric Bechet, Dilek Z. Hakkani-Tür, Michael McTear, Giuseppe Riccardi, and Gokhan Tur. 2008. Spoken language understanding. *IEEE Signal Processing Magazine*, 25(3):50–58, May.

David Nadeau and Satoshi Sekine. 2007. A survey of named entity recognition and classification. *Linguisticæ Investigationes*, 30(1):3–26.

Tomoko Ohta. 2002. The GENIA corpus: An annotated research abstract corpus in molecular biology domain. In *Proc. of the Human Language Technology Conference*, pages 73–77.

David D. Palmer, John D. Burger, and Mari Ostendorf. 1999. Information extraction from broadcast news speech data. In *Proc. of the DARPA Broadcast News Workshop*.

Sophie Rosset, Olivier Galibert, Gilles Adda, and Eric Bilinski. 2007. The LIMSI participation to the QAst track. In *Working Notes for the CLEF 2007 Workshop*, Budapest, Hungary, September.

Erik Tjong Kim Sang and Fien De Meulder. 2003. Introduction to the CoNLL-2003 shared task: Language-independent named entity recognition. In *Proc. of CoNLL*.

Satoshi Sekine. 2004. Definition, dictionaries and tagger of extended named entity hierarchy. In *Proc. of LREC*, Lisbon, Portugal.

Jordi Turmo, Pere R. Comas, Sophie Rosset, Olivier Galibert, Nicolas Moreau, Djamel Mostefa, Paolo Rosso, and Davide Buscaldi. 2009. Overview of QAST 2009 - question answering on speech transcriptions. In *CLEF 2009 Working Notes*, Corfu, Greece.

Cornelis Joost van Rijsbergen. 1979. *Information Retrieval*. Butterworths, London. `http://www.dcs.gla.ac.uk/Keith/Preface.html`.

Ellen M. Voorhees and Donna Harman. 2000. Overview of the ninth text retrieval conference. In *Proc. of TREC-9*.

Normalising Audio Transcriptions for Unwritten Languages

Adel Foda* and **Steven Bird**[†]
*Department of Mathematics and Statistics
[†]Department of Computer Science and Software Engineering
University of Melbourne, Victoria 3010, Australia

Abstract

The task of documenting the world's languages is a mainstream activity in linguistics which is yet to spill over into computational linguistics. We propose a new task of transcription normalisation as an algorithmic method for speeding up the process of transcribing audio sources, leading to text collections of usable quality. We report on the application of sentence and word alignment algorithms to this task, before describing a new algorithm. All of the algorithms are evaluated over synthetic datasets. Although the results are nuanced, the transcription normalisation task is suggested as an NLP contribution to the grand challenge of documenting the world's languages.

1 Introduction

The majority of the world's 6800 languages are relatively unstudied. Although some of the world's languages have been carefully described and analysed, most of them have not yet even been documented. Such documentation consists of 'comprehensive and transparent records supporting wide ranging scientific investigations of the language' (Woodbury, 2010). In this context then, it is striking that 50 years of research in computational linguistics have so far only touched about 1% of the world's languages. In 100 years, 90% will be extinct or on the way out (Krauss, 2007). Accordingly, we set ourselves the following question: what can computational linguistics offer to support the urgent task of documenting and analyzing the world's endangered languages? There have been other recent efforts to address this question, focussing on interlinear text (Xia and Lewis, 2007; Baldridge and Palmer, 2009). Our focus is different, being concerned with creating the unannotated text that is presupposed by this earlier work. We also differentiate our work from more general computational support for documentary and descriptive linguistics, such as tools for transcribing audio or editing lexicons.

Recently, Abney and Bird (2010) have proposed to incorporate *machine translation* (MT) into the workflow of language documentation. However, a significant challenge for this program is posed by the fact that the majority of the world's languages are not written. How can NLP techniques be applied to improve the speed and efficiency of audio transcription for unwritten languages?

The task of transcription differs from transliteration (Knight and Graehl, 1998) in several ways. Transliteration is required in the context of machine translation for dealing with proper names, which are a common source of out-of-vocabulary items. The goal is to make the words pronounceable in a target language having a different inventory of sounds and syllables, and having different grapheme-to-phoneme rules. Since the source and target languages have established orthographies, the correct placement of word boundaries is never in question.

Transcription, on the other hand, involves representing spoken utterances in written form. In the absence of a standard orthography or lexicon, two transcribers will usually represent sounds using different symbols, and will often disagree on the placement of word boundaries. Transcribers may use a mixture of conventions from other languages, e.g. "vowels as in Italian, consonants as in English", and may invent their own system of diacritics. The goal is to faithfully capture all of the significant aspects of pronunciation. By obtaining many independent transcriptions of the same utterance, we can hope that the most consistent practices will come to dominate, giving rise to a collectively-defined system of normalized transcriptions.

This paper reports on an investigation into algorithmic methods for normalising sets of transcriptions of an audio recording. We begin by describing the role that MT could yet play in language documentation efforts, and discuss the initial challenge of audio transcription (section 2). Next, we observe that the problem of aligning the words of two audio transcriptions is analogous to sentence-by-sentence alignment of two documents: there is no-reordering, and only contiguous material needs to be split or merged. In section 3, we perform transcription alignment and evaluate its effectiveness by adapting two existing algorithms. In section 4 we describe a novel method using an extension of Hidden Markov Models in order to infer the hidden 'sound' sequence heard by transcribers. This permits each transcription to be normalised into a sequence of 'sounds'. Each of the methods is evaluated using synthetic data (section 5), data that has been generated in order to have known ground truths on which to evaluate the methods.

2 MT for unwritten languages

Recently, Abney and Bird (2010) have proposed to incorporate MT into the workflow of language documentation. MT supports the task of ensuring interpretability of the language records. It is not feasible to construct richly annotated resources, such as treebanks, for low-density languages. Instead, as argued by Abney and Bird (2010), we should take translation into English (or some other reference language) to be an adequate representation of the meaning of source language texts. Furthermore, also following (Abney and Bird, 2010), we assume that a language documentation is only complete if an adult who is already proficient in one of the world's major languages is able to acquire fluency in the language using only the archived bilingual resources. Obviously, such a test would take years to perform, and would need to be done again, each time the resources for a language are updated. However, a statistical machine translation (SMT) system can attempt this acquisition automatically, and its mistakes highlight any shortcomings in the documentation while there is still time to collect more. All that is required then, is substantial quantities of bilingual text, or n-lingual text in the general case, in machine-readable format. A structure that has been proposed to accommodate this data is the *Universal Corpus*.

A significant challenge for this program is posed by the fact that the majority of the world's languages are not written. Amongst the remaining languages that have a writing system, the majority do not have widespread literacy. Even where literacy is widespread, the majority of languages do not have a substantial community of writers. Finally, the presence of an orthography and users of the orthography does not ensure consistent spelling. How then, could we hope to obtain significant quantities of text in such languages?

Substantial efforts are already underway to record the oral literature of endangered languages while there is still time. This is painstaking work, and transcription is usually a slow process given the issues with orthography just identified. However, such transcriptions are an essential step to the creation of other language resources such as lexicons and grammars. This leads to a more narrowly focussed question: how can NLP techniques be applied to improve the speed and efficiency of audio transcription for unwritten languages?

Let us suppose that, for a given language, several native speakers were available to transcribe large quantities of audio recordings. We can be sure that no two speakers will transcribe the same source recording the same way. There will be variations in spelling, word segmentation, capitalisation, punctuation, and so forth. These variations will stem from varying levels of education, and varying experience of literacy in other languages. With enough resources, we could arrange for each source to be transcribed by more than one speaker. What would it take to automatically combine and normalise these transcriptions to produce a single transcription per source, of sufficient quality to be useful for downstream language technologies? These normalised transcriptions could then be aligned with manually supplied translations, leading to a bitext collection.

3 Existing methods

3.1 The Gale-Church Algorithm

The Gale-Church Algorithm (GCA) aligns the sentences of a document with those of its translation in a foreign language (Gale and Church, 1993). The algorithm exploits the fact that longer sentences in one language tend to correspond to longer sentences in the other. A pair of documents is aligned into cliques of zero, one or two consecutive sentences from each language.

Model Description. The model assumes that for a sentence of length L_1, the length of the corresponding clique of sentences in the foreign language is distributed as:

$$L_2 \sim N(cL_1, s^2L_1) \tag{3.1}$$

where c represents the mean number of characters emitted in the foreign language for each character in the source language, and s^2 is the variance per translated character. Empirical studies on European languages determined the optimal parameters to be $c = 1, s^2 = 6.8$ (Gale and Church, 1993).

The best alignment between paragraphs is determined by minimising a cost metric for alignments, based on the distribution given in Equation 3.1, and prior probabilities for different alignment types. Specifically, the cost of an alignment between a set of sentences E (of total length L_1) and a foreign set F (of total length L_2) is defined by

$$D(F, E) = -\log P(\#F|\#E)P(L_2|L_1) \tag{3.2}$$

$P(L_2|L_1)$ is calculated by integrating the normal distribution given in Equation (3.1) over all values more extreme (further from the mean) than

Alignment	0-1	1-1	2-1	2-2
Prior	0.010	0.890	0.089	0.011

Table 1: Original prior probabilities for alignment types in the GCA (Gale and Church, 1993).

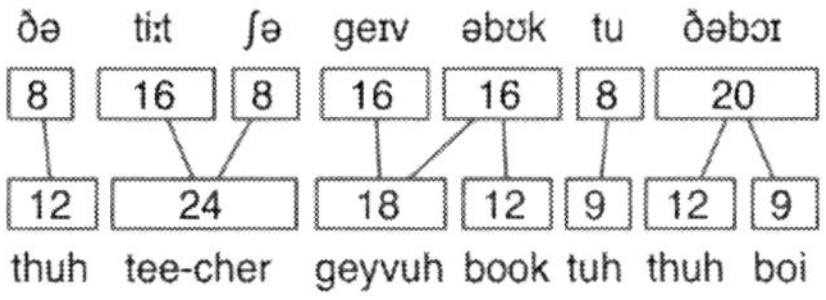

Figure 1: Aligning words from non-standard orthographic transcriptions with the Gale-Church Algorithm, using normalised word lengths.

L_2. $P(\#F|\#E)$ is the prior probability of alignment between sentence sets of sizes $|F|$ and $|E|$. The priors for alignment types used in the original algorithm are given in Table 1.

Then, for two paragraphs with numbers of sentences L_1 and L_2, their highest-probability alignment is derived using the following procedure. Denote the probability of the best alignment between the sentences $1 \dots i \leq I$ and $1 \dots j \leq J$ by $P(i,j)$, and the alignment itself by $B(i,j)$. Then $B(i,j)$ is determined by:

$$\arg\max_{b \in \{0,1,2\}^2} \big[P(i-b_1, j-b_2) \times D(\{i-b_1+1,...,i\},\{j-b_2+1,...,j\})\big]$$

Application to transcription normalisation. The GCA can be applied to align transcriptions at the level of words, rather than sentences, without violating the assumptions of the model (see Figure 1). In this way, the algorithm may be used to pre-process documents by splitting them into smaller pieces – aligned words – for further character-level processing such as alignment and transliteration.

The algorithm as defined is only applicable to aligning two sentences at a time. However, it has a simple extension to allow alignments of N transcriptions simultaneously. The best alignment between sentences $\{1,...,i_1\}$, ..., $\{1,...,i_N\}$ is determined by:

$$\arg\max_{b \in \{0,1,2\}^N} \big[P(i_1-b_1,...,i_N-b_N) \times D(\{i_1-b_1+1,...,i_1\},\dots,\{i_N-b_N+1,...,i_N\})\big]$$

where the distance function D is defined as an N-dimensional generalisation of the original GCA distance function.

Limitations. The GCA only uses the information about the lengths of the word fragments. Hence it ignores other useful information such as the characters used in the word fragments. A tightly coupled character pair, e.g. characters corresponding to a rare sound, may strongly indicate the true fragment alignment. In determining the most likely alignment between sentences, the algorithm uses predefined prior probabilities of alignment types, based on European languages. In order to apply the algorithm to word fragment alignments, these prior probabilities should be re-estimated. Since the GCA is only applied to synthetic data in this work, we will retain the original priors and generate data according to them.

3.2 Moses

In order to perform a system-level evaluation of the GCA as a transcription pre-processor for character-based aligners, we require an established alignment system. For this purpose we use Moses, which is an SMT system designed to extend the IBM Models for unsupervised phrase-based translation (Koehn, 2010).

Model description. Moses uses a mathematical model to determine a probability distribution over possible translations of a sentence. Given a source language sentence e, a foreign language sentence f, and a division of the sentences into I phrases (blocks of consecutive words), the probability of the foreign sentence given the source sentence is defined as follows (Koehn, 2010):

$$p(f^I|e^I) = \prod_{i=1}^{I} \phi(f_i|e_i) d(\text{start}_i - \text{end}_{i-1} - 1) \quad (3.3)$$

where e_i and f_i are the ith phrases in the source and foreign languages, $\phi(f|e)$ is the probability of translating the phrase e into f, start_i is the position of the first word in the ith phrase, end_i is the position of the last word in the ith phrase, and d is a function that penalises re-ordering (when $\text{start}_i - \text{end}_{i-1} - 1 \neq 0$).

Application to transcription problem. To apply Moses to the transcription normalisation problem, we adopt the basic unit of characters instead of words. In this context, a "phrase" corresponds to a word fragment, or sequence of characters.

The first step of Moses training uses GIZA++ (Och and Ney, 2003) to establish likely word alignments. We use the HMM model for word alignment (Vogel et al., 1996), since the IBM models encompass reorderings which are not relevant for transcription alignment. An example of training Moses to detect regular sound correspondences between Portuguese and Spanish from a comparative wordlist (Wagner, 2010) is shown in Table 2.

4 HMM method

In this section a new method for transcription normalisation based on Hidden Markov Models is in-

ES	PT	ϕ(ES|PT)	N
ie	e	0.72	50
rse	r se	0.93	28
rs	r se	0.81	32
ón	ão	0.71	24

Table 2: Sample of results from training Moses on a Spanish-Portuguese comparative wordlist. ϕ is the proportion of instances of the ES fragment aligning with the PT fragment. N is the number of samples of the ES fragment.

troduced. This method aims to address the problem of N-way transcription normalisation.

4.1 Model description

The leading idea in the new model is that whatever orthography is used, the sequence of characters in a transcription corresponds closely to the sequence of sounds heard by the transcriber. This suggests a model in which the characters are treated as emissions and the sounds are treated as hidden states in a modified version of a Hidden Markov Model. Our goal is to infer the most likely hidden state (sound) sequence given a set of N transcriptions of the same audio, and to use this as a normalised form.

Each hidden state (sound) is associated with a probability distribution over all possible emissions. Emissions are character sequences ranging in length from 0 up to some maximum, denoted LE. Hence, denoting the emission probability distribution for hidden state element s by ϕ_s,

$$\phi_s(e) : \bigcup_{i=0}^{LE} \{c_1, c_2, ..., c_N\}^i \to [0, 1] \tag{4.1}$$

where the $\{c_i\}$ is an inventory of all the characters used in the orthography.

This setup would be sufficient if character emissions occur in a strict linear order with respect to the hidden states emitting them, but that is not always true. A counter-example is given by the English word *date*. In Figure 2, the last three sounds together cause the emission *ate*: the emission of the character *e* is unique to the *combination* of the sounds. This phenomenon is not modelled sufficiently by, say, adding some probability of emitting the characters *te* from the *t* sound; the extra letter is only emitted when the sounds occur together.

To address this problem, we allow emissions from *blocks* of hidden states acting in unison, referred to as **source blocks** or just **sources**. A source block, s, is defined by:

$$s \in \bigcup_{i=1}^{LB} \{h_1, h_2, ..., h_M\}^i \tag{4.2}$$

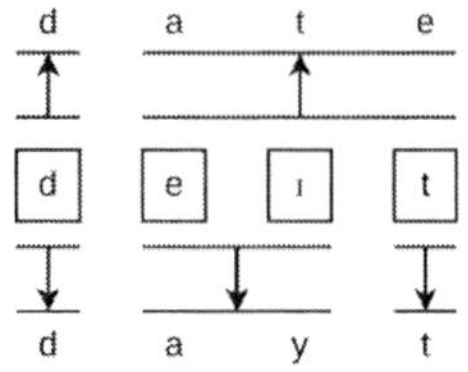

Figure 2: Transcriptions of the word *date* using English orthography and a hypothetical phonetic orthography. The true sequence of sounds is shown in IPA in the center. The correspondence between sounds and orthographic representation is indicated using arrows. Note that the last three sounds together are responsible for the emission of the characters *ate* in English orthography.

where LB is the length of the longest source block allowed by the model, and the h_i are the hidden states of the model, of which there are M in total. Each block has its own emission probability distribution which treated as being independent from the emission distributions of its components. In Figure 2, the last three sounds act as a block in the top transcription language. Apart from block emissions, no other provisions are made for out-of-order emissions.

Given a set of N transcriptions assumed to be of the same audio, we can compute its probability with respect to a given hidden state sequence using the ideas of source blocks and emissions. A **model** is a pair composed of a hidden state sequence $S = (h_1, h_2, ..., h_{|S|})$ and an **alignment** ψ of the state sequence to the characters in the transcriptions. The alignment is constructed by splitting each transcription into emissions, and splitting the hidden state sequence into source blocks, which are assigned to the emissions in order (hence, for each transcription, there must be an equal number of source blocks and emissions). Note that the hidden state sequence may be split into source blocks differently for each transcription. Hence, the complete alignment is a vector of independent per-transcription alignments, $\psi = (\psi_i)$. An alignment ψ_i of a hidden state sequence of length $|S|$ to a particular transcription of length L_i is defined as a vector of pairs (see Figure 3):

$$\psi_i = [([s_1, s_2), [t_1, t_2)), ([s_2, s_3), [t_2, t_3)), \ldots, ([s_J, |S|), [t_J, L_i + 1))] \tag{4.3}$$

where $s_1 = t_1 = 1$, $J = |\psi_i|$ is the number of source blocks, and t_i may equal t_{i+1} in the case of a zero-length emission. Then, the probability of an observed set of M transcriptions given a state

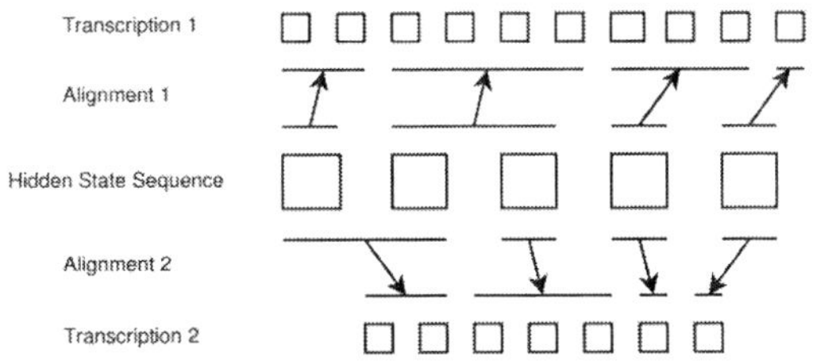

Figure 3: Sample alignment of a hidden state sequence of length 5 to two transcriptions. In transcription 1, sounds [2, 3] emit characters [3, 6] as a block, and in transcription 2, sounds [1, 2] emit characters [1, 2] as a block. The alignment for Transcription 1 as defined in (4.3) is: $\psi_1 = (([1,2),[1,3)),([2,4),[3,7)),([4,5),[7,10)),([5,6),[10,11)))$.

sequence and alignment is given by:

$$P(T_1, T_2, ..., T_M|S, \psi) = \prod_{i=1}^{M}\prod_{j=1}^{J} \phi^i([t_j, t_{j+1})|[s_j, s_{j+1})) \quad (4.4)$$

where we have defined $\phi^i(e|s)$ to be the probability of emitting the emission e from the source block s in the ith transcription language. For the purpose of inferring the most likely hidden state sequence, we use Bayes' Theorem: the probability of a model given a set of transcriptions is proportional to:

$$P(S, \psi|T_1, T_2, ..., T_M) \propto P(S, \psi)P(T_1, T_2, ..., T_M|S, \psi) \quad (4.5)$$

where to calculate $P(S, \psi)$, we use a first order Markov Model on the hidden state sequence, and make no relative penalties for different alignments:

$$P(S, \psi) = P(S) = \prod_{(S_i, S_{i+1})} P(S_{i+1}|S_i) \quad (4.6)$$

4.2 Model Implementation

The model and an EM training procedure were implemented in C++.

Training. Training follows a modified Expectation Maximisation format. The emission distributions and bigram model for the hidden states are initialised randomly, then the following process is looped over a fixed number of iterations:

1. Model fitting:
   (a) State sequences are sampled randomly for each sentence group in the corpus.
   (b) Random alignments to the transcriptions are generated for each state sequence.
   (c) Probability of the random fits calculated.
2. Model re-estimation:
   (a) Count for each emission event and state sequence event are weighted by probability of the sample in which they occur and added to running totals.
   (b) Weighted counts for each event are normalised and smoothing is applied.
   (c) Pairs of sources with low information radii are merged.

Sampling Strategy. We use a greedy sampling strategy to ensure that some high likelihood models are included in the sample. Specifically, the process is as follows:

1. Choose a random number of sounds for the state sequence.
2. Choose a (uniformly) random alignment to the transcriptions.
3. For each state sequence position, randomly select sounds and evaluate the probability of the partial model.
4. Choose the sound that had the highest probability.

The number of times random sounds are drawn in step 3 is equal to the number of hidden states used by the model. This ensures a good chance of a higher-probability sound being chosen, while preventing lower probability samples from being unrepresented.

Clustering. The last part of the E-step in the main training procedure is a form of clustering. The two most similar source blocks (defined by similarity of their emission distributions) are combined. One source block takes on the average distribution of the two, while the other is re-initialised with a uniform distribution. This leaves one source block free to acquire a new emission probability distribution, which may lead to a better overall modelling of the data. Hence, the clustering step provides a way for the training to jump out of local maxima. Clustering may be repeated a variable number of times, to merge multiple similar source pairs in a single training iteration. The similarity measure over emission distributions used to determine which source pairs to merge is the *information radius* (Manning and Schütze, 1999).

Length normalisation. Longer sentences naturally correspond to longer state sequences. Hence there are more possible models for a longer sentence, and therefore the probability of any given model is lower. This reduces the weight associated with a longer sentence when training. In fact, given two sentences, one twice as long as the other, the weight of the longer sentence will be roughly the square of the weight of the shorter one. Since the event counts are weighted by the probability of the sample containing them (and hence weights are < 1), longer sentences will contribute less data when training. This bias can be prevented using length normalisation. Length normalisation scales the weight of a sample according to its length. The length normalised weight for a sample is given by $w^* = \sqrt[|S|]{w}$ where $|S|$ is the length of the state sequence and w is the model probability computed using Equation (4.4).

4.3 Limitations

While the hidden state sequence is a natural normalised form for transcriptions, it is not enlightening when inspected. Hidden states are labelled only by integers, hence there is no immediate indication of what sound a particular hidden state may represent. Thus, a further decoding procedure may be needed to convert the true normalised form to a human-readable form.

Another limitation of the method is that it does not consider previously-known correspondences between transcription styles. For example, transcribers using similar character sets would be likely to use the same characters to mean the same sounds. The algorithm converts each data set into a list of integers, where each unique character has a single entry in a map. The maps for each transcription language are independent. Taking this type of information into account in advance may speed up the training process and improve its accuracy.

A further limitation is that the emission distribution associated with a source block is treated as being independent from the emission distributions of its constituent sounds. This is unrealistic; for example, if a source block in English contains the sound *t*, it is very likely that the emission produced by that source block will contain the letter *t*, but this is not captured in the model.

5 Evaluation

In the first sections we outline two synthetic data generation methods. These are designed to allow evaluation of character-based aligners based on the ground truth emission correspondences in the generated corpora. A metric quantifying the difference between the emission distributions learned by the character aligner and the ground-truth distributions is also defined. The evaluation is limited to the case of two parallel transcriptions. Evaluation of a character-based aligner involves an 18 part test performed for each data generation method: combinations of 3 sentence lengths (5, 10, and 15 words), and 3 corpus sizes (10, 25, 50 sentences), with and without GCA pre-processing of the corpus. Each test was performed 3 times with different randomly generated corpora and the results were averaged to give the presented value.

The next section involves an evaluation of GCA for the purpose of pre-processing transcriptions for normalisation. For this purpose, we outline a simple data generation scheme to produce parallel corpora with known ground truth alignments. Furthermore, the efficacy of the GCA as a preprocessor for character-based alignment tools is examined by studying the effect of GCA pre-processing on alignments learnt by the well-known Moses SMT system.

5.1 Synthetic method 1

This method is intended to produce corpora with character-aligned text in two randomly generated 'languages'. First, a set E of random possible emissions are generated in the first language. For each emission $e \in E$, a probability distribution over emissions in the second language, $\phi_e(f)$, is randomly generated. The support of each $\phi_e(f)$ distribution includes a small number of emissions, uniformly chosen between 1 and 5.

To generate words, a random integer is chosen from a gamma distribution, and that number of emissions are drawn uniformly from the set E of possible emissions in the first language. For each emission e included in the word, a corresponding emission f is drawn from the $\phi_e(f)$ distribution. The emissions are concatenated to form the words. An alignment type is then drawn from the GCA priors (Table 1). The corresponding words are split according to the alignment type, where split points are chosen uniformly along the length of the words. Sentences are generated by stringing together series of words generated in this way. Hence the true emission correspondence distributions ϕ_e are known and can be compared to those learnt by an aligner.

5.2 Synthetic method 2: Block-based HMM

The second synthetic method involves generation of parallel corpora under the assumptions of the HMM method. This method may be used to generate any number of transcriptions simultaneously, but for this application we limit generation to two languages at a time. The data generation process is as follows:

1. A random language model for hidden states is generated, a random set of valid source blocks is generated, and random emission distributions for all valid source blocks are generated as in Synthetic Method 1.
2. For each individual word, a state sequence length is drawn from a gamma distribution.
3. For each word, a random sequence of sounds of that length is generated according to the language model, with initial probabilities equal to the stationary probabilities of the chain.
4. Starting with the longest block length, LE, and working back to blocks of length 1, emissions are chosen for any valid blocks appearing

in the state sequence.

5. The resulting emissions are concatenated to form the words for each transcription.
6. An alignment type is chosen from the GCA priors and the words are split according to that alignment, uniformly along their length.
7. Words formed this way are strung together to form sentences.

To calculate the true correspondence distributions between emissions we use Bayes' Theorem. Let f be an emission in the second language, and e an emission in the first language. Then the probability of an instance of e corresponding to f in the corpus is:

$$P(f|e) = \sum_{s \in S} P(f, s|e) \propto \sum_{s \in S} P(s)P(e|s)P(f|s) \tag{5.1}$$

Where S is the set of possible source blocks. Note that emissions selected for the different transcriptions from a common source are independent, so that $P(f|s, e) = P(f|s)$. Note also that the division of the hidden state sequence into blocks is common to both transcription languages. To calculate Equation (5.1), $P(e|s)$ and $P(f|s)$ are taken directly from the emission distributions. $P(s)$ is calculated using the stationary properties of the Markov chain used in sequence generation. Writing $s = s_1, s_2, ..., s_N$, we have the approximation:

$$P(s) = \alpha(s_1)P(s_1|s_2) \ldots P(s_{N-1}|s_N) \tag{5.2}$$

where $\alpha(s_1)$ is the stationary probability of the first sound of the source block. Equation (5.2) is only correct if word boundaries are treated as states in the HMM, which they are not; state sequence lengths are pre-drawn from a gamma distribution. However, the assumption becomes more accurate as the mean word length increases, and the average source block length decreases. Keeping block lengths short (maximum of 2-sound blocks) mitigates the effects of this inaccuracy, and the assumption will be kept.

5.3 Evaluation metric

For each of the data generation methods explained above, we have access to ground truth distributions for regular emission correspondences between the two languages. We define an accuracy metric based on the information radii between the true correspondence distributions (produced during corpus generation) and those produced by the aligners. Moses automatically produces emission correspondence distributions, and for the HMM method they are calculated using Equation (5.1).

Although information radius is only defined for two distributions, we can define a new metric quantifying the distance between a set of paired distributions. Let the paired distribution sets be $\{P_i$

Align	P	R	F-score	N
0 - 1	0.00	0.00	0.00	104
1 - 1	0.90	0.95	0.93	8886
1 - 2	0.82	0.67	0.74	893
2 - 2	0.00	0.00	0.00	117

Table 3: Results of running GCA on a corpus

and $\{Q_i\}$, $i \in E$, (E is the set of all emissions observed in the first language). Then we will use the metric:

$$D = \sum_{i \in I} w_i \text{IRad}(P_i, Q_i) \tag{5.3}$$

where IRad is the information radius (Manning and Schütze, 1999), and the weight w_i is the proportion of occurrences of the ith emission in the corpus, relative to all other emissions.

5.4 Gale-Church evaluation

For evaluation of the GCA, parallel corpora were generated using the following procedure:

1. A random sequence of alignments (0-1,1-1, etc.) was drawn with probabilities equal to the priors in the GCA (Table 1).
2. For each alignment, a random word length was drawn from a gamma distribution to form the first corpus. The parameters of the gamma distribution were chosen to be similar to those in the distribution of lengths of English words (West, 2008).
3. Each such word was randomly 'translated' under the assumptions of the GCA; the corresponding word length was drawn from a normal distribution according to the assumptions of the GCA (Gale and Church, 1993).
4. Each word pair in both corpora was then split according to their associated alignment type. Word splitting was distributed uniformly along the length of the word.

The parallel corpora generated were aligned using the unmodified GCA, and the accuracy of the resulting alignment was quantified using an F-score.

Results of running the GCA on a corpus generated using the above method are presented in Table 3. The algorithm did not correctly identify any 0-1 or 2-2 alignments. This effect occurs when aligning short (word size of less than 10 characters) fragments; increasing the word lengths to sentence size (~100 characters) causes the alignments to be picked up by the algorithm. The effect likely relates to the very low priors assigned to those alignment types (see Table 1). On the other alignment categories, the algorithm performs well.

The results of running Moses on corpora generated using synthetic methods 1 and 2 are shown in Tables 4 and 5 respectively. For both data generation methods it is clear that pre-processing using

M/+G		#Sentences		
		10	25	50
#Words	5	0.33/0.27	0.28/0.16	0.31/0.15
	10	0.46/0.29	0.46/0.16	0.30/0.10
	15	- /0.31	- /0.22	- /0.16

Table 4: Moses accuracy scores calculated using (5.3) (lower is better), for Synthetic Method 1. M: Moses alone, M+G: corpus pre-processed using the GCA. A dash represents failure of Moses to train (common with long sentences).

M/+G		#Sentences		
		10	25	50
#Words	5	0.18/0.06	0.05/0.03	0.03/0.03
	10	0.29/0.04	0.18/0.01	0.32/0.05
	15	0.28/0.03	0.33/0.04	0.21/0.02

Table 5: Moses accuracy scores calculated using (5.3) (lower is better), for Synthetic Method 2. M: Moses alone, M+G: corpus pre-processed using the GCA.

GCA improves the ability of Moses to learn emission correspondences. The effect of using GCA as a pre-processor is especially pronounced in the case of synthetic method 2, where dramatic decreases in the evaluation metric are observed. In addition to improving the accuracy of the training, the GCA also makes training possible on corpora which include longer sentences.

5.5 HMM Method

The results of running the HMM Method on corpora generated using synthetic methods 1 and 2 are shown in Tables 6 and 7 respectively. GCA preprocessing appears to have little effect on accuracy for this method. The method performs extremely well on corpora generated using synthetic method 2, which uses the assumptions of the HMM model. Comparing the results of training across the two data generation methods, it is clear that while the HMM method performs exceptionally on corpora generated using its assumptions, the implementation cannot yet achieve similar results on corpora which are generated differently.

H/+G		#Sentences		
		10	25	50
#Words	5	0.18/0.18	0.42/0.43	
	10	0.12/0.12	0.22/0.22	
	15	0.21/0.22	0.25/0.25	

Table 6: HMM Method accuracy scores calculated using (5.3) (lower is better), for Synthetic Method 1. H: HMM Method alone, H+G: corpus pre-processed using the GCA. Not all evaluations were completed due to prohibitive running times on large corpora.

H/+G		#Sentences		
		10	25	50
#Words	5	0.00/0.00	0.00/0.00	
	10	0.00/0.00	0.00/0.00	
	15	0.00/0.00	0.01/0.01	

Table 7: HMM Method accuracy scores calculated using (5.3) (lower is better), for Synthetic Method 2. H: HMM Method alone, H+G: corpus pre-processed using the GCA. Not all evaluations were completed due to prohibitive running times on large corpora.

6 Conclusion

We have introduced the transcription normalisation problem, and have tested the application of new and existing computational methods to it, with mixed results.

The evaluation of the Gale-Church Algorithm showed that it has a significant positive impact on subsequent training of character aligners. Hence the GCA will be useful in preparing texts so that they may be subject to character level processing, such as alignment and transliteration.

Regrettably, the implementation of the HMM method could not be fully developed in the available time. Features such as greedy sampling of the alignment space remain to be implemented. The method displayed promising results on corpora generated under HMM assumptions, however it is not yet versatile enough to achieve similar results when modelling corpora generated under different assumptions.

The results of the evaluation, while illustrating some interesting comparisons, are difficult to interpret. For instance, it is unclear what value of the accuracy metric a system would have to produce before it could be declared accurate enough to be useful in the transcription normalisation problem. Such investigations would require human evaluators.

Acknowledgements

We are grateful to David Chiang and three anonymous reviewers for helpful comments on the work reported here.

References

Steven Abney and Steven Bird. 2010. The human language project: Building a universal corpus of the world's languages. In *Proceedings of the 48th Annual Meeting of the Association for Computational Linguistics*, pages 88–97. Association for Computational Linguistics.

Jason Baldridge and Alexis Palmer. 2009. How well does active learning *actually* work? Time-based evaluation of cost-reduction strategies for language documentation. In *Proceedings of the 2009 Conference on Empirical Methods in Natural Language Processing*, pages 296–305. Association for Computational Linguistics.

William A. Gale and Kenneth W. Church. 1993. A program for aligning sentences in bilingual corpora. *Computational Linguistics*, 19:75–90.

Kevin Knight and Jonathan Graehl. 1998. Machine transliteration. *Computational Linguistics*, 24.

Philipp Koehn. 2010. *Statistical Machine Translation*. Cambridge University Press.

Michael E. Krauss. 2007. Mass language extinction and documentation: the race against time. In Osahito Miyaoka, Osamu Sakiyama, and Michael E. Krauss, editors, *The Vanishing Languages of the Pacific Rim*. Oxford University Press.

Christopher D. Manning and Hinrich Schütze. 1999. *Foundations of Statistical Natural Language Processing*. MIT Press.

Franz Josef Och and Hermann Ney. 2003. A systematic comparison of various statistical alignment models. *Computational Linguistics*, 29:19–51, March.

Stephan Vogel, Hermann Ney, and Christoph Tillmann. 1996. HMM-based word alignment in statistical translation. *COLING'96: The 16th International Conference on Computational Linguistics*, pages 836–841, August.

Jennifer Wagner. 2010. Romance languages vocabulary lists. http://www.ielanguages.com/romlang.html, December.

Marc West. 2008. The mystery of zipf. http://plus.maths.org/content/mystery-zipf, August.

Anthony C. Woodbury. 2010. Language documentation. In Peter K. Austin and Julia Sallabank, editors, *The Cambridge Handbook of Endangered Languages*. Cambridge University Press.

Fei Xia and William D. Lewis. 2007. Multilingual structural projection across interlinearized text. In *Proceedings of the Meeting of the North American Chapter of the Association for Computational Linguistics*, pages 452–459. Association for Computational Linguistics.

Similarity Based Language Model Construction for Voice Activated Open-Domain Question Answering

István Varga Kiyonori Ohtake Kentaro Torisawa Stijn De Saeger
Teruhisa Misu Shigeki Matsuda Jun'ichi Kazama
Institute of Information and Communications Technology (NICT)
3-5 Hikaridai, Seika-cho, Soraku-gun, Kyoto, 619-0289 Japan
{istvan, kiyonori.ohtake, torisawa, stijn, teruhisa.misu, shigeki.matsuda, kazama}@nict.go.jp

Abstract

This paper describes a novel method of constructing a language model for speech recognition of inputs with a particular style, using a large-scale Web archive. Our target is an open domain voice-activated QA system and our speech recognition module must recognize relatively short, domain independent questions. The central issue is how to prepare a large scale training corpus with low cost, and we tackled this problem by combining an existing domain adaptation method and distributional word similarity. From 500 seed sentences and 600 million Web pages we constructed a language model covering 413,000 words. We achieved an average improvement of 3.25 points in word error rate over a baseline model constructed from randomly sampled Web sentences.

1 Introduction

This paper presents a novel language model construction method for speech recognition, which is to be utilized by *Ikkyu*, an open-domain voice-activated Japanese QA system. Ikkyu takes relatively short spoken questions concerning a broad range of topics as input through a smartphone and provides the answers retrieved from a large scale Web archive. The challenge we tackle here is to provide a language model for a large-vocabulary speech recognition module to recognize such questions.

The widespread practice in language model construction is to train the model with a corpus that matches the domain and style of the target application. "Domain" usually refers to a set of utterances that are strongly related to a particular topic (e.g., travel). Ikkyu does not have any domain in this sense. The final QA system is expected to answer all the questions concerning every possible topic as far as our QA module can find the answers from the Web.

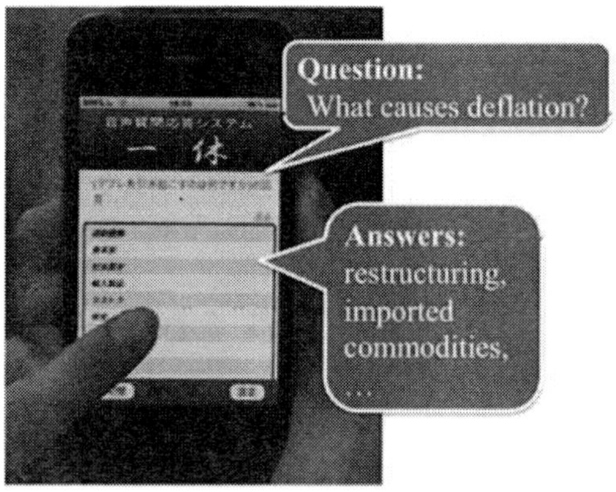

Figure 1: Screenshot of our QA system (*Ikkyu*) with the answers for *"What causes deflation?"*.

Since current state-of-the-art speech recognition systems cannot recognize long sentences through a smartphone with a high sentence accuracy, we decided to focus on relatively short questions, roughly consisting of a noun, an interrogative pronoun, and a predicate. Also, our current QA module can deal with only relatively short questions and this restricts the answerable questions. We call the restrictions on possible questions due to these factors *style* hereafter. (See Section 2 for a detailed description of style.) Our challenge is to prepare a large number of questions over various topics that match this style. Manual construction of such a corpus is impossible considering the necessary vocabulary coverage, thus an automatic method for collecting questions is needed.

Our method starts from an extremely small seed

(1)	Hayabusa ha nannen buri ni chikyuu ni kikan shita? *After how many years did Hayabusa (Japanese space probe) return to the Earth?*
(2)	Saikin hatsubai sareta Sony no gakushuu rimokon no kataban ha? *What's the model ID of Sony's recent universal remote control device?*
(3)	Itazuke iseki ha doko ni arimasu ka? *Where are the Itazuke ruins?*
(4)	Minamoto Yoritomo no otouto no namae ha nani desu ka? *What is the name of the brother of Yoritomo Minamoto (Japanese feudal lord)?*
(5)	Tokyo Disneyland no moyori no eki ha doko desu ka? *Which station is closest to Tokyo Disneyland?*
(6)	Gogatsu no tanjouseki wo oshiete kudasai. *Tell me the birthstones of May.*
(7)	Netchuushou no shoki shoujou ha? *(What is) the first symptom of hyperthermia?*
(8)	Kokusei chousa ha nannen oki ni jisshi sareru? *How long is the interval (in year) between each national census?*
(9)	Suteroido no fukusaiyou ni ha donna mono ga arimasu ka? *What are the side effects of steroids?*
(10)	Kaiketsu Zorori no sakusha ha dare? *Who is the author of Kaiketsu Zorori (cartoon)?*
(11)	Wimbledon de yuushou ssita hito ha dare? *Who is the champion at Wimbledon?*
(12)	Rui 14 sei no gyouseki ha nan desu ka? *What are the achievements of Louis XIV?*
(13)	Nihon de iPhone ha dore kurai urete imasu ka? *How many iPhones have been sold in Japan?*
(14)	Posutomodan to ha nani desu ka? *What is postmodern?*
(15)	Java no saishin baajon ha? *What is the latest version of Java?*

Table 1: Correctly recognized question examples from the test data. (May contain questions that can not be answered by our QA module.)

corpus consisting of hundreds of sentences that are manually tailored so that they match the style while also covering a wide range of topics. Next it selects sentences similar to ones in the seed corpus from a large Web archive (Shinzato et al., 2008). The selection is done by a combination of distributional similarity for nouns (Kazama et al., 2010) and an existing automatic *domain* adaptation method, intended to construct a relatively large *in-domain* training corpus (Misu and Kawahara, 2006). We show that this adaptation technique can be useful even in constructing an open-domain but style restricted corpus.

The major problem we tackle is the following: since constructing a large seed corpus is not affordable, we need to deal with the inevitable sparsity of a smaller seed corpus. Since this seed corpus needs to cover as many topics as possible, the number of questions for each topic is too scarce. Although the domain adaptation method is designed to deal with a similar problem, i.e., data sparseness caused by small seed corpora, it is questionable whether it would be equally efficient in domain independent, style restricted settings with a seed corpus of the same size. Our basic idea to overcome this difficulty is to expand the

(1)	Defure wo hikiokosu no ha nani desu ka. *What causes deflation?*
(2)	Yanaacheku ga sakkyoku shita no ha nan desu ka? *What [musical pieces] are composed by Janáček?*
(3)	Heisokusei doumyaku koukashou wo fusegu no ha nan desu ka? *With what can peripheral artery disease be prevented?*
(4)	Kawazugawa de nani ga tsuremasu ka? *What [kind of fish] can you catch in the Kawazu river?*

Table 2: Answerable questions of the QA module.

seed corpus by replacing nouns with distributionally similar nouns in the seed corpus, adding the resulting new sentences to the seed corpus. As a result, the domain adaptation method can pick up sentences referring to a wider range of topics from the Web more efficiently.

In the experiments using an existing speech recognition engine, ATRASR (Matsuda et al., 2006), our proposal's best model covering 413,000 words achieved an average word error rate of 15.49% and an average sentence error rate of 54.73%. The obtained improvement by our method over a baseline language model constructed from randomly sampled Web sentences was 3.25 points in word error rate and 4.28 points in sentence error rate.

Table 1 shows some questions correctly recognized by our best model. These suggest that our speech recognition module can actually recognize questions concerning a wide range of topics.

2 Our Open-Domain QA System *(Ikkyu)*

Before presenting the proposed method, we explain about Ikkyu, our open domain QA system, to clarify the motivation behind the task settings and the requirements for our speech recognition module. Figure 1 is a screenshot of Ikkyu, answering the question *"What causes deflation?"*. The answers are extracted from a large Web archive (6.0×10^8 Web pages) (Shinzato et al., 2008) in just a few seconds and each answer is linked to the original Web page from which it is extracted. Users can check more information regarding the answers just by following these links. Table 2 lists some examples of the questions the current prototype can actually answer.

For the example question of Figure 1 (*"What causes deflation?"*), the system unexpectedly presented a major Japanese automobile manufacturer as an answer. The blog entry, from which the system extracted the answer, claimed that the company kept its huge profit (more than tens of billion US dollars) and this shrinked public demand and worsened the deflation. The same story was reported in an authoritative economic magazine after we found this answer.

The ultimate objective in this speech driven QA project is to offer a platform with which users can easily broaden their viewpoint by discovering valuable information including unexpected ones, like the example above, at any time, any place, which may result in more efficient decision making in all circumstances. In achieving this goal, we believe flexible speech recognition can be a great help since it can allow users to ask anytime, anywhere, any questions that come to mind.

The QA module is an extension of a pattern-based relation extraction method (De Saeger et al., 2009). It converts the input question, such as *"What causes deflation?"*, into the lexico-syntactic binary pattern "X causes Y" and automatically computes its paraphrases as well, such as "X triggers Y" and "Y is a cause of X". X and Y are variables, corresponding to the topic and interrogative pronoun of the question. These patterns are then matched against the Web archive after one of the variables is filled with the corresponding noun in the original question (Y = "deflation" in the above example). The nouns matching the unfilled variable (X) are provided as answers.

An important point here is that the form of the answerable questions are restricted by the patterns utilized by the QA module. These were automatically extracted beforehand from frequently observed dependency paths of a Web archive, amounting to 70 million in number, thus covering virtually all topics found in the archive. Because of this pattern extraction scheme, most patterns consist of a predicate, two variables (to be filled with nouns) and some postpositions connecting the predicate and the variables. Due to this tendency in the patterns, most answerable questions consist of a predicate, a noun, an interrogative pronoun and some additional function words. This is the *style* we assumed for our QA system.

Further elaboration of this notion of *style* may lead to the idea that the language model may be derived by converting all possible patterns into questions. We attempted this approach, but found that it was extremely difficult, as will be discussed in Section 5.3.

Instead, we start from a small corpus prepared in a relatively independent way from the architecture of our QA module. A positive side-effect of this approach is that it can be applied to speech recognition for other QA systems as far as the style of the questions match that of our QA module.

3 Background

This section describes the statistical domain adaptation method and the distributional word similarity to be used in the proposed method.

3.1 Statistical adaptation method

We combine our similarity based expansion method with an existing statistical adaptation method proposed by Misu and Kawahara (2006). In their method a seed corpus S is used to generate search queries for retrieving similar, relevant text from the Web. The search queries are generated by automatically extracting keywords with large TF-IDF values. Next, for each sentence from the retrieved text a $score$ is calculated, i.e. the word perplexity relative to the seed language model.

$$score = 2^{-\frac{1}{n}\sum_{i=1}^{n}\log_2 p(w_i|w_{i-1},w_{i-2})}$$

Here w_i represents the i-th word in a sentence with n words. For trigrams that contain unknown words, the minimum trigram probability of the seed language model is assigned as a penalty. The sentences whose $score$ is smaller than a threshold θ are selected to form the training corpus T, together with the seed corpus.

Note that this method selects sentences from Web search results using the keyword queries determined according to TF-IDF. However, our main goal is to efficiently identify questions covering a wide range of topics while matching a certain style, often represented by colloquial textual fragments and therefore consisting of frequent words. We judged that Web search using TF-IDF score is harmful because it is likely to filter out such frequent words, therefore we skipped it. Instead, $score$ was computed for all the sentences of the Web archive and sentences were selected solely based on the $score$ values. We fixed the unknown trigram probability at 10^{-10}. Compound nouns (or noun sequences) are treated as single noun.

We call our implementation of this statistical adaptation method "Misu's method" hereafter.

3.2 Distributional word similarity

Distributional word similarity measures the semantic similarity between words based on the distributional hypothesis (Harris, 1954), which states that words that occur in the same contexts tend to have similar meanings. Based on this hypothesis, many similarity measures have been proposed. We adopt a recent method of Kazama et al. (2010).

Kazama et al. (2010) applied the Bayesian approach for the similarity calculation to alleviate the problem of data sparseness. The method starts from the base similarity measure, the Bhattacharyya coefficient, which is defined over probability distributions p_1 and p_2 as follows:

$$BC(p_1, p_2) = \sum_{k=1}^{K} \sqrt{p_{1k} \times p_{2k}}$$

p_1 and p_2 are the conditional context distributions for two given words, $p(f_k|w_1)$ and $p(f_k|w_2)$. The contexts, f_k, used in (Kazama et al., 2010) are dependency relations such as "subj-of-swim" for the word "tuna". Instead of using $p(f_k|w_1)$ directly, their method estimates the distribution of $p(f_k|w_1)$ itself using the Bayesian method to capture the unreliability of data and calculates the expectation of the above base similarity under those distributions. They showed that this method outperforms many existing similarity measures through the experiments using large-scale Japanese Web data.

4 Proposed Method

The proposed method can be described as follows. The inputs are the seed corpus S and a Web archive W.

Step 1 For each sentence s in S, pick up every noun w that is not in a stop-word list L and replace w in s with the most similar k words according to Kazama's distributional similarity (Kazama et al., 2010). The resulting sentences are added to S.

Step 2 Apply Misu's method (Misu and Kawahara, 2006) to S and W and construct a training corpus T.

Step 3 Construct a language model from T using existing tools for speech recognition.

Assume the question *"What are the symptoms of gout?"* is in S, "gout" and "symptom" are not in L, "osteoporosis" and "cause" are among the k most similar words to "gout" and "symptom" respectively. Then, in Step 1 the new sentences *"What are the symptoms of osteoporosis?"* and *"What are the causes of gout?"* are added to the seed corpus S. In Step 2, we can expect that Misu's method picks up sentences such as *"What are the treatments of osteoporosis?"* in the Web archive and adds it to the training corpus T. This is because the new question shares two trigrams ("What are the" and "of osteoporosis ?") with the newly added seed sentence *"What are the causes of osteoporosis?"*, and is likely to have a relatively low (thus better) *score* value. Note that the question is less likely to be added to the training corpus if the noun replacement of "gout" with "osteoporosis" was not conducted since it has less common trigrams with the original seed question. This is a benefit obtained by our method.

In our experiments, we used approximately 500 questions as seed corpus S. These were manually crafted according to the instructions described in Section 5.1.2. The Web archive W consists of 6.0×10^8 Japanese Web pages (Shinzato et al., 2008). The distributional similarity between nouns was computed from another Web archive consisting of 1.0×10^8 Japanese Web pages. The stop-word list L contains about 2,000 nouns whose frequency exceed 10^7 in our Web archive. This list was devised because highly frequent nouns often behave as function words, and replacing such nouns often yield ill-formed sentences.

While the style of the initial seed corpus necessarily reflects the underlying task (i.e. recognizing question sentences), the various steps of our proposed method do not rely on any explicit or implicit stylistic elements of the input seed corpus, so we consider our method to be task-independent.

5 Evaluation

5.1 Evaluation settings

5.1.1 Corpora

We prepared two Web archives as the starting point of language modeling: the first (`www`) is unfiltered in regards of style, while the second (`wwwq`) is a subset of the first, attempting to follow the style requirements of the QA system.

- **www** The first archive consists of 6.0×10^8 Web pages (Shinzato et al., 2008). We use this Web archive as training data for language modeling. After sanity check, we retained a corpus of 1.79×10^{10} words in 1.35×10^9 sentences. We call this corpus `www`.

- **wwwq** While the `www` corpus preserves the open-domain characteristics of the Web archive, it completely ignores the requirements of Ikkyu regarding style, containing various sentence types besides questions. Using simple heuristics, we selected questions from www. Since Japanese doesn't necessarily use question marks with questions, we identified questions as sentences that end with question marks or question markers (ka, kai, kashira, kana). We also extracted requests, which end with kudasai (≈*please*) or continuative verb + gerund te (≈Japanese colloquial request). This filtering retained a question corpus of 1.23×10^9 words in 1.01×10^8 sentences. We call this corpus wwwq.

Note that these regular expressions allow many sentences that don't match the style of Ikkyu, such as *why*, *how* or polar questions. Removing such problematic sentences from the corpus is not a trivial task in Japanese. For instance, interrogative pronouns can be omitted in Japanese.

The benefit of our proposed method is that we can rely on statistics and a small seed corpus without dealing with such numerous minor problems.

5.1.2 Evaluation sets

We recorded the questions uttered by 50 people (25 female and 25 male). Each subject was presented with 100 questions that Ikkyu can accept as input, after which each subject uttered approximately 50 of her/his own spontaneous questions which were recorded using smartphones. They were instructed to formulate simple questions, consisting of a noun, a predicate and an interrogative pronoun ("what", "who", "where" or "when") for a wide range of topics as far as possible, with the interrogative pronoun possibly being replaced by an expression to formulate a request, or being omitted altogether. Note that in spite of these instructions the recorded data contains some questions which do not conform.

The group was randomly split into three, with g0 containing 10 speakers, g1 and g2 containing 20 speakers each. Table 3 shows their details. The corpus of g0 was used as seed corpus, whereas g1 and g2 were used for two-fold cross validation.

Group	g0 (S)	g1	g2
# of sentences	498	1000	999
# of words	4043	7671	8322
average sentence length	8.118	7.671	8.330

Table 3: Seed corpus and evaluation data.

5.2 Results

5.2.1 Best distributional similarity rank (k)

Firstly, we tried to find the best similarity rank k and training data size combination in terms of word-error-rate (WER), using the following values: k=1, 2, 3, 4, 5, 10, 15, 20, 100. After the seed corpus expansion, we incrementally increased the size of the training data, starting from a 10 million word corpus, gradually changing the threshold θ on Misu's score. We determined the best setting by two-fold cross validation, that is, we used the g1 set as development set with g2 as evaluation set, and vice versa. Figure 2 presents the WER curves for each parameter k, trained on the www corpus. Training on the www corpus provided with the best absolute performances, with $k = 10$ being the best setting in terms of WER consistently in both evaluation data, when the corpus size was approximately 160 million words (Figure 2). The vocabulary of this model has 413,000 entries. Note that $k = 10$ achieved best or 2nd best WER at most data points. This consistency suggests the effectiveness of our noun replacement. An interesting point is that the performance is saturated when k is relatively small, suggesting that the noun replacement is a relatively sensitive operation.

Note that when $k = 0$, the method is equivalent to Misu's method. The difference in WER between the best performance of Misu's method and our method when $k = 10$ is 0.19 points in g1 and 0.72 points in g2. Using McNemar's test (McNemar, 1947), we found that these differences are statistically significant ($p < 0.05$). Although the difference in g1 is quite small, (1) the best performance of our method is achieved using a smaller training corpus (50% of Misu's method); (2) if we use the same corpus size achieving the best performance in all the settings, i.e., 160 million words, the difference between Misu's method and $k = 10$ is even larger: 0.66 points in g1 and 0.95 points in g2; (3) there is also a large difference between the peak performances regarding sentence error rate (SER) in both of g1 and g2 (0.90 and 1.90 points). These observations suggest that our method is more effective than Misu's original method.

When we used the question archive wwwq instead of www, the same tendency was observed. The best performance was obtained when $k = 10$ for both g1 and g2. The peak performance was obtained when the corpus size had 80 million words consistently in both test data. However, the best

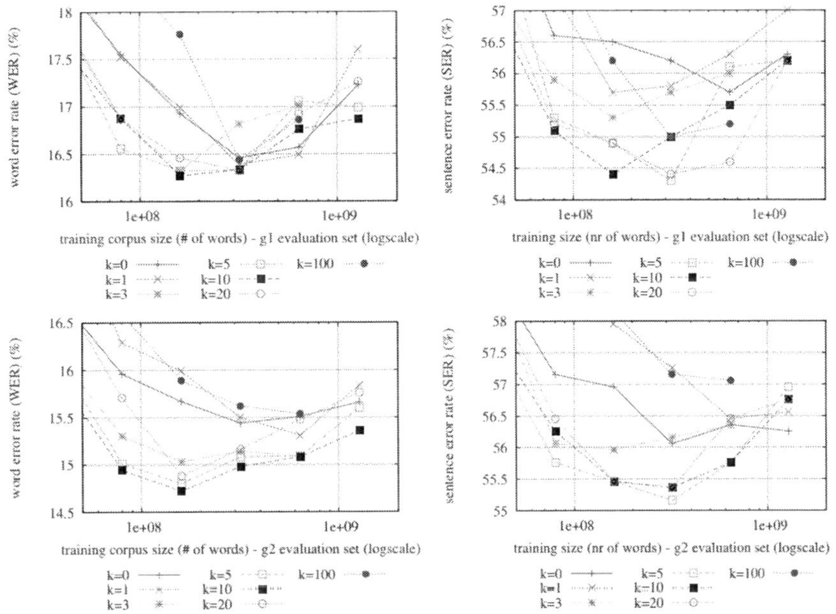

Figure 2: WER curves with various distributional similarity rank k, trained on the `www` corpus.

performance was worse than when we trained on `www` (16.35% in g1 and 15.28% in g2).

5.2.2 Comparison with the baselines

Next, we confirm that our method with the best setting ($k = 10$, 160 million words, trained on `www`) outperforms other baseline methods by comparing the following methods:

- **www.X** Our method applied to `www`.
- **wwwq.X** Our method applied to `wwwq`.
- **www.R** Random sampling from `www`.
- **wwwq.R** Random sampling from `wwwq`.

The results are presented in Figure 4.

Here we must mention that due to memory constraints, our language model training module (ATRASR) could not handle the entire `www` corpus. (We used machines with 72 GB memory.) The largest training data we could experiment on was 3.10×10^9 words. In case of the `wwwq` corpus such limitations don't apply, since 1.23×10^9 words can be handled by the module.

The peak performance of the baselines were achieved when the training data was largest, with `wwwq` showing lower WERs. Our method outperformed both baselines: regarding WER, we achieved 16.27% and 14.72% on g1 and g2, with an average improvement of 3.25 points, over the best baseline (`www`). These differences are also statistically significant ($p < 0.01$). Regarding SER, we achieved 54.30% and 55.16% on g1 and g2, respectively, with an average improvement of 4.28 points over the best baseline (`wwwq`), with the difference being statistically significant ($p < 0.01$). The performances of the baseline methods are not saturated and it may show much lower WER and SER if we can avoid the memory limitation problem somehow. However, the corpus size becomes so large (about 8 times the size of our best method), that would cause a significant slowdown of speech recognition. Figure 3 shows the real time factor[1] measured in our experiments. The best baseline method (trained on `www`) is already 2.8 times slower than the proposed method with the best setting. These observations suggest that our method is most suitable for our purpose.

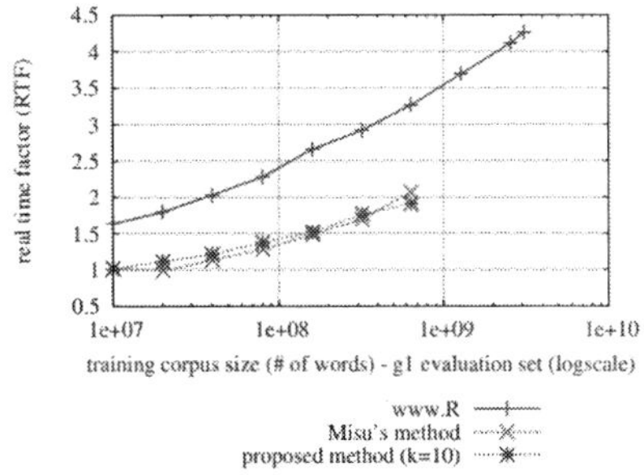

Figure 3: RTF in function of training corpus size.

[1] RTF ("real time factor"): defined as the processing time of the input divided by the duration of the input.

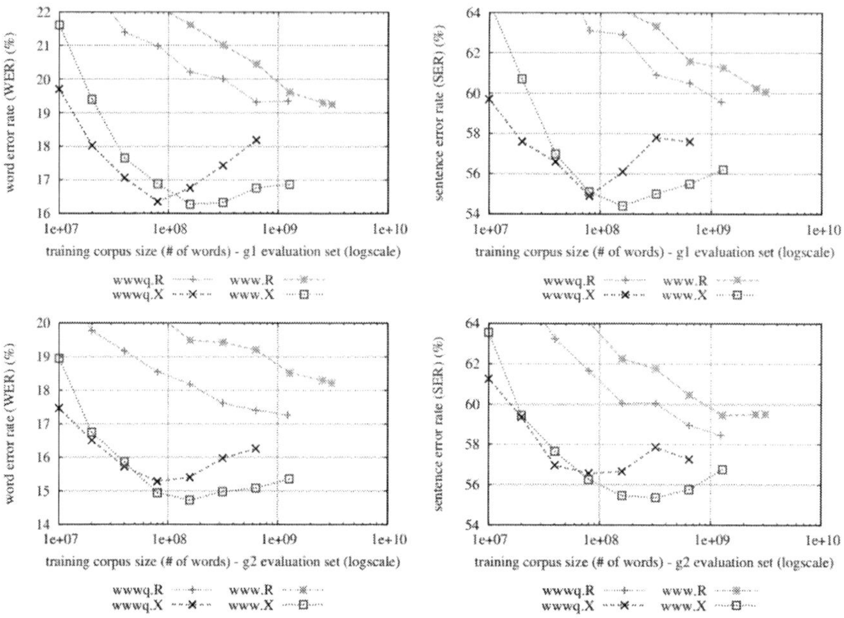

Figure 4: Our proposal versus the baselines.

5.2.3 N-best evaluation

The user interface of our QA system on smartphones has a user-friendly editing environment for word lattices provided by the speech recognition module. The user can correct the recognition results just by selecting some alternative words if the correct ones are included in the best N recognition results. The chance of a correct recognition is estimated as the probability of the correct question being in the N-best recognition results. We calculated SER over the top 100 recognition results. We found that between 59% and 62% (on g2 and g1, respectively) of speech inputs can be easily retrieved either by the top speech recognition result, or utilizing the error-recovery interface. This is important for the QA module in order to properly interpret and answer the questions.

5.3 Discussions

A concern is whether noun replacement really works as we intended. The improvement may have been achieved only for the words other than nouns, particularly the ones frequently observed in questions, such as verb suffixes indicating interrogative mood. This would not lead to topic expansion, as we intended. We conducted another series of experiments to investigate this supposition. Figure 5 shows the WER and SER of only nouns in the test data. Regarding noun-SER, a sentence is correct if all its nouns are correctly recognized. Interrogative pronouns were not considered. Using two-fold cross validation, on both g1 and g2 our method consistently achieved a lower noun-WER and noun-SER than Misu's method (without noun replacement), resulting in more accurate noun recognition. The difference between the best performances was 0.70 and 0.56 points in terms of noun-WER (on g1 and g2, respectively); 1.20 and 1.80 points in terms of noun-SER. These differences are statistically significant ($p < 0.05$). This implies that our concern was unfounded. Another observation is that the performance of the noun recognition does not saturate as the corpus size grows as far as we have tested. Analyzing this phenomenon more deeply and further improving the performance is our future work.

Another point is whether the noun replacement must be done before applying Misu's method. We may be able to achieve the same effect by performing noun replacement on the corpus obtained by Misu's method only using the original seed corpus. We experimentally confirmed this is not the case, although we don't present the experimental results for the sake of space. A possible explanation is that noun replacement generates many semantically ill-formed questions. If these are used as training corpus, they may be harmful. However, as seeds they only derive trigram probabilities for sentence selection, the selected sentences being natural, real life sentences from the Web.

We also attempted to build a language model by converting the patterns used by the QA module

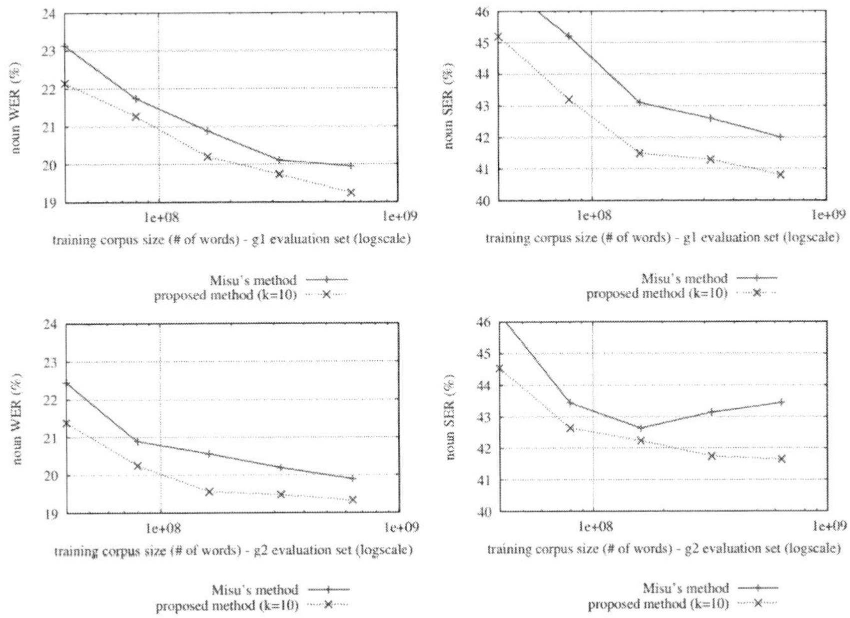

Figure 5: Noun evaluation on www.

to questions by replacing one of its variables with interrogative pronouns and attach some words indicating the interrogative mood. For instance, we could generate *"What causes deflation?"* from the pattern "X causes Y", but also less natural questions, such as *"What causes destruction?"*, which is extremely vague and is unlikely to be asked without a specific context. The conversion procedures generated a large number of such unnatural questions, and the resulting speech recognition performance was worse than that obtained by a corpus randomly sampled from our Web archive. To achieve the performance compatible to our method, thorough research must be conducted on generating only natural questions.

6 Related Work

The Web has been used as a relatively inexpensive source of large-scale data. "Just-in-time" language modeling (Berger et al., 1998) submits content words from previous user sentences as queries to a web search engine, Zhu et al. (2001) use a search engine to update the probabilities of already existing n-grams. More recently Bulyko et al. (2003) use frequent n-grams of the seed corpus as queries to retrieve similar text from the Web. Sarikaya et al. (2005) retrieves relevant text based on the BLEU score. Word perplexity is another frequently used similarity measure (Misu and Kawahara, 2006; Creutz et al., 2009). Some of these frameworks can be substituted for Misu's method in our framework, such replacement being a primary candidate of our future work.

Another category of related work relevant to our method is class-based language modeling (Brown et al., 1992). Many attempts refine this framework (Yamamoto et al., 2001; Chen and Chu, 2010; Emami et al., 2010). By replacing word trigrams in Misu's method by class trigrams, we may be able to achieve an effect similar to that obtained by our method without conducting noun replacement as additional procedure. However, the granularity of word classes may be a problem, considering that, in our framework, the optimal number of similar nouns replacing a noun in the seed corpus is relatively small (just 10). The comparison of class-based language models and our framework would be an interesting future work.

7 Conclusions

We have proposed a similarity based language model construction method for Ikkyu, a voice driven open-domain QA system. We used the combination of a distributional similarity based noun replacement method and a statistical domain adaptation method. Our best language model outperformed the baseline model constructed from random sampling of a Web archive by 3.25 points in word error rate and 4.28 points in sentence error rate, while using 8 times less training data.

References

Adam Berger, Robert Miller. 1998. Just-in-time language modeling. In *Proceedings of ICASSP-98*, pages 705–708.

Peter F. Brown, Vincent J. Della Pietra, Peter V. deSouza, Jenifer C. Lai, Robert L. Mercer. 1992. Class-Based n-gram Models of Natural Language. *Computational Linguistics* 18(4), pages 467–479.

I. Bulyko, M. Ostendorf, A. Stolcke. 2003. Getting more mileage from web text sources for conversational speech language modeling using class-dependent mixtures. In *Proceedings of Human Language Technology 2003 (HLT2003)*, pages 7–9.

Stanley F. Chen, Stephen M. Chu. 2010. Enhanced Word Classing for Model M. In *Proceedings of Interspeech 2010*, pages 1037–1040.

Mathias Creutz, Sami Virpioja, Anna Kovaleva. 2009. Web augmentation of language models for continuous speech recognition of SMS text messages. In *Proceedings of the 12th Conference of the European Chapter of the ACL*, pages 157–165.

Stijn De Saeger, Kentaro Torisawa, Jun'ichi Kazama, Kow Kuroda, Masaki Murata. 2009. Large Scale Relation Acquisition using Class Dependent Patterns. In *Proceedings of the IEEE International Conference on Data Mining (ICDM'09)*, pages 764–769.

Ahmad Emami, Stanley F. Chen, Abraham Ittycheriah, Hagen Soltau, Bing Zhao. 2010. Decoding with shrinkage-based language models. In *Proceedings of Interspeech 2010*. pages 1033–1036.

Zellig Harris. 1954. Distributional Structure. In *Word* 10(23), pages 142–146.

Jun'ichi Kazama, Stijn De Saeger, Kow Kuroda, Masaki Murata, Kentaro Torisawa. 2010. A Bayesian Method for Robust Estimation of Distributional Similarities. In *Proceedings of ACL 2010*, pages 247–256.

S. Matsuda, T. Jitsuhiro, K. Markov, S. Nakamura. 2006. ATR Parallel Decoding Based Speech Recognition System Robust to Noise and Speaking Styles *IEEE Transactions on Information and Systems* vol. E89-D(3), pages 989–997.

I. McNemar. 1947. Note on the sampling error of the difference between correlated proportions or percentages. In *Psychometrika* 12, pages 153–157.

Teruhisa Misu and Tatsuya Kawahara. 2006. A Bootstrapping Approach for Developing Language Model of New Spoken Dialogue Systems by Selecting Web Texts. In *Proceedings of Interspeech 2006*. pages 9–13.

R. Sarikaya, A. Gravano, Y. Gao. 2005. Rapid Language Model Development Using External Resources for New Spoken Dialog Domains. In *Proceedings of ICASSP 2005*, vol I, pages 573–576.

Keiji Shinzato, Tomohide Shibata, Daisuke Kawahara, Chikara Hashimoto, Sadao Kurohashi. 2008. TSUBAKI: An open search engine infrastructure for developing new information access. In *Proceedings of IJCNLP*, pages 189–196.

Xiaojin Zhu, R. Rosenfeld. 2001. Improving trigram language modeling with the world wide web. In *Proceedings of ICASSP*, pages 533–536.

Hirofumi Yamamoto, Shuntaro Isogai, Yoshinori Sagisaka. 2001. Multi-Class Composite N-gram Language Model for Spoken Language Processing Using Multiple Word Clusters. In *Proceedings of ACL-2001*, pages 6–11.

The application of chordal graphs to inferring phylogenetic trees of languages

Jessica Enright and **Grzegorz Kondrak**
Department of Computing Science
University of Alberta
Edmonton, AB, T6G 2E8, Canada
{enright,kondrak}@cs.ualberta.ca

Abstract

Phylogenetic methods are used to build evolutionary trees of languages given character data that may include lexical, phonological, and morphological information. Such data rarely admits a perfect phylogeny. We explore the use of the more permissive conservative Dollo phylogeny as an alternative or complementary approach. We propose a heuristic search algorithm based on the notion of chordal graphs. We test this approach by generating phylogenetic trees from three datasets, and comparing them to those produced by other researchers.

1 Introduction

Reconstructing the histories of language families is one of the principal tasks of historical linguistics. A linguistic phylogenetic tree conveys the evolution of a language family. The family tree can be constructed on the basis of characteristics that are common to sets of languages. which include lexical, phonological, and morphological affinities. Of particular importance are cognates — words that originate from the same ancestral word, and are distinct from words that are "borrowed", i.e. transferred between languages at some point in history. For example, English *brother* is cognate with German *bruder* and Russian *brat*, all of which come from a Proto-Indo-European word reconstructed as *bhrāter*, while *cousin* is a borrowing from French.

The task of inferring phylogenetic trees of languages is complicated by the pervasiveness of borrowings, which frequently occur when languages are in close contact. For example, English is a Germanic language but the majority of its vocabulary is borrowed from other branches of Indo-European. Several approaches have been proposed to incorporate borrowings into the tree building process (Minett and Wang, 2003). In particular, Nakhleh et al. (2005a) introduce the concept of a phylogenetic *network*, which is obtained by augmenting a putative tree with edges representing contact between languages. They present a method to calculate the minimum number of borrowings required to admit that tree. However, the method does not actually construct a tree from the data, and it may be computationally intractable when the number of borrowings is large.

In this paper, we propose to apply a conservative Dollo phylogeny (CDP) as a model of linguistic phylogenetics. The approach was originally developed by Przytycka et al. (2006) in computational biology. Since it is NP-Hard to compute the minimum number of deletions required for a dataset to conform to a CDP (Lewis and Yannakakis, 1980), we propose a heuristic search algorithm based on the notion of chordal graphs. Our algorithm produces an output tree that minimizes the number of borrowings directly from the data. In addition, it has the potential of being significantly faster to compute than the more commonly known perfect phylogeny. Our approach produces plausible phylogenetic trees on three different datasets.

This paper is structured as follows. In Section 2, we outline the required background, including several graph theoretic notions and alternative phylogenies. In Section 3, we describe our heuristic search algorithm to compute the minimum set of data entries that are inconsistent with a CDP. We also describe a number of preprocessing steps that we take in order to make our problem more computationally feasible. In Section 4, we describe the experiments on three datasets, and compare the resulting phylogenetic trees to those produced by other researchers. In Section 5, we describe an extension to our heuristic search. We conclude with future work and a summary in Sections 6 and 7.

2 Background

In this section, we outline the notions of perfect and Dollo phylogenies, and several graph-theoretic notions, including intersection graphs and chordal graphs.

2.1 Perfect phylogeny

A *character* represents a property of languages. In this paper, we consider only binary characters, which have two possible states: 1 and 0. For example, a presence or absence of a particular cognate can be considered a character. The information encoded by a set of characters is used for constructing phylogenetic trees. We say that a character *back evolved* if after evolving from 0 state to 1 state, it subsequently is lost and switches back on the tree from 1 state to 0 state. We say that a character has *parallel evolution* if it evolves twice on the tree from state 0 to state 1 independently. We say that a character is *borrowed* if it has been transferred from one branch to another by contact between linguistic groups.

Given a set of binary characters, we say that a rooted tree with languages as the leaf nodes is a *perfect phylogeny* if for each character there exists a binary labeling such that the root node is labeled with a zero, and all nodes sharing the same label are connected. This implies that each character evolves exactly once, and that there is no back-mutation or borrowing. For example, the tree in Figure 1 is not a perfect phylogeny because characters one and two back-evolve. It is possible to recognize whether a set of characters admits a perfect phylogeny in polynomial time (Felsenstein, 2004).

The character data representing actual languages rarely admit a perfect phylogeny because back mutation, parallel evolution, and borrowing often occur in the course of linguistic evolution. Instead, we are usually interested in establishing for a given character data how far away it is from admitting a perfect phylogeny. *Maximum parsimony* attempts to minimize the overall number of evolutionary events required on a tree to explain the character data, where an evolutionary event is a switch of a character from one state to another (Felsenstein, 2004). Because maximum parsimony is NP-Hard (Day et al., 1986), many approximate approaches have been proposed for this task. Nakhleh et al. (2005b) provide an excellent survey of linguistic phylogenetic methods.

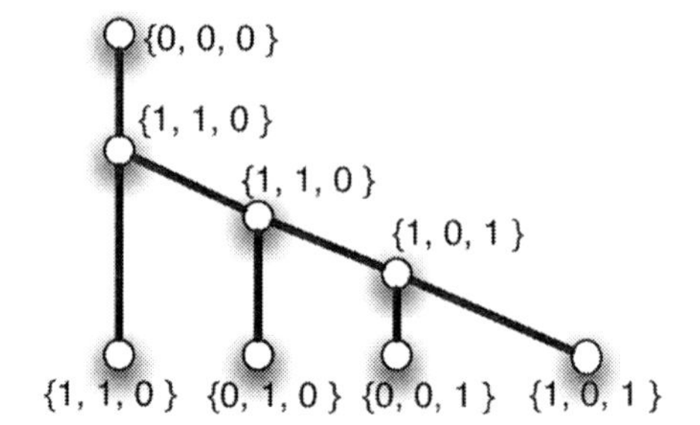

Figure 1: An example of a tree with three characters that is a conservative Dollo phylogeny (CDP), but not a perfect phylogeny.

Nakhleh et al. (2005a) propose perfect *phylogeny networks* as a way of simplifying the phylogeny problem. A perfect phylogeny network is a graph (not necessarily a tree) such that every character exhibits a perfect phylogeny on at least one of the subtrees of that graph. This approach is particularly powerful in modeling borrowing; however, it requires the underlying genetic tree to be defined beforehand. The edges added to the tree represent contact between languages. Unfortunately, even given a phylogenetic tree and character data, determining the minimum number of edges one must add to produce a perfect phylogeny network is NP-Hard (Day et al., 1986). Nakhleh et al. (2005a) mention that applying the perfect phylogeny network approach to their Indo-European language dataset is tractable only because very few edges need to be added to their tree to produce a perfect phylogeny network.

2.2 Dollo phylogenies

Given a set of binary characters, we say that a rooted tree with languages as the leaf nodes is a *Dollo phylogeny* if for each character there exists a binary labeling such that the root node is labeled with a zero, and all nodes sharing the label 1 are connected (Farris, 1977). In essence, each character evolves exactly once, but, in contrast to a perfect phylogeny, an arbitrary number of back-mutations are allowed. Unfortunately, every set of character data admits a Dollo phylogeny. Clearly, the notion of Dollo phylogeny is too permissive to be useful in linguistic phylogenetics.

Przytycka et al. (2006) propose the notion of a *conservative Dollo phylogeny* (CDP), which is a Dollo phylogeny satisfying an additional condition: any two characters that occur together in their 1 states at an internal node must also occur together in their 1 states at some leaf node. For example, the tree in Figure 1 is a CDP.

In the context of language evolution, the CDP condition implies that for any two characters in some ancestral language, there exist corresponding evidence in the form of a known language possessing both of those characters. This is a very strong requirement for which numerous linguistic counter-examples can be found, but it is much less strong, and therefore more more likely to be satisfied, than the requirement for a perfect phylogeny. We expect the CDP condition to guide our heuristic search algorithm towards more realistic phylogenetic reconstructions, especially in cases where a number of diverse languages share a relatively small set of reliable characters.

Few non-trivial datasets representing language families admit a CDP. This may be attributed either to borrowing or to the violation of the CDP condition. Since we have no way distinguish between the two explanations, in the remainder of this paper we will simply refer to such events as borrowings. In most cases, our objective is to establish the minimum number of those instances.

2.3 Chordal graphs

In this section we define the notions of chordal and intersection graphs that underlie our heuristic search algorithm.

Graph $G = (V, E)$, where E is the set of edges, and V is the set of vertices, is an *intersection graph* of a family of sets $\mathcal{R}$ if there is a one-to-one and onto function (*bijection*) $\mathcal{F}$ between V and $\mathcal{R}$ such that

$$\forall s, t \in R : (F(s), F(t)) \in E \text{ iff } s \cap t \neq \emptyset \quad (1)$$

Informally, each vertex in the intersection graph represents a set, and two vertices are connected by an edge if and only if the two corresponding sets intersect. Figure 2 shows an example of an intersection graph. Given sets, we can compute their intersection graph in linear time.

A *chord* of a cycle is an edge between two non-consecutive vertices of a cycle. A *chordless cycle* is a cycle with no chords. A *chordal graph* is a graph with no chordless cycles of length greater than three. Figure 3 shows an example of a chordal graph. Rose et al. (1976) provide a linear-time recognition algorithm for chordal graphs.

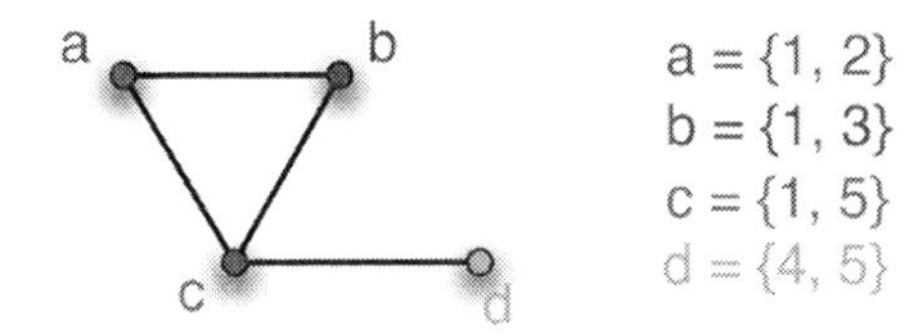

Figure 2: An example of a family of sets on the right and an intersection graph of those sets on the left.

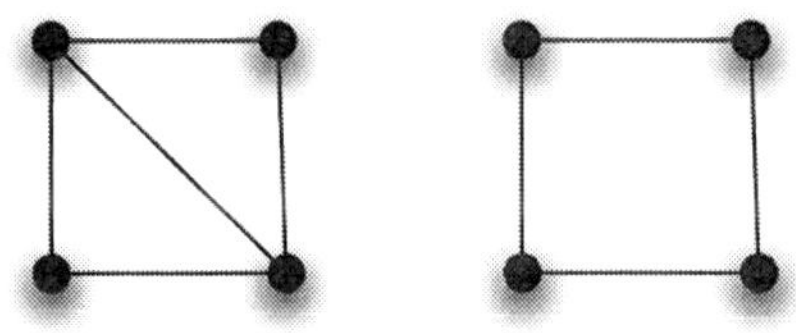

Figure 3: An example chordal graph on the left, and a graph that is not chordal on the right.

We can consider a character in phylogeny data as a set composed of the individuals or languages that possess that character. For example, the set for a cognate is the set of languages that contain that cognate. Przytycka et al. (2006) prove that a set of characters admits a CDP if and only if their intersection graph is chordal. Therefore, it is possible to determine whether a set of characters admits a CDP in linear time. We employ this result in order to infer phylogenetic trees of languages.

3 Heuristic search

Our search algorithm takes the intersection graph of the character data as input, and finds the minimum number of vertices (characters, in this case) that must be removed to produce a chordal graph. We take advantage of the fact that a character dataset admits a CDP if and only if the intersection graph of the character data is chordal. Our heuristic breadth-first search is guaranteed to find the minimum number of the inconsistent vertices.

One key observation allows this search to execute in reasonable time:

Observation 1. *Let $G = (V, E)$ be a graph. Let C be a chordless cycle of G. Let V' be a set of vertices such that removing V' from G results in a chordal graph. Then V' must include at least one vertex on C.*

Algorithm 1 Our main heuristic search algorithm.
search(Graph $G = (V, E)$, List *currentSolution*)

Vertex v $\leftarrow$ isChordal(G);
if v = null **then**
    Print *currentSolution*
    return
end if
Vector candidates $\leftarrow$ *getCandidates*(G, v)
for all Vertex u in candidates **do**
    Add u to *currentSolution*
    Graph $G' \leftarrow G[V \backslash \{u\}]$
    search$(G',$ *currentSolution*$)$
    Remove u from *currentSolution*
end for

Algorithm 2 Candidate generator.
getCandidates(Graph $G = (V, E)$, Vertex v)

Cycle $C \leftarrow$ the vertices of the shortest chordless cycle of length ≥ 4 containing v
if $|C| > 4$ **then**
    Cycle $C_4 \leftarrow$ a chordless cycle of length 4 if one exists in G
    if C_4 is not null **then**
        return C_4
    end if
end if
return C

Proof. Assume that V' contains none of the vertices in C. Then all vertices of C are in $V \backslash V'$. Therefore C is present in the graph obtained by removing V' from G, which is chordal by definition of V', a contradiction. □

By applying the above observation inductively, at each stage of our search, we need only consider as successor states the states produced by removing a vertex in a chordless cycle of our graph.

The pseudo-code of our heuristic search is shown in Algorithm 1. Subroutine *isChordal* takes a graph as a parameter, and returns a vertex that belongs to a chordless cycle, or *null* if G is chordal. The subroutine implements the algorithm based on lexicographic breadth-first search proposed by Rose et al. (1976). The subroutine *getCandidates* for selecting the candidate nodes to be considered in the search is formalized in Algorithm 2. It gets all vertices on a chordless cycle, and identifies them as candidates for removal. In order to guarantee optimality, we need to recursively consider removing each of these vertices. Observation 1 makes this search computationally feasible in experimental data. In the worst case, the algorithm has exponential running time in the size of the input data, which is what we expect in the case of an exact algorithm applied to an NP-complete problem.

3.1 Language grouping

In order to make our experiments computationally tractable, we follow Nakhleh et al. (2005a) in combining sets of languages into single units. For example, we consider the Germanic languages as a single group because we are confident that their most recent common ancestor is not an ancestor of any other language. The operation of language grouping is performed as a preprocessing step to the construction of the intersection graph of the characters.

Beyond achieving the goal of decreasing computation time, we expect that the application of language grouping will actually make our data closer to admitting a CDP in a way consistent with true evolutionary history. Consider two characters s and t that intersect in the context of language grouping L, but not without. Then s and t are not present in any of the same languages, but there are two languages $l_i, l_j \in L$ such that l_i has character s but not t, and language l_j has character t but not s. If s and t are only present within the language grouping, they are not informative when language family grouping is used. However, if both s and t are present at an internal node ancestral to language grouping L, then this will make the data closer to admitting a CDP by decreasing the number of borrowings that we need to posit.

3.2 Tree extraction

Once our search has found a minimum set of vertices to remove from our graph in order to make it chordal, we extract a phylogenetic tree from the resulting graph. Gavril (1974) shows that chordal graphs are the intersection graphs of subtrees of a tree, and gives a polynomial-time algorithm to build a corresponding family of subtrees. Following Przytycka et al. (2006), we use the union of those subtrees as a phylogenetic tree for our languages.

Figure 4: The tree given by our algorithm for Chinese dialect cognate data.

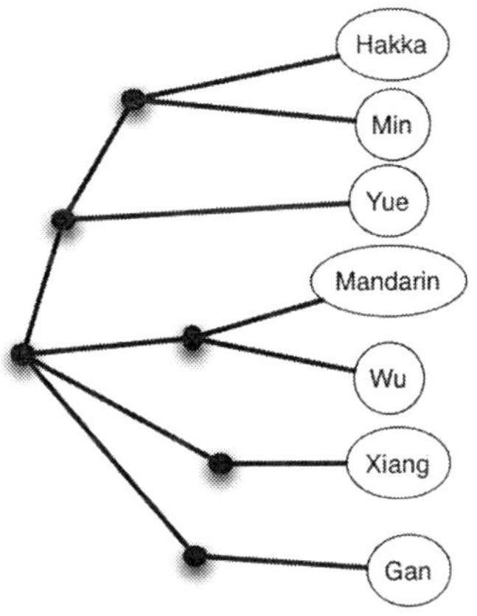

4 Experiments

In order to assess the suitability of the CDP approach to linguistic phylogeny we performed experiments on three datasets.

4.1 Chinese dialects

The data consist of 15 cognates across seven Chinese dialects compiled by Minett and Wang (2003). The set can be characterized as relatively small and clean.

The tree produced by our algorithm (Figure 4, which is non-binary, is completely consistent with one of the five binary trees (Type III) of Minett and Wang (2003). Also, our tree shares the grouping of Hakka and Min with all five of their proposed trees.

Minett and Wang (2003) show that in order to explain their data, at least seven borrowings must have occurred. Our algorithm gives the same number.

The experiment confirms that our method is sound, and produces results that are open to further elucidation.

4.2 CPHL subset

The dataset consists of 22 phonological characters and 13 morphological characters for 24 Indo-European languages from the Computational Phylogenetics in Historical Linguistics (CPHL) project[1]. We decided to exclude the lexical characters which are the most likely to be borrowed.

For example, one phonological character identifies languages that underwent the loss of initial y when it was followed by e. Three languages (Hittite, Luvian, and Lycian) which exhibit that sound change are encoded as character 1, while the remaining Indo-European languages are encoded as character 2.

Figure 5 shows the tree produced by our method on the CPHL subset. No characters needed to be removed from the intersection graph of the characters to yield a chordal graph, which can be interpreted that our CDP assumption is reasonable.

There are several differences between the tree in Figure 5 and the tree presented on the website of the CPHL project. First, Albanian is grouped with the Armenian and Greek languages rather than with the Germanic languages. Second, there is a node of high degree linking four language subfamilies. This result implies that the character set is not sufficiently large to establish a more detailed relationship between those subfamilies.

Nakhleh et al. (2005a) use the CPHL dataset to build perfect phylogenetic networks. However, their approach requires a phylogenetic tree as input, and minimizes borrowing events over only that tree. In contrast, our approach minimizes borrowing events over all possible phylogenetic trees without enumerating them.

4.3 Comparative Indo-European Data Corpus

The dataset consists of 84 Swadesh 200-word lists representing contemporary Indo-European languages (Dyen et al., 1992). We used only the most reliable cognate sets numbered between 002 and 099, which contain forms that are cognate with each other and not cognate with the forms belonging to other sets. Each cognate set is treated as a separate character. For grouping purposes, we divided the languages into the following ten groups: Celtic, Romance, Germanic, Baltic, Slavic, Indic, Greek, Armenian, Iranian, and Albanian.

As a further simplifying step, we identified all cases where the same language group contains multiple cognate sets representing the same Swadesh meaning. For example, consider the words for 'neck': Nepali *manto* is cognate with Irish *muineal*, while Gujarati *gerden* is cognate with Macedonian *vrat*. In such cases, we removed all but one of the cognate sets involved, provided they are found in only two language families. In our example, we therefore remove the cognate set

[1] http://www.cs.rice.edu/~nakhleh/CPHL/

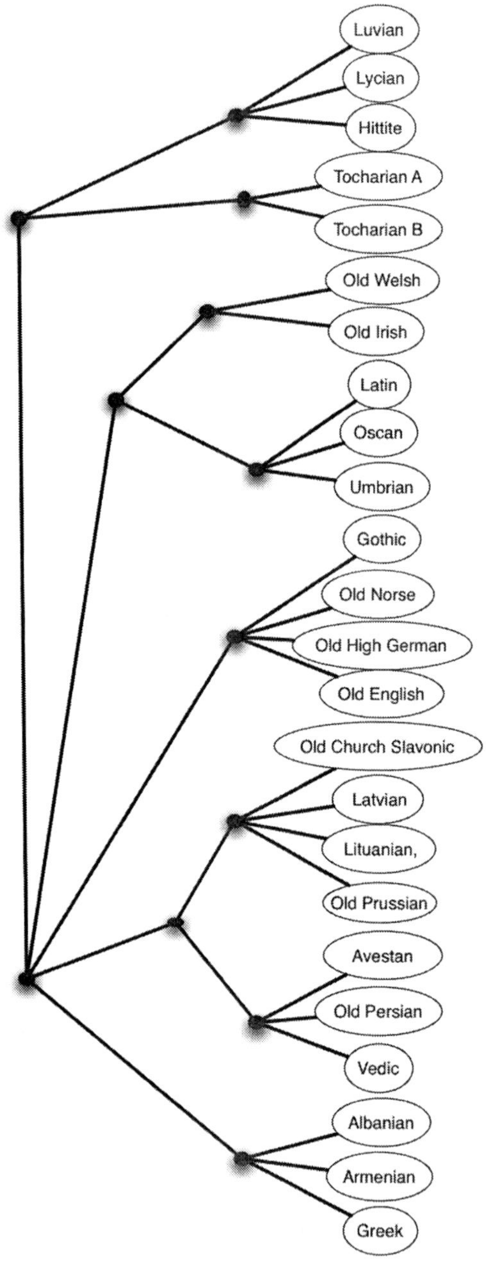

Figure 5: The tree given by our algorithm for the CPHL dataset, morphological and phonological characters only, with no language grouping.

shared between the Celtic and Indic families. This does not affect the total number of required borrowings.

Figure 6 shows the tree obtained when we ran our search on the Comparative Indo-European Data Corpus with language grouping. To construct this tree, our search found a minimum set of eight inconsistent cognates. We have analyzed these cognates, and while a few are inherited, most are either borrowings or annotation errors (e.g., Slovenian *jagat* 'to hunt' or Albanian *tuti* 'all').

Although the consensus about the exact form of the Indo-European language phylogeny is yet to be reached in spite of many decades of research, our tree conforms to several well-established facts, including the affinity betwen Baltic and Slavic, Indic and Iranian, and the *Satem core*. However, there are some differences in comparison with the tree proposed by the CPHL project.

In Figure 6, the Albanian and Germanic languages are more closely grouped with the Celtic and Romance languages than the Baltic, Slavic, Indic, Greek and Armenian Languages. The opposite is true in the tree proposed by Nakhleh et al. (2005a). However, they note that the Germanic languages seem to have exhibited a large amount of borrowing compared to the other languages they considered, and mention that on their trees the position of Albanian is uncertain. If Germanic has undergone a substantial amount of non-tree-like evolution, then it is unsurprising that it is the major source of disagreement between our and their trees.

Our tree in Figure 6 also differs from our tree in Figure 5, in which a single vertex branches to many groups of languages. Another difference is the placement of Albanian.

Gray and Atkinson (2003) also built a phylogenetic tree for the Indo-European languages using the Comparative Indo-European Data Corpus. Their tree differs significantly from that proposed by Nakhleh et al. (2005a). The tree produced by Gray and Atkinson (2003) does not group Balto-Slavic with Indo-Iranian, while both our tree and the tree in (Nakhleh et al., 2005a) do. Gray and Atkinson (2003) instead groups Balto-Slavic with the Germanic, Romance, and Celtic language families. The placement of Albanian is different in all three trees. All three trees group Baltic with Slavic, Armenian with Greek, and Indic with Iranian.

Figure 6: The tree given by our algorithm for the Comparative Indo-European Data Corpus with language grouping.

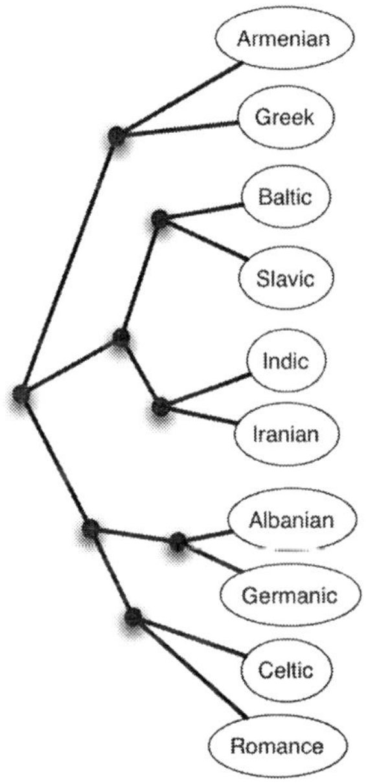

5 Tiered search

We noticed when running experiments that characters that are thought in the literature to be borrowed are often present in few language families, whereas characters that are thought to be ancestrally inherited are often present in a larger number of language families. We therefore devised a tiered version of our heuristic search. In this version, we first run the search on only the characters that are present at more than two language families. We find the minimum number of these characters that must be removed to result in a chordal graph, remove that minimum set from the overall dataset, and run a subsequent search on this set in which the only vertices that are allowed to be removed are present at exactly two language families. We finally concatenate the minimum set of vertices that this search finds with the minimum set found in the earlier search to produce our overall minimal set of borrowing events.

We tested tiered search on the Comparative Indo-European Data Corpus. Our results were negative. In particular, the resulting tree fails to group Baltic and Slavic together, which is universally accepted in historical linguistics. This suggests that the observation is not sufficiently general to improve the proposed method.

6 Future work

We plan to extend our research on several directions.

First, our heuristic search could likely be made more efficient, though not asymptotically. Apart from the careful selection of nodes to evaluate as noted in Observation 1, we perform no search tree pruning. There are likely choices of nodes to be evaluated that are strictly dominated by other nodes. For example, consider two vertices u, v in a chordless cycle C of length greater than three such that the only neighbors of u are in C, but v is also in other chordless cycles, and has neighbors outside C. Then the choice to remove v strictly dominates the choice to remove u.

Second, we plan to modify our search procedure to minimize the total number of borrowings. rather than the total number of borrowed characters. We have found that in our experiments that minimizing the later has always minimized the former, but this may not be the case in all datasets.

Finally, we intend to improve the speed of the heuristic search, which would enable us to run tests on larger and more inconsistent datasets.

7 Conclusion

We have proposed conservative Dollo-phylogeny as a model for linguistic phylogenetics. We devised and tested an algorithm for calculating the minimum number of inconsistent characters within a dataset over all possible phylogenetic trees without enumerating those trees. We tested this approach on three datasets with positive results.

The main advantage of this approach is its speed. All computations took very little time - on the order of seconds. Previous approaches have been much slower. The trees produced by our method are therefore useful not only in their own right, but also as a very rapid initial stage of a computation. One possible approach would be to quickly generate trees with our method, and then use them as input to a more exhaustive algorithm.

Our approach calculates the minimum number of characters that are inconsistent with CDP across all possible phylogenetic trees without actually considering these trees individually. The CDP model and our heuristic algorithm may be particularly useful in cases where the number of languages is large, or where not even a partial tree is known.

Acknowledgements

This research was supported by the Natural Sciences and Engineering Research Council of Canada. The authors thank Dr. Lorna Stewart for cooperation.

References

William Day, David Johnson, and David Sankoff. 1986. The computational complexity of inferring rooted phylogenies by parsimony. *Mathematical Biosciences*, 81:33–42.

Isidore Dyen, Joseph B. Kruskal, and Paul Black. 1992. An Indoeuropean classification: A lexicostatistical experiment. *Transactions of the American Philosophical Society*, 82(5).

James S. Farris. 1977. Phylogenetic analysis under Dollo's law. *Systematic Zoology*, 26(1):77–88.

Joseph Felsenstein. 2004. *Inferring Phylogenies*. Number 1. Sinauer Associates, Massachusetts, USA.

Fanica Gavril. 1974. The intersection graphs of subtrees in trees are exactly the chordal graphs. *Journal of Combinatorial Theory (B)*, 16:47–56.

Russell D. Gray and Quentin D. Atkinson. 2003. Language-tree divergence times support the anatolian theory of Indo-European origin. *Nature*, 426(6965):435–439, November.

John M. Lewis and Mihalis Yannakakis. 1980. The node-deletion problem for hereditary properties is NP-complete. *Journal of Computer and System Sciences*, 20:219–230.

James W. Minett and William S.-Y Wang. 2003. On detecting borrowing: Distance-based and character-based approaches. *Diachronica*, 20:289–331(43).

Luay Nakhleh, Don Ringe, and Tandy Warnow. 2005a. Perfect phylogenetic networks: A new methodology for reconstructing the evolutionary history of natural languages. *Language (Journal of the Linguistic Society of America)*, 81(2):382–420.

Luay Nakhleh, Tandy Warnow, Don Ringe, and Steven N. Evans. 2005b. A comparison of phylogenetic reconstruction methods on an IE dataset. *The Transactions of the Philological Society*, 3(2):171 – 192.

Teresa Przytycka, George Davis, Nan Song, and Dannie Durand. 2006. Graph theoretical insights into evolution of multidomain proteins. *Journal of computational biology*, 13(2):351–363.

Donald J. Rose, R. Endre Tarjan, and George S. Leuker. 1976. Algorithmic aspects of vertex elimination on graphs. *SIAM Journal of Computing*, 5(2):266–283.

Cross-domain Feature Selection for Language Identification

Marco Lui and Timothy Baldwin
NICTA VRL
Department of Computer Science and Software Engineering
University of Melbourne, VIC 3010, Australia
saffsd@gmail.com, tb@ldwin.net

Abstract

We show that transductive (cross-domain) learning is an important consideration in building a general-purpose language identification system, and develop a feature selection method that generalizes across domains. Our results demonstrate that our method provides improvements in transductive transfer learning for language identification. We provide an implementation of the method and show that our system is faster than popular standalone language identification systems, while maintaining competitive accuracy.

1 Introduction

Language identification (LangID) is the task of determining the language(s) that a text is written in. It is considered by some researchers to be a solved task, because previous research has reported near-perfect accuracy (Cavnar and Trenkle, 1994). Hughes et al. (2006) elaborated a number of simplifying assumptions that have made this the case, and Baldwin and Lui (2010a) showed that when some of these assumptions are relaxed to make the task closer to the actuality of open-web LangID, it becomes considerably harder. In this paper, we demonstrate that the style of evaluation used by Baldwin and Lui (2010a) performs well in-domain but badly cross-domain, and develop a novel method for preserving high in-domain accuracy, while significantly boosting cross-domain accuracy. Similarly to Baldwin and Lui (2010a), we make the simplifying assumption that all documents are monolingual, despite recent work on multilingual LangID (Baldwin and Lui, 2010b).

LangID is usually formulated as a supervised machine learning problem and evaluated in an offline setting (Cavnar and Trenkle, 1994; Baldwin and Lui, 2010a). However, its primary use is online without any additional configuration, optimized for maximal cross-domain accuracy. A number of such standalone LangID systems are available, notable among which is `TextCat` (van Noord, 1997). `TextCat` has been the LangID solution of choice in research, and is the basis of language identification/filtering in the ClueWeb09 Dataset (Callan and Hoy, 2009) and Corpus-Builder (Ghani et al., 2004). Elsewhere, Google provides LangID as a web service via its Google Language Detect API (`GoogleAPI`). While it has much higher accuracy than `TextCat` (as we show in Section 6.1), research applications contravene the service's terms of use, and moreover the service is rate-limited.

Our ideal system should offer the same advantages as `TextCat` in terms of licensing and run-time speed, while matching the open-domain accuracy and ease-of-use of an API such as `GoogleAPI`. To this end, we release the optimized final LangID system described in this paper, and benchmark it against `TextCat` and `GoogleAPI`. Our major contributions are: (1) we show that negative transfer occurs when training a classifier over a combined set of LangID datasets; (2) we show that language models learned in a particular domain do not always generalize to other domains; (3) we develop a method for extracting features for LangID that are not tied to a particular domain, and show that our method mitigates negative transfer and provides improvements in cross-domain LangID; (4) we show that our method can incorporate additional languages without a penalty in performance on existing languages; and (5) we provide an implementation of our method that is faster than state-of-the-art LangID systems while maintaining competitive accuracy.

2 Background

LangID as a computational task is usually attributed to Gold (1967), who sought to investigate language learnability from a language theory perspective. However, its current form is much more recognizable in the work of Cavnar and Trenkle (1994), where the authors classified documents according to rank order statistics over byte n-grams between a document and a global language profile. Since the 1990s, LangID has been formulated as a supervised machine learning task, and has been greatly influenced by text categorization in general. Monolingual LangID of a test document D_i takes the form of a mapping onto a unique language from a closed set of languages C, i.e. $\mathcal{I} : D_i \rightarrow c_i \in C$.

Statistical approaches applied to LangID include the use of Markov models over n-gram frequencies (Dunning, 1994) and dot products of word frequency vectors (Darnashek, 1995). Kernel methods have also been applied to the task of LangID (Kruengkrai et al., 2005). Linguistically motivated models for LangID have also been proposed, such as stop word list overlap (Johnson, 1993), where a document is classified according to its overlap with lists for different languages. There has also been work on word and part of speech correlation (Grefenstette, 1995), cross-language tokenisation (Giguet, 1995) and grammatical-class models (Dueire Lins and Gonçalves, 2004).

LangID has been applied in a variety of domains, including USENET messages (Cavnar and Trenkle, 1994), web pages (Kikui, 1996; Martins and Silva, 2005; Liu and Liang, 2008), and web search queries (Hammarstrom, 2007; Ceylan and Kim, 2009). It has been shown to improve performance of other tasks such as parsing (Alex et al., 2007) and multilingual text retrieval (McNamee and Mayfield, 2004). It has also been used for gathering data for linguistic corpus creation (Ghani et al., 2004; Baldwin et al., 2006; Xia et al., 2009; Xia and Lewis, 2009), and is an important area of research for supporting low-density languages (Hughes et al., 2006; Abney and Bird, 2010).

Transfer learning refers to the use of data from external domains to improve task performance on a target domain. Pan and Yang (2010) provide a survey, in which they define *transductive* transfer learning, where labels are available in source domain(s) but not in the target domain. This corresponds exactly to our task, where we wish to train a classifier using language-labelled data from a variety of sources, and apply this classifier to target data without making any assumptions about its domain. Pan and Yang (2010) also discuss the phenomenon of *negative transfer*, whereby including data from the source domain(s) results in reduced performance in the target domain.

Other work has used the term *domain adaptation* to refer to *inductive* transfer learning, where labels are available in both the source and target domains, and the goal is to improve the performance in the target domain (Daumé III and Marcu, 2006; Daumé III, 2007). Daumé III and Marcu (2006) tackle this problem by using a mixture model, where data in a specific domain is modelled as coming from a mixture of domain-specific and general components, and the linkage between domains is achieved by sharing a single general component. In our task, we have no labels in the target domain, and thus know nothing about the domain-specific component. Thus, our challenge is to build a suitable model of the general component, which we do by eliminating features that make minimal contribution to the general component. This approach makes the conversion of documents to a standardized representation much simpler than a model that decomposes individual features into general and domain-specific components.

Dataset	Docs	Langs	Doc Length (bytes)
JRC-ACQUIS	20000	22	18478.5±60836.8
CLUEWEB09	20000	10	36909.0±20735.2
DEBIAN	21735	89	12329.8±30902.7
RCV2	20000	13	3382.7±1671.8
WIKIPEDIA	20000	68	7531.3±16522.2
N-EUROGOV	1500	10	17460.5±39353.4
N-TCL	3174	60	2623.2±3751.9
N-WIKIPEDIA	4963	67	1480.8±4063.9

Table 1: Summary of the LangID datasets

3 Data Sources

For this work, we collected language-labelled development data from five sources of diverse origin, and use these as the basis of our examination of in-domain, inductive (all-domain) and transductive (cross-domain) learning. We additionally use three independent test data sets to validate the effectiveness of the final methodology. Statistics of all datasets are provided in Table 1.

3.1 Development data sets

JRC-ACQUIS: JRC-ACQUIS is an aligned multilingual parallel corpus (Steinberger et al., 2006) totalling 463792 documents in 22 languages. From the corpus, we randomly selected 20000 documents without replacement, maintaing the relative skew of languages. For each document, only the text enclosed in the <body> tags was retained.

CLUEWEB09: The ClueWeb09 dataset (Callan and Hoy, 2009) consists of about 1 billion web pages in 10 languages.[1] The language of each document was automatically detected using `TextCat`, an implementation of the algorithm of Cavnar and Trenkle (1994). We sampled 20000 instances from the dataset by selecting the first instance in each of 20000 files selected without replacement. Because the language labels are automatically assigned, they do not constitute a true gold-standard, and we thus use CLUEWEB09 exclusively as a training dataset in Section 6.

WIKIPEDIA: Wikimedia provides dumps of the complete contents of all Wikipedia wikis.[2] Individual languages have their own wiki, usually under the corresponding ISO 639-1 code. We obtained XML dumps of the wikis with valid ISO 639-1 codes. From these dumps, we selected 20000 pages in a skew-preserving fashion. In order to ensure that each language contained at least 20 documents, we limited selection to the 68 largest wikis by page count. The data we used was obtained from July–August 2010.

RCV2: Reuters RCV2[3] consists of over 487000 Reuters News stories in 13 languages. We randomly selected 20000 documents in a skew-preserving fashion.

DEBIAN: The Debian Project maintains manual translations of the content strings of a large number of software packages.[4] We obtained all translations with codes corresponding to valid ISO 639-1 codes. This resulted in 21735 language-package pairs in 89 languages.

For each dataset, we randomly divided the documents into two equal-sized partitions. One partition was used for selecting language features and for training, and the other was used for testing. To distinguish between them, we label the partitions A and B, respectively. For example, DEBIAN_A is the partition of the DEBIAN dataset used to compute feature weights and language models, and DEBIAN_B is the partition used for testing. We also make frequent use of the union of the A partitions across all datasets, and will refer to this as UNION_A.

[1]`http://boston.lti.cs.cmu.edu/clueweb09/`

[2]`http://dumps.wikimedia.org/backup-index.html`

[3]`http://trec.nist.gov/data/reuters/reuters.html`

[4]`http://i18n.debian.net/material/po/unstable/main/`

3.2 Test data sets

In order to evaluate accuracy in the transductive learning setting, we make use of N-EUROGOV, N-TCL and N-WIKIPEDIA, the three datasets described in detail by Baldwin and Lui (2010a). N-EUROGOV was sourced from the EuroGOV collection used in the 2005 Web-CLEF task, N-TCL was manually sourced by the Thai Computational Linguistics Laboratory (TCL) in 2005 from online news sources, and N-WIKIPEDIA is drawn from a 2008 dump of Wikipedia, with normalization.

4 Learning Algorithms

In this work, we use a multinomial naive Bayes learner. For brevity, we only give a short sketch of the technique; it is described in much more detail by McCallum and Nigam (1998). The crux of the method is to compute the probability that an instance belongs to a class C_i from a given closed set C, and hence assign the most probable class to a document D, consisting of a vector of n features $x_1 \ldots x_n$:

$$c = argmax_{C_i \in C} P(C_i|D)$$

Bayes' theorem allows us to re-express this as:

$$c = argmax_{C_i \in C} \frac{P(D|C_i)P(C_i)}{P(D)}$$

where $P(D)$ is a normalizing constant independent of C_i. Thus for classification, we only need to estimate $P(D|C_i)$ and $P(C_i)$. C is modelled as a categorical distribution over classes, and so $P(C_i)$ is obtained via a maximum likelihood estimate. In order to estimate $P(D|C_i)$, we make the naive assumption that each term is conditionally independent, hence:

$$P(D|C_j) = \prod_{i=1}^{n} \frac{P(t_i|C_j)^{N_{D,t_i}}}{N_{D,t_i}!}$$

where N_{D,t_i} is the frequency with which term t_i occurs in D.

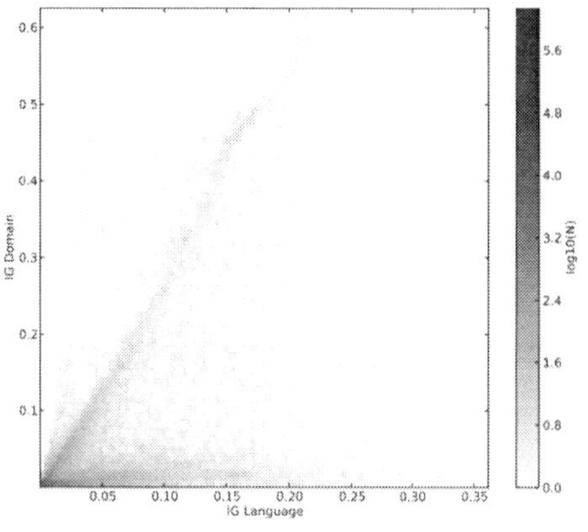

Figure 1: Scatter plot of IG for language vs. IG for domain (byte trigrams)

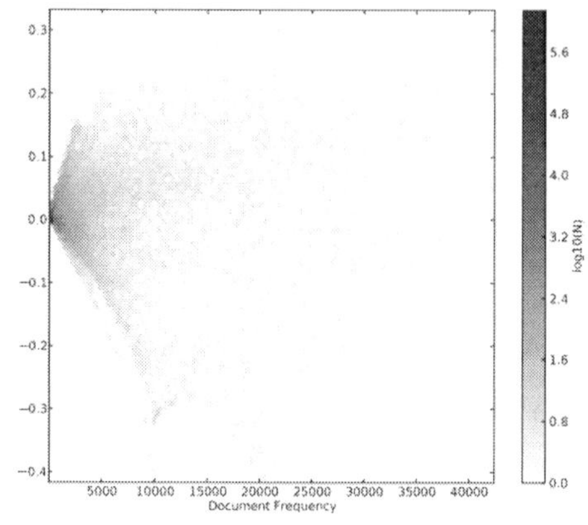

Figure 2: Scatter plot of DF vs. $\mathcal{LD}$ (byte trigrams)

The reason we select multinomial naive Bayes is that it is relatively lightweight and has been shown to be highly accurate when combined with feature selection (McCallum and Nigam, 1998; Manning et al., 2008). To establish the generalizability of our results, we also experimented with a nearest prototype classifier based on skew divergence (Lee, 2001), based on the findings of Baldwin and Lui (2010a). However, when combined with feature selection, we found it was consistently outperformed by the naive Bayes classifier, and thus omit results from this paper. We also experimented with a linear-kernel SVM learner, but once again omit results as we found it to be comparable in accuracy to naive Bayes when combined with feature selection, but much slower to retrain.

5 Feature Selection

The document representation that we use is a mixture of byte n-grams (Cavnar and Trenkle, 1994; Baldwin and Lui, 2010a), as it is language-neutral in that it does not make any assumptions about the language or language type of each document. In particular, we make no assumptions about word delimitation (e.g. via white space) in each language. Results from Baldwin and Lui (2010a) additionally suggest that explicit encoding detection is not necessary in LangID, and that the simple byte tokenization strategy also used in this work is superior to encoding-aware codepoint-based tokenization. Where we have data in more than one encoding, we do not transcode it; instead we simply extract byte features across all the encodings. In practice this is not an issue as the data that we use is mostly UTF8-encoded, with small quantities of other encodings (esp. in N-TCL). We make no further mention of encoding as it is not the focus of this work.

Cavnar and Trenkle (1994) perform feature selection over such a mixture of n-grams, where $1 \leq n \leq 5$. Their feature selection method is based on the frequency of terms, where the N most frequent terms for each language are retained in the global feature set. Related to term frequency is document frequency, where rather than counting individual terms in a class, we count the number of documents that a particular term appears in. Feature selection based on document frequency has been shown to be inferior to other methods. Generally it has been found that Information Gain ($\mathcal{IG}$: Quinlan (1986)) is particularly suited to feature selection in multiclass problem settings such as LangID (Yang and Pedersen, 1997; Forman, 2003).

The novel aspect of our research is that we consider $\mathcal{IG}$ of particular n-gram features along multiple dimensions: (1) with respect to the set of all languages; (2) with respect to a given language; and (3) with respect to the domain the data was obtained from. We are interested in identifying features that have high $\mathcal{IG}$ with respect to language but low $\mathcal{IG}$ with respect to domain.

For each of 1-grams, 2-grams and 3-grams we computed the $\mathcal{IG}$ of each feature with respect to the set of all languages in our development datasets (97 languages), as well as with respect to the set of 5 domains. A scatter plot of $\mathcal{IG}$ for language vs. domain for 3-grams is presented in Figure 1. From this analysis, it is clearly visible that there are two distinct groups of features: one where the $\mathcal{IG}$ for language is strongly correlated with that for domain, and one where the $\mathcal{IG}$ for language is largely independent of that for domain. We are interested in identifying features in the second group, and so for each feature we compute a $\mathcal{LD}$ ($\mathcal{L}$anguage-$\mathcal{D}$omain) score, defined as:

$$\mathcal{LD}^{all}(t) = \mathcal{IG}^{all}_{lang}(t) - \mathcal{IG}_{domain}(t)$$

The number of features to consider grows exponentially with n-gram order. This makes calculating the $\mathcal{IG}$ for higher token n-gram orders computationally infeasible. Yang and Pedersen (1997) found that document frequency ($\mathcal{DF}$) and $\mathcal{IG}$ were strongly correlated. Thus, we studied the relationship between $\mathcal{LD}$ and $\mathcal{DF}$ in our data, and found that low $\mathcal{DF}$ is a good predictor of low $\mathcal{LD}$ score, but not vice versa, as seen in Figure 2. As $\mathcal{DF}$ is much cheaper to compute than $\mathcal{IG}$, we first identify the 15000 features with highest $\mathcal{DF}$ for a given n-gram order, and assign a $\mathcal{LD}$ score of 0 to all features outside this set.

We also consider an alternative formulation of $\mathcal{LD}$. Due to skews between the quantities of data for each language, the highest-ranked features by $\mathcal{LD}$ tend to be biased towards the more common languages. In order to mitigate this, we also consider a formulation whereby we compute a $\mathcal{LD}^{bin}$ score for each feature conditioned on each language l:

$$\mathcal{LD}^{bin}(t|l) = \mathcal{IG}^{bin}_{language}(t|l) - \mathcal{IG}_{domain}(t)$$

In order to give better representaiton to less-frequent languages, we then select the top-scoring features from each language, and define the $\mathcal{LD}^{bin}$ feature set as the union of these features.

The number of features N is a parameter in both methods that we will investigate empirically in Section 6.

6 Experimental Setup and Results

The results presented in Baldwin and Lui (2010a) are based on cross-validation within datasets, without considering the applicabiliy of a model learned in one domain to LangID in another domain. Baldwin and Lui (2010a) also presented preliminary results with regards to feature selection, based on the Cavnar and Trenkle (1994) method. We first compare results with and without feature selection using our $\mathcal{LD}^{bin}$ and $\mathcal{LD}^{all}$ metrics, as well as $\mathcal{IG}^{all}_{lang}$—where we select the top features according to their information gain with the set of all languages—and finally $\mathcal{IG}^{bin}_{lang}$—where we select a fixed number of features per language, according to their information gain with the language.

Baldwin and Lui (2010a) found that byte bigrams performed well as a feature set for LangID, so we use them for this initial experiment. Tokenizing across all of our datasets results in 57160 unique bigrams. For $\mathcal{IG}^{all}_{lang}$ and $\mathcal{LD}^{all}$, we consider the top 2000 to 10000 features, in increments of 1000. For the per-language metrics, we experiment with selecting 100 to 800 features per langauge, in increments of 100.

We perform this experiment in two settings: (1) the supervised learning setting, where we use training and test data from the same domain; and (2) the inductive transfer learning setting, where we train a single classifier on UNION_{A}—the union of the A partitions across the five domains—and use this to classify partition B from each of the five domains in turn. We found that for $\mathcal{IG}^{all}_{lang}$, 10000 features produced the best results; for $\mathcal{IG}^{bin}_{lang}$, it was 100 features per class, corresponding to 4078 features; for $\mathcal{LD}^{all}$, it was 3000 features; and for $\mathcal{LD}^{bin}$ it was 200 features per class, corresponding to 3086 features. We report the results for the best parametrization of each feature selection metric in Tables 2 and 3. In each case, we present the classification accuracy for the full feature set ("Full"), followed by the classification accuracy for feature selection over the same combination of training and test dataset, as the Δ over Full. In all our experiments, the language skew present in each domain is preserved in both the training and the test partitions.

In the supervised case, the accuracy attained is similar when using the full feature set as for the respective reduced feature sets. This shows that utilizing the reduced feature sets does not harm in-domain classification accuracy, implying that we are able to preserve the key features required for classifying the data.

In the case of inductive transfer learning, we observe negative transfer: the greater amount of training data causes the accuracy to drop. This is particularly evident over RCV2, where adding in data from the other four domains results in a drop in accuracy from 0.973 to 0.576. We find that the $\mathcal{LD}$ features are generally able to better mitigate this than the $\mathcal{IG}_{lang}$ features. $\mathcal{LD}^{bin}$ features pro-

Train	Eval	Full	$\mathcal{IG}^{all}_{lang}$	$\mathcal{IG}^{bin}_{lang}$	$\mathcal{LD}^{all}$	$\mathcal{LD}^{bin}$
JRC-ACQUIS$_A$	JRC-ACQUIS$_B$	0.985	+0.000	+0.007	+0.007	+0.005
DEBIAN$_A$	DEBIAN$_B$	0.963	+0.003	+0.002	−0.001	−0.016
RCV2$_A$	RCV2$_B$	0.973	−0.017	−0.016	−0.003	+0.026
WIKIPEDIA$_A$	WIKIPEDIA$_B$	0.935	+0.017	+0.020	+0.030	+0.001

Table 2: In-domain supervised learning accuracy, relative to all features ("Full")

Train	Eval	Full	$\mathcal{IG}^{all}_{lang}$	$\mathcal{IG}^{bin}_{lang}$	$\mathcal{LD}^{all}$	$\mathcal{LD}^{bin}$
UNION$_A$	JRC-ACQUIS	0.931	−0.001	+0.039	+0.060	+0.062
	DEBIAN	0.817	−0.031	+0.049	+0.122	+0.127
	RCV2	0.576	−0.048	+0.129	+0.347	+0.410
	WIKIPEDIA	0.739	−0.150	−0.070	+0.179	+0.179

Table 3: Inductive Transfer Learning (all-domain) accuracy, relative to all features ("Full")

vide the best accuracy over each dataset in the inductive transfer learning setting, increasing accuracy over RCV2 to 0.986, exceeding the accuracy of the in-domain classification on the full feature set. We find that $\mathcal{LD}^{bin}$ features can also improve accuracy for in-domain classification, increasing accuracy on RCV2 to a near-perfect 0.999. These results validate the choice of $\mathcal{LD}^{bin}$ as a suitable metric for selecting general features for LangID.

Since our aim is to build a classifier in a transductive transfer learning setting, we examined the behaviour of the $\mathcal{LD}^{bin}$ features in such a setting over our 5 datasets. For each dataset, we trained a classifier on the A partitions, and evaluated the classifier on the B partition of each of the other datasets. Since each dataset covers a different set of languages, there may be languages in the evaluation dataset that are not present in the training dataset. It makes no sense to attempt to classify documents in these languages since we will by definition misclassify them, so the results reported in Table 4 are only over languages in the evaluation set that are also present in the training set. As a result, caution must be exercised in naively comparing accuracy figures across different combinations of training and test datasets.

In Table 4, we see several examples of language models not generalizing to other domains. For example, we see that when using all features, the language models learned from RCV2 classify data from the RCV2 domain with accuracy 0.973, but this drops to 0.838, 0.889 and 0.796 in other domains. We also find that language models from other domains have reduced accuracy when classifying RCV2 data. We find that in all these cases, using the $\mathcal{LD}^{bin}$ features mitigates this loss in accuracy. On RCV2 in particular, use of the $\mathcal{LD}^{bin}$ features results in over 0.95 accuracy when training with any of the 5 domains.

There is a number of domains where the use of the $\mathcal{LD}^{bin}$ features results in a loss in accuracy relative to the full feature set. This contrasts with our results in the inductive learning setting. We hypothesize that this is due to the $\mathcal{LD}^{bin}$ features having been selected from the union of all 5 datasets. While this feature set represents a general model across these 5 domains, for a specific pair of domains there will be some additional features that are strong predictors of language.

Preliminary work by Baldwin and Lui (2010a) suggested that feature selection over a mixture of n-grams yielded promising results. This is also supported by Cavnar and Trenkle (1994), who use a mixture of 1- to 5-grams. We thus investigated the interaction between the range of n-gram orders used for feature selection, the number of features selected per language and classification accuracy. Based on the results in Tables 2, 3 and 4, we used the $\mathcal{LD}^{bin}$ metric exclusively.

We conducted a parameter search for maximum token order M (e.g. $M = 3$ would mean all 1-, 2- and 3-grams) and number of features per language N. We considered $1 \leq M \leq 9$ and $100 \leq N \leq 800$ in increments of 100 features. We tested all combinations exhaustively in a supervised learning task across the union of all 5 datasets. We found that the best results are obtained for $M \geq 4$ and $N \geq 300$. In order to maximize classification rate we need to minimize the number of features used, so we chose $M = 4$ and $N = 300$, producing a feature set consisting of 7480 features.

In building a universal LangID tool, we need to quantify the effect of training on languages extraneous to the target domain. To investigate this, we perform experiments over the datasets of Baldwin and Lui (2010a) using two different classifiers: a reference classifier trained on all languages

Training	Test Dataset: JRC-ACQUIS Full	JRC-ACQUIS $\mathcal{LD}^{bin}$	DEBIAN Full	DEBIAN $\mathcal{LD}^{bin}$	RCV2 Full	RCV2 $\mathcal{LD}^{bin}$	WIKIPEDIA Full	WIKIPEDIA $\mathcal{LD}^{bin}$
JRC-ACQUIS	0.985	+0.005	0.979	−0.055	0.812	+0.174	0.977	−0.026
CLUEWEB09	0.981	−0.005	0.989	−0.010	0.925	+0.069	0.927	−0.039
DEBIAN	0.983	−0.003	0.963	−0.016	0.689	+0.261	0.937	−0.058
RCV2	0.838	+0.148	0.889	−0.003	0.973	+0.026	0.796	+0.154
WIKIPEDIA	0.837	+0.141	0.863	+0.011	0.561	+0.407	0.935	+0.001

Table 4: Transductive transfer learning (cross-domain) accuracy relative to all features ("Full")

Test Dataset	langid.py Accuracy	langid.py docs/s	TextCat ΔAcc	TextCat Slowdown	TextCat (retrained) ΔAcc	TextCat (retrained) Slowdown	GoogleAPI ΔAcc	GoogleAPI Slowdown
JRC-ACQUIS	0.991	69.8	−0.164	18.5×	−0.075	11.1×	+0.004	7.0×
DEBIAN	0.969	94.1	−0.305	25.1×	−0.129	14.2×	−0.043	9.4×
RCV2	0.992	146.6	−0.642	34.9×	−0.922	19.1×	+0.005	14.6×
WIKIPEDIA	0.959	102.7	−0.210	26.2×	−0.365	14.9×	−0.012	10.3×
N-EUROGOV	0.987	68.5	−0.046	18.1×	−0.083	11.1×	+0.006	6.9×
N-TCL	0.904	172.1	−0.299	38.8×	−0.232	22.5×	+0.018	17.2×
N-WIKIPEDIA	0.913	209.2	−0.207	45.9×	−0.227	25.7×	−0.010	20.9×

Table 5: Comparison of standalone classification tools, in terms of accuracy and speed (documents/second), relative to `langid.py`

present in the training set, and a domain-specific classifier trained only on languages in the test set. The reference classifier is trained on 1–4-grams, selecting 300 features per language on the full 97 languages, whereas each domain-specific classifier is trained only on the subset of languages present in the target domain.

Figure 3 shows a scatter plot of the per-language accuracy over the different datasets. Rather than harming performance, we find that adding languges extraneous to the target domain generally has no impact on accuracy over the languages in the dataset. In fact, it occasionally positively impacts on accuracy (points to the left of the diagonal), and for the rare instances where it hurts accuracy (points to the right of the diagonal), the difference is relatively modest.

6.1 Comparison to existing tools

Our ultimate interest is in building a standalone classifier that is fast and accurate. For comparison to existing tools, we implemented our method as a Python module (`langid.py`), in the form of a single Python file with pre-trained models for 97 languages. It can act as a standalone LangID system, an embedded Python module, or a web service with an AJAX API.[5]

We compared the speed and accuracy of our system to `TextCat`, as well as `GoogleAPI`. `GoogleAPI` is constrained to: (1) limit the classification rate to 10 documents/second, and (2) base the classification only on the first 500 bytes of the document. These constraints are imposed by the service's terms of use. For `TextCat`, we test it: (1) off-the-shelf using the pre-trained language models, and (2) after retraining it over the same training data as `langid.py`.

Table 5 shows the accuracy of each system across 7 test datasets, as well as the speed in documents per second. We present absolute accuracy and speed for `langid.py`, and relative accuracy and slowdown for the other classifiers. The machine used to perform this experiment was a commodity desktop-class machine, with an Intel Q9400 4-Core CPU, 4GB of RAM and a 7200RPM SATA II hard drive. The slowdown for `GoogleAPI` is reported based on a classification rate of 10 documents per second.

We find that in general, `langid.py` is faster and more accurate than `TextCat` (both off-the-shelf and re-trained). The difference is smallest over a "traditional" LangID dataset like N-EUROGOV which contains only 10 languages, and is much more pronounced over a dataset like N-TCL which has a much larger variety of languages. Comparing `langid.py` and `GoogleAPI`, the two systems are evenly matched in accuracy, but again, `langid.py` is significantly faster. All differences in accuracy are statistically significant (McNemar's test, $p < 0.01$).

We note that the accuracy of `langid.py` is slightly lower on N-TCL than on other datasets. N-TCL has a high proportion of non-UTF8 doc-

[5]The code is available for public download from `http://www.csse.unimelb.edu.au/research/lt/resources/langid/`

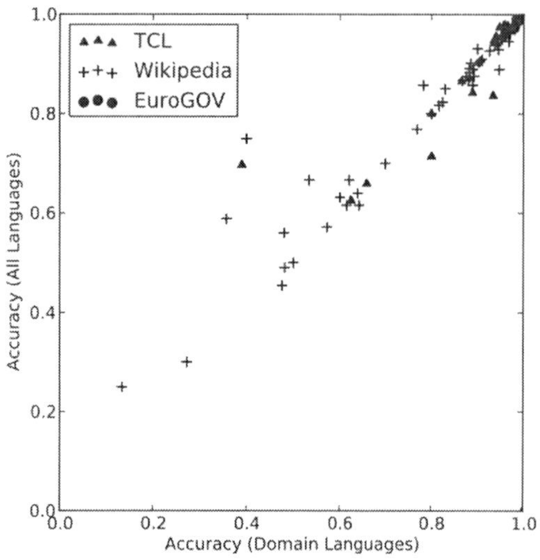

Figure 3: Per-language accuracy of a classifier trained only on languages present in the evaluation domain (x-axis) vs. all languages (y-axis)

Test dataset	Feature selection		
	TextCat	$\mathcal{CT}$	$\mathcal{LD}^{bin}$
N-EuroGOV	0.904	+0.067	+0.083
N-TCL	0.672	+0.016	+0.227
N-Wikipedia	0.686	+0.084	+0.223

Table 6: Comparison of `TextCat` to a `NB` classifier using $\mathcal{CT}$ and $\mathcal{LD}^{bin}$ for feature selection, using UNION_A as the training data

uments (57%). To quantify the effect of this, we transcoded all the documents in N-TCL to UTF8 and repeated the experiment. We found that after transcoding, the accuracy of `langid.py` increased from 0.904 to 0.947. This indicates that unsupported encodings have a small impact on accuracy, though it is relatively minor considering that the majority of the data is not UTF8-encoded.

The are two key conceptual differences between `TextCat` and `langid.py`: feature selection and learning algorithm. `TextCat` ($\mathcal{CT}$) selects features per language by term frequency, whereas `langid.py` uses $\mathcal{LD}^{bin}$ (the focus of this work). On the other hand, the learning algorithm used by `TextCat` is a nearest-prototype method using the token rank difference metric of Cavnar and Trenkle (1994), whereas `langid.py` uses multinomial naive Bayes. In order to consider these differences independently, we combine the $\mathcal{CT}$ feature selection with the multinomial naive Bayes learner, selecting the union of the top-300 features per language by document frequency over 1- to 5-grams, yielding 10846 features. For comparison, we also selected the top 300 features by $\mathcal{LD}^{bin}$ over 1- to 5-grams, yielding 8166 features. We then trained a naive Bayes classifier over UNION_A using the respective feature sets, and used it to classify each of N-EuroGOV, N-TCL and N-Wikipedia. In Table 6, we compare the accuracy of these two classifiers to (retrained) `TextCat`. Across all datasets, $\mathcal{LD}^{bin}$ is superior to $\mathcal{CT}$. Additionally, `NB` with $\mathcal{CT}$ is superior to `TextCat` (which uses the same feature selection strategy, with the nearest prototype learner), although the difference here is much smaller. This suggests that the bulk of the improvement of `langid.py` over `TextCat` is due to the use of $\mathcal{LD}^{bin}$, as developed in this research.

7 Conclusion

We demonstrated the problem of negative transfer in training a LangID system using language-labelled data from a variety of domains. We developed a method for identifying features that are strongly predictive of language across multiple domains by examining the difference in information gain of each feature with language and with the source domain. We used this method to compile a feature set from 50,000 documents in 97 languages across 5 datasets, and implemented this as a standalone LangID system using a naive Bayes classifier. We empirically compared our system to state-of-the-art LangID systems, and found our system to be faster whilst maintaining competitive accuracy.

Acknowledgments

The authors wish to thank Google for providing increased access to the Google AJAX Language Identification API for the purposes of this research. The first author was additionally a recipient of travel support from Google Australia.

NICTA is funded by the Australian Government as represented by the Department of Broadband, Communications and the Digital Economy and the Australian Research Council through the ICT Centre of Excellence program.

References

Steven Abney and Steven Bird. 2010. The human language project: building a Universal Corpus of the world's languages. In *Proceedings of the 48th Annual Meeting of the Association for Computational Linguistics*, pages 88–97, Uppsala, Sweden.

Beatrice Alex, Amit Dubey, and Frank Keller. 2007. Using foreign inclusion detection to improve parsing performance. In *Proceedings of the Joint Conference on Empirical Methods in Natural Language Processing and Computational Natural Language Learning 2007 (EMNLP-CoNLL 2007)*, pages 151–160, Prague, Czech Republic.

Timothy Baldwin and Marco Lui. 2010a. Language identification: The long and the short of the matter. In *Proceedings of Human Language Technologies: The 11th Annual Conference of the North American Chapter of the Association for Computational Linguistics (NAACL HLT 2010)*, pages 229–237, Los Angeles, USA.

Timothy Baldwin and Marco Lui. 2010b. Multilingual language identification: ALTW 2010 shared task dataset. In *Proceedings of the Australasian Language Technology Workshop 2010 (ALTW 2010)*, pages 5–7, Melbourne, Australia.

Timothy Baldwin, Steven Bird, and Baden Hughes. 2006. Collecting low-density language materials on the web. In *Proceedings of the 12th Australasian Web Conference (AusWeb06)*. `http://www.ausweb.scu.edu.au/ausweb06/edited/hughes/`.

Jamie Callan and Mark Hoy. 2009. *ClueWeb09 Dataset*. Available at `http://boston.lti.cs.cmu.edu/Data/clueweb09/`.

William B. Cavnar and John M. Trenkle. 1994. N-gram-based text categorization. In *Proceedings of the Third Symposium on Document Analysis and Information Retrieval*, Las Vegas, USA.

Hakan Ceylan and Yookyung Kim. 2009. Language identification of search engine queries. In *Proceedings of the Joint Conference of the 47th Annual Meeting of the ACL and the 4th International Joint Conference on Natural Language Processing of the AFNLP*, pages 1066–1074, Singapore.

Marc Darnashek. 1995. Gauging similarity with n-grams: Language-independent categorization of text. *Science*, 267:843–848.

Hal Daumé III and Daniel Marcu. 2006. Domain adaptation for statistical classifiers. *Journal of Artificial Intelligence Research*, 26(1):101–126.

Hal Daumé III. 2007. Frustratingly easy domain adaptation. In *Proceedings of the 45th Annual Meeting of the Association for Computational Linguistics (ACL 2007)*, pages 256–263, Prague, Czech Republic.

Rafael Dueire Lins and Paulo Gonçalves. 2004. Automatic language identification of written texts. In *Proceedings of the 2004 ACM Symposium on Applied Computing (SAC 2004)*, pages 1128–1133, Nicosia, Cyprus.

Ted Dunning. 1994. Statistical identification of language. Technical Report MCCS 940-273, Computing Research Laboratory, New Mexico State University.

George Forman. 2003. An Extensive Empirical Study of Feature Selection Metrics for Text Classification. *Journal of Machine Learning Research*, 3(7-8):1289–1305.

Rayid Ghani, Rosie Jones, and Dunja Mladenic. 2004. Building Minority Language Corpora by Learning to Generate Web Search Queries. *Knowledge and Information Systems*, 7(1):56–83.

Emmanuel Giguet. 1995. Categorization according to language: A step toward combining linguistic knowledge and statistic learning. In *Proceedings of the 4th International Workshop on Parsing Technologies (IWPT-1995)*, Prague, Czech Republic.

E. Mark Gold. 1967. Language identification in the limit. *Information and Control*, 5:447–474.

Gregory Grefenstette. 1995. Comparing two language identification schemes. In *Proceedings of Analisi Statistica dei Dati Testuali (JADT)*, pages 263–268.

Harald Hammarstrom. 2007. A Fine-Grained Model for Language Identication. In *Proceedings of Improving Non English Web Searching (iNEWS07)*, pages 14–20.

Baden Hughes, Timothy Baldwin, Steven Bird, Jeremy Nicholson, and Andrew MacKinlay. 2006. Reconsidering language identification for written language resources. In *Proceedings of the 5th International Conference on Language Resources and Evaluation (LREC 2006)*, pages 485–488, Genoa, Italy.

Stephen Johnson. 1993. Solving the problem of language recognition. Technical report, School of Computer Studies, University of Leeds.

Genitiro Kikui. 1996. Identifying the coding system and language of on-line documents on the internet. In *Proceedings of the 16th International Conference on Computational Linguistics (COLING '96)*, pages 652–657, Kyoto, Japan.

Canasai Kruengkrai, Prapass Srichaivattana, Virach Sornlertlamvanich, and Hitoshi Isahara. 2005. Language identification based on string kernels. In *Proceedings of the 5th International Symposium on Communications and Information Technologies (ISCIT-2005)*, pages 896–899, Beijing, China.

Lillian Lee. 2001. On the effectiveness of the skew divergence for statistical language analysis. In *Proceedings of Artificial Intelligence and Statistics 2001 (AISTATS 2001)*, pages 65–72, Key West, USA.

Jicheng Liu and Chunyan Liang. 2008. Text Categorization of Multilingual Web Pages in Specific Domain. In *Proceedings of the 12th Pacific-Asia Conference on Advances in Knowledge Discovery and Data Mining*, PAKDD'08, pages 938–944, Osaka, Japan.

Christopher D. Manning, Prabhakar Raghavan, and Hinrich Schütze. 2008. *Introduction to Information Retrieval*. Cambridge University Press, Cambridge, UK.

Bruno Martins and Mário J. Silva. 2005. Language identification in web pages. In *Proceedings of the 2005 ACM Symposium on Applied Computing (SAC '05)*, page 764.

Andrew McCallum and Kamal Nigam. 1998. A comparison of event models for Naive Bayes text classification. In *Proceedings of the AAAI-98 Workshop on Learning for Text Categorization*, Madison, USA.

Paul McNamee and James Mayfield. 2004. Character N-gram Tokenization for European Language Text Retrieval. *Information Retrieval*, 7(1–2):73–97.

Sinno Jialin Pan and Qiang Yang. 2010. A Survey on Transfer Learning. *IEEE Transactions on Knowledge and Data Engineering*, 22(10):1345–1359, October.

J.R. Quinlan. 1986. Induction of Decision Trees. *Machine Learning*, 1(1):81–106, October.

Ralf Steinberger, Bruno Pouliquen, Anna Widiger, Camelia Ignat, Tomaž Erjavec, Dan Tufis, and Dániel Varga. 2006. The JRC-Acquis: A multilingual aligned parallel corpus with 20+ languages. In *Proceedings of the 5th International Conference on Language Resources and Evaluation (LREC'2006)*, Geona, Italy.

Gertjan van Noord, 1997. *TextCat*. Software available at `http://odur.let.rug.nl/~vannoord/TextCat/`.

Fei Xia and William Lewis. 2009. Applying NLP technologies to the collection and enrichment of language data on the web to aid linguistic research. In *Proceedings of the EACL 2009 Workshop on Language Technology and Resources for Cultural Heritage, Social Sciences, Humanities, and Education (LaTeCH – SHELT&R 2009)*, pages 51–59, Athens, Greece.

Fei Xia, William Lewis, and Hoifung Poon. 2009. Language ID in the context of harvesting language data off the web. In *Proceedings of the 12th Conference of the EACL (EACL 2009)*, pages 870–878, Athens, Greece.

Yiming Yang and Jan O. Pedersen. 1997. A comparative study on feature selection in text categorization. In *Proceedings of the 14th International Conference on Machine Learning*.

A Wikipedia-LDA Model for Entity Linking with Batch Size Changing Instance Selection

Wei Zhang[†] **Jian Su**[‡] **Chew Lim Tan**[†]

[†]School of Computing
National University of Singapore
{z-wei,tancl}@comp.nus.edu.sg

[‡] Institute for Infocomm Research
sujian@i2r.a-star.edu.sg

Abstract

Entity linking maps name mentions in context to entries in a knowledge base through resolving the name variations and ambiguities. In this paper, we propose two advancements for entity linking. First, a Wikipedia-LDA method is proposed to model the contexts as the probability distributions over Wikipedia categories, which allows the context similarity being measured in a semantic space instead of literal term space used by other studies for the disambiguation. Furthermore, to automate the training instance annotation without compromising the accuracy, an instance selection strategy is proposed to select an informative, representative and diverse subset from an auto-generated dataset. During the iterative selection process, the batch sizes at each iteration change according to the variance of classifier's confidence or accuracy between batches in sequence, which not only makes the selection insensitive to the initial batch size, but also leads to a better performance. The above two advancements give significant improvements to entity linking individually. Collectively they lead the highest performance on *KBP-10* task. Being a generic approach, the batch size changing method can also benefit active learning for other tasks.

1 Introduction

Knowledge base population (KBP)[1] involves gathering information scattered among the documents of a large collection to populate a knowledge base (KB) (e.g. Wikipedia). This requires either linking entity mentions in the documents with entries in the KB or highlighting these mentions as new entries to current KB.

Entity linking (McNamee and Dang, 2009) involves both finding name variants (e.g. both *"George H. W. Bush"* and *"George Bush Senior"* refer to the 41st U.S. president) and name disambiguation (e.g. given *"George Bush"* and its context, we should be able to disambiguate which president it is referring to).

Compared with Cross-Document Coreference (Bagga and Baldwin, 1998) which clusters the articles according to the entity mentioned, entity linking has a given entity list (i.e. the reference KB) to which we disambiguate the entity mentions. Moreover, in the articles, there are new entities not present in KB.

For name disambiguation in entity linking, there has been much previous work which demonstrates modeling context is an important part of measuring document similarity. However, the traditional approach for entity linking treats the context as a bag of words, n-grams, noun phrases or/and co-occurring named entities, and measures context similarity by the comparison of the weighted literal term vectors (Varma *et al.*, 2009; Li *et al.*, 2009; McNamee *et al.*, 2009; Zhang *et al.*, 2010; Zheng *et al.*, 2010; Dredze *et al.*, 2010). Such literal matching suffers from sparseness issue. For example, consider the following four observations of *Michael Jordan* without term match:

1) Michael Jordan is a leading researcher in machine learning and artificial intelligence.

2) Michael Jordan is currently a full professor at the University of California, Berkeley.

3) Michael Jordan (born February, 1963) is a former American professional basketball player.

4) Michael Jordan wins NBA MVP of 91-92 season.

To measure the similarity of these contexts, the semantic knowledge underlying the words is needed.

Furthermore, current state-of-the-art entity linking systems (Dredze *et al.*, 2010; Zheng *et al.*, 2010) are based on supervised learning approach requiring lots of annotated training instances to achieve good performance. However, entity linking annotation is highly dependent on the KB. When a new KB comes, the annotating process needs to be repeated. We have tried to automate this annotating process (Zhang *et al.* 2010). However, as discussed in that paper, the distribution of the auto-generated data is not con-

[1] http://nlp.cs.qc.cuny.edu/kbp/2010/

sistent with the real dataset, because only some types of instances can be generated.

In this paper, we propose two approaches: (1) a Wikipedia-LDA model to effectively mine the semantic knowledge from the contexts of the mentions. Such topic model allows us to measure the similarity between articles and KB entries in the semantic space of Wikipedia category. (2) An instance selection strategy to effectively utilize the auto-generated annotation through an iterative process of selecting a representative, informative and diverse batch of instances at each iteration. The batch sizes at each iteration change according to the variance of classifier's confidence or accuracy between batches in sequence, which makes selection insensitive to the initial batch size and performs better than fixed size.

We conduct evaluation on *KBP-10* data (Ji *et al.*, 2010). Experiments show that the Wikipedia-LDA model is able to effectively capture the underlying semantic information and produce statistically significant improvement over literal matching alone. Correspondingly, instance selection can make the dataset more balanced and it also produces a significant gain in entity linking performance. Collectively, the two advancements lead the highest performance on *KBP-10* task. Being a generic approach, the batch size changing method proposed in this paper can also benefit active learning for other tasks.

The remainder of this paper is organized as follows. Section 2 introduces the framework for entity linking. We present our Wikipedia-LDA model in Section 3, and the instance selection in Section 4. Section 5 shows the experiments and discussions. Section 6 concludes our work.

2 Entity Linking Framework

Entity linking is done through two steps: name variation resolution and name disambiguation. Name variation resolution finds variants for each entry in KB and then generates the possible KB candidates for the given name mention by string matching. Name disambiguation is to map a mention to the correct entry in the candidate set.

2.1 Name Variation Resolution

Wikipedia contains many name variants of entities like confusable names, spelling variations, nick names, etc. We extract the name variants of an entry in KB by leveraging the knowledge sources in Wikipedia: "titles of entity pages", "disambiguation pages"[2], "redirect pages"[3] and "anchor texts". With the acquired name variants for entries in KB, the possible KB candidates for a given name mention can be retrieved by string matching. If the given mention is an acronym, we will expand it from the given article, and then use entity linking process.

2.2 Name Disambiguation

First, using a learning to rank method, we rank all the retrieved KB candidates to identify the most likely candidate. In this learning to rank method, each name mention and the associated candidates are formed by a list of feature vectors. During linking, the score for each candidate entry is given by the ranker. The learning algorithm we used is ranking SVM (Herbrich *et al.*, 2000).

Next, the preferred KB candidate is presented to a binary classifier (Vapnik, 1995) to determine if it is believed as the target entry for a name mention. From here, we can decide whether the mention and top candidate are linked. If not, the mention has no corresponding entry in KB (*NIL*). The base features adopted for both learning to rank and classification include 15 feature groups divided to 3 categories. A summary of the features is listed in Table 1. Due to the space limit, we only show the feature name, leaving out the feature details which can be found in (Dredze *et al.*, 2010; Zheng *et al.*, 2010).

Categories	Feature Names
Surface	Exact Equal Surface, Start With String of Query, End With String of Query, Equal Word Num, Miss Word Num
Contextual	TF-IDF Similarity, Similarity Rank, All Words in Text, NE Number Match, Country in Text Match, Country in Text Miss, Country in Title Match, Country in Title Miss, City in Title Match
Others	NE Type

Table 1: Base Feature Set

3 Wikipedia-LDA Model

In the similar task cross-document coreference (Han and Zhao 2009) and other tasks (e.g. text classification) (Wang and Domeniconi, 2008), Wikipedia concepts are used to model the text. Wikipedia concept is a kind of entity-level topic. In our approach, we use the cross-entity topic Wikipedia Categories to represent the semantic knowledge.

[2] http://en.wikipedia.org/wiki/Wikipedia:Disambiguation
[3] http://en.wikipedia.org/wiki/Wikipedia:Redirect

Thus, we model the contexts as the distributions over Wikipedia categories. Then, the similarity between the contexts can be measured in a semantically meaningful space. Finally, such semantic similarity, together with other base features, is incorporated in the trainable models to learn the ranker and classifier.

3.1 Modeling the Contexts as Distributions over Wikipedia Categories

Wikipedia requires contributors to assign categories to each article, which are defined as "major topics that are likely to be useful to someone reading the article". Thus, Wikipedia can serve as a document collection with multiple topical labels, where we can learn the posterior distribution over words for each topical label (i.e. Wikipedia category). Then, from the observed words in the mention's context and KB entry, we can estimate the distribution of the contexts over the Wikipedia categories. To obtain this distribution, we use a supervised Latent Dirichlet Allocation (LDA) model – labeled LDA defined by Ramage *et al.* (2009), which represents state-of-the-art method for multi-labeled text classification. It performs better on collections with more semantically diverse labels, which we need in order to leverage on the large semantically diverse categories from Wikipedia as the topical labels.

Figure 1 shows us a graphical representation of the labeled LDA for the multi-labeled document collection. Labeled LDA is a three level hierarchical Bayesian model. β is the multinomial distribution over words for a Wikipedia category, which has a Dirichlet prior with hyperparameter η. Both the category set Λ as well as the topic prior α influence the topic mixture θ. These distributions can be used to generate documents in the form of a collection of words (w). D is the number of documents, N is the document length and K is the number of categories.

After the model is trained by Wikipedia data, the distributions of KB entry and the article over K categories are estimated by calculating the topic proportions θ. θ is given by an EM procedure that treats θ as a parameter with Z missing.

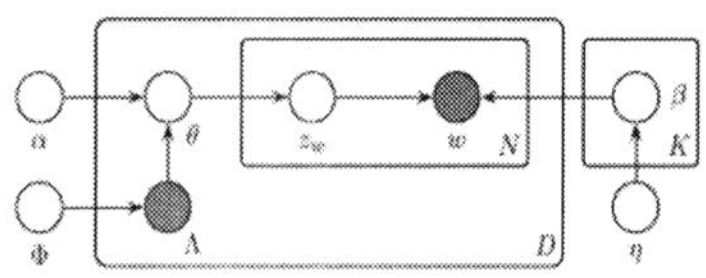

Figure 1: Graphical model of Labeled LDA

3.2 Context Similarity

We have mapped the contexts to a K-dimensional semantic space. Thus, we can calculate the context similarity by their distance in this space. To measure the context similarity in the K-dimensional topical space, we calculate the Cosine value as below:

$$Similarity_{d,e} = \frac{\sum_{k=1}^{K} \theta_{d,k} \times \theta_{e,k}}{\sqrt{\sum_{k=1}^{K} (\theta_{d,k})^2} \times \sqrt{\sum_{k=1}^{K} (\theta_{e,k})^2}} \quad (1)$$

Where d means the document with the name mention and e means the KB entry.

Such semantic similarity can be further combined with other term matching features for SVM ranker and classifier of entity linking.

3.3 Wikipedia Category Selection

Each article in Wikipedia is assigned several categories by the contributors as requested. However, from our observation some categories in Wikipedia may not be suitable to model the topics of a document. Thus, we shall consider selecting an appropriate subset from the Wikipedia categories to effectively model the contexts. We examined five possible category subsets: **All**, **All-admin**, **isa_all**, **isa_class**, and **isa_instance**.

Wikipedia contains 165,744 categories. This is the set **All.**

There are some meta-categories used for encyclopedia management in Wikipedia, e.g. "*Wikipedia editing guidelines*", which are unsuitable to describe the topics of a document. Thus, we remove the categories which contain any of the following strings: *wikipedia, wikiprojects, lists, mediawiki, template, user, portal, categories, articles* and *pages*. This leaves 127,325 categories (**All-admin**).

However, some categories such as "*people by status*" and "*Geography by place*" in the **All-admin** set cannot serve as the topics of a document properly. Thus, we need to remove them from the category set. From our observation, the topical categories are usually in *is-a* relation. For example, the relation between the two topical categories "*Olympic basketball players*" and "*Olympic competitors*" is an *is-a* relation, while the categories to be removed "*people by status*" and "*Geography by place*" are not in any *is-a* relation. We thus only select the categories connected by *is-a* relation to **isa_all** subset.

Since the categories are connected by unlabeled links in Wikipedia, we need to identify *is-a* relation links. We use the four methods as below proposed by Ponzetto and Strube (2007) to distinguish *is-a* and *not-is-a* relation links.

We first use a syntax-based method: assign *is-a* to the link between two categories if they share the same lexical head lemma (e.g. "*British Computer Scientists*" and "*Computer Scientists*").

Then, we use structural information from the category network: (1) for a category *c*, look for a Wikipedia article *P* with the same name. Take all *P*'s categories whose lexical heads are plural nouns $CP = \{cp_1, cp_2, ..., cp_n\}$. Take all supercategories of *c*, $SC=\{sc_1, sc_2, ...,sc_k\}$. If the head lemma of one of cp_i matches the head lemma of sc_j, label the relation between *c* and sc_j as *is-a*. (2) assign *is-a* label to the link between two categories if a Wikipedia article is redundantly categorized under both of them. For example, "*Internet*" is categorized under both "*Computer networks*" and "*Computing*" and there is a link between "*Computer networks*" and "*Computing*". Then this link is assigned *is-a*.

Next, we use lexical-syntactic patterns in a corpus. This method uses two sets of patterns. One set is used to identify *is-a* relations (Caraballo, 1999; Hearst, 1992), for example "*such* NP_1 *as* NP_2", NP_1 and NP_2 are the values of categories and their subcategories respectively. The second set is used to identify *not-is-a* relations. For example "NP_1 *has* NP_2", where the link between NP_1 and NP_2 will be assigned *not-is-a*. These patterns are used with a corpus built from Wikipedia articles, and separately with the Tipster corpus (Harman and Liberman, 1993). The label is assigned by majority voting between the frequency counts for the two types of patterns.

Finally, we assign *is-a* labels to links based on transitive closures - all categories along an *is-a* chain are connected to each other by *is-a* links.

Another fact is that the categories defined by Wikipedia are not all classes. For example, "*Microsoft*" is an instance of the class "*Computer and Video Game Companies*", and it appears both as an article page and as a category in Wikipedia. We would like to further examine the two different subsets: **isa_class**, and **isa_instance** in **isa_all** set for entity linking. To distinguish instance and class in **isa_all** set, we use a structure-based method (Zirn *et al.*, 2008). The categories which have other subcategories or Wikipedia articles connected to them by *is-a* relation are assigned *class* label. In our problem, the remaining categories are approximately regarded as instances.

4 Instance Selection Strategy

In this section, we explore a method to effectively utilize a large-scale auto-generated data for entity linking.

In our pervious work (Zhang *et al.* 2010), we proposed automatically gathering large-scale training instances for entity linking. The basic idea is to take a document with an unambiguous mention referring to an entity *e1* in KB and replace it with its variation which may refer to *e1*, *e2* or others. For example, a mention "*Abbott Laboratories*" in a document only refers to one KB entry "*Abbott Laboratories*". "*Abbott Laboratories*" in the document is replaced with its ambiguous synonyms, including "*Abbott*" "*ABT*", etc. Following this approach, from the 1.7 million documents in *KBP-10* text collection, we generate 45,000 instances.

However, the distribution of the auto-generated data is not consistent with the real dataset, since the data generation process can only create some types of training instances. In the case of "*Abbott Laboratories*", more than ten "*Abbott*" mentions are linked to "*Abbott Laboratories*" entry in KB, but no "*Abbott*" example is linked to other entries like "*Bud Abbott*" "*Abbott Texas*", etc. Thus, we need an instance selection approach to reduce the effect of this distribution problem. However, the traditional instance selection approaches (Brighton and Mellish, 2002; Liu and Motoda, 2002) only can solve two problems: 1) a large dataset causes response-time to become slow 2) the noisy instances affect accuracy, which are different from our needs here. We thus propose an instance selection approach to select a more balanced subset from the auto-annotated instances. This instance selection strategy is similar to active learning (Shen *et al.*, 2004; Brinker, 2003) for reducing the manual annotation effort on training instances through proposing only the useful candidates to annotators. As we already have a large set of auto-generated training instances, the selection here is a fully automatic process to get a useful and more balanced subset instead.

We use the SVM classifier mentioned in Section 2.2 to select the instances from the large dataset. The initial classifier can be trained on a set of initial training instances, which can be a small part of the whole auto-generated data, or the limited manual annotated training instances available, e.g. those provided by *KBP-10*.

Our instance selection method is an iterative process. We select an informative, representative and diverse batch of instances based on current hyperplane and add them to the current training instance set at each iteration to further adjust the hyperplane for more accurate classification.

We use the distance as the measure to select informative instances. The distance of an instance's feature vector to the hyperplane is computed as follows:

$$Dist(w) = \left|\sum_{i=1}^{N} \alpha_i y_i k(s_i, w) + b\right| \qquad (2)$$

Where w is the feature vector of the instance, α_i, y_i and s_i correspond to the weight, class and feature vector of the ith support vector respectively. N is the number of the support vectors.

Next, we quantify the representativeness of an instance by its density. Such density is defined as the average similarity between this instance and all other instances in the dataset. If an instance has the largest density among all the instances in the dataset, it can be regarded as the centroid of this set and also the most representative instance.

$$Density(w_i) = \frac{\sum_{j \neq i} Sim(w_i, w_j)}{N-1} \qquad (3)$$

Where w is the instance in the dataset and N is the size of dataset. *Sim* is cosine similarity.

We combine the informativeness and representativeness by the function $\lambda(1 - Dist(w)) + (1 - \lambda)Density(w)$, in which *Dist* and *Density* are normalized first. The individual importance of each part in this function is adjusted by a tradeoff parameter λ (set to 0.5 in our experiment). The instance with the maximum value of this function will be selected first to the batch. This instance will be compared individually with the selected instances in current batch to make sure their similarity is less than a threshold β. This is to diversify the training instance in the batch to maximize the contribution of each instance. We set β to the average similarity between the instances in the original dataset. When a batch of α instances is selected, we add them to the training instance set and retrain the classifier.

Such a batch learning process will stop at the peak confidence of the SVM classifier, since Vlachos (2008) shows that the confidence of the SVM classifier is consistent with its performance. The confidence can be estimated as the sum of the distances to hyperplane for the instances of an un-annotated development set. The development set guides the selection process to solve the distribution problem mentioned above. Alternatively, we can also leverage on some annotated development data and use accuracy instead to guide the selection process. We explore both approaches for different application scenarios in our experiments.

We now need to decide how to set the batch size α at each iteration. It is straightforward to set a fixed batch size α (**Fixed Number**), which never changes during the process. However, there are some limitations as demonstrated in our experiment in this paper. First, the performance is sensitive to the batch size. Second, if we set the batch size too big, it will impede further improvement allowed by small batch size. But if we set the batch size too small from the beginning, it will dramatically increase the number of iterations needed which will make the selection too slow. To resolve the above issues, we change the batch size according to the variance of classifier's confidence on an un-annotated set. Thus, we assign an integer to α_1 and α_2 in the first two iterations, and α_i $(i > 2)$ in the ith iteration is computed as below (**Flexible Number**):

$$\alpha_i = \frac{\alpha_{i-1} * (con_{i-1} - con_{i-2})}{con_{i-2} - con_{i-3}} \qquad (4)$$

where con_i is the confidence of the classifier on the un-annotated dataset at i^{th} iteration.

Figure 2 summarizes the selection procedure.

Given: Initial Training Set $T=\{T_1, T_2 \ldots T_m\}$,
Original Set to be selected $A=\{A_1, A_2 \ldots A_n\}$,
Batch Set with the maximal size α.
Initialization: *Batch Set* = $\emptyset$
Loop until the confidence/accuracy of the classifier on a development set does not increase
  Train a Classifier on T
  Batch Set=$\emptyset$
  Update α according to Equation 4
  Loop until *Batch Set* is full
  - Select A_i with the maximal value P from A
    $P = \lambda(1 - Dist(w)) + (1 - \lambda)Density(w)$
  - RepeatFlag=false;
  - **Loop** for each A_k in *Batch Set*
      If $Sim(A_i, A_k) > \beta$ **Then**
        RepeatFlag=true
        Stop the Loop
  - **If** RepeatFlag==false **Then**
      Add A_i to *Batch Set*
  - Remove A_i from A

  $T = T \cup Batch\ Set$

Figure 2: Instance Selection Strategy

5 Experiments and Discussions

5.1 Experimental Setup

In our study, we use *KBP-10* knowledge base and document collection to evaluate our approach for entity linking. The KB is autogenerated from Wikipedia. The KB contains

Features	ALL	NIL	Non-NIL	ORG	GPE	PER
Base Features	83.2	88.2	77.2	82.1	75.1	92.5
Base + All	84.0	88.6	78.5	84.0	76.0	92.1
Base + All - admin	84.9	88.9	80.0	84.9	76.9	92.8
Base + isa_all	**85.9**	89.1	82.0	85.2	78.6	93.8
Base + isa_class	85.5	88.8	81.3	84.9	78.0	93.2
Base+isa_instance	83.9	88.9	77.8	82.9	76.6	92.1

Table 2: Results of Entity Linking for Semantic Features

818,741 different entries and the document collection contains 1.7 million documents. Each KB entry consists of the Wikipedia Infobox[4] and the corresponding Wikipedia page text. The test data has 2,250 mentions across three named entity types: Person (PER), Geo-Political Entity (GPE) and Organization (ORG). The documents containing these mentions are from newswire and blog text. The training set consists of 3,904 newswire mentions and 1,500 web mentions. In order to leverage name variant information mentioned in Section 2.1 and category network mentioned in Section 3.3, we further get Wikipedia data directly from Wikipedia website[5]. The version we use is released on Oct. 08, 2008.

For pre-processing, we perform sentence boundary detection derived from Stanford parser (Klein and Manning, 2003), named entity recognition using a SVM based system trained and tested on ACE 2005 with 92.5(P) 84.3(R) 88.2(F), and co-reference resolution using a SVM based resolver trained and tested on ACE 2005 with 79.5%(P), 66.7%(R) and 72.5%(F). In our implementation, we use the binary SVM[Light] developed by Joachims (1999) and SVM[Rank] developed by Joachims (2006). The classifier and ranker are trained with default parameters. The Stanford Topic Model Toolbox[6] is used for Labeled-LDA with default learning parameters.

We adopt micro-averaged accuracy used in *KBP-10* to evaluate our Entity Linker, i.e. the number of correct links divided by the total number of mentions.

5.2 System with Wikipedia-LDA

Table 2 lists the performance of entity linking with overall accuracy (*ALL*) as well as accuracy on subsets (*Nil, Non-Nil, ORG,GPE* and *PER*) of the data. In the first row, only base features described in Section 2.2 are used. This baseline system models the contexts with literal terms. The second to sixth rows report the results combining base features with semantic knowledge (i.e. the context similarity is computed by the five different subsets of Wikipedia categories mentioned in Section 3.3).

American novels	American film actors	Members of the National Academy of Sciences	American basketball players
novel	role	prize	**nba**
book	actor	**researcher**	**basketball**
story	films	**professor**	points
paperback	appeared	science	rebounds
plot	actress	nobel	games
print	television	institute	draft
edition	hollywood	theory	guard
isbn	california	physics	overall
hardback	roles	received	coach
characters	movie	sciences	**professional**
published	acting	medal	assists
man	married	chemistry	play
father	death	academy	**season**
love	character	award	forward
written	starred	ph. d	ncaa

Table 3: Sample Wikipedia Categories and Corresponding Top 15 Words

We see that all the five systems with semantic features perform better than the baseline system, which models the context similarity as literal term matching. Especially, the **isa_all** and **isa_class** can achieve significantly better result than the baseline ($\rho < 0.05$, χ^2 test). These results prove that the semantic knowledge underlying the contexts has good disambiguation power for entity linking. Table 3 tells the reason of the improvements. Table 3 shows us four sample Wikipedia categories and top 15 highly probable words identified by the topic model for these categories. The topic model successfully assigns a high probability to the words *"researcher"* and *"professor"* in the category *"Members of the National Academy of Sciences"*, and assign a high probability to the words "*nba*" "*basketball*" "*professional*" and "*season*" in the category *"American basketball players"*. Such semantic

[4] http://en.wikipedia.org/wiki/Template:Infobox
[5] http://download.wikipedia.org
[6] http://nlp.stanford.edu/software/tmt/tmt-0.3/

Methods	ALL	NIL	Non-NIL	ORG	GPE	PER
Auto_Gen	81.2	81.8	80.5	80.8	72.5	90.3
Auto_Gen+IS	**85.2**	87.5	82.5	84.4	78.5	92.8
KBP	83.2	88.2	77.2	82.1	75.1	92.5
KBP+Auto_Gen	82.2	83.8	80.4	81.7	75.6	89.5
KBP+Auto_Gen+IS	**85.5**	87.7	82.9	84.7	78.9	92.8

Table 4: Results of Entity Linking for Instance Selection

knowledge learned from Wikipedia data is helpful in the example of *"Michael Jordan"* mentioned in Section 1. This shows that entity linking can benefit from the semantic information underlying the words and overcome the shortcomings of literal matching.

We further compare the performances of the five different category subsets. From the last five rows of Table 2, we can see that **isa_all** subset performs best among the five subsets for disambiguation. This should be because **isa_all** includes more categories than **isa_class** and **isa_instance**, and thus can capture more semantic information. However, although **All** and **All-admin** include even more categories, they introduce many categories which are unsuitable to model the topics of a news article or blog text, such as the two categories mentioned in Section 3.3, "*people by status*" which is not in an *is-a relation* and "*Wikipedia editing guidelines*" which is used for encyclopedia management.

5.3 System with Instance Selection

Table 4 shows the results for evaluating our instance selection strategy. These experiments use the base features (Section 2.2).

5.3.1 With and Without Manual Annotated Data

We want to find out the effectiveness of our instance selection strategy if no manually annotated data is available. In the first block of Table 4, we compare the performances of the systems with and without instance selection. "*Auto_Gen*" uses the auto-generated dataset described at the beginning of Section 4 as the training set directly, and "*Auto_Gen+IS*" applies our instance selection to the auto-generated data for training. In the instance selection process, we use the KB entries with more than 15 linked documents in the auto-generated data as our Initial Training Set (1,800 instances) to train a classifier, and then use this classifier to select instance from the auto-generated dataset. The first block of Table 4 shows that our instance selection gives significant improvements ($\rho < 0.05$, χ^2 test). These improvements show our selection strategy makes the training set more balanced and it can effectively reduce the effect of distribution problem in the large scale dataset.

We further evaluate our instance selection strategy when a large manually annotated data is available in the second block of Table 4. *"KBP"* is trained on the manually annotated *KBP-10* training set. "*KBP+Auto_Gen*" is trained on *KBP-10* set and the auto-generated set. *"KBP+Auto_Gen+IS"* uses *KBP-10* training set as the Initial Training Set, and applies instance selection process to the auto-generated data. Comparing "*KBP+ Auto_Gen*" with "*KBP*", we can see that the unbalanced distribution caused serious problem which even pull down the performance achieved by the large manual annotation alone. The experiment results of "*KBP*" and "*KBP+Auto_Gen+IS*" show that our instance selection strategy appears very necessary to bring further improvements over the large manually annotated dataset (5,404 instances). These significant ($\rho < 0.05$, χ^2 test) improvements are achieved by incorporating more training instances in a reasonable way.

Comparing the performance of "*Auto_Gen+IS*" with *"KBP"* in Table 4, we can find that our method performs better without hard intensive work on annotating 5,404 articles. This proves that using our instance selection can save labor without compromise of entity linking accuracy. The pretty much same performance of "*Auto_Gen+IS*" with *"KBP +Auto_Gen+IS"* also confirms the above conclusion.

5.3.2 Fixed Size Vs. Changing Size

We are also interested in the effectiveness of the two schemes (i.e. Fixed Number and Flexible Number) of setting the batch size α mentioned in Section 4. In Figure 3, we set the batch size α in Fixed Number scheme and α_1 α_2 in Flexible Number scheme, to different numbers from 50 to 140 increasing 10 each time. We conduct instance selection to the auto-generated data. Figure 3 shows that flexible batch size outperforms the fixed size for entity linking. Especially, the improvement at α=50, 60 and 70 is significant ($\rho < 0.05$, χ^2 test). This proves that batch size should be in line with the variance of the classifier's confidence at each iteration of instance selection. Furthermore, in this Figure, the performance of flexible batch size is more stable than the Fixed Number scheme. This shows that Flexible Number scheme makes the entity linking system insensitive to the initial batch size during instance selection process. Thus the initial batch size of the experiments in Table 4 is set to 80, which we believe that very similar performance can be achieved even with a different initial size. Another fact is that the selection process is similar to active learning, which needs to manually annotate the selected instances in each batch. Thus, being a generic approach, the batch size changing method proposed in this paper can also benefit active learning for other tasks.

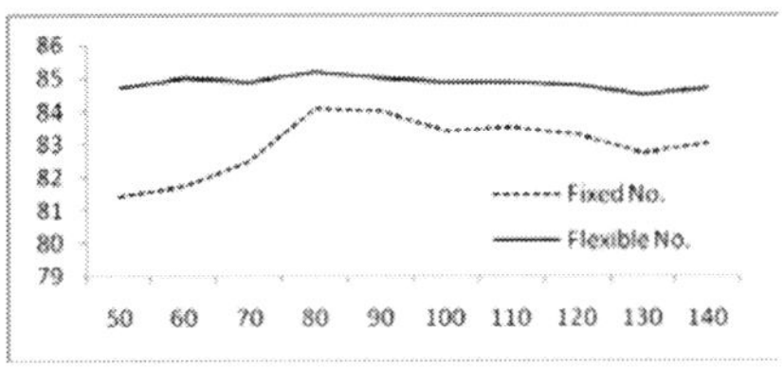

Figure 3: Performance Curves for Two Batch Size Schemes

5.3.3 (Un-)Annotated Development Set

In the above study, we directly use the test set without annotations as the development set for instance selection to optimize our solution to the application data. Such an approach will be useful when the application set is available in advance as in the case with *KBP* benchmarks.

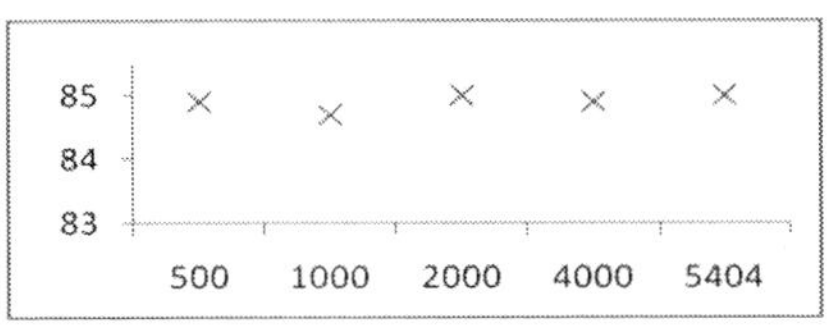

Figure 4: Annotated Development data

When the application set is unavailable beforehand, in other words, the articles to be linked only arrive one after the other in linking stage, we leverage on the accuracy on annotated development set for the instance selection. Figure 4 shows the performances on different sizes of annotated development set. The results show that the different sizes contribute more or less same performances. We only need to use a small amount of annotated development data, 500 articles in our study to guide the instance selection to achieve similar performance as with unannotated test set being development data.

5.4 Overall Result Combining Two Approaches

We also evaluate our model which combines the Wikipedia- LDA and Instance Selection together on *KBP-10* data, and compare our method with the top 7 systems in *KBP-10* shared task (Ji *et al.*, 2010). As shown in Figure 5, the first column is the performance of our system for entity linking, which outperforms the best solution[7] in *KBP-10* shared task.

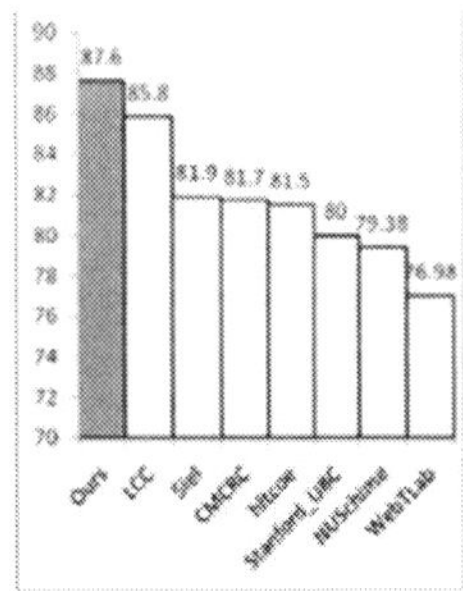

Figure 5: A Comparison with *KBP-10* Systems

6 Conclusion

In our paper, we explored using two innovative approaches for entity linking. We proposed a Wikipedia-LDA to entity linking, which can discover the semantic knowledge underlying the contexts. We also investigated the effectiveness of five subsets of Wikipedia categories to model the contexts. Furthermore, we proposed a batch size changing instance selection strategy to reduce the effect of distribution problem in the auto-generated data. It makes entity linking system achieve state-of-the-art performance without hard labor. Meanwhile, the flexible batch size not only makes the selection insensitive to the initial batch size, but also leads to a better performance than the fixed batch size. The above two advancements significantly improve entity linking system individually, and collectively they lead the highest performance on *KBP-10* task.

Acknowledgment

This work is partially supported by Microsoft Research Asia eHealth Theme Program.

[7] Another system submission shows 86.8%. However, it accesses web which is not allowed in *KBP* benchmark as the purpose to develop a standalone system, which is our focus here as well.

References

A. Bagga and B. Baldwin. 1998. Entity-Based Cross-Document Coreferencing Using the Vector Space Model. *36th Annual Meeting of the Association of Computational Linguistics*. 1998.

H. Brighton and C. Mellish. 2002. Advances in Instance Selection for Instance-Based Learning Algorithms. *Data Mining and Knowledge Discovery*.

K. Brinker. 2003. Incorporating Diversity in Active Learning with Support Vector Machines. In *Proceeding of ICML*. 2003.

S. A. Caraballo. 1999. Automatic construction of a hypernym-labeled noun hierarchy from text. In *Proceedings of the 37th Annual Meeting of the Association for Computational Linguistics*, College Park, Md., 20-26 June. 1999.

M. Dredze, P. McNamee, D. Rao, A. Gerber and T. Finin. 2010. Entity Disambiguation for Knowledge Base Population. *23rd International Conference on Computational Linguistics (COLING 2010)*, August 23-27, 2010, Bejing, China

X. Han and J. Zhao. 2009. Named Entity Disambiguation by Leveraging Wikipedia Semantic Knowledge. *Proceeding of the 18th ACM conference on Information and knowledge management* (2009).

D. Harman and M. Liberman. 1993. *TIPSTER Complete. LDC93T3A, Philadelphia, Penn. Linguistic Data Consortium*, 1993.

M. A. Hearst. 1992. Automatic acquisition of hyponyms from large text corpora. In *Proceedings of the 15th International Conference on Computational Linguistics*, Nantes, France, 23-28 August 1992.

R. Herbrich, T. Graepel and K. Obermayer. 2000. Obermayer. Large Margin Rank Boundaries for Ordinal Regression. *Advances in Large Margin Classifiers (pp. 115-132)*. 2000.

H. Ji, R. Grishman, H. Dang, K. Griffitt, and J. Ellis. 2010. Overview of the TAC 2010 Knowledge Base Population Track. In Proceedings of *Text Analysis Conference 2010*.

T. Joachims. 1999. Making large-Scale SVM Learning Practical. *Advances in Kernel Methods - Support Vector Learning*, MIT Press, 1999.

T. Joachims. 2006. Training Linear SVMs in Linear Time, *The ACM Conference on Knowledge Discovery and Data Mining (KDD)*, 2006.

D. Klein and C. D. Manning. 2003. Fast Exact Inference with a Factored Model for Natural Language Parsing. In *Advances in Neural Information Processing Systems 15 (NIPS 2002)*, Cambridge, MA: MIT Press, pp. 3-10.

F. Li, Z Zheng, F Bu, Y Tang, X Zhu, and M Huang. 2009. THU QUANTA at TAC 2009 KBP and RTE Track. *Text Analysis Conference 2009 (TAC 09)*.

H. Liu and H. Motoda. 2002. On Issues of Instance Selection. 2002. *Data Mining and Knowledge Discovery*, 6, 115-130. 2002.

P. McNamee and H. T. Dang. 2009. Overview of the TAC 2009 Knowledge Base Population Track. In *Proceeding of Text Analysis Conference 2009*

P. McNamee *et al.* 2009. HLTCOE Approaches to Knowledge Base Population at TAC 2009. *In Proceedings of Text Analysis Conference 2009 (TAC 09)*.2009.

S. P. Ponzetto and M. Strube. 2007. Deriving a Large Scale Taxonomy from Wikipedia. In *Proceedings of the 22nd National Conference on Artificial Intelligence*, Vancouver, B.C., 22-26 July, 2007, pp. 1440-1447.

D. Ramage, D. Hall, R. Nallapati and C. D. Manning. 2009. Labeled LDA: A supervised topic model for credit attribution in multi-labeled corpora. In Proceedings *of the 2009 Conference on Empirical Methods in Natural Language Processing*, 2009.

D. Shen, J. Zhang, J. Su, G. D. Zhou and C. L. Tan. 2004. Multi-Criteria-based Active Learning for Named Entity Recognition. In *Proceedings of the ACL 2004*.

V. Vapnik. 1995. The Nature of Statistical Leaning Theory. *Springer-Verlag, New York. 1995*

V. Varma *et al.* 2009. IIIT Hyderabad at TAC 2009. In *Proceedings of Text Analysis Conference 2009 (TAC 09)*.

A. Vlachos. 2008. A Stopping Criterion for Active Learning. *Computer Speech and Language*. 22(3):295-312. 2008.

P. Wang and C. Domeniconi. 2008. Building Semantic Kernels for Text Classification Using Wikipedia. 14th ACM SIGKDD International Conference on Knowledge Discovery and Data Mining. 2008

W. Zhang, J. Su, C. L. Tan and W. T. Wang. 2010. Entity Linking Leveraging Automatically Generated Annotation. *23rd International Conference on Computational Linguistics*, August 23-27, 2010.

Z Zheng, F Li, X Zhu and M Huang. 2010. Learning to Link Entities with Knowledge Base. In Proceedings of *the 11th Annual Conference of the North American Chapter of the Association for Computational Linguistics (NAACL)*. 2010. Los Angeles, CA

C. Zirn, V. Nastase and M. Strube. 2008. Distinguishing Between Instances and Classes in the Wikipedia Taxonomy. In *Proceedings of the 5th European Semantic Web Conference*, Tenerife, Spain, 1-5 June 2008.

Discovering Latent Concepts and Exploiting Ontological Features for Semantic Text Search

Vuong M. Ngo[1,2,3] and **Tru H. Cao**[1,2]

[1]HCMC University of Technology and [2]John von Neumann Institute, VNU-HCM, and [3]VNG Corporation

{vuong,tru}@cse.hcmut.edu.vn

Abstract

Named entities and WordNet words are important in defining the content of a text in which they occur. Named entities have ontological features, namely, their aliases, classes, and identifiers. WordNet words also have ontological features, namely, their synonyms, hypernyms, hyponyms, and senses. Those features of concepts may be hidden from their textual appearance. Besides, there are related concepts that do not appear in a query, but can bring out the meaning of the query if they are added. The traditional constrained spreading activation algorithms use all relations of a node in the network that will add unsuitable information into the query. Meanwhile, we only use relations represented in the query. We propose an ontology-based generalized Vector Space Model to semantic text search. It discovers relevant latent concepts in a query by relation constrained spreading activation. Besides, to represent a word having more than one possible direct sense, it combines the most specific common hypernym of the remaining undisambiguated multi-senses with the form of the word. Experiments on a benchmark dataset in terms of the MAP measure for the retrieval performance show that our model is 41.9% and 29.3% better than the purely keyword-based model and the traditional constrained spreading activation model, respectively.

1. Introduction

With rapid development of the World Wide Web and e-societies, Information Retrieval (IR) has many challenges in discovering and exploiting those rich and huge information resources. Semantic search improves search precision and recall by understanding user's intent and the contextual meaning of concepts in documents and queries (Huston and Croft, 2010; Losada, et al, 2010; Egozi, et al, 2011).

Concepts are named entities or WordNet words (unnamed entities). Named entities are those that are referred to by names such as people, organizations, and locations (Sekine, 2004) and could be described in ontologies. Each fully recognized named entity (NE) has three features, namely, name, class, and identifier. WordNet words are words in a lexical database (e.g. WordNet database). Each fully recognized WordNet word (WW) has three features, namely, form, direct hypernym, and sense.

Lexical search is not adequate to represent the semantics of queries referring to NEs or WWs. Some examples of NE-based queries are: (1) Search for documents about "*football clubs*"; (2) Search for documents about "*Barcelona*"; (3) Search for documents about "*Paris City*"; (4) Search for documents about "*Paris City, Texas, USA*". In fact, the first query searches for documents containing NEs of the class *Football Club*, e.g. *Chelsea* or *Barcelona*, rather than those containing the keywords "*football club*". For the second query, target documents may mention *Football Club Barcelona* under other names, i.e., the football club's aliases, such as *Football Club Barca*. Besides, documents containing *Barcelona City* or *Barcelona University* are also suitable. In the third query, users do not expect to receive answer documents about entities that are also named "*Paris*", e.g. the actress *Paris Hilton* or *University of Paris* but are not cities. Meanwhile, the fourth query requests documents about a precisely identified named entity, i.e., the *Paris City in Texas, USA*, not the one in France. That are, entity aliases, classes, and identifiers have to be taken into account.

Some examples about WW-based queries are: (1) Search for documents about "*movement*"; (2) Search for documents about "*movement belonging to change*"; and (3) Search for documents about "*movement belonging to the act of changing location from one place to another*". That is because the word *movement* has many different senses. In fact, the first query searches for documents containing not only the word *movement* but also its synonyms, e.g. *motion*, *front*, *cam-*

paign, and *trend*, or its hypernyms, e.g. *change*, *occurrence*, *social group*, *venture*, and *disposition*. For the second query, users do not expect to receive answer documents about words that are also labelled "*movement*", e.g. *movement belonging to a natural event* and *movement belonging to a venture*, but do not express changes. Meanwhile, the third query requests documents about a precisely identified word sense. The word *movement* means not only the action of changing something but also the act of changing location from one place to another, e.g. *the movement of people from the farms to the cities*.

Moreover, queries may contain both named entities and WordNet words. Some examples of NE-WW based queries are "*temblor in USA*" or "*natural calamity in USA*", for which documents about "*earthquake in United States of America*" are truly relevant answers.

Besides, there are latent concepts that do not appear in queries but present user's intent. Intuitively, adding correct related concepts to a query will increase the recall and the precision of searching. In contrast, adding incorrect related concepts will decrease performance of IR system. For examples, consider the following queries: (1) Search for documents about "*cities that are tourist destinations of Thailand*"; (2) Search for documents about "*tsunami in Southeast Asia*"; (3) Search for documents about "*settlements are built in west of Jerusalem*"; and (4) Search for documents about "*Barack Obama uses high-tech defences*". For the first query, Chiang Mai and Phuket should be added into the query, because they belong to class *City* and are *tourist destinations of Thailand*. For the second query, countries having relation "*is part of*" with *Southeast Asia* in the exploited ontology should be added into the query, e.g. *Indonesia* or *Philippine*. However, added countries should be those that were actually hit by at least one tsunami, according to the given ontology. So, *Laos* should not be added into the query. For the third query, if there are facts that *settlements are built in* the locations in the *west of Jerusalem*, e.g. *Givat Zeev* and *Pisgat Zeev*, then those locations should add into the query. For the fourth query, bullet-resistant suit should be added into the query; because it *is hyponym of high-tech defences* and the President *Barack Obama have used* a bullet-resistant suit.

In this paper, we propose a new ontology-based text search model with two key ideas as our two contributions. First, it exploits different ontological features of NE and WW existing in documents and queries. Until now, there is no other text search model that formally exploits and presents in documents and queries all above-mentioned NE features or all above-mentioned WW features. Specifically, in a context, after a disambiguation process, if a WordNet word has more than one sense with the equally highest rank, then the most specific common hypernym (msc_hypernym) of those senses will be chosen and the word will be represented by the pair of that hypernym and the form of the word. Meanwhile, other WordNet-based text search models choose one of those senses randomly or all of the senses (Vooheres, 1994; Liu, et al., 2004; Zaihrayeu, et al., 2007; Hsu, et al., 2008; Giunchiglia, et al., 2009). Second, our model expands a query by latent concepts relating to concepts and relations in the original query as asserted in employed ontologies. Our proposal is more general than Fu, et al. (2005), which considered only spatial relations.

In the next section, we discuss related works. Section 3 describes the proposed system architecture and detailed model. Section 4 presents evaluation of the proposed model and discussion on experiment results in comparison to other models. Finally, section 5 gives some concluding remarks.

2 Related Works

2.1 Exploiting Named Entities

There are works exploiting NEs but not for document search. The Falcons system described in Cheng, et al. (2008) is assisted by users to determine clearly the meaning of queries. In Cheng, et al. (2007), the authors use classes of NEs associated with keywords in a query. However, they are for entity search.

Vallet and Zaragoza (2008), Santos, et al. (2010), Demartini, et al. (2010), and Kaptein, et al. (2010) use only names and classes of NEs, and they are for entity ranking (Balog, et al. 2009).

Gupta and Ratinov (2008), Chang, et al. (2008), Wang, et al. (2009), and Jing, et al. (2010) use only labels of concepts (NE names or WW forms) to represent documents and queries. Moreover, they are for document classification, not document search.

There are some papers using named entity for document search. Bast et al. (2007) considers only entity classes in combination with keywords. In Ahn, et al. (2010), the NameSieve system uses only names and classes of NEs, and limits in four entity class: who, where, when and what. Beside, the system is helped by users to determine clearly the meaning of queries. In Egozi, et al. (2011), the authors use only names of concepts to present documents and queries.

2.2 Exploting WordNet

Voorhees (1994), Liu, et al. (2004) and Hsu, et al. (2008) use all forms of a sense and all forms of every hyponym of a sense in a query. Meanwhile, Zaihrayeu, et al. (2007) uses all forms of a sense to expand a document, and Wang, et. al. (2004) and Giunchiglia, et al. (2009) additionally use all forms of every hypernym of a sense in a document. Mihalcea and Moldovan (2000) use senses in both queries and documents, and all forms of every hypernym of a sense in a document.

Moreover, since the above-surveyed papers, except for Mihalcea and Moldovan (2000), use word forms to represent word senses, it may reduce the precision of system. Indeed, a query containing a word having form f and sense x could also match to documents containing a word having the same form f but different sense y. The drawback is similar with using only word forms of hypernyms and hyponyms of senses.

Especially, in case a word has more than one sense determined by a Word Sense Diambiguation (WSD) algorithm, the above works choose randomly one sense from those senses, which may decrease the retrieval performance if that is a wrong choice. In contrast, in our system, such a word is represented by the combination of its form and the most specific common hypernym of the senses.

2.3 Exploiting Latent Concepts

Some systems improve document retrieval performance by expanding queries with user's participation, such as Sanderson (2004), Balog, et al. (2008), Castellani, et al. (2009), Meij, et al. (2009) and Ahn, et al. (2010). Whereas, Bendersky and Croft (2008), and Huston and Croft (2010) identify key concepts in queries to remove unimportant words.

In Wang and Zhai (2008), the authors exploit synonyms or co-occurring relations in search engine logs for repairing or expanding queries. In Losada, et al. (2010), the system uses pseudo-relevance feedback to expand queries. However, the two systems do not take account relations in a query.

In Tran, et al. (2007), the authors map concepts of a query to an ontology to find suitable related concepts. In Cheng, et al. (2007), the target problem is to search for named entities of specified classes associated with keywords in a query. Different from our model, the two systems do not take account relations in queries and they are for question-and-answering but not document search.

In Castells, et al. (2007), the system finds identified named entities belonging to a class of NE in a query, after the query's vector is constructed by the NEs. This step is unnecessarily time consuming. In our proposed models, the query and document vectors having the entity class can be constructed and matched right away. Beside, its queries must be specified by RDQL. Similarity, in Kasneci, et al. (2008), queries must be written by SPARQL. Concepts and relations must be clearly specified by users. Whereas, this need not in our system. Moreover, the work is for question-and-answering, not document retrieval.

Spreading Activation (SA) is a popular algorithm for query expansion. But pure-SA would return most results irrelevant to queries (Berthold, et al., 2009). So, SA algorithms have been constrained by some methods to improve retrieval performance.

In Rocha, et al. (2004), the authors propose a hybrid spread activation algorithm that combined SA algorithm together with ontology based information retrieval. In Aswath, et al. (2005), the system uses a two-level SA network to activate strongly positive and strongly negative matches based on keyword search results.

In Schumacher, et al. (2008), the system finds answers of given query and added into the query before using an SA algorithm. Besides, Hsu, et al (2008) expands query by using SA on all relations in WordNet and only selecting kernel words that are activated and represent the content of a query by some rules.

In Jiang and Tan (2009), the authors map the original query to a keyword set and searches for documents relating to the keyword set. After that, the documents are pre-annotated with information of an ontology and the initial concepts are extracted from the retrieved documents. An SA algorithm is used to find concepts semantically relating to the concepts in the ontology. Finally, the activated concepts are used to rerank the documents to present for user. In Lee, et al. (2010), the system sets up an associative network with nodes being web pages and links between the nodes being relations between the web pages. Initial nodes of SA algorithm are web pages that are strongly associated to given query.

Next, other nodes (web pages) of their network are activated.

However, the above Constrained-SA (CSA) models do not use relations in a given query to constrain spreading. Meanwhile, our relation-CSA method activates concepts relating to concepts and relations in queries. In Fu, et al. (2005), the authors use the relations in a query to expand the query. However, the work only exploits spatial relations (e.g. near, inside, north of). In contrast, in this paper, we propose more general rules for query expansion.

3 Ontology-based Text Search

3.1 System Architecture

Our proposed system architecture of semantic text search is shown in Figure 1. It has two main parts. Part 1 presents document and query annotation and expansion. Part 2 presents the query expansion module using a relation-CSA (RCSA) method.

Our proposed model needs an ontology having: (1) a comprehensive class catalog with a large concept population for expressing clearly information of documents and queries; and (2) a comprehensive set of relations between concepts and facts for expanding queries with latently related concepts. Since no single ontology is rich enough for every domain and application, merging or combining multiple ontologies are reasonable solutions (Choi, et al. 2006). So we have combined 3 ontologies, namely, KIM, WordNet, and YAGO to have a rich ontology for our model.

In this work we employ KIM (Kiryakov, et al. 2005) for automatic NE recognition and semantic annotation of documents and queries. The KIM PROTON ontology contains about 300 classes and 100 attributes and relations. KIM World Knowledge Base (KB) contains about 77,500 entities with more than 110,000 aliases. NE descriptions are stored in an RDF(S) repository. Each NE has information about its specific class, aliases, and attributes (i.e., its own properties or relations with other NEs). The average precision and recall of the NE recognition engine are about 90% and 86%, respectively[1].

WordNet (Fellbaum, 1998) is a lexical database for English organized in synonym sets (synsets). There are various semantic relations between these synonym sets, such as hypernym, hyponym, holonym, meronym, and similarity. WordNet version 3.0 contains about 155,000 words organized in over 117,000 synsets.

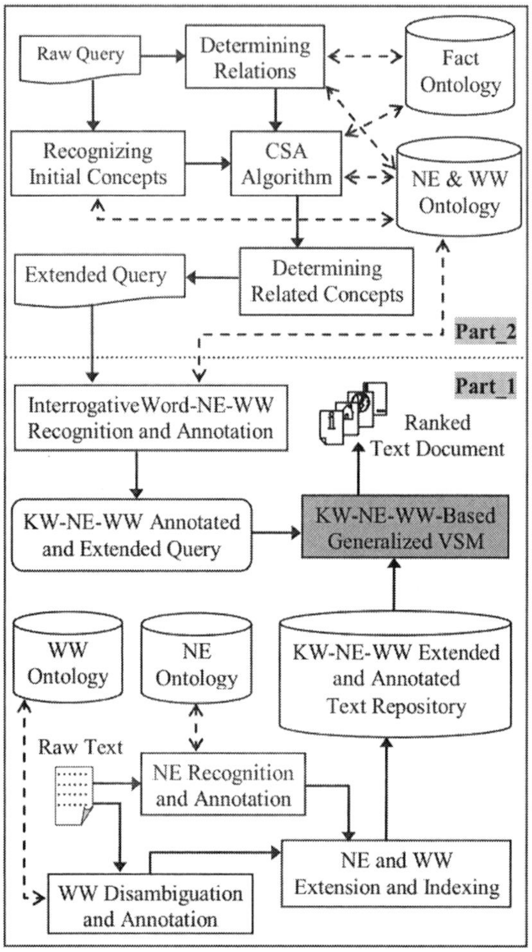

Figure 1. System architecture for semantic search

Since KIM ontology and WordNet define only a small number of relations, and KIM KB contains a limited number of facts, we employ YAGO (Yet Another Great Ontology) (Suchanek, et al. 2007; Suchanek, et al. 2008) for an ontology of relations in the system. It contains about 1.95 millions entities, 93 different relation types, and 19 millions facts about specific relations between entities. The correctness of the facts is about 95%. In addition, with logical extraction techniques and a flexible architecture, YAGO can be further extended in future. Note that, to have more relation types and facts for experiments, we can manually combine it with Wikipedia. We use KIM, WordNet, YAGO as the NE, WW, and Fact ontologies in our system, respectively.

The NE Recognition-and-Annotation module and WW Disambiguation-and-Annotation module extract and embed NE features and WW features in a raw text, respectively. The text is then indexed by contained NE features, WW features,

[1] It is reported at http://www.ontotext.com/kim/performance.html.

and keywords, and stored in the Extended KW-NE-WW Annotated Text Repository. Meanwhile, the InterrogativeWord-NE-WW Recognition-and-Annotation module extracts and embeds the most specific NE features and WW features in the extended query, and replaces the interrogative word if existing by a suitable class. Semantic document search is performed via the KW-NE-WW-Based Generalized Vector Space Model (VSM) module.

3.2 Word Sense Disambiguation

To choose the intended sense of a word in a context, a WSD algorithm is employed. Supervised WSD systems have high accuracy (Pradhan, et al. 2007) but need manually sense-tagged corpora for training. In IR, training corpora of a supervised WSD algorithm need to be large which are usually laborious and expensive to construct. Knowledge-based WSD systems (Liu, et al. 2005; Sinha and Mihalcea, 2007; Navigli and Lapata, 2007; Agirre and Soroa, 2009a) are developed to overcome the knowledge acquisition bottleneck and avoid manual effort. Besides, for specific domains, knowledge-based WSD systems have better performance than generic supervised WSD systems trained on balanced corpora (Agirre, et al. 2009b). We use Personalizing PageRank algorithm of Agirre and Soroa (2009a) having 56.8% accuracy for our WordNet based WSD. Moreover, we enhance it by using Pos-Tagger and Lemmatization in Toutanova, et al. (2003) having 97.24% accuracy. However, if a word has two or more probable senses, then our WSD algorithm will choose the most specific common hypernym of the senses in hypernym hierarchy of WordNet. We use WordNet version 3.0 for the WSD algorithm. Figure 2 describes the difference between the traditional KB-based WSDs and our KB-based WSD.

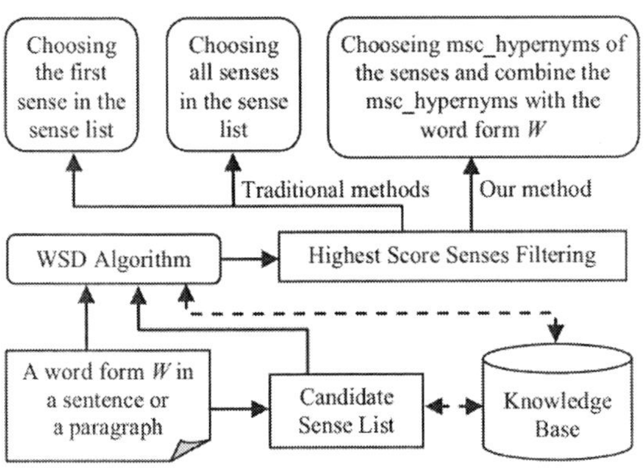

Figure 2. Difference between the traditional KB-based WSDs and our KB-based WSD

3.3 Annotating and Expanding in Queries and Documents

We propose a generalized VSM in which a document or a query is represented by a vector over a space of generalized terms. Each term is a NE feature, a WW feature, or a keyword. As usual, similarity of a document and a query is defined by the cosine of the angle between their representing vectors. Our work has implemented the model by developing a platform modified from Lucene[2]. The system automatically processes documents for KW-NE-WW-based searching in the following steps:

1. Removing stop-words in the documents.
2. Recognizing and annotating NEs in the documents using KIM[3].
3. Disambiguating and annotating WWs that are not NEs in the document using the WSD algorithm mentioned in section 3.2.
4. Words not defined in KIM and WordNet are treated as plain keywords.
5. Extending the documents with implied NE features. That is, for each entity named n possibly with class c and identifier id in a document, the triples (n/*/*), (*/c/*), (n/c/*), (alias(n)/*/*), (*/super(c)/*), (n/super(c)/*), (alias(n)/c/*), (alias(n)/ super(c)/*), and (*/*/id) are virtually added to the document. Here $alias(n)$, $super(c)$, $syn(w)$ and $super(h)$ respectively denote any alias of n, any super class of c, any synonym of w, and any super hypernym of h in the ontology and knowledge base of discourse.
6. Extending the document with implied WW features:
   - If the sense s of the word is determined, then s and its expanded features *form(s)*, *hypernym(s)*, *form(hypernym(s))*, *form(s)/ hypernym(s)* are added into the document.
   - If the word has more than one sense with f and *msc_hypernym(possible_senses(f))* as its apparent form and the most specific common hypernym, respectively, then f *and* *f/msc_hypernym(possible_senses(f))* and their expanded features:

     form(msc_hypernym(possible_senses(f))),

     msc_hypernym(possible_senses(f)),

     form(hypernym(msc_hypernym(possible_senses(f)))),

     hypernym(msc_hypernym(possible_senses (f))),

---

[2] http://lucene.apache.org/

[3] http://www.ontotext.com/kim/

f/hypernym(msc_hypernym(possible_senses (f))) are virtually added to the document.

7. Original and implied features of NE and WW, and plain keywords are indexed by S-Lucene.

A query is also automatically processed in the following steps:

1. Removing stop-words in the query.
2. Recognizing and annotating NEs in the query.
3. Disambiguating and annotating WWs that are not NEs in the query.
4. Words not defined in KIM and WordNet are treated as plain keywords.
5. Representing each recognized entity named *n* possibly with class *c* and identifier *id* by the most specific and available triple among (*n*/*/*), (*/*c*/*), (*n*/*c*/*), and (*/*/*id*).
6. Representing each recognized WordNet word:
   - If the sense *s* of the word is determined, then the word is represented by *s*.
   - If the word has more than one sense with *f* and *msc_hypernym(possible_senses(f))* as its apparent form and the most specific common hypernym, respectively, then the word is represented by *f/msc_hypernym (possible_senses(f))*.

Besides, there is latent information of the interrogative words *Who, What, Which, When, Where*, or *How* in a query. For example, given the query "*Where was George Washington born?*", the important terms are not only the NE *George Washington* and the WW "*born*", but also the interrogative word *Where*, which is to search for locations or documents mentioning them. For instance, *Where* in this example should be mapped to the class *Location* of NE. The mapping could be automatically done with high accuracy using the method proposed in (Cao, et al. 2008).

3.4 Discovering Latent Concepts in Queries

The followings are the six main steps of our RCSA method to determine relevant latent related concepts for a query:

1. Recognizing relation phrases: Relation phrases are prepositions, verbs, and other phrases representing relations, such as *in, on, is, near, north of, live in, located near, was actress in, is author of*, and *was born*. We have implemented a relation phrase recognition using the ANNIE tool of GATE (Cunningham, et al. 2006).
2. Determining relations: Each relation phrase recognized in step 1 is mapped to the corresponding relation in fact ontology or NE ontology by a manually built dictionary. For example, "*was actress in*" is mapped to *actedIn*, "*is author of*" is mapped to *wrote*, and "*nationality is*" is mapped to *isCitizenOf*.
3. Recognizing initial concepts: we find concepts in the query by mapping the words expressed in the query to entity names or word forms in the exploited ontologies. These are original concepts in the query and initial concepts of the method.
4. Presenting each relation in the query in the form C_1RC_2, where R is a relation found in step 2, and C_1 and C_2 are initial concepts found in step 3.
5. Determining related concepts. Let C_4 be a latent concept derived from a relation C_1RC_2.
   - If C_2 is a NE having identifier and belonging to class *Location*:
     - If R is described by a verb and a spatial relation phrase, e.g. "born in the north of", find C_4 that satisfies $C_4R_SC_2$ in the employed NE ontology and $C_1R_FC_4$ in the Fact ontology, where R_S is the relation expressed by the verb and R_F is the relation expressed by the spatial relation phrase.
     - Otherwise, find C_4 that satisfies C_4 *is_part_of* C_2 in the NE ontology and C_1RC_4 in the Fact ontology.
   - If C_2 is a NE class only, find C_4 that satisfies C_4 *is_subClass_of* C_2 in the NE ontology and C_1RC_4 in the Fact ontology.
   - If C_2 is a WW, find C_4 that satisfies C_4 *is_hyponym_of* C_2 in the WW ontology and C_1RC_4 in the Fact ontology.
6. Before being added into the query, the latent concepts are represented by their main entity aliases or word forms.

Comparing with pure-SA algorithm, the RCSA algorithm has two constraints as follows: (1) distance constraint: only concepts having direct relations, in accordance to the exploited ontology, with original nodes in queries are activated; and (2) relation constraint: relations used for spreading in the Fact ontology must appear in the query.

For the computational cost, we note that document annotation is performed offline, while queries are typically short and thus query annotation and expansion could be done quickly. Therefore, the query answering time is not a problem.

4 Experiments

Evaluation of a retrieval method requires two components being a test dataset and quality measures (Baeza-Yates and Ribeiro-Neto, 1999; Manning, et al. 2008). The L.A. Times document collection is employed, which was used by 15 papers among the 33 full-papers of SIGIR-2007 and SIGIR-2008 about text IR using TREC dataset. The L.A. Times consists of more than 130,000 documents in nearly 500MB. Next, queries in the QA Track-1999, which have answer documents in this document collection, are used. So, there are 124 queries of 200 queries in this Track chosen.

Table 1. MAPs and two-sided p-values of the Lexical, NE+KW, WW+KW and NE+WW+KW models.

Model A and **MAP**	Model B and **MAP**	Improvement	Two-Sided P-Value
NE+WW +KW **0.6024**	Lexical **0.5099**	18.1%	0.02004
	NE+KW **0.5652**	6.6%	0.03359
	WW+KW **0.5391**	11.7%	0.04118

Table 2. MAPs and two-sided p-values of the Lexical, CSA and RCSA models.

Model A and **MAP**	Model B and **MAP**	Improvement	Two-Sided P-Value
RCSA **0.6594**	Lexical **0.5099**	29.3%	0.02952
	CSA **0.5592**	17.9%	0.04987

We have evaluated and compared the IR models in average Precision-Recall (P-R) curves, average F-measure-Recall (F-R) curves, and mean average precision (MAP) values (Baeza-Yates and Ribeiro-Neto, 1999; Manning, et al. 2008). Because, average P-R curves and average F-R curves represent commonly the retrieval performance and allow comparison of those of different systems. The closer the curve is to the right top corner, the better performance it represents (Manning, et al. 2008). Whereas, MAP is a single measure of retrieval quality across recall levels and considered as a standard measure in the TREC community (Voorhees and Harman, 2005). Obtained values of the measures presented above might occur by chance. Therefore, a statistical significance test is required (Hull, 1993). We use Fisher's randomization (permutation) test for evaluating the significance of the observed difference between two systems, as recommendation of Smucker, et al. (2007). As shown Smucker, et al. (2007), 100,000 permutations were acceptable for a randomization test and the threshold 0.05 of the two-sided significance level, or two-sided p-value, could detect significance.

We conduct experiments to compare the results obtained by the following seven different search models:

1. Lexical: This is the Lucene text search engine as a tweak of the traditional keyword-based VSM.
2. NE+KW: This is the model only exploiting features of NEs to annotate and expand documents and queries.
3. WW+KW: This is the model only exploiting features of WW to annotate and expand documents and queries.
4. NE+WW+KW: This is the model combining NE+KW and WW+KW, as presented in section 3.3.
5. CSA: This is the model using the traditional constrained SA algorithm. It expands queries by broadcasting all direct-links to original concepts in the Fact ontology to find related concepts. The expanded queries and documents of the CSA model are represented by keywords.
6. RCSA (6): This is the model improving the above CSA model. The RCSA model only uses links presented in a query to find related concepts, as presented in section 3.4.
7. Semantic Search: This is the model combining RCSA and NE+WW+KW, as presented in section 3.

The MAP values of the models and two-sided p-values of randomization tests between them in Table 1 show that taking into account ontological features in queries and documents does enhance text retrieval performance; NE+WW+KW performs about 18.1%, 6.6%, and 11.7% better than the Lexical, NE+KW and WW+KW models in terms of the MAP measure, respectively.

In Table 2, we see that RCSA model really performs about 29.3% and 17.9% better than the Lexical and CSA models in terms of the MAP measure, respectively. So, discovering latent concepts in a query does enhance text retrieval performance.

Finally, Table 3 and Figure 3 show that text retrieval performance is improved by the combination of discovering latent concepts and exploiting logical feature in documents and queries. In terms of the MAP measure, Semantic Search performs about 41.9% and 29.3% better than the Lexical and CSA models, respectively. Beside, Semantic Search also performs about 28%, 34.2%, 20.1%, and 9.7% better than the NE+KW, WW+KW, NE+WW+KW and RCSA models, respectively.

Table 3. MAPs and two-sided p-values of the Semantic Search model and the other six models.

Model A and MAP	Model B and MAP	Improvement	Two-Sided P-Value
Semantic Search 0.7233	Lexical **0.5099**	41.9%	0.01071
	NE+KW **0.5652**	28.0%	0.00313
	WW+KW **0.5391**	34.2%	0.00845
	NE+WW+KW **0.6024**	20.1%	0.01791
	CSA **0.5592**	29.3%	0.01255
	RCSA **0.6594**	9.7%	0.04516

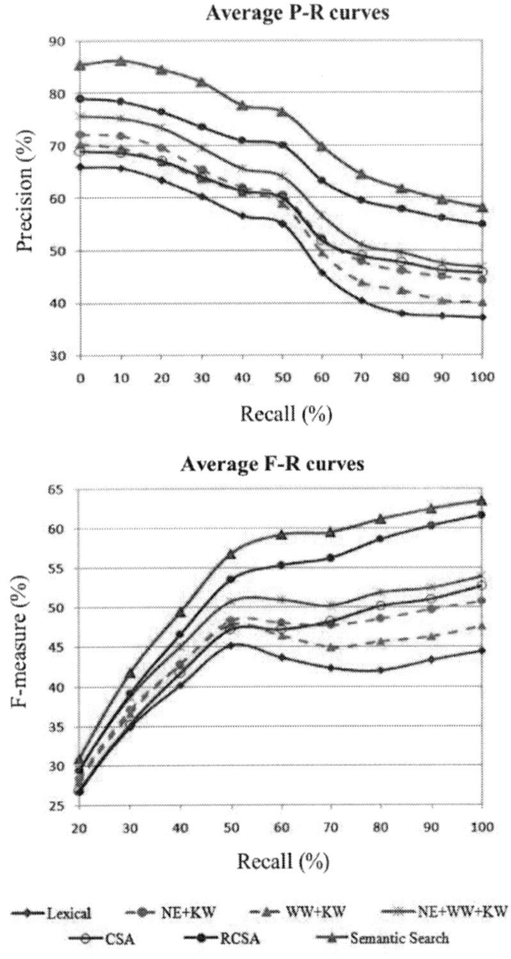

Figure 3. Average P-R and F-R curves of the seven search models on 124 queries of TREC

5 Conclusion

We have presented the generalized VSM that exploits and annotates ontological features of named entities and WordNet words in documents and queries for semantic text search. In case a word has more than one sense determined by a WSD algorithm, the word is represented by the combination of its form and the most specific common hypernym of those senses. Besides, our model expands a query by discovering relevant latent concepts in the query by constrained spreading activation using relations in the query.

The conducted experiments on a TREC dataset have showed that our semantic search improves the search quality in terms of the precision, recall, F, and MAP measures. Although this work uses VSM for proving the advantage of exploiting the proposed ontological features and discovering latent concepts in text search, it could be adapted for other information retrieval models as well.

References

Agirre, E.; Soroa, A. 2009a. *Personalizing PageRank for Word Sense Disambiguation*. In EACL-2009, pp.33-41.

Agirre, E.; Lopez De Lacalle, O.; Soroa, A. 2009b. *Knowledge-Based WSD on Specific Domains: Performing better than Generic Supervised WSD*. In IJCAI-2009, pp. 1501-1506.

Ahn, J. W., et al. 2010. *Semantic annotation based exploratory search for information analysts*. In International Journal of Information Processing and Management, Vol. 46, No. 4, pp. 383-402.

Aswath, D., et al. 2005. *Boosting Item Keyword Search with Spreading Activation*. In WI-2005, pp. 704-707.

Baeza-Yates, R.; Ribeiro-Neto, B. 1999. *Modern Information Retrieval*. ACM Press, New York.

Balog, K., et al. 2009. *Overview of the TREC 2009 entity track*. In TREC-2009.

Balog, K.; Weerkamp, W.; Rijke, M. D. 2008. *A few examples go a long way: constructing query models from elaborate query formulations*. In SIGIR-2008, pp. 371-378.

Bast, H., et al. 2007. *ESTER: Efficient Search on Text, Entities, and Relations*. In SIGIR-2007, pp. 671-678.

Bendersky, M.; Croft, B. W. 2008. *Discovering key concepts in verbose queries*. In SIGIR-2008, pp. 491-498.

Berthold, M. R., et al. 2009. *Pure spreading activation is pointless*. In CIKM-09, pp. 1915-1918.

Chang, M. W., et al. 2008. *Importance of semantic representation: dataless classification*. In AAAI-2008, pp. 830-835.

Cao, T. H.; Cao, T. D.; Tran, T. L. 2008. *A Robust Ontology-Based Method for Translating Natural Language Queries to Conceptual Graphs*. In ASWC-2008, LNCS, Vol. 5367, pp. 479-492.

Castells, P.; Vallet, D.; Fernández, M. 2007. *An Adaptation of the Vector Space Model for Ontology-Based Information Retrieval*. IEEE Transactions of Knowledge and Data Engineering, Vol. 19, No. 2, pp. 261-272.

Castellani, S., et al. 2009. *Creation and Maintenance of Query Expansion Rules*. In ICEIS-2009, LNBIP, Vol. 24, pp. 819-830.

Cheng, G., et al. 2008. *Searching Semantic Web Objects based on Class Hierarchies*. In WWW-2008 Workshop on Linked Data on the Web, pp. 199-226.

Cheng, T., et al. 2007. *EntityRank: Searching Entities Directly and Holistically*. In VLDB-2007, pp. 387-398.

Choi, N.; Song, I. Y.; Han, H. 2006. *A Survey on Ontology Mapping*. In ACM SIGMOD Record, Vol. 35, No. 3, pp. 34-41.

Cunningham, H., et al. 2006. *Developing Language Processing Components with GATE Version 4*. User Guide. http://gate.ac.uk/sale/tao.

Demartini, G., et al. 2010. *Why finding entities in wikipedia is difficult, sometimes*. In Journal of formation Retrieval, Vol. 13, No. 5, pp. 534-567.

Egozi, O.; Markovitch, S.; Gabrilovich, E. 2011. *Concept-Based Information Retrieval Using Explicit Semantic*. In Journal ACM Transactions on Information Systems. Vol 29, No. 2.

Fellbaum, C. 1998. WordNet: *An Electronic Lexical Database*, MIT Press, Cambridge MA.

Fu, G.; Jones, C. B.; Abdelmoty, A. I. 2005. *Ontology-based Spatial Query Expansion in Information Retrieval*. In Proceedings of On the Move to Meaningful Internet Systems: ODBASE-2005, LNCS, Vol. 3761, pp. 1466-1482.

Giunchiglia, F.; Kharkevich, U.; Zaihrayeu, I. 2009. *Concept Search*. In ESWC-2009, pp. 429-444.

Gupta, R.; Ratinov, L. A. 2008. *Text categorization with knowledge transfer from heterogeneous data sources*. In AAAI-2008, pp. 842–847.

Hsu, M. H.; Tsai, M. F.; Chen, H. H. 2008. *Combining WordNet and ConceptNet for Automatic Query Expansion- A Learning Approach*. In AIRS-2008, LNCS, Springer, Vol. 4993, pp. 213-224.

Hull, D. 1993. *Using Statistical Testing in the Evaluation of Retrieval Experiments*. In SIGIR-1993, pp. 329-338.

Huston, S.; Croft, W. B. 2010. *Evaluating Verbose Query Processing Techniques*. In SIGIR-2010, pp. 291-298.

Jiang, X.; Tan, A. H. 2009. *Learning and Inferencing in User Ontology for Personalized Semantic Web Search*. Information Sciences (Elsevier Journal), Vol. 179, No. 16, pp. 2794-2808.

Jing, L.; Michael, K. Ng.; Huang, J. Z. 2010. *Knowledge-Based Vector Space Model for Text Clustering*. In Knowledge and Information Systems, Vol. 25, No.1 pp. 35-55.

Kaptein, R., et al. 2010. *Entity ranking using Wikipedia as a pivot*. In CIKM-2010, pp. 69-78.

Kasneci, G., et al. 2008. *The YAGO-NAGA Approach to Knowledge Discovery*. In SIGMOD-2008, pp. 41-47.

Kiryakov, A., et al. 2005. *Semantic Annotation, Indexing, and Retrieval*. In Elsevier's Journal of Web Semantics, Vol. 2, No. 1, pp. 49-79.

Lee, M.; Kim, W.; Wang, T. G. 2010. *An Explorative Association-Based Search for the Semantic Web*. In ICSC-2010, pp. 206-211.

Liu, S., et al. 2004. *An effective approach to document retrieval via utilizing WordNet and recognizing phrases*. In SIGIR-2004, pp. 266-272.

Liu, S.; Yu, C.; Meng, W. 2005. *Word Sense Disambiguation in Queries*. In CIKM-2005, pp. 525-532.

Losada, D. E. 2010. *Statistical query expansion for sentence retrieval and its effects on weak and strong queries*. In Information Retrieval, Vol. 13, No. 5, pp. 485-506.

Manning, C. D.; Raghavan, P.; Schütze, H. 2008. *Introduction to Information Retrieval*, Cambridge University Press.

Meij, E.; Weerkamp, W.; Rijke, M. D. 2009. *A Query Model Based on Normalized Log-Likelihood*. In CIKM-2009, pp. 1903-1906.

Mihalcea, R.; Moldovan, D. 2000. *Semantic Indexing using WordNet Senses*. In ACL-2000 workshop on Recent Advances in Natural Language Processing and Information Retrieval, pp. 35 – 45.

Navigli, R.; Lapata, M. 2007. *Graph connectivity measures for unsupervised word sense disambiguation*. In IJCAI-2007, pp. 1683-1688.

Pradhan, S., et al. 2007. *Semeval-2007 task-17: English lexical sample srl and all words*. In SemEval-2007, pp. 87-92.

Rocha, C.; Schwabe, D.; Aragao, M. P. 2004. *A Hybrid Approach for Searching in the Semantic Web*. In WWW-2004, pp. 374-383.

Sanderson, M. 2004. *A study of user interaction with a concept based interactive query expansion support tool (CiQuest) which is integrated into Okapi*. In ECIR-2004, LNCS, Vol. 2997, pp. 42-56.

Santos, R. L. T.; Macdonald, C.; Ounis, I. 2010. *Voting for related entities*. In Proceedings of RIAO '10 Adaptivity, Personalization and Fusion of Heterogeneous Informa, pp. 1-8.

Schumacher, K.; Sintek, M.; Sauermann, L. 2008. *Combining Fact and Document Retrieval with Spreading Activation for Semantic Desktop Search*. In ESWC-2008, LNCS, Vol. 5021, pp. 569-583.

Sekine, S. 2004. *Named Entity: History and Future*. Proteus Project Report.

Smucker, M. D.; Allan, J.; Carterette, B. 2007. *A comparison of statistical significance tests for information retrieval evaluation Export*. In CIKM-2007, pp. 623-632.

Sinha, R.; Mihalcea, R. 2007. *Unsupervised graph based word sense disambiguation using measures of word semantic similarity*. In ICSC-2007, pp. 363-369.

Suchanek, F. M.; Kasneci, G.; Weikum, G. 2007. *YAGO - A Core of Semantic Knowledge. Unifying WordNet and Wikipedia*. In WWW-2007, pp. 697-706.

Suchanek, F. M.; Kasneci, G.; Weikum, G. 2008. *YAGO - A Large Ontology from Wikipedia and Wordnet*. In Journal of Semantic Web, Vol. 6, No. 3, pp. 203-217.

Toutanova, K., et al. 2003. *Feature-Rich Part-of-Speech Tagging with a Cyclic Dependency Network*. In HLT-NAACL-2003, pp. 252-259.

Tran, T., et al. 2007. Ontology-Based Interpretation of Keywords for Semantic Search. In ISWC-2007, LNCS, Vol. 4825, pp. 523-536.

Vallet, D.; Zaragoza, H. 2008. *Inferring the most important types of a query: a semantic approach*. In Proceedings of SIGIR-2008, pp. 857-858.

Voorhees, E. M.; Harman, D. K. 2005. TREC- *Experiment and Evaluation in Information Retrieval*. MIT Press.

Wang, P.; Hu, J.; Zeng, H. J.; Chen, Z. 2009. *Using Wikipedia Knowledge to Improve Text Classification*. Knowledge and Information Systems, Vol.19, pp. 265-281.

Wang, B.; Brookes, B. R. 2004. *A semantic approach for Web indexing*. In Proceedings of APWeb-2004, LNCS, Springer, Vol. 3007, pp. 59-68.

Wang, X.; Zhai, C. 2008. *Mining term association patterns from search logs for effective query reformulation*. In CIKM-2008, pp. 479-488.

Zaihrayeu, I., et al. 2007. *From web directories to ontologies: Natural language processing challenges*. In ISWC-2007 + ASWC-2007, LNCS, Vol. 4825, pp. 623-636.

CLGVSM: Adapting Generalized Vector Space Model to Cross-lingual Document Clustering

Guoyu Tang[1,2], Yunqing Xia[1], Min Zhang[2], Haizhou Li[2],Fang Zheng[1]
[1]Dept. of Comp. Sci. & Tech., Tsinghua University, Beijing 100084, China
sweetyuer@gmail.com,{yqxia,fzheng}@tsinghua.edu.cn

[2]Institute for Infocomm Research, A-STAR, Singapore
{mzhang, hli}@i2r.a-star.edu.sg

Abstract

Cross-lingual document clustering (CLDC) is the task to automatically organize a large collection of cross-lingual documents into groups considering content or topic. Different from the traditional hard matching strategy, this paper extends traditional generalized vector space model (GVSM) to handle cross-lingual cases, referred to as CLGVSM, by incorporating cross-lingual word similarity measures. With this model, we further compare different word similarity measures in cross-lingual document clustering. To select cross-lingual features effectively, we also propose a *soft-matching* based feature selection method in CLGVSM. Experimental results on benchmarking data set show that (1) the proposed CLGVSM is very effective for cross-document clustering, outperforming the two strong baselines vector space model (VSM) and latent semantic analysis (LSA) significantly; and (2) the new feature selection method can further improve CLGVSM.

1 Introduction

The globalization of business environment urges organizations to maintain documents in different language. Obviously, organizations and research communities nowadays encounter the challenge of cross-lingual document clustering (CLDC). Document clustering seeks to automatically organize a large collection of documents into groups of similar documents. Various document clustering technologies have been proposed to deal with monolingual documents.

The classical solution to monolingual document clustering is vector space model (VSM), which explores bag of words (BOW) to construct feature space. Each document is converted to a VSM vector. Serious problem occurs when words are matched to the features using the hard matching strategy. For example, when the word *coast* is selected as a feature, word *seashore* will not contribute to hard matching unless it is also selected as a feature.

Different semantic document representation models have been proposed to address the shortcoming of VSM. Some semantic document representing models such as Latent Semantic Analysis (LSA) (Landauer et al., 1998) and Latent Dirichlet Allocation (Blei et al., 2003) implicitly capture statistical semantics by mapping documents to a lower dimension space. Other models such as Generalized Vector Space Model (GVSM) (Wang et al., 1985) extract statistical semantics in an explicit way by directly estimating measures of correlations between words.

The above models are designed for monolingual document sets and cannot be applied to cross-lingual scenario unless a bridge is created to connect cross-lingual features. Carbonell et al. (1997) use semantic models in parallel corpus. As features are selected from a common parallel/comparable corpus, which is usually different from the test cross-lingual document, over-fitting problem inevitably happens.

Other researchers propose to translate features or documents with bilingual dictionary or machine translation tools (Mathieu et al., 2004).However, ambiguity happens constantly and it is difficult to determine translation of a word. Meanwhile, if one translation of a word is selected as feature, the hard matching problem still occurs and becomes more serious.

In this paper, we extend the monolingual GVSM to handle cross-lingual cases, referred to as Cross-lingual GVSM (CLGVSM). Besides term correlation, we make use of word similarity in CLGVSM. For the cross-lingual we use statistical word similarity measure with the parallel corpus. We further improve cross-lingual word similarity by incorporating dictionary or translation probability. Experimental results show that the best result is achieved when combining the Second Order Co-occurrence Pointwise Mutual Information (SOCPMI) measure on the test dataset and translation probability in development dataset.

Selecting cross-lingual features is a key issue in cross-lingual document clustering. In this work, we propose a *soft-matching* based feature selection method in CLGVSM. In the new feature selection method, most representative terms are selected in semantic space according to Soft Term Frequency and Soft Document Frequency. In this way, a non-feature word can improve weight of the semantically similar features and make contribution to document clustering. Experimental results show that CLGVSM outperforms both LSA and VSM significantly with the help of proper word similarity measure.

The rest of this paper is organized as follows. In section 2, related work is surveyed. In section 3, the CLGVSM model is discussed. Experimental results as well as discussion are presented in Section 4. We conclude this paper in Section 5.

2 Related work

2.1 Monolingual Document Representation Models

The most commonly used model for document representation is the vector space model (VSM). It is assumed in VSM that terms are independent of each other and thus any semantic relations between them are ignored. Proposed by Landauer et al. (1998), LSA seeks to decompose the term-document matrix using singular value decomposition, in which each feature is a linear combination of all words.

Proposed by Wang et al. (1985) and further improved by Farahat and Kamel (2010), GVSM is proved an effective document representation model to address limitation of VSM. The model estimates similarity between documents based on how much their terms are related. Wang et al. (1985) pointed out orthonormal basis in VSM and proposed a new model to remove the assumption. Farahat and Kamel (2010) improved GVSM by developing better estimation of term correlation and applying dimension reduction techniques in a semantic space. Results show that the improved GVSM is advantageous over other representation models such as LSA.

Other document representation models are based on lexical ontologies such as WordNet, to represent documents in the concept space (Hotho et al., 2003). Similar representation models are seeks to exploit knowledge within an encyclopedia. Explicit Semantic Analysis (Cimiano et al., 2009) is a famous model that represents words as vectors in a space of concepts represented by articles from Wikipedia.

Most of those semantic models are designed for monolingual document sets, and cannot be used in cross-lingual scenario directly.

2.2 Cross-lingual Document Clustering

The difficulty of CLDC is how to deal with cross-language issue. The straightforward solution is document translation. In TDT3[1], four systems attempted to used Machine Translation systems (Leek et al., 1999). The results show that using a machine translation tool leads to around 50% performance loss, compared with monolingual topic tracking. This ascribed mainly to the poor accuracy of machine translation systems.

Dictionary and corpus are two popular ways to get cross-language information. Some researches (Evans and Klavans, 2003) use dictionary to translate documents. Others (Mathieu et al., 2004) use dictionary to translate features or keywords. But it is hard to select proper translation of ambiguous words. Mathieu et al. (2004) use bilingual dictionaries to translate named entities and keywords and modify the cosine similarity formula to calculate similarity between bilingual documents. Pouliquen et.al (2004) rely on a multilingual thesaurus called Eurovoc to create cross-lingual article vectors.

Wei et al. (2008) use LSA to construct a multilingual semantic space onto which words and document in either language can be mapped and dimensions are reduced again according to documents to be cluster. Yogatama and Tanaka-Ishii (2009) use propagation algorithm to merge multilingual spaces from comparable corpus and spectral method to cluster documents. Li et al. (2007) use Kernel Canonical Correlation Analysis, a method of finding the maximally correlated projections of documents in two languages for cross-language Japanese-English patent retrieval and document classification. Unlike document classification, document clustering lacks training data. So semantic space is constructed from the parallel/comparable corpus, and the dimensions are selected on the basis of their importance in parallel/comparable corpus, which is usually different from the target multilingual documents.

[1]http://www.itl.nist.gov/iad/mig//tests/tdt/1999/index.html

In this work, our proposed CLGVSM use semantic similarity to solve word matching problem caused by different languages. Semantic space is constructed based on word similarity and in our feature selection method, features are select on the basis of their importance in documents to be clustered.

2.3 Cross-lingual Word Similarity

In both monolingual GVSM (Wang et al, 1985) and improved GVSM (Farahat and Kamel, 2010), correlation, correlation between words is computed in documents to be clustered and correlation of the best performance in document clustering is calculate as covariance of words with the assumption that words are random variables with Gaussian distributions. In this work we use word similarity which is calculated as cosine similarity of term vector covariance. This measure can be called as COV measure.

But this similarities method is estimated in test documents which lacks cross-lingual information.

Various measures for cross-lingual word semantic similarity have been proposed to explore statistical techniques and semantic network.

Research works propose to use *WordNet* by Resnik (1999) to measure similarity between English words. Liu and Li (2002) adopt HowNet calculate word similarity in machine translation. Xia et al. (2011) propose to explore cross-lingual word similarity by observing concept definition provided by HowNet.

Corpus-based measures for semantic similarity are found more interesting. The classical method is Pointwise Mutual Information (PMI) (Church and Hanks, 1990). Many researches are based on PMI, such as PMI-IR (Turney, 2001) and Second Order Co-occurrence PMI (SOCPMI) (Islam and Inkpen, 2006). SOCPMI is proved better than PMI-IR and some other similarity measures (Islam and Inkpen, 2006).

In this work, we implement three representative measures: HowNet-based measure (Xia et al., 2011), SOCPMI measure (Islam and Inkpen, 2006) and COV measure (Farahat and Kamel, 2010).

3 Cross-Lingual Generalized VSM

3.1 Generalized VSM

Let $D=\{d_j; j=1,...N\}$ be a set of N documents which contain M terms, X be a $M\times N$ matrix whose element x_{ij} represents the weight of term t_i in document d_j. GVSM (Wang et al, 1985) estimates correlation between documents based on how their terms are related. The GVSM model presents document in a non-orthogonal space and similarity between two documents is calculated as follows.

$$Sim^{\mathrm{GVSM}}(d_1,d_2)=\frac{d_1^T G d_2}{\sqrt{d_1^T G d_1}\sqrt{d_2^T G d_2}}, \quad (1)$$

where G is an $M\times M$ association matrix which represents correlations between terms and is usually computed as inner-products of term vectors in some space. An example of 3×3 association matrix is given as follows.

$$\begin{array}{c} \\ t_1 \\ t_2 \\ t_3 \end{array} \begin{array}{c} \begin{array}{ccc} t_1 & t_2 & t_3 \end{array} \\ \begin{pmatrix} 0.1 & 0.2 & 0.3 \\ 0.4 & 0.5 & 0.3 \\ 0.4 & 0.2 & 1 \end{pmatrix}_{3\times 3}, \end{array}$$

where every row and column represents a term, respectively.

In tradition GVSM (Wang et al, 1985), terms are represented as vectors in the dual space of documents and the association measures between terms are calculated as the cosine of the angle between their vectors in the dual space. Accordingly, G can be calculated as:

$$G=L^{-1/2}XX^TL^{-1/2} \quad (2)$$

where L is a diagonal matrix whose elements are the lengths of term vectors in the dual space.

And in improved GVSM (Farahat and Kamel, 2010), the best G which is covariance matrix of terms is calculated as

$$G_{\mathrm{COV}}=\frac{1}{n_c-1}QHQ^T \quad (4)$$

where Q is random sample of X and

$$H=1-\frac{1}{n_c}ee^T \quad (5)$$

G_{COV} maps uncorrelated terms to near-orthogonal directions and negatively correlated terms to opposite directions in the semantic space, while traditional G maps both uncorrelated terms and negatively correlated terms to near-orthogonal directions. Thus we use cosine similarities between term vectors in case of G_{COV} as one of our similarity measures. As the GVSM models proposed, G is estimated from documents to be clustered; they cannot acquire cross-lingual information and cannot deal with cross-lingual issues directly. So we extend GVSM to cross-lingual GVSM by using cross-lingual word similarity measures in section 3.2

3.2 Cross-Lingual GVSM

Note that before (Farahat and Kamel, 2010); term correlation was used in GVSM to construct association matrixes G with the inner-product of term vectors in some semantic space. Length of term vectors quantifies how important of the term in the documents. Thus correlation of terms is not totally the same with similarity of terms. But it is difficult for term correlation to adapt into cross-lingual case. Term vectors generated from test data lack cross-lingual information. Carbonell et.al (1997), generate term vectors from development data. Noise occurs because term importance differs in two dataset.

For those reasons mentioned above, we choose word similarity instead of term correlation to construct word association matrix. And the other advantage of using word similarity is that we can ignore noisy similarity values which contribute little to document similarity calculation. In that case, the associate matrix becomes sparse and computational time can be saved. Therefore in this work, we explore the following several word similarity measures in constructing word association and setup a similarity threshold.

Knowledge-based Similarity Measures

We choose to use cross-lingual word similarity based on HowNet (Xia et al., 2011) which makes use of concept graph in HowNet. HowNet is concept based and the atom unit is sememe, so similarity between words is actually reflected by the sememes they carry. The key idea of cross-lingual word similarity calculation is to locate bilingually definitions for given words so that the language barrier is overcome. For details please refer to Xia et al. (2011).

Statistical Similarity Measures

Statistical similarity actually reflects conceptual relevance between words as it considers merely word co-occurrences within a corpus. We evaluate two statistical similarity measures: SOCPMI and COV in this work.

SOCPMI was proposed by Islam and Inkpen (2006), in which PMI is applied to rank the neighboring words with in a corpus. The measure is proved accurate because it calculates relevance between two words that do not co-occur frequently. Note that the original SOCPMI measure is designed to deal with monolingual word similarity. We extend this measure in this work to calculate similarity between cross-lingual words. The goal is achieved by counting neighboring words with the same language in the corpus and computing the cross-lingual PMI in a parallel corpus.

As we mentioned above, associate matrix G constructed by covariance of term vectors achieve the best performance in monolingual document clustering. In this paper we use the cosine similarity instead of inner-product in COV similarity measure.

The two above word similarity measures both need to be calculated in a cross-lingual parallel/comparable corpus.

Combining Similarity with Dictionary or Translation probability

The statistical word similarity measures are developed with general development corpus. However, we believe word co-occurrence in the test documents is also very useful. Thus we improve cross-lingual word similarity in the following way: statistical monolingual word similarity is computed from test documents first and a dictionary or translation probability as a bridge is used to get cross-lingual word similarity.

When using dictionary as bridge, assuming word w_i which has a translation list $T_i^{\mathrm{T}}=\{t_{i_k}^{\mathrm{T}}; k = 1...N_i^{\mathrm{T}}\}$ and word w_j which has a translation list $T_j^{\mathrm{T}}=\{t_{j_k}^{\mathrm{T}};k = 1...N_j^{\mathrm{T}}\}$, we choose the highest value between similarities of w_i and each words in T_j^{T} and similarities of w_j and each words in T_i^{T} as similarity between w_i and w_j.

When using translation probability as bridge, assuming word w_i which has a translation probability list $P_i^{\mathrm{T}}=\{t_{i_k}^{\mathrm{T}}: p_{i_k};k = 1...N_i^{\mathrm{W}}\}$ and word w_j which has a translation list $P_j^{\mathrm{T}}=\{ t_{i_k}^{\mathrm{T}} : p_{j_k} ; k = 1...N_j^{\mathrm{W}}\}$, the similarity of w_i and w_j can be calculated as follows:

$$Sim^{\mathrm{PR}}(w_i \rightarrow w_j) = \sum_k p_{i_k} \times Sim^{\mathrm{Mono}}(w_j, t_{i_k}^{\mathrm{W}}) \quad (6)$$

$$Sim^{\mathrm{PR}}(w_j \rightarrow w_i) = \sum_k p_{j_k} \times Sim^{\mathrm{Mono}}(w_j, t_{i_k}^{\mathrm{W}}) \quad (7)$$

$$Sim^{\mathrm{PR}}(w_i, w_j) = \max\{Sim^{\mathrm{PR}}(w_i \rightarrow w_j), Sim^{\mathrm{PR}}(w_i \leftarrow w_j)\} \quad (8)$$

where Sim^{Mono} returns monolingual word similarity.

3.3 Feature selection for GVSM

Term Importance based on GVSM

In the VSM model, importance of a term is proportional to Term Frequency (*TF*) in a single document, and inversed proportional to Document Frequency (*DF*) in a document set. We argue that the theory can be improved.

Consider a document that contains term *criminal* for 3 times and term *imprisonment* for 10 time. We find that term *criminal* is still very important though its *TF* is low. This is because term *imprisonment* is semantically similar to *criminal* and it appears many times. If the classical term matching method is named *hard matching*, we can call our method *soft matching*. We incorporate the *soft-matching* idea to the GVSM model.

In the GVSM model, importance of a term can be reflected by the following statistics.

(1) Soft Term Frequency

The soft term frequency (TF^s) considers the term and the semantically similar terms. Given term$t$ and document d, we first retrieve the semantically similar terms $T=\{t_i\}_{i=1...M^T}$ from document$d$. We define the soft term frequency (TF^s) as follows.

$$TF^s(t,d) = \sum_i TF_i \times Sim(t,t_i) \quad (9)$$

where TF_i denotes term frequency of term t_i within document d.

Note that the soft term frequency is calculated within a single document.

(2) Soft Document Frequency

The soft document frequency (DF^s) considers not only number of documents that contain the term, but also the number of documents that contains the semantically similar terms. Given term$t$ and document set $D=\{d_j\}_{j=1...N}$. Let $d_j=\{t_{i,j}\}_{i=1...M^D}$ denote terms within documentd_j. We define the soft document frequency (DF^s) as follows.

$$DF^s(t) = \sum_{d_j \in D} \max_i\{Sim(t,t_{i,j}))\} \quad (10)$$

Note that the soft document frequency is calculated within a document set. We use maximum instead of summation in order to reduce the effects of word pairs with low similarities.

Feature Selection in GVSM

With GVSM-based term importance, features can be selected appropriately. Following the idea of TF-IDF, we refine inverse document frequency as follows.

$$IDF^s(t) = log\left(\frac{N}{DF^s(t)}\right), \quad (11)$$

where Ndenotes number of documents.

The soft weighting equation of term t in document$d$is as follows.

$$w^s(t,d) = TF^s(t,d)IDF^s(t) \quad (12)$$

If we select features for a document based solely on term weight, some semantically similar terms might be selected because they hold close weights. This results in fewer representatives feature set. Before feature selection we update term TF^sas follows:

1) Setup an initial term list.
2) Sort terms in the list according to their TF^sin descending order.
3) Move the first term$t_0$into the tentative feature list.
4) For each remaining term in the list, update its TF^x using the following equation.

$$TF^s_{g+1}(t,d) = TF^s_g(t,d) - \sum_{t_k \in d}(Sim(t,t_k)Sim(t_0,t_k)TF^s(t_k,d), \quad (13)$$

wheret_k denotes a term in document d, and g the iteration round number.

5) Delete terms a weight less than 0in the list.
6) Repeat step 2) ~ 5) until the term list becomes empty.

Once the tentative feature list is obtained, we then calculate weight for each candidate features using Eq (12). The features of each document are then ranked according to the weight and joined together to represent document set.

Document representation in GVSM

With the feature set available, we describe how a document is represented with the features. Let$F=\{f_i\}_{i=1...M^F}$denote the feature set, and $T=\{t_j\}_{j=1...M^D}$ denote terms within document$d$. We now try to map d to the feature space.

For each feature, it should be mapped no matter whether it appears in the document set. But in order to avoid redundant information, we map only one term with each feature.

So for feature list F sort by TF^s in document d, the actually weight of feature f_i in document d is as follows:

First, retrieve the most similar term t^* which is not included in T^M, which stores terms that have been matched.

$$t^* = argmax_{t_i \in d, t_i \notin T_M} Sim(t,f_i) \quad (14)$$

Then we re-calculate weight $w^a$of term $f_i$as follows.

$$w^a(f_i,d) = TF(t^*)IDF^s(f_i) \quad (15)$$

Finally, put t^*into T^M and repeat until all features are matched once.

3.4 Document Clustering based on GVSM

With document similarity, we employ certain clustering algorithm to manage the cross-lingual documents with a few clusters. As clustering algorithm is not core of this work, we simply choose the classic document clustering algorithm, i.e., HAC (Hierarchical Agglomerative Clustering) algorithm (Voorhees, 1986). To measure cluster-cluster similarity, we adopt the group-average link algorithm (Voorhees, 1986). The merging procedure repeats until a desired number of clusters are obtained.

4 Evaluation

4.1 Setup

Development dataset: We randomly extract 1M parallel sentence pairs from LDC corpora (i.e., LDC2004E12, LDC2004T08, LDC2005T10, LDC2003E14, LDC2002E18m LDC2005T06, LDC2003E07 and LDC2004T07) as our development data to train the bilingual corpus-based term similarity and get translation probability.
Dictionary: Translation pairs are extracted from HowNet.
Translation Probability: We compute translation probability by Giza++ (Och and Ney, 2000) in development data.
Test dataset: Four datasets are tested in this paper.

Corpus	TDT41 (2002) (Topic#/Story#)	TDT42 (2003) (Topic#/Story#)
English	38/1270	33/617
Chinese	37/657	32/560
Common	40/1927	37/1177

Table1. Statistics on the twoTDT4 datasets.

Corpus	CLTC1 (Topic#/Story#)	CLTC2 (Topic#/Story#)
English	20/200	20/600
Chinese	20/200	20/600
Common	20/400	20/1200

Table2. Statistics on the two CLTC datasets.

TDT4 datasets

We first extract two datasets from the TDT4 evaluation dataset (see statistics in Table 1).

CLTC datasets

The second dataset is extracted from our own cross-lingual topic corpus (CLTC). The news articles are retrieved from Gigaword (English and Chinese), and the topics are labeled by human (see statistics in Table 2).

Evaluation criteria

We adopt the evaluation criteria proposed by Steinbach et al. (2000). The calculation starts from maximum F-measure of each cluster. Let A_i represent the set of articles managed in a system-generated cluster c_i, A_j the set of articles managed in a human-generated cluster c_j. F-measure of the system-generated cluster c_i is calculated as follows.

$$\begin{aligned} p_{i,j} &= \frac{|A_i \cap A_j|}{|A_j|} & p_i &= \max_j\{p_{i,j}\} \\ r_{i,j} &= \frac{|A_i \cap A_j|}{|A_i|} & r_i &= \max_j\{r_{i,j}\} \\ f_{i,j} &= \frac{2 \cdot p_{i,j} \cdot r_{i,j}}{p_{i,j} + r_{i,j}} & f_i &= \max_j\{f_{i,j}\} \end{aligned} \quad (16)$$

where $p_{i,j}$, $r_{i,j}$ and $f_{i,j}$represent precision, recall and measure of cluster when compared with clusterc_j , respectively.

We also use relative F-measure to compare systems over all dataset which is used by Farahat and Kamel (2010).In this approach, the F measure for a particular data set are normalized relative to the best value obtained using different representation models when applying the same clustering algorithm to the same data set:

$$F_r = \frac{F}{\max_i\{F_i\}}, \quad (17)$$

where F_i denotes F-measure values obtained using different representation models.

The relative F measures are then averaged for different data sets.

4.2 Evaluation

Experiment 1: Different word similarity calculation measures

This experiment seeks to compare different cross-lingual word similarity (CLWS) measures. Seven CLWS measures are implemented:
HN: HowNet-based cross-lingual word similarity measure.
SOCPMI^DEV: SOCPMI similarity measure learned from development data.
SOCPMI&DIC: SOCPMI similarity measure calculated in test documents and dictionary as cross-lingual bridge.
SOCPMI&TranPro: SOCPMI similarity measure directly computed in test documents and translation probability on development set as cross-lingual bridge.
COV^DEV: COV similarity measure learned from development data.
COV&DIC: COV similarity measure computed in test documents and dictionary as cross-lingual bridge.

System / Dataset	HN	SOCPMI ^DEV	SOCPMI &DIC	SOCPMI &TranPro	COV ^DEV	COV &DIC	COV &TranPro
TDT41	0.783	0.880	0.854	0.892	0.824	0.868	0.907
TDT42	0.797	0.880	0.835	0.880	0.860	0.840	0.851
CLTC1	0.764	0.818	0.834	0.877	0.782	0.854	0.874
CLTC2	0.667	0.856	0.804	0.839	0.805	0.833	0.840

Table 3. Highest F-measure of CLDC systems with different CLWS measures.

System	HN	SOCPMI ^DEV	SOCPMI &DIC	SOCPMI &TranPro	COV ^DEV	COV &DIC	COV &TranPro
ARF	0.855	0.976	0.945	**0.991**	0.929	0.965	0.986

Table 4. Average of relative F-measure (ARF) of CLDC systems with different CLWS measures.

COV&TranPro: COV similarity measure in test documents and translation probability as cross-lingual bridge.

All the CLDC systems use HAC algorithm to do clustering documents. The thresholds of similarity measures in this paper is all set 0.4 based on our empirical study. Experiment results on four datasets are as Table 3. Table 4 computed from Table 3 shows the average of relative F-measure (ARF) over all data sets for different CLWS measures.

We can observe from Table 3 and Table 4 that the performance of HowNet is much worse than other systems in all dataset. We look into the intermediate results to check the reasons. We find semantic similarities between words computed based on HowNet are too high. For example, word similarity between *Federal Reserve* and *bank* is assigned 1 by HowNet. Error analysis shows that HowNet-based CLWS measure puts much emphasis upon the semantic property of given word rather than semantic itself. So it tends to assign bigger CLWS values to semantically similar word pairs, no matter how semantically relevant they are. This would obviously jeopardize document clustering. With such an observation, we conclude that HowNet-based CLWS measure is not suitable for document clustering.

We can also observe that systems with translation probability outperform those with dictionary when the same monolingual word similarity measures are used. For instance, SOCPMI&TranPro outperforms SOCPMI&DIC by 4.5% on average on relative F-measure and COV&TranPro outperforms COV&DIC by 1.9%. Two reasons are worth noting. First, dictionary extracted from HowNet have more OOV than translation probability computed from development corpus. Translation probability is more discriminative than dictionary when word is ambiguous. It tries to get word similarity from the most frequency translation.

Seen from Table 4 that SOCPMI&TranPro outperforms SOCPMI^DEV by 1.5% on average relative F-measure and COV&TranPro outperforms COV^DEV by 5.5% on average relative F-measure. As both systems use the same development data to get cross-lingual information and the different is that systems computed word similarity in test dataset take use of word occurrence information in test dataset so we can conclude that with combining word similarity in test dataset and translation probability can is useful in cross-lingual document clustering.

And over all seven systems, SOCPMI&TRAN achieves the best result on average, so we select SOCPMI&TRAN as our word similarity measures and next experiments both use this word similarity measure.

Experiment 2: Different feature selection vs. dimension reduction methods

This experiment aims to compare the proposed feature selection method and the existing ones. Three CLDC systems are implemented.

SFS: feature selection we proposed by TF^s-$IDF^s$and soft matching is used in GVSM.

HFS: feature selection by TF-IDF and hard matching is used in GVSM.

NFS: feature selection is not used, which equals to system SOCPMI&TranPro in Experiment 1.

System / Dataset	SFS	HFS	NFS
TDT41	0.900	0.903	0.892
TDT42	0.899	0.881	0.880
CLTC1	0.876	0.869	0.877
CLTC2	0.891	0.847	0.839

Table5. Highest F-measure of CLDC systems with/without feature selection.

System	SFS	HFS	NFS
F-measure	**0.998**	0.980	0.976

Table6. Average of relative F-measure of CLGVSM systems with/without feature selection.

Experiment results on four test datasets are given in Table 5. Table 6 computed from Table 5 shows the ARF over all data sets for different feature selection methods.

Seen from Table 6, system with feature selection we proposed using soft matching outperforms system with feature selection using hard matching by 1.8% on average relative F-measure It also outperforms system without feature selection by 2.2% on average relative F-measure.

This reveals that feature selection does improve GVSM. The reason why it works is that with TF^sandDF^s, it can select the most representative terms as feature set and with proper document representation method, documents are properly matched into feature space.

Experiment 3: Different document representation models

This experiment aims to compare CLGVSM with VSM and LSA. Three CLDC systems are implemented:

CLGVSM: Our system, which equals FS system in Experiment 2.

VSM: A baseline system that uses VSM to represent documents and cosine similarity to compute document systems. HowNet dictionary is used to match terms in different languages.

LSA: LSA uses dictionary to match terms in different languages and make use of LSA in test dataset. The number of LSA dimensions is set to 200,

Experiment results on two data sets are given in Table 7. Table 8 computed from Table 7 shows the ARF over all data sets for different document representation models.

System	CLGVSM	VSM	LSA
TDT41	0.900	0.877	0.885
TDT42	0.899	0.835	0.881
CLTC1	0.876	0.792	0.867
CLTC2	0.891	0.776	0.841

Table7. Highest F-measure of CLDCsystems with different document representation models.

System	CLGVSM	VSM	LSA
F-measure	**1**	0.920	0.974

Table8. Average of relative F-measure of CLDCsystems with different document representation models.

We can observe from Table 8 that CLGVSM outperforms VSM by 8.0% on average relative F-measure. It means CLGVSM improve cross-lingual document clustering by using SOCPMI^TRAN similarity measure. Observation shows that the word similarity measure makes significant contribution to document clustering. Using second order co-occurrence information of words, SOCPMI assigns word pair with higher PMI a higher similarity. This coincides perfectly with the real demand in word similarity measuring. For example, word similarity between 犯罪分子 (*criminal*) and *imprisonment* is assigned 0.49 by SOCPMI. When 犯罪分子 is chosen as a feature, document containing *imprisonment* holds a reasonable similarity with document containing 犯罪分子 even though they do not contain common word.

Results also show that CLGVSM outperforms LSA by 2.6% on average relative F-measure. It means CLGVSM is better than LSA in cross-lingual document clustering by using SOCPMI^TRAN similarity measure. The follow reason is worth noting. When dictionary is used to match words in LSA, the semantic relation between different translations of one term in one document is added and this brings much noise. While in CLGVSM, cross-lingual terms are soft matched by SOCPMI^TRAN term similarity.

5 Conclusion

In this paper, we extend monolingual generalized VSM (GVSM) to handle cross-lingual cases, referred to as CLGVSM, by incorporating cross-lingual word similarity measures.Under GVSM, we compare different word similarity measures in cross-lingual document clustering. We propose new feature selection method for CLGVSM and experiments show it improves document clustering. We also compare CLGVSM and other well-known document representation models such as VSM and LSA and experiments show it outperform both VSM and LSA significantly.

Three conclusions can be drawn in this paper. Firstly, HowNet-based word similarity method is less suitable for document clustering. Secondly, translation probability computed from a development dataset as a cross-lingual bridge performs better than HowNet dictionary. At last, combining word similarity in test dataset and translation probability in development dataset can help cross-lingual document clustering.

In the future, we will apply CLGVSM in more languages pairs and extend it in more than two languages. As GVSM represents document with semantic space, we can utilize GVSM to handle sparse data problem in short text clustering.

Acknowledgment

This work is partially supported by NSFC (60703051) and MOST (2009DFA12970). We thank the reviewers for the valuable comments.

References

D. M. Blei, A. Y. Ng, and M.I. Jordan. 2003. Latent dirichlet allocation. J. Machine Learning Research (3):993-1022.

K. W. Church and P. Hanks. 1990. Word association norms, mutual information, and lexicography. Computational Linguistics, 16(1):22-29.

P. Cimiano, A. Schultz, S. Sizov, P. Sorg, and S. Staab. Explicit vs. latent concept models for cross-language information retrieval. Proc. of IJCAI'09, 2009.

C. Corley and R. Mihalcea. 2005. Measuring the semantic similarity of texts, Proc. of the ACL Workshop on Empirical Modeling of Semantic Equivalence and Entailment, p.13-18, June 30-30, 2005, Ann Arbor, Michigan

Z. Dong and Q. Dong. 2006. HowNet and the Computation of Meaning. World Scientific Publishing Co. Inc., River Edge, NJ, USA.

D. K. Evans and J. L. Klavans. 2003. A Platform for Multilingual News Summarization, Technical Report. Department of Computer Science, Columbia University.

A. K. Farahat, M. S.Kamel.2010. Statistical semantic for enhancing document clustering. Knowledge and Information Systems.

A. Hotho, S. Staab,G. Stumme. 2003. WordNet improves text document clustering. Proc. of SIGIR2003 semantic web workshop.ACM, New York, pp. 541-544.

A. Islam and D. Inkpen. 2006. Second order co-occurrence PMI for determining the semantic similarity of words. Proc. LREC'2006: 1033-1038

A. Islam and D. Inkpen. 2008 Semantic text similarity using corpus-based word similarity and string similarity, ACM Transactions on Knowledge Discovery from Data (TKDD) v.2 (2), pp.1-25, July 2008

T. K. Landauer and S. T. Domais. 1997. A Solution to Plato's Problem: The Latent Semantic Analysis Theory of Acquisition, Induction and Representation of Knowledge. Psychological Review. 104(2):211-240.

T. Landauer, P. W. Foltz and D. Laham. 1998. Introduction to Latent Semantic Analysis. Discourse Processes 25: 259-284.

T. Leek, H. Jin, S. Sista, and R. Schwartz. 1999. The BBN cross-lingual topic detection and tracking system. Proc. of TDT' 1999.

Y. Li, J. Shawe-Tylor, 2007, Advanced learning algorithms for cross-language patent retrieval and classification. Information Processing and Management v.43(5), pp 1183-1199, September, 2007.

Q Liu, S Li. 2002.Word similarity computing base don Hownet. Computational Linguistics and Chinese Language Processing. (in Chinese)

B. Mathieu, R. Besancon and C. Fluhr. 2004. Multilingual Document Clusters Discovery. Proc. of RIAO'2004: 1-10.

F. J. Och, H. Ney. 2000. Improved Statistical Alignment Models. Proc. of the 38th Annual Meeting of the Association for Computational Linguistics: 440-447.

B. Pouliquen, R. Steinberger, C. Ignat, E. Käsper, I. Temnikova. 2004. Multilingual and cross-lingual news topic tracking. Proc. of COLING'2004:959-965.

P. Resnik. 1999. Semantic similarity in a taxonomy: An information based measure and its application to problems of ambiguity in natural language. Journal of Artificial Intelligence Research, V.11:95–130.

R. Rosenfeld. 1996. A maximum entropy approach to adaptive statistical language modeling. Computer speech and language. 10:187-228.

P. D. Turney. 2001. Mining the Web for Synonyms: PMI-IR versus LSA on TOEFL. Proc. of ECML'2001: 491-502.

E. M. Voorhees. 1986. Implementing Agglomerative Hierarchic Clustering Algorithms for Use in Document Retrieval. Information Processing and Management, 22(6): 465-76.

C-P. Wei, C. C. Yang and C-M. Lin. 2008. A Latent Semantic Indexing Based Approach to Multilingual Document Clustering. Decision Support System. 45(3):606-620.

S. K. M. Wong, W. Ziarko, P. C. N. Wong. 1985 Generalized vector model in information retrieval. Proc. of the 8th ACM SIGIR:18-25

Y. Xia, T. Zhao, and P. Jin. 2011. Measuring Chinese-English Cross-lingual Word Similarity with HowNet and Parallel Corpus. Proc. of CICling'2011(II):221-233.

D. Yogatamaan, K.Tanaka. 2009. Multilingual Spectral Clustering Using Document Similarity Propagation. Proc. of EMNLP'2009: 871-879.

Thread Cleaning and Merging for Microblog Topic Detection

Jianfeng Zhang[1,2], Yunqing Xia[1], Bin Ma[1,2], Jianmin Yao[2], and Yu Hong[2]
[1]Dept. of Comp. Sci. & Tech., Tsinghua University, Beijing 100084, China
yqxia@tsinghua.edu.cn
[2]School of Comp. Sci. & Tech., Soochow University, Suzhou 215104, China
{jfzhang, bma, jyao, hongy}@suda.edu.cn

Abstract

As a classic natural language processing technology, topic detection recently attracts more research interests due largely to the rapid development of microblog. The most challenging issue in microblog topic detection is sparse data problem. In this paper, the temporal-author-topic (TAT) model is designed to accomplish microblog topic detection in two phases. In the first phase, the TAT model is applied to clean the thread, namely, to filter noisy microblog texts out of each thread. In the second phase, microblog texts within each thread are merged to form the thread text so that the TAT model is applied to find global topics. The new approach differs from the Hierarchical Agglomerative Clustering (HAC) algorithm by making use of microblog threads to overcome the sparse data problem. Experimental results justify our claims.

1 Introduction

Topic detection is the technique that discovers the latent topics from the given collection of text. Originated from the famous TDT evaluation workshop[1], topic detection research has attracted intensive and persistent interests from governments with security purpose. With the rapid advance of the Internet, the Web content becomes so plentiful that people start to explore how to make good use of the content with commercial purpose. Very recently, microblog becomes surprisingly popular. According to the recent Twitter statistics, 155 million tweets are created per day on average[2]. This leads to huge research passion on the microblog content.

Theoretically, topic detection from microblog text is similar to that from news articles. However, the microblog text is rather different from news articles. According to Ellen et al. (2011), microblog text is a typical microtext. Compared to regular long text such as news article, the microblog text exhibits the following characteristics.

- **Short**. Every microblog text finishes in less than 140. In fact, most texts are only a sentence or even a phrase.
- **Informal**. Spoken language is typically used, usually containing abbreviations and misspellings.
- **Semi-structured.** Each microblog text contains text as well as author and time.
- **Highly contextual**. Most microblog texts are created by replying or evaluating the existing texts. Meanwhile, they are replied or evaluated by others.
- **Conversational.** The microblog texts are usually naturally organized by thousands of conversation threads. In the thread, we name the top text by *head posting*, and the remaining texts by *followup postings*.

The following challenges in microblog text processing are worth noting. Firstly, microblog texts, especially the *followup postings*, contain very few characters. This inevitably leads to serious sparse data problem when machine learning algorithms are adopted to handle the microblog texts. Secondly, grammar is usually informal in microblog texts. Abbreviations and misspellings are constant. This makes standard language processing tools inapplicable on microblog texts. Thirdly, in the *followup postings*, anaphora and ellipsis are constantly used. This makes topic analysis rather difficult.

Some related work has been reported on microtext such as chat language and short messages (Dyke et al., 1999; Zhou et al., 2005; Shen et al., 2006; Peng et al., 2007). An earlier attempt on microblog text processing is Shen et al. (2009), which adopts TFIDF algorithm to analyze the Chinese microblog texts. Ramage et al. (2010) maps Twitter texts to four potential

[1] http://projects.ldc.upenn.edu/TDT/
[2] http://techcrunch.com/2011/04/06/twitter-q1-stats/

dimensions by labeled LDA, then sorts and recommends Twitter based on the result of LDA. However, the common drawback of the related work is sparse data problem because each posting is viewed as an individual text.

We argue that each microblog thread maintains a dominating topic, and that the thread structure plays an important role in microblog topic detection. In this work, the temporal-author-topic (TAT) model is designed to accomplish microblog topic detection in two phases. In the first phase, the TAT model is applied on each thread to organize the intra-thread postings into a few clusters, in which the cluster containing the head posting should dominate. The intention is to exclude the *followup postings* that are irrelevant to the head *posting* from the thread. In this way, the thread is made cleaner. In the second phase, postings within each cleaned thread are merged to form a bigger text, referred to as thread text. The TAT model is then applied on the thread texts to find global topics.

The new approach makes use of microblog threads to address the sparse data problem, which makes the approach different from any hierarchical text clustering approaches, e.g., Hierarchical Agglomerative Clustering (HAC). As it contains all relevant postings in the thread, the thread text is longer that any individual posting. In this manner, the sparse data problem can be relieved to great extent. Contributions of this work are summarized as follows.

(1) The thread structure in microblog is investigated in this work to address the sparse data problem in microblog topic detection. We argue cleaning and merging are crucial.

(2) A benchmark dataset is developed, which can be used by researchers to evaluate microblog topic detection approaches.

(3) The temporal-author-topic (TAT) model is proposed to model microblog text.

(4) A two-phase approach is designed to accomplish microblog topic detection. In the first phase, the thread structure is used to clean every thread. In the second phase, each cleaned thread is merged to form a bigger text so that microblog topic detection is made more accurate.

The rest of this paper is organized as follows. In Section 2, related work is summarized. In Section 3, the principle of our approach is given. In section 4, the temporal-author-topic model is described. Section 5 presents the two-phase topic detection approach. Section 6 presents experimental results as well as discussions. We conclude this paper in Section 7.

2 Related Work

2.1 Topic Detection

Topic detection (TD) appeared as a subtask in TDT (topic detection and tracking) evaluation workshops. Since 1998, many research efforts have been made. The earlier work is carried out under TDT evaluation. Many famous universities and companies such as IBM Watson, BBN, CMU and CUHK, have participated in TDT workshop. TDT has been more and more important.

Two subtasks are included in TD evaluation, i.e., online topic detection and hierarchical topic detection. Online topic detection (OTD) is to detect new topic and collect the subsequent relevant news. The OTD systems usually focus on selection and combination of the clustering methods. Generally, k-means clustering algorithm is adopted by researchers. Yang et al. (1998) first adopted the hierarchy clustering to detect topics, but the results can be further enhanced. Therefore, Xu et al. (1999) and Wartena et al. (2008) used k-means to cluster the news streams to realize the topic detection, and the results are better than previous work. Papka et al. (1999) compared different clustering algorithms and attempted to combine the advantage of each algorithm. The results show the combination is efficient.

TDT 2004 defines a new TD task: hierarchical topic detection (HTD)[3]. HTD presents that the theme and topic of the news reports usually distribute in different levels. For example, *Financial Crisis in Wall Street* and *Rise of Gold Price* both belong to the topic *The 10 Financial Events in 2009*, but the emphasis of the theme makes two reports in different levels. Cutting et al. (1992) proposed a hybrid clustering algorithm to improve traditional HAC (Hierarchical Agglomerative Clustering). Trieschnigg et al. (2004) adopted incremental hierarchical clustering to implement HTD. Complexity of TD is decreased in this approach, on condition that remaining efficiency of clustering. All proposed TD approaches can achieve good performance in regular texts. However, it is not known whether the clustering algorithms are effective in microblog TD.

[3] http://ciir.cs.umass.edu/pubfiles/ir-389.pdf

Our approach is similar to HAC in nature. However, two differences are worth noting. First, each microblog thread is viewed as a priori cluster in our approach. The intra-thread topic detection helps to clean the thread. In contrast, the HAC approach does not use the thread structure. Second, the irrelevant postings are excluded in forming the thread text, which is used in higher level topic clustering. Differently, the HAC approach excludes no text.

2.2 Mircoblog Text Processing

Microblog is a user-relationship based platform to assist user sharing and gaining information. As microblog booms, microtext is made large scale. Microblog text processing has thus become an important topic. In this paper, we mainly summarize the related work on microblog topic detection. Microblog topic detection exhibits profound significance. Two functions are interesting. Firstly, it is able to remind users of the important events that has happened or is happening in a period. Sharifi et al. (2010) proposed a method to summarize the topic in microblog. Microblog texts were detected if they contain the same maximum common substring, and the substring is regarded as the title of microblog topic. Nevertheless, there exists much noise in the microblog postings. Thus, the maximum common substring might be a meaningless phrase or sentence. O'Connor et al. (2010) used document clustering and text summarization techniques to induce topics that are relevant to the query[4]. The main idea of the method is still to match the microblog texts that contain the key words or phrases, making the results less accurate.

Secondly, irrelevant texts can be filtered out with topic detection approach. Wang et al. (2010) proposed a TwitterRank algorithm, which sorts the returned microblog texts by relevance score. In Liu et al. (2010), a feature selection method based on part-of-speech and HowNet is proposed, which can improve the performance of microblog classification. Similarly, Sriram et al. (2010) classified tweets into five categories, i.e. News, Events, Opinions, Deals and Private Messages by making use of author information within the tweets. With such a system, user can choose to view tweets based on their interest. Unfortunately, every posting is regarded as an individual text in previous methods, suffering the serious sparse data problem.

[4] http://tweetmotif.com/

3 The Principle

3.1 The Idea

To illustrate our idea, we take a *head posting* and its *followup postings* as a Twitter example in Figure 1.

With thousands of samples like Figure 1, we make observations and come up with the corresponding arguments as follows.

Figure 1. A Twitter head posting and its *followup* postings

Observation 1: The *followup postings* are created to reply the head posting directly or indirectly.

Argument 1: Postings in one thread are usually topic-relevant.

For example, the three *followup postings* in Figure 1 are all topic-relevant.

Observation 2: There exist a few irrelevant postings, e.g., spam and meaningless postings.

Argument 2: The irrelevant postings can be distinguished from the relevant ones considering content similarity.

Observation 3: The individual postings are very short, i.e., up to 140 characters, while a thread usually contains more than 20 postings, which add up to more than 200 words.

Argument 3: The topic-relevant postings in a thread can be merged to form a bigger text so as to relieve sparse data problem.

With above arguments, we propose a two-phase microblog topic detection approach, in which irrelevant postings are filtered out of the threads in the first phase and relevant postings in each thread are merged to form a bigger thread text.

3.2 Definitions

For description convenience, we first give some definitions being related to microblog text.

***Definition* 1: Posting**. A *posting* is a piece of semi-structured microblog text that covers author, time and textual content, denoted with d.

***Definition* 2: Head Posting**. A *head posting* is a piece of microblog text that is spontaneously delivered, denoted with d^H.

***Definition* 3: Followup Posting**. A *followup posting* is a piece of microblog text that replies to another piece of microblog text, denoted with d^F.

***Definition* 4: Thread**. A *thread* is a set of microblog texts that contains the head posting and the *followup postings*, denoted with $T=(V,E)$. The thread complies with the tree structure.

***Definition* 5: Forest**. A *forest* is a set of microblog threads, denoted with $F=(V^{\cup},E^{\cup})$.

An example microblog forest is given in Figure 2, in which three threads maintains three head postings and fourteen *followup postings*.

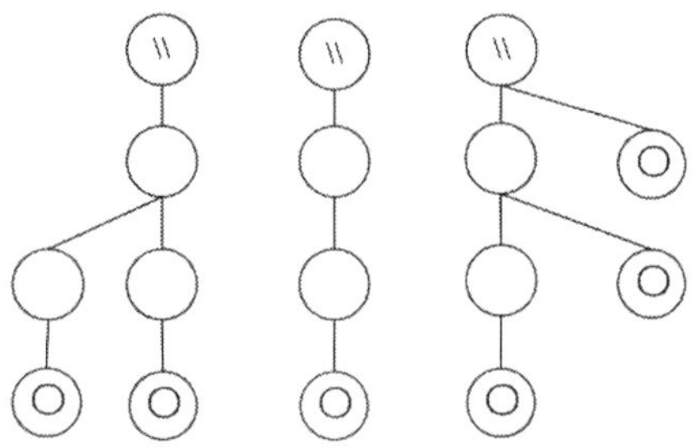

Figure 2. The example microblog forest contains three threads, where ◎ represents the *head posting*, ○ the non-leaf *followup postings*, and ◎ the leaf *followup postings*.

The forest structure discloses some important information. As shown in Figure 2, every thread begins with a head posting and contains a few *followup postings*.

3.3 The Workflow

The workflow of our two-phase topic detection approach is given in Figure 3. In the first phase, intra-thread topic detection is run locally to find irrelevant *followup postings* within each thread. In the second phase, the relevant postings in each thread are merged to form a thread text so that the global topic detection is achieved with the thread texts. As thread texts are bigger in size, global topic detection can thus yield better results. In this way, sparse data problem in microblog topic detection can be alleviated to great extent.

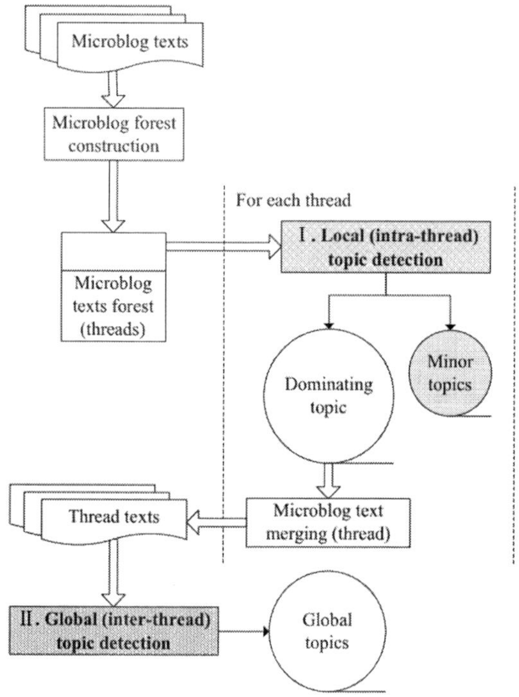

Figure 3. The workflow of our approach.

4 The Approach

Topic detection relies on a topic models. In this work, the temporal-author-topic model (TAT) is proposed to handle microblog texts. For description convenience, we first give the probabilistic topic model.

4.1 Probabilistic Topic Model

The common topic model used in topic detection is probabilistic topic model. Three distributions are given as follows:

(1) Word-topic distribution: $P(w,z)=\varphi(z)$;

(2) Word-topic dispatch: $P(w|z)=\delta(w)$

(3) Word-document distribution: $P(w,d)=\psi(d)$;

where z represents a topic, and w a word. The topic analysis actually judges the topic distribution $\theta(d)$ of document d.

4.2 Temporal-Author-Topic Model

As a kind of Internet microtext, the microblog text is intentional, conversational and

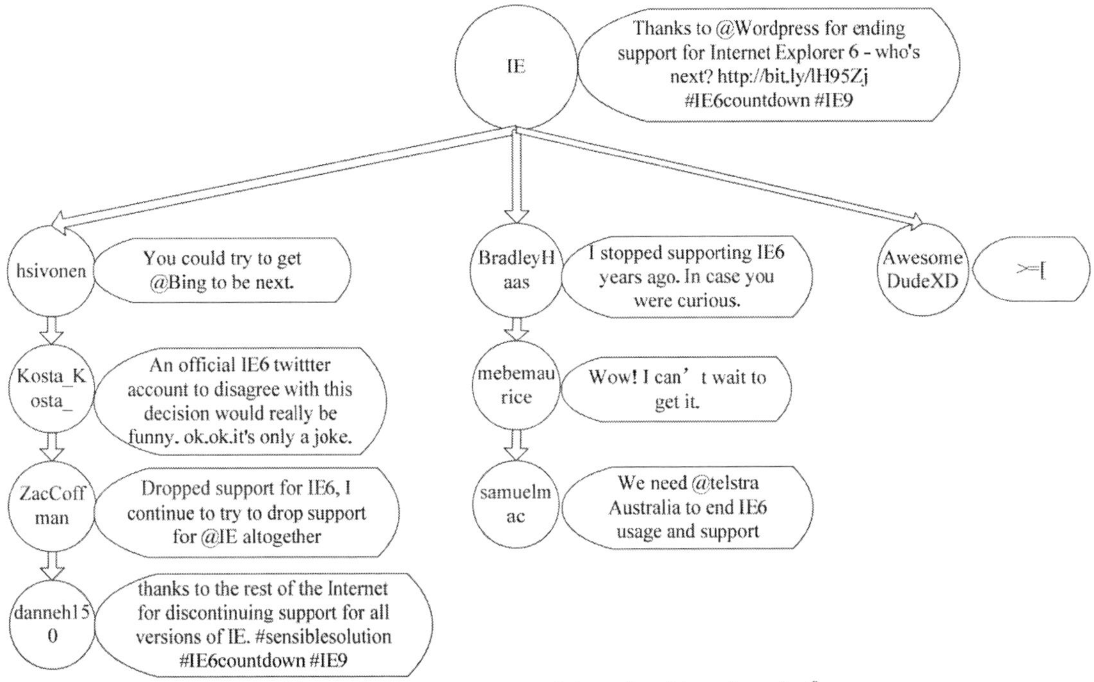

Figure 4. Tree structure of the microblog thread T^O

personalized. The topic model for the microblog texts should reflect above characteristics. We consider the following information as the features in microblog topic detection.

- **Author**: In the microblog texts, author is a prominent feature. Observations show that one author usually participates in a limited number of topics. In this work, the author information is added in the common topic model, and the author-topic (AT) model is formed.
- **Timestamp**: We also find out that, if an author delivers several statements within a short period, these statements probably focus on a limited number of topics. Thus we define the interval as one hour, which means two posts are probably related to the same topic if they are delivered within one hour. Considering the temporal information, the AT model then evolves to the temporal-author-topic (TAT) model.
- **Thread**: Thread information is very important to microblog topic detection. Suppose a set of postings belong to the same conversation thread, they are assumed to talk about the same topic, which is initiated by the *head posting*. In this work, thread information is viewed as a key feature.

Finally, based on the common topic model, TAT adds in the following distributions:

(4) Temporal-Author-Topic distribution: $P(t,a,w,z)=\rho(z)$;

(5) Temporal-Author-Topic dispatch: $P(t,a,w|z)=\sigma(w)$;

where t is timestamp, a the author.

The distribution can be obtained from microblog text development dataset.

4.3 Local Topic Detection

Local topic detection, also called intra-thread topic detection, is the first phase in microblog topic detection. In this phase, the topic analysis is one-cluster based, which means that a dominating topic will be detected while the texts in the other topics are deemed irrelevant to the dominating topic.

Figure 4 gives a tree structure of the microblog thread T^O in Figure 1. The thread tree has three sub-trees, namely, there are three subtopics within thread T^O. However, seen from Figure 4, the right sub-tree is obviously not relevant to the dominating topic. Thus in this thread, the posting in the right sub-tree is deemed a spam posting. We adopt topic detection to filter such spam postings in every microblog thread.

The TAT model is used in thread topic detection in this work. We further consider more heuristics. In microblog threads, there exist many *followup postings*.

Given a pair of postings, in which one posting replies the other, the two postings P_1 and P_2 hold *A-reply-B* relation. They are assumed to talk about the same topic. The *A-reply-B* relation plays an important role in thread topic detection. We define that, if two postings hold the *A-reply-B* relation, in clustering, the similarity of two postings is increased by a parameter λ. The similarity formula is given as follows.

$$Sim(P_1, P_2) = \lambda + Sim(P_1, P_2),$$
$$\lambda = \frac{1}{|N|} \quad , \quad (1)$$

where $Sim(P_1, P_2)$ represents the posting similarity calculated with VSM model, and $|N|$ is the number of postings in the thread.

Due to the quantity of spam postings is small, after calculating the similarity, the cluster which has the least postings may be filtered as the spam. As a result, a clean and topic-related thread T^R is obtained from thread T^O.

4.4 Global Topic Detection

Global topic detection, also referred to as inter-thread topic detection, is conducted on forest level. Microblog texts are usually very short, i.e., less than 140 characters. We propose to make use of thread structure to address the sparse data problem. We merge microblog texts in every clean thread to form a bigger thread text. Then the global topic detection is achieved with thread texts. Once a thread text is assigned a topic label, microblog texts in this thread are all assign the label. In this way, the ultimate goal of microblog topic detection is achieved.

Denote thread text being generated with thread T^R by X_i, which is combination of all the posts in thread T^R. Now we convert the microblog text into a set of thread texts $X_{i=1,...,N}$. The global topic detection is executed on $X_{i=1,...,N}$ to find microblog topics.

4.5 LDA-based Feature Weighting

TFIDF (term frequency and inverse document frequency) is widely used to calculate feature weights. In this paper, we also evaluate the Latent Dirichlet Allocation (LDA) in feature selection. LDA is proven better than TFIDF in regular texts (Madsen et al., 2005; Krestel et al., 2009). In this work, we evaluate how it works on microblog texts.

LDA is an unsupervised model proposed by Blei et al. (2003). It views every text as the combination of topics, and transfers the dimension of words into topics.

To be specific, LDA models document as a mixture of *K* latent topics, each of which is a multinomial distribution over a word vocabulary *W*. For document j, we first draw a mixed proportion $\theta_{k|j}$ from a Dirichlet with parameter α. For the ith word in the document, a topic z_{ij} is drawn with topic k chosen with probability $\theta_{k|j}$. Then word x_{ij} is drawn from the z_{ij}^{th} topic by taking on value *w* with probability $\phi_{w|k}$. Finally, a Dirichlet prior with parameter β is placed on the topics $\phi_{w|k}$. Thus, the generative process is given as follows.

$$\phi_{k|j} \sim D[\alpha] \quad \phi_{w|k} \sim D[\beta]$$
$$z_{ij} \sim \theta_{k|j} \quad x_{ij} \sim \phi_{w|z_{ij}} \quad (2)$$

Given the observed words $X = \{x_{ij}\}$, Bayesian inference seeks to compute the posterior distribution over the latent topic indices $Z = \{z_{ij}\}$, the mixed proportion $\theta_{k|j}$, and the topics $\phi_{w|k}$. An efficient procedure is to use collapsed Gibbs sampling, where θ and ϕ are marginalized out, and the latent variables Z are sampled. Given the current state of all but one variable z_{ij}, the conditional probability of z_{ij} is given below.

$$p(z_{ij} = k | z^{\neg ij}), x, \alpha, \beta) \propto$$
$$(\alpha + n_{k|j}^{\neg ij})(\beta + n_{x_{ij}|k}^{\neg ij})(w\beta + n_k^{\neg ij}) \quad , \quad (3)$$

where the superscript $\neg ij$ means that the corresponding data-item is excluded in the count values, and $n_{jkw} = \#\{i : x_{ij} = w, z_{ij} = k\}$. We use the convention that missing indices are summed out: $\sum_w n_{jkw}$ and $n_{w|k} = \sum_j n_{jkw}$.

4.6 VSM-based Document Similarity

Vector Space Model (VSM) is a widely used document representation model. Let *d* represent a document and $\{t_i\}_{i=1,...,K}$ feature terms appearing in document *d*. Then document *d* can be represented by the following text vector V_d according to the TFIDF or LDA.

$$V_d = (t_1 : w_1^s; ...; t_K^s),$$

where w_i^s is weight of feature term t_i.

In VSM, document similarity is usually measured using the cosine function, which is given as follows.

$$Sim(d_1, d_2) = \frac{D_1^T, D_2}{\sqrt{D_1^T, D_1}\sqrt{D_2^T, D_2}}, \quad (4)$$

where D_1 and D_2 denote the two document vectors.

4.7 Text Clustering

Any clustering algorithms can be used in our algorithm. In this work, but we choose K-means (Duda et al., 1973) and HAC (Voorhees, 1986).

HAC is similar to our approach due to the hierarchical nature. So we intend to compare our approach against HAC. We select K-means because it is a classical clustering algorithm.

5 Experiment

5.1 Data Preparation

There is no benchmark dataset that fits into our scenario. We have to compile the gold standard by ourselves.

We use SINA microblog API[5] to extract Chinese microblog texts. Then the gold standard is compiled by six human annotators. The annotation scheme complies with the TDT4 annotation guideline.

Finally, we constructed a microblog dataset containing 1,100 threads and 16,500 postings (i.e., 15 postings in each thread on average). The postings are managed in 100 topics.

5.2 Evaluation Metrics

We adopted the evaluation metrics proposed by Steinbach et al. (2000). The calculation starts from the maximum *F*-measure in each cluster. Let A_i represent the set of articles that are managed in a system-generated cluster c_i, A_j is the set of articles managed in a human-generated cluster c_j. *F* measure of the system-generated cluster c_i is calculated as follows.

$$
\begin{aligned}
p_{i,j} &= \frac{|A_i \cap A_j|}{|A_j|} & p_i &= \max_j\{p_{i,j}\} \\
r_{i,j} &= \frac{|A_i \cap A_j|}{|A_i|} & r_i &= \max_j\{r_{i,j}\}, \\
f_{i,j} &= \frac{2 \cdot p_{i,j} \cdot r_{i,j}}{p_{i,j} + r_{i,j}} & f_i &= \max_j\{f_{i,j}\}
\end{aligned}
\quad (5)
$$

where $p_{i,j}$, $r_{i,j}$ and $f_{i,j}$ represent precision, recall and *F* measure of cluster c_i when compared with cluster c_j, respectively.

5.3 The Approaches

Three baseline approaches are developed in this work. The intention is to evaluate the influence of author, timestamp and thread information on topic analysis, respectively.

Baseline B1: Only posting text is used in topic detection. All postings are used equally in topic detection.

Baseline B2: Author information is added to the baseline system B1 and the author-topic (AT) model is formed. All postings are used equally in topic detection.

Baseline B3: Timestamp is added to baseline system B2 and the temporal-author-topic (TAT) model is formed. All postings are used equally in topic detection.

Our approach OUR: The TAT model is used in topic modeling. The thread information is considered, and topics within microblog texts are detected in two phases.

Note that TFIDF or LDA are adopted for feature selection and HAC or K-means for text clustering in all systems. To evaluate how topic number influences the approach, six predefined class numbers are defined in this experiment, ranging from 50 to 100.

5.4 Results and Discussions

Table 1 reports the experimental results of our approach and the baselines on gold-standard dataset of predefined cluster number of 100, which use TFIDF or LDA feature selection and HAC or K-means clustering algorithm.

	K-means + TFIDF (%)	K-means + LDA (%)	HAC + TFIDF (%)	HAC + LDA (%)
B1	21.1	23.2	17.2	21.7
B2	25.5	26.4	22.2	25
B3	25.2	27	21.8	25.4
OUR	26.6	31.2	24.7	27.5

Table 1. F measure values of approaches with predefined topic number 100.

Three observations are made on the experiment results. Firstly, according to Table 1, system B2 outperforms B1 by 4.6%, system B3 outperforms B2 by 1.1%, and our system outperforms B3 by 2.8% on average. It is thus proven that author, timestamp and thread information are important in microblog topic detection.

The significant outperformance can be explained by two types of errors that constantly happen in baseline systems but not in our system. Errors of the first type come from the conversation threads. In the baseline systems, each posting is considered as an individual text. The contextual information is ignored in the clustering process. For example, one posting reads: *It's really cute*! It is difficult for the baseline systems to figure out which topic it belongs to. In contrast, our approach can merge the posting to the head posting reads: *Beijing Kennel Club adopts six stray dogs*. It is no longer for our system to detect what is really cute.

[5] http://open.weibo.com/wiki/index.php/SDK

The second typical error comes from the sparse data problem. As aforementioned, a posting is considered as an individual text in baseline systems. When we use TFIDF or LDA in feature selection and adopt VSM to represent the posting, the data sparseness is serious. For instance, a text vector V_i looks like

$$V_i = (t_1 : 0; t_2 : 0; ...; t_{k-1} : 1, t_k : 0),$$

where only the feature t_{k-1} appears in the posting. We even find some extreme postings that contain no feature at all. It is difficult to calculate the similarity between two such postings.

In our approach, thread is viewed as a whole, and thread text is used to find global topics. The sparse data problem is alleviated to great extent. This is the major reason that leads to significant outperformance.

Secondly, we compare feature selection algorithms, i.e. TFIDF and LDA, in all experiments. LDA is demonstrated to be better than TFIDF in regular texts. In this work, we try to prove this conclusion with microblog texts. As shown in Table 1, the system using LDA outperforms that uses TFIDF. We thus conclude that the conclusion made by Madsen, et al. (2005) and Krestel et al. (2009) is also true on microblog texts.

Thirdly, we compare different clustering algorithms, i.e. HAC and K-means, in our experiments. Seen from Table 1, the system using K-means outperforms that uses HAC. We can conclude that K-means algorithm fits into our approach better than HAC.

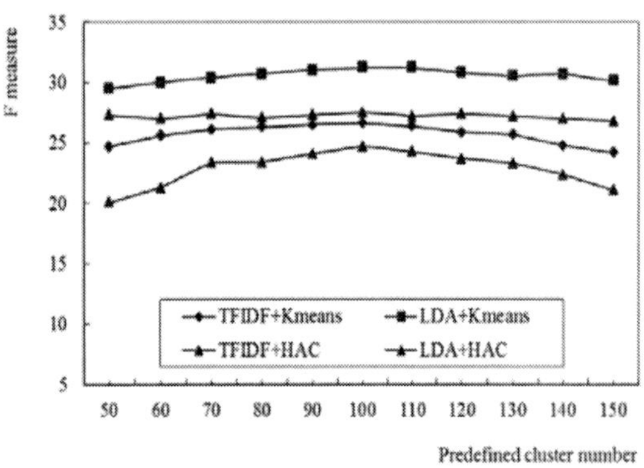

Figure 4. F measure curves of our approach with various topic numbers.

Finally, we evaluate how the predefined topic number influences the clustering algorithm. Seen from Figure 4, the approaches with LDA perform stably with different topic number. But for the approaches with TFIDF, different trend is disclosed. Performance of the approaches climbs gradually. Shown in Figure 4, our approach improves less when topic number is closer to 100. When the topic number is bigger than 100, F measure of our approach starts to drop. It can thus be concluded that TFIDF is sensitive to topic number than LDA. Note that the topic number in the gold standard dataset is 100. We thus conclude that the approach fits to the datasets well.

6 Conclusion and Future Work

In this paper, the Temporal-Author-Topic (TAT) model is proposed for microblog topic detection. Experimental results show that, the new model fits specially into microblog when information about timestamp and author is incorporated. We further make use of the thread information and propose a two-phase approach. Intra-thread topic detection is first executed to clean every thread, and then inter-thread topic detection is run to find global topics more precisely with bigger thread texts. The notable contribution lies in that the serious sparse data problem in microblog processing is alleviated to great extent.

However, the reported work is still preliminary. In the future, we will conduct full evaluation with microblog text in multiple languages. Meanwhile, we are aware that the maximum F measure (i.e., 31.2%) of the approach is rather low. We will incorporate various word similarity measures to achieve feature selection and document similarity in concept level.

Acknowledgments

This work is partially supported by NSFC (60703051, 60970057, 61003152), MOST (2009DFA12970) and Suzhou Municipal Foundation (SYG201030). We thank the reviewers for the valuable comments.

References

M. Blei, Y. Ng, I. Jordan. 2003. Latent Dirichlet Allocation. *Journal of Machine Learning Research 3 (2003)*: 993-1022.

D. Cutting, D. Karger, J. O. Pedersen, and J. W. Tukey. 1992. A cluster-based approach to browsing large document collections. In *Proceedings of the 15th annual international ACM SIGIR conference on Research and development in information retrieval*. NY: ACM, 1992, 318–329.

R. Duda and P. Hart. 1973. Pattern Classification and Scene Analysis. *John Wiley and Sons, Inc.*, New York, NY.

N. Dyke, H. Lieberman, P. Maes. 1999. Butterfly: A Conversation-Finding Agent for Internet Relay Chat. *Proc. of the 4th international conference on Intelligent User Interfaces, 1999.*

J. Ellen. 2011. All about microtext: A working definition and a survey of current microtext research within artificial intelligence and natural language processing. *Proc. of ICAART-11.*

R. Krestel, P. Fankhauser, W. Nejdl. 2009. Latent dirichlet allocation for tag recommendation. *Proceedings of the third ACM conference on Recommender system*, 2009.

Z. Liu, W. Yu, W. Chen, S. Wang, F. Wu. 2010. Short Text Feature Selection and Classification for Micro Blog Mining. *Proceedings of International Conference on Computational Intelligence and Software Engineering (CISE 2010)*, pp.1-4, 2010.

R. E. Madsen, D. Kauchak, C. Elkan. 2005. Modeling word burstiness using the Dirichlet distribution. *ICML '05 Proceedings of the 22nd international conference on Machine learning, ACM, New York,* 2005.

B. O'Connor, M. Krieger and D. Ahn. 2010. TweetMotif: Exploratory Search and Topic Summarization for Twitter. *Proc. of ICWSM 2010.*

R. Papka. 1999. On-line New Event Detection, Clustering and Tracking. *Amherst: Department of Computer Science, UMASS.*

J. Peng, D. Yang, S. Tang, Y. Fu, H. Jiang. 2007. A Novel Text Clustering Algorithm Based on Inner Product Space Model of Semantic. Computer Journal, 2007, 8 (30): 1354-1363.

D. Ramage, S. Dumais and D. Liebling. 2010. Characterizing Microblogs with Topic Models. *In ICWSM'2010.*

B. Sharifi, M.-A. Hutton and J. Kalita. 2010. Summarizing Microblogs Automatically. *Proc. of NAACL-HLT'2010*: 685-688.

D. Shen, Q. Yang, J. Sun, Z. Chen. 2006. Thread Detection in Dynamic Text Message Streams. *Proc. of SIGIR'06*: 35-42.

Y. Shen, C. Tian, S. Li, S. Liu. 2009. The Grand Information Flows in Micro-blog. *Journal of Information & Computational Science 6*: 2 (2009): 683-690.

B. Sriram, D. Fuhry, E.Demir, H. Ferhatosmanoglu. 2010. Short Text Classification in Twitter to Improve Information Filtering. In Sigir'10, Performance Evaluation, 841-842.ACM.

M. Steinbach, G. Kapypis and V. Kumar. 2000. A Comparison of Document Clustering Techniques. *KDD Workshop on Text Mining*, 2000:109-111.

D. Trieschnigg and W Kraaij. 2004. TNO hierarchical topic detection report at TDT 2004. *The 7th Topic Detection and Tracking Conf.*

E. M. Voorhees. 1986. Implementing Agglomerative Hierarchic Clustering Algorithms for Use in Document Retrieval. *Information Processing and Management*, 22(6): 465-76.

J. Wang, E.-P. Lim, J. Jiang, Qi He. 2010. TwitterRank: Finding Topic-sensitive Influential Twitterers. In *WSDM'10.*

C. Wartena and R. Brussee. 2008. Topic detection by clustering keywords. *In Proceedings of the 19th International Conference on Database and Expert Systems Application:* 54–58.

J. Xu and W. Croft. 1999. Cluster-based language models for distributed retrieval. *In Proceedings of the SIGIR 1999*: 254-261.

Y. Yang, T Pierce and J Carbonell. 1998. A study on Retrospective and On-Line Event detection. *Proceedings of the 21st annual international ACM SIGIR conference on Research and development in information retrieval*: 28-36.

L. Zhou and E. Hovy. 2005. Digesting Virtual "Geek" Culture: *The Summarization of Technical Internet Relay Chats. ACL 2005*: 298-305.

Training a BN-based user model for dialogue simulation with missing data

Stéphane Rossignol[†,‡], **Olivier Pietquin**[†,‡], **Michel Ianotto**[†,‡]
[†]SUPELEC - IMS Research Group
2 rue Édouard Belin, Metz
France
[‡]UMI 2958 (GeorgiaTech - CNRS)
{forename.surname}@supelec.fr

Abstract

The design of a Spoken Dialogue System (SDS) is a long, iterative and costly process. Especially, it requires test phases on actual users either for assessment of performance or optimization. The number of test phases should be minimized, yet without degrading the final performance of the system. For these reasons, there has been an increasing interest for dialogue simulation during the last decade. Dialogue simulation requires simulating the behavior of users and therefore requires user modeling. User simulation is often done by statistical systems that have to be tuned or trained on data. Yet data are generally incomplete with regard to the necessary information for simulating the user decision making process. For example, the internal knowledge the user builds along the conversation about the information exchanged while interacting is difficult to annotate.

In this contribution, we propose the use of a previously developed user simulation system based on Bayesian Networks (BN) and the training of this model using algorithms dealing with missing data. Experiments show that this training method increases the simulation performance in terms of similarity with real dialogues.

1 Introduction

The design of a Spoken Dialogue System (SDS) is a long, iterative and costly process. Although several attempts exist to simplify this design such as the VoiceXML language (W3C, 2008), graphical interfaces (McTear, 1998) or machine-learning-based methods (Pietquin and Dutoit, 2003), it remains an expert job. Especially, it requires test phases on actual users either for assessment of performance (Eckert et al., 1997; López-Cózar et al., 2006) or strategy optimization by means of reinforcement learning (Levin et al., 1997; Pietquin and Dutoit, 2006a). The number of test phases should be minimized, yet without degrading the final performance of the system. One solution to this problem is the use of Wizard-of-Oz methods (Kelley, 1984; Rieser, 2008). Although this doesn't require a real implementation of the dialogue system to be tested, this is still time and money consuming. For these reasons, there has been an increasing interest for dialogue simulation during the last decade (Eckert et al., 1997; Pietquin and Dutoit, 2006a; Schatzmann et al., 2006; López-Cózar et al., 2006). Dialogue simulation requires simulating the behavior of users and therefore requires user modeling as well as error modelling (Pietquin and Dutoit, 2006b; Schatzmann et al., 2007b). Most often, dialogue simulation takes place at the intention level (Eckert et al., 1997; Pietquin and Dutoit, 2006a; Schatzmann et al., 2007c) but can take place at the speech signal level (López-Cózar et al., 2006). This paper focuses on the former solution and more specifically on statistical user simulation (Eckert et al., 1997; Cuayáhuitl et al., 2005; Pietquin and Dutoit, 2006a; Schatzmann et al., 2007c). Statistical models are generally parametric generative models where parameters are conditional probabilities that can either be hand-tuned (estimated by experts) because of the complexity of the model (Pietquin, 2006; Schatzmann et al., 2007a), trained on actual man-machine dialogue data (Eckert et al., 1997; Cuayáhuitl et al., 2005; Pietquin et al., 2009; Syed and Williams, 2008) or a mix of both (Scheffler and Young, 2001; Keizer et al., 2010) so as to deal with parameters which are not directly accessible in a database. Indeed, data are often incomplete with regard to the necessary information for simulating the user decision making process. For example, the internal knowledge the user builds along the conversation about the dialogue context is difficult to annotate.

In this contribution, we propose the use of a previously developed user simulation system based on Bayesian Networks (BN) described in Section 2 and the training of this model using algorithms dealing with missing data. As said before, in the case of man-machine dialogues data, some information is often missing in the annotations. This paper focuses on the user's internal representation of the dialogue context which is referred to as the *knowledge* of the user. This is a major difference with other papers of the literature such as (Syed and Williams, 2008) where transition probabilities are estimated according to the history of system and user acts. Taking into account the incremental knowledge of the user about previous exchanges is important to ensure the consistency of the dialogue during the interaction (Pietquin, 2006). Although it is a difficult task, the knowledge of the user could be inferred from the data itself, by a human expert, a set of rules, or a trained classification algorithm dedicated to this task. In Section 4, this approach is followed, the knowledge (or an accurate estimate) is supposed to be known and the derived training methods for learning the BN parameters are explained. Alternatively, the knowledge of the user can be treated as hidden and the BN parameters can be learned using corresponding Expectation-Maximization algorithms. This approach is described in Section 5, both within a statistical framework (expected-likelihood maximization) and within a Bayesian framework (starting from some prior distribution over parameters). The experiments described in Section 6 show that this training method increases the simulation performance in terms of similarity with real dialogues.

2 BN-based user simulation

The user simulation method studied in this paper is based on the probabilistic model of a man-machine dialog proposed in (Pietquin, 2005; Pietquin and Dutoit, 2006a). The interaction between the user and the dialog manager is seen as a sequential transfer of intentions thanks to dialog acts organized in turns noted t. At each turn t the dialog manager selects a system act a_t conditionally to its internal state s_t and according to its strategy. The user answers by a user act u_t which is conditioned by the goal g_t s/he is pursuing and the knowledge k_t s/he has about the dialog (what has been exchanged before reaching turn t). So, at a given turn, the information exchange can be modeled thanks to the joint probability $p(a, s, u, g, k)$ of all these variables. This joint probability can be factored as:

$$p(a, s, u, g, k) = p(u|g, k, a, s)p(g|k, a, s)p(k|s, a)p(a|s)p(s)$$

Given that :

- since the user doesn't have access to the SDS state, u, g and k cannot depend on s,
- the user's goal can only be modified according to his/her knowledge of the dialog,

this expression can be simplified:

$$p(a, s, u, g, k) = \underbrace{p(u|g, k, a)}_{\text{User act}} \overbrace{p(g|k)}^{\text{Goal Modif.}} \underbrace{p(k|a)}_{\text{Know. update}} \overbrace{p(a|s)}^{\text{DM Policy}} p(s)$$

This can be expressed by the Bayesian network depicted on Fig. 1.

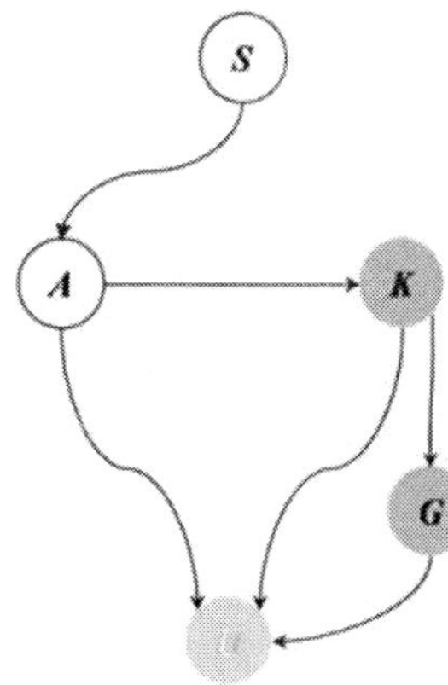

Figure 1: Bayesian Network-based Simulated User

As explained in (Pietquin and Dutoit, 2006a), the practical use of this kind of BN requires a tractable representation of the stochastic variables $\{a, s, u, g, k\}$. Variables are therefore considered as vectors of either boolean either symbolic values which makes them discrete in any case and limits the number of conditional probabilities which are the parameters Θ of this model (see (Pietquin, 2005; Pietquin and Dutoit, 2006a) for more details).

In this BN, nodes represented as empty circles o are input variables of the simulator (actually the outputs of the SDS), the light-gray circle ● is the output variable (user's utterance) and the dark-gray circles ● are internal variables (knowledge and goal). The parameters linked to these internal variables are generally hard to obtain from data collection since it is hard to infer what are the user knowledge and goal from the transcripts of interactions. The most difficult is probably to infer the knowledge of the user since in data collection settings or Wizard-of-Oz experiments, the user goal can be imposed on test users while the knowledge is built during the interaction and depends on it.

3 Dialogue example within the TownInfo domain

A dialogue example between the simulated user and the HIS dialogue manager (Young et al., 2009) is shown below. The user has the goal to get the name, phone number and address of a restaurant that serves Italian food and beer. The dialogue shows both system (SYS) and user (USR) acts. At the start of the dialogue, the simulator is initialised with a (randomly generated) user goal. Some of the slots are constrained by the user (G_C) and other are requested by him (G_R).

```
G_R> name, phone, addr
G_C> type=restaurant, food=italian, drinks=beer

Sys> hello() [Greet]
Usr> hello() {1.00}
.
Sys> repeat() [Repeat]
Usr> hello(type=restaurant) {1.00}
--
Sys> request(near) [Request]
Usr> inform(food=italian,drinks=beer) {1.00}
--
Sys> inform(name=none,type=restaurant,
     food=italian) [Offer]
Usr> reqalts(food=indian) {1.00}
--
Sys> inform(name="Carnaby Street",type=restaurant,
     drinks=beer,food=indian) [Offer]
Usr> deny(drinks=wine,drinks=beer) {1.00}
--
Sys> inform(name="The Parrot",type=bar,drinks=beer,
     food=indian) [Offer]
Usr> request(phone) {1.00}
--
Sys> inform(name="The Parrot",
     phone="728-66-32") [Inform]
Usr> request(addr) {1.00}
--
Sys> inform(name="The Parrot",
     addr="Art Square") [Inform]
Usr> bye()
--

End> --
```

In the next sections, the training methods used for estimating the parameters of the BN-based user simulation described in Section 2 are described.

4 Training methods with complete data

4.1 Maximum likelihood

When all variables in a dataset are observed, a statistical framework can be used, in which the frequencies of events appearing in the database are computed. This is known as the *maximum likelihood* approach:

$$\Theta_{i,j,k}^{ML} = \hat{p}\left(X_i = x_k \mid pa(X_i) = x_j\right) = \frac{N_{i,j,k}}{\sum_k N_{i,j,k}}$$

where the set of $\Theta_{i,j,k}^{ML}$ are the BN parameters that need to be learned, $N_{i,j,k}$ is the number of events in the database for which the variable X_i is in the state x_k and its parents in the network (pa) in the configuration x_j.

4.2 Bayesian training

Bayesian estimation of the parameters is slightly different. It actually aims at estimating the probability distribution over parameters and estimates the parameters using either a *maximum a posteriori* (MAP) approach or the parameters' expectation given this distribution. This is done knowing that the variables have been observed and requires some prior on the parameters. Using a Dirichlet distribution prior (standard choice for multivariate distributions), it is possible to derive an analytical formula for the expected parameters which is similar to the one obtained in the previous section. Using the MAP approach:

$$\Theta_{i,j,k}^{MAP} = \hat{p}\left(X_i = x_k \mid pa(X_i) = x_j\right) = \frac{N_{i,j,k} + \alpha_{i,j,k} - 1}{\sum_k N_{i,j,k} + \alpha_{i,j,k} - 1}$$

where the $\alpha_{i,j,k}$ are the coefficients of the Dirichlet distribution.

Using the *a priori* expectation approach (AEP) instead of the MAP, one gets:

$$\Theta_{i,j,k}^{AEP} = \hat{p}\left(X_i = x_k \mid pa(X_i) = x_j\right) = \frac{N_{i,j,k} + \alpha_{i,j,k}}{\sum_k N_{i,j,k} + \alpha_{i,j,k}}$$

4.3 Priors on parameters

The $\alpha_{i,j,k}$ are priors on parameters' distribution (Dirichlet distribution coefficients), as they are set by an expert. It is thus possible to give to these coefficients more or less importance, given the confidence of the expert. This will result in different trained BN/retrained BN user simulators. Fine-tuning the $\alpha_{i,j,k}$ will allow us to get simulators behaving more or less like the human users which produced the database, as shown in Section 6. Of course, if nothing is known (no expert available), a uniform distribution over parameters (all coefficient being equal) can be taken as a prior and the method can still be used.

5 Training methods with missing data

5.1 Expectation-Maximization algorithm

The *Expectation-Maximization* (EM) algorithm (Dempster et al., 1977) allows estimating the BN parameters even when the data corresponding to some of the parameters is missing.

EM is a recursive algorithm applied until convergence as explained hereafter.

Let us assume that:

- $X_\nu = \left\{X_\nu^{(l)}\right\}_{l=1\ldots N}$ is the set of the N observable data.
- $\Theta^{(t)} = \left\{\Theta_{i,j,k}^{(t)}\right\}$ are the estimations of the parameters of the BN at iteration t.

EM is a recursive algorithm, initialized with arbitrary $\Theta^{(0)}$ values, consisting of two steps:

- **Expectation (E)** step: the missing data $N_{i,j,k}$ are estimated, by computing their expectation conditionally to the data and to the current parameter estimates (i.e., to the current distribution estimate):

$$N_{i,j,k}^* = E[N_{i,j,k}] = \sum_{l=1}^{N} \hat{p}\left(X_i = x_k \mid pa(X_i) = x_j, X_\nu^{(l)}, \Theta^{(t)}\right)$$

  This consists in doing inference using the current parameter values, and in replacing the missing values by the probabilities obtained by inference.

- **Maximization (M)** step: replacing the missing $N_{i,j,k}$ by their expected value computed in the previous step, it is possible to compute the new parameter values $\Theta^{(t+1)}$, using maximum likelihood:

$$\Theta_{i,j,k}^{(t+1)} = \frac{N_{i,j,k}^*}{\sum_k N_{i,j,k}^*}$$

5.2 Expectation-Maximization algorithm and Bayesian training

The EM algorithm can be used within the Bayesian framework as well. In that case, the maximum likelihood estimation used in the **M** step must be replaced by an *a posteriori* maximum. Using the *a posteriori* expectation, one gets:

$$\Theta^{(EM)} = \Theta_{i,j,k}^{(t+1)} = \frac{N_{i,j,k}^* + \alpha_{i,j,k}}{\sum_k N_{i,j,k}^* + \alpha_{i,j,k}}$$

6 Experiment

6.1 Dialogue task and data

To test the different training algorithms, the user simulator parameters have been learnt on a database containing 1234 actual man-machine dialogues in the domain of tourist information. The dialogue system is a large-scale application aiming at retrieving information about user's interests in a city (about restaurants, hotels, *etc.*) so as to provide relevant propositions of venues as described in (Keizer et al., 2010). The venues can be of different types such as bar, restaurants and hotels. Each venue is described by a set of features (type of cuisine, location in the city *etc.*). The hierarchical structure of the task makes it relatively complex as well as the high number of slots (13). The data contains transcripts and semantic annotations in terms of dialogue act. The BN-based user simulator has been tested against the HIS Dialogue Manager developed at Cambridge University (Young et al., 2009).

6.2 Training methods

Six training setups for the BN-based user simulator were tested. 1000 dialogues were generated for each configuration after training. The six setups are described below:

- "ori-T-BN": the knowledge parameters were estimated on the database and the BN parameters were learned using the results by a Maximum Likelihood method ($\Theta_{i,j,k}^{ML}$) (see Section 4).

- "mod-T-BN": the knowledge parameters were estimated on the database and the BN parameters were learned with a Bayesian learning method (AEP method) and using priors fixed by an expert, reasonably taken into account ($\Theta_{i,j,k}^{AEP}$) (see Section 4).
- "H-BN": the BN parameters were hand-coded by an expert (Heuristics).
- "mod-T1-BN": the knowledge was supposed missing and the BN parameters were learned using the database by Bayesian EM and priors fixed by an expert; first version: expert almost not taken into account ($\Theta^{(EM)}$) (see Section 5).
- "mod-T2-BN": the knowledge was supposed missing and the BN parameters were learned using the database by Bayesian EM and priors fixed by an expert; second version: expert reasonnably taken into account ($\Theta^{(EM)}$).
- "mod-T3-BN": the knowledge was supposed missing and the BN parameters were learned using the database by Bayesian EM and priors fixed by an expert; third version: expert much taken into account ($\Theta^{(EM)}$).

The last three configurations are the most realistic ones.

6.3 Evaluation methods

Four dissimilarity measures have been computed: the Precision, the Recall, the symmetric Kullback-Leibler dissimilarity DS and the average number of turns per dialog (Pietquin and Hastie, 2011).

Precision:

$$P = 100 \times \frac{\text{Correctly predicted actions}}{\text{All actions in simulated response}}$$

Recall:

$$R = 100 \times \frac{\text{Correctly predicted actions}}{\text{All actions in real response}}$$

$$DS(P||Q) = \frac{D_{KL}(P||Q) + D_{KL}(Q||P)}{2}$$

where

$$D_{KL}(P||Q) = \sum_{i=1}^{M} p_i log(\frac{p_i}{q_i}),$$

and where p_i (resp. q_i) is the frequency of dialogue act a_i in the histogram of distribution P (resp. Q) obtained on the database (resp. on the generated data). The simulated dialogues are compared to the dialogues from the database on this basis. Notice that the Precision and the Recall must be as high as possible, the Kullback-Leibler as low as possible and the average number of turns per dialogue as close to the average number of turns per dialogue in the database (which is 8.185).

	ori-T-BN	mod-T-BN	H-BN
Precision:	47.11	50.62	63.63
Recall:	57.89	60.68	53.20
DS:	0.7292	0.6712	0.8803
Nturns/diag:	18.19	15.15	5.283

Table 1: Dissimilarities using the first three BN configurations

	mod-T1-BN	mod-T2-BN	mod-T3-BN
Precision:	63.71	64.60	67.13
Recall:	61.84	63.83	69.27
DS:	0.6674	0.7864	0.5288
Nturns/diag:	7.690	7.980	8.703

Table 2: Dissimilarities using the last three BN configurations

6.4 Results

The results are provided in Tables 1 and 2. Table 1 clearly indicates that the first configurations do not provide realistic dialogues. Considering the Recall, the DS and the number of turns, the mod-T-BN gives the best results. The fact that ori-T-BN gives bad results indicates that the database is not large enough, and/or that the inferred knowledge is not very accurate. The H-BN was designed to give as short as possible dialogues: this can be seen in the dissimilarity measures.

Table 2 indicates that the training techniques with missing data are efficient, allowing not to use the error-prone (automatic or manual) knowledge inference. Taking the expert information into account allows to improve the performance to some extent, considering the Precison, the Recall and the number of turns per dialogue dissimilarity measures. The DS dissimilarity measure gives more uncertain results.

7 Conclusions

In this paper, the problem of user simulation in spoken dialogue systems is addressed and particularly the training of statistical user simulation systems on actual data. Most often, actual man-machine dialogue corpora annotations do not contain all the required information for simulating the user's decision-making process. For instance, the knowledge of the dialogue context which is incrementally built by the user during the interaction is very difficult to annotate. To tackle this problem, this contribution proposes the use of expectation-maximization algorithms (in a Maximum Likelihood setting or a Bayesian setting) to learn parameters of a BN-based user model. Experimental results show that this method improves significantly the similarity of automatically generated dialogues.

In the future, this user model will be used to train a reinforcement-learning-based dialogue manager so as to optimize the dialogue strategy. Also, the extension of this user simulation technique to other tasks is envisioned. The simulation of the grounding process which is possible thanks to this kind of model (Rossignol et al., 2010) should also benefit from this training method to generate more realistic dialogues. Finally, we want to compare the performance of this user model to newly proposed models such as in (Chandramohan et al., 2011) according to several metrics (Pietquin and Hastie, 2011).

Acknowledgement

The work presented here has been done during the CLASSiC project (Grant No. 216594, www.classic-project.org) funded by the European Commission's 7th Framework Programme (FP7).

References

Senthilkumar Chandramohan, Matthieu Geist, Fabrice Lefèvre, and Olivier Pietquin. 2011. User Simulation in Dialogue Systems using Inverse Reinforcement Learning. In *Proceedings of the 12th Annual Conference of the International Speech Communication Association (Interspeech 2011)*, Florence (Italy), August.

Heriberto Cuayáhuitl, Steve Renals, Oliver Lemon, and Hiroshi Shimodaira. 2005. Human-Computer Dialogue Simulation Using Hidden Markov Models. In *Proceedings of the IEEE Workshop on Automatic Speech Recognition and Understanding (ASRU 2005)*, pages 290–295.

A.P. Dempster, N.M. Laird, and D.B. Rubin. 1977. Maximum Likelihood from Incomplete Data via the EM Algorithm. *Journal of the Royal Statistical Society. Series B (Methodological)*, 39(1):1–38.

Wieland Eckert, Esther Levin, and Roberto Pieraccini. 1997. User Modeling for Spoken Dialogue System Evaluation. In *Proceedings of the IEEE Workshop on Automatic Speech Recognition and Understanding (ASRU'97)*, pages 80–87.

Simon Keizer, Milica Gašić, Filip Jurčíček, François Mairesse, Blaise Thomson, Kai Yu, and Steve Young. 2010. Parameter estimation for agenda-based user simulation. In *Proceedings of the SIGdial Conference on Discourse and Dialogue (SIGdial 2010)*, Tokyo, Japan, September.

John Kelley. 1984. An Iterative Design Methodology for User-Friendly Natural Language Office Information Applications. *ACM Transactions on Office Information Systems*, 2(1):26–41.

Ester Levin, Roberto Pieraccini, and Wieland Eckert. 1997. Learning Dialogue Strategies within the Markov Decision Process Framework. In *Proceedings of the IEEE Workshop on Automatic Speech Recognition and Understanding (ASRU'97)*, December.

Ramón López-Cózar, Zoraida Callejas, and Michael F. McTear. 2006. Testing the performance of spoken dialogue systems by means of an artificially simulated user. *Artificial Intelligence Review*, 26(4):291–323.

Michael McTear. 1998. Modelling spoken dialogues with state transition diagrams: experiences with the cslu toolkit. In *Proc 5th International Conference on Spoken Language Processing*, pages 1223–1226.

Olivier Pietquin and Thierry Dutoit. 2003. Aided Design of Finite-State Dialogue Management Systems. In *Proceedings of the 4th IEEE International Conference on Multimedia and Expo (ICME 2003)*, volume III, pages 545–548, Baltimore (USA, MA), July.

Olivier Pietquin and Thierry Dutoit. 2006a. A Probabilistic Framework for Dialog Simulation and Optimal Strategy Learning. *IEEE Transactions on Audio, Speech and Language Processing*, 14(2):589–599, March.

Olivier Pietquin and Thierry Dutoit. 2006b. Dynamic Bayesian Networks for NLU Simulation with Application to Dialog Optimal Strategy Learning. In *Proceedings of the 31st IEEE International Conference on Acoustics, Speech and Signal Processing (ICASSP 2006)*, volume I, pages 49–52, Toulouse (France), May.

Olivier Pietquin and Helen Hastie. 2011. A survey on metrics for the evaluation of user simulations. *Knowledge Engineering Review*. Accepted for Publication.

Olivier Pietquin, Stéphane Rossignol, and Michel Ianotto. 2009. Training Bayesian networks for realistic man-machine spoken dialogue simulation. In *Proceedings of the 1rst International Workshop on Spoken Dialogue Systems Technology (IWSDS 2009)*, Irsee (Germany), December. 4 pages.

Olivier Pietquin. 2005. A Probabilistic Description of Man-Machine Spoken Communication. In *Proceedings of the 5th IEEE International Conference on Multimedia and Expo (ICME 2005)*, pages 410–413, Amsterdam (The Netherlands), July.

Olivier Pietquin. 2006. Consistent Goal-Directed User Model for Realistic Man-Machine Task-Oriented Spoken Dialogue Simulation. In *Proceedings of the 7th IEEE International Conference on Multimedia and Expo*, pages 425–428, Toronto (Canada), July.

Verena Rieser. 2008. *Bootstrapping Reinforcement Learning-based Dialogue Strategies from Wizard-of-Oz data*. Ph.D. thesis, Saarland University, Department of Computational Linguistics, Saarbrucken, July.

Stéphane Rossignol, Olivier Pietquin, and Michel Ianotto. 2010. Grounding Simulation in Spoken Dialog Systems with Bayesian Networks. In G. Geunbae Lee et al., editor, *Proceedings of the International Workshop on Spoken Dialogue Systems (IWSDS 2010)*, volume 6392 of *Lecture Notes in Artificial Intelligence (LNAI)*, pages 110–121, Gotemba (Japan), October. Springer-Verlag, Heidelberg-Berlin.

Jost Schatzmann, Karl Weilhammer, Matt Stuttle, and Steve Young. 2006. A survey of statistical user simulation techniques for reinforcement-learning of dialogue management strategies. *Knowledge Engineering Review*.

Jost Schatzmann, Blaise Thomson, Karl Weilhammer, Hui Ye, and Steve Young. 2007a. Agenda-Based User Simulation for Bootstrapping a POMDP Dialogue System. In *Proceedings of the Annual Meeting of the Association for Computational Linguistics (ACL) with Human Language Technology Conference (HLT 2007)*, Rochester.

Jost Schatzmann, Blaise Thomson, and Steve Young. 2007b. Error Simulation for Training Statistical Dialogue Systems. In *Proceedings of the International Workshop on Automatic Speech Recognition and Understanding (ASRU'07)*, Kyoto (Japan).

Jost Schatzmann, Blaise Thomson, and Steve Young. 2007c. Statistical User Simulation with a Hidden Agenda. In *Proceedings of the SIGDial Workshop on Discourse and Dialogue (SIGdial'07)*, Anvers (Belgium).

Konrad Scheffler and Steve Young. 2001. Corpus-Based Dialogue Simulation for Automatic Strategy Learning and Evaluation. In *Proc. NAACL Workshop on Adaptation in Dialogue Systems*.

Umar Syed and Jason D. Williams. 2008. Using Automatically Transcribed Dialogs to Learn User Models in a Spoken Dialog System. In *Proceedings of the Annual Meeting of the Association for Computational Linguistics (ACL) with Human Language Technology Conference (HLT 2008)*, Columbus, Ohio, USA.

W3C, 2008. *VoiceXML 3.0 Specifications*, December. http://www.w3.org/TR/voicexml30/.

Steve Young, Milica Gašić, Simon Keizer, François Mairesse, Blaise Thomson, and Kai Yu. 2009. The Hidden Information State Model: a practical framework for POMDP based spoken dialogue management. *Computer Speech and Language*, 24(2):150–174, April.

Automatic identification of general and specific sentences by leveraging discourse annotations

Annie Louis
University of Pennsylvania
Philadelphia, PA 19104
lannie@seas.upenn.edu

Ani Nenkova
University of Pennsylvania
Philadelphia, PA 19104
nenkova@seas.upenn.edu

Abstract

In this paper, we introduce the task of identifying general and specific sentences in news articles. Given the novelty of the task, we explore the feasibility of using existing annotations of discourse relations as training data for a general/specific classifier. The classifier relies on several classes of features that capture lexical and syntactic information, as well as word specificity and polarity. We also validate our results on sentences that were directly judged by multiple annotators to be general or specific. We analyze the annotator agreement on specificity judgements and study the strengths and robustness of features. We also provide a task-based evaluation of our classifier on general and specific summaries written by people. Here we show that the specificity levels predicted by our classifier correlates with the intuitive judgement of specificity employed by people for creating these summaries.

1 Introduction

Sentences in written text differ in how much specific content they have. Consider the sentences in Table 1 from a news article about the Booker prize. The first one is specific and details the issues surrounding the books chosen for the award. The second sentence is general, it states that the prize is controversial but provides no details. In this work, we present the first analysis of properties associated with general and specific sentences and introduce an approach to automatically identify the two types.

The novel, a story of Scottish low-life narrated largely in Glaswegian dialect, is unlikely to prove a popular choice with booksellers who have damned all six books shortlisted for the prize as boring, elitist and - worst of all - unsaleable.
...
The Booker prize has, in its 26-year history, always provoked controversy.

Table 1: General (in italics) and specific sentences

The distinction between general and specific sentences would be beneficial for several applications. Prescriptive books on writing advise that sentences that make use of vague and abstract words should be avoided or else immediately followed by specific clarifications (Alred et al., 2003). So our classifier could be useful for the prediction of writing quality. Other applications include text generation systems which should control the type of content produced and information extraction systems can use the distinction to extract different types of information.

Our definition of general/specific is based on the level of detail present in a sentence. This definition contrasts our work from some other recent studies around the idea of generic/specific distinctions in text. Reiter and Frank (2010) present an automatic approach to distinguish between noun phrases which describe a class of individuals (generic) versus those which refer to a specific individual(s). In Mathew and Katz (2009), the aim is to distinguish sentences which relate to a specific event (called episodic) from those which describe a general fact (habitual sentences). Our focus is on a different and broader notion of general/specific which is motivated by potential applications in summarization and writing feedback. The task of identifying these types of sentences has not been addressed in prior work.

We present a supervised classifier for detecting general and specific sentences. We obtain our training data from the Penn Discourse Treebank (PDTB), where relevant distinctions have been annotated in the larger context of discourse relation analysis. We show that classification accuracies as high as 75% can be obtained for distinguishing sentences of the two types compared with a random baseline of 50%. We also perform an annotation study to obtain direct judgements from people about general/specific sentences in news articles from two corpora and use this dataset to validate the accuracy of our features and their robustness across genre. Finally, we train a classifier on the combined set of all annotated data.

We also present a task-based evaluation of our classifier using a large corpus of summaries written by people. For some of the topics, people were instructed to write specific summaries that focus on details, for others they were asked to include only general content. We find that our classifier successfully predicts the difference in specificity between these two types of summaries.

2 A general vs. specific sentence classifier based on discourse relations

The task of differentiating general and specific content has not been addressed in prior work, so there is no existing corpus annotated for specificity. For this reason, we first exploit indirect annotations of these distinctions in the form of certain types of discourse relations annotated in the Penn Discourse Treebank (PDTB) (Prasad et al., 2008). The discourse relations we consider are Specification and Instantiation. They are defined to hold between adjacent sentences. The definitions of the relations do not talk directly about the specificity of sentences, but they seem to indirectly indicate that the first one is general and the second is specific. The exact definitions of these two relations in the PDTB are given in (Prasad et al., 2007). Some examples are shown in Table 2.

The PDTB annotations cover 1 million words from Wall Street Journal (WSJ) articles. Instantiations and Specifications are fairly frequent (1403 and 2370 respectively). In contrast to efforts in automatic discourse processing (Marcu and Echihabi, 2001; Sporleder and Lascarides, 2008), in our work we are not interested in identifying adjacent sentences between which this relation holds. Our idea is to use the *first* sentences in these relations as general sentences and the *second* as specific sentences.[1] Although the definitions of these relations describe the specificity of one sentence relative to the other, we do not focus on this pairwise difference in specificity. We believe that the realization of a general sentence should have some unique properties regardless of the particular sentence that precedes or follows it.

We use these relations to study the properties of general and specific sentences and to test the feasibility of differentiating these two types. We obtain good success on this task and equipped with the knowledge from our study, we collect direct judgements of general/specific notion from annotators on a smaller set of sentences. Using these annotations, we confirm that our classifier learnt on the discourse relations generalizes without noticeable compromise in accuracy. We describe our classifier based on discourse relations here, the annotation study is detailed in the next section.

2.1 Features

Based on a small development set of 10 examples each of Instantiation and Specification, we came up with several features that distinguished between the specific and general sentences in the sample. Some of our features require syntax information. We compute these using the manual parse annotations for the articles from the Penn Treebank corpus (Marcus et al., 1994).

Sentence length. We expected general sentences to be shorter than the specific ones. So we introduced two features—the number of words in the sentence and the number of nouns.

Polarity. Sentences with strong opinion are typical in the general category in our examples in Table 2. For instance, the phrases "publishing sensation", and "very slowly–if at all" are evaluative while the specific sentences in these relations present evidence which justify the general statements. So, we record for each sentence the number of positive, negative and polar (not neutral) words using two lexicons—The General Inquirer (Stone et al., 1966) and the MPQA Subjectivity Lexicon (Wilson et al., 2005). We also add another set of features where each of these counts is normalized by the sentence length.

Specificity. Specific sentences are more likely to contain specific words and details. We use two sets of features to capture specificity of words in the sentence. The first of these is based on WordNet (Miller et al., 1990) and is motivated by prior work by Resnik (1995) where hypernym relations from WordNet were used to compute specificity. For each noun and verb in a sentence, we record the length of the path from the word to the root of

[1] We use only the *implicit* relations from the PDTB; ie, the sentences are not linked by an explicit discourse connective such as 'because' or 'but' that signals the relation.

Instantiations
[1] *The 40-year-old Mr. Murakami is a publishing sensation in Japan.* A more recent novel, " Norwegian Wood " (every Japanese under 40 seems to be fluent in Beatles lyrics), has sold more than four million copies since Kodansha published it in 1987.
[2] *Sales figures of the test-prep materials aren't known, but their reach into schools is significant.* In Arizona, California, Florida, Louisiana, Maryland, New Jersey, South Carolina and Texas, educators say they are common classroom tools.
[3] *Despite recent declines in yields, investors continue to pour cash into money funds.* Assets of the 400 taxable funds grew by $ 1.5 billion during the last week, to $ 352.7 billion.
Specifications
[4] *By most measures, the nation's industrial sector is now growing very slowly—if at all.* Factory payrolls fell in September.
[5] *Mrs. Hills said that the U.S. is still concerned about 'disturbing developments in Turkey and continuing slow progress in Malaysia.'* She didn't elaborate, although earlier U.S. trade reports have complained of videocassette piracy in Malaysia and disregard for U.S. pharmaceutical patents in Turkey.
[6] *Alan Spoon, recently named Newsweek president said Newsweek's ad rates would increase 5% in January.* A full, four-color page in Newsweek will cost $100,980

Table 2: Examples of general (in italics) and specific sentences from the PDTB

the WordNet hierarchy through the hypernym relations. The longer this path, we would expect the words to be more specific. The average, min and max values of these distances are computed separately for nouns and verbs and are used as features.

Another measure of word specificity is the inverse document frequency (idf) for a word w (Joho and Sanderson, 2007), defined as $\log \frac{N}{n}$. Here N is the number of documents in a large collection, and n is the number of documents that contain the word w. We use articles from one year (87,052 documents) of the New York Times (NYT) corpus (Sandhaus, 2008) to compute idf. Words not seen in the NYT corpus were treated as if they were seen once. The features for a sentence are the average, min and max idfs for words in the sentence.

NE+CD. In news articles, especially the WSJ, specific sentences often contain numbers and dollar amounts. So we add as features the count of numbers (identified using the part of speech), proper names and dollar signs. The performance of these features, however, is likely to be genre-dependent. We also introduce another entity-related feature—the number of plural nouns. From our example sentences, we notice that plural quantities or sets are a property of general sentences.

Language models. General sentences often contain unexpected, catchy words or phrases. Consider the phrase "pour cash" in example [3] (Table 2); it is figurative and informal in the context of finance reports. When one reads the second sentence in the relation and observes the actual rise in funds investments, we understand why such a figurative phrase was used to introduce this fact. We expected that language models would capture this aspect by assigning a lower likelihood to unexpected content in the general sentences. We build unigram, bigram and trigram language models using one year of news articles from the NYT corpus. Using each model, we obtain the log probability and perplexity of the sentences to use as features. The unigram language model captures the familiarity of individual words. On the other hand, we expect the perplexity computed using higher order models to distinguish between common word transitions in the domain, and those that are unexpected and evoke surprise.

Syntax. We also noted frequent usage of qualitative words such as adjectives and adverbs in general sentences. So we include some syntax based features: counts of adjectives, adverbs, adjective phrases and adverbial phrases. We also record the number of verb phrases and their average length in words and the number of prepositional phrases. We expect that longer verb phrases would be associated with more specific sentences.

Words. We also add the count of each word in the sentence as a feature. Numbers and punctuations were removed but all other words were included. Only words seen in the training set are valid features. New words in the test sentences are ignored.

2.2 Results

We build two classifiers for distinguishing general and specific sentences: one trained on sentences from Instantiation relations, and one on sentences from Specification. The first sentence in the relation was considered an example of general sentence, and the second of specific one. No pairing information was preserved or exploited. We train a logistic regression classifier[2] with each set of features described above and evaluate the predictions

[2] http://www.csie.ntu.edu.tw/ cjlin/liblinear/

Features	Instantiations	Specifications
NE+CD	68.6	56.1
language models	65.8	55.7
specificity	63.6	57.2
syntax	63.3	57.3
polarity	63.0	53.4
sentence length	54.0	57.2
all non-lexical	75.0	62.0
lexical (words)	74.8	59.1
all features	75.9	59.5

Table 3: Classifier accuracy (baseline 50%)

using 10-fold cross validation.

We choose logistic regression for our task because we expected that a probability measure would be more appropriate to associate with each sentence rather than hard classification into the two classes. We provide further analysis of the classifier confidence in the next section. Here for reporting results, we use a threshold value of 0.5 on the confidence score. There are equal number of positive and negative examples, so the baseline random accuracy is 50%. Table 3 shows the accuracy of our features.

The classifiers trained on Instantiation examples are promising and better than those trained on Specifications. The highest accuracy on Instantiations-based classifier comes from combining all features, reaching 75.9% which is more than 25% absolute improvement over the baseline. The individually best class of features are the words with 74.8% accuracy showing that there are strong lexical indicators of the distinction.

Among the non-lexical features, the NE+CD class is the strongest with an accuracy of 68%. Language models, syntax, polarity and specificity features are also good predictors, each outperforming the baseline by over 10% accuracy. The sentence length features are the least indicative. These non-lexical feature classes though not that strong individually, combine to give the same performance as the word features. Moreover, one would expect that non-lexical features would be more robust across different types of news and topics compared to the lexical ones and would have fewer issues related to data sparsity. We analyse this aspect in the next section.

For the Specifications-based classifier, the highest performance is barely 10% above baseline. The best accuracy (62%) is obtained with a combination of all non-lexical features. In contrast to the Instantiations case, language models and entities features sets are less accurate in making the general-specific distinction on the Specification examples. Polarity is the worst set of features with only 53% accuracy.

A possible explanation of the difference in results from the two types of training data is that in Specification relations, the specificity of the second sentence is only relative to that of the first. On the other hand, for Instantiations, there are individual characteristics related to the generality or specificity of sentences. We confirm this hypothesis in Section 3.2.

2.3 Feature analysis

In this section, we take a closer look at the features that most successfully distinguished specific and general sentences on the *Instantiation* dataset. Given that words were the most predictive feature class, we identified those with highest weight in the logistic regression model. Here we list the top word features for the two types of sentences and which appear in at least 25 training examples.

General number, but, also, however, officials, some, what, prices, made, lot, business, were

Specific one, a, to, co, i, called, we, could, get, and, first, inc

Discourse connectives such as 'but', 'also' and 'however', and vague words such as 'some' and 'lot' are top indicators for general sentences. Words indicative of specific sentences are 'a', 'one' and pronouns. However, a large number of other words appear to be domain specific indicators—'officials', 'number', 'prices' and 'business' for general sentences, and 'co.', 'inc' for the specific category.

The weights associated with non-lexical features conformed to our intuitions. Mentions of numbers and names are predictive of specific sentences. Plural nouns are a property of general sentences. However, the dollar sign, which we expected is more likely with specific sentences turned out to be more frequent in the other category. As for the language model features, general sentences tended to have lower probability and higher perplexity than specific ones. General sentences also have greater counts of polarity words (normalized by length) and higher number of adjectives and adverbs and their phrases. At the same time, these sentences have fewer and shorter verb phrases and fewer prepositional phrases.

3 Testing the classifier on new sentences

So far, we have used discourse relations as sources of general and specific sentences. Here we present an annotation study where we asked people to directly judge a sentence as general or specific. We use these annotations to validate our classifier based on discourse relations and to ascertain whether these distinctions can be performed intuitively by people. So we only elicit annotations on a small set of examples rather than build a large corpus for training.

We also use sentences from articles from different news sources, enabling us to study the robustness of the classifier for news in general, beyond the more domain specific materials from the Wall Street Journal. Further we highlight a useful aspect of our predictions. We find that the confidence (probability from logistic regression) with which our classifier predicts the class for a sentence is correlated with the level of annotator agreement on the sentence. This finding suggests that the confidence scores can be used successfully to assign a graded level of specificity.

3.1 Annotations for general/specific

For our initial study outlined above, we have used the Instantiation and Specification sentences from Wall Street Journal texts in the PDTB. So we chose three WSJ articles from the PDTB corpus for further annotation, each around 100 sentences long. These articles were the ones with maximum number of Instantiations because we wanted to test whether people would judge the two sentences in Instantiations in the same manner as we have used them (the first general and the second specific).

We also chose articles from another corpus, AQUAINT (Graff, 2002), to compare the effect of corpus specifics on the classifier performance. These are a set of 8 news articles, six published by the Associated Press (AP) and two by Financial Times and are around 30 sentences each. Overall, there were 294 sentences from the WSJ and 292 from AP. Both sets of articles are about news, but the WSJ contains mainly financial reports.

We used Amazon's Mechanical Turk (MTURK)[3] to obtain annotations. We presented a user with one sentence at random and three options for classifying it: general/ specific/ can't decide. We provided minimal instructions[4]

	WSJ articles			AP articles		
Agree	**total**	**gen**	**spec**	**total**	**gen**	**spec**
5	96	51	45	108	33	75
4	102	57	45	91	35	56
3	95	52	43	88	49	39
undecided	1			5		
Total	294	160	133	292	117	170

Table 4: Annotator agreement

and annotators were encouraged to use their intuition to choose a judgement.

We obtained judgements from 5 unique users for each sentence. However, it is not the case that all sentences were judged by the *same* 5 annotators. So we do not compute the standardly reported Kappa measures for annotator agreement. Rather, we present statistics on the number of sentences split by how many annotators agreed on the sentence class. We also indicate the number of sentences where the majority decision was general or specific (Table 4).

As we can see from the table, there were only very few cases (6 out of $\sim$600) where no majority decision was reached by the 5 annotators. For about two-thirds of the examples ($\sim$400) in both the WSJ and AP, there was either full agreement among the five annotators or one disagreement. These results are high for a new task where annotators mainly relied on intuition. Some examples of sentences with different agreement levels are shown in Table 5.

Here we can notice why the examples with low agreement could be confusing. Sentence [S2] judged as specific (by three annotators) contains details such as the exact quantities of rainfall. At the same time, it contains the vague phrase "still had only". The remaining two annotators could have seen these general properties as more relevant for their judgement. Sentence [G2] which also had low agreement, has some general properties but also specific information, such as the phrase describing the word "companies".

In terms of the distribution of general and specific sentences, the two sets of articles differ. In the WSJ, there are more general (55% of total) than specific sentences. In the AP articles, specific sentences form the majority (60%) and there is a wider gap between the two types. One reason for this difference could be the length of the ar-

[3]http://sites.google.com/site/amtworkshop2010/

[4]"Sentences could vary in how much detail they contain. One distinction we might make is whether a sentence is general or specific. General sentences are broad statements made about a topic. Specific sentences contain details and can be used to support or explain the general sentences further. In other words, general sentences create expectations in the minds of a reader who would definitely need evidence or examples from the author. Specific sentences can stand by themselves. For example, one can think of the first sentence of an article or a paragraph as a general sentence compared to one which appears in the middle. In this task, use your intuition to rate the given sentence as general or specific."

	Agree = 5	[G1] The conditions necessary for a dollar crisis had been building up in currency markets for some time.
General	Agree = 3	[G2] The flip side of the hurricane's coin was a strong showing from the stocks of home construction companies expected to benefit from demand for rebuilding damaged or destroyed homes.
	Agree = 5	[S1] By midnight, 119 mph winds were reported in Charleston.
Specific	Agree = 3	[S2] But the weather service said all Mississippi farm communities still had only 30 percent to 50 percent of normal moisture.

Table 5: Example general and specific sentences with agreement 5 and 3

	General	**Specific**
Sent1	29 L5(14), L4(9), L3(6)	3 L5(1), L4(1), L3(1)
Sent2	6 L5(1), L4(3), L3(2)	26 L5(13), L4(9), L3(4)

Table 6: Annotator judgements on instantiation sentences

	General	**Specific**
Sent1	10 L5(4), L4(3), L3(3)	6 L5(1), L4(1), L3(4)
Sent2	8 L5(5), L4(3), L3(0)	8 L5(5), L4(2), L3(1)

Table 7: Annotator judgements on specification sentences

ticles. Those from WSJ are much longer than the AP articles and probably longer articles have more topics and corresponding general statements.

3.2 Results on Instantiation examples

We have assumed from the definitions of Instantiation and Specification relations, that their first sentences (*Sent1*) are general and their second (*Sent2*) specific. Further, we used these two sentences independently in two different classes. Now we test this intuition directly. Would people given only one of these sentences in isolation, give it the same judgement of generality as we have assumed?

There were 32 Instantiations and 16 Specification relations in the three WSJ articles we annotated and each of these relations is associated with two sentences, *Sent1* and *Sent2*. In Tables 6 and 7, we provide the annotator judgements and agreement levels on these sentences. The number of sentences x in each category with a certain level of agreement y is indicated as Ly(x). So L5(3) means that three sentences had full agreement 5.

For Instantiations, we find that the majority of *Sent1* are judged as general and the majority of *Sent2* are specific, 80% in each case. But for both *Sent1* and *Sent2*, there is one sentence which all the annotators agreed should be in the opposite class than assumed. So there are some cases where without context, the judgement can be rather different. But such examples are infrequent in the Instantiation sentences.

On the other hand, Specifications show a weaker pattern. For *Sent1*, still a majority (62.5%) of the sentences are called as general. However, for *Sent2*, the examples are equally split between general and specific categories. Hence it is not surprising that the Instantiation sentences have more detectable properties associated with the first general sentence and the second specific sentence and the classifier trained with these examples obtains better performance compared with training on Specifications.

3.3 Classifier accuracy and confidence

Now we test our classifier trained on Instantiation relations on the new annotations we have obtained on WSJ and AP articles. The parse trees for sentences in the test set were obtained using the Stanford Parser (Klein and Manning, 2003). Since our classifier was trained on Instantiations sentences from the WSJ, when testing on the new WSJ annotations, we retrained the classifier after excluding sentences that overlapped with the test set.

Our goal here is to a) understand the performance and genre independence of our features on the new test set b) explore the accuracy on examples with different levels of annotator agreement c) build a combined classifier using both discourse relations and direct annotations.

In each line of Table 8, we report the performance on examples from the specified agreement levels. A '+' sign indicates that examples from multiple agreement levels were combined.

Non-lexical features give the best performance on both sets of articles. The word features trained on WSJ Instantiations give more than 10% lower accuracy than non-lexical features, even on the WSJ articles. So lexical features probably do not cover all example types but non-lexical features provide better abstraction and portability across corpora. The accuracy of the non-lexical features on all directly annotated examples (*Agreement 3+4+5*) is 76% on WSJ and 81% on AP, similar to results on the Instantiation sentences.

But the accuracy increases on examples with

Examples	WSJ sentences Size	All features	Nonlexical	Words	AP sentences Size	All features	Nonlexical	Words
Agreement 5	96	90.6	96.8	84.3	108	69.4	94.4	78.7
Agreement 4 + 5	198	80.8	88.8	77.7	199	65.8	89.9	74.8
Agreement 3 + 4 + 5	293	73.7	76.7	71.6	287	59.2	81.1	67.5

Table 8: Accuracy of classifier on annotated examples

higher agreement and is over 90% for sentences with full agreement. The sentences with more agreement appear to have easily detectable properties for the respective class and so the classifier produces accurate predictions for them. As we saw, examples with low annotator agreement (Table 5) probably have a mix of properties from both classes. We further analyze the relationship between agreement and classifier performance by studying the classifier confidence scores.

In Table 9, we report the mean value of the classifier confidence for predicting the *correct class* for sentences having different agreement levels. A correct prediction occurs when the confidence is above 0.5 for the target class, so all the values we consider here are above 0.5. We now want to study when the correct prediction is made, how large is the confidence on examples with different annotator agreement levels. When the mean value of confidence scores at a particular agreement level was significantly better than another (determined by a two-sided t-test), those levels with lower confidence are indicated within parentheses.

As expected, the confidence of the classifier is significantly higher at greater levels of agreement again proving that the examples with higher annotator agreement are easier to classify automatically. So, the probability value produced by the classifier could be a better metric to use than the hard classification into classes. Further, since humans do have a low agreement on one-third of the sentences, a graded value is probably more suitable for the prediction of generality of a sentence.

We now have a larger set of annotated examples, so we combine the sentences from these two corpora with the Instantiation examples and build a combined classifier. Here the total general sentences is 1648 and there are 1674 specific sentences. So the distribution is almost equal and the baseline random performance would be 50% accuracy. The 10-fold cross validation accuracies from non-lexical, word and 'all features' on this full set are shown below.

Nonlexical : 72.36
Words : 72.36
All features: 74.68

Agreement	WSJ	AP
5	0.77 (4, 3)	0.78 (4,3)
4	0.70	0.70 (3)
3	0.67	0.66

Table 9: Mean value of confidence score on correct predictions

Here, after combining the examples, the classifier learns the lexical features indicative of both types of articles. So we end up with a similar trend as on the Instantiations based classifer. Both non-lexical and word features individually obtain 72% accuracy. Their combination is slightly better with 75% accuracy. So word features only when trained on both types of data again end up becoming good predictors and complementary with non-lexical features. So for new domains, the non-lexical features would be more robust.

Overall, we have provided a classifier that has high accuracy on a diverse set of examples.

4 Task based evaluation

So far we have tested our classifier on individual sentences which were judged as general or specific. Now we provide a task-based evaluation on news summaries. Here people were asked to write general or specific summaries for a set of articles, in the first type conveying only the general ideas and in the second providing specific details about the topic. We show that our classifier successfully distinguishes these two types of summaries.

Summarization is one task where the distinction between general and specific content is relevant. The space available for summary content is limited. So authors include some specific detail but at the same time have to generalize other content to stay within the space limit. Early work in Jing and McKeown (2000) report that when people create summaries, they generalize some of the sentences from the source text, others are made more specific. From the point of view of automatic systems, Haghighi and Vanderwende (2009) developed a topic model-based summarization system which learns the topics of the input at both overall document level as well as specific subtopics. Sentences are assumed to be generated by a combination of the general and specific topics in the input texts. However, since the preference of such sentences is not known, only heuristics were applied to choose the proportions. We expect our classifier to be useful in such cases.

4.1 Data

We use summaries and source texts from the Document Understanding Conference (DUC) organized by NIST in 2005.[5] The task in 2005 was to create summaries that are either general or specific. Each input consists of 25 to 50 news articles on a common topic. A topic statement is provided for *each input* which states the user's information need. Gold standard summaries for evaluation are created by human assessors for all these inputs. A length limit of 250 words is enforced.

During the creation of input sets, the annotators were asked to specify for each input, the type of summary that would be appropriate. So annotators provided a desired *summary granularity* for each input: either *general* or *specific*. There were a total of 50 inputs, 24 of them were marked for general summaries, the remaining for specific.

Next these input texts and topic statements were given to trained NIST assessors for writing summaries.[6] For some inputs (20), 9 summaries each were provided by the assessors, other inputs had 4 summaries. Considering the granularity of inputs, there is a roughly equal distribution of general (146) and specific (154) summaries. We now test if our classifier predictions can distinguish between these general and specific summaries where people relied on an intuitive idea of general and specific content overall in the summary.

4.2 Difference in specificity

For this analysis, we use the combined classifier from the Instantiation relations and extra annotations. We used the combination of all features since it gave the best performance for this setup.

Next we assigned a specificity level for each summary in the following way. For each sentence in the summary, we obtained the classifier confidence for predicting the sentence to be "specific". Each token in the summary was assigned the confidence of the sentence in which it appeared. Then the *average specificity of words* in the summary was computed as the average value of this confidence measure over all the tokens in the summary.

[5] `http://duc.nist.gov/duc2005/`

[6] The guidelines and example summaries can be found at `http://duc.nist.gov/duc2005/`.

Text	**General category**	**Specific category**
Summaries	0.55 (0.15)	0.63 (0.14)
Inputs	0.63 (0.06)	0.65 (0.04)

Table 10: Mean value (and standard deviation) of specificity levels for inputs and summaries

The statistics for this score in the general and specific categories are shown in Table 10.

For specific summaries, the mean specificity is 0.63, while for general ones it is only 0.55. The difference is also statistically significant under a two sided t-test (p-value of 1.5e-06). This result shows that our predictions are able to distinguish the two types of summaries.

We also computed the specificity scores for inputs in the same manner. Here the mean value is around 0.63 and does not vary significantly between the two classes (pvalue = 0.275). So while the inputs do not vary in specificity for the two categories, the summary authors have injected the required granularity during summary creation. To emulate the human summaries, systems would need to optimize for a measure of general/specific rather than use a generic strategy. Our classifier's predictions could be combined with other content selection features for such purposes.

5 Conclusion

We have introduced a new task—identification of general and specific sentences. We have shown how certain discourse relations involve these two types of sentences and can be used as training data for the task. We introduced features such as polarity, word specificity, language models, entity-related and lexical features which resulted in high classification performance, 25% absolute increase over the baseline. Our classifier also provides a graded score for specificity and can distinguish general and specific summaries written by people.

With this success, for future work, we plan to investigate the use of our classifier in applications which can use the general/specific notion. One task is providing feedback during writing. By learning patterns of use of general and specific sentences, we can use our predictions to annotate sentences which need more support from the writer. We also plan to explore pairs of general and specific sentences for the task of question generation. Specific sentences with important content can be treated as a potential answer, while a general sentence on the same subtopic can be used to generate the question.

References

G.J. Alred, C.T. Brusaw, and W.E. Oliu. 2003. *Handbook of technical writing*. St. Martin's Press, New York.

D. Graff. 2002. The aquaint corpus of english news text. *Corpus number LDC2002T31, Linguistic Data Consortium, Philadelphia.*

A. Haghighi and L. Vanderwende. 2009. Exploring content models for multi-document summarization. In *Proceedings of NAACL-HLT*, pages 362–370.

H. Jing and K. McKeown. 2000. Cut and paste based text summarization. In *Proceedings of NAACL*.

H. Joho and M. Sanderson. 2007. Document frequency and term specificity. In *Proceedings of RIAO*.

D. Klein and C.D. Manning. 2003. Accurate unlexicalized parsing. In *Proceedings of ACL*, pages 423–430.

D. Marcu and A. Echihabi. 2001. An unsupervised approach to recognizing discourse relations. In *Proceedings of ACL*, pages 368–375.

M.P. Marcus, B. Santorini, and M.A. Marcinkiewicz. 1994. Building a large annotated corpus of english: The penn treebank. *Computational Linguistics*, 19(2):313–330.

T. Mathew and G. Katz. 2009. Supervised categorization for habitual versus episodic sentences. In *Sixth Midwest Computational Linguistics Colloquium. Indiana University Bloomington, May*, pages 2–3.

G.A. Miller, R. Beckwith, C. Fellbaum, D. Gross, and K. J. Miller. 1990. Introduction to wordnet: An online lexical database. *International Journal of Lexicography (special issue)*, 3(4):235–312.

R. Prasad, E. Miltsakaki, N. Dinesh, A. Lee, A. Joshi, L. Robaldo, and B. Webber. 2007. The penn discourse treebank 2.0 annotation manual. *http://www.seas.upenn.edu/ pdtb*.

R. Prasad, N. Dinesh, A. Lee, E. Miltsakaki, L. Robaldo, A. Joshi, and B. Webber. 2008. The penn discourse treebank 2.0. In *Proceedings of LREC*.

N. Reiter and A. Frank. 2010. Identifying generic noun phrases. In *Proceedings of ACL*, pages 40–49.

P. Resnik. 1995. Using information content to evaluate semantic similarity in a taxonomy. In *Proceedings of IJCAI*, pages 448–453.

E. Sandhaus. 2008. The new york times annotated corpus. *Corpus number LDC2008T19, Linguistic Data Consortium, Philadelphia.*

C. Sporleder and A. Lascarides. 2008. Using automatically labelled examples to classify rhetorical relations: An assessment. *Natural Language Engineering*, 14:369–416.

P.J. Stone, J. Kirsh, and Cambridge Computer Associates. 1966. *The General Inquirer: A Computer Approach to Content Analysis*. MIT Press.

T. Wilson, J. Wiebe, and P. Hoffmann. 2005. Recognizing contextual polarity in phrase-level sentiment analysis. In *Proceedings of HLT-EMNLP*, pages 347–354.

A POS-based Ensemble Model for Cross-domain Sentiment Classification

Rui Xia and **Chengqing Zong**

National Laboratory of Pattern Recognition
Institute of Automation, Chinese Academy of Sciences
rxia.cn@gmail.com, cqzong@nlpr.ia.ac.cn

Abstract

In this paper, we focus on the tasks of cross-domain sentiment classification. We find across different domains, features with some types of part-of-speech (POS) tags are domain-dependent, while some others are domain-free. Based on this finding, we proposed a POS-based ensemble model to efficiently integrate features with different types of POS tags to improve the classification performance. Weights are trained by stochastic gradient descent (SGD) to optimize the perceptron and minimal classification error (MCE) criteria. Experimental results show that the proposed ensemble model is quite effective for the task of cross-domain sentiment classification.

1 Introduction

In recent years, transfer learning and domain adaptation, the task aiming to utilize labeled data from the other domains (source domain) to help learning for current domain (target domain), has attracted more and more attention in the fields of both machine learning and natural language processing, including sentiment classification. The task of sentiment classification is supposed to be domain-specific. Classifiers trained on the source domain usually perform poorly in the target domain. This is quite reasonable since the word distribution changes from one domain to another, and some words that are positive in one domain may express an opposite meaning in another one. Therefore, it is challenging to transfer a classifier trained on the source domain to the target domain.

Methodology to solve this problem can be divided into three major categories (Pan and Yang, 2009): the instance-based transfer, the feature-based transfer and the parameter-based transfer. The instance-based transfer learns the importance of labeled data in the source domain by instance re-weighting and importance sampling. These reweighed instances are then used for learning in the target domain. Feature-based transfer aims to learn a good feature representation for the target domain using labeled data in the source domain with the help of a large number of unlabeled data in the target domain. The parameter-based transfer mostly assumes that individual models for related tasks share some parameters or prior distribution of hyper-parameters. The shared part is then added to the cost function for transfer learning.

In this paper, we propose a POS-based ensemble model for cross-domain sentiment classification. Other than the above-mentioned methodology, the transfer procedure in our approach is neither instance re-weighting nor feature representation. Broadly speaking, our approach belongs to the parameter-based transfer, but different from the traditional ways, the transfer procedure is embodied in an ensemble manner.

By observing the K-L distance of multi-domain datasets, we find that cross different domains, the distribution of features with some types of POS tags, such as adjectives and adverbs, has little change; while some other parts, for example, nouns, vary sharply. Furthermore, we investigate the most significant features ranked by information gain (IG). We find that the significance of adjectives and adverbs increases from in-domain to cross-domain tasks, while nouns become less important.

Based on these findings, we infer that an efficient ensemble of features according to their POS tags, may benefit more from the domain-free parts and overcome the drawbacks of domain-dependent parts, and finally enhance the overall cross-domain sentiment classification performance. We proposed two methods, namely the average perceptron (Perc) and the minimal classification error (MCE) criterion, to learn the weights of base-classifiers.

The remainder of this paper is organized as follows. Section 2 reviews related work. In Section 3, we introduce our motivation with detailed investigation. In Section 4, we propose our ensemble model for cross-domain sentiment classification. Experimental results are reported and discussed in Section 5 and 6 respectively. Section 7 draws conclusions and outlines directions for future work.

2 Related Work

2.1 Domain Adaptation

Existing approaches for cross-domain sentiment classification mostly belong to the feature-based transfer. Among them, the structural correspondence learning (SCL) algorithm proposed by (Blitzer et al., 2007) is the representative one. SCL tries to get the mapping matrix from non-pivot feature space to pivot feature space. Non-pivot features are then transferred though a projection over the principle components of the mapping matrix. (Li et al., 2009b) proposed to transfer lexical prior knowledge across domains via matrix factorization techniques. (Pan et al., 2010) proposed cross-domain sentiment classification via spectral feature alignment and compared their method with SCL.

Another work (Aue and Gamon, 2005) combined small amounts of labeled data with large amounts of labeled data in target domain to learn the model parameters for a generative naïve Bayes classifier using the Expectation Maximization (EM) algorithm.

The above work all need a large amount of unlabeled data in the target domain to help building the transfer procedure. Our approach does not need those unlabeled data. Nevertheless, we do need a small amount of labeled data from target domain, say, 50-200 instances, to help transfer learning.

2.2 Ensemble Techniques

Several researchers have achieved improvements in sentiment classification accuracy via the ensemble techniques. The work (Whitehead and Yaeger, 2008) conducted four ensemble algorithms (bagging, boosting, random subspace and bagging random subspaces) for sentiment classification. In the work by (Li et al., 2007), different classifiers were generated with different sets of features according to their POS tags. Those component classifiers are then selected and combined using several fixed rules. Experimental results showed that sum rule achieves the best performance.

We made a comparative study (Xia et al., 2011) about the effectiveness of ensemble techniques for sentiment classification. Two schemes of feature set were designed at first. Three well-known classification algorithms were then employed as base-classifiers for each of the feature sets. Three types of ensemble models were finally conducted for three ensemble strategies, with the emphasis on the evaluation of the effectiveness of ensemble techniques for sentiment classification.

Different from above methods, our focus in this paper is cross-domain sentiment classification. Compared to our former reports, we prove that the ensemble model is more effective for cross-domain tasks than for the in-domain ones.

3 Problem Investigation

3.1 POS Tag Groups

The POS information is supposed to be a significant indicator of sentiment expression. The work on subjectivity detection (Hatzivassiloglou and Wiebe, 2000) revealed a high correlation between the presence of adjectives and sentence subjectivity, yet this may not be taken to mean that other POS tags do not contribute. Indeed, it was resulted in (Pang et al., 2002; Benamara et al., 2007) that using only adjectives as features actually results in much worse performance than using the same number of most frequent unigrams. Other researchers (Riloff et al., 2003) pointed out that certain verbs and nouns are also strong indicators of sentiment. According to their significance to sentiment classification, we categorize the POS tags into four groups, as shown in Table 1.

Group	Contained POS tags
J	adjectives, adverbs
V	verbs
N	nouns
O	the other POS tags

Table 1. Four groups of POS tags

3.2 Cross-domain K-L Distances

When conducting transfer learning, it is crucial to find that from one domain to another, which part of knowledge changes and which part of knowledge remains similar. Then the "unchanged" part of knowledge should be kept during the learning process, while the "changed" part should be transferred. Our intuition is that from one domain to another, nouns change the most, because domains (or topics) are mostly denoted by nouns; while adjectives and adverbs change less, for example, "*great*" and "*love*" always express the meaning that something is good, no matter the domain is Book or Movie.

Holding this belief, we observe the cross-domain K-L distance (also called relative entropy) of the class-conditional distribution of each type of POS tags. We use the Multi-Domain Sentiment Dataset[1] for statistics. This dataset was introduced by (Blitzer et al., 2007) and then widely used in the field of cross-domain sentiment classification. It contains product reviews taken from Amazon.com from four product types (domains) – Book (B), DVD (D), Electronics (E) and Kitchen (K). Each of these contains 1000 positive and 1000 negative reviews.

We use the term "X-Y" to denote the task computing K-L distance of domain X and Y. For example, "B-D" denotes the K-L distance between the Book domain and DVD domain. We compute the K-L distance of two domains for each class based on the assumption that the class-conditional distribution is the multinomial distribution. The results are presented in Table 2.

We focus on the comparison between different types of POS tags. The K-L distance of N is the largest in all cross-domain tasks, significantly larger than the other POS types and Uni (unigrams). It indicates that from one domain to another, the change of N is the biggest part. On the contrary, the distribution of O changes the least. It is reasonable that the POS tags contained in O, such as prepositions, pronouns, etc., are mostly domain-free. The K-L distance of J is larger than that of O, but significantly smaller than that of N. The value is also smaller compared to that of all unigrams. V gives the comparable K-L distance. We may conclude that most features in J and V are partially domain-free. It also coincides with our intuition that "*great*" and "*love*" always express a positive meaning in whatever domains.

Generally, the cross-domain K-L distances of different types of POS tags can be ranked as: N>>Uni>V>J>O.

Task	Class	J	V	N	O	Uni
B-D	Pos	0.1608	0.2022	0.5420	0.0197	0.1968
	Neg	0.1427	0.1632	0.5149	0.0144	0.1779
B-E	Pos	0.4353	0.3752	1.2125	0.1329	0.4738
	Neg	0.3585	0.3414	1.1787	0.1221	0.4416
B-K	Pos	0.4487	0.4255	1.2059	0.1146	0.4752
	Neg	0.3348	0.3770	1.2620	0.1298	0.4690
D-E	Pos	0.3983	0.3614	1.1751	0.1281	0.4579
	Neg	0.3430	0.3429	1.1850	0.0905	0.4279
D-K	Pos	0.4028	0.4125	1.2587	0.1168	0.4820
	Neg	0.3372	0.3687	1.3352	0.0921	0.4686
E-K	Pos	0.2428	0.1934	0.9310	0.0208	0.3093
	Neg	0.1856	0.1836	0.7791	0.0153	0.2592

Table 2: Cross-domain K-L distance

3.3 Most Significant Cross-domain Features

Furthermore, we investigate the most significant cross-domain features. We choose the top-N features that are ranked by information gain (IG) which was proved to be an effective feature selection method for sentiment classification (Li et al.,

[1] http://www.cs.jhu.edu/~mdredze/datasets/sentiment/

2009a). In table 3, we report the number of different POS tags from top-50, 100, 200, 500 and 1000 features respectively. "In" denotes the average result of four individual domains. "Share" denotes the number of features shared by all of the four groups of top-*N* features.

We first observe the average results of four individual top-100 features. The number of J, V, N and O cover the percentage of 42.0, 24.0, 24.0 and 9.0 respectively. Among the four groups of top-100 features, only 11 words appear in all of them. These features are "*great*", "*love*", "*unfortunately*", "*money*", "*highly*", "*bad*", "*worst*", "*excellent*", "*not*", "*waste*" and "*best*", where adjectives, verbs and nouns cover 81.8%, 9.1% and 9.1% respectively. In the case of individual top-200 features, the number of shared words by four domains is 19, 63.2% of which are adjectives.

As *N* increases, the percentage of four groups of POS tags in shared features can be generally ranked as: J>V>N>O. This has confirmed our intuition that nouns are the most domain-specific, while adjectives and adverbs are especially good cross-domain features.

Top-*N*	In/Share	Num	J (%)	V (%)	N (%)	O (%)
100	In	100	42.0	24.0	24.0	9.0
	Share	11	81.8	9.1	9.1	0.0
200	In	200	35.0	27.5	28.0	19.5
	Share	19	63.2	15.8	10.5	10.5
500	In	500	30.4	26.6	33.6	9.4
	Share	35	54.3	20.0	14.3	11.4
1000	In	1000	27.4	26.8	37.8	8.0
	Share	67	44.8	22.4	20.9	11.9

Table 3: Top-features by feature selection

4 The Ensemble Model

4.1 A POS-based Weighted Combination

The pursuit of POS-based weighted combination is motivated by the intuition that an appropriate integration of different participants might leverage distinct strengths. For example, the weights assigned to adjectives and adverbs are supposed to be higher than that of nouns.

We first build a new meta-feature vector $\hat{\mathbf{x}} = [o_{11}, \ldots, o_{kj}, \ldots, o_{DC}]$, where $o_{kj}(\mathbf{x})$ denotes the predicted score of the *k*th base-classifier for the *j*th class, C is the number of classes and D is the number of base-classifiers (in our approach C equals 2 and D equals 4). Then, the weighted combination could be represented by

$$O_j = \sum_{k=1}^{D} \omega_k o_{kj} = \sum_{k=1}^{D} \omega_k \hat{\mathbf{x}}_{k \times D + j}, \quad (1)$$

where $\hat{\mathbf{x}}_{k \times D + j}$ denotes the score for the *j*th class of the *k*th base-classifier.

4.2 Weight Optimization

To learn the weights in Equation (1) , we propose to use stochastic gradient descent (SGD) to optimize some criteria. We consider two criteria in our approach, namely the perceptron (Perc) model, and minimal classification error (MCE) criterion.

The cost function of Perc in multi-class case is given by

$$J_p = \frac{1}{N} \sum_{i=1}^{N} \left[\max_{j=1,\ldots,C} g_j(\hat{\mathbf{x}}_i) - g_{y_i}(\hat{\mathbf{x}}_i) \right]. \quad (2)$$

Note that in implementation, we utilize the average perceptron, a variation of perceptron that averages weights of all iterations, to improve the robustness.

The MCE criterion proposed by (Juang and Katagiri, 1992) is supposed to be more relevant to the classification error. In their approach, a simple version of misclassification measure of the instance $\hat{\mathbf{x}}_i$ from the *j*th class is defined by

$$d_j(\hat{\mathbf{x}}_i) = -g_{y_i}(\hat{\mathbf{x}}_i) + \max_{h \neq j}\{g_h(\hat{\mathbf{x}}_i)\}. \quad (3)$$

Based on this measure, the cost function of MCE is given by

$$J_{mce} = \frac{1}{N} \sum_{i=1}^{N} \sum_{j=1}^{C} I(y_i = j) \delta(d_j(\hat{\mathbf{x}}_i) + \alpha), \quad (4)$$

where $\delta(\bullet)$ is the sigmoid function, and α is the hyper-parameter.

SGD uses approximate gradients estimated from subsets of the training data and updates the parameters in an online manner:

$$w_k(t+1) = w_k(t) - \eta(t)\frac{\partial J}{\partial w_k}, \quad (5)$$

where t denotes the iteration step and $\eta(t)$ denotes the learning rate. Compared to standard gradient descent, SGD is much faster and more efficient, especially for large datasets.

5 Experiments

5.1 Experimental Settings

We use the Multi-domain dataset for experiments, which was already introduced in Section 3.2. The term "source→target" is used to denote the cross-domain tasks. For example, "D→B" represents the task that is trained in the DVD domain but the tested in the Book domain.

In our experiments, each dataset is split into a training set of 1600 instances, and a test set of 400 instances. The NLTK toolkit[2] is used for word tokenization. The MXPOST[3] tool is chosen as our POS tagger. Features with the term frequency no less than four are selected for classification.

Since it was reported that Naïve Bayes performs the best among three classifiers (Naïve Bayes, MaxEnt and SVM) on Multi-Domain Sentiment Dataset (Xia et al., 2011), we choose it as the base classification algorithm. We use the tool OpenPR-NB[4] in our experiments, with the settings of multinomial event model and Laplace smoothing.

After base-classification, the predicted score of the test set is randomly split to a meta-development set and meta-test set. The ensemble systems are trained on the meta-development set to classify the meta-test set to get the final prediction. The learning rate of SGD is set to be one and the maximal iteration number is set to be 100.

The process of meta-learning and test is randomly repeated for 100 times. All of the following results are in terms of an average of the 100 repeats.[5]

[2] http://www.nltk.org/

[3] http://www.inf.ed.ac.uk/resources/nlp/local_doc/MXPOST.html

[4] http://www.openpr.org.cn/

[5] The leave-one-out cross validation procedure was used in some previous work. In our experiments, since the size of development set is required to be comparatively small, cross validation is not quite suitable.

5.2 Results of Uni-based Ensemble

Table 4 reports the performance of Uni-based ensemble. Unigrams are categorized into four groups according to Table 1, denoted by Uni-J, Uni-V, Uni-N and Uni-O respectively. The perforamce of using all unigrams without transfer (denoted by Uni) is taken as the baseline. In ensemble approaches, we report results of three rules, i.e., the Sum rule, Perc and MCE criteria. Perc and MCE are trained by 200 labeled data in the target domain.

At first, we focus on the comparison of Uni and Uni-J. Uni-J performs consistently better than Uni in most of the cross-domain tasks (71.40% vs. 70.54%). This is opposite to the conclusion in in-domain tasks that using only adjectives as features results in much worse performance than using the same number of most frequent unigrams (Pang et al., 2002; Benamara et al., 2007). It also confirms our intuition that adjectives and adverbs are more effective feature for cross-domain tasks, and an efficient ensemble of these POS tags may be more effective.

Secondly, we observe the performance of Sum rule. We have drawn the conclusion in (Xia et al., 2011) that Sum rule is a low-cost yet effective approach for sentiment classification. However, this conclusion may not hold in the cross-domain tasks. Sum rule performs significantly worse than the best base-classifier (Uni-J). This is quite reasonable that assigning equal weights to unbalanced component base-classifiers will reduce the effect of ensemble.

Finally, we observe the results of weighted combination. Their performance is consistently higher than Uni and Uni-J, except for the task E→K (a slight decline). In average of 12 tasks, Perc and MCE outperform the Uni baseline by 3.01% and 3.94% respectively. Comparing Perc and MCE, the performance of MCE is more attractive, 0.93% higher than Perc in average.

Tasks	Uni-J	Uni-V	Uni-N	Uni-O	Uni	Ensemble		
						Sum	Perc	MCE
D→B	75.50	62.00	62.00	56.00	73.25	74.75	77.87	**78.88**
E→B	72.75	59.50	59.75	57.00	69.75	71.25	**72.35**	**72.35**
K→B	68.75	59.50	57.75	54.50	67.75	66.75	69.59	**70.47**
B→D	74.75	64.00	65.00	66.75	74.50	75.00	77.46	**77.81**
E→D	70.25	57.25	52.50	56.50	67.50	66.75	71.47	**72.66**
K→D	71.25	60.25	58.50	56.75	73.75	73.50	76.28	**77.25**
B→E	67.50	56.50	53.00	55.50	63.25	63.75	68.36	**69.26**
D→E	66.00	56.75	58.50	48.50	61.75	63.50	67.21	**68.71**
K→E	77.50	67.00	63.25	60.25	74.75	75.00	77.79	**79.74**
B→K	69.50	60.50	60.75	55.00	69.00	70.50	70.14	**71.14**
D→K	67.75	62.25	61.00	52.75	71.00	70.25	74.67	**75.86**
E→K	75.25	68.25	67.50	57.00	**80.25**	77.50	79.39	79.65
Average	71.40	61.15	59.96	56.38	70.54	70.71	73.55	**74.48**

Table 4. Performance (%) of Uni-based Ensemble

5.3 Results of UB-based Ensemble

We still consider using unigrams and bigrams together as candidate features for ensemble. Unigrams and bigrams are divided into four subsets (UB-J, UB-V, UB-N and UB-O), according to the POS tags of its headword. The performance of unigrams and bigrams without transfer is used as the baseline (denoted by UB). The reported ensemble results are also with the help of 200 labeled data from the target domain. Detailed results are presented in Table 5.

We still first compare UB-J and UB. This time, UB-J beats UB in some tasks, but it does not show general superiority. It is probably due to that some adjective information has coupled with other POS tags, such as J-N. Nevertheless, its performance is still comparative higher compared with the other three types of POS tags.

With regard to the ensemble methods, the performance of sum rule is not so sound, the same as before. The weighted combination still gains significant improvements over the UB baseline. In average, Prec and MCE outperform the UB baseline by 3.01% and 3.94% respectively. Overall, the ensemble model is quite effective for cross-domain sentiment classification. Among them, MCE is the most effective.

6 Discussion

6.1 Ensemble Model Revisited

In this section, we try to give some explanations about why the ensemble model is effective for cross-domain sentiment classification.

In traditional linear classifiers, the weights assigned to each feature are trained on the source-domain labeled data. Each weight thus embodies the significance of its responding feature to the source-domain classification. Transferring from one domain to another, those weights need to be adapted to the target domain.

Based on the observation that some parts of the feature are domain-dependent and some parts are domain-free, an efficient ensemble may be an effective way to adapt those weights to the target-domain. The behind transferring procedure can be interpreted as:

$$\begin{aligned}&\log P(c_j \mid d)\\ &\propto \log P(c_j) + \sum_i \log P(t_i \mid c_j)\\ &= \log P(c_j) + \omega_1 \sum_{i_1 \in J} \log P(t_{i_1} \mid c_j) + \omega_2 \sum_{i_2 \in V} \log P(t_{i_2} \mid c_j)\\ &\quad + \omega_3 \sum_{i_3 \in N} \log P(t_{i_3} \mid c_j) + \omega_4 \sum_{i_4 \in O} \log P(t_{i_4} \mid c_j),\end{aligned} \tag{6}$$

Tasks	UB-J	UB-V	UB-N	UB-O	UB	Ensemble		
						Sum	Perc	MCE
D→B	78.00	64.25	65.75	59.00	76.25	77.00	79.51	**81.01**
E→B	72.50	64.75	64.75	62.75	77.75	76.50	77.09	**77.80**
K→B	70.25	61.00	65.00	55.75	72.25	72.25	73.37	**74.06**
B→D	75.00	70.75	67.25	65.50	77.00	78.25	78.21	**79.03**
E→D	71.00	62.75	58.00	55.75	73.25	72.75	73.98	**74.77**
K→D	72.25	59.00	60.75	61.00	73.00	76.00	75.66	**77.14**
B→E	67.25	62.50	58.00	59.00	68.50	69.00	70.78	**72.27**
D→E	69.00	60.75	58.25	49.50	65.50	66.50	69.29	**70.34**
K→E	77.25	73.50	69.00	61.50	81.25	80.25	81.71	**82.87**
B→K	72.50	63.50	62.50	58.25	74.50	74.75	73.87	**75.02**
D→K	70.00	67.75	60.50	53.75	74.75	74.75	77.37	**78.68**
E→K	78.50	70.50	67.75	57.75	79.75	79.50	80.34	**81.13**
Average	72.79	65.08	63.13	58.29	74.48	74.79	75.93	**77.01**

Table 5. Performance (%) of UB-based Ensemble

where the conditional word probability is transferred from $P(t_i|c_j)$ to $P(t_i|c_j)^{\omega_i}$, which encodes information of both the sentiment significance and cross-domain ability.

In table 6, we present the average weights trained by MCE across all tasks. We can see that the weight of J is the largest in four parts, generally a half percentage. Thereby, the conditional probability of features in J will get a comparatively larger value. Such re-assignments of parameters will be good for cross-domain tasks.

Ensemble Tasks	J	V	N	O
Uni-based	0.52	0.20	0.16	0.12
UB-based	0.45	0.21	0.16	0.18

Table 6. Average weights trained by MCE

6.2 Sensitivity on Parameter Tuning

In this section, we test the sensitivity on parameter tuning. For simplicity, we fix the weights of V and O to be 0.20 and 0.15 respectively. We use ω to denote the weight of J, and the weight of N is thus $(0.65-\omega)$. We tune the value of ω from 0 to 0.65, and observe the average accuracy of ensemble. The curve is displayed in Fig. 1.

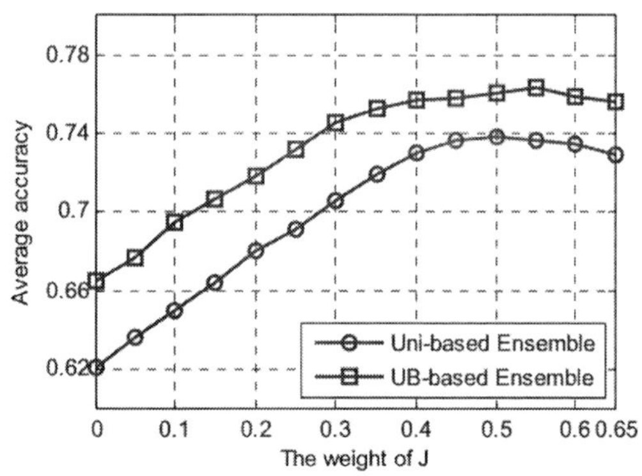

Fig. 1. Parameter sensitivity test

We can conclude from Fig. 1 that the ensemble performance is quite sensitive to the weights assigned to base-classifiers. When ω is close to 0, the weight of N is comparatively larger, and the ensemble performance drops sharply. The best result was obtained when ω locates at the area close to 0.5. The golden weights are quite similar to the results trained by MCE (Table 6). This shows that MCE is effective at parameter tuning.

Moreover, these weights can also be regarded as the empirical values when performing POS-based ensemble, in case that there is no or very few labeled data available in the target domain.

6.3 Dependency on the Size of Labeled Data in the Target Domain

Finally, we discuss the dependency of our approach on the size of labeled data in the target domain. In Fig. 2, we observe the performance of our ensemble model as the size of labeled data from the target domain increases from 50 to 300. "In-domain" denotes the accuracy trained on those labeled data for in-domain classification. "No transfer" denotes the result trained on 1600 labeled data in the source domain without transfer. Two ensemble approaches are also displayed for comparison. The reported accuracy is the average of 12 cross-domain tasks.

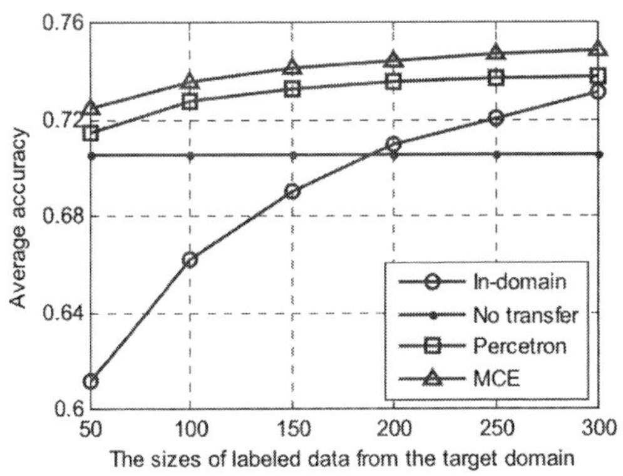

Fig. 2. Performance as labeled data in target domain increase

From Fig. 2, we can see that when the size of labeled data is small, the in-domain performance is fairly poor. At this time, the ensemble model could substantially improve the performance. As the size of labeled data increases, all of the systems yield higher performance. When the size increases to 300, the ensemble model shows limited superiority. It is reasonable that the in-domain learning is always the best if labeled data is enough.

Although the improvements of the ensemble model gained over the in-domain system become less as the size of labeled data increases, we could still conclude that in the case that there is only few labeled data in the target domain, the ensemble model is quite effective, to take the advantage of a large number of labeled data from the source domains, to help improving sentiment classification performance in the target domain.

7 Conclusion

In this paper, we propose a POS-based ensemble model for cross-domain sentiment classification. The motivation is based on the observation that some types of POS tags are domain-free, while some others are domain-dependent. Therefore, an efficient ensemble of them would leverage distinct strengths and improve the classification performance. Experimental results show that when the labeled data in the target is few, the proposed ensemble model is quite effective to make use of the labeled data from the source domain to improve the classification performance in the target domain.

We also update our previous conclusion drawn regarding the effectiveness of ensemble for in-domain sentiment classification (Xia and Zong, 2010; Xia et al., 2011). We conclude that the POS-based ensemble model is more effective for cross-domain sentiment classification than in-domain tasks.

In the future, we plan to extend the ensemble model to the tasks of cross-domain sentiment classification with multiple source domains. We also wish to make use of a large amount of unlabeled data in the target domain to help assist the ensemble performance for cross-domain sentiment classification in the framework of ensemble learning.

Acknowledgment

The research work has been funded by the Natural Science Foundation of China under Grant No. 60975053 and 61003160, and supported by the External Cooperation Program of the Chinese Academy of Sciences.

References

Anthony Aue and Michael Gamon, 2005. Customizing Sentiment Classifiers to New Domains: A Case Study. In Proceedings of Recent Advances in Natural Language Processing (RANLP).

Farah Benamara, Carmine Cesarano, Antonio Picariello, Diego Reforgiato and V. S. Subrahmanian, 2007. Sentiment Analysis: Adjectives and Adverbs are Better than Adjectives Alone. In Proceedings of the International Conference on Weblogs and Social Media (ICWSM).

John Blitzer, Mark Dredze and Fernando Pereira, 2007. Biographies, Bollywood, Boom-boxes and Blenders:

Domain Adaptation for Sentiment Classification. In Proceedings of the Association for Computational Linguistics (ACL).

Vasileios Hatzivassiloglou and Janyce Wiebe, 2000. Effects of Adjective Orientation and Gradability on Sentence Subjectivity. In Proceedings of the International Conference on Computational Linguistics (COLING), pages 299-305.

BH Juang and S Katagiri, 1992. Discriminative learning for minimum error classification. IEEE Transactions on Signal Processing, 40 (12). pages 3043-3054.

Shoushan Li, Rui Xia, Chengqing Zong and Chu-Ren Huang, 2009a. A framework of feature selection methods for text categorization. In Proceedings of the Annual Meeting of the Association for Computational Linguistics (ACL), pages 692-700.

Shoushan Li, Chengqing Zong and Xia Wang, 2007. Sentiment Classification through Combining Classifiers with Multiple Feature Sets. In Proceedings of the IEEE International Conference on Natural Language Processing and Knowledge Engineering (NLP-KE), pages 135-140.

Tao Li, Yi Zhang and Vikas Sindhwani, 2009b. A non-negative matrix tri-factorization approach to sentiment classification with lexical prior knowledge. In Proceedings of the Annual Meeting of the Association for Computational Linguistics (ACL), pages 244-252.

Jialin Pan, Xiaochuan Ni, Jiantao Sun, Qiang Yang and Zheng Chen, 2010. Cross-domain sentiment classification via spectral feature alignment. In Proceedings of the International World Wide Web Conference (WWW), pages 751-760.

Jialin Pan and Qiang Yang, 2009. A survey on transfer learning. IEEE Transactions on Knowledge and Data Engineering, 22 (10). pages 1345-1359.

Bo Pang, Lillian Lee and Shivakumar Vaithyanathan, 2002. Thumbs up? Sentiment Classification using Machine Learning Techniques. In Proceedings of the Conference on Empirical Methods in Natural Language Processing (EMNLP), pages 79-86.

Ellen Riloff, Janyce Wiebe and Theresa Wilson, 2003. Learning Subjective Nouns using Extraction Pattern Bootstrapping. In Proceedings of the Conference on Natural Language Learning (CoNLL), pages 25-32.

Matthew Whitehead and Larry Yaeger, 2008. Sentiment Mining Using Ensemble Classification Models. In the International Conference on Systems, Computing Sciences and Software Engineering (CISSE).

Rui Xia, Chengqing Zong and Shoushan Li, 2011. Ensemble of Feature Sets and Classification Algorithms for Sentiment Classification. Information Sciences, 181 (6). pages 1138-1152.

Rui. Xia and Chengqing. Zong, 2010. Exploring the use of word relation features for sentiment classification. In Proceedings of the 23rd International Conference on Computational Linguistics (COLING), pages 1336-1344.

Ensemble-style Self-training on Citation Classification

Cailing Dong **Ulrich Schäfer**
German Research Center for Artificial Intelligence (DFKI) GmbH
Language Technology Lab, Campus D 3 1, D-66123 Saarbrücken, Germany
cherinedong@gmail.com ulrich.schaefer@dfki.de

Abstract

Classification of citations into categories such as use, refutation, comparison etc. may have several relevant applications for digital libraries such as paper browsing aids, reading recommendations, qualified citation indexing, or fine-grained impact factor calculation. Most citation classification approaches described so far heavily rely on rule systems and patterns tailored to specific science domains. We focus on a less manual approach by learning domain-insensitive features from textual, physical, and syntactic aspects. Our experiments show the effectiveness of this feature set with various machine learning algorithms on datasets of different sizes. Furthermore, we build an ensemble-style self-training classification model and get better classification performance using only few training data, which largely reduces the manual annotation work in this task.

1 Introduction

Still in the current age of Semantic Web, structured repositories, ontologies and huge databases, scientific knowledge is preserved and transported in rather unstructured pieces of information, vulgo scientific papers or other similar, textual representations. Except bibliographical metadata, (manually) assigned keywords or coarse-grained classifications, there is no further, general method to unlock the written treasures without tedious reading, while full-text search is generally considered too imprecise and may be misleading.

Citations, spread over scientific text, are important anchors that help to structure the broad publication space. They are of invaluable importance to beginners in a scientific field as they ultimately point to seminal, original work and knowledge not explicitly available or repeated in every publication. Citations are also the primary discourse links in scientific discussion which typically span over years or even decades. Furthermore, citations are helpful to understand and reproduce findings. Thus, they form a predominant text feature for every reader. Wan et al. (2009), e.g., present a study on user needs for browsing scientific publications and show that citations play an important role, Schäfer and Kasterka (2010) suggest a novel user interface for navigating in typed citation graphs.

Garfield (1965) is probably the first to discuss an automatic computation of a citation classification. Many studies on citation classification are generally derived from the four-dimensional citation schema proposed by Moravcsik and Murugesan (1975). They distinguish between confirmative vs. negational; conceptual (theory) vs. operational (method); evolutionary (build on cited work) vs. juxtapositional (alternative to cited work); and organic (necessary to understand, reproduce) vs. perfunctory (citation out of politeness, policy, piety). The number of different proposed classes (also called citation *functions*) varies from 3 to 35 (Garfield, 1965; Garzone, 1996; Mercer and DiMarco, 2004; Teufel et al., 2006; Harwood, 2009). Most approaches try to identify more detailed dimensions and mutually exclusive classes by making use of many different features, such as the location of the *citation sentence*[1], surrounding POS tags, and the Boolean information indicating self-citation. In (Teufel et al., 2006), POS tags were employed to find grammatical subjects and further classified as specific agent types, while Mercer and DiMarco (2004) proved the efficiency of rhetoric cues in citation classification. Both studies suggest the potential capability of syntactic features in classifying citations.

Differently from previous work that mainly focuses on cue words and depends on large training sets, our work has the following contributions:

1. *Small but comprehensive feature set:* we only use a small set of features to describe a cita-

[1] We call the exact single sentence which contains the citation the *citation sentence*. There may be several citation sentences for each *reference* listed at the end of a paper.

tion sentence. It covers textual, physical and syntactic aspects and is domain-independent, which could help to make the adaptation to different science domains minimal.
2. *Robust supervised classification model:* we compare the performance of different machine learning algorithms with various sizes of training data. The results show the robustness of the classifiers on our feature set even with a small training set.
3. *Ensemble-style self-training classification model:* we design a semi-supervised learning algorithm to make use of unlabeled data. Differently from standard self-training algorithms, we use an ensemble learning model to choose more reliable new labeled data and achieve good performance. This approach helps to reduce the manual annotation effort.

The paper is structured as follows. We describe our corpus and annotation schema in Section 2, the definition of features will be elaborated in Section 3. We explain the classification experiments in Section 4 and finally conclude in Section 5.

2 Corpus and Annotation

2.1 Definition of Citation Functions

In this paper, we focus on the dimension of "organic or perfunctory" citations in Moravcsik and Murugesan (1975)'s schema and divide the citations into the following four general categories:

- **Background *(class0)***: citations which describe background of the main topic on the whole, or provide recent studies and state-of-the-art approaches in a general way.
- **Fundamental idea *(class1)***: citations about main previous work which inspired or gave specific hints on the current work.
- **Technical basis *(class2)***: citations of important tools, methods, data and other resources used or adapted in the current work.
- **Comparison *(class3)***: citations comparing methods or results with the current work.

We build these citation categories mainly due to the following reasons. First of all, these categories cover the most general and mutually exclusive citation functions. One could easily sketch a picture of a typical, arbitrary scientific publication based on citations from these categories. Secondly, rhetorical and syntactic characteristics are comparatively obvious in terms of functions in this basic level. Thus, our strategy might be valuable for the construction of further detailed automatic citation classification models with more fine-grained categories.

2.2 Corpus

Our corpus comes from the ACL (Association for Computational Linguistics) Anthology[2] (Bird et al., 2008), a comprehensive collection of scientific conference and workshop papers in the area of computational linguistics and language technology. We randomly chose papers from proceedings of the ACL conference in 2007 and 2008. Detailed information on our corpus is provided in Table 1. Corpus pre-processing and the annotation schema will be elaborated in the next subsections.

2.3 Corpus Pre-processing

For each paper in the corpus, we extract citation and reference information from the original PDF file by employing the citation parsing tool ParsCit (Councill et al., 2008). The *citation text* (a text snippet surrounding a citation) delivered by ParsCit is usually not sensitive to paragraph and sentence boundaries and may contain noise such as page number and footnotes. Therefore, we designed a text parser to get better citation sentences and related information by the following steps:

1. From the HTML output of a commercial PDF-to-text extraction tool, we generate a well-organized file with explicit paragraph and sentence boundaries.
2. We extract the titles of each section and its corresponding subsections, and map them into one of six predefined *section categories*[3]: ***Introduction***, ***Related work***, ***Method***, ***Experiment***, ***Evaluation***, and ***Conclusion***. We assign each sentence in the paper its corresponding section category.
3. We extract the corresponding correct citation sentence for a given reference based on its *citation marker* (denoted by authors and publishing year) and *citation text* from ParsCit.

2.4 Annotation Schema

Two annotators annotated the papers independently following our guidelines. The annotators not only focused on each citation sentence separately, but also read the paragraph and the whole section where the sentence is located, then made

[2] `http://aclweb.org/anthology`

[3] We associate section categories by means of synonyms which usually occur in the corresponding section titles.

ACL paper ID	# of distinct citation sentences	citation function distribution (class0 : class1 : class2 : class3)	remarks
P08-1009 ~ P08-1050	731	485 : 160 : 52 : 34	long-paper set1
P07-1001 ~ P07-1050	784	492 : 196 : 67 : 29	long-paper set2
P08-2001 ~ P08-2030	253	173 : 65 : 8 : 7	short-paper set

Table 1: Annotated corpus

a decision on the function of the citation over the whole paper, trying to be in the same perspective as the authors. The inter-annotator agreement between these two annotators is 0.757 measured by Cohen's kappa coefficient (Cohen, 1960), with parameter $n = 4$, $N = 1768$, and $k = 2$. This is quite high given the fact that a kappa value of 0.69 is considered as marginally stable, and 0.8 is considered as stable (Teufel et al., 2006).

3 Feature Set Construction

In this work, we consider the features of each citation sentence in three views: textual, physical and syntactic.

3.1 Textual Features

From the perspective of natural language processing, without any external information, the words in a citation sentence provide the textual distinction in classification. That's the reason why most of the previous work on citation classification is dominated by cue words. We also extract cue words representing certain citation functions, which are listed in Table 2.

From the table, one can observe that firstly only a few cue words exist in each group. Secondly, most cue words in the same group are synonyms. Thirdly, these cue words are domain-independent. We define subject_{cue} to indicate if the agent of the action described in the given citation sentence is related to the current work. It plays an important role in improving the distinguishing capability of other cue words. Besides, as mentioned before, DiMarco et al. (2006) showed the frequency of hedging cues in citation contexts and their importance in citation classification. We also observe that some hedging words listed in hedge_{cue} and suggest_{cue} occur more often in the class Background compared to other classes.

The textual features we defined are as follows:

- a Boolean feature for each group in Table 2, which indicates the existence of *any* cue word from the group in the citation sentence.
- a numerical weight for each group in Table 2, denoting the number of cue words from the group occurring in the citation sentence.
- a Boolean feature and corresponding weight feature for subject_{cue} in *neighbor sentences*[4]. Normally, the more frequently subject_{cue} occurs in consecutive sentences, the more likely the corresponding citation sentence is related to the current work.

3.2 Physical Features

As observed by other researchers on this topic, e.g. Teufel et al. (2006), the sentence location is an important feature, since it might be the most reliable information on citation function one could obtain from the paper directly. Specifically, we take the following physical features into account to distinguish between different citation functions:

- *Location*: section category, belonging to one of the predefined six categories described in Section 2.3.
- *Popularity*: number of references cited in the same sentence.
- *Density*: number of different references in the citation sentence and its neighbor sentences.
- *AvgDens*: average of *Density* among neighbor sentences surrounding the citation sentence.

3.3 Syntactic Features

During annotation, we found that the sentence structure of citation sentences varies according to their function. For example, citation sentences describing background of work are usually in active voice, while basic methods or tools used in the papers are in most cases introduced in passive voice. When the authors review some previous work in a general way, they tend to use present perfect tense, while using simple present tense to elaborate on their own work. These syntactic and writing styles can be extracted based on the POS sequences of citation sentences. In our work, the POS tags are generated by TreeTagger (Schmid, 1994), trained on the Penn Treebank (Marcus et al., 1994).

The typical syntactic patterns we defined are listed as follows. All examples are extracted from papers in our corpus, and the source paper id (ACL

[4]We define *neighbor sentences* as the sentences right before and after the given citation sentence.

Function	Group	Cue words
	subject$_{cue}$	we, our, us, table, figure, paper, algorithm, here
Background *(class0)*	**quantity**$_{cue}$	many, some, most, several, number of, numerous, variety, range of
	frequency$_{cue}$	usually, often, common(ly), typical(ly), traditional(ly)
	tense$_{cue}$	recent(ly), prior, previous, early
	example$_{cue}$	such as, for example, for instance, e.g.
	suggest$_{cue}$	may, might, could, would, will, can, should
	hedge$_{cue}$	suppose, conjecture, want, possible
Fundamental idea *(class1)*	**idea**$_{cue}$	following, similar to, motivate, inspired, idea, spirit
Technical basis *(class2)*	**basis**$_{cue}$	provided by, taken from, extracted from, based on, use, run, apply, extend, measure, evaluate, modify, extract
Comparison *(class3)*	**compare**$_{cue}$	compare, differ, deviate, contrast, exceed, outperform, opposed, consistent with, significant
	result$_{cue}$	result, accuracy, precision, performance, baseline

Table 2: Group of cue words corresponding to citation functions

ID) is denoted in square brackets following each example sentence. We also mark the text corresponding to each specific syntactic structure by underlines. For the POS sequence of each citation sentence, we delete the citation marker in parentheses for convenience.

1. **".*\\(\\) VV[DPZN].*":** *Fox <u>() showed</u> that cohesion is held in the vast majority of cases for English-French* [P08-1009]
2. **".*(VHP|VHZ) VV.*":** *while Cherry and Lin () <u>have shown</u> it to be a strong feature for word alignment* [P08-1009]
3. **".*VH(D|G|N|P|Z) (RB)*VBN.*":** *Inducing features for taggers by clustering <u>has been</u> tried by several researchers ().* [P08-1048]
4. **".*MD (RB)*VB(RB)* VVN.*":** *For example, the likelihood of those generative procedures <u>can be accumulated</u> to get the likelihood of the phrase pair ().* [P08-1010]
5. **"[^IW.]*VB(D|P|Z) (RB)*VVND.*":** *Our experimental set-up <u>is modeled</u> after the human evaluation presented in ().* [P08-1009]
6. **"(RB)*PP (RB)*V.*":** *<u>We use</u> Conditional Random Fields (CRFs) () to perform this tagging.* [P08-1047]
7. **".*VVG (NP)*(CC)*(NP).*":** *<u>Following ()</u>, we provide the annotators with only short sentences: those with source sentences between 10 and 25 tokens long.* [P08-1009]

Figure 1 illustrates the distribution of these patterns in different classes (we consider class1 and class2 together, denoted as class1+2) in long-paper set1 and short-paper set (long-paper set2 is used separately for further validating the feature sets). Among these syntactic patterns, the figures showed that the distribution of these patterns in the set of short papers and the set of long papers are consistent, i.e., the first 4 patterns are representative for class Background, while the other 3 patterns are typical for the other 3 classes.

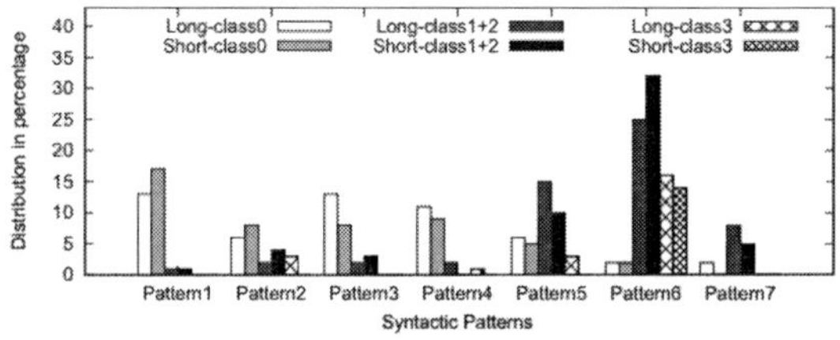

Figure 1: Distribution of syntactic patterns

We define a Boolean feature for each syntactic pattern indicating whether the pattern matches the POS sequence of the citation sentence. Combined with the cue words defined in Table 2, especially with subject$_{cue}$ and typical verbs in class1 to class3, the contribution of these patterns to overall performance increases significantly.

Thus, our final feature set is the collection of these textual, physical and syntactic features.

4 Citation Classification

4.1 Effectiveness of Syntactic Features

First of all, we build a set of experiments to test the effectiveness of syntactic features in citation classification. We compare the classification performance of our feature set with and without syntactic features on different machine learning algorithms, and with various training-testing ratios. We employ the meta class *AttributeSelectedClassifier* in Weka (Hall et al., 2009), and set *ChiSquaredAttributeEval* and *Ranker* (threshold 0) as evaluator and search method for attribute selection. The following 5 machine learning algorithms provided in Weka are employed as basic classifiers: *BayesNet*, *NaiveBayes*, *SMO* (*PolyKernel* is chosen as support vector kernel), *J48* and *RandomForest*.

We randomly split our whole corpus (including long-paper set2) into training dataset and test dataset with training instance ratios of 80%, 60%, 20% and 10%, respectively. For each of these four training-testing ratio configurations, we use 20 different random seeds to generate 20 different datasets. With each dataset, we measure the testing result by Macro-F (the mean of the F-measures of all classes), following Teufel et al. (2006). Then the final performance is measured by the average Macro-F of these 20 experiments with the same training-testing ratio configuration.

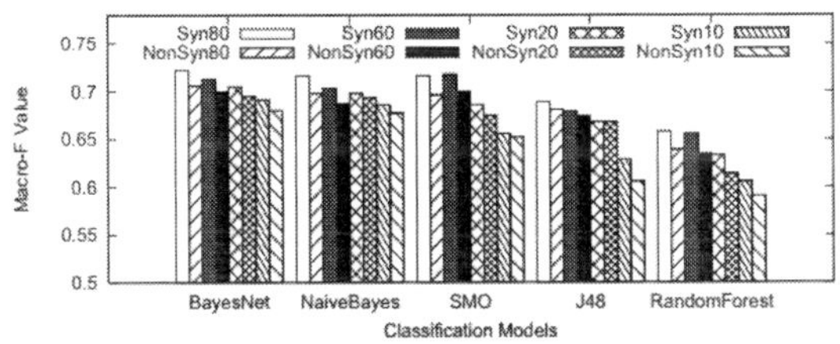

Figure 2: Performance of feature sets with and without syntactic features

Figure 2 illustrates the performance of feature sets with and without syntactic features on different sizes of training data. *Syn80* and *NonSyn80* denote feature sets with and without syntactic features when the ratio of training data is 80% respectively, analogously for other training data ratios. We can see that the feature sets with syntactic features can always beat the ones without syntactic features for all the datasets with different sizes of training data, independently of the classification model used. Besides, for all these datasets in different configurations, BayesNet and NaiveBayes are not very sensitive to the size of the training data. That is, these two supervised classification models can well learn our feature sets and make a good classification performance with only few training data (training ratio as 10% here, about 170 instances). It proves the effectiveness of our feature set to some extent.

4.2 Ensemble-style Self-training for Citation Classification

As in many other natural language processing tasks, large training datasets need to be annotated manually in order to improve the performance of citation classification. That is, a good annotation schema and abundant annotated training data are the basis for building a good automatic citation classification model. Because annotation is time-consuming, we design a semi-supervised learning algorithm to make use of unlabeled data under small training datasets in citation classification. Specifically, we adopt the idea of self-training (Zhu and Goldberg, 2009) to employ unlabeled data, but select new labeled data in the process of self-training in a more reliable way by taking advantage of the ensemble learning (Opitz and Maclin, 1999) algorithm.

4.2.1 Basic Self-training Algorithm

As a typical algorithm in semi-supervised learning, the self-training algorithm tries to extend the training dataset by changing some unlabeled data to labeled data with its own current predicted labels. We describe the basic self-training process in detail in Algorithm 1[5]. There are two main approaches to select the unlabeled data: one is to select the instances with highest predictive confidence *(prob-selfTrain)*, which is the original approach; the other is to randomly select some instances from unlabeled dataset *(random-selfTrain)*, which has been shown to be effective in some applications. As shown in line 6 and line 7, we implement these two approaches in parallel. Three different basic classifiers are used in this algorithm. From the main procedure of this algorithm, one can see that each classifier maintains its own labeled and unlabeled datasets in each iteration independently. This algorithm is set to be our baseline algorithm.

4.2.2 Ensemble-style Self-training Algorithm

Every supervised learning algorithm tries to search for the best hypothesis through a hypothesis space, therefore makes good predictions with a particular problem, i.e, based on given training data. Taking advantage of this property, ensemble learning tries to improve the prediction accuracy by combining different supervised learning algorithms. In self-training, each prediction process is actually supervised learning, therefore the quality of the training data is very important. Furthermore, self-training is based on the assumption that one's own high confidence predictions are correct, i.e. the final results could be worse if the model repeatedly learns from its own previous wrong decisions. To avoid such a situation, we devise an ensemble-style self-training algorithm by using ensemble learning to choose reliable new labeled

[5]Set $\{a,b,c,d\}$ denotes the number of instances in class0, class1, class2 and class3 as a, b, c, d, respectively. Analogously for set $\{m,n,p,q\}$ for indicating the number of added instances in each iteration.

Algorithm 1 Baseline: basic self-training algorithm

Require:
Whole dataset D ; training set ratio α ; Basic classifiers *Base1, Base2, Base3*;
Iteration times K; Initial number of labeled instances $\{a,b,c,d\}$;
Number of instances added to labeled dataset in each loop: $\{m,n,p,q\}$;

Pre-process:
Training dataset *Train* with number of instances $|D| * \alpha$; Test dataset *Test* with instances $\{D\} - \{Train\}$;
Labeled dataset L with initial number of instances $\{a,b,c,d\}$ randomly selected from *Train*;
Unlabeled dataset U with instances $\{Train\} - \{L\}$;
Labeled dataset $L_1 = L$, L_2=L and L_3=L; Unlabeled dataset $U_1 = U$, U_2=U and U_3=U;

Procedure:
for $k = 0$ **to** K **do**
  for each classifier $Base_i$ $(i = 1,2,3)$ **do**
    Use L_i to train classifiers $Base_i$
    Obtain the test results on *Test* by classifier $Base_i$
    Make prediction for each instance in U_i by classifier $Base_i$
    a. prob-selfTrain: Select $\{m,n,p,q\}$ instances which have highest prediction confidence from U, denoted as L_{i-add}
    b. random-selfTrain: Randomly select $\{m,n,p,q\}$ instances from U, denoted as L_{i-add}
    $L_i = L_i + L_{i-add}$; $U_i = U_i$ - L_{i-add}
  end for
end for

Algorithm 2 Ensemble-style self-training algorithm

Require: configuration of *Train, Test, L, U*, and value of parameters $\{a,b,c,d\}$, $\{m,n,p,q\}$, K as well as basic classifiers *Base1, Base2, Base3* are the same as those in Algorithm 1;

Procedure:
1: **for** $k = 0$ **to** K **do**
2: Use L to train classifiers *Base1, Base2, Base3*, respectively
3: Obtain the test results on *Test* by classifier *Base1, Base2, Base3* respectively
4: Obtain the test results on *Test* by ensemble model *Ensemble*, consist of *Base1, Base2* and *Base3*
5: Make prediction for each instance in U by *Ensemble*
6: Randomly select $\{m,n,p,q\}$ instances from U, denoted as L_{add}
7: $L = L + L_{add}$; $U = U$ - L_{add}
8: **end for**

data in each iteration. The detailed procedure is displayed in Algorithm 2. Here, the datasets and parameters are set to be the same as those in Algorithm 1, in order to compare the performance of both algorithms. In this ensemble-style self-training algorithm, one can see that all the basic classifiers and ensemble model *Ensemble* share the same labeled dataset L and unlabeled dataset U, which is maintained by *Ensemble* via choosing new labeled data in ensemble way (line 5 and 6).

4.2.3 Ensemble Learning

Normally, there are two main combination rules in ensemble learning to make the final prediction for a given instance. One is probability-based, that is, choosing the decision of the basic classifier which produces the highest prediction confidence for the instance. Another is to use majority voting. In our experiments, we choose BayesNet, SMO and NaiveBayes as the basic classifiers in our ensemble model and adopt the majority voting combination rule, due to the following reasons: 1) these three models have better overall performance according to Figure 2; 2) Usually, the more diverse the member algorithms, the more effective their ensemble model can be (Rokach, 2010). The classification mechanisms of BayesNet and SMO are totally different, which can ensure the performance of the ensemble model to some extent; 3) it is impossible to use probability-based combination rules due to the uninterpretable prediction probability in SMO. Thus, using a classifier with good overall performance such as NaiveBayes in majority vote could ensure the accuracy of ensemble learning to a certain degree.

4.2.4 The Class Imbalance Problem

From previous research on citation classification, independently of how many different functions were defined, one can observe that the dataset is class-imbalanced. For example, in a sentiment-oriented classification schema, negative citations are much less frequent than positive citations. Conversely, a high volume of citations actually is used to describe the background. Thus, class imbalance is actually a key issue in automatic citation classification. Previous research often ignored this fact, possibly because pattern-driven or rule-based models are less sensitive to such a distribution of datasets. Usually, standard classifiers try to get the overall accuracy with the cost of misclassifying the instances in small classes (Zhou and

Liu, 2006), while small classes are always those classes people are most interested in. Taking our citation classification as an example, "organic" citations are more attractive than the "perfunctory" ones. In our experiments, we try to balance the instances of these classes to protect small classes.

4.2.5 Experiments

In this set of experiments, we also wrap these three base classifiers with the meta class *AttributeSelectedClassifier* in the same configuration as in the last experiments in Section 3.1. As listed in Table 1, the average ratios among these 4 classes are imbalanced, around *16:6:1.8:1*. On the one hand, we try to keep the natural distribution to some extent (number of instances in the two bigger classes: class0:class1≈2:1; number of instances in the two smaller classes: class2:class3≈2:1). On the other hand, we slightly reduce the intensity of the class imbalance to avoid misclassifying too many instances from the small classes (here, we limit the ratio of class0 and class3 to be less than 5). To protect the small classes, we set the distribution of the initial labeled dataset to around *5:2.5:2:1*. A few new labeled data with similar distributions are added in each iteration to avoid introducing too much noise. We conduct two experiments.

Exp-a: We set the number of instances in the smallest class class3 as 5, in order to ensure the accuracy. The iteration time K is 10. So α is set to be 0.3 in case insufficient unlabeled data to be added as labeled data. That is, 30% of the instances are randomly extracted as training set and the remaining instances are set as test data. Thus, according to our predefined class distribution, we set initial labeled data $\{20, 10, 8, 5\}$, and the rest of the training data are regarded as unlabeled data. The number of new labeled data in each iteration is $\{6, 4, 3, 1\}$.

Exp-b: In this experiment, we use 3 labeled instances in class3 to conduct the self-training process, initial labeled data $\{a, b, c, d\}$ is set to be $\{15, 8, 6, 3\}$ following predefined class distribution. Less new labeled data is added each time, $\{m, n, p, q\}$=$\{5, 3, 2, 1\}$ with more iterations, K=30. α is set to 0.3 due to the long iterations.

As mentioned before, self-training has a high demand on training data, especially initial labeled data. That is, the quality of the initial labeled data can largely affect the final overall performance. In order to obtain fairly general results, we repeat each experiment described above 10 times

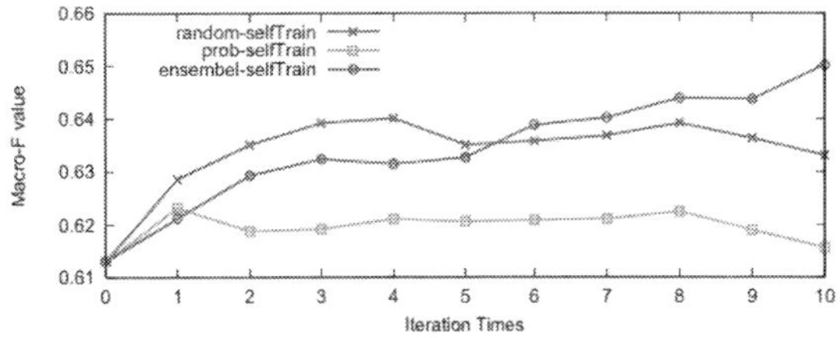

(a) SMO

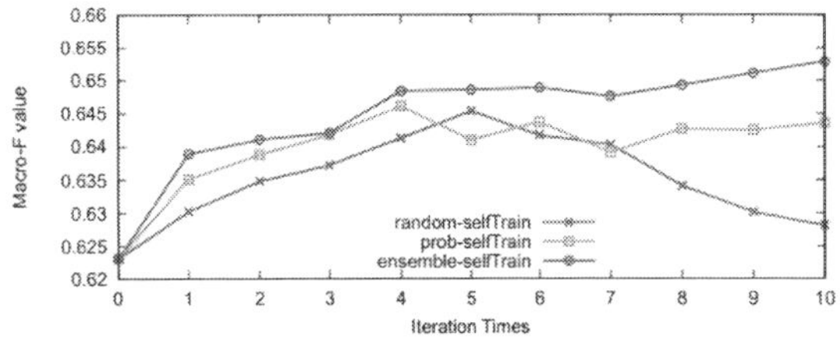

(b) BayesNet

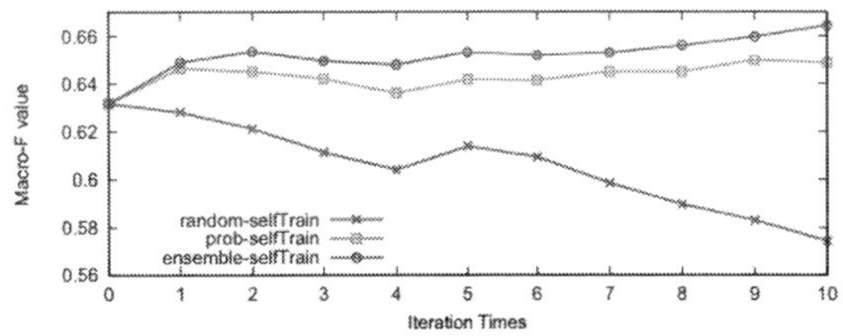

(c) NaiveBayes

Figure 3: *Exp-a:* Basic self-training vs. ensemble-style self-training with different basic classifiers

with different seeds, splitting the dataset into training set and test set and therefore the initial labeled data each time are different. The final results are measured by the average value of Macro-F in these ten experiments. Figure 3 and Figure 4 illustrate the final average Macro-F values obtained by different basic classifiers with parameters given in *Exp-a* and *Exp-b*, respectively. Here, Macro-F in iteration 0 is obtained based on initial labeled data, so the algorithms with *prob-selfTrain*, *random-selfTrain* and ensemble-style self-training (denoted as *ensemble-selfTrain*) start at the same point for the same basic classifier.

From Figure 3 and Figure 4, we can observe that for the two probability-driven classifiers BayesNet and NaiveBayes, their *prob-selfTrain* process is better than *random-selfTrain* on the whole. We observe the opposite for classifier SMO since its prediction confidence is meaningless. In general, our ensemble-style self-training algorithm outperforms both kinds of basic self-training algorithms independently of the basic classifier used. Its self-training process is quite stable due to the relatively reliable new labeled data ensured by ensemble learning strategies. Among all three basic clas-

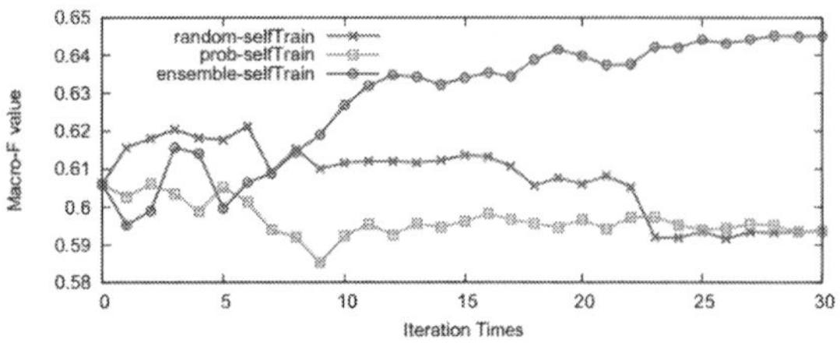

(a) SMO

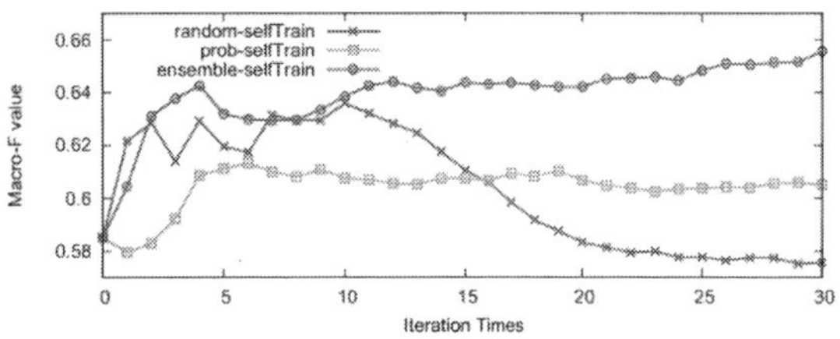

(b) BayesNet

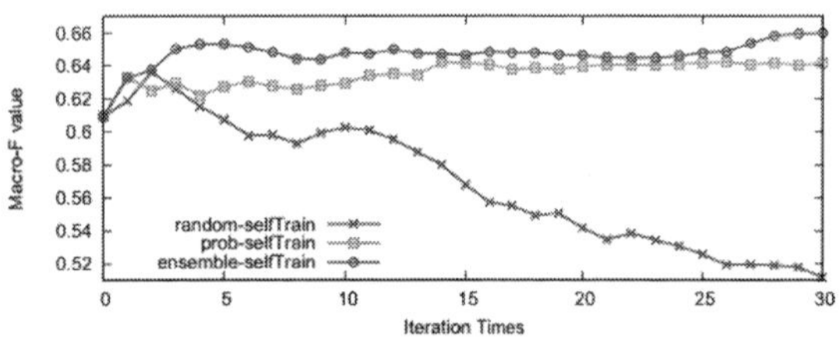

(c) NaiveBayes

Figure 4: *Exp-b:* Basic self-training vs. ensemble-style self-training with different basic classifiers

sifiers with the same experimental setup, NaiveBayes has the best performance not only at the starting point (iteration 0), but also in the whole ensemble-style self-training process.

In our ensemble-style self-training algorithm, we also build an ensemble model *Ensemble*. In Figure 5, we compare the performance of ensemble-style self-training with basic classifier *Ensemble* (denoted as *ensembleSelfTrain-Ensemble*) and NaiveBayes under experimental setup *Exp-a* and *Exp-b*, respectively.

Based on the observation, we found that although *Ensemble* is a good guide on selecting new labeled data, its self-training performance is not as good as NaiveBayes. There might be two main reasons. First of all, without self-training, NaiveBayes itself fits our feature sets quite well and shows the best performance among all the classifiers. Combining with other classifier as done in model *Ensemble* could affect its good performance. Secondly, ensemble models tend to be over-fitting to the training data. During the self-training process, the training data changes slightly by adding few new labeled data each time, so the over-fitting problem occurs soon. Thus, we choose

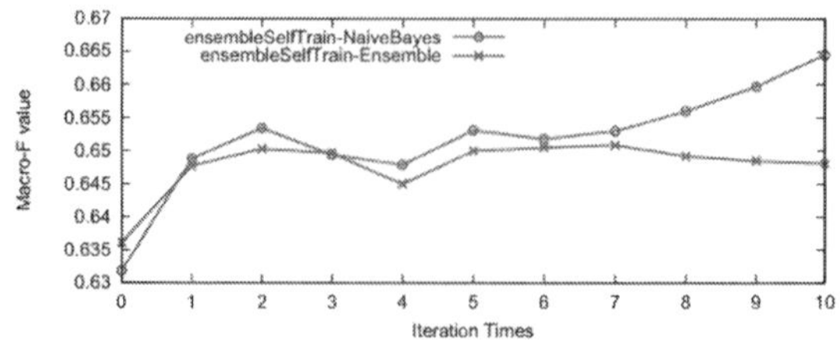

(a) *Exp-a*

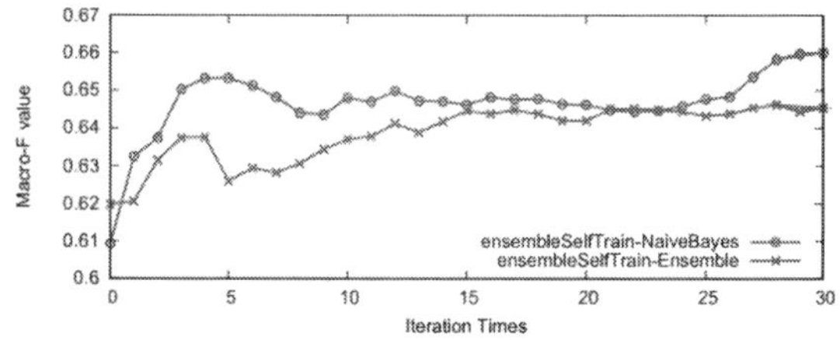

(b) *Exp-b*

Figure 5: Ensemble-style self-training on NaiveBayes vs. *Ensemble*

ensemble-style self-training with main basic classifier NaiveBayes as our final classifier for citation classification.

5 Summary

In this work, we defined a citation classification schema to better sketch the skeleton of a scientific paper from its background, fundamental ideas, technical basis and performance comparison. These citation functions are distinguished by features from textual, physical and syntactic aspects, which are simple but comprehensive, and domain-independent. Using different supervised learning classifiers on various sizes of training datasets, we improved and demonstrated the efficiency of our feature set by adding syntactic patterns extracted from POS tags. The supervised classification models NaiveBayes and BayesNet have shown their robustness on our feature set, with only about 170 training instances. Furthermore, we built an ensemble-style self-training algorithm to better use and extend training data. Using about only 40 labeled instances, our final classifier can improve the Macro-F value by almost 5%. This model could largely alleviate manual annotation in citation classification.

Acknowledgments

This research has been funded by the German Federal Ministry of Education and Research under contract 01IW08003 (project TAKE). We thank the anonymous reviewers for insightful comments.

References

Steven Bird, Robert Dale, Bonnie Dorr, Bryan Gibson, Mark Joseph, Min-Yen Kan, Dongwon Lee, Brett Powley, Dragomir Radev, and Yee Fan Tan. 2008. The ACL anthology reference corpus: A reference dataset for bibliographic research. In *Proceedings of the Language Resources and Evaluation Conference (LREC-2008)*, pages 1755–1759, Marrakesh, Morocco.

Jacob Cohen. 1960. A coefficient of agreement for nominal scales. *Educational and Psychological Measurement*, 20:37–46.

Isaac G. Councill, C. Lee Giles, and Min-Yen Kan. 2008. ParsCit: An open-source CRF reference string parsing package. In *Proceedings of the Language Resources and Evaluation Conference (LREC-2008)*, pages 661–667, Marrakesh, Morocco.

Chrysanne DiMarco, Frederick Kroon, and Robert Mercer. 2006. Using hedges to classify citations in scientific articles. In *Computing Attitude and Affect in Text Theory and Applications*, pages 247–263.

Eugene Garfield. 1965. Can citation indexing be automated? In Mary Elizabeth Stevens, Vincent E. Giuliano, and Laurence B. Heilprin, editors, *Statistical Association Methods for Mechanical Documentation*. National Bureau of Standards, Washington, DC. NBS Misc. Pub. 269.

Mark Garzone. 1996. Automated classification of citations using linguistic semantic grammars. Master's thesis, Dept. of Computer Science, The University of Western Ontario, Canada.

Mark Hall, Eibe Frank, Geoffrey Holmes, Bernhard Pfahringer, Peter Reutemann, and Ian H. Witten. 2009. The WEKA data mining software: An update. *SIGKDD Explorations*, 11(1).

Nigel Harwood. 2009. An interview-based study of the functions of citations in academic writing across two disciplines. *Journal of Pragmatics*, 41(3):497–518.

Mitchell P. Marcus, Beatrice Santorini, and Mary Ann Marcinkiewicz. 1994. Building a large annotated corpus of English: The Penn treebank. *Computational Linguistics*, 19(2):313–330.

Robert E. Mercer and Chrysanne DiMarco. 2004. A design methodology for a biomedical literature indexing tool using the rhetoric of science. In Lynette Hirschman and James Pustejovsky, editors, *HLT-NAACL 2004 Workshop: BioLINK 2004, Linking Biological Literature, Ontologies and Databases*, pages 77–84, Boston, Massachusetts, USA.

Michael J. Moravcsik and Poovanalingam Murugesan. 1975. Some results on the function and quality of citations. *Social Studies of Science*, 5:86–92.

David Opitz and Richard Maclin. 1999. Popular ensemble methods: an empirical study. *Journal of Artificial Intelligence Research*, 11:169–198.

Lior Rokach. 2010. Ensemble-based classifiers. *Artificial Intelligence Review*, 33:1–39, February.

Ulrich Schäfer and Uwe Kasterka. 2010. Scientific authoring support: A tool to navigate in typed citation graphs. In *Proceedings of the NAACL-HLT 2010 Workshop on Computational Linguistics and Writing*, pages 7–14, Los Angeles, CA.

Helmut Schmid. 1994. Probabilistic part-of-speech tagging using decision trees. In *Proceedings of International Conference on New Methods in Language Processing*, Manchester, UK.

Simone Teufel, Advaith Siddharthan, and Dan Tidhar. 2006. Automatic classification of citation function. In *Proceedings of the 2006 Conference on Empirical Methods in Natural Language Processing (EMNLP)*, pages 103–110, Sydney, Australia.

Stephen Wan, Cécile Paris, Michael Muthukrishna, and Robert Dale. 2009. Designing a citation-sensitive research tool: an initial study of browsing-specific information needs. In *Proceedings of the 2009 Workshop on Text and Citation Analysis for Scholarly Digital Libraries*, NLPIR4DL '09, pages 45–53, Suntec, Singapore.

Zhihua Zhou and Xuying Liu. 2006. On multi-class cost-sensitive learning. In *Proceedings of the 21st National Conference on Artificial Intelligence (AAAI)*, pages 567–572.

Xiaojin Zhu and Andrew B. Goldberg. 2009. *Introduction to Semi-Supervised Learning*. Morgan and Claypool.

Back to the Roots of Genres: Text Classification by Language Function

Henning Wachsmuth
University of Paderborn, s-lab
Paderborn, Germany
hwachsmuth@s-lab.upb.de

Kathrin Bujna
University of Paderborn
Paderborn, Germany
kabu@mail.upb.de

Abstract

The term "genre" covers different aspects of both texts and documents, and it has led to many classification schemes. This makes different approaches to genre identification incomparable and the task itself unclear. We introduce the linguistically motivated text classification task *language function analysis*, LFA, which focuses on one well-defined aspect of genres. The aim of LFA is to determine whether a text is predominantly expressive, appellative, or informative. LFA can be used in search and mining applications to efficiently filter documents of interest. Our approach to LFA relies on fast machine learning classifiers with features from different research areas. We evaluate this approach on a new corpus with 4,806 product texts from two domains. Within one domain, we correctly classify up to 82% of the texts, but differences in feature distribution limit accuracy on out-of-domain data.

1 Introduction

Text classification has been successfully applied to various natural language processing tasks, among which some of the most popular are topic detection, authorship attribution, sentiment analysis, and genre identification. While the first three refer to single aspects of a text, genres cover different properties of both documents and texts, such as their form, function, purpose, and target audience. As a consequence, many different genre classification schemes exist, which makes most approaches to genre identification badly comparable as a recent study showed (Sharoff *et al.*, 2010). Correspondingly, the question which features work best in genre identification still remains open. We argue that one major reason behind is a missing common understanding of genres and that we need to focus on the single aspects of genres in order to overcome this situation.

In this paper, we investigate *why* a text was written. Therefore, we introduce the ambitious task *language function analysis*, abbreviated as LFA, i.e., to classify the predominant function of a text as intended by its author. In line with the work of the psychologist Karl Bühler (1934), we distinguish three abstract and very general classes, namely, *expressive*, *appellative*, and *informative* texts. Several search and text mining applications can benefit from applying LFA as a document filtering step with respect to both efficiency and effectiveness. A search engine, for instance, might restrict its result list to hits that mainly serve an informative purpose. Similarly, LFA can be used in opinion mining to cancel out promotional texts in favor of personal attitudes. While, of course, LFA does not replace genre identification, we think that language functions constitute one root of a common and clear genre concept.

Language functions are well-studied in linguistic pragmatics, but we analyze whether they also correlate with statistical text characteristics. For this purpose, we built a manually annotated corpus with 4,806 product-related texts from two separated domains (music and smartphones) in close collaboration with industry. Each text is tagged as *personal*, *commercial*, or *informational*, which can be seen as an application-specific classification by language function. Also, the texts have been categorized by sentiment polarity.

Our approach to LFA relies on machine learning of lexical and shallow linguistic features from different research areas. We evaluate this approach both for classification within one corpus domain and for the transfer to another domain. With respect to the in-domain task, our results indicate that a text collection of homogeneous quality and style allows for high accuracy. In particular, we correctly classify 81.9% of the music texts using a very efficiently computable feature set. This makes our approach suitable for document filtering purposes. However, classification of out-of-domain data seems difficult because of the *covariate shift* (Shimodaira, 2000) in feature distribution between domains. Interestingly, though, the best-performing features for this task come from the area of authorship attribution.

1.1 Summary of Contributions

Altogether, the main contributions of this paper are the following:

- We introduce the linguistically motivated text classification task language function analysis, which addresses one well-defined aspect of genres (Section 2).
- We provide a corpus for language function analysis and sentiment analysis with product-related texts that were manually annotated by one of our industrial partners (Section 4).
- We analyze the impact of machine learning features from different research areas on the language function analysis of texts from two domains (Sections 5 and 6).

2 Language Function Analysis

One of the most influential attempts to categorize language functions was introduced by the famous psychologist Karl Bühler (1934). In his *Organon model*, which is rooted in Plato's view of language as a tool, Bühler identifies and interrelates three fundamental functions of natural language in communication: the *expression* of the speaker, the *appeal* to the receiver, and the *representation* of the object or state of affair being communicated. As illustrated in Figure 1 they all refer to a linguistic sign, which can be understood as the unit of all forms of language.

Based on the three language functions, Katharina Reiß (1971) defined a classification of text types, which relates to the intention of the author of a text. In particular, she distinguished between the form-focused expression of the author's attitudes in *expressive* texts, the aim of making an appeal to the reader in *appellative* (or *operative*) texts, and the content-focused description of objects and facts in *informative* texts. Reiß assigned several concrete text types such as "report" (informative), "novel" (expressive), or "comment" (in-

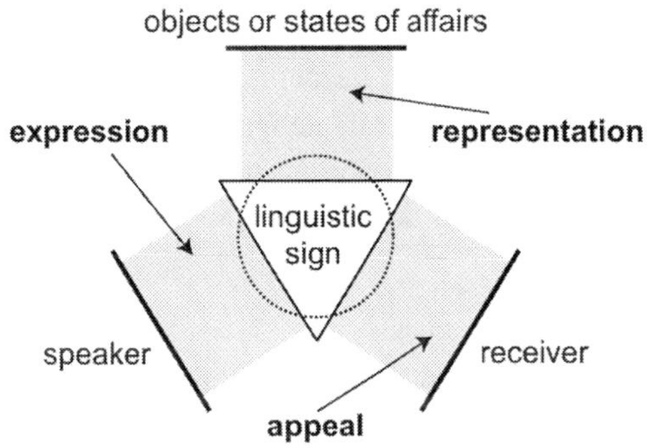

Figure 1: The organon model, formulated by Karl Bühler (1934), with its three language functions expression, appeal, and representation.

formative and appellative) to one or more of these classes. While she claimed that a hybrid type is the regular case, she observed that one function is predominant in most texts. We adopt Reiß' typology to define the language function analysis task.

Definition 1 (Language Function Analysis) *Let $C = \{expressive, appellative, informative\}$ be the set of abstract language functions and let d be a text. Then the task of language function analysis, LFA, is to find the mapping $d \mapsto c \in C$ such that c is the predominant language function of d.*

We argue that LFA can help in many practical problems where document filtering is needed, especially because of its generic nature. For product-related texts, the use of LFA emerges, when we map the abstract functions in C to the following concrete language function classes of text:

- *personal (expressive).* Text that aims to express the personal attitude of an individual towards a product of interest.
- *commercial (appellative).* Text that follows commercial purposes with respect to a product of interest.
- *informational (informative).* Text that reports on a product of interest in an objective and journalistic manner.

Another example for a set of concrete language function classes might be *review* (expressive), *proposal* (appellative), and *report* (informative) in the research project context. Notice, though, that the mapping from abstract functions to concrete classes of text is meant to be an interpretation for a concrete learning situation rather than a redefinition of the task. In the remaining sections, we use the classes *personal*, *commercial*, and *informational* for a first evaluation of LFA. Our intuition is that, statistically, language functions imply shallow linguistic features, such as certain parts-of-speech or writing style characteristics.

3 Related Work

Classification by intention has been recently addressed in (Kröll and Strohmaier, 2009). The authors infer a subset of 145 intentions from the transcriptions of speeches based on actions mentioned *within* the text. Similar problems refer to the analysis of speaker intentions in conversation (Kadoya *et al.*, 2005) and to the area of textual entailment (Michael, 2009), which is about the information implied by text. In contrast, LFA is about the question why a text was written and, thus, refers to the authorial intention *behind* a text.[1]

In that, our work resembles (Santini, 2005) where a linguistic expert system analyzes the gradation of four text types that convey the purpose and function of a text. Two of these types fit to the abstract functions introduced in Section 2, namely, the types "explicatory/informational" and "argumentative/persuasive". However, the other types ("descriptive/narrative" and "instructional") seem quite arbitrary and appear to intersect with the first type. Moreover, a class for the expression of personal views is missing. This might result from the used SPIRIT corpus (Clarke et. al., 2002), which was created for question answering purposes. Besides, language functions constitute a general classification scheme that may be concretized for a task at hand, while Santini regards text types only as input to web genre identification.

In terms of the communicative purpose of a text, language functions can be considered as the most abstract view on genres. Indeed, Kessler *et al.* (1997) argue that the class of texts that aim at persuading someone would not be seen as a genre merely because that class is too generic. While the authors simply define a genre to refer to a certain functional trait as well as to some formal properties, several abstract and concrete classification schemes have been proposed for genre identification. In a pioneer study on genres, Biber (1986) analyzes basic textual dimensions, such as "informative vs. involved", while Karlgren and Cutting (1994) try to automatically separate informative from imaginative texts. Stamatatos *et. al.* (2000) rely on more concrete press-related genres (e.g. "Letter to the editor" or "Spot news"), and Garera and Yarowsky (2009) investigate modern conversational genres, such as "Email".

The two latter show that genres do not only describe the function and purpose of a text, but also its form and target audience and, thus, also represent concepts orthogonal to language functions. Correspondingly, a great deal of genre research in the last decade focused on web genres as surveyed in (Stein *et al.*, 2010). Two standard corpora for web genre identification, KI-04 (Meyer zu Eissen and Stein, 2004) and SANTINIS (Santini, 2010), illustrate a common situation in genre research: Their classification schemes partly overlap, e.g. the class "Help" from KI-04 can be mapped to "FAQ" in SANTINIS, but partly also contain unique and quite specific classes, such as "Search pages" in SANTINIS. Moreover, Sharoff *et. al.* (2010) found out that seemingly similar classes ("Portrayal" and "Personal home page") differ strongly in terms of discriminative features. This supports our argumentation that there is neither a clear common understanding of genres, nor a well-defined genre concept. Additionally, Boese and Howe (2005) recognized that, in the web, genres may evolve over time to other genres.

However, language functions still represent one important aspect of genres. Accordingly, genre identification and LFA have similarities with respect to both practical applications (e.g. document filtering) and potentially helpful features. Since our focus is on a text itself as opposed to a document, we follow Webber (2009) who emphasizes the importance of text-internal and linguistic features, such as particular parts-of-speech. Also, we investigate both character-based and word-based n-grams, which were most successful in the above-mentioned evaluation of genre collections of Sharoff *et al.* (2010).

Further promising features relate to sentiment analysis and authorship attribution. Like LFA, sentiment analysis covers the issue of subjectivity (Pang and Lee, 2008), but it addresses *what* is said. Correspondingly, research in sentiment analysis often focuses only on characteristic terms as in (Prettenhofer and Stein, 2010). In contrast, approaches to authorship attribution aim at measuring the writing style of a text; sometimes based on

[1] While literature theory also addresses the intention of the reader and the intention of the text itself (Eco, 1990), only authorial intention is relevant for the purpose of this paper.

lexical and shallow linguistic information (Luyckx and Daelemans, 2008), sometimes using deeper analyses like parsing (Raghavan *et al.*, 2010). We adopt some of these features in Section 5 and 6.

4 The LFA-11 Corpus

To evaluate LFA, we built the LFA-11 corpus with manually annotated German texts from two separated domains: *music* and *smartphones*. The purpose of the corpus is to provide textual data for the development and evaluation of approaches to LFA and sentiment analysis. The corpus is freely available at http://infexba.upb.de.

The music collection of LFA-11 contains 2,713 promotional texts, professional and user reviews that were taken from a social network platform. Accordingly, these texts are well-written and of homogeneous style. In contrast, a set of 2,093 blog posts from the *Spinn3r corpus*[2] addresses smartphones. The Spinn3r project aims at crawling and indexing the whole blogosphere. Hence, the texts in the smartphone collection vary strongly in quality and writing style. While the music texts span 9.4 sentences with 23.0 tokens on average, the blog posts have an average length of 11.8 sentences but only 18.6 tokens per sentence.

4.1 Annotations

The corpus consists of UTF-8 encoded XMI files preformatted for the Apache UIMA framework[3], which implements the *Unstructured Information Management Architecture* (Ferrucci and Lally, 2004). Each file includes the text together with one of the language function annotations *personal*, *commercial*, and *informational*. Also, the texts have been classified by sentiment polarity as positive, negative, or neutral. Tagging was done by two employees of the *Digital Collections Verlagsgesellschaft mbH*, a leading supplier of digital asset management systems.

Figure 2 shows excerpts from three texts of the music collection, one out of each language function class. The excerpts have been translated to English for clarity. While some indicators of language functions might have been lost due to translation, the examples underline the strong connection of the concrete language function classes to the abstract functions from Section 2. In order to support a consistent categorization, the following

personal. ... *How did Alex recently ask when he saw Kravitz' latest best-of collection: Is it his own liking, the voting on his website, or the chart position what counts? Good question. However, in our case, there is nothing to argue about: 27 songs, all were number one. The Beatles. Biggest band on the globe.* ...

commercial. ... *The sitars sound authentically Indian. In combination with the three-part harmonious singing and the jingle-jangle of the Rickenbacker guitars, they create an oriental flair without losing their Beatlesque elegance. If that doesn't make you smile!* ...

informational. ... *"It's All Too Much"? No, no, still okay, though an enormous hype was made for decades about the seemingly new Beatles song. The point is that exactly this song "Hey Bulldog" has already been published long time ago, most recently on a reprint of "Yellow Submarine" in the year 1987.* ...

Figure 2: Translated excerpts from three texts of the music collection. Note that the translation to English might have affected the indicators of the corresponding language functions.

guidelines were given to the two employees for the language function annotations:

- *personal.* "Use this annotation if the text seems not to be of commercial interest, but probably represents the personal view on the product of a private individual."
- *commercial.* "Use this annotation if the text is of obvious commercial interest. The text seems to predominantly aim at persuading the reader to buy or like the product."
- *informational.* "Use this annotation if the text seems not to be of commercial interest with respect to the product. Instead, it predominantly appears to be informative in a journalistic manner."

About 20% of the music texts and 40% of the smartphone texts were tagged twice in order to compute inter-annotator agreement. The resulting values $\kappa_m = 0.78$ (music) and $\kappa_s = 0.67$ (smartphone) of Cohen's Kappa (Carletta, 1996) for the language function annotations constitute "substantial agreement". Especially κ_s is far from perfect, which can be problematic for text classification purposes. Under consideration of the hybridity of language functions in texts (cf. Section 2), κ_m and κ_s appear to be quite high, though.

[2] Spinn3r corpus, http://www.spinn3r.com

[3] Apache UIMA, http://uima.apache.org

Set	personal	commercial	informational
music collection			
Training	521 (38.5%)	127 (9.4%)	707 (52.2%)
Validation	419 (61.7%)	72 (10.6%)	188 (27.7%)
Test	342 (50.4%)	68 (10.0%)	269 (39.6%)
smartphone collection			
Training	546 (52.1%)	90 (8.6%)	411 (39.3%)
Validation	279 (53.3%)	36 (6.9%)	208 (39.8%)
Test	302 (57.7%)	28 (5.4%)	193 (36.9%)

Table 1: Distribution of language function classes in the music and smartphone sets of the corpus.

Set	positive	neutral	negative
music collection			
Training	1003 (74.0%)	259 (19.1%)	93 (6.9%)
Validation	558 (82.2%)	82 (12.1%)	39 (5.7%)
Test	514 (75.7%)	115 (16.9%)	50 (7.4%)
smartphone collection			
Training	205 (19.6%)	738 (70.5%)	104 (9.9%)
Validation	110 (21.0%)	343 (65.6%)	70 (13.4%)
Test	84 (16.1%)	359 (68.6%)	80 (15.3%)

Table 2: Distribution of sentiment polarity classes in the music and smartphone sets of the corpus.

4.2 Evaluation Sets

We created splits for each domain with half of the texts in the training set and each one fourth in the validation set and test set, respectively. Table 1 and Table 2 show the class distributions of language functions and sentiment polarities. The distributions indicate that the training, validation, and test sets differ significantly from each other. Also, Table 1 and 2 give a first hint that the correlation between language functions and sentiment is low. With regard to the distribution of language functions, we observe a large imbalance between the three classes. In case of double-annotated texts, we chose the annotations of the employee who categorized more texts as *commercial*. Still, this class remains by far the minority class with only about 5% to 10% of the texts in all sets. This, of course, makes the task at hand more difficult.

5 Features

To investigate whether LFA has correlations with other text classification tasks, we experimented with several lexical and shallow linguistic features that relate to some of the research areas mentioned in Section 3. For a concise evaluation, we organized these features into the following six types.

1. *Simple genre features.* Simple approaches from genre identification: the frequency of each part-of-speech tag that occurs at least 15 times in the training set, the average word length, and the *Lix* readability index (Anderson, 1983).

2. *Text type.* Features inspired by linguistic expert knowledge from (Santini, 2005), namely, the frequency of time and money entities as well as the frequency of two sets of part-of-speech tags: a) personal and possessive pronouns, b) nouns and adjectives.

3. *Writing style.* A selection of measures used in authorship attribution (Stamatatos, 2009): the frequency of the most common words, part-of-speech trigrams, and character trigrams as well as the frequency of capitalized, upper-case, and lower-case words. The same for parentheses, punctuation and quotation marks, and the portion of "?" and "!" under all sentence delimiters.

4. *Sentiment.* Indicators for sentiment, namely, the frequency of 15 common emoticons such as ";-)" and the sentiment polarity of the text.

5. *Core trigrams.* The frequency of the most discriminative part-of-speech and character trigrams of each language function class. Similar features performed best in (Sharoff *et al.*, 2010). Here, we use all trigrams that occur over six times as often in one class c as in any other class $c' \neq c$.

6. *Core vocabularies.* The frequency of the most discriminative words, introduced as a genre feature by Lee and Myaeng (2002). We define such a word to occur at least in 15 training texts of class c and over six times as often in c as in any other class $c' \neq c$.

6 Experiments

We now report on an evaluation of our approach to text classification by language function. As text classification often suffers from domain dependency, i.e., effective results are only achieved in the learning domain, we experimented with both corpus domains. The goal of our evaluation can be seen as three-fold: first, to evaluate the effectiveness of an LFA classifier on in-domain and out-of-domain data, second, to analyze the impact of each single feature type from Section 5, and third,

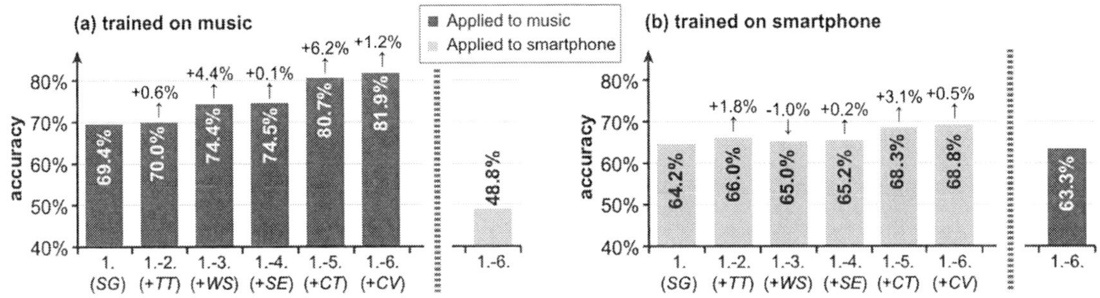

Figure 3: Classification accuracy in the LFA task for a stepwise integration of the six feature types and the transfer to another domain: (a) Training on the music training set, application to the music test set, and transfer to the smartphone test set. (b) Training on the smartphone training set, application to the smartphone test set, and transfer to the music test set.

to check whether LFA based on supervised learning qualifies for document filtering purposes.[4]

6.1 Experimental Set-up

Since commercial texts are largely underrepresented in the music and the smartphone collection, the two training sets were balanced with oversampling. After sentence splitting and tokenization, we applied the highly efficient *TreeTagger* (Schmid, 1995) for part-of-speech tagging and we extracted time and money entities with fast regular expressions. Regarding sentiment polarity, we used the corpus annotations for simplicity.

For the writing style features, we determined the 48 most common words, the 55 most common part-of-speech trigrams, and the 35 most common character trigrams on the training set of each collection. Accordingly, we computed the most discriminative trigrams for feature type 5. The core vocabularies sum up to 30 words for the music collection and to 36 words for the smartphone collection (proper names were discarded). Some of these words are quite specific, e.g. "single" in the music domain (an indicator for *commercial*), while others seem less domain-dependent such as "zumindest" ("at least", *informational*).

Altogether, the six feature types were instantiated by 299 music and 373 smartphone features, respectively. On both training sets, we trained one linear multi-class support vector machine (hereafter called SVM) using feature type 1 to m for each $m \in [1, 6]$ as well as one such SVM using only type m. For this, we applied the *LibSVM* integration in *Weka* (Hall et. al., 2009; Fan et. al., 2001), where we selected the cost parameters of all SVMs on the validation sets. Finally, we analyzed the impact of the resulting classifiers on both test sets. We measured their effectiveness in terms of accuracy, precision, and recall and their efficiency in milliseconds per processed input text.

6.2 Results

Effectiveness of the classifiers. Figure 3a illustrates classification accuracy on the music test set for a stepwise integration of feature type 1 to 6 into an SVM trained on the music training set. Additionally, the accuracy for the transfer of the SVM with all features to the smartphone domain is depicted. The simple genre features (*SG*) already achieved 69.4%. While text type (*TT*) and sentiment (*SE*) contributed only little, the writing style features (*WS*) and the core trigrams (*CT*) boosted accuracy by 4.4% and 6.2%, respectively. At last, the core vocabularies (*CV*) added 1.2 percentage points to the resulting overall accuracy of 81.9% (86.7% on the validation set).

When we applied the SVM with all features to the smartphone test set, its accuracy dropped to 48.8%. To find out whether this dramatic decrease indicates a covariate shift in the feature distribution between the two domains, we retrained the SVM on the smartphone training set. Indeed, its accuracy was re-increased to 68.8%, as shown in Figure 3b. Interestingly, though, the domain transfer worked fine in the opposite direction, i.e., the SVM trained on smartphone texts still correctly classified 63.3% of the texts in the music test set. We suppose that this effect originates from the heterogeneity of the smartphone texts, which prevented the learning of features from being biased towards a certain style of speech. Such a bias naturally exists in music reviews and the like.

[4]The Java source code and the feature files used for evaluation can be accessed at http://infexba.upb.de.

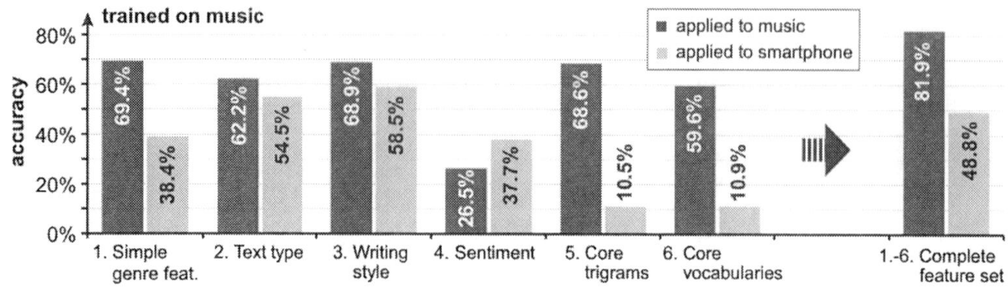

Figure 4: Classification accuracy of each feature type trained on the music training set and applied to both the music test set and the smartphone test set. The accuracy of all features is given on the right.

Domain	Class	Precision	Recall	F_1
music	personal	88.7%	84.8%	86.7%
	commercial	61.9%	88.2%	72.7%
	informational	80.8%	76.6%	78.6%
smartphone	personal	83.5%	68.5%	75.3%
	commercial	23.2%	46.4%	31.0%
	informational	63.9%	72.5%	68.0%

Table 3: Precision, recall and F_1-score for the three language function classes on the in-domain test sets using the SVM with all six feature types.

Nevertheless, Figure 3b also conveys that we achieved 13.1% less accuracy in the smartphone domain than in the music domain (68.8% vs. 81.9%). The accuracy of *SG*, 64.2%, was over five points lower, and only the integration of *TT* (+1.8%) and *CT* (+3.1%) yielded notable improvements afterwards. Adding *WS* even led to a decrease of one percentage point. However, this does not mean that the writing style features failed, as we see later on, but seems to be only noise from the optimization process of the SVM.

While a kappa value of 0.67 (cf. Section 4) renders high accuracy difficult, in general, one reason for the weak performance on the smartphone test set can be inferred from Table 3. This table lists effectiveness results of the SVMs with all features for each class. On the music test set, we observe a recall of more than 75% for all three classes. Though precision significantly dropped for *commercial*, given a class imbalance of 1:9 (commercial:rest), 61.9% is still over five times better than the expected precision of guessing. In contrast, the recognition of commercial texts failed on the smartphone test set with an F_1-score of only 31.0%. Apparently, the SVM did not determine meaningful features for *commercial*, probably because of the small number of commercial texts (cf. Table 1) in combination with the heterogeneity of the smartphone collection. This, in turn, also affected the effectiveness of the other classes.

Effectiveness of the feature types. We measured the effectiveness of each feature type in isolation in order to investigate their impact on LFA. Within music, the simple genre features, the writing style type, and the core trigrams did best, each of them with nearly 70% accuracy as shown in Figure 4. However, there is not *one* discriminative type, i.e., the complete feature set clearly outperformed all single types. Under the transfer to the smartphone domain, only the text type and writing style features reasonably maintained effectiveness. The core vocabularies failed on out-of-domain data, and also the core trigrams did unexpectedly bad, dropping from 68.6% to 10.5%.

With regard to sentiment, our evaluation underpins the observation from Section 4 that sentiment polarities and language functions hardly correlate: the according features learned on the music training set did not work out on both test sets, and the same holds for the opposite direction in Figure 5. There, we see that feature type 1, 3, and 5 also performed best within the smartphone domain. In particular, the writing style type (64.8%) is only 4% worse than the complete feature set. Moreover, while the domain transfer worked well in general, again the most impact was achieved by the text type features with 59.8% accuracy and by the writing style features with 58.9%. This suggests that the distribution of these features is only weakly domain-dependent in LFA. With respect to the writing style type, this is an interesting result, as it indicates that the genre-related task LFA significantly benefits from features that are most prominent in the area of authorship attribution.

Efficiency. We measured the run-time of the classifier with the complete feature set ten times on the music test set using a *2 GHz Intel Core*

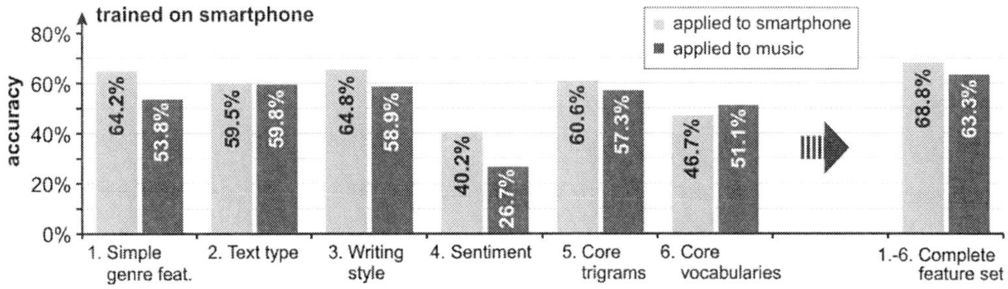

Figure 5: Classification accuracy of each feature type trained on the smartphone training set and applied to both the smartphone test set and the music test set. The accuracy of all features is given on the right.

2 Duo MacBook with *4 GB RAM*. Including all processing steps (sentence splitting, tokenization, part-of-speech tagging, entity recognition, feature extraction, and classification), the average runtime was 37.0 ms per text (σ = 0.6 ms) compared to 6.2 ms needed for tokenization alone. At least for the homogeneous music domain, where we achieved high accuracy, we thus claim that our approach is suitable for fast document filtering.

7 Conclusion

We presented the text classification task language function analysis, LFA, which addresses *why* a text was written and which is motivated by Karl Bühler's functions of natural language. We see language functions as one root of a well-defined genre concept and we argue that a common understanding of such a concept is needed in order to achieve real progress in genre research.

For evaluation of LFA, we provide the LFA-11 corpus with product-related texts from two very different domains that was developed in collaboration with industry. Each text in the corpus has been manually classified by its concrete language function. Approaching LFA with machine learning, we achieved promising results within one homogeneous domain. Moreover, we found out that features commonly used in authorship attribution have the most impact on LFA in both evaluated domains and that they also qualify for domain transfer. This indicates that language functions relate to the writing style of a text. In contrast, the correlation with sentiment appeared to be low.

However, in general, both the language function analysis of more heterogeneous texts and the domain transfer remain unsolved. In future work, we hence aim to investigate the use of sentence-level classification and domain adaptation techniques to further improve our approach to LFA.

Acknowledgments

This work was partly funded by the German Federal Ministry of Education and Research (BMBF) under contract number 01IS08007A.

References

Jonathan Anderson. 1983. Lix and Rix: Variations on a Little-known Readability Index. *Journal of Reading*, 26(6):490–496.

Douglas Biber. 1986. Spoken and Written Textual Dimensions in English: Resolving the Contradictory Findings. *Language*, 62(2):384–413.

Elizabeth S. Boese and Adele E. Howe. 2005. Effects of Web Document Evolution on Genre Classication. In *Proceedings of the 14th ACM International Conference on Information and Knowledge Management*, pages 639–646, Bremen, Germany.

Karl Bühler. 1934. *Sprachtheorie. Die Darstellungsfunktion der Sprache*. Verlag von Gustav Fischer, Jena, Germany.

Jean Carletta. 1996. Assessing Agreement on Classification Tasks: The Kappa Statistic. *Computational Linguistics*, 22: 249–254.

Charles L. A. Clarke, Gordon V. Cormack, M. Laszlo, Thomas R. Lynam, and Egidio L. Terra. 2002. The Impact of Corpus Size on Question Answering Performance. In *Proceedings of the 25th Annual International ACM SIGIR Conference on Research and Development in Information Retrieval*, pages 369–370, Tampere, Finland.

Umberto Eco. 1990. *I Limiti dell'Interpretazione*. Bompiani, Milano, Italy.

Rong-En Fan, Pai-Hsuen Chen, and Chih-Jen Lin. 2001. Working Set Selection Using Second Order Information for Training Support Vector Machines. *Journal of Machine Learning Research*, 6:1889–1918.

David Ferrucci and Adam Lally. 2004. UIMA: An Architectural Approach to Unstructured Information

Processing in the Corporate Research Environment. *Natural Language Engineering*, 10(3–4):327–348.

Nikesh Garera and David Yarowsky. 2009. Modeling Latent Biographic Attributes in Conversational Genres. In *Proceedings of the Joint Conference of the 47th Annual Meeting of the Association for Computational Linguistics and the 4th International Joint Conference on Natural Language Processing*, pages 710–718, Suntec, Singapore.

Mark Hall, Eibe Frank, Geoffrey Holmes, Bernhard Pfahringer, Peter Reutemann, and Ian H. Witten. 2009. The WEKA Data Mining Software: An Update. *SIGKDD Explorations*, 11(1).

Yuki Kadoya, Kazuhiro Morita, Masao Fuketa, Masaki Oono, El-Sayed Atlam, Toru Sumitomo, and Jun-Ichi Aoe. 2005. A Sentence Classification Technique using Intention Association Expressions. *International Journal of Computer Mathematics*, 82(7):777–792.

Jussi Karlgren and Douglass Cutting. 1994. Recognizing Text Genres with Simple Metrics using Discriminant Analysis. In *Proceedings of the 15th International Conference on Computational Linguistics*, pages 1071–1075, Kyoto, Japan.

Brett Kessler, Geoffrey Numberg and Hinrich Schütze. 1997. Automatic Detection of Text Genre. In *Proceedings of the 35th Annual Meeting of the Association for Computational Linguistics and Eighth Conference of the European Chapter of the Association for Computational Linguistics*, pages 32–38, Madrid, Spain.

Mark Kröll and Markus Strohmaier. 2009. Analyzing Human Intentions in Natural Language Text. In *Proceedings of the Fifth International Conference on Knowledge Capture*, pages 197–198, Redondo Beach, CA.

Yong-Bae Lee and Sung Hyon Myaeng. 2002. Text Genre Classification with Genre-Revealing and Subject-Revealing Deatures. In *Proceedings of the 25th Annual International ACM SIGIR Conference on Research and Development in Information Retrieval*, pages 145–150, Tampere, Finland.

Loizos Michael. 2009. Reading between the Lines. In *Proceedings of the 21st International Joint Conference on Artifical intelligence*, pages 1525–1530, San Francisco, CA.

Kim Luyckx and Walter Daelemans. 2008. Authorship Attribution and Verification with Many Authors and Limited Data. In *Proceedings of the 22nd International Conference on Computational Linguistics*, pages 513–520, Manchester, UK.

Sven Meyer zu Eissen and Benno Stein. 2004. Genre Classification of Web Pages: User Study and Feasibility Analysis. In *Proceedings of the 27th German Conference on Artificial Intelligence*, pages 256–269, Ulm, Germany.

Bo Pang and Lillian Lee. 2008. Opinion Mining and Sentiment Analysis. *Foundations and Trends in Information Retrieval*, 2(1–2):1–135.

Peter Prettenhofer and Benno Stein. 2010. Cross-Language Text Classification using Structural Correspondence Learning. In *Proceedings of the 48th Annual Meeting of the Association of Computational Linguistics*, pages 1118-1127, Uppsala, Sweden.

Sindhu Raghavan, Adriana Kovashka, and Raymond Mooney. 2010. Authorship Attribution using Probabilistic Context-Free Grammars. In *Proceedings of the ACL 2010 Conference Short Papers*, pages 38–42, Uppsala, Sweden.

Katharina Reiß. 1971. *Möglichkeiten und Grenzen der Übersetzungskritik*. Max Hueber Verlag, Munich, Germany.

Marina Santini. 2005. Automatic Text Analysis: Gradations of Text Types in Web Pages. In *Proceedings of the Tenth ESSLLI Student Session*, pages 276–285, Edinburgh, UK.

Marina Santini. 2010. Cross-testing a Genre Classication Model for the Web. *Genres on the Web: Computational Models and Empirical Studies*, Springer.

Serge Sharoff, Zhili Wu, and Katja Markert. 2010. The Web Library of Babel: Evaluating Genre Collections. In *Proceedings of the Seventh Language Resources and Evaluation Conference, LREC 2010*, pages 3063–3070, Malta.

Hidetoshi Shimodaira. 2000. Improving Predictive Inference under Covariate Shift by Weighting the Log-Likelihood Function. *Journal of Statistical Planning and Inference*, 90(2):227–244.

Helmut Schmid. 1995. Improvements in Part-of-Speech Tagging with an Application to German. In *Proceedings of the EACL SIGDAT-Workshop*, pages 47–50, Dublin, Ireland.

Efstathios Stamatatos, Nikos Fakotakis, and George K. Kokkinakis. 2000. Text Genre Detection using Common Word Frequencies. In *Proceedings of the 18th International Conference on Computational Linguistics*, pages 808–814, Saarbrücken, Germany.

Efstathios Stamatatos. 2009. A Survey of Modern Authorship Attribution Methods. *Journal of the American Society for Information Science and Technology*, 60(3):538–556.

Benno Stein, Sven Meyer zu Eißen, and Nedim Lipka. 2010. Web Genre Analysis: Use Cases, Retrieval Models, and Implementation Issues. *Text, Speech and Language Technology*, 42:167–190.

Bonnie Webber. 2009. Genre Distinctions for Discourse in the Penn TreeBank. In *Proceedings of the 47th Annual Meeting of the Association for Computational Linguistics and the 4th International Joint Conference on Natural Language Processing*, pages 674–682, Suntec, Singapore.

Transductive Minimum Error Rate Training for Statistical Machine Translation

Yinggong Zhao[1]*, **Shujie Liu**[2], **Yangsheng Ji**[1], **Jiajun Chen**[1], **Guodong Zhou**[3]
[1]State Key Laboratory for Novel Software Technology at Nanjing University
Nanjing 210093, China
{zhaoyg,jiys,chenjj}@nlp.nju.edu.cn
[2]School of Computer Science and Technology, Harbin Institute of Technology
Harbin, China
shujieliu@mtlab.hit.edu.cn
[3]School of Computer Science and Technology, Soochow University
Suzhou, China
gdzhou@suda.edu.cn

Abstract

This paper investigates parameter adaptation in Statistical Machine Translation(SMT). To overcome the parameter bias-estimation problem with Minimum Error Rate Training(MERT), we extend it under a transductive learning framework, by iteratively re-estimating the parameters using both development and test data, in which the translation hypotheses of the test data are used as pseudo references. Furthermore, in order to overcome the over-training and unstableness problems respectively in employing such pseudo references, a termination criterion using a hyper-parameter and a Minimum Bayes Risk(MBR)-based hypothesis selection method are proposed in our work. Experimental results show that the transductive MERT method could yield significant performance improvements over a strong baseline on a large-scale Chinese-to-English translation task.

1 Introduction

Machine translation (MT) is the automatic translation from one natural language into another using computer, while SMT is an approach to MT that is characterized by the use of machine learning methods (Lopez, 2008). Nowadays, SMT is usually built on a log-linear model (Och and Ney, 2002), which can be abstracted into two steps: the first one is model training, i.e., learning features from large collection of bilingual parallel corpus; and the other is parameter estimation, in which the feature weight is tuned on an independent development dataset.

More specifically, for each source sentence f, we search for its final translation e^* among all possible translations based on the following equation:

$$P(e^*|f) = \arg\max_{e} Pr(e|f) \quad (1)$$

Under the log-linear model, the posterior probability $Pr(e|f)$ can be decomposed as:

$$Pr(e|f) = p_\lambda(e|f)$$
$$= \frac{\exp(\sum_{m=1}^{M}(\lambda_m \cdot h_m(e,f)))}{\sum_{e'}\exp(\sum_{m=1}^{M}(\lambda_m \cdot h_m(e',f)))} \quad (2)$$

where each $h_m(e,f)$ is a feature function and λ_m is the corresponding weight for m=1,...,M.

In SMT, there are three sections of data: the training data for feature estimation, the development data for weight tuning, and the test data for final evaluation. However, these three parts may belong to different domains, leading to distribution variations, which indicates that the features and weights learned from the data may be bias-estimated. As a result, the adaptation for features and their corresponding weights are both important issues in SMT.

In this article we focus on the latter issue, i.e., the model parameter adaptation. From the viewpoint of machine learning, development data is labeled data used for parameter learning, while test data is unlabeled and applied for evaluation. In

*Part of this work is done during the first author's internship at Microsoft Research Asia.

the previous works of transductive learning(Liu et al., 2010; Chan and Ng, 2007), the unlabeled data can be used to improve the model training so as to tackle the bias-estimation problem. Under such framework, the weight learned on both development and test dataset, in which the test dataset is constructed using n-best translations as pseudo references, moves towards the test data with regularization of development data, which alleviates the overtraining in normal MERT and matches the test data better.

The remainder of this paper is structured as follows: Related works on model adaptation in SMT are presented in Section 2, and our transductive MERT is proposed in Section 3. Experimental results are shown in Section 4, followed by conclusions and future work in the last section.

2 Related Work

Model adaptation in SMT has attracted increasing attentions in recent years. As mentioned in the previous section, corresponding to the two steps in SMT pipeline, there are two directions for adaptations.

The first one is feature adaptation, which tries to build model (translation model & language model) that could fit the development or test dataset better. This direction includes data selection (Lü et al., 2007; Hildebrand et al., 2005) and data weighting (Foster and Kuhn, 2007; Matsoukas et al., 2009). However, efficiency is the main obstacle for these methods (esp. data selection approach) since model building is time consuming.

The second direction is model parameter adaptation, which includes the transductive MERT method we propose in this article. Nevertheless, little attention has been paid to this direction to date. Mohit et al (2009) tried to build a classifier to predict whether or not a phrase is difficult. The language model weight is then adapted for each phrase segment based on this difficulty. In Li et al (2010), a related subset of development dataset is extracted for given test dataset. The test dataset is then translated under weight learned on this subset. Besides, Sanchis-Trilles and Casacuberta (2010) propose Bayesian adaptation for weight optimization based on a small amount of labeled test data, which is not necessary in our work.

The most similar previous work with ours is Ueffing et al (2007), who also propose a transductive learning framework for SMT. However, our method is different from their in the following three aspects:

Firstly, our method focuses on model parameter adaptation, while Ueffing et al (2007) pays attention to feature adaptation. In their work, the training model is rebuilt by combining original training data with n-best translation outputs of development and test data, in order to overcome the data sparseness problem. In contrast, we try to solve the parameter bias-estimated problem using the information of both development and test data.

Secondly, the parameter adaptation problem is more complicated in SMT, since overtraining is serious due to the limited size of development data. In this work, we use hyper-parameter to indicate the overtraining in the estimation step.

Finally, our method is more efficient than adaptation on the translation & language model. In Ueffing et al.(2007), training model building is necessary for each round, which is time consuming. By comparison, the running time is much shorter for our method, since no model building is required, although it is still longer than simple one-pass translation under baseline.

3 Transductive MERT for Machine Translation

3.1 Minimum Error Rate Training

In SMT, given a development dataset containing source sentences F_1^S with corresponding reference translations R_1^S, the purpose of MERT (Och, 2003) is to find a set of parameters λ_1^M which optimizes an automated evaluation metric (e.g., BLEU) under a log-linear model:

$$\hat{\lambda}_1^M = \arg\min_{\lambda_1^M} \sum_{s=1}^{S} (Err(R_s, \hat{E}(F_s; \lambda_1^M))) \quad (3)$$

in which the number of errors in sentence E is obtained by comparing it with a reference sentence R using function $Err(R, E)$ and

$$\hat{E}(F_s; \lambda_1^M) = \arg\max_{E} \sum_{s=1}^{S} (\lambda_m h_m(E, F_s)) \quad (4)$$

As shown in Algorithm 1, the decoder translates development dataset under current weight(default weight for first round), and generates N-best translation hypotheses for each sentence. The weight is then updated according to equation 3. This procedure repeats until performance converges.

Algorithm 1 MERT for SMT

Input: Development data :$\{F_1^S, R_1^S, C_1^S\}$
Set λ= init-weight and C_1^S={}
Translate F_1^S and get N-Best list L_1^S
while C_1^S != $C_1^S \bigcup L_1^S$ **do**
  $C_1^S = C_1^S \bigcup L_1^S$
  Update λ using translation candidates C_1^S
  Translate F_1^S using λ to generate N-Best list L_1^S
end while

3.2 Transductive MERT

The basic idea of transductive learning is to use predicted labels from unlabeled data to improve learning performance. Based on the this assumption and normal MERT method, our transductive MERT (T-MERT) works as follows: Firstly, the feature weight is estimated on the development data with references. Test dataset is then translated using current weight. For each source sentence of test data, its 4-best translations are used as pseudo references. The feature weight is further re-estimated based on both the development dataset and the test dataset with pseudo references. Meanwhile, the pseudo references of test dataset are replaced in each round, while the development dataset is fixed throughout the procedure. The whole process runs M rounds so that we could get M different results, which are used in the hypothesis selection step (discussed in section 3.4).

As shown in Algorithm 2, the T-MERT algorithm could be divided into two loops: in the outer loop (outer-translation step), the test dataset is translated under current weight and new pseudo labeled test dataset is constructed; while in inner loop (inner-MERT step), the parameter weight is learned from the combined dataset. Meanwhile, there still remains two problems in algorithm 2: when the loop will terminate in inner-MERT step, and how we can select final hypothesis from the multiple results for test data T. These two issues will be discussed respectively in following parts of this section.

3.3 Stop Criterion

In MERT, the loop terminates until the performance converges. While in T-MERT, the weight would be overtrained to the pseudo references of the test data, which could not guarantee that the translations obtained in each iteration are good enough. Here we introduce a hyper-parameter H to indicate the overtraining. In each inner round i, let SD_i stands for the BLEU score of development data D, SpT_i represents the BLEU score of test data T under pseudo references and $SDpT_i$ indicates the BLEU score of combined dataset L , then we define the hyper-parameter H_i as follows:

Algorithm 2 Transductive MERT for SMT

Input: Development data $\{D_1^S, R_1^S, C_1^S\}$, Test data $\{T_1^W\}$, total round M
Let $L=\{D_1^S, R_1^S, C_1^S\}$ and $U=\{T_1^W\}$
Do MERT based on L and get weight λ
Let C_1^S={}
Translate U under λ and get N-Best list N_1^W
for $i = 1$ **to** M **do**
  Select 4-best translations to build $\tilde{U}_1^W$ from N_1^W
  Let $L = \{\{D_1^S, R_1^S, C_1^S\} \bigcup \{T_1^W, \tilde{U}_1^W, N_1^W\}\}$
  Set λ= init-weight
  repeat
    Translation L and get N-Best translations LB_1^{S+W}
    Let $L = L \bigcup LB_1^{S+W}$
    Update λ on L
  until Certain condition satisfies(Section 3.3)
  Translate U under λ and get N-Best list N_1^W, in which we select 1-best translation as T_i
end for
Select final translation(Section 3.4) from collections T_i (i=1, ..., M)

$$H_i = \frac{SD_i}{SD_{i-1}} \cdot exp\frac{SpT_i}{SpT_{i-1}} \cdot exp\frac{SDpT_i}{SDpT_{i-1}} \quad (5)$$

Here, H_i represents the relative improvement between the performance of inner round i and that of the previous round. A smaller H_i value indicates the inner-MERT turns to be converged on combined dataset L, showing that the weight would be overtrained. Due to the fact that the test dataset owns no references, we cannot attain its BLEU score in each round. As an alternative, we could only obtain SD_i, SpT_i and $SDpT_i$, as shown in above equation. In optimization step of normal MERT, what we need to do is to update the parameter to maximize the score on development data. While here we encounter the overtraining, we use ratio of scores to indicate the training. Instead of maximizing the score, we want to optimize the relative improvement of the system performance. In

T-MERT, we observe that the performance is always the best when the inner-MERT terminates as H_i reaches peak[1].

3.4 Hypothesis Selection with Minimum Bayes Risk(MBR)

From T-MERT algorithm, we can get M different results from M outer-translation rounds. Due to intrinsic property and the randomness in MERT, the results from outer-translation step of T-MERT are not quite stable, making the hypotheses selection a necessity.

According to (Ehling et al., 2007), for each source sentence with N different translations, we could select the final translation based on the following Minimum Bayes Risk principal:

$$\hat{e} = \arg\min_{e}\{\sum_{e'}(Pr(e'|f)\cdot(1-BLEU(e',e)))\} \quad (6)$$

Here $Pr(e'|f)$ denotes the posterior probability for translation e' and $BLEU(e', e)$ represents the sentence-level BLEU score for e' using e as reference.

However, since the translation hypotheses are generated under different groups of weights, the corresponding posterior probability is no longer comparable. Here we simplify this problem under the assumption that all available translations are generated equally. Then equation 6 could be converted into:

$$\hat{e} = \arg\min_{e}\{\sum_{e'}(1 - BLEU(e', e))\} \quad (7)$$

Based on equation 7, we can select the hypothesis from the collections of translations efficiently. And the primary purpose of using MBR selection in this work is to stabilize the translation performance, as we select final result using only sentence-level BLEU scores between different hypotheses.

4 Experimental Results

4.1 Experimental Setup

In the experiments, we re-implement a hierarchical phrase-based decoder based on (Chiang, 2005). The word alignment is trained by GIZA++ under an intersect-diag-grow heuristics refinement. The plain phrases are extracted from all bilingual training data available from LDC, including LDC2002E18, LDC2003E07, LDC2003E14,

[1]And we find that in experiments, hyper-parameter H_i of the second round is always maximal.

Table 1: Statistics on development and test data sets.

DATA SET	#SENTENCE	#WORD
MT03	919	36,021
MT05	1,082	43,765
MT06	1,664	38,209
MT08	1,357	33,042

LDC2004E12, LDC2004T08, LDC2005E83, LDC2005T06, LDC2005T10, LDC2006E26, LDC2006E34, LDC2006E85, LDC2006E92, and LDC2007T09, which consists in total of about 8.5M sentence pairs while hierarchical rules are only extracted from selected data sets, including LDC2003E14, LDC2003E07, LDC2005T10, LDC2006E34, LDC2006E85, and LDC2006E92, which contain about 467K sentence pairs. We build the 5-gram language model on the English section of all bilingual training data together with the Xinhua portion of the English Gigaword corpus.

The development and test dataset pairs are selected from NIST2003 (MT03), NIST2005 (MT05), NIST2006 (MT06) and NIST2008 (MT08). The data statistics are shown in Table 1. In the experiments, all translation results are measured in case-insensitive BLEU scores (Papineni et al., 2002).

4.2 Results under Transductive MERT

Figure 1 and Figure 2 show the hyper-parameter $H(iter_{number})$ for each iteration in the 10-round inner-MERT step. In both figures, MT03 is development dataset while MT05 & MT08 are test datasets. We find that the hyper-parameter H always reaches the peak at the 2nd iteration, showing fast convergence during parameter estimation on the combination of development data and pseudo labeled test data. Similar phenomenon could also be observed on other dataset pairs.

Here, the reason might be that the pseudo translate references for the test data are generated with the current SMT model and its parameters. So the newly generated translation references on the test data are intuitively similar to translations obtained using the current model parameters. When we re-estimate the parameters on the combined dataset starting from the initial parameters, the learning procedure can quickly fit the newly generated data. While parameter estimation step continues iteratively, the learning algorithm may favor those incorrectly generated translation references, which makes the overtraining more serious and hurts the final performance. By applying the hyper-parameter as the stop metric, we could control the learning procedure to avoid the overtraining.

We can also review the roles that the development and test datasets play in the procedure of avoiding over-training. The reason for that we transductively generate translations as pseudo references for test data is that we expect the estimation procedure biases towards the test data when incorporated in the learning procedure. Meanwhile, the development data also plays an important role in the learning process. Because development data owns true references, it acts as a regularization term to ensure that the feature weight will not excessively biased toward the test data with generated pseudo references in the learning procedure.

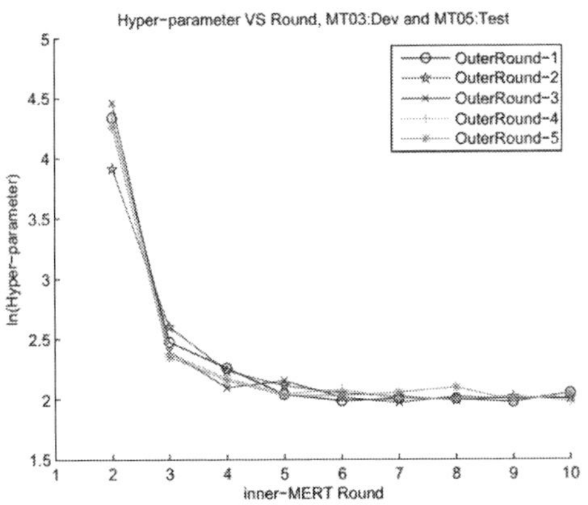

Figure 1: Hyper-parameter of 10 inner-MERT loops under 5 outer-translation rounds(OutRound-i) in T-MERT algorithm(without MBR), MT03:Dev and MT05:Test.

Based on the above discussion, we also compare results under different rounds for inner-MERT to verify the role of the hyper-parameter. As shown in figure 3(MT03 development and MT05 test) and figure 4(MT03 development and MT08 test), the results under T-MERT with 2-rounds inner-MERT are always best among different rounds, which is close to the baseline in figure 3 and much better in figure 4. Here the baseline for the test dataset is translated under weight learned from normal MERT on the development data, and remains constant for the following parts. For both

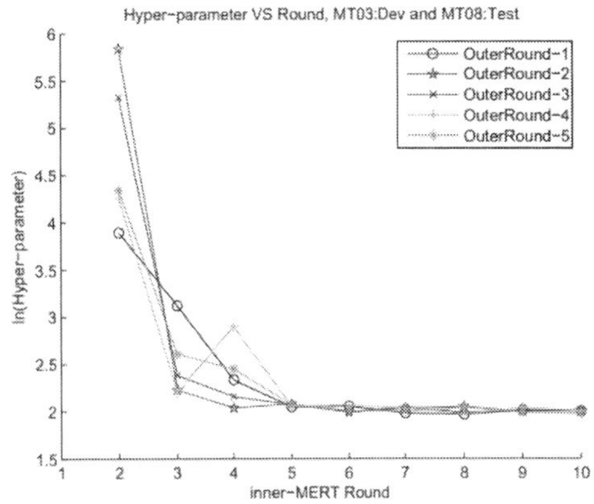

Figure 2: Hyper-parameter of 10 inner-MERT loops under 5 outer-translation rounds in T-MERT algorithm(without MBR), MT03:Dev and MT08:Test.

figures, we observe that 1-round inner-MERT is not sufficient to learn the weight well, while inner-MERT using more than 2 rounds leads to significant overtraining, which is consistent with the results obtained from the hyper-parameter.

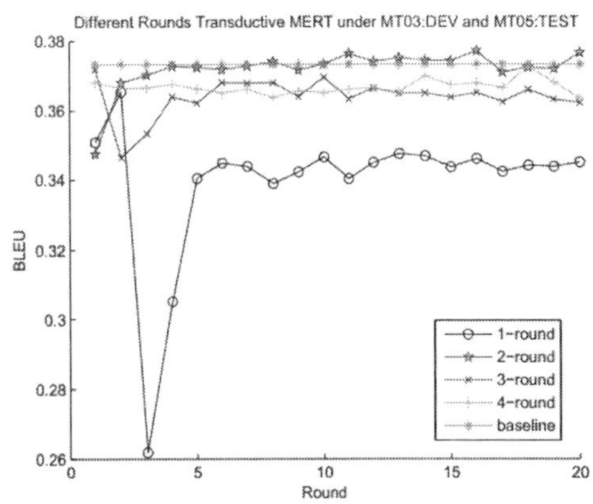

Figure 3: Results under T-MERT algorithm(without MBR) with fixed inner-MERT loops from 1 to 4, 20 outer-translation rounds, and baseline. MT03:Dev and MT05:Test.

Although the score of T-MERT under 2-round inner-MERT is comparable to or even better than baseline, the performance is still unstable, changing drastically for different rounds of outer-translation step (over 4 BLEU points for MT03:Dev and MT05:Test, and even larger for MT03:Dev and MT08:Test). We use the MBR s-

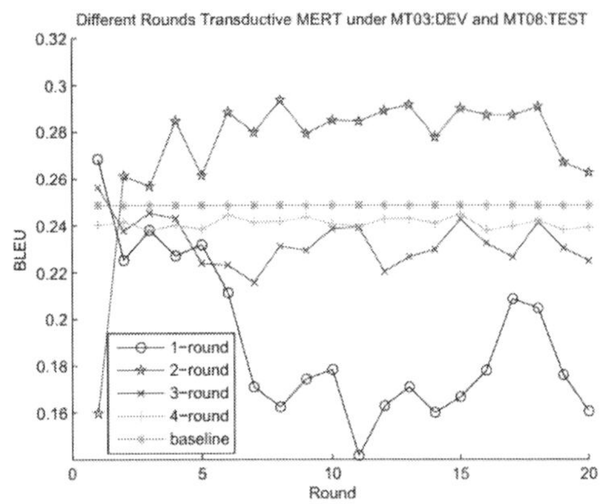

Figure 4: Results under T-MERT algorithm(without MBR) with fixed inner-MERT loops from 1 to 4, 20 outer-translation rounds, and baseline. MT03:Dev and MT08:Test.

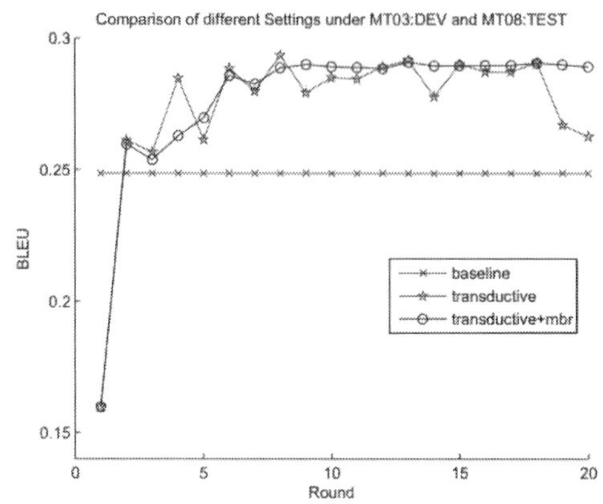

Figure 6: Result of baseline,T-MERT under 2 inner rounds without and with MBR selection. MT03:DEV and MT08:Test.

election proposed in section 3.4 to choose a suitable hypothesis, and the corresponding results are shown in figure 5 and figure 6. It could be found that as the number of outer-translation rounds increases, the algorithm generates more groups of translation outputs, from which the performance under MBR selection turns to be more and more stable.

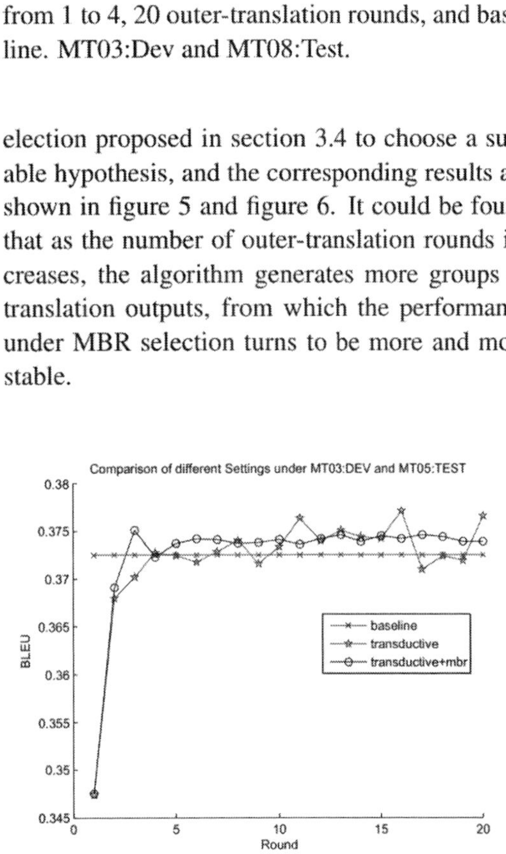

Figure 5: Result of baseline,T-MERT under 2 inner-MERT rounds without and with MBR selection. MT03:DEV and MT05:Test.

The above parts discuss two solutions for the problems we encounter in the transductive MERT, i.e., the inner-MERT stop criterion and MBR selection. We further evaluate our method (under 2 round inner-MERT and MBR selection) on all dataset pairs, which is any pair of MT03, MT05, MT06 and MT08. The final results are shown in table 2, from which we observe that for the dataset pair MT03 and MT05 the result under T-MERT is close to baseline, while for the pair MT03 and MT08, the improvement is significant in both directions. The result is similar with the observation on these evaluation datasets, i.e., MT03 and MT05 are under similar distribution, while MT03 and MT08 are quite different. Generally speaking, MT03 and MT05 are both composed of only news data, while MT06 and MT08 are consisted of news and web-blog data. As we know, the news data is significantly different from the web-blog data. We can find that our method could achieve significant improvement on 9 of total 12 dataset pairs, indicating that the distribution variation between dataset pairs is quite a common phenomenon. For datasets under similar distribution, the baseline performance is close to oracle, which means that potential space for improvement under the adaptation is limited; while for datasets that are quite different, there is much room for further increase in performance, since the baseline weight estimated on development is seriously biased for the test.

Besides, we try one extra comparison, i.e., using same dataset for both development and test under T-MERT. The result is also shown in table 2. We find that for MT03 and MT05, the result under T-MERT is close to baseline (a little higher), while for MT06 and MT08, the result is fairly lower. The reason that the adapted result on MT03 is slightly higher than baseline is that the result in

Table 2: Results of baseline and T-MERT under MBR Selections for different dataset pairs. Here symbol ↑ shows that the improvement is significant, ↓ indicates decrease is significant, and | means no significant changes

DEV	MT03		MT05		MT06		MT08	
TEST	BASELINE	T-MERT	BASELINE	T-MERT	BASELINE	T-MERT	BASELINE	T-MERT
MT03	0.3914	0.3933(|)	0.3861	0.3908(|)	0.3731	0.3830(↑)	0.3586	0.3704(↑)
MT05	0.3733	0.3739(|)	0.3687	0.3724(|)	0.3592	0.3700(↑)	0.3414	0.3576(↑)
MT06	0.3358	0.3582(↑)	0.3344	0.3569(↑)	0.3636	0.3579(↓)	0.3504	0.3653(↑)
MT08	0.2486	0.2892(↑)	0.2543	0.2755(↑)	0.2774	0.2768(|)	0.2929	0.2809(↓)

each round is close to baseline, making it possible for the selection performance to be slightly higher than baseline, while for others the result in each round is lower than baseline. However, we do not hope that our method could be significantly better than baseline in this case, as baseline performance is also the oracle performance for the test dataset. We assume that we know the development and the test datasets are distinct in advance before applying the T-MERT algorithm.

5 Conclusion and Future Work

In this paper, we investigate the parameter adaptation issue in SMT. In particular, a transductive MERT algorithm is proposed to better explore both development and test datasets. Besides, a hyper-parameter is proposed to control the over-training problem in the parameter estimation step and a Minimum Bayes Risk (MBR)-based hypothesis selection method is adopted to stabilize the final performance. Compared with a state-of-the-art baseline, our method achieves significant and sustainable improvement.

In future, we plan to incorporate better hypothesis selection algorithms to choose high quality sentences from the test dataset, since sentences with bad translations would bring side effect during the learning procedure. Besides, we plan to further investigate the mechanism of transductive MERT in boosting the performance of SMT.

Acknowledgments

We thank Ning Xi and Shujian Huang for their meaningful suggestions. We would also like to thank the anonymous reviewers for their helpful comments. This work is supported by the National Natural Science Foundation of China (No.61003112) and the National Fundamental Research Program of China (2010CB327903)

References

Yee S. Chan and Hwee T. Ng. 2007. Domain adaptation with active learning forword sense disambiguation. In *In Proceedings of the 45th Annual Meeting of the Association of Computational Linguistics*, pp. 49–56, Prague, Czech Republic, 2007.

David Chiang. 2005. A hierarchical phrase-based model for statistical machine translation. In *In Proceedings of the 2010 Conference on Empirical Methods in Natural Language Processing*, pp. 263–270, Ann Arbor, 2005.

Nicola Ehling, Richard Zens and Hermann Ney. 2007. Minimum bayes risk decoding for bleu. In *In Proceedings of the ACL 2007 Demo and Poster Sessions*, pp. 101–104, Prague, 2007.

George Foster and Roland Kuhn. 2007. Mixture-model adaptation for smt. In *In Proceedings of the Second ACL Workshop on Statistical Machine Translation*, Prague, Czech Republic, 2007.

Almut Silja Hildebrand, Matthias Eck, Stephan Vogel and Alex Waibel. 2005. Adaptation of the translation model for statistical machine translation based on information retrieval. In *In Proceedings of EAMT*, Budapest, Hungary, 2005.

Philipp Koehn. 2004. Statistical significance tests for machine translation evaluation. In *In Proc. of the Conference on Empirical Methods in Natural Language Processing*, pp. 160–167, 2004.

Mu Li, Yinggong Zhao, Dongdong Zhang and Ming Zhou. 2010. Adaptive development data selection for log-linear model in statistical machine translation. In *In Proceedings of the 23rd International Conference on Computational Linguistics (Coling 2010)*, pp. 662–670, Beijing, 2010.

Yang Liu, Steve Hanneke and Jaime Carbonell. 2010. A theory of transfer learning with applications to active learning. Technical report, Machine Learning Department, Carnegie Mellon University, New Brunswick, MA, 2010.

Adam Lopez. 2008. Statistical machine translation. *ACM Computing Surveys*, 40(3), 2008.

Yajuan Lü, Jin Huang, and Qun Liu. 2007. Improving statistical machine translation performance by training data selection and optimization. In *In Proceedings of the 2007 Joint Conference on Empirical Methods in Natural Language Processing*, pp. 343–350, Czech Republic, 2007.

Spyros Matsoukas and Antti-Veikko I. Rosti and Bing Zhang. 2009. Discriminative corpus weight estimation for machine translation. In *In Proc. of the Conference on Empirical Methods in Natural Language Processing*, pp. 160–167, 2009.

Behrang Mohit, Frank Liberato and Rebecca Hwa. 2009. Language model adaptation for difficult to translate phrases. In *In Proceedings of the 13th Annual Conference of the EAMT*, pp. 160–167, 2009.

Franz Och. 2003. Minimum error rate training in statistical machine translation. In *In Proceedings of the 41th Annual Meeting of the Association for Computational Linguistics (ACL)*, Sapporo, Japan, 2003.

Franz Och and Hermann Ney. 2002. Discriminative training and maximum entropy models for statistical machine translation. In *In Proceedings of the 40th Annual Meeting of the Association for Computational Linguistics (ACL)*, pp. 295–302, Philadelphia, 2002.

Kishore Papineni, Salim Roukos, Todd Ward, and Wei-Jing Zhu. Bleu: a method for automatic evaluation of machine translation. In *In Proceedings of the 40th Annual Meeting of the Association for Computational Linguistics (ACL)*, pp. 311–318, Philadelphia, 2002.

German Sanchis-Trilles and Francisco Casacuberta. 2010. Log-linear weight optimisation via bayesian adaptation in statistical machine translation. In *In Proceedings of the 23rd International Conference on Computational Linguistics (Coling 2010)*, pp. 662–670, Beijing, 2010.

Nicola Ueffing, Gholamreza Haffari and Anoop Sarkar. 2007. Transductive learning for statistical machine translation. In *In Proceedings of the 45th Annual Meeting of the Association of Computational Linguistics*, pp. 25–32, Czech Republic, 2007.

Distributed Minimum Error Rate Training of SMT using Particle Swarm Optimization

Jun Suzuki, Kevin Duh, and Masaaki Nagata
NTT Communication Science Laboratories, NTT Corp.
2-4 Hikaridai, Seika-cho, Soraku-gun, Kyoto, 619-0237 Japan
{suzuki.jun, kevin.duh, nagata.masaaki}@lab.ntt.co.jp

Abstract

The direct optimization of a translation metric is an integral part of building state-of-the-art SMT systems. Unfortunately, widely used translation metrics such as BLEU-score are non-smooth, non-convex, and non-trivial to optimize. Thus, standard optimizers such as minimum error rate training (MERT) can be extremely time-consuming, leading to a slow turnaround rate for SMT research and experimentation. We propose an alternative approach based on particle swarm optimization (PSO), which can easily exploit the fast growth of distributed computing to obtain solutions quickly. For example in our experiments on NIST 2008 Chinese-to-English data with 512 cores, we demonstrate a speed increase of up to 15x and reduce the parameter tuning time from 10 hours to 40 minutes with no degradation in BLEU-score.

1 Introduction

Recent statistical machine translation (**SMT**) systems employ a linear combination of several model components, such as translation models, language models, and reordering models. Translation is performed by selecting the most-likely translation, which is the candidate translation with the highest score based on the different model components. We usually refer to this search process as 'decoding'. Although the development of decoding algorithms is a key topic in SMT research, if we are to construct better SMT systems it is also important to find a way to determine the weights of different model components. We refer to this process as 'parameter tuning'.

The current standard strategy for tuning the parameters of SMT systems is to search for the weights that maximize a given translation quality metric such as BLEU-score (Papineni et al., 2002). In fact, minimum error rate training (MERT) proposed by (Och, 2003) is the most widely used parameter tuning method in SMT community. This is because, empirically, we obtain better translation system performance by directly optimizing the translation metric than by maximizing the likelihood function. However, translation metrics such as BLEU-score are often non-smooth, non-convex, and non-trivial to optimize, and direct maximization does not allow us simply to apply well-known fast and robust optimization techniques such as the gradient-ascent method. This restriction makes the parameter tuning process extremely slow.

In this paper, we propose a novel distributed MERT framework based on particle swarm optimization (**PSO**) (Kennedy and Eberhart, 1995), a population based stochastic optimization technique, to improve the slow parameter tuning process. The main characteristics of our method are that: (1) it directly optimizes a metric such as BLEU-score, (2) it greatly reduces the parameter tuning time compared with the conventional MERT, and (3) it is highly scalable, meaning that additional distributed processors lead to better and faster performance.

Our main motivation is to *improve the experiment turn-around time* for SMT system development. A faster parameter tuning algorithm would have a positive impact on research on all the components of the SMT system. Imagine a researcher designing a new pruning algorithm for decoding, a new word alignment model, or a new domain adaptation method. Any of these methods need to be evaluated in the context of a full SMT system, which requires parameter tuning. If we can reduce the parameter tuning time from 10 hours to 1 hour, this can greatly increase the pace of innovation. Thus our motivation is orthogonal to recent research on improving MERT, such as efforts to escape local maxima problems (Cer et al., 2008;

Foster and Kuhn, 2009; Moore and Quirk, 2008), or incorporate lattices (Macherey et al., 2008).

2 Parameter Tuning for SMT Systems

Most recently developed SMT systems consist of several model components, such as translation models, language models, and reordering models. To combine evidence obtained from these different components, we often define a discriminative (log-)linear model.

Suppose the SMT system has D components. The log probabilities of the components are usually treated as features in the discriminative model. We denote the d-th feature, or log probability of the d-th component given a source sentence $\mathbf{f}$ and its translation $\mathbf{e}$, as $\phi_d(\mathbf{e}, \mathbf{f})$. We also denote the d-th weight as λ_d. Then, finding the most likely translation $\hat{\mathbf{e}}$ of a given source sentence $\mathbf{f}$ with the SMT system can be written in the following maximization problem:

$$\hat{\mathbf{e}} = \arg\max_{\mathbf{e}} \sum_{d=\{1,\dots,D\}} \lambda_d \phi_d(\mathbf{e}, \mathbf{f}). \quad (1)$$

This process is called 'decoding' in SMT.

Next, to obtain better translation quality for any translations, we need somehow to tune the component weights λ_d for all d. The current standard strategy for parameter tuning is to directly maximize a translation quality measure such as BLEU-score rather than likelihood.

Suppose we have a dataset consisting of S sentences. Let $\mathbf{f}_s$ be the s-th input sentence (source language) in the tuning dataset. We also suppose that each $\mathbf{f}_s$ has Q reference translations that are usually generated by hand. Thus, let $\mathbf{r}_{s,q}$ be the q-th reference translation of $\mathbf{f}_s$. We write the weights in the vector representation as, for example, $\boldsymbol{\lambda} = \{\lambda_d\}_{d=1}^{D}$, and a system translation of $\mathbf{f}_s$ obtained when the weights are $\boldsymbol{\lambda}$ as $\hat{\mathbf{e}}(\mathbf{f}, \boldsymbol{\lambda})$ to provide a better explanation. Then, the direct maximization of a translation metric $\mathcal{M}$ can be written in the following form:

$$\boldsymbol{\lambda}^* = \arg\max_{\boldsymbol{\lambda}} \mathcal{M}(\{\mathbf{f}_s, \{\mathbf{r}_{s,q}\}_{q=1}^{Q}, \hat{\mathbf{e}}_s(\mathbf{f}_s, \boldsymbol{\lambda})\}_{s=1}^{S}). \quad (2)$$

where $\boldsymbol{\lambda}^*$ represents the optimal solution.

2.1 Outline of Och's MERT

The most widely used parameter tuning framework for solving Equation 2 in SMT is MERT proposed by (Och, 2003). There are several variations for updating weights during the iterative tuning process in MERT. The most commonly used algorithm for MERT is usually called Koehn-coordinate descent (KCD), which is used in the MERT utility packaged in the popular Moses statistical machine translation system (Koehn et al., 2007). Another choice is Powell's method that was advocated when MERT was first introduced for SMT (Och, 2003). Since KCD tends to be marginally more effective at optimizing the MERT objective, and is much simpler to implement than Powell's method, this paper focuses only on KCD.

KCD is a variant of a coordinate ascent (or descent) algorithm. At each iteration, it moves along the coordinate, which allows for the greatest progress of the maximization. The routine performs a trial line maximization along each coordinate to determine which one should be selected. It then updates the weight vector with the coordinate that it found to be the best objective in the trial.

To perform an iterative parameter update with MERT, it is necessary to evaluate the system translation quality given by the current weights by the translation metric to be optimized. This process obviously requires us to perform decoding (Equation 1), and decoding is usually a very expensive process. Thus, it often becomes infeasible to undertake decoding every iteration if the size of the tuning dataset is relatively large. To overcome this issue, Och (2003) has also introduced the N-best approximation method. This method separates decoding and the parameter tuning process into an outer and an inner loop. The outer loop first runs the decoder over the source sentences in the tuning dataset with the current weights to generate N-best lists of translations. Then, the method employs the inner loop procedure to optimize the weights based on those N-best lists instead of decoding the tuning dataset. After obtaining the optimal weights from the inner loop, we repeat the outer loop to generate a new N-best list. Figure 1 shows the system outline, which is described in detail elsewhere (Bertoldi et al., 2009).

We note here that the method proposed in this paper essentially involves the replacement of the inner loop algorithm of the conventional MERT.

3 Particle Swarm Optimization (PSO)

Particle Swarm Optimization (PSO) is an (iterative) stochastic optimization technique proposed

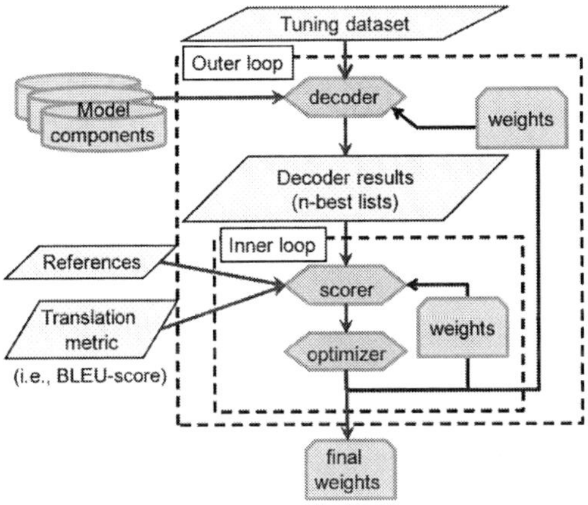

Figure 1: System outline of MERT proposed by (Och, 2003); This system diagram was first published in (Bertoldi et al., 2009)

in (Kennedy and Eberhart, 1995). This optimization technique is explained in terms of emulating the social behavior of flocks of birds and shoals of fish, or taking advantage of the concept of the social sharing of information.

The basic strategy of this optimization technique is that each particle flies individually through the search space to find the best position in the search space. By this iterative search process, each particle can learn from the experience of other particles in the same population (called a swarm). In other words, each particle in the iterative search process would adjust its flying velocity as well as position based on both its own acquaintance and the flying experience of other particles in the swarm. PSO has been shown to be effective in solving a variety of complex optimization problems in practice. Thus, PSO may also work relatively well in MERT since optimizing translation metric such as BLEU-score is also a complex optimization problem.

3.1 Basic definition

Suppose we have a D-dimensional problem space (search space) given by the task at hand. Then, we also assume that we have an objective function F, which is generally called a fitness function in the context of PSO, to evaluate the solution. Basically, solving the task is equivalent to either maximizing or minimizing the objective function. For example, with the parameter tuning of SMT systems, the objective function F is BLEU-score, and the solution should be the parameter set that maximizes the BLEU-score over a given tuning dataset. Hereafter, we assume a maximization problem.

For PSO, we assume that the swarm consists of K particles. Each individual particle P_k, where $k \in \{1, \dots, K\}$, can be represented as a three-tuple $P_k = (\mathbf{x}_k, \mathbf{v}_k, \mathbf{b}_k)$, where $\mathbf{x}_k$ is the current position in the search space, $\mathbf{v}_k$ is the current velocity, and $\mathbf{b}_k$ is the personal best position in the search space. Note that $\mathbf{x}_k$, $\mathbf{v}_k$,and $\mathbf{b}_k$ are all represented as D-dimensional vectors. As briefly explained in Section 3, PSO is an iterative optimization technique. The personal best position, $\mathbf{b}_k$, corresponds to the position in the search space where particle k has the largest value of objective function F over all the past iterations. Hereafter, let t represent the PSO iteration counter, where $t \in \{1, \dots, T\}$, and T represents the maximum iteration number given by a user, or is possibly set at infinity. In our case, we set $T = 100,000$.

Formally, the personal best values for the k-th particle at the t-th iteration, $\mathbf{b}_k(t)$, is updated by the following equation:

$$\mathbf{b}_k(t+1) = \begin{cases} \mathbf{x}_k(t+1) & \text{if } F(\mathbf{x}_k(t+1)) > F(\mathbf{b}_k(t)) \\ \mathbf{b}_k(t) & \text{otherwise} \end{cases} ,\quad (3)$$

where we set $\mathbf{b}_k(0) = \mathbf{x}_k(0)$ for all k.

The position yielding the largest objective among all the particles in the swarm is called the global best position. We denote this global best position as $\mathbf{g}$, and denote the global best position at t-iteration as $\mathbf{g}(t)$. $\mathbf{g}(t)$ can be easily obtained by finding the $\mathbf{b}_k(t)$ that has the largest objective, which is written as follows:

$$\mathbf{g}(t) = \operatorname*{arg\,max}_{\mathbf{b} \in \{\mathbf{b}_1(t), \mathbf{b}_2(t), \dots, \mathbf{b}_K(t)\}} F(\mathbf{b}). \quad (4)$$

We assume $U(a, b)$ is a function that returns a value between a and b drawn from a uniform distribution. We denote $\mathbf{U}(a, b)$ as a D-dimensional vector all of whose elements are $U(a, b)$. Then, the iterative PSO tuning process is mainly built on the following equations:

$$\begin{aligned} \mathbf{v}_k(t+1) = & \xi(t)\mathbf{v}_k(t) \\ & + c_1 \mathbf{U}(0,1)(\mathbf{b}_k(t) - \mathbf{x}_k(t)) \\ & + c_2 \mathbf{U}(0,1)(\mathbf{g}(t) - \mathbf{x}_k(t)), \end{aligned} \quad (5)$$

$$\mathbf{x}_k(t+1) = \mathbf{x}_k(t) + \mathbf{v}_k(t+1). \quad (6)$$

where ξ is the inertia weight of the past velocity, and c_1 and c_2 are acceleration constants regulating the relative velocities with respect to the best personal and global positions. We use $c_1 = 2.0$,

$c_2 = 2.0$, and $\xi(t) = 1.0 - t/T$, which are one standard setting for PSO. We also define $\mathbf{v}_k(0) = \mathbf{U}(-1, 1)$ and $\mathbf{x}_k(0) = \mathbf{U}(-1, 1)$ for all k.

To summarize the process, the velocities $\mathbf{v}_k$ for all particles P_k are individually updated at the beginning of each iteration t by using the (personal) past velocity, and information about the personal and global best position. The new velocity for each particle is then added to its own current position $\mathbf{x}_k$ to obtain the next position of the particle. After that, each particle updates its personal best position by using Equation 3, and finally the global best position of the swarm is updated by the mutual sharing of the personal best positions. PSO performs the above process iteratively until convergence is reached or iterations attain the maximum number T defined by the user.

The key feature of the PSO architecture is that information regarding the global best position g is shared by all particles as shown in Equation 5.

3.2 Extension to guarantee local convergence

The standard PSO algorithm described in the previous section does not guarantee convergence on a local maximum. It merely means that all the particles have converged on the best position discovered so far by the swarm. To address this issue, we use the modified version of PSO proposed in (van den Bergh and Engelbrecht, 2002) that can guarantees convergence to a local maximum. The basic idea of the modification is allow the global best particle to move until it has reached a local maximum. To achieve this, they introduced a new velocity update equation for the global best particle. Note that particles other than the global best particle in the swarm continue to use the usual velocity update as shown in Equation 5.

Let τ be the index of the global best particle. Then, we use the following equation to update the velocity of the global best particle at the t-th iteration:

$$\begin{aligned}\mathbf{v}_\tau(t+1) = &-\mathbf{x}_\tau(t) + \mathbf{g}(t) + \xi(t)\mathbf{v}_\tau(t) \\ &+\rho(t)\mathbf{U}(-1, 1),\end{aligned} \tag{7}$$

where ρ is a scaling factor of the stochastic term $\mathbf{U}(-1, 1)$, which is defined as follows:

$$\rho(t+1) = \begin{cases} 2\rho(t) \text{ if } \#S > T_s \\ 0.5\rho(t) \text{ if } \#F > T_f \\ \rho(t) \text{ otherwise} \end{cases}, \tag{8}$$

where $\#S$ and $\#F$, respectively, denote the number of consecutive failures or successes in finding a new global best point where a failure is defined as $f(\mathbf{g}(t)) = f(\mathbf{g}(t-1))$.

Then, in the same manner as Equation 6, the new position can be calculated by adding the new velocity:

$$\begin{aligned}\mathbf{x}_\tau(t+1) &= \mathbf{x}_\tau(t) + \mathbf{v}_\tau(t+1) \\ &= \mathbf{g}(t) + \xi(t)\mathbf{v}_\tau(t) + \rho(t)\mathbf{U}(-1, 1).\end{aligned} \tag{9}$$

The $-\mathbf{x}_\tau(t)$ term in the velocity update is canceled when updating the position. This means that a new position is always updated from the global best position $\mathbf{g}(t)$. This is one of the key tricks of the modification; the global best particle always searches for a new position around the current best position until new global best position is found. ρ also plays an important role in guaranteeing the locally convergence of the method. The diameter of this search area is controlled by the parameter ρ. The updating of ρ means that if the global best objective function value does not change, then ρ shrinks to half its original size and the search space around the global best position becomes smaller. The initial default value of $\rho(0) = 1.0$.

Finally, if we cannot find a new global best position around the current global best position in a certain number of iterations T_c then the current global best position can be considered a local maximum. We use $T_c = 15$.

A proof of guaranteed convergence to local maxima for this algorithm can be found in (van den Bergh and Engelbrecht, 2002). Note that this modification still does not guarantee convergence to the global optimum position unless the objective function is a convex function.

4 MERT-PSO for SMT

This section describes a way to incorporate PSO into the MERT framework. First, the position x in PSO corresponds to the component weights in the SMT system $\boldsymbol{\lambda}$. Next, the objective function F in PSO can be defined as a translation metric such as BLEU-score $\mathcal{M}$ shown in Equation 2. Therefore, in our case, F is calculated by using a tuning dataset $\mathcal{D}$ and system translations of the tuning dataset given by the current weight (position) x. We denote a translation metric such as BLEU-score as $F(\mathbf{x}, \mathcal{D})$ for MERT-PSO.

In PSO, each particle can individually update its velocity, position and personal best position. Thus, we design MERT-PSO to work in a parallel computing environment. Basically, we uti-

Algorithm: MERT-PSO

Input: K: number of particles, D: degree of parameter dimension, T: maximum number of iterations, T_c: threshold of convergence evaluation, I: iteration number for update trial, $\mathcal{D}$: tuning dataset, F: objective function.

Main procedure:

initParticle(P_k) $\forall k$ in parallel processing
$(\tau, \mathbf{g}(0)) \leftarrow$ Eq. 4
$T' \leftarrow 0$
for t in $0, \ldots, T-1$
  execParticle(t, P_k, τ) $\forall k$ in parallel processing
  $(\tau, \mathbf{g}(t+1)) \leftarrow$ Eq. 4
  $T' = T' + 1$ if $F(\mathbf{g}(t+1), \mathcal{D}) = F(\mathbf{g}(t), \mathcal{D})$, or $T' = 0$ otherwise
  break if $T' \geq T_c$
end_for
output $\mathbf{g}(t+1)$

procedure: **initParticle**(P_k)

$\mathbf{v}'_k \leftarrow \mathbf{U}(-1,1)$ and $\mathbf{x}'_k \leftarrow \mathbf{U}(-1,1)$
$\mathbf{v}_k(0) \leftarrow \mathcal{P}(\mathbf{v}'_k)$ and $\mathbf{x}_k(0) \leftarrow \mathcal{P}'(\mathbf{x}'_k)$
$\mathbf{b}_k(0) \leftarrow \mathbf{x}_k(0)$

procedure: **execParticle**(t, P_k, τ)

for i in $1, \ldots, I$
  $\mathbf{v}' \leftarrow \mathbf{V}(k,t)$ or $\mathbf{V}'(k,t)$ if $k = \tau$ (Eq. 5 or 7)
  $\mathbf{v}^{\text{tmp}} \leftarrow \mathcal{P}(\mathbf{v}')$ (Eq. 10)
  $\mathbf{x}' \leftarrow \mathbf{x}_k(t) + \mathbf{v}^{\text{tmp}}$ (Eq. 6)
  $\mathbf{x}^{\text{tmp}} \leftarrow \mathcal{P}'(\mathbf{x}')$ (Eq. 11)
  if $F(\mathbf{x}^{\text{tb}}, \mathcal{D}) < F(\mathbf{x}^{\text{tmp}}, \mathcal{D})$
    $\mathbf{x}^{\text{tb}} \leftarrow \mathbf{x}^{\text{tmp}}$ and $\mathbf{v}^{\text{tb}} \leftarrow \mathbf{v}^{\text{tmp}}$
  end_if
end_for
$\mathbf{x}_k(t+1) \leftarrow \mathbf{x}^{\text{tb}}$, and $\mathbf{v}_k(t+1) \leftarrow \mathbf{v}^{\text{tb}}$
$\mathbf{b}_k(t+1) \leftarrow$ Eq. 3 using $\mathcal{D}$

Figure 2: MERT-PSO algorithm implemented in the inner loop of MERT.

lize a master-slave architecture for parallelization. We simply allocate one particle to one slave node (or processor), and the master node manages the global best position and the convergence test.

4.1 Extensions

This section describes our four proposed extensions for PSO that make it possible to fit PSO to parameter tuning for SMT systems.

The value of each dimension of every velocity is usually clamped to the range $[-v_{\max}, v_{\max}]$ to avoid having too large an absolute velocity and thus realizing better convergence. Here, we introduce another procedure that can also avoid having velocities that are too large. Our proposed procedure is well-known as a 'norm projection' in the discriminative machine learning community, *i.e.*, (Shalev-Shwartz et al., 2007), which can be defined as follows:

$$\mathcal{P}(\mathbf{v}) = \min\left\{1, \frac{\beta}{||\mathbf{v}||_p}\right\}\mathbf{v}, \qquad (10)$$

where β represents the radius of L_p-norm ball. In our experiments, we set $\beta = 1$ and $p = 1$. We project the velocity vector into the L_p-norm ball immediately after we update the velocities.

Next, in a similar manner to Equation 10, we also project the current positions for all particles 'onto' L_p-norm ball after updating. We use the following function:

$$\mathcal{P}'(\mathbf{x}) = \frac{1}{||\mathbf{x}||_p}\mathbf{x}, \qquad (11)$$

Suppose $\mathbf{x}' = \mathcal{P}(\mathbf{x})$, then note that $\hat{\mathbf{e}}(\mathbf{f}, \mathbf{x})$ and $\hat{\mathbf{e}}(\mathbf{f}, \mathbf{x}')$ for any $\mathbf{f}$ can be identical. This is because we assume the translation models used in our method to be the linear model described by Equation 1. This assumption guarantees that any system translation $\hat{e}$ given by Equation 1 is never changed as a result of this position projection. This fact implies that we can find the solution onto an L_p-norm ball with a fixed radius. Thus, this projection may lead to faster convergence since it enables us to reduce the search space of PSO.

Third, for each iteration, we update the velocity and position of each particle to those with the best objective value among I trials, in our case $I = 10$. Let the right-hand side of Equations 5 and 7 be $\mathbf{V}(k,t)$ and $\mathbf{V}'(\tau,t)$, respectively, that is $\mathbf{V}(k,t) = \xi(t)\mathbf{v}_k(t) + c_1\mathbf{U}(0,1)(\mathbf{b}_k(t) - \mathbf{x}_k(t)) + c_2\mathbf{U}(0,1)(\mathbf{g}(t) - \mathbf{x}_k(t))$, and $\mathbf{V}'(\tau,t) = -\mathbf{x}_\tau(t) + \mathbf{g}(t) + \xi(t)\mathbf{v}_\tau(t) + \rho(t)\mathbf{U}(-1,1)$. Both $\mathbf{V}(k,t)$ and $\mathbf{V}'(\tau,t)$ have randomness characterized by $\mathbf{U}$. Therefore, we select the best position and velocity in I random trials as the position and velocity of $t+1$ in t iterations. This extension reduces the number of inefficient searches (and also the communication cost between particles). Thus, this may also lead to a faster tuning process.

Finally, we slightly modify the update scheme of ρ explained in Equation 8 to simplify the process as follows:

$$\rho(t+1) = \begin{cases} 0.5\rho(t) & \text{if } F(\mathbf{g}(t)) = F(\mathbf{g}(t-1)) \\ 1.0 & \text{otherwise} \end{cases}.$$

To summarize our method, Figure 2 shows its overall algorithm.

4.2 Implementations

Basically, we implemented the PSO algorithm described above in Moses, one of the leading open source implementations of phrase-based machine translation (Koehn et al., 2007). More specifically, we substituted our PSO method for the inner loop

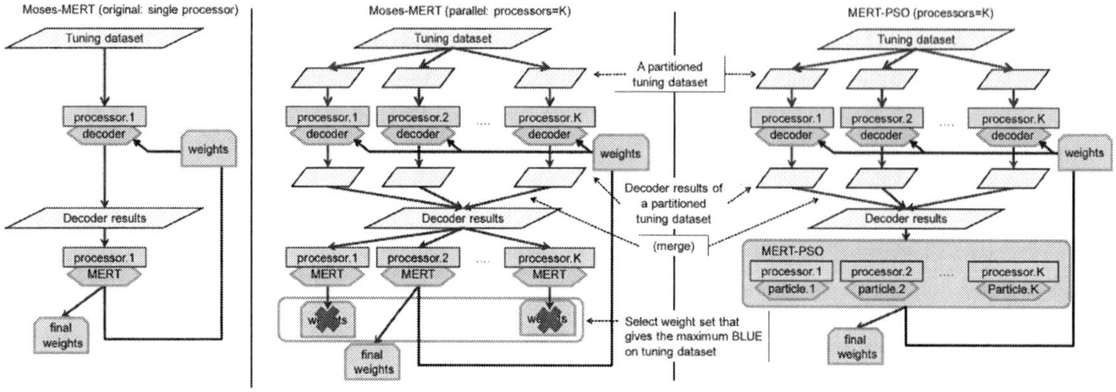

Figure 3: Outline process images (a) Moses-MERT (original), (b) Moses-MERT (our parallel version), and (c) MERT-PSO

	NIST-08	WMT-10
Source lang.	Chinese	German
Target lang.	English	English
# of sent. in tuning dataset (S)	2679	2524
# of reference per sent. (Q)	4	1
# of dimensions (D)	8	14
# of N-best per sent. (N)	100	100

Table 1: Details of data used in our experiments.

of Moses MERT. The source code was written in C++ with boost:::MPI libraries for parallelization.

Moreover, we also substituted the code we developed for the outer loop code to run a decoder in parallel to work on a large number of computational resources such as cluster PCs. This is simply accomplished by separating the tuning dataset, and then each computational resource executes the decoder independently to decode part of the partitioned dataset.

Additionally, in our experiments, we also implemented a parallel version of Moses-MERT as a competitor for comparison with our method. In this case, we independently performed the inner-loop algorithm of the original Moses-MERT in many computers with randomly selected initial weights. After completing all the Moses-MERT procedures, we selected a weight set that provided the best BLED-score.

Outline process images for three different implementations are shown in Figure 3.

5 Experiments

In our experiments, we evaluated the effectiveness of the proposed MERT-PSO in terms of both performance and runtime by comparison with a MERT package in Moses (Moses-MERT), and our parallel extended version of Moses (Moses-MERT parallel). All three algorithms use the Moses decoder (Koehn et al., 2007) to select the best translation given a source sentence (Equation 1).

We conducted our experiments on NIST-08 and WMT-10 datasets. Table 1 summarizes the data statistics used in our experiments. Note that the tuning datasets are formed from NIST-04 and NIST-05 test data for NIST-08, and WMT-09 test data for WMT-10. For both tasks, we train phrase tables from the provided training data using the standard GIZA++ pipeline and train language models using SRILM. The feature set consists of the standard 5 translation model probabilities, 1 language model probability, 1 distortion feature and 1 word penalty feature for 8 features, and an additional 6 reordering models for 14 features.

6 Results and Discussion

6.1 Evaluations for overall tuning process

Tables 2, and 3 show the results of our experiments comparing the parameter tuning qualities of the original Moses-MERT, Moses-MERT (parallel) and MERT-PSO. All the experiments were performed ten times using different random seeds for each trial. We assumed the number of available computational resources, which we refer to as '#PN', to be 512 in these experiments. In the tables, Ave, Max., Min., and Std. represent the average, maximum, minimum and standard deviation of ten trials, respectively.

Clearly, MERT-PSO greatly reduced the total runtime compared with the original Moses-MERT. Although MERT-PSO used a lot more computational resources than the original Moses-MERT, the original Moses-MERT can never achieve the tuning speed of MERT-PSO.[1] Additionally, we

[1] It should be noted that Moses-MERT (parallel) is our

		Moses-MERT (original)	Moses-MERT (#PN=512)	MERT-PSO (#PN=512)
BLEU score	Ave.	30.18	**30.26**	**30.26**
	Max.	30.25	30.28	**30.30**
	Min.	30.06	**30.24**	30.20
	Std.	.0033	**.0003**	.0008
#.of outer loop	Ave.	9.9	9.0	**7.1**
	Min.	7	**6**	**6**
	Max.	17	11	**8**
	Std.	2.03	1.61	**0.73**
inner loop total time (hh.mm.ss)	Ave.	01.00.16	01.01.45	**00.05.21**
	Min.	00.26.48	00.26.06	**00.03.40**
	Max.	02.31.39	01.31.09	**00.07.14**
opt. total time (hh.mm.ss)	Ave.	09.40.08	01.40.40	**00.36.41**
	Min.	06.44.39	00.51.58	**00.27.26**
	Max.	13.28.29	02.19.26	**00.43.20**

Table 2: Results for NIST-08 dataset.

		Moses-MERT (original)	Moses-MERT (#PN=512)	MERT-PSO (#PN=512)
BLEU score	Ave.	20.17	20.21	**20.23**
	Max.	20.21	20.24	**20.26**
	Min.	20.06	20.13	**20.19**
	Std.	.0552	.0331	**.0245**
#.of outer loop	Ave.	13.0	12.5	**7.4**
	Min.	10	10	**5**
	Max.	17	16	**9**
	Std.	2.06	1.80	**1.20**
inner loop total time (hh.mm.ss)	Ave.	03.40.22	03.18.43	**00.09.09**
	Min.	02.02.11	02.12.57	**00.04.11**
	Max.	05.55.01	05.14.53	**00.13.23**
opt. total time (hh.mm.ss)	Ave.	25.40.38	07.14.40	**02.07.12**
	Min.	20.08.22	05.20.47	**01.15.40**
	Max.	37.51.22	10.04.13	**02.23.24**

Table 3: Results for WMT-10 dataset.

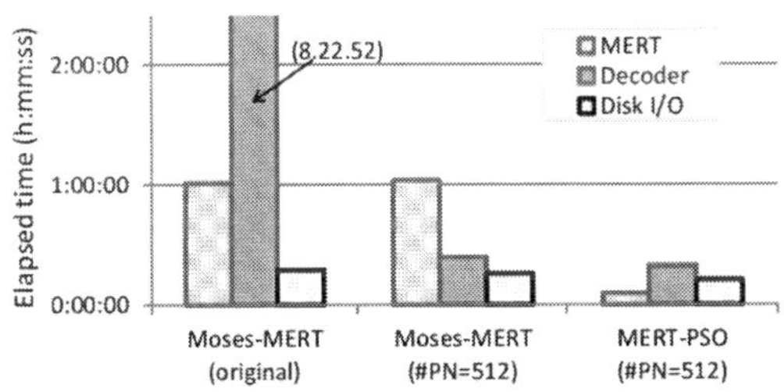

Figure 4: Detailed rates of parameter tuning process (inner loop), decoding (outer loop), and disk I/O times in total runtimes for NIST-08 dataset.

can find the tendency that the standard deviations of the BLEU-scores for MERT-PSO are relatively small. This implies that MERT-PSO has the power to produce a robust solution. This property is important for stochastic optimization algorithms.

The results of our developed parallel Moses-MERT are largely similar to those obtained by MERT-PSO in terms of BLEU-scores. However, the average runtimes of MERT-PSO are at least three times faster than those of Moses-MERT (parallel). These observations may be interesting; PSO searches almost randomly for the model component weights during the parameter tuning process, but it can still find good weights sufficiently quickly. The faster runtime of MERT-PSO is also explained by this simple randomized update procedure of PSO in contrast to KCD used in Moses-MERT, which tries to find the optimal coordinate by using an iterative line search.

Another interesting finding is that MERT-PSO tends to reduce the number of outer loops. This can be a good characteristic for the current MERT framework since decoding (outer loop) is usually expensive.

own developed system that is not implemented in the original Moses open source software.

Figure 4 summarizes the parameter tuning process (inner loop), decoding (outer loop), and disk I/O times for each method for NIST-08 dataset. Most SMT researchers would agree that the most of the MERT runtime is spent on decoding (outer loop). As shown in this figure, this is basically true for Moses-MERT (original) when the tuning dataset is large. However, with the parallel method, it appears not always to be true. For example, the dominant process of Moses-MERT (parallel) is parameter tuning process (inner loop). Thus, developing a faster parameter tuning algorithms is still meaningful.

6.2 Evaluations for inner loop process

This section evaluates the compared methods in terms of single inner loop process. To allow fair comparisons, all the methods are evaluated using the same N-best lists, even though running multiple iterations of MERT would normally produce different N-best lists. To perform this experiment, we first constructed models using the original Moses. Then, we utilized the generated intermediate files for the experiments described in this section.

6.2.1 Effect of parallelization

Figure 5 shows the effect of parallelization in terms of BLEU-score and runtime. It is clear that smaller #PN provided lower BLEU-score in MERT-PSO. MERT-PSO generally requires a certain number of particles (processors) to work well. It seems that we need at least 64 particles for a stable tuning in our setting. However, when MERT-PSO employed sufficiently many particles, it outperformed Moses-MERT and provided stable convergence even though MERT-PSO is a stochastic optimization method.

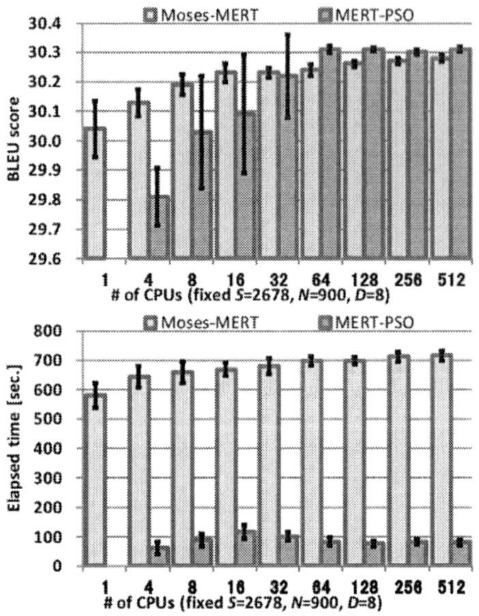

Figure 5: Runtimes and BLEU-score of changing parallelization number in a single inner loop process for NIST-08 dataset (vertical line at each bar represents Std.).

Note that larger #PN provided better BLEU-score but slower runtime in Moses-MERT. This is because Moses-MERT (parallel) runs the original MERT processes individually on every processors. Thus, the runtime of Moses-MERT depends on the slowest MERT process for all MERT processes. Instead, it can select the weights that provide the best BLEU score among all the results of the MERT processes. This is the reason of this observation.

6.2.2 Robustness against S and N

Figure 6 shows the runtimes against the average number of N-best lists in a single inner loop, where the number of sentences in a tuning set is fixed, and runtimes against the sentences in a single inner loop, where the average number of N-best list is fixed.

We can find MERT-PSO has an almost linear relation in both figures in the same way as Moses-MERT. These figures also clarified that MERT-PSO is very robust as regards increasing the number of sentences and the average N-best list size per sentence.

6.3 Test data performance

Table 4 shows the average BLEU-scores provided by ten models of Moses-MERT and MERT-PSO with 512 parallel processing for the test data. We

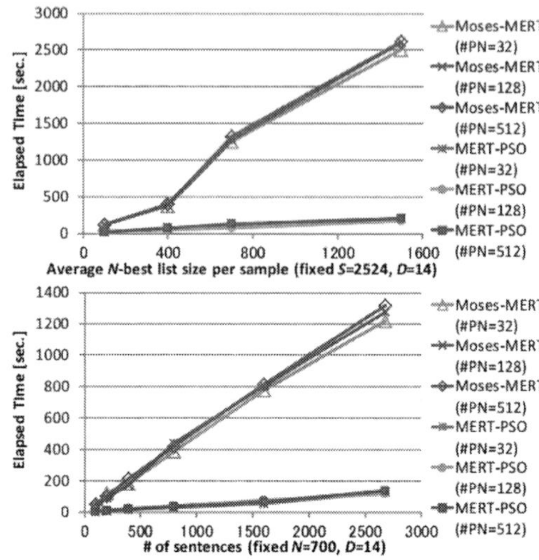

Figure 6: Runtimes vs. average N-best list size per sentence (top), and number of sentences in tuning dataset (bottom) in a single inner loop process for WMT-10 dataset.

		Moses-MERT (#PN=512)	MERT-PSO (#PN=512)
NIST-08 (Ch-En)	Ave.	21.32	**21.40**
WMT-10 (Ge-En)	Ave.	**21.25**	21.22

Table 4: Results for test data comparing Moses-MERT (parallel: #PN=512) and MERT-PSO (#PN=512).

confirmed that the translation qualities of MERT-PSO for unseen sentences are nearly the same level as those of Moses-MERT in terms of BLEU-score. This empirical evidence encourage us to use MERT-PSO as a replacement of Moses-MERT: MERT-PSO can provide the same quality level models as those provided by Moses-MERT with much faster runtime.

7 Conclusion

Our main goal was to provide a method to *improve the experiment turn-around time* for SMT system development. This paper proposed a novel distributed MERT framework based on particle swarm optimization (MERT-PSO). When there are abundant computational resources such as cluster PCs, our method can provide very much faster parameter tuning for SMT systems while maintaining the translation quality provided by the standard parameter tuning algorithms such as BLEU-score. Even though MERT-PSO is a stochastic approach, the experimental results showed that MERT-PSO is very robust, and in most cases, provides better results than the original Moses-MERT.

References

Nicola Bertoldi, Barry Haddow, and Jean-Baptiste Fouet. 2009. Improved Minimum Error Rate Training in Moses. *Prague Bulletin of Mathematical Linguistics*, No. 91:7–16.

Daniel Cer, Dan Jurafsky, and Christopher D. Manning. 2008. Regularization and search for minimum error rate training. In *Proceedings of the Third Workshop on Statistical Machine Translation*, pages 26–34, Columbus, Ohio, June. Association for Computational Linguistics.

George Foster and Roland Kuhn. 2009. Stabilizing minimum error rate training. In *Proceedings of the Fourth Workshop on Statistical Machine Translation*, pages 242–249, Athens, Greece, March. Association for Computational Linguistics.

James F. Kennedy and Russell C. Eberhart. 1995. Particle Swarm Optimization. In *Proceedings of IEEE International Conference on Neural Networks*, pages 1942–1948.

Philipp Koehn, Hieu Hoang, Alexandra Birch, Chris Callison-Burch, Marcello Federico, Nicola Bertoldi, Brooke Cowan, Wade Shen, Christine Moran, Richard Zens, Chris Dyer, Ondrej Bojar, Alexandra Constantin, and Evan Herbst. 2007. Moses: Open source toolkit for statistical machine translation. In *Proceedings of the 45th Annual Meeting of the Association for Computational Linguistics Companion Volume Proceedings of the Demo and Poster Sessions*, pages 177–180, Prague, Czech Republic, June. Association for Computational Linguistics.

Wolfgang Macherey, Franz Och, Ignacio Thayer, and Jakob Uszkoreit. 2008. Lattice-based minimum error rate training for statistical machine translation. In *Proceedings of the 2008 Conference on Empirical Methods in Natural Language Processing*, pages 725–734, Honolulu, Hawaii, October. Association for Computational Linguistics.

Robert C. Moore and Chris Quirk. 2008. Random restarts in minimum error rate training for statistical machine translation. In *Proceedings of the 22nd International Conference on Computational Linguistics (Coling 2008)*, pages 585–592, Manchester, UK, August. Coling 2008 Organizing Committee.

Franz Josef Och. 2003. Minimum error rate training in statistical machine translation. In *Proceedings of the 41st Annual Meeting of the Association for Computational Linguistics*, pages 160–167.

Kishore Papineni, Salim Roukos, Todd Ward, and Wei-Jing Zhu. 2002. Bleu: a method for automatic evaluation of machine translation. In *Research Report RC22176, IBM Research Division, Thomas J. Watson Research Center*, pages 311–318.

Shai Shalev-Shwartz, Yoram Singer, and Nathan Srebro. 2007. Pegasos: Primal Estimated sub-GrAdient SOlver for SVM. In *Proceedings of the Twenty-Fourth International Conference on Machine Learning*, pages 807–814.

Frans van den Bergh and Andries P. Engelbrecht. 2002. A new locally convergent particle swarm optimizer. In *Proceedings of IEEE International Conference on Systems, Man, and Cybernetics*, pages 96–101.

Going Beyond Word Cooccurrences in Global Lexical Selection for Statistical Machine Translation using a Multilayer Perceptron

Alexandre Patry
KeaText
845 Blvd. Décarie, Suite 202
Montréal, Canada H4L 3L7
alexandre.patry@keatext.com

Philippe Langlais
DIRO/RALI
Université de Montréal
Montréal, Canada H3C 3J7
felipe@iro.umontreal.ca

Abstract

Phrase-based statistical machine translation (PBSMT) decoders translate source sentences one phrase at a time using strong independence assumptions over the source phrases. Translation table scores are typically independent of context, language model scores depend on a few words surrounding the target phrase and distortion models do not influence directly the choice of target phrases.

In this work, we propose to condition the selection of each target word on the whole source sentence using a multilayer perceptron (MLP). Our interest in MLP lies in their hidden layer which encodes source sentences in a representation that is not directly tied to the notion of word.

We evaluated our approach on an English to French translation task. Our MLP model was able to improve BLEU scores over a standard PBSMT system.

1 Introduction

Phrase-based statistical machine translation systems translate source sentences step by step, starting with an empty sentence and ending when all source words have been translated (Koehn et al., 2003). At each step, an untranslated phrase is selected and one of its translation is appended at the end of the translation.

In this work, we are interested in the selection of a target phrase to translate a given source phrase. This selection is usually guided by three families of models. Translation models evaluate the intrinsic quality of a given phrase pair using evidences such as cooccurrence statistics between source and target words or phrases. These models always compute the same scores for a given pair of phrases, wherever it is used. A second family are language models, which evaluate the likeliness of target n-grams[1] independently from the source sentence. A third family are distortion models, whose main purpose is to evaluate the likelihood of phrase reorderings.

All these models only consider a fraction of the information available at a time. Figure 1 presents a partial translation that could be encountered by a decoder where these fractions of information are not enough to make a good decision. In this example, the decoder has already translated all but the last source word and it must decide if *plant* is translated by *usine* (a building) or *plante* (the botanic sense). As the position of the source word is fixed, the distortion model will not be of any help. If the system uses a 3-gram, only the last two words (*de cette*) of the partial hypothesis will be considered. Finally, the translation model will score the two options considering only *plant*. Therefore, the word *leaves* is never considered and the final decision largely depends on whether the training corpus is more biased toward one translation or the other.

This problem is not new and has even been addressed by the creators of CANDIDE (Berger et al., 1994), one of the first SMT system. We know of three groups of approaches for tackling it.

A first group of approaches acknowledge the bias of the system and use it at its advantage by customizing the training corpus for each source sentence. This bias can be introduced with thematic training corpora (Xu et al., 2007; Lü et al., 2007) or with custom corpora built dynamically to

[1] Sequences of n words where n usually varies between 3 and 5.

Source	~~the leaves of this~~ plant
Partial target	les feuilles de cette
Pair 1	plant → usine
Pair 2	plant → plante

Figure 1: An example state where the selection of a target phrase depends mostly on the bias of the training corpus (words already translated are strike through).

be similar to the source sentence (Hildebrand et al., 2005; Lü et al., 2007).

A second group of approaches cast the target phrase selection problem in a word sense disambiguation setting where source phrases are considered as ambiguous words and their translations as different meanings (Vickrey et al., 2005). This usually boils down to training one classifier per source phrase. These classifiers use a variety of features like surrounding source words, target words, part-of-speech or lemmas(Berger et al., 1994; Carpuat and Wu, 2007; Stroppa et al., 2007; Chan et al., 2007). Instead of training one classifier per source phrase, Gimpel and Smith (2008) use the same contextual scores for all the source phrases. The weights of those scores are then optimized with the other weights of the decoder.

Finally a third group of approaches assign a probability to every words in the target vocabulary given a source sentence (Venkatapathy and Bangalore, 2009; Mauser et al., 2009; Patry and Langlais, 2009). This predicted vocabulary can guide the decoder at translation time.

Our approach stands in this last group and we present its general idea in section 2. While previous approaches used linear or logistic regression models, we opted for the multilayer perceptron presented in section 3. Section 4 motivates this choice with a simple example. Section 5 details the algorithm to train our MLP. Experimental results, previous works and conclusion then follow in sections 6, 7 and 8 respectively.

2 Target vocabulary prediction

Standard PBSMT systems condition their translation on one source phrase at a time. In this work, we propose a new model conditioning its score on the complete source sentence. We treat the prediction of each target word as a Bernouilli trial where the presence of a word is a success and its absence a failure. The probability of a target sentence can thus be evaluated with:

$$\Pr(\mathbf{t} \mid \mathrm{s}) = \overbrace{\prod_{t \in \mathbf{t}} \Pr(t \mid \mathrm{s})}^{\text{Present}} \overbrace{\prod_{t \notin \mathcal{T} - \mathbf{t}} 1 - \Pr(t \mid \mathrm{s})}^{\text{Absent}} \quad (1)$$

where t is a target word, $\mathbf{t}$ a target sentence, $\mathcal{T}$ the target vocabulary and s the source sentence.

We are now left with the problem of evaluating $\Pr(t \mid \mathrm{s})$, the probability of a target word given a source sentence. Previous work have modelled this distribution with linear models like IBM Model 1 (Mauser et al., 2009):

$$\Pr_{\text{IBM1}}(t \mid \mathrm{s}) = \frac{1}{|\mathrm{s}|} \sum_{s \in \mathrm{s}} \Pr(t \mid s) \quad (2)$$

or a logistic regression model (Venkatapathy and Bangalore, 2009; Mauser et al., 2009):

$$\Pr_{lr}(t \mid \mathrm{s}) = \mathrm{sigmoid}\left(\sum_{s \in \mathrm{s}} w_{t,s}\right) \quad (3)$$

$$\mathrm{sigmoid}(z) = \frac{1}{1 + e^{-z}} \quad (4)$$

where $w_{t,s}$ is a weight between the tokens s and t.

Both models assign weights directly between source and target words. We opted instead for a multilayer perceptron where source and target words are connected indirectly through an hidden layer.

3 Multilayer perceptrons

Instead of assigning weights between source and target words, our MLP project the source words in an artificial representation offered by the hidden layer, and then project this artificial representation on the target vocabulary. The architecture of our MLP is as follow:

$$\vec{h} = \tanh(W\vec{s}) \quad (5)$$

$$\vec{y} = \mathrm{tsigmoid}(V\vec{h}) \quad (6)$$

$$\mathrm{tsigmoid}(z) = \mathrm{sigmoid}(z - 4.6) \quad (7)$$

where V and W are weight matrices to optimize, $\vec{s}$ the source sentence encoded in an one-hot vector, $\vec{h}$ contains the values of the hidden units and $\vec{y}$ contains the prediction probabilities of all target words in $\mathcal{T}$.

We use a sigmoidal activation function on the output layer (eq. 6) because it returns values between 0 and 1 that can be interpreted as probabilities. Sigmoid returns 0.5 when its input is 0,

Source	Target
the floor of the plant	le plancher de l'usine
the stem of the plant	la tige de la plante
the leaves and stem of the flower	les feuilles et la tige de la fleur
the floors and walls of the house	les planchers et les murs de la maison

Figure 2: Training corpus for our motivating example.

meaning that empty sentences encoded by vectors containing only zeros yield probabilities of 0.5 for all target word. It is clearly not what we want, so we use instead a modified sigmoid function (eq. 7) where empty sentences entail small probabilities for all target words (0.01 in our case). We could have used the same function for the hidden layer, but we opted for the hyperbolic tangent as it is known to shorten training time (LeCun et al., 1998).

More details on the training of our MLP are given in section 5.

4 Motivating Example

Conditioning the translation on the whole source sentence has already been studied. Previous approaches used linear or logistic regression models assigning a weight between every pair of source and target words. The number of connections in those models is thus quadratic in the size of the source and target vocabularies. Figure 3 shows the weight matrix of a logistic regression models trained by gradient descent on the sentences of Figure 2. The matrix is displayed in an Hinton diagram where white squares represent positive weights and black squares represent negative weights. The size of the squares are proportional to the absolute value of the weights.

Only pairs of words cooccurring in the training corpus get a weight different from zero, making the weight matrix sparse. This sparsity helps the model to scale well to larger vocabulary, but it cannot model relations in translation beyond word cooccurrences.

On the other hand, a MLP where source words are first projected into an artificial representation, and then on the target words, is not sparse. Figure 4 presents the weight matrices that were learnt from our training corpus. Any source word can thus contribute to the probability of any target word even when both words do not cooccur in the

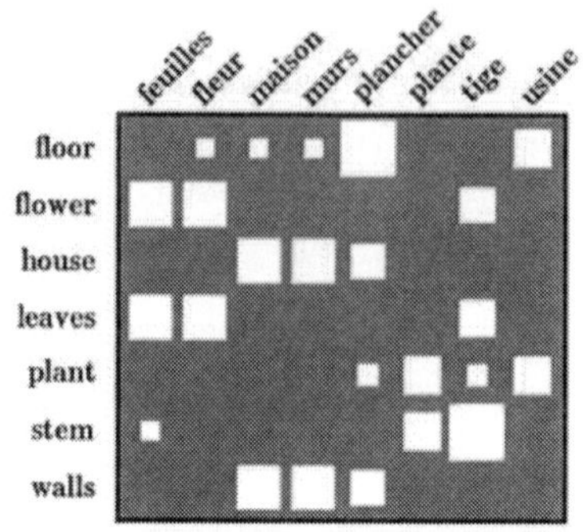

Figure 3: Weights learned for a logistic regression model optimized by gradient descent.

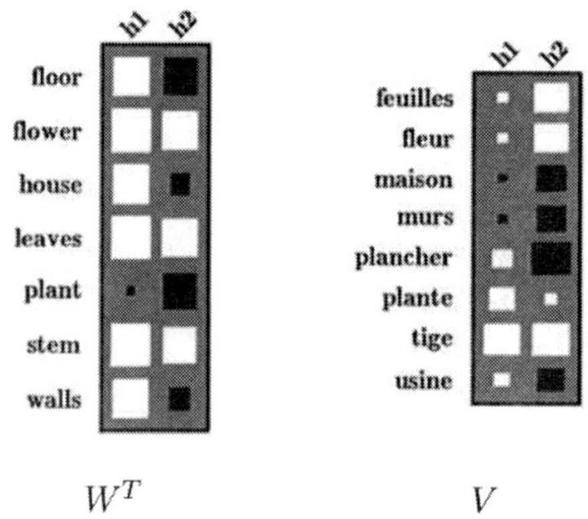

Figure 4: Weights learned for a MLP.

training corpus.

To show this fundamental difference between both kinds of models, we trained a logistic regression model and a MLP on the training corpus presented in Figure 2. We used these two models to predict the French words from the content words of *the leaves of the plant*. Both set of predictions are presented in Figure 5.

The regression model is unable to favour *plante* over *usine* because both words cooccur the same number of times with *plant* but do not cooccur with *leaves*. On the other hand, the MLP is able to favour *plante* because its artificial representation can separate words related to botanic (white squares in h_2 columns of Figure 4) from words related to buildings (black squares in h_2 columns of Figure 4).

Figure 6 shows the projection of four sentences on the artificial representation. Even if the four sentences share all the same words but one, the MLP is able to group sentences about botanic and

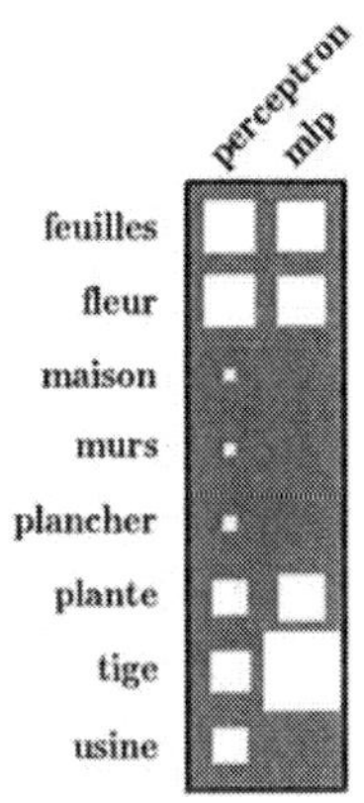

Figure 5: Predictions of the logistic regression model and the MLP for *the leaves of this plant.*

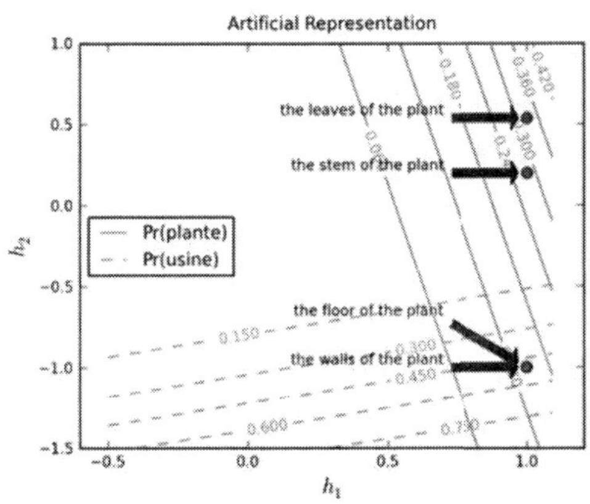

Figure 6: Projection of four sentences on the artificial representation.

buildings in different zones.

Leveraging the artificial representation offered by MLP to overcome data sparsity is not a novel idea: Bengio et al. (2003) and Schwenk (2007) trained state-of-the-art language models for speech recognition and machine translation using MLP.

5 MLP Training

To train our MLP, we must select values for V and W that will optimize the likelihood of our training data (eq. 1). We do so by minimizing the following error function using a gradient descent algorithm:

$$E(\mathbf{s},\mathbf{t}) = \sum_{t \in \mathcal{T}-\mathbf{t}} \log\left(1 - y_{t|\mathbf{s}}\right) - \sum_{t \in \mathbf{t}} \log y_{t|\mathbf{s}} \quad (8)$$

1. Initialize V and W with $U(-0.05, 0.05)$.
2. For iterations 1 to 20:
   (a) For each batch of 100 sentences pairs:
      i. Compute the gradients of V and W with respect to eq. 8.
      ii. Test the following learning rates in orders 0.5, 0.05, 0.01 and select the first that decreases the error (eq. 9).
      iii. When such a learning rate exists, update V and W in the direction of their negative gradients multiplied by the learning rate.
3. Return V and W.

Figure 7: Gradient descent algorithm that we used to train our MLP.

where $y_{t|\mathbf{s}}$ is the probability that t appears in a translation of $\mathbf{s}$ according to our MLP. Gradient descent algorithms for MLP are already covered in many textbooks (Bishop, 1995), but because our models contain millions of weights, we had to develop some heuristics in order to keep the training time reasonable. Our modified gradient descent algorithm is presented in Figure 7.

This algorithm starts by initializing the values of V and W with a uniform between $(-0.05, 0.05)$. We varied the range of this uniform without notable variations in the results.

Computing gradients on the whole dataset before each update is too time consuming. Therefore, we computed the gradients on mini-batch of 100 sentence pairs instead. We could have used a stochastic gradient descent as well (mini-batches of size 1), but mini-batches are an opportunity to easily parallelize the training algorithm. We can encode all the source sentences of a mini-batch in a matrix where each sentence stands on a column, thus ending up with matrices-matrices multiplications instead of matrices-vectors multiplications in equations 5 and 6. This is desired as the former are faster to compute than the latter for modern linear algebra toolkit like ATLAS (Whaley and Petitet, 2005).

Once the gradients are computed, we must select a learning rate. We found this step to be critical to the success of our models. We first tried with a fixed learning rates, but the results were disappointing. We then implemented Brent line search algorithm (Press et al., 1992, §10.2), but it was painfully slow. We finally ended up with the line search algorithm described on lines 2(a)ii and 2(a)iii. Even though this algorithm is simple, it did as well as Brent line search to optimize the log-likelihood in our experiments but it was faster.

We added a L1 regularizer to the error function during the line search to penalize big updates that bring small improvements:

$$E_{\text{L1}}(\mathbf{s},\mathbf{t}) = E(\mathbf{s},\mathbf{t}) + 0.1\left(\sum_{ki}|w_{ki}| + \sum_{jk}|v_{jk}|\right) \quad (9)$$

However, we did not used this regularized error to compute the gradients because it tends to push all weights toward zero at each update. This behaviour is not desired in our setting because only the weights associated to present source words are updated in W. Many words only appear in a couple of batches and their weights would all be pushed toward zero if we would include the regularizer when computing the gradients.

6 Experiments

We integrated our prediction models (see section 6.1) in an in house multi-stack phrase-based decoder which has performances similar to those of PHARAOH (Koehn, 2004a) when used in the same conditions.

We trained our phrase-table using TRAIN-FACTORED-MODEL.PERL, a script available with the MOSES PBSMT (Koehn et al., 2007). We optimized the weights of our log-linear model to maximize BLEU on our development set with the Nelder-Mead algorithm (Press et al., 1992) on n-best lists of 2000 sentences. To keep the decoding time reasonable, we limited the number of translations per source phrase to 30 and the number of hypotheses per stack to 50. We conducted our experiments with a trigram language model.

We are aware that our system could be enhanced in several ways. The distortion models embedded in MOSES are known to improve quality upon the translations produced by PHARAOH, and larger n-gram models, such as 5-gram models, might deliver as well slightly better results. This is left as future work. As will be discussed in section 6.5, our system performs comparably to other state-of-the-art systems tested in similar settings, and therefore, the gains we observed by integrating our prediction model into the decoder are representative.

6.1 Prediction scores

We investigated two ways (scores) to integrate our trained prediction models to the decoder.

As our MLP are trained to maximize the likelihood of the training data (eq. 1), it would be natural to add the likelihood score to the log-linear model optimized by the decoder. Likelihood is however heavy to compute because it sums over the complete target vocabulary. We followed Mauser et al. (2009) who suggested to use the *odd* score instead:

$$odd(\mathbf{t}|\mathbf{s}) = \prod_{t\in\mathbf{t}} \frac{y_{t|\mathbf{s}}}{1 - y_{t|\mathbf{s}}} \quad (10)$$

An odd of x for a given word means that this word is x times more likely to be present in the translation than to be absent from it. An interesting property of this score is that it is proportional to eq. 1 once the source sentence is known.

We evaluated a second score that counts the number of target words with a probability higher than a given threshold α:

$$pred(\mathbf{t} \mid \mathbf{s}) = \left|\{t \in \mathbf{t} \mid y_{t|\mathbf{s}} > \alpha\}\right| \quad (11)$$

We selected the threshold to maximize the f-measure when the predicted words are compared against the reference translation of our development corpus, as suggested in (Patry and Langlais, 2009).

A convenient property of these scores is that they can be computed one target word at a time. Each time a new phrase is appended to a partial translation, the decoder can thus compute *odd* and *pred* on this new phrase and update the partial translation score accordingly.

6.2 Models and data

We evaluated our system on a French-English translation task. We used corpora that were made available for the *Fourth Workshop on Machine Translation* (Callison-Burch et al., 2009). We trained our models on EUROPARL and the NEWS-COMMENTARY sections. We used TEST2007 as our development corpus, TEST2008 as our in-domain test corpus and NEWSTEST2009 as our out-of-domain test corpus.

We used those data to train three prediction models:

IBM1 An IBM1 model (eq. 2) trained with GIZA++ (Och and Ney, 2003).

PERCEPTRON A perceptron with a translated sigmoidal activation function:

$$\Pr_{\text{PERCEPTRON}}(t \mid \mathbf{s}) = \text{tsigmoid}(U\vec{s}) \qquad (12)$$

where U is a sparse matrix linking each source word with its 10 best translations according to IBM1.[2] This model is equivalent to logistic regression (eq. 12).

MLP-64 A MLP with 64 hidden units. This number of hidden units was selected after informal experiments on the development corpus.

Both MLP-64 and PERCEPTRON were trained using the algorithm of Figure 7. In our first attempts, we observed that our prediction models caused the decoder to include many spurious stop words in the translations. We thus restricted their source and target vocabulary to content words.

MLP-64 and perceptron do not handle large vocabulary as easily as IBM1, we thus limited their vocabulary to words appearing at least 20 times in the training corpus. The English vocabulary diminished from 133 141 to 21 915 words and the French vocabulary from 143 980 to 28 095 words. This simplification allowed us to trained our MLP in less than 3 hours on an Intel Xeon quad-core processor with a clock-rate of 2.8 GHz.

6.3 In-domain

The results of the in-domain evaluation are presented in Table 1. We first observe that all models predicting a target vocabulary get better BLEU than the baseline. Those improvements are statistically significant with a confidence of 95% according to our bootstrap resampling with replacement tests (Koehn, 2004b). We also observed that MLP-64 systems are significantly better than all the other three systems.

We compared MLP-64 translation against those of our baseline and noticed that both systems agree for one sentence out of four. The other translations usually differ in one or two words having similar senses, but MLP-64 tends to select translations that are closer to the reference translations.

[2]We limited the number of links because our training algorithm implementation had a hard time without it.

System	BLEU (%)	
	odd	pred
baseline	30.06	30.06
+ IBM1	30.32	30.65
+ PERCEPTRON	30.68	30.71
+ MLP-64	**30.86**	**31.00**

Table 1: In-domain evaluation. Bold scores are significantly better than the other scores of their column.

System	BLEU (%)	
	odd	pred
baseline	19.05	19.05
+ IBM1	20.00	**19.92**
+ PERCEPTRON	19.93	**19.82**
+ MLP-64	**20.45**	**19.89**

Table 2: Out-of-domain evaluation.

6.4 Out-of-domain

The results for news translations are presented in Table 2.

We first observe a decrease of 10 BLEU point when compared against the results of the in-domain translation. This decrease asserts the challenge we face when designing a system that should translate many genres of documents. We still observe that all models predicting a target vocabulary are better than the baseline.

The best system is MLP-64 combined with *odd* score. The translations of the system are significantly better than the translations of all the other systems according to BLEU. We observe modest gains for *pred* scores where IBM1 is the best system, but there are no significant differences among all the models predicting a target vocabulary.

6.5 Comparison to state-of-the-art

The best SMT systems of the *Fourth Workshop on Machine Translation* (Callison-Burch et al., 2009) for the English-French translation task were evaluated at 28 BLEU points comparatively to our best system which got 20.45. This is a huge difference, but news translation was the main task of this workshop and participant used much more data than we used in our experiments. It is thus not fair to compare our out-of-domains results against those ones.

We can however compare our results to those

of the *Third Workshop on Machine Translation* (Callison-Burch et al., 2008) where a news corpus was translated by systems tuned to translate parliament proceedings. The best systems for in-domain English-French translations obtained 32 BLEU points and the best systems for out-of-domain translations 20 BLEU points. Our results are thus competitive with those of state-of-the-art systems in a comparable situation.

7 Previous Works

To our knowledge, IBM1 is the first target vocabulary prediction models that was used in SMT. It was one of the best model among many others in a rescoring module for a PBSMT (Och et al., 2004).

The term *global lexical selection* was coined by Bangalore et al. (2007) who pushed the idea of target vocabulary prediction further than us. They devised a system that first predicted a set of target words and then reordered those words to produce a final translation. This system is particularly suited for languages that are not sensitive to word reordering like Hindi (Venkatapathy and Bangalore, 2009). Their system use a logistic regression model to predict the target words from the set of n-grams in the source sentence. Our *pred* score is a softer version of this idea. It encourages the decoder to select the predicted words without forcing it and it allows the reordering to take place in the PBSMT.

Mauser et al. (2009) integrated a logistic regression model predicting target words from all the source words in a PBSMT. Using this model, they gained one BLEU point over their baseline on a Chinese to English translation task.

IBM1 is a linear regression model over probability of target words given each source words individually. Mauser et al. (2009) extended this model to condition it on source word cooccurrences (word and trigger pairs). This models improved BLEU score of one point over their baseline system. Note that our MLP consider all source words jointly, word cooccurrences are thus automatically modelled.

Patry and Langlais (2009) were the first to use a MLP to predict target words, but they did not tested it in a SMT system. They got their best results when they added a bilingual lexicon to their MLP. We tested this extension in our system but it did not improve over MLP-64.

8 Conclusion

Phrase-based statistical machine translation systems condition their scores on few source words at a time to produce their translations. While previous works used linear or logistic regression models to capture broader dependencies on the source sentence, we presented, motivated and evaluated the use of a multilayer perceptron for such a task. We opted for MLP because of their hidden units which offer an artificial representation of source sentences.

We compared three different models for target words prediction: IBM1, PERCEPTRON and MLP-64. In all our experiments, we observed a significant improvement for all these models over the baseline system, but the best of our contextual model was MLP-64 with improvements of 0.94 and 1.4 BLEU points on in-domain and out-of-domain translations respectively. These results are encouraging, especially since several choices have been made that we could revisit, thus leaving an open space for further improvements.

In this study, we controlled the size of the source and target vocabularies by selecting only words appearing at least 20 times. Since translation systems are usually good with frequent words, we would like to select our vocabularies in order to maximize the gains of the translation system.

We selected a L1 regularizer because it is known to be efficient and simple to implement. We would however like to devise another regularizer that would encourage the MLP to group together artificial representations of source sentences having similar translations.

Also, we would like to validate our model on other language pairs and other corpora and we plan to investigate the influence of the corpus size and the number of hidden units on the translation quality.

An important limitation of our MLP is their ignorance of sentence structures. One partial solution to this problem is to model source n-grams instead of source words like Venkatapathy and Bangalore (2009) suggested. This approach has its limitation because it only captures local structures and cannot consider grammatical or semantic relations. We are thus thinking about alternative ways to encode the source sentences and how these new representations could be included to our model.

References

Srinivas Bangalore, Patrick Haffner, and Stephan Kanthak. 2007. Statistical machine translation through global lexical selection and sentence reconstruction. In *ACL*.

Yoshua Bengio, Réjean Ducharme, Pascal Vincent, and Christian Janvin. 2003. A neural probabilistic language model. *The Journal of Machine Learning Research*, 3:1137–1155.

Adam L. Berger, Peter F. Brown, Stephen A. Della Pietra, Vincent J. Della Pietra, John R. Gillett, John D. Lafferty, Robert L. Mercer, Harry Printz, and Luboš Ureš. 1994. The candide system for machine translation. In *HLT '94: Proceedings of the workshop on Human Language Technology*, pages 157–162. Association for Computational Linguistics.

Christopher M. Bishop. 1995. *Neural Networks for Pattern Recognition*. Oxford University Press.

Chris Callison-Burch, Philipp Koehn, Christof Monz, Josh Schroeder, and Cameron Shaw Fordyce, editors. 2008. *Proceedings of the Third Workshop on Statistical Machine Translation*. Association for Computational Linguistics, June.

Chris Callison-Burch, Philipp Koehn, Christof Monz, and Josh Schroeder, editors. 2009. *Proceedings of the Fourth Workshop on Statistical Machine Translation*. Association for Computational Linguistics, March.

Marine Carpuat and Dekai Wu. 2007. Improving statistical machine translation using word sense disambiguation. In *Proceedings of the 2007 Joint Conference on Empirical Methods in Natural Language Processing and Computational Natural Language Learning (EMNLP-CoNLL)*, pages 61–72.

Yee Seng Chan, Hwee Tou Ng, and David Chiang. 2007. Word sense disambiguation improves statistical machine translation. In *Proceedings of the 45th Annual Meeting of the Association of Computational Linguistics*, pages 33–40. Association for Computational Linguistics, June.

Kevin Gimpel and Noah A. Smith. 2008. Rich source-side context for statistical machine translation. In *Proceedings of the Third Workshop on Statistical Machine Translation*, StatMT '08, pages 9–17. Association for Computational Linguistics.

Almut Silja Hildebrand, Matthias Eck, Stephan Vogel, and Alex Waibel. 2005. Adaptation of the translation model for statistical machine translation based on information retrieval. In *Proceedings of the European Association for Machine Translation 10th Annual Conference*, May.

Philipp Koehn, Franz Josef Och, and Daniel Marcu. 2003. Statistical phrase-based translation. In *NAACL '03: Proceedings of the 2003 Conference of the North American Chapter of the Association for Computational Linguistics on Human Language Technology*, pages 48–54. Association for Computational Linguistics.

Philipp Koehn, Hieu Hoang, Alexandra Birch, Chris Callison-Burch, Marcello Federico, Nicola Bertoldi, Brooke Cowan, Wade Shen, Christine Moran, Richard Zens, Chris Dyer, Ondrej Bojar, Alexandra Constantin, and Evan Herbst. 2007. Moses: Open source toolkit for statistical machine translation. In *Proceedings of the 45th Annual Meeting of the Association for Computational Linguistics Companion Volume Proceedings of the Demo and Poster Sessions*, pages 177–180. Association for Computational Linguistics, June.

Philipp Koehn. 2004a. Pharaoh: A beam search decoder for phrase-based statistical machine translation models. In *AMTA*, pages 115–124.

Philipp Koehn. 2004b. Statistical significance tests for machine translation evaluation. In Dekang Lin and Dekai Wu, editors, *Proceedings of EMNLP 2004*, pages 388–395. Association for Computational Linguistics, July.

Y. LeCun, L. Bottou, G. Orr, and K. Muller. 1998. Efficient backprop. In G. Orr and Muller K., editors, *Neural Networks: Tricks of the trade*. Springer.

Yajuan Lü, Jin Huang, and Qun Liu. 2007. Improving statistical machine translation performance by training data selection and optimization. In *Proceedings of the 2007 Joint Conference on Empirical Methods in Natural Language Processing and Computational Natural Language Learning (EMNLP-CoNLL)*, pages 343–350.

Arne Mauser, Saša Hasan, and Hermann Ney. 2009. Extending statistical machine translation with discriminative and trigger-based lexicon models. In *Conference on Empirical Methods in Natural Language Processing*, August.

Franz Josef Och and Hermann Ney. 2003. A systematic comparison of various statistical alignment models. *Computational Linguistics*, 29(1):19–51.

Franz Josef Och, Daniel Gildea, Sanjeev Khudanpur, Anoop Sarkar, Kenji Yamada, Alexander Fraser, Shankar Kumar, Libin Shen, David Smith, Katherine Eng, Viren Jain, Zhen Jin, and Dragomir R. Radev. 2004. A smorgasbord of features for statistical machine translation. In *HLT-NAACL*, pages 161–168.

Alexandre Patry and Philippe Langlais. 2009. Prediction of words in statistical machine translation using a multilayer perceptron. In International Association for Machine Translation (IAMT), editor, *Proceedings of the Twelfth Machine Translation Summit*, aug.

William H. Press, Saul A. Teukolsky, William T. Vetterling, and Brian P. Flannery. 1992. *Numerical recipes in C (2nd ed.): the art of scientific computing*. Cambridge University Press.

Holger Schwenk. 2007. Continuous space language models. *Comput. Speech Lang.*, 21(3):492–518.

Nicolas Stroppa, Antal van den Bosch, and Andy Way. 2007. Exploiting source similarity for smt using context-informed features. In *Proceedings of the 11th International Conference on Theoretical and Methodological Issues in Machine Translation*, pages 231–240, September.

Sriram Venkatapathy and Srinivas Bangalore. 2009. Discriminative machine translation using global lexical selection. *ACM Trans. Asian Lang. Inf. Process.*, 8(2).

David Vickrey, Luke Biewald, Marc Teyssier, and Daphne Koller. 2005. Word-sense disambiguation for machine translation. In *HLT '05: Proceedings of the conference on Human Language Technology and Empirical Methods in Natural Language Processing*, pages 771–778. Association for Computational Linguistics.

R. Clint Whaley and Antoine Petitet. 2005. Minimizing development and maintenance costs in supporting persistently optimized BLAS. *Software: Practice and Experience*, 35(2):101–121, February.

Jia Xu, Yonggang Deng, Yuqing Gao, and Hermann Ney. 2007. Domain dependant statistical machine translation. In *Proceedings of MT Summit XI*, pages 515–520, September.

System Combination Using Discriminative Cross-Adaptation

Jacob Devlin and **Antti-Veikko I. Rosti** and
Shankar Ananthakrishnan and **Spyros Matsoukas** *
Raytheon BBN Technologies, 10 Moulton St, Cambridge, MA 02138, USA
{jdevlin,arosti,sanantha,smatsouk}@bbn.com

Abstract

Cross-adaptation (CA) based methods of machine translation (MT) system combination work by adapting the decoding step of a baseline system using information from alternate systems. Generally, the required information is very deep, such as a full decoding forest. In this paper, we describe a method of cross-adaptation based system combination which only requires the final output from each alternate system. This is achieved by adding a discriminatively weighted n-gram confidence feature to our decoder. In order to optimize the confidence weight of each system, we present a novel procedure called *non-linear Expected-BLEU optimization* that can be used to optimize arbitrary non-linear parameters for any decoding feature. We also describe a method for explicitly creating an adapted system that is *dissimilar* from each particular input system, which we have found to be useful in combination. Although our new method does not outperform a state-of-the-art confusion network (CN) based combination system on its own, we obtain statistically significant gains of 0.21-0.45 BLEU when the CA output is used as an additional system in CN combination.

*This work was supported by DARPA/I2O Contract No. HR0011-06-C-0022 under the GALE program (Approved for Public Release, Distribution Unlimited). The views, opinions, and/or findings contained in this article/presentation are those of the author/presenter and should not be interpreted as representing the official views or policies, either expressed or implied, of the Defense Advanced Research Projects Agency or the Department of Defense.

1 Introduction

In general terms, *system combination* is the task of using multiple machine translation (MT) systems to produce an output that is better than any input system could produce by itself. The method for doing this is largely shaped by the information available: some require an actual MT decoder for each system (Li et al., 2009), some require a full forest of derivations (DeNero et al., 2010), and some only require the final output translations from each system (Rosti et al., 2009). Our research was done as part of a project where multiple sites develop their decoding systems independently, and then these outputs are combined together to produce a "team" output. Because these systems widely differ in structure, the only information we have available for system combination is an n-best list of hypotheses. No source-side correspondences are available, and some systems are only capable of producing a 1-best list.

Additionally, in this procedure, we assume that a strong baseline decoding system is available for each condition where system combination is performed. The general principle behind this procedure is to run a baseline decoding system with the output *adapted* towards the output of the other systems. In this case, we perform the adaptation by effectively increasing the probability of language model n-grams that are seen in other systems' outputs, as well as including translation rules extracted from the other systems' outputs. The relative weight of each system is estimated discriminatively using a novel extension to the Expected-BLEU optimization procedure which allows for the tuning of non-linear feature weights.

Currently, we use a state-of-the-art confusion network based procedure for system combination based on (Rosti et al., 2009). Although our new method *does* produce a significant gain over the best single system, it does not perform as well as our confusion network decoding on any condition that we tried. However, this new procedure was not designed to replace our existing method, but rather to complement it. When we used the output of the adaptation-based combination as an additional system in our standard confusion network decoding, we obtained a moderate gain in Arabic web, and a smaller gain on Arabic newswire.

2 Related Work

Existing research in MT system combination can generally be divided into two major approaches: confusion networks and cross-adaptation.[1] Confusion network based methods align the various input hypotheses against one another to form the confusion network, and then generate the most likely path through this network to produce a combined 1-best (Bangalore et al., 2001). However, as mentioned previously, we already have state-of-the-art confusion network system in place, which is based on (Rosti et al., 2007; Rosti et al., 2009). It is known that combining the outputs of multiple system combination procedures can produce further gains. Therefore, our goal was to design a *complementary* combination system which could be used in conjunction with our current system to produce better results than either could independently.

In automated speech recognition (ASR), generalized forms of adaptation have widely been used for a number of years (Rozzi and Stern, 1991) and more recently, cross-adaptation has been used as a method of ASR system combination (Stüker et al., 2006; Gales et al., 2007). In machine translation, a number of cross-adaptation based combination methods have been developed under a multitude of names. However, nearly all of these methods require rich information about each system which is not available for our task. Collaborative decoding (Li et al., 2009) requires that each system's decoder be run multiple times in an iterative fashion. DeNero's model combination (DeNero et al., 2010) requires a full decoding forest from each system. Joint optimization (He and Toutanova, 2009) and hybrid decoding (Cui et al., 2010) require that the input models[2] for each system be available to the combination decoder.

Crego et al. (2010) describes a method for LM-based combination which is most similar to the work presented in this paper, but their method does not discriminatively estimate weights for an arbitrary number of input systems.[3] In fact, they only present results where their main system is adapted using the output of a *single* other systems. By contrast, we present results where our main system is adapted by 7-14 other systems, and the weight for each of these is estimated discriminatively. As far as we know, there has been no previous work in developing a method of cross-adaptation which (a) requires only the final output from each system, and (b) discriminatively estimates the adaptation weight for each system. The latter is highly desirable when combining a large number of systems of varying quality, as with our task.

In order to discriminatively estimate the adaptation weight of each input system, we use a highly-scalable MT-specific optimization procedure called *Expected-BLEU* (Devlin, 2009; Rosti et al., 2010). The Expected-BLEU procedure is very similar to the Co-BLEU metric (Pauls et al., 2009), and is more distantly related to earlier work such as Tromble's linear approximation of BLEU (Tromble et al., 2008) and Smith's minimum risk annealing (Smith and Eisner, 2006). In this paper, we describe a novel extension to Expected-BLEU that allows for the optimization of arbitrary non-linear feature parameters. This allows for any feature parameters that are differentiable with respect to the feature score to be optimized alongside the normal log-linear decoding weights during the standard optimization procedure.

3 Description of MT System

Our baseline machine translation system, which is also used to perform the cross-adaptation, is a state-of-the-art hierarchical decoder based on (Shen et al., 2008) and (Chiang, 2007). Bottom-up chart parsing is performed to produce a shared forest of derivations, and possible path through the

[1] There is a third approach, known as "hypothesis selection," which simply selects the best input hypotheses as the "combined" output, based on some features (Hildebrand and Vogel, 2008). However, there has been comparatively little research on this method due to its simplicity and lack of room for improvement.

[2] Such as the set of translation rules and the language model.

[3] The *adaptation weight* represents how much each system should influence the adaptation process.

forest defines one hypothesis h.[4] The decoder uses a log-linear translation model, so the score of hypothesis h is defined as:

$$S_h(\vec{w}) = \sum_{i=1}^{m} w_i \sum_{r \in R(h)} F_{ri} \quad (1)$$

where $R(h)$ is the set of translation rules that make up hypothesis h, m is the number of features, F_{ri} is the score of the ith feature in rule r, and w_i is the weight of feature i. This weight vector is optimized discriminatively to maximize BLEU score on a tuning set, using the Expected-BLEU optimization procedure.

Our decoder uses all of the standard statistical MT features, such as:

- $P(T|S)$ = forward rule translation
- $P(S|T)$ = backward rule translation
- $LS(T|S)$ = lexical smoothing
- $P(q_j|q_{j-1},...)$ = language model

Additionally, we use approximately 50,000 sparse, binary-valued features which model specific events such as "Is the bigram 'united states' seen in the target side of the translation rule?" These features do cause some amount of overfitting on the tuning set, but we have not found this to be harmful to the test sets. However, this also causes a certain amount of variability on the tune set results, so minor variations in BLEU score on the tuning set from condition to condition are to be expected.

The cross adaptation models described below are used as standard log-linear feature scores, and the weights are optimized jointly with the normal decoding features.

4 Discriminative Model Adaptation

In this section, we describe how the cross-adaptation is actually implemented in our system. We perform the adaptation by defining additional decoding features which affect both the language model and the translation model, in order to make the MT output appear more like the output of the other systems.

4.1 Discriminative Language Model Adaptation

We perform language model adaptation by effectively increasing the language model probability of n-grams that are seen in the other systems' outputs. Since we use a 3-gram decoder, we adapt the probability of all 1-grams, 2-grams, and 3-grams.

In the past, Snover et al. (2008) performed language model adaptation using simple linear interpolation:

$$P(q_j|q_{j-1},...) = \sum_{i=1}^{K} v_i P_i(q_j|q_{j-1},...) \quad (2)$$

where K is the number of models, $q = (q_j, q_{j-1}, ...)$ is the n-gram in question, and v_i is the weight for model i, constrained so that $\sum_i v_i = 1$. This formula replaces the standard language model probability in the log-linear decoding model. When this feature was used by Snover, it combined the standard language model with a test-sentence-specific language model that was trained on several hundred documents. However, in the case of system combination, we are adapting towards a much smaller amount of data, so $P(q_j|q_{j-1},...,q_{j-n+1})$ will not be well estimated. Therefore, we use a modified formula which uses a binary function $\delta(q)$ to indicate the presence or absence of the n-gram q. This formula is used as an additional feature in the log-linear decoding model:[5]

$$F(q, \vec{v}) = \log(\epsilon + \frac{\sum_{i=1}^{K} e^{v_i} G_i(q)}{\epsilon + \sum_{i=1}^{K} e^{v_i}}) \quad (3)$$

$$G_i(q) = \frac{\sum_{j=1}^{H_i} b_{ij} \delta_{ij}(q)}{\sum_{j=1}^{H_i} b_{ij}} \quad (4)$$

where K is the number of systems, ϵ is a small positive value fixed at 10^{-8}, and v_i is the discriminatively estimated weight for system i.[6] If an n-gram is seen in exactly *zero* system outputs, it does *not* receive a score of $\log(\epsilon)$, but instead receives a score of $\log(1)$ and triggers an additional binary feature. This additional feature acts as a discriminative backoff log-probability for unseen n-grams, and generally optimizes to a large negative value in the range of -10 to -15.

The function $G_i(q)$ represents the "count" of n-gram q in system i's n-best list. In it, H_i is the number of hypotheses in system i, $\delta_{ij}(q)$ is a binary "occurrence function" that returns 1 if n-gram q is seen in hypothesis ij, and b_{ij} is a

[4] In this case, *hypothesis* refers to a specific path through the shared forest, rather than a specific output string.

[5] Therefore, the standard language model probability remains unchanged.

[6] ϵ is used to prevent log() underflow or divide-by-zero errors, since v_i is unbounded.

hypothesis-specific positive weighting which assigns mass to each hypothesis as a function of its rank. Obviously, if q is seen in every hypothesis of system i, $G_i(q) = 1$. Note that $\delta_{ij}(q)$ does not return the actual *count* of q, because we never want $G_i(q)$ or $F(q, v)$ to return a value over 1 (or $\log(1)$).

Theoretically, b_{ij} could be estimated discriminatively, but for simplicity we use the following formula which assigns mass to each hypothesis based on its rank in the n-best list:

$$b_{ij} = H_i - j + 1 \quad (5)$$

As an example, if system i has a 5-best output, and n-gram q is seen in hypotheses 1 and 4, then $G_i(q) = \frac{5+2}{5+4+3+2+1} = 0.467$.

Equation 3 can be thought of as the log-confidence that n-gram q is consistent with the other systems' outputs. Note that $F(q, \vec{v})$ is continuous and differentiable with respect to the weights $\vec{v}$, and $F(q, \vec{v})$ returns a value in the range $[\log(\epsilon), 0]$ for all values of $\vec{v}$. These properties make it possible to discriminatively estimate $\vec{v}$ within our standard optimization framework, which is discussed in Section 5.

4.2 Discriminative Translation Model Adaptation

We extract adapted translation rules using the method described in (Snover et al., 2008). Essentially, for each source phrase s, we consider every target phrase t from each of the input system hypotheses as a possible translation of s.[7] We limit the maximum length of s and t to 3 and 5, respectively. Clearly, this produces many extraneous rules. We prune these rules only keeping the top 20 most likely target translations of each s, sorted by the "noisy-or" lexical smoothing score between s and t (Zens and Ney, 2004). This lexical smoothing score is used as an additional decoding feature.

The formula for the discriminative adapted rule confidence is exactly the same as Equation 3:

$$H(r, \vec{z}) = \log(\epsilon + \frac{\sum_{i=1}^{K} e^{z_i} G_i(r)}{\epsilon + \sum_{i=1}^{K} e^{z_i}}) \quad (6)$$

$$G_i(r) = \frac{\sum_{j=1}^{H_i} b_{ij} \delta_{ij}(r)}{\sum_{j=1}^{H_i} b_{ij}} \quad (7)$$

where r is the adapted rule and $\vec{z}$ are the discriminative system weights. The "occurrence function" $\delta_{ij}(r)$ function returns 1 when the rule r's target phrase $\vec{t}$ is seen *anywhere* in hypothesis ij.

[7]This adaptation performed independently for each test sentence.

5 Parameter Optimization

In this section, we describe a novel procedure for discriminatively optimizing the non-linear parameters $\vec{v}$ and $\vec{z}$ used in Equations 3 and 6. These parameters are jointly optimized alongside the standard log-linear decoding weights to directly maximize BLEU score on a tuning set. In order to perform this optimization, we use a modified version of *maximum BLEU* tuning, called *Expected-BLEU* (Rosti et al., 2010). For the benefit of the reader, we will first give a brief overview of maximum BLEU and Expected-BLEU optimization. Afterwards, we will describe a novel extension to Expected-BLEU which allows for the optimization of non-linear feature parameters.

5.1 Expected-BLEU Optimization

Standard maximum BLEU optimization attempts to find the set of weights $\vec{w}$ that maximizes the 1-best BLEU score over an n-best list, with BLEU (Papineni et al., 2002) defined as:

$$BLEU(\vec{w}) = \left(\prod_{m=1}^{4} \frac{\sum_{i=1}^{N} c_{ib_i(\vec{w})}^{(m)}}{\sum_{i=1}^{N} t_{ib_i(\vec{w})}^{(m)}} \right)^{1/4} \cdot \theta \left(1 - \frac{\sum_i r_{ib_i(\vec{w})}}{\sum_{i=1}^{N} h_{ib_i(\vec{w})}} \right) \quad (8)$$

$$b_i(\vec{w}) = \text{argmax}_{h \in H_i}(S_h(\vec{w})) \quad (9)$$

where $\theta(x) = \min(1.0, e^x)$, N is the number of test sentences, b_i is the 1-best hypothesis of the ith sentence selected using weights $\vec{w}$, and $\{c_{b_i}^{(1)}, c_{b_i}^{(2)}, ...h_{b_i}\}$ are the 10 pre-computed BLEU statistics for hypothesis b_i.[8] Crucially, the selection of 1-best hypotheses with respect to $\vec{w}$ is *discrete*, and therefore the max BLEU function is non-differentiable. Because of this, a line search algorithm such as Powell's method (Powell, 1964) must be used to optimize the weights, which does not perform well when more than few dozen weights are optimized simultaneously.

Expected-BLEU optimization seeks to approximate max BLEU using a continuous objective function. The advantage of this is that it quickly

[8]$c^{(m)}$ is the number of matching m-grams, $t^{(m)}$ is the number of total hypothesis m-grams, r is the reference length, h is the hypothesis length, and $\theta(x)$ is a "brevity penalty" which penalizes short hypotheses.

converges even when tens of thousands of weights are estimated simultaneously. Therefore, instead of discretely selecting a 1-best hypothesis from each of the m test sentences, the BLEU statistics are summed over *every* hypothesis weighted by its corresponding posterior probability. Note that we compute the expectation of each of the 10 BLEU statistics *independently*, so the Expected-BLEU formula is not technically equivalent to the "expected value of BLEU." However, in practice this has not been an issue.

The posterior probability for hypothesis ij is simply the normalized decoding probability:

$$p_{ij}(\vec{w}) = \frac{e^{\gamma S_{ij}(\vec{w})}}{\sum_{k=1}^{n} e^{\gamma S_{ik}(\vec{w})}} \quad (10)$$

The free parameter γ controls the shape of the distribution, with a higher γ shifting more mass towards the 1-best hypothesis.

As a final step, we replace Equation 8's "brevity penalty" $\theta(x) = \min(1, e^x)$ with a differentiable approximate over the range $0.9 \leq x \leq 1.1$. The function is defined as:

$$\phi(x) = \frac{e^x - 1}{e^{1000x} + 1} + 1 \quad (11)$$

The final Expected-BLEU objective function is then:

$$ExpBLEU(\vec{w}) = \left(\prod_{m=1}^{4} \frac{\sum_i \sum_j p_{ij} c_{ij}^{(m)}}{\sum_i \sum_j p_{ij} t_{ij}^{(m)}} \right)^{1/4} \cdot \phi \left(1 - \frac{\sum_i \sum_j p_{ij} r_{ij}}{\sum_i \sum_j p_{ij} h_{ij}} \right) \quad (12)$$

where p_{ij} is short for $p_{ij}(\vec{w})$, as defined in Equation 10. The values $\{c_{ij}^{(m)}, ...\}$ are the same pre-computed BLEU statistics as in Equation 8.

The differentiation of this function with respect to $\vec{w}$ can be performed in a fairly small number of steps using basic calculus, the details of which are provided in (Devlin, 2009). The functions $ExpBLEU(\vec{w})$ and $\frac{dExpBLEU}{dw}$ are used with LBFGS (Liu and Nocedal, 1989) to perform n-best based parameter optimization. We use a standard iterative optimization procedure: (1) Decode tuning set with initial weights $\vec{w}$ and generate n-best list, (2) Optimize $\vec{w}$ on n-best list, (3) Repeat (1) and (2) until convergence, (4) Decode validation set.

In order to prevent over-fitting, we add a standard $L2$-norm regularization term to our objective function:

$$Obj(\vec{w}) = ExpBLEU(\vec{w}) - \alpha ||\vec{w} - \vec{w}'||^2 \quad (13)$$

where $\vec{w}'$ is the initial weight vector at the current iteration of optimization, and α is the regularization term, fixed at 10^{-5}.

5.2 Non-Linear Feature Optimization

The previous section describes the optimization procedure for standard linear decoding weights, but it can also be extended to optimize non-linear weights, as in Equation 3 and Equation 6. We simply modify Equation 1 so that F_i is a function of parameters $\vec{v}_i$:

$$S_h(\vec{w}, \vec{v}) = \sum_{i=1}^{m} w_i \sum_{r \in R_h} F_{ri}(\vec{v}_i) \quad (14)$$

For each non-linear feature type, we must implement $\frac{dF_{ri}}{d\vec{v}_i}$. Then, we can "generically" compute $\frac{dExpBLEU}{dF_{ri}}$ inside of the optimizer and apply the chain rule to compute:

$$\frac{dExpBLEU}{d\vec{v}_i} = \sum_h \sum_{r \in R_h} \frac{dExpBLEU}{dF_{ri}} \frac{dF_{ri}}{d\vec{v}_i} \quad (15)$$

where R_h is the set of rules associated with hypothesis h. This information is usually not available to the optimizer, so this functionality must be added.

The non-linear weights $\vec{v}$ are jointly optimized with the standard decoding weights $\vec{w}$ using the function $ExpBLEU(\vec{w}, \vec{v})$.

5.3 Dissimilarity Optimization

Because the ultimate goal of the cross-adaptation combination is to use it as an additional system in confusion network decoding, it would be beneficial if we could ensure that it contains complementary information. In the past, we have seen that that system combination performs best when the input systems have similar performance but are very different from one another. We model this difference or *dissimilarity* between two sentences using the TER metric, which measures the normalized number of "edits" required to transform the one sentence into another (Snover et al., 2006). Normally, TER is computed on an MT hypothesis against its reference translation. In this case, we instead measured the TER of the cross-adaptation output against the external input system hypotheses.[9]

We attempted to explicitly increase TER dissimilarity by discriminatively optimizing against the input system hypotheses.[10] In other words, we used the input hypotheses as reference translation and optimized in the *opposite* direction that we normally would. We added this as a linear term in our existing Expected-BLEU objective function. Note that Expected-BLEU is computed against the reference translations and Expected TER is computed against the external input systems:

$$\begin{aligned} Obj(\vec{w}, \vec{v}) = & ExpBLEU_{Ref}(\vec{w}, \vec{v}) \\ & +0.1 \cdot ExpTER_{ExSys}(\vec{w}, \vec{v}) \\ & -\alpha ||\vec{w} - \vec{w}'||^2 \end{aligned} \quad (16)$$

The dissimilarity term is weighted at 0.1 in order to prevent the BLEU score from degrading by a significant amount. Note that it is not contradictory to adapt *towards* the input hypotheses while simultaneously optimizing *against* those same hypotheses, because the adaptation is done at the n-gram level and TER is computed on the sentence level. We want to use words and phrases from the input systems, but we don't want the final sentence to be too similar to any one particular input hypothesis.

6 Experiments

The input to our system combination procedure consists of output from 14 different machine translation systems developed independently at 5 different sites. Of these, 7 were "internal" systems developed at our site, while 7 were "external" systems developed at the 4 outside sites. The 7 internal systems all used the same hierarchical decoder and feature set described in Section 3, but varied by source tokenization and method of word alignment. The 7 external systems include a phrasal system, two hierarchical systems, a syntax system, a tree-to-string system, a string-to-tree system, and a hand-crafted rule based system. We will present results on Arabic-to-English web and newswire.

Our parallel training data and development sets consist of publicly available LDC/NIST data, as well as data specific to DARPA's Global Autonomous Language Exploitation (GALE) project. The publicly available training data consists of 3.3 million words of newswire/treebank LDC-released data as well as 118 million words of LDC-released UN data. The GALE-only training data consists of 46 million words of LDC-released data plus 30 million words released by Sakhr Software. The monolingual LM training consists of 4 billion words from the GigaWord corpus and 4 billion words from various other sources such as Google News and New York Times. We use a 3-gram LM for decoding and 5-gram LM for rescoring.

Our development sets were constructed using the NIST MT04, MT05, MT06, and MT08 data sets, as well as the GALE Phase1-Phase4 development/evaluation sets. We use one tuning set, referred to as "Tune," to optimize both the cross-adaptation and confusion network based systems. Our validation set is referred to as "Test." [11]

Our cross-adaptation system uses the features described in Section 4 to actually perform the adaptation, but is otherwise identical to our baseline system, referred to as "Best Single System" or "Internal Best."

Because we use a large number of discriminative features in our baseline MT system, there is a moderate-to-significant over-fitting effect when optimizing on any new set. However, in the past we have found that even a large amount of over-fitting (e.g., 3-4 BLEU points) on the tuning set does *not* have a negative affect on the test set results. Here, we see less than 1.0 BLEU over-fitting during cross-adaptation and less than 0.5 BLEU on the final combination, so we did not take any steps to mitigate it. The proper solution would likely be to use separate sets to optimize the cross-adaptation and the confusion network. The descriptions of the "Tune" and "Test" sets are shown in Table 1.

	Tune		*Test*	
	# sents	# refs	# sents	# refs
ara nw	5456	2.1	1986	1.4
ara web	5454	2.3	2276	2.4

Table 1: "Number of sentences" and "average number of references per sentence" for the development sets.

[9] The "external" input systems are those that were developed at outside sites. Since our internal system is used to perform the cross-adaptation, we do not perform dissimilarity optimization against its baseline output.

[10] Alternately, we could optimize against the confusion network baseline output, but we found that this did not perform well.

[11] The input systems were optimized on a third set, which is not used here.

Since it is not practical to present the scores on all input systems, Table 2 shows BLEU scores for the best internal system as well as the top three external systems. In both cases, the best internal system outperforms all of the external systems. It is interesting to note that the best internal system outperforms the top two external systems by a greater margin on Arabic web than Arabic newswire.

	ara nw		**ara web**	
	Tune	*Test*	*Tune*	*Test*
	BLEU	BLEU	BLEU	BLEU
Internal Best	48.48	45.00	39.77	41.44
External 1st	47.74	44.35	38.27	40.20
External 2nd	47.71	44.20	37.49	39.01
External 3rd	44.84	42.29	36.77	38.54

Table 2: Comparison of best internal system vs. top three external systems. Here, "Tune" is a valid test set, since none of the *input* systems were optimized on it.

One final detail to note is that on Arabic web we performed adaptation using all 14 input systems, while on Arabic newswire we only used the 7 external systems. The reason is that on newswire we encountered an optimization issue where the weights for the internal systems would receive a large value during the first few iterations of tuning, which would cause the optimization to converge at a sub-optimal local maximum. However, even when we manually finessed the optimization, we did not see a gain on cross-adaptation from using all 14 systems on newswire. Because the weights are estimated discriminatively, it should theoretically never be harmful to include additional systems,[12] so we plan to experiment with different types of regularization to solve this optimization issue. On Arabic web, this issue did not occur, so we were able to use all 14 systems without any "manual finessing."

6.1 Cross-Adaptation Results

Tables 3 and 4 show the effect of using the cross-adaptation features from Equations 3 and 6. We use separate weights for each n-gram order as well as the adapted rules, which results in $4K$ total weights, where K is the number of systems.[13]

On Arabic web, our optimized cross-adaptation system (*CA*) gains 3.1 BLEU over our best single system (*BSS*), and gets within 0.4 BLEU of our confusion network baseline (*CN*). When the cross-adaptation output is used as an additional system during confusion network decoding, we see a gain of 0.37 BLEU (*CN w/ CA*). Using the dissimilarity cross-adaptation as a second additional system helps slightly more, bringing the total gain to 0.45 BLEU (*CN w/ CA+DCA*). In both cases, the gain is statistically significant.

	ara web			
	Tune		*Test*	
	BLEU	TER	BLEU	TER
BSS	39.77	47.81	41.44	46.69
BSS w/ "Tune"	42.41	46.39	41.69	46.61
CA, No Opt	43.32	45.55	43.95	44.75
CA	43.52	45.27	44.58	44.49
DCA	41.88	46.44	43.15	45.48
CN	43.10	45.52	45.00	44.56
CN w/ CA	43.70	45.20	45.37*	44.46
CN w/ DCA	43.47	45.27	45.12	44.27*
CN w/ CA+DCA	43.76	45.23	45.45*	44.36*

Table 3: Combination results on Arabic web using 14 input system. * indicates that the system is significantly better than *CN* using a 95% confidence interval, as defined in (Koehn, 2004). Significance is only shown on the Test set. **BSS** = Best single system. **BSS w/ "Tune"** = Tuning on "Tune" using only standard features, instead of the normal decoding tuning set. **CN** = Confusion network baseline. **CA, No Opt** = Cross-adaptation, fixing all of the non-linear system weight to $a_i = 0$, but the standard linear feature weights optimized as normal. **CA** = Cross-adaptation, allowing the non-linear system weights to optimize. **CN w/ CA** = Using the output of *CA* as an additional input in *CN*. **DCA** = Cross adaptation with dissimilarity optimization. **CN w/ DCA** = Using the output of *DCA* as an additional input in *CN*. **CN w/ CA+DCA** = Using the output of both *CA* and *DCA* as an additional input in *CN*.

On Arabic newswire, the optimized cross-adaptation system gains 2.3 BLEU over the best single system, but performs 0.8 BLEU worse than our confusion network baseline. Using the cross-adaptation output as an additional system yields no gain, while using the dissimilarity optimized cross-adaptation output as an additional system yields a minor gain of 0.2 BLEU. However, the gain on BLEU is statistically significant.

We also provide the results on two additional test conditions for Arabic web. The condition *BSS*

[12]It should never harm the results on the tuning set, although it could be harmful on the test set.

[13]We estimate a separate set of weights for (1) unigrams, (2) bigrams, (3) trigrams, and (4) adapted rules.

	ara nw			
	Tune		*Test*	
	BLEU	TER	BLEU	TER
BSS	48.48	38.59	45.00	38.51
CA	51.54	36.37	47.30	36.72
DCA	49.94	37.33	46.27	37.35
CN	51.67	35.87	48.07	35.87
CN w/ CA	52.03	35.91	48.05	35.87
CN w/ DCA	51.81	35.95	48.27*	35.77
CN w/ CA+DCA	52.06	35.84	48.28*	35.71

Table 4: Combination results on Arabic newswire using 7 input systems. Conditions have same meaning as in Table 3.

w/ "Tune" shows the results of optimizing on the system combination tuning set, as opposed to the standard tuning set which all of the input systems were optimized on. We can see that the gain on "Test" is very small, meaning that this difference was not an issue. For the condition *CA, No Opt* we set all of the adaptation weights to a fixed value of $a_i = 0$, so all systems receive an equal "vote" in the adaptation features.[14] As expected, this has a detrimental effect on the results, losing 0.6 BLEU compared to *CA*.

6.2 Dissimilarity Optimization Results

The previous tables demonstrate that although dissimilarity optimization performs worse than standard cross-adaptation, it is still beneficial to use it as an additional system in the confusion network decoding. Table 5 shows how dissimilar the *DCA* output is from the input systems compared to *CA*. The *DisTER* score is computed on the MT output of each condition against the 7 external input systems. We see that on newswire the *DCA* output is 4.5 TER points more dissimilar than the *CA* output, while on web it is 3.1 TER more dissimilar. At the same time, both *DCA* conditions gains 1.0-1.5 BLEU points over the best single system.

	ara nw		ara web	
	Test		*Test*	
	BLEU	DisTER	BLEU	DisTER
BSS	45.00	23.16	41.44	29.65
CA	47.30	15.63	44.58	22.38
DCA	46.27	20.17	43.15	25.50

Table 5: **BSS** = Best single system. **CA** = Cross-adaptation. **DCA** = Cross-adaptation with dissimilarity optimization. **BLEU** is computed against the reference translations, while **DisTER** is computed against the input systems.

[14]Recall that the true weight is e^{a_i}

7 Conclusions and Future Work

In this paper, we presented a novel method of cross-adaptation based system combination which obtains statistically significant BLEU gains over best single system. The advantages of this method are that it can be implemented using only simple decoding features, and that it requires just an n-best list from the input systems, as opposed to alternate cross-adaptation methods that require deeper information. Although this new method does not perform as well as our existing confusion network based combination, we showed that it is beneficial when used as additional system in the confusion network decoding.

We also showed that it is possible to explicitly create a system with complementary information by using *dissimilarity optimization*, where the TER score between the cross adaptation output and the input systems is used as part of the optimization objective function. Although this method of optimization degrades the BLEU score compared to standard cross-adaptation, we showed that it is useful to use this output as a second additional system during confusion network decoding.

In the future, we plan to use the dissimilarity optimization procedure to produce multiple input systems which are explicitly optimized to be different from one another. We already know that it is beneficial to combine multiple systems that use the same decoder/feature set but vary by tokenization/alignment/etc. If we can discriminatively optimize these systems so that they have higher pair wise TER scores without harming their BLEU scores, it may be possible to obtain a larger gain during combination.

Additionally, we presented a highly-scalable, robust method for optimizing arbitrary non-linear feature parameters alongside the standard log-linear decoding weights. We have already used this method to explore many types of new features, such as using a neural net based language model and discriminatively optimizing sentence-level confidence weights on the training data. We plan to further refine our optimization procedure to use additional regularization and normalization, so that very high-dimensional non-linear feature sets can be used without any issues.

References

S. Bangalore, G. Bordel, and G. Riccardi. 2001. Computing consensus translation from multiple machine translation systems. In *ASRU*, pages 351–354.

D. Chiang. 2007. Hierarchical phrase-based translation. *Computational Linguistics*, 33(2):201–228.

J.M. Crego, A. Max, and F. Yvon. 2010. Local lexical adaptation in machine translation through triangulation: SMT helping SMT. In *COLING*, pages 232–240.

L. Cui, D. Zhang, M. Li, M. Zhou, and T. Zhao. 2010. Hybrid decoding: decoding with partial hypotheses combination over multiple SMT systems. In *COLING*, pages 214–222.

J. DeNero, S. Kumar, C. Chelba, and F. Och. 2010. Model combination for machine translation. In *NAACL-HLT*, pages 975–983.

J. Devlin. 2009. Lexical features for statistical machine translation. Master's thesis, University of Maryland.

M.J.F. Gales, X. Liu, R. Sinha, P.C. Woodland, K. Yu, S. Matsoukas, T. Ng, K. Nguyen, L. Nguyen, J.-L. Gauvain, L. Lamel, and A. Messaoudi. 2007. Speech recognition system combination for machine translation. In *ICASSP*, pages 1277–1280.

X. He and K. Toutanova. 2009. Joint optimization for machine translation system combination. In *EMNLP*, pages 1202–1211.

A.S. Hildebrand and S. Vogel. 2008. Combination of machine translation systems via hypothesis selection from combined n-best lists. In *AMTA*, pages 254–261.

P. Koehn. 2004. Statistical significance tests for machine translation evaluation. In *EMNLP*, pages 388–395.

M. Li, N. Duan, D. Zhang, C.-H. Li, and M. Zhou. 2009. Collaborative decoding: partial hypothesis re-ranking using translation consensus between decoders. In *ACL-IJCNLP*, pages 585–592.

D.C. Liu and J. Nocedal. 1989. On the limited memory BFGS method for large scale optimization. *Mathematical Programming*, 45(3):503–528.

K. Papineni, S. Roukos, T. Ward, and W.-J. Zhu. 2002. BLEU: a method for automatic evaluation of machine translation. In *ACL*, pages 311–318.

A. Pauls, J. DeNero, and D. Klein. 2009. Consensus training for consensus decoding in machine translation. In *EMNLP*, pages 1418–1427.

M.J.D. Powell. 1964. An efficient method for finding the minimum of a function of several variables without calculating derivatives. *Computer Journal*, 7(2):155–162.

A.-V.I. Rosti, S. Matsoukas, and R. Schwartz. 2007. Improved word-level system combination for machine translation. In *ACL*, pages 312–319.

A.-V.I. Rosti, B. Zhang, S. Matsoukas, and R. Schwartz. 2009. Incremental hypothesis alignment with flexible matching for building confusion networks: BBN system description for WMT09 system combination task. In *WMT*, pages 61–65.

A.-V.I. Rosti, B. Zhang, S. Matsoukas, and R. Schwartz. 2010. BBN system description for WMT10 system combination task. In *WMT/MetricsMATR*, pages 321–326.

W.A. Rozzi and R.M. Stern. 1991. Speaker adaptation in continuous speech recognition via estimation of correlated mean vectors. In *ICASSP*, pages 865–868.

L. Shen, J. Xu, and R. Weischedel. 2008. A new string-to-dependency machine translation algorithm with a target dependency language model. In *ACL-HLT*, pages 577–585.

D.A. Smith and J. Eisner. 2006. Minimum risk annealing for training log-linear models. In *ACL-COLING*, pages 787–794.

M. Snover, B. Dorr, R. Schwartz, L. Micciula, and J. Makhoul. 2006. A study of translation edit rate with targeted human annotation. In *AMTA*, pages 223–231.

M. Snover, B. Dorr, and R. Schwartz. 2008. Language and translation model adaptation using comparable corpora. In *EMNLP*, pages 857–866.

S. Stüker, C. Fügen, S. Burger, and M. Wölfel. 2006. Cross-system adaptation and combination for continuous speech recognition. In *INTERSPEECH*, pages 521–524.

R. Tromble, S. Kumar, F. Och, and W. Macherey. 2008. Lattice minimum Bayes-risk decoding for statistical machine translation. In *EMNLP*, pages 620–629.

R. Zens and H. Ney. 2004. Improvements in phrase-based statistical machine translation. In *HLT-NAACL*, pages 257–264.

Word Sense Disambiguation by Combining Labeled Data Expansion and Semi-Supervised Learning Method

Sanae Fujita
NTT Communication Science Lab.
fujita.sanae@lab.ntt.co.jp

Akinori Fujino
NTT Communication Science Lab.
fujino.akinori@lab.ntt.co.jp

Abstract

Lack of training data is one of the severest problems facing word sense disambiguation (WSD). To overcome the problem, we propose a method that combines automatic labeled data expansion (Step-1) and semi-supervised learning (Step-2). The Step-1 and 2 methods are both effective, but their combination has a synergistic effect.

In this paper, in Step-1, we automatically extract reliable labeled data from raw corpora using dictionary example sentences, even for infrequent and unseen senses (which do not appear in training data, but appear in a dictionary). Then, in Step-2, we apply a semi-supervised classifier and obtain a improvement using easy-to-get unlabeled data. In this step, we also show that we can guess even unseen senses.

We target a SemEval-2010 Japanese lexical sample WSD task. Both the Step-1 and Step-2 methods performed better than the best published result (76.4 %). Furthermore, the combined method achieved much higher accuracy (84.2 %).

1 Introduction

Many words have multiple meanings that change depending on the context. Recently, it has been confirmed that word sense disambiguation (WSD) improves certain NLP applications such as parse selection (Fujita et al., 2007) or Machine Translation (Chan et al., 2007). In international WSD competitions such as SemEval, many tasks have been proposed, which shows that WSD is a problem that attracts a lot of interest. In this paper, we experiment on the Japanese WSD task from the most recent competition, SemEval-2010 (Okumura et al., 2010).

Various methods have been proposed for WSD (Navigli, 2009). Unsupervised approaches such as clustering based methods (Pedersen, 2006) and extended Lesk (Lesk, 1986) have been shown to do well (Baldwin et al., 2010), although in general, they are beaten by supervised approaches if training data are provided (Tanaka et al., 2007). With the Japanese WSD tasks at SENSEVAL-2 and SemEval-2010, supervised approaches achieved the best results (Murata et al., 2003; Okumura et al., 2010). However, the lack of training data is a severe problem with non-English languages. Also in the Japanese WSD task, there are only 50 given training instances for each target word and this is insufficient.

Two main types of methods have been proposed to compensate for a lack of training data. One type is the semi-supervised learning method (Niu et al., 2005; Pham et al., 2005) or bootstrapping (Mihalcea, 2002, 2004; Yarowsky, 1995). These methods use labeled data and unlabeled data, and this is beneficial because unlabeled training data is easy to obtain. These methods are effective and have high applicability, but unfortunately, there is one problem in that this method cannot obtain training data for senses in the lexicon that do not appear in the training data (we call this an **unseen sense**).

Another type of method designed to make up for a lack of training data, is automatic labeled data expansion (Mihalcea and Moldovan, 1999; Agirre and Martinez, 2000) . They proposed expanding the amount of labeled data through a Web search using monosemous synonyms or unique expressions in definitions from `WordNet` (Fellbaum, 1998). These methods are also effective, and may be able to obtain labeled data even for unseen senses. But one expected problem will be that the performance is influenced by a sense bias (that is sense frequency) that varies with corpora (Agirre and Martinez, 2004).

Therefore, in this paper, we propose a method

ID 37713	Headword とる【取る・採る・執る・捕る】 *toru "take/pick/collect/do/catch"*
0-0-1-0	置いてあったものなどを手に持つ。*"to get something left into one's hand."*
0-0-1-1	手で握り持つ。*"take and hold by hand."*「手に取って見る」*"pick up and see"*
0-0-1-2	手に持ってそれを使って仕事をする。*"hold something in one's hand, and work with it."* 「筆を取る」*"start writing"*
...	...
0-0-8-0	直接に手がけてする意を添える。*"add emphasis of undertaking some action directly."* 「式を取り行う」*"perform a ceremony"*

Figure 1: Simplified Entry from Iwanami Dictionary: とる *toru* "take"

that combines automatic labeled data expansion and semi-supervised learning aiming a synergistic effect. That is, we propose a two-step approach: in the first step (Step-1), we automatically expand the labeled training data from raw corpora. In this step, we aim to expand the labeled training data even for unseen and infrequent senses.

Then, in the second step (Step-2), we apply a semi-supervised classifier. In this step, we aim to achieve on improvement using easy-to-get unlabeled data. In this step, we also compare the results obtained using given training data only and show the benefits of our combination method. We also show its effectiveness for unseen senses.

This paper is structured as follows. We describe the target task in § 2. We describe our automatic labeled data expansion method (Step-1) in § 3, the evaluate the data quality using an experiment and human evaluation in § 4. Then we apply a semi-supervised learning method (Step-2) in § 5. We conclude the paper in § 6.

2 SemEval-2010: Japanese WSD

In this paper, we experiment on the SemEval-2010 Japanese WSD task. The sense inventory used in this task was the `Iwanami` Japanese Dictionary (Nishio et al. (1994)). `Iwanami` was originally paper dictionary. We show an example entry for `Iwanami` in Figure 1. As shown in Figure 1, each entry in `Iwanami` has POS information and definition sentences, and most of entries have example sentences. `Iwanami` has four hierarchical layers in word sense descriptions. In this task, senses at the third layer are used at the evaluation phase. For example, 0-0-1 and 0-0-8 in Figure 1. `Iwanami` includes 60,321 entries split into 85,870 senses, which are merged into 79,611 senses at the third layer. For this task, 50 words (22 nouns, 23 verbs, and 5 adjectives) are selected as the targets, which are split into 219 senses at the third layer; of these, 144 senses appear in the training data. On the other hand, 9 senses are unseen senses that appear in both `Iwanami` and the test data, but do not appear in the training data.

Both the training and test data are part of the Balanced Corpus of Contemporary Japanese: `BCCWJ`[1], which is morphologically analyzed by `UniDic`[2] and hand-corrected. For each target word, 50 instances are provided in both the training and test data. We show an example of the given training data in (1). The given training data are morphologically analyzed, but have no information about the base forms, therefore we added the base forms (lemma) automatically. The given data are also partly tagged with sense IDs of `Iwanami`.

(1) <mor pos=' 動詞-一般' rd=' トッ' bfm=' トル' sense='37713-0-0-1-1' lemma=' 取る'> 取っ</mor>

One feature of this task is that the training and test data come from heterogeneous corpora. The training data include books or magazines (`PB`), newspaper articles (`PN`), and government white papers (`OW`). The test data also include documents from a Q&A site on the WWW (`OC`). However, in this paper, we do not focus on domain adaptation, because 50 instances are insufficient, especially for investigating domain adaptation as reported by Fujita et al. (2010) and Shirai and Nakamura (2010).

3 Method for Automatic Labeled Data Expansion: Step-1

In this section, we introduce our automatic labeled data expansion method (Step-1). The main aim of this step is to obtain reliable labeled data even for unseen and infrequent senses.

[1] http://www.ninjal.ac.jp/kotonoha/

[2] http://www.tokuteicorpus.jp/dist/

As mentioned in § 1, several labeled data expansion methods have been proposed such as Mihalcea and Moldovan (1999) and Agirre and Martinez (2000, 2004). They mainly used `WordNet`'s monosemous synsets (for example, *"recollect"* for *remember*$_1$) for Web search. This kind of method is effective, and offers the possibility of supplying training data for unseen senses. But unfortunately, we cannot obtain monosemous synonyms because our target task is not tagged with `WordNet`.

Therefore, in this paper, instead of these methods, we propose a method that provides reliable training data using example sentences from a dictionary. Such sentences are informative, but in most case of paper dictionaries such as `Iwanami`, the examples are fragmentary to save spaces (in `Iwanami`, an average of 4 words). Therefore, we attempt to extract longer, more natural and high quality labeled data from the raw corpus, under strict conditions using fragmentary examples.

That is, first, we extract example sentences (`EX`) from `Iwanami`. Then, we collect sentences that include an exact match for `Iwanami`'s example for sense (s_k) of headword (h). Finally, we morphologically analyze the candidate sentences, and if both the base form and the coarse POS correspond to those of h, we tag the words with s_k and add the sentences to the labeled data.

For example, we can extract an example sentence as in (2), from 37713-0-0-1-2 in Figure 1. In (2), the headword is in **boldface** and is tagged with '37713-0-0-1-2' (at the third layer, '37713-0-0-1').

(2) 筆 を **取る**
pens ACC pick up
"(I) start writing"

The data used in the Japanese WSD task is part of the `BCCWJ` corpus. Therefore, we use the remainder of the `BCCWJ` to extract the training data. Note that its morphological information is not hand-corrected. According to the readme file that comes with the `BCCWJ`, it includes about 43 million words.

We show an example of extracted labeled data in (3). The underlined part is exactly the same as the example sentence in (2). Therefore we tag 取る *toru* "pick up/take" with 37713-0-0-1-2 and add this entire sentence to the labeled training data.

(3) 筆 を **取る** 気 は 起ら なかっ た
pens ACC pick up feel TOP become not did
"(I) did not get into start writing"

Because of our strict condition, the size and variation of the extracted labeled data are limited. However, this method gave us longer and more natural reliable labeled data. Besides, most languages have dictionaries, and most of these dictionaries include examples, we expect our method to be applicable to other languages and dictionaries.

We show the size of the extracted and given training data (`Trn`) in Table 1. As shown in Table 1, the extracted labeled data give less coverage of sense types to the given training data, but give them many more instances. On average, 130 labeled sentences were extracted per example, for 326 example sentences. And training instances for 9 unseen senses were extracted from `Iwanami`'s `EX`, and 5 unseen senses were extracted from `BCCWJ`.

	Sense Types		Instances	
Corpus	All	Unseen	All	Unseen
`Trn`	144	-	2,500	-
`EX`	156	9	1,450	46
`BCCWJ`	114	5	42,430	94

Table 1: Size of extracted and given training data

4 Evaluation of our Labeled Data Expansion Method: Step-1

In this section, we investigate the reliability and effectiveness of our automatic labeled data expansion. For this purpose, in § 4.1, we investigate the performance over the Japanese WSD task when we apply the supervised learning approach with and without the extracted labeled data. Then in § 4.2, we also provide a quantitative analysis of the extracted training data.

4.1 Performance over Japanese WSD Task

4.1.1 System Description

Machine Learning Methods We constructed supervised and semi-supervised WSD classifiers for each target word, based on machine learning methods. The classifiers for a target word were designed to select a sense from pre-defined senses for an instance of the target word.

In Step-1, we employed a *Maximum Entropy Model (*MEM*)* (Nigam et al., 1999) to design the supervised WSD classifier. Let x denote the feature vector for an instance of a target word and $s \in \{s_1, \ldots, s_k, \ldots, s_K\}$ denote a sense of the target word. For the supervised WSD classifier, for the target words, the conditional probability of s given x is modeled as

$$P(s_k|x;W) = \frac{\exp(w_k^T x)}{\sum_{k'=1}^{K} \exp(w_{k'}^T x)}, \forall k, \quad (4)$$

where $W = [w_1, \ldots, w_k, \ldots, w_K]$ is a parameter matrix and w_k^T represents the transposed vector of w_k. We estimated the parameter matrix value by using labeled data.

Features For each target word w, we used the surface form, the base form, the POS tag, and the coarse POS categories, such as nouns, verbs, and adjectives of w. Then we also used bag-of-words in the same sentence. Here the target is the ith word, so we also used the same information for the $i-2, i-1, i+1$, and $i+2$nd words. We used bigrams, trigrams, and skipbigrams back and forth within three words. And we also used domain type PB, PN, OW, and OC as features.

Analytical Setting One anticipated problem with our expanding method in Step-1 is that the extracted data may have a different sense distribution from test data. Therefore, to investigate trends based on sense distribution, we employed the entropy $E(w)$ of the frequency distribution in given training data, which is given by

$$E(w) = -\sum_{k=1}^{K} p(s_k|w) \log p(s_k|w), \quad (5)$$

where $p(s_k|w)$ is the probability that word w will be sense s_k. In other words, $p(s_k|w)$ and then $E(w)$ reflect sense frequency bias. Note that $p(s_k|w)$ differs from $P(s_k|x)$, which is the probability of sense given *each instance* of the target word.

The entropy $E(w)$ will be lower if one paticular sense appears more frequently. Therefore, following the SENSEVAL-2 Japanese WSD task (Shirai, 2003), we divided the target words into three classes: difficult (D_{diff}: $E(w) \geq 1$), middle (D_{mid}: $0.5 \leq E(w) < 1$), and easy (D_{easy}: $E(w) < 0.5$). There were 9 target words for D_{diff}, 20 for D_{mid}, and 21 for D_{easy}.

4.1.2 Results and Discussion

Learning Curves Because of our strict condition, the variation in the extracted labeled data is limited, therefore, the system may cause over-learning. So first, we investigate the learning curves by limiting the number of added training instances for each Iwanami example.

Table 2 shows average accuracies over target words obtained with various number of added labeled instances per example. $L\#$ in the table shows the upper-bound for adding labeled instances per example. We used all extracted labeled instances when the number was less than #.

We adjusted the parameters based on a 5-fold cross-validation of the given training data. The best result (RALI-2, Brosseau-Villeneuve et al. (2010)) in a formal run of SemEval-2010 is also shown in Table 2 for reference, and the system uses the most frequent sense as a baseline.

	D_{easy}	D_{mid}	D_{diff}	Total
Base Line	**91.5**	67.0	51.3	69.0
RALI-2	-	-	-	76.4
Trn (No expansion)	90.6	70.9	61.1	77.4
+ $L1$	90.7	72.0	64.7	78.5†
+ $L5$	**90.8**	72.1	65.8	78.8†
+ $L10$	90.7	72.9	67.3	79.4 †
+ $L30$	90.7	73.8	68.2	**79.9**†
+ $L50$	90.5	**74.0**	68.0	79.8†
+ $L100$	90.3	73.4	68.2	79.6†
+ $L300$	90.4	73.5	68.2	79.6†
+ All extracted instances	89.7	73.6	**68.9**	79.5
+ EX	89.8	72.2	64.9	78.3
+ $L30$ + EX	90.1	73.3	68.4	79.5
+ $L30$ + EXrL	90.5	**74.8**	**68.4**	**80.2**†

Table 2: Results for given training data (Trn) or with extracted labeled data (by MEM) : where † shows that there is significant improvement over Trn by t-test at 5 % level of significance.

Using only the given training data (we call this Trn, 77.4 %), we achieved an improvement over the best published method (76.4 %). Even only one labeled instance per example gave better results (78.5 %) than the given training data alone, and 30 labeled instances gave the best result (79.9 %) in total[3].

Table 2 shows the accuracy per entropy based difficulty band. We found an interesting trend, namely that expanding the training data tended

[3]All results except "+All extracted instances" significantly improved over Trn.

to degrade the accuracy for easy words (D_{easy}), but improved it for the middle (D_{mid}) and difficult words (D_{diff}). With easy words, the best result (91.5 %) was provided by the selection of the most frequent sense. On the other hand, especially for difficult words, expansion was very effective, and using All extracted instances gave a +7.8 % (= 68.9 − 61.1) improvement over `Trn`. Difficult word means that many more senses appear in corpus. In other words, more instances are needed to guess the sense correctly, that is the reason for our method is especially effective for such difficult words.

Adding Original Example Sentences Then, we investigated other conditions. As shown in § 3, in `Iwanami`, there are 1,450 original example sentences, such as in a sentence (2), for the target words. However we could use only 362 example sentences to extract labeled instances, such as in a sentence (3). Therefore, 1,088 (=1,450-362) example sentences did not used to extract labeled data.

So, we also added original example sentences in 3 patterns: that is adding [1] all the original example sentences (EX), [2] 30 extracted labeled instances (*L30*) and EX, and [3] *L30* and unused example sentences (`EXrL`) that could not be used to obtain labeled data. These results are also shown at the bottom of Table 2[4].

As shown in Table 2, the third pattern (+*L30* +`EXrL`) gave the best results (80.2 %), and it is superior to the patterns using all original examples. The original examples tend to be short, but because shorter examples are easier to match to the raw corpus, we can filter out examples in `EXrL` that are too short.

4.2 Human Evaluation of Extracted Training Data

We also provide a quantitative analysis of the extracted training data. The first 5 sentences extracted from `BCCWJ` were checked manually. Which included 1,038 sentences for 47 words split into 114 senses. Of which 979 sentences (94.3 %) were considered correct.

Because `Iwanami` was different from `WordNet`, we could not make a direct comparison with another expansion method such as (Mihalcea and Moldovan, 1999). But the quality of this manual evaluation result is comparable to that (95.7 %) reported in (Mihalcea and Moldovan, 1999).

4.3 Conclusion in Step-1

In this step, we extracted labeled data automatically using example sentences from `Iwanami`. This method gave us longer, more natural and higher quality labeled data from the raw corpus, and we could obtain the labeled data even for unseen and infrequent senses.

Step-1 provided superior performance (80.2 %) to the state-of-the-art result (76.4 %), and the high effectiveness of this method is proved.

However, it may be difficult to achieve any further improvement because the extracted data may have an unnatural sense distribution and limited variations. Therefore, to realize an improvement, we employ a semi-supervised learning method in Step-2.

5 Employing Semi-supervised Learning Method: Step-2

In Step-2, we constructed a semi-supervised WSD classfier for each target word by using a successful semi-supervised learning method called *Maximum Hybrid Log-likelihood Expectation* (MHLE) (Fujino et al., 2010). It was reported that the MHLE method was useful for obtaining better classification performance especially when there was a large difference between the distributions of the labeled and test data. As mentioned in § 2, the data of the Japanese WSD task is across very different types of corpus; ranging from formal government paper to rough Web data. That was the reason that we employed the MHLE method.

In this section, we first describe the outline of the MHLE-based semi-supervised WSD classifier (in § 5.1), and then we present our method for extracting unlabeled data (in § 5.2). Finally, we undertake an experiment and investigate the effectiveness of our combination of semi-supervised learning and labeled data expansion (in § 5.3).

5.1 MHLE-based semi-supervised WSD classifier

In the MHLE-based semi-supervised WSD classifier for a taget word, the conditional probability, $P(s|x)$, of sense $s \in \{s_1, \ldots, s_k, \ldots, s_K\}$ given the feature vector x of a word instance is modeled by a combination of discriminative and generative models, $P_d(s|x;W)$ and $p_g(x,s;\Theta)$, where W and Θ

[4]Only one result using `EXrL` significantly improved over `Trn`.

are the parameters of these models. By applying the classifier form and training method presented in Fujino et al. (2010), we defined $P(s|x)$ as

$$P(s_k|x;W,\Theta,\beta) = \frac{P_d(s_k|x;W)p_g(x,s_k;\Theta)^\beta}{\sum_{k'=1}^{K} P_d(s_{k'}|x;W)p_g(x,s_{k'};\Theta)^\beta}, \forall k. \quad (6)$$

We also provided the objective function, J for the parameter estimation of $P(s_k|x;W,\Theta,\beta)$ by using labeled and unlabeled datasets, $L = \{(x_n,s_n)\}_{n=1}^{N}$, and $U = \{x_m\}_{m=1}^{M}$ as

$$\begin{aligned} J &= \sum_{n=1}^{N} \log P_d(s_n|x_n;W)p_g(x_n,s_n;\Theta)^\beta \\ &+ \sum_{m=1}^{M} \log \sum_{k=1}^{K} P_d(s_k|x_m;W)p_g(x_m,s_k;\Theta)^\beta \\ &+ \log p(W) + \beta \log p(\Theta). \end{aligned} \quad (7)$$

Here, $\beta(>0)$ is a combination weight. W and Θ can be estimated as the values that maximize J for a fixed β value. The local optimal solution of W and Θ around an initial value can be obtained by an iterative computation such as the EM algorithm (Dempster et al., 1977). Namely, the MHLE-based semi-supervised WSD classifier is constructed by combining the discriminative and generative models trained on both labeled and unlabeled samples (See Fujino et al. (2010) for the details of the combination and training methods).

We employed a maximum entropy model (multinomial logistic regression model) and a naive Bayes model as $P_d(s|x;W)$ and $p_g(x,s;\Theta)$, as well as the text classifier presented in Fujino et al. (2010). In the naive Bayes model, the probability distribution of $x = (x_1,\dots,x_i,\dots,x_V)$ given s is regarded as a multinomial distribution: $p_g(x|s;\Theta) \propto \prod_{i=1}^{V}(\theta_{si})^{x_i}$, and the joint probability distribution of x and s is modeled as $p_g(x,s;\Theta) = p_g(x|s;\Theta)P(s)$. Here, $\theta_{si} > 0$ and $\sum_{i=1}^{V}\theta_{si} = 1$. V represents the dimension of feature vector x, and θ_{si} is the probability that the ith feature appears in an instance whose sense is s. $\Theta = \{\theta_{si}\}_{s,i}$ is the paremeter set of the naive Bayes model. In our experiments, we set $P(s) = 1/K$. We used Gaussian and Dirichlet priors as $p(W)$ and $p(\Theta)$, respectively. We tuned the β ($\in 0.5, 1, 2, 5, 10$) value with a 5-fold cross-validation of the labeled data.

5.2 Extracting Unlabeled Data

As unlabeled data, we extract sentences that include the target words from BCCWJ corpus. We show an example in (8), the **boldface** part indicates the target word.

(8) 年貢 に **取る** べし
annual tax as assess should
"(You) should assess annual tax"

Because of the looser restriction, we can extract many more sentences than the labeled data in § 3. For example, from BCCWJ alone, we can extract more than 10,000 instances for 22 words and more than 1,000 instances for the remaining words except for one (一つ *hitotsu* "one").

5.3 Experiment and Evaluation: Step-2

In this section, we describe an experiment in which we employed a semi-supervised classifier based on MHLE.

This experiment has two purposes; that is to investigate the effectiveness of (a) MHLE based semi-supervised WSD, and (b) automatically expanded data as labeled data.

5.3.1 Results and Discussion

Table 3 shows the results we obtained using unlabeled data extracted from BCCWJ. *U#* in the table shows the number of used unlabeled instances. In this experiment, we limited the unlabeled data to 10, 100, 200, 300, 500 and 1000. The smaller unlabeled data are subsets of the larger unlabeled data. We also use the given training data and several types of expanded data as labeled data.

Effectiveness of MHLE When we used only the given training data as labeled data (Trn), 300 unlabeled data gave the best performance (82.8 %), and it achieved a +5.4 % (= 82.8 − 77.4) improvement.

In addition, in contrast with the results in § 4, some improvements were achieved even for easy words. As described in § 5.1, it has been reported that the MHLE was robust even when the labeled and test data were very different, as with the Japanese WSD task, which came from heterogeneous corpus. Therefore, we can say that this semi-supervised WSD using a hybrid generative/discriminative approach (MHLE) is effective (with respect to purpose (a) above).

Effectiveness of Automatically Expanded Labeled Data We used several types of expanded data as labeled data; that is, Trn +EX, +*L*1, +*L*30, +*L*1 +EXrL, and +*L*30 +EXrL. Note that Trn +*L*30 +EXrL gave the best result in Step-1.

As shown in Table 3, all of the automatically expanded labeled data provided better results than the given training data alone. Therefore, we can say that these automatically expanded data are better than the given training data as labeled data (as regards purpose (b) above).

The labeled data Trn +L30 +ExrL gave the best results in Step-1, but the data that achieved the best result overall was Trn +L1. This shows that ultimately the original (fragmentary) example sentences are no match for the real world sentences extracted from raw corpora. By comparing +L1 with L30, for easy words in particular, +L1 produced better results than +L30 probably because of the sense bias. But for difficult words, +L30 produced better results than +L1.

In conclusion, also in our combination method, larger labeled data expansion was effective for more difficult words.

Learning Curves for Sample Words As shown above, MHLE works very effectively, however, that's not to say that the larger unlabeled data give better results. We show some learning curves for sample target words in D_{mid}, using Trn +L1 as the labeled data in Figure 2. As this figure shows, the behavior is very different from that of the target words.

For some words, the accuracy still is not saturated (For example, 良い *yoi* "good"), but for some words, the accuracy is decreasing (For example, 持つ *motu* "have"). In future work, we will investigate the causes of improvement or degradation.

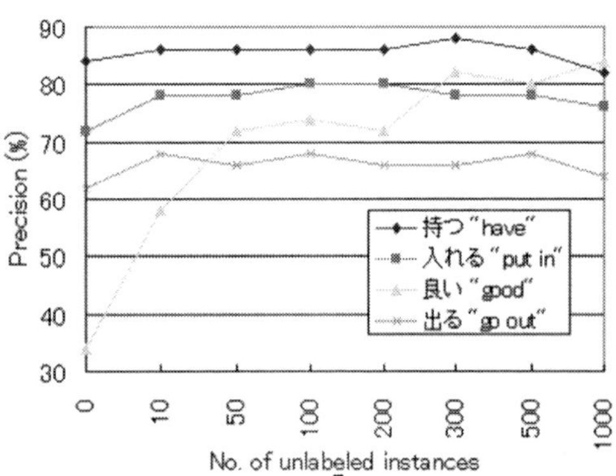

Figure 2: Learning curves for sample target words using expanded training data (Trn +L1) as the labeled data (MHLE) (%)

	D_{easy}	D_{mid}	D_{diff}	Total
Trn	90.6	70.9	61.1	77.4
+U10	91.2	76.7	68.2	81.3
+U100	91.3	78.2	68.4	82.0
+U200	91.9	79.1	69.1	82.7
+U300	91.9	79.6	68.9	**82.8**
+U500	91.3	78.9	68.0	82.2
+U1000	90.9	79.0	68.0	82.0
Trn + EX	89.8	72.2	64.9	78.3
+U10	91.8	77.5	70.4	82.2
+U100	91.9	79.7	70.9	83.2
+U200	92.3	80.4	72.2	**83.9**†
+U300	92.4	80.6	71.1	83.8†
+U500	92.0	80.4	72.2	83.8†
+U1000	91.6	80.6	70.0	83.3
Trn +L30 +ExrL	90.5	74.8	68.4	80.2†
+U10	91.7	78.1	71.1	82.6
+U100	91.8	79.6	72.9	83.5
+U200	91.8	80.3	72.7	**83.8**
+U300	91.9	80.0	71.8	83.5
+U500	91.4	80.5	72.2	83.6†
+U1000	91.4	80.5	72.2	83.4
Trn +L1 +ExrL	90.6	72.9	62.9	78.5†
+U10	91.7	76.2	67.8	81.2
+U100	**92.5**	79.8	70.0	83.4†
+U200	92.3	80.6	70.9	**83.8**†
+U300	92.3	80.4	70.0	83.5
+U500	91.9	81.3	70.4	**83.8**†
+U1000	91.7	80.6	70.0	83.4
Trn + L30	90.7	73.8	68.2	79.9†
+U10	91.6	78.5	71.8	82.8
+U100	91.8	79.2	72.2	83.2
+U200	92.1	79.9	73.1	83.8
+U300	92.2	80.0	**73.6**	**84.0**
+U500	91.5	79.8	72.4	83.4
+U1000	91.0	80.0	72.7	83.3
Trn + L1	90.7	72.0	64.7	78.5†
+U10	92.1	77.1	70.7	82.2
+U100	92.2	79.7	71.1	83.4†
+U300	92.4	**80.9**	72.2	**84.2**†
+U500	92.1	80.8	73.1	**84.2**†
+U1000	91.4	79.7	70.4	83.0

Table 3: Results of semi-supervised learning (MHLE), using given/expanded training data as the labeled data (%): where † shows that there is significant improvement over results using Trn as labeled data by t-test at 5 % level of significance; that is we compared Trn +L1 to Trn, Trn +L1 +U10 to Trn + U10, and so on.

5.3.2 Effectiveness for Unseen Senses

One of the advantages of our method is that it can provide training data even for unseen senses (which did not appear in the given training data but were in the dictionary). Therefore, we investigated the accuracy for unseen senses. In the Japanese WSD task, there are 18 instances for 9 unseen senses (See § 3). Table 4 shows the result for the 18 instances.

When we use expanded labeled data, the system can sometimes guess the unseen senses. The best performance (9 correct (50.0 %)) was achieved by +L30, because more labeled data were provided even for unseen senses. But also with +L1, 6 instances (33.3 %) were correct.

Of course, these unseen senses have no given training data (Trn), so the accuracy is 0 % on Trn. Therefore, no method based on given training data alone (Trn) can guess these senses correctly. So this constitutes a significant improvement.

	No.	%
Trn	0	0.0
Trn + EX	0	0.0
+*U*10 - *U*1000	5	27.8
Trn + *L*30 + EXrL	0	0.0
+*U*10	3	16.7
+*U*100	7	38.9
+*U*200 - *U*1000	**9**	50.0
Trn +*L*1 +EXrL	0	0.0
+*U*10 - *U*1000	2	11.1
Trn + *L*30	0	0.0
+*U*10	2	11.1
+*U*100	5	27.8
+*U*200 - *U*500	**9**	50.0
+*U*1000	4	22.2
Trn + *L*1	0	0.0
+*U*10	2	11.1
+*U*100	4	22.2
+*U*200, *U*300,*U*1000	5	27.8
+*U*500	6	33.3

Table 4: Effectiveness for unseen senses (9 senses, 18 instances)

6 Conclusion

In this paper, we proposed a combination WSD method consisting of automatic labeled data expansion (Step-1) and semi-supervised learning (Step-2). We targeted the SemEval-2010 Japanese WSD task, and showed the effectiveness of our proposed method.

In Step-1, we automatically extracted labeled data from raw corpora. We could extract longer, more natural and higher quality labeled data even for unseen senses, with a strict condition using the fragment examples.

In this step, we had already achieved a better performance (80.2 %) than the best result (76.4 %) in the formal run of the Japanese WSD task.

In Step-2, we employed semi-supervised learning. As the semi-supervised learning method, we employed the hybrid generative/discriminative approach (MHLE), because this method has been reported to be robust even when the labeled and test data were very different as in the Japanese WSD task, which came from heterogeneous corpus.

As a result, in this step MHLE achieved a good improvement (82.8 %), even when using only given training data as labeled data. Moreover, we showed the effectiveness of our expanded data as labeled data. We investigated which type of expanded data was the best as labeled data, then showed that adding only one sentence per original example was the best as labeled data (84.2 %), and could make it possible for the system to guess even unseen senses (33.3 %). In other words, when using labeled data for semi-supervised learning, minimum expansion provides the best performance, and protects the system against sense bias.

In feature work, we intend to investigate the reasons for improvement or degradation. We also intend to perform experiments in which we change the amount of expanded labeled data based on entropy based difficulties.

References

Eneko Agirre and David Martinez. 2000. Exploring Automatic Word Sense Disambiguation with Decision Lists and the Web. *CoRR*, pp. 11–19.

Eneko Agirre and David Martinez. 2004. Unsupervised WSD based on Automatically Retrieved Examples: The Importance of Bias . In *Proceedings of the 2004 Conference on Empirical Methods in Natural Language Processing: EMNLP-2004*, pp. 25–32.

Timothy Baldwin, Su Nam Kim, Francis Bond, Sanae Fujita, David Martinez, and Takaaki Tanaka. 2010. A Reexamination of MRD-based Word Sense Disambiguation. *Transactions on Asian Language Information Process, Association for Computing Machinery (ACM)*, 9(1):1–21.

Bernard Brosseau-Villeneuve, Noriko Kando, and Jian-Yun Nie. 2010. RALI: Automatic Weighting of Text Window Distances. In *Proceedings of the 5th International Workshop on Semantic Evaluation*, pp. 375–378. Association for Computational Linguistics.

Yee Seng Chan, Hwee Tou Ng, and David Chiang. 2007. Word sense disambiguation improves statistical machine translation. In *Proceedings of the 45th Annual Meeting of the Association for Computational Linguistics: ACL-2007*, pp. 33–40.

A. P. Dempster, N. M. Laird, and D. B. Rubin. 1977. Maximum likelihood from incomplete data via the EM algorithm. *Journal of the Royal Statistical Society, Series B*, 39:1–38.

Christine Fellbaum. 1998. A semantic network of English verbs. In Christine Fellbaum, editor, *WordNet: An Electronic Lexical Database*, chapter 3, pp. 70–104. MIT Press.

Akinori Fujino, Naonori Ueda, and Masaaki Nagata. 2010. A robust semi-supervised classification method for transfer learning. In *Proceedings of the 19th ACM International Conference on Information and Knowledge Management (CIKM'10)*, pp. 379–388.

Sanae Fujita, Francis Bond, Stephan Oepen, and Takaaki Tanaka. 2007. Exploiting Semantic Information for HPSG Parse Selection. In *Proceedings of ACL-2007 Workshop on Deep Linguistic Processing*, pp. 25–32.

Sanae Fujita, Kevin Duh, Akinori Fujino, Hirotoshi Taira, and Hiroyuki Shindo. 2010. MSS: Investigating the Effectiveness of Domain Combinations and Topic Features for Word Sense Disambiguation. In *the 5th International Workshop on Semantic Evaluation*, pp. 383–386. Association for Computational Linguistics.

Michael Lesk. 1986. Automatic Sense Disambiguation using Machine Readable Dictionaries: How to Tell a Pine Cone from an Ice Cream Cone. In *Proceedings of the 5th Annual International Conference on Systems documentation*, pp. 24–26.

Rada Mihalcea. 2002. Bootstrapping Large Sense Tagged Corpora. In *Proceedings of the 3rd International Conference on Language Resources and Evaluation: LREC-2002*, pp. 1407–1411.

Rada Mihalcea. 2004. Co-training and Self-training for Word Sense Disambiguation. In *Proceedings of the Conference on Natural Language Learning (CoNLL-2004)*, pp. 33–40.

Rada Mihalcea and Dan Moldovan. 1999. An Automatic Method for Generating Sense Tagged Corpora. In *Proceedings of the American Association for Artificial Intelligence (AAAI-1999)*, pp. 461–466.

Masaaki Murata, Masao Utiyama, Kiyotaka Uchimoto, Qing Ma, and Hitoshi Isahara. 2003. CRL at Japanese dictionary-based task of SENSEVAL-2. *Journal of Natural Language Processing*, 10(3):115–143. (in Japanese).

Roberto Navigli. 2009. Word sense disambiguation: A survey. *ACM Comput. Surv.*, 41(2):1–69.

Kamal Nigam, John Lafferty, and Andrew McCallum. 1999. Using maximum entropy for text classification. In *IJCAI-99 Workshop on Machine Learning for Information Filtering*, pp. 61–67.

Minoru Nishio, Etsutaro Iwabuchi, and Shizuo Mizutani. 1994. *Iwanami Kokugo Jiten Dai Go Han [Iwanami Japanese Dictionary Edition 5]*. Iwanami Shoten, Tokyo. (in Japanese).

Zheng-Yu Niu, Dong-Hong Ji, and Chew Lim Tan. 2005. Word sense disambiguation using label propagation based semi-supervised learning. In *Proceedings of the 43rd Annual Meeting of the Association for Computational Linguistics: ACL-2005*, pp. 395–402.

Manabu Okumura, Kiyoaki Shirai, Kanako Komiya, and Hikaru Yokono. 2010. SemEval-2010 Task: Japanese WSD. In *Proceedings of the 5th International Workshop on Semantic Evaluation*, pp. 69–74. Association for Computational Linguistics.

Ted Pedersen. 2006. *Word Sense Disambiguation: Algorithms and Applications*, volume 33, chapter 6, pp. 133–166. Springer.

Thanh Phong Pham, Hwee Tou Ng, and Wee Sun Lee. 2005. Word Sense Disambiguation with Semi-Supervised Learning. In *Proceedings of the Twentieth National Conference on Artificial Intelligence: AAAI-2005*, pp. 1093–1098.

Kiyoaki Shirai. 2003. SENSEVAL-2 Japanese dictionary task. *Journal of Natural Language Processing*, 10(3):3–24. (in Japanese).

Kiyoaki Shirai and Makoto Nakamura. 2010. JAIST: Clustering and Classification Based Approaches for Japanese WSD. In *Proceedings of the 5th International Workshop on Semantic Evaluation*, pp. 379–382. Association for Computational Linguistics.

Takaaki Tanaka, Francis Bond, Timothy Baldwin, Sanae Fujita, and Chikara Hashimoto. 2007. Word Sense Disambiguation Incorporating Lexical and Structural Semantic Information. In *Proceedings of the 2007 Joint Conference on Empirical Methods in Natural Language Processing and Computational Natural Language Learning: EMNLP-CoNLL-2007*, pp. 477–485.

David Yarowsky. 1995. Unsupervised word sense disambiguation rivaling supervised methods. In *Proceedings of the 33rd Annual Meeting of the Association for Computational Linguistics: ACL-93*, pp. 189–196.

Combining ConceptNet and WordNet for Word Sense Disambiguation

Junpeng Chen
Computer School, Wuhan University,
Wuhan, P. R. China
chenjp@whu.edu.cn

Juan Liu*
Computer School, Wuhan University,
Wuhan, P. R. China
liujuan@whu.edu.cn

Abstract

Knowledge-based Word sense Disambiguation (WSD) methods heavily depend on knowledge. Therefore enriching knowledge is one of the most important issues in WSD. This paper proposes a novel idea of combining WordNet and ConceptNet for WSD. First, we present a novel method to automatically disambiguate the concepts in ConceptNet; and then we enrich WordNet with large amounts of semantic relations from the disambiguated ConceptNet for WSD. The evaluation experiments on the Semeval-2007 coarse-grained all-words disambiguation task show that the enriched WordNet can significantly improve the performance of knowledge-based WSD methods.

1 Introduction & Motivation

1.1 Introduction

Word sense Disambiguation (WSD) is a task of selecting the proper sense of ambiguous terms in the text. WSD is an intermediary step within many Natural Language Processing (NLP) applications, such as text summarization, machine translation, text processing, and so on. Finding a solution to the WSD problem is essential or even compulsory for such NLP applications.

There are two main classes of WSD approaches: supervised WSD, and knowledge-based WSD. The former employs statistical learning to learn a classifier from training data. The preparation for these training data may be laborious and erroneous. Moreover, building a manually annotated corpus, as required by supervised WSD methods, to cover all word senses in lexicon is expensive, and even infeasible. In contrast, knowledge-based WSD methods rely on the use of wide-coverage knowledge resources. These methods do not need the human labeled training data. The widely used knowledge resource in such methods is WordNet (Fellbaum, 1998). However, WordNet-based WSD methods usually achieved lower performance compared to supervised methods, mainly due the fact that the lexical and semantic knowledge contained in WordNet is not sufficient for WSD.

Therefore, many methods (see Section2) have emerged to enrich WordNet with the lexical and semantic knowledge for WSD purpose, such as by using Wikipedia, on-line lexicons, domain, and so on. The literature research results show that the use of enriched knowledge does improve the performance of WordNet based WSD systems, in terms of both accuracy and coverage.

However, most of the present methods mainly focus on enriching WordNet with limited lexical and taxonomic knowledge. Though Wikipedia contains many semantic relations, the knowledge extracted from Wikipedia may contain noises, for some of them are derived from weak semantic links, and lack of confidence.

In this paper, we propose to use ConceptNet (Havasi&Alonso, 2007) with the large amounts of semantic relations between concepts, to enrich WordNet. For there are many ambiguous concepts existed, ConceptNet cannot be directly used to enrich WordNet. Thus, we develop a novel methodology to automatically disambiguate the ambiguous ConceptNet concepts. By using the disambiguated ConceptNet, we can enrich semantic relations in WordNet. To evaluate performance of WSD based on the extended WordNet, we implement a simple knowledge-based algorithm and its extension, embedded with WordNet, WordNet+ConceptNet, respectively. The comparison results show that using WordNet along with disambiguated ConceptNet can make even simple knowledge-based algorithms achieve state-of-the-art performances.

*the corresponding author

1.2 ConceptNet

ConceptNet is a large collaborative Web knowledge resource, which encompasses commonsense knowledge about the spatial, physical social, temporal and psychological aspects of everyday life (e.g., airplane is capable of flight, plane relates to geometry). It is useful in a wide variety of applications such as speech recognition (Lieberman et al., 2005), intelligent user interface (Speer et al., 2009), machine translation (Caseli et al., 2010), and so on.

Until 2011, ConceptNet contains nearly one million of assertions represented as triplets like *<concpet1, relation, concept2>*, to define the concrete semantic relations between two specific concepts. All the assertions are organized as a semantic network, where a node stands for a concept, and an edge stands for a relation between two concepts. There are above 400,000 concepts in ConceptNet, each of them are denoted as either a word or a phrase, and labeled by a unique identifier. In addition, ConceptNet defines nearly thirty kinds of semantic relations, such as CapableOf (agent's ability), SubeventOf (event hierarchy), MotivationOf (affect), DesireOf (want to), and so on, most of which are not included in WordNet. Therefore, if extending WordNet with the large amounts of semantic relations contained in ConceptNet, it is desirable to improve the performances of WordNet-based WSD methods.

However, ConceptNet cannot be directly used for WSD purpose due to the existence of polysemy and synonymy of the concepts in it.

Polysemy is the tendency for ConceptNet concepts to have multiple senses. For example, a ConceptNet concept *plane* has two word senses: "a fixed-wing aircraft", or "an unbounded two-dimensional shape". Which sense should be used depends on the considered assertion including the concept. Therefore, we should first assign the correct senses for those concepts in the assertions before using them to enrich WordNet.

Synonymy is another tendency for the concepts in ConceptNet to have a common word sense. For example, the concept *airplane* has only one sense: "a fix-wing aircraft", which is also the first sense of the concept *plane*. It is obvious that the concepts related to *airplane* should have the same relation with *plane*. However, it is not the case in ConceptNet. Concept *airplane* has an atLocation relation with the concept *airplane hangar*, whereas *plane* has not such relation with *airplane hangar*. This leads to the inconsistency of knowledge base. Therefore assigning the correct senses for the ambiguous concepts in the assertions to find the synonym concepts will improve the quality of the knowledge base.

2 Related Work

Up to now, there are many approaches to enrich the knowledge of WordNet for WSD tasks. For instances, Magnini&Cavaglià (2000) proposed to use domain knowledge to assign domain labels to most WordNet synsets. Some researchers (Mihalcea&Moldovan, 2001; Navigli, 2009; Hwang et al., 2011) proposed to enrich semantic relations by means of the disambiguation of the glosses of WordNet or other machine-readable dictionaries. Some other researches (Agirre et al., 2000; Cuadros&Rigau, 2008) extract semantic relations from Web to enrich WordNet. However, all above methods mainly aim to enrich lexical and taxonomic resources. Therefore some recent work (Mihalcea, 2007; Ponzetto&Navigli, 2010) exploits Wikipedia, a large collaborative Web encyclopedia, to extract the knowledge for WSD. However, the type of semantic relations extracted from Wikipedia is uncertain. Moreover, it is hard to know which semantic relations are transitive or belong to the same type (e.g. isA, part of).

Different with the existed methods, we propose to use Conceptnet to enrich the knowledge in WordNet, which has several advantages over previous works. First, ConceptNet is a large-scale commonsense knowledge base for many aspects of everyday life, such as spatial, physical social, temporal, psychological, and so on. Injecting such knowledge from ConceptNet into WSD system can effectively relieve the knowledge acquisition problem in WSD. Second, the semantic relations from some of the previous work such as Wikipedia are extracted in an indirect way, each of which has no a clear relation type. Thus some of those semantic relations are too weak to be filtered (Ponzetto&Navigli, 2010). In contrast, the semantic relations in ConceptNet are directly defined as assertions, each of which has a very clear relation type. Therefore, the semantic relations in ConceptNet are expected to be more robust than the others.

3 Disambiguating ConceptNet

For there are many ambiguous concepts existed in ConceptNet, it cannot be directly used to enrich WordNet for WSD. It is necessary to disambiguate the ambiguous ConceptNet concepts.

Assume concept *plane* have two senses. The first one is "a fixed-wing aircraft"; and the second one is "an unbounded two-dimensional shape". Given a ConceptNet assertion *<plane, usedFor, fly>*, one can easily judge the appropriate sense of *plane* in this assertion to be the first sense of *plane*. That is because people do not simply regard a sense of a word as an abstract symbol, but a concrete entity that has many properties. For the first sense of *plane*, people may think that it is an *aircraft*, also named *airplane*, and has *wings*, etc. For the second sense of *plane*, people may think that it is a *shape*, or a *form*, and relates to *mathematics*, etc. The concepts *aircraft*, *airplane*, and *wing* relate to *fly* more closely than *shape*, *form*, and *mathematics*. By integrating such information, people can easily know the correct sense of *plane* in the assertion *<plane, usedFor, fly>*.

We propose a method to simulate the human's processing of disambiguating ambiguous concepts by three steps. Given a ConceptNet assertion *<c, relation, d>*, where concept *c* is ambiguous (the cases of *d* being ambiguous or both *c* and *d* being ambiguous are the similar), in order to disambiguate *c* in this assertion, firstly, we construct a word sense profile (WSP) for each sense of *c*. A WSP is a set of terms (words) relating to a sense, it describes the sense in a whole (Section 3.1). Secondly, we measure the relatedness between the terms in WSP with *d* in the same assertion based on NGD (Section 3.2). Thirdly, we filter out the noisy terms in WSP, which would decrease the performance of ConceptNet disambiguating (Section 3.3).

As a result, we calculate the score of the WSP for each sense, and choose the sense with the lowest WSP score as appreciated one for the ambiguous concept in the assertion. Therefore, for each ambiguous concept of every ConceptNet assertion, we can assign the appropriate sense to it according to the WSP scores; and the resulted ConceptNet can be used to extend WordNet.

3.1 Constructing Word Sense Profile

As we all know, WordNet is structured as a semantic network in which nodes stand for a concept **sense**, and are linked by a small set of semantic relations such as hypernymy, hyponymy, meronymy, and so on. For ambiguous concepts with multiple senses, there are multiple nodes in the network. The concept sense is represented by a **synset** (a set of words sharing a common meaning, each word is called a synonymy in the synset). For an example, for concept *plane*, we can use plane_n^1 as the label of one of its senses, in which the subscript and superscript indicate its part of speech (e.g. "n" stands for noun) and sense no., respectively; and its synset is denoted as plane_n^1 = (airplane, aeroplane, plane), illustrating that this synset is consist of three synonymys: *airplane*, *aeroplane* and *plane*. Moreover, each synset has a textual definition, namely **gloss**. For instance, the gloss of synset plane_n^1 is "an aircraft that has a fixed wing and is powered by propellers or jets".

Given a WordNet synset *S*, we make use of the following knowledge resources to construct its **Word Sense Profile**, WSP(*S*).

Synonymy: all synonyms in *S*. For an example, three synonyms in the synset plane_n^1 will all be included in the WSP(plane_n^1).

Hypernymy/Hyponymy: all synonyms in the hypernym synset *H* of *S* (e.g., *S* is a kind of *H*) or in the hyponym synset *H* of *S* (e.g., *H* is a kind of *S*). For instance, the hypernym of synset plane_n^1 is $\text{heavier-than-air craft}_n^1$ = (heavier-than-air craft), then the synonym *heavier-than-air craft* will also be included in WSP(plane_n^1).

Meronymy/Holonymy: all synonyms in synsets *M* which has a meronymy (e.g., *M* is a part of *S*) or a holonymy (e.g., *S* is a part of *M*) relation with *S*, will be containd in WSP of S. For example, given a synset plane_n^1, one of the meronymies plane_n^1 is pod_n^4=(pod, fuel pod), so *pod* and *fuel pod* will also be included in WSP(plane_n^1).

Gloss: the set of words in the gloss of *S*. For example, the gloss of synset plane_n^1 is "an aircraft that has a fixed wing and is powered by propellers or jets". After removing the stop words, the remaining words will be included in WSP(plane_n^1).

Indirect Resources: Besides above direct relations in WordNet, we also use some indirect ones that are derived from the transitivity of WordNet semantic relations, to construct the WSP. Given a synset *A*, if *A* has a direct relation with synset *B*, *B* has a direct relation with synset *C*, and then *A* has an indirect relation with *C*. Therefore, *C* is regarded as an indirect resources for *A* and all synonyms of *C* are also added in the WSP(*A*).

For a synset *S*, WSP(*S*) is defined as the set of words obtained from direct or indirect resources.

3.2 Measuring Relatedness

Given a ConceptNet assertion *<c, relation, d>*, after getting the WSP of each sense of the ambiguous concept *c*, we need to know which sense is the most likely one in this assertion by calculating a score for the WSP. To do so, we first measure the relatedness between a term in the WSP and *d*, and then compute the arithmetic mean of the values as the score of the WSP.

Normalized Google Distance (NGD) (Cilibrasi et al., 2007) was proposed to measure semantic relatedness between two terms using the vast available knowledge on the Web. Concretely, NGD takes advantage of the number of hits returned by search engine such as Google, to compute the distance between terms. Small NGD value indicates close relatedness, while large value suggests the opposite. Given a term pair <*x*, *y*>, the normalized Google distance between *x* and *y*, NGD(*x*, *y*), can be obtained as follows:

$$NGD(x,y)=\frac{\max\{\log f(x),\log f(y)\}-\log f(x,y)}{\log N-\min\{\log f(x),\log f(y)\}} \quad (1)$$

Where *f(x)* is the number of Google hits for the term *x*, *f(y)* is the number of Google hits for the term *y*, *f(x, y)* is the number of Google hits for both terms *x* and *y*, and *N* is the number of web pages indexed by Google. The smaller the NGD score, the more related the two terms are.

According to the definition, it is desirable to use NGD to measure the relatedness between any term in the WSP and *d*.

Note that we always compute the NGD scores in the context of ConceptNet assertion <*c, relation, d*>. That is, we only need to consider the relatedness between *d* and the term in WSP(*c*). Therefore, we sometimes simply say the NGD score of a term in this paper without confusion.

3.3 Filtering the Noise Terms

Ideally, the NGD score of any term in the WSP of the correct sense is lower than that in the WSP of incorrect sense, thus we can simply use the arithmetic mean of the scores to evaluate the relatedness of WSP and the assertion. However, it is inevitable that there are some noisy terms in WSPs, which will dramatically decrease the performance of disambiguating ConceptNet. Therefore, we need to pay efforts to reduce such noises.

There are two kinds of noises: those from WSP of the correct sense, and those from WSP of the wrong sense(s). Suppose we have an assertion <*c, relation, d*>, where concept *c* is ambiguous and has two senses c_n^1 and c_n^2. Corresponding to the assertion, the correct sense of *c* is c_n^1, and a wrong sense of *c* is c_n^2.

Then the first kind of noises are from WSP(c_n^1), which do not have close relation to *d*. Thus their NGD scores should be high, though they have a WordNet relation to c_n^1. For an example, given a ConceptNet assertion <*plane, isA, vehicle*>, the correct sense of *plane* is plane_n^1 (a fixed-wing aircraft). Term *navigation light* is in WSP(plane_n^1), however there is no close relatedness between *navigation light* and *vehicle*, resulting that it is a noisy term in WSP(plane_n^1), belonging to the first group. Obviously, this kind of noises have high NGD scores and would increase the score of the WSP of the correct sense, thus correspondingly decrease the probability of selecting the correct sense as the appreciated sense of ambiguous concept.

The second kind of noises are from WSP(c_n^2), which have close relation to *d* whereas occur in the incorrect WSP. Since they are closely related to *d*, their NGD scores are usually low, hence lower the score of the WSP of the wrong sense, which may lead to selecting the wrong sense as the appreciated one for ambiguous concept. Such noises mainly come from the ambiguous terms contained in the WSPs. For an instance, *basketball* has two word senses: basketball_n^1 ("a game played on a court by two opposing teams of 5 players"), or basketball_n^2 ("an inflated ball used in playing basketball"). Based on WordNet, it is easy to get WSP(basketball_n^1) = (game, handball,...), and WSP(basketball_n^2) = (ball, handball,...). We can see that *handball* occurs in both WSPs. In fact, *handball* is itself ambiguous and has two senses: handball_n^1 ("a small rubber ball used in playing the game of handball"), handball_n^2 ("a game played in a walled court"). Given a ConcepNet assertion <*basketball, isA, popular sport*>, it is clear that the correct sense of *basketball* should be basketball_n^1, while basketball_n^2 is not the appropriate one for this assertion. It is desirable that all terms in WSP(basketball_n^2) have high NGD scores. However, it is not the case for term *handball*. According to handball_n^1, we know that the NGD score of *handball* should be low, for *handball* and *popular sport* frequently cooccur in the Web. There is no problem for the occurrence of *handball* in WSP(handball_n^1). However, it is because the computation of NGD score does not consider different senses of the same term in different occurrences, different *handballs* in different WSPs actually have the same NGD scores though they correspond to different senses. As a result, the term "*handball*" in WSP(basketball_n^2) becomes a noise to the assertion *<basketball, isA, popular sport>* for it improperly lower the score of WSP(basketball_n^2) and increase the risk of assigning the sense basketball_n^2 to concept *basketball* in the assertion.

Of course, in real applications, it is impossible to know which kind of noises exist and where they are in advance. Moreover, whether a term in a WSP is a noise may depend on the specific ConceptNet assertion, just as the *handball* in above example. We simply try three filters by using different strategies in the calculation of WSP scores: TopN filter, Threshold filter and Top r% filter.

TopN filter only selects the top *n* terms with the smallest NGD scores to take part in the calculation of WSP score. Threshold filter only retains the terms with NGD scores lower than a predetermined threshold value *t* to compute WSP score. Top r% filter supposes that the number of noise terms may be proportionate to the size of WSP, and only selects the top *r%* terms with the smallest NGD scores to compute the WSP score.

Obviously, all of above strategies aim to reducing the first kind of noises by disregarding the terms with larger NGD scores. In fact, it is hard to filter out the second kind of noises for most of them are related to the specific concept sense, which keeps unknown before the calculation of WSP scores. Furthermore, there is also the dilemma due to the filtering that the second kind of noises are more likely to be retained for they have lower NGD scores.

Nevertheless, we could still avert the second kind of noises to some extent, not by filtering, but by preventing them from being added into the WSP. Now that the second kind of noises mainly comes from the ambiguous terms, we can analyze which relationships defined in Section 3.1 may introduce more ambiguous terms thus could not be taken into consideration. We will address this problem in Section 4.1.3.

4 Experiments

Our evaluation experiments consist of two steps. The first step is to evaluate the intrinsic quality of the disambiguated ConceptNet (Section 4.1), including the selection of the noise filters and analysis of effects of different combinations of WordNet relationships on the disambiguation results. The second step is to evaluate the impact of combining disambiguated ConceptNet and WordNet for coarse-grained WSD by comparing different methods (Section 4.2).

4.1 Evaluation of the Disambiguating ConceptNet

To our best knowledge, there is no literature work for ConceptNet disambiguation before. So we first generate the test bed as the gold standard for evaluations; and then compare our disambiguated concepts to this gold standard to see how many of them are matched. We also compare different noise filtering strategies mentioned in Section 3.3 and accordingly choose the best one as the final noise filter. To avoid introducing more second kind of noises when generating WSPs, we also investigate different combinations of WordNet relationships mentioned in Section 3.1 by comparing by disambiguating accuracies.

4.1.1 Gold Standard Generation

To evaluate our ConcepNet disambiguating methods, we created a gold standard data as follows. First, we randomly selected a set of 1,000 assertions from the ConceptNet, and checked whether the included concepts have multiple senses in WordNet. By doing so, we found 425 ambiguous concepts with more than one WordNet senses, which are contained in 365 of the 1,000 assertions. Then we asked a language expert to annotate the WordNet senses for the ambiguous concepts in these ConceptNet assertions. To see whether the annotations are convincible, we asked a different expert to tag the same 425 ambiguous concepts in the 365 assertions independently. The kappa coefficient (Carletta, 1996), which is used to calculate the inter-annotator agreement, show that the two annotations achieved a perfect agreement with coefficient as 0.9. Therefore, we use the first annotation results as the gold standard to evaluate our methods.

4.1.2 Comparison of Three Filter Methods

To compare different filtering strategies mentioned in Section 3.3, we first construct WSP for each sense of the 425 concepts, and then calculating the WSP scores after noise filtering by different strategies separately; finally, we annotate each concept with a sense according to the WSP scores. We also did the concept annotation by calculating the WSP scores without noise filtering for reference. In the construction of WSP, we made use of the following six WordNet resources: synonymy, hypernymy, hyponymy, meronymy/holonymy, gloss, and hyponymy→ gloss (the gloss of the hyponymy; the similar denotations are also used in the following). Section 4.1.3 will show the reason.

To investigate the significance of the WSP score based annotation method against the random or dominant annotation, we also assigned a sense to each concept, by randomly selecting one from the available senses and by selecting the most frequent sense, respectively.

Table 1 shows annotation accuracies of different methods, where "MFS BL" and "Random BL" correspond to the performances of random and dominant annotation respectively. In the experiments, we set n=10 for TopN filter, t=0.2 for Threshold filter, and r=20 for Top r% filter. These parameter values were set by our experience, to achieve the best performances on the 425 concepts.

Filter	Accuracy
TopN Filter	**82.4%**
Threshold Filter	61.4%
Top r% Filter	60.5%
No Filter	44.0%
MFS BL	57.4%
Random BL	20.8%

Table1. Performance of the disambiguating ConceptNet using different filter methods

From Table 1 we can see that, the annotation results of WSP based methods are much more significant than the random method, and the use of noise filtering can significantly enhance the accuracy of the annotation. Without noise filtering, the WSP based method shows even worse performance than the MFS baseline (-17.4%), which demonstrates that there are actually some noise terms in WSP that decrease the performance of ConceptNet disambiguating.

In addition, we also see that though all of the filter methods can effectively filter out the noise terms from the WSP thus improve the performance of WSP method, TopN filter is significantly better than the other two (+21.9% and +21.0% compared to Top r% Filter and Threshold Filter respectively). This suggests that TopN would be the most appropriate filter method for removing the noise terms from WSPs. We think the result might due to the following factors. Firstly, Threshold filter cannot effectively remove the second kind of noise terms, because it may filter out too much right terms from the WSP of a wrong sense, while remain terms belonging to the second kind of noise. Therefore, there are not enough right terms to relieve the second kind of noise terms for the wrong sense. Secondly, the sizes of the WSPs may vary wildly. For the senses whose WSP size are small, Top r% filter may remain too few terms (e.g. only two or three terms), thus the WSP scores are very sensitive to the remain noises. Finally, for each sense, TopN filter remains a fixed number of terms. If the second kind of noise terms exists, there might be enough right terms to relieve the impact of those noise terms if we set the proper value to parameter n.

Therefore, in the comparative experiments, we only consider the TopN filter. In order to get a proper value of n, we investigated the performance of the filter by ranging n from 1 to 50 stepped by one and found that it is appropriate for TopN filter to set n in [6, 11]. In our work, we set n=10.

4.1.3 Investigation on the Resources Combination

Just mentioned in Section 3.3, WordNet resources defined in Section 3.1 may introduce the second kind of noises. Due to the fact that this kind of noises is hard to be filtered out, we should prevent such noises from entering the WSPs as possible as we can. Therefore, we tried different combinations and evaluate our ConceptNet disambiguating method, to investigate which combination is the best for our task.

Although hypernymy, hyponymy, and meronymy/holonymy are transitive, and can generate the indirect WordNet resources, the number of meronymy/holonymy is far below than those of the other two in the WordNet. Thus, we ignore the indirect WordNet resources derived from meronymy/holonymy. As a result, ten WordNet resources are used as the candidate resources to construct WSP. Five of them are direct WordNet resources (synonymy, hypernymy, hyponymy, meronymy/holonymy, and gloss), and five are indirect WordNet resources: hypernymy → hyponymy, hypernymy → gloss, hypernymy → hypernymy, hyponymy→hyponymy, and hyponymy→gloss.

Table 2 summarizes the highest accuracies of our ConceptNet disambiguating method with different combinations of WordNet resources against the 425 annotated concepts. The results show that our method achieves the highest accuracy with the six WordNet resources: hyponymy → gloss, gloss, hyponymy, hypernymy, meronymy/holonymy, and synonymy. The combination of the six resources is abbreviated as "six resources" (We also tried to combine the direct resources with any of other four indirect resources, the results show that they cannot improve and even decrease the performance. Especially, hypernymy→hyponymy dramatically decreases accuracy (-8.94% compared to the "six resources"). Therefore, we do not list the accuracies of combining other indirect resources with the direct ones). We also noticed that based on the "six resources", the accuracy will be decreased by adding any new indirect WordNet resource. All of above facts imply that the indirect WordNet semantic resources except hyponymy→gloss may contain much more noise terms than the direct resources, especially the second kind of noises. Therefore, in order to avoid introducing too many noises, we chose the combination of "six resources" to construct WSP, and then disambiguate the ConceptNet for extending WordNet purpose.

Resources combination	**Accuracy**
Hyponymy→gloss	68.2%
Hyponymy→gloss + gloss	73.4%
Hyponymy→gloss + gloss + hyponymy	76.2%
Hyponymy→gloss + gloss + hyponymy+ Hypernymy	78.1%
Hyponymy→gloss + gloss + hyponymy+ hypernymy+ meronymy/holonymy	80.7%
Hyponymy→gloss + gloss + hyponymy+ hypernymy+ meronymy/holonymy+ synonymy	**82.4%**
Six resources+ hyponymy→hyponymy	80.5%
Six resources+ hypernymy→hypernymy	80.2%
Six resources+ hypernymy→gloss	79.8%
Six resources+ hypernymy→hyponymy	73.4%

Table2. The highest accuracies of disambiguating ConceptNet with different size of WordNet resources

4.2 Evaluation of WSD Methods

After disambiguated, the ConceptNet can be used to extend WordNet for WSD. In order to evaluate the impact of combining disambiguated ConceptNet and WordNet, we performed the comparative experiments on the Semeval-2007 coarse-grained all-words WSD dataset (Navigli et al., 2007) . We have chosen coarse-grained word sense disambiguation because the meanings of the ambiguous concepts in the ConceptNet assertions are naturally coarser than those in WordNet are. For example, given a ConceptNet assertion <*rain, isA, water*>, assigning either the first sense ("water falling in drops from vapor condensed in the atmosphere") or the second sense ("drops of fresh water that fall as precipitation from clouds") in WordNet to *rain* is suitable.

Since the aim of our experiment is to evaluate the impact of extended knowledge resource on WSD performance, the WSD algorithm is not the core of our work. Anyway, we implemented a simple knowledge-based algorithm, namely GM (Galley&McKeown, 2003), and our extending version. GM algorithm processes text sequentially, and compares current word to all of the previous words. If one of the senses of the current word has a semantic relation (synonymy, hypernym, hyponym, hypernymy→hyponymy) with any senses of previous words, then there is a weighted semantic edge between these two senses. After processing the whole text, a disambiguated graph is built, whose nodes represent the word senses and edges stand for the four kinds of semantic relations. Finally, for each sense of a target word, all scores of the edges linked to it are summed up as its score. The sense with the highest score is chosen as the correct sense for the target word.

In addition, we simply extend GM algorithm by considering more semantic relations. The extended algorithm is called as ExtGM. In details, in the semantic network of WordNet, if the length of the shortest path between two senses is not greater than four, we also consider that there exists a semantic relation between them, and assign the weight of this semantic relation as the inverse of the length. Since we did not focus on the WSD algorithms, the values of the two parameters (length, weight) of the implemented algorithms were not optimized.

Resource	**Method**	**P**	**R**	**F_1**
WordNet	GM	86.9	55.0	67.4
	ExtGM	**87.4**	70.6	78.0
WordNet + ConceptNet	GM	83.7	73.6	78.3
	ExtGM	85.5	**79.9**	**82.6**
WordNet + Wikipedia	Degree	87.3	72.7	79.4
	MFS BL	77.4	77.4	77.4
	Random BL	63.5	63.5	63.5

Table3. Performance on Semeval-2007 coarse-grained all words WSD (nouns only subset)

Table 3 shows the evaluation results of GM and ExtGM on Semeval-2007 coarse-grained all-words dataset, by using different knowledge resources: WordNet, WordNet+CocneptNet, where

P, R, and F_1 represent precision, recall and F1-measure respectively. We also use the random chosen sense (Random BL) and the most frequent sense (MFS BL) as baselines.

From this table, we can see that enriching WordNet with semantic relations from ConceptNet yields a significantly improvement against only using WordNet.

We also listed the result of Degree on WordNet+Wikipedia (Ponzetto&Navigli, 2010) in Table 3, from which we can see that compared to Degree, our method attains a slight variation in precision, but a significantly high increase in recall. The result shows that ConceptNet can increase recall for WSD more effectively than Wikipedia, though the size of Wikipedia is larger than that of ConceptNet. The reason may be that ConceptNet focuses on basic, unspoken knowledge which is obvious or common sense, therefore knowledge in ConceptNet may be more frequently used than those in Wikipedia.

Resource	Method	P	R	F_1
ConceptNet	ExtGM	**85.4**	**46.4**	**60.1**
ConceptNet(MFS)	ExtGM	80.9	43.4	56.5
	MFS BL	77.4	77.4	77.4

Table4. Performance on Semeval-2007 coarse-grained all words WSD (nouns only subset, and ConceptNet Only)

We further evaluate ExtGM on the two different ConceptNet: ConceptNet disambiguated by our method; ConceptNet disambiguated by MFS strategy, which assigns the most frequent sense to each ambiguous ConceptNet concept. The results are shown in Table 4, which illustrates that our method can attain significantly high increase in precision and recall. This proves that our ConceptNet disambiguating method is effective.

Algorithm	Nouns only F_1	All word F_1
ExtGM	**84.1**	**82.8**
SUSSX-FR	81.1	77.0
NUS-PT	82.3	**83.2**
MFS BL	77.4	78.9
Random BL	63.5	62.7

Table5. Performance on Semeval-2007 coarse-grained all-words WSD with MFS as a back-off strategy when no sense is assigned

Finally we compare the ExtGM with WordNet+ConceptNet to state-of-the-art WSD systems: SUSSX-FR (Koeling&McCarthy, 2007) and NUS-PT (Chan et al., 2007), which are the best unsupervised and supervised WSD systems participating in the Semeval-2007 coarse-grained all-words WSD task, respectively. Since the Semeval-2007 organizers allowed the algorithms to use the MFS as a back-off strategy when they did not return an answer, we apply this rule to ExtGM. Table 5 shows the results for nouns (1,108) and all words (2,269). The performance of ExtGM with WordNet+ConceptNet is significantly better than the best unsupervised system, and is not statistically different from the best supervised system NUS-PT. The result shows that enriching WordNet with the disambiguated ConceptNet can effectively improve the performance of knowledge-based WSD algorithms. In addition, using such enriched WordNet, even a simple knowledge-based algorithm can achieve state-of-the-art performance.

5 Conclusions

In this paper, we first proposed a novel method for the automatic disambiguation of a large-scale common sense knowledge base, namely ConceptNet. Then we used the disambiguated ConceptNet to enrichment WordNet. Our experiments show that enriching WordNet with the disambiguated ConceptNet can significantly improves the performance of knowledge-based WSD methods. On one hand, even a simple knowledge-based WSD algorithm using the enriched WordNet can perform as well as the highest-performing supervised ones. On the other hand, more sophisticated approaches (Agirre&Soroa, 2009; Navigli&Lapata, 2010) may achieve even higher performance by using such enriched WordNet. Moreover, the proposed ConceptNet disambiguating method can be easily applied for other knowledge resources to improve their quality too. We notice that ConceptNet is a multilingual common sense knowledge base, while we only concentrate on English Word Sense Disambiguation in this paper. It would be interesting to explore the impact of this knowledge resource in a multilingual setting.

Acknowledgements

The work was partially supported by the National Natural Science Foundation of China (60970063, 60773010), the Ph.D. Programs Foundation of Ministry of Education of China (20090141110026), and the Fundamental Research Funds for the Central Universities (6081007).

References

Agirre, E., O. Ansa, et al. 2000. Enriching very large ontologies using the WWW. Proceedings of the ECAI 2000 workshop "Ontology Learning".

Agirre, E. and A. Soroa 2009. Personalizing PageRank for word sense disambiguation. Proceedings of the 12th Conference of the European Chapter of the Association for Computational Linguistics. Athens, Greece, Association for Computational Linguistics: 33-41.

Carletta, J. 1996. "Assessing agreement on classification tasks: the kappa statistic." Comput. Linguist. **22**(2): 249-254.

Caseli, H. d. M., B. A. Sugiyama, et al. 2010. Using common sense to generate culturally contextualized machine translation. Proceedings of the NAACL HLT 2010 Young Investigators Workshop on Computational Approaches to Languages of the Americas. Los Angeles, California, Association for Computational Linguistics: 24-31.

Chan, Y. S., H. T. Ng, et al. 2007. NUS-PT: exploiting parallel texts for word sense disambiguation in the English all-words tasks. Proceedings of the 4th International Workshop on Semantic Evaluations. Prague, Czech Republic, Association for Computational Linguistics: 253-256.

Cilibrasi, R.L., et al. 2007. "The Google Similarity Distance." IEEE Transactions on Knowledge and Data Engineering **19**(3): 370-383.

Cuadros, M. and G. Rigau 2008. KnowNet: building a large net of knowledge from the web. Proceedings of the 22nd International Conference on Computational Linguistics - Volume 1. Manchester, United Kingdom, Association for Computational Linguistics: 161-168.

Fellbaum, C., Ed. 1998. WordNet. An electronic lexical database, MIT Press.

Galley, M. and K. McKeown 2003. Improving Word Sense Disambiguation in Lexical Chaining. In Proceedings of the 18th International Joint Conference on Artificial Intelligence. Acapulco, Mexico: 1486--1488.

Havasi, C. and R. S. a. J. Alonso 2007. ConceptNet 3: a Flexible, Multilingual Semantic Network for Common Sense Knowledge. In Proceedings of Recent Advances in Natural Languge Processing 2007.

Hwang, M., C. Choi, et al. 2011 "Automatic Enrichment of Semantic Relation Network and Its Application to Word Sense Disambiguation." IEEE Transactions on Knowledge and Data Engineering **23**(6): 845 - 858

Koeling, R. and D. McCarthy 2007. Sussx: WSD using automatically acquired predominant senses. Proceedings of the 4th International Workshop on Semantic Evaluations. Prague, Czech Republic, Association for Computational Linguistics: 314-317.

Lieberman, H., A. Faaborg, et al. 2005. How to wreck a nice beach you sing calm incense. Proceedings of the 10th international conference on Intelligent user interfaces. San Diego, California, USA, ACM: 278-280.

Magnini, B. and G. Cavaglià 2000. Integrating subject field codes into WordNet In Proceedings of the second International Conference on Language Resources and Evaluation 1413--1418.

Mihalcea, R. 2007. Using Wikipedia for automatic Word Sense Disambiguation. NAACLHLT-07: 196-203.

Mihalcea, R. and D. I. Moldovan 2001. eXtended WordNet: progress report in Proceedings of NAACL Workshop on WordNet and Other Lexical Resources 95--100.

Navigli, R. 2009. Using cycles and quasi-cycles to disambiguate dictionary glosses. Proceedings of the 12th Conference of the European Chapter of the Association for Computational Linguistics. Athens, Greece, Association for Computational Linguistics: 594-602.

Navigli, R. and M. Lapata 2010. "An Experimental Study of Graph Connectivity for Unsupervised Word Sense Disambiguation." IEEE Trans. Pattern Anal. Mach. Intell. **32**(4): 678-692.

Navigli, R., K. C. Litkowski, et al. 2007. SemEval-2007 task 07: coarse-grained English all-words task. Proceedings of the 4th International Workshop on Semantic Evaluations. Prague, Czech Republic, Association for Computational Linguistics: 30-35.

Ponzetto, S. P. and R. Navigli 2010. Knowledge-rich Word Sense Disambiguation rivaling supervised systems. Proceedings of the 48th Annual Meeting of the Association for Computational Linguistics. Uppsala, Sweden, Association for Computational Linguistics: 1522-1531.

Speer, R., J. Krishnamurthy, et al. 2009. An interface for targeted collection of common sense knowledge using a mixture model. Proceedings of the 14th international conference on Intelligent user interfaces. Sanibel Island, Florida, USA, ACM: 137-146.

It Takes Two to Tango: A Bilingual Unsupervised Approach for Estimating Sense Distributions Using Expectation Maximization

Mitesh M. Khapra **Salil Joshi** **Pushpak Bhattacharyya**
Department Of Computer Science and Engineering,
IIT Bombay,
Powai,
Mumbai, 400076.
{miteshk,salilj,pb}@cse.iitb.ac.in

Abstract

Several bilingual WSD algorithms which exploit translation correspondences between parallel corpora have been proposed. However, the availability of such parallel corpora itself is a tall task for some of the resource constrained languages of the world. We propose an ***unsupervised*** bilingual EM based algorithm which relies on the counts of translations to estimate sense distributions. ***No parallel or sense annotated corpora are needed***. The algorithm relies on a synset-aligned bilingual dictionary and in-domain corpora from the two languages. A symmetric generalized Expectation Maximization formulation is used wherein the sense distributions of words in one language are estimated based on the raw counts of the words in the aligned synset in the target language. The overall performance of our algorithm when tested on 4 language-domain pairs is better than current state-of-the-art knowledge based and bilingual unsupervised approaches.

1 Introduction

Word Sense Disambiguation (WSD) is one of the central and most widely investigated problems in Natural Language Processing (NLP). A wide variety of approaches ranging from supervised to unsupervised algorithms have been proposed. Of these, supervised approaches (Ng and Lee, 1996; Lee et al., 2004) which rely on sense annotated corpora have proven to be more successful, and they clearly outperform knowledge based and unsupervised approaches (Lesk, 1986; Walker and Amsler, 1986; Agirre and Rigau, 1996; Rada, 2005; Agirre and Soroa, 2009; McCarthy et al., 2004). However, creation of sense annotated corpora has always remained a costly proposition, especially for some of the resource deprived languages.

In this context, *"Disambiguation by Translation"* is a popular paradigm which tries to obviate the need for sense annotated corpora without compromising on accuracy. Such algorithms rely on the frequently made observation that a word in a given source language tends to have different translations in a target language depending on its sense. Given a sentence-and-word-aligned parallel corpus, these different translations in the target language can serve as automatically acquired sense labels for the source word. Although these algorithms (*e.g.*, (Diab and Resnik, 2002; Ng et al., 2003)) give high accuracies, the requirement of a significant amount of bilingual parallel corpora may be an unreasonable demand for many language pairs (perhaps more unreasonable than collecting sense annotated corpora itself).

Recent work by Khapra et al. (2009) has shown that, within a domain, it is possible to leverage the annotation work done for WSD on one language (L_2) for the purpose of another language (L_1), by projecting parameters learned from wordnet and sense annotated corpus of L_2 to L_1. This method does not require a parallel corpus. However, it requires sense marked corpus for one of the two languages. In this work, we focus on scenarios where no sense marked corpus is available in either language. Our method requires only untagged in-domain corpora from the two languages. Given such bilingual in-domain corpora (non-parallel) the counts of different translations appearing in the other language can be used to estimate the sense distributions in one language.

For example, consider the word *facility* which has two senses, *viz.*, "a building used for a particular industry" and "a service (*e.g., gym/internet facility*)". Given a set of documents from the Sports domain, it is intuitive to expect that the second sense would be more prevalent. Similarly, if we are given a corpus of another language (say, Hindi) belonging to the same domain (*i.e.*, Sports) then we would expect to see more words which are manifestations of the second sense than the first sense. Thus, we can estimate the probabilities of different senses of the word *'facility'* by looking at the counts of its translations in different senses. In this case, the count of the translations belonging to the second sense would be more and hence this sense would emerge as the winner sense. However, the catch here is that the translations themselves might be ambiguous and hence simply relying on their counts would lead to errors. Hence, we propose a generalized Expectation Maximization based formulation where the counts get weighted by the sense probabilities estimated in the previous iteration.

The overall performance of our algorithm, when tested in an all-words scenario (as opposed to testing on specific target words) for two languages across two domains, is better than state-of-the-art knowledge based and bilingual unsupervised approaches. Further, when the evaluation is restricted to only those words which have different translations across senses, the overall performance of our algorithm is better than the wordnet first sense baseline for 2 out of the 4 language-domain pairs. Such words account for 82-83% of the total test words. This is appreciable as the wordnet first sense baseline is often *hard-to-beat* for an unsupervised approach even when restricted to specific domains. For example, in the SEMEVAL-2010 task on *"All Words WSD on a specific domain"* (Agirre et al., 2010), no unsupervised system was able to perform better than the wordnet first sense baseline.

The remainder of this paper is organized as follows. In section 2 we present related work. Section 3 describes the Synset aligned multilingual dictionary which lies at the heart of our work. In section 4 we discuss the EM formulation used for estimating sense distributions with the help of a motivating example. Section 5 presents the experimental setup. In section 6 we give the results followed by discussions in section 7. Section 8 concludes the paper.

2 Related Work

Monolingual approaches to Word Sense Disambiguation are abundant ranging from supervised, semi-supervised to unsupervised methods. Supervised approaches such as SVM (Lee et al., 2004) and k-NN (Ng and Lee, 1996) give high accuracies, but the requirement of large annotated corpora renders them unsuitable for resource scarce languages. On the other hand, Knowledge based approaches (Lesk, 1986; Walker and Amsler, 1986; Agirre and Rigau, 1996; Rada, 2005; Agirre and Soroa, 2009) which use wordnet, and unsupervised approaches (McCarthy et al., 2004) which use untagged corpus, are less demanding in terms of resources but fail to deliver good results. This situation underlines the need for high accuracy resource conscious approaches to WSD.

In this context, usupervised Word Sense Induction (WSI) methods (Jean, 2004; Klapaftis and Manandhar, 2008) which induce corpus senses by partitioning the co-occurrence graph of a target word have shown promise. One drawback of these approaches is that they require a large number of untagged instances (typically, collected from the web) for every target word to induce meaningful partitions in the co-occurrence graph. Collecting such target-word specific instances is a difficult proposition (especially in an all-words scenario) for resource constrained languages such as Hindi and Marathi which have very poor web presence. Further, in a bilingual setting where parameters need to be ported from one language to another, it is important to associate labels with the clusters induced from the graph partitions so that these clusters can be aligned across languages. This is a difficult proposition and does not fall under the purview of WSI. Hence, in this work we stick to dictionary defined senses as opposed to corpus induced senses.

Disambiguation by Translation (Gale et al., 1992; Dagan and Itai, 1994; Resnik and Yarowsky, 1999; Ide et al., 2001; Diab and Resnik, 2002; Ng et al., 2003; TufiŞ et al., 2004; Apidianaki, 2008) is another paradigm which attempts at reducing the need for annotated corpora, while ensuring high accuracy. The idea is to use the different target translations of a source word as automatically acquired sense labels. A severe drawback of these algorithms is the requirement of a significant amount of parallel corpora which may be difficult to obtain for many language pairs.

Li and Li (2004) proposed an approach based on bilingual bootstrapping which does not need parallel corpora and relies only on in-domain corpora from two languages. However, their approach is semi-supervised in contrast to our approach which is unsupervised. Further, they focus on the more specific task of Word Translation Disambiguation (WTD) as opposed to our work which focuses on the broader task of WSD.

Kaji and Morimoto (2002) proposed an unsupervised bilingual approach which aligns statistically significant pairs of related words in language L_1 with their cross-lingual counterparts in language L_2 using a bilingual dictionary. This approach is based on two assumptions (i) words which are most significantly related to a target word provide clues about the sense of the target word and (ii) translations of these related words further reinforce the sense distinctions. The translations of related words thus act as cross-lingual clues for disambiguation. This algorithm when tested on 60 polysemous words (using English as L_1 and Japanese as L_2) delivered high accuracies (coverage=88.5% and precision=77.7%). However, when used in an all-words scenario on our dataset, this algorithm performed poorly (see section 6).

Our work focuses on a bilingual approach for estimating sense distributions and the only resources required for our work are in-domain corpora from two languages and a synset aligned multilingual dictionary which is described in the next section.

3 Synset Aligned Multilingual Dictionary

A novel and effective method of storage and use of dictionary in a multilingual setting was proposed by Mohanty et al. (2008). For the purpose of current discussion, we will refer to this multilingual dictionary framework as *MultiDict*. One important departure in this framework from the traditional dictionary is that **synsets are linked, and after that the words inside the synsets are linked.** The basic mapping is thus between synsets and thereafter between the words.

Concepts	L1 (English)	L2 (Hindi)	L3 (Marathi)
04321: a youthful male person	{malechild, boy}	{लड़का *(ladkaa)*, बालक *(baalak)*, बच्चा *(bachchaa)*}	{मुलगा *(mulgaa)*, पोरगा *(porgaa)*, पोर *(por)*}

Table 1: Multilingual Dictionary Framework

Table 1 shows the structure of MultiDict, with one example row standing for the concept of *boy*. The first column is the pivot describing a concept with a unique ID. The subsequent columns show the words expressing the concept in respective languages (in the example table, *English, Hindi and Marathi*). The pivot language to which other languages link is Hindi. This approach of creating wordnet for a new language by linking to the synsets of a pivot language - more popularly known as the expansion approach - has several advantages over creating a wordnet from scratch as discussed in Mohanty et al. (2008).

Note that every word in the Marathi synset is considered to be a translation of the corresponding words in the Hindi synset. Thus, the Marathi words *mulgaa*, *porgaa* and *por* are translations of the Hindi word *ladakaa* and so on. These synset-specific translations play a very important role in our work as explained in the next section.

4 Bilingual EM for estimating sense distributions

We first explain the intuition behind our approach and then derive the E and M steps of our algorithm with the help of an example.

4.1 Intuition

Our work relies on the key observation of Khapra et al. (2009) that within a domain, the co-occurrence counts of *(word, sense)* in one language can be used to estimate the sense distributions of their translations in another language. For example, consider two languages, say $L_1 = Hindi$ and $L_2 = Marathi$. Now, for a given word u in L_2 if a particular sense (say S_1) is more prevalent in a domain then a target language (L_1) corpus from the same domain will contain more words which are translations of sense S_1 as compared to words which are translations of other senses of this word. For example, the Marathi word *maan*, when used in the sense of *"body part (neck)"* gets translated in Hindi as *gardan* or *galaa* whereas when it is used in the sense of *"prestige"*, it gets translated as *aadar* or *izzat*. Now consider that corpora for the two languages are available from the Health domain. Since, in the Health domain, the *"body part (neck)"* sense is more prevalent we can expect the words *gardan* or *galaa* to be more prevalent in a Hindi Health corpus as compared to *aadar* or *izzat*. The probability of the dif-

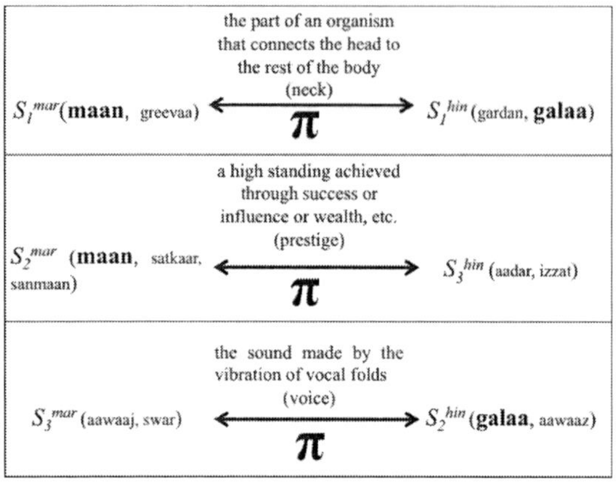

Figure 1: Alignment between different synsets of *maan* and *galaa*

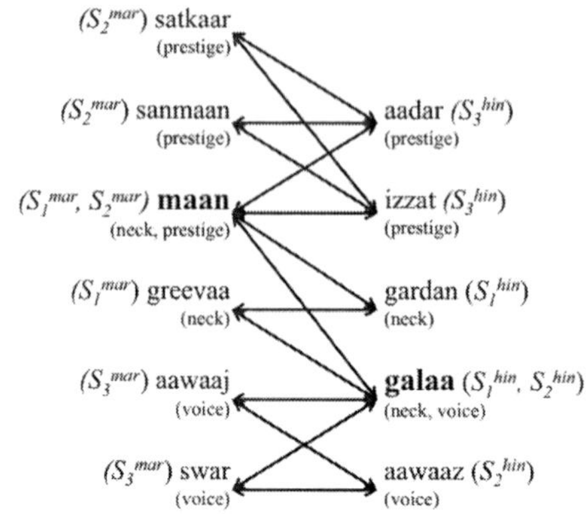

Figure 2: A bipartite graph of translation correspondences

ferent senses of *maan* can thus be estimated based on the counts of {*gardan, galaa*} and {*aadar, izzat*}. However, since the words {*gardan, galaa*} and {*aadar, izzat*} may themselves be ambiguous, their raw counts cannot be used directly for estimating the sense distributions of *maan*. Instead, these counts are refined iteratively using an EM algorithm as explained in the next subsection.

4.2 Derivation with illustration

With the basic intuition provided above, we can now start deriving the EM formulation for estimating sense distributions. For ease of understanding we present the derivation with the help of an illustration. We use the following notations,

- L_1 = first language (say, Hindi)
- L_2 = second language (say, Marathi)
- $synsets_L(word) = \{S^L | word \in S^L\}$ where, S^L denotes a synset in language L
- $words(S^L) = \{word | word \in S^L\}$
- $\pi_{L_2}(S^{L_1}) = S^{L_2}$ s.t. $Sense(S^{L_1}) = Sense(S^{L_2})$ *i.e.*, S^{L_1} & S^{L_2} represent the same concept in L_1 and L_2 respectively. The synsets S^{L_1} and $\pi_{L_2}(S^{L_1})$ will thus be aligned in the *MultiDict*.
- $translations_{L_2}(word, S^{L_1}) = words(\pi_{L_2}(S^{L_1}))$.The function $translations$ thus gives the translations of a $word \in S^{L_1}$ in the corresponding projected synset in L_2.

Now, consider the word $maan \in S_1^{mar}$ and the word $galaa \in S_1^{hin}$ where $\pi_{hin}(S_1^{mar}) = S_1^{hin}$ and vice versa. Further, $galaa \in translations_{hin}(maan, S_1^{mar})$ and $maan \in translations_{mar}(galaa, S_1^{hin})$. The different synsets to which these words belong and the corresponding aligned synsets in the other language are shown in Figure 1. The complete set of translations of these words are shown in Figure 2. We are now interested in estimating $P(S_1^{mar}|maan)$ and $P(S_1^{hin}|galaa)$. Figures 1 and 2 should be referred to while reading the derivation below.

Using the basic definition of probability, we have,

$$P(S_1^{mar}|maan) = \frac{\#(S_1^{mar}, maan)}{\#(S_1^{mar}, maan) + \#(S_2^{mar}, maan)}$$

where,

$\#(S_i^{mar}, maan)$ = *no. of times maan appears with sense* S_i^{mar}

Following the approach of Khapra et al. (2009) we replace the counts of $(S_i^{mar}, maan)(i \in \{1,2\})$ by the collective counts of the translations in the aligned synsets. The rationale behind the above substitution is that if $v \in L_2$ is a translation of $u \in L_1$ in sense S then the co-occurrence count of (v, S) gives a good approximation for the co-occurrence count of (u, S). Thus,

$$P(S_1^{mar}|maan)$$
$$\approx \frac{\#(S_1^{hin}, gardan) + \#(S_1^{hin}, galaa)}{\#(S_1^{hin}, gardan) + \#(S_1^{hin}, galaa) + \#(S_3^{hin}, aadar) + \#(S_3^{hin}, izzat)}$$

where,

$S_1^{hin} = \pi_{hin}(S_1^{mar})$ (*see Figure* 1)

$S_3^{hin} = \pi_{hin}(S_2^{mar})$ (*see Figure* 1)

$(gardan, galaa) \in translations_{hin}(maan, S_1^{mar})$ (*see Figure* 2)

$(aadar, izzat) \in translations_{hin}(maan, S_2^{mar})$ (*see Figure* 2)

If we had a sense annotated corpus in Hindi then we could have easily estimated the above probability as shown by Khapra et al. (2009). We propose that even in the absence of such annotated corpus we can still estimate the sense distributions using the expected value of the terms in the above equation as shown below,

E-step

$$P(S_1^{mar}|maan) \approx \frac{P(S_1^{hin}|gardan) \cdot \#(gardan) + P(S_1^{hin}|galaa) \cdot \#(galaa)}{Z}$$

$$\begin{aligned} \textit{where, } Z = & P(S_1^{hin}|gardan) \cdot \#(gardan) \\ & + P(S_1^{hin}|galaa) \cdot \#(galaa) \\ & + P(S_3^{hin}|aadar) \cdot \#(aadar) \\ & + P(S_3^{hin}|izzat) \cdot \#(izzat) \end{aligned}$$

The above equation takes care of the fact that the different translations of $maan$ would themselves be ambiguous and hence their raw counts (*e.g,* $\#(gardan)$, $\#(galaa)$, *etc.*) cannot be used directly for estimations. Instead, these counts are weighted with the appropriate probability to calculate the expected count (*e.g.,* $E[\#(S_1^{hin}, galaa)] = P(S_1^{hin}|galaa) \cdot \#(galaa)$). The parameters $P(S_1^{hin}|galaa)$, $P(S_1^{hin}|gardan)$, $P(S_3^{hin}|aadar)$ and $P(S_3^{hin}|izzat)$ above are unknown and can in turn be estimated using the counts of the corresponding translations of these words (see Figure 2) as shown below:

M-step

$$P(S_1^{hin}|galaa) \approx \frac{P(S_1^{mar}|maan) \cdot \#(maan) + P(S_1^{mar}|greeva) \cdot \#(greeva)}{Z}$$

$$\begin{aligned} Z = & P(S_1^{mar}|maan) \cdot \#(maan) \\ & + P(S_1^{mar}|greeva) \cdot \#(greeva) \\ & + P(S_3^{mar}|aawaaj) \cdot \#(aawaaj) \\ & + P(S_3^{mar}|swar) \cdot \#(swar) \end{aligned}$$

$$\begin{aligned} & \textit{where,} \\ & S_1^{mar} = \pi_{hin}(S_1^{hin}) \ (see\ Figure\ 1) \\ & S_3^{mar} = \pi_{mar}(S_2^{hin}) \ (see\ Figure\ 1) \\ & (maan, greeva) \in translations_{mar}(galaa, S_1^{hin}) \ (see\ Figure\ 2) \\ & (aawaaj, swar) \in translations_{mar}(galaa, S_2^{hin}) \ (see\ Figure\ 2) \end{aligned}$$

Similarly, the other parameters (*i.e.,* $P(S_1^{hin}|gardan)$, $P(S_3^{hin}|aadar)$ and $P(S_3^{hin}|izzat)$) can be estimated. The overall process of estimating sense distributions in the two languages can thus be considered to be a back-and-forth traversal over translation correspondences as shown in Figure 2. The two languages thus mutually help each other in estimating sense distributions. In general, for a word $u \in L_1$ and a word $v \in L_2$ the E and M steps can be written as shown below.

E-Step:

$$P(S_k^{L_1}|u) \approx \frac{\sum_{v} P(\pi_{L_2}(S_k^{L_1})|v) \cdot \#(v)}{\sum_{S_i^{L_1}} \sum_{y} P(\pi_{L_2}(S_i^{L_1})|y) \cdot \#(y)}$$

$$\begin{aligned} \textit{where, } & S_k^{L_1}, S_i^{L_1} \in synsets_{L_1}(u) \\ & v \in translations_{L_2}(u, S_k^{L_1}) \\ & y \in translations_{L_2}(u, S_i^{L_1}) \end{aligned}$$

M-Step:

$$P(S_j^{L_2}|v) \approx \frac{\sum_{a} P(\pi_{L_1}(S_j^{L_2})|a) \cdot \#(a)}{\sum_{S_i^{L_2}} \sum_{b} P(\pi_{L_1}(S_i^{L_2})|b) \cdot \#(b)}$$

$$\begin{aligned} \textit{where, } & S_j^{L_2}, S_i^{L_2} \in synsets_{L_2}(v) \\ & a \in translations_{L_1}(v, S_j^{L_2}) \\ & b \in translations_{L_1}(v, S_i^{L_2}) \end{aligned}$$

Note that the E and M steps are symmetrical except for the change in languages. Either of them could be the E-step, making the other as the M-step. Once the sense distributions have been estimated using the above EM algorithm, each word in the test corpus is disambiguated by assigning it the most frequent sense as learned from the sense distributions.

4.3 Problematic cases in estimating sense distributions using EM (non-progressiveness estimation)

Some words have the same translations in the target language across senses. For example, the word *samudra* in Marathi has two senses, *viz.*, S_1 = *a large water body* and S_2 = *a limitless quantity*, which is a metaphorical sense (*e.g.*, a *sea* of opportunities). The corresponding Hindi synsets contain the same word, *viz.*, *saagar*. In other words, *samudra* in Marathi gets translated as *saagar* in Hindi irrespective of its sense. Further, the back-translation of *saagar* in Marathi is *samudra* in both the senses. These words thus form a closed loop of translations. In such cases the algorithm

Category	Polysemous words Tourism	Polysemous words Health	Monosemous words Tourism	Monosemous words Health
Noun	62336	24089	35811	18923
Verb	6386	1401	3667	5109
Adjective	18949	8773	28998	12138
Adverb	4860	2527	13699	7152
All	92531	36790	82175	43322

Table 2: Polysemous and Monosemous words per category in each domain for Hindi

Category	Polysemous words Tourism	Polysemous words Health	Monosemous words Tourism	Monosemous words Health
Noun	45589	17482	27386	11383
Verb	7879	3120	2672	1500
Adjective	13107	4788	16725	6032
Adverb	4036	1727	5023	1874
All	70611	27117	51806	20789

Table 3: Polysemous and Monosemous words per category in each domain for Marathi

Category	Avg. degree of wordnet polysemy for polysemous words: Tourism	Health
Noun	3.02	3.17
Verb	5.05	6.58
Adjective	2.66	2.75
Adverb	2.52	2.57
All	3.09	3.23

Table 4: Average degree of wordnet polysemy per category in the 2 domains for Hindi

Category	Avg. degree of wordnet polysemy for polysemous words: Tourism	Health
Noun	3.06	3.18
Verb	4.96	5.18
Adjective	2.60	2.72
Adverb	2.44	2.45
All	3.14	3.29

Table 5: Average degree of wordnet polysemy per category in the 2 domains for Marathi

will not progress and get stuck with the initial values. It will thus fail to produce better estimates in successive iterations.

Further, for some language-specific words appearing in L_1 (or L_2), no projected synsets were available in L_2 (or L_1 respectively). As evident from the E and M steps, in the absence of such synsets, the algorithm will assign zero probabilities to all the senses of such words.

5 Experimental Setup

We used the publicly available dataset[1] described in Khapra et al. (2010) for all our experiments. The data was collected from two domains, *viz.*, Tourism and Health. The data for Tourism domain was collected by manually translating English documents downloaded from Indian Tourism websites into Hindi and Marathi. Similarly, English documents for Health domain were obtained from two doctors and were manually translated into Hindi and Marathi. The entire data was then manually annotated by three lexicographers adept in Hindi and Marathi. To calculate the inter-tagger agreement (ITA), we we got a small portion (around 5%) of the corpus annotated by two annotators[2]. The ITA on this small corpus was found to be around 85%.

Since ours is an unsupervised algorithm, we refer to the manually assigned sense labels only for evaluation and do not use them during training. The various statistics pertaining to the total number of words, number of words per POS category and average degree of polysemy are described in Tables 2 to 5. Although Tables 2 and 3 also report the number of monosemous words, we would like to clearly state that we do not include monosemous words while evaluating the performance of our algorithms (such words do not need any disambiguation).

We did a 2-fold cross validation of our algorithm using this corpus. The unsupervised parameter estimation was done using 1 fold and testing was done on the remaining fold. Each word in the test corpus is disambiguated by assigning it the most frequent sense as learned from the estimated sense distributions. Note that even though the corpora were parallel we have not used this property in any way in our experiments or EM formulation. In fact, the documents in the two languages were arbitrarily split into 2 folds so that the parallel documents do not fall in the same folds for the two languages. Further, we observed that whether the documents are split arbitrarily (such that parallel documents do not lie in the same fold) or carefully (such that parallel documents lie in the same fold) the overall F-scores remain comparable (within $\pm$ 0.5%). Also note that there was sufficient variety in our corpus as the Tourism documents were related to places from all over India. Similarly, the Health documents were related to a wide range of diseases from common cold to cancer.

6 Results

We report the results using following algorithms:

a. Wordnet first sense ***(WFS)***: The F-score obtained by selecting the first sense of every word. This is a typically reported baseline for supervised approaches as the WFS of a word in

[1] http://www.cfilt.iitb.ac.in/wsd/annotated_corpus

[2] It is very expensive to get the entire corpus tagged by 2 annotators. Hence, we calculated the ITA based on the agreement between two lexicographers on a small portion of the corpus

Algorithm	Average				
	N	R	A	V	O
WFS	60.00	68.64	52.39	39.65	57.29
EM	53.35	56.95	51.39	29.98	51.26
PPR	56.17	0.00	38.94	29.74	48.88
RB	34.74	44.32	39.38	17.21	34.79
MI	10.97	3.89	10.07	5.63	9.97

Table 6: Average 2-fold cross validation results averaged over all Language-Domain pairs for all words

Algorithm	Average				
	N	R	A	V	O
WFS	60.86	65.00	52.64	42.00	57.70
EM	57.78	61.28	54.16	31.87	54.98
PPR	58.03	0.00	40.91	30.58	50.42
RB	34.17	43.37	39.21	15.64	34.13
MI	9.62	4.69	8.96	4.17	8.78

Table 7: Average 2-fold cross validation results averaged over all Language-Domain pairs for words which do not face the problem of non-progressiveness estimation

Algo-rithm	HINDI-HEALTH					MARATHI-HEALTH					HINDI-TOURISM					MARATHI-TOURISM				
	N	R	A	V	O	N	R	A	V	O	N	R	A	V	O	N	R	A	V	O
WFS	52.12	73.59	50.79	22.06	52.12	58.52	68.00	44.29	47.91	55.43	64.22	75.66	51.13	33.30	59.99	58.97	57.36	58.26	44.65	57.16
EM	50.87	54.30	55.05	5.87	50.43	56.78	54.96	50.33	41.93	53.81	54.02	57.88	49.88	20.09	51.07	52.44	58.35	51.52	37.57	50.95
PPR	44.82	0.00	40.56	20.66	41.22	54.88	0.00	38.04	39.94	48.32	58.44	0.00	36.44	24.06	50.11	59.55	0.00	41.8	31.92	51.49
RB	34.31	45.01	40.72	9.10	35.65	37.33	44.34	38.42	20.68	36.05	34.20	44.62	39.37	12.62	34.33	34.71	43.51	38.86	20.99	34.46
MI	12.73	6.5	11.13	5.65	11.69	9.78	4.65	10.16	5.16	9.01	11.07	2.11	9.41	3.27	9.77	10.37	4.09	10.28	7.73	9.72

Table 8: Average 2-fold cross validation results for each Language-Domain pair for all words

Algo-rithm	HINDI-HEALTH					MARATHI-HEALTH					HINDI-TOURISM					MARATHI-TOURISM				
	N	R	A	V	O	N	R	A	V	O	N	R	A	V	O	N	R	A	V	O
WFS	54.25	69.17	50.77	21.21	52.95	61.50	67.86	44.27	52.30	57.68	64.50	69.45	50.14	34.61	59.46	58.98	57.73	61.02	47.34	57.85
EM	56.39	56.54	57.35	4.70	54.64	62.58	58.99	53.78	45.24	58.72	57.47	65.22	51.09	20.70	53.87	57.09	61.19	56.78	40.01	55.20
PPR	47.07	0.00	40.50	18.80	42.68	57.98	0.00	39.79	44.11	51.27	59.65	0.00	37.88	23.10	51.12	61.54	0.00	46.30	33.29	53.19
RB	34.14	46.43	40.76	6.54	35.54	35.86	45.38	38.65	18.35	34.96	33.99	40.01	38.57	11.31	33.67	33.79	43.92	39.30	19.45	33.71
MI	11.96	8.23	10.20	3.73	10.98	9.17	5.42	9.69	2.97	8.38	9.08	2.66	7.91	2.52	8.13	9.32	4.33	9.43	5.93	8.64

Table 9: Average 2-fold cross validation results for each Language-Domain pairs for words which do not face the problem of non-progressiveness estimation

Hindi and Marathi wordnets is determined manually by a lexicographer based on his/her native speaker intuition.

b. Random Baseline ***(RB)***: The F-score obtained by selecting a random sense of every word. This is a typically reported baseline for unsupervised approaches.

c. Bilingual Expectation Maximization ***(EM)***: The F-score obtained by using our approach.

d. Personalized PageRank ***(PPR)***: The F-score obtained by using a state-of-the-art knowledge based approach (Agirre and Soroa, 2009).

e. Mutual Information ***(MI)***: The F-score obtained by using the bilingual unsupervised approach of Kaji and Morimoto (2002) which uses cross-lingual clues based on in-domain corpora and aligned synsets.

6.1 A note on other state-of-the-art approaches

The unsupervised algorithm by McCarthy et al. (2004) which uses in-domain corpora to estimate predominant senses would have been more appropriate for comparison with our approach as it is a corpus based approach as opposed to PPR which is a wordnet based approach. However, this approach requires a dependency parser to extract syntactic relations to construct a feature vector for identifying the nearest neighbors of a target word. Unfortunately, such parsers are not available for Hindi and Marathi and hence we could not compare our algorithm with this approach. Further, there are other unsupervised approaches (see section 2) which use corpus induced senses and/or parallel corpora. However, our work focuses on dictionary defines senses and does not need parallel corpora. Hence we did not find it appropriate to present a comparison with these algorithms.

6.2 Non-progressiveness estimation

We observed that around 17-18% of the total words in the corpus face the problem discussed in section 4.3. Hence we report 2 sets of results:

(i) only for those words which do not face the problem of non-progressiveness estimation.

(ii) for all words.

The first set of results thus covers 82-83% of the words in the corpus depending on the language and the domain.

All the results are summarized in Tables 6 to 9. Table 6 gives the overall average F-score for all-words over all language domain pairs. Similarly, Table 7 gives the overall average F-score for only those words which do not face the problem of non-progressiveness estimation. Tables 8 and 9 give the average F-score for each language-domain pair for all words and for words which do not face the problem of non-progressiveness estimation respectively. In all tables, we report F-scores for each POS category (N:-nouns, R:-adverbs, A:-adjectives, V:-verbs, O:-all).

7 Discussions

We discuss the important observations made from Tables 6 to 9.

7.1 Performance on all words

The overall performance of our algorithm (see Table 6) is better than state-of-the-art knowledge based approach (PPR) by 3%, bilingual unsupervised approach (MI) by 41% and random baseline (RB) by 17%. These results are consistent across all language-domain pairs except for MARATHI-TOURISM where the performance of PPR is better than our algorithm by 0.5%. On an average the performance of PPR on nouns is better than our algorithm by 3%. However, in 2 out of the 4 language-domain pairs our algorithm does better on nouns than PPR (by 6% in HINDI-HEALTH and 2% in MARATHI-HEALTH - see Table 8). PPR gives an F-score of 0% for adverbs in all language-domain pairs because Hindi and Marathi wordnets do not have any synset relations defined for adverbs.

The performance of all the algorithms is less than the wordnet first sense baseline. As stated earlier, this is a hard baseline for unsupervised approaches (Agirre et al., 2010). Note that the wordnet first sense baseline is more like a supervised approach because the first sense of a word is either determined manually by a lexicographer or by using counts from a mixed domain sense marked corpus. This is a laborious and expensive task which is difficult to do for wordnets of resource deprived languages.

7.2 Performance on words not facing the problem of non-progressiveness estimation

When the performance is restricted to words which do not face the problem of non-progressiveness estimation our approach still does better than PPR, MI and random baseline (see Table 7). Here, the results are consistent across all language-domain pairs (see Table 9). In addition, for two language-domain pairs (*viz.*, MARATHI-HEALTH and HINDI-HEALTH) our algorithm does better than the wordnet first sense baseline. Even though the overall improvement over WFS is small (1-2%) it is still appreciable for an unsupervised approach. Note that none of the other approaches (PPR, MI) are able to perform better than WFS in any language-domain pair.

7.3 Poor performance on verbs

Amongst all the POS categories, the performance of our algorithm is lowest for verbs. We observed that there are two main reasons for this. Firstly, the polysemy of verbs is much higher than that of other POS categories (see Tables 4 & 5). This is a commonly observed problem for all algorithms. Secondly, we observed that many verbs have very fine senses because of which they tend to have overlapping sets of translations across senses. Even though they do not form a closed loop of translations they share many translations across senses. For example, the Hindi word *karna* has the same Marathi translation *karne* in 8 out of the 21 senses that it appears in. Due to these shared translations, the approach of "disambiguation by translation" does not have much scope in the case of such verbs.

8 Conclusions

We presented an unsupervised bilingual approach for estimating sense distributions of words. The algorithm does not require any parallel corpora and uses only in-domain corpora from the two languages. The sense distributions are estimated using a novel bilingual EM formulation by performing a back-and-forth traversal over translation correspondences in the two languages. The algorithm consistently beats the random baseline and state-of-the-art knowledge based and unsupervised approaches. Further, when tested on words which have different translations across senses, the algorithm gives slight improvement over the wordnet first sense baseline in 2 out of the 4 language-domain pairs.

As future work, we would like to test our algorithm on language pairs which belong to distant families so that the number of words having same translations across senses would be less.

References

Eneko Agirre and German Rigau. 1996. Word sense disambiguation using conceptual density. In *In Proceedings of the 16th International Conference on Computational Linguistics (COLING)*.

Eneko Agirre and Aitor Soroa. 2009. Personalizing pagerank for word sense disambiguation. In *EACL*, pages 33–41.

Eneko Agirre, Oier López de Lacalle, Christiane Fellbaum, Shu-Kai Hsieh, Maurizio Tesconi, Monica Monachini, Piek Vossen, and Roxanne Segers. 2010. Semeval-2010 task 17: All-words word sense disambiguation on a specific domain. In *Proceedings of the 5th International Workshop on Semantic Evaluation*, pages 75–80, Uppsala, Sweden, July. Association for Computational Linguistics.

Marianna Apidianaki. 2008. Translation-oriented word sense induction based on parallel corpora. In *LREC*.

Ido Dagan and Alon Itai. 1994. Word sense disambiguation using a second language monolingual corpus. *Comput. Linguist.*, 20:563–596, December.

Mona Diab and Philip Resnik. 2002. An unsupervised method for word sense tagging using parallel corpora. In *Proceedings of the 40th Annual Meeting on Association for Computational Linguistics*, ACL '02, pages 255–262, Morristown, NJ, USA. Association for Computational Linguistics.

William Gale, Kenneth Church, and David Yarowsky. 1992. A method for disambiguating word senses in a large corpus. *Computers and the Humanities*, 26:415–439. 10.1007/BF00136984.

Nancy Ide, Tomaž Erjavec, and Dan TufiŞ. 2001. Automatic sense tagging using parallel corpora. In *In Proceedings of the 6 th Natural Language Processing Pacific Rim Symposium*, pages 212–219.

Véronis Jean. 2004. Hyperlex: Lexical cartography for information retrieval. In *Computer Speech and Language*, pages 18(3):223–252.

Hiroyuki Kaji and Yasutsugu Morimoto. 2002. Unsupervised word sense disambiguation using bilingual comparable corpora. In *Proceedings of the 19th international conference on Computational linguistics - Volume 1*, COLING '02, pages 1–7, Stroudsburg, PA, USA. Association for Computational Linguistics.

Mitesh M. Khapra, Sapan Shah, Piyush Kedia, and Pushpak Bhattacharyya. 2009. Projecting parameters for multilingual word sense disambiguation. In *Proceedings of the 2009 Conference on Empirical Methods in Natural Language Processing*, pages 459–467, Singapore, August. Association for Computational Linguistics.

Mitesh Khapra, Saurabh Sohoney, Anup Kulkarni, and Pushpak Bhattacharyya. 2010. Value for money: Balancing annotation effort, lexicon building and accuracy for multilingual wsd. In *Proceedings of the 23rd International Conference on Computational Linguistics*.

Ioannis P. Klapaftis and Suresh Manandhar. 2008. Word sense induction using graphs of collocations. In *Proceeding of the 2008 conference on ECAI 2008: 18th European Conference on Artificial Intelligence*, pages 298–302, Amsterdam, The Netherlands, The Netherlands. IOS Press.

K. Yoong Lee, Hwee T. Ng, and Tee K. Chia. 2004. Supervised word sense disambiguation with support vector machines and multiple knowledge sources. In *Proceedings of Senseval-3: Third International Workshop on the Evaluation of Systems for the Semantic Analysis of Text*, pages 137–140.

Michael Lesk. 1986. Automatic sense disambiguation using machine readable dictionaries: how to tell a pine cone from an ice cream cone. In *In Proceedings of the 5th annual international conference on Systems documentation*.

Hang Li and Cong Li. 2004. Word translation disambiguation using bilingual bootstrapping. *Comput. Linguist.*, 30:1–22, March.

Diana McCarthy, Rob Koeling, Julie Weeds, and John Carroll. 2004. Finding predominant word senses in untagged text. In *ACL '04: Proceedings of the 42nd Annual Meeting on Association for Computational Linguistics*, page 279, Morristown, NJ, USA. Association for Computational Linguistics.

Rajat Mohanty, Pushpak Bhattacharyya, Prabhakar Pande, Shraddha Kalele, Mitesh Khapra, and Aditya Sharma. 2008. Synset based multilingual dictionary: Insights, applications and challenges. In *Global Wordnet Conference*.

Hwee Tou Ng and Hian Beng Lee. 1996. Integrating multiple knowledge sources to disambiguate word sense: an exemplar-based approach. In *Proceedings of the 34th annual meeting on Association for Computational Linguistics*, pages 40–47, Morristown, NJ, USA. Association for Computational Linguistics.

Hwee Tou Ng, Bin Wang, and Yee Seng Chan. 2003. Exploiting parallel texts for word sense disambiguation: an empirical study. In *Proceedings of the 41st Annual Meeting on Association for Computational Linguistics - Volume 1*, ACL '03, pages 455–462, Morristown, NJ, USA. Association for Computational Linguistics.

Mihalcea Rada. 2005. Large vocabulary unsupervised word sense disambiguation with graph-based algorithms for sequence data labeling. In *In Proceedings of the Joint Human Language Technology and Empirical Methods in Natural Language Processing Conference (HLT/EMNLP)*, pages 411–418.

Philip Resnik and David Yarowsky. 1999. Distinguishing systems and distinguishing senses: new evaluation methods for word sense disambiguation. *Nat. Lang. Eng.*, 5:113–133, June.

Dan TufiŞ, Radu Ion, and Nancy Ide. 2004. Fine-grained word sense disambiguation based on parallel corpora, word alignment, word clustering and aligned wordnets. In *Proceedings of the 20th international conference on Computational Linguistics*, COLING '04, Stroudsburg, PA, USA. Association for Computational Linguistics.

D. Walker and R. Amsler. 1986. The use of machine readable dictionaries in sublanguage analysis. In *In Analyzing Language in Restricted Domains, Grishman and Kittredge (eds), LEA Press*, pages 69–83.

Dynamic and Static Prototype Vectors for Semantic Composition

Siva Reddy
University of York, UK
siva@cs.york.ac.uk

Ioannis P. Klapaftis
University of York, UK
giannis@cs.york.ac.uk

Diana McCarthy
Lexical Computing Ltd, UK
diana@dianamccarthy.co.uk

Suresh Manandhar
University of York, UK
suresh@cs.york.ac.uk

Abstract

Compositional Distributional Semantic methods model the distributional behavior of a compound word by exploiting the distributional behavior of its constituent words. In this setting, a constituent word is typically represented by a feature vector conflating all the senses of that word. However, not all the senses of a constituent word are relevant when composing the semantics of the compound. In this paper, we present two different methods for selecting the relevant senses of constituent words. The first one is based on Word Sense Induction and creates a static multi prototype vectors representing the senses of a constituent word. The second creates a single dynamic prototype vector for each constituent word based on the distributional properties of the other constituents in the compound. We use these prototype vectors for composing the semantics of noun-noun compounds and evaluate on a compositionality-based similarity task. Our results show that: (1) selecting relevant senses of the constituent words leads to a better semantic composition of the compound, and (2) dynamic prototypes perform better than static prototypes.

1 Introduction

Vector Space Models of lexical semantics have become a standard framework for representing a word's meaning. Typically these methods (Schütze, 1998; Pado and Lapata, 2007; Erk and Padó, 2008) utilize a bag-of-words model or syntactic dependencies such as subject/verb, object/verb relations, so as to extract the features which serve as the dimensions of the vector space. Each word is then represented as a vector of the extracted features, where the frequency of co-occurrence of the word with each feature is used to calculate the vector component asociated with that feature. Figure 1 provides an example of two nouns assuming a bag-of-words model.

	vector dimensions					
	animal	buy	apartment	price	rent	kill
house	⟨ 30	60	90	55	45	10 ⟩
hunting	⟨ 90	15	12	20	33	90 ⟩

Figure 1: A hypothetical vector space model.

Compositional Distributional Semantic methods formalise the meaning of a phrase by applying a vector composition function on the vectors associated with its constituent words (Mitchell and Lapata, 2008; Widdows, 2008). For example, the result of *vector addition* to compose the semantics of *house hunting* from the vectors **house** and **hunting** is the vector $\langle 120, 75, 102, 75, 78, 100\rangle$.

As can be observed the resulting vector does not reflect the correct meaning of the compound *house hunting* due to the presence of irrelevant co-occurrences such as *animal* or *kill*. These co-occurrences are relevant to one sense of *hunting*, i.e. (*the activity of hunting animals*), but not to the sense of *hunting* meant in *house hunting*, i.e. *the activity of looking thoroughly*. Given that *hunting* has been associated with a single prototype (vector) by conflating all of its senses, the application of a composition function $\oplus$ is likely to include irrelevant co-occurrences in $\mathbf{house} \oplus \mathbf{hunting}$.

A potential solution to this problem would involve the following steps:

1. build separate prototype vectors for each of the senses of *house* and *hunting*
2. select the relevant prototype vectors of *house* and *hunting* and then perform the semantic composition.

In this paper we present two methods (section 3) for carrying out the above steps on noun-noun compounds. The first one (section 3.1) applies Word Sense Induction (WSI) to identity different senses (also called static multi prototypes) of the constituent words of a compound noun and then applies composition by choosing the relevant senses. The second method (section 3.2) does not identify a fixed set of senses. Instead, it represents each constituent by a prototype vector which is built dynamically (also called as a dynamic prototype) by activating only those contexts considered to be relevant to the constituent in the presence of the other constituent, and then performs the composition on the dynamic prototypes. For performing composition, we use vector composition functions.

Our evaluation (section 5) on a task for rating similarity between noun-noun compound pairs shows: (1) sense disambiguation of constituents improves semantic composition and (2) dynamic prototypes are better than static multi prototypes for semantic composition.

2 Related work

Any distributional model that aims to describe language adequately needs to address the issue of compositionality. Many distributional composition functions have been proposed in order to estimate the semantics of compound words from the semantics of the constituent words. Mitchell and Lapata (2008) discussed and evaluated various composition functions for phrases consisting of two words. Among these, the simple additive (ADD) and simple multiplicative (MULT) functions are easy to implement and competitive with respect to existing sophisticated methods (Widdows, 2008; Vecchi et al., 2011).

Let us assume a target compound noun N that consists of two nouns n and n'. Bold letters represent their corresponding distributional vectors obtained from corpora. $\oplus(\mathbf{N})$ denotes the vector of N obtained by applying the composition function $\oplus$ on $\mathbf{n}$ and $\mathbf{n}'$. Real number v_i denote the ith co-occurrence in $\mathbf{v}$. The functions ADD and MULT following Mitchell and Lapata (2008) are defined as follows:

$$\begin{aligned} \text{ADD:} \quad & \oplus(\mathbf{N}) = \alpha\,\mathbf{n} + \beta\,\mathbf{n}' \\ & \text{i.e. } \oplus(\mathbf{N})_i = \alpha\,\mathrm{n}_i + \beta\,\mathrm{n}'_i \\ \text{MULT:} \quad & \oplus(\mathbf{N}) = \mathbf{n}\mathbf{n}' \\ & \text{i.e. } \oplus(\mathbf{N})_i = \mathrm{n}_i \,.\, \mathrm{n}'_i \end{aligned} \qquad (1)$$

where α and β are real numbers.

Relevant to our work is the work of Erk and Padó (2008) who utilize a structured vector space model. The prototype vector of a constituent word is initially built, and later refined by removing irrelevant co-occurrences with the help of the selectional preferences of other constituents. The refined vectors are then used for the semantic composition of the compound noun. The results are encouraging showing that polysemy is a problem in vector space models. Our approach differs to theirs in the way we represent meaning - we experiment with static multi prototypes and dynamic prototypes. Our vector space model is based on simple bag-of-words which does not require selectional preferences for sense disambiguation and can be applied to resource-poor languages.

There are several other researchers who tried to address polysemy for improving the performance of different tasks but not particularly to the task of semantic composition. Some of them are Navigli and Crisafulli (2010) for web search results clustering, Klapaftis and Manandhar (2010b) for taxonomy learning, Reisinger and Mooney (2010) for word similarity and Korkontzelos and Manandhar (2009) for compositionality detection. In all cases, the reported results demonstrate that handling polysemy lead to improved performance of the corresponding tasks. This motivates our research for handling polysemy for the task of semantic composition using two different methods described in the next section.

3 Sense Prototype Vectors for Semantic Composition

In this section we describe two approaches for building sense specific prototype vectors of constituent words in a noun-noun compound. The first approach performs WSI to build static multi prototype vectors. The other builds a single dynamic prototype vector for each constituent by activating only the relevant exemplars of the constituent with respect to the other constituent. An exemplar is defined as a corpus instance of a target word.

These sense specific prototype vectors are then used for semantic composition. Let N be the compound noun with constituents n and n'. Our aim is to select the relevant senses of n and n'.

3.1 Static Multi Prototypes Based Sense Selection

In the first stage (section 3.1.1), a WSI method is applied to both n and n'. The outcome of this stage is a set of clusters (senses). Each of these clusters is associated with a prototype vector taking the centroid of the cluster. Following Reisinger and Mooney (2010) we use the terminology *multi prototype vectors* in the meaning of *sense clusters*. Let $S(n)$ (resp. $S(n')$) be the set of prototypes of n, where each $s_i^n \in S(n)$ denotes the ith sense of the noun n. Since these prototypes of constituents are static and do not change when the compound changes we refer to them as *static multi prototypes*.

In the next stage (section 3.1.2), we calculate all the pairwise similarities between the clusters of n and n', so as to select a pair of clusters with the highest similarity. The selected clusters are then combined using a composition function, to produce a single vector representing the semantics of the target compound noun N.

3.1.1 Graph-based WSI

Word Sense Induction is the task of identifying the senses of a target word in a given text. We apply a graph-based sense induction method, which creates a graph of target word instances and then clusters that graph to induce the senses. We follow the work of Klapaftis and Manandhar (2010a) for creating the graph and apply *Chinese Whispers* (CW) (Biemann, 2006), a linear graph clustering method that automatically identifies the number of clusters.

Figure 2 provides a running example of the different stages of the WSI method. In the example, the target word *mouse* appears with the *electronic device* sense in the contexts *A*, *C*, and with the *animal* sense in the contexts *B* and *D*.

Corpus preprocessing: Let bc denote the base corpus consisting of the contexts containing the target word tw. In our work, a context is defined by a set of words in a window of size 100 around the target.

Target word: *mouse*	
Extracted nouns & verbs	**Extracted collocations**
A: device, windows, move, pc, **mouse**,...	A: {1, 2, 3, 4, 5, 6}
B: animal, move, cat, tail, **mouse**,.......	B: {7, 8, 9, 10, 11, 12}
C: computer, pc, windows, **mouse**,.......	C: {5, 13, 14}
D: mousetrap, catch, tail, **mouse**,.......	D: {15, 16, 17}
Collocations index	
1:device_windows, 2:device_move, 3:device_pc, 4:windows_move, 5:windows_pc, 6:move_pc, 7:animal_move, 8:animal_cat, 9:animal_tail, 10:move_tail, 11:move_cat, 12:cat_tail, 13: computer_pc, 14:computer_windows, 15: mousetrap_catch, 16:mousetrap_tail, 17:catch_tail	
Graph	

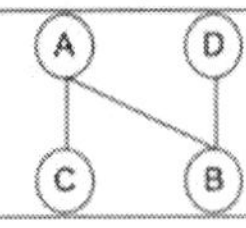

Figure 2: Running example of WSI

The aim of this stage is to capture words contextually related to tw. In the first step, the target word is removed from bc and part-of-speech tagging is applied to each context. Only nouns and verbs are kept and lemmatised. In the next step, the distribution of each word in the base corpus is compared to the distribution of the same noun in a reference corpus using the log-likelihood ratio (G^2) (Dunning, 1993). Words that have a G^2 below a pre-specified threshold (parameter p_1) are removed from each context of the base corpus. The result of this stage is shown in the upper left part of Figure 2.

Graph creation & clustering: Each context $c_i \in bc$ is represented as a vertex in a graph G. Edges between the vertices of the graph are drawn based on their similarity, defined in Equation 2, where $sm_{cl}(c_i, c_j)$ is the *collocational weight* of contexts c_i, c_j and $sm_{wd}(c_i, c_j)$ is their bag-of-words weight. If the edge weight $W(c_i, c_j)$ is above a prespecified threshold (parameter p_3), then an edge is drawn between the corresponding vertices in the graph.

$$W(c_i, c_j) = \frac{1}{2}(sm_{cl}(c_i, c_j) + sm_{wd}(c_i, c_j)) \quad (2)$$

Collocational weight: The limited polysemy of collocations is exploited to compute the similarity between contexts c_i and c_j. In this setting, a collocation is a juxtaposition of two words within the same context. Given a context c_i, a total of $\binom{N}{2}$ collocations are generated by combining each word with any other word in the context. Each collocation is weighted using the log-likelihood ratio (G^2) (Dunning, 1993) and is filtered out if the G^2

is below a prespecified threshold (parameter p_2). At the end of this process, each context c_i of tw is associated with a set of collocations (g_i) as shown in the upper right part of Figure 2 . Given two contexts c_i and c_j, the Jaccard coefficient is used to calculate the similarity between the collocational sets, i.e. $sm_{cl}(c_i, c_j) = \frac{|g_i \cap g_j|}{|g_i \cup g_j|}$.

Bag-of-words weight: Estimating context similarity using collocations may provide reliable estimates regarding the existence of an edge in the graph, however, it also suffers from data sparsity. For this reason, a bag-of-words model is also employed. Specifically, each context c_i is associated with a set of words (g_i) selected in the corpus preprocessing stage. The upper left part of Figure 2 shows the words associated with each context of our example. Given two contexts c_i and c_j, the bag-of-words weight is defined to be the Jaccard coefficient of the corresponding word sets, i.e. $sm_{wd}(c_i, c_j) = \frac{|g_i \cap g_j|}{|g_i \cup g_j|}$.

Finally, the collocational weight and bag-of-words weight are averaged to derive the edge weight between two contexts as defined in Equation 2. The resulting graph of our running example is shown on the bottom of Figure 2. This graph is the input to CW clustering algorithm. Initially, CW assigns all vertices to different classes. Each vertex i is processed for an x number of iterations and inherits the strongest class in its local neighborhood LN in an update step. LN is defined as the set of vertices which share a direct connection with vertex i. During the update step for a vertex i: each class C_k receives a score equal to the sum of the weights of edges (i, j), where j has been assigned class C_k. The maximum score determines the strongest class. In case of multiple strongest classes, one is chosen randomly. Classes are updated immediately, which means that a node can inherit classes from its LN that were introduced in the same iteration.

Experimental setting The parameters of the WSI method were fine-tuned on the nouns of the SemEval-2007 word sense induction task (Agirre and Soroa, 2007) under the second evaluation setting of that task, i.e. supervised (WSD) evaluation. We tried various parameter combinations shown in Table 1. Specifically, we selected the parameter combination p_1=15, p_2=10, p_3= 0.05 that maximized the performance in this evaluation. We use ukWaC (Ferraresi et al., 2008) corpus to retrieve all the instances of the target words.

Parameter	Range
G^2 word threshold (p_1)	15,25,35,45
G^2 collocation threshold (p_2)	10,15,20
Edge similarity threshold (p_3)	0.05,0.09,0.13

Table 1: WSI parameter values.

3.1.2 Cluster selection

The application of WSI on the nouns $n \in N$ and $n' \in N$ results in two sets of clusters (senses) $S(n)$ and $S(n')$. Cluster $S(n)$ is a set of contexts of the word n. Each context is represented as an exemplar $\mathbf{e}$, a vector specific to the context. Only the 10000 most frequent words in the ukWaC (along with their part-of-speech category) are treated as the valid co-occurrences i.e. the dimensionality of the vector space is 10000. For example, the exemplar of *hunting* in the context *"the-x purpose-n of-i autumn-n hunting-n be-v in-i part-n to-x cull-v the-x number-n of-i young-j autumn-n fox-n"* is ⟨ purpose-n:1, autumn-n:2, part-n:1, cull-v, number-n:1, young-j:1, fox-n:1 ⟩

For every cluster s_i^n in $S(n)$ we construct a prototype vector $\mathbf{v}^{\mathbf{s_i^n}}$ by taking the centroid of all the exemplars in the cluster. Following Mitchell and Lapata (2008), the context words in the prototype vector are set to the ratio of probability of the context word given the target word to the overall probability of the context word[1].

The next step is to choose the relevant sense of each constituent for a given compound. We assume that the meaning of a compound noun can be approximated by identifying the most similar senses of each of its constituent nouns. Accordingly all the pairwise similarities between the $\mathbf{v}^{\mathbf{s_i^n}}$ and $\mathbf{v}^{\mathbf{s_i^{n'}}}$ are calculated using cosine similarity and the pair with maximum similarity is chosen for composition.

3.2 Dynamic Prototype Based Sense Selection

Kilgarriff (1997) argues that representing a word with a fixed set of senses is not a good way of modelling word senses. Instead word senses should be defined according to a given context. We propose a dynamic way of building word senses for the constituents of a given compound.

We use an exemplar-based approach to build the dynamic sense of a constituent with the help of other constituent. In exemplar-based modelling

[1]This is similar to pointwise mutual information without logarithm

followed by huge tarpon that like to use the	**light**	of your torch to help them hunt. At the
the Christmas trade this year or the	**lights**	will be off, probably for ever. The Merrymen
embrace better health - but doing so in the	**light**	of real and trusted information about the
present your organisation in a professional	**light**	and in a way our all our clients value.
continues to be significant, together with other	**light**	industries such as electrical engineering
and near-infrared light, along with red	**light**	emitted by hydrogen atoms and green light

Figure 3: Six random sentences of *light* from ukWaC

(Erk and Padó, 2010; Smith and Medin, 1981), each word is represented by all its exemplars without conflating them into a single vector. Depending upon the purpose, only relevant exemplars of the target word are activated. Exemplar-based models are more powerful than just prototype based ones because they retain specific instance information. As described in the previous section, an exemplar is a vector that represents a single instance of a given word in the corpus.

Let E_n be the set of exemplars of the word n. Given a compound N with constituents n and n', we remove irrelevant exemplars in E_n creating a refined set $E_n^{n'} \subset E_n$ with the help of the other constituent word n'. The prototype vector $\mathbf{n}^{\mathbf{n}'}$ of n is then built from the centroid of the refined exemplar set $E_n^{n'}$. The vector $\mathbf{n}^{\mathbf{n}'}$ represents the relevant prototype vector (sense) of n in the presence of the other constituent word n'. Unlike the static prototypes defined in the previous section, the prototype vectors of n and n' are built dynamically based on the given compound. Therefore, we refer to them as dynamic prototype vectors.

3.2.1 Building Dynamic Prototypes

We demonstrate our method of building dynamic prototypes with an example. Let us take the compound *traffic light*. Let **Traffic**, **Light** and **TrafficLight** denote the prototype vectors of *traffic*, *light* and *traffic light* respectively. Word *light* occurs in many contexts such as quantum theory, optics, lamps and spiritual theory. In ukWaC, *light* occurs with 316,126 exemplars. Figure 3 displays 6 random sentences of *light* from ukWaC. None of these exemplars are related to the target compound *traffic light*. When a prototype vector of *light* is built from all its exemplars, irrelevant exemplars add noise increasing the semantic differences between *traffic light* and *light* and thereby increasing the semantic differences between **TrafficLight** and **Traffic** $\oplus$ **Light**. This is not desirable. The cosine similarity sim(**Light**, **TrafficLight**) is found to be 0.27.

We aim to remove irrelevant exemplars of *light* with the help of the other constituent word *traffic* and then build a prototype vector of *light* which is related to the compound *traffic light*. Our intuition and motivation for exemplar removal is that it is beneficiary to choose only the exemplars of *light* which have context words related to *traffic* since the exemplars of *traffic light* will have context words related to both *traffic* and *light*. For example car, road, transport will generally be found within the contexts of all the words *traffic*, *light* and *traffic light*.

We rank each exemplar of *light* with the help of collocations of *traffic*. Collocations of *traffic* are defined as the context words which frequently occur with *traffic*, e.g. car, road etc. The exemplar of *light* representing the sentence "*Cameras capture cars running red* ***lights*** ..." will be ranked higher than the one which does not have context words related to *traffic*. We use Sketch Engine[2] (Kilgarriff et al., 2004) to retrieve the collocations of *traffic* from ukWaC. Sketch Engine computes the collocations using Dice metric (Dice, 1945). We build a collocation vector $\mathbf{Traffic}^{\mathbf{colloc}}$ from the collocations of *traffic*.

We also rank each exemplar of *light* using the distributionally similar words to *traffic* i.e. words which are similar to *traffic* e.g. transport, flow etc. These distributionally similar words helps to reduce the impact of data sparseness and helps prioritize the contexts of *light* which are semantically related to *traffic*. Sketch Engine is again used to retrieve distributionally similar words of *traffic* from ukWaC. Sketch Engine ranks similar words using the method of Rychlý and Kilgarriff (2007). We build the vector $\mathbf{Traffic}^{\mathbf{similar}}$ which consists of the similar words of *traffic*.

Every exemplar **e** from the exemplar set E_{light} [3] is finally ranked by

$$sim(\mathbf{e}, \mathbf{Traffic}^{\mathbf{colloc}}) + sim(\mathbf{e}, \mathbf{Traffic}^{\mathbf{similar}})$$

[2]Sketch Engine `http://www.sketchengine.co.uk`

[3]In E_{light}, we do not include the sentences which have the compound noun *traffic light* occurring in them.

We choose the top n% of the ranked exemplars in E_{light} to construct a refined exemplar set $E_{\text{light}}^{\text{traffic}}$. A prototype vector $\mathbf{Light}^{\mathbf{Traffic}}$ is then built by taking the centroid of $E_{\text{light}}^{\text{traffic}}$. $\mathbf{Light}^{\mathbf{Traffic}}$ denotes the sense of *light* in the presence of *traffic*. Since sense of *light* is built dynamically based on the given compound (here *traffic light*), we define $\mathbf{Light}^{\mathbf{Traffic}}$ as the dynamic prototype vector. The similarity sim($\mathbf{Light}^{\mathbf{Traffic}}$, **TrafficLight**) is found to be 0.47 which is higher than the initial similarity 0.27 of **Light** and **TrafficLight**. This shows that our new prototype vector of *light* is closer to the meaning of *traffic light*.

Similarly we build the dynamic prototype vector $\mathbf{Traffic}^{\mathbf{Light}}$ of *traffic* with the help of *light*. The dynamic prototypes $\mathbf{Traffic}^{\mathbf{Light}}$ and $\mathbf{Light}^{\mathbf{Traffic}}$ are used for semantic composition to construct $\mathbf{Traffic}^{\mathbf{Light}} \oplus \mathbf{Light}^{\mathbf{Traffic}}$

4 Composition functions

Given a compound, we perform composition using the sense based prototypes selected in the above section. We use the composition functions ADD and MULT described in Equation 1.

For the function ADD, we use equal weights for both constituent words i.e. $\alpha = \beta = 1$. For the function MULT there are no parameters.

5 Evaluation

Mitchell and Lapata (2010) introduced an evaluation scheme for semantic composition models. We evaluate on their dataset, describe the evaluation scheme, and present the results of various models.

5.1 Dataset

Mitchell and Lapata (2010) prepared a dataset[4] which contains pairs of compound nouns and their similarity judgments. The dataset consists of 108 compound noun pairs with each pair having 7 annotations from different annotators who judge the pair for similarity. A sample of 5 compound pairs is displayed in Table 2.

5.2 Evaluation Scheme

For each pair of the compound nouns, the mean value of all its annotations is taken to be the final similarity judgment of the compound.

[4]We would like to thank Jeff Mitchell and Mirella Lapata for sharing the dataset.

Annotator	N	N'	rating
4	phone call	committee meeting	2
25	phone call	committee meeting	7
11	football club	league match	6
11	health service	bus company	1
14	company director	assistant manager	7

Table 2: Evaluation dataset of Mitchell and Lapata (2010)

Let N and N' be a pair. To evaluate a model, we calculate the cosine similarity between the composed vectors $\oplus(\mathbf{N})$ and $\oplus(\mathbf{N'})$ obtained from the composition on sense based prototypes generated by the model. These similarity scores are correlated with human mean scores to judge the performance of the model.

5.3 Models Evaluated

We evaluate all the models w.r.t. the composition functions ADD and MULT.

Static Single Prototypes: This model does not perform any sense disambiguation and is similar to the method described in (Mitchell and Lapata, 2008). The prototype vector of each constituent formed by conflating all its instances is used to compose the vector of the compound.

Static Multi Prototypes: In the method described in section 3.1, word sense induction produces a large number of clusters i.e. static multi prototypes. We tried various parameters like choosing the target prototype of a constituent only from the top 5 or 10 large clusters.

Dynamic Prototypes: In the method described in section 3.2, the dynamic prototype of a constituent is produced from the top n% exemplars of the ranked exemplar set of the constituent. We tried various percent activation (n%) values - 2%, 5%, 10%, 20%, 50%, 80%.

Compound Prototype: We directly use the corpus instances of a compound to build the prototype vector of the compound. This method does not involve any composition. Ideally, one expects this model to give the best performance.

Static Multi Prototypes with Guided Selection: This is similar to Static Multi Prototypes model except in the way we choose the relevant prototype for each constituent. In section 3.1.2 we described an unsupervised way of prototype selection from multi prototypes. Unlike there, here we choose the constituent prototype (sense) which has the highest similarity to the prototype vector of the

Parameter Description	ADD	MULT
Static Single Prototypes		
	0.5173	0.6104
Static Multi Prototypes		
Top 5 clusters	0.1171	0.4150
Top 10 clusters	0.0663	0.2655
Dynamic Prototypes		
Top 2 % exemplars	0.6261	**0.6552**
Top 5 % exemplars	0.6326	0.6478
Top 10 % exemplars	**0.6402**	0.6515
Top 20 % exemplars	0.6273	0.6359
Top 50 % exemplars	0.5948	0.6340
Top 80 % exemplars	0.5612	0.6355
Static Multi Prototypes with Guided Selection		
Top 5 clusters	0.2290	0.4187
Top 10 clusters	0.2710	0.4140
Compound Prototype		
	0.4152	

Table 3: Spearman Correlations of Model predictions with Human Predictions

compound. This is a guided way of sense selection since we are using the compound prototype vector which is built from the compound's corpus instances. The performance of this model gives us an idea of the upper boundary of multi prototype models for semantic composition.

5.4 Results and Discussion

All the above models are evaluated on the dataset described in section 5.1. Table 3 displays the Spearman correlations of all these models with the human annotations (mean values).

The results of Static Single Prototypes model are consistent with the previous findings of Mitchell and Lapata (2010), in which MULT performed better than ADD.

All the parameter settings of Dynamic Prototypes outperformed Static Single Prototypes. This shows that selecting the relevant sense prototypes of the constituents improve semantic composition. We also observe that the highest correlation is achieved by including just the top 2% exemplars for each constituent. It seems that as the sample of exemplars increases, noise increases as well, and this results in a worse performance.

The comparison between Static Single Prototypes and Static Multi Prototypes shows that the former performs significantly better than the latter. This is not according to our expectation. The possible reason for poor performance could be because of the sense selection process (section 3.1.2) which might have failed to choose the relevant sense of each constituent word.

However, Static Multi Prototypes with Guided Sense Selection still fail to perform better than Static Single Prototypes. Therefore, we can conclude that the lower performance of Static Multi Prototypes cannot be attributed to the sense selection process only. Despite that, the applied graph clustering method results in the generation of a very large number of clusters, some of which refer to the same word usage with subtle differences. Hence, our future work focuses on a selection process that chooses multiple relevant clusters of a constituent word. Additionally, our ongoing work suggests that the use of verbs as features in the graph creation process (section 3.1.1) causes the inclusion of noisy edges and results in worse clustering.

Our evaluation also shows that Dynamic Prototypes provide a better semantic composition than Static Multi Prototypes. The main reason for this result stems from the fact that Dynamic Prototypes explicitly identify the relevant usages of a constituent word with respect to the other constituent and vice versa, without having to deal with a set of issues that affect the performance of Static Multi Prototypes such as the clustering and the sense selection process.

The performance of Compound Prototype is lower than the compositional models. The reason could be due to the data sparsity. Data sparsity is known to be a major problem for modelling the meaning of compounds. In a way, the results are encouraging for compositional models.

In all these models, the composition function MULT gave a better performance than ADD.

6 Conclusions

This paper presented two methods for dealing with polysemy when modeling the semantics of a noun-noun compound. The first one represents senses by creating static multi prototype vectors, while the second represents context-specific sense of a word by generating a dynamic prototype vector. Our experimental results show that: (1) sense disambiguation improves semantic composition, and (2) dynamic prototypes are a better representation of senses than static multi prototypes for the task of semantic composition.

In future, we would like to explore other static multi prototype approaches of Reisinger and Mooney (2010) and Klapaftis and Manandhar (2010a) in comparison with dynamic prototypes. Dynamic prototypes are found to be particularly encouraging since they present a different mechanism for sense representation unlike traditional methods.

Acknowledgements

The authors are grateful to Lexical Computing Ltd for providing a free installation of Sketch Engine at University of York. The authors would like to thank anonymous reviewers for their excellent feedback. This work is supported by the European Commission via the EU FP7 INDECT project, Grant No.218086, Research area: SEC-2007-1.2-01 Intelligent Urban Environment Observation System.

References

Eneko Agirre and Aitor Soroa. 2007. Semeval-2007 task 02: Evaluating word sense induction and discrimination systems. In *Proceedings of the Fourth International Workshop on Semantic Evaluations (SemEval-2007)*, pages 7–12, Prague, Czech Republic, June. Association for Computational Linguistics.

Chris Biemann. 2006. Chinese Whispers - An Efficient Graph Clustering Algorithm and its Application to Natural Language Processing Problems. In *Proceedings of TextGraphs*, pages 73–80, New York, USA.

Lee R. Dice. 1945. Measures of the amount of ecologic association between species. *Ecology*, 26(3):pp. 297–302.

Ted Dunning. 1993. Accurate Methods for the Statistics of Surprise and Coincidence. *Computational Linguistics*, 19(1):61–74.

Katrin Erk and Sebastian Padó. 2008. A structured vector space model for word meaning in context. In *Proceedings of the Conference on Empirical Methods in Natural Language Processing*, EMNLP '08, pages 897–906, Stroudsburg, PA, USA. Association for Computational Linguistics.

Katrin Erk and Sebastian Padó. 2010. Exemplar-based models for word meaning in context. In *Proceedings of the ACL 2010 Conference Short Papers*, ACLShort '10, pages 92–97, Stroudsburg, PA, USA. Association for Computational Linguistics.

Adriano Ferraresi, Eros Zanchetta, Marco Baroni, and Silvia Bernardini. 2008. Introducing and evaluating ukWaC, a very large web-derived corpus of english. In *Proceedings of the WAC4 Workshop at LREC 2008*, Marrakesh, Morocco.

Adam Kilgarriff, Pavel Rychly, Pavel Smrz, and David Tugwell. 2004. The sketch engine. In *Proceedings of EURALEX 2004.*

Adam Kilgarriff. 1997. I don't believe in word senses. In *Computers and the Humanities, 31(2):91-113.*

Ioannis Klapaftis and Suresh Manandhar. 2010a. Word sense induction & disambiguation using hierarchical random graphs. In *Proceedings of the 2010 Conference on Empirical Methods in Natural Language Processing*, pages 745–755, Cambridge, MA, October. Association for Computational Linguistics.

Ioannis P. Klapaftis and Suresh Manandhar. 2010b. Taxonomy Learning Using Word Sense Induction. In *Proceedings of NAACL-HLT-2010*, pages 82–90, Los Angeles, California, June. ACL.

Ioannis Korkontzelos and Suresh Manandhar. 2009. Detecting compositionality in multi-word expressions. In *Proceedings of the ACL-IJCNLP 2009 Conference Short Papers*, ACLShort '09, pages 65–68, Stroudsburg, PA, USA. Association for Computational Linguistics.

Jeff Mitchell and Mirella Lapata. 2008. Vector-based models of semantic composition. In *Proceedings of ACL-08: HLT*, pages 236–244, Columbus, Ohio.

Jeff Mitchell and Mirella Lapata. 2010. Composition in distributional models of semantics. *Cognitive Science.*

Roberto Navigli and Giuseppe Crisafulli. 2010. Inducing word senses to improve web search result clustering. In *EMNLP*, pages 116–126.

Sebastian Pado and Mirella Lapata. 2007. Dependency-based construction of semantic space models. *Computational Linguistics*, 33(2):161–199.

Joseph Reisinger and Raymond J. Mooney. 2010. Multi-prototype vector-space models of word meaning. In *HLT-NAACL*, pages 109–117.

Pavel Rychlý and Adam Kilgarriff. 2007. An efficient algorithm for building a distributional thesaurus (and other sketch engine developments). In *Proceedings of the 45th Annual Meeting of the ACL on Interactive Poster and Demonstration Sessions*, ACL '07, pages 41–44, Stroudsburg, PA, USA. Association for Computational Linguistics.

Hinrich Schütze. 1998. Automatic Word Sense Discrimination. *Computational Linguistics*, 24(1):97–123.

Edward E. Smith and Douglas L. Medin. 1981. *Categories and concepts / Edward E. Smith and Douglas L. Medin*. Harvard University Press, Cambridge, Mass. :.

Eva Maria Vecchi, Marco Baroni, and Roberto Zamparelli. 2011. (linear) maps of the impossible: Capturing semantic anomalies in distributional space. In *Proceedings of the Workshop on Distributional Semantics and Compositionality*, pages 1–9, Portland, Oregon, USA, June. Association for Computational Linguistics.

Dominic Widdows. 2008. Semantic vector products: Some initial investigations. In *Second AAAI Symposium on Quantum Interaction, Oxford*, March.

Using Prediction from Sentential Scope to Build a Pseudo Co-Testing Learner for Event Extraction

Shasha Liao
Computer Science Department
New York University
liaoss@cs.nyu.edu

Ralph Grishman
Computer Science Department
New York University
grishman@cs.nyu.edu

Abstract

Event extraction involves the identification of instances of a type of event, along with their attributes and participants. Developing a training corpus by annotating events in text is very labor intensive, and so selecting informative instances to annotate can save a great deal of manual work. We present an active learning (AL) strategy, *pseudo co-testing*, based on one view from a classifier aiming to solve the original problem of event extraction, and another view from a classifier aiming to solve a coarser granularity task. As the second classifier can provide more graded matching from a wider scope, we can build a set of pseudo-contention-points which are very informative, and can speed up the AL process. Moreover, we incorporate multiple selection criteria into the pseudo co-testing, seeking training examples that are informative, representative, and varied. Experiments show that pseudo co-testing can reduce annotation labor by 81%; incorporating multiple selection criteria reduces the labor by a further 7%.

1 Introduction

The goal of event extraction is to identify instances of a class of events in text. There can be many event types; for example, the ACE 2005 event extraction task involved a set of 33 generic event types and subtypes appearing frequently in the news. A typical event extraction task, in addition to identifying the event itself, also identifies all of the participants and attributes of the event; these are the entities that are involved in that event. Annotating a corpus in order to train an event tagger is a costly task.

First of all, event extraction is difficult and requires substantial training data. The same event might be presented in various expressions, and an expression might represent different events in different contexts. For example, "retire" and "resign" can both represent an *End-Position* event, while "leave" can represent either an *End-Position* or *Move* event in different contexts. Moreover, for each event type, the event participants and attributes may also appear in multiple forms and exemplars of the different forms may be required.

Furthermore, compared to other tasks like name tagging or part of speech tagging, events of a particular type appear relatively rarely in a document. One document might only contain one or two events of a given type, or even none at all. For the ACE 2005 event extraction task, *Attack* events have the highest frequency in the training corpus (2240 times, an average of 4 events per document), while *Start-Position* events only appear 232 times (an average of 1/3 event per document). As a result, to acquire enough training samples, we need to annotate a lot of documents. If we can predict which documents, or even which sentences to annotate, we can save a lot of time.

Considering the complexity of event extraction and the labor of annotating an event, providing the annotator with an informative sample to annotate is especially important. Active learning (AL) is a good way to do so because it aims to keep the human annotation effort to a minimum, only asking for advice where the training utility of the result of such a query is high.

Active learning is a supervised machine learning technique in which the learner is in control of the selection of data used for learning. The intent is to ask an *oracle* - typically a human with extensive knowledge of the domain at hand

- about the classes of instances for which the model trained so far makes unreliable predictions. Selective sampling methods, introduced by Cohn, Atlas and Ladner (1994), made the learner query the oracle about data that is likely to be misclassified. This is the crucial aspect of AL – finding "good" instances for a human to annotate.

In this paper, we investigate the use of AL in event extraction. In particular, we apply the active learning approach to the *Attack* event, because it is the most frequent event type in the ACE corpus, and is particularly challenging because of the large number of different expressions: there are 312 different words in the corpus that serve at least once as the main word (the "trigger") of an *Attack* event,

After studying several sampling strategies, we settled upon a *pseudo co-testing* approach where a second classifier which solves a coarser variant of the original task is used. Furthermore, we incorporate multiple selection criteria into the pseudo co-testing, not only selecting more informative sentences, but also considering their distribution in the sample pool, and the diversity of the instances added to the training set at the same time.

2 Event Extraction

2.1 Task Description

ACE defines an event as a specific occurrence involving participants[1], and it annotates 8 types and 33 subtypes of events. In this task, an *event mention* is a phrase or sentence within which an event is described, including trigger and arguments. An event mention must have one and only one trigger, and can have an arbitrary number of arguments. The *event trigger* is the main word that most clearly expresses an event occurrence. The *event mention arguments (roles)*[2] are the *Entity/Timex mentions*[3] that are involved in an event mention, and their relation to the event. For example, an *Attack* event might include participants like *Attacker* or *Target*, or attributes like *Time-Within* and *Place*. Arguments will be taggable only when they occur within the scope of the corresponding event, typically the same sentence.

Consider the sentence:

*(1) This Friday in France, **Bob Cole** was on his way home when **he** was **attacked**...*

Event extraction depends on previous phases like name identification, entity mention classification, and entity mention coreference. Table 1 shows the results of this preprocessing. Note that entity mentions that share the same EntityID are coreferential and treated as the same object.

Entity/Timex mention		Head	Entity ID	Type
1-1-1		France	1-1	GPE
1-T1-1		Friday	1-T1	Timex
1-2-1		Bob Cole	1-2	PER
1-2-2		He	1-2	PER
Event type	**Trigger**	**Role**		
		Place	**Target**	**Time**
Attack	attacked	1-1-1	1-2-2	1-T1-1

Table 1. An example of Entity /Timex mentions, and Attack events

In this example, there is one *Attack* event, which contains attributes and participants including place, target and time.

2.2 Baseline Event Tagger

Identifying a potential trigger – the word most clearly expressing the event – is essential for event extraction. Usually, the trigger itself is the most important clue in detecting and classifying the type of an event; for example, words like "attack", "conflict", and "beat" are more likely to represent an *Attack* event, while "meet", "eat", and "shopping" are not likely to be triggers of *Attack* events. Then, once we find possible triggers, we can apply the argument / role identification to find the participants or attributes of the event. For example, the subject of the trigger word "attack" is usually the *Attacker* argument, while the object is the *Target* argument.

However, although the trigger itself is crucial to determine whether or not there is a reportable event, it is not always sufficient. As a result, most current event extraction systems consider trigger and argument information together to tag a reportable event.

[1] See http://projects.ldc.upenn.edu/ace/docs/English-Events-Guidelines_v5.4.3.pdf for a description of this task.

[2] Note that we do not deal with event mention coreference in this paper, so each event mention is treated as a separate event.

[3] An *Entity mention* is a reference (typically, a noun phrase) to an object or a set of objects in one of the semantic categories of interest. A *Timex mention* is a reference to a time expression.

In this paper, we adapted an existing state-of-the-art English IE system [Grishman et al. 2005][4] to serve as our baseline system. This system extracts events independently for each sentence, because the definition of event mention argument constrains them to appear in the same sentence.

In the training process, a pattern collector is first applied to all annotated events to build features used in later classifiers, and then three Maximum Entropy-based classifiers are trained. For each word (trigger candidate) in the training data, if it is a verb, noun or adjective (the three possible parts-of-speech for a trigger in ACE), we update the following three classifiers:

- **Argument Classifier:** Given the trigger candidate and a *Entity / Timex mention* in the sentence, to distinguish whether the mention is a possible argument of a specific event type;
- **Role Classifier:** for each argument identified by the argument classifier, to determine its role with respect to a specific event type;
- **Trigger Classifier:** Given the trigger candidate, the pattern representing the local syntactic context, and a set of roles identified by the role classifier, to determine whether this word is a true trigger, and this is a reportable event.

In the test procedure, for each word (each potential trigger), the argument / role classifier is applied to collect the possible arguments/roles connected to this word, and then the trigger classifier is used to decide whether it is a trigger or not. If it is, an event mention including the trigger and all its roles will be reported, else the word will not be tagged as a trigger, and all the arguments/roles collected by previous classifiers are discarded.

3 Active Learning for Event Extraction

Active learning has been successfully applied to a number of natural language processing tasks, such as named entity recognition (Shen et al. 2004; Hachey, Alex and Becker 2005; Kim et al. 2006), text categorization (Schohn and Cohn 2000; Tong and Koller 2002; Hoi, Jin & Lyu 2006), part of speech tagging (Ringger et al. 2007), parsing (Osborne and Baldridge 2004; Becker and Osborne 2005; Reichart and Rappoport 2007), and word sense disambiguation (Chen et al. 2006; Zhu and Hovy 2007). However, there have not yet been any studies to use active learning in event extraction.

There are several sampling methods in active learning; the most commonly used ones include uncertainty-based sampling, committee-based sampling, and co-testing. Co-testing (Muslea et al. 2000) involves two (or more) redundant views; it simultaneously trains a separate classifier for each view, and the system selects a query based on the degree of disagreement among the learners. Because well-informed classifiers for the two views should agree, co-testing will select an example which is informative for at least one of the classifier models.

In theory, co-testing has some advantages over uncertainty sampling and committee-based sampling. However, the disadvantage of co-testing is that it has more constraints: the two views should be disjoint and each sufficient to learn a classifier. As discussed above, event extraction is complicated and involves several classifiers on different levels interacting together. This makes it difficult to split the feature set into two views. In particular, the identity of the trigger will be a critical feature for any successful classifier. Committee-based sampling faces similar problem as co-testing: it is hard to generate several classifiers that are consistent with the training set or sub-samples of it, respectively.

This leaves uncertainty-based sampling as an attractive option. Although Muslea (2000) points out that uncertainty sampling may make queries that lead to minimal improvements of the classifier, and therefore require more queries to build an accurate classifier, it is simple and can be applied to almost all kinds of statistical models.

We could do active learning at the token level: – asking the *oracle* whether a specific token triggers an event – but that is not very practical. Rather, for each query, we return a sentence that might contain an event to ask the oracle to annotate. We do so because the oracle needs to read the whole sentence to decide whether it is a reportable event, and annotate all its arguments. Thus, a sentence-based sampling pool is built where each sentence is treated as a sample query.

3.1 Applying Uncertainty-based Sampling

Event extraction is a compound classification task, which involves the identification of argu-

[4] The existing system had both pattern matching and statistical components; we integrated these components so that the resulting system would have a uniform probabilistic model suitable for the active learning strategies we employed.

ments/roles, and the event trigger. These classifiers are separately trained, but not independent; results from previous classifiers are used as features for the following classifier, and the decision by the following classifier will affect the previous results (arguments confidently tagged by the argument/role classifier will be discarded if the trigger labeling treats it as not a event). Because the final classifier – the trigger classifier – takes all the considerations we mentioned above as input, and makes a final decision of a reportable event, we use its output as the probability of the event tagger. The traditional approach in uncertainty sampling (Lewis and Gale 1994) queries one of the samples on which the classifier is the least confident. In our case, the greatest uncertainty regarding the presence of an event corresponds to the trigger probability closest to 0.5. We treat the uncertainty of the sentence as the maximum of the uncertainties of the constituent words (i.e., the uncertainty attributable to the word with probability closest to 0.5):

$$e\_Info(S_i) = 1 - \min_{w_j \in S_i} |0.5 - prob\_e(w_j)|$$

where $prob\_e(w_j)$ is the trigger probability of the word w_j in S_i, as returned by the event tagger.

3.2 Problems with Uncertainty-based Sampling

However, the results of uncertainty-based sampling are somewhat disappointing (see Figures 3, 4, and 5 in section 5.3). It performs quite well at first: within a few iterations, trigger labeling (event detection) quickly achieves a performance (F score) of 65%, but beyond that point the gain is very slow. At this point there is still a 7% gap between its performance and that of a classifier trained on the whole sampling pool.

Why does uncertainty-based AL perform this way? The event tagger depends primarily on the particular trigger and secondarily on its local structure, for example, the potential arguments in the immediate vicinity of the trigger and the dependency paths between them. Such information is effective at identifying the trigger and arguments, but is responsive only to particular words and patterns. Triggers and structures which have not been seen in the training data will be assigned uniformly low probabilities. When trained on the whole ACE 2005 corpus (in a supervised training scenario) this is appropriate behavior: we don't want to report an event in testing if we haven't seen the trigger before.[5] However, for active learning, the inability to differentiate among potential new triggers and local structures is critical. Only a few words ever serve as possible triggers for a specific event type. For the *Attack* event, only 2.0% of the words in the ACE training data ever act as an event trigger. The uncertainty of the event tagger, by itself, does not provide useful guidance regarding possible additional triggers the user should be asked about, and the system might query a lot of irrelevant sentences with unseen words before a sentence with a new trigger is found.

We can see this as an instance of a more general problem. Our goal in AL is to select for labeling those data points which are most likely to improve the accuracy of the model. Methods like uncertainty-based sampling are heuristics towards that end, but are not always effective; their success depends on characteristics of the classifier and the feature space. For event extraction, the classifier is most likely to benefit from finding *new*, *frequently-occurring* triggers. We need a way of identifying likely candidates.

Furthermore, we note that – while the final trigger classifier which we train from the labeled data must operate at the token level – we will be presenting the user with a sentence to label, so it is sufficient for the classifier we use for AL to operate at the sentence level.

3.3 Another View from Sentential Scope

Can we find a classifier which suits the needs of our active learner by identifying sentences which are likely to contain an event? A simple (bag-of-words) classifier based on the words in the sentence can do quite well at this task. For example, a sentence with "troops", "victim", "bloody" and "soldier" might be more likely to contain an *Attack* event, even if these words might not be elements of the event.

These bag-of-words features are not particularly helpful for the original task of identifying an event (trigger and arguments) – they don't pinpoint a particular word as the trigger. But that's not a problem if the data selection for AL is operating at a coarser level.[6]

[5] Unlike some other tasks such as named entity and part-of-speech tagging, local contextual clues by themselves are generally not strong enough to reliably tag an event.
[6] Note that some active learners for tasks such as named entities and part-of-speech which also train token-level annotators choose to present data to the user at the sentence level, because it is more convenient and efficient for the user. These taggers could select data at the token level using

3.4 Pseudo Co-Testing

The sentence-level bag-of-words classifier is far from perfect – the predictions at the sentence level are somewhat noisy. But considering that only 6.5% of the sentences in the ACE data contain an *Attack* event, returning a possibly relevant sentence is much more useful than returning a totally irrelevant sentence. If a sentence S in the sample pool shares many words with another sentence in the training data known to contain an event, and the event tagger does not find a trigger word in S, there is a good chance that S contains a new (previously unseen) trigger word and new local structure, because the two sentences may be describing the same event, but using different verbs and word sequences.

Thus, we apply a pseudo co-testing algorithm with one view from an event tagger based on local information, and another view, which aimed to solve an approximate task: whether there is a possible event in a sentence.

We call this algorithm "*pseudo* co-testing" because one of the views is not sufficient to solve the target problem, but is sufficient to solve a subproblem at a coarser granularity, in contrast to traditional co-testing. People might argue that when a *pseudo contention point* is found in this algorithm, it means that at least one of the classifiers is wrong, but we do not know (until we query the oracle) which one. If it is the event tagger, this sample is informative for the event tagger and adding this sample will improve the performance; if it is the sentence classifier, it is not guaranteed that this sample is informative for the event tagger. However, since the updated sentence classifier will serve to select subsequent queries, samples informative for the sentence classifier should accelerate subsequent active learning. Furthermore, the event tagger and the sentence classifier each have their own advantages in finding an event to query. The event tagger prefers sentences with already-known local patterns, like a trigger and its arguments, although the overall sentence (the choice of words and wider structure) might be very different. The sentence classifier prefers sentences sharing the same words, but which may have different local structures. Together they offer the potential for finding new triggers which do not appear in the existing training data (via the sentence classifier) and then acquiring event and non-event exemplars of these triggers (through the event tagger).

In pseudo co-testing, we use the probabilities from the event tagger and sentence classifier to build a contention set consisting of those sentences where the event tagger and sentential event recognizer make different predictions. Among these sentences, we assume that the larger the margin between the event tagger and sentential event recognizer, the less certain the sample is. So, instead of randomly choosing samples from the contention set, we order the samples by their margins between the event tagger and sentential event recognizer, and pick the ones with largest margin:

$$co\_Info(S_i) = \underset{w_j \in S_i \& isCP}{Max} \left| prob\_e(w_j) - prob\_s(S_i) \right|$$

where $prob\_s(S_i)$ is the probability from the sentence classifier; while $prob\_e(w_j)$ is the trigger probability from the event tagger for the word w_j in sentence S_i, and w_j is a *contention point* (CP) where the event tagger's prediction is opposite that of the sentence classifier.

4 Multi-criteria-based AL

Normally active learning only considers the *informativeness* of the sample. In uncertainty-based query, *informativeness* is represented by the least confident sample; in committee-based querying, it is represented by the samples on which the committee vote is the most equally split; in co-testing, it is represented by the contention sample. Shen et al. (2004) pointed out that we should maximize the contribution of the selected instances based on multiple criteria besides *informativeness.* For example, the *representativeness* and *diversity* of the sentence should also be considered. In this way, we not only consider whether the current model contains enough information to classify this sentence (as containing an event), but also consider the distribution of this sample in the whole sampling pool (*representativeness*), and moreover, insure that we select different kind of samples in a batch to make the selection more diverse (*diversity*).

4.1 Features used in Similarity of Samples

To evaluate the *representativeness* and *diversity*, we first need to calculate the similarity between two samples, in our case, two sentences. In general, a sentence will be represented as a vector of features $S_1 = \{f_{11}, f_{12}, f_{13}, \ldots\ldots, f_{1n}\}$ and

---

two views based on the identity of a token and its immediate context. We share these user considerations, but in addition selecting data at the sentence level enables us to create effective complementary views for event extraction not available at a finer (token) level.

the similarity is calculated based on the feature vectors of the two sentences. Thus, the essential problem becomes how to build the feature vector for a sentence. Since there are two classifiers in the pseudo co-testing, we use features from both classifiers, and measure the similarity using a cosine measure, following Shen et al (2004):

$$Sim(S_1,S_2) = \frac{\sum_{f_i \in S_1} \sum_{f_j \in S_2} sim(f_i,f_j)}{|S_1| \ |S_2|}$$

where $sim(f_i,f_j)$ is 1 when f_i and f_j are the same, otherwise 0.

4.2 Representativeness

A few prior studies have considered this selection criterion (McCallum and Nigam 1998; Tang et al. 2002; Shen et al. 2004). The *representativeness* of a sample can be evaluated based on how many samples are similar to this sample. Adding samples which are more representative to the training set will have an effect on a larger number of unlabeled samples.

For every sentence in the sampling pool, we measure its *representativeness* based on its average similarity to other sentences in the sampling pool:

$$Represent(S_i) = \frac{\sum_{S_j \in P, i \neq j} sim(S_i,S_j)}{|P|-1}$$

where P is the current sampling pool. In this way, we will filter out the samples that are rare in the whole sampling pool, and focus our effort on the samples that appear more frequently in the whole corpus.

In addition to favoring the most informative example, we also prefer the most representative example. To combine scores from *informativeness* and *representativeness*, we followed Shen et al (2004)'s metric:

$$Score(S_i) = \lambda \cdot co\_Info(S_i) + (1-\lambda) Represent(S_i)$$

where the relative importance of each criterion is determined by the parameter λ ($0 \leq \lambda \leq 1$). In our experiment, λ is set to 0.7.

4.3 Diversity

The role of the *diversity* criterion is to maximize the training utility of a batch of samples. As we add a batch of samples into the training data in one iteration (for efficiency in updating the model), we want to make sure we provide various types of sentences, which provide the most information as a whole, and avoid selecting very similar sentences for a single batch. To this end, after we rank the sentences in the sampling pool, based on the different strategies mentioned above, we skip over any sentence whose similarity to one already selected in the same batch exceeds a threshold (see Figure 2).

The diversity metric is involved in selecting a batch of instances, as follows:

```
====================
Given: SenSet = (S1,...,SN) and the BatchSet with the
maximal size K.
Initialization: BatchSet = empty
Loop until BatchSet is full
        Select Si based on some measure from SenSet;
        RepeatFlag = false;
        Loop from j = 1 to CurrentSize of BatchSet
                If Score(Si, Sj) > threshold Then
                        RepeatFlag = true;
                        break;
        If RepeatFlag == false Then
                Add Si into BatchSet.
======================
```

Figure 2. Diversity criterion in batch-based active learning

5 Experiments

We use the ACE 2005 training corpus, which contains in total 598 annotated documents, to simulate the active learning process. For evaluation, we conduct a blind test on a set of 54 randomly chosen documents. For each active learning strategy, we make 4 runs and use the average scores as our final results. For each run, 10 documents are randomly chosen as the initial training data, and the rest (534 documents) are used to build the sampling pool. Overall, the average initial training set contains 369 sentences, and the sampling pool contains an average of 12074 sentences.

A Maxent model based on bag-of-words features serves as the sentence classifier. To reduce data sparseness, all inflected words are changed to their lemma form (e.g. "attackers"→"attacker"). A list of stop words is also applied.

For each iteration, we picked 50 sample sentences at the top of the ranked list based on different query strategies. To simulate the user queries, annotations extracted from the key annotations are returned as user feedback, and added into the training data.

5.1 Query Strategies

In the following sections, we compare the performance of the query strategies mentioned above – uncertainty-based query (*Uncertainty*), pseudo co-testing (*pCT*), and multi-criteria pseudo co-testing(*multi_pCT*). We employ a random sampling (*Random*) method as a baseline, where samples are selected randomly to add to the training data. Also, to assess the benefit of active learning, we report the performance from the event tagger trained on the entire ACE2005 data except for the test set (*Full_Corpus*).

5.2 Results

The performances (F-measure) of different strategies are evaluated based on three metrics: argument/role labeling (Figures 3 & 4) and trigger labeling (Figure 5).

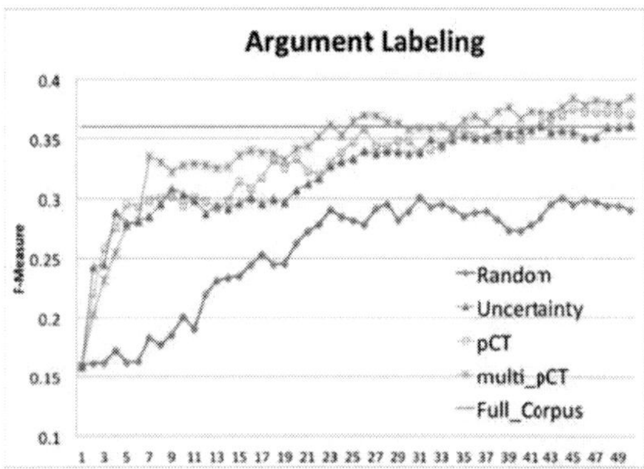

Figure 3. Performance (F-Measure) of argument labeling

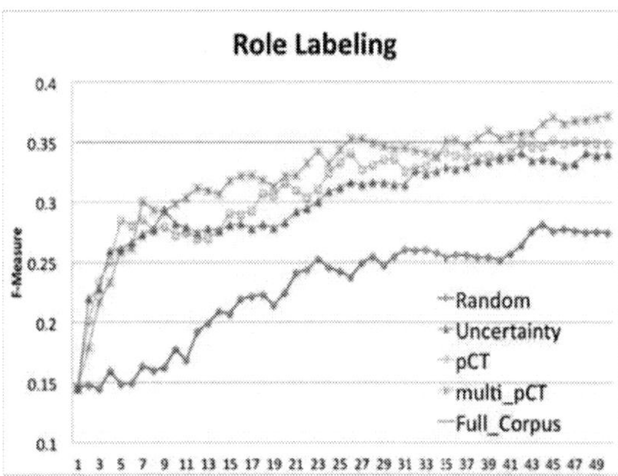

Figure 4. Performance (F-Measure) of role labeling

Uncertainty-based querying (*Uncertainty*) yields poorer results than the other active learning strategies, because of the event tagger's relatively rigid matching procedure. Thus, it lacks the ability to recognize new potential triggers or patterns. For example, if we have pattern *A* which is very similar to some event-bearing patterns in the training data, and pattern *B* which is quite different from any pattern in the training data, the event tagger will treat them the same. However, the sentence classifier provides more graded matching, and gives the sentence containing pattern *A* higher score because they share a lot of words. Thus, the pseudo co-testing (*pCT*) would give a higher score to pattern *A*, and achieve better performance. Also, we observed that multi-criteria pseudo co-testing (*multi_pCT)* performs best in all three evaluations.

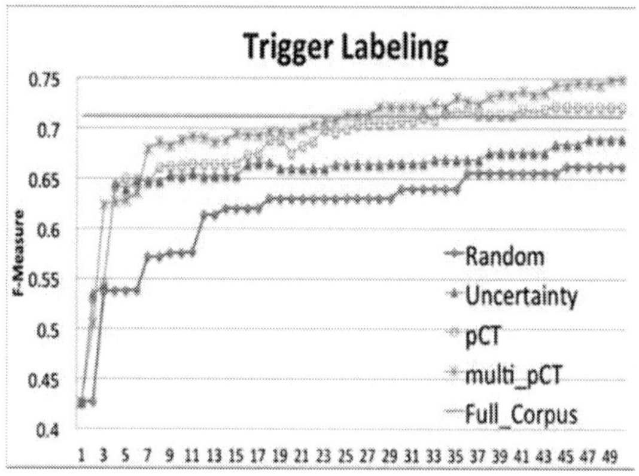

Figure 5. Performance (F-Measure) of trigger labeling

The differences between the approaches are particularly marked for trigger labeling after just a few iterations. Consider how much data must be annotated to get to 95% of full corpus score for trigger labeling (F-Measure 67.5%): *multi_pCT* only takes 7 iterations; *pCT* takes 17 iterations; *Uncertainty* takes 38 iterations. In other words, 5.8%, 9.8%, 18.2% of the whole corpus needs to be annotated to reach the same performance. Thus, using *pCT* is almost twice as fast as *Uncertainty* to reach a reasonable performance, while *multi_pCT* will shorten this process by half again. The benefits of better query selection are clearest for the first few batches of queries, which may be the range of greatest practical import for developers wanting to quickly add new event types.

Overall, we observe that pseudo co-testing performs better on all three evaluation measures than uncertainty-based active learning. Uncertainty-based active learning requires more than 100 iterations before it reaches the level of performance on all three measures achieved by the supervised system, trained on the entire corpus (*Full_Corpus*). *pCT* takes 41 iterations to reach this level. At this point, there are in total 369+2050 = 2419 sentences in the training data; this represents a reduction in labor over sequential annotation of 80.6%. Applying the multi-criteria-based strategy (*multi_pCT*), we can reach this point even earlier, in iteration 23, where the labor is reduced by 87.8%[7].

6 Related Work

Many existing active learning methods are based on selecting the most uncertain examples using various measures (Thompson et al. 1999; Schohn and Cohn 2000; Tong and Koller 2000; Engelson and Dagan 1999; Ngai and Yarowsky 2000). (McCallum and Nigam 1998; Tang et al. 2002) proposed methods that consider the representativeness criterion in active learning. (Tang et al. 2002) use the density information to weight the selected examples but do not use it to select a sample. (Brinker 2003) first incorporated diversity in active learning for text classification. Shen et al. (2004) proposed a multi-criteria-based active learning approach and applied it to named entity recognition. They jointly consider multiple criteria, including *informativeness*, *representativeness* and *diversity*. Experiments showed that incorporating all the criteria together is more efficient than single-criterion-based methods.

Traditional active learning with redundant views splits the feature set into several sub-sets or views, each of which is enough, to some extent, to describe the underlying problem. Muslea et al. (2000) presented an approach in which two classifiers are trained only on labeled data, then run over the unlabeled data. A contention set of examples is then created, consisting of all unlabeled examples on which the classifiers disagree. Samples are randomly selected from this set for query, and then both classifiers are retrained.

To the best of our knowledge, there is no study yet of active learning in event extraction. However, Patwardhan and Riloff (2009) presented a model for role filling in event extraction that jointly considers both the local context around a phrase and the wider sentential context in a probabilistic framework. They used a sentential event recognizer and a plausible role-filler recognizer to jointly make decisions on a sentence, and find the roles of the events. Although it is not a co-testing process, it gave us the intuition of using a sentential view to predict possible events in a sentence.

7 Conclusion

In this paper, we investigate strategies of active learning for event extraction, and propose a novel way of selecting good samples to be added to the training pool. Experiments show that a classifier for a coarser task can provide an extra view to build a pseudo co-testing strategy. Although the ultimate goal involves training the original (fine-grained) classifier, the coarser task can provide useful information for query selection. In the special case of event extraction, we find that a sentence classifier can help an event tagger select a better query, because it is not only good at finding new trigger and local structures from graded matching over a wider scope, but also provides a better way of judge the representativeness and diversity of the samples. In our experiment, we reduced human labor by 80.6% to 87.8%.

Acknowledgments

Supported by the Intelligence Advanced Research Projects Activity (IARPA) via Air Force Research Laboratory (AFRL) contract number FA8650-10-C-7058. The U.S. Government is authorized to reproduce and distribute reprints for Governmental purposes notwithstanding any copyright annotation thereon. The views and conclusions contained herein are those of the authors and should not be interpreted as necessarily representing the official policies or endorsements, either expressed or implied, of IARPA, AFRL, or the U.S. Government.

References

Markus Becker and Miles Osborne 2005. A two-stage method for active learning of statistical grammars. *In Proceedings of the Nineteenth International Joint Conference on Artificial Intelligence. Edinburgh, Scotland, UK.*

K. Brinker. 2003. Incorporating Diversity in Active Learning with Support Vector Machines. *In Proceedings of ICML, 2003.*

[7] We observe that the AL can perform better than training on the whole corpus; we believe that this is a result of AL selecting more positive training data. After 50 iterations of *multi-pcT*, 31.4% of the selected sentences have positive *Aattack* examples, whereas only 6.1% of the entire corpus has such positive examples. Separate experiments suggest that using a corpus richer in positive examples can produce a small improvement in performance.

Jinying Chen, Andrew Chein, Lyle Ungar and Martha Palmer. 2006. An empirical study of the behavior of active learning for word sense disambiguation. *In Proceedings of the HLT-NAACL 2006. New York, USA.*

S. A. Engelson and I. Dagan. 1999. Committee- Based Sample Selection for Probabilistic Classifiers. *Journal of Artifical Intelligence Research.*

Ralph Grishman, David Westbrook and Adam Meyers. 2005. NYU's English ACE 2005 System Description. *In Proc. ACE 2005 Evaluation Workshop, Gaithersburg, MD.*

B. Hachey, B. Alex, and M Becker. 2005. Investigating the effects of selective sampling on the annotation task.. *In proceedings of the Ninth Conference on Computational Natural Language Learning (CoNLL-2005), 144-151. ACL, Ann Arbor, Michigan, USA.*

Steven C.H Hoi, Rong Jin and Michael R. Lyu. 2006. Large-scale text categorization by batch mode active learning. *Proceedings of the 15th International World Wide Web Conference (WWW 2006). Edinburgh, Scotland.*

R. Jones, R. Ghani, T. Mitchell, and E. Riloff. 2003. Active Learning for Information Extraction with Multiple View Feature Sets, *ECML-03 Workshop on Adaptive Text Extraction and Mining*

Seokhwan Kim, Yu Song, Kyungduk Kim, Jeong-won Cha, and Gary Geunbae Lee. 2006. MMR-based active machine learning for bio named entity recognition. *In Proceedings of the HLT-NAACL 2006. New York, USA.*

A. McCallum and K. Nigam. 1998. Employing EM in Pool-Based Active Learning for Text Classification. *In Proceedings of ICML, 1998.*

Muslea, I., Minton, S., & Knoblock, C. (2000) Selective sampling with redundant views. *Proc. Of National Conference on Artificial Intelligence (pp. 621-626)*

Miles Osborne and Jason Baldridge. 2004. Ensemble-based active learning for parse selection. *In Proceedings of Human Language Technology Conference- the North American Chapter of the Association for Computational Linguistics Annual Meeting. (HLT-NAACL 2004). Boston, Massachusetts, USA.*

S. Patwardhan and E. Riloff. 2009. A Unified Model of Phrasal and Sentential Evidence for Information Extraction. *Proceedings of the 2009 Conference on Empirical Methods in Natural Language Processing (EMNLP-09)*

Roi Reichart and Ari Rappoport 2007. An ensemble method for selection of high quality parses. *In Proceedings of the 45th Annual Meeting of the Association for Computational Linguistics (ACL 2007).*

Eric Ringger, Peter McClanahan, Robbie Haertel, George Busby, Marc Carmen, James Carroll, Kevin Seppi and Deryle Lonsdale 2007. Active Learning for part-of-speech tagging: Accelerating corpus annotation. *In proceedings of the Linguistic Annotation Workshop. ACL, Prague, Czech Republic. 2007.*

Greg Schohn and David Cohn. 2000. Less is more: Active learning with support vector machines. *In Proceedings of the Seventeenth International Conference on Machine Learning (ICML-2000). Stanford, California, USA.*

D Shen, J Zhang, J Su, and G Zhou. 2004. Multi-Criteria-based Active Learning for Named Entity Recognition. *Proceedings of the 42nd Annual Meeting on Association for Computational Linguistics, 2004.*

M. Tang, X. Luo and S. Roukos. 2002. Active Learning for Statistical Natural Language Parsing. *In Proceedings of the ACL 2002.*

C. A. Thompson, M. E. Califf and R. J. Mooney. 1999. Active Learning for Natural Language Parsing and Information Extraction. *In Proceedings of ICML 1999.*

Simon Tong and Daphne Koller 2002. Support vector machine active learning with applications to text classification. *Journal of Machine Learning 2 (Match): 45-66*

Jingbo Zhu and Eduard Hovy 2007. Active Learning for word sense disambiguation with methods for addressing the class imbalance problem. *In Proceedings of the 2007 Joint Conference on Empirical Methods in Natural Language Processing and Computational Natural Language Learning.*

Text Segmentation and Graph-based Method for Template Filling in Information Extraction

Ludovic Jean-Louis, Romaric Besançon, Olivier Ferret
CEA, LIST, Vision and Content Engineering Laboratory
Fontenay-aux-Roses, F-92265 France
{ludovic.jean-louis,romaric.besancon,olivier.ferret}@cea.fr

Abstract

In event-based Information Extraction systems, a major task is the automated filling from unstructured texts of a template gathering information related to a particular event. Such template filling may be a hard task when the information is scattered throughout the text and mixed with similar pieces of information relative to a different event. We propose in this paper a two-step approach for template filling: first, an event-based segmentation is performed to select the parts of the text related to the target event; then, a graph-based method is applied to choose the most relevant entities in these parts for characterizing the event. An evaluation of this model based on an annotated corpus for earthquake events shows that we achieve a 77% F1-measure for the template-filling task.

Text	Template
[EV1]There are no reports of damage or injuries after a small **earthquake** rattled the Chino Hills area Tuesday morning. [EV1]The 3.1-magnitude **quake** hit at 6:40 a.m. and was centered about two miles west of Chino Hills. [EV1]It was felt in several surrounding communities.	*EV1* • **EVENT**: earthquake • DATE: Tuesday morning • TIME: 6:40 a.m • MAGNITUDE: 3.1 • LOCATION: Chino Hills
[EV2]Last July, a 5.4-magnitude **quake** hit the same area. [EV2]That **quake** resulted in cracked walls and broken water and gas lines.	*EV2* • **EVENT**: quake • DATE: Last July • TIME: • MAGNITUDE: 5.4 • LOCATION:

Figure 1: Example of template filling

1 Introduction

Information Extraction (IE) is a process that aims at extracting pieces of information from texts. Following the paradigm defined in the Message Understanding Conferences (MUC) (Grishman and Sundheim, 1996), IE systems focus on extracting structured information concerning events to fill predefined *templates*. These templates make it possible to highlight the information that is specific to a type of events and to discard pieces of information that are not relevant in this respect. Figure 1 gives an example of the filling of a template by information extracted from a news article.

Common issues addressed by IE systems for filling a template include identifying named entities, finding relations between these entities, resolving entity coreference, gathering scattered information, etc. (Turmo et al., 2006).

Currently, there is no standard approach for filling templates. However, most IE systems have been relying on a sentence-oriented approach: first, domain-specific patterns or classifiers are used to process sentences separately; then, ad-hoc strategies for merging these local results into templates are applied. Even if such approach has been used widely, it does not take into account two important problems: *(i)* events can be described in more than one sentence; *(ii)* patterns/classifiers mainly capture binary relations among entities while events are not limited to binary relations.

An illustration of the first problem is given by Figure 1, where information relative to the event *EV1* is expressed beyond the sentence scope. This problem raises more generally the question of defining event-related spans of text or, in other words, determining whether a sentence refers to an event, and eventually the type of this event. In this article, we tackle this issue through the means of discourse segmentation. More specifically, we propose segmenting texts according to the events they refer to. Our objective is to narrow the span of text to explore in order to link a named entity to an event mention. As time is an important feature for discriminating events, we chose to perform this segmentation by relying on temporal cues.

Concerning the second problem, we can observe in Figure 1 that most of the sentences comprise an event mention with more than 2 related entities: the first sentence involves 3 entities while the second one involves 4 entities. Similarly to (McDonald et al., 2005), we refer to such relations as *complex relations*, namely any n-ary relation among n typed entities. In this context, each event can be seen as a complex relation where the arity of the relation n is equal to the number of entity types that should be filled in the template (n=5 in the previous example). Several methods were proposed for extracting complex relations such as graph-based methods (McDonald et al., 2005; Wick et al., 2006) or inference-based methods (Goertzel et al., 2006). In this article, we tackle the complex relation extraction by proposing a graph-based method. We start by building an entity graph based on the result of text segmentation; then we use several domain-independent strategies for the reconstruction of the complex relation.

The remainder of this article is organized as follows: the next section discusses related work while Section 3 presents a general overview of our approach. Sections 4 and 5 detail the methods used for the two steps: event segmentation and template filling. Finally, Section 6 gives the results of the evaluation of each step.

2 Motivation and Related Work

Template filling is a central task for IE systems and has been the object of numerous studies. For instance, in the context of the MUC (Message Understanding Conferences) and ACE (Automatic Content Extraction) (Doddington et al., 2004) evaluation campaigns, one of the objectives assigned to the systems was to fill predefined templates with a static/fixed structure. Although this is the most widespread approach, a work such as (Chambers and Jurafsky, 2011) adopts a different view and proposes an unsupervised approach for filling templates without prior knowledge about their structure: they rely on clustering techniques for learning the structure of templates and on syntactic patterns for extracting their fillers.

A wide range of IE systems, particularly those based on learning approaches, have been relying on the idea that an event is often described within a single sentence, which leads to the hypothesis that pieces of information across sentences are less important. This idea is called the *single sentence assumption* by Stevenson (2006), who reported that only 60% of the facts mentioned in three MUC corpora (MUC 4-6-7) could be identified following this hypothesis. More recently, Ji et al. (2010) showed that around 40% of relations among entities require using cross-sentence inference techniques for their extraction.

Few approaches have been proposed for information extraction at a discourse level. Among them, (Gu and Cercone, 2006) and (Patwardhan and Riloff, 2007) are the closest to ours. (Gu and Cercone, 2006) is a segment-based HMM (Hidden Markov Model) approach. It relies on a first HMM model for identifying text units (sentences) that are relevant for the extraction of template fillers and on another HMM to extract the fillers from the retrieved sentences. Similarly, Patwardhan and Riloff (2007) proposed first to identify relevant sentences by using a self-trained SVM (Support Vector Machine) and then, to apply extraction patterns (primary and secondary patterns) to find the template fillers.

One of the first successful approach for the extraction of n-ary relations came from the biomedical community (McDonald et al., 2005) and was later applied to the domain of corporate management successions (Afzal, 2009). Other works tackled the complex relation problem in the context of *database record extraction*. They proposed to focus on the compatibility of a set of entities rather than on the compatibility of pairs of entities, which led them to take into account intersentential relations between entities (Wick et al., 2006; Mansuri and Sarawagi, 2006; Feng et al., 2007).

3 Overview

Event extraction as presented in this article takes place in a wider context of technology watch in which users are mainly interested in the most recent events. In this context, our goal is to synthesize from news articles the information about such recent events into a dashboard. However, news articles often refer to several comparable events, generally for pointing out the similarities and differences between a recent event and past events. In our specific application, we are not interested in the past events and we consider them as a source of noise for extracting information about the main event of a news article. We made the assumption, as in (Feng et al., 2007), that one document is associated with one record (event in our case). We adopted a two-step strategy to tackle this problem:

- segmenting texts into events: events might

be described over a single sentence. Therefore, we need to segment texts according to the events they refer to. These segments are frequently discontinuous as the structure of news articles is often dominated by moves between the main event and past similar events;

- filling event templates from relations: since event segments go beyond the sentence level, they are even more likely to contain complex relations than sentences. Therefore, we have to verify which entities mentioned in these segments are eligible to be part of the complex relation.

4 Segmenting Texts into Events

The goal of our segmentation of texts is to delimit segment units in relation with a target event. In previous work such as (Gu and Cercone, 2006; Patwardhan and Riloff, 2007), the methods for identifying such segments relied on fully lexicalized models that were learned using word surface forms. (Naughton, 2007) adopted a more generic approach by exploiting text structure. Our proposal is based on the idea that using temporal cues can help discriminate events, in particular similar events. In the example of Figure 2 for instance, two kinds of temporal cues can be used for this task: date values and verb tenses.

> {MAIN} An earthquake measuring 5.6 on the Richter scale hit Jayapura, Papua, shortly after midnight on **Sunday**.
> {SUB} Previously on **Saturday** the agency recorded a magnitude 5.6 earthquake had hit Melonguane in North Sulawesi.
> {OUT} Indonesia, sits on a vulnerable quake-hit zone called the Pacific Ring of Fire.

Figure 2: Example of text segmentation: {MAIN}=Main event, {SUB}=Secondary event, {OUT}=Background

Our segmentation approach is based on an event-oriented representation of texts: a text is viewed as a sequence of sentences in which each sentence is characterized by the presence or the absence of an event. As in previous work, we have made the hypothesis that one sentence is linked to one event[1]. Hence, we tackle the segmentation task as a classification problem where each sentence of a text must be associated with an event type.

We classify sentences according to the following three categories. **Main event**: all sentences referring to the main event of the text; **Secondary event**: all sentences containing data that are related to an event different from the *Main Event*; **Background**: all sentences that belong neither to the *Main Event* nor a *Secondary Event*. An example for each category is given in Figure 2.

Our intuition is that for segmenting texts, the most interesting criteria rely not only on the nature of sentences but also on their linking at a discourse level, with the idea that categories of events don't follow one another in an arbitrary way. For instance, in the example of Figure 2, the shift from one event to another is associated with the change of verb tense *preterit/past perfect*. Our focus compared to previous segmentation approaches is to capture the dependencies between the shifts of temporal frames and the shifts of events.

For this purpose, we trained a linear Conditional Random Field (CRF) model (Lafferty et al., 2001) using the following temporal cues as features. *verb tenses*: a binary feature is associated with each possible verb tense (feature is 1 if at least one verb of the sentence has the considered tense); *presence of dates*: if a sentence contains a date, it is likely to refer to an event different from the previous sentence (except for the first occurrence of a date); *temporal expressions*: this feature accounts for the presence of temporal expressions in a sentence, such as *"over the past two weeks, in recent years"*, often related to generalities. The dependencies between successive event types are taken into account by the linear structure of our CRF model. More details about this segmentation model can be found in (Jean-Louis et al., 2010).

5 Filling Event Templates from Relations

For the filling of event templates, we propose a graph-based approach relying on the paradigm of complex relation extraction. Its first step (*graph construction*) detects relations between entity pairs in the same sentence to build an entity graph. The second step (*template filling*) applies generic strategies for selecting the most relevant entities associated with the template by exploiting the entity graph. These two steps are described in more details in the following sections.

[1]This hypothesis is not verified for all texts but can be considered as a reasonable simplification in the context of our study.

5.1 Graph Construction

The entity graph we build in this first step characterizes at the document level the presence/absence of semantic relations between each pair of entities. For building such a graph, we propose to rely on the most relevant text segments in relation to the target event instead of considering the entire document. In our case, these segments are those built from the sentences classified as {MAIN} by the segmentation model presented in Section 4.

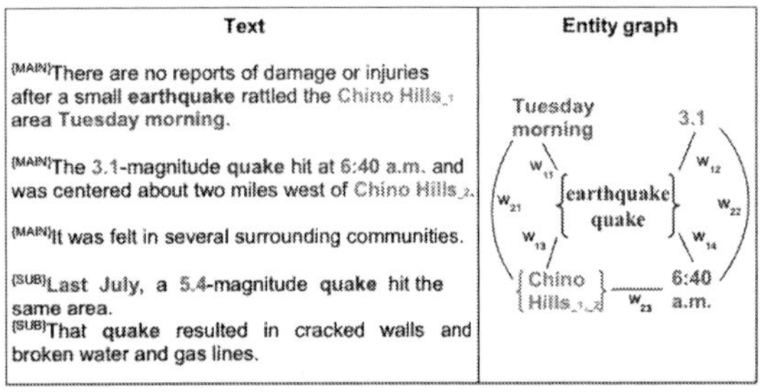

Figure 3: Example of entity graph

The entity graph is a weighted graph whose nodes are associated with named entity mentions while edges are associated with the relations between these mentions. The weight associated with each edge measures the confidence that a semantic relation exists between its two entities in a sentence. The graph is undirected as we mainly rely on relation confidence, a symmetric notion in our case, for filling templates. Figure 3 shows an example of such entity graph. Note that we assume that all entity mentions having the same value are equivalent (as the two mentions of *Chino Hills*) since they are located in the same event segment. Similarly, we consider all event mentions as equivalent (as *earthquake* in the first sentence and *quake* in the second sentence).

The presence of a relation between two entities in a sentence is classically determined by a statistical classifier. Following the standard approach of (McDonald et al., 2005) or (Liu et al., 2007), the weight of a relation is evaluated by the confidence score of this classifier and ranges in [0,1] in all the experiments of Section 6.3. In most previous works, such classifier mainly relies on a set of lexicalized features, without any syntactic feature (Afzal, 2009; Gu and Cercone, 2006; Wick et al., 2006). In (Liu et al., 2007), syntactic features are used in addition to lexicalized features. In contrast, our aim is to build a model that only makes use of syntactic features and does not rely on lexical information (such as inflected forms or lemma) in order to have a more generic model that can be easily adapted to another domain. For evaluating the contribution of lexicalized features compared to syntactic features, we trained different classifiers based on three distinct sets of features, detailed in Table 1:

Features description	FEAT-BASE	FEAT-LEX	FEAT-NOLEX
Entity type of E1 and E2	✓	✓	✓
POS of E1 and E2	✓	✓	✓
Words in E1 and E2	✓		
Word bigrams in E1 and E2	✓	✓	✓
Words between E1 and E2	✓	✓	
Word bigrams between E1 and E2	✓	✓	
POS between E1 and E2	✓	✓	✓
# words between E1 and E2	✓	✓	✓
POS bigrams between E1 and E2		✓	✓
# synt. relations between E1 and E2		✓	✓
Syntactic path between E1 and E2		✓	✓
Relative position and POS[2]		✓	✓
# entities between E1 and E2		✓	✓
# event mentions between E1 and E2		✓	✓
POS of two words after/before E1		✓	✓
POS of two words after/before E2		✓	✓

Table 1: Features for relation classification

- *FEAT-BASE*: same feature set as (Afzal, 2009), based on lexicalized features;
- *FEAT-LEX*: a feature set that contains lexicalized features, and syntactic features inspired by (Liu et al., 2007)[3];
- *FEAT-NOLEX*: same feature set as *FEAT-LEX*, but without the lexicalized features.

5.2 Template Filling

Template filling aims at selecting the best entities for the template slots. In our approach, this selection relies on the relations between entities in the entity graph. Note that we are trying to fill domain-specific templates that have a fixed number of slots though it is not mandatory that every slot gets a value. As every slot is associated with an entity type, we need to select (when it is possible) one entity value for each slot. This problem can be seen as the complex relation reconstruction task described in (Afzal, 2009; McDonald et al., 2005). We compared several approaches to tackle this issue:

[2]If either E1 or E2 is an event mention, indicate whether the other entity is after/before its POS.

[3]Some of their features are not relevant in our context since they are only applicable in the biomedical domain.

Heuristic is a simple but efficient approach that selects for each entity type the first entity mention occurring in the main event segment.

Confidence is an approach that selects, for each entity type, the entity connected to the event mention with the highest confidence weight.

PageRank is a link analysis based approach that relies on the PageRank algorithm (Brin and Page, 1998). The idea is to use the graph structure to rank entities according to their importance in the graph and to select, for each entity type, the entity mention with the highest PageRank score.

Vote is a voting-based approach exploiting the output of the *Confidence*, *PageRank* and *Heuristic* approaches: a majority vote is performed for each entity type and the entity mention with the highest number of votes (one vote by approach) is chosen.

Hybrid is an hybrid approach that applies for each entity type the best selection approach for this type. The main idea is to increase overall performance by allowing one entity type to be selected with one approach and another entity type to be selected by a different approach. For instance, the best selection approach for dates is *Confidence* whereas it is *Heuristic* for geographical coordinates.

Except for the first approach, the output is complemented by the use of the heuristic approach as back-off when no entity has been retrieved for a given entity type. Such a situation happens when a template filler is the only entity of a sentence and therefore, cannot be extracted by the binary relation classifier.

6 Evaluation

This section provides details concerning the experimental evaluation of our template-filling process. We present the corpus in Section 6.1 and the individual results for the different steps of our process in Sections 6.2, 6.3 and 6.4. We also evaluate the impact of the segmentation step on the final results in Section 6.5 and finally propose an analysis of errors in Section 6.6.

6.1 Corpus

The work presented in this paper was developed for an application dedicated to the surveillance of earthquake event mentions in news articles. The earthquake event template summarizes the main characteristics of a seismic event, namely its date, time, location, magnitude, geographical coordinates and its mention (earthquake, afterquake, etc.)[4]. An example of such template is provided in Figure 1, knowing that our target application is not interested in the secondary event *EV2*.

We carried out all the experiments on a corpus of 501 French news articles concerning earthquakes. These articles were collected between February 2008 and early September 2008 from a *Agence France Presse* (AFP) newswire (1/3 of the corpus) and from Google News (2/3 of the corpus). The corpus was manually annotated by domain analysts for filling the earthquake event template. The annotators identified a total of 2,775 entities divided into 6 entity types: event mention (18%), location (34%), date (17%), time (12%), magnitude (17%) and geo-coordinates (1%)[5].

Each document was preprocessed by the LIMA linguistic analyzer (Besançon et al., 2010), performing tokenization, sentence boundary detection, part-of-speech tagging, verb tense analysis, named entity recognition and dependency parsing.

6.2 Segmenting Text into Events

We used a subset of 140 articles from our corpus as training data for the CRF-based segmentation model. These articles were manually annotated into 1,659 segments according to the categories defined in Section 4: *Main event (70%), Secondary event (17%), Background (13%).* Most of these articles contain a main event and at least one secondary event (short articles might not refer to a secondary event). Note that the *Secondary event* class includes without distinction all secondary events. The implementation was achieved using the CRF++[6] toolkit. We report in Table 2 results of our CRF model (*CrfSeg*) compared to a baseline (*ParaSeg*) in terms of F1-measure using a 5-fold cross-validation. The baseline *ParaSeg* is a paragraph-based heuristic that assigns *Main event* category to all the sentences in the first two paragraphs and considers others

[4]Casualties were not considered here because their correct identification would require a chunker.

[5]Several entities could be annotated for the same slot when variants or different levels of granularity were present: for locations, both a city and a country name for instance.

[6]http://crfpp.sourceforge.net

as secondary event[7]. Results in Table 2 show

Event type	ParaSeg (%)	CrfSeg (%)
Main event	11.14	92.71
Secondary event	21.7	67.91
Background	0	79.42

Table 2: Results of text segmentation into events (F1-Measure)

that our model obtains fairly good classification performance for all categories and is particularly suited for identifying the main event section. They also show the impact of taking temporal cues into account compared to relying on text structure only. Note that the poor results of our baseline partly come from its ignorance of the *Background* category. The *Relevant Sentence Classifier* of (Patwardhan and Riloff, 2007) has a goal similar to our segmentation with Recall|Precision|F1-Measure scores of 63%|46%|53% on terrorism documents and 72%|41%|52% on disease outbreak documents. We provide these figures as indicative results but not for direct comparison since their approach is different: they used a SVM classifier with lexicalized features and not temporal cues, classified sentences according to two classes (Irrelevant, Relevant) and performed their evaluation for English, on the MUC-4 terrorism and ProMed corpora.

6.3 Graph Construction

Our graph construction method relies on a binary relation classifier for assessing the existence of a semantic relation between two entities in a sentence. We experimented several types of statistical classifiers with the three sets of features (*FEAT-BASE, FEAT-LEX, FEAT-NOLEX*) presented in Section 5.1. A set of 44 articles from our corpus was used to annotate binary relations. Among the 5,000 binary relations in these articles, 969 were in-sentence relations. 43 relations were discarded because one of their entities was actually included in the span of a larger entity not recognized because of its type (such as organizations), the rest was used for training the classifiers: 690 in the *POSITIVE* class, in which the two entities of the candidate relation refer to the same earthquake event, and 236 in the *NEGATIVE* class, where the two entities are associated with different earthquake events. The following sentence contains examples of both *POSITIVE* and *NEGATIVE* relations:

[POSITIVE]: The first *quake*, with a magnitude of *5.3*, struck at about 11.05am and was followed a few minutes later by a stronger quake with a 6.5 magnitude...

[NEGATIVE]: The first *quake*, with a magnitude of 5.3, struck at about 11.05am and was followed a few minutes later by a stronger quake with a *6.5* magnitude...

We tested three types of learning algorithms with these quite unbalanced training data by relying on the Mallet toolkit[8] for their implementation: Naive Bayes (*NB*), Maximum Entropy (*ME*), Decision Tree (*DT*). We report in Table 3 the results obtained for each feature set and algorithm in terms of recall (*R*), precision (*P*) and F1-Measure (*F*) using a 5-fold cross-validation. The results of a simple baseline that assigns the *POSITIVE* category to each relation are also given.

Feature set	Algo.	R(%)	P(%)	F(%)
FEAT-LEX	ME	96.30	95.92	96.10
FEAT-BASE	ME	91.22	96.09	93.57
FEAT-NOLEX	ME	91.66	94.99	93.26
FEAT-LEX	DT	89.01	96.45	92.55
FEAT-LEX	NB	93.44	90.69	92.02
FEAT-NOLEX	DT	91.17	88.74	89.83
FEAT-NOLEX	NB	89.58	89.23	89.37
FEAT-BASE	DT	84.35	94.70	89.16
FEAT-BASE	NB	86.73	87.86	87.27
Baseline	–	100.00	25.50	40.49

Table 3: Results for binary relation classifiers

Table 3 first shows the interest of using syntactic features as FEAT-LEX outperforms FEAT-BASE. Moreover, the non-lexicalized feature set FEAT-NOLEX obtains results equivalent to the lexicalized feature set FEAT-BASE. Concerning the learning algorithms, we observe the following hierarchy: ME > DT > NB. (Afzal, 2009) observes a different hierarchy, DT > ME > NB, but on a different corpus and a different language, which makes the comparison difficult. In terms of general performances, our results are in the same range as those reported in (Afzal, 2009), his best score being R=0.95%|P=0.87%|F=0.91% with a decision tree. Finally, we adopted the Maximum Entropy model trained with the FEAT-NOLEX feature set instead of FEAT-LEX. This choice is motivated by the fact that FEAT-NOLEX obtains

[7] We experimented other learning approaches such as HMM and Maximum Entropy models but we only provide results for the best approach, that is to say, CRF.

[8] http://mallet.cs.umass.edu

reasonable results without relying on strongly domain-dependent information such as lexicalized features.

6.4 Template Filling

As we mentioned in Section 5.2, our approach for template filling relies on the selection of relevant entities from the entity graph. Our idea is to compute for each entity a weight that quantifies its importance in the graph and consequently, makes it possible to rank the entities. We assume that the best ranked entities are more likely to be good fillers than others.

Before applying the entity selection strategies described in Section 5.2 to the entity graph, we apply a node merging step. The goal of this step is, on the one hand, to identify all the nodes that refer to the same entity value and remove duplicates and, on the other hand, to establish cross-sentence relations between entities. In our case, we used the node merging step for event mentions and date and location entity types: all dates having the same normalization and all locations having the same surface form are considered equivalent.

All annotated documents in our corpus were used for evaluating the different entity selection strategies. We report in Table 4 the results of template filling in terms of recall (*R*), precision (*P*) and F1-Measure (*F*), aggregated for all entity types.

Approach	R(%)	P(%)	F(%)
Hybrid	77.55	76.87	77.15
Vote	74.93	74.27	74.54
Confidence	74.89	74.16	74.47
Heuristic	73.40	73.06	73.17
PageRank	72.41	71.73	72.01

Table 4: Association of entities to events

These results confirm that the basic heuristic strategy is a powerful approach since it performs slightly better than the PageRank strategy. As the PageRank strategy only relies on the graph structure without considering the weight of the edges, its highest ranked entities are those that are highly connected regardless of the weight of the edges. As a consequence, if several non fillers entities are strongly linked, they get better scores than the others. Mihalcea (2004) proposed a weighted version of the PageRank algorithm that deals with this issue and should be tested in this context. Table 4 also shows that the best strategy is the *Hybrid* approach, which associates each entity type with a given selection approach: this method corrects the fact that an approach can perform well on a given entity type but poorly on another type.

6.5 Impact of Event Segmentation

In this section, we propose to evaluate the impact of our text segmentation procedure on the template filling task. Our text segmentation method focuses on identifying relevant text spans for the extraction. However, all documents do not mention several earthquake events and some only focus on a single event. In the latter case, our temporal segmentation might seem less relevant since all the sentences refer to the same event.

Our purpose in this section is to evaluate the impact of the segmentation on documents that mention a single event compared to those that mention multiple events. Our intuition is that the temporal segmentation should have a limited effect on single event documents and improve results on multiple event documents. In order to verify this hypothesis, we manually split the initial corpus into two sets according to the number of earthquake events they discuss. We obtained 227 multi-event documents (*M*) and 274 single-event documents (*S*). Finally, we applied each template-filling strategy on both (*M*) and (*S*) document sets, including the segmentation step or not. We report the results in Table 5 in terms of F1-Measure aggregated for all entity types.

	Without segmentation		With segmentation	
Approach	S(%)	M(%)	S(%)	M(%)
Hybrid	79.20	73.61	78.34	75.61
Vote	77.67	68.68	76.89	71.81
Confidence	72.55	66.07	71.79	69.10
Heuristic	73.96	73.16	73.07	73.10
PageRank	70.92	59.72	70.67	65.32

Table 5: Impact of segmentation on single/multi-event texts (F1-Measure)

Concerning single-event documents, results in Table 5 show that the best performing strategies do not use segmentation though the global difference is not highly significant (+0.71% in average). At the opposite, strategies based on segmentation perform better on multi-event documents (+2.74% in average). Moreover, our best strategy (hybrid approach with segmentation) outperforms our baseline (heuristic without segmentation) on both document sets. Globally, these findings demonstrate that our temporal segmentation preserves results on single-event documents and improves results on multi-event documents.

6.6 Error Analysis

In order to have a more comprehensive view of the performance of our method for template filling, we performed an analysis of errors. The idea of this analysis is to identify the reason why a given entity filler is not found. In this context we identified three major types of errors:

- named entity recognition errors (*NE-err*): the entity is not identified by the linguistic pre-processing;
- event segmentation errors (*Seg-err*): the entity is identified by the linguistic pre-processing but its sentence is not tagged as part of a {MAIN} segment;
- template filling errors (*Fill-err*): the entity was identified in the correct event segment but was not selected as a template filler;
- *Correct*: the entity was correctly identified and selected as a template filler.

Figure 4 presents the percentage of each type of errors on all our evaluation corpus for two template filling strategies[9]: one without segmentation, the heuristic strategy *(Heuristic)*, and the other with segmentation, the hybrid strategy *(Hybrid)*. The

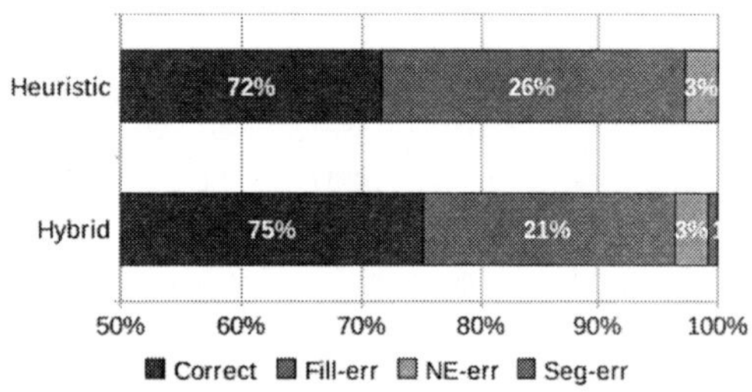

Figure 4: Classification of errors

graph shows that the baseline heuristic strategy achieves a high level of correctly identified entities (*72%*) but a significant level of template filling errors (*26%*). Our best strategy reduces this type of errors while it increases the percentage of correct fillers. Moreover, it only induces a limited number of errors due to event segmentation (*1%*).

[9]The percentages on the graph are rounded up, which explains why they do not sum to 100%.

7 Conclusion

Most of IE approaches focus on sentence-based evidences for filling templates and rely on few discourse level information. In this article, we have presented an approach for template filling based on event segmentation and graph-based entity selection. Our event segmentation takes place at the discourse level and relies on temporal cues. It uses a CRF model to find the sentences that are most relevant for filling the event template. These sentences are then used to build an entity graph from which template filler entities are selected. We have proposed several strategies for selecting the entities – heuristic, confidence-based, PageRank-based – and various ways of combining these strategies: vote and hybrid approaches.

We have presented detailed results of our IE approach on a corpus of French news articles about earthquake events. Our experiments have shown that this approach improves the simple, but powerful heuristic in this field, that always selects the first entity found in a document for each type of fillers. These results have also shown that our approach is well suited for documents that mention several comparable events. Finally, our analysis of errors have demonstrated that there is still room for improvement since 21% of remaining errors are due to incorrect entity selection.

Concerning future work, our next experiments will be dedicated to the generalization of our template filling method to different contexts and more precisely, to other languages and domains. We have already obtained promising results by testing our event segmentation module on a set of English news articles in the seismic domain with only a limited effort of adaptation. For domain generalization, we are planning experiments in the financial domain.

Acknowledgment

This work was partly supported by the FP7 Virtuoso project under the grant agreement 242352. The European Commission contribution is eight million euros in the Virtuoso project : `http://www.virtuoso.eu`

References

Naveed Afzal. 2009. Complex Relations Extraction. In *Conference on Language & Technology 2009 (CLT09)*, Lahore, Pakistan.

Romaric Besançon, Gaël de Chalendar, Olivier Ferret, Faiza Gara, and Nasredine Semmar. 2010. LIMA: A Multilingual Framework for Linguistic Analysis and Linguistic Resources Development and Evaluation. In 7th *Conference on Language Resources and Evaluation (LREC 2010)*, Valletta, Malta.

Sergey Brin and Lawrence Page. 1998. The anatomy of a large-scale hypertextual web search engine. In *Proceedings of the seventh international conference on World Wide Web 7*, WWW7, pages 107–117, Amsterdam, The Netherlands. Elsevier Science Publishers B. V.

Nathanael Chambers and Dan Jurafsky. 2011. Template-Based Information Extraction without the Templates. In 49th *Annual Meeting of the Association for Computational Linguistics: Human Language Technologies*, pages 976–986, Portland, Oregon, USA.

George Doddington, Alexis Mitchell, Mark Przybocki, Lance Ramshaw, Stephanie Strassel, and Ralph Weischedel. 2004. The Automatic Content Extraction (ACE) Program – Tasks, Data, and Evaluation. In 4th *Conference on Language Resources and Evaluation (LREC 2004)*, pages 837–840, Lisbon, Portugal.

Donghui Feng, Gully Burns, and Eduard Hovy. 2007. Extracting Data Records from Unstructured Biomedical Full Text. In *EMNLP-CoNLL'07*, pages 837–846, Prague, Czech Republic.

Ben Goertzel, Hugo Pinto, Ari Heljakka, Michael Ross, Cassio Pennachin, and Izabela Goertzel. 2006. Using Dependency Parsing and Probabilistic Inference to Extract Relationships between Genes, Proteins and Malignancies Implicit Among Multiple Biomedical Research Abstracts. In *HLT-NAACL BioNLP Workshop on Linking Natural Language and Biology*, pages 104–111, New York, USA.

Ralph Grishman and Beth Sundheim. 1996. Message Understanding Conference-6: A Brief History. In 16th *International Conference on Computational linguistics (COLING'96)*, pages 466–471, Copenhagen, Denmark.

Zhenmei Gu and Nick Cercone. 2006. Segment-based hidden Markov models for information extraction. In 21st *International Conference on Computational Linguistics and* 44th *Annual Meeting of the Association for Computational Linguistics*, pages 481–488, Sydney, Australia.

Ludovic Jean-Louis, Romaric Besançon, and Olivier Ferret. 2010. Using temporal cues for segmenting texts into events. In Hrafn Loftsson, Eiríkur Rögnvaldsson, and Sigrún Helgadóttir, editors, 7th *International Conference on Natural Language Processing (IceTAL 2010)*, volume 6233 of *Lecture Notes in Computer Science*, pages 150–161. Springer Berlin / Heidelberg.

Heng Ji, Ralph Grishman, and Hoa Trang Dang. 2010. Overview of the TAC 2010 Knowledge Base Population Track. In *Third Text Analysis Conference (TAC 2010)*, Gaithersburg, Maryland, USA.

John D. Lafferty, Andrew McCallum, and Fernando C. N. Pereira. 2001. Conditional Random Fields: Probabilistic Models for Segmenting and Labeling Sequence Data. In *Eighteenth International Conference on Machine Learning (ICML'01)*, pages 282–289, San Francisco, CA, USA.

Yudong Liu, Zhongmin Shi, and Anoop Sarkar. 2007. Exploiting Rich Syntactic Information for Relationship Extraction from Biomedical Articles. In *NAACL-HLT'07, short paper session*, pages 97–100, Rochester, New York.

Imran R. Mansuri and Sunita Sarawagi. 2006. Integrating unstructured data into relational databases. In 22nd *International Conference on Data Engineering (ICDE'06)*, pages 29–40, Washington, DC, USA.

Ryan McDonald, Fernando Pereira, Seth Kulick, Scott Winters, Yang Jin, and Pete White. 2005. Simple algorithms for complex relation extraction with applications to biomedical IE. In *ACL 2005*, pages 491–498, Ann Arbor, Michigan, USA.

Rada Mihalcea. 2004. Graph-based Ranking Algorithms for Sentence Extraction, Applied to Text Summarization. In 42st *Annual Meeting of the Association for Computational Linguistics (ACL 2004)*, Barcelona, Spain.

Martina Naughton. 2007. Exploiting Structure for Event Discovery Using the MDI Algorithm. In 45th *Annual Meeting of the Association for Computational Linguistics (ACL 2007)*, pages 31–36, Prague, Czech Republic.

Siddharth Patwardhan and Ellen Riloff. 2007. Effective Information Extraction with Semantic Affinity Patterns and Relevant Regions. In *EMNLP-CoNLL'07*, pages 717–727, Prague, Czech Republic.

Mark Stevenson. 2006. Fact distribution in Information Extraction. *Language Resources and Evaluation*, 40(2):183–201.

Jordi Turmo, Alicia Ageno, and Neus Català. 2006. Adaptive information extraction. *ACM Computer Surveys*, 38(2):1–47.

Michael Wick, Aron Culotta, and Andrew McCallum. 2006. Learning Field Compatibilities to Extract Database Records from Unstructured Text. In *EMNLP'06*, pages 603–611, Sydney, Australia.

Joint Distant and Direct Supervision for Relation Extraction

Truc-Vien T. Nguyen and **Alessandro Moschitti**
Department of Information Engineering and Computer Science
University of Trento
38123 Povo (TN), Italy
{nguyenthi,moschitti}@disi.unitn.it

Abstract

Supervised approaches to Relation Extraction (RE) are characterized by higher accuracy than unsupervised models. Unfortunately, their applicability is limited by the need of training data for each relation type. Automatic creation of such data using Distant Supervision (DS) provides a promising solution to the problem. In this paper, we study DS for designing end-to-end systems of sentence-level RE. In particular, we propose a joint model between Web data derived with DS and manually annotated data from ACE. The results show (i) an improvement on the previous state-of-the-art in ACE, which provides important evidence of the benefit of DS; and (ii) a rather good accuracy on extracting 52 types of relations from Web data, which suggests the applicability of DS for general RE.

1 Introduction

Automatic Relation Extraction (RE) as defined in ACE (Doddington et al., 2004) achieves the highest accuracy when supervised approaches are applied, e.g., (Zelenko et al., 2002). Unfortunately, they require labeled data and tend to be domain-dependent as different domains involve different relations. Distant supervision (DS), e.g., using Wikipedia (Banko et al., 2007; Mintz et al., 2009; Hoffmann et al., 2010), can be applied for automatically acquiring relation types and their training data.

The main idea behind DS is to exploit (i) relation repositories, e.g., the *Infobox*, x, of Wikipedia to define a set of relation types $RT(x)$ and (ii) the text of the page associated with x to produce the training sentences, which are supposed to express instances of $RT(x)$.

Previous work has applied DS to RE at *corpus level*, e.g., (Banko et al., 2007; Mintz et al., 2009): relation extractors are (i) learned using such not completely accurate data and (ii) applied to extract relation instances from the whole corpus. The multiple pieces of evidence for each relation instance are then exploited to recover from errors of the automatic extractors. Additionally, a recent approach, i.e., (Hoffmann et al., 2010), has shown that DS can be also applied at level of Wikipedia article: given a target *Infobox* template, all its attributes[1] can be extracted from a given document matching such template.

Sentence-level RE (SLRE) has been typically modeled with the traditional supervised approach, e.g., using the data manually annotated in ACE (Culotta and Sorensen, 2004; Kambhatla, 2004; Bunescu and Mooney, 2005; Zhang et al., 2005; Zhang et al., 2006; Bunescu and Mooney, 2007; Nguyen et al., 2009). The resulting extractors are very valuable as they find rare relation instances that might be expressed in only one document. For example, the relation *President(Barrack Obama, United States)* can be extracted from thousands of documents thus there is a large chance of acquiring it. In contrast, *President(Eneko Agirre, SIGLEX)* is probably expressed in very few documents (if not just one sentence), increasing the complexity for obtaining it.

In (Nguyen and Moschitti, 2011), we firstly used DS from Wikipedia for SLRE by exploiting state-of-the-art models based on Support Vector Machines (SVMs) and kernel methods (KM). The experiments showed that our approach is robust to Web documents and can achieve high accuracy, i.e., an F1 of 74.29% on 52 YAGO relations.

In this paper, to accurately assess the benefit of using DS for SLRE, we manually mapped relations from YAGO to ACE based on their descrip-

[1]This is a simpler tasks as one of the two entity is fixed.

tions. Then, we designed a joint RE model combining DS and ACE data and tested it on ACE gold standard. This way the results are validated with the data provided by the expert linguistic annotators of ACE. The improvement produced by DS in these tests provides a strong evidence of the benefits of our joint model.

Additionally, since our aim is to produce RE for real-world applications, we experimented with end-to-end systems, which use Named Entity Recognizers (NERs). For this purpose, we also exploited Freebase for creating DS data for our robust NER (Nguyen et al., 2010). The results show that our RE systems can be applied to any document/sentence achieving an appreciable F1 of 67%.

In the remainder of this paper, Section 2 presents the related work, Section 3 describes the datasets for distant and direct supervision and the mapping between ACE and YAGO relations, Section 4 illustrates our RE models, including the joint ACE-Wikipedia model, Section 5 reports on all experiments with our models and finally Section 6 summarizes the conclusions.

2 Related Work

The extraction of relational data from text has drawn popularity for its potential application in a broad range of tasks. It refers to the automated extraction of relational facts, or world knowledge from the Web (Yates, 2009). To identify semantic relations using machine learning, three learning settings have mainly been applied, namely supervised methods (Zelenko et al., 2002; Culotta and Sorensen, 2004; Kambhatla, 2004; Zhou et al., 2005), semi supervised methods (Brin, 1998; Agichtein and Gravano, 2000), and unsupervised methods (Hasegawa et al., 2004; Banko et al., 2007).

Early work on Relation Extraction has mostly employed kernel-based approaches (Zelenko et al., 2002; Culotta and Sorensen, 2004; Bunescu and Mooney, 2005; Zhang et al., 2005). Structural kernels on parse trees were proposed in (Collins and Duffy, 2001) for parse reranking and (Culotta and Sorensen, 2004) extended them for RE using augmented dependency trees. Recent literature has shown that efficient and appropriate kernels can be used to solve the RE problem, exploiting constituency trees (Zhang et al., 2006) and their combination with dependency trees (Nguyen et al., 2009)

Traditional relation classifiers use only labeled data for training. However, these are expensive to obtain, as they require efforts of experienced human annotators. In contrast, unlabeled data is relatively easy to collect, but its use is still an open problem. (Bunescu and Mooney, 2007) proposed a way of using a handful training set for RE. However, such model was applied to very few relation types. Distant supervised learning (Mintz et al., 2009) addresses this problem by using large amount of data to build classifiers.

The DS algorithm creates training data by selecting sentences that probably contain the target relation type. For example, suppose that $r(e1, e2)$ expresses one relation between pair of entities $e1$ and $e2$, then all sentences containing both $e1$ and $e2$ could be useful training examples. (Riedel et al., 2010) improved the DS assumption by only requiring that at least one of the sentences containing $e1$ and $e2$ expresses $r(e1; e2)$. They achieved a substantial improvement in extraction performance.

The most similar model to our DS algorithm is the method in (Hoffmann et al., 2010), which extracts relations from Wikipedia pages by using supervision from the page's infobox. In contrast, our approach allows for acquiring training data for relations defined in different sources.

3 Resources for designing and evaluating Generalized Distant Supervision

The resources we used to implement DS are YAGO, a large knowledge base of entities and relations, and Freebase, a collection of Wikipedia news articles. Our procedure uses entities and facts from YAGO to provide relation instances. For each pair of entities that appears in some YAGO relations, we retrieve all the sentences of the Freebase documents that contain such entities.

Additionally, as DS data is noisy, for accurately evaluating our extractors, we (i) manually annotated a small dataset and (ii) mapped some YAGO relations to ACE. This way we can measure the impact of Wikipedia training data on the ACE data.

3.1 ACE (Automatic Content Extraction)

The ACE effort (Doddington et al., 2004) aims at developing technology for automatically carrying out inference in natural language text. The data includes the entities being mentioned, the relations among these entities that are directly expressed, and the events in which these entities participate. Moreover, data includes various source types (image, audio, text) and languages (English, Arabic). We use the ACE 2004 corpus with seven relation types: Physical (PHYS), Person/Social (PER-SOC), Employment/Membership/Subsidiary (EMP-ORG), Agent-Artifact (ART), PER/ORG Affiliation (Other-AFF), GPE Affiliation (GPE-AFF), and Discourse (DISC). These relationships are explicitly described in the ACE document guidelines.

RE, as defined in ACE, is the task of finding relevant semantic relations between pairs of entities in texts. For example, the following sentence from the ACE 2004 corpus:

> ***Tara Singh Hayer**, editor of **The Indo-Canadian Times.***

expresses the employee/organization relation (EMP-ORG) between the first entity, i.e., *Tara Singh Hayer* (of type *person*) and the second entity, i.e., *The Indo-Canadian Times* (of type *organization*).

3.2 YAGO

This is a huge semantic knowledge base derived from WordNet and Wikipedia. It comprises about more than 2 million entities (like *persons*, *organizations*, *cities*, etc.) and 20 million facts connecting such entities. These include the taxonomic Is-A hierarchy as well as semantic relations between entities. The facts of YAGO have been extracted from the category system and the *Infoboxes* of Wikipedia and have been combined with taxonomic relations from Wordnet.

We use the YAGO ontology and the knowledge base, version *2008-w40-2*, whose validation has shown an accuracy of 95% for 99 relations. However, some of them are (a) rather trivial, e.g. *familyNameOf* or *givenNameOf*; (b) describe numerical attributes that change over time, e.g. *hasBudget*, *hasGDP* or *hasPopulation*; (c) symmetric, e.g. *hasPredecessor* and *hasSuccessor*; and (d) used for data management and do not convey semantics, e.g. *describes* or *foundIn*. Therefore, we removed trivial relations, unstable relations, and those used for data management. We obtained 1,489,156 instances of 52 relation types to be used with our DS approach. Some examples are shown in Table 1.

Algorithm 3.1: ACQUIRE_LABELED_DATA()

$DS = \emptyset$
$YAGO(R)$: *Instances of Relation R*
for each $\langle Wikipedia\ article : W \rangle \in Freebase$
do {
 $S \leftarrow set\ of\ sentences\ from\ W$
 for each $s \in S$
 do {
  $\mathcal{E} \leftarrow set\ of\ entities\ from\ s$
  for each $E_1 \in \mathcal{E}$ **and** $E_2 \in \mathcal{E}$ **and** $R \in YAGO$
  do {
   if $R(E_1, E_2) \in YAGO(R)$
   then $DS \leftarrow DS \cup \{s, R^+\}$
   else $DS \leftarrow DS \cup \{s, R^-\}$

return $(\mathcal{DS})$

3.3 Freebase

To access to the Wikipedia documents, we used Freebase (version March 27, 2010), which is a dump of the full text of all Wikipedia articles. It has been sentence-tokenized by Metaweb Technologies. For our experiments, we used 100,000 articles of which only 28,074 contain at least one relation for a total of 68,429 of relation instances. These connect 744,060 entities, 97,828 dates and 203,981 numerical attributes. Statistics are shown in Table 2.

In Freebase articles, Wikipedia entities like *Person*, *Organization* or *Location* are marked whereas numbers or dates are not. This prevents to extract interesting relations between entities and dates, e.g. *John F. Kennedy was born on May 29, 1917* or between entities and numerical attributes, e.g. *The novel Gone with the wind has 1037 pages.* Thus, we designed 18 regular expressions to extract dates and other 25 rules to extract numerical attributes, which range from integer numbers to ordinal numbers, percentage, monetary, speed, height, weight, area, time, and ISBN.

3.4 Distant Supervision

DS for RE is based on the following assumption, if (i) a sentence is connected *in some way* to a database of relations and (ii) it contains the pair of entities participating in such relation then it is likely that such sentence expresses the relation. For our DS, we relax (i) by allowing for the use of an external DB of relations such as YAGO and any document of Freebase. The alignment between YAGO and Freebase is implemented by the Wikipedia page link: for example the

Relation name	Size	Example
actedIn	28,836	George Clooney, Batman & Robin
bornIn	36,189	Alan Turing, London
created	95,248	Apple Inc., Dylan
diedIn	13618	Leonhard Euler, Saint Petersburg
directed	23,723	Mel Gibson, Braveheart
hasChild	4,454	Nero Claudius Drusus, Claudius
hasSuccessor	55,535	Jimmy Carter, Ronald Reagan
isAffiliatedTo	13,038	George W. Bush, Republican Party
isCitizenOf	4,865	Paul Cézanne, France
livesIn	14,710	Isaac Newton, England
locatedIn	60,261	Philadelphia, Pennsylvania
produced	41,747	Francis Ford Coppola, Apocalypse Now

Table 1: Some of selected YAGO relation types and their number of instances.

link *http://en.wikipedia.org/wiki/James_Cameron* refers to the entity *James_Cameron*.

A simplified version of our approach is the following: for any YAGO relation instance, scan all the sentences of all Wikipedia articles to test point (ii). Unfortunately, this procedure is impossible in practice since there are millions of relation instances in YAGO and millions of Wikipedia articles in Freebase, i.e. an order of magnitude of 10^{14} iterations[2]. Thus we use a more efficient procedure formally described in Alg. 3.1: for each Wikipedia article in Freebase, we scan all of its NEs. Then, for each pair of entities seen in the sentence, we query YAGO to retrieve the relation instance connecting these entities.

It should be noted that, our approach solves most of the problems for DS pointed out in (Bunescu and Mooney, 2007). Indeed, such issues are due to the sampling method used to acquire DS sentences: NEs were used as query to a search engine, whose weighting schemes introduce a bias. As, we utilize whole documents randomly drawn from Freebase and extract from them all possible positive and negative relation instances, no artificial feature (e.g. word) distribution is generated.

	Docs	Entities		Relations
ACE	443	Entities	12,037	5,784
DS	28,074	Entities	744,060	68,429
		Dates	97,828	
		Numbers	203,981	

Table 2: Statistics on the ACE and the DS datasets.

3.5 Mapping relations between YAGO-ACE

The YAGO knowledge base created from Wordnet and Wikipedia contains 99 relations whereas the ACE 2004 corpus only defines 7 relation types between 7 entity types. To further measure the impact of our Wikipedia dataset and the relations learnt, we mapped 33 relations of YAGO into those of ACE 2004. Surprisingly, we have found a fair correlation between the two different sources, which can help to validate our DS approach. The projection is shown in Table 3.

YAGO relations	Projection
actedIn	ART
bornIn	PHYS
created	ART
dealsWith	EMP-ORG
diedIn	PHYS
directed	ART
discovered	ART
graduatedFrom	EMP-ORG
happenedIn	PHYS
hasAcademicAdvisor	PER-SOC
hasCapital	PHYS
hasChild	PER-SOC
hasCurrency	ART
hasOfficialLanguage	ART
hasProduct	ART
hasProductionLanguage	ART
hasSuccessor	PER-SOC
hasWonPrize	ART
influences	PER-SOC
interestedIn	ART
isAffiliatedTo	EMP-ORG
isCitizenOf	GPE-AFF
isLeaderOf	EMP-ORG
isMarriedTo	PER-SOC
livesIn	PHYS
locatedIn	PHYS
madeCoverFor	ART
originatesFrom	PHYS
participatedIn	ART
politicianOf	Other-AFF
produced	ART
worksAt	EMP-ORG
wrote	ART

Table 3: 33 YAGO relation types projected into ACE.

[2]Assuming 100 sentences for each article.

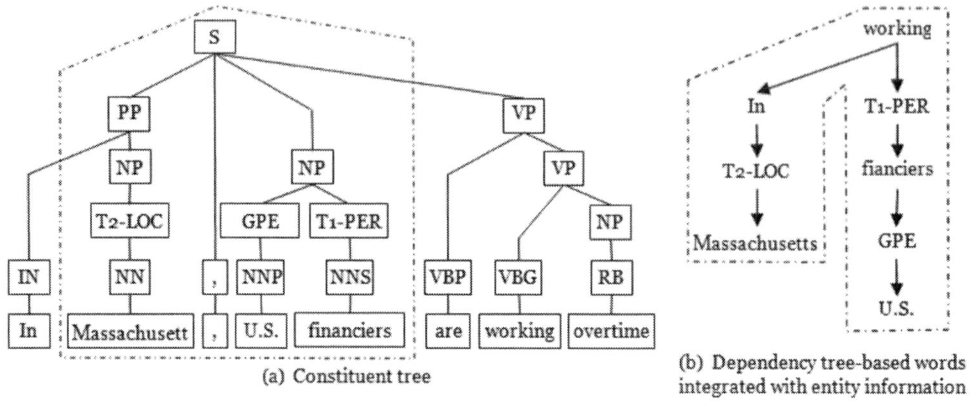

Figure 1: The constituent and dependency parse trees integrated with entity information

4 Direct, distant and joint supervised learning

We model RE using state-of-the-art kernel methods: syntactic structures are used to represent relation instances whereas kernel functions measure the similarity between pairs of them. Such functions correspond to scalar products between implicit feature vectors in the space of substructures. Additionally, we define a joint model between the RE classifier trained on ACE and trained on DS data such that we can merge together the information from the two datasets on similar relation type.

4.1 RE based on Kernel Methods

State-of-the-art ACE RE, i.e. (Zhang et al., 2006; Nguyen et al., 2009), uses tree kernels applied to constituent and dependency syntactic structures, extracted from the sentences expressing the target relations. Given a parse tree, the path-enclosed tree (PET) is used as input of a tree kernel function. PET is the smallest common subtree including the two entities of a relation. Figure 1.a shows the constituent tree and figure 1.b shows a fragment of the dependency tree of the sentence: *In Massachussets, U.S. financiers are working overtime*. The dashed frame in Figure 1.a surrounds PET associated with the two mentions, *financiers* and *Massachussets*. Moreover, to improve the representation, two extra nodes T1-PER and T2-LOC, denoting the type PERSON and LOCATION, are added to the parse tree, above the two target NEs, respectively.

In our experiments, we use the model defined in (Zhang et al., 2006), which combines a syntactic tree kernel applied to constituent parse trees and a polynomial kernel over feature extracted from the entities:

$$CK_1 = \alpha \cdot K_P + (1 - \alpha) \cdot TK, \quad (1)$$

where α is a coefficient to give more or less impact to the polynomial kernel, K_P, and TK is the syntactic tree kernel (Collins and Duffy, 2001) applied to PET.

We also use the best model in (Nguyen et al., 2009), which combines the advantages of the two parsing paradigms by adding six sequence kernels. These are applied to paths derived from the dependency tree and enriched with node labels of the constituent tree as follows:

$$CSK = \alpha \cdot K_P + (1 - \alpha) \cdot (TK + \sum_{i=1,..,6} SK_i), \quad (2)$$

where SK_i are the sequence kernels applied to the structure i defined in (Nguyen et al., 2009).

In our application domain there are many different categories of name entities, e.g. Editor, President, Employer, and so on. Thus the typically available NE types, e.g. Person, Organization, Location, Time, Numbers, do not provide much selective information. For this purpose, we also provide adapted kernels by simply removing the category label in the nodes of the trees and in the sequences. This data transformation corresponds to define different kernel functions (Cristianini and Shawe-Taylor, 2000).

4.2 Joint Model for Distant and Direct Supervision

An interesting test of the quality of our DS data can be carried out by using it for ACE RE experiments. This way, we can use the gold and well annotated dataset of ACE to accurately measure the impact of DS data. For this purpose, we define a joint model as follows: first, we select the portion of hand-labeled ACE 2004 corpus containing common relations (see the mapping in Section 3.5).

Second, we create a huge labeled dataset under distant supervision assumption (described in Section 3.4) from Wikipedia news articles and YAGO knowledge base. Thanks to the projection from YAGO to ACE relations, we generate the two datasets under the same set of labels. This way, labeled data can be automatically acquired from a huge corpus and used to enrich ACE relation extractors.

Third, we train (i) the M_{ace} RE model on ACE dataset and (ii) the M_{mixed} model on ACE dataset mixed with the labeled data from Wikipedia (by using for example CSK).

Next, as standard SVM classifiers do not provide calibrated posterior probabilities we apply Platt transformation (Platt, 2000) improved by (Lin et al., 2007) with an additional sigmoid function. This allows us to map the SVM outputs of the two models M_{ace} and M_{mixed} into probabilities.

Finally, we linearly combine the probability of the two classifiers as follows:

$$P(C|r) = \alpha \cdot P(C|r, C_1) + \beta \cdot P(C|r, C_2), \quad (3)$$

where C_i is the output of classifier i, α and β are the weights learned from a validation set to encode the importance of the classifier for detecting the relation r. This combination provides a more robust model with respect to domain change.

5 Experiments

The aim of the experiments is to demonstrate that our DS produces reliable and practical usable relation extractors. For this purpose, we test SLRE trained with DS and with the joint DS and ACE data. We also test end-to-end RE, which also requires the experimentation of our automatic Named Entity Recognizer.

5.1 Experimental setting

We used the English portion of the ACE 2004 corpus including 443 documents, annotated with seven entity types and seven relation types. We obtained 5,784 positive and 55,650 negative examples when generating pairs of entity mentions as candidate relations. We employed the Stanford Parser (Klein and Manning, 2003) to produce parse trees. The candidate relations are generated by iterating all pairs of entity mentions in the same sentence.

Regarding the DS data extraction (see Table 2), we used two PCs, one with Intel X5270 3.50GHz CPU, 32GB RAM, another with 3.40GHz CPU and 8GB RAM to run the Algorithm 3.1. We processed about 25,000 Wikipedia documents per day per machine. When we added the generation of structures and features, the whole procedure required one day to process 5,000 Wikipedia documents (per machine). Thus, it took about 10 days to create the dataset and the computational learning files.

To train and test our binary relation classifier, we used SVMs, where relation detection is formulated as a multiclass classification problem. We employed *one vs. rest*, selecting the instance with largest margin as the final label. We used the Tree Kernel toolkit[3] (Moschitti, 2004; Moschitti, 2006; Moschitti, 2008) as SVM platform to implement CK_1 and CSK (see Section 4.1). The training phase with convolution kernels on syntactic parse tree and diverse sequence kernels on the large DS data took 3 days.

For testing on ACE data, we applied 5-fold cross-validation and evaluated single classifiers with the average of Precision, Recall and F1 on the 5-folds. The overall accuracy is measured with the mean of the Micro-Average (All) over the 5-folds.

For testing on Wikipedia, as DS data may be incorrect, we created a test set by sampling 200 articles from Freebase (these articles are not used for training). An expert annotator then examined one sentence at a time and took all possible pairs of entities, where the latter were already marked in the sentence. For each pair of entities, the considered 52 relations from YAGO (and used in our RE system) are marked as positive or negative, respectively. The annotator obtained 2,601 relation instances used for evaluation.

Regarding NE recognition, we applied CRFs to Wikipedia data but we could not use the whole amount of data. Thus we sampled 18,198 Wikipedia articles, selecting 4/5 for training and the rest for testing. The training phase took 14 hours and 30 minutes, whereas the classification took less than 10 minutes.

[3]http://disi.unitn.it/ moschitt/Tree-Kernel.htm

Class	PHYS		EMP-ORG		GPE-AFF		All	
Precision	72.06	72.46	85.71	90.00	78.95	83.33	72.41	80.16
Recall	67.12	68.49	80.00	81.82	75.00	75.00	75.54	72.66
F1	69.50	70.42	82.76	85.71	76.92	78.95	73.94	76.23

Table 4: RE from ACE 2004 of three relations between named entities: for each PHYS, EMP-ORG and GPE-AFF, the left and right columns report our best relation extractor only using ACE and ACE+Wikipedia data.

Class	PHYS	PER-SOC	EMP-ORG	ART	Other-AFF	GPE-AFF	DISC	All
ACE data								
Precision	56.28	88.12	80.82	80.68	62.73	76.55	80.15	74.47
Recall	44.51	59.80	76.73	39.20	17.11	32.32	59.85	57.26
F1	49.71	71.25	78.72	52.76	26.89	45.45	68.53	64.74
ACE + Wikipedia data								
Precision	58.22	91.06	81.76	80.68	62.73	78.49	80.15	77.65
Recall	48.44	64.74	76.66	37.14	17.11	32.26	59.85	59.84
F1	52.88	75.68	79.13	50.86	26.89	45.73	68.53	67.59

Table 5: Results on ACE 2004 considering all the type of entities and all the 7 ACE relations.

5.2 Using Wikipedia Relational Extractors to improve on ACE

In the ACE program, relations are defined between pairs of entities. These not only refer to NEs but also to mentions, e.g. indicated by a common noun or noun phrase, or represented by a pronoun. In contrast, Wikipedia instances mainly refer to NEs, e.g. *Leonardo Da Vinci*, *Canada* or *Titanic*, and we do not use pronominal references for building RE instances. Thus, we carried out two kinds of experiments: using (i) RE task as defined in ACE with all kind of entities and (ii) only relations between named entities. We have observed that the NE relations only exist for the classes: Physical (PHYS), Employment/Membership/Subsidiary (EMP-ORG) and GPE Affiliation (GPE-AFF).

Table 5 presents the combination results. Overall, using Wikipedia data improves the state-of-the-art of standard RE from 64.74% to 67.59%. Moreover, if we focus on *proper* NE relations, i.e. of the type indicated in point (ii), the relation extractors improve from 73.94% to 76.23%. These results are interesting as show that (a) we can improve the best systems with DS and (b) relations learned from Wikipedia can be mapped into those defined by expert linguists on ACE. We also tested a model learned from only DS data. For space reason, we do not report the complete results: as expected, its overall F1 is lower than the model trained on only ACE (about 10 absolute percent points less).

5.3 End-to-end Relation Extraction

In this section, we describe the experiments using automatic NEs. Previous work, e.g. (Zhang et al., 2006; Zhou et al., 2007; Nguyen et al., 2009) performed extraction using gold entity features such as entity types (*Person*, *Location*, *Organization*), entity subtypes (*Nation*, *Population-Center* for *GPE*). For example, in the sentence *Bush went to Washington*, the type of the first named entity, *Bush*, is PERSON and for the second named entity, *Washington*, is LOCATION. When accurate, such features improve performance. In case of fully automatic systems they introduce noise and in Wikipedia they are not available. Thus, we removed all gold entity features (entity type, entity subtype, mention type, and LDC mention type) from ACE annotations. We modeled tree and sequence kernels based on constituent and dependency parse trees along with a few features that can be extracted automatically such as the string and the head word of the entity. Note that in (Nguyen et al., 2009; Zhou et al., 2007; Zhang et al., 2006), even for tree kernels, the tree structures were also integrated with entity types (see Figure 1 as an example). Therefore, in the parse trees in Figure 1, we replaced entity types PER, ORG, LOC with a generic type ETYPE.

5.3.1 Entity Extraction from ACE and Wikipedia

For entity extraction, we followed the design in (Nguyen et al., 2010) by applying CRF++ [4]. We

[4] http://crfpp.sourceforge.net

Corpus	ACE	Wikipedia
Precision	77.84	68.84
Recall	70.26	64.56
F1	73.85	66.63

Table 6: Results of entity extraction from ACE and entity detection from Wikipedia.

Setting	Gold NEs	Automatic NEs
Precision	91.42	82.16
Recall	62.57	56.57
F1	74.29	67.00

Table 8: Results on end-to-end RE from Wikipedia.

performed automatic entity extraction from seven classes from ACE 2004 and entity detection from Wikipedia. While ACE documents have been annotated with seven classes *Person, Organization, Facility, Location, GPE, Vehicle, Weapon*, for Wikipedia, we used Freebase as learning source, where entities have been annotated in each Wikipedia article. Note that for Wikipedia, the entity detection has been done for only entities, like *Person, Organization, Location*. For dates and numerical attributes, we used the extraction patterns described in Section 3.4. The results reported in Table 6 are rather lower than in standard NE recognition. We should consider that our NER also tags mentions in ACE, which is a hard task whereas for Wikipedia, the entity instances from YAGO potentially belong to thousands of different categories. Although we do not categorize entities, it makes the complexity of detecting of NE boundaries higher.

5.3.2 RE from Automatic Entity Extraction

Web data entities are often not annotated and not available as in hand-labeled corpora like ACE or in Wikipedia pages. In this new experiment, we move to a novel task where entities are detected and classified automatically from a classifier. This way, we aim at designing an end-to-end RE system, where entities are not known beforehand. We also introduce a new task, that is the extraction of Wikipedia relations from any web text, i.e. detection of Wikipedia instances from any web page and not only from Wikipedia articles (where links often exist for Wikipedia instances).

Setting	Gold Features/ Gold NEs	No gold Features/ Gold NEs	No gold Features/ Auto NEs
Precision	76.60	74.47	70.27
Recall	67.00	57.26	47.52
F1	71.50	64.74	56.70

Table 7: Results on end-to-end RE from ACE.

The results are shown in Table 7 and Table 8. We note that the gold entity features lead to very good F1. When we remove these, the F1 decreases from 71.50% to 64.74%. Nevertheless, without gold entity features, RE from Wikipedia still achieves very good performance, i.e. an F1 of 74.29%.

6 Conclusion

In this paper, we proposed a study on novel training methods using semi-structured resources such as Wikipedia. As the NLP field always requires new methods to leverage the ever-increasing amounts of user-generated data available on the web, ours is a particularly important achievement for RE. We presented adaptation and experimentation of state-of-the-art RE models also exploiting a mapping between Wikipedia and ACE relations. We also extensively experimented with end-to-end systems applicable both to Wikipedia pages as well as to any natural language text. Our method is general and we suggest that it could be applicable to other external resources or other NLP tasks.

Acknowledgments

This research has been partly supported by the European Community Seventh Framework Programme (FP7/2007-2013) under the grant 247758: Trustworthy Eternal Systems via Evolving Software, Data and Knowledge (EternalS).

References

Eugene Agichtein and Luis Gravano. 2000. Snowball: Extracting relations from large plain-text collections. In *Proceedings of the Fifth ACM International Conference on Digital Libraries*.

Michele Banko, Michael J. Cafarella, Stephen Soderland, Matt Broadhead, and Oren Etzioni. 2007. Open information extraction from the web. In *Proceedings of IJCAI*, pages 2670–2676, San Francisco, CA, USA. Morgan Kaufmann Publishers Inc.

Sergey Brin. 1998. Extracting patterns and relations from world wide web. In *Proceeding of WebDB Workshop at 6th International Conference on Extending Database Technology*, pages 172–183.

Razvan Bunescu and Raymond Mooney. 2005. A shortest path dependency kernel for relation extraction. In *Proceedings of HLT-EMNLP*, pages 724–731, Vancouver, British Columbia, Canada, October.

Razvan Bunescu and Raymond Mooney. 2007. Learning to extract relations from the web using minimal supervision. In *Proceedings of ACL*, pages 576–583, Prague, Czech Republic, June.

Michael Collins and Nigel Duffy. 2001. Convolution kernels for natural language. In *Proceedings of NIPS*, pages 625–632.

Nello Cristianini and John Shawe-Taylor. 2000. *An Introduction to Support Vector Machines and Other Kernel-based Learning Methods*. Cambridge University Press, Cambridge, United Kingdom.

Aron Culotta and Jeffrey Sorensen. 2004. Dependency tree kernels for relation extraction. In *Proceedings of ACL*, pages 423–429, Barcelona, Spain, July.

George Doddington, Alexis Mitchell, Mark Przybocki, Lance Ramshaw, Stephanie Strassel, and Ralph Weischedel. 2004. The automatic content extraction (ACE) programtasks, data, and evaluation. In *Proceedings of LREC*, pages 837–840, Barcelona, Spain.

Takaaki Hasegawa, Satoshi Sekine, and Ralph Grishman. 2004. Discovering relations among named entities from large corpora. In *Proceedings of ACL*, pages 415–422, Barcelona, Spain, July.

Raphael Hoffmann, Congle Zhang, and Daniel S. Weld. 2010. Learning 5000 relational extractors. In *Proceedings of ACL*, pages 286–295, Uppsala, Sweden, July.

Nanda Kambhatla. 2004. Combining lexical, syntactic, and semantic features with maximum entropy models for information extraction. In *Proceedings of ACL*, pages 178–181, Barcelona, Spain.

Dan Klein and Christopher D. Manning. 2003. Accurate unlexicalized parsing. In *Proceedings of ACL*, pages 423–430, Sapporo, Japan, July.

Hsuan-Tien Lin, Chih-Jen Lin, and Ruby C. Weng. 2007. A note on platts probabilistic outputs for support vector machines. *Machine Learning*, 68(3):267–276.

Mike Mintz, Steven Bills, Rion Snow, and Daniel Jurafsky. 2009. Distant supervision for relation extraction without labeled data. In *Proceedings of ACL-AFNLP*, pages 1003–1011, Suntec, Singapore, August.

Alessandro Moschitti. 2004. A study on convolution kernels for shallow statistic parsing. In *Proceedings of ACL*, pages 335–342, Barcelona, Spain, July.

Alessandro Moschitti. 2006. Efficient convolution kernels for dependency and constituent syntactic trees. In *Proceedings of ECML*, pages 318–329, Berlin, Germany, September.

Alessandro Moschitti. 2008. Kernel methods, syntax and semantics for relational text categorization. In *Proceedings of CIKM*, pages 253–262, New York, NY, USA. ACM.

Truc Vien T. Nguyen and Alessandro Moschitti. 2011. End-to-end relation extraction using distant supervision from external semantic repositories. In *Proceedings of ACL-HLT*, pages 277–282, Portland, Oregon, USA, June.

Truc-Vien T. Nguyen, Alessandro Moschitti, and Giuseppe Riccardi. 2009. Convolution kernels on constituent, dependency and sequential structures for relation extraction. In *Proceedings of EMNLP*, pages 1378–1387, Singapore, August.

Truc-Vien T. Nguyen, Alessandro Moschitti, and Giuseppe Riccardi. 2010. Kernel-based reranking for named-entity extraction. In *Proceedings of COLING*, pages 901–909, Beijing, China, August.

John C. Platt. 2000. Probabilities for sv machines. *Advances in Large Margin Classifiers*, pages 61–74.

Sebastian Riedel, Limin Yao, and Andrew McCallum. 2010. Modeling relations and their mentions without labeled text. In *Proceedings of ECML-PKDD*, pages 148–163.

Alexander Yates. 2009. Extracting world knowledge from the web. *IEEE Computer*, 42(6):94–97, June.

Dmitry Zelenko, Chinatsu Aone, and Anthony Richardella. 2002. Kernel methods for relation extraction. In *Proceedings of EMNLP*, pages 71–78, July.

Min Zhang, Jian Su, Danmei Wang, Guodong Zhou, and Chew Lim Tan. 2005. Discovering relations between named entities from a large raw corpus using tree similarity-based clustering. In *Proceedings of IJCNLP*, pages 378–389.

Min Zhang, Jie Zhang, Jian Su, and GuoDong Zhou. 2006. A composite kernel to extract relations between entities with both flat and structured features. In *Proceedings of COLING-ACL*, pages 825–832, Sydney, Australia, July.

GuoDong Zhou, Jian Su, Jie Zhang, and Min Zhang. 2005. Exploring various knowledge in relation extraction. In *Proceedings of ACL*, pages 427–434, Ann Arbor, USA, June.

GuoDong Zhou, Min Zhang, DongHong Ji, and QiaoMing Zhu. 2007. Tree kernel-based relation extraction with context-sensitive structured parse tree information. In *Proceedings of EMNLP-CoNLL*, pages 728–736, Prague, Czech Republic, June.

A Cross-lingual Annotation Projection-based Self-supervision Approach for Open Information Extraction

Seokhwan Kim, Minwoo Jeong[†], Jonghoon Lee, Gary Geunbae Lee
Department of Computer Science and Engineering,
Pohang University of Science and Technology
{megaup, stardust, jh21983, gblee}@postech.ac.kr

Abstract

Open information extraction (IE) is a weakly supervised IE paradigm that aims to extract relation-independent information from large-scale natural language documents without significant annotation efforts. A key challenge for Open IE is to achieve self-supervision, in which the training examples are automatically obtained. Although the feasibility of Open IE systems has been demonstrated for English, utilizing such techniques to build the systems for other languages is problematic because previous self-supervision approaches require language-specific knowledge. To improve the cross-language portability of Open IE systems, this paper presents a self-supervision approach that exploits parallel corpora to obtain training examples for the target language by projecting the annotations onto the source language. The merit of our method is demonstrated using a Korean Open IE system developed without any language-specific knowledge.

1 Introduction

The objective of information extraction (IE) is to generate structured information representing semantic relationships among a set of arguments from natural language documents. Although many supervised machine learning approaches have been successfully applied to IE tasks, applications of these approaches are still limited because large amounts of training data are required to achieve good extraction results. Because manual annotation for training examples is very expensive, weakly-supervised techniques to learn the IE system without significant annotation efforts have been sought (Zhang, 2004; Chen et al., 2006).

Open IE is an alternative weakly-supervised IE paradigm (Banko et al., 2007). The goal of Open IE is to yield both domain-independent and relation-independent extractions from a large amount of natural language text without requiring hand-crafted rules or hand-annotated training examples. A key challenge to implementing Open IE is to learn extractors without manually annotated training examples. Self-supervised learning approaches have allowed Open IE systems such as TextRunner (Banko et al., 2007) and WOE (Wu and Weld, 2010) to extract relations from large-scale English text with automatically annotated training examples obtained using external knowledge.

However, applying the self-supervision approaches adopted by previously reported Open IE systems to build a new system is problematic in languages other than English, because these approaches mainly depend on language-specific knowledge for English. For example, TextRunner obtains training examples from the English Penn Treebank by triggering a set of hand-written heuristics denoting syntactic structural constraints to decide whether or not a given instance has a semantic relationship. To learn an extractor for a new language, this approach requires a syntactically annotated corpus and language-specific heuristics for the target language. WOE achieves self-supervised learning of Open IE by using heuristic matches between attribute values in Wikipedia infoboxes and their corresponding sentences. This method can reduce the cost of

[†] Now at Microsoft Bing

building an Open IE system for a new language, because Wikipedia articles and their infoboxes are available not only for English, but also for most other languages. But differences among languages in the amount of available resources from Wikipedia are still severe; for example, English Wikipedia includes about 3.5 million articles, but Korean Wikipedia includes only about 150,000 articles as of January 2011.

In this paper, we propose a cross-lingual annotation projection-based self-supervision approach to improve the cross-language portability of Open IE systems. This method exploits parallel corpora to obtain training examples in the target language by projecting the annotations generated by the Open IE system for the source language. The goal is to determine whether a semantic relationship in a pair of noun phrases in the target language L_T is the same as in the corresponding pair of noun phrases in the source language L_S; this process is called cross-lingual annotation projection. Using our self-supervision approach, we developed the first English-to-Korean Open IE system that does not require any language-specific knowledge. We use an English-Korean parallel corpus to project the results of an English Open IE system onto training examples for the target Korean system.

We present the definition of Open IE problem in Section 2, describe our cross-lingual annotation projection-based self-supervision approach for Open IE in Section 3, present details about implementation of the Korean Open IE system developed based on our proposed approach in Section 4, report the evaluation result of the system in Section 5, present related work in Section 6, and conclude this paper in Section 7.

2 Open Information Extraction

The problem of Open IE is to learn a function $f : D \rightarrow \{\langle e_i, r_{i,j}, e_j \rangle | 1 \leq i,j \leq N\}$, where D is a given natural language document, e_i and e_j are entities which have a semantic relationship that is explicitly expressed in a contextual subtext $r_{i,j}$, and N is the total number of entities in D. For example, the output of an Open IE system for an input sentence *"Obama was born in Hawaii."* will be a tuple ⟨ *Obama, was born in, Hawaii* ⟩. Whereas traditional relation extraction problems such as ACE RDC have attempted to process both explicit and implicit relationships, Open IE aims to only extract explicit relationships $r_{i,j}$ in the context (Banko et al., 2007). Following Banko (2007), this paper concerns semantic relationships between entity pairs within a single sentence and considers each base noun phrase as an entity candidate.

Because the goal of Open IE paradigm is to eliminate direct human supervision, an extractor should be learned from the training examples obtained automatically without requiring hand-crafted rules or hand-labeled annotations: this process is called self-supervised learning. Self-supervised learning for Open IE is performed in two steps: (1) self-supervision and (2) extractor learning. In the self-supervision step, the training examples to learn an extractor are generated for each instance, i.e., pair of noun phrases in the given sentence. Next, self-supervised learning determines whether or not each instance is semantically related. The key to achieving self-supervision is to determine how to automatically identify the existence of a semantic relationship between noun phrases. Whereas previously reported Open IE systems have performed this determination based on syntactic structural heuristics or structured information from Wikipedia, our proposed self-supervision approach utilizes the projected annotations from the results of Open IE system developed for another language. Details about our self-supervision approach are provided in Section 3.

In the learning step, a set of training examples obtained from self-supervision is utilized to learn an extractor f. The extractor has been successfully implemented using statistical models such as the Naive Bayes classifier (Banko et al., 2007) and conditional random fields (CRF) (Banko et al., 2008).

3 Cross-Lingual Annotation Projection-Based Self-Supervision

Cross-lingual annotation projection is an approach to obtain training examples for L_T by projecting the annotations for L_S using parallel corpora between L_T and L_S. This approach has been applied for several natural language processing tasks which have differences in the amounts of available resources among target languages (Yarowsky and Ngai, 2001; Yarowsky et al., 2001; Merlo et al., 2002; Hwa et al., 2002; Zitouni and Florian, 2008; Pado and Lapata, 2009). A premise of our method is that parallel corpora between L_T and L_S are much easier to obtain than is a task-specific training dataset for L_T: this premise is generally reasonable because large numbers of parallel corpora for various language pairs are available.

We consider the Open IE as a task with an imbalance problem in resource according to the target language, because most reported systems for Open IE were developed only for English and because they depend on language-specific knowledge. We propose a cross-lingual annotation projection-based self-supervision method of obtaining training examples for Open IE. The cross-lingual annotation projection for self-supervision can be performed for each bi-sentence pair $\langle S_S^i, S_T^i \rangle$ in parallel corpora between L_T and L_S as follows:

1) **Annotation:** Given an input sentence S_S^i, a set of extracted tuples O_S^i is yielded by the extractor f_s for the source language L_S.

2) **Projection:** The annotations O_T^i for the sentence S_T^i are generated by projecting from O_S^i based on word alignment between S_S^i and S_T^i.

3.1 Annotation

The first step in projecting annotations from L_S onto L_T is to obtain annotations for the sentences in L_S, as follows:

1) A set of entities $\{e_S^1, \cdots, e_S^N\}$ in the given sentence S_S^i is identified using a base phrase chunker in L_S. Each base noun phrase is considered as an entity candidate.

2) Each instance is composed of a pair of entities $\langle e_S^l, e_S^m \rangle$ in S_S^i, where $1 \leq l < m \leq N$.

3) For each instance $\langle e_S^l, e_S^m \rangle$, the extractor f_s for the source language L_S outputs the existence of semantic relation between e_S^l and e_S^m and the textual fragment $r_S^{i,j}$ indicating the detected relationship.

As an example of annotation projection for self-supervision of Korean Open IE with a bi-text in an L_T Korean and an L_S English (Figure 1), the annotation of the sentence in English shows that the pair of entities "Barack Obama" and "Honolulu" has a semantic relationship and "was born in" indicates the relationship between two entities.

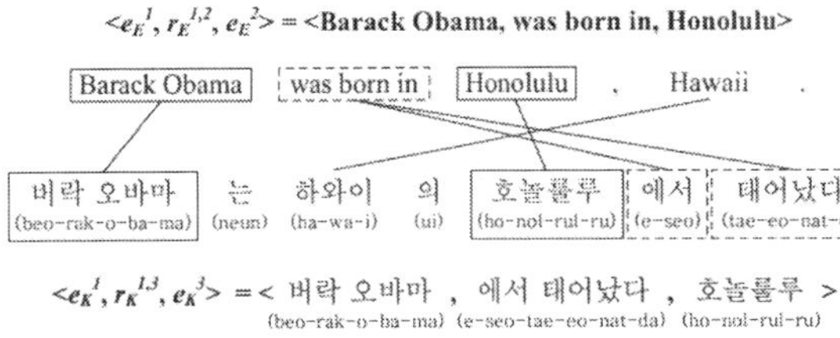

Figure 1: An example of cross-lingual annotation projection for Open IE of a bitext in English and Korean

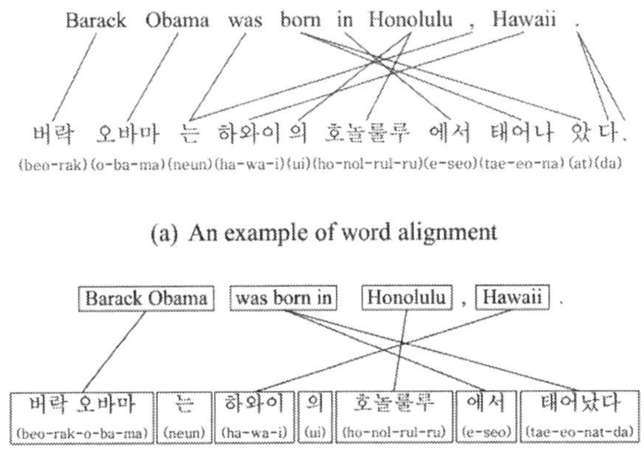

(a) An example of word alignment

(b) An example of chunk alignment

Figure 2: Comparision between word and chunk alignments

3.2 Projection

To use cross-lingual annotation projection to project the annotations from the sentences in L_S onto the sentences in L_T, we utilize word alignment information, which is an important component of statistical machine translation techniques. The objective of the word alignment task is to identify translational relationships among the words in a bi-text, and to produce a bipartite graph with a set of edges between words with translational relationships (Figure 2(a)). However, the results of automatic word alignment may include incorrect alignments because of technical difficulties. For example, the alignments (Figure 2(a)) have some errors such as ⟨Honolulu, ui⟩, ⟨COMMA, neun⟩ and ⟨PERIOD, da⟩.

The success of annotation projection is highly dependent on the quality of word alignment, to obtain quality results, the efforts to minimize harmful effects of erroneous word alignments should be minimized. In this work, we use alignments (Fig-

$A_P \leftarrow \vec{C}_S \times \vec{C}_T$
$A_C \leftarrow \emptyset$
for all $\left(C_S^i, C_T^j\right) \in A_P$ **do**
  $M(i,j) \leftarrow$ # of aligned words among C_S^i and C_T^j
end for
while $A_P \neq \emptyset$ **do**
  $(i,j) \leftarrow \underset{(i',j')}{\text{argmax}} \left(M(i',j') | (C_S^{i'}, C_T^{j'}) \in A_P\right)$
  if $(i,*) \notin A_C$ and $(*,j) \notin A_C$ **then**
    $A_C \leftarrow A_C \bigcup \{(i,j)\}$
  else if $(i, \vec{j_i}) \in A_C$ and j is adjacent to $\vec{j_i}$ **then**
    $A_C \leftarrow \left(A_C - (i, \vec{j_i})\right) \bigcup \left\{\left(i, \vec{j_i} \bigcup \{j\}\right)\right\}$
  else if $(\vec{i_j}, j) \in A_C$ and i is adjacent to $\vec{i_j}$ **then**
    $A_C \leftarrow \left(A_C - (\vec{i_j}, j)\right) \bigcup \left\{\left(\vec{i_j} \bigcup \{i\}, j\right)\right\}$
  end if
  $A_P \leftarrow A_P - (C_S^i, C_T^j)$
end while
return A_C

Figure 3: A chunk alignment algorithm

ure 3) between pairs of base phrase chunks instead of between pairs of words. For a given bi-text $\langle S_S^i, S_T^i \rangle$, a base phrase chunker for corresponding language produces chunk lists $\vec{C}_S$ for the source language and $\vec{C}_T$ for the target language. To identify the translational alignment between each pair of chunks C_S^i and C_T^j, the algorithm is performed in a simple greedy manner, i.e., a chunk pair that includes more word alignments is aligned before a chunk pair with few alignments, and a series of adjacent chunks aligned with the same counterpart can be merged. Chunk-based reorganization (Figure 3) of the word alignment in Figure 2(a) reduced the number of erroneous word alignments (Figure 2(b)).

Using chunk alignment, the annotations in the target language sentence S_T^i are projected from the annotations in the source language sentence S_S^i as follows:

1) As in the annotation phase, each instance is composed of a pair of base noun phrases $\langle e_T^l, e_T^m \rangle$ in S_T^i, where $1 \leq l < m \leq N$.

2) For each instance $\langle e_T^l, e_T^m \rangle$, its translational instance $\langle e_S^o, e_S^p \rangle$ in S_S^i is explored based on the result of chunk alignment.

3) The existence of semantic relationship in $\langle e_T^l, e_T^m \rangle$ is determined by projection.

4) If $\langle e_T^l, e_T^m \rangle$ is projected as a positive instance, the contextual subtext in S_T^i aligned with $r_S^{o,p}$ in S_S^i is extracted as $r_T^{l,m}$, and the final annotation $\langle e_T^l, r_T^{l,m}, e_T^m \rangle$ is produced.

In the Figure 1, an instance $\langle e_K^1, e_K^3 \rangle = \langle$ beo-rak-o-ba-ma, ho-nol-rul-ul $\rangle$ in the Korean sentence is aligned with the instance $\langle e_E^1, e_E^2 \rangle = \langle$ Barack Obama, Honolulu $\rangle$ in the English sentence. Because $\langle e_E^1, e_E^2 \rangle$ is predicted as a positive instance in the annotation phase, $\langle e_K^1, e_K^3 \rangle$ can be also considered to be a semantically related instance. Then, "e-seo-tae-eo-nat-da" in the Korean sentence is identified as $r_K^{1,3}$ which is aligned to $r_E^{1,2}$ = "was born in" in S_E^i, and finally, $\langle e_K^1, r_K^1, 3, e_K^3 \rangle$ = $\langle$beo-rak-o-ba-ma, e-seo-tae-eo-nat-da, ho-nol-rul-ul$\rangle$ is yielded.

4 Implementation

We developed a Korean Open IE system (Figure 4) based on our proposed cross-lingual annotation projection-based self-supervised learning. Our system is operated with no language-specific knowledge or resource for the target language, Korean. It requires only an Open IE system for another source language and a parallel corpus between source and target languages. In this system, we have used English as the source language, because most reported techniques for Open IE were developed for English. According to the advantages of English Open IE systems, the objective of our system is to perform domain-independent and relation-independent extraction. Furthermore, the fact that manual annotations are not needed to obtain training examples is also valid for applying the system to a new language. The system consists of three parts: self-supervision, learning and extraction.

4.1 Self-supervision

The sole input of our self-supervision method is a parallel corpus of L_S and L_T. We used an English-Korean parallel corpus [1] which consists of 266,892 bi-sentence pairs in English and Korean. Each sentence in the corpus was processed for POS tagging and base phrase chunking using OpenNLP [2]

[1] The parallel corpus collected is available in our website http://isoft.postech.ac.kr/~megaup/ijcnlp/datasets

[2] http://incubator.apache.org/opennlp/

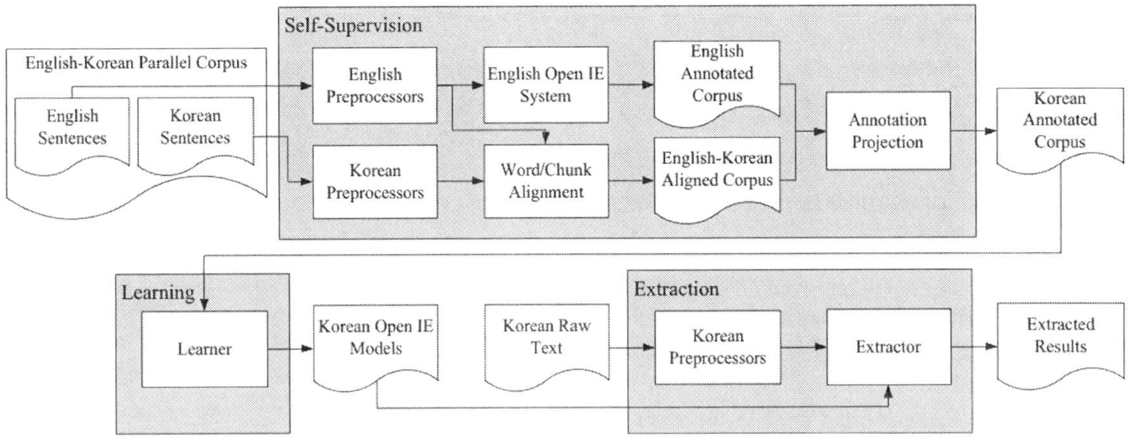

Figure 4: Overall architecture of the Korean Open IE system

for English sentences and Espresso [3] for Korean sentences.

For each preprocessed bi-sentence, word alignment was performed using GIZA++ software [4] (Och and Ney, 2003) in the standard configuration in both English-Korean and Korean-English directions. The bi-directional alignments were joined using the grow-diag-final algorithm (Koehn et al., 2003). The results of word alignment were reorganized by the chunk alignment algorithm 3.

The other prerequisite of the self-supervision in our system is that the Open IE system for the source language should obtain the annotations for source language sentences in the parallel corpus. We used our own implementation of the English Open IE system (Banko et al., 2007). We obtained a set of training examples to learn the extractor by applying a series of heuristics to the WSJ part of the Penn Treebank. From 49,208 sentences, 1,028,361 instances were generated; 9.0% of them were determined to be positive instances by the heuristic-based self-supervision. Using these instances, lexical and POS tag features were used to learn a CRF model. The CRF++ toolkit [5] was used to learn the extractor for English.

For the given preprocessed parallel corpus and Open IE system for the source sentences, annotation projection was performed. First, each English sentence in the parallel corpus was analyzed using the English Open IE system. Of 598,115 acquired instances, 169,771 positive annotations were produced by the annotation phase. These annotations were projected to the corresponding instances in the Korean part of the parallel corpus. This operation was performed based on the information obtained from chunk alignment. Finally, a set of training examples for the Korean Open IE system was projected. The projected dataset included 278,730 instances; 89,743 were positive.

4.2 Learning

Using training examples obtained by self-supervision, an extractor for Korean Open IE was generated. The extractor is composed of two statistical models. One is a maximum entropy (ME) classifier to detect whether or not each given instance is positive; the other is a CRF model to identify the contextual subtext indicating the semantic relationship for each positive instance. Both models utilized lexical and POS tag features in the node sequence of the dependency path between two entities organizing a given instance. The dependency path for each instance was generated using MSTParser (McDonald et al., 2005) [6] with a model trained on the Sejong corpus (Kim, 2006). The extractor was implemented using CRF++ and Maximum Entropy Modeling toolkits [7].

4.3 Extraction

During execution, the input of the system is raw text in Korean and the output is a set of extractions

[3] http://air.changwon.ac.kr/AIR/entry/Espresso_POS_K

[4] http://code.google.com/p/giza-pp/

[5] http://crfpp.sourceforge.net/

[6] http://sourceforge.net/projects/mstparser/

[7] http://homepages.inf.ed.ac.uk/lzhang10/maxent_toolkit.html

Model	P	R	F
Heuristic	47.7	20.1	28.3
Projection	33.6	49.0	39.8
Heuristic + Projection	41.9	46.4	44.1

Table 1: Comparison of performances among heuristic-based, projection-based and the merged models.

for the given text. The input text should be preprocessed by the analyzers for Korean sentences in the previously mentioned parts of the system. Then the instances and their features are extracted for each preprocessed sentence. The two models (Section 4.2) are operated in a cascaded manner for a given instance and its features: first the ME model identifies the existence of semantic relationship in a given instance, then the CRF model explores the context indicator only for instances determined to be positive by the ME model. Based on the results of two cascaded models, the system outputs the extracted results in the form of a triple, $\langle e_i, r_{i,j}, e_j \rangle$.

5 Evaluation

To evaluate our Korean Open IE system introducing cross-lingual annotation projection-based self-supervision, extractions were performed for two types of datasets. One dataset was built by annotating the semantic relationships denoted in a small number of sentences randomly selected from Korean Wikipedia articles. The dataset consists of 250 sentences and 1,434 instances, 308 of which were annotated to be positive instances. To compare with our system, we built a heuristic-based Korean Open IE system considered as a baseline. The baseline model was trained on the corpus automatically obtained from Sejong treebank corpus using a set of heuristics which were utilized for the English Open IE system except language-specific rules. On the test dataset, we measured the performances of three models: heuristic-based model, projection-based model, and the merged model trained on the mixture of both training datasets. Precision, Recall and F-measure were adopted for our evaluation.

Table 1 compares the performances of three models. The baseline model using only language-independent heuristics achieves poor performance, especially in recall. On the other hand, our proposed projection-based model outperforms

Type	Newswire		Wikipedia	
	prec.	# of extr.	prec.	# of extr.
Birth Place	65.2	256	69.1	971
Won Award	57.4	824	63.3	286
Acquisition	67.0	1112	50.3	143
Invent Of	53.1	32	47.6	103

Table 2: Evaluation results for four relation types

Error Type	# of errors
Chunking Error	364 (26.9%)
Dependency Parsing Error	461 (34.1%)
Extracting Error	527 (39.0%)

Table 3: Distribution of the errors

the baseline model, due to largely increased recall. Moreover, the projected instances helps to improve the performance of the heuristic-based approach by merging the training datasets. The results show that our proposed projection-based method is more effective than the previous approach to build an Open IE system for a new language.

The second evaluation was performed on the extractions of our system for the large amount of documents. We used two datasets: one dataset consists of 2,565,487 sentences in 302,276 documents obtained from Korean Newswire Second Edition published by LDC; the other contains 1,342,003 sentences in 123,000 articles from Korean Wikipedia.

The evaluation was performed manually for the extracted results annotated by four relation types {BIRTH_PLACE, WON_AWARD, ACQUISITION, INVENT_OF}. The relation type of each extracted result was determined by manual clustering based on its contextual indicator $r_{i,j}$. Our system output 3,727 extractions with an average precision of 63.7% for four relation types (Table 2).

To investigate the reason for erroneous extractions, a qualitative analysis of 1,352 errors was performed (Table 3). Errors were classified into three categories: chunking errors and dependency parsing errors (both caused by the preprocessors), and extracting errors (caused by the extractor for well-preprocessed instances). About 60% of the errors were caused by preprocessors including base phrase chunking and dependency parsing. Because our system is highly dependent on the result of preprocessors, the performance of the extractor can be increased by reducing its sensitivity to preprocessor errors; this is a topic for future work.

6 Related Work

Many supervised machine learning approaches have been successfully applied to solve traditional relation extraction tasks (Kambhatla, 2004; Zhou et al., 2005; Zelenko et al., 2003; Culotta and Sorensen, 2004; Bunescu and Mooney, 2005; Zhang et al., 2006), but these approaches require a large number of training examples to achieve high performance. To reduce the annotation cost, weakly-supervised techniques have been designed (Zhang, 2004; Chen et al., 2006).

Open IE pioneered by TextRunner (Banko et al., 2007) is an alternative weakly-supervised IE paradigm. TextRunner aims to perform relation-independent extraction by introducing the self-supervision approach based on a small set of heuristics about syntactic structural constraints. The performance of TextRunner was further improved using O-CRF and casting the Open IE task as a kind of sequential labeling problem (Banko et al., 2008). Wu and Weld (2010) presented another Open IE system WOE which utilizes an alternative self-supervision approach based on Wikipedia infoboxes. The main difference between our work and previous Open IE approaches is that we did not use language-dependent knowledge or resources for self-supervision, but implemented it using cross-lingual annotation projection techniques.

Early studies of cross-lingual annotation projection considered lexically-based tasks, e.g., part-of-speech tagging (Yarowsky and Ngai, 2001), named-entity tagging (Yarowsky et al., 2001), and verb classification (Merlo et al., 2002). Recently, applications of annotation projection such as dependency parsing (Hwa et al., 2002), mention detection (Zitouni and Florian, 2008), and semantic role labeling (Pado and Lapata, 2009) have been studied. To the best of our knowledge, no work has reported on the Open IE task.

7 Conclusions

This paper presented a novel self-supervision approach for Open IE. Our approach uses cross-lingual annotation projection to automatically obtain training examples for a target language by propagating annotations generated by an existing Open IE system for a source language via a parallel corpus between two languages. The main advantage of our method is that no language-dependent knowledge is required to learn the extractor. Our method can contribute to improving the cross-language portability of the Open IE paradigm.

The feasibility of our approach was demonstrated by our Korean Open IE system. The system was developed using only an English Open IE system and an English-Korean parallel corpus; the system never utilized any language specific knowledge or resources for the target language Korean. Furthermore, the system operated in fully unsupervised manner, because all components including prerequisites do not require hand-labeled annotations or hand-crafted rules for the target task. The system outperformed the baseline system based on the language-independent heuristics. For large amount of documents, the system produced 3,727 extractions with a precision of 63.7% for four relation types.

However, our method can still be improved. Many erroneous extractions were caused by errors committed by preprocessors. To reduce sensitivity to these kinds of errors, we plan to introduce assessment techniques which are not included in this work. Another direction of our future work is to investigate a hybrid approach to self-supervision considering not only cross-lingual projected annotations, but also various external knowledge source such as Wikipedia and WordNet. We expect that this fusion approach can help to improve the quality of extracted results, because the effectiveness of each approach has been demonstrated for IE tasks.

Acknowledgments

This research was supported by the MKE(The Ministry of Knowledge Economy), Korea, under the ITRC(Information Technology Research Center) support program supervised by the NIPA(National IT Industry Promotion Agency) (NIPA-2011-(C1090-1121-0008))

References

M. Banko, M. J Cafarella, S. Soderland, M. Broadhead, and O. Etzioni. 2007. Open information extraction from the web. In *Proceedings of the IJCAI-07*, pages 2670–2676.

M. Banko, O. Etzioni, and T. Center. 2008. The tradeoffs between open and traditional relation extraction. In *Proceedings of the ACL-08:HLT*, pages 28–36.

R. C Bunescu and R. J Mooney. 2005. A shortest path dependency kernel for relation extraction. In *Proceedings of the HLT/EMNLP 2005*, pages 724–731.

Jinxiu Chen, Donghong Ji, Chew Lim Tan, and Zhengyu Niu. 2006. Relation extraction using label propagation based semi-supervised learning. In *Proceedings of the COLING/ACL 2006*, pages 129–136.

A. Culotta and J. Sorensen. 2004. Dependency tree kernels for relation extraction. In *Proceedings of the ACL 2004*, pages 423–429.

Rebecca Hwa, Philip Resnik, Amy Weinberg, and Okan Kolak. 2002. Evaluating translational correspondence using annotation projection. In *Proceedings of the ACL 2002*, pages 392–399.

N. Kambhatla. 2004. Combining lexical, syntactic, and semantic features with maximum entropy models for information extraction. In *Proceedings of the ACL 2004*, pages 178–181.

H. Kim. 2006. Korean national corpus in the 21st century sejong project. In *Proceedings of the 13th NIJL International Symposium*, pages 49–54.

Philipp Koehn, Franz Josef Och, and Daniel Marcu. 2003. Statistical phrase-based translation. In *Proceedings of the HLT-NAACL 2003*, volume 1, pages 48–54.

R. McDonald, F. Pereira, K. Ribarov, and J. Hajič. 2005. Non-projective dependency parsing using spanning tree algorithms. In *Proceedings of the HLT/EMNLP 2005*, pages 523–530.

Paola Merlo, Suzanne Stevenson, Vivian Tsang, and Gianluca Allaria. 2002. A multilingual paradigm for automatic verb classification. In *Proceedings of the ACL 2002*, pages 207–214.

Franz Josef Och and Hermann Ney. 2003. A systematic comparison of various statistical alignment models. *Computational Linguistics*, 29(1):19–51, March.

S. Pado and M. Lapata. 2009. Cross-lingual annotation projection of semantic roles. *Journal of Artificial Intelligence Research*, 36(1):307–340.

F. Wu and D. Weld. 2010. Open information extraction using wikipedia. In *Proceedings of the ACL 2010*, pages 118–127.

David Yarowsky and Grace Ngai. 2001. Inducing multilingual POS taggers and NP bracketers via robust projection across aligned corpora. In *Proceedings of the NAACL 2001*, pages 1–8.

David Yarowsky, Grace Ngai, and Richard Wicentowski. 2001. Inducing multilingual text analysis tools via robust projection across aligned corpora. In *Proceedings of the HLT 2001*, pages 1–8.

Dmitry Zelenko, Chinatsu Aone, and Anthony Richardella. 2003. Kernel methods for relation extraction. *J. Mach. Learn. Res.*, 3:1083–1106.

Min Zhang, Jie Zhang, Jian Su, and Guodong Zhou. 2006. A composite kernel to extract relations between entities with both flat and structured features. In *Proceedings of the COLING/ACL 2006*, pages 825–832.

Zhu Zhang. 2004. Weakly-supervised relation classification for information extraction. In *Proceedings of the CIKM 2004*, pages 581–588.

Guodong Zhou, Jian Su, Jie Zhang, and Min Zhang. 2005. Exploring various knowledge in relation extraction. In *Proceedings of the ACL 2005*, page 434.

Imed Zitouni and Radu Florian. 2008. Mention detection crossing the language barrier. In *Proceedings of the EMNLP 2008*, pages 600–609.

Exploring Difficulties in Parsing Imperatives and Questions

Tadayoshi Hara
National Institute of Informatics, Japan
harasan@nii.ac.jp

Takuya Matsuzaki
University of Tokyo, Japan
matuzaki@is.s.u-tokyo.ac.jp

Yusuke Miyao
National Institute of Informatics, Japan
yusuke@nii.ac.jp

Jun'ichi Tsujii
Microsoft Research Asia, China
jtsujii@microsoft.com

Abstract

This paper analyzes the effect of the structural variation of sentences on parsing performance. We examine the performance of both shallow and deep parsers for two sentence constructions: imperatives and questions. We first prepare an annotated corpus for each of these sentence constructions by extracting sentences from a fiction domain that cover various types of imperatives and questions. The target parsers are then adapted to each of the obtained corpora as well as the existing query-focused corpus. Analysis of the experimental results reveals that the current mainstream parsing technologies and adaptation techniques cannot cope with different sentence constructions even with much in-domain data.

1 Introduction

Parsing is a fundamental natural language processing task and essential to various NLP applications. Recent research on parsing technologies has achieved high parsing accuracy in the same domain as the training data, but once we move to unfamiliar domains, the performance decreases to unignorable levels.

To address this problem, previous work has focused mainly on adapting lexical or syntactic preferences to the target domain, that is, on adding lexical knowledge or adjusting probabilistic models for the target domain using available resources in the target domain (see Section 2). Underlying the previous approaches, there seems to be the assumption that grammatical constructions are not largely different between domains or do not affect parsing systems, and therefore the same parsing system can be applied to a novel domain.

However, there are some cases where we cannot achieve such high parsing accuracy as parsing the Penn Treebank (PTB) merely by re-training or adaptation. For example, the parsing accuracy for the Brown Corpus is significantly lower than that for the Wall Street Journal (WSJ) portion of the Penn Treebank, even when re-training the parser with much more in-domain training data than other successful domains.

This research attempts to identify the cause of these difficulties, and focuses on two types of sentence constructions: imperatives and questions. In these constructions, words in certain syntactic positions disappear or the order of the words changes. Although some recent works have discussed the effect of these sentence constructions on parsing, they have focused mainly on more well-formed or style-restricted constructions such as QA queries, etc. This research broadens the target scope to include various types of imperatives and questions. We analyze how such sentences affect the parsing behavior and then attempt to clarify the difficulties in parsing imperatives and questions. To do so, we first prepare an annotated corpus for each of the two sentence constructions by borrowing sentences from fiction portion of the Brown Corpus.

In the experiments, parsing accuracies of two shallow dependency parsers and a deep parser are examined for imperatives and questions, as well as the accuracy of their part-of-speech (POS) tagger. Since our focus in this paper is not on the development of a new adaptation technique, a conventional supervised adaptation technique was applied to these parsers and the tagger. Our aim is rather to clarify the difficulties in parsing imperatives and questions by analyzing the remaining errors after the adaptation.

2 Related work

Since domain adaptation is an extensive research area in parsing research (Nivre et al., 2007), many ideas have been proposed, including un- or semi-supervised approaches (Roark and Bacchiani, 2003; Blitzer et al., 2006; Steedman et al., 2003; McClosky et al., 2006; Clegg and Shepherd, 2005; McClosky et al., 2010) and supervised approaches (Titov and Henderson, 2006; Hara et al., 2007). The main focus of these works is on adapting parsing models trained with a specific genre of text (in most cases the Penn Treebank WSJ) to other genres of text, such as biomedical research papers and broadcast news. The major problem tackled in such tasks is the handling of unknown words and domain-specific manners of expression. However, parsing imperatives and questions involves a significantly different problem; even when all words in a sentence are known, the sentence has a very different structure from declarative sentences.

Compared to domain adaptation, structural types of sentences have received little attention to date. A notable exception is the work on QuestionBank (Judge et al., 2006). This work highlighted the low accuracy of state-of-the-art parsers on questions, and proposed a supervised parser adaptation by manually creating a treebank of questions.[1] The question sentences are annotated with phrase structure trees in the Penn Treebank scheme, although function tags and empty categories are omitted. QuestionBank was used for the supervised training of an LFG parser, resulting in a significant improvement in parsing accuracy. Rimell and Clark (2008) also worked on the problem of question parsing in the context of domain adaptation, and proposed a supervised method for the adaptation of the C&C parser (Clark and Curran, 2007). In this work, question sentences were collected from TREC 9-12 competitions and annotated with POS and CCG lexical categories. The authors reported a significant improvement in CCG parsing without phrase structure annotations.

Our work further extends Judge et al. (2006) and Rimell and Clark (2008), while covering a wider range of sentence constructions. Although QuestionBank and the resource of Rimell and Clark (2008) claim to be corpora of questions, they are biased because the sentences come from QA queries. For example, such queries rarely include yes/no questions or tag questions. For our study, sentences were collected from the Brown Corpus, which includes a wider range of types of questions and imperatives. In the experiments, we also used QuestionBank for comparison.

[1]QuestionBank contains a small number of imperative and declarative sentences, details of which are given in Section 4.

3 Target Parsers and POS tagger

We examined the performance of two dependency parsers and a deep parser on the target text sets. All parsers assumed that the input was already POS-tagged. We used the tagger in Tsuruoka et al. (2005).

3.1 MST and Malt parsers

The MST and Malt parsers are dependency parsers that produce non-projective dependency trees, using the spanning tree algorithm (McDonald et al., 2005a; McDonald et al., 2005b)[2] and transition-based algorithm (Nivre et al., 2006)[3], respectively. Although the publicly available implementation of each parser also has the option to restrict the output to a projective dependency tree, we used the non-projective versions because the dependency structures converted from the question sentences in the Brown Corpus included many non-projective dependencies. We used the `pennconverter` (Johansson and Nugues, 2007) [4] to convert a PTB-style treebank into dependency trees [5]. To evaluate the output from each of the parsers, we used the labeled attachment accuracy excluding punctuation.

3.2 HPSG parser

The Enju parser (Ninomiya et al., 2007)[6] is a deep parser based on the HPSG (Head Driven Phrase Structure Grammar) formalism. It produces an analysis of a sentence including the syntactic structure (i.e., parse tree) and the semantic structure represented as a set of predicate-argument dependencies. We used the toolkit distributed with the Enju parser to train the parser with a PTB-style treebank. The toolkit initially converts a PTB-style treebank into an HPSG treebank and then trains the parser on this. The HPSG treebank converted from the test section was used as the gold-standard in the evaluation. As evaluation metrics for the parser, we used labeled and un-

[2]http://sourceforge.net/projects/mstparser/

[3]http://maltparser.org/

[4]http://nlp.cs.lth.se/software/treebank_converter/

[5]We used the `-conll2007` option for the data extracted from the Brown Corpus and the `-conll2007` and `-raw` options for the QuestionBank data.

[6]http://www-tsujii.is.s.u-tokyo.ac.jp/enju

Genre	Total	Imperatives (*S-IMP*)		Questions (*SBARQ*)		Questions (*SQ*)	
		Top / embedded	Total	Top / embedded	Total	Top / embedded	Total
Popular lore	3,164	50 / 20	70 (2.21%)	40 / 11	51 (1.61%)	32 / 11	43 (1.36%)
Belles lettres	3,279	16 / 22	38 (1.16%)	51 / 9	60 (1.83%)	62 / 13	75 (2.29%)
General fiction	3,881	72 / 46	118 (3.04%)	76 / 42	118 (3.04%)	71 / 24	95 (2.45%)
Mystery / detective fiction	3,714	83 / 54	137 (3.69%)	78 / 20	98 (2.64%)	91 / 20	111 (2.99%)
Science fiction	881	17 / 18	35 (3.97%)	24 / 6	30 (3.41%)	24 / 6	30 (3.41%)
Adventure / western fiction	4,415	101 / 77	178 (1.25%)	55 / 39	94 (2.13%)	71 / 33	104 (2.36%)
Romance / love story	3,942	80 / 63	143 (3.63%)	68 / 48	116 (2.94%)	100 / 47	147 (3.73%)
Humor	967	10 / 21	31 (3.21%)	15 / 11	26 (2.69%)	25 / 18	43 (4.45%)
Total (all of the above)	24,243	429 / 321	750 (3.09%)	407 / 186	593 (2.45%)	476 / 172	648 (2.67%)

(%: ratio to all sentences in a parent genre)

Table 1: Numbers of extracted imperative and question sentences

Imperatives

- Let 's face it ! !
- Let this generation have theirs .
- Believe me .
- Make up your mind to pool your resources and get the most out of your remaining years of life .
- Believe me ! !
- Find out what you like to do most and really give it a whirl .

Questions

- Why did he want her to go to church ? ?
- Could he honestly believe it would be good for Carla to have those old prophets gripping her imagination now ? ?
- What was the matter with him that they all wearied him ? ?
- How could a man look to any one of them for an enlargement of his freedom ? ?
- Did many of Sam 's countrymen live in boxcars in the bush ? ?
- Had Sam ever lived in a boxcar ? ?

Figure 1: Example sentences extracted from Brown Corpus

labeled precision/recall/F-score of the predicate-argument dependencies produced by the parser.

4 Preparing treebanks of imperatives and questions

This section explains how we collected the treebanks of imperatives and questions used in the experiments in Section 5.

4.1 Extracting imperatives and questions from Brown Corpus

The Penn Treebank 3 contains treebanks of several genres of texts. Although the WSJ treebank has been used extensively for parsing experiments, we used the treebank of the Brown Corpus in our experiments. As the Brown Corpus portion includes texts of eight different genres of literary works (see the first column in Table 1), it is expected to contain inherently a larger number of imperatives and questions than the WSJ portion.

The Brown Corpus portion of the Penn Treebank 3 is annotated with phrase structure trees as in the Penn Treebank WSJ. Interrogative sentences are annotated with the phrase label *SBARQ* or *SQ*, where *SBARQ* denotes wh-questions, while *SQ* denotes yes/no questions. Imperative sentences are annotated with the phrase label *S-IMP*. All sentences annotated with these labels were extracted. Imperatives and questions appear not only at the top level but also as embedded clauses. We extracted such embedded imperatives and questions as well. However, if these were embedded in another imperative or question, we only extracted the outermost one. Extracted sentences were post-processed to fit the natural sentence form; that is, with first characters capitalized and question marks or periods added as appropriate.

As a result, we extracted 750 imperative sentences and 1,241 question sentences from 24,243 sentences. Examples of extracted sentences are shown in Figure 1. Table 1 gives the statistics of the extracted sentences, which show that each genre contains top-level / embedded imperative and question sentences to some extent.[7]

As described below, we also used QuestionBank in the experiments. The advantage, however, of using the Brown treebank is that it includes annotations of function tags and empty categories, and therefore, we can apply the Penn Treebank-to-HPSG conversion program of Enju (Miyao and Tsujii, 2005), which relies on function tags and empty categories. Hence, we show experimental results for Enju only with the Brown data. It should also be noted that, a constituency-to-dependency converter, `pennconverter` (Johansson and Nugues, 2007), provides a more accurate conversion when function tags and empty categories are available (see footnote 4).

4.2 Extracting questions from QuestionBank

QuestionBank consists of question sentences as well as a small number of imperative and declarative sentences. We extracted 3,859 sentences annotated with *SBARQ* or *SQ*. During the exper-

[7]Although we also applied a similar method to the WSJ portion, we only obtained 115 imperatives and 432 questions. This data was not used in the experiments.

Target	Total	Division
WSJ	43,948	39,832 (Section 02-21) for training / 1,700 (Section 22) for development test / 2,416 (Section 23) for final test
Brown overall	24,243	19,395 for training / 2,424 for development test / 2,424 for final test (randomly divided)
Brown imperatives	750	65 × 10 for ten-fold cross validation test / 100 for error analysis (chosen evenly from each genre)
Brown questions	1,240	112 × 10 for ten-fold cross validation test / 141 for error analysis (chosen evenly from each genre)
QuestionBank questions	3,859	1,000 for final test / 2,560 for training / 299 for error analysis (from the top of the corpus)

(# of sentences)

Table 2: Experimental datasets for each domain

iments, we found several annotation errors that caused fatal errors in the treebank conversion. We manually corrected the annotations of twelve sentences.[8] Examples of the annotation errors include brackets enclosing empty words and undefined or empty tags. We also found and corrected obvious inconsistencies in the corpus: character “ ’ “ replaced by “<” (737 sentences), token “?” tagged with “?” instead of “.” (2,051 sentences), and phrase labels annotated as the POS (one sentence).

5 Exploring difficulties in parsing imperatives and questions

We examined the performance of the three parsers and the POS tagger with Brown imperatives and questions, and QuestionBank questions. By observing the effect of the parser or tagger adaptation in each domain, we can identify the difficulties in parsing imperative and question sentences. We also examined the portability of sentence construction properties between two similar domains: questions in Brown and in QuestionBank.

5.1 Experimental settings

Table 2 shows the experimental datasets we created for five domains: WSJ, Brown overall, Brown imperatives, Brown questions, and QuestionBank questions. Each of the parsers and the POS tagger was adapted to each target domain as follows:

POS tagger - For Brown overall, we trained the model with the combined training data of Brown overall and WSJ. For Brown imperatives / questions and QuestionBank, we replicated the training data a certain number of times and utilized the concatenated replicas and WSJ training data for training. The number of replicas of training data was determined from among 1, 2, 4, 8, 16, 32, 64, and 128, by testing these numbers on the development test sets in three of the ten datasets for cross validation.

MST and Malt parser - For Brown overall and QuestionBank questions, we trained the model on combined data for the target domain and the original model. For Brown imperatives and questions, we replicated the training data ten times and utilized the concatenated replicas and WSJ training data for training.

Enju parser - We used the adaptation toolkit in the Enju parser (Hara et al., 2007), which is based on the idea of reference distribution (Jelinek, 1998). The parser was trained on the same training data set as the MST and Malt parser for each of the target domains .

[8] We intend making these corrections publicly available.

Target	WSJ tagger	Adapted tagger
WSJ	97.53%	-
Brown overall	96.15%	96.68%
Brown imperatives	92.36%	93.96%
Brown questions	94.69%	95.80%
QuestionBank questions	93.14%	95.69%

Table 3: Accuracy of each POS tagging system for imperatives and questions

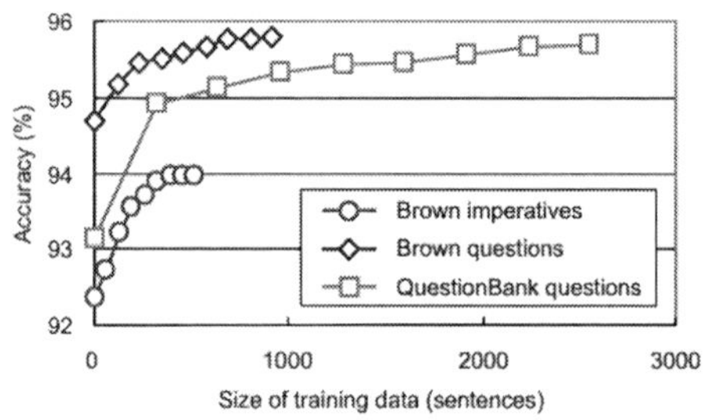

Figure 2: POS tagging accuracy vs. corpus size

5.2 Overview of POS tagging accuracy

Table 3 gives the POS tagging accuracy for the target domains. When we applied the WSJ tagger to other domains, the tagging accuracy basically decreased. For Brown overall, compared with the WSJ, the accuracy did not decrease much. However, for imperatives and questions, the POS tagger accuracy decreased significantly. The table shows that the adaptation improved the tagging accuracy to some extent, but that the improved accuracy for imperatives and questions was still below that of the adapted tagger for Brown overall.

Figure 2 shows the POS tagging accuracy for

Target	Correct → Error	WSJ tagger	Adapted tagger
Brown imperatives	VB → NN / NNP	13	9
	VB → VBP	8	2
	RB → RP	4	2
	UH → RB	3	1
	RB → IN	3	1
	IN → RP	3	3
	NN → NNP	2	3
	RB → DT	2	3
Brown questions	VB → VBP	16	2
	NN → JJ	3	3
	JJ → VBN	3	3
	IN → RB	2	3
QuestionBank questions	WDT → WP	28	0
	NN → NNP	17	12
	JJ → NNP	9	7
	VB → VBP	8	1
	VB → NN / NNP	7	6
	NN → JJ	6	4

(# of errors)

Table 4: Main tagging errors for each construction

the target domains for varying sizes of the target training data. This graph shows that for both types of sentences, the first 300 training sentences greatly improved the accuracy, but thereafter, the effect of adding training data declined. It indicates the inherent difficultly in parsing imperatives and questions; to match the tagging accuracy of the WSJ tagger for the WSJ (97.53% in Table 3), just using much more training data does not appear to be enough. In particular, the problem is more serious for imperatives.

5.3 Error analysis in POS tagging

Next, we explored the tagging errors in each domain to observe the types of errors from the WSJ tagger and which of these were either solved by the adapted taggers or remain unsolved.

Table 4 shows the most frequent tagging errors given by the WSJ tagger / adapted tagger for Brown questions, Brown imperatives, and QuestionBank questions, respectively. From the results, we found that the main errors of the WSJ tagger for the Brown domains were mistagging of verbs, that is, "VB → ***". We then analyzed why each of these errors had occurred.

For Brown imperatives, the WSJ tagger gave two main tagging errors: "VB → NN(P)" and "VB → VBP". These two types of errors arise from the differences in sentence constructions between Brown imperatives and WSJ. First, the WSJ tagger, trained mainly on declarative sentences, prefers to give noun phrase-derived tags at the beginning of a sentence, whereas an imperative sentence normally begins with a verb phrase. Second, the main verb in an imperative sentence takes a base form, whereas the WSJ tagger trained mainly on tensed sentences prefers to take the verb as a present tense verb.

After adapting the tagger to Brown imperatives, the tagger would have learned that the first word in a sentence tends to be a verb, and that the main verb tends to take the base form. Table 4 shows that the above two types of errors decreased to some extent as expected, although a few mistags of verbs still remained.

By investigating the remaining errors associated with VB, we found that several errors still occurred even in simple imperative sentences such as "VB → NN" for "Charge" in "Charge something for it", and that some errors tended to occur after a to-infinitive phrase or conjunction, such as "VB → NN" for "subtract" in "To find the estimated net farm income, subtract ...". The former type could be solved by increasing the training data, whereas the latter error type cannot easily be solved with a model based on a word N-gram since it cannot recognize the existence of a long advervial phrase, etc. preceding the main verb.

We also analyzed the errors in Brown questions and QuestionBank questions, and again found that many errors were due to the fact that the WSJ tagger was trained on a corpus consisting mainly of declarative sentences. After the adaptation, although some of the errors, such as the special use of wh-words, i.e., "WDT → WP", were corrected, other kinds of errors related to the global change in sentence structure still remained.

To tag words correctly both in imperatives and questions, we may have to consider richer information than only N-gram based features, such as dependency or phrasal structures. Context information may also help; if the tagger knows that a sentence is uttered in a sequence of conversation, the tagger can consider the higher possibility of the sentence being an imperative or question.

5.4 Overview of parsing accuracy

Table 5 gives the parsing accuracy of MST (first order), MST (second order), Malt, and the Enju parser for WSJ, Brown overall, Brown imperatives, Brown questions, and QuestionBank questions. Figure 3 plots the parsing accuracy against the training data size of the four parsers for Brown imperatives, Brown questions, and QuestionBank questions. The bracketed numbers give the accuracy improvements from "WSJ parser + WSJ tagger". Note that, since the training of the MST

Parser	Target	WSJ parser + WSJ tagger	WSJ parser + Adapted tagger	WSJ parser + Gold POS	Adapted parser + WSJ tagger	Adapted parser + Adapted tagger	Adapted parser + Gold POS
MST parser (1st order)	WSJ	87.08	-	88.54 (+1.46)	-	-	-
	Brown overall	80.83	81.14 (+0.31)	82.20 (+1.37)	82.49 (+1.66)	83.00 (+2.17)	84.30 (+3.47)
	Brown imperatives	76.60	78.34 (+1.74)	81.16 (+4.56)	78.62 (+2.02)	80.86 (+4.26)	83.40 (+6.80)
	Brown questions	75.91	77.57 (+1.66)	79.83 (+3.92)	78.67 (+2.76)	80.28 (+4.37)	82.75 (+6.84)
	QuestionBank questions	59.58	60.67 (+1.09)	61.54 (+1.96)	83.25 (+23.67)	85.41 (+25.83)	86.75 (+27.17)
MST parser (2nd order)	WSJ	88.22	-	89.74 (+1.52)	-	-	-
	Brown overall	81.60	81.83 (+0.23)	83.14 (+1.54)	(-)	(-)	(-)
	Brown imperatives	76.64	78.35 (+1.71)	81.17 (+4.53)	79.44 (+2.80)	81.39 (+4.75)	84.04 (+7.40)
	Brown questions	75.92	77.65 (+1.73)	79.86 (+3.94)	(-)	(-)	(-)
	QuestionBank questions	59.63	60.60 (+0.97)	61.64 (+2.01)	(-)	(-)	(-)
Malt parser	WSJ	87.46	-	88.99 (+1.53)	-	-	-
	Brown overall	79.50	79.76 (+0.26)	80.95 (+1.45)	82.28 (+2.78)	82.59 (+3.09)	83.84 (+4.34)
	Brown imperatives	73.37	74.62 (+1.25)	77.57 (+4.20)	77.91 (+4.54)	79.92 (+6.55)	83.18 (+9.81)
	Brown questions	71.12	72.41 (+1.29)	75.25 (+4.13)	78.73 (+7.61)	80.03 (+8.91)	82.72 (+11.60)
	QuestionBank questions	58.75	59.82 (+1.07)	60.42 (+1.67)	89.28 (+30.53)	92.55 (+33.80)	93.87 (+35.12)
Enju parser	WSJ	89.56	-	90.52 (+0.96)	-	-	-
	Brown overall	81.19	81.61 (+0.42)	82.63 (+1.44)	83.70 (+2.51)	84.29 (+3.10)	85.37 (+4.18)
	Brown imperatives	74.82	76.68 (+1.86)	80.52 (+5.70)	79.91 (+5.09)	81.53 (+6.71)	84.29 (+9.47)
	Brown questions	76.88	79.45 (+2.57)	80.75 (+3.87)	80.10 (+3.22)	82.24 (+5.36)	83.55 (+6.67)

(Enju: F-score of predicate-argument relations / MST, Malt: Accuracy of labeled attachments (%))

Table 5: Accuracy of each parsing system for the Brown Corpus and QuestionBank

parser (second order) on Brown overall, Brown questions, and QuestionBank could not be completed in our experimental environment[9], the corresponding parsing accuracies denoted by bracketed hyphens in Table 5 could not be measured, and consequently, we could not plot complete graphs of the second order MST for Brown questions and QuestionBank questions in Figure 3.

After adaptation (see "Adapted parser" columns in Table 5), the parser achieved two to eight percent higher accuracy for each of the Brown domains compared to the WSJ parser. For QuestionBank, 25 to 35 percent improvement in accuracy was observed. Figure 3 shows that the improvement is generally proportional to the size of the training data and that this tendency does not seem to converge, except for the Malt parser for QuestionBank. This would suggest that lower accuracy than that of the WSJ parser for the WSJ could still be as a result of a lack of training data. In Figure 3, the parser accuracy for QuestionBank, for which we could use much more training data than for Brown questions, approaches or even exceeds that of the WSJ parser for WSJ. However, as there is no more training data for Brown imperatives and questions, we need to either prepare more training data or explore approaches that enable the parsers to be adapted with small amounts of training data.

5.5 Error analysis on parsing

To capture an overview of the adaptation effects, we observed the error reduction in the Malt parser.

[9]The reason is a crash of the learning program, presumably caused by huge memory consumption and/or huge intermediate files.

Target	Dependency	WSJ parser	Adapted parser
Brown imperatives	ADV	39	32
	ROOT	33	9
	COORD	26	22
	NMOD	25	26
	OBJ	22	19
Brown questions	ADV	43	33
	NMOD	37	34
	SBJ	32	24
	ROOT	24	9
	COORD	21	12

(# of recall errors)

Table 6: Main parsing errors of Malt parser for Brown imperatives and questions

Table 6 gives the recall errors on labeled dependencies, which were observed more than ten times for 100 analysis sentences in each domain. For each dependency shown in the second column, the third and fourth columns show the number of parsing errors by the WSJ parser with gold tags and the adapted parser with gold tags, respectively. Since ROOT dependencies, that is, heads of sentences, are critical to the construction of sentences, we focus mainly on this type of error.

For Brown imperatives and questions, the reduction in ROOT dependency accuracy was prominent. On investigation, we found that the WSJ parser often made mistakes in parsing sentences which began or ended with the name of the person being addressed. For example, in Brown imperatives, for the sentence "See for yourself, Miss Zion.", the WSJ parser mistook the name "Zion" to be ROOT, and the main verb "See" to be a modifier of the name. The adapted parser correctly assigned ROOT to the main verb.

We also found that the WSJ parser often made mistakes in parsing sentences containing quota-

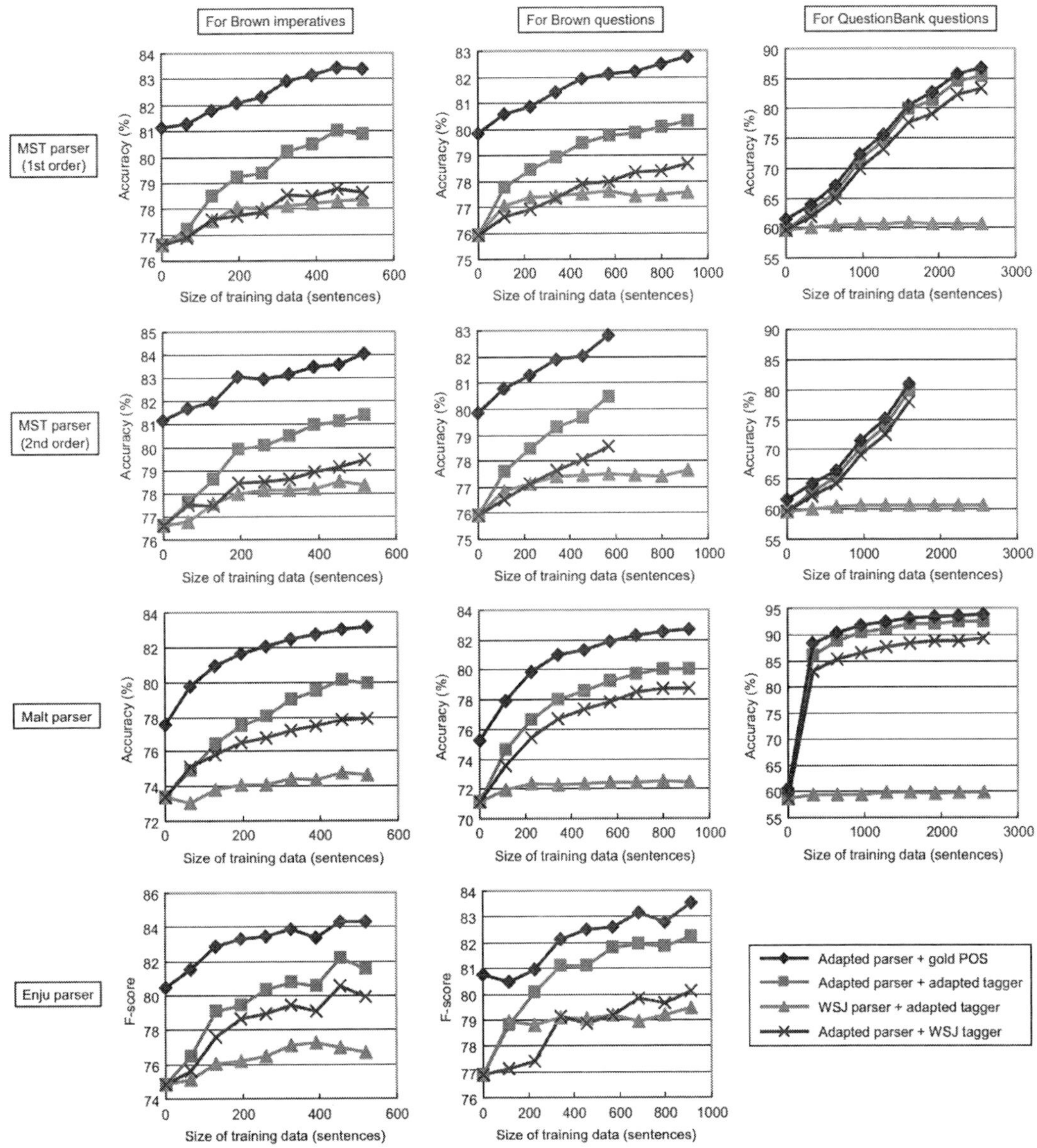

Figure 3: Learning curve of various parsers for Brown Corpus and Question Bank

tion, exclamation, or question marks, such as " "Hang on" !!" " or " "Why did you kill it" ??". For such sentences, the WSJ parser regarded the first "!" or "?" as ROOT, and "Hang" or "did" as the modifier of the punctuation. A possible reason for this type of error could be that the Brown Corpus places exclamation or question marks outside, instead of inside the quotation. The adapted parser could handle this dubious construction and assigned ROOT to the main verbs as the corpus required. [10]

On the other hand, we also observed some unsolved errors, of which we discuss two. First, Brown imperatives and questions, include many colloquial sentences, which have rather flexible constructions, especially imperatives, such as "Lift, don't shove lift!", "Come out, come out in the meadow!", etc. The parsing models based on the plausibility of constructions were not able to capture such sentences.

Second, having different sentence constructions within a single sentence, such as, where a to-infinitive phrase or subordinate clause precedes an imperative or question, often confused the parser. For example, for the imperative sentence, "To find the estimated net farm income, subtract

[10] We may have to correct the corpus.

Parser	WSJ parser + Gold POS	WSJ parser + WSJ tagger	WSJ parser + Adapted tagger	Adapted parser + Gold POS	Adapted parser + WSJ tagger	Adapted parser + Adapted tagger
Adapted to Brown questions → tested on QuestionBank questions						
MST parser (1st order)	61.54	59.58	59.65	63.06	61.07	61.07
MST parser (2nd order)	61.64	59.63	59.58	(-)	(-)	(-)
Malt parser	60.42	58.75	58.64	62.12	60.54	60.48
(POS tagger)	100	93.14	92.97	100	93.14	92.97
Adapted to QuestionBank questions → tested on Brown questions						
MST parser (1st order)	79.83	75.91	76.30	72.26	69.02	69.07
MST parser (2nd order)	79.86	75.92	76.11	(-)	(-)	(-)
Malt parser	75.25	71.12	71.15	67.70	63.98	63.43
(POS tagger)	100	94.69	94.69	100	94.69	94.69

(Parser: Accuracy of labeled attachments (%) / POS: Accuracy of tagged labels (%))

Table 7: Accuracy of each parsing system adapted to one question domain and tested on another question domain

Target	yes-no questions	wh-questions WP	WDT	WRB
Brown questions	59	18	2	22
QuestionBank questions	0	48	31	21

(# of sentences in the analyzed data)

Table 8: Distribution of question types

the estimated annual farming expenditure...", both the WSJ and adapted parsers regarded "find" as ROOT, because the parsers regarded the words following "find" as a that-clause complementing "find", as in "To find [(that) the estimated net farm income, subtract the estimated annual farming ...]". It would be difficult for the parsers to know which is the main clause in such complex sentences. This type of error cannot be solved merely by increasing the training data.

Imperative or question sentences typically consist not only of a pure imperative or question clause, but also of other constructions of phrases or clauses. These complex sentences were parsed without being partitioned into separate constructions, and as a result the parser sometimes became confused.

5.6 QuestionBank vs. Brown questions

Both the Brown questions and QuestionBank are in the question domain. In this section, we examine whether a parser adapted to one domain could be ported to another domain.

QuestionBank does not provide function tags, and therefore in training and evaluation of the parsers, abstracted dependencies were extracted from the corpus. As a result, a parser adapted to one domain could not provide correct dependency labels on functions for the other domain. However, we would expect that sentence constructions are basically common and portable between two domains, which would provide a correct boundary for phrases and therefore, the correct dependencies in phrases would be introduced by the adaptation.

Table 7 gives the parsing or tagging accuracy of each parser and the POS tagger for Brown questions and QuestionBank. These results differ from those in Table 5 in that the parsers and the tagger have been adapted to another question domain. The table shows that the parsers adapted to the Brown questions improved their parsing accuracy with QuestionBank, whereas the parsers adapted to QuestionBank decreased in accuracy. Table 8 could explain this result. Using Brown questions, many wh-questions were learnt, which is what QuestionBank mainly contains. On the other hand, despite yes-no questions constituting more than half the Brown Corpus, these were not learnt using QuestionBank for training.

A question domain contains various types of questions with various sentence constructions. In order to parse questions correctly, we need to capture each of these correctly. This type of problem was not so obvious when we were working mainly with declarative sentences.

6 Conclusion

Through experiments with various parsers we observed that simple supervised adaptation methods are insufficient to achieve parsing accuracy comparable with that of declarative sentences. This observation holds both for POS tagging and parsing, and indicates that the parsers need to be fundamentally improved, such as re-constructing feature designs or changing parsing models.

Following on from this study, future work includes investigating parsing frameworks that are robust for sentences with different constructions, and/or methods that can effectively adapt a parser to different sentence constructions including imperatives and questions, among others.

References

John Blitzer, Ryan Mcdonald, and Fernando Pereira. 2006. Domain adaptation with structural correspondence learning. In *Proceedings of the 2006 Conference on Empirical Methods in Natural Language Processing*, pages 120–128, Sydney, Australia.

Stephen Clark and James R. Curran. 2007. Wide-coverage efficient statistical parsing with CCG and log-linear models. *Computational Linguistics*, 33(4):493–552.

A. B. Clegg and A. Shepherd. 2005. Evaluating and integrating treebank parsers on a biomedical corpus. In *Proceedings of the ACL 2005 Workshop on Software*, Ann Arbor, Michigan.

Tadayoshi Hara, Yusuke Miyao, and Jun'ichi Tsujii. 2007. Evaluating impact of re-training a lexical disambiguation model on domain adaptation of an HPSG parser. In *Proceedings of 10th International Conference on Parsing Technologies (IWPT 2007)*, pages 11–22.

Frederick Jelinek. 1998. *Statistical Methods for Speech Recognition*. The MIT Press, Cambridge, MA, USA.

Richard Johansson and Pierre Nugues. 2007. Extended constituent-to-dependency conversion for english. In *Proceedings of NODALIDA 2007*.

John Judge, Aoife Cahill, and Josef van Genabith. 2006. Questionbank: Creating a Corpus of Parsing-Annotated Questions. In *Proceedings of the 21st International Conference on Computational Linguistics and 44th Annual Meeting of the ACL*, pages 497–504.

David McClosky, Eugene Charniak, and Mark Johnson. 2006. Reranking and self-training for parser adaptation. In *Proceedings of the 21st International Conference on Computational Linguistics and the 44th annual meeting of the Association for Computational Linguistics*, pages 337–344, Sydney, Australia.

David McClosky, Eugene Charniak, and Mark Johnson. 2010. Automatic Domain Adaptation for Parsing. In *Proceedings of the 2010 Annual Conference of the North American Chapter of the ACL*, pages 28–36, Los Angeles, California.

Ryan McDonald, Koby Crammer, and Fernando Pereira. 2005a. Online large-margin training of dependency parsers. In *Proceedings of ACL-2005*.

Ryan McDonald, Fernando Pereira, Kiril Ribarov, and Jan Hajič. 2005b. Non-projective dependency parsing using spanning tree algorithms. In *Proceedings of HLT/EMNLP-2005*.

Yusuke Miyao and Jun'ichi Tsujii. 2005. Probabilistic disambiguation models for wide-coverage HPSG parsing. In *Proceedings of the 43rd Annual Meeting on Association for Computational Linguistics (ACL)*, pages 83–90.

Takashi Ninomiya, Takuya Matsuzaki, Yusuke Miyao, and Jun'ichi Tsujii. 2007. A log-linear model with an n-gram reference distribution for accurate hpsg parsing. In *Proceedings of IWPT 2007*, June. Prague, Czech Republic.

Joakim Nivre, Johan Hall, and Jens Nilsson. 2006. MaltParser: A data-driven parser-generator for dependency parsing. In *Proceedings of LREC*, pages 2216–2219.

Joakim Nivre, Johan Hall, Sandra Kübler, Ryan McDonald, Jens Nilsson, Sebastian Riedel, and Deniz Yuret. 2007. The CoNLL 2007 shared task on dependency parsing. In *Proceedings of the CoNLL Shared Task Session of EMNLP-CoNLL 2007*, pages 915–932, Prague, Czech Republic, June. Association for Computational Linguistics.

Laura Rimell and Stephen Clark. 2008. Adapting a Lexicalized-Grammar Parser to Contrasting Domains. In *Proceedings of the 2008 Conference on Empirical Methods in Natural Language Processing*, pages 475–584.

Brian Roark and Michiel Bacchiani. 2003. Supervised and unsupervised PCFG adaptation to novel domains. In *Proceedings of the 2003 Conference of the North American Chapter of the Association for Computational Linguistics on Human Language Technology*, pages 126–133, Edmonton, Canada.

Mark Steedman, Miles Osborne, Anoop Sarkar, Stephen Clark, Rebecca Hwa, Julia Hockenmaier, Paul Ruhlen, Steven Baker, and Jeremiah Crim. 2003. Bootstrapping statistical parsers from small datasets. In *Proceedings of the tenth conference on European chapter of the Association for Computational Linguistics*, pages 331–338, Budapest, Hungary.

Ivan Titov and James Henderson. 2006. Porting statistical parsers with data-defined kernels. In *Proceedings of the Tenth Conference on Computational Natural Language Learning*, pages 6–13, New York City.

Yoshimasa Tsuruoka, Yuka Tateishi, Jin-Dong Kim, Tomoko Ohta, John McNaught, Sophia Ananiadou, and Jun'ichi Tsujii. 2005. Developing a robust part-of-speech tagger for biomedical text. In *Advances in Informatics - 10th Panhellenic Conference on Informatics*, volume LNCS 3746, pages 382–392, Volos, Greece, November. ISSN 0302-9743.

A Discriminative Approach to Japanese Zero Anaphora Resolution with Large-scale Lexicalized Case Frames

Ryohei Sasano
Precision and Intelligence Laboratory
Tokyo Institute of Technology
sasano@pi.titech.ac.jp

Sadao Kurohashi
Graduate School of Informatics
Kyoto University
kuro@i.kyoto-u.ac.jp

Abstract

We present a discriminative model for Japanese zero anaphora resolution that simultaneously determines an appropriate case frame for a given predicate and its predicate-argument structure. Our model is based on a log linear framework, and exploits lexical features obtained from a large raw corpus, as well as non-lexical features obtained from a relatively small annotated corpus. We report the results of zero anaphora resolution on Web text and demonstrate the effectiveness of our approach. In addition, we also investigate the relative importance of each feature for resolving zero anaphora in Web text.

1 Introduction

Zero anaphora resolution is the task of detecting and identifying the omitted arguments of a predicate. Since arguments are often omitted in Japanese, zero anaphora resolution plays an important role in the analysis of Japanese predicate-argument structures. For example, in the following text:

(i)	*Musuko-wa*	*itazura-ga*	*sukide*	
	son-TOP	mischief-NOM	like	
	watashi-mo	*(ϕ-ni)*	*te-wo*	*yaiteiru.*
	I	ϕ-DAT	hands-ACC	burn (have difficulty)

(My son likes mischief, so I have difficulty with ϕ.)

the dative argument of the predicate '*yaku*[1] (burn)' has been omitted. The omitted element is called a zero pronoun, and in this example it refers to '*musuko* (son).' Although most previous work has focused on zero anaphora in newspaper articles, this paper aims to resolve zero anaphora in Web text, since this involves a wider range of writing styles and is thus considered to be a more practical setting.

Reference resolution systems generally require a variety of information sources ranging from syntactic and discourse preferences to semantic preferences (Ng and Cardie, 2002; Haghighi and Klein, 2010). Since syntactic and discourse preferences are not word-specific, they can be learned from a relatively small annotated corpus. Semantic preferences, on the other hand, represent highly lexicalized knowledge, and hence it is difficult to learn these from a small annotated corpus. In some cases, knowledge of the relations between a predicate and its particular argument is insufficient, particularly for zero anaphora resolution. For example, although the dative argument of the predicate '*yaku* (bake/burn)' is generally filled by a *disk*, such as a CD or DVD, it is often filled by a *person*, such as '*musuko* (son),' if the accusative argument is filled by '*te* (hands)' as in the example (i).[2] Thus, knowledge of relations among a predicate and its multiple arguments is required to take such preferences into account.

Sasano et al. (2008) exploited large-scale case frames that were automatically constructed from 1.6 billion Web sentences as such a lexical resource, and proposed a probabilistic model for Japanese zero anaphora resolution. Their model demonstrated moderate performance, but it could not easily introduce new features, especially overlapping ones, nor take into consideration the importance of each feature, due to the assumption of independence in estimating probability. However, we think a variety of clues can be useful for zero anaphora resolution, where it is important to exploit overlapping features and consider the importance of each feature.

[1] '*Yaku*' is the original form of '*yaiteiru*.'

[2] '*Te-wo yaku*' (literally 'burn hands') is a Japanese idiom, which means 'have difficulty' in English.

Therefore, in this paper, we extend Sasano et al. (2008)'s model by incorporating it into a log-linear framework, and introduce overlapping features such as lexical features with different granularities. In addition, we also investigate the relative importance of each feature for resolving zero anaphora in Web text.

2 Related Work

Several approaches to Japanese zero anaphora resolution have been proposed. Seki et al. (2002) proposed a probabilistic model for zero pronoun detection and resolution that used hand-crafted case frames. Kawahara and Kurohashi (2004) introduced wide-coverage case frames that were automatically constructed from a large corpus to alleviate the sparseness of hand-crafted case frames. They used the case frames as selectional restrictions for zero pronoun resolution. Iida et al. (2006) explored a machine learning method using rich syntactic pattern features that represented the syntactic relations between a zero-pronoun and its candidate antecedent.

Since predicate-argument structure analysis and zero anaphora resolution are closely related, several approaches have simultaneously solved these two tasks. Sasano et al. (2008) proposed a lexicalized probabilistic model for zero anaphora resolution, which adopted an entity-mention model and simultaneously resolved predicate-argument structures and zero anaphora. Taira et al. (2008) proposed a model for analyzing predicate-argument structures by using decision lists, which integrated the tasks of semantic role labeling and zero-pronoun identification. Imamura et al. (2009) proposed a discriminative model for analyzing predicate-argument structures that simultaneously conducted zero anaphora resolution.

For languages other than Japanese, Ferrandez and Peral (2000) proposed a hand-engineered rule-based method for both determining anaphoricity and identifying antecedents in Spanish zero pronoun resolution. Zhao and Ng (2007) proposed feature-based methods to Chinese zero anaphora resolution. Kong and Zhou (2010) proposed a tree kernel-based unified framework for Chinese zero anaphora resolution, which dealt with three subtasks: zero anaphora detection, anaphoricity determination, and antecedent identification.

3 Case Frames

3.1 Lexicalized case frames

Our model exploits lexicalized case frames that are automatically constructed from 1.6 billion Web sentences by using Kawahara and Kurohashi (2002)'s method. Case frames are constructed for each predicate like PropBank frames (Palmer et al., 2005), and for each meaning of the predicate like FrameNet frames (Fillmore et al., 2003). However, neither pseudo-semantic role labels such as Arg1 in PropBank nor information about frames defined in FrameNet are included in the case frames. Each case frame describes surface cases that each predicate has and examples that can fill a case slot, which is fully-lexicalized like the subcategorization lexicon VALEX (Korhonen et al., 2006).

Note that case frames offer not only knowledge of the relations between a predicate and its particular case slot, but also knowledge of the relations among a predicate and its multiple case slots. Table 1 shows examples of constructed case frames.[3] A different case frame is constructed for each meaning of '*yaku* (bake/burn),' such as 'bake foods,' 'have difficulty,' and 'burn on a disk.'

3.2 Generalization of examples

The data sparseness problem is alleviated to some extent but not eliminated by using case frames that are automatically constructed from a large corpus. For instance, there are thousands of named entities (NEs) that cannot intrinsically be covered. Sasano et al. (2008) generalized examples of case slots based on 22 common noun categories defined in the Japanese morphological analyzer JUMAN,[4] and 8 NE classes defined by the IREX Committee (1999) to deal with this problem.

In addition, we generalized case slot examples based on automatically acquired multi-word noun clusters. Kazama and Torisawa (2008) proposed the parallelization of EM-based clustering with the aim of enabling large-scale clustering and using the resulting clusters in NE recognition. We used the resulting 2,000 clusters acquired from 1 million unique multi-word nouns.

Table 2 lists examples of the resulting 2,000 clusters.[3] As well as common noun categories and NE classes, we calculated the average of the probabilities that each case slot example belonged to

[3] We use English examples for the sake of readability.
[4] http://nlp.kuee.kyoto-u.ac.jp/nl-resource/juman-e.html

	Case slot	Examples:#	Generalized examples:%
yaku (1) (bake)	*ga* nominative	I:39, owner:26, daughter:22, mother:19, ···, Asako:2, ···	[CT:PERSON]:0.620, [NE:PERSON]:0.116, [CL:887]:0.070, ···
	wo accusative	bakery:9265, cake:4495, meat:4057, fish:2002, ···	[CT:FOOD]:0.711, [CL:883]:0.221, [CT:BODY PART]:0.105, ···
	ni dative	snack:35, breakfast:33, birthday:29, gift:21, ···	[CT:ABSTRACTION]:0.233, [CT:FOOD]:0.171, [CL:624]:0.076, ···
	de tools/methods	frying pan:894, moderate heat:425, ···	[CT:ARTIFACT]:0.356, [CL:291]:0.252, ···
		⋮	
yaku (2) (have difficulty)	*ga* nominative	who:7, teacher:7, everyone:5, family:4, government:3, ···	[CT:PERSON]:0.372, [NE:PERSON]:0.128, [CT:ORGANIZATION]:0.128, ···
	wo accusative	hand:6864	[CT:BODY PART]:1.000
	ni dative	child:52, attack:43, treatment:40, provision:32, daughter:30, ···	[CT:ABSTRACTION]:0.432, [CT:PERSON]:0.172, [NE:PERSON]:0.060, [CL:32]:0.016, ···
		⋮	
yaku (3) (burn)	*ga* nominative	I:1, husband:1,	[CT:PERSON]:1.000
	wo accusative	file:20, tune:14, music:9, image:8, video:4, ···	[CT:ABSTRACTION]:0.645, [CT:ARTIFACT]:0.273, ···
	ni dative	CD:3106, DVD:2066, ···	[CL:70]:0.829, ···
	de tools	machine:21, writing soft:10, PC:5, iTunes:4, ···	[CT:ABSTRACTION]:0.294, [CT:ARTIFACT]:0.191, [NE:ARTIFACT]:0.054, ···
		⋮	
		⋮	

Table 1: Example case frames for '*yaku* (bake / have difficulty / burn).'

Cluster	Nouns
CL:32	child (0.974), infant (0.738), kid (0.727), babies and infant (0.436), ···
CL:70	CD (0.896), DVD (0.837), CD-ROM (0.603), cassette (0.512), ···
CL:291	low heat (0.720), slow fire (0.715), moderate heat (0.681), distant fire (0.678), ···
CL:624	dinner (0.926), supper (0.925), lunch (0.882), breakfast (0.868), ···
CL:883	Chinese noodles (0.860), noodles (0.801), curry (0.793), cake (0.749), ···
CL:887	mother (0.909), parents (0.875), mom (0.838), husband (0.775), father (0.774), ···

Table 2: Examples of resulting 2,000 clusters (Kazama and Torisawa, 2008). Nouns that have high probabilities of belonging to target clusters are shown with probabilities.

the target cluster, and added it to the case slot. For example, if examples of a case slot include 'CD:3106,' 'DVD:2066,' and 271 other examples that have no probability of belonging to cluster 70, the average for cluster 70 is calculated as:

$$\frac{0.896 \times 3106 + 0.837 \times 2066}{3106 + 2066 + 271} \approx 0.829.$$

This type of generalized example represents more fine-grained semantic categories compared with examples that are generalized by using common noun categories and NE classes. The generalized examples are also included in Table 1, such as "[CL:70]:0.829" in the dative case slot of '*yaku* (3).' CT, NE, and CL in generalized examples denote common noun category, named entity class, and multi-word noun cluster, respectively.

4 A Discriminative Model for Zero Anaphora Resolution

4.1 Overview

Our model basically follows that of Sasano et al. (2008), except for the method of estimating possible combinations of case frames and predicate-argument structures. We also limited the target cases for zero anaphora resolution to '*ga*' (nominative), '*wo*' (accusative), and '*ni*' (dative) cases. The outline of our model is as follows:

1. Parse an input text and recognize NEs.
2. Resolve coreference and link each mention to a discourse entity or create a new entity.
3. From the end of each sentence, analyze the predicate-argument structure for each verb or adjective using the following steps:

1.	< cf ='*yaku*'(1), s =[NOM:'*watashi*' (I), ACC:'*te*' (hands), DAT:'*musuko*' (son)]>
2.	< cf ='*yaku*'(1), s =[NOM:'*watashi*' (I), ACC:'*te*' (hands), DAT:NULL']>
3.	< cf ='*yaku*'(1), s =[NOM:NULL, ACC:'*te*' (hands), DAT:'*watashi*' (I)]>
4.	< cf ='*yaku*'(1), s =[NOM:'*musuko*' (son), ACC:'*te*' (hands), DAT:NULL>
5.	**< cf ='*yaku*'(2), s = [NOM:'*watashi*' (I), ACC:'*te*' (hands), DAT:'*musuko*' (son)]>**
6.	< cf ='*yaku*'(2), s =[NOM:'*watashi*' (I), ACC:'*te*' (hands), DAT:NULL']>
	⋮

Table 3: Examples of possible combinations of case frame cf and predicate-argument structure s for the predicate '*yaku*' in the example (i) in Section 1. Bold font indicates the proper combination for this example.

(a) Select a case frame temporarily.

(b) List possible predicate-argument structures including omitted arguments.

(c) Estimate possible combinations of case frames and predicate-argument structures, and select the one with the highest estimate.

In 3-(b), we first consider only the overt arguments and prune away improbable structures to reduce the search space. We apply a log-linear framework to estimating a combination of a case frame and a predicate-argument structure to introduce overlapping features and take into consideration the relative importance of each feature.

Note that the estimation is not separately conducted for each argument, but for all arguments including overt and omitted arguments. For examples, when we analyze the predicate '*yaku*' in the example (i) in Section 1, we consider the various combinations as listed in Table 3, and choose the combination with the highest estimate.

4.2 Log-linear model

When text t and target predicate p are given, we choose the combination of case frame cf and predicate-argument structure s with the highest conditional probability,

$$(cf_{best}, s_{best}) = \arg\max_{cf,s} P(cf, s|p, t).$$

We model the conditional probability, using a log-linear framework:

$$P(cf, s|p, t; \Lambda) = \frac{1}{Z(p,t)} \exp\{\Lambda \cdot \boldsymbol{F}(cf, s, p, t)\},$$

$$Z(p,t) = \sum_{\{cf,s\} \in C(p,t)} \exp\{\Lambda \cdot \boldsymbol{F}(cf, s, p, t)\},$$

where $\boldsymbol{F} = (f_1, \ldots, f_K)$ is a feature vector whose elements represent K feature functions, $\Lambda = (\lambda_1, \ldots, \lambda_K)$ denotes a weight vector (parameter vector) for the feature functions, and $C(p,t)$ yields a set of possible combinations of case frame cf and predicate-argument structure s for given predicate p and text t.

4.3 Parameter estimation

We now describe how parameter vector Λ is estimated from a set of training data. When the training set consisting of N instances $\{(s^{(1)}, p^{(1)}, t^{(1)}), (s^{(2)}, p^{(2)}, t^{(2)}), \ldots, (s^{(N)}, p^{(N)}, t^{(N)})\}$ is given, we choose the combination of CF and Λ that maximize the posterior probability:

$$\max_{CF,\Lambda} \left\{ \sum_{n=1}^{N} \log P(cf^{(n)}, s^{(n)}|p^{(n)}, t^{(n)}; \Lambda) - \alpha||\Lambda||^2 \right\},$$

where α is a regularization parameter for the L2 norm, and $CF = (cf^{(1)}, cf^{(2)}, \ldots, cf^{(N)})$ is a combination of possible case frames, i.e. $cf^{(n)}$ is a candidate case frame for the given instance $(s^{(n)}, p^{(n)}, t^{(n)})$. Since the appropriate case frames are not annotated in the training set, we choose an appropriate case frame in estimating parameters with the following algorithm:

1. Initialize parameter Λ to a random value in the range [0,1].

2. For each training instance, update $cf^{(n)}$ that maximizes $P(cf, s|p, t; \Lambda)$ with current parameter Λ:

$$\hat{cf}^{(n)} = \arg\max_{cf^{(n)}} P(cf^{(n)}, s^{(n)}|p^{(n)}, t^{(n)}; \Lambda)$$

   If $CF = (cf^{(1)}, cf^{(2)}, \ldots, cf^{(N)})$ is not updated, we determine current parameter Λ as the resulting parameter.

3. If CF is updated, we renew parameter Λ that maximizes the posterior probability with N training instances $\{(cf^{(1)}, s^{(1)}, p^{(1)}, t^{(1)}), \ldots, (cf^{(N)}, s^{(N)}, p^{(N)}, t^{(N)})\}$,

$$\mathcal{L}_\Lambda = \sum_{n=1}^{N} \log P(cf^{(n)}, s^{(n)} | p^{(n)}, t^{(n)}; \Lambda) - \alpha ||\Lambda||^2,$$

and go back to step 2. To avoid overfitting, we include an L2-regularization term in the objective.[5] $\mathcal{L}_\Lambda$ is maximized by the Limited memory BFGS (L-BFGS) algorithm (Nocedal, 1980).[6]

In both steps 2 and 3, the log-likelihood increases monotonically, and this algorithm thus always converges to an optimal solution but does not ensure the global maximum parameter will be assigned. That is, we can obtain convergence to different local optima. Therefore, we test several initial values and adopt the resulting parameter that maximizes posterior probability.

5 Features

5.1 Lexical features

We exploit six types of lexical features: word PMI (Pointwise Mutual Information), cluster PMI, category PMI, NE PMI, occupancy of a case slot, and overt argument assignment score. Their values are real values that are calculated by using case frames. Since our model is based on the entity-mention model that assigns zero pronouns not to a certain mention but to an entity, several values can be calculated for a certain lexical feature by taking coreferential mentions into consideration. In such cases, we choose the highest value as a corresponding lexical feature.

Word PMI Each case slot of a case frame has typical words that are often assigned to the slot. We use the PMI features between a slot of a case frame and its antecedent candidate to reflect such preferences:

e.g.

- $\log\{P(child|\text{cf=}yaku(2)\text{,case=}ni)/P(child)\}$

As well as most other features, this type of features is distinguished by the case of zero pronouns: '*ga*,' '*wo*,' and '*ni*,' respectively.

Cluster, Category, and NE PMI We also use generalized example versions of word PMI to alleviate the data sparseness problem in word PMI:

[5]We set α to 1.0 in all our experiments.

[6]We used libLBFGS 1.9: http://www.chokkan.org/software/liblbfgs/.

e.g.

- $\log\{P([\text{CL:32}]\ |yaku(2), ni)/P([\text{CL:32}])\}$
- $\log\{P([\text{CT:PERSON}]|yaku(2), ni)/P([\text{CT:PERSON}])\}$
- $\log\{P([\text{NE:PERSON}]|yaku(2), ni)/P([\text{NE:PERSON}])\}$

After this, we will generically call these three features **GE PMI**. All the features described above overlap, and only their granularities are different.

Occupancy of case slot We believe that there is a relation between the occupancy of a case slot and its generativity of zero pronouns. For example, since the *ni* (dative) case of '*yaku* (3)' often appears, we assume this slot is just omitted as a zero pronoun even if there is no overt argument. However, since the *ni* (dative) case of '*yaku* (1)' rarely appears, we assume there is no case slot if there is no overt argument.

Therefore, we use the log occupancy of the case slot, whose value is the same as the log of the generative probability of a case slot in Kawahara and Kurohashi (2006)'s model and estimated from case structure analysis of a large raw corpus:

e.g.

- $\log P(A(cs) = 1|\text{cf=}yaku(2)\text{,case=}ni)$,

  where $A(cs) = 1$ denotes that the target case slot is occupied by an overt argument.

Overt argument assignment score Our model not only takes into account the correspondence between a case slot and its omitted argument, but also the correspondence between a case slot and its overt argument. The score for overt argument assignment reflects the likelihood of an overt argument assignment, and this is the same as the score for the predicate-argument structure in Kawahara and Kurohashi (2006)'s model, which does not take into consideration zero anaphoric relations.

e.g.

- $\log P(\text{cf=}yaku(2), ga_{ov}{:}watashi, wo_{ov}{:}te|yaku)$

Only this feature is not separately calculated for each case, but for the whole overt predicate-argument structure. Note that, this feature also includes non-lexical preferences in the analysis of a predicate-argument structure.

5.2 Non-lexical features

We also exploit three types of non-lexical features, which are binary features to reflect syntactic and

Intra sentential (64 categories)	
Itopic:	Mentioned with **topic** marker
IP-self:	Mentioned at **parent** node
IC-self:	Mentioned at **child** node
IGP-self:	Mentioned at **grand-parent** node
IGC-self:	Mentioned at **grand-child** node
⋮	⋮
IB-self:	Mentioned at a preceding node in the sentence except above (**before**)
IA-self:	Mentioned at a following node in the sentence except above (**after**)
IP-*ga*-ov:	Overt nominative argument of a predicate in **parent** node
IP-*ga*-om:	Omitted nominative argument of a predicate in **parent** node
IP-*wo*-ov:	Overt accusative argument of a predicate in **parent** node
IP-*wo*-om:	Omitted accusative argument of a predicate in **parent** node
⋮	⋮
IGP-*ga*-ov:	Overt nominative argument of a predicate in **grand-parent** node
⋮	⋮
Inter sentential (21 categories)	
B1:	Mentioned in the adjacent sentence
B1-*ga*-ov:	Overt nominative argument of a predicate in the adjacent sentence
B1-*ga*-om:	Omitted nominative argument of a predicate in the adjacent sentence
B1-*wo*-ov:	Overt accusative argument of a predicate in the adjacent sentence
⋮	⋮
B2:	Mentioned in two sentences before
B2-*ga*-ov:	Overt nominative argument of a predicate in the two sentence before
⋮	⋮
B3:	Mentioned in more than two sentences before
⋮	⋮

Table 4: Examples of case/location categories.

discourse preferences. Since Web text slightly adheres to formal grammar and thus rich syntactic preferences are not considered very important for resolution of zero anaphora in Web text, we only introduce simple features as non-lexical features.

Case/location We use case/location features to reflect syntactic, functional, and locational preferences. We considered 85 case/location categories, examples of which are summarized in Table 4. If an antecedent candidate appears in a certain case/location category, the corresponding feature value is 1; otherwise 0. These features are made for each case, respectively, i.e. there are a total of 255 case/location features.

Salience Previous work has reported the usefulness of salience in anaphora resolution (Lappin and Leass, 1994; Mitkov et al., 2002; Sasano et al., 2008). We introduce salience features to take into account the salience of each discourse entity. First, we apply the following simple rules to estimating the salience of each entity, and we then set salience features, whose value is 1 if the salience of an antecedent candidate is no less than 1.0; otherwise 0.

- +2: mentioned with topical marker "*wa*."
- +1: mentioned without topical marker "*wa*."
- ×0.5: beginning of each sentence.

Case assigned features We introduce case assigned features for each case type. The value is 1 if the corresponding zero pronoun is assigned to an antecedent; otherwise 0.

If the weights for these features become larger, corresponding zero pronouns are assigned to antecedents more often. Thus, the weights for these features are regarded as parameters to control the recall/precision trade-off. Although we mainly evaluate our system by using the F-measure, the algorithm mentioned in Section 4.3 does not select a parameter that maximizes the F-measure. Thus, after parameters are estimated by the algorithm, we adjust the weights for these features to maximize the F-measure by using training or development data.

6 Experiments

6.1 Setting

We used the same data set as described in (Sasano et al., 2009). This data set consisted of 186 Web documents (979 sentences, 19,677 morphemes), in which all predicate-argument relations were manually annotated. There were 2,137 predicates in this corpus, and 683 zero anaphoric relations were annotated. We call this data set a Web Corpus after this. We performed 6-fold cross-validation. We used correct morphemes, named entities, dependency structures, and coreference relations that were manually annotated to concentrate on zero anaphora resolution. We tested 10 initial values as parameter Λ. Since the parameters converged to almost the same value for each initial value, we considered that our model achieved the global maximum parameters in most cases.

We applied two baseline models for comparison. The first was the model proposed by Sasano et al. (2008), which did not use a log-linear framework but exploited almost the same clues. In addition, we also conducted an experiment with merged case frames to verify the usefulness of the

	Recall	Precision	F-measure
Sasano et al. (2008)'s model	0.341 (233/683)	0.306 (233/762)	0.322
Proposed model with merged case frames	0.334 (228/683)	0.412 (228/553)	0.369
Proposed model	0.379 (259/683)	0.403 (259/642)	**0.391**

Table 5: Experimental results of zero anaphora resolution on Web Corpus.

Case	Type	Recall	Precision	F-measure
NOM	Intra-sentential	0.504 (120/238)	0.460 (120/261)	0.481
	Inter-sentential	0.460 (104/226)	0.387 (104/269)	0.420
ACC	Intra-sentential	0.250 (17/68)	0.447 (17/38)	0.321
	Inter-sentential	0.163 (7/43)	0.194 (7/36)	0.177
DAT	Intra-sentential	0.105 (6/57)	0.316 (6/19)	0.158
	Inter-sentential	0.098 (5/51)	0.263 (5/19)	0.143

Table 6: Detailed experimental results for the proposed model on the Web Corpus.

Removed feature type	Recall	Precision	F-measure
None (Use all features)	0.379 (259/683)	0.403 (259/642)	**0.391**
(Lexical features)			
– Word PMI	0.363 (248/683)	0.378 (248/656)	*0.370*
– Cluster PMI	0.375 (256/683)	0.401 (256/638)	0.387
– Category PMI	0.367 (251/683)	0.423 (251/593)	**0.393**
– NE PMI	0.381 (260/683)	0.389 (260/668)	0.385
– GW PMI (Clust. + Cat. + NE)	0.350 (239/683)	0.413 (239/579)	*0.379*
– All PMI (Word + GW)	0.325 (222/683)	0.391 (222/567)	*0.355*
– Occupancy of case slot	0.365 (249/683)	0.404 (249/617)	0.383
– Overt argument assignment score	0.411 (281/683)	0.350 (281/804)	*0.378*
(Non-lexical features)			
– Case/location	0.264 (180/683)	0.346 (180/520)	*0.299*
– Salience	0.376 (257/683)	0.411 (257/626)	**0.393**
– All non-lexical (Case/loc. + Salience)	0.250 (171/683)	0.312 (171/545)	*0.279*

Table 7: Performance by removing one feature type at a time from feature sets. Bold font indicates higher F-measures than 0.390 and italics indicate F-measures lower than 0.380.

case frames that had been constructed for each meaning of each verb/adjective. We merged all case frames of a certain verb/adjective in this experiment, and thus each predicate only had one case frame. As a result, this model only took into account knowledge of the relations between two terms, i.e. a predicate and its particular argument. For example, while the model with the case frames in Table 1 considers the dative case of '*te-wo yaku*' would be filled by a *person*, the model with the merged case frame considers the case would be filled by a *disk* with high probability.

6.2 Experimental Results

Table 5 summarizes the experimental results of zero anaphora resolution on the Web Corpus. The results indicate that our proposed model outperformed both Sasano et al. (2008)'s model[7] and the model with merged case frames, which demonstrates the effectiveness of the log-linear framework and the usefulness of the case frames that were constructed for each meaning of each verb/adjective.

Table 6 shows the performance of the proposed model for each case and for each of intra- and inter-sentential zero anaphoric relations. Since the Web Corpus consists of relatively short sentences, there are many inter-sentential zero anaphora. Compared with previous work (Taira et al., 2008; Imamura et al., 2009), our model can resolve inter-sentential zero anaphora in the Web Corpus with comparatively good performance.

6.3 Contribution of features

We eliminated feature types one by one to investigate the contribution each made. Table 7 presents the eliminated feature types and the performance without each type. This table indicates the importance of word PMI and case/location features, since we obtained 0.021 and 0.092 lower F-measures without these features, respectively.

On the other hand, generalized example versions of word PMI did not affect performance much. However, when all generalized example PMIs were eliminated, performance worsened. Therefore, we considered that cluster PMI, category PMI, and NE PMI could be clues for zero anaphora resolution, and confirmed that zero anaphora resolution could benefit from overlap-

[7]For the same 20 articles that were used for testing in (Sasano et al., 2008), our model achieved a recall of 0.525 (64/122), a precision of 0.615 (64/104), and an F-measure of 0.566, while they obtained a recall of 0.410 (50/122), a precision of 0.373 (50/134), and an F-measure of 0.391.

Feature	Weight		
	ga nominative	*wo* accusative	*ni* dative
Occupancy of case slot	0.292	**0.531**	**0.723**
Word PMI	0.154	**0.299**	0.211
Cluster PMI	0.005	**0.347**	0.058
Category PMI	**0.844**	**0.617**	0.391
NE PMI	**0.563**	-0.119	-0.444

Table 8: Weights of lexical features. The Bold font indicates that value of weight is larger than average of weights in the same row.

Case	Type	Imamura et al. (2009) R	P	F	Our model R	P	F
NOM	Intra	0.434	0.588	**0.500**	0.400	0.390	0.395
	Inter	0.076	0.475	0.131	0.221	0.273	**0.244**
ACC	Intra	0.216	0.537	**0.308**	0.169	0.181	0.175
	Inter	0.004	0.250	0.007	0.050	0.101	**0.066**
DAT	Intra	0.000	0.000	0.000	0.098	0.082	**0.089**
	Inter	0.000	0.000	0.000	0.030	0.023	**0.026**

Table 9: Experimental results on the NAIST Text Corpus. R, P, and F denote recall, precision, and F-measure, respectively.

ping features. Salience features did not contribute to performance when using case/location features. We think this is because case/location features involve salience information.

Table 8 lists the weights of the lexical features in the proposed model. Since the variance in each type of feature is different, it is not very meaningful to compare different feature types. However, we can find a tendency for each case type by comparing the weights of the same feature types. In fact, we have obtained several interesting findings.

The weights of the case slot occupancy features, which denote how often the target slot is occupied by an overt argument, are large for the *wo* (accusative) and *ni* (dative) cases, but small for the *ga* (nominative) case. This means that there are tight relations between occupancy of the case slot and the generativity of the slot in the accusative and dative cases, but not in the case of the nominative.

We also found differences between the nominative and the accusative cases in the PMI features. The weights of course-grained lexical knowledge, such as category and NE PMIs, are relatively large in the nominative case. However, the weights of fine-grained lexical knowledge are relatively large in the accusative case. This means that the lexical preference for the nominative is coarser than that for the accusative case.

6.4 Comparison with previous work

We also conducted experiments on the NAIST Text Corpus version 1.4β (Iida et al., 2007) to compare our results with those from previous work. We used articles from January 1st to 11th and editorials from January to August for training, articles on January 12th and 13th and the September editorials for development, and articles from January 14th to 17th and editorials from October to December for testing. While the NAIST Text Corpus has the predicate-argument structure of the original form annotated even for predicates that appear in passive or causative voice, our model outputs the surface predicate-argument structure. Therefore, we excluded such predicates. Table 9 summarizes the performance of our model on the NAIST Text Corpus with the performance of Imamura et al. (2009)'s model. Although these experiments did not use the exact same data, we can see that our model achieved comparable performance even for newspaper articles.

Compared with Iida et al. (2006)'s model, which exploited rich syntactic patterns, our model did not seem to perform as well for the NAIST Text Corpus.[8] We conjectured that this was because the NAIST Text Corpus consisted of newspaper articles that included relatively long sentences with formal grammar, and thus rich syntactic patterns were quite effective. Our model also took into account syntactic clues by using case/location features. However, since we basically focused on the zero anaphora in Web text that only adhered slightly to formal grammar, we did not give priority to exploring effective syntactic patterns.

7 Conclusion

This paper presented a discriminative model for Japanese zero anaphora resolution that can exploit large-scale lexicalized case frames, as well as non-lexical features obtained from a relatively small annotated corpus. Experimental results on a Web text revealed that our model could effectively resolve zero anaphora. We plan to investigate new features for zero anaphora resolution including richer syntactic patterns and global constraints in future work.

[8] Note that, their experiment was conducted on a small and relatively reliable subset of the NAIST Text Corpus, and thus we could not directly compare the results.

References

A. Ferrandez and J. Peral. 2000. A computational approach to zero-pronouns in spanish. In *Proc. of ACL'00*, pages 166–172.

C. J. Fillmore, C. R. Johnson, and M. R.L. Petruck. 2003. Background to framenet. *International Journal of Lexicography*, 16(3):235–250.

Aria Haghighi and Dan Klein. 2010. Coreference resolution in a modular, entity-centered model. In *Proc. of NAACL-HLT'10*, pages 385–393.

Ryu Iida, Kentaro Inui, and Yuji Matsumoto. 2006. Exploiting syntactic patterns as clues in zero-anaphora resolution. In *Proc. of COLING-ACL'06*, pages 625–632.

Ryu Iida, Mamoru Komachi, Kentaro Inui, and Yuji Matsumoto. 2007. Annotating a japanese text corpus with predicate-argument and coreference relations. In *Proc. of ACL'07 Workshop: Linguistic Annotation Workshop*, pages 132–139.

Kenji Imamura, Kuniko Saito, and Tomoko Izumi. 2009. Discriminative approach to predicate-argument structure analysis with zero-anaphora resolution. In *Proc. of ACL-IJCNLP'09*, pages 85–88.

IREX Committee, editor. 1999. *Proc. of the IREX Workshop*.

Daisuke Kawahara and Sadao Kurohashi. 2002. Fertilization of case frame dictionary for robust Japanese case analysis. In *Proc. of COLING'02*, pages 425–431.

Daisuke Kawahara and Sadao Kurohashi. 2004. Zero pronoun resolution based on automatically constructed case frames and structural preference of antecedents. In *Proc. of IJCNLP'04*, pages 334–341.

Daisuke Kawahara and Sadao Kurohashi. 2006. A fully-lexicalized probabilistic model for Japanese syntactic and case structure analysis. In *Proc. of HLT-NAACL'06*, pages 176–183.

Jun'ichi Kazama and Kentaro Torisawa. 2008. Inducing gazetteers for named entity recognition by large-scale clustering of dependency relations. In *Proc. of ACL-HLT'08*, pages 407–415.

Fang Kong and Guodong Zhou. 2010. A tree kernel-based unified framework for chinese zero anaphora resolution. In *Proc. of EMNLP'10*, pages 882–891.

Anna Korhonen, Yuval Krymolowski, and Ted Briscoe. 2006. A large subcategorization lexicon for natural language processing applications. In *Proc.of LREC'06*, pages 3000–3006.

Shalom Lappin and Herbert J. Leass. 1994. An algorithm for pronominal anaphora resolution. *Computational Linguistics*, 20(4):535–562.

Ruslan Mitkov, Richard Evans, and Constantin Orăsan. 2002. A new, fully automatic version of Mitkov's knowledge-poor pronoun resolution method. In *Proc. of CICLing'02*, pages 168–186.

Vincent Ng and Claire Cardie. 2002. Improving machine learning approaches to coreference resolution. In *Proc. of ACL'02*, pages 104–111.

Jorge Nocedal. 1980. Updating quasi-newton matrices with limited storage. *Mathematics of Computation*, 35(151):773–782.

Martha Palmer, Dan Gildea, and Paul Kingsbury. 2005. The proposition bank: A corpus annotated with semantic roles. *Computational Linguistics*, 31(1):71–105.

Ryohei Sasano, Daisuke Kawahara, and Sadao Kurohashi. 2008. A fully-lexicalized probabilistic model for japanese zero anaphora resolution. In *Proc. of COLING'08*, pages 769–776.

Ryohei Sasano, Daisuke Kawahara, and Sadao Kurohashi. 2009. The effect of corpus size on case frame acquisition for discourse analysis. In *Proc. of NAACL-HLT'09*, pages 521–529.

Kazuhiro Seki, Atsushi Fujii, and Tetsuya Ishikawa. 2002. A probabilistic method for analyzing Japanese anaphora integrating zero pronoun detection and resolution. In *Proc. of COLING'02*, pages 911–917.

Hirotoshi Taira, Sanae Fujita, and Masaaki Nagata. 2008. A japanese predicate argument structure analysis using decision lists. In *Proc. of EMNLP'08*, pages 523–532.

Shanheng Zhao and Hwee Tou Ng. 2007. Identification and resolution of Chinese zero pronouns: A machine learning approach. In *Proc. of EMNLP-CoNLL'07*, pages 541–550.

Author Index

Association for Computational Linguistics
209 N. Eighth Street
Stroudsburg, Pennsylvania 18360

5th International Joint Conference on Natural Language Processing 2011

(IJCNLP 2011)

Chiang Mai, Thailand
8-13 November 2011

Volume 2 of 2

ISBN: 978-1-62276-505-8

Printed from e-media with permission by:

Curran Associates, Inc.
57 Morehouse Lane
Red Hook, NY 12571

Some format issues inherent in the e-media version may also appear in this print version.

Printed by Curran Associates, Inc. (2013)

Association for Computational Linguistics
209 N. Eighth Street
Stroudsburg, Pennsylvania 18360

Phone: 1-570-476-8006
Fax: 1-570-476-0860

acl@aclweb.org

Additional copies of this publication are available from:

Curran Associates, Inc.
57 Morehouse Lane
Red Hook, NY 12571 USA
Phone: 845-758-0400
Fax: 845-758-2634
Email: curran@proceedings.com
Web: www.proceedings.com

Table of Contents

Part A: Full Papers

Part B: Short Papers

An Empirical Comparison of Unknown Word Prediction Methods

Kostadin Cholakov[†], **Gertjan van Noord**[†], **Valia Kordoni**[‡], **Yi Zhang**[‡]

† University of Groningen, The Netherlands
‡ Saarland University and DFKI GmbH, Germany
{k.cholakov,g.j.m.van.noord}@rug.nl
{kordoni,yzhang}@coli.uni-sb.de

Abstract

We compare two types of methods which deal with unknown words in the context of computational grammars. Methods of the first type are based on the idea of *supertagging* and use a tagger to predict lexical descriptions for unknown tokens in a given input. The second type of methods perform *lexical acquisition* (LA) which, in the context of this paper, refers to the automatic acquisition of new lexical entries for the lexicon of a given grammar. The methods are compared based on the effect their application has on the parsing coverage and accuracy of the GG grammar of German (Crysmann, 2003). In particular, we adapt the LA method of Cholakov and van Noord (2010) which was originally developed for the Dutch Alpino system to be used with the GG. Its impact on coverage and accuracy on a test corpus of German newspaper texts is compared to the results reported previously on the same corpus for methods which employed a tagger. Furthermore, in a smaller experiment, we show that the linguistic knowledge this LA method provides can also be used for sentence realisation.

1 Introduction

Computational grammars of natural language which rely on hand-crafted lexicons containing elaborate linguistic descriptions usually have low lexical coverage. This is due to the fact that it is impossible to list every word in a language in the lexicon. If a word is unknown to the grammar, or its description in the lexicon is wrong or incomplete, the grammar might fail to produce a (correct) analysis.

In this paper, we compare two types of approaches for dealing with unknown words. The first type is based on the concept of supertagging while the second one performs LA. Generally, supertagging refers to the process of applying a sequential tagger to assign lexical descriptions associated with each word in an input string, relative to a given grammar. It was introduced as a means to reduce parsing ambiguity of LTAG grammars (Bangalore and Joshi, 1999), and has since been applied within CCG (Clark, 2002; Clark and Curran, 2004) and HPSG (Dridan et al., 2008; Zhang et al., 2010) grammars. Supertagging has also been employed for dealing with unknown words. However, in such methods, the tagger is used to assign lexical descriptions **only** to the unknown tokens in a given sentence. It is important to note here that henceforth, we will use the term *supertagging* in this narrow sense of tagging unknown words only. Supertagging methods often work *online*. The unknown words are assigned lexical entries when they are encountered in the input during parsing. Therefore, the focus is primarily on improving the parsing coverage and accuracy of the grammar for a particular input. The performance of such methods is usually evaluated in terms of *token accuracy*, that is the proportion of correctly tagged unknown lexical tokens in the input.

LA, on the other hand, aims at learning automatically new lexical entries and thus, at extending the lexicon of a given grammar. The strategy is to improve the parsing coverage and accuracy by improving the quality and the coverage of the lexicon of the grammar. While suppertagging methods are concerned with a particular form of the unknown word within the particular context this form occurs in the input, LA techniques look at various forms and contexts of the unknown word and use more detailed linguistic information to learn a new lexical entry for it. This makes LA methods more complex and time-consuming. That is why, they are often applied *offline*. LA methods are usually evaluated in terms of *type precision* and *type recall*. For a given LA method, type precision indicates the proportion of correctly predicted lexical entries and type recall indicates how many of the correct lexical entries for a given word are actually found.

Both supertagging and LA have been successfully used. For instance, Blunsom and Baldwin (2006) employ a conditional random field-based tagger to predict lexical entries for large-scale HPSG grammars of English (ERG; (Copestake and Flickinger, 2000)) and Japanese (JACY; (Siegel and Bender, 2002)). Zhang and Kordoni (2006) and Dridan et al. (2008) have developed a maximum entropy-based (ME) tagger and investigate the effect its application has on the parsing performance of the ERG and the GG. Other methods which apply the same tagger to the GG include Nicholson et al. (2008) and Cholakov et al. (2008). The ERG, the GG and JACY are part of the DELPH-IN collaboration[1] and as such, they share the same grammar design and parsing architecture which facilitates the application of the same tagger. Baldwin (2005) presents a LA approach where various secondary resources (POS taggers, chunkers, etc.) are used to create an abstraction of words unknown to the ERG and then binary classifiers are employed to learn lexical entries for those words. However, learning is done based on incomplete information obtained by the various resources used. Further, no evaluation of the effect the method has on the parsing performance of the ERG is provided. Cholakov and van Noord (2010) describe a LA method where a ME-based classifier is used to acquire lexical entries for all forms in the paradigms of words, unknown to the large-scale Dutch Alpino grammar (van Noord, 2006). The paper also shows that the application of LA improves the parsing accuracy of Alpino on open-domain texts.

For our purpose of comparing supertagging and LA, we investigate how methods implementing these strategies affect the parsing coverage and accuracy when applied with the same grammar, namely the GG. Our choice of German and the GG as a platform for comparison is motivated by the fact that German has richer morphology and a more free word order than both English and Dutch which makes unknown word handling more challenging. We adapt the LA method of Cholakov and van Noord (2010) – henceforth C&vN– and applied with the GG. Then, we compare the parsing coverage and accuracy the GG achieves on a German newspaper corpus to those reported for supertagging methods applied previously with the GG on the same corpus. For all techniques, the experiments show that their application leads to an increase in coverage compared to the baseline, that is the standard GG setup. However, the supertagging methods achieved this at the price of having lower accuracy than the baseline. The application of the adapted C&vN method, on the other hand, increases parsing accuracy compared to the baseline. This difference in quality might not always be crucial since less accurate parses produced by the grammar can still be used successfully in many NLP applications. In such cases, the less complex supertagging methods might be the preferred choice. However, through a small sentence realisation experiment, we give an example of an application where high-quality LA is a prerequisite.

Other kinds of LA techniques have also been proposed. Cussens and Pulman (2000) used a symbolic approach employing *inductive logic programming*, while Erbach (1990), Barg and Walther (1998) and Fouvry (2003) followed a unification-based approach. However, it is doubtful if those methods are scalable since they have not been applied to large-scale grammars and no meaningful evaluation has been provided.

The remainder of the paper is organised as follows. Section 2 describes the resources we employ. Section 3 gives an overview of the supertagging methods previously applied with the GG. Section 4 describes the adaptation of the C&vN method to the GG. Section 5 gives details on the training procedure for the ME-based classifier used in the C&vN technique. Section 6 evaluates the parsing coverage and accuracy on the German newspaper corpus when this technique is applied with the GG and compares the results to the results reported previously for the suppertagging methods for this corpus. Section 7 explores the possibility of using newly acquired lexical entries in a small sentence realisation task. Section 8 concludes the paper.

2 Resources

The GG (Crysmann, 2003) is an HPSG grammar based on typed feature structures. The GG types are strictly defined within a type hierarchy. The

[1] `http://wiki.delph-in.net/`

grammar contains constructional and lexical rules, as well as a lexicon where words are assigned lexical types. Currently, it consists of 5K types, 115 rules and the lexicon contains approximately 55K entries. There are 411 distinct lexical types which words can be mapped onto. Below is an example of a GG lexical entry, namely the entry for the word *Aufgabe* (a task):

```
aufgabe-n := count-noun-le &
 [ MORPH.LIST.FIRST.STEM < "Aufgabe" >,
   SYNSEM.LKEYS [ --SUBJOPT -,
          KEYAGR c-n-f,
          KEYREL "_aufgabe_n_rel",
          KEYSORT abstract,
          MCLASS nclass-9 ] ].
```

The lexical type 'count-noun-le' shows that the word is a countable noun[2]. The STEM type feature specifies the stem of the word. The stem for nouns is the singular nominative noun form, for adjectives– the base noninflected form and for verbs– the root form. Adverbs in German have a single form which is used as the value of the STEM feature in adverb entries. Some nouns (e.g., *Baukosten* (building costs)) do not have all forms typical for German nouns. In such cases, the word itself is set as the value of the STEM feature. The KEYAGR feature indicates case, number and gender. In the example above, case and number are left underspecified while the gender is set to feminine. The value of SUBJOPT shows that this noun is always used with an article and MCLASS indicates its morphological paradigm. The KEYREL and KEYSORT features define the semantics of the word.

Further, we employ the PET system (Callmeier, 2000) to parse with the GG. PET is a system for efficient processing of unification-based grammars. The system comprises a sophisticated preprocessor, a bottom-up chart parser and a grammar compiler. For our purposes, we should note that the parser has a built-in unknown word guesser which, based on some simple heuristics, assigns generic types to the unknown words. Most of the features in these types are left underspecified.

We compare the results of the various methods based on how they affect the parsing coverage and accuracy of the GG on the Frankfurter Rundschau (FR) newspaper corpus. The corpus contains 614K sentences and the articles in it deal with various domains.

[2] *le* stands for lexeme.

3 Suppertagging Methods

Here, we give an overview of supertagging methods applied previously with the GG. Typically, the unknown words are assigned *open-class* lexical types. In the case of the GG, open-class lexical types are those assigned to nouns, adjectives, verbs and adverbs. It is assumed that closed-class words are already handled by the grammar.

Dridan et al. (2008) adopts the method proposed in Zhang and Kordoni (2006) for English and the ERG and applies it to the GG. A ME-based tagger is trained on features extracted from the context of the unknown word– four characters from the beginning and the end of the word, and two words of context (where available) either side of the target word together with their POS tags[3]. The application of the tagger led to an improved parsing coverage on a test corpus containing 700 short German questions from the CLEF competition. No evaluation in terms of accuracy is provided for German. For the same experiment with the ERG, the accuracy achieved with the tagger was below the baseline accuracy (the standard ERG setup).

Nicholson et al. (2008) employs the same ME-based tagger but the paper examines its performance more closely. The tagger is evaluated by performing a 10-fold cross-validation on the treebank associated with the GG. Words which appeared only in the test fold were considered unknown. Since the sentences in the treebank are annotated, the method is able to use the lexical types of the context words as features instead of their POS tags. The achieved token accuracy is 58%. Then, the tagger is used to predict lexical types for unknown words in a random sample of 1000 sentences extracted from the FR corpus. However, since no annotation is available for the test corpus, the tagger is run with the same features as in Dridan et al. (2008) but without the POS tags of the context words.

The results are given in Table 1. Coverage increased by 8% for the test corpus. An estimation of the parsing accuracy is also given. Parsing accuracy is measured as the proportion of sentences for which a correct parse is produced, among the set of parses. 87 sentences were randomly selected and manually examined. The baseline accuracy was 85%. When suppertagging is applied accuracy drops to 84%. This is consistent with the re-

[3] The corpora used had been POS tagged with the TreeTagger (Schmid, 1994).

sults reported in Dridan et al. (2008) for the ERG.

Cholakov et al. (2008) develops further the idea of using lexical types as features in the tagger. The paper presents the same system setup as Nicholson et al. (2008) but with one crucial difference. The tagset used in the experiments consists of more detailed descriptions of the GG lexical types. In this new tagset, the values of some of the morphosyntactic features from the lexical entries are attached to the type definition, thus making the information they carry accessible to the tagger. For example, according to the guidelines given in Cholakov et al. (2008), the lexical type of *Aufgabe* would become *count-noun-le_-_f* after attaching the values of the SUBJOPT and KEYAGR features to the type definition[4]. Having this additional information, the token accuracy of the tagger increases to 73.54%. The effect the method has on the parsing coverage and accuracy is shown in Table 1. The experiment is done on a random sample of 10K sentences from the FR with the corpus POS tagged and the tags of the context words used as features in the tagger instead of lexical types. Parsing accuracy is measured as the proportion of 100 randomly selected sentences with at a correct parse produced. Again, accuracy decreases in comparison to the baseline (the standard GG setup).

It is important to note that the lexical entries created by the aforementioned methods for unknown words are sort of generic due to the inability of those methods to access the values of the type features defined in the entries. In Nicholson et al. (2008) only the type of the word can be specified and the word is set as the value of the STEM feature. Every other feature in the entry is either underspecified or assigned some default value. The technique of Cholakov et al. (2008) can define more features in the created lexical entry due to the detailed tagset used. However, accuracy still decreased.

4 Lexical Acquisition with The GG

In this section, we describe the adaptation of the C&vN LA method to the GG. This adaptation raises the important question about portability of LA. Because of their complexity and dependence on a particular grammar, LA methods have been applied within a single parsing system, in a single framework, and mostly for a single language. So, it is unclear to what extent the various techniques can be used for a different language or parsing architecture. However, the C&vN method is claimed explicitly to be portable to other systems and languages provided some conditions are met. These include: a finite set of labels which unknown words are mapped onto, a syntactic parser, and a morphological component which generates the paradigm(s) of a given unknown word.

Similar to Cholakov et al. (2008), we created a set of labels which consists of more refined definitions of the GG lexical types. Accordingly, we attach the values of some of the type features defined in the relevant lexical entries to the type definitions of those entries. However, for reasons of data sparseness, we choose to exclude some of the features which Cholakov et al. (2008) considered relevant. Experiments with different sets of features have shown that the best results are achieved when only features designating morphosyntactic agreement are considered. For all noun types and predicative adjectives this is the KEYAGR feature and for verb types allowing for prepositional complements– the COMPAGR and the OCOMPAGR features which indicate the case of the the (oblique) complement. For instance, the lexical type of *Aufgabe* will become *count-noun-le_f* after the gender value of the KEYAGR feature is attached.

C&vN propose a method for the generation of the paradigm(s) of a given unknown Dutch word (Cholakov and van Noord, 2009). The type of word form predicted by the paradigm for that word is used as a feature in the ME-based classifier employed in C&vN for learning unknown words. For example, the paradigm of *Aufgabe* will indicate that the word is a singular feminine noun and this information will be passed on to the classifier. Further, unlike the Dutch Alpino grammar, the GG does not have a full form lexicon. All word forms are derived by applying various morphological rules defined in the GG to the word stem. Therefore, we need to add only the correct stem of the unknown word the lexicon. Then, all forms of the word will automatically be recognised by the grammar. That is why, in the case of the GG, we use the generated paradigms to perform the mapping between unknown words and their stems. For instance, if *Aufgaben* (tasks) is an unknown word, we will add *Aufgabe*, the stem

[4]The values for case and number for nouns are almost always left underspecified; that is why only the value of the gender is attached to the type definition.

Method	Coverage (%)		Accuracy (%)	
	Baseline (standard GG)	GG + tagger	Baseline (standard GG)	GG + tagger
Lexical	12	20	85	84
Lexical+POS	8.9	21.1	85	83

Table 1: Coverage and accuracy results for the GG and the FR corpus. *Lexical* refers to Nicholson et al. (2008) where only affixes and context words are used as features. The last row refers to Cholakov et al. (2008) where the POS tags of the context words are also employed.

indicated by its paradigm, to the lexicon.

Due to the GG design, it is not straightforward to use the morphological rules of the grammar for paradigm generation. Following the C&vN technique developed for generating the paradigms of Dutch words, we created a German finite state morphology. The morphology does not have access to any linguistic information and thus, it generates all possible paradigms allowed by the word orthography. Then, the number of search hits Yahoo! returns for each form in a given paradigm is combined with some simple heuristics to disambiguate the output of the morphology and to determine the correct paradigm(s). We also apply heuristics to guess the gender for words with generated noun paradigms and to determine if a word which is assigned a verb paradigm starts with a separable particle.

One could argue that there is a simpler approach for mapping the various forms of the unknown word to its stem. For instance, the TreeTagger provides both POS and stem information with high accuracy. However, the generation of the paradigms allows us to consider contexts in which other forms of a given unknown word occur and thus, to have access to much more and linguistically diverse data. Further, using the paradigms, we are able to determine which of the morphological classes defined within the GG a given unknown word belongs to and specify the value of the MCLASS type feature in the lexical entry generated for this word. We are also able to determine the value of the VCOMPFORM type feature which indicates the separable particle in verb entries. However, those are not crucial for the classification process and they are likely to cause data sparseness. That is why, those type features are assigned their values after the lexical type of a given word has been predicted. The semantic features in the lexical entries for newly acquired words, as well as the other features whose values are not learnt via LA are assigned default values or left underspecified.

We adopted the ME-based classifier[5] and the features used for unknown word prediction as described in C&vN. The probability of a lexical type t, given an unknown word and its context c is:

$$(1) \qquad p(t|c) = \frac{exp(\sum_i \Theta_i f_i(t,c))}{\sum_{t' \in T} exp(\sum_i \Theta_i f_i(t',c))}$$

where $f_i(t,c)$ may encode arbitrary features from the context and $< \Theta_1, \Theta_2, ... >$ can be evaluated by maximising the pseudo-likelihood on a training corpus (Malouf, 2002).

Table 2 shows the features for *Aufgabe*. Since the stem of the unknown word is added to the lexicon, we also experimented with prefix and suffix features extracted from the stem. We assumed that those could allow for a better generalization of morphological properties but they proved to be less informative for LA.

Features
i) A, Au, Auf, Aufg
ii) e, be, abe, gabe
iii) hyphen_no
iv) noun_feminine #predicted by the paradigm
v) count-noun-le_f, mass-noun-le_f
vi) noun⟨f⟩

Table 2: Features for *Aufgabe* (a task)

Rows **(v)** and **(vi)** show syntactic features obtained from what C&vN refer to as 'parsing with universal types'. In C&vN, each unknown word is assigned all target lexical types, i.e. it is treated as being maximally ambiguous. However, to reduce ambiguity and make the parsing computationally feasible, we use the generated paradigms as a filtering mechanism and assign a given word only those types which belong to the POS of the paradigm(s) generated for this word. That is why, *Aufgabe* is assigned all noun lexical types. Sentences containing morphological forms of *Aufgabe*

[5]The classifier is developed using the TADM tool; `http://tadm.sourceforge.net/`

are then parsed with PET in best-only mode. For each sentence only the best parse selected by the disambiguation model of the parser is preserved. Then, the lexical type that has been assigned to the form of *Aufgabe* occurring in this parse is stored.

We employ the most frequently used type(s), based on an empirical threshold (80% for the GG), as features in the classifier (row **v**). Further, as illustrated in row **(vi)**, each piece of information attached to the type definitions (the part after the underscore) is also taken as a separate feature. By considering these syntactic features, we manage to involve the grammar directly in the prediction process, unlike the methods discussed in the previous section where only lexical features and POS tags were used. Here, the grammar can decide which lexical type(s) are best suited for a given unknown word. This is an effective way to include the syntactic constraints imposed on the unknown word into the prediction process.

5 Training of The Classifier

In order to train the classifier, we need annotated data. That is why, we temporarily remove some words from the GG lexicon and use them for training and tuning the various parameters of the classifier. The lexical entries of the removed words are used as gold standard.

We remove only words belonging to open-class lexical types. Each such type has at least 10 lexical entries in the lexicon mapped onto it and it is assigned to at least 15 distinct words occurring in large corpora parsed with PET and the GG. The parsed corpus we use consists of roughly 2.5M sentences randomly selected from the German part of the Wacky project (Kilgarriff and Grefenstette, 2003). Following these criteria, we have selected 39 open-class types out of the 411 lexical types defined in the GG. The expansion of the type definitions of the 39 types with the values of the relevant type features resulted in the creation of 68 *expanded* types. Table 3 gives more details about the type distribution.

2400 words are removed from the lexicon of the GG. Of these, 2000 are used for training, and 400 words are used as a test set to give an idea about the performance of the classifier. We assume that less frequent words are typically unknown and, in order to simulate their behaviour, all 2400 words have between 40 and 100 occurrences in the parsed corpus. Experiments with a minimum lower than 40 occurrences have shown that this is a reasonable threshold to filter out typos, tokenization errors, etc. The distribution of the parts-of-speech for the 2400 words and the evaluation of the paradigm generation component are shown in Table 4 (some words have more than a single part-of-speech). Accuracy indicates how many of the generated paradigms are correct.

	Original types	Expanded types
Total	39	68
-nouns	5	15
-verbs	28	45
-adjectives	4	6
-adverbs	2	2

Table 3: Distribution of the target lexical types

	overall	nouns	adj	verbs
total	2954	1196	651	694
accuracy(%)	96.45	91.09	100	99.54

Table 4: Paradigm generation results

In the paradigms generated for verbs there were three mistakes. However, the generated verb stems were all correct. Similarly, the stems for all nouns were correct, including the stems of 98 nouns which contained a mistake in their paradigm. In 91 cases the singular genitive form was incorrect, in another 12 cases the predicted gender was wrong. The mapping of the words to their correct stems is correct in all cases.

We allow for multiple types per word to be predicted but we discard the types accounting together for less than 5% of probability mass. Additionally, there are four baseline methods. The ***naive*** one assigns the most frequent expanded type in the lexicon, *count-noun-le_f*, to each unknown word. In the ***naive POS*** baseline each word is given the most frequent expanded type for the POS of each paradigm generated for it. The ***GG*** baseline predicts for the unknown word the target type(s) used as features for this word in the classifier (e.g., for *Aufgabe*, these are the types from row (v) in Table 2). For the ***TnT*** baseline, we used the treebank available for the GG to train the TnT POS tagger (Brants, 2000) with the tagset consisting of all lexical types in the GG. The sentences extracted for each unknown word are then tagged in best-only mode. Similarly to the GG baseline, the unknown word is given the type(s) most frequently assigned to it (80% threshold). The average type precision and type recall for the 400 test words are given in Table 5. Table 6 shows the F-measure per POS for the LA model.

Model	Prec(%)	Rec(%)	F-meas(%)
Naive	21.75	21.07	21.41
Naive POS	58.96	47.65	52.7
GG	55.03	57.12	56.06
TnT	61.21	49.17	54.53
LA with the GG	82.04	86.5	84.21

Table 5: Results on the 400 test words

POS	nouns	adj	verbs	adv
F-meas (%)	92.4	90.93	67.25	75.82

Table 6: F-measures per POS for the LA model

The LA model improves upon the baselines. The F-measure reaches 80% when 300 words are used for training and the learning curve flattens out at 1600 training words. The method performs very similar to the results reported for Dutch and Alpino, which demonstrates that it can be successfully applied outside the environment it was primarily developed for.

Predicting lexical entries for verbs is the hardest task for the LA model. The classifier has a strong bias towards assigning transitive and intransitive verb types. It either fails to predict infrequent frames or it wrongly predicts a transitive type for intransitive verbs and vice versa. Another difficulty for the model is the distinction which the GG makes between ergative and non-ergative verbs. The main issue with adverbs is that many of them can be used as adjectives as well. As a consequence, the classifier has a strong bias towards predicting an adverb type for words for which an adjective type has also been predicted. No pattern in the errors for nouns and adjectives can be identified.

6 Parsing Coverage and Accuracy

Having adapted the C&vN method to be used with the GG, we can now compare it with the supertagging methods by investigating how its application affects parsing coverage and accuracy on the FR corpus. We were not able to obtain the sentence sets used in Nicholson et al. (2008) and Cholakov et al. (2008), so we created a test set of 450 sentences randomly extracted from the FR corpus. All sentences contained at least one unknown word. The average sentence length is 17.16 tokens, with a ratio of 1.09 unknown words per sentence. For this experiment, we parse the 450 sentences with PET, under three conditions. In the first case, the standard configuration of the GG is used where the unknown word guesser assigns generic types to the unknown words. Dridan et al. (2008) report that passing a POS tagged input to the guesser enhances its performance and improves parsing coverage. That is why, in the second case, the 450 sentences were tagged with TnT outputting all POS tags with non-zero probabilities for each word. Then, the tagged sentences are parsed with PET. In the third case, we add to the GG lexicon lexical entries acquired offline by the adapted C&vN method.

The results are given in Table 7. The models employing POS tags and LA have practically the same coverage performance. The *GG+POS* one produced at least one parse for 113 sentences and the LA model produced analyses for those 113 sentences plus 4 more, thus giving a total of 117 parsed sentences. The standard GG model was able to cover 57 sentences. The parsed sentences for all models are manually examined and accuracy is again measured as the percentage of those parsed sentences which had a correct parse produced among the set of parses. There were 99 such sentences for the model which employs LA and 89 and 47 for the *GG+POS* and the *GG-standard* model, respectively. The drop in the accuracy for the *GG+POS* model compared to the standard GG one is consistent with the accuracy results reported in Dridan et al. (2008) for the ERG. We should note, though, that both the LA and *GG+POS* models also produced a correct parse for the 47 sentences for which the standard model delivered a correct analysis.

Model	Cov (%)	Acc (%)	LB Acc (%)
GG-standard	12.67	82.46	92.87
GG + POS	25.11	78.76	92.51
GG + LA	26	84.62	94.71

Table 7: Coverage and accuracy results for FR. *LB Acc* stands for labelled brackets accuracy.

The better accuracy result achieved by the LA model has to do mainly with the fact that the built-in guesser assigns noun types to the vast majority of the unknown words. The underspecified features in those entries create a lot of ambiguity and make it harder for the parser disambiguation model to select the correct analysis. The LA method, on the other hand, supplies the parser with more detailed and linguistically accurate lexical entries which facilitates ambiguity resolution.

The results differ from the ones reported on the FR corpus for the suppertagging methods (Table 1) where the application of the tagger increased coverage but the price was lower accuracy. We attribute this to the bigger amount of features used in the classifier in the C&vN method which enabled the learning of more detailed lexical entries.

However, the estimation used up till now for accuracy is a rather crude one. Another way of looking at accuracy is to measure how close the top ranked parse for a given sentence is to the correct parse produced for this sentence. We selected the 47 sentences for which all three models have produced the correct parse and used them as our gold standard, to be able to report accuracy numbers, for the best parse.[6] Accuracy is measured in terms of labelled brackets. The results given in Table 7 show that not only the LA model produces a correct parse for more sentences but also the top ranked analysis is of better quality.

7 LA for Text Generation

As a further evaluation, we also investigate how the lexical entries acquired with LA affect sentence realisation. While in parsing the ambiguity in such less constrained lexical entries dissolves quickly in its context, there is a potential risk of overgeneration in the reverse process.

We selected 14 words assigned verb types by the tagger in the experiment with the FR corpus. Then, 64 sentences, each of which contains one of those 14 words, are extracted from corpora. We construct manually another sentence set where these words are replaced by verbs from the GG lexicon with a similar lexical type. This comparison set indicates what the performance of the GG would be with fully constrained, but otherwise similar lexical entries.

Realisation with the GG is performed within the LKB grammar engineering platform which provides a chart-based generator with various optimisations for packed parse forest (Carroll and Oepen, 2005). We parsed the two sentence sets and then used the best analysis to generate a realisation for each sentence. There were 3.28 realisations per sentence for the test set versus 3.16 for the comparison one. As for accuracy, a realisation is considered correct if it is an exact match of the original sentence (excluding punctuation). Despite the higher number for realisations per sentence for the test set, the quality of the realisations is the same for both sets– for 60 sentences a correct realisation is produced. Thus, the entries acquired with LA can be employed for both parsing and realisation.

We should note that realisation with the generic lexical entries acquired by the unknown word guesser of the parser is computationally not feasible because of the many underspecified features in those entries. Nicholson et al. (2008) and Cholakov et al. (2008) did not perform any experiments on realisation but we assume that the underspecification in the entries those methods produce would also make sentence realisation practically impossible.

8 Conclusion

Two types of methods for dealing with unknown words were compared. The application of methods, where a tagger was used to predict lexical descriptions for words unknown to the GG grammar of German, led to an increase in parsing coverage on a German newspaper corpus. However, accuracy was below the baseline, that is the accuracy of the standard GG setup. The other type of methods employ LA techniques to extend the lexicon of a grammar with new lexical entries for unknown words. We adapted one such method, namely the one of Cholakov and van Noord (2010), which has been primarily developed for the Dutch Alpino grammar, to be used with the GG. The application of the method led to an increase in both parsing coverage and accuracy on the same newspaper corpus. We attributed the better performance of the C&vN technique to the fact that it had access to more features during prediction, including such which came directly from the grammar, and it was able to assign more linguistically accurate entries to the unknown words. Last, in a smaller experiment, we showed that those entries can be successfully used for sentence realisation.

References

Tim Baldwin. 2005. Bootstrapping deep lexical resources: Resources for courses. In *Proceedings of*

[6] That is why, the reported accuracy numbers are rather high.

the ACL-SIGLEX 2005 Workshop on Deep Lexical Acquisition, Ann Arbor, USA.

Srinivas Bangalore and Aravind Joshi. 1999. Supertagging: An approach to almost parsing. In *Computational Linguistics*, volume 25(2), pages 237–65.

Petra Barg and Markus Walther. 1998. Processing unknown words in HPSG. In *Proceedings of the 36th Conference of the ACL*, Montreal, Quebec, Canada.

Phil Blunsom and Timothy Baldwin. 2006. Multilingual deep lexical acquisition for HPSGs via supertagging. In *Proceedings of EMNLP 2006*, Sidney, Australia.

Thorsten Brants. 2000. TnT– a statistical part-of-speech tagger. In *Proceedings of the Sixth Conference on Applied Natural Language Processing ANLP-2000*, Seattle, WA.

Ulrich Callmeier. 2000. PET– a platform for experimentation with efficient HPSG processing techniques. In *Journal of Natural Language Engineering*, volume 6, pages 99–107. Cambridge University Press.

John Carroll and Stephan Oepen. 2005. High efficiency realization for a wide-coverage unification grammar. In *Proceedings of the 2nd International Joint Conference on Natural Language Processing (IJCNLP 2005)*, pages 165–176, Jeju Island, Korea.

Kostadin Cholakov and Gertjan van Noord. 2009. Combining finite state and corpus-based techniques for unknown word prediction. In *Proceedings of the 7th Recent Advances in Natural Language Processing (RANLP) conference*, Borovets, Bulgaria.

Kostadin Cholakov and Gertjan van Noord. 2010. Acquisition of unknown word paradigms for large-scale grammars. In *Proceedings of the 23rd International Conference on Computational Linguistics (COLING-2010)*, Beijing, China.

Kostadin Cholakov, Valia Kordoni, and Yi Zhang. 2008. Towards domain-independent deep linguistic processing: Ensuring portability and re-usability of lexicalised grammars. In *Proceedings of COLING 2008 Workshop on Grammar Engineering Across Frameworks (GEAF08)*, Manchester, UK.

Stephen Clark and James Curran. 2004. The importance of supertagging for wide-coverage CCG parsing. In *Proceedings of the 20th International Conference on Computational Linguistics (COLING'2004)*, Geneva, Switzerland.

Stephen Clark. 2002. Supertagging for combinatory categorical grammar. In *Proceedings of the 6th International Workshop on Tree Adjoining Grammar and Related Frameworks*, Venice, Italy.

Ann Copestake and Dan Flickinger. 2000. An open-source grammar development environment and broad-coverage English grammar using HPSG. In *Proceedings of LREC 2000*, Athens, Greece.

Berthold Crysmann. 2003. On the efficient implementation of German verb placement in HPSG. In *Proceedings of RANLP 2003*, Borovets, Bulgaria.

James Cussens and Stephen Pulman. 2000. Incorporating linguistic constraints into inductive logic programming. In *Proceedings of the Fourth Conference on Computational Natural Language Learning*.

Rebecca Dridan, Valia Kordoni, and Jeremy Nicholson. 2008. Enhancing perfomrmance of lexicalised grammars. In *Proceedings of ACL-08: HLT*, Columbus, Ohio.

Gregor Erbach. 1990. Syntactic processing of unknown words. IWBS report 131. Technical report, IBM, Stuttgart.

Frederik Fouvry. 2003. Lexicon acquisition with a large-coverage unification-based grammar. In *Companion to the 10th Conference of EACL*, pages 87–90, Budapest, Hungary.

Adam Kilgarriff and G Grefenstette. 2003. Introduction to the special issue on the web as a corpus. In *Computational Linguistics*, volume 29, pages 333–347.

Robert Malouf. 2002. A comparison of algorithms for maximum entropy parameter estimation. In *Proceedings of the 6th conference on Natural Language Learning (CoNLL-2002)*, pages 49–55, Taipei, Taiwan.

Jeremy Nicholson, Valia Kordoni, Yi Zhang, Timothy Baldwin, and Rebecca Dridan. 2008. Evaluating and extending the coverage of HPSG grammars: A case study for German. In *Proceedings of LREC-2008*, Marakesh, Morocco.

Helmut Schmid. 1994. Probabilistic part-of-speech tagging using decision trees. In *Proceedings of the International Conference on New Methods in Language Processing*, Manchester, UK.

Melanie Siegel and Emily Bender. 2002. Efficient deep processing of Japanese. In *Proceedings of the 3rd Workshop on Asian Language Resources and International Standardization*, Taipei, Taiwan.

Gertjan van Noord. 2006. At last parsing is now operational. In *Proceedings of TALN*, Leuven, Belgium.

Yi Zhang and Valia Kordoni. 2006. Automated deep lexical acquisition for robust open text processing. In *Proceedings of the Fifth International Conference on Language Resourses and Evaluation (LREC 2006)*, Genoa, Italy.

Yaozhong Zhang, Takuya Matsuzaki, and Jun'ichi Tsujii. 2010. A simple approach for HPSG supertagging using dependency information. In *Proceedings of 11th Annual Conference of the North American Chapter of the Association for Computational Linguistics (NAACL-HLT'10)*, Los Angeles, CA.

Training Dependency Parsers from Partially Annotated Corpora

Daniel Flannery[1], **Yusuke Miyao**[2], **Graham Neubig**[1], **Shinsuke Mori**[1]
[1]Graduate School of Informatics, Kyoto University
Yoshida Honmachi, Sakyo-ku, Kyoto, Japan
[2]National Institute of Informatics
2-1-2 Hitotsubashi, Chiyoda-ku, Tokyo, Japan
flannery@ar.media.kyoto-u.ac.jp, yusuke@nii.ac.jp,
neubig@ar.media.kyoto-u.ac.jp, forest@i.kyoto-u.ac.jp

Abstract

We introduce a maximum spanning tree (MST) dependency parser that can be trained from partially annotated corpora, allowing for effective use of available linguistic resources and reduction of the costs of preparing new training data. This is especially important for domain adaptation in a real-world situation. We use a pointwise approach where each edge in the dependency tree for a sentence is estimated independently. Experiments on Japanese dependency parsing show that this approach allows for rapid training and achieves accuracy comparable to state-of-the-art dependency parsers trained on fully annotated data.

1 Introduction

Parsing is one of the fundamental building blocks of natural language processing, with applications ranging from machine translation (Yamada and Knight, 2001) to information extraction (Miyao et al., 2009). However, while statistical parsers achieve higher and higher accuracies on in-domain text, the creation of data to train these parsers is labor-intensive, which becomes a bottleneck for smaller languages. In addition, it is also a well known fact that accuracy plummets when tested on sentences of a different domain than the training corpus (Gildea, 2001; Petrov et al., 2010), and that in-domain data can be annotated to make up for this weakness.

In this paper, we propose a maximum spanning tree (MST) parser that helps ameliorate these problems by allowing for the efficient development of training data. This is done through a combination of an efficient corpus annotation strategy, and a novel parsing method. For corpus construction, we use partial annotation, which allows an annotator to skip annotation of unnecessary edges, focusing their efforts only on the ones that will provide the maximal gains in accuracy.

While partial annotation has been shown to be an effective annotation strategy for a number of tasks (Tsuboi et al., 2008; Sassano and Kurohashi, 2010; Neubig and Mori, 2010), traditional MST parsers such as that of McDonald et al. (2005) cannot be learned from partially annotated data. The reason for this is that they use structural prediction methods that must be learned from fully annotated sentences. However, a number of recent works (Liang et al., 2008; Neubig et al., 2011) have found that it is possible to ignore structure and still achieve competitive accuracy on tasks such as part-of-speech (POS) tagging.

Similarly, recent work on dependency parsing (Spreyer and Kuhn, 2009; Spreyer et al., 2010) has shown that training constraints can be relaxed to allow MST parsers to be trained from partially annotated sentences, with only a small reduction in parsing accuracy. In this approach the scoring function used to evaluate potential dependency trees is modified so that it does not penalize trees consistent with the partial annotations used for training. Our formulation of an MST parser is based on an even stronger independence assumption, namely that the score of each edge is independent of the other edges in the dependency tree. While this does have the potential to decrease accuracy, it has a number of advantages such as the ability to use partially annotated data, faster speed, and simple implementation.

We perform an evaluation of the proposed method on a Japanese dependency parsing task. First, we compare the proposed method to both a traditional MST parser (McDonald et al., 2005), and a deterministic parser (Nivre and Scholz, 2004). We find that despite the lack of structure in our prediction method, the proposed method is still able to achieve accuracy similar to that of the traditional MST parser, while training and testing speeds are similar to that of the deterministic parser.

In addition, we perform a case-study of the use of partial annotation in a practical scenario, where we have data that follows a segmentation standard that differs from the one we would like to follow. In Japanese dependency parsing, traditionally phrase segments (*bunsetsu*) have been used instead of words as the minimal unit for parsing (Kudo and Matsumoto, 2002; Sassano and Kurohashi, 2010), but these segments are often too large or unwieldy for applications such as information extraction and machine translation (Nakazawa and Kurohashi, 2008). In our case-study, we demonstrate that a corpus labeled with phrase dependencies can be used as a partially annotated corpus in the development of a word-based parser that is more appropriate for these applications. The use of a phrase-labeled corpus allows us to increase the accuracy of a word-based parser trained on a smaller word-labeled data set by 2.75%.

2 Pointwise estimation for dependency parsing

This work follows the standard setting of recent work on dependency parsing (Buchholz and Marsi, 2006). Given as input a sequence of words, $\boldsymbol{w} = \langle w_1, w_2, \ldots, w_n \rangle$, the goal is to output a dependency tree $\boldsymbol{d} = \langle d_1, d_2, \ldots, d_n \rangle$, where $d_i \equiv j$ when the head of w_i is w_j.[1] We assume that $d_i = 0$ for some word w_i in a sentence, which indicates that w_i is the head of the sentence.

2.1 A Pointwise MST Parser

The parsing model we pursue in this paper is McDonald et al. (2005)'s edge-factored model. A score, $\sigma(d_i)$, is assigned to each edge (i.e. dependency) d_i, and parsing finds a dependency tree, $\hat{\boldsymbol{d}}$, that maximizes the sum of the scores of all the edges.

$$\hat{\boldsymbol{d}} = \mathop{\mathbf{argmax}}_{\boldsymbol{d}} \sum_{d \in \boldsymbol{d}} \sigma(d). \quad (1)$$

It is known that, given $\sigma(d)$ for all possible dependencies in a sentence, $\hat{\boldsymbol{d}}$ can be computed by the maximum spanning tree algorithm such as Chu-Liu/Edmonds' algorithm.

An important difference from McDonald et al. (2005) is in the estimation of $\sigma(d)$. McDonald et al. (2005) applied a perceptron-like algorithm that optimizes the score of entire dependency trees. However, we stick to pointwise prediction: $\sigma(d_i)$ is estimated for each w_i independently. A variety of machine-learning-based classifiers can be applied to the estimation of $\sigma(d)$, because it is essentially an n-class classification problem.

In the experiments, we estimate a log-linear model (Berger et al., 1996). We calculate the probability of a dependency labeling $p(d_i = j)$ for a word w_i from its context, which is a tuple $x = \langle \boldsymbol{w}, \boldsymbol{t}, i \rangle$, where $\boldsymbol{t} = \langle t_1, t_2, \ldots, t_n \rangle$ is a sequence of POS tags assigned to $\boldsymbol{w}$ by a tagger. The conditional probability $p(j|x)$ is given by the following equation.

$$p(j|x, \boldsymbol{\theta}) = \frac{\exp(\boldsymbol{\theta} \cdot \boldsymbol{\phi}(x, j))}{\sum_{j' \in \mathcal{J}} \exp(\boldsymbol{\theta} \cdot \boldsymbol{\phi}(x, j'))} \quad (2)$$

The feature vector $\boldsymbol{\phi} = \langle \phi_1, \phi_2, \ldots, \phi_m \rangle$ is a vector of non-negative values calculated from features on pairs (x, j), with corresponding weights given by the parameter vector $\boldsymbol{\theta} = \langle \theta_1, \theta_2, \ldots, \theta_m \rangle$. We estimate $\boldsymbol{\theta}$ from sentences annotated with dependencies. It should be noted that the probability $p(d_i)$ depends only on i, j, and the inputs $\boldsymbol{w}$, $\boldsymbol{t}$, which ensures that it is estimated independently for each w_i. Because parameter estimation does not involve computing $\hat{\boldsymbol{d}}$, we do not apply the maximum spanning tree algorithm in training.

2.2 Features

Our current implementation uses the following features for $\boldsymbol{\phi}$.

F1: The distance between a dependent word and its candidate head.

F2: The surface forms of the dependent and head words.

F3: The parts-of-speech of the dependent and head words.

F4: The surface forms of up to three words to the left of the dependent and head words.

F5: The surface forms of up to three words to the right of the dependent and head words.

[1] While we describe unlabeled dependency parsing for simplicity, it is trivial to extend it to labeled dependency parsing.

i	1	2	3	4	5	6	7	8	9
w_i	政府	は	投資	に	つなが	る	と	歓迎	し
Eng.	Gov.	*subj.*	investment	to	leads	*ending*	that	welcomes	do
t_i	noun	part.	noun	part.	verb	infl.	part.	noun	verb
d_i		8							
F1		6							
F2		は						歓迎	
F3		part.						noun	
F4		政府						つなが, る, と	
F5		投資, に, つなが						し	
F6		noun						verb, infl., part.	
F7		noun, part., verb						verb	

The second word, case marker は (*subj.*), has two grammatically possible heads: the verb つなが (leads) and the verb 歓迎 (welcomes). In our framework, only this word needs to be annotated with its head.

Figure 1: An example of a partially annotated sentence and the features for a dependency between case marker は (*subj.*) and the verb 歓迎 (welcomes).

F6: The parts-of-speech of the words selected for F4.

F7: The parts-of-speech of the words selected for F5.

Figure 1 shows the values of these features for a partially annotated example sentence where one word, case marker は (*subj.*), has been annotated with its head, the verb 歓迎 (welcomes).

Pointwise prediction rather than structured prediction has the potential to hurt parsing accuracy. However, our method can enjoy greater flexibility, which allows for training from partially annotated corpora as will be described in Section 3. It also simplifies the implementation and reduces the time necessary for training.

2.3 Solution Search

In the experiments, we target Japanese parsing. Because Japanese is a head-final language, we assume $d_i > i$ for all $i \neq n$ and $d_n = 0$. This assumption reduces the maximum spanning tree algorithm to a simpler algorithm: for each word we select the dependency with the maximum score. As this never creates a loop of dependencies, a recursive process as in Chu-Liu/Edmonds' algorithm is not necessary.

3 Domain Adaptation for MST Parsing

Assuming that the cost of annotation corresponds roughly to the number of annotations performed, out of all possible annotations to have annotators perform for a target domain corpus we want to select the ones which provide the greatest benefit to accuracy when training. The high cost of annotation work is the primary motivation for this approach.

3.1 Partial Annotation for a Parser

In the context of dependency parsing, partial annotation refers to annotating only certain dependencies between words in a sentence. Dependencies which are assumed to have little to no value for training are left unannotated. Figure 1 shows an example of a partially annotated sentence that can be used as training data by our system.

Before text can be annotated with dependencies for use in our system, it must first be tokenized and labeled with POS tags.[2] We assume that the results of this tokenization and POS tagging are accurate enough that we need to manually annotate only the dependencies between the tokenized words.

3.2 Learning Feature Weights from Partial Annotations

As explained in Section 2.1, edge scores, $\sigma(d_i)$, are estimated for each w_i independently. This means that the estimation of $\sigma(d_i)$ requires only a gold dependency of w_i, and the other dependencies in a sentence are not necessary. This allows us to learn weights $\boldsymbol{\theta}$ for features from partially annotated corpora. When training data includes a gold

[2] We take a language-independent approach that does not make any assumptions about the unit of tokenization or the meaning of tags used.

phrase-based dependency corpus (fully annotated)

ID	head	phrase
01	02	党内/noun の/part.
02	07	議論/noun は/part.
03	04	「/symbol 保守/noun
04	05	二/noun 党/suff. 論/noun は/part.
05	06	よろし/adj. く/infl. な/adj. い/infl. 。/symbol 」/symbol と/part.
06	07	い/verb う/infl.
07	–	もの/noun だ/aux. 。/symbol

Figure 2: An example of phrase-based dependency annotation for a sentence.

dependency that w_i depends on w_j, a discriminative classifier can be trained by regarding $d_i = j$ as a positive sample and $d_i = j'$ s.t. $j' \neq j$ as negative samples.

In the case of Japanese parsing, because $j > i$ for all $d_i = j$, negative samples are $d_i = j'$ s.t. $j' \neq j \wedge j' > i$. For example, from the partial annotation given in Figure 1, we can create a training instance for w_2, は (*subj.*), where the positive sample is $d_2 = 8$ and the negative samples are $d_2 = 3, 4, \ldots, 7, 9$.

3.3 Domain Adaptation with a Partially Annotated Training Corpus

As a case study, we show how partial annotation can be used as a low-cost method of converting the annotation standard of an existing linguistic resource. As we mentioned in Section 1, traditional frameworks for Japanese dependency parsing are phrase-based. Many existing dependency corpora use phrases as the unit of annotation, and these resources are a valuable potential source of data for mining word dependencies. However, phrase dependencies alone do not provide enough information for an automatic conversion to word dependencies. One of the advantages of our parser is that it can be trained on a partially annotated corpus, so if we can derive even some word dependencies from phrase dependencies we can quickly and easily make use of existing resources.

To take advantage of these linguistic resources, we created a number of rules to derive word-based dependency annotations from phrase-based annotations. Instead of trying to convert all phrase dependencies, we focused on heuristics that provide only reliable word dependencies. The word-based dependency set produced by these rules is a partial annotation of the original corpus.

For the domain adaptation experiments described in Section 4, we used this procedure on the NAIST Text Corpus (NTC) (Iida et al., 2007) to create a small partially-annotated target domain corpus. The NTC consists of newspaper articles from the Mainichi Shimbun.[3] Figure 2 shows an example sentence from this corpus annotated with phrase dependencies.

To aid the construction of conversion rules, we chose three broad categories of words - content words, function words, and punctuation symbols - that provide clues to the structure of a phrase. Before we explain our rules, we will give a short explanation of these three categories.

We defined content words as nouns, verbs, adjectives, interjections, prenominal adjectives, suffixes, and prefixes. Function words are auxiliary verbs, particles, inflections, and conjunctions. In this context, punctuation symbols are both the English and Japanese versions of period and comma characters. These three categories are used to determine phrases which can be mined for relatively accurate word dependencies.

Figure 3 shows an example of how the rules explained below are used to derive word-based dependencies from phrase-based dependencies for the sentence given in Figure 2.

The first two rules are inter-phrase rules, which are concerned with the relationship between words located in different phrases.

1. LAST: Given a dependent phrase and its head phrase in the original annotation, set the head of the last word in the dependent phrase to the last content word in the head phrase. Note, we only apply this rule if the head phrase consists of a content word followed by zero or more function words, followed by an optional punctuation symbol.

[3] In addition to phrase dependency annotations, the NTC also contains predicate-argument and coreference tags that are useful for deriving reliable word dependencies.

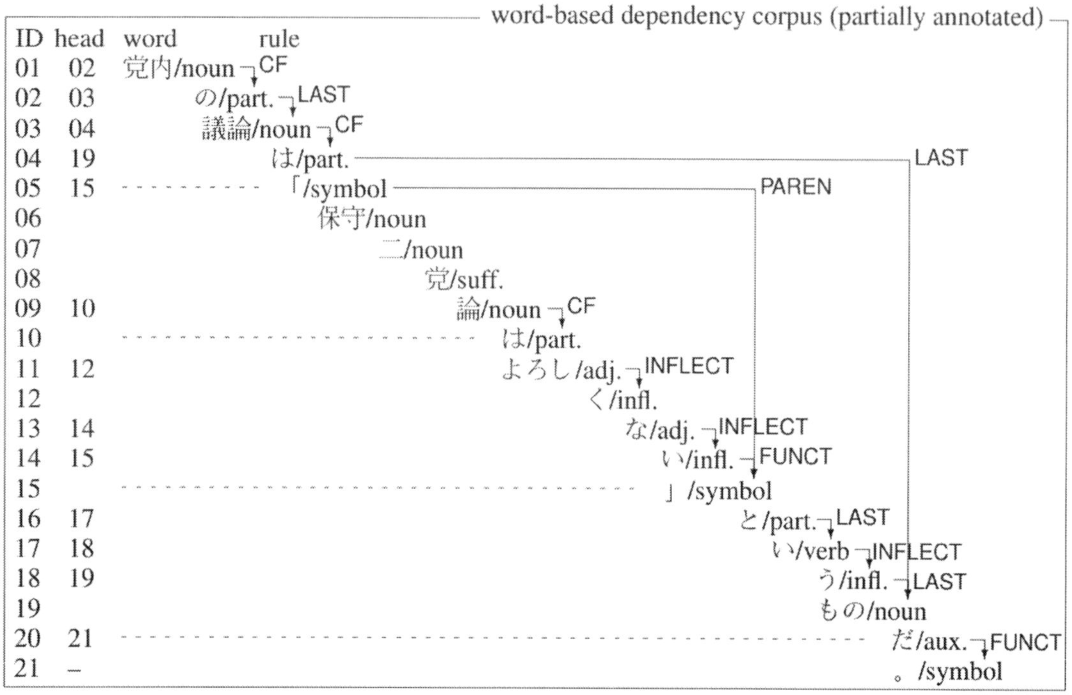

Figure 3: An example of word-based dependencies derived from phrase-based dependencies for a sentence.

2. PAREN: Set the head of a left parenthesis (or left bracket) word to the first right parenthesis (or right bracket) that follows it in the sentence.

The last four rules are intra-phrase rules that are concerned with the dependencies between words in the same phrase. The following rules were found to be effective.

3. FFS: If a phrase consists of zero or more content words, function words, or punctuation symbols followed by a sequence of two function words and a punctuation symbol, then set the head of the first function word in the sequence to the second function word and the head of the second function word to the punctuation symbol.

4. CF: If a phrase consists of zero or more content words followed by a sequence of a content word and a function word, then set the head of the content word to the function word.

5. INFLECT: If a word that is inflected in Japanese (verb, auxiliary verb, or adjective[4]) is followed by an inflection, the first word depends on the inflection.

6. FUNCT: If a function word is followed by a punctuation symbol, set the head of the function word to the punctuation symbol.

[4]In Japanese there are two types of adjectives, *i*-type adjectives and *na*-type adjectives. Both types are inflected.

4 Evaluation

As an evaluation of our parser, we measured parsing accuracies of several systems on test corpora in two domains: one is a general domain in which a corpus fully annotated with word boundary and dependency information is available, and the other is a target domain assuming an adaptation situation in which only a partially annotated corpus is available for quick and low-cost domain adaptation.

4.1 Experimental Settings

In the experiments we used example sentences from a dictionary (Keene et al., 1992) as the general domain data, and newspaper articles as the target domain data. We used business newspaper articles (Nikkei), similar to the Wall Street Journal, for the target domain test set. For the domain adaptation experiments, we used the partially-annotated corpus mentioned in Section 3.3 as a

Table 1: Sizes of Corpora.

ID	source	usage	#sentences	#words	#chars
EHJ-train	example sentences	training	11,700	145,925	197,941
EHJ-test	from a dictionary	test	1,300	16,348	22,207
NTC-train	newspaper articles	training	34,712	1,045,328	1,510,618
NKN-test	newspaper articles	test	1,002	29,038	43,695

NTC-train is a partially annotated corpus derived from phrase-based dependency annotations.

target domain training corpus. This corpus consists of newspaper articles that are similar to the target domain test set.

Usages and specifications of the various corpora are shown in Table 1. All the sentences are segmented into words manually and all the words are annotated with their heads manually. The Japanese data provided by the CoNLL organizers (Buchholz and Marsi, 2006) are the result of an automatic conversion from phrase (*bunsetsu*) dependencies. For a more appropriate evaluation we have prepared a word-based dependency data set.

The dependencies have no labels because almost all nouns are connected to a verb with a case marker and many important labels are obvious. The words are not annotated with POS tags, so we used a Japanese POS tagger, KyTea (Neubig et al., 2011), trained on about 40k sentences from the BCCWJ (Maekawa, 2008).

For the general domain experiments we compared the following systems, using projective parsing algorithms for training because of the assumptions about Japanese parsing outlined in Section 2.1.

1. **Malt**: Nivre et al. (2006)'s MaltParser, using Nivre's arc-eager algorithm and the option for strict root handling.
2. **MST**: McDonald et al. (2005)'s MST Parser, using k-best parse size with k=5.
3. **PW**: Our system, where pointwise estimation is used to estimate dependencies. Stochastic gradient descent training was used to train log-linear models.

4.2 With a Fully Annotated Training Corpus

For the first experiment, we measured the accuracy of each system on an in-domain test set when training on a fully annotated corpus. The results are shown in Table 2. Malt and MST have similar accuracy. PW has slightly higher accuracy than both of these systems, but the difference in accuracy is not statistically significant. We also measured the training time and the parsing speed of each system. Table 3 shows the results. From this table, first we see that MST is much slower than Malt, as is well known. Our method, however, is much faster than MST and the parsing speed is approximately the same as the shift-reduce-based Malt.

Theoretically the training time of our method is proportional to the number of annotated dependencies. In line with Kudo and Matsumoto (2002), we make two assumptions about Japanese dependency parsing. First, because Japanese is a head-final language we assume that every word except the final one in a sentence depends on one of the words located to its right. Second, we assume that all dependencies are projective, in other words that edges in the dependency tree do not cross each other. These assumptions limit the number of candidate heads for a word, reducing the training time.

Because all parsers were trained with projective algorithms, the first assumption is most likely the main reason for the difference in training times between PW and MST. For other languages where possible heads can be located both to the left and right of a word, we expect training times to increase. Our pointwise approach can be extended to handle these languages by changing the constraint on heads from $j > i$ to $j \neq i$ for all $d_i = j$. This is an important direction for future work now that we have confirmed that this approach is effective for Japanese.

We performed a second experiment in the general domain to measure the impact of the training corpus size on parsing accuracy. To make smaller training corpora, we set a fixed number of dependency annotations and then sequentially selected sentences from EHJ-train until the desired number of dependency annotations were collected. The re-

Table 2: Parsing Accuracy on EHJ-test.

method	EHJ-test
Malt	96.63%
MST	96.67%
PW	96.83%

All systems were trained on EHJ-train.

Table 3: Training Time and Parsing Speed.

method	training time	parsing speed
Malt	14[s]	1.3[ms/sent.]
MST	1901[s]	32.7[ms/sent.]
PW	125[s]	2.8[ms/sent.]

All systems were trained on EHJ-train and tested on EHJ-test. The machine used had a 3.33GHz processor and 12GB of RAM.

sults are shown in Figure 4. Though PW achieves the highest accuracy when the full training corpus is used, Malt has higher accuracy than both of the MST-based systems when the training corpus is one-third or less the size of the full training corpus. It can also be shown that both MST-based systems improve at a similar rate for all sizes of training corpora.

4.3 Domain Adaptation with a Partially Annotated Training Corpus

Tasks that make use of parsers, such as machine translation (Yamada and Knight, 2001), often require word-based models. However, because phrase-based approaches have traditionally been used for Japanese dependency parsing (Kudo and Matsumoto, 2002; Sassano and Kurohashi, 2010), word-based linguistic resources for Japanese are scarce. Preparing the fully annotated corpora required by existing word-based parsers such as McDonald et al. (2005)'s MST Parser is an expensive and laborious task.

Our parser attempts to address these problems by introducing a word-based framework for dependency parsing that can use partially annotated training data. Partial annotation is one way to efficiently make use of existing resources in the target domain without incurring high annotation costs.

We used each rule described in Section 3.3 individually to convert the annotations in the NTC-train and produce a pool of word-based dependencies. We then selected 5k of those dependencies to add to EHJ-train, and measured the results on NKN-test. We also used all rules simultaneously to produce word-based dependencies and measured the results in the same way as the individual rules. The total size of the partial annotation pool produced by using all rules was 248,148 dependencies out of 1,010,648 annotation candidates (not counting the last word of sentences, which has no dependency). The baseline case only used the EHJ-train with no partial annotations from the pool. The results are shown in Figure 5.

It can be seen that the LAST rule is the most effective, followed by the PAREN rule. This suggests that the long-distance dependencies provided by these rules are more useful for domain adaptation than the short-distance dependency information that the intra-phrase rules provide.

Combining all of the rules increases the accuracy on NKN-test to 88.44%, an increase of 2.75% over the baseline. This combination of rules results in lower accuracy gains than the sum of the gains from individual rules because different rules may convert the same phrase dependencies. These results show that our pointwise approach allows for effective use of existing target domain resources and increased parsing accuracy in the target domain through partial annotation.

5 Related Work

There has been a significant amount of work on how to utilize in-domain data to improve the accuracy of parsing. The majority of this work has focused on using unlabeled data in combination with self-training (Roark and Bacchiani, 2003; McClosky et al., 2006) or other semi-supervised learning methods (Blitzer et al., 2006; Nivre et al., 2007; Suzuki et al., 2009).

Roark and Bacchiani (2003) also present work on supervised domain adaptation, although this focuses on the utilization of an already-existing in-domain corpus.

There has also been some work on efficient annotation of data for parsing (Tang et al., 2002; Osborne and Baldridge, 2004; Sassano and Kurohashi, 2010). Most previous work focuses on picking efficient sentences to annotate for parsing, but Sassano and Kurohashi (2010) also present a method for using partially annotated data with deterministic dependency parsers, which can be trivially estimated from partially annotated data.

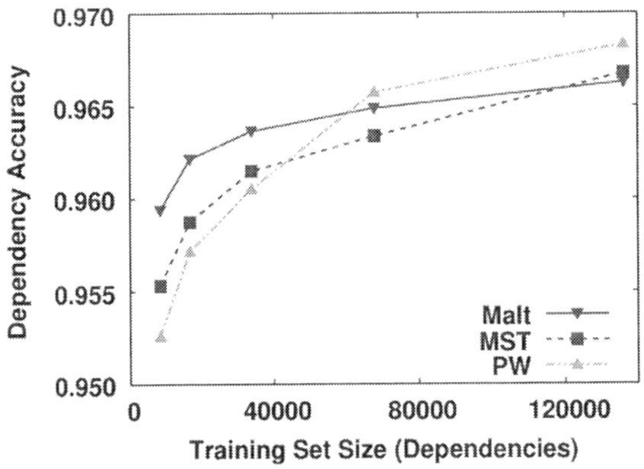

Figure 4: Comparison of parsing accuracy for different parsers.

Other recent work (Spreyer and Kuhn, 2009; Spreyer et al., 2010) has shown how both Nivre et al. (2006)'s MaltParser and McDonald et al. (2005)'s MST can be adapted to use partially annotated training data.

Traditional MST parsers such as McDonald et al. (2005)'s use structured prediction methods. Wang et al. (2007) showed that local classification methods can be used to train structured predictors. Their approach also uses "dynamic" features, where the predictions for some surrounding edges are used as features when estimating a possible edge between a dependent and head word.

Our parser also makes use of local classification methods for training, but in contrast to Wang et al. (2007) we take a pointwise approach based on the assumption that edge scores can be estimated independently. This work follows in the thread of Liang et al. (2008) and Neubig et al. (2011), who demonstrated that these assumptions can be made without a significant degradation in accuracy for POS tagging. Here we demonstrated that the same approach can be used for MST-based dependency parsing.

6 Conclusion

We introduced an MST parser that evaluates the score for each edge in a dependency tree independently, which allows for the use of partially annotated corpora in training. We demonstrated that target domain data annotated in this way can be combined with available general domain data to increase parsing accuracy in the target domain.

We evaluated state-of-the-art dependency parsers on a Japanese dependency parsing task,

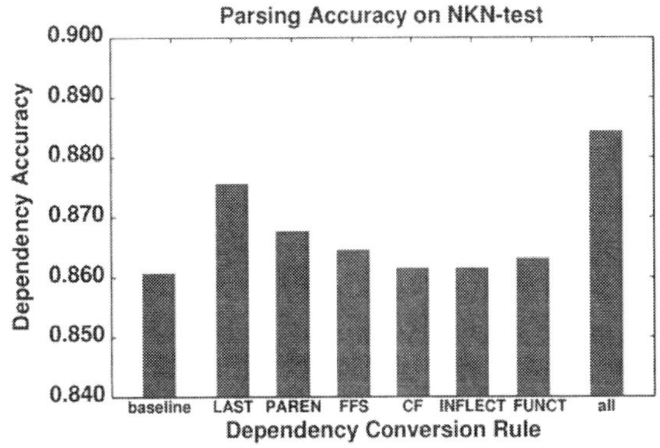

Figure 5: Parsing Accuracy on NKN-test.

and found that our parser achieves accuracy comparable to that of a traditional MST parser. Additionally, the training and parsing speed of our parser is much faster than the traditional one, which allows it to be used for active learning in a real-world domain adaptation situation.

References

Adam L. Berger, Vincent J. Della Pietra, and Stephen A. Della Pietra. 1996. A maximum entropy approach to natural language processing. *Computational Linguistics*, 22(1):39–71.

John Blitzer, Ryan McDonald, and Fernando Pereira. 2006. Domain adaptation with structural correspondence learning. In *Proceedings of the 2006 Conference on Empirical Methods in Natural Language Processing*, pages 120–128.

Sabine Buchholz and Erwin Marsi. 2006. CoNLL-X shared task on multilingual dependency parsing. In *Proceedings of the Tenth Conference on Computational Natural Language Learning (CoNLL-X)*, pages 149–164.

Daniel Gildea. 2001. Corpus variation and parser performance. In *Proceedings of the 2001 Conference on Empirical Methods in Natural Language Processing*, pages 167–202.

Ryu Iida, Mamoru Komachi, Kentaro Inui, and Yuji Matsumoto. 2007. Annotating a Japanese text corpus with predicate-argument and coreference relations. In *Proceedings of the Linguistic Annotation Workshop*, pages 132–139.

Donald Keene, Hiroyoshi Hatori, Haruko Yamada, and Shouko Irabu. 1992. *Japanese-English Sentence Equivalents (in Japanese)*. Asahi Press, Electronic book edition.

Taku Kudo and Yuji Matsumoto. 2002. Japanese dependency analysis using cascaded chunking. In *Proceedings of the Sixth Conference on Computational Natural Language Learning*, volume 25, pages 1–7.

Percy Liang, Hal Daumé III, and Dan Klein. 2008. Structure compilation: trading structure for features. In *Proceedings of the 25th International Conference on Machine Learning*, pages 592–599.

Kikuo Maekawa. 2008. Balanced corpus of contemporary written Japanese. In *Proceedings of the 6th Workshop on Asian Language Resources*, pages 101–102.

David McClosky, Eugene Charniak, and Mark Johnson. 2006. Reranking and self-training for parser adaptation. In *Proceedings of the 44th Annual Meeting of the Association for Computational Linguistics*, pages 337–344.

Ryan McDonald, Fernando Pereira, Kiril Ribarov, and Jan Hajič. 2005. Non-projective dependency parsing using spanning tree algorithms. In *Proceedings of the 2005 Conference on Empirical Methods in Natural Language Processing*, pages 523–530.

Yusuke Miyao, Kenji Sagae, Rune Saetre, Takuya Matsuzaki, and Jun'ichi Tsujii. 2009. Evaluating contributions of natural language parsers to protein-protein interaction extraction. *Bioinformatics*, 25(3):394–400.

Toshiaki Nakazawa and Sadao Kurohashi. 2008. Linguistically-motivated tree-based probabilistic phrase alignment. In *In Proceedings of the Eighth Conference of the Association for Machine Translation in the Americas (AMTA2008)*.

Graham Neubig and Shinsuke Mori. 2010. Word-based partial annotation for efficient corpus construction. In *Proceedings of the Seventh International Conference on Language Resources and Evaluation*.

Graham Neubig, Yosuke Nakata, and Shinsuke Mori. 2011. Pointwise prediction for robust, adaptable Japanese morphological analysis. In *The 49th Annual Meeting of the Association for Computational Linguistics: Human Language Technologies Short Paper Track*.

Joakim Nivre and Mario Scholz. 2004. Deterministic dependency parsing of English text. In *Proceedings of the 20th International Conference on Computational Linguistics*.

Joakim Nivre, Johan Hall, and Jens Nilsson. 2006. Maltparser: A data-driven parser-generator for dependency parsing. In *Proceedings of the Fifth International Conference on Language Resources and Evaluation*.

Joachim Nivre, Johan Hall, Sandra Kübler, Ryan McDonald, Jens Nilsson, Sebastian Riedel, and Deniz Yuret. 2007. The CoNLL 2007 shared task on dependency parsing. In *Proceedings of the CoNLL Shared Task Session of EMNLP-CoNLL 2007*.

Miles Osborne and Jason Baldridge. 2004. Ensemble-based active learning for parse selection. In *Proceedings of the Human Language Technology Conference of the North American Chapter of the Association for Computational Linguistics*, pages 89–96.

Slav Petrov, Pi-Chuan Chang, Michael Ringgaard, and Hiyan Alshawi. 2010. Uptraining for accurate deterministic question parsing. In *Proceedings of the 2010 Conference on Empirical Methods in Natural Language Processing*, pages 705–713.

Brian Roark and Michiel Bacchiani. 2003. Supervised and unsupervised PCFG adaptation to novel domains. In *Proceedings of the 2003 Human Language Technology Conference of the North American Chapter of the Association for Computational Linguistics*, pages 126–133.

Manabu Sassano and Sadao Kurohashi. 2010. Using smaller constituents rather than sentences in active learning for Japanese dependency parsing. In *Proceedings of the 48th Annual Meeting of the Association for Computational Linguistics*, pages 356–365.

Kathrin Spreyer and Jonas Kuhn. 2009. Data-driven dependency parsing of new languages using incomplete and noisy training data. In *Proceedings of the Thirteenth Conference on Computational Natural Language Learning (CoNLL-2009)*, pages 12–20.

Kathrin Spreyer, Lilja Øvrelid, and Jonas Kuhn. 2010. Training parsers on partial trees: a cross-language comparison. In *Proceedings of the Seventh International Conference on Language Resources and Evaluation*.

Jun Suzuki, Hideki Isozaki, Xavier Carreras, and Michael Collins. 2009. An empirical study of semi-supervised structured conditional models for dependency parsing. In *Proceedings of the 2009 Conference on Empirical Methods in Natural Language Processing*, pages 551–560.

Min Tang, Xiaoqiang Luo, and Salim Roukos. 2002. Active learning for statistical natural language parsing. In *Proceedings of the 40th Annual Meeting of the Association for Computational Linguistics*, pages 120–127.

Yuta Tsuboi, Hisashi Kashima, Shinsuke Mori, Hiroki Oda, and Yuji Matsumoto. 2008. Training conditional random fields using incomplete annotations. In *Proceedings of the 22th International Conference on Computational Linguistics*.

Qin Iris Wang, Dekang Lin, and Dale Schuurmans. 2007. Simple training of dependency parsers via structured boosting. In *Proceedings of the TwentiethInternational Joint Conference on Artificial Intelligence*, pages 1756–1762.

Kenji Yamada and Kevin Knight. 2001. A syntax-based statistical machine translation model. In *Proceedings of the 39th Annual Meeting of the Association for Computational Linguistics*, pages 523–530.

A Breadth-First Representation for Tree Matching in Large Scale Forest-Based Translation

Sumukh Ghodke **Steven Bird** **Rui Zhang**
Department of Computer Science and Software Engineering
University of Melbourne, Victoria 3010, Australia
{sghodke,sb,rui}@csse.unimelb.edu.au

Abstract

Efficient data structures are necessary for searching large translation rule dictionaries in forest-based machine translation. We propose a breadth-first representation of tree structures that allows trees to be stored and accessed efficiently. We describe an algorithm that allows incremental search for trees in a forest and show that its performance is orders of magnitude faster than iterative search. A B-tree index is used to store the rule dictionaries. Prefix-compressed indexes with a large page size are found to provide a balance of fast search and disk space utilisation.

1 Introduction

Statistical machine translation (SMT) uses machine learning and parallel corpora to perform translations automatically. Syntax based SMT systems can be broadly classified into two types based on the input to the system: tree-based and string-based (Mi et al., 2008). In a tree-based system, the input is a parse tree of the source language, whereas in the latter, the input is a sequence of words that is simultaneously parsed and translated. Forest-based translation employs multiple parse trees for each source language sentence.

Forest-based translation can be performed in three main steps. First, the input sentence is parsed into a packed forest, which is then pruned. Next, for each tree in the packed forest, all matching translation rules are found. These translation rules are then combined to form a translation forest. The translation forest is finally decoded to produce a sentence in the target language.

The second step – finding all matching translation rules for each tree in the source sentence forest – is a complex task in itself. It could be performed by enumerating all trees in the forest and then searching for those trees in the translation rule dictionary. Of the enumerated trees, those that are present in the rule dictionary produce the translation forest. However, enumerating all possible trees from a forest incurs an exponential cost and many or most of those generated trees may not exist in the rule dictionary. Hence, a common approach in MT research is to perform the inverse task, and iterate over all the rules to check whether each rule matches anywhere in the source forest. This is a relatively easy task, especially if the rule dictionary is not large. In experimental setups a subset of rules may be used based on the prior knowledge of the rules required for the given test sentences. While that method works for research experiments on translation methods, no prior knowledge is available for online MT systems, and iterating over all rules will not be efficient for large rule dictionaries. Another method used to quicken the search is to limit the depth of the rules. Shallower rule trees are lesser in number. However, the reduction in depth can lower the translation quality.

This paper's contribution is in the second step of forest-based translation. We propose a breadth-first representation of translation rule trees and a sorted index architecture to store and retrieve translation rules efficiently. Together, they allow all translation trees to be discovered at each node in the forest, incrementally. Each node in the forest is expanded to form trees that are present in the rule dictionary. This allows the rule dictionary to contain all rules without any restriction on the depth of the rule or the size of the collection.

Translation rules are stored in the BerkeleyDB (Olson et al., 1999) B-tree index structure. Section 3 describes the breadth-first representation used to store trees in the index. The architecture of the translation system and the method of incremental tree expansion are described in Section 4. Section 4 also discusses the significance of the breadth-first over a depth-first tree storage approach.

Section 5 describes our experimental setup. The experiments measure the total time to construct a translation forest from a pruned source forest. An iterative search over the rule dictionary is the baseline performance measure. In addition to comparing the indexed search with the baseline, this section also analyses the effect of page size and compression on search performance. Multiple rule indexes are created to test the effect of the database parameter settings. The operating system disk cache and the database cache are cleared to simulate a fresh start before operating on each forest. The experiments are conducted on two rule dictionaries and three forest collections. The first rule dictionary has 11.8M rule trees and the second has 33.1M rules. The rules are extracted from NIST (2010a) data while the forest collections are extracted from NIST (2010a; 2010b) data.

2 Background

In this section we present the fundamentals of packed forests and forest-based translation before briefly describing the B-tree index structure.

2.1 Packed Forest

Packed forests or forests are directed hypergraphs and have been used to model and represent several applications in computer science and discrete mathematics (Klein and Manning, 2001).

Directed hypergraphs can be defined as a pair: $H = (V, E)$ where $V = \{v_1, v_2, \cdots, v_n\}$ is the set of nodes and $E = \{E_1, E_2, \cdots, E_m\}$ is the set of hyperedges. Each hyperedge can be defined as a pair: $E_i = (X_i, Y_i) \mid X_i,\ Y_i \subseteq V,\ i = 1, 2, \cdots, m$.

Packed forests have been used in NLP in the area of sentence parsing (Gallo et al., 1993) where the propositions of a parse analysis correspond to the nodes in the hypergraph and rules are represented as hyperedges. A similar model is used in forest based machine translation, where multiple parses of the input sentence are modelled as a forest. In NLP applications, the head of a hyperedge is usually a single node. This allows a single hyperedge to be semantically equivalent to a tree node with its children.

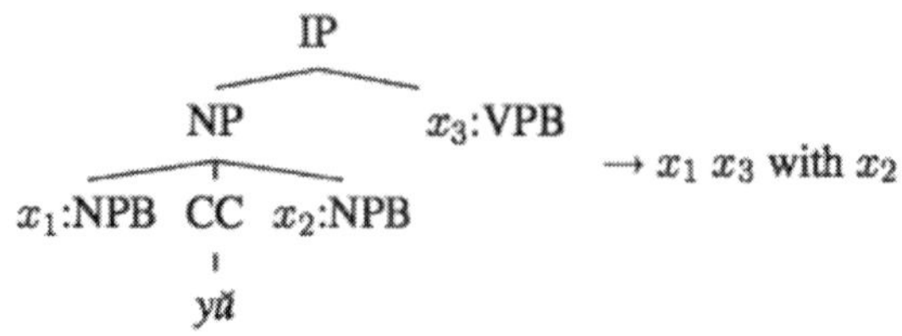

Figure 1: A translation rule reproduced from (Mi and Huang, 2008)

2.2 Forest Based Translation

Forest-based SMT overcomes the limitations of parse errors in tree-based translation and has been shown to be faster than k-best tree-based translation (Mi et al., 2008). For translating a sentence using the forest-based translation technique, we require a parser that can process a source language sentence and produce a packed forest and a translation rule dictionary, or database, which is a collection of *tree-to-string* translation rules (Huang et al., 2006; Liu et al., 2006).

A translation rule is a mapping from a source language tree to a string in the target language. An example translation rule from Chinese to English is shown in Figure 1. The left-hand-side is the source language tree. The Chinese word *yǔ* is translated to *with* in the target side on the right. The x_i variables on the right-hand-side are placeholders for the corresponding elements in the tree. Other numerical parameters associated with each translation rule are not shown here. Note that there may be several rules in the rule dictionary that have identical source language trees but different translations.

Once a source language sentence is parsed into a packed forest and pruned, the next step is to find trees in the forest that have matching rules in the translation rule dictionary. Matching rules are used to produce a translation forest for decoding into a target language string. The forest is a hypergraph made up of hyperedges where each hyperedge has a single source node, while the rules in the rule dictionary are trees.

Recent work by Huang and Mi (2010) has shown that forest expansion can be done in decoders using beam search (Koehn, 2004). However, to the best of our knowledge, no index-based search structures for incrementally finding trees have been proposed to date.

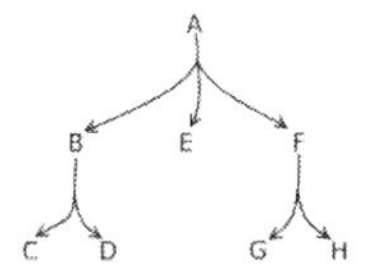

(a)

A(B(C D) E F(G H))

(b)

A3B2C0D0E0F2G0H0

(c)

A3B2E0F2C0D0G0H0

(d)

ABEFCDGH32020000

(e)

Figure 2: Transforming a tree into a breadth-first format

2.3 Indexing Methods

Data structures for indexing can be broadly classified into either memory based or disk based. Memory based indexes are not considered here since an online SMT system with a large translation rule dictionary requires disk based storage.

B-trees are balanced search trees that are designed to work efficiently from the disk. They minimise disk I/O and provide an insert and delete time complexity of *O(log n)*, where *n* is the number of objects in the database. The keys in a B-tree are always in sorted order, therefore providing a guarantee of proximity for comparable keys.

The B-tree implementation in BerkeleyDB is used in our experiments. Since the keys are sorted, consecutive keys often share a common prefix. BerkeleyDB allows the compression of keys in a database via user-defined compress and decompress functions. If no such functions are supplied, it performs prefix compression. Our experiments test the performance of search with page size and compression of keys. Other settings such as the minimum number of keys for each leaf page and cache size allow us to fine tune the performance of the system, but we do not report experiments on those for lack of space.

3 Breadth-first Representation

The storage and efficient retrieval of the left-hand-side of translation rules is closely linked to the format in which they are stored. This section describes the format we use to represent trees both in queries and for rules in the index.

Trees can be represented linearly in several ways. As mentioned in Section 2.2, although a forest is a hypergraph made up of hyperedges, the left-hand-sides of rules in the rule dictionary are actually trees. Each node in a forest can have zero or more outgoing hyperedges. A hyperedge is be treated as a tree node with its children. Source sentence trees are constructed by recursively expanding nodes in the forest.

Figure 2a shows a tree constructed with three hyperedges, having head nodes A, B and F. Figure 2b shows the typical string representation of the tree where a node's descendants are scoped by an open and close bracket. The bracketed format, although visually intuitive, is not efficient for storage and processing. There has been much research on succinct representation of tree structures. Succinct representations encode trees in the most compact fashion by either using a balanced bracket representation or depth first unary degree sequences (Jansson et al., 2007). Such methods often represent the open and close brackets of a tree in bit notations. However, braces can only be matched when the trees are stored in a depth-first format and it cannot be applied to breadth-first representations.

Figure 2c represents the tree as a sequence of label and integer pairs. The labels represent node labels in the tree in a depth first format and the integers that follow each node label give the number of children at that node. Figure 2d shows a similar encoding scheme, but with the tree traversed in a breadth-first format. Finally, Figure 2e shows the format used in this paper. In our format, we separate the node labels and the integers representing the number of child nodes. When using this representation in the index, each node label is represented by a unique integer, which occupies four bytes, whereas the integer representing the number of child nodes is restricted to a maximum value of 255, and can therefore be represented in one byte.

Separating the node labels from integers representing the number of child nodes gives us a greater prefix overlap between consecutive expansions. For example, if we were to use the interleaved expansion method shown in Figure 2d on the hyperedge with head A and then expand the hyperedge with head B, the breadth-first representation of the trees would be A3B0E0F0 and A3B2E0F0C0D0. We can see that the expansion of the node B has resulted in its number of children being updated to 2 from 0. Since, each label is encoded using 4 bytes and the child count using 1 byte, the overlap between the expanded sequences is 9 bytes. With the separated breadth-first format (Figure 2e) the two trees are ABEF3000 and ABEFCD320000, an overlap of 4 node labels or 16 bytes. The separated form helps in increasing the prefix overlap of expanded tree structures.

If, instead, the depth-first notation is used, then the second tree is represented as A3B2C0D0E0F0. Then, even if the integers are separated, the prefix shared by the two queries is only 9 bytes.

To generalise the breadth-first representation and the prefix overlap, consider a tree T containing k nodes, denoted here as an ordered sequence $N = (n_1, n_2, \cdots, n_k)$ in breadth-first order. Each node is either fully expanded or is collapsed, therefore, if k is greater than 1, then the first node, being the root, must be fully expanded. Let the labels of nodes in N be a sequence $L = (l_1, l_2, \cdots, l_k)$ and let $C = (c_1, c_2, \cdots, c_k)$ denote the sequence of the number of children of each node in N. The separated breadth-first representation of T, which is used in this paper, is the sequence $B = (l_1, l_2, \cdots, l_k, c_1, c_2, \cdots, c_k)$. In a tree T, the number of nodes that can be expanded is equal to the number of leaves p, where $p \leq k$. Each expansion of a leaf node in T produces a new tree. Let $S = \{T_i \mid i \in \{1, 2, \cdots, k\}\}$ be the set of all trees produced as a result of the expansion, where $|S| = p$ and each tree, T_i, is an expansion of node n_i in T and its separated breadth-first representation is B_i. Let $N_i' = \{n_j \mid depth(n_j) \leq depth(n_i)\}$ be a set of all nodes of depth less than or equal to node n_i's depth in T. Then, B_i shares a prefix of at least $4\,|N_i'|$ bytes with B.

Now, each node n_i has been considered to have either no child or one ordered set of children. While this is true in a tree, a forest is different. Each node in a forest can have multiple expansions, or hyperedges. The algorithm discussed in the next section therefore iterates over all possible hyperedges at a node.

4 Index Architecture

This section explains the structure of the index and the incremental search algorithm. To present a broader picture of where the index and search components fit within a larger online MT system, a representative block diagram of a complete forest-based MT system is provided in Figure 3. We focus only on the the incremental search algorithm

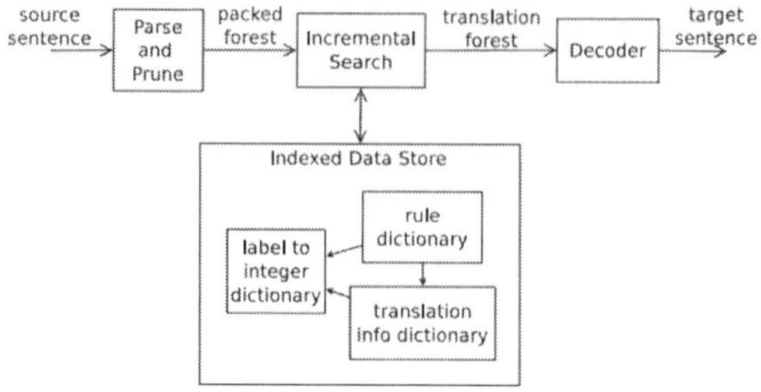

Figure 3: Architecture for an online forest-based translation system

and the rule dictionary in this section. The function of other components in the indexed data store is only briefly explained as they are not critical to the operation of the search algorithm.

The indexed data store is composed of three dictionaries. The first is a label to integer mapper. It assigns an integer identifier to all unique labels in the system. All tree node labels, including words, that appear on both sides of translation rules are indexed within this dictionary. The integer id for a label can be looked up using the label string as the key while encoding a tree query or while creating the other two dictionaries. A reverse mapping from the integer id to the label is used while constructing the translation forest from encoded rule trees. Any key-value data-structure could be used for the label mapper. It could even be a memory based hash table if it fits in memory.

The other two dictionaries, the rule dictionary and the translation info dictionary, contain the information about translation rules. The rule dictionary or database is a collection of left-hand-sides of translation rule trees accessible by a tree as the key. Each tree in the rule database has a unique integer id as its value. The integer id is the reference to a position in the translation info dictionary. Each rule tree may have one or more target language translations. Hence, each entry in the translation info database is a list of translations. Each element in the list is a tuple of the target language strings and the parameters defining the statistics of that translation. The target language strings are stored as a sequence of integer ids and the parameters are stored in a pre-defined binary format. The translation info database uses a simple record list structure from the BerkeleyDB library.

A large rule dictionary, requires a disk-resident index to support efficient access. The B-tree data-structure is used as the rule database because of its scaling capabilities and its sorted key storage property which is critical to the operation of the incremental search algorithm.

4.1 Incremental Forest Exploration

The incremental search algorithm finds trees within a forest that are also present in the rule dictionary. Nodes are expanded incrementally to ensure that expansions occur only where there is a possibility of a translation rule when expanded. This section also explains the significance of the breadth-first representation to the working of the algorithm and the reason why depth-first encoding will not work.

The algorithm works on a given source language forest where each node has one or more hyperedges. The function Process_Node in Pseudocode 1 iterates over each node in a forest in order to find the trees originating at that node. The incremental search itself is detailed in function Find_Tree_Increment in Pseudocode 1. The increment finding function is now explained here by assuming that a tree is being processed. It can be extended to work with forests as shown in the pseudocode.

Consider the tree T with k nodes, of which p nodes are leaves, as described in Section 3. The separated breadth-first representation of T, B, is essentially made up of two halves. The first half of B contains node label identifiers while the latter half contains child counts. This is true when the elements of B are considered as integers only, but the ratio is different in the binary form of B where the first half is represented using 4 bytes and the second half uses only 1 byte each. Nevertheless, both halves represent the information of nodes in sequence N, where N is in breadth-first order. To find a tree T in the rule dictionary, the tree has to be translated to the binary encoding of B to be searched in the index. Then, the tree would need to be expanded at p nodes to check if there are any possible rules that match when expanded. The process of finding any expansions of a tree is performed recursively in the function Find_Tree_Increment of Pseudocode 1.

When expanding trees, the data-structure needs to be an efficient one to operate on, since this is a recursive task. The algorithm should also facilitate a simple way of tracking the position in the tree where the expansion is taking place. This can be performed very easily because of a prop-

Pseudocode 1 Incremental search for trees

```
proc Get_Translation_Forest sourceForest
  RuleDB points to the translation rule database
  for node in sourceForest do
    call Process_Node with node
  end for

proc Process_Node node
  if node doesn't have hyperedges then
    label ← node's label
    word ← child of node
    # the only tree possible is 'label(word)'
    query ← call Separated_Breadth_First with label(word)
    if query is present in RuleDB then
      add query to translation forest
    end if
    return
  end if
  hyperedges ← all hyperedges at node
  for hyperedge in hyperedges do
    query ← call Separated_Breadth_First with hyperedge
    if query is found in RuleDB then
      add query to translation forest
    end if
    if query is found or (query is not found but prefix of
    query is found) then
      call Find_Tree_Increment with query
    end if
  end for

proc Find_Tree_Increment sbfArray
  labels ← first half of sbfArray
  childCounts ← second half of sbfArray
  lastNd ← node corresponding to labels' last element
  startNd ← node imm. after node corresponding to
  childCounts's last non-zero entry
  # startNd contains the node after the last expanded node
  # in breadth-first order
  for node from startNd to lastNd do
    if node doesn't have hyperedges then
      word ← child of node
      appLabel ← labels + [word's label]
      appChild ← childCounts + [0]
      appChild[node] ← the number of children of node
      query ← appLabel + appChild
      if query is present in RuleDB then
        add query to translation forest
      end if
      continue
    end if
    hyperedges ← all hyperedges at node
    for hyperedge in hyperedges do
      numTails ← number of hyperedge's tail nodes
      appLabel ← labels + [hyperedge's tail labels]
      arrayOfZeroes ← [0] * numTails
      appChild ← childCounts + arrayOfZeroes
      appChild[node] ← numTails
      query ← appLabel + appChild
      if query is found in RuleDB then
        add query to translation forest
      end if
      if query is found or (query is not found but prefix of
      query is found) then
        call Find_Tree_Increment with query
      end if
    end for
  end for

proc Separated_Breadth_First tree
  return the separated breadth first representation of tree
```

erty of the breadth-first representation. The property is that, when we expand node n_i in a tree T, and the $depth(n_i) = depth(T)$ or $depth(n_i) = depth(T) - 1$ and $\nexists$ n_j where $j > i$ and n_j is expanded, then, the child nodes of node n_i can simply be appended to N. In the function Find_Tree_Increment, the $startNd$ and $lastNd$ variables point to the start and end of expandable nodes in the tree represented by $sbfArray$. The $startNd$ node is located by finding the node immediately after the last expanded node when traversing the sequence N from k to 1. A node n_i is expanded if c_i is greater than 0. Hence, since this pattern exists, the recursive function treats its input parameter as a list and ignores the fact that it's operating on a tree.

A depth-first representation does not support such a property that allows expansions of nodes to be appended at the end of the list. This is because the tree expansion for searching rules is such that when a node is expanded, all its children have to be included at once, due to which expansions of trees in the depth-first method will almost always have child nodes appear in-between the original sequence of nodes. The only exception is when the very last node in the depth-first sequence is expanded. Having successive expansions differ from one another reduces their proximity in the index.

5 Experiments

5.1 Data

We use two rule collections in our experiments. The rules are extracted from 1.5M word-aligned sentence pairs of Chinese and English from the NIST (2010a) machine translation corpus. The first rule collection contains 11.8M Chinese translation rules, of which about 7.8M are for unique trees. All trees are limited to a depth of five levels. The second rule collection contains 33.1M rules, of which 23.9M are unique. The rules in the second collection are binarized but not limited by depth. The rule collections are 285MB and 2.5GB on disk, respectively, when gzipped.

In total, we use three forest collections. The first forest collection contains 254 forests from NIST (2010a) data. The second forest collection contains 288 forests, also obtained by parsing NIST (2010a) data, but they are binarized to work with the second rule collection. The third forest collection contains 348 binarized forests obtained by parsing NIST (2010b) data.

rule set	page size	regular	compressed
1	4K	1001MB	569MB
1	8K	947MB	537MB
1	16K	960MB	525MB
1	32K	954MB	496MB
2	4K	3.1GB	1.6GB
2	8K	3.0GB	1.5GB
2	16K	3.0GB	1.3GB
2	32K	3.0GB	1.2GB

Table 1: Size of B-tree indexes

5.2 Setup

The experiments are run on an Intel Core2Duo processor (2.4GHz; 4MB cache) desktop machine with 2GB of RAM. The operating system is Ubuntu desktop edition version 10.04.2. The index and program are installed on two different hard disks, both having a disk speed of 5400 rpm. The disk on which the code is installed has a page size of 4KB while the index disk has a page size of 8KB.

The index is created using B-tree index structures in the BerkeleyDB (version 5.1) library. The search algorithm is coded in Python and is open sourced[1]. Database accesses from the python program are through a python wrapper for BerkeleyDB called bsddb3[2]. The B-tree indexes are created with and without prefix compression. We also create indexes with four different page sizes (4K, 8K, 16K, and 32K) to analyse the effect of page size on performance. The sizes of the B-tree rule dictionaries are shown in Table 1.

Caching has a significant impact on performance measurements for disk-based searching. There are a minimum of 2 levels of caching while performing the tests. One cache is handled by the database while the other is a disk level cache managed by the operating system. We clear the database cache by choosing an in-memory cache and re-starting the database process when required. The commands *sync;* followed by *echo 3 > /proc/sys/vm/drop_caches;* are used to clear the operating system cache.

Search time is measured using the *datetime* package in Python version 2.6 and cache performance of the database is measured using BerkeleyDB tools. Every test is run three times and the average time is reported. The exact search process

[1] https://bitbucket.org/leopardspot/forest-search
[2] http://pybsddb.sourceforge.net/bsddb3.html

rule set	forest set	baseline	breadth-first
1	1	$\sim$ 23min	1.55sec
2	2	$\sim$ 80min	15.71sec
2	3	$\sim$ 80min	11.49sec

Table 2: Average time to search a forest

is explained in the specific experiment's sections.

5.3 Incremental Tree Matching

Experiment 1: Comparison with baseline

This experiment compares the performance of the baseline system with the breadth-first index based approach. The baseline checks if each rule in the rule dictionary is found in the forest being translated. If found, the rule is added to the translation forest. Almost one-third of the rules in the full rule collection have a common left-hand side. Also, rules with the same left-hand-side have been found to be consecutive in the collection. Therefore, the outcome of previous rule's check is reused if the current rule is same as the previous one.

The average forest search time with the baseline setup is compared with the best breadth-first index based search method in Table 2. The times reported for the incremental breadth-first search are obtained when using a regular 32K page size index. The average time is the ratio of the total time required to search all forests in a forest set, and the number of forests in the set.

Experiment 2: Page size and compression

This experiment compares the effects of page size and compression on the search time in a breadth-first index. For each forest in a forest collection, the time to search the forest is measured. An average of those times across all forests in the collection is shown in Table 3 for indexes of various page sizes, with and without compression.

Experiment 3: Cache utilisation

In order to measure the cache utilisation of the indexes, the forests are searched sequentially without closing the database or clearing the disk cache. A BerkeleyDB utility is then used to obtain the memory usage statistics which displays the cache hit ratio. The cache usage will depend on the order in which the forests are searched and also on the content of the forests. However, the forests are searched in the same order across all indexes, therefore, their relative cache performances can be meaningfully compared.

rule set	forest set	page size	regular (s)	compressed (s)
1	1	4K	2.35	2.09
1	1	8K	2.01	1.93
1	1	16K	1.69	1.86
1	1	32K	1.55	2.01
2	2	4K	20.86	22.90
2	2	8K	25.42	18.52
2	2	16K	17.73	18.69
2	2	32K	15.71	19.62
2	3	4K	14.13	15.03
2	3	8K	17.86	12.78
2	3	16K	12.63	13.16
2	3	32K	11.49	14.03

Table 3: Average time for breadth-first search

5.4 Analysis

From Table 2, it is clear that the baseline method is more than an order of magnitude slower. It can also be observed that forest sets 2 and 3 take about the same amount of time on average over rule set 2. It is therefore clear that the search time for the baseline method is primarily determined by the size of the rule set and not on the size of the forest. Table 3 shows that the best performance in B-tree indexes is always obtained in the uncompressed, or regular, index and when using the 32K page size. However, the performance of the compressed index seems to stabilise and not deteriorate much beyond the 8K page size. Considering that the compressed indexes are almost half the size of the regular index – or even smaller than half in the case of rule set 2 with 16K and 32K page sizes – they might be the better option to consider for very large collections.

The average run times on a collection of forests depend on the properties of individual forests in the collection. A histogram of the number of forests searched in time intervals shows us that when searching a compressed index the search operates faster on already fast searches and slower on the initially-slow searches. Figure 4 and Figure 5 show the histograms for the third set of forests searched using a compressed and an uncompressed index, respectively, each with a page size of 8K. From the figures, it is evident that the number of forests translated in less than 5s – the first stick in the figures – increase in the compressed index, while the slower forests which take about 200s on a regular index take about 250s or

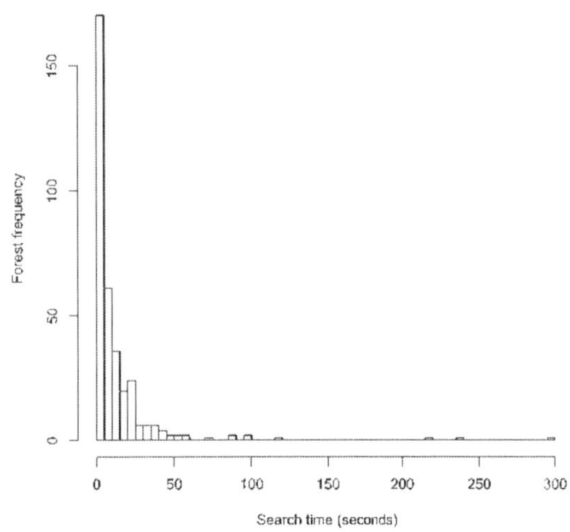

Figure 4: Distribution of forests searched in an 8K compressed index

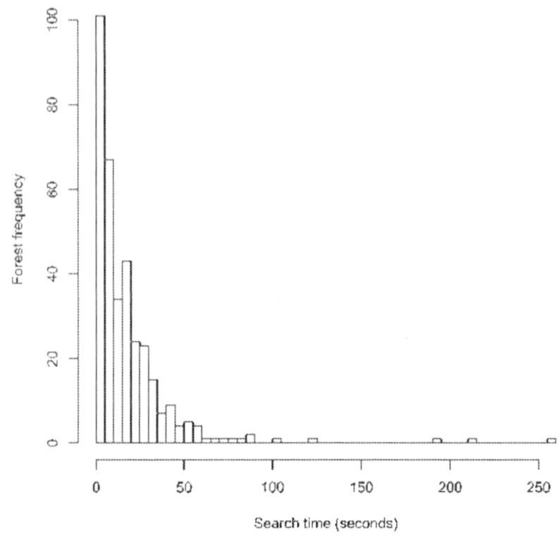

Figure 5: Distribution of forests searched in an 8K uncompressed index

longer on the compressed index. This is true even in other page sizes. Histograms for the 32K page size index – omitted here for lack of space – look similar to Figure 4 and Figure 5, but the compressed index shows a very marginal increase in the number of faster forests and a clear increase in the time for the slower forests. But, even without compression, the 32K index has about the same number of forests translated in less than 5s as the faster 8K compressed index.

Cache utilisation is found to be very high in all cases. The number of pages retrieved from a compressed index is always lower than that for an uncompressed one. Cache misses are clearly not the cause for the slowdown in the compressed indexes. The decompress operation is the most likely reason. However, with compression, more queries, or keys, would fit in one page which may causes a speedup when fewer queries are required while searching a forest.

Another observation is that although rule set 2 is about 3 times as large as rule set 1– both in the number of rules and in the size of the index – the search times do not show a 3-fold increase. This could be the result of various factors. One, the rule set 1 might have more pages cached than rule set 2, because it's a smaller index. Two, the depth of the rules in rule set 1 are limited to 5 whereas the depth is not limited in set 2. We feel that the most likely reason in this case is the first one. However, to verify we would have to test with a larger dataset which is limited in depth.

6 Conclusion and Future Work

We propose a breadth first representation for trees and use that representation in an algorithm to incrementally find all trees in a forest that are also present in a rule dictionary. We compare the performance of the algorithm on two different rule sets and three forest collections. We find our method to outperform an exhaustive search baseline by more than an order of magnitude. We find that the a compressed index provides a balance of fast search and less disk space, but uncompressed indexes are faster with large B-tree page sizes.

In the future, we would like to explore the properties of forests that influence their search time. We would also like to perform more experiments with depth limitation to ascertain if a depth limit improves performance.

Acknowledgements

We thank Dr. Liang Huang from ISI, USA and Dr. Haitao Mi from ICT, China, for their feedback and technical discussions during this research. We also thank Google for their travel scholarship awarded to the first author.

References

Giorgio Gallo, Giustino Longo, Stefano Pallottino, and Sang Nguyen. 1993. Directed hypergraphs and applications. *Discrete Applied Mathematics*, 42:177–201, April.

NIST Multimodal Information Group. 2010a. NIST 2006 Open Machine Translation (OpenMT) Evaluation, Linguistic Data Consortium, Philadelphia.

NIST Multimodal Information Group. 2010b. NIST 2008 Open Machine Translation (OpenMT) Evaluation, Linguistic Data Consortium, Philadelphia.

Liang Huang and Haitao Mi. 2010. Efficient incremental decoding for tree-to-string translation. In *Proceedings of the 2010 Conference on Empirical Methods in Natural Language Processing*, EMNLP '10, pages 273–283, Stroudsburg, PA, USA. Association for Computational Linguistics.

Liang Huang, Kevin Knight, and Aravind Joshi. 2006. A syntax-directed translator with extended domain of locality. In *Proceedings of the Workshop on Computationally Hard Problems and Joint Inference in Speech and Language Processing*, CHSLP '06, pages 1–8, Stroudsburg, PA, USA. Association for Computational Linguistics.

Jesper Jansson, Kunihiko Sadakane, and Wing-Kin Sung. 2007. Ultra-succinct representation of ordered trees. In *Proceedings of the eighteenth annual ACM-SIAM symposium on Discrete algorithms*, SODA '07, pages 575–584, Philadelphia, PA, USA. Society for Industrial and Applied Mathematics.

Dan Klein and Christopher D. Manning. 2001. Parsing and hypergraphs. In *Seventh International Workshop on Parsing Technologies (IWPT- 2001)*, pages 123–134, Beijing, China, October.

Philipp Koehn. 2004. Pharaoh: a beam search decoder for phrase-based statistical machine translation models. In *Proceedings of the Sixth Conference of the Association for Machine Translation in the Americas*, pages 115–124.

Yang Liu, Qun Liu, and Shouxun Lin. 2006. Tree-to-string alignment template for statistical machine translation. In *Proceedings of the 21st International Conference on Computational Linguistics and the 44th annual meeting of the Association for Computational Linguistics*, ACL-44, pages 609–616, Stroudsburg, PA, USA. Association for Computational Linguistics.

Haitao Mi and Liang Huang. 2008. Forest-based translation rule extraction. In *Proceedings of the Conference on Empirical Methods in Natural Language Processing*, EMNLP '08, pages 206–214, Stroudsburg, PA, USA. Association for Computational Linguistics.

Haitao Mi, Liang Huang, and Qun Liu. 2008. Forest-based translation. In *Proceedings of ACL-08: HLT*, pages 192–199, Columbus, Ohio, USA, June. Association for Computational Linguistics.

Michael A. Olson, Keith Bostic, and Margo Seltzer. 1999. Berkeley DB. In *Proceedings of the annual conference on USENIX Annual Technical Conference*, pages 43–43, Berkeley, CA, USA. USENIX Association.

Bayesian Subtree Alignment Model based on Dependency Trees

Toshiaki Nakazawa **Sadao Kurohashi**
Graduate School of Informatics, Kyoto University
Yoshida-honmachi, Sakyo-ku
Kyoto, 606-8501, Japan
nakazawa@nlp.kuee.kyoto-u.ac.jp kuro@i.kyoto-u.ac.jp

Abstract

Word sequential alignment models work well for similar language pairs, but they are quite inadequate for distant language pairs. It is difficult to align words or phrases of distant languages with high accuracy without structural information of the sentences. In this paper, we pro- pose a Bayesian subtree alignment model that incorporates dependency relations be- tween subtrees in dependency tree struc- tures on both sides. The dependency re- lation model is a kind of tree-based re- ordering model, and can handle non-local reorderings, which sequential word-based models often cannot handle properly. The model is also capable of handling multi-level structures, making it possible to find many-to-many correspondences automatically without any heuristic rules. The size of the structures is controlled by non-parametric Bayesian priors. Experimental alignment results show that our model achieves 3.5 points better alignment error rate for English-Japanese than the word sequential alignment model, thereby verifying that the use of dependency information is effective for structurally different language pairs.

1 Introduction

Alignment accuracy is crucial for providing high quality corpus-based machine translation systems because translation knowledge is acquired from an aligned training corpus. For similar language pairs, alignment accuracy is high, and the state-of-the-art word alignment tool GIZA++ has a smaller than 10% alignment error rate (AER) for French-English. GIZA++ is an implementation of the alignment models called the IBM models (Brown et al., 1993), which handle sentences as sequences of words, usually followed by some heuristic symmetrization rules to combine the alignment results in both directions. Since the accuracy is to some extent good for some language pairs, many researchers focus not on alignment, but on translation with more linguistic information incorporated in the models. Phrase-based SMT (Koehn et al., 2003) uses units larger than words, whereas Hiero (Chiang, 2005) used a kind of sentence structure. Various other studies tried incorporating additional linguistic knowledge such as syntactic trees (Chiang, 2010), dependency trees (Menezes and Quirk, 2008), or packed-forests (Tu et al., 2010) in their translation models. Note that all these works are based on the word sequential alignment models.

However, for distant language pairs such as English-Japanese or Chinese-Japanese, the word sequential model is quite inadequate (about 20 to 30 % AER), and therefore it is important to improve the alignment accuracy itself. The differences between languages can be seen in Figure 1, which shows an example of English-Japanese. The word or phrase order is quite different for these languages. Another important point is that there are often many-to-one or many-to-many correspondences. For example, the Japanese noun phrase "受 光 素子" is composed of three words, whereas the corresponding English phrase consists of only one word "photodetector", and the English function word "for" corresponds to two Japanese function words "に は". In addition, there are basically no counterparts for the English articles (a, an, the). Figure 2 shows the alignment results from bi-directional GIZA++ together with a combination heuristic called grow-diag-final-and[1] for the same sentence pair given in Figure 1. The system failed to align some words in the Japanese noun

[1]This is trained on the same corpus used in Section 4.

phrase, and incorrectly aligned "the ↔ は ". The word sequential model is prone to many such errors even for short simple sentences of a distant language pair.

Even if the word order differs greatly between languages, phrase dependencies tend to hold between languages. This is also true in Figure 1. Therefore, incorporating dependency analysis into the alignment model is useful for distant language pairs. Cherry and Lin (2003) proposed a model that uses a source side dependency tree structure and constructs a discriminative model. However, the drawback is that the alignment unit is the word, and thus, it can only find one-to-one alignments. The capability of generating many-to-many correspondences is also important because one or more words often correspond to more than one word on the other side.

Nakazawa and Kurohashi (2009) also proposed a model focusing on dependency relations. They modeled phrase dependency relations in dependency trees on both sides. The model is also capable of estimating many-to-many correspondences automatically without any heuristics through maximum likelihood estimation. One serious drawback of their model is that it tends to acquire incorrect larger subtrees. For models that can handle multiple levels (or sizes) of structures, larger structures always defeat smaller ones in maximum likelihood estimation, and the best solution is to align one sentence as a structure with the other for all sentence pairs. Although Denero et al. (2008) solved this degeneracy by placing a Dirichlet process prior over the parameters that can control the size of phrases properly, their Bayesian model again only handles sentences as sequences of words. In this paper, we take advantage of the two studies by Nakazawa et al. and Denero et al., and propose a Bayesian subtree alignment model based on dependency trees to improve alignment accuracy for distant language pairs.

2 Dependency Tree-based Alignment Model

Our model is an extension of the one proposed by Denero et al. (2008). Two main drawbacks of the previous model are the lack of structural information and a naive distortion model. For similar language pairs such as French-English (Marcu and Wong, 2002) or Spanish-English (DeNero et al., 2008), even a simple model that handles sentences as a sequence of words works adequately. This does not hold for distant language pairs such as English-Japanese or Chinese-Japanese, in which word orders differ greatly. We incorporate dependency relations of words into the alignment model and define the reorderings on the word dependency trees. Figure 1 shows an example of the dependency trees for Japanese and English.

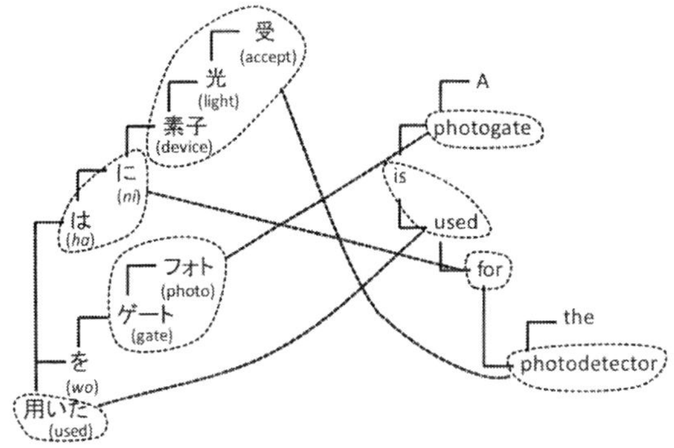

Figure 1: Example of dependency trees and alignment of subtrees. The root of the tree is placed at the extreme left and words are placed from top to bottom.

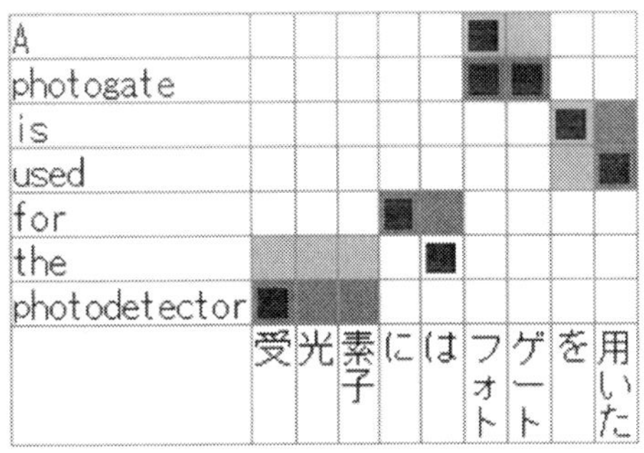

Figure 2: Alignment results from bi-directional GIZA++. Black boxes depict the system output, while dark (Sure) and light (Possible) gray cells denote gold-standard alignments.

2.1 Generative Story Description

Similar to the previous works (Marcu and Wong, 2002; DeNero et al., 2008), we first describe the generative story for the joint alignment model.

1. Generate ℓ concepts from which subtree pairs are generated independently.

2. Combine the subtrees in each language so as to create parallel sentences.

Here, subtrees are equivalent to phrases in the previous works. One subtree in a concept can be NULL, which represents an unaligned subtree. We restrict the unaligned subtrees to be composed of exactly one word, because of our model simplicity (NULL-alignment restriction).

The number of concepts ℓ is parameterized using a geometric distribution:

$$P(\ell) = p_c \cdot (1 - p_c)^{\ell - 1}. \quad (1)$$

Each concept c_i generates a subtree pair $\langle e_i, f_i \rangle$ from an unknown distribution θ_T, and then they are combined in each language. We denote the combinations of subtrees in English as $D_E = \{(j \rightarrow k)\}$, where $(j \rightarrow k)$ denotes that subtree e_j depends on subtree e_k, and in the foreign language as D_F. D refers to D_E and D_F as a whole.

With these notations, the joint probability for a sentence pair is defined as:

$$P(\{\langle e, f \rangle\}, D) = P(\ell) \cdot P(D|\{\langle e, f \rangle\}) \cdot \prod_{\langle e, f \rangle} \theta_T(\langle e, f \rangle). \quad (2)$$

2.2 Subtree Generation

When generating subtrees, we first decide whether to generate an unaligned subtree (with probability p_ϕ) or an aligned subtree pair (with probability $1 - p_\phi$). DeNero et al. (2008) used $p_\phi = 10^{-10}$ to strongly discourage NULL alignment, but this is not reasonable for some language pairs. Taking Japanese and English as an example, English determiners (a, an, the) and Japanese case markers (*ha*, *ga*, *wo*, etc.) rarely have counterparts. In addition, if the corpus is less clean and sentence pairs often contain a different amount of information, the strict restriction may lead to alignment errors. Therefore, we use $p_\phi = 0.33$.

Aligned subtree pairs are generated from an unknown probability distribution θ_A, which obeys the Dirichlet process (DP):

$$\theta_A(\langle e, f \rangle) \sim DP(M_A, \alpha_A), \quad (3)$$

where M_A is the base distribution and α_A is a concentration parameter. The base distribution is defined as:

$$\begin{aligned} M_A(\langle e, f \rangle) &= [P_f(f) P_{WA}(e|f) \cdot P_e(e) P_{WA}(f|e)]^{\frac{1}{2}} \\ P_f(f) &= p_t \cdot (1 - p_t)^{|f|-1} \cdot \left(\frac{1}{n_f}\right)^{|f|} \\ P_e(e) &= p_t \cdot (1 - p_t)^{|e|-1} \cdot \left(\frac{1}{n_e}\right)^{|e|}, \end{aligned} \quad (4)$$

where P_{WA} is the IBM model1 likelihood (Brown et al., 1993), and n_f and n_e are the numbers of word types in each language. θ_A gives a non-zero weight to aligned subtree pairs only.

Unaligned subtrees are generated from another unknown probability distribution θ_N:

$$\begin{aligned} \theta_N(\langle e, f \rangle) &\sim DP(M_N, \alpha_N) \\ M_N(\langle e, f \rangle) &= \begin{cases} P_{WA}(e|\text{NULL}) & \text{if } f = \text{NULL} \\ P_{WA}(f|\text{NULL}) & \text{if } e = \text{NULL} \end{cases}. \end{aligned} \quad (5)$$

θ_N gives a non-zero weight to unaligned subtrees only. Note that unaligned subtrees are always composed of only one word in our model. Finally, θ_T can be decomposed as:

$$\theta_T(\langle e, f \rangle) = p_\phi \theta_N(\langle e, f \rangle) + (1 - p_\phi)\theta_A(\langle e, f \rangle). \quad (6)$$

2.3 Dependency Relation Probability

Instead of the naive reordering model in the previous work, our model considers dependency relations between subtrees and assigns a weight to each relation. Suppose subtree f_j depends on subtree f_k (parent subtree), which means $(j \rightarrow k) \in D_F$, and both f_j and f_k are aligned subtrees. Their counterparts, e_j and e_k respectively, are somewhere on the dependency tree of the other side. We can assume that e_j tends to depend on e_k because the dependencies between concepts hold across languages. The dependency relation probability reflects this tendency.

Formally, we extract a tuple $(N(f_j), rel(f_j, f_{j'}))$ for subtree f_j, and assign the dependency relation probability to that tuple. For unaligned subtrees, the dependency relation probability is not taken into consideration. If the parent subtree is an unaligned subtree, we ascend the dependency tree to the root node until an aligned subtree is found. We call the nearest aligned subtree a *pseudo parent*. The pseudo parent for subtree f_j is denoted as $f_{j'}$, and the number of unaligned subtrees from f_j to $f_{j'}$ is denoted as $N(f_j)$. We consider an imaginary root node as a pseudo parent for the root subtree. For example, the parent subtree of "フォト ゲート (photogate)" is "を (accusative)" which is unaligned in Figure 1. The pseudo parent is "用いた (used)" and the number of unaligned subtrees $N = 1$. Japanese function words are often unaligned, similar to this example, but the dependency relations between subtrees stepping over the function words are assumed to hold on the other side. Therefore we introduce a pseudo parent to capture the relations.

Function $rel(f_j, f_{j'}))$ returns a dependency relation between the counterparts of the two arguments. Note that the counterparts of f_j and $f_{j'}$ are e_j and $e_{j'}$, respectively. We express a dependency relation as the shortest path from one subtree to another. For simplicity, we indicate the path with a pair of non-negative integers, where the first is the number of steps going up (Up) the dependency tree and the other is the number going down ($Down$). It also requires one additional step for going through unaligned subtrees. For example, in Figure 1, traveling from "A photogate" to "photodetector" requires 1 step going up (to reach "is used") and 2 steps going down (via "for"), so the dependency relation is $(Up, Down) = (1, 2)$. Consequently, the tuple is represented as a triplet of non-negative integers $R_f = (N, Up, Down)$.

The dependency relation probabilities for the foreign language side are drawn from an unknown probability distribution θ_{fe} and for the English side from θ_{ef}, with both obeying the DP:

$$\begin{array}{rcl} \theta_{fe}(R_f) & \sim & DP(M_{fe}, \alpha_{fe}) \\ M_{fe}(R_f) & = & p_{fe} \cdot (1 - p_{fe})^{N+Up+Down-1} \\ \theta_{ef}(R_e) & \sim & DP(M_{ef}, \alpha_{ef}) \\ M_{ef}(R_e) & = & p_{ef} \cdot (1 - p_{ef})^{N+Up+Down-1}. \end{array} \quad (7)$$

Using the notations and definitions above, the dependency tree-based reordering model $P(D|\{\langle e, f\rangle\})$ is decomposed as:

$$P(D|\{\langle e, f\rangle\}) = \prod_{\langle e,f\rangle} \theta_{fe}(R_f) \cdot \theta_{ef}(R_e). \quad (8)$$

3 Model Training

We train the model by means of a collapsed Gibbs sampling, which has been used in some recent NLP works (DeNero et al., 2008). In a Gibbs sampling, we first need to initialize the states of the training data, such as the boundaries between subtrees and their alignments, and also initialize the latent variables according to the initial states of the data. Starting with the initial state, we generate many samples in order from the last state by changing a small local point. Normalizing the counts in the samples yields the parameter estimations.

3.1 Initialization

We initialize the states of the training data by heuristically merging bi-directional alignment results of the standard word alignment tool GIZA++. Many machine translation studies use heuristics to combine the two alignment results, one of which is called grow-diag-final-and (Koehn et al., 2007). Our heuristic is similar to this, but the difference is that we combine the two results based on dependency trees, and not on word sequences. The initialization is carried out by the following steps:

1. Take the intersection of the two results.

2. Add alignment points connected to at least one accepted point in terms of the dependency tree (corresponds to grow-diag).

3. Add alignment points between two unaligned words (corresponds to final-and).

Initial boundaries of subtrees and their alignments, and also the counts of subtree pairs and dependency relations are thus acquired.

3.2 Sampling Operators

Our sampler uses three operators repeatedly to generate samples. The operators are illustrated in Figure 3. A solid circle represents a single word, while a subtree is depicted as the part surrounded by a dotted line. Alignment links between subtrees are represented by broken lines.

Each application of an operator generates one new sample, and of course we could use all the generated samples. However, successive samples are almost the same, except for one local part. It is no use keeping all the samples, so we keep only one sample, which is the final outcome after applying all the operators to all the possible points in all the sentence pairs in the training corpus.

SWAP

The SWAP operator exchanges the counterparts of two subtrees with each other. Boundaries between subtrees and the number of aligned subtrees in the sentence pair are fixed. There are two cases for SWAP:

1. Both of the subtrees are aligned (SWAP-1).

2. One of the two subtrees is unaligned and the other is composed of only one word (SWAP-2).

An illustration of the result of the SWAP operator is shown at the top of Figure 3.

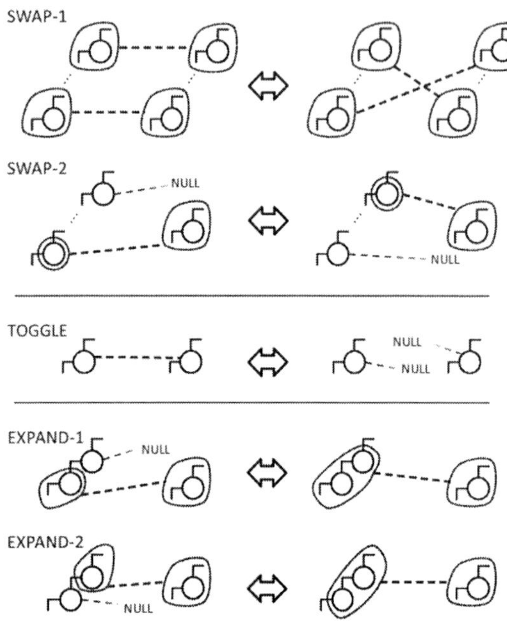

Figure 3: Illustration of the operators.

TOGGLE

The TOGGLE operator adds or removes an alignment. If f_j and e_k are both unaligned subtrees, TOGGLE links these two subtrees. Alternatively, if f_j and e_j are aligned, TOGGLE cuts the link and makes each of the subtrees unaligned. Because of the NULL-alignment restriction, TOGGLE does nothing if f_j or e_j is composed of more than one word. Boundaries between subtrees are fixed. An illustration of the TOGGLE operation is shown in the middle of Figure 3.

EXPAND

The EXPAND operator expands or contracts an aligned subtree. If an unaligned subtree is next to an aligned one, EXPAND tries to merge the unaligned and aligned subtrees. It also tries to exclude a marginal node from a subtree, and to make the excluded node unaligned. There are two cases for EXPAND:

1. A node is added to a subtree as a new leaf node, or a leaf node of a subtree is excluded (EXPAND-1).

2. A node is added to a subtree as the new root node, or the root node of a subtree is excluded (EXPAND-2).

EXPAND-1 does not have any restrictions on its operation. However, for EXPAND-2, if the root node has more than one child node inside the subtree, it cannot exclude the root node, because the subtree will be divided into two subtrees by the exclusion, and it is impossible to return to the previous state. Operators in a Gibbs sampler must be able to return the same status by immediately reapplying the same operator to the same point. An illustration of the EXPAND operation is shown in Figure 3.

3.3 Computational Complexity and Parallel Sampling

The distortion model of the previous work does not consider any relations to neighboring phrases, so any operation does not affect the distortions of neighboring phrases. On the contrary, our proposed model considers the relations, and this leads to an increase in the computational complexity for one operation. For example, swapping two aligned subtree pairs requires re-calculation of the dependency relation probabilities for not only the four focused subtrees, but also subtrees whose pseudo parent is one of the focused subtrees. This is the same for the TOGGLE operation.

To make matters worse, the EXPAND operator requires much more. All the subtrees that traverse the locally changed subtree, 1) in finding a pseudo parent, and 2) in finding the dependency relations, need re-calculation of the dependency relation probabilities, because the number of steps (N, Up and $Down$) will change.

This increase in computational complexity makes the training time much longer, so that it is impossible to train using a single CPU. To alleviate this problem somewhat, we divide the training data into several parts and execute sampling in parallel. The overall flow of model training is summarized as follows:

1. Initialize the training corpus and current counts of subtree pairs and dependency relations, and divide the corpus into several sections.

2. Start sampling in parallel using the same current counts, and generate one sample from each section. A sample is the final state of the section.

3. Gather samples and update the current counts by counting subtree pairs and dependency relations in the samples.

4. Go back to step 2.

4 Alignment Experiments

We conducted alignment experiments on English-Japanese and Chinese-Japanese corpora to show the effectiveness of the proposed model.

4.1 Settings

For English-Japanese, the JST[2] paper abstract corpus was used. This corpus was created by NICT[3] from JST's 2M English-Japanese paper abstract corpus using the method of Utiyama and Isahara (2007). For Chinese-Japanese, we used the paper abstract corpus provided by JST and NICT. This corpus was developed during a project in Japan called the "Development and Research of Chinese-Japanese Natural Language Processing Technology". The statistics of these corpora are shown in Table 4.1. Unfortunately, these two corpora are not freely available now, but they will become available to everyone in near future.

As gold-standard data, we used 479 sentence pairs of English-Japanese and 510 sentence pairs of Chinese-Japanese. These were annotated by hand using two types of annotations: sure (S) alignments and possible (P) alignments (Och and Ney, 2003). The unit of evaluation was the word for all the languages. We used precision, recall, and alignment error rate (AER) as evaluation criteria. All the experiments were run on the original forms of words. The hyper parameters for our model used in the experiments are summarized in Table 4.1.

Japanese sentences were converted into dependency structures using the morphological analyzer JUMAN (Kurohashi et al., 1994), and the dependency analyzer KNP (Kawahara and Kurohashi, 2006). For English sentences, Charniak's nlparser was used to convert them into phrase structures (Charniak and Johnson, 2005), and then they were transformed into dependency structures by rules defining head words for phrases. Chinese sentences were converted into dependency trees using the word segmentation and POS-tagging tool by Canasai et al. (2009) and the dependency analyzer CNP (Chen et al., 2008).

For comparison, we used GIZA++ (Och and Ney, 2003) which implements the prominent sequential word-based statistical alignment model

[2]http://www.jst.go.jp/

[3]http://www.nict.go.jp/

	En-Ja		Zh-Ja	
	En	Ja	Zh	Ja
# of sentences	996K		680K	
# of words	24.7M	27.5M	18.8M	22.3M
ave. sent. length	24.8	27.6	27.7	32.9

Table 1: Statistics of the training corpus.

	α_A	α_N	p_t	α_{fe}, α_{ef}	p_{fe}, p_{ef}
En-Ja	100	100	0.8	100	0.5
Zh-Ja	10	100	0.8	100	0.5

Table 2: Hyper parameters used in experiments.

of the IBM Models. We conducted word alignment bidirectionally with the default parameters and merged them using the grow-diag-final-and heuristic (Koehn et al., 2003). Furthermore, we used the BerkeleyAligner[4] (DeNero and Klein, 2007) with default settings for unsupervised training. Experimental results for English-Japanese are shown in Table 4.1, and those for Chinese-Japanese are shown in Table 4.1. The alignment accuracy of the initialization described in Section 3.1 is indicated as "Initialization", while the accuracy after conducting Gibbs sampling is indicated as "Proposed".

4.2 Discussion

For English-Japanese, our proposed model achieved reasonably high alignment accuracy compared with that of GIZA++ and the BerkeleyAligner. Using tree structures combined with the bi-directional alignment results leads to better accuracy than the original sequential heuristic (indicated as Initialization). We also give the alignment accuracy obtained by Nakazawa and Kurohashi (2009) (indicated as Nakazawa+ in Table 4.1, and applicable only to the English-Japanese corpus)[5]. Their model suffered from a degeneracy in acquiring larger phrases caused by maximum likelihood estimation, and this led to low precision and high recall. Compared with their model, our proposed model overcomes the degeneracy and outperforms in terms of both precision and recall. Figure 4 shows an example of the improvement in alignment. GIZA++ aligned function words incorrectly because of the lack of structural information. For example, GIZA++ aligned the English "of" and the Japanese "の"

[4]http://code.google.com/p/berkeleyaligner/

[5]They used 475 sentence pairs instead of 479 sentence pairs of ours. The difference comes from the inconsistency of word segmentations of Japanese, but it is negligibly small.

	Pre.	Rec.	AER
grow-diag-final-and	81.17	62.19	29.25
BerkeleyAligner	85.00	53.82	33.72
Nakazawa+	80.28	63.85	28.67
Initialization	82.39	61.82	28.99
Proposed	**85.93**	**64.71**	**25.73**

Table 3: Results of English-Japanese alignment experiments.

	Pre.	Rec.	AER
grow-diag-final-and	83.77	75.38	20.39
BerkeleyAligner	**88.43**	69.77	21.60
Initialization	84.71	**75.46**	19.90
Proposed	85.52	74.71	**19.89**

Table 4: Results of Chinese-Japanese alignment experiments.

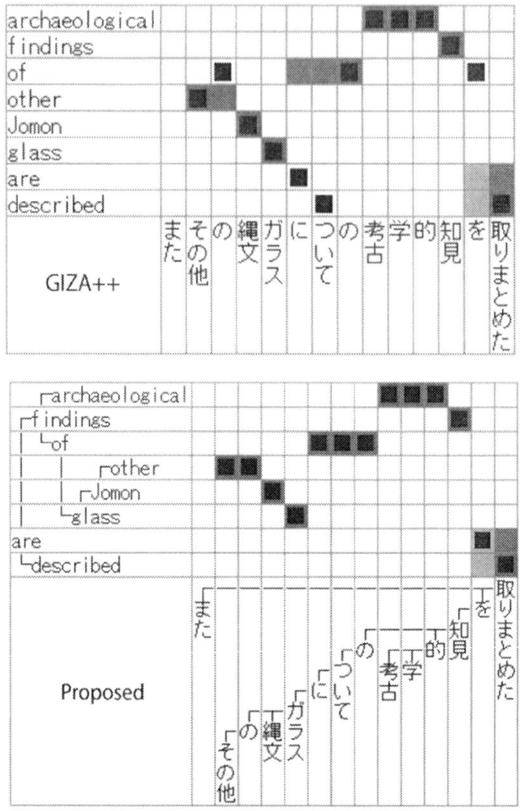

Figure 4: Alignment results from bi-directional GIZA++ (top) and proposed model (bottom).

in the third word. This was incorrectly derived from the combination heuristic: English posterior word "other" and Japanese prior word "その他" are aligned by intersection, and thus, "of ↔ の" is also aligned through the grow-diag heuristic. This could be avoided by introducing dependency trees: the English words "of" and "other" are not contiguous in the dependency tree. In addition, there is no correspondence between "に ついて の ↔ of". This is a rare translation for "of", which is most frequently translated as "の", so GIZA++ aligned "の ↔ of" only. A nonparametric Bayesian model is capable of finding the correct alignment with the support of occurrences of the subtree pair elsewhere in the training corpus.

The reasons for recall being significantly lower than precision in all the models are summarized in the two points. One is the separation between gold-standard criteria and system output. In Figure 4, "are described" and "を 取りまとめた" are aligned in their entirety, but the system found one-to-one alignments, which are also acceptable. The other is that it is sometimes hard to align part of a sentence in a smaller unit for distant language pairs, because the expressions are quite different. In such cases, the system is obliged to align expressions enmasse, which leads to low recall.

For Chinese-Japanese, we failed to improve alignment accuracy greatly. A major cause of this undesirable result could be the accuracy of the Chinese parser. Both the English and Japanese parsers used in the experiments can analyze sentences with over 90% accuracy, whereas the accuracy of the Chinese parser is less than 80% despite it being state-of-the-art in the world (Chen et al., 2008). The parsing accuracy reported in this paper was obtained from an experiment using gold-standard word segmentation and POS-tags. Starting with raw sentences results in about 77.4% accuracy. This information was obtained from communication with the authors. Fundamental NLP technologies in each language must be improved in the long term, and sophisticated models, which use deeper analysis of sentences like our model, should become effective in the near future. One possible short-term solution for the parsing problem is to use the n-best parsing results in the model. Another kind of solution was proposed by Burkett et al. (2010), who described a joint parsing and alignment model that can exchange useful information between the parser and aligner.

However, even in the case of Chinese-Japanese alignment, we achieved higher precision than GIZA++. For translation, precision is more im-

	BLEU
grow-diag-final-and	24.59
Initialization	**25.33**
Proposed	24.50

Table 5: BLEU results for Japanese-to-English translation experiments.

portant than recall. The BerkeleyAligner showed much higher precision than GIZA++ and, in Chinese-Japanese alignment, than our model as well. However, recall was quite low compared with all the other models. Lower recall results in a large translation table because the phrase extraction heuristics 'grow' over each unaligned word.

5 Translation Experiments

We conducted Japanese-to-English translation experiments on the same corpus used in the alignment experiment. We translated 500 paper abstract sentences from the JST corpus. Note that these sentences were not included in the training corpus. We used the state-of-the-art phrase-based SMT toolkit Moses(Koehn et al., 2007) with default options, except for the distortion limit ($6 \rightarrow 20$). It was tuned by MERT using another 500 development sentence pairs.

Table 5 shows the BLEU scores for the translations. Although the difference in alignment accuracy between grow-diag-final-and and Initialization is small, the BLEU score was improved by 0.74 point. This is because syntactic information reduced incorrect alignment points and the quality of translation table becomes better. This result provided evidence that syntactic knowledge is useful for distant language pairs. However, the BLEU score decreased after iterations of our alignment model. The main reason is that the alignment result of our model is not compatible with Phrase-based SMT. Our model often output sequentially discontiguous alignments which are harmful for PSMT to create fine-grained phrase table. We need to use other decoders which is compatible with our alignment model (Nakazawa and Kurohashi, 2010), and we believe that our model leads to better translation quality.

6 Conclusion

In this paper, we proposed a linguistically-motivated nonparametric Bayesian subtree alignment model based on dependency tree structures for distant language pairs. The model incorporates the tree-based reordering model. It also solves the degeneracy of the maximum likelihood estimation for models capable of handling multiple levels of structures by placing a Dirichlet process prior over parameters. Experimental results show that a word sequential model does not work well for distant language pairs, but that this can be addressed by using syntactic information. Our proposed model achieved a lower AER by about 3.5 points compared with GIZA++.

To support allegation that syntactic information is important for distant language pairs, it is necessary to compare our model with the original word sequential study (DeNero et al., 2008), which was consulted often. It is also important to apply our model not only to other distant language pairs, but also to similar language pairs, and to investigate the results. We are planning to use standard data set such as NIST or IWSLT. Also, we could use the n-best parsing results in our model to alleviate the error propagation from parsing, especially for Chinese.

References

Peter F. Brown, Stephen A. Della Pietra, Vincent J. Della Pietra, and Robert L. Mercer. 1993. The mathematics of statistical machine translation: Parameter estimation. *Association for Computational Linguistics*, 19(2):263–312.

David Burkett, John Blitzer, and Dan Klein. 2010. Joint parsing and alignment with weakly synchronized grammars. In *Human Language Technologies: The 2010 Annual Conference of the North American Chapter of the Association for Computational Linguistics*, pages 127–135, Los Angeles, California, June. Association for Computational Linguistics.

Eugene Charniak and Mark Johnson. 2005. Coarse-to-fine n-best parsing and maxent discriminative reranking. In *Proceedings of the 43rd Annual Meeting of the Association for Computational Linguistics (ACL'05)*, pages 173–180.

Wenliang Chen, Daisuke Kawahara, Kiyotaka Uchimoto, Yujie Zhang, and Hitoshi Isahara. 2008. Dependency parsing with short dependency relations in unlabeled data. In *In Proceedings of the 3rd International Joint Conference on Natural Language Processing (IJCNLP-08)*, pages 88–94.

Colin Cherry and Dekang Lin. 2003. A probability model to improve word alignment. In *Proceedings of the 41st Annual Meeting of the Association of Computational Linguistics*, pages 88–95.

David Chiang. 2005. A hierarchical phrase-based model for statistical machine translation. In *Proceedings of the 43rd Annual Meeting of the Association for Computational Linguistics (ACL'05)*, pages 263–270.

David Chiang. 2010. Learning to translate with source and target syntax. In *Proceedings of the 48th Annual Meeting of the Association for Computational Linguistics*, pages 1443–1452, Uppsala, Sweden, July. Association for Computational Linguistics.

John DeNero and Dan Klein. 2007. Tailoring word alignments to syntactic machine translation. In *Proceedings of the 45th Annual Meeting of the Association of Computational Linguistics*, pages 17–24, Prague, Czech Republic, June. Association for Computational Linguistics.

John DeNero, Alexandre Bouchard-Côté, and Dan Klein. 2008. Sampling alignment structure under a Bayesian translation model. In *Proceedings of the 2008 Conference on Empirical Methods in Natural Language Processing*, pages 314–323, Honolulu, Hawaii, October. Association for Computational Linguistics.

Daisuke Kawahara and Sadao Kurohashi. 2006. A fully-lexicalized probabilistic model for japanese syntactic and case structure analysis. In *Proceedings of the Human Language Technology Conference of the NAACL, Main Conference*, pages 176–183, New York City, USA, June. Association for Computational Linguistics.

Philipp Koehn, Franz J. Och, and Daniel Marcu. 2003. Statistical phrase-based translation. In *HLT-NAACL 2003: Main Proceedings*, pages 127–133.

Philipp Koehn, Hieu Hoang, Alexandra Birch, Chris Callison-Burch, Marcello Federico, Nicola Bertoldi, Brooke Cowan, Wade Shen, Christine Moran, Richard Zens, Chris Dyer, Ondrej Bojar, Alexandra Constantin, and Evan Herbst. 2007. Moses: Open source toolkit for statistical machine translation. In *Annual Meeting of the Association for Computational Linguistics (ACL), demonstration session*.

Canasai Kruengkrai, Kiyotaka Uchimoto, Jun'ichi Kazama, Yiou Wang, Kentaro Torisawa, and Hitoshi Isahara. 2009. An error-driven word-character hybrid model for joint chinese word segmentation and pos tagging. In *Proceedings of the Joint Conference of the 47th Annual Meeting of the ACL and the 4th International Joint Conference on Natural Language Processing of the AFNLP*, pages 513–521, Suntec, Singapore, August. Association for Computational Linguistics.

Sadao Kurohashi, Toshihisa Nakamura, Yuji Matsumoto, and Makoto Nagao. 1994. Improvements of Japanese morphological analyzer JUMAN. In *Proceedings of The International Workshop on Sharable Natural Language*, pages 22–28.

Daniel Marcu and Daniel Wong. 2002. A phrase-based,joint probability model for statistical machine translation. In *Proceedings of the 2002 Conference on Empirical Methods in Natural Language Processing*, pages 133–139. Association for Computational Linguistics, July.

Arul Menezes and Chris Quirk. 2008. Syntactic models for structural word insertion and deletion during translation. In *Proceedings of the 2008 Conference on Empirical Methods in Natural Language Processing*, pages 734–743, Honolulu, Hawaii, October. Association for Computational Linguistics.

Toshiaki Nakazawa and Sadao Kurohashi. 2009. Statistical phrase alignment model using dependency relation probability. In *In Proceedings of the third Workshop on Syntax and Structure in Statistical Translation (SSST-3)*, pages 10–18, Boulder, Colorado, June.

Toshiaki Nakazawa and Sadao Kurohashi. 2010. Fully syntactic ebmt system of kyoto team in ntcir-8. In *In Proceedings of the 8th NTCIR Workshop Meeting on Evaluation of Information Access Technologies (NTCIR-8)*, pages 403–410.

Franz Josef Och and Hermann Ney. 2003. A systematic comparison of various statistical alignment models. *Association for Computational Linguistics*, 29(1):19–51.

Zhaopeng Tu, Yang Liu, Young-Sook Hwang, Qun Liu, and Shouxun Lin. 2010. Dependency forest for statistical machine translation. In *Proceedings of the 23rd International Conference on Computational Linguistics (Coling 2010)*, pages 1092–1100, Beijing, China, August. Coling 2010 Organizing Committee.

Masao Utiyama and Hitoshi Isahara. 2007. A japanese-english patent parallel corpus. In *MT summit XI*, pages 475–482.

Enriching SMT Training Data via Paraphrasing

Wei He[1], **Shiqi Zhao**[12], **Haifeng Wang**[2], **Ting Liu**[1]
[1]Research Center for Social Computing and Information Retrieval, Harbin Institute of Technology
{whe,tliu}@ir.hit.edu.cn
[2]Baidu
{zhaoshiqi,wanghaifeng}@baidu.com

Abstract

This paper proposes a novel method to resolve the coverage problem of SMT system. The method generates paraphrases for source-side sentences of the bilingual parallel data, which are then paired with the target-side sentences to generate new parallel data. Within a statistical paraphrase generation framework, we employ an object function, named Sentence Novelty, to select paraphrases which having the most novel information to the bilingual training corpus of the SMT model. Meanwhile, the context is considered via a language model in the source language to ensure the fluency and accuracy of paraphrase substitution. Compared to a state-of-the-art phrase based SMT system (Moses), our method achieves an improvement of 1.66 points in terms of BLEU on a small training corpus which simulates a resource-poor environment, and 1.06 points on a training corpus of medium size.

1 Introduction

Current statistical machine translation (SMT) systems learn how to translate by analyzing bilingual parallel corpora. Generally speaking, high-quality translations can be produced when ample training data is available. Previous studies have indicated that the translation quality can be improved by 2 points of BLEU (Papineni et al., 2002) when the size of the parallel data is doubled (Koehn et al., 2003). However, for the so called *low density* language pairs that do not have large-scale parallel corpora, limited amount of training data usually leads to a problem of low coverage in that many phrases encountered at run-time have not been observed in the training data. According to Callison-Burch et al. (2006), for a training corpus containing 10,000 words, translations will have been learned for only 10% of the unigrams in the test set. For a training corpus containing 100,000 words this increases to 30%. This problem becomes more serious for higher-order n-grams, and for morphologically richer languages.

To overcome the coverage problem of SMT, besides the efforts of mining larger parallel corpora from various resources, some researchers have investigated to use paraphrasing approaches. The studies can be classified into two categories by the target of paraphrasing: (1) paraphrasing the input source sentences; (2) paraphrasing the training corpus. In the first category, the proposed approaches mainly focus on handling n-grams that are unknown to the SMT model. Callison-Burch et al. (2006) and Marton et al. (2009) paraphrase unknown terms in the input sentences using phrasal paraphrases extracted from bilingual and monolingual corpora. Mirkin et al. (2009) rewrite unknown terms with entailments and paraphrases acquired from WordNet. Onishi et al. (2010) and Du et al. (2010) build paraphrase lattices for input sentences and select the best translations using a lattice-based SMT decoder. In the second category of paraphrasing training corpus, Bond et al. (2008) and Nakov (2008) paraphrase the source side of training corpus using hand-crafted rules.

In this paper, we propose a method that enriches SMT training data using a statistical paraphrase generating (SPG) model. The method generates paraphrases for the source-side sen-

This work was partially done when the first author was visiting Baidu.

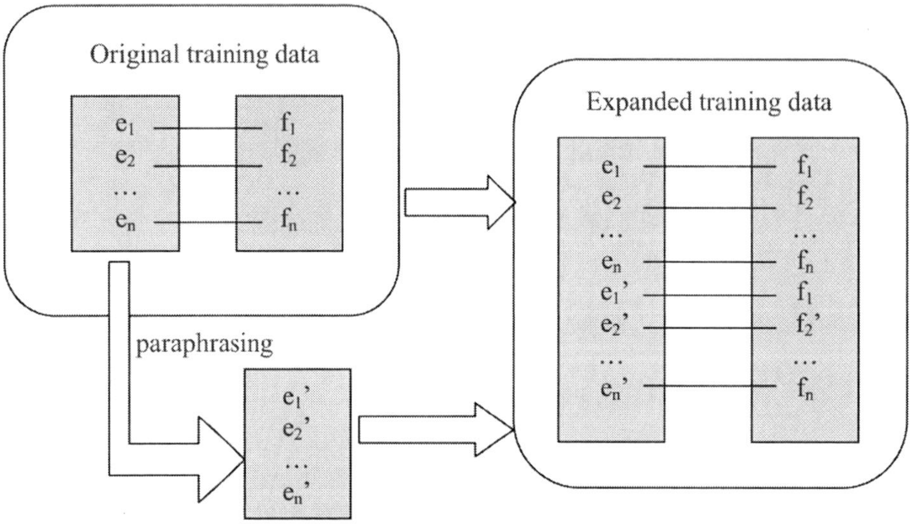

Figure 1. Sketch map of the paraphrasing based translation corpus expansion.

tences of the bilingual parallel data, which are then paired with the target-side sentences to generate new parallel data. The procedure is illustrated in Figure 1. The SPG framework can be considered as an application-specific source-to-source translating procedure (Zhao et al. 2009) which is similar to phrase based statistical machine translation. We employ an object function, named *Sentence Novelty*, to select paraphrases that introduce the most novel information to the bilingual training corpus. In our approach, the context of paraphrasing substitution is considered during generating paraphrasing sentences, which yields paraphrases with higher precision. Experimental results show that the performance of a state-of-the-art phrase based SMT system (Moses in this work) can be improved from 17.91 to 19.57 in terms of BLEU on a small training set, and from 25.46 to 26.52 on a training corpus of medium size. Results also indicate that our method gains a significant improvement over the method of Callison-Burch et al. (2006).

The rest of this paper is structured as follows. We review related work on improving SMT through paraphrasing in Section 2. The proposed statistical paraphrase generation model is described in Section 3. Section 4 presents our method of enlarging training data via paraphrasing. Section 5 and 6 present the experiments and results. We discuss our work in Section 7 and conclude the paper in Section 8.

2 Related Work

Previous studies on improving SMT through paraphrasing input sentences mainly focus on finding translations for unknown terms using phrasal paraphrases. In these methods, an unknown term can be paraphrased to a known term which has translations in the phrase table. Callison-Burch et al. (2006) acquire phrasal paraphrases from bilingual parallel corpora based on a pivot approach. The main idea is that phrases aligned with the same foreign phrase in a bilingual corpus may be paraphrases. The learned paraphrases are applied in a SMT system in the following manner. Suppose e_1 is an unknown source phrase, e_2 is a paraphrase of e_1, which can be translated as f in the phrase table, the method simply takes f as e_1's translation. A new phrase pair (e_1, f) is added to the phrase table with an additional feature $h(f, e_1)$ to distinguish the original phrase pairs and the newly generated ones, which is defined as:

$$h(f, e_1) = \begin{cases} p(e_2 \mid e_1) & \text{If phrase table entry } (f, e_1) \text{ is generated from } (f, e_2) \\ 1 & \text{Otherwise} \end{cases}$$

where $p(e_2 \mid e_1)$ denotes the paraphrase probability.

Marton et al. (2009) propose a method similar to that of Callison-Burch et al. (2006). The only difference is that the paraphrases are extracted from monolingual corpora based on distributional hypothesis. Compared with bilingual corpora, it is easier to acquire monolingual corpora, especially for resource-poor languages.

Mirkin et al. (2009) utilize paraphrases and entailment rules, namely the synonyms and hyponyms from WordNet, to substitute unknown terms in source sentences. Some context models are also used for ranking and filtering the paraphrases and entailments before feeding them to the SMT engine.

Onishi et al. (2010) and Du et al. (2010) build paraphrase lattices for the input sentences. In this scenario, paraphrases are in fact competing with each other. All possible paraphrases are kept and finally selected by the SMT decoder.

Experimental results in these works have proved that the methods that paraphrase input sentences indeed improve SMT results by increasing coverage, especially on small training sets. However, the approaches have two problems. The first one is efficiency. All of the methods that improve SMT through paraphrasing input sentences can be considered as a two-stage procedure, i.e., collecting paraphrases for unknown terms and then translating. Obviously, low efficiency is the bottleneck for this kind of method, since it goes through decoding twice, one for paraphrasing and one for translating. The other problem is that the context is not considered during phrasal paraphrase substitution, which causes a low paraphrasing accuracy. Notice that many paraphrase substitutions are acceptable only in specific contexts. For example, *bank* and *shore* are paraphrases, but we can only substitute *bank* with *shore* in a context related to rivers. Without considering the paraphrase's context, the paraphrasing substitution has a relatively low accuracy, which limits the effect of these methods. The only exception is the work of Mirkin et al. (2009), which uses context models for ranking paraphrases. However, the generated paraphrases without paraphrasing probabilities are difficult to be incorporated with a statistical context model. As described in Mirkin et al. (2009), the main contribution of context models was to reduce the number of paraphrase candidates and improve the efficiency of the system. In contrast, in our method, all the work that enriches SMT with paraphrases is conducted in the training step, which avoids affecting the decoding procedure. Meanwhile, the context of paraphrase substitution is considered using a source language model in our method.

Other researches directly enlarge SMT training corpora based on paraphrase techniques. Nakov (2008) employs six rules for paraphrasing the training corpus. Here we list two rules as examples:

1. $[_{NP}$ **NP$_1$** ***of*** **NP$_2$**$]$ → $[_{NP}$ **NP$_2$ gen NP$_1$**$]$
the lifting of the beef import ban → the beef import ban's lifting
2. **NP$_{gen}$ → NP**
Commissioner's statement→Commissioner statement

where: gen is a genitive marker: ' or 's; NP_{gen} is an NP with an internal genitive marker.

Bond et al. (2008) use grammars to paraphrase the source side of training data, covering aspects like word order and minor lexical variations (tenses etc.) but not content words. The paraphrases are added to the source side of the corpus and the corresponding target sentences are duplicated.

The above-mentioned methods that expand training data via paraphrasing have two disadvantages: (1) hand-crafted paraphrasing rules are language-dependent; (2) to ensure the paraphrase accuracy, only some simple paraphrase rules are used. Our work should be classified into this category. But a clear difference is that our paraphrase generation method is a statistical one without any language specific feature, which (1) utilizes paraphrase resources extracted from large-scale corpora; (2) balances the accuracy and variation rate of paraphrases with a decoding algorithm that searches for the optimal path among all the paraphrasing candidates.

3 Paraphrase Generation

3.1 Paraphrasing Framework

We employ an application-driven statistical paraphrase generation framework which is proposed by Zhao et al. (2009). The framework is based on a log-linear model in which three submodels are defined, namely, a paraphrase model, a language model and a usability model, which control the adequacy, fluency and usability of the paraphrases, respectively.

Paraphrase generation is a decoding process similar to SMT. The input sentence S is first segmented into a sequence of I units $\bar{s}_1^I$, which are then paraphrased to a sequence of units $\bar{t}_1^I$. Let $(\bar{s}_i, \bar{t}_i)$ be a pair of paraphrase units, their paraphrase likelihood is computed using a score function $\varphi_{pm}(\bar{s}_i, \bar{t}_i)$. Thus the paraphrase score $p_{pm}(\bar{s}_1^I, \bar{t}_1^I)$ between S and T is decomposed into:

$$p_{pm}(\bar{s}_1^I, \bar{t}_1^I) = \prod_{i=1}^{I} \varphi_{pm}(\bar{s}_i, \bar{t}_i)^{\lambda_{pm}}$$

where λ_{pm} is the weight of the paraphrase model.

A four-gram language model is employed to ensure the fluency and eliminate the ambiguity of paraphrase. The language model based score for the paraphrase T is computed as:

$$p_{lm}(T) = \prod_{j=1}^{J} p(t_j \mid t_{j-3} t_{j-2} t_{j-1})^{\lambda_{lm}}$$

where J is the length of T, t_j is the j-th word of T, and λ_{lm} is the weight for the language model.

The usability model prefers paraphrase units that are more suitable for the application. The usability of T depends on paraphrase units it contains. We propose a specific usability model to enrich SMT training corpus, which is described in chapter 3.2.

3.2 Sentence Novelty Model

In this paper, we do not limit our method to handling unknown terms. Instead, our goal is to grub knowledge from paraphrases and enrich the translation corpora. Therefore, within the application-driven paraphrase generation framework, we propose a specific paraphrasing usability model, *sentence novelty*, for selecting paraphrases which contain the most novel n-grams to the translation model. Given a paraphrased sentence T, which consists of J words, the novelty function $Novel(TM,T,n,j)$ judges whether the occurrence of t_j generates a new n-gram to the translation model (TM) according to the prior n-1 words of t_j. Formally, the novel function for position j can be defined as:

$$Novel(TM,T,n,j)\begin{cases} 1 & \text{If } t_{j-n+1}\ldots t_j \text{ is a new n-gram to } TM \\ 0 & \text{otherwise} \end{cases}$$

Thus the novelty model for a paraphrased sentence T, considering the novelty of 1-gram to N-gram (N=4 in this work), is computed as:

$$p_{nm}(t) = \exp\left(\sum_{j=1}^{J}\sum_{n=1}^{N} Novel(TM,t,n,j)\right)^{\lambda_{nm}}$$

where λ_{nm} is the weight for the novelty model,

Now we can describe the complete formula of the SPG framework as:

$$p(T \mid S) = \lambda_{pm}\sum_{i=1}^{I}\log\varphi_{pm}(\bar{s}_i,\bar{t}_i) + \lambda_{lm}\sum_{j=1}^{J}\log p(t_j \mid t_{j-3}t_{j-2}t_{j-1}) + \lambda_{nm}\sum_{j=1}^{J}\sum_{n=1}^{N} Novel(TM,T,n,j)$$

4 Expanding SMT Training Corpus

4.1 Corpus Expansion

We enhance the SMT model by expanding the training corpus using paraphrases. Firstly, the sentence-level paraphrases are generated on the source side (English in our experiments) of the training bi-texts. Then the paraphrased sentences and the corresponding translations on the target side (Chinese in this work) which align with the original sentences compose new bilingual sentence pairs.

To grub knowledge from paraphrases as much as possible, we exploit two different strategies for paraphrase generation in the experiments: (1) generating 1-best paraphrase for every source sentence in the training corpus, and (2) generating k-best paraphrases for a source sentence and selecting m sentences from them which have the most novel n-grams. Thus we get two paraphrased bilingual corpora besides the original corpus. Sentence pairs generated by the two strategies are shown in Table 1. From the table, it can be seen that on the source side the 1-best paraphrase sentence has a relatively high quality, while the sentences selected from k-best paraphrase results have lower accuracy but higher coverage. On the target side, the original Chinese sentence is just copied to align with the generated paraphrase sentences.

4.2 Paraphrase Selecting Strategy

As mentioned above, in strategy (2) we selected m paraphrases in the generated top-k results, which have the most different n-grams. The reason of not using all the k-best results for improving SMT is that the top-k paraphrases generated for a sentence are generally very similar, if we train the SMT model on all these sentences, it would be quite time-consuming and much of the computation is vain. Therefore we propose an algorithm to select a subset from all the paraphrase sentences, which can cover most of the newly introduced information while dramatically reduce the numbers of paraphrases. The algorithm is described in Figure 2.

```
procedure SENTENCE_SELECTION
input: m, set S {k-best paraphrase sen-
tences:S1,…,Sk}
todo: select m sentences from set S
  M := {S1}, remove S1 from S
  while (|M| < m)
    MAX_DISTANCE := 0
    i-max := 0
    for Si := each sentences in S
       Ai := AVERAGE_EDIT_DISTANCE(Si,M)
       if Ai > MAX_DISTANCE
         MAX_DISTANCE := Ai
         i-max = i
    M := M ∪ {Si-max}, remove Si-max from S
  return M
```

Figure 2: The algorithm for paraphrase selection.

	Source sentences	Target sentences
original	Solving environmental problems is a big and urgent mission.	解决环境问题已经为刻不容缓的重大任务。
1-best	**The resolution of** environmental problems is a **large** and urgent **task**.	解决环境问题已经为刻不容缓的重大任务。
selected k-best	**The resolution of** environmental problems is a **large** and urgent **task**.	解决环境问题已经为刻不容缓的重大任务。
	The solution to environmental problems is **high** and urgent **task**.	解决环境问题已经为刻不容缓的重大任务。
	The resolution of environmental problems is a **major** urgent and mission.	解决环境问题已经为刻不容缓的重大任务。
	Solving environmental problems **are** a big and urgent **task**.	解决环境问题已经为刻不容缓的重大任务。
	…	…

Table 1: Examples of generated sentence pairs.

At the beginning of the algorithm, the selected sentence set M is empty. In each iteration, we select a sentence $S_{i\text{-}max}$ from the k-best paraphrase sentence set S and add it to M. In the selection of $S_{i\text{-}max}$, we calculate the average Edit Distance (ED) between each candidate sentence S_i and all sentences in M by the function of AVERAGE_EDIT_DISTANCE(S_i,M). The sentence most different (with the largest average ED) from the already selected sentences in M is selected. In the algorithm, the edit distance among the sentences in M has been considered as the optimization objective function, which ensures the sentences with most novel n-grams are selected.

4.3 Model Integrating

After corpus expansion, we get three bilingual corpora for SMT training: (1) the original corpus, (2) corpus of 1-best paraphrases on the source side and original translations on the target side, (3) corpus of selected m paraphrases on the source side and original translations on the target side. Notice that the reliability of the three corpora is in a descending order. The original corpus which is produced by human can be considered as golden standard corpus. The quality of corpus consisting of 1-best paraphrases (*1-PARA* corpus in the following context) is lower than the original corpus. The corpus of m paraphrase sentences which were selected from the k-best paraphrase results by the algorithm described in 4.2 (namely, *M-PARA* corpus) may be the most noisy.

Considering the different reliabilities of these corpora, simply merging them into a new corpus and train a translation model is not the optimal solution. Therefore, within a phrase-based SMT framework, we train three phrase tables from these corpora, and then integrate these phrase tables with different weights. The integration is a procedure of linear interpolation which can be described in the following formula:

$$PT = \sum_{i=1}^{n} \lambda_i PT_i$$

where λ_n is weight of PT_n, which is set up empirically.

We first merge the phrase tables trained from the original corpus and *1-PARA* corpus, and get a new phrase table (Original + *1-PARA*). Then we integrate the Original + *1-PARA* phrase table with the phrase table trained from the *M-PARA* corpus and get another phrase table (Original + *1-PARA + M-PARA)*. The effectiveness of these enriched phrase tables is tested in the experimental section.

5 Experimental Setup

5.1 Paraphrase Resources

The paraphrase generating framework we used is not limited to a certain type of paraphrase resource. Any paraphrase resources with paraphrasing probability can be integrated into the framework. We simply choose phrasal paraphrases acquired from the Europarl corpus using Callison-Burch's paraphrase extracting toolkit[1]. The toolkit supports extraction of both phrasal paraphrases and syntactically constrained paraphrases. In this paper, we only use the phrasal paraphrase extracting part of the toolkit which extracts paraphrases from bilingual corpus using

[1] http://cs.jhu.edu/~ccb/howto-extract-paraphrases.html

pivot method (Colin Bannard and Chris Callison-Burch. 2005).

We extract phrasal paraphrases for all n-grams ($n \leq 6$) in the source sentences in the training data. Some operations are performed on the extracted phrasal paraphrases to ensure the accuracy: (1) paraphrases with score < .03 are filtered out, (2) paraphrases consisting of nothing but stop-words are removed.

5.2 SMT Data

For the baseline system, we trained on the Sinorama and FBIS corpora (LDC2005T10 and LDC2003E14). After tokenization and filtering, this bilingual corpus contained 319,694 lines (7.9M tokens on Chinese side and 9.2M tokens on English side). We trained a 4-gram language model on the Chinese side of the bi-text. Then we randomly selected 29,000 lines form the bi-text, and constructed a reduced training corpus to simulate a resource-poor language. We tested the system using the English-Chinese NIST MT 2008 evaluation set. The test set contains 1859 English sentences, each of which has four human references for automatic evaluation. For development, we used the Chinese-English NIST MT 2005 evaluation set, taking one of the English references as source, and the Chinese source as a single reference translation. All the Chinese sentences in the training corpora were segmented with the word segmentation tool from Language Technology Platform (LTP)[2]. We used two metrics, BLEU[3] and TER[4] (Snover et al., 2005), for automatic evaluation. Following the evaluation standard of NIST, the system translations and references were split into Chinese characters in automatic evaluation.

5.3 Translation Model

We used Moses, a state-of-the-art phrase-based SMT model (Koehn et al., 2007), in decoding. In Moses, the generated translation hypotheses are scored mainly based on a translation model, a language model, and a reordering model. These components are deemed as features and combined within a log-linear framework:

$$e^* = aug \max_{e} \{\sum_{i=1}^{n} \lambda_i h_i(e,f)\}$$

where $h_i(e,f)$ is a feature function with λ_i as the weight. The feature weights can be trained with Minimum Error Rate Training (MERT) (Och, 2003) on the development set using BLEU as the objective function.

[2] http://ir.hit.edu.cn/ltp/

[3] ftp://jaguar.ncsl.nist.gov/mt/resources/mteval-v13a.pl

[4] http://www.umiacs.umd.edu/~snover/terp/

	29k	**Full**
Ori.	324k	3603k
+1-PARA	507k(+56%)	4514k(+25%)
+1-PARA+M-PARA	878k(+171%)	8359k(+132%)

Table 2: Number of phrase pairs in different phrase tables.

Set	**Model**	**BLEU-4**	**TER**
29k	Baseline	17.91	66.83
	CB	18.75	66.68
	Ori.+1-PARA	19.26***	65.98
	Ori.+1-PARA +M-PARA	**19.57*****	**65.88**
Full	Baseline	25.46	62.36
	Callison-Burch	25.76	61.62
	Ori.+1-PARA	**26.52*****	**61.36**
	Ori.+1-PARA +M-PARA	26.33***	61.47

Table 3: Experimental results: "***" means that the method performs significantly better than both the baseline and Callison-Burch with $\rho < 0.01$, using Koehn's (2004) pair-wise bootstrap test for BLEU with 95% confidence interval.

	1gram	2gram	3gram	4gram
Baseline	50.4%	17.9%	3.9%	0.6%
+1-PARA	54.2%	21.5%	5.0%	0.9%
+1-PA.+M-PA.	56.3%	24.7%	6.2%	1.1%
CB	56.8%	26.3%	6.4%	1.5%

Table 4: Coverage rate of phrase tables trained from 29k training set.

6 Results and Analysis

After corpus expansion and model integrating, the size of the original phrase table is increased. The number of phrase pairs in the original PT and the merged PTs which are extracted from 29k and full corpora are shown in Table 2.

As can be seen, the number of phrase pairs is significantly increased after corpus expansion. Specifically, the sizes of the augmented phrase tables are increased by 56% and 171% for the 29k set, 25% and 132% for the full set, which prove that our sentence novelty model has made considerable contributions to the enrichment of phrase tables.

We evaluated the effectiveness of the enriched phrase tables in translation. In order to conduct a direct comparison with the existing techniques, we took Moses trained with the original bi-text

1	Source sentence	cyber experts said the investigations in india will take time
	Baseline result	**网络**版**专家说，在印度将**把**时间调查。**
	Our result	**网络**版**专家说，在 印度的调查需要 时间。**
2	Source sentence	it happens again and again .
	Baseline result	它再**次**与再**次发生。**
	Our result	**发生这** 一次 又一次。
3	Source sentence	people just talk about cars and stuff .
	Baseline result	**人们只谈车和材料。**
	Our result	**人只谈**公园**和材料。**

Table 5: Translation examples on 29k-bitext systems. The n-grams that match the references are highlighted in bold. Here *our result* refers to the system of Original+1-PARA+M-PARA.

as a baseline. We also developed another comparison system by re-implementing the method proposed by Callison-Burch et al. (2006) (CB for short hereafter), which used the same paraphrase resource as described above to paraphrase unknown phrases (up to 6-gram) of the test sentences. The feature weights for the model of Callison-Burch et al. (2006) were trained with MERT on the development set.

The evaluation results are shown in Table 3. We can see that our method outperforms both the baseline and CB models under both evaluation metrics. On the 29k subset, the improved model using only 1-best paraphrases has a significant 1.35 BLEU points gain over its baseline, and the model integrated with both 1-best and m-best paraphrases has a further improvement of 1.66 points. On the full set, the model augmented by 1-best paraphrases achieves the best performance, which gained 1.06 BLEU points over the baseline; the model augmented by 1-best and m-best selected paraphrases got an improvement of 0.87 points. A possible reason is that for small training data, the increment of coverage is more important for improving the translation model; while on a larger training corpus, the accuracy of paraphrases plays a more important role.

Notice that the training set, test set and development set in this work are the same as (Marton et al. 2009), which reported a negative result on the full training set. In contrast, our method outperformed the baseline on both small and full training sets.

We further compared the coverage rate of different models on the test set. The result of 29k training set is shown in Table 4. It can be seen that the coverage of 1-gram, 2-grams, 3-grams and 4-grams on the test set is increased by our Ori.+1-PARA. And the method Ori.+1-PARA+M-PARA has further improved the coverage. It is not surprising that the phrase table of Callison-Burch (CB) has the best coverage on the test set among all the compared models, since their method targets on paraphrasing unknown terms of the test set at run-time. While our method does not target on unknown terms, our goal is enriching the knowledge of SMT system using paraphrases with novel information. Therefore given a specific test set, the unknown terms covered by our method are just a subset of CB's method. However, on such a subset, our method gains significant improvement in translation quality over CB's approach. A possible reason that can explain this is that CB's method only considers the paraphrase probability which controls the adequacy, while in our method, the adequacy, fluency and novelty of the generated paraphrase sentences are well balanced by the SPG framework which can produce paraphrases of better quality.

7 Discussion

We have shown that the SPG framework with an object function of sentence novelty can improve the performance of SMT on both training corpus of small and medium size. Although the experiments are performed on a resource-rich language pair, i.e. English-to-Chinese, the method is portable to other language pairs because our approach is language-independent. No language-specific features are used in the SPG framework. Our proposed method has another advantage of not relying on certain paraphrase resources, and therefore can use any type of training data for paraphrasing. This advantage is important for those resource-poor language pairs.

We further examine the translation results of the baseline and our method. Some examples are shown in Table 5. In row 1 and row 2, the baseline results are improved by our method mainly in the translation of *will take time* and *again and again*. The phrases can only be translated word by word in the baseline model. But in our augmented model, the phrases can match complete translation phrases which are extracted from the paraphrase-expanded training data. The paraphrase quality remains an issue with this method. A negative example is shown in row 3, which is caused by a wrong paraphrase substitution *cars* → *park*.

8 Conclusions and Future Work

This paper proposes a novel method for enriching SMT training data by paraphrasing the source-side sentences of the bilingual parallel data through a statistical paraphrase generation framework. Within the framework, a paraphrase model and a language model in the source language are employed to ensure the accuracy of paraphrase. And a proposed object function, named sentence novelty, is used to select paraphrases which have the most novel information for SMT system. Experimental results demonstrate that our method significantly improves the baseline by 1.66 and 1.06 on small and medium size training corpora in terms of BLEU. We have also proved in experiments that our method significantly outperforms the model proposed by Callison-Burch et al. (2006). In the future work, we will plan to test the effectiveness of our method on a large-scale corpus.

Acknowledgement

This work was supported by National Natural Science Foundation of China (NSFC) via grant 61073126, 61133012, 60803093.

References

Colin Bannard and Chris Callison-Burch. 2005. Paraphrasing with bilingual parallel corpora. In *Proceedings of ACL*.

Francis Bond, Eric Nichols, Darren Scott Appling, and Michael Paul. 2008. Improving Statistical Machine Translation by Paraphrasing the Training Data. In *Proceedings of the IWSLT*, pages 150–157.

Chris Callison-Burch, Philipp Koehn, and Miles Osborne. 2006. Improved Statistical Machine Translation Using Paraphrases. In *Proceedings of NAACL*, pages 17-24.

Jinhua Du, Jie Jiang, Andy Way. 2010. Facilitating Translation Using Source Language Paraphrase Lattices. In *Proceedings of EMNLP*, pages 420-429.

Philipp Koehn, Franz Josef Och, and Daniel Marcu. 2003. Statistical Phrase-Based Translation. In *Proceedings of HLT/NAACL*, pages 48–54

Philipp Koehn. 2004. Statistical significance tests for machine translation evaluation. In *Proceedings of EMNLP*, pages 388-395.

Philipp Koehn, Hieu Hoang, Alexandra Birch, Chris Callison-Burch, Marcello Federico, Nicola Bertoldi, Brooke Cowan, Wade Shen, Christine Moran Richard Zens, Chris Dyer, Ondrej Bojar, Alexandra Constantin, and Evan Herbst. 2007. Moses: Open source toolkit for statistical machine translation. In *Proceedings of the ACL Demo and Poster Sessions*, pages 177–180.

Yuval Marton, Chris Callison-Burch, and Philip Resnik. 2009. Improved Statistical Machine Translation Using Monolingually-Dervied Paraphrases. In *Proceedings of EMNLP*, pages 381-390.

Shachar Mirkin, Lucia Specia, Nicola Cancedda, Ido Dagan, Marc Dymetman, Idan Szpektor. 2009. Source-Language Entailment Modeling for Translation Unknown Terms. In *Proceedings of ACL*, pages 791-799.

Preslav Nakov. 2008. Improved Statistical Machine Translation Using Monolingual Paraphrases. In *Proceedings of ECAI*, pages 338-342.

Fanz Josef Och. 2003. Minimum Error Rate Training in Statistical Machine Translation. In *Proceedings of ACL*, pages 160-167.

Takashi Onishi, Masao Utiyama, Eiichiro Sumita. 2010. Paraphrase Lattice for Statistical Machine Translation. In *Proceedings of ACL*, pages 1-5.

Kishore Papineni, Salim Roukos, Todd Ward, Wei-Jing Zhu. 2002. BLEU: a Method for Automatic Evaluation of Machine Translation. In *Proceedings of ACL*, pages 311-318.

Matthew Snover, Bonnie J. Dorr, Richard Schwartz, John Makhoul, Linnea Micciulla, and Ralph Weischedel. 2005. A study of translation error rate with targeted human annotation. *Technical Report LAMP-TR-126, CS-TR-4755, UMIACS-TR-2005-58*, University of Maryland, July, 2005.

Shiqi Zhao, Xiang Lan, Ting Liu, and Sheng Li. 2009. Application-driven Statistical Paraphrase Generation. *In Proceedings of ACL*, pages 834-842.

Translation Quality Indicators for Pivot-based Statistical MT

Michael Paul and Eiichiro Sumita
National Institute of Information and Communications Technology
MASTAR Project
Kyoto, Japan
michael.paul@nict.go.jp

Abstract

Recent research on multilingual statistical machine translation focuses on the usage of *pivot languages* in order to overcome resource limitations for certain language pairs. This paper provides new insights into what factors make a good pivot language and investigates the impact of these factors on the overall pivot translation performance. Pivot-based SMT experiments translating between 22 Indo-European and Asian languages were used to analyze the impact of eight factors (*language family*, *vocabulary*, *sentence length*, *language perplexity*, *translation model entropy*, *reordering*, *monotonicity*, *engine performance*) on pivot translation performance. The results showed that 81% of system performance variations can be explained by these factors.

1 Introduction

The translation quality of statistical machine translation (SMT) approaches heavily depends on the amount and coverage of bilingual language resources available to train the statistical models. There exist several data collection initiatives[1] amassing and distributing large amounts of textual data. For frequently used language pairs like *French-English*, large text data sets are readily available. However, for less frequently used language pairs only a limited amount of bilingual resources are available, if any at all.

In order to overcome language resource limitations, recent research on SMT focuses on the usage of *pivot languages* (de Gispert and Marino, 2006; Utiyama and Isahara, 2007; Wu and Wang, 2007; Bertoldi et al., 2008). Instead of a direct translation between two languages where only a limited amount of bilingual resources is available, the *pivot translation* approach makes use of a third language that is more appropriate due to the availability of more bilingual corpora and/or its relatedness towards either the source or the target language. For most recent research efforts, *English* is the pivot language of choice due to the richness of available language resources. However, recent research on pivot translation has shown that the usage of non-English pivot languages can improve translation quality for certain language pairs (Paul et al., 2009; Leusch et al., 2010).

Concerning the contribution of aspects of different language pairs on the quality of machine translation, (Birch et al., 2008) identified three features (*morphological complexity*, *amount of reordering*, *historical relatedness*) for predicting success of MT in translations between the official languages of the European Union. Moreover, (Koehn et al., 2009) investigated an additional feature (*translation model complexity*) using the JRC-Aquis corpus covering not only Indo-European languages, but also one semitic and three Finno-Ugric languages.

This paper differs from previous research in the following aspects: we focus on the framework of *pivot translation*, where a target language translation of a source language input is obtained through an intermediate (*pivot*) language, investigate what factors make a good pivot language and what impact these factors have on the overall translation quality of language pairs not only including Indo-Euopean languages, but also a large variety of Asian languages. In Section 2, we report on pivot-based SMT experiments translating between 22 Indo-European as well as Asian languages in order to provide new insights into how much language diversity affects the translation performance of pivot translation approaches. In Section 3, eight factors (*language family*, *vocabulary*, *sentence length*, *language perplexity*,

[1] LDC: http://www.ldc.upenn.edu, ELRA: http://www.elra.info

translation model entropy, reordering, monotonicity, engine performance) are investigated to determine the significance of each factor in predicting translation quality using linear regression analysis.

2 Pivot Translation

Pivot translation is a translation from a source language (SRC) to a target language (TRG) through an intermediate *pivot* (or *bridging*) *language* (PVT). Within the SMT framework, various coupling strategies like *cascading*, *phrase-table composition*, and *pseudo-corpus generation* have been proposed. For the experiments reported in this paper, we utilized the *cascading* approach because it is computational less expensive, but still performs comparably well compared to the other, more sophisticated pivot translation approaches. Pivot translation using the *cascading* approach requires two translation engines where the first engine translates the source language input into the pivot language and the second engine takes the obtained pivot language output as its input and translates it into the target language. Given N languages, a total of $2*N*(N-1)$ SMT engines have to be built in order to cover all $N*(N-1)*(N-2)$ SRC-PVT-TRG language pair combinations.

The importance of translation quality factors in pivot translation are investigated using the multilingual *Basic Travel Expressions Corpus* (BTEC), which is a collection of sentences that bilingual travel experts consider useful for people going to or coming from another country (Kikui et al., 2006). The sentence-aligned corpus consists of 160k sentences pairs covering 22 Indo-European and Asian languages which belong to a variety of language families including *Germanic* (da,de,en,nl), *Romance* (es,fr,it,pt,ptb), *Slavic* (pl,ru), *Indo-Iranian* (hi), *Semitic* (ar), *Austronesian* (id,ms,tl), *Tai* (th), *Mon-khmer* (vi), and *Sinitic* (zh,zht) languages. The corpus statistics are summarized in Table 1, where *Voc* specifies the vocabulary size and *Len* the average sentence length of the respective data sets. These languages differ largely in word order (*Order*: subject-object-verb (*SOV*), subject-verb-object (SVO), verb-subject-object (*VSO*)), segmentation unit (*Unit*: phrase, word, none), and degree of inflection (*Inflection*: high, moderate, light). Very similar characteristics can be seen for *Indo-European* languages and for certain subsets of *Asian languages* (*ja, ko*; *id, ms*). In addition, *Indo-European* languages have, in general, a higher degree of inflection compared to Asian languages. Concerning word segmentation, the corpora were preprocessed using language-specific word-segmentation tools for languages that do not use white-space to separate word/phrase tokens (ja,ko,th,zh,zht). For all other languages, simple tokenization tools were applied. All data sets were case-sensitive with punctuation marks preserved.

Table 1: Language Resources

(European Languages)

Language		Voc	Len	Order	Unit	Inflection
Danish	da	26.5k	7.2	SVO	word	high
German	de	25.7k	7.1	SVO	word	high
English	en	15.4k	7.5	SVO	word	moderate
Spanish	es	20.8k	7.4	SVO	word	high
French	fr	19.3k	7.6	SVO	word	high
Hindi	hi	33.6k	7.8	SOV	word	high
Italian	it	23.8k	6.7	SVO	word	high
Dutch	nl	22.3k	7.2	SVO	word	high
Polish	pl	36.4k	6.5	SVO	word	high
Portuguese	pt	20.8k	7.0	SVO	word	high
Brazilian Portuguese	ptb	20.5k	7.0	SVO	word	high
Russian	ru	36.2k	6.4	SVO	word	high

(Asian Languages)

Language		Voc	Len	Order	Unit	Inflection
Arabic	ar	47.8k	6.4	VSO	word	high
Indonesian	id	18.6k	6.8	SVO	word	high
Japanese	ja	17.2k	8.5	SOV	none	moderate
Korean	ko	17.2k	8.1	SOV	phrase	moderate
Malay	ms	19.3k	6.8	SVO	word	high
Thai	th	7.4k	7.8	SVO	none	light
Tagalog	tl	28.7k	7.4	VSO	word	high
Vietnamese	vi	9.9k	9.0	SVO	phrase	light
Chinese	zh	13.3k	6.8	SVO	none	light
Taiwanese	zht	39.5k	5.9	SVO	none	light

The language resources were randomly split into three subsets for the evaluation of translation quality (*eval*, 1000 sentences), the tuning of the SMT model weights (*dev*, 1000 sentences) and the training of the statistical models (*train*). However, in a real-world application, identical language resources covering three or more languages are not necessarily to be expected. In order to avoid a trilingual scenario for the pivot translation experiments, the *train* corpus was randomly split into two subsets of 80k sentences each, whereby the first set of sentence pairs was used to train the SRC-PVT translation models and the second subset of sentence pairs was used to train the PVT-TRG translation models. In total, 924 SMT translation engines were built to cover all 9,240 language pair combinations.

For the training of the SMT models, standard

Table 3: Oracle Pivot Translation Quality (BLEU)

	TRG → / ↓ SRC	da	de	en	es	fr	hi	it	nl	pl	pt	ptb	ru	ar	id	ja	ko	ms	th	tl	vi	zh	zht
		(European Languages)												(Asian Languages)									
(European Languages)	da	–	53.9 (en)	60.3 (nl)	59.1 (en)	57.6 (en)	45.3 (en)	53.4 (en)	57.6 (en)	49.8 (en)	57.8 (ptb)	57.8 (en)	49.5 (en)	48.8 (en)	52.5 (ms)	37.5 (ko)	36.9 (en)	51.9 (id)	51.6 (en)	47.7 (en)	52.6 (en)	34.2 (en)	39.9 (en)
	de	57.2 (en)	–	61.3 (nl)	59.3 (en)	57.3 (en)	45.6 (en)	53.6 (en)	58.5 (en)	49.7 (en)	59.2 (ptb)	58.3 (pt)	49.1 (en)	47.8 (en)	52.1 (ms)	37.8 (en)	36.8 (en)	51.5 (en)	51.8 (en)	48.3 (en)	52.2 (en)	33.3 (en)	41.1 (en)
	en	59.8 (es)	55.5 (nl)	–	62.7 (pt)	60.7 (es)	45.8 (es)	56.9 (es)	60.1 (es)	49.9 (es)	65.7 (ptb)	65.5 (pt)	50.7 (es)	50.1 (es)	57.2 (ms)	39.4 (ko)	38.0 (ja)	56.8 (id)	51.3 (es)	49.4 (es)	53.6 (es)	33.6 (es)	40.4 (es)
	es	59.0 (en)	54.4 (en)	63.3 (pt)	–	59.4 (en)	45.6 (en)	55.7 (en)	58.6 (en)	51.7 (en)	64.7 (ptb)	64.6 (pt)	50.5 (en)	50.1 (en)	55.3 (ms)	38.5 (ko)	37.7 (en)	54.4 (id)	52.5 (en)	49.6 (en)	54.0 (en)	34.1 (en)	40.4 (en)
	fr	56.4 (en)	50.9 (en)	58.8 (es)	58.2 (en)	–	43.2 (en)	52.4 (en)	54.8 (en)	47.3 (en)	58.7 (ptb)	57.9 (pt)	47.3 (en)	48.2 (en)	52.5 (ms)	37.8 (en)	37.6 (ja)	51.1 (id)	49.5 (en)	46.6 (en)	50.5 (en)	33.4 (es)	39.9 (en)
	hi	50.3 (en)	47.4 (en)	50.5 (ptb)	51.8 (en)	50.8 (en)	–	47.9 (en)	50.2 (en)	44.4 (en)	51.5 (ptb)	51.6 (pt)	44.6 (en)	44.7 (en)	50.3 (ms)	35.7 (ko)	34.6 (en)	50.8 (id)	48.1 (en)	43.6 (en)	48.2 (en)	30.8 (en)	36.9 (en)
	it	56.7 (en)	52.8 (en)	60.6 (pt)	59.5 (en)	58.1 (en)	44.8 (en)	–	55.7 (en)	48.8 (en)	60.5 (ptb)	60.2 (pt)	48.1 (en)	47.1 (en)	52.5 (ms)	38.1 (en)	36.8 (en)	52.1 (id)	50.6 (en)	47.3 (en)	51.6 (en)	32.3 (es)	40.5 (en)
	nl	60.3 (en)	55.8 (en)	60.9 (es)	61.5 (en)	59.6 (en)	46.3 (en)	55.0 (en)	–	51.1 (en)	60.0 (ptb)	59.5 (en)	50.3 (en)	49.7 (en)	52.6 (ms)	37.7 (en)	36.8 (en)	51.9 (en)	52.0 (en)	49.0 (en)	53.3 (en)	33.3 (en)	39.9 (en)
	pl	54.7 (en)	51.1 (en)	56.1 (ptb)	56.2 (en)	54.0 (en)	44.2 (en)	51.2 (en)	53.5 (en)	–	56.1 (ptb)	56.6 (pt)	48.7 (en)	46.4 (en)	52.3 (ms)	37.4 (ko)	37.6 (en)	51.6 (id)	50.1 (en)	47.3 (en)	50.5 (en)	32.7 (en)	39.7 (en)
	pt	60.6 (ptb)	55.8 (ptb)	68.7 (ptb)	67.0 (ptb)	63.6 (ptb)	47.3 (ptb)	58.8 (ptb)	60.1 (ptb)	51.8 (ptb)	–	67.8 (es)	52.2 (ptb)	52.4 (ptb)	54.8 (ms)	38.1 (ko)	37.3 (en)	53.6 (id)	53.5 (ptb)	50.1 (ptb)	54.8 (ptb)	34.1 (ptb)	42.6 (ptb)
	ptb	60.4 (pt)	56.5 (pt)	68.9 (pt)	66.9 (pt)	62.8 (pt)	47.9 (pt)	59.1 (pt)	60.0 (pt)	52.8 (pt)	70.0 (es)	–	51.5 (pt)	52.2 (pt)	54.9 (pt)	38.7 (ko)	37.2 (en)	54.2 (pt)	52.9 (pt)	50.5 (pt)	54.8 (pt)	34.8 (pt)	42.2 (pt)
	ru	51.6 (en)	47.6 (en)	53.6 (ptb)	53.8 (en)	51.5 (en)	42.2 (en)	47.5 (en)	51.2 (en)	46.8 (en)	53.2 (ptb)	53.8 (pt)	–	44.8 (en)	50.3 (ms)	36.7 (en)	35.8 (en)	50.3 (id)	47.4 (en)	44.2 (en)	49.1 (en)	32.0 (en)	37.0 (en)
(Asian Languages)	ar	54.7 (en)	51.3 (en)	56.5 (pt)	57.1 (en)	56.1 (en)	44.9 (en)	51.7 (en)	54.4 (en)	47.2 (en)	55.7 (ptb)	55.6 (pt)	47.9 (en)	–	52.0 (ms)	36.4 (en)	36.1 (en)	52.0 (en)	49.2 (en)	45.6 (en)	51.8 (en)	32.4 (en)	38.7 (en)
	id	52.0 (ms)	48.5 (ms)	56.7 (ms)	54.0 (ms)	51.9 (ms)	46.1 (ms)	49.2 (ms)	51.7 (ms)	48.4 (ms)	51.3 (ptb)	51.3 (pt)	46.9 (ms)	47.8 (ms)	–	39.1 (ms)	37.5 (ja)	59.6 (en)	51.7 (ms)	47.8 (ms)	52.7 (ms)	34.6 (ms)	41.5 (ms)
	ja	33.5 (en)	31.9 (en)	38.8 (ko)	37.9 (ko)	38.6 (en)	29.3 (ko)	33.0 (en)	34.1 (en)	31.1 (en)	35.8 (ptb)	36.3 (pt)	30.7 (en)	29.8 (ko)	35.5 (ko)	–	46.7 (zh)	33.9 (id)	37.9 (ko)	33.7 (ko)	35.5 (ko)	46.9 (ko)	33.1 (ko)
	ko	33.2 (ja)	31.8 (ja)	38.7 (ja)	37.1 (ja)	38.8 (ja)	28.8 (ja)	32.4 (ja)	32.7 (ja)	30.7 (ja)	34.5 (ja)	36.3 (ja)	29.5 (ja)	29.7 (ja)	35.2 (ja)	45.8 (zh)	–	34.2 (id)	38.1 (ja)	32.4 (ja)	33.7 (ja)	47.2 (ja)	32.9 (ja)
	ms	53.1 (id)	50.5 (id)	57.8 (id)	55.1 (id)	53.8 (id)	47.3 (id)	49.5 (id)	53.0 (id)	49.3 (id)	52.3 (id)	53.2 (id)	48.7 (id)	48.5 (id)	60.2 (en)	39.8 (id)	37.0 (id)	–	53.2 (id)	48.7 (id)	53.4 (id)	35.1 (id)	42.9 (id)
	th	49.5 (en)	45.0 (en)	50.1 (ptb)	49.2 (en)	48.5 (en)	40.6 (en)	45.1 (en)	47.9 (en)	43.2 (en)	50.1 (ptb)	49.8 (pt)	40.8 (en)	41.4 (en)	48.5 (ms)	36.1 (ko)	36.8 (ja)	47.9 (id)	–	41.7 (en)	47.5 (en)	31.4 (id)	37.0 (en)
	tl	53.6 (en)	50.2 (en)	54.5 (pt)	55.6 (en)	53.7 (en)	43.7 (en)	49.7 (en)	51.8 (en)	47.0 (en)	53.5 (ptb)	53.1 (pt)	46.0 (en)	45.4 (en)	52.5 (ms)	37.5 (ko)	36.7 (en)	50.8 (id)	50.2 (en)	–	51.3 (en)	33.0 (en)	39.3 (en)
	vi	53.2 (en)	48.8 (en)	53.7 (pt)	53.8 (en)	52.6 (en)	42.8 (en)	48.8 (en)	51.8 (en)	46.4 (en)	52.2 (ptb)	53.3 (pt)	45.4 (en)	46.0 (en)	53.0 (ms)	36.8 (ko)	35.4 (ja)	52.8 (id)	49.3 (en)	45.2 (en)	–	31.6 (ms)	38.3 (en)
	zh	31.7 (en)	31.2 (nl)	35.4 (zht)	35.8 (en)	34.9 (en)	27.9 (ja)	31.5 (en)	32.1 (en)	29.1 (en)	33.1 (ptb)	33.4 (ja)	27.7 (ms)	27.0 (nl)	34.3 (ms)	47.4 (ko)	47.6 (ja)	32.3 (id)	36.3 (en)	30.9 (en)	33.2 (en)	–	33.8 (ja)
	zht	44.1 (en)	41.4 (en)	44.5 (pt)	45.4 (en)	44.5 (en)	36.8 (en)	40.8 (en)	43.5 (en)	39.4 (en)	44.6 (ptb)	44.3 (pt)	39.5 (en)	38.2 (en)	44.5 (ms)	40.8 (zh)	38.5 (zh)	44.0 (id)	43.0 (en)	39.4 (en)	42.8 (en)	35.0 (ja)	–

Table 2: Pivot Language Dependency

(European Languages)

PVT	BLEU (%) *low*		*high*
da	24.2	~	60.2
de	25.1	~	61.8
en	26.2	~	67.7
es	24.9	~	70.0
fr	24.5	~	62.3
hi	23.7	~	53.1
it	23.7	~	65.8
nl	26.2	~	61.6
pl	25.2	~	56.8
pt	25.8	~	68.9
ptb	24.9	~	68.8
ru	22.6	~	56.9

(Asian Languages)

PVT	BLEU (%) *low*		*high*
ar	23.3	~	57.1
id	25.6	~	57.9
ja	26.8	~	59.4
ko	25.7	~	58.3
ms	25.5	~	57.3
th	23.3	~	52.3
zht	23.7	~	44.7
vi	23.6	~	55.3

word alignment (Och and Ney, 2003) and language modeling (Stolcke, 2002) tools were used. Minimum error rate training (MERT) was used to tune the decoder's parameters, and was performed on the *dev* set using the technique proposed in (Och and Ney, 2003). For the translation, an in-house multi-stack phrase-based decoder was used. For the evaluation of translation quality, we applied the standard automatic evaluation metric BLEU which calculates the geometric mean of n-gram precision by the system output with respect to reference translations multiplied by a brevity penalty to prevent very short candidates from receiving too high a score. Scores range between 0 (worst) and 1 (best) (Papineni et al., 2002). For our experiments, single translation references were used.

Table 2 summarizes the BLEU score ranges of all pivot translation experiments obtained for a given pivot language. The results show a large variation in BLEU scores for all pivot languages indicating that the best pivot choice largely depends on the respective source and target language. For European pivot languages, the best language combination scores are in general much higher than the ones obtained for Asian pivot languages.

Table 3 lists the highest BLEU scores of the pivot translation experiments obtained for all language pair combinations. The pivot language achieving

Table 4: Changes in Pivot Selection for Non-English European and Asian Language Pairs (BLEU)

(Non-English European Language Pairs)

TRG → ↓ SRC	da	de	es	fr	hi	it	nl	pl	pt	ptb	ru
da	–	51.7 **(nl)**	56.0 **(nl)**	56.2 **(es)**	43.1 **(es)**	50.6 **(es)**	55.2 **(es)**	46.7 **(pt)**	57.8 (ptb)	57.6 **(pt)**	47.5 **(es)**
de	55.4 **(nl)**	–	57.1 **(ptb)**	55.4 **(ptb)**	43.3 **(nl)**	51.9 **(ptb)**	54.8 **(es)**	47.3 **(nl)**	59.2 (ptb)	58.3 (pt)	47.8 **(nl)**
es	57.0 **(pt)**	52.9 **(pt)**	–	58.4 **(pt)**	43.9 **(pt)**	54.7 **(pt)**	56.0 **(ptb)**	48.8 **(pt)**	64.7 (ptb)	64.6 (pt)	48.4 **(ptb)**
fr	53.2 **(pt)**	50.1 **(nl)**	57.2 **(pt)**	–	41.6 **(es)**	50.7 **(es)**	53.4 **(es)**	45.0 **(es)**	58.7 (ptb)	57.9 (pt)	45.8 **(es)**
hi	47.3 **(ptb)**	45.6 **(nl)**	49.6 **(ptb)**	48.4 **(ptb)**	–	45.2 **(ptb)**	47.6 **(de)**	41.4 **(es)**	51.5 (ptb)	51.6 (pt)	41.7 **(es)**
it	53.8 **(pt)**	50.4 **(nl)**	58.5 **(pt)**	56.4 **(ptb)**	42.4 **(pt)**	–	53.8 **(es)**	46.8 **(pt)**	60.5 (ptb)	60.2 (pt)	47.3 **(es)**
nl	55.5 **(es)**	51.6 **(da)**	57.7 **(ptb)**	56.7 **(es)**	43.9 **(es)**	52.0 **(es)**	–	47.7 **(pt)**	60.0 (ptb)	59.5 **(pt)**	47.9 **(es)**
pl	51.8 **(pt)**	47.9 **(pt)**	53.9 **(ptb)**	51.8 **(pt)**	41.9 **(pt)**	49.6 **(ptb)**	51.3 **(es)**	–	56.1 (ptb)	56.6 (pt)	45.6 **(es)**
pt	60.6 (ptb)	55.8 (ptb)	67.0 (ptb)	63.6 (ptb)	47.3 (ptb)	58.8 (ptb)	60.1 (ptb)	51.8 (ptb)	–	67.8 (es)	52.2 (ptb)
ptb	60.4 (pt)	56.5 (pt)	66.9 (pt)	62.8 (pt)	47.9 (pt)	59.1 (pt)	60.0 (pt)	52.8 (pt)	70.0 (es)	–	51.5 (pt)
ru	50.0 **(pt)**	46.8 **(nl)**	52.5 **(pt)**	50.6 **(pt)**	40.7 **(es)**	46.9 **(ptb)**	49.7 **(es)**	44.2 **(pt)**	53.2 (ptb)	53.8 (pt)	–

(Asian Language Pairs)

TRG → ↓ SRC	ar	id	ja	ko	ms	th	tl	vi	zh	zht
ar	–	52.0 (ms)	35.6 **(id)**	33.9 **(id)**	52.0 **(id)**	46.1 **(ms)**	41.3 **(id)**	46.7 **(ms)**	31.1 **(id)**	36.4 **(id)**
id	47.8 (ms)	–	39.1 (ms)	37.5 (ja)	54.9 **(vi)**	51.7 (ms)	47.8 (ms)	52.7 (ms)	34.6 (ms)	41.5 (ms)
ja	29.8 (ko)	35.5 (ko)	–	46.7 (zh)	33.9 (id)	37.9 (ko)	33.7 (ko)	35.5 (ko)	46.9 (ko)	33.1 (ko)
ko	29.7 (ja)	35.2 (ja)	45.8 (zh)	–	34.2 (id)	38.1 (ja)	32.4 (ja)	33.7 (ja)	47.2 (ja)	32.9 (ja)
ms	48.5 (id)	53.8 **(ar)**	39.8 (id)	37.0 (id)	–	53.2 (id)	48.7 (id)	53.4 (id)	35.1 (id)	42.9 (id)
th	39.4 **(ms)**	48.5 (ms)	36.1 (ko)	36.8 (ja)	47.9 (id)	–	40.5 **(id)**	44.3 **(ms)**	31.4 (id)	34.7 **(ms)**
tl	40.8 **(id)**	52.5 (ms)	37.5 (ko)	36.7 **(ja)**	50.8 (id)	46.5 (ms)	–	47.0 **(ms)**	32.3 **(id)**	36.5 **(ms)**
vi	42.5 **(ms)**	53.0 (ms)	36.8 (ko)	35.4 (ja)	52.8 (id)	48.6 **(ms)**	43.6 **(ms)**	–	31.6 (ms)	37.0 **(ms)**
zh	26.9 **(zht)**	34.3 (ms)	47.4 (ko)	47.6 (ja)	32.3 (id)	35.9 **(ja)**	30.8 **(ko)**	32.6 **(zht)**	–	33.8 (ja)
zht	35.9 **(id)**	44.5 (ms)	40.8 (zh)	38.5 (zh)	44.0 (id)	40.6 **(id)**	36.8 **(id)**	40.5 **(ms)**	35.0 (ja)	–

the highest scores (*oracle pivot*) for translating the source (S) language into the target (T) language are given in parantheses. Non-English oracle pivot languages are highlighted in boldface. The figures show that the *English* pivot approach still achieves the highest scores for the majority of the examined language pairs. However, in 49.8% (230 out of 462) of the cases, a non-English pivot language, mainly *Portuguese*, *Brazilian Portuguese*, *Malay*, *Indonesian*, *Japanese*, *Korean*, is preferable. For languages that are closely related like Portuguese vs. Brazilian Portuguese and Malay vs. Indonesian, the related language should be chosen as the pivot language when either translating from or into the respective language for 88.7% (71 out of 80) and 85.0% (68 out of 80) of the privot translation experiments, respectively. Moreover, *Japanese* is the dominant pivot language when translating from Korean into an other language (95.0%, 19 out of 20) , but not for the translation into Korean (30.0%, 6 out of 20). These results suggest that in general pivot languages closely related to the source language have a larger impact on the overal pivot translation quality than pivot languages related to the target language.

Interestingly, for European-only language pairs, only European languages are the oracle pivot language, the majority of which is English. In addition, Spanish is the pivot language of choice when translating from English into another European language and the Dutch pivot achieved the highest BLEU scores for Germanic-only language pairs. On the other hand, when translating between Asian languages, 65.6% (59 out of 90) of the oracle pivot languages are Asian languages. The Spanish (Chinese) oracle pivot languages for translations between Portuguese and Brazilian Portuguese (Japanese and Korean) also stresses the importance of language relatedness.

In order to investigate the dependency of pivot language selection and language families further, Table 4 summarizes the BLEU scores of pivot translations between only (a) non-English European and (b) Asian language pairs. The results of the European-only language pairs in the table on the left confirm the findings of Table 3. *Portuguese* and *Brazilian Portuguese* are still the dominant pivot languages for non-English European language pairs. An increase of Spanish/Dutch oracle pivot language pairs can be seen for the translation between only Romance/Germanic languages, respectively. Similarly, Malay and Indonesian are the dominant pivot languages, followed by Japanese and Korean, for Asian-only language pairs, most of which achieve BLEU scores that are only slightly lower than the ones for the English oracle pivot language experiments reported in Table 3.

Table 5 summarizes the percentages for the language pairs where the respective pivot language achieved the highest automatic evaluation score for the pivot translation experiments summarized in Table 3 (all language pairs) and Table 4 (non-English European language pairs, Asian language pairs). The results show that English is indeed the pivot language of choice for the majority of the investigated translation directions, but for almost half of the language pairs a non-English pivot language is preferable.

In order to investigate how much improvement

Table 5: Oracle Pivot Language Distribution

(All Language Pairs)

PVT	usage (%)		PVT	usage (%)	
en	232	(50.2)	ko	21	(4.5)
pt	40	(8.7)	es	19	(4.1)
ptb	38	(8.2)	nl	5	(1.1)
id	37	(8.0)	zh	4	(0.9)
ms	36	(7.8)	zht	1	(0.2)
ja	29	(6.3)			

(Non-English European Language Pairs)

PVT	usage (%)		PVT	usage (%)	
pt	40	(36.3)	nl	10	(9.1)
ptb	32	(29.1)	de	1	(0.9)
es	26	(23.7)	da	1	(0.9)

(Asian Language Pairs)

PVT	usage (%)		PVT	usage (%)	
id	28	(31.1)	zh	4	(4.4)
ms	27	(30.0)	zht	2	(2.2)
ja	15	(16.6)	vi	1	(1.1)
ko	12	(13.3)	ar	1	(1.1)

Table 6: Gain of non-English Pivot Languages

PVT	(oracle)	Gain in BLEU (%) avg	min	max
zh	(4)	4.7	3.2	6.1
ja	(27)	2.5	0.1	13.3
id	(35)	2.4	0.6	5.4
pt	(31)	2.3	0.3	4.6
ptb	(32)	2.1	0.3	4.9
ko	(19)	1.9	0.1	11.4
ms	(34)	1.8	0.1	3.9
es	(4)	0.8	0.1	2.4
nl	(2)	0.6	0.5	0.8

in pivot translation performance can be achieved by using non-English pivot languages instead of an English pivot, we calculated the difference in BLEU scores for all 188 non-English language pairs where the non-English pivot language improved translation quality. Table 6 summarizes the average, minimal and maximal gains in BLEU scores for the respective pivot language translation experiments. The pivot languages are sorted according to the highest average increase in translation performance and the amount of improved language pairs are given in parantheses. In total, an average gain of 2.2 BLEU points were obtained for the investigated language pairs. The highest gains (13.4/11.4 BLEU points) were achieved for the Japanese/Korean pivots when translating Korean/Japanese into Chinese, respectively.

3 Indicators of Pivot Translation Quality

The diversity of the pivot language selection reported in the last section rises the question of what makes a language a good pivot language for a given language pair.

We investigated the following eight factors (comprised of a total of 45 distinct features) based on the language resources and SMT engines (SRC-PVT, PVT-TRG) used for the pivot translation experiments described in Section 2 where the total number of features of each factor is given in brackets. For SMT-engine-related features, both translation directions (SRC-PVT, PVT-TRG) are taken into account.

- *language family* [2]: a binary feature verifying whether the source and target languages of the SMT engines belong to the same family or not.
- *vocabulary* [15]: the training data vocabulary size of source and target languages, the ratio of source and target vocabulary sizes, and the overlap between source and target vocabulary.
- *sentence length* [12]: the average sentence length of source and target training sets and the ratio of source and target sentence length.
- *reordering* [6]: the amount and span of word order differences (reordering) in the training data and the *Reordering Quantity* score as proposed in (Birch et al., 2008).
- *language perplexity* [4]: perplexity of the utilized language models measured on the *dev*/*eval* data sets.
- *translation model entropy* [2]: amount of uncertainty involved in choosing candidate translation phrases as proposed in (Koehn et al., 2009).
- *engine performance* [2]: the BLEU scores of the respective SMT engine used for the pivot translation experiments.
- *monotonicity* [2]: the BLEU score difference of a given SMT engine for decoding with and without a reordering model.

The impact of the above factors in isolation on the translation performance is measured using linear regression which models the relationship between a response variable and one or more explanatory variables. Data sets are modeled using linear functions and unknown model parameters are estimated from the data. In this paper, the response variable is defined by the BLEU metric (measuring the pivot translation performance) and the explanatory variables are given by the feature values obtained for each of the respective language pair combinations. Figure 1 gives an example for a simple linear regression using the *reordering quantity* feature as the explanatory variable for (a) all language pairs, (b) European languages only, and (c) Asian languages only. The "goodness of

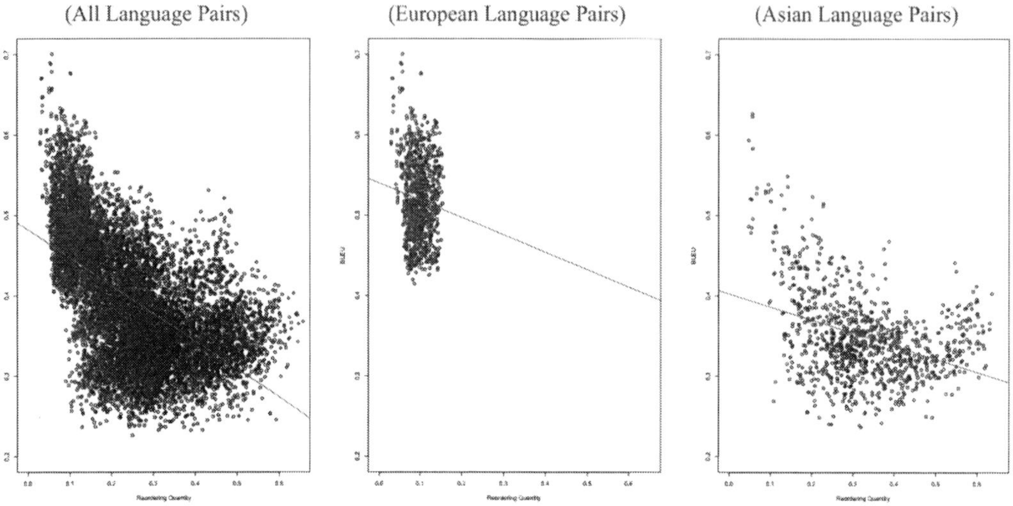

Figure 1: Linear Regression Example (*Reordering Quantity*)

fit" of the explanatory variable(s) is calculated using the R^2 coefficient of determination, which is a statistical measure of how well the regression line approximates the real data points. An R^2 of 1.0 indicates that the regression line perfectly fits the data. For the *translation model entropy* factor, for example, we obtain an R^2 of 0.4604 for all language pairs, which indicates that 46.04% of the differences in translation performance can be explained by this factor.

3.1 Predictive Power of Single Factors

Table 7 summarizes the R^2 scores of the multiple linear regression analysis of the respective investigated factors, i.e. all features of a given factor are combined and treated as multiple explanatory variables. In total, 81% of the system performance variations can be explained when all investigated factors are taken into account. For European language pairs, the impact is even larger (91%). However, for Asian language pairs, the investigated factors have much less correlation (R^2 of 0.5888) with the overall pivot translation translation quality, indicating the difficulty of selecting an appropriate pivot language for translation tasks including Asian languages.

The impact of each factor on the translation performance is also given in Table 7. The results show that *engine performance* is the most correlated factor, followed by *translation model entropy* and *reordering* when all language combinations are taken into account. *Language family* and *language perplexity* seems to have the least impact on translation performance. However, when applying linear regression on language subsets (only European vs. only Asian languages), the impact of factors largely differs. Similar to all language pairs, the *engine performance* factor is most relevant for both European and Asian language subsets.

Table 7: Impact on Translation Performance

Explanatory Variable	R^2 All	R^2 European	R^2 Asian
all factors	0.8102	0.9106	0.5880
engine performance	0.7438	0.7906	0.5151
translation model entropy	0.4604	0.3669	0.1661
reordering	0.4383	0.4593	0.1806
vocabulary	0.3112	0.3867	0.2389
monotonicity	0.2682	0.0149	0.1323
sentence length	0.1717	0.6052	0.0724
language family	0.1204	0.1280	0.0982
language perplexity	0.0826	0.1100	0.0337

For pivot translations between European languages, *sentence length*, *reordering* and *vocabulary* are more predictive than the *translation model entropy* factor. Moreover, the *monotonicity* factor obtains the lowest R^2 score indicating that word order differences between European languages occur mainly on the phrase-level (*local reordering*) and that only minor gains can be achieved when reordering successive phrases. The high R^2 score for *sentence length* also suggests that the ratio of sentence length is an important feature when selecting an appropriate pivot language for closely related languages.

On the other hand, looking at the Asian language pair regression results, the lower R^2 scores underline the large diversity between the Asian languages. Relatively high R^2 scores for *reordering* and *monotonicity* are obtained for Asian lan-

Table 8: Factor Contribution

Explanatory Variable	R^2 All	European	Asian
all factors	0.8102	0.9106	0.5880
w/o engine performance	0.5621	0.8755	0.3683
w/o language perplexity	0.7734	0.8895	0.5488
w/o sentence length	0.7856	0.8989	0.5501
w/o reordering	0.7958	0.8999	0.5712
w/o vocabulary	0.7961	0.8766	0.5669
w/o translation model entropy	0.8004	0.9024	0.5748
w/o monotonicity	0.8026	0.9024	0.5768
w/o language family	0.8035	0.9022	0.5793

guages, indicating that structural differences between the pivot language and the source/target language largely affects the overal pivot translation quality.

3.2 Contribution of Single Factors

Besides the predictive power of each factor, we calculated the R^2 scores of all the factors besides one (*leave-one-out*) in order to investigate the contribution of each factor to the multiple linear regression analysis. In general, the smaller the R^2 score after omitting a given factor, the larger the contribution of this factor on the explanation of the overall translation performance is supposed to be.

The results summarized in Table 8 show that the largest contribution for all language pairs is obtained for the *engine performance* factor, followed by *language perplexity* and *sentence length*. Interestingly, the *vocabulary* factor contributes as much as the *engine performance* factor for European languages, but not for Asian languages. This confirms that morphological similarities between highly inflected languages are important to identify an appropriate pivot language. Moreover, for European-only and Asian-only language pairs, the omission of any of these factors led to lower R^2 scores, but the difference towards the complete factor set is much smaller. This shows the importance of all the investigated features for the task of pivot language selection, especially if languages of large diversity are to be taken into account.

3.3 Translation Direction Dependency

In order to investigate whether the selection of a pivot language depends more on its relationship towards the source language or the target language, we carried out a linear regression analysis based on all factors using (a) only source-language-related features (*SRC-PVT only*) and (b) only target-language-related features (*PVT-TRG only*). The results are summarized in Table 9.

Table 9: Source vs. Target Language Dependency

Explanatory Variable	R^2 All	European	Asian
all factors	0.8102	0.9106	0.5880
SRC-PVT only	0.4923	0.3125	0.2805
PVT-TRG only	0.4732	0.6505	0.2986

In order to distinguish between languages of large diversity, the source language features seem to be more predictive than the target language features. However, for more coherent language pairs, like in the case of European languages, the impact on how much language diversity affects pivot translation performance shifts towards target-language-related features. However, the restriction to either the source or the target features leads to a large decrease in the R^2 scores for all language data sets, underlining the importance of both source-language-related and target-language-related feature sets to identify an appropriate pivot language for a given language pair.

4 Conclusion

We investigated the impact of eight translation quality indicators for the task of pivot translation between 22 languages covering a large diversity of language characteristics. A linear regression analysis showed that 81% of the variation in translation performance differences can be explained by the combination of these factors. The most informative factor in identifying the best pivot language is *engine performance*, i.e., the translation quality of the SMT engines used to translate (a) the source input into the intermediate language and (b) the intermediate language MT output into the target language. In addition, the highest correlation of the investigated factors towards pivot translation performance was obtained when both source-language-related and target-language-related features were combined. The importance of source vs. target language features largely depends on the diversity of the investigated language pairs, i.e., source language features are preferable for heterogenous language pairs whereas the focus shifts towards target-language-related features for more coherent language pairs. In addition, the differentiation between European and Asian languages revealed that the task of identifying a pivot language for new language pairs largely depends on the availability of structurally similar languages.

As future work, we are planning to investigate the importance of the factors analyzed in Section 3 in the selection of pivot languages for new language pairs by applying a machine learning algorithm like *Support Vector Machines* (SVM) to train discriminative models for the task of predicting a pivot language that achieves the highest translation performance for a given translation task.

References

Nicola Bertoldi, Madalina Barbaiani, Marcello Federico, and Roldano Cattoni. 2008. Phrase-Based Statistical Machine Translation with Pivot Languages. In *Proceedings of the 5th International Workshop on Spoken Language Translation (IWSLT)*, pages 143–149, Hawaii, USA.

Alexandra Birch, Miles Osborne, and Philipp Koehn. 2008. Predicting success in machine translation. In *Proceedings of the Conference on Empirical Methods in Natural Language Processing (EMNLP)*, pages 745–754, Honolulu, Hawaii.

Adria de Gispert and Jose B. Marino. 2006. Catalan-english statistical machine translation without parallel corpus: bridging through spanish. In *Proceedings of 5th International Conference on Language Resources and Evaluation (LREC)*, pages 65–68, Genoa, Italy.

Genichiro Kikui, Seiichi Yamamoto, Toshiyuki Takezawa, and Eiichiro Sumita. 2006. Comparative study on corpora for speech translation. *IEEE Transactions on Audio, Speech and Language*, 14(5):1674–1682.

Philipp Koehn, Alexandra Birch, and Ralf Steinberger. 2009. 462 Machine Translation Systems for Europe. In *Proceedings of the Machine Translation Summit XII*, Ottawa, Canada.

Gregor Leusch, Aurélien Max, Josep Maria Crego, and Hermann Ney. 2010. Multi-Pivot Translation by System Combination. In *Proceedings of 7th International Workshop on Spoken Language Translation (IWSLT)*, pages 299–306, Paris, France.

Franz Josef Och and Hermann Ney. 2003. A Systematic Comparison of Various Statistical Alignment Models. *Computational Linguistics*, 29(1):19–51.

Kishore Papineni, Salim Roukos, Todd Ward, and Wei-Jing Zhu. 2002. BLEU: a Method for Automatic Evaluation of Machine Translation. In *Proceedings of the 40th Annual Meeting of the Association for Computational Linguistics (ACL)*, pages 311–318, Philadelphia, USA.

Michael Paul, Hirofumi Yamamoto, Eiichiro Sumita, and Satoshi Nakamura. 2009. On the Importance of Pivot Language Selection for Statistical Machine Translation. In *Proceedings of the North American Chapter of the Association for Computational Linguistics - Human Language Technologies (NAACL/HLT)*, pages 221–224, Boulder, USA.

Andreas Stolcke. 2002. SRILM - an extensible language modeling toolkit. In *Proceedings of the 7th International Conference on Spoken Language Processing (ICSLP)*, pages 901–904, Denver.

Masao Utiyama and Hitoshi Isahara. 2007. A comparison of pivot methods for phrase-based statistical machine translation. In *Proceedings of Human Language Technologies (HLT)*, pages 484–491, New York, USA.

Hua Wu and Haifeng Wang. 2007. Pivot Language Approach for Phrase-Based Statistical Machine Translation. In *Proceedings of 45th Annual Meeting of the Association for Computational Linguistics (ACL)*, pages 856–863, Prague, Czech Republic.

Source Error-Projection for Sample Selection in Phrase-Based SMT for Resource-Poor Languages

Sankaranarayanan Ananthakrishnan, Shiv Vitaladevuni, Rohit Prasad, and Prem Natarajan
Raytheon BBN Technologies
10 Moulton Street
Cambridge, MA 02138, U.S.A.
{sanantha,svitalad,rprasad,pnataraj}@bbn.com

Abstract

The unavailability of parallel training corpora in resource-poor languages is a major bottleneck in cost-effective and rapid deployment of statistical machine translation (SMT) technology. This has spurred significant interest in active learning for SMT to select the most informative samples from a large candidate pool. This is especially challenging when irrelevant outliers dominate the pool. We propose two supervised sample selection methods, viz. greedy selection and integer linear programming (ILP), based on a novel measure of benefit derived from error analysis. These methods support the selection of diverse and high-impact, yet relevant batches of source sentences. Comparative experiments on multiple test sets across two resource-poor language pairs (English-Pashto and English-Dari) reveal that the proposed approaches achieve BLEU scores comparable to the full system using a very small fraction of all available training data (ca. 6% for E-P and 13% for E-D). We further demonstrate that the ILP method supports global constraints of significant practical value.

1 Introduction

The laborious and time-consuming nature of producing parallel training corpora for the development of high-quality SMT systems cannot be overstated. Barring a few mainstream languages, the vast majority of language pairs can be classified as "resource-poor" as far as availability of a usable SMT system is concerned. Active learning can reduce human labor, turn-around time and monetary cost of developing SMT systems with little or no loss in translation accuracy.

In its simplest form, active learning for building parallel corpora involves selecting "high-value" samples from a large monolingual corpus of source sentences (the *candidate pool*) for translation by a bilingual human expert. The notion of "value" depends on the selection method, and can be derived using unsupervised, semi-supervised, or supervised techniques. For instance, Eck et al. (2005) define high-value source sentences as those that contain a large number of previously unseen n-grams. While it aims to increase coverage of the training set, the main deficiency of this approach is its tendency to pick irrelevant outliers if the candidate pool contains data from unrelated regimes.

Haffari et al. (2009) propose a number of features, such as similarity to the seed corpus, translation probability, n-gram and phrase coverage as unsupervised measures of the value of candidate samples. Additionally, a linear combination of these features is proposed as a supervised measure of value for ranking candidate sentences. The parameters of this model are optimized on two separate held-out bilingual development sets. The disadvantage of this approach is that it relies on the candidate pool having the same distributional characteristics as the development sets used for parameter estimation. Haffari and Sarkar (2009) explore active learning in a multilingual setting (different source languages f_d to be translated to a single target language e) using disagreement between target hypotheses generated by each of the SMT systems. For single language active learn-

This paper is based upon work supported by the DARPA TRANSTAC Program. The views expressed are those of the author and do not reflect the official policy or position of the Department of Defense or the U.S. Government.

ing, they use OOV phrases, i.e. source n-grams without translation choices.

Ananthakrishnan et al. (2010) propose an error-driven approach that identifies translation errors on a held-out development set, and uses this to train a discriminative pairwise comparator function that preferentially selects candidate sentences with constructs that are incorrectly translated in the development set. The chosen sentences provide maximum potential reduction in translation error. The advantage of this method over other unsupervised and semi-supervised selection strategies is that it favors domain-relevant sentences that are difficult to translate. However, its granularity is low, because it considers errors only at the sentence level. Further, the diversity constraint is implemented in a non-optimal, ad-hoc manner by deleting feature functions from the pairwise classification model.

Bloodgood and Callison-Burch (2010) explored active learning to augment training data for *high resource* language pairs. They experimented with random, shortest, and longest sentence selection, as well as a technique they refer to as *Vocab-Growth*. The latter prefers a candidate sentence that contains the most frequent n-gram not seen in the labeled training data. Again, this approach is unsuitable if the pool contains a lot of irrelevant sentences. Moreover, their system is based entirely on source language statistics, and does not use any feedback from the SMT system. As one of their examples indicates, this makes it susceptible to selecting sentences containing n-grams that were already correctly translatable.

This paper introduces a novel, fine-grained, error-driven measure of value for candidate sentences obtained by translation error analysis on a domain-relevant held-out development set. Errors identified in translation hypotheses are projected back on to the corresponding source sentences through phrase derivations from the SMT decoder. This projected error is used to obtain a "benefit value" for each source n-gram that serves as a measure of its translation difficulty. Sentence selection is posed as the problem of choosing K sentences from the candidate pool that maximize the sum of the benefit values of n-grams covered by the choice. This is a generalization of the set-covering problem, known to be NP-Complete. We present two approximate solutions: (a) an efficient greedy algorithm and (b) an integer linear programming (ILP) formulation. We compare these two methods and demonstrate their superiority to numerous competing selection strategies described in the literature.

2 Translation Error Projection

The principal advantage of error-driven sample selection (Cohn et al., 1996; Meng and Lee, 2008) over traditional unsupervised or semi-supervised active learning (Hwa, 2004; Tang et al., 2002; Shen et al., 2004) is its ability to choose instances, which, when annotated, potentially maximize error reduction of the learner on a reference set.

We assume the following data configuration for error-driven sample selection for SMT. A seed parallel corpus $\mathbf{S}$ is required to bootstrap an initial translation system. However, we do not require that this corpus be drawn from the same distribution as the testing condition. This relaxed assumption is particularly useful for developing SMT systems for resource-poor language pairs for which in-domain parallel training data may not be readily available, but a (low quality) translation system may be built using data from other domains, genres or dialects. We also assume a phrase-based SMT architecture (Koehn et al., 2003).

A held-out development (tuning) set $\mathbf{D}$ is used for optimizing the parameters of the SMT system using MERT (Och, 2003), as well as for error-analysis in guiding the proposed sample selection algorithms. System performance is evaluated on a fair test set $\mathbf{T}$. We assume that the tuning set is derived from the same distribution as the test set. The selection algorithms operate on a large pool of monolingual source sentences $\mathbf{P}$ to extract high-value samples for translation by a human expert. The candidate pool may contain any mixture of relevant and irrelevant sentences, and may also possess significant redundancy.

2.1 Error Analysis

The SMT system is bootstrapped using the seed training corpus $\mathbf{S}$. The held-out set $\mathbf{D}$ is decoded by the SMT to obtain 1-best translation hypotheses. Translation edit rate (TER) analysis (Snover et al., 2006) is used to identify errors in the hypotheses by aligning them to the target references. The TER alignment identifies a set of insertions, substitutions, deletions, and shifts that is required to transform a hypothesis to its corresponding reference. Large values of TER indicate greater dis-

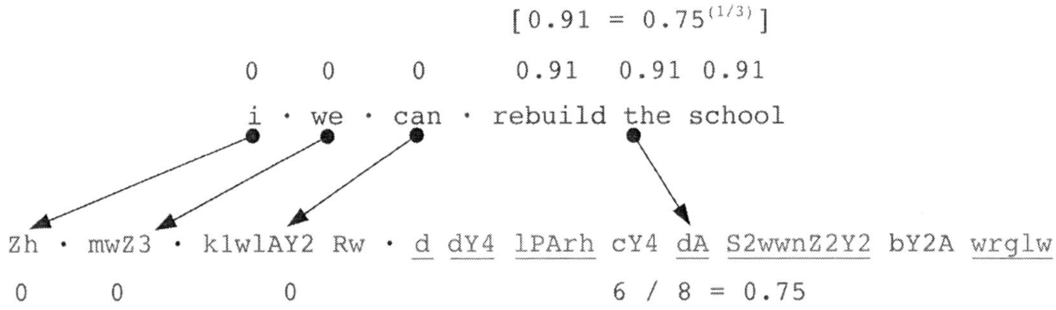

Figure 1: Example illustrating evaluation of back-projected error for a source sentence given phrase derivations and error analysis of its translation hypothesis (English-Pashto). Incorrectly hypothesized words are underlined in red.

similarity between hypotheses and references, corresponding to poor translations.

An individual target word in the hypothesis is deemed "correct" if it aligns to itself in the TER alignment. Conversely, hypothesized words corresponding to substitution or insertion errors are considered "incorrect" translations, while deletion errors are ignored. Thus, each hypothesized word can be labeled "correct" or "incorrect" based on the TER alignment, providing a fine-grained view of translation difficulty on the held-out set.

2.2 Benefit/Objective Function

TER analysis enables us to label errors at the word level for each SMT hypothesis. However, it is the knowledge of which *source words* were translated incorrectly that is useful for sample selection. Assuming there is a way to attach a label (or real value) to each source word in the held-out set $\mathbf{D}$ indicating whether it was correctly translated (or to what degree it was translated), we can compute a *benefit value* over each source n-gram. The sum of benefit values over all source n-grams can be used as an objective function that must be maximized by selecting suitable samples from the candidate pool.

The SMT decoder produces *phrase derivations* specifying the origin of each target phrase in a hypothesis, providing a convenient mechanism for approximate projection of target error labels back on to the source words. We refer to this as error back-projection. We compute, for each target phrase in the phrase derivations, the *target phrase error* as a ratio of the number of words labeled "incorrect" to the total number of words within that phrase. This quantity is then equally distributed among constituent source words using the geometric mean with respect to the number of words in the containing source phrase (obtained from the phrase derivation), to give us a back-projected error at the level of individual source words. Since the phrase derivations form a mutually exclusive partition over the source sentence, we can compute an unambiguous back-projected error value for each source word in the held-out set $\mathbf{D}$. Figure 1 illustrates this procedure with an example.

We then compute a benefit value for each source n-gram as the sum of back-projected error of the constituent source words. The set of source phrases in the SMT decoder derivations is typically a very small subset of the set of all possible n-grams of equal length. By distributing back-projected phrase error over individual target words, we are able to compute benefit values for n-grams not covered by the phrase table inventory. Finally, we sum the benefit values of source n-grams that occur multiple times in $\mathbf{D}$ to generate a table of benefit values hashed by the corresponding n-grams.

3 Sentence Selection Problem

Given a set of n-grams $\mathcal{N} = \{n_i\}_{i=1}^{m}$ from source sentences in $\mathbf{D}$ and associated benefit values $b_i \geq 0$ computed by error back-projection, the goal of sample selection is to choose a batch of K sentences that maximizes the cumulative benefit value of n-grams covered by the chosen sentences. The contribution of each sentence towards the objective function is equal to the sum of benefit values of all unique n-grams it contains.

The sentence selection problem is closely related to the classical set covering problem, one of 21 NP-complete problems described in Karp's seminal paper on reducibility (Karp, 1972). The decision version of set covering is as follows: given a set of elements T and a set of subsets within T, say $\mathcal{T} = \{T_j \subseteq T\}$, is it possible to select k subsets such that their union is the superset T? This problem is known to be NP-Complete.

To visualize the similarity of set covering to the sentence selection problem, note that the elements of T are akin to n-grams, and the subsets T_j's correspond to sentences. It is easy to show that the set covering problem can be reduced to the sentence selection problem. Thus, there does not exist a polynomial time algorithm for optimal sentence selection unless $P = NP$.

There is a standard greedy approximation algorithm for the minimum set covering problem (Cormen et al., 2001): at each iteration, choose the subset T_j that has the largest number of as yet uncovered elements of T. The procedure is repeated until all elements in T are covered. We next present a variant of this algorithm for the sentence selection problem. Our algorithm address two differences between sentence selection and set covering: (a) each n-gram provides a distinct benefit value on covering, and (b) we must select only K sentences and maximize the cumulative benefit.

4 Greedy Sample Selection

The greedy solution constructs batches iteratively by choosing, at each step, the sentence whose total current benefit is the largest. Each sentence in the candidate pool is decomposed into its constituent n-grams, and the sum of benefit values of these n-grams is computed. The sentence that scores highest on this criterion is chosen. Resetting the benefit values of n-grams in previously chosen sentences ensures diversity. The greedy selection technique is illustrated in Algorithm 1. Each iteration of the master loop selects one sentence based on the local maximum of the objective function. The indicator function $\mathcal{I}_i(\cdot)$ returns unity if n-gram n_i is present in the argument sentence, and zero otherwise.

The greedy algorithm provides a highly-scalable approximation to the solution and can be applied to systems with millions of n-grams and candidate sentences. It is, however, sub-optimal in general; potentially better solutions can be obtained by casting it in an integer linear programming (ILP) framework, as discussed below.

Algorithm 1 Greedy Sample Selection

```
B ← ()
for k = 1 to K do
    p* ← arg max_{p∈P} Σ_{i=1}^{m} b_i I_i(p)
    B(k) ← p*
    P ← P − {p*}
    b_i ← 0 ∀ {i | I_i(p*) = 1}
end for
return B
```

5 Integer Linear Programming (ILP)

We define a set of indicator variables, x_j, for the sentences, $x_j = 1$ if sentences p_j is selected and 0 otherwise. Similarly, there are a set of indicator variables, y_i, for the n-grams, $y_i = 1$ if n-gram n_i is covered by some selected sentence and 0 otherwise. Sentence selection can be expressed as the following integer linear program (ILP):

$$\begin{aligned} \max: & \sum_i b_i y_i \\ \text{subj. to.}: & \; y_i \leq \sum_{j|\mathcal{I}_i(p_j)=1} x_j \;\; \forall i \\ & \sum_j x_j \leq K \\ & 0 \leq y_i \leq 1 \;\forall i \;,\; x_j \in \{0,1\} \;\forall j \end{aligned} \tag{1}$$

Notice that since $b_i \geq 0$, in order to maximize the optimization function each y_i will be set to 1 whenever at least one of the sentence covering its n-gram is selected, $x_j = 1$.

In general, exact optimization of ILP is NP-Hard. However, there are several publicly available solvers for ILPs with thousands of variables. For instance, the open-source *lp-solve* program uses the Branch-and-Bound technique to solve ILPs and in our experiments handles systems with thousands of sentences.

5.1 Including Application Constraints

Unlike greedy selection, ILP allows us to impose additional application or domain specific global constraints within the optimization framework. One example is to bound the total number of words in the selected sentences rather than number of chosen sentences. This is useful because when the number of sentences is constrained, the system is biased to choose longer sentences as they would cover more n-grams. Assuming manual translation cost to be linear in the number of words, we can put a bound on the total length of the chosen sentences. Let l_j be the length of sentence p_j. We can put a bound $\sum_j l_j x_j \leq L$. Imposing such a bound is similar to the Knapsack problem, a standard NP-Complete problem (Cormen et al., 2001). We can also incorporate prior information on the goodness of sentences by including sentence costs (e.g. syntactic well-formedness, length, etc.), c_j's, within the optimization function: $\sum_i b_i y_i + \sum_j c_j x_j$. In contrast to the greedy algorithm, ILP provides a natural framework to perform *joint* optimization over multiple types of constraints.

5.2 Solving the ILP for Practical Problems

Even moderate size SMT applications involve tens of thousands of n-grams and sentences, e.g., one of our test conditions has approximately $79,000$ n-grams and $100,000$ sentences. Each sentence would result in an integer variable in the ILP. State-of-the-art solvers have difficulty handling such large problems, e.g., *lp-solve* was unable to solve the ILP for a system with $100,000$ sentences. We propose a two-step solution to achieve scalability. If k sentences must be selected in a given active learning iteration, we use the greedy algorithm to prune the problem by choosing $k' > k$ sentences from the corpus, and subsequently construct the ILP on this smaller problem to select the required k sentences. While ILP is optimal, greedily pruning the problem for ILP may result in sub-optimality.

We observed the run time and optimization value computed by ILP for different k', keeping k constant at 16. We chose smaller (k', k) for these simulations to allow ILP to run to completion. Figure 2 summarizes our findings. Note that the optimum improves with larger prune size and requires more iterations. Larger prune sizes allow the ILP to choose from a larger pool of sentences, and are therefore likely to improve the optimum. However, these typically require more iterations. In this paper, we used the greedy algorithm to prune the problem to $K' = 1000$ sentences, and then select $K = 400$ sentences using ILP (we restricted ILP run-time to 20 minutes per batch).

6 Experimental Results

We demonstrate the effectiveness of greedy and ILP-based sample selection by conducting simulation experiments on two resource-poor lan-

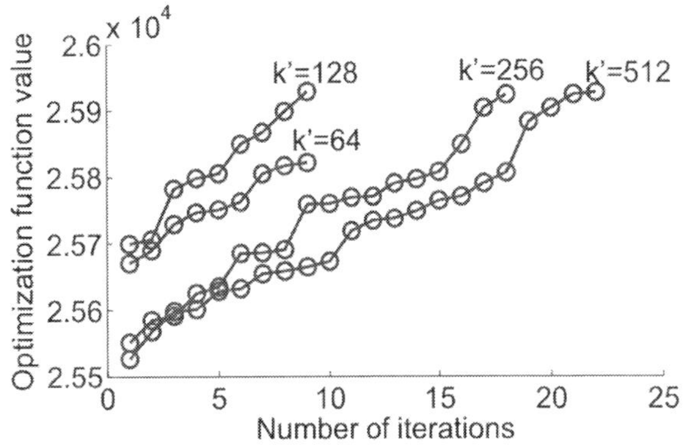

Figure 2: Optimization function value for different iterations of ILP branch-and-bound, for different sizes of pruned problems ($k' = 64, 128, 256, 512$) for constant choice cardinality, $k = 16$.

guage pairs commissioned under the DARPA Transtac speech-to-speech translation initiative, viz. English-Pashto (E2P) and English-Dari (E2D). In both cases, only a small fraction of the available training data is pertinent to the translation task. This simulates a condition where a large source language corpus (e.g. English) is harvested from the Web, of which only a small fraction is relevant to the target SMT system.

We simulate low-resource conditions by sequestering the majority of available parallel training data. A seed translation model is bootstrapped with a very small subset of the training corpus; source sentences of the remainder constitute the candidate pool. Because obtaining monolingual text in the target language is usually not a constraint, we train the target language model (LM) from all available target language sentences in the training corpus.

We then apply the proposed selection algorithms to choose fixed-size batches from the pool. Translations for the selected sentences are obtained from the sequestered parallel corpus (thus simulating a human oracle). The chosen batch and its translation is appended to the seed corpus S for retraining the SMT. At each iteration, we independently decode the test set and evaluate translation accuracy in order to compare the trajectory of BLEU for these and other competing selection strategies:

- *Random*: Source sentences are uniformly sampled from the candidate pool $\mathbf{P}$.
- *Dissimilarity*: Select sentences from $\mathbf{P}$ with the largest number of n-grams not seen in S

(Eck et al., 2005; Haffari et al., 2009).

- *Longest*: Pick the longest sentences from the candidate pool **P**.
- *Discriminative*: Choose sentences that potentially minimize translation error using a maximum-entropy pairwise comparator (Ananthakrishnan et al., 2010).
- *Greedy*: Simple greedy selection with proposed error-projection benefit objective.
- *ILP*: Integer linear programming optimization with error-projection benefit objective.

English-to-Pashto Simulation: The E2P data originates from a two-way collection of spoken dialogues, and consists of two parallel sub-corpora: a directional E2P corpus and a directional Pashto-English (P2E) corpus. Each sub-corpus has its own independent training, development, and test partitions. The directional E2P training, development, and test sets consist of 33.9k, 2.4k, and 1.1k sentence pairs, respectively. The directional P2E training set consists of 76.5k sentence pairs. In addition, DARPA has made available to all Transtac participants an open 564-sentence E2P test set with four target references for each input.

We trained a baseline E2P SMT system from all available E2P and reversed P2E data. The full-system BLEU scores on the single-reference internal test set and on the multi-reference DARPA evaluation test set were 10.8 and 24.4, respectively. We set up active learning simulation by randomly sampling 1,000 sentence pairs from the directional E2P training partition to obtain the seed training corpus. The remainder of this set, and the entire reversed P2E training partition were combined to create the pool. The reversed directional P2E data is considered irrelevant as far as the E2P test sets are concerned. The pool thus consists of 30% in-domain and 70% irrelevant sentence pairs. We simulated 35 iterations with batches of 400 sentences each; the seed corpus grows to 15,000 sentence pairs at the end of the simulation.

English-to-Dari Simulation: The E2D data is also derived from a two-way collection of spoken dialogues. The directional E2D training, development, and test sets consist of 11.6k, 3.2k, and 2.8k sentence pairs, respectively. The directional D2E training set consists of 52.9k sentence pairs. The full-system BLEU on the E2D test set was 15.1.

As with E2P, the seed training corpus was obtained by randomly sampling 1,000 sentence pairs from the directional E2D training partition. All remaining parallel training data were designated as the candidate pool. Thus, only about 17% of the candidate pool is considered relevant with respect to the E2D test set. Again, we simulated 35 iterations with batches of 400 sentences each.

BLEU Trajectories: The trajectories of BLEU scores for the E2P and E2D test sets are shown in Figures 3(a), 3(b), and 3(c), respectively. The horizontal line near the top of each plot represents the corresponding full-system BLEU score. The following observations are noteworthy:

- BLEU scores using the proposed greedy and ILP-based selection methods ramp up very quickly to the full-system level using a small fraction of available training data. On the E2P single-reference test set, the top-line BLEU score of 10.8 is attained after just 12 iterations (5.8k sentence pairs), as against 100k sentence pairs for the full system (**6%** of the corpus). Likewise for E2D, the full-system BLEU score of 15.1 is attained after only 18 iterations (8.2k sentence pairs), as opposed to 65k sentence pairs for the full system (**13%** of the corpus).
- In some cases, BLEU scores with training corpora constructed using active learning exceed those obtained with the full system. This is because our selection algorithms are biased to choose relevant, in-domain sentences from the candidate pool. Initially, the training corpus is kept free of outliers that cause performance degradation in the full system. With more iterations of selection, the latter eventually find their way into the training set, causing translation performance to settle around the top-line BLEU scores.
- Under identical initial conditions at the first iteration of active learning, the ILP benefit optimum exceeds the greedy optimum by 444.5 units for E2P, and by 420.3 units for E2D. This confirms the theoretical superiority of ILP over greedy selection.

We computed total area under the BLEU curves for the various selection techniques as a single figure of merit. Summarized in Table 1, the BLEU-Iteration product shows source error-projection with the ILP selection algorithm outperforming all competing techniques, including discriminative sample selection (Ananthakrishnan et al., 2010).

Global Length Constraint: The above simula-

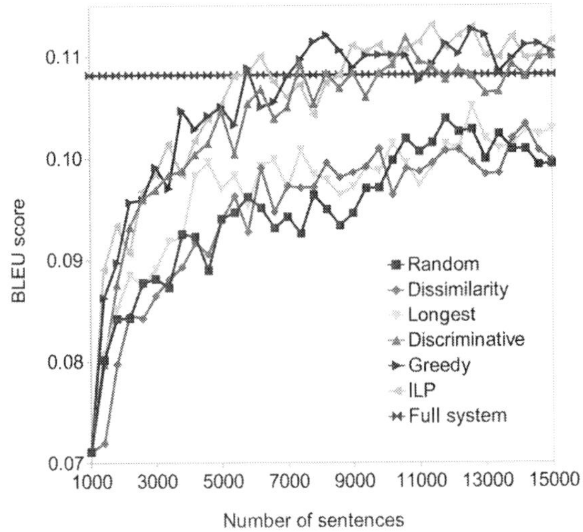

(a) Trajectory of BLEU (E2P-SingleRef)

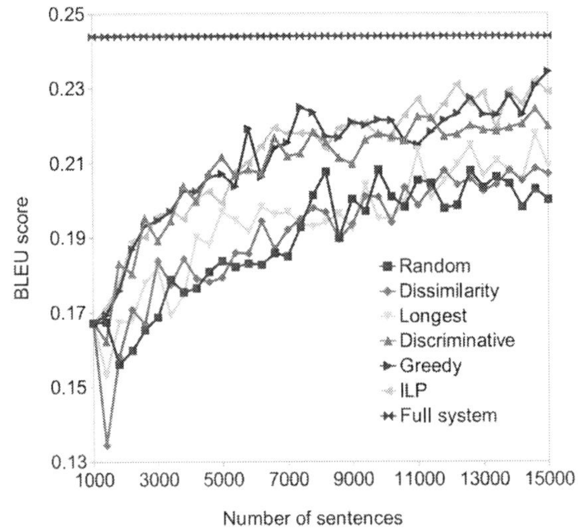

(b) Trajectory of BLEU (E2P-MultiRef)

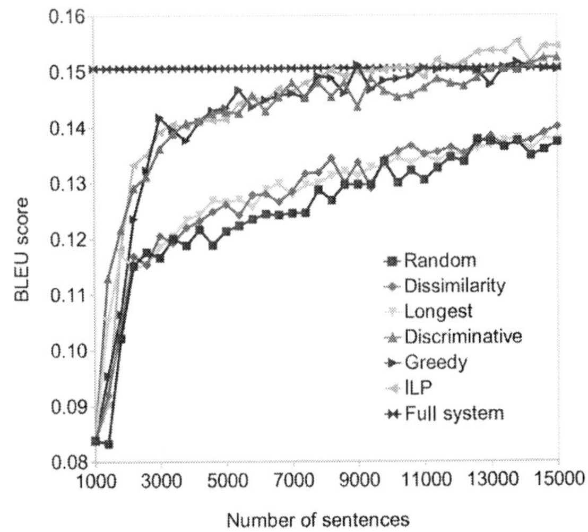

(c) Trajectory of BLEU (E2D-SingleRef)

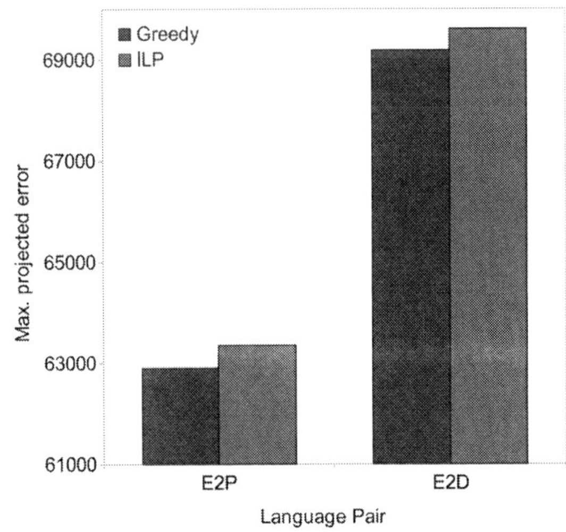

(d) Maximum benefit for greedy and ILP selection

Figure 3: Simulation results for E2P and E2D.

Method	E2P-SR	E2P-MR	E2D-SR
Random	83.03	78.76	144.65
Dissim.	82.34	81.18	154.17
Longest	89.89	93.65	155.72
Discrim.	113.54	145.32	205.56
Greedy	120.83	155.64	204.95
ILP	**121.16**	**156.70**	**210.51**

Table 1: Area under the BLEU curve with respect to 0-th iteration baseline.

tions choose a fixed number of sentences at each iteration. However, the ILP optimization framework also permits the integration of global constraints, such as the number of words in a batch. This is an important practical benefit, as most professional translators charge by word rather than by sentence. Other selection methods can only support such constraints in an ad-hoc fashion. To evaluate this feature of ILP selection, we implemented a variant of the greedy algorithm where the stopping criterion is number of words selected. We then imposed a global length constraint for ILP as described in Section 5.1, and compared BLEU scores across 35 simulation iterations for E2P with a limit of 5,000 words per batch (Figure 4(a)). The trend in BLEU indicates that ILP provides a better framework for integration of such constraints.

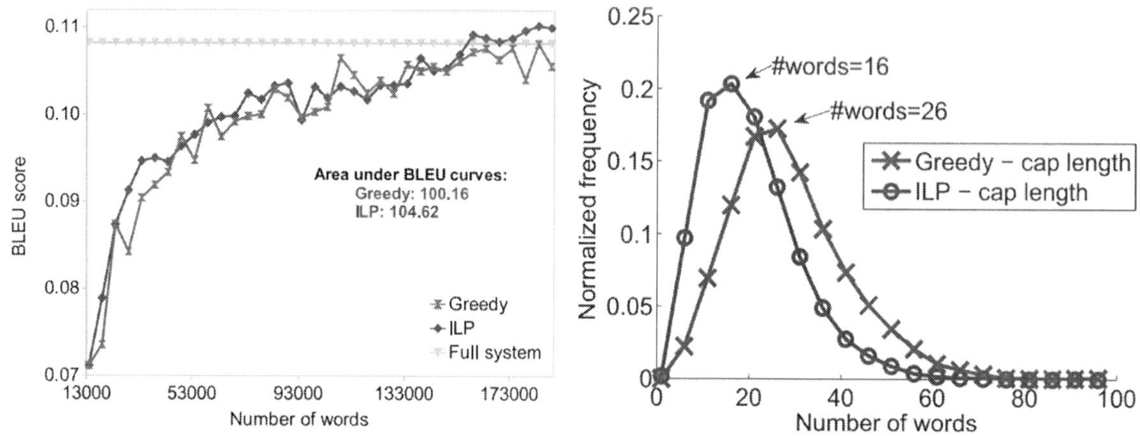

(a) Length-capped BLEU trajectory (E2P-SingleRef). Full system training data contains 1.46M source words.

(b) Normalized histogram of sentence length

Figure 4: Comparison of greedy and ILP with global length constraint of 5,000 words per batch.

Moreover, the overall sentence length distribution shown in Figure 4(b) indicates that the greedy algorithm prefers a smaller number of very long sentences, whereas ILP prefers a larger number of shorter sentences. The latter is an important practical benefit for applications such as crowdsourcing, because annotators often find it difficult to translate long sentences. Secondly, automatic word alignment quality for long sentence pairs is often poor. Finally, larger number of sentences in the training pool is likely to increase diversity.

7 Discussion and Future Work

Active learning provides a useful framework for alleviating the significant costs associated with developing SMT systems for resource-poor language pairs. In this paper, we introduced a novel criterion for active sample selection, viz. back-projected translation error. Candidate instances that score well on this criterion are chosen for translation by a bilingual human expert. We showed that the problem of maximizing the error-projection objective function is closely related to the set-covering problem, known to be NP-complete.

We used a simple greedy selection algorithm as a first approximation to the solution. BLEU trajectories from simulation experiments demonstrated the superiority of this scheme to competing active learning algorithms. We then proposed an optimization framework to maximize the objective function for sample selection, and provided a solution via ILP. The ILP-based selection algorithm also supports global constraints on the optimization problem, e.g. overall corpus size in words, which neither greedy selection nor other competing strategies can implement in a principled fashion. We also showed that ILP was superior to the greedy approach when constraining selected batches by total number of words, rather than by number of sentences.

The proposed approach is shown to outperform competing active learning strategies when the candidate pool contains a small number of high-impact samples buried within a large corpus of mostly irrelevant text. Guided by an in-domain development set, our approach always selects relevant samples that are likely to provide maximal benefit to the SMT system. Pilot experiments suggest that this approach may not be as effective when the candidate pool is completely task-relevant. Another weakness of our technique is the reliance on a relatively small development set to guide selection. Performance may saturate once all sentences in the development set can be translated accurately. Generally, a large, rich development set will tend to give better results. In the future, we plan to experiment with random sampling to vary the development set at each active learning iteration.

We have shown the effectiveness of our approach in the context of phrase-based SMT systems. The same principles can be extended to hierarchical or syntax-based SMT architectures with minimal effort.

References

Sankaranarayanan Ananthakrishnan, Rohit Prasad, David Stallard, and Prem Natarajan. 2010. Discriminative sample selection for statistical machine translation. In *Proceedings of the 2010 Conference on Empirical Methods in Natural Language Processing*, EMNLP '10, pages 626–635, Morristown, NJ, USA. Association for Computational Linguistics.

Michael Bloodgood and Chris Callison-Burch. 2010. Bucking the trend: large-scale cost-focused active learning for statistical machine translation. In *Proceedings of the 48th Annual Meeting of the Association for Computational Linguistics*, ACL '10, pages 854–864, Stroudsburg, PA, USA. Association for Computational Linguistics.

David A. Cohn, Zoubin Ghahramani, and Michael I. Jordan. 1996. Active learning with statistical models. *Journal of Artificial Intelligence Research*, 4(1):129–145.

Thomas H. Cormen, Charles E. Lerserson, and Ronald L. Rivest. 2001. *Introduction to Algorithms*. Prentice Hall of India.

Matthias Eck, Stephan Vogel, and Alex Waibel. 2005. Low cost portability for statistical machine translation based in N-gram frequency and TF-IDF. In *Proceedings of IWSLT*, Pittsburgh, PA, October.

Gholamreza Haffari and Anoop Sarkar. 2009. Active learning for multilingual statistical machine translation. In *Proceedings of the Joint Conference of the 47th Annual Meeting of the ACL and the 4th International Joint Conference on Natural Language Processing of the AFNLP: Volume 1 - Volume 1*, ACL '09, pages 181–189, Stroudsburg, PA, USA. Association for Computational Linguistics.

Gholamreza Haffari, Maxim Roy, and Anoop Sarkar. 2009. Active learning for statistical phrase-based machine translation. In *NAACL '09: Proceedings of Human Language Technologies: The 2009 Annual Conference of the North American Chapter of the Association for Computational Linguistics*, pages 415–423, Morristown, NJ, USA. Association for Computational Linguistics.

Rebecca Hwa. 2004. Sample selection for statistical parsing. *Computational Linguistics*, 30:253–276.

Richard M. Karp. 1972. Reducibility among combinatorial problems. In R. E. Miller and J. W. Thatcher, editors, *Complexity of Computer Computations*, pages 85–103. Plenum.

Philipp Koehn, Franz Josef Och, and Daniel Marcu. 2003. Statistical phrase-based translation. In *NAACL '03: Proceedings of the 2003 Conference of the North American Chapter of the Association for Computational Linguistics on Human Language Technology*, pages 48–54, Morristown, NJ, USA. Association for Computational Linguistics.

Qinggang Meng and Mark Lee. 2008. Error-driven active learning in growing radial basis function networks for early robot learning. *Neurocomputing*, 71(7-9):1449–1461.

Franz Josef Och. 2003. Minimum error rate training in statistical machine translation. In *ACL '03: Proceedings of the 41st Annual Meeting on Association for Computational Linguistics*, pages 160–167, Morristown, NJ, USA. Association for Computational Linguistics.

Dan Shen, Jie Zhang, Jian Su, Guodong Zhou, and Chew-Lim Tan. 2004. Multi-criteria-based active learning for named entity recognition. In *ACL '04: Proceedings of the 42nd Annual Meeting on Association for Computational Linguistics*, page 589, Morristown, NJ, USA. Association for Computational Linguistics.

Matthew Snover, Bonnie Dorr, Richard Schwartz, Linnea Micciulla, and John Makhoul. 2006. A study of translation edit rate with targeted human annotation. In *Proceedings AMTA*, pages 223–231, August.

Min Tang, Xiaoqiang Luo, and Salim Roukos. 2002. Active learning for statistical natural language parsing. In *ACL '02: Proceedings of the 40th Annual Meeting on Association for Computational Linguistics*, pages 120–127, Morristown, NJ, USA. Association for Computational Linguistics.

A Named Entity Recognition Method based on Decomposition and Concatenation of Word Chunks

Tomoya Iwakura† Hiroya Takamura‡ Manabu Okumura‡
†Fujitsu Laboratories Ltd.
iwakura.tomoya@jp.fujitsu.com
‡Precision and Intelligence Laboratory, Tokyo Institute of Technology
{takamura,oku}@pi.titech.ac.jp

Abstract

We propose a Named Entity (NE) recognition method in which word chunks are repeatedly decomposed and concatenated. We can obtain features from word chunks, such as the first word of a word chunk and the last word of a word chunk, which cannot be obtained in word-sequence-based recognition methods. However, each word chunk may include a part of an NE or multiple NEs. To solve this problem, we use the following operators: SHIFT for separating the first word from a word chunk, POP for separating the last word from a word chunk, JOIN for concatenating two word chunks, and REDUCE for assigning an NE label to a word chunk. We evaluate our method on a Japanese NE recognition data set that includes about 200,000 annotations of 191 types of NEs from over 8,500 news articles. The experimental results show that the training and processing speeds of our method are faster than those of a linear-chain structured perceptron and a semi-Markov perceptron while high accuracy is maintained.

1 Introduction

Named Entity (NE) recognition is a process by which the names of particular classes and numeric expressions are recognized in text. NEs include person names, locations, organizations, dates, times, and so on. NE recognition is one of the basic technologies used in text processing, including Information Extraction (IE), Question Answering (QA), and Information Retrieval (IR).

Supervised learning algorithms have been applied successfully to create NE recognizers. In the early stages, algorithms for training classifiers, including Maximum Entropy Models (Uchimoto et al., 2000), AdaBoost (Carreras et al., 2002), and Support Vector Machines (Yamada, 2007) were widely used. Recently, learning algorithms for structured prediction, such as linear-chain Conditional Random Fields (CRFs) (Lafferty et al., 2001), linear-chain structured perceptron (Collins, 2002a), semi-Markov perceptron (Cohen and Sarawagi, 2004), and semi-Markov Conditional Random Fields (Sarawagi and Cohen, 2004), have been widely used because of their good performances in terms of accuracy.

However, the computational cost of using these algorithms for structured prediction can become problematic when we handle a large number of types of NE classes. The computational cost of learning first-order-Markov models with linear-chain CRFs or structured perceptron is $O(K^2N)$, where K is the number of types of classes and N is the length of the sentence. Semi-Markov-based algorithms, such as semi-Markov perceptron and semi-Markov CRFs, enumerate NE candidates represented by word chunks in advance for capturing features such as the first word of a chunk and the last word of a chunk. Therefore, the computational cost of a semi-Markov perceptron is $O(KLN)$, where L is the upper bound length of the entities.

The computational cost might not be a big problem, when we use these learning algorithms to recognize a small number of types of NEs, such as the seven types in MUC (Grishman and Sundheim, 1996), the eight types in IREX (Committee, 1999), and the four types in the CoNLL shared task (Tjong Kim Sang and De Meulder, 2003). However, the computational cost will be higher than ever, when we recognize a large types of classes like Sekine's extended NE hierarchy that includes about 200 types of NEs for covering several types of needs of IE, QA, and IR (Sekine et al., 2002).

This paper proposes a word-chunk-based NE recognition method for creating fast NE recognizers while high accuracy is maintained by capturing rich features extracted from word chunks. Our method recognizes NEs from word-chunk sequences identified by a base chunker. When we use a base chunker with a computational cost of $O(KN)$ or lower than it, we can maintain the computational cost of our method as $O(KN)$. This is because the length of the word-chunk sequences is less than or equal to the sentence length N. In addition, our method can use features extracted from word chunks that cannot be obtained in word-based NE recognitions.

However, each word chunk may include a part of an NE or multiple NEs. To solve this problem, we use the following operators: SHIFT for separating the first word from a word chunk, POP for separating the last word from a word chunk, JOIN for concatenating two word chunks, and REDUCE for assigning an NE class label to a word chunk. Therefore, we call our method SHIFT-POP-JOIN-REDUCE parser (SPJR for short).

We demonstrate experimentally that the training and processing speeds of SPJR-based NE recognizers can be considerably faster than those of a linear-chain-perceptron and a semi-Markov-perceptron, while high accuracy is maintained.

2 SHIFT-POP-JOIN-REDUCE Parser

This section describes our method that recognizes NEs from word chunk sequences. We assume word chunk sequences are given by a base chunker which is described in Section 3.4.

2.1 Operators for Word Chunks

To recognize NEs from word chunks, we use SHIFT and POP for decomposing word chunks, JOIN for concatenating two word chunks, and REDUCE for assigning one of the defined NE class labels. In the following, $C = \langle C_1, ..., C_{|C|}\rangle$ denotes a word chunk sequence. cbw_j is the first word of C_j, and cew_j is the last word of C_j.

- REDUCE: This operator assigns one of the NE labels to a word chunk.

- POP: This operator separates the last word from a word chunk, and the separated word is treated as a new word chunk. POP is only applied to a word chunk consisting of more than one word. When POP is applied to C_j, the last word cew_j is separated from C_j. Indices of the following word chunks C_k $(j + 1 \leq k \leq |C|)$ are incremented by 1, and the separated word cew_j becomes new C_{j+1}. There is one exceptional procedure for POP to use as much initial chunk information as possible. If POP is successively applied to the j-th chunk, the separated words are concatenated and regarded as the $(j + 1)$-th chunk. For example, if C_j consists of words "w x y z" and POP is applied to both y and z, then the C_{j+1} will be considered to be "y z".

- SHIFT: This operator separates the first word from a word chunk, and the separated word is treated as a new word chunk. SHIFT is only applied to a word chunk consisting of more than one word. When SHIFT is applied to C_j, the first word cbw_j is separated from C_j. Indices of the word chunks C_k $(j \leq k \leq |C|)$ are incremented by 1, and the separated word cbw_j becomes new C_j.

- JOIN: This operator concatenates two adjacent word chunks. When JOIN is applied to C_j and C_{j+1}, C_j and C_{j+1} are concatenated for creating new C_j. Indices of the word chunks C_k $(j + 2 \leq k \leq |C|)$ are decremented by 1. To avoid an endless loop by generating previously processed word chunks, we forbid JOIN from occurring immediately after POP or SHIFT.

2.2 Training an NE Recognizer

The input to our training procedure is the word chunks of a base chunker along with the NE labels on those correct word chunks. To train an NE recognizer, we first generate training samples, and then run a machine-learning algorithm over the training samples. Figure 1 shows a pseudo-code of the procedure for generating training samples from the i-th input. $\{T_1, ... T_M\}$ is a set of training data consisting of M sentences.

$T_i = \langle T_{i,1}, ..., T_{i,M_i}\rangle$ $(1 \leq i \leq M)$ is the i-th training input. $T_{i,j}$ $(1 \leq j \leq M_i)$ is the j-th chunk of T_i, and $l(T_{i,j})$ is the NE label of $T_{i,j}$. If $T_{i,j}$ is not an NE, $l(T_{i,j})$ is O. The procedure runs as follows:

- (S0) We generate initial word chunks C from the word-sequence consisting of T_i with the given base chunker. We start to check the following steps from (S1) to (S5) for generating samples. The following process continues until all word chunks in T_i are processed.

```
# T_i = {T_{i,1}, ... T_{i,M_i}}: an input
# T_{i,j} (1 ≤ j ≤ M_i): a word chunk
# l(T_{i,j}): T_{i,j}'s NE label
# W_i: words in T_i
# C = {C_1, ... C_{|C|}}: word chunks
# l(cbw_j): the NE label of the last word of C_j
# l(cew_j): the NE label of the first word of C_j
# gen(C_j, OP): generate a training sample
#        for OPERATOR (OP) applied to C_i
# (S0) to (S5) correspond to those of Sec. 2.2.
GenerateTrainingSample(T_i)
# (S0) Generate a word chunk-sequence
# with a base chunker.
C = Chunking(W_i); j = 1;
while j ≤ M_i do
  if C_j == T_{i,j} then # (S1)
    gen(C_j, REDUCE = l(T_{i,j})); j++;
  else if l(cew_j) == O then # (S2)
    gen(C_j, POP); C = POP(C, j);
  else if l(cbw_j) == O then # (S3)
    gen(C_j, SHIFT); C = SHIFT(C, j);
  else if ( a word or words included in C_j
    are not the constituents of T_j) then # (S4)
    gen(C_j, POP); C = POP(C, j);
  else # (S5)
    gen(C_j, JOIN); C = JOIN(C, j);
  end if
end while
```

Figure 1: A pseudo code of the generation of training samples.

- (S1) If the current chunk C_j is equivalent to the correct chunk $T_{i,j}$, we generate a training sample for REDUCE=$l(T_{i,j})$. This means REDUCE for annotating a word chunk with $l(T_{i,j})$. Then we move to the next word chunk. ($j++$)

- (S2) If the label of the last word of the current chunk cew_j is "O", a training sample for applying POP to C_j is generated. Then POP is applied to C_j.

- (S3) If the label of the first word of the current chunk cbw_j is "O", a training sample for applying SHIFT to C_j is generated. Then SHIFT is applied to C_j.

- (S4) If a word or words included in C_j are not the constituents of $T_{i,j}$, a training sample for applying POP to C_j is generated.

- (S5) If all the above steps are not executed, the correct NE exists across more than one chunk. Therefore, we generate a sample of current word chunk for JOIN.

After generating training samples for all the inputs, we train a model from the training samples with a machine-learning algorithm.

2.3 An Example of Training

Consider the following training data T_i.

- [Mr.]$_O$ [Ken Ono]$_{PER}$ [went]$_O$ [skiing]$_O$

We first identify base chunks, and the result is as follows:

- [Mr. Ken] [Ono went] [skiing]

We denote this base chunking result as C. Word chunks are indicated by bracketing, and a current chunk is underlined.

We first compare $T_{i,1}$ and C_1. C_1 is not equivalent to $T_{i,1}$, and the NE label of the first word of C_1, "Mr.", is "O". Therefore, we generate a training sample for applying SHIFT to C_1 by (S3), and apply SHIFT to C_1. The current C would be the following.

- [Mr.] [Ken] [Ono went] [skiing]

We compare C_1 and $T_{i,1}$ again, and C_1 is equivalent to $T_{i,1}$. Therefore, we generate a training sample for applying REDUCE=O to C_1 by (S1), and move to the next word chunk.

- [Mr.] [Ken] [Ono went] [skiing]

C_2 is not equivalent to $T_{i,2}$, and C_2 does not satisfy (S1) to (S4). We generate a training sample of JOIN for C_2 by (S5), and apply JOIN to C_2 and C_3.

- [Mr.] [Ken Ono went] [skiing]

C_2 is still not equivalent to $T_{i,2}$, and the NE label of the last word "went" is "O". Therefore, we generate a training sample for applying POP to C_2 by (S2), and apply POP to C_2.

- [Mr.] [Ken Ono] [went] [skiing]

C_2 is equivalent to $T_{i,2}$, and a training sample for REDUCE=PER is generated. The remaining C_3 and C_4 are also equivalent to $T_{i,3}$ and $T_{i,4}$, respectively. Thus, two training samples for REDUCE=O are generated.

2.4 NE Recognition

Figure 2 shows a pseudo-code of our NE recognition method. When recognizing NEs from a given word sequence, we first identify an initial word

W: an input word-sequence
$C = \{C_1, ... C_{|C|}\}$: word chunks
$L = \{L_1, ... L_{|C|}\}$: NE class labels of word chunks
$Model$: a trained model
NERecognition(W, $Model$)
  # Generate a word chunk-sequence
  # with a base chunker. j is for C.
  $C = Chunking(W)$; $j = 1$;
  while $j \leq |C|$ **do**
    # Select an operation. If REDUCE is
    # selected, selectOP returns an NE label l.
    (op, l) = selectOP(C_j,$Model$);
    if op == REDUCE **then**
      $L_j = l$ # keep C_j's NE label
      $j++$ # Move to the next word chunk
    else if op == POP **then**
      $C = POP(C, j)$;
    else if op == SHIFT **then**
      $C = SHIFT(C, j)$;
    else if op == JOIN **then**
      $C = JOIN(C, j)$;
    end if
  end while
  return C and L

Figure 2: A pseudo code of NE recognition.

chunk sequence of the input with a base chunker as in the training.

Then we process each word chunk from the beginning of the sentence to the end of the sentence. An operator to use on the current word chunk is decided upon with a trained model, and each word chunk is processed according to the selected operator. If all the word chunks are processed, we return word chunks with their NE labels.

2.5 An Example of Recognition

Consider the following input data:
`-Mr. Jim Ji goes to U.K`

We identify base chunks of the input as follows.
`-[Mr. Jim Ji] [goes] [to] [U.K]`

We denote this base NE chunking result as C. An operator for each word chunk in C is selected with a trained model $Model$. Here, we assume SHIFT is selected and apply SHIFT to C_1. After applying SHIFT to C_1, C_1 becomes [Mr.], and C_2 becomes [Jim Ji].
`-[Mr.] [Jim Ji] [goes] [to] [U.K]`

We start to select an operator for the new C_1, and REDUCE=O is selected. We keep O as the NE class of C_1, and move to the next chunk C_2.
`-[Mr.] [Jim Ji] [goes] [to] [U.K]`

Next, we select an operator for the C_2, and REDUCE=PER is selected. We keep PER as the NE class of C_2, and move to the next chunk C_3. We continue this NE recognition process for the remaining word chunks. When we process all the word chunks, we return C with their NE labels.

3 Experimental Settings

3.1 Data Set and Evaluation Metrics

We used an extended NE corpus for our evaluation (Hashimoto et al., 2008). This Japanese corpus consists of about 8,500 articles from 2005 Mainichi newspaper. NE tags on this corpus is based on the extended NE hierarchy introduced by Sekine et al (Sekine et al., 2002). The corpus includes 240,337 tags for 191 types of NEs. To segment words from Japanese sentences, we used ChaSen.[1] We created the following sets for this experiment.

- training data: news articles from January to October 2005 in the corpus. The training data includes 1,806,772 words and 205,876 NEs.
- development data: news articles from November 2005 in the corpus. The development data includes 145,635 words and 15,405 NEs.
- test data: news articles from December 2005 in the corpus. The test data includes 177,159 words and 19,056 NEs.

Recall, precision, and F-measure are our evaluation metrics. Recall is defined to be the number of correctly recognized NEs divided by the number of all NEs. Precision is defined to be the number of correctly recognized NEs divided by the number of all recognized NEs. F-measure (FM) is defined as follows:

FM = 2 × recall × precision / (recall + precision).

[1] We use ChaSen-2.4.2 with Ipadic-2.7.0. ChaSen's web page is http://chasen-legacy.sourceforge.jp/. Words may include partial NEs because words segmented with ChaSen do not always correspond with NE boundaries. If such problems occur when we segment the training data, we annotated a word chunk with the type of the NE included in the word chunk. We did not deal with the difference between NE boundaries and word boundaries in this experiment.

3.2 Algorithms to be Compared

The following algorithms are compared with our method.

- Linear-chain structured perceptron (**Linear-Chain**, for short) (Collins, 2002a): This is a perceptron-based algorithm for labeling tags to word-sequences. In this algorithm, features are only generated from each word and its surrounding words.

- Semi-Markov perceptron (**Semi-Markov**, for short) (Cohen and Sarawagi, 2004): This algorithm is based on sequentially classifying chunks of several adjacent words, rather than single words. Ideally, all the possible word chunks of each input should be considered for this algorithm. However, the training of this algorithm requires a great deal of memory. Therefore, we limit the maximum length of the word-chunks. We use word chunks consisting of up to five or ten words. [2]

- NE Chunking and Classification (**NECC**, for short) (Carreras et al., 2002): This method consists of two parts. The first part is a base NE recognition as in our method. The second part is NE classification. Unlike in our method, this method just classifies given word chunks without decomposing and concatenating them. This method was used in the best system of the shared task of CoNLL 2002 (Tjong Kim Sang, 2002).

- Shift-Reduce Parser for NE Recognition (**SR**, for short) (Yamada, 2007): This algorithm is based on shift-reduce parsing for word-sequences. It uses two operators. The first one is shift which concatenates a word and its following word chunk. The other is reduce for annotating an NE label to current word chunk.[3] The algorithm is different from ours in that the initial inputs of their method are word sequences. Thus, each word chunk is constructed little by little. Therefore, the algorithm cannot use features obtained from word chunks at the early stage.

[2]This is because when we ran Semi-Markov without the chunk length constraint, it used 72GB memory, which is our machine memory size, and 1 GB swap region on its hard disc.

[3]To compare the performance under the same conditions, we did not use the operator to separate characters from words to recognize partial NEs in words.

We use the multiclass perceptron algorithm for NECC, SR and SPJR. Thus all of the algorithms are based on perceptron (Rosenblatt, 1958). We apply the averaged perceptron (Collins, 2002a) for all the training algorithms. All the learners and NE recognizers were implemented with $C++$. We used perceptron-based algorithms because perceptron-based algorithms usually show the faster training speed and lower usage of memory than training algorithms, such as MEMM (McCallum et al., 2000), CRFs (Lafferty et al., 2001), and so on. Actually, when we applied a CRFs implementation based on LBFGS (Liu and Nocedal, 1989) to the training data, the implementation consumed 72GB memory which is our machine memory size.

We select the number of the iteration that shows the highest F-measure in the development data for each NE recognizer. We set the maximum iteration number at 50.

3.3 Features

The features used in our experiment are shown in Table 1. As features for Linear-Chain perceptron, we used the following. Here, k denotes the current word position. w_k is the k-th word, and p_k is the Part-Of-Speech (POS) tag of k-th word. We used the word and the POS of the k-th word and the words in 2-word windows before and after the k-th word with the current NE-tag t_k and the NE tag t_{k-1} of the previous word. Each NE tag is represented as IOB1 (Ramshaw and Marcus, 1995). This representation uses three tags I, O and B, to represent the inside, outside and beginning of a chunk. B is only used at the beginning of a chunk which immediately follows another chunk that NE class is the same. Each tag is expressed with NE classes, like I-CL, B-CL, where CL is an NE class.[4] To realize a fast training speed for Linear-Chain, we only used the valid combination of t_k and t_{k-1} in terms of the chunk representation.

[4]We compared five types of chunk representation: IOB1 , IOB2, IOE1, IOE2 (Tjong Kim Sang and Veenstra, 1999) and Start/End (SE) (Uchimoto et al., 2000) in terms of the number of the NE tags. The number of the NE tags for each representation is as follows; IOB1 is 202, IOB2 is 377, IOE1 is 202, IOE2 is 377, and SE is 730. This experiment uses IOB1 because IOB1 has one of the lowest number of NE tags. The number of NE tags is related to the training speed of Linear-Chain. Actually, Linear-Chain using IOB1-based training data was about 2.4 times faster than Linear-Chain using SE-based training data in our pilot study with small training data.

Table 1: Features. k denotes a word positions for Linear-Chain. w_k is the k-th word surface, and p_k is the POS tag of the k-th word. t_k is the tag of the k-th word. TT_k is t_k or the combination of t_k and t_{k-1}. bp is the position of the first word of the current chunk. ep indicates the position of the last word of the current chunk. ip is the position of words inside the current chunk. ($bp < ip < ep$). If the length of the current chunk is 2, we use features that indicate there is no inside word as the features of ip-th words. t_j is the NE class label of j-th chunk. CL_j is the length of the current chunk, whether it be 1, 2, 3, 4, or longer than 4. WB_j indicates word bigrams, and PB_j indicates POS bigrams inside the current chunk.

Without chunk (Linear-Chain)
$[TT_k, w_k], [TT_k, w_{k-1}], [TT_k, w_{k-2}],$ $[TT_k, w_{k+1}], [TT_k, w_{k+2}], [TT_k, p_k],$ $[TT_k, p_{k-1}], [TT_k, p_{k-2}], [TT_k, p_{k+1}],$ $[TT_k, p_{k+2}], [TT_k, p_{k-2}, p_{k-1}],$ $[TT_k, p_{k+1}, p_{k+2}], [TT_k, p_{k-2}, p_{k-1}, p_{k+}],$ $[TT_k, p_k, p_{k+1}, p_{k+2}]$
With chunk (Semi-Markov, NECC, SR, SPJR)
$[t_j, CL_j], [t_j, WB_j], [t_j, PB_j],$ $[t_j, w_{bp}], [t_j, p_{bp}], [t_j, w_{ep}], [t_j, p_{ep}],$ $[t_j, w_{ip}], [t_j, p_{ip}], [t_j, w_{bp}, w_{ep}], [t_j, p_{bp}, p_{ep}],$ $[t_j, w_{bp}, p_{ep}], [t_j, p_{bp}, w_{ep}],$ $[t_j, w_{bp-1}], [t_j, p_{bp-1}], [t_j, w_{bp-2}], [t_j, p_{bp-2}],$ $[t_j, w_{ep+1}], [t_j, p_{ep+1}], [t_j, w_{ep+2}], [t_j, p_{ep+2}],$ $[t_j, p_{bp-2}, p_{bp-1}], [t_j, p_{ep+1}, p_{ep+2}],$ $[t_j, p_{bp-2}, p_{bp-1}, p_{bp}], [t_j, p_{ep}, p_{ep+1}, p_{ep+2}]$

Semi-Markov, NECC, SR, and SPJR, using word chunks, used features extracted from words in a word chunk and the words in two-word windows before and after the word chunk. The features extracted from chunks differ from those of Linear-Chain.

3.4 Base Chunkers

NECC and SPJR require a base chunker. To compare performances obtained with different base chunkers, we used a rule-based chunker and a machine-learning-based chunker.

We used a chunker that concatenates successive words with noun or unknown POS tags, or words existing in brackets, for the rule based chunker (**RC**, for short). This identification is fast because the chunker only checks POS tags.

Our machine-learning-based base chunker is the SR-based chunker trained to distinguish just two chunks: NE and non-NE. To train a machine-learning-based chunker, we first converted the given training data into a training data for base chunkers. There are only two classes for the training data used for base chunking: NE or not.

For example, the following labeled input,

`Dr. [Toru Tanaka]`$_{PER}$ `goes to [Kyoto]`$_{LOC}$

is converted as follows.

`[Dr.]`$_O$ `[Toru Tanaka]`$_{BNE}$ `[goes]`$_O$ `[to]`$_O$ `[Kyoto]`$_{BNE}$

BNE indicates that the word chunk becomes NE, and O indicates non-NE.

The converted training data are used for training a base NE chunker that identifies base NEs and non-NEs. Words identified as non-NEs are treated as word chunks consisting of a word.

Then we split the converted training data into five portions. To obtain a training set for recognizing NEs, we repeated the following process for all the five portions. We trained a base NE chunker with four out of five the portions of the converted training data. The base NE chunker identified base NEs from the remaining portion. After all the portions were processed, we trained the SPJR- or NECC-based NE recognizer from the five portions along with the NE labels on those correct word chunks.

For recognizing NEs in the test phase, we used a base NE chunker trained with all the given training data converted by the method. To examine whether we can attain high accuracy while maintaining fast training and processing speed, we used SR, the fastest algorithm among our compared algorithms, for training base NE chunkers.

4 Experimental Results

Table 2 shows the experimental results.[5] The NE recognizers based on our method showed good performance. SPJR with RC is the second, and SPJR with SR is the fourth best F-measure on test data. The best and the third systems are Semi-Markov-based ones. These results indicate that features extracted from word chunks contributed to improved accuracy.

To compare the results of SPJR (RC) with the others, we employed a McNemar paired test on the labeling disagreements as was done in (Sha and

[5]We used a machine with Intel(R) Xeon(R) CPU X5680 @ 3.33GHz and 72 GB memory.

Table 2: Experimental results. FM, RE, and PR indicate F-measure Recall, and Precision, obtained with each algorithm, respectively. The dev. and test indicate the results for the development data, and the results for the test data. MEM. indicates the amount of memory size (GB) for the training of each algorithm. TRAIN. indicates the training time for each algorithm (in hours). PROC. indicates the processing speed of the development data for each algorithm (in seconds). (SR) and (RC) indicate NECC or SPJR that uses a SR-based chunker or RC, respectively. The numbers after L= indicate the maximum length of the word-chunks for Semi-Markov perceptron.

Algorithm	FM (RE,PR) for dev.	FM (RE,PR) for test	MEM.	TRAIN.	PROC.
Linear-Chain	78.95 (75.53, 82.68)	80.62 (77.36, 84.18)	12.9	23.54	81.27
Semi-Markov (L=5)	79.46 (76.78, 82.34)	80.90 (78.39, 83.58)	9.8	0.97	41.06
Semi-Markov (L=10)	80.54 (77.46, 83.86)	81.95 (79.04, 85.08)	18.3	1.98	62.96
SR	78.66 (74.53, 83.28)	79.89 (75.84, 84.39)	0.78	0.12	3.54
NECC (SR)	78.81 (72.02, 87.01)	80.61 (73.98, 88.55)	0.76	0.26	5.75
NECC (RC)	51.56 (36.73, 86.49)	50.00 (35.09, 86.93)	0.73	0.08	2.98
SPJR (SR)	79.30 (76.06, 82.82)	80.83 (77.85, 84.05)	0.76	0.29	5.86
SPJR (RC)	79.48 (76.05, 83.23)	81.09 (77.76, 84.71)	3.05	0.27	3.02

Pereira, 2003). We compared results on test data by character units because the ends or beginnings of Japanese NEs do not always correspond with word boundaries. All the results except for Semi-Markov (L=10) indicate that there is a significant difference ($p < 0.01$). This result shows that SPJR (RC) showed high accuracy.

Our method also showed faster training and processing speeds than those of Linear-Chain and Semi-Markov. Specifically, our proposed method with RC showed about a 87 times faster training speed and about a 27 times faster processing speed than those of Linear-Chain. Our method showed about a 7 times faster training speed and about a 21 times faster processing speed than those of Semi-Markov (L=10). In addition, our algorithm requires a lower maximum memory size than Linear-Chain and Semi-Markov.

5 Discussion

5.1 Comparison with Linear-Chain

Our algorithm showed much faster speed than Linear-Chain. This is because the difference of computational procedure. Linear-Chain-based ones run Viterbi algorithm to select the best labeled sequence in terms of the scores assigned by a trained model for each input in both training and testing. When running Viterbi algorithm, Linear-Chain-based ones have to check the connections of class labels. The number of connections is up to K^2, where K is the number of types of class labels. On the other hand, SPJR-based ones greedily recognize NEs.

5.2 Comparison with Semi-Markov

Since the maximum length of the word-chunks affects the performance of Semi-Markov, we evaluated Semi-Markov using two types of the maximum lengths of the word-chunks. Semi-Markov (L=5) showed faster training and processing speed than Semi-Markov (L=10). However, SPJR-based ones still showed much faster training and processing speed than Semi-Markov (L=5). In addition, compared with Semi-Markov (L=5), SPJR (RC) showed higher accuracy and SPJR (SR) showed competitive accuracy. This result indicates that SPJR-based ones show faster speed than Semi-Markov giving up accuracy for improving speed.

5.3 Comparison with SR

SR showed faster training and processing speeds than those of SPJR and NECC using the SR-based base NE chunker. Specifically, SR showed about a 2.4 times faster training speed and about a 1.6 times faster processing speed than those of SPJR. This is because SPJR and NECC require training for the SR-based NE chunker and base NE recognition. However, SPJR showed better accuracy than SR. In addition, SPJR with RC showed faster processing speed than SR. These results indicate that our method using an appropriate base chunker realizes fast processing speed while maintaining accuracy.

5.4 Comparison with NECC

SPJR with RC showed much higher accuracy than NECC with RC. This is because the accuracy of RC-based NEs recognition is low. The SR-based base NE chunker identifies 86.56% of word chunks that become NEs in development data. However, RC identified only 50.75%. NECC can only identify correct NEs from correct chunks. Therefore, NECC with RC showed low accuracy. These results indicate our method based on decomposition and concatenation of word chunks contributed to improving accuracy.

However, SPJR (RC) showed more memory usage than SPJR (SR) and NECC-based ones. This is also related to the accuracy of each base chunker. To correctly recognize NEs from word chunks wrongly identified by the rule-based chunker, more training samples for decomposition or concatenation were generated. NECC showed slightly faster training and processing speeds than SPJR. This may be because NECC identifies the NE class of each word chunk without decomposition or concatenation.

5.5 Computational Efficiency

Our algorithm showed faster training and processing speeds than Linear-Chain and Semi-Markov. Formally, the computational cost of Semi-Markov is $O(KLN)$, where L is the upper bound length of word chunks, N is the length of the sentence and K is the size of the label set. As for Semi-Markov, L is 10 and K is 191 in this experiment. And that of the first order Linear-Chain perceptron is $O(K^2N)$, and K is 202 in this experiment. In contrast, the computational cost of NECC, SR, and SPJR is $O(KN)$ and K is 191.

Semi-Markov required more memory usage than the other algorithms. The number of word chunks of each sentence in Semi-Markov is roughly LN. In contrast, the number of word chunks or words of each sentence for Linear-Chain, NECC, SR, and SPJR are up to N. This indicates that Semi-Markov handles about L times larger space than the other algorithms in terms of the number of nodes. Therefore, it requires more memory usage than the others.

6 Related Work

There have been methods proposed to improve the training speed for semi-Markov-based models and perceptron-based methods. With regard to reducing the space of lattices built into the Semi-Markov-based algorithms, a method was proposed to filter nodes in the lattices with a naive Bayes classifier (Okanohara et al., 2006). To improve training speed of the structured perceptron, distributed training strategies and convergence bounds for a particular mode of distributed the structured perceptron training are provided in (McDonald et al., 2010).

While the formulation is different, SPJR shares similar idea with transformation based learning (Brill, 1995). For example, a transformation-based POS tagging alters the POS tag of each word with an ordered list of transformations. These transformations alter the POS tag of each word based on contextual cues.

Methods using rich information other than semi-Markov-based algorithms are proposed as well. Previous works use N-best outputs to obtain rich features. For example, a boosting-based algorithm and a perceptron-based algorithm for reranking N-best outputs were proposed (Collins, 2002b). Another approach uses feature forests generated from N-best outputs (Huang, 2008). This method merges N-best outputs into a single lattice. In contrast with these methods, which require a computational cost for processing N-best outputs, our method only handles an output.

Our proposed method showed good performance in this experiment, however, there is a drawback due to our recognizing strategy. Since NE recognizers based on our proposed method recognizes NEs greedily, only a mistake may affect later recognition process. In the future, we consider methods to incorporate techniques used in shift-reduce parsing (Huang and Sagae, 2010), like beam search or dynamic programming, into our recognition method for solving the problem.

7 Conclusion

We proposed a method for recognizing NEs from word chunk sequences. Our method uses operators for decomposing and concatenating word chunks. Experimental results showed training and processing speeds of our method are faster than those of linear-chain structured perceptron and semi-Markov perceptron while high accuracy is maintained. In the future we would like to evaluate our method with other tasks, such as NP chunking, and Text Chunking. We would also like to evaluate our method with different base chunkers.

References

Eric Brill. 1995. Transformation-based error-driven learning and natural language processing: A case study in part-of-speech tagging. *Computational Linguistics*, 21(4):543–565.

Xavier Carreras, Lluís Màrques, and Lluís Padró. 2002. Named entity extraction using adaboost. In *Proc. of CoNLL'02*, pages 167–170.

William W. Cohen and Sunita Sarawagi. 2004. Exploiting dictionaries in named entity extraction: combining semi-markov extraction processes and data integration methods. In *Proc. of KDD'04*, pages 89–98.

Michael Collins. 2002a. Discriminative training methods for Hidden Markov Models: theory and experiments with perceptron algorithms. In *Proc. of EMNLP'02*, pages 1–8.

Michel Collins. 2002b. Ranking algorithms for named-entity extraction: Boosting and the voted perceptron. In *In Proc. of ACL'02*, pages 489–496.

IREX Committee. 1999. *Proc. of the IREX workshop*.

Ralph Grishman and Beth Sundheim. 1996. Message understanding conference- 6: A brief history. In *Proc. of COLING'06*, pages 466–471.

Taiichi Hashimoto, Takashi Inui, and Koji Murakami. 2008. Constructing extended named entity annotated corpora. *IPSJ SIG Notes*, 2008(113):113–120.

Liang Huang and Kenji Sagae. 2010. Dynamic programming for linear-time incremental parsing. In *Proc. of ACL'10*, pages 1077–1086.

Liang Huang. 2008. Forest reranking: Discriminative parsing with non-local features. In *Proc. of ACL'08*, pages 586–594.

John D. Lafferty, Andrew McCallum, and Fernando C. N. Pereira. 2001. Conditional random fields: Probabilistic models for segmenting and labeling sequence data. In *Proc. of ICML'01*, pages 282–289.

Dong C. Liu and Jorge Nocedal. 1989. On the limited memory bfgs method for large scale optimization. *Mathematical Programming*, 45:503–528.

Andrew McCallum, Dayne Freitag, and Fernando C. N. Pereira. 2000. Maximum entropy markov models for information extraction and segmentation. In *ICML*, pages 591–598.

Ryan McDonald, Keith Hall, and Gideon Mann. 2010. Distributed training strategies for the structured perceptron. In *Proc. of NAACL HLT'10*, pages 456–464.

Daisuke Okanohara, Yusuke Miyao, Yoshimasa Tsuruoka, and Jun ichi Tsujii. 2006. Improving the scalability of semi-markov conditional random fields for named entity recognition. In *Proc. of ACL'06*.

Lance Ramshaw and Mitch Marcus. 1995. Text chunking using transformation-based learning. In *Proc. of the Third Workshop on Very Large Corpora*, pages 82–94. Association for Computational Linguistics.

Frank Rosenblatt. 1958. The perceptron: A probabilistic model for information storage and organization in the brain. 65(6):386–408.

Sunita Sarawagi and William W. Cohen. 2004. Semi-markov conditional random fields for information extraction. In *Proc. of NIPS'04*.

Satoshi Sekine, Kiyoshi Sudo, and Chikashi Nobata. 2002. Extended named entity hierarchy. In *Proc. of LREC'02*.

Fei Sha and Fernando Pereira. 2003. Shallow parsing with conditional random fields. In *Proc. of NAACL HLT'03*, pages 134–141.

Erik F. Tjong Kim Sang and Fien De Meulder. 2003. Introduction to the conll-2003 shared task: Language-independent named entity recognition. In *Proc. of CoNLL-2003*, pages 142–147.

Erik Tjong Kim Sang and Jorn Veenstra. 1999. Representing text chunks. In *Proc. of EACL '99*, pages 173–179.

Erik F. Tjong Kim Sang. 2002. Introduction to the conll-2002 shared task: Language-independent named entity recognition. In *Proc. of CoNLL'02*, pages 155–158.

Kiyotaka Uchimoto, Qing Ma, Masaki Murata, Hiromi Ozaku, Masao Utiyama, and Hitoshi Isahara. 2000. Named entity extraction based on a maximum entropy model and transformation rules. In *Proc. of ACL 2000*, pages 326–335.

Hiroyasu Yamada. 2007. Shift-reduce chunking for japanese named entity extraction. *IPSJ SIG Notes*, 2007(47):13–18.

Extract Chinese Unknown Words from a Large-scale Corpus Using Morphological and Distributional Evidences

Kaixu Zhang† and **Ruining Wang**† and **Ping Xue**‡ and **Maosong Sun**†
†State Key Laboratory on Intelligent Technology and Systems
Tsinghua National Laboratory for Information Science and Technology
Department of Computer Science and Technology
Tsinghua University, Beijing 100084, China
{kareyzhang,wangruining.student,sunmaosong}@gmail.com
‡The Boeing Company
ping.xue@boeing.com

Abstract

The representative method of using morphological evidence for Chinese unknown word (UW) extraction is Chinese word segmentation (CWS) model, and the method of using distributional evidence for UW extraction is accessor variety (AV) criterion. However, neither of these methods has been verified on large-scale corpus. In this paper, we propose extensions to remedy the drawbacks of these two methods to handle large-scale corpus: (1) for CWS, we propose a generalized definition of word to improve the recall; and (2) for AV, we propose a restricted version to decrease noise. We carry out experiments on a Chinese Web corpus with approximate 200 billion Chinese characters. Experimental results show that our methods outperform the baselines, and the combination of the two evidences can further improve the performance. Moreover, our methods can also efficiently segment the corpus on the fly, which is especially valuable for processing large-scale corpus.

1 Introduction

A Chinese word is constructed with one or more Chinese characters. Chinese characters can ambiguously combine to form Chinese words, and there are no explicit delimiters in the text to indicate word boundaries. It is thus crucial for most Chinese natural language processing tasks to maintain a large word list. Given that Chinese language has several productive word creation mechanisms, identification and extraction of UW is an important task for or Chinese NLP tasks.

Chinese unknown word (UW) extraction aims to extract UWs from a given corpus and enrich the word list. Two types of information can be used to determine whether a string of characters in question is a Chinese UW or not, namely the characters that construct the string in question, and the neighbors that this string of characters appears with. The first type of information can be regarded as the morphological evidence, while the second can be viewed as the distributional evidence.

The representative method of using morphological evidence is Chinese word segmentation (CWS) model. CWS is to identify every word token in a given sentence. Using the CWS model, we can define the word-string ratio (WSR) to extract UWs. The representative method of using distributional evidence is the accessor variety (AV) criterion (Feng et al., 2004a).

WSR is directly derived from the CWS method based on character tagging (Xue, 2003). This CWS method is based on the morphological information of the strings in question and their context. Strings with high WSR are considered as words, for high WSR indicates that the corresponding string is segmented as a word by this CWS method with high probability. Though the performance of the CWS method is relatively high, it leaves a number of UWs unrecognized or incorrectly recognized due to erroneous segmentation.

The AV criterion (Feng et al., 2004a) is based on the distributional information. Strings that have various contexts can be considered as words. It is shown that this method works well even for UWs with frequency of about 10. But both words and non-words with high frequency tend to have high AV. This brings noise for UW extraction in a large-scale corpus.

However, neither of these methods has been verified on large-scale Web corpus. In fact, as we observe, they both show certain deficiencies when dealing with large-scale corpus.

The emergence of online documents that contain various UWs poses challenges to UW extraction and other Chinese NLP tasks, but also provides a rich resource to make the UW extraction more meaningful.

Taking the two methods above as baselines, we propose two new methods, namely, generalized word string ratio (GWSR), and restricted accessor variety (RAV), by extending the current methods respectively, in order to overcome the relevant problems for large-scale corpus.

For GWSR, we propose a sophisticated way to generalize the definition of word in the CWS model. This method can extract more UWs that cannot be correctly segmented as words. For RAV, as opposed to AV, we restricted the accessors to be a small set of word pairs $(\mathbf{w}_l, \mathbf{w}_r)$ such that $\mathbf{w}_l$ appears right before the string in question and, at the same time, $\mathbf{w}_r$ appears right after the string in question. RAV is especially suitable for a large-scale corpus in which UWs occur with relatively high frequency.

We carry out experiments on a Chinese Web corpus with approximate 200 billion Chinese characters. Experiment results show that our methods outperform the corresponding baselines, and the combination of our methods can further improve the performance. Some examples are shown in the experiments section.

We further investigate the effect of corpus size to UW extraction. The numbers of Chinese characters in corpora range from 20 million to 200 billion. Moreover, our methods can also efficiently segment the corpus on the fly, which is practical for processing large-scale corpus.

The contribution of this paper is twofold. First, we proposed two UW extraction methods which outperform the baselines based on morphological and distributional evidence. Second, our experiments were conducted on corpora with up to 200 billion Chinese characters and provided insights about the effect of corpus size on UW extraction.

2 Background

2.1 CWS as Character Tagging

CWS aims to segment Chinese sentences into words. A practical CWS model needs to handle UWs, which are also named as out-of-vocabulary (OOV) words. If a corpus is perfectly segmented, the UW extraction task is also accomplished.

Xue (2003) proposed a character sequence tagging framework for CWS. Comparing to other methods, it has better performance on dealing with the UWs (Ling et al., 2003; Peng et al., 2004). The sequence tagging framework is also used for named entity identification in English (McCallum and Li, 2003), which is related to Chinese UW extraction.

In this framework, the input is a raw Chinese sentence s, denoted as a sequence of characters c_i:

$$\mathbf{s} = \overline{c_1 \dots c_n} \quad (1)$$

The output of the character sequence tagging is a sequence $\mathbf{t}$ of tags t_i corresponding to the input characters:

$$\mathbf{t} = \overline{t_1 \dots t_n} \quad (2)$$

where $t_i \in \{\mathrm{B}, \mathrm{M}, \mathrm{E}, \mathrm{S}\}$. The tags B / M / E indicate that the corresponding character is at the beginning / middle / end position of a multi-character word. The tag S indicates that the corresponding character is a single character word. The segmentation result of this sentence can thus be determined by the tag sequence.

Given an input sentence s, the output sequence of tags t is calculated as

$$\mathbf{t} = \arg\max_{\mathbf{t}'} W^T \Phi(\mathbf{s}, \mathbf{t}') \quad (3)$$

where Φ returns a feature vector of the pair $(\mathbf{s}, \mathbf{t}')$, and W is a vector of feature weights. The decoding is to find a $\mathbf{t}$ that maximizes the objective function.

Machine learning methods such as maximum entropy (Ng and Low, 2004), conditional random field model (Peng et al., 2004) and perceptron (Jiang et al., 2009) have been used for this framework.

The features in this framework are mainly composed by character unigrams, character bigrams and tag bigrams. In Chinese, a character is usually a morpheme. Therefore the CWS model based on the character tagging framework can be regarded as a UW extraction method using morphological information.

However, in contrast to CWS, UW extraction focuses on identifying substrings in a corpus that are potential words independent of the environments where they may occur. Though the performance of the CWS method is relatively high, the poor recall of UWs 'is still the Achilles heel of segmentation systems' (Emerson, 2005). The

CWS methods also fails to capture distributional information of the strings in question.

2.2 UW Extraction and the Accessor Variety Criterion

There are methods proposed for UW extraction based on morphological evidence, distributional evidence, or both (Chen and Ma, 2002; Ma and Chen, 2003; Feng et al., 2004a; Hong et al., 2009).

Some methods can be used for both UW extraction and CWS (Sun et al., 1998; Feng et al., 2004b; Jin and Tanaka-Ishii, 2006; Zhao and Kit, 2008). But for CWS, these methods are not comparable with the character tagging based CWS methods (Zhao and Kit, 2008), because the character tagging based CWS methods can better capture the morphological information.

We focus on a UW extraction method based on the distributional information, namely the accessor variety (AV) criterion (Feng et al., 2004a).

Assuming that a string is likely a meaningful unit if it occurs in different linguistic environments (Feng et al., 2004a), AV is defined as:

$$\mathrm{AV}(\mathbf{v}) = \min\{\mathrm{L_{av}}(\mathbf{v}), \mathrm{R_{av}}(\mathbf{v})\} \quad (4)$$

The $\mathrm{L_{av}}(\mathbf{v})$ is defined as the number of distinct Chinese characters that precede $\mathbf{v}$ plus the number of times that $\mathbf{v}$ appears at the beginning of a sentence. The $\mathrm{R_{av}}(\mathbf{v})$ is defined as the number of distinct Chinese characters that succeed $\mathbf{v}$ plus the number of times that $\mathbf{v}$ appears at the end of a sentence. The larger the $\mathrm{AV}(\mathbf{v})$ is, the more likely $\mathbf{v}$ is a word.

In order to fulfill this method, an extra dictionary is needed. And three ad hoc rules are used to discard strings which contain adhesive characters and cannot be words. The details can be found in (Feng et al., 2004a).

This method works well even for strings with low frequency because any distinct character is regarded as an accessor. However, when applying the method to a large-scale corpus in which strings in question are of high frequency, the noise increases considerably due to the lenient definition of the accessor.

3 Our Model

In this section, first we will introduce two UW extraction methods based on a character tagging based CWS model. Then we propose a UW extraction method called restricted accessor variety based on the distributional evidence. Finally, we discuss the combination of these methods.

3.1 Morphological Evidence

3.1.1 Word-string Ratio

A character tagging based CWS model, which is based on the morphological evidence, can be directly used to extract UWs in a corpus. The Word-string ratio (WSR) provides a straightforward way to determine whether a string in question is a word or not. Strings with high WSR are regarded as UWs.

WSR is defined as the ratio of the frequency of $\mathbf{v}$ that is segmented as a word to the frequency $\mathbf{v}$ that occurs as a string in the corresponding corpus:

$$\mathrm{WSR}(\mathbf{v}) = \frac{\mathrm{WF}(\mathbf{v})}{\mathrm{SF}(\mathbf{v})} \quad (5)$$

where word frequency $\mathrm{WF}(\mathbf{v})$ is the number of times that string $\mathbf{v}$ is segmented by the CWS model as a word in the corpus, and string frequency $\mathrm{SF}(\mathbf{v})$ is the number of times that string $\mathbf{v}$ appears in the corpus.

Now we discuss how to define the words in the CWS model. Since the tag sequence $\mathbf{t}$ in the character tagging framework may contain conflicts (e.g., the tag sequence "B B" means that two immediately connected characters are both at the beginning of multi-character words, which is impossible), we use an alternative way to define the words in the output. This new definition is also a preparation for the definition of the generalized word that we will propose.

Recall the decoding process of the CWS model in the character tagging framework described in Equation 3. Given a sentence $\mathbf{s} = \overline{c_1 \ldots c_n}$, we define $\mathrm{Conf}(m)$ as the confidence that there is a word boundary after the m-th character c_m ($t_m \in \{\mathrm{E}, \mathrm{S}\}$):

$$\mathrm{Conf}(m) = \max_{t_m \in \{\mathrm{E,S}\}} W^T \Phi(\mathbf{s}, \mathbf{t}) - \max_{t_m \in \{\mathrm{B,M}\}} W^T \Phi(\mathbf{s}, \mathbf{t}) \quad (6)$$

Obviously, $\mathrm{Conf}(m) > 0$ indicates that there is more likely a word boundary after the m-th character, while $\mathrm{Conf}(m) < 0$ indicates that there is less likely a word boundary after the m-th character.

If the string in question $\overline{c_i \cdots c_j}$ in s is a word, two confidences of the string boundaries $\mathrm{Conf}(i -$

1) and $\text{Conf}(j)$ should be positive and the confidences inside the string $\text{Conf}(k)$ should be negative for $k = i, \cdots, j-1$. In other words, the string $\overline{c_i \cdots c_j}$ is regarded as a word if and only if:

$$\text{Conf}_o(\overline{c_i \cdots c_j}) > 0 > \text{Conf}_i(\overline{c_i \cdots c_j}) \quad (7)$$

where $\text{Conf}_o(\overline{c_i \cdots c_j})$ and $\text{Conf}_i(\overline{c_i \cdots c_j})$ are defined as:

$$\text{Conf}_o(\overline{c_i \cdots c_j}) = \min\{\text{Conf}(i-1), \text{Conf}(j)\} \quad (8)$$

$$\text{Conf}_i(\overline{c_i \cdots c_j}) = \max_{k=i,\cdots,j-1} \text{Conf}(k) \quad (9)$$

Roughly speaking, words defined according to tag sequence $\overline{t_i \cdots t_j}$ and words defined according to the definition above are identical. In a test set of 107 thousand words, there are only 6 sentences of which the results are not identical.

3.1.2 Generalized Word-String Ratio

Although the CWS model can achieve relatively high performance. It fails to segment many instances of UWs correctly. This makes them hard to be extracted based on WSR.

In order to address this deficiency, we define a notion of generalized word, and we use the Generalized Word-String Ratio (GWSR) to extract UWs as a modified version of WSR. This idea is derived from Liu et al. (2008) and Zhang et al. (2010). For convenience, the term "word" in the rest part of this subsection always refers to a string that is segmented as a word by CWS model.

We define a cost function of string $\mathbf{v} = \overline{c_i \cdots c_j}$ based on the confidence function:

$$\text{Cost}(\mathbf{v}) = \max\{0 - \text{Conf}_o, \text{Conf}_i - 0\} \quad (10)$$

If a string $\mathbf{v}$ is segmented as a single word, the cost function returns a non-positive value; otherwise, it returns a positive value. The larger this value is, the less likely this string can be regarded as a word.

Now we can define GWSR of string $\mathbf{v}$:

$$\text{GWSR}_{\text{th\_LW}}(\mathbf{v}) = \frac{\text{GWF}_{\text{th\_LW}}(\mathbf{v})}{\text{SF}(\mathbf{v})} \quad (11)$$

where the generalized word frequency $\text{GWF}_{\text{th\_LW}}(\mathbf{v})$ is the number of times that string $\mathbf{v}$ appears with $\text{Conf}_o(\mathbf{v}) > \text{Conf}_i(\mathbf{v})$ and $\text{Cost}(\mathbf{v}) \leq \text{th\_LW}$ in a certain sentence. Here th_LW is a threshold. The inequality $\text{Conf}_o(\mathbf{v}) > \text{Conf}_i(\mathbf{v})$ should be always satisfied. Otherwise it will bring in noise.

Note that $\text{WF}(\mathbf{v}) = \text{GWF}_0(\mathbf{v})$ means that when $\text{th\_LW} = 0$ only words are regarded as generalized words.

The GWSR provides a way to allow UWs which are incorrectly segmented by the CWS model to be extracted. As a side effect, more noise may be brought in.

3.2 Distributional Evidence

The AV criterion is a method to extract UWs based on the distributional evidence. Here we propose a new version of the distribution-based criterion called restricted accessor variety (RAV) which is more suitable for the extraction from a large-scale corpus. We will describe this method and then discuss the difference between RAV and AV.

The RAV method can be divided into two steps. First, we identify the restricted contexts that words tend to appear in. Second, we count the number of distinct restricted contexts that the string in question appears in.

We define a restricted accessor pair as a pair of words that has the ability to match the majority of words. First, we define the matching between a pair of words $(\mathbf{w}_l, \mathbf{w}_r)$ and a string $\mathbf{v}$. We say that $(\mathbf{w}_l, \mathbf{w}_r)$ and $\mathbf{v}$ match if:

$$\frac{t(\mathbf{w}_l, \mathbf{v}, \mathbf{w}_r)}{f(\mathbf{v})} > \text{th\_RAV} \quad (12)$$

where th_RAV is a threshold. $f(\mathbf{v})$ is the number of times that $\mathbf{v}$ appears as a word or a sequence of words in the corpus segmented by our CWS model. $t(\mathbf{w}_l, \mathbf{v}, \mathbf{w}_r)$ is the number of times that the string $\mathbf{v}$ appears right after $\mathbf{w}_l$ and before $\mathbf{w}_r$ where $\mathbf{w}_l$ and $\mathbf{w}_r$ are also segmented as words.

Given a dictionary, we can find m word pairs which are most likely to match words in the dictionary. These pairs construct a set of restricted accessor pairs $\mathbf{R}$.

The RAV of a string v is defined as the number of restricted accessor pairs that match this string:

$$\text{RAV}(\mathbf{v}) = \sum_{(\mathbf{w}_l, \mathbf{w}_r) \in \mathbf{R}} 1_{[\text{th\_RAV}, \infty)} \left(\frac{t(\mathbf{w}_l, \mathbf{v}, \mathbf{w}_r)}{f(\mathbf{v})} \right) \quad (13)$$

where $1_{[\text{th\_RAV}, \infty)}$ is an indicator function to indicate whether $(\mathbf{w}_l, \mathbf{w}_r)$ and $\mathbf{v}$ match:

$$1_{[\text{th\_RAV}, \infty)}(x) = \begin{cases} 1 & x \in [\text{th\_RAV}, \infty) \\ 0 & \text{otherwise.} \end{cases} \quad (14)$$

The more restricted accessor pairs a string matches, the more likely it is a word.

Notice that the distribution-based method is usually used to measure the semantic distance between words. In our approach, by setting m (the number of restricted accessor pairs) to a relatively small number, the restricted accessor pairs can match any UW, no matter what meaning the word has or what word category it belongs to. Examples of the restricted accessor pairs will be shown in Section 4.3.

RAV is different from AV in at least four ways.

First, RAV is normalized. This prevents RAV from possible noise in the large-scale corpus. In such a corpus, a high frequency string tends to have more accessors which will bring noise to the AV criterion. In contrast, noise may be filtered out by a threshold in Eq. 13.

Second, RAV only considers restricted accessor pairs rather than any characters that precede or succeed the strings. This is also designed to further decrease the noise from a large-scale corpus.

Third, RAV does not need an ad hoc procedure to discard strings with adhesive characters, which prevents RAV from improperly discarding UWs. These adhesive characters in Chinese may also have the ability to be as a morpheme in a word. For example, "地" can be used as a function mark following an adverb, while it can also be a morpheme with the meaning "ground/territory" to form many UWs like "飞地" (enclave, literally "flying territory").

Last but not least, as RAV only concerns with a small number of restricted accessor pairs, RAV is more effective and efficient than AV in a large-scale corpus.

3.3 Combine Morphological and Distribu-tional Evidences

The morphological evidence and the distributional evidence represent the properties of different aspects of the "wordhood". The morphology-based method concerns with the possible character sequence that forms the string in question, and treats each occurrence of the string independently. The distribution-based method is not concerned with how a string is made up by characters, but with the context the string is in.

Evidence shows that these two methods are complementary; we expect to get a better performance by combining them. In this paper we only propose a simple way of linear combination.

4 Experiments

4.1 Dataset and Evaluation Method

A dictionary is needed to distinguish unknown words from known words. We used the same dictionary that Feng et al. (2004a) used. Totally 119,803 words in this downloaded dictionary are used as the known words.

SogouT corpus is an open and free large-scale Web corpus . This Web corpus was also used by Li and Sun (2009) in their semi-supervised CWS model. After certain process to remove non-text content such as the HTML tags, we obtained 119 million web pages consisting of 203 billion Chinese characters.

The whole corpus is denoted as LARGE. We sampled about one percent of these pages as a smaller corpus called MIDDLE, and further sampled about one percent of these pages in MIDDLE as SMALL. Corpora with different sizes are used to investigate how the size of the corpus influences the performances of different UW extraction methods.

It is difficult to evaluate the performance of UW extraction directly on such a large corpus. We used a partial evaluation method similar to the method used by Feng et al. (2004a). We sampled 2000 sentences from a balanced corpus (YUWEI corpus) consisting of news articles, academic articles, textbook articles, novels and other types of texts. Various UWs appear in these sentences. Since Chinese words commonly consist of 2, 3 or 4 characters (Chang and Su, 1997), only strings with length of 2, 3 or 4 in these sentences are considered as the UW candi-dates (strings in question). After filtering the strings that already appear in the dictionary, the remaining 111,536 strings are used as the test set.

In order to annotate these strings in the test set, we used the record of a Chinese input method software as an auxiliary data . We selected strings that are frequently inputted by users and manually annotated 1,630 of them as UWs. The annotation may have bias because the low frequency words tend to be ignored for the manually annotation. But the annotation is still independent of these UW extraction methods we use. Some of the UWs are 小诸葛 (nickname of a Chinese general Bai Chongxi), 二氯甲烷 (methylene chloride), 冬修 (to build in the winter by peasants in their slack

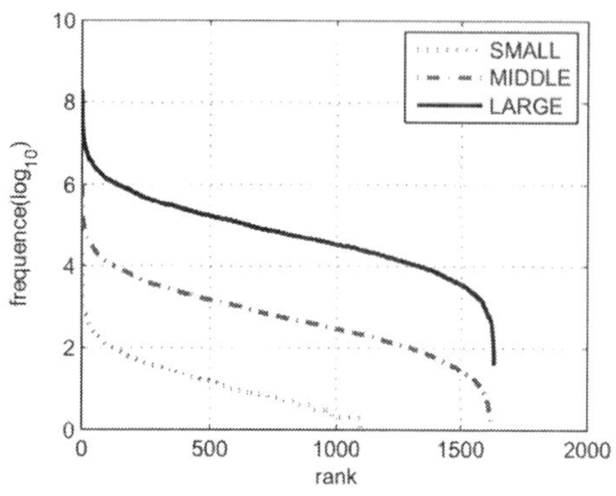

Figure 1: The frequencies of UWs in three corpora

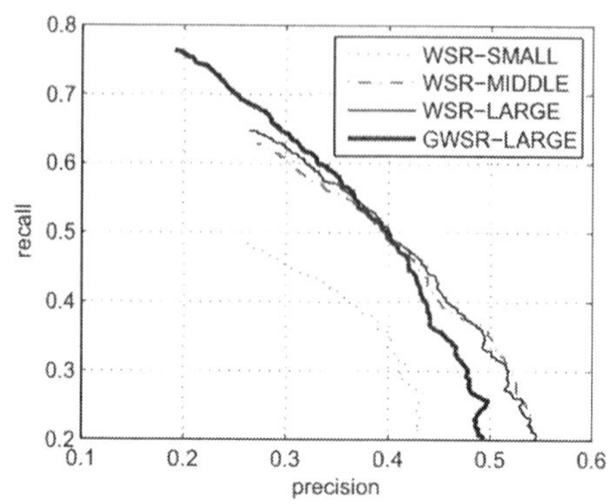

Figure 2: The precision-recall curves for WSR and GWSR on three corpora. The curves of GWSR on the SMALL and MIDDLE corpora are not showed due to the limitation of space.

season) and 官印 (official seal).

Figure 1 is an overview of the frequencies of the UWs in the corpora we used. We can observe the differences between these corpora. A number of UWs even do not appear in the SMALL corpus, while most of the UWs appear with a frequency higher than 10,000 in the LARGE corpus.

We use precision and recall as the evaluation measures:

$$\text{precision} = \frac{\text{\# of retrieved unknown words}}{\text{\# of retrieved words}} \quad (15)$$

$$\text{recall} = \frac{\text{\# of retrieved unknown words}}{\text{\# of annotated unknown words}} \quad (16)$$

The precision-recall curves of every method are drawn for the comparison. For each of these methods, a single threshold can be used to control the number of strings that are extracted. The precision-recall curves are drawn according to these thresholds.

Notice that in the evaluation, all the known words (words that are already in the dictionary) are not counted.

4.2 Morphological Evidence: WSR and GWSR

In this subsection we describe the implementation of our character tagging based CWS model, and the experiment results of the WSR and GWSR methods.

Template
$c_{i-1}t_i$, c_it_i, $c_{i+1}t_i$
$c_{i-2}c_{i-1}t_i$, $c_{i-1}c_it_i$, $c_ic_{i+1}t_i$, $c_{i+1}c_{i+2}t_i$
$t_{i-1}t_i$

Table 1: The feature templates for the CWS model

The CWS model we use is based on the averaged perceptron (Collins, 2002). The features templates are listed in Table 1, which are similar to the templates used for a CRF-based model (Tseng et al., 2005).

The training set provided by Microsoft Research in SIGHAN bake-off 2005 (Emerson, 2005) is used to train our CWS model. The F-measure on the test set was 0.963. This is comparable with the reported best 0.964, which is from a CRF-based model (Tseng et al., 2005).

Additional techniques were used to speed up the decoding of our CWS model. A modified double-array trie (Aoe et al., 1992) data structure was implemented to store and retrieve the feature values. Fix-point numbers (integer) rather than floating point numbers are used for the calculation without losing accuracy. With some other minor improvements, the decoding speed of one process is up to 2 million characters per second. This makes it possible to segment the large-scale Web corpus on the fly.[1]

Since the WSR and GWSR for strings with low string frequency are not precise enough, we discard strings with low string frequency using the thresholds 0, 15 and 1,500 for the SMALL, MIDDLE and LARGE corpora, respectively. The threshold th_LW discussed in Section 3 for GWSR is set to 2.

Figure 2 shows the precision-recall curves for WSR and GWSR on three corpora.

On the SMALL corpus, the performance of

[1]The modified version is available at http://code.google.com/p/perminusminus/

WSR is poor, for the majority of UWs appear with a low frequency or even do not appear in this corpus. On the MIDDLE corpus, the performance is better than the one on the SMALL corpus. But on the LARGE corpus, the performance improvement is not observable comparing to the performance on the MIDDLE corpus. The GWSR behaves similarly to WSR when we enlarge the corpus. This phenomenon indicates that the methods based on the morphological evidence cannot benefit from a larger corpus if the frequencies of corresponding strings are high enough.

Consider this with Figure 1, we find that a frequency of about 100 is enough for WSR and GWSR to determine whether the corresponding string is a word or not.

Now we compare GWSR with WSR on the LARGE corpus in Figure 2. GWSR has a better performance in the left part of the precision-recall curve but a poorer performance in the right part of this curve. We can say that GWSR has a better recall but a poorer precision, which is consistent with our discussion in Section 3.1. Comparing to WSR, the GWSR can extract more UWs, while it brings in more noise as a side effect. The advantage of simply using GWSR instead of WSR is not obvious.

4.3 Distributional Evidence: AV and RAV

The words used to induce the restricted accessor pairs set are all the known words that appear in the 2,000 sentences we sampled from YUWEI corpus. We induce a restricted accessor pairs set of 50 word pairs, which are most likely to match these words. Some of the pairs are (#,#), (#, 和), (到, 的) and (没有,#). # is used as a special word to denote the beginning and the end of a sentence.

Among these 50 word pairs, only 3 pairs contain words with 2 characters. Other words are all single character words. Nearly all the words are function words. 和 (and), 到 (to), 的 (a particle) and 没有 ('no' or 'do not') which are in the pairs we showed are all frequently used function words.

We found that the word with the highest frequency in these pairs is "#", which is consistent with the claim by Li and Sun (2009) that punctuation marks are useful for CWS.

All these pairs have the ability to match a majority of words in different word categories or with different meanings. This result also benefits from the fact that Chinese words do not have inflection

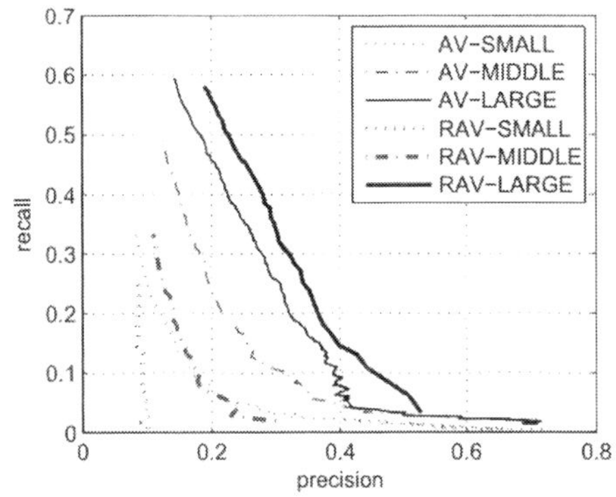

Figure 3: precision-recall curves for AV and RAV on three corpora

and agglutination. For example, an adjective like 幸福 (happy) can be used as a noun (happiness), a verb (be happy) or an adverb (happily) without changing the form.

We calculated AV and RAV for the strings in the test set on these three corpora. We found that RAV is more efficient than AV. According to the formulas, RAV only needs to assign a vector of 50 integers (we use 50 restricted accessor pairs in the experiments) for each string, while AV needs to assign a hash table for each string. Plus, the additional process for AV to discard strings with adhesive characters is also implemented according to the instruction in (Feng et al., 2004a).

Results are shown in Figure 3. Notice that the precision and recall for AV are lower than those reported by Feng et al. (2004a), for in our experiments the known words are not counted. Counting known words, the precision and recall are comparable with those reported by them.

We see that for both methods, larger size of the corpus improves the performances. We can even expect that more data can further enhance these methods.

AV and RAV behave differently when we enlarge the corpus. On both the SMALL and MIDDLE corpus, the AV method is better than the RAV method, whereas on the LARGE corpus, RAV outperforms AV. The reason is that the RAV method strongly depends on the size of corpus. Even 1000 occurrences may not be enough for a relatively accurate RAV of a string. This characteristic is also quite different from the WSR and LWSR methods.

Thus RAV is more suitable than AV when we have a large-scale corpus. Plus RAV does not need an ad hoc process to discard strings with adhesive characters.

4.4 Combine Morphological and Distribu-tional Evidences

In this subsection we first show the differences of the errors made by the methods based on morphological and distributional evidences, respectively. Then we combine these two kinds of methods and show that the performance will be further improved.

(G)WSR and RAV are based on different evidences. The errors of these methods are thus quite different.

Non-words	GWSR	RAV
逍遥法 (part of "逍遥法外")	0.879	6
脱但 (off but)	0.817	2
一书里 (in a book of)	0.671	10
一个女孩 (a girl)	0	50
实验结果 (experiment result)	0	49
严格把关 (to strictly check)	0	43

Table 2: Some false positive examples for GWSR and RAV in the LARGE corpus

Table 2 shows some non-words that are incorrectly regarded as UWs by GWSR or RAV. Some non-words sun as 逍遥法 have high GWSR values, for they tend to be segmented as words by the CWS models. But they may have low RAV values for they are hard to be used as single syntactic units. Multi-word compounds such as 一个女孩 have high RAV for they have similar distribution as words. But they may have low GWSR because the CWS model tends to segment them into smaller parts with high confidence.

We linearly combine the scores of the morphological and distributional evidences. WSR and GWSR are used as the morphological evidence, respectively. For the AV method contains a filtering process, we cannot assign a value for every string. Only the RAV is used as the distributional evidence.

WSR and GWSR range from 0 to 1, while RAV ranges from 0 to 50. In our experiments, the weights for the morphological and distributional evidences are 50 and 0.8, respectively.

Two thick lines in Figure 4 show the performances of the combinations of the evidences. The precision of combing WSR and RAV (dashed thick line) is increased comparing to WSR. If we replace WSR by GWSR in the combined method

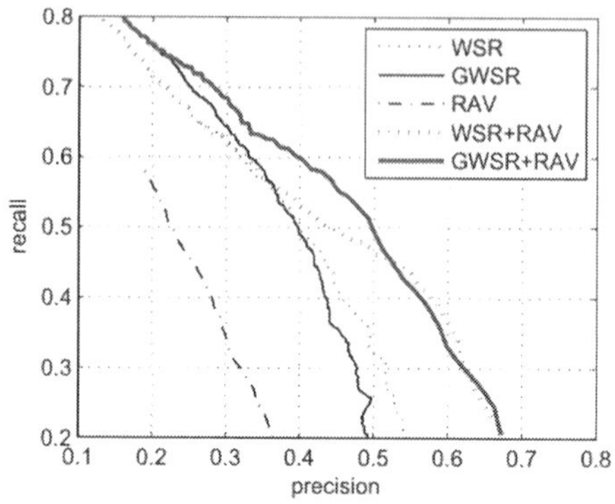

Figure 4: The combination of the morphological evidence and the distributional evidence on the LARGE corpus

(solid thick line), the recall is further increased without observably losing the precision. So the combination of GWSR and RAV outperforms the combination of WSR and RAV.

5 Conclusion

We discussed two UW extraction methods, namely morphology based and distribution based methods. The WSR based on morphological evidence has a relative high performance, while it does not benefit from the use of a large-scale corpus. The performance of the accessor variety (AV) based on distributional evidence improves gradually as we enlarge the corpus. We also proposed two extended methods. The method based on generalized word-string ratio (GWSR) has higher recall comparing to WSR. The restricted accessor variety (RAV) is specially designed for the large-scale web corpus in which the UWs are with high frequency.

Our methods outperformed the baselines, and the combination of the two methods can further improve the performance.

In the future, we will explore how to optimize the combination of GWSR and RAV to further improve UW extraction and the performance of the CWS models in general.

Acknowledgments

This work is suooprted by the Tsinghua-Boeing Joint Research Project.

The author would like to thank Dr. Zhiyuan Liu for his helpful discussion, and Jianzhi Zeng for the proofreading of this paper.

References

J. Aoe, K. Morimoto, and T. Sato. 1992. An efficient implementation of trie structures. *Software: Practice and Experience*, 22(9):695–721, September.

J. S Chang and K. Y Su. 1997. An unsupervised iterative method for chinese new lexicon extraction. *International Journal of Computational Linguistics & Chinese Language Processing*, 1(1):101 - 157.

K. J. Chen and W. Y. Ma. 2002. Unknown word extraction for chinese documents. In *Proceedings of the 19th international conference on Computational linguistics-Volume 1*, pages 1–7. Association for Computational Linguistics.

M. Collins. 2002. Discriminative training methods for hidden markov models: Theory and experiments with perceptron algorithms. In *Proceedings of the ACL-02 conference on Empirical methods in natural language processing-Volume 10*, page 1 - 8.

T. Emerson. 2005. The second international chinese word segmentation bakeoff. In *Proceedings of the Fourth SIGHAN Workshop on Chinese Language Processing*, pages 123–133. Jeju Island, Korea.

H. Feng, K. Chen, X. Deng, and W. Zheng. 2004a. Accessor variety criteria for chinese word extraction. *Computational Linguistics*, 30(1):75–93.

H. Feng, K. Chen, C. Kit, and X. Deng. 2004b. Unsupervised segmentation of chinese corpus using accessor variety. *Natural Language Processing - IJCNLP 2004*, pages 694–703.

C. M Hong, C. M Chen, and C. Y Chiu. 2009. Automatic extraction of new words based on google news corpora for supporting lexicon-based chinese word segmentation systems. *Expert Systems with Applications*, 36(2):3641 - 3651.

W. Jiang, L. Huang, and Q. Liu. 2009. Automatic adaptation of annotation standards: Chinese word segmentation and POS tagging ⊢a case study. In *Proceedings of the 47th ACL*, page 522 - 530, Suntec, Singapore, August. Association for Computational Linguistics.

Z. Jin and K. Tanaka-Ishii. 2006. Unsupervised segmentation of chinese text by use of branching entropy. In *Proceedings of the COLING/ACL on Main conference poster sessions*, pages 428–435. Association for Computational Linguistics.

Z. Li and M. Sun. 2009. Punctuation as implicit annotations for chinese word segmentation. *Computational Linguistics*, 35(4):505–512.

G. O.H.C Ling, M. Asahara, and Y. Matsumoto. 2003. Chinese unknown word identification using character-based tagging and chunking. In *Proceedings of the 41st Annual Meeting on Association for Computational Linguistics-Volume 2*, page 197 - 200.

Y. Liu, B. Wang, F. Ding, and S. Xu. 2008. Information retrieval oriented word segmentation based on character associative strength ranking. In *Proceedings of the Conference on Empirical Methods in Natural Language Processing*, pages 1061–1069. Association for Computational Linguistics.

W. Y. Ma and K. J. Chen. 2003. A bottom-up merging algorithm for chinese unknown word extraction. In *Proceedings of the second SIGHAN workshop on Chinese language processing-Volume 17*, pages 31–38. Association for Computational Linguistics.

A. McCallum and W. Li. 2003. Early results for named entity recognition with conditional random fields, feature induction and web-enhanced lexicons. In *Proceedings of the seventh conference on Natural language learning at HLT-NAACL 2003-Volume 4*, page 188 - 191.

H. T. Ng and J. K. Low. 2004. Chinese part-of-speech tagging: one-at-a-time or all-at-once? word-based or character-based. In *Proc of EMNLP*.

F. Peng, F. Feng, and A. McCallum. 2004. Chinese segmentation and new word detection using conditional random fields. In *Proceedings of the 20th international conference on Computational Linguistics*, page 562. Association for Computational Linguistics.

M. Sun, D. Shen, and B. K Tsou. 1998. Chinese word segmentation without using lexicon and hand-crafted training data. In *Proceedings of the 17th international conference on Computational linguistics-Volume 2*, pages 1265–1271. Association for Computational Linguistics Morristown, NJ, USA.

H. Tseng, P. Chang, G. Andrew, D. Jurafsky, and C. Manning. 2005. A conditional random field word segmenter for sighan bakeoff 2005. In *Proceedings of the Fourth SIGHAN Workshop on Chinese Language Processing*, pages 168–171. Jeju Island, Korea.

N. Xue. 2003. Chinese word segmentation as character tagging. *Computational Linguistics and Chinese Language Processing*, 8(1):29–48.

K. Zhang, M. Sun, and P. Xue. 2010. A local generative model for chinese word segmentation. *Information Retrieval Technology*, pages 420–431.

H. Zhao and C. Kit. 2008. An empirical comparison of goodness measures for unsupervised chinese word segmentation with a unified framework. In *The Third International Joint Conference on Natural Language Processing (IJCNLP-2008), Hyderabad, India.*

Entity Disambiguation Using a Markov-Logic Network

Hong-Jie Dai[1,2] **Richard Tzong-Han Tsai**[3*] **Wen-Lian Hsu**[1,2*]

[1]Department of Computer Science, National Tsing Hua University,
300 No. 101, Section 2, Kuang-Fu Road, Hsinchu, Taiwan, R.O.C.
[2]Intelligent Agent Systems Lab., Institute of Information Science, Academia Sinica,
128 Academia Road, Sec.2, Nankang, Taipei, Taiwan, R.O.C.
[3]Department of Computer Science & Engineering, Yuan Ze University
135 Yuan-Tung Road, Chungli, Taoyuan, Taiwan, R.O.C.
hongjie@iis.sinica.edu.tw
thtsai@saturn.yzu.edu.tw
hsu@iis.sinica.edu.tw

Abstract

Entity linking (EL) is the task of linking a textual named entity mention to a knowledge base entry. It is a difficult task involving many challenges, but the most crucial problem is entity ambiguity. Traditional EL approaches usually employ different constraints and filtering techniques to improve performance. However, these constraints are executed in several different stages and cannot be used interactively. In this paper, we propose several disambiguation formulae/features and employ a Markov logic network to model interweaved constraints found in one type of EL, gene mention linking. To assess our systems effectiveness in different applications, we adopt two evaluation schemes: article-wide and instance-based precision/recall/F-measure. Experimental results show that our system outperforms the baseline systems and state-of-the-art systems under both evaluation schemes.

1 Introduction

Entity linking (EL) is the task of linking a textual named entity mention to a knowledge base (KB) entry, such as linking a person/organization mention to its Wikipedia entry (Kulkarni, Singh et al. 2009; McNamee and Dang 2009). This task has broad applications and is important in information extraction (IE) and text mining.

EL involves many challenges, but the most crucial problem in EL is *entity ambiguity*. Take the name John A. Smith for example. It might appear in KB as John Alexander Smith, John Blair Smith, John D. Smith, etc. Entity disambiguation determines which of all the possible John Smith KB entries a given "John Smith" refers to. Several disambiguation approaches have been proposed to address the entity ambiguity problem. For example, Dredze et al. (2010) formulated the disambiguation task as a ranking problem and developed features to link entities to Wikipedia entries. Zhang et al. (2010) used an automatically generated corpus to train a binary classifier to reduce ambiguities. Dai et al. (2010) collected external knowledge for each entity and calculated likelihoods stating the similarity of the current text with the knowledge to improve the disambiguation performance.

In addition to the entity ambiguity problem, the EL task in Text Analysis Conference (TAC) 2009 introduce the absence issue (McNamee and Dang 2009): for entities that have no corresponding entry in the KB a NIL should be returned. To deal with the absence issue, Bunescu and Pasca (2006) filtered out linked mentions whose scores are less than a fixed threshold. Li et al. (2009) trained a separate binary classifier to validate linked mentions. Dredze et al. (2010) treated the NIL as another KB entry candidate to train their EL ranking model.

Most previous works employed separate stages to execute NIL-filtering and disambiguation. However, a separate-stage approach ignores possible dependencies between NIL-filtering and disambiguation can result in error propagation. Figure 1 illustrates the problem. It shows a biomedical abstract, which discusses the relationship of the gene "CD59" to

*Corresponding author

TITLE: Structure of the **CD59**-encoding gene: further evidence of a relationship to *murine* lymphocyte antigen Ly-6 protein
ABSTRACT: The gene for **CD59** [**membrane inhibitor of reactive lysis** (**MIRL**), **protectin**], a phosphatidylinositol-linked surface glycoprotein that regulates the formation of the polymeric **C9 complex** of complement and that is deficient on the abnormal hematopoietic cells of *patients* with paroxysmal nocturnal hemoglobinuria, consists of four exons spanning 20 kilobases. ...
PMID [1381503]

Figure 1: An Example of Entity Linking.

other lymphocyte antigens. An EL system must link the human gene entity "CD59" and all its instances in the body of the abstract (including "membrane inhibitor of reactive lysis", "protectin", and "MIRL", in the first sentence) to the EntrezGene database entry ID:966. However, the same name "CD59" in the title refers to a murine gene and, therefore, must be linked to ID:12509 instead. A separate-stage approach is likely to run into trouble with this example. In the EL stage, "MIRL" can be unambiguously linked to ID:996 with high confidence, because a search for the name in EntrezGene returns only one match. Linking the other mentions (e.g. "CD59" and "protectin") to ID:996 is not as easy. For example, "CD59" alone has 18 candidate entries. However, because we know that these names are synonyms of MIRL, we can then link them more easily. Unfortunately, a separate NIL-filtering stage may filter out the entity mention "MIRL" because it is listed as an abbreviation of organization names, such as Mineral Industry Research Laboratory. With a joint inference process we can carry out both tasks simultaneously to avoid this type of error propagation (Poon and Domingos 2007).

Joint inference has become popular recently, because they make it possible for features and constraints to be shared among tasks. For example, Che and Liu (2010) created a joint model for word sense disambiguation (WSD) and semantic role labeling, and Finkel and Manning (2009) integrated parsing and named entity recognition in a joint model. In this paper, we use the Markov Logic Network (MLN) (Richardson and Domingos 2006), a joint model which combines first order logic (FOL) and Markov networks, to unify the NIL-filtering and entity disambiguation stages. The model captures the contextual information of the recognized entities for entity disambiguation as well as the constraints when linking an entity mention to a KB entry—for example, an entity mention can only be linked to a database entry when the mention has not been recognized as an NIL.

Another advantage of employing MLN in our EL disambiguation model is that it is easy to model arbitrary longer range dependencies among entities. For example, the saliency of a given entity in a given discourse is one property that can be modeled with MLN. This property was defined by Gale et al. (1992) in WSD, but has not been applied to EL disambiguation. It states that in a given discourse, there is precisely one entity that is the center of attention. This entity is mentioned over and over again, makes it more salient than others. We can utilize this phenomenon to improve the disambiguation confidence. Continuing with the example shown in Figure 1, ID:996 is a candidate KB entry for the entity "CD59" and all its instances, including "membrane inhibitor of reactive lysis", "protectin", and "MIRL" in the first sentence, we can then assume that ID:996 is more salient than other candidate KB entries. As described in the previous paragraph, we can link the entity "MIRL" to ID:996 with high confidence. Therefore, we are more likely to be able to link all the other entities to ID:996 as well.

Finally, existing EL approaches in biomedical domain assess system performance in terms of the effectiveness of database curation (Morgan, Wellner et al. 2007). In addition, we evaluate our system at a fine-grained resolution, entity by entity. Such an evaluation is more relevant to IE tasks such as the bio-molecular event extraction.

2 Markov Logic

In FOL, formulae are constructed using four types of symbols: constants, variables, functions, and predicates. *Constants* represent objects in a domain of discourse (e.g. people: **Ann**, **John**, etc., or database entries). *Variables* (e.g., x, y) range over the objects. *Predicates* represent the relations among objects (e.g. $correlates$), or attributes of objects (e.g. $hasTitle$). Variables and constants may be typed. An *atom* is a predicate symbol applied to a list of arguments, which may be variables or constants (e.g. $hasTitle(\mathbf{John}, x)$). A *ground atom* is an atom all of whose arguments are constants (e.g. $hasTitle(\mathbf{John}, \mathbf{Mr.})$). A *world* is an assignment of truth values to all possible ground atoms. A KB is a partial specification of a world; each atom in it is true, false or (implicitly) unknown.

A Markov network represents the joint distribution of a set of variables $X = (X_1, \ldots, X_n) \in \mathcal{X}$ as a product of factors: $P(\mathbf{X} = \mathbf{x}) = \frac{1}{Z}\prod_k f_k(\mathbf{x}_k)$, where each factor f_k is a non-negative function of a subset of the variables $\mathbf{x}_k$, and Z is a normalization constant. As long as $P(\mathbf{X} = \mathbf{x}) > 0$ for all $\mathbf{x}$, the distribution can be equivalently represented as a log-linear model: $P(\mathbf{X} = \mathbf{x}) = \frac{1}{Z}\exp(\sum_i w_i g_i(\mathbf{x}))$, where the features $g_i(\mathbf{x})$ are arbitrary functions of (a subset of) the variables' state.

An MLN L is a set of pairs (F_i, w_i), where F_i is a formula in FOL and w_i is a real number represented a weight. Together with a finite set of constants C, it defines a Markov network $M_{L,C}$, where $M_{L,C}$ contains one node for each possible grounding of each predicate appearing in L. The value of the node is 1 if the ground predicate is true, and 0 otherwise. The probability distribution over possible worlds x is given by $P(X = x) = \frac{1}{Z}\exp\left(\sum_{i \in F}\sum_{j \in G_i} w_i g_j(x)\right)$ where Z is the partition function, F is the set of all first-order formulae in the MLN, g_i is the set of groundings of the ith first-order formula, and $g_j(x) = 1$ if the jth ground formula is true and $g_j(x) = 0$ otherwise. General algorithms for inference and learning in Markov logic are discussed in Richardson and Domingos (2006). We employ thebeast toolkit (downloaded from http://code.google.com/p/thebeast/) to implement our MLN model. It uses 1-best MIRA online learning method for learning weights and employs cutting plane inference (Riedel 2008) with integer linear programming as its base solver for inference at test time and the MIRA online learning process.

3 Methods

In this paper, we tackle one type of EL, gene mention linking, which links each gene entity mention to one EntrezGene ID. EntrezGene (Maglott, Ostell et al. 2006) is the most popular large scale gene database. Generally speaking, the EL task can be separated into four steps: (1) identifying entities in a given article, (2) filtering NIL entity mentions, (3) finding candidate KB entries (or database IDs) for the remaining entity mentions, and (4) picking one KB entry for each entity mention. To concentrate on EL's major challenge, our MLN-based system only focuses on steps 2 and 4. In the following section, we define the main formulae used in our MLN-based EL system.

3.1 Linking Constraints Formulae

First, we illustrate a basic formula for the assumption that if an entity is mapped to only one KB entry, it should be linked to the entry:

Formula L.1

$\exists! \, id.\, hasCandidate(i, id) \Rightarrow isLinkedTo(i, id)$

where $hasCandidate(i, id)$ represents that the ith entity mention has a candidate entry id; and $isLinkedTo(i, id)$ represents that i is linked to id.

Note that we refer to an entity by its order in the article (e.g., the ith entity) for several reasons. One, not all names can be found in the training data. Secondly, even if two entities have the same surface string, they may link to different KB entries. Lastly, this allows us to model the order information and dependency among all entities.

Because the objective of the EL task is to discover a unique KB entry for each entity, we must define a formula to ensure that the constraint is satisfied. We use the following formula to prevent an entity associating with more than two entries.

Formula L.2 $isLinkedTo(i, id_1) \wedge id_1 \neq id_2 \Rightarrow \neg isLinkedTo(i, id_2)$

Formula L.2 is a hard constraint that must always hold whereas the others are soft and can be violated.

3.2 Saliency Formula

The saliency property can be written as follows:

Formula S.1: Saliency:

$$i < j \wedge isLinkedTo(i, id) \wedge hasCandidate(j, id) \Rightarrow isLinkedTo(j, id)$$

In other words, if the KB entry id is linked to an entity i that precedes the current mention j, and id is a candidate KB entry of j, then the current entity j should also be linked to id.

3.3 Disambiguation Formulae

As shown in Table 1, there are numerous observed predicates defined for the disambiguation process. Before diving into the details of all the formulae, we summarize the basic idea and describe how one could apply it to other EL tasks.

In our disambiguation approach, we rely on background knowledge k, such as an entity's inhabited location, or an entity's skill or functionality. k describes various aspects of the entity i's ambiguous KB entry, id. Whenever the entity is discussed, some of these aspects will be mentioned as well. Using k, we can write formulae like the following for disambiguation:

	hasCandidate(i, id)
	hasChromosomeInfo(i, id, sd)
	hasWord(w): the abstract contain a word *w*.
	PPIKeyword(w), *isPPIPartner(id_1, id_2)*
	hasPPIPartnerRank (i, id, r), *hasGOTermRank(i, id, r)*,
	hasTissueTermRank(i, id ,r)
	hasPrecedingWord(i, w, l), *hasFollowingWord(i, w, l)*
	hasUnigramBetween(i, j, w)
Variable Type	*i*: an integer, which refers to the *i*th gene mention in the given article (similarly *j* refers to the *j*th mention)
	id: an EntrezGene ID, which refers to a linked KB entry.
	sd: an integer, which refers to the sentence distance.
	w: a word.
	r: an integer, which refers to the rank of the matching.
	l: an integer, which refers to a context window length.

Table 1: Main Predicates for Disambiguation.

$$Content\_Knowledge(i, id, k) \Longrightarrow isLinkedTo(i, id)$$

The formula shows that if the context of the entity i, which has a linking candidate KB entry id , contains the background knowledge information k, the entity i should be linked to id.

In this paper, we define four predicates to capture the recognized genes' background information, including chromosome location, protein-protein interaction (PPI), tissue type and gene ontology. For example, the predicate $hasChromosomeInfo(i, id, sd)$ indicates that the chromosome location information of the i th entity, which has the KB entry id as its linked candidate entry, can be found in the surrounding text in the range sd. Applying this predicate to the sentence: "The human **UBQLN3** gene was mapped to the *11p15* region of chromosome 11," the entity mention UBQLN3 must be linked to the KB entry ID:50613 because 50613's chromosome location, *11p15*, is found in the same sentence. The formula describing the relation of $hasChromosomeInfo$ and $isLinkedTo$ is defined as follows:

$$hasChromosomeInfo(i, id, +sd) \Longrightarrow isLinkedTo(i, id)$$

Here, we can see that there is an additional parameter ($+sd$) in $hasChromosomeInfo$. sd indicates where the chromosome information corresponding to id locates. The "+" notation in the above formula indicates that we must learn a separate weight for each grounded variable (sd). For example, $hasChromosomeInfo(i, id, 0)$ and $hasChromosomeInfo(i, id ,1)$ are given two different weights in our MLN model after training.

Correlation information, such as "KB entry id_1 usually interacts with an entry id_2", can be used in disambiguating an entity i as follows. The PPI information recorded in the database can provide the correlation information. Based on the correlation information as well as the candidate KB entry distribution in the current context, the id that correlated with the most unambiguous entries is the most likely id to be linked to i. We define the predicate $hasPPIPartnerRank(i, id, r)$ to represent this concept. The formula defining the relationship between $hasPPIPartnerRank$ and $isLinkedTo$ is:

$$\exists! \, id. hasPPIPartnerRank(i, id, 1) \wedge \exists w. hasWord(w) \wedge PPIKeyword(w) \Longrightarrow isLinkedTo(i, id)$$

One can see that there are two predicates, $hasWord$ and $PPIKeyword$, in this formula that check if the article contains PPI keywords. Two similar predicates, $hasGOTermRank$ and $hasTissueTermRank$, represent the concept that i should be linked to the id with the largest number of corresponding gene ontology terms (entity's function) or tissue terms (entity's location) found in the context.

For the correlation information, we further define the following formula to capture the dependency that an entity j should be linked to id_2 if another entity i has been linked to id_1, and id_1 forms a correlation with id_2:

Formula D.1

$$\exists w. hasWord(w) \wedge PPIKeyword(w) \wedge isLinkedTo(i, id_1) \wedge hasCandidate(j, id_2) \wedge isPPIPartner(id_1, id_2) \Longrightarrow isLinkedTo(j, id_2)$$

This formula shows another long range dependency among entities used in our MLN model (The first long dependency formula is S.1).

Finally, an entity mention j may sometimes be followed by its variant i (abbreviation or full name). Usually, the variant i is put in parentheses. If i can be uniquely linked to id, it is very likely that j is also linked to id. An example formula is shown as follows:

$$hasPrecedingWord(i, "(", 1) \wedge hasFollowingWord(i, ")", 1) \wedge \exists! \, u. hasUnigramBetween(i, j, u) \wedge \exists! \, id. hasCandidate(i, id) \wedge u = "(" \Longrightarrow isLinkedTo(j, id)$$

3.4 NIL-filtering Formulae

We approach the absence issue by filtering the following mention type: those belonging to classes that are not in the database curation target; called NILs. In linking gene mentions to KB entries, NILs appear when the gene mentions are protein families or complexes, or in a specific organism that is not considered. For example, in Figure 1, an EL system must return NIL for "C9

	hasName(*i*, *n*) *hasFirstWord*(*i*, *w*), *hasLastWord*(*i*, *w*), *isBlacklisted*(*w*): the word sequence *w* is blacklisted, *containsMoreSpecificMentions*(*i*): the *i*-th gene mention collocates with more specific gene mentions in the current context. *SpeciesTerm*(*w*), *AllUpperCase*(*i*), *hasPartOfSpeech*(*i*, *k*, *p*)
Variable Type	*n*: a word or a sequence of words that refer to the surface name of a gene mention. *ch*: characters. *d*: an integer. *k*: the *k*th index of the gene mention. *p*: a part-of-speech

Table 2: Main Predicates for NIL-filtering.

complex" in the first sentence, because the mention is a protein complex that is not EntrezGene's curation target. The predicate $isSuitableForLinking$ describes this concept.

We then employ the following formula to ensure that, whenever the ith entity is linked to a KB entry id, it must be an entity suitable for linking.

$$isLinkedTo(i, id) \Longrightarrow isSuitableForLinking(i)$$

The formula models the stage decisions determined by traditional EL systems. The KB entry id does not have to be linked to the entity i proposed by the entity recognition/classification stage; however, the id cannot be assigned to the ith gene mention that has not been proposed as a potential entity. The formula is a hard constraint.

The initial formula containing $isSuitableForLinking$ treats any entity i with surface name n as a potential entity:

$$hasName(i, +n) \Longrightarrow isSuitableForLinking(i)$$

Again, the "+" notation in the above formula indicates that the MLN must learn a separate weight for each entity name n.

In person name EL, for example, one could define $hasTitle$ to indicate that a title, such as Mr. or Mrs., appears in the ith entity's context and apply the formula for the $isSuitableForLinking$ predicate:

$$hasTitle(i, +t) \Longrightarrow isSuitableForLinking(i).$$

In our work, we construct our formulae by using the observed predicates defined in Tables 1 and 2 to determine whether or not i is a NIL by checking i's context. For example:

$$hasFirstWord(i, +w) \wedge SpeciesTerm(+w) \Longrightarrow isSuitableForLinking(i)$$

implies that a certain gene mention i's suitability for linking depends on whether or not i's first word is a certain species keyword w.

4 Results

4.1 Evaluation Metrics

We use two metrics to evaluate our approach and compare it with other EL disambiguation methods. Both use the standard precision, recall, and F-measure metrics (PRF) at two resolutions (article and instance).

Article-wide evaluation is based on the standard used in the BioCreative challenge (Morgan, Lu et al. 2008), which was designed to determine an EL system's performance as an aid for the curation of biological databases. The EL system outputs a list of EntrezGene IDs for a given article. The list is then compared to the gold standard IDs list for the article. The PRF scores are calculated based on the sums of true/false positives/negatives (TP, TN, FP, FN).

Instance-based evaluation measures the EL performance at a fine-grained IE resolution, which can support the development of advanced IE tasks. In contrast to the first metric, the PRF scores are calculated based on the sums of TP, TN, FP and FN for all instances in the test dataset; we further consider whether the boundary matches that of the linked KB entry's mention. Therefore, under this criterion, an FP could link a true entity to the wrong KB entry or link a false entity to any KB entry; while an FN could link a true entity to the wrong KB entry or fail to recognize a true entity. In cases where a true entity is linked to the wrong KB entry, both the FN and FP are increased by 1.

For TP/FP/FN, we need to determine when the predicted boundary matches that of the gold standard. Most entity recognition tasks use "exact-matching" as the primary criterion. Under this criterion, a candidate entity can only be counted as a TP if both its left and right boundaries fully coincide with the gold answer. However, in a real scenario, a gene mention can be tagged in several ways (e.g., "... between serum <entity>LH</entity>" and "... between <entity>serum LH</entity>" are both correct). Furthermore, for the EL task, the correctness of the linked KB entry is more important than its boundaries. Therefore, we use approximate-matching (Subramaniam, Mukherjea et al. 2003) to determine the boundary criterion. For example, a TP is counted when a machine-linked gene mention is a substring of the gold standard-linked gene mention or vice versa, and the linked KB entry is equal to the gold entry.

4.2 Dataset

In the experiments we used the training and test sets released by the BioCreative II gene normalization (GN) task (Morgan, Lu et al. 2008). The dataset provides a list of human gene EntrezGene database entries (IDs) that appear in each abstract. Although the gold standard answers contain each EntrezGene database entry's surface name shown in the abstract, they do not give the exact location of the corresponding entity mention in the abstract. So the original BioCreative II dataset can only be used to evaluate article-wide EL performance.

To obtain instance-based evaluation results, we need to expand the original annotation of the dataset. Our in-lab biologists annotated the exact locations and boundaries of the KB entries' gene mentions in a semi-automated manner. The automated annotation process used the entry's surface name provided by the gold standard to tag the entire corpus. Human annotators then corrected the recognized entities and linked results based on the context.

To compile the EL training corpus for our EL models, we employed a state-of-the-art gene mention linking system released by Lai et al. (2009) to recognize all gene mentions and generate candidate KB entries for each entity. For each mention *m* in a sentence *s* recognized by Lai's system and the set of KB entry candidates for *m* output by Lai's system, we searched *s* for the first human annotated mention *n* overlapping with *m* and set *n*'s KB entry as *m*'s true KB entry. Other candidates were set as *m*'s incorrect KB entries.

For the NIL-filtering corpus (NIL corpus), again, for each mention *m* in a sentence *s* recognized by Lai's system, we checked whether or not the boundary of the mention *m* match with the human annotated boundary. All matched mentions are regarded as true positives while the others are negative instances.

4.3 Model Configurations

For our experiments, we constructed four MLN-based configurations. In addition, separate-stage models for NIL-filtering and disambiguation were also constructed.

$\mathbf{MLN_{LINK}}$: To assess baseline performance without disambiguation and NIL-filtering, we constructed an MLN-based configuration, MLN_{LINK}, only employing formulae related to linking constraints (refer to section 3.1). We compared its performance with that of a modified version of Lai's system, for which all mentions with only one KB entry were directly treated as answers, and entities with more than one candidate KB entry were discarded. This system is referred to as $\mathbf{Lai_{NO\_DIS}}$.

$\mathbf{MLN_{SAL}}$: To assess the performance gain from the saliency property, we constructed a second MLN-based configuration, MLN_{SAL}, by adding the formula corresponding to the saliency property (Formula S.1) to the MLN_{LINK} configuration.

$\mathbf{MLN_{DIS}}$: This configuration uses the constraints defined in Section 3.1, the saliency property in Section 3.2, and the disambiguation formulae defined in Section 3.3. We compared it with two other previous approaches: Lai et al.'s rule-based approach and Crim et al.'s (2005) supervised learning approach, which treated the EL disambiguation task as a classification problem and solved by employing the maximum entropy (ME) model. For Lai et al.'s approach, denoted as $\mathbf{Lai_{DIS}}$, we directly employed Lai et al.'s original system, which had been well-tuned on the BioCreative II GN dataset. One can refer to their work (Lai, Bow et al. 2009) for more details. For the supervised learning approach, denotes as $\mathbf{ME_{DIS}}$, we transformed the formulae described in Section 3.3 to binary feature functions in ME.

$\mathbf{MLN_{JOINT}}$: The final MLN-based configuration (MLN_{JOINT}) was constructed by adding the NIL-filtering formulae to MLN_{DIS}. That is, all formulae introduced in Section 3 were employed.

$\mathbf{ME_{NF}}$ for separate NIL-filtering: To simulate and compare the separate-stage NIL-filtering and EL disambiguation approach with MLN_{JOINT}, we developed a separate NIL-filtering model for Lai_{DIS} and ME_{DIS}, denoted as $\mathbf{ME_{NF}}$. The ME_{NF} model was executed before the disambiguation step. We formulated the NIL-filtering task as a classification problem and used the features equivalent to the formulae described in Section 3.4 to train a ME-based classifier.

We employed the greedy backward sequential selection algorithm (Aha and Bankert 1995) to select the optimized feature sets for ME_{NF} with ten-fold cross validation on the training dataset. The algorithm starts from all features transformed from NIL-filtering formulae and repeatedly removes a feature whose removal yields the maximal performance improvement in the overall EL task. Note that the feature selection procedure is designed for optimizing the performance of EL not NIL-filtering. We will discuss this in Section 5.3.

In the next sub-section, we discuss the instance-based IE results. Then, we derive BioCreative's evaluation results by merging the linked KB entries in all indexes and removing duplicated entries.

4.4 Experiment Results

Table 3 shows the instance-based and article-wide results evaluated on the test set. The first three columns show each system's PRF. The last column shows the relative advantage of F-score over the rule-based baseline ($\text{Lai}_{\text{NO\_DIS}}$).

In the second row, we can see that MLN_{LINK} achieves exactly the same performance as $\text{Lai}_{\text{NO\_DIS}}$, indicating that the MLN-based system can simulate $\text{Lai}_{\text{NO\_DIS}}$ by only employing the linking constraints. In the third row, we can observe that, by adding S.1, the recall rate is improved by 2.7% which results in an improved F-score. This shows that the saliency property is effective in instance-based evaluation. However, MLN_{SAL} performs slightly worse than MLN_{LINK} in the article-wide evaluation, the reason for which is explained in Section 5.1.

From the fourth to the sixth row, we can see that MLN outperforms the other two models. Adding disambiguation formulae also further boost the EL performance in both instance-based and article-wide evaluations by an apparent large margin (3.6% and 13.7%).

Finally, in the last configuration set (7th, 8th, and 9th row), we can see that $\text{MLN}_{\text{JOINT}}$ does better than the compared separate-stage methods under both evaluation metrics. $\text{MLN}_{\text{JOINT}}$ also achieves the best performance among all MLN-based models under both instance-based and article-wide evaluations.

5 Discussion

5.1 Model Long-range Dependencies

One advantage of employing MLN in our EL modeling is that it is easy to model arbitrary longer range dependencies, as expressed by the formula S.1 and D.1. It is difficult to model such dependencies using ME. As shown in Table 3 (MLN_{SAL}), adding the S.1 dependency improves instance-based EL performance without any domain knowledge. A similar result is achieved by adding D.1 with PPI—instance-based performance can be improved by 1.1%/0.6% on the training/test set, respectively. We also observe that adding Linking formulae with S.1

Metrics	Instance-based (%)				Article-wide (%)			
Config.	P	R	F	Adv	P	R	F	Adv
$\text{Lai}_{\text{NO\_DIS}}$	80.7	56.3	66.3	-	77.3	71.5	74.3	-
$\mathbf{MLN}_{\mathbf{LINK}}$	80.7	56.3	66.3	-	77.3	71.5	74.3	-
$\mathbf{MLN}_{\mathbf{SAL}}$	79.5	59.0	67.7	+2.1	77.2	71.3	74.1	-0.2
Lai_{DIS}	72.9	63.9	68.1	+2.7	82.6	83.4	83.0	+11.7
ME_{DIS}	79.2	58.2	67.1	+1.2	88.8	79.0	83.6	+12.5
$\mathbf{MLN}_{\mathbf{DIS}}$	73.8	64.3	68.7	+3.6	86.1	83.0	84.5	+13.7
ME_{NF}+Lai_{DIS}	73.7	64.2	68.7	+3.6	84.1	83.7	83.9	+12.9
ME_{NF}+ME_{DIS}	80.2	58.4	67.6	+2.0	90.2	79.0	84.3	+13.4
$\mathbf{MLN}_{\mathbf{JOINT}}$	77.5	63.7	70.0	+5.6	87.7	83.8	85.7	+15.3

Table 3: Instance-/Article-wide Results on the BioCreative Test Set.

reduces the recall rate in the article-wide evaluation. According to our analysis, S.1 improves the recall in the instance-based evaluation. In contrast, for article-wide, S.1 slightly reduces the recall. This is because after adding S.1, mentions tend to be linked to "salient" KB entries. In instance-based evaluation, the salient KB entries have higher frequency; therefore, the improvement of linking salient entries can cover the losses caused by disregarding the un-salient entries. However, in the article-wide evaluation, all entries in an article are counted equally; therefore, the improvement of instance-based evaluation does not transfer to article-wide evaluation.

5.2 Linking to Multiple KB Entries

Another advantage of our model is its flexibility. The EL task is usually defined as linking an entity to a unique KB entry. However, in some cases, there are entities that cannot be uniquely linked. For example, the "ABCB9 protein" in the sentence "**ABCB9 protein** appears to be most highly expressed in the Sertoli cells of the seminiferous tubules in *mouse and rat testes*."

The EL system cannot link each of the gene mentions in the above sentences to just one EntrezGene KB entry. Our model can deal with the issue easily by modifying the constraint in L.2 with a larger cardinality, or introducing additional formulae to determine the cardinal constraint dynamically.

5.3 Joint Model vs. Separate-stage Models

Compared with the two separate-stage approaches, $\text{MLN}_{\text{JOINT}}$ has the following two advantages: (1) it performs several functions using one model, and (2) it finds the optimal solution for the integrated stages. The first advantage has been illustrated by Meza-Ruiz et al. (2009). This is to be contrasted with separate-stage systems where several components need to be trained and integrated by different strategies.

The second advantage is based on our observation on the training set, employing all features transformed from NIL-filtering formulae in the ME_{NF} model might be able to achieve the best NIL-filtering performance, but it does not guarantee that the final integrated EL performance can also be the best. This is the reason why we need to employ the backward feature selection algorithm to optimize EL performance for the separate-stage systems as described in Section 4.3.

5.4 Boundary Issue in EL

Our experiment results raise an interesting question: What causes absolute score differences between the instance-based and article-wide evaluations. Several works have studied the boundary issue in entity recognition (Finkel, Dingare et al. 2005; Tsai, Wu et al. 2006). We observe that the issue also has a significant effect on the performance of EL. For example, consider the following sentence in the training set (PMID: 9346890): "<entity id=3083>Hepatocyte growth factor (HGF) activator</entity> is a serine protease responsible for proteolytic activation of <entity id=3082>HGF</entity> in response to tissue injury"

We found that Lai et al.'s system and the three publically available gene mention recognition systems[1] all separate the first gene mention (ID:3083) into at least one mention, ("hepatocyte growth factor" or "HGF"). The incorrect boundary leads to errors in EL, and could result in the extraction of an incorrect self-activation event: <entity id=3082>HGF</entity> activates <entity id=3082>HGF</entity>. An experiment conducted on the test set shows that our MLN model can achieve an F-score 79.4% in instance-based evaluation if we replaced the predicted mentions' boundaries with their corresponding overlapping gold boundaries.

5.5 Related Works

The EL problem comes up in many fields of research. Among database researchers, this problem is described as data de-duplication (Sarawagi and Bhamidipaty 2002). In the AI community, the same EL problem is described as entity resolution (Singla and Domingos 2006; Bhattacharya and Getoor 2007). In the biomedical field, term identification (Krauthammer and Nenadic 2004) or normalization (Hirschman, Colosimo et al. 2005) are used to refer to the same concepts.

Several approaches had been proposed to deal with EL tasks. The following four points explain the distinctiveness of our work. The first is that, as the names of different database entries might be identical, techniques based purely on character/token-based similarity metrics do not work well. The second is that, in our task, all KB entries in the database are unique while it is not true in the tasks tackled by previous works. Third, in our EL task, measuring the similarity between a KB entry and an entity mention requires comparing their related information (fields). The former's can be acquired from the KB while the latter's should be extracted from its context. The latter's is hard to extract because the context is written in natural language, which is unstructured and some information may not appear in the context. This phenomena is against the assumption most previous EL approaches (Fellegi and Sunter 1969; Elmagarmid, Ipeirotis et al. 2007) based on: entities should have the same set of fields. Finally, as described in Section 1, our work needs to consider the absence issue to filter out NIL entities, which are not considered in the most previous EL approaches.

6 Conclusion

In this paper, we present a novel approach that employs MLN to model the constraints and decisions in the EL task. The contribution of this paper is threefold. First, we propose several features for EL disambiguation and NIL-filtering and demonstrate a feasible approach for modeling them by using an MLN. Second, unlike existing EL disambiguation approaches, which do not model the dependencies among entities, the proposed approach learns to model the dependencies, including the saliency and interaction among KB entries, and the performance improvement is promising. Third, we describe a new evaluation scheme that use the BioCreative corpus to analyze EL tasks from an additional perspective, instance-based evaluation, which have not yet been applied in the EL field thus far.

Acknowledgement

This research was supported in part by the National Science Council under grant NSC99-3112-B-001-005 and NSC98-2221-E-155-060-MY3, the Academia Sinica Investigator Award 95-02 and the research center for Humanities and Social Sciences under grant IIS-50-23.

[1]ABNER, GENIA tagger and BANNER.

Reference

Bhattacharya, I. and L. Getoor. 2007. Collective entity resolution in relational data. *ACM Transactions on Knowledge Discovery from Data (TKDD)*, 1(1): 5.

Bunescu, R and M Pasca. 2006. Using encyclopedic knowledge for named entity disambiguation. In: *European Chapter of the Assocation for Computational Linguistics*.

Che, Wanxiang and Ting Liu. 2010. Jointly Modeling WSD and SRL with Markov Logic. In: *Proceedings of the 23rd International Conference on Computational Linguistics*, Beijing, China.

Crim, Jeremiah, Ryan McDonald and Fernando Pereira. 2005. Automatically Annotating Documents with Normalized Gene Lists. *BMC Bioinformatics*, 6(Suppl 1): S13.

Dai, Hong-Jie, Po-Ting Lai and Richard Tzong-Han Tsai. 2010. Multistage Gene Normalization and SVM-Based Ranking for Protein Interactor Extraction in Full-Text Articles. *IEEE TRANSACTIONS ON COMPUTATIONAL BIOLOGY AND BIOINFORMATICS*, 7(3): 412-420.

Dredze, Mark, Paul McNamee, Delip Rao, Adam Gerber and Tim Finin. 2010. Entity Disambiguation for Knowledge Base Population. In: *Proceedings of the 23rd International Conference on Computational Linguistics (Coling 2010)*, Beijing.

Elmagarmid, Ahmed K., Panagiotis G. Ipeirotis and Vassilios S. Verykios. 2007. Duplicate Record Detection: A Survey. *IEEE Trans. on Knowl. and Data Eng.*, 19(1): 1-16.

Fellegi, I.P. and A.B. Sunter. 1969. A theory for record linkage. *Journal of the American Statistical Association*, 64(328): 1183-1210.

Finkel, Jenny, Shipra Dingare, Christopher Manning, Malvina Nissim, Beatrice Alex and Claire Grover. 2005. Exploring the boundaries: gene and protein identification in biomedical text. *BMC Bioinformatics*, 6(Suppl 1): S5.

Finkel, Jenny Rose and Christopher D. Manning. 2009. Joint parsing and named entity recognition. In: *Proceedings of NAACL 2009*.

Gale, WA, KW Church and D Yarowsky. 1992. A method for disambiguating word senses in a large corpus. *Computers and the Humanities*, 26(5): 415-439.

Hirschman, Lynette, Marc Colosimo, Alexander Morgan and Alexander Yeh. 2005. Overview of BioCreAtIvE task 1B: normalized gene lists. *BMC Bioinformatics*, 6(Suppl 1): S11.

Krauthammer, Michael and Goran Nenadic. 2004. Term identification in the biomedical literature. *Journal of Biomedical Informatics*, 37(6): 512-526.

Kulkarni, Sayali, Amit Singh, Ganesh Ramakrishnan and Soumen Chakrabarti. 2009. Collective annotation of wikipedia entities in web text. In: *Proceeding of the 17th ACM SIGKDD Conference on Knowledge Discovery and Data Mining (KDD)* Paris, France, ACM.

Lai, Po-Ting, Yue-Yang Bow, Chi-Hsin Huang, Hong-Jie Dai, Richard Tzong-Han Tsai and Wen-Lian Hsu. 2009. Using Contextual Information to Clarify Gene Normalization Ambiguity. In: *The IEEE International Conference on Information Reuse and Integration (IEEE IRI 2009)*, Las Vegas, USA, IEEE Press.

Li, Fangtao, Zhicheng Zheng, Fan Bu, Yang Tang, Xiaoyan Zhu and Minlie Huang. 2009. THU QUANTA at TAC 2009 KBP and RTE Track. In: *Proceedings of Test Analysis Conference 2009 (TAC 09)*, Gaithersburg, Maryland USA.

Maglott, Donna, Jim Ostell, Kim D. Pruitt and Tatiana Tatusova. 2006. Entrez Gene: gene-centered information at NCBI. *Nucleic Acids Research*, 35(suppl 1): D26-D31.

McNamee, Paul and Hoa Trang Dang. 2009. Overview of the TAC 2009 Knowledge Base Population Track. In: *Proceedings of the Second Text Analysis Conference (TAC 2009)*, Gaithersburg, Maryland.

Meza-Ruiz, Ivan and Sebastian Riedel. 2009. Jointly identifying predicates, arguments and senses using Markov logic. In: *Proceedings of Human Language Technologies: The 2009 Annual Conference of the North American Chapter of the Association for Computational Linguistics*, Boulder, Colorado, Association for Computational Linguistics.

Morgan, AA, B Wellner, JB Colombe, R Arens, ME Colosimo and L Hirschman. 2007. Evaluating the automatic mapping of human gene and protein mentions to unique identifiers. In: *Pac Symp Biocomput.*

Morgan, Alexander, Zhiyong Lu, Xinglong Wang, Aaron Cohen, Juliane Fluck, Patrick Ruch, Anna Divoli, Katrin Fundel, Robert Leaman, Jorg Hakenberg, Chengjie Sun, Heng-hui Liu, Rafael Torres, Michael Krauthammer, William Lau, Hongfang Liu, Chun-Nan Hsu, Martijn Schuemie, K Bretonnel Cohen and Lynette Hirschman. 2008. Overview of BioCreative II gene normalization. *Genome Biology*, 9(Suppl 2): S3.

Poon, H and P Domingos. 2007. Joint inference in information extraction. In, Menlo Park, CA; Cambridge, MA; London; AAAI Press; MIT Press; 1999.

Richardson, Matthew and Pedro Domingos. 2006. Markov logic networks. *Machine Learning*, 62(Special Issue: Multi-Relational Data Mining and Statistical Relational Learning): 107-136.

Riedel, Sebastian. 2008. Improving the accuracy and efficiency of map inference for markov logic. In: *Proceedings of UAI 2008*, AUAI Press.

Sarawagi, Sunita and Anuradha Bhamidipaty. 2002. Interactive deduplication using active learning. In: *Proceedings of the eighth ACM SIGKDD international conference on Knowledge discovery and data mining*, Edmonton, Alberta, Canada, ACM.

Singla, Parag and Pedro Domingos. 2006. Entity Resolution with Markov Logic. In: *Proceedings of the Sixth International Conference on Data Mining*, IEEE Computer Society.

Subramaniam, L. Venkata, Sougata Mukherjea, Pankaj Kankar, Biplav Srivastava, Vishal S. Batra, Pasumarti V. Kamesam and Ravi Kothari. 2003. Information extraction from biomedical literature: methodology, evaluation and an application. In: *Proceedings of the twelfth international conference on Information and knowledge management*, New Orleans, LA, USA, ACM.

Tsai, Richard Tzong-Han, Shih-Hung Wu, Wen-Chi Chou, Chun Lin, Ding He, Jieh Hsiang, Ting-Yi Sung and Wen-Lian Hsu. 2006. Various criteria in the evaluation of biomedical named entity recognition. *BMC Bioinformatics*, 7(92): 14.

Zhang, Wei, Jian Su, Chew Lim Tan and Wen Ting Wang. 2010. Entity Linking Leveraging Automatically Generated Annotation. In: *Proceedings of the 23rd International Conference on Computational Linguistics (Coling 2010)*, Beijing.

Named Entity Recognition in Chinese News Comments on the Web

Xiaojun Wan[a], Liang Zong[b], Xiaojiang Huang[c], Tengfei Ma, Houping Jia, Yuqian Wu and Jianguo Xiao
Institute of Compute Science and Technology, The MOE Key Laboratory of Computational Linguistics, Peking University, Beijing 100871, China
{[a]wanxiaojun, [c]huangxiaojiang}@icst.pku.edu.cn
[b]zongliang.cn@gmail.com

Abstract

News comment is a new text genre in the Web 2.0 era. Many people often write comments to express their opinions about recent news events or topics after they read news articles. Because news comments are freely written without checking, they are very different from formal news texts. In particular, named entities in news comments are usually composed of some wrongly written words, informal abbreviations or aliases, which brings great difficulties for machine detection and understanding. This paper addresses the task of named entity recognition in Chinese news comments on the Web. We propose to leverage the entity information in the referred news article to improve named entity recognition in the news comments. Three different schemes are investigated to find useful entities in the news article for new feature generation in the CRFs model. Finally, a dictionary-based correction step is employed to further improve the results. We manually labelled a benchmark dataset with 60 pieces of news and 6000 comments downloaded from a popular Chinese news portal – www.sina.com.cn. The experimental results on the dataset show that our method is effective for this special task.

1 Introduction

Named entity recognition (NER) is one of the fundamental tasks in the field of natural language processing. It has been widely used in the areas of information retrieval, machine translation, question answering, and so on. In most literatures, named entities are defined as entity names (person names, location names and organization names). With the advent of MUC, CONLL, ACE and SIGHAN evaluations, NER has received much attention of the researchers and hence achieved great development.

News comment is a new text genre in the Web 2.0 era, and many people often write and post comments to express their opinions on recent news events or topics after they read news articles. As the roles which people play on the internet have gradually changed from acquirers to suppliers, news comments have become one of the most valuable information resources. For example, on one of the popular Chinese news portals – sina.com.cn, every piece of hot news is associated with over 500 comments. Named entity recognition is the basis of many other news comments understanding and mining applications, including entity relation extraction, opinion holder and target extraction in news comments, and so on.

Because news comments are freely written by different persons with different education backgrounds and writing styles, they are very different from formal news texts. In particular, Chinese news comments have the following properties:

1) The texts in news comments are very informal and noisy, especially for entity names. There are always many noisy pieces of texts in the comments because the comments are written by various users, e.g., wrongly written words, extra spaces, meaningless characters, or informal names, etc. For example, "汇源/Huiyuan" may be wrongly written to the word "汇圆/Huiyuan".

2) News comments are written with various styles. Since the comments are written by different users with different backgrounds, each one has its own writing style. Different users may use different words and phrases to express the same entities. For example, "八一队/Bayi Team" may be written as "81 队".

3) The texts in news comments are usually very short and concise. The average length of each comment is about 20~25 characters in our dataset. Many entity names in news comments are abbreviated in various ways. For example, "信息科学技术学院/School of Electronics En-

gineering and Computer Science" may be abbreviated as "信院", "信科" or "信息".

4) Most news comments are relevant to the news topics in the referred news article. There is usually a strong relationship between news comments and the news article. Most news comments are focusing on the entities or events introduced in the news article, or related entities and events. For example, given an news article about "姚明/Yao Ming", some news comments may talk about the players and teams explicitly mentioned in the news article, such as"姚明/Yao Ming" or "休斯敦火箭队/Houston Rockets", and other news comments may talk about related players and teams in NBA, such as "奥尼尔/O'Neal" and "菲尼克斯太阳队/Phoenix Suns".

The first three properties bring great challenges for named entity recognition from Chinese news comments. But the fourth property brings very useful knowledge for the task. In this study, we focus on the task of named entity recognition in Chinese news comments on the web, which has not been investigated yet. Considering the close relationships between named entities in the referred news article and named entities in the news comments, we propose to leverage the entity information in the news article to improve named entity recognition in the news comments. Three schemes are exploited for collecting useful entities from the news article, and then the entity information is incorporated into the CRF-based algorithm for recognizing named entities in the news comments. Finally, an additional correction step is used to further improve the performance.

We manually labeled an evaluation dataset with 60 pieces of news and 6000 news comments from a popular Chinese news portal (www.sina.com.cn). Experimental results on the dataset show that our proposed approach is effective for the task of NER in news comments. The use of focused entities and related entities in the referred news article is very beneficial for the task.

The rest of this paper is organized as follows. Section 2 introduces related work. Section 3 presents our proposed approach. Section 4 shows the experimental setup and results. Finally, Section 5 summarizes the conclusions.

2 Related Work

Traditional named entity recognition systems use linguistic grammar-based techniques as well as statistical models. The techniques can be categorized into rule-based (Sekine and Nobata, 2004; Chiticariu et al., 2010), machine learning-based (including unsupervised, supervised and semi-supervised methods) (Bikel et al., 1999; Mayfield et al., 2003; McCallum and Li, 2003; Bender and Ney, 2003; Florian et al., 2003; McCallum and Li, 2003; Etzioni et al., 2005; Klementiev and Roth, 2006; Okanohara et al., 2006; Finkel and Manning, 2009; Singh et al., 2010) and hybrid models (Srihari et al., 2001). The most popular statistical models for named entity recognition include Support Vector Machine, Hidden Markov Model, Maximum Entropy Model, Conditional Random Fields, and so on. Background knowledge derived from Wikipedia and WordNet has been used for improving the NER task (Kazama and Torisawa, 2007; Richman and Schone, 2008; Pennacchiotti and Pantel, 2009). Most previous works have investigated the NER task over formal text such as news articles. These kinds of texts are written by professional writers, and thus they are well organized and well-structured, and they have seldom grammatical and spelling errors and noises.

Recently, a few works have investigated the task over informal English texts such as emails and blogs. Huang et al. (2001) address the problem of extracting identity and phone number of the caller from voicemail messages, and they present three typical information extraction methods: hand-crafted rule-based method, maximum entropy models, and probabilistic transducer induction. Jansche and Abney (2002) present a two-phase procedure consisting of a hand-crafted component and a classifier for information extraction from voicemail. Minkov et al. (2005) propose to use email-specific structural features and a recall-enhancing method for improving person name recognition from email. Gruhl et al. (2009) explore the application of restricted relationship graphs and statistical techniques to improve named entity annotation in on-line forum texts discussing popular music.

Generally speaking, the Chinese NER task is harder because Chinese texts have no explicit word segmentation information, and Chinese named entities lacks the capitalization information that plays an important role in signaling named entities, and moreover, the structures of Chinese named entities are more complicated, especially for entity abbreviations. Most Chinese NER systems adopt statistical models or hybrid solutions. Sun et al. (2002) consider the problem of Chinese named entity identification using statistical language model, and they integrate word segmentation and NE identification into a unified framework that consists of several class-based language models. Fang and Sheng (2002) present a hybrid approach, which combines a machine learning method and a rule based method, to improve the Chinese NE system's efficiency. Zhu et al. (2003) adopt the source-channel model framework for the single character named entity recognition. Gao et al. (2005) propose a pragmatic mathematical framework in which segmenting known words and detecting unknown words of different types can be performed simultaneously in a unified way. Wu et al. (2005) present a statistical model with human knowledge which treats NER as a probabilistic tagging problem. Fu and Luke (2005) present a lexicalized HMM-based approach to Chinese NER. Yu et al. (2008) use a Markov Logic Network to combine various types of domain knowledge to correct the output of the Conditional Random Fields model. Zhao and Kit (2008) propose a supervised learning model which combines the unsupervised segmentation results to improve performance. Most of the researches in this field are restricted to formal text corpus, such as newswire articles. To our knowledge, our work is the first attempt to investigate the named entity recognition task over the informal Chinese news comments.

3 Our Proposed Approach

3.1 Overview

As mentioned earlier, named entities in Chinese news comments are more difficult to recognize than those in formal text corpus because of the informal written style of the comments. Given a Chinese news article and its associated comments, our task aims to recognize all named entities (person names, location names and organization names) in the comments.

The basic idea of our proposed approach is to leverage the close relationships between named entities in the news comments and named entities in the news article. We first find a few useful named entities in the news article and then incorporate the entity information into the basic NER tagging algorithm. Finally, we use an additional correction step to further improve the performance. Our approach adopts the CRF-based algorithm for named entity recognition, and we focus on how to find useful entity information from the news article for improving NER in the news comments. Figure 1 shows the framework of our proposed approach. The three key components will be presented in next sections, respectively.

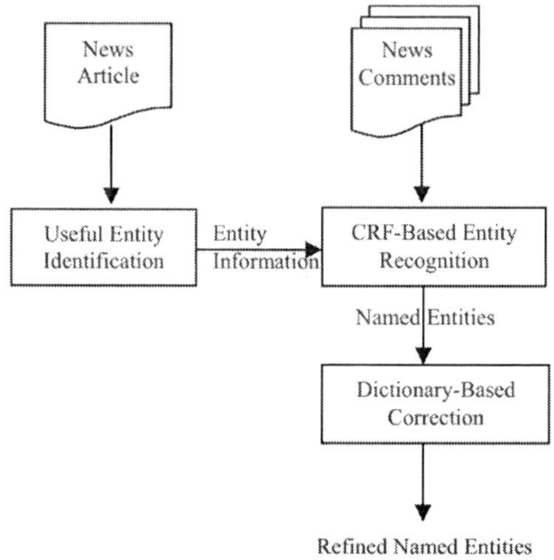

Figure 1: The framework of our proposed approach

3.2 The CRF-Based Entity Recognition Algorithm

The Conditional Random Fields (Lafferty et al., 2001) model is a probabilistic framework to segment and label sequence data, and it has been successfully used in many NLP tasks, including word segmentation, POS tagging, named entity recognition, and so on. The CRFs model defines the conditional distribution $p(Y|X)$ of the labels Y given the observations X with the following formula:

$$P_\lambda(Y \mid X) = \frac{1}{Z(X)} exp(\sum_{c \in C} \sum_k \lambda_k f_k(Y_c, X, c))$$

Y is the label sequence; X is the observation sequence; $Z(X)$ is a normalization term; f_k is a feature function; λ_k is the weight of feature function f_k; C is the set of cliques in the undirected graphic model. Given the training data with a set of sentences (characters with their corresponding tags), the parameters of the model are trained by maximizing the conditional log-likelihood. In the testing phase, given a test sentence x, the tagging sequence y is given by $Argmax_y P(y|x)$.

CRFs has been shown to perform well on the task of Chinese named entity recognition (Zhou et al, 2006, Chen et al, 2006, Yu et al, 2008). We treat the Chinese NER task as a character-based sequence labeling problem and use the CRFs model for learning and inference. In this study, we use the linear-chain CRFs model implemented in the CRF++ toolkit[1]. We use four tags (B - beginning of an entity, I - inside of an entity, E – end of an entity, S – a single character entity) for tagging each type of named entity, and thus we have totally 13 tags (including the tag O- outside of any entity). Standard features used in our basic method are listed in Table 1. The segmentation features and POS features are given by our in-house Chinese word segmentation and POS tagging tools. The segmentation features indicate the positions of the Chinese characters in the corresponding Chinese words after word segmentation, and the position of each Chinese character is represented by three types: the first character in a word, the last character in a word, and the middle character in a word. For the POS features, the POS tag of each Chinese character is the same with that of the Chinese word which the character belongs to.

Character features	$C_n, n \in [-3,3]$
	$C_nC_{n+1}, n \in [-3,2]$
Segmentation features	$S_n, n \in [-2,2]$
	$S_nS_{n+1}, n \in [-2,1]$
POS features	$P_n, n \in [-2,2]$
	$P_nP_{n+1}, n \in [-2,1]$

Table 1: Standard features used in the baseline method

Entity features	$F_n, n \in [-2,2]$
	$F_nF_{n+1}, n \in [-2,1]$

Table 2: Entity-based features used in our proposed method

The basic method using the above standard features does not work well because the standard features rely only on the news comments, while the named entities in the news comments may appear in different informal or erroneous forms. Since the comments have a very close relationship with the corresponding news article, how to effectively use the named entities' information in the news article is the primary problem in our proposed method. After we extract a few useful entities from the news article, we propose to generate new entity features and add them to the CRFs model.

For each entity type, we collect one prefix list and one suffix list by extracting the prefixes and suffixes from the useful entities. Based on these lists, we assign additional tags to the characters in the news comments to indicate whether the characters are included in a particular list. For instance, the character "刘" \ "Liu" in a person name "刘翔" \ "LiuXiang" is extracted as a prefix of the person name. When a character in a comment is included in a person prefix list, we assign a tag of "Per_Prefix_1", otherwise, we assign a tag of "Per_Prefix_0". The new entity features are listed in Table 2.

The key issue in this study is how to find useful entities from the news article, and we propose three schemes for addressing this problem in next sections.

3.3 Useful Entity Identification

In this section, we propose three schemes for finding useful entities in the news article. The first scheme aims to recognize and use all named entities in the news article. The second scheme aims to extract and use only focused named entities in the news article. The third scheme aims to expand the focused named entities by using web search results.

3.3.1 All NE Recognition

This scheme is the simplest scheme based on the assumption that all the named entities in the news article are useful clues for the NER task in the associated news comments. In this study, we use our in-house Chinese NER tool to tag all named entities in the news article and use all the named entities as useful entities for new feature generation, as mentioned in Section 3.2. Our in-house Chinese NER tool is based on the CRFs model. The F-measure values of the tool over the MSR NER news corpus are 94.14% for person entities, 87.03% for location entities and 84.97% for organization entities.

3.3.2 Focused NE Extraction

This scheme advances the first scheme by finding only a few important named entities in the news article. There are usually many named entities in the news article, and the named entities are unequally important. The associated comments usually focus on discussing a few important entities, which are called focused named entities. The use of all the named entities may introduce some noises, and instead we use only the focused named entities in this scheme.

Focused entities refer to the named entities which are most relevant to the main topic of a news article. Similar to Zhang et al. (2004), we consider the task of focused named entity extraction as a binary classification problem. Given a named entity in the news article, we use a classi-

[1] http://crfpp.sourceforge.net/

fication model to classify it as focused entity or not. For a named entity A, the features used in our classification model are listed in Table 3.

Feature Name	Feature Value	Feature Description
Entity Type	Integer (0,1,2)	Entity type of A
Entity Frequency	Positive Integer	Occurrence number of A in news article
In Title or Not	Boolean (T, F)	Whether A appears in the title or not
Entity Document Frequency	Positive Integer	Number of news articles contain A
Entity Distribution	Positive Float	The distribution of A in news article

Table 3: Features used for focused NE extraction

In Table 3, the first four features are easy to understand. The entity distribution feature measures how evenly an entity is distributed in a document. The motivation is that if a named entity occurs in many different parts of a document, it is more likely to be an important entity. We use the entropy of the probability distribution to measure it. Considering a document which is divided into m sections with equal length, a named entity's probability distribution is represented by $\{p_1, p_2, \ldots, p_i, \ldots, p_m\}$, where

$$p_i = \frac{\textit{occurrence number in the i-th section}}{\textit{total occurrence number in the document}}$$

The entity distribution feature value is then computed by $entropy = -\sum_{i=1}^{m} p_i \log p_i$. In our experiments, we simply set $m = 5$.

In the experiments, we used the SVMLight toolkit for classification. We collected 1000 news articles from a popular Chinese news portal - news.sohu.com. Each news article was manually annotated with its focused named entities, and there were totally 1447 focused entities (i.e. 1.4 focused entities per article). We performed 5-fold cross-validation on the dataset and the mean F-measure was 81%.

After we use the classification model to classify all the named entities in the news article into focused entities or not, we do not directly use the classified focused entities, because the number of focused entities is very small. Instead, in order to leverage more useful entities for feature generation, we select the top K percent named entities, which are the most confidently classified focused entities in the news article, as useful name entities. K is a parameter in our study. We use the output value of the SVM classification model to indicate the classification confidence level.

3.3.3 Related NE Expansion

The above two schemes find useful entities only from the particular news article. However, according to our observation, some named entities in the news comments do not appear in the particular news article at all, but they are closely related to some entities in the news article. This phenomenon is called "topic shifting". For example, when a news article is talking about "中国联通"\"China Unicom", related entities such as "中国移动"\"China Mobile", "中国电信"\"China Telecom", which do not appear in the news article, may be talked about in the associated comments. There related entities are also very useful clues and thus we develop a related NE expansion tool to discover the related entities by using web mining techniques. We use the focused name entities extracted from each news article in Section 3.3.2 as seeds and use our tool to discover related entities for each focused entity. Finally, we use these entities as useful entities for feature generation.

There have been a few researches (Ohshima et al., 2006; Wang and Cohen, 2007, Vyas and Pantel, 2009) related to named entity expansion. One of the most famous online services is *Google Sets*[2]. Motivated by these related researches, our tool consists of the following two key steps for NE expansion of each single focused entity.

1) Given a focused entity e, we first submit four queries ["*e* 和"] / ["e and"], ["和 *e*"] / ["and e"], ["*e* 比"] / ["e than"] and ["比 *e*"] / ["than e"] to the Google web search engine and get the top 100 results for each query[3]. Then we split the snippets in the search result into sentences. The character sequences that occur both immediately before the two queries (["和 *e*"] and ["比 *e*"]) and immediately after the two queries (["*e* 和"] and ["*e* 比"]) are extracted as initial candidates, and they are ranked by the geometric mean of the times each one appears immediately before the two queries (["和 *e*"] and ["比 *e*"]) and the times each one appears immediately after the two queries (["*e* 和"] and ["*e* 比"]). The top five candidates with high ranks are selected as the initial expansion results. In this step, we emphasize more on the precision of the candidates by using

[2] http://labs.google.com/sets

[3] The string in [ ] is the complete query string. Note that quotation marks ("") are used in each query string to guarantee that the query characters appear consecutively in the results.

only two strong indicator words "和" / "and" and "比" / "than".

2) For each candidate e' obtained in step 1), we submit a query ["e" "e'"] to the Google search engine and obtain the top 100 results and the corresponding whole web pages[4]. Similar to Wang and Cohen (2007), in each semi-structured web page, we find the common HTML contexts of the two entities e and e' as wrappers and use these wrappers to extract more candidates from the page. A graph $G = <V, E>$ is built, where V includes all wrappers and candidates and $E = \{(w, c)|$ if candidate c is extracted by wrapper $w\}$. The weight for each edge in E was set to 1. A random graph walk with restart (RWR) is then applied to the graph to score the candidates. Finally, the top ranked candidates whose normalized scores are greater than 0.05 are selected as the expansion results. The precision value can reach 75% based on analysis of the expansion results for five focused entities.

The example expansion results by using our tool and *Google Sets* are shown in Table 4 when the seed entity is "休斯顿火箭"\"Houston Rocket".

Query: 休斯顿火箭(Houston Rocket)	
Google Sets	Our tool
火箭季后赛 (Rockets Playoffs) 火箭 vs (Rockets vs) 火箭迷来踩 (Rockets fans come to see) 火箭的 (Rockets') 仓储管理 (Storage Management) 迈阿密热火 (Miami Heat) ……	洛杉矶湖人 (LA Lakers) 圣安东尼奥马刺 (San Antonio Spurs) 达拉斯小牛 (Dallas Mavericks) 波士顿凯尔特人 (Boston Celtics) 底特律活塞 (Detroit Pistons) 丹佛掘金 (Denver Nuggets) 芝加哥公牛 (Chicago Bulls) 菲尼克斯太阳 (Phoenix Suns) 奥兰多魔术 (Orlando Magic) 波特兰开拓者 (Portland Trail Blazers) 金州勇士 (Golden State Warriors) 犹他爵士 (Utah Jazz) ……

Table 4: Related NE expansion results

3.4 Dictionary-based Correction

In this section, we present a dictionary-based correction step to address the following two issues:

1) As compared with named entities in news articles, a few named entities in news comments may have different spellings with the same or similar pronunciations, e.g., "谢亚龙" / "Xieyalong" in a news article and "谢鸭龙" / "Xieyalong" in a news comment, "刘翔" / "Liuxiang" in a news article and "刘降" / "Liuxiang" in a news comment.

2) As compared with named entities in news articles, a few named entities in news comments may be replaced with some concise English expressions, e.g., "易趣" / "Yiqu" in a news article and "ebay" in a news comment, "周杰伦" / "Zhoujielun" in a news article and "JAY" in a news comment.

For addressing the first case, we use a Chinese Pinyin dictionary to correct the results. If a Chinese character sequence in a news comment has the same pronunciation as some named entity in the news article, the character sequence is tagged as a named entity with the same type. For example, the character sequence "谢鸭龙" / "Xieyalong" in a news comment has the same pronunciation as the person name "谢亚龙" / "Xieyalong" in the news article, and thus we tag "谢鸭龙" / "Xieyalong" as a person name in our correction step.

For addressing the second case, we use an online English-Chinese bilingual dictionary (http://dict.youdao.com) for correction. The online dictionary can return the translations for most new words, such as "Jay", "ebay", and such translations can not be found in traditional dictionaries. For each sequence of continuous non-Chinese characters, we submit the string to the online dictionary, and a list of Chinese translations is returned. We then compare the translations and the entities in the news article, and if a match is found, the correction is performed.

4 Experiment and Analysis

4.1 Experiment Setup

There are no public benchmark datasets for evaluation of named entity recognition in Chinese news comments. Therefore, we manually labeled our dataset for evaluation. We downloaded 60 pieces of news and their associated comments from a popular Chinese news portal – www.sina.com.cn in October, 2008. They belonged to five different domains: politics, economics, sports, entertainment and technology. For each piece of news, we selected the first 100 comments. We then manually annotated the named entities (person name, location name and organization name) in the comments. Two annotators were employed and the conflicting annotations were resolved by discussion. Figure 2 gives

[4] Note that quotation marks ("") are used for each entity (e, e'), but not for the whole query string.

two examples in our dataset and Table 5 shows the entity distribution in our dataset. The dataset will be freely downloaded from our website.

①全国绝大多数城市房价暴涨的时候，为什么 <ne type="org" ref="中国房地产协会">**中房协** </ne>不站出来建议<ne type="org">**国务院**</ne>调整房地产调控政策？？？
When housing price kept soaring in most cities, why <ne type="org" ref="China Real Estate Association"> **zhongfangxie** </ne> didn't stand out to suggest <netype="org"> **the State Department** </ne> changing the tactics of adjustment and control of the real estate.
②<ne type="per" ref="周杰伦">**JAY**</ne> 是最棒的．永远支持<ne type="per" ref="周杰伦">**杰伦** </ne>!
<ne type="per" ref="zhoujielun"> **JAY** </ne> is the best one, we will stand for <ne type="per" ref="zhoujielun"> **jielun** </ne> forever.

Figure 2: Two examples in our dataset

	Per	Loc	Org	Total
Number	3295	3758	2780	9833

Table 5: Entity distribution in our dataset

In the experiments, we use 5-fold cross validation for evaluation. In each fold, 80% is used for training and the remaining 20% is used for testing. We use the standard F-measure for evaluation.

Finally, the performance values are averaged over the five folds.

4.2 Results and Discussions

Table 6 shows the comparison results for baselines and our proposed methods with different settings. Baseline1 directly uses a public available Chinese NER tool – S-MSRSeg[5] developed by MSR to tag the comments, and it is based on the linear mixture model framework. Baseline2 directly uses our in-house NER tool to tag the comments. Baseline3 uses only the standard features in the CRFs model, which is trained on the comments data via cross-validation, and it does not make use of any entity information in the news article. Different settings are investigated in our proposed method when K is simply set to 50.

We can see that Baseline1 and Baseline2 do not perform well, because the two baselines are developed for NER in formal news texts. Though Baseline3 does not use complex features, it performs much better than the first two baselines, which demonstrates the big difference between news texts and news comments.

The use of the entity information in the referred news article can much improve the performance, especially for person names and organization names. All the three schemes for finding useful entities in the news article are helpful to the task. In particular, the use of focused entities in the news article (Baseline3 + FocusedNE) can much outperform Baseline3 and the method using all named entities (Baseline3 + All NE) for person name recognition and organization name recognition. The results show that not all the named entities in the news article can provide important clues for NER in the news comments, and using all entities' information may cause some noises. We give an example in the news of "SPORTS_12" in our dataset. "SPORTS_12" talks about Liu Xiang withdrawing from the Olympics. There are totally five different named entities in the news article. Our focused NE extraction model marks "刘翔" / "Liuxiang" and "北京" / "Beijing" as focused NEs when the parameter $K = 50$. In the associated comments, there are totally 216 NEs. Among them, 112 NEs refer to the two focused NEs, and less than 10 NEs in the comments refer to the other three NEs in the news article. Using these three NEs' information for NER in comments may cause some noises.

Furthermore, the use of related named entities (Baseline3 + FocusedNE + RelatedNE) can further improve the performance. The F-measure for organization name recognition receives an improvement of 2.3%, while the F-measures for person and location recognition do not change significantly. This is because our related NE expansion tool works very well with an organization name as input. But when the input entity is a person or location name, a few of the expansion results are not named entities, which may introduce many noises to the CRFs model.

Lastly, we can see that the correction step can improve the performance for person name recognition and organization name recognition. Overall, the use of focused entities and related entities as useful entities, together with the correction step, can achieve the best performance in our experiments. The performance for location name recognition cannot be improved very much because the number of location name variants in the news comments is very limited.

[5] The tool can be downloaded from http://research.microsoft.com/en-us/um/people/jfgao/

	Per (%)	Loc (%)	Org (%)
Baseline1 (S-MSRSeg)	60.93	86.13	26.26
Baseline2 (Our In-house NER Tool)	73.61	80.75	37.28
Baseline3 (CRF with Standard Features)	73.73	88.92	59.63
Baseline3 + All NE	74.78	89.40	61.18
Baseline3 + Focused NE	80.53	90.12	65.02
Baseline3 + Focused NE + Related NE	80.80	90.15	67.31
Baseline3 + Focused NE + Correction	82.83	90.30	68.77
Baseline3 + Focused NE + Related NE + Correction	**83.06**	**90.32**	**70.87**

Table 6: Experimental results (F-measure)

In order to better understand the contribution of the focused named entity extraction step, we show the experiment results for the overall method (Baseline3 + FocusedNE + RelatedNE + Correction) with different values for the parameter K in Table 7. K is varying from 0 to 100 with a step size of 25. K=0 means that no name entity information in the news article is used, and K = 100 means that all the name entities in the news article are considered. We can see that in our dataset when K is set to a number around 50 (between 25 and 75), the overall performance does not change much. Using no entities (K=0) and using all entities (K=100) will much lower the overall performance, which demonstrates that it is important to leverage appropriate named entities for feature generation in our proposed method.

K	Per (%)	Loc (%)	Org (%)
K = 0	76.71	89.16	65.37
K = 25	81.57	90.21	71.38
K = 50	83.06	90.32	70.87
K = 75	81.16	89.85	69.53
K =100	77.31	89.56	67.59

Table 7: Overall results (F-measure) vs. K

5 Conclusion and Future Work

In this paper, we propose to leverage the entity information in the referred news article to improve named entity recognition in the news comments. Three schemes for finding useful entities are presented. Experimental results demonstrate the effectiveness of each component in our proposed method.

In future work, we will explore new features based on the relationships between news article and news comments, and the relationships between news comments. We will also address the co-reference resolution task in news comments.

Acknowledgments

This work was supported by NSFC (60873155), Beijing Nova Program (2008B03) and NCET (NCET-08-0006). We thank the anonymous reviewers for their useful comments.

References

O. Bender, F. J. Och and H. Ney. 2003. Maximum entropy models for named entity recognition. In CoNLL.

D. M. Bikel, R. L. Schwartz, and R. M. Weischedel. 1999. An algorithm that learns what's in a name. In Machine Learning, volume 34, pages 211–231.

A. Chen, F. Peng, R. Shan, and G. Sun. 2006. Chinese named entity recognition with conditional probabilistic models. In 5th SIGHAN Workshop on Chinese Language Processing.

L. Chiticariu, R. Krishnamurthy, Y. Li, F. Reiss and S. Vaithyanathan. 2010. Domain adaptation of rule-based annotators for named-entity recognition tasks. In Proceedings of EMNLP2010.

O. Etzioni, M. Cafarella, D. Downey, A.-M. Popescu, T. Shaked, S. Soderland, D. S.Weld, and A. Yates. 2005. Unsupervised Named-Entity Extraction from the Web: An Experimental Study. Artif. Intell., 165 (2005) (1), pp. 91–134.

X. Fang and H. Sheng. 2002. A hybrid approach for Chinese named entity recognition. In Proceedings of Discovery Science'02.

J. R. Finkel and C. D. Manning. 2009. Nested named entity recognition. In EMNLP.

R. Florian, A. Ittycheriah, H. Jing, and T. Zhang. 2003. Named entity recognition through classifier combination. In CoNLL.

G. Fu and K.-K. Luke. 2005. Chinese named entity recognition using lexicalized HMMs. ACM SIGKDD Explorations Newsletter – Natural Language Processing and Text Mining, 7(1).

J. Gao, M. Li, A. Wu, and C.-N. Huang. 2005. Chinese Word segmentation and named entity recognition: a pragmatic approach. Computational Linguistics, 31(4).

D. Gruhl, M. Nagarajan, J. Pieper, C. Robson, and A. Sheth. 2009. Context and domain knowledge enhanced entity spotting in informal text. In ISWC.

J. Huang, G. Zweig, and M. Padmanabhan. 2001. Information extraction from voicemail. In ACL.

M. Jansche and S. Abney. 2002. Information extractionfrom voicemail transcripts. In EMNLP.

J. Kazama and K. Torisawa 2007. Exploiting-Wikipedia as External Knowledge for Named Entity Recognition. Proceedings of EMNLP2007.

A. Klementiev and D. Roth. 2006.Weakly Supervised Named Entity Transliteration and Discovery from Multilingual Comparable Corpora. In Proceeding of ACL2006.

J. Lafferty, A. McCallum, and F. Pereira. 2001. Conditional random fields: Probabilistic models for segmenting and labeling sequence data. In Proceedings of ICML01.

J. Mayfield, P. McNamee and C. Piatko. Named Entity Recognition using Hundreds of Thousands of Features. In: Proceedings of CoNLL-2003.

A. McCallum and W. Li. 2003. Early results for named entity recognition with conditional random fields, feature induction and web-enhanced lexicons. In CoNLL.

E. Minkov, R. C. Wang, and W. W. Cohen. 2005. Extracting personal names from emails: Applying named entity recognition to informal text. In HLT/EMNLP.

H. Ohshima, S. Oyama, and K. Tanaka. 2006. Searching Coordinate Terms with Their Context from the Web. Proceeding of WISE2006.

D. Okanohara, Y. Miyao, Y. Tsuruoka; J. Tsujii. 2006. Improving the Scalability of Semi-Markov Conditional Random Fields for Named Entity Recognition. In Proceeding of ACL2006.

M. Pennacchiotti and P. Pantel. 2009. Entity extraction via ensemble semantics. In Proceedings of EMNLP2009.

A. E. Richman and P. Schone 2008. Mining Wiki Resources for Multilingual Named Entity Recognition. In Proceeding of ACL2008.

S. Sekine and C. Nobata. 2004. Definition, dictionaries and tagger for extended named entity hierarchy. In Proceedings of Conference on Language Resources and Evaluation.

S. Singh, D. Hillard, and C. Leggeteer. 2010. Minimallysupervised extraction of entities from text advertisements. In NAACL-HLT.

R. Srihari, C. Niu, and W. Li. 2001. A hybrid approachfor named entity and sub-type tagging. In ANLP.

J. Sun, J. Gao, L. Zhang, M, Zhou, and C. Huang. 2002. Chinese named entity identification using class-based language model. In Proceedings of COLING2002.

R. C. Wang, and W. W. Cohen. 2007. Language-Independent Set Expansion of Named Entities using the Web. Proceeding of ICDM2007.

V. Vyas, P. Pantel. 2009. Semi-automatic entity set refinement. Proceedings of HLT-NAACL2009.

Y. Wu, J. Zhao, B. Xu, and H. Yu. 2005. Chinese named entity recognition based on multiple features. In Proceedings of HLT-EMNLP2005.

X. Yu, W. Lam, S.-K. Chan, Y. K. Wu, B. Chen. 2008. Chinese NER Using CRFs and Logic for the Fourth SIGHAN Bakeoff. The Sixth SIGHAN Workshop on Chinese Language Processing.

L. Zhang, Y. Pan, T. Zhang. 2004. Focused named entity recognition using machine learning. In Proceedings of SIGIR2004.

H. Zhao and C. Kit, 2008. Unsupervised Segmentation Helps Supervised Learning of Character Tagging for Word Segmentation and Named Entity Recognition. The Sixth SIGHAN Workshop on Chinese Language Processing.

J. Zhou, L. He, X. Dai, and J. Chen. 2006. Chinese named entity recognition with a multi-phase model. In 5th SIGHAN Workshop on Chinese Language Processing.

X. Zhu, M. Li, J. Gao and C.-N. Huang. 2003. Single character Chinese named entity recognition. In Proceedings of SIGHAN2003.

Clustering Semantically Equivalent Words into Cognate Sets in Multilingual Lists

Bradley Hauer and Grzegorz Kondrak
Department of Computing Science
University of Alberta
Edmonton, Alberta, Canada, T6G 2E8
{bmhauer,gkondrak}@ualberta.ca

Abstract

Word lists have become available for most of the world's languages, but only a small fraction of such lists contain cognate information. We present a machine-learning approach that automatically clusters words in multilingual word lists into cognate sets. Our method incorporates a number of diverse word similarity measures and features that encode the degree of affinity between pairs of languages. The output of the classification algorithm is then used to generate cognate groups. The results of the experiments on word lists representing several language families demonstrate the utility of the proposed approach.

1 Introduction

Cognates are words with a shared linguistic origin, such as English *father* and French *père*. Identification of cognates is essential in historical linguistics, and cognate information has been successfully applied to natural language processing tasks, such as sentence alignment in bitexts (Simard et al., 1993), and statistical machine translation (Kondrak et al., 2003). The problem of automatically identifying pairs of cognates has been addressed previously (Frunza and Inkpen, 2009; Kondrak, 2009). The process of identification is usually based on the combination of the following three types of evidence: phonetic similarity, semantic similarity, and recurrent sound correspondences. The input data include dictionaries, multilingual word lists, and bitexts. The objective can be finding pairs of cognates among two related languages, or finding groups of cognates among multiple languages.

In this paper, we focus on the task of identifying cognate groups (clusters) in word lists on the basis of word similarity and language relationships. Word lists are now available for most of the world's languages (Wichmann et al., 2011). However, only a fraction of such lists contain cognate information. Methods proposed for pairwise cognate identification are of limited utility for such data because they fail to consider the transitivity property of the cognation relationship. Cognate groups are also more useful than cognate pairs as the input to algorithms for reconstructing phylogenetic trees (Bouchard-Côté et al., 2007).

A number of word similarity measures have been applied to the problem of cognate identification (Frunza et al., 2005). Kondrak and Dorr (2004) report that a simple average of various measures outperforms any individual measure of phonetic similarity. We propose to combine measures using a machine-learning approach based on support vector machines (SVMs). The SVMs are trained on both positive and negative examples, and allow for a seamless combination of a number of diverse similarity measures.

In addition to word similarity features, we include a set of language-pair features that incorporate information regarding the degree of relatedness between languages. We develop a way to self-train these features in the absence of pre-existing cognate information. We also present a novel clustering algorithm for defining cognate groups, which utilizes the classification decisions generated by the SVM classifier. We evaluate our method on two sets of word lists representing several language families. The results demonstrate the utility of the proposed techniques.

This paper is structured as follows. In Section 2, we define the task that we address in this work. In Section 3, we discuss relevant previous work. In Section 4, we describe our method of clustering cognates. Section 5 explains our evaluation methodology. Sections 6 and 7 report the results of our experiments. We conclude with a discussion of our work, its implications, and the potential for further research.

2 Problem definition

There are over five thousand languages in the world, which are grouped into dozens of language families (Lewis, 2009). Some language families, such as Indo-European and Austronesian, are very well documented. There are many languages, however, for which the only available data are relatively short vocabulary lists. For example, most languages in the Automated Similarity Judgement Program database (Wichmann et al., 2011) are represented by word list composed of only 40 meanings. Other lists of the most stable meanings range from 15 to 200 (Dyen et al., 1992).

	ALL	AND	ANIMAL	...
Irish	uile	agus	ainhme	...
Welsh	pob	a	anifail	...
Breton	holl	hag	aneval	...
Rumanian	toti	iar	animal	...
Italian	tutto	ed	animale	...
...	...	...	...	...

Table 1: A sample of the Indo-European Database used in our experiments.

Table 1 visualizes a small part of the typical dataset as a two-dimensional $m \times n$ table, in which rows represent n individual languages and columns represent m distinct meanings. The meanings are limited to the basic vocabulary that is relatively resistant to lexical replacement, and present in most of the world's languages (Swadesh, 1952). The task that we address in this paper is the identification of cognate groups (clusters) within each column. The number of clusters can range between 1 and n. Since many datasets contain either orthographic forms or use an approximate phonetic encoding, we do not require the words to be fully phonetically transcribed. If the data contains multiple words per language/meaning slot, we randomly pick one of the forms and discard the others. We will evaluate our methods by comparing the generated clusters to cognate judgements made by linguists that are experts in language families represented by the datasets.

3 Previous work

Frunza et al. (2005) experiment with several Weka classifiers (Hall et al., 2009) that combine various orthographic similarity measures for the pairwise identification of cognates and false friends[1] as aids to second-language learners. Datasets were extracted from various sources: a manually aligned bitext, lists of cognates and false friends, and exercises for language learners. No single classifier is reported as the most accurate on all tasks. Our approach differs in the focus on identifying cognate groups for the purpose of classifying related languages.

Mulloni (2007) applies the SVMTool tagger (Giménez and Màrquez, 2004) to automatically generate words in one language from their cognates in a related language. He reports a 30-35% accuracy on an English-German cognate list. A relatively large list of cognates (1683 entries) was used for training the SVMTool. This underlines the inherent problem with the proposed methods: in order to identify or generate cognates between languages, a substantial number of cognates must have already been identified. We are interested in a more realistic scenario where *no* cognate pairs are available.

Bouchard-Côté et al. (2007) present a unified stochastic model of diachronic phonology aimed at the automatic reconstruction of proto-forms and deriving phylogenetic trees. They assume the cognate groups to be the input to their model. In the actual experiments on four closely-related Romance languages they filtered out non-cognates by thresholding the normalized edit distance scores. They consider the joint modelling of phonology with the determination of cognates as "an interesting direction for future work." We include edit distance as one of the features in our SVM model.

Hall and Klein (2010) point out the limitations of pairwise cognate identification, and present a generative phylogenetic model for determining cognate groups from unaligned word lists. However, their method requires the language family tree to be known beforehand. This is a difficult prerequisite to satisfy as phylogenetic trees are rarely uncontroversial even in the case of well-studied families. In their experiments, they also disregard the semantic information, instead applying their method to randomly scrambled cognate groups from three closely related Romance languages. In contrast, our experimental setup emulates a much more realistic scenario.

[1] False friends are words that are orthographically similar but historically unrelated, such as English *dinner* and Spanish *dinero*.

4 Clustering cognates

We propose a discriminative approach to clustering cognates. We start by formulating cognate identification as a binary classification task on pairs of words that have the same meaning in different languages. Our model is trained on annotated data from a subset of the dataset, and applied to a different, disjoint subset. The classification results are then used to cluster words into cognate sets. In this section we discuss various features used for training the binary classifier, as well as the details of our clustering approach.

The principal idea for cognate identification follows from the observation that, on average, cognate pairs display higher word similarity that non-cognates. Since no single word similarity measure may be sufficient, we want to utilize a combination of measures. We opt for a feature-based approach because it is more principled and flexible than a simple average or a linear combination of scores. It also allows us to seamlessly incorporate a set of language-pair features that provide additional context for the classification.

We considered various software packages, including Weka (Hall et al., 2009), SVM-light (Joachims, 1999), Liblinear (Fan et al., 2008), and LibSVM (Chang and Lin, 2011). We ultimately selected LibSVM for our experiments due to its higher overall performance in development.

4.1 Word similarity features

We selected the following word similarity features on the basis of the results of our preliminary development experiments:

- minimum edit distance
- the longest common prefix length
- number of common bigrams
- the length of each word (2 separate features)
- the difference in length between the longer and the shorter word

During development, we also experimented with other features, but decided not to include them in the final system for various reasons. The longest common subsequence length was considered redundant with edit distance; longest common substring length and the number of common trigrams were mostly subsumed by bigrams; and shared first letter was generalized by the prefix length.

We decided to exclude features based on phonetic similarity in order to ensure the applicability to datasets that contain only orthographic forms.

4.2 Language-pair features

A limitation of the word similarity features is their strictly local application to pairs of words. However, it is useful to consider not only the words, but also the languages they come from. Intuitively, if we observe that two language lists contain a large number of similar word pairs, we would expect the languages to be closely related, and therefore share many cognates. Conversely, if there is little overall similarity, we may suspect that that cognates will be rare or non-existent.

As an example, consider the average value of the normalized minimum edit distance computed between semantically equivalent words across pairs of word lists. For French and Italian, which are closely related Romance languages, the value is 0.44. In contrast, for French and German, which are more remotely related, the value is only 0.18. Indeed, among 199 word pairs each, there are 155 cognate pairs between French and Italian, and only 48 between French and German. The similarity between cognates is also expected to be greater between strongly related languages, as there would, on average, have been less divergence due to the more recent linguistic split. Once again, our example supports this idea: the average similarity between French/Italian cognates is 0.52, while the average similarity between French/German cognates is 0.22. We would like our classifier to take advantage of this tendency.

Our solution is to introduce a set of binary language pair features, one for each pair of languages in the data. For example, any instance consisting of a German word and an English word has a feature corresponding to that language pair set to '1', and all other language-pair features set to '0'. The language-pair features elevate the learned classification model from a local model to a global one, allowing it to make connections between languages, rather than words alone. For example, if relatively many training instances that have the German-English feature set to '1' are cognate, this information is expected to increase cognate recognition accuracy for this language pair at test time.

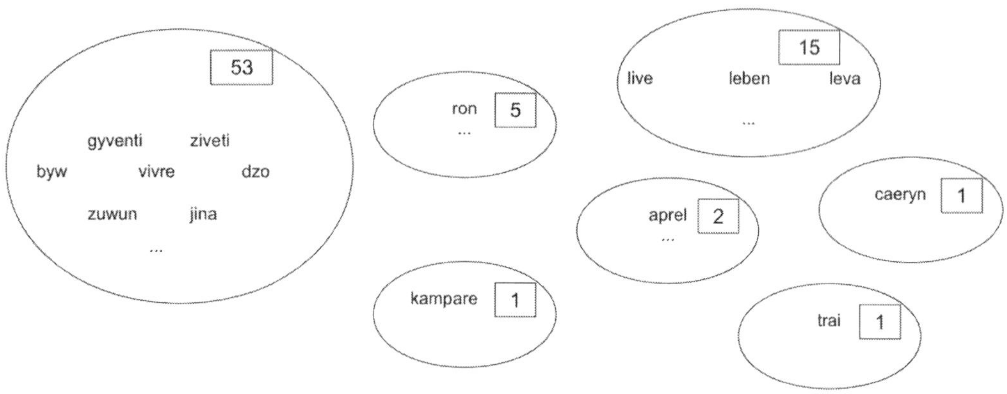

Figure 1: A cognate clustering of of the words with the meaning "to live". The boxed numbers are the total number of words in that cluster.

4.3 Self-training the language-pair features

As with any features, the weights for language-pair features must be derived from annotated training data. For example, in order to derive a useful weight for the German-English feature, we need training instances consisting of English and German words, which are annotated either as cognates or as non-cognates. However, in a realistic scenario of our approach being applied to a previously unanalyzed family of languages, no cognate information may be available. Thus we are faced with a circular problem: language-pair features are likely to improve cognate identification accuracy, but we need to have at least some cognates already identified in order to train the language-pair features.

Our proposed solution to the problem is to train the weights of the language-pair features on our own classifications. We adopt a two-pass approach. We first train a model and classify the data without the language-pair features; language information from the training data is not used in any way. These initial classifications of the test data are then treated as correct, thus providing a 'best guess' at what the cognate classifications would be, were they available. Next, we re-train the model using the initial classification, but this time utilizing the language-pair features. The second and final classification is obtained with the new model, which is expected to be more accurate. This method allows the language-pair features to be used to good effect on any set of languages, using only information locally available in the data to be classified.

4.4 Clustering

After the pairwise cognate classification is completed, the final task is the formation of cognate groups, or clusters. An example of such a clustering is shown in Figure 1, wherein words from various languages for the meaning "to live" have been correctly placed in cognate groups. Each ellipse is a cluster; two words are cognate if and only if they are in the same cluster. Obtaining clusterings such as these for arbitrary data is one objective of our research.

Because of the transitivity property of cognates, there is often no clustering that is completely consistent with the pairwise classification decisions. Each triple of words x, y, and z involves three binary classification instances: $x - y$, $y - z$, and $x - z$. The contradiction arises if two instances are classified as positive, and the remaining one is classified as negative. Consider, for example, the words *beva*, *bivi*, and *vivir*, all of which mean "to live" in Breton, Sardinian, and Spanish, respectively. It is reasonable to expect that *beva* and *bivi* will be identified as cognate, as will *bivi* and *vivir*, due to the similarity between these two pairs. The remaining pair, *beva* and *vivir*, have much lower similarity, and could reasonably be identified as non-cognate. In fact, all three of these words are cognate with each other. A clustering approach would first put two of the words into a single cluster; the remaining word would be added due to its similarity with one of the first two words. Thus, even though the cognate relationship between *beva* and *vivir* may not be found directly, the links *beva-bivi* and *bivi-vivir* are enough; our clustering method finds a cognate pair that would otherwise have been overlooked.

In order to come up with a clustering, we typically need to override some of the binary classifications. Blindly following the transitivity property is likely to result in clusters that are excessively large, since some positive classifications are caused by accidental similarities between non-cognate words. Consider another pair of words with the meaning "to live": Breton *beva* and Swedish *leva*. While obviously similar (differing by only a single letter substitution), they are, in fact, not cognate. This presents a challenge: finding a proper additional condition that should be satisfied before merging clusters, in order to avoid such accidental merges.

The solution employed by our clustering method is based on the notion of *average similarity* between clusters. Initially, each word corresponding to a particular meaning is placed in its own cluster. We then consider each word pair that has been classified as cognate, and for each pair decide whether the corresponding clusters should be merged. We compute the average value of cognate judgements between the two clusters, which is a measure of how similar the two clusters are. If this value is less than a certain threshold (optimized during development), the merge is aborted, and clustering continues as it would had the two words been judged non-cognate. Otherwise, the clusters containing each word are merged.

5 Evaluation of clustering quality

Pairwise classification is typically evaluated by some combination of the following four well-known measures: accuracy (correct classifications divided by all classifications), precision (true positives divided by all positive classifications), recall (true positives divided by actual positives), and F-score (the harmonic average of precision and recall). However, evaluating clustering is a more complex problem than evaluating pairwise classifications. Pairwise metrics have significant weaknesses when applied to clustering, where a word is proposed to be cognate with all words in its cluster. Incorrectly assigning a word to a large cluster will generate a large number of false positives, while incorrectly assigning a word to a smaller cluster would generate fewer false positives. On the other hand, incorrectly positing two clusters instead of one is penalized proportionally to the square of the size of the cluster. In short, the number of false positives and false negatives an error creates may not be balanced or consistent.

We considered a number of alternative metrics, eventually deciding on the B-Cubed measure. B-Cubed metrics assign a precision and recall to each item in a set of clusters — in our case, to each word. The item precision is the ratio of the number of its cognates in its cluster to the number of items in its cluster. The item recall is the ratio of the number of cognates in its cluster to the total number of its cognates. A B-Cubed F-score is computed from the B-Cubed precision and recall, analogously to pairwise F-score. Amigó et al. (2009) show that B-Cubed metrics satisfy four constraints deemed critical to a valid clustering evaluation metric, while all other metrics investigated, including pairwise metrics, fail at least one of these criteria.

For an illustrative example, consider again the words shown in Figure 1. The gold standard indicates one large cluster (53 words), one medium sized cluster (15 words), and several smaller clusters. In this case, incorrectly assigning (or failing to assign) a single word to the large cluster produces many false positives (or false negatives), while exchanging a word between two smaller clusters has a minimal effect. In order to verify the inconsistency of pairwise metrics on clustering, we analyzed two different clusterings of these words; one was an excessively aggressive clustering, in which the medium-sized cluster was almost entirely subsumed into the larger cluster. The other was a more conservative clustering which formed the medium-sized cluster comparatively well, and generally better recovered the overall structure of the actual clusters. The pairwise metrics reported the more aggressive clustering to be significantly better than the more conservative result; the B-Cubed metrics did not display this anomalous behavior.

The above example demonstrates that pairwise metrics can, under realistic conditions, report a much worse clustering to be significantly better, demonstrating their intrinsic volatility: a single error can have dramatic, unpredictable effects that depend more on chance similarities than on the quality of the clustering or classification process. B-Cubed metrics do not have this problem; being an average of item-based measurements, errors will have consistent effects, balanced against the resulting quality of the clusters. We therefore adopt B-Cubed metrics as the preferred measure of clustering performance.

6 The Indo-European experiments

Our first experiment involves an extremely well-studied family, for which we also have access to relatively long and complete lists of basic words. We divide the data into training and test sets along different sets of meanings. The same languages appear in both sets.

6.1 Data

The publicly-available Comparative Indo-European Database (Dyen et al., 1992) contains words for 200 different meanings in 95 languages of the Indo-European family. The words in each meaning are grouped in cognate sets. We used a pre-processed version of the data which places each meaning in an individual file, for a total of 200 files. Each word is labelled with the number of the cognate set that it belongs to.[2] We randomly selected 20 out of 200 meanings data as a development set. We also created a separate held-out test set of 20 meanings, roughly 10% of the data. We performed two tests: one with a small 20-meaning training set, and the other with a large 180-meaning training set, which also included the development set. In both cases, the test set was the same. We made sure that the sets of meanings in the training and test data were disjoint.

6.2 Classification methods

We tested three methods of classification, each making different use of language-pair features (LPF):

- NO LPF: a strictly "local" method that considers only the pair of words in question, and utilizes no language-pair features.
- SUPERVISED LPF: the weights of language-pair features are trained on the annotated instances in the training set.
- SELF-TRAINED LPF: the two-pass approach described in section 4.3. No cognate information for the language pairs in the test set is assumed to be in the training set.

[2]This processed data is available on request.

Method	Size of Training Set	
	20	180
Baseline	0.623	0.623
NO LPF	0.642	0.687
SELF-TRAINED LPF	0.656	0.687
SUPERVISED LPF	0.677	0.677

Table 2: Average B-Cubed F-Scores for the Indo-European data.

For the baseline, we adopt a simple but surprisingly effective method of grouping words according to their first letter or phoneme. Two cognates maintaining their common initial sound are assigned to the same cluster by this baseline. However, unrelated words that accidentally share the same first letter are also marked as cognate. In the example shown in Figure 1, the baseline correctly identifies the middle-sized cluster of words from 15 Germanic languages, but splits the largest cluster into several smaller ones, containing words starting with b, d, g, j, and z, respectively.

6.3 Results

Table 2 shows the results in terms of average B-Cubed F-score. Our methods consistently outperform the first-letter baseline regardless of the size of the training set. When the 20 meaning training subset was used, the results rank the SELF-TRAINED LPF method between the SUPERVISED LPF and NO LPF methods. When the 180 meaning training set was used, the NO LPF and SELF-TRAINED LPF models achieved substantial improvement voer the baseline; however, somewhat surprisingly, the SUPERVISED LPF model obtained a smaller improvement. This suggests that the SUPERVISED LPF model may have issues with overspecialization, or may not be able to make use of data past a certain point. The improvement exhibited by the SELF-TRAINED LPF model suggest that the two-pass method makes greater use of additional training data, and is capable of producing even better clusters than the SUPERVISED LPF model.

7 The ASJP experiments

This set of experiments involved some of the relatively short lists from a comprehensive database that contains most of the world's languages. This time, we divided the data into the training and test sets by languages, rather than by meanings.

Baseline	0.653
NO LPF	0.662
SELF-TRAINED LPF	0.714
SUPERVISED LPF	0.703

Table 3: Average B-Cubed F-Scores for ASJP data, with languages grouped by family.

Baseline	0.660
NO LPF	0.724
SELF-TRAINED LPF	0.701
SUPERVISED LPF	0.665

Table 4: Average B-Cubed F-Scores for ASJP data, with languages ordered alphabetically.

7.1 Data

Our second dataset consists of word lists from the Automated Similarity Judgement Program (ASJP) project, which represent 92 languages belonging to 5 language families: Austro-Asiatic, Hmong-Mien, Mixe-Zoque, Sino-Tibetan, and Tai-Kadai. Each list contains 40 basic meanings transcribed in a phonetic notation devised for the ASJP.

We performed two experiments on this data. In each experiment, the first 46 languages were used for training, and the other 46 were used for testing. For the first experiments, the languages were grouped according to language families, ensuring that most families appeared exclusively either in the training or the test set (one group was split between the two sets). For the second test, we sorted the languages alphabetically, essentially shuffling different language families. One of our objectives was to determine how the distribution of the languages affects the results. The first experiment adopts natural divisions between language families, emulating a realistic scenario where a model is trained on well-studied families and applied to the data representing less-studied families. The second experiment represents the situation where we have annotation for some of the languages in a family, and aim to discover cognates among other languages in the same family. The alphabetic ordering is akin to random shuffling of languages, but has the advantage of being easy to replicate.

7.2 Results on the data grouped by family

In this experiment, languages were naturally arranged into language families. That is, all languages in the same language family, such as Sino-Tibetan and Tai-Kadai, are adjacent in the data. This provides a realistic testing environment, wherein one set of language families (with known cognate data) is used to obtain cognate information for another set of language families.

Table 3 shows that the SELF-TRAINED LPF model obtains the best results in this experiment. The model appears able to generalize well, though it is not trained on any of the language pairs it is tested on. The NO LPF method and the baseline method are less effective. The SUPERVISED LPF method is again less effective that the SELF-TRAINED LPF method. This is likely caused by the lack of training data that contains the information for the language pairs that it encounters in the test set.

7.3 Results on the data sorted alphabetically

This experiment is based on the same ASJP dataset, with the exception that the languages are sorted alphabetically. This strengthens the relationship between the training and test sets (as languages from all families can be found in each), while reducing the similarities within them.

The results of this test are presented in Table 4. The NO LPF approach was a surprise winner this time. It appears that the presence of more linguistic relationships between the training and testing sets was the deciding factor. We conjecture that the relationship between the training and test sets was sufficiently strong for a locally trained model to provide very good results.

On the other hand, the SUPERVISED LPF approach performed much worse, only barely exceeding the baseline results. This likely occurs for the same reason that the NO LPF method does better — there are not enough similarities between the training and the test data to use global features accurately.

Notably, the SELF-TRAINED LPF approach still does quite well, even with fewer similarities to use. This demonstrates high reliability, as all other methods do poorly on at least one test; only the SELF-TRAINED LPF method provides high quality clusterings throughout all experiments.[3]

8 Discussion

Based on our results, we are able to conclude that our methods can consistently and accurately

[3]We also considered training on the Indo-European data and testing on ASJP data, but unfortunately the two datasets use entirely different notations: Romanized orthography versus specialized phonetic encoding. No simple method exists for converting between the two.

identify and cluster cognates, exceeding the performance of a strong baseline method. We have shown how SVMs can produce accurate cognate classifications; we have also shown how these classifications can be systematically used to create cognate groups. Evaluated with the B-Cubed metrics, these clusters are demonstrated to be of high quality compared to known cognate groups.

Language pairs appear to be most useful as binary features in a supervised SVM model if the data to be classified are from a small number of language families. In cases where there are fewer similarities in the data, fewer connections between languages can be learned. Relying on the cognate annotations substantially lowers the quality of the results in such situations, as the data it requires is not available. We thus find the SUPERVISED LPF method not only impractical, but also rather unreliable.

In contrast, our SELF-TRAINED LPF approach has been demonstrated to be a reliable, high-performing method, which produces good classifications in all of our experiments, throughout which the size of the training data and the distribution of the languages to be classified varies significantly. While not always yielding the best clusters overall, the SELF-TRAINED LPF method has been shown to consistently yield very good results across all tests. It functions well under realistic conditions, as it does not require cognate information on the languages to be classified. Furthermore, it can find global connections between languages that do not have cognate information available. We thus take our results as a recommendation for the use of the SELF-TRAINED LPF approach, and for the further investigation of language-pair features in cognate identification in general.

9 Conclusion

We have proposed an effective new method of identifying cognates that can make useful global connections from local data. Our demonstration that SVMs can make use of language information to improve cognate classifications lays a foundation for the use of cognate judgements in language classification and provides insight into how machine learning methods can be used successfully for the purposes of cognate identification.

Further work in this area might process language pairs directly using a method similar to our own, developing a machine learning, cognate based method for language classification. Brown et al. (2008) notes that cognate judgements could be used to compare and classify languages, but that this is yet to be done. Our use of relationships between language pairs to assist in classification sets a strong precedent for cognate-based language classification. In addition, other machine learning algorithms, such as Bayesian classifiers, as well as sophisticated phonetic similarity measures, may produce more accurate cognate classifications and clusters, and could be tested in future studies.

Acknowledgements

We thank Eric Holman, Søren Wichmann, and other members of the ASJP project for sharing their cognate-annotated data sets. We also thank Shane Bergsma for insightful comments. Format conversion of the Comparative Indo-European Database was performed by Qing Dou. This research was partially funded by the Natural Sciences and Engineering Research Council of Canada.

References

Enrique Amigó, Julio Gonzalo, Javier Artiles, and Felisa Verdego. 2009. A comparison of extrinsic clustering evaluation metrics based on formal constraints. *Information Retrieval*, pages 461–486.

Alexandre Bouchard-Côté, Percy Liang, Thomas Griffiths, and Dan Klein. 2007. A probabilistic approach to diachronic phonology. *Proceedings of the 2007 Conference on Empirical Methods on Natural Language Processing (EMNLP07)*.

Cecil H. Brown, Eric W. Holman, Søren Wichmann, and Viveka Velopillai. 2008. Automated classification of the World's languages: A description of the method and preliminary results. *Language Typology and Universals 61:4*, pages 285–308.

Chih-Chung Chang and Chih-Jen Lin. 2011. LIBSVM: A library for support vector machines. *ACM Transactions on Intelligent Systems and Technology*, 2:27:1–27:27. Software available at `http://www.csie.ntu.edu.tw/~cjlin/libsvm`.

Isidore Dyen, Joseph Kruskal, and Paul Black. 1992. An indoeuropean classication: A lexicostatistical experiment. *Transactions of the American Philosophical Society*.

Rong-En Fan, Kai-Wei Chang, Cho-Jui Hsieh, Xiang-Rui Wang, and Chih-Jen Lin. 2008. LIBLINEAR: A library for large linear classification. *Journal of Machine Learning Research*, 9:1871–1874.

Oana Frunza and Diana Inkpen. 2009. Identification and disambiguation of cognates,false friends, and partial cognates using machine learning techniques. *International Journal of Linguistics, Vol. 1, No. 1.*

Oana Frunza, Diana Inkpen, and David Nadeau. 2005. A text processing tool for the romanian language. *Proceedings of the EuroLAN 2005 Workshop on Cross-Language Knowledge Induction.*

Jesús Giménez and Lluís Màrquez. 2004. Svmtool: A general pos tagger generator based on support vector machines. *Journal of Machine Learning Research.*

David Hall and Dan Klein. 2010. Finding cognate groups using phylogenies. *Proceedings of the 48th Annual Meeting of the Association for Computational Linguistics*, pages 1030–1039.

Mark Hall, Eibe Frank, Geoffrey Holmes, Bernhard Pfahringer, Peter Reutemann, and Ian H. Witten. 2009. The weka data mining software: An update. *SIGKDD Explorations, Volume 11, Issue 1.*

T. Joachims. 1999. Making large-scale svm learning practical. *Advances in Kernel Methods - Support Vector Learning.*

Grzegorz Kondrak and Bonnie J. Dorr. 2004. Identification of confusable drug names: A new approach and evaluation methodology. *Proceedings of the Twentieth International Conference on Computational Linguistics (COLING 2004)*, pages 952–958.

Grzegorz Kondrak, Daniel Marcu, and Kevin Knight. 2003. Cognates can improve statistical translation models. *Proceedings of the 2003 Conference of the North American Chapter of the Association for Computational Linguistics on Human Language Technology*, pages 46–48.

Grzegorz Kondrak. 2009. Identification of cognates and recurrent sound correspondences in word lists. *TAL Volume 50*, pages 201–235.

M. Paul Lewis. 2009. *Ethnologue: Languages of the World, 16th edition.* Dallas, Tex.: SIL International.

Andrea Mulloni. 2007. Automatic prediction of cognate orthography using support vector machines. *Meeting of the ACL: Student Research Workshop, 2007.*

Michel Simard, George F. Foster, and Pierre Isabelle. 1993. Using cognates to align sentences in bilingual corpora. *CASCON '93 Proceedings of the 1993 conference of the Centre for Advanced Studies on Collaborative research: distributed computing - Volume 2.*

Morris Swadesh. 1952. Lexico-statistic dating of prehistoric ethnic contacts. *Proceedings of the American philosophical society*, 96:452–463.

Soren Wichmann, Andre Muller, Viveka Velupillai, Annkathrin Wett, Cecil H. Brown, Zarina Molochieva, Sebastian Sauppe, Eric W. Holman, Pamela Brown, Julia Bishoffberger, Dik Bakker, Johann-Mattis List, Dmitry Egorov, Oleg Belyaev, Matthias Urban, Robert Mailhammer, Helen Geyer, David Beck, Evgenia Korovina, Pattie Epps, Pilar Valenzuela, Anthony Grant, and Harald Hammarstrom. 2011. The ASJP Database (version 14). `http://email.eva.mpg.de/~wichmann/ASJPHomePage.htm`.

Extending WordNet with Hypernyms and Siblings Acquired from Wikipedia

Ichiro Yamada[†‡] **Jong-Hoon Oh**[†] **Chikara Hashimoto**[†] **Kentaro Torisawa**[†]
Jun'ichi Kazama[†] **Stijn De Saeger**[†] **Takuya Kawada**[†]
[†]Information Analysis Laboratory, National Institute of
Information and Communications Technology, 619-0289 Kyoto, Japan
{rovellia,ch,torisawa,kazama,stijn,tkawada}@nict.go.jp
[‡]NHK Science & Technology Research Laboratories, 157-8510 Tokyo, Japan
yamada.i-hy@nhk.or.jp

Abstract

This paper proposes a method for extending WordNet with terms in Wikipedia. Our method identifies a WordNet synset by integrating evidence derived from the structure of an article in Wikipedia and distributional similarity of terms. Unlike previous methods, utilizing the hypernym and siblings of the target term acquired from Wikipedia, the proposed method can deal with terms other than Wikipedia article titles and can work well even when reliable distributional similarity of a target term is unavailable. Experiments show that the proposed method can identify synsets for 2,039,417 inputs at precision rate of 84%. Furthermore, it is estimated from the experimental results that there should be 328,572 terms among all the inputs whose synset our method can correctly identify, while previous methods relying only on distributional similarity and lexico-syntactic patterns cannot.

1 Introduction

As a comprehensive repository of word senses, WordNet (Fellbaum, 1998) has played an important role in many natural-language-processing (NLP) tasks. Hand-crafted semantic knowledge, however, has low coverage of named entities and domain-specific knowledge. To address this issue, many researchers have proposed methods for extending WordNet by mapping new terms to a WordNet "synset."[1]

In this paper, we propose a novel method that extends WordNet by integrating the *Wikipedia article structure* and *distributional similarity*. With this method, an appropriate synset for a term in Wikipedia is identified by using the distributional similarity of the term and that of the term's hypernym and siblings, which are automatically acquired from Wikipedia. (Hereafter, **trg** is used for a target term for which we identify the appropriate synset, **hyper** is used for the hypernym of **trg** and **sib** is used for the sibling of **trg**.)

The reason for using **hyper** and **sib** can be explained as follows. In general, when an unknown term is encountered, its context helps in interpreting the term. Especially, if the unknown term's hypernym and/or its semantically similar terms (its **sibs**) were somehow learned as context, it would often be possible to successfully guess its meaning. In WordNet expansion, **trg** may correspond to terms for which reliable distributional similarity is unavailable. In such cases, the distributional similarity of **hyper** and **sib** can help. Even when the distributional similarity of **trg** is available, that of **hyper** and **sib** can boost the performance of synset identification by providing additional sources of information.

In this study, **trg**, **hyper** and **sib** are derived from hyponymy relation instances acquired from Wikipedia. Acquisition of hyponymy relations from Wikipedia is based on the internal structure of Wikipedia articles. For example, the Wikipedia article "Jack Black" is composed of the article title "Jack Black", section titles "Career" and "Films", and an itemized list under the "films" section as shown in Fig. 1. Hyponymy relation instances like (films, *Kung Fu Panda*), (films, *Airborne*) and (films, *Johnny Skidmarks*) can be acquired from this structure (Sumida et al., 2008). Most hyponyms in these hyponymy relation instances are not in WordNet and thus should be added to WordNet.

Trg, **hyper** and **sib** obtained from Wikipedia are the inputs ($\mathcal{I}$s. See Section 3) to candidate generation of appropriate synset for **Trg**, whose outputs, in turn, become the inputs to candidate selection (Figure 2). The candidate generation relies on multiple *synset identification modules*.

[1]A synset is a set of cognitive synonyms, each expressing a distinct concept.

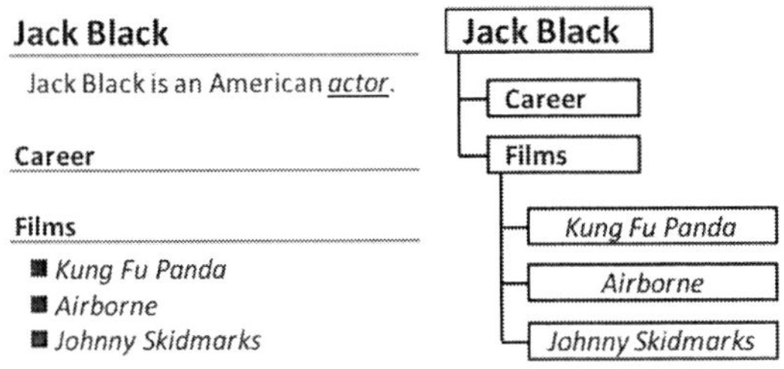

Figure 1: Internal structure of Wikipedia article "Jack Black".

Each module uses a different combination of information sources for generating appropriate synset candidates. This difference between the modules makes it possible to generate diverse synset candidates from the different viewpoint of each module. The most appropriate synset is selected by the candidate selection using a classifier that can discriminate better synset candidates from worse ones among outputs of the multiple synset identification modules. The candidate selection is expected to improve the precision of synset identification.

Experiments show that the proposed method can identify synsets for 2,039,417 $\mathcal{I}$s with 84% precision rate. In contrast, our implementation of Yamada et al. (2009), which uses the distributional similarity of **trg** only, has a precision rate of only 50.3% and covers less than half of the whole input from Wikipedia. Furthermore, it is estimated from the experimental results that there should be 328,572 terms among all the 1,231,172 unique **trg**s in the 2,039,417 $\mathcal{I}$s whose synset can be correctly identified by our method, but not by previous methods relying only on distributional similarity and lexico-syntactic patterns (Snow et al., 2006; Yamada et al., 2009).

2 Related Work

As a resource for extending WordNet, Wikipedia has recently received growing interest (Ruiz-Casado et al., 2005; Suchanek et al., 2007; Toral et al., 2008; Wu and Weld, 2008; Toral et al., 2009; Ponzetto and Navigli, 2009). These studies link a Wikipedia article title to a WordNet synset by using the Wikipedia category system, Wikipedia infoboxes, or similarity between Wikipedia article contents as evidence. However, these methods cannot handle terms that are not Wikipedia-article titles, and thus their coverage is limited.

On the other hand, distributional similarity between terms has been used in extending an existing taxonomy like WordNet (Snow et al., 2006; Yamada et al., 2009). Snow et al. (2006) identified a hypernym for a target term by using lexico-syntactic patterns and distributionally similar terms of the target term. Then the target term is linked to a WordNet synset by using its hypernym and distributionally similar terms as evidence. Yamada et al. (2009) linked a target term to its hypernym in a given taxonomy by using distributional similarity between the target term and terms in the taxonomy.

However, it is often the case that we cannot obtain reliable distributional similarity of a term and we cannot acquire hypernyms of a term co-occurring with lexico-syntactic patterns, especially when the term is infrequent in a corpus. As a result, we can hardly expect that the previous methods (Snow et al., 2006; Yamada et al., 2009) work well for this infrequent term. Nonetheless, we believe that it is important to deal with such infrequent terms, since they constitute the long-tail of the Web. Our method exploits not only the distributional similarity of a target term but also that of hypernym and siblings of the target term. Accordingly, as indicated by the experimental results in Section 4, our method achieves a higher precision and a broader coverage.

Many researchers have proposed methods for hyponymy relation acquisition from texts (Hearst, 1992; Shinzato and Torisawa, 2004; Sumida and Torisawa, 2008; Sumida et al., 2008; Oh et al., 2009; Oh et al., 2010). Recently, Wikipedia has gained attention as a source for hyponymy relations (Sumida and Torisawa, 2008; Sumida et al., 2008; Oh et al., 2009; Oh et al., 2010). Hyponymy relation instances acquired from Wikipedia are relevant to hypernyms and siblings of a term in our proposed method and the method of Sumida and Torisawa (2008) is used for preprocessing in the proposed method.

3 Proposed Method

The proposed method is overviewed in Figure 2. In the preprocessing stage (Section 3.1), hyponymy relation instances are acquired by using a method of acquiring hyponymy relations (proposed by Sumida et al. (2008)) from Wikipedia articles. From these relations, **trg**, **hyper** and **sib**, which are denoted as $\mathcal{I} =<$ target term, hypernym, siblings $>$ or $\mathcal{I} =< trg, hyp, N_{sib}(trg) >$ in short, are obtained. In

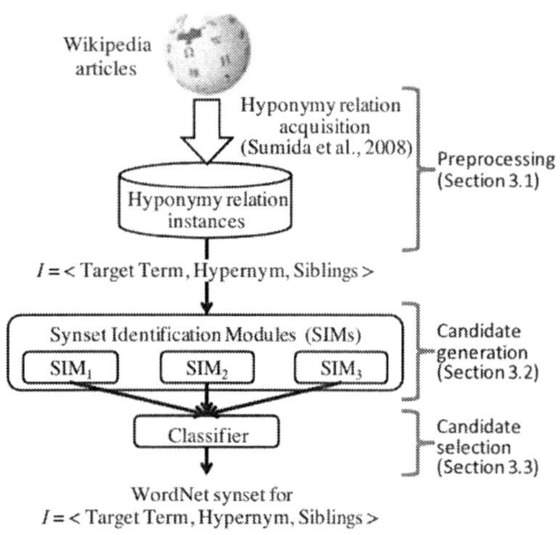

Figure 2: Overview of proposed method.

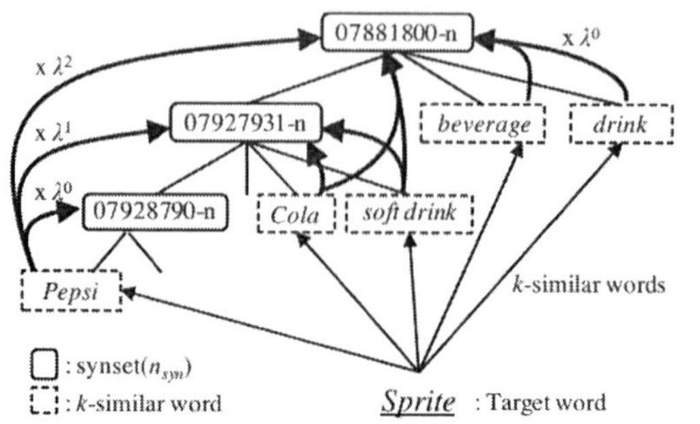

Figure 3: Example of score propagation by **trg** *Sprite* and its **sib** *Coke*.

the candidate-generation stage (Section 3.2), three synset identification modules (SIMs) generate candidates of appropriate synsets for a given $\mathcal{I}$. Finally, in the candidate-selection stage (Section 3.3), a classifier produces the final output by selecting the best one among the output of the three SIMs. In our task, "one sense per one hyponymy relation instance" is assumed. For example, *Airborne* in Fig. 1 represents the meaning of "film", while the term itself has several other meanings.

3.1 Acquisition of Hypernyms (hyper) and Siblings (sibs)

A set of hyponymy relation instances are acquired by using "A tool for hyponymy relation acquisition from Wikipedia"[2] (Sumida et al., 2008). This tool extracts hyponymy-relation candidates from a Wikipedia article structure and then applies SVM to select the correct hyponymy relation instances from the candidates. Among the resulting hyponymy relation instances, reliable ones are selected by using a threshold value for a SVMs score with 90% precision [3]. Furthermore, hyponymy relation instances are restricted to ones whose hyponym comes from leaf nodes in the hierarchical layout of Wikipedia articles (i.e., *Kung Fu Panda* in Fig. 1). By means of this restriction, terms that are not named entities are filtered out. The method used for acquisition of hyponymy relations is explained in detail in Sumida et al. (2008).

[2]Available at `http://alaginrc.nict.go.jp/hyponymy/index.html`

[3]To ensure the results had 90% precision, an SVM score (distance from hyperplane) of 0.49 was used as the threshold value.

Some **hyper**s in hyponymy relations extracted from Wikipedia are often very long noun sequences like *wild south-China tiger*. Consequently, their reliable distributional similarity is unavailable owing to their low-frequency or their absence in corpora. This problem is addressed by applying a longest-suffix match against frequently-appearing terms in a corpus for which reliable distributional similarity is measured (Section 3.2.2) under the assumption that the longest suffix can be regarded as the superordinate concept of **hyper**. For example, *south-China tiger* is the longest-suffix match result for *wild south China tiger*. If the longest suffix for **hyper** cannot be found, the hyponymy relation instances containing **hyper** are ignored.

Sibs are extracted from a Wikipedia article structure under the condition that their **hyper**s are the same.

3.2 Synset Identification Modules

Each synset identification module (SIM) generates synset candidates for a given $\mathcal{I} =< trg, hyp, N_{sib}(trg) >$. The candidates are determined by a *score propagation method*. A WordNet synset gets a higher score if it is considered to be the appropriate synset for trg.

3.2.1 Scoring by Propagation

The score for input $\mathcal{I} =< trg, hyp, N_{sib}(trg) >$ and WordNet synset syn is defined as $PS(\mathcal{I}, syn)$ in Eq. (1), which represents the weighted sum of the sub-scores for target term trg, its hypernym hyp, and a set of siblings, $N_{sib}(trg)$. Each sub-score, $S(n, syn)$ (Eq. (2)), is computed by score propagation through the hierarchical structure of WordNet synsets, where n is either **trg**, **hyper** or **sib**. Figure 3 illustrates the score propagation. It is assumed that "*Sprite*" is a **trg** and "07881800-

$$PS(\mathcal{I}, syn) = \alpha \times S(trg, syn) + \beta \times S(hyp, syn) + \gamma \times \sum_{sib \in N_{sib}(trg)} \frac{S(sib, syn)}{|N_{sib}(trg)|} \quad (1)$$

$$S(n, syn) = \sum_{n_k \in TopK(n)} \sum_{syn_k \in SYN(n_k)} \lambda^{d(syn, syn_k)} \times sim(n, n_k) \quad (2)$$

n" is a synset for which the sub-score $S(n, syn)$ is computed. First, a set of k terms in the Japanese WordNet that is the most similar to **trg** is obtained. This set is extracted by using the distributional similarity measure mentioned in Section 3.2.2 and is denoted by $TopK(n)$ in Eq. (2). Second, the synset *receives* the penalized distributional similarity from the k terms ($n_k \in TopK(n)$ in Eq. (2)). The score propagation is controlled by $\lambda^{d(syn, syn_k)}$, where $0 < \lambda < 1$, $d(syn, syn_k)$ is the distance between two synsets syn and syn_k in the WordNet hierarchy, and syn_k is a synset to which $n_k \in TopK(n)$ belongs. More precisely, $d(syn, syn_k)$ is the minimum length of any ancestral path between syn and syn_k, and $d(syn, syn_k) = 0$ if $syn = syn_k$.

Note that as distance $d(syn, syn_k)$ increases, $\lambda^{d(syn, syn_k)}$ becomes smaller and $sim(n, n_k)$ therefore makes less contribution to $S(n, syn)$. On the other hand, $S(n, syn)$ tends to *recieve* a penalized similarity from more synsets distant from syn than those close to syn. The score therefore has the largest value when these two tendencies are balanced.

The score propagation for **trg** and **sib**, in Figure 3, is done only in the direction to ancestors in the Wordnet hierarchy. On the contrary, the score propagation for **hyper** is done in a slightly different way. That is, the penalized distributional similarity is propagated to not only the ancestors but also the descendants.

The final score value, $PS(\mathcal{I}, syn)$, is the sum of sub-score values S for **trg**, **hyper**, and **sib** weighted by constants α, β, and γ, where $\alpha + \beta + \gamma = 1$. These constants are optimized in the experiment, which is described in Section 4.1. This score-propagation scheme is an extension of Yamada et al. (2009).

3.2.2 Measuring Distributional Similarity

The distributional similarity between two terms (n_1 and n_2) is defined as

$$sim(n_1, n_2) = 1 - D_{JS}(P(a|n_1) \| P(a|n_2)) \quad (3)$$

where a denotes a class to which the term belongs, and $D_{JS}(P(a|n_1) \| P(a|n_2))$ is the Jensen-Shannon divergence between two probability distributions, $P(a|n_1)$ and $P(a|n_2)$.

To calculate probability distribution $P(a|n)$, Torisawa (2001) conducted noun clustering using the triple $< v, p, n >$ obtained from a parsed corpus, where v, n, and p represent a verb, a noun, and a postposition that attaches to the noun. The noun and the postposition constitute a phrase that depends on the verb. The probability of occurrence of the triple $< v, p, n >$ is defined as

$$\begin{aligned} & P(< v, p, n >) \\ & =_{def} \sum_{a \in A} P(< v, p > |a) P(n|a) P(a) \end{aligned} \quad (4)$$

where a denotes a class of $< v, p >$ and n. $P(< v, p > |a)$, $P(n|a)$, and $P(a)$ are estimated by the EM-based clustering method, which estimates these probabilities by using a given corpus. In the E-step, probability $P(a| < v, p >)$ is calculated. In the M-step, probabilities $P(< v, p > |a)$, $P(n|a)$, and $P(a)$ are updated to arrive at the maximum likelihood using the results of the E-step. From the results of estimation by this EM-based clustering method, probabilities $P(< v, p > |a)$, $P(n|a)$, and $P(a)$ for $< v, p >$, n, and a are obtained. $P(a|n)$ is then calculated by the following equation:

$$P(a|n) = \frac{P(n|a)P(a)}{\sum_{a \in A} P(n|a)P(a)} \quad (5)$$

With the aim of enabling large-scale clustering and using the resulting clusters in named entity recognition, Kazama and Torisawa (2008) proposed parallelization of this EM-based clustering method. Kazama et al. (2009) then reported the calculation of distributional similarity by using the clustering results. We applied their method to the TSUBAKI corpus (Shinzato et al., 2008), a collection of 100-million Japanese Web pages containing 6×10^9 sentences. We prepared about 1,000,000 terms for calculating the distributional similarity. These one million terms consist of the following three sets of terms: (1) sets of hyponymy relation instances extracted from Wikipedia, (2) sets in WordNet, and (3) sets from the TSUBAKI corpus that are neither (1) nor (2). Terms in sets (1) or (2) were required to syntactically depend on 10 different $< v, p >$ in the TSUBAKI corpus for reliably calculating the distributional similarities. Terms in set (3) have been chosen from those that have the largest number of dependency relations in the corpus, so the total number of terms is one million.

3.2.3 Definition of SIMs

Three synset identification modules (SIMs), namely, SIM_1, SIM_2, and SIM_3, were developed. These three modules make it possible to generate diverse candidates of an appropriate synset by using different evidence derived from **trg**, **hyper**, and **sib**. Table 1 summarizes the information that each SIM uses as a trigger for score propagation. SIM_1 relies on $PS(\mathcal{I}, syn)$, whose β and γ are zero, while SIM_2 is defined by $PS(\mathcal{I}, syn)$, whose γ is zero.

Information sources	SIM_1	SIM_2	SIM_3
Target term (**trg**)	✓	✓	✓
Hypernym (**hyper**)		✓	✓
Sibling (**sib**)			✓

Table 1: Information sources used in each module.

Basically, each SIM generates top-n synsets that maximize $PS(\mathcal{I}, syn)$ over all WordNet synsets. Here, one heuristics is used for SIM_2 and SIM_3 when **hyper** is available. When **hyper** belongs to WordNet synsets, one of the synsets is usually the appropriate synset of the **trg**. According to this observation, the top-n synsets among the synsets that contain **hyper** are generated. However, if the hyponymy relation is wrong (like *musician* as a hypernym of *acoustic guitars*), this heuristics will have a negative effect on the performance of synset identification.

To avoid this effect, the following additional condition is set: At least one of the synsets to which **hyper** belongs has score $PS(\mathcal{I}, syn) > 0$. Under this condition, the synset which contains the **hyp** but is not supported by the **trg** and its **sibs** is not preferred in generating candidates of an appropriate synset.

3.3 Selecting Appropriate Synset among Outputs of Multiple SIMs

Once SIMs generate WordNet synset candidates for a **trg**, to select the most appropriate synset, a classifier is applied to these candidates. As the classifier, SVMs trained with a polynomial kernel of degree 2 are used[4]. Moreover, the following features are used for training SVMs, which are selected by the ablation test reported in Section 4.4.

f1: **hyper**

f2: Name of SIM used for generating appropriate synset candidates

f3: Value of $PS(\mathcal{I}, syn)$ given by each SIM

f4: Synset ID of WordNet synset candidate

f5: Suffix of **trg**

f6: Suffix of **hyper**

Regarding f5 and f6, the suffixes are obtained in the same way as the procedure for longest-suffix matching described in Section 3.1. Finally, the synset which has the largest SVM score is selected as appropriate synset for **trg**.

4 Experiments

4.1 Experimental Set up

For our experiments, 4,057,879 hyponymy relation instances were acquired from the 2009-09-27 version of the Japanese Wikipedia dump (containing about 0.9 million articles). Hyponymy relation instances whose hyponyms are not found in the Japanese WordNet and are from a leaf node in a layout structure of a Wikipedia article (which usually corresponds to an itemized list like the movie names in Fig. 1) were then selected. After these processes, 2,039,417 hyponymy relation instances containing 1,231,172 unique hyponyms (**trg**), of which about 80% are not Wikipedia article titles, were acquired. **Sibs** for each hyponym (**trg**) were then acquired from the hyponymy relation instances. Finally, 2,039,417 $\mathcal{I}$s (note that $\mathcal{I} =< trg, hyp, N_{sib}(trg) >$ composed of **trg**, **hyper**, and **sibs**) were used for the experiments.

800 $\mathcal{I}$s were randomly selected for development data, and 1,800 $\mathcal{I}$s were selected for test data from the 2,039,417 $\mathcal{I}$s, where a **trg** in the selected $\mathcal{I}$s is unique over both development and test data. Candidate generation was applied to these development and test data, and the appropriate synsets

[4]TinySVM, available at `http://chasen.org/taku/software/TinySVM`, wasused

among candidates for each $\mathcal{I}$ were then manually labeled. In the labeling, three judges were asked to mark synset candidates as the correct synset for $\mathcal{I}$ if one of terms in the synset candidate is an appropriate hypernym[5]. Finally, the correct synset for $\mathcal{I}$ was determined by the judges' majority vote. The interrater agreement between the three judges (Siegel's Kappa) was 0.785, indicating substantial agreement.

We performed parameter optimization by using the development data. The parameters used in our method showing the best performance for development data were used in our experiments, namely, the number of similar terms $k = 60$, the parameter for score propagation $\lambda = 0.6$, and weights for $S(n, syn)$ in $PS(\mathcal{I}, syn)$ ($\alpha = 0.6$ and $\beta = 0.4$ for SIM_2 and $\alpha = 0.5$, $\beta = 0.4$, and $\gamma = 0.1$ for SIM_3).

4.2 Results

In the experiment, the eleven systems listed as follows (ten baseline systems and our proposed system) were evaluated.

- $B1$–$B3$: Bi represents a system that outputs the best candidate of SIM_i $(1 \leq i \leq 3)$.
- $SB1$–$SB3$: SBi represents a system based on a classifier that selects the best synset among the top-5 candidates of SIM_i $(1 \leq i \leq 3)$
- $CB1$: randomly selects one of the outputs of B1–B3 as the appropriate synset.
- $CB2$: selects the most frequently observed synset in the training data among the outputs of B1–B3.
- $EB1$: randomly selects one of synsets, which contains a **hyper** in $\mathcal{I}$.
- $EB2$: selects the most frequently observed synset in the training data among synsets, which contains a **hyper** in $\mathcal{I}$.
- Proposed method: The proposed method using B1–B3

$B1$ is our implementation of the method proposed by Yamada et al. (2009). Evaluation of B1–B3 shows the performance of candidate generation by SIM_1, SIM_2, and SIM_3. $EB1$ and $EB2$ can be considered simple extensions of an existing research of Sumida et al. (2008) for estimating Wordnet synsets.

Table 2 shows the precision rate of each system. We could not evaluate all 1,800 samples for $B1$, $SB1$, $EB1$ and $EB2$. $B1$ and $SB1$ were able to generate outputs for 614 $\mathcal{I}$s, where trg in $\mathcal{I}$s was included in the target terms for calculating the distributional similarity. $EB1$ and $EB2$ can select the synset when **hyper** or the suffix of **hyper** is registered in WordNet. For this reason, it was not possible to select a synset for 174 **trg**s out of the 1,800 samples in $EB1$ and $EB2$. As a result, we used 1,636 samples in evaluating $EB1$ and $EB2$. $SB1$–$SB3$, $CB2$, $EB2$, and the proposed method were evaluated by five-fold cross validation with test data because these systems need training data for learning their classifier or finding the most frequently observed synset.

The precision rate of the proposed method is the highest among those of all the systems in Table 2. Comparison of the proposed method and one of $SB1$–$SB3$ shows the effectiveness of integration of different information generated by multiple SIMs. In the results for $B1$–$B3$ and $SB1$–$SB3$, $SB1$ and $SB2$ (which use a classifier), respectively, attain higher precision than systems $B1$ and $B2$ (which do not use a classifier). The precision of $SB3$ is, however, lower than that of $B3$, indicating that using a classifier is not always effective for synset identification.

System	Precision
$B1$	50.3 (309/ 614)
$B2$	70.9 (1,276/1,800)
$B3$	78.2 (1,408/1,800)
$SB1$	59.3 (364/ 614)
$SB2$	72.4 (1,303/1,800)
$SB3$	76.3 (1,374/1,800)
$CB1$	71.9 (1,294/1,800)
$CB2$	80.2 (1,444/1,800)
$EB1$	56.5 (924/1,636)
$EB2$	79.2 (1,296/1,636)
Proposed method	84.2 (1,515/1,800)

Table 2: Experimental results of each system.

4.3 Evaluation by Ranking

Figure 4 shows precision rates by their ranking for the system outputs of $B1$–$B3$, $SB1$–$SB3$, and the proposed method. The vertical axis indicates precision rate; the horizontal axis indicates the rank

[5] Judges were required to label the following ten synsets (00001740, 00001930, 00002137, 00002684, 00003553, 00004258, 00004475, 00023100, 00007347, and 00021939) as wrong one. These synsets were selected in descending order of the number of their lower nodes in the WordNet hierarchy.

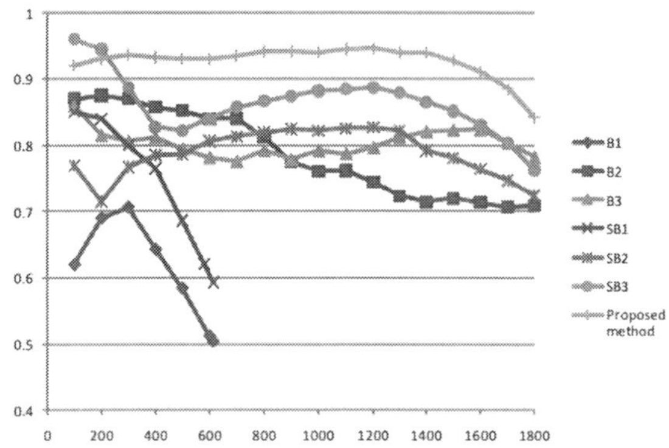

Figure 4: Precision rate by ranking.

of **trg** in scores, i.e., all the outputs are sorted in the descending order of scores. For $B1$, $B2$, and $B3$, $PS(\mathcal{I}, syn)$ is used as a score, while for $SB1$, $SB2$, $SB3$, and the proposed method, the distance from the hyperplane of an SVM is used as a score. For $SB1$, $SB2$, $SB3$, and the proposed method, averaged scores over the five folds were used.

It should be noted that the proposed method outperforms the other methods for almost all the ranks and keeps a precision rate of about 84%. This result implies that the method can identify synsets with a precision rate of about 84% for all 2,039,417 $\mathcal{I}$s.

Note also that the proposed method keeps a precision rate of about 91% until the top 88.9% (1600/1800). From this result, it is estimated that the method can identify synsets for 1,813,042 $\mathcal{I}$s (88.9% of all 2,039,417 $\mathcal{I}$s) with a precision rate of about 91%.

4.4 Contribution of Each Feature

To examine the effectiveness of each of the six features used for the classifier, ablation tests using the development data (which examined the change in the performance of the classifier when one of the features was ignored) were conducted. Table 3 lists the results of these tests. This table shows that

Feature set	Precision
All	82.6 (661/800)
w/o **Hyper** (f1)	82.1 (657/800)
w/o Name of SIM (f2)	82.5 (660/800)
w/o Value of $PS(\mathcal{I}, syn)$ (f3)	82.0 (656/800)
w/o Synset ID (f4)	81.1 (649/800)
w/o Suffix of the **trg** (f5)	82.1 (657/800)
w/o Suffix of the **hyper** (f6)	82.4 (659/800)

Table 3: Results of ablation test.

f4 (the synset ID of a WordNet synset candidate) is the most effective for the classifier.

4.5 Distribution of Output Synset IDs

freq.	Synset ids	Example terms in WordNet
336	04599396	work, piece of work
336	00007846	someone, person
132	06613686	moving picture,movie
68	06619428	broadcast, programme
44	08237863	cast, cast of characters
44	08008335	organisation, organization
28	06376154	drama
25	08276720	school
25	03315023	installation, facility
23	06616806	docudrama, documentary
22	07020895	music
22	04341686	construction, structure
19	00455599	game
17	06362953	writing, piece of writing
17	03129123	creation

Table 4: Distribution of output synset IDs.

Table 4 lists the distribution of output synset IDs determined by our method. About two-thirds of the results were assigned a very specific synset. The remaining terms were all assigned to the two most-frequent synsets: 04599396 or 00007846. In the case when a term was assigned to these most-frequent synsets, a more specific synset, like 06613686 (moving picture, movie) or 09765278 (actor), should have been chosen. However, our current scoring process does not take the synsets' granularity into account, so it sometimes favors the more general synsets, like 06613686 or 00007846. Fine-tuning our algorithm to compensate for this tendency will be an important future work.

4.6 Analysis

4.6.1 Advantage of Proposed Method

The advantage of the proposed method compared to previous methods that use nothing but either distributional similarity of a **trg** or co-occurrence with their hypernyms via lexico-syntactic patterns (Snow et al., 2006; Yamada et al., 2009) (or both) was demonstrated as follows. Specifically, it was shown that many terms do not have reliable distributional similarity (owing to their infrequency in a corpus) and do not co-occur with their hypernyms via any lexico-syntactic pattern in a sentence. Even so, our method can correctly identify the synset of such terms thanks to their **hy-**

pers and **sibs** acquired from the internal structure of Wikipedia articles.

First, 1,515 terms were extracted from all 1,800 $\mathcal{I}$s whose synset our method could correctly identify. The occurrence of each term in a corpus that consists of 600 million Japanese Web pages (a super set of the one-million-page TSUBAKI corpus) was then counted. According to the result of this counting, 430 terms occur less than 10 times. We believe that it is not possible to obtain reliable distributional similarity for these terms owing to their infrequency. Note that the distributional similarity of the suffix of **hyper** was used instead of that of the **hyper** itself. (Section 3.1). If the suffix of a term is used, it might be possible to obtain reliable distributional similarity even for the 430 terms. Accordingly, it was determined whether the suffix of a term can help the synset identification for each of the 430 terms by checking whether the suffix of each of the 430 terms is actually its subordinate concept. According to the results of this checking, 342 terms out of the 430 do not have a suffix that is their correct subordinate concept. Reliable distributional similarity is thus not available for them even when the suffix technique is used.

Next, the co-occurrence of each of the 342 terms and its **hyper** via some lexico-syntactic pattern within a sentence was checked by using the 600-million-page Japanese Web corpus. According to the results of this check, 290 terms out of 342 do not co-occur with their **hyper** within a sentence; thus, the co-occurrence with their **hyper** cannot be used to identify their synset.

In conclusion, it is difficult for the previous methods to correctly identify the synset of the 290 terms that do not co-occur with their **hyper** within a sentence, while our method can. From this result, it is estimated that the number of such terms in all the 2,039,417 $\mathcal{I}$s is 328,572.

4.6.2 Error Analysis

From the 285 incorrect synsets output by the proposed method, 124 were selected from B3, 110 were selected from B2, and 51 were selected from B1. For 232 of these 285 errors, all outputs of B1, B2, and B3 were judged incorrect. Because the proposed method's classifier chooses the final result from the outputs of B1, B2, and B3, it cannot help selecting the wrong candidate in these cases. 100 erroneous synsets were randomly selected from our results, and the following three types of error were found.

Missing terms for some senses in the Japanese WordNet (20/100): For instance, the Japanese term *anime* is defined in synset *06616464-n* as *animation originating in Japan*, but no term in the Japanese WordNet is linked to this synset (Bond et al., 2009). The Japanese WordNet does contain other meanings for the term *anime*, such as *a hard copal derived from an African tree* (synset *14896018-n*) and *any of various resins or oleoresins* (synset *14766265-n*). As a result, Japanese animation films with the hypernym *anime* are linked to either *14896018-n* or *14766265-n*. This type of error should be avoidable by adding such missing terms to the Japanese WordNet.

Terms incorrectly identified as persons (16/100): Many named entities such as companies or movie titles are often mistaken for references to people. For example, a movie titled "BROTHER" is distributionally similar to other movies as well as family terms like "sister" and "mother". Moreover, WordNet does not contain many movie titles, so the "family term" sense is selected as the dominant sense, and "BROTHER" was given the synset of *person*. We expect such problems can be alleviated by adding more named entities to WordNet.

Hyponymy relation acquisition error (10/100): The precision of hyponymy-relation acquisition was 90%, which accounted for the remaining 10% of the errors. For example, the term *acoustic guitar* was given the wrong hypernyms, namely, *musician*, which results in misclassification.

5 Conclusion

This paper proposed a method for extending WordNet with terms in Wikipedia, by exploiting hypernyms (**hyper**s) and siblings (**sib**s) of target terms (**trg**s) acquired from Wikipedia as additional sources of information. Experimental results showed that the proposed method could identify synsets for 2,039,417 inputs at precision rate of 84%. Furthermore, it was estimated that there were 328,572 terms among all the inputs whose synsets the proposed method could correctly identify. In contrast, previous methods relying on distributional similarity and lexico-syntactic patterns only could not identify these synsets.

References

Francis Bond, Hitoshi Isahara, Sanae Fujita, Kiyotaka Uchimoto, Takayuki Kuribayashi, and Kyoko Kanzaki. 2009. Enhancing the Japanese WordNet. In *Proceedings of the 7th Workshop on Asian Language Resources*, pages 1–8.

Christiane Fellbaum. 1998. *WordNet: An Electronical Lexical Database*. The MIT Press.

Marti A. Hearst. 1992. Automatic acquisition of hyponyms from large text corpora. In *Proceedings of the 14th International Conference on Computational linguistics (COLING-92)*, pages 539–545.

Jun'ichi Kazama and Kentaro Torisawa. 2008. Inducing gazetteers for named entity recognition by large-scale clustering of dependency relations. In *Proceedings of the 46th Annual Meeting of the Association for Computational Linguistics: Human Language Technologies (ACL-08:HLT)*, pages 407–415.

Jun'ichi Kazama, Stijn De Saeger, Kentaro Torisawa, and Masaki Murata. 2009. Generating a large-scale analogy list using a probabilistic clustering based on noun-verb dependency profiles. In *15th Annual Meeting of the Association for Natural Language Processing, C1-3 (in Japanese)*, pages 84–87.

Jong-Hoon Oh, Kiyotaka Uchimoto, and Kentaro Torisawa. 2009. Bilingual co-training for monolingual hyponymy-relation acquisition. In *Proceedings of the Joint Conference of the 47th Annual Meeting of the ACL and the 4th International Joint Conference on Natural Language Processing of the AFNLP (ACL-IJCNLP 2009)*, pages 432–440.

Jong-Hoon Oh, Ichiro Yamada, Kentaro Torisawa, and Stijn De Saeger. 2010. Co-star: A co-training style algorithm for hyponymy relation acquisition from structured and unstructured text. In *Proceedings of the 23rd International Conference on Computational Linguistics (COLING 2010)*, pages 842–850.

Simone Paolo Ponzetto and Roberto Navigli. 2009. Large-scale taxonomy mapping for restructuring and integrating wikipedia. In *Proceedings of the 21th International Joint Conference on Artificial Intelligence (IJCAI 2009)*, pages 2083–2088.

Maria Ruiz-Casado, Enrique Alfonseca, and Pablo Castells. 2005. Automatic assignment of wikipedia encyclopedic entries to wordnet synsets. In *Advances in Web Intelligence, volume 3528 of Lecture Notes in Computer Science*, pages 380–386.

Keiji Shinzato and Kentaro Torisawa. 2004. Acquiring hyponymy relations from web documents. In *Proceedings of the Human Language Technology Conference and North American chapter of the Association for Computational Linguistics annual meeting (HLT-NAACL04)*, pages 73–80.

Keiji Shinzato, Tomohide Shibata, Daisuke Kawahara, Chikara Hashimoto, and Sadao Kurohashi. 2008. Tsubaki: An open search engine infrastructure for developing new information access. In *Proceedings the Third International Joint Conference on Natural Language Processing (IJCNLP 2008)*, pages 189–196.

Rion Snow, Daniel Jurafsky, and Andrew Y. Ng. 2006. Semantic taxonomy induction from heterogenous evidence. In *Proceedings of the 43nd Annual Meeting of the Association for Computational Linguistics (ACL-06)*, pages 801–808.

Fabian M. Suchanek, Gjergji Kasneci, and Gerhard Weikum. 2007. Yago: A Core of Semantic Knowledge. In *Proceedings of the 17th international conference on World Wide Web (WWW '07)*, pages 697–706.

Asuka Sumida and Kentaro Torisawa. 2008. Hacking Wikipedia for hyponymy relation acquisition. In *Proceedings of the Third International Joint Conference on Natural Language Processing (IJCNLP 2008)*, pages 883–888.

Asuka Sumida, Naoki Yoshinaga, and Kentaro Torisawa. 2008. Boosting precision and recall of hyponymy relation acquisition from hierarchical layouts in Wikipedia. In *Proceedings of the 6th International Conference on Language Resources and Evaluation (LREC 2008)*.

Antonio Toral, Rafael Munoz, and Monica Monachini. 2008. Named entity wordnet. In *Proceedings of the Sixth International Conference on Language Resources and Evaluation (LREC 2008)*, pages 741–747.

Antonio Toral, Oscar Ferrandez, Eneko Agirre, and Rafael Munoz. 2009. A study on linking Wikipedia categories to WordNet using text similarity. In *Proceedings of Recent Advances in Natural Language Processing (RANLP 2009)*, pages 449–454.

Kentaro Torisawa. 2001. An unsuperveised method for canonicalization of Japanese postpositions. In *Proceedings of the 6th Natural Language Processing Pacific Rim Symposium (NLPRS 2001)*, pages 211–218.

Fei Wu and Daniel S. Weld. 2008. Automatically refining the wikipedia infobox ontology. In *Proceeding of the 17th international conference on World Wide Web (WWW '08)*, pages 635–644.

Ichiro Yamada, Kentaro Torisawa, Jun'ichi Kazama, Kow Kuroda, Masaki Murata, Stijn De Saeger, Francis Bond, and Asuka Sumida. 2009. Hypernym discovery based on distributional similarity and hierarchical structures. In *Proceedings of the 2009 Conference on Empirical Methods in Natural Language Processing (EMNLP 2009)*, pages 929–937.

What Psycholinguists Know About Chemistry: Aligning Wiktionary and WordNet for Increased Domain Coverage

Christian M. Meyer and **Iryna Gurevych**
Ubiquitous Knowledge Processing Lab
Technische Universität Darmstadt
Hochschulstraße 10, 64289 Darmstadt, Germany
http://www.ukp.tu-darmstadt.de

Abstract

By today, no lexical resource can claim to be fully comprehensive or perform best for every NLP task. This caused a steep increase of resource alignment research. An important challenge is thereby the alignment of differently represented word senses, which we address in this paper. In particular, we propose a new automatically aligned resource of Wiktionary and WordNet that has (i) a very high domain coverage of word senses and (ii) an enriched sense representation, including pronunciations, etymologies, translations, etc. We evaluate our alignment both quantitatively and qualitatively, and explore how it can contribute to practical tasks.

1 Introduction

Though WordNet has been extensively used in knowledge-rich natural language processing (NLP) systems, there is no best lexical resource for all purposes. Jarmasz and Szpakowicz (2003), for example, found better results for solving word choice problems when using Roget's thesaurus instead of WordNet. There is indeed a large number of different lexical resources: The ACL Special Interest Group on the Lexicon[1] lists, for instance, more than 40 different lexical resources on their homepage that have been proposed as a source of background knowledge for different NLP tasks.

These resources typically differ in two ways: (i) They have a different coverage of words and word senses, and (ii) they encode heterogeneous types of information that is attached to their words and word senses. This heterogeneity ranges from very fundamental differences, like the distinction between lexicographic and encyclopedic knowledge to more specific ones, such as one resource encodes semantic frames, while another focuses on subsumption relations between word senses. Using WordNet without further considerations thus limits the performance of a system, since each resource has its individual advantages.

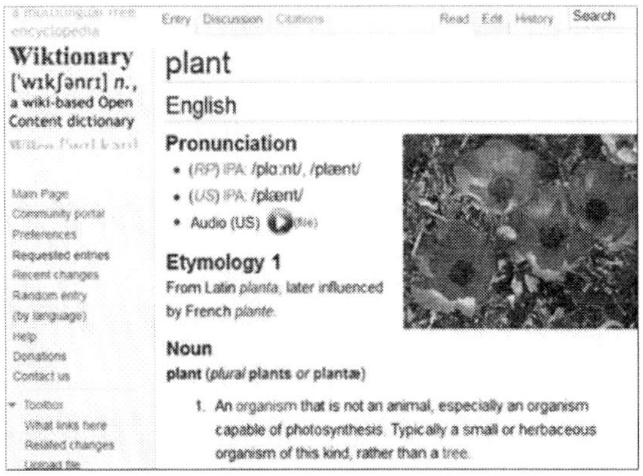

Figure 1: Wiktionary article *'plant'*

This has caused increasing research in the area of lexical resource alignment. It has been shown that aligned resources yield synergies, which lead to better performance than using the resources individually. For instance, Shi and Mihalcea (2005) improve semantic parsing using the knowledge of an aligned resource of FrameNet, WordNet, and VerbNet. Recently, Ponzetto and Navigli (2010) observed improvements for coarse-grained and domain-specific word sense disambiguation using an alignment between WordNet and Wikipedia for adding new relations to WordNet.

In another line of research, the community based online dictionary Wiktionary has been successfully applied in several NLP tasks, such as cross-lingual image retrieval (Etzioni et al., 2007), named entity recognition (Richman and Schone, 2008), or synonymy mining (Navarro et al., 2009; Sajous et al., 2010). Zesch et al. (2008b) compare different semantic relatedness measures using either WordNet, Wikipedia, or Wiktionary and find

[1]http://www.siglex.org/, accessed 2011-05-10

the best results for Wiktionary. Besides its large coverage, Wiktionary also offers a great variety of linguistic information, such as pronunciations, etymologies, glosses, related words, translations, and many others. De Melo and Weikum (2010) exploit, for instance, alternative spellings and etymologies to enrich their lexical database.

In this work, we propose aligning WordNet and Wiktionary at the level of word senses. The resulting alignment has two important properties that go substantially beyond previous alignments: (i) increased domain coverage and (ii) enriched representation of senses. While Wiktionary is larger in size than most other previously aligned resources, such as Roget's thesaurus, Meyer and Gurevych (2010) analyze some word senses from WordNet and Wiktionary and come to the conclusion that certain domains are better covered by only one of the resources. This leads us to assume a very high domain coverage in our aligned resource.

Much work on lexical resource alignment involves Wikipedia, which contains lots of information about named entities. Wiktionary, in contrast, encodes common words and is not restricted to nouns. This opens up new possibilities for tasks including verbs, adjectives, or multiwords. Regarding the representation of senses, Wiktionary contains a great variety of linguistic information, like pronunciations or etymologies that are not found in previously aligned lexical resources.

The contributions of our work are threefold: (i) We present an automatic word sense alignment between the entire WordNet and Wiktionary, which we make publicly available. (ii) For evaluating the quality of our alignment, we introduce a new dataset based on human judgments to allow for future comparability of our results. (iii) We analyze the characteristics of our aligned resource, and how it can benefit different NLP tasks. We particularly point out that our resource has a much broader coverage of domain-specific word senses, which is important for processing real world data.

2 Notation and Lexical Resources

We first define the terminology used throughout the paper and introduce the two lexical resources WordNet and Wiktionary that are the subjects of our word sense alignment.

Lexical resources. By *lexical resource*, we mean a list of words and word senses. Our notion of *word* also includes multiwords, idioms, inflected forms, etc. Each word can have multiple *word senses*, which is one of multiple possible meanings for a word. A good illustration for this notion of words are the headwords in dictionaries, whereby the different meanings of the headword correspond to our notion of word sense.[2]

WordNet (Fellbaum, 1998) is a lexical resource for the English language that has been created by psycholinguists at the Princeton University. The resource is organized in synsets (i.e., sets of synonymous words) that are connected in a clear-cut subsumption hierarchy. The latest version 3.0 encodes 117,659 synsets. Each synset is represented by a gloss that is often followed by a short usage example. The synset {*plant, works, industrial plant*} is, for instance, represented by the gloss *"buildings for carrying on industrial labor"*.

Wiktionary[3] is a freely available, multilingual online dictionary. Similar to Wikipedia, the contents in Wiktionary can be edited by every Web user, which causes the resource to grow very quickly: by April 2010, the English Wiktionary contained over 1,700,000 article pages with linguistic knowledge about words in over 100 languages. For each word, multiple word senses can be encoded. Like in WordNet, they are represented by a gloss and example sentences illustrating the usage of a word sense. Additionally, there are hyperlinks to synonyms, hypernyms, meronyms, etc. Figure 1 shows the Wiktionary article *'plant'* as an example. For extracting the knowledge from Wiktionary, we use the Java-based Wiktionary Library (Zesch et al., 2008a). Using a Wiktionary dump of April 3, 2010, we counted 335,748 English words and 421,847 word senses.

Word sense alignment. A *word sense alignment*,[4] or *alignment* for short, is a list of pairs of word senses from two lexical resources. A pair of word senses that are aligned in a word sense alignment denote the same meaning. In WordNet, there is, for instance, a synset *"buildings for carrying on industrial labor"* for the word *'plant'*, which denotes the same meaning as the Wiktionary word

[2]Note that there is no commonly accepted standardized terminology in the field. Our notion of word is thus sometimes called *lemma* or *lexeme*; a *word sense* is also called *lexical unit*; whereas a lexical resource is also referred to as *sense inventory* or *(computational) lexicon*.

[3]`http://www.wiktionary.org`

[4]Other terms for *(word sense) alignment* are *mapping* or *matching*. This notion of alignment is not to be mixed up with *word alignment* or *sentence alignment*, which are used for processing parallel texts as in machine translation.

sense *"a factory or other industrial or institutional building or facility"*. Another Wiktionary sense *"an organism that is not an animal [...]"*, however, clearly denotes a different meaning and should thus not be aligned to the WordNet synset.

3 Related Work

In the last twenty years, there have been many works on aligning lexical resources at the level of word senses. Almost all alignment approaches for the English language include WordNet, which is the *de facto* standard resource in the field. Early works address the alignment of WordNet with: Roget's thesaurus and the Longman Dictionary of Contemporary English (Kwong, 1998) [K98], the HECTOR corpus (Litkowski, 1999) [L99], the Unified Medical Language System (Burgun and Bodenreider, 2001) [BB01], CYC (Reed and Lenat, 2002) [RL02], VerbNet and FrameNet (Shi and Mihalcea, 2005) [SM05], as well as the Oxford Dictionary of English (Navigli, 2006) [N06].

The great potential of the collaborative resource Wikipedia in many NLP applications, such as semantic relatedness (Gabrilovich and Markovitch, 2007; Milne and Witten, 2008), word sense disambiguation (Mihalcea, 2007; Ponzetto and Navigli, 2010), or named entity recognition (Bunescu and Paşca, 2006), motivates aligning WordNet and Wikipedia to benefit from the advantages of both these resources. One line of research is thereby the alignment of WordNet synsets and Wikipedia categories, which has been done based on the shared taxonomic structure (Toral et al., 2008) [T08], textual entailment and semantic relatedness methods (Toral et al., 2009) [T09], as well as graph algorithms (Ponzetto and Navigli, 2009) [PN09].

Since the vast majority of knowledge is encoded in the Wikipedia article pages, also those have been aligned to WordNet synsets. The first work in this direction has been carried out by Ruiz-Casado et al. (2005) [R05] for the Simple Wikipedia, which is a smaller version of the full Wikipedia. Most of the published work, however, focuses on the articles in the full Wikipedia and their alignment to WordNet synsets. This task has been done based on: human judgments (Mihalcea, 2007) [M07], giving preference to WordNet's first sense (Suchanek et al., 2008) [S08], word overlap (de Melo and Weikum, 2010; Navigli and Ponzetto, 2010) [MW10,NP10], and using semantic relatedness measures (Niemann and Gurevych, 2011) [NG11]. Each approach has been evaluated on a separate, manually annotated dataset: De Melo and Weikum (2010) report a precision of $P = .85$, Navigli and Ponzetto (2010) observe $F_1 = .79$, and the alignment described by Niemann and Gurevych (2011) evaluates to $F_1 = .78$. It should be noted that these numbers are not comparable to each other, since they are based on different datasets and annotation schemes.

Work	Method	Resource	Full
[K98]	overlap	LDOCE & Roget	–
[L99]	syntax	HECTOR	–
[BB01]	overlap	UMLS	–
[RL02]	manual	CYC	–
[SM05]	structure	VerbNet & FrameNet	√
[N06]	relatedness	Oxford Dictionary	√
[T08]	structure	Wikipedia categories	√
[T09]	relatedness	Wikipedia categories	√
[PN09]	structure	Wikipedia categories	√
[R05]	overlap	Simple Wikipedia art.	√
[M07]	manual	Wikipedia articles	–
[S08]	mfs	Wikipedia articles	√
[MW10]	overlap	Wikipedia articles	√
[NP10]	overlap	Wikipedia articles	√
[NG11]	relatedness	Wikipedia articles	√
[MG10]	manual	Wiktionary senses	–
This work	relatedness	Wiktionary senses	√

Table 1: Previous work on aligning WordNet

Recently, also Wiktionary has been found to be a very promising resource for NLP tasks. So far, Wiktionary knowledge has been used for image search (Etzioni et al., 2007), calculating semantic relatedness (Zesch et al., 2008b), information retrieval (Müller and Gurevych, 2009), and synonymy detection (Navarro et al., 2009). An alignment has been done manually for a small number of word senses shared by Wiktionary and WordNet (Meyer and Gurevych, 2010) [MG10], but to the best of our knowledge, there is yet no word sense alignment covering the full resources. For applying an aligned resource in a practical system, such as word sense disambiguation, we, however, need a full alignment of the two resources. This is the subject of our work.

Table 1 shows an overview of related work on aligning WordNet with different lexical resources. Besides the resource that it is aligned to and whether the full resources have been processed, the table shows the utilized methods, which we classified into methods: aligning the first sense [mfs], counting weighted or normalized word overlaps (including the cosine measure) [overlap], using syntactic patterns [syntax], considering the (graph) structure of the resource [structure], utilizing measures of semantic relatedness, such as semantic vectors or personalized PageRank [relatedness], and aligning senses manually [manual].

4 Word Sense Alignment

Most previous alignments are based on a one-to-one alignment assumption – i.e., that each sense is aligned with exactly one sense in the other resource. Niemann and Gurevych (2011), however, argue that there are senses requiring none, one, or multiple aligned senses.

This also holds for alignments of Wiktionary and WordNet. For example, the Wiktionary word sense *"the people who decide on the verdict; the judiciary"* for the word *'bench'* can be aligned to the two WordNet synsets *"persons who administer justice"* and *"the magistrate or judge or judges [...]"*. Accordingly, the Wiktionary word sense *"the bottom part of a sand casting mold"* for the noun *'drag'* is not covered by any WordNet synset and should thus not be aligned.

Therefore, we follow the alignment approach by Niemann and Gurevych (2011), which includes a state-of-the-art word sense disambiguation method by Agirre and Soroa (2009) that is known to outperform word overlap based measures. The method consists of the two steps (i) candidate extraction and (ii) candidate alignment that we briefly review in the following.

In the *candidate extraction* step, the algorithm iterates over all word senses in one lexical resource and extracts suitable candidates within the other resource that *might* form a valid alignment. In our case, we iterate over all synsets in WordNet and extract all word senses from Wiktionary that are encoded for one of the synset's synonymous words. For example, we extract all 9 Wiktionary word senses from the article *'plant'* and all 4 word senses from *'works'* for the WordNet synset {*plant, works, industrial plant*}. The word *'industrial plant'* is not encoded in Wiktionary. In the *candidate alignment* step, each candidate is then scored with two similarity measures:

(i) The *cosine similarity* (COS) calculates the cosine of the angle between a vector representation of the two senses s_1 and s_2:

$$\mathrm{COS}(s_1, s_2) = \frac{\mathrm{BoW}(s_1) \cdot \mathrm{BoW}(s_2)}{||\mathrm{BoW}(s_1)||\ ||\mathrm{BoW}(s_2)||}$$

To represent a sense as a vector, we use a bag-of-words approach – i.e., a vector $\mathrm{BoW}(s)$ containing the term frequencies of all words in the definition of s. Note that there are different options for choosing the definition of sense s: For WordNet, the gloss of the synset can be used alone or in combination with its hyponyms and/or hypernyms. For Wiktionary, we can choose between gloss, usage examples, and related words of the word sense. We will discuss the best configuration during our evaluation in the following section.

(ii) The *personalized PageRank based measure* (PPR) estimates the semantic relatedness between two word senses s_1 and s_2 by representing them in a semantic vector space and comparing these semantic vectors $\mathbf{Pr}_{s_1}$ and $\mathbf{Pr}_{s_2}$ by computing

$$\mathrm{PPR}(s_1, s_2) = 1 - \sum_i \frac{(\mathbf{Pr}_{s_1,i} - \mathbf{Pr}_{s_2,i})^2}{\mathbf{Pr}_{s_1,i} + \mathbf{Pr}_{s_2,i}},$$

which is a χ^2 variant introduced in Niemann and Gurevych (2011). The main idea of choosing $\mathbf{Pr}$ is to use the personalized PageRank algorithm for identifying those synsets that are central for describing a sense's meaning. The sense *"buildings for carrying on industrial labor"* is, for instance, well represented by the WordNet noun synsets {*plant, works, industrial plant*}, {*building complex, complex*}, or the adjective synset {*industrial*}. These synsets should have a high centrality (i.e., a high PageRank score), which is calculated as

$$\mathbf{Pr} = cM\mathbf{Pr} + (1 - c)\mathbf{v},$$

with the damping factor c controlling the random walk, the transition matrix M of the underlying semantic graph, and the probabilistic vector $\mathbf{v}$, whose i^{th} component $\mathbf{v}_i$ denotes the probability of randomly jumping to node i in the next iteration step.[5] Unlike in the traditional PageRank algorithm, the components of the jump vector $\mathbf{v}$ are not uniformly distributed, but personalized to the sense s by choosing $\mathbf{v}_i = \frac{1}{m}$ if at least one synonymous word of synset i occurs in the definition of sense s, and $\mathbf{v}_i = 0$ otherwise. The normalization factor m is set to the total number of synsets that share a word with the sense definition, which is required for obtaining a probabilistic vector.

Having calculated the similarity scores, we add the pair of the WordNet synset and the Wiktionary

[5] We use the publicly available UKB software (Agirre and Soroa, 2009) for calculating the PageRank scores and utilize the WordNet 3.0 graph augmented with the Princeton Annotated Gloss Corpus as M. The damping factor c is set to 0.85.

```
function ALIGN(WordNet, Wiktionary)
  alignment := ∅;
  for each synset ∈ WordNet.getSynsets() do
    // Candidate extraction
    candidates := ∅;
    for each word ∈ synset.getWords() do
      candidates := candidates
          ∪ Wiktionary.getWordSenses(word);
    // Candidate alignment
    for each candidate ∈ candidates do
      sim_cos := COS(synset, candidate);
      sim_ppr := PPR(synset, candidate);
      if sim_cos ≥ τ_cos ∧ sim_ppr ≥ τ_ppr then
        alignment := alignment
            ∪ (synset, candidate);
  return alignment;
end.
```

Figure 2: Pseudo code of the alignment algorithm

sense to our alignment if both similarity scores are above a certain threshold τ_{cos} and τ_{ppr}. We learned these thresholds in a 10 fold cross validation on our dataset that is explained in the following section. The optimal thresholds have been determined independently from each other using a simple binary split of the fold's items. The final thresholds are $\tau_{cos} = .13$ and $\tau_{ppr} = .49$.

Figure 2 shows the alignment algorithm in pseudo-code. Further details can be found in (Niemann and Gurevych, 2011).

5 Evaluation

To evaluate our WordNet–Wiktionary alignment, we follow the methodology of previous approaches and compare the result of our automatic alignment algorithm with human judgments. Therefore, we create a new manually annotated dataset, as we are not aware of any other datasets that could be used for this task. Our dataset is publicly available for future work on aligning WordNet and Wiktionary.

Dataset creation. Niemann and Gurevych (2011) introduce a well-balanced dataset for the alignment of WordNet and Wikipedia. Their sampled WordNet synsets are uniformly distributed in the number of synonyms, distance to the root node, and unique beginners. This way, a quantitative judgment of the alignment quality is as unbiased as possible. Since lexical resources are known to be very diverse (e.g., in terms of domain coverage (Burgun and Bodenreider, 2001; Meyer and Gurevych, 2010)), this is very important to get an impression about the alignment in general. Therefore, we reuse 320 synsets from their dataset as a primer for our evaluation dataset. For each synset, we extract all possible Wiktionary senses according to the candidate extraction step introduced in the previous section. This results in 2,423 sense pairs.

We asked 10 annotators to rate each sense pair as describing the same meaning (class 1) or describing a different meaning (class 0). The annotators are students in computer science, math, or linguistics, whereby two of them had previous experience with annotation studies. We described the annotation task in an annotation guidebook[6] and trained the annotators with some example cases.

Inter-rater agreement. To ensure the reliability of our annotated dataset, we calculate the inter-rater agreement between the annotators using the measures described by Artstein and Poesio (2008). The average observed agreement is $A_O = .93$ and the multi-rater chance-corrected agreement is $\kappa = .70$. Table 2 shows the pairwise κ for each pair of raters. The annotators C and F have the lowest inter-rater agreement between each other (.58) and with all other raters (.62 and .65). These two raters are thus on the opposite sides of the scale. Further analysis reveals that C is biased towards class 0 (different meaning) and F is biased towards class 1 (same meaning). We removed the annotations of these two raters, which yields an inter-rater agreement of $\kappa = .74$.

A dataset with such an agreement is considered reliable and allows to draw tentative conclusions (Krippendorff, 1980), although its agreement is lower than for WordNet–Wikipedia alignment datasets. More precisely, Niemann and Gurevych (2011) report $\kappa = .87$ and Navigli and Ponzetto (2010) measure $\kappa = .9$. Since even the two skilled annotators I and J only obtained an agreement of .80, we conclude that the alignment task of WordNet and Wiktionary is harder than the alignment of WordNet and Wikipedia. This does not come as a surprise, because Wikipedia contains encyclopedic knowledge that is largely complementary to the linguistic knowledge in WordNet and thus does not require to make fine-grained sense distinctions. WordNet and Wiktionary, however, both encode lexicographic knowledge about common words of the English language and thus require the distinction of very subtle differences in

[6] Available from our homepage: `http://www.ukp.tu-darmstadt.de/data/sense-alignment/`

κ	A	B	C	D	E	F	G	H	I	J
B	.72									
C	.60	.64								
D	.72	.75	.60							
E	.73	.72	.63	.74						
F	.64	.65	**.58**	.65	.68					
G	.75	.72	.66	.73	.75	.64				
H	.67	.72	.60	.72	.68	.64	.68			
I	.75	.74	.64	.77	.76	.67	.79	.73		
J	.72	.75	.62	.77	.77	.67	.76	.73	**.80**	
∅	.70	.71	**.62**	.72	.72	**.65**	.72	.69	.74	.73

Table 2: Pairwise κ of our annotation study

Method	A	P	R	F_1
RAND	.662	.212	.594	.313
MFS	.802	.329	.508	.399
COS only	.901	.598	**.703**	.646
PPR only	**.915**	**.684**	.636	.659
COS&PPR	**.914**	.674	.649	**.661**

Table 3: Performance of our alignment algorithm

the word sense definitions. We will discuss some examples during our error analysis.

Alignment quality. From our annotated data, we create a gold standard using majority vote of the remaining 8 annotators. An additional rater is asked to break the 27 ties. Following Navigli and Ponzetto (2010), we compare our automatic sense alignment with the gold standard using accuracy A, precision P, recall R, and the $F_1 = \frac{2PR}{P+R}$ score.

As baseline approaches, we implemented a first sense heuristic (MFS) and a method making a random selection (RAND). Table 3 shows the results of these baselines as well as our COS and PPR measures and their combination (COS&PPR). As noted in the previous section, there are multiple options for representing a sense. For WordNet, the synonyms, the gloss of the synset, and its direct hypernym and hyponyms have been tried as features. For Wiktionary, we experimented with the word, its gloss, usage examples, and synonyms. We tried all possible combinations and found the best result for using the synonyms and the gloss of the WordNet synset and its hypernym together with all four Wiktionary features. The table shows only the results for these features.

Our COS, PPR, and COS&PPR methods outperform the baseline by far. The difference is statistically significant at the 1% level in each case.[7] While COS has the highest recall and PPR has the highest precision, COS&PPR is a reasonable trade-off yielding the highest F_1 score. The difference of PPR and COS&PPR over COS is again statistically significant at the 1% level. The difference between PPR and COS&PPR is not statistically significant, which leads us to the conclusion that the PPR and COS&PPR methods perform equally well for our alignment task.

When analyzing the dataset, we observed a lower inter-rater agreement than for WordNet–Wikipedia alignments. This effect also becomes visible in our evaluation results: While Niemann and Gurevych (2011) measure an F_1 score of .53 for their MFS baseline and .78 for their COS&PPR method, the results are between .12 to .14 lower for the WordNet–Wiktionary alignment, which again shows that the word sense alignment between WordNet and Wiktionary is a more complex task than for WordNet and Wikipedia.

Error analysis. We carried out a detailed error analysis to identify the main types of errors made by our algorithm. Of the 2,423 sense pairs in the dataset, our COS&PPR algorithm yields 98 false positives and 110 false negatives.

Regarding the false negatives (i.e., the sense pairs that the method could not align, although they represent the same meaning), we found three main error classes: (i) The sense definitions were very different in their choice of words, such as in *"good discernment"* and *"ability to notice what others might miss"* for the word *'eye'*. These errors are hard to resolve, as they require a deep understanding and world knowledge. (ii) The sense definitions are very similar (e.g., *"any of various plants of the genus Centaurea* [...]*"* and *"any of various common weeds of the genus Centaurea"* for the word *'knapweed'*), but the similarity scores of the two measures were slightly below the chosen thresholds. These errors are caused by our choice of fixed similarity thresholds, which could, for instance, be improved by using machine learning for aligning the sense pairs. (iii) References to derived words occur in the sense definitions. An example is the word *'pacification'*, which is described as *"the process of pacifying"* and thus refers to the definition of *'pacifying'*. Such errors might be alleviated by taking the definitions of the derived words into account. This, however, raises again a word sense disambiguation challenge for finding the correct word sense of the derived word.

Amongst the false positives (i.e., the automatically aligned sense pairs with different meanings), we mainly found (i) highly related senses, such

[7] We use McNemar's test with Yates' correction.

as *"a computer that provides client stations with access to files and printers as shared resources to a computer network"* and *"any computer attached to a network"* for *'host'*, which are clearly related, but differ in their specification. The latter word sense does not require the host to provide file access or resources, but the former does. Although these two senses do not represent exactly the same meaning, their alignment is very useful for many NLP applications; e.g., for a semantic information retrieval system, which usually does not require to make subtle sense distinctions when searching relevant documents. Future work could distinguish between sense alignments sharing the same meaning and sharing a highly related meaning. (ii) Another large class of errors is due to an erroneous interpretation of a definition's meaning. Consider again the computing related sense of *'host'*. This sense is also aligned to *"any organization that provides resources and facilities for a function or event"*, because the words *resource, facility, function*, and *event* also frequently occur in the computer science domain. These errors are hard to tackle, but we plan to further investigate the influence of a sense's position in the taxonomy of a lexical resource.

6 Characteristics of the Wiktionary–WordNet Alignment

Aligning lexical resources is only one side of the coin. Another one is the question, how the aligned resource can be applied in practice and which NLP tasks can benefit from it. Our alignment of Wiktionary and WordNet yields a new resource with (i) increased coverage and (ii) an enriched representation of word senses.

Increased coverage. Coverage is crucial for almost every NLP task. Our final Wiktionary–WordNet alignment consists of 315,583 candidates, of which 56,970 pairs are marked as alignments. For 60,707 WordNet synsets there has been no corresponding word sense found in Wiktionary, and, vice versa, there are 371,329 Wiktionary word senses that have not been aligned with any WordNet synset. The word *'devisor'* is, for instance, only found within WordNet, and *'libero'* merely has an entry in Wiktionary. The new aligned lexical resource contains 488,988 word senses.

Table 4 shows the number of word senses per part of speech (POS) that are shared by both resources and that have no alignment with the respective other resource. The high number of word senses only occurring in Wiktionary can be explained by the 106,328 inflected word forms that are not encoded by WordNet. While the vast majority of encoded senses are nouns, also the coverage of other parts of speech benefits from the alignment of the two resources. This is a clear advantage over Wikipedia–WordNet alignments, which usually focus on nouns only. Besides verbs, adjectives, and adverbs that are also encoded by WordNet, Wiktionary additionally contains pronouns, phrases, idioms, sayings, etc.

	Overlap	only Wiktionary	only WordNet
Nouns	34,464	158,085	47,651
Verbs	8,252	29,119	5,515
Adj./Adv.	14,236	60,977	7,541
Other POS	0	16,778	0
Inflected Forms	0	106,328	0
Biology	4,465	4,067	12,869
Chemistry	2,561	8,260	2,268
Engineering	1,108	940	1,080
Geology	2,287	2,898	2,479
Humanities	4,949	2,700	5,060
IT	439	3,032	557
Linguistics	1,249	1,011	1,576
Math	615	2,747	483
Medicine	3,613	3,728	3,058
Military	574	426	585
Physics	1,246	2,835	1,252
Religion	733	1,154	781
Social Sciences	3,745	2,907	4,458
Sport	905	2,821	807

Table 4: POS and domains of our aligned resource

Pantel and Lin (2002) note that manually compiled lexicons are often missing domain-specific word senses, which is an important aspect for domain-aware NLP tools. In their manual Wiktionary–WordNet alignment, Meyer and Gurevych (2010) come to the conclusion that WordNet has a focus on humanities and social sciences, while Wiktionary has a higher coverage of natural sciences and sports. Their findings are, however, limited to a very small set of word senses and thus might not hold for the entire resources. Therefore, we analyze the encoded domains for the whole aligned resource. To identify the domain of a sense, we use WordNet Domains (Bentivogli et al., 2004) to classify the WordNet synsets into 157 domains (e.g., *'biology'*). For Wiktionary, we use the domain markers encoded in the glosses. An example is the sense *"(snooker) A play in which the cue ball knocks one (usually red) ball onto another* [...]*"* of the word *'plant'*, labeled with the *'snooker'* domain. We count 714 different labels in Wiktionary.[8] For being able to relate WordNet's and Wiktionary's labels, we manually grouped them into 14 general classes listed in Table 4. The specialized domains *'genetics'* and *'botany'*, for instance, have been grouped together in a more general domain *'biology'*. For each of these general domains, we count the number of word senses that are either overlapping between the resources or found in only one of them.

In the analysis, we confirm the findings of Meyer and Gurevych (2010): WordNet encodes a larger number of word senses from humanities and social sciences. About twice as many senses are only found in WordNet compared to the respective number in Wiktionary. Moreover, word senses from natural sciences and information sciences are, in general, better represented by Wiktionary. In particular, word senses related to chemistry, math, and IT are almost exclusively found in Wiktionary. Examples are the computer science related sense of *'host'* discussed above or the chemistry related sense *"an intramolecular valence bond, atom or chain of atoms that connects two different parts of a molecule"* of *'bridge'*, which both have no counterpart in WordNet. The situation is, however, different for the biology domain. WordNet covers the entire taxonomy of plants and animals, which is only fragmentarily found in Wiktionary. A high overlap between the two resources can be observed for linguistics and medicine. Aligning Wiktionary and WordNet hence allows for fast adaptation to a certain domain and fosters the development of high quality cross-domain applications.

Enriched sense representation. Besides its coverage, Wiktionary is also very rich in its lexical semantic information, which includes etymologies, alternative spellings, pronunciations, glosses, related words, translations, and many more. De Melo and Weikum (2010) exploit, for example, alternative spellings and etymologies for enriching their lexical database. They, however, do not align their resource with Wiktionary and thus cannot make use of the semantic information contained in glosses or related words. WordNet, on the other hand, is known for its rigid subsumption hierarchy and contains a large number of synonyms that proved useful for many NLP tasks.

[8]To avoid noise, we only consider labels occurring at least 10 times and manually filter register or style labels, such as *'poetic'* or *'archaic'*.

Applicability. The potential of aligned resources has been previously shown by many researchers: Shi and Mihalcea (2005), for instance, align FrameNet and VerbNet with WordNet and obtain improved results for semantic parsing. A similar approach has been followed by Loper et al. (2007), who align VerbNet and PropBank for improving semantic role labeling. Recently, Ponzetto and Navigli (2010) have used their Wikipedia–WordNet alignment to improve a knowledge-based word sense disambiguation system.

Our alignment of Wiktionary and WordNet now allows for further work in these directions by (i) exploiting the high coverage of our aligned resource, and (ii) using the enriched representation of senses. Apart from semantic parsing and word sense disambiguation noted above, also semantic relatedness is an interesting task, since Zesch et al. (2008b) found very good results using Wiktionary alone. This might be even surmounted by using our aligned resource. In our future work, we plan to investigate these applications in greater detail.

7 Conclusion

In this paper, we propose a novel word sense alignment between the entire WordNet and the collaborative online dictionary Wiktionary. This work goes beyond previous research efforts in aligning WordNet with Wikipedia, FrameNet, VerbNet and similar lexical resources, as Wiktionary allows for (i) an increased coverage of word senses and (ii) an enriched representation of senses, including pronunciations, etymologies, translations, etc. In our analysis, we particularly found a higher coverage of technical domains in Wiktionary and of humanities and social sciences in WordNet, which are consolidated in our aligned resource. For our alignment, we follow the method by Niemann and Gurevych (2011). We create a well-balanced evaluation dataset, which we make publicly available together with the entire aligned resource.[9]

Acknowledgments. This work has been supported by the Volkswagen Foundation as part of the Lichtenberg-Professorship Program under grant No. I/82806. We thank Elisabeth Niemann, Christian Kirschner, Christian Wirth, and Dr. Judith Eckle-Kohler for their contributions to this paper, and the IXA group at the University of the Basque Country for sharing their UKB software.

[9]`http://www.ukp.tu-darmstadt.de/data/sense-alignment/`

References

Eneko Agirre and Aitor Soroa. 2009. Personalizing PageRank for Word Sense Disambiguation. In *Proceedings of the 12th Conference of the European Chapter of the Association for Computational Linguistics*, pages 33–41, Athens, Greece.

Ron Artstein and Massimo Poesio. 2008. Inter-Coder Agreement for Computational Linguistics. *Computational Linguistics*, 34(4):555–596.

Luisa Bentivogli, Pamela Forner, Bernardo Magnini, and Emanuele Pianta. 2004. Revising WordNet Domains Hierarchy: Semantics, Coverage, and Balancing. In *Proceedings of the COLING '04 Workshop on 'Multilingual Linguistic Resources'*, pages 101–108, Geneva, Switzerland.

Razvan Bunescu and Marius Paşca. 2006. Using Encyclopedic Knowledge for Named Entity Disambiguation. In *Proceedings of the 11th Conference of the European Chapter of the Association for Computational Linguistics*, pages 9–16, Trento, Italy.

Anita Burgun and Olivier Bodenreider. 2001. Comparing Terms, Concepts and Semantic Classes in WordNet and the Unified Medical Language System. In *Proceedings of the NAACL '01 Workshop 'WordNet and Other Lexical Resources: Applications, Extensions and Customizations'*, pages 77–82, Pittsburgh, PA, USA.

Gerard de Melo and Gerhard Weikum. 2010. Providing Multilingual, Multimodal Answers to Lexical Database Queries. In *Proceedings of the 7th International Conference on Language Resources and Evaluation*, pages 348–355, Valletta, Malta.

Oren Etzioni, Kobi Reiter, Stephen Soderland, and Marcus Sammer. 2007. Lexical Translation with Application to Image Search on the Web. In *Proceedings of Machine Translation Summit XI*, Copenhagen, Denmark.

Christiane Fellbaum, editor. 1998. *WordNet: An Electronic Lexical Database (Language, Speech, and Communication)*. Cambridge, MA: MIT Press.

Evgeniy Gabrilovich and Shaul Markovitch. 2007. Computing Semantic Relatedness using Wikipedia-based Explicit Semantic Analysis. In *Proceedings of the 20th International Joint Conference on Artificial Intelligence*, pages 1606–1611, Hyderabad, India.

Mario Jarmasz and Stan Szpakowicz. 2003. Roget's Thesaurus and Semantic Similarity. In *Proceedings of the International Conference on Recent Advances in Natural Language Processing*, pages 212–219, Borovets, Bulgaria.

Klaus Krippendorff. 1980. *Content Analysis: An Introduction to Its Methodology*. Thousand Oaks, CA: Sage Publications.

Oi Yee Kwong. 1998. Aligning WordNet with Additional Lexical Resources. In *Proceedings of the COLING-ACL '98 Workshop 'Usage of WordNet in Natural Language Processing Systems'*, pages 73–79, Montreal, QC, Canada.

Kenneth C. Litkowski. 1999. Towards a Meaning-Full Comparison of Lexical Resources. In *Proceedings of the ACL Special Interest Group on the Lexicon Workshop on Standardizing Lexical Resources*, pages 30–37, College Park, MD, USA.

Edward Loper, Szu-ting Yi, and Martha Palmer. 2007. Combining Lexical Resources: Mapping Between PropBank and VerbNet. In *Proceedings of the Seventh International Workshop on Computational Semantics*, Tilburg, The Netherlands.

Christian M. Meyer and Iryna Gurevych. 2010. How Web Communities Analyze Human Language: Word Senses in Wiktionary. In *Proceedings of the Second Web Science Conference*, Raleigh, NC, USA.

Rada Mihalcea. 2007. Using Wikipedia for Automatic Word Sense Disambiguation. In *Proceedings of the Conference of the North American Chapter of the Association for Computational Linguistics*, pages 196–203, Rochester, NY, USA.

David Milne and Ian H. Witten. 2008. Learning to Link with Wikipedia. In *Proceedings of the 17th ACM International Conference on Information and Knowledge Management*, pages 509–518, Napa Valley, CA, USA.

Christof Müller and Iryna Gurevych. 2009. Using Wikipedia and Wiktionary in Domain-Specific Information Retrieval. In *Evaluating Systems for Multilingual and Multimodal Information Access: Proceedings of the 9th Workshop of the Cross-Language Evaluation Forum*, volume 5706 of *Lecture Notes in Computer Science*, pages 219–226. Berlin/Heidelberg: Springer.

Emmanuel Navarro, Franck Sajous, Bruno Gaume, Laurent Prévot, ShuKai Hsieh, Ivy Kuo, Pierre Magistry, and Chu-Ren Huang. 2009. Wiktionary and NLP: Improving synonymy networks. In *Proceedings of the ACL '09 Workshop 'The People's Web Meets NLP: Collaboratively Constructed Semantic Resources'*, pages 19–27, Suntec, Singapore.

Roberto Navigli and Simone Paolo Ponzetto. 2010. BabelNet: Building a Very Large Multilingual Semantic Network. In *Proceedings of the 48th Annual Meeting of the Association for Computational Linguistics*, pages 216–225, Uppsala, Sweden.

Roberto Navigli. 2006. Meaningful Clustering of Senses Helps Boost Word Sense Disambiguation Performance. In *Proceedings of the 21st International Conference on Computational Linguistics and the 44th Annual Meeting of the Association for Computational Linguistics*, pages 105–112, Sydney, Australia.

Elisabeth Niemann and Iryna Gurevych. 2011. The People's Web meets Linguistic Knowledge: Automatic Sense Alignment of Wikipedia and WordNet. In *Proceedings of the Ninth International Conference on Computational Semantics*, pages 205–214, Oxford, UK.

Patrick Pantel and Dekang Lin. 2002. Discovering Word Senses from Text. In *Proceedings of the Eighth ACM SIGKDD International Conference on Knowledge Discovery and Data Mining*, pages 613–619, Edmonton, AB, Canada.

Simone Paolo Ponzetto and Roberto Navigli. 2009. Large-Scale Taxonomy Mapping for Restructuring and Integrating Wikipedia. In *Proceedings of the 21st International Joint Conference on Artificial Intelligence*, pages 2083–2088, Pasadena, CA, USA.

Simone Paolo Ponzetto and Roberto Navigli. 2010. Knowledge-Rich Word Sense Disambiguation Rivaling Supervised Systems. In *Proceedings of the 48th Annual Meeting of the Association for Computational Linguistics*, pages 1522–1531, Uppsala, Sweden.

Stephen L. Reed and Douglas B. Lenat. 2002. Mapping Ontologies into Cyc. In *Proceedings of the AAAI '02 Workshop 'Ontologies and the Semantic Web'*, pages 1–6, Edmonton, AB, Canada.

Alexander E. Richman and Patrick Schone. 2008. Mining Wiki Resources for Multilingual Named Entity Recognition. In *Proceedings of the 46th Annual Meeting of the Association for Computational Linguistics: Human Language Technologies*, pages 1–9, Columbus, OH, USA.

Maria Ruiz-Casado, Enrique Alfonseca, and Pablo Castells. 2005. Automatic Assignment of Wikipedia Encyclopedic Entries to WordNet Synsets. In *Advances in Web Intelligence: Proceedings of the Third International Atlantic Web Intelligence Conference*, volume 3528 of *Lecture Notes in Computer Science*, pages 380–386. Berlin/Heidelberg: Springer.

Franck Sajous, Emmanuel Navarro, Bruno Gaume, Laurent Prévot, and Yannick Chudy. 2010. Semi-automatic Endogenous Enrichment of Collaboratively Constructed Lexical Resources: Piggybacking onto Wiktionary. In *Advances in Natural Language Processing: Proceedings of the 7th International Conference on NLP*, volume 6233 of *Lecture Notes in Artificial Intelligence*, pages 332–344. Berlin/Heidelberg: Springer.

Lei Shi and Rada Mihalcea. 2005. Putting Pieces Together: Combining FrameNet, VerbNet and WordNet for Robust Semantic Parsing. In *Computational Linguistics and Intelligent Text Processing: 6th International Conference*, volume 3406 of *Lecture Notes in Computer Science*, pages 100–111. Berlin/Heidelberg: Springer.

Fabian Suchanek, Gjergji Kasneci, and Gerhard Weikum. 2008. YAGO — A Large Ontology from Wikipedia and WordNet. *Web Semantics: Science, Services and Agents on the World Wide Web*, 6(3):203–217.

Antonio Toral, Rafael Muñoz, and Monica Monachini. 2008. Named Entity WordNet. In *Proceedings of the Sixth International Conference on Language Resources and Evaluation*, pages 741–747, Marrakech, Morocco.

Antonio Toral, Óscar Ferrández, Eneko Agirre, and Rafael Muñoz. 2009. A study on Linking Wikipedia categories to Wordnet synsets using text similarity. In *Proceedings of the 7th International Conference on Recent Advances in Natural Language Processing*, pages 449–454, Borovets, Bulgaria.

Torsten Zesch, Christof Müller, and Iryna Gurevych. 2008a. Extracting Lexical Semantic Knowledge from Wikipedia and Wiktionary. In *Proceedings of the 6th International Conference on Language Resources and Evaluation*, pages 1646–1652, Marrakech, Morocco.

Torsten Zesch, Christof Müller, and Iryna Gurevych. 2008b. Using Wiktionary for Computing Semantic Relatedness. In *Proceedings of the Twenty-Third AAAI Conference on Artificial Intelligence*, pages 861–867, Chicago, IL, USA.

From News to Comment: Resources and Benchmarks for Parsing the Language of Web 2.0

Jennifer Foster[1], **Özlem Çetinoğlu**[1], **Joachim Wagner**[1], **Joseph Le Roux**[2]
Joakim Nivre[3], **Deirdre Hogan**[1] and **Josef van Genabith**[1]
[1,3]NCLT/CNGL, Dublin City University, Ireland
[2]LIF - CNRS UMR 6166, Université Aix-Marseille, France
[3]Department of Linguistics and Philology, Uppsala University, Sweden
[1]{jfoster,ocetinoglu,jwagner,dhogan,josef}@computing.dcu.ie
[2]joseph.le-roux@lif.univ-mrs.fr, [3]joakim.nivre@lingfil.uu.se

Abstract

We investigate the problem of parsing the noisy language of social media. We evaluate four Wall-Street-Journal-trained statistical parsers (Berkeley, Brown, Malt and MST) on a new dataset containing 1,000 phrase structure trees for sentences from microblogs (tweets) and discussion forum posts. We compare the four parsers on their ability to produce Stanford dependencies for these Web 2.0 sentences. We find that the parsers have a particular problem with tweets and that a substantial part of this problem is related to POS tagging accuracy. We attempt three retraining experiments involving Malt, Brown and an in-house Berkeley-style parser and obtain a statistically significant improvement for all three parsers.

1 Introduction

With the explosive growth in social media, natural language processing technologies, including parsers, need to adapt to reflect the linguistic changes brought about by new forms of online communication. The availability of the Penn Treebank has encouraged much research in supervised parsing for English and facilitated comparision between parsers. This has led to impressive performance for in-domain parsing. Some progress has also been achieved in adapting parsers to new domains using semi-supervised and unsupervised approaches involving some labelled source domain training data, little, if any, labelled target domain data and large quantities of unlabelled target domain data. Much of the work on parser adaptation has focused on biomedical text and questions - very little has focused on the informal language prevalent in much of the user-generated content of Web 2.0. Domain adaptation to the language of social media is particularly challenging since Web 2.0 is not really a domain, consisting, as it does, of utterances from a wide variety of speakers from different geographical and social backgrounds.

Foster (2010) carried out a pilot study on this topic by investigating the performance of the Berkeley parser (Petrov et al., 2006) on sentences taken from a sports discussion forum. Each misparsed sentence was examined manually and a list of problematic phenomena identified. We extend this work by looking at a larger dataset consisting not only of discussion forum posts but also microblogs or tweets. We extend the parser evaluation to the Brown reranking parser (Charniak and Johnson, 2005), MaltParser (Nivre et al., 2006) and MSTParser (McDonald et al., 2005), and we examine the ability of all four parsers to recover typed Stanford dependencies (de Marneffe et al., 2006). The relative ranking of the four parsers confirms the results of previous Stanford-dependency-based parser evaluations on other datasets (Cer et al., 2010; Petrov et al., 2010). Furthermore, our study shows that the sentences in tweets are harder to parse than the sentences from the discussion forum, despite their shorter length and that a large contributing factor is the high part-of-speech tagging error rate.

Foster's work also included a targeted approach to improving parser performance by modifying the Penn Treebank trees to reflect observed differences between Wall Street Journal (WSJ) sentences and discussion forum sentences (subject ellipsis, non-standard capitalisation, etc.). We approach the problem from a different perspective, by seeing how far we can get by exploiting unlabelled target domain data. We employ three types of parser retraining, namely, 1) the McClosky et al. (2006) self-training protocol, 2) uptraining of Malt using dependency trees produced by a slightly more accurate phrase structure parser (Petrov et al., 2010), and 3) PCFG-LA self-training (Huang and Harper, 2009). We combine the benefits of the dependency parsing uptraining work of Petrov et al. and the self-training protocol of McClosky et al. by retraining Malt on trees produced by a self-trained version of the Brown parser.

We find that considerable improvements can be obtained when discussion forum data is used as the source of additional training material, and more modest improvements when Twitter data is used. Grammars trained on the discussion forum data perform well on Twitter data, but the reverse is not the case. For Malt, we obtain an absolute LAS increase of 8.8% on the discussion forum data and an improvement of 5.6% on the Twitter data. For Brown, we obtain an absolute f-score improvement of 2.4% on the discussion forum data and an increase of 1.7% on Twitter. For the Berkeley-style parser that we use in the PCFG-LA self-training experiment, the f-score improvements are 4.7% and 1.2% respectively.

The novel contributions of the paper are:

1. A new dataset consisting of 1,000 hand-corrected phrase structure parse trees for sentences from two types of social media (discussion forums and tweets).
2. A detailed evaluation of four popular WSJ-trained parsers on this new dataset.
3. An investigation of how well the most successful unsupervised parser adaptation methods perform on this new dataset. Since Web 2.0 is not really a domain, it is important not to assume that the methods that have been developed for more clearly defined domains will work without carrying out the experiments.
4. A discussion of the main issues involved in parsing Web 2.0 text.

The new dataset is discussed in §2 and the baseline parser evaluation is detailed in §3. The retraining experiments are described in §4. §5 contains a discussion of how this work could be extended.

2 Web 2.0 Data

Our Web 2.0 dataset, summarised in Table 1, consists of a small treebank of 1,000 hand-corrected phrase structure parse trees and two larger corpora of unannotated sentences. The sentences in the treebank originate from discussion forum comments and microblogs (tweets). The sentences in the larger corpora are taken from the same sources as the treebank sentences.

2.1 Tweets

Hand-Corrected Parse Trees 60 million tweets on 50 topics encompassing politics, business, sport and entertainment, were collected using the public Twitter API between February and May 2009 (Bermingham and Smeaton, 2010). The microblog section of the Web 2.0 treebank contains 519 sentences taken from this corpus. The development set contains 269 sentences and the test set contains 250. Hyperlinks and usernames were replaced by the generic names *Urlname* and *Username* respectively, and the tweets were split by hand into sentences. Tweets containing just a hyperlink were not included in the treebank. For the rest of this paper, we refer to the development set as *TwitterDev* and the test set as *TwitterTest*.

Unannotated Sentences From the full Twitter corpus, we constructed a sub-corpus of approximately 1 million tweets. As with the treebank tweets, hyperlinks were replaced by the term *Urlname* and usernames by *Username*. Tweets with more than one non-ASCII character were removed, and the remaining tweets were passed through our in-house sentence splitter and tokeniser, resulting in a corpus of 1,401,533 sentences. We refer to this as the *TwitterTrain* corpus.

2.2 Discussion Forum Comments

Hand-Corrected Parse Trees The discussion forum section of the Web 2.0 treebank is an extension of that described in Foster (2010). It contains 481 sentences taken from two threads on the BBC Sport 606 discussion forum in November 2009.[1] As with the tweets, the discussion forum posts were split into sentences by hand. The development set contains 258 sentences and the test set 223. For the remainder of the paper, we use the term *FootballDev* to refer to this development set and the term *FootballTest* to refer to the test set.

Unannotated Sentences The same discussion forum that was used to create *FootballDev* and *FootballTest* was scraped during the final quarter of 2010. The content was stripped of HTML markup and passed through an in-house sentence splitter and tokeniser, resulting in a corpus of 1,009,646 sentences. We call this the *Football-Train* corpus.

[1] `http://www.bbc.co.uk/dna/606/F15264075?thread=7065503&show=50` and `http://www.bbc.co.uk/dna/606/F15265997?thread=7066196&show=50`

Corpus Name	*#Sen*	*SL Mean*	*SL Med.*	σ
TwitterDev	269	11.1	10	6.4
TwitterTest	250	11.4	10	6.8
TwitterTrain	1,401,533	8.6	7	6.1
FootballDev	258	17.7	14	13.9
FootballTest	223	16.1	14	9.7
FootballTrain	1,009,646	15.4	12	13.3

Table 1: Basic Statistics on the Web 2.0 datasets: number of sentences, average sentence length, median sentence length and standard deviation

2.3 Annotation

The sentences in the Web 2.0 treebank (*TwitterDev/Test* and *FootballDev/Test*) were first parsed automatically using an implementation of the Collins Model 2 generative statistical parser (Bikel, 2004). They were then corrected by hand by one annotator, using as a reference the Penn Treebank (PTB) bracketing guidelines (Bies et al., 1995) and the PTB trees themselves. For structures which do not appear in the PTB, new annotation decisions needed to be made. An example is the annotation of hyperlinks in tweets. These were annotated as proper nouns in a single word noun phrase, and, if occurring at the end of a tweet, were attached in the same way as a nominal adverbial.

The annotator went through the dataset twice, and a second annotator then annotated 10% of the sentences (divided equally between discussion forum posts and tweets). Agreement between the two annotators on labelled bracketing is 94.2%. The sources of the disagreements involved 1) the PTB bracketing guidelines leaving open more than one annotation option (usually placement of adverbs), 2) (almost) agrammatical fragments (e.g. *USA, USA, USA* or *Wes Brown > Drogba*) and 3) multiword expressions (e.g. *in fairness*).

3 Baseline Evaluation

We first evaluate four widely used WSJ-trained statistical parsers on our new Web 2.0 datasets:

Berkeley (Petrov et al., 2006) We train a PCFG-LA using 6 iterations and we run the parser in *accurate* mode.

Brown (Charniak and Johnson, 2005) We employ this parser in its out-of-the-box settings.

Malt (Nivre et al., 2006) We use the *stacklazy* algorithm described in Nivre et al. (2009). We train a linear classifier where the feature interactions are modelled explicitly.

Parser	F-Score	POS Acc.
WSJ22		
Berkeley Own Tagging	90.0	96.5
Berkeley Predicted Tags	89.0	96.6
Berkeley Gold Tags	90.0	99.7
Brown	91.9	96.3
FootballDev		
Berkeley Own Tagging	79.0	92.2
Berkeley Predicted Tags	78.8	92.7
Berkeley Gold Tags	81.5	98.0
Brown	79.7	93.5
TwitterDev		
Berkeley Own Tagging	71.1	84.1
Berkeley Predicted Tags	70.1	84.1
Berkeley Gold Tags	76.5	97.2
Brown	73.8	85.5

Table 2: Evalb Results for Berkeley and Brown

MST (McDonald et al., 2005) We use the settings described in Nivre et al. (2010).

Our training data consists of §02-21 of the WSJ section of the PTB (Marcus et al., 1994). Although our main aim in this experiment is to establish how well WSJ-trained parsers perform on our new Web 2.0 dataset, we also report performance on §22 as a reference. We use Parseval labelled f-score to compare the two phrase structure parsers. We then compare all four parsers by training the dependency parsers on WSJ phrase structure trees converted to labelled dependency trees and by converting the output of the two phrase structure parsers to labelled dependency trees. For the dependency evaluation, we use the CoNLL evaluation metrics of labelled attachment score (LAS) and unlabelled attachment score (UAS).

The labelled dependency scheme that we use is the Stanford basic dependency scheme (de Marneffe et al., 2006). We experiment with the use of gold POS tags, POS tags obtained using a POS tagger (Giménez and Màrquez, 2004) and, for the phrase structure parsers, POS tags produced by the parsers themselves. The Brown parser always performs its own POS tagging. The Berkeley parser can be supplied with POS tags but it is not guaranteed to use them – trees containing the supplied POS tag for a given word may be removed from the chart during coarse-to-fine pruning.[2]

3.1 Results

Table 2 shows the Parseval f-score and part-of-speech (POS) tagging accuracy for the Berkeley

[2]In the interest of replicability, detailed information on experimental settings is available at `http://nclt.computing.dcu.ie/publications/foster_ijcnlp11.html`.

Parser	LAS	UAS	LAS	UAS	LAS	UAS
	WSJ22		*FootballDev*		*TwitterDev*	
Berk O	90.5	93.2	79.8	84.8	68.9	75.1
Berk P	89.9	92.5	80.1	84.9	68.2	74.2
Brown	91.5	94.2	82.0	86.3	71.4	77.3
Malt P	88.0	90.6	76.1	81.5	67.3	73.6
MST P	88.8	91.3	76.4	81.1	68.1	73.8
Berk G	91.6	93.4	83.1	86.4	76.8	80.8
Malt G	90.0	91.6	80.4	83.7	78.3	81.6
MST G	90.7	92.3	80.8	83.4	78.4	81.3

Table 3: Dependency Evaluation Results: O (Own Tagging), P (Predicted Input from POS Tagger), G (Gold Tags)

and Brown parsers on the three development sets.[3] We observe the following: Twitter data is harder to parse than the discussion forum data; parsing accuracy is slightly higher when the Berkeley parser does its own POS tagging than when a pipeline model is employed; POS errors are a bigger problem for the Web 2.0 datasets than for the in-domain test set, particularly for *TwitterDev*.

The LAS and UAS scores for all four parsers are presented in Table 3. The relative ranking of the four parsers is the same as that reported in Cer et al. (2010). One striking aspect of the results is the bigger performance discrepancy between the phrase structure and dependency parsers for the discussion forum data than for the Twitter data. There is also a bigger performance discrepancy between LAS and UAS for the Web 2.0 data than for the WSJ data — this could be related to the fact that the Stanford converter has been developed using Penn Treebank trees, and it is certainly related to POS tagging accuracy since the difference is less pronounced when the input to the parsers is gold POS tags. In gold tag mode, the dependency parsers achieve slightly higher performance than the Berkeley parser for the Twitter data. This might have something to do with the 97% POS tagging accuracy for Berkeley gold tagging mode (see Table 2) but this cannot be the whole story since we do not see the same trend for the discussion forum data even though POS tagging accuracy is not 100% here either.

3.2 Error Analysis

In order to better understand the results in Tables 2 and 3, we examine POS confusions for the three datasets and we provide a breakdown of parsing performance by dependency type.

[3]The Brown parser makes use of non-PTB tags to mark auxiliary verbs (AUX and AUXG). We take this difference into account when calculating POS tagging accuracy.

3.2.1 POS Tagging

Something we notice in Tables 2 and 3 is the difference in parsing accuracy between the scenario in which the parser is supplied with the correct POS tag for each word in the input string and the realistic scenarios in which it is supplied with POS tags produced by a POS tagger or in which it produces the POS tags as part of the parsing process. It is clear from this difference that a proportion of the parsing errors can be attributed to POS tagging errors, and it is also clear that this proportion is greater for the out-of-domain Web 2.0 text than it is for the in-domain WSJ text. The proportion of unknown words in the development sets already tells us something: 2.8% of the tokens in *WSJ22* do not occur in *WSJ2-21* compared to 6.8% for *FootballDev* and 16.6% for *TwitterDev*.[4]

We look in more detail at the POS tagging errors produced by the Berkeley parser in own tagging mode, the Brown parser and SVMTool (the POS tagger used in the Malt, MST and Berkeley pipelines). Instead of looking at the most common POS tagging errors, we attempt to locate the tagging errors that are associated with inaccurate phrase structure trees. For each POS confusion that occurs more than 5 times in the particular development set, we find the relative frequency of this confusion in sentences receiving a Parseval f-score under 70.0. We then order the POS confusions by these relative frequencies. The top-ranking confusions (gold/system) common to all three systems are as follows:

1. *WSJ22*: `NNS/VBZ`, `VBZ/NNS`
2. *FootballDev*: `RB/JJ`, `RB/RP`, `VB/VBP`
3. *TwitterDev*: `JJ/NNP`, `NN/VB`, `NNP/VB`, `NNP/JJ`, `VBZ/NNS`

The tendency for the noun/verb confusion that we see in *WSJ22* and *TwitterDev* to affect parser accuracy has been documented before (Dalrymple, 2006). The following is a *TwitterDev* example:

```
(FRAG
   (NP (JJ Username)
       (S (NP (JJ fantastic))
          (VP (VB win))))
  (. !) (. !))
```

The *RB/JJ* confusion in *FootballDev* can be explained by the tendency of some posters to drop the *-ly* suffix on adverbs (e.g. *played **bad***). The

[4]The tokens *Username* and *Urlname* are unknown and occur repeatedly. But even discounting these, the ratio is 14.0%.

prominence of *NNP* in *TwitterDev* is interesting and suggests, for one thing, that less emphasis should be placed on capitalisation in the tagging of unknown words:

```
(S
   (NP (NNP grrr))
   (: ...)
   (VP (VB spotify)
       (PP (IN in)
           (NP some kind of
           infinite update loop))))
```

3.2.2 Stanford Dependencies

We analyse the deprel+attachment f-scores of the best non-gold-tagged configuration of each parser. This means that for the Berkeley parser we use the version that performs its own tagging.

For most of the dependency types there is a general trend as exemplified in Figure 1: for each of the three datasets, the relation Brown > Berk > MSTParser > MaltParser holds. The *WSJ22* results are around 5-10% absolute better than the *FootballDev* results while the drop for *TwitterDev* is in the 15-20% range on average. Frequent dependencies like nominal subjects (`nsubj`), direct objects (`dobj`), adverbial clauses (`advcl`), `copulars`, open complements (`xcomp`), `prepositional` modifiers follow this trend. The relations `det`, `root`, `aux`, `pobj`, `poss`, `possessive`, `neg` are easy to recover in all datasets, with no big drops observed for *FootballDev* or *TwitterDev*. For adjectival modifiers (`amod`), adverbial modifiers (`advmod`), and complements (`complm`), the decreasing pattern over the three datasets holds but the dependency parsers outperform the constituency parsers.

Coordination is one of the harder relations to recover. According to the Stanford scheme, the first conjunct is the head of the coordination. The conjunction is attached to the head via the `cc` relation and the other conjuncts are attached via the `conj` relation. For *WSJ22*, the phrase structure parser scores are around 85% for `cc` and slightly lower for `conj`, and the dependency parsers scores are around 80% for `cc` and 71% for `conj`. For the Web 2.0 data the scores decrease from *WSJ22* to *FootballDev* but increase again for *TwitterDev*. The drop in performance for *FootballDev* is in line with Foster's (2010) observation that the discussion forum data contain difficult coordination cases involving coordination of unlike constituents. It is possible that the length of the Twitter sentences acts as a natural inhibitor to such

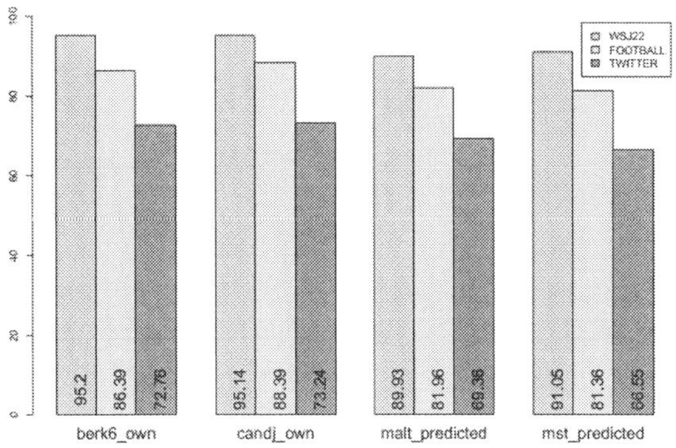

Figure 1: F-scores for `nsubj`

cases. We also note that Brown clearly outperforms the other parsers on *TwitterDev*.

4 Making Use of Unlabelled Data

One approach to the parser domain adaptation problem is to train a new system using large quantities of automatically parsed target domain text. We experiment with two retraining methods: *self-training* in which the training data of the parser we are attempting to adapt is augmented by adding trees produced by the same parser for the sentences in our unannotated target domain corpus, and *uptraining*, in which the training set of a less accurate parser is augmented with trees for the unannotated corpus sentences produced by a more accurate parser.

4.1 Charniak and Johnson Self-Training

McClosky et al. (2006) demonstrate that a WSJ-trained parser can be adapted to the fiction domains of the Brown corpus by performing a type of self-training that involves the use of the Brown parser. Their training protocol is as follows: sentences from the LA Times are parsed using the first-stage parser and reranked in the second stage. These parse trees are added to the original WSJ training set and the *first-stage* parser is retrained. The sentences from the target domain, in this case, Brown corpus sentences are then parsed using the newly trained first-stage parser and reranked using the original reranker, resulting in a performance jump from 85.2% to 87.8%. One of the factors that make this training protocol effective are the non-generative features in the discriminative reranker (McClosky et al., 2008), and the use of the reranker means that this method is not a pure

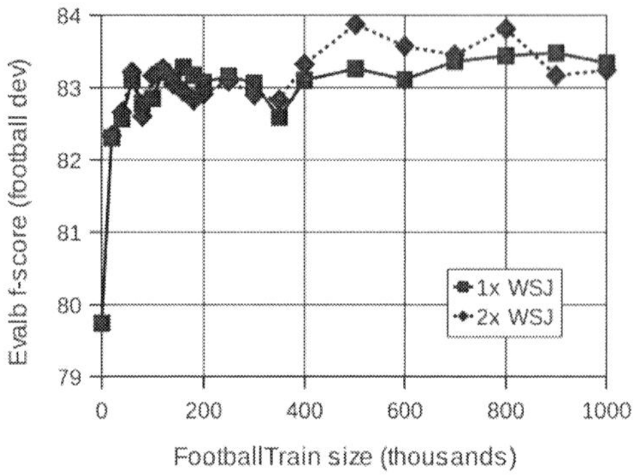

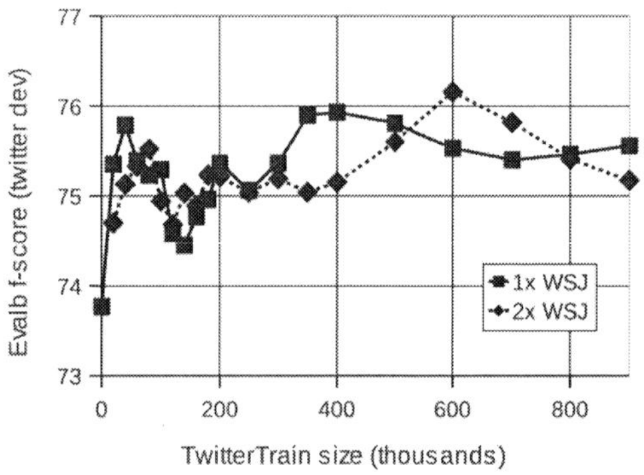

Figure 2: Brown self-training results

self-training one, but rather a type of uptraining.

We apply the procedure McClosky at el. to determine whether the performance of Brown can be improved on Web 2.0 data. The top graph in Figure 2 shows the results obtained for *FootballDev* when the first-stage parser is retrained on various combinations of *WSJ02-21* and parse trees produced by the reranking parser for sentences in *FootballTrain*. The bottom graph represents the f-scores for *TwitterDev* using *TwitterTrain* instead of *FootballTrain*. It is clear from the top graph that adding material from *FootballTrain* results in a significant improvement over the baseline f-scores of 79.7. The highest f-score is 83.8, obtained using two copies of *WSJ2-21* and 500,000 *FootballTrain* trees. The improvements achieved using *TwitterTrain* are less pronounced, with an absolute improvement of 2.4% obtained using 600,000 *TwitterTrain* trees and two copies of *WSJ02-21*.

4.2 Malt Uptraining

Petrov et al. (2010) perform a Stanford-dependency-based parser evaluation, with sentences from QuestionBank (Judge et al., 2006) as their test data. They find that deterministic dependency parsers such as MaltParser suffer more from the domain differences between QuestionBank and WSJ than phrase structure parsers such as the Berkeley parser. They then attempt to improve the accuracy of MaltParser on questions by training it on questions parsed by the Berkeley parser, arguing that the linear time complexity of a parser such as Malt is needed for real-time processing of web data. They demonstrate that the same improvement in accuracy can be obtained by using 100,000 automatically parsed questions as can be obtained using 2,000 manually parsed QuestionBank trees.

We perform two uptraining experiments. In the first, we retrain MaltParser using a combination of *WSJ02-21* and trees produced by Brown for sentences in the *FootballTrain* or *TwitterTrain* corpora (we call this *vanilla uptraining*). In the second and novel approach, we use a *self-trained* Brown grammar to parse the trees for uptraining (we call this *domain-adapted uptraining*).[5] For all configurations, the POS tagger, SVMTool, is retrained on the same data as MaltParser.

The results of the uptraining experiments show that significant improvements are obtained for both types of uptraining, but as expected, the domain-adapted uptraining is superior. The graph in Fig. 3 shows that the best *FootballDev* grammar is obtained using domain-adapted uptraining with 350,000 *FootballTrain* trees and one copy of *WSJ02-21* (an improvement of 5.7% over the baseline). The corresponding Twitter graph (not shown due to lack of space) shows that an improvement of 4.6% can be obtained on *TwitterDev* using domain-adapted uptraining with 200,000 *TwitterTrain* trees and one copy of *WSJ02-21*.

4.3 Latent Variable Self-Training

Experiments with pure self-training, i.e. training a parser on its own output, have had mixed results over the years. Charniak (1997), Steedman et al. (2003) and Plank (2009) provide evidence that it is not effective, whereas the experiments of Reichart and Rappoport (2007), Huang and Harper (2009) and Sagae (2010) suggest that it can be useful. Huang and Harper (2009) are the first to ap-

[5]The Brown grammar used for domain-adapted uptraining is trained on the first half of *FootballTrain* and *TwitterTrain*. We parse the second half of *FootballTrain* and *TwitterTrain* for both types of uptraining.

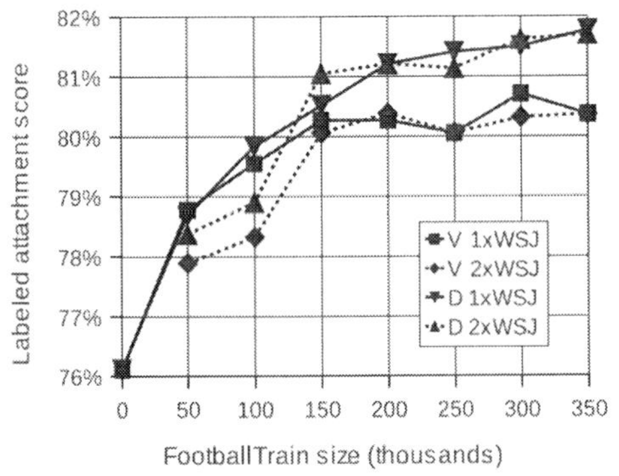

Figure 3: Malt uptraining LAS results for *FootballDev*: V stands for Vanilla Uptraining and D for Domain-Adapted Uptraining

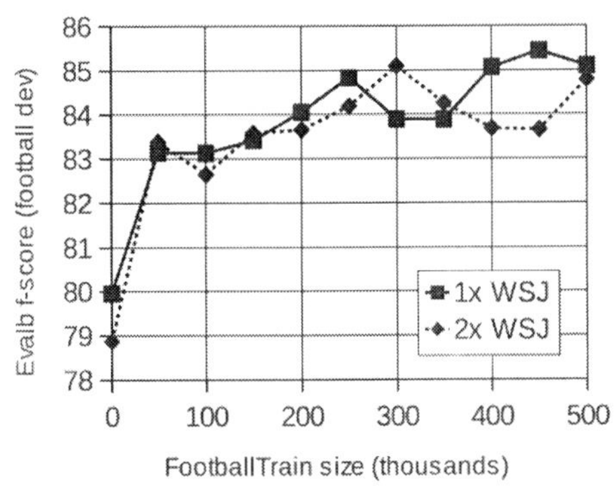

Figure 4: PCFG-LA self-training results

ply self-training using a PCFG-LA — with positive results. They argue that self-training works in this scenario because the additional training data prevents the split-merge process from overfitting.

We apply the self-training method of Huang and Harper to our new datasets. Like Huang and Harper, we use our own PCFG-LA parser because the trainer is multi-threaded, allowing us to handle the computation needed to train a PCFG-LA on large corpora. We train a 6-iteration PCFG-LA using *WSJ02-21* and use it to parse the *FootballTrain* and *TwitterTrain* corpora. We then add the automatically parsed material to our WSJ training set and retrain more 6-iteration PCFG-LAs. The result for *FootballDev* using *FootballTrain* is shown in Table 4. We achieve an absolute f-score improvement of 5.5% on *FootballDev*. The corresponding *TwitterTrain* graph is not shown for space reasons. The *TwitterTrain* improvements are more modest, with an f-score increase of approximately 2% on *TwitterDev*.

Grammar	*FootballTest*	*TwitterTest*	*WSJ23*
Charniak and Johnson self-training (F-Score)			
Baseline	81.2	73.3	91.4
Best FootballDev	83.6*	75.0*	91.1*
Best TwitterDev	81.0	74.7*	91.1*
Latent variable PCFG self-training (F-Score)			
Baseline	77.7	69.5	89.8
Best FootballDev	82.4*	70.6*	89.4*
Best TwitterDev	81.7*	70.7	89.6
Malt uptraining (LAS)			
Baseline	71.8	64.1	87.7
Best FootballDev	80.6*	69.7*	86.5*
Best TwitterDev	76.7*	68.2*	87.1*

Table 4: Test Set Results

4.4 Test Set Results

For each of our three retraining experiments, we take the best grammar for *FootballDev* and the best grammar for *TwitterDev* and apply them to the three test sets. In the PCFG-LA self-training experiments, a *FootballTrain* grammar actually outperforms all *TwitterTrain* grammars on *TwitterDev* and so we use this for final testing. The results are provided in Table 4. Statistically significant differences between the relevant baseline are marked with an asterisk.

5 Discussion

Parser retraining The variance in the size of improvements between the development and test sets (a greater improvement for Malt uptraining and a smaller improvement for Brown self-training) and the fact that, for Brown and Malt, the best grammar on *TwitterDev* is outperformed on *TwitterTest* by the best grammar on *FootballDev* is most likely due to the small size of the datasets. However, the results are promising, and clearly demonstrate that unlabelled user-generated content can be used to improve parser accuracy.

The reasons for the improvements yielded by the three types of retraining need to be determined.[6] The underperformance of the *TwitterTrain* material in comparison to the *FootballTrain* material suggests that sample selection involving language and topic identification needs to be applied before parser retraining. We also intend to test the combination of PCFG-LA self-training

[6]See Foster et al. (2011) for a preliminary analysis of the effect of Malt uptraining on sentences from *TwitterDev*.

and product grammar parsing described in Huang et al. (2010) on our Web 2.0 dataset.

Combination Parsing Several successful parsing methods have employed multiple parsing models, combined using techniques such as voting, stacking and product models (Henderson and Brill, 2000; Nivre and McDonald, 2008; Petrov, 2010). An ensemble approach to parsing seems particularly appropriate for the linguistic melting pot of Web 2.0, as does the related idea of selecting a model based on characteristics of the input. For example, a preliminary error analysis of the Malt uptraining results shows that coordination cases in *TwitterDev* are helped more by grammars trained on *FootballTrain* than on *TwitterTrain*, suggesting that sentences containing a conjunction should be directed to a *FootballTrain* grammar. McClosky et al. (2010) use linear regression to determine the correct mix of training material for a particular document. We intend to experiment with this idea in the context of Web 2.0 parsing.

Preprocessing Foster (2010) and Gadde et al. (2011) report improved parsing and tagging performance when the input data is normalised before processing, This work employs very little data cleaning and future work will involve exploring the interaction between preprocessing and parser retraining. Hyperlinks and usernames in tweets were replaced by the terms *Urlname* and *Username* respectively — to make life easier for parsers and POS taggers, proper nouns that are in the systems' lexicons should be used. The automatic sentence splitter and tokeniser that was used to create the Web 2.0 training sets makes use of abbreviation statistics in order to determine sentence boundaries. We compiled an abbreviation table using football discussion forum data but made no attempt to modify it for Twitter data. What is needed is a sentence-splitter tuned to the punctuation conventions of Twitter. However, more fundamental question remain: what is the correct unit of analysis for tweets and does it even make sense to talk about sentences in the context of Twitter? Our next step in this direction is to experiment with the Twitter-specific resources (tagset, tagger, tokeniser) described in Gimpel et al. (2011).

More Datasets We have focused on WSJ material as the source for our labelled training data. Future work will involve the use of other syntactically annotated resources including Brown and Switchboard, as well as Ontonotes 4.0, which has recently been released and which contains syntactically annotated web text (300k words).

More Parser Evaluation The cross-parser evaluation we have presented in the first half of the paper is by no means exhaustive. For example, to measure the positive effect of discriminative reranking, the first-stage Brown parser should also be included in the evaluation. Other statistical parsers could be evaluated, and it would be interesting to examine the performance of systems which employ hand-crafted grammars and treebank-trained disambiguators in order to determine whether a system less tuned to the PTB is more appropriate for this kind of heterogeneous data (Plank and van Noord, 2010). We have employed the Stanford dependencies in this work — other labelled dependency schemes are available and it might be informative to examine the relative performance of the parsers from the perspective of many such schemes rather than just one. Gold standard dependency annotations for the new sentences would also be a bonus.

Acknowledgements

This research has been supported by Enterprise Ireland (CFTD/2007/229) and by Science Foundation Ireland (Grant 07/CE/ I1142) as part of the CNGL (www.cngl.ie) at School of Computing, DCU, and by the French Agence Nationale pour la Recherche, through the SEQUOIA project (ANR-08-EMER-013). We thank the reviewers for their helpful comments.

References

Adam Bermingham and Alan Smeaton. 2010. Classifying sentiment in microblogs: Is brevity an advantage? In *Proceedings of CKIM.*

Ann Bies, Mark Ferguson, Karen Katz, and Robert MacIntyre. 1995. Bracketing guidelines for Treebank II style. Technical report, University of Pennsylvania.

Daniel Bikel. 2004. Intricacies of Collins parsing model. *Computational Linguistics*, 30(4).

Daniel Cer, Marie-Catherine de Marneffe, Daniel Jurafsky, and Christopher D. Manning. 2010. Parsing to Stanford dependencies: Trade-offs between speed and accuracy. In *Proceedings of LREC.*

Eugene Charniak and Mark Johnson. 2005. Course-to-fine n-best-parsing and maxent discriminative reranking. In *Proceedings of the 43rd ACL.*

Eugene Charniak. 1997. Statistical parsing with a context-free grammar and word statistics. In *Proceedings of AAAI*.

Mary Dalrymple. 2006. How much can part-of-speech tagging affect parsing? *Natural Language Engineering*, 12(4).

Marie-Catherine de Marneffe, Bill MacCartney, and Christopher D. Manning. 2006. Generating typed dependency parses from phrase structure parses. In *Proceedings of LREC*.

Jennifer Foster, Özlem Çetinoğlu, Joachim Wagner, Joseph Le Roux, Stephen Hogan, Joakim Nivre, Deirdre Hogan, and Josef van Genabith. 2011. #hardtoparse: Pos tagging and parsing the twitterverse. In *Proceedings of the AAAI Workshop on Analysing Microtext*.

Jennifer Foster. 2010. "cba to check the spelling" investigating parser performance on discussion forum posts. In *Proceedings of NAACL-HLT*.

Phani Gadde, L. V. Subramaniam, and Tanveer A. Faruquie. 2011. Adapting a wsj trained part-of-speech tagger to noisy text: Preliminary results. In *Proceedings of Joint Workshop on Multilingual OCR and Analytics for Noisy Unstructured Text Data*.

Jesús Giménez and Lluís Màrquez. 2004. Svmtool: A general pos tagger generator based on support vector machines. In *Proceedings of LREC*.

Kevin Gimpel, Nathan Schneider, Brendan OConnor, Dipanjan Das, Daniel Mills, Jacob Eisenstein, Michael Heilman, Dani Yogatama, Jeffrey Flanigan, and Noah A. Smith. 2011. Part-of-speech Tagging for Twitter: Annotation, Features and Experiments. In *Proceedings of ACL:HLT*.

John C. Henderson and Eric Brill. 2000. Exploiting diversity in natural language processing: Combining parsers. In *Proceedings of EMNLP*.

Zhongqiang Huang and Mary Harper. 2009. Self-training PCFG grammars with latent annotations across languages. In *Proceedings of EMNLP*.

Zhongqiang Huang, Mary Harper, and Slav Petrov. 2010. Self-training with products of latent variable grammars. In *Proceedings of EMNLP*.

John Judge, Aoife Cahill, and Josef van Genabith. 2006. Questionbank: Creating a corpus of parse-annotated questions. In *Proceedings of ACL*.

Mitchell Marcus, Grace Kim, Mary Ann Marcinkiewicz, Robert MacIntyre, Ann Bies, Mark Ferguson, Karen Katz, and Britta Schasberger. 1994. The Penn Treebank: Annotating predicate argument structure. In *Proceedings of the ARPA Speech and Natural Language Workshop*.

David McClosky, Eugene Charniak, and Mark Johnson. 2006. Reranking and self-training for parser adaptation. In *Proceedings of ACL*.

David McClosky, Eugene Charniak, and Mark Johnson. 2008. When is self-training effective for parsing? In *Proceedings of COLING*.

David McClosky, Eugene Charniak, and Mark Johnson. 2010. Automatic domain adaptation for parsing. In *Proceedings of NAACL-HLT*.

Ryan McDonald, Koby Crammer, and Fernando Pereira. 2005. Online large-margin training of dependency parsers. In *Proceedings of ACL*.

Joakim Nivre and Ryan McDonald. 2008. Integrating graph-based and transition-based dependency parsers. In *Proceedings of ACL-HLT*.

Joakim Nivre, Johan Hall, and Jens Nilsson. 2006. Maltparser: A data-driven parser-generator for dependency parsing. In *Proceedings of LREC*.

Joakim Nivre, Marco Kuhlmann, and Johan Hall. 2009. An improved oracle for dependency parsing with online reordering. In *Proceedings of IWPT*.

Joakim Nivre, Laura Rimell, Ryan Mc Donald, and Carlos Gómez-Rodríguez. 2010. Evaluation of dependency parsers on unbounded dependencies. In *Proceedings of COLING*.

Slav Petrov, Leon Barrett, Romain Thibaux, and Dan Klein. 2006. Learning accurate, compact and interpretable tree annotation. In *Proceedings of ACL*.

Slav Petrov, Pi-Chuan Chang, Michael Ringgaard, and Hiyan Alshawi. 2010. Uptraining for accurate deterministic question parsing. In *Proceedings of EMNLP*.

Slav Petrov. 2010. Products of random latent variable grammars. In *Proceedings of NAACL-HLT*.

Barbara Plank and Gertjan van Noord. 2010. Grammar-driven versus data-driven: Which parsing system is more affected by domain shifts? In *Proceedings of the ACL Workshop on NLP and Linguistics: Finding the Common Ground*.

Barbara Plank. 2009. A comparison of structural correspondence learning and self-training for discriminative parse selection. In *Proceedings of the NAACL-HLT Workshop on Semi-supervised Learning for Natural Language Processing*.

Roi Reichart and Ari Rappaport. 2007. Self-training for enhancement and domain adaptation of statistical parsers trained on small datasets. In *Proceedings of ACL*.

Kenji Sagae. 2010. Self-training without reranking for parser domain adapation and its impact on semantic role labelling. In *Proceedings of the ACL Workshop on Domain Adaptation for NLP*.

Mark Steedman, Miles Osbourne, Anoop Sarkar, Stephen Clark, Rebecca Hwa, Julia Hockenmaier, Paul Ruhlen, Steven Baker, and Jeremiah Crim. 2003. Boot-strapping statistical parsers from small datasets. In *Proceedings of EACL*.

Toward Finding Semantic Relations not Written in a Single Sentence: An Inference Method using Auto-Discovered Rules

Masaaki Tsuchida†§* **Kentaro Torisawa**‡ **Stijn De Saeger** ‡
Jong-Hoon Oh‡ **Jun'ichi Kazama**‡ **Chikara Hashimoto**‡ **Hayato Ohwada**§
† Information and Media Processing Laboratories, NEC Corporation, Nara, Japan
m-tsuchida@cq.jp.nec.com
‡ Information Analysis Laboratory, National Institute of
Information and Communications Technology, Kyoto, Japan
{torisawa,stijn,rovellia,kazama,ch}@nict.go.jp
§ Graduate school of Science and Technology, Tokyo University of Science, Chiba, Japan.
ohwada@ia.noda.tus.ac.jp

Abstract

Recent advances in automatic knowledge acquisition methods have enabled us to construct massive knowledge bases of semantic relations. Most previous work has focused on semantic relations explicitly expressed in single sentences. Our goal in this work is to obtain valid *non-single sentence* relation instances, which are not written in any single sentence and may not be even written in a large corpus. We develop a method to infer new semantic relation instances by applying auto-discovered inference rules, and show that our method inferred a considerable number of valid instances that were not written in single sentences even in 600 million Web pages.

1 Introduction

Recent advances in automatic relation acquisition methods (Agichtein and Luis, 2001; Etzioni et al., 2004; Pantel and Pennacchiotti, 2006; Paşca et al., 2006; Banko and Etzioni, 2008; De Saeger et al., 2009) have opened the way to build large knowledge bases containing a huge number of semantic relation instances such as "CAUSE(*allergen*, *allergy*)" and "PREVENTION(*coffee*, *drowsiness*)". Such a massive knowledge base is valuable for applications like innovation and risk management (Torisawa et al., 2010), like finding potential and unexpected causes of a disease, unknown side-effects of a drug, and so on. In such tasks overlooking a small piece of information can have grave consequences.

In this work, our goal is to acquire *Non-single Sentence relation instances* (**NS instances**), which are not written in any single sentences, in order to reduce the possibility of overlooking valuable information. More precisely, if the two nouns in an instance (e.g., "allergen" and "allergy" in "CAUSE(*allergen*, *allergy*)") do not appear in any single sentences in a given corpus together with the other clues indicating the relation type (e.g., the verb "cause"), the instance is an NS instance. *NS instances* may be *indirectly* written in a sequence of several sentences using anaphora or may not be written at all even in a given corpus. In the following, we call the complement of NS instances *Single Sentence relation instances* (**SS instances**), which consist of two nouns that co-occur in some single sentences in a given corpus together with some evidence for a relation type.

Most existing relation acquisition methods acquire relation instances using lexico-syntactic patterns (Pantel and Pennacchiotti, 2006; Paşca et al., 2006; De Saeger et al., 2009) such as "X causes Y" or probabilistic sequence labeling models (Banko and Etzioni, 2008). These methods basically rely on the structure of single sentences and they are for acquiring SS instances. Thus we consider that NS instances are practically beyond their reach. A few attempts to overcome this limitation include inference-based methods. These methods take SS instances provided by other methods as input and infer relation instances including NS ones using auto-discovered inference rules (Schoenmackers et al., 2010; Carlson et al., 2010) or distributional similarities (Tsuchida et al., 2010). We consider such inference approaches to be promising for acquiring NS instances.

This paper proposes an inference-based method for acquiring NS instances. We start from a set of *seed relation instances* of a target relation, which are acquired by an existing semi-supervised

*This work was done when the author was at the National Institute of Information and Communications Technology.

pattern-based method (De Saeger et al., 2009), and induce a large number of *recursive* inference rules to infer new relation instances. The instances inferred by the rules are ranked based on the scores assigned to the rules and the top instances are produced as final output.

Specifically, our method infers new instances of particular *target* relations by applying the following type of *recursive rules* to large corpora.

$$\text{"X } \textit{pattern} \text{ Y"} \wedge R_{\text{SEED}}(Y,Z) \rightarrow R_{\text{HYPO}}(X,Z)$$

Here, "X *pattern* Y" indicates that X and Y co-occur in a certain lexico-syntactic pattern, R_{SEED} (Y,Z) is one of the seed relation instances, and an inferred instance of the target relation is denoted by R_{HYPO} (X,Z). Though we distinguish R_{SEED} (Y,Z) and R_{HYPO} (X,Z) by the subscripts "SEED" and "HYPO", they are supposed to be the same target relation, and thus the rules are recursive. Note that this type of recursive rules could not be employed in an existing inference-based method (Schoenmackers et al., 2010) as described in Section 4.1.

For acquiring *NS instances*, rules combine patterns and relation instances ("X *pattern* Y" and R_{SEED} (Y,Z)) scattered throughout many distinct documents. The following is an example rule learned by our method.

$$\text{"X } \textit{is rich in} \text{ Y"} \wedge \text{PREVENTION}_{\text{SEED}}(Y,Z) \rightarrow \text{PREVENTION}_{\text{HYPO}}(X,Z)$$

This can be interpreted as: "If X *is rich in* Y and Y *prevents* Z, then X *prevents* Z.", and seems valid in many cases. An interesting example is that the rule generated the relation instance "PREVENTION(*X=blue-backed fish, Z=cerebral thrombosis*)" where "*Y=eicosapentaenoic acid*". This is a rather well-known fact in Japan these days, and you can find many Web pages stating this fact in early 2011. However, the words "*blue-backed fish*" and "*cerebral thrombosis*" do not co-occur in any four sentence window in the 600M Web page corpus used in our experiments, which was crawled in 2008. Thus, "PREVENTION(*blue-backed fish, cerebral thrombosis*)" is an NS instance and exemplifies the importance and necessity of inferring NS instances.

This example also introduces the idea underlying our evaluation scheme. Proper evaluation of new relation hypotheses that are not mentioned together in the extraction corpus would require verification by domain experts, which is clearly beyond our resources. We therefore evaluate new relation hypotheses using a larger and newer corpus (i.e. a commercial search engine), under the naive assumption that *correct* instances will be found in this bigger corpus. We realize this evaluation scheme cannot do justice to genuinely unknown instances but only gives a lowerbound of the true precision.

Through a series of experiments for acquiring three semantic relations, *causality*, *prevention*, and *material*, from a 600 million page Japanese Web corpus, we show that our method can infer *valid* NS instances. We also compare our method to the markov logic inference algorithm introduced in Schoenmackers et al. (2010) and show that our procedure, while considerably simpler, outperforms it.

2 Related Work

Previous work can be categorized into three groups: 1) methods for *extracting* SS instances (Etzioni et al., 2004; Pantel and Pennacchiotti, 2006; Paşca et al., 2006; Banko and Etzioni, 2008; De Saeger et al., 2009), 2) methods for *inferring* relation instances (Carlson et al., 2010; Schoenmackers et al., 2010; Tsuchida et al., 2010), and 3) work in bioinformatics aiming at helping users to discover unseen relation instances as novel knowledge (Swanson, 1986; Srinivasan, 2004; Hu et al., 2006; Hristovski et al., 2008).

The methods in the first category aim at extracting a large number of instances by employing automatically induced *paraphrases* of lexico-syntactic patterns or probabilistic sequence labeling methods. In this category, we focus on De Saeger et al. (2009), which is the seed instance extractor employed in this work. This takes *seed patterns*, such as "X causes Y", as input and learns a large amount of *paraphrase patterns* to extract relation instances from a corpus. Unlike other pattern-based methods, De Saeger et al. (2009) learns *class dependent paraphrase patterns*, which place semantic word class restrictions on the noun pairs they may extract, like "*X*:`chemical` causes *Y*:`disease`". These class restrictions enable to distinguish between multiple senses of frequent but highly ambiguous patterns. For instance, given a class *independent* pattern "X causes Y" as seed, if we restrict X and Y in "Y from X" to the classes of chemicals and diseases (as in "*cancer* from *cadmium*"), the class dependent pattern "*Y*:`disease` from *X*:`chemical`" becomes a valid paraphrase of "X causes Y". Note that, other class restrictions of the same pattern (e.g., "*Y*:`products` from *X*:`company`", as in "iPhone from Apple") may not yield a valid paraphrase of "X causes Y". To obtain word classes they use a large-scale word clustering algorithm (Kazama and Torisawa, 2008), and rank each instance in the corpus according to a score based on the semantic similarity between the seed patterns and each class dependent pattern the instance co-occurs with.

Although much work in this category successfully extracts the instances *implicitly* written in a single sentence based on a wide range of non-trivial evidence including paraphrases (e.g., "Y by X" for causality), the applicability of these methods is restricted to SS instances.

In the second category, Schoenmackers et al. (2010), which is the most relevant to our work, takes relation instances provided by TextRunner (Banko and Etzioni, 2008) as input and induces Horn clauses as inference rules. The weights of the rules and the probabilities of the hypothesized instances are estimated by a markov logic network (Richardson and Domingo, 2006; Huynh and Mooney, 2008). They also proposed a weighted counting method for discounting the effects of uncertain (or infrequent) instances, and a method for discounting weights of longer rules by strong Gaussian prior.

The goal of Schoenmackers et al. (2010) was to acquire *implicit* relation instances. Note that their "implicit" instances cover what we call SS and NS instances, while our target are only NS instances. For instance, they regarded the instances acquired by simple paraphrase rules such as "CAN_CAUSE(X,Y) $\rightarrow$ CAUSE(X,Y)" as *implicit instances*. For "CAUSE(a,b)" to be inferred by this rule, "CAN_CAUSE(a,b)" must be written in single sentences so that TextRunner can recognize it. This means that such instances are SS instances.

Actually their algorithm was tuned to prefer SS instances and around 70% of the acquired valid instances were in this category. Certainly, their method uses more complex rules that can infer NS instances, but the precision of the instances inferred by such non-paraphrase rules is quite low (around 20%) [1]. Also they have not empirically examined how many NS instances are actually found in their output.

In contrast, we focus on more complex rules that can infer NS instances. An important point is that their method cannot deal with considerable parts of our complex rules because their inference algorithm for markov logic network (Huynh and Mooney, 2008) poses some restrictions on recursive rules as discussed in Section 4.1. We also empirically show that their scoring mechanism does not lead to higher precision at least in our setting, although we have not checked whether this is due to the restrictions on recursive rules or is due to some other reasons.

Another work in this category, Carlson et al. (2010) hypothesized instances using Horn clauses discovered by Inductive Logic Programming (Quinlan and Cameron-Jones, 1993). Tsuchida et al. (2010) generates hypothesized relation instances by substituting words in seed instances with distributionally similar words.

In bioinformatics, there are attempts to develop methods to help discoveries of relation instances by linking clues from different literatures (Swanson, 1986; Srinivasan, 2004; Hu et al., 2006; Hristovski et al., 2008). These methods cannot be easily adapted to other domains, because they require heavily engineered resources like databases of MEDLINE records and hand-annotation with MeSH [2] metadata. These also require some input and/or interactions to capture the interests of the human expert. Our aim is to infer unseen NS instances without such resources and human effort.

Recently, De Saeger et al. (2011) have shown that it is possible to acquire SS instances from highly complex and infrequent expressions, using word classes and lexico-syntactic pattern fragments, which they call *partial patterns*. Such approach may prove useful for acquiring NS instances too, as the method can acquire relation instances without considering any pattern connecting the two words of the instance. Yet their work focused only on SS instances.

3 Proposed Method

Our method takes a set of seed relation instances and a large corpus as input. The seed instances are obtained using De Saeger et al. (2009), after some rudimentary cleaning (Section 4). Then, our method induces possible inference rules, and assigns scores to the instances inferred by the rules. The high-ranked instances are provided as output.

[1] They acquired a total 2.6M instances with 50% precision for a variety of relation types. Also, about 1.25M SS instances in those were inferred by simple paraphrase rules with 80% precision. The precision of the instances inferred by non-paraphrase rules can be estimated as the solution for $0.50 = \frac{1.25\times0.80+(2.6-1.25)\times x}{2.6}$ as x $(= 0.22)$.

[2] `http://www.nlm.nih.gov/mesh/`

In the following, we describe the details of each step. Note that the algorithm presented here can produce SS instances as well as NS instances. In the evaluation, *potential* SS instances are excluded from the output by checking the co-occurrence of the word pairs in the instances in single sentences.

3.1 Inducing Inference Rules

We consider inference rules (a special case of Horn-clauses) that have the following form:

$$\text{"X } \textit{pattern} \text{ Y"} \wedge \text{R}_{\text{SEED}}(\text{Y,Z}) \rightarrow \text{R}_{\text{HYPO}}(\text{X,Z})$$

This rule hypothesizes relation instances by substituting the first argument Y of a seed instance with X where the connection between X and Y is provided by "X *pattern* Y". [3] To handle multi-word expressions such as "*red wine*", we allow NP chunks to fill the slots of the X, Y or Z variables. Our motivation here is to have a more exhaustive set of relation instances for a given relation type. As a starting point we focus on the simple rules as the one above, although a wide range of other forms are possible. Sharing a variable (i.e. Y) guarantees that at least some relationship between X and Z holds and reduces the risk of generating meaningless rules, while the arbitrariness of the pattern allows us to consider a broad range of evidence to find new instances.

For inducing inference rules, first we find two seed instances that have the same second argument. Suppose that the target relation is causality, and we have two seed instances, CAUSE(*bronchitis*, *cough*) and CAUSE(*mold*, *cough*), with common second argument "*cough*". Then, we can search for "X *pattern* Y", which informs us of a certain relation between the first arguments of the two seed instances, *bronchitis* and *mold* in this example. We may be able to find "X causes Y" from the expression ".. *mold* causes *bronchitis* .." and induce the following rule that infers one seed instance from another seed instance.

$$\text{"}\textit{mold} \text{ causes } \textit{bronchitis}\text{"} \wedge \text{CAUSE}_{\text{SEED}}(\textit{bronchitis,cough}) \rightarrow \text{CAUSE}_{\text{HYPO}}(\textit{mold, cough})$$

By generalizing *mold*, *bronchitis*, and *cough* to variables X, Y and Z, we can obtain the following acceptable rule that can be interpreted as "if X is a cause of a cause (Y) of Z, X is a cause of Z".

$$\text{"X causes Y"} \wedge \text{CAUSE}_{\text{SEED}}(\text{Y,Z}) \rightarrow \text{CAUSE}_{\text{HYPO}}(\text{X,Z})$$

Here, by assuming that $\text{CAUSE}_{\text{HYPO}}$ (*bronchitis*, *cough*) is inferred from $\text{CAUSE}_{\text{SEED}}$ (*mold*, *cough*), we also obtain the following unacceptable rule, which contradicts with common sense.

$$\text{"Y causes X"} \wedge \text{CAUSE}_{\text{SEED}}(\text{Y,Z}) \rightarrow \text{CAUSE}_{\text{HYPO}}(\text{X,Z})$$

We can say that the former is a *swapped rule* of the latter and vice-versa. The above rule can be interpreted as "If Y is a cause of X and Z, then X is a cause of Z", which is nonsense. In Section 3.2.1, we introduce a heuristic to remove such unacceptable swapped rules.

To alleviate pattern ambiguity, all the patterns in the rules are *class dependent patterns* (Section 2). The induced rules are augmented with class restrictions on the variables in the pattern:

$$\text{"X:}\texttt{virus}\text{ causes Y:}\texttt{sickness}\text{"} \wedge \text{CAUSE}_{\text{SEED}}(\text{Y,Z}) \rightarrow \text{CAUSE}_{\text{HYPO}}(\text{X,Z})$$

As word classes for the class restrictions, we used a word clustering result obtained by applying a probabilistic word clustering algorithm (Kazama and Torisawa, 2008) to dependency relations extracted from 100M Web pages. The results are represented by the probability distribution $P(c|w)$ where w is a word (the number of words is 1M in this paper) and c is a class identifier, which is a hidden variable in a predefined set C.

To have a *discrete* boundary of class membership, we assume w belongs to class c if and only if $P(c|n) \geq 0.2$ or $c = \arg\max_{c \in C} P(c|n)$. We set $|C|$ to 500, following De Saeger et al. (2009). Also, the classes are just class identifiers (i.e., integers). To simplify the explanation, we omit these class restrictions in the rest of our paper.

Finally, to discard unproductive rules, all the rules that cannot generate more than M seed relation instances using the other seed instances are discarded. In this work, we set M to 10.

3.2 Scoring Hypothesized Instances

After inducing the rules, we hypothesize relation instances by applying the rules to an input corpus, and assign scores to the instances. *Instance score* for a hypothesized instance is defined as the sum of the scores of the rules that generated the instance. Rule score $r\_score(r)$ is an approximated precision of the instances inferred by the rule, assuming that the seed instances are *correct* relations and the others are not.

$$r\_score(r) = \frac{\text{\# of seeds in hypotheses by } r}{\text{\# of hypotheses by } r}$$

[3]We also consider the rules where Z appears as the first arguments, i.e., "X *pattern* Y" $\wedge$ $\text{R}_{\text{SEED}}(\text{Z,Y}) \rightarrow \text{R}_{\text{HYPO}}(\text{Z,X})$.

Here, r is an inference rule.

Instance score h_score is defined as the sum of the applicable rule scores.

$$h\_score(h) = \sum_{r \in \mathbf{Irules}(h,\mathbf{Seeds},\mathbf{Rules})} r\_score(r)$$

Here, h is a hypothesized instance, and **Rules** is a set of inference rules. **Seeds** is a set of seed relation instances, and **Irules** is a set of rules in **Rules** that infer h from **Seeds**.

We use the following additional heuristics during this ranking scheme.

3.2.1 Removing unacceptable swapped rules

The first heuristic is introduced for removing unacceptable swapped rules. Recall that our inference rule always has its swapped rule like the following two example rules.

A "X causes Y" $\wedge$ $\text{CAUSE}_{\text{SEED}}$ (Y, Z) $\rightarrow$ $\text{CAUSE}_{\text{HYPO}}$ (X, Z)

B "Y causes X" $\wedge$ $\text{CAUSE}_{\text{SEED}}$ (Y, Z) $\rightarrow$ $\text{CAUSE}_{\text{HYPO}}$ (X, Z)

Here, we have three observations: 1) if one rule is acceptable, its swapped rule is not (e.g., rule A is acceptable but rule B is not), 2) if a rule often generates reflexive relation instances, i.e., R_{HYPO} (x,x) for some word "x", the rule is likely to be unacceptable, and 3) the swapped rule of such an unacceptable rule (like rule B) often represents a transitive relation. For example, above rule A represents a transitive relation for causality (X $\rightarrow$ Y $\rightarrow$ Z then X $\rightarrow$ Z). On the other hand, the seed instance and the pattern in rule B represent that the same cause Y results in X and Z. If the seed instance and the pattern represents the same causal relation instance, $\text{CAUSE}_{\text{HYPO}}$ (X,Z) becomes $\text{CAUSE}_{\text{HYPO}}$ (x,x).

We found that rules generating many R_{HYPO} (x,x) attain a high score in our rule scoring. To remedy this we set $r\_score(r)$ to 0 if r generates more R_{HYPO} (x,x) than its swapped version. If the two rules do not generate R_{HYPO} (x,x) or the number of R_{HYPO} (x,x) by the two rules are the same, this is not applied. We refer to this as (X,X)-based rule filtering hereafter.

3.2.2 Excluding highly vague words

Our inference rules are based on *pivot* words, i.e., the shared variable Y in "X pattern Y $\wedge$ R_{SEED}(Y,Z) $\rightarrow$ R_{HYPO}(X,Z)". If the pivot is so vague that it likely refers to different objects in the seed and the pattern, the inference would be wrong (Schoenmackers et al., 2010). For example, we can generate false hypothesis $\text{CAUSE}_{\text{HYPO}}$ (*cerebral stroke*, *pneumonia*) from "*cerebral stroke* causes *disease*" and $\text{CAUSE}_{\text{SEED}}$ (*disease*, *pneumonia*). Here "*disease*" is highly vague, and likely refers to different types of diseases in different texts.

To address this problem we prepared a stop word list and discarded relation instances that contain one of these stop words. We calculate the document frequency of each word in the 600M page Web corpus, and regard a word whose document frequency is higher than threshold T as a stop word. We set T to 400,000 and obtain about 15,000 stop words in our experiments.

4 Evaluation

Our evaluation focuses on three main questions: 1) How accurate are the *NS instances* hypothesized by our method? 2) How accurate are all the instances hypothesized by our method? 3) Does our method infer relation instances with higher precision than competing methods? After explaining the experimental setting we answer each question from our experimental results. We also analyze the cause of errors at the end of this section.

4.1 Experimental Setting

We evaluated our results on the three relations:

***Causality*(X,Y):** X can directly or indirectly cause Y. e.g., CAUSE(*allergen*, *allergy*).

***Prevention*(X,Y):** X can directly or indirectly help to avoid the occurrence of Y. e.g., PREVENTION(*coffee*, *drowsiness*).

***Material*(X,Y)** X is a material or ingredient of Y. e.g., MATERIAL(*grape*, *wine*).

We employed the evaluation scheme introduced in Tsuchida et al. (2010). To evaluate the correctness of a given hypothesized instance, we presented three human judges with short texts as possible evidence. For each hypothesized instance, we collected up to 20 short texts from the search results provided by Yahoo! API [4] for a query consisting of the two nouns and a priming term for each target relation, i.e., the Japanese word for "*cause*", "*material*" or "*prevention*". All texts were collected from February to the middle of March in 2011.

The expectation behind this scheme is that many of correct *NS instances* in a smaller corpus,

[4] http://developer.yahoo.co.jp/webapi/search/

i.e., the 600M page Web corpus, can be found with explicit evidence in a larger corpus, i.e., pages accessible through a commercial search engine.

In our evaluation scheme, our three annotators mark a hypothesized instance as correct if they find "sufficient evidence" (see below) in at least one of the presented text snippets. We say a text snippet contains "sufficient evidence" if it either explicitly asserts the target relation between the word pair, or implicitly presupposes it. A hypothesized instance is judged incorrect when 1) the provided texts do not present sufficient evidence, or 2) a relation instance is not informative enough without further context (e.g., CAUSE(*insulin, change*), we don't know what *change* can be caused by *insulin* without further context). Correctness of a hypothesized instance is determined by the judges' majority vote. The inter-rater agreement (Fleiss' kappa) was 0.57 for causality, 0.56 for prevention and 0.57 for material, indicating the judgements are reasonably stable.

For each relation, the seed instances were the top 20,000 instances given by our implementation of De Saeger et al. (2009) with the class-based cleaning that took about 15 minutes. More precisely, we discarded inappropriate instances by manually identifying and removing semantic classes that are inappropriate for the target relation. The precision of the seed instances was 81% for *causality* , 78% for *material* and 44% for *prevention*. We used about 25 seed patterns for each relation, which were created by one of the authors with one hour tuning. We show some examples of the seed patterns (translated from Japanese).

***Causality*(X,Y)** "X causes Y", "Y caused by X", "X that causes Y", ...

***Prevention*(X,Y)** "X prevents Y", "Y prevented by X", "X that prevents Y", ...

***Material*(X,Y)** "X is material of Y", "Y made from X", "X that is material of Y", ...

From the seed instances, our method induced 24,044 rules for causality, 17,868 for prevention and 14,978 for material, and obtained 3.04M hypothesized instances for causality, 2.44M for prevention and 2.17M for material. These hypothesized instances do not include the seed instances. Table 1 shows some hypothesized instances.

In our experiments we compared three systems.

SUM: Proposed method.

MLN: Markov logic network based scoring method of Schoenmackers et al. (2010).

MLN(X,X): MLN with the weight of the rules removed by (X,X)-based rule filtering set to 0.

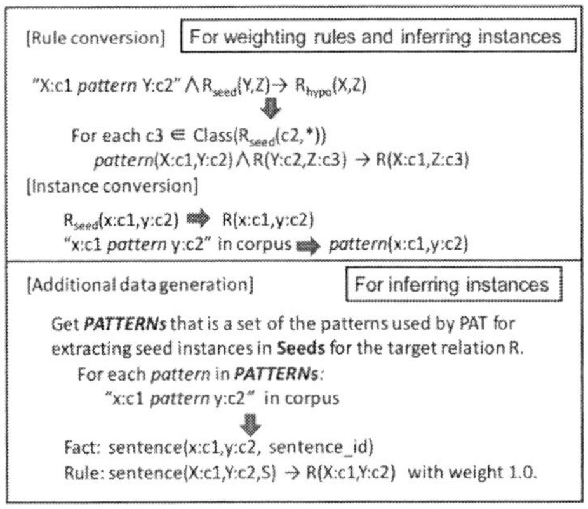

Figure 1: Data generation for MLN. X, Y and Z are variables, x, y and z are nouns. c1, c2 and c3 are noun classes, and Class(R_{SEED} $(c, *)$) is a set of classes, c_i, for which some R_{SEED} (y:c, z:c_i) exists. "x:c" indicates that x belongs to class c, and "X:c" means that X restricts possible nouns by class c.

We do not compare our method to Carlson et al. (2010), since Schoenmackers et al. (2010) already showed that MLN outperforms that method.

In preparing MLN, we converted our rules to the format used in Schoenmackers et al. (2010) as shown in Figure 1. Unlike our method, all rule variables in their work have class (or hypernym) restrictions, and predicates with different argument classes are treated as different. Truly recursive rules that have the same predicate with the same class restrictions in both head and body were removed due to limitations in their inference algorithm.[5] We removed 10,944 rules for causality (46% of all rules), 8,614 (48%) for prevention and 7,074 (47%) for material, respectively. When inferring instances, we also generated the additional rules and facts (lower half of Figure 1) that reflect their assumption that an instance frequently extracted from single sentences is likely to be true. Also, we empirically set the standard deviations of the Gaussian prior for learning rule weights and the prior weight of all unknown facts for inference to 2.0 and -3.0. We did not use the variable Gaussian prior to discount the weights of longer rules, because the lengths of all our rules are the same.

4.2 Evaluation Results

For SUM, MLN and MLN(X,X), we investigated the precision of the top 10,000 *NS instances* —

[5] The freely available inference system for markov logic Alchemy (`http://alchemy.cs.washington.edu/`) allows recursive rules, but turned out to be too slow for practical use. In our experiments we gave up on it after waiting more than a week for the program to finish.

Table 1: Examples of evaluated hypothesized instances and the rules that inferred the instances (translated from Japanese). The meaning of "N4S" is described in Section 4.2. All the instances marked with"NS", "N4S" and "SS" were judged as *correct*. "*UR" marks incorrect instances generated by *unacceptable rules*. "*AR" denotes incorrect instances generated by *acceptable rules*. "*NE" denotes instances having *no evidence* in the provided texts, though we expected that the instances may be correct based on their original rules and seed instances. For simplicity, we omit the class restrictions of rules.

	Label	Inferred instance	Samples of rules that generated the left hypothesized instance.
Causality	N4S	CAUSE$_{HYPO}$ (Z=*SO2 gas*, X=*allergy symptoms*), Y= *asthma*	CAUSE$_{HYPO}$ (Z,X) ← **X** *is caused by* **Y** ∧ CAUSE$_{SEED}$ (Z,Y) CAUSE$_{HYPO}$ (Z,X) ← **X** *gets worse by* **Y** ∧ CAUSE$_{SEED}$ (Z,Y)
	NS	CAUSE$_{HYPO}$ (X=*reactive oxygen species*, Z=*aneurysm*), Y=*high blood pressure*	CAUSE$_{HYPO}$ (X,Z) ← **X**'*s increase causes* **Y** ∧ CAUSE$_{SEED}$ (Y,Z) CAUSE$_{HYPO}$ (X,Z) ← **X** *is a cause of* **Y** ∧ CAUSE$_{SEED}$ (Y,Z)
	SS	CAUSE$_{HYPO}$ (X=*pesticide*, Z=*colorectal cancer*), Y=*harmful substance*	CAUSE$_{HYPO}$ (X,Z) ← **Y** *is contained in* **X** ∧ CAUSE$_{SEED}$ (Y,Z) CAUSE$_{HYPO}$ (X,Z) ← **X** *is called* **Y** ∧ CAUSE$_{SEED}$ (Y,Z)
	*UR	CAUSE$_{HYPO}$ (X=*bilirubin*, Z=*colorectal cancer*) Y=*bile*	CAUSE$_{HYPO}$ (X,Z) ← **X** *is contained in* **Y** ∧ CAUSE$_{SEED}$ (Y,Z) CAUSE$_{HYPO}$ (X,Z) ← **X** *is excreted in* **Y** ∧ CAUSE$_{SEED}$ (Y,Z)
	*AR	CAUSE$_{HYPO}$ (Z=*potato crisp*, X=*atherosclerosis*) Y=*lifestyle diseases*	CAUSE$_{HYPO}$ (Z,X) ← **Y** *is a cause of* **X** ∧ CAUSE$_{SEED}$ (Z,Y) CAUSE$_{HYPO}$ (Z,X) ← **X** *caused by* **Y** ∧ CAUSE$_{SEED}$ (Z,Y)
	*AR	CAUSE$_{HYPO}$ (X=*tobacco*, Z=*food poisoning*) Y=*harmful component*	CAUSE$_{HYPO}$ (X,Z) ← **Y** *contained in* **X** ∧ CAUSE$_{SEED}$ (Y,Z) CAUSE$_{HYPO}$ (X,Z) ← **X** *contains* **Y** ∧ CAUSE$_{SEED}$ (Y,Z)
	*NE	CAUSE$_{HYPO}$ (Z=*magnesium chloride*, X=*atherosclerosis*) Y=*high blood pressure*	CAUSE$_{HYPO}$ (Z,X) ← **X** *gets worse by* **Y** ∧ CAUSE$_{SEED}$ (Z,Y) CAUSE$_{HYPO}$ (Z,X) ← **Y** *triggers* **X** ∧ CAUSE$_{SEED}$ (Z,Y)
Prevention	N4S	PREVENTION$_{HYPO}$ (X=*blue-backed fish*, Z=*cerebral thrombosis*), Y=*eicosapentaenoic acid*	PREVENTION$_{HYPO}$ (X,Z) ← **Y** *is extracted from* **X** ∧ PREVENTION$_{SEED}$ (Y,Z) PREVENTION$_{HYPO}$ (X,Z) ← **X** *is rich in* **Y** ∧ PREVENTION$_{SEED}$ (Y,Z)
	NS	PREVENTION$_{HYPO}$ (Z=*sunflower oil*,X=*heart disease*), Y=*high blood pressure*, Y1=*linoleic acid*	PREVENTION$_{HYPO}$ (Z,X) ← **X** *is caused by* **Y** ∧ PREVENTION$_{SEED}$ (Z,Y) PREVENTION$_{HYPO}$ (Z,X) ← **Y1** *is contained in* **Z** ∧ PREVENTION$_{SEED}$ (Y1,X)
	SS	PREVENTION$_{HYPO}$ (X=*sesame lignan*, Z=*cerebral stroke*), Y=*antioxidant effects*,Y1=*high blood pressure*	PREVENTION$_{HYPO}$ (X,Z) ← **X** *having* **Y** ∧ PREVENTION$_{SEED}$ (Y,Z) PREVENTION$_{HYPO}$ (X,Z) ← **Y1** *gives rise to* **Z** ∧ PREVENTION$_{SEED}$ (X,Y1)
	*UR	PREVENTION$_{HYPO}$ (Z=*niacin*, X=*kidney disease*), Y=*high blood pressure*	PREVENTION$_{HYPO}$ (Z,X) ← **Y** *is accompanied by* **X** ∧ PREVENTION$_{SEED}$ (Z,Y) PREVENTION$_{HYPO}$ (Z,X) ← **X** *is a cause of* **Y** ∧ PREVENTION$_{SEED}$ (Z,Y)
	*NE	PREVENTION$_{HYPO}$ (Z=*egg*, X=*dizziness*), Y=*anemia*, Y1=*iron*	PREVENTION$_{HYPO}$ (Z,X) ← **X** *is caused by* **Y** ∧ PREVENTION$_{SEED}$ (Z,Y) PREVENTION$_{HYPO}$ (Z,X) ← **Z** *contains* **Y1** ∧ PREVENTION$_{SEED}$ (Y1,X)
Material	N4S	MATERIAL$_{HYPO}$ (X=*red grape*, Z=*cuvee*), Y=*pinot noir*	MATERIAL$_{HYPO}$ (X,Z) ← **X** *such as* **Y** ∧ MATERIAL$_{SEED}$ (Y,Z) MATERIAL$_{HYPO}$ (X,Z) ← **X** *including* **Y** ∧ MATERIAL$_{SEED}$ (Y,Z)
	NS	MATERIAL$_{HYPO}$ (Z=*sugar beet*, X=*hydrogen*), Y=*ethanol*	MATERIAL$_{HYPO}$ (Z,X) ← **X** *is extracted from* **Y** ∧ MATERIAL$_{SEED}$ (Z,Y) MATERIAL$_{HYPO}$ (Z,X) ← **Y** *is converted into* **X** ∧ MATERIAL$_{SEED}$ (Z,Y)
	SS	MATERIAL$_{HYPO}$ (Z=*corn*, X=*ethylene*), Y=*ethanol*	MATERIAL$_{HYPO}$ (Z,X) ← **X** *is made from* **Y** ∧ MATERIAL$_{SEED}$ (Z,Y) MATERIAL$_{HYPO}$ (Z,X) ← **Y** *is material of* **X** ∧ MATERIAL$_{SEED}$ (Z,Y)
	*UR	MATERIAL$_{HYPO}$ (Z=*blueberry*, X= *plain yogurt*), Y=*blueberry jelly*	MATERIAL$_{HYPO}$ (Z,X) ← **Y** *is mixed in* **X** ∧ MATERIAL$_{SEED}$ (Z,Y) MATERIAL$_{HYPO}$ (Z,X) ← *put* **Y** *in* **X** ∧ MATERIAL$_{SEED}$ (Z,Y)
	*AR	MATERIAL$_{HYPO}$ (X=*sugarcane*, Z= *zero-emisions vehicle*), Y=*ethanol*	MATERIAL$_{HYPO}$ (X,Z) ← **Y** *extracted from* **X** ∧ MATERIAL$_{SEED}$ (Y,Z) MATERIAL$_{HYPO}$ (X,Z) ← **Y** *made from* **X** ∧ MATERIAL$_{SEED}$ (Y,Z)

Table 2: Results from the binomial one-tailed test between SUM and the other methods. The significance level is 0.05. For each relation, cells show the number of data points (8 max) in the precision graph (like Figure 3) where "SUM wins / SUM loses / no significant difference".

	MLN(X,X)	MLN	MAX	No (X,X) filtering	No rule score
Causality	0 / 0 / 8	6 / 0 / 2	8 / 0 / 0	6 / 0 / 2	3 / 0 / 5
Prevention	8 / 0 / 0	7 / 0 / 1	6 / 0 / 2	0 / 0 / 8	0 / 0 / 8
Material	7 / 0 / 1	7 / 0 / 1	1 / 0 / 7	8 / 0 / 0	2 / 0 / 6

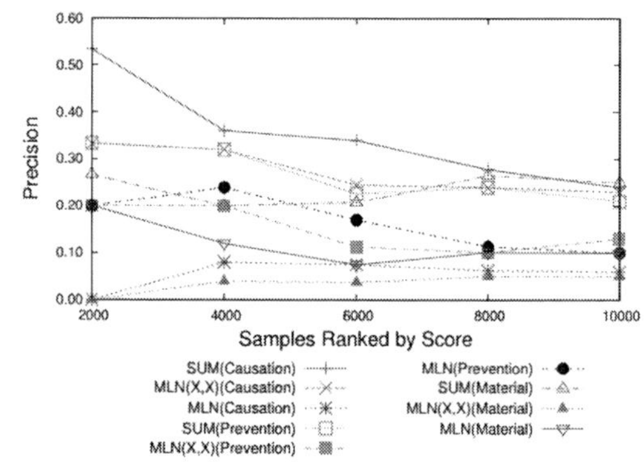

Figure 2: Precision of the top 10,000 NS instances.

word pairs that do not co-occur in any single sentence — using 100 random samples. The precision curves in Figure 2 show that SUM outperforms both MLN and MLN(X,X). Although the precision of the top 10,000 NS instances obtained by SUM is relatively low (20% to 30%), we do think this is a promising result given the difficulty of the task. In tasks such as innovation support and risk management, one must explore the border between the known and unknown. We expect even hypothesized instances with 20 to 30% precision can be useful in such contexts.

Next, we would like to address the question of how many acquired NS instances are not written in our corpus at all. Answering this question precisely is difficult because of anaphora and ellipsis. Therefore we assume that if the two nouns of an NS instance do not co-occur in any four sentence window ("N4S") in the corpus, the instance is unlikely to be mentioned explicitly in any form in the corpus. For causality, 44 of the 100 evaluated samples were N4S instances, 8 of which were correct

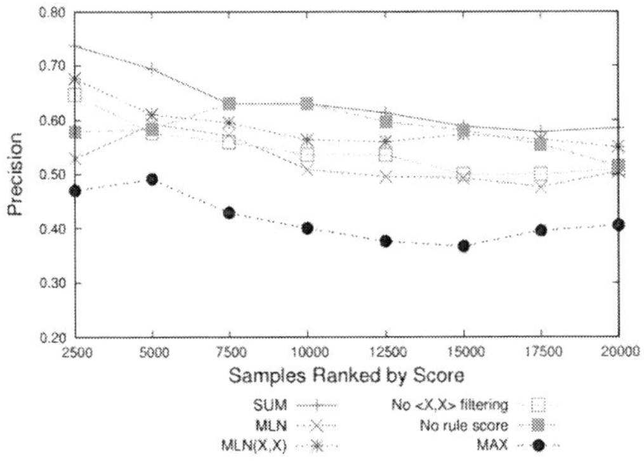

Figure 3: Causality: top 20,000 results' precision

(18% precision). The evaluated prevention and material samples respectively contained 22 and 35 N4S instances, with 2 and 8 correct ones (9% and 23% precision). We expect that at least some of these instances are not mentioned in our corpus.

To confirm the superiority of the proposed method, we investigated the precision of the top 20,000 instances of each method without removing SS instances from the evaluation data using 200 random samples. Our method showed 59% for causality (Fig. 3), 46% for prevention and 43% for material of the top 20,000 in precision, which is considerably higher than the precision of the NS samples only.

In addition to MLN and MLN(X,X) we also evaluated the following three baseline methods to confirm that all the design choices effectively contribute to the performance of our method.

No (X,X) filtering: SUM without (X,X)-based filtering.
No rule score: SUM, where all rule scores are constant.
MAX: A variant of the instance scoring function, $\max_{r \in \mathbf{Irules}(h,\mathbf{Seeds},\mathbf{Rules})} r\_score(r)$.

Figure 3 shows the precision curves for causality. In all relations SUM outperforms MLN, MLN(X,X) and all baseline methods. Table 2 shows the results of the binomial one-tailed test between SUM and each compared method, and suggests that SUM had statistically significant improvements in many cases. SUM showed only minor improvements compared with "No rule score". This suggests that the instances inferred by *many* rules tend to be correct, irrespective of the rule scores. We think this is due to the overall quality of the rules, as this would not be the case if many rules were invalid. Table 2 also shows that for transitive relations (causality and material), (X,X)-based rule filtering is effective.

4.3 Error Analysis

Table 1 shows some instances hypothesized by the proposed method. We distinguish between incorrect instances generated by unacceptable rules (marked "*UR" in Table 1) and others. We found that about 60% of incorrect instances are generated by unacceptable rules. For example, "$\text{CAUSE}_{\text{HYPO}}$ (X=*bilirubin*, Z=*colorectal cancer*)" was generated by the rule "$\text{CAUSE}_{\text{HYPO}}$ (X,Z) ← X *is contained in* Y ∧ $\text{CAUSE}_{\text{SEED}}$ (Y,Z)".

Incorrect instances generated by seemingly correct rules are marked with "*AR" in Table 1. These can further be categorized into three types (examples of each are in Table 1).

Type A: Uninformative instances for our evaluation criteria (See Section 4.1).
e.g., $\text{CAUSE}_{\text{HYPO}}$ (Z=*potato crisps*, X=*atherosclerosis*). The validity of this instance depends on context, i.e., the amount of potato crisps that one eats.

Type B: Instances generated with vague pivot words (See Section 3.2.2).
e.g., $\text{CAUSE}_{\text{HYPO}}$ (X=*tobacco*, Z=*food poisoning*), Y=*harmful component*. *harmful component* is vague.

Type C: Instances generated from incorrect seed instances.
e.g., $\text{MATERIAL}_{\text{HYPO}}$ (X=*sugarcane*, Z=*zero-emissions vehicle*), derived from the incorrect seed instance $\text{MATERIAL}_{\text{SEED}}$ (Y=*ethanol*, Z=*zero-emisions vehicle*).

The ratio was roughly 10% for type **A**, 5% for type **B** and 5% for type **C** for all the relation types. For the remaining incorrect instances (about 20%), the judges could not find sufficient evidence in the presented text snippets, although some such instances do appear to be valid. Such instances are marked "*NE". This suggests our evaluation scheme may be underestimating the true precision.

5 Conclusion

This paper introduced an inference-based method that takes a set of seed relation instances as input, and outputs hypothesized instances using inference rules induced from these seed instances.

We showed that our method can infer valid relation instances whose component nouns do not cooccur in any single sentence or any four sentence window even in a 600M page Web corpus. We expect this result is promising for inferring new knowledge, because such instances may contain instances not mentioned in the context of that particular semantic relation even in 600M Web pages.

Acknowledgments

The authors thank Dr. Tuyen N. Huynh of SRI International, who kindly provided the source code of Huynh and Mooney (2008) for our experiments.

References

Eugene Agichtein and Gravano Luis. 2001. Snowball: Extracting Relations from Large Plain-Text Collections. In *Proc. of the 5th ICDL*, pages 85–94.

Michele Banko and Oren Etzioni. 2008. The tradeoffs between open and traditional relation extraction. In *Proc. of the 46th ACL-08:HLT*, pages 28–36.

Andrew Carlson, Justin Betteridge, Bryan Kisiel, Burr Settles, Estevam R. Hruschka Jr., and Tom M. Mitchell. 2010. Toward an architecture for never-ending language learning. In *Proc of the 24th AAAI*, pages 1306–1313.

Stijn De Saeger, Kentaro Torisawa, Jun'ichi Kazama, Kow Kuroda, and Masaki Murata. 2009. Large Scale Relation Acquisition Using Class Dependent Patterns. In *Proc. of the 9th ICDM*, pages 764–769.

Stijn De Saeger, Kentaro Torisawa, Masaaki Tsuchida, Junfichi Kazama, Chikara Hashimoto, Ichiro Yamada, Jong-Hoon Oh, Istvan Varga, and Yulan Yan. 2011. Relation Acquisition using Word Classes and Partial Patterns. In *Proc. of the EMNLP2011*, pages 825–835.

Oren Etzioni, Michael Cafarella, Doug Downey, Stanley Kok, Ana-Maria Popescu, Tal Shaked, Stephen Soderland, Daniel S. Weld, and Alexander Yates. 2004. Web-Scale Information Extraction in Knowitall (Preliminary Results). In *Proc. of the 13th WWW*, pages 100–110.

D. Hristovski, C. Friedman, T. C. Rindflesch, and B. Peterlin. 2008. Literature-Based Knowledge Discovery using Natural Language Processing. *Literature-based Discovery, Information Science and Knowledge Management*, 15:133–152.

Xiaouha Hu, Xiaodan Zhang, Illhoi Yoo, and Yanqing Zhang. 2006. A semantic approach for mining hidden links from complementary and non-interactive biomedical literature. In *Proc. of the 6th SDM*, pages 200–209.

Tuyen N. Huynh and Raymond J. Mooney. 2008. Discriminative structure and parameter learning for markov logic networks. In *Proc. of the 25th ICML*, pages 416–423.

Jun'ichi Kazama and Kentaro Torisawa. 2008. Inducing Gazetteers for Named Entity Recognition by Large-scale Clustering of Dependency Relations. In *Proc. of the 46th ACL*, pages 407–415.

Marius Paşca, Dekang Lin, Jeffrey Bigham, Andrei Lifchits, and Alpa Jain. 2006. Names and Similarities on the Web: Fact Extraction in the Fast Lane. In *Proc. of the COLING-ACL06*, pages 809–816.

Patrick Pantel and Marco Pennacchiotti. 2006. Espresso: Leveraging generic patterns for automatically harvesting semantic relations. In *Proc. of the COLING-ACL06*, pages 113–120.

J. R. Quinlan and R. M. Cameron-Jones. 1993. FOIL: A Midterm Report. In *Proc. of the ECML*, pages 3–20.

Matthew Richardson and Pedro Domingo. 2006. Markov logic networks. *Machine Learning*, 26:107–136.

Stefan Schoenmackers, Oren Etzioni, Daniel S. Weld, and Jesse Davis. 2010. Learning first-order horn clauses from web text. In *Proc. of EMNLP2010*, pages 1088–1098.

Padmini Srinivasan. 2004. Text mining: generating hypotheses from medline. *Journal of the American Society for Information Science and Technology*, 55(5):396–413.

Don R. Swanson. 1986. Undiscovered public knowledge. *Library Quarterly*, 56(2):103–118.

Kentaro Torisawa, Stijn De Saeger, Jun'ichi Kazama, Asuka Sumida, Daisuke Noguchi, Yasunari Kakizawa, Masaaki Murata, Kow Kuroda, and Ichiro Yamada. 2010. Organizing the web's information explosion to discover unknown unknowns. *New Generation Computing*, 28(3):217–236.

Masaaki Tsuchida, Stijn De Saeger, Kentaro Torisawa, Masaki Murata, Jun'ichi Kazama, Kow Kuroda, and Hayato Ohwada. 2010. Large scale similarity-based relation exapnsion. In *Proc of the 4th IUCS*, pages 140–147.

Fleshing it out: A Supervised Approach to MWE-token and MWE-type Classification

Richard Fothergill and Timothy Baldwin
Department of Computer Science and Software Engineering
The University of Melbourne
VIC 3010 Australia
r.fothergill@student.unimelb.edu.au, tb@ldwin.net

Abstract

Although some multiword expressions (MWEs) like *How do you do?* have exclusively idiomatic meaning, other MWE-types like the phrase *kick the bucket* may be idiomatic or literal depending on context. The recently developed *OpenMWE* corpus provides the largest freely available collection of annotated MWE-tokens suitable for supervised classification, but so far its potential has only been superficially investigated and only for classification of MWE-types in the corpus. Instead, we train and evaluate classifiers for crosstype classification and introduce novel features specialised to this task. Our best crosstype classifiers performed as well on non-trained MWE-types as a majority class baseline which has knowledge of the MWE-type.

1 Introduction

A **multiword expression (MWE)** is an idiosyncratically interpreted linguistic unit which consists of more than a single word (or "crosses word boundaries") (Sag et al., 2002; Baldwin and Kim, 2009). The nature of these idiosyncrasies can vary greatly — from *traffic light* and *street light* which are remarkable only in that they are not interchangeable — to *how do you do?*, the meaning of which is non-compositional in modern English.

MWEs will typically resist lexico-syntactic variation to some extent (Fazly et al., 2009). For example, the phrase *a picture is worth a thousand words* does not allow the freedom of lexical substitution and modification that its constituent words would usually enjoy, making otherwise equivalent variations — *an image is worth fifty score words*, *a picture is worth approximately a thousand words* — sound wrong or at least unnatural to a native speaker.

The meaning of a MWE as a whole may not derive literally from the composition of its constituent words (Baldwin et al., 2003). For example, the English expression *kick the bucket* may be used to refer to *death* in any number of ways unrelated to either kicking or buckets. In these cases we say the MWE has an idiomatic interpretation.

When talking about MWEs we make a distinction between an MWE lexeme out of context, which we call an **MWE-type**, and specific instances of the MWE in context, which we call an **MWE-token**.

Some MWE-types have only an idiomatic meaning, such as the English greeting *How do you do?*, interpretation of which can be perplexing if attempted literally. However for others, the literal uses are still perfectly valid, and individual MWE-tokens may be ambiguous between an idiomatic and literal meaning. For example, *kick the bucket* may indeed refer to a violent act against a bucket and have nothing to do with death at all.

Relation to Word Sense Disambiguation

MWE-token disambiguation can be approached as if it were a word sense disambiguation (WSD) task where the MWE-types correspond to word types and MWE-tokens to word tokens (Hashimoto and Kawahara, 2009). In this conception, the analogue of word senses are the idiomatic and literal classes for an MWE-type.

In WSD, supervised methods are by far the most successful but large amounts of data are required for *each* word type to be disambiguated (Navigli, 2009). However, unlike in WSD, we can expect to find *some* linguistic commonality between the idiomatic senses of distinct MWE-types. This leads us to hope for more general **crosstype** classification algorithms, which might alleviate the knowledge acquisition bottleneck. In this paper we will refer to WSD (more specifically "word expert") style classification of ambiguous MWE-tokens as **type-specialised** classification.

The **first sense** or **majority class** baseline, in which a word is always labelled with its predominant sense, is known to perform very well at WSD due to a Zipfian distribution of senses (Preiss et al., 2009). We expect no different for the MWE-token disambiguation task where the two-class problem is virtually guaranteed a majority class baseline accuracy of over 50%. There has been work in unsupervised first sense learning for WSD using lexical resources (McCarthy et al., 2007), but the de facto baseline in WSD is a supervised first sense baseline (Navigli, 2009). We make use of a **type-specialised baseline**, which is a supervised majority class baseline modelled on the WSD first sense baseline. We also introduce a **corpus baseline** which, calculated based on idiomatic and literal counts of a collection of MWE-types, is the type-specialised baseline's crosstype analogue.

Our Contribution

In this paper we explore the supervised classification of ambiguous MWE-tokens using the *OpenMWE* corpus of Japanese idioms (Hashimoto and Kawahara, 2009). We introduce new features tailored to the crosstype classification task and refine features for type-specialised classification. To our knowledge, our experiments are the largest in supervised MWE-token classification to date. We explore more deeply the interaction between several aspects of the task, including differences between crosstype and type-specialised classification; combinations of major classes of features; and finally, the size of the training corpus.

We find that:

1. Our new WSD inspired features offer consistent improvements in performance, and our new idiom features usually offer marginal improvements. The extended WSD and idiom features used together for type-specialised classification yield state-of-the-art results in terms of raw performance.

2. Our new features for crosstype classification interact with the task and with other features in interesting ways, and in some cases give substantial improvements to performance.

3. Our best results in crosstype classification use *only* our extended WSD features. Despite using no tagged data for the target MWE-types, they achieved a performance in excess of the (supervised) type-specialised baseline.

This last result is significant because it demonstrates the readiness of our crosstype classifiers to work on previously unseen MWE-types. It is also interesting because it uses only semantic features and none of the lexico-syntactic fixedness features widely expected to be effective for MWE classification (Fazly et al., 2009; Hashimoto et al., 2006; Li and Sporleder, 2010).

2 Related Work

The *OpenMWE* corpus was compiled by Hashimoto and Kawahara (2009). To our knowledge it is by far the largest freely available gold-standard corpus of ambiguous MWE-tokens in any language, comprising 146 ambiguous MWE-types with 102,856 annotated MWE-tokens in total.

Apart from the enormous task of constructing the *OpenMWE* corpus, Hashimoto and Kawahara (2009) also used it to perform some experiments with supervised MWE-token classification. Noting the similarities between this task and WSD, they employed the most effective WSD features and machine learning algorithm surveyed by Lee and Ng (2002). They also included linguistic features explored by Hashimoto et al. (2006) designed to capture the relative fixedness of Japanese idioms, which we will refer to as idiom features. The machine learning algorithm used was *Support Vector Machines* and models were trained on the WSD features with various combinations of the idiom features. Type-specialised classifiers were trained for the 90 MWE-types which were deemed to have sufficient idiomatic and literal examples in the corpus. The model trained on WSD features was found to improve greatly on the type-specialised baseline, with some additional performance added by one of the idiom features.

Only being able to classify MWE-tokens of the 90 MWEs with sufficient training examples is a severe limitation on the usefulness of type-specialised classifiers in natural language processing applications. Our goal is to escape this limitation by training classifiers which work on MWE-types on which they have not been trained. To that end, we have extended the features used by Hashimoto and Kawahara (2009) with complementary features and introduced a new class of features designed for crosstype classification.

Li and Sporleder (2010) conducted a thorough investigation of features used for supervised MWE-token classification. Context features similar to the WSD features of Hashimoto and Kawahara (2009) were used, as were a number of linguistically motivated features. Like us, Li and Sporleder (2010) performed crosstype classification. Unfortunately many of the features were too sparse to have a significant effect and only the context features produced significant results. This may have been due to the relatively small size of the corpus used, which comprised around 4000 MWE-tokens across 13 MWE-types. In our results the context features still dominate, but the effects of idiom based features can be seen and those features hold up well on their own as well.

Diab and Bhutada (2009) described a novel supervised MWE-token classification system based on a sequence labelling model. Unlike our method, their model identifies the position of the token in the text as part of the process. Like Li and Sporleder (2010), the size of the corpus is small (2500 MWE-tokens of 53 MWE-types), and classifiers were trained on collections of MWE-types. Anecdotally, the classifiers were able to pick some MWEs out of running text without even knowing their constituents beforehand, however their performance at this was not tested. A major finding of Diab and Bhutada (2009) was that reducing the feature space of context features by replacing word lemmas with their named-entity category had a significant positive effect on classification performance, a finding that is consolidated by Diab and Krishna (2009).

Fazly et al. (2009) observed that idiomatic uses of MWEs tend to occur in one of a small set of canonical forms, and developed an unsupervised method for learning these canonical forms, based on a set of linguistically-motivated features which built on the work of Cook et al. (2007). They applied the learned set of canonical forms to the task of MWE-token identification with remarkable success. Our method similarly uses linguistically-motivated features to perform MWE-token identification, but using a cross-type supervised model.

3 Feature Extraction

We extracted features in three main groups: WSD features, idiom (token) features and idiom type features. The first two categories include the features used by Hashimoto and Kawahara (2009) and our own extensions. The third category was introduced by us and is specialised to crosstype classification.

3.1 Preprocessing

Our feature extraction makes extensive use of the Japanese dependency parser *KNP* (Kurohashi and Nagao, 1994),[1] however features should be reproducible in other languages with a suitable dependency parser, morphological analyser, and electronic thesaurus or ontology. Each instance in the corpus was preprocessed by running it through *KNP* to extract specific linguistic information.[2] To help elucidate both the details of our feature extraction and how it might be replicated for another language, we will look at the information extracted for the sentence in Example (1):

(1) 桂子さんは、 サッカーの 腕を
keiko-saN-wa, sakkā-no ude-o
Keiko-TOPIC soccer-GEN arm-OBJ
上げた。
ageta.
raised.

"Keiko raised her soccer arm." (literal)

"Keiko improved her skills at soccer." (idiomatic)

Japanese is a non-segmenting language in that it has no clearly marked word boundaries. In Figure 1, Example (1) has been segmented by *KNP* into tokens[3] which are then grouped into chunks. Each chunk has a *parent* link to a higher chunk describing the dependency parse of the sentence. In the conventional word order for Japanese, dependency links are always forwards so the head of a phrase is also its rightmost (final) chunk. From Figure 1, we see that *keiko* "Keiko" and *ude* "arm" are the dependents of *ageta* "raised", with *sakkā* "soccer" modifying *ude* "arm". This gives rise

[1] http://nlp.ist.i.kyoto-u.ac.jp/EN/?KNP

[2] *KNP*'s memory usage is high and on some sentences exceeded the available memory in our machine (32GB). Those instances were excluded from our analysis.

[3] In fact, *KNP* delegates the initial segmentation and token feature annotation to the morphological analyser *Juman*.

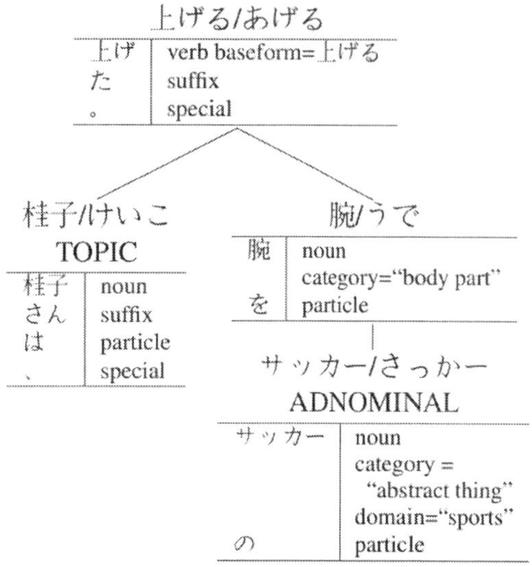

Figure 1: English summary of the select parts of the output of *KNP* when run on the sentence in Example (1)

to the incorrect literal interpretation *#Keiko raised her soccer arm*. In fact, *ude-o ageru* "to improve one's skills" is an ambiguous MWE.

In this paper when we refer to *words* we are in fact referring to the chunks returned by *KNP*. This is the most appropriate level of segmentation for our purposes because it is the level at which the dependency parse exists and because the tokenisation level includes affixes and particles which would need filtering. *KNP* labels each chunk with a normalised form, which we use as the *lemma* of the word for our feature extraction. We also extract the part of speech, category and domain of tokens corresponding most closely to the lemma, as additional features of the word.

The category and domain information performs a similar function to the named entity information used by Diab and Bhutada (2009): it collapses classes of words into a single feature while retaining relevant semantic information. An information source such as an ontology or thesaurus could be substituted for use in other languages. Hashimoto and Kawahara (2009) translate the *category* output of *KNP* as *hypernym*, and we will adopt the same terminology hereafter.

Returning to Figure 1, take note of the *TOPIC* flag on the first chunk and the ADNOMINAL flag on the second. *KNP* produces many chunk annotations; we made use of five main kinds:

ADNOMINAL appearing on adnominal modifiers;

TOPIC appearing on sentential topics and emphasised chunks;

VOICE of inflected verbs;

NEGATED denoting negation; and

VOLITIONAL denoting a volitional modality.

For all but the volitional modality group, *KNP* outputs only one or two annotation variants (e.g. there are two voices in Japanese: passive and causative). For the volitional modality, Hashimoto and Kawahara (2009) used five classes: request, invitation, order, volition and prohibition. We made use of the same subset of modalities output by *KNP*.

The *KNP* chunk annotations we used chiefly capture inflections on words in the text, something which Diab and Bhutada (2009) approximate with a character n-gram feature. For implementation in other languages, the n-gram heuristic or any available morphological analyser might be used.

3.2 Word sense disambiguation features

We adopted the WSD inspired features of Hashimoto and Kawahara (2009) and extended them with our own new features.

Hashimoto and Kawahara (2009) features

Hashimoto and Kawahara (2009) put together a set of features based on WSD best practice as espoused by Lee and Ng (2002). They included:

1. full context, in the form of bag features for lemma, hypernym and domain of single words in the full surrounding context.[4]

2. local context, in the form of part of speech and lemma features for indexed word offsets to each side of the MWE.

3. syntactic context, in the form of lemmas and POS for context words in a syntactic relationship with either the first or last constituent word of the MWE.

For more details on implementation of these features, see Hashimoto and Kawahara (2009).

[4]Note that due to the way the corpus was constructed, the full context is a single sentence, albeit a long one.

full context features

lemma keiko, majime, ...
hypernym abstract thing, body part, person.
domain sports, familial associations.

local context features

lemma majime_{-3}, reNshū_{-2}, sakkā_{-1}, ...
$(\text{majime}, \text{sakkā})_{-3,-1}$, ...
POS adjective_{-3}, noun_{-2}, noun_{-1}, ...
$(\text{adjective}, \text{noun})_{-3,-1}$, ...
hypernym $\text{abstract thing}_{-2}$, $\text{abstract thing}_{-1}$, ...
$(\text{NULL}, \text{abstract thing})_{-3,-1}$, ...
domain sports_{-1}, ...
$(\text{NULL}, \text{sports})_{-3,-1}$, ...

syntactic context features

lemma $\text{sakkā}_{\text{child}}$
POS $\text{noun}_{\text{child}}$
hypernym $\text{abstract thing}_{\text{child}}$
domain $\text{sports}_{\text{child}}$

Figure 2: A sample of the WSD inspired features extracted for Example (2).

New WSD features

We introduce hypernym and domain features for the local and syntactic contexts. Use of hypernym and domain features in the syntactic context is particularly interesting. The intent of the syntactic features is to capture selectional restrictions involving constituents of the MWE. Violation of selectional restrictions for or by constituents of the MWE leads us to strongly suspect an idiomatic usage. In the case of Example (2) we see that having *sakkā* "soccer" modifying *ude* "arm" is strongly indicative of the idiomatic *ude-o ageru* "to raise skills". For this MWE, any sport has the same implication. We can see from Figure 1 that *KNP* has extracted the domain *sports* for *sakkā* "soccer" so a classification algorithm can use this feature to make a valid generalisation. Our local context hypernym and domain features are less targeted, but we consider them to be worthwhile in light of the success of named-entity features in the literature (Diab and Bhutada, 2009).

Note that we use the same definitions of local and syntactic context as Lee and Ng (2002), with the specialisations to MWEs outlined by Hashimoto and Kawahara (2009).

Figure 2 contains a sample of all original and new WSD features, extracted for the MWE-token in Example (2), which expands Example (1):

(2) 桂子さんは　真面目に 練習して、
keiko-saN-wa majime-ni reNshū-shite,
Keiko-TOPIC diligent-ly practice,
サッカーの 腕を　　上げた。
sakkā-no　ude-o　ageta.
soccer-GEN arm-OBJ raised.
お母さんは　喜んだ。
okāsan-wa　yorokoNda.
Mother-TOPIC pleased.

"Keiko practised diligently and improved her skills at soccer. Her mother was pleased."

3.3 Idiom token features

As with the WSD features, we adopted the idiom features of Hashimoto and Kawahara (2009) with additional features of our own.

Hashimoto and Kawahara (2009) features

The idiom features of Hashimoto and Kawahara (2009) included a single binary feature for each of the *KNP* chunk annotation groups listed at the end of Section 3.1. For each of the groups, the feature fires if one of the annotations appears on a relevant word in the MWE. Details of each are given in the outline of our extensions below.

The final idiom feature of Hashimoto and Kawahara (2009) was the adjacency feature. This feature fires if the constituents of the MWE are contiguous, i.e., there are no intervening chunks. They found that this feature had a greater impact on classification performance than the other idiom features combined.

New idiom features

Each of the boolean idiom features of Hashimoto and Kawahara (2009) captures some variation of the form of the MWE. We introduce features capturing details on the kind of variation:

- The ADNOMINAL modification feature fires if a non-constituent adnominal modifies a noun in the MWE. We include features for the lemma, POS, hypernym and domain of such a modifier whenever it exists.

- The TOPIC feature fires if a constituent noun is marked as a sentential topic. In this case we include features for the lemma, POS, hypernym and domain of the constituent.

- The VOICE, NEGATION and VOLITIONAL features fire if the MWE has a head verb and it has voice marking or is negated. We include features specifying what for of voice, negation or volitional marking is used.

- Finally for the adjacency feature, we include lemma, POS, hypernym and domain features from a single intervening chunk where any existed. When more than one is found, we take the rightmost.

In the sentence of Example (2), features only fire for adnominal modification. Since *sakkā* "soccer" modifies the constituent *ude* "arm", the adnominal modification boolean feature fires, as do our lemma, POS, hypernym and domain features for the modifier: *sakkā*, *noun*, *abstract thing* and *sports* respectively. As was the case when *sakkā* "soccer" was considered in its role as a modifier of *ude* "arm", we note that it is in fact informative that the adnominal modifier is a sport and not, for example, a person.

3.4 Type features

The features we have discussed so far have, for the most part, ignored the constituent words of the MWE-type itself. For type-specialised classifiers this is inconsequential since the constituents are constant. However features of the MWE-type may be important for crosstype classification where similarities between different MWEs could be leveraged. Therefore, for each MWE-type, we use the lemma, POS, hypernym and domain of the headword in particular and a bag feature for each across all words in the MWE.

One motivation for these features is to allow a crosstype classifier to make more informed decisions when confronted with tokens of types it was trained on. For example, if a collection of constituents has been encountered in training, a supervised statistical classifier may capture the prior probability for idiomaticity of the training MWE-type. For crosstype classification, some constituents — in particular the headword — may be indicative of the relative idiomaticity of an idiom. For example, common verbs such as *take* and *make* are common in idioms such as *take a shot* and *make a stand*.

4 Results

We evaluated classifiers using combinations of the three main classes of features. For all tasks, a tenfold cross-validation partitioning was used, and a

Feature Types			Accuracy	
idiom	*type*	*wsd*	*basic*	*extended*
	*		0.623	–
*			0.630	0.627
*	*		0.626	0.651
		*	0.737	0.745
	*	*	0.736	0.743
*		*	0.738	0.746
*	*	*	0.739	0.745
corpus baseline			0.612	–
type-specialised baseline			0.741	–

Table 1: Results of combining different features for crosstype classification. "Basic" results restrict the idiom and WSD features to those of Hashimoto and Kawahara (2009); "extended" results include our extensions.

feature count cutoff of one was used to filter out uninformative features. Given the binary classification nature of the task we used accuracy as our performance metric, microaveraging across all instances in the corpus.

For statistical significance we used the sign test because our crosstype classification testing partitions were unevenly weighted, making a t-test inappropriate. Unless otherwise stated, comparisons were significant with $p < 0.05$.

We constructed two kinds of majority class baseline using class counts from the corpus: the corpus baseline, which achieved an accuracy of 0.612, and the type-specialised baseline, with an accuracy of 0.741. All other systems were linear kernel *Support Vector Machine* models trained using the *libSVM* package.[5]

4.1 Crosstype classification

For the purposes of testing crosstype classification we partitioned the set of 90 MWE-types for cross-validation. Thus classifiers were trained on the instances of 81 types and tested on the instances of the 9 unseen types. Note that since the corpus contains a different number of instances for each type, the partition size was not strictly constant. Results across all feature combinations appear in Table 1.

The idiom type and token features did manage to improve on the corpus baseline by a little over one percentage point each. However, this is over

[5]We initially used the *TinySVM* package and quadratic kernels of Hashimoto and Kawahara (2009) for comparability reasons, but eventually changed system and kernel for consistency and speed of convergence.

Feature Types			Accuracy	
idiom	*type*	*wsd*	*basic*	*extended*
	*		0.741	–
*	*		0.748	0.752
*			0.630	0.639
		*	0.844	0.847
	*	*	0.851	0.854
*		*	0.847	0.849
*	*	*	0.854	0.856
corpus baseline			0.612	–
type-specialised baseline			0.741	–

Table 2: Results for classification of MWE-tokens of MWE-types seen in the training corpus. As in Table 1, "Basic" results restrict the idiom and WSD features to those of Hashimoto and Kawahara (2009).

ten percentage points behind the results when using WSD features alone. In fact, the WSD features *with our extensions* achieved effectively our best results. The addition of idiom features with our extensions achieved fractionally better performance without statistical significance and all feature combinations which did not include our full complement of WSD features had lower performance. The WSD features' performance exceeds even the type-specialised baseline, which was built on gold-standard data which the crosstype classifier has no access to.

It is a surprising result, for two reasons: first, that idiom features are widely assumed to be a key information source, particularly for unsupervised disambiguation (Cook et al., 2007), and second, that WSD features — paragraph context in particular — are typically used as a model of the *meaning* of a token. It is counterintuitive that models of semantics are more informative than models of lexico-syntactic variations when the testing and training sets that are explicitly disjoint with respect to MWE-type.

The idiom token or type features alone did not stand up well in comparison. However, we note that combining our type features with the complete idiom token features provided a disproportionate boost to a classification accuracy of almost four percentage points above the baseline.

What happens when a nominally crosstype classifier encounters an instance of a MWE-type which it *has* seen in its training set? To test this, we partitioned the corpus stratified across types.

Feature Types		Accuracy	
idiom	*wsd*	*basic*	*extended*
*		0.768	0.769
	*	0.882	0.886
*	*	0.886	0.890
type-specialised baseline		0.741	–

Table 3: Results of combining different features for type-specialised classifiers. "Basic" results restrict the idiom and WSD features to those of Hashimoto and Kawahara (2009); "extended" results include our extensions.

That is, classifiers were trained on 90% of instances from *all* MWE-types in the corpus and tested on the remaining 10%. The results are shown in Table 2.

The idiom features once again improved a couple of percentage points on the baseline. In this instance, the type features produced much better results, achieving the same results as the type-specialised majority class baseline. It is not possible for any deterministic classifier to do better on the same input because the idiom type features are constant across all instances of a MWE-type.

Once again the WSD features did far better than any of the others at 23 percentage points over the corpus baseline and over ten points above even the type-specialised baseline. This is more to be expected than the equivalent result for crosstype classification since, by their origin, WSD features are designed to capture differences in semantics for known types.

The indisputable dominance of WSD features observed in these experiments warrants further investigation, which we leave for future work.

4.2 Type-specialised classification

If a known MWE-type can be explicitly detected, the general crosstype classifier need not be used: we can fall back on type-specialised classifiers like those of Hashimoto and Kawahara (2009). To see how much better we can do by selecting an appropriate type-specialised classifier, we trained and tested classifiers on the same partitioning as the previous task but restricted to instances of one MWE-type at a time. The results appear in Table 3.

In this case the idiom features improved a little even on the type-specialised baseline. This indicates that the idiom features do contain information about MWE-token idiomaticity even if it does

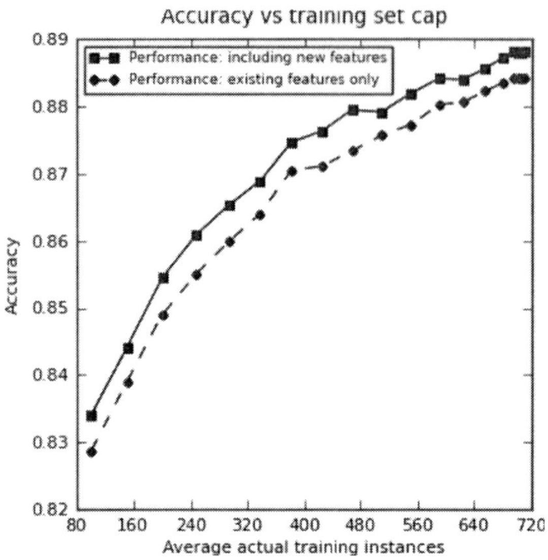

Figure 3: Results for type-specialised classifiers with capped training set sizes.

not generalise well across types.

The WSD features achieved close to the best results seen across all our experiments. An improvement of four percentage points is seen compared to the previous task, which is indicative of the noise introduced by simultaneously training on data of 90 idioms. Our best results were achieved using all of the idiom and WSD features together, hitting an even 0.890.

Finally, we used the type-specialised task to investigate the significance of the size of the *Open-MWE* corpus. To do this we measured cross-validation accuracy while limiting the total number of training instances. Training set size caps ranging between 100 and 1000 instances were used, but in practice most of the MWE-types had between 500 and 1000 available training instances, so the average actual training instances used was less than the cap. We performed these experiments using our complete WSD and idiom features and, for comparison, with the original features of Hashimoto and Kawahara (2009). The results appear in Figure 3.

Even with 100 instances per MWE-type, we achieved an accuracy of 0.834, which is an appreciable improvement on the type-specialised baseline. However the data show a definite positive trend with the number of instances, reaching 0.884 under a cap of 650 instances (and 589 average actual instances) per MWE-type.

Setting the maximum number of instances per MWE-type to 1000 achieved an accuracy of 0.888. Additionally, when restricted to the original features used by Hashimoto and Kawahara (2009) a performance of 0.884 is observed. Since Hashimoto and Kawahara (2009) also capped instance counts at 1000 this is our most comparable result to their best of 0.893. We note that with our new features, results were consistently around half a percentage point higher, so consider this to be state of the art performance.

5 Conclusions

We have shown that crosstype classification of ambiguous MWE-tokens can surpass the type-specialised baseline while alleviating the requirement on labelled token instances, thus enabling classification of tokens of previously unseen MWE-types.

Our type features and new idiom features, working in concert with the idiom features of Hashimoto and Kawahara (2009), substantially increase crosstype classification performance over the baseline. However their effect is wholly subsumed by the inclusion of WSD features. On type-specialised classification, our new idiom and WSD features achieve more consistent gains.

Finally, we conclude that the size of the *Open-MWE* corpus raises potential performance by leaps and bounds, but additional performance is still to be had by more data.

For future work we would like to investigate the dominance of WSD features at crosstype classification. The success of semantic features where the training and test sets have — by design — different semantics, making this an intriguing counter-intuitive result, as does the relatively poor performance of features targeted at linguistic properties of MWEs.

Acknowledgements

This research was supported by Australian Research Council grant no. DP0988242.

References

Timothy Baldwin and Su Nam Kim. 2009. Multiword expressions. In Nitin Indurkhya and Fred J. Damerau, editors, *Handbook of Natural Language Processing*, pages 267–292. CRC Press, Boca Raton, USA, 2nd edition.

Timothy Baldwin, Colin Bannard, Takaaki Tanaka, and Dominic Widdows. 2003. An empirical model of multiword expression decomposability. In *Proceedings of the ACL 2003 Workshop on Multiword Expressions: Analysis, Acquisition and Treatment*, pages 89–96, Sapporo, Japan.

Paul Cook, Afsaneh Fazly, and Suzanne Stevenson. 2007. Pulling their weight: Exploiting syntactic forms for the automatic identification of idiomatic expressions in context. In *Proceedings of the Workshop on A Broader Perspective on Multiword Expressions*, pages 41–48, Prague, Czech Republic.

Mona T. Diab and Pravin Bhutada. 2009. Verb noun construction MWE token supervised classification. In *MWE '09: Proceedings of the Workshop on Multiword Expressions*, pages 17–22, Singapore.

Mona T. Diab and Madhav Krishna. 2009. Handling sparsity for verb noun MWE token classification. In *GEMS '09: Proceedings of the Workshop on Geometrical Models of Natural Language Semantics*, pages 96–103, Athens, Greece.

Afsaneh Fazly, Paul Cook, and Suzanne Stevenson. 2009. Unsupervised type and token identification of idiomatic expressions. *Computational Linguistics*, 35(1):61–103.

Chikara Hashimoto and Daisuke Kawahara. 2009. Compilation of an idiom example database for supervised idiom identification. *Language Resources and Evaluation*, 43:355–384.

Chikara Hashimoto, Satoshi Sato, and Takehito Utsuro. 2006. Detecting Japanese idioms with a linguistically rich dictionary. *Language Resources and Evaluation*, 40:243–252.

Sadao Kurohashi and Makoto Nagao. 1994. KN parser: Japanese dependency/case structure analyzer. In *Proceedings of the Workshop on Sharable Natural Language Resources*, Nara, Japan.

Yoong Keok Lee and Hwee Tou Ng. 2002. An empirical evaluation of knowledge sources and learning algorithms for word sense disambiguation. In *EMNLP '02: Proceedings of the 2002 Conference on Empirical Methods in Natural Language Processing*, pages 41–48, Philadelphia, USA.

Linlin Li and Caroline Sporleder. 2010. Linguistic cues for distinguishing literal and non-literal usages. In *Coling 2010: Posters*, pages 683–691, Beijing, China.

Diana McCarthy, Rob Koeling, Julie Weeds, and John Carroll. 2007. Unsupervised acquisition of predominant word senses. *Computational Linguistics*, 33(4):553–590.

Roberto Navigli. 2009. Word sense disambiguation: A survey. *ACM Computing Surveys*, 41(2).

Judita Preiss, Jon Dehdari, Josh King, and Dennis Mehay. 2009. Refining the most frequent sense baseline. In *Proceedings of the Workshop on Semantic Evaluations: Recent Achievements and Future Directions*, pages 10–18, Boulder, USA.

Ivan Sag, Timothy Baldwin, Francis Bond, Ann Copestake, and Dan Flickinger. 2002. Multiword expressions: A pain in the neck for NLP. In *Computational Linguistics and Intelligent Text Processing*, pages 189–206, Mexico City, Mexico.

Identification of relations between answers with global constraints for Community-based Question Answering services

Hikaru Yokono
Precision and Intelligence Laboratory,
Tokyo Institute of Technology
yokono@lr.pi.titech.ac.jp

Takaaki Hasegawa
NTT Cyber Space Laboratories,
NTT Corporation
hasegawa.takaaki@lab.ntt.co.jp

Genichiro Kikui*
NTT Cyber Space Laboratories,
NTT Corporation
kikui.genichiro@lab.ntt.co.jp

Manabu Okumura
Precision and Intelligence Laboratory,
Tokyo Institute of Technology
oku@pi.titech.ac.jp

Abstract

Community-based Question Answering services contain many threads consisting of a question and its answers. When there are many answers for a question, it is hard for a user to understand them all. To address this problem, we focus on logical relations between answers in a thread and present a model for identifying the relations between the answers. We consider that there are constraints among the relations, such as a transitive law, and that it might be useful to take these constraints into account. To consider these constraints, we propose the model based on a Markov logic network. We also introduce super-relations to give additional information for logical relation identification into our model. Through the experiment, we show that global constraints and super-relations make it easier to identify the relations.

1 Introduction

Community-based Question Answering services, such as Yahoo! Answers[1], OKWave[2] and Baidu Zhidao[3], have become popular web services. In these services, a user posts a question and other users answer it. The questioner chooses one of the answers as the best answer. These services have many threads consisting of one question and a number of answers, and the number of threads grows day by day. The threads are stored and anyone can read them. When a user has a question, if there is a similar question in the service, he or she can refer to the answers to the similar question. Herefrom, these services are useful for not only the questioner but also other users having a similar question.

When more answers get posted for a question, the answers in the thread might become more diverse. Some of these answers will be similar or oppositional to each other. Also, when a question tends to have various answers, e.g. the questioner asks for opinions (e.g. "What are your song recommendations?"), it is insufficient to read only the best answer. Generally, as the only one best answer is chosen from the answers, a user may miss other beneficial answers. When a user checks these services with a mobile device, its small display is inefficient to browse all answers.

To alleviate these problems, it would be useful to get an overview of answers in a thread, such as by identifying the relations between the answers or by summarizing them (Jimbo et al., 2010; Liu et al., 2008). The purpose of this study is to identify logical relations between answers with a high degree of accuracy, as a basis of these methods.

We propose an identification model with global constraints on logical relations between answers. Among the relations, there are some constraints like a transitive law. To this end, it is necessary to identify relations in a thread at once, and identified relations need to satisfy as many of these constraints as possible. Our model is based on a Markov logic network and incorporates these constraints as formulas of first order logic.

Also, we group logical relations on the basis of semantic similarity and transitivity and call these grouped relations "coarse relations" and "transi-

*Current affiliation is Faculty of Computer Science and System Engineering, Okayama Prefectural University.

[1] http://answers.yahoo.com/

[2] http://okwave.jp/

[3] http://zhidao.baidu.com/

tive relations", respectively. We consider that these relations might be useful for identification of logical relations and that identification of these relations is easier than that of logical relations. Thus, we incorporate identification of these super-relations into our model.

We briefly describe our related work in section two. Then, we show the logical relations between answers in section three and present our model with global constraints using a Markov logic network in section four. We explain the experiment and the results in section five and conclude our paper in section six.

2 Related Work

The growing popularity of Community-based Question Answering services has prompted many researchers to investigate their characteristics and to propose models for applications using them.

Question search and ranking answers are an important application because there are many threads in these services. Jeon et al. discussed a practical method for finding existing question and answer pairs in response to a newly submitted question (Jeon et al., 2005). Surdeanu et al. proposed an approach for ranking the answers retrieved by Yahoo! Answers (Surdeanu et al., 2008). Wang et al. proposed the ranking model for answers (Wang et al., 2009). Wang et al. proposed a model based on a deep belief network for the semantic relevance of question-answer pairs (Wang et al., 2010).

The user's qualifications affect the quality of his or her answer. For example, an IT expert may provide a good answer to a question about computers. Jurczyk and Agichtein proposed a model to estimate the authority of users as a means of identifying better answers (Jurczyk and Agichtein, 2007). Pal and Konstan proposed the expert identification model (Pal and Konstan, 2010) .

Each user has a background. If a user is an amateur in some field, he or she cannot understand a difficult question of the field. For a user-oriented question ranking, Chen and Kao proposed a model to classify a question as easy or difficult (Chen and Kao, 2010).

When there are many answers in a thread, multi-answer summarization is a good way to understand the answers. Liu et al. proposed taxonomies for a question and answers, and automatic summarization model for answers (Liu et al., 2008). Their best answer taxonomy is based on reusability for similar questions, factuality and so on, and their question type taxonomy is based on the expected answer. Achananuparp et al. proposed a model to extract a diverse set of answers (Achananuparp et al., 2010). Their approach is based on a graph whose edges have weight about similarity and redundancy.

Meanwhile, identification of discourse relations in meetings or dialogs was tackled by some researchers. Hillard et al. demonstrated that automatic identification of agreement and disagreement is feasible by using various textual, durational, and acoustic features (Hillard et al., 2003). Galley et al. described a statistical approach for modeling agreements and disagreements in conversational interaction, and classified utterances as agreement or disagreement by using the adjacency pairs and features that represent various pragmatic influences of previous agreements or disagreements to the target utterance (Galley et al., 2004).

Jimbo et al. proposed a model of relation identification for Community-based Question Answering services (Jimbo et al., 2010). Their model identified relations using Support Vector Machines with various features. We think considering constraints among relations might contribute to improve the performance of identifying relations. Therefore, we realize it with a Markov logic network.

Relation identification is considered as a problem to find labeled edges between pairs of nodes, where a node is an answer in a thread. Structured output learning is a method to predict such a structure (Tsochantaridis et al., 2004; Crammer et al., 2006). Morita et al. proposed a model based on structured output learning to identify agreement and disagreement relations in a discourse (Morita et al., 2009). Yang et al. used structured Support Vector Machines to extract contexts and answers for questions in threads of online forums (Yang et al., 2009).

3 Logical Relations between Answers

A thread consists of a question and some answers and the answers are sorted in order of posted time. Thus, in this paper, we try to identify to which preceding answer and in what relation an answer is related. However, some answers are irrelevant to a question and these answers might be unnecessary for an overview of a thread. Therefore, we consider not only answer-answer relations, but also question-answer relations. We consider two relations for question-answer pairs, and seven relations for answer-answer pairs.

3.1 Relations for Question-Answer Pairs

The relations for question-answer pairs are "answer" and "unrelated". The "answer" relation is that the answer answers the question directly and is beneficial for the questioner. The "unrelated" relation is that the answer has no relation with the expected answer for the question.

The reason why we consider the "unrelated" relation is that some answers are replies to other answers or questions to the original questioner to ask for further details.

3.2 Relations for Answer-Answer Pairs

We define the logical relations for answer-answer pairs according to Radev's work that defines 24 types of relations between texts for multi-document summarization (Radev, 2000). Table 1 shows the relations we consider.

Table 1: Logical relations between answers

Relation	Description
equivalence	Two answers have same contents.
elaboration	The content of the latter includes that of the former.
subsumption	Two answers do not have same contents directly, but they are related to each other.
summary	The content of the latter is a summary of the former.
partial	Two answers have partially-duplicated contents, and they also have mutually different contents.
contradiction	Two answers are completely inconsistent with each other.
unrelated	The contents of two answers have no relation. For example, two answers are different answers for the question.

Figure 1 shows an example of a thread.

Answers (a1) and (a2) include the same content, i.e. they recommend XXX, while answer (a3) expresses a different opinion. Answer (a4) mentions about XXX as well as answers (a1) and (a2), but contains the opposite opinion.

Hence, the relation between (a1) and (a2) is "equivalence" and the relations between (a1) and (a3) and between (a2) and (a3) are "unrelated". The relations between (a1) and (a4) and between (a2) and (a4) are "contradiction" and the relation between (a3) and (a4) is "unrelated".

Question (q). Can anyone recommend me a good internet provider?
Answer 1 (a1). XXX is good, though I use only this provider.
Answer 2 (a2). I prefer XXX. It is cheap and fast.
Answer 3 (a3). I use YYY and it is no problem.
Answer 4 (a4). The customer support of XXX is the worst.

Figure 1: Example of a QA thread

Here, since the relation between (a1) and (a2) is "equivalence" and the relation between (a1) and (a4) is "contradiction", we expect that the relation between (a2) and (a4) will be the same as the one between (a1) and (a4). This type of constraint is what we incorporate into the model.

4 Relation Identification Model with Global Constraints

We propose a joint identification model of logical relations between answers in a thread.

We consider that there are some constraints between logical relations. However, since not all relations satisfy a same constraint, we group logical relations into two types of super-relations on the basis of two kinds of commonality; transitivity and semantic similarity.

To incorporate constraints between relations, we try to identify relations for all pairs in a thread jointly. For these purposes, we take an approach with a Markov logic network.

4.1 Super-Relations for Answer-Answer Relations

We consider two kinds of super-relations for answer-answer relations; coarse relations and transitive relations. Coarse relations are based on semantic similarity and transitive relations are based on transitivity, that is, whether a transitive law is satisfied for relations.

Tables 2 and 3 show the correspondences between coarse relations and logical relations and between transitive relations and logical relations, respectively.

It might be easier to identify these two super-relations than logical relations, because these relations are coarser than logical relations. Furthermore, these information might be useful for identification of logical relations.

Table 2: Coarse relations

Relation	Logical relation
similar	equivalence, subsumption, elaboration, summary, partial
contradiction	contradiction
unrelated	unrelated

Table 3: Transitive relations

Relation	Logical relation
transitive	equivalence, subsumption, elaboration, summary
intransitive	contradiction, partial, unrelated

4.2 Markov Logic Network

A Markov logic network (MLN, in short) is a model combining first order logic and a Markov network (Richardson and Domingos, 2006). In this framework, we can take account of domain knowledge as formulas of first order logic. In first order logic, if there is at least one predicate that violates formulas in a possible world[4], the world is not valid. Therefore, a model with first order logic can only have strict constraints.

On the other hand, a MLN assigns a weight to each formula and can tolerate violation of the formula.

A MLN L is defined as a set of tuples $(\{F_i, w_i\})$, where F_i is a formula of first order logic and w_i is its weight. The distribution for a possible world x is as follows:

$$P(X = x) = \frac{1}{Z} \exp\left(\sum_i w_i n_i(x)\right)$$

where $n_i(x)$ is the number of F_i's ground formulas which are true on x, and Z is a normalization factor. A ground formula is a formula whose terms are constants.

The advantage of this model is that it can treat not only multiple relation identification tasks but also constraints between relations.

In this paper, according to the terminology of *markov thebeast*[5] (Riedel, 2008), which is one of the implementations of a MLN, we call the predicates that indicate aspects obtained from input data as **observed predicates**, the predicates that indicate aspects to be estimated as **hidden predicates**. The observed predicate corresponds to a feature in a general machine learning framework, and the hidden predicate corresponds to a label.

In addition, we call the formulas that express relations between observed predicates and a hidden predicate **local formulas** and formulas that express relations between hidden predicates **global formulas**.

4.3 Proposed Model

To identify the logical relation, our model consists of five subtasks: identification of question-answer relations, identification of whether two answers have a relation, identification of coarse relations, transitive relations, and logical relations. Table 4 shows the hidden predicates corresponding to these subtasks. For the question-answer relation, the relation between question i and answer j is "answer" if the predicate $hasqarelation(i, j)$ is true, and "unrelated" otherwise. For the answer-answer relation, the term l of the predicate $aarelation(i, j, l)$ corresponds to the logical relation to be identified originally.

Table 4: Hidden predicates

Predicate	Description
$hasqarelation(i, j)$	Answer j replies question i directly.
$hasaarelation(i, j)$	There is a relation between answer i and answer j.
$coarserelation(i, j, c)$	The coarse relation between i and j is c.
$transrelation(i, j, t)$	The transitive relation between i and j is t.
$aarelation(i, j, l)$	The logical relation between i and j is l.

In our model, when an answer is "unrelated" to the question, we exclude it from the identification of the answer-answer relation.

4.3.1 Local Formulas

In a MLN, there is only one hidden predicate in a local formula. We describe the relation between observed predicates and a hidden predicate on local formulas. For observed predicates, based on Jimbo et al.'s model (Jimbo et al., 2010), we consider thread features (e.g. order of answers and question type), n-gram features (e.g. word unigram and word bigram), semantic features, named-entity features, and similarity features. Table 5 lists some of the observed predicates. Since our model uses these features both for question-answer relations and answer-answer

[4]A possible world is a set of ground atoms. A ground atom is a predicate whose term is constant.

[5]http://code.google.com/p/thebeast/

relations, we use a term "article" for a question and an answer in this section.

Table 5: Some of the observed predicates

Predicate	Description
$question(i)$	Article i is a question.
$questiontype(q)$	The question type of the thread is q.
$first(i)$	Article i is the first answer in the thread.
$neighbor(i, j)$	Article j adjoins article i.
$longer(i, j)$	Article i is longer than article j.
$timegap(i, j, t)$	A time interval between article i and j is t.
$antonym(i, j)$	Article i and j contain antonyms.
$sameurl(i, j)$	Article i and j include a same URL.
$unigram(i, u)$	Article i contains word unigram u.
$bigram(i, b)$	Article i contains word bigram b.
$questionfocus(i)$	Article i contains the question-focus.
$samefocus(i, j)$	Article i and j contain the same question-focus.
$focusedneclass(i)$	Article i contains a word of the focused NE class.
$namedentity(i)$	Article i contains a named entity.
$samene(i, j)$	Article i and j contain the same named entities.
$samequoted(i, j)$	Article i and j contain the same quoted expression.
$scosine(i, j, c)$	Cosine similarity between article i and j in terms of sentences is c

For identification of relations between articles, the information obtained from the question, such as a class of an expected answer for a question, might be useful.

A question usually consists of multiple sentences such as in Figure 2. In this example, the essential question is the latter sentence. Therefore, we extract the core sentence and the question-focus and estimate the question type, on the basis of Tamura et al.'s model (Tamura et al., 2005).

Question.
I'm planning a journey to Hokkaido.
Can you suggest some good sightseeing places?

Figure 2: Example of a question

The core sentence is the most important sentence, that is, the one requiring an answer in the question. Usually, the core sentence is an interrogative one such as "Where is the most famous place in Hokkaido?". But questioners sometimes ask questions without an interrogative form, such as "Please tell me some good sightseeing places in Hokkaido.". To cope with this diversity, a machine learning approach is taken to extract the core sentence.

The question-focus is then extracted from the core sentence. The question-focus is the word that determines the answer class of the question. For example, the question-focus in Figure 2 is "places".

We extract the question-focus according to the following steps[6]:

step 1. Find the phrase including the last verb of the sentence or the phrase with "?" at the end.

step 2. Find the phrase that modifies the phrase found in step 1.

step 3. Output the nouns and the unknown words in the phrase found in step 2.

Question types are categorized in terms of the expected answer into the thirteen types in table 6.

Table 6: Question types

Nominal answer	Non-nominal answer
Person	Reason
Product	Way
Facility	Definition
Location	Description
Time	Opinion
Number	Other (text)
Other (noun)	

We use a model based on Support Vector Machines (SVM, in short) to identify the question type for the question. In this model, the feature vector is obtained from the core sentence.

The question types whose answers are nouns require a specific class of named entity for the answer, e.g. the class of named entity, PERSON for the question type, Person. We call this class **focused NE class**. Table 7 shows the correspondence between a question type and a named entity class.

Table 7: Question type and focused NE class

Question type	Focused NE class
Person	PERSON
Product	ARTIFACT
Facility	LOCATION, ORGANIZATION
Location	LOCATION
Time	DATE, TIME
Number	MONEY, PERCENT

For n-gram features, we also consider unigram and bigram for the first five words and the last five

[6]This procedure is specific to Japanese.

words in each article. For similarity features, we also consider cosine similarities in terms of word unigram, word bigram, phrase unigram, noun unigram, and noun category unigram.

The score c for sentence-based cosine similarity is calculated as follows:

$$c = \max_{s_{i_m} \in S_i, s_{j_n} \in S_j} \mathrm{sim}_{\cos}(s_{i_m}, s_{j_n})$$

where s_{i_m} is a m-th sentence of article i and S_i is a set of sentences in article i. $\mathrm{sim}_{\cos}(x, y)$ means a cosine similarity between sentence x and y. For the predicate about similarity like $scosine(i, j, c)$, we do not use the score itself for c but rather a value from 0 to 1 divided up into tenths.

For t in the predicate $timegap(i, j, t)$, we choose the one from {"less than an hour", "an hour ~ 3 hour", "3 hour ~ 6 hour", "6 hour ~ 12 hour", "12 hour ~ 24 hour", "24 hour ~ 48 hour", "48 hour ~ 72 hour", "more than 72 hour"} for the actual time gap between article i and j.

We consider the same pattern of local formulas for each hidden predicate. Some examples of local formulas are:

$$question(i) \wedge first(j) \Rightarrow hasqarelation(i, j) \quad (1)$$

$$bigram(i, +w_1) \wedge bigram(j, +w_2) \Rightarrow hasaarelation(i, j) \quad (2)$$

$$samequoted(i, j) \Rightarrow coarserelation(i, j, +c) \quad (3)$$

$$scosine(i, j, +v) \Rightarrow transrelation(i, j, +t) \quad (4)$$

$$lastunigram(i, +u_1) \Rightarrow aarelation(i, j, +l) \quad (5)$$

where "+" indicates that the weight of the formula depends on each constant to be grounded. For example, formula (1) has one weight in spite of values for i and j, but formula (3) has a separate weight for each value of c.

4.3.2 Global Formulas

Global formulas have more than one hidden predicates, and we can use these formulas to incorporate constraints between hidden predicates into the model. Figure 3 shows some global formulas that we consider.

There are two kinds of formulas in a MLN: hard constraints and soft constraints. Hard constraints are formulas that must be satisfied in a possible world. This kind of constraint is realized by assigning a huge value for its weight. For a possible world where a formula of hard constraints is false, its probability is almost zero. In our model, formulas from (6) to (12) are hard constraints.

We describe preconditions for each hidden predicate (formulas (6)-(10)) and correspondences between super-relations and logical relations (formulas (11) and (12)) as hard constraints. For example, formula (10) represents that if there is any transitive relation between answer i and j, there needs to be any logical relation between the answers.

Soft constraints are formulas that are allowed to be false in a possible world. It is obvious that a possible world where soft constraints are satisfied is more probable than a world where soft constraints are not satisfied. Thus, the model identifies relations to satisfy as many of these constraints as possible. In our model, formulas from (13) to (16) are soft constraints. We describe soft constraints for relations among three answers i, j, and k.

Formula (13) represents a semantic relevancy and formula (14) represents a transitive law. As shown in the example in Figure 1, when a relation between two answers is "equivalence", it is reasonable to assume that logical relations from these answers to other answers are identical with each other. Formula (15) represents this situation, and formula (16) represents the opposite direction of formula (15), that is, relations from other answers to these answers.

5 Experiment

To evaluate our model, we conducted an experiment with annotated question-answers threads in Japanese.

5.1 Experimental Settings

We used 299 threads of three genres from Yahoo! Chiebukuro[7], which is a Japanese Community-based Question Answering service. Table 8 shows the statistics of the data we used.

Table 8: Statistics of the data

Genre	the number of threads	the number of answers	Average number of answers in a thread
Cook	99	776	7.83
PC	100	618	6.13
Love	100	813	8.13

For each question-answer pair and answer-answer pair, five annotators annotated a relation. In annotating relations, answers whose question-answer relation had been annotated with "unre-

[7]http://chiebukuro.yahoo.co.jp/

$$
\begin{aligned}
\neg hasqarelation(i,j) &\Rightarrow \neg hasaarelation(j,k) && (6)\\
\neg hasqarelation(i,k) &\Rightarrow \neg hasaarelation(j,k) && (7)\\
hasaarelation(i,j) &\Rightarrow \exists t(transrelation(i,j,t)) && (8)\\
hasaarelation(i,j) &\Rightarrow \exists c(coarserelation(i,j,c)) && (9)\\
transrelation(i,j,t) &\Rightarrow \exists l(aarelation(i,j,l)) && (10)\\
coarserelation(i,j,\text{"similar"}) &\Rightarrow \neg(aarelation(i,j,\text{"contradiction"}) \lor \\
& \quad aarelation(i,j,\text{"unrelated"})) && (11)\\
transrelation(i,j,\text{"transitive"}) &\Rightarrow \neg(aarelation(i,j,\text{"partial"}) \lor \\
& \quad aarelation(i,j,\text{"contradiction"}) \lor \\
& \quad aarelation(i,j,\text{"unrelated"})) && (12)\\
coarserelation(i,j,\text{"similar"}) &\land coarserelation(j,k,\text{"similar"}) \\
&\Rightarrow coarserelation(i,k,\text{"similar"}) && (13)\\
transrelation(i,j,\text{"transitive"}) &\land transrelation(j,k,\text{"transitive"}) \\
&\Rightarrow transrelation(i,k,\text{"transitive"}) && (14)\\
aarelation(i,j,\text{"equivalence"}) &\Rightarrow aarelation(i,k,+l) \land aarelation(j,k,+l) && (15)\\
aarelation(j,k,\text{"equivalence"}) &\Rightarrow aarelation(i,j,+l) \land aarelation(i,k,+l) && (16)
\end{aligned}
$$

Figure 3: Some of the global formulas

lated" were excluded from the annotation of the answer-answer relation. We considered only relation labels that more than two annotators agreed on the experiment. The number of pairs that we used and the distributions of relations are shown in Tables 9 and 10, respectively.

Table 9: Number of pairs

	Cook	PC	Love
question-answer	775	616	811
answer-answer	2194	1012	1626

Table 10: Distribution of relations

	Relation	Cook	PC	Love
question-answer	answer	0.925	0.924	0.905
	unrelated	0.075	0.076	0.095
answer-answer	equivalence	0.115	0.186	0.192
	elaboration	0.026	0.083	0.033
	subsumption	0.000	0.009	0.008
	summary	0.012	0.033	0.025
	partial	0.073	0.078	0.113
	contradiction	0.055	0.084	0.187
	unrelated	0.716	0.528	0.442

To acquire the semantic category for nouns, we utilized a Japanese thesaurus, Nihongo-Goi-Taikei (Ikehara et al., 1997). For antonyms, we used the Japanese dictionary, Kadokawa-Ruigo-Shin-Jiten (Ohno and Hamanishi, 1981).

For dependency parsing, we used Japanese dependency parser CaboCha[8]. For named entities, we utilized CaboCha's output.

We used SVM^{light}[9] for the implementation of SVM and *markov thebeast* for a MLN.

5.2 Results

For each genre, we performed 10-fold cross validation and evaluated the F-value.

The baseline model was one using SVM based on (Jimbo et al., 2010). In this model, we used the observed predicates for our model as features and trained a binary classifier for the question-answer relation and a one-versus-rest classifier for the answer-answer relation. The algorithm for the baseline model is as follows:

step 1. Identify the question-answer relation between the question and each answer.

step 2. For answers to be identified as an "answer", identify the answer-answer relation.

Our work is different from Jimbo et al.'s work with respect to the number of relations. We considers seven relations for answer-answer pairs, while they consider four relations. Also, we used a different data from their experiment. Therefore, we could not conduct an accurate comparison experiment between our model and their model.

Table 11 shows the results. Bold face indicates that F-value of our model was higher than the baseline model and symbols $^{**}(p < 0.01)$ and $^{*}(p < 0.05)$ indicate the F-value was significantly different from the baseline with a sign test. Compared with the baseline model, our model was better for most relations.

[8]http://chasen.org/~taku/software/cabocha/

[9]http://www.cs.cornell.edu/people/tj/svm_light/

Table 11: Results for each relation (F-value)

Relation	Cook SVM	Cook MLN	PC SVM	PC MLN	Love SVM	Love MLN
QArelation	0.961	0.956*	0.959	0.958	0.949	0.945*
AArelation	0.793	**0.796****	0.470	**0.653****	0.326	**0.612****
Coarse (similar)	0.018	**0.246****	0.315	**0.326****	0.176	**0.266****
Coarse (contradiction)	0.000	**0.025**	0.000	**0.033**	0.000	**0.091****
Coarse (unrelated)	0.636	**0.642****	0.423	0.378**	0.301	**0.312****
Trans (transitive)	0.000	**0.094****	0.000	**0.309****	0.000	**0.120****
Trans (intransitive)	0.712	0.712	0.498	**0.506****	0.497	0.495
Logical (equivalence)	0.000	**0.062****	0.164	**0.245****	0.019	**0.116****
Logical (elaboration)	0.000	0.000	0.000	**0.022**	0.000	0.000
Logical (subsmption)	0.000	0.000	0.000	0.000	0.000	0.000
Logical (summary)	0.000	0.000	0.000	**0.014**	0.000	0.000
Logical (partial)	0.000	**0.141****	0.000	**0.098****	0.000	**0.102****
Logical (contradiction)	0.000	**0.025**	0.000	**0.033**	0.000	**0.094****
Logical (unrelated)	0.636	**0.637****	0.406	0.380**	0.311	0.306**

While the baseline model considered only the target pair in identification, our model considers the relations of all pairs at the same time and identifies relations to satisfy as many constraints as possible. These constraints on relations contribute to improve the performance for the identification of relations.

Also, to evaluate the effectiveness of introducing the super-relations, we evaluated the model without coarse relations and transitive relations (w/o-super).

Table 12 shows the results for the data for PC. Bold face indicates the best value for each relation. For most relations, the w/o-super model was better than the baseline model. Although the w/o-super model does not leverage global formulas about super-relations (e.g. formula (13)), it leverages global formulas about logical relations (e.g. formula (16)) as well as the MLN model. We consider that the reason why the w/o-super model outperformed the SVM model is that these constraints worked well.

Table 12: Results for the model w/o super (F-value)

Relation	SVM	w/o-super	MLN
QArelation	**0.959**	0.952**	0.958
AArelation	0.470	0.546**	**0.653****
Coarse (similar)	0.315	–	**0.326****
Coarse (contradiction)	0.000	–	**0.033**
Coarse (unrelated)	**0.423**	–	0.378**
Trans (transitive)	0.000	–	**0.309****
Trans (intransitive)	0.498	–	**0.506****
Logical (equivalence)	0.164	**0.264****	0.245**
Logical (elaboration)	0.000	0.000	**0.022**
Logical (subsmption)	0.000	0.000	0.000
Logical (summary)	0.000	0.000	**0.014**
Logical (partial)	0.000	0.044	**0.098****
Logical (contradiction)	0.000	0.018	**0.033**
Logical (unrelated)	**0.406**	0.251**	0.380**

Furthermore, the MLN model is better than the w/o-super model. Because super-relations focus on transitivity and semantic similarity, identifying these relations is easier than the logical relations and the information about these relations is useful for identifying the logical relations.

In our model, there are some constraints between the predicate $aarelation$ and the other predicates. When the performances for the identifications of auxiliary relations (i.e. $hasaarelation$, $coarserelation$, $transrelation$) are worse, the performance of the identification of logical relations would be worse too. Therefore, in order to improve the performance of logical relation identification, it is necessary to improve the performance of identifying these auxiliary relations.

6 Conclusion

We proposed a logical relation identification model with a Markov logic network. There are constraints between relations and we incorporated them into the model. These constraints may be violated and a MLN permits violation of them.

Through the experiment, we showed that our model is better than a baseline model using SVM and that incorporating super-relations improves the performance. However, since the accuracy was not so high, we need to improve our model.

The relation between answers is the effective information for understanding the overview of a thread. Our future work is to propose answers summarization model and thread visualization model, based on these logical relations.

References

Palakorn Achananuparp, Xiaohua Hu, Tingting He, Christopher C. Yang, Yuan An, and Lifan Guo. 2010. Answer diversification for complex question answering on the web. In *Proceedings of The 14th Pacific-Asia Conference on Knowledge Discovery and Data Mining*, pages 375–382.

Ying-Liang Chen and Hung-Yu Kao. 2010. Finding hard questions by knowledge gap analysis in question answer communities. In *Proceedings of the 6th Asia Information Retrieval Societies Conference.*, pages 370–378.

Koby Crammer, Ofer Dekel, Joseph Keshet, Shai Shalev-Shwartz, and Yoram Singer. 2006. Online passive-aggressive algorithms. *Journal of Machine Learning Research*, 7:551–585.

Michel Galley, Kathleen McKeown, Julia Hirchberg, and Elizabeth Shriberg. 2004. Identifying agreement and disagreement in conversational speech: Use of baysian networks to model pragmatic dependencies. In *Proceedings of the 42nd Annual Meeting on Association for Computational Linguistics*, pages 669–676.

Dustin Hillard, Mari Ostendorf, and Elizabeth Shriberg. 2003. Detection of agreement vs. disagreement in meetings: training with unlabeled data. In *Proceedings of the North American Chapter of the Association for Computational Linguistics*, pages 34–36.

Satoru Ikehara, Masahiro Miyazaki, Satoshi Shirai, Akio Yokoo, Hiromi Nakaiwa, Kentarou Ogura, Yoshifumi Ooyama, and Yoshihiko Hayashi. 1997. *Nihongo-Goi-Taikei*. Iwanami Shoten. (In Japanese).

J. Jeon, W.B. Croft, and J. Lee. 2005. Finding semantically similar questions based on their answers. In *Proceedings of the SIGIR'05*.

Kazuki Jimbo, Hiroya Takamura, and Manabu Okumura. 2010. Identification of relations between utterances in question answering communities. In *Proceedings of The 24th Annual Conference of the Japanese Society for Artificial Intelligence 3D3-3*. (In Japanese).

Pawel Jurczyk and Eugene Agichtein. 2007. Discovering authorities in question answer communities by using link analysis. In *Proceedings of 16th ACM International Conference on Information and Knowledge Management*, pages 919–922.

Yuanjie Liu, Shasha Li, Yunbo Cao, Chin-Yew Lin, Dingyi Han, and Yong Yu. 2008. Understanding and summarizing answers in community-based question answering services. In *Proceedings of the 22nd International Conference on Computational Linguistics*, pages 497–504.

Hajime Morita, Hiroya Takamura, and Manabu Okumura. 2009. Structured output learning with polynomial kernel. In *Proceedings of the International Conference RANLP-2009*, pages 281–286.

Susumu Ohno and Masato Hamanishi. 1981. *Kadokawa-Ruigo-Shin-Jiten*. Kadokawa Shoten. (In Japanese).

Aditya Pal and Joseph A. Konstan. 2010. Expert identification in community question answering: Exploring question selection bias. In *Proceedings of 19th ACM International Conference on Information and Knowledge Management*, pages 1505–1508.

Dragomir Radev. 2000. A common theory of information fusion from multiple text sources step one: Cross-document structure. In *Proceedings of 1st SIGdial Workshop on Discourse and Dialogue*, pages 74–83.

Matthew Richardson and Pedro Domingos. 2006. Markov logic networks. *Machine Learning*, 62(1-2):107–136.

Sebastian Riedel. 2008. Improving the accuracy and efficiency of map inference for markov logic. In *Proceedings of the 24th Annual Conference on Uncertainty in AI (UAI '08)*, pages 468–475.

Mihai Surdeanu, Massimiliano Ciaramita, and Hugo Zaragoza. 2008. Learning to rank answers on large online qa collections. In *Proceedings of the ACL'08*, pages 719–727.

Akihiro Tamura, Hiroya Takamura, and Manabu Okumura. 2005. Classification of multiple-sentence questions. In *Proceedings of the Second International Joint Conference on Natural Language Processing*, pages 426–437.

Ioannis Tsochantaridis, Thomas Hofmann, Thorsten Joachims, and Yasemin Altun. 2004. Support vector learning for interdependent and structured output spaces. In *Proceedings of the 21st International Conference on Machine Learning*, pages 823–830.

Xin-Jing Wang, Xudong Tu, Dan Feng, and Lei Zhang. 2009. Ranking community answers by modeling question-answer relationships via analogical reasoning. In *Proceedings of the 32nd Annual ACM SIGIR Conference*, pages 179–186.

Baoxun Wang, Xiaolong Wang, Chengjie Sun, Bingquan Liu, and Lin Sun. 2010. Modeling semantic relevance for question-answer pairs in web social communities. In *Proceedings of the 48th Annual Meeting of the Association for Computational Linguistics*, pages 1230–1238.

Wen-Yun Yang, Yunbo Cao, and Chin-Yew Lin. 2009. A structural support vector method for extracting contexts and answers of questions from online forums. In *Proceedings of the 2009 Conference on Empirical Methods in Natural Language Processing*, pages 514–523.

Automatically Generating Questions from Queries for Community-based Question Answering

Shiqi Zhao[1,2], **Haifeng Wang**[1], **Chao Li**[2], **Ting Liu**[2], **Yi Guan**[2]
[1]Baidu, Beijing, China
{zhaoshiqi,wanghaifeng}@baidu.com
[2]Harbin Institute of Technology, Harbin, China
beyondlee2008@yahoo.cn, tliu@ir.hit.edu.cn, guanyi@hit.edu.cn

Abstract

This paper proposes a method that automatically generates questions from queries for community-based question answering (cQA) services. Our query-to-question generation model is built upon templates induced from search engine query logs. In detail, we first extract pairs of queries and user-clicked questions from query logs, with which we induce question generation templates. Then, when a new query is submitted, we select proper templates for the query and generate questions through template instantiation. We evaluated the method with a set of short queries randomly selected from query logs, and the generated questions were judged by human annotators. Experimental results show that, the precision of 1-best and 5-best generated questions is 67% and 61%, respectively, which outperforms a baseline method that directly retrieves questions for queries in a cQA site search engine. In addition, the results also suggest that the proposed method can improve the search of cQA archives.

1 Introduction

In recent years, community-based question answering (cQA) services become popular, such as Yahoo! Answers (answers.yahoo.com) in English and Zhidao (zhidao.baidu.com) in Chinese. In cQA, people can have their questions answered by other people rather than by automatic QA systems, which usually better guarantee the answer quality. Till Oct. 2010, Zhidao has accumulated over 100 million answered questions, which form an extremely large and valuable knowledge base.

Lin (2008) first proposed the idea of automatically generating questions from queries. The underlying assumption is that when a user issues a query to a search engine, he could have a question in mind but it is more convenient and efficient for him to realize the question as a query. This technique could have a great impact on cQA services.

First, it can improve the search of cQA archives. As we know, most of cQA resources can be searched with general search engines like Google and Baidu (www.baidu.com). Many of them also have their own site search engines. However, since user queries are mostly short and incomplete, it is quite often that many less relevant questions are retrieved when searching cQA archives. By generating questions from short queries, we can expand the queries and estimate questions that are more likely to be interested in, which could help to retrieve more related questions from cQA archives.

Second, this technique can be useful in enlarging cQA resources. For example, in some search engines like Baidu, if a query is found to be frequently searched, the query will be automatically submitted to a cQA site and expected to be answered by some users. However, a problem is that the frequent queries are usually short and incomprehensible, which makes it hard for users to understand and answer the queries. If we can generate questions from queries, it will become more natural for users to answer the questions, thus contribute new data to the cQA resources[1].

Third, the technique can also be used in query analysis. Through reformulating queries to well-formed questions, it will get easier to analyze the relationship of the query terms as well as the focus of the users' requirement.

In this paper, we follow the proposal of (Lin, 2008) and put forward a novel method for query-to-question generation. The method includes two stages, i.e., template acquisition and question generation. In the former stage, the method collects query-to-question pairs from search engine query

[1]The generated incorrect questions will be ignored by users, which will not evidently influence the performance.

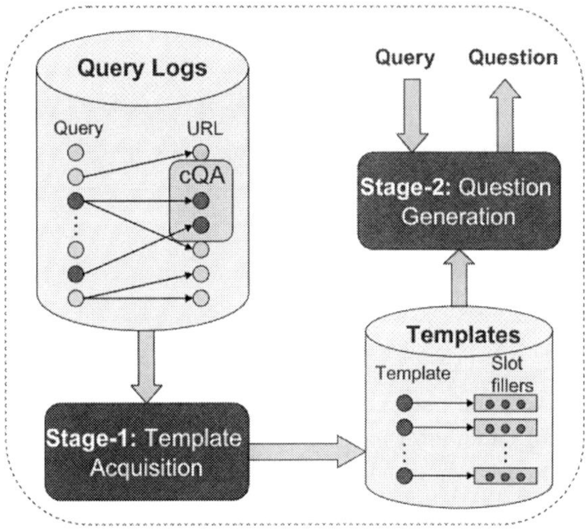

Figure 1: Overview of the method.

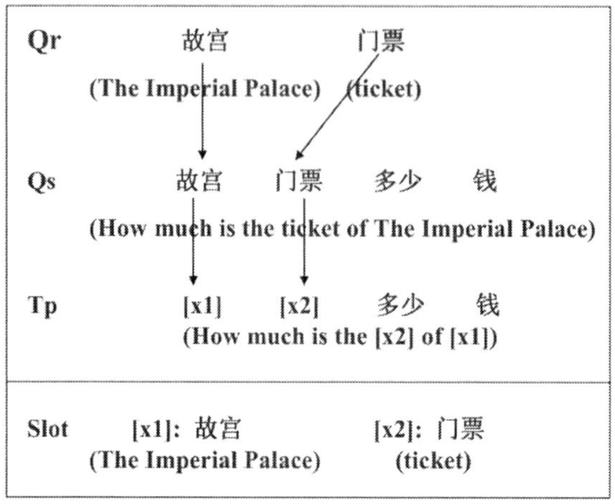

Figure 2: An example of Qr, Qs, and Tp.

logs and further extracts question generation templates. In the latter stage, it generates questions for input queries using the obtained templates. Figure 1 illustrates these two stages.

We conducted experiments on a set of 1000 short queries randomly selected from Baidu's query logs. The results show that our method is effective. Specifically, the method generates questions for 76.5% test queries. The precision of 1-best and 5-best questions is 67% and 61%, respectively, which evidently outperforms a baseline that directly retrieves questions for queries using a cQA site search engine. In addition, we designed a strategy to improve the search of cQA archives through query-to-question generation, and the result is quite promising. Although our experiments were carried out in Chinese, the method can be extended to other languages in which cQA archives exist.

2 Proposed Method

2.1 Template Acquisition

As mentioned above, the cQA archives are frequently searched and viewed through search engines. Therefore, we can find a large number of records in search engine query logs, in which users searched a query Qr and clicked on a question Qs from the cQA archives. Such $\langle Qr, Qs\rangle$ pairs can be collected and used for training question generation models. In our method, we mine $\langle Qr, Qs\rangle$ pairs from Baidu's query logs. In detail, suppose a user issued a query Qr in Baidu and clicked on a search result with the title T, then $\langle Qr, T\rangle$ will be extracted as a $\langle Qr, Qs\rangle$ pair if it meets the following constraints:

- Qr is not a question[2], and it contains at most three terms. Our intuition is that long queries might be clear enough which need not to be expanded into questions.
- T should be a question Qs and must be from a cQA web site (Zhidao in our experiments).
- Qr should be subsumed in Qs. This constraint limits that Qr can only be *extended* to questions, whose terms are not allowed to be transformed or deleted during question generation.

From the identified $\langle Qr, Qs\rangle$ pair, we can induce a template Tp by substituting query terms in the question Qs with slots $\{[x_i]|1 \leq i \leq n\}$, where n is the number of query terms of Qr. An example is shown in Figure 2. In what follows, we term Qs as an *instantiation* of Tp.

In our experiments, we obtained over 15 million $\langle Qr, Qs\rangle$ pairs from the query logs used, and accordingly extracted 547,325 templates. To eliminate templates that are rarely instantiated, we filtered those templates with less than 10 unique instantiations. 18,929 templates were left after filtering, each with 80 unique instantiations on average. Analysis result reveals that 80% of the eliminated templates are those long and complicated ones, which may seldom be used in practice.

[2]We developed a rule-based tool to identify whether a Chinese word sequence is a question.

Note that a query could instantiate more than one templates. For example, query "故宫 门票 *(The Imperial Palace / ticket)*" can instantiate "*[x1] [x2] 多少 钱 (How much is the [x2] of [x1])*", "*[x1] [x2] 价格 是 多少 (What is the price of [x1]'s [x2])*", and "*[x1] [x2] 贵 吗 (Is the [x2] of [x1] expensive)*", etc. We therefore need to compute the likelihood that a query instantiates each template, which can be used in template ranking and selecting during question generation. In our work, given query Qr and all templates it can instantiate $\{Tp_1, ..., Tp_n\}$, we compute the likelihood of Qr instantiating $Tp_i (1 \leq i \leq n)$ based on maximum likelihood estimation:

$$p(Tp_i|Qr) = \frac{c(Qr, Tp_i)}{c(Qr)} \quad (1)$$

where $c(Qr, Tp_i)$ is the frequency that Qr instantiates Tp_i in the query logs, $c(Qr)$ is the frequency that Qr occurs in the query logs. The acquired templates along with the queries that can instantiate each template are stored in a database D_{Tp}.

2.2 Question Generation

With the induced templates, we can generate questions for any input query qr[3]. Since most of the templates are unsuitable for qr, we need a strategy to select the templates and only retain the useful ones. Our observation is that similar queries usually have close search intent. They may tend to instantiate identical templates and generate similar questions. For example, we found that queries about the tickets of something are mostly interested in the price and instantiate template "*[x1] [x2] 多少 钱 (How much is the [x2] of [x1])*". Thus when we get a new query qr about tickets, it is reasonable for qr to instantiate the same template and generate a question qs asking about the price.

Guided by this intuition, we generate questions for query qr using the templates of qr's similar queries. In practice, we first retrieve qr's similar queries from D_{Tp}, each of which must contain the same number of terms and share at least one identical term with qr. After that, we collect all templates that can be instantiated by the retrieved similar queries, which are then instantiated by qr to generate a list of questions. All the generated questions are ranked and the top-N are returned. The example in Figure 3 illustrates this process.

We take two factors into account when ranking the generated questions. The first is the likelihood that query qr instantiates template Tp, and the second is the fluency of the generated question qs. Hence we define:

$$\begin{aligned} \hat{qs} &= \arg\max_{qs} f(qs, Tp, qr) \quad (2) \\ &= \arg\max_{qs}\{\lambda f_{TP}(Tp, qr) + (1-\lambda) f_{LM}(qs)\} \end{aligned}$$

where $f(qs, Tp, qr)$ is the score function for question ranking, which is decomposed into two parts, i.e., $f_{TP}(Tp, qr)$ and $f_{LM}(qs)$. The former computes the likelihood that qr instantiates Tp, while the latter measures the fluency of qs generated by instantiating Tp with qr.

Definition of $f_{TP}(Tp, qr)$. Let $\{Qr_i | 1 \leq i \leq I\}$ be the similar queries of qr that can instantiate template Tp, we define $f_{TP}(Tp, qr)$ as:

$$f_{Tp}(Tp, qr) = \log \sum_{i=1}^{I} p(Tp|Qr_i) p(Qr_i|qr) \quad (3)$$

where $p(Tp|Qr_i)$ is the probability that Qr_i instantiates Tp, which has been defined in Equ. (1). $p(Qr_i|qr)$ reflects the degree that qr resembles Qr_i, which is defined as the query similarity $sim(qr, Qr_i)$ and is computed as:

$$sim(qr, Qr_i) = \prod_{j=1}^{J} sim(t_{qr\_j}, t_{Qri\_j}) \quad (4)$$

where $sim(t_{qr\_j}, t_{Qri\_j})$ is the similarity between the j-th term of qr and Qr_i, and J is the number of terms in both qr and Qr_i[4]. According to Equ. (4), qr and Qr_i are deemed similar only when they are similar term by term. This guarantees that each term of qr can safely fill in the slot induced from the corresponding term of Qr_i. The similarity between two terms t_1 and t_2 is computed based on distributional hypothesis, which assumes that words occurring in similar contexts tend to have similar meanings (Harris, 1985). We therefore define $sim(t_1, t_2)$ as the similarity of the context words of the two terms:

$$sim(t_1, t_2) = \cos(V_{ctx}(t_1), V_{ctx}(t_2)) \quad (5)$$

[3]Here we use qr and qs to denote a new query and its generated question, so as to differentiate from Qr and Qs that represent query and question mined from query logs.

[4]Recall that each similar query of qr must have the same number of terms as qr.

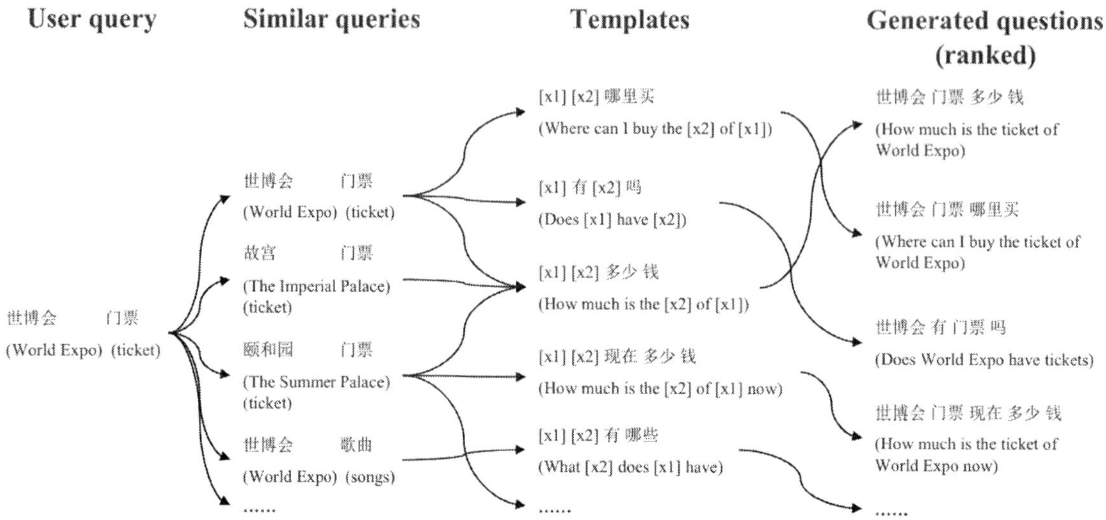

Figure 3: Generating questions from queries with templates induced from search engine query logs.

where $\cos(.,.)$ is the cosine similarity between two vectors. $V_{ctx}(t)$ is the vector of context words of t, which is constructed using Baidu query logs. Specifically, words occurring within the same queries as t are extracted as t's context words. The weight of each context word w is computed in a similar way as tf-idf:

$$W_t(w) = tf_t(w) \times \log \frac{N}{n(w)} \quad (6)$$

where $tf_t(w)$ is the frequency that w occurs in the contexts of t. $n(w)$ is the number of terms whose context words contain w. N is the total number of terms, i.e., the size of vocabulary.

Definition of $f_{LM}(qs)$. The other score function $f_{LM}(qs)$ is designed to measure the fluency of the generated questions, which is defined based on a tri-gram language model:

$$f_{LM}(qs) = \frac{1}{L} \log(p_{LM}(qs)) \quad (7)$$

in which L is the number of terms in qs, and $p_{LM}(qs)$ is the language model score of qs:

$$p_{LM}(qs) = \prod_{l=1}^{L} p(t_l|t_{l-2}t_{l-1}) \quad (8)$$

In our experiments, the language model was trained using over 15 million questions from the collected $\langle Q_r, Q_s \rangle$ pairs. We estimated the parameter λ in Equ. (2) using a development set with 247 random queries. In detail, we generated questions for each query and had all questions manually annotated (Section 3.1). We then examined λ ranging from 0 to 1 and evaluated $P@5$ precision (Section 3.2) under each setting. The setting that obtained the highest performance was selected, which was $\lambda = 0.3$.

3 Evaluation

Our experiments contain two parts. In the first part, we evaluated the precision of the generated questions based on human annotation. In the second part, we used the query-to-question generation algorithm to improve the search of cQA archives.

3.1 Experimental Setup

Comparison method. To our knowledge, there is no existing system that can automatically generate questions from queries. We therefore design a baseline method for comparison, which retrieves questions from cQA archives (termed as RcQA hereafter). Given a query qr, RcQA searches qr in Zhidao site search engine and retrieves questions containing qr[5]. The questions are ranked according to the orders assigned by the site search engine. We compare our query-to-question generation method (QtQG for short) and RcQA on precision. The reason why we employ the cQA site

[5]The retrieved titles from Zhidao are not necessarily questions. We ignored the non-question results when collecting questions from Zhidao.

search engine in the baseline instead of computing the similarity between queries and questions by ourselves is that we believe the cQA site search engine has adopted a state-of-the-art method when computing query-question similarity.

Experiment data. To construct a test set, we randomly sampled 1000 queries from Baidu query logs, each of which contains no more than 3 terms. The test queries cover a variety of domains, including *health*, *food*, *sport*, *music*, *movie*, *software*, *computer game*, etc. As described in Section 2, we used our method to generate questions for each test query, which were ranked according to Equ. (2). We kept up to top-5 questions of each query for evaluation. Meanwhile, we also retrieved up to top-5 questions for each query from Zhidao with RcQA.

Human annotation. Questions produced with both QtQG and RcQA were evaluated based on human annotation. We had two annotators, both of whom are native Chinese speakers. The questions produced with two methods were mixed before being presented to the annotators, so as to avoid bias during annotation. Two annotators evaluated the questions separately. For a query qr, a generated question qs is annotated as *correct* if it is fluent, comprehensible, and likely to be asked by people when they search qr. Otherwise, qs is annotated as *incorrect*. For instance, for the query "世博会 门票 (*World Expo / ticket*)", question "世博会 门票 多少钱 (*How much is the ticket of the World Expo*)" was annotated as correct whereas "世博会 门票 哪里 可以 下载 (*Where can I download the ticket of the World Expo*)" was annotated as incorrect. In addition, a question was annotated as incorrect if it contains too much extra information that is impossible to be induced from the query[6]. For instance, question "在 昆山 怎么 买 世博会 门票 (学生票) (*How can I buy student tickets of Word Expo in Kunshan*)" was judged as incorrect for the above query, since "学生票 (*student tickets*)" and "在 昆山 (*in Kunshan*)" cannot be induced from the query.

After the first round of annotation, we calculated the kappa statistic between two annotators. The result shows that kappa $K = 0.78$, indicating a substantial agreement (K: 0.61-0.8) according to (Landis and Koch, 1977). Data with different annotations were then annotated by a third-party judge, so as to get the final annotations.

[6]Note that question descriptions written by question askers to further explain the questions are not extracted and evaluated together with questions, thus our evaluation metrics are not biased against questions with long and verbose descriptions.

	$P@1$	$P@2$	$P@3$	$P@4$	$P@5$
QtQG	0.67	0.66	0.64	0.62	0.61
RcQA	0.47	0.44	0.42	0.40	0.40

Table 1: $P@N$ results of QtQG and RcQA.

3.2 Evaluation of Precision

Experimental results show that, QtQG can generate at least one question for 765 queries, while RcQA can retrieve at least one question from Zhidao for 660 queries. It suggests that QtQG achieves a larger coverage than RcQA. After the questions were manually annotated, we computed the precision at top-N results ($P@N$):

$$P@N = \frac{|S_{CQs}(N) \cap S_{Qs}(N)|}{|S_{Qs}(N)|} \quad (9)$$

where $S_{Qs}(N)$ denotes the set of top-N questions and $S_{CQs}(N)$ denotes the set of correct ones. Table 1 summarizes the $P@N$ results ($1 \leq N \leq 5$) averaged on the test set for the two methods, from which we can see that QtQG significantly outperforms RcQA. Especially, we observed the results and found that QtQG can generate correct questions for some unpopular queries, about which we cannot even find questions from the web. For example, query "昆明 KTV 沙发 (*Kunming / KTV / sofa*)" can retrieve no question from the web, but our method can generate question "昆明 哪里 有 卖 KTV 沙发 的 (*Where to Buy KTV sofa in Kunming*)", which makes perfect sense and is quite likely to reflect users' requirement. Please note that some of the learned templates can reorder the query terms when generating questions. For example, for the query "门票 颐和园 (*ticket / the Summer Palace*), the template "*[X2]* 的 *[X1]* 多少钱" can be matched and the correct question "颐和园 的 门票 多少钱 (*How much is the ticket of the Summer Palace*)" can be generated.

We then conducted error analysis on the data set. Specifically, we sampled 100 incorrect questions produced with QtQG and RcQA, respectively. Analysis results reveal that 84% of incorrect questions generated with QtQG are those incomprehensible or not fluent questions, such as question "德州 到 天气预报 怎么走 (*How can I get to weather forecast from Dezhou*)" for query "德

州天气预报 (*Dezhou / weather forecast*)". The rest errors are questions that are well formed but less likely to be asked by people. On the other hand, for RcQA, 91% errors are questions containing too much extra information. For example, for query "温州 歌曲 (*Wenzhou / songs*)", RcQA retrieves the question "谁 能 提供 给 我 一些 关于 温州小吃 的 诗歌， 歌曲 或者 趣味 知识 (*Who can give me some poems, songs, or interesting knowledge about Wenzhou snacks*)" . Obviously, it is too specific and not so good as the question generated with QtQG "关于 温州 的 歌曲 有 哪些 (*Are there any songs about Wenzhou*)".

Further more, we also analyzed queries for which QtQG or RcQA failed to generate questions. We sampled 100 such queries for the two methods and had them manually annotated. Results show that, 84% queries for which QtQG cannot generate questions are single-word queries. This is due to our limitation when searching similar queries for a new query qr (Section 2.2), that the similar queries for qr must share at least one identical word with qr. This constraint is designed to restrict search space when looking for similar queries. However it also limits that a single-word query can find similar queries and be rewritten as questions only when the same query has appeared in the D_{Tp} database (Section 2.1). This is a drawback of our method, which will be addressed in the future work. On the other hand, 82% queries for which RcQA did not retrieve questions are because the queries are unpopular. No question about them has been asked in Zhidao.

3.3 Improving cQA Search

As mentioned above, one application of query-to-question generation is to improve the search of cQA archives. We therefore carried out an experiment to examine its effectiveness. We design a strategy to integrate the QtQG module into the cQA site search engine. The basic idea is that, given a query qr, its generated question qs, and a cQA site search engine CQA, if qr's search result in CQA is unsatisfactory, but qs's result is good, then we can return qs's result for qr. The strategy is formally described in Table 2. The key problem here is how to estimate the quality of the search results. This is an interesting research topic but out of the scope of this paper. In our experiment, we adopted a simple criterion, namely, computing the similarity between the query and the title of the search result. The larger the similarity, the better the result. This criterion is naive, but our experiment result below shows that it is enough to verify the effectiveness of QtQG in cQA search.

Input:	qr: user query
	qs: generated question for qr
	CQA: cQA site search engine
Output:	$RST(qr)$: search result of qr in CQA
1. Search qr in CQA, get result $R(qr)$	
2. Search qs in CQA, get result $R(qs)$	
3. Estimate the quality of $R(qr)$, get $E(R(qr))$	
4. Estimate the quality of $R(qs)$, get $E(R(qs))$	
5. **If** $E(R(qr)) = BAD$ and $E(R(qs)) = GOOD$	
6. Return $RST(qr) = R(qs)$	
7. **Else**	
8. Return $RST(qr) = R(qr)$	

Table 2: Strategy for improving cQA search with automatically generated questions.

We experimented with the 765 test queries for which at least one question can be generated with our method. We only examined the 1-best question generated for each query. The cQA site search engine used is Zhidao. In addition, when evaluating and comparing the search results of the original query and generated question, we just considered the top-1 search result, which is not only for convenience, but also because the top-1 result usually means more to users in a search engine. The practical strategy used in the experiment is shown in Table 3, in which $sim(qr, R(qr))$ denotes the similarity between the query qr and the title of the top-1 search result $R(qr)$. The similarity is computed based on word overlap rate. $sim(qs, R(qs))$ is computed in the same way. Thresholds T_1 and T_2 were empirically set as 0.7 and 0.8, respectively.

Experimental results show that the top-1 search results for 65 (out of 765) test queries were changed using the above strategy, which means that our method has replaced the original search results of these queries with that of the generated questions. We asked the annotators to compare the search results before and after using the strategy. A query is annotated as *Good* if its new result is better than the old one, *Bad* if the new result is worse than the old one, and *Same* if the quality of the result is not evidently changed. Annotation result is shown in the first line of Table 4. As can be seen, the top-1 search results for 27

Input:	qr: user query
	qs: generated 1-best question for qr
	ZD: Zhidao cQA archive
Output:	$RST(qr)$: top-1 search result of qr in ZD

1. Search qr in ZD, get top-1 result $R(qr)$
2. Search qs in ZD, get top-1 result $R(qs)$
3. Compute similarity $sim(qr, R(qr))$
4. Compute similarity $sim(qs, R(qs))$
5. **If** $sim(qr, R(qr)) < T_1$ and $sim(qs, R(qs)) > T_2$
6. Return $RST(qr) = R(qs)$
7. **Else**
8. Return $RST(qr) = R(qr)$

Table 3: Strategy used in the experiments.

	Good	Same	Bad	Total
All que.	27	31	7	65
Correct que.	26	23	4	53
Incorrect que.	1	8	3	12

Table 4: Evaluating the effectiveness of query-to-question generation in cQA search.

queries get better, while that for only 7 queries get worse. This result demonstrates that our question generation technique can improve the performance of cQA search. Take the following case for example. The original query is " 读后感 (*book review*)", whose top-1 search result is "假如给我三天光明的读后感 (*book review of 'Three Days to See'*)". Our method can generate a question "读后感怎么写 (*How to write a book review*)" for the query and accordingly retrieve this question as the top-1 result from Zhidao. It is obvious that the new result is much more likely to be looked for by users than the old one.

We also analyzed the search results that got worse after using our strategy. It is found that 6 of the 7 are still correct but not so good as the old ones. There is only one search result becomes unrelated to the query. Moreover, we should note that the 1-best questions used for improving cQA search are not necessarily correct. Hence we further evaluated the performance when only considering the correct or incorrect 1-best questions. The evaluation results are depicted in line 2 and 3 of Table 4. It is interesting to find that the performance did not evidently decrease when we only used the incorrect 1-best questions in our strategy. This result indicates that the performance of the query-to-question generation module in cQA search is not sensitive to the generation errors if we adopt a proper strategy to integrate it into the cQA site search engine.

4 Related Work

4.1 Research on cQA

Several studies have been carried out on cQA. Some of them have focused on retrieval and recommendation on cQA archives. For example, Xue et al. (2008) designed a retrieval model for cQA search, which considers both question and answer parts when measuring the relatedness between queries and cQA resources. Wang et al. (2009) presented a syntactic tree matching method for finding similar questions. Cao et al. (2008) proposed a question recommendation method based on tree cut model. Wang et al. (2010) proposed a graph-based approach to segmenting multi-sentence questions, so as to improve search performance. Another category of studies on cQA aims to estimate the quality of questions, answers, and users. For example, Song et al. (2008) examined the utility of questions in the cQA archives. Liu et al. (2008) presented a classification-based method to automatically predict whether a question-asker will be satisfied with the answers. Jurczyk and Agichtein (2007) tried to identify experts in a cQA community.

4.2 Question Generation

Question generation is a branch of natural language generation, which is defined as the task of automatically generating questions from some form of input (Rus and Graesser, 2009). The input may vary from a deep semantic representation to a raw text. Previous studies on question generation have mostly focused on text-to-question generation, which generates questions from declarative sentences or paragraphs. This technique is useful in education, especially in reading tutoring. Most previous studies employed rule-based methods in their text-to-question generation systems (Ali et al., 2010; Kalady et al., 2010; Mannem et al., 2010; Pal et al., 2010; Piwek and Stoyanchev, 2010; Varga and Ha, 2010).

Query-to-question generation is a sub-task of question generation, which was first proposed by Lin (2008). Lin has suggested to learn query-to-question generation models with query logs. However, no detail method or evaluation has been presented. There has been no other research since, either, which may be mainly because few researchers can access the query log data.

4.3 Query Reformulation

Query reformulation is an important topic in the IR community, since it can improve users' search experience. Query reformulation mainly involves query reduction, expansion, and spelling correction. Query-to-question generation is closely related to query expansion. However, its goal is not only expanding useful information for the original query, but also organizing the information to produce a question, with which one can better understand the query's structure and the user's intent.

Several techniques have been proposed for query reformulation, which are mostly based on relevance feedback (Xu and Croft, 1996; Mitra et al., 1998) and query log analysis. Especially, the studies based on query logs can be divided into three categories. In the first one, researchers learn related query pairs from query sessions. The basic idea is that queries from the same session are more likely to be related to each other (Fonseca et al., 2005; Jones et al., 2006; Zhang and Nasraoui, 2006). The second kind of method identifies related queries using click-through information. They assume that queries leading to similar clicks are related in meaning (Wen et al., 2002; Baeza-Yates and Tiberi, 2007). The third category of method directly learns expansion terms from the clicked documents of the query. Their hypothesis is that terms in a query and a user-clicked document might be related (Cui et al., 2002; Riezler et al., 2008).

4.4 Template Induction

Template induction has been widely researched in NLP community, in which the following studies are close to our work. (1) Answer template learning in QA. Some QA systems use templates in answer extraction, which can be learned from large Web corpora or Web search results with handcrafted seed tuples (Ravichandran and Hovy, 2002). (2) Query template acquisition. For example, Agarwal et al. (2010) mine templates from search engine query logs with the goal of query interpretation. Szpektor et al. (2011) extract templates for long-tail queries so as to improve query recommendation. (3) Paraphrase template learning. Paraphrase templates are templates that can convey identical information when the variables are instantiated with the same contents. Paraphrase templates can be learned from monolingual corpora based on distributional hypothesis (Lin and Pantel, 2001), from comparable news articles based on alignment (Barzilay and Lee, 2003), or from bilingual corpora based on pivot approaches (Zhao et al., 2008). The above-mentioned studies are all related to our work. However, none of the previous work addresses the problem of query-to-question template generation.

5 Conclusions and Future Work

This paper addresses the problem of query-to-question generation for cQA and proposes a method based on search engine query logs. Several conclusions can be drawn from the experimental results. First, search engine query logs are powerful data for the research of query-to-question generation, from which we have acquired a large volume of question generation templates. Second, the proposed method is effective, which achieves promising precision and outperforms a baseline method. Third, the query-to-question generation technique can be used to improve the search of cQA archives.

In our future work, we will exploit larger-scale query logs for acquiring question generation templates. We will also improve the similar query retrieval strategy (Section 2.2), which underperforms now on single-word queries. In addition, we will have a deeper insight into the applications of question-to-query generation in cQA services.

Acknowledgments

This work was supported by (1) China Postdoctoral Science Foundation (No.20100480100), and (2) Beijing Postdoctoral Research Foundation.

References

Ganesh Agarwal, Govind Kabra, and Kevin Chen-Chuan Chang. 2010. Towards Rich Query Interpretation: Walking Back and Forth for Mining Query Templates. In *Proceedings of WWW*, pages 1-10.

Husam Ali, Yllias Chali, and Sadid A. Hasan. 2010. Automation of Question Generation From Sentences. In *Proceedings of the Third Workshop on Question Generation*, pages 58-67.

Ricardo Baeza-Yates and Alessandro Tiberi. 2007. Extracting Semantic Relations from Query Logs. In *Proceedings of KDD*, pages 76-85.

Regina Barzilay and Lillian Lee. 2003. Learning to Paraphrase: An Unsupervised Approach Using

Multiple-Sequence Alignment. In *Proceedings of HLT-NAACL*, pages 16-23.

Yunbo Cao, Huizhong Duan, Chin-Yew Lin, Yong Yu, and Hsiao-Wuen Hon. 2008. Recommending Questions Using the MDL-based Tree Cut Model. In *Proceedings of WWW*, pages 81-90.

Hang Cui, Ji-Rong Wen, Jian-Yun Nie, Wei-Ying Ma. 2002. Probabilistic Query Expansion Using Query Logs. In *Proceedings of WWW*, pages 325-332.

Bruno M. Fonseca, Paulo Golgher, Bruno Pôssas, Berthier Ribeiro-Neto, Nivio Ziviani. 2005. Concept-based Interactive Query Expansion. In *Proceedings of CIKM*, pages 696-703.

Zellig Harris. 1985. Distributional Structure. In *The Philosophy of Linguistics*, pages 26-47.

Rosie Jones, Benjamin Rey, Omid Madani, and Wiley Greiner. 2006. Generating Query Substitutions. In *Proceedings of WWW*, pages 387-396.

Pawel Jurczyk and Eugene Agichtein. 2007. Hits on Question Answer Portals: Exploration of Link Analysis for Author Ranking. In *Proceedings of SIGIR*, pages 845-846.

Saidalavi Kalady, Ajeesh Elikkottil, Rajarshi Das. 2010. Natural Language Question Generation Using Syntax and Keywords. In *Proceedings of the Third Workshop on Question Generation*, pages 1-10.

J. R. Landis and G. G. Koch. 1977. The Measurement of Observer Agreement for Categorical Data. In *Biometrics* 33(1): 159-174.

Chin-Yew Lin. 2008. Automatic Question Generation from Queries. In *Proceedings of Workshop on the Question Generation Shared Task and Evaluation Challenge*.

De-Kang Lin and Patrick Pantel. 2001. Discovery of Inference Rules for Question Answering. In *Natural Language Engineering* 7(4): 343-360.

Yandong Liu, Jiang Bian and Eugene Agichtein. 2008. Predicting Information Seeker Satisfaction in Community Question Answering. In *Proceedings of SIGIR*, pages 483-490.

Prashanth Mannem, Rashmi Prasad, and Aravind Joshi. 2010. Question Generation from Paragraphs at UPenn: QGSTEC System Description. In *Proceedings of the Third Workshop on Question Generation*, pages 84-91.

Mandar Mitra, Amit Singhal, and Chris Buckley. 1998. Improving Automatic Query Expansion. In *Proceedings of SIGIR*, pages 206-214.

Santanu Pal, Tapabrata Mondal, Partha Pakray, Dipankar Das and Sivaji Bandyopadhyay. 2010. QGSTEC System Description - JUQGG: A Rule based approach. In *Proceedings of the Third Workshop on Question Generation*, pages 76-79.

Paul Piwek and Svetlana Stoyanchev. 2010. Question Generation in the CODA project. In *Proceedings of the Third Workshop on Question Generation*, pages 29-34.

Deepak Ravichandran and Eduard Hovy. 2002. Learning Surface Text Patterns for a Question Answering System. In *Proceedings of ACL*, pages 41-47.

Stefan Riezler, Yi Liu, and Alexander Vasserman. 2008. Translating Queries into Snippets for Improved Query Expansion. In *Proceedings of COLING*, pages 737-744.

Vasile Rus and Arthur C. Graesser. 2009. Workshop Report: The Question Generation Task and Evaluation Challenge. Institute for Intelligent Systems, Memphis, TN, ISBN: 978-0-615-27428-7.

Idan Szpektor, Aristides Gionis, and Yoelle Maarek. 2011. Improving Recommendation for Long-tail Queries via Templates. In *Proceedings of WWW*, pages 47-56.

Young-In Song, Chin-Yew Lin, Yunbo Cao and Hae-Chang Rim. 2008. Question Utility: A Novel Static Ranking of Question Search. In *Proceedings of AAAI*, pages 1231-1236.

Andrea Varga and Le An Ha. 2010. WLV: A Question Generation System for the QGSTEC 2010 Task B. In *Proceedings of the Third Workshop on Question Generation*, pages 80-83.

Kai Wang, Zhaoyan Ming, Tat-Seng Chua. 2009. A Syntactic Tree Matching Approach to Finding Similar Questions in Community-based QA Services. In *Proceedings of SIGIR*, pages 187-194.

Kai Wang, Zhaoyan Ming, Xia Hu, Tat-Seng Chua. 2010. Segmentation of Multi-Sentence Questions: Towards Effective Question Retrieval in cQA Services. In *Proceedings of SIGIR*, pages 387-394.

Ji-Rong Wen, Jian-Yun Nie, and Hong-Jiang Zhang. 2002. Query Clustering Using User Logs. In *ACM Transactions on Information Systems* 20(1): 59-81, 2002.

Jinxi Xu and W. Bruce Croft. 1996. Query Expansion using Local and Global Document Analysis. In *Proceedings of SIGIR*, pages 4-11.

Xiaobing Xue, Jiwoon Jeon, W. Bruce Croft. 2008. Retrieval Models for Question and Answer Archives. In *Proceedings of SIGIR*, pages 475-482.

Zhiyong Zhang and Olfa Nasraoui. 2006. Mining Search Engine Query Logs for Query Recommendation. In *Proceedings of WWW*, pages 1039-1040.

Shiqi Zhao, Haifeng Wang, Ting Liu, and Sheng Li. 2008. Pivot Approach for Extracting Paraphrase Patterns from Bilingual Corpora. In *Proceedings of ACL-08:HLT*, pages 780-788.

Question Classification Based on an Extended Class Sequential Rule Model

Zijing Hui, Juan Liu*, Lumei Ouyang
Computer School, Wuhan University, Wuhan 40072, P. R. China
{zijinghui, liujuan, ouyanglumei}@whu.edu.cn

Abstract

Question classification is a crucial preprocessing for question answering system; it can help to make sure the user's intention. Most of previous researches focus on the feature driven methods that represent a question with a bag of features, which ignore the important information contained in the words order and distance. To take such information into account, this paper proposes to describe the questions via the ExCSR (Extended Class Sequential Rule) model. To mine ExCSR rules, a method based on PrefixSpan, called DS-SRM (Distance Sensitive Sequential Rule Miner), is presented as well. Due to the existence of redundancy in the mined rules, a rule selection algorithm MCRSelection (Most Cover Rule Selection) is also proposed to find the most interesting rules. Experiments results on UIUC question set[1] show that the proposed method can achieve the accuracy of 90.6%, which outperforms the previously reported results.

1 Introduction

Question classification, i.e., classifying questions into predetermined types, is quite an important problem in question answering (QA) system, it helps to make clear the intention of users so that the system can choose the appropriate strategies of answers searching and ranking. Similar to other classification problems, question classification usually needs to build the classifier from the training data which contains a set of labeled questions; the classifier is then used to classify the unlabeled questions.

Although questions are special kinds of texts, question classification is more challenging than text classification. Compared to normal texts, a question is usually a very short sentence (some even with few of words), and mostly one word just occurs once in one question, which results that the widely used vector space model (mainly based on TF/IDF) fails to work. To address this problem, researchers usually develop a lot of features, such as location, organization, name, etc., to annotate the words/phrases in the questions, and then use the bag of features to represent the questions. However, such methods still suffer some problems. (1) To get the satisfactory classification performances, they usually need an extremely large amount of features. For example, Li et al. used more than 200,000 features (Li et al., 2006) to represent questions in UIUC question set, while Huang et al. used 13,697 binary features in their best feature space (Huang et al., 2008). (2) The bag of features representation ignores the relationship and the order information among words within the questions, which will cause the misclassification. For example, "Which city is famous for rose?" and "Which rose is famous for city?" belong to two different classes (the former one asks about the <location>, while the later one is about the <entity> or <plant>), due to that "rose" and "city" have different orders. (3) The information of word distance is valuable in question classification yet is not considered by the present methods. For example, "How many people did Randy Craft kill?" asks about the <number>, while "How Randy Craft killed many people?" is about the <description>. The difference of the distances between "how" and "many" plays a role on the types of the questions. CSRs (Class Sequential Rules) originally proposed for opinion extraction (Hu and Liu, 2006) take the word sequences into account. However, it still ignores the distance information between words.

In this paper, we extend the representation of CSRs by integrating the distance information into it, and propose the ExCSR (Extended Class Sequential Rule) model. To mine the ExCSRs, we further propose an algorithm, called DS-SRM (Distance Sensitive Sequential Pattern Miner), based on PrefixScan (Pei et al., 2004). To remove the redundancy of the mined rules, we present an efficient rule selection method, MCRSelection (Most Cover Rule Selection). The remainder of this paper is organized as follows: section 2 introduces the related works; section 3

* the corresponding author
[1] http://cogcomp.cs.illinois.edu/Data/QA/QC/

describes the CSR and its extension ExCSR; the rule mining and selection algorithms are presented in section 4; section 5 is the evaluation experiments and results; the paper ends with the concluding remarks in the last section.

2 Related Works

Question classification is a process that assigns a question to a single category or a set of categories. The categories can be organized as either flat or hierarchical taxonomies. Li & Roth (2002) defined a two-layered taxonomy shown in Table 1. The taxonomy consists of six coarse categories and a total of 50 finer categories. Since this taxonomy has been regarded as somewhat informal standard and has been used in much other work on question classification, it is also used in our paper. Given the taxonomy, the classification machinery is then needed to put the questions into specific category or categories. There are two main machineries for the classification, i.e., manual and automatic. The manual methods (Hermjakob, 2001) use hand-written rules and heuristics to do the classification, thus it is time consuming and hard to extend to new question categories; while the automatic methods classify the questions based on machine learning technologies or statistical methods, thus are much more efficient and easy to extend to new question types. Therefore, most of the work follows the automatic methods, which will be also adopted in our work. There are many machine learning methods have been proposed for automatic question classification. Radev et al. (2002) proposed to learn rules by using decision tree method, after trained on TREC-8 and TREC-9, it reached an accuracy of around 70% on TREC-10. Li and Roth (2002) reported a hierarchical approach based on the SNoW learning architecture. By trained on 5500 questions and tested on 500 questions from TREC-10, which are collected in UIUC dataset, it reached an accuracy of 84.2%. Zhang and Lee (2003) used linear SVMs with all possible question word grams, and obtained accuracy of 79.2%. Krishnan et al. (2005) used a short sequence called informer span as important features that are identified by the Conditional Random Field (CRF), and built a meta-classifier using a linear SVM on the features. Their model got the accuracy of 86.2% on UIUC question set. Li and Roth (2006) used more semantic information in WordNet, plus their originally proposed syntactic ones (Li & Roth, 2002), after being trained on 21500 questions, their model achieved an accuracy of 89.3% on a test set of 1000 questions. Li et al. (2008) propose to classify what-type questions by head noun tagging and achieve 85.60% accuracy. Huang et al. (2008; 2009) used much more compact feature set than Li and Roth's work, by taking the head words and their hypernyms as features, with other standard features such as unigrams, they obtained accuracy of 89.2% using linear support vector machine (SVMs), and 89.0% using Maximum Entropy (ME) model. Ray et al. (2010) used the semantic features of the WordNet and the vast knowledge repository in Wikipedia to build the classification model. They trained their model over 5500 questions in UIUC, and tested it over 2393 questions from five TREC collections, and got the average precision of 89.55%. However, to our best knowledge, all of the present works seldom consider the word sequence and word distance for question classification problem. In this paper, we exploit the information of word sequence and word distance in the questions and develop an efficient classification method. The details of the proposed methods will be provided in the next sections.

Coarse Class	Fine Class
ABBREVIATION	abbreviation, exp
DESCRIPTION	definition, description, manner, reason
ENTITY	animal, body, color, creative, currency, disease/medicine, event, food, instrument, language, letter, other, plant product, religion, sport, substance, symbol, technique, term, vehicle, word
HUMAN	group, individual, title, description
LOCATION	city, country, mountain, other, state
NUMERIC	code, count, date, money, order, other, period, percent, speed, temperature, volume/size, weight

Table 1. Two-layered taxonomy proposed by Li & Roth (2002)

3 Class Sequential Rule Model and Its Extension

Class sequential rule (CSR) model was originally proposed to represent the labeled sequences in the research of opinion feature extraction (Hu & Liu, 2006). For the completeness of this paper, we first introduce CSR model, then state its extension model ExCSR in this section.

3.1 Class Sequential Rule Model

Let $I = \{i_1, i_2, ..., i_n\}$ be a set of items, and an *element* or *itemset* be a non-empty set of items. A *sequence* is defined as an ordered list of elements, denoted by $\langle e_1 e_2 ... e_r \rangle$, where e_i is an *element* (Liu,

2007). An item can occur only once in an element of a sequence, but can occur multiple times in different elements.

A sequence $s_1 = \langle a_1a_2...a_r\rangle$ is a *subsequence* of another sequence $s_2 = \langle b_1b_2...b_m\rangle$ or s_2 *contains* s_1, if there exist integers $1 \leq j_1 < j_2 < ... < j_{r-1} < j_r \leq m$ such that $a_1 \subseteq b_{j1}$, $a_2 \subseteq b_{j2}$, ..., $a_r \subseteq b_{jr}$.

Let $D = \{(s_1, y_1), (s_2, y_2), ..., (s_n, y_n)\}$ be the input data of labeled sequences, where s_i is a sequence and $y_i \in Y$ is its class, Y is the set of all classes, $I \cap Y = \emptyset$. A CSR is a production rule $X \rightarrow y$, where X is a sequence, and $y \in Y$.

Table 2 lists some examples of CSRs, where each English word is an item and the class label is in the right side.

Id	Sequence	Class
1	<What difference between>	Desc:desc
2	<Who>	Human:ind
3	<How much weight>	Count:weight
4	<How much>	Count:money
5	<What be NN>	Desc:def

Table 2. Examples of CSRs

A data instance (s_i, y_i) in D is said to cover the CSR $X \rightarrow y$ if s_i contains X. A data instance (s_i, y_i) is said to satisfy *t*he CSR if s_i contains X and $y_i = y$. The *support* of the CSR is the total instances in D that covers the rule. Given the minimum support threshold *min_sup*, a sequence X is called a *sequential pattern* in D if $support(X) \geq min\_sup$. The *confidence* of the CSR is the proportion of instances in D that covers the rule also satisfies the rule.

3.2 Extended Class Sequential Rule Model

Although the CSR takes the word sequence into account, it still ignores the distance information between words/phrases which should be also important to question classification. Therefore, we extend the representation of CSRs by considering the distance information. The extended class sequential rule model is called ExCSR hereinafter.

First, we define three simple kinds of distance constraints, shown in Table 3.

Index	Distance Constraint	Description
1	[NEIGH]	Two elements are neighbored. Used to extract the phrase, like "how [NEIGH] much"
2	[NEAR]	Two elements are not more than a give threshold away.
3	[ANY] or blank	Two elements can be of any distance, [ANY] can be omitted.

Table 3. Definition of distance labels

Suppose $<x_1x_2 \ldots x_r> \rightarrow y$ be a CSR rule, then we define an ExCSR as $<d_1x_1d_2x_2 \ldots d_rx_rd_{r+1}> \rightarrow y$, where d_i takes one of the distance constraints in Table 3, which limits the occurring distance between elements x_{i-1} and x_i when the rule is selected to match an instance for classification. For d_1, we can image that there is a special element "x_0" representing the beginning of a sentence, therefore, d_1 is used to constrain the occurring distance of x_1 apart from the beginning of a sentence. Similarly, d_{r+1} constrains the occurring distance of x_r to the end of a sentence.

Then, taking the CSR rules in Table 2 as examples, their extended ExCSR rules might be in the forms listed in Table 4. The support and confidence of an ExCSR is just the same as its original CSR.

Id	Sequence	Class
1	<[NEIGH] What [NEAR] difference [NEAR] between [ANY]>	Desc: desc
2	<[NEIGH] who [ANY]>	Human: ind
3	<[NEIGH] How [NEIGH] much [ANY] weight [NEIGH]>	Count: weight
4	<[NEIGH] How [NEIGH] much [ANY]>	Count: money
5	<[NEIGH] What [NEAR] be [NEAR] NN [NEIGH]>	Desc: def

Table 4. Possible ExCSR examples originated from CSRs in Table 2.

It is noticeable that if only [ANY] is used, then the ExCSR model is actually the same as CSR model. Furthermore, by using ExCSR model, more compact rules that are usually ignored in CSRs mining but play important roles in question classification will be considered. For example, the CSR "<in what year> → date" is too short that it may cover many questions belonging to different classes which causes its confidence may be lower than the threshold; while its corresponding ExCSR "< [NEIGH] in [NEIGH] what [NEIGH] year [ANY] > → date" cannot cover so many questions with conflicted classes as the CSR due to the distance constraint, thus it should have higher confidence and be included in the final classification model.

4 DS-SRM: ExCSRs Mining Method

DS-SRM consists of three parts: preprocessing, mining and rules filtering, shown in Figure 1.

Given a set of question texts, the preprocessing step parses every sentence and translates it into a sequence of elements labeled with semantic information, and the mining step generates a set of ExCSRs satisfying the minimum support (*min_sup*) and minimum confidence (*min_conf*) requirements from the sequences. Since the distance label [ANY] covers [NEIGH] and [NEAR], the mined ExCSR set should contains a lot of redundant rules with the same element sequences but different distance labels. Therefore, the filtering step is required to remove the redundancy of the rule set. The filtered ExCSRs are to be used to classify the unseen question sentences.

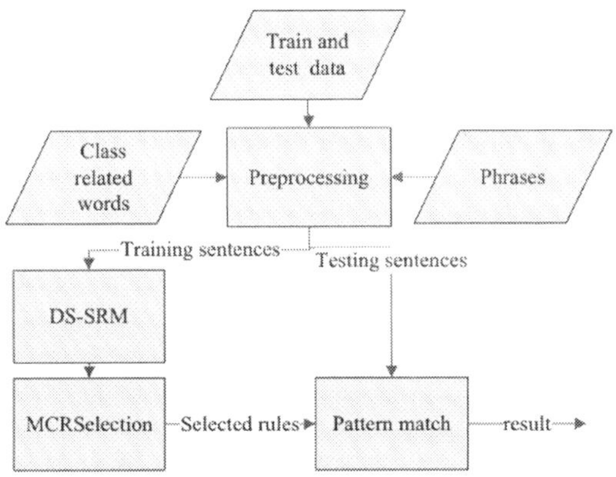

Figure 1. The workflow of DS-SRM

4.1 Preprocessing the Question Texts

Now that the question sentences are in the form of raw texts and cannot be directly used for the rules mining purpose, it's necessary to do the preprocessing by scanning each sentence to do annotation, chunking, and so on. By doing this, each sentence is re-organized by a set of elements with semantic information, especially with the words related to class information. This paper performs the following main preprocessing:

(1) Phrases recognition

There are some phrases consisting of several noun words, which can represent entity classes as a whole, yet each word of it may has different meanings. For example, "*state flower*" denotes a kind of "plant" where "state" is just as a modifier of "flower". While "state" could be regarded as a "location" and "flower" is a kind of "plant" if "state" and "flower" are separately considered. Therefore, we need to recognize such kinds of phrases to avoid ambiguity. We first collect a lot of frequent phrases by grouping the adjacently occurring words from the web pages according to the mutual information statistics. And then locate the ambiguous phrases within the question sentences and manually annotate them with the related class labels (It should be noticed that this processing just recognizes out the phrases of ambiguity, not all phrases or the name entities).

(2) Named entities recognition

A named entity recognizer (NER) of Stanford (Finkel et al., 2005) which defines four types of entities is used to assign a semantic type to noun phrases in a sentence.

For example, a question "*What was W.C. Fields ' real name?*" will be changed into "*What was [person_name] ' real name?*" after the using NER, which will be helpful to assign this question to correct class. However, if we do not tag "*W.C. Fields*" as a person's name, it will be difficult to correctly identify the question's class.

(3) Part-Of-Speech (POS) tagging

POS is important syntactic information in text preprocessing, and it allows us to generate general rules. In our wok, we have used the Stanford Log-linear Part-Of-Speech (Toutanova et al., 2003) to do POS tagging.

(4) Chunking

Besides POS tagging, we also use a chunker, also called as shallow parser, to find out some special structures and phrases and then to eliminate the adjunct words which may have bad impacts on the classification.

For example, in the following question: *What is a group of turkeys called?* (Huang, et al. 2008)

The word "*turkeys*" acts as the central word and contributes to classifying question as "animal", however, the phrase "*a group of*" would introduce ambiguity to misclassify this question to "human group". Therefore, we need to deal with such kinds of phrases. In this work, we adopt the Illinois chunker package (Mavronicolas et al., 1991).

(5) Class related words tagging

For each type of question, there are usually some words related to the question class. Li et al., (2002) have built a list of related words for each question class in their research. For example, for class "*food*", the related words set would be {*alcoholic, apple, beer, berry, breakfast, brew, butter, candy, cereal, champagne, cook, eat, sweat...*}. Using the class label to tag such related words would be very useful for the question classification. However, the class related words may be nouns, verbs and adjectives, and we have found that the verbs and adjectives would cause the ambiguity in our test. Therefore, we only use the nouns in the class related word sets collected by Li et al. (2002). Nevertheless, there still maybe exist the word ambiguity problem. At present, we just ignore it for it has less impact on the performance of our ExCSR rules.

After the preprocessing, the each question sentence will be transformed into a sequence of triplets <[pos], word, [cid]>, where "pos" and "cid" are the POS and class tags of the word respectively. For those *wh* words ("what", "when", "who", "how"...), the "pos" in the triplet is left blank; for any words except those class related nouns, the "cid" is left blank. From the sequences, we can mine out the ExCSRs.

4.2 Mining the ExCSR Rules

The mining procedure is extended from PrefixSpan (Pei et al., 2004), an efficient sequence rule mining method. We will not introduce the PrefixSpan method itself, which is beyond the topic of this paper. Instead, we present our modified version based on the framework of PrefixSpan. The mining algorithm, called DS-SRM (Distance Sensitive Sequential Rule Miner), is shown in Algorithm 1, which is composed of a recursive procedure DS-SPM (Distance Sensitive Sequential Pattern Mining).

It is noticeable that the imported distance information [NEIGH], [NEAR] and [ANY] are not exclusive: [ANY] covers [NEIGH] and [NEAR]; and [NEAR] covers [NEIGH]. Therefore, when counting the occurrence for each item in Step 1 of Procedure DS-SPM, if the current item is (NEIGH, b), then the counters for (NEIGH, b), (NEAR, b), (ANY, b) increase one; if the current item is (NEAR, b), then the counters for (NEAR, b), (ANY, b) increase one.

Algorithm 1: (DS-SRM)Distance Sensitive Sequential Rule Miner

Input: The training set $D = \{(s_1, y_1), (s_2, y_2), ..., (s_n, y_n)\}$, where each s_i is the preprocessed sequence;
The minimum support threshold: *min_sup*;
The minimum confidence threshold: *min_conf*.
//Rules with the confidence below *min_conf* or support below *min_sup* will be disregarded.

Output: A set of ExCSRs satisfying the support and confidence requirements

Parameters: Λ - a sequential pattern set;
α - a sequential pattern in Λ;.

Step 1: $S = \{s_1, s_2, \ldots, s_n\}$; $Y = \{y_1, y_2, \ldots, y_n\}$

Step 2: Λ = DS-SPM(<>, 0, S);

Step 3: for each α in Λ

(a) count the frequencies of all covered classes (the classes that the covered sequences belong to), and find the most frequent class label $y \in Y$;

(b) if support($\alpha \rightarrow$y) $\geq$ *min_sup* and confidence($\alpha \rightarrow$y) $\geq$ *min_conf* then output $\alpha \rightarrow$y.

Procedure DS-SPM (α, *len*, $S|_\alpha$)

Input: A sequence set S;
The minimum support threshold: *min_sup*;

Output: The complete set of sequential patterns

Parameters: α - a sequential pattern, where each element is a triplet originated from section 4.1 and have attached the distance information in the form of [(*d*, *pos*), (*d*, *word*), (*d*, *cid*)] (*d* is the distance information and initially is blank), each pair in a triplet is regarded as an item;
len - the length of α;
$S|_\alpha$ - the α-projected sequence set, the collection of labeled suffixes of sequences in S with regards to prefix α. If α is empty, then $S|_\alpha$= S.
Tnear - the threshold to indicate whether two triplets are NEAR.

Step 1: Scan $S|_\alpha$ once to find each frequent item, (d_b,b), such that

a) (d_b,b) can be assembled to the last element of α to form a sequential pattern; or

b) $<(d_b,b)>$ can be appended to the last item of α to form a sequential pattern ($<(d_b,b)>$ denotes the triplet containing (d_b,b)).

Step 2: for each frequent item (d_b,b), append it to α to form a sequential pattern α', and output α'.

Step 3: for each α', construct α'-projected set $S|_{\alpha'}$ by the following ways:

(a) $S|_{\alpha'}$ = set of suffixes of sequences in S with regards to prefix α';

(b) For each item (d_c,c) in $S|_{\alpha'}$, revising its distance information by one of the following ways:
  (i) if (d_c,c) is in the same triplet with (d_b,b), then modify (d_c,c) to (b,c);
  (ii) if (d_c,c)'s triplet is neighbor to (d_b,b)'s triplet, then modify (d_c,c) to (*NEIGH*, *c*);
  (iii) if (d_c,c)'s triplet is near to (d_b,b)'s triplet with regards of *Tnear*, then modify (d_c,c) to (*NEAR*, *c*);
  (iv) OTHERWISE, modify (d_c,c) to (*ANY*, *c*);

Step 4: call DS-SPM(α',*len*+1, $S|_{\alpha'}$).

Algorithm 1. The flow of DS-SRM algorithm

4.3 Filtering out Redundant ExCSR Rules

Since [NEIGH], [NEAR], and [ANY] are not exclusive, Algorithm 1 may generate quite a lot of redundant rules. In order to remove the redundancy, we first define the interestingness of a rule *r* as Equation (1):

$$\text{Interestingness}(r)=\text{support}(r)*\text{confidence}(r) \quad (1)$$

Then we can rank the rules according to their interestingness. Rules with high interestingness score tend to have high support as well as high confidence, thus should be remained.

Due to the use of overlapping constraints, there are usually some rules with the same support and confidence, exemplified in Table 5.

Rule Id	Class	Conf.	Sup.	Rule
1	DESC :desc	100%	32	<[what][be][difference][between]>
2	DESC :desc	100%	32	<[what][be][difference][NEAR][between]>

Table 5. Example rules with same support and confidence

Rule 1 and 2 are with the same confidence 100% and support 32 thus have the same interestingness. However, rule 1 is more general than rule 2 for it uses less distance constraints, so we prefer to remain rule 1 and discard rule 2. For this purpose, we further to define a measure as Equation (2):

$$\text{Distance\_Constraint}(r) = \sum_{i=1}^{k} \text{label\_value}(i) \quad (2)$$

Where *label_value(i)* denotes the value of the *i-th* distance label (the value of [NEIGH], [NEAR], [ANY] is set to 2, 1, 0.5 separately), and *k* is the total number of distance labels used in rule *r*.

Obviously, shorter rules with simpler distance constraint are more general and preferred.

Therefore, we propose a rule selection algorithm MCRSelection illustrated in Algorithm 2, which will be used iteratively for all classes, one run for one class, to remove the redundant rules.

5 Experiments and Discussions

In order to evaluate our proposed method, we have compared our method to other art-of-state methods on the UIUC question set. We first describe the data sets used in our experiments. In order to investigate which combination of the distance information is optimal to our method, we then test our method with different distance combination. Finally, we compare our method with the optimal distance combination to other representative methods. In the experiments, we set the threshold values of parameters *min_sup*, *min_conf* and *Tnear* as 3, 0.75 and 2 respectively by experience.

Algorithm 2: MCRSelection

Input: rule set R = $\{r_1, r_2 \ldots r_n\}$ for specific class;
The training question set D.

Output: rule set R' without redundancy

Step 1: R' = ∅;

Step 2: Calculate interestingness for each rule in R;

Step 3: Rank rules according to the interestingness and find the rule r with the highest interestingness. If there are one more than such rules, then choose the one with the least Distance-Constraint value;

Step 4: R' = R' ∪ {r}; R = R – {r};

Step 5: D = D- {instances satisfied by r};

Step 6: if D is empty, then return R';

Step 7: For each r∈R, update support(r) with regards to the updated D;

Step 8: go to **step 2**.

Algorithm 2. The flow of MCRSelection algorithm

5.1 Data Set

Class	Question Num.	Class	Question Num.
ABBR	9	desc	7
abb	1	manner	2
exp	8	reason	6
ENTITY	94	**HUM**	65
animal	16	group	6
body	2	ind	55
color	10	title	1
creative	0	desc	3
currency	6	**LOC**	81
dis.med.	2	city	18
event	2	country	3
food	4	mount	3
instrument	1	other	50
language	2	state	7
letter	0	**NUM**	113
other	12	code	0
plant	5	count	9
product	4	date	47
religion	0	distance	16
sport	1	money	3
substance	15	order	0
symbol	0	other	12
technique	1	period	8
term	7	percent	3
vehicle	4	speed	6
word	0	temp	5
DESC	138	size	0
def	123	weight	4

Table 6. The composition of TREC 10 test set

In order to facilitate the comparison, similar to previously reported results, we also use the same benchmark UIUC question training and test sets in our experiments, where the questions are labeled as six coarse categories and a total of 50 finer categories. Concretely, we train our model with training set containing 5500 labeled questions and test it on the TREC 10 question set with 500 questions. The composition of the test set is listed in Table 6.

5.2 Investigation on the Distance Combinations

In section 3.2, we have introduced three kinds of distance: [NEIGH], [NEAR] and [ANY]. In order to know whether all of them are necessary in our method, we have tested our method with different distance combination on the same data sets. Table 7 shows the overall performances on 6 coarse classes and 50 fine classes with different combinations separately; and Table 8 presents more details on the six coarse categories.

	ANY	NEAR+ ANY	NEIGH+ ANY	All
6 classes	90.6%	92.8%	92.1%	93.6%
50 classes	83.8%	87.8%	86.8%	90.6%

Table 7. Performances of our method with different distance constration combinations

	ABBR	ENTITY	DESC	HUMAN	LOC	NUM
ANY	81.8%	73%	82%	95%	86%	92.6%
NEAR+ ANY	90%	76%	87%	97%	87%	93%
NEIGH+ ANY	90%	75%	84%	95%	89%	93%
All	90%	79%	95%	98%	90%	95%

Table 8. More detailed investigation on the distance combinations

Obviously, with all of the three kinds of distance information, our method reaches the best performance. In fact, if only [ANY] is considered, our ExCSR model is just the CSR model without the distance constraints, with which the overall accuracies are 90.6% in coarse classes, and 83.3% in fine grained classes respectively, which are lower than the cases that the distance constraints are considered.

The more detailed results in Table 8 also show that including all of the distance information can get the highest prediction accuracies on all of the six categories. Especially for the DESC class, the previously feature bag based methods usually perform not very good due to the fact that question classes are distance sensitive, while our method with all distance information included can get 95% overall accuracy. For example, "What foods contain vitamin B12?" is labeled as "ENTY: food", while "What is fiber in food?" belongs to "DESC: define" in UIUC data sets. The main difference between above question texts is the distance between two words "what" and "food" that are critical to the classification. Due to ignoring the distance information, the feature-bag based method usually cannot correctly classify the second question and may label it as "ENTY: food". While our method can properly distinguish these two questions for they correspond to different ExCSRs. The similar cases occur in questions of class "DESC: desc".

All in all, our proposed ExCSR including all of the three distance constraints is an effective model to the question classification. Thus in the comparison experiment, we consider all of the distance constraints.

5.3 Comparing with other Methods

By considering all of the distance constraints, the performances on different categories of our method are listed Table 9.

Class	Pre.	Rec.	F	Class	Pre.	Rec.	F
ABBR	90	100	94.7	desc	100	85.7	92.3
abb	100	100	100	manner	100	100	100
exp	100	100	94.1	reason	85.7	83.3	83.3
ENTITY	78.8	87.2	82.8	**HUM**	98.3	87.7	92.7
animal	93.3	87.5	90.3	group	71.4	66.7	72.7
body	100	100	100	ind	94.8	90.9	95.2
color	100	100	100	title	/	/	/
creative	/	/	/	desc	100	100	100
currency	100	83.8	90.9	**LOC**	90.2	91.4	90.8
dis.med.	66.7	100	80	city	100	100	100
event	66.7	100	80	country	100	100	100
food	100	75	85.7	mount	100	100	100
instrument	100	100	100	other	83.9	50	85.1
language	100	100	100	state	85.7	100	100
letter	/	/	/	**NUM**	94.5	92	93.2
other	41.7	50	48	code	/	/	/
plant	83.3	100	90.9	count	81.8	100	100
product	75	75	75	date	95.9	100	100
religion	/	/	/	distance	100	93.8	93.8
sport	100	100	100	money	100	33.3	40
substance	73.7	93.3	82.3	order	/	/	/
symbol	/	/	/	other	85.7	66.7	72.7
technique	100	100	100	period	72.7	75	80
term	58.3	100	73.7	percent	75	100	85.7
vehicle	100	100	100	speed	100	100	100
word	/	/	/	temp	100	100	100
DESC	94.8	92	93.4	size	/	/	/
def	95	92.7	93.8	weight	100	100	100

Table 9. The performances on different categories of our method

In order to know what is the rank of our method, we compare our methods with other representative methods: Zhang and Lee (2003); Huang et al., (2008); Krishnan et al., (2005). Since

Huang et al. (2008) have compared their method with Li et al. (2006) and show that their method is superior, we don't consider Li et al., (2006) method in this work.

The comparison results are shown in Table 10, showing that our method achieves the best accuracy. Although the results of Huang's method are competitive to our method, however, they use some manual regular expression patterns. Moreover, Huang et al. used a large amount of features 13697 to construct their model, while our ExCSRs model are more compact and final classifier only has 412 rules with length less than 4.

Method	6 classes	50 classes
Zhang & Lee, Linear SVM	87.4%	79.2%
Krishnan et al., SVM+ CRF	93.4%	86.2%
Huang et al., Maximum Entropy Model	93.6%	89%
Our method	93.6%	90.6%

Table 10. Overall comparison results with other three methods

Now that the results of Huang's method are competitive to ours, we further compare it with ours on each fine grained class, and the accuracies are shown in Table 11.

Class	Huang Method	Our Method	Class	Huang Method	Our Method
ABBR			desc	75	100
abb	100	100	manner	100	100
exp	88.9	100	reason	85.7	85.7
ENTITY			**HUM**		
animal	94.1	93.3	group	71.4	71.4
body	100	100	ind	94.8	94.8
color	100	100	title	/	/
creative	/	/	desc	100	100
currency	100	100	**LOC**		
dis.med.	40	66.7	city	100	100
event	100	66.7	country	100	100
food	100	100	mount	100	100
instrument	100	100	other	83.9	83.9
language	100	100	state	85.7	85.7
letter	/	/	**NUM**		
other	45.5	41.7	code	/	/
plant	100	83.3	count	81.8	81.8
product	100	75	date	95.9	95.9
religion	/	/	distance	100	100
sport	100	100	money	100	100
substance	88.9	73.7	order	/	/
symbol	/	/	other	85.7	85.7
technique	100	100	period	72.7	72.7
term	100	58.3	percent	75	75
vehicle	100	100	speed	100	100
word	/	/	temp	100	100
DESC			size	/	/
def	89	95	weight	100	100

Table 11. Precisions for fine grained question categories with Huang's method and our method

Table 11 shows that our method can achieve better results on most classes, especially for DESC coarse class that is considered to be difficult to identify (Li et al., 2006). By investigating the questions in that class we found that the question classes are sensitive to the word order and distance. Huang represents a sentence as a bag of features and ignore the relative order and of words their distances, thus performed not very well.

Of course, both our method and Huang's method show bad performance on Entity: other class, which is also shown to be difficult to identify, for the question texts in "other" class is quite fuzzy, we will put emphasis on this kind of class.

We also analyzed the incorrectly identified questions, and found that there are inherently ambiguity in training and testing questions (see examples in Table 12), which also conforms to Huang et al (2008)'s analysis.

Class	Rule
ENTITY:animal	What is a group of frogs called ?
ENTITY:termeq	What are the spots on dominoes called ?
ENTITY:termeq	What 's the term for a young fox ?
ENTITY:animal	What is the scientific name for elephant ?

Table 12. Ambiguous questions in testing set

6 Conclusion

In this paper, we first present ExCSR model for question classification, which is extended from the CSR model by integrating the distance information. Compared to CSR model, ExCSR is more compact intuitive, yet effective; then we describe the ExCSR mining algorithm, DS-SRM, and the rule filtering algorithm MCRSelection. By MCRSelection algorithm, we can keep the most interesting rules with less redundancy. Experiment results on the UIUC question set show that our method outperforms previously reported results.

In the future, we will consider more sophisticated method to address the questions with fuzzy information such as those of "other" class in UIUC data set.

Acknowledgements

The work was partially supported by the National Natural Science Foundation of China (60970063, 60773010), the Ph.D. Programs Foundation of Ministry of Education of China

(20090141110026), and the Fundamental Research Funds for the Central Universities (6081007).

References

Xin Li and D. Roth. 2006. Learning Question Classifiers: the Role of Semantic Information. *Natural Language Engineering*, 12(3):229–249.

Zhiheng Huang, M. Thint, and Z. Qin. 2008. Question classification using head words and their hypernyms. *In Proc. of the EMNLP*. pp.927-936

Minqing Hu and Bing Liu. 2006. Opinion Feature Extraction Using Class Sequential Rules. *In Proc. of AAAI-06.*

Pei, J. Han, J., Mortazavi-Asl, B., Wang, J., Pinto, H., Chen, Q., Dayal, U., and Hsu, M.-C. 2004. Mining Sequential Patterns by Pattern-Growth: The PrefixSpan Approach. *IEEE Transactions on Knowledge and Data Engineering,* 16(10):1-17.

Li, X. and D. Roth. 2002. Learning Question Classifiers. *In Proc. of the 19th international conference on Computational linguistics (COLING '02),* vol. 1: 556–562.

Hermjakob, U. 2001. Parsing and question classification for question answering. *In Proc. of ACL-2001 Workshop on Open-Domain Question Answering.*

Radev, D., Fan, W., Qi, H.,Wu, H. & Grewal, A. 2002. Probabilistic question answering on the web. *In Proc. of the 11th international conference on World Wide Web (WWW2002), Hawaii.*

Zhang D. and W. S. Lee. 2003. Question Classification using Support Vector Machines. *In Proc. of the ACM SIGIR conference on information retrieva l(SIGIR'03)*: 26–32.

V. Krishnan, S. Das, and S. Chakrabarti. 2005. Enhanced answer type inference from questions using sequential models. *In Proc. of the HLT/EMNLP'2005.*

Fangtao Li, Xian Zhang, Jinhui Yuan and Xiaoyan Zhu. 2008. Classifying What-Type Questions by Head Noun Tagging. *In Proc. of the 22nd International Conference on Computational Linguistics (COLING 2008)*, pp. 481-488

Zhiheng Huang, Marcus Thint, Asli Celikyilmaz. 2009. Investigation of Question Classifier in Question Answering. *In Proc. of the 2009 Conference on Empirical Methods in Natural Language Processing*. pp. 543–550.

Santosh Kumar Ray, Shailendra Singh, B.P. Joshi. 2010. A semantic approach for question classification using WordNet and Wikipedia. *Pattern Recognition Letters*: 1935-1943.

Bing Liu. 2007. Web data mining: Exploring hyperlinks, contents, and usage data. *Springer-Verlag,* Berlin, Heiderlberg.

Jenny Rose Finkel, Trond Grenager, and Christopher Manning. 2005. Incorporating Non-local Information into Information Extraction Systems by Gibbs Sampling. *In Proc. of the 43nd Annual Meeting of the Association for Computational Linguistics (ACL 2005).* pp.363-370.

Kristina Toutanova, Dan Klein. 2003. Christopher Manning, and Yoram Singer. Feature-Rich Part-of-Speech Tagging with a Cyclic Dependency Network. *In Proc. of HLT-NAACL.* pp.252-259.

M. Mavronicolas and D. Roth. 1991. Sequential Consistency and Linearizability: Read/Write Objects. *In Proc. of the 29th Annual Allerton Conference on Communication, Control and Computing.* pp.683-692.

K2Q: Generating Natural Language Questions from Keywords with User Refinements

Zhicheng Zheng
Tsinghua University
zhengzc04@gmail.com

Xiance Si
Google Inc.
sxc@google.com

Edward Y. Chang
Google Inc.
edchang@google.com

Xiaoyan Zhu
Tsinghua University
zxy-dcs@tsinghua.edu.cn

Abstract

Garbage in and garbage out. A Q&A system must receive a well formulated question that matches the user's intent or she has no chance to receive satisfactory answers. In this paper, we propose a keywords to questions (K2Q) system to assist a user to articulate and refine questions. K2Q generates candidate questions and refinement words from a set of input keywords. After specifying some initial keywords, a user receives a list of candidate questions as well as a list of refinement words. The user can then select a satisfactory question, or select a refinement word to generate a new list of candidate questions and refinement words. We propose a User Inquiry Intent (UII) model to describe the joint generation process of keywords and questions for ranking questions, suggesting refinement words, and generating questions that may not have previously appeared. Empirical study shows UII to be useful and effective for the K2Q task.

1 Introduction

Keyword search has long been considered an unnatural undertaking task, but it works well with search engines. When entering a question to a Q&A system such as Yahoo! Answers and Quora, however, the keyword paradigm simply does not work. A question must be articulated specifically in the form of natural language. For instance, keywords such as *New York restaurant* is ambiguous in its intent. The user may want restaurants in New York, or want to know the tipping practice at New York restaurants, or something else under the myriad other possible interpretations. For a question to be answered, the asker must articulate her intent with sufficient specificity. Partly because we have been detrained by search engine from writing a question in a complete sentence, and partly because a question is hard to articulate completely when the asker is in a learning mode, a Q&A system should provide tools to users to help them clarify their questions so as to get good answers.

In this paper, we propose K2Q, a system that converts keywords to questions by considering both query history and user feedback. More specifically, given a set of keywords, K2Q generates a list of ranked questions as well a list of refinement words. A user can select a satisfactory question, or she can select a refinement word to generate a new list of candidate questions and refinement words. This process iterates until the user finds a good question matching her intent or quits.

To build an effective K2Q system, there are three aspects that need to be researched. A user issues a question typically because the desired information cannot be found. Our first task, therefore, is in the generation of unseen questions (*unseen questions* refer to those questions which are not known in advance by a K2Q system). After all, popular questions being asked before can be searched via search engines. Second, we must address the challenge of ranking candidate questions. Questions, unlike keywords, rarely repeat. (The same question can be asked in many different forms.) Among the questions we have collected, only occur more than once. Therefore, a simple ranking scheme based on frequency is not feasible. Third, the suggestion scheme of refinement words must consider maximizing information gain. It is thus desirable to generate diverse refinement words. An intuitive method is to use the most frequent words in candidate questions (after the removal of functional words). However, this method only considers the strength of relatedness between the words and the candidate questions, and may generate several refinement words indicating the same subtopic. For example, when a user inputs *cat feed*, if we simply use the most frequent words as refinement words, we will suggest both *food* and *eat* which indicate the same topic of *feed cat*. Diverse refinement words lead to more efficient feedbacks, and thus produce a fewer number of iterations before getting a satisfactory question.

To overcome the aforementioned three challenges, we propose a User Inquiry Intent (UII) model, which describes the joint generation process of keywords and questions. We employ an adaptive language model to describe the process of forming questions, and use automatically induced question templates to create unseen questions. Candidate questions are sorted by their fluency, i.e., the probability of being seen in a Q&A system. We compute the entropy on the distribution of the user's intent and generate refinement words. We then suggest refinement words that maximize entropy gain. Consequently, a satisfactory question can be generated in fewer iterations. Our experiments show that: 1) a template-based approach improves the coverage of suggestions; 2) compared with the baseline method, our UII model improves the ranking of the suggested questions; and 3) the UII model generates better refinement words than the baseline method of suggesting most frequent words. The results suggest that our proposed UII model is effective.

The contributions of this paper can be summarized as follows:

1. We propose a K2Q system, which benefits users to articulate and refine their questions to be more specific and more overtly express their intent.
2. To address the technical challenges of developing K2Q, we propose the UII model, which models the joint generation process of keywords and questions.
3. We show that the UII model is effective in both generating and refining questions by experiments conducted with real-world query logs.

This paper proceeds as follows. Section 2 presents a brief survey of related work. Section 3 details the UII model, which describes the joint generation of both search keywords and natural language questions. Experiments are described in Section 4 and conclusions are given in Section 5.

2 Related Work

To the best of our knowledge, there is no direct research on the K2Q problem. However, query suggestion and question recommendation are among the most relevant tasks that have been researched.

Query suggestion aims to suggest related refined query words to users, and is employed by most modern search engines. Many research efforts have been devoted to query suggestion (Ma et al., 2010; Chirita et al., 2007a) and other, similar tasks such as query expansion (Chirita et al., 2007b; Cui et al., 2003; Theobald et al., 2005; Xu and Croft, 1996) and query refinement (Kraft and Zien, 2004). Applying query suggestion to K2Q is problematic for two reasons: 1) Query suggestion makes heavy use of the query log information such as click sessions. However, less than 1% of queries are questions, and even less of those repeat more than twice. The sparsity of questions renders query suggestion algorithms ineffective when applied to K2Q. 2) To propose new query suggestions, keyword-level editing operations such as *add, delete or change* are used (Jones et al., 2006). These operations do not take grammar into consideration, and are too simple to be applied to whole, complete sentences.

Question recommendation suggests questions which are related to the initial question (Cao et al., 2008; Wu et al., 2008). By treating the initial keywords as a question, question recommendation algorithms can also be used to suggest questions for K2Q. However, question recommendation focuses on proposing existing questions, which fails at the first challenge of generating unseen questions.

Researchers have worked on solving individual challenges posed by K2Q. For question generation, Lin (2008) proposed an "automatic question generation from queries" task in 2008, but no technical approaches were discussed. Kotov and Zhai (2010) proposed to organize search results by corresponding questions. They employed some manually created templates to transform normal sentences into questions. Their work was to generate questions from a paragraph or a sentence, but not according to keywords. In addition, since producing templates requires human effort, it is difficult to achieve high coverage. In IR field, some researchers automatically generate query templates (Agarwal et al., 2010; Szpektor et al., 2011). Inspired by their work, we try to generate templates automatically.

For question ranking, Wu et al. (2008) calculated user-to-question similarity and question-to-question similarity by employing the PLSA model, then ranked candidate questions by combining the two similarity scores. However, it is difficult to model users in K2Q, so this algorithm is not suitable for our purpose. Cao et al. (2008) proposed an "MDL-based Tree Cut Model" to rank candidate questions. They organized the candidate questions in a tree, then defined question similarity based on both *specificity* and *generality*. They ranked the candidate questions by combining the two similarity scores. Their work aimed to suggest interesting questions to the user, but K2Q proposes to recommend questions with high popularity in order to make correct predictions. Sun et al. (2009) ranked questions with several CQA specific features. However, since the candidate questions in K2Q come from different CQA sites, and some candidates are even unseen questions, it is difficult to apply these features in K2Q. In this paper, we rank questions according to their popularity, which is measured by including an adaptive language model in UII model.

For the generation of refinement words, the most relevant task is query suggestion. Diversity is an important factor in query suggestion, and most of the related works exploited the information of query logs in order to diversify the query suggestion results. Wang et al. (2009) extracted subtopics of a query by mining query reformulations in user session logs. Ma et al. (2010) proposed a method based on Markov random walks and hitting time analysis on a query-URL bipartite graph. Sadikov et al. (2010) clustered query refinements by performing multiple random walks on a Markov graph that approximates user search behavior. However, in K2Q, we cannot get sufficient click information between keywords and questions due to its sparsity in the query logs. In this paper, we use click information to evaluate our methods, but not for training since the total amount is small.

3 User Inquiry Intent Model

When a user inputs a query or posts a question, she wants to get some information. We will refer to the information need as user intent. Both the query and the question are generated from the user intent. We will use an example to illustrate the generative process. A user wants to know what the hot research topics in natural language processing are. If she employs search engines, she might create a query *hot research topics NLP* from her intent. If she wants to post a question in the community, she might choose a way to express her intent. She may choose *What are hot research topics in [subject_areas]*, or *Which research topics are hot in [subject_areas]*. Different ways of posting her intent generate different questions. In this example, let the corresponding final questions be *What are hot research topics in NLP* and *Which research topics are hot in NLP*. The replaceable part (such as *[subject_areas]*) can be considered as slots for concrete words. Generally, a slot can be interpreted as a word or a word cluster. A word cluster is a set of words which can be used in similar contexts. For example, *Beijing* and *Paris* are in the same cluster since they are both suitable to be used in the context *in [cities]*. We obtain the word clusters by using k-means as was shown in (Lin and Wu, 2009).

Here, we propose a User Inquiry Intent model to describe the process of generating queries and questions from the user intent.

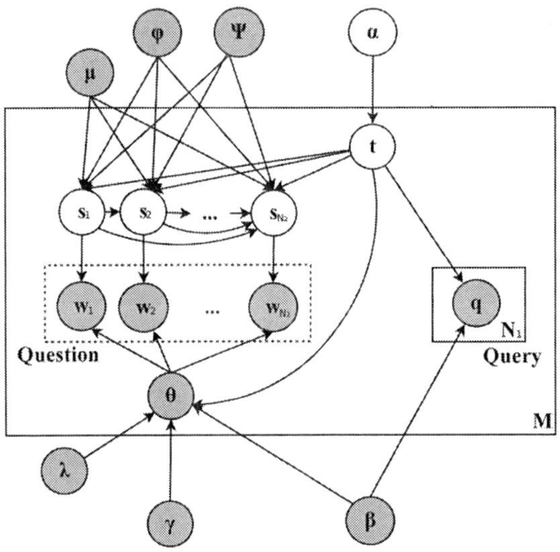

Figure 1: The plate representation of the UII model. (as in Probabilistic Graphical Models)

The plate representation of UII model is shown in Figure 1. In the model:

is the index of user intents, ranging from to (is the number of different user intents). A user intent not only corresponds to a distribution over all words but also corresponds to a distribution over the slots .

and are both indices of words, ranging from to (is the number of different words). In Figure 1, the left group of is the question which is able to express the user intent . The right group of is the query which is also able to express .

is the index of slots, ranging from to

*** Formatting Issue - Best Available Paper/Graphic ***

. Besides the slots which are reserved for exact words, there are an additional more slots for word clusters.

is the prior parameter of the distribution of user intents. is a vector of length :

, .

is the prior parameter of the word distribution on each user intent . is a matrix of size

: , , .

is the prior parameter of the slot transition. is a matrix. Denote the preceding slots of as . Since there are too many possible values of , in practice we only reserve the frequent N-grams as possible values of . The size of is then , where is the size of frequent N-grams. ,

, .

is the prior parameter of the word distribution on each slot . is a matrix of size

. , ,

.

is the prior parameter of the slot distribution on each user intent . is a matrix of size . , ,

.

is a matrix. Each row of is the word distribution on a slot under a particular user intent.

and are two mixture weights of prior distributions. Under user intent , , follow the Dirichlet distribution with parameters . Under user intent , the slot transition probability is calculated by Eq. 1, which is an adaptive language model (Kneser et al., 1997).

(1)

We refer the generative process as Algorithm 1. The process is illustrated with the same example as in the beginning of this section. The user intent has high probabilty on the words *hot*, *research*, *topic*, *NLP*, and hence generates the set of query words *hot research topic NLP*. Assuming that the probability of seeing a slot is determined by two preceding slots, then by considering both the slot distribution on the user intent and the slot transition probability, the user intent first generates *What* from a *START* slot; then *are* from *START What*; *hot* from *What are*; *research* from *are hot*; *topics* from *hot research*; *in* from *research topics*; *[subject_areas]* from *topics in*; and finally an *END* slot from *in [subject_areas]*. Under the user intent, we generate question words from the slots in the slot sequence *What are hot research topics in [subject_areas]*, and form the question word sequence *What are hot research topics in NLP*.

```
Choose ;
for each word in the query do
  | Choose ;
end
Choose , where
  ;
for each word in the question do
  | Choose ,
  | is calculated as Eq. 1 ;
  | Choose ;
end
```

Algorithm 1: The algorithm for UII model

3.1 Inference

Given prior parameters (for convenience, we denote all prior parameters as , and all other variables as), the joint distribution is calculated as:

We integrate out to calculate :

The right side of the equation is separated into four parts: (1) ; (2) ; (3) , is calculated by Eq. 1; (4) The integration is solved by:

Here, is a matrix, is the count of slot generating words in the question. Function is the gamma function.

3.2 Parameter Estimation

As the complexity of the UII model is non-trivial, in this work we choose to estimate the parameters of different components separately instead of performing a global joint optimization.

and are weight parameters for combining different distributions. We set them empirically.

We estimate the other prior parameters with a given question set (we refer to these questions as known questions). is the prior word distribution of slots. There are two kinds of slots, one can be filled with exactly one word, and the other can be filled with any words from the corresponding word cluster. Hence, we estimate as:

Here is the probability of the -th word in the -th word cluster. We set the history to be the preceding slots, which allows the slot sequence to be an -order Markov chain. We obtain from statistics on the known questions.

In order to estimate , and , we cluster the known questions, where the questions in the same cluster contain the same bag of words (We only exclude the stopwords). Suppose we obtain question clusters such that each cluster contains questions, then we estimate as: . According to the statistics of word distributions on each question cluster, we estimate and as: , .

3.3 Question Generation

In order to reduce the computational complexity of the model, we do not actually generate all possible questions that the UII model is capable of. Instead, we use a template based method to generate the candidate questions, which are subsequently ranked by the UII model.

Question Templates Generation

To generate unseen questions, we generate question templates from known questions. A question template is a sequence of slots, where each slot is a word or a word cluster. If there are cluster slots in a template, we refer to it as a -variable template. Given a set of questions, we initialize a set of -variable templates. By replacing one word of a -variable template with a corresponding cluster, we obtain a -variable template. By merging all the same -variable templates, we get a set of -variable templates with their support numbers (the support number is the number of -variable templates employed to generate the -variable template). By increasing the threshold of the minimum support number (denoted as), we filter out those templates with low quality.

Question Generation from Initial Keywords

Firstly, we search for known questions that contain all the keywords and use them as suggestion candidates (We search for at most questions). For popular keywords such as *New York steakhouse*, we have enough known questions covering all aspects of the inquiry intents. However, for rare keywords such as *Tangshan*[1] *steakhouse*, performing a search in the known questions might yield only a few or no candidates.

Secondly, we generate unseen questions by the use of question templates. By replacing one of the initial keywords with its cluster, we search for -variable templates that contain both the cluster and the rest keywords (We search for at most -variable templates). Then, we replace the cluster slot in the templates with the actual initial keyword, creating a new question.

Both known and generated questions are added into the final candidate question set.

3.4 Question Ranking

With the candidate question set, we use the UII model to rank the candidates by , the probablity of the question was generated given the keywords. The probability is calculated as:

(2)

We could perform exact computation (i.e. Dynamic Programming) to compute the sum over all possible , however, since each suggestion should be finished in a timely fashion, the complexity of exact computation is not acceptable. Recall the process where we generated candidate questions, we only consider all the question templates that we obtained as all possible slot permutations. Then we only need to sum up all these to calculate the probability, which makes it possible to finish in real-time.

3.5 Refinement Word Generation

The goal of refinement words is to reduce the number of interactions required to reach the desired

[1]A city in China.

*** Formatting Issue - Best Available Paper/Graphic ***

question. With the UII model, we use an information theory based approach to select refinement words. We define the entropy on the distribution of the user intents given the initial keywords as:

Here, ———, and is calculated as:

Then, if the user selects a refinement word , the resulted entropy gain is:

Entropy gain measures the reduced uncertainty that results by adding . As we aim to reduce the number of interaction steps in K2Q, we select those refinement words that maximize the expected entropy gain in each step. The expected entropy gain of a refinement words set R is:

Here is the probability that a user will choose from when a set of refinement words is given to query . is calculated as:

If the user does not select any refinement words from R, then the expectation of entropy gain on R is meaningless. Hence we define our optimization function as Eq. 3:

(3)

Here ———, where is the number of candidate questions when giving query , and is the number of the candidate questions which contain at least one refinement word in R.

The optimization problem is an NP-complete problem, hence in practice, we use a greedy strategy described by Algorithm 2.

```
Initialize      ,         = true;
while                  and        do
    Select   =
                                  ;
    if
                then
                    ;
                = true;
    else
                = false;
    end
end
```

Algorithm 2: Greedy strategy algorithm of refinement words generation

4 Experiments

In the section, we use real world questions and Web queries to evaluate the performance of candidate question generation, question ranking and refinement word generation.

4.1 Data Sets

We use a large set of English questions as the training set to generate question templates and estimate the prior parameters in the UII model. There are questions in the question set, which are obtained from popular CQA sites such as Yahoo! Answers. Notice that questions from WikiAnswers[2] are intentionally excluded from the training set, as we want to use WikiAnswers' questions as samples of unseen questions to evaluate the performance of question ranking when faced with unseen questions.

To evaluate the performance of K2Q, we need to know the mapping relationship between query and question. To this end, we use Web query logs to create the data set. After the user inputs a query, she will click a result if she thinks it is satisfactory. By only considering the clicked results that are from CQA sites, we collect pairs of queries and their target questions. We employ a one week query log from Google. To avoid data noise, we collect only those query-question pairs which occur at least times in the query log. Under these conditions, we get approximate query-question pairs.

4.2 Evaluation of Candidate Question Generation

First, we show the number of templates under different support numbers ( ) in Figure 2. As the figure shows, the number of 1-variable templates drops significantly when we need more supports. According to our observation, suffices as a good balance point between quantity and quality.

[2]http://wiki.answers.com

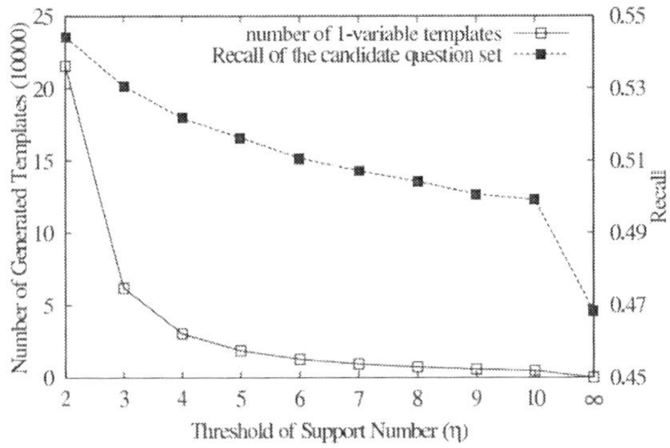

Figure 2: Number of -variable templates and recall of candidate questions with different . The templates help improve the recall (Note: means no template is used)

Second, we set up an experiment to evaluate the coverage of candidate questions generated by K2Q. We select the top most frequent query-question pairs as the test set. For each query-question pair, we generate candidate questions for the query. We define the query-question pair to be *recalled* in a candidate question set if the set contains the target question in the query-question pair. We use recall to measure the performance of our candidate question generation algorithm, which is defined as:

$$\frac{\textit{recalled query-question pair}}{\textit{query-question pairs}} \quad (4)$$

Recall measures the coverage of the candidate question set. The higher the recall, the more target questions are included in the candidate question sets. Figure 2 also shows the results under different (means no 1-variable template is used). Compared to the case when 1-variable templates are not used, our candidate question generation algorithm improved the recall by % %.

4.3 Evaluation of Question Ranking

The baseline method that we compare our approach to is the language model (denoted as LM). The language model ranks the candidate questions according to the probability that it would generate the question. Since a popular question tends to contains popular N-grams, the language model also measures the popularity of the question. Specifically, we use the same question set as that in Section 4.1 to train a -gram language model.

To construct the test set, we select query-question pairs that satisfy the following conditions: 1) the target question in the query-question pair is generated as a candidate question; 2) the target question comes from WikiAnswers, as we are more concerned with the ranking performance on unseen questions. The results in Table 1 show that the UII model provides a better ranking of the candidate questions when compared to the language model. We argue this improvement results from two aspects of the UII model: 1) The UII model introduces word clusters, which smooths the probability of rare N-grams. This is important in ranking since the generated unseen questions always contain several rare N-grams. 2) The UII model generates slot sequences via an adaptive langugage model, which helps adjust slot transition probabilities under different user intents.

We select two examples (shown in Table 2) to illustrate the aforementioned aspects of our UII model's superiority to the conventional language model. The target question of the first query is *what is the meaning of advocacy*. Since the 3-gram *meaning of advocacy* never occurs in the training set, LM does not rank the target question as the top 1 best candidate. However, the 3-gram *meaning of WordCluster* occurs frequently in the training set, so the UII model ranks the target question as the top 1 best candidate. The target question of the second query is *what are the different types of Google*. In the training set, the phrases *how many* occurs more frequently than the phrase *what are the different*, so LM does not rank the target question as its number 1 candidate. However, the corresponding user intent has high probability to generate the slot *different*, so the target question is ranked as the best candidate by the UII model.

Recall at	**LM**	**UII model**	Improvement
top 1	37.5%	43.5%	+16.0%
top 2	54.2%	58.0%	+7.0%
top 3	64.1%	66.6%	+4.1%

Table 1: The UII model performs better on the most frequent query-question pairs set

4.4 Evaluation of Refinement Word Generation

We use the query-question pairs to evaluate the performance of the generation of refinement words. We compare the UII model with an intuitive method which selects the most frequent words in the candidate questions as refinements (denoted as MF). The goal of refinement words is to interact with the user in those cases

Query	Question at top 3	
	UII model	LM
advocacy meaning	**What is the meaning of advocacy?** The meaning of advocacy? What is meaning of advocacy?	What is the meaning advocacy? **What is the meaning of advocacy?** What is the meaning of the advocacy?
Google types	**What are the different types of Google?** What are the types of Google? How many types of Google?	How many types of Google? Different types of Google? **What are the different types of Google?**

Table 2: Two examples of top 3 suggestions by UII model and LM (The target questions of the queries are shown in bold)

when the initial keywords are too simple to express the user intent. Since one word queries are often too simiple to express the user intent, we use one word queries as the test set. These query-question pairs also satisfy the following two conditions: 1) the target question in the query-question pair is generated as a candidate question; 2) the UII model ranks the target question not to be among the top ten.

We use such query-question pairs as the test set. For each method, we generate a list of refinement words. We use each of the refinement words to refine the query, and then subsequently re-rank the candidate questions and create a new set of 10 refinement words. By exploring all possible choices of refinement words among the list of 10 in each interaction, we find the minimal number of interaction steps that lead to the target questions. We search for at most steps. If K2Q ranks the target question among the top 10 within these interactions, then set the query cost to be the minimal interaction number in which this occured; otherwise, let the query cost be . We consider two metrics: 1) the number of query-question pairs where K2Q ranks the target question among the top ten within interactions (denoted as RN); 2) the reciprocal average query cost (denoted as RAQC). The larger RAQC is, the fewer the number of interactions K2Q requires to successfully rank the target question.

	MF	UII model	Improvement
RN	363	409	+12.7%
RAQC	0.258	0.265	+2.63%

Table 3: UII model performs better than the baseline method on refinement words generation

From the results in Table 3, we find that: 1) With refinement words, K2Q is more effective of suggesting the target questions. 2) With refinement words generated by the UII model, K2Q gets more efficient feedback, which leads to better performance when compared to the intuitive method. MF only considers the frequency of the words, not the diversity. In contrast, the UII model is effective in suggesting those refinement words that maximally reduce the entropy of the distribution of user intents. It is clear that the UII model suggests a better list of refinement words than the intuitive method.

5 Conclusion

In this paper, we propose the UII model to solve the K2Q problem. The UII model exhibits a simultaneous process of generating both questions and queries based on the user intents. UII model utilizes existing questions on the Web, and leverages templates to generate and rank unseen questions. This model is also equipped with the ability to suggest refinement words that maximize the entropy gain of inferred intent distribution. Experiments show that: 1) using templates improves the coverage of suggestions by % %; 2) the UII model improves the ranking of suggestions over conventional language models with recall at top ranked questions increased over ; 3) the UII model suggests better refinement words when compared to a baseline method of suggesting words based on frequency. By interacting via these refinement words, K2Q is able to rank target questions within top ten, higher than the baseline method. These results show that our proposed UII model yields better suggestions than separated methods in K2Q.

The UII model is a generative model. In this paper, we estimate all the prior parameters without using query-question pairs. Since there are mountains of query-question pairs from query logs, we plan to better estimate the prior parameters with these pairs in future work. Another important direction is to use real-world feedback to evaluate the model, as our current evaluation does not consider real users.

*** Formatting Issue - Best Available Paper/Graphic ***

References

G. Agarwal, G. Kabra, and K.C.C. Chang. 2010. Towards rich query interpretation: Walking back and forth for mining query templates. In *Proc. of WWW*. ACM.

Y. Cao, H. Duan, C.Y. Lin, Y. Yu, and H.W. Hon. 2008. Recommending questions using the mdl-based tree cut model. In *Proc. of WWW*, pages 81–90. ACM.

P.A. Chirita, C.S. Firan, and W. Nejdl. 2007a. Personalized query expansion for the web. In *Proc. of SIGIR*, pages 7–14. ACM.

Paul Alexandru Chirita, Claudiu S. Firan, and Wolfgang Nejdl. 2007b. Personalized query expansion for the web. In *Proc. of SIGIR*, SIGIR '07, pages 7–14, New York, NY, USA. ACM.

Hang Cui, Ji-Rong Wen, Jian-Yun Nie, and Wei-Ying Ma. 2003. Query expansion by mining user logs. *IEEE Transactions on Knowledge and Data Engineering*, 15:829–839.

R. Jones, B. Rey, O. Madani, and W. Greiner. 2006. Generating query substitutions. In *Proc. of WWW*, pages 387–396. ACM.

R. Kneser, J. Peters, and D. Klakow. 1997. Language model adaptation using dynamic marginals. In *Fifth European Conference on Speech Communication and Technology*.

A. Kotov and C.X. Zhai. 2010. Towards natural question guided search. In *Proc. of WWW*, pages 541–550. ACM.

R. Kraft and J. Zien. 2004. Mining anchor text for query refinement. In *Proc. of WWW*, pages 666–674. ACM.

D. Lin and X. Wu. 2009. Phrase clustering for discriminative learning. In *Proc. of ACL*, pages 1030–1038. Association for Computational Linguistics.

C.Y. Lin. 2008. Automatic question generation from queries. In *Workshop on the Question Generation Shared Task*.

H. Ma, M.R. Lyu, and I. King. 2010. Diversifying Query Suggestion Results. In *Proc. of AAAI*.

E. Sadikov, J. Madhavan, L. Wang, and A. Halevy. 2010. Clustering query refinements by user intent. In *Proc. of WWW*, pages 841–850. ACM.

K. Sun, Y. Cao, X. Song, Y.I. Song, X. Wang, and C.Y. Lin. 2009. Learning to recommend questions based on user ratings. In *Proc. of CIKM*, pages 751–758. ACM.

I. Szpektor, A. Gionis, and Y. Maarek. 2011. Improving recommendation for long-tail queries via templates. In *Proc. of WWW*, pages 47–56. ACM.

M. Theobald, R. Schenkel, and G. Weikum. 2005. Efficient and self-tuning incremental query expansion for top-k query processing. In *Proc. of SIGIR*, pages 242–249. ACM.

X. Wang, D. Chakrabarti, and K. Punera. 2009. Mining broad latent query aspects from search sessions. In *Proc. of SIGKDD*, pages 867–876. ACM.

H. Wu, Y. Wang, and X. Cheng. 2008. Incremental probabilistic latent semantic analysis for automatic question recommendation. In *Proceedings of the 2008 ACM conference on Recommender systems*, pages 99–106. ACM.

J. Xu and W.B. Croft. 1996. Query expansion using local and global document analysis. In *Proc. of SIGIR*, pages 4–11. ACM.

Answering Complex Questions via Exploiting Social Q&A Collection

Youzheng Wu Chiori Hori Hisashi Kawai Hideki Kashioka
Spoken Language Communication Group, MASTAR Project
National Institute of Information and Communications Technology (NiCT)
2-2-2 Hikaridai, Keihanna Science City, Kyoto 619-0288, Japan
{youzheng.wu, chiori.hori, hisashi.kawai, hideki.kashioka}@nict.go.jp

Abstract

This paper regards social Q&A collections, such as Yahoo! Answer as a knowledge repository and investigates techniques to mine knowledge from them for improving a sentence-based complex question answering (QA) system. In particular, we present a question-type-specific method (QTSM) that studies at extracting question-type-dependent cue expressions from the social Q&A pairs in which question types are the same as the submitted question. The QTSM is also compared with question-specific and monolingual translation-based methods presented in previous work. Thereinto, the question-specific method (QSM) aims at extracting question-dependent answer words from social Q&A pairs in which questions are similar to the submitted question. The monolingual translation-based method (MTM) learns word-to-word translation probabilities from all social Q&A pairs without consideration of question and question type. Experiments on extension of the NTCIR 2008 Chinese test data set verify the performance ranking of these methods as: QTSM > {QSM, MTM}. The largest F_3 improvements of the proposed QTSM over the QSM and MTM reach 6.0% and 5.8%, respectively.

1 Introduction

Research on the topic of QA systems has mainly concentrated on answering factoid, definitional, reason and opinion questions. Among the approaches proposed for answering these questions, machine learning techniques have been found more effective in constructing QA components from scratch. Yet these supervised techniques require a certain scale of question and answer (Q&A) pairs as training data. For example, Echihabi et al. (2003) and Sasaki (2005) respectively constructed 90,000 English and 2,000 Japanese Q&A pairs for their factoid QA systems. Cui et al. (2004) collected 76 term-definition pairs for their definitional QA system. Higashinaka and Isozaki (2008) used 4,849 positive and 521,177 negative examples in their reason QA system. Stoyanov et al. (2005) required a known subjective vocabulary for their opinion QA system. This paper is concerned with answering complex questions which answers generally consists of a list of nuggets (Voorhees, 2003; Mitamura et al., 2008). Apart from definitional and opinion (TAC, 2008) complex questions, many other types of complex questions have not yet to be thoroughly studied[1]. To answer these complex questions via supervised techniques, we need to collect training Q&A pairs for each type of complex question, though this is an extremely expensive and labor-intensive task.

This paper is to explore the possibility of automatic learning of training Q&A pairs and mining needed knowledge from social Q&A collections such as Yahoo! Answer[2]. That is to say, we are interested in whether or not millions of, possible noisy, user-generated Q&A pairs can be exploited for automatic QA system. This is a very important question because a positive answer can indicate that a plethora of training Q&A data is readily available to QA researchers.

Many studies, such as (Riezler et al., 2007; Surdeanu et al., 2008; Duan et al., 2008; Wang, 2010a) have addressed retrieving of similar Q&A pairs from social QA websites as answers to test questions; thus answers cannot be generated for questions that have not been answered on such

[1]Most complex questions have generally been called what-questions in previous studies. This paper argues that it is helpful to treat them discriminatively.

[2]`http://answers.yahoo.com/`

sites. Our study, however, regards social Q&A websites as a knowledge repository and aims at exploiting knowledge from them for synthesizing answers to questions, which have not been answered on these sites. Even for questions that have been answered, it is necessary to perform answer summarization as (Liu et al., 2008) indicated. Our approach can also be used for this purpose. To the best of our knowledge, there appears to be very little literature on this aspect.

Various kinds of knowledge can be mined from social Q&A collections for supporting complex QA system. In this paper, we present a question-type-specific method (QTSM) to mine question-type-specific knowledge and compare it with question-specific and monolingual translation-based methods proposed in related work. Given a question Q, the three methods can be summarized as follows: (1) The proposed QTSM studies at recognizing question type Q_t from the Q; collecting Q&A pair in which question types are the same as Q_t; extracting salient cue expressions that are indicative of answers to the question type Q_t; and using the expressions and Q&A pairs to train a binary classifier for removing noise candidate answers. (2) The question-specific method (QSM) tries to collect Q&A pairs that are similar to Q from social Q&A collection, and extract question-dependent (Q-specific in this case) answer words to improve complex QA system. (3) The monolingual translation-based method (MTM) employs all social Q&A pairs and learns word-to-word translation probabilities from them without consideration of question Q and question type Q_t to solve the lexical gap problem in complex QA system. The three methods are evaluated in terms of the extension of the NTCIR 2008 test data set. The Pourpre v.0c evaluation tool (Lin and Demner-Fushman, 2006) is employed, which is also adopted to evaluate TREC QA systems. The experiments show that the proposed QTSM is most effective, for instance, the largest F_3/NR improvements of QTSM over the baseline, QSM, and MTM models reach 8.6%/12.6%, 6.0%/6.7%, and 5.8%/7.1%, respectively. The ranking of the methods was: QTSM > {QSM, MTM}.

2 Social Q&A Collection

Social QA websites such as Yahoo! Answer and Baidu Zhidao[3] provide an interactive platform for users to post questions and answers. After questions are answered by users, the best answer can be chosen by the asker or nominated by the community. Table 1 demonstrates an example of these Q&A pairs, the number of which has risen dramatically on such sites. The pairs could collectively form a source of training data needed in supervised machine-learning-based QA systems.

Question	What do you think is the main cause of global warming?
Best Answer	The primary cause of global warming is the emission of green house gases like carbon dioxide, methane, nitrous oxide...
Other Answer	...What is NOT at all clear is whether human-activity is causing for the current warming trend...
Other Answer	First of all, it is damaging outcome of man-made faults...

Table 1: Example of social Q&A pairs

This paper aims at exploiting such user-generated Q&A collections for improving complex QA systems via automatic learning of Q&A training pairs and mining needed knowledge from them. Social collections, however, have two salient characteristics: textual mismatch between questions and answers (i.e., question words are not necessarily used in answers), and user-generated spam or flippant answers, which are unfavorable factors in our study. We only crawl questions and their best answers to form Q&A pairs, wherein the best answers are longer than the empirical threshold (20 words). Finally, about 40 million Q&A pairs were crawled from Chinese social QA websites and will be used as a source of training data.

3 Complex QA System

The typical complex QA system architecture is a cascade of three modules. The Question Analyzer analyzes test question and identifies type of question. The Document Retriever & Answer Candidate Extractor retrieves documents related to questions from the given collection (*Xinhua* and *Lianhe Zaobao* newspapers from 1998-2001 were used in this study) for consideration, and segments them into sentences as answer candidates. The Answer Ranker applies state-of-the-art IR formulas (e.g., KL-divergence language model) to estimate "similarities" between sentences (we used 1,024 sentences) and question and ranks sentences according to their similarities. Finally, the top N sentences are deemed the final answers.

Given question Q_1 = "What are the hazards of global warming?" and its three answer candidates, a_1 = "Solutions to global warming range from changing a light bulb to engineering giant reflec-

[3]http://zhidao.baidu.com/

tors in space ...," a_2 = "Global warming will bring bigger storms and hurricanes that hold more water ...," and a_3 = "nuclear power has relatively low emission of carbon dioxide (CO_2), one of the major causes of global warming", it is hard for the above architecture to correctly select a_2 as answer, because the three candidates contain the same keywords in question Q_1. To improve this architecture, external knowledge must be incorporated. As introduced in section 2, social Q&A collection is a good choice for mining needed knowledge. In this paper, we propose a question-type-specific technique of exploiting social Q&A collection (as introduced in section 4) to mine the knowledge, and compare it with question-specific (section 5.1) and monolingual translation-based (section 5.2) methods in experiments.

4 QTSM

Based on our observation, that is, answers to a type of complex question usually contain question-type-dependent cue expressions that are helpful in answering complex questions, we propose the QTSM that aims to learn these cue expressions for each type of question and utilize them to improve complex QA systems.

For each test question, the QTSM performs the following steps: (1) Recognizing the type of test question by identifying the *question focus* of question. (2) Collecting positive and negative training Q&A pairs of the type of question from the social Q&A collection. (3) Extracting question-type-specific salient cue expressions from the Q&A pairs. (4) Utilizing the cue expressions and Q&A pairs to build a binary classifier of the type of the test question. (5) Employing the classifier to remove noise from candidate answers before using the Answer Ranker to select final answers to the question.

4.1 Question Type

Earlier work on factoid QA systems tried to recognize question types via classification techniques (Li, et al., 2002), which require taxonomy of question types such as location, organization, person and training instances for each type. This algorithm may be inappropriate to complex QA systems due to there are hundreds of question types and we have little prior knowledge about defining complex QA-oriented taxonomy. This paper recognizes type of complex question by identifying its question focus. Question focus is defined as a short subsequence of tokens (typically 1-3 words) in a question that are adequate for indicating its question type. Take Q_1 = "What are the hazards of global warming?" and Q_2 = "What disasters are caused due to global warming?" as examples, *hazard* and *disaster* are their corresponding question focuses.

To recognize question type, we simply assume that type of complex question is only determined by its question focus; that is to say, question-type and question focus can be used interchangeably in this paper. Based on this assumption, question Q_1 and Q_2 belong to the hazard-type and disaster-type questions, respectively. Krishnan (2005) has showed that (a) the accuracy of recognizing question types reached 92.2% by using only question focuses and (b) the accuracy of recognizing question focuses was 84.6%. This indicates that most questions contain question focuses and it is practicable to represent question types by question focuses. Thereby, the task of recognizing question types shifts to recognizing question focuses from questions.

We regard question focus recognition as a sequence-tagging problem and employ conditional random fields (CRFs) because many studies have proven a consistent advantage of CRFs in sequence tagging. We manually annotate 4,770 questions with question focuses to train a CRF model, which classifies each question word into a set of tags $O = \{I_B, I_I, I_O\}$: I_B for a word that begins a focus, I_I for a word occuring in the middle of a focus and I_O for a word outside of a focus. In the following feature templates used in the CRF model, w_n and t_n refer to word and part-of-speech (PoS), respectively, and n refers to the relative position from the current word n=0. The feature templates contain four types: unigrams of w_n and t_n, where $n = -2, -1, 0, 1, 2$; bigrams of $w_n w_{n+1}$ and $t_n t_{n+1}$, where n=$-1, 0$; trigrams of $w_n w_{n+1} w_{n+2}$ and $t_n t_{n+1} t_{n+2}$, where $n = -2, -1, 0$; and bigrams of $O_n O_{n+1}$, where n=$-1, 0$.

Among 4,770 questions, 1,500 are held out as test set, the others are used for training. The experiment shows that precision of the CRF model on the test set is 89.5%. At offline, the CRF model is used to recognize question focuses from questions of social Q&A pairs. Finally, we recognize 103 question focuses for which frequencies are larger than 10,000. Moreover, the numbers of question focuses for which frequencies are larger than 100, 1,000, and 5,000 are 4,714, 807, and 194, respectively. Among 4,714 recognized question focuses, 87% are not included in the question focus training questions. At online phrase, the CRF model is used to identify question focus of test question.

4.2 Q&A Pairs

It is necessary to manually annotate question focuses for identifying question types, however, training Q&A pairs for the question types can be automatically leant as follows once question types are determined.

4.2.1 Basic Positive Q&A Pairs

For question-type X, social Q&A pairs for which question focuses are the same as X are regarded as basic positive Q&A pairs QA_{basic} of X-type questions. Formally, $QA_{basic} = \{QA_i | AT_i = X\}$, where QA_i denotes a Q&A pair, and AT_i denotes question focus of QA_i. Table 2[4] reports the number of Q&A pairs for each type of question in the extension of the NTCIR 2008 test set (discussed in the experimental section). For example, 10,362 Q&A pairs are leant for answering hazard-type questions. Table 3 lists questions which, together with their best answers, are utilized as basic positive training pairs of the corresponding type of complex questions.

Qtype	#	Qtype	#
Hazard-type	10,362	Function-type	41,005
Impact-type	35,097	Significance-type	14,615
Attitude-type	1,801	Measure-type	3,643
Reason-type	50,241	Casualty-type	102
Event-type	5,871	Scale-type	642

Table 2: Numbers of basic positive Q&A pairs learned (#)

4.2.2 Bootstrapping Positive Q&A Pairs

For question types like casualty(伤亡)-type for which only a few basic positive Q&A pairs are learnt, Q&A pairs for similar question types like fatality(死伤)-type can be used. Hownet (Dong, 1999), a lexical knowledge base with rich semantic information and which serves as a powerful tool for meaning computation, is adopted for bootstrapping the basic positive Q&A pairs. In Hownet, a word may represent multiple concepts, and each concept consists of a group of sememes. For example, the Chinese word for "伤亡(casualty)" is described as: "phenomena|现象, wounded|受伤, die|死, undesired|莠". The similarity between two words can be estimated by,

$$sim(w_1, w_2) = \max_{1 \le i \le |w_1|; 1 \le j \le |w_2|} sim(c_i, c_j)$$

$$sim(c_i, c_j) = \frac{\sum\limits_{1 \le k \le |c_i|} \max\limits_{1 \le z \le |c_j|} sim(se_{i,k}, se_{j,z})}{|c_i|}$$

where c_i and c_j represent the i-th and j-th concept of word w_1 and w_2, respectively, $|w_1|$ is the number of concepts that w_1 represents, $se_{i,k}$ denotes the k-th sememe of concept c_i, $|c_i|$ is the number of sememes of concept c_i, and $sim(se_{i,k}, se_{j,z})$ is 1 if they are same, otherwise the value is set to 0.

Accordingly, the bootstrapping positive Q&A pairs QA_{boot} of X-type questions is composed of the Q&A pairs in which question focuses are similar to X. Formally, $QA_{boot} = \{QA_j | sim(AT_j, X) > \theta_1\}$, where, AT_j is question focus of QA_j, θ_1 is the similarity threshold.

Qtype	Questions of Q&A pairs
Hazard -type	What are the **hazards** of the trojan.psw.misc.kah virus?
	List the **hazards** of smoking.
	What are the **hazards** of contact lenses?
Casualty -type	What were the **casualties** of the Sino-French War?
	What were the **casualties** of the Sichuan earthquake?
	What were the **casualties** of the Indonesian Tsunami?
Reason -type	What are the main **reasons** for China's water shortage?
	What are the **reasons** for asthma?
	What are the **reasons** for air pollution?

Table 3: Questions (translated from Chinese) of Q&A pairs (words in bold are question focuses).

4.2.3 Negative Pairs & Preprocessing

For each type of question, we also randomly select some Q&A pairs that do not contain question focuses and their similar words in questions as negative training Q&A pairs.

Preprocessing of the training data, including word segmentation, PoS tagging, named entity (NE) recognization (Wu et al., 2005), and dependency parsing (Chen, 2009), is conducted. We also replace each NE with its tag type.

4.3 Extracting Cue Expressions and Building Classifiers

In this paper, we extract two kinds of cue expressions: n-grams at the sequential level and depen-

[4] Function-type: What are the **functions** of the United Nations? Impact-type: List the **impact** of the 911 attacks on the United States. Significance-type: List the **significance** of China's accession to the WTO. Attitude-type: List the **attitudes** of other countries toward the Israel-Palestine conflict. Measure-type: What **measures** have been taken for energy-saving in Japan? Event-type: List the **events** in the Northern Ireland peace process. Scale-type: Give information about the **scale** of the Kunming World Horticulture Exposition. Refer to Table 3 for other types of questions.

dency patterns at the syntactic level. The purpose of cue expression mining is to extract a set of frequent lexical and PoS-based subsequences that are indicative of answers to a type of question.

The n-gram cue expressions include (1) 3,000 lexical unigrams selected using the formula: $score_w = tf_w \times log(\frac{N}{df_w})$, where tf_w denotes the frequency of word w, df_w denotes the frequency of Q&A pairs in which w appears, and N is the total number of the Q&A pairs; (2) lexical bigrams and trigrams that contain the selected unigrams and their frequencies are larger than the empirical thresholds; (3) PoS-based unigrams; and (4) PoS-based bigrams with frequencies larger than the threshold. The dependency pattern is defined as relation between words of a dependency tree. Figure 1 shows an example. Both lexical and PoS patterns with frequencies larger than the threshold are selected.

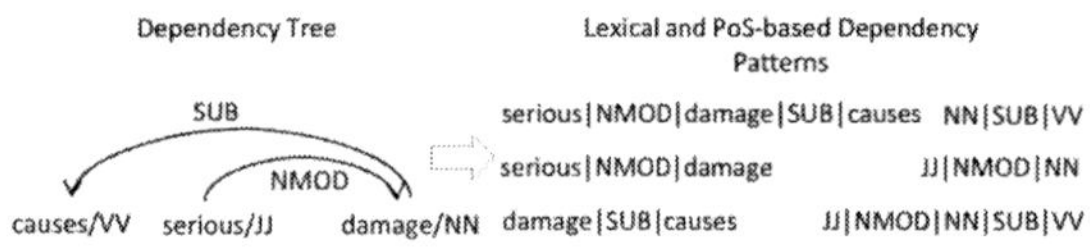

Figure 1: Example of dependency patterns

We also assign each extracted cue expression ce_i a weight calculated using the equation $weight_{ce_i} = c_1^{ce_i}/(c_1^{ce_i} + c_2^{ce_i})$, where, $c_1^{ce_i}$ and $c_2^{ce_i}$ denote its frequencies in positive and negative training Q&A pairs, respectively. The weights are used as values of features in SVM classifier.

The extracted cue expressions and collected Q&A pairs are used to build a question-type-specific classifier for each type of question, which is then used to remove noise sentences from answer candidates. For classifiers, we employ multivariate classification SVMs (Thorsten Joachims, 2005) that can directly optimize a large class of performance measures like F_1-Score, prec@k (precision of a classifier that predicts exactly k = 100 examples to be positive) and error-rate (percentage of errors in predictions).

5 Comparison Models

5.1 QSM

The QSM (question-specific method) first learns potential answer words to the question, and then re-ranks candidates by incorporating their "similarities" to the answer words. For each submitted question, the following four steps are performed. (1) An IR algorithm is used to retrieve the most similar Q&A pairs (top 50 in our experiments) to the question from the social Q&A collection. (2) All non-stop words from the retrieved Q&A pairs are weighted using a TFIDF score and the top M words are selected to form an answer profile Ap. (3) Answer candidates are re-ranked according to the similarity formula $sim(a_i) = \gamma sim(Q, a_i) + (1-\gamma)sim(a_i, Ap)$, where $sim(Q, a_i)$ denotes the similarity between question Q and candidates a_i, $sim(a_i, Ap)$ means the similarity between candidates and the answer profile Ap, γ is the weight. Both $sim(Q, a_i)$ and $sim(a_i, Ap)$ are estimated using cosine similarity in this paper. (4) Finally, the top N candidates are selected as answers to Q.

QSM is also widely used in answering definitional questions and TREC QA "other" questions (Kaisser et al., 2006; Chen, et al., 2006), which, however, learn answer words from the most relevant snippets returned by a Web search engine. Section 6 compares QSM based on 50 most relevant social Q&A pairs and that based on 50 most relevant snippets returned by Yahoo!.

5.2 MTM

The MTM learns word-to-word translation probability from all social Q&A pairs without consideration of the question and question type to improve complex QA system. The monolingual translation-based method treats Q&A pairs as the parallel corpus, with questions corresponding to the "source" language and answers to the "target" language. Monolingual translation models have recently been introduced to solve the lexical gap problem in IR and QA systems (Berger et al., 1999; Riezler et al., 2007; Xue, et al., 2008; Bernhard et al., 2009). A monolingual translation-based method for our complex QA system can be expressed by:

$$P(Q|a_i) = \prod_{w \in Q} ((1-\gamma)P_{mx}(w|a_i) + \gamma P_{ml}(w|C))$$
$$P_{mx}(w|a_i) = (1-\zeta)P_{ml}(w|a_i) + \zeta \sum_{t \in S} P(w|t)P_{ml}(t|a_i) \quad (1)$$

where Q is the question, a_i the candidate answer, γ the smoothing parameter for the whole Q&A collection, $P(w|t)$ the probability of translating an answer term t to a question term w, which is obtained by using the GIZA++ (Och and Ney, 2003), the impact of the translation probabilities is controlled by ζ (=0.6 in this paper).

As in the common practice in translation-based retrieval, we utilize IBM model 1 for obtaining word-to-word probability $P(w|t)$ from 6.0 million social Q&A pairs. Preprocessing of the Q&A pairs only involves word segmentation (Wu et al., 2005) and stop word removal.

6 Experiments

As Section 4.1 shows, there exist hundreds of types of complex questions, it is hard to evaluate our approach on all of them. In this paper, question types contained in the NTCIR 2008 test set (Mitamura et al., 2008) are used. The NTCIR 2008 test data set contains 30 complex questions[5] that we discuss here. However, a small number of test questions are included for certain question types; e.g., it contains only one hazard-type, one scale-type, and three significance-type questions. To form a more complete test set, we create another 57 test questions to be released with this paper. The test data used in this paper therefore includes 87 questions and is called an extension of the NTCIR 2008 test data set. For each test question we also provide a list of weighted answer nuggets, which are used as the gold standard answers for evaluation. The evaluation is conducted by employing Pourpre v1.0c tool that uses the standard scoring methodology for TREC "other" questions (Voorhees, 2003). Each question is scored using nugget recall NR, nugget precision NP, and a combination score F_3 of NR and NP. Refer to (Lin and Demner-Fushman, 2006) for the detailed computation. The final score of a system run is the mean of the scores across all test questions.

6.1 Overall Results

Table 4 summarizes the evaluation results of the systems. The baseline refers to the conventional method in which the similarity is the same as $sim(Q, a_i)$ in section 5.1. QSM_{web} and QSM_{qa} indicate QSM that learns answer words from the Web and the social Q&A pairs, respectively. $QTSM_{prec}$ denotes QTSM based on the classifier optimizing performance prec@k.

This table indicates that the complex QA performance can be clearly improved by exploiting social Q&A collection. In particular, we observe that: 1) QTSM obtains the best performance; e.g., the F_3 improvements of $QTSM_{prec}$ over MTM and QSM_{qa} in terms of N=10 are 5.8% and 6.0%, respectively. 2) QSM_{qa} outperforms QSM_{web} by 2.0% when N=10. Further analysis shows that the average number of the gold standard answer words learned in QSM_{web} (42.9%) are fewer than that learned in QSM_{qa} (58.1%). The reason may lie in: Q&A pairs are more complete and complementary than snippets that only contain length-limited contexts of question words. This proves that learning answer words from social Q&A pairs is superior to that from the snippets returned by a Web search engine. 3) The performance ranking of these models is: $QTSM_{prec}$ > {MTM, QSM_{qa}} > QSM_{web}. QSM_{qa} depends on very specific knowledge, i.e. answer words to each question, which may fail when social Q&A collection does not contain similar Q&A pairs, or similar Q&A pairs do not contain answer words to the question. MTM learns very general knowledge from social Q&A collection, i.e., word-to-word translation probability, which is not apt to any question, any type of question, or any domain question. $QTSM_{prec}$, however, learns question-type-specific salient expressions, which granularity is between QSM_{qa} and MTM. This may be the reason that $QTSM_{prec}$ achieves better performance.

Figure 2 displays how well $QTSM_{prec}$ performs for each type of question when N=10 for further comparison. This figure indicates that our method improves QSM_{qa} on most types of test questions; e.g., the F_3 improvements on function-type and hazard-type questions are 20.0% and 14%, respectively. It is noted that QSM_{qa} achieves better performance than $QTSM_{prec}$ on event-type questions. We interpret this to mean that the extracted salient cue expressions may not characterize answers to event-type questions. More complex features such as templates used in MUC-3 (MUC, 1991) may be needed. Figure 3 shows NR recall curves of the three models, which characterize the amount of relevant information contained within a fixed-length text segment (Lin, 2007). We observe that $QTSM_{prec}$ can greatly improve MTM and QSM_{qa} at every answer length. For example, the improvement of $QTSM_{prec}$ over MTM is about 10.0% when the answer length is 400 words. Yet there is no distinct difference between MTM and QSM_{qa}.

[5]Because definitional, biography, and relationship questions in the NTCIR 2008 test set are not discussed here.

	F_3 (%)		NR (%)		NP (%)	
	$N=5$	$N=10$	$N=5$	$N=10$	$N=5$	$N=10$
Baseline	18.18	21.95	19.85	27.64	25.32	18.96
QSM_{web}	20.36	22.57	23.47	29.63	22.30	13.57
QSM_{qa}	$21.28^{\dagger}$	$24.63^{\dagger}$	24.60	33.49	22.99	15.47
MTM	20.47	$24.76^{\dagger}$	19.85	33.10	21.73	13.57
$QTSM_{prec}$	$23.47^{\flat}$	$30.58^{\flat}$	26.68	40.22	27.65	20.33

Table 4: Overall performance for the test data when outputting the top N sentences as answers. Significance tests are conducted on the F_3 scores. †: significantly better than Baseline at the $p = 0.1$ level using two-sided t-tests; $^{\flat}$: significantly better than QSM_{qa} at the 0.005 level.

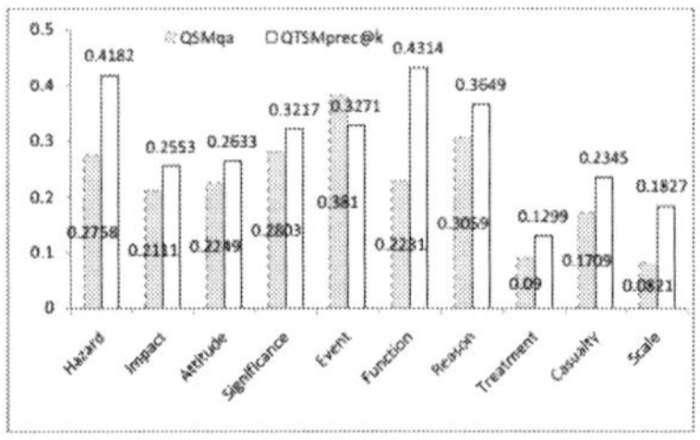

Figure 2: F_3 performance by type of question

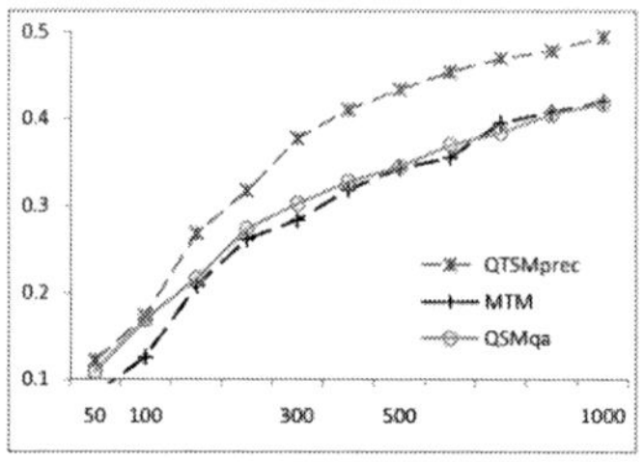

Figure 3: Recall over various answer lengths

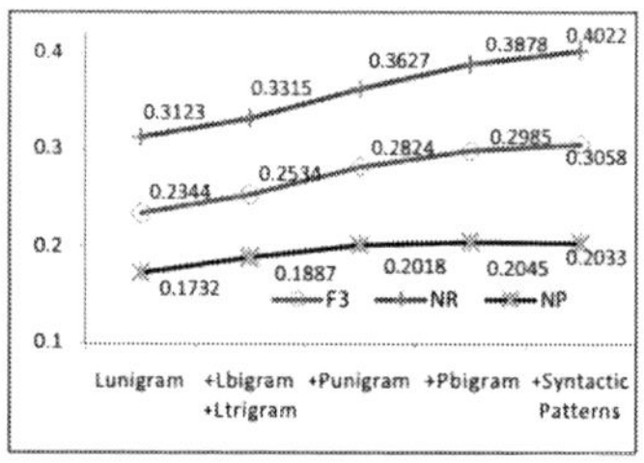

Figure 4: Impact of features on $QTSM_{prec}$

6.2 Impact of Features

To evaluate the contributions of individual features to the QTSM, this experiment gradually adds them. Figure 4 shows the performance of $QTSM_{prec}$ on different sets of features, L and P represent lexical and PoS-based n-gram cue expressions, respectively. This table demonstrates that all the lexical and PoS features can positively impact $QTSM_{prec}$. The contribution from dependency patterns is, however, not significant, which may be due to the limited number of dependency patterns learned.

6.3 Subjective evaluation

Pourpre v1.0c evaluation is based on n-gram overlap between the automatically produced answers and human-generated reference answers. Thus, it is not able to measure the conceptual equivalent. In subjective evaluation, the answer sentences returned by QA systems are labeled by two native Chinese assessors. Given a pair of answers for each question, the assessors are asked to determine which summary has better content for the question, or whether both are equally responsive. If their judgements are different, they will discuss a final judgement. This kind of evaluation is also used in (Biadsy et al., 2008; Liu et al., 2008).

Table 6 indicates that $QTSM_{prec}$ is much better than MTM and QSM_{qa}. For example, 56.3% of these judgements preferred the answers produced by $QTSM_{prec}$ over those produced by MTM. Table 5 compares the top 3 answers to question Q_1 answered by MTM and $QTSM_{prec}$.

$QTSM_{prec}$	Better	Equal	Worse
$QTSM_{prec}$ vs. MTM	56.3%	12.6%	31.1%
$QTSM_{prec}$ vs. QSM_{qa}	55.2%	13.8%	31.0%

Table 6: Results of subjective evaluation

7 Related Work

Some pioneering studies on social Q&A collection have recently been conducted. Much of the research aims at retrieving answers to queried questions from social Q&A collection. For example, Surdeanu et al. (2008) proposed an answer-ranking engine for non-factoid questions by incorporating textual features into a machine learning approach. Duan et al. (2008) retrieved questions semantically equivalent or close to the queried question for a question recommendation system. Agichtein et al. (2008) investigated techniques for finding high-quality content in social Q&A collection, and indicated that 94% of answers to questions have high quality. Xue, et al. (2008) proposed a retrieval model that combines a translation-based language model for the question part with a query likelihood approach for the

MTM	...非洲将是最易受全球气候变暖危害冲击的大陆.../...Africa will be most vulnerable to the impacts of global warming...
	...全球气候变暖将会对全球不同地区气候变化产生更为严重的影响。/...global warming will more seriously impact climate change in different regions of the world...
	...气候变暖对非洲造成的严重负面影响.../...global warming had a serious negative impact on Africa...
$QTSM_{prec}$	...全球气候变暖将给生态环境带来严重破坏, 致使自然灾害频繁发生, 而受其影响最为严重的当属非洲大陆。/...global warming will bring serious damage to the ecological environment, and result in frequent occurrences of natural disasters. There is no doubt that Africa is the most seriously impacted continent.
	全球气候变暖将会使非洲大陆的干旱地区, 特别是非洲中部和南部的干旱、半干旱地区更加缺水, 耕地退化和荒漠化现象越来越严重。/Global warming will cause more serious water shortages in the arid areas of the African continent, especially in central and southern arid and semi-arid areas. Land degradation and desertification will become increasingly serious.
	此外, 全球变暖还会导致极端气候现象频繁发生, 如寒潮、热浪、暴雨、龙卷风等, 对人类社会构成极大威胁。/Global warming will also lead to frequent extreme weather phenomena such as cold waves, heat waves, storms, and tornados, which poses a great threat to human beings.

Table 5: Top 3 answers to question, "What are the hazards of global warming?" returned by MTM and $QTSM_{prec}$

answer part. Wang (2010a) proposed an effective question retrieval in social Q&A collections.

Another category of study regards social Q&A collection as a kind of knowledge repository and aims to mine knowledge from it for generating answers to questions. To the best of our knowledge, there appears to be very limited work addressing this aspect. Mori et al. (2008) proposed a QSM method for improving complex Japanese QA systems, which collect Q&A pairs using 7-grams for which centers are interrogatives.

This paper is also related to query-based summarization of DUC (Dang, 2006; Harabagiu et al., 2006), which aims at synthesizing a fluent, well-organized 250-word summary for a given topic description and a collection of relevant documents generated manually. The topic descriptions usually consist of several complex questions such as "*Describe theories on the causes and effects of global warming and arguments against them.*" Thus, many approaches such as LexRank (Erkan and Radev, 2004) focus on compressing the relevant documents. We implement a LexRank method for our task, for which performance is even worse than the baseline. Our observation is that a query-based summarization task is given a set of manually generated relevant documents, but our QA systems need to retrieve relevant documents automatically, and there exist a great deal of noise.

8 Conclusion

This paper investigated techniques for mining knowledge from social Q&A websites for improving a sentence-based complex QA system. The proposed QTSM (question-type-specific method) explored social Q&A collection to automatically learn question-type-specific training Q&A pairs and cue expressions, and create a question-type-specific classifier for each type of question to filter out noise sentences before answer selection. Experiments on the extension of NTCIR 2008 test questions indicate that QTSM is more effective than QSM (question-specific method) and MTM (monolingual translation-based method) methods; e.g., the largest improvements in F_3 over QSM and MTM reaches 6.0% and 5.8%, respectively.

In the future, we will endeavor to: (1) reduce noise in the training Q&A pairs, and design more characteristic cue expressions to various types of questions such as event-templates for event-type question (MUC, 1991); (2) adapt QTSM to summarize answers in social QA sites (Liu et al., 2008); (3) learn paraphrases to recognize types of questions that do not contain question focuses such as "What causes global warming?"; (4) adapt the QA system to a topic-based summarization system, which will, for instance, summarize accidents according to "casualty" and"reason", and events according to "reason", "measure" and "impact".

References

Abdessamad Echihabi and Daniel Marcu. 2003. A Noisy-Channel Approach to Question Answering. In *Proc. of ACL 2003*, Japan.

Adam Berger and John Lafferty. 1999. Information Retrieval as Statistical Translation. In *Proc. of SIGIR 1999*, pp222-229.

Delphine Bernhard and Iryna Gurevych. 2009. Combining Lexical Semantic Resources with Question & Answer Archives for Translation-based Answer Finding. In *Proc. of ACL-IJCNLP 2009*, pp728-736.

Ellen M. Voorhees. 2003 Overview of the TREC 2003 Question Answering Track. In *Proc. of TREC 2003*, pp54-68, USA.

Eugene Agichtein, Carlos Castillo, Debora Donato. 2008 Finding High-Quality Content in Social Media. In *Proc. of WSDM 2008*, California, USA.

Fadi Biadsy, Julia Hirschberg, Elena Filatova. 2008. An Unsupervised Approach to Biography Production using Wikipedia. In *Proc. of ACL2008.*

Franz J. Och and Hermann Ney. 2003. A systematic Comparison of Various Statistical Alignment Models. In *Computational Linguistics*, 29(1):19-51.

Gunes Erkan and Dragomir Radev. 2004. LexRank: Graph-based Lexical Centrality as Salience in Text. In *Journal of Artificial Intelligence Research*,22:457-479.

Hang Cui, Min Yen Kan, and Tat Seng Chua. 2004. Unsupervised Learning of Soft Patterns for Definition Question Answering. In *Proc. of WWW 2004.*

Hoa Trang Dang. 2006. Overview of DUC 2006. In *Proc. of TREC 2006.*

Huizhong Duan, Yunbo Cao, Chin Yew Lin, and et al. 2008. Searching Questions by Identifying Question Topic and Question Focus. In *Proc. of ACL 2008.*

Jimmy Lin. 2007. Is Question Answering Better Than Information Retrieval? Toward a Task-based Evaluation Framework for Question Series. In *Proc. of HLT/NAACL2007*, pp 212-219.

Jimmy Lin and Dina Demner-Fushman. 2006. Will Pyramids Built of Nuggets Topple Over. In *Proc. of HLT/NAACL2006*, pp 383-390.

Kai Wang, Zhao-Yan Ming, Xia Hu, Tat-Seng Chua. 2010a. Segmentation of Multi-Sentence Questions: Towards Effective Question Retrieval in cQA Services. In *Proc. of SIGIR 2010*, pp 387-394.

Michael Kaisser, Silke Scheible, and Bonnie Webber. 2006. Experiments at the University of Edinburgh for the TREC 2006 QA track. In *Proc. of TREC2006.*

Mihai Surdeanu, Massimiliano Ciaramita, and Hugo Zaragoza. 2008. Learning to Rank Answers on Large Online QA Collections. In *Proc. of ACL 2008.*

Ryuichiro Higashinaka and Hideki Isozaki. 2008. Corpus-based Question Answering for why-Questions. In *Proc. of IJCNLP 2008*, pp 418-425.

Sanda Harabagiu, Dan Moldovan, Christine Clark, Mitchell Bowden, Andrew Hickl, 2005. Employing Two Question Answering Systems in TREC-2005. In *Proc. of TREC2005.*

Sanda Harabagiu, Finley Lacatusu, Andrew Hickl. 2006. Answering Complex Questions with Random Walk Models. In *Proc. of SIGIR 2006*, pp 220-227.

Stefan Riezler, Er Vasserman, Ioannis Tsochantaridis, Vibhu Mittal, Yi Liu. 2007. Statistical Machine Translation for Query Expansion in Answer Retrieval. In *Proc. of the ACL-2007*, pp 464-471.

Tatsunori Mori, Takuya Okubo, and Madoka Ishioroshi. 2008. A QA system that can answer any class of Japanese non-factoid questions and its application to CCLQA EN-JA task. In *Proc. of NTCIR2008*, Tokyo, pp 41-48.

Teruko Mitamura, Eric Nyberg, Hideki Shima, Tsuneaki Kato, and et al. 2008. Overview of the NTCIR-7 ACLIA Tasks: Advanced Cross-Lingual Information Access. In *Proc. of NTCIR 2008.*

Thorsten Joachims. 2005. A Support Vector Method for Multivariate Performance Measures. In *Proc. of ICML2005*, pp 383-390.

Ves Stoyanov, Claire Cardie, and Janyce Wiebe. 2005. Multi-Perspective Question Answering Using the OpQA Corpus. In *Proc. of HLT/EMNLP 2005.*

Vijay Krishnan, Sujatha Das and Soumen Chakrabarti. 2005. Enhanced Answer Type Inference from Questions using Sequential Models. In *Proc. of EMNLP 2005*, pp 315-322.

Vladimir Vapnik 1998. Statistical learning theory. John Wiley.

Wenliang Chen, Jun'ichi Kazama, Kiyotaka Uchimoto, and Kentaro Torisawa. 2009. Improving Dependency Parsing with Subtrees from Auto-Parsed Data. In *Proc. of EMNLP 2009*, pp 570-579.

Xiaobing Xue, Jiwoon Jeon, and W.Bruce Croft. 2008. Retrieval Models for Question and Answer Archives. In *Proc. of SIGIR 2008*, pp 475-482.

Xin Li and Dan Roth. 2002. Learning question classifiers. In *Proc. of COLING 2002*, pp 556-562.

Yi Chen, Ming Zhou, and Shilong Wang. 2006. Reranking Answers for Definitional QA Using Language Modeling. In Proc. of ACL/COLING2006.

Youzheng Wu, Jun Zhao, Bo Xu, and Hao Yu. 2005. Chinese Named Entity Recognition Model based on Multiple Features. In *Proc. of HLT/EMNLP 2005.*

Yuanjie Liu, Shasha Li, Yunbo Cao, and et al. 2008. Understanding and Summarizing Answers in Community-Based Question Answering Services. In *Proc. of COLING 2008.*

Yutaka Sasaki. 2005. Question Answering as Question-biased Term Extraction: A New Approach toward Multilingual QA. In *Proc. of ACL 2005.*

Dong Zhendong, Dong Qiang. 1999. Hownet. `http://www.keenage.com`.

Message Understanding Conference (MUC) `http://www-nlpir.nist.gov/related_projects/muc/index.html`.

TAC (Text Analysis Conference) 2008 Question Answering Track. `http://www.nist.gov/tac/2008/qa/`.

Safety Information Mining — What can NLP do in a disaster —

Graham Neubig
Kyoto University
Yoshida Honmachi, Sakyo-ku, Kyoto, Japan

Yuichiroh Matsubayashi
National Institute of Informatics
Chiyoda-ku, Tokyo

Masato Hagiwara, Koji Murakami
Rakuten Institute of Technology
New York

Abstract

This paper describes efforts of NLP researchers to create a system to aid the relief efforts during the 2011 East Japan Earthquake. Specifically, we created a system to mine information regarding the safety of people in the disaster-stricken area from Twitter, a massive yet highly unorganized information source. We describe the large scale collaborative effort to rapidly create robust and effective systems for word segmentation, named entity recognition, and tweet classification. As a result of our efforts, we were able to effectively deliver new information about the safety of over 100 people in the disaster-stricken area to a central repository for safety information.

1 Introduction

On March 11, 2011 at 14:46[1], a massive earthquake of Magnitude 9.0 struck off the coast of Japan. The earthquake and the ensuing Tsunami caused damage across the entire eastern coast of the country, with homes destroyed, roads impassible, and large swaths of the disaster-stricken area losing electricity and the ability to communicate.

Figure 1 shows the death toll and the number of missing people from tsunami and earthquake, presented by the Japanese National Police Agency. The number of missing people reached its peak on March 25th, indicating that the government took 2 weeks to fully grasp the total number of victims, although they began gathering information about the whereabouts of victims and survivors as soon as the earthquake hit. One of the main reasons for this delay was that prefectures could not effectively collect the information from municipal governments or police stations because many of them were extensively damaged or destroyed by the disaster (Anonymous, 2011)[2]. Furthermore, damage to communication equipment, power outages, and inundation of the air waves prevented the use of mobile phones, which are generally the most important tool for communication during a disaster.

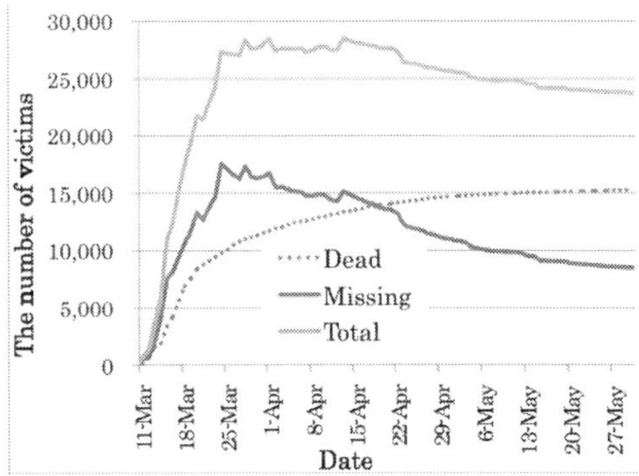

Figure 1: Change of overall death toll and missing people

As a result, Twitter or social network services (SNS) such as mixi[3] played an important role for propagating safety information among people. However, with SNSs flooded with information about the disaster, it was difficult to ensure that people would be properly connected with the information they were seeking. Soon after the disaster struck, many NLP researchers, engineers, and students from all over Japan (including the authors), spontaneously created a working group called "ANPI_NLP"[4] to try to organize this information into a form that would be useful. In particular, we focused on mining and organizing information on Twitter regarding safety of individuals in the disaster-stricken area, as people are initially more concerned about the safety of their family or

[1] All the dates and times in this paper are in JST.

[2] `http://www.asahi.com/special/10005/TKY201103120549.html`

[3] `http://mixi.jp/`

[4] The word "ANPI" means "safety" in Japanese.

friends than anything else.

There were three major elements to this process:

- Separating the tweets that contained safety information from the huge number of irrelevant tweets.
- Extracting important information, such as person names and locations from highly domain-specific text included in the tweets.
- Verifying and delivering this information to the people that need it.

The working group tackled these issues in safety information extraction from Twitter, preparing resources, building tools, and connecting the extracted information with Google Person Finder (GPF)[5], a central location for safety information that was widely publicized through the Japanese news media. Our priorities were not only the accuracy, but also the speed with which we could provide the information.

In this paper, we report the process of building an information extraction system in a disaster-response situation within a matter of days. The challenges involved included organizing volunteers (§2), building resources for out-of-domain, noisy internet data (§3), and applying these volunteers and resources to the construction of NLP tools (§4 and §5). We also describe the final results of the project, the provision of new information about missing persons to GPF (§6), and summarize related work (§7). Finally in §8 we discuss what went right and what went wrong with the project, and provide some insight into what can be done to prepare for similar situations in the future.

2 Organization and Communication

The project began with a single Twitter post soon after the earthquake hit, imploring NLP researchers and engineers to think about what they could do to help in the time of need. In particular, the creation of resources and tools that could be used to process information about the earthquake was cited as one example. In under an hour, the first responders to this call had started creating the language resources described in §3.

Given the public nature of Twitter, word of the efforts spread, and the number of participants quickly increased. With the large number of weakly connected participants, there was no clear power structure in place to delegate authority. Instead, several leaders spontaneously emerged, centered around people who joined the project early, had large Twitter followings, or were experts in a specific area (such as the creation of data or domain adaptation of tools). In addition to the discourse on Twitter, a publicly available Wiki page was created to gather information about the project in a single place[6]. Overall, we believe that the existing online communication framework proved quite effective in rallying and organizing members for the project.

On the other hand, the largest challenge in the project organization was the initial underestimation of the outpouring of support that the project would see. In the end, over 65 volunteers joined the project, and it was often difficult for the few main organizers to rapidly design and delegate tasks to such a large number of volunteers. This resulted in an over-concentration of effort in some areas, and lack of effort in others. We hope that this paper will help provide a road-map for the type of tasks that may be necessary in rapid-response NLP situations, and prompt discussion on what other tasks may be taken on in a disaster.

3 Language Resources and Tweet Corpus

The earliest stage of the project focused on sharing linguistic resources. These included dictionaries, which were used to improve various text analyzers and classifiers. At the same time, we also made efforts towards building a labeled corpus of tweets containing safety information, with the final goal of extracting information from unlabeled tweets.

3.1 Text Analysis Resources

Among the earliest contributions to the project were dictionaries, especially those containing person and place names specific to the Tohoku region. These were generally contributed by people directly familiar with the resources, the creators or maintainers of the dictionaries themselves.

As time was critical, the linguistic analysis tools actually used in the project were based on widely available general domain resources, as well as domain-specific resources gathered within the very early stages of the project. The general domain language resources consisted of the Balanced Corpus of Contemporary Written Japanese

[5] http://japan.person-finder.appspot.com/

[6] http://trans-aid.jp/ANPI_NLP (in Japanese).

(BCCWJ) (Maekawa, 2008) and the UniDic dictionary (Den et al., 2008), which are high quality and annotated with a variety of tags.

The domain-specific resources gathered specifically for the project and used in the analysis tools described in §4 included:

- The dictionary used in the open source Mozc Japanese Input method, which contained 50,848 first names and 26,519 last names and was provided by the maintainer of the project.

- A name list that contains last names specific to northeast Japan[7]. These resources were publicly available on the web.

- A location name list of Iwate, Miyagi, Fukushima, and Ibaraki prefectures created by downloading a database of postal code information and manually checking the data.

A number of other resources were created by volunteers, including a list of all the station names in Japan, station location information, landmark names in Kanto and Tohoku extracted from Wikipedia, a list of geopolitical entities, and a list of abbreviated school names and places. While these resources were certainly significant, it was the resources that were prepared early on in the process that provided the most aid to the project as a whole. This indicates that for similar situations in the future, it is essential to have as many resources as possible immediately available, and preferably familiar to the people in the project to facilitate rapid processing and dispersal.

3.2 Tweet Corpus Construction

As Twitter contained a wide variety of earthquake-related posts including information about the safety of people in the disaster-affected area, we decided to create a corpus of disaster-related tweets to aid our information extraction efforts. The first tweet corpus shared was the collection of 469,504 tweets containing the word "地震" (earthquake) from March 11th 16:09 to March 13th 8:59. We also collected tweets with the hash tags "#anpi" (safety information) such as "#hinan" (evacuation), "#j_j_helpme" (help request), and "#save_"+ location names. Tweets containing RT (re-tweets) and QT (quote tweets) were removed to eliminate duplication. As a result, 61,376 tweets were collected from March 13th 1:37am until March 14th 16:45pm.

A typical tweet containing safety information looked like the following [8]:

> 気仙沼市の田中太郎・花子さんと連絡が取れません！どなたか消息をご存知ありませんでしょうか？
> TANAKA Taro and Hanako who lived in Kesennuma City can't be reached. Does anybody know where they are?

From the large corpus of tweets, we hope to discover two pieces of information. First, we must recognize the *topic* of the tweet, in this case that the tweet is asking for information about missing people (tweet classification). Second, we need to recognize that the people in question are "TANAKA, Taro" and "Hanako," both of whom live in "Kesennuma City" (NE recognition).

In order to create data to train tools to perform both tweet classification and NE recognition, volunteers began to perform tagging as soon as the tweet collection was finished. First, we defined nine kinds of tweet labels specifying the tweet topics, which are listed in Table 1. The distinction among S/O/U was sometimes unclear and went under extensive discussion among volunteers. In practice, the distinction of I/L/P/M from others (S/O/U) is of the highest importance.

One example is shown below:

```
<person type="M">TANAKA Taro</person> and
<person type="M">Hanako</person> living in
<location>Kesennuma city</location> can't
be reached.
```

Safety information is optionally added to every person tag, specifying the object of the safety information, as shown in the above example. Also multiple tags are permitted when multiple types of safety information are contained in a single tweet.

Utilizing Twitter, word was spread about the tagging task force, gathering a large number of volunteers, most of whom were NLP researchers, engineers, or students. In order to facilitate the task-force, several people with annotation experience responded to questions in real-time, and various tools were created and shared among the annotators. Over 65 volunteers gathered to tag the corpus with class and NE tags over the course of two days, resulting in a total of 33,242 tweet annotated.

[7] http://platinum22000.fc2web.com/{miyagi,fukushima,iwate,tochigi}.htm

[8] The actual person and place names have been replaced with pseudonyms to preserve anonymity.

Label	Definition	Example	Count
I	Him/Herself is alive	I'm XXX in YYY City. I'm all right.	405
L	Alive	Mr./Ms. XXX in YYY City is at ZZZ Shelter. He/She is alive.	1,154
P	Passed away	—	93
M	Missing	The safety of Mr./Ms. XXX living in YYY City is unknown.	4,438
H	Help Request	Mr./Ms. XXX is left in YYY and needs help!	280
		My relatives/parents/... staying in South XXX City are missing.	
S	Information request	Refugees at XXX School are provided enough daily supplies? (Safety information of unspecific individual, region, etc.)	1,903
O	Not safety information	You can post safety information on this site!	24,035
R	External link	Survivor list of XXX City: http://...	773
U	Unknown	(Non-Japanese or nonsense postings)	1,235

Table 1: Safety information tags on tweets

While the annotators were generally more skilled and motivated than those in previous attempts to create language resources using crowdsourcing (Callison-Burch and Dredze, 2010; Finin et al., 2010), given the rapid nature by which the project developed, annotation started before tagging standards were put in place, leading to some inconsistency in the tagged corpus. In retrospect, despite the speed of the project, it would have been helpful to spend some more time thinking about what information was really necessary for the task, and have more experienced annotators do a quick test run before opening annotation to the broader volunteer base. In addition, as many of the annotators were less experienced, explicitly allowing the annotators to "pass" on difficult instances would have reduced the amount of time wasted on difficult or ambiguous cases.

4 Text Analysis

Before mining the tweets for useful information, it was necessary to create text analysis tools that were capable of handling this very specialized data set. The main objective of text analysis was named entity recognition (NER), which would allow for the identification of names and locations.

4.1 Morphological Analysis and NER

The first step in Japanese text processing is morphological analysis (MA), which splits raw Japanese text into words and assigns POS tags to each word. While previous research in tagging for Twitter has profited by building a custom NLP pipelines over the course of several months (Gimpel et al., 2011; Ritter et al., 2011) or by building semi-supervised learning systems (Liu et al., 2011), it was necessary to create a morphological analyzer in the course of several hours. This is due to the fact that all other components of the system depend on MA, and cannot be developed until MA is in place. Thus, we utilized existing general domain resources, and added new resources as they were collected in a domain-adaptation framework.

For this task we used KyTea[9], an open source morphological analysis tool notable for being relatively robust to out-of-domain data, and being able to flexibly incorporate a variety of language resources (Neubig et al., 2011).

We trained a word segmentation (WS) and POS tagging model for KyTea using the BCCWJ and UniDic as a base. We trained the POS tagging model, but in order to facilitate NE recognition farther down the pipeline, we replaced all proper nouns with their subcategory tag ("first name," "place name," etc.). We also added a corpus of conversational and news text (CN Corpus) that was only annotated with word boundaries, and a large list of Japanese first and last names. We indicate the model trained with all of these resources as ORIG.

While the POS tagger works on a word-by-word basis, most named entities consist of multiple words. Previous work has developed linguistic resources for English NE tagging on Twitter (Finin et al., 2010), but again considering the short time frame, we developed a simple rule-based system to connect multiple words into single named entities. Rules scanned the corpus in order, finding the first of three POS tags: "first name (FNAME)," "last name (LNAME)," or "place name (PNAME)." These words are labeled with PERSON, PERSON, or LOCATION NE tags respectively. Continuing in the order of the corpus, all words directly following a marked NE are merged if marked with one of the three previously mentioned POS tags, or as a "suffix (SUF)[10]". An example of the three step

[9] Available at http://www.phontron.com/kytea.

[10] A small set of suffixes that are used in conjunction with person names such as "*-san*" or "*-kun*" were omitted.

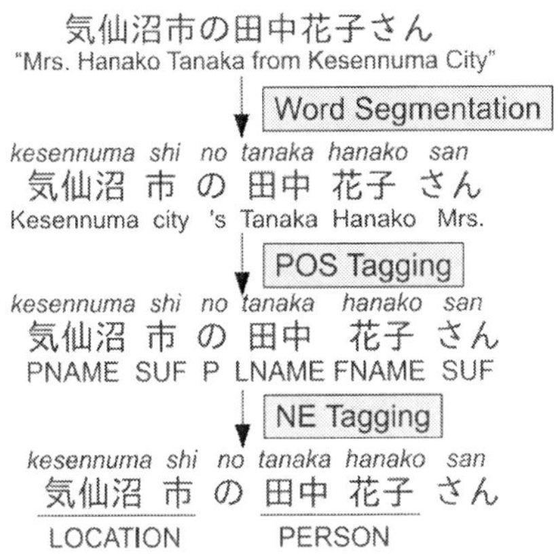

Figure 2: An example of the three steps of named entity recognition. Pronunciations and English translations are also provided for reference.

Name	Words	WS	POS	Group
BCCWJ	997k	○	○	ORIG
CN Text	503k	○		ORIG
UniDic	217k	○	○	ORIG
Names	144k	○	○	ORIG
Address	73.4k	○	○	+DICT
+Names	29.4k	○	○	+DICT
Active	10.2k	○		+ACTIVE

Table 2: Resources used in building the model with names, word counts, whether each corpus is annotated with WS and POS information, and which group the resource was added in.

NE tagging process is shown in Figure 2.

4.2 Domain Adaptation

While this classifier worked well on general domain data, it is known that accuracy greatly decreases for text in different domains or styles than the training data (Finin et al., 2010; Neubig et al., 2011; Ritter et al., 2011). In the tweet data there were a large number of place and person names specific to the disaster-stricken region, as well as a large number of linguistic phenomena specific to tweets, and thus it was necessary to add a number of language resources (summarized in Table 2) to adapt the text processing tools to the new domain.

To improve the accuracy on person and place names, we added the language resources previously described in section 3. The combination of these dictionaries is indicated by "+Names" in Table 2, and a model trained adding these resources is indicated with +DICT.

Finally, to handle the the large number of Twitter-related linguistic phenomena such as the word "tweet" or hash tags, we annotated word boundaries using the active-learning/partial-annotation method described by Neubig et al. (2011). For each round of active learning, we chose the 100 words for which the morphological analyzer was least confident, and had a single human annotator correct the word boundaries for these words. This was repeated for 4 rounds (400 words), which took approximately 1.5 hours total. The model trained by adding this data to +DICT is indicated as +ACTIVE.

		ORIG	+DICT	+ACTIVE
WS	F	97.3%	97.3%	97.7%
Lab. NE	P	53.9%	69.6%	69.2%
	R	55.6%	71.7%	72.7%
Unlab. NE	P	70.6%	80.4%	80.8%
	R	72.7%	82.8%	84.9%

Table 3: Word segmentation F-measure and NE precision (P) and recall (R) for both labeled and unlabeled evaluation.

4.3 Result Analysis

In order to demonstrate the necessity and effectiveness of domain adaptation, we present results of a quantitative and qualitative analysis of WS and NER for ORIG, +DICT, and +ACTIVE.

Table 3 shows results for a quantitative analysis of WS and NE tagging results on a manually annotated corpus of 50 tweets. Labeled NE accuracy indicates that the NE is only considered correct if both its span and its label (PERSON/LOCATION) are correct, and unlabeled NE accuracy indicates that the NE is considered correct if the span is matched, regardless of the label. It can be seen that the addition of dictionaries for the target domain greatly increased the NE accuracy, up to 16% for labeled tagging. The active-learning-based annotation further improved the WS accuracy by 0.42%, resulting in gains of NE recall of 1-2%.

The main reason for the improvement between the ORIG and +DICT was the proper handling of place names in the disaster-stricken area. ORIG would split long addresses into several NEs, some of which were mistakenly recognized as as person names. For example, "気仙沼_市" (Kesennuma city) was mistakenly split into "気仙_沼_市" (Kesen swamp city) and "気仙" was recognized as a person name. Further, the active learning for WS fixed segmentation errors such as correcting the improperly segmented "平浄_水場" to the properly segmenting "平_浄水_場" (Taira water purifying plant). This, in turn, allowed for "平" (Taira) to be properly recognized as a location name.

The largest remaining challenge for the fully adapted system was the distinction between last names and place names, which are highly ambiguous in Japanese. The use of the address information corpus greatly improved the NE tagging results, but also biased the classifier heavily towards place names. In a rapid-response situation it is necessary to use any and all of the resources available, even if they are known to be biased. This sample-bias problem can likely be ameliorated by recent progress in machine learning techniques (Huang et al., 2007).

5 Safety Information Classifier

Next, we describe the classifier that we built to find tweets containing safety information out of all the tweets in the corpus.

5.1 Model 1

Our first classifier, which we will call Model 1, was developed in several hours by oversimplifying the classification problem and using a very limited feature set.

While, as explained in §3.2, a single tweet could be assigned multiple labels, for Model 1 we simply took the first label that each annotator assigned to be true, and trained a one-vs.-rest classifier on this data. We used two types of features for the classification, bag-of-character-n-gram features, and NE features. The bag-of-character-n-gram features created a separate feature for each character n-gram from unigram to trigrams. As most Japanese words are relatively short, this is able to capture the most important words while not requiring word segmentation and thus being relatively robust. Second, we used the counts of each type of named entity tag, which are generally larger in tweets that contained useful information.

We trained all models using the default SVM solver of LIBLINEAR (Fan et al., 2008). 10-fold cross validation on the test set showed that the classifier achieved a tag accuracy of 86.13%.

5.2 Model 2

After few days, we created Model 2 as an extension of Model 1. Model 2 used a multi-class and multi-label classifier which output all the labels each of whose score exceeds a threshold t.

We extended the feature set for Model 2. Model 2 includes the same features as Model 1, but for n-grams, Model 2 does not count duplicated sequences. As NE features, co-occurrence information of PERSON and LOCATION in a single tweet was added as tweets for safety confirmation should generally include both of them. Combination of character 3-grams and the appearance of a PERSON was also added to capture a tweet's intention for that person. We also used existence of the hash tag "#anpi" and the total number of appearance of hash tags except for "#anpi" as clues for dividing tweets not related to safety confirmation (label O, U, S) from the others. Finally, we used the existence of the string "http(s)" and combination of existence of "http(s)" and NE as clues for the label R (external lists).

5.3 Evaluation

We evaluated the Model 2 classifier in detail using the corpus from the 17th of March, which contained 9,812 tweets. We divided the corpus into three sets: 80% for training, 10% for development, and the other 10% for test. For comparison, we also developed Model 1′ which is a multi-label model using the same feature set as Model 1.

Table 4 shows the results of the two models. The performance is not significantly different in terms of accuracy, but Model 2 obtained higher recall than Model 1′. The thresholds here were empirically determined to the one that maximize the F1-scores on the development set.

We described the result for each label with Model 2 in Table 5. Good performance was obtained for the O and M that comparatively have a larger number of instances. However, the recalls for the labels having few instances were lower. Especially, most of the label L were still missing. The most frequent mis-prediction was occurred between U, S and O. This is not a big problem since all these three labels are unrelated to safety confirmation. However, by analyzing errors, we found that there are a significant number of inconsistencies for these three labels depending on the annotators due to the inconsistent annotation standards mentioned in Section 2. A promising solution for situations like these is the recent development of methods and publicly available tools for extremely efficient active learning for text classification (Tong and Koller, 2002; Settles, 2011). These would allow for similar final results to be

		Dev				Test			
Model	t	P	R	F	Acc.	P	R	F	Acc.
Model 1′	0.55	87.8%	84.3%	86.0%	96.8%	87.9%	84.9%	86.4%	96.9%
Model 2	0.45	86.1%	85.7%	85.9%	96.7%	87.1%	86.4%	86.8%	97.0%

Table 4: Micro-averaged precision (P), recall (R), F-score (F), and accuracy (Acc.) achieved by Model 1′ and Model 2. For the evaluation, we transformed the gold and predicted data from multi-labeled instances to nine sets of binary-labeled instances.

Label	#samples	P	R	F
O	719	88.4%	98.3%	93.1%
M	134	91.2%	93.3%	92.3%
S	51	72.5%	56.9%	63.7%
L	45	50.0%	11.1%	18.2%
R	32	76.9%	31.3%	44.4%
U	22	0.0%	0.0%	0.0%
I	12	50.0%	58.3%	53.9%
H	6	100.0%	50.0%	66.7%
P	4	0.0%	0.0%	0.0%

Table 5: Precision (P), recall (R) and F-score (F) for each labels using Model 2 ($t = 0.45$).

Gold	Predict	#err.	Gold	Predict	#err.
U	O	22	LR	OR	2
S	O	17	R	LR	2
L	O	13	O	LR	2
LR	O	11	S	OS	2
R	O	9	MS	S	2
O	S	7	LPR	O	2
L	M	5	LM	M	2
M	IM	5	LM	IM	2
M	O	4	IM	M	2
R	OR	3			
H	O	3	Others		16
M	S	3	Total		136

Table 6: Label sequences where the errors occurred with Model 2 ($t = 0.45$).

achieved by a fewer number of annotators, reducing inconsistency issues.

6 Application of the System

The final step was verifying that the information was in fact reliable, and then matching PERSON and LOCATION tokens from tweets, which were classified as "L" (the person is alive) to the information of Google Person Finder (GPF). We chose to verify and match the information by hand to prevent the provision of misinformation on a sensitive topic such as safety of earthquake victims.

GPF contained several columns, such as the first name and last name of the person, home neighborhood, home city and home prefecture. The manually corrected NE information was matched with GPF data, and we were able to update the personal information of more than a hundred individuals that were confirmed to be alive in tweets.

However, many tokens extracted from tweets had problems, including:

- **Incomplete** LOCATION **information:** The tokens lacked a couple of information such as city, or neighborhood. "I was able to contact Taro Tanaka, who lives in Miyagi prefecture! [宮城県の田中太郎と無事に連絡が取れました！]". In this case, there may be many Taro Tanakas living in the prefecture, so a single individual cannot be identified.
- **Incomplete** PERSON **names:** a) Last or first names were be omitted when describing people of the same family. "I found Taro, Jiro, and Hanako Tanaka of Sendai at an evacuation shelter. [仙台市に住む田中太郎、次郎、花子が避難所にいました。]" or "The Tanaka family who live in Sendai has been reached! [仙台市に住む田中一家の安否が確認できました。]" b) Many person names that are likely written in logographic *kanji* in normal text were instead written phonetically (using *katakana* or *hiragana*).

While we focused mainly on extracting information about missing people, it has also been noted that Twitter is a source of other information in disaster situations (Corvey et al., 2010; Vieweg et al., 2010). For example, "50 people in Kesennuma city have evacuated to a hill behind the city hall. [気仙沼で被災し、市民会館の裏山に 50 人避難しています]" includes the number of people (50) and a concrete location (a hill behind the city hall), and could be a good indicator of where to concentrate rescue efforts. This could be an area of very practical application for recent research in verifying reliability of information on Twitter (Kawahara et al., 2008; Qazvinian et al., 2011).

7 Related Work

Besides the safety information mining task which we described in the previous sections, we observed many other efforts to help the earthquake victims via NLP technologies as sub-projects of ANPI_NLP. Prominent ones include:

- **Association of tweets to evacuation shelter locations:** This includes geo-coding location names extracted from tweets and associating them with the evaluation shelter lists, which are also geo-coded.
- **Visualization of tweets on a map:** This includes mapping geo-tagged tweets on a map so that they can be searched easily.
- **Translation of information to foreign languages:** This includes compilation and sharing of technical term multilingual dictionaries, automatic translation of earthquake information, and provision of the translated information in four major languages spoken by foreigners in Japan.

We are definitely not the first to focus on the disaster-related natural language processing. Lewis (2010) reports the development project of Haitian Creole translation system in rapid response to the Haiti earthquake in 2010. While their motivations have a lot in common with ours, such as the necessity to set up a deployable system in a very short time span. Corvey et al. (2010) describe the annotation of a corpus about the Oklahoma wildfires, aiming at provision of broad-scale information as opposed to safety information mining about individuals. There have also been a number of works on detecting general trends from twitter, including work by Sakaki et al. (2010), who detect earthquakes based on Twitter postings. There are many other systems designed for information sharing in emergency, including the one described in (Hasegawa et al., 2005).

8 Conclusion

In this paper we presented a description of the efforts of a group of volunteers to create a useful NLP system in a short time frame in response to a natural disaster.

On the whole, we believe the project was a success. In an extremely short time-frame, we were able to design, implement, and run a system for extracting useful information from a highly unorganized and difficult-to-process information source. In the short term, this allowed us to provide information about the safety of over 100 people. In addition, this allowed us to clarify the framework required, and develop tools that can be used to allow for provision of information on an even larger scale in future disaster situations. On a more abstract level, we were able to show that NLP has the potential to make a contribution in a disaster-response situation, which we hope will provide an impetus for similar future projects.

However, a number of challenges remain, and we conclude by summarizing the major lessons learned in the project.

- **Speed is everything:** Gathering data, making analysis tools, creating a classifier, and providing information to the public all needed to be performed on a limited time frame. As each of these steps must be completed in order, a delay in any part would result in delays for the overall process. Thus, it was necessary to create working tools as fast as possible, even if this meant making sacrifices in accuracy and refining later.
- **A better annotation framework is needed:** To resolve the challenges posed by annotation in such a short time frame, we must focus on create of better standards considering only the necessary information, do test annotation runs to work out the kinks, and allow annotators to "pass" on difficult annotations.
- **Human resources must be used effectively:** The project summoned an outpouring of support much larger than originally expected. To harness all of the people that are willing to help, it is important to have an overall project vision, and be able to quickly identify new projects for volunteers to work on.

Disasters such as earthquakes are tragic, overwhelming times, with too much information coming in for any individual to handle. We hope that our work has demonstrated that there is a need and a means for processing of this information, and will motivate similar projects in the future.

Acknowledgments

While too numerous to list here, the authors would like to sincerely thank all of the over 65 participants in the project. Without their generous contributions of time, resources, and expertise, the work described here would have never been possible. Finally, we thank Taiichi Hashimoto, Atsushi Fujita, Shinsuke Mori, and anonymous reviewers for their helpful comments on this manuscript.

References

Anonymous. 2011. Yakusho/keisatsu kinou daun, anpi kakunin susumazu, higashinihon daishinsai (In Japanese). In *the Asahi Shimbun*, page 20. March 13.

Chris Callison-Burch and Mark Dredze. 2010. Creating speech and language data with amazon's mechanical turk. In *NAACL HLT 2010 Workshop on Creating Speech and Language Data with Amazon's Mechanical Turk*, pages 1–12.

William J. Corvey, Sarah Vieweg, Travis Rood, and Martha Palmer. 2010. Twitter in mass emergency: What NLP can contribute. In *NAACL HLT 2010 Workshop on Computational Linguistics in a World of Social Media*, pages 23–24, Los Angeles, California, USA, June. Association for Computational Linguistics.

Yasuharu Den, Junpei Nakamura, Toshinobu Ogiso, and Hideki Ogura. 2008. A proper approach to Japanese morphological analysis: Dictionary, model, and evaluation. In *6th International Conference on Language Resources and Evaluation (LREC)*.

Rong-En Fan, Kai-Wei Chang, Cho-Jui Hsieh, Xiang-Rui Wang, and Chih-Jen Lin. 2008. LIBLINEAR: a library for large linear classification. *The Journal of Machine Learning Research*, 9:1871–1874.

Tim Finin, William Murnane, Anand Karandikar, Nicholas Keller, Justin Martineau, and Mark Dredze. 2010. Annotating named entities in Twitter data with crowdsourcing. In *NAACL HLT 2010 Workshop on Creating Speech and Language Data with Amazon's Mechanical Turk*, pages 80–88, Los Angeles, June. Association for Computational Linguistics.

Kevin Gimpel, Nathan Schneider, Brendan O'Connor, Dipanjan Das, Daniel Mills, Jacob Eisenstein, Michael Heilman, Dani Yogatama, Jeffrey Flanigan, and Noah A. Smith. 2011. Part-of-speech tagging for Twitter: Annotation, features, and experiments. In *49th Annual Meeting of the Association for Computational Linguistics: Human Language Technologies*, pages 42–47, Portland, Oregon, USA, June. Association for Computational Linguistics.

Satoshi Hasegawa, Kumi Sato, Shohei Matsunuma, Masaru Miyao, and Kohei Okamoto. 2005. Multilingual disaster information system: information delivery using graphic text for mobile phones. *AI & Society*, 19(3):265–278.

Jiayuan Huang, Alexander J. Smola, Arthur Gretton, Karsten M. Borgwardt, and Bernhard Scholkopf. 2007. Correcting sample selection bias by unlabeled data. *Advances in neural information processing systems*, 19:601.

Daisuke Kawahara, Sadao Kurohashi, and Kentaro Inui. 2008. Grasping major statements and their contradictions toward information credibility analysis of web contents. In *2008 IEEE/WIC/ACM International Conference on Web Intelligence and Intelligent Agent Technology*, pages 393–397. IEEE.

William D. Lewis. 2010. Haitian Creole: how to build and ship an MT engine from scratch in 4 days, 17 hours, & 30 minutes. In *14th Annual Conference of the European Association for Machine Translation*.

Xiaohua Liu, Shaodian Zhang, Furu Wei, and Ming Zhou. 2011. Recognizing named entities in tweets. In *49th Annual Meeting of the Association for Computational Linguistics: Human Language Technologies*, pages 359–367, Portland, Oregon, USA, June.

Kikuo Maekawa. 2008. Balanced corpus of contemporary written Japanese. In *6th Workshop on Asian Language Resources*, pages 101–102.

Graham Neubig, Yosuke Nakata, and Shinsuke Mori. 2011. Pointwise prediction for robust, adaptable japanese morphological analysis. In *The 49th Annual Meeting of the Association for Computational Linguistics: Human Language Technologies (ACL-HLT) Short Paper Track*, Portland, Oregon, USA, 6.

Vahed Qazvinian, Emily Rosengren, Dragomir R. Radev, and Qiaozhu Mei. 2011. Rumor has it: Identifying misinformation in microblogs. In *2011 Conference on Empirical Methods in Natural Language Processing*, pages 1589–1599, Edinburgh, Scotland, UK., July. Association for Computational Linguistics.

Alan Ritter, Sam Clark, Mausam, and Oren Etzioni. 2011. Named entity recognition in tweets: An experimental study. In *Conference on Empirical Methods in Natural Language Processing*.

Takeshi Sakaki, Makoto Okazaki, and Yutaka Matsuo. 2010. Earthquake shakes Twitter users: real-time event detection by social sensors. In *19th international conference on World wide web*, pages 851–860. ACM.

Burr Settles. 2011. Closing the loop: Fast, interactive semi-supervised annotation with queries on features and instances. In *2011 Conference on Empirical Methods in Natural Language Processing*, pages 1467–1478, Edinburgh, Scotland, UK., July. Association for Computational Linguistics.

Simon Tong and Daphne Koller. 2002. Support vector machine active learning with applications to text classification. *Journal of Machine Learning Research*, 2:45–66, March.

Sarah Vieweg, Amanda L. Hughes, Kate Starbird, and Leysia Palen. 2010. Microblogging during two natural hazards events: what twitter may contribute to situational awareness. In *28th international conference on Human factors in computing systems*, pages 1079–1088. ACM.

A Character-Level Machine Translation Approach for Normalization of SMS Abbreviations

Deana L. Pennell
The University of Texas at Dallas
800 W. Campbell Road
Richardson, TX 75080
deana@hlt.utdallas.edu

Yang Liu
The University of Texas at Dallas
800 W. Campbell Road
Richardson, TX 75080
yangl@hlt.utdallas.edu

Abstract

This paper describes a two-phase method for expanding abbreviations found in informal text (*e.g.*, email, text messages, chat room conversations) using a machine translation system trained at the character level during the first phase. In this way, the system learns mappings between character-level "phrases" and is much more robust to new abbreviations than a word-level system. We generate translation models that are independent of the way in which the abbreviations are formed and show that the results show little degradation compared to when type-dependent models are trained. Our experiments on a large data set show our proposed system performs well when tested both on isolated abbreviations and, with the incorporation of a second phase utilizing an in-domain language model, in the context of neighboring words.

1 Introduction

Text messaging (SMS) is a rapidly growing form of alternative communication for cell phones. This popularity has caused safety concerns leading many US states to pass laws prohibiting texting while driving. The technology is also difficult for users with visual impairments or physical handicaps to use. We believe a text-to-speech (TTS) system for cell phones can decrease these problems to promote safe travel and ease of use for all.

Text normalization is the usual first step for TTS. Text message lingo is also similar to the chatspeak that is prolific on forums, blogs and chatrooms. Screen readers will thus benefit from such technology, enabling visually impaired users to take part in internet culture. In addition, normalizing informal text is important for various language processing tasks, such as information retrieval, summarization, and keyword, topic, sentiment and emotion detection, which are currently receiving a lot of attention for informal domains.

Normalization of informal text is complicated by the large number of abbreviations used. Some previous work on this problem used phrase-based machine translation (MT) for SMS normalization; however, a large annotated corpus is required for such a supervised learning method since the learning is performed at the word level. By definition, this method cannot make a hypothesis for an abbreviation it did not see in training. This is a serious limitation in a domain where new words are created frequently and irregularly.

We propose a two-phase approach. In the first phase, an MT model is trained at the character-level rather than the word- or phrase-level, allowing recognition of common abbreviation patterns regardless of the words in which they appear. We decode the hypotheses in the second phase using a language model for the final prediction.

2 Related Work

Text normalization is an important first step for any text-to-speech (TTS) system and has been widely studied in many formal domains. Sproat et al. (2001) provides a good resource for text normalization and its associated problems. Spell-checking algorithms are mostly ineffective on this type of data because they do not account for the phenomena in informal text. Some prior work instead focused on single typographic errors using edit distance (Kukich, 1992), perhaps combined with pronunciation modeling, such as (Toutanova and Moore, 2002).

One line of research views normalization as a noisy channel problem. Choudhury et al. (2007) describe a supervised noisy channel model using HMMs for SMS normalization. Cook and Stevenson (2009) extend this work to create an unsupervised noisy channel approach using probabilistic models for common abbreviation types and choosing the English word with the highest probability after combining the models. Deletion-based abbreviations were addressed in our past work using statistical models (maximum entropy and conditional random fields) combined with an in-domain language model (LM) (Pennell and Liu, 2010; Pennell and Liu, 2011). Liu et al. (2011) extend the statistical model to be independent of abbreviation type with good results.

Whitelaw et al. (2009) used a noisy channel model based on orthographic edit distance using the web to generate a large set of automatically generated (noisy) pairs to be used for training and for spelling suggestions. Although they use the web for collection, they do not focus on informal text but rather on unintentional spelling mistakes. Beaufort et al. (2010) combine a noisy channel model with a rule-based finite-state transducer and got reasonable results on French SMS, but have not tried their method on English text. Han and Baldwin (2011) first determine whether a given out-of-vocabulary (OOV) word needs to be expanded or is some other type of properly-formed OOV. For those predicted to be ill-formed, a confusion set of possible candidate words is generated based on a combination of lexical and phonetic edit distance and the top word is chosen in context using LM and dependency parse information.

Machine translation (MT) techniques trained at the word- or phrase-level are also common. Translation of SMS from one language to another led Bangalore et al. (2002) to use consensus translations to bootstrap a translation system for instant messages and chat rooms where abbreviations are common. Aw et al. (2006) view SMS lingo as if it were another language with its own words and grammar to produce grammatically correct English sentences using MT. Q. and H. (2009) trained an MT system using three on-line SMS dictionaries for normalizing chat-like messages on Twitter. Kobus et al. (2008) incorporate a second phase in the translation model that maps characters in the texting abbreviation to phonemes, which are viewed as the output of an automatic speech recognition (ASR) system. They use a non-deterministic phonemic transducer to decode the phonemes into English words. The technical paper of Raghunathan and Krawczyk (2009) details an explicit study varying language model orders, distortion limit and maximum phrase length allowed by the MT system during decoding. Contractor et al. (2010) also uses an SMT model; however, in an attempt to get around the problem of collecting and annotating a large parallel corpus, they automatically create a noisy list of word-abbreviation pairs for training using some heuristics. As far as we know, we are the first to use an MT system at the character-level for this task.

3 Data

Due to the lack of a large parallel corpus suitable for our study, we are building a corpus using status updates from twitter.com. Twitter allows users to update status messages by sending an SMS message to a number designated for the Twitter service. To ensure that our corpus is representative of the domain we are modeling, we use Twitter's meta-data to collect only messages sent via SMS. Some examples of highly abbreviated messages from our corpus are shown below.

(a) `Aye.oops,dat was spose to be a txt`

(b) `Rndm fct bout wife: n the past 10 yrs I can cnt on one hand the num Xs she's 4gotn to unlock my car door`

(c) `OMG I LOVE YOU GUYS. You pwn :) !!!`

(d) `i need to qo to bedd qotta wakee up at 7am for school....`

(e) `heard it again! xD 3 TIMES.a sng i nvr hear!`

3.1 Choosing Messages for Annotation

An annotator's time is wasted if he is presented with many messages containing no abbreviations, or with sentences all containing the same, very common abbreviations. A scoring system was thus devised using the following metrics:

1. **Word Count Index.** A low word count index indicates that a message is close to the mean message length. Messages with fewer than five words are removed from consideration. We calculate the index as $|N-E(N)|/\sigma(N)$, where N is the number of words in the message and mean and standard deviation are calculated over the entire corpus.
2. **Perplexity Scores.** Two perplexity scores are calculated against character-level language

models. A low perplexity of the message compared to standard English text indicates that the message is less likely to be in a foreign language or jibberish. Similarly, a low perplexity of the message compared to our corpus indicates that the message is more representative of the domain. A sentence is removed if in either case the perplexity value is greater than a threshold (1000 in our study).

3. **OOV Count.** This is a simple count of the number of out of vocabulary (OOV) words in the message compared to an English dictionary, which we denote N_{OOV}. This metric helps guarantee that we select messages containing many OOV words. We remove the sentence completely when $N_{OOV} = 0$.

4. **OOV Percentages.** This metric consists of two scores: the first is N_{OOV}/N; the second is a non-duplicate OOV percentage, where we remove all repeated words and then recalculate the percentage. If the first score is greater than 0.5 but the second is not, we remove the message from consideration.

5. **OOV Frequency Scores.** For each OOV token (including emoticons) we find the frequency of the token across the entire corpus. This ensures that we annotate those abbreviations that are commonly used.

A sorted list is generated for each metric. The final score for each sentence is a weighted average of its position in each list, with more weight given to the non-duplicate OOV percentage and less weight given to the OOV frequency scores. The sentences are ranked in a penultimate list based on this final score. Finally, a post processing step iterates through the list to remove sentences introducing no new OOV words compared to higher-ranked sentences. Messages were annotated in the order of rank.

3.2 Annotation

Five undergraduate students were hired for the annotation task. In total, 4661 twitter status messages were annotated. Of these, 74 were given to multiple annotators so that we can calculate inter-annotator agreement. All 74 of these messages were also annotated by the first author as a standard for comparison. There were 7769 tokens annotated as an abbreviation by at least one annotator with 3761 (48%) unique to a single annotator.

We calculate pairwise agreement for whether or not a token is an abbreviation for all tokens given to each pair, including those that both agreed were not abbreviations. The Fleiss' Kappa $\kappa = 0.891$ for these pairwise values is quite high so the number of annotators can be reduced without negative effects to the project as long as they are familiar with the domain.

4 Normalization Approach

We describe a two-phase approach for SMS normalization. The first phase uses a character-level MT system to generate possible hypotheses for each abbreviation. The second uses a language model (LM) to choose a hypothesis in context.

Typically, an SMT system translates a sentence from one language to another. An alignment step learns a mapping of words and phrases between the two languages using a training corpus of parallel sentences. During testing, this mapping is used along with LMs to translate a sentence from one language to another. While researchers have used this method to normalize abbreviations (Bangalore et al., 2002; Aw et al., 2006; Kobus et al., 2008; Q. and H., 2009; Contractor et al., 2010), it is not robust to new words and leads to poor accuracy in this domain where new terms are used frequently and inconsistently.

Our system differs in that we train the MT model at the character-level during the first phase; that is, rather than learning mappings between words and phrases we instead map characters to other characters in what can be a many-to-many mapping. For example, the ending "-er" (as in "teacher" or "brother") is often abbreviated with the single character 'a'. Characters may also be mapped to symbols ("@" for "at"), numbers ("8" for "ate") or nothing at all (deletions).

Formally, for an abbreviation $a : c_1(a), c_2(a), ..., c_m(a)$ (where $c_i(a)$ is the ith character in the abbreviation), we use an MT system to find the proper word hypothesis:

$$\begin{aligned} \hat{w} &= \arg\max p(w|a) \quad (1)\\ &= \arg\max p(w)p(a|w)\\ &= \arg\max p(c_1(w), ...c_n(w))\\ &\quad \times p(c_1(a), ..., c_m(a)|c_1(w), ...c_n(w)) \end{aligned}$$

where $c_i(w)$ is a character in the English word w, $p(c_1(w), ...c_n(w))$ is obtained using a character LM, and $p(c_1(a), ..., c_m(a)|c_1(w), ...c_n(w))$ is based on the learned phrase translation table.

Pairs of words from our annotated data are used for training: the original token (which may or may not be an abbreviation) and its corresponding English word. We removed tokens which the annotators were unable to translate and those marked as sound effects (*e.g.*, ahhhhh, zzzzz, blech, hrmpf, etc.). Punctuation was removed from the remaining data, excluding that found in emoticons (which we treat as words) and apostrophes in common contractions and possessive forms. To facilitate character-level training, we insert a space between each character and replace any spaces with the underscore character.

Because training is done at the character-level, each hypothesis (w) for an abbreviation (a) is a sequence of characters, which may or may not be a valid word. To see why, examine the partial phrase-table shown in Figure 1[1]; using this table, "hab" could be translated to "hib", "habulary" or "habou" as well as the word "have". It is also very likely that a hypothesis will appear many times in the hypothesis list due to different segmentation (two characters may be generated by a single phrase mapping or by two different mappings, one for each character). We generate 20 *distinct* hypotheses for each token and then eliminate hypotheses that do not occur in the CMU Lexicon.

Until this point, we have only normalized a single abbreviation without context. In a realistic setting contextual information is available to help with translation. We thus introduce a second phase using a word-level LM to disambiguate hypotheses when context is available. This is the typical noisy channel model used for speech recognition or MT decoding and is comparable to equation 1.

Determining the standard English sentence, $W = w_1 w_2 ... w_n$, from a given informal sentence, $A = a_1 a_2 ... a_n$, can be formally described as:

$$\begin{aligned}\widehat{W} &= \arg\max P(W|A) \qquad (2)\\ &= \arg\max P(W)P(A|W)\\ &\approx \arg\max \prod P(w_i|w_{i-n+1}...w_{i-1})\\ &\quad \times \prod P(a_i|w_i)\\ &= \arg\max(\sum \log P(w_i|w_{i-n+1}...w_{i-1})\\ &\quad + \sum \log P(a_i|w_i))\end{aligned}$$

where the approximation is based on the assumption that each abbreviation depends only on the corresponding word (we are not considering one-to-many mappings in this study), and a word is dependent on its previous $(n-1)$ words. In other words, this probability is represented by a traditional n-gram LM.

The abbreviation score in Equation 2, $P(a_i|w_i)$, represents the likelihood that abbreviation a_i is derived from word w_i, and can be obtained from:

$$p(a_i|w_i) \propto \frac{p(w_i|a_i)}{p(w_i)} \qquad (3)$$

where $p(w_i|a_i)$ is the abbreviation model (AM) score from the character-level MT system, and $p(w_i)$ is from the character LM we used in MT decoding. In this study, we just use the score from the MT system as the likelihood score, without dividing by the character-level LM contribution. This is equivalent to using both character- and a word-level LMs during decoding.

Equation 2 assumes that the AM and LM should be weighted equally, but in actuality one model may prove to be more helpful than the other. For this reason, we allow the terms from equation 2 to be weighted differently, yielding the final equation

$$\begin{aligned}\widehat{W} &= \arg\max(\alpha \sum \log P(w_i|w_{i-n+1}...w_{i-1})\\ &\quad +\beta \sum \log P(a_i|w_i)) \qquad (4)\end{aligned}$$

where α and β are determined empirically.

5 Experiment 1: Evaluation on Isolated Abbreviations

We use the Moses MT system (Koehn et al., 2007) in all our experiments, including Giza++ for alignment. The score assigned to a translation is derived from four models: the phrase translation table, the language model, the reordering model,

[1]Aside from the possible translations, the phrase table also shows five values for each word. They correspond to the inverse phrase translation probability $\phi(f|e)$, the inverse lexical weighting $lex(f|e)$, the direct phrase translation probability $\phi(e|f)$, the direct lexical weighting $lex(e|f)$ and the phrase penalty (always $exp(1) = 2.718$), where e and f are the English and foreign phrases, respectively. We do not currently make use of these values.

```
a b ||| _ a b ||| 0.714286 0.880834 0.018315 0.164514 2.718
a b ||| a _ b ||| 0.5 0.880834 0.010989 0.164514 2.718
a b ||| a b b ||| 0.181818 0.880834 0.00732601 0.905748 2.718
a b ||| a b o u ||| 0.00714286 0.880834 0.003663 0.00346958 2.718
a b ||| a b o ||| 0.00662252 0.880834 0.003663 0.0690538 2.718
a b ||| a b u l a r y ||| 1 0.440819 0.003663 4.55505e-08 2.718
a b ||| a b ||| 0.894737 0.880834 0.934066 0.934993 2.718
a b ||| a p ||| 0.00956938 0.000874125 0.00732601 0.000887968 2.718
a b ||| a v e ||| 0.00249377 0.000970303 0.003663 3.35128e-05 2.718
a b ||| b ||| 0.000325839 0.308415 0.003663 0.968721 2.718
a b ||| i b ||| 0.0238095 0.308415 0.003663 0.077216 2.718
```

Figure 1: An excerpt from a phrase table showing possible translations when the character sequence "ab" is found in a message.

and a word length penalty. We use Moses' default weights for these models, but plan to adjust the weights in the future to determine each model's contribution to a good translation. For each abbreviation we generate 20 distinct hypotheses. We finally remove non-word hypotheses using the CMU lexicon. Note that occasionally Moses generates a positive score (impossible for a real log-probability). When this occurs, we use the value -0.1 instead, indicating that this pair is very likely.

Note that our accuracy is bounded from above by the percentage of pairs in testing that appear in the 20-best hypotheses generated by Moses. For this reason, we first wish to find a setup to maximize the upper bound on our performance.

5.1 Experimental Variations

There are different factors that may affect the performance of our system for individual words: the character-level LM used for decoding, the way the models are trained, and the data used to train those models. We thus evaluate different experimental variations, described below.

Training/Testing Configuration

To test the effect of using more specific versus more general data when training the MT system, we used the following training sets:

1. **General Setup:** Training and testing are both done using all of the annotated data, including words that are already in standard form in the message.
2. **Single-word Abbreviation Setup:** In training, we remove those abbreviations corresponding to multiple words (for example, "brb" representing "be right back") and those words already in standard form. Again we test the system using all of the annotated data.
3. **Type-dependent Setup:** We train a separate model for each major abbreviation type (see Table 1) except insertions. The type of each abbreviation in the test set has been annotated so we use its respective model for testing. We assumed that knowledge about the abbreviation formation method would increase the model's ability to translate the abbreviation. Currently there is no known procedure for automatically determining the abbreviation type without having prior knowledge of its translation, so this setup is just for comparison purpose to evaluate how well the more general methods are performing.

Formation Method	Example
Deletions	ppl (people)
Substitutions	2nite (tonight)
Repetitions	yeeeeesssss (yes)
Swaps	tounge (tongue)
Insertions	borded (bored)

Table 1: Examples of major abbreviation types.

Language Model (LM) Order

We wanted to determine how the order of the character-level LM used by Moses affected performance. A smaller order model may not capture larger phrases or long distance dependencies, but the smaller model may generalize better due to the sparseness of many high-order phrases.

We explore different character LMs used in decoding to generate word hypotheses, including character-based 3-, 5-, and 7-gram LMs. These are trained on a subset of 16,543,813 messages from the Edinburgh Twitter corpus (Petrovic et al., 2010) containing no OOV words compared to an English dictionary. Each model is used in the above training/testing configurations.

	Order 3		Order 5		Order 7	
	Top-1	**Top-20**	**Top-1**	**Top-20**	**Top-1**	**Top-20**
All (14611)	59.30	81.32	62.62	81.49	63.30	81.95
Abbreviations (2842)	11.75	53.24	30.33	62.95	33.04	63.83
Standard Form (10629)	76.89	94.39	75.86	91.55	75.91	91.81
Deletions (1406)	8.68	52.63	31.58	62.87	34.71	63.51
Substitutions (620)	9.35	37.91	22.58	51.94	25.32	52.58
Repetitions (510)	23.14	81.37	32.55	79.02	34.90	79.80
Swaps (106)	33.02	70.75	69.81	86.79	66.04	90.57
Insertions (55)	0.00	27.27	14.55	49.09	20.00	56.36
Combination (140)	0.71	23.57	21.43	43.57	25.00	43.57

Table 2: Accuracy using the General setup (%).

	Order 3		Order 5		Order 7	
	Top-1	**Top-20**	**Top-1**	**Top-20**	**Top-1**	**Top-20**
All (14611)	75.97	91.23	75.75	92.50	75.57	92.53
Abbreviations (2842)	14.53	63.16	36.45	72.31	37.40	72.38
Standard Form (10629)	92.47	98.79	86.31	97.93	85.84	97.95
Deletions (1406)	11.38	64.15	39.90	74.04	40.61	74.11
Substitutions (620)	11.13	48.23	25.48	60.80	27.42	61.45
Repetitions (510)	28.24	84.31	37.45	82.75	38.24	82.55
Swaps (106)	35.85	91.51	76.42	96.23	73.58	95.28
Insertions (55)	0.00	36.36	18.18	54.55	20.00	58.18
Combination (140)	1.43	33.57	25.00	59.29	27.14	57.14

Table 3: Accuracy using the Single-word setup (%).

5.2 Results

The results from different training/testing configurations and LM orders are shown in Tables 2, 3 and 4. We use a cross-validation setup where we train the MT system using the annotations from four annotators and test on the data from the fifth. The mean score from the five runs is reported here. In all three tables, we show top-1 and top-20 accuracy. For top-1 accuracy, the system is considered correct if and only if the top hypothesis given by Moses exactly matches the standard English form. If the correct standard English form is listed anywhere in the 20 hypotheses generated by Moses, we count it correct in top-20 accuracy. The top 20-accuracy represents the possible gain we can achieve by re-ranking the lists using context.

We break down the results by abbreviation type to determine any performance difference. The top portion of Tables 2 and 3 shows results for all 14611 unique pairs in the annotated data, including words already in standard form and abbreviations corresponding to multiple words. The following two rows show results on abbreviations of single words and words already in standard form, respectively. The lower portion breaks down the results by abbreviation type. The rows listing specific types include those abbreviations using *only* that abbreviation method. The final row lists results for those abbreviations formed using multiple methods. The type-dependent setup (Table 4) reports results for each type when using the model trained for that specific type.[2]

Removing multi-word abbreviations and words already in standard form from training generally increases accuracy. The type-dependent model usually outperforms the single-word model, as expected. Comparing Tables 3 and 4 shows that performance decrease using the type-independent single-word model is usually small, helping avoid costly human annotation of types in the future. Contrary to expectations, the type-independent

[2]We do not train a separate model for the insertions due to the small number of abbreviations of that type in our data. Looking at those marked as insertions, most of them appear to be typographical errors caused by "fat fingering" a keypad (*e.g.* "jusyt" for "just"), although a few appear stylistic in nature, *e.g.*,"confrused" for "confused".

	Order 3		Order 5		Order 7	
	Top-1	Top-20	Top-1	Top-20	Top-1	Top-20
Deletions (1406)	11.45	64.08	38.98	73.33	40.11	73.47
Substitutions (620)	12.26	55.48	27.58	62.58	27.74	63.06
Repetitions (510)	28.63	84.51	39.02	83.33	39.61	83.53
Swaps (106)	35.85	97.17	77.36	97.17	77.36	97.17

Table 4: Accuracy using the type-dependent training and testing (%).

model outperformed the type-dependent model for the deletion type. Examining the abbreviations formed by combining at least two methods helps explain why this occurs. Of the 140 abbreviations combining abbreviation types, 102 contain at least one deletion. Adding these abbreviations in training yields additional examples for the model to learn from.

There is a large increase in accuracy between using a 3-gram versus a 5-gram model. However, the jump from 5-gram to 7-gram is much smaller, and in some cases it even decreases performance. We thus recommend using a 5-gram character model and training using only single-word abbreviations.

6 Experiment 2: Incorporation of Contextual Information

In many cases, there are many word hypotheses for a given abbreviation. Without contextual information the top hypothesis is static. In some cases the system can use contextual information to suggest the correct word even when it may not be the most likely choice using the AM alone. To evaluate the effect of context on normalization, we create a test set containing trigrams using one word of context on either side of each abbreviation. If an abbreviation falls at the beginning or end of a message we use <s> and </s> for the left or right context, respectively. We replace OOV context words with their annotated standard forms.

The top performing setup from Section 5 is used to build the AM, which is then combined with a bigram LM for decoding using equation 2. The LM uses Kneser-Ney smoothing and was trained on the same portion of the Edinburgh corpus as used for the character-level models. We do not include the <unk> token in the LM because its probability is quite high and preliminary tests (not included here) show a degradation in performance when it is utilized. Instead, we use a log probability of -99 for all unknown terms seen in testing.

LM-only	Full	Partial	Section 5.2[3]
13.5	69.7	69.3	36.45

Table 5: Accuracy on tests using context (%).

We performed three types of tests in order to determine the best setup for decoding using context.

1. **LM-only.** This system serves as a baseline for comparison. We eliminate the abbreviation model completely and use only the LM for decoding. In this case, all unigrams in the LM are considered to be possible candidates for each abbreviation.

2. **Full.** We use the LM in combination with the abbreviation model using equation 2 with $\alpha = 1.0$ and $\beta = 0.1$ (found empirically).

3. **Partial.** Due to the small weight found for the abbreviation model in the previous setup, we wish to show that the abbreviation score is helpful for decoding. We use the abbreviation model to generate the candidate words for each abbreviation, but we do not use the abbreviation score in decoding.[4]

We again performed cross validation by first training an AM using the data from four of the annotators and then testing on the trigrams formed from the final annotator's data. In total there were 4415 context trigrams used in testing. This is larger than the 2842 abbreviations shown in the previous section because the previous tests used unique abbreviations, which may in reality correspond to multiple words and unique contexts. Table 5 shows the normalization results. As a basis of comparison, the state-of-the-art Jazzy spell-

[3]Using single-word training and 5-gram character LM.

[4]We eliminate the AM term from equation 4, yielding $\widehat{W} = \arg\max_{w_i \in S}(\sum \log P(w_i|w_{i-n+1}...w_{i-1})$ where the candidate set S is generated by the MT system. Equivalently, we set $\beta = 0$.

	Top-1	Top-3	Top-10	Top-20
Jazzy (Idzelis, 2005)	49.86	53.13	54.78	55.44
(Choudhury et al., 2007)	59.9	–	84.3	88.7
(Cook and Stevenson, 2009)	59.4	–	83.8	87.8
(Liu et al., 2011)[a]	58.09	70.96	–	–
(Liu et al., 2011)[b]	62.05	75.91	–	–
This Work	60.39	74.58	75.57	75.57

Table 6: System comparison on the 303-term test set from (Choudhury et al., 2007).

[a]LetterTran.
[b]LetterTran + Jazzy.

checker (Idzelis, 2005) achieves 38% accuracy on this dataset.

It is clear that the LM-only setup is not sufficient for this task and that our AM is necessary. The **Full** and **Partial** setups perform similarly; while the **Full** model consistently performs slightly better for all annotators, it is probably not a significant difference. We hope that by optimizing Moses' parameters we can obtain higher performance from the AM.

Compared to the 1-best results from Section 5.2 we see that incorporating contextual information yields significant gain. Our performance is bounded from above by the percentage of correct solutions that appear in our candidate lists. For the contextual task, 77.2% of the correct words appear in the lookup lists after the AM is applied, showing that we can still improve the decoding process. Fully 91.7% of the correct words appear in the LM, meaning that the AM is still eliminating many correct answers from consideration. We are investigating methods to address these shortcomings for our future work.

7 Comparison to Past Work

Although there has been very little work on this task until quite recently, multiple studies have been done using the small 303-term dataset first used by (Choudhury et al., 2007). For this reason, we run our system on this small data set. We also use the state-of-the-art Jazzy spell-checker (Idzelis, 2005) as a baseline.

System comparisons are shown in Table 6. The results shown for other systems (except Jazzy) are those reported in their respective papers; we did not re-implement their systems. Our system performs comparably to the work of (Liu et al., 2011) on this dataset. Although we outperform both (Choudhury et al., 2007) and (Cook and Stevenson, 2009) in top-1, they outperform our system at top-10 and top-20. With better re-ranking, their systems have the potential to outperform ours. One of our goals is thus to obtain better coverage.

8 Conclusions and Future Work

In this paper we presented a two-phase approach using character-level machine translation for informal text normalization. When combined with contextual information at the word level, our results are state-of-the art, but there is still some room for improvement.

Although they are far more common, abbreviations formed by deletion and substitution method have worse performance compared to those formed by repetition or swap. It may be useful to create systems specific to those formation types, such as the deletion system from (Pennell and Liu, 2010). Provided that these systems are not trained using the MT approach, it is likely that they contain complementary (rather than redundant) information. Combining hypotheses from multiple sources may increase performance on these abbreviation types.

Although we incorporate contextual information in Section 6, the setup is not entirely realistic. We test only on abbreviations, assuming that we know which words are abbreviations and which are not. A simple heuristic of only applying our system to OOV words (compared to a dictionary) may not perform well. Proper nouns are often OOV and should not be expanded, but we *would* like to expand "off" ("office") or "cat" ("category"), which are also dictionary words. We also assume there are not other abbreviations to be expanded in the context. In reality, many users write highly abbreviated messages, posing greater difficulties for sentence-level decoding. We will address sentence-level decoding in future work.

References

AiTi Aw, Min Zhang, Juan Xian, and Jian Su. 2006. A phrase-based statistical model for SMS text normalization. In *COLING/ACL*, pages 33–40, Sydney, Australia.

Srinivas Bangalore, Vanessa Murdock, and Giuseppe Riccardi. 2002. Bootstrapping bilingual data using consensus translation for a multilingual instant messaging system. In *19th International Conference on Computational Linguistics*, pages 1–7, Taipei, Taiwan.

R. Beaufort, S. Roekhaut, L.A. Cougnon, and C. Fairon. 2010. A hybrid rule/model-based finite-state framework for normalizing SMS messages. In *Proceedings of the 48th Annual Meeting of the Association for Computational Linguistics*, pages 770–779, Uppsala, Sweden. Association for Computational Linguistics.

Monojit Choudhury, Rahul Saraf, Vijit Jain, Animesh Mukherjee, Sudeshna Sarkar, and Anupam Basu. 2007. Investigation and modeling of the structure of texting language. *International Journal of Document Analysis and Recognition*, 10:157–174.

Danish Contractor, Tanveer A. Faruquie, and L. Venkata Subramaniam. 2010. Unsupervised cleansing of noisy text. In *Proceedings of the 23rd International Conference on Computational Linguistics: Posters*, COLING '10, pages 189–196, Stroudsburg, PA, USA. Association for Computational Linguistics.

Paul Cook and Suzanne Stevenson. 2009. An unsupervised model for text message normalization. In *NAACL HLT Workshop on Computational Approaches to Linguistic Creativity*, pages 71–78, Boulder, CO.

B. Han and T. Baldwin. 2011. Lexical normalisation of short text messages: Makn sens a# twitter. In *Proceedings of the 49th Annual Meeting of the Association for Computational Linguistics: Human Language Technologies. Association for Computational Linguistics.*

Mindaugas Idzelis. 2005. Jazzy: The java open source spell checker.

Catherine Kobus, François Yvon, and Géraldine Damnati. 2008. Normalizing SMS: Are two metaphors better than one? In *22nd International Conference on Computational Linguistics*, pages 441–448, Manchester, UK.

Philipp Koehn, Hieu Hoang, Alexandra Birch, Chris Callison-Burch, Marcello Federico, Nicola Bertoldi, Brooke Cowan, Wade Shen, Christine Moran, Richard Zens, Chris Dyer, Ondřej Bojar, Alexandra Constantin, and Evan Herbst. 2007. Moses: open source toolkit for statistical machine translation. In *Proceedings of the 45th Annual Meeting of the ACL on Interactive Poster and Demonstration Sessions*, ACL '07, pages 177–180, Stroudsburg, PA, USA. Association for Computational Linguistics.

Karen Kukich. 1992. Technique for automatically correcting words in text. *ACM Computing Surveys*, 24(4):377–439.

F. Liu, F. Weng, B. Wang, and Y. Liu. 2011. Insertion, deletion, or substitution? normalizing text messages without pre-categorization nor supervision. *Proc. of ACL-HLT.*

Deana Pennell and Yang Liu. 2010. Normalization of text messages for text-to-speech. In *ICASSP*, pages 4842–4845, Dallas, Texas, USA.

Deana Pennell and Yang Liu. 2011. Toward text message normalization: Modeling abbreviation generation. In *ICASSP*, Prague, Czech Republic, May.

Saša Petrovic, Miles Osborne, and Victor Lavrenko. 2010. The edinburgh twitter corpus. In *NAACL-HLT Workshop on Computational Linguistics in a World of Social Media*, pages 25–26, Los Angeles, California, USA.

Carlos A. Henríquez Q. and Adolfo Hernández H. 2009. A ngram-based statistical machine translation approach for text normalization on chat-speak style communications. In *Content Analysis for the Web 2.0 (CAW2.0 2009)*, Madrid, Spain.

K. Raghunathan and S. Krawczyk. 2009. Cs224n: Investigating sms text normalization using statistical machine translation.

Richard Sproat, Alan Black, Stanley Chen, Shankar Kumar, Mari Ostendorf, and Christopher Richards. 2001. Normalization of non-standard words. *Computer Speech and Language*, 15(3):287–333.

Kristina Toutanova and Robert C. Moore. 2002. Pronunciation modeling for improved spelling correction. In *ACL*, pages 144–151, Philadelphia, Pennsylvania.

C. Whitelaw, B. Hutchinson, G.Y. Chung, and G. Ellis. 2009. Using the web for language independent spellchecking and autocorrection. In *Proceedings of the 2009 Conference on Empirical Methods in Natural Language Processing: Volume 2-Volume 2*, pages 890–899. Association for Computational Linguistics.

Using Text Reviews for Product Entity Completion

Mrinmaya Sachan Tanveer Faruquie L. V. Subramaniam Mukesh K. Mohania
IBM Research India
New Delhi, India
{mrsachan, ftanveer, lvsubram, mkmukesh}@in.ibm.com

Abstract

In this paper we address the problem of obtaining structured information about products in the form of attribute-value pairs by leveraging a combination of enterprise internal product descriptions and external data. Product descriptions are short text strings used internally within enterprises to describe a product. These strings usually comprise of the Brand name, name of the product, and its attributes like size, color, etc. Existing product data quality solutions provide us the capability to standardize and segment these descriptions into their composing attributes using domain specific rulesets. We provide techniques that can leverage the supervision provided by these existing rulesets for extracting missing values from other external text data sources accurately. We use a large real life data collection to demonstrate the effectiveness of our approach.

1 Introduction

Enterprises usually store information of its products in the form of unstructured text strings. Such product descriptions contain the name of the product and its specific attributes. These product descriptions are usually written by multiple people and could contain overlapping information or even the same information written differently. For example, a superstore may source the same product from many different vendors and each vendor may give varying descriptions of the same product. Information could be scattered through various departments and held by certain employees or systems instead of being available centrally. This results into varying standards and vocabulary.

Consider the following product descriptions obtained from an enterprise selling cameras. They are provided by different vendors supplying the cameras to the enterprise:
Nikon D90 4288×2848 703 g Digicam F/1.8
Nikon Digital 90 Cam 12.3MP 1.8 F-Len(1.55lb)
Nikon D-90 Camera with Nikkor 50mm 1.8D
Expert knowledge specific to the domain (that D90, D-90 and Digital 90, 4288 × 2848 and 12.3 MP, F-number 1.8 and 1.8 D focal length, and 703 g and 1.55lbs are same) is required to conclude that the entries above are the same product. Coupled with data entry errors, the problem of identifying a standard representation of the product becomes even harder.

The problem of obtaining a structured representation of such product descriptions is similar to the 'Attribute-Value pair' mining problem. Attribute represents an aspect of the product. It could be anything from a manufacturing detail like model number to information like color, size and weight.

Due to its practical applications, the problem has drawn interest from the research community as well as the industry. There are many products which provide solutions for standardizing, matching, merging and validating such descriptions. Popular ones include Oracle middleware, Silvercreek, Ethoscontent product-copy, Trilliumsoftware and IBM Data Stage-Quality Stage. Since rules are easy to understand, manage and give good accuracies in practice, they are widely used by these solutions. Overall, the product data cleansing solution is achieved by a collection of rule sets, each tackling a given product vertical. A ruleset scales to descriptions within its vertical.

Often, the product descriptions are very brief and do not convey the entire information about the product. Critical information about the product could be missing. Because of this, an enterprise does not have a complete view of its products and services. Suppose an enterprise wants to have manufacturer wise information about its products for making important demand-supply decisions. If the manufacturer information is erroneously captured or missing, it wouldn't be possible. This lack of information makes it difficult for a potential customer to compare products and make an informed decision about it. At the same time, low data quality impedes business. An enterprise may loose its competitive edge due to poor customer service and advertising resulting from incorrect reporting and incomplete view of its products and services. Having a standard and complete structured representation of a product can help in consolidation and is useful in various business intelligence applications. Given the purchasing history of its customers, a better view of enterprise products would result into a host of benefits like better targeted advertising, better recommender systems and reduced maintenance effort.

At the same time, as more and more people are beginning to write reviews, blogs and opinions about their experiences in using products, it is possible to obtain a lot of information about the products on the web. Popular merchant sites like Ebay and Amazon contain a large number of product reviews from its customers. These reviews not only contain reviewer sentiments but also contain key information which can be used to create an enriched view of the products. Our goal is to obtain a complete view of the products by extracting attribute values from such sources.

Here we note that existing rulesets used by data cleansing solutions can give us critically important supervision to drive the attribute-value extraction. This would not only help us in achieving greater accuracy but also allow us to extract true product values. Infact, a key differentiator that puts this work apart from its peers is that the supervision provided by the rules allows us to extract attribute 'values' in the real sense and not merely sentiment words as in most previous works.

Overall, the task of creating a complete view of the products comprises of standardization of appropriate features present in the product descriptions along with enrichment using web data. We carry out product description segmentation by writing handcrafted rules on top of a domain specific dictionary. Then, we show that the same rules can be reused on web data to fill-in missing values for many of the product attributes. Our paper is organized as follows. Section 2 gives us the necessary background and describes related work. Then, Section 3 describes our approach in detail. In Section 4, we report experimental results on real datasets. Finally, Section 5 concludes.

2 Related Work and Background

There has been significant work in information extraction from text data for products. In particular the extraction of product attributes and user sentiments has received wide attention. One of the methods (Hu and Liu, 2004) is to use frequent item sets of nouns along with the opinion words to mine infrequent product attributes. This method is further improved (Zhuang et al., 2006) by using domain knowledge along with noun phrases for attribute extraction. Another refinement (Qiu et al., 2009) uses extraction rules based on different relations existing between opinion words and attribute words. These relations are syntactic and are propagated in an iterative manner.

Some approaches detect product attributes along with opinion extraction. (Liu et al., 2005) first detects attributes by using a rule miner to find noun phrases. Further, it finds polarity descriptors for these noun phrases. (Popescu and Etzioni, 2005) computes the point wise mutual information between noun phrases and product class specific discriminators to determine whether a noun phrase is a product attribute. It finds part-whole patterns by querying the web and uses a part-whole pattern for attribute mining. It further finds the sentiments of these attributes. In contrast, our work finds actual values for the attributes and not merely sentiments expressed by users.

An approach to finding attributes and sentiments jointly is to mine patterns of aspects-evaluation (Kobayashi et al., 2007) using statistical and contextual cues. Here aspects are attributes for a particular product and evaluations are the opinions expressed. The significance of discovered patterns are computed based on their statistical strength. (Wang and Wang, 2008) uses iterative boot strapping to find opinion words from attributes and then finding attributes from opinion words in an alternating fashion. It uses mutual information to measure association between them and linguistic rules to identify infrequent attributes and opinion words. In one of the most interesting works of its kind, (Zhai et al., 2010) groups domain synonyms to form feature groups using a naive Bayesian EM formulation iteratively on the labeled and unlabeled data. It leads to each unlabeled example being assigned a posterior proba-

Table 1: Sample Segmented Product Descriptions

Description	BrandName	ProductName	Product	Lens	Resolution	Price
Fujifilm Quick Snap Single Use Camera	Fujifilm	Quick Snap	Camera	NULL	NULL	NULL
$25 cannon EF f/2.8 USM Lens	Canon	EF	Lens	f/2.8 USM	NULL	$ 25
Sony DSCP 8 3.2 MP Camra	Sony	DSCP 8	Camera	NULL	3.2 MP	NULL

bility of belonging to a group giving it the ability to find multigram attribute terms. However, these methods concentrate on detecting product attributes and do not find associated values.

Among machine learning approaches CRF (Peng and McCallum, 2006) (Stoyanov and Cardie, 2008) has been effective if we have training data and want to extract template attributes and values. However, we do not always have a pre-defined list of explicit attributes and values which have to be extracted and populated. The method in (Ghani et al., 2006) finds attributes and values together using a naive bayes algorithm combined with EM. This method requires labeled training data which is often difficult and expensive to produce. Also, since both the attribute and value extraction is automatic, the accuracy is low and hence, not useful for most business applications. Our method differs from it as we propose an automatic approach to detect potential attributes and a combination of rules and semi-supervised learning to extract values. Our method also has the flexibility to detect values of pre-defined attributes.

3 Our Approach

We pose the problem of Product Entity Completion as two sub-problems: Product description segmentation and Enrichment. The segmentation problem simulates the product data standardization done in the industry. It constructs a standard attribute value representation using product descriptions found in the enterprise database. A set of attributes $\{A_1 \ldots A_n\}$ is decided by applying some initial domain knowledge. We are given a set of product descriptions comprising of values for one or more attributes. Our task is to segment these descriptions and put each segment into one of the n attribute bins. Since the descriptions are incomplete, large number of attribute values are null after the segmentation step. Enrichment task leverages the supervision provided by the rules to extract unknown or missing values from external web data.

3.1 Product Description Segmentation

Enterprise descriptions of products are short strings containing information about one or more attributes like "Brand Name", "Product Name", "Model Number", "Manufacturer" and few other product specific attributes. To attain a standard view of products and to conform to organization-wide specifications, product data cleansing solutions are used to segment the descriptions into these product attributes. Non-standard representations are converted to standard forms and misspellings, etc are corrected. Some typical examples of product descriptions and their corresponding standardized forms are shown in Table 1.

To begin with, the enterprise or a domain expert ascertains the attributes comprising the descriptions. To perform the task of moving free-form descriptions into these pre-determined fixed attribute columns, a dictionary classification for generic tokens like involved brand names and product names is maintained from various intellectual property organizations like UNSPSC[1] and WIPO[2], and common metric units and currency symbols from common knowledge. This dictionary of standards is often stored in the form of rich taxonomies and is fixed. Each token is assigned a classification symbol depending on its type. To account for all misspellings ("Camera", "Camcorder" and "Camrecorder"), difference in vocabularies("Oz" and "Ounces"), classifications, synonyms and abbreviations, and other non-standard representations, the native forms(like Camrecorder) are mapped to a standard form (Camcorder) using signature clustering techniques as described in (Prasad et al., 2011). This is conveniently achieved by popular string similarity measures and by looking at context of these native forms in the input descriptions. Such data driven context mining approaches to find various ways in which similar words (which often have the same classification entry) like "Camera", "Camcorder" and "Camrecorder", and "LCD", "CFD" and "TFT" help reduce the manual effort in rule writing and dictio-

[1] http://www.unspsc.org/

[2] http://www.wipo.int/portal/index.html.en

nary building. Despite this, suitable additions to these dictionaries are sometimes needed from domain experts. Example classification for our running example is given in Table 2.

Table 2: Classification Entries

NativeForm	StandardForm	Classification	Symbol
Canon	CANON	Brand	B
Cannon	CANON	Brand	B
Sony	SONY	Brand	B
Fujifilm	FUJIFILM	Brand	B
Quick Snap	QUICK SNAP	Product Name	N
Camera	CAMERA	Product	P
Camra	CAMERA	Product	P
USM	USM	Lens Property	L
$	$	Currency	C
MP	MEGAPIXEL	Metric	M
F	F	Alphabet	A

Also, we generate symbols for each number or unknown word to help us make use of the context to write rules. The classifications lead to a pattern of symbols for every product description entry.

For the following product description,
"Canon Powershot SD1200IS 10 MPIXEL Digital Cam $f/3.5 - 6.3$ $8''$ LCD Screen $123"
the corresponding pattern would be:
"$B + @\#M + PA/\# - \#\#M + +C\#$"
Here, B is a brand name and P is a product name recognized from one of the catalogues lying with the enterprise or some intellectual property database. M is a metric unit and C is a currency symbol lying in the dictionary of metric standards and currencies, respectively. Other symbols include $+$ for an unknown word, $\#$ for a number and @ for an alphanumeric. Finally, a domain expert writes rules to move entries into appropriate database columns and complete the standardization. Rules are written to process important subpatterns from the left or the right and capture attribute values in one pass. Table 3 lists some hand crafted segmentation rules to capture Resolution, Focal Length and Price. People invest a great amount of time, effort and money in building and maintaining these rules for extracting information from product descriptions. The output of these rules are used to populate Data Warehouses and Product Information Management (PIM) systems. However, these rules are applied only to short product descriptions which do not lead to a complete view of the product. In the subsequent step, we provides techniques that employ these rules to discover missing values of existing attributes. Doing so reuses the time and effort spent in building

Table 3: Rules for Segmentation Process

Subpattern	Rule[a]
# | M="MP"	COPY [1][2] "Resolution";
A="F" | / | # | - | #	COPY [1][2][3][4][5] "FocalLength";
C | #	COPY [1] "Currency"; COPY [2] "Price";

[a][N] represents the Nth token in the subpattern
"Resolution", "FocalLength" and "Price" are Attribute columns
| represents a token separator

the rules on external content which otherwise is very expensive and time consuming to build.

3.2 Missing Value Filling

We observe that the product descriptions after standardization have missing values for many predefined attributes (Nambiar et al., 2011). Next, to obtaining a complete view of the product we extract these values from the product reviews available on the web. Our approach is general and can be extended to other data sources like Sales and Marketing data, Product Catalogs, Website Product Listings and so on. Unlike many previous attempts, we extract meaningful 'values' of interesting attributes such as the shape, size and manufacturer's name and not merely use sentiments. We make use of the supervision provided by already existing rulesets frequently used for standardization to get a handle of such values. However as the reviews are verbose and noisy, these values too contain a lot of noise. Hence some text processing heuristics are used to choose most appropriate values.

However, we should note that the rules are meant for short product descriptions and not the user reviews. Due to high degree of verbosity and possibility of competing product talk in the reviews, direct rule application on the reviews yields many candidate values for each attribute. Hence, we devise a strategy to prune inappropriate candidates. Our approach to prune out unimportant candidates assesses the affinity of all the candidate values with their corresponding product descriptions and calculates a confidence level for each of them. Confidence level intuitively measures the likelihood that the candidate is a true value of the attribute and product in question. For each product and each of its attributes, the enterprise can then choose the value with the highest confidence (if its confidence is above a certain threshold).

Table 4: Sample Standardized Product Descriptions

Brand Name	Product Name	Product	Focal Length	Lens Diameter	Price	Weight
Canon	EF	Lens	2.8D	70-200mm	-	-

Table 5: Sample Product Reviews

... I bought a *Canon 2.8D lens*...certainly worth each of the **1369 bucks**.....**2.9 pounds** is a bit heavier...
... new *Nikon AF f/3.5-5.6G* ... fair price deal of **$ 685** ...

We compute the affinity for a candidate by looking at the appearances of known attribute values(values obtained by segmentation of the product description strings) of the product in its context. The 'known attribute values' are assigned certain weights and the confidence score for the candidate is computed using the weights carried by the 'known attribute values' in its context. Assuming all weights to be equal, the following example explains the idea in detail:
Consider the product description "Canon EF 70-200mm f/2.8D Lens" and its corresponding segmented output in table 4. Here - represents the missing values to be filled using the reviews. Consider the two reviews given in table 5. Out of the candidates "1369 bucks " and "$ 685" for the price attribute, "1369 bucks" is chosen as it contains more known attribute values (Canon, 2.8D, lens) in its context in review 1. On the other hand as "$ 685" has many competing attribute values (which do not match the known values) in its context (Nikon, AF, f/3.5-5.6G), it is rejected. Similarly, "2.9 pounds" being the only candidate for the weight attribute is accepted due to the presence of many matching known values in its context.

In the above example, we simply counted the number of known attribute values in each candidate's context to compute its confidence score. All the known values carried equal weights.

However, certain values occur much more rarely than others in free text. Hence, matching a rarer value in a candidate's context should give us more confidence that the review author is talking about the same product (as in the product description string) than one which occurs more frequently. For example, matching a value Focal length '18-55 mm' (which occurs rarely) instills more confidence than if the value color 'black' (a value which should occurs very frequently) is matched. We quantify this idea by assigning an 'importance' measure to all known values. The importance $I(v)$ of a known value v can be decided by the proportion of distinct product entities in the database(output of the standardization phase) that contain the value v. Since we wish to weigh rarer values more as they signify more importance, we use the inverse document frequency(IDF) formulation popularly used in previous text mining works to define:

$$I(v) = \begin{cases} log(\frac{N}{n(v)}) & \text{if n(v) >0} \\ 0 & \text{otherwise} \end{cases}$$

where, N is the total number of distinct entities for the attribute in the database, and $n(v)$ is the number of distinct product entities that contain the value v.

We also note that matching the value for a certain attribute can signify greater confidence than others. For instance, if the "Product:Camera" or "Brand:Nikon" matches we still cannot be very sure because the author can be comparing two different cameras or two Nikon products. However if a value mentioning weight or lens of the camera matches, we can be more certain as it is unlikely to have two cameras with exactly the same weight or the same lens.

With this intuition in mind, we also give different weights to each 'attribute' in the standardization schema for matching. These weights intuitively signify our confidence on a value of the given attribute towards matching. In our running example, intuitively we should give more weight to 'Weight' or 'Lens' attributes than 'Product' and'Brand'. Weight of the attributes can be expressed by the domain expert during the schema decision process. Please note that this schema decision and weight assignment needs to be done only once per product vertical. For the matching to be effective, all real numbers were morphed to a common representation '#' and misspellings were corrected for terms known in the dictionary.

Finally, these weights and importance measures are tied together to estimate the confidence for each candidate value. We introduce a distance metric to quantify the distance between two words in a review. The effect of a value on the confidence of a candidate dies off with its distance from the candidate. A formal description of the idea is given below.

Given: Attribute schema $A=\{A_1 \dots A_N\}$, set of products P and set of reviews R_p for each $p \in P$,

$$R = \bigcup_{p \in P} R_p$$

Let $A_i(p)$ be the value of attribute A_i for the product $p \in P$ from the segmentation step. Let $I_p(A_i, r)$ be the set of index positions at which $A_i(p)$ occurs in the review $r \in R_p$. Define:

$$B_p(A_i) = \begin{cases} 1 & \text{if } A_i(p) \text{ is known} \\ 0 & \text{otherwise} \end{cases}$$

Let attribute value A_j be missing for some product p after the segmentation step i.e. $B_p(A_j) = 0$ for some $j \in \{1 \dots n\}$. Given a set of candidates $C_p(A_j, r)$ (obtained by applying rules on a product review $r \in R_p$) for attribute A_j and product p, we define:

$$Q_p(c,r) = \sum_{x=1}^{n} \left(B_p(A_x) W(A_x) \sum_{i \in I_p(A_x, r)} I(i) d_r(i,c) \right)$$
$$\forall c \in C_p(A_j, r)$$

where d_r is a distance metric defined over every pair of words in a given review r.

In similar lines to the idea presented so far, occurrence of a value that contests a value already known from the standardization stage(segmentation output of the product description) can be used as an indicator that the author is talking of some other product or attribute. Hence, we have a case to reject candidates in its vicinity. Also, often people compare two products or brands while writing a review. Use of comparative adjective forms or coordinating conjunctions like "but, whereas, while, although, etc." that express a contrast mark such cases. To incorporate both of the above ideas, we can easily extend the objective function Q_p to account for these contingencies by adding terms to the summation that reduce the score of a candidate if conflicting attribute values and active comparison is found in its vicinity.

Consider the following review:

I love the Point and Shoot mode in my new camera X. I was bored of using the same auto mode in my old cam Y. Though it lacks the auto-program feature, still it's worth its price in gold. While auto mode in Camera Y was a sham, night mode was a cool addition. A f/1.8 lens , preferably brand Z would just be the icing on the cake.

Here the author compares his old camera with the one he just purchased and finally talks about buying a different product (a lens). A naive extraction scheme will extract features for each of cameras X and Y, and lens Z. The problem could be further compounded if the author swings back and forth comparing two products leading us to the deep waters of Pronoun Resolution and Attribute Coreference Resolution. However, we easily find a way around them with the assumption that the switch will not happen too frequently in most reviews.

Finally, as the descriptions are often sparse, we do not have all representative values for an attribute. A better 'importance' measure for a value ($I(v)$) can be obtained from the reviews. Also, in the above description, Q_p values can be arbitrarily large or small. Hence, we translate this idea in the probabilistic sense to a scale between 0 and 1. In an informal manner, the affinity of each candidate with the product can be treated as a confidence measure (represented by $P(c)$ instead of discrete Q_p values) in a scale of 0 to 1.

We also give a linear time algorithm based on the above idea. The algorithm iterates over all the candidates, modifying their affinity and dispersing the change to all other candidates in the review.

Given:- A set of products P and a set of reviews R_p for every product $p \in P$. Let $C_{p,r}$ be the set of candidates for product p in review r. Let A be the set of attributes. $W_{sim}(A_k)$ and $W_{diff}(A_k)$ are the weights of the attribute A_k for a matching value and a competing value, respectively. Weight W_{comp} penalizes a comparative sentence in the affinity calculation. $d_r(c, c')$ is some distance metric defined on all candidate pairs in a review r. We set the distance between two candidates as the number of words between their occurrence in the review in our simulations.

for each $p \in P$:
  for each $r \in R_p$:
    for $c \in C_{p,r}$:
      Compute: $I(c)$
      Initialize: $P(c) = \frac{1}{2}$
      Init_value=P(c)
      for $k \in 1 \dots n$:
        if $c = A_k(p)$:
          $P(c) := W_{sim}(A_k) * P(c) + (1 - W_{sim}(A_k))$

```
        end if
        else if c = A_k(p'), p' ∈ P, p'! = p:
            P(c) := W_diff(A(k)) * P(c)
        end elseif
        end for
        if c lies in a comparative sentence:
            P(c) := W_comp * P(c)
        end if
        Change(c)=P(c)-Init_value
        for c' ∈ C_{p,r}, c'! = c:
            P(c)+ = Change(c') × I(c') × e^{-d_r(c',c)}
        end for
        Normalize P
      end for
    end for
end for
```

Selection:- Finally for each product p and attribute A_j that misses a value for p, we choose the candidate with maximum affinity($P(c)$) i.e. choose c^*_{p,A_j} such that,

$$c^*_{p,A_j} = \underset{c' \in C_p(A_j,r), r \in R_p}{\text{argmax}} \quad P(c',r).$$

Finally, c^*_{p,A_j} is filled in as a value for A_j if $P(c^*_{p,A_j}, r))(r$ is the review containing $c_{p,A_j})$ is above a certain threshold. The algorithm runs with a complexity of $O(N+C^2)$ where N is the size of the reviews(number of words) and C is the number of candidates generated by applying rules on them. Since C is generally small, this is effectively linear with respect to size.

4 Evaluation

4.1 Dataset

The algorithms were tested on a real life dataset crawled from 'Amazon'. It contains reviews and short descriptions of 996 products in the Camera and Accessories space (Cameras, lenses, filters, etc). The total number of reviews was 23,337 leading to reviews per product ratio of about 24. Average number of words per review was around 40. Each product has a minimum of 20 reviews.

4.2 Experimental Setup

4.2.1 Product Description Segmentation

The experiments were carried out by first identifying the appropriate schema and 12 attributes were identified for description segmentation. They are given in Table 6. Rules (as described in Section 4.1) were used to standardize the descriptions into the composing attributes. The dictionary augmentation and rule writing together took nine man-hours. This is much lower than usual since we used Intellectual Property datasets on Brands and Products and clustering used to detect misspellings and varying vocabulary.

Table 6: Attributes guessed by the Rule Writer

Attribute	Value	Attribute	Value
Brand	Nikon	Product Type	Digital
Zoom	True	Color	Black
Lens	F/2.8 D	Retail Price	$ 250
Model	D 90	Product	Camera
Filter	UV	Size	Compact
Resolution	12MP	Features	Point&Shoot

4.2.2 Missing Value Filling

It was observed that around 60% of the attributes after the segmentation stage were null. So we used the reviews to fill in these missing values. Reusing the rules on the reviews led to a whopping 8434 candidates for the 12 attribute places in 969 products, which on using the confidence score based pruning scheme reduced to 5321. We set 0.5 as the weights for Brand Name, Product Name, Product Type and Color; and 1 for the remaining attributes. Recall that this is in-line with our arguments that there can be many products with the same Brand name, Product name, type and color but it is less likely for two products to have the same value for other attributes (say Retail Price or Weight). This choice of weights is done once and can be done at the time of the initial schema selection. Finally to select or reject candidates, we use a threshold. We used 0.4 times the mean(of the candidate confidence values) as the threshold for selection in our experiments. The threshold can be chosen based on the general confidence that the enterprise has on the correctness of the reviews. As the threshold is decreased, the number of values filled in increases but the precision-recall (and thereby F-Score) decreases.

4.3 Results

To evaluate our work, we also compute the entire attribute values view manually. Using this as ground truth, we calculate the Precision, Recall and F-Score of the overlap it has with our proposed techniques. Sometimes the values extracted are only partially correct for example, if the measurement unit is missing for the weight attribute.

Table 7: Evaluation Metrics for each Stage

Evaluation Stages	100 Cameras			100 Lenses		
Partially Correct	**Precision**	**Recall**	**F-Score**	**Precision**	**Recall**	**F-Score**
1.Standardization	1.000	0.909	0.952	1.000	0.925	0.961
2.Missing Value Extraction	0.888	0.705	0.786	0.837	0.700	0.762
Baseline 1	0.728	0.682	0.704	0.706	0.676	0.691
Baseline 2	0.771	0.709	0.739	0.741	0.703	0.712
Completely Correct	**Precision**	**Recall**	**F-Score**	**Precision**	**Recall**	**F-Score**
1.Standardization	0.998	0.901	0.947	1.000	0.917	0.957
2.Missing Value Filling	0.773	0.613	0.683	0.721	0.632	0.674
Baseline 1	0.644	0.607	0.625	0.618	0.596	0.607
Baseline 2	0.613	0.534	0.571	0.578	0.527	0.551

Hence, we evaluate results for both cases (when the values match perfectly or only partially).

4.3.1 Product Description Segmentation

As the Standardization stage is rule based, with time, close to perfect precision and recall can be achieved. In nine man-hours of effort, we achieved very high precision and recall as shown in Table 7.

4.3.2 Missing Value Filling

In Table 7, we give the precision and recall for the Enrichment phase. Here, we also draw two baseline comparisons for our work.

Baseline 1 is drawn by using the values extracted by the standardization stage from a training set (remaining 886 cameras) as seeds to train a CRF. The value extraction task is treated as a multi-class classification problem where each word is to be classified as a value to one of the attributes $(A_1 \ldots A_n)$ or as a "not a value" class. To generate a training set, every word is represented as a feature vector of $n + 20$ features. First n features are boolean entries and represent if the word matches an already known attribute value of the product. If the word matches with a value for A_j, then j^{th} feature is set to true and the rest to false. 10 words in the context of that word and their POS tags are remaining 20 features. The seeds are used to assign class labels to the training set. State of the art CRF is used for value extraction in a 10-fold setting. Please note that drawing the seeds from the standardization stage (which was rule based) gives this baseline the supervision provided by the rules. This is done to make a comparison with our approach fair. Recall that our technique for missing value Assignment leverages the supervision of existing rules to come up with meaningful values for the attributes.

(Ghani et al., 2006) laid down an ingenious technique to automatically extract candidate attribute-value seeds. They considered all pair of consecutive words (w_i, w_{i+1}) where w_i is a candidate value for the attribute w_{i+1}. Next, they computed the mutual information between all such candidate attribute-value pairs to prune down to fewer but cleaner seeds. Baseline 2 generates seeds by their technique and filters them for the attributes $\{A_1 \ldots A_n\}$. Again, CRF is trained with the same feature space.

It can further be observed that due to rule based cues, our techniques do well even when completely correct values are expected. However, Baseline 2 (projection of (Ghani et al., 2006) on the attribute set) falls apart as most extracted values are incomplete and partial.

The entire experiment is also carried out on a similar dataset of 100 lenses to prove the generalization ability of our technique within the product domain(Photography). Results on the lens dataset (shown in Table 7) are very close to the camera dataset, and occasionally better.

5 Conclusion

In this work, we tackle the problem of creating the complete view of an enterprise's products and services. We utilize the rulesets developed by existing product data cleansing solutions for value extraction from unstructured text media. Hereby, we escaped the laborious process of writing annotators. Supervision provided by the rules helped us uncover values which can give us a better view of the product and not merely sentiments.

References

Rayid Ghani, Katharina Probst, Yan Liu, Marko Krema, and Andrew Fano. 2006. Text mining for product attribute extraction. *SIGKDD Explorations Newsletter*, 8(1):41–48.

Minqing Hu and Bing Liu. 2004. Mining and summarizing customer reviews. In *Proceedings of the International Conference on Knowledge discovery and data mining*, pages 168–177.

Nozomi Kobayashi, Kentaro Inui, and Yuji Matsumoto. 2007. Extracting aspect-evaluation and aspect-of relations in opinion mining. In *Proceedings of the Joint Conference on Empirical Methods in Natural Language Processing and Computational Natural Language Learning*.

Bing Liu, Minqing Hu, and Junsheng Cheng. 2005. Opinion observer: analyzing and comparing opinions on the web. In *Proceedings of the International Conference on World Wide Web*, pages 342–351.

U. Nambiar, A. Faruquie, K. H. Prasad, L. V. Subramaniam, and M. K. Mohania. 2011. Data augmentation as a service for single view creation. In *Proceedings of IEEE International Conference on Services Computing (SCC)*.

Fuchun Peng and Andrew McCallum. 2006. Information extraction from research papers using conditional random fields. *Information Processing Management*, 42(4):963–979.

Ana-Maria Popescu and Oren Etzioni. 2005. Extracting product features and opinions from reviews. In *Proceedings of the conference on Human Language Technology and Empirical Methods in Natural Language Processing*, pages 339–346.

K. H. Prasad, T.A. Faruquie, S. Joshi, S. Chaturvedi, L. V. Subramaniam, and M. K. Mohania. 2011. Data cleansing techniques for large enterprise datasets. In *Proceedings of SRII Global Conference (SRII)*.

Guang Qiu, Bing Liu, Jiajun Bu, and Chun Chen. 2009. Expanding domain sentiment lexicon through double propagation. In *Proceedings of the International joint Conference on Artifical intelligence*, pages 1199–1204.

Veselin Stoyanov and Claire Cardie. 2008. Topic identification for fine-grained opinion analysis. In *Proceedings of International Conference on Computational Linguistics*, pages 817–824, Morristown, NJ, USA.

B. Wang and H. Wang. 2008. Bootstrapping Both Product Features and Opinion Words from Chinese Customer Reviews with Cross-Inducing. *Proceedings of International Joint Conference on Natural Language Processing*.

Zhongwu Zhai, Bing Liu, Hua Xu, and Peifa Jia. 2010. Grouping product features using semi-supervised learning with soft-constraints.

Li Zhuang, Feng Jing, and Xiao-Yan Zhu. 2006. Movie review mining and summarization. In *Proceedings of the International Conference on Information and knowledge management*, pages 43–50.

Mining bilingual topic hierarchies from unaligned text

Sumit Negi
IBM Research India
Vasant Kunj, Institutional Area
New Delhi, India
sumitneg@in.ibm.com

Abstract

Recent years have seen an exponential growth in the amount of multilingual text available on the web. This situation raises the need for novel applications for organizing and accessing multilingual content. Common examples of such applications include Multilingual Topic Tracking, Cross-Language Information retrieval systems etc. Most of these applications rely on the availability of multilingual lexical resources which require significant effort to create. In this paper we present an unsupervised method for building *bilingual topic hierarchies*. In a *bilingual topic hierarchy*, topics (where a topic is a distribution over words) are arranged in a hierarchical fashion with abstract topics appearing near the root of the hierarchy and more concrete topics near the leaves. Such bilingual topic hierarchies can be useful for organizing bilingual corpus based on common topics, cross-lingual information retrieval and cross-lingual text classification. Our method builds upon the prior work done on Bayesian non-parametric inferencing of topic hierarchies and multilingual topic modeling to extract bilingual topic hierarchies from unaligned text. We demonstrate the effectiveness of our algorithm in extracting such topic hierarchies from a collection of bilingual text passages and FAQs.

1 Introduction

The last few decades have seen an explosive growth in Internet accessibility in developing regions of the world. A significant part of this growth has been in countries that use languages other than English as their primary language (Chinese, Spanish, Arabic, Hindi etc). The increasing number of multilingual Internet users has resulted in a tremendous increase in the amount multilingual content that is available on the Web. This situation raises the need for novel ways of organizing and accessing multilingual content. Work done on Cross Language Information Retrieval (CLIR) (Xu et al., 2001) i.e. retrieving information written in a language different from the language of the user's query is one key attempt in this very direction. Similarly, there has been increased interest in multilingual text mining applications such as sentiment detection (Boiy and Moens, 2008), mining multilingual news feeds, cross lingual text categorization (Bel et al., 2003) etc. Most of these applications use bilingual dictionaries or lexical databases to perform such tasks. For instance, (Pouliquen et al., 2004) use the *Eurovoc* multilingual thesaurus for cross-lingual news topic tracking. (Mihalcea et al., 2007) use a bilingual dictionary to generate subjectivity analysis resources for a given language. Similarly, CINDOR (Ruiz et al., 2000) uses interlingua resources to address the cross language information retrieval problem.

Considering the importance of multilingual lexical resources efforts to (semi) automatically build/populate such resources from Web or other large text collections have gained prominence. For example, (Nagata et al., 2001) build a bilingual dictionary of English-Japanese technical term by collecting and scoring translation candidates from the Web. (Widdows et al., 2002; Nerima et al., 2003) describe similar initiatives related to building multilingual lexical resources from large text corpora.

The work presented in this paper is similar in spirit i.e. it presents an automated way of building and populating a lexical resource given a text corpus. In this paper we propose an unsupervised method of building *bilingual topic hierarchies* using Topic models (Blei et al., 2003). In a topic hierarchy, topics (where a topic is a distribution over words) are arranged in a hierarchical fashion with abstract topics appearing near the root of the hierarchy and more concrete topics near the leaves. Figure 1 is an example of a bilingual topic hierarchy. Such topic hierarchies can be useful for organizing/navigating bilingual corpus based on common topics, cross-lingual information retrieval and multilingual text categorization.

Motivating Example: Consider a corpus containing medical documents from two different languages on a common set of topics (e.g. genetics, pharmacology, toxicology etc). The documents in this corpus are not aligned in anyway i.e. there is no document or sentence level alignment between documents of the two languages in the corpus. Let us assume that the goal is to organize this bilingual corpus in such a way that it is easy to locate documents of a certain topic/sub-topic irrespective of the language in which the document was authored. One way of achieving this would be to arrange the document from the corpus in some sort of a hierarchy where (a) documents pertaining to different topics appear in different subtrees of the hierarchy and (b) within a given subtree documents belonging to abstract topics appear at higher levels of the subtree than documents belonging to concrete subtopics.

Organizing documents in such a fashion could be aided by the availability of a bilingual topic hierarchy as shown in Figure 1 in which topics (where a topic is a collection of words) are arranged in a hierarchical fashion with abstract topics appearing near the root of the hierarchy and more concrete topics near the leaves. Moreover, using a data-driven approach (as proposed by our method) for building such a bilingual topic hierarchy ensures that the hierarchy is representative of the structure present in the data. Note, that the hierarchy shown in Figure 1 was generated by our proposed method from a corpus containing English and Hindi medical documents on topics such as Behavior (MeSH [1]Category F01.145), Alcohol Drinking (MeSH Category F01.145.317.269) etc.

2 Prior Work

Topic models have been used for analyzing topic trends in research literature, inferring captions for images, social network analysis in email, and expanding queries with topically related words in information retrieval. Most of the topic modeling

[1]Medical Subject Headings

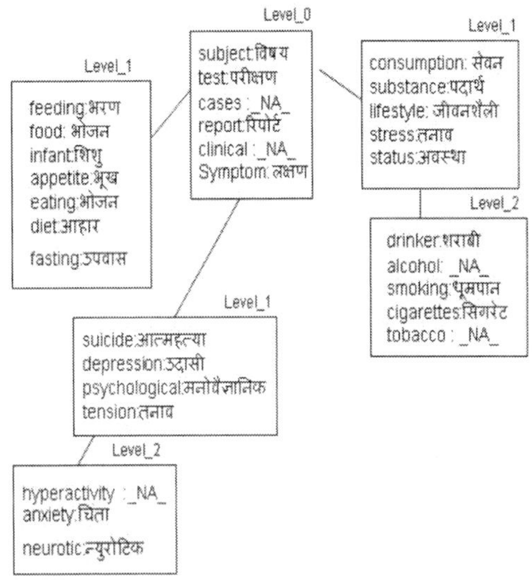

Figure 1: Bilingual Topic Hierarchy

work on text has occurred in the monolingual context. *Multilingual topic models* (MTM) is a relatively new area of research as compared to Topic modeling on monolingual corpus. In their work (Jagarlamudi and Daum III, 2010) (Boyd-Graber and Blei, 2009) demonstrate how a monolingual topic model, which groups together semantically similar words based on similar context, cannot be used directly on a multilingual corpus. This is because of the fact that almost all documents are written in a single language hence similar meaning words from different languages will never share similar context. Consequently, even though a topic model applied on a bilingual corpus will find coherent topics (for each language independently) it will bifurcate the topic space between the two languages.

In Figure 2 we show a few topics discovered by Latent Dirichlet Allocation (Blei et al., 2003) on a bilingual corpus containing Hindi and English documents. The outcome is similar to what was demonstrated by (Jagarlamudi and Daum III, 2010) on the Europarl[2] parallel corpus i.e. LDA bifurcates the topics between the two languages despite their being striking similarity between topics in the two languages. For instance, Topic *C1* and *C3* should be merged together as they form one coherent topic cluster (both these clusters have

[2]http://www.statmt.org/europarl/

words relevant to *'crop-disease'*). Similarly, Topic *C2* and *C5* should be merged together as they form one coherent topic cluster (both these clusters have words relevant to *'agriculture'*).

In order to discover coherent topics across languages, most multilingual topic models take the document's language into consideration. Previous work on Multilingual Topic Modeling connects the languages by assuming parallelism at either the sentence level or document level. (Zhao and Xing, 2006) propose BiTAM (Bilingual topic admixture models) and HM-BiTAM (Hidden Markov Bilingual topic admixture model), bilingual topic model for Statistical Machine Translation that assume sentence level alignment. Work done by (Kim and Khudanpur, 2004; Tam and Schultz, 2007; Ni et al., 2009) relax the sentence level alignment but require document level alignment. These requirements, namely sentence/document level alignment are too restrictive as finding parallel corpus for all possible domains and languages is difficult. Recent work by (Jagarlamudi and Daum III, 2010) and (Boyd-Graber and Blei, 2009) relax these restrictions by proposing multilingual topic models that work on unaligned text in multiple languages. MuTo (Multilingual Topic Model) (Boyd-Graber and Blei, 2009) does away with the alignment requirement by assuming that similar themes and ideas appear in both languages. The JointLDA model (Jagarlamudi and Daum III, 2010) , which can be seen as a generalization of MuTo, uses a bilingual dictionary to mine bilingual topics from an unaligned corpus. As JointLDA requires only a bilingual dictionary, which is easy to obtain for most pair of languages, we use this model for extracting bilingual topic hierarchies. Please note that the JointLDA model cannot be used directly to infer topic hierarchies. This is because like LDA, JointLDA treats topics as a flat set of probability distributions, with not direct relationship between topics. To discover relationships between topics the Hierarchical Latent Dirichlet Allocation (Blei et al., 2010) is used.

To the best of our knowledge our work of discovering bilingual topic hierarchies using Topic models is a first. Our generative model uses the JointLDA (a multilingual topic modeling approach) and hLDA (a hierarchial topic modeling approach) models to discover bilingual topic hierarchies from an unaligned bilingual corpus. Combining these two models gives us an unsupervised mechanism of discovering bilingual topic hierarchies. Moreover, in this setup no assumption about the topics or hierarchy structure (there are no limitation such as maximum depth or maximum branching factor) needs to be made.

The paper is organized as follows. In Section 3 we provide a short overview of the Hierarchical Latent Dirichlet Allocation and JointLDA. Section 4 provides details of the proposed generative model for extracting bilingual topic hierarchies from an unaligned bilingual corpus. Experiments and conclusion are provided in Section 5 and Section 6 respectively.

3 Hierarchical Latent Dirichlet Allocation and JoinLDA models

For ease of exposition, we first describe the basics of the Hierarchical Latent Dirichlet Allocation and JoinLDA models. Topic models such as Latent Dirichlet Allocation (LDA) treat topics as a flat set of probability distributions, with no direct relationship between topics. While such models can be used to discover set of topics from a corpus they fail to detect the level of abstraction of a topic, or how topics are related. Blei et al. propose a *hierarchical topic model* hLDA (Blei et al., 2010) that learns such relations between topics. Given a collection of documents each of which contains a set of words, hLDA discovers topics in the documents and organizes these topics into a hierarchy. More general topics appear near the root whereas more specialized topics appear near the leaf of the hierarchy. In the hierarchy each node is associated with a topic, where topic is distribution over words. Under this generative model a document is generated by choosing a path from the root to a leaf, repeatedly sampling topics along the path, and sampling the words from the selected topics. Blei et al. define a *nested Chinese restaurant process* which is used as a prior distribution over the possible hierarchies (a hierarchy can be thought of as a infinitely-deep and infinitely-branching tree).

In hLDA each document is assigned a single path in the hierarchy. The first level, which is directly below the root, induces a coarse partition on the documents. Topics at this level place high probability on words that are useful within the corresponding subset/partition. The nested partitions of documents become finer as one moves down the hierarchy. Consequently, the corresponding topics (and the words associated with those topics) be-

C1	C2	C3	C4	C5	C6	C7	C8
pesticide	soil	बीमारी	कीटनाशक	फसल	market	disease	मंडी
pest	harvest	टीका	छिड़कना	गेहूँ	wholesale	vaccine	थोक
blight	grain	परजीवी	बिमारी	चावल	storage	viral	वितरण
rust	cultivate	लक्षण	मिलाना	कपास	district	bacterial	गाँव
parasite	rice	खाल	परजीवी	मौसम	price	symptoms	दाम
	wheat			खेती		influenza	

Figure 2: Topics extracted by LDA from a bilingual Hindi-English corpus

come more specialized to the particular documents in those paths. As mentioned in (Blei et al., 2010) the goal of finding a topic hierarchy at different levels of abstraction is distinct from the problem of hierarchical clustering. Hierarchical clustering treats each data point as a leaf in a tree, and merges similar data points up the tree until all are merged into a root node. Thus, the internal nodes formed during the hierarchical clustering process shares words with their children. In contrast, in the hierarchical topic model the internal nodes are not summaries of their children. Rather, the internal nodes reflect the shared terminology of the documents assigned to the paths that contains them.

We extend the hLDA model to extract *bilingual topic hierarchies* from unaligned bilingual corpus. Even though there has been some attempts to extract topics (not topic hierarchies) from cross-lingual corpus, these approaches assume either explicit or indirect clues about document alignment. In order to overcome such restrictions, namely sentence/document alignment, we use the JointLDA model proposed by (Jagarlamudi and Daum III, 2010). The JointLDA model is an extension of the LDA model which uses bilingual dictionaries to generate documents in different languages. The JointLDA model, like LDA, models a document as a mixture over T topics, where the mixture weight (θ_d) is drawn from a Dirichlet distribution. JointLDA introduces an additional hidden variable called *concepts*, in defining a topic distribution. Each topic is now a distribution over concepts rather than words, where the topic distribution is also drawn from a Dirichlet distribution. Finally, a *concept* can be realized in different ways depending on the choice of the document's language (l_d). This additional layer of language independent abstraction over the words allows the model to capture common topics in different languages effectively. JointLDA use bilingual dictionary entries as substitute for these concepts. Out-of-dictionary words are handled by adding artificial dictionary entries to the dictionary. For more details on the JointLDA model readers should see (Jagarlamudi and Daum III, 2010).

In the next section we describe in detail our proposed bilingual-topic hierarchy generative model.

4 Generative Process

In the bilingual-topic hierarchy model for a given document d a path $\mathbf{c}_d$ (where a path denotes a collection of topics) is drawn from a nested Chinese Restaurant Process (nCRP). Given a choice of a path, or in other words a collection of topics, the GEM (Pitman, 2002) distribution is used to define a probability distribution on the topics along that path. Given a draw from a GEM distribution, a document for language l_d is generated by first repeatedly selecting topics according to the probabilities defined by that draw, followed by selecting a *concept* from a multinomial distribution, and then selecting a word given the *concept* and language of the document. The generative process can thus be summarized as

1. For each table $k \in T$ in the infinite tree
   (a) draw a topic $\beta_k \sim \mathrm{Dir}(\eta)$
2. For each doc $d \in \{1,2....D\}$
   (a) draw $\mathbf{c}_d \sim \mathrm{nCRP}(\gamma)$
   (b) draw a distribution over levels in the tree, $\theta_d|\{\mathrm{m},\pi\} \sim \mathrm{GEM}(\mathrm{m},\pi)$
   (c) for each word in the document
      i. choose level $z_{d,n}|\theta \sim \mathrm{Mult}(\theta_d)$
      ii. select a concept (dictionary entry) $v_{d,n} \sim \mathrm{Mult}(\beta_{\mathbf{c}_d}[z_{d,n}])\Psi(v_{d,n},\mathrm{l}_d)$
      iii. select a word from $\mathrm{p}(w_{d,n}|\ v_{d,n},\mathrm{l}_d)$

Where the function $\Psi(v_{d,n},\mathrm{l}_d)$ is 1 if the dictionary entry $v_{d,n}$ can generate a word from language l_d

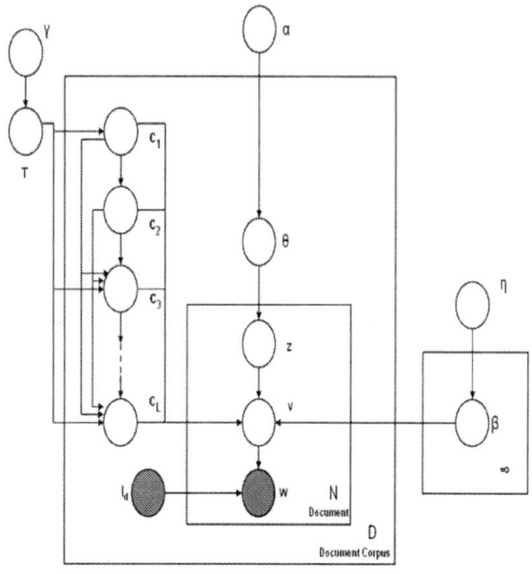

Figure 3: bilingual-topic hierarchy model

and otherwise 0. Given a dictionary entry and language there is only one possibility for a word and hence p($w_{d,n}$| $v_{d,n}$,l_d) = 1 (Jagarlamudi and Daum III, 2010). Figure 3 illustrates the bilingual-topic hierarchy generative process using the plate model notation.

4.1 Approximate Inference

Given the bilingual-topic hierarchy model the goal is to perform *posterior inference* i.e. to invert the generative process of documents for estimating the hidden topical structure of a bilingual document collection. The posterior distribution gives us the distribution of the underlying topic structure that might have generated an observed collection of bilingual documents. Finding this posterior distribution is a key problem in Bayesian statistics. Since the posterior distribution does not have a closed form we employ an approximate inferencing technique namely a variant of Markov Chain Monte Carlo (MCMC) technique called *collapsed Gibbs sampling* (Liu, 1994). In a Gibbs sampler each latent variable is iteratively sampled conditioned on the observations and all other latent variables. To speed up convergence the collapsed Gibbs sampler marginalize out some of the latent variables. Collapsed Gibbs sampling for topic models has been widely used in topic modeling applications (McCallum et al., 2004; Mimno and McCallum, 2007; Rosen-Zvi et al., 2004).

The variables needed by the sampling algorithm are: $w_{d,n}$: the *n*th word in document *d* (observed), l_d : document *d*'s language (observed), $c_{d,l}$: the *l*th topic in document *d*, $v_{d,n}$: the *concept* (dictionary entry) associated with the *n*th word in document *d* and $z_{d,n}$: the assignment of the *n*th word in document *d* to one of the L available topics. The Gibbs sampler integrates out all the other variables in the model to assess the values of $z_{d,n}$, $c_{d,l}$ and $v_{d,n}$.

We approximate the posterior $p(\mathbf{c}_{1:D}, \mathbf{z}_{1:D}, \mathbf{v}_{1:D} \mid \eta, \gamma, \mathrm{m}, \pi, \mathbf{w}_{1:D}, \mathbf{l}_{1:D})$ where hyper-parameter γ reflects the likelihood that documents will choose new paths when traversing the nested CRP, η reflects the expected variance of the underlying topics ($\eta \ll 1$ will tend to choose topics with fewer high probability words), and m and π reflect our expectation about the allocation of words to levels within a document. Bold fonts $\mathbf{c}_{1:D}$, $\mathbf{z}_{1:D}$, $\mathbf{v}_{1:D}$ denote vector of level allocations, topic allocations and concept allocation respectively. The variable $\mathbf{c}_d$ denotes the per-document path, $z_{d,n}$ denotes per-word level allocation to topics in those paths (as mentioned in Section 3, a path in a tree picks out a collection of topics) and $v_{d,n}$ denotes *concept* for the *n*th word in document *d*. Next, we describe in detail how level allocations, concepts and paths are sampled.

4.1.1 Sampling

In this section Equation (1), (2), (3) detail how the level allocation variable $z_{d,n}$ is sampled. Given the current path assignments, we sample the level allocation variable $z_{d,n}$ for word *n* in document *d* from its distribution given the current value of all other variables

$$p(z_{d,n}|\mathbf{z}_{-(d,n)}, \mathbf{c}, \mathbf{v}, m, \pi, \eta) \propto p(z_{d,n}|\mathbf{z}_{d,-n}, m, \pi).p(v_{d,n}|\mathbf{z}, \mathbf{c}, \mathbf{v}_{-(d,n)}, \eta) \quad (1)$$

Where $\mathbf{z}_{-(d,n)}$ and $\mathbf{v}_{-(d,n)}$ are vectors of level allocations and concepts leaving out $z_{d,n}$ and $v_{d,n}$ respectively. The first term in (1) is a distribution over levels.

$$p(z_{d,n} = k \mid \mathbf{z}_{d,-n}, m, \pi) = \frac{(1-m)\pi + \#[\mathbf{z}_{-(d,n)} = k]}{\pi + \#[\mathbf{z}_{-(d,n)} \geq k]} \prod_{j=1}^{k-1} \frac{m\pi + \#[\mathbf{z}_{d,-n} > j]}{\pi + \#[\mathbf{z}_{d,-n} \geq j]} \quad (2)$$

Where #[..] counts the elements of an array satisfying a given condition. Interested readers are requested to refer to (Blei et al., 2010) for detailed derivation. The second term in (1) is the probability of a given concept based on possible assignment. From the assumption that the topic parameter β_i are generated from a dirchilet distribution with hyper-parameter η we obtain

$$p(v_{d,n} = j \mid \mathbf{z}, \mathbf{c}, \mathbf{v}_{-(d,n)}, \eta) \propto \\ \#[\mathbf{z}_{-(d,n)} = z_{d,n}, \mathbf{c}_{z_{d,n}} = c_{(d,z_{d,n})}, \mathbf{v}_{-(d,n)} = j] + \eta \quad (3)$$

Where (3) gives the smoothed frequency of the number of times concept *j* is allocated to topic at level $z_{d,n}$ of the path c_d.

Given level allocation, in order to sample the path associated with each document conditioned on all other paths and concept assignments (4), (5) is used. Where

$$p(\mathbf{c}_d \mid \mathbf{c}_{-d}, \mathbf{v}, \mathbf{z}, \eta, \gamma) \propto \\ p(\mathbf{c}_d \mid \mathbf{c}_{-d}, \gamma).p(\mathbf{v}_d \mid \mathbf{c}, \mathbf{z}, \mathbf{v}_{-d}, \eta). \quad (4)$$

The probability of *concept* is obtained by integrating over the multinomial parameters.

$$p(\mathbf{v}_d \mid \mathbf{c}, \mathbf{z}, \mathbf{v}_{-d}, \eta) = \\ \prod_{l=1}^{max(z_d)} \frac{\Gamma(\sum_v \#[\mathbf{z}_{-d} = l, \mathbf{c}_{-d,l} = c_{d,l}, \mathbf{v}_{-d} = v] + V\eta)}{\prod_v \Gamma(\#[\mathbf{z}_{-d} = l, \mathbf{c}_{-d,l} = c_{d,l}, \mathbf{v}_{-d} = v] + \eta)} \times \\ \frac{\prod_v \Gamma(\#[\mathbf{z} = l, \mathbf{c}_l = c_{d,l}, \mathbf{v} = v] + \eta)}{\Gamma(\Sigma_v \#[\mathbf{z} = l, \mathbf{c}_l = c_{d,l}, \mathbf{v} = v] + V\eta)} \quad (5)$$

For each document *d* the topic and concept assignments for each word i.e. ($z_{d,n}$,$v_{d,n}$) is sampled from the probability distribution given by

$$p(z_{d,n} = k, v_{d,n} = j \mid \mathbf{z}_{-(d,n)}, \mathbf{v}_{-(d,n)}, \mathbf{w}, \mathbf{l}) \propto \\ \frac{n^d_{-(d,n),k} + \gamma}{n^d_{-(d,n),(.)} + L\gamma} \cdot \frac{n^j_{-(d,n),k} + \eta}{n^{(.)}_{-(d,n),k} + V\eta} \quad (6)$$

In (6) $n^j_{-(d,n),k}$ ($n^{(.)}_{-(d,n),k}$) is the number of times the dictionary entry *j* (any dictionary entry) is used along with topic *k* for sampling any word excluding the word $w_{d,n}$. Similarly, $n^d_{-(d,n),k}$ ($n^d_{-(d,n),(.)}$) is the number of words in document *d* that are assigned to topic *k* (any topic) excluding the word $w_{d,n}$. Note, L is the number of topics (levels in the hierarchy) and V the vocabulary size. Figure 4 provides an overview of the sampling algorithm.

```
Given the current state of the sampler [ c_{1:D}, z_{1:D}, v_{1:D} ]
Begin
  For each document d ∈ {1,......,D}
    Draw c_d using (4)
    For each word in document d draw z_{d,n} using (1)
    For each word in document d draw v_{d,n} using (6)
End
```

Figure 4: Gibbs Sampling Algorithm

5 Experiments

To demonstrate that the bilingual-topic hierarchy model extracts meaningful topic hierarchies the model was applied on two real world data-sets. The first data-set is a collection of 2000 questions on the following three topics: *health insurance*, *auto insurance* and *passport/visa* queries. This data set was built by crawling government and insurance company web sites. The average length of a question in this corpus is eleven words. The question corpus contains 1200 questions in Hindi and 800 question in English. Further details of this data-set, henceforth referred to as *Data-Set A*, is provided in Table 1. The extracted bilingual topic hierarchy is shown in Figure 5. For our experiments we used *Shabdanjali*[1] as our bilingual (Hindi-English) dictionary. Since the coverage of a bilingual dictionary will be limited we add artificial entries ($\_NA\_$) for out-of-dictionary words. This is similar to the approach adopted by (Jagarlamudi and Daum III, 2010) in their JointLDA work.

Language	Health	Auto	Passport/Visa	Total
Hindi	440	330	430	1200
English	280	350	170	800

Table 1: Data-Set A.

We apply our algorithm on a second data set which is a collection of text passages on *agricultural* and *animal rearing*. This data-set, henceforth referred to as *Data-Set B*, is a collection of 1100 passages, 700 of which are in Hindi and the rest 400 in English. The average length of a passage in this data-set is 221 words. The extracted bilingual topic hierarchy is shown in Figure 6.

In order to facilitate the visualization of extracted topic hierarchies we restrict the number of levels to three. As is evident from Figure 5, Figure 6 the model was able to successfully extract the underlying bilingual-hierarchical struc-

[1]http://www.shabdkosh.com/content/category/downloads/

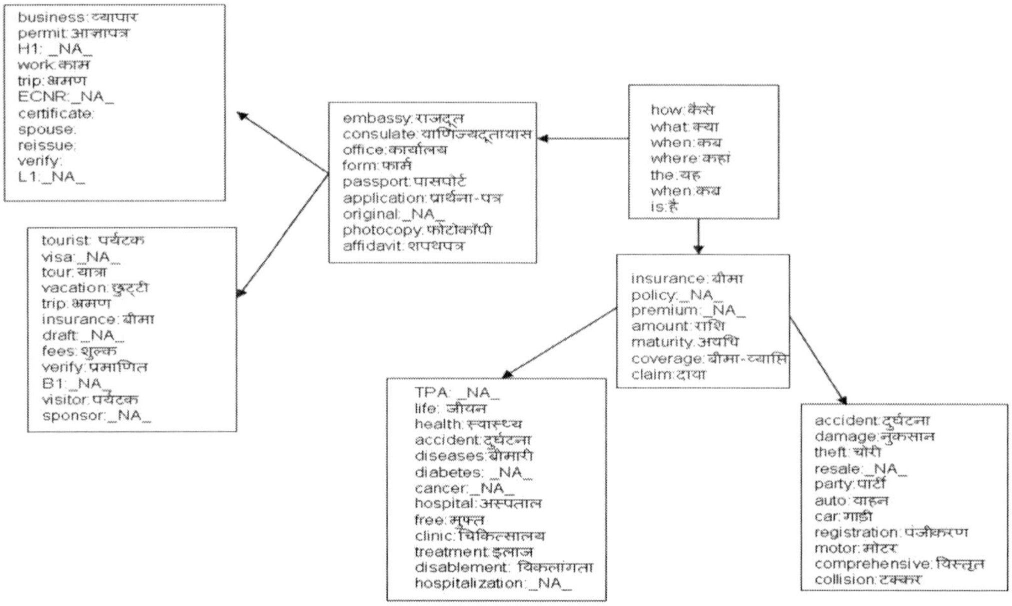

Figure 5: Bilingual Topic Hierarchy: Data-Set A

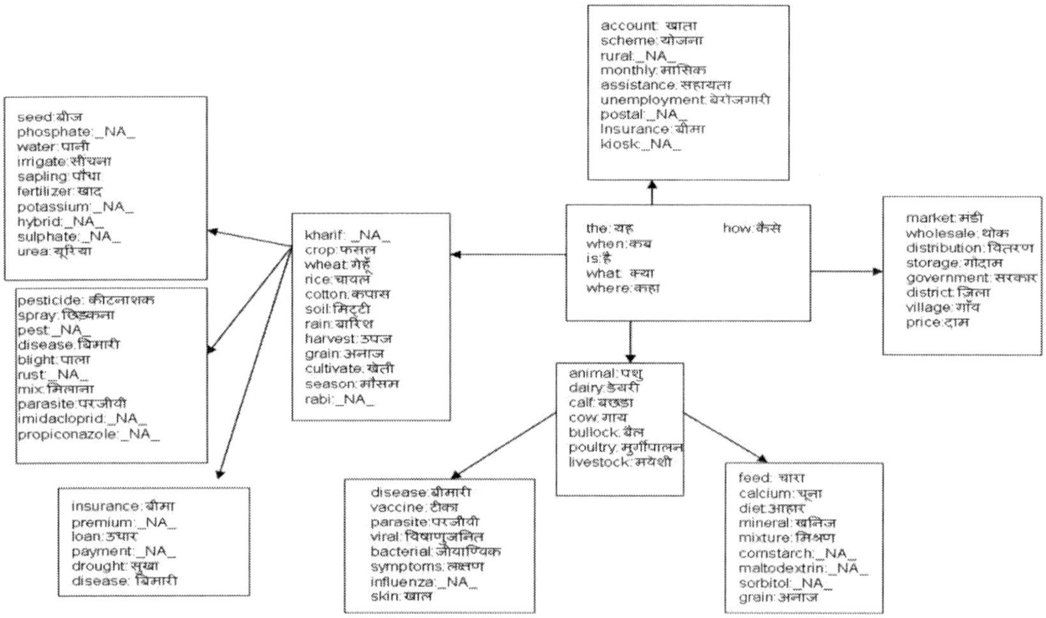

Figure 6: Bilingual Topic Hierarchy: Data-Set B

ture from the two document collections. For example for *Data-Set B* (Figure 6) the second level of the hierarchy captures the two prominent topics (where a topic is a distribution over words) present in the document collection namely that related to agriculture and animal rearing. The third level of this hierarchy further refines these topics. The *agriculture* topic is further split into subtopics related to crop-disease, crop-cultivation and crop-insurance. Similarly, the *animal-rearing* topic cluster is split into subtopic related to animal-disease and animal-feed. For a quantitative evaluation of our method we use predictive held-out likelihood as a measure of performance. Fig-

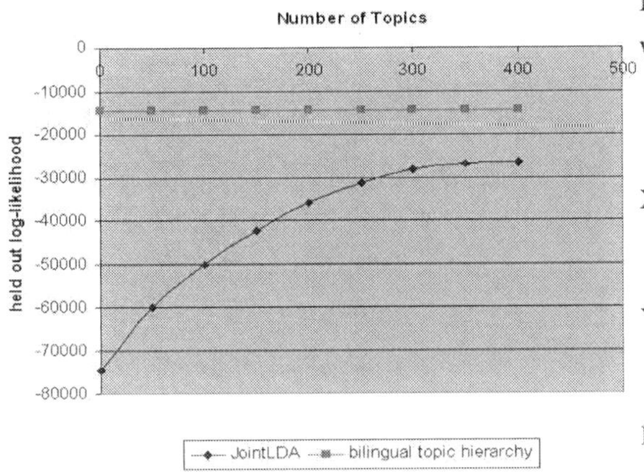

Figure 7: Held out log-likelihood vs Number of topics

ure 7 illustrates the five-fold cross-validated held-out likelihood for JointLDA and bilingual topic hierarchy on the test corpus. It is evident from this experiment that for topic cardinalities in the range 0 to 400, bilingual topic hierarchy provides significantly better predictive performance than JointLDA.

6 Conclusion

In this paper we presented an unsupervised method for building *bilingual topic hierarchies.* In a topic hierarchy, topics (where a topic is a distribution over words) are arranged in a hierarchical fashion with abstract topics appearing near the root of the hierarchy and more concrete topics near the leaves. Such bilingual topic hierarchies can be useful for organizing bilingual corpus based on common topics, cross-lingual information retrieval and cross-lingual text classification. We propose a generative model that employs Bayesian non-parametric inferencing of topic hierarchies and multilingual topic modeling to extract such bilingual topic hierarchies from unaligned text. The effectiveness of the algorithm in extracting bilingual topic hierarchies is demonstrated on a collection of bilingual text passages and FAQs. As part of future work we plan to use the extracted bilingual topic hierarchies for cross-lingual text classification and information retrieval tasks.

References

W. Kim and S. Khudanpur. 2004. *Lexical triggers and latent semantic analysis for cross-lingual language model.* ACM Transactions on Asian Language Information Processing.

X. Ni and J.T Sun and J. Hu and Z. Chen. 2009. *Mining multilingual topics from Wikipedia.* In International World Wide Web Conference.

Y. C Tam and T. Schultz. 2007. *Bilingual LSA-based translation lexicon adaptation for spoke language translation.* In INTERSPEECH.

B. Zhao and E.P Xing. 2006. *Bilingual topic admixture models for word alignment.* Association for Computational Linguistics.

B. Pouliquen and R. Steinberger and C. Ignat and E. Kasper and I. Temnikova. 2004. *Multilingual and Crosslingual News Topic Tracking.* In COLING 2004.

J. Xu and R. Weischedel and R. Nguyen. 2001. *Evaluating a probablistic model for cross-lingual information retrieval.* In SIGIR 2001.

N. Bel and C.H.A Koster and M. Villegas. 2003. *Cross-lingual text categorization.* In ECDL 2003.

E. Boiy and M. Moens. 2008. *A machine learning approach to sentiment analysis in multilingual Web texts.* Information Retrieval, 2008.

M. Nagata and T. Saito and K. Suzuki. 2001. *Using the web as a bilingual dictionary.* In Proceedings of the workshop on Data-driven methods in machine translation.

D. Widdows and B. Dorow and C. Chan. 2002. *Using parallel corpora to enrich multilingual lexical resources.* In Third International Conference on Language Resources and Evaluation.

L. Nerima and V. Seretan and E. Wehrli. 2003. *Creating a multilingual collocation dictionary from large text corpora.* In Research Note Sessions of the 10th Conference of the European Chapter of the Association for Computational Linguistics.

J. Bernardo and A. Smith. 1994. *Bayesian Theory.* John Wiley & Sons Ltd.

D. Blei and T. Griffiths and M. Jordan. 2010. *The nested Chinese restaurant process and Bayesian nonparametric inference of topic hierarchies.* Journal of the ACM.

J. Jagarlamudi and H. Daum. 2010. *Extracting Multilingual Topics from Unaligned Comparable Corpora.* 32nd European Conference on IR Research,ECIR.

J. Boyd-Graber and D. M. Blei. 2009. *Multilingual Topic Models for Unaligned Text.* Uncertainty in Artificial Intelligence.

J. Pitman. 2002. *Combinatorial Stochastic Processes.* Lecture Notes for St. Flour Summer School.

J. Liu. 1994. *The collapsed Gibbs sampler in Bayesian computations with application to a gene regulation problem.* Journal of the American Statistical Association.

A. McCallum and A. Corrada-Emmanuel and X. Wang. 2004. *The author-recipient-topic model for topic and role discovery in social networks: Experiments with Enron and academic email.* Tech. report, University of Massachusetts, Amherst.

D. Mimno and A. McCallum. 2007. *Organizing the OCA: Learning faceted subjects from a library of digital books.* In Proceedings of the 7th ACM/IEEE-CS Joint Conference on Digital libraries.

M. Rosen-Zvi and T. Griffiths and M. Steyvers and P. Smith. 2004. *The author-topic model for authors and documents.* In Proceedings of the 20th Conference on Uncertainity in Artificial Intelligence.

M. Ruiz and A. Diekema and P. Sheridan. 2000. *CINDOR Conceptual Interlingua Document Retrieval: TREC-8 Evaluation.* In Proceedings of the Eighth Text Retrieval Conference (TREC8).

R. Mihalcea and C. Banea and J. Wiebe. 2007. *Learning multilingual subjective language via cross-lingual projections.* In Proceedings of the Association for Computational Linguistics (ACL).

D. M. Blei and A. Y. Ng and M. I. Jordan. 2003. *Latent dirichlet allocation.* Journal of Machine Learning Research.

Efficient Near-Duplicate Detection for Q&A Forum

Yan Wu, Qi Zhang, Xuanjing Huang
Fudan University
School of Computer Science
{10210240075,qz,xjhuang}@fudan.edu.cn

Abstract

This paper addresses the issue of redundant data in large-scale collections of Q&A forums. We propose and evaluate a novel algorithm for automatically detecting the near-duplicate Q&A threads. The main idea is to use the distributed index and Map-Reduce framework to calculate pairwise similarity and identify redundant data fast and scalably. The proposed method was evaluated on a real-world data collection crawled from a popular Q&A forum. Experimental results show that our proposed method can effectively and efficiently detect near-duplicate content in large web collections.

1 INTRODUCTION

There is a rise in popularity of Question and Answering forums in recent years. The forums allow users to post, browse, search and answer questions. Q&A forum acts not only as a medium for knowledge sharing , but also as a place in which one can seek advice, and satisfy others' curiosity about a countless number of things (Adamic et al., 2008). However, because of the ever-increasing growth of it, and the fact that users are not always experts in the areas they post threads on, duplicate content becomes a serious issue. And, most of the current Q&A forums haven't had a efficient mechanism to identify threads with near-duplicate content. As a consequence, users have to go through different versions of duplicate or near-duplicate content, and are often frustrated by it. Baidu Zhidao[1] is one of the largest Q&A forums in China. It contains more than 100 million question and answer pairs. Because of the increasing popularity and the number of users, it also encounters the long-standing problem – content duplication. For example, there are more than four hundred question-answer pairs which contain the same content "When is the birthday of Jay?" Other Q&A forums are facing the similar problem.

Along with the increasing requirements and the limitations of manual methods, there have been growing research activities in duplicate detection, during the past few years. Common automatical methods to detect duplicates are copy detection or near-duplicate detection (Gionis et al., 1999; Muthmann et al., 2009; Shivakumar and Garcia-Molina, 1995; Shivakumar and Garcia-Molina, 1999; Theobald et al., 2008; Zhang et al., 2010). Most of the current near-duplication detection approaches usually focus on the document level to figure out the web pages with different framing, navigation bar, and advertisements, but duplicate content. However, unlike duplicated web-pages, forum threads have the following differences:

1. Forum threads contain additional structured meta information, e.g. title, tags, external/internal links, etc. So, the method used to detect near-duplicate of the forum thread is to the web-page.

2. The average length of threads is usually less than the news articles. Adamic et al. reported that most of the thread lengths are less than 400 words in Yahoo! Answers(Adamic et al., 2008).

3. The number of threads grows in a significant pace compare to other media. Thus a more efficient method need to be used to handle millions of content.

[1] http://zhidao.baidu.com

In this paper we propose a novel algorithm for detecting near-duplicate threads in the Q&A forums. Threads with similar content can be identified. The proposed algorithm completes the pairwise similarity comparisons in two steps: inverted index building and then similarity computations with it. Thread content and other meta information can be represented by signature/feature sets. As the Web collections contain hundreds of millions pages, this algorithm is done through MapReduce (Dean and Ghemawat, 2004), which is a framework for large-scale distributed computing. We implement our method and compare it with the state-of-the-art approaches on a real-world data crawled from a Q&A web forum and one manually labeled evaluation corpus. From the experimental results, we can observe that both effectiveness and efficiency are significantly improved. The major contributions of this work are as follows:

- We analyze the common structure of threads in Q&A forums, and give a definition of near-duplicate thread.
- We propose efficient solutions, which use distributed inverted index and are implemented under Map-Reduce framework, for calculating pairwise similarity and identifying redundant data fast and scalably.
- We describe a number of signatures for unstructured content and other meta information, and experimentally evaluate them.
- A tight upper bound of Jaccard coefficient is given and used in the to speed up the similarity calculation.
- We evaluate our method on a real-world corpus crawled from Baidu Zhidao. Experimental results showed that our algorithm can achieve better result than the state-of-the-art algorithms for detecting near-duplicate web pages on forum content.

The rest of the paper is structured as follows: In Section 2, a number of related work and the state-of-the-art approaches in related research areas are briefly described. Section 3 defines the problem we try to deal with and gives the introduction of MapReduce framework. In Section 4, we present the proposed methods. Experimental results in testing collections and performance evaluation are shown in Section 5. Finally, Section 6 concludes this paper.

2 RELATED WORK

Near-duplicate detection has been widely studied over the past several years. Previous works on duplicate and near-duplicate detection can be roughly divided into two research ares: document representation and efficiency. The first one focuses on how to represent a document with or without linguistic knowledge. The second area, which focuses on how to handle hundreds of millions of documents, has also received lots of attentions. The technique of estimating similarity among pairs of documents was presented by Broder et al. (Broder, 1997). They used *shingles*, which does not rely on any linguistic knowledge, to represent documents and Jaccard overlap to calculate the similarity. I-Match (Chowdhury et al., 2002) divided the duplicate detection into two tasks: 1) filtering the input document based on collection statistics; 2) calculating a single hash value for the remainder text. The documents with same hash value are considered as duplicates. SpotSigs was proposed in 2008 by Theobald et al. (Theobald et al., 2008), which combines stopword antecedents with short chains of adjacent content terms. Hajishirzi et al. (Hajishirzi et al., 2010) presented an adaptive near-duplicate detection method, which can achieve high accuracy across different target domains. Besides the approaches focused on Web pages or documents, Muthmann et al. (Muthmann et al., 2009) proposed their work to identify threads with near-duplicate content and to group these threads in the search results.

3 PRELIMINARIES

Although there are several different websites which provide the Q&A service, their question-answer thread structure are very similar. Usually, each thread includes a question (Title), none or several sentences used to describe the question (*Description*), a best answer, and a number of other answers. Based on the common structure of Q&A forum threads, we will use the following definition to capture near-duplicate threads:

Definition 1 *Near-Duplicate Thread – Two threads are near-duplicate with each other in Q&A forum: (1) if both of their question and answer parts are the same with each other, or (2) if their question parts are same and one of the answers contains additional information compare to another answer.*

Consider the following examples:

Example 1
Question: *When is the birthday of Jay?*
Description: The birthday of Jay.
Best Answer: January 18th, 1979

Example 2
Question: *Who can tell me what's the Jay's birthday?*
Description: Jay "male, top R&B singer", I want to know when he was born.
Best Answer: 18/1/1979

Since the question part of example 1 and example 2 have the same meaning and answer parts are also the same, they are near-duplicate threads according to our definition, although the two threads use different words and expressions in the question parts and different date formats in the answer parts.

4 OUR APPROACH

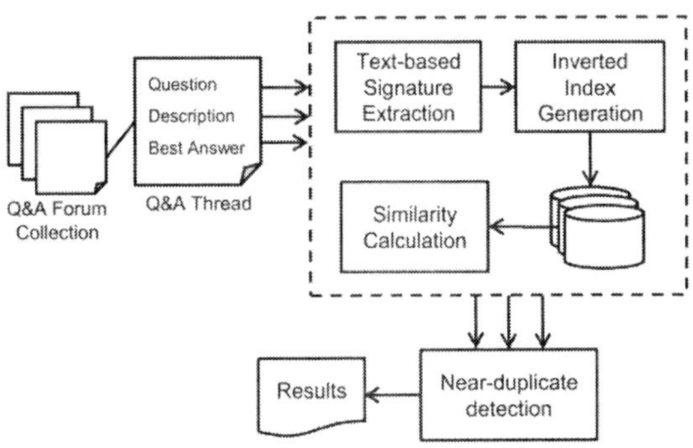

Figure 1: Process for detecting near-duplicate threads

Figure 1 shows the process for identifying near-duplicate threads in Q&A forums. The process consists of four stages:

Stage 1. Text-based Signature extraction produces signatures for each thread. Signatures for different parts are separately extracted. We only consider three parts including "Question", "Description", and "Best Answer" in this paper.

Stage 2. Inverted index generation treats signatures as terms and builds distributed inverted indexes for collections.

Stage 3. Similarity Calculation solves the pairwise similarity comparison problem with the generated distributed inverted indexes.

Stage 4. Near-duplicate detection identifies near-duplicate threads based on the calculated similarities among Q&A threads in different parts.

In Stage 1, we try to use several types of signatures extracted from different meta-information to partially overcome the problem of word-overlap limitation. The efficient pairwise similarity comparison problem is captured in Stage 2 and 3. This section describes two algorithms for solving the similarity calculation problem with two kinds of distributed inverted index: *Term-based Index* and *Doc-based Index*. These two algorithms are described in turn. Both term-based and doc-based algorithms follow the unified framework. Based on the similarities among different parts, the near-duplicate detection is done in Stage 4.

4.1 Upper Bound of Jaccard Similarity

Jaccard coefficient is widely used to measure the similarities among sets. In this work, we use it to measure the similarities among forum threads, which are represented by a group of signatures. $J(A,B) = \frac{|A \bigcap B|}{|A \bigcup B|}$ is the default Jaccard similarity defined for two sets. Theobald et al. described the bounds of it (Theobald et al., 2008), which is

$$\begin{aligned} J(A,B) &= \frac{|A \bigcap B|}{|A \bigcup B|} = \frac{|A \bigcap B|}{|A| + |B| - |A \bigcap B|} \\ &\leq \frac{\min(|A|,|B|)}{\max(|A|,|B|)} \end{aligned} \quad (1)$$

For $|A| \leq |B|$, we can get:

$$J(A,B) \leq \frac{|A|}{|B|} \quad (2)$$

With the upper bound and vector representation of threads, we observe that near-duplicated threads have the similar length. If

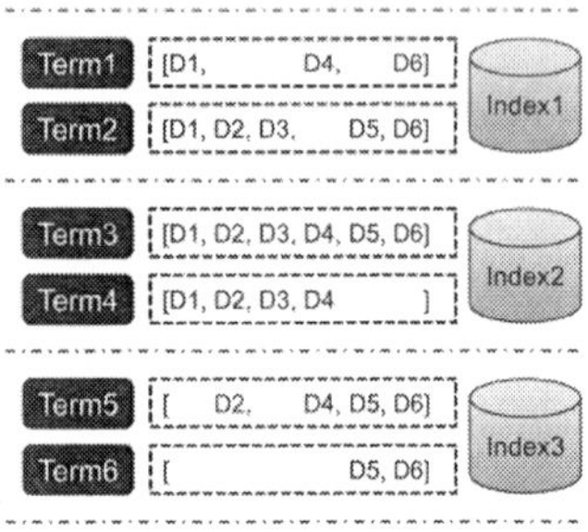

Figure 2: Example of term-based distributed index

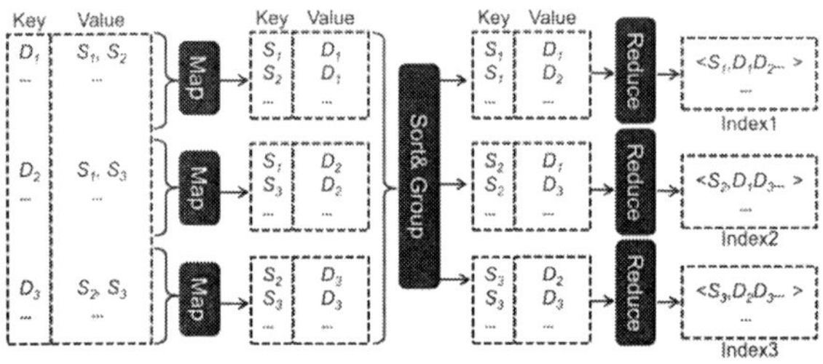

Figure 3: Data flow of term-based distributed index generation

we set the threshold to τ, thread pairs where $\frac{|A|}{|B|} \leq \tau$ can be safely removed.

Inspired by Eq.2, we further propose a more tightly upper bound of Jaccard similarity as follows:

$$J(A,B) = \frac{|A \bigcap B|}{|A \bigcup B|} = \frac{|A| - |A-B|}{|B| + |A-B|} \leq \frac{|A| - |C|}{|B| + |C|}, C \subseteq A - B \quad (3)$$

It can be easily proofed that this bound 3 is tighter than the upper bound of Eq. 2. If the set C can be detected, more calculation can be reduced with it. In this work, both of the upper bounds are used to reduce the size of intermediate data. In algorithm 1, the Eq.2 is used. While the more tightly bound Eq.3 is used in the algorithm 2.

4.2 Term-based approach

Inverted index is an index data structure storing a mapping from terms (signatures in this work) to its documents. In order to distributedly calculate the pairwise similarity, the inverted index should be split into multiple parts, which can be parallelly processed in the further steps. The term-based distributed index splits the inverted index according to the rows. Each partition of the distributed index only contains a number of terms and their corresponding posting list. Figure 2 shows an example of it. In the figure, "Index 1" contains posting lists of "Term 1" and "Term 2". Other terms are separately stored in "Index 2" and "Index 3".

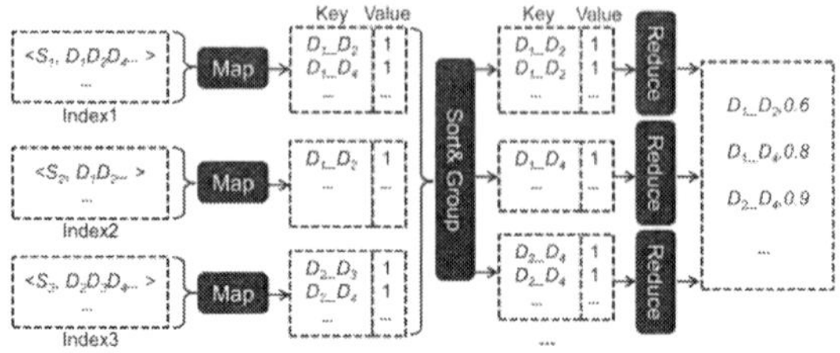

Figure 4: Data flow of similarity calculation based on term-based distributed index

Algorithm 1 Pseudo-code of term-based algorithm

MAP$(S_i, [D_1, D_2, ...])$

```
for all D_i ∈ [D_1, D_2, ...] do
    for all D_j ∈ [D_1, D_2, ...] do
        if ( |D_i| ≥ |D_j| and |D_j|/|D_i| ≥ τ )
        or ( |D_i| ≤ |D_j| and |D_i|/|D_j| ≥ τ ) then
            EMIT(⟨D_i, D_j⟩, S_i)
        end if
    end for
end for
```

REDUCE$(\langle D_i, D_j \rangle, [S_1, S_2, ...])$

```
if |D_i ∩ D_j| / |D_i ∪ D_j| ≥ τ then
    EMIT(⟨D_i, D_j⟩)
end if
```

The data flow of term-based distributed index generation using MapReduce is shown in Figure 3. Input to the distributed indexer consists of thread ids as key and extracted signatures as terms. In each mapper operation, all signatures are iteratedly processed. For each signature, a pair consisting of the signature id as key and the thread id as value is created. The mapper emits those key-value pairs as intermediate data. After grouping and sorting, thread ids which contain the same signature are grouped together. The reducer gets a part of key-value pairs (term and associate posting list) as input and emits them as a partition of the distributed index.

Based on the term-based distributed index, the data flow of near-duplicate detection algorithm is shown in Figure 4. The input of the procedure *map* is the signature id (S_i) and associated postings list ($[D_1, D_2, ...]$, where D_i represents thread id). Inside each mapper, all candidate thread pairs which fit the the Eq. 2 , the upper bound of the Jaccard similarity, are emitted to the key-value pair ($(\langle D_i, D_j \rangle, S_i)$. After grouping and sorting, all signature ids belonging to the same thread pair are brought together. With the list, Jaccard similarity can be easily calculated. The procedure *reduce* takes the thread pair and corresponding list as input and emits the Jaccard similarity (the predefined threshold τ is used to reduce the size of output). The pseudo-code of this algorithm is shown in Algorithm 1. The line 4 in the algorithm is based on the upper bound of Jaccard similarity and used to reduce the size of intermediate data.

However, in practical terms, the term-based method can not be directly used to process the collection which contains more than one million threads. Too many intermediate outputs will cause problem. In this work, we limit the maximum number of intermediate output as the approximation method, which is proposed by Lin (Lin, 2009). This approximation can improve the efficiency of the term-base algorithm, based on which the term-based method can process large collections. However the calculated similarities may not reflect the real similarities with this approximation method.

4.3 Doc-based approach

Different to the term-based distributed index, doc-based distributed index splits the inverted index according to the columns. Each partition of doc-based distributed index only contains a number of threads and their corresponding terms. Figure 6 shows an example of it. In the figure, "Index 1" contains terms which are contained in the "D_1" and "D_2"and their corresponding posting lists.

Figure 5 shows two kinds of doc-based distributed index generation data flows using MapReduce. Input to both of the distributed indexers is the same as the term-based one, which consists of thread ids as key and extracted signatures as terms. Figure 5(a) shows a standard inverted index generation procedure using MapReduce. Different with the standard one, only a partition of forum threads collection are input to the MapReduce job at each time. And the procedure is iterated over the entire collection. An alternative method is shown in Figure 5(b). The entire collection is processed with a MapReduce job. In each mapper operation, a partition of doc-based distributed index is generated and is written to the disk. No reducers are required in the job. Although the second approach is simple and no iteration is required, the size of the input collection is much smaller compare to the first one, because of the memory limitation.

Algorithm 2 Pseudo-code of doc-based algorithm

MAP($S_i, [D_1, D_2, ...]$)

for all $D_i \in InitializedIndex$ **do**
  for all $D'_i \in InputIndex$ **do**
    if ($|D_i| \geq |D'_i|$ **and** $\frac{|D'_i|}{|D_i|} \leq \tau$)
    or ($|D_i| \leq |D'_i|$ **and** $\frac{|D_i|}{|D'_i|} \leq \tau$) **then**
      continue
    end if
    $C \leftarrow \emptyset$
    $\delta \leftarrow 0$
    for all $S_{ij} \in D_i$ **do**
      if $S_{ij} \in D'_i$ **then**
        $\delta \leftarrow \delta + 1$
      else
        $C \leftarrow C \bigcup S_{ij}$
        if $\frac{|D_i|-|C|}{|D'_i|+|C|} \leq \tau$ **then**
          continue
        end if
      end if
    end for
    $sim(D_i, D'_i) \leftarrow \frac{\delta}{|D_i|+|D'_i|-\delta}$
    EMIT($\langle D_i, D'_i \rangle, sim(D_i, D'_i)$)
  end for
end for

REDUCE($\langle D_i, D'_i \rangle, sim(D_i, D'_i)$)

EMIT($\langle D_i, D'_i \rangle$)

The data flow of similarity calculation algorithm based on the doc-based distributed

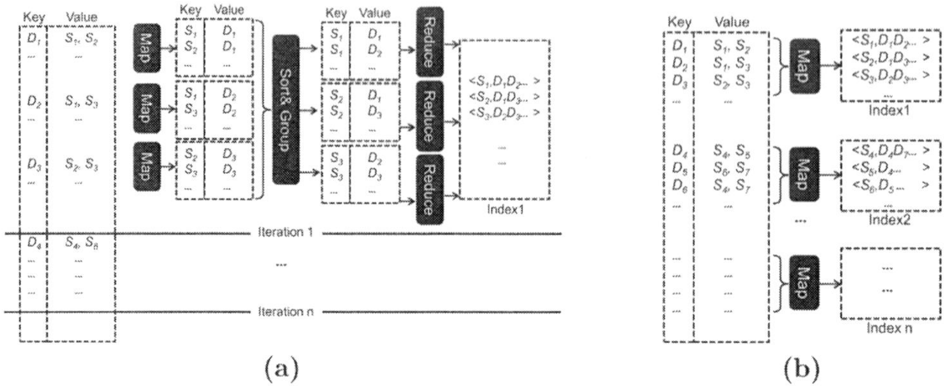

Figure 5: Data flow of doc-based distributed index generation

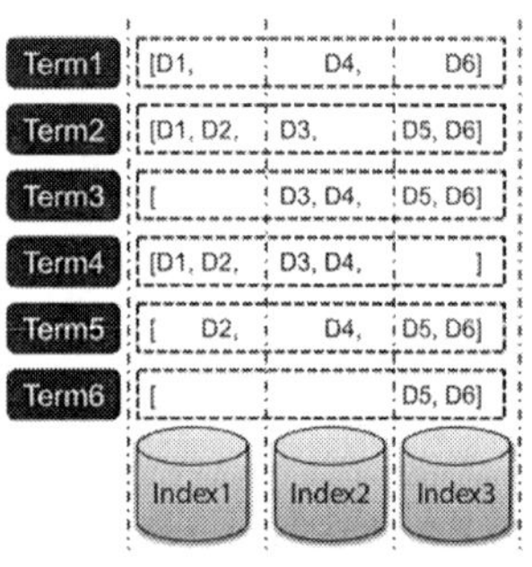

Figure 6: Example of doc-based distributed index

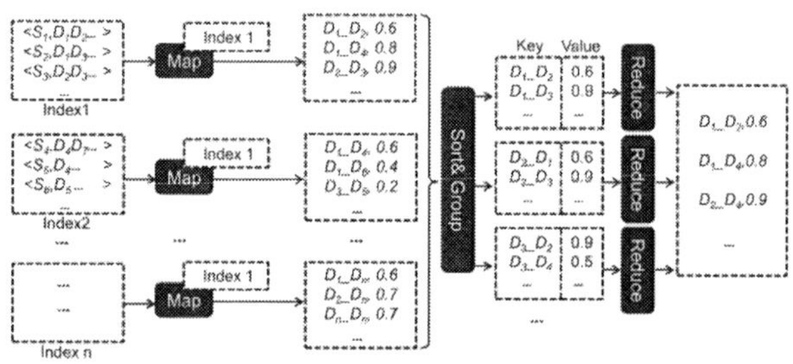

Figure 7: Data flow of one iteration of the similarity calculation based on doc-based distributed index

index is shown in Figure 7. The whole procedure should be iterated until all partitions of the distributed index have been processed. At the each iteration, all mappers are initialized with a same partition of distributed index (E.g. "Index 1" in the figure). The input of the procedure *map* is the signature id (S_i) and associated postings list ($[D_1, D_2, ...]$, where D_i represents thread id). Different mappers will get different partitions of the index as input. Inside each mapper, a inverted-index based algorithm is used to calculate the similarities between the initialized index and the input index. The pseudo-code of this algorithm is shown in Algorithm 2.

4.4 Near-Duplicate Detection

Based on the definition of near-duplicate thread, the final stage, near-duplicate detection, tries to combine the similarities calculated through the previous steps and other information extracted from threads to determine whether threads are near-duplicate or not. Obviously, most of the popular machine learning methods (e.g. Support Vector Machines, Maximum Entropy, AdaBoost, and so on) can be used to solve the problem with the calculated similarities and extracted information as feature sets. However, for simplification, in this paper we use linear combination of different parts' similarities and a predefined threshold τ to do that. If the similarities $S(T_i, T_j)$ calculated through the Eq. 4 are bigger than τ, those Q&A pairs are emitted as near-duplicates.

$$S(T_i, T_j) = \theta_t S_T(T_i, T_j) + \theta_d S_D(T_i, T_j) + \theta_a S_A(T_i, T_j),$$
$$\text{where } \theta_t + \theta_d + \theta_a = 1, \textit{and } \theta_t, \theta_d, \theta_a \geq 0 \qquad (4)$$

S_T,S_D, and S_A respectively represent similarities calculated through different parts. θ_t, θ_d, and θ_a represent the weights of similarities between different parts, and are roughly tuned based on a small number of manually labeled corpus.

Table 1: Summarization of F_1 scores of different signatures in different parts

Signature	Question	Description	Answer
2-Shingles	59.33%	**99.54%**	90.74%
3-Shingles	**60.29%**	**99.54%**	**95.05%**
4-Shingles	58.33%	**99.54%**	91.58%
Winnowing($k = 3, w = 3$)	52.06%	97.24%	85.30%
Winnowing($k = 5, w = 3$)	52.62%	97.16%	87.69%
I-Match([0.10, 0.90])	53.59%	95.31%	44.16%
I-Match([0.20, 0.80])	51.82%	93.95%	44.95%
SpotSigs(# Antecedent=50)	20.77%	13.70%	74.56%
SpotSigs(# Antecedent=100)	34.06%	18.75%	75.54%

5 EXPERIMENTS

In this section, we detail experimental evaluations of the proposed method on both effectiveness and efficiency. We crawled a portion of the Baidu Zhidao, resulting in a local archive of about 28.6 million questions, all of which have user-labeled "best answers". The corpus covers more than 100 categories. From this set we manually selected 2000 question-answer threads as "Gold-Standard". Four individuals were asked to label the duplications among question-answer threads. Meanwhile, the duplications between threads in different parts have also been manually judged. The average kappa statistic among them is around 73.2%, which shows good agreement.

We ran experiments on a 15-node cluster. Each node contains two Intel Xeon processor E5430 2.66GHz with four cores, 32GB RAM, and 128GB hard disk. We used an extra node for running the master daemons to manage the Hadoop job and distributed file system. Software stack of the experiments used Java 1.6 and Hadoop version 0.20.2. All the MapReduce jobs were implemented in Java for Hadoop framework. HDFS was used to provide the distributed storage.

5.1 Comparison of Signatures

In order to compare the performance of different signatures in the Q&A domain, the "Gold-Standard" serves in the following experiments, since these near-duplicates have been manually judged by humans. Performance comparison of different signatures with various parameters in question, description, and answer parts is shown in this section.

Table 1 summarizes the best result of different signatures in question, description and answer parts (the main parameters are shown in the bracket). We observe that 3-Shingles achieve the best result in all three parts. However, the performances of 2-Shingles, 4-Shingles are comparable. I-Match and SpotSigs achieve worse result than other methods. The possible reasons are given in the previous of the section. We also observe that although all signature extraction methods are highly tunable, the results are stable with a large range of parameters' values. With all different signatures, the performance of question part is not very satisfactory. After carefully examining the results, we observe that questions with same meaning often differ significantly in syntax and language. In (Jeon et al., 2005; Muthmann et al., 2009), it is also mentioned that two threads that have the same meaning may use different wording. Most of the signatures used for near-duplicate detection can not process this kind of issue very well. We think that it is also the main reason of the low performance of I-Match. The best F_1 score of question part is only 60.29%, however, the precision can achieve 96.46%. It indicates that although not all the duplications can be detected, most of the duplications we extracted are right. For answer part, since the average length is more than 200 characters, the performance of it is satisfactory.

5.2 Performance of Near-Duplicate Detection Stage

To investigate the parameters used in the Eq.3 and the threshold τ, hill climbing algorithm is used for tuning the four parameters. We randomly selected 100 initial seeds. Table 2 shows a number of F_1 score with different parameters. The best F_1 score of the near-duplicate thread detection is 66.22% (P=94.98%, R=50.83%) in this domain with parameters $\theta_t = 0.4$, $\theta_t = 0.2$, $\theta_t = 0.4$, and $\tau = 0.5$. Based on the definition of near-duplicate threads, question parts should have the same intuition. Because of this, the final detection performance is highly impacted by the performance of question part. More natural language processing techniques would improve the detection recall. While it may also consume much more computational time.

5.3 Term-based V.S. Doc-based

To judge and compare the efficiency and scalability of doc-based and term-based distributed

Table 2: Performance of near-duplicate detection stage with different parameters

θ_t	θ_d	θ_a	τ	P	R	F_1-Score
0.2	0	0.8	0.1	10.73%	**96.90%**	19.32%
0.3	0.6	0.1	0.1	17.30%	69.01%	27.66%
0.5	0.3	0.2	0.2	24.82%	62.40%	35.51%
0.4	0.5	0.1	0.2	35.88%	54.34%	43.22%
0.7	0.1	0.2	0.3	46.49%	57.44%	51.39%
0.6	0.2	0.2	0.3	65.01%	56.82%	60.64%
0.5	0.3	0.2	0.3	77.26%	54.75%	64.09%
0.4	0.2	0.4	0.5	**94.98%**	50.82%	**66.22%**
0.4	0.3	0.3	0.4	89.93%	51.65%	65.62%
0.4	0.4	0.2	0.3	40.50%	53.31%	46.03%
0.6	0	0.4	0.5	80.24%	54.55%	64.94%

index, it is best to evaluate them in a real-world data set. Figure 8 summaries the efficiency comparison between the two distributed indexing methods. 3-Shingles method is used to extract signatures from all three parts of the input corpus. In near-duplicate detection stage, parameters is set as follows: $\theta_t = 0.4$, $\theta_t = 0.2$, $\theta_t = 0.4$, and $\tau = 0.5$. The x-axis represents the size of the corpus, the total number of processing time is represented in y-axis. The doc-based method is much efficient than the term-based method when the size of the corpus is smaller than 2 million. Because of the approximation used in the term-based method, the slope of the term-based method's curve is lower than doc-based method ones when the size of the corpus is bigger than 2 million. However, the approximation also made the impact on the number of near-duplicates extracted by term-based method to be much lower than the doc-based method.

Figure 9 shows the number of detected near-duplicate threads through term-based method versus doc-based method. The total number of threads which are near-duplicate with one or more threads is shown in the figure. We observe that there are about 0.473 million (15.78%) threads which can be found one or more near-duplications in the corpus. We observe that although the corpus we used in this experiment only contain 3 million threads, 4.25 million of near-duplicate threads pairs are

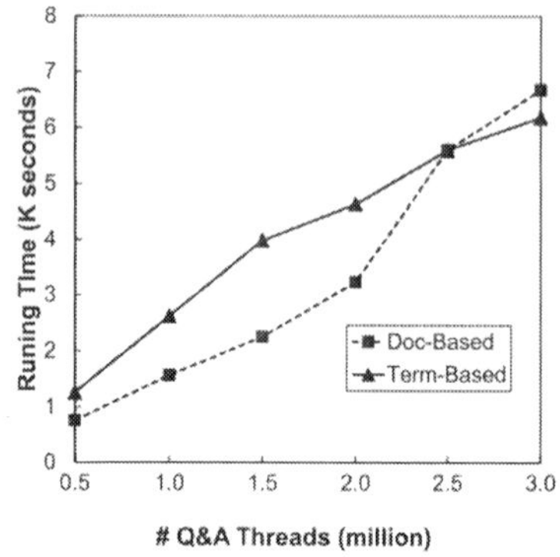

Figure 8: Term-based V.S. Doc-based in Efficiency

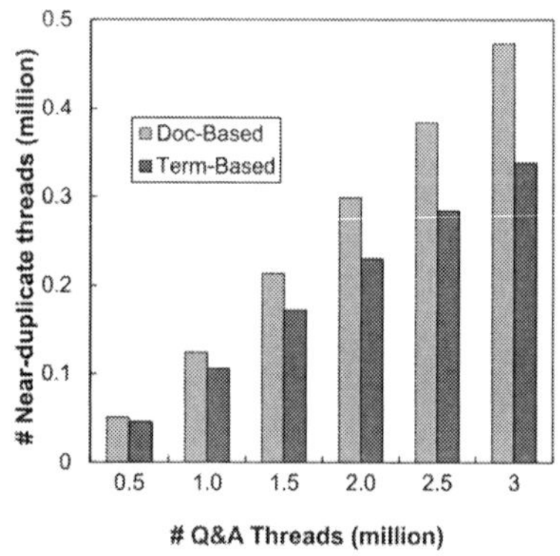

Figure 9: Number of detected Near-duplicated threads

extracted from it. It means that some popular questions have a huge number of near-duplicated ones.

6 CONCLUSION AND FUTURE WORK

In this paper we studied the problem of near-duplicate detection for Q&A forums. We proposed two distributed inverted index methods to calculate similarities in parallel using MapReduce framework. We defined the near-duplicate Q&A thread and used the evaluated signatures, parallel similarity calculating and a liner combination method to extract near-duplications. Experimental results in the real-world collection show that the proposed method can be effectively and efficiently used to detect near-duplicates. About 15.78% of Q&A threads contain more than one near-duplicates in the collection.

Acknowledgments

The author wishes to thank the anonymous reviewers for their helpful comments. This work was partially funded by 973 Program (2010CB327906), National Natural Science Foundation of China (61003092, 61073069), Shanghai Science and Technology Development Funds(10dz1500104), Doctoral Fund of Ministry of Education of China (200802460066), Shanghai Leading Academic Discipline Project (B114), and Key Projects in the National Science & Technology Pillar Program(2009BAH40B04).

References

Lada A. Adamic, Jun Zhang, Eytan Bakshy, and Mark S. Ackerman. 2008. Knowledge sharing and yahoo answers: everyone knows something. In *WWW '08: Proceeding of the 17th international conference on World Wide Web*, pages 665–674, New York, NY, USA. ACM.

Andrei Z. Broder. 1997. On the resemblance and containment of documents. In *Proceedings of SEQUENCES 1997*, page 21, Washington, DC, USA. IEEE Computer Society.

Abdur Chowdhury, Ophir Frieder, David Grossman, and Mary Catherine McCabe. 2002. Collection statistics for fast duplicate document detection. *ACM Trans. Inf. Syst.*, 20(2):171–191.

Jeffrey Dean and Sanjay Ghemawat. 2004. Mapreduce: Simplified data processing on large clusters. In *Proceedings of OSDI 2004*, San Francisco, CA, USA.

Aristides Gionis, Piotr Indyk, and Rajeev Motwani. 1999. Similarity search in high dimensions via hashing. In *VLDB '99*, pages 518–529, San Francisco, CA, USA. Morgan Kaufmann Publishers Inc.

Hannaneh Hajishirzi, Wen-tau Yih, and Aleksander Kolcz. 2010. Adaptive near-duplicate detection via similarity learning. In *SIGIR '10: Proceeding of the 33rd international ACM SIGIR conference on Research and development in information retrieval*, pages 419–426, New York, NY, USA. ACM.

Jiwoon Jeon, W. Bruce Croft, and Joon Ho Lee. 2005. Finding similar questions in large question and answer archives. In *CIKM '05: Proceedings of the 14th ACM international conference on Information and knowledge management*, pages 84–90, New York, NY, USA. ACM.

Jimmy Lin. 2009. Brute force and indexed approaches to pairwise document similarity comparisons with mapreduce. In *Proceedings of SIGIR '09*, pages 155–162, New York, NY, USA. ACM.

Klemens Muthmann, Wojciech M. Barczyński, Falk Brauer, and Alexander Löser. 2009. Near-duplicate detection for web-forums. In *IDEAS '09: Proceedings of the 2009 International Database Engineering & Applications Symposium*, pages 142–151, New York, NY, USA. ACM.

Narayanan Shivakumar and Hector Garcia-Molina. 1995. Scam: A copy detection mechanism for digital documents. In *Digitial Library*.

Narayanan Shivakumar and Hector Garcia-Molina. 1999. Finding near-replicas of documents and servers on the web. In *Proceedings of WebDB 1998*, pages 204–212, London, UK. Springer-Verlag.

Martin Theobald, Jonathan Siddharth, and Andreas Paepcke. 2008. Spotsigs: robust and efficient near duplicate detection in large web collections. In *SIGIR '08*, pages 563–570, New York, NY, USA. ACM.

Qi Zhang, Yue Zhang, Haomin Yu, and Xuanjing Huang. 2010. Efficient partial-duplicate detection based on sequence matching. In *SIGIR '10: Proceeding of the 33rd international ACM SIGIR conference on Research and development in information retrieval*, pages 675–682, New York, NY, USA. ACM.

A Graph-based Method for Entity Linking

Yuhang Guo, Wanxiang Che, Ting Liu*, Sheng Li
Research Center for Social Computing and Information Retrieval
MOE-Microsoft Key Laboratory of Natural Language Processing and Speech
School of Computer Science and Technology
Harbin Institute of Technology, China
{yhguo, car, tliu*, sli}@ir.hit.edu.cn

Abstract

In this paper, we formalize the task of finding a knowledge base entry that a given named entity mention refers to, namely entity linking, by identifying the most "important" node among the graph nodes representing the candidate entries. With the aim of ranking these entities by their "importance", we introduce three degree-based measures of graph connectivity. Experimental results on the TAC-KBP benchmark data sets show that our graph-based method performs comparably with the state-of-the-art methods. We also show that using the name phrase feature outperforms the commonly used bag-of-word feature for entity linking.

1 Introduction

Entity linking is the task of computationally mapping a named entity mention in given context to the intended entry in a referential knowledge base. Large-scale knowledge bases have been proved to be valuable for many natural language processing applications such as question answering (MacKinnon and Vechtomova, 2008), information extraction (Paşca, 2009), information retrieval (Santamaría et al., 2010), coreference resolution (Ponzetto and Strube, 2007) and word sense disambiguation (Fogarolli, 2009). And entity linking is a natural way to access these knowledge bases.

Mention ambiguity is prevalent in language use. For example, in the following two sentences

- "Mount Bromo is one of Java's most popular tourist attractions."
- "Candidates must have technical skills in JSP, ASP, Java, HTML."

the named entity mention *Java* refers to *an island in Indonesia* and *a programming language* respectively.

In this paper, we focus on the named entity disambiguation in entity linking and approach this problem from a graphical perspective. We begin by building a graph in which nodes correspond to the context around the target mention and the candidate entries from the knowledge base, whereas directed edges represent the reference dependency between nodes. Then we calculate the "importance" score for each candidate node and assign the most "important" candidate to the target mention. Here we compare three degree-based measures of graph connectivity that assess the node importance. Through experiments performed on benchmark data sets, we show that the graph-based method achieves comparable performance to the state-of-the-art in the entity linking task. The result also indicates that to build linkage between nodes, name phrase (i.e. n-gram of name words) performs better than the traditional bag-of-word feature. Our contributions are threefold: introducing an entity linking method under the graph-based framework, a novel in-degree graph connectivity measure for entity disambiguation, and an empirical comparison of the bag-of-word and the name phrase feature.

This paper is organized as follows. Section 2 gives a brief overview of the related work. Section 3 introduces the Wikipedia encyclopedia and our graph-based method. Section 4 describes each components of our entity linking system, especially the disambiguation algorithm. Experimental settings, results and analysis are presented in

*Corresponding author

Section 5. The last section offers some concluding remarks.

2 Related Work

Linking name mentions to knowledge base entries has attracted more and more attentions in these years. As an open available resource, Wikipedia is a natural choice of knowledge source for its large scale and good quality. Early work mainly focused on the usage of the structure information in Wikipedia. Bunescu and Pasca (2006) trained a taxonomy kernel on Wikipedia data to disambiguate named entities in open domain. Cucerzan (2007) integrated Wikipedia's category information in their vector space model for named entity disambiguation. Mihalcea and Csomai (2007) extracted sentences from Wikipedia, regarding the linking information as sense annotation, and used supervised machine learning models to train a classifier for disambiguation. Similarly, Milne and Witten (2008) adopted a learning approach for the disambiguation in Wikipedia. Their method is to balance the prior probability of a sense with its relatedness to the surrounding context.

Recently, an Entity Linking task in the Knowledge Base Population (KBP) track evaluation (McNamee and Dang, 2009) provided a benchmark data set. The first KBP track was held at the Text Analysis Conference (TAC)[1], aiming to explore information about entities for Question Answering and Information Extraction. The knowledge base in the evaluation data is also based on Wikipedia. Many information retrieval based models have been proposed on this data set. For example, Dredze et al. (2010) presented a maximum margin approach to rank the candidates. They combined rich features including Wikipedia structure and entity's popularity. Zheng et al. (2010) proposed learning to rank models for the entity linking problem and obtained high accuracy.

One of the most important component of entity linking is to compute the relatedness between entities. Some of the previous works use vector space model and calculate the cosine similarity over the bag-of-word feature vectors (Mihalcea and Csomai, 2007) or the category feature vectors (Cucerzan, 2007). Others take into account citation overlap of the relevant Wikipedia entry (Milne and Witten, 2008; Kulkarni et al., 2009; Radford et al., 2010), which implies the co-occurrence of the entities. These methods work when significant overlap can be observed between the entities or their features. For example, the co-occurrent frequency of *Java (programming language)* and *HTML* is higher than *Java (island)* and *HTML* in the Wikipedia articles. Hence the *Java* probably means the programming language rather than the island when its context contains *HTML*. However, entities like *human* and *homo* are seldom cited in the same article. Although they are highly related. In fact, their relatedness can be easily captured through their mutual citations. In this paper, we compute the entity relatedness by using the direct citation in the Wikipedia.

Graph-based approaches are proved useful in the research of word sense disambiguation. Sinha and Mihalcea (2007) compared several measures of word semantic similarity and algorithms for graph centrality for word sense disambiguation. They found that the performances of their graph-based algorithms are competitive to the unsupervised state-of-the-art ones. Navigli and Lapata (2009) investigated several graph connectivity measures for word sense disambiguation. They found the best measures are degree and PageRank (Brin and Page, 1998). In this paper, we approach entity linking by leveraging graph-based methods.

3 Graph-based Entity Linking

As defined in the TAC-KBP track, the input of the entity linking task includes:

- a Knowledge Base $KB \subseteq \mathcal{E}$, where $KB = \{e_i | 1 \le i \le n\}$, e_i is the ith entity in *KB* and $\mathcal{E}$ is the set of all entities around the world, and
- a query that consists of a mention string $m \in \mathcal{L}$ and the background document $D \in \mathbb{D}$ it appears in, where $\mathcal{L}$ is a lexicon which is composed of words and phrases, and $\mathbb{D}$ is a collection of documents.

The output is

- the entity e_i that m refers to in the context of D, where $e_i \in KB$, and
- `NIL` if such an entity is absent from the *KB*.

We formalize the task as a function:

$$\textsc{Link}(m, D) = \begin{cases} e_i & \text{if } 1 \le i \le n \\ \texttt{NIL} & \text{otherwise} \end{cases}$$

[1]http://www.nist.gov/tac

where $e_i = \textsc{Entity}(m, D)$ and

$$\textsc{Entity} : \mathcal{L} \times \mathbb{D} \rightarrow \mathcal{E}$$

is the function to find the corresponding entity for a query.

In our experiments we use Wikipedia as the knowledge base. In the following, we first briefly introduce the structure of Wikipedia. Next we describe our entity linking method. Note that although we use the Wikipedia in the experiments, our method is not limited to this knowledge source.

3.1 Wikipedia

Wikipedia is an online encyclopedia written by volunteers around the world. Its English version contains more than 3,400,000 articles [2]. Each article in the Wikipedia consists of a unique title and a main body which includes descriptions of the concerned entity. Articles are usually titled by the formal name of the entities, which sometimes are suffixed with a discriminative string on condition that another entity also share the same name. In the latter situation, the namesakes will be listed in a **Disambiguation Page**[3]. As an example, consider two entities of the same name *Java*, "the most populous island in Indonesia,", and "an object-oriented high-level programming language." In the page of *Java (disambiguation)*, the corresponding titles are represented as:

1. *Java (island)*,
2. *Java (programming language)*.

The main body of an article consists of descriptive words for the entity. In this text, many related entities are mentioned and some of the entities' titles are further wrapped with brackets to link to the corresponding articles with the aim of facilitating the access to those articles. For instance, in the following fragment of the article *Java (programming language)*,

> "Sun relicensed most of its Java technologies under the [[GNU General Public License]].[4]"

[2]Throughout our experiment, we will use the English version of Wikipedia snapshotted in January, 2010.

[3]See: http://en.wikipedia.org/wiki/Wikipedia:Disambiguation for detail

[4]In our experiment the main body text we use is the source of the article, which is encoded in the wiki markup language. See: http://en.wikipedia.org/wiki/Wiki_markup

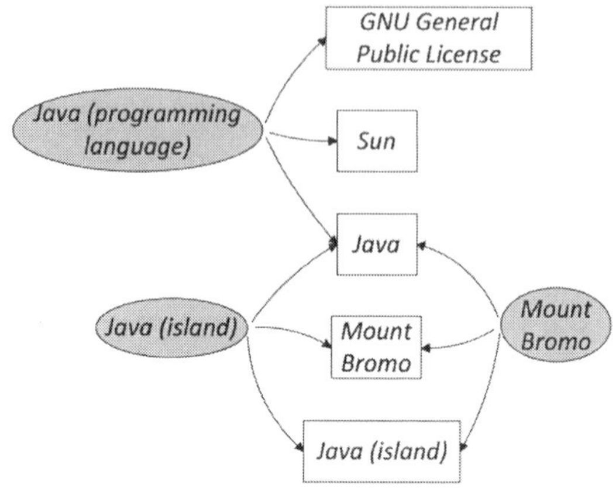

Figure 1: An example of the Wikipedia graph.

The entities: *Sun*, *Java*, and *GNU General Public License* are mentioned, where the square brackets "[[]]" will generate a cross reference link to the article of *GNU General Public License*.

We can view the Wikipedia as a graph with two types of nodes: the article nodes and the name nodes. A directed edge from an article node to a name node represents that the name appears in the article.

Figure 1 shows a partition of the Wikipedia graph. In this graph, the dark gray ellipse nodes correspond to articles which we tag with their titles and the white square nodes correspond to name strings. *Sun*, *Java*, and *GNU General Public License* are mentioned in the article of *Java (programming language)*, and hence we draw directed edges from the article to them.

3.2 The Disambiguation Method

In this paper, we approach to the entity linking task in two stages. The first stage is to find the candidate entities to the target name string. And the second stage is to estimate the "importance" of each candidate according to the context of the mention and select the most "important" one. Here we focus on the second stage. The steps of our candidate extraction will be described in section 4. In this section, we will introduce a disambiguation method based on out-degree and in-degree measures of graph connectivity .

We build a graph $G = (V, E)$ corresponding to the context where the target name appears in. For the out-degree connectivity measure, the node set in the graph consists of the names that are mentioned in the context and the articles of the corre-

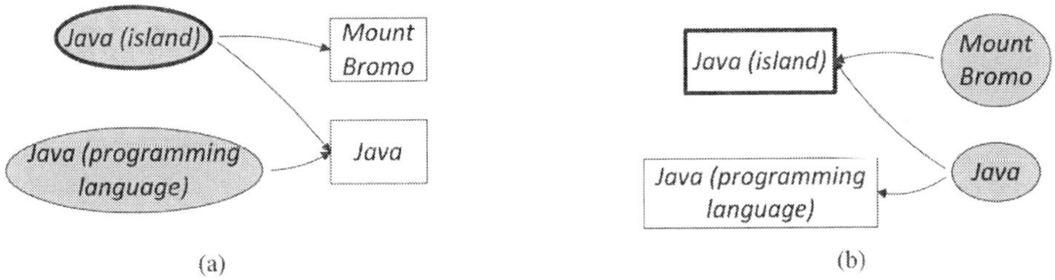

Figure 2: An example of the graph-based named entity disambiguation method.

sponding candidates (i.e. context: name nodes and candidate: article nodes). There exists a directed edge from an article node to a name node when the name is mentioned in the article. The article node of the highest out-degree is considered as the most "important" one in this graph and the corresponding entity to this article node is then selected for the queried mention. For the in-degree measure, the node set consists of the names of the candidate entities and the articles of the context entities that mentioned in the context (i.e. context: article nodes and candidate: name nodes). There is an edge that linked to a candidate name node when a context article contains that name. This time name node with the highest in-degree is considered most "important" and we assign the corresponding entity of this name node to the queried mention.

Here we give a simplified example. Consider of a context fragment:

> "Mount Bromo is one of Java's most popular tourist attractions."

and candidates of a query name *Java*:

1. *Java (island)*,

2. *Java (programming language)*.

The graphs for the out-degree and the in-degree measures are illustrated in Figure 2. In Figure 2(a) we can see the article nodes are *Java (island)* and *Java (programming language)*, and the name nodes are *Mount Bromo*[5] and *Java*. The node of *Java (island)* has 2 outer links which is higher than any other nodes and therefore *Java (island)* is assigned to the query *Java*. In Figure 2(b) *Java (island)* will also be selected because its in-degree is the highest.

[5]Anchor text *Bromo* appears in the Wikipedia page of *Java (island)*. In the source of the article, we can find the target *Mount Bromo*

Formally, the above method can be represented as to find the node:

$$u^* = \arg\max_u imp(u). \quad (1)$$

For the out-degree measure,

$$imp(u) = deg_{out}(u) = |(u, v) \in E : v \in V|.$$

And for the in-degree measure,

$$imp(u) = deg_{in}(u) = |(v, u) \in E : v \in V|.$$

We can combine the out-degree and in-degree measures and get:

$$imp(u) = (1-\lambda)ndeg_{out}(u) + \lambda ndeg_{in}(u), \quad (2)$$

where

$$ndeg_{out}(u) = \frac{deg_{out}(u)}{\sum_{u \in V} deg_{out}(u)}$$

and

$$ndeg_{in}(u) = \frac{deg_{in}(u)}{\sum_{u \in V} deg_{in}(u)}$$

are normalized degree scores. In our experiment, when there are two tied candidates, we choose a random one.

4 An Entity Linking System

In this section, we will introduce an entity linking system. This system includes 2 components: candidate selection and disambiguation, in which the disambiguation part is based on the graphical method we described in section 3.2.

4.1 Candidate Selection

As described in (Dredze et al., 2010), usually an entity has three kinds of name variations, including acronyms (e.g. *American Broadcasting Company* vs. *ABC*), aliases (e.g. *Robert Gates* vs. *Bob Gates*), and alternate spellings (e.g. *Air Macau* vs. *Air Macao*) etc.

1) For an acronym, we try to find its full form in the context through the following rules:

- If the acronym is bracketed, we extract the name phrase immediately before the capitalized letter nearby (e.g. "... *The Mexican Football Federation (FMF) on Monday* ...").
- If the acronym is followed by a bracket, we extract the phrase in the bracket (e.g. "... *From the PRC (People's Republic of China) we get much benefit.* ...").
- Or else, we just find the phrase in the context with the same capitalized letter as the acronym (e.g. "... *he told the Australian Broadcasting Corporation.* ..." vs. *ABC*).

When the full form of the acronym is found, we substitute the target mention string with its full form.

2) The Wikipedia provides the most common alias names for entities through the **Redirect Pages**[6], which maps an alias to the corresponding article titled with the formal name. By this mechanism we can access the candidate with the formal name from an alias name (e.g. *Bob Gates* $\rightarrow$ *Robert Gates*), or find several candidates listed in a disambiguation page (e.g. *Gates* $\rightarrow$ *Gates (disambiguation)*).

3) However, name variations which are not included in the Wikipedia's redirect pages (e.g. *Air Macao*) could not be found by the above function. We invoke web search engines to find the most relevant term of the name string in the Wikipedia using the "within a site" search function. We construct and submit a search query like "*Air Macao site:en.wikipedia.org*" and extract the first returned entity (i.e. *Air Macau*) as a candidate.

4.2 Disambiguation

To build a graph for the disambiguation, we need to extract names from the context of the query (either as the name node or the article node). We use a segmentation technique which is inspired from a Chinese word segmentation algorithm, the forward maximum matching algorithm (Guo, 1997) on the context to find all the names which are included in the Wikipedia title list (i.e. all the name phrases in our Wikipedia graph are the Wikipedia article titles). This algorithm prefers to find the longest names that match with the string. Here we refer the context name as neighboring name and the corresponding entity as neighboring entity of the target name string.

For the out-degree measure (as described in Section 3.2), we search for each neighboring name in the article of each candidate. If there is a match, we draw a directed edge from the candidate node to the neighboring name node. This procedure can be represented as Algorithm 1, where C_a is the article node set of the candidate entities, N_n is the node set of the neighboring names, and $Article(a)$ is the main body text of an article node a.

Algorithm 1 Out-degree measure based graph construction

Require: C_a and N_n
Ensure: Graph $G = (V, E)$

$V := C_a \cup N_n$
$E := \emptyset$
for all $c \in C_a$ **do**
  for all $n \in N_n$ **do**
    if $n \in Article(c)$ **then**
      $E := E \cup (c, n)$
    end if
  end for
end for
return (V, E)

Similarly, for the in-degree measure we build the graph in Algorithm 2, where C_n is the name node set of the candidate entities and N_a is the article node set of the neighboring entities.

Algorithm 2 In-degree measure based graph construction

Require: C_n and N_a
Ensure: Graph $G = (V, E)$

$V := C_n \cup N_a$
$E := \emptyset$
for all $c \in C_n$ **do**
  for all $n \in N_a$ **do**
    if $c \in Article(n)$ **then**
      $E := E \cup (n, c)$
    end if
  end for
end for
return (V, E)

For the combined measure we build both of the above graphs. And then we normalize the measures and combine them with a λ parameter (see

[6] See http://en.wikipedia.org/wiki/Wikipedia:Redirect for detailed instructions

Equation 2) for each candidate node.

When the graph is constructed, we then select the candidate node with the maximum out-degree or in-degree or the combined degree based measure. In our method, if the maximum out-degree or in-degree of the candidate nodes is zero, which means for all the candidate nodes there is no edges out or in, then the system will return `NIL` to assert the corresponding entity is not included in the knowledge base.

5 Experiment

5.1 Data set

We evaluated our disambiguation method on two benchmark data sets. Specifically, we use the entity linking data from TAC-KBP track in 2009 (McNamee and Dang, 2009) and the same track in 2010 (Ji et al., 2010).

The TAC-KBP 2009 data set includes 3,904 queries for 560 distinct entities and a track knowledge base (TKB) which contains 818,741 entities. The knowledge base were derived from a snapshot of English Wikipedia in October, 2008. Each query is comprised of a target name mention and a context document where the name occurs. These documents are mainly newswire documents. Over a half (2229) of the queries could not be linked to any entity in the TKB and should be tagged with `NIL`.

The TAC-KBP track in 2010 inherit the knowledge base used in the TAC-KBP 2009 and its test data set contains 2,250 queries. Similar to the track in 2009, Over a half (1230) of the entities are absent from the knowledge base. In this data set, a third (750) of the context documents are from weblog texts and the rest are from newswire documents.

In our system, we use Wikipedia as the knowledge base (KB). The result of our system can be easily mapped to the TKB entries because the KB is a superset of the TKB. In the entity linking, if the selected entity in the Wikipedia KB is not included in the TKB, our system will return `NIL`. We used the snapshot of English Wikipedia in January, 2010 and employed a Java based application programming interface (Zesch et al., 2008) to access this archive. The Wikipedia dump is open available in the web site: http://dumps.wikimedia.org/enwiki/.

TAC-KBP track	2009	2010
candidates/query	6.36	4.55
coverage	0.8083	0.7862

Table 1: Data sets and the result of the candidate selection.

# sentence	1	3	5	7	9	all
# neighbor	6	10	14	16	18	36

Table 2: The average number of the neighboring names for each query with different context window sizes in the TAC-KBP 2009 data set.

5.2 Candidate Coverage

As a result of the candidate selection (see Section 4.1), we obtained 6.36 candidates for each query on average from TAC-KBP track 2009 and 4.55 from TAC-KBP track 2010. In order to isolate the impact of the disambiguation method, we evaluated the coverage of the candidate set, which is the percentage of the intended queries that fall into the candidate set. Formally,

$$coverage = \frac{\sum_{q \in Q} |\{e_q \in C_q \cap \mathit{TKB}\}|}{\sum_{q \in Q} |\{e_q \in \mathit{TKB}\}|},$$

where Q is the set of the queries, e_q is the corresponding entity for the query q, C_q is the candidate entity set of q, and *TKB* is the track knowledge base, which is a set of entities here. In Table 1, we show the result of the candidate selection for the two data sets.

5.3 Entity Linking

We segment the context document into word or name phrase fragments and filter out stop words (e.g. *about*, *have*, *the*, etc.). In order to evaluate our graph-based method in different scales, we select nodes of neighboring entities from these fragments in several context window sizes around the target mention name: the sentence where the target name appears in, plus the immediately adjacent sentence before and after the sentence containing the target name, and plus the adjacent two sentences before and after, etc. From Table 2 we can see that in the data set of TAC-KBP 2009, the average number of the neighbor nodes per query we extracted increases as the context range increases.

Figure 3 shows the micro-averaged accuracies of our graph-based method on the TAC-KBP 2009

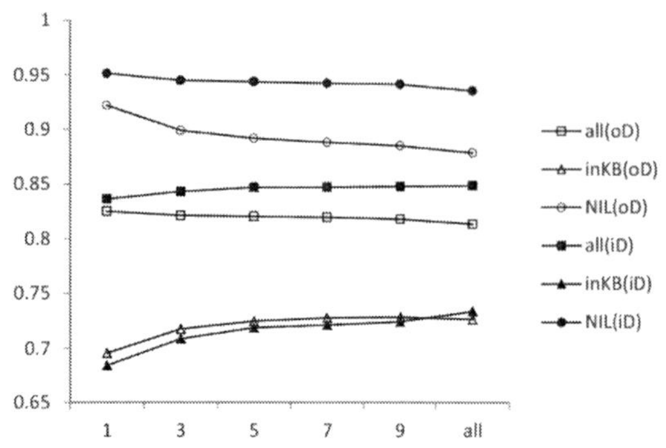

Figure 3: Accuracies for the out-degree based algorithm (oD) and the in-degree based algorithm (iD) on TAC-KBP 2009 data with different number of sentences around the target name mention as context.

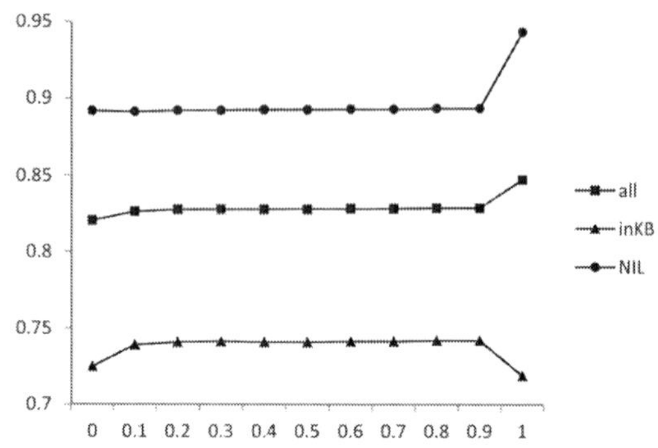

Figure 4: Accuracies for the combined measure with the λ parameter.

data set. Our evaluation metric includes the accuracy of all queries (all), the accuracy of the queries that are in KB (inKB), and the accuracy of identifying the out-of-KB entities (NIL). The horizontal axis is the number of the sentences around the target mention name (i.e. context window size), where "all" means that all the sentences in the document are included. From this figure, we can see that the inKB accuracies of the out-degree measure and the in-degree measure increase and portray a similar trend as more neighbor nodes imported. On the contrary, the NIL accuracies decrease and the overall accuracies have no obvious changes. The accuracies of the two measures for the inKB queries are very close, but for the NIL queries the in-degree measure outperforms the out-degree significantly (z test with p=0.01). This results in that for all queries the accuracies of the in-degree measure (i.e. all(iD)) are higher than the out-degree measure (i.e. all(oD)) in all the context ranges. We find that among the candidate nodes for each query, more than 2 nodes have non-zero out-degree on average, whereas less than 0.5 node has non-zero in-degree, which means that the in-degree measure returns more NIL entities, resulting in higher precision on NIL queries in this data set.

We combine the out-degree measure and the in-degree measure through Equation 2. The system performance with the λ parameter is illustrated in Figure 4. Here we set the context window size as 5. Note that when $\lambda = 0$ or $\lambda = 1$, the method reduces to the pure out-degree measure or in-degree based measure. In Figure 4 we can see that for the non-trivial combination (i.e. $\lambda \neq 0$ and 1) the accuracies have no obvious changes with the λ parameter. The NIL accuracies of the combined method are nearly the same as the out-degree ones and significantly lower than the in-degree measure. For the inKB queries, the combined method performs better than the other two methods. For all queries, the accuracy of the combined method is lower than the in-degree but higher than the out-degree ones. The reason for the higher accuracy of the in-degree measure than the combined measure is that in the combined measure the candidates of zero score are fewer than that in the in-degree measure even if λ is near to 1. So that the accuracy for NIL queries of the combined measure is lower than the in-degree measure.

In Table 3 we show the results of our graph based method on TAC-KBP 2009 and TAC-KBP 2010 data set. A number of the state-of-the-art system results are compared. According to our experiment on TAC-KBP 2009 data set, here we set the context window size as 1 for the out-degree measure (oD), as "all" for the in-degree measure (iD) and as 5 for the linear combined measure (Comb.), and set $\lambda = 0.5$.

We list the results of the top 3 systems in the TAC-KBP track 2009 and 2010. Most of them used sophisticated feature or labeled data for training. On the contrary, our graph-based methods need no feature other than the named phrases. Besides, our system has few parameters to tune. Among these system results, our graph-based method with in-degree measure outperform-

	TAC-KBP 2009			TAC-KBP 2010		
Acc.	all	inKB	NIL	all	inKB	NIL
Rank 1	0.8217	0.7654	0.8641	0.8680	0.8059	0.9195
Rank 2	0.8033	0.7725	0.8264	0.8373	0.7520	0.9081
Rank 3	0.7984	0.7063	0.8677	0.8191	0.7373	0.8870
sLesk	0.8066	0.7075	0.8811	0.7938	0.7059	0.8667
oD	0.8248	0.6955	0.9219	0.8169	0.7059	0.9089
iD	0.8489	0.7337	0.9354	0.8240	0.7127	0.9163
Comb.	0.8276	0.7409	0.8928	0.8160	0.7402	0.8789

Table 3: System accuracies on TAC-KBP 2009 and 2010 data sets. Rank 1-3 are top 3 systems in the TAC-KBP track 2009 and 2010, sLesk is the simplified Lesk algorithm based system, oD and iD are the out-degree based and the in-degree based systems and Comb. is the system that combined the out-degree and in-degree measure.

s the best system in TAC-KBP 2009 significantly (z test, p=0.01) and can outperform the third rank system in TAC-KBP 2010.

Simplified Lesk algorithm (sLesk) (Lesk, 1986; Banerjee and Pedersen, 2002; Agirre and Edmonds, 2006) is a well-known disambiguation algorithm which is similar to our graph-based method with in-degree measure. This algorithm is usually used as the baseline for word sense disambiguation. The main idea of this algorithm is to find the sense, the glossary of which has the most overlap with the context of the target multi-meaning word. The difference between these two algorithms is that our method uses name phrases as the feature other than the bag-of-word feature used in sLesk. Here we set the context window size of sLesk the same as the out-degree measure. The result shows that on both data sets our method with out-degree measure outperforms the simplified Lesk algorithm by a significant margin (z test, p=0.05).

From the last three rows in Table 3 we can see that in our graph based methods, the in-degree measure performs best among the three measures for all queries. The combined measure has a higher accuracy in inKB queries. The high NIL accuracy of the in-degree measure makes it to be suitable for the task of identifying novel concepts such as knowledge base population.

6 Conclusion

In this paper, we presented a preliminary study of graph based method for entity linking. We evaluated three degree-based measures to find the most suitable entity node for the target name mention. Our experimental results on two benchmark data sets show that our simple but effective method performs comparably to the sophisticated state-of-the-art methods and the in-degree measure outperforms the other two measures.

Based on the comparison between the simplified Lesk algorithm and our out-degree based method, we also conclude that the name phrase feature is better than the common used bag-of-words.

Acknowledgments

This work was supported by National Natural Science Foundation of China (NSFC) via grant 60803093, 60975055, 61073126, 61133012 Natural Scientific Research Innovation Foundation in Harbin Institute of Technology (HIT.NSRIF.2009069), and Fundamental Research Funds for the Central Universities (HIT.KLOF.2010064).

References

Eneko Agirre and Philip Edmonds, editors. 2006. *Word Sense Disambiguation: Algorithms and Applications*, volume 33 of *Text, Speech and Language Technology*. Springer, July.

Satanjeev Banerjee and Ted Pedersen. 2002. An adapted lesk algorithm for word sense disambiguation using wordnet. In *CICLing '02: Proceedings of the Third International Conference on Computational Linguistics and Intelligent Text Processing*, pages 136–145, London, UK. Springer-Verlag.

Sergey Brin and Lawrence Page. 1998. The anatomy of a large-scale hypertextual web search engine. In *Proceedings of the seventh international conference on World Wide Web 7*, WWW7, pages 107–117, Amsterdam, The Netherlands, The Netherlands. Elsevier Science Publishers B. V.

Razvan C. Bunescu and Marius Pasca. 2006. Using encyclopedic knowledge for named entity disambiguation. In *EACL*. The Association for Computer Linguistics.

Silviu Cucerzan. 2007. Large-scale named entity disambiguation based on Wikipedia data. In *Proceedings of the 2007 Joint Conference on Empirical Methods in Natural Language Processing and Computational Natural Language Learning (EMNLP-CoNLL)*, pages 708–716, Prague, Czech Republic, June. Association for Computational Linguistics.

Mark Dredze, Paul McNamee, Delip Rao, Adam Gerber, and Tim Finin. 2010. Entity disambiguation for knowledge base population. In *Proceedings of the 23rd International Conference on Computational Linguistics (Coling 2010)*, pages 277–285, Beijing, China, August. Coling 2010 Organizing Committee.

Angela Fogarolli. 2009. Word sense disambiguation based on wikipedia link structure. *International Conference on Semantic Computing*, 0:77–82.

Jin Guo. 1997. Critical tokenization and its properties. *Comput. Linguist.*, 23:569–596, December.

Heng Ji, Ralph Grishman, Hoa Trang Dang, Kira Griffitt, and Joe Ellis. 2010. Overview of the tac 2010 knowledge base population track. In *Proceedings of the Third Text Analysis Conference (TAC2010)*.

Sayali Kulkarni, Amit Singh, Ganesh Ramakrishnan, and Soumen Chakrabarti. 2009. Collective annotation of wikipedia entities in web text. In *Proceedings of the 15th ACM SIGKDD international conference on Knowledge discovery and data mining*, KDD '09, pages 457–466, New York, NY, USA. ACM.

Michael Lesk. 1986. Automatic sense disambiguation using machine readable dictionaries: how to tell a pine cone from an ice cream cone. In *Proceedings of the 5th annual international conference on Systems documentation*, SIGDOC '86, pages 24–26, New York, NY, USA. ACM.

Ian MacKinnon and Olga Vechtomova. 2008. Improving complex interactive question answering with wikipedia anchor text. In *Proceedings of the IR research, 30th European conference on Advances in information retrieval*, ECIR'08, pages 438–445, Berlin, Heidelberg. Springer-Verlag.

P. McNamee and H.T. Dang. 2009. Overview of the tac 2009 knowledge base population track. In *Proceedings of the Second Text Analysis Conference (TAC2009)*.

Rada Mihalcea and Andras Csomai. 2007. Wikify!: linking documents to encyclopedic knowledge. In *CIKM '07: Proceedings of the sixteenth ACM conference on Conference on information and knowledge management*, pages 233–242, New York, NY, USA. ACM.

David Milne and Ian H. Witten. 2008. Learning to link with wikipedia. In *CIKM '08: Proceeding of the 17th ACM conference on Information and knowledge management*, pages 509–518, New York, NY, USA. ACM.

Roberto Navigli and Mirella Lapata. 2009. An experimental study of graph connectivity for unsupervised word sense disambiguation. *IEEE Transactions on Pattern Analysis and Machine Intelligence*, 99(1):1–1.

Marius Paşca. 2009. Outclassing Wikipedia in open-domain information extraction: Weakly-supervised acquisition of attributes over conceptual hierarchies. In *Proceedings of the 12th Conference of the European Chapter of the ACL (EACL 2009)*, pages 639–647, Athens, Greece, March. Association for Computational Linguistics.

Simone Paolo Ponzetto and Michael Strube. 2007. Knowledge derived from wikipedia for computing semantic relatedness. *J. Artif. Int. Res.*, 30:181–212, October.

Will Radford, Ben Hachey, Joel Northman, Matthew Honnibal, and James R. Curran. 2010. Document-level entity linking: Cmcrc at tac 2010. In *Proceedings of the Text Analysis Conference*, Gaithersburg, MD, USA.

Celina Santamaría, Julio Gonzalo, and Javier Artiles. 2010. Wikipedia as sense inventory to improve diversity in web search results. In *Proceedings of the 48th Annual Meeting of the Association for Computational Linguistics*, pages 1357–1366, Uppsala, Sweden, July. Association for Computational Linguistics.

Ravi Sinha and Rada Mihalcea. 2007. Unsupervised graph-based word sense disambiguation using measures of word semantic similarity. In *International Conference on Semantic Computing*, volume 0, pages 363–369, Los Alamitos, CA, USA. IEEE Computer Society. unread.

Torsten Zesch, Christof Müller, and Iryna Gurevych. 2008. Extracting lexical semantic knowledge from wikipedia and wiktionary. In *LREC*. European Language Resources Association.

Zhicheng Zheng, Fangtao Li, Minlie Huang, and Xiaoyan Zhu. 2010. Learning to link entities with knowledge base. In *Human Language Technologies: The 2010 Annual Conference of the North American Chapter of the Association for Computational Linguistics*, pages 483–491, Los Angeles, California, June. Association for Computational Linguistics.

Harvesting Related Entities with a Search Engine*

Shuqi Sun[1], Shiqi Zhao[2,1], Muyun Yang[1], Haifeng Wang[2], and Sheng Li[1]
[1]Harbin Institute of Technology, Harbin, China
{sqsun,ymy}@mtlab.hit.edu.cn, lisheng@hit.edu.cn
[2]Baidu, Beijing, China
{zhaoshiqi,wanghaifeng}@baidu.com

Abstract

This paper addresses the problem of related entity extraction and focuses on extracting related persons as a case study. The proposed method builds on a search engine. Specifically, we mine candidate related persons for a query person q using q's search results and the query logs containing q. The acquired candidates are then automatically rated and ranked using a SVM regression model that investigates multiple features. Experimental results on a set of 200 randomly sampled query persons show that the precision of the extracted top-1, 5, and 10 related persons exceeds 91%, 90%, and 84%, respectively, which significantly outperforms a state-of-the-art baseline.

1 Introduction

Facilitating efficient navigation in the knowledge space is essential to satisfying the current Web search demands. Named entities are vital building blocks of such a space, and retrieving related entities provides an efficient way of navigation. Related entity extraction refers to mining from text resources named entities with certain relationships between them, e.g. *person-affiliation* and *organization-location*. To this end, great efforts have been made recently in both academic (Banko et al., 2007; Wu and Weld, 2010) and industry (Zhu et al., 2009; Shi et al., 2010) circles.

A wide range of NLP applications could benefit from the high-quality repository of related entities. For query suggestion in Web search and e-business, given a query concerning some entity e, one can suggest entities related to e, in which users may also have interest. This could be regarded as a remarkable complement to the current techniques suggesting queries that merely contain the entity e or are similar in wording with e (Boldi et al., 2009). In online encyclopedia (e.g. Wikipedia) construction, linking together related entities can facilitate the users for effective navigation. Additionally, related entity extraction also allows us to automatically construct social networks.

In this paper, we focus on related person extraction, though our proposed techniques can be extended to other types of entities. Here, we provide a comprehensive definition of related persons, which fall into the following four categories.

- **Persons with definite relationships.** The relationships in this category can be explicitly represented with definite concepts, e.g. *parent*, *friend*, *colleague*, etc. Most previous literature focuses on such definite relationships between persons (Brin,1998; Etzioni et al.,2005; Banko et al.,2007; Zhu et al.,2009).

- **Persons related in certain events.** In the second category, the related persons interact with the query person in certain events, such as *co-starring* in the same movie or *co-authoring* in the same scientific paper.

- **Persons with similar identities** may also be of interest. In the case of query recommendation, for instance, when users query some particular type of persons, such as *actors* or *singers*, it is highly informative to recommend other similar persons of the same type.

- **Persons having other relationships** with the query person that do not fall into the three main categories above. For instance, given a person q, characters played by q (an actor) in a movie or created by q (an author) in her fiction belong to this category.

* This work was done when the first author was visiting Baidu.

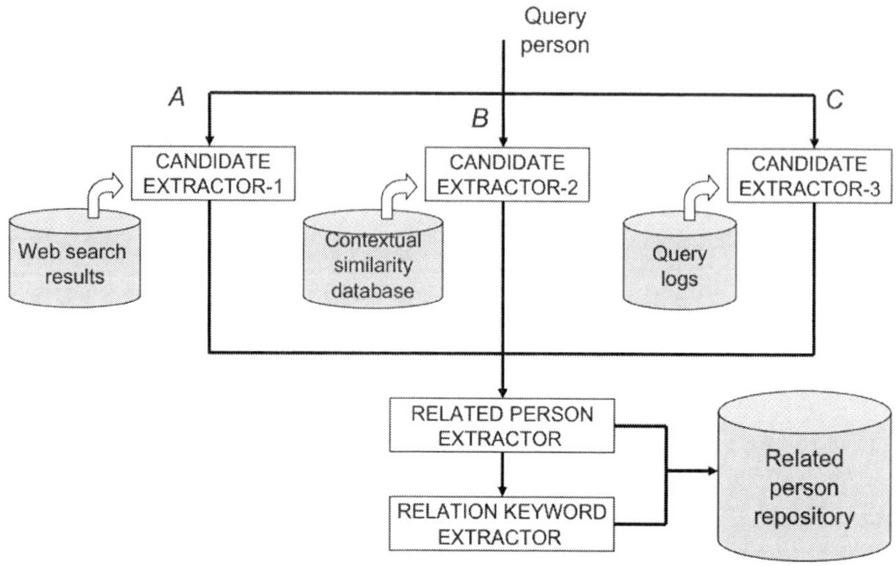

Figure 1: Overview of the proposed method.

Figure 1 illustrates the overview of our method. Our work is motivated by related entry suggestion in online encyclopedia construction and query suggestion in Web search. Thus, we are interested in finding related persons given a query person q. We employ a search engine SE to facilitate the extraction of related persons. In particular:

- We directly extract related persons from q's context in its search results returned by SE (flow A);
- Guided by distributional hypothesis (Harris, 1985), we mine q's related persons appearing in similar contexts (also collected from search results) with q (flow B);
- In addition, we exploit the query logs of SE, and extract q's related persons that co-occur with q in the same queries (flow C).

Extracting related persons aided by search engines has the following advantages. First, it can easily pinpoint web documents containing the query person, so that we can efficiently extract co-occurring persons and collect context information. Second, search results provided by search engines always contain the latest information, from which we can identify the newly emergent related persons. Third, the tremendous amount of search engines' indexed Web pages dramatically broadens the scope of the query person's context. Fourth, by exploiting search engine query logs, we can capture the related persons that the Web users are most interested in.

Using each of the three resources above, we aggregate up to 10 candidate related persons for each query person, and re-rank them with a Support Vector Machine (SVM) regression model that exploits multiple features, which finally outputs the top 10 related persons for each query person.

We evaluated our method with a set of 200 query persons randomly selected from Baidu[1] query logs, and compare it with Renlifang[2], a well known system developed for related person extraction. Experiment results show that our approach consistently outperforms Renlifang with a gap of 8%-13% in terms of averaged $Precision@K$. Specifically, 8.28% (0.915 vs. 0.845), 12.9% (0.9 vs. 0.797), and 9.73% (0.846 vs. 0.771) improvement has been achieved at rank 1, 5, and 10 respectively.

2 Related Work

Our work has its roots in both relation extraction and thesaurus construction. For relation extraction, the main approaches focus on binary relations between entities. These works use classifiers (Jiang and Zhai, 2007; Wang, 2008), extraction templates (Brin, 1998; Etzioni et al., 2005) or formulae (Agichtein and Gravano, 2000) to iden-

[1] http://www.baidu.com. Baidu is the largest commercial Chinese search engine in China.

[2] http://renlifang.msra.cn/

tify whether certain relations exist between pairs of entities. Supervised approaches view relation extraction as a classification problem, using either prior-designed feature sets (Jiang and Zhai, 2007) or kernel-based similarities (Wang, 2008) in classification. On the other hand, semi-supervised approaches avoid the heavy human labor in providing training examples by using bootstrapping techniques. For instance, DIPRE (Brin, 1998), Snowball (Agichtein and Gravano, 2000), and KNOWITALL (Etzioni et al., 2005) all adopt seed-pattern iterations to aggregate related entities.

Besides the works on traditional relation extraction, studies on open information extraction (Open IE) have emerged recently, which avoid pre-defining types of relations, and enjoy the capability of mining arbitrary types of semantic relations from both document collections (Shinyama and Sekine, 2006) and Web environment (Banko et al., 2007). Banko et al. (2007) build an Open IE system, TEXTRUNNER, that trains a Naïve Bayes classifier under the supervision of dependency rules. WOE (Wu and Weld, 2010) improves the precision and recall of TEXTRUNNER by mining clues from semi-structured texts in online encyclopedia and adopting different learning algorithms. Another descendent of TEXTRUNNER is the work of Mintz et al. (2009), which uses Freebase tuples as initial supervising information for training extractors. It is worth noting that building the learners is not mandatory. For example, Eichler et al. (2008) directly use syntactic patterns to perform Open IE.

There are also approaches that combine traditional relation extraction and Open IE together. Banko and Etzioni (2008) present H-CRF combining the two types of systems' output. StatSnowBall (Zhu et al., 2009) also performs both relation-specific extraction and Open IE. Like the technique proposed in (Banko and Etzioni, 2008), it formalizes the extraction problem as sequence labeling, but uses Markov Logic Networks (MLN) instead of Conditional Random Field (CRF).

In thesaurus construction, mainstream efforts related to our work consist of synonym / comparable entities clustering (Lin, 1998; Pantel, 2003; Wang and Cohen, 2007). Lin (1998) popularized the automatic clustering of similar words using distributional similarity. Pantel (2003) presents a more sophisticated clustering algorithm that first collects a small set of representative elements for each concept and then assigns words to their most-similar concept. Wang and Cohen (2007) alternatively investigate set expansion problem, that is, how to retrieve similar entities given a small number of seeds. With flexible matching patterns and random walk based ranking algorithm, their system outperforms Google Sets^{TM} in terms of Mean Average Precision (MAP). There are also researches forcusing on the relationship between verbs or adjectives, such as (Turney et al., 2003) and (Chklovski and Pantel, 2004).

In comparison to previous works on relation extraction, our work does not restrict itself to identifying pairs of entities whose relation is explicitly described by "infix"-like patterns, such as "Louis XVI *was born in* 1754". Alternatively, we mine related entities from context similarity and co-occurrence points of views. Moreover, through empirical studies, we find that query log is an effective data source in the extraction of related entities. On the other hand, different from synonym / comparable entities mining, our work retrieves a more extensive scope of results. In addition to entities similar or comparable to the query, we also extract those having more complicated relationships with the query, such as entities that interact with each other in certain events. Our work is also different from social network construction (Kautz et al., 1997), in that the evidences we use are also applicable to other types of named entities besides person.

3 Proposed Method

Our method for extracting related persons consists of two main stages. First, we generate candidate related persons in three fashions, based on context co-occurrence, contextual similarity, and query text co-occurrence, respectively. We collect up to 10 candidates from each source and combine them together. Second, we apply a SVM regression model to rate and rank the candidates and retain top 10 related persons for each query person. Five features are investigated, three of which are corresponding to the candidate extraction methods noted above, while the other two are based on joint-search of the query and each candidate.

3.1 Candidate Extraction

3.1.1 Context Co-occurrence

Co-occurrence is a traditional knowledge source for relation extraction (Church and Hanks, 1990).

In comparison to previous studies, we utilize a search engine to efficiently traverse the enormous Web corpus. In detail, we submit each query person q to a search engine and collect top 200 search results. We recognize co-occurred persons of q in the content of the search results within a window of limited length centered at each occurrence of q. The NER tool we used is based on a large NE table and a set of specific rules. In our experiments, the search engine we used is Baidu, and the length of the window is 5 words on both sides of the query. As a filtering step, we weed out persons that co-occur with the query for less than 3 times. Finally, we rank the co-occurred persons in descending order by their frequency, and keep up to top 10 as candidates.

3.1.2 Contextual Similarity

The distributional hypothesis presumes that words occurring in similar contexts tend to have similar meanings (Harris, 1985). In the scenario of related entity extraction, entities share similar contexts involve not only those with similar identities, e.g., two famous *pop stars*, but also those interacting with each other in the same event, e.g. two actors *co-starring* in the same movie. In this paper, we assemble in advance a large collection of persons, which contains approximately 160K person entities. For each person in the collection, we submit it to Baidu and extract its context words from its top 200 search results within the same text window (5 words on both sides) as above. The volume of the whole search result set is around 400GB In this manner, we generate a context word vector $v = (w_1, w_2, ..., w_K)$ for each person, in which w_i is a context word, and K is the total number of unique context words over the whole collection. The weight of w_i is calculated as:

$$W(w_i) = log(1 + tf_i) \cdot log(\frac{N}{qf_i}) \quad (1)$$

where tf_i denotes the frequency of w_i in the context of the given person, qf_i denotes the number of persons in the collection whose context words contain w_i, and N denotes the total number of persons in the collection. We use logarithm on the frequency tf_i to reduce the influence of the words with extremely high frequency.

We extract candidate related persons for each query person q via selecting top 10 persons from the collection according to the contextual similarity with q. We compute the similarity between two context vectors v_i and v_j using Jensen-Shannon divergence (JSD), as it performs better than some other similarity computation methods, such as cosine similarity, in our experiments. We first normalize the input vectors by the sum of their components, and calculate the JSD as described in (Lee, 1999):

$$JSD(v_i, v_j) = \frac{1}{2}[KL(v_i \| v') + KL(v_j \| v')] \quad (2)$$

where KL denotes the Kullback-Leibler divergence between two vectors, and $v' = (v_i + v_j)/2$. Note that the larger the JSD is, the less similar two vectors are. Thus the similarity between vectors v_i and v_j is computed as $1 - JSD(v_i, v_j)$.

3.1.3 Query Text Co-occurrence

Web search queries represent the demand of information from the users. Queries are known to be noisy and of little syntactic structure. However, previous works have demonstrated that there is sufficient knowledge encoded in the query texts to perform information extraction tasks (Paca, 2007), and that extracting information within query logs can better represent the users' interests (Jain and Pennacchiotti, 2010).

We found from Baidu query logs that related persons are often searched together for users' curiosity about their relationships. Such pairs of persons consist of not only those with persistent relationships like *couples* and *friends*, but also those related in certain events, especially some hot news. In this spirit, we employ a Baidu query log containing approximately 9.08 billion raw queries to extract candidate related persons. For each query person q, we traverse the query log and extract persons that co-occur with q in the same queries. We filter out the persons that co-occur with q for less than N times (N is set 20 empirically in the experiments), and sort the left ones in descending order by the frequency of co-occurrence. Top 10 candidates are kept thereby.

3.2 Features for Regression

This paper recasts related person extraction as a regression problem. Given the candidates extracted as above, we train a regression model to score all the candidates and accordingly select the top-ranking ones as related persons. In this work, we investigate five features in the regression model.

Feature 1: Context Co-occurrence Feature (CCF). We design the first feature CCF to measure the co-occurring frequency of the query person q and a candidate related person c_j:

$$CCF(q, c_j) = \frac{Cooc(q, c_j)}{K} \quad (3)$$

where $Cooc(q, c_j)$ is the co-occurring frequency of q and c_j in the top K ($K = 200$) search results of q. Intuitively, the feature CCF is the average number of co-occurrences in each kept search result. We would like to stress that the feature computation is independent of candidate extraction, i.e., the feature CCF is available for all candidates extracted in the three manners above. This is also the case with the following features.

Feature 2: Contextual Similarity Feature (CSF). The contextual similarity described above is also taken as a feature. Given the context vectors v_q and v_j for the query person q and a candidate related person c_j, we devise the CSF feature as:

$$CSF(q, c_j) = 1 - JSD(v_q, v_j) \quad (4)$$

Feature 3: Query text Co-occurrence Feature (QCF). The QCF feature is designed to measure the frequency that the query person q and a candidate c_j are searched in the same queries. Here we define the QCF feature as the conditional probability of observing c_j in queries containing q:

$$QCF(q, c_j) = p(c_j|q) = n_{qj}/n_q \quad (5)$$

where n_q denotes the number of queries in the query log containing q, and n_{qj} denotes the number of queries containing both q and c_j.

In addition to the three features above, we also design two *joint-search* based features. Our motivation is that we can gather more clues about the relationship between two persons by searching them together and analyzing the search results. In practice, for each query person q and a candidate related person c_j, we form a joint-search query "q c_j" and submit it to Baidu. Roughly speaking, Baidu will first return results containing both q and c_j and then those containing either q or c_j. We keep top 200 search results and define the following two features:

Feature 4: Joint-search Co-occurrence Feature (JCF). A pair of related persons is supposed to co-occur in the joint-search results frequently. We thus use the JCF feature to measure the co-occurrence frequency of q and c_j in their joint-search results, which is defined as:

$$JCF(q, c_j) = \frac{2 \times s(q, c_j)}{s(q) + s(c_j)} \quad (6)$$

where $s(q)$ and $s(c_j)$ denote the numbers of sentences in the joint-search results that contain q and c_j respectively. $s(q, c_j)$ denotes the number of sentences containing both q and c_j.

Feature 5: Joint-search Distance Feature (JDF). The JDF feature takes the distance between q and c_j in the joint-search results into account. The underlying consideration is that related entities might appear closer to each other than irrelated ones. In practice, we only consider the cases in which q and c_j appear within the same sentences. The JDF feature is defined as:

$$JDF(q, c_j) = exp[-\frac{1}{S}\sum_{i=1}^{S} d_i(q, c_j)] \quad (7)$$

where S is the number of sentences in which q and c_j co-occur. $d_i(q, c_j)$ is their distance, i.e., the minimum number of words between them, in the i-th sentence they occur. We use the natural exponential function to restrict the range of the feature value.

3.3 SVM Regression Model

The judgment of the relatedness between persons is not binary. Closely related persons should receive more credit than loosely related ones. Thus we choose the regression scheme, which fits a continuous scoring function towards human annotated scores. We build SVM regression models using Gaussian kernel. The SVM toolkit we use in the experiments is SVM-Light v6.01[3], with its parameters at default setting. From the perspective of real application, for each new query person, we could generate its candidates as well as the features, and score them with the learned SVM regression model. However, in our experiments, we adopt 5-fold cross validation to validate the performance of the model. We will introduce the construction of the data sets in section 4.

[3]http://svmlight.joachims.org/

4 Experiments

4.1 Experimental Settings

4.1.1 Data Preparation

To construct the data set for model training and testing, we randomly sampled 200 Chinese query persons (i.e. queries that exclusively contain a single person entity) from the query logs of Baidu. For each query person, we extracted candidate related persons from the exploited resources as described in Section 3.1. In total, we acquired 4177 candidate related persons for the 200 sampled query persons, each of which has 20.9 candidates on average. We also obtained the top 10 related persons for the 200 queries produced by Renlifang for our comparison experiments. Renlifang is developed based on approximately 1 billion Web pages and object-level retrieval techniques (Nie et al., 2005; Nie et al., 2007; Nie et al., 2007), and is one of the most famous entity search engines in Chinese. Two native Chinese speakers were asked to rate all the candidates extracted by our approach as well as Renlifang results on a 4-point scale, i.e., 0,1,2,3. Specifically, a potential related person p of a query person q gets the rating 0 if p and q are not related. Ratings ranging from 1 to 3 correspond to relationships of different strengths, namely, *mild*, *moderate*, and *strong*. The raters were given instructions and examples that explained how to decide the relation strength between two persons. Two raters each labeled half of the data and checked the labeling results for each other. Those labeling results that had not reached an agreement would be discussed together, so as to generate a final rating.

4.1.2 Evaluation Metrics

To examine the performance of the SVM regression model, we randomly split the 200 query persons, along with their candidate related persons, in to 5 equal-size subsets, and performed 5-fold cross validation. In each run, four subsets are used for training and the other one is used for testing. The candidate related persons of each test person were automatically rated by the regression model, and top 10 of them were kept for evaluation. We adopt two metrics in the evaluation. In the first one, all the system outputs with a rating larger than 0 (i.e., 1,2,3) are counted as correct related persons of the test person q, without regard to the difference in relation strength. We calculate $Prec@K$ $(1 \leq K \leq 10)$ for the list of ranked related persons L_q of q and report the average $Prec@K$ on the whole data set:

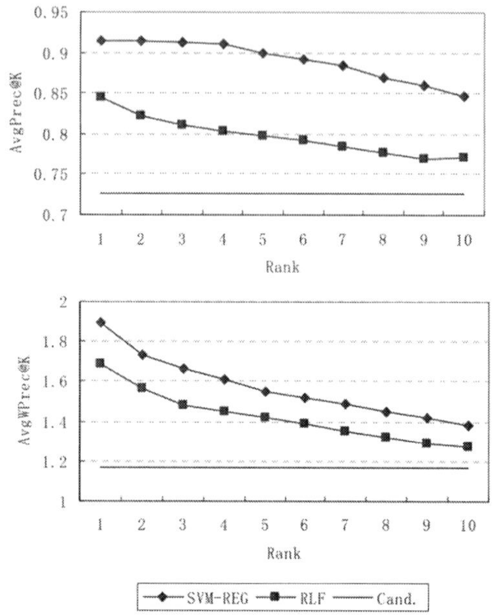

Figure 2: The comparison with Renlifang.

$$AvgPrec@K = \frac{1}{N}\sum_{N}\frac{\sum_{k=1}^{K}\mathbf{1}(R_{L_q}(k) > 0)}{K} \quad (8)$$

where $R_{L_q}(k)$ is the human-assigned rating of the k-th related person for q, $\mathbf{1}(\cdot)$ is the indicator function that yields 1 if $R_{L_q}(k) > 0$ and 0 otherwise, N is the total number of test persons that have at least one candidate related person extracted.

The second evaluation metric takes relation strength difference into consideration and assesses the system outputs based on an average weighted $Prec@K$, which is defined as:

$$AvgWPrec@K = \frac{1}{N}\sum_{N}\frac{\sum_{k=1}^{K} R_{L_q}(k)}{K} \quad (9)$$

4.2 Overall Comparison

In our experiments, we first compared the performances of our method and Renlifang according to $AvgPrec@K$ and $AvgWPrec@K$. The comparison results are depicted in Figure 2. In detail, the upper part of Figure 2 shows the performances of two systems in terms of $AvgPrec@K$. As can be seen, our method (SVM-REG) consistently outperforms Renlifang (RLF) by 8%-13%. Specifically, the performance gaps between these two

Rank	Related Entity (Translation)	Relationship
1	巩俐 (Gong Li)	Co-starring; Similar identity
2	姜文 (Jiang Wen)	Co-starring; Similar identity
3	葛优 (Ge You)	Co-starring; Similar identity
4	朱军 (Zhu Jun)	In certain event
5	吴宇森 (John Woo)	Actor-Director; In certain event
6	陈玉莲 (Idy Chan)	Love affair; In certain event
7	成龙 (Jackie Chan)	Comparative; Similar identity
8	钟楚红 (Cherie Chung)	Co-starring; Similar identity
9	刘德华 (Andy Lau)	Comparative; Similar identity
10	周星驰 (Stephen Chow)	Comparative; Similar identity

Table 1: Example of top-10 related persons for query person "周润发".

methods are 8.28% (0.915 vs. 0.845), 12.9% (0.9 vs. 0.797), and 9.73% (0.846 vs. 0.771) at rank 1, 5, and 10. The comparison of $AvgWPrec@K$ (lower part of Figure 2) shows the same trend. At all ranks from 1 to 10, our approach significantly outperforms Renlifang by 9%-12%. Table 1 shows an example of the ranked results for query person "周润发" (Chow Yun-fat, Hong Kong actor).

To verify the effectiveness of the regression features, we carried out another series of experiments, eliminating one feature each time. The results are summarized in Figure 3. We can see that eliminating features CSF and JCF both result in a sharp decrease in the performance, which demonstrates the effectiveness of these two features. The performance also decreases when we ignore the QCF feature, but the drop is not evident. The other two features, namely CCF and JDF, seem useless in regression, since the performance is even slightly enhanced when they are eliminated.

Through observing the data, we find that the CCF feature seriously suffers from sparseness problem. In our experiments, only 2051 of the 4177 candidates have non-zero CCF value. Sparseness should be the main reason that invalidates the CCF feature. As to the JDF feature, throughout our analysis, there is no obvious correspondence between person relationship and their distance in the joint-search results, which means that the JDF feature is not discriminative.

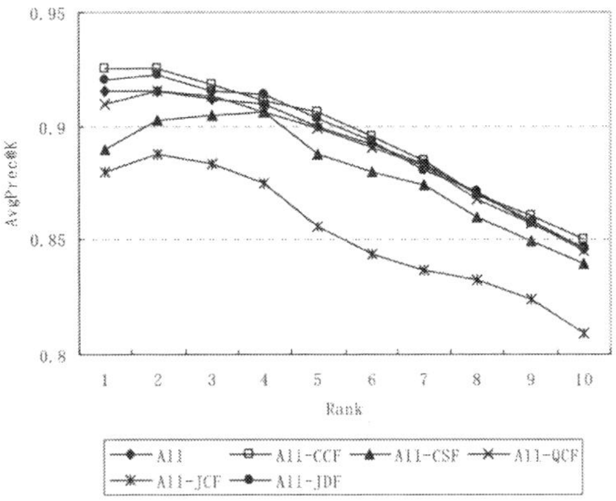

Figure 3: Evaluation of Feature Contribution.

	Con.	Sim.	Que.	All
# of test persons	196	200	178	200
# of candidates	1454	2000	1599	4177
# of cor. cands.	1229	1283	1359	3031

Table 2: Statistics of the candidate related persons extracted from three resources.

4.3 Contribution of Individual Resources

Recall that, in this work, the candidate related persons are acquired from three resources, based on contextual co-occurrence (Con.), contextual similarity (Sim.), and query text co-occurrence (Que.), respectively. It is therefore necessary to examine the contribution of each individual resource. Table 2 tabulates some statistics of candidate related persons extracted from three resources. Specifically, the first line of the table shows the number of test persons for which each resource can provide candidate related persons. The second line gives the total number of candidates yielded from each resource. The last line shows the number of correct candidates, namely, the candidates with ratings larger than 0.

We can find that each resource can provide a considerable number of candidate related persons. However, the qualities of the candidates differ a lot. In particular, the resource based on contextual similarity provides 10 candidate related persons for all the 200 test persons, but the precision is below 65%, which is the lowest. The other two

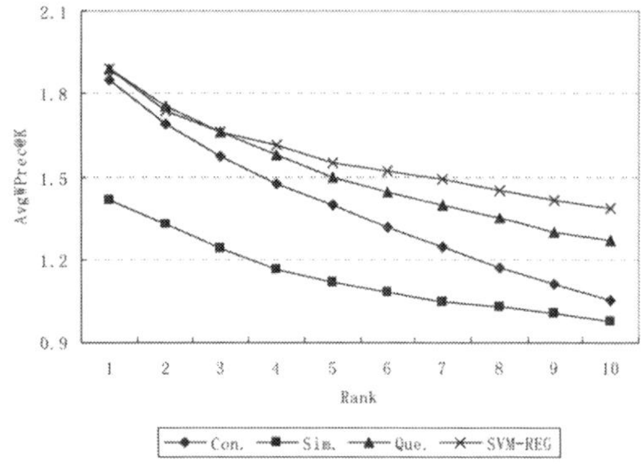

Figure 4: $AvgWPrec@K$ of ranked lists returned by individual resources and SVM regression model.

resources fail to provide candidates for some of the test persons, but their precisions are much higher, both of which exceed 84%. The last column of Table 2 shows the numbers of overall unique candidates and the correct ones. We can see that the overlap among three candidate sets is not large, indicating that all the three resources are contributing to the acquisition of candidate related persons.

To further investigate the quality, especially the relation strength, of the candidates acquired from each resource, we report $AvgWPrec@K$ of the raw ranked list of top 10 candidates from each resource in Figure 4. For the sake of comparison, we also include the $AvgWPrec@K$ results achieved by the SVM regression model using the whole feature set. The comparison results suggest that the $AvgWPrec@K$ scores of Que. and Con. come close to that of our SVM regression model when we only compare the top 3 or 4 candidates. However, the performance gap becomes larger as K grows. This is because the SVM regression model benefits from a much larger pool of candidates, from which it can select related persons of stronger relationships. We can also see that Sim. evidently underperforms Que. and Con., which is in accordance with the results reported in Table 2. In summary, the resource of Sim. assures the recall, while Que. and Con. provide relatively high-quality candidates, and the SVM regression model combines all evidences effectively.

5 Conclusions

In this paper, we make use of multiple resources provided by a search engine for acquiring related persons. The acquired candidates are rated and ranked with a SVM regression model that exploits various features. The following conclusions can be drawn from the experimental results:

First, the search engine facilitates the collection of needed resources in related entity extraction, with which we can easily collect ample web pages and query logs containing the queries of interest.

Second, the task of related entity extraction evidently benefits from the combination of multiple resources. We have observed significant improvement over the methods using each single resource.

Third, the SVM regression model is effective for rating and filtering the candidate related entities given discriminative features.

Our future work will be carried out along several directions. First of all, we will address the coreference resolution issue. The regression model will also be strengthened by employing more features. In addition, we will extend the method to other entity categories beyond person. We will also consider to extract cross-category related entities in the following work.

Acknowledgments

This work was supported by (1) China Postdoctoral Science Foundation (No.20100480100), (2) Beijing Postdoctoral Research Foundation, and (3) the Key Project of Natural Science Foundation of China (Grant No. 60736044). The authors are grateful for the anonymous reviewers for their valuable comments.

References

Eugene Agichtein and Luis Gravano. 2000. Snowball: Extracting Relations from Large Plain-text Collections. In *Proceedings of the Fifth ACM Conference on Digital Libraries*, pages 85-94.

Michele Banko, Michael J Cafarella, Stephen Soderland, Matt Broadhead and Oren Etzioni. 2007. Open Information Extraction from the Web. In *Proceedings of IJCAI*, pages 2670-2676.

Michele Banko and Oren Etzioni. 2008. The Tradeoffs Between Open and Traditional Relation Extraction. In *Proceedings of ACL-08:HLT*, pages 28-36.

Paolo Boldi, Francesco Bonchi, Carlos Castillo, Debora Donato, and Sebastiano Vigna. 2009. Query Suggestions Using Query-Flow Graphs. In *Proceedings of the 2009 Workshop on Web Search Click Data*, pages 56-63.

Sergey Brin. 1998. Extracting Patterns and Relations from the World Wide Web. In *WebDB Work-*

shop at 6th International Conference on Extending Database Technology, EDBT '98, pages 172-183.

Timothy Chklovski and Patrick Pantel. 2004. VerbOcean: Mining the Web for Fine-Grained Semantic Verb Relations. In *Proceedings of EMNLP*, pages 33-40.

Kenneth Ward Church and Patrick Hanks. 1990. Word Association Norms, Mutual Information, and Lexicography. *Computational Linguistics*, 16(1):22-29.

Kathrin Eichler, Holmer Hemsen and Günter Neumann. 2008. Unsupervised Relation Extraction from Web Documents. In *Proceedings of LREC*, pages 1674-1679.

Oren Etzioni, Michael Cafarella, Doug Downey, Ana-Maria Popescu, Tal Shaked, Stephen Soderland, Dan-iel S. Weld, and Alexander Yates. 2005. Unsupervised Named-Entity Extraction from the Web: An Experimental Study. *Artificial Intelligence*, 165(1): 91-134.

Zellig Harris. 1985. Distributional Structure. In Katz, J. J. (ed.), *The Philosophy of Linguistics*. New York: Oxford University Press. pages 26-47.

Alpa Jain and Marco Pennacchiotti. 2010. Open Entity Extraction from Web Search Query Logs. In *Proceedings of COLING*, pages 510-518.

Jing Jiang and Chengxiang Zhai. 2007. A Systematic Exploration of the Feature Space for Relation Extraction. In *Proceedings of HLT/NAACL*, pages 113-120.

Henry Kautz, Bart Selman, and Mehul Shah. 1997. Referral Web: Combining Social Networks and Collaborative Filtering. *Communications of the ACM*, 40(3): 63-65.

Lillian Lee. 1999. Measures of Distributional Similarity. In *Proceedings of ACL*, pages 25-32.

Dekang Lin. 1998. Automatic Retrieval and Clustering of Similar Words. In *Proceedings of COLING-ACL*, pages 768-774.

Mike Mintz, Steven Bills, Rion Snow, and Dan Jurafsky. 2009. Distant Supervision for Relation Extraction without Labeled Data. In *Proceedings of ACL-IJCNLP*, pages 1003-1011.

Zaiqing Nie, Yuanzhi Zhang, Ji-Rong Wen, and Wei-Ying Ma. 2005. Object-Level Ranking: Bringing Order to Web Objects. In *Proceedings of WWW*, pages 567-574.

Zaiqing Nie, Ji-Rong Wen, and Wei-Ying Ma. 2007a. Object-Level Vertical Search. In *Proceedings of the 3rd Biennial Conference on Innovative Data Systems Research*, pages 235-246.

Zaiqing Nie, Yunxiao Ma, Shuming Shi, Ji-Rong Wen, and Wei-Ying Ma. 2007b. Web Object Retrieval. In *Proceedings of WWW*, pages 81-90.

Patrick Pantel. 2003. Clustering by Committee. *Doctoral Dissertation, Department of Computing Science, University of Alberta.*

Marius Paşca. 2007. Organizing and Searching the World Wide Web of Facts - Step Two: Harnessing the Wisdom of the Crowds. In *Proceedings of WWW*, pages 101-110.

Shuming Shi, Huibin Zhang, Xiaojie Yuan, and Ji-Rong Wen. 2010. Corpus-based Semantic Class Mining: Distributional vs. Pattern-Based Approaches. In *Proceedings of COLING*, pages 993-1001.

Yusuke Shinyama and Satoshi Sekine. 2006. Preemptive Information Extraction using Unrestricted Relation Discovery. In *Proceedings of HLT/NAACL*, pages 304-311.

Peter D. Turney, Michael L. Littman, Jeffrey Bigham, and Victor Shnayder. 2003. Combining Independent Modules to Solve Multiple-choice Synonym and Analogy Problems. In *Proceedings of RANLP*, pages 482-489.

Richard C. Wang and William W. Cohen. 2007. Language-Independent Set Expansion of Named Entities using the Web. In *Proceedings of ICDM*, pages 342-350.

Mengqiu Wang. 2008. A Re-examination of Dependency Path Kernels for Relation Extraction. In *Proceedings of IJCNLP*, pages 841-846.

Fei Wu and Daniel S. Weld. 2010. Open Information Extraction using Wikipedia. In *Proceedings of ACL*, pages 118-127.

Jun Zhu, Zaiqing Nie, Xiaojiang Liu, Bo Zhang, and Ji-Rong Wen. 2009. StatSnowball: a Statistical Approach to Extracting Entity Relationships. In *Proceedings of WWW*, pages 101-110.

Acquiring Strongly-related Events using Predicate-argument Co-occurring Statistics and Case Frames

Tomohide Shibata and **Sadao Kurohashi**
Graduate School of Informatics, Kyoto University
Yoshida-honmachi, Sakyo-ku, Kyoto, 606-8501, Japan
{shibata,kuro}@i.kyoto-u.ac.jp

Abstract

This paper proposes a method for automatically acquiring strongly-related events from a large corpus using predicate-argument co-occurring statistics and case frames. The strongly-related events are acquired in the form of strongly-related two predicates with their relevant arguments. First, strongly-related events are acquired from predicate-argument co-occurring statistics. Then, the remaining argument alignment is performed by using case frames. We conducted experiments using a Web corpus consisting of 1.6G sentences. The accuracy for the extracted event pairs was 96%, and the accuracy of the argument alignment was 79%. The number of acquired event pairs was about 20 thousands.

1 Introduction

Natural language understanding requires a wide variety of knowledge. One is the relation between predicate and argument. This relation has been automatically acquired in the form of case frames from a large corpus, and is utilized for parsing (Kawahara and Kurohashi, 2006). Another is the relation between events. The relation between events includes temporal relation, causality, and so on, and is useful for coreference resolution (Bean and Riloff, 2004) and anaphora resolution (Gerber and Chai, 2010).

This paper extracts two strongly-related events. Since the meaning of a predicate itself is often ambiguous, an event is treated as predicate-argument structure, namely the predicate with their relevant arguments. An example of two strongly-related events is shown below[1]:

PA_1		PA_2
P_1: pick up nom A_1:{man, person} acc A_2:{purse}	$\Rightarrow$	P_2: bring nom A_1:{man, person} acc A_2:{purse} dat A_3:{police}

In the above example, while the argument A_1 and A_2 appear both in PA_1 and PA_2, the argument A_3 appears only in PA_2. The argument A_3 works for specifying the meaning of the predicate P_2. The method that automatically extracts sets of events from unlabeled corpora (Chambers and Jurafsky, 2008; Chambers and Jurafsky, 2009) relies on the coreference relation of arguments, and thus cannot extract an argument such as A_3.

In languages where an argument is often omitted, such as Japanese, sentences illustrating the above two events usually occur in the following form (for simplicity, the sentences are explained in English):

(1) a. A man picked up a purse and brought (ϕ) to the police.

b. (ϕ) picked up a purse and brought (ϕ) to the police.

In the sentence (1-a), the argument A_1 and A_2 are omitted in PA_2. Moreover, as an agent is specifically omitted, in the sentence (1-b), the argument A_1 in PA_1 is also omitted. The coreference-based method (Chambers and Jurafsky, 2008; Chambers and Jurafsky, 2009) is hard to be applied to such a language since an argument rarely appears in both PA_1 and PA_2.

Our proposed method extracts strongly-related events in a two-phrase construct. First, since the arguments, such as A_2 and A_3, which specify the meaning of the predicate occur in at least one predicate-argument structure, the co-occurrence measure between "pick up purse" and "bring to police" can be calculated from their occurrences. Thus, we can regard "pick up purse" and "bring to police", whose mutual information is high, as strongly-related events.

[1] nom, acc, dat denotes nominative, accusative, dative, respectively.

Next, we identify the remaining arguments by using case frames (Kawahara and Kurohashi, 2006). Case frames describe what kinds of arguments each predicate takes and what kinds of nouns can fill a case slot. With the similarity of noun distribution between an argument in a case frame assigned to PA_1 and an argument in a case frame assigned to PA_2, the remaining arguments can be aligned. In the above example, acc A_2 ("purse") in PA_1 corresponds to acc A_2 in PA_2, and nom A_1 ("man", "person") in PA_1 corresponds to nom A_1 in PA_2.

The rest of this paper is organized as follows: Section 2 reviews related work. Section 3 describes an overview of our proposed method. Section 4 describes predicate-argument structure pairs extraction. Section 5 explains co-occurrence statistics calculation between predicate-argument structures using an association rule mining, and Section 6 describes argument alignment based on case frames. Section 7 reports on our experiments.

2 Related Work

We describe manually constructed resources for event relations, and then explain automatic acquisition methods from a corpus.

2.1 Manually Constructed Resource

Singh and Williams constructed a common sense knowledge base concerned with ordinary human activity (Singh and Williams, 2003). The knowledge base consists of 80,000 propositions with 415,000 temporal and atemporal links between propositions. Espinosa and Lieberman proposed an EventNet, a toolkit for inferring temporal relations between commonsense events from the Openmind Commonsense Knowledge Base (Espinosa and Lieberman, 2005).

Recently, Regneri et al. collect natural language descriptions from volunteers over the Internet, and compute a temporal script graph (Regneri et al., 2010). They collected 493 event sequence descriptions for the 22 scenarios such as "eating in a fast-food restaurant" using the Amazon Mechanical Turk.

2.2 Automatic Acquisition of Event Relation from Corpus

There are several types in the event relation acquisition. One is the inference rule acquisition. Lin and Pantel extended the distributional hypothesis on words, and calculated two paths in a dependency tree (Lin and Pantel, 2001). If two paths tend to link the same sets of words, these are regarded as being similar. For example, they calculated the similarity between "X is the author of Y" and "X wrote Y".

Another type is the script-like knowledge acquisition. Chambers and Jurafsky learn narrative schemas, which mean coherent sequences or sets of events, from unlabeled corpora (Chambers and Jurafsky, 2008; Chambers and Jurafsky, 2009). This method extracts two events that share a participant, called a *protagonist*. Since these methods rely on the coreference analysis result, they are hard to be applied to languages where omitted arguments or zero anaphora are often utilized.

Kasch and Oates proposed a method for extracting script-like structures from collections of Web documents (Kasch and Oates, 2010). Their method is topic-driven, and the experiment was performed on only one situation *eating at a restaurant*.

There is some work for acquiring two related events taking argument sharing approach (Torisawa, 2006; Abe et al., 2008). Torisawa proposed a method for acquiring inference rules with temporal constrains by using verb-verb co-occurrences in Japanese coordinated sentences and verb-noun co-occurrences (Torisawa, 2006). Abe et al. acquire semantic relations between events by coupling the pattern-based relation-oriented approach and the anchor-based argument-oriented approach (Abe et al., 2008). Their method first acquires candidate predicate pairs by exploiting a pattern-based method, and then seeks anchors indicative of the shared argument. If anchors are found, the predicate pair is verified. These methods can acquire only event relations that have a shared argument.

3 Overview of Our Proposed Method

This paper focuses on Japanese, and extracts two strongly-related events in the form as shown in Figure 1. Figure 2 depicts an overview of our proposed method. First, pairs of predicate-argument structures (PAs) that have a dependency relation are extracted from a Web corpus. Then, from a large number of extracted pair of PAs, strongly-related two predicates with their relevant arguments are extracted. Since the meaning of a predicate itself is often ambiguous, the predicate with

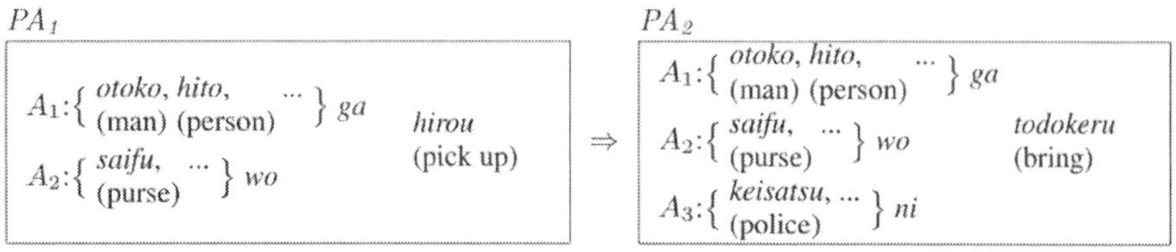

Figure 1: An example of strongly-related events. (*ga* (nom), *wo* (acc), and *ni* (dat) are Japanese case markers.)

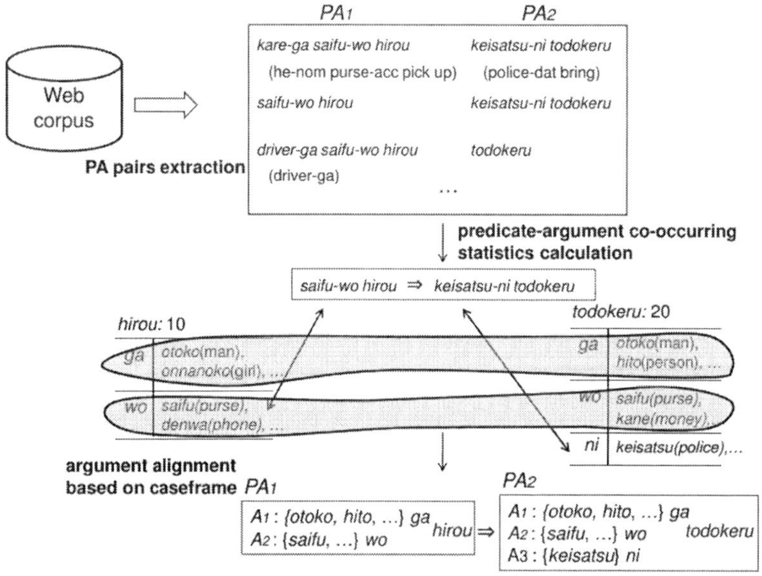

Figure 2: An overview of our proposed method.

their relevant arguments is extracted. For example, whereas the pair between "*hirou* (pick up)" and "*todokeru* (bring)" is not strongly related, the pair between "*saifu-wo* (purse-acc) *hirou*" and "*keisatsu-ni* (police-dat) *todokeru*" is. To extract the predicate with relevant arguments, the pointwise mutual information of the pair of arbitrary *PAs* is calculated, and the pair whose pointwise mutual information is high is regarded as strongly-related events. We adopt *association rule mining* (Agrawal et al., 1993) for the calculation of co-occurrence statistics between *PAs* effectively.

Next, the remaining arguments are identified using case frames. For the predicate "*hirou*(pick up)" whose argument takes "*saifu*(purse)-*wo*", what kinds of arguments are taken can be obtained from case frames. As shown in Figure 2, in the case frame 10 of "*hirou*"[2], where the argument *wo* takes "*saihu*", "*denwa*", the argument *ga* takes "*otoko*", "*onnanoko*", and so on. Similarly, in the case frame 20 of "*todokeru*", where the argument *ni* takes "*keisatsu*", the argument *ga* takes "*otoko*", "*onnanoko*", and so on, and the argument *wo* takes "*saihu*" and so on. With the similarity of noun distribution between an argument in PA_1 and one in PA_2, the remaining arguments can be aligned.

[2]Each predicate has several case frames, and case frame 10 of "*hirou*" means 10th case frame for the predicate "*hirou*".

4 Predicate-Argument Structure Pairs Extraction

Strongly-related events appear in the form where they have a dependency relation with a variety of expressions (especially clause relation) in a text. For example, the event "*saifu*(purse)-*wo hirou*(pick up)" and the event "*keisatsu*(police)-*ni todokeru*(bring)" appear as follows:

(2) *saifu-wo hiro-te* *keisatsu-ni todoke-ta*
purse-acc pick up and police-dat brought

((A man) picked up a purse, and brought it to a police.)

We extract two strongly-related events from a large number of pairs of two *PAs* that have a dependency relation. From parsing results, a pair of *PAs* that have a dependency relation is first extracted. The extracted arguments are *ga* (nom), *wo* (acc), and *ni* (dat). If a predicate has an at-

Table 1: Examples of clause relation and predicate-argument structure extraction.

clause relation	example sentence	PA_1	PA_2
sequence	*hachi-ni sa-sare **te** hareta* (bee-dat)(bitten) (swollen)	*hachi-ni sa-sareru*	*hareru*
cause	*hachi-ni sa-sareta **node** hareta*	*hachi-ni sa-sareru*	*hareru*
condition	*hachi-ni sa-sareru **to** hareta*	*hachi-ni sa-sareru*	*hareru*
purpose	*suibun-wo tobasu **tame-ni** kanetsu-suru* (water-acc) (drain) (heat)	*kanetsu-suru*	*suibun-wo tobasu*
contradiction	*hachi-ni sa-sareta **keredo** hare-nakatta*	*hachi-ni sa-sareru*	*hareru*
simultaneous	shower-*wo abi **nagara** ha-wo migaku* (take) (teeth-acc) (brush)	shower-*wo abi*	*ha-wo migaku*

Table 2: Examples of word class and its words.

class	words
77	*hachi* (bee), *ka* (mosquito), ···
105	dress, *ishou* (cloth), suit, ···
502	address, *bangou* (number), ID, ···
956	*juugeki*(shooting), *shuugeki*(attack), ···
1829	*kenshuu* (training), intern, ···
1901	*douro* (road), *kokudou* (national highway), ···

tribute, such as negation, causative, and passive, the attribute is attached to the predicate as a flag. Table 1 shows examples of clause relation and predicate-argument structure extraction.

We consider PA pairs that occur with a clause relation sequence as standard. In the case of clause relation purpose, PA pairs occur in the following form: PA_2 *tame-ni* PA_1, and so PA_1 and PA_2 are transposed. In the case of the clause relation contradiction, the negation flag in the predicate of PA_2 is reversed.

Argument Generalization

An argument is generalized to its word class so as to alleviate the problem of data sparseness. As a word class, a large-scale clustering result of verb-noun dependency relations (Kazama and Torisawa, 2008) is used. The number of word class is 2,000, and this word class covers one million noun phrases. Table 2 shows examples of a word class and its words.

In pairs of the extracted PAs, the noun n is replaced with the word class $\langle c \rangle$ for which the probability $P(c|n)$ is maximal. For example, "PA_1: *ka*(mosquito) *ni sa-sareru* (bitten), PA_2: *hareru* (swollen)" is changed to "PA_1: $\langle 77 \rangle$ *ni sa-sareru*, PA_2: *hareru*" since "*ka*" belongs to the word class $\langle 77 \rangle$. In the same way, "PA_1: *hachi*(bee) *ni sa-sareru*, PA_2: *hareru*" is changed to "PA_1: $\langle 77 \rangle$ *ni sa-sareru*, PA_2: *hareru*", and thus, these two PAs can be identical.

5 Co-occurrence Statistics Calculation between Predicate-Argument Structures

Given a lot of PAs, as extracted in Section 4, the co-occurrence statistics between PAs is calculated. Since the number of pairs of arbitrary PAs is enormous, a question that arises is how to obtain related PAs effectively. To solve this problem, we adopt *association rule mining* (Agrawal et al., 1993) for the calculation of co-occurrence statistics between PAs. The association rule mining method can efficiently seek candidate items that satisfy specific conditions.

5.1 Association Rule Mining

Association rule mining is a method for discovering significant rules in a large database (Agrawal et al., 1993). This method is originally designed to discover rules such as "a customer who buys diapers tends to buy beer" in customer transactions.

Let $I = I_1, I_2, \cdots, I_m$ be a set of binary attributes, called items. Transaction t is defined as a set of items ($t \subseteq I$), and transaction database T is defined as a set of transactions ($T = t_1, t_2, \cdots, t_n$).

A *rule* is defined as an implication of the form $X \Rightarrow Y$ where $X, Y \subseteq I$ and $X \cap Y = \phi$. This signifies "if X occurs, Y tends to occur". The set of items X and Y are called antecedent (left-hand side, lhs) and consequent (right-hand side, rhs) of the rule respectively. For every rule, the following three measures are defined:

$$support(X \Rightarrow Y) = \frac{C(X \cup Y)}{|T|} \quad (1)$$

$$confidence(X \Rightarrow Y) = \frac{support(X \Rightarrow Y)}{support(X)} \quad (2)$$

$$lift(X \Rightarrow Y) = \frac{confidence(X \Rightarrow Y)}{support(Y)}, \quad (3)$$

Table 3: Examples of transaction data. (One line represents a transaction.)

PA_1		PA_2	
arguments	predicate	arguments	predicate
saifu(purse)-*wo*	*hirou* (pick up)	*keisatsu*(police)-*ni*	*todokeru* (bring)
kare(he)-*ga*, *saifu-wo*	*hirou*	*keisatsu-ni*	*todokeru*
saifu-wo	*hirou*		*todokeru*
	hirou	*keisatsu-ni*	*todokeru*
	...		
saifu-wo	*hirou*		*tewatasu* (hand)
saifu-wo	*hirou*	*kare*(he)-*ni*	*tewatasu*
otoko(man)-*ga*, *saifu-wo*	*hirou*		*tewatasu*
	...		

where $C(X)$ represents the number of transactions containing the item X.

The *support* is defined as the fraction formed the number of transactions that contain the item-set X and the total number of transactions in the database. The *confidence* is defined as the fraction formed from the transactions that contain $X \cup Y$ and the transactions that contain X. The *lift* corresponds to pointwise mutual information between X and Y.

Apriori algorithm (Borgelt and Kruse, 2002) is one of the well-known implementations for association rule mining. This algorithm exploits the observation that no superset of an infrequent item-set can be frequent, and uses breadth-first search and a tree structure to seek candidate items.

The input for Apriori algorithm is transaction data, the minimum support, and minimum confidence, and the algorithm enumerates all rules that satisfy the specified conditions.

5.2 Apriori Algorithm Application to Co-occurrence Calculation

The Apriori algorithm is applied to the calculation of co-occurrence statistics between PAs. An item introduced in Section 5.1 corresponds to a predicate or an argument, and a transaction is obtained from a pair of PAs. Examples of transaction data are shown in Table 3.

Since the rules we want to extract are supposed to satisfy the following conditions:

- X (left-hand side) consists of a predicate of PA_1, and zero or more arguments in PA_1
- Y (right-hand side) consists of a predicate of PA_2, and zero or more arguments in PA_2,

all the rules that do not satisfy these conditions are discarded. Among those that do, the rule for which the lift is higher than *lift-min* and less than *lift-max* is adopted. It is well-known that the pointwise mutual information (which corresponds to lift) for which the frequency is low gets extremely high, and thus rules for which the lift is greater than *lift-max* are discarded.

The Apriori algorithm naturally judges which argument is relevant for each predicate pair. For example, from the transaction data shown in Table 3, the following rule is obtained:

1. *saifu-wo hirou* $\Rightarrow$ *keisatsu-ni todokeru*

2. *saifu-wo hirou* $\Rightarrow$ *tewatasu*

The first rule implies that for the predicate pair "*hirou*" and "*todokeru*", "*saifu-wo*" for the predicate in PA_1 and "*keisatsu-ni*" for the predicate in PA_2 are relevant. Similarly, the second rule implies that for the predicate pair "*hirou*" and "*tewatasu*", "*saifu-wo*" for the predicate in PA_1 is relevant.

6 Argument Alignment based on Case Frames

As mentioned in Introduction, since an argument is often omitted in the extracted predicate-argument pairs, there is usually a lack of arguments in the extracted rules as described in the previous section. In the following rule, the argument of the *wo* case in PA_1 corresponds to the *wo* case in PA_2, and the argument that includes nouns such as "*otoko*(man)", "*hito*(person)" acts for the *ga* case both in PA_1 and PA_2.

saifu-wo hirou $\Rightarrow$ *keisatsu-ni todokeru*

Such alignment between arguments can be performed by case frames. The case frames are constructed automatically by clustering similar predicate usages from a raw corpus, and thus each predicate has several case frames. Examples of the case frames are shown in Table 4. When both a

Table 4: Examples of the automatically constructed case frames.

verb	case marker	examples
hirou:1 (pick up)	*ga*	*josei*(lady), *hito*(person), ···
	wo	taxi, *kuruma*(car), ···
···		
hirou:10 (pick up)	*ga*	*otoko*(man), *onnanoko*(girl), ···
	wo	*saifu*(purse), *denwa*(phone) ···
···		
todokeru:1 (deliver)	*ga*	staff, *syokuin*(staff), ···
	wo	*jyohou*(information), news, ···
···		
todokeru:20 (bring)	*ga*	*otoko*(man), *hito*(person), ···
	wo	*saifu*(purse), *kane*(money), ···
	ni	*keisatsu*(police), ···
···		

case in cf_1 assigned to PA_1 and a case in cf_2 assigned to PA_2 have a similar distribution of examples, the case in PA_1 and the case in PA_2 can be aligned.

The best combinations of the case frame in both PA_1 and PA_2 and the best alignment of cases are determined as follows:

1. If there is an argument, select case frames corresponding to the argument, otherwise, all case frames are candidates. In the above example, while in PA_1 the case frame 10 is selected according to the argument for the case *wo* ("*saifu*"), in PA_2 the case frame 20 is selected according to the case *ni* ("*keisatsu*").
2. Choose the best case frame pairs that maximize the following score:

$$\underset{cf_1,cf_2}{\text{argmax}}\; max_{\mathbf{a}} \sum_{a\in\mathbf{a}} sim(arg_1, a(arg_1)) \quad (4)$$

   where $\mathbf{a}$ denotes the alignment of case components between PA_1 and PA_2, arg_1 denotes an argument in PA_1, $a(arg_1)$ denotes an argument in PA_2 that aligned with arg_1, and sim denotes the cosine similarity of the case components distribution between arg_1 and $a(arg_1)$. In the example, the alignment between the case *ga* of the case frame 10 in PA_1 and the case *ga* of the case frame 20 in PA_2, and the case *wo* in PA_1 and the case *wo* in PA_2 is performed.

7 Experiments

7.1 Settings

Approximately 100 million Japanese Web pages were used to extract strongly-related events. These pages include 6 billion sentences, containing 100 billion words. Owing to the presence of many duplicate pages on the Web, such as mirror pages, duplicate sentences were discarded. Thus, 1.6 billion sentences containing approximately 25 billion words were acquired. The average number of characters and words in a sentence were 28.3 and 15.6, respectively.

The Web corpus was processed using the Japanese Morphological Analyzer JUMAN[3] and the Japanese parser KNP[4], and pairs of PAs were extracted. The number of extracted PAs was approximately 400 million.

In the application of Apriori algorithm explained in Section 5.2, the minimum support, confidence was set to 1.0×10^{-7}, 1.0×10^{-3} respectively, and *lift-min*, *lift-max* was set to 10, 10,000 respectively.

The case frames were automatically constructed from the Web corpus consisting 1.6G sentences with a method proposed by (Kawahara and Kurohashi, 2006). For 31,000 predicates, case frames were constructed; the average number of case frames of a predicate was 25; the average number of case slots of a case frame was 4.7.

Table 5: Accuracy of extracted rule and the argument alignment.

	correct		incorrect
extracted rule	96(96.0%)		4(4.0%)
	correct	incorrect	
argument alignment	76(79.1%)	20(20.8%)	–

7.2 Result and Discussion

7.2.1 Evaluation of Co-occurrence Statistics Calculation

We acquired approximately 20,000 rules described in Section 5, and evaluated the acquired rules. We chose 100 rules at random, and evaluated whether each is valid. The upper part in Table 5 shows the accuracy, and we found 96 valid rules of the 100, and the accuracy was 0.96. Examples of the extracted rules and its evaluation are shown in Table 6. A major error is the parsing error. In the example (8) in Table 6, the predicate "*ataru*" in PA_1 is correctly a part of function expressions.

7.2.2 Evaluation of Argument Alignment

We chose 96 instances that were judged as correct in the previous section, and calculated the accu-

[3]http://nlp.kuee.kyoto-u.ac.jp/nl-resource/juman-e.html
[4]http://nlp.kuee.kyoto-u.ac.jp/nl-resource/knp-e.html

Table 6: Examples of acquired rules by the association rule mining method (Section 5).

	PA₁ argument	*PA₁* predicate		*PA₂* argument	*PA₂* predicate	evaluation
(1)	*teiin*(capacity) *ni*	*tassuru*(reach)	⇒		*shimekiru*(close)	correct
(2)	*daigaku*(university) *wo*	*sotsugyo*(graduate)	⇒	*kaisha*(company) *ni*	*shuusyoku*(get a job)	correct
(3)		*tentou*(fall down)	⇒		*kossetsu*(fracture)	correct
(4)		*nominate-sareru*(nominate)	⇒		*jusyo*(win an award)	correct
(5)		*tazuneru*(visit)	⇒	*hanashi*(talk) *wo*	*ukagau*(hear)	correct
(6)		*purezento*(present)	⇒		*yorokoba-reru*(delighted)	correct
(7)		*kekkon*(get married)	⇒	*kodomo*(child)-*ga*	*iru*(have)	correct
(8)	*riyou*(use)-*ni*	*ataru* (at)	⇒	*touroku*(registration)-*ga*	*hitsuyou*(necessary)	incorrect

Table 7: Examples of acquired strongly-related events. (The underlined arguments indicate the one acquired by the association rule mining method. Ids in the left column correspond to ones in Table 6.)

	PA₁ argument	*PA₁* predicate		*PA₂* argument	*PA₂* predicate	evaluation
(1)	A_1:{ *boshuu*, *moushikomi*, ... (invitation) (application) } *ga* A_2:{ *teiin* (capacity) } *ni*	*tassuru* (reach)	⇒	A_1:{ *boshuu*, *moushikomi*, ... (invitation) (application) } *wo*	*shimekiru* (close)	correct
(2)	A_1:{ *watashi*, *kodomo*, ... (I) (child) } *ga* A_2:{ *daigaku* (university) } *wo*	*sotsugyo* (graduate)	⇒	A_1:{ *watashi*, *kodomo*, ... (I) (child) } *ga* A_3:{ *kaisha* (company) } *ni*	*shuusyoku* (get a job)	correct
(3)	A_1:{ *musuko*, *kodomo*, ... (son) (child) } *ga*	*tentou* (fall down)	⇒	A_1:{ *musuko*, *kodomo*, ... (son) (child) } *ga*	*kossetsu* (fracture)	correct
(4)	A_1:{ *sakuhin*, ... (product) } *ga* A_2:{ *sho*, *yuushuu-sho*, ... (prize) (grand prix) } *ni*	*nominate-sareru* (nominate)	⇒	A_1:{ *sakuhin*, ... (product) } *ga* A_2:{ *sho*, *yuushuu-sho*, ... (prize) (grand prix) } *wo*	*jusyo* (win an award)	correct
(5)	A_1:{ *watashi*, *hito*, ... (I) (person) } *ga* A_2:{ *sensei*, *shachou*, ... (teacher) (chief) } *wo*	*tazuneru* (visit)	⇒	A_1:{ *watashi*, *hito*, ... (I) (person) } *ga* A_2:{ *sensei*, *shachou*, ... (teacher) (chief) } *ni* A_3:{ *hanashi*, ... (talk) } *wo*	*ukagau* (hear)	correct
(6)	A_1:{ *kanojo*, *josei*, ... (she) (lady) } *ga* A_2:{ *shouhin*, *hana*, ... (goods) (flower) } *wo*	*purezento* (present)	⇒	A_2:{ *shouhin*, *hana*, ... (goods) (flower) } *ga* A_1:{ *kanojo*, *josei*, ... (she) (lady) } *ni*	*yorokoba-reru* (delighted)	incorrect
(7)	A_1:{ *kodomo*, ... (child) } *ga*	*kekkon* (get married)	⇒	A_1:{ *kodomo*, ... (child) } *ga*	*iru* (have)	incorrect

racy of the argument alignment. The bottom part in Table 5 shows the accuracy, and we found 76 of 94 were valid, and the accuracy was 0.791. Table 7 shows examples of acquired strongly-related events. A major error is that the case component distribution between two cases in a *PA* is very similar. In the example (6), the alignment shown in Figure 3 is correct. This error was caused by the fact that the case *ga* and the case *ni* in PA_1 and the case *ga* and the case *ni* in PA_2 include nouns representing an agent.

Another error is that some constructed case frames do not have an indispensable case slot. In the example (7), the alignment shown in Figure 4 is correct. This error is due to the fact that the assigned case frame to PA_2 does not have the *ni* case. To cope with this problem, we are planning to increase the size of Web corpus for the case frames compilation.

7.2.3 Comparison with Coreference-based Method

Our method was compared with the coreference-based method (Chambers and Jurafsky, 2008). Since the accuracy of coreference resolution is not high (Sasano et al. report an F-score of approximately 0.75 in a newspaper domain (Sasano et al., 2007)), if a noun appears twice in a Web page, and it fills a syntactic relation of the predicate w and the predicate v, the noun is regarded as a corefer-

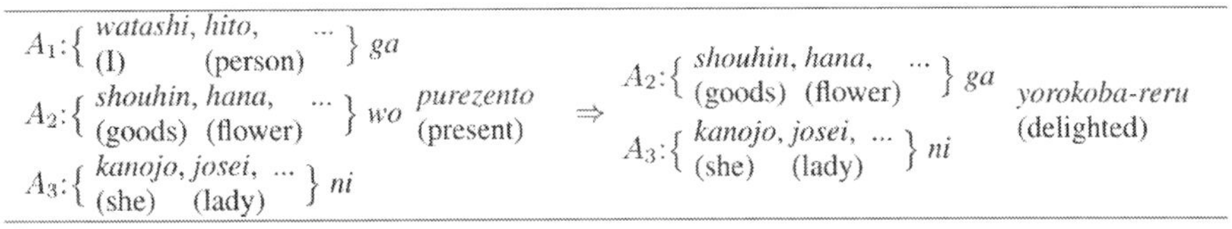

Figure 3: The correct alignment of (6) in Table 7.

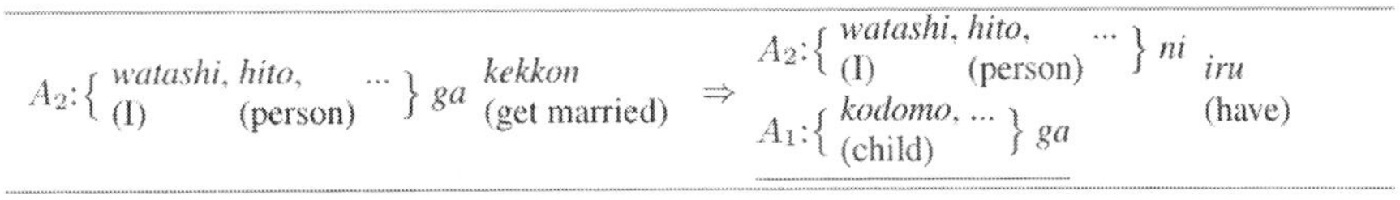

Figure 4: The correct alignment of (7) in Table 7.

Table 8: Comparison of our method with the coreference-based method. (The covered ratio is the fraction formed the number of the acquired noun by the coreference-based method and the number of the nouns in the aligned argument by our method.)

case in PA_1	case in PA_2	covered ratio	
ga	*ga*	0.163	(3,768 / 23,180)
ga	*wo*	0.282	(549 / 1,944)
ga	*ni*	0.176	(474 / 2,689)
wo	*ga*	0.272	(753 / 2,764)
wo	*wo*	0.483	(7,106 / 14,713)
wo	*ni*	0.321	(1,054 / 3,284)
ni	*ga*	0.163	(344 / 2,113)
ni	*wo*	0.338	(1,042 / 3,086)
ni	*ni*	0.282	(549 / 1,944)

ence, following the method proposed by (Abe et al., 2008). The PMI score was calculated as follows:

$$pmi(e(w,d), e(v,g)) = \log \frac{P(e(w,d), e(v,g))}{P(e(w,d))P(e(v,g))} \quad (5)$$

where $e(w,d)$ is the verb/dependency pair w and d, and d and g have the coreferent relation.

In our acquired rules, we examined whether the k-most frequent noun in the aligned argument can be covered by the coreference-based method. In our experiment, k was set to be 5. The result is shown in Table 8. The number was classified according to the case in PA_1 and in PA_2. We found that most of the nouns in aligned argument cannot be acquired by the coreference-based method. Especially, the covered ratio of the pair of the case *ga* in PA_1 and the case *ga* in PA_2 was relatively low, which often corresponds to *agent*. In Japanese, since an *agent* is often omitted, it is hard to be acquired by the coreference-based method. However, our method can identify its use by using case frames.

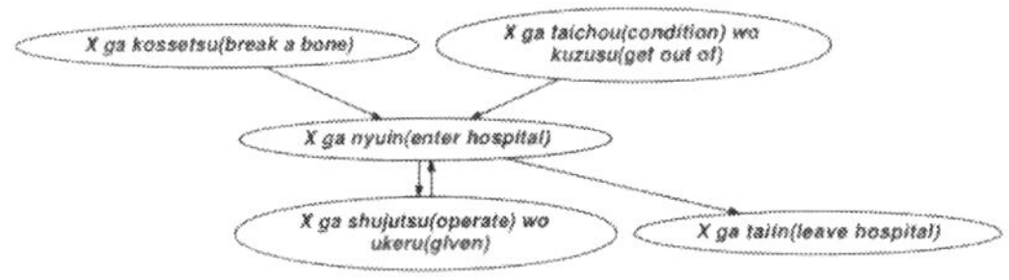

Figure 5: Network structure between events concerned with "enter hospital". (X: {*kodomo*(child), *musume*(daughter), $\cdots$})

7.2.4 Event Network Structure

Figure 5 is an example of a network structure between events concerned with "enter hospital", which is constructed from strongly-related events obtained by our proposed method. Anchor/coreference-based method cannot acquire the argument "*taichou*(condition)-*wo*" that presents in one node (which means this argument is shared by no events). In contrast, our proposed method can acquire such an argument.

8 Conclusion

This paper proposed a method for automatically acquiring strongly-related events from a large corpus using predicate-argument co-occurring statistics and case frames. Our method first extracted pairs of predicate argument structures that have a dependency relation are extracted from a Web corpus. Then, two events whose pointwise mutual information is high is extracted as strongly-related. We adopt association rule mining for the calculation of co-occurrence statistics between predicate-argument structures effectively. Then, the argument alignment was performed by using case frames.

For future work, since the acquired events include several relations such as temporal relation, causality, and means, we are planning to classify the relations automatically. Acquired event relations would then be utilized in Recognizing Textual Entailment (RTE) and Question Answer (QA) tasks.

References

Shuya Abe, Kentaro Inui, and Yuji Matsumoto. 2008. Two-phased event relation acquisition: coupling the relation-oriented and argument-oriented approaches. In *Proceedings of the 22nd International Conference on Computational Linguistics (Coling 2008)*, pages 1–8.

Rakesh Agrawal, Tomasz Imielinski, and Arun Swami. 1993. Mining association rules between sets of items in large databases. In *Proceedings of the ACM-SIGMOD 1993 International Conference on Management of Data (1993)*, pages 207–216.

David Bean and Ellen Riloff. 2004. Unsupervised learning of contextual role knowledge for coreference resolution. In *HLT-NAACL 2004: Main Proceedings*, pages 297–304.

Christian Borgelt and Rudolf Kruse. 2002. Induction of association rules: Apriori implementation. In *Proceedings of 15th Conference on Computational Statistics*, pages 395–400.

Nathanael Chambers and Dan Jurafsky. 2008. Unsupervised learning of narrative event chains. In *Proceedings of ACL-08: HLT*, pages 789–797.

Nathanael Chambers and Dan Jurafsky. 2009. Unsupervised learning of narrative schemas and their participants. In *Proceedings of the Joint Conference of the 47th Annual Meeting of the ACL and the 4th International Joint Conference on Natural Language Processing of the AFNLP*, pages 602–610.

Jose Espinosa and Henry Lieberman. 2005. EventNet: Inferring temporal relations between commonsense events. In *Proceedings of the 4th Mexican International Conference on Artificial Intelligence*, pages 61–69.

Matthew Gerber and Joyce Chai. 2010. Beyond NomBank: A study of implicit arguments for nominal predicates. In *Proceedings of the 48th Annual Meeting of the Association for Computational Linguistics*, pages 1583–1592.

Niels Kasch and Tim Oates. 2010. Mining script-like structures from the web. In *Proceedings of the NAACL HLT 2010 First International Workshop on Formalisms and Methodology for Learning by Reading*, pages 34–42.

Daisuke Kawahara and Sadao Kurohashi. 2006. A fully-lexicalized probabilistic model for japanese syntactic and case structure analysis. In *Proceedings of the HLT-NAACL2006*, pages 176–183.

Jun'ichi Kazama and Kentaro Torisawa. 2008. Inducing gazetteers for named entity recognition by large-scale clustering of dependency relations. In *Proceedings of ACL-08: HLT*, pages 407–415.

Dekang Lin and Patrick Pantel. 2001. Discovery of inference rules for question answering. *Natural Language Engineering*, 7(4):343–360.

Michaela Regneri, Alexander Koller, and Manfred Pinkal. 2010. Learning script knowledge with web experiments. In *Proceedings of the 48th Annual Meeting of the Association for Computational Linguistics*, pages 979–988.

Ryohei Sasano, Daisuke Kawahara, and Sadao Kurohashi. 2007. Improving coreference resolution using bridging reference resolution and automatically acquired synonyms. In *Discourse Anaphora and Anaphor Resolution Colloquium*, pages 125–136.

Push Singh and William Williams. 2003. Lifenet: A propositional model of ordinary human activity. In *Proceedings of Workshop on Distributed and Collaborative Knowledge Capture*.

Kentaro Torisawa. 2006. Acquiring inference rules with temporal constraints by using japanese coordinated sentences and noun-verb co-occurrences. In *Proceedings of Human Language Technology Conference/North American chapter of the Association for Computational Linguistics annual meeting (HLT-NAACL06)*, pages 57–64.

Relevance Feedback using Latent Information

Jun Harashima
Graduate School of Informatics,
Kyoto University,
Yoshida-honmachi, Sakyo-ku,
Kyoto, 606-8501, Japan
harashima@nlp.kuee.kyoto-u.ac.jp

Sadao Kurohashi
Graduate School of Informatics,
Kyoto University,
Yoshida-honmachi, Sakyo-ku,
Kyoto, 606-8501, Japan
kuro@i.kyoto-u.ac.jp

Abstract

We present a novel relevance feedback (RF) method that uses not only the surface information in texts, but also the latent information contained therein. In the proposed method, we infer the latent topic distribution in user feedback and in each document in the search results using latent Dirichlet allocation, and then we modify the search results so that documents with a similar topic distribution to that of the feedback are re-ranked higher. Evaluation results show that our method is effective for both explicit and pseudo RF, and that it has the advantage of performing well even when only a small amount of user feedback is available.

1 Introduction

The main purpose of information retrieval (IR) is to provide the user with documents that are relevant to his/her information needs. However, it is difficult to achieve this by one-off retrieval, since user queries are typically short and often ambiguous (Jansen et al., 2000).

Relevance feedback (RF) is a technique to solve this problem. The basic procedure of RF is as follows. First, a system obtains initial search results for a given query, and presents them to the user. The user then annotates some of the documents in the search results as being relevant or not, and the system modifies the search results using this feedback.

There are a variety of RF methods that depend on different retrieval models. Rocchio's algorithm (Rocchio, 1971) and the Ide dec-hi method (Ide, 1971) are well-known RF methods for the vector space model (Salton et al., 1975). In the probabilistic model (Spärck Jones et al., 2000), the weight of terms can be modified by feedback. For language modeling approaches (Ponte and Croft, 1998), Zhai and Lafferty (2001) proposed a fundamental RF method.

As described above, many methods have been proposed for RF. However, most of the previous methods use only the surface information in texts. That is, they ignore the latent information in texts, which could assist in improving IR performance. For example, they do not and cannot use the information of words for RF that do not appear in user feedback even if these words are highly probable from the latent topics of the feedback.

In this paper, we explore a novel RF method for language modeling approaches. In the proposed method, we use not only the surface information in texts, but also the latent information contained therein. More specifically, we infer the latent topic distribution in user feedback and in each document in the search results using latent Dirichlet allocation (LDA), and then we modify the search results so that documents with a similar topic distribution to that of the feedback are re-ranked higher. Evaluation results show that our method is effective for both explicit and pseudo RF, and that it has the advantage of performing well even when only a small amount of user feedback is available.

2 Language Modeling Approaches to IR

In this section, we describe the language modeling approaches to IR that form the basis of our method.

2.1 Overview

Language modeling approaches can be classified into three types: the query likelihood model

(Ponte and Croft, 1998), the document likelihood model (Lavrenko and Croft, 2001), and the Kullback-Leibler (KL) divergence retrieval model (Lafferty and Zhai, 2001). In the query likelihood model, a document language model is constructed for each document in the collection. When a query is submitted by a user, the query likelihood is computed using the document model for each document. Then, the documents in the collection are ranked according to their likelihoods. In the document likelihood model, a query language model is constructed for a given query, and this is then used to compute the document likelihood for each document in the collection. The documents are then ranked by their likelihoods. In the KL-divergence retrieval model, both a query model and a document model are constructed, and the documents in the collection are ranked according to the KL-divergence between these models.

2.2 Language Model Construction

There are several ways of constructing a query model and a document model. One method is maximum likelihood estimation (MLE). The MLE of a word w_j with respect to a text $\boldsymbol{t}$ (e.g., query, document) is computed as

$$P_{\boldsymbol{t}}^{MLE}(w_j) = \frac{tf(w_j, \boldsymbol{t})}{|\boldsymbol{t}|}, \tag{1}$$

where $tf(w_j, \boldsymbol{t})$ represents the frequency of w_j in $\boldsymbol{t}$.

Dirichlet smoothed estimation (DIR) (Zhai and Lafferty, 2004) is also a well-known construction method. The DIR of w_j with respect to $\boldsymbol{t}$ is computed as follows.

$$P_{\boldsymbol{t}}^{DIR}(w_j) = \frac{tf(w_j, \boldsymbol{t}) + \mu P_{\boldsymbol{D}_{all}}^{MLE}(w_j)}{|\boldsymbol{t}| + \mu} \tag{2}$$

where $\boldsymbol{D}_{all}$ represents a collection, and μ represents the smoothing parameter that controls the degree of confidence in the frequency in $\boldsymbol{D}_{all}$ rather than in the frequency in $\boldsymbol{t}$.

2.3 RF for Language Modeling Approaches

Zhai and Lafferty proposed a fundamental RF method for the language modeling approaches (Zhai and Lafferty, 2001). When user feedback is given, they construct a language model for the feedback. Then, a new query model is constructed by interpolating the feedback model with the original query model, which is used to obtain the initial search results. Finally, they modify the search results using the new query model. They show the effectiveness of their method through their experiments, and report that the performance is better than that of Rocchio's algorithm.

3 LDA

In this section, we explain LDA, which is employed in the proposed method.

3.1 Overview

LDA (Blei et al., 2003) is one of the most popular topic models, and is viewed as an Bayesian extension of Probabilistic Latent Semantic Indexing (PLSI) (Hofmann, 1999). In PLSI, it is assumed that each document has a unique topic proportion $\boldsymbol{\theta} = (\theta_1, \ldots, \theta_K)$. In contrast, LDA posits that $\boldsymbol{\theta}$ can take any values in the $(K-1)$ simplex, a topic proportion that means a point of the simplex is drawn from a Dirichlet distribution $\mathrm{Dir}(\boldsymbol{\alpha})$. Note that the parameter $\boldsymbol{\alpha}$ is a K-vector with components $\alpha_k > 0$. In LDA, the probability of a document $\boldsymbol{d}_i$ in the training data is calculated as follows.

$$P(\boldsymbol{d}_i|\boldsymbol{\alpha}, \boldsymbol{\beta})$$
$$= \int P(\boldsymbol{\theta}|\boldsymbol{\alpha}) \left(\prod_{j=1}^{J} \left(\sum_{k=1}^{K} P(w_j|z_k, \boldsymbol{\beta}) \, P(z_k|\boldsymbol{\theta}) \right)^{tf(w_j, \boldsymbol{d}_i)} \right) d\boldsymbol{\theta}$$

where $z_k (k = 1, \ldots, K)$ represents a topic, and $\boldsymbol{\beta} = (\boldsymbol{\beta}_1, \ldots, \boldsymbol{\beta}_K)$ represents the distributions over words for each topic z_k.

3.2 Parameter Estimation

In LDA, the expectation-maximization algorithm cannot be used to estimate the parameters, since the computation of the posterior distribution of latent variables is intractable. Thus, a wide variety of techniques using the variational method and Gibbs sampling, have been proposed to estimate the parameters (Blei et al., 2003; Griffiths and Steyvers, 2004). Here, we explain the technique using the variational method, as this is employed in the proposed method.

First, variational parameters $\boldsymbol{\gamma}_i = (\gamma_{i1}, \ldots, \gamma_{iK})$ and $\boldsymbol{\phi}_i = (\phi_{i1}, \ldots, \phi_{iJ})$ are introduced for each document $\boldsymbol{d}_i$ in the training data. Then, the optimal values of these are found by repeatedly computing the following pair of update equations:

$$\phi_{ijk} \propto \beta_{kj} \exp\Big(\Psi(\gamma_k) - \Psi\Big(\sum_{k'=1}^{K} \gamma_{k'}\Big)\Big) \quad (3)$$

$$\gamma_{ik} = \alpha_k + \sum_{j=1}^{J} \phi_{ijk}\, tf(w_j, \boldsymbol{d}_i) \quad (4)$$

where Ψ is the first derivative of the log Γ function.

Next, $\boldsymbol{\alpha}$ and $\boldsymbol{\beta}$ are updated using $\boldsymbol{\gamma}_i$ and $\boldsymbol{\phi}_i$ for each $\boldsymbol{d}_i$. In the original paper, a Newton-Raphson method was used to estimate $\boldsymbol{\alpha}$ (Blei et al., 2003). However, estimation with the Newton-Raphson method has the disadvantages that it takes a long time and each estimated α_k can be a negative value under certain circumstances. It is known that the fixed-point iteration method (Minka, 2000) is a better estimation technique, and hence, we present the update equations based on this method. The update equations for $\boldsymbol{\alpha}$ and $\boldsymbol{\beta}$ are given below.

$$\beta_{kj} \propto \sum_{i=1}^{I} \phi_{ijk}\, tf(w_j, \boldsymbol{d}_i)$$

$$\alpha_k = \frac{\sum_{i=1}^{I}\{\Psi(\alpha_k + n_{ik}) - \Psi(\alpha_k)\}}{\sum_{i=1}^{I}\{\Psi(\alpha_0 + |\boldsymbol{d}_i|) - \Psi(\alpha_0)\}}\, \alpha_k^{old}$$

where $n_{ik} = \sum_{j=1}^{J} \phi_{ijk}\, tf(w_j, \boldsymbol{d}_i)$, $\alpha_0 = \sum_{k'=1}^{K} \alpha_{k'}$, and α_k^{old} represents α_k before the update.

Finally, the updates of $\boldsymbol{\gamma}_i$ and $\boldsymbol{\phi}_i$ for each $\boldsymbol{d}_i$ and those of $\boldsymbol{\alpha}$ and $\boldsymbol{\beta}$ are iterated until convergence. Once all the parameters have been estimated, we can obtain the probability of a word w_j given a document $\boldsymbol{d}_i$ as

$$P_{\boldsymbol{d}_i}^{LDA}(w_j) \simeq \frac{\sum_{k=1}^{K} \beta_{kj}\gamma_{ik}}{\sum_{k=1}^{K} \gamma_{ik}}. \quad (5)$$

3.3 Inference of Unseen Texts

One major advantage of LDA over PLSI is that it has a natural way of inferring the probabilities of unseen texts, which are not included in the training data. When we compute the probabilities of an unseen text $\boldsymbol{t}$, the variational parameters $\boldsymbol{\gamma}_t$ and $\boldsymbol{\phi}_t$ are estimated using Eqs.(3) and (4). Then, for example, the probabilities of words given $\boldsymbol{t}$ can be obtained using Eq.(5).

3.4 LDA in IR

Certain works using LDA for IR are closely related to our work. Wei and Croft (2006) incorporate LDA into a query likelihood model, while Zhou and Wade's work can be viewed as a study that incorporates LDA into a KL-divergence retrieval model (Zhou and Wade, 2009). Such works successfully utilize the latent information in texts through LDA, and report that the latent information is effective for ad-hoc retrieval. Although there are many differences between our work and those mentioned above, one of the biggest differences is that whereas the other works explored the effectiveness of the latent information for ad-hoc retrieval, we explore it for RF beyond ad-hoc retrieval.

4 Proposed Method

4.1 Overview

An overview of the proposed method is illustrated in Figure 1. First, when a query is submitted by a user, we obtain the initial search results (Step 1). Next, for each document in the search results, we construct a hybrid language model that contains not only the surface information, but also the latent information in the document (Step 2). Then, when user feedback is given, we also construct a hybrid language model for it (Step 3). Finally, we construct a new query model by interpolating the original query model with the feedback model. We also re-rank the initial search results using this new model so that documents with a similar topic distribution to that of the user feedback are re-ranked higher (Step 4). In the following subsections, we describe each step in detail.

4.2 Acquisition of Initial Search Results

In the proposed method, we employ a KL-divergence retrieval model (Lafferty and Zhai, 2001) to obtain the initial search results for a given query. First, we construct the MLE-based query model $P_{\boldsymbol{q}}^{MLE}(\cdot)$ for a query $\boldsymbol{q}$ using Eq.(1). Then, for each document containing $\boldsymbol{q}$ in the collection, the KL-divergence between the DIR-based document model and the MLE-based query model is computed. That is, the score of a document $\boldsymbol{d}$ for a query $\boldsymbol{q}$ is defined as follows.

$$initial\_score(\boldsymbol{d}, \boldsymbol{q}) = -KL(P_{\boldsymbol{q}}^{MLE}(\cdot)||P_{\boldsymbol{d}}^{DIR}(\cdot))$$

Finally, the initial search results $\boldsymbol{D_q} = (\boldsymbol{d}_1, \ldots, \boldsymbol{d}_{|\boldsymbol{D_q}|})$ are obtained by ranking the documents according to their scores.

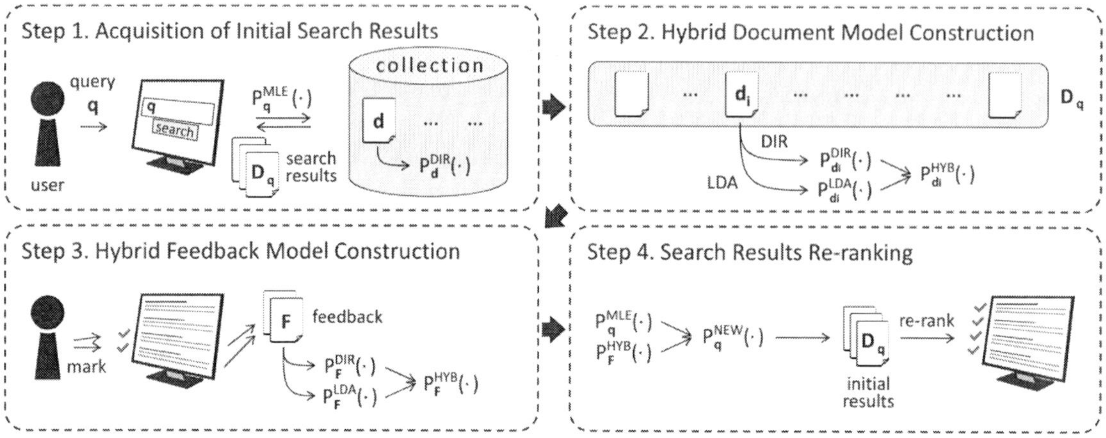

Figure 1: Overview of the proposed method.

4.3 Hybrid Document Model Construction

For each document in the search results, we construct a hybrid language model, which we call the HYB-based language model. In this model, we take into account the latent information in documents as well as the surface information.

First, an LDA-based document model that contains the latent information in the document is constructed for each document. We perform LDA on $\boldsymbol{D_q}$ to infer the topic distribution in each document $\boldsymbol{d}_i$, and estimate the parameters $\boldsymbol{\alpha}$, $\boldsymbol{\beta}$ and γ_i for each $\boldsymbol{d}_i$ as described in Section 3.2. Then, the LDA-based document model is constructed by computing the probabilities of words given $\boldsymbol{d}_i$ using Eq.(5). In this model, we can allocate high probability to words that are highly probable from the latent topic distribution of a document.

Next, for each $\boldsymbol{d}_i$, we construct an HYB-based document model $P^{HYB}_{\boldsymbol{d}_i}(\cdot)$ by interpolating the DIR-based document model with the LDA-based document model as follows.

$$P^{HYB}_{\boldsymbol{d}_i}(w_j) = (1-a)P^{DIR}_{\boldsymbol{d}_i}(w_j) + aP^{LDA}_{\boldsymbol{d}_i}(w_j)$$

where a is a parameter that controls the reliability of the LDA-based document model.

This interpolation is motivated by significant improvements reported in (Wei and Croft, 2006). They also interpolate a DIR-based document model with an LDA-based document model, and perform LDA on the whole collection to construct the LDA-based document model. However, executing LDA throughout the whole collection requires high computational cost. In the proposed method, we can avoid this problem by performing LDA only on the set of search results, which is much smaller than the whole collection.

4.4 Hybrid Feedback Model Construction

When feedback is given, we also construct an HYB-based language model for it. First, we obtain feedback $\boldsymbol{F} = (\boldsymbol{f}_1, \ldots, \boldsymbol{f}_{|\boldsymbol{F}|})$ that is relevant to the user's information need. Note that, in this study, we are not concerned with whether $\boldsymbol{F}$ is explicit, implicit, or pseudo feedback. Moreover, we have no preference of whether each $\boldsymbol{f}_i$ is a whole document or part of a document (e.g., title, snippet).

Next, we perform LDA on $\boldsymbol{F}$ to infer the topic distribution in $\boldsymbol{F}$, and construct the LDA-based feedback model $P^{LDA}_{\boldsymbol{F}}(\cdot)$. To be more precise, we generate a virtual relevant document $\boldsymbol{f}$ by combining each $\boldsymbol{f}_i$, and infer the variational parameter $\gamma_{\boldsymbol{f}}$ as described in Section 3.3. Then, $P^{LDA}_{\boldsymbol{F}}(\cdot)$ is constructed using Eq.(5).

Finally, we construct the HYB-based feedback model $P^{HYB}_{\boldsymbol{F}}(\cdot)$, which contains the surface and latent information in $\boldsymbol{F}$. $P^{HYB}_{\boldsymbol{F}}(\cdot)$ is constructed in the same manner as $P^{HYB}_{\boldsymbol{d}_i}(\cdot)$. That is,

$$P^{HYB}_{\boldsymbol{F}}(w_j) = (1-a)P^{DIR}_{\boldsymbol{F}}(w_j) + aP^{LDA}_{\boldsymbol{F}}(w_j)$$

where $P^{DIR}_{\boldsymbol{F}}(\cdot)$ is constructed using Eq.(2).

4.5 Search Results Re-ranking

We construct a new query model, which is used to re-rank the initial search results. The new query model $P^{NEW}_{\boldsymbol{q}}(\cdot)$ is constructed by interpolating the original query model $P^{MLE}_{\boldsymbol{q}}(\cdot)$ with the hybrid feedback model $P^{HYB}_{\boldsymbol{F}}(\cdot)$ as follows.

$$P^{NEW}_{\boldsymbol{q}}(w_j) = (1-b)P^{MLE}_{\boldsymbol{q}}(w_j) + bP^{HYB}_{\boldsymbol{F}}(w_j)$$

where b is a parameter that controls the reliability of the feedback model. This interpolation is based on Zhai and Lafferty's linear combination method (see Section 2.3).

Then, for each document $\boldsymbol{d}_i$ in the search results $\boldsymbol{D}_{\boldsymbol{q}}$, we compute the KL-divergence between $P^{HYB}_{\boldsymbol{d}_i}(\cdot)$ and $P^{NEW}_{\boldsymbol{q}}(\cdot)$. That is, the score of document $\boldsymbol{d}_i$ for query $\boldsymbol{q}$ and feedback $\boldsymbol{F}$ is defined as

$$\begin{aligned} &re\text{-}ranking\_score(\boldsymbol{d}_i, \boldsymbol{q}, \boldsymbol{F}) \\ &\qquad = -KL(P^{NEW}_{\boldsymbol{q}}(\cdot) || P^{HYB}_{\boldsymbol{d}_i}(\cdot)). \end{aligned}$$

Finally, we obtain the revised search results by re-ranking the documents in $\boldsymbol{D}_{\boldsymbol{q}}$ according to their re-ranking scores.

5 Experiments

5.1 Overview

We conducted three experiments to evaluate the performance of our method. An overview of each experiment is given below.

Experiment 1. Effectiveness with Respect to Explicit and Pseudo RF

We examined how well our method performed in re-ranking the initial search results using explicit and pseudo feedback. In the experiment with explicit RF, we obtained the top 100 documents with the highest initial scores as the initial search results for a given query, and re-ranked them using our method with two relevant documents that were given explicitly. In our experiments, we employed the queries and the relevant documents provided by NTCIR (see Section 5.3). Then, we compared the results with the following three (re-)ranking results.

INIT This is the ranking of the initial search results obtained based on the KL-divergence retrieval model.

WORD This is the ranking of the search results obtained after simple RF, where we used only the surface information (i.e., words) in the feedback and the documents in the search results. This ranking is equivalent to the ranking obtained using our method with $a = 0$.

REPR This is the re-ranking result obtained using Zhai and Lafferty's RF method (Zhai and Lafferty, 2001). The process of the method is almost the same to that of WORD. The main difference is that it modifies the probabilities of words in feedback by a background word distribution (see their paper). We chose their method as it is a representative RF method for language modeling approaches.

Our method can also be applied to pseudo RF. Hence, we also explored the effectiveness of our method in this regard. With pseudo RF, the top n documents in the initial search results are assumed to be relevant, and the search results are re-ranked based on this assumption. We implemented pseudo RF using our method for $n = 10$, and compared the results with the three (re-)ranking results described above.

Experiment 2. Effect of the Amount of Feedback

It is important to know how well our method performs when only a small amount of feedback is obtained, because in practice users generally cannot be bothered to provide feedback, and thus sufficient feedback is rarely obtained. We investigated how the amount of explicit feedback affected the performance of our method. To be more precise, we reduced the amount of available explicit feedback little by little, and observed the change in precision at 10 top re-ranked documents (P@10). For this experiment, we used seven different amounts of explicit feedback: 2^1, 2^0, 2^{-1}, 2^{-2}, 2^{-3}, 2^{-4}, and 2^{-5} relevant documents. Note that, for example, 2^{-1} documents means that we used half a document's worth of words in the relevant documents given as explicit feedback. In this case, half the words were sampled randomly from the feedback, and only these words were used for RF.

Experiment 3. Sensitivity to Parameters

It is also important to know how the reliability of the LDA-based document model and the HYB-based feedback model affect the performance of our method. Hence, we investigated how sensitive our method is to parameters a and b. We re-ranked the initial search results using different values for these parameters ranging from 0 to 1 in steps of 0.1, and measured how the performance of our method changed according to these values.

5.2 Configuration of Our Method

The configuration of our method is given below. For the DIR estimation, we set the smoothing parameter $\mu = 1,000$. This setting was also employed in other works (Zhai and Lafferty, 2001; Wei and Croft, 2006). The number of topics K for LDA was set to 20, since with this setting we obtained better results in the preliminary experiments, in which we performed LDA with K ranging from 10 to 100 in steps of 10. We set the initial values of $\alpha_k (k = 1, \ldots, K)$ to 1, and the initial values of $P(w_j|z_k, \boldsymbol{\beta})$ to random values. The number of iterations for the variational parameters and that for $\boldsymbol{\alpha}$ and $\boldsymbol{\beta}$ were set to 10. Additionally, we limited the size of the vocabulary in LDA, designated as J in Section 3, to $1,000$. We selected $1,000$ words based on their importance to the search results. Note that the importance of a word w_j to the search results $\boldsymbol{D_q}$ is defined as $df(w_j, \boldsymbol{D_q}) * \log(|\boldsymbol{D}_{all}|/df(w_j, \boldsymbol{D}_{all}))$, where $df(w_j, \boldsymbol{D})$ represents the document frequency of w_j in documents $\boldsymbol{D}$.

5.3 Data Set

In our experiments, we employed the test collection used in the Web Retrieval Task in the Third NTCIR Workshop (Eguchi et al., 2002). The NTCIR Workshops are a series of evaluation workshops designed to enhance research in information access technologies. The test collection consists of $11,038,720$ Japanese Web pages and 47 information needs. For each information need, about $2,000$ documents are rated as highly relevant, fairly relevant, partially relevant, or irrelevant. We used only 40 information needs in our experiments. The remaining 7 (with identification numbers: 0011, 0018, 0032, 0040, 0044, 0047, and 0061) were not used, because we could not retrieve 100 documents for each (see Section 5.1).

Figure 2 gives an example of an information need for the Web Retrieval Task in the Third NTCIR Workshop. The meaning of each element is given below.

⟨NUM⟩ gives the identification number of the information need.

⟨TITLE⟩ provides up to three terms that are similar to the actual query submitted to a real search engine.

⟨DESC⟩ describes the user's information need in a single sentence.

⟨RDOC⟩ provides up to three identification numbers of examples of relevant documents for the information need.

We employed the terms in the ⟨TITLE⟩ tag as the query, and the documents in the ⟨RDOC⟩ tag as explicit feedback. Note that since the numbers of terms and documents differed depending on the information need, we employed the first two terms in the ⟨TITLE⟩ tag and the first two documents in the ⟨RDOC⟩ tag for each information need.

5.4 Evaluation Method

We used P@10, mean average precision (MAP), normalized discounted cumulative gain at 10 top (re-)ranked documents (NDCG@10), and NDCG@100 (Järvelin and Kekäläinen, 2002) in the evaluation. In the calculation of P@10 and MAP, documents that were rated as highly relevant, fairly relevant and partially relevant were regarded as relevant, while documents rated as irrelevant and unrated documents were regarded as irrelevant. Note that MAP was calculated using all the (re-)ranked documents (i.e., 100 documents). In calculating NDCG, we assessed the relevance score of documents rated highly relevant, fairly relevant and partially relevant as 3, 2, and 1 respectively.

To evaluate the effectiveness of explicit RF, we decided in advance which documents would be used as explicit feedback as described in Section 5.3, and if these were included in the initial search results and the re-ranked results, we removed them from both sets of results. One common problem in the evaluation of the effectiveness of explicit RF is how to handle documents that users have marked as relevant (i.e., the input to RF methods) (Hull, 1993). If the initial search results and the re-ranked results are compared in a straightforward manner, the latter have an advantage. This is due to the fact that documents that are known to be relevant tend to be re-ranked higher. However, if we remove them from the re-ranked results, they have a disadvantage. This is especially true if there are few relevant documents. Therefore, we removed the documents used as explicit feedback from both the initial search results and the re-ranked results in the experiments with explicit RF.

In contrast, we did not apply extra care in Experiment 1 with pseudo RF, and measured the performance of each method using its raw (re-)ranked results.

5.5 Experimental Results

Experiment 1. Effectiveness with Respect to Explicit and Pseudo RF

Table 1 gives the results for explicit RF. Owing to space limitations, we only show the optimal results in terms of P@10 for each method. The optimal results for WORD were obtained using our

⟨NUM⟩ 0008 ⟨/NUM⟩
⟨TITLE⟩ Salsa, learn, methods ⟨/TITLE⟩
⟨DESC⟩ I want to find out about methods for learning how to dance the salsa ⟨/DESC⟩
⟨RDOC⟩ NW011992774, NW011992731, NW011992734 ⟨/RDOC⟩

Figure 2: Example of an information need for a Web Retrieval Task in the Third NTCIR Workshop.

Table 1: Effectiveness with respect to explicit RF.

	P@10	MAP	NDCG@10	NDCG@100
INIT	0.278	0.106	0.220	0.249
WORD	0.310	0.111	0.228	0.250
REPR	0.303	0.107	0.236	0.249
OURS	0.383	0.117	0.284	0.255

Table 2: Effectiveness with respect to pseudo RF.

	P@10	MAP	NDCG@10	NDCG@100
INIT	0.298	0.112	0.243	0.268
WORD	0.303	0.111	0.258	0.274
REPR	0.300	0.112	0.250	0.270
OURS	0.330	0.112	0.283	0.278

method with $a = 0$ and $b = 0.7$, while those for OURS (our method) were obtained with $a = 0.2$ and $b = 0.7$.

Based on this table, we can confirm that our method is effective with respect to explicit RF. Our method significantly improved the initial search results across all metrics. Additionally, it outperformed two other baseline RF methods, with the differences in all metrics being statistically significant (Wilcoxon signed-rank test, $p < 0.05$). There were no significant differences between the baseline methods, since they were similar in process to each other. These results suggest that the latent information in the user feedback and each document in the search results is useful for explicit RF.

As a result of the investigation, we found that our method made good use of the words that did not appear in the feedback but were highly probable from the latent topic distribution of the feedback. Consider the information need in Figure 2 as an example. The documents employed as user feedback did not contain the words "technique" or "level", which are related to the information need. As such, the baseline methods could not use these words. In contrast, our method allocated a certain degree of probability to these highly probable words using LDA, despite the words not appearing in the feedback, and hence raised the score of relevant documents in the search results containing these words.

Table 2 gives the results for pseudo RF. The values of the parameters for WORD and OURS were determined as: $a = 0, b = 0.7$, and $a = 0.1, b = 0.6$, respectively. Note that the results of INIT in Table 2 differ from those in Table 1. This is because although we removed the documents used as user feedback from the initial search results (and the re-ranked results) in the experiment with explicit RF, we did not remove them from any of the results in this experiment.

From this table, we can see that our method significantly improved the initial search results. Additionally, our method outperformed the baseline methods. From these results, we can conclude that our method is also effective with respect to pseudo RF.

Experiment 2. Effect of the Amount of Feedback

Figure 3 shows the effect of the amount of explicit feedback on the performance of our method. For comparison with baseline methods, we also present their results. The parameters for each method were identical to those used in Experiment 1 with explicit RF.

From this figure, we can see that our method achieved consistently high performance. For example, when 2^0 relevant documents (i.e., one relevant document) were given as user feedback, our method improved the initial search results by about 35% in P@10. Additionally, a notable feature is that although the improvements in the baseline methods almost disappeared, our method performed well when only a small amount of feedback was obtained. For example, improvement of about 18% was achieved even with only 2^{-5} documents, which constituted an average of 52 words in our experiment. The reason for this is, once again, that our method is able to use not only the surface words in the feedback, but also the highly probable words from its latent topic distribution.

As described above, our method can re-rank search results using a small amount of feedback. This suggests that our method is practically useful, and that it performs well even if only a part of a document (e.g., title, snippet), the relevance of which is easier to determine than that of the whole document, are given as user feedback.

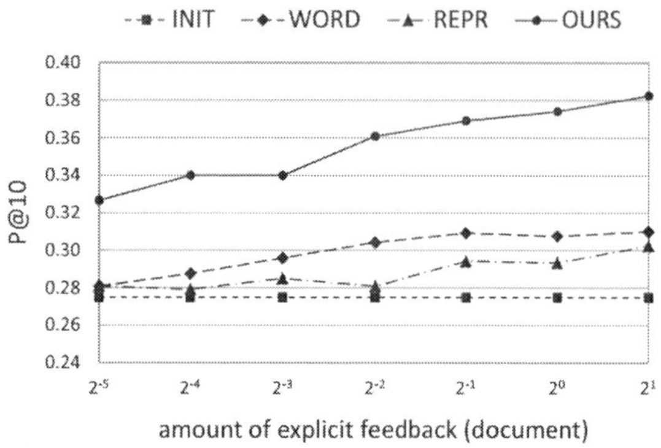

Figure 3: Effect of the amount of feedback.

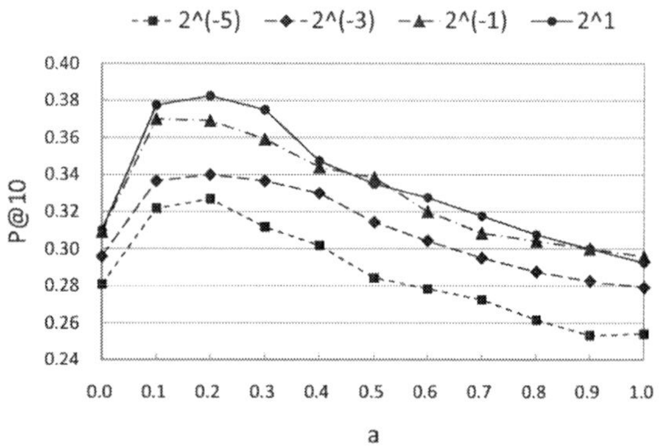

Figure 4: Sensitivity to parameter a.

Experiment 3. Sensitivity to Parameters

The sensitivity of the performance to a is illustrated in Figure 4. Each line in the figure represents the results with different amounts of explicit feedback: 2^{-5}, 2^{-3}, 2^{-1}, and 2^{1} relevant documents. The value of the other parameter b was fixed to 0.7. From this figure, we can see that the performance of our method is sensitive to the value of a, and that the optimal value is about 0.2. Despite the goal and setting being different to ours, this optimal value is similar to that reported in (Wei and Croft, 2006), where the DIR- and LDA-based document models were interpolated as in our work.

The sensitivity to b is depicted in Figure 5. The value of a was fixed to 0.2. According to this figure, we can see that the setting of b also affected the performance of our method. Additionally, this figure shows that if we set the value appropriately, the interpolated new query model is more effective than both the original query model on its own (i.e., $b = 0.0$) and the feedback model on its own (i.e., $b = 1.0$). These findings concur approximately with the results presented in (Zhai and Lafferty, 2001).

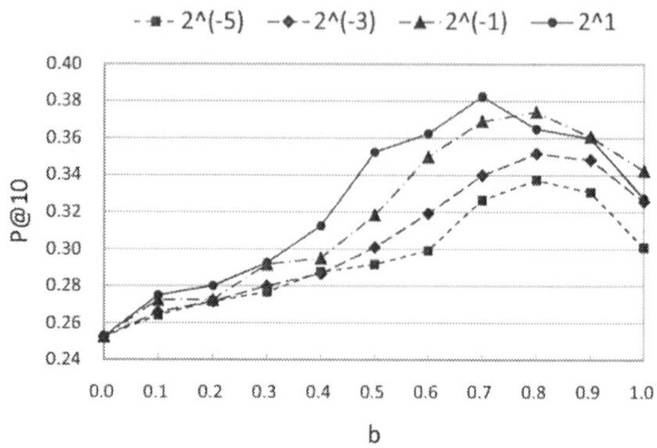

Figure 5: Sensitivity to parameter b.

5.6 Discussion

Although our method achieved good performance in our experiments, we also encountered a problem in that the method took a long time to execute. More specifically, our method required about one minute to estimate the parameters of LDA in Step 2. (On the other hand, the time required for Steps 1, 3, and 4 was only a few seconds.) Thus, we need to explore ways of reducing the time for parameter estimation so that our method can be used in real situations. One way of doing this is to choose a faster estimation technique. For example, collapsed variational methods may provide a viable solution (Teh et al., 2006; Asuncion et al., 2009). Another alternative is to decrease the size of the vocabulary, designated as J in Section 3. For example, we conducted an additional experiment, in which we set $J = 100$, and confirmed that the time for parameter estimation fell to about 10 seconds without any significant change in performance.

6 Conclusion

In this paper, we proposed a novel RF method using latent information, and discussed the effectiveness thereof. Using LDA, our method infers the distributions over latent topics in the feedback and in each document in the search results. Then, documents whose topic distribution resembles that of the feedback are regarded as being relevant to the user's information need, and are re-ranked higher. Through our experiments, we confirmed that our method achieves good performance for both explicit and pseudo RF, and that it provides the benefit of performing well even when only a small amount of feedback can be obtained. As future work, we aim to explore ways of reducing the execution time of our method so that it can be used in practical situations.

References

Arthur Asuncion, Max Welling, Padhraic Smyth, and Yee Whye Teh. 2009. On smoothing and inference for topic models. In *Proceedings of UAI 2009*.

David M. Blei, Andrew Y. Ng, and Michael I. Jordan. 2003. Latent dirichlet allocation. *Jounal of Machine Learning Research*, 3:993–1022.

Koji Eguchi, Keizo Oyama, Emi Ishida, Kazuko Kuriyama, and Noriko Kando. 2002. The web retrieval task and its evaluation in the third ntcir workshop. In *Proceedings of SIGIR 2002*, pages 375–376.

Thomas L. Griffiths and Mark Steyvers. 2004. Finding scientific topics. In *Proceedings of NAS 2004*, pages 5228–5235.

Thomas Hofmann. 1999. Probabilistic latent semantic indexing. In *Proceedings of SIGIR 1999*, pages 50–57.

David Hull. 1993. Using statistical testing in the evaluation of retrieval experiments. In *Proceedings of SIGIR 1993*, pages 329–338.

Eleanor Ide. 1971. New experiments in relevance feedback. In *The SMART Retrieval System: Experiments in Automatic Document Processing*, pages 337–354. Prentice-Hall Inc.

Bernard James Jansen, Amanda Spink, and Tefko Saracevic. 2000. Real life, real users, and real needs: a study and analysis of user queries on the web. *Information Processing and Management*, 36(2):207–227.

Kalervo Järvelin and Jaana Kekäläinen. 2002. Cumulated gain-based evaluation of ir techniques. *ACM Transactions on Information Systems*, 20(4):422–446.

John Lafferty and Chengxiang Zhai. 2001. Document language models, query models, and risk minimization for information retrieval. In *Proceedings of SIGIR 2001*, pages 111–119.

Victor Lavrenko and W. Bruce Croft. 2001. Relevance-based language models. In *Proceedings of SIGIR 2001*, pages 120–127.

Thomas P. Minka. 2000. Estimating a dirichlet distribution. Technical report, Microsoft.

Jay M. Ponte and W. Bruce Croft. 1998. A language modeling approach to information retrieval. In *Proceedings of SIGIR 1998*, pages 275–281.

Joseph John Rocchio. 1971. Relevance feedback in information retrieval. In *The SMART Retrieval System: Experiments in Automatic Document Processing*, pages 313–323. Prentice-Hall Inc.

Gerard Salton, Anita Wong, and Chung-Shu Yang. 1975. A vector space model for automatic indexing. *Communications of the ACM*, 18(11):613–620.

Karen Spärck Jones, S. Walker, and Stephen E. Robertson. 2000. A probabilistic model of information retrieval: Development and comparative experiments. *Information Processing and Management*, 36(6):779–808,809–840.

Yee Whye Teh, David Newman, and Max Welling. 2006. A collapsed variational bayesian inference algorithm for latent dirichlet allocation. In *Proceedings of NIPS 2006*.

Xing Wei and W.Bruce Croft. 2006. Lda-based document models for ad-hoc retrieval. In *Proceedings of SIGIR 2006*, pages 178–185.

Chengxiang Zhai and John Lafferty. 2001. Model-based feedback in the language modeling approach to information retrieval. In *Proceedings of CIKM 2001*, pages 403–410.

Chengxiang Zhai and John Lafferty. 2004. A study of smoothing methods for language models applied to information retrieval. *ACM Transactions on Information Systems*, 22(2):179–214.

Dong Zhou and Vincent Wade. 2009. Latent document re-ranking. In *Proceedings of EMNLP 2009*, pages 1571–1580.

Passage Retrieval for Information Extraction using Distant Supervision

Wei Xu° Ralph Grishman° Le Zhao*

°New York University
New York, NY, USA
xuwei,grishman@cs.nyu.edu

*Carnegie Mellon University
Pittsburgh, PA, USA
lezhao@cs.cmu.edu

Abstract

In this paper, we propose a keyword-based passage retrieval algorithm for information extraction, trained by distant supervision. Our goal is to be able to extract attributes of people and organizations more quickly and accurately by first ranking all the potentially relevant passages according to their likelihood of containing the answer and then performing a traditional deeper, slower analysis of individual passages. Using Freebase as our source of known relation instances and Wikipedia as our text source, we collected a weighted set of keywords indicative of each relation and then use it to re-rank the passages retrieved by the Lemur search engine. Experiments show that our algorithm significantly outperforms state-of-the-art passage retrieval techniques in evaluations of both individual passage retrieval and end-to-end information extraction.

1 Introduction

Large-corpus information extraction involves the extraction of pre-specified types of relations and events from large corpora. For example, the Knowledge Base Population (KBP) slot-filling task (Ji et al., 2010) involves finding, from a large corpus, a few dozen attributes of a specified person or organization.

In many cases we do not have the time to perform in-depth extraction for all attributes over the entire corpus. Consequently, addressing this task typically involves a blend of traditional question answering (QA) and information extraction (IE) methods. Like QA, we need to begin with passage retrieval, where a passage can range from a sentence to a piece of text or a document. However, unlike QA, we have a fixed inventory of relations and a fixed set of expected answer types (e.g. employer of a person). This allows us to bring to bear the more specialized learning methods of IE to tune the passage retrieval for each relation of interest.

To the best of our knowledge, we are the first to systematically study the passage retrieval algorithm for information extraction and propose a novel distant supervision approach to obtain a list of weighted keywords for each relation. Distant supervision (Mintz et al., 2009) makes use of noisy training data generated automatically from a related, but different, type dataset to solve problems on another type of data. Instead of a handful of human-selected keywords, we automatically learn hundreds or thousands of indicative keywords from a freely available online resource, Freebase, which is similar to Wikipedia Infoboxes. Passages are ranked and retrieved based on these keywords indicative of certain relations. We then feed individual passages to a traditional IE system or to an answer extraction component as used in QA systems to obtain the final outputs. Both the training and testing procedures of our method require only statistics of surface words and named entities in the text and thus are time efficient.

This paper addresses the following questions:

1) How can we tune passage retrieval for a particular relation?

2) How do distant learning methods apply to the passage retrieval task?

3) How much do these methods improve over typical QA passage retrieval?

We will measure the improvement in two ways:

1) ability to find a relevant passage, such as reduction in the number of passages the system must examine and increase in the proportion of relevant passages in top-ranked ones;

2) improvement in the precision and recall of information extraction by taking passage relevance into account.

2 Previous Work

Relatively little work has been done to investigate in detail the quality of the IR for large-corpus IE and take advantage of the more constrained relations of interest compared to traditional QA. The Knowledge Base Population (KBP) track at TAC 2010 (Ji et al., 2010) evaluates the ability of automated systems to discover information about named entities. Its slot-filling task is to find answers to queries asking a few dozen attributes of a specified entity, such as the 'employee_of' attribute of a given PERSON entity. We refer to the given entity as the *target entity*, and the attributes of entities as *slot types*. In past KBP competitions, many participants (Li et al., 2009; Byrne and Dunnion, 2010; Chen et al., 2010) exploited a QA system to fill slots by constructing queries based on target entities and slot types. However, their query templates contain only a few additional query terms other than the target entity name, which are mostly obtained manually.

Most of QA systems use the question words as-is or with expansion to form the retrieval system query. Various query expansion approaches have been used to tackle the passage-query mismatch problem, including relevance feedback (Derczynski et al., 2008), ontologies (Bhogal et al., 2007), semantic lexica (Ofoghi et al., 2006), etc. As a data-driven approach, relevance feedback is sensitive to the quality of first time retrieval. Our use of Freebase, a freely available large semantic database, to provide distant supervision requires neither labeled data nor costly constructed knowledge models.

Some researchers (Grishman and Min, 2010; Chrupala et al., 2010; Surdeanu et al., 2010) integrated IR and IE together. Surdeanu et al. (2010) coupled the entity name with a handful of hand-selected trigger words for each slot type as queries to IR system in an effort to boost the ranking of sentences likely to contain the relations of interest. Chrupala et al. (2010) proposed one of the most customized passage retrieval components for large-corpus IE. Besides the target name entity, they take into account the type of expected named entity (such as ORGANIZATION for the 'employee_of' relation) and expand queries by predefined words that are predictive for specific slot types (such as 'work' for the 'employee_of' relation). There are also relevant works emerging from the IR community in the Related entity Finding (REF) task in the TREC Entity Track (Balog et al., 2010), which is to return a ranked list of related entities given an expected type of entity and a brief description (query) of the relation in free text. Fang et al. (2010) ranked entities by their relevance to the query at the document, passage and entity level, primarily based on the similarity between terms.

In all this previous work, the limited number of query terms has become the performance bottleneck of the passage retrieval for large-corpus information extraction.

Perhaps most similar to our distant supervision keyword learning approach for passage retrieval is the semi-automatic method of Nguyen et al. (2007), who extract only several keywords for each relation from Wikipedia and study only the dependency subtrees that contain those keywords. In contrast to their tf-idf model followed by a manual selection step, our algorithm allows us to fully automatically extract hundreds or even thousands of keywords with a weight indicating their relevance to each relation.

Mintz et al. (2009) proposed a distant supervision approach for relation extraction using a rich-featured logistic regression model. Like us, they used Freebase as a source of known relation instances and Wikipedia as a text source to create noisy training data and tested on the Wikipedia data. Our approach differs from theirs in several ways. First, our main concern is the speed required for large-corpus IE and reducing the amount of text to process by passage retrieval, while they use deep NLP features such as parsing and process the whole corpus. Second, we assure the quality of output by using a supervised information extraction system trained on golden data, while their performance is constrained by noisy training data. Third, we evaluate on a corpus that consists of news and web data, while they test on Wikipedia data that is from the same source as the training data. We prove that our method is adaptive to new domains because it is based on lexical statistics and thus tolerant to noise in the training data.

3 Freebase and Wikipedia

Freebase[1] is a freely available online database of structured knowledge. It collects information about approximately 20 million entities (such as

[1] http://www.freebase.com

people, places, books, etc.) from a wide variety of sources, including Wikipedia, MusicBrainz (music), NNDB (biographical information), user editing, etc.

Following the literature (Mintz et al., 2009), we refer to each attribute of a person or organizations as an ordered, binary 'relation' between entities. We refer to individual entity pairs in a relation as relation instances. For example, the 'employee_of' relation indicates a person's employment history with zero to many companies, of which an instance can be <Steve Jobs, employee_of , Apple Inc.>.

Freebase provides us a set of relations and entity pairs that participate in those relations. Often understood as a Wikipedia-turned-database, Freebase also distinguishes similar names and includes exact wiki articles for many entities, and thus forms a perfect source for training texts. We will later discuss the effectiveness and adaptivity of using Wikipedia as training corpus at the end of Section 4 and in Section 7.

4 Learning Indicative Keywords for Relations from Freebase

Our intuition in this research is that there exist some keywords that provide clues to the text passages containing the relationship. For example, a sentence or a couple of successive sentences which contain words like 'hire', 'work', 'appoint', and so on, are highly likely to express the 'employee_of' relation.

We identify such keywords using a distant supervision approach. First, we obtain entity pairs for a certain relation and the Wiki articles of these entities from Freebase. Then we locate the entities in the training corpus to collect sample sentences for each relationship. Finally, we rank the words based on their frequency in those sample sentences versus all sentences in the training corpus.

Like previous work (Nguyen et al., 2007; Mintz et al., 2009), our distant supervision assumption is that if two entities participate in a relation, a sentence that contains those two entities might express that relation. For our training corpus, we choose Wikipedia in this paper since it well supports Freebase data and is believed to have high grammatical correctness compared to that of the web overall. It is also feasible to use another corpus as long as it potentially contains text about the relationships of interest and the known entity pairs.

Unlike (Mintz et al., 2009), which considers any sentences containing the pair of entities, we take advantage of the fact that Wikipedia records only one article per language for a real world entity. Any sentences in the person's Wiki article that contains the person name or pronouns ('she' or 'he') and his/her employer name are considered positive examples, others as negative examples. This setting can capture more true positive examples. What is more, Freebase includes name variants of a real world entity and thus gives a better chance to match the person name back to his/her Wiki pages.

We then determine if a word is indicative and to what degree for a certain type of relation based on its occurrence in positive and negative examples. We use the morphological base forms to replace their inflectional variants in the process. The indicative score I of word w for relation R is calculated by the following formula:

$$I(w,R) = \frac{Pos}{Pos + Neg} \times \frac{Pos}{Pos + \alpha} \qquad (1)$$

where $Pos = |S_{pos}(w,R)|$ and $Neg = |S_{neg}(w,R)|$, $S(w,R)$ are all the positive/negative sentences for relation R which contain word w. The larger the weight the more likely the word indicates the relationship. The first factor $Pos/(Pos + Neg)$ favors words which are more frequent in positive sentences versus all sentences. The factor $Pos/(Pos + \alpha)$ is used to reduce low frequency word noise, where α is a constant to be set experimentally. All the words with $Pos > Neg$ are extracted to form a weighted keyword list for each relation.

Table 1 shows the top-weighted keywords learned for the 'employee_of' and 'member_of' relations, using the January 2011 data dump of Freebase. The Freebase contains 10702 instances of 'employee_of' relation (named '/business/ employment_tenure/' in Freebase), among which 4497 are found in its corresponding Wikipedia articles. In total, 6574 positive, 93756 negative examples and a weighted set of 2436 keywords indicative of the relation are extracted. For 'member_of' relation (named '/organization/ organization_membership/' in Freebase), there are 586 instances in Freebase, 244 positive and 13749 negative examples extracted from Wikipedia pages. With many fewer training examples provided by Freebase for the 'member_of' relation, only 290 keywords are learned, but they proved to be effective in the experiments in Section 7.

employee_of		
1-10	**11-20**	**21-30**
faculty	currently	headquarter
professor	chairman	since
emeritus	join	housemaster
chancellor	founder	dynamo
teach	chief	yesterday
executive	department	retail
dean	conglomerate	officer
rector	head	merger
lecturer	subsidiary	director
therapeutics	company	president
31-40	**41-50**	**51-60**
shareholder	appointment	appoint
at	physiology	instructor
chain	professorship	merge
position	retailer	zoology
supermarket	owner	former
psychology	until	current
creative	acquisition	studio
associate	holding	adjunct
chair	developer	found
teaching	assistant	vice

member_of		
1-5	**6-10**	**11-15**
fraternity	gradual	president
sorority	elect	peaceful
fraternal	guerrilla	founder
member	carve	fellow
membership	hence	sector

Table 1. List of top-weighted keywords

It is very interesting that many keywords found may not be intuitive, such as "currently", "until", and "supermarket" for the 'employee_of' relation. Though they do not directly imply the occurrence of the relations, they tend to co-occur with the relations, thus helpful in retrieval. Moreover, our system does not rely on only one keyword to make decisions and thus is robust. We also notice that the 'member_of' relation in Freebase has a bias towards the education domain; however, this has little impact in general performance, as shown in Section 7, because the keyword set still covers the most common keywords such as 'member' and 'founder' while the more domain-specific words are rarely seen in the text. This is likely because usually the queried entity helps in disambiguating the relation words and focusing on the right subset of the relation words.

5 Passage Retrieval for Information Extraction

5.1 Lemur

Our goal is to develop a speedy passage retrieval model for the IE task without using complex NLP techniques.

We first employ the high-performance Lemur passage retrieval engine to select relevant passages about the target named entity from a large corpus. Lemur (Metzler and Croft, 2004) implements a model combining language modeling and an inference network and has been widely used in large-corpus IE and QA systems. We define a passage as a natural paragraph in the texts and use Lemur's default setting, which shows a satisfactory capability to retrieve most passages containing a given entity in experiments.

Then, we re-rank the retrieved passages in descending order of their probability of containing the target relation R (e.g. 'employee_of').

5.2 Baseline

Our baseline passage retrieval algorithm for information extraction is derived from the state-of-the-art methods used in the IE community (Chrupala et al., 2010; Surdeanu et al., 2010), IR community (Zhao and Callan, 2008) and Question Answering community (Tellex et al., 2003; Hickl et al., 2007; Moldovan et al., 2007; Gómez et al., 2007). The baseline (and our proposed approach) are intended to involve minimal human-constructed knowledge, annotated data and complex NLP processing.

In the baseline method, the ranking score B of a passage P, with respect to relation R and target entity E, consists of four elements:

$$B(P,R,E) = W_1(P,E) + W_2(P,R) + W_3(P,R) + W_4(P,E) \quad (2)$$

Please note that the constants c in each scoring functions $\boldsymbol{W}$ are only used to define cascading criteria, e.g. any passage that contains the target named entity will be ranked higher than those do not, and thus can be set rather arbitrarily.

1) **The target named entity ($\boldsymbol{W_1}$):** We ensure that passages that (partly) include the string of entity names rank higher than those only containing pronouns.

$$W_1(P,E) = \begin{cases} c_{1a}, if\ P\ contains\ E \\ c_{1b}, if\ P\ partly\ contains\ E \\ c_{1c}, if\ P\ contains\ pronouns \\ 0,\ otherwise \end{cases} \quad (3)$$

where $c_{1a} > c_{1b} > c_{1c}$ are arbitrary constants larger than any possible value of $W_2 + W_3 + W_4$. The passage partly contains the entity when it shares at least a word in common with the entity name.

2) **The named entity of the expected type (W_2):** The named entity of the type that is to be found for the relation is called the expected named entity, (e.g. 'ORGANIZATION' for relation 'employee_of'). We run the Stanford Named Entity Recognizer (Finkel et al., 2005) on Lemur's passage retrieval outputs, preferring passages that contain a named entity of the sought type, and more strongly preferring names that have not appeared in previously retrieved passages (novel names).

$$W_2(P,R) = \begin{cases} c_2 + c_3, if\ P\ contains\ novel\ expected\ entity \\ c_3, if\ P\ contains\ expected\ entity \\ 0, otherwise \end{cases} \quad (4)$$

where c_2 and c_3 are arbitrary constants larger than any possible value of $W_3 + W_4$.

3) **The expansion terms (W_3):** The expansion terms include predefined words that are predictive of or related to a specific relation. We adapt the indicative word list used by Surdeanu et al. (2010) in their KBP system, which include several words for each relation. We also use a list containing 635 common title words as related terms for the 'employee_of' relation. This effort is to simulate the usage of WordNet and ontologies for term expansions but is considered to be more accurate and comprehensive since these terms are collected for the purpose of these particular relations.

$$W_3(P,R) = \begin{cases} c_4, if\ P\ contains\ related\ terms\ of\ R \\ 0, otherwise \end{cases} \quad (5)$$

where c_4 is a arbitrary constant set not less than 1 (thus W_4).

4) **The original rank in Lemur (W_4):** We also take into account the rank from Lemur's passage retrieval.

$$W_4(P,E) = \frac{1}{LemurRank(P,E)} \quad (6)$$

where $LemurRank(P,E)$ is the rank of the passage P as returned from Lemur when querying for entity name E.

5.3 Passage Retrieval using Indicative Keywords Learned from Freebase (IKFB)

As in the baseline, we give top priority to the passages that contain the target named entity and at least a named entity of the expected type for the relation. We discard other weighting schema in Section 5.2 but apply our learned list of weighted indicative keywords instead.

$$K(P,R,E) = W_1(P,E) + W_2(P,R) + W_5(P,R) \quad (7)$$

5) The indicative keywords (W_5):

$$W_5(P,R) = \sum_{w \in L_{distant}(R) \cap w \in Top_n(P)} I(w,R) \quad (8)$$

where $L_{distant}(R)$ is the set of indicative keywords obtained by the approach described in Section 4, $Top_n(P)$ is the set of top n words weighted by $I(w,R)$ which appears in passage P. The number n is experimentally set as 5 in this paper; it serves to prevent preferring longer passages while decreasing the relevance of extremely short passages.

6 Evaluation Issues

6.1 Test Data

In this paper, we use the KBP corpus as test data, which includes about 1.3 million documents of newswire and 0.5 million of web data.

We evaluate passage retrieval algorithms on one of the most frequent relations in the KBP task (Ji et al., 2010; Chen et al., 2010): 'employee_of'. We also experiment on 'member_of' relation, but due to limitations of space we only present MRR values for this relation. The KBP 2010 training data prepared by the Linguistic Data Consortium and by the participants, including 67 person entities, 54 instances each for 'employee_of' and 'member_of' relation, are used as test data in our experiments. Please note that one entity may be involved in multiple relation instances, e.g. a person may have multiple employers.

6.2 Evaluation Metrics

We evaluate the passage retrieval algorithms in two ways. First, we measure the performance of passage retrieval as an independent system, in the context of IR and QA. Second, we examine its impact on the end-to-end information extraction pipeline, in the context of IE.

6.2.1 Evaluation of Individual PR system

Following the literature of passage retrieval (Gómez et al., 2007; Roberts and Gaizauskas, 2004) and question answering, we use three metrics in the experiments, *Coverage*, *Redundancy* and *Mean Reciprocal Rank (MRR)*.

Let Q be the relation query set, D all possible passages which are retrieved by Lemur, $A_{D,q}$ the subset of D which contains correct answers for $q \in Q$, and $F^S_{D,q,n}$ the n top-ranked passages in D retrieved by a retrieval system S responding to query q.

The *coverage* of a retrieval system S for a query set Q and passage collection D at rank n is defined as:

$$coverage^S(Q, D, n) \equiv \frac{\left|\{q \in Q | F^S_{D,q,n} \cap A_{D,q} \neq \emptyset\}\right|}{|Q|} \quad (9)$$

The *answer redundancy* (or simply redundancy) is defined as:

$$redundancy^S(Q, D, n) \equiv \frac{\sum_{q \in Q} \left|F^S_{D,q,n} \cap A_{D,q}\right|}{|Q|} \quad (10)$$

The *Mean Reciprocal Rank (MRR)* (Voorhees, 1999) is defined as:

$$mrr^S(Q, D, n) \equiv \frac{\sum_{q \in Q} rr\left(q, F^S_{D,q,n}\right)}{|Q|} \quad (11)$$

where rr is the Reciprocal Rank which is the inverse of the rank of the first returned passage which contains the answer; or 0 if the answer is not found in the top n retrieved passages. The function is defined as:

$$rr\left(q, F^S_{D,q,n}\right) \equiv \begin{cases} 1/k, if\ \exists k{:}\ k = \underset{1 \le i \le n}{\operatorname{argmin}}\left(F^S_{D,q,i} \cap A_{D,q} \neq \emptyset\right) \\ 0, otherwise \end{cases} \quad (12)$$

The coverage gives the proportion of relation instances (correct answers to the query) that can be found within the top n passages retrieved for each query. The redundancy gives the average number, per question, of passages within the top n ranks retrieved which contain a correct answer. The MRR is the average of the reciprocal ranks of the first ranked passage containing a correct answer.

6.2.2 Evaluation of End-to-End IE system

We also evaluate the impact of the passage retrieval algorithm on the final output of a large-corpus information extraction system.

6.2.2.1 Traditional IE Pipeline

We exploit a simple two-stage pipeline architecture for the KBP task. First, we retrieve passages related to the target entity. Then we apply to those passages a traditional information extraction system (Grishman et al., 2005; Ji and Grishman, 2008) to extract relations, which was originally created for the NIST Automatic Content Extraction (ACE) Evaluations. Its relation extraction component uses maximum entropy models, incorporating diverse lexical, syntactic, semantic and ontological knowledge.

To generate the final results, there could be different strategies. We use a simple strategy in this paper, which suffices to show the capability of our system, outputting the answers of the m top-ranked passages that provide an answer (possibly duplicate). A more delicate design is not a focus of this research.

6.2.2.2 QA-like Pipeline

The new passage retrieval IKFB system also allows us to create a QA-like pipeline for large-scale information extraction. Besides applying a sophisticated IE system to the retrieved passages using deep NLP techniques, such as coreference resolution, we can exploit answer extraction/selection components similar to many QA systems. Some common answer extraction/selection approaches, e.g. using distance from keywords, can possibly boost the speed by avoiding deep analysis and improve recall/precision by finding answers that the traditional IE system misses.

Consider the target entity "John Dewey" for example; the IE system failed to extract any employment information from the corpus. Our IKFB algorithm assigns top rank to the following passage:

"An institution that sees itself as an unconventional alternative to other colleges, the New School was founded in 1919 by a group of professors, including the philosopher and education reformer John Dewey, who had resigned in protest from Columbia. They could not abide by a stance taken by Columbia's president at the time, Nicholas Murray Butler, that faculty members had to support America's entry into World War I."

We investigate the potential value of passage ranking by implementing a simple answer extraction component and using its output when the IE pipeline failed to provide any answers to the probe query. The primitive method is to find the organization name that is closest to the target entity in the first top ranked passage, e.g. "Columbia" for the above passage (note: "New School" is missed by the Stanford named entity tagger). A distance-based answer extraction component is good at dealing with complicated language phenomena, since it is less likely to face data sparsity problem or syntactic analysis errors than many IE approaches do.

6.2.2.3 Measurement Metrics

In this framework, we use the traditional measures for evaluating IE, *precision* and *recall*. Following the symbols defined in section 6.2.1, *precision* and *recall* are defined as:

$$precision^S(Q,D,m) \equiv \frac{\sum_{q\in Q}|T^S_{D,q,m} \cap B_{D,q}|}{\sum_{q\in Q}|T^S_{D,q,m}|} \quad (14)$$

$$recall^S(Q,D,m) \equiv \frac{\sum_{q\in Q}|T^S_{D,q,m} \cap B_{D,q}|}{\sum_{q\in Q}|B_{D,q}|} \quad (15)$$

where m is as mentioned in Section 6.2.2.1 about the output generating strategies, $T^S_{D,q,m}$ are the system output, and $B_{D,q}$ are the golden answers.

7 Experiment Results

As we described in Section 6, we carry out experiments for the "employee_of" relation on the training data from KBP 2010, which includes 67 entities and 54 instances of the relation (involving 30 entities) as keys. Using the January 2011 data dump of Freebase as our sources of known relation instances and Wikipedia as out text source, we collect a weighted set of keywords indicative of the relation and then use it to re-rank the passages retrieved by the Lemur engine.

Three passage retrieval algorithms are compared:

- **Lemur**: the passage retrieval functionality provided by Lemur using only the target entity name. An example query looks like this: #combine[p](#5(John Dewey).
- **Baseline**: a baseline approach that prioritizes the passages retrieved by Lemur which contain the expected answer type, relevant terms of the relation, etc.
- **IKFB**: our proposed approach using the weighted keywords learned by distant supervision on Freebase data.

The constants in the ranking formulas were set as follows: $c_{1a} = 30000$, $c_{1b} = 20000$, $c_{1c} = 10000$, $c_2 = 1000$, $c_3 = 100$, $c_4 = 1$. Other values of these constants would be equally effective, as long as they distinguish the priority of each scoring criteria.

7.1 Performance of Individual Passage Retrieval

In Figure 1, we can see the improvement of our passage retrieval algorithm for information extraction usage with respect to the Lemur search engine and baseline system.

The coverage gives the proportion of correct answers that can be found within the top n passages retrieved for each query, if using a perfect information extraction system. For 31.5% of relation instances, only one passage had to be examined to retrieve the employment information using IKFB, while this number is 16.7% for the baseline system, 9.3% for Lemur. The coverage of the baseline and IKFB converge as the number

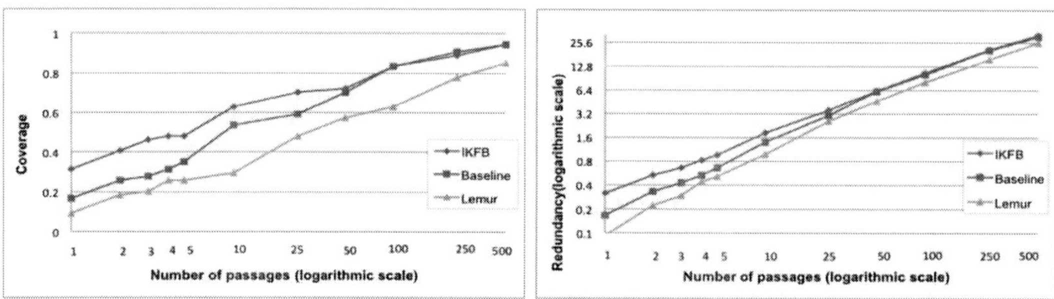

Figure 1. Performance of Individual Passage Retrieval Systems

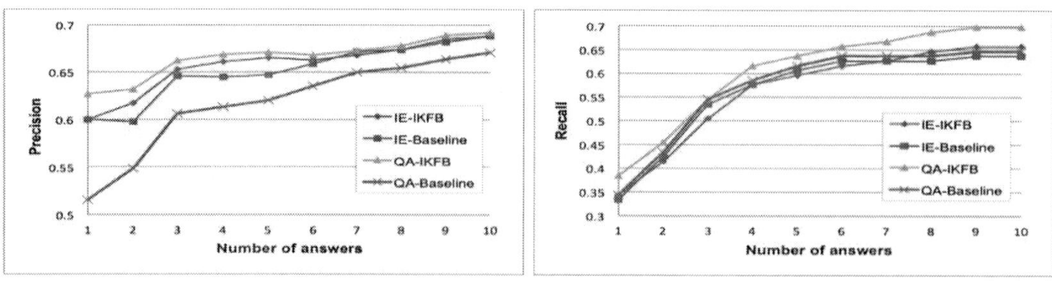

Figure 2. Performance of End-to-End IE extracting answers for top-ranked passages for each target entity

of passages retrieved increases.

The redundancy gives the average number of passages within the top n retrieved passages which contain a correct answer. On average 18.7% of the top 10 ranked passages by IKFB contain answers, while the number is 5.93% for baseline system.

Table 2 represents the Mean Reciprocal Rank of all three systems and evaluations for all passages ($n = \infty$ in Formula 11). In the previous figure, we can appreciate that the difference in both coverage and redundancy decreases with the number of passages.

System	employee_of	member_of
IKFB	0.409	0.260
Baseline	0.269	0.149
Lemur	0.180	0.079
p-value	0.0092	0.0044

Table 2. Comparision of MRR
p-value: comparing IKFB to Baseline

The paired, two-tailed Student's t test (Smucker et al., 2007) shows that our proposed algorithm IKFB is significantly superior to the baseline in terms of MRR.

7.2 Impact of Passage Retrieval on Information Extraction

Figure 2 represents the performance of an end-to-end information extraction system that extracts the top m ($m = 1{\sim}10$) answers using different passage retrieval algorithms. Both QA and IE pipelines are shown.

Because the information in the training data is incomplete, the output answers were examined manually; another 45 relation instances were discovered besides the given 54 keys in KBP data. IKFB achieves somewhat higher precision with similar recall. It ranks the passages containing the answer higher, while ranking the passages containing the correct answers ahead of those which may suggest wrong answers to the IE system.

There is great room for improvement on answer extraction, such as using a QA-pipeline. It is not uncommon that the information extraction system fails to extract the right answers even when the passages containing them are retrieved and ranked at top. The IE system can only successfully locate 7 out of the 54 given keys in 2.4% of the top 10 ranked passages by IKFB, although 17 keys are contained in 18.7% of these retrieved passages.

Of the total 67 person entities in our test data, the IE-pipeline is not able to extract any employment information for 12 of them. However, using the primitive QA-pipeline, we are able to recover 4 of them while introducing 6 new errors. As shown in Figure 2, the integration of the QA-pipeline to the IE-pipeline improves the end-to-end system performance by 3-5%, since low recall is the most crucial problem of traditional IE systems. Good ranking is particularly important to the IE+QA pipeline; as Figure 2 shows, adding QA to the baseline produces a considerable loss of precision.

8 Conclusions and Future Work

We have presented a novel method to extract keywords from Wikipedia articles and rank passages for information extraction. The key features of our method includes: (1) combining the advantages of question answering and information extraction techniques; (2) involving no complicated or time consuming processes; (3) requiring no costly annotation but making use of freely available Wikipedia and Freebase.

Given the success of our primitive QA-pipeline, we plan to implement a more competitive and customized question answering system for information extraction tasks. We also consider looking more deeply into the adaptiveness from Wikipedia to texts from other sources in order to further improve the quality of weighted keywords.

Acknowledgments

Supported by the Intelligence Advanced Research Projects Activity (IARPA) via Air Force Research Laboratory (AFRL) contract number FA8650-10-C-7058. The U.S. Government is authorized to reproduce and distribute reprints for Governmental purposes notwithstanding any copyright annotation thereon. The views and conclusions contained herein are those of the authors and should not be interpreted as necessarily representing the official policies or endorsements, either expressed or implied, of IARPA, AFRL, or the U.S. Government.

We wish to thank Adam Meyers and Satoshi Sekine of New York University and Heng Ji of the City University of New York for their advice.

References

Krisztian Balog, Pavel Serdyukov and Arjen P. de Vries. 2010. Overview of the TREC 2010 Entity Track. In *TREC 2010*.

J. Bhogal, A. Macfarlane and P. Smith. 2007. A review of Ontology Based Query Expansion. *Information Processing and Management*, 43(4), 866-886.

Lorna Byrne and John Dunnion. 2010. *UCD IIRG at TAC 2010 KBP Slot Filling Task*. In *TAC 2010 Workshop*.

Zheng Chen, Suzanne Tamang, Adam Lee, Xiang Li, Wen-Pin Lin, Matthew Snover, Javier Artiles, Marissa Passantino, Heng Ji. 2010. CUNY-BLENDER TAC-KBP2010 Entity Linking and Slot Filling System Description. In *TAC 2010 Workshop*.

Grzegorz Chrupala, Saeedeh Momtazi, Michael Wiegand, Stefan Kazalski, Fang Xu, Benjamin Rogh, Alexandra Balahur and Dietrich Klakow. 2010. Saarland University Spoken Language Systems at the Slot Filling Task of TAC KBP 2010. In *TAC 2010 Workshop*.

Leon Derczynski, Jun Wang, Robert Gaizauskas and Mark A. Greenwood. 2008. A Data Driven Approach to Query Expansion in Question Answering. In *COLING 2008 Workshop on Information Retrieval for Question Answering*.

Yi Fang, Luo Si, Zhengtao Yu, Yantuan Xian and Yangbo Xu. 2009. Entity Retrieval by Hierarchical Relevance Model, Exploiting the Structure of Tables and Learning Homepage Classifiers. In *TREC 2009*.

Jenny Rose Finkel, Trond Grenager, and Christopher Manning. 2005. Incorporating Non-local Information into Information Extraction Systems by Gibbs Sampling. In *ACL 2005*.

José Manuel Gómez, Paolo Rosso and Emilio Sanchis. 2007. Re-ranking of Yahoo Snippets with the JIRS Passage Retrieval System. In *IJCAI 2007 Workshop on Cross Lingual Information Access*.

Ralph Grishman and Bonan Min. 2010. New York University KBP 2010 Slot-Filling System. In *TAC 2010 Workshop*.

Ralph Grishman, David Westbrook and Adam Meyers. 2005. NYU's English ACE 2005 System Description. In *ACE 2005 Workshop*.

Andrew Hickl, Kirk Roberts, Bryan Rink, Jeremy Bensley, Tobias Jungen, Ying Shi and Johan Williams. 2007. Question Answering with LCC's CHAUCER-2 at TREC 2007. In *TREC 2007 Workshop*.

Heng Ji and Ralph Grishman. 2008. Refining Event Extraction Through Cross-document Inference. In *ACL 2008*.

Heng Ji, Ralph Grishman, H.T. Dang, K. Griffitt and J. Ellis. 2010. Overview of the TAC 2010 Knowledge Base Population Track. In *TAC 2010 Workshop*.

Fangtao Li, Zhicheng Zheng, Fan Bu, Yang Tang, Xiaoyan Zhu and Minlie Huang. 2009. THU QUANTA at TAC 2009 KBP and RTE Track. In *TAC 2009 Workshop*.

Donald Metzler and W. Bruce Croft. 2004. Combining the Language Model and Inference Network Approaches to Retrieval. *Information Processing and Management Special Issue on Bayesian Networds and Information Retrieval*, 40(5), 735-750.

Mike Mintz, Steven Bills, Rion Snow and Dan Jurafsky. 2009. Distant Supervision for Relation Extraction without Labeled Data. In *ACL 2009*.

Dan Moldovan, Christine Clark and Mitchell Bowden. 2007. Lymba's Power Answer 4 in TREC 2007. In *TREC 2007 Workshop*.

Dat P.T. Nguyen, Yutaka Matsuo and Mitsuru Ishizuka. 2007. Relation Extraction from Wikipedia Using Subtree Mining. In *AAAI 2007*.

Bahadorreza Ofoghi, John Yearwood and Ranadhir Ghoshi. 2006. A Semantic Approach to Boost Passage Retrieval Effectiveness for Question Answering. In *ASCS 2006*.

Ian Roberts and Robert Gaizauskas. 2004. Evaluating Passage Retrieval Approaches for Question Answering. In *ECIR 2004*.

Mark D. Smucker, James Allan and Ben Carterette. 2007. A Comparison of Statistical Significance Tests for Information Retrieval Evaluation. In *CIKM 2007*.

Mihai Surdeanu, David McClosky, Julie Tibshirani, John Bauer, Angel X. Chang, Valentin I. Spitkovsky, Christopher D. Manning. 2010. A Simple Distant Supervision Approach for the TAC-KBP Slot Filling Task. In *TAC 2010 Workshop*.

Stefanie Tellex, Boris Katz, Jimmy Lin, Aaron Fernandes and Gregory Marton. 2003. Quantitative Evaluation of Passage Retrieval Algorithms for Question Answering. In *SIGIR 2003*.

Ellen M. Voorhees. 1999. The Trec-8 Question Answering Track Report. In *TREC 1999 Workshop*.

Le Zhao and Jamie Callan. A Generative Retrieval Model for Structured Documents. In *CIKM 2008*.

Using Context Inference to Improve Sentence Ordering for Multi-document Summarization

Peifeng Li **Guangxi Deng** **Qiaoming Zhu**

School of Computer Science and Technology, Soochow University

1 Shizi St, Suzhou, China, 215006

{pfli,gxdeng,qmzhu}@suda.edu.cn

Abstract

In this paper, we propose a novel context inference-based approach for sentences ordering in multi-document summarization application. Our method first detects whether or not two summarization sentences should be adjacent according to the similarity between one summarization sentence and the context of the other one, and then it computes the reliability of the adjacent summarization sentences based on the similarity and their relative position. To be specific, the first sentence will be selected according to features of sentence, and the second sentence will be selected if and only if it has the maximum reliability with previous sentence. Evaluation result shows that our method outperforms the state-of-the-art ones on DUC2004 corpus.

1 Introduction

Multi-document summarization is an automatic procedure aimed at extraction of information from multiple texts written about the same topic. Whereas, sentence ordering, the last task of multi-document summarization, will finally affect the quality of summarization. Furthermore, the task of sentence ordering in multi-document summarization is harder than that in single document summarization because multiple documents are created by different authors who have different writing styles and backgrounds. Therefore, no natural order of texts can be extracted as the basis of sentence ordering judgment. How to conduct an efficient and effective method for sentences ordering is a difficult but important task for both multi-document summarization and other text processing job, e.g. Question Answering.

Currently, a variety of studies have been reported on sentence ordering. Some methods adopted chronological information (McKeown et al., 1999; Lin et al., 2001; Barzilay et al., 2002; Okazaki et al., 2004) while others learned the natural order of sentences from source documents or large corpus (Lapata, 2003; Barzilay and Lee, 2004; Nie et al., 2006; Ji and Nie, 2008). However, chronological information cannot be easily extracted from those non-news documents and constructing a large corpus also is not so easy. Furthermore, those results of all above methods are far from satisfactory. Therefore, how to achieve coherent summarization still is an issue for us.

This paper proposes a novel method to infer the order of summarization sentences for multi-document summarization according to their context. We first judge whether or not two summarization sentences should be adjacent based on the similarity between one summarization sentence and the context of the other one, and then compute the reliability based on the similarity and relative position of the adjacent summarization. To be specific, the first sentence will be selected based on its features, and the second sentence will be selected if and only if it has the maximum adjacency reliability with previous sentence. The experimental results on DUC2004 corpus show that our method outperforms state-of-the-art ones.

The reminder of this paper is organized as follows. In Section 2, the related work is introduced. The motivation of our method is discussed in Section 3. In Section 4, the context inference-based sentence ordering algorithm is described. In Section 5, the experiments and evaluation are presented. Conclusions and future work are given in Section 6.

2 Related Work

So far many studies on sentence ordering have

been proposed. They can be divided into two categories: chronology-based method and natural order-based method. To be specific, chronology-based methods determine sentence ordering according to the chronological order of events while natural order-based methods infer sentence ordering according to some cues that are learned from source documents and corpus.

Barzilay et al. (2002) proposed a chronology-based method to sort sentence, they assumed the theme of sentences were the cues of sentence ordering. Based on it, they presented a strategy according to the first published date of the theme; then sorted sentences based on their order of presentation in the same article.

Okazaki et al. (2004) proposed an approach to improve the chronological sentence ordering method by using precedence relation technology. They assumed the presupposed information should be transferred to reader in advance before the sentence was interpreted. They first arranged sentences in a chronological order and then estimated the presupposed information for each sentence by using the content of the sentences located in before each sentence in its original article.

Generally speaking, the articles in news domain usually contain descriptions of date and events accompanying the publication sequences. Therefore, chronology-based method is practical for news domain. However, chronological information is not ubiquitous in a large number of multi-document summarization tasks. So, some studies began to focus on general domain, and they sorted sentences according to the source documents and corpus.

McKeown et al. (2001) and Barzilay et al. (2001) presented a majority ordering algorithm to sort sentences. They classified sentences of source documents into different themes or topics using summarization sentences. If sentences from theme 1 preceded sentences from theme 2 when they appeared in same text, then putted theme 1 was preceding theme 2. The order of summarization sentences was determined by the order of themes. However, there were some potential issues in this kind of method. Firstly, it was not easy to correctly cluster sentences into topics. Secondly, some summarization sentences may belong to a same topic. Finally, the relative order between two topics may be not steady.

Lapata (2003) provided an unsupervised probabilistic model for sentence ordering. The model assumed that sentences were represented as a set of features that could be automatically extracted from the corpus without manual annotation. The conditional probability of sentence pairs can be learned from a training corpus. By computing conditional probability of each sentence pairs, the approximate optimal global sentence ordering can be achieved using a simple greedy algorithm.

Bollegala et al. (2005) combined three ordering methods together, said chronological ordering, probabilistic ordering and topic relatedness ordering, and adopted a machine learning approach for sentence ordering. The mixed system can achieve better performance than any of the three individual one. To be extended, they also proposed a bottom-up approach for sentence ordering (Bollegala et al., 2010). They defined four criteria (chronology, topical-closeness, precedence and succession) between two textual segments, and adopted SVM classifier to learn the relative order of them. They repeatedly concatenated two textual segments into one segment based on the relative order until all sentences were arranged.

Nie et al. (2006) adopted adjacency of sentence pairs to sort sentences. Sentence adjacency was calculated based on adjacency of features of each sentence pairs. Adjacency between two sentences represented how closely they should be putted together in a set of summarization sentences. Ji et al. (2008) extended the above adjacency model. They proposed a cluster-adjacency based method to map each sentence of source documents to a theme by using semi-supervised classification method. The adjacency of sentences pair was learned from source documents according to adjacency of clusters they belonged to.

Our method is different from above ones in two aspects. First, we try to find the indirect relations of summarization sentences according to source documents. Second, the source documents are topic-related and most summarization sentences or their similar ones appear in more than one source document. Meanwhile, there are more than two summarization sentences or their similar ones may co-occur in a source document. Therefore, we can infer the order of summarization sentences by using the indirect relation between summarization sentences.

3 Motivation

Different documents have different writing styles and backgrounds. Besides, sentences that used to describe a same topic may have different forms. Therefore, source documents maybe cannot provide the direct information for sentence ordering. However, they still provide some indirect information which can be used to infer the order of summarization sentences.

Each source document for multi-document summarization is not an information island. They may have some overlapped information. For example, there are three documents to report a same news event. The first document describes its background and cause. The second one describes the origin, process and result. The third one describes the effect and comment. Each document has its own key point, but they have some overlapped information. The first and the second one report the cause in both while the second and the third one report the effect in both.

Each summarization sentence is extracted from a source document even though it is created or rewritten manually, it also can link to one or more sentences in source documents. Therefore, each summarization sentence is also not isolated and there are many sentences surrounding them in the source document. We call these sentences as the context of the summarization sentence. Furthermore, the source documents are in same topic and most of summarization sentences are presented in more than one document. In a word, a summarization sentence may have some similar sentences in source documents.

Accordingly, we provide a method to infer the order of summarization sentences by using their context. Let us consider an example: there are two documents, d_1 and d_2, sketched in Figure 1, where ss_1 and ss_2 are two summarization sentences or their similar ones in source documents, $s1_i$ and $s2_i$ are the context sentence of ss_1 and ss_2 respectively.

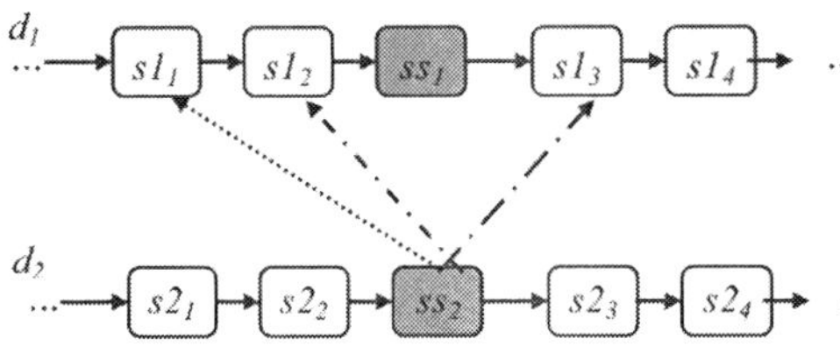

Figure 1. An example of summarization sentences and their context

If ss_2 is similar to $s1_1$, we have reason to believe that ss_2 and ss_1 should be adjacent and ss_2 should be in front of ss_1 because $s1_1$ is front of ss_1. The highly similarity between ss_2 and $s1_1$, the highly probability that ss_2 is in front of ss_1.

If ss_2 is not similar to $s1_1$, but it is similar to $s1_2$, we also consider ss_2 should be in front of ss_1, but the probability will higher because $s1_2$ is closer to ss_1 than $s1_1$. Similarly, if ss_2 is similar to $s1_3$, ss_1 should be in front of ss_2.

4 Context Inference-based Sentence Ordering Algorithm

From the analysis in section 3, we can infer the order of sentence by using the similarity between summarization sentences and their context. We compute the adjacent credibility of two sentences and then use a directed graph with weight to represent the order of summarization sentences. A vertex denotes a sentence. If two sentences are adjacent then an edge exists of them. The weight of edge is the adjacency credibility of two sentences. Figure 2 shows the order relation among summarization sentences, there is an edge from s_1 to s_3 and the weight is 0.5, which means s_1 and s_3 are adjacent, and the credibility of them is 0.5. From figure 2, we can find a path contained all vertexes, which has the maximum weight. The order of the path is considered as the best logical order of summarization sentences.

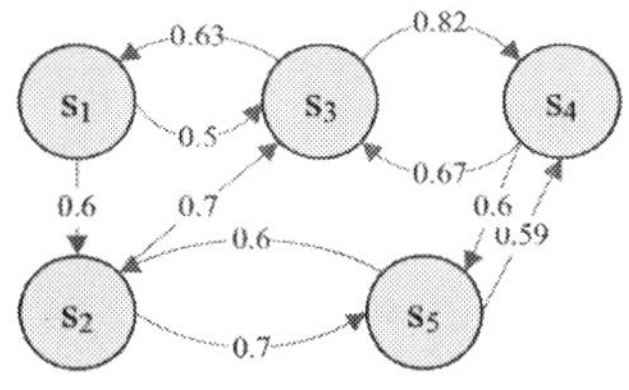

Figure 2. Graph of summarization sentences and their relation

Due to finding an optimal path in a graph is a typical NP problem; we will use an algorithm to find an approximate optimal path. We assume that the document set $D=\{d_1, d_2 ... d_n\}$, a document $d_j=\{s_{j,1}, s_{j,2}, ..., s_{j,m}\}$ where $s_{j,i}$ is the ith sentence in d_j, the summarization sentences set $SS=\{ss_1, ss_2, ..., ss_k\}$, the Graph $G=NULL$. For a sentence ss_i in d_j, its context sentence set is $\{d_j - ss_i\}$. The algorithm is described as follows.

Input: D, SS and G

Output: P, an ordered list that contains all summarization sentences.

BEGIN

Step 1: For each ss_i in SS, add a vertex to graph G;

Step 2: For each ss_i in d_j, compute the similarity $sim(ss_k, s_{j,l})$ between each ss_k ($ss_k \in \{SS - ss_i\}$) and each s_{jl}

($s_{j,l} \in \{d_j - ss_i\}$) respectively. ss_i and ss_k are directed adjacent if existing a $sim(ss_k, s_{j,l})>\theta$ where $s_{j,l} \in \{d_j - ss_i\}$.

If $s_{j,l}$ is in front of ss_i, the credibility $weight(ss_i, ss_k)$ that ss_k is in front of ss_i is computed as follow:

$$weight(ss_i, ss_k) = w * sim(ss_k, s_{j,l}) + (1-w) * \frac{rank(s_{j,l})}{rank(ss_i)} \quad (1)$$

where $rank(ss_i)$ is the sequence of ss_i in the document it belongs to (e.g. the rank of second sentence of document is 2), w is the contribution of sentence similarity to the credibility, $sim(ss_k, s_{j,l})$ is the similarity between ss_k and $s_{j,l}$. If there is no edge from ss_k to ss_i in G, then add an edge to G; else if $weight(ss_i, ss_k)$ is greater than the weight of existing edge, then update the edge.

If ss_i is in front of $s_{j,l}$, the credibility $weight(ss_i, ss_k)$ is computed as follows:

$$weight(ss_i, ss_k) = w * sim(ss_k, s_{j,l}) + (1-w) * \frac{Len(d_j) - rank(s_{j,l})}{Len(d_j) - rank(ss_i)} \quad (2)$$

where $len(d_j)$ is the total number of sentences contained in d_j. If there is no edge from ss_i to ss_k in G, then add an edge to G; else if $weight(ss_i, ss_k)$ is greater than the weight of the existing edge, update the edge.

Sentence similarity between sentences s_1 and s_2 can be computed based on TF-IDF or WordNet (Achananuparp, 2008). Sentences similarity based TF-IDF can be calculated as follow:

$$sim(s_1, s_2) = \vec{V_1} \cdot \vec{V_2} = \frac{\sum_{i=1}^{n} x_i \cdot y_i}{\sqrt{\sum_{i=1}^{n} x_i^2} * \sqrt{\sum_{i=1}^{n} y_i^2}} \quad (3)$$

where $V_1 = \{x_1, x_2 ... x_n\}$, $V_2 = \{y_1, y_2 ... y_n\}$, V_1, V_2 are TF-IDF vectors of sentences s_1 and s_2.

Sentence similarity $sim(s_1, s_2)$ based on WordNet is defined as

$$sim(s_1, s_2) = \frac{\sum_{w \in s1} Sim(w, s_2) + \sum_{w \in s2} Sim(w, s_2)}{length(s_1) + length(s_2)} \quad (4)$$

where $sim(w, s_i)$ is the maximum semantic similarity between word w and sentence s_i, $length(s_i)$ is the length of sentence s_i.

Step 3: We use a feature-based method to find the first sentence, assume that there is a null sentence at the beginning of each source document and it contains a null feature (Nie, 2006). The probability of a sentence ss_i is the first one is defined as follow:

$$\text{Prob}_i = \frac{1}{K} \sum_{t=1}^{K} \frac{freq(feature_t, nullfeature)}{freq(feature_t)} \quad (5)$$

where K is the number of features in sentence s_i. $freq()$ is the frequency function, $freq(feature_t)$ denotes the frequency of $feature_t$ in the source documents, $freq(feature_t, nullfeature)$ denotes the frequency of $feature_t$ and the *null feature* co-occurring in the source documents within a limited range (one or several sentences, we assign 3 to the range). Select the sentence with the maximum probability as the first sentence. Add the first sentence to P.

Step 4: Get the trail sentence of P, select the next sentence and add it to P. Given an already ordered sentence serial P: $ss_1, ss_2 ... ss_i$ which is a subset of the summarization sentences set SS. The next sentence can be found by formula (6):

$$\text{ss}_j = \arg\max_{s_j \in SS-P} (weight(ss_i, ss_j)) \quad (6)$$

Step 5: If P contains all summarization sentences then exit; otherwise go to step 4.

END

5 Experiments and Evaluation

5.1 Test Set and Evaluation Metrics

Due to current methods provided their experiment results using DUC04 corpus, we also use it to conduct our experiment. DUC04 provide 50 source document sets and four manual summaries for each document set in its Task2. Each document set consists of 10 documents. In the DUC04, sentences in summaries are not directly come from the source documents and they are created by manually. Therefore, we need map them back to the sentences in source documents. For each manual summarization sentence, we find a sentence in source document sets that has the maximal similarity with it as its source sentence. These source sentences of each summarization are taken as inputs to ordering model, but sequential information is neglected. The output ordering of various models are compared with the specified ones in manual summaries. A number of metrics can be used to evaluate the difference between two orderings. In this paper, we adopt Kendall's τ (Lebanon, 2002), which was defined as:

$$\tau = 1 - \frac{2(number\_of\_inversions)}{N(N-1)/2} \quad (7)$$

where N is the number of objects to be ordered (i.e., sentences), $number\_of\_inversions$ is the minimal number of interchanges of adjacent objects to transfer an ordering into another. Intuitively, τ can be considered as how easily an ordering can be transferred to another. The value of τ varies from -1 to 1, where 1 denotes the best situation where two orderings are the same, and -1 denotes the worst situation where two orderings are completely reversed. Given a standard ordering, randomly produced orderings of the same objects would get an average τ of 0. For example, Table 1 lists three numbers of sequences, their natural sequences and the corresponding τ values.

Examples	Natural sequences	τ values
1 2 4 3	1 2 3 4	0.67
1 5 2 3 4	1 2 3 4 5	0.40
2 1 3	1 2 3	0.33

Table 1: Ordering Examples

5.2 Experimental Results

In order to get the best performance, we adjusted the parameters of our approach (θ and w). We adopted DUC02 as the development set to adjust parameters θ and w. In DUC02, it provide 60 document sets of approximately 10 documents each and one manual summarization of about 100 words for each document set in Task2. Figure 3 show the experiment results, from it, we can finally get the optimal value of θ and w (0.3 and 0.6 respectively).

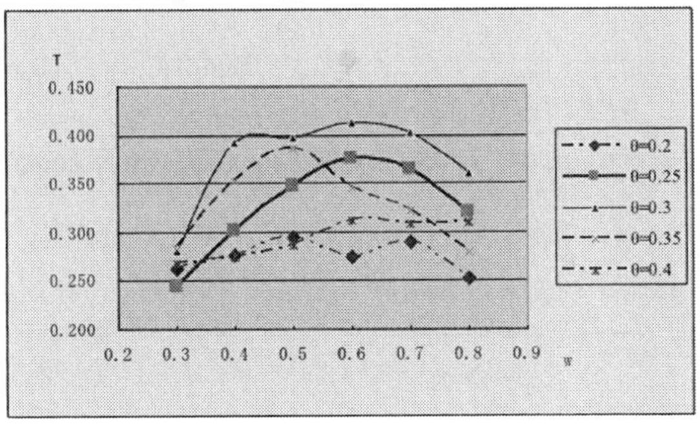

Figure 3. Graph of adjusting parameters

We assume Rd, Mo, Pr, Fa and Ca to denote random ordering, majority ordering, probabilistic model, feature-adjacency based model and cluster-adjacency based model which have been mentioned in section 2 respectively. Due to other methods didn't report their results on DUC04 corpus; we do not compare our method with them in this paper. We define our Context-based approach as Co. Table 2 shows the results of different methods. The τ value of our approach reaches 0.43, which outperforms other approaches. Also, the performance of WordNet-based similarity measure is slightly better than the TF-IDF based one. The reason may be that some authors will express the same meaning by using some different but synonymous words.

Models	τ	Similarity Measure
Rd	-0.007	
Mo	0.143	
Pr	0.144	
Fa	0.316	
Ca	0.415	
Co	0.424	TF-IDF
Co	0.432	WordNet

Table 2: Experimental results (θ=0.3, w=0.6 in Co)

We conduct another experiment, correction ratio of sentence inference from correctly ordered previous sentences, to see why our method gets better performance. The result is listed in table 3.

Models	1st sentence →2nd sentence	2nd sentence →3rd sentence
Mo	24.4%	10%
Pr	25.0%	25%
Fa	31.8%	50%
Ca	56.2%	61.6%
Co (TF-IDF)	62.5%	64.2%
Co (WordNet)	63.2%	65.4%

Table 3. Comparison of correct sentence inference

From table 3, our method has the highest correction ratio of sentence inference, which mean that our method's strategy to choose next sentence is reasonable than that of others. Probabilistic ordering, a statistical method, tries to find the ordering clue from the corpus, but they ignore the importance of source documents. Basically, we know that people can easily find the order of summarization sentences according to the source documents. But it's difficult to give the order for the sentence base on a corpus without the source documents even for a knowledgeable man. Therefore, we believe the source documents can give us some effective and efficient information. Fa and Ca models sort sentences by using sentence adjacency, which is calculated based on adjacency of feature pairs. However, how to choose effective features is a potential issue of this kind of method. Besides, it doesn't always mean two sentences are likely to be adjacent when some words of them are adjacent. Our method is different from other ones in that we find the indirect relations between summarization sentences based on the context and make full use of the information which provided by source documents.

Table 4 shows a further comparison among all methods. "Positive ordering" means that the result of ordering is better than that of random ordering and "Negative ordering" denotes the output ordering which gets a negative τ. From it, we can review that our method generates the most positive orderings while with the least negative orderings. Precision of first sentence of our method is less than that of Ca. If we assume the first sentence of summarization is known in advance, experiments show that the average τ value of our method could reach 0.562.

Models	Precision of 1st sentence	Positive Orderings	Negative Orderings
Rd	14.0%	48.4%	44.6%
Mo	21.6%	61.8%	31.8%
Pr	40.8%	62.5%	29.5%
Fa	59.5%	71.5%	19.0%
Ca	65.5%	81.0%	15.5%
Co (TF-IDF)	59.5%	84.5%	10.5%
Co (WordNet)	59.5%	84.8%	10.1%

Table 4. Correction ratio of 1st sentence ranking

6 Conclusion and Future Work

This paper presents a novel method for sentence ordering in multi-document summarization application. The proposed method first computes the similarity between summarization sentences and context of other summarization sentences, judge whether or not two sentences should be adjacent, and then compute the reliability according to the similarity. The experimental results review that our method outperforms other sentence ordering methods on DUC04 corpora.

For further work, we will change the strategy to improve the accuracy of first summarization sentence; therefore, the τ value could have an obvious improvement. In addition, we will conduct more experiments to verify the effectiveness and efficient of our method using manual evaluation.

Acknowledgments The authors would like to thank the anonymous reviewers for their comments on this paper. This research was supported by the National Natural Science Foundation of China under Grant No. 61070123 and No. 60970056, The Research Fund for the Doctoral Program of Higher Education of China under Grant No. 20093201110006, the Natural Science Major Fundamental Research Program of the Jiangsu Higher Education Institutions under Grant No. 08KJA520002.

References

Danushka Bollegala, Naoaki Okazaki, Mitsuru Ishizuka. 2005. A Machine Learning Approach to Sentence Ordering for Multi-document Summarization and Its Evaluation. In *IJCNLP 2005, LNAI 3651*. pages 624-635.

Danushka Bollegala, Naoaki Okazaki, Mitsuru Ishizuka. 2010. A bottom-up approach to sentence ordering for multi-document summarization, *Information Processing & Management*. 46:89-109.

Ji Donghong and Nie Yu. 2008. Sentence Ordering based on Cluster Adjacency in Multi-Document Summarization. In *IJCNLP 2008*, pages 745-750.

Guy Lebanon and John Lafferty. 2002. Cranking: Combining Rankings Using Conditional Probability Models on Permutations. In *ICML 2002*, Morgan Kaufmann Publishers, San Francisco, CA, pages 363-370.

Kathleen R. Mckeown, Regina Barzilay, David Evans, Vasileios Hatzivassiloglou, Simone Teufel. 2001. Columbia Multi-document Summarization: Approach and Evaluation. In *DUC01*.

Mirella Lapata. 2002. Automatic Evaluation of Information Ordering: Kendall's Tau. *Computational Linguistics*, 32(4): 471-484.

Mirella Lapata. 2003. Probabilistic Text Structuring: Experiments with Sentence Ordering. In *ACL 2003*. pages 545–552.

Naoaki Okazaki, Yutaka Matsuo, Mitsuru Ishizuka. 2004. Improving chronological sentence ordering by precedence relation, In *COLING 2004*, pages 750-756.

Nie Yu, Ji Donghong and Yang Lingpeng. 2006. An Adjacency Model for Sentence Ordering in Multi-document. In *AIRS 2006*.

Palakorn Achananuparp, Xiaohua Hu, Xiajiong Shen. 2008. The Evaluation of Sentence Similarity Measures. In *Proceedings of the 10th international conference on Data Warehousing and Knowledge Discovery*, Berlin, Heidelberg, Springer-Verlag, pages 305–316.

Regina Barzilay, Noemie Elhadad, McKeown R. Kathleen. 2002. Inferring Strategies for Sentence Ordering in Multi-document News Summarization.

Journal of Artificial Intelligence Research, 17:(35–55).

Regina Barzilay, Noemie Elhadad and Kathleen R. McKeown. 2001. Sentence Ordering in Multi-document Summarization. In *HLT 2001*, San Diego, CA, pages 149-156.

Enhancing extraction based summarization with outside word space

Christian Smith, Arne Jönsson
Santa Anna IT Research Institute AB
Linköping, Sweden
christian.smith@liu.se, arnjo@ida.liu.se

Abstract

We present results from improving vector space based extraction summarizers. The summarizer uses Random Indexing and Page Rank to extract those sentences whose importance are ranked highest for a document, based on vector similarity. Originally the summarizer used only word vectors based on the words in the document to be summarized. By using a larger word space model the performance of the summarizer was improved. Along with the performance, robustness was improved as random seeds did not affect the summarizer as much as before, making for more predictable results from the summarizer.

1 Introduction

Many persons have, for various reasons, problems assimilating long complex texts. Not only persons with visual impairments or dyslexia, but also, for instance, those having a different mother tongue or persons in need of a quick summary of a text. A tool for automatic summarization of texts from different genres as an aid in reading can thus be useful for many persons and purposes.

Automatic summarization can be done in various ways. A common distinction is extract versus abstract summaries. An extract summary is created by extracting the most important sentences from the original text so that the result is a shorter version of the original text with some information still present, for instance the most important sentences or words. An abstract summary on the other hand is a summary where the text has been broken down and rebuilt as a complete rewrite to convey a general idea of the original text. Furthermore, the summaries can be indicative (for instance only providing keywords as central topics) or informative (content focused) (Firmin and Chrzanowski, 1999). The former might be more usable when a reader needs to decide whether or not the text is interesting to read and the latter when a reader more easily needs to get a grasp of the meaning of a text that is supposed to be read.

In this paper we will examine and try to increase the performance of an automatic extraction-based summarizer. Previously, the summarizer has been functioning without aid of outside corpora or training material. While the performance have been good, some improvements utilizing an outside corpus can be achieved.

The technique behind the summarizer will first be described in more detail, after which some results are presented which indicates that the performance can be enhanced by using outside training material.

2 The word space model

The word space model, or vector space model (Eldén, 2007), is a spatial representation of a word's meaning that can reduce the linguistic variability and capture semantically related concepts by taking into account the positioning of words in a multidimensional space, instead of looking at only shallow linguistic properties. This facilitates the creation of summaries, since the positioning in the word space can be used to evaluate the different passages (words or sentences for instance) in relation to a document with regards to informational and semantic content.

Every word in a given context occupies a specific point in the space and has a vector associated to it that can be used to define its meaning.

Word spaces are constructed according to the distributional hypothesis and the proximity hypothesis. In the distributional hypothesis, words that occur in similar contexts have similar meanings so that a *word* is the sum of its contexts and the *context* is the sum of its words, where the *con-*

text can be defined as the surrounding words or the entire document. The proximity hypothesis states that words close to each other in the word space have similar meaning while those far from each other have dissimilar meaning.

The word space can be constructed from a matrix where text units are columns and the words in all text units are rows in the matrix. A certain entry in the matrix is nonzero iff the word corresponding to the row exists in the text unit represented by the column. The resulting matrix is very large and sparse which makes for the usage of techniques for reducing dimensionality and get a more compact representation. Latent Semantic Analysis is one such technique that, however, can be computationally expensive unless used with alternative algorithms (Gorrell, 2006). Random Indexing (Sahlgren, 2005; Kanerva, 1988) is another dimension reduction technique based on sparse distributed representations that provide an efficient and scalable approximate solution to distributional similarity problems.

3 The summarizer

CogSum is an extraction based summarizer, using the word space model Random Indexing (RI), c.f. Hassel (2007) and a modified version of PageRank (Brin and Page, 1998).

In Random Indexing context vectors are accumulated based on the occurrence of words in contexts. Random Indexing can be used with any type of linguistic context, is inherently incremental, and does not require a separate dimension reduction phase as for instance Latent Semantic Analysis.

Random Indexing can be described as a two-step operation:

Step 1 A unique d-dimensional *index vector* is assigned and randomly generated to each context (e.g. each document or each word). These index vectors are sparse and high-dimensional. They consist of a small number, ρ, of randomly distributed +1s and -1s, with the rest of the elements of the vectors set to 0.

Step 2 *Context vectors* are produced on-the-fly. As scanning the text, each time a word occurs in a context, that context's d-dimensional index vector is added to the context vector for the word. The context window defines a region of context around each word, and the number of adjacent words in a context window is called the context window size, w. For example, with $w = 2$, i.e. a 2x2 context window, the word o_n is represented by the context window c_m as:

$$c_m = [(o_{n-2})(o_{n-1})o_n(o_{n+1})(o_{n+2})],$$

and the context vector of o_n in c_m would be updated with:

$$C_m = R(o_{n-2}) + R(o_{n-1}) + R(o_{n+1}) + R(o_{n+2}),$$

where $R(x)$ is the random index vector of x. This process is repeated every time we observe o_n in our data, adding the corresponding information to its existing context vector C. If the context c_m is encountered again, no new index vector will be generated. Instead the existing index vector for c_m is added to C to produce a new context vector for o_n.

Words are thus represented by d-dimensional context vectors that are effectively the sum of the index vectors of all the contexts in which the word appears.

Additionally, the vectors within the sliding contex window can be weighted according to the distance to the focus word. One example is $2^{(1-distance)}$, or $[0.5, 1, 0, 1, 0.5]$ for a 2x2 context window providing a larger weight for words closest to the focus word (Karlgren and Sahlgren, 2001).

After the creation of word context vectors, the similarity between words could be measured by calculating the cosine angle between their word vectors, by taking the scalar product of the vectors and dividing by their norms such as:

$$cos(x, y) = \frac{x \cdot y}{|x|\,|y|} \quad (1)$$

Random Indexing is useful for acquiring the context vectors of terms, it is however not clear how a bigger context, such as a sentence, could be built from the word vectors. A crude way of creating sentence vectors from word vectors would be to simply summarize the vectors of the words in the sentence after they have been normalized to unit length. However, as the number of words in a sentence increases, so will the sentence similarity to the mean vector. Comparing sentences or documents in this way using cosine will make for larger similarity just by a larger number of words, regardless of relatedness. To alleviate this problem, the mean document vector is subtracted from each of the sentence's word vectors before summarizing the vectors (Higgins and Burstein, 2007), see Equation 2.

$$\vec{sent}_j = \frac{1}{S}\sum_{i=1}^{S}(\vec{w}_i - \vec{doc}) \quad (2)$$

where S denotes the number of words, w, in sentence j and $\vec{doc}$ is calculated as in Equation 3.

$$\vec{doc} = \frac{1}{N}\sum_{i=1}^{N}\vec{w}_i \quad (3)$$

where N denotes the number of unique words.

Words that are similar to the document vector will come closer to the zero vector, while those dissimilar to the document vector will increase in magnitude. When later summarizing the vectors, those of greater magnitude will have increased impact on the total sentence vector so that common, non-distinct, words not contribute as much to the sentence vector. As this reduces the impact of common non-distinct words, there is essentially no need for a stop word list.

COGSUM also uses the Weighted PageRank algorithm in conjunction to its RI-space to rank the sentences (Chatterjee and Mohan, 2007).

The method of using graph-based ranking algorithms for extracting sentences in summarization purposes was proposed by Mihalcea (2004), who introduce the TextRank model. In graph-based algorithms such as TextRank the text need to be represented as a graph, where each vertex depicts a unit of text and the edges between the units represent a connection between the corresponding text units. Graph-based ranking algorithms may be used to decide the importance of a vertex within a graph, by taking into account global information from the entire graph, rather than from only the local context of the vertices. The ranks are thus recursively computed so that the rank of a vertex depends on all the vertices' ranks. In TextRank, PageRank is used to rank the sentences, although it is noted that other ranking algorithms are possible. PageRank is a graph-based ranking algorithm which originally was used to rank home pages automatically and objectively in the Google search engine (Brin and Page, 1998). In TextRank, for the task of sentence extraction, each sentence in a text is represented as a vertex and the relation between sentences are based on their overlap or "similarity", denoted by Equation 4.

$$Similarity(S_i, S_j) = \frac{|\{w_k | w_k \in S_i \& w_k \in S_j\}|}{log(|S_i|) + log(|S_j|)} \quad (4)$$

Thus, if a sentence adresses certain concepts, the other sentences that share content will get recommended by that sentence in the recursive fashion provided by PageRank.

To use PageRank and Random Indexing for summaries an undirected fully connected graph is created where a vertex depicts a sentence in the current text and an edge between two different vertices is assigned a weight that depicts how similar these are based on a cosine angle comparison of their meaning vectors, see Figure 1. As it is fully connected, all vertices are connected with each other and all out-links are also considered as in-links.

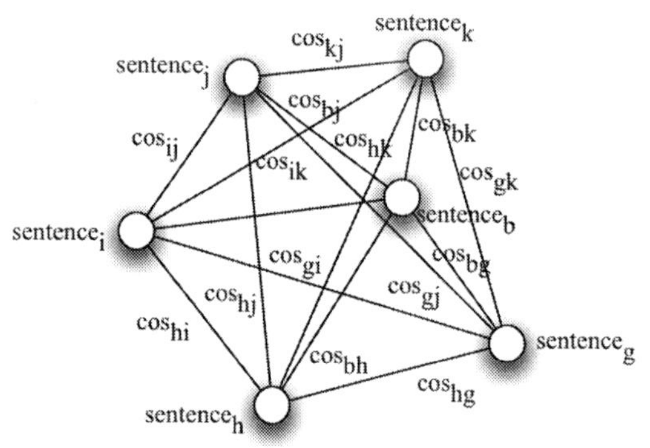

Figure 1: A simplified graph where sentences are linked and weighted according to the cosine values between them.

The algorithm rank ingoing and outgoing links to pages depending on the number of links as follows, Equation 5:

$$PR^W(s_i) = (1-d) + d * \sum_{s_j In(s_i)} w_{ji} \frac{PR^W(s_j)}{\sum_{s_k \in Out(s_j)} w_{kj}} \quad (5)$$

where s_i is the sentence under consideration, $In(s_i)$ is the set of sentences that link to s_i, $Out(s_j)$ is the set of sentences that link from s_i and d is the damping factor.

The damping factor was originally set to account for the possibility of a surfer clicking a random web link when (s)he gets bored (Brin and Page, 1998). With regards to the ranking of sentences, we see the damping factor as the possibility of a sentence containing some implicit information that a certain reader might consider more important at the time, following an analogy by Mihalcea and Tarau (2004). The PageRank-algorithm utilizes the "random surfer model" and using weighted PageRank in text comparison utilizes "text surfing" in the context of text cohesion. The links in the sentence graph might be attributed to links between connected concepts or topics semantically, creating a "web" of understanding on which a reader might surf.

The computation is carried out on all sentences iteratively until node weights converge, see Figure 2.

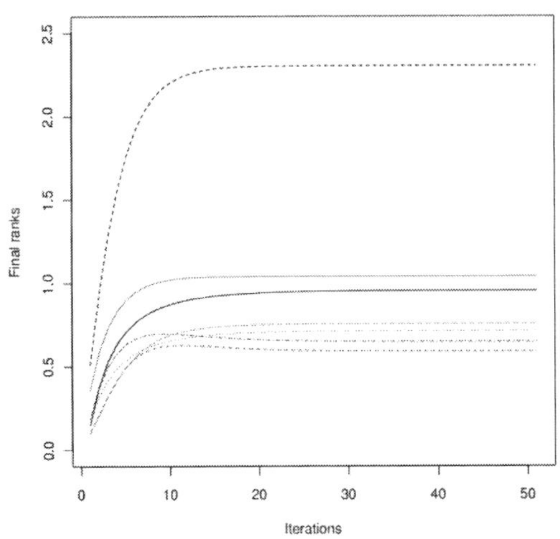

Figure 2: Each line represents a sentence from a single text with its weight plotted on the y-axis on each iteration on the x-axis. 50 iterations are plotted.

The ranking algorithm does not rely only on local context information (vertex) but draws information recursively from the entire graph. Sentences with similar content will then contribute with positive support to each other through a recommendation process, where the sentences' ranks are increased or decreased each iteration. This does not exclusively depend on the number of sentences supporting a sentence, but also on the rank of the linking sentences. This means that a few high-ranked sentences provide bigger support than a greater number of low-ranked sentences. This leads to a ranking of the sentences by their importance to the document at hand and thus to a summary of desired length only including the most important sentences.

When the text has been processed using RI and PageRank, the most important sentences are extracted using the final ranks on the sentences, for instance 30% of the original text, resulting in a condensed version of the original text with the most important information intact, in the form of extracted sentences. Since all sentences are ranked, the length of the summary is easy to specify, in COGSUM this is implemented as a simple slider. COGSUM is designed for informative summaries, but it is also possible to have indicative summaries by clicking a "keywords" check box.

COGSUM is written in Java and utilizes a Random Indexing toolkit available at Hassel (2011a). No outside material is used which makes the summarizer highly portable and usable for several languages and domains.

Previous evaluations of COGSUM with human users show that summaries produced by COGSUM are useful, considered informative enough and readable (Jönsson et al., 2008). COGSUM has also been evaluated on gold standards for news texts and authority texts showing that it is better than another Swedish summarizer, SweSum, (Dalianis, 2000) on authority texts and almost as good on news texts, texts that the other summarizer was especially adapted to handle (Gustavsson and Jönsson, 2010).

4 Multi-document word vectors

COGSUM has previously worked without aid from any outside source making it highly portable and more or less language independent. However, some problems have been detected. We identified some abruptness in the resulting summaries, affected by the random factor of the index vectors. This was regardless of setting of dimensionality and other parameters.

To investigate the effect of randomness several summaries with different index vectors were created. The final ranks of the sentences in a text after the summarization process were calculated and plotted on each random seed that held its own distribution of the ones in the index vectors, Figure 3. The figure shows 10 different summaries with their own seeds. The final values after the ranking are plotted on the y-axis mapped to each seed on the x-axis. A straight line would mean that the results are predictable and not affected as much by randomness. As can be seen in Figure 3 there is quite some randomness in which sentences that are chosen depends on the seed to the Random Indexing algorithm.

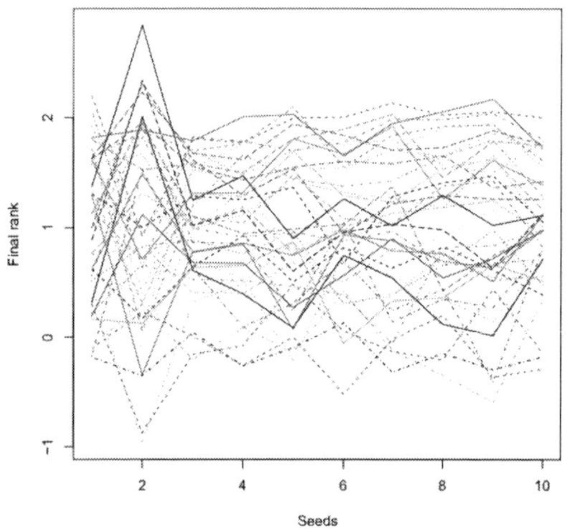

Figure 3: Ten different seeds without pretrained space. Each series represents a sentence in a text. The values on the y-axis are the final values of each sentence after the PageRank-algorithm.

For COGSUM, we wanted to extend the method by using an outside larger RI-space. Using a large RI-space, a better semantic representation of the words can be acquired (Sahlgren, 2006). By extending the method to use an outside training space we thus believe that the quality and robustness of the summaries can be improved.

COGSUM takes as input the text to be summarized, but now also a previously trained RI-space is supplied, containing the semantic vectors of the words.

The RI-space was created from several Swedish texts from different genres, all in all approximately 240 000 words. The articles consisted of a number of novels in a subset of the Stockholm-Umeå Corpus (Ejerhed et al., 2006), a set of newspaper articles available at the concordances of Språkbanken, specifically from the Parole corpus (Ridings, 2011), and some popular science articles from the same place.

The text is processed by assigning each of the words the corresponding semantic vector from the space. Sentence vectors are constructed as proposed by Chatterjee and Mohan (2007) and Higgins and Burstein (2007), i.e. the words in a sentence are summarized after the subtraction of the mean space vector, and divided by the number of words in the sentence, as in Equation 2.

To investigate the effect on randomness we created 10 summaries with different seeds, the same way as in Figure 3. Figure 4 shows 10 trials on different seeds as before on the same text, but using the larger outside RI-space described above. Comparing figures 3 and 4 reveals a more straight line when using a large RI-space. Thus, by using an outside RI-space, the effect of randomness is reduced and a more predictable result between seeds is achieved.

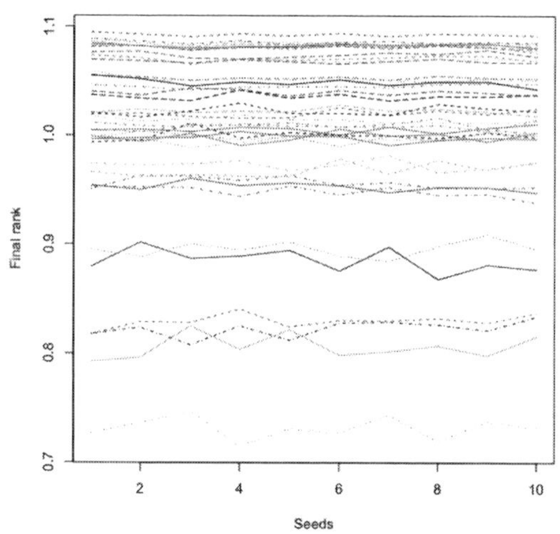

Figure 4: Ten different seeds with pretrained space, each line representing a sentence in a text. The values are the final ranks of each sentence after the PageRank algorithm.

Another problem that has emerged is that the weighted PageRank sometimes fail to converge. This might happen in the original PageRank when the number of outlinks from a vertex is zero (Eldén, 2007). The corresponding phenomenon in the weighted PageRank-algorithm is when the sum of the out weights from a given sentence is zero or close to zero. One reason is that since sentence similarity can be both positive and negative it is possible that they even out. Also, nearly orthogonal sentence vectors makes for weights around zero. This only happens when not using an outside space. Since a small document does not contain the distribution of words across a large number of context, it is likely that several sentences contain words that occur only in that sentence. When the context vectors for the sentences thereby are created, their vectors may be too sparse and the angle between them becomes nearly orthogonal, and the weights sum up to zero.

Figure 5 is produced similar to Figure 2 , where each line represents a sentence. The ranks in the graph are plotted on the y-axis and each iteration on the x-axis. It is clear that the values fail to converge and stabilize which might be a problem when extracting sentences based on the ranks. This does not happen when using a large RI-space, since the sentence vectors are built from context vectors using a large number of contexts.

The problem can be alleviated simply by redoing the random indexing-phase using a different random seed, which is what is done in the current implementation when not using any outside source.

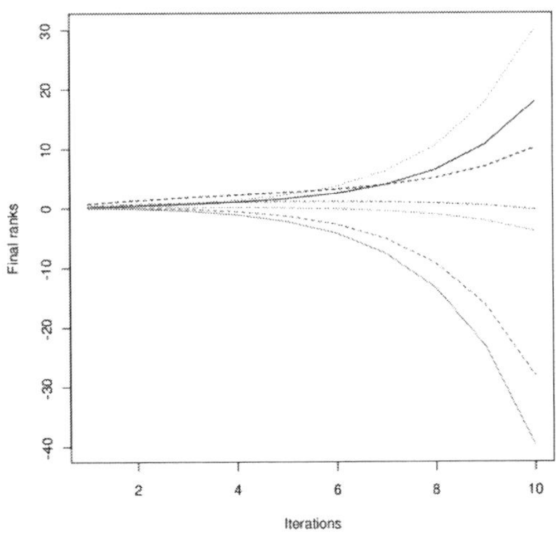

Figure 5: No convergence during the weighted PageRank-algorithm. Each line represents a sentence in a text with the rank plotted on the y-axis and the corresponding iteration during the PageRank on the x-axis. The first ten iterations are plotted.

5 Evaluation

By equipping the summarizer with a better semantic understanding an evaluation was also performed investigating the information quality of the summarizer.

By using a pre-trained RI-space it was hypothesized not only that the random factor could be eliminated, but also that the quality of the summaries would improve. A comparison was made between using an outside text source and using only the document to be summarized to build the RI-space. Since several random seeds provided different summaries on the same text, the average performance measure of 10 seeds for each text was calculated when not using an outside random index space.

The pre-trained RI-space used a dimensionality of 1800, a window size, $w = 2$ with a weighting of $[0.5, 1, 0, 1, 0.5]$, and 8 non-zeroes in the index vectors, similar to Karlgren and Sahlgren (2001).

Using no pre-trained space, the dimensionality was set to 100, window size, $w = 2$ with the same weighting as above, and 4 non-zeroes, to account for a much smaller space, as in Chatterjee and Mohan (2007).

For the evaluation 13 Swedish newspaper articles with a length ranging from 100 to 800 words, see Table 1, were summarized to 30% and compared to human created gold standard summaries of the same length, available at KTHeXtractCorpus (Hassel, 2011b).

Several automatic evaluation packages are available, most notably ROUGE (Lin, 2004). We used, however, also the more recent package AutoSummENG (Giannakopoulos et al., 2008) since it is reported as having a higher correlation with human evaluations than ROUGE (Giannakopoulos, 2009). For AutoSummENG, the comparison was performed by means of graph-value similarity taking content similarity between different texts on character level into consideration. The texts are represented as graphs where each vertex depicts a character n-gram. The graphs from the model and system summaries are then compared resulting in a similarity measure denoting the performance of the system.

It should be noted that no preprocessing in terms of stop word removal and stemming were performed during the ROUGE evaluation since the package is tuned for English and no Swedish lexicon for that purpose were available at the time.

Table 2 shows the values acquired using AutoSummENG for each text and we see that for most texts the summaries produced using the larger RI-space are better than the ones without RI-space.

	Words	Sentences
Text1	110	7
Text2	688	40
Text3	701	37
Text4	400	27
Text5	227	13
Text6	153	9
Text7	441	24
Text8	179	10
Text9	483	33
Text10	838	67
Text11	388	24
Text12	169	9
Text13	471	32

Table 1: Text characteristics, the number of words and sentences on each text.

AutoSummEnG	Without space	With space
Text1	0.301	0.751
Text2	0.484	0.484
Text3	0.497	0.509
Text4	0.569	0.447
Text5	0.276	0.556
Text6	0.321	0.520
Text7	0.510	0.502
Text8	0.239	1.000
Text9	0.340	0.465
Text10	0.347	0.419
Text11	0.487	0.556
Text12	0.574	0.384
Text13	0.520	0.517
Mean	**0.420**	**0.547**

Table 2: Evaluation of each summary. Each summary has been compared to a gold standard created by humans. The left column shows the values acquired for the summaries using no outside random indexing-space and the right column shows the values after using an outside space. The values are acquired by means of graph value similarity using AutoSummENG.

Using no space, the mean value from all texts of the comparison was 0.420. By using an outside space, the mean value was 0.547 which is a significant improvement ($p < .05$).

As a comparison, evaluations using the more known ROUGE package was performed. When using ROUGE a similar result is obtained, see table 3. Comparing the results of AutoSummENG and ROUGE yields a correlation of $\approx .96$.

6 Conclusion

By using a large word space model the performance of the extraction based summarizer CogSum could be improved. Along with the performance, robustness was improved, as the random factor between seeds was reduced, making for more predictable results from the summarizer. The performance was evaluated using AutoSummENG, a tool to compare generated texts with gold standard texts created by humans. The evaluation was performed without input from humans, although humans created the gold standard and thus affected the results indirectly, no measures regarding readability were taken. Thus, the measure does not capture readability, only that the extracted sentences can be seen as the most important for the document and that they correspond to human created gold standards.

Evaluations were also performed using ROUGE to have a point of reference since AutoSummENG is a lesser known method of evaluation and the results from these two different packages correlated strongly.

ROUGE-1	Without space	With space
Text1	0.386	0.695
Text2	0.538	0.551
Text3	0.570	0.540
Text4	0.647	0.522
Text5	0.290	0.590
Text6	0.368	0.599
Text7	0.600	0.573
Text8	0.359	0.975
Text9	0.452	0.541
Text10	0.454	0.560
Text11	0.574	0.665
Text12	0.682	0.369
Text13	0.599	0.625
Mean	**0.502**	**0.600**

Table 3: Evaluation of each summary using ROUGE-1 n-gram. Each summary has been compared to a gold standard created by humans. The left column shows the ROUGE scores acquired for the summaries using no outside random indexing-space and the right column shows the scores after using an outside space.

Further improvements can be seen with regards to stabilizing weights in the weighted PageRank-algorithm. By using a large word space the sentence vectors become more dense since they are built from context vectors from a large number of contexts. The sentence vectors are thus not as likely to be nearly orthogonal which becomes a problem when summarizing the weights as outlinks, since the sum then might be close to zero.

An increased quality in semantic representation however comes with some tradeoffs. A large word space reduces the portability somewhat, and increases the computational effort since a large space uses a much larger dimensionality. Also, the word space makes it language dependent, a previously strong argument for this method. Creating a larger RI-space for a new language is, however, not such a difficult task if a large enough corpus is available.

The word space that was used was produced from rather general texts and it would be interesting for the future to investigate the effect of different RI-spaces on different genres and domains, both in terms of training material but also on the quality of the summaries. Since Random Indexing is incremental, it is easy to add documents to the semantic space.

Although previous work (Smith and Jönsson, 2011) have looked at readability and concluded that the readability may be increased using extraction based summarization, it is still unclear exactly how cohesive they are. Mihalcea and Tarau (2004) draws an analogy between the PageRank "random surfer model" and "text surfing" which relates to the concept of text cohesion. The links in the graph might be attributed to links between connected concepts or topics in a semantic way so it would not be surprising to find that the summaries have acceptable cohesion. Future research will have to conclude the cohesiveness of the summaries and how they may need to be improved.

We have, however, shown that the quality and robustness can be improved by using an outside previously trained random indexing space in the process of vector space model extraction based automatic summarization.

Acknowledgments

This research was partly supported by a research grant from The Swedish Post and Telecom Agency (PTS).

References

Sergey Brin and Lawrence Page. 1998. The anatomy of a large-scale hypertextual web search engine. *Computer Networks and ISDN Systems*, 30(1-7):107–117.

Nilhadri Chatterjee and Shiwali Mohan. 2007. Extraction-based single-document summarization using random indexing. In *Proceedings of the 19th IEEE international Conference on Tools with Artificial intelligence – (ICTAI 2007)*, pages 448–455.

Hercules Dalianis. 2000. Swesum – a text summarizer for swedish. Technical Report TRITA-NA-P0015, IPLab-174, NADA, KTH, Sweden.

Eva Ejerhed, Gunnel Källgren, and Benny Brodda. 2006. Stockholm umeå corpus version 2.0.

Lars Eldén. 2007. *Matrix Methods in Data Mining and Pattern Recognition*. Society for Industrial & Applied Mathematics (SIAM).

Thérese Firmin and Michael J Chrzanowski, 1999. *An Evaluation of Automatic Text Summarization Systems*, volume 6073, pages 325–336. SPIE.

George Giannakopoulos, Vangelis Karkaletsis, George Vouros, and Panagiotis Stamatopoulos. 2008. Summarization system evaluation revisited: N-gram graphs. *ACM Transactions on Speech Language Processing*, 5(3):1–39.

George Giannakopoulos. 2009. *Automatic Summarization from Multiple Documents*. Ph.D. thesis, University of the Aegean.

Genevieve Gorrell. 2006. *Generalized Hebbian Algorithm for Dimensionality Reduction in Natural Language Processing*. Ph.D. thesis, Linköping University.

Pär Gustavsson and Arne Jönsson. 2010. Text summarization using random indexing and pagerank. In *Proceedings of the third Swedish Language Technology Conference (SLTC-2010), Linköping, Sweden.*

Martin Hassel. 2007. *Resource Lean and Portable Automatic Text Summarization*. Ph.D. thesis, ISRN-KTH/CSC/A–07/09-SE, KTH, Sweden.

Martin Hassel. 2011a. Java random indexing toolkit, January 2011. `http://www.csc.kth.se/~xmartin/java/`.

Martin Hassel. 2011b. Kth extract corpus (kthxc), January 2011. `http://www.nada.kth.se/~xmartin/`.

Derrick Higgins and Jill Burstein. 2007. Sentence similarity measures for essay coherence. In *Proceedings of the 7th International Workshop on Computational Semantics (IWCS), Tilburg, The Netherlands.*

Arne Jönsson, Mimi Axelsson, Erica Bergenholm, Bertil Carlsson, Gro Dahlbom, Pär Gustavsson, Jonas Rybing, and Christian Smith. 2008. Skim reading of audio information. In *Proceedings of the The second Swedish Language Technology Conference (SLTC-08), Stockholm, Sweden.*

Pentii Kanerva. 1988. *Sparse distributed memory.* Cambridge MA: The MIT Press.

Jussi Karlgren and Magnus Sahlgren. 2001. From words to understanding. In Y. Uesaka, P.Kanerva, and H. Asoh, editors, *Foundations of Real-World Intelligence*, chapter 26, pages 294–308. Stanford: CSLI Publications.

Chin-yew Lin. 2004. Rouge: a package for automatic evaluation of summaries. pages 25–26.

Rada Mihalcea and Paul Tarau. 2004. TextRank: Bringing order into texts. In *Conference on Empirical Methods in Natural Language Processing*, Barcelona, Spain.

Rada Mihalcea. 2004. Graph-based ranking algorithms for sentence extraction, applied to text summarization. In *Proceedings of the ACL 2004 on Interactive poster and demonstration sessions*, ACLdemo '04, Morristown, NJ, USA. Association for Computational Linguistics.

Daniel Ridings. 2011. Parole corpus at språkbanken. `http://spraakbanken.gu.se/parole/`.

Magnus Sahlgren. 2005. An Introduction to Random Indexing. *Methods and Applications of Semantic Indexing Workshop at the 7th International Conference on Terminology and Knowledge Engineering, TKE 2005.*

Magnus Sahlgren. 2006. *The Word-Space Model: Using distributional analysis to represent syntagmatic and paradigmatic relations between words in high-dimensional vector spaces.* Ph.D. thesis, Stockholm University, Department of Linguistics.

Christian Smith and Arne Jönsson. 2011. Automatic summarization as means of simplifying texts, an evaluation for swedish. In *Proceedings of the 18th Nordic Conference of Computational Linguistics (NoDaLiDa-2010), Riga, Latvia.*

Shallow Discourse Parsing with Conditional Random Fields

Sucheta Ghosh Richard Johansson Giuseppe Riccardi
Department of Information Engineering and Computer Science, University of Trento
{ghosh, johansson, riccardi}@disi.unitn.it

Sara Tonelli
FBK-IRST
satonelli@fbk.eu

Abstract

Parsing discourse is a challenging natural language processing task. In this paper we take a data driven approach to identify arguments of explicit discourse connectives. In contrast to previous work we do not make any assumptions on the span of arguments and consider parsing as a token-level sequence labeling task. We design the argument segmentation task as a cascade of decisions based on conditional random fields (CRFs). We train the CRFs on lexical, syntactic and semantic features extracted from the Penn Discourse Treebank and evaluate feature combinations on the commonly used test split. We show that the best combination of features includes syntactic and semantic features. The comparative error analysis investigates the performance variability over connective types and argument positions.

1 Introduction

Automatic discourse processing is considered one of the most challenging NLP tasks due to its dependency on lexical and syntactic features and on the inter-sentential relations. While automatic discourse processing of structured documents or free text is still in its infancy, a number of applications of this technology in practical NLP systems have been proposed. For instance, Somasundaran et al. (2009) describe the use of discourse structure for opinion analysis. Other applications include conversational analysis and dialog systems (Tonelli et al., 2010).

In this work we divide the whole task of discourse parsing into two sub-tasks: connective classification and argument segmentation and classification. Several successful attempts have already been made in the direction of automatic classification of connectives, while token-level argument segmentation has not been explored. Therefore in this paper we will focus on the segmentation and labeling of discourse arguments (`Arg1` and `Arg2`) with full spans, as defined in the annotation protocol of the Penn Discourse Treebank (PDTB) (Prasad et al., 2008).

We present a methodology that, given explicit discourse connectives, automatically extracts discourse arguments by identifying `Arg1` and `Arg2` including the corresponding text spans. We call this approach *shallow* following Prasad et al. (2010) as opposed to tree-like representations of discourse, as in Rhetorical Structure Theory (Mann and Thompson, 1988). Indeed, we provide a flat chunk classification of discourse relations, building a non-hierarchical representation of the relations in a text.

The discourse parser is designed as a cascade of argument-specific CRFs trained on different sets of lexical, syntactic and semantic features. The evaluation is made in terms of exact and partial match of arguments. The partial match condition may be useful in the case of noisy input or for applications that do not require exact alignment.

The paper is structured as follows: in Section 2 we present related work to discourse parsing. In Section 3 we detail argument annotation in PDTB and we report some statistics about the PDTB corpus. In Section 4 the pipeline implemented for the argument segmentation and classification task is presented while in Section 5 two different feature sets used for classification are detailed and compared. In Section 6 the experimental setup is described, together with an extensive evaluation and error analysis. Finally, we draw some conclusions in Section 7.

2 Related Work

The task that we address in this paper – automatic extraction of discourse arguments for given explicit discourse connectives – has been attempted a number of times. Soon after the initial release of the PDTB, it was realized that sentence-internal arguments may be located and classified using techniques similar to semantic role detection and classification methods. Wellner and Pustejovsky (2007) were the first to carry out such an experiment on the PDTB, and Elwell and Baldridge (2008) later improved over their results. However, their task was limited to retrieving the argument *heads*. In contrast, we integrate discourse segmentation in the parsing pipeline because we believe that spans are necessary when using the discourse arguments as input to applications such as opinion mining, where attributions need to be explicitly marked. Besides, no gold data are available for head-based discourse parsing evaluation and they have to be automatically derived from parse trees with a further processing step. With our approach, instead, we can directly use PDTB argument spans both for training and for testing.

Dinesh et al. (2005) extracted complete arguments with boundaries, but only for a restricted class of connectives. The recent work by Prasad et al. (2010) is also limited, since their system only extracts the *sentences* containing the arguments.

In our work, we assume that explicit discourse connectives are given beforehand, either taken directly from a gold standard or automatically identified. The second task based on PDTB was tackled among others by Pitler et al. (2008) and Pitler and Nenkova (2009).

In addition to the work on finding explicit connectives and their arguments, there has been recent work on classification of *implicit* discourse relations, see for instance Lin et al. (2009). In a similar classification experiment, Pitler et al. (2009) investigated features ranging from low-level word pairs to high-level linguistic cues, and demonstrated that it is useful to model the sequence of discourse relations using a sequence labeler. Although they both outperformed their respective baselines, this task is very difficult and performances are still very low.

3 The Penn Discourse Treebank (PDTB)

The Penn Discourse Treebank (Prasad et al., 2008) is a resource including one million words from the Wall Street Journal (Marcus et al., 1993), annotated with discourse relations.

Based on the observation that "no discourse connective has yet been identified in any language that has other than two arguments" (Webber et al. (2010), p. 15), connectives in the PTDB are treated as discourse predicates taking two text spans as *arguments*, i.e. parts of the text that describe events, propositions, facts, situations. Such two arguments in the PDTB are just called `Arg1` and `Arg2` and are chosen according to syntactic criteria: `Arg2` is the argument syntactically bound to the connective, while `Arg1` is the other one. This means that the numbering of the arguments does not necessarily correspond to their order of appearance in text.

In the PDTB, discourse relations can be overtly expressed either by *explicit* connectives, or by *alternative lexicalizations* (AltLex). The first group of connectives corresponds primarily to a few well-defined syntactic classes, while alternative lexicalizations are generally non-connective phrases used to express discourse relations, such that the insertion of an explicit connective would lead to redundancy. There is also a third type of relations - the *implicit* ones - which can be inferred between adjacent sentences, even if no discourse connective is overtly realized.

Every kind of relation (i.e. explicit, implicit and AltLex) in the PDTB is assigned a sense label based on a three-layered hierarchy: the top-level *classes* are the most generic ones and include EXPANSION, CONTINGENCY, COMPARISON and TEMPORAL labels (see below resp. examples from *a* to *d*). Then, each class is further specified at *type* and *subtype* level. Since the state of the art in automatic surface-sense classification (at *class* level) has already reached the upper bound of inter-annotator agreement (Pitler and Nenkova, 2009), we do not include this task in our pipeline. Instead, we use the *class* label as one of our features, because we can expect to achieve similar performance both with gold standard and with automatically assigned classes.

As for the relations considered, we focus here exclusively on *explicit* connectives and the identification of their arguments, including the exact spans. This kind of classification is very complex, since `Arg1` and `Arg2` can occur in many different configurations. Consider for example the following explicit relations annotated in the PDTB[1]:

[1] In all examples of this paper, `Arg1` is reported in italics, `Arg2` appears in bold and discourse connectives are underlined. At the end of the sentence we specify the *class* label

(a) *I never gamble too far.* In particular **I quit after one try, whether I win or lose.** [EXPANSION]

(b) Since **McDonald's menu prices rose this year**, *the actual deadline may have been more.* [CONTINGENCY]

(c) As an indicator of the tight grain supply situation in the U.S., market analysts said **that late Tuesday the Chinese government**, *which often buys U.S. grains in quantity*, **turned** instead **to Britain to buy 500,000 metric tons of wheat.** [COMPARISON]

(d) When **Mr. Green won a $240,000 verdict in a land condemnation case against the State in June 1983**, he says, *Judge O'Kicki unexpectedly awarded him an additional $100,000.* [TEMPORAL]

An explicit connective can occur between two arguments (a) or before them (b). It can also appear inside the argument as shown in (c), where Arg2 is composed of three discontinuous text spans and Arg1 is interpolated. Furthermore, Arg1 and Arg2 need not to be adjacent, as shown in (d), where "he says" does not belong to any argument span. The latter case is annotated as an *Attribution* in the PDTB, because it ascribes the assertion in text to the agent making it. Attributions occur in 34% of all explicit relations in the PDTB, and represent one of the major challenges in identifying exact argument spans, especially for Arg2. However, given the fact that Arg2 is syntactically bound to the connective, its identification is generally considered an easier task than the detection of Arg1 (Prasad et al., 2010). As shown in Table 1, the position of Arg1 w.r.t. the discourse connective is highly variable and, when it does not occur in the same sentence of the connective, it can be very distant from Arg2, even in a preceding paragraph.

Explicit connectives (tokens)	18,459
Explicit connectives (types)	100
Arg1 in same sentence as connective	60.9%
Arg1 in previous, adjacent sentence	30.1%
Arg1 in previous, non adjacent sentence	9.0%

Table 1: Statistics about PDTB annotation from Prasad et al. (2008).

Another element increasing the complexity of Arg1 and Arg2 identification is the fact that discourse connectives can be expressed by subordinating and coordinating conjunctions as well as by discourse adverbials, and each type is subject to different discourse constraints. Furthermore, argument spans range from clauses, even single verb phrases, to multiple sentences, and they do not necessarily match single constituents in the syntax because they can be discontinuous. For all these reasons, the identification of Arg1 has been only partially addressed in previous works (see for instance Prasad et al. (2010).

The PDTB achieved high-valued inter-annotator agreement. Overall agreement for identifying both the arguments (Arg1 and Arg2) of explicit connectives reached 90.2%, with a general tendency of lower scores for Arg1 and higher scores for Arg2. When considering a matching technique that gives credit also to partial overlap, the agreement reaches 94.5% for explicit connectives (Wellner, 2009).

4 Processing pipeline

We show that discourse annotation can be performed *in a pipeline* handling all types of explicit connectives and argument positions. The fundamental idea is to divide the whole complex task into several small and simpler independent subtasks, in order to feed the output of each step into the following one. An overview of the pipeline is given in Fig. 1. Note that, this representation includes data pre-processing, training and testing.

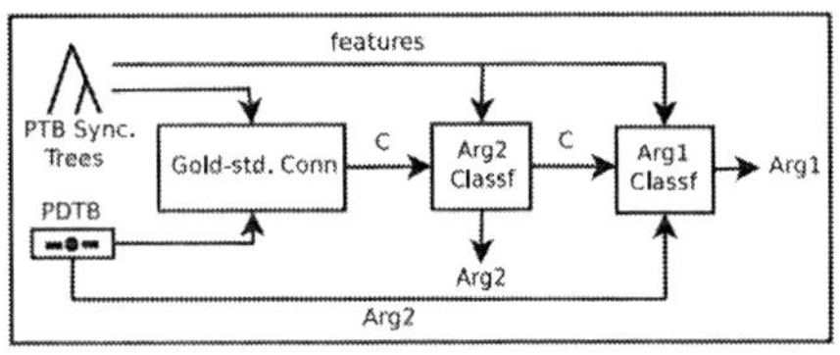

Figure 1: Argument parsing pipeline given Gold-Std Connective(C)

In contrast to previous works, our shallow parsing strategy combines the identification of non-overlapping sequences as connective arguments and the tagging of such text chunks with Arg1 and Arg2 labels.

Since our experiments are based on gold-standard parse trees, we take advantage of the overlap between the PDTB and the Penn Treebank documents (Marcus et al., 1993) in order to map PDTB discourse annotation onto PTB parse trees. We extract the gold-standard connectives with the corresponding top-level sense label from PDTB relations, since this sense label is also one of the features used by our system. This feature is denoted as C in Fig. 1. Besides, we also extract from the PTB trees all syntactic features needed by the system for the first parsing subtask, which is the identification of `Arg2`.

After the identification of `Arg2` given the connective sense label and feature(s) from the gold parse trees, we proceed with the classification of `Arg1`. This step-by-step methodology is different from previous approaches like the one by Wellner and Pustejovsky (2007), where the authors select *pairwise* the best heads of `Arg1` and `Arg2` in order to capture their dependencies, and also by Elwell and Baldridge (2008), who additionally develop *connective-specific* models. Our approach is motivated by two intuitions: first, the identification of `Arg2` and `Arg1` may require different features, since the two arguments have different syntactic and discourse properties, as discussed in Section 3. Second, the identification of `Arg2` is much easier than the identification of `Arg1`, because the former is syntactically bound to the connective. For this reason, a two-step decision architecture seems more appropriate, because we can start with the easier classification task and then exploit additional output information to tackle the second task.

5 Feature description

We report in Table 2 the list of all features considered in the argument labeling task and we explain them in the light of the example in Fig. 2.

Despite the complex task, the feature set is quite small for both arguments. For the identification of `Arg1`, we include one additional features which corresponds to `Arg2` gold standard labels. Note that the best performing set of features does not include all those listed in the table (see feature analysis in Tables 4 and 5).

Features used for `Arg1` and `Arg2` segmentation and labeling.	
F1.	Token (T)
F2.	Sense of Connective (CONN)
F3.	IOB chain (IOB)
F4.	PoS tag
F5.	Lemma (L)
F6.	Inflection (INFL)
F7.	Main verb of main clause (MV)
F8.	Boolean feature for MV (BMV)
F9.	Previous sentence feature (PREV)
Additional feature used only for `Arg1`	
F10.	`Arg2` Labels

Table 2: Feature sets for `Arg1` and `Arg2` segmentation and labeling.

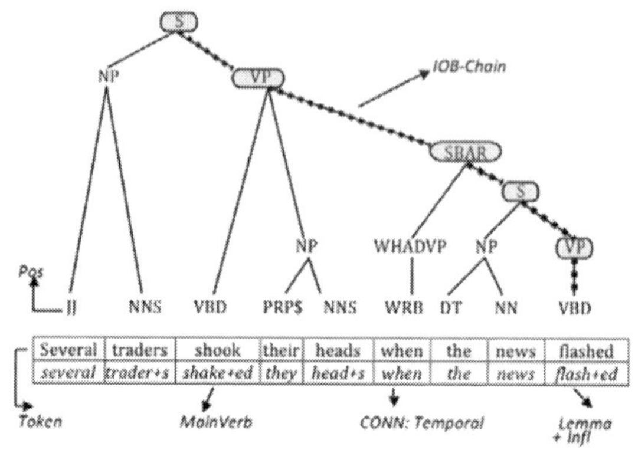

Figure 2: Example sentence with system features

The sense of the connective (F2) refers to one of the four top-level classes in PDTB sense hierarchy, namely TEMPORAL, COMPARISON, CONTINGENCY and EXPANSION. In the sentence reported in Fig. 2, for example, only "when" bears the *temporal* label, while all other tokens are assigned as a "null".

The IOB(Inside-Outside-Begin) chain[2] (F3) is extracted from a full parse tree and corresponds to the syntactic categories of all the constituents on the path between the root note and the current leaf node of the tree. Experiments with other syntactic features proved that IOB chain conveys all deep syntactic information needed in the task, and makes all other syntactic information redundant, for example clause boundaries, token distance from the connective, constituent label, etc. In Fig. 2 the path between "flashed" and the root node is highlighted. The corresponding feature would be *I-S/E-VP/E-SBAR/E-S/C-VP*, where B-, I-, E- and C- indicate whether the given token is respectively at the beginning, inside, at the end of the constituent, or a single token chunk. In this case, "flashed" is at the end of every constituent in the chain, except for the last VP, which dominates one single leaf.

In order to extract the morphological features needed, we use the *morpha* tool (Minnen et al., 2001), which outputs lemma (F5) and inflection information (F6) of the candidate token. The latter is the ending usually added to the word root to convey inflectional information. It includes for example the *-ing* and *-ed* suffixes in verb endings as well as the *-s* to form the plural of nouns. In our

[2]We extracted this feature using the Chunklink.pl script made available by Sabine Buchholz at `http://ilk.uvt.nl/team/sabine/chunklink/README.html`

example sentence, this feature would be for example *s* for "traders" and "heads", etc.

As for features (F7) and (F8), they rely on information about the main verb of the current sentence. More specifically, feature (F7) is the main verb token (i.e. *shook* in our example), extracted following the head-finding strategy by Yamada and Matsumoto (2003), while feature (F8) is a boolean feature that indicates for each token if it is the main verb in the sentence or not.[3]

The previous sentence feature "Prev" (F9) is a connective-surface feature and is used to capture if the following sentence begins with a connective. Our intuition is that it may be relevant to detect `Arg1` boundaries in inter-sentential relations. The feature value for each candidate token of a sentence corresponds to the connective token that appears at the beginning of the following sentence, if any. Otherwise, it is equal to 0.

We also add gold-standard `Arg2` labels (F10) as an extra information for `Arg1` identification.

6 Experiments

All data used in our experiments are taken from PTB and PDTB. In particular, folders 02 – 22 are used to train the model, while folders 00 – 01 belong to the development set, and folders 23 and 24 are meant for testing. Our goal is to classify discourse arguments given the connectives by focusing on one relation at time. Since this results in a large search space for the classifier, we prune the search space trying to preserve the relevant contextual information related to the arguments. For this reason, the data given as input to the classifier include a window of two sentences before and after the given connective. This allows us to reduce the search space by more than 90%. In Table 3 we give the statistics of the explicit relation instances for the whole PDTB corpus and span limit sets. Most of the explicit relations (95%) occur within the five sentence window (two preceding and two following the sentence including the connective token).

We use the CRF++ tool (`http://crfpp.sourceforge.net/`) for sequence labeling classification (Lafferty et al., 2001), with second-order Markov dependency between tags. Beside the individual specification of a feature in the feature description template, the features in various combinations are also represented. We used this tool because the output of CRF++ is compatible to CoNLL 2000 chunking shared task, and we view our task as a discourse chunking task. On the other hand, linear-chain CRFs for sequence labeling offer advantages over both generative models like HMMs and classifiers applied at each sequence position. Also Sha and Pereira (2003) claim that, as a single model, CRFs outperform other models for shallow parsing.

Number of all explicit relations in PDTB	18459
Number of explicit relations with `Arg1` entirely *inside* the window	94%
Number of explicit relations with `Arg1` entirely *inside or overlapping* the window	95%

Table 3: Statistics about explicit relations and `Arg1` extension.

6.1 Evaluation methodology

We present our results using precision, recall and F1 measures. Following Johansson and Moschitti (2010), we use three scoring schemes: *exact*, *intersection* (or *partial*), and *overlap* scoring. In the exact scoring scheme, a span extracted by the system is counted as correct if its extent exactly coincides with one in the gold standard. However, we also use the two other scoring schemes since exact scoring may be uninformative in some situations where it is enough to have a rough approximation of the argument spans. In the overlap scheme, an expression is counted as correctly detected if it overlaps with a gold standard argument, i.e. if their intersection is nonempty. The intersection scheme assigns a score between 0 and 1 for every predicted span based on how much it overlaps with a gold standard span, so unlike the other two schemes it will reward close matches.

6.2 Feature analysis

Our feature set includes a small set of lexical, syntactic and semantic features, which convey the essential information needed to represent the arguments' position and the clausal boundaries, as well as the internal clause structure. We first take into account the features commonly used in similar works, for example by Wellner and Pustejovsky (2007) and Elwell and Baldridge (2008), and then carry out a selection step in order to identify only the feature combination that performs best in our parsing task. Note that both Wellner and Puste-

[3]We used the head rules by Yamada & Matsumoto (`http://www.jaist.ac.jp/~h-yamada/`)

jovsky (2007) and Elwell and Baldridge (2008) limit their classification to argument heads, thus they may employ features that are not very relevant to our approach.

We follow the hill-climbing (greedy) feature selection technique proposed by Caruana and Freitag (1994). In this optimization scheme, the best-performing set of features is selected on the basis of the best F1 "exact" scores. Therefore, we increase the number of features at each step, and report the corresponding performance. In order to understand better the contribution of each feature and also to avoid sub-optimal solutions, we also run an ablation test by leaving out one feature in turn from the best-performing set. We use the development split to generate results for the feature analysis to find the best performing feature set, whereas the train split is used to built model. Final results are generated using only the test split.

The results of our feature analysis are reported in Table 4 for `Arg2` and Table 5 for `Arg1`. We do not report the scores having zero as F1-measure.

Features	P	R	F1
Features in Isolation			
Token (T)	0.25	0.08	0.13
Connective (CONN)	0.58	0.50	0.54
IOB_Chain (IOB)	0.22	0.06	0.10
PoS	0.26	0.03	0.05
Lemma (L)	0.26	0.09	0.13
Morph(L+INFL)	0.27	0.05	0.09
Hill-Climbing Feature Analysis			
T+CONN	0.80	0.73	0.76
T+CONN+IOB	0.83	0.75	0.79
T+CONN+IOB+Morph	**0.84**	**0.76**	**0.80**
T+CONN+IOB+Morph+Prev	0.83	0.75	0.79
T+CONN+IOB+Morph+Prev+PoS	0.85	0.75	0.79
Token+CONN+IOB+PoS +Morph+BMV+Prev	0.84	0.74	0.78
Token+CONN+IOB+PoS +Morph+MV+BMV+Prev	0.82	0.72	0.77
Feature Ablation			
T+CONN+IOB	0.83	0.75	0.79
T+CONN+Morph	0.80	0.69	0.74
IOB+CONN+Morph	0.84	0.72	0.77
T+IOB+Morph	0.29	0.16	0.20

Table 4: Results with Single and Combined Features for `Arg2`

Both the feature-in-isolation procedure and the ablation test show that the connective sense feature is the most relevant feature for `Arg1` and `Arg2`, whereas the analysis results for `Arg1` show that the "Prev" feature is also important.

We observe that the performance of the lemma increases if integrated with the inflection feature, while inflection in isolation scores a null Precision, Recall and F1. Therefore, we consider lemma and inflection together as a single feature, which we call *Morph*.

We show that the best performing set for `Arg1` includes eight features, whereas the best feature combination for `Arg2` classification is achieved using only four features, namely token, IOB chain, connective sense and *Morph*.

Features	P	R	F1
Features in Isolation			
Token (T)	0.29	0.03	0.05
Connective (CONN)	0.40	0.08	0.14
IOB_Chain (IOB)	0.18	0.04	0.06
PoS	0.14	0.00	0.01
Lemma (L)	0.26	0.03	0.05
Morph(L+INFL)	0.27	0.02	0.03
Prev_feat(PREV)	0.57	0.09	0.16
Hill-Climbing Feature Analysis			
T+CONN	0.62	0.30	0.40
T+CONN+IOB	0.65	0.32	0.44
T+CONN+IOB+Prev	0.69	0.45	0.55
T+CONN+IOB+Arg2+Prev	0.69	0.50	0.58
T+CONN+IOB+BMV+Arg2+Prev	0.70	0.50	0.58
T+CONN+IOB+BMV +Arg2+Prev+Morph	**0.73**	**0.50**	**0.60**
T+CONN+IOB+BMV+Prev +Morph+PoS+Arg2	0.72	0.51	0.59
Token+CONN+IOB+PoS+Prev +Morph+MV+BMV+Arg2	0.69	0.50	0.58
Feature Ablation			
T+CONN+IOB+BMV+Morph+Prev	0.70	0.44	0.54
T+CONN+IOB+BMV+Prev+Arg2	0.70	0.50	0.58
T+CONN+IOB+BMV+Morph+Arg2	0.69	0.38	0.50
T+CONN+IOB+Prev+Morph+Arg2	0.72	0.51	0.60
T+CONN+BMV+Morph+Prev+Arg2	0.69	0.46	0.55
T+IOB+BMV+Morph+Prev+Arg2	0.62	0.36	0.45
CONN+IOB+BMV+Morph+Prev+Arg2	0.70	0.50	0.59

Table 5: Results with Single and Combined Features for `Arg1`

The best combination for `Arg1` classification includes all features from our initial set described in Table 2, except MV and PoS. This is probably due to the fact that PoS information becomes redundant for the classifier and BMV and MV convey the same kind of information.

6.3 Results

We compute a baseline (Table 6 between parenthesis) for each parsing subtask, i.e. `Arg1` and `Arg2` identification with the test dataset. To obtain this baseline, we take into account that *i)* `Arg2` is the argument immediately adjacent to the connective and *ii)* 90% of the relations in PDTB are either intra-sentential or involve two contiguous sentences. Thus, Arg2 baseline is computed by labeling as Arg2 the text span between the connective and the beginning of the next sentence. The other baseline, on the other hand, is computed by labeling as Arg1 all tokens in the text span from the end of the previous sentence to the connective position. In case the connective occurs at the beginning of a sentence, then the baseline classifier tags the previous sentence as Arg1.

		P	R	F1
Arg2	**Exact**	**0.83** (0.53)	**0.75** (0.46)	**0.79** (0.49)
	Partial	0.93 (0.80)	0.84 (0.85)	0.88 (0.82)
	Overlap	0.97 (0.98)	0.88 (0.85)	0.92 (0.91)
Arg1 +Prev	**Exact**	**0.70** (0.19)	**0.48** (0.19)	**0.57** (0.19)
	Partial	0.83 (0.50)	0.62 (0.68)	0.71 (0.58)
	Overlap	0.91 (0.70)	0.63 (0.68)	0.74 (0.69)
Arg1 -Prev	**Exact**	**0.70** (0.19)	**0.38** (0.19)	**0.50** (0.19)
	Partial	0.83 (0.50)	0.49 (0.68)	0.62 (0.58)
	Overlap	0.92 (0.70)	0.50 (0.68)	0.65 (0.69)

Table 6: Results of Arg1 and Arg2 extraction with test dataset. Baseline results between parentheses.

In Table 6 we report for each parsing subtask Precision, Recall and F1 achieved with the best performing feature set (see Section 6.2) using the test split, with the corresponding baseline between parenthesis. Note that before evaluation, all spans were normalized by removing leading or trailing punctuation. The best results and features are highlighted in Table 4 and 5 for Arg2 and Arg1 respectively.

We compute the confidence intervals using a resampling method (Hjorth, 1993). For Arg1 identification, we observe that the confidence interval (95%) without "Prev" feature ranges from 0.48 to 0.52 and the same interval is between 0.55 and 0.59 with "Prev" feature, if the exact F1 measure is taken into account. For Arg2 identification the confidence interval (95%) is between 0.78 and 0.81, when the exact F1 measure is taken into account. A statistical significance test run on previous and current results of Arg1 identification shows also that the difference is significant ($p < 0.0001$).

We observe in the results that recall is consistently lower than precision in all tables. This is probably due to the fact that CRF is more conservative while tagging data with argument label compared to other classifiers, which may lead to a lower coverage.

As expected, Arg2 parsing subtask achieves a better performance than Arg1 subtask because Arg2 position and extension are easier to predict. This is confirmed by the fact that the baseline precision of Arg2 *overlap* is 0.98. Also, the major improvement w.r.t. the baseline is achieved in the *exact* setting.

6.4 Error Analysis

We carry out a further analysis on the test set in order to characterize parser errors on different test set partitions. Since Arg1 may occur in a previous sentence w.r.t. the connective, we want to assess the impact of Arg1 position on the parsing task. Therefore, we separately evaluate Arg1 precision, recall and F1 on intra-sentential and inter-sentential discourse relations. Results are reported in Table 7. We also show the changes before and after adding the lexical feature targeting inter-sentential cases.

		Arg1-Results		
		P	R	F1
Intra-Sentential w/o Prev_feat	Exact	0.73	0.61	0.66
	Partial	0.86	0.77	0.81
	Overlap	0.95	0.78	0.86
Inter-Sentential w/o Prev_feat	Exact	0.19	0.01	0.02
	Partial	0.27	0.02	0.04
	Overlap	0.31	0.02	0.04
Intra-Sentential with Prev_feat	Exact	0.77	0.61	0.68
	Partial	0.88	0.79	0.81
	Overlap	0.96	0.77	0.85
Inter-Sentential with Prev_feat	Exact	0.52	0.27	0.36
	Partial	0.68	0.40	0.50
	Overlap	0.79	0.40	0.54

Table 7: Results of Arg1 parsing for intra- and inter- sentential partitions. In the test set, the number of intra- and inter- sentential relations are 1028 and 617 respectively.

The "Prev" feature is critical to the parser to achieve reasonable baseline Arg1 performance for the inter-sentential partition of the test set.

We also carry out a comparative analysis of the parsing performance in the *exact* evaluation setting by considering separately coordinating, subordinating and adverbial connectives. We make the above-mentioned distinction following the suggestion by Elwell and Baldridge (2008), because each connective type has a different behavior w.r.t. its arguments: coordinating connectives (e.g. *and, but*) usually have syntactically similar arguments, subordinating ones (e.g. *since, before*) are dominated or adverbially linked to Arg1 and are syntactically bound to Arg2, while adverbial connectives (i.e. *nevertheless, for instance*) can occur in different positions in the sentence and are not necessarily bound to Arg1.

The evaluation results are presented in Table 8.

In previous works, e.g. Elwell and Baldridge (2008), adverbial connectives were usually considered the most difficult connective type to classify. This is confirmed by our results obtained on `Arg1`, which show that adverbial connectives negatively affect both precision and recall, with a higher impact on recall. As for `Arg2`, the parsing results on the three connective types are more homogeneous.

We also observe that the "Prev" feature significantly improves `Arg1` parsing with any connective type because it increases recall, while precision decreases with coordinating and adverbial connectives.

Conn. Type	P	R	F1
Results for Arg2			
Coordinating	0.81	0.75	0.78
Subordinating	0.86	0.78	0.82
Adverbial	0.83	0.74	0.78
Results for Arg1(w/o Prev)			
Coordinating	0.73	0.42	0.54
Subordinating	0.73	0.45	0.56
Adverbial	0.68	0.26	0.37
Results for Arg1 (with Prev)			
Coordinating	0.69	0.59	0.64
Subordinating	0.76	0.50	0.61
Adverbial	0.64	0.34	0.44

Table 8: Exact evaluation for each connective type. Coordinating connectives appear in around 40% of the relations, while subordinating and adverbials are respectively 25% and 35% of all connectives.

In order to understand the most common mistakes done by the classifier, we present two example relations where resp. `Arg1` (e) and `Arg2` (f) are wrongly identified[4]. Note that in example (f) `Arg1` appears in the previous sentence, which we do not report here.

(e) Many analysts said the September increase was a one-time event, *coming* <u>as</u> **dealers introduced their 1990 models** [CONTINGENCY]

(f) <u>However</u>, Jeffrey Lane, president of Shearson Lehman Hutton, said **that Friday's plunge is "going to set back" relations with customers**, "because it reinforces the concern of volatility [COMPARISON]

In (e), the classifier tagged the whole text from "the September" to "coming" as `Arg1` instead of only "coming", since it takes clausal boundaries as a relevant factor for identifying the argument spans. In (f) the classifier is unable to detect `Arg2` probably because the argument does not occur immediately next to the connective.

A manual inspection of misclassified relations confirms that the parser is more accurate in the identification of the sentences containing the arguments rather than in the detection of their exact spans. Also, mistakes concern mostly the classification of inter-sentential relations (especially as regards the `Arg1` classifier), thus we will need to focus on these specific cases for future improvements.

7 Conclusions

We cast the complex task of discourse argument parsing as a set of cascading subtasks to be tackled in sequence, and we showed that in this way we achieved a reasonable parser accuracy by handling the whole labeling process in a pipeline.

Since we consider this discourse parsing task as a token-level sequence-labeling task, we were able to detect connective arguments and the corresponding boundaries avoiding the computationally complex approaches described in previous works.

We trained a CRF classifier with lexical, syntactic and semantic features extracted from PDTB and PTB gold annotation. We tested these features both in isolation and in different combinations in order to achieve an optimized performance. To make training time manageable, we pruned the search space by 90%, though leaving out only around 5% of all `Arg1` in PDTB.

We also presented a comparative error analysis (subsection 6.4), where we showed that `Arg1` classification on intra-sentential relations achieves a performance comparable to `Arg2` classification (Table 6). Since the main open issue in our approach is the correct classification of `Arg1` in inter-sentential relations, we plan to improve it through more feature engineering. We already extended our experimental framework by including automatically annotated parse trees and connectives in the pipeline (Ghosh et al., 2011).

8 Acknowledgements

This work was partially funded by the LiveMemories project (www.livememories.org). Richard Johansson was funded by the EC FP7 under grant 231126: LivingKnowledge – Facts, Opinions and Bias in Time.

[4]The examples show the gold standard annotation.

References

Rich Caruana and Dayne Freitag. 1994. Greedy attribute selection. In *Proceedings of the Eleventh International Conference on Machine Learning*.

Nikhil Dinesh, Alan Lee, Eleni Miltsakaki, Rashmi Prasad, Aravind Joshi, and Bonnie Webber. 2005. Attribution and the (non-)alignment of syntactic and discourse arguments of connectives. In *Proceedings of the Workshop on Frontiers in Corpus Annotations II: Pie in the Sky*, pages 29–36, Ann Arbor, Michigan, June.

Robert Elwell and Jason Baldridge. 2008. Discourse connective argument identification with connective specific rankers. In *Proceedings of ICSC-2008*, Santa Clara, United States.

Sucheta Ghosh, Sara Tonelli, Giuseppe Riccardi, and Richard Johansson. 2011. End-to-end discourse parser evaluation. In *Proceedings of 5th IEEE International Conference on Semantic Computing*, Palo Alto, CA, USA.

J. S. Urban Hjorth. 1993. *Computer Intensive Statistical Methods*. Chapman and Hall, London.

Richard Johansson and Alessandro Moschitti. 2010. Syntactic and semantic structure for opinion expression detection. In *Proceedings of the Fourteenth Conference on Computational Natural Language Learning*, pages 67–76.

John Lafferty, Andrew McCallum, and Fernando Pereira. 2001. Conditional random fields: Probabilistic models for segmenting and labeling sequence data. In *18th International Conf. on Machine Learning*. Morgan Kaufmann.

Ziheng Lin, Min-Yen Kan, and Hwee Tou Ng. 2009. Recognizing implicit discourse relations in the Penn Discourse Treebank. In *Proceedings of the 2009 Conference on Empirical Methods in Natural Language Processing*, pages 343–351, Singapore.

William Mann and Sara Thompson. 1988. Rhetorical structure theory: Toward a functional theory of text organization. *Text*, 8(3):243–281.

Mitchell P. Marcus, Beatrice Santorini, and Mary Ann Marcinkiewicz. 1993. Building a Large Annotated Corpus of English: the Penn Treebank. *Computational Linguistics*, 19(2):313–330.

Guido Minnen, John Carroll, and Darren Pearce. 2001. Applied morphological processing of English. *Natural Language Engineering*.

Emily Pitler and Ani Nenkova. 2009. Using syntax to disambiguate explicit discourse connectives in text. In *Proceedings of the 47th Annual Meeting of the Association for Computational Linguistics and the 4th International Joint Conference on Natural Language Processing*.

Emily Pitler, Mridhula Raghupathy, Hena Mehta, Ani Nenkova, Alan Lee, and Aravind Joshi. 2008. Easily identifiable discourse relations. In *Proceedings of the 22nd International Conference on Computational Linguistics (Coling 2008)*, pages 87–90, Manchester, United Kingdom.

Emily Pitler, Annie Louis, and Ani Nenkova. 2009. Automatic sense prediction for implicit discourse relations in text. In *Proceedings of the Joint Conference of the 47th Annual Meeting of the ACL and the 4th International Joint Conference on Natural Language Processing of the AFNLP*, pages 683–691, Suntec, Singapore.

Rashmi Prasad, Nikhil Dinesh, Alan Lee, Eleni Miltsakaki, Livio Robaldo, Aravind Joshi, and Bonnie Webber. 2008. The Penn Discourse Treebank 2.0. In *Proceedings of the 6th International Conference on Languages Resources and Evaluations (LREC 2008)*, Marrakech, Morocco.

Rashmi Prasad, Aravind Joshi, and Bonnie Webber. 2010. Exploiting scope for shallow discourse parsing. In *Proceedings of the Seventh conference on International Language Resources and Evaluation (LREC'10)*, Valletta, Malta.

Fei Sha and Fernando Pereira. 2003. Shallow parsing with conditional random fields. In *Proceedings of HLT/NAACL*, pages 213–220.

Swapna Somasundaran, Galileo Namata, Janyce Wiebe, and Lise Getoor. 2009. Supervised and unsupervised methods in employing discourse relations for improving opinion polarity classification. In *Proceedings of the 2009 Conference on Empirical Methods in Natural Language Processing*, pages 170–179, Singapore.

Sara Tonelli, Giuseppe Riccardi, Rashmi Prasad, and Aravind Joshi. 2010. Annotation of discourse relations for conversational spoken dialogs. In *Proceedings of the Seventh conference on International Language Resources and Evaluation (LREC'10)*, Valletta, Malta.

Bonnie Webber, Markus Egg, and Valia Kordoni. 2010. Discourse Structure and Language Technology. *Natural Language Engineering*, 1(1):1–49.

Ben Wellner and James Pustejovsky. 2007. Automatically identifying the arguments of discourse connectives. In *Proceedings of the 2007 Joint Conference on Empirical Methods in Natural Language Processing and Computational Natural Language Learning (EMNLP-CoNLL)*, pages 92–101, Prague, Czech Republic.

Ben Wellner. 2009. *Sequence Models and Ranking Methods for Discourse Parsing*. Ph.D. thesis, Brandeis University.

Hiroyasu Yamada and Yuji Matsumoto. 2003. Statistical dependency analysis with support vector machines. In *Proceedings of 8th International Workshop on Parsing Technologies*.

Relational Lasso
—An Improved Method Using the Relations among Features—

Kotaro Kitagawa **Kumiko Tanaka-Ishii**
Graduate School of Information Science and Technology,
The University of Tokyo
kitagawa@cl.ci.i.u-tokyo.ac.jp kumiko@i.u-tokyo.ac.jp

Abstract

Relational lasso is a method that incorporates feature relations within machine learning. By using automatically obtained noisy relations among features, relational lasso learns an additional penalty parameter per feature, which is then incorporated in terms of a regularizer within the target optimization function.

Relational lasso has been tested on three different tasks: text categorization, polarity estimation, and parsing, where it was compared with conventional lasso and adaptive lasso (Zou, 2006) when using a multi-class logistic regression optimization method. Relational lasso outperformed these other lasso methods in the tests.

1 Introduction

As machine learning methods scale up and now deal with millions of features, we ideally want to add all possible features without having to manually verify or consider the effectiveness of each feature with respect to the performance. In other words, we need an automatic way to exploit any usable information that can be obtained from features. However, with current machine learning methods, adding noisy features could lower performance, so the user still has to decide which features are worth adding.

Regularization methods have recently received greater interest because of this need. Regularization is expressed as a constraint term within an optimization function, where the term is given as a function regarding the importance weight of each feature. Regularization provides a means of importance control embedded within the target optimization problem. Among the various regularizers, *lasso*, proposed by (Tibshirani, 1996) is the most widely used because of its mathematical comprehensiveness.

This paper describes a method, which we call *relational lasso*, that improves upon the conventional lasso method. We show that relational lasso improves the overall performance of classification compared with that of other lasso methods. This study was motivated through a limitation we observed in conventional lasso: that features could be inter-related, but such dependences are not incorporated within the current regularization. Therefore, the conventional method tends to favor correlated features, which can lead to the importance of non-correlated features being neglected.

Relational lasso overcomes this limitation of conventional lasso by introducing an additional penalty parameter for each feature; this parameter is estimated automatically given the noisy relations among features, where the relations are also automatically generated. While the proposed method does not add to the computational complexity of the conventional regularization method, it improves the quality of classification. We explain the method and show empirical results from tests based on three different text classification and parsing tasks.

Regularization was originally proposed as a way to avoid over-fitting by favoring some small number of features. Our method presented in this article exploits this approach further and attempts to estimate the importance of each feature within the relations it has with other features. As explained in more detail in the following section, attempts along the same line have been made to incorporate underlying relations among features, such as by *fused lasso* through the ordering among features (Tibshirani et al., 2005), or by *group lasso* through groups among features (Yuan and Lin, 2006). However, fused lasso assumes problems with features that can be ordered in some meaningful way, and group lasso requires underlying group information to be configured before the method is applied. The closely related work to ours is *adaptive lasso* (Zou, 2006), which introduces an additional parameter per feature. However, since adaptive lasso does not explicitly process relations among features, the estimation of this additional parameter is completely different from our method. Moreover, as will be empirically shown, our method outperforms adaptive lasso, which in fact performed worse than even the conventional method.

Related work on regularization techniques has shown the potential of regularization not only to prevent over-fitting, but also to serve as a kind of feature selection. Relational lasso provides another step along this line. Here, we show that our method outperforms other lasso methods in different classification tasks. Moreover, it works well even when noisy features are added, something that degrades the performance of other lasso methods.

2 Related Work

As explained, feature selection is the key to our method's effectiveness, and here we summarize the related work done along this line. A substantial number of studies have been done on feature selection techniques, and these techniques can be classified into three categories according to (Guyon and Elisseeff , 2003): wrapper methods, filter methods and embedded methods.

The wrapper is the most naïve way of selecting a subset of features through predictive accuracy (Kohavi and John, 1997). The user searches the possible feature space greedily using an induction algorithm and selects the best subset with the best predictive accuracy. Wrappers with greedy algorithms can be computationally expensive and the stepwise selection is often trapped into a local optimal solution. Since the possible number of subsets for a set is exponential to the number of features in the original set, in practice the user typically defines the subset arbitrarily depending on the category of features, as was tested by (Scott and Matwin , 1999). This makes impossible any fine adjustment as to which individual features to use.

Filter methods, on the other hand, select good features according to some criteria, thus providing the means for selecting individual features. These methods have been extensively studied, and a good overview is available in (Manning, 1999). The representatives of the evaluation function for choosing good/bad features are chi-squares and mutual information, and features having higher scores for these functions are considered good features. While filtering methods are effective and therefore often used, these methods are independent of the learning method that they are used with. Moreover, the performance is not guaranteed to improve even though feature selection is used.

The last category is embedded methods, where the feature selection is embedded within the overall classification problem. The decision tree is an example of an embedded method, and machine learning techniques using pruning steps have been studied (Perkins et al., 2003). *Lasso*, an acronym for "least absolute shrinkage and selection operator", using the L_1 norm (Tibshirani, 1996) is a computationally efficient method for simultaneously achieving the estimation and feature selection.

Although lasso helps achieve an effective model, the L_1 norm could cause biased estimation among features (Knight and Fu, 2000) by not being able to distinguish between truly significant and noisy features.

To cope with this problem, (Zou and Hastie, 2005) proposed the *elastic net* method, which is expressed as the conjunct of L_1 and L_2 norms of the feature weights. They show that this method works when the number of features substantially exceeds the number of learning data, and also when there is strong correlation between some features. Another proposal is *fused lasso*, which incorporates the order of features (as found in their numbers, such as found in the case when each image pixel value forms a feature) (Tibshirani et al., 2005). Here, the target application is protein mass spectroscopy and gene expression data, and the method is only applicable to a target where the order among features is explicit, as in the case of gene or image pixels. (Yuan and Lin, 2006) proposed *grouped lasso*, which incorporates underlying groups among features. The fused and grouped lasso methods require configuration of the structure among features.

Recently, a new approach called *weighted lasso* is proposed which calculates the L_1 norm on features, each of which is weighted. As one method, (Zou, 2006) proposed a two-step approach called *adaptive lasso*. This paper proposes an alternative weighted lasso method, in which the estimation of the weights is processed differently from that of adaptive lasso. Although the procedure of adaptive lasso is closest to relational lasso, the learning of adaptive lasso does not explicitly handle the relations among features.

All these methods are attempts to incorporate the relations, or structure, among features —such as dependence, ordering and groups— into machine learning through the framework of regularization. Although such dependence is not always given or tractable, we believe this information can be learned from some automatically generated noisy relation among features.

3 L1-Regularization of Multi-Class Logistic Regression

Before going on to the main points of relational lasso, let us summarize the regularization framework that we adopt. Regularization is the general method used in classification. The target function has two terms, one for fitting and another for regularization. This second term penalizes the weights acquired by each feature, typically by incorporating the addition of their norms into a target function for the classifier. This prevents the target function becoming too over-fitted by favoring some specific sets of features. In this sense, the regularization term can be considered as serving for feature selection.

Of the various ways to define the target function, in this paper we focus on the multi-class logistic regression model and L1-regularization; namely, the lasso method.

The fitting function adopted in this paper is a multi-class logistic regression model, denoted as LR in the following. LR is used to model the relationship between the input vectors $\boldsymbol{x} = \mathbb{R}^n$ and labels $y \in \boldsymbol{Y}$. The conditional probability for a label y given x is defined as

$$\begin{aligned} p(y|x;\boldsymbol{w}) &= \frac{1}{Z(\boldsymbol{x})}\exp\left(\boldsymbol{w}^T\phi(\boldsymbol{x},y)\right) \\ Z(x) &= \sum_{y'}\exp\left(\boldsymbol{w}^T\phi(\boldsymbol{x},y')\right), \end{aligned}$$

where $\phi(\boldsymbol{x},y) \in \mathbb{R}^m$ is the feature vector and $\boldsymbol{w} \in \mathbb{R}^m$ is the weight vector. When the training examples $\{(x_i, y_i)\}(i = 1, \cdots, l)$ are given, minimization of the loss function

$$L(\boldsymbol{w}) = -\sum_i \log p(y_i|\boldsymbol{x}_i;\boldsymbol{w}),$$

is equivalent to the maximum likelihood estimation.

Regularization makes it possible to obtain a good model for LR, without restricting the number of features, by imposing appropriate restrictions on weight $\boldsymbol{w}$. Of the different ways of regularization, in this paper we adopt (Tibshirani, 1996)'s method of imposing an L_1 norm on parameters because of its mathematical simplicity, especially when applied with LR. This method is called lasso and facilitates both estimation and automatic variable selection. When applying this lasso to logistic regression, the MAP estimation of weights for each feature is given by the following formula, the target function to be optimized:

$$\boldsymbol{w}^* = \arg\min_{\boldsymbol{w}} L(\boldsymbol{w}) + \lambda\sum_i |w_i|, \qquad (1)$$

where λ is the parameter defining the strength of the regularization term's influence on the optimization.

Although our proposal applies in general to various types of target function, in this paper we examine its effectiveness within this particular target function. This target function was chosen because the target function of LR-lasso is mathematically comprehensive, so multi-class logistic regression and lasso are widely applied. Further investigation to determine whether our method works well for other target functions will be part of our future work.

4 Relational Lasso —The Proposed Method

The limitation of conventional lasso is that relations among features cannot be incorporated. For example, highly correlated features which lead towards a higher performance could all acquire relatively large weights. This would lead to favoring a single aspect that counts for the classification and neglecting other minor but still important aspects which would enable better classification. This happens when a high correlation is found among features. Therefore, when one feature is favored, the other correlated features must be heavily penalized, so that features which count for classification from a different aspect are more favored.

To express this, we adopt the weighted lasso approach, so an additional penalizing parameter α_i for each feature i is introduced in the second term of formula (1):

$$\boldsymbol{w}^* = \arg\min_{\boldsymbol{w}} L(\boldsymbol{w}) + \lambda \sum_i \alpha_i |w_i|. \tag{2}$$

The solution found here, subject to the L_1 regularizer, is equivalent to the solution obtained from the constrained optimization problem:

$$\begin{aligned} &\underset{\boldsymbol{w}}{\text{minimize}} \quad L(\boldsymbol{w}), \\ &\text{s.t.} \qquad\quad \sum_i \alpha_i |w_i| \leq \gamma. \end{aligned}$$

The parameter γ corresponds to λ of formula (2). Each parameter α_i determines the penalty for w_i and directly affects the importance of the ith feature.

Previous work on adaptive lasso (Zou, 2006) also introduces an additional parameter, such as α_i, in addition to the weight parameter. Adaptive lasso focuses on the presence of oracle properties[1], and works in two stages of optimization. First weight w_i is learned with conventional lasso. Second, L_1 norm is re-weighted with the parameters α_i as $\alpha_i = 1/|\hat{w}_i|^\delta$ being set from initial lasso estimator $\hat{\boldsymbol{w}}$ using a parameter δ, and the optimization problem is processed using $\boldsymbol{\alpha}$. Therefore, their way of learning this additional parameter does not explicitly concern the exploitation of additional information different from the original weight w_i. On the other hand, our α is estimated given a noisy relation among features, thus it plays a different role from w. In this sense, the way to handle this additional parameter for relational lasso is completely different from adaptive lasso. In other words, the originality of our method lies in using α to express the relations between underlying features.

The relations between features are denoted as R, which is provided to the proposed algorithm and used to estimate α. R denotes a pairwise dependence relation between features. That is, if there are m features in total, $R \subset (1, \cdots, m) \times (1, \cdots, m)$. Unlike previous work such as fused (Tibshirani et al., 2005) and grouped lasso (Yuan and Lin, 2006), R in our work is a noisy relation which can be automatically obtained by scanning through features.

Although there are various possibilities for obtaining R, one way is through the *inclusion* relation among features. Given a pair of features p and q, the feature q *includes* p, if in every data of the learning data, when the value of feature q is non-zero, the value of feature p is always non-zero. For example, for the case of the adjective "economic" and its stem "econom", the latter includes the former while also being a stem for other terms such as "economy" and "economist". In the final classification, it is unknown which of "econom" and "economic" counts. For part-of-speech tagging, "econom" would not provide much information since it does not have a complete form, but for topic estimation, "econom" might provide sufficient information by representing the terms "economic", "economy" and "economist". In both cases, when the two words appear as features, they share a tight relation and when one is given high importance, the other will as well in conventional lasso. In relational lasso, if one representative is selected, then other similar features in the same group will acquire less importance by having a larger penalty.

The overall procedure is shown in Procedure 1. The procedure obtains three kinds of learning data input, a relation among features, and parameter values. Before optimizing the target function, denoted in the second line from the bottom, the procedure calculates α depending on the given relation R among features. This procedure is expressed in terms of a while-structure, which enables the adjustment of penalty parameters for highly correlated features. The processed feature is held in set F to avoid any duplicate processing of features.

In the while-structure, features are selected one at a time in the order of larger values of $\frac{\partial L(\boldsymbol{w})}{\partial \boldsymbol{w}}$, with $\boldsymbol{w}$ being the zero vector[2]. The number of the selected feature is denoted as k^*. Then, for all ks which are related to k^* in R, the α is enlarged by a

[1]Oracle property (Fan and Li , 2001) is satisfied if the optimization problem can correctly select the nonzero weights with probability converging to one and the estimators of the nonzero weights are asymptotically normal with the same means and covariance that they would have if the zero coefficients were known in advance.

[2]There are other possibilities for this order of processing features, such as randomizing the order. In the Grafting method (Perkins et al., 2003), the processed feature is selected by calculating $\frac{\partial L(\boldsymbol{w})}{\partial \boldsymbol{w}}$ every time in the while-structure, which is also possible with relational lasso. This however remains as future work.

Procedure 1 Relational Lasso

Input:

- $(x_i, y_i)(i = 1, \cdots, n)$
- Parameters λ, a_1, a_2
- Relation among m features $R \subset (1, \cdots, m) \times (1, \cdots, m)$

$\boldsymbol{\alpha} = \mathbf{1}, \boldsymbol{w} = \mathbf{0}, F = \{\}$
$\boldsymbol{v} = \frac{\partial L(\boldsymbol{w})}{\partial \boldsymbol{w}}$
while $|F| < m$ **do**
  $k^* = \arg\max_{k \notin F} |v_k|$
  for all $k \notin F$ and $(k^*, k) \in R$ **do**
    $\alpha_k = \alpha_k + a_1$
  end for
  for all $k \notin F$ and $(k, k^*) \in R$ **do**
    $\alpha_k = \alpha_k + a_2$
  end for
  $F = F \cup k^*$
end while
$\boldsymbol{w} = \arg\min_{\boldsymbol{w}} L(\boldsymbol{w}) + \lambda \sum_k \alpha_k |w_k|$
return $\boldsymbol{w}$

certain constant a_1 and a_2, depending on whether the feature k is included or k^* is included. When the while procedure ends, F includes all the features. Finally, $\boldsymbol{w}$ is estimated in terms of LR-lasso, where the second term is weighted further with the thus estimated α. When some specific w_k becomes zero, this means that the weight is considered as not selected for the classification task.

One further improvement that might be possible for the above procedure is to repeat the while-structure and the estimation of w, so that α and w perform co-training; this also remains for our future work. Moreover, the procedure presented here remains an ad hoc modification of conventional lasso based on our motivation. A more proper mathematical reformulation of this method will be part of our future work.

5 Evaluation

5.1 Experimental Settings

We will consider the following two feature sets.

- Standard features
- Standard and additional features

Here, an additional feature set is introduced so that it can be noisy with respect to the classification. Therefore, the interest lies in whether the performance is better when we have the additional features than it is when we have only the standard features.

We consider three methods:

- Conventional lasso (Tibshirani, 1996)
- Adaptive lasso (Zou, 2006)
- Relational lasso (proposed method)

We are interested in whether relational lasso performs better than the other methods. In practice we can select the best λ parameter used for lasso methods, using cross-validation, although we examined multiple λs, which determine the strength of the regularizers' influence as shown in formulas (1) and (2) of Sections 3 and 4.

The other parameters introduced in Section 4 are set as follows. Adaptive lasso has the parameter $\delta = 1$, which is set as the common choice in (Krämer et al., 2009) and the parameter α_i is defined from initial estimator $\hat{\boldsymbol{w}}$ as follows:

$$\alpha_i = \max\left\{\frac{1}{|\hat{w}_i|}, 1\right\}.$$

For relational lasso, parameters a_1 and a_2 were each set to 1. For L_1 regularized LR, a coordinate descent method is implemented by modifying LIBLINEAR[3]. Coordinate descent methods have been widely applied elsewhere because of their suitability for application to higher-order problems (Yuam et al., 2010).

For each pair of a feature and a method, we considered the following three problems of text classification, polarity estimation, and statistical parsing. The next three sections explain the standard and additional feature sets, the relation among features R, and the evaluation scores.

Task 1: Text Classification

Twenty Newsgroups (20NG)[4] were used as the dataset for text classification. This collection contains 18,846 English documents partitioned across 20 different news groups.

The data was sorted by date, with the first 60% used as a training set and the remaining 40% used as a test set. A simple bag of words was used

[3]http://www.csie.ntu.edu.tw/~cjlin/liblinear/

[4]provided by Jason Rennie, http://people.csail.mit.edu/jrennie/20Newsgroups/

Table 1: Features used for dependency parsing

unigram	for w in $w_{i-1}, w_i, w_j, w_{j+1}, w_{j+2}, w_{j+2}$	pos(w), lex(w)
	for w in w_{i-1}, w_i, w_j,	pos(w^{left}), lex(w^{left})
	for w in w_{i-1}, w_i,	pos(w_i^{right}), lex(w_i^{right}), pos(w_i^{head}),lex(w_i^{head})
bigram	for (v, w) in $(w_i, w_j), (w_{i-1}, w_j)$	pos(v)pos(w),pos(v)lex(w),lex(v)pos(w),lex(v)lex(w)
add bigram	for (v, w) in $(w_i, w_{j+1}), (w_j, w_{j+1})$	pos(v)pos(w),pos(v)lex(w),lex(v)pos(w),lex(v)lex(w)
add preposition	for w in $w_{j+1}, w_{j+2}, w_{j+3}$ (if w_j is a preposition)	lex(w_i)lex(w_j)pos(w), pos(w_i)lex(w_j)lex(w)

as the standard feature sets, whereas all stems of all words were used as additional features. R was defined as the relation between each word and its stems.

A multi-class classification task is typically evaluated by macro and micro F1 values, so we also provided these values.

Task 2: Polarity Estimation

Polarity dataset v2.0[5] was used as the second data set. The content of each data was a movie review in text, tagged with the sentiment of positive or negative. The data consisted of 1,000 positive and 1,000 negative reviews. Since the data set was small, the average accuracy was obtained through 10-fold cross validation.

Feature sets were basically the same as for Task 1, where the standard was a bag of words, the additional set consisted of word stems, and relation R was the relation among words and their stems.

The evaluation was based on the accuracy of the binary classification of positive/negative.

Task 3: Parsing

We also tested the methods on a parsing task, which was a task drastically different from tasks 1 and 2. We used CoNLL-X formatted sentences from the Wall Street Journal section of the Penn Tree-bank. Sections 2-21 were used as training data (39,832 sentences), and section 23 was used as test data (2,416 sentences).

The parsing algorithm we tested is the standard shift-reduce parsing proposed by (Nivre, 2003), where the parsing proceeds by successive determination of the relation between two words (denoted as w_i and w_j). Such a determination is considered a 4-class classification problem that is modeled and learned by LR, augmented by the three lasso methods being evaluated.

[5]provided by Bo Pang, `http://www.cs.cornell.edu/people/pabo/movie-review-data/`

The standard features used are listed in Table 1. Here, pos(w) indicates the part of speech of the word w, where w_i indicates the ith word of a given sentence, and w_i^{left} indicates the already parsed dependent word of w_i placed to its farthest left side. The additional feature set included all dependent words involving w_i and w_j, and all bi-grams concerning words used as features in the standard set. In our dependency parsing task, we measured the word accuracy which was defined as the ratio of words assigned correct heads divided by the total of all words.

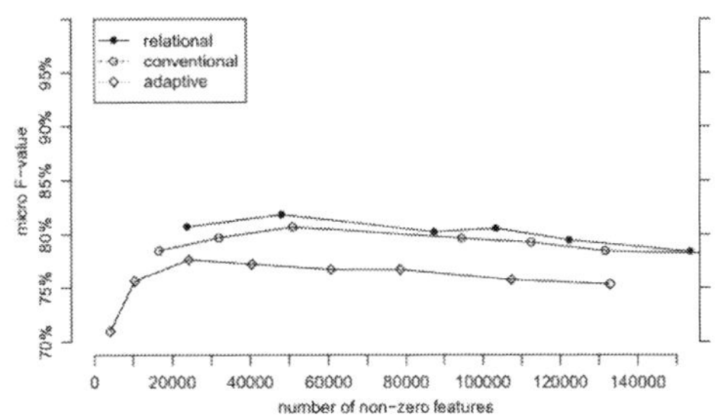

Figure 1: Task 1: Micro F1 values for the number of non-zero features

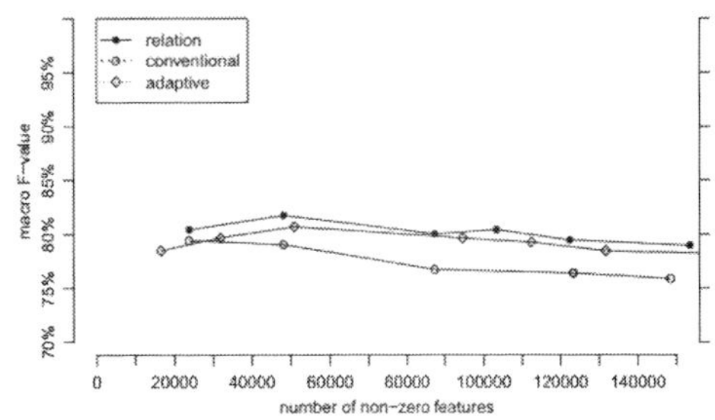

Figure 2: Task 1: Macro F1 values for the number of non-zero features

5.2 Results

Figures 1 and 2 show the results for Task 1, Figure 3 those for Task 2, and Figure 4 those for Task 3. Horizontal axes show the number of features and vertical axes show accuracy. Each graph has three lines, indicating the conventional, adaptive and relational lasso methods applied to the standard and additional features all together. Each line has five points, each corresponding to a different value of λ. The horizontal coordinate was determined by counting how many features remained non-zero for each value of λ.

Overall, all figures, except for Figure 3 show that relational lasso outperformed the adaptive and conventional lasso methods. This was to be expected, since relational lasso has the relation R as input, unlike the conventional lasso method. This confirms that information from the underlying R does improve lasso performance. Curiously, the performance of adaptive lasso for some figures was lower than that of the conventional method. The reason for this will be given later in this section.

As Figure 3 and Figure 4 show, the performance was competitive among the three lasso methods, when the number of features were small. However, with a large number of features, relational lasso generally outperforms the other lassos.

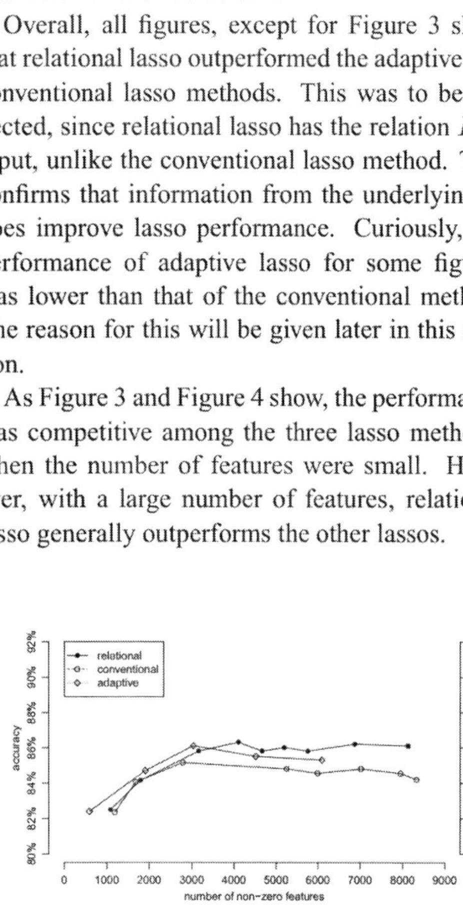

Figure 3: Task 2: Accuracy for the number of non-zero features

It is difficult to compare the performance since different λ values lead to different levels of performance, so the maximum performance obtained by changing the λ value is shown in Table 2. Columns are for different lasso methods with standard and additional feature sets, whereas rows represent different tasks. Note that the best values of λ differ depending on the pairs of methods and features.

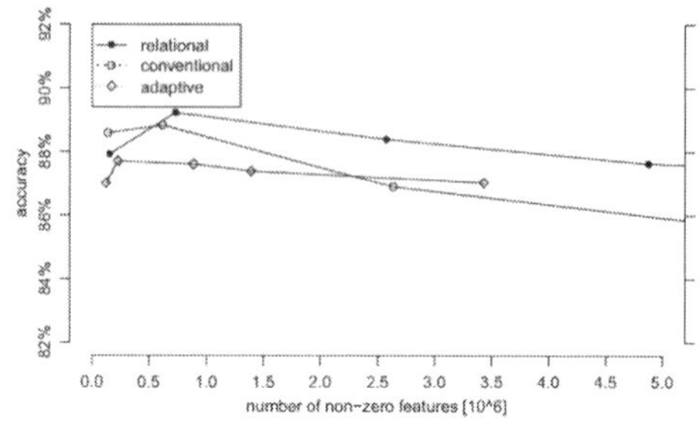

Figure 4: Task 3: Word accuracy for the number of non-zero features

Overall, the last column presents the highest performance in each row, thus suggesting the effectiveness of relational lasso.

For Task 2, when features of standard and additional sets were used, the performance of the conventional method decreased compared to that when only the standard set was used. This could happen if the additional feature set is noisy and the regularizer cannot exploit the useful information from the additional set of features. On the other hand, the performance of relational and adaptive lasso for the same task was improved by extracting the useful information; that is, the performance was higher than when using only the standard features. This shows that the use of underlying information among features enhances the overall performance.

For Tasks 1 and 3, adding features led to better performance than when using only the standard set. Note, though, that the performance increase was greatest for relational lasso. Thus, relational lasso is the best among the three lasso methods at exploiting information, and thus performs better in terms of accuracy.

In this table, too, we see that for Task 2, the performance of adaptive lasso is below that of the conventional lasso. We consider the reason for this to be as follows. Since the optimization for adaptive lasso is done in two stages, some of the features are dropped within the first stage. In the second stage, these features will never re-acquire any importance. In other words, the feature selection must be done at the very end in order to preserve the possibility of some features to re-acqure the importance through learning.

Before ending, we must note the impact of relational lasso on the speed of overall processing.

Table 2: Maximum Performance among Various Values of λ for Three Lasso Methods

Lasso Methods	Conventional		Adaptive		Relational	
Feature Sets	Std	Std+Add	Std	Std+Add	Std	Std+Add
Task 1 (micro)	79.67%	81.03%	76.78%	77.16%	78.87%	**81.81%**
Task 1 (macro)	79.43%	80.69%	76.53%	77.67%	78.52%	**81.72%**
Task 2	85.81%	84.95%	85.56%	86.1%	84.82%	**86.45%**
Task 3	75.87%	88.81%	74.64%	87.71%	75.97%	**89.23%**

The pre-processing to obtain α is very fast, since it only scans the number of features once. The bottleneck of the procedure lies in the estimation of w since this requires convergence through a repetitive procedure. Therefore, the computational complexity of relational lasso will not change even with α within the regularizer, and the overall speed of relational lasso is almost the same as that of the conventional method. In contrast, adaptive lasso requires twice as much time since the bottleneck part is done twice. In this sense, our method outperforms adaptive lasso in speed and is not significantly slower than conventional, at least for the settings we have examined in this section.

6 Conclusion

Relational lasso utilizes relations among features to better exploit information through regularization, especially through lasso methods. The conventional lasso method is not designed to incorporate relations among features, and this leads to biased weighting of a group of features having similar behavior. Relational lasso controls such relations underlying features by introducing a penalty parameter for each feature. The penalty increases when a feature is related to some other feature having less of a penalty. This parameter score is incorporated as the regularization term of the target machine learning function for the optimization objective.

We compared relational lasso to the conventional method and the adaptive lasso proposed by (Zou, 2006), which also uses an additional parameter per feature. We evaluated the methods based on how well they performed three tasks of text categorization, polarity estimation, and parsing. Relational lasso outperformed the other lasso methods in these tasks. Moreover, the performance of the conventional lasso methods deteriorated when noisy features were added, while relational lasso successfully extracted useful information from these features and its performance improved.

As part of our future work, we plan to investigate whether our method works for other tasks such as tagging, and with other target functions. Moreover, there are many directions we can take to further improve the method, such as through co-training. Last, it will be interesting to see how our method can be mathematically reformulated.

References

Jianqing Fan, Runze Li. 2001. Variable selection via nonconcave penalized likelihood and its oracle properties. *Journal of the American Statistical Association*, vol.96, pp.1348–1360.

Isabelle Guyon, André Elisseeff. 2003. An introduction to variable and feature selection. *The Journal of Machine Learning Research*, vol.3, pp.1157–1182.

G. V. Kass. 1980. An exploratory technique for investigating large quantities of categorical data. *Journal of the Royal Statistical Society. Series C*, vol.29, pp.119–127.

Keith Knight, Wenjiang Fu. 2000. Asymptotics for lasso-type estimators. *The Annals of Statistics*, vol.28, pp.1356–1378.

Ron Kohavi, George H. John. 1997. Wrappers for feature subset selection, *Artificial intelligence*, vol.97, pp.273–324.

Nicole Krämer, Juliane Schäfer, Anne-Laure Boulesteix. 2009. Regularized estimation of large-scale gene association networks using graphical Gaussian models. *BMC Bioinformatics*, vo.10.

Christopher Manning, Hinrich Schuetze. 1999. *Foundations of Statistical Natural Language Processing*. MIT Press.

Joakim Nivre. 2003. An efficient algorithm for projective dependency parsing. *Proceedings of the 8th International Workshop on Parsing Technologies*, pp. 149-160.

Simon Perkins, Kervin Lacker, and James Theiler. 2003. Grafting: Fast, Incremental Feature Selection by Gradient Descent in Function Space. *The Journal of Machine Learning Research*, vol.3, pp.1333–1356.

Yvan Saeys, Iñaki Inza, and Pedro Larrañaga. 2007. A review of feature selection techniques in bioinformatics. *Bioinformatics*, vol.23, num.19, pp.2507–2517.

Sam Scott, Stan Matwin. 1999. Feature engineering for text classification. *Proceedings of ICML-99, 16th International Conference on Machine Learning*, pp.379–388.

Robert Tibshirani. 1996. Regression shrinkage and selection via the lasso. *Journal of the Royal Statistical Society*, Series B, vol.58, pp.267–288.

Robert Tibshirani, Michael Saunders, Saharon Rosset, Ji Zhu, and Keith Knight 2005. Sparsity and smoothness via the fused lasso. *Journal of the Royal Statistical Society*, Series B, vol.67, pp.91–108.

Guo-Xun Yuan, Kai-Wei Chang, Cho-Jui Hsieh, Chih-Jen Lin. 2010. A comparison of optimization methods and software for large-scale l1-regularized linear classification. *The Journal of Machine Learning Research*, vol.11, pp.3183–3234.

Ming Yuan, Yi Lin. 2006. Model selection and estimation in regression with grouped variables. *Journal of the Royal Statistical Society*, Series B, vol.68, pp.49–67.

Ying Yang, Jan O. Pedersen. 1997. A comparative study on feature selection in text categorization. *Proceedings of the Fourteenth International Conference on Machine Learning*, pp.412–420.

Hui Zou. 2006. The adaptive lasso and its oracle properties. *Journal of the American Statistical Association*, vol.101, pp.1418–1429.

Hui Zou, Trevor Hastie. 2005. Regularization and variable selection via the elastic net. *Journal of the Royal Statistical Society*, Series B, vol.67, pp.301–320.

Enhance Top-down method with Meta-Classification for Very Large-scale Hierarchical Classification *

Xiao-Lin Wang[1,2], Hai Zhao[1,2], Bao-Liang Lu[1,2†]
[1]Center for Brain-Like Computing and Machine Intelligence
Department of Computer Science and Engineering, Shanghai Jiao Tong University
[2]MOE-Microsoft Key Laboratory for Intelligent Computing and Intelligent Systems
Shanghai Jiao Tong University
800 Dong Chuan Rd., Shanghai 200240, China
arthur.xl.wang@gmail.com, {zhaohai; blu}@cs.sjtu.edu.cn

Abstract

Recent large-scale hierarchical classification tasks typically have tens of thousands of classes as well as a large number of samples, for which the dominant solution is the top-down method due to computational complexity. However, the top-down method suffers from accuracy deficiency, that is, its accuracy is generally lower than that of the flat approach of 1-vs-Rest. In this paper, we employ meta-classification technique to enhance the classifying procedure of the top-down method. We analyze the proposed method on the aspect of accuracy, and then test it with two real-world large-scale data sets. Our method both maintains the efficiency of the conventional top-down method and provides competitive classification accuracies.

1 Introduction

Test categorization, as a key technology of data mining, has received intensive study for decades. Recently, real-world applications have raised some large-scale tasks that typically have tens of thousands of classes, where many established techniques such as the 1-vs-Rest multiclass classification fail due to computational complexity. Meanwhile, those large-scale tasks usually employ hierarchies to organize the huge number of classes that they have, which provides a clue to solve them. Such kind of tasks include categorizing patent documents into the taxonomy of International Patent Classification (IPC) (Fall et al., 2003; Fujii et al., 2007) and categorizing web pages into the directories of Open Directory Project (ODP) or Yahoo! (Labrou and Finin, 1999; Liu et al., 2005).

The existing approaches to hierarchical classification mainly fall into two categories. One category aims at raising classification accuracy, which generally takes hierarchies as additional clue for classifying a sample besides its content. Such researches include hierarchical support vector machines (SVM) (Cai and Hofmann, 2004; Tsochantaridis et al., 2005), hierarchical Rocchio-like classifiers (Labrou and Finin, 1999), min-max modular network (Lu and Ito, 2002; Lu and Wang, 2009) and ensemble classifications (Punera and Ghosh, 2008).

The other category aims at reducing computational complexity. The main approach in this category is an ensemble classification method called top-down method (Bennett and Nguyen, 2009; Ceci and Malerba, 2007a; Koller and Sahami, 1997; Liu et al., 2005; Montejo-Ráez and Ureña-López, 2006; Sun and Lim, 2001; Xue et al., 2008; Yang et al., 2003). Top-down method builds a tree of classifiers which is isomorphic with the hierarchy of classes.

Top-down method classifies a test sample as follows. The sample is filtered down the tree of classifiers from the root node. For each parent node that the sample reaches, those child nodes whose confidence values predicted by the base-classifiers exceed a predefined threshold are invoked to carry the sample on. When the sample reaches the bottom leaf nodes eventually, the predictions can be made (Liu et al., 2005; Montejo-Ráez and Ureña-López, 2006; Yang et al., 2003). As this classifying process employs the threshold strategy of comparing the scores with thresholds, which is named score-cut (S-cut) in the context of flat multiclass classification (Yang, 2001), we call this kind of

* This work was partially supported by the National Natural Science Foundation of China (Grant No. 60903119, Grant No. 61170114 and Grant No. 90820018), the National Basic Research Program of China (Grant No. 2009CB320901), the Science and Technology Commission of Shanghai Municipality (Grant No. 09511502400), and the European Union Seventh Framework Programme (Grant No. 247619).

† Corresponding author

conventional top-down method the S-CUT Top-Down method (ScutTD) so as to distinguish it from the later variant top-down methods in this paper.

ScutTD is far more efficient than the normal flat approach of 1-vs-Rest in handling the classification tasks that has a large number of classes. The computational complexity of 1-vs-Rest is linear to the number of classes, while that of ScutTD is approximately logarithmic (Ceci and Malerba, 2007a; Liu et al., 2005; Wang and Lu, 2010; Yang et al., 2003). As an practical example, in an classification experiment on 492 617 training documents, 275 364 test documents and 132 199 categories of Yahoo!, ScutTD costs only 2.1 hours on training and 0.12 hours on classifying, while 1-vs-Rest costs 310 hours on training and 54 hours on classifying (Liu et al., 2005).

However, ScutTD has a well-known deficiency of classification accuracy, that is, its performance is generally worse than the flat 1-vs-Rest approach (Bennett and Nguyen, 2009; Ceci and Malerba, 2007a; Wang and Lu, 2010; Xue et al., 2008). As a persuasive evidence, in the 2009 PASCAL challenge on large-scale hierarchical text [1], flat methods rank highest, hybrid methods rank next and top-down methods rank lowest.

The main reason for the accuracy deficiency of ScutTD is that its classifying procedure actually consists of cascaded decisions about which child nodes should be invoked from a parent node. Each of these decisions is made upon the score of local base-classifiers only, and not changeable after that. Thus a wrong decision inevitably leads to a group of wrong predictions. This problem is usually called error propagation (Wang and Lu, 2010; Xue et al., 2008). Sun et al. study a special case of this problem, the wrong decision of rejecting a child node at high layers, and call it the blocking problem (Sun et al., 2004). Liu et al. compare this classifying procedure to a Pachinko-machine (Liu et al., 2005). As a solution, Ceci and Malerba has proposed a bottom-up thresholding strategy (Ceci and Malerba, 2007a)

In this paper, we propose a 'global' classifying method for top-down method to reduce its error propagation. The idea is to treat combining the predictions of the base-classifiers as a meta-classification task, for which we name our method Meta-classification Top-down method (MetaTD).

[1] http://lshtc.iit.demokritos.gr/

There is one point that needs to be clarified. There are two kinds of hierarchical classification tasks in real-world applications. One kind is mandatory leaf-node classification where only the leaf nodes are the validate labels or classes (Dumais and Chen, 2000; Freitas and de Carvalho, 2007; Silla and Freitas, 2010). In contrast, the other is non-mandatory leaf-node classification correspondingly, where both the internal nodes and the leaf nodes are validate labels (Lewis et al., 2004; Liu et al., 2005). In this paper, we handle the first kind of hierarchical classification – mandatory leaf-node classification.

The rest of paper is organized as follows. The proposed MetaTD as well as the conventional ScutTD is formally presented in Sec. 2. We then provide some ideas on the classification accuracy of MetaTD in Sec. 3. After that we test MetaTD with two real-world data sets in Sec. 4. Finally we conclude this paper in Sec. 5.

2 Methods

In this section, we present the formal descriptions of the proposed MetaTD. We first review the conventional ScutTD. We then present MetaTD in detail. After that an example is given to illustrate MetaTD.

2.1 S-cut Top-down Method

Suppose H is a hierarchy of classes which records all the relations of parent nodes and their children,

$$H = \{(p, c) | p \text{ is a parent node}, \; c \text{ is one of its children}\}$$

where (p, c) is called a parent-child relation. Suppose T,D and E are the training, development and test sets respectively.

Applying ScutTD consists of the following three steps.

First, train base-classifiers. One classifier will be trained for each parent-child relation (p, c) of the hierarchy H, noted as f_c, through the following local training set,

$$T_{pc} = \{(x, y) | x \in T_p, y = +1 \text{ if } x \in T_c, \; y = -1 \text{ otherwise}\} \quad (1)$$

where T_* is the subset of training samples that belong to the node $*$.

Second, find optimal thresholds for the base-classifiers. The approaches to this step actually have alternatives. Micro-F_1 is taken as the criterion optimization target which balances both precision and recall, as follows (Bennett and Nguyen, 2009; Liu et al., 2005).

$$
\begin{aligned}
t_c &= \underset{t}{argmax}\, F_1(D_{pc}, f_c, t) \\
&= \underset{t}{argmax} \frac{2P(D_{pc}, f_c, t)R(D_{pc}, f_c, t)}{P(D_{pc}, f_c, t) + R(D_{pc}, f_c, t)},
\end{aligned}
\tag{2}
$$

$$
\begin{aligned}
P(D_{pc}, f_c, t) &= \frac{n_r}{|\{x|(x,y) \in D_{pc}, f_c(x) \geq t\}|}, \\
R(D_{pc}, f_c, t) &= \frac{n_r}{|D_{pc}|}, \\
n_r &= |\{x|(x,y) \in D_{pc}, f_c(x) \geq t, y = 1\}|,
\end{aligned}
$$

where t_c and f_c are the local threshold and base-classifier, D_{pc} is the local development subset which is similar with the T_{pc} defined by Eq. 1), P and R are the precision and recall, and n_r is the number of correct predict labels.

Third, classify the test instances. The algorithm of this step is presented in Fig. 1. With the trained base-classifiers f_c and the thresholds t_c, the test set E can be classified.

Require: a test instance x
 a hierarchy H={$(p, c)|(p, c)$ is a parent-child }
 base-classifiers $\{f_c|(p, c) \in H\}$
 thresholds $\{t_c|(p, c) \in H\}$
Ensure: a predicted label set y
 $q \leftarrow [Root]$, $y \leftarrow \{\}$
 while q is not empty **do**
  $p \leftarrow$ pop out the first item of q
  if p is a leaf node **then**
   $y \leftarrow y \cup \{p\}$
  else
   for all c, $(p, c) \in H$ **do**
    $s_c \leftarrow f_c(x)$
    if $s_c \geq t_c$ **then**
     append c into p
    end if
   end for
  end if
 end while
 return y

Figure 1: ScutTD algorithm

2.2 Meta-classification Top-down method

To describe the proposed MetaTD, we first introduce the definition of meta-samples as follows,

$$
\mathcal{M}(u, l, f_*) = (\mathcal{M}_x(u_x, l, f_*), \mathcal{M}_y(u_y, l, f_*))
\tag{3}
$$

$$
\begin{aligned}
\mathcal{M}_x(u_x, l, f_*) &= \{(n_i, f_{n_i}(u_x))|n_i \in p_l\} \\
\mathcal{M}_y(u_y, l, f_*) &= \begin{cases} +1, & l \in u_y \\ -1, & l \notin u_y \end{cases}
\end{aligned}
$$

where $\mathcal{M}$ is the meta-mapping that consists of meta-input $\mathcal{M}_x$ and meta-output $\mathcal{M}_y$, H is a hierarchy, $u = (u_x, u_y)$ is a base-sample where u_x is the input part and u_y is the label set, l is a leaf node (or a label), that is, a validate label for base-samples, $p_l = (n_0, n_1, \ldots, n_k)$ is a path from the root to l where $n_0 = root$, $n_k = l$, $(n_i, n_{i+1}) \in H$, and f_* are base-classifiers.

However, the above definition yields one meta-sample for each class, which may cause a problem of computational complexity on large-scale tasks. Hence a method of selecting label candidates for each base-sample is employed so that only a small fraction of labels need to be delivered into meta-classification. We note this selection method as $L(u_x, f_*, H)$.

MetaTD is based on the above two settings, and its workflow is described in Fig. 2.

The training phase consists of three steps as follows,

1. Train base-classifiers f_* on a training data set T, which is the same with ScutTD.
2. Construct a meta-training set with the base-classifiers and a development set D, $M_T = \cup_{u \in D}\{\mathcal{M}(u, l, f_*, H)|l \in L(u_x, f_*, H)\}$.
3. Train a meta-classifier g on M_T.

The whole training phase requires the base-level training set T and development set D, the description of the hierarchy H, and produces a set of base-classifiers f_* and a meta-classifier g.

The classifying phase also consists of three steps as follows,

1. Construct a group of meta-samples from a test base-sample u_x (its label u_y is unknown), $M_E = \{\mathcal{M}_x(u_x, l, f_*)|l \in L(u_x, f_*, H)\}$.
2. Present these meta-samples to the meta-classifier g,
$$
\begin{aligned}
g(M_E) &= \{g(\mathcal{M}_x(u_x, l, f_*))|l \in L(u_x, f_*, H)\} \\
&= \{g_{u_x, l}|l \in L(u_x, f_*, H)\}.
\end{aligned}
$$
3. Interpret the predictions into base-level labels. The interpretation is generally simple and

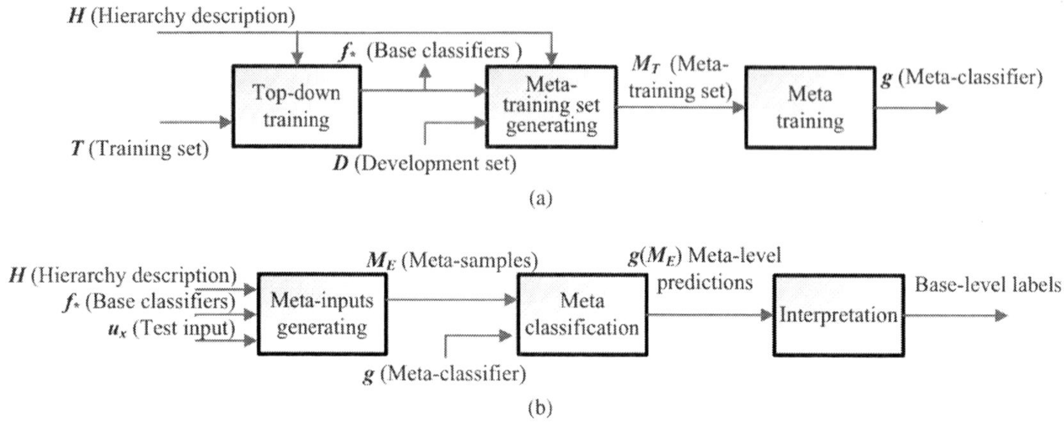

Figure 2: Workflows of meta-classification top-down method: (a) training phase; (b) classifying phase.

straightforward, and just outputs the labels with large scores. The practical interpretation depends on the data sets, and will be described in the section of experiments.

The remained problems now are how to implement meta-sample representations $\mathcal{M}_x(u_x, l, f_*)$ and selection of label candidates $L(u_x, f_*, H)$, which are solved in the next two subsections.

2.2.1 Representations of Meta-samples

In this subsection, the meta-samples will be made into real numerical vectors that are ready to be used by meta-classifiers. We use sparse vector to represent meta-samples through the following steps:

First, encode the scores of the related base-classifiers into a sparse vector. All the nodes except the root are numbered with integers, which serve as the dimensions of the sparse vector.

Second, augment the representations with the features about the global attributes of the root-to-leaf paths in the hierarchy. The purpose of this step is to raise classification accuracy, as these global attributes may be helpful to decide whether a path is true. The following three additional features are used according to our pilot experiments,

1. the *average* score of nodes along a path;
2. the *minimum* score of nodes along a path;
3. the fraction of nodes whose scores exceed the thresholds employed in ScutTD, named *pass-rate*.

In the end, the values of meta features are transferred into a sensible interval in order to fit the training of meta-classifiers (Liu, 2005; Liu et al., 2004). Two types of transformation functions are used according to our pilot experiments. For the additional features, the following standard scaling function is used,

$$z_s = \frac{s - \mu_s}{\sigma_s}$$

where s is the value of an additional feature, μ_s and σ_s are the corresponding mean and variance.

For the basic features, the following sigmoid function is used,

$$z_s = \frac{1}{1 + e^{-(s-\mu_s)}}$$

where s is a score at a node n, and μ_s is the average score at node n. This function is a simplification of the Platt' sigmoid fitting (Platt, 1999; Cesa-Bianchi et al., 2006), and it is more robust than the original one in the context of hierarchical classification according to our pilot experiements.

2.2.2 Selection of Label Candidates

How should label candidates be selected? In fact, the method of selecting label candidates is kind of like a classification method as both of them take in samples and give out the labels most likely to be right. However, the method of selecting label candidates should output more labels than a normal classifying method, in order to provide a wider coverage on truly correct ones. To find such a 'loose' classifying method, we refer to flat multi-class classification where another threshold strategy of Rank-cut (R-cut), besides the S-cut introduced above, is also widely used (Montejo-Ráez and Ureña-López, 2006; Yang, 2001). R-cut is to accept the top r labels with the highest confident scores, where r is a predefined integer.

Applying R-cut to the context of the top-down method is straightforward. The top-r children are

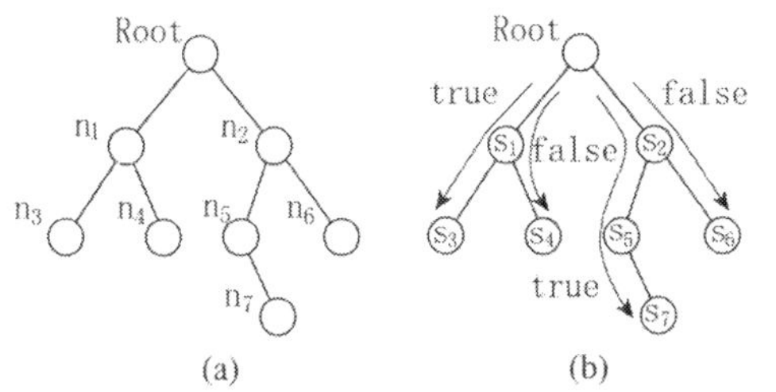

Figure 3: An illustration of solving hierarchical classification with MetaTD: (a) the class hierarchy; (b) the paths as meta-samples.

invoked from their parent node regardless of their scores, and the rest procedure is the same with S-cutTD (see Fig. 1). We name this method RcutTD, and employ it to select label candidates in the proposed MetaTD. Note that RcutTD has been discussed before and is considered improper for the classifying procedure of the top-down method (Li-u et al., 2005).

2.3 Illustration of Meta-classification Top-down Method

In this subsection we illustrate MetaTD with an example. Suppose a hierarchical classification task has the hierarchy of classes shown by Fig. 3a, where n_0 is the root, and the leaf nodes n_3, n_4, n_6 and n_7 are validate labels.

Further suppose that a tree of base-classifiers have been built through the top-down training. Here comes a sample with n_3 and n_7 as its correct labels. Fig. 3b shows that each base-classifier yields a relevant score s_i.

MetaTD converts each possible label (or leaf n-ode) into a meta-sample – the target is whether this leaf node is a correct label and the features are the scores of the base-classifiers along the path (Fig. 3b). For this example, the following four meta-samples can be generated,

$$\begin{array}{ll} \text{true} & n_0 \rightarrow (n_1, s_1) \rightarrow (n_3, s_3) \\ \text{false} & n_0 \rightarrow (n_1, s_1) \rightarrow (n_4, s_4) \\ \text{true} & n_0 \rightarrow (n_2, s_2) \rightarrow (n_5, s_5) \rightarrow (n_7, s_7) \\ \text{false} & n_0 \rightarrow (n_2, s_2) \rightarrow (n_6, s_6). \end{array} \tag{4}$$

These meta-samples are then interpreted into numerical sparse vectors. Suppose that n_1 to n_7 are numbered with integers 1–7, then the numerical sparse vectors can be generated (see Tab. 1).

With more meta-samples like above, a meta-classifier can be trained. Later this meta-classifier can be applied to the meta-samples made from a base-level test sample to pick out the right labels. In this way, MetaTD fulfills the original base-level classifying task.

No.	Basic			Extension		
1	1:s_1 [a]	3:s_3		8:a_{13} [b]	9:m_{13}	10:p_{13}
2	1:s_1	4:s_4		8:a_{14}	9:m_{14}	10:p_{14}
3	2:s_2	5:s_5	7:s_7	8:a_{257}	9:m_{257}	10:p_{257}
4	2:s_2	6:s_6		8:a_{26}	9:m_{26}	10:p_{26}

[a] dimension:value
[b] $a_{i_1 i_2 \ldots i_k}$, $m_{i_1 i_2 \ldots i_k}$, $p_{i_1 i_2 \ldots i_k}$ denote the average, minimum, and pass-rate of $s_{i_1}, s_{i_2} \ldots s_{i_k}$ respectively.

Table 1: Representing meta-samples with sparse vectors

3 Accuracy Analysis

The classification accuracy of top-down method-s is actually not very clear or predictable. To our best knowledge, no strict accuracy analyses on the conventional ScutTD have been reported yet. Here we just provide some general ideas about the comparison of accuracy between MetaTD and ScutTD.

First, whether pruning possible labels with R-cutTD or not has minor impact on the overall classification result. The labels rejected by RcutTD all have quite low scores on some parent-child relations and are very likely to be filtered out by the successive meta-classifier.

Second, ignoring the impact of selecting label candidates, the conventional top-down method of ScutTD can be actually seen as a weak meta-classifier in the framework of MetaTD. Suppose here is a meta-sample (a sparse vector),

$(n_1{:}z_1,\ n_2{:}z_2,\ \ldots,\ n_k{:}p_k,\ n_a{:}z_a,\ n_m{:}z_m,\ n_p{:}z_p)$ where n_i and p_i are a node number and its value, and n_a,n_m,n_p are the additional features. Then ScutTD works like,

$$\text{Output} = \begin{cases} \text{True} & \text{if } p_i > t_i \text{ for all } i = 1 \ldots k \\ \text{False} & \text{otherwise} \end{cases}$$

where t_i is the threshold of node n_i. Clearly this formula is a cascaded of binary decisions, which is weaker than some common classifiers such as weighted voting.

4 Experiments

In this section, after describing the experimental settings, we present the performance comparisons between MetaTD and baseline methods as well as historical records on the entire data sets. We then

Data	No. Sample			Feature		Class	
	Train.	Dev.	Test	No.	Avg.[a]	No.	Avg.[b]
LSHTC	93k	34k	34k	381k	173	12k	1.0
NTCIR	2 762k	374k	359k	694k	108	49k	2.7

[a] average features per sample, that is, average unique terms per document.
[b] average labels per sample.

Table 2: Statistical information of data sets

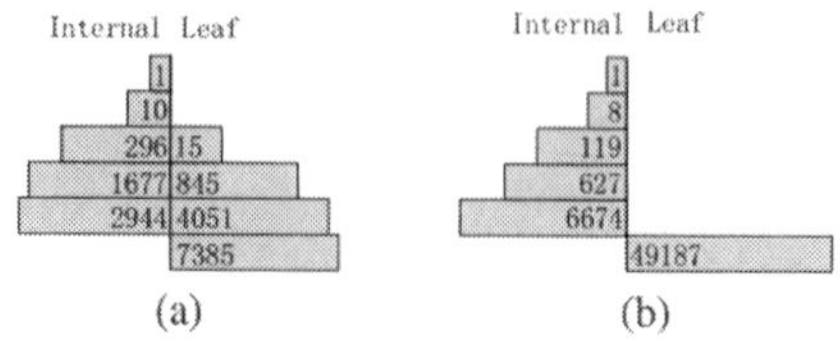

Figure 4: Number of internal and leaf nodes at each level of the hierarchy: (a) LSHTC; (b) NTCIR.

report the comparison with flat 1-vs-Rest approach on several subsets.

4.1 Experimental Settings

4.1.1 Data Sets

Two real-world data sets, the data set of web pages in the PASCAL2 Large-scale Hierarchical Text Classification challenge (LSHTC)[2] and the data set of patent documents from NII Test Collection for IR Systems Project (NTCIR)[3], are used in our experiments.

The PASCAL2 Large-scale Hierarchical Text Classification (LSHTC) challenge is held at 2009, aimed at promoting the study of classification methods for large hierarchies. The challenge attracts 19 participants with a variety of approaches (Kosmopoulos et al., 2010).

International Patent Classification (IPC) is a real-world taxonomy maintained by World Intellectual Property Organization (WIPO) [4]. The data set that we use is provided by NTCIR which is freely available for research purpose (Fall et al., 2003; Fujii et al., 2007). This data set consists of 3 496 137 Japanese patent documents submitted to Japan Patent Office from 1993 to 2002.

The statistics of two data sets and their hierarchies are presented in Tab. 2 and Fig. 4. Note that LSHTC's is a single-labeled task while NTCIR's is a multi-labeled ones.

4.1.2 Performance Measurement and Baseline Methods

Different performance measurements and baseline methods are adopted for the two data sets due to their difference of single-label and multi-label. NTCIR is multi-labeled, so the most commonly used criterion for general multi-labeled classifications, micro-F_1, is taken as the performance measurement. ScutTD is taken as the baseline method.

LSHTC is single-labeled, so accuracy is taken as the performance measurement. However, there is a problem about baseline method as ScutTD is not proper for single-labeled task. As a matter of fact, single-labeled hierarchical classifications are easier than multi-labeled ones, and it is natural to activate the child node with the largest score during top-down classification, like (Koller and Sahami, 1997). This method happens to be RcutTD with the parameter r=1. In addition to this baseline method, the evaluation records of LSHTC are also used for comparison.

4.1.3 Settings of MetaTD

The representation of meta-samples follows the description in Sec. 2.2.1. RcutTD is employed to select label candidates as described in Sec. 2.2.2. We set the parameter r=2 due to a trade-off between classification accuracy and time cost according to several pilot experiments.

The recent implement of SVM, Liblinear, is adopted as the meta-classifier (Fan et al., 2008).

Meta-to-base interpreters are needed to transfer the meta-level predictions into base-level labels. LSHTC is single-labeled, so it's natural to take the label with the largest meta-level scores. NTCIR is multi-labeled, and the strategy of S-cut in flat multi-class classification is employed.

4.1.4 Other Settings

The bag-of-word model with the term weight of TFIDF is adopted as the base-level sample representation in this paper (Sebastiani, 2002). To handle the Japanese text in the NTCIR's data set, we use the segment tool of Chasen [5] (Jin et al., 2010), and remove the function words from the result.

The base-level classifier is SVM^{light} with linear kernel. The default cost factor of SVM^{light} is used on NTCIR, while the cost factors are tuned by the development sets on LSHTC.

[2] `http://lshtc.iit.demokritos.gr/`

[3] `http://research.nii.ac.jp/ntcir/index-en.html`

[4] `http://www.wipo.int/classifications/ipc/en/`

[5] `http://chasen.naist.jp/hiki/ChaSen/`

LSHTC, 12 294 classes			
Rank	Method	Acc.	Group
1	Not reported	0.4676	alpaca
2	Committees of flat approaches	0.4632	jhuang
	MetaTD	**0.4513**	
3	Flattened Top-down method	0.4433	arthur.
4	Centroid-based classifier	0.4431	XipengQiu
5	Deep Classification	0.4317	Turing
6	Not reported	0.4270	Dyakonov
	RcutTD	**0.4262**	
7	Flattened Top-down method	0.4152	logicators
11	k-NN	0.4023	NakaCristo

Table 3: Classification accuracies on single-labeled LSHTC as well as its challenge records

NTCIR, 49 187 classes	
Method	Micro-F_1
ScutTD	0.272
MetaTD	**0.426**

Table 4: Classification accuracies on the multi-labeled data set of NTCIR

The experiments are run on four 64-bit computers with multi-core 1.9*GHz* AMD CPUs. All the experiments require actually up to 8*G* memory according to our observation.

4.2 Performance on Entire Data Sets

In this subsection we compare MetaTD with baseline methods on the entire data sets of LSHTC and NTCIR from the aspects of accuracy and efficiency.

4.2.1 Accuracy Comparisons

The experimental results on the single-labeled LSHTC as well as the challenge records are presented in Tab. 3. MetaTD turns out to be between the second and third place, while the baseline method of RcutTD ranks between the sixth and seventh place. The method at the second place is a committee of two flat approaches – variants of the OOZ algorithm (Madani and Huang, 2008) and the passive-aggressive algorithm (Crammer et al., 2006). The methods at both the third and seventh places are both top-down methods enhanced by flattening the original hierarchy. Deep classification ranks at the fifth place (Xue et al., 2008). In short, MetaTD outperforms the conventional and several variant top-down methods.

The results on the multi-labeled NTCIR are presented in Tab. 4. MetaTD achieves a much higher micro-F_1 than the baseline method of ScutTD.

Method	Training		Classify.[a]
	LSHTC, 12 294 classes		
RcutTD	Train base-classifiers	$10h$	0.108
MetaTD	Train base-classifiers	$17h$	0.131
	Prepare meta-train. set	$1h$	
	Meta-training	$18s$	
	NTCIR, 49 187 classes		
Scut/MetaTD	Train base-classifiers	$261h$	
ScutTD	Find optimal thresholds	$4h$	0.029
Meta-learning	Prepare training set	$12h$	0.062
	Meta-training	$466s$	

[a] seconds per sample

Table 5: Time costs of training and classifying with conventional top-down methods and MetaTD.

No. Class.	LSHTC			NTCIR		
	Train.	Dev.	Test	Train.	Dev.	Test
$1k$	$7k$	$2k$	$2k$	$38k$	$16k$	$17k$
$5k$	$39k$	$12k$	$12k$	$155k$	$64k$	$68k$
$10k$	$76k$	$23k$	$23k$	$253k$	$102k$	$104k$
$15k$	–[a]	–	–	$320k$	$129k$	$129k$

[a] there is not enough classes in the original data set.

Table 6: Numbers of classes and samples at the subsets of LSHTC and NTCIR

4.2.2 Efficiency Comparisons

The training and classifying time costs of MetaTD and baseline methods are presented in Tab. 5. In the training phrase, training base-classifiers causes most time cost. The additional cost of meta-classification MetaTD is only 5%–10% of that cost. Meta-training unexpectedly costs very little time, while preparing meta-training sets costs most additional time cost.

On the aspect of classifying, the time cost of MetaTD is about twice as much as the conventional top-down methods. According to our observation, considerable time is spent on reading samples and loading classifiers.

4.3 Comparison with Flat Approach of 1-vs-Rest on Subsets

In this subsection we compare the performance of top-down methods with the flat approach of 1-vs-Rest multiclass classification. Given the great computational complexity of the flat approach, several subsets are made from the entire data sets of LSHTC and NTCIR through randomly picking up classes and samples (see Tab. 6).

All the experimental settings here are consistent with previous experiments on the entire data sets. For the flat approach of 1-vs-Rest, the SVM^{light} is

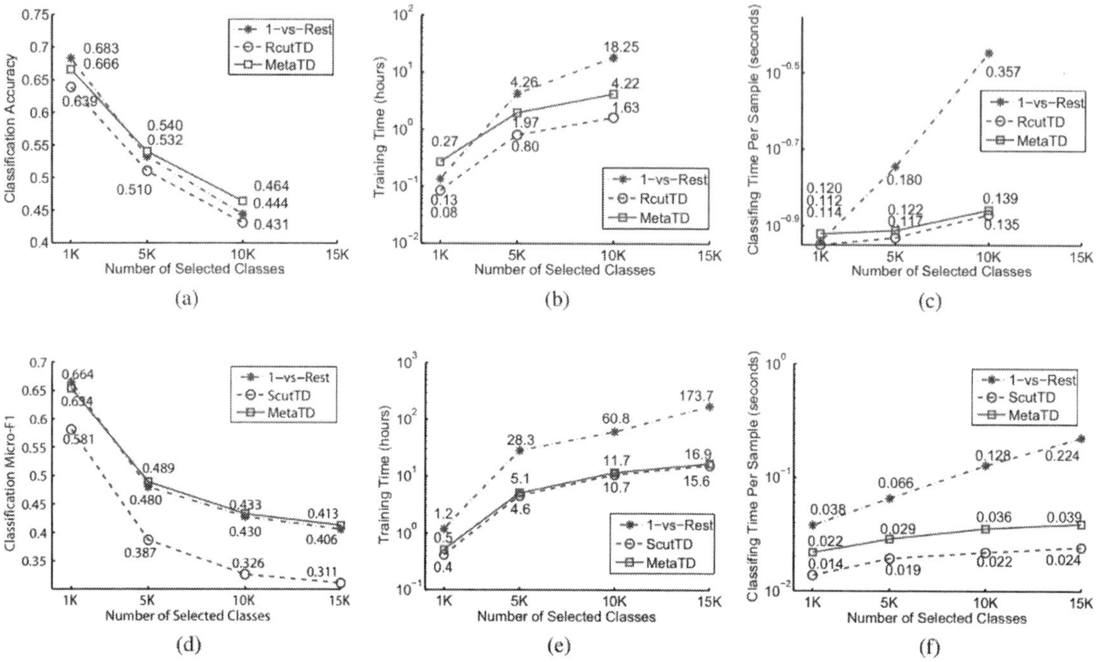

Figure 5: Performance comparison of flat 1-vs-Rest approach, conventional top-down methods and MetaTD on subsets of various sizes: (a) through (c) for LSHTC; (d) through (f) for NTCIR.

taken as the base-classifier.

The experiment results are presented in Fig. 5. On the aspect of classification accuracy, MetaTD catches up with the 1-vs-Rest approach. In particular, MetaTD slightly outperforms 1-vs-Rest approach on both data sets when the number of classes exceeds 5 thousands.

On the aspect of computational complexity, MetaTD is close to the conventional top-down methods, and they all show a great superiority over the 1-vs-Rest approach on both training and classifying as expected.

5 Conclusions

In this paper, we propose a meta-learning top-down method (MetaTD) in order to reduce the error propagation of the conventional ScutTD while remain its capability for large-scale hierarchical classification. In the experiments, MetaTD outperforms ScutTD and catches up with the flat 1-vs-Rest approach on classification accuracy. On the aspect of computational complexity, MetaTD only costs 5%-10% extra time in training and classifying, so it is suitable for most applications where ScutTD are being used.

References

P.N. Bennett and N. Nguyen. 2009. Refined experts: improving classification in large taxonomies. In *Proc. of SIGIR'09*, pages 11–18. ACM.

L. Cai and T. Hofmann. 2004. Hierarchical document categorization with support vector machines. In *Proc. of ACM international conference on information and knowledge management*, pages 78–87. ACM.

M. Ceci and D. Malerba. 2007a. Classifying web documents in a hierarchy of categories: a comprehensive study. *Journal of Intelligent Information Systems*, 28(1):37–78.

M. Ceci and D. Malerba. 2007b. Classifying web documents in a hierarchy of categories: a comprehensive study. *Journal of Intelligent Information Systems*, 28(1):37–78.

N. Cesa-Bianchi, C. Gentile, and L. Zaniboni. 2006. Hierarchical classification: combining Bayes with SVM. In *Proc. of ICML'06*, pages 177–184. ACM.

K. Crammer, O. Dekel, J. Keshet, S. Shalev-Shwartz, and Y. Singer. 2006. Online passive-aggressive algorithms. *Journal of Machine Learning Research*, 7:551–585.

S. Dumais and H. Chen. 2000. Hierarchical classification of Web content. In *Proc. of SIGIR'00*, pages 256–263. ACM.

C.J. Fall, A. Törcsvári, K. Benzineb, and G. Karetka. 2003. Automated categorization in the international patent classification. In *ACM SIGIR Forum*, volume 37, pages 10–25. ACM.

R.E. Fan, K.W. Chang, C.J. Hsieh, X.R. Wang, and C.J. Lin. 2008. LIBLINEAR: A library for large linear classification. *Journal of Machine Learning Research*, 9:1871–1874.

AA Freitas and A.C. de Carvalho, 2007. *A Tutorial on Hierarchical Classification with Applications in Bioinformatics.*, pages 175–208. IGI Publishing.

A. Fujii, M. Iwayama, and N. Kando. 2007. Introduction to the special issue on patent processing. *Information Processing & Management*, 43(5):1149–1153.

Gang Jin, Qi Kong, Jian Zhang, Xiaolin Wang, Cong Hui, Hai Zhao, and Bao-Liang Lu. 2010. Multiple strategies for NTCIR-08 patent mining at BCMI. In *Proc. of the 8th NTCIR workshop meeting on evaluation of information access technologies*, pages 303–308.

D. Koller and M. Sahami. 1997. Hierarchically classifying documents using very few words. In *Proc. of ICML'97*, pages 170–178.

A. Kosmopoulos, E. Gaussier, G. Paliouras, and S. Aseervatham. 2010. The ECIR 2010 large scale hierarchical classification workshop. In *ACM SIGIR Forum*, volume 44, pages 23–32. ACM.

Y. Labrou and T. Finin. 1999. Yahoo! as an ontology: using Yahoo! categories to describe documents. In *Proc. of the eighth international conference on Information and knowledge management*, pages 180–187. ACM.

D. D. Lewis, Y. Yang, T. G. Rose, and F. Li. 2004. Rcv1: A new benchmark collection for text categorization research. *Journal of Machine Learning Research*, 5:361–397.

C. L. Liu, H. Hao, and H. Sako. 2004. Confidence transformation for combining classifiers. *Pattern Analysis & Applications*, 7(1):2–17.

T. Y. Liu, Y. Yang, H. Wan, H. J. Zeng, Z. Chen, and W.Y. Ma. 2005. Support vector machines classification with a very large-scale taxonomy. *ACM SIGKDD Explorations*, 7(1):36–43.

C. L. Liu. 2005. Classifier combination based on confidence transformation. *Pattern Recognition*, 38(1):11–28.

B.L. Lu and M. Ito. 2002. Task decomposition and module combination based on class relations: A modular neural network for pattern classification. *IEEE Tran. on Neural Networks,*, 10(5):1244–1256.

B.L. Lu and X.L. Wang. 2009. A Parallel and Modular Pattern Classification Framework for Large-Scale Problems. *Chen C. H. editor, Handbook of Pattern Recognition and Computer Vision (4th Edition)*, pages 725–746.

O. Madani and J. Huang. 2008. On updates that constrain the features' connections during learning. In *Proceeding of SIGKDD'08*, pages 515–523. ACM.

A. Montejo-Ráez and L. Ureña-López. 2006. Selection strategies for multi-label text categorization. *Advances in Natural Language Processing*, pages 585–592.

J. Platt. 1999. Probabilistic outputs for support vector machines. *Bartlett P., Schoelkopf B., Schurmans D., Smola, A. J. editor, Advances in Large Margin Classifiers*, pages 61–74.

K. Punera and J. Ghosh. 2008. Enhanced hierarchical classification via isotonic smoothing. In *Proceeding of the 17th international conference on World Wide Web*, pages 151–160. ACM.

F. Sebastiani. 2002. Machine learning in automated text categorization. *ACM computing surveys (CSUR)*, 34(1):1–47.

C. N. Silla and A. A. Freitas. 2010. A survey of hierarchical classification across different application domains. *Data Mining and Knowledge Discovery*, pages 1–42.

A. Sun and E. P. Lim. 2001. Hierarchical text classification and evaluation. In *Proc. of the ICDM'01*, pages 521–528. IEEE.

A. Sun, E. P. Lim, W. K. Ng, and J. Srivastava. 2004. Blocking reduction strategies in hierarchical text classification. *IEEE Tran. on Knowledge and Data Engineering*, pages 1305–1308.

I. Tsochantaridis, T. Joachims, T. Hofmann, and Y. Altun. 2005. Large margin methods for structured and interdependent output variables. *Journal of Machine Learning Research*, 6(2):1453.

X. L. Wang and B. L. Lu. 2010. Flatten hierarchies for large-scale hierarchical text categorization. In *Proc. of fifth international conference on digital information management*, pages 139–144.

G. R. Xue, D. Xing, Q. Yang, and Y. Yu. 2008. Deep classification in large-scale text hierarchies. In *Proc. of SIGIR'08*, pages 619–626. ACM.

Y. Yang, J. Zhang, and B. Kisiel. 2003. A scalability analysis of classifiers in text categorization. In *Proc. of SIGIR'03*, pages 96–103. ACM.

Y. Yang. 2001. A study of thresholding strategies for text categorization. In *Proc. of SIGIR'01*, pages 137–145.

*** Formatting Issue - Best Available Paper/Graphic ***

Using Syntactic and Shallow Semantic Kernels to Improve Multi-Modality Manifold-Ranking for Topic-Focused Multi-Document Summarization

Yllias Chali
University of Lethbridge
Lethbridge, AB, Canada
chali@cs.uleth.ca

Sadid A. Hasan
University of Lethbridge
Lethbridge, AB, Canada
hasan@cs.uleth.ca

Kaisar Imam
University of Lethbridge
Lethbridge, AB, Canada
imam@uleth.ca

Abstract

Multi-modality manifold-ranking is recently used successfully in topic-focused multi-document summarization. This approach is based on Bag-Of-Words (BOW) assumption where the pair-wise similarity values between sentences are computed using the standard cosine similarity measure (TF*IDF). However, the major limitation of the TF*IDF approach is that it only retains the frequency of the words and disregards the syntactic and semantic information. In this paper, we propose the use of syntactic and shallow semantic kernels for computing the relevance between the sentences. We argue that the addition of syntactic and semantic information can improve the performance of the multi-modality manifold-ranking algorithm. Extensive experiments on the DUC benchmark datasets prove the effectiveness of our approach.

1 Introduction

Text summarization is a good way to compress a huge amount of information into a concise form by selecting the most important information and discarding redundant information. According to Mani (2001), automatic text summarization takes a partially-structured source text from multiple texts written about the same topic, extracts information content from it, and presents the most important content to the user in a manner sensitive to the user's needs. In contrast to summarizing one document that is termed as single document summarization, multi-document summarization deals with multiple documents as sources that are related to one main topic under consideration. As compared to generic summarization that must contain the core information central to the source documents, the main goal of topic-focused multi-document summarization (i.e. query-based multi-document summarization) is to create from the documents a summary that can answer the need for information expressed in the topic or explain the topic (Wan et al., 2007). In this paper, we consider the problem of producing extraction-based[1] topic-focused multi-document summaries given a collection of documents.

In recent years, a variety of manifold-ranking based methods are applied successfully to topic-focused multi-document summarization. The basic manifold-ranking method is a typical graph-based summarization method that makes uniform use of the sentence-to-sentence relationships and the sentence-to-topic relationships in a manifold-ranking process (Wan et al., 2007). In the multi-modality manifold-ranking algorithm, sentence relationships are classified into within-document relationships and cross-document relationships, and each kind of relationships are considered as a separate modality (graph) (Wan and Xiao, 2009). These methods are based on Bag-Of-Words (BOW) assumption where the pair-wise similarity values between the sentences are computed using the standard cosine measure (TF*IDF). The major limitation of the TF*IDF approach is that it only retains the frequency of the words and does not take into account the sequence of them (word ordering). It ignores the syntactic and semantic structure of the sentences and thus, cannot distinguish between "The police shot the gunman" and "The gunman shot the police". Traditionally, information extraction techniques are based on the BOW approach augmented by language modeling. But when the task like *multi-document summarization* requires the use of more

[1] An extract summary consists of sentences extracted from the document while an abstract summary employs words and phrases not appearing in the original document (Mani and Maybury, 1999).

complex semantics, the approaches based on only BOW are often inadequate to perform fine-level textual analysis. Although some improvements on BOW are given by the use of dependency trees and syntactic parse trees (Hirao et al., 2004), (Punyakanok et al., 2004), (Zhang and Lee, 2003b), but these too are not adequate in terms of documents having very long and articulated sentences or even paragraphs. Shallow semantic representations could prevent the sparseness of deep structural approaches and the weakness of BOW models (Moschitti et al., 2007). Thus, attempting an application of syntactic and semantic information in measuring the relevance between the sentences seems natural and hardly controversial.

In this paper, we extensively study the impact of syntactic and semantic information in computing the similarity between the sentences in the multi-modality manifold learning framework for topic-focused multi-document summarization. We believe that the augmentation of the similarity measures based on the syntactic and semantic information could be helpful to characterize the relation between the sentences in a more effective way than the traditional TF*IDF based similarity measures alone. To include syntactic and semantic information into the multi-modality manifold-ranking framework, we apply the tree kernel functions (Collins and Duffy, 2001) and re-implement the syntactic and shallow semantic tree kernel model according to Moschitti et al. (2007). We run our experiments on the DUC[2]-2006 benchmark dataset, and the results show that the addition of syntactic and semantic information improves the performance of the BOW-based multi-modality manifold-ranking approach. The rest of this paper is organized as follows: Section 2 focuses on the related work, Section 3 describes the multi-modality manifold ranking model, Section 4 discusses the syntactic and shallow semantic kernels, Section 5 presents the experimental details with evaluation results and finally, Section 6 concludes the paper.

2 Related Work

In recent years, researchers have become more interested in topic-focused summarization and hence, different methods have been proposed ranging from heuristic extensions of generic summarization schemes (by incorporating topic-biased information) to novel ones. For instance, Nastase (2008) expands the query by using encyclopedic knowledge in Wikipedia and use the topic expanded words with activated nodes in the graph to produce an extractive summary. Hal Daumé and Marcu (2006) present BAYESUM ("Bayesian summarization"), a sentence extraction model for query-focused summarization.

Wan et al. (2007) propose a manifold-ranking method to make uniform use of sentence-to-sentence and sentence-to-topic relationships whereas the use of multi-modality manifold-ranking algorithm is shown in Wan and Xiao (2009). However, these methods use the standard cosine similarity measure to compute the relatedness between the sentences ignoring the syntactic and semantic information. The importance of syntactic and semantic features in finding textual similarity is described by Zhang and Lee (2003a), Moschitti et al. (2007), and Moschitti and Basili (2006). An effective way to integrate syntactic and semantic structures in machine learning algorithms is the use of *tree kernel* functions (Collins and Duffy, 2001) which has been successfully applied to question classification (Zhang and Lee, 2003a; Moschitti and Basili, 2006). In this paper, we use the tree kernel functions and to the best of our knowledge, no study has used tree kernel functions before to encode syntactic/semantic information for more complex tasks such as computing the relatedness between the sentences in the multi-modality manifold ranking algorithm for topic-focused multi-document summarization.

3 Multi-Modality Manifold-Ranking Model

In this section, we present the theoretical details of the manifold-ranking method (Zhou et al., 2003a; Zhou et al., 2003b), a universal ranking algorithm. This method is employed to rank data points and has been successfully applied in topic-focused document summarization in Wan et al. (2007) where the data points refer to the topic description and all the sentences in the documents. The manifold-ranking process for the summarization task can be formalized as follows (Wan and Xiao, 2009):

Given a set of data points , the first point represents the topic description (query point) and

[2]http://duc.nist.gov/

the rest points represent all the sentences in the documents (data points to be ranked). The basic manifold-ranking algorithm treats the sentence relationships in a single modality (Wan et al., 2007) whereas, in Wan and Xiao (2009), the relationships between the sentences in a document set are classified as either within-document relationship or cross-document relationship to form two separate modalities to reflect the local information channel and the global information channel between the sentences, respectively. The two modalities are applied in the multi-modality manifold-ranking algorithm for ranking the sentences effectively. Based on each kind of modality, an undirected graph is built to reflect each kind of sentence relationships. Let be the within-document affinity matrix containing only the within-document links for the data points, where is the cosine similarity[3] value between and if and belong to the same document or one of and is ; Otherwise, is set to . Similarly, let be the cross-document affinity matrix containing the cross-document links, where is the cosine similarity value between and if and belong to different documents or one of and is ; Otherwise, is set to . All the relationships between the topic, and any document sentence are included in both and . Then, and are normalized by and , respectively, where and are the diagonal matrices with - element equal to the sum of the th row of and , respectively. Then the multi-modality learning task for topic-focused summarization is to infer the ranking function from , and : .

Linear Fusion: For fusing the two modalities, we use the linear fusion scheme as this was shown to perform the best in Wan and Xiao (2009). This scheme fuses the constraints from , and simultaneously by a weighted sum. The cost function associated with is defined as:

(1)

where , , and capture the trade-off between the constraints[4].

As discussed previously, the basic multi-modality manifold-ranking model lacks sensitivity to the context in which the words appear since it is solely based on the BOW assumption. It ignores the internal structure of the sentences and does not consider word orders. Our aim in this paper is to propose a similarity measure in which syntactic and/or semantic information can be added to enhance the multi-modality manifold-ranking model by encoding the relational information between the words in sentences. We claim that for a complex task like topic-focused multi-document summarization where the relatedness between the document sentences is an important factor, the multi-modality manifold algorithm for ranking sentences would perform more effectively if we could incorporate the syntactic and semantic information with the standard cosine measure (i.e. TF*IDF) in calculating the similarity between sentences. In the next section, we describe how we can encode syntactic and semantic structures in calculating the similarity between sentences.

4 Syntactic and Shallow Semantic Structures

Given a sentence (or query[5]), we first parse it into a syntactic tree using a parser like (Charniak, 1999) and then, calculate the similarity between the two trees using the *tree kernel* (discussed in Section 4.1). However, syntactic information is often not adequate when dealing with long and articulated sentences or paragraphs. Shallow semantic representations, bearing a more compact information, could prevent the sparseness of deep structural approaches (Moschitti et al., 2007). Initiatives such as PropBank (PB) (Kingsbury and Palmer, 2002) have made possible the design of accurate automatic Semantic Role Labeling (SRL) systems like ASSERT (Hacioglu et al., 2003).

[3] We augment syntactic and/or semantic information with this measure in our proposed model using the syntactic and/or shallow semantic kernels described in Section 4 and argue that the combined measure performs better.

[4] The first two terms of the right-hand side in the cost function are the smoothness constraints for the two modalities while the last term denotes the fitting constraint.

[5] The query is denoted as the first point in the data space of the manifold ranking framework and represented by .

*** Formatting Issue - Best Available Paper/Graphic ***

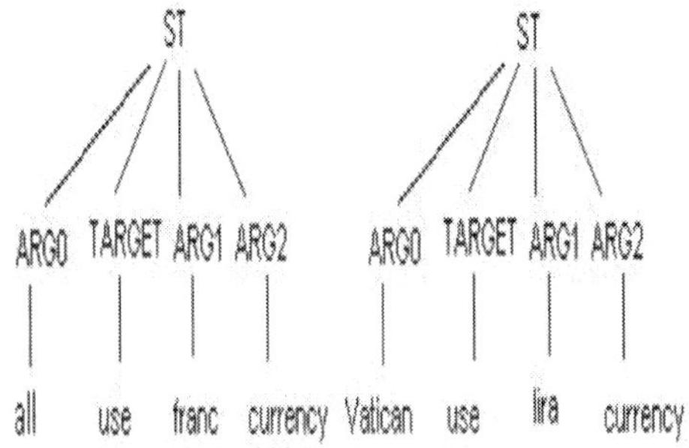

Figure 1: Example of semantic trees

For example, consider the PB annotation:

```
[ARG0 all][TARGET use][ARG1
the french franc][ARG2
as their currency]
```

Such annotation can be used to design a shallow semantic representation that can be matched against other semantically similar sentences, e.g.

```
[ARG0 the Vatican][TARGET use]
[ARG1 the Italian lira][ARG2
as their currency]
```

In order to calculate the semantic similarity between the sentences, we first represent the annotated sentence (or query) using the tree structures like Figure 1 which we call Semantic Tree (ST). In the semantic tree, arguments are replaced with the most important word-often referred to as the semantic head. We look for noun first, then verb, then adjective, then adverb to find the semantic head in the argument. If none of these is present, we take the first word of the argument as the semantic head. This reduces the data sparseness with respect to a typical cosine measure representation used in the basic multi-modality manifold-ranking model.

4.1 Tree Kernels

Once we build the trees (syntactic or semantic), our next task is to measure the similarity between the trees. For this, every tree is represented by an dimensional vector , where the i-th element is the number of occurrences of the i-th tree fragment in tree . The tree fragments of a tree are all of its sub-trees which include at least one production with the restriction that no production

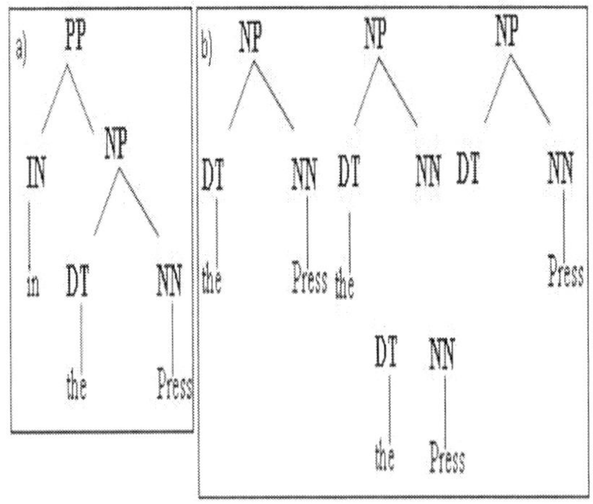

Figure 2: (a) An example tree (b) The sub-trees of the NP covering "the press".

rules can be broken into incomplete parts. Figure 2 shows an example tree and a portion of its subtrees.

Implicitly we enumerate all the possible tree fragments . These fragments are the axis of this m-dimensional space. Note that this needs to be done only implicitly, since the number is extremely large. Because of this, (Collins and Duffy, 2001) defines the tree kernel algorithm whose computational complexity does not depend on .

The tree kernel of two trees and is actually the inner product of and :

(2)

We define the indicator function to be 1 if the sub-tree is seen rooted at node and 0 otherwise. It follows:

where, and are the set of nodes in and respectively. So, we can derive:

(3)

where, we define = .
Next, we note that can be computed in polynomial time, due to the following recursive definition:

1. If the productions at and are different then
2. If the productions at and are the same, and and are pre-terminals, then
3. Else if the productions at and are not pre-terminals,

(4)

where, is the number of children of in the tree; because the productions at and are the same, we have . The i-th child-node of is . *TK* is the similarity value (tree kernel) between the sentences (and/or the query sentence) based on the syntactic structure. For example, for the following sentence and query we get the following score:

Query (q): Describe steps taken and worldwide reaction prior to introduction of the Euro on January 1, 1999. Include predictions and expectations reported in the press.

Sentence (s): Europe's new currency, the euro, will rival the U.S. dollar as an international currency over the long term, Der Spiegel magazine reported Sunday.

Score: 65.5

4.2 Shallow Semantic Tree Kernel (SSTK)

The tree kernel (TK) function computes the number of common subtrees between two trees. Such subtrees are subject to the constraint that their nodes are taken with all or none of the children they have in the original tree. Though, this definition of subtrees makes the TK function appropriate for syntactic trees but at the same time makes it not well suited for the semantic trees (ST). The critical aspect of steps (1), (2) and (3) of the TK function is that the productions of two evaluated nodes have to be identical to allow the match of further descendants. This means that common substructures cannot be composed by a node with only some of its children as an effective ST representation would require. (Moschitti et al., 2007) solve this problem by designing the Shallow Semantic Tree Kernel (SSTK) which allows to match portions of a ST. The SSTK is based on two ideas: first, it changes the ST by adding *SLOT* nodes. These accommodate argument labels in a specific order i.e. it provides a fixed number of slots, possibly filled with *null* arguments, that encode all possible predicate arguments. Leaf nodes are filled with the wildcard character * but they may alternatively accommodate additional information. The slot nodes are used in such a way that the adopted TK function can generate fragments containing one or more children. As previously pointed out, if the arguments were directly attached to the root node, the kernel function would only generate the structure with all children (or the structure with no children, i.e. empty). Second, as the original tree kernel would generate many matches with slots filled with the null label, we have set a new step 0 in the TK calculation:

(0) if (or) is a pre-terminal node and its child label is *null*, ;
and subtract one unit to , in step 3:

The above changes generate a new *C* which, when substituted (in place of original *C*) in Eq. 3, gives the new SSTK. For example, for the following sentence and query we get the semantic score:

Query (q): Describe steps taken and worldwide reaction prior to introduction of the Euro on January 1, 1999. Include predictions and expectations reported in the press.

Sentence (s): The Frankfurt-based body said in its annual report released today that it has decided on two themes for the new currency history of European civilization and abstract or concrete paintings.

Score: 9

5 Experiments and Results

5.1 Task Description

In this paper, we re-implement the multi-modality manifold ranking algorithm for topic-focused multi-document summarization by encoding the syntactic and semantic information to measure sentence relationships. We use the linear approach for fusing the modalities as this was shown to perform the best (Wan and Xiao, 2009). The purpose of our experiments is to study the impact of the syntactic and semantic representation in the multi-modality manifold-ranking framework.

Over the past three years, complex questions have been the focus of much attention in both the automatic question-answering and multi-document summarization (MDS) communities. While most current complex QA evaluations (including the 2004 AQUAINT Relationship QA Pilot, the 2005 Text Retrieval Conference (TREC) Relationship QA Task, and the 2006 GALE Distillation Effort) require systems to return unstructured lists of candidate answers in response to a complex question, recent MDS evaluations (including the 2005, 2006 and 2007 Document Understanding Conferences (DUC)) have tasked systems with returning paragraph-length answers to complex questions that are responsive, relevant, and coherent. The DUC conference series is run by the National Institute of Standards and Technology (NIST) to further progress in summarization and enable researchers to participate in large-scale experiments. We use the main task of DUC 2006 for evaluation. The task was: "Given a complex question (topic description) and a collection of relevant documents, the task is to synthesize a fluent, well-organized 250-word summary of the documents that answers the question(s) in the topic". To accomplish this task, we generate summaries for a subset of 10 topics of DUC 2006 dataset by each of our six systems as defined below:

(1) COSINE: This system is the original multi-modality manifold ranking method described in Section 3 that uses the standard cosine similarity measure based on TF*IDF and does not consider the syntactic/semantic information.

(2) SYN: This system measures the similarity between the sentences using the *syntactic tree* and the *general tree kernel* function defined in Section 4.1.

(3) SEM: This system measures the similarity between the sentences using the *shallow semantic tree* and the *shallow semantic tree kernel* function defined in Section 4.2.

(4) COSINE+SYN: This system measures the similarity between the sentences using both standard cosine similarity measure and the syntactic tree kernel.

(5) COSINE+SEM: This system measures the similarity between the sentences using both standard cosine similarity measure and the shallow semantic tree kernel.

(6) COSINE+SYN+SEM: This system measures the similarity between the sentences using standard cosine similarity measure, syntactic tree kernel, and shallow semantic tree kernel.

5.2 Automatic Evaluation

We carried out automatic evaluation of our candidate summaries using ROUGE (Lin, 2004) toolkit, which has been widely adopted for automatic summarization evaluation. *ROUGE* stands for "Recall-Oriented Understudy for Gisting Evaluation". It is a collection of measures that determines the quality of a summary by comparing it to reference summaries created by humans. The measures count the number of overlapping units such as n-gram, word-sequences, and word-pairs between the system-generated summary to be evaluated and the ideal summaries created by humans. For all our systems, we report the widely accepted important metrics: ROUGE-2 and ROUGE-SU. We also present the ROUGE-1 scores since this has a high correlation with the human judgement. All the ROUGE measures were calculated by running ROUGE-1.5.5 with stemming but no removal of stopwords. ROUGE run-time parameters were set as the same as DUC 2007 evaluation setup. They are:

ROUGE-1.5.5.pl -2 -1 -u -r 1000 -t 0 -n 4 -w 1.2 -m -l 250 -a

Table 1 to Table 3 show the ROUGE-1, ROUGE-2, and ROUGE-SU scores of our six different systems. In the experiments, the regularized parameter for the fitting constraint is fixed at 0.4, as in Wan et al. (2007). We kept as it was shown to be the most effective choice for the linear fusion scheme in Wan and Xiao (2009).

Systems	Recall	Precision	F-score
COSINE	0.3619	0.3043	0.3305
SYN	0.3571	0.3105	0.3320
SEM	0.3814	0.2909	0.3299
COSINE+SYN	0.3627	0.3105	0.3346
COSINE+SEM	0.3737	0.3140	0.3412
COSINE+SYN+SEM	0.3648	0.3117	0.3360

Table 1: ROUGE-1 measures

Systems	Recall	Precision	F-score
COSINE	0.0584	0.0488	0.0532
SYN	0.0638	0.0558	0.0595
SEM	0.0732	0.0555	0.0631
COSINE+SYN	0.0611	0.0522	0.0563
COSINE+SEM	0.0691	0.0581	0.0631
COSINE+SYN+SEM	0.0658	0.0560	0.0605

Table 2: ROUGE-2 measures

Systems	Recall	Precision	F-score
COSINE	0.1262	0.0890	0.1043
SYN	0.1190	0.0903	0.1025
SEM	0.1406	0.0818	0.1033
COSINE+SYN	0.1278	0.0937	0.1081
COSINE+SEM	0.1334	0.0944	0.1104
COSINE+SYN+SEM	0.1282	0.0939	0.1083

Table 3: ROUGE-SU measures

For all the systems, Table 4 shows the F-scores of the reported ROUGE measures. From these results, we clearly see the positive impact of syntactic and semantic information in the multi-modality manifold ranking method for topic-focused multi-document summarization. The SYN system improves the ROUGE-1 and ROUGE-2 scores over the COSINE system by 0.45%, and 11.84% while underperforms the ROUGE-SU score by 1.75% respectively. The SEM system improves the ROUGE-2 scores over the COSINE system by 18.60% while underperforms the ROUGE-1 and ROUGE-SU scores by 0.18%, and 0.96% respectively. The COSINE+SYN system improves the ROUGE-1, ROUGE-2, and ROUGE-SU scores over the COSINE system by 1.24%, 5.82%, and 3.64% respectively. The COSINE+SEM system improves the ROUGE-1, ROUGE-2, and ROUGE-SU scores over the COSINE system by 3.23%, 18.60%, and 5.84% respectively. Lastly, the COSINE+SYN+SEM system improves the ROUGE-1, ROUGE-2, and ROUGE-SU scores over the COSINE system by 1.66%, 13.72%, and 3.83% respectively. Deep analysis of all these results yields that the proposed systems (that encode the syntactic and/or semantic information in the multi-modality manifold ranking framework) considerablely outperform the standard cosine similarity based manifold approach. The results also denote that encoding the syntactic and/or semantic information on top of the standard cosine similarity measure often outperform the systems that consider only syntactic and/or semantic information. From all our six systems, we can see that the *SEM* and *COSINE+SEM* are the best performing systems on average while performance of the *COSINE+SYN+SEM* decreases a bit indicating the fact that encoding both syntactic and semantic information on top of the standard cosine similarity measure has a negative impact on the multi-modality manifold ranking method. This may be due to the fact that the SYN system does not perform too well as seen from the results and thus deteriorates the performance of the COSINE+SYN+SEM system.

Systems	R-1	R-2	R-SU
COSINE	0.3305	0.0532	0.1043
SYN	0.3320	0.0595	0.1025
SEM	0.3299	0.0631	0.1033
COSINE+SYN	0.3346	0.0563	0.1081
COSINE+SEM	0.3412	0.0631	0.1104
COSINE+SYN+SEM	0.3360	0.0605	0.1083

Table 4: ROUGE F-scores for different systems

In Table 5, the proposed methods are compared with the NIST baseline. The NIST baseline is the official baseline system established by NIST that generated the summaries by returning all the leading sentences (up to 250 words) in the
field of the most recent document(s). We also list the average ROUGE scores of all the participating systems for DUC-2006 (i.e. AverageDUC). From the tables, we can see that the proposed multi-modality manifold ranking methods based on the syntactic and semantic measures mostly outperform the NIST baseline system. They can also achieve higher ROUGE scores as comparable to the average scores of all the participating systems of DUC-2006.

Confidence Intervals We also show 95% confidence interval of the important evaluation metrics for our systems to report significance for doing meaningful comparison. We use the ROUGE tool for this purpose. ROUGE uses a randomized method named bootstrap resampling to com-

*** Formatting Issue - Best Available Paper/Graphic ***

Systems	ROUGE-1	ROUGE-2
COSINE	0.3305	0.0532
SYN	0.3320	0.0595
SEM	0.3299	0.0631
COSINE+SYN	0.3346	0.0563
COSINE+SEM	0.3412	0.0631
COSINE+SYN+SEM	0.3360	0.0605
Baseline	0.3209	0.0526
AverageDUC	0.3778	0.0748

Table 5: System comparison (F-scores)

pute the confidence interval. Bootstrap resampling has a long tradition in the field of statistics (Efron and Tibshirani, 1994). We use 1000 sampling points in the bootstrap resampling. Table 6 reports the 95% confidence intervals of the important ROUGE measures.

Systems	R-2	R-SU
COSINE	0.0401 - 0.0682	0.0854 - 0.1207
SYN	0.0439 - 0.0802	0.0845 - 0.1313
SEM	0.0530 - 0.0753	0.0928 - 0.1128
COSINE+SYN	0.0366 - 0.0805	0.0918 - 0.1286
COSINE+SEM	0.0499 - 0.0799	0.0873 - 0.1328
COSINE+SYN+SEM	0.0436 - 0.0795	0.0949 - 0.1205

Table 6: 95% confidence intervals for different systems

5.3 Manual Evaluation

Even if the ROUGE scores had significant improvement, it is possible to make bad summaries that get state-of-the-art ROUGE scores (Sjöbergh, 2007). So, we conduct an extensive manual evaluation in order to analyze the effectiveness of our systems. Two university graduate students judged the summaries for linguistic quality and overall responsiveness according to the DUC-2007 evaluation guidelines[6]. The given score is an integer between 1 (very poor) and 5 (very good) and is guided by consideration of the following factors: 1. Grammaticality, 2. Non-redundancy, 3. Referential clarity, 4. Focus and 5. Structure and Coherence. They also assigned a content responsiveness score to each of the automatic summaries. The content score is an integer between 1 (very poor) and 5 (very good) and is based on the amount of information in the summary that helps to satisfy the information need expressed in the topic. Table 7 presents the average linguistic quality and overall responsive scores of all our systems. These results also justify our claim by showing positive impacts of encoding syntactic and/or semantic information in the multi-modality manifold ranking framework. From these results, we can see that the proposed syntactic and/or semantic measure based systems outperform the COSINE system by a considerable margin.

Systems	Lin. Quality	Responsiveness
COSINE	2.50	3.60
SYN	3.40	3.80
SEM	4.10	4.40
COSINE+SYN	3.50	4.00
COSINE+SEM	2.60	3.40
COSINE+SYN+SEM	4.00	4.30

Table 7: Linguistic quality and responsiveness scores

6 Conclusion

In this paper, we proposed to encode the syntactic and semantic information for measuring sentence relationships in the multi-modality manifold ranking algorithm for topic-focused multi-document summarization and reported that adding syntactic and/or semantic information on top of the standard cosine measure improves the performance over the cosine measure alone. We parsed the sentences into the syntactic trees using the Charniak parser and applied the general tree kernel functions to measure the similarity between sentences. We used the shallow semantic tree kernel to measure the semantic similarity between two semantic trees. To the best of our knowledge, no other study has used syntactic and semantic information in the multi-modality manifold ranking model to improve its performance. We evaluated our systems automatically using ROUGE and conducted an extensive manual evaluation. Experimental results proved our claim by showing the effectiveness of the proposed methods.

Acknowledgments

We thank the anonymous reviewers for their useful comments. The research reported in this paper was supported by the Natural Sciences and Engineering Research Council (NSERC) of Canada – discovery grant and the University of Lethbridge.

[6]http://www-nlpir.nist.gov/projects/duc/duc2007/quality-questions.txt

References

E. Charniak. 1999. A Maximum-Entropy-Inspired Parser. In *Technical Report CS-99-12*, Brown University, Computer Science Department.

M. Collins and N. Duffy. 2001. Convolution Kernels for Natural Language. In *Proceedings of Neural Information Processing Systems*, pages 625–632, Vancouver, Canada.

H. Daumé III and D. Marcu. 2006. Bayesian query-focused summarization. In *Proceedings of the 21st International Conference on Computational Linguistics and the 44th annual meeting of the Association for Computational Linguistics*, pages 305–312.

B. Efron and R. J. Tibshirani. 1994. *An Introduction to the Bootstrap*. CRC Press.

K. Hacioglu, S. Pradhan, W. Ward, J. H. Martin, and D. Jurafsky. 2003. Shallow Semantic Parsing Using Support Vector Machines. In *Technical Report TR-CSLR-2003-03*, University of Colorado.

T. Hirao, , J. Suzuki, H. Isozaki, and E. Maeda. 2004. Dependency-based Sentence Alignment for Multiple Document Summarization. In *Proceedings of COLING 2004*, pages 446–452, Geneva, Switzerland. COLING.

P. Kingsbury and M. Palmer. 2002. From Treebank to PropBank. In *Proceedings of the International Conference on Language Resources and Evaluation*, Las Palmas, Spain.

C. Y. Lin. 2004. ROUGE: A Package for Automatic Evaluation of Summaries. In *Proceedings of Workshop on Text Summarization Branches Out, Post-Conference Workshop of Association for Computational Linguistics*, pages 74–81, Barcelona, Spain.

I. Mani and M. Maybury, 1999. *Advances in Automatic Text Summarization*. MIT Press.

I. Mani, 2001. *Automatic Summarization*. John Benjamins Co, Amsterdam/Philadelphia.

A. Moschitti and R. Basili. 2006. A Tree Kernel Approach to Question and Answer Classification in Question Answering Systems. In *Proceedings of the 5th International Conference on Language Resources and Evaluation*, Genoa, Italy.

A. Moschitti, S. Quarteroni, R. Basili, and S. Manandhar. 2007. Exploiting Syntactic and Shallow Semantic Kernels for Question/Answer Classificaion. In *Proceedings of the 45th Annual Meeting of the Association of Computational Linguistics*, pages 776–783, Prague, Czech Republic. ACL.

V. Nastase. 2008. Topic-driven multi-document summarization with encyclopedic knowledge and spreading activation. In *Proceedings of the Conference on Empirical Methods in Natural Language Processing (EMNLP-08)*, pages 763–772.

V. Punyakanok, D. Roth, and W. Yih. 2004. Mapping Dependencies Trees: An Application to Question Answering. In *Proceedings of AI & Math*, Florida, USA.

J. Sjöbergh. 2007. Older Versions of the ROUGEeval Summarization Evaluation System Were Easier to Fool. *Information Processing and Management*, 43:1500–1505.

X. Wan and J. Xiao. 2009. Graph-based multimodality learning for topic-focused multi-document summarization. In *Proceedings of the 21st international jont conference on Artifical intelligence (IJCAI-09)*, pages 1586–1591.

X. Wan, J. Yang, and J. Xiao. 2007. Manifold-ranking based topic-focused multi-document summarization. In *Proceedings of the 20th international joint conference on Artifical intelligence (IJCAI-07)*, pages 2903–2908.

A. Zhang and W. Lee. 2003a. Question Classification using Support Vector Machines. In *Proceedings of the Special Interest Group on Information Retrieval*, pages 26–32, Toronto, Canada. ACM.

D. Zhang and W. S. Lee. 2003b. A Language Modeling Approach to Passage Question Answering. In *Proceedings of the Twelfth Text REtreival Conference*, pages 489–495, Gaithersburg, Maryland.

D. Zhou, O. Bousquet, T. Navin Lal, J. Weston, and B. Schölkopf. 2003a. Learning with local and global consistency. In *Proceedings of NIPS-03*.

D. Zhou, J. Weston, A. Gretton, O. Bousquet, and B. Schölkopf. 2003b. Ranking on data manifolds. In *Proceedings of NIPS-03*.

Automatic Determination of a Domain Adaptation Method for Word Sense Disambiguation Using Decision Tree Learning

Kanako Komiya
Tokyo University of Agriculture and Technology
2-24-16 Naka-cho, Koganei
Tokyo, 184-8588 Japan
kkomiya@cc.tuat.ac.jp

Manabu Okumura
Tokyo Institute of Technology
4259 Nagatsuta Modori-ku
Yokohama 226-8503 Japan
oku@pi.titech.ac.jp

Abstract

Domain adaptation (DA), which involves adapting a classifier developed from source to target data, has been studied intensively in recent years. However, when DA for word sense disambiguation (WSD) was carried out, the optimal DA method varied according to the properties of the source and target data. This paper describes how the optimal method for DA was determined depending on these properties using decision tree learning, given a triple of the target word type of WSD, the source data, and the target data, and discusses what properties affected the determination of the best method when Japanese WSD was performed.

1 Introduction

Classifiers in standard supervised machine learning have been trained for data in domain A using manually annotated data in domain A, e.g., to train classifiers for newswires using newswires. However, classifiers for data in domain B have sometimes been necessary when there have been no or few manually annotated data, and there have only been manually annotated data in domain A, which have been related to domain B. Domain adaptation (DA) involves adapting the classifier that have been trained from data in domain A (source domain) to data in domain B (target domain). This has been studied intensively in recent years.

However, the optimal method of DA varied according to the properties of the data in the source domain (the source data) and the data in the target domain (the target data) when DA for word sense disambiguation (WSD) was carried out. (We will show it in Section 4.)

We define a case as a triple of the target word type of WSD, the source data, and the target data. This paper describes how the optimal method for DA was determined depending on these properties using decision tree learning given a case and discusses what properties affected the determination of the best method when Japanese WSD was performed.

This paper is organized as follows. Section 2 reviews related works on DA and Section 3 explains how a DA method is automatically determined. Section 4 describes the data we used. How to label the data and how to train the classifiers using these are explained in Section 5. We present the results in Section 6 and discuss them in Section 7. Finally, we conclude the paper in Section 8.

2 Related Work

The DA problem can be categorized into three types depending on the information for learning, i.e., supervised, semi-supervised, and unsupervised approaches. A classifier in a supervised approach is developed from a large amount of labeled source data and a small amount of labeled target data with the aim of classifying target data better than a classifier developed only from the target data. A classifier in a semi-supervised approach is developed from large amounts of labeled source data and unlabeled target data with the aim of classifying target data better than a classifier developed only from the source data. Finally, a classifier is developed from a large amount of labeled source data with the aim of classifying target data accurately in the unsupervised approach. We focused on the supervised DA of WSD in this paper.

Many researchers have investigated DA within or outside the area of natural language processing. Chan and Ng (2006) carried out the DA of WSD by estimating class priors using an EM algorithm. Chan and Ng (2007) also conducted the DA of WSD by estimating class priors using the EM algorithm, but this was supervised DA using active learning.

In addition, Daumé III (2007) worked on the supervised DA. He augmented an input space and made triple length features that were general, source-specific, and target-specific. This was easy to implement, could be used with various DA methods, and could easily be extended to multi-domain adaptation problems. Daumé III et al. (2010) extended the work in (Daumé III, 2007) to semi-supervised DA. It inherited the advantages of the supervised version and outperformed it by using unlabeled target data.

Agirre and de Lacalle (2008) worked on the semi-supervised DA of WSD. They applied singular value decomposition (SVD) to a matrix of unlabeled target data and a large amount of unlabeled source data, and trained a classifier with them. Agirre and de Lacalle (2009) worked on the supervised DA using almost the same method, but they used a small amount of labeled source data instead of the large amount of unlabeled source data.

Jiang and Zhai (2007) demonstrated that performance increased as examples were weighted when DA was applied. This method could be used with various other supervised or semi-supervised DA methods. In addition, they tried to identify and remove source data that misled DA, but they concluded that it was only effective if examples were not weighted.

Zhong et al. (2009) proposed an adaptive kernel approach that mapped the marginal distribution of source and target data into a common kernel space. They also conducted sample selection to make the conditional probabilities between the two domains closer.

Raina et al. (2007) proposed self-taught learning that utilized sparse coding to construct higher level features from the unlabeled data collected from the Web. This method was based on unsupervised learning.

Tur (2009) proposed a co-adaptation algorithm where both co-training and DA techniques were used to improve the performance of the model.

The research by Blitzer et al. (2006) involved work on semi-supervised DA, where they calculated the weight of words around the pivot features (words that frequently appeared both in source and target data and behaved similarly in both) to model some words in one domain that behaved similarly in another. They applied SVD to the matrix of the weights, generated a new feature space, and used the new features with the original features.

The closest work to ours is that by McClosky et al. (2010) who focused on the problem where the best model for each document is not obvious when parsing a document collection of heterogeneous domains. They studied it as a new task of *multiple source parser adaptation*. They proposed a method of parsing a sentence that first predicts accuracies for various parsing models using a regression model, and then uses the parsing model with the highest predicted accuracy. The main difference is that their work was about parsing but ours discussed here is about Japanese WSD. They also assumed that they had labeled corpora in heterogeneous domains but we have not. We determined the best DA method using the decision tree learning given a triple of the target word type of WSD, the source data, and the target data and found what features affected the determination of the best method.

Harimoto et al. (2010) measured the distance between domains to conduct DA using a suitable corpus in parsing. In addition, van Asch and Daelemans (2010) reported that performance in DA could be predicted depending on the similarity between source and target data using automatically annotated corpus in parsing. They focused on how corpora were selected for use as source data according to the distance between domains, but here we focus on how to select a method of DA depending on properties such as the distance between domains.

3 Automatic determination of DA method

We expected the average accuracy of WSD, when DA methods that were determined automatically were used for all cases, to be higher than when the original methods were used collectively. Hence, we would be able to determine the best DA method automatically using decision tree learning. A decision tree would indicate what features affect the determination of the optimal method of DA.

3.1 DA methods for WSD

Two methods were used as the DA methods for WSD in this study.

- *Target Only*: Train a classifier with a small amount of target data that are randomly selected and manually labeled but without source data.

- *Random Sampling*: Train a classifier with source data and a small amount of target data that are randomly selected and manually labeled.

Ten word tokens of the target data were randomly selected and manually labeled in all the experiments.

Libsvm (Chang and Lin, 2001), which supports multi-class classification, was used as the classifier for WSD. A linear kernel was used according to the results obtained from preliminary experiments. Seventeen features were introduced to train the classifier.

- Morphological features
  - Bag-of-words (4 features)
  - Part-of-speech (POS) (4 features)
  - Finer subcategory of POS (4 features)
- Syntactic feature (1 feature)
  - If the POS of a target word is a noun, the verb which the target word modifies
  - If the POS of a target word is a verb, the case element of "ヲ" (wo, objective) for the verb
- Semantic features
  - Semantic classification code (4 features)

Morphological features and semantic features were extracted from the surrounding words (two words to the right and left) of the target word. POS and finer subcategory of POS can be obtained using a morphological analyzer. We used ChaSen [1] as a morphological analyzer, the Bunruigoihyo thesaurus (National Institute for Japanese Language and Linguistics, 1964) for semantic classification codes, and CaboCha [2] as a syntactic parser. Five-fold cross validation was used in the experiments.

3.2 Labels of Decision Tree

One of the following labels was given to every case depending on the most accurate method and as we shall explain later, two labels (TO and RS) or three labels (TO, RS, and SA) were used for classification. Note that the decision tree determines which DA method should be used, *Random Sampling* or *Target Only*, given the properties of the source and target data for each case.

- TO: The cases in which *Target Only* had higher accuracy than *Random Sampling*.
- RS: The cases in which *Random Sampling* had higher accuracy than *Target Only*.
- SA: The cases in which *Random Sampling* and *Target Only* had the same accuracy.

3.3 Features of Decision Tree

We think the optimal method for DA varies depending on the distribution of the source data and the target data, the distance between them, and so on. The following 40 features (consisting of 24 types) in total were used for decision tree learning.

1. Simulation accuracy of *theOther*: The accuracy of WSD when a classifier was trained with the source data and tested with ten labeled word tokens of the target data.
2. Simulation accuracy of *Target Only*: The accuracy of WSD when a classifier was trained with ten labeled word tokens of the target data and tested using a leave-one-out cross-validation method.
3. Ratio of two simulation accuracies: (1) / (2).
4. Number of source data: The number of word tokens in the whole source data.
5. Number of target data: The number of word tokens in the whole target data.
6. Number of source data / target data: (4) / (5).
7. The number of word senses that appeared in the whole source data set.
8. The number of word senses that appeared in ten word tokens of the target data.
9. The number of word senses of the WSD target words in the dictionary.
10. The number of word tokens of the most frequent sense (MFS) of the whole source data.
11. The number of word tokens of MFS in the ten labeled word tokens of the target data.

[1] http://sourceforge.net/projects/masayu-a/

[2] http://sourceforge.net/projects/cabocha/

12. Whether the MFS of the whole source data and the ten labeled word tokens of the target data were the same or not.

13. Percentage of MFS in source data: (10) / (4).

14. Percentage of MFS in ten word tokens of target data: (11) / the number of word tokens in the labeled target data (=10).

15. Percentage of MFS in ten word tokens of target data in source data: The number of source data word tokens with MFS in ten labeled word tokens of the target data / (4).

16. Percentage of MFS of source data in ten word tokens of target data: The number of word tokens with MFS in the source data in ten labeled word tokens of the target data / the ten word tokens.

17. The JS divergence between the distribution of word sense IDs of 4/5 of the whole source data and the distribution of word sense IDs of ten labeled word tokens of target data. Abbreviated as "JSD (word sense)".

18. The JS divergence between the feature distributions for WSD of the whole source and the whole target data (17 kinds, cf. Section 3.1) Abbreviated as "JSD (*)". *is a feature name in Section 3.1.

19. The summation of 17 kinds of JS divergences (18). Abbreviated as "JSD (Feature_plus)".

20. The JS divergence between the distribution of the whole source data and the whole target data feature units, when a unit is the sequence of 17 kinds of WSD features. Abbreviated as "JSD (Feature_all)".

21. The number of word senses that did not appear in ten labeled word tokens of the target data but did in the whole source data.

22. The number of common word senses between the whole source data and ten labeled word tokens of the target data.

23. Percentage of common word senses between whole source data and ten word tokens of target data in ten word tokens: the number of word tokens whose word senses appeared in both the whole source data and ten labeled word tokens of the target data in the ten word tokens / the ten word tokens.

24. Percentage of common word senses between whole source data and ten word tokens of target data in source data: the number of word tokens whose word senses appeared in both the whole source data and ten labeled word tokens of the target data in the source data/ (4).

The C4.5 of Quinlan (1993) was used as the algorithm for decision tree learning and a binary tree was generated. The experiments were conducted with five-fold cross validation. The threshold values for pruning were optimized with preliminary experiments using 1/4 of the training data set as a development data set. Here, the entropy of a node was tuned as the threshold value in 0.1 increments. The value of a smaller tree was used when more than one threshold value gave the same accuracy.

4 Data

Three data were used for the experiments: (1) the sub-corpus of white papers in the Balanced Corpus of Contemporary Japanese (BCCWJ) (Maekawa, 2008), (2) the sub-corpus of documents from a Q&A site on the WWW of BCCWJ, and (3) Real World Computing (RWC) text databases (newspaper articles) (Hashida et al., 1998). DAs were conducted in six directions according to various source and target data. Word senses were annotated in these corpora according to a Japanese dictionary, i.e., the Iwanami Kokugo Jiten (Nishio et al., 1994). It has three levels for sense IDs, and we used the fine-level sense in the experiments. Multi-sense words that appeared equal or more than 50 times in both source and target data were selected as the target words in the experiment. There were 24 word types for white papers ⇔ Q&A site, 22 for white papers ⇔ newspaper articles, and 26 for Q&A site ⇔ newspaper articles. Twenty-eight word types and 144 cases were used in the experiments in total. Table 1 lists the minimum, maximum, and average number of word tokens in each case. Table 2 shows the list of target words.

Table 3 summarizes the results from the DA experiments when the source data and the target data were swapped [3]. These results were the av-

[3]Multi-sense words that appeared less than 50 times in source or target data were included as the target words in the

Table 1: Minimum, maximum, and average number of word tokens in each case

Genre	Min.	Max.	Ave.
BCCWJ white papers	58	7,610	2074.50
BCCWJ Q&A site	82	13,976	2300.43
RWC newspaper	50	374	164.46

erage accuracies of all the target words of WSD. *Self*, which is standard supervised learning with the target data, assuming that fully annotated data were obtained and could be used for learning and *theOther*, which is standard supervised learning only with the source data, were tested as references. We found that the optimal method of DA varied depending on the corpora that were used as the source and target data.

5 Labeling of data and learning of decision tree

We tried to generate decision trees in various ways and compared their accuracies to find the most effective way of generating the best decision tree.

5.1 Labeling of data

TO, RS, or SA was given to every case depending on the most accurate method. SA was particularly given to cases in which *Random Sampling* and *Target Only* had the same accuracy.

The difference between accuracies and the definition of SA was treated in two ways.

- *Equal*: The SA label was assigned when the WSD accuracies of *Target Only* and *Random Sampling* were totally equal.
- *Chi-square*: The SA label was assigned when the WSD accuracies of *Target Only* and *Random Sampling* were not significantly different according to a chi-square test. The level of significance in the test was 0.05.

Table 4 indicates the number of cases and the total word types given TO or RS labels according to *Equal* and *Chi-square*.

5.2 Treatment of SA in decision tree learning

The third label, SA, was assigned to cases with no difference between the accuracies of *Random Sampling* and *Target Only* and was treated in two ways in the experiments.

experiment of this figure.

Table 2: The list of target words

Number of senses	Target words (in Japanese)	Sense example in English
2	場合	case
	自分	self
3	事業	project
	情報	information
	地方	area
	社会	society
	思う	suppose
	子供	child
4	分かる	understand
	考える	think
5	含む	contain
	使う	use
	技術	technique
6	関係	connection
	時間	time
	一般	general
	現在	present
	作る	make
7	今	now
8	前	before
10	持つ	have
11	進む	advance
12	見る	see
14	入る	enter
16	言う	say
21	出す	serve
22	手	hand
	出る	leave

- *Ternary classification with SA*: Perform ternary classification of TO, RS, and SA in training and the testing.
- *Binary classification without SA*: Remove cases with SA labels from training data set and perform binary classification of TO and RS. All the cases are used for the testing.

Figure 1 shows the frame format for five-fold cross validation of decision tree learning when *Binary classification without SA* was used. There was a total of 144 cases, and only data with TA or RS labels were used as a training data set for decision tree learning. There were 129 cases when *Equal* was used and 69 cases when *Chi-square* was used (dark gray parts). A classifier was developed from 4/5 of the training data set (white

Table 3: Results from DA experiments when source and target data were swapped

DA method	Accuracy	
Source data	Q&A site	white papers
Target data	white papers	Q&A site
theOther	79.65%	83.35%
Random sampling	85.40%	83.86%
Target Only	88.20%	77.74%
self	95.97%	91.65%

Table 4: Number of cases and total word types given TO or RS labels according to *Equal* and *Chi-square*

Source data	Target data	*Equal*	*Chi*
white papers	Q&A site	21	13
white papers	newspaper	18	9
Q&A site	newspaper	25	12
Q&A site	white papers	25	12
newspaper	white papers	20	11
newspaper	Q&A site	20	12
Total cases		129	69
Total word types		27	20

parts) and tested using 1/5 of the whole cases (light gray part) in one execution of five-fold cross validation. (Three-quarter of the training data (3/5 of the whole data set) and 1/4 of the training data (1/5 of the whole data set) was used for the training data and the test data of the parameter tuning respectively.)

We calculated the accuracies of WSD using the DA method for the labels (*Target Only* for TO and *Random Sampling* for RS). We used *Random Sampling* for cases with SA labels when *Ternary classification with SA* was used. When *Binary classification without SA* was used, we had no correct answers for the cases of SA in the test phase. However, either label could be given to them because they were cases in which *Random Sampling* and *Target Only* had the same accuracy. Therefore, we assigned TO or RS to them depending on the decision tree that was generated.

5.3 Classification

As Table 1 indicates, some cases had many word tokens and some had few. For example, a case had 58 word tokens when the source data were from the RWC newspaper articles, the target data were from the BCCWJ white papers, and the target

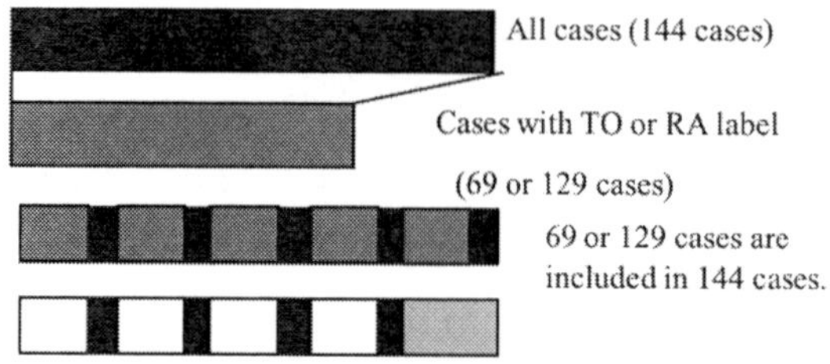

Figure 1: Five-fold cross validation of decision tree learning when *Binary classification without SA* was used

word type was "言う". (This case had 58 word tokens because the word appeared 58 times). Therefore, the average accuracy of WSD could be improved if cases that had more word tokens could be predicted more precisely. We also classified cases with weighted word tokens, as well as just classified cases, in two ways.

- *Case classification*: Perform decision tree learning on the assumption that every case has the same weight.
- *Classification with weighting of word tokens*: Perform decision tree learning with weighting on the assumption that every case has the weight of the number of word tokens in the case.

The weights of the cases were used to calculate entropy.

6 Results

Table 5 lists the average accuracies of WSD when the original methods were used collectively. The average accuracies were calculated from 232,116 word tokens in 144 cases. (They were micro-averaged over the word tokens.) Table 5 indicates that *Target Only* outperformed *Random Sampling* and its accuracy was 81.23%. Here, *Selected Source Only* is a DA method where train a classifier with only selected source data that are similar to the target data. We used 0.8 of cosine distance as a threshold value. We did not include this method as a DA method that is automatically determined but showed as reference.

Table 6 summarizes the average accuracies of WSD when the DA methods that were determined were used for every case. There were nine ways of determining the DA methods: eight automatic and one manual. The eight automatic approaches

Table 5: Average accuracy of WSD when methods were used collectively

DA method	Accuracy of WSD
Target Only	81.23 %
Random Sampling	80.28 %
Selected Source Only	82.27 %

Table 6: Average accuracy of WSD when methods that were determined automatically were used

Way to determine a method	Accuracy of WSD
Equal_3_case	82.36%
Equal_3_token	82.44%
Chi_3_case	83.49%
Chi_3_token	83.42%
Equal_2_case	**83.50%**
Equal_2_token	81.88%
Chi_2_case	82.55%
Chi_2_token	82.92%
manually	85.25%

were all combinations of the two choices in Sections 5.1, 5.2, and 5.3. Abbreviations of the ways in Table 6 are in the format of a_b_c where a is the choice for Section 5.1, b is that for Section 5.2 and c is that for Section 5.3. The "3" and "2" represent *Ternary classification with SA* and *Binary classification without SA*, and "case" and "token" represent *Case classification* and *Classification with weighting of word tokens*, respectively. When the manual approach was used, the DA method with the highest accuracy was chosen manually for every case. Its average accuracy was in the upper bound for our proposed method.

Table 6 shows that the automatic way with the highest average accuracy was Equal_2_case. The accuracy was 83.50%, and it significantly outperformed *Target Only* and *Selected Source Only* in Table 5 (81.23% and 82.27%) . This means that the average accuracy of WSD when DA methods that were determined automatically were used was higher than when the original methods were used collectively.

7 Discussion

7.1 Comparison of ways of determining DA methods

We compare the results for ways of determining DA methods in this section. First, usually *Chi-square* was better for labeling of data, but *Equal* was better when *Binary classification without SA* and *Case classification* were used simultaneously. Second, usually *Ternary classification with SA* was better for treating SA in decision tree learning, but *Binary classification without SA* was better when *Equal* and *Case classification* were used simultaneously. Finally, we could not find any patterns of the results for *Case classification* or *Classification with weighting of word tokens*.

The approach with the highest accuracy in the eight automatic ways was where SA labels were applied when the accuracies of WSD for the two methods were totally equal, binary classification was performed without SA, and cases were classified without weighted word tokens (Equal_2_case). Significant differences were found in the three comparisons above when they were evaluated with a Chi-square test when the other conditions were the same.

The accuracy of decision tree learning was 60.42% when the Equal_2_case was used. This value was not very high, which may be due to the optimizing threshold value of pruning with a development data set. We think the reason low classification accuracy with decision trees did not critically influence the average accuracy of WSD was that most errors were for cases where *Random Sampling* and *Target Only* had almost the same accuracy.

7.2 Discussion on learned decision tree

We present the decision tree with the highest accuracy in an appendix in five executions of five-fold cross validation in the decision tree learning of the Equal_2_case, whose average WSD accuracy was the highest in the eight automatic ways of learning, and we discuss the features and their values that contributed to the generation of the tree.

First, TO was assigned when the "ratio of two simulation accuracies >= 0.40" was false in the root node of the decision tree. Therefore, TO was assigned to cases whose ratio of "Simulation accuracy of *theOther* / Simulation accuracy of *Target Only*" was lower than 0.40. That is, TO was assigned to the cases when the accuracy of WSD when a classifier was trained with ten labeled word tokens of the target data and tested using a leave-one-out cross-validation method was higher than the accuracy of WSD when a classifier was trained with the source data and tested using ten labeled word tokens of the target data. In other words, this indicates that the simulation using ten manually labeled word tokens of the target data was an important clue in predicting the optimal DA method.

Next, TO was selected when JSD (bag-of-words of one word to the left of the target word) was equal to or more than 0.61 in the node with level one. This indicated that a classifier should only be trained with ten labeled word tokens of target data, without source data, when the distributions of the feature of bag-of-words of one word to the left of the WSD target word differed between the source and target data.

Moreover, TO was selected when JSD (semantic classification code of one word to the right of the target word) was equal to or more than 1.00 in the node with level two. This indicated that a classifier should only be trained with ten labeled word tokens of target data, without source data, when the distributions of the semantic classification code features of one word to the right of the WSD target word differed between the source and target data.

The decision tree in the appendix is small and simple, but the second best tree (there is a difference in only one case) consists of 13 questions. According to the tree, TO tends to be assigned when JS divergences such as JSD (word sense), JSD (Feature_plus), and JSD (Syntactic feature) are large, and RS tends to be assigned when they are small. Large JS divergence indicates that the distributions of a feature are different, and small JS divergence indicates that the distributions of a feature are close. This indicates that when the distributions of the important feature for WSD are different and the source data are not sufficiently close to the target data, the source data should not be used.

8 Conclusion

We described how the optimal method of DA could be determined depending on the properties of the source and target data using decision tree learning and found what properties affected the determination of the best method when Japanese WSD was performed. We defined a case as a triple of the target word type of WSD, the source data, and the target data, all of which were classified into two labels (TO and RS) or three labels (TO, RS, and SA). Here, the case with TO should only be trained with a small amount of target data, the case with RS should be trained with source data and a small amount of target data, and SA represents a case with no difference between the accuracies for the two methods. The average accuracy of WSD when the DA methods that were determined automatically were used was significantly higher than when the original methods were used collectively. We automatically generated a decision tree in eight ways, the most accurate of which was with SA label when the WSD accuracies of the two methods were totally equal, performed binary classification without SA, and classified cases without weighted word tokens. The top node in the tree that was generated indicated that simulation using ten manually labeled word tokens of the target data was an important clue enabling the optimal DA method to be predicted.

Acknowledgments

We would like to thank the reviewers for very constructive and detailed comments. This research is supported by Grants-in-Aid for Scientific Research, Priority Area "Japanese Corpus".

A Generated decision tree

Upper edge represents true and lower edge represents false.

```
          ┌─TO: 3 cases
     ┌─JSD (bag-of-words of one word to the left
     │  │   of the target word) >= 0.61
     │  │     ┌─TO: 3 cases
     │  └─JSD (semantic classification code
     │        │ of one word to the right of
     │        │ the target word) >= 1.00
     │        └─TO: 28 cases RS: 62 cases
Ratio of two simulation accuracies >= 0.40
     └─TO: 7 cases
```

References

Eneko Agirre and Oier Lopez de Lacalle. 2008. On robustness and domain adaptation using svd for word sense disambiguation. In *Proceedings of the 22nd International Conference on Computational Linguistics*, pages 17–24.

Eneko Agirre and Oier Lopez de Lacalle. 2009. Supervised domain adaption for wsd. In *Proceedings of the 12th Conference of the European Chapter of the Association of Computational Linguistics*, pages 42–50.

John Blitzer, Ryan McDonald, and Fernando Pereira. 2006. Domain adaptation with structural coppespondence learning. In *Proceedings of the 2006 Conference on Empirical Methods in Natural Language Processing*, pages 120–128.

Yee Seng Chan and Hwee Tou Ng. 2006. Estimating class priors in domain adaptation for word sense disambiguation. In *Proceedings of the 21st International Conference on Computational Linguistics and 44th Annual Meeting of the Association for Computational Linguistics*, pages 89–96.

Yee Seng Chan and Hwee Tou Ng. 2007. Domain adaptation with active learning for word sense disambiguation. In *Proceedings of the 45th Annual Meeting of the Association of Computational Linguistics*, pages 49–56.

Chih-Chung Chang and Chih-Jen Lin, 2001. *LIBSVM: a library for support vector machines*. Software available at http://www.csie.ntu.edu.tw/ cjlin/libsvm.

Hal Daumé III, Abhishek Kumar, and Avishek Saha. 2010. Frustratingly easy semi-supervised domain adaptation. In *Proceedings of the 2010 Workshop on Domain Adaptation for Natural Language Processing, ACL 2010*, pages 23–59.

Hal Daumé III. 2007. Frustratingly easy domain adaptation. In *Proceedings of the 45th Annual Meeting of the Association of Computational Linguistics*, pages 256–263.

Keiko Harimoto, Yusuke Miyao, and Jun'ichi Tsujii. 2010. Kobunkaiseki no bunyatekiou ni okeru seido teika youin no bunseki oyobi bunyakan kyori no sokutei syuhou, in japanese. In *Proceedings of NLP2010*, pages 27–30.

Koichi Hashida, Hitoshi Isahara, Takenobu Tokunaga, Minako Hashimoto, Shiho Ogino, and Wakako Kashino. 1998. The rwc text databases. In *Proceedings of the First International Conference on Language Resource and Evaluation*, pages 457–461.

Jing Jiang and ChengXiang Zhai. 2007. Instance weighting for domain adaptation in nlp. In *Proceedings of the 45th Annual Meeting of the Association of Computational Linguistics*, pages 264–271.

Kikuo Maekawa. 2008. Balanced corpus of contemporary written japanese. In *Proceedings of the 6th Workshop on Asian Language Resources (ALR)*, pages 101–102.

David McClosky, Eugene Charniak, and Mark Johnson. 2010. Automatic domain adaptation for parsing. In *Proceedings of the 2010 Annual Conference of the North American Chapter of the Association for Computational Linguistics*, pages 28–36.

National Institute for Japanese Language and Linguistics. 1964. *Bunruigoihyo*. Shuuei Shuppan, In Japanese.

Minoru Nishio, Etsutaro Iwabuchi, and Shizuo Mizutani. 1994. *Iwanami Kokugo Jiten Dai Go Han*. Iwanami Publisher, In Japanese.

John Ross Quinlan. 1993. *C4.5: Programs for Machine Learning*. Morgan Kaufmann Publishers.

Rajat Raina, Alexis Battle, Honglak Lee, Benjamin Packer, and Andrew Y. Ng. 2007. Self-taught learning: Transfer learning from unlabeled data. In *ICML '07: Proceedings of the 24th international conference on Machine learning*, pages 759–766.

Gokhan Tur. 2009. Co-adaptation: Adaptive cotraining for semi-supervised learning. In *Proceedings of the IEEE International Conference on Acoustics, Speech and Signal Processing, 2009. ICASSP 2009.*, pages 3721–3724.

Vincent van Asch and Walter Daelemans. 2010. Using domain similarity for performance estimation. In *Proceedings of the 2010 Workshop on Domain Adaptation for Natural Language Processing, ACL 2010*, pages 31–36.

Erheng Zhong, Wei Fan, Jing Peng, Kun Zhang, Jiangtao Ren, Deepak Turaga, and Olivier Verscheure. 2009. Cross domain distribution adaptation via kernel mapping. In *Proceedings of the 15th ACM SIGKDD international conference on Knowledge discovery and data mining*, pages 1027–1036.

*** Formatting Issue - Best Available Paper/Graphic ***

Learning from Chinese-English Parallel Data for Chinese Tense Prediction

Feifan Liu
The University of Wisconsin-Milwaukee
liuf@uwm.edu

Fei Liu and Yang Liu
The University of Texas at Dallas
feiliu,yangl @hlt.utdallas.edu

Abstract

Tense prediction can be useful for many language processing tasks, such as temporal inference and machine translation. In this paper, we investigate using diverse contextual features for Chinese tense prediction under a statistical learning framework. Because of lack of annotated training data, we propose to leverage Chinese-English parallel corpora to automatically generate reference tense for model training. We also propose to use an iterative learning framework to deal with the noisy reference data to improve learning. Evaluation is performed using both automatically generated reference data and a manually annotated set with verb tense. Our results demonstrate the effectiveness of our proposed learning framework that maps annotation from one language to another using parallel data. Furthermore, we show better performance using our proposed iterative bootstrapping learning method compared to using the original automatically created training data.

1 Introduction

Tense is used in languages to indicate the time at which an action or event described by the sentence takes place. Lacking correct tense information can cause confusion and misunderstanding in communication. Predicting tense information is very useful for different natural language processing tasks: both monolingual applications such as speech recognition (Karlgren, 1996) and multilingual applications such as machine translation (MT) (Buschbeck et al., 1991).

In inflectional languages like English, tense is often expressed by verb inflections, which can be easily recognized. For example, "*I worked till 5pm yesterday*" uses the past-tense verb "*worked*" to describe an event in the past. However, in languages such as Chinese, no verb inflections exist to indicate any tense information (Xiao and McEnery, 2002). The morphology of a verb itself never changes when used to express different tenses. The following examples (1a) and (1b) indicate a past-tense sentence and a future-tense sentence respectively; however, the form of the Chinese verb "到(arrive)" is the same in the two cases.

Example 1:
1a. 几天前(several days ago)我(I)到(arrive) 了(n/a) 上海(Shanghai).
I arrived at Shanghai several days ago. (past)
1b. 今天晚上(tonight)7点(7 pm)我(I)将(will) 到(arrive)上海(Shanghai).
I will arrive at Shanghai at 7 pm tonight. (future)

This lack of inflections in Chinese verbs imposes some challenges in many applications. For instance, in a Chinese-English machine translation (MT) system, it is almost impossible to determine the tense for the corresponding English verb if solely based on the Chinese verb morphology. However, tense information does exist in Chinese language, and it is expressed lexically instead of morphologically. There are useful contextual cues that can help determine the tense for the whole Chinese sentence or individual verbs, such as temporal adverbs or phrases, aspect auxiliary words and prepositions. For instance, in example (1a), the aspect particle "了(a particle word in Chinese, there is no literal translation to English)" and temporal phrase "几天前(several days ago)" together indicate the past tense of the sentence, and thus the correct translation of the sentence is "*I arrived at Shanghai several days ago*".

Most of the previous work on tense prediction (Li et al., 2004; Cao et al., 2004; Ye and Zhang, 2005; Lin, 2006) has been conducted using relatively small data sets (e.g., hundreds of

Chinese sentences) and typically news article domain. They often require hand crafted rules in the systems. In this paper, we adopt a statistical classification framework for Chinese tense prediction. This study is different from previous work in that (a) we propose to utilize the parallel Chinese-English corpora to automatically generate reference tense information, which overcomes the limitation of insufficient training data as in previous work; (b) we evaluate a variety of linguistic contextual features for this task; and (c) we propose to use a modified bootstrapping iterative learning method in order to select more reliable and informative instances, which addresses the problem that the automatically derived training data is noisy. We evaluate our system by comparing with the automatically derived references as well as human annotations. Our experimental results have shown that our tense prediction system performs reasonably well, suggesting we can leverage the parallel data to learn information for one language from the other language, and that the iterative learning approach we proposed is effective.

2 Related Work

Time Expression Recognition and Normalization (TERN) was a task evaluated in the Automatic Content Extraction (ACE) program. It requires that certain temporal expressions mentioned in the documents be detected and recognized. Such temporal expressions include both absolute and relative expressions, durations, event-anchored expressions, and sets of times. The tense prediction task we investigate in this paper is related to the TERN task in that identifying temporal expressions may be helpful to determine the verb tense. Lin (Lin, 2003; Lin, 2006) outlined a framework for temporal interpretation in Chinese from a theoretical perspective. Hundreds of rules and situations were induced to determine the appropriate tense for Chinese sentences, based on information such as viewpoint aspect, verbal semantics, temporal adverbials, and complement and relative clauses. (Li and Wong, 2002; Li et al., 2001) used a rule-based approach to combine different types of temporal indicators for temporal relation classification. These indicators include time word, time position word, temporal adverb, auxiliary word, preposition word, auxiliary verb, trend verb, and some special verbs. (He et al., 2008) explored an error-driven strategy to derive heuristic rules to recognize time expression. (Cheng, 2008) investigated using dependency structure analysis for temporal relation identification.

Machine learning methods have been adopted for the tense prediction task in recent years. (Li et al., 2004) and (Cao et al., 2004) investigated linguistic features including eleven temporal indicators and one event class, and compared several classifiers (e.g., decision trees, naive Bayes classifier). Their results showed that adopting collaborative bootstrapping approach was able to reduce the human efforts required for the task, though it also degraded the classification accuracy. (Ye and Zhang, 2005) applied conditional random fields for tense classification on Chinese news documents, and reported an overall sentence and paragraph level accuracy of around 58%.

In this paper, we attempt to automatically predict tense information using a classification framework with diverse contextual information, especially around the verbs in the sentence. To address the problem of lacking annotated data, we develop effective methods that leverage the aligned English sentences to obtain reference tense for Chinese. Similar mapping methods have been investigated recently for some natural language processing applications (Bentivogli et al., 2004; Ye and Zhang, 2005; Feldman et al., 2006; Pado and Lapata, 2009; Chen and Ji, 2009; Schwarck et al., 2010), where there are parallel corpora and annotation is only available for one language, thus allowing us to derive information for the other language based on the alignment. Since such automatically extracted labels are noisy, we further adopted a modified bootstrapping method for more effective learning. Bootstrapping or self-training has shown promising results in many different tasks by utilizing labeled and unlabeled data, such as named entity classification (Collins and Singer, 1999), parsing (McClosky et al., 2006), web page classification (Blum and Mitchell, 1998), relation and pattern extraction (Ravichandran and Hovy, 2002; Pasca et al., 2006), machine translation (Ueffing, 2006) and ontology population (Carlson et al., 2009).

3 Approaches for Chinese Tense Prediction

In this study, we focus on the prediction of absolute tense information, which indicates the relationship between the speech time and the event time under the Reichenbachian theory (Thompson, 2005). We consider four basic tenses: present, past, future, and infinitive. Other detailed tense and aspect information such as progressive and perfect is not used in this paper.

3.1 Problem Definition

The tense prediction task can be formulated as a classification task. We use a verb-based tense prediction setup, where our goal is to develop a classification system to assign each verb in the sentence a tense tag (from 4 basic tenses mentioned above). As illustrated in Example 2, tags of "1,2,3,4" denote infinitive, past, present, future tense respectively. Note that in the example the aspect particle "了(a particle word in Chinese, there is no literal translation to English)" not only is the indicator of past tense (as in Example 1), but also is used in the context of future tense. This shows the ambiguity and the challenges of the tense prediction problem.

Example 2:
上星期(last week) 没有(not) **完成(finish)/2** 任务(the task)，我们(we) **计划(plan)/3** **招募(recruit)/1** 更多(more) 人(people)，因为(because) 下周五(next Friday) 我们(we) 就要(will) **汇报(submit)/4** 结果(the results) 了。

Last week we did not finish the task, we plan to recruit more people because we will submit the results next Friday.

Compared to sentence-based framework, this verb-based setting is more flexible and has advantages especially for complex sentences. In addition, we expect that the verb-based setup is more beneficial for other applications, such as providing richer annotation for machine translation.

3.2 Leveraging Contextual Features for Tense Prediction

We use a supervised learning framework for tense classification of every verb. In this initial study, we investigate using some basic lexical features (i.e., words) and simple syntactic features (POS tags). The following lists all the features we used.

Bag of words (BOW) features: For each verb, we consider words before and after that verb within a predefined window length (5 in our experiments).

Words and POS patterns (WP): These include combinations of the word/POS tag of the current verb and those from either the previous or the following adjacent word. These features are expected to capture some expression patterns unique to some tense class. For example, the pattern "verb+了(a particle word with no literal translation to English)" means a verb followed by a word "了", which is often a good indicator of past tense.

Local bigram features: We hypothesize that in addition to information from the immediate previous and the following words of the verb, other adjacent words and patterns around the verb may also be good indicators for tense. They may form a temporal expression or part of it, such as "几天前(several days ago)". We thus extract the word bigrams before and after the verb within a 3-word window.

Global bigram features: We observe that useful cues to predict a verb's tense can appear anywhere in a sentence, therefore, we include all the bigrams in the sentence as the global feature.

Dependency features (DEP): We automatically derived dependency features for each verb as features, which are expected to capture long-distance temporal evidence through dependency relation.

Note that we limited the feature scope to within one sentence since we noticed that information from other sentences is often noisy and not helpful to determine the tense for verbs in the current sentence.

3.3 Automatic Extraction of Tense Reference based on Parallel Data

An important part of supervised learning is the collection of labeled data. For the tense prediction task, we need reference tense information for each Chinese verb. Currently there is no labeled data publicly available for this task. To avoid the time-consuming manual labeling efforts, we propose to leverage the parallel Chinese-English corpus to automatically obtain the tense annotation for Chinese verbs using the corresponding English data. The following describes our procedure.

POS tag and parse the English sentences, and generate tense information for each verb.

POS tag the Chinese sentences.

Align the English and Chinese sentences at the word level.

For each identified verb in the Chinese sentences, if it is aligned to one English verb, or if it is aligned to multiple English verbs but with no conflicting tense types, then we use the corresponding English verb tense as the reference tag for that Chinese verb; otherwise, we do not include that Chinese verb in the training set.

This process of generating reference tense for the Chinese verbs is not perfect due to errors in English parsing and tense assignment, word alignment between Chinese and English, and Chinese POS tagging. In addition, tenses are not always well-alignable between two different languages. However, it can effectively make use of the large amount of existing parallel corpora and provides an efficient way to create a large set of labeled data automatically. In addition, most learning frameworks have the potential power to deal with noisy data and thus we expect this data set may still allow us to build an effective model for tense prediction. Furthermore, since one of our future plans is to use tense information in Chinese to help Chinese to English machine translation, we believe that using information derived from English suits this goal. (Ye and Zhang, 2005) also used a parallel Chinese-English corpus to obtain tense information, however, it was done manually. In contrast, our method is automated, which allows us to utilize a large amount of existing parallel data.

3.4 Iterative Learning Using Noisy Training Data

Since the reference data automatically derived from parallel corpora is noisy, we propose to use an iterative method to address this problem for more effective learning. Our method is similar to bootstrapping (or self-training), but different in that: (i) we do not have a gold-standard seed set to start with; (ii) our data is not fully unlabeled, instead it has the labels obtained from the mapping process using parallel data; and (iii) we use different data labeling and selection methods in the iterative learning process. Our algorithm is shown in Algorithm 1, with more detailed description below.

Create an initial set.

Unlike self-training, we do not have an initial human annotated seed set. Therefore we will select a reliable small set from our noisy data for iterative learning. Our expectation is that when testing the classifier on the data set used for training, the noisy data points

Algorithm 1 Iterative learning algorithm from noisy data

Let be the automatically labeled training data
Train classifier on
Select initial training set based on self-testing using
for to **do**
  Train classifier on
  Classify using
  Assign a label to each instance in
  Rank instances in each class
  Select top data samples in each class,
  Update training data,
end for

(i.e., instances with incorrect initial labels) are likely to have wrong predictions or low confidence (note that there are other impacting factors such as the features and the classifier used). We define the confidence score for the classifier's output as the ratio between the probability of the predicted label and the probability of the second most probable label. Using this measure, we created an initial set containing 10% of the entire data that have the highest confidence scores. We also compared this confidence measure with using the standard posterior probabilities from the classifier, and found this performed better.

In each iteration, assign labels to instances in the set of unselected samples.

In each iteration, we first apply the currently trained classifier to label each instance that is not yet selected by the iterative process, and then assign a final label to an instance using information based on the current iteration classifier ( ) and the initially self-trained classifier (, which is trained using the entire data set). This is different from traditional bootstrapping where there is only one classifier during the iterations. When the two classifiers agree on the most likely tag for an instance, it is straightforward to assign this tag. When there is a disagreement, we need to resolve the conflict. For this, we use confidence score from each classifier (the same confidence measure as used above), and use the label from the classifier with a higher confidence score. To take into account of the difference of the score range, we normalize the

confidence score: .
Rank instances.

This is needed for better selection of reliable and informative instances for model training. We rank instances in each tense category (their labels are determined from the previous step) based on the confidence score from the current classifier . We found this performed better than other metrics, such as Kullback-Leibler distance and Gap ratio.

Select top-ranked instances to add to the training set.

Based on the above ranking, we selected the top (p is empirically set to 0.5 in this work) of instances in each class and added them to the training set for next iteration training. Some previous studies (e.g., (Carlson et al., 2009)) showed that constraints are useful for self-learning or semi-supervised learning in terms of quality control. Therefore, in addition to the ranking scores above, during the selection process we consider more constraints. Specifically, for each instance we compare the labels generated based on three sources: original automatically derived label, prediction from the current classifier, and prediction from the initial self-trained classifier. We filter out cases using two different constraints: (a) Constraint I: neither the prediction from the current classifier nor the self-trained one is the same as the automatically derived label. (b) Constraint II: none of those three labels agree with others, that is, they are all different.

4 Experiments and Results

4.1 Data and Experimental Setup

The training data we used is from the Chinese-English parallel MT data collection provided by LDC for the DARPA GALE program. It comes from various domains: broadcast news, broadcast conversation, newswire, weblog, and newsgroup. We split the data into sentences when there is a period, question mark, or exclamation mark. All of the English sentences were parsed using the Charniak parser (Charniak and Johnson, 2005). The English verbs were then labeled with tense tags based on the parses. We used the Chinese POS tagger from (Huang et al., 2007) and Chinese dependency parser from (Chang et al., 2009). After preprocessing the source and target language data (mainly word segmentation for Chinese and tokenization for English), we used GIZA++ (Och and Ney, 2003) to obtain a word-level alignment. After applying heuristic rules to eliminate verbs that have no aligned English verbs or are aligned to multiple verbs with conflicting tenses (see Section 3.3 for reference tense creation), we finally created a training set consisting of 279,379 verb instances and 38,087 sentences.

We chose the maximum entropy (ME) model as the classifier for tense prediction, because ME can effectively utilize many features and performs competitively with other approaches in many classification tasks. We used the ME implementation from (Zhang, 2006) with a Gaussian prior of 0.1 and 100 iterations in the model training.

4.2 Cross Validation Evaluation Using Automatically Generated Reference

First we directly use the automatically created training set and measure the cross validation performance, mainly to evaluate the modeling approach and features for tense prediction. We use classification accuracy as the performance measurement in this experiment. Table 1 shows the 5-fold cross validation results using different feature sets described in Section 3.2. The baseline is calculated when assigning the majority tag in the training set to all the test instances.

Features	Accuracy (%)
Baseline	34.70
BOW	56.89
+ WP	63.13
+ Local-Bigram	63.39
+ Global-Bigram	64.90
+ Dependency	65.02

Table 1: Classification accuracy using different feature sets for verb-based tense prediction. Results are based on 5-fold cross-validation using automatically generated tense labels.

We found that adding contextual feature sets improves performance incrementally. When only bag of words (BOW) features are used, the accuracy is 56.89%, substantially better than the baseline of 34.70%. Adding "word and POS pattern" (WP) around verbs yields significant improvement, resulting in the accuracy of 63.13%, 7.8% gain compared to using BOW features only. This suggests that such combination of word and POS may represent some syntactic characteristics and is more indicative of tense information. As expected, adding local bigram features slightly improves the performance and global bigram features can further boost the tense classification performance, yielding an accuracy of 64.90%. This shows that for verb tense prediction, global bigrams can provide some helpful information complementary to local features in recognizing tense information. Interestingly, adding dependency features only slightly improved the performance, which could be due to the low quality of dependency extraction on speech data. On the other hand, incrementally adding features might not clearly indicate the contribution of each feature type due to overlap problem. We further conducted experiments to see the effects of excluding each feature type at one time. The results show similar patterns to the above, showing the "BOW" and "Global-Bigram" features are most important features, and "Local-Bigram" and "Dependency" features are least important features.

Note that the training data is noisy due to the automatic process. To have a better understanding of the data quality, we decided to sample a small subset of the data and create human annotation. We randomly selected 2 files in the training data and asked a native Chinese speaker to manually label the first 150 utterances of each file. The annotator was asked to decide which verbs to label and assign the appropriate tense labels. No other explicit instructions were provided. During annotation, the human annotator found that many cases are ambiguous and felt tense labeling is quite subjective, suggesting creating human annotation for tense is very challenging as investigated in (Xue et al., 2008). Using this small data set, we found that the percentage of correct tense labels by the automatic alignment process was 78.52% (329 out of 419 instances), which seems quite satisfying, although further inspection is still needed.

4.3 Evaluation on Human Annotated Data

Another setting we use to evaluate the automatic tense prediction performance is by comparing to human annotation. We performed a pilot annotation for verb tense. The same native Chinese speaker as that who created the small sample training set manually annotated the verbs with tense types using 900 utterances from 6 randomly selected files in the GALE MT 2007 development set. In total, 2484 verbs were labeled by the human annotator, and these are used as the references to measure the performance of our automatic tense prediction system.

Because the POS tagger may miss some verbs and thus there will be no system hypothesis for those verbs, two different metrics are used in this evaluation. One is the labeled recall rate, defined as the percentage of the correctly labeled verbs out of the human labeled verbs; the other metric is the tense classification accuracy measured using only those verbs that are identified by both the POS tagger and the human annotator. As dependency features do not seem to be reliable enough, we trained two models from the automatically generated data set to validate its effectiveness on test data: one is using all the features (ALL) and the other one excludes dependency features (W/O Dependency). The results are shown in Table 2. To make a more competitive baseline system, instead of using the majority category of all the verbs on the training set, we used the majority tag for each individual verb.

System	Recall(%)	Accuracy(%)
Baseline	52.79	56.52
ALL	71.50	74.80
W/O Dependency	73.09	76.49

Table 2: Verb tense prediction performance on the human annotated test data.

We can see that the POS tagging errors (i.e., missing verbs) have a noticeable impact on system performance. Note that there is a difference between the baseline performance using the human annotation vs. the automatically created data set. There are two reasons for this. First is the different class distributions in the two data sets, for example, about 28%, 34%, 32%, and 16% for infinitive, past, present, and future tense respectively in the automatically labeled set, and 15%, 35%, 42%, and 8% in human annotation. Second, the baseline results in Table 2 are word-based, rather than the majority class for the entire set.

Our results show that using parallel data to derive reference annotations is a promising approach for a statistical learning framework, achieving the best performance of 76.49% compared with the baseline of 56.52%. Although adding dependency features obtained small improvement for the cross validation result, it degraded the performance on test set (see last row in Table 2). Therefore we exclude that feature for subsequent experiments. We also observe that the performance is much better compared to Table 1, even though the class distributions are different in training and testing (which may affect statistical learning). One explanation might be that noisy labels from automatically generated training data may harm the cross validation performance. In addition, statistical learning can deal with the noisy data for training a robust model on unseen test data. We will show how the effects of noisy labels can be further reduced by iterative learning in next section.

4.4 Iterative Learning Results

Table 3 shows the best results for three iterative learning settings evaluated using the human annotated data set. These are from different numbers of iterations with different combinations of label assignment and instance ranking methods. We can see that using iterative learning generally improved tense classification in different settings – achieving the best accuracy of 77.49% compared to the original 76.49%, and the best recall rate of 74.02% compared to the original 73.09%. It suggests that our proposed learning method can effectively overcome some negative impact of the noisy training data, by iteratively selecting more likely trustworthy instances for model training. The best performance was obtained by applying constraint II (74.02%/77.49%), while adding constraint I degraded the performance a lot, which could be because using constrain I mislead the iterative process as more rules would miss out some useful training instances in the early stage. It suggests that adding appropriate constrains in the iterative bootstrapping process can provide better quality control for improved performance.

Selection Constraint	Recall (%)	Accuracy (%)
W/O Constraints	73.85	77.31
Constraint I	72.31	75.72
Constraint II	74.02	77.49

Table 3: Verb tense prediction performance on the human annotated test data using iterative learning. The results using the original training data are 73.09 and 76.49 for recall and accuracy.

For the iterative learning algorithm, we also examined its learning curve. Figure 1 shows the curves for the above best system using Constraint II. The horizontal dotted line is the baseline result when we just use the original data without iterative learning. We notice that performance in the early iterations generally increases (with some fluctuations) as more data samples are added for model training. After certain number of iterations, the performance starts dropping, since some added instances are noisy and do not help learning. Based on the trend shown in the curve, we expect that when the classifier itself improves, such as when incorporating more discriminative features, the learning curve could potentially increase further. The curves for other settings show similar patterns, with the best results achieved at different number of iterations.

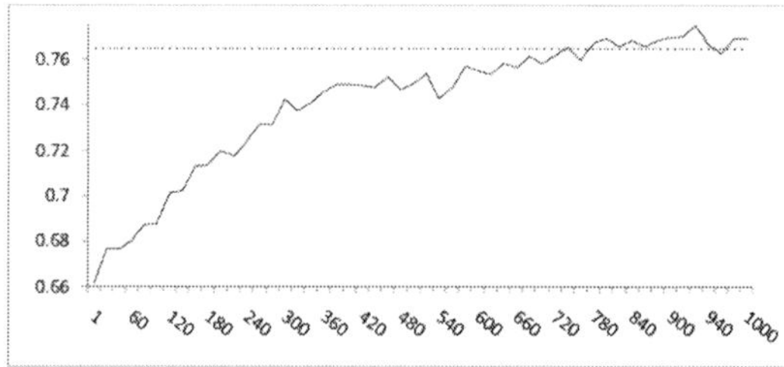

Figure 1: Learning curve of the iterative learning approach.

Another question we try to answer is how much we can attribute the performance improvement to iterative learning, or whether simply resampling can achieve similar performance. We examined re-sampling methods based on confidence measure (as described in iterative learning) to select similar number of samples as used in the iterative learning system above (using its optimal number of iterations), and then evaluated the classifier trained using this subset of the data. The results shows that simple re-sampling only obtained the accuracy of 74.58%, which is even worse than using the entire data set. Therefore we can conclude that the improvement we observe is mainly from the iterative learning method.

4.5 Error Analysis

Example 3 illustrates some examples of errors from our analysis. We identified several reasons causing the errors of our tense prediction system:

> Imperfect Chinese word segmentation and POS tagging results can directly affect the correct identification of Chinese verbs. In example (3a), the named entity "戴尔(Dell)" was incorrectly segmented as two Chinese words, and "戴" was further tagged as a verb due to its verb meaning "wear". In

Example 3:
3a) 戴/3 尔(Dell) 公司(Inc.) 新闻(media) 发言人 (spokesman) JessBlackburn 表示(indicate)/2， 该(the) 公司 (company) 正在(is) 评估(evaluating)/3 Google 的 软件 (software)。

The spokesman of Dell Inc. indicated that, the company is evaluating the software from Google.

3b) 小时(hour) 工部(department) 分(divide)/3 职位(position) 技能(skill) 要求(require)/3 不(not) 高(high)/1， 如(such as) 食品(food) 促销 员(salesman)/3 、 理 货 员(shelf stockers) 等(etc)， 失业(unemployment) 人员(people) 经过(by) 简单 (simple)/3 的 培训(training) 即可(can) 上(take)/3 岗(job)。

Some positions for hourly workers require less job skills, such as the food salesman, shelf stockers, etc., the unemployed can take the job after simple training.

3c) 负责人(manager) 称(claim)/2， 他们(they) 会(will) 在 (by) 2005 年(year) 底(end) 完成(finish)/4 这项(the) 工程 (project)。

The manager claimed that they would finish the project by the end of 2005.

example (3b), the phrase "小时工(hourly worker)部分(some)职位(position)" was incorrectly segmented and the resulting word "分(divide)" was incorrectly tagged as a verb. In addition, some adjectives were also wrongly recognized as verbs, such as "高(high)", "简单(simple)".

There is limitation using our current feature set and it needs deep understanding to derive the correct tense. In example (3c), the system assigns future tense to the Chinese verb "完成(finish)" mainly because of the evidence "会(will)". To correct this, the system needs to determine that "the end of 2005" already passed based on knowledge or other long distance context (e.g., "But they didn't." in the following sentence).

The Chinese verb may not always be translated into English verbs, and vice versa. Training noises plus the imperfect alignment tools and other propagated errors from other preprocessing modules contributed another portion of errors.

Human annotation is not perfect. In some cases, both the system's output and human annotation are acceptable but they are not consistent. On the one hand, it shows the challenges of this task; on the other hand it suggests that investigation of inter-agreement among human subjects is needed in the future.

5 Conclusion and Future Work

In this paper, we have developed a classification approach to predict tense for Chinese verbs. We proposed an automatic mechanism to generate reference tense for the Chinese verbs that utilizes the Chinese-English parallel corpora, thus can efficiently create a large training set without relying on the time-consuming human annotation efforts. Our experimental results have shown that various contextual features around verbs can be effectively used to determine tense information, and this method of leveraging parallel corpora is feasible for Chinese tense prediction. In addition, the bootstrapping approach we explored in this paper further improves performance, proving to be an effective way to select training samples iteratively from noisy data.

In our future work, we will refine the process to automatically create the training set to better deal with problems from POS tagging, parsing, and alignment. A better data set will likely improve the tense prediction model. In addition, inter-agreement of human annotation on tense information is worth studying, especially for conversational style data. Finally, we will investigate using richer syntactic information and other semi-supervised methods (e.g. co-training in (Bergsma et al., 2011)) for tense prediction, and more importantly, develop methods using tense information derived in our system for machine translation and other applications.

Acknowledgments

We thank Eugene Charniak for providing his tools to obtain the tense information for the English verbs, Mary Harper for providing the parses for English and POS tagger for Mandarin, and Mari Ostendorf for useful discussions. This work was supported by DARPA under Contract No. HR0011-06-C-0023. Distribution is unlimited.

References

Luisa Bentivogli, Pamela Forner, and Emanuele Pianta. 2004. Evaluating cross-language annotation transfer in the multisemcor corpus. In *Proceedings of COLING*.

S. Bergsma, D. Yarowsky, and K. Church. 2011. Using large monolingual and bilingual corpora to improve coordination disambiguation. In *Proceedings of ACL/HLT*.

Avrim Blum and Tom Mitchell. 1998. Combining labeled and unlabeled data with co-training. In *Proceedings of COLT*, pages 92–100.

Bianka Buschbeck, Renate Henschel, Iris Höser, Gerda Klimonow, Andreas Küstner, and Ingrid Starke. 1991. Limits of a sentence based procedural approach for aspect choice in German-Russian MT. In *Proceedings of EACL*, pages 269–274.

Guihong Cao, Wenjie Li, Kam-Fai Wong, and Chunfa Yuan. 2004. Combining linguistic features with weighted bayesian classifier for temporal reference processing. In *Proceedings of COLING*, pages 702–708.

Andrew Carlson, Justin Betteridge, Estevam R. Hruschka, Jr., and Tom M. Mitchell. 2009. Coupling semi-supervised learning of categories and relations. In *Proceedings of the NAACL HLT 2009 Workshop on Semi-Supervised Learning for Natural Language Processing*, pages 1–9.

P. Chang, H. Tseng, D. Jurafsky, and C.D. Manning. 2009. Discriminative reordering with chinese grammatical relations features. In *Proceedings of the Third Workshop on Syntax and Structure in Statistical Translation*.

Eugene Charniak and Mark Johnson. 2005. Coarse-to-fine n-best parsing and maxent discriminative reranking. In *Proceedings of ACL*, pages 173–180.

Zheng Chen and Heng Ji. 2009. Can one language bootstrap the other: A case study on event extraction. In *Proceedings of HLT-NAACL 2009 Workshop on Semi-supervised Learning for Natural Language Processing*.

Y. Cheng. 2008. Constructing a temporal relation identification system of Chinese based on dependency structure analysis. Thesis in Nara Institute of Science and Technology.

M. Collins and Y. Singer. 1999. Unsupervised models for named entity classification. In *Proceedings of EMNLP*.

Anna Feldman, Jirka Hana, and Chris Brew. 2006. A cross-language approach to rapid creation of new morpho-syntactically annotated resources. In *Proceedings of LREC*.

R. He, B. Qin, T. Liu, Y. Pan, and S. Li. 2008. A novel heuristic Error-Driven learning for recognizing Chinese time expression. *Journal of Chinese Language and Computing*, 18(4):139 - 159.

Zhongqiang Huang, Mary Harper, and Wen Wang. 2007. Mandarin part-of-speech tagging and discriminative reranking. In *Proceedings of EMNLP*.

Jussi Karlgren. 1996. Tense prediction for speech recognition purposes. Technical Report in New York University.

Wenjie Li and Kam-Fai Wong. 2002. A word-based approach for modeling and discovering temporal relations embedded in Chinese sentences. *ACM Transactions on Asian Language Information Processing (TALIP)*, 1(3):173–206.

Wenjie Li, Kam-Fai Wong, and Chunfa Yuan. 2001. A model for processing temporal references in Chinese. In *Proceedings of the workshop on Temporal and spatial information processing*, pages 1–8.

Wenjie Li, Kam-Fai Wong, Guihong Cao, and Chunfa Yuan. 2004. Applying machine learning to Chinese temporal relation resolution. In *Proceedings of ACL*, pages 582–588.

JoWang Lin. 2003. Temporal reference in mandarin Chinese. *Journal of East Asian Linguistics*, 12(3):259–311.

JoWang Lin. 2006. Time in a language without tense: The case of Chinese. *Journal of Semantics*, 23(1):1–53.

David McClosky, Eugene Charniak, and Mark Johnson. 2006. Effective self-training for parsing. In *Proceedings of HLT-NAACL*, pages 152–159.

Franz Josef Och and Hermann Ney. 2003. A systematic comparison of various statistical alignment models. *Computational Linguistics*, 29(1):19–51.

Sebastian Pado and Mirella Lapata. 2009. Cross-lingual annotation projection of semantic roles. *Journal of Artificial Intelligence Research*, 26:307–340.

Marius Pasca, Dekang Lin, Jeffrey Bigham, Andrei Lifchits, and Alpa Jain. 2006. Names and similarities on the web: fact extraction in the fast lane. In *Proceedings of ACL*, pages 809–816.

Deepak Ravichandran and Eduard Hovy. 2002. Learning surface text patterns for a question answering system. In *Proceedings of ACL*, pages 41–47.

Florian Schwarck, Alexander Fraser, and Hinrich Schuetze. 2010. Bitext-based resolution of german subject-object ambiguities. In *Proceedings of HLT/NAACL*.

Ellen Thompson. 2005. *Time in Natural Language: Syntactic Interfaces with Semantics and Discourse*. Walter de Gruyter.

Nicola Ueffing. 2006. Self-training for machine translation. In *Proceedings of NIPS workshop on Machine Learning for Multilingual Information Access*.

R. Z. Xiao and A. M. McEnery. 2002. A corpus-based approach to tense and aspect in English-Chinese translation. In *The 1st International Symposium on Contrastive and Translation Studies between Chinese and English*.

N. Xue, H. Zhong, K. Y Chen, and M. Marrakech. 2008. Annotating "tense" in a tense-less language. In *Proceedings of the Fifth International Conference on Language Resources and Evaluation*.

Yang Ye and Zhu Zhang. 2005. Tense tagging for verbs in cross-lingual context: A case study. In *Proceedings of IJCNLP*, pages 885–895.

Le Zhang. 2006. Maximum entropy modeling toolkit for Python and C++. http://homepages.inf.ed.ac.uk/s0450736/maxent_toolkit.html.

Jointly Extracting Japanese Predicate-Argument Relation with Markov Logic

Katsumasa Yoshikawa, Masayuki Asahara and Yuji Matsumoto
Graduate School of Information Science,
Nara Institute of Science and Technology
8916-5, Takayama-cho, Ikoma, Nara 630-0192, Japan
{katsumasa-y,masayu-a,matsu}@is.naist.jp

Abstract

This paper describes a new Markov Logic approach for Japanese Predicate-Argument (PA) relation extraction. Most previous work built separated classifiers corresponding to each case role and independently identified the PA relations, neglecting dependencies (constraints) between two or more PA relations. We propose a method which collectively extracts PA relations by optimizing all argument candidates in a sentence. Our method can jointly consider dependency between multiple PA relations and find the most probable combination of predicates and their arguments in a sentence. In addition, our model involves new constraints to avoid considering inappropriate candidates for arguments and identify correct PA relations effectively. Compared to the state-of-the-art, our method achieves competitive results without large-scale data.

1 Introduction

Predicate-argument (PA) relation extraction is one of the challenging problems in Natural Language Processing. The analysis extracts semantic information such as "who did what to whom", which is often useful to various applications like information extraction, document summarization, and machine translation.

Predicate-argument relation extraction is often called semantic role labeling. In English, it has been researched on large corpora such as FrameNet (Fillmore et al., 2001) and PropBank (Palmer et al., 2005). CoNLL Shared Task 2008 (Surdeanu et al., 2008) is a representative work of semantic role labeling based on these corpora. Japanese PA relation extraction is a kind of semantic role labeling but an argument is often called *case*. A typical example of Japanese PA relation is shown in Figure 1. In this example, "行った (went)" is a predicate and there are two arguments for the predicate, that is, a nominative case role (ga) is "彼 (He)" and a dative case role (ni) is "図書館 (library)".

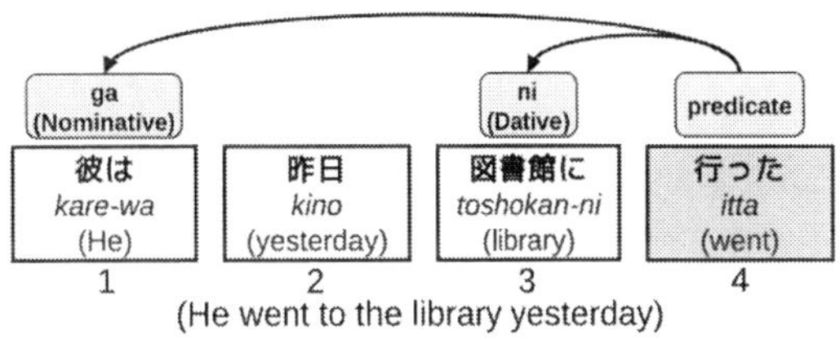

Figure 1: Example of Predicate-Argument Structure

In Japanese, Taira et al. (2008) and Imamura et al. (2009) tackled PA relation extraction on NAIST Text Corpus (Iida et al., 2007). They created three separated models corresponding to each of the case; ga (Nominative), wo (Accusative), and ni (Dative).

Even though some English semantic role labeler apply global models, most of them solve problems on a *per-predicate* basis (Toutanova et al., 2008; Watanabe et al., 2010). In this work, we propose an approach to Japanese PA relation extraction on a *per-sentence* basis and utilize important dependencies between one PA relation and another in the same sentence. In order to use such dependencies as global constraints, we apply a Markov Logic approach to Japanese PA relation extraction. In recent years, in English semantic role labeling, a Markov Logic model has achieved one of the state-of-the-art results (Meza-Ruiz and Riedel, 2009a). With global constraints between multiple PA relations, a Markov Logic model can avoid inconsistencies between several PA relations and improve performance of extraction.

In addition, we introduce new global constraints to effectively delete inappropriate argument candidates which are unrelated to PA relations. We consider that extraction of PA relations and dele-

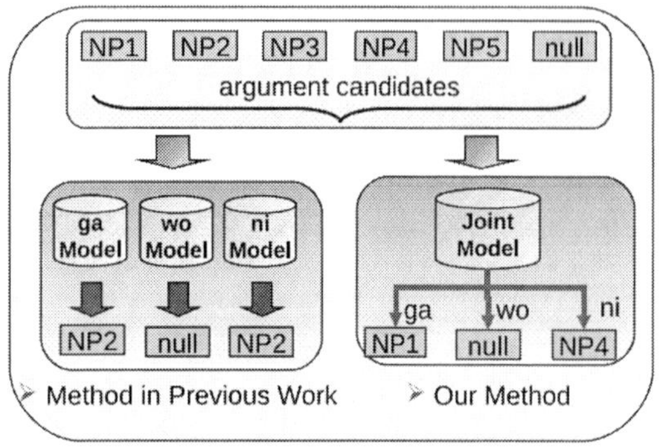

Figure 2: Difference in Methods

tion of the other phrases are two sides of the same coin. We jointly perform such extraction and deletion with Markov Logic.

Through our experiments, we report the effectiveness of the Markov Logic approach to Japanese PA relation extraction in detail. We show that our model with global constraints outperforms the model without them. Comparison with previous work shows that our Markov Logic approach achieves competitive results without selectional preference features obtained from large-scale unlabelled data. In qualitative analysis, we find that our global model resolves some difficult cases such as PA relations in relative clauses.

The remainder of this paper is organized as follows: Section 2 describes related work; Section 3 introduces Markov Logic; Section 4 explains our proposed Markov Logic Network; Section 5 presents and discusses the experimental setting and the results; and in Section 6 we conclude and present ideas for future research.

2 Related Work

In Japanese, PA annotated corpora such as Kyoto Text Corpus (KTC) (Kawahara et al., 2002) and NAIST Text Corpus (NTC) (Iida et al., 2007) have been developed and utilized. [1] CoNLL Shared Task 2009 (Hajič et al., 2009) included Japanese PA relation extraction on the data from KTC.

The data we used in this work is from NTC. NTC is based on the same text as KTC, which contains 38,384 sentences from 2,929 news articles. [2] The annotation in NTC has the three case roles: "ga (Nominative)", "wo (Accusative)", and "ni (Dative)". The predicate-argument annotation in NTC is based on deep cases and is more difficult to analyze than the surface case annotations which KTC employs. Note that KTC includes morphological information, base phrase segmentation, and syntactic dependency structure. We can merge these annotation from KTC and deep case annotation from NTC.

There are two main previous work with NTC. First, Taira et al. (2008) researched extraction of PA relations by SVM classifiers and decision lists. Their approach focused on not only verbal predicates but also nominal predicates. Secondly, Imamura et al. (2009) combined a Maximum Entropy model with a language model learned from large-scale corpora and achieved the state-of-the-art results.

Both Taira et al. and Imamura et al. created an independent model for each of the cases *ga, wo,* and *ni* (the left box in Figure 2). So, their models neglect the dependencies between cases. For example, the method in previous work produces "NP2" for both ga and ni cases. Though it is unlikely that the same noun phrase occupies two argument positions of a predicate, it is possible with their models.

However, our Markov Logic approach creates a joint model for the three cases and finds the most probable assignments taking into consideration the dependency between them. As a result, our model can prevent such an unlikely result (See the right box in Figure 2).

Moreover, in contrast to Imamura's work, our method does not exploit large-scale corpora. They depended on their language model derived from large-scale corpora to decide the selectional preference between a predicate and an argument. On the other hand, we handle the problem by global optimization *per-sentence* without using large-scale corpora.

In the CoNLL Shared Task 2009 (Hajič et al., 2009), a competition of multilingual semantic role labeling was held and Japanese was one of the target languages. In the shared task, Meza-Ruiz and Riedel (2009b) proposed a joint approach with Markov Logic. They also reported their Markov Logic approach for English semantic role labeling in detail (Meza-Ruiz and Riedel, 2009a). Their method divided the problem into four subtasks: predicate identification, argument identification, sense disambiguation, and role labeling. The subtasks are solved jointly. [3] We adapt their model to

[1] KTC is annotated with surface cases and NTC is annotated with deep cases

[2] These articles are from a Japanese newspaper, "Mainichi Shinbun"

[3] Note, in the CoNLL *2009* Shared Task, predicate identification is not necessary. So, they used the CoNLL *2008* Shared Task data in their work.

Japanese PA relation extraction on NTC. In order to compare with Taira et al. (2008) and Imamura et al. (2009), we perform only argument identification and role labeling.

About joint models of semantic role labeling without using Markov Logic, there are various previous work on CoNLL Shared Task Data. For example, Toutanova et al. (2008) and Watanabe et al. (2010) proposed joint models on the data of CoNLL Shared Task 2005 and 2009, respectively. While their models solve the problem on a *per-predicate* basis, our Markov Logic model solves it on a *per-sentence* basis. An optimization on a per-sentence basis is necessary and desirable for PA relation extraction on NTC since NTC has deep case annotations without case-frame dictionaries corresponding to them.

3 Markov Logic

It has long been clear that local classification alone cannot adequately solve all prediction problems we encounter in practice. This observation motivated a field within machine learning, often referred to as Statistical Relational Learning (SRL), which focuses on the incorporation of global correlations that hold between statistical variables (Getoor and Taskar, 2007).

One particular SRL framework that has recently gained momentum as a platform for global learning and inference in AI is Markov Logic (Richardson and Domingos, 2006), a combination of first-order logic and Markov Networks. It can be understood as a formalism that extends first-order logic to allow formulae that can be violated with some penalty. From an alternative point of view, it is an expressive template language that uses first order logic formulae to instantiate Markov Networks of repetitive structure. In the field of NLP, the Markov Logic approach has been applied to various tasks such as entity resolution (Singla and Domingos, 2006), information extraction (Poon and Domingos, 2007), and coreference resolution (Poon and Domingos, 2008), among others.

From a wide range of SRL languages we chose Markov Logic because it supports discriminative training (as opposed to generative SRL languages such as PRM (Koller, 1999)). Moreover, several Markov Logic software libraries exist and are freely available (as opposed to other discriminative frameworks such as Relational Markov Networks (Taskar et al., 2002)).

A *Markov Logic Network* (MLN) M is a set of pairs (ϕ, w) where ϕ is a first order formula and w is a real number (the formula's weight). It defines a probability distribution over sets of ground atoms, or so-called *possible worlds*, as follows:

$$p(\mathbf{y}) = \frac{1}{Z}\exp\left(\sum_{(\phi,w)\in M} w \sum_{\mathbf{c}\in C^{\phi}} f_{\mathbf{c}}^{\phi}(\mathbf{y})\right) \quad (1)$$

Here each $\mathbf{c}$ is a binding of free variables in ϕ to constants in our domain. Each $f_{\mathbf{c}}^{\phi}$ is a binary feature function that returns 1 if in the possible world $\mathbf{y}$ the *ground formula* we get by replacing the free variables in ϕ with the constants in $\mathbf{c}$ is true, and 0 otherwise. C^{ϕ} is the set of all bindings for the free variables in ϕ. Z is a normalization constant. Note that this distribution corresponds to a Markov Network (the so-called *Ground Markov Network*) where nodes represent ground atoms and factors represent ground formulae.

Designing formulae is only one part of the game. In practice, we also need to choose a training regime (in order to learn the weights of the formulae we added to the MLN) and a search/inference method that picks the most likely set of ground atoms (PA relations in our case) given our trained MLN and a set of observations. However, implementations of these methods are often already provided in existing Markov Logic interpreters such as *Alchemy* [4] and *Markov thebeast*. [5]

4 Proposed Markov Logic Network

This section describes our Markov Logic model for Japanese PA relation extraction. We will describe our proposed Markov Logic Network (MLN) in detail. First, let us define logical predicates for our MLN. The three *hidden* predicates are listed in Table 1.

predicate	definition
$isArg(i)$	Bunsetsu i is an argument
$delete(i)$	Bunsetsu i is deleted
$role(i, j, r)$	Bunsetsu i has an argument j with role r

Table 1: Hidden Predicates

Note that Japanese dependency parsing is based on *bunsetsu* units, which are similar in concept to English base phrases. In order to exploit information parsed in this way, we handle all logical predicates by bunsetsu phrases (not tokens).

The hidden predicates model the decisions we

[4]http://alchemy.cs.washington.edu/

[5]http://code.google.com/p/thebeast/

logical predicate	description	example
$word(i,w)$	Bunsetsu i has word form w	行った (went), 彼 (he)
$stem(i,s)$	Bunsetsu i has stem s	行く (go)
$pos(i,p)$	Bunsetsu i has POS tag p (coarse-grained)	名詞 (noun)
$dpos(i,p)$	Bunsetsu i has POS tag p (fine-grained)	名詞-一般 (noun-general)
$ne(i,n)$	Bunsetsu i has named entity tag n (from NE tagger)	PERSON, LOCATION
$kana(i,k)$	Bunsetsu i has kana (Romanization) k	itta, kare
$isPred(i)$	Bunsetsu i is a predicate	True or False
$numeric(i)$	Bunsetsu i has a number character	True or False
$definite(i)$	Bunsetsu i contains the article corresponding to DEFINITE "the", such as "sore" or "sono"	True or False
$demonstrative(i)$	Bunsetsu i contains the article corresponding to DEMONSTRATIVE "this" or "that", such as "kono" or "ano"	True or False
$particle(i)$	Bunsetsu has a particle such as "wa","ga","wo", "ni"	True or False
$goiCate(i,g)$	Bunsetsu i has lexical category tag g in Nihongo Goi Taikei (Ikehara et al., 1997)	スポーツ (sport), 女性 (female)
$goiMatch(i,j)$	Bunsetsu phrases i and j satisfy the selectional restriction of Nihongo Goi Taikei	True or False
$dep(i,j,d)$	Dependency label between i and j is d	True or False
$path(i,j,l)$	Syntactic path between i and j is l	↑↓ (sibling), ↑↑ (ancestor)

Table 2: Observed Predicates

need to make: whether a bunsetsu phrase i is an argument of some predicate (argument identification); whether a bunsetsu phrase i is deleted (phrase deletion); whether a bunsetsu phrase j is an argument of the predicate i with semantic role r (role labeling).

Here the first two types of decision can be modeled through unary logical predicates $isArg(a)$ and $delete(i)$, while the other type can be represented by a ternary logical predicate $role(p,a,r)$. Because we do not know their information at test time, we call them *hidden*.

Our Markov Logic approach is based on English semantic role labeling with Markov Logic as proposed by Meza-Ruiz and Riedel (2009a). As mentioned earlier, they divided the problem into four subtasks and defined five hidden predicates (*isPredicate, isArgument, hasRole, role*, and *sense*). In order to be comparable with the previous work in Japanese PA relation extraction (Taira et al., 2008; Imamura et al., 2009), we deal with only argument identification and role labeling in our research. Therefore, we define only the three hidden predicates in Table 1.

In addition to the hidden predicates, we define *observed* logical predicates representing information at test time. For example, in our case we could introduce a predicate $word(i,w)$ which indicates that a phrase i has the word form w. We list the all observed predicates in Table 2.

With our predicates defined, we can now go on to incorporate our intuition about the task using weighted first-order logic formulae. In the following we will explain the formulae of our proposed MLN. Sections 4.1 and 4.2 describe our local and global formulae for *isArg* and *role*, respectively. Section 4.3 mentions the formulae for deletion.

4.1 Local Formulae

We say that a formula is *local* if its groundings relate any number of observed ground predicates to exactly one hidden ground predicate. Local formulae are defined with some observed predicates from Table 2 and a hidden predicate from Table 1.

The local formulae for *isArg* and *delete* capture the relation of the bunsetsu phrases with their lexical and syntactic properties (simple phrase property). The formula describing a local property of word form is

$$word(a,+w) \Rightarrow isArg(a) \quad (2)$$

which implies that a bunsetsu a is an argument with a weight that depends on the word form. Note, the + notation indicates that the MLN contains one in-

Type	Formula	Description
hard	$isArg(a) \Rightarrow \exists p.\exists r.role(p, a, r)$	Every argument must relate to at least one predicate
hard	$role(p, a, r) \Rightarrow isArg(a)$	If a plays the role r for p, then a has to be an argument
hard	$role(p, a, r_1) \wedge r_1 \neq r_2 \Rightarrow \neg role(p, a, r_2)$	There is exact one case role between a predicate and an argument

Table 3: Global Formulae for *isArg* and *role*

stance of the rule, with a separate weight, for each assignment of the variables with a plus sign.

The local formulae for *role* represent properties between two bunsetsu phrases (linked phrases property). For example, the following formula

$$ne(a, +n) \wedge dep(p, a, +d) \Rightarrow role(p, a, +r) \quad (3)$$

denotes a local property of named entity and syntactic dependency.

As in Formula (3), some observed predicates (*goiMatch, dep*, and *path*) in Table 2 construct formulae using other observed predicates in this table.

First-order logical formulae such as Formulae (2) and (3) become the feature templates of MLN. Each template produces several instantiations. An example of a template instantiation based on Figure 1 is

$$ne(1, PERSON) \wedge dep(4, 1, \text{“}D\text{”}) \Rightarrow role(4, 1, \text{ga}) \quad (4)$$

which is a typical expansion from Formula (3).

4.2 Global Formulae

The intuition behind the previous formulae can also be captured using a local classifier. However, Markov Logic also allows us to say more:

$$isArg(a) \Rightarrow \exists p.\exists r.role(p, a, r) \quad (5)$$

In this formula, we made a statement about more global properties of a PA relation extraction that cannot be captured with local classifiers. This formula ensures the consistency between predicate and argument, that is, arguments belong to at least one predicate. This type of rule forms the core idea of our global model.

Global formulae involve two or more atoms of hidden predicates and enable us to jointly deal with argument identification, phrase deletion, and role labeling. With global formulae, our MLN considers not only a single decision at a time but also handles several decisions, simultaneously. Our global formulae for argument identification and role labeling are shown in Table 3.

All the formulae in Table 3 are hard constraints which enforce consistency between the hidden predicates. In MLN, formulae of hard constraint are defined as special formulae with *infinite* weights. A possible world which violates hard constraints is never chosen as a correct answer. For example, Formula (5) is such a global formula. Another formula ensuring the consistency between *role* and *isArg* is

$$role(p, a, r) \Rightarrow isArg(a) \quad (6)$$

which indicates “If a phrase a plays the role r for p, then a must be an argument”.

The last global formula

$$role(p, a, r_1) \wedge r_1 \neq r_2 \Rightarrow \neg role(p, a, r_2) \quad (7)$$

implies that there is only one case role between a predicate p and an argument a. Formula (7) enables us to prevent the contradiction shown in Figure 2.

4.3 Deletion Formulae

Let us explain formulae for deletion in this section, independently. The main idea of our deletion is to delete bunsetsu phrases which are unrelated to PA relations and to help extract correct arguments. Extraction of correct arguments and deletion of non-arguments are two sides of the same idea. An example is shown in Figure 3. We have a main verb “行った (went)” as a predicate and there are five argument candidates for it. We want to extract correct arguments, “彼は (He)” for ga-case and “図書館 (library)” for ni-case among the five candidates. Here, if we can remove an instrumental case, “母の新しい車で (by mother’s new car)”, extracting the correct arguments becomes much easier.

Notably, our significant contribution is doing this deletion processes with extraction of PA relations, simultaneously. Deleting too many bunsetsu phrases often hurts the recall because it often deletes correct arguments. We call this phenomena *over-deletion*. Performing extraction and deletion by one joint model prevents over-deletion and improves the performance of PA relation extraction.

Deletion formulae are also divided into local and global. However, local formulae implement the same properties for *isArg* we mentioned in Section 4.1. As an exception, a characteristic local formula

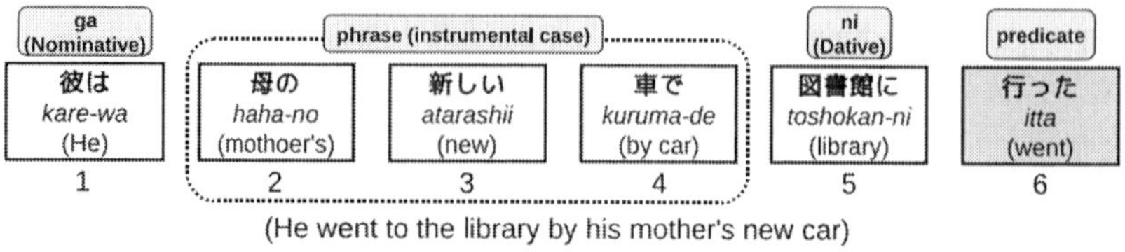

Figure 3: Example of PA Relation with Instrumental Case

is

$$dep(i, j, +d) \wedge isPred(j) \Rightarrow \neg delete(i). \quad (8)$$

which implies the PA relations with syntactic dependencies are not deleted. It implements the fact that PA relations often have syntactic dependency relations. Actually, we can find that dependency relations are dominant in Table 5 and Formula (8) contributes to improve performance.

However, the local formulae address the deletion of a single bunsetsu phrase and we cannot expect a large improvement by adding *delete*. The main contributions of *delete* come from the global deletion formulae.

The global formulae for *delete* have three hard and one soft constraints. We show the global formulae in Table 4. The first three formulae in this table show the hard constraints which ensure the consistency between *delete* and the other two hidden predicates (*isArg* and *role*). The most important formula of them is

$$delete(i) \Rightarrow \neg isArg(i) \quad (9)$$

which implies that the deleted phrase does not become an argument.

The last formula in Table 4 is defined as a soft constraint:

$$word(h, +w) \wedge pos(h, +p) \wedge dep(h, m, +d)$$
$$\wedge delete(h) \Rightarrow delete(m) \quad (10)$$

which denotes "if a head phrase h is removed, then the child phrases m should be deleted". This formula does not always hold but the remaining uncertainty with regard to this formula is captured by a weight trained from corpora. This constraint implements the important deletion concept as we mentioned earlier.

Considering the example in Figure 3, Formula (10) is grounded as,

$$word(4, \text{“車で”}) \wedge pos(4, \text{NOUN+PARTICLE})$$
$$\wedge dep(4, 2, \text{“}D\text{”}) \wedge delete(4) \Rightarrow delete(2) \quad (11)$$

which implies that "if '車で (by car)' is removed, '母の (mother's)' should be also removed". Figure 4 shows the dependency parsed tree extracted from

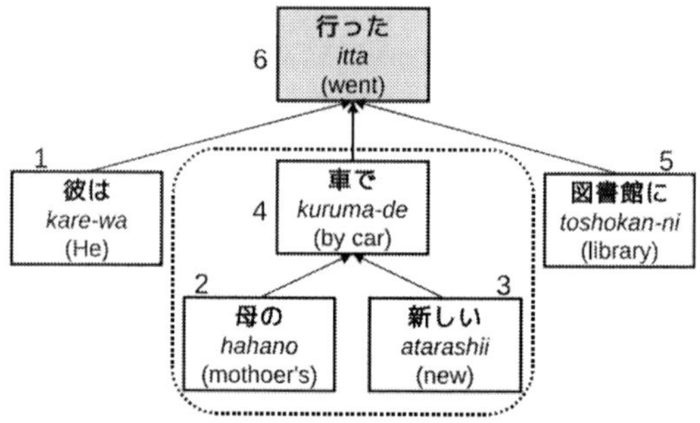

Figure 4: Deletion of Instrumental Case

the sentence in Figure 3. The subtree under "車で (by car)" should be deleted by Formula (11).

Note that Japanese dependency parsing usually targets only unlabeled parsing. Almost all labels are "D". [6] Therefore, we exploit the *word* and *pos* of head bunsetsu phrases as a substitution. In Japanese, word form and POS implicitly give us information similar to dependency labels. However, if we exploit our method in English, labeled information such as *probj* or *amod* should be helpful to train proper weights for Formula (10).

5 Experimental Results

5.1 Experimental Setup

Our experimental setting is based on previous work (Taira et al., 2008; Imamura et al., 2009) which was performed on NAIST Text Corpus.

Let us summarize our used data and tools. The data used, NAIST Text Corpus version 1.4β, has news articles and editorials. As training examples, we use articles published from January 1st to January 11th and editorials from January to August. As development data, we use articles published on January 12th and 13th and editorials in September. For evaluation, we use articles dated January 14th to 17th and editorials dated October to December. This way to split the data is same as Taira et al. (2008). We show the statistics of the evaluation data in Table 5.

As seen in this table, "ga-case" is dominant. PA relations which have syntactic dependency re-

[6] We sometimes have "P", "A", and "I" labels but it is not enough to model our deletion idea.

Type	Formula	Description
hard	$isArg(a) \Rightarrow \neg delete(a)$	If a is an argument then it is not deleted.
hard	$delete(i) \Rightarrow \neg isArg(i)$	If a bunsetsu i is deleted then it is not an argument.
hard	$role(p, a, r) \Rightarrow \neg delete(p) \wedge \neg delete(a)$	If a is an argument of p with the role r then neither p nor a is deleted.
soft	$word(h, +w) \wedge pos(h, +p) \wedge dep(h, m, +d) \wedge delete(h) \Rightarrow delete(m)$	If a head phrase h is deleted with word w and POS p then a child phrase m is deleted.

Table 4: Global Deletion Formulae

	ga	wo	ni
Dep.	13,086	5,192	3,645
Zero-Intra	4,556	376	231
Total	17,642	5,568	3,876

Table 5: Statistics in Evaluation Data

	Local			*Global*		
	P	R	F	P	R	F
isArg	79.2	71.4	75.1	94.6	84.2	89.1
delete	86.6	90.4	88.4	94.3	97.9	96.1
role	86.3	72.5	78.8	85.5	**77.7**	81.4

Table 6: Local vs Global

lations (Dep.) are much more common than intra-sentential zero-anaphoric PA relations (Zero-Intra). However, in Japanese, we often find zero-anaphoric PA relations called *case ellipsis*. More detailed descriptions of PA relation types are shown in (Iida et al., 2006). Note that we target only PA relations which occur in a sentence (*intra-sentential* PA relations). The joint approach using Markov Logic is computationally hard even if it targets only *intra-sentential* PA relations. Therefore, extraction of *inter-sentential* PA relations which are crossing sentence boundaries is intractable. Moreover, our approach finds the most optimized PA assignments in a whole sentence. To keep consistency in a sentence, we delete the sentences which have inter-sentential PA relations.

For extracting features, we exploit the annotation of Kyoto Text Corpus as the POS and the syntactic dependency of bunsetsu phrases. We perform named entity tagging using CaboCha version 0.53. [7] Based on Taira's work, we introduce selectional restriction features from a Japanese Thesaurus, Nihongo Goi Taikei (Ikehara et al., 1997). Learning and inference algorithms for our joint model are provided by Markov thebeast, a Markov Logic engine tailored for NLP applications.

5.2 Results

First, let us show the comparison between the models with/without global constraints in Table 6. ***Global*** is the model with global constraints and ***Local*** is without them. Note that the local and global formulae of deletion are also included in ***Local*** and ***Global***, respectively. Table 6 shows Precision (P), Recall (R), and F1-value (F) of each hidden predicate. We can find that ***Global*** yielded clear improvements for all hidden predicates. These improvements are statistically significant. [8] These results suggest that the three target subtasks (argument identification, phrase deletion, and role labeling) can cooperate with each other. For PA relation extraction (*role*), the recall was mainly improved (the value in bold type).

We perform a simple analysis of hidden predicate removal. For each hidden predicate, a model was trained with that predicate removed and all other predicates retained. For PA relation extraction (*role*), Table 7 shows the model performance with removal of the *isArg* and *delete* predicates.

The removal of *delete* drops the model performance larger than that of *isArg*. While the removal of *isArg* drops the precision and saves the recall, the removal of *delete* is the other way around.

Next, we evaluate the results of PA relation extraction (*role*) by each case, "ga (Nominative)", "wo (Accusative)", and "ni (Dative)" in Table 8. All scores in the table are F1-value. Our ***Global*** model is more advantageous in "Zero-Intra" than ***Local*** model. Especially, in ga-case of Zero-Intra the score jumped from 42.1pt to 54.1pt (+12pt). Again, with global constraints, our global model finds the most probable state in the sentence. It is often difficult to extract Zero-Intra PA relations with only local features because syntactic dependencies between them are weak. Therefore, our global constraints contribute to find correct assignments of PA relations and we got a large improvement in Zero-Intra.

Let us compare our results with the state-of-the-art (Taira et al., 2008; Imamura et al., 2009). In Table 8, we show the best scores in bold types for

[7] http://code.google.com/p/cabocha/

[8] $p < 0.01$, McNemar's test 2-tailed

	Local			*Global*			[Taira, 2008]			[Imamura, 2009]		
	ga	wo	ni	ga	wo	ni	ga	wo	ni	ga	wo	ni
Dep.	85.7	91.2	79.5	**88.8**	91.3	79.7	75.6	88.2	**89.5**	87.0	**93.9**	80.8
Zero-Intra	42.1	7.3	0.0	**54.1**	10.3	0.0	30.2	11.4	**3.7**	50.0	**30.8**	0.0

Table 8: Comparison to the State-of-the-Art (F1)

Predicate Removed	P	R	F
No removal (***Global***)	85.5	77.7	81.4
-isArg	**84.8**	77.9	81.2
-delete	85.3	**76.8**	80.8
-isArg-delete (***Local***)	86.3	72.5	78.8

Table 7: Effect of Hidden Predicate Removal

each case. For ga-case, our model, ***Global***, outperformed the others. On the other hand, for wo-case and ni-case, our results were relatively lower than them. Because our approach deals with the all three cases by one joint model and ga-case is dominant in the data, it extracts more numbers of ga-case than the others. However, ga-case is often the most important for PA relation extraction and sometimes called *indispensable case*. Our method can extract such important information better than previous work. Although our model did not exploit large-scale corpora, our results are competitive to the results of Imamura et al. (2009).

Error Analysis

(this)	(reason)		(Gray Wolf)	(**revival in the US**)
この	ため	,	灰色狼の	米復活を
1	2		3	4

(plan)	(**FWS**)	(in Canada)	(capture)
進める	魚類野生動物局が	カナダで	捕獲した
5	6	7	8

(wild)	(**twelve wolves**)	(transport by air)	
野性の	十二匹を	空輸	.
9	10	11	

(Form this reason, FWS which plans to revive Gray Wolf in the US captured twelve wolves in Canada and transported them by air.)

In the above sentence, we have three predicates (gray boxed) and three arguments (underlined). The relations between predicates and arguments are complex with relative clause and often cause misunderstandings.

About this sentence, our ***Local*** model output:

$$\left\{role(5,6,ga), role(5,4,wo), role(8,6,ga), \underline{role(11,2,ga)}, role(11,10,wo)\right\}$$

It did not output wo-case of "捕獲した (capture)". Because we do not have case-frame dictionary in NTC, our models did not know that "捕獲した" usually requires wo-case (Accusative).

Another error is underlined that ga-case of "空輸 (transport by air)" is identified as "ため (reason)", because "ため" is only a phrase dependent on "空輸".

On the other hand, ***Global*** improved the errors as

$$\left\{role(5,6,ga), role(5,4,wo), role(8,6,ga), \underline{role(8,10,wo)}, \underline{role(11,6,ga)}, role(11,10,wo)\right\}.$$

By global optimization in a sentence, our ***Global*** model overcame the lack of semantic features and successfully identified "十二匹を" as wo-case of "捕獲した". This PA relation is in a relative clause and often hard to identify. Though Abekawa and Okumura (2005) resolved Japanese PA relations in relative clauses by exploiting large-scale corpora, our Markov Logic approach handles this problem by global optimization. Moreover, in global model, $\{delete(1), delete(2), delete(7)\}$ are also output and "この" and "ため" did not become argument candidates. As a result, "魚類野性動物局が" was correctly selected as a ga-case of "空輸".

6 Conclusion

In this paper, we proposed a new Markov Logic approach for Japanese predicate-argument (PA) relation extraction. Our model exploited global constraints between multiple PA relations and introduced phrase deletion. Our global constraints successfully improved the performance of PA relation extraction. In comparison to the state-of-the-art, our approach achieved competitive results with no large-scale data.

As future work, we will introduce utilizing features derived from large-scale data following Imamura's work. Selectional preference features from large-scale corpora are expected to improve the performance for extracting wo-case and ni-case. We will also investigate the state-of-the-art technique of sentence compression in related to our deletion approach. It might be interesting to evaluate our approach in sentence compression tasks. Adding sentence compression might make the PA relation extractor more efficient and allow us to extract *inter-sentential* PA relations, too.

References

Takeshi Abekawa and Manabu Okumura. 2005. Corpus-based analysis of japanese relative clause constructions. In *Proceedings of 2nd International Joint Conference on Natural Language Processing (IJCNLP)*, pages 46–57, Jeju Island, Korea.

Charles J. Fillmore, Charles Wooters, and Collin F. Baker. 2001. Building a large lexical databank which provides deep semantics. In *Proceedings of the Pacific Asian Conference on Language, Information and Computation(PACLIC)*, Hong Kong.

Lise Getoor and Ben Taskar, 2007. *Introduction to Statistical Relational Learning*, chapter 12, pages 339–371. The MIT Press, Cambridge Massachusetts 02142.

Jan Hajič, Massimiliano Ciaramita, Richard Johansson, Daisuke Kawahara, Maria Antònia Martí, Lluís Màrquez, Adam Meyers, Joakim Nivre, Sebastian Padó, Jan Štěpánek, Pavel Straňák, Mihai Surdeanu, Nianwen Xue, and Yi Zhang. 2009. The conll-2009 shared task: Syntactic and semantic dependencies in multiple languages. In *Proceedings of the Thirteenth Conference on Computational Natural Language Learning (CoNLL 2009): Shared Task*, pages 1–18, Boulder, Colorado, June. Association for Computational Linguistics.

Ryu Iida, Kentaro Inui, and Yuji Matsumoto. 2006. Exploiting syntactic patterns as clues in zero-anaphora resolution. In *Proceedings of the 21st International Conference on Computational Linguistics and the 44th annual meeting of the Association for Computational Linguistics*, ACL-44, pages 625–632, Stroudsburg, PA, USA. Association for Computational Linguistics.

Ryu Iida, Mamoru Komachi, Kentaro Inui, and Yuji Matsumoto. 2007. Annotating a japanese text corpus with predicate-argument and coreference relations. In *Proceedings of the Linguistic Annotation Workshop*, LAW '07, pages 132–139, Stroudsburg, PA, USA. Association for Computational Linguistics.

Satoru Ikehara, Masahiro Miyazaki, Satoshi Shirai, Akio Yokoo, Hiromi Nakaiwa, Kentaro Ogura, Yoshifumi Ooyama, and Yoshihiko Hayashi. 1997. *Nihongo Goi Taikei, A Japanese Lexicon*. Iwanami Shoten, Tokyo.

Kenji Imamura, Kuniko Saito, and Tomoko Izumi. 2009. Discriminative approach to predicate-argument structure analysis with zero-anaphora resolution. In *Proceedings of the Joint Conference of the 47th Annual Meeting of the ACL and the 4th International Joint Conference on Natural Language Processing of the AFNLP (ACL-IJCNLP), Conference Short Papers*, pages 85–88, Suntec, Singapore, August. Association for Computational Linguistics.

Daisuke Kawahara, Sadao Kurohashi, and Koichi Hashida. 2002. Construction of japanese relevance-tagged corpus (in japanese). In *the 8th Annual Meeting of the Association for Natural Language Processing*, pages 495–498.

Daphne Koller, 1999. *Probabilistic Relational Models*, pages 3–13. Springer, Berlin/Heidelberg, Germany.

Ivan Meza-Ruiz and Sebastian Riedel. 2009a. Jointly identifying predicates, arguments and senses using markov logic. In *Proceedings of Human Language Technologies: The 2009 Annual Conference of the North American Chapter of the Association for Computational Linguistics*, pages 155–163, Boulder, CO, USA, June. Association for Computational Linguistics.

Ivan Meza-Ruiz and Sebastian Riedel. 2009b. Multilingual semantic role labelling with markov logic. In *Proceedings of the Thirteenth Conference on Computational Natural Language Learning (CoNLL 2009): Shared Task*, pages 85–90, Boulder, Colorado, June. Association for Computational Linguistics.

Martha Palmer, Paul Kingsbury, and Daniel Gildea. 2005. The proposition bank: An annotated corpus of semantic roles. *Computational Linguistics*, 31.

Hoifung Poon and Pedro Domingos. 2007. Joint inference in information extraction. In *Proceedings of the Twenty-Second National Conference on Artificial Intelligence*, pages 913–918, Vancouver, Canada. AAAI Press.

Hoifung Poon and Pedro Domingos. 2008. Joint unsupervised coreference resolution with Markov Logic. In *Proceedings of the 2008 Conference on Empirical Methods in Natural Language Processing*, pages 650–659, Honolulu, Hawaii, October. Association for Computational Linguistics.

Matthew Richardson and Pedro Domingos. 2006. Markov logic networks. *Machine Learning*, 62(1-2):107–136.

Parag Singla and Pedro Domingos. 2006. Entity resolution with markov logic. In *Proceedings of the Sixth International Conference on Data Mining (ICDM)*, pages 572–582, Washington, DC, USA. IEEE Computer Society.

Mihai Surdeanu, Richard Johansson, Adam Meyers, Lluís Màrquez, and Joakim Nivre. 2008. The conll 2008 shared task on joint parsing of syntactic and semantic dependencies. In *CoNLL 2008: Proceedings of the Twelfth Conference on Computational Natural Language Learning*, pages 159–177, Manchester, England, August. Coling 2008 Organizing Committee.

Hirotoshi Taira, Sanae Fujita, and Masaaki Nagata. 2008. A japanese predicate argument structure analysis using decision lists. In *Proceedings of the Conference on Empirical Methods in Natural Language Processing (EMNLP)*, pages 523–532, Honolulu, HI, USA. Association for Computational Linguistics.

Ben Taskar, Abbeel Pieter, and Daphne Koller. 2002. Discriminative probabilistic models for relational data. In *Proceedings of the 18th Annual Conference on Uncertainty in Artificial Intelligence (UAI-02)*, pages 485–492, San Francisco, CA. Morgan Kaufmann.

Kristina Toutanova, Aria Haghighi, and Christopher D. Manning. 2008. A global joint model for semantic role labeling. *Computational Linguistics*, 34:161–191, June.

Yotaro Watanabe, Masayuki Asahara, and Yuji Matsumoto. 2010. A structured model for joint learning of argument roles and predicate senses. In *Proceedings of the ACL 2010 Conference Short Papers*, pages 98–102, Uppsala, Sweden, July. Association for Computational Linguistics.

Word Meaning in Context: A Simple and Effective Vector Model

Stefan Thater and **Hagen Fürstenau** and **Manfred Pinkal**
Department of Computational Linguistics
Saarland University
{stth, hagenf, pinkal}@coli.uni-saarland.de

Abstract

We present a model that represents word meaning in context by vectors which are modified according to the words in the target's syntactic context. Contextualization of a vector is realized by reweighting its components, based on distributional information about the context words. Evaluation on a paraphrase ranking task derived from the SemEval 2007 Lexical Substitution Task shows that our model outperforms all previous models on this task. We show that our model supports a wider range of applications by evaluating it on a word sense disambiguation task. Results show that our model achieves state-of-the-art performance.

1 Introduction

Distributional vector-space models of word meaning have proven helpful for a number of basic natural language processing tasks, such as word sense discrimination (Schütze, 1998) and disambiguation (McCarthy et al., 2004), or modeling of selectional preferences (Erk, 2007), and have been successfully used in a variety of applications like information retrieval (Manning et al., 2008) or question answering (Tellex et al., 2003). Standard distributional models of meaning are attractive because they are simple, have wide coverage, and, in particular, can be acquired using unsupervised methods at virtually no cost. Vector-space models of meaning lend themselves as a basis for determining a soft and gradual concept of semantic similarity (e.g., through the *cosine* measure), which does not rely on a fixed set of dictionary senses with their well-known problems (Kilgarriff, 1997).

The sensitivity of word meaning to the context of use, however, poses a major challenge for distributional semantics. Meaning vectors are based on co-occurrence counts for *words* across all word senses and usages. This means that, for instance, any occurrence of the verb *charge*, such as in the expressions *charge a fee* or *charge a battery*, is assigned the same vector representation, ignoring the difference of word sense. On the other hand, the fact that *charge* and *impose* are near-synonyms in *charge/impose a fee* will not be properly reflected in their respective meaning vectors, since the former, but not the latter, includes (context words reflecting) the "supply electricity" sense of *charge*.

The problem of modeling context-sensitivity in a distributional framework has first been addressed in the seminal paper of Schütze (1998), who uses second-order bag-of-words vectors for the task of word sense discrimination. Recently, the issue has been taken up by several approaches that include some kind of syntactic information, in part under the heading of "distributional compositionality" (Mitchell and Lapata, 2008; Erk and Padó, 2008), in part as "syntax-sensitive contextualization" (Thater et al., 2010). These approaches have in common that the contextual influence on the meaning of a target word w is modeled through vector composition: The meaning of w in context c is represented by a vector obtained by combining the vectors of w and c using some operation such as component-wise multiplication or addition.

The results published during the last couple of years show a considerable increase of performance, but at the price of an increasing complexity and lack of intuitive transparency of the models. In this paper, we will demonstrate that one can keep the model simple and at the same time outperform the state of the art. We achieve this as follows: First, we take a different, more general view on the basic operation of contextualization. Like the aforementioned approaches, we model contextualization as modification of the target vector, but we do not restrict this operation to variants of vector composition, but consider a broader range of operations, which *re-weight* individual vector components. Second, we identify the distributional similarity score between the words defining the vector components on the one hand, and the actual context words in a given syntactic position on the other hand as the most effective basis for this re-weighting.

We evaluate our method on two different tasks: *paraphrase ranking* and *word sense disambiguation*. The paraphrase ranking task has been used in several approaches and provides benchmarks for our system, and the controlled conditions of the experiment make it easy to assess the influence of different design decisions on the performance. In practical terms, we will use a paraphrase ranking task derived from the SemEval 2007 Lexical Substitution Task (McCarthy and Navigli, 2007). We exceed the state of the art by almost 6% in terms of generalized average precision.

The application to word sense disambiguation (WSD) demonstrates that our model is more generally applicable. We phrase the WSD task as a paraphrase ranking task: Roughly speaking, finding the contextually appropriate word sense amounts to identifying the WordNet synset containing the best paraphrase candidate for the target. We evaluate our system on the SemEval 2007 coarse-grained unsupervised WSD task (Navigli et al., 2007). Our results are competitive to the results reported in the literature.

Plan of the paper. We will first review related work in Section 2, before we present our model in Section 3. We evaluate our model's performance on a paraphrase ranking task in Section 4 and on the task of word sense disambiguation in Section 5. Section 6 concludes.

2 Related work

Inspired by earlier work of Kintsch (2001), who proposes a network algorithm to extract context-specific vector representations for words in context, Mitchell and Lapata (2008) investigate the systematic combination of distributional representations of word meaning along syntactic structure. They propose to represent the meaning of a complex expression that consists of two syntactically related words w and w' by a vector obtained by combining the word vectors of w and w', and find that component-wise multiplication performs best for the task under consideration. They consider their proposal primarily under the aspect of compositionality, but it can also be taken to be a method to contextualize a target word through its dependents.

Erk and Padó (2008) propose structured vector representations, where each word is characterized by a standard co-occurrence vector, plus separate vector representations for the (inverse) selectional preferences for subject, object, and other syntactic relations. Contextualization is modeled by combining, e.g., the basic vector of the target verb with the selectional preferences of subject and object.

Thater et al. (2010) propose a similar approach, where word meaning is modeled as a second-order vector obtained by summing over first-order vectors representing the inverse selectional preferences of a word's syntactic arguments. Contextualization is modeled as above in terms of vector composition. Among the aforementioned approaches, their proposal performs best, but at the cost of a rather complex and unintuitive concept of second-order co-occurrence vectors.

Other approaches achieve good results without using vector composition. Dinu and Lapata (2010) represent word meaning in context by using a latent variable model, where context-dependence is modeled by conditioning the latent variable on the context in which a word occurs. Similar proposals have been made by Reisinger and Mooney (2010a) and Li et al. (2010).

A different approach has been taken by Erk and Padó (2010) and Reisinger and Mooney (2010b). Instead of "refining" vector representations ranging over all words in a corpus by means of vector composition, they start out from "token" vectors for individual instances of words in context, and then group these token vectors into different sense-specific clusters.

3 The model

We propose a model of word meaning that allows the computation of vector representations for *individual uses* of words, characterizing the specific meaning of a word in its sentential context. For instance, the vector of the verb *charge* in the expression *charge a tax* should reflect its monetary sense, while its vector in the expression *charge a battery* should be representative of its "supply electricity" sense.

We derive a *contextualized* vector from the basic meaning vector of a target word by *reweighting* its components on the basis of the context of the occurrence, where we take the context to be made

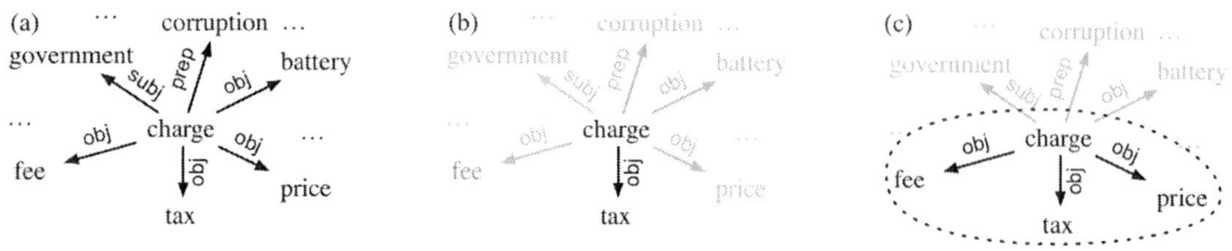

Figure 1: Graphical representation for a basic vector for *charge* (a), and two contextualized vectors for *charge* in context *charge a tax*, obtained by (b) a strict and (c) our more sophisticated contextualization method based on semantic similarity.

up of the direct syntactic dependents of the target (and its direct inverse dependents). The dimensions of both basic and contextualized vectors represent co-occurring words in specific syntactic relations. Fig. 1a shows the basic vector for *charge* as an example, where we use arrows to indicate the internal structure of the vector; the weights of the vector components are omitted for simplicity.

The operation of contextualization reinforces those dimensions of the basic vector that are licensed by the context of the specific instance under consideration. The easiest way of adapting the vector of a word to its context of use is to retain only those dimensions corresponding to its syntactic neighbors, which results in an extremely sparse vector with zero values for most of its dimensions. For instance, contextualizing the vector for *charge* in *charge a tax* (Fig. 1b) would zero out all (r,w) components with $r \neq$ OBJ or $w \neq tax$, retaining only one non-zero dimension (the one for *tax*).

As we will see in Section 4, this simple approach is surprisingly successful. However, we achieve substantially better results by leveraging *semantic similarity information* about the context words. Instead of considering only the dimensions of the context words themselves, we retain dimensions of those words that are distributionally similar to the context words, weighted by their similarity score. The vector for *charge* in *charge a tax* will then contain additional non-zero dimensions for all words similar to *tax* (Fig. 1c). In a way, similarity-based contextualization is a formalization of the intuitive concept of "the meaning of w in the context of a word *like* w'."

Formal description. We assume a set W of words and a set R of syntactic relations. The latter includes dependency relation labels such as SUBJ or OBJ for *subject* and *object*, as well as the corresponding inverse relations such as SUBJ^{-1}. We represent the meaning of any word $w \in W$ by a vector in the vector space V spanned by the set of basis vectors $\{\mathbf{e}_{(r,w')} \mid r \in R, w' \in W\}$. Such a vector records the association strength between w and any context word w' occurring in relation r. Specifically, we associate a word $w \in W$ with a vector $\mathbf{v}(w) \in V$ by setting

$$\mathbf{v}(w) := \sum_{r \in R, w' \in W} f(w,r,w') \cdot \mathbf{e}_{(r,w')}$$

where f is a function that assigns a weight to the dependency triple (w,r,w'). In the simplest case, this could be the frequency of w occurring together with w' in relation r in a corpus of dependency trees. In the experiments reported below, we use *pointwise mutual information* (Church and Hanks, 1990) instead, as it proved superior to raw frequency counts:

$$PMI(w,r,w') = \log \frac{p(w,w' \mid r)}{p(w,\cdot \mid r)p(\cdot,w' \mid r)}$$

Here the dots stand for marginalization over the relevant variables.

Given an occurrence of a word w in the context of another word w_c, related by the syntactic relation r_c, we now define a contextualized version of $\mathbf{v}(w)$ by *reweighting* the vector components. We set

$$\mathbf{v}_{r_c,w_c}(w) := \sum_{r \in R, w' \in W} \alpha_{r_c,w_c,r,w'} \cdot f(w,r,w') \cdot \mathbf{e}_{(r,w')}$$

Here, the weights $\alpha_{r_c,w_c,r,w'}$ quantify the degree to which a vector dimension (r,w') is compatible with the observed context (r_c,w_c). We consider three alternative definitions of these weights, corresponding to the three cases shown in Figure 1:

No contextualization: $\alpha_{r_c,w_c,r,w'} := 1$

In this case the definition of $\mathbf{v}_{r_c,w_c}(w)$ coincides with that of $\mathbf{v}(w)$.

Strict contextualization:

$$\alpha_{r_c,w_c,r,w'} := \delta_{r_c,r}\delta_{w_c,w'} = \begin{cases} 1 & \text{if } r_c = r \text{ and } w_c = w' \\ 0 & \text{else} \end{cases}$$

Here, we only retain the one dimension (r_c, w_c) that is licensed by the context and set all other dimensions to 0.

Similarity-based contextualization:

$$\alpha_{r_c,w_c,r,w'} := \delta_{r_c,r} \cdot \text{sim}(w_c, w') = \begin{cases} \text{sim}(w_c, w') & \text{if } r_c = r \\ 0 & \text{else} \end{cases}$$

Here, we generalize over the surface context and license all words w' that are semantically similar to the context word w_c.

While any measure of semantic similarity can be employed, in the experiments reported below we compute the similarity between w_c and w' as the cosine of the angle between their basic vector representations $\mathbf{v}(w_c)$ and $\mathbf{v}(w')$.

Of course, we want to take into account more than a single context word for a given occurrence of w. Given context words $w_1, \ldots, w_n$ and corresponding syntactic relations $r_1, \ldots, r_n$, we obtain a contextualized vector of w by superimposing the vectors $\mathbf{v}_{r_i,w_i}$ $(1 \leq i \leq n)$ through vector addition:

$$\mathbf{v}_{r_1,w_1,\ldots,r_n,w_n}(w) := \sum_{i=1}^{n} \mathbf{v}_{r_i,w_i}(w)$$

The resulting vector $\mathbf{v}_{r_1,w_1,\ldots,r_n,w_n}(w)$ is our completely contextualized representation for the word w that contains information about all context words.

4 Ranking Paraphrases

In this section, we evaluate to what extent our model supports the choice of contextually appropriate paraphrases for different uses of a target word. We follow previous work (Thater et al., 2010; Erk and Padó, 2010; Dinu and Lapata, 2010) and consider the following task: We are given a target word w in a sentential context and a set of reference words $w_1, \ldots, w_k$, where each w_i is a lexical paraphrase of w in one of w's senses. The task is to rank the candidate words w_i according to their appropriateness as paraphrases of *w in the given context*. Ideally, the model will rank, for instance, *levy* higher than *recharge* as a paraphrase of *charge* in *charge a fee*, and lower in *charge the battery*.

4.1 Experimental Set-up

Gold standard. We derive our gold standard from the SemEval 2007 lexical substitution task dataset (McCarthy and Navigli, 2007). The original dataset contains 10 instances for each of 201 target words (nouns, verbs, adjectives and adverbs) in different sentential contexts. For each instance, five subjects were asked to name appropriate paraphrases. Table 1 shows an example of three instances of *charge* together with their gold standard paraphrases. Each paraphrase comes with a weight, which corresponds to the number of times it was chosen by the different subjects.

The original task addresses two subtasks: identifying paraphrase candidates and ranking them according to the context. Here, we restrict ourselves to the second subtask. Following previous work, we pool all annotated gold-standard paraphrases of a target word w across all contexts into a set of *paraphrase candidates* for w, which our model is supposed to rank with respect to contextual appropriateness for the individual instances of w. We do not extract multi-word expressions, for which our model cannot compute vector representations, and obtain a dataset consisting of 1986 instances for 197 different words. In our derived dataset, each word type has an average of 17 paraphrases, 3.5 of which are correct (on average) for individual instances of the word.

Vector space. We draw on dependency trees obtained by parsing the English Gigaword corpus (LDC2003T05) to build our vector space model. The corpus consists of news from several newswire services, and contains over four million documents. We used the Stanford parser (de Marneffe et al., 2006) to parse the corpus. The resulting dependency trees were modified in a post-processing step by folding prepositions into edge labels to make the relation between a head word and the head noun of a prepositional phrase explicit. Furthermore, we collapsed particle verb constructions into single nodes. To facilitate processing and reduce noise, we excluded all dependency triples that occurred less than 3 times or had a PMI score below 0, which resulted in a corpus of about 888 million dependency triples accounting for 28 million triple types.

To further reduce computational costs, we set higher frequency and PMI thresholds for the computation of the similarity scores used in the contextualization of vectors: in the experiments reported

Sentence	Substitution candidates
Annual fees are *charged* on a pro-rata basis [...]	levy 2; require 1; impose 1; demand 1
Plug in you h 10 in the usb outlet and it will *charge* without the plug in adaptor.	recharge 2; supply electricity 1; charge up 1
Pauline Gilmore, 32, was *charged* with possessing a blast bomb.	indict 3; accuse of 2; accuse 1

Table 1: Three examples from the lexical substitution task data set for the target word *charge*.

below, we consider only (vectors based on) dependency triples that occur at least 5 times and have a PMI score of at least 2. Note that these thresholds are used only to speed up processing. The effect on the overall performance is minimal: an experiment on a randomly chosen 10% subset of the test set shows that we obtain almost identical scores, but runtime is reduced by a factor of more than 35.

Scoring. We rank the paraphrase candidates for a target word in context by the similarity of their basic vectors to the contextualized vector of the target. Contextualizing both the target and the paraphrase candidate has been observed to reduce performance (Thater et al., 2010; Dinu and Lapata, 2010). Similarity is measured in terms of the dot product of the vectors. In cases where the Stanford parser produced dependency trees that are inconsistent with the information about the target word in the gold standard, or where the contextualized vector is zero, we use the basic vector of the target as a fallback. This fallback method applies to 7% of all instances in the dataset.

Evaluation method. Following previous work (Thater et al., 2010; Erk and Padó, 2010), we use *Generalized Average Precision* (Kishida, 2005) to compare the ranking predicted by our model with the gold standard. GAP takes values between 1.0 and 0.0, where a value of 1.0 indicates that all correct items are ranked before all incorrect ones, and that higher-weighted items are ranked before lower-weighted ones. Statistical significance of differences in performance are computed by approximate randomization (Chinchor et al., 1993).

4.2 Results

Table 2 shows results for three versions of our model, corresponding to the three definitions of the weighting factors that were detailed in Section 3:

(a) No contextualization

POS	Random	No context	Strict	Sim.-based
Verb	27.4	38.4	41.6	48.8
Noun	30.1	45.2	47.3	52.9
Adj	28.4	42.2	45.8	51.1
Adv	36.4	51.6	50.6	55.3
All	30.0	43.7	46.0	51.7

Table 2: Results for our model using different contextualization methods, compared to a random baseline.

(b) Strict contextualization

(c) Similarity-based contextualization

In addition, we show the performance of a baseline that ranks paraphrase candidates randomly.

We observe that similarity-based contextualization is very effective, improving performance by 8% compared to the "no context" variant, and still by almost 6% compared to the strict variant that uses surface context only. The differences are statistically significant ($p < 0.001$).

Figure 2 provides a different view on system performance. It shows how often the k first candidates in the ranking contain at least one gold standard paraphrase. In particular, we can observe that similarity-based contextualization predicts a good top-ranked candidate in 55% of the cases; the top three contain a correct paraphrases in more than 80% of the cases.

Table 3 compares our model to previous models that have been evaluated using the Lexical Substitution Task (LST) dataset. Our model outperforms all previously proposed methods. Although all models have been evaluated on test-sets derived from the LST dataset in essentially the same way, the datasets differ slightly due to technical details, so strictly speaking the results cannot be compared directly. However, since all authors report similar

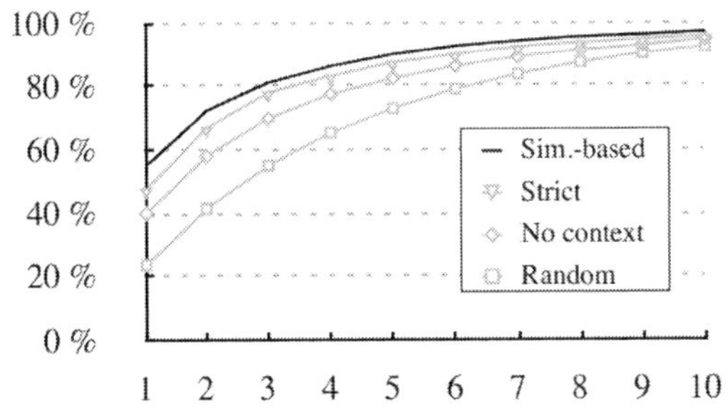

Figure 2: The figure shows how often the k first candidates in the ranking contain at least one gold standard paraphrase (for $k \leq 10$).

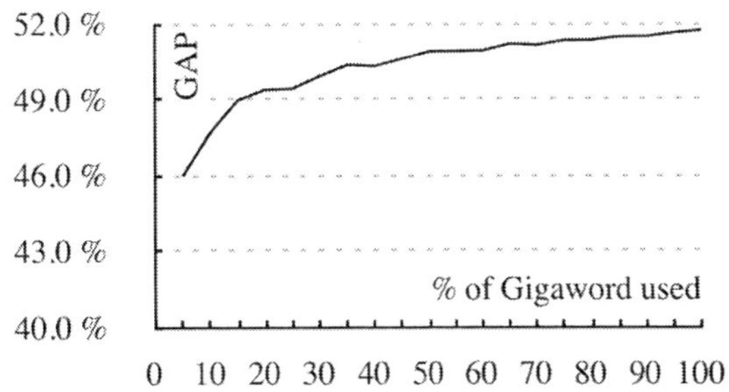

Figure 3: Learning curve: GAP with varying corpus size.

Model	GAP	Random
Erk and Padó (2008)	27.4†	N/A
Erk and Padó (2010)	38.6‡	28.5
Dinu and Lapata (2010)	42.9	30.3
Thater et al. (2010)	46.0	30.0
Our model	51.7	30.0

† Cited from Erk and Padó (2010). The result refers to a small subset of the Lexical Substitution Task dataset.

‡ Evaluated on nouns, verbs, and adjectives (not adv.).

Table 3: Comparison to previous work

scores for the random baselines, we assume that the complexity of the subsets used in previous work is more or less comparable.

Learning curve. The corpus used in our study is much larger than the British National Corpus (BNC) that has been used, for instance, in Erk and Padó's (2008; 2010) models. To assess the contribution of the corpus size to the performance of our model, we randomized the order of dependency trees in the parsed Gigaword corpus and constructed vector space models using increasing subsets of the complete corpus with a step size of 5%. The resulting learning curve is shown in Figure 3. We see that our model performs well even on small subsets of Gigaword. When we use only 5% of the dependency trees, which is roughly two third of the size of BNC, we already obtain a GAP score of 46.0%, which is 5.7% less than our result with full Gigaword, but 7.4% more than the best reported BNC-based model.

Syntactic information. Finally, we investigated the impact of syntactic information by comparing our model against two variants: (i) a "bag of words" variant that does not use syntactic information at all and (ii) a "syntactically filtered" variant similar to Padó and Lapata (2007) that uses syntactic information but does not explicitly represent syntactic role information in the vector representations. Variant (i) is based on co-occurrence statistics on pairs (w, w') of content words within a five-word window; for variant (ii) we consider all pairs (w, w') such that w and w' are linked by some syntactic relation. Technically, we represent these pairs as dependency triples involving some arbitrary fixed syntactic role label.

We observe that syntactic information contributes to the success of our approach both by selecting relevant context words and by characterizing their syntactic relations: In terms of GAP, the "bag of words" variant achieves 48.7%, the "syntactically filtered" variant 50.9%, and our full model 51.7%. The relatively small difference between the two syntactic variants, while maybe surprising at first sight, is explained by the fact that in most cases the syntactic role of a dependency triple is predictable from the words it connects: For more than 88% of all dependency triples in Gigaword, the syntactic role is actually the most frequent one for the respective pair of words. Yet, the difference between the two variants is statistically significant ($p < 0.05$): The model supports correct decisions in those cases where syntactic role information matters.

5 Word Sense Disambiguation

In a second experiment, we applied our model to the task of word-sense disambiguation. For an individual instance of a word, we predict the correct WordNet sense (Fellbaum, 1998) of the target based on its immediate syntactic context, without relying on any manually annotated training data. Our system is *knowledge-based*, according to the classification of WSD approaches proposed in McCarthy

(2009) and Navigli (2009). It is a *knowledge-lean* system, in contrast to many other systems that exploit external resources, since it uses only a small subset of the structural information provided by WordNet – just as much as is required to adapt our contextualization model to the WSD task.

The state of the art in knowledge-based WSD systems not trained on annotated data is defined by the models of Navigli and Velardi (2005), Ponzetto and Navigli (2010) and Li et al. (2010). The former two rely on a rich inventory of additional knowledge resources. Li et al. (2010) restricts itself to WordNet information in a similar way as our approach, and therefore is our natural benchmark.

5.1 Method

We frame the task of choosing the right WordNet sense as a paraphrase ranking task like the one considered in Section 4, with all possible synonyms of the target word constituting the set of (lexical) paraphrase candidates. The basic idea for predicting a sense of the target word is to choose the synset that contains the most similar paraphrase. As the WordNet synsets of the target word are often singletons, just containing the target itself, we additionally include all words from direct hypernym, hyponym, and similar synsets (WordNet relation "similar to"). We ignore multiword expressions since our model does not provide vector representations for them.

While we generally found the richer collection of candidates to improve system performance, the inclusion of hypernyms can have a negative effect on sense discrimination, since different word senses frequently share the same hypernym. To counter this effect, we consider the average similarity scores of the best two paraphrase candidates of each sense rather than relying on the most similar candidate alone. More technically speaking, we collect all relevant sense paraphrases $c_{i,1}, \ldots, c_{i,k_i}$ for each sense s_i of the target word. We compare the contextualized vector of the target word to the basic meaning representations of these candidate words, obtaining a similarity score for each of them. The score of the sense s_i is then defined as the average of the scores of the two top-scoring candidate words, and the sense with the highest such score is predicted. Our model fails to predict a sense for an ambiguous target if the candidate set of any sense is empty, which can happen in cases where all applicable sense paraphrases are multiword expressions.

We will experiment with two instantiations of this model: the basic version described above, and a version that additionally integrates information about prior sense distributions by multiplying the score of each synset with its prior probability, and falls back to the most frequent sense in cases where the basic model fails to make a prediction. Prior probabilities are estimated by using sense frequency information from WordNet.

5.2 Experimental setup

Gold standard. We evaluate our model on the SemEval 2007 Coarse-grained English All-words Task (Navigli et al., 2007) test set. The test set consists of 5,377 words of running text from five documents from different genres. All open-class words in this corpus are annotated with coarse-grained sense labels, which are defined as clusters of WordNet senses and are obtained by mapping WordNet 2.1 senses to the Oxford Dictionary of English (Soanes and Stevenson, 2003). On a subset of 710 instances an inter-annotator agreement of 93.80% was reported, which can be considered the upper bound for any WSD system on the data set.

Predicting coarse-grained senses. The method described in Section 5.1 predicts (fine-grained) WordNet senses. It can be straightforwardly extended to the coarse-grained WSD task by picking the sense cluster containing the top-ranked synset. We achieved slightly better results by applying a different method: We normalize the scores of all synsets so that they sum up to 1, which allows us to interpret them as a probability distribution. We then compute probabilities for each sense cluster by aggregating over its constituent synsets, and predict the most probable one (which need not be the one containing the most probable synset).

Baselines. We compare our model against a random baseline and the most frequent sense (MFS) baseline that always predicts the sense with the highest sense frequency according to WordNet.

5.3 Results

Table 4 summarizes results on the test set in terms of precision, and compares them to two baselines and the state-of-the-art system of Li et al. (2010). Except in the case of our basic system (-MFS) without prior information, which cannot use information about most frequent senses as fallback and covers only 74.6% of the test cases, coverage is 100% and therefore precision coincides with recall.

Model	+MFS	-MFS
Random	52.4	52.4
Most frequent sense (MFS)	78.9	—
Li et al. (2010)	81.3‡	78.8‡
Our Model	80.9	78.7†
Combined system	82.2	78.9

† Covers 74.6% of the dataset.

‡ Results reported here are higher than the results reported by Li et al. (2010). Our results are based on the scoring script provided by the organizers of the SemEval 2007 shared task. Differences are due to details such as sensitivity to capitalization when system predictions are compared with the gold standard.

Table 4: Precision of our model on the WSD task, with (+MFS) and without (-MFS) prior knowledge about sense distributions, compared to the state-of-the-art system by Li et al.

We can see that our model's performance is competitive with the state of the art: In both settings our model outperforms the two baselines, and reaches the performance level of the benchmark system of Li et al. (2010).

Interestingly, the strengths of our and Li el al.'s systems are complementary. For example, in the sentence "The *diners* at my table simply lit more Gauloises [...]," our model correctly predicts the sense "person eating a meal" of the target *diners*, based on the leading sense paraphrase *eater*. The system by Li et al. (2010), on the other hand, predicts the sense "passenger car where food is served", which fits the general topic similarly well, but is highly implausible in the given syntactic context. However, in the sentence "The program text, or source, was converted into machine instructions using a special program called a *compiler*," the system by Li et al. (2010) is able to leverage topical clues to correctly predict the software sense of *compiler*, whereas our system ranks the sense paraphrase *author* over *program* and thus incorrectly predicts the sense "person who compiles encyclopedias."

Given this complementary nature of the two systems, we tried to combine them in a straightforward way, by averaging their predicted probability distributions (defaulting to Li et al. for instances not covered by our model). Table 4 shows that the combined system outperforms both individual systems both with and without MFS information. In the former case (with MFS), the improvement of 0.9% is statistically significant ($p < 0.01$) according to McNemar's test.

6 Conclusions and Future Work

We have presented a technically simple and intuitively transparent vector space model of word meaning in context. Contextualization of a vector is realized by reweighting its components, using semantic similarity information about the words occurring in the target's local syntactic context.

We evaluated our method on a paraphrase ranking task derived from the SemEval 2007 Lexical Substitution Task dataset and showed that it substantially outperforms all previous approaches, exceeding the state of the art by almost 6% in terms of generalized average precision. We showed that our model supports a wider range of application by evaluating it on a word sense disambiguation task. The model reaches the performance level of the state-of-the-art benchmark system of Li et al. (2010). The combination of the two systems performs significantly better than either system used in isolation, and outperforms the most-frequent-sense baseline by over 3%.

The contextualization operation takes only the *words* in the targets *local* syntactic context into account. A natural direction for future research is to generalize the contextualization operation so that the context words themselves can be contextualized in a recursive fashion and all words in the target's complete syntactic environment can contribute information.

Our present model incorporates syntactic relations, although semantic information should ideally be expressed in terms of underlying semantic roles. We have seen that the use of syntactically structured vector representations leads to a relatively small, but statistically significant increase in performance, compared to variants of our model that do not represent rich syntactic information. We expect that further progress can be made by integrating semantic role information.

Acknowledgments. We would like to thank Georgiana Dinu and Linlin Li for their support and helpful comments. This work was supported by the Cluster of Excellence "Multimodal Computing and Interaction", funded by the German Excellence Initiative, and the project SALSA, funded by DFG (German Science Foundation).

References

Nancy Chinchor, David D. Lewis, and Lynette Hirschmant. 1993. Evaluating message understanding systems: An analysis of the third message understanding conference (MUC-3). *Computational Linguistics*, 19(3):409–449.

Kenneth W. Church and Patrick Hanks. 1990. Word association, mutual information and lexicography. *Computational Linguistics*, 16(1):22–29.

Marie-Catherine de Marneffe, Bill MacCartney, and Christopher D. Manning. 2006. Generating typed dependency parses from phrase structure parses. In *Proceedings of the fifth international conference on Language Resources and Evaluation (LREC 2006)*, Genoa, Italy.

Georgiana Dinu and Mirella Lapata. 2010. Measuring distributional similarity in context. In *Proceedings of the 2010 Conference on Empirical Methods in Natural Language Processing*, Cambridge, MA.

Katrin Erk and Sebastian Padó. 2008. A structured vector space model for word meaning in context. In *Proceedings of the 2008 Conference on Empirical Methods in Natural Language Processing*, Honolulu, HI, USA.

Katrin Erk and Sebastian Padó. 2010. Exemplar-based models for word meaning in context. In *Proceedings of the ACL 2010 Conference Short Papers*, Uppsala, Sweden.

Katrin Erk. 2007. A simple, similarity-based model for selectional preferences. In *Proceedings of the 45th Annual Meeting of the Association of Computational Linguistics*, Prague, Czech Republic.

Christiane Fellbaum, editor. 1998. *Wordnet: An Electronic Lexical Database*. Bradford Book.

Adam Kilgarriff. 1997. I don't believe in word senses. *Computers and Humanities*, 31(2):91–113.

Walter Kintsch. 2001. Predication. *Cognitive Science*, 25:173–202.

Kazuaki Kishida. 2005. Property of average precision and its generalization: An examination of evaluation indicator for information retrieval experiments. *NII Technical Report*.

Linlin Li, Benjamin Roth, and Caroline Sporleder. 2010. Topic models for word sense disambiguation and token-based idiom detection. In *Proceedings of the 48th Annual Meeting of the Association for Computational Linguistics*, Uppsala, Sweden.

Christopher D. Manning, Prabhakar Raghavan, and Hinrich Schütze. 2008. *Introduction to Information Retrieval*. Cambridge University Press.

Diana McCarthy and Roberto Navigli. 2007. SemEval-2007 Task 10: English Lexical Substitution Task. In *Proceedings of SemEval*, Prague, Czech Republic.

Diana McCarthy, Rob Koeling, Julie Weeds, and John Carroll. 2004. Finding predominant word senses in untagged text. In *Proceedings of the 42nd Meeting of the Association for Computational Linguistics (ACL'04)*, Barcelona, Spain.

Diana McCarthy. 2009. Word sense disambiguation: An overview. *Language and Linguistics Compass*, 3(2):537–558.

Jeff Mitchell and Mirella Lapata. 2008. Vector-based models of semantic composition. In *Proceedings of ACL-08: HLT*, Columbus, OH, USA.

Roberto Navigli and Paola Velardi. 2005. Structural semantic interconnections: a knowledge-based approach to word sense disambiguation. *IEEE Transactions on Pattern Analysis and Machine Intelligence*, 27(7):1075–1088.

Roberto Navigli, Kenneth C. Litkowski, and Orin Hargraves. 2007. Semeval-2007 task 07: Coarse-grained English all-words task. In *Proceedings of the Fourth International Workshop on Semantic Evaluations (SemEval-2007)*, Prague, Czech Republic.

Roberto Navigli. 2009. Word Sense Disambiguation: a survey. *ACM Computing Surveys*, 41(2):1–69.

Sebastian Padó and Mirella Lapata. 2007. Dependency-based construction of semantic space models. *Computational Linguistics*, 33(2):161–199.

Simone Paolo Ponzetto and Roberto Navigli. 2010. Knowledge-rich word sense disambiguation rivaling supervised systems. In *Proceedings of the 48th Annual Meeting of the Association for Computational Linguistics*, Uppsala, Sweden.

Joseph Reisinger and Raymond Mooney. 2010a. A mixture model with sharing for lexical semantics. In *Proceedings of the 2010 Conference on Empirical Methods in Natural Language Processing*, Cambridge, MA.

Joseph Reisinger and Raymond J. Mooney. 2010b. Multi-prototype vector-space models of word meaning. In *Human Language Technologies: The 2010 Annual Conference of the North American Chapter of the Association for Computational Linguistics*, Los Angeles, California.

Hinrich Schütze. 1998. Automatic word sense discrimination. *Computational Linguistics*, 24(1):97–124.

Catherine Soanes and Angus Stevenson, editors. 2003. *Oxford Dictionary of English*. Oxford University Press.

Stefanie Tellex, Boris Katz, Jimmy Lin, Aaron Fernandes, and Gregory Marton. 2003. Quantitative evaluation of passage retrieval algorithms for question answering. In *Proceedings of the 26th Annual International ACM SIGIR Conference on Research and Development in Information Retrieval (SIGIR)*.

Stefan Thater, Hagen Fürstenau, and Manfred Pinkal. 2010. Contextualizing semantic representations using syntactically enriched vector models. In *Proceedings of the 48th Annual Meeting of the Association for Computational Linguistics*, Uppsala, Sweden.

Automatic Analysis of Semantic Coherence in Academic Abstracts Written in Portuguese

Vinícius Mourão Alves de Souza
State University of Maringá
Maringá, PR, Brazil, 87020-900
vsouza@din.uem.br

Valéria Delisandra Feltrim
State University of Maringá
Maringá, PR, Brazil, 87020-900
valeria.feltrim@din.uem.br

Abstract

SciPo is a system whose ultimate goal is to support novice writers in producing academic texts in Brazilian Portuguese through presentation of critiques and suggestions. Currently, it focuses on the rhetorical structure of texts, being capable of automatically detecting and criticizing the rhetorical structure of Abstract sections. We describe a system that enhances SciPo's functionality by evaluating aspects of semantic coherence in academic abstracts. This system identifies features of sentences based on semantic similarity measures and rhetorical structure. Different machine learning algorithms were trained and evaluated with these features, resulting in three classifiers capable of detecting specific coherence issues on sentences with regard to a rhetorical structure model for abstracts. Results indicate that the system yields higher performance than the baseline for all classifiers.

1 Introduction

This research has been motivated by a need for advanced discourse analysis capabilities for writing tools such as SciPo (short for Scientific Portuguese). SciPo (Feltrim et al., 2006) is a system whose ultimate goal is to support novice writers in producing academic texts in Brazilian Portuguese. Currently, it focuses on Computer Science academic texts and supports the writing of abstracts and introductions. Its functionalities are based on the use of structure models — in terms of schematic structure, rhetorical strategies and lexical patterns — similar to the ones proposed by Swales (1990) and Weissberg and Buker (1990), and authentic examples organized as case bases. Although SciPo provides feedback with regard to the text rhetorical structure in the form of critiques and suggestions, it does not provide considerations about the text semantics, such as aspects related to its coherence, which is a fundamental characteristic for text legibility and interpretability.

We understand coherence as what makes a group of words or sentences semantically meaningful. We assume that coherence refers to the establishment of a logical sense among different sentences of a text. Thus, it is a principle of interpretability related to the communicational situation and to the capability of the reader in calculating the meaning of the text. Therefore, it is bounded to the text, but it does not depend only on the text (van Dijk, 1981).

Aiming at complementing SciPo's functionalities, we have developed classifiers for the automatic detection of specific semantic relations in academic texts in Portuguese, then it can be used by SciPo for providing feedback referring to text coherence. Based on textual features that can be readily read off the text, the classifiers present indications related to semantic aspects that contribute to a high level of coherence.

We believe that our work brings innovative contributions due to the nature of the analyzed corpus, especially by language and rhetorical structure of the texts, and the kind of application to which we intend to apply coherence analysis. As mentioned by Burstein et al. (2010), there is a small body of work that has investigated the problem of identifying coherence in student essays. None of the work cited by Burstein et al. (2010) is focused on academic writing, but on essays written by English writers that may be native/non-native and have different writing skills. This kind of text tends to present more explicit coherence problems than the ones that may occur on a academic writing corpus, as the one used in this work. Academic texts are usually written by students who have domain, at a certain level, on the language (in our case, Portuguese) and on the genre, which can make structure and coherence problems subtle. The more subtle a problem is, more difficult it is to be automatic treated.

Besides the corpus differences, most of systems presented in the literature that realize coherence analysis are in the context of Automatic Essay Scoring (Lapata and Barzilay, 2005), which is also different from our context of work. We cite three scoring systems which considers aspects of coherence when grading essays: *Criterion* (Burstein et al., 2003; Higgins et al., 2004; Burstein et al., 2010), *Intelligent Essay Assessor* (Landauer et al., 2003), and *Intellimetric* (Elliot, 2003). Unlike these systems, SciPo is a writing support system, which means that we are not interested in to ascribe a score to it, but we want the system to be able to detect a possible structure and coherence issues and give some comprehensible feedback to the writer. The three cited systems employ the Latent Semantic Analysis (Landauer et al., 1998) to extract text features related to coherence aspects, and the results reported by them have motivated their use in our work .

2 Corpus and Annotation

In order to analyze coherence issues that may occur in academic texts written in Portuguese by undergraduate students, we have collected 385 abstracts of monographs written as part of the requirements for achieving a BS degree in Computer Science. The corpus annotation was processed in two distinctive parts: (i) rhetorical structure annotation and (ii) coherence annotation, as following described.

2.1 Rhetorical Structure Annotation and Analysis

Each abstract has the correspondent work's title attached to it. Also, each sentence was previously delimitated with appropriate beginning/ending tags. Then, we used AZPort (Feltrim et al., 2006) to label each sentence accordingly to its rhetorical status (Teufel and Moens, 2002). AZPort is a Naive Bayesian classifier that renders each input sentence a set of six possible categories, namely Background, Gap, Purpose, Methodology, Result, and Conclusion. These categories correspond to the components that make up the rhetorical structure model proposed by Feltrim et al. (2006) to academic abstracts.

We manually revised the resulting annotated corpus and corrected possible mistakes made by AZPort. Thus, the noise from the automatic annotation of rhetorical structure does not interfere in the coherence annotation. A total of 2,293 sentences were automatically annotated and manually revised. The distribution of categories in the annotated corpus is presented in Table 1.

Categories	Sentence (N)	Distribution(%)
Background	808	35.23
Gap	215	09.38
Purpose	426	18.58
Methodology	273	11.90
Result	451	19.67
Conclusion	120	05.24
Total	2,293	100

Table 1: Rhetorical categories distribution.

It can be observed in Table 1 that Background is the most frequent category (34.78% of all sentences). The prevalence of category can be explained by the corpus nature. When writing monographs abstracts, writers usually are not limited to a fixed maximum of words, thus they tend to write more sentences contextualizing the work. This is not true for papers abstracts, which tend to be limited in length and, therefore, leading writers to focus on Purpose and Result (Feltrim et al., 2003). In our corpus, Purpose and Result are also frequent categories, accounting for 19.63% and 19.41% of all sentences, respectively. Methodology, Gap and Conclusion categories were less frequent.

2.2 Coherence Annotation and Analysis

Following Higgins et al. (2004), we have tried to identify and annotate semantic relations among specific rhetorical categories, but taking into consideration that we are dealing with abstract sections of academic texts and that we want to use the resulting information as a resource to formulate useful feedback to SciPo users. We came up with an adaptation of the four dimensions proposed by Higgins et al. (2004), resulting in four kinds of relations that we also called dimensions: (i) Dimension Title, (ii) Dimension Purpose, (iii) Dimension Gap-Background, and (iv) Dimension Linearity-Break. Each dimension is described as follows.

2.2.1 Dimension Title

We assume that the title of an academic text should reveal the main topics treated in it. We also assume that the abstract of an academic text should inform the reader about these topics, even though in a summarized form. The lack of relationship between the abstract sentences and the title may be an evidence of two possible situations: (i) the title is inappropriate for the abstract or (ii) the abstract has coherence problems.

In order to proceed with the corpus annotation, we have assumed that the abstracts titles were always appropriate and then we verified the semantic similarity between each sentence in the abstract and its title. Each sentence was labeled as *high* if it is strongly related to the title. Otherwise, it was labeled as *low*. We have decided to use a binary scale rather than a finer grained one due to the subjective nature of the task. Even with only two possible labels, the agreement between two human annotators measured by the Kappa statistics over a randomly selected subset of 209 sentences of the corpus and was around 0.6 (see Table 4).

Over a total of 2,293 sentences, 1,050 (46.80%) were ranked as been weakly related to the title (*low* sentences) and 1,243 (54,20%) as been strongly related (*high* sentences). The distribution of *high* and *low* sentences among the six possible rhetorical categories is presented in Table 2.

	Sentences	
Categories	High	Low
Background	364	444
Gap	104	111
Purpose	355	071
Methodology	139	134
Result	220	231
Conclusion	061	059
Total	1,243	1,050

Table 2: Dimension Title annotation.

It can be observed in Table 2 that Purpose sentences tend to have a strong level of relatedness to the title, since 83.33% of such sentences were ranked as *high*. It is much higher than the average of *high* sentences for other categories, which is 48.79%. Background sentences are the less related to the title, having more than half of the total of sentences (54.95%) ranked as *low*. In fact, these are not surprising results. Background sentences usually appears at the beginning of the abstract with the purpose of establishing the context of the research and, therefore, may not be directly related to the main topics of the research being presented. Instead, it may address questions or state facts of a broader area of study, which will prepare the reader to understand the motivations that led to the presented work. Thus, the detection of a weak relationship between the title and a Background sentence cannot be assumed as a coherence problem. On the other hand, Purpose sentences are expected to address directly the main topics treated by the research and then to be strongly related to the title. This is in accordance with the traditional "general — specific — general" model accepted as standard for scientific texts (Swales, 1990; Weissberg and Buker, 1990), especially introduction and abstract sections. Therefore, the existence of a weak relationship between Purpose sentences and the title probably indicates a coherence issue. With respect to the remaining rhetorical categories (Gap, Methodology, Result, and Conclusion), its relatedness to the title is quite balanced, with an average of 50.5% of *low* sentences and 49.5% of *high* sentences over a total of 1,059 sentences. In our observations, the relatedness of these categories of sentences to the title depends on other aspects than coherence, like the very nature of the research being reported. Thus, we cannot assume that the lack of a strong relationship between a sentence of these categories and the title may indicate a coherence problem.

Taking into account these results, we have concluded that the analysis of this dimension can be used as an indicative of a possible coherence problem in the Purpose rhetorical component of the abstract.

2.2.2 Dimension Purpose

The relationship between a rhetorical component and other components dictates the global coherence of the text (Higgins et al., 2004). Therefore, for an abstract to be easy to follow and understand, the rhetorical components must be related. Taking into consideration the rhetorical structure model used for the annotation of the corpus, it is expected the Purpose component to be related to Methodology, Result and Conclusion components. Thus, we understand that the absence of relationship between each of these components and the Purpose component can be an indication of a coherence problem.

For.each abstract in the corpus, we have verified the semantic similarity between the sentences labeled as Purpose and the remaining sentences of the abstract. Each non-Purpose sentence was labeled as *high* if it is strongly related to Purpose; otherwise, it was labeled as *low*. The label *n/a* was assigned to sentences of abstracts which do not have Purpose sentences. We have measured the agreement between two human annotators by the Kappa statistics over a randomly selected subset of 167 sentences of the corpus and was around 0.8 (see Table 6).

Apart from 573 sentences (426 Purpose sentences and 147 *n/a* sentences distributed among the other five categories), 1,720 sentences were labeled as *high/low* for this dimension. Over this total of sentences, 704 (40.93%) were ranked as been weakly related to the Purpose (*low* sentences) and 1,016 (59,07%) as been strongly related to the Purpose (*high* sentences). The distribution of *high* and *low* sentences among the rhetorical categories is presented in Table 3.

	Sentences	
Categories	High	Low
Background	378	380
Gap	129	079
Methodology	171	082
Result	264	135
Conclusion	074	028
Total	1,016	704

Table 3: Dimension Purpose annotation.

As it can be observed in Table 3, the sentences most related to the Purpose indeed are those labeled as Conclusion, Methodology, and Result. The percentages of *high* sentences for these categories are 72.55%, 67.59%, and 66.17%, respectively. It is worth noticing that the percentage of *high* sentences for Methodology, and Result categories could be even higher, as many sentences of these categories restate the content of the Purpose component by the use of anaphoric expressions, which decreases the level of semantic relationship between the sentences.

Once again, the general nature of Background sentences have placed them as the higher percentage of *low* sentences (50.13%). In fact, Background sentences tend to be closely related to Gap sentences then to Purpose ones, so the low level of relationship between Background and Purpose sentences cannot be assumed as a possible coherence problem.

We have concluded that the analysis of the Dimension Purpose for Methodology, Result, and Conclusion sentences can be used to detect possible coherence problems involving these rhetorical components.

2.2.3 Dimension Gap-Background

As noted earlier, Background sentences tend to be closely related to Gap sentences then to Purpose ones. Thus, it is expected that the Gap component is related with at least one sentence of Background. Therefore, we understand that the absence of relationship between these components can be an indication of a coherence problem.

For each abstract with Gap and Background sentences in the corpus, we have verified the semantic relationship between the sentences of these categories. Each Gap sentence was labeled as *yes* if it is strongly related with some Background sentence; otherwise, it was labeled as *no*.

Apart from 32 sentences belonging to abstracts which do not have Gap/Background sentences, 183 sentences were labeled as *yes/no* for this dimension. Over this total of sentences, 74.86% were ranked as *yes* and 24.14% were ranked as *no*. We have measured the agreement between two human annotators by the Kappa statistics over a randomly selected subset of 46 sentences of the corpus and was around 0.7 (see Table 8).

Taking into consideration the annotation results for this dimension, we have concluded that the analysis of the Dimension Gap-Background can be used to detect possible coherence problems involving the relationship between the rhetorical components Gap and Background.

2.2.4 Dimension Linearity-break

This dimension focuses on detecting linearity breaks between adjacent sentences. Unlike to the other dimensions, Linearity-break is independent of the rhetorical structure of the abstract. A human annotator was instructed to label sentences *yes* when there was a difficulty in establishing a logical connection between the current sentence and its previous and/or its following sentence. Otherwise, the annotator was instructed to label sentences *no*.

Over a total of 2,293 sentences, only 153 were ranked as *yes* (7.14%). This indicates that it is relatively rare to find a sentence which is not related to its adjacencies, as 92.86% of all sentences in our corpus were ranked as *no* with respect to this dimension. In fact, the analysis of this dimension indicates very local coherence issues, which we believe to be more frequent in texts with more serious writing problems than the ones observed in the texts of our corpus.

3 Automatic Analysis of Coherence

As previously stated, the purpose of this work is to develop complementary functionalities for the SciPo system to be capable of identifying semantic coherence related aspects in academic abstracts written in Portuguese. The feedback to be provided by the new functionalities proposed in this work aims at highlighting the presence of potential issues related to semantic coherence in academic abstracts, especially the ones related to Dimension Title, Dimension Purpose, and Dimension Gap-Background.

3.1 Development

For performing the automatic analysis of Dimension Title, Purpose and Gap-Background, we developed classifiers induced by machine learning algorithms and based on features extracted from the text surface and from LSA processing.

The first stage is the annotation of the rhetorical structure of the abstract. In our experiments, we have used abstracts whose automatically assigned rhetorical labels were manually revised. As noted earlier, this is necessary so that the noise from the automatic annotation of rhetorical structure does not interfere in predicting coherence judgments. Nevertheless, in a final version of the semantic coherence analysis module we would use the rhetorical labels assigned by AZPort, and further evaluation of the effect of using these automatically assigned labels is necessary.

The next stage for the semantic coherence analysis concerns the LSA processing. Some preprocessing was required and it proceeds in three steps for all sentences in the corpus: (i) case folding (for data standardization), (ii) stop words removal, and (iii) stemming. These three steps contribute to a better performance of the attributes extracted based on LSA. After data pre-processing and build of a significant semantic space, LSA allows to make comparisons between sentences in order to extract features of the texts. The comparisons took in to account the semantic relation between each pair of sentences based on the LSA model, where the level of similarity is given by the frequency of sentences occurring in similar contexts. For each of the 385 abstracts, we performed all possible comparisons between pairs of sentences within a same abstract, including the abstract title sentences.

3.2 Attribute Extraction

We extracted a set of 13 features for each sentence in the corpus. We have used the features proposed by Higgins et al. (2004) as a starting point for our owns. All features were automatically extracted and used in the induction of the classifiers. The complete set of features is:

1. Rhetorical category of the target sentence;
2. Rhetorical category of the sentence that precedes the target sentence;
3. Rhetorical category of the sentence that follows the target sentence;
4. Presence of words that may characterize an anaphoric element;
5. Position of the sentence within the abstract, computed based on the beginning of the abstract;
6. Presence of words that may characterize some kind of transition;
7. Length of the target sentence measured in words;
8. Length of the title measured in words;
9. LSA similarity score of the target sentence with its preceding sentence;
10. LSA similarity score of the target sentence with its following sentence;
11. LSA similarity score of the target sentence with the entire abstract title;
12. LSA similarity score of the target sentence with all the sentences of the abstract classified as Purpose; and
13. Maximum LSA similarity score of the target Gap sentence with some Background sentence of the abstract.

Features 1 to 8 are based on the abstract rhetorical structure and other shallow measures. Features 9 to 13 are based on LSA processing. Features 1 to 10 compose our basic pool of features and were used in the induction of all classifiers. Feature 11 was added to the basic pool of features when inducting Dimension Title classifier. For each sentence in an abstract, Dimension Title classifier uses the extracted features to predict whether it is strongly/weakly related to the title (*high/low* categories). Similarly, feature 12 was added to the basic pool of features for the induction of Dimension Purpose classifier. This classifier uses the extracted features to predict, for each sentence in an abstract, whether it is strongly/weakly related to the Purpose sentences of the target abstract (also *high/low* categories). Feature 13 is extracted only of Gap sentences in abstracts that also have Background sentences. Thus, Dimension Gap-Background classifier uses the basic pool of features plus feature 13 to predict, for each Gap sentence in an abstract, whether it is related with at least one Background sentence (*yes/no* categories).

4 Evaluation of Classification Models

Based on the extracted features, we generated and evaluated classification models for Dimension Title, Purpose and Gap-Background. For each dimension, we trained and tested 15 different machine learning algorithms using the implementations provided by the WEKA (Witten and Frank, 2005), resulting on a total of 45 classifiers. Among the classes of algorithms that we evaluated are decision trees, rule induction, probabilistic models, support vector machines, linear regression, and others. All the classifiers were inducted using 10-fold stratified cross-validation and the set of features. The performance was measured by comparing the system's prediction with one human annotation. We assumed the annotation performed by one of the subjects in the previous annotation experiment as our "gold standard" and used it as training material. The best model for each dimension was used for further experiments and evaluation.

For each dimension, we also report the performance of a simple baseline measure, which always assigns the prevalent category (*high/low* or *yes/no*) to every sentence.

4.1 Classification Model for Dimension Title

Among the evaluated learning algorithms for Dimension Title, MultiBoostAB implemented based on Webb (2000) presented the best performance. Using C4.5 (Quinlan, 1993) as the base learning algorithm, MultiBoostAB combines boosting and wagging techniques for forming decision committees. The MultiBoostAB classifier achieved F-measure of 0.811 for the *high* category, and 0.782 for the *low* category. We also evaluated the performance of each of our features for this dimension. As expected, feature 11 (LSA similarity score of the target sentence with the entire abstract title) achieved the best performance.

In order to analyze the performance of the classification model with regard to each rhetorical category, we inducted and evaluated six different classifiers, one for each rhetorical category. Each of these classifiers was trained using the abstracts titles and a set of sentences of the target category. Baselines classifiers were also evaluated for each category. The baseline performance for all the Dimension Title classifiers in terms of Precision, Recall, F-measure, accuracy, and Kappa is presented in Table 4. The performance of each Dimension Title classifier also in terms of Precision, Recall, F-measure, Accuracy, and Kappa is presented in Table 5. The Kappa measure shown in Table 4 refers to the agreement between two human annotators. In Table 5, refers to the agreement among each classifier and our "gold-standard".

As shown by the results reported on Table 4 and Table 5, all our MultiBoostAB classifiers outperform the baseline. The best performance, both in terms of F-measure and Kappa, was achieved by the Purpose classifier. The Kappa above 0.8 indicates high agreement between classifier and human annotator.

Looking at the performance of the classifiers for *high* and *low* sentences, it can be observed that most of them perform better for *high* sentences. We ascribe this to the lower level of ambiguity in assigning a sentence as *high*. In fact, our human annotators have found more difficulties in ranking a sentence as being weakly related to the title (*low* sentences) than in ranking it as strongly related (*high* sentences). They claim the existence of a higher level of ambiguity in *low* sentences than in *high* sentences.

As for the superior performance of the Purpose classifier, we attribute that to the strong relationship between the content of Purpose sentences and the title, as previously discussed, and to the fact that Purpose sentences usually are clear and objective, presenting well defined lexical and syntactic markers. In general, it is possible to say that there is less ambiguity in ranking a Purpose sentence as strongly/weakly related to the title than ranking the relationship of a Background sentence to thc title.

Both the evaluation results for the classification model and the semantic content of Purpose sentences leads us to employ the Dimension Title automatic evaluation only to sentences rhetorically categorized as Purpose.

	High			Low			Total	
	Precision	Recall	F-measure	Precision	Recall	F-measure	Acc	Kappa (N)
Background (N=808)	0.000	0.000	0.000	0.549	1.000	0.708	0.549	0.750 (87)
Gap (N=215)	0.000	0.000	0.000	0.516	1.000	0.680	0.516	0.577 (46)
Purpose (N=426)	0.833	1.000	0.908	0.000	0.000	0.000	0.833	0.696 (42)
Methodology (N=273)	0.509	1.000	0.674	0.000	0.000	0.000	0.509	0.512 (14)
Result (N=451)	0.000	0.000	0.000	0.512	1.000	0.677	0.512	0.625 (16)
Conclusion (N=120)	0.508	1.000	0.673	0.000	0.000	0.000	0.508	0.500 (4)
All sentences (N=2,293)	0.542	1.000	0.702	0.000	0.000	0.000	0.542	0.610 (209)

Table 4: Baseline performance on Dimension Title.

	High			Low			Total	
	Precision	Recall	F-measure	Precision	Recall	F-measure	Acc	Kappa
Background (N=808)	0.761	0.742	0.751	0.792	0.809	0.800	0.774	0.551
Gap (N=215)	0.748	0.856	0.798	0.844	0.730	0.783	0.790	0.582
Purpose (N=426)	0.977	0.961	0.969	0.818	0.887	0.851	0.948	0.820
Methodology (N=273)	0.703	0.835	0.763	0.787	0.634	0.702	0.736	0.470
Result (N=451)	0.824	0.700	0.757	0.750	0.857	0.800	0.780	0.559
Conclusion (N=120)	0.729	0.836	0.779	0.800	0.678	0.734	0.758	0.515
All sentences (N=2,293)	0.820	0.801	0.811	0.771	0.792	0.782	0.797	0.592

Table 5: MultiBoostAB performance on Dimension Title.

4.2 Classification Model for Dimension Purpose

Among the evaluated learning algorithms for Dimension Purpose, SimpleLogistic, an algorithm of logistic regression implemented based on Sumner et al. (2005), presented the best performance. The SimpleLogistic classifier achieved F-measure of 0.868 for the *high* category, and 0.801 for the *low* category. Once again, the strongest feature was one of the LSA set, feature 12 (LSA similarity score of the target sentence with all the sentences of the abstract classified as Purpose).

In order to analyze the performance of the classification model with regard to each rhetorical category, we inducted and evaluated five different classifiers, one for each rhetorical category except Purpose. Each of these classifiers was trained using Purpose sentences and a set of sentences of the target category. Baselines classifiers were also evaluated for each category. The baseline performance for all the Dimension Purpose classifiers in terms of Precision, Recall, F-measure, Accuracy, and Kappa is presented in Table 6. The performance of each Dimension Purpose classifier also in terms of Precision, Recall, F-measure, Accuracy, and Kappa is presented in Table 7. The Kappa measure shown in Table 6 refers to the agreement between two human annotators. In Table 7, refers to the agreement among each classifier and our "gold-standard".

The results reported on Table 6 and Table 7 show that all our SimpleLogistic classifiers outperform the baseline. The best performance, both in terms of F-measure and Kappa, was achieved by the Gap classifier. The Kappa for this classifier is 0.754, which indicates a good level of agreement between classifier and human annotator. Apart from Background classifier, all four classifiers performed well. As discussed earlier, it is not surprising that the Background classifier present a weaker performance, as the semantic content of Background sentences usually are general, and, therefore, semantically distant from the Purpose.

Taking into account the F-measure values only for *high* sentences, the best performance was achieved by the Conclusion classifier. In most cases, Conclusion sentences that are strongly related to Purpose, reintroduce the topics stated in the Purpose, even if in a broader context. Again, it is accordance with "general—specific—general" model for scientific texts.

It can also be observed on Table 7 that the Methodology classifier presents the second worse performance on this dimension (it outperforms only the Background classifier), despite the strong relationship between the Methodology and Purpose components. We ascribe this to the characteristics of Methodology sentences, which usually introduce new nouns to the abstract, such as names of techniques, metrics, and other. These newly introduced nouns cause a low LSA score between Methodology and Purpose sentences, contradicting the human annotator whose analysis considers more than just the text surface.

	High			Low			Total	
	Precision	Recall	F-measure	Precision	Recall	F-measure	Acc	Kappa (N)
Background (N=758)	0.000	0.000	0.000	0.501	1.000	0.667	0.501	0.644 (87)
Gap (N=208)	0.620	1.000	0.765	0.000	0.000	0.000	0.620	0.804 (46)
Methodology (N=253)	0.675	1.000	0.805	0.000	0.000	0.000	0.675	0.811 (14)
Result (N=399)	0.661	1.000	0.795	0.000	0.000	0.000	0.661	0.818 (16)
Conclusion (N=102)	0.725	1.000	0.840	0.000	0.000	0.000	0.725	1.000 (4)
All sentences (N=1,720)	0.592	1.000	0.742	0.000	0.000	0.000	0.592	0.815 (167)

Table 6: Baseline performance on Dimension Purpose.

	High			Low			Total	
	Precision	Recall	F-measure	Precision	Recall	F-measure	Acc	Kappa
Background (N=758)	0.786	0.804	0.795	0.801	0.782	0.791	0.792	0.586
Gap (N=208)	0.901	0.915	0.908	0.857	0.835	0.846	0.884	0.754
Methodology (N=253)	0.879	0.895	0.887	0.772	0.744	0.758	0.845	0.645
Result (N=399)	0.889	0.909	0.899	0.814	0.778	0.795	0.864	0.694
Conclusion (N=102)	0.897	0.946	0.921	0.833	0.714	0.769	0.882	0.691
All sentences (N=1,720)	0.852	0.885	0.868	0.824	0.778	0.801	0.841	0.669

Table 7: SimpleLogistc performance on Dimension Purpose.

Both the evaluation results for the classification model and the results from the manual annotation process leads us to employ the Dimension Purpose automatic evaluation to sentences categorized Methodology, Result, and Conclusion.

4.3 Classification Model for Dimension Gap-Background

Considering the evaluated learning algorithms for Dimension Gap-Background, DecisionTable implemented based on Kohavi (1995) presented the best performance. The classifier achieved F-measure of 0.935 for the *yes* category, and 0.795 for the *no* category. We evaluated the performance of each of our features and feature 13 (Maximum LSA similarity score of the target sentence with some Background sentence of the abstract) achieved the best performance. The baseline performance and the DecisionTable classifier in terms of Precision, Recall, F-measure, Accuracy, and Kappa is shown in Table 8.

As shown the Table 8, our classifier outperforms the baseline. Furthermore, the Kappa measured between the classifier and our "gold-standard" was 0.731, which indicates high agreement between the classifier and the human annotator.

Looking at the performance of the classifier, it can be observed that most of them perform better for *yes* sentences. We ascribe this to the presence of anaphoric references in Gap sentences, which decrease the level of semantic relationship. Furthermore, we have a smaller number of sentences ranked as *no* (24.14%).

Evaluation results for the classification model and the results from the manual annotation process encourage us to employ the automatic evaluation of Dimension Gap-Background to sentences rhetorically categorized as Gap in abstracts that have both Background and Gap sentences.

5 Conclusions and Future Work

This work mainly proposes to present four coherence-related dimensions that can be incorporated to the SciPo system. We believe such a proposal to be novel in the context of academic writing, especially in Portuguese.

We also presented how the three dimensions can be automated by using classification models. Dimension Title, Purpose and Gap-Background models present good results and should be incorporated to SciPo as new functionalities. On the other hand, taking into consideration the annotation process, we observed difficulties to label the sentences with regard to the Dimension Linearity-break. Therefore, due to the annotation ambiguity and the low number of examples found, we do not present the classification model for Linearity-break in this work. We believe that such a dimension can be applied to future works in a corpus with can provide more examples of linearity break as, for instance, texts generated by automatic summarizers. In addition, an alternative to be considered in analyzing Dimension Linearity-break is the use of the Entity-grid model proposed by Barzilay and Lapata (2008), which treats local coherence aspects.

	Yes			No			Total	
	Precision	Recall	F-measure	Precision	Recall	F-measure	Acc	Kappa (N)
Baseline (N=183)	0.748	1.000	0.855	0.000	0.000	0.000	0.748	0.725 (46)
DecisionTable (N=183)	0.922	0.949	0.935	0.833	0.761	0.795	0.906	0.731 (183)

Table 8: Baseline performance versus DecisionTable classifier on Dimension Gap-Background.

References

Regina Barzilay and Mirella Lapata. 2008. Modeling local coherence: An entity-based approach. *Computational Linguistics*, 34(1):1–34.

Jill Burstein, Martin Chodorow, and Claudia Leacock. 2003. Criterion online essay evaluation: An application for automated evaluation of student essays. In *Proceedings of the Fifteenth Annual Conference on Innovative Applications of Artificial Intelligence*. Association for the Advancement of Artificial Intelligence.

Jill Burstein, Joel Tetreault, and Slava Andreyev. 2010. Using entity-based features to model coherence in student essays. In *Human Language Technologies: The 2010 Annual Conference of the North American Chapter of the Association for Computational Linguistics*, pages 681–684. Association for Computational Linguistics.

Scott Elliot. 2003. Intellimetric: From here to validity. In M.D. Shermis and Jill Burstein, editors, *Automatic Essay Scoring: A Cross-Disciplinary Perspective*, pages 71–86, Mahwah, NJ. Lawrence Erlbaum Associates.

Valéria D. Feltrim, Sandra Maria Aluísio, and Maria das Graças Volpe Nunes. 2003. Analysis of the rhetorical structure of computer science abstracts in portugese. In Dawn Archer, Paul Rayson, Andrew Wilson, and Tony McEnery, editors, *Proceedings of Corpus Linguistics 2003*, volume 16, part 1, special issue of *UCREL Technical Papers*, pages 212–218.

Valéria D. Feltrim, Simone Teufel, Maria das Graças Volpe Nunes, and Sandra Maria Aluísio. 2006. Argumentative zoning applied to criquing novices scientific abstracts. In James G. Shanahan, Yan Qu, and Janyce Wiebe, editors, *Computing Attitude and Affect in Text: Theory and Applications*, pages 233–246, Dordrecht, The Neherlands. Springer.

Derrick Higgins, Jill Burstein, Daniel Marcu, and Claudia Gentile. 2004. Evaluating multiple aspects of coherence in student essays. In *Human Language Technologies: The 2004 Annual Conference of the North American Chapter of the Association for Computational Linguistics*. Association for Computational Linguistics.

R. Kohavi. 1995. The power of decision tables. *Machine Learning: ECML-95*, pages 174–189.

Thomas K. Landauer, Peter W. Foltz, and Darrell Laham. 1998. Introduction to latent semantic analysis. *Discourse Processes*, 25:259–284.

Thomas K. Landauer, Darrell Laham, and Peter W. Foltz. 2003. Automated essay scoring and annotation of essays with the intelligent essay assessor. In M.D. Shermis and Jill Burstein, editors, *Automated Essay Scoring: A Cross Disciplinary Perspective*, pages 87–112, Mahwah, NJ. Lawrence Erlbaum Associates.

Mirella Lapata and Regina Barzilay. 2005. Automatic evaluation of text coherence: Models and representations. In *In the Intl. Joint Conferences on Artificial Intelligence*, pages 1085–1090.

Ross Quinlan. 1993. *C4.5: Programs for Machine Learning*. Morgan Kaufmann Publishers, San Mateo, CA.

Marc Sumner, Eibe Frank, and Mark A. Hall. 2005. Speeding up logistic model tree induction. In Alípio Jorge, Luís Torgo, Pavel Brazdil, Rui Camacho, and João Gama, editors, *Proceedings of the 9th European Conference on Principles and Practice of Knowledge Discovery in Databases (PKDD 2005)*, volume 3721 of *Lecture Notes in Computer Science*, pages 675–683. Springer.

John Swales. 1990. *Genre Analysis: English in Academic and Research Settings*. Cambridge University Press, Cambridge, UK.

Simone Teufel and Marc Moens. 2002. Summarising scientific articles — experiments with relevance and rhetorical status. *Computational Linguistics*, 28(4):409–446.

Teun A. van Dijk. 1981. *Studies in the Pragmatics of Discourse*. Mouton, The Hague/Berlin.

Geoffrey I. Webb. 2000. Multiboosting: A technique for combining boosting and wagging. *Machine Learning*, 40:159–196.

Robert Weissberg and Suzanne Buker. 1990. *Writing up Research: Experimental Research Report Writing for Students of English*. Prentice Hall.

Ian Witten and Eibe Frank. 2005. *Data Mining: Practical Machine Learning Tools and Techniques*. Morgan Kaufmann, San Francisco, CA, 2nd edition.

Sentence Subjectivity Detection with Weakly-Supervised Learning

Chenghua Lin[1,2], Yulan He[2] and Richard Everson[1]

[1]Department of Computer Science, University of Exeter, Exeter, EX4 4QF, UK
[2]Knowledge Media Institute, The Open University, Milton Keynes, MK7 6AA, UK
{C.Lin,Y.He}@open.ac.uk, R.M.Everson@exeter.ac.uk

Abstract

This paper presents a hierarchical Bayesian model based on latent Dirichlet allocation (LDA), called subjLDA, for sentence-level subjectivity detection, which automatically identifies whether a given sentence expresses opinion or states facts. In contrast to most of the existing methods relying on either labelled corpora for classifier training or linguistic pattern extraction for subjectivity classification, we view the problem as weakly-supervised generative model learning, where the only input to the model is a small set of domain independent subjectivity lexical clues. A mechanism is introduced to incorporate the prior information about the subjectivity lexical clues into model learning by modifying the Dirichlet priors of topic-word distributions. The subjLDA model has been evaluated on the Multi-Perspective Question Answering (MPQA) dataset and promising results have been observed in the preliminary experiments. We have also explored adding neutral words as prior information for model learning. It was found that while incorporating subjectivity clues bearing positive or negative polarity can achieve a significant performance gain, the prior lexical information from neutral words is less effective.

1 Introduction

Subjectivity detection seeks to identify whether the given text expresses opinions (subjective) or reports facts (objective). Such a task of distinguishing subjective information from objective is useful for many natural language processing applications. For instance, sentiment classification often assumes that the input documents are opinionated, and ideally only contain subjective statements. Document summarization systems need to summarize different perspectives and opinions. For question answering systems, extracting and presenting information of the appropriate type, i.e., opinions or facts, is imperative according to the specific question being asked (Yu and Hatzivassiloglou, 2003; Wiebe and Riloff, 2005; Pang and Lee, 2008).

Work on sentence-level subjectivity detection is relatively sparse compared to document-level sentiment classification. Early work used a bootstrapping algorithm to learn subjective (Riloff and Wiebe, 2003) or both subjective and objective (Wiebe and Riloff, 2005) expressions for sentence-level subjectivity detection. In contrast to bootstrapping, there has been some recent attempts exploring various n-gram features and different level of lexical instantiation for detecting subjective utterance from conversation data (Wilson and Raaijmakers, 2008; Raaijmakers et al., 2008; Murray and Carenini, 2009).

However, the aforementioned line of work tackled subjectivity detection either as supervised or semi-supervised learning, requiring labelled data and extensive knowledge which are expensive to acquire. On the other hand, both subjectivity and sentiment are context sensitive and in general quite domain dependent (Pang and Lee, 2008), so that classifiers trained on one domain often fail to produce satisfactory performance when shifted to new domains (Gamon et al., 2005; Blitzer et al., 2007). Moreover, user generated content from web are often massive and evolve rapidly over time, which imposes more challenges to the subjectivity detection task. These observations have thus motivated us to develop a subjectivity detection algorithm that is relatively simple compared to existing methods (e.g., based on bootstrapping or n-gram features), and yet can easily be transferred between domains through unsupervised or weakly-supervised learning without using any labelled data.

In this paper, we focus on the problem of weakly-supervised sentence-level subjectivity detection. Instead of learning subjective extraction patterns or exploring various n-gram features, we view the problem as generative model learning with the proposed subjectivity detection LDA (subjLDA) model. In this model, the generative process involves: (1) three subjectivity labels for sentences (i.e., sentence expresses subjective opinions as being positive/negative, or states facts as being objective); (2) a sentiment label for each word in the sentence (either positive, negative, or neutral), and (3) the words in the sentences.

We test the subjLDA model on the publicly available Multi-Perspective Question Answering (MPQA) dataset. Two lists of domain independent subjectivity lexicons, namely the subjClue and SentiWordNet lexicons (Esuli and Sebastiani, 2006), were incorporated as prior knowledge for subjLDA model learning. Preliminary results show that the weakly-supervised subjLDA model is able to significantly outperform baseline. Furthermore, it was found that while incorporating subjectivity clues bearing positive or negative polarity can achieve a significant performance gain, the prior lexical information from neutral words is less effective for improving the classification accuracy.

The rest of the paper is organized as follows. Section 2 reviews the previous work on subjectivity classification. Section 3 presents the subjLDA model. Experimental setup and results on the MPQA dataset are discussed in Sections 4 and 5, respectively. Finally, Section 6 concludes the paper and outlines the future work.

2 Related Work

2.1 Subjectivity Detection

While sentiment classification and subjectivity detection are closely related to each other, it has been reported that separating subjective and objective instances from text is more difficult than sentiment classification, and the improvement of subjectivity detection can benefit the latter as well (Mihalcea et al., 2007).

Early work by Riloff and Wiebe (2003) focused on a bootstrapping method for sentence-level subjectivity detection. They started with high-precision subjectivity classifiers which automatically identified subjective and objective sentences in un-annotated texts. The subjective expression patterns were learned from syntactic structure output from the previously labelled high confidence texts. The learned patterns were used to automatically identify additional subjective sentences, which enlarged the training set, and the entire process was then iterated. Wiebe and Riloff (2005) used very similar method for subjectivity detection as Riloff and Wiebe (2003). But they moved one step forward that they also learned objective expressions apart from subjective expressons. As the subjective/objective expression patterns are based on syntactic structures, they are more flexible than single words or n-grams.

Wilson and Raaijmakers (2008) compared the performance of classifiers trained using word n-grams, character n-grams, and phoneme n-grams for recognizing subjective utterances in multiparty conversation. Raaijmakers et al. (2008) extended the work in (Wilson and Raaijmakers, 2008) by further analyzing the performance of detecting subjectivity in meeting speech by combining a variety of multimodal features including additional prosodic features. More recently, Murray and Carenini (2009) proposed to learn subjective expression patterns from both labeled and unlabeled data using n-gram word sequences. Their approach for learning subjective expression patterns is similar to (Raaijmakers et al., 2008) which relies on n-grams, but goes beyond fixed sequences of words by varying levels of lexical instantiation as in (Riloff and Wiebe, 2003).

2.2 Weakly-supervised Sentiment Classification

In this section, we first review some work in sentiment analysis using generative models as it partly inspires our work of viewing subjectivity detection as generative model learning. We then discuss other weakly-supervised sentiment classification approaches which also use prior word knowledge.

Intuitively, sentiment or subjectivity are context dependent. Therefore, modelling topic coupled with sentiment should serve a critical function in sentiment analysis. There has seen several lines of work pursuing this direction. Eguchi and Lavrenko (2006) considered the topic dependence of sentiment and combined sentiment models with topic models for sentiment retrieval. Mei et al. (2007) proposed the topic-sentiment mixture (TSM) model for capturing mixture of topics and sentiment simultaneously on Weblogs. The multi-aspect sentiment (MAS) model by Titov and McDonald (2008) focused on aggregating sentiment text for sentiment summary of rating aspects.

The more recently proposed joint sentiment-topic (JST) model (Lin and He, 2009; Lin et al., 2010) holds the closest paradigm to the proposed subjLDA model. They targeted document-level sentiment detection with weakly-supervised generative model learning, where the only knowledge being incorporated was from generic sentiment lexicons. In the JST model, topics are assumed to be generated dependent on sentiment distributions and then words are generated conditioned on sentiment-topic pairs. However, there are several intrinsic differences between JST and subjLDA: (1) JST mainly focused on document-level sentiment classification, while, in contrast, subjLDA has a different scope of targeting sentence-level subjectivity detection; (2) in JST the prior knowledge was encoded during the Gibbs sampling by assigning a word with its prior sentiment label if that word appears in the sentiment lexicon. This essentially places hard sentiment label to words and can not resort the situation when words have ambiguous sentiment polarity. Our proposed approach incorporates sentiment prior knowledge in a more principled way, in that we use sentiment lexicons to modify the topic-word Dirichlet priors and essentially create an informed prior distribution for the sentiment labels.

Another common solution to weakly-supervised sentiment classification is to make use of prior word polarity knowledge, where one uses a small number of seed words with known polarity to infer the polarity of a large set of unidentified terms. Turney and Littman (2002) classified the sentiment orientation of other terms in the corpus through mutual information, based on a small set of positive/negative paradigm words. Starting with a single seed word meaning "*good*" and a negation check, Zagibalov and Carroll (2008) derived a classifier through iteratively retraining, and treated sentiment and subjectivity as a continuum rather than distinct classes.

3 The SubjLDA Model

As shown in Figure 1(b), subjLDA is essentially a four-layer Bayesian model. In order to generate a word $w_{d,m,t}$ (i.e., the tth word token of sentence m within document d), one first chooses a subjectivity label[1] $s_{d,m} \in [1, K]$ for each sentence in document d from the per-document subjectivity distribution π_d. Following that, one chooses a sentiment label $l_{d,m,t} \in [1, S]$ for each word in the sentences from the per-sentence sentiment distribution $\theta_{s_{d,m}}$. Finally, one draws a word from the per-corpus word distribution $\varphi_{l_{d,m,t}}$ conditioned on the corresponding sentiment label. The classification of sentence subjectivity in subjLDA is determined directly from the sentence subjectivity label $s_{d,m}$. The formal definition of the subjLDA generative process is as follows:

- For each sentiment label $l \in [1, S]$
  - Draw $\boldsymbol{\varphi}_l \sim \text{Dir}(\boldsymbol{\lambda}_l \times \boldsymbol{\beta}_l^T)$.
- For each document $d \in [1, D]$, choose distributions $\pi_d \sim \text{Dir}(\gamma)$.
- For each sentence $m \in [1, M_d]$ in document d,
  - Sample a subjectivity label $s_{d,m} \sim \text{Mult}(\pi_d)$,
  - Choose a distribution $\theta_{d,m} \sim \text{Dir}(\alpha_{s_{d,m}})$,
  - For each of the $N_{d,m}$ word position,
    - ∗ Choose a sentiment label $l_{d,m,t} \sim \text{Mult}(\theta_{s_{d,m}})$,
    - ∗ Choose a word $w_{d,m,t} \sim \text{Mult}(\varphi_{l_{d,m,t}})$.

In practice, it is quite intuitive that one classifies a sentence as subjective if it contains one or more strongly subjective clues (Riloff and Wiebe, 2003). However, the criterion for classifying objective sentences could be rather different, because a sentence is likely to be objective if there are no strongly subjective clues. In order to encode this knowledge into the subjLDA model learning, during the model initialization step, we initialized sentence subjectivity label s based on the aforementioned criterion with prior knowledge input from the sentiment lexicon. If a sentence does not match any sentiment words, its subjectivity label will be randomly sampled.

[1] We have conducted another set of experiments modelling only subjective and objective labels. It was found that subjLDA performed slightly better with 3 subjectivity labels than with binary labels. We do not report the binary label results here due to page limit.

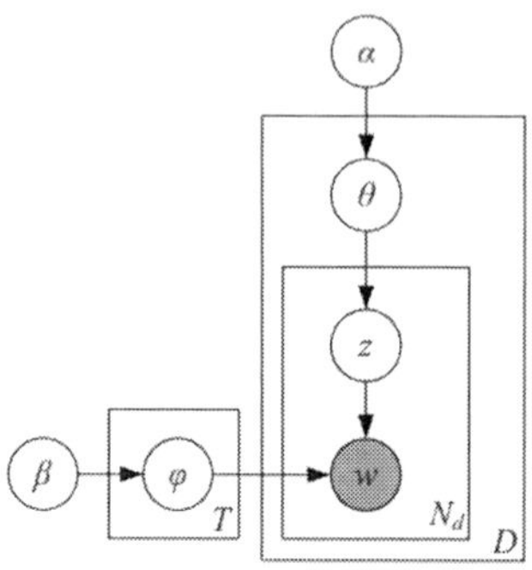

(a)

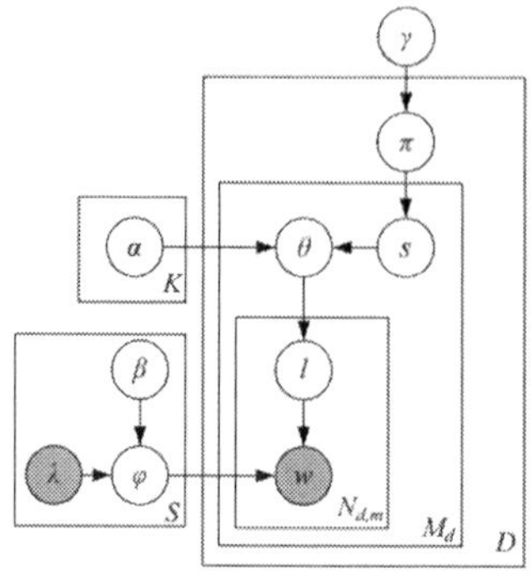

(b)

Figure 1: (a) LDA model; (b) subjLDA model.

3.1 Incorporating Model Prior

Compared to the LDA model, besides adding a sentence-level subjectivity label generation layer, we also add an additional dependency link of $\boldsymbol{\varphi}$ on the matrix $\boldsymbol{\lambda}$ of size $S \times V$ which we use to encode word prior sentiment information. The matrix $\boldsymbol{\lambda}$ can be considered as a transformation matrix which modifies the Dirichlet priors $\boldsymbol{\beta}$ so that the word prior sentiment polarity can be captured.

Intuitively, $\boldsymbol{\lambda}$ is firstly initialized as a matrix with all the elements taking a value of 1. Given a sentiment lexicon, for each term $w \in \{1, ..., V\}$ in the corpus vocabulary, if w is found in the sentiment lexicon, then for each $l \in \{1, ..., S\}$, the element λ_{lw} is updated as follows

$$\lambda_{lw} = \begin{cases} 0.9 & \text{if } S(w) = l \\ 0.05 & \text{otherwise} \end{cases}, \quad (1)$$

where the function $S(w)$ returns the prior sentiment label of w in a sentiment lexicon, i.e., positive, negative or neutral. For example, the word "*excellent*" with index w_t has a positive sentiment polarity. The corresponding row vector λ_{w_t} is $[0.05, 0.9, 0.05]$ with its elements representing neutral, positive, and negative prior polarity. Multiplying $\boldsymbol{\beta}$ with $\boldsymbol{\lambda}$, we can enforce that the word "*excellent*"has much higher probability of being drawn from the positive topic word distributions generated from a Dirichlet distribution with parameter $\beta_{l_{pos}w_t}$.

The previously proposed DiscLDA (Lacoste-Julien et al., 2008) and Labeled LDA (Ramage et al., 2009) also utilize a transformation matrix to modify Dirichlet priors by assuming the availability of document class labels. In contrast, we use word prior sentiment as supervised information to modify the topic-word Dirichlet priors.

3.2 Model Inference

The total probability of the model is

$$P(\boldsymbol{w}, \boldsymbol{l}, \boldsymbol{s}, \boldsymbol{\theta}, \boldsymbol{\varphi}, \boldsymbol{\pi}; \alpha, \beta, \gamma) = \prod_{j=1}^{S} P(\varphi_j; \boldsymbol{\lambda} \times \boldsymbol{\beta}) \cdot \prod_{d=1}^{D} P(\pi_d; \gamma) \prod_{m=1}^{M_d} P(s_{d,m}|\pi_d) P(\theta_{d,m}; \alpha_{s_{d,m}}) \cdot \prod_{t=1}^{N_{d,m}} P(l_{d,m,t}|\theta_{d,m}) P(w_{d,m,t}|\varphi_{l_{d,m,t}}), \quad (2)$$

where the bold-font variables denote vectors.

We use Gibbs sampling to estimate the posterior of subjLDA by sequentially sampling each variable of interest, $l_{d,m,t}$ and $s_{d,m}$ here, from the distribution over that variable given the current values of all other variables and the data. Letting the index $x = (d, m)$ and the subscript $-x$ denote a quantity that excludes counts in sentence m of document d, the conditional posterior for s_x is

$$P(s_x = k|\boldsymbol{s}_{-x}, \boldsymbol{l}, \boldsymbol{w}, \alpha, \beta, \gamma) \propto \frac{(N_{d,k} + \gamma_k) - 1}{(N_d + \sum_{k=1}^{K} \gamma_k) - 1} \cdot \frac{\prod_{j=1}^{S} \prod_{b=0}^{N_{d,m,j}-1} (b + \alpha_{s_x,j})}{\prod_{b=0}^{N_{d,m}-1} (b + \sum_{j=1}^{3} \alpha_{s_x,j})}, \quad (3)$$

where $N_{d,k}$ denotes the frequency of sentences assigned to subjectivity label k in document d; N_d is the total number of sentences in document d; $N_{d,m,j}$ is the total number of words in sentence m of document d associated with sentiment label j; $N_{d,m}$ is the total number of words in sentence m of document d.

In terms of the sentiment label, letting the index $y = (d, m, t)$ denote t^{th} word in sentence m of document d and the subscript $-y$ denote a quantity that excludes data from t^{th} word position, the conditional posterior for l_t is

$$P(l_y = j | \boldsymbol{s}, \boldsymbol{l}_{-y}, \boldsymbol{w}, \alpha, \beta, \gamma) \propto \frac{N_{d,m,j} + \alpha_{s_{d,m},j} - 1}{N_{d,m} + \sum_{j=1}^{S} \alpha_{s_{d,m},j} - 1} \cdot \frac{Y_{j,w_t} + \lambda_{j,w_t}\beta_{j,w_t} - 1}{Y_j + \sum_{r=1}^{V} \lambda_{j,r}\beta_{j,r} - 1} \quad (4)$$

where Y_{j,w_t} denotes the frequency of word w_t associated with sentiment label j in the document collection; Y_j is the total number of words associated with sentiment label j in the document collection.

Equations 3-4 are the conditional probabilities derived by marginalizing out the random variables π, θ, and φ. Samples obtained from the Markov chain are used to approximate the per-document subjectivity distribution

$$\pi_{d,k} = \frac{N_{d,k} + \gamma_k}{N_d + \sum_{k=1}^{K} \gamma_k}. \quad (5)$$

The approximated per-sentence sentiment distribution is

$$\theta_{d,m,j} = \frac{N_{d,m,j} + \alpha_{s_{d,m},j}}{N_{d,m} + \sum_{j=1}^{S} \alpha_{s_{d,m},j}}. \quad (6)$$

Finally, the per-corpus sentiment-word distribution is

$$\varphi_{j,r} = \frac{Y_{j,r} + \lambda_{j,r}\beta_{j,r}}{Y_j + \sum_{r=1}^{V} \lambda_{j,r}\beta_{j,r}}. \quad (7)$$

4 Experimental Setup

4.1 Dataset

We tested our model on the MPQA dataset[2] version 1.2, which is derived from a variety of foreign news documents. The whole corpus consists of 535 documents with a total number of 6,111 subjective and 5,001 objective sentences. We performed a two-stage preprocessing on the dataset by first removing stop words and non-word characters, followed by standard stemming for reducing vocabulary size and minimizing sparse data problems. After preprocessing, the MPQA dataset contains 131,220 words with 10,511 distinct terms (cf. the original dataset with 264,808 words and a vocabulary size of 31,201 without any preprocessing).

4.2 Lexical Prior Knowledge

We explored incorporating two subjectivity lexicons as prior knowledge for subjLDA model learning, namely, the subjClue[3] and SentiWordNet[4] lexicons. We point out that the subjClue lexicon is not related to the MPQA dataset as it was collected from a number of sources, where some were culled from manually developed resources and others were identified automatically using both annotated and unannotated data (Wiebe and Riloff, 2005). We only extract the lexical clues that are considered strongly subjective, with the weakly subjective clues being discarded. The rationale behind the filtering is that while a strongly subjective clue is seldom used without a subjective meaning, weakly subjective clues are ambiguous, often having both subjective and objective uses. After stemming, removing the duplicated lexical terms and retaining those that have appeared in the corpus, we finally obtained a lexicon subset of 477 positive and 917 negative words.

SentiWordNet provides a wide coverage of lexical terms by tagging all the synsets of WordNet with three sentiment labels, i.e., positive, negative and neutral. In our experiment, we only use the neutral words from SentiWordNet for investigating how neutral words would affect the subjLDA model performance. After the same preprocessing as performed on the subjClue lexicon, a total of 193,871 neutral words were extracted. Further mapping the extracted neutral words with the corpus results in 6,457 neutral words.

5 Experimental Results

In this section, we first present the experimental results of sentence-level subjectivity classification on the MPQA dataset, and subsequently evaluate the impact on the classification performance by varying the proportion of prior information being incorporated. All the results reported here are averaged over 5 runs with 800 Gibbs sampling iterations.

5.1 Overall Results

The baseline is calculated by counting the overlap of the prior lexicon with the dataset. We classify a sentence as subjective if it contains one or more positive/negative sentiment words; if there is no matching, the sentence will be classified as

[2] http://www.cs.pitt.edu/mpqa/databaserelease/

[3] http://www.cs.pitt.edu/mpqa/

[4] http://sentiwordnet.isti.cnr.it/

Table 1: Subjectivity classification results. (Boldface indicates the best results.)

Model	Objective (%)			Subjective (%)			Overall (%)
	Recall	Precision	F-measure	Recall	Precision	F-measure	Accuracy
Baseline	46.5	74.1	57.1	76.7	63.7	69.6	63.1
subjLDA	59.7	**71.6**	**65.1**	**80.9**	**71.0**	**75.6**	**71.2**
LDA (Sent.)	**60.5**	65.7	63.0	74.2	69.7	72.0	68.1
LDA (Doc.)	51.4	68.7	58.8	80.6	67.0	73.2	67.6
Wiebe 05	77.6	68.4	72.7	70.6	79.4	74.7	73.8

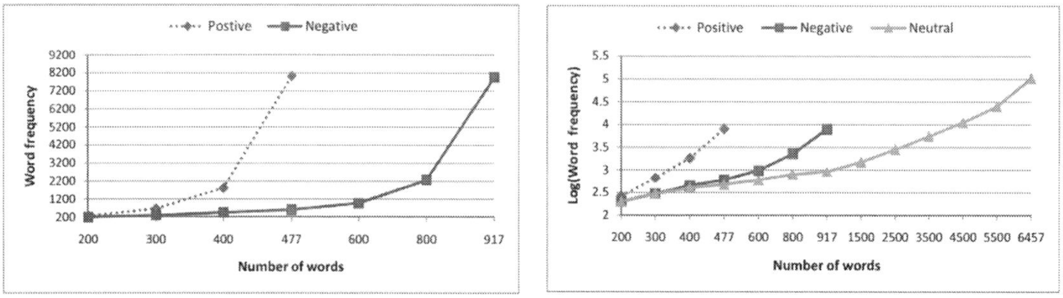

(a)

(b)

Figure 2: (a) Positive and negative lexicon statistics; (b) Positive, negative and neutral lexicon statistics.

objective. The improvement over this baseline will reflect how much subjLDA can learn from data. The LDA model (Blei et al., 2003), as shown in Figure 1(a), has been used as baseline in document-level sentiment classification in previous research (Lin et al., 2010). Thus, we also evaluated LDA on the sentence-level subjectivity detection task by modelling a mixture of three sentiment topics, i.e., positive, negative and neutral. For fair comparison, we encoded prior knowledge of sentiment lexicon into LDA as identical to subjLDA. Thus the LDA model here can be considered as a weakly-supervised version. Moreover, we tested LDA under two different modes, i.e., modelling a normal document vs. treating each individual sentence as a separate document. The sentence sentiment is determined as follows.

(a) LDA in document mode: sentiment of sentence m in document D is calculated using

$$P(l|m) \propto P(m|l)P(l|d) = \prod_{w_t \in m} P(w_t|l)P(l|d). \quad (8)$$

We define that sentence m is classified as an objective sentence if its probability of neutral label given sentence $P(l = neu.|m)$, is greater than both $P(l = pos.|m)$ and $P(l = neg.|m)$. Otherwise, the sentence is classified as subjective.

(b) LDA in sentence mode: sentence subjectivity is directly determined based on the per-sentence sentiment distribution θ, using identical classification metrics to the document mode.

As can be seen from Table 1, a significant performance gain was observed for both subjLDA and LDA over the baseline. Particularly, more than 8% gain was observed for subjLDA, giving the best overall accuracy of 71.2% which is 3.1% and 3.6% higher than LDA(Sent.) and LDA(Doc.), respectively. In addition, except for objective recall, subjLDA outperforms LDA in both the sentence and document modes for all the other evaluation metrics, with more balanced objective and subjective F-measures being attained compared to the other two models. On the other hand, it was observed that while LDA(Doc.) can achieve a comparable subjective F-measure to LDA(Sent.), its objective F-measure is nearly 5% lower, resulting in worse overall performance. This is probably due to the fact that by treating each individual sentence as a document, LDA(Sent.) can avoid inferencing global sentiment topics and thus capture more accurate sentiment information from local topics. We measured the overall accuracy significance with paired t-Test (critical P=0.01). Results show that the improvements of subjLDA over both LDA(sent.) and LDA(doc.) are highly statistically significant. Thus, we conclude that subjLDA is superior than LDA in the subjectivity detection task.

When compared to the previous proposed boot-

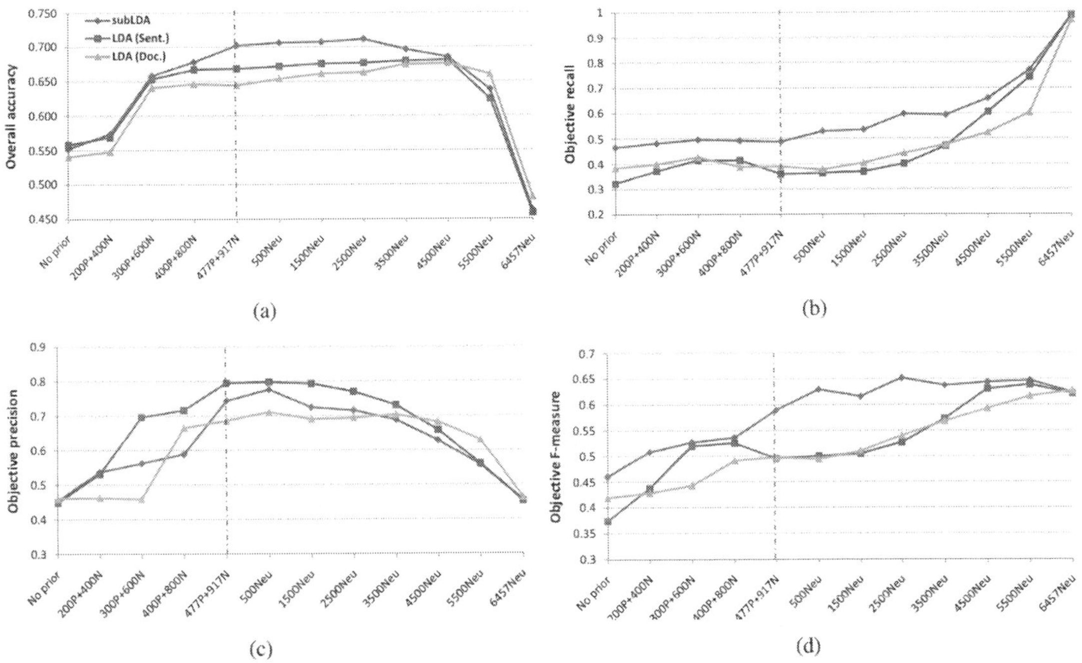

Figure 3: Subjectivity classification performance vs. different prior information by gradually adding the subjective and neutral words. The vertical dashed line denotes the point where all the positive and negative words have been incorporated into the model; 200P+400N denotes adding the least frequent 200 positive and 400 negative words; 500Neu denotes adding the least frequent 500 neutral words in addition to all the positive and negative words.

strapping approach (Wiebe and Riloff, 2005), subjLDA is about 2% lower in terms of overall accuracy. However, it should be noted that, their approach used a much larger training set for self-training which consists of more than 100,000 sentences. Moreover, apart from subjectivity clues, they also used additional features such as subjective/obejctive pattern and POS for the Naive Bayes sentence classifier training. In contrast, the proposed subjLDA model is relatively simple with only a small set of subjectivity clues being incorporated as prior knowledge.

5.2 Classification Results with Different Priors

While positive/negative sentiment lexicon is commonly used in lexical approaches to sentiment classification, the impact of incorporating neutral words remains relatively unexplored. In this experiment, we investigated the impact on the model performance by incorporating additional knowledge from neutral words. We started by first considering the positive and negative words only and gradually increased the number of words starting with the lowest frequency words. After all the positive and negative words have been incorporated, we then gradually added additional neutral words into the model also from the lowest frequency to the highest. Figure 2 shows the lexicon statistics of all the positive, negative and neutral words, where the value on the x-axis represents the number of words sorted by word frequency and the corresponding y-axis value indicates the total number of times those words appear in the corpus. For instance, the 400 least frequent positive words appear a total of 1,826 times in the corpus as shown in Figure 2(a).

Figure 3 depicts the subjectivity classification results of subjLDA and LDA by varying the proportion of lexical terms being incorporated. It is quite obvious from the overall accuracy shown in the figure that both subjLDA and LDA benefit from incorporating the information of subjective words, and in general, the more lexical items the better the results. Without using any neutral words, all the three models achieved the best results when all the subjective words were incorporated. It was noted that subjLDA performed similar to LDA when only a small number of low frequency subjective words were used. However, with more higher frequency subjective words being incorporated, subjLDA shows stronger performance boosting over LDA and gives the best accuracy of 70.2% when all the subjective words were incorporated, being 3.4% and 5.8% better than LDA(Sent.) and LDA(Doc.), respectively, as indicated by the vertical dashed line in the figure.

On the other hand, adding neutral words is also beneficial, where performance gain was observed for all the 3 models in addition to the best results using subjective words only (i.e., subjLDA by 1%, LDA(Sent.) by 1.6% and LDA(Doc.) by 2.9%). Analyzing the objective recall and precision shown in Figure 3(b) and 3(c) reveals that, while incorporating the 4,500 least frequent neutral words considerably increases the objective recall, the objective precision does not drop much which eventually leads to the overall improvement of all the three models.

However, compared to the subjective words, the classification improvements by incorporating additional neutral words are less significant. This is probably due to the fact that while the presence of positive/negative words conveys clear subjective meanings, neutral words are relatively vague which could bear objective or subjective sense under different contexts. Furthermore, all three models experience a significant performance drop after the point of (4500Neu). Examining Figure 2 reveals that, while the 4,500 least frequent neutral words appear 11,142 times in the corpus, the 1,957 most frequent words (i.e., from 4500 to 6457) appear 93,036 times, nearly 10 times as much as the former. Thus, the high frequency neutral words become dominant in the model and result in severe classification bias towards the objective class. Therefore, appropriate filtering of neutral words is necessary in order to avoid introducing bias into model learning.

5.3 Sentiment Topics

In subjLDA, we model three topics in the per-corpus word distribution, each of which corresponds to neutral, positive and negative sentiment. Figure 4 shows the top 15 topic words of the sentiment topics extracted from the MPQA dataset by subjLDA. It can be easily observed that while the positive and negative sentiment topics consist of clear sentiment bearing words, the neutral topic contains mostly theme words with no sentiment, which illustrates the effectiveness of subjLDA in extracting sentiment bearing topics from text.

Sentiment topics		
Neutral	Positive	Negative
countri	state	terror
presid	right	opposit
unit	support	concern
govern	gener	evil
intern	want	critic
bush	interest	question
report	posit	mean
elect	move	protest
china	remark	violat
militari	hope	accus
war	alli	refus
prison	agre	despit
taiwan	live	reject
minist	provid	fail
foreign	consent	impos

Figure 4: Sentiment topics extracted by subjLDA.

6 Conclusions and Future Work

This paper presents the subjectivity detection LDA Model (subjLDA) for sentence-level subjectivity classification. In contrast to most of the existing approaches requiring labelled corpora or linguistic pattern extraction, we view this problem as weakly-supervised generative model learning where the only input to the model is a small amount of domain independent subjective/neutral words. The subjLDA model has been evaluated on the MPQA dataset. Preliminary results show that except slightly lower in objective recall, subjLDA outperformed LDA over all other evaluation metrics, and is comparable to the previously proposed bootstrapping approach using a much larger training set. Moreover, it was found that while incorporating more subjective words can generally yield better results, the performance gain by employing extra neutral words is less significant.

There are several directions we would like to pursue in the future. While word lexical prior information is incorporated by modifying the Dirichlet prior for topic-word distributions here, it is also possible to explore other mechanisms to define expectation or posterior constraints. In addition, the current subjLDA model only models bag-of-words features, another future step would be extending subjLDA to include higher order information such as bigrams for improving model performance.

Acknowledgements

This work was supported in part by the EC-FP7 projects ROBUST (grant number 257859) and VPH-Share (grant number 269978).

References

David M. Blei, Andrew Y. Ng, and Michael I. Jordan. 2003. Latent Dirichlet allocation. *J. Mach. Learn. Res.*, 3:993–1022.

John Blitzer, Mark Dredze, and Fernando Pereira. 2007. Biographies, bollywood, boom-boxes and blenders: Domain adaptation for sentiment classification. In *Proceedings of the Association for Computational Linguistics (ACL)*, pages 440–447.

Koji Eguchi and Victor Lavrenko. 2006. Sentiment retrieval using generative models. In *Proceedings of the Conference on Empirical Methods in Natural Language Processing (EMNLP)*, pages 345–354.

A. Esuli and F. Sebastiani. 2006. SentiWordNet: A publicly available lexical resource for opinion mining. In *Proceedings of LREC*.

M. Gamon, A. Aue, S. Corston-Oliver, and E. Ringger. 2005. Pulse: Mining customer opinions from free text. *Lecture Notes in Computer Science*, 3646:121–132.

S. Lacoste-Julien, F. Sha, and M.I. Jordan. 2008. DiscLDA: Discriminative learning for dimensionality reduction and classification. In *NIPS*.

Chenghua Lin and Yulan He. 2009. Joint sentiment/topic model for sentiment analysis. In *Proceedings of the ACM conference on Information and knowledge management (CIKM)*.

Chenghua Lin, Yulan He, and Richard Everson. 2010. A comparative study of Bayesian models for unsupervised sentiment detection. In *Conference on Computational Natural Language Learning (CoNLL)*.

Qiaozhu Mei, Xu Ling, Matthew Wondra, Hang Su, and ChengXiang Zhai. 2007. Topic sentiment mixture: modeling facets and opinions in weblogs. In *Proceedings of the 16th international conference on World Wide Web (WWW)*, pages 171–180.

R. Mihalcea, C. Banea, and J. Wiebe. 2007. Learning multilingual subjective language via cross-lingual projections. In *In Proceedings of the Association for Computational Linguistics (ACL)*, page 976.

G. Murray and G. Carenini. 2009. Predicting subjectivity in multimodal conversations. In *Proceedings of the Conference on Empirical Methods in Natural Language Processing (EMNLP)*, pages 1348–1357.

Bo Pang and Lillian Lee. 2008. Opinion mining and sentiment analysis. *Found. Trends Inf. Retr.*, 2(1-2):1–135.

S. Raaijmakers, K. Truong, and T. Wilson. 2008. Multimodal subjectivity analysis of multiparty conversation. In *Proceedings of the Conference on Empirical Methods in Natural Language Processing (EMNLP)*, pages 466–474.

D. Ramage, D. Hall, R. Nallapati, and C.D. Manning. 2009. Labeled LDA: A supervised topic model for credit attribution in multi-labeled corpora. In *Proceedings of the Conference on Empirical Methods in Natural Language Processing (EMNLP)*, pages 248–256.

E. Riloff and J. Wiebe. 2003. Learning extraction patterns for subjective expressions. In *Proceedings of the conference on Empirical methods in natural language processing (EMNLP)*, pages 105–112.

Ivan Titov and Ryan McDonald. 2008. A joint model of text and aspect ratings for sentiment summarization. In *Proceedings of the Aunal Meeting on Association for Computational Linguistics and the Human Language Technology Conference (ACL-HLT)*, pages 308–316.

Peter D. Turney and Michael L. Littman. 2002. Unsupervised learning of semantic orientation from a hundred-billion-word corpus. *ArXiv Computer Science e-prints*, cs.LG/0212012.

J. Wiebe and E. Riloff. 2005. Creating subjective and objective sentence classifiers from unannotated texts. In *Proceedings of the Conference on Computational Linguistics and Intelligent Text Processing (CICLing)*, volume 3406, pages 486–497. Springer.

T. Wilson and S. Raaijmakers. 2008. Comparing word, character, and phoneme n-grams for subjective utterance recognition. In *Proceedings of INTERSPEECH*, pages 1614–1617.

Hong Yu and Vasileios Hatzivassiloglou. 2003. Towards answering opinion questions: Separating facts from opinions and identifying the polarity of opinion sentences. In *Proceedings of the Conference on Empirical Methods in Natural Language Processing (EMNLP)*, pages 129–136.

T. Zagibalov and J. Carroll. 2008. Automatic seed word selection for unsupervised sentiment classification of Chinese text. In *Proceedings of the International Conference on Computational Linguistics (COLING)*, pages 1073–1080.

Opinion Expression Mining by Exploiting Keyphrase Extraction

Gábor Berend
Department of Informatics,
University of Szeged
2. Árpád tér, H-6720, Szeged, Hungary
berendg@inf.u-szeged.hu

Abstract

In this paper, we shall introduce a system for extracting the keyphrases for the reason of authors' opinion from product reviews. The datasets for two fairly different product review domains related to movies and mobile phones were constructed semi-automatically based on the pros and cons entered by the authors. The system illustrates that the classic supervised keyphrase extraction approach – mostly used for scientific genre previously – could be adapted for opinion-related keyphrases. Besides adapting the original framework to this special task through defining novel, task-specific features, an efficient way of representing keyphrase candidates will be demonstrated as well. The paper also provides a comparison of the effectiveness of the standard keyphrase extraction features and that of the system designed for the special task of opinion expression mining.

1 Introduction

The amount of community-generated contents on the Web has been steadily growing and most of the end-user contents (e.g. blogs and customer reviews) are likely to deal with the author's emotions and opinions towards some subject. The automatic analysis of such material is useful for both companies and consumers. Companies can easily get an overview of what people think of their products and services and what their most important strengths and weaknesses are while users can have access to information from the Web before purchasing some product.

In this paper we will introduce a system which assigns pro and con keyphrases (free-text annotation) to product reviews. When dealing with product reviews, our definition of keyphrases is the set of phrases that make the opinion-holder feel negative or positive towards a given product, i.e. they should be the reason why the author likes or dislikes the product in question (e.g. *cheap price, convenient user interface*). Here, we adapted the general keyphrase extraction procedure from the scientific publications domain (Witten et al., 1999; Turney, 2003) to the extraction of opinion-reasoning features. However, our task is rather different since we aim at identifying the reasons for opinions, instead of keyphrases that represent the content of the whole document.

The supervised keyphrase extractor to be introduced here was trained on the pros and cons assigned to the reviews by their authors on the epinions.com site. These pros and cons are ill-structured free-text annotations and their length, depth and style are extremely heterogeneous. In order to have clean gold-standard corpora, we manually revised the segmentation and the contents of the pros and cons, and obtained sets of tag-like keyphrases.

2 Related work

There have been many studies on opinion mining (Turney, 2002; Pang et al., 2002; Titov and McDonald, 2008; Liu and Seneff, 2009). Our approach relates to previous work on the extraction of reasons for opinions. Most of these papers treat the task of mining reasons from product reviews as one of identifying sentences that express the author's negative or positive feelings (Hu and Liu, 2004a; Popescu and Etzioni, 2005). This paper is clearly distinguishable from them as our goal is to find the reasons for opinions expressed by phrases and we aim the task of phrase extraction instead of sentence recognition.

This work differs in important aspects even from the frequent pattern mining-based approach of (Hu and Liu, 2004b) since they regarded the main task of mining opinion features with respect to a group of products, not individually at review-level as we did. Even if an opinion feature phrase is feasible for a given product-type, it is not necessary that all of its occurrence are accompanied with sentiments expressed towards it (e.g. *The phone comes in red and black colors*, where *color* could be an appropriate product feature, but not an opinion-forming phrase).

A similar task to pro and con extraction gathers the key aspects from document sets, which has also gained interest recently (Sullivan, 2008; Branavan et al., 2008; Liu and Seneff, 2009). Existing aspect extraction systems first identify a number of aspects throughout the whole review set, then they automatically assign items from this pre-recognized set of aspects to each unseen review. Hence, they work at the corpus level and restrict themselves to using only a pre-defined number of aspects.

The approach presented here differs from these studies in the sense that it looks for the reason phrases themselves review by review, instead of multi-labeling some aspects. These approaches are intended for applications used by companies who would like to obtain a general overview about a product or would like to monitor the polarity relating to their products in a particular community. In contrast, we introduce here a keyphrase extraction-based approach which works at the document level as it extracts keyphrases from reviews which are handled independently of each other. This approach is more appropriate for the consumers, who would like to be informed before purchasing some product.

The work of Kim and Hovy (2006) lies probably the closest to our one. They addressed the task of extracting con and pro sentences, i.e. the sentences on why the reviewers liked or disliked the product. They also note that such pro and con expressions can differ from positive and negative opinion expressions as factual sentences can also be reason sentences (e.g. *Video drains battery.*). Here the difference is that they extracted sentences, but we targeted phrase extraction.

Most of the keyphrase extraction approaches (Witten et al., 1999; Turney, 2003; Medelyan et al., 2009; Kim et al., 2010) work on the scientific domain and extract phrases from one document that are the most characteristic of its content. In these supervised approaches keyphrase extraction is regarded as a classification task, in which certain n-grams of a specific document function as keyphrase candidates, and the task is to classify them as proper or improper keyphrases. Here, our task formalization of keyphrase extraction is adapted from this line of research for opinion mining and we focus on the extraction of phrases from product reviews that also bear subjectivity and induce sentiments in its author. As community generated pros and cons can provide abundant training samples and our goal is to extract the users' own words, here we also follow this supervised keyphrase extraction procedure.

3 Opinion Phrase Extraction Framework

Here, we employed a supervised machine learning approach for the extraction of reason keyphrases from a given review. Candidate terms were extracted from the text of the review and those present in the extracted set of pros and cons were regarded as positive examples during training and evaluation. Maximum Entropy classifiers were trained and the keyphrase candidates with the highest posteriori probabilities were selected to be keyphrases for a review of a test document in question. In the following subsections we will describe how keyphrase candidates and the feature space representing them were constructed.

3.1 Candidate term generation

One key aspect in keyphrase extraction is the way keyphrase candidates are selected and represented. As usually the number of potentially extracted n-grams and that of genuine keyphrases among them show high imbalancedness, keyphrase candidates are worth to be filtered, instead of using any successive n-grams. For this reason we limited the maximal length of the extracted phrases to at most 4 tokens and also required that the phrases should begin with either a non-stopword adjective, verb or noun and should end to either a non-stopword noun or adjective.

As for the filtration of the candidate set, a new step is introduced here, which omits normalized phrases that had only such occurrences which contained stopwords. This simple step proved effective in excluding many non-proper opinion phrases (i.e. increasing the maximal precision achievable) at the cost of discarding only a small proportion of proper phrases (i.e. slightly decreasing the best recall achievable).

Once we had the keyphrase candidates, they had

to be brought to a normalized form. The normalization of an n-gram consisted of lowercasing and Porter-stemming each of the lemmatized forms of its tokens, then putting these stems into alphabetical order (while omitting the stems of stopword tokens). With this kind of representation it was then possible to handle two orthographically different, but semantically equivalent phrases, such as '*the screen is tiny*' and '*TINY screen*' in the same way.

Previous works on keyphrase extraction also usually carry out this step of normalization, however, here we did it in such a manner that a mapping to each of the original orthographic forms of a normalized form and its corresponding context (i.e. the sentences containing it) was preserved at the same time and that could be successfully utilized at later processing steps.

To provide an alternative way of normalizing phrases, experiments relying on the usage of WordNet (Fellbaum, 1998) were also conducted. In these settings the normalized form of a single token was determined by first searching for all its synsets (in the case of verbs, these were such noun synsets that were in derivative relation with the synsets of the verb word form). Then instead of Porter-stemming the original token, its most frequent word form was stemmed, based on the estimated frequencies of WordNet for all the word forms of the synsets of the original token. In this way two – originally differently stemmed – word forms, such as *decide* and *decision* could be stemmed to the same root forms. Another advantage of this procedure is that it is able to handle semantic similarity to some extent.

The remaining parts of the normalization procedure were left unchanged (i.e. lowercasing and alphabetical ordering of the normalized forms of the individual tokens). Later, in the Results section, the effect of this kind of normalization will be shown.

Candidate terms were handled at the review level instead of occurrence level. This means that each normalized occurrence of a keyphrase candidate was gathered from the document and the feature values for the candidate term aggregate over its occurrences.

3.2 Feature representation

We constructed a rich feature set to represent the review-level keyphrase candidates. The feature space incorporates features calculated on the basis of the normalized phrases themselves, but more importantly, thanks to the mapping between the normalized phrase forms and their original occurrences, new contextual and orthographic features were possible to incorporate.

Features that could be generally used for any kind of keyphrase extracting task (e.g. that makes use of multiword expressions or character suffixes in a special way) and ones designed especially for the novel task of opinion phrase extraction (e.g. that uses SentiWordNet to determine polarity) as well as the standard features of keyphrase extraction are both introduced in the following.

Standard Features Since we assumed that the underlying principles of extracting opinionated phrases are quite similar to that of extracting standard (most of the time scientific) keyphrases, features of the standard setting were applied in this task as well. The most common ones, introduced by KEA (Witten et al., 1999) are the **Tf-idf** value and the **relative position** of the first occurrence of a candidate phrase within a document. We should note that KEA is primarily designed for keyphrase extraction from scientific publications and whereas the position of the first occurrence might be indicative in research papers, product reviews usually do not contain a summarizing "abstract" at the beginning. For these reasons we chose these features as the ones which form our baseline system. **Phrase length** is also a common feature, which was defined here as the number of the non-stopword tokens of an opinion phrase candidate.

Linguistic and orthographic features Since certain POS-codes are more frequent than others among genuine keyphrases, features generated by POS-codes belonging to an occurrence of a normalized phrase were applied. As **POS-code** sequences seem to be more informative, instead of simply indicating which POS-codes were assigned to any orthographic alternation of a normalized keyphrase candidate, it would be desirable to store the POS-code sequences in their full length as well. However, doing so might affect dimensionality in a negative way (especially when having few training data), i.e. the number of all the possible POS-code sequences ranging from lengths of 1 to 4 is too much. To overcome this issue, positional information was added to the POS-code features derived from the tokens of an n-gram. Features of POS-codes that were assigned to a token being itself a 1-token long keyphrase candidate, at the beginning, at the end, in between an n-gram, got a prefix `S-`, `B-`, `E-` and `I-`, respectively. For instance, the phrase *cheap/JJ phone/NN* induces the features {*B-JJ*, *E-NN*}, whereas the 1-token-long phrase *cheap/JJ* induces the feature {*S-JJ*}. Finally, numeric values for a normalized candidate phrase were assigned based on the distribution of the different POS-related features of all the running-text forms of a normalized phrase.

We introduced features exploiting the syntactic context of a candidate with parse trees. For an n-gram with respect to all the sentences it was contained in a given document, this feature stored the average and the minimal depths of those **NP-rooted trees** that contained the whole n-gram in its yield. These features are intended to express the "noun phraseness" of the phrase.

Features generated from the **character suffixes** of the individual tokens of the occurrences of a normalized keyphrase candidate were also employed. Character suffix features also incorporated positional information, similarly as it was done in the case of POS features. The suffixes themselves came from the last 2 and 3 characters of the tokens constructing an n-gram. For instance, the features induced by (and thus assigned with true value) for the phrase *cheap phone* are {*B-eap*, *B-ap*, *E-one*, *E-ne*}.

Opinionated phrases often bear special orthographic characteristics, e.g. in the case of *so slooow* or *CHEAP*. Due to the fact that the original forms of the phrases are stored in our representation, it was possible to construct two features for this phenomenon: the first feature is responsible for **character runs** (i.e. more than 2 of the same consecutive characters), and an other is responsible for **strange capitalization** (i.e. the presence of uppercase characters besides the initial one). The S-,B-,E-,I- prefixes were applied here as well, just like in the case of the **Named Entity** feature, which represented if a token was part of NE (with its type as well).

World knowledge-based features Features relying on the outer resources of Wikipedia and SentiWordNet were also exploited during our experiments. They were useful as world knowledge could be incorporated by their means.

Multiword expressions are lexical items that can be decomposed into single words and display idiosyncratic features (Sag et al., 2002), in other words, they are lexical items that contain space.

To measure the added value of MWEs in the task of opinion phrase extraction, a set of features was designed that indicated whether a certain phrase candidate (1) is an MWE on its own (e.g. *ease of use*), (2) can be composed from more MWEs on the list (e.g. *mobile internet access*), or is just the (3) superstring of at least one MWE from the list (e.g. *send text messages*). In order to be able to make such decisions, a wide list of MWEs was constructed from Wikipedia (dump 2011-01-07): all the links and formatted (i.e. bold or italic) text were gathered that were at least two tokens in length, started with lowercase letters and contained only English characters or some punctuation. Finally, an alignment of the elements of the list and the contexts of the reviews of the dataset was carried out (taking care of linguistic alternations and POS-tag matchings).

A more sophisticated surface-based feature used external information as well on the individual tokens of a phrase. It relied on the **sentiment scores** of SentiWordNet (Esuli et al., 2010), a publicly available database that contains a subset of the synsets of the Princeton Wordnet with positivity, negativity and neutrality scores assigned to each one, depending on the use of its sentiment orientation (which can be regarded as the probability of a phrase belonging to a synset being mentioned in a positive, negative or neutral context). These scores were utilized for the calculation of the sentiment orientations of each token of a keyphrase candidate. Surface-based SentiWordnet-calculated feature values for a keyphrase candidate included the *maximal positivity and negativity and subjectivity* scores of the individual tokens and the *total sum* over all the tokens of one phrase.

Sentence-based features were also defined based on SentiWordNet as it was also used to check for the presence of **indicator terms** within the sentences containing a candidate phrase. Those word forms were gathered from SentiWordNet, for which the sum of the average positivity and negativity sentiments scores among all its synsets were above 0.5 (i.e. the ones that are more likely to have some kind of polarity). Then for a given keyphrase candidate of a given document, a true value was assigned to the SentiWordNet-derived indicator features that had at least one co-occurrence within the same sentence with the keyphrase candidate in the same document.

SentiWordnet was also used to investigate the entire sentences that contained a phrase candidate. This kind of feature calculated the sum of every sentiment score in each sentence where a given phrase candidate was present. Then the mean and the deviation of the sum of the sentiment scores were calculated for each token of the phrase-containing sentences and assigned to the phrase candidate. The mean of the sentiment scores of the individual sentences yielded a general score on the **sentiment orientation** of the sentences containing a candidate phrase, while higher values for the **deviation** was intended to capture cases when a reviewer writes both factual (i.e. uses few opinionated words) and non-factual (i.e. uses more emotional phrases and opinions) sentences about a product.

Finally, Wikipedia was also used to incorporate semantic features from its category hierarchy. (Wikipedia categories form a taxonomy, indicating which article belongs to which (sub)category). In the case of a candidate phrase all the nominal parts of the normalized titles of **Wikipedia categories** for its related Wikipedia articles were added as separate binary features to the feature space. The normalization of the Wikipedia category names was similar to that of keyphrase candidates. For instance, given the candidate phrase '*service quality*' the feature *wiki_control_qual* is set to true since the Wikipedia article named *Service quality* is in the category *Quality control*.

Document and corpus-level features Among document-level features, the **standard deviation of the relative positions** compared to the document length was a measure to be computed. Higher values of the deviation in the position means that the reviewer keeps repeating some phrase from the beginning to the end of the review, which might indicate that this phrase is of higher importance for them.

As verbs often contribute to the sentiment polarity of the noun phrases they accompany (e.g. '*I adore its fancy screen.*' versus '*I bought this phone one year ago.*'), a set of features was introduced to deal with the **indicative verbs** in the context of candidate phrase occurrences within their document. For this feature to be calculated we took those verbs as indicators that occurred at least 100 times in the whole training dataset. When calculating a feature value for an opinionated-phrase candidate, the algorithm matched all of its occurrences in a document against every indicator verb. For the calculation of the feature value for a given phrase candidate – indicator verb pair, a syntactic distance value was first defined. This syntactic distance was equal to the minimal height of the subtree which contained both the keyphrase candidate and the indicator verb itself to the left among all the sentences associated with a document that contained the keyphrase candidate. The feature value was then determined by simply taking the reciprocal of this semantic distance. This way, the feature value was scaled between 0 and 1. (Note that for indicator verbs that were not present in any of the sentences containing a phrase candidate associated with a document, the semantic distance value was defined to be infinity, the limit value of the reciprocal of which is 0.)

Quite general characteristics of reason-expressing phrases can also be captured at the corpus level. Simply using the number of times an argument phrase aspirant was assigned to a review as a proper phrase on the training dataset was also taken into account as a **corpus-level** feature since the same proper opinion phrases can easily reoccur regarding products of the same type.

4 Experiments

Experiments were carried out on two fairly different types of product reviews, namely mobile phones and movies. We use standard keyphrase extraction evaluation metrics and baselines for evaluating our pros and cons extractor system.

4.1 Datasets

In our experiments, we crawled two quite different domains of product reviews, i.e. mobile phone and movie reviews from the review portal `epinions.com`. For both domains, 2000 reviews were crawled from `epinions.com` and an additional of 50 and 75 reviews for measuring inter-annotator agreement, respectively. This corpus is quite noisy (similarly to other user-generated contents); run-on sentences and improper punctuation were common, as well as grammatically incorrect sentences since reviews were often written by non-native English speakers. [1]

[1]All the data used in our experiments are available at `http://rgai.inf.u-szeged.hu/proCon`

	Mobiles	Movies
Number of reviews	2009	1962
Avg. sentence/review	31.9	29.8
Avg. tokens/sentence	16.1	17.0
Avg. keyphrases/review	4.7	3.2
Avg. keyphrase candidates/review	130.38	135.89

Table 1: Size-related statistics of the corpora

The list of pros and cons was inconsistent too in the sense that some reviewers used full sentences to express their opinions, while usually a few token-long phrases were given by others. The segmentation of their elements was marked in various ways among reviews (e.g. comma, semicolon, ampersand or the *and* token) and even differed sometimes within the very same review. There were many general or uninformative pros and cons (like *none* or *everything* as a pro phrase) as well.

In order to have a consistent gold-standard annotation for training and evaluation, we manually refined the pros and cons of the reviews in the corpora. In the first step, the automatic preprocessing of the segmentation of pros and cons was checked by human annotators. Our automatic segmentation method split the lines containing pros and cons along the most frequent separators. This segmentation was corrected by the annotators in 7.5% of the reviews. Then the human annotators also marked the general pros and cons (11.1% of the pro and con phrases) and the reviews without any identified keyphrases were discarded.

4.2 Evaluation issues

Keyphrase extraction systems are traditionally evaluated on the top-n ranked keyphrase candidates for each document by F-score (Kim et al., 2010), which combines the precision and recall of the correct keyphrases' class. Evaluation is carried out in a strict manner as a top-ranked keyphrase candidate is accepted if it has exactly the same standardized form as one of the keyphrases assigned to the review. The ranking of the phrase candidates was based on a probability estimation of a candidate belonging to the positive keyphrase class. Results reported here were obtained using 5-fold cross validation using Maximum Entropy classifier.

As we treated the mining of pros and cons as a supervised keyphrase extraction task, we conducted measurements with KEA (Witten et al., 1999), which is one of the most cited publicly available automatic keyphrase extraction system. However, we should note that due to the fact that our phrase extraction and representation strategy (and even the determination of true positive instances to some extent) slightly differs from that of KEA, the added values of our features should rather be compared to our second Baseline System (BL_{WN}) which uses WordNet for candidate phrase normalization. The baseline systems use our framework, with the feature set of KEA, which consists of tf-idf feature and the relative first occurrence of a keyphrase candidate. The only difference among the two baseline systems is that BL does not apply the WordNet-based normalization of phrase candidates introduced in Section 3.1.

Since we had the same findings as Branavan et al. (2008) that authors often omit several opinion forming aspects from their pros and cons listings that they later include in their review, we decided to determine the complete lists of pros and cons manually, that is, to compose pro and con phrases on the basis of the reviews. Due to the highly subjective nature of sentiments, the determination of sentiment-affecting pro and con phrases was carried out by three linguists, who were asked to annotate a 25-document subset of the mobile phone dataset. Their averaged agreements for the determination of pro phrases are 0.701 and 0.533 for Dice's coefficient and Jaccard index, and 0.69 and 0.526 for cons, respectively.

4.3 Results

In our experiments all the linguistic processing of the product reviews were carried out using Stanford CoreNLP. It uses the Maximum Entropy POS-tagger of Toutanova and Manning (2000) and syntactic parsing works on the basis of Klein and Manning (2003). The ranking of the candidate keyphrases was based on the posteriori probabilities of the MALLET implementation (McCallum, 2002) of Maximum Entropy classifier (le Cessie and van Houwelingen, 1992).

During the fully automatic evaluation, we followed strict evaluation (see 4.2) that is commonly utilized in scientific keyphrase extraction tasks. Table 2 contains the results of the strict evaluation for both domains. However, since strict evaluation is more likely to suit the evaluation of scientific keyphrase extraction better, i.e. semantically equivalent but different word forms are less common at that domain, we conducted human evaluation on the 25-document subset of the mobile

Feature	Mobiles Top-5	Mobiles Top-10	Mobiles Top-15	Movies Top-5	Movies Top-10	Movies Top-15
KEA	1.72/1.84/1.77	1.42/3.04/1.94	1.39/4.48/2.12	1.21/1.93/1.49	0.98/3.13/1.5	0.89/4.26/1.48
BL	2.6/2.8/2.73	2.6/5.5/3.54	2.6/8.2/3.93	1.6/2.5/1.95	1.5/4.9/2.34	1.6/7.4/2.58
BL_{WN}	2.7/2.9/2.8	2.7/5.8/3.68	2.7/8.7/4.12	1.7/2.8/2.14	1.7/5.4/2.61	1.7/8.2/2.88
IV	3.1/3.4/3.25§	2.9/6.2/3.92	2.8/9.1/4.31	2.4/3.7/2.9†	2.0/6.3/3.04§	1.9/8.8/3.09
KF	2.6/2.8/2.71	2.7/5.9/3.73	2.7/8.7/4.11	1.7/2.7/2.09	1.7/5.4/2.59	1.7/8.2/2.87
$Length$	3.2/3.4/3.26 §	3.1/6.6/4.18†	2.9/9.3/4.4	2.1/3.3/2.6	2.0/6.4/3.08§	2.0/9.1/3.22§
MWE	4.7/5.0/4.88‡	3.8/8.0/5.11‡	3.4/10.8/5.12‡	2.3/3.6/2.81†	2.0/6.3/3.06†	1.9/9.1/3.18§
POS	4.6/4.9/4.71‡	4.2/9.0/5.77‡	3.9/12.6/5.98‡	2.9/4.6/3.57‡	2.8/8.7/4.18‡	2.5/11.7/4.1‡
SWN	6.0/6.4/6.2‡	4.9/10.4/6.65‡	4.3/13.6/6.49‡	3.7/6.0/4.6‡	3.1/9.8/4.73‡	2.8/13.1/4.59‡
$StDev$	3.9/4.2/4.06‡	3.8/8.1/5.15‡	3.5/11.2/5.33‡	2.9/4.6/3.59‡	2.6/8.1/3.9‡	2.5/11.6/4.07‡
$Orth.$	3.2/3.4/3.28§	3.1/6.7/4.27†	2.9/9.5/4.49	3.0/4.7/3.65‡	2.5/7.8/3.76‡	2.3/10.9/3.82‡
$Suffix$	11.5/12.2/11.83‡	8.6/18.2/11.66‡	6.9/22.0/10.54‡	6.8/10.7/8.34‡	5.2/16.4/7.91‡	4.3/20.1/7.08‡
$Syntax$	3.5/3.7/3.61‡	3.0/6.4/4.06	2.8/9.1/4.33	2.3/3.6/2.78†	2.0/6.1/2.97§	1.9/9.1/3.2§
$Wiki$	11.9/12.7/12.25‡	8.1/17.4/11.09‡	6.3/20.1/9.63‡	8.8/13.9/10.78‡	6.3/19.8/9.59‡	4.8/22.5/7.9‡
$COMB$	**14.8/15.7/15.27**‡	10.4/22.0/14.11‡	8.0/25.4/12.17‡	**10.0/15.8/12.22**‡	7.0/21.9/10.63‡	5.3/24.6/8.67‡

Table 2: Performance using different features in the form of Precision/Recall/F-score obtained. IV, KF, SWN and Orth. stands for indicator verbs, corpus-level keyphrase frequency, SentiWordNet and orthography-driven features, respectively. Symbols §, † and ‡ in the upper index of a result indicates that it is significantly better compared to the baseline system which uses the WordNet based candidate phrase normalization (BL_{WN}) at confidence levels of 0.1, 0.05 and 0.01, based on Student's t-test, respectively. As it was only the KF feature which did not yield any significant improvement at all, the combined system (COMB) incorporated all the features but KF.

phone domain. The results of the manual evaluation is shown in 3.

4.4 Discussion

The fact that the highest F-scores for keyphrases are achieved when the number of extracted phrases is around the average number of pro and con phrases per reviews (i.e. between 3 and 5) suggests that our ordering of keyphrase candidates is quite effective (since once we find the number of keyphrases a document has, performance cannot really grow anymore).

Comparing the nature of the task of extracting keyphrases from scientific publications and that of product reviews, we shall take two observations: firstly, keyphrases of scientific documents are more universal, i.e. once we have the knowledge that the expression *distributed computing* was a good keyphrase for one scientific document, we can be more confident about it being a proper keyphrase for other documents within the same domain as well, whereas in the case of opinion phrases such as *pink color* can easily be mentioned in either opinionated and non-opinionated contexts. Secondly, besides scientific keyphrases being more ***universal***, they are more ***deterministic*** in the sense that there are fewer ways to express good keyphrases, e.g. suppose *simulated annealing* is a proper keyphrase for a scientific document, it is unlikely that an automatic system would extract *imitated annealing*, whereas in the case of product review the gold standard keyphrases often differ from their mention in the text (e.g. *tiny keys* and *small keys*).

The above mentioned examples suggest that opinion phrase extraction is more difficult to be performed and evaluated compared to scientific keyphrase extraction. We should note that the best performing system at SemEval-2010 (Kim et al., 2010) that dealt with the much simpler task of scientific keyphrase extraction achieved an F-score of 19.3 when evaluated against author keywords at the top-15 level.

It should be also added here, that among the keyphrases regarded as false positives in our evaluations, there were many near misses due to synonymy, e.g. *tiny keys* and *small keys* or *slow Web* and *slow WAP*. To overcome the synonymy issue to some extent the WordNet-based rewriting of tokens was introduced, which brought improvement in the case of the baseline systems for both domains (so it was employed in the later experiments as well). Another source of false positive classifications was due to the incompleteness of the opinion aspect entered by the user, i.e. not all the important aspects are necessarily listed among the

	Top-5			Top-10			Top-15		
	Prec.	Recall	F-score	Prec.	Recall	F-score	Prec.	Recall	F-score
∪	72.8	20.63	32.14	66.8	33.54	44.66	63.47	46.88	53.92
∩	46.4	27.81	34.77	41.6	44.92	43.2	37.07	56.68	44.82
Author	34.4	22.29	27.05	31.6	35.43	33.4	28.8	45.14	35.17

Table 3: Results of the human evaluation. ∪, ∩ and Author means when the automatic keyphrases were matched against the union, intersection of the keyphrases of three independent annotators and the keyphrases of the original author, respectively.

pros and cons section, as described earlier. On the other side, many of the author-entered keyphrases were absent in the contents of a review in their same form: only 34,8% and 23,9% of gold standard keyphrases could be found in the texts having the same normalized form for the mobile phone and the movie domains, respectively, setting an upper bound for the recall values when evaluating based on strict matching.

To overcome all the previously mentioned shortcoming during automatic evaluation, human evaluation was performed and it showed that real life application of opinion phrase extraction could be of much higher utility than strict evaluation would suggest. This is due to the fact that human annotators had access to common sense knowledge and during the inspection of keyphrases they could resolve such cases that were impossible during automatic evaluation.

All the features were effective in the sense that expanding the baseline feature set by them separately resulted in better results. Moreover, in the majority of the cases improvements were of high significance (see Table 2). The added value of Wikipedia features (that are likely to work well in other domains as well) should be highlighted as well as the relatively poor effect of keyphrase frequency feature which normally works better in the case of standard scientific keyphrase extraction tasks. A possible reason for keyphrase frequency feature not being that effective in the opinion domain is that in the case of opinionated keyphrases, the presence of such a phrase that was marked as positive in one document is not necessarily marked the same way in other documents, e.g. because one author may write about the feature objectively while the other may write his strong opinions about the very same feature, using similar wording.

5 Conclusions

In this paper, we presented a pros and cons extraction system by pointing out the parallelism between the keyphrases of scientific papers – given by their author – and the pros and cons phrases – given by product reviewers. The WordNet-based phrase normalization and an extended stopword-based filtration of keyphrase candidates introduced here could be of possible use for any kind of phrase extraction tasks. Besides demonstrating their similarity, the main differences of the two tasks were also highlighted, and several ways to adopt to the specialties of opinion phrase extraction have been suggested by introducing a rich feature set, some of which could also be widely used (e.g. Wikipedia-based ones), and others are specifically designed to the special task of opinion phrase extraction (e.g. SentiWordNet-related ones).

Among the most important differences of opinion phrase extraction from scientific keyphrase extraction we should note that for product reviews the pure occurrence of a single phrase is less deterministic to be a keyphrase, i.e. some emotional context is necessary to treat them as genuine ones. Also, the language of reviews is more special since it tends to contain elements that are not present in other genres of documents, such as irony and sarcasm and offers more possibility to express identical things in different ways. In total, our results are competitive with those of other standard keyphrase extraction tasks even when applying strict normalized form matching evaluation. Moreover, human evaluation showed that when semantics are involved into the evaluation, results are significantly better than it is suggested by automatic evaluations.

Acknowledgments

This work was supported by the Project "TÁMOP-4.2.1/B-09/1/KONV-2010-0005 – Creating the Center of Excellence at the University of Szeged", supported by the European Union and co-financed by the European Regional Development Fund and by the project BELAMI financed by the National Innovation Office of the Hungarian government.

References

S.R.K. Branavan, Harr Chen, Jacob Eisenstein, and Regina Barzilay. 2008. Learning document-level semantic properties from free-text annotations. In *Proceedings of ACL-08: HLT*, pages 263–271, Columbus, Ohio. ACL.

Andrea Esuli, Stefano Baccianella, and Fabrizio Sebastiani. 2010. Sentiwordnet 3.0: An enhanced lexical resource for sentiment analysis and opinion mining. In *Proceedings of the Seventh conference on International Language Resources and Evaluation (LREC'10)*, Valletta, Malta. ELRA.

Christiane Fellbaum, editor. 1998. *WordNet An Electronic Lexical Database*. The MIT Press, Cambridge, MA ; London.

Minqing Hu and Bing Liu. 2004a. Mining and summarizing customer reviews. In *Proceedings of the tenth ACM SIGKDD international conference on Knowledge discovery and data mining*, KDD '04, pages 168–177, New York, NY, USA. ACM.

Minqing Hu and Bing Liu. 2004b. Mining opinion features in customer reviews. In *Proceedings of the 19th national conference on Artifical intelligence*, AAAI'04, pages 755–760. AAAI Press.

Soo-Min Kim and Eduard Hovy. 2006. Automatic identification of pro and con reasons in online reviews. In *Proceedings of the COLING/ACL 2006 Main Conference Poster Sessions*, pages 483–490, Sydney, Australia. ACL.

Su Nam Kim, Olena Medelyan, Min-Yen Kan, and Timothy Baldwin. 2010. Semeval-2010 task 5: Automatic keyphrase extraction from scientific articles. In *Proceedings of the 5th International Workshop on Semantic Evaluation*, SemEval '10, pages 21–26, Morristown, NJ, USA. ACL.

Dan Klein and Christopher D. Manning. 2003. Accurate unlexicalized parsing. In *Proceedings of the 41st ACL*, pages 423–430.

S. le Cessie and J.C. van Houwelingen. 1992. Ridge estimators in logistic regression. *Applied Statistics*, 41(1):191–201.

Jingjing Liu and Stephanie Seneff. 2009. Review sentiment scoring via a parse-and-paraphrase paradigm. In *Proceedings of the 2009 Conference on Empirical Methods in Natural Language Processing*, pages 161–169, Singapore. ACL.

Andrew Kachites McCallum. 2002. Mallet: A machine learning for language toolkit. http://mallet.cs.umass.edu.

Olena Medelyan, Eibe Frank, and Ian H. Witten. 2009. Human-competitive tagging using automatic keyphrase extraction. In *Proceedings of the 2009 Conference on Empirical Methods in Natural Language Processing*, pages 1318–1327, Singapore. ACL.

Bo Pang, Lillian Lee, and Shivakumar Vaithyanathan. 2002. Thumbs up?: sentiment classification using machine learning techniques. In *EMNLP '02: Proceedings of the ACL-02 conference on Empirical methods in natural language processing*, pages 79–86, Morristown, NJ, USA. ACL.

Ana-Maria Popescu and Oren Etzioni. 2005. Extracting product features and opinions from reviews. In *Proceedings of Human Language Technology Conference and Conference on Empirical Methods in Natural Language Processing*, pages 339–346, Vancouver, British Columbia, Canada. ACL.

Ivan A. Sag, Timothy Baldwin, Francis Bond, Ann Copestake, and Dan Flickinger. 2002. Multiword Expressions: A Pain in the Neck for NLP. In *Proceedings of CICLing-2002*, pages 1–15, Mexico City, Mexico.

Todd Sullivan. 2008. Pro, con, and affinity tagging of product reviews. Technical Report 224n, Stanford CS.

Ivan Titov and Ryan McDonald. 2008. A joint model of text and aspect ratings for sentiment summarization. In *Proceedings of ACL-08: HLT*, pages 308–316, Columbus, Ohio. ACL.

Kristina Toutanova and Christopher D. Manning. 2000. Enriching the knowledge sources used in a maximum entropy part-of-speech tagger. In *Proceedings of the 2000 Joint SIGDAT conference on Empirical methods in natural language processing and very large corpora*, EMNLP '00, pages 63–70, Stroudsburg, PA, USA. ACL.

Peter Turney. 2002. Thumbs up or thumbs down? semantic orientation applied to unsupervised classification of reviews. In *Proceedings of the 40th Annual Meeting of the Association for Computational Linguistics (ACL)*, pages 417–424.

Peter Turney. 2003. Coherent keyphrase extraction via web mining. In *Proceedings of IJCAI*, pages 434–439.

Ian H. Witten, Gordon W. Paynter, Eibe Frank, Carl Gutwin, and Craig. 1999. Kea: Practical automatic keyphrase extraction. In *ACM DL*, pages 254–255.

Extracting Resource Terms for Sentiment Analysis

Lei Zhang
Department of Computer Science
University of Illinois at Chicago
851 S. Morgan St, Chicago IL 60607
lzhang3@cs.uic.edu

Bing Liu
Department of Computer Science
University of Illinois at Chicago
851 S. Morgan St, Chicago IL 60607
liub@cs.uic.edu

Abstract

Existing research on sentiment analysis mainly uses sentiment words and phrases to determine sentiments expressed in documents and sentences. Techniques have also been developed to find such words and phrases using dictionaries and domain corpora. However, there are still other types of words and phrases that do not bear sentiments on their own, but when they appear in some particular contexts, they imply positive or negative opinions. One class of such words or phrases is those that express resources such as water, electricity, gas, etc. For example, "*this washer uses a lot of electricity*" is negative but "*this washer uses little water*" is positive. Extracting such resource words and phrases are important for sentiment analysis. This paper formulates the problem based on a bipartite graph and proposes a novel iterative algorithm to solve the problem. Experimental results using diverse real-life sentiment corpora show good results.

1 Introduction

Sentiment analysis or opinion mining has been an active research area in recent years (e.g., Pang and Lee 2008; Turney, 2002; Wiebe *et al.* 2004; Hu and Liu, 2004; Kim and Eduard, 2004; Wilson *et al.* 2005; Popescu and Etzioni, 2005; Riloff *et al.* 2006; Esuli and Fabrizio, 2006; Mei et al, 2007; Stoyanov and Cardie; 2008). Researchers have studied the problem at the document level, sentence level and aspect level to determine the sentiment polarity expressed in a document, in a sentence and on an aspect of an entity (see the surveys (Pang and Lee, 2008) and (Liu, 2010)). One type of key information used in almost all existing sentiment analysis techniques is a list of sentiment words (or opinion words). Positive sentiment words are words expressing desired states or qualities, e.g., *good*, *amazing*, and *excellent*, and negative sentiment words are words expressing undesirable states or qualities, e.g., *bad*, *crappy*, and *ugly*.

A key characteristic of these words is that they themselves bear sentiments. They are frequently used in sentiment analysis tasks. However, it is also important to recognize that sentiment analysis based only on these words (or phrases) is far from sufficient. There are still many other types of expressions that do not bear sentiments on their own, but when they appear in some particular contexts, they imply sentiments. In (Liu, 2010), several such expressions and their corresponding opinion/sentiment rules are introduced. We believe that all these expressions have to be extracted and associated problems solved before sentiment analysis can achieve the next level of accuracy. One such type of expressions involves resources, which occur frequently in many application domains. For example, *money* is a resource in probably every domain ("*this phone costs a lot of money*"), *gas* is a resource in the car domain, and *ink* is a resource in the printer domain. If a device consumes a large quantity of resource, it is undesirable. If a device consumes little resource, it is desirable. For example, the sentences, "*This laptop needs a lot of battery power*" and "*This car uses a lot of gas*" imply negative sentiments on the laptop and the car. Here, "gas" and "battery power" are resources, and we call these words *resource terms* (which cover both *words* and *phrases*).

In terms of sentiments involving resources, the rules in Figure 1 are applicable (Liu, 2010). Rules 1 and 3 represent normal sentences that involve resources and imply sentiments, while rules 2 and 4 represent comparative sentences that involve resources and also imply sentiments, e.g., "*this washer uses much less water than my*

1.	Positive	←	consume no or little resource
2.		|	consume less resource
3.	Negative	←	consume a large quantity of resource
4.		|	consume more resource

Figure 1: Sentiment polarity of statements involving resources.

old GE washer". To the best of our knowledge, there is no reported algorithm that extracts resource terms. In this paper, we propose an iterative algorithm to extract them from a domain corpus, e.g., a set of product reviews. In the above example sentence, we want to extract "*water*" as a resource term.

The most related work to ours is the product aspect/feature extraction (e.g., Hu and Liu, 2004, Popescu and Etzioni, 2005, Kobayashi *et al.* 2007, Scaffidi *et al.* 2007, Titov and McDonald, 2008, Stoyanov and Cardie. 2008, Wong *et al.*, 2008, Zhao *et al.*, 2010). A resource in a domain is often an aspect or implies an aspect. For example, in "*this camera uses a lot of battery power*", "battery power" clearly indicates *battery life*, which is an aspect of the camera entity. However, there are some important differences between resources and other types of aspects. The key difference is that resource terms often contribute directly to sentiments (e.g., based on the quantity that is consumed), while other aspects may not. e.g., "picture quality" in "*the picture quality of this camera is great*," where "great" solely determines the sentiment of the sentence. Thus, resource terms require special treatments in sentiment analysis. In this paper, we focus on identifying and extracting resource terms.

This paper models the extraction problem with a bipartite graph and proposes a novel circular definition to reflect a special reinforcement relationship between *resource usage verbs* (e.g., *consume*) and resources (e.g., *water*) for resource extraction. We call the proposed method MRE (*M*utual *R*einforcement based on *E*xpected values). Based on the definition, the problem is solved using an iterative algorithm. To initialize the iterative computation, some global *seed resources* are employed to find and to score some strong resource usage verbs. These scores are applied as initialization for the iterative computation in the bipartite graph for any application domain. When the algorithm converges, we obtain a ranked list of candidate resource terms. Our experimental results based on 7 real-life data sets show the effectiveness of the proposed method. It outperforms 5 strong baselines.

2 Related work

As we discussed in the introduction, this work is mainly related to product aspect extraction. Hu and Liu (2004) proposed a technique based on association rule mining to extract frequent nouns and noun phrases as product aspects. They also introduced the idea of using sentiment words to find additional (infrequent) aspects. Popescu and Etzioni (2005) improved the precision of this method by determining whether a noun/noun phrase is indeed a product aspect by computing the pointwise mutual information (PMI) score between the phrase and class discriminators, e.g., "*xx has*", "*xx comes with*", etc., where *xx* is a product class word, and using Web search.

A dependency based method is proposed in (Zhuang *et al.*, 2006) to extract aspects for a movie review application. Dependency relations are also used in (Qiu *et al.* 2011) to extract both aspects and sentiment words. Zhang *et al.* (2010) augmented this method by introducing aspect ranking. Wang and Wang (2008) proposed a similar bootstrapping method but not based on dependencies. In (Kobayashi *et al.* 2007), a pattern mining method was proposed to find extraction patterns. Statistics from the corpus are employed to determine the extraction confidence.

Other works on aspect extraction use topic modeling and probabilistic modeling to capture and group aspects at the same time (e.g., Mei *et al.*, 2007; Titov and McDonald, 2008; Lu *et al.* 2009; Zhao *et al.*, 2010; Wang *et al.* 2010; Jo and Oh, 2011). In (Su *et al.*, 2008), a clustering method was also proposed with mutual reinforcement to identify aspects.

However, all these existing works focused on extracting aspects in general. They do not specifically identify resource terms, which are a special type of aspects, and need additional techniques to recognize them.

Our work is also related to the general information extraction problem. There are two main approaches to information extraction: rule-based and statistical. Early extraction systems are mainly based on rules (e.g., Riloff, 1993). In statistical methods, the most popular models are Hidden Markov Models (HMM) (Rabiner, 1989;

Jin *et al.*, 2009), and Conditional Random Fields (CRF) (Lafferty *et al.*, 2001). CRF has been used in extracting aspects and topics (e.g., Stoyanov *et al.*, 2008, Jakob and Gurevych, 2010). However, a limitation of CRF is that it only captures local patterns rather than long range patterns. Also, CRF is a supervised method, but our method is a bootstrapping method which needs no supervision but only a few initial global resource seeds.

Our proposed method is also related to the Web page ranking algorithm HITS (Kleinberg, 1999), which finds hub and authority pages based on the hyperlink structure of the Web pages. However, our method is quite different as we have a different formulation. We will discuss the details in Section 3. HITS is also one of the baseline methods that will be compared with the proposed MRE technique in the evaluation section. Our method outperforms HITS considerably.

3 The Proposed Method

In this section, we present the proposed technique. Let us use the following two example sentences to develop the idea and the algorithm:

1. *This car uses a lot of gas.*
2. *This car uses less gas than Honda Civic.*

We call the first sentence a *normal sentence*, and the second sentence a *comparative sentence.*

From these two sentences, we can make the following observation:

Observation: The sentiment expressed in a sentence about resource usage is often determined by the triple,

(verb, quantifier, noun_term),

where *noun_term* is a noun or a noun phrase

In the first sentence, "uses" is the main verb, "a lot of" is a quantifier phrase, and "gas" is a noun representing a resource. In the second sentence, "uses" is also the main verb, "less" is a comparative quantifier, and "gas" is again a resource as a noun. We want to use such triples to help identify resources in a domain.

We notice that using only a pair,

(verb, noun_term), or
(quantifier, noun_term)

is not sufficient. The pair (verb, noun_term) is unsafe because such pairs are very common since subject-verb-object (SVO) is the most common English sentence structure, and the object is usually a noun term. Using (quantifier, noun_term) is also unsafe as the meaning of the noun terms following quantifiers can be diverse.

By no means do we say that any above triple implies the last noun term is a resource. For example, "colors" is not a resource in "*this car got many colors*". The triples only find candidate resources, which need to be further analyzed (see Section 3.2).

Since it is unsafe to use the pair (verb, noun_term) or (quantifier, noun_term), we use only triples for candidate resource extraction. Due to the fact that it is easy to compile the main expressions of quantifiers, we just need to extract verbs and noun terms to discover candidate resources which are the noun terms. The quantifiers that we use in this work are listed in Table 1.

Quantifiers
some, several, numerous, many, much, more, most, less, least a large/huge/small/tiny number of a large/huge/small/tiny quantity/amount of lot/lots/tons/ton/plenty/deal/load/loads of [a] few/little

Table 1: A list of quantifiers

3.1 Extract Triples and Build a Graph

Since our algorithm is based on triples, we now discuss how to extract them. To extract triples from a corpus, part-of-speech (POS) tagging is first performed on each sentence. Verbs and nouns are then identified based on their POS tags. Verbs are words tagged as VB, VBD, VBZ, VBG, VBN, and VBP. Nouns are words tagged as NN and NNS. In addition, we regard a phrase with continuous POS tags of NN and NNS as a noun phrase, e.g., "spray/NN gel/NN" is seen as a single noun phrase "spray gel". In English grammar, quantifiers usually precede and modify noun terms. Thus, after locating a quantifier in a sentence, we extract its associated noun term, which directly follows the quantifier. After obtaining the noun term, we further exploit the dependency relation to find the associated verb in the sentence, since there is an assumed *verb-object* relationship between the verb and the noun. The relationship can be determined by a dependency parser. In our work, we approximate the dependency by making use of a text window in the sentence. It works quite well. Thus we did not use a dependency parser, which tends to be inefficient. We choose the closest verb in a text window (e.g., 10 words) before the noun as the verb part of the triple. Note that verbs such as "*is*", "*was*", "*am*" "*are*", "*were*" "*have*", "*has*", and "*had*" are not used since they usually do not express resource usages. Finally, we lemmatize both the verb and the noun and store them only in the lemmatized format in a triple.

With all extracted triples, we build a bipartite graph based on the verb set V, the noun set N, and the set of links L between V and N. A link (i, j) is in L if there is a triple involving a verb $i \in V$ and a noun term $j \in N$. Note that in this graph, we do not use quantifiers, which are only used to identify candidate verbs and nouns.

3.2 The Proposed Algorithm

We now present the proposed algorithm, which relies on the bipartite graph to encode a special kind of mutual enforcement relationship between resource usage verbs and resource terms. Before diving into the details of the algorithm, we define the following concepts.

Definition (Resource Term): A resource term represents a physical or virtual entity that can be consumed or obtained in order to benefit from it.

Some resources are general, which exist in many different application domains, i.e., "money" in "*this TV costs me a lot of money*". Other resources are more domain-specific, e.g., "onboard memory" in "*the phone uses more onboard memory*".

Definition (Resource Usage Verb): A resource usage verb (or *resource verb* for short) is a verb that can express resource usage.

Likewise, some resource verbs are general and can modify many different resource terms, e.g., "uses" in "*this car uses much more gas*", "*this washer uses a lot of water*", and "*this program uses a lot of memory.*" Many others are more resource-specific, and tend to frequently co-occur with specific resources, e.g., "*spent*" in "*I spent too much money to buy the car*".

It seems that we can solve the problem of extracting resource terms using a simple graph propagation strategy. That is, given an application domain corpus, the user first provides a few seed resource terms. Using the bipartite graph, we can identify some resource verbs by following the links of the graph. The newly identified resource verbs are then used to identify new resource terms. The process continues until no more resource terms or verbs can be found.

However, this simple strategy has some major problems. First, as many resource verbs and terms are domain-specific, asking the user to provide some seeds for each domain is non-trivial. Second, many nouns (or verbs) in the triples may not be resources (or resource usage verbs), e.g., "*this car comes with many colors.*" Any error resulted in the propagation can generate more errors subsequently.

With these concerns in mind, we propose a more sophisticated iterative algorithm. To solve the first problem above, we take a global approach. Instead of asking the user to provide some seed resources for each domain, we simply provide some global resource seeds, e.g., *water*, *money*, and *electricity*. Then in each application, the user does not need to do anything. Using these global resource seeds, we want to identify some good resource usage verbs. These verbs act as the initialization for the discovery of additional resource terms in each domain based on the domain corpus. The proposed method thus consists of two main stages. The first stage is only done once and the results are used for individual application domains as the initialization.

Stage 1: *Identifying Global Resource Verbs*

Global resource verbs are those verbs that can express resource usage of many different resources, e.g., *use* and *consume*. We can use a bipartite graph constructed from a large data set to find them. The following observations help us formulate the solution:

1. A global resource verb has links to many different resource terms. The more diverse the resource terms that a verb can modify, the more likely it is a good global resource verb.
2. Conversely, the more global resource verbs a resource term is associated with, the more likely it is a genuine resource term.

These two observations indicate that the global resource verbs and the resource terms have a mutual enforcement relationship, which can be modeled by the Web page ranking algorithm HITS exactly. We give a brief introduction to the HITS algorithm (Kleinberg, 1999) below.

The objective of HITS (Hyperlink-induced topic search) is to find Web pages that are authorities and hubs. A good authority page is a page pointed to by many pages, and a good hub is a page that points to many pages. There is a mutual reinforcement relationship between authority pages and hub pages.

Given a set of Web pages S, HITS computes an *authority score* and a *hub score* for each page in S. Let the number of pages to be studied be n. We use $G = (S, E)$ to denote the (directed) link graph of S, where E is the set of directed edges (or links) among the pages in S. We use M to denote the adjacency matrix of the graph.

$$M_{ij} = \begin{cases} 1 & if (i,j) \in E \\ 0 & otherwise \end{cases} \quad (1)$$

Let the authority score of page i be $A(i)$, and the hub score of page i be $H(i)$. The mutual reinforcing relationship in HITS is defined as follows:

$$A(i) = \sum_{(j,i) \in E} H(j) \quad (2)$$

$$H(i) = \sum_{(i,j) \in E} A(j) \quad (3)$$

We can write them in a matrix form. We use **A** to denote the column vector with all authority scores, and use **H** to denote the column vector with all hub scores:

$$\mathbf{A} = M^T\mathbf{H} \quad (4)$$

$$\mathbf{H} = M\mathbf{A} \quad (5)$$

To solve the equations, the widely used method is power iteration, which starts with some random values for the vectors, e.g., $\mathbf{A}^0 = \mathbf{H}^0 = (1, 1, \ldots 1)^T$. It then continues to compute iteratively till convergence. Note that the initial values do not generally affect the final ranking of authorities and hubs.

In our scenario, global resource verbs act as hubs and resource terms act as authorities. We provided a list of common resources (seeds) (see Section 4). Using these seeds, we extract triples from the corpus and produce a link graph as discussed in Section 3.1. The noun term set N consists of only these seed resource terms, and the V set consists of only those verbs which form triples with the N set. HITS is then applied on the graph. After HITS converges, each candidate resource verb has a hub score. We normalize them to the 0-1 interval. The resulting values are used to initialize the system for discovering resource terms from each application domain. That is, we do not need to execute stage 1 anymore.

Stage 2: *Discovering Resource Terms in a Domain Corpus*

Given the global resource verb values from stage 1 and a domain corpus, the stage 2 system identifies resource terms from the domain corpus.

In this stage, we still start with a bipartite graph as in the first stage. The graph can be constructed as discussed in Section 3.1 by extracting triples from the domain corpus. On one side of the bipartite graph, it is the set of candidate resource terms N (noun terms) and on the other side, it is the set of candidate resource (usage) verbs V. For each $i \in V$, we want to compute its likelihood of being a resource verb, denoted by $u(i)$, and for each noun term $j \in N$, we want to compute its likelihood of being a resource term, denoted by $r(j)$. If i and j are in a triple, a link (i, j) is in the link set L.

An obvious question is: Can we use HITS here as in stage 1? The answer is no. Unlike stage 1, the N set here is no longer a set of true resources, but only a list of noun terms, which are just candidate resources. A verb modifying multiple noun terms does not necessarily indicate that the verb is a resource usage verb. For example, it could be a general verb like "get". Also, as mentioned earlier, it is not always the case that if a noun term is modified by many verbs, it is a resource term. For example, it could be a topic word like "car" for the car domain. Applying the simple reinforcement relation in HITS is ineffective as we will see in the experiment section. To introduce the proposed technique, we make the following observations:

1. If a noun term is *frequently* associated with a verb (including quantifiers), the noun term is more likely to be a genuine resource term.
2. If a verb is *frequently* associated with a noun term (including quantifiers), it is more likely to be a genuine resource verb.

These two observations indicate that we should take verb and noun term co-occurrence frequency into consideration, which cannot be used in HITS. To consider frequency, we turn the frequency into a probability and make use of the expected value to compute scores for the verbs and noun terms, rather than summation in HITS.

In probability, given a random variable X, its *expected value* is defined as

$$E[X] = \sum_i p_i x_i \quad (6)$$

where x_i is a possible outcome of the random variable X and p_i is the probability of x_i.

For our case, we have the following definitions for $u(i)$ and $r(j)$.

$$u(i) = \sum_{(i,j) \in L} p_{ji} r(j) \quad (7)$$

$$r(j) = \sum_{(i,j) \in L} p_{ij} u(i) \quad (8)$$

where

$$p_{ij} = \frac{c(i,j)}{\sum_{(k,j)\in L} c(k,j)} \text{ and}$$

$$p_{ji} = \frac{c(i,j)}{\sum_{(i,k)\in L} c(i,k)}$$

$c(i, j)$ is the frequency count of the link (i, j) in our corpus. p_{ij} is thus the probability of link (i, j) among all links from different verbs i to a noun j. p_{ji} is the probability of link (i, j) among all links from different nouns j to a verb i. We called this proposed algorithm MRE (*M*utual *R*einforcement based on *E*xpected values)

Smoothing the Probabilities

Although the idea is reasonable, we found an important issue when computing expected values. If a noun term j occurs only once, and it is connected with a strong resource verb i, its ranking value becomes very high. Due to its low frequency, the expected value of $r(j)$ is just the value of $u(i)$. In many cases, the value may be even higher than some frequent noun terms, whose value may be reduced by being associated with some non-resource verbs. This situation is not desirable. Since for sentiment analysis application, we should rank those frequent resource terms at the top instead of the terms which only occur once in the corpus.

The problem is that the probabilities of verbs or nouns are not reliable due to limited data. In order to handle infrequent verbs or noun terms, we smooth the probabilities to avoid probabilities of 0 or 1. The standard way of doing this is to augment the count of each distinctive verb/term with a small quantity λ ($0 \le \lambda \le 1$) or a fraction of a verb or noun term in both the numerator and denominator. Thus any verb and noun term will have a smoothed probability as follows.

$$p_{ij} = \frac{\lambda + c(i,j)}{\lambda |N| + \sum_{(k,j)\in L} N(k,j)} \quad (9)$$

$$p_{ji} = \frac{\lambda + c(i,j)}{\lambda |V| + \sum_{(i,k)\in L} N(i,k)} \quad (10)$$

This is called the *Lidstone smoothing* (Lidstone's law of succession) (Lidstone, 1920). We use λ to 0.01, which performs well. In the equations, $|V|$ is the total number of verbs and $|N|$ is the total number of noun terms in the graph.

Algorithm: MRE (Q, G)
Input: A global resource verb set Q with their hub scores computed from HITS in stage 1, and G is the bipartite graph
Output: a ranked list of candidate resource terms

1. $u^0(i) \leftarrow H(i)$ of verb i, if *verb* $i \in Q$
2. $u^0(i) \leftarrow \arg\min_{r\in Q}\{H(r)\}$, if *verb* $i \notin Q$
3. **Repeat** till convergence
4. $\quad r^{n+1}(j) = \sum_{(i,j)\in L} p_{ij} u^n(i)$
5. $\quad u^{n+1}(i) = \sum_{(i,j)\in L} p_{ji} r^n(j)$
6. $\quad$ normalize $r(j)$ and $u(i)$
7. Output the ranked candidate resource terms based on their $r(j)$ score values.

Figure 2: The proposed MRE algorithm

Note that with smoothing, the original bipartite graph becomes a complete bipartite graph. Each added link is given a very small probability as computed using Equations (9) and (10).

The Computation Algorithm

The computation algorithm for the proposed method MRE is given in Figure 2. Q is the set of verbs from stage 1, and G is the bipartite graph. To initialize the iterative computation, we assign the hub score from stage 1 to each verb $i \in V$ as its initial score $u^0(i)$ if i is in Q (line 1). If i is not in Q, $u^0(i)$ is given the minimum value of the hub scores of all verbs in Q (line 2).

After this initialization, the algorithm proceeds iteratively until convergence. We will describe the convergence characteristic of the algorithm in Section 4.5.

Finally, we note that unlike HITS, which converges to the same hub and authority (steady-state) scores regardless the initialization. For MRE, the initialization makes a big difference as we will see in the evaluation section.

4 Evaluation

We now evaluate the proposed MRE method. We first describe the data sets, evaluation metrics, and then the experimental results. We also compare MRE with 5 baseline methods.

4.1 Data Sets and Global Resource Seeds

We used seven (7) diverse data sets to evaluate our technique. These data sets were crawled from the Web. Table 2 shows the domains (based on their names) and the number of sentences in each

Data sets	Car	Washer	Paint	Printer	Haircare	Mobile	TV
# of Sent.	56880	9997	1655	16314	29347	25354	23901

Table 2. Experimental data sets

Data sets	Car	Washer	Paint	Printer	Haircare	Mobile	TV	Ave.
TF	0.40	0.20	0.60	0.80	0.40	0.40	0.20	0.43
TFR	0.40	0.40	0.40	0.80	0.40	0.40	0.60	0.49
HITS	0.60	0.40	0.20	0.80	0.60	0.40	0.40	0.49
MRE-NI	0.20	0.80	0.20	0.60	0.60	0.60	0.80	0.54
MRE-NS	0.60	0.60	0.60	0.80	0.60	0.40	0.40	0.57
MRE	1.00	0.80	0.60	0.80	0.60	0.80	0.80	0.77

Table 3. Experimental results: Precision@5

Data sets	Car	Washer	Paint	Printer	Haircare	Mobile	TV	Ave.
TF	0.40	0.20	0.70	0.60	0.30	0.50	0.50	0.46
TFR	0.30	0.50	0.60	0.50	0.40	0.40	0.50	0.46
HITS	0.50	0.60	0.50	0.70	0.50	0.50	0.40	0.53
MRE-NI	0.30	0.80	0.40	0.40	0.30	0.70	0.60	0.50
MRE-NS	0.70	0.60	0.70	0.60	0.60	0.70	0.40	0.61
MRE	0.90	0.80	0.80	0.60	0.70	0.80	0.60	0.74

Table 4. Experimental results: Precision@10

Data sets	Car	Washer	Paint	Printer	Haircare	Mobile	TV	Ave.
TF	0.40	0.30			0.20	0.35	0.35	0.32
TFR	0.30	0.50			0.30	0.20	0.40	0.34
HITS	0.55	0.65			0.50	0.50	0.35	0.51
MRE-NI	0.30	0.70			0.45	0.50	0.45	0.48
MRE-NS	0.60	0.65			0.50	0.55	0.45	0.55
MRE	0.75	0.70			0.65	0.60	0.55	0.65

Table 5. Experimental results: Precision@20

data set ("Sent." means the sentence). Each data set contains a mixture of reviews, blogs, and forum discussions about one type of product. We split each posting into sentences and the sentences are POS-tagged using the Brill's tagger (Brill, 1995). The tagged sentences are the input to our system MRE.

The global resource terms (resource seeds) used in the first stage of our method are: "gas", "water", "electricity", "money", "ink", "shampoo", "detergent", "room" "fabric softener", and "soap". In stage 1 of our algorithm, we used the combined data set of those in Table 2 to compute the hub scores for global resources usage verbs found to be associated with the resource seeds through some quantifiers.

4.2 Evaluation Metrics

We adopt the rank precision, also called **precision@N** metric for the experimental evaluation. It gives the percentage of correct resource terms (precision) at different rank positions. This is a popular method used in search ranking evaluation because one does not know all the relevant pages. This is also the case in our work as we do not know how many resource terms have been mentioned in each of the data set.

4.3 Baseline Methods

TF (Triple Frequency): This method finds all triples of the form (verb, quantifier, noun_term), and then ranks them according to their frequency counts. This basically corresponds to the methods used in (Hu and Liu 2004; Popescu and Oren, 2005; Zhuang *et al.* 2006; Qiu *et al.* 2011) as it combines the frequency and dependency patterns of the triples. This method is reasonable because many triples are indeed resource usage descriptions, and those more frequent ones (ranked high) are more likely to be genuine ones.

TFR (Triple Frequency Ratio): This method is similar to the above method but it divides TF by the number of pairs (verb, noun_term) with the same verb and the same noun term as in the triple. The reason for doing so is that such pairs are very common because **subject-verb-object (SVO)** is the most common English sentence structure, and object is usually a noun term. If the ratio of the occurrences of the triple is small, it may not be a resource usage description and then should be ranked low because sentences containing resources are usually talking about resource usages.

HITS: This method simply runs the HITS algorithm in the second stage for each data set. In this case, the global initialization is not useful as HITS will reach a steady state regardless of the initialization.

MRE-NI: Our MRE method without initialization by the global resource usage verbs.

MRE-NS: Our MRE method without the probability smoothing.

4.4 Results and Discussions

Tables 3-5 give the precision results for top 5, top 10, and top 20 ranked candidate resource terms. Each value in the last column gives the average precision for the corresponding row. We note that in Table 5, there are no results for "Paint" and "Printer" because no resources were found by any algorithm beyond top 10 as there are not many resources in these domains. It is also important to note that those resources that have been used as global seeds in stage 1 of our algorithm are not counted in the precision computation for the results in the tables. In other words, the discovered resource terms are all new. From the tables, we can make the following observations:

1. TF and TRF perform poorly. We believe the reason is that frequent triples or frequent triple ratio do not strongly indicate resource usages.
2. The performance of the HITS algorithm is also inferior. For only two data sets (out of 7), it performs similarly to MRE for the top 5 results. Its average results are all much worse than those of MRE.
3. Global resource verbs are very useful. As we can see, without using them (MRE-NI), the results are dramatically worse.
5. Probability smoothing also helps significantly. Without it, MRE-NS produces worse results consistently compared with MRE.
6. MRE is the best method overall. On average, it consistently outperforms every baseline method. Moreover, it does better than the 5 baseline methods on every data set at every rank position except for the data set "Printer" for the top 10 results, for which HITS is better.

From these observations, we can conclude that our proposed MRE algorithm is highly effective and it outperforms all 5 baseline methods.

4.5 Algorithm Convergence

In this sub-section, we show the convergence characteristic of the proposed MRE algorithm.

Figure 3 shows the convergence behavior of MRE for the car data set, where the x-axis is the number of iterations, and the y-axis is the difference of the average 1-norm values of the vector r and vector u in two consecutive iterations. We can see that the algorithm converges quite fast, i.e., in about 8 iterations. For other data sets, they behave similarly. All of them converge within 6-9 iterations. In all experiments, the algorithm stops when the 1-norm difference is less than 0.01.

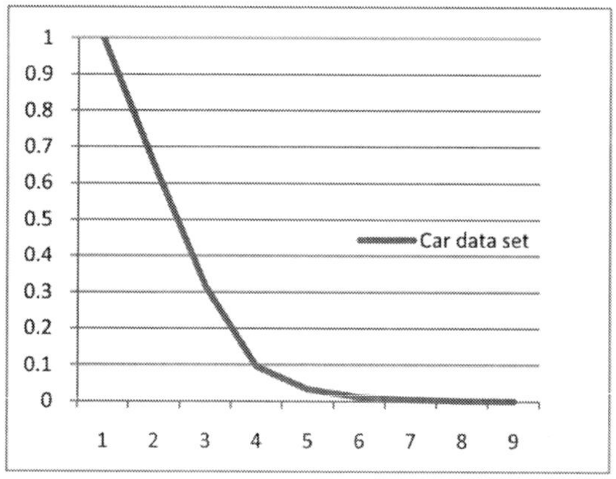

Figure 3: Convergent rate for car data

5 Conclusion

This paper proposed the problem of extracting resource words and phrases in opinion documents. They are a class of terms that are important for sentiment analysis. As we explained in the introduction section, when such resource terms appear with certain verbs and quantifiers, they often imply positive or negative sentiments or opinions. To the best of our knowledge, this work is the first attempt to discover such words and phrases. A novel iterative algorithm based on a circular definition of resource words and their corresponding verbs has been proposed. It was modeled on a bipartite graph and a special reinforcement relationship between resource usage verbs and resource terms. Experimental results based on 7 real-world opinion data sets showed that the proposed MRE method was effective. It outperformed 5 baseline methods. In our future work, we plan to improve the algorithm to make it more accurate, and also study sentiment analysis involving resource words or phrases

References

Brill, Eric. 1995. Transformation-Based Error-Driven Learning and Natural Language Processing: a case study in part of speech tagging. *Computational Linguistics, 1995.*

Esuli, Andrea and Fabrizio Sebastiani 2006. SentiWordNet: A Publicly Available Lexical Resouce for Opinion Mining. *LREC 2006*

Hu, Minqing and Bing Liu. 2004. Mining and Summarizing Customer Reviews. *KDD 2004*

Jakob, Niklas and Iryna Gurevych. 2010. Extracting Opinion Targets in a Single- and Cross-Domain Setting with Conditional Random Fields. In *Proceedings of EMNLP 2010*

Jin, Wei, Hung Hay Ho, and Rohini K. Srihari. 2009. A Novel Lexicalized HMM-based Learning Framework for Web Opinion Mining. *ICML 2009*

Jo, Yohan and Alice Oh. 2011. Aspect and Sentiment Unification Model for Online Review Analysis. In *Proceedings of WSDM 2011*

Kim, Soo-Min and Eduard H, Hovy. 2004. Determining the sentiment of opinions. *COLING-2004*, 2004.

Kleinberg, Jon. 1999. "Authoritative sources in hyperlinked environment" *Journal of the ACM 46 (5): 604-632 1999*

Kobayashi, Nozomi, Kentaro Inui, and Yuji Matsumoto. 2007. Extracting Aspect-Evaluation and Aspect-of Relations in Opinion Mining. *EMNLP.*

Lafferty, John, Andrew McCallum and Fernando Pereira. 2001 Conditional Random Fields: Probabilistic Models for Segmenting and Labeling Sequence Data. In *Proceedings of ICML*, 2001.

Lidstone, J. George. 1920. Note on the General Case of the Bayes-Laplace Formula for Inductive or a Posteriori Probabilities. *Transactions of the Faculty of Actuaries 1920*

Liu, Bing. 2010. Sentiment analysis and subjectivity. *Handbook of Natural Language Processing, second edition*, 2010.

Lu, Y., C. Zhai, and N. Sundaresan. Rated aspect summarization of short comments. In *Proceedings of International Conference on World Wide Web (WWW-2009)*, 2009.

Mei, Qiaozhu, Ling Xu, Matthew Wondra, Hang Su, and ChengXiang Zhai. 2007. Topic Sentiment Mixture: Modeling Facets and Opinions in Weblogs. In *Proceedings of WWW, 2007.*

Pang, Bo and Lillian Lee. 2008. Opinion Mining and Sentiment Analysis. *Foundations and Trends in Information Retrieval pp. 1-135 2008.*

Popescu, Ana-Maria and Oren Etzioni. 2005. Extracting product features and opinions from reviews. In *Proceedings of EMNLP, 2005.*

Qiu, Guang, Bing Liu, Jiajun Bu and Chun Chen. 2011. Opinion Word Expansion and Target Extraction through Double Propagation. *Computational Linguistics*, Vol. 37, No. 1: 9.27.

Rabiner, Lawrenence. 1989. A Tutorial on Hidden Markov Models and Selected Applications in Speech Recognition. In *Proceedings of the IEEE, 77(2), 1989.*

Riloff, Ellen. 1993. Automatically Constructing a Dictionary for Information Extraction Tasks. In *Proceedings of AAAI 1993.*

Riloff, Ellen, Siddharth Patwardhan and Janyce Wiebe. 2006. Feature Subsumption for Opinion Analysis. In *Proceedings of EMNLP 2006*

Stoyanov, Veselin and Claire Cardie. 2008. Topic Identification for Fine-grained Opinion Analysis. In *Proceedings of COLING 2008*

Su, Qi, Xinying Xu, Honglei Guo, Zhili Guo, Xian Wu, Xiaoxun Zhang, Bin Swen and Zhong Su. 2008. Hidden Sentiment Association in Chinese Web Opinion Mining. *WWW 2008.*

Titov, Ivan and Ryan McDonald. 2008. Modeling Online Reviews with Multi-grain Topic Models. In *Proceedings of WWW* 2008.

Turney, Peter. 2002. Thumbs up or thumbs down?: semantic orientation applied to unsupervised classification of reviews. In *Proceedings of ACL-2002*, 2002.

Wang, Bo and Houfeng Wang. 2008. Bootstrapping both Product Features and Opinion Words from Chinese Customer Reviews with Cross-Inducing In *Proceedings of IJCNLP 2008.*

Wang, Hongning, Yue Lu, and Chengxiang Zhai. 2010. Latent Aspect Rating Analysis on Review Text Data: A Rating Regression Approach. In *Proceedings of KDD 2010.*

Wiebe, Janyce, T. Wilson, R. Bruce, M. Bell, and M. Martin. 2004. Learning subjective language. *Computational Linguistics*, 30(3): p. 277-308.

Wilson, Theresa, Janyce Wiebe and Paul Hoffmann. 2005. Recognizing Contextual Polarity in Phrase-Level Sentiment Analysis. *HLT/EMNLP 2005*

Zhang, Lei, Bing Liu., Suk Hwan Lim, Eamonn O'Brien-Strain. 2010. Extracting and Ranking Product Features in Opinion Documents. In *Proceedings of COLING 2010*

Zhao, Xin. Jing Jiang, Hongfei Yan, Xiaoming Li. 2010. Jointly Modeling Aspects and Opinions with a MaxEnt-LDA Hybrid. *EMNLP, 2010.*

Zhuang, Li, Feng Jing, Xiao-yan Zhu. 2006. Movie Review Mining and Summarization. *CIKM 2006.*

Towards Context-Based Subjectivity Analysis

Farah Benamara
IRIT-CNRS
Toulouse
benamara@irit.fr

Baptiste Chardon
Synapse Développement
Toulouse
baptiste.chardon@synapse-fr.com

Yannick Mathieu
LLF-CNRS
Paris
yannick.mathieu@linguist.jussieu.fr

Vladimir Popescu
IRIT-CNRS
Toulouse
popescu@irit.fr

Abstract

We propose a new subjectivity classification at the segment level that is more appropriate for discourse-based sentiment analysis. Our approach automatically distinguish between subjective non-evaluative and objective segments and between implicit and explicit opinions, by using local and global context features.

1 Introduction

Subjectivity and polarity classification is one of the most studied research area in opinion analysis (Pang and Lee, 2004; Wiebe and Riloff, 2005; Wilson et al., 2009). The first task generally distinguish between objective and subjective statements. Polarity classification is then performed in order to extract positive, negative and possibly neutral statements. These two tasks are co-dependent, since subjectivity analysis filters out statements that contain no opinion.

A common approach in these tasks is to rely on the prior polarity of words and expressions as encoded in external lexical resources. However, as (Polanyi and Zaenen, 2006) stated, identifying prior polarity alone may not suffice to improve sentiment analysis at a finer grain, we need both *local* and *global* context. Context provided *locally* can help in two ways. First, it can be used in subjectivity word sense disambiguation (SWSD) in order to determine if a given word has a subjective or an objective sense (Akkaya et al., 2009). It can also be used to identify valence shifters (viz. negations, modalities and intensifiers) that strengthen, weaken or reverse the prior polarity of a word or an expression (Kennedy and Inkpen, 2006; Wilson et al., 2009). *Global* context on the other hand can be used to identify implicit opinions and to improve the recognition of the overall stance.

Few research efforts have been undertaken on using discourse as features for sentence / clause-based opinion analysis. Among them, (Pang and Lee, 2004) assume that subjective and objective sentences are more likely to appear together, (Asher et al., 2008) have developed an annotation schema for a fine-grained contextual opinion analysis using discourse relations, (Taboada et al., 2008) have used a Rhetorical Structure Theory discourse parser in order to calculate semantic orientation by weighting the nuclei more heavily, and finally, (Somasundaran, 2010) has proposed a discourse-level treatment to improve sentence-based polarity classification and to recognize the overall stance. More recently, (Zhou et al., 2011) proposed an unsupervised method to recognize RST-based discourse relations for eliminating intra-sentence polarity ambiguities. However, no work has investigated so far how discourse structure can be used to enhance subjectivity analysis (SA).

Using discourse for SA raises new issues: *Is sentence/clause subjectivity-based analysis appropriate? Is binary subjective vs. objective classification enough for capturing how opinions are expressed within discourse?* and finally, *how can rhetorical relations help to correctly identify subjective orientation at a finer-grained level?* In this paper, we aim to answer these questions.

2 Context-Based SA: New Challenges

2.1 Segment-Based SA

The sentence level is not appropriate for context-based SA, since, in addition to objective clauses, a single sentence may contain several opinion clauses that can be connected by rhetorical relations. Moving to the clause level is also not appropriate, since several opinion expressions can be discursively related as in *The movie is great but too long* where we have a *Contrast* relation or as in *Mr. Dupont, a rich business man, has been savagely killed* where we have an *Elaboration* because the appositive gives further information about the eventuality introduced in the main clause. Therefore, we need to move to a finer-grained analysis, at the segment level. (Somasundaran et al., 2007) have used a similar level to detect the presence of sentiment and arguing in dialogues. However, segment annotations were provided by their corpus, whereas in our case, segments are defined according to the Segmented Discourse Representation Theory (SDRT) (Asher and Lascarides, 2003) and are automatically detected.

2.2 Beyond Binary Classification

SA can not be simply reduced to binary subjective vs. objective classification. The following examples extracted from our corpus of French movie reviews illustrate this (they are translated in English and discourse segments are between []):

(1) [The movie is not bad,]$_a$ [although some persons left the auditorium]$_b$
(2) [Laborious]$_a$ [and copy/paste of the first part.]$_b$
(3) [This movie is poignant,]$_a$ [and the actors excellent.]$_b$ [It will remain in your DVD closet.]$_c$
(4) [I suppose]$_a$ [that the government policy failed]$_b$

Segments (1.a), (2.a), (3.a), (3.b) and (4.b) are *explicit opinions*. (1.b), (2.b) and (3.c) convey *implicit opinions* and (4.a) is *subjective*, but *non-evaluative*. (Wiebe et al., 2005) have already proposed an expression-level annotation scheme that distinguishes between explicit mentions of private states, speech events expressing private states, and expressive subjective elements. (Liu, 2010) has also observed that subjective sentences and opinionated sentences (which are objective or subjective sentences that express implicit positive or negative opinions) are not the same, even though opinionated sentences are often a subset of subjective sentences. We follow the same observations and we propose a new subjectivity classification at the segment level that is more appropriate for discourse-based sentiment analysis. We automatically classify each segment into four classes, namely *S*, *OO*, *O* and *SN*, as defined below.

Definition 1. *S segments* are segments that contain explicitly lexicalized *subjective and evaluative* expressions. Their polarity can be positive (as in (1.a)), negative (as in (2.a)) or neutral in the sense that their positivity/negativity depends on the context (as in (3.a)).

Definition 2. *OO segments* are positive or negative opinions implied in an objective segment. They do not contain any explicit subjective clues and are objective out of context [1].

Definition 3. *O segments* do not contain any lexicalized subjective term, neither do an implied opinion.

Definition 4. *SN segments* are subjective, but non-evaluative segments that are used to introduce opinions. In general, these segments contain verbs that are used to report the speech and opinions of others. It is important to note that *SN* does not cover the cases of neutral opinion.

These classes have several advantages over standard binary classification. First, they allow us to distinguish between purely subjective expressions (*S*) and implicit subjective expressions (*OO*). Secondly, our classes can be used to enhance polarity classification, since they allow for the removal of the *O* and *SN* segments, which do not convey any positive, negative or neutral opinion. Finally, our classes can also be used to enhance the overall opinion strength assessment. *SN* segments, especially in news articles, can play an important role since they convey the degree of veracity of the information and the degree of the commitment of the author and of the writer.

Recently, some efforts have been done on the automatic identification of implicit sentiments. For example, (Greene and Resnik, 2009) used lexical semantics and syntax. (Muşat and Trăuşan-Matu, 2010) investigated the influence of valence shifters on the identification of implicit sentiment in economic texts. However, to our knowledge, as yet no work proposed to automatically distinguish between evaluative and non-evaluative segments on the one hand, and between implicit and explicit opinions on the other hand, by using contextual features.

2.3 Rhetorical relations and SA

Using SDRT as a formal framework, we have the following discourse relations: *Contrast*(*a*,*b*) in (1) marked by *although*, *Continuation*(*a*,*b*) in

[1]This definition does not take into account implicit opinions conveyed in subjective segments, such as metaphors.

(2) marked by *and*, and *Attribution*(a,b) in (4).We observe in our corpus that segments related by a *Contrast* or *Continuation* relation often share the same subjective orientation (about 80 %). However, discourse connectors are not the only indicator for deciding whether a segment is opinionated or not. Indeed, some connectors can introduce several discourse relations. In addition, relations are not always explicitly marked, as in (3) where the implicit opinion conveyed in segment c is linked to the subjective segments a and b by a *Result* relation. Another problem is how segments are attached within the discourse structure. In (3), we have *Continuation*(a,b) and *Result*([a,b], c) where [a,b] is a complex segment. Therefore, the subjectivity of segment c depends on [a,b].

Using discourse in opinion analysis is thus a complex task. As a preliminary step, we propose to study the influence of contextual features using mostly lexically-marked discourse relations, and, crucially, without relying on any existing discourse relation annotated corpora. We do not use complex segments and we assume that each segment is only attached to the nearby segment on the left or on the right. In the next sections, we first present the data and our subjective lexicon. Sections 5 and 6 detail respectively the segmentation algorithm and the classification strategies. Section 7 presents the experiments we carried out and discusses the results.

3 Data and Annotations

Our corpus is composed of 136 French movie reviews extracted from the Allô Ciné web site (115 are used for development (our gold) and 21 for test). Three judges performed a two step annotation: first segmentation and then segment classification. Segmentation consists in finding elementary discourse units (EDUs). EDUs typically correspond to verbal clauses, but also to other syntactic units describing eventualities, adjuncts (like appositions or frame adverbials), non-restrictive relatives and appositions (for embedded EDUs). In case of *S* EDUs, we observe that several opinion expressions (often conjoined NPs or APs clauses) can be related by discourse relations.We resegment such EDUs into separate clauses – for instance [*the film is beautiful and powerful*] is taken to express two segments: [*the film is beautiful*][*and powerful*]. For segment annotation, we rely on an already existing annotation guide elaborated during the ANNODIS project (Afantenos et al., 2010) that shows that segmentation is a relatively easy task even for naives. In order to avoid errors in determining the basic units, segmentation relies on annotation consensus.

For segment classification, we elaborated a specific annotation guide where we ask the judges to annotate each EDU into *S*, *OO*, *O* and *SN* according to the definitions given in Section 2.2. First, the judges were trained to the task and discussed while annotating the same documents (10 reviews that were subsequently discarded from the gold). Then, they separately doubly-annotated each review. This yielded an average Cohens kappa of 0.7 for *S*, 0.72 for *O*, 0.61 for *SN* and 0.54 for *OO*. The latter two are moderate agreements and figure, we believe, an artifact of the length of the texts. Indeed, the longer a text is, the higher difficulty for human subjects is in detecting discourse context in longer texts. However, the study of this hypothesis falls out of the scope of this paper and is therefore left for future work. Nonetheless, these figures are well in the range of state-of-the-art research reports in distinguishing between explicit and implicit opinions (Toprak et al., 2010). For our experiments, the conflicting cases were resolved through discussion between annotators.

4 Subjective Lexicon

Our lexicon is composed of 270 verbs, 632 adjectives, 296 nouns, 594 adverbs, 51 interjections, 178 opinion expressions, with 95 modalities among all these. Since there is no existing free subjective lexicon for French, we have manually built our own lexicon from the study of a wide variety of corpora.Following the opinion categorization described in (Asher et al., 2008), each entry (except for adverbs) is associated to four high-level semantic categories (namely *reporting*, *judgement*, *sentiment* and *advice*) and to 24 subcategories. For adverbs, we use additional categories: *negation, affirmation, doubt, intensifier* and *manner*. Only adverbs of manner express opinions, the other adverbs are used as valence shifters.

We manage both polarity and sense ambiguities. We do not fix the polarity of entries that may have context-dependent polarity orientations. Instead, we list all possible orientations (for example, the entry *long* has both a positive and a negative polarity). In order to detect if a subjective entry from our lexicon is employed in an objective sense, we coupled our lexicon to an external French dictionary D that manually encodes the senses of more than 77 678 words and expressions depending on syntactic configurations For example, the French adjective "*noble*" (noble) has three senses: (a) "noblesse" (pertaining to the aristocracy), (b) "précieux" (precious) and (c) "élevé" (lofty). For each entry E_L in our lexicon, we manually look for its corresponding senses in D as follows: if $E_L \in D$ then if $SubjSense_{E_L} \subseteq Sense_{E_L}$ then add to our lexicon the set $SubjSense_{E_L}$. Thus, for *noble* we only retain (b) and (c) as subjective senses. This dictionary is used by the Cordial syntactic parser (Laurent et al., 2009) in order to perform SWSD. If the identified sense found by the parser is encoded in our lexicon, then the word has a subjective sense; otherwise, it has an objective sense.

5 Automatic Discourse Segmentation

The segmentation is carried out using a set of lexical and syntactic features as described in (Afantenos et al., 2010). These features include the distance from sentence boundaries, the dependency path, and the chunk start/end. Since we used a different syntactic parser, we modified certain features accordingly, and discarded others. We performed a two-level segmentation. First, we constructed a feature vector for each word token, which is classified into: R (Right) for words starting an EDU, L (Left) for tokens ending an EDU, N (Nothing) for words completely inside its EDUs, and B (Both) for tokens which constitute the only word of an EDU.

In the second step, the EDUs which contain at least one token that belongs to our subjective lexicon were retained for a further segmentation. The latter is easier than the segmentation performed at the first level, because we do not encounter embedded segments. Thus, the second-level segmentation of EDUs comes down to searching for one or more "cut points" therein. Since the proportion of EDUs that need to be resegmented is relatively low (about 12 % in the gold standard), we carried out this step by using symbolic rules. These are mainly based on discourse markers.

We performed a supervised learning by using the MegaM software package[2], based on the Maximum Entropy model (Berger et al., 1996) in order to classify each segment into the R, L, Nothing or Both classes, as described above. We carried out a 10-fold cross-validation on our gold standard and an evaluation on the Test data. Table 1 shows first-level EDUs segmentation results for the Right, the Left and Nothing boundaries. For the symbolic segmentation, we evaluated our results (i) on the gold and (ii) on the Test data. The F-measures for boundary recognition are 97.88 % in (i) and 98.65 % in (ii); for the internal-boundaries, we have 84.17 % in (i) and 84.68 % in (ii). Finally, for the new EDU recognition we obtain 77.23 % in (i) and 76.31 % in (ii).

6 Classifiers

The classes, *S*, *O*, *SN* and *OO* are unbalanced in the development corpus. Besides, getting the *OO* segments right is far from obvious, sometimes even for humans. This is why we have defined two orthogonal binary sets of classes:

(a) S_NC vs. O_NC where S_NC = $S \cup SN$ and O_NC = $O \cup OO$ which distinguish between *subjective non-contextual* segments, which are intrinsically subjective, irrespective of their context of occurrence and *objective non-contextual* segments, which, in the absence of any context, are intrinsically objective.

(b) Eval_Op vs. Non_EvalOp where Eval_Op = $S \cup OO$ and Non_EvalOp = $O \cup SN$ which distinguish between *evaluative* and *opinionated* segments, which, given the appropriate context, contain an explicit or an implicit opinion and *non-evaluative* and *non-opinionated* segments, which, irrespective to the context, are not evaluative.

On the gold standard, this grouping yields 919 S_NC EDUs, 511 O_NC EDUs and 1083 Eval_Op EDUs, 347 Non_EvalOp EDUs. Two binary classifiers are constructed, one for each of the two binary sets of classes, defined above: an "S" classifier for **(a)** and an "Op" classifier for **(b)**. Given that the binary sets of classes represent two mutually independent re-partitionings of the segment space, the classifiers are independent of one another. Hence, they can be run in parallel. Then, their outputs are used, via a simple set of four rules, to yield the original four EDU classes. The rules are:

- IF an EDU is S_NC AND Eval_Op, then it is *S*;
- IF an EDU is S_NC AND Non_EvalOp, then it is *SN*;
- IF an EDU is O_NC AND Eval_Op, then it is *OO*;
- IF an EDU is O_NC AND Non_EvalOp, then it is *O*.

The two orthogonal classifiers introduced above

[2]http://www.cs.utah.edu/~hal/megam/

	Precision			Recall			F-measure		
	R	L	Nothing	R	L	Nothing	R	L	Nothing
Gold	94.97	93.80	97.88	93.41	94.14	98.10	94.18	93.97	97.99
Test	92.61	93.47	94.05	81.79	78.69	98.15	86.86	85.45	96.06

Table 1: First-level EDU segmentation results (in percents)

operate on the same input text. Hence, to get the class of each EDU in the input text, it suffices to perform a fusion of the results of these classifiers, via the four rules shown above. Each classifier is based on SVMs ("Support Vector Machines") (Burges, 1998). From each EDU a distinct feature vector is computed for each classifiers.

6.1 Feature Set

The features used are described in Table 2. They have been grouped in "Local" and "Contextual" features, according to whether they rely on adjacent EDUs or not. All the features are binary.

Local Features. They have been grouped in "Lexical", "Stylistic" and "Syntactic", according to whether they rely on lexical information only, on stylistic or on syntactic information. We have three lexical features. The first one concerns the presence in an EDU of a noun, adjective, adverb of manner, verb, expression or interjection that belongs to the lexicon, excluding entries expressing modalities and negations. The second feature refines the previous one by taking into account only those lexical entries that have subjective senses as described in section 4. The last lexical feature checks the presence of modals in the lexicon.

"Stylistic" features look for emoticons, words in capital letters and for specific punctuation marks. For emoticons, we rely on a dictionary of 79 emoticons. Capitalization is extracted by taking care to filter out certain standard acronyms, such as DVD. For punctuations, we look for sequences of punctuation marks, such as "??", "!!", "?!", or "!?".

We have five "syntactic" features. The first one looks for comparatives and relative superlatives using a set of manually-built French language-specific comparative and superlative patterns. The second one checks the presence of verbs in the "reporting" category, or in the "advice" category that do not have prior polarity, and by seeing whether the arguments the verbs are in the EDUs or not. The next feature gets the scoping of the modals via a syntactic (dependence) analysis of the EDU. The fourth local syntactic feature is extracted by using a set of manually-built typical French syntactic patterns that bear a subjective meaning. These patterns also allow for some flexibility since other words might be intercalated. The last feature is also detected via a syntactic analysis of the text in order to check if an EDU is left-detached place or time (circumstantial) complement (CC) since these EDUs are mainly objective.

Contextual Features. These features have been grouped in two subtypes, "Non-discursive" and "Discursive". Non-discursive features test the presence of a reporting or non-polar advice verband we test it on the EDU that occurs *before* (i.e., to the left of) the current EDU. The second group of contextual features refer to discourse constraints. The first one checks for the *unmarked Commentary* relation between the current EDU and the next one, when the latter contains an emoticon. If this happens, then that previous EDU is Eval_Op. The next feature checks for the simultaneous presence of two marked SDRT rhetorical relations, in the set {*Continuation*, *Parallel*, *Contrast*, *Alternation*}, one between the current EDU and the previous one, and the other between the current EDU and the next one, with the previous and the next EDUs being in the Eval_Op class. In order to determine the presence of these rhetorical relations, we rely on a French lexicon of discourse connectors, developed with the SDRT rhetorical relations in mind (Roze et al., 2010). The feature that follows is a relaxation of the previous one, in that it applies when at least one marked rhetorical relation is found, between the previous EDU and the current one, or between the latter and the next one. The last feature is based on the empirically-motivated intuition that, in general, in reviews, the last EDU tends to be the second argument of a *Result* relation between (some EDUs in) the rest of the document and itself. As such, this last EDU tends to be in the Eval_Op class.

6.2 Getting the Discursive Features

For computing the two discursive features in a current EDU that are based on discourse markers (henceforth, "DFM"), we rely on an already

Scope	Type	Description	S	Op
Local	Lexical	Subjective expression from the lexicon	√	√
		Semantically-disambiguated subjective expression	√	√
		Modal	—	√
	Stylistic	Emoticon	√	√
		Punctuation marks	—	√
		Word in capital letters	—	√
	Syntactic	Relative superlative or comparative	—	√
		Reporting, or non-polar advice verb, with the argument not in the EDU	√	√
		Word modified by a modal	—	√
		Syntactic pattern	—	√
		EDU left-detached place or time complement	—	√
Contextual	Non-discursive	Reporting, or non-polar advice verb, in the *previous* EDU	—	√
	Discursive	Emoticon in the *next* EDU	—	√
		(Discourse marker in the current EDU and *previous* EDU is Eval_Op) and (discourse marker in the *next* EDU and the *next* EDU is Eval_Op)	—	√
		(Discourse marker in the current EDU and *previous* EDU is Eval_Op) or (discourse marker in the *next* EDU and the *next* EDU is Eval_Op)	—	√
		Current EDU is the last in a document	—	√

Table 2: Features for the two classifiers: S and Op

available Op classification of the previous and/or next EDUs. Of course, for a raw input text, such a classification is not available. Hence, we have devised an iterative procedure for the Op classifier, which first starts with an Op classification by using all the features in Table 2, except for DFM. This provides a first Op classification of the input EDUs, which is used for *bootstrapping* a second iterative Op classification of the EDUs, this time by using all the features in Table 2.

In order to guarantee the convergence of the procedure, we rely on the idea that the goal of the Op classification is mainly to detect *OO* EDUs among intrinsically *O* EDUs. Thus, from the perspective of the Op partitioning of the EDU space, the classification is supposed to start with all the input EDUs as Non_EvalOp, and then to move the appropriate ones into the Eval_Op class. This boils down to imposing a constraint on the second Op classification in the iterative procedure, namely, that it does not alter the class of the EDUs which had already been classified as Eval_Op. The stopping criterion consists in the stabilization of the F-measure of the classifier with respect to the initial test data. The procedure assumes that both classifiers (the bootstrapping one and the iterative one) have been trained on the same data, except that the feature vectors are defined as appropriate for each classifier; the DFM features are determined, in the training phase, by relying on the gold annotation of the training EDUs.

The procedure goes as described below, where $bootstrp\_vs$ is the set of bootstrapping feature vectors, and $curr\_vs(i)$ is the set of input feature vectors at iteration i. $preds(i)$ are the predicted class labels of the respective SVM classifier, at iteration i; $\leftarrow$ is the assignment operator; $F\_score(A, B)$ is the F-measure between the class labellings of a list of feature vectors, A, and a list of class labels, B, both lists having the same length. $\oplus$ is an operator that takes the same types of arguments as F_score, A and B, and implements the filter on the Eval_Op EDUs ensuring the convergence of the iterative procedure ($length(A)$ is the number of elements in list A). It is defined as:

$A \oplus B ::=$ for i from 0 to $length(A)$:
  if $class(A[i]) =$ Non_EvalOp:
    $class(A[i]) \leftarrow B[i]$.

We call ϵ the "convergence factor", a threshold of the F-measure variation from one iteration to another. MAX_ITER is the maximum number of iterations if convergence is not achieved before. The procedure is:

for an input test document $test$:

1. compute $bootstrp\_vs$, with all features except for DFM;
2. apply the bootstrapping classifier on $bootstrp\_vs$; obtain thus $preds(0)$ and $F\_score(0) \leftarrow F\_score(bootstrp\_vs, preds(0))$;
3. compute DFM by using $preds(0)$; obtain thus $curr\_vs(0)$;
4. for n from 1 to MAX_ITER:
   4.1 $curr\_vs(n) \leftarrow curr\_vs(n-1) \oplus preds(n-1)$
   4.2 apply the iterative classifier on $curr\_vs(n)$; obtain thus $preds(n)$ and $F\_score(n)$ $\leftarrow$

$F\_score(curr\_vs(n), preds(n))$;

4.3 if $||F\_score(n) - F\_score(n-1)|| \leq \epsilon$: STOP

5. compute $F\_score(preds(n), test)$.

7 Experiments and Results

Several experiments were performed for testing the validity of our subjectivity classification approach, and especially of the contextual features. Thus, first the two classifiers are assessed in a 10-fold cross-validation on the development corpus. Secondly, the two classifiers are evaluated on the 21-document test corpus, with the entire development corpus used for training. For both setups, we have used the SVM-light software package[3]. Due to the fact that the feature vector spaces were found to be non-linearly-separable for both the S and Op classifiers, training was performed by using polynomial kernels. The Op classifier is evaluated in two manners when DFM features are used: first, the values of these features are drawn from the class annotation of the EDUs as given in the manually annotated corpus. Secondly, the iterative approach has been used, in order to test the approach in the real-life scenario when the contextual features cannot be detected by relying on a prior annotation of the input data. In all situations, the four rules introduced in Section 6 are used on the results of the two classifiers for inferring the finer-grained class of each EDU.

7.1 Evaluation of the Classifiers

We first present, in Table 3 the results of both classifiers, both in 10-fold cross-validation on the development corpus ("Gold"), and on the test data ("Test"). We first start with baseline feature sets, to which several features are progressively added; this is marked by the "+" sign. The best performances are marked in boldface. For the S classifier, our baseline considers only emoticons, all entries from the lexicon, except adverbs of manner or negation as well as modalities, along with the presence of a reporting verb with no argument. We observe that when adverbs of manner are added, all the performance figures improve, on both Gold and Test data (although a slight loss in precision is noticed on the new data). We also observe that adding SWSD yields the best performance figures for S.

For the Op classifier, our baseline uses local and syntactic features which rely on our lexicon: the presence of a subjective word or an emoticon or a modal or a word in the scope of a modal. Adding stylistic features provides a slight improvement of all the performance figures on the Gold but a slight degradation on the Test data. This might be due to a less regular way of using punctuation marks. The use of the feature referring to the presence of comparative and superlative patterns in the Gold slightly degrades precision, but provides the best recall of all the feature combinations for the Op classifier. On the Test data, no change in the measures is recorded. When syntactic patterns are added the recall slightly degrades but the accuracy and precision improve, thus providing the best F-score of all the feature combinations on the Gold. However, on the Test data all performance figures slightly degrade. Adding SWSD degrades the recall and, slightly, the F-measure but improves the accuracy and precision; this is true for the Gold and for the Test data. Adding contextual features that do not rely on a prior classification of the context slightly degrades accuracy and precision in the Gold, but provides a more significant improvement in the recall and yields a slightly higher F-score than without these features.

On the Test data, contextual features detect more subjective (explicit or implicit) EDUs than without them. Adding contextual features that rely on a prior classification of the EDUs, provides the best accuracy and precision of all our feature sets which shows their added value. The recall however, worsens on both the Gold and on the Test data (and so does the F-measure), because of the sparseness of the discourse markers in our corpus. Indeed, these last contextual features rely on surface cues which mark only a slight proportion of the discourse relations considered (cf. Section 2.3). This shows that although discourse information seems to be useful in detecting (mostly implicit) subjective EDUs that cannot be detected by other surface means, providing a good coverage is a caveat that could be solved, we believe, through a deeper level of analysis (for example lexical semantic). Finally, adding syntactic information pertaining the EDU being a left-detached CC, and to the presence of a reporting or non-polar advice verb without argument, yields only an improvement of the recall and F-measure, but the accuracy and precision worsen.

In the iterative Op classifier, for the convergence factor $\epsilon = 0.01$, the iterative procedure stops af-

[3] http://svmlight.joachims.org/

Classif.	Feature set	Accuracy		Precision		Recall		F-measure	
		Gold	Test	Gold	Test	Gold	Test	Gold	Test
S	Baseline	74.3	68.79	77.82	65.5	83.35	79.39	80.49	71.77
	+ Adverbs	74.68	70	77.85	66.18	84.25	81.82	80.92	73.17
	+ Semantic disambiguation	**82.31**	**70.91**	**87.54**	**67.69**	84.08	80	85.77	73.33
non-iter. Op	Baseline	75.82	**73.33**	76.25	73.56	98.93	99.59	86.12	84.61
	+ Capitalized words and punctuation marks	76.51	72.73	76.8	73.39	98.94	98.77	86.48	84.2
	+ Superlatives and comparatives	76.52	72.73	76.73	73.39	99.13	98.77	86.5	84.2
	+ Syntactic patterns	76.66	72.42	76.94	73.31	98.84	98.35	86.53	84
	+ Semantic disambiguation	**77.39**	**73.33**	**81.14**	**78.6**	91.98	87.65	86.22	82.87
	+ Contextual features, no discourse markers	77.32	**75.15**	80.35	79.49	93.31	89.3	86.35	84.1
	+ Contextual features, discourse markers	**78.35**	**75.15**	**83.74**	**85.15**	88.33	80.25	85.97	82.62
	+ EDU left-detached and CC	77.18	74.55	79.15	77.89	94.71	91.36	86.23	84.08
iter. Op	+ Contextual features, discourse markers	77.68	75.45	82.78	84.32	89.02	81.89	85.79	83.08

Table 3: Results (in percents) for the S and Op classifiers

Configuration	*S*		*SN*		*O*		*OO*	
	Gold	Test	Gold	Test	Gold	Test	Gold	Test
Best S / best non-iterative non-contextual Op	80.83	70.6	97.58	96.06	79.35	75.75	72.64	66.06
Best S / best non-iterative contextual Op	81.38	73.33	97.57	92.72	79.96	74.54	79.02	72.12
Best S / best iterative (contextual) Op	81.45	73.03	97.64	93.03	79.21	74.54	77.88	70.9

Table 4: Accuracies (in percents) for the four-class classification

ter at most 2 iterations on the Gold data, and at most 3 iterations on the Test data. As expected, the accuracies and precisions worsen slightly (by around 1 %) on the Test data, since the classes of the adjacent EDUs are not provided beforehand by the gold standard. However, on the Test data the accuracy (but not the precision) very slightly improves (by less than 0.5 %). The recall increases slightly as well on both data sets (by around 1 % as well), which means that the imperfections of the iteratively-obtained classification of the adjacent EDUs somewhat compensates for the limits of these two features themselves.

7.2 Evaluation of the Four Classes

We now show the results of the classification of the EDUs in the four classes *S*, *OO*, *SN* and *O*, obtained by applying the four rules described in Section 6 on the outputs of the S and Op classifiers with the feature sets providing the best performance figures, according to the boldface results in Table 3. For the contextual Op configuration we analyze both the non-iterative (non-iter. Op) and iterative (iter. Op) performance effects on the four classes. The accuracies are synthesized in Table 4. We observe that adding contextual features improves the performance figures, except for the *SN* class, where they degrade by 0.01 % for the non-iterative contextual Op, and, only on the Test data, for the *O* class, where they degrade by 0.21 %. We especially notice the dramatic improvements, on both the Gold and the Test data, for the *OO* class, of implicit subjective EDUs. We thus see that the contextual features provide an improvement of around 5–6 % for the accuracy. The improvements are, as expected, less marked in iter. Op. However, the degradation is rather slight: less than 2 % for the *OO* class and even less for the other classes. Nonetheless, even with the iter. Op, the performance figures remain higher than with the non-contextual Op classifier. Interestingly, in iter. Op, performance figures for the *S* (on the Gold only) and *SN* classes slightly improve.

8 Conclusion and Further Work

In this paper, we have assessed a discourse-based approach to SA. We have proposed a method to distinguish between four types of discourse units, by using both local and global context features. In the future, we plan to annotate opinion documents with SDRT-inspired relations, in order to learn them automatically from several cues other than discourse markers. We believe that the real strength of the discourse-based approach to opinion analysis appears when assessing the global polarity of documents.

Acknowledgements

This work was supported by a DGA-RAPID project under grant number 0102906143. We also thank Stergos Afantenos for his useful help on automatic discourse segmentation.

References

Stergos D. Afantenos, Pascal Denis, Philippe Muller, and Laurence Danlos. 2010. Learning recursive segments for discourse parsing. In *Proceedings of the Language Resources and Evaluation Conference (LREC)*, pages 3578–3584.

Cem Akkaya, Janyce Wiebe, and Rada Mihalcea. 2009. Subjectivity word sense disambiguation. In *Proceedings of Empirical Methods in Natural Language Processing (EMNLP)*, pages 190–199, Stroudsburg, PA, USA. Association for Computational Linguistics.

Nicholas Asher and Alex Lascarides. 2003. *Logics of Conversation*. Cambridge University Press.

Nicholas Asher, Farah Benamara, and Yvette Yannick Mathieu. 2008. Distilling opinion in discourse: A preliminary study. In *Proceedings of Computational Linguistics (CoLing)*, pages 7–10, Manchester, UK. Association for Computational Linguistics.

Adam L. Berger, Stephen A. Della Pietra, and Vincent J. Della Pietra. 1996. A maximum entropy approach to natural language processing. *Computational Linguistics*, 22:39–71.

Christopher J. C. Burges. 1998. A tutorial on support vector machines for pattern recognition. *Data mining and knowledge discovery*, 2(2):121–167.

Stephan Greene and Philip Resnik. 2009. More than words: syntactic packaging and implicit sentiment. In *Proceedings of Human Language Technologies: The Annual Conference of the North American Chapter of the Association for Computational Linguistics (HLT – NAACL)*, pages 503–511.

Alistair Kennedy and Diana Inkpen. 2006. Sentiment classification of movie and product reviews using contextual valence shifters. *Computational Intelligence*, 22(2):110–125.

Dominique Laurent, Sophie Nègre, and Patrick Séguéla. 2009. L'analyseur syntaxique Cordial dans Passage. In *Proceedings of Traitement Automatique des Langues Naturelles (TALN)*, Senlis, France.

Bing Liu. 2010. Sentiment analysis and subjectivity. In Nitin Indurkhya and Fred J. Damerau, editors, *Handbook of Natural Language Processing, Second Edition*. CRC Press, Taylor and Francis Group, Boca Raton, FL.

Claudiu Muşat and Ştefan Trăuşan-Matu. 2010. The impact of valence shifters on mining implicit economic opinions. *Lecture Notes in Computer Science*, 6304:131–140.

Bo Pang and Lillian Lee. 2004. A sentimental education: sentiment analysis using subjectivity summarization based on minimum cuts. In *Proceedings of the 42nd Annual Meeting on Association for Computational Linguistics*, pages 271–278, Stroudsburg, PA, USA. Association for Computational Linguistics.

Livia Polanyi and Annie Zaenen. 2006. Contextual valence shifters. In *Computing Attitude and Affect in Text: Theory and Applications*, volume 20 of *The Information Retrieval Series*, pages 1–10, Berlin-Heidelberg. Springer-Verlag.

Charlotte Roze, Laurence Danlos, and Philippe Muller. 2010. LEXCONN: a french lexicon of discourse connectives. In *Proceedings of Multidisciplinary Approaches to Discourse (MAD)*, pages 114–125, Moissac, France.

Swapna Somasundaran, Josef Ruppenhofer, and Janyce Wiebe. 2007. Detecting arguing and sentiment in meetings. In *Proceedings of the SIGdial Workshop on Discourse and Dialogue*, pages 26–34. Association for Computational Linguistics.

Swapna Somasundaran. 2010. *Discourse-level relations for Opinion Analysis*. PhD Thesis, University of Pittsburgh.

Maite Taboada, Kimberly Voll, and Julian Brooke. 2008. Extracting sentiment as a function of discourse structure and topicality. In *School of Computing Science Technical Report 2008-20*.

Cigdem Toprak, Niklas Jakob, and Iryna Gurevych. 2010. Sentence and expression level annotation of opinions in user-generated discourse. In *Proceedings of the 48th Annual Meeting of the Association for Computational Linguistics*, ACL '10, pages 575–584, Stroudsburg, PA, USA. Association for Computational Linguistics.

Janyce Wiebe and Ellen Riloff. 2005. Creating subjective and objective sentence classifiers from unannotated texts. In *Proceedings of the International Conference on Intelligent Text Processing and Computational Linguistics (CICLing)*, volume 3406 of *Lecture Notes in Computer Science*, pages 486–497, Berlin, Heidelberg. Springer-Verlag.

Janyce Wiebe, Theresa Wilson, and Claire Cardie. 2005. Annotating expressions of opinions and emotions in language. *Language Resources and Evaluation*, 39(2–3):165–210.

Theresa Wilson, Janyce Wiebe, and Paul Hoffmann. 2009. Recognizing contextual polarity: An exploration of features for phrase-level sentiment analysis. *Computational Linguistics*, 35(3):399–433.

Lanjun Zhou, Binyang Li, Wei Gao, Zhongyu Wei, and Kam-Fai Wong. 2011. Unsupervised discovery of discourse relations for eliminating intra-sentence polarity ambiguities. In *Proceedings of the 2011 Conference on Empirical Methods in Natural Language Processing*, pages 162–171, Edinburgh, Scotland, UK., July. Association for Computational Linguistics.

Compression Methods by Code Mapping and Code Dividing for Chinese Dictionary Stored in a Double-Array Trie

Huidan Liu
Institute of Software,
Chinese Academy of Sciences;
Graduate University of the
Chinese Academy of Sciences
huidan@iscas.ac.cn

Minghua Nuo
Institute of Software,
Chinese Academy of Sciences;
Graduate University of the
Chinese Academy of Sciences
minghua@iscas.ac.cn

Longlong Ma
Institute of Software,
Chinese Academy of Sciences
longlong@iscas.ac.cn

Jian Wu
Institute of Software,
Chinese Academy of Sciences
wujian@iscas.ac.cn

Yeping He
Institute of Software,
Chinese Academy of Sciences
yeping@iscas.ac.cn

Abstract

There is serious data sparseness problem in Chinese dictionary stored in a double-array trie. This paper proposes six compression methods by code mapping and code dividing to make it more compact, and a metric called Resource Consumption Ratio is proposed to evaluate these methods. Under the proposed criteria, five of the six methods are better than the baseline. The best method maps the character code into its frequency order, and then divides it into two jump codes. It achieves a space usage reduction of 39.88% and takes only 0.20% time of the baseline on the construction while it takes 13.21% more time on the retrieval. As preprocessing methods, these methods can be used to reduce more space by combining to other compression method which improves the double-array structure itself.

1 Introduction

In many applications of processing strings, a trie search is very useful because it enables fast retrieval and longest prefix matching with a small dictionary (Fredkin, 1960). Tries are used in a broad range of applications to represent a set of strings in fields such as information retrieval systems (Brain and Tharp, 1994; Nelson, 1997; Okada et al., 2001), lexical analyses (Aho et al., 2007; Lesk, 1975), morphological analyses (Aoe et al., 1996), natural language processing (Baeza-Yates and Gonnet, 1996; Peterson, 1980), bibliographic search (Aho et al., 1975), pattern matching (Flajolet and Puech, 1986), for IP address routing tables (Fu et al., 2007; Nilsson and Karlsson, 1999; Pao and Li, 2003), and text indexing (Navarro, 2004).

Double-array is a trie implementation which is proposed by (Aoe, 1989), and it is widely used in many applications at present because it combines the fast access of a matrix form with the compactness of a list form. However, there is a serious data sparseness problem when the double-array is used to store Chinese dictionary (Chinese double-array, hereafter, and similarly, English double-array for English dictionary). For a typical English dictionary with 45,373 words, the compression ratio of the double-array reaches 94.48%, but for a Chinese dictionary with 343,103 words, it's only 43.95%. In this paper, we analyze the reasons which lead to the data sparseness, and propose several methods to reduce the space usage of the Chinese double-array.

This paper is organized as follows: Section 2 introduces related work. Section 3 describes the outline of the double-array. In Section 4, we analyze the reasons resulting in the data sparseness. In Section 5, we give a baseline double-array, and propose six methods to make the double-array more compact. We propose the evaluation metric in Section 6. We make experiment and evaluate the six methods in Section 7. Section 8 concludes this paper.

2 Related work

Aoe (1989) presented an efficient digital search algorithm by introducing the structure called a double-array, which combines the fast access of a matrix form with the compactness of a list form.

Aoe (1992) proposed an implementation of the double-array which stores only as much of the prefix in the trie as is necessary to disambiguate the key, and the tail of the key is stored in a string array, denoted as TAIL. This structure is called a minimal prefix (MP) double-array.

Andersson and Nilsson (1993) introduced level-compressed (LC) trie to compress parts of the trie that are densely populated (Nilsson and Karlsson, 1999). A recent improvement in the LC trie is proposed by Fu et al. (2007).

Bentley and Sedgewick (1997) first presented the Ternary Search Tree (TST). TST combines the attributes of binary search trees and digital search tries.

Heinz (2002) proposed the burst trie, which is a collection of "containers" that are accessed via a conventional trie. It achieves high space efficiency by selectively collapsing chains of trie nodes into small containers of strings that share a common prefix. Askitis and Sinha (2007) proposed an improvement of burst trie called the HAT-trie which uses cache-conscious hash tables. Compared with a TST, the burst trie is 25% faster and uses only 50% of the memory, though it was found to be slower than TST with genomic data (Heinz et al., 2002).

Oono (2003) presented a method of dividing a key into several parts and defining link information between keys. It turned out that the double-array is 30% smaller than old method.

Wang (2006) proposed an improved strategy for the double-array. The node with most child nodes is inserted firstly while constructing, which reduces the data sparseness and keeps the search efficiency. Li (2006) designed and implemented a Chinese dictionary based on the double-array. Wang et al. (2009) introduced the idea of Sherwood random thoughts and mutation of genetic algorithms to improve the performance of the method proposed by Wang (2006) to avoid catching the trap of local optimal solution.

Yata (2007) presented two compaction methods for a static MP double-array, an element compaction and a trie compaction. The element compaction reduces the size of each element. The trie compaction reduces the number of nodes (a descended trie) and the length of the array keeping suffixes. The space usage for the new double-array is under the half of that for the original one, but the compaction methods little degrade the retrieval speed of the double-array.

Dorji (2010) presented three methods to compress the MP double-array. The first two methods accommodate short suffixes inside the leaf nodes, and prune leaf nodes corresponding to the end marker symbol. They achieve size reduction of up to 20%, making insertion and deletion faster at the same time while keeping the retrieval time of $O(1)$. The third method eliminates empty spaces in the array that holds suffixes, and improves the size reduction further by about 5% at the cost of increased insertion time. Compared to a TST, the key retrieval of the compressed double-array is 50% faster and its size is 3-5 times smaller.

All the compression methods are focusing on the corresponding trie or the double-array structure itself. However, the space usage of a double-array is very relevant to the content which is stored in it. We will compress the double-array by preprocessing the content.

3 Outline of double-array

A double-array is an array form of a trie (Aoe, 1989). It uses two one-dimensional arrays, named BASE and CHECK, to represent a trie. An element of the trie consists of the two array units with the same index in BASE and CHECK. Every element corresponds to a node of the trie, except empty elements, and we will also take the nonempty element as a node in this paper. For a certain node, the unit in BASE indicates the offset to child nodes, while the unit in CHECK normally stores the index of the parent node.

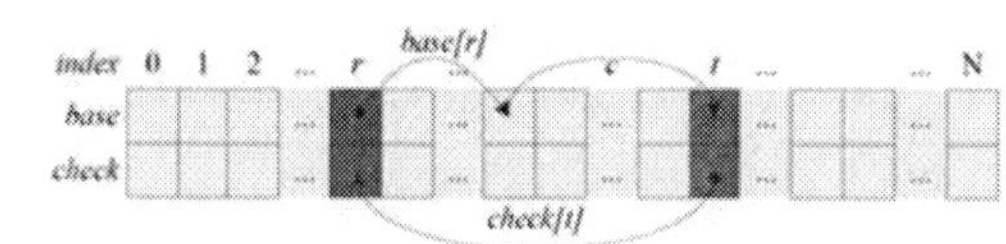

Figure 1: Relation between a node t and its parent node r in the double-array

As shown in Figure 1, in a double-array, a node t is a child of another node r, if and only if there is a relation between the two nodes.

$$\begin{cases} BASE[r] + c & = t \\ CHECK[t] & = r \end{cases} \quad (1)$$

where c is a numerical value corresponding to a character in a key, which we call "jump code" because it leads to a jump (state transition) from a node to its child node.

The retrieval of a key is just a walk from the root node to a leaf node, which is done fast by array operations in the double-array. The time complexity for a state transition from node r to its child node t is $O(1)$ in the double-array, thus the time complexity for retrieving a key is $O(k)$ for the length k of that key.

4 Data sparseness problem analysis

Unlike alphabetic writing script, Chinese is an ideographic script which has a large character set. There are more than 70,000 coded Chinese characters in Unicode 6.0. Although most of them are historic characters, there are still a large amount of characters that are frequently used. As in the Chinese dictionary mentioned above, there are more than 14,000 characters used.

The data sparseness problem of Chinese double-array mainly results from the large character set. First, jump codes vary in a large interval. In Unicode 6.0, the code of Chinese character varies from 3400 to 9FCB, and there are still a large amount of characters out of the range because they are out of the basic multilingual plane and should be represented by surrogate pairs which are in the interval from D800 to DFFF. But, not all of the characters are used in the dictionary. As a result, there are many empty elements between the most left child node and the most right one from the same parent in the double-array while inserting, although some of them may be used to store other nodes soon after. Second, a node has much more child nodes in Chinese trie than in English. In the Chinese dictionary, there are more than 800 words which begin with the same character "" meaning "one", which indicates that the corresponding node will have more than 800 children. However, in an English trie, the number of child nodes for any node doesn't exceed 52 for there are only 26 letters in the alphabet. More child nodes lead to more collision, which results in more empty elements indirectly.

5 Compression of Chinese double-array

In this section, we first present a baseline double-array, and then propose six methods of compaction. For each method, we only focus on the space usage, and compare it with the baseline from node count (NC), array length (AL), auxiliary space and compression ratio (CR). CR is the ratio of the number of non-empty elements to the total number of elements in the double-array. It represents the compactness of the double-array. We will use it to estimate how much room there is to apply compression method to reduce the space usage. We evaluate each method by calculating the space reduction rate (SRR), which is the ratio of the total space usage of each method to that of the baseline.

5.1 Baseline

Simply, we take the double-array proposed by (Aoe, 1989) which uses directly the code of a character as the as the baseline. Generally, there is an array called TAIL (Aoe et al., 1992) which stores suffix strings in the MP double-array. But we use the original double-array which store all the whole keys rather than only the minimal prefixes as the baseline to compute the space usage conveniently. As each unit in the array is an integer which takes up 4 bytes memory, the total space usage can be calculated as follow: $8bytes \times len$, where len is the length of the double-array.

We use the character code as the jump code in the baseline. For the key set K={"中国", "中国象棋", "中间", "上海", "上浮"} in which it means "China", "Chinese chess", "middle", "Shanghai" (a city of China), "floating upward" respectively, the corresponding trie is as shown in Figure 2. Note that a node with two concentric circles corresponds to an acceptance state which indicates the end of a word.

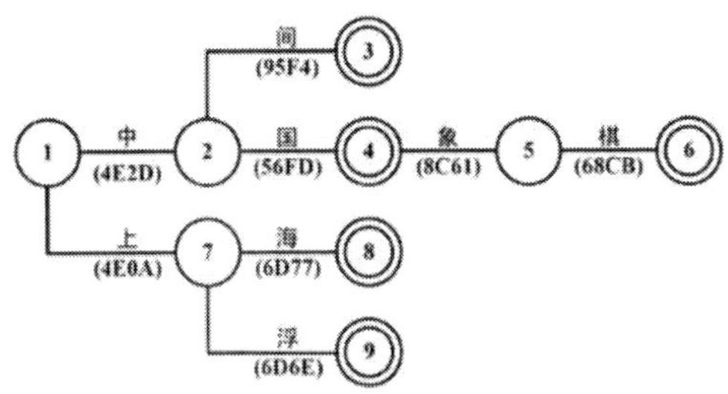

Figure 2: The trie of the key set K.

Based on the trie shown in Figure 2, a Chinese double-array is built to store the Chinese dictionary. As it will be represented by a surrogate pair if a character is out of the basic multilingual plane, we will take it as two characters for convenience. The baseline takes 1,714,339 units for the BASE and CHECK respectively, in which only 753,412 units are not empty, and the CR is 43.95%. As we analyzed in the former section, the first method we can think out is mapping the jump codes into a small interval.

5.2 Code mapping methods

As shown in Figure 3, this method maps the codes of all characters used in the dictionary into a small continuous interval. BASE stores the offsets from each node to its child nodes, and different start points only lead to different offsets, which hardly affect the space usage. So the start point of the interval is not very important. In this paper, we take 80 (hex) as the start point to make it compatible with English script. The mapping just changes the value of each jump code, while the trie keeps unchanged.

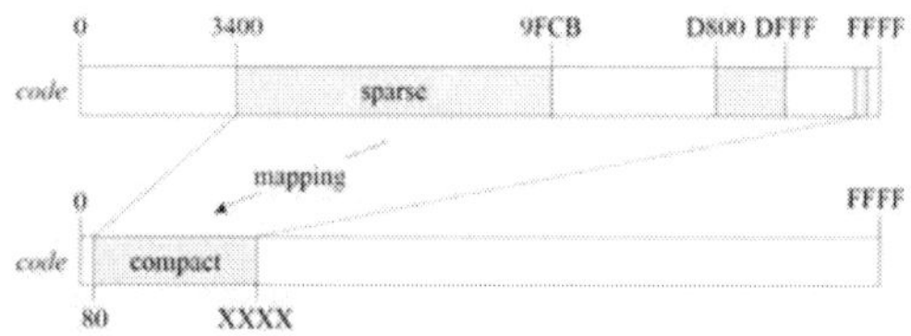

Figure 3: Code mapping.

We have to use another array to store the mapping table. Each unit takes 2 bytes, and 65536 (10000 in hex) units are needed to include all codes in basic multilingual plane. The auxiliary space is: $2\ bytes \times 65536 = 131072\ bytes$.

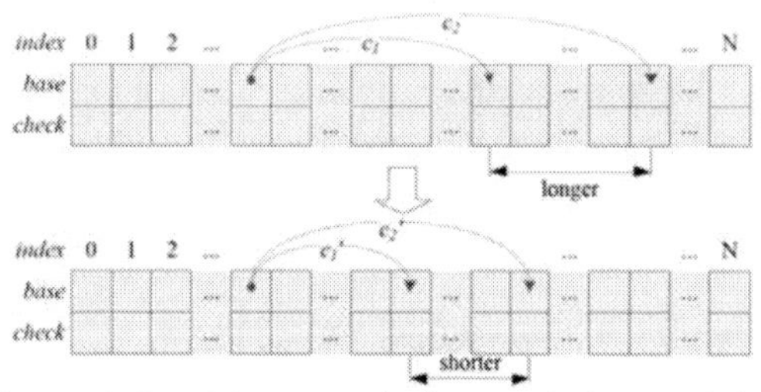

Figure 4: Double-arrays before and after applying code mapping method.

As shown intuitively in Figure 4, before applying code mapping method, for every node in the trie, there is a long distance between the most left child node and the most right one. After apply the method, the distance becomes much shorter. The number of child nodes keeps the same, data is more compact for the parent node, and the collision is controlled in a small range in the double-array while inserting other nodes. As child nodes for every intermediate node are arranged more compactly, it alleviates the data sparseness problem more or less.

Based on code mapping, we introduce the following two methods:

Method 1: Mapping each character code to its original order number in Unicode. The method takes the order number as the jump code for each character used in the dictionary, and keeps their original codes for others during the retrieval process. The relation between the target jump code c' and the original jump code c can be represented by the following formula:

$$c' = order(c) + C \tag{2}$$

where $order(c)$ is the order number of c among all the Chinese characters used in the dictionary when they are sorted in ascending order by code, and C is a constant which indicates the start point of the target interval. We set C equal to 80 (hex).

This method is already used by many people (Aoe, 1989; Aoe et al., 1992; Wang et al., 2006; Li et al., 2006; Dorji et al., 2010). Wang (2006) and Li (2006) used this method in their dictionary, but they just simply map the Chinese characters coded in the Chinese standard GB 2312 to 1~6763.

As shown in Table 1, after the mapping, the CR is improved to 47.49%, and it reduces the space usage of the double-array by 6.51% in total considering the auxiliary space. As the CR is still very low, there is much room for improvement.

	NC	AL	AS (bytes)	CR	SRR
Baseline	753412	1714339	0	43.95%	
Method 1	753412	1586337	131072	47.49%	6.51%

Table 1: Space usage of Method 1 compared with the baseline.

In Method 1, we make code mapping according to their original order in Unicode. However, different characters have different frequencies in the dictionary, then what will happen if we map two characters with the same frequency to two target jump codes of which the numerical difference is as small as possible?

Method 2: Mapping the jump codes to their frequency orders. Then, all high frequency characters will be mapped into a small interval. If two characters leading to state transitions from the same node to its two child nodes are both frequency used in the dictionary, then the distance between the two child nodes will be shorter than in Method 1. The relation between the target jump code c' and the original one c is represented by the following formula:

$$c' = freqorder(c) + C \tag{3}$$

where $freqorder(c)$ is the order number of c among all the Chinese characters used in the dictionary when they are sorted by frequency in descending order.

As shown in Table 2, after the mapping, the CR is improved to 58.56%, and it reduces the space usage of the double-array by 23.99% in total.

	NC	AL	AS (bytes)	CR	SRR
Baseline	753412	1714339	0	43.95%	
Method 2	753412	1286622	131072	58.56%	23.99%

Table 2: Space usage of Method 2 compared with the baseline.

Compared with Method 1, Method 2 makes a significant improvement, but there is still room for improvement.

5.3 Code dividing methods

We make all jump codes varying in a small interval by code mapping, but the interval is still much larger than that in the English double-array. It spreads from 80 (hex) to 3730 (hex), for there are more than 14,000 Chinese characters are used in the dictionary. However, in a English double-array, the jump codes vary in a much smaller interval, which is from 41 (hex of letter "A") to 7A (hex of letter "z") originally. To compress the interval equivalent to that of English, we divide each original jump code into two or more jump codes to break a long jump in the original double-array into two much shorter jumps.

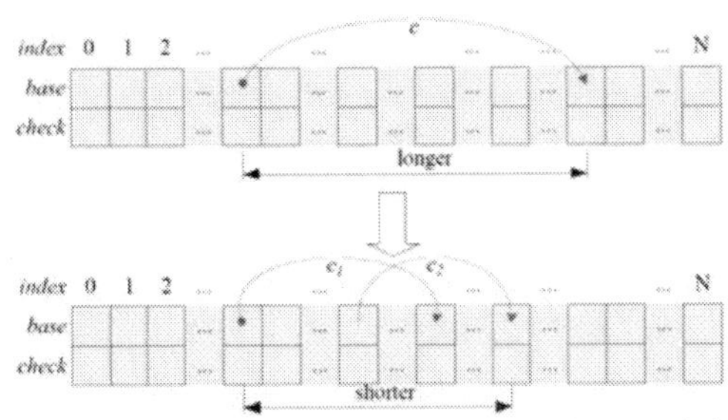

Figure 5: Double-arrays before and after applying code dividing methods.

As shown in Figure 5, every original jump code is divided into two jump codes. A state transition in the original double-array becomes two state transitions in the new double-array. The node (state) count increases. But it becomes more compact, it's still possible to reduce the space usage.

Method 3: Divide the code of a Chinese character into two small codes. To ensure that the two codes vary in equivalent interval, we take the high byte of the code as the first target code, and the low byte as the second. To make it compatible with English, we also change the start point of the interval to 80 (hex) as we do in Method 1. The relation between the two target jump codes c1, c2 and the original jump code c can be represented by Formula 4.Note that in the formula, $(c \gg 8)$ and $(c\&FF)$ are just the high/low byte of the c.

$$\begin{cases} c1 &= (c \gg 8) &+ C \\ c2 &= (c \,\&\, FF) &+ C \end{cases} \tag{4}$$

Generally, the sum of c1 and c2 is much smaller than c. For example, for a certain Chinese character "一", $c = 4E00$, then $c1 = CE(hex), c2 = 80(hex)$, and $c1 + c2 = 014E(hex)$, which is much smaller than c1. It results in shorter distance between a parent node and its child nodes, and shorter distance between different child nodes from the same parent.

As every original jump code is divided into two jump codes, the corresponding trie changes. For the key set K, the corresponding trie is shown in Figure 6. Although each jump code is divided into two, the total node count is smaller than the twice of the original trie's, because some nodes are shared, just like the nodes 2 in Figure 6 because "中" and "上" have the same high byte. It's similar to node 13.

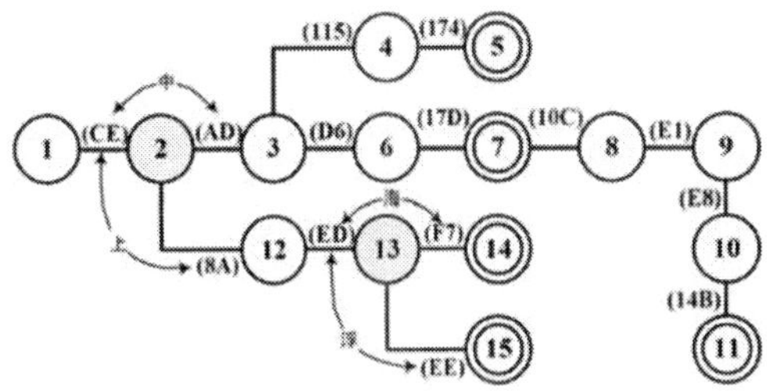

Figure 6: The new trie of key set K.

	NC	AL	AS (bytes)	CR	SRR
Baseline	753412	1714339	0	43.95%	
Method 3	998995	1043342	0	95.75%	39.14%

Table 3: Space usage of Method 3 compared with the baseline.

As shown in Table 3,every original code is divided into two codes, the node count of the double-array increases by 32.60% from 753412, but the CR is improved to 95.75%, which is similar to English double-array. So the length of the double-array is still smaller than the baseline. Meanwhile, Method 3 doesn't use a mapping table. It needs no auxiliary space. Thus, the space reducing rate reaches 39.14% in total.

Then what will happen if we divide the original code into 3 or more codes?

Method 4: Take the UTF-8 sequence of Chinese character as the corresponding jump codes.

	NC	AL	AS (bytes)	CR	SRR
Baseline	753412	1714339	0	43.95%	
Method 3	998995	1043342	0	95.75%	39.14%
Method 4	1200403	1264949	0	94.90%	26.21%

Table 4: Space usage of Method 3 and Method 4 compared with the baseline.

As shown in Table 4, after applying Method 4, the node count increases nearly 60% compared with the baseline, which leads to more space usage than Method 3. The CR of Method 4 is a little smaller than that of Method 3. The space usage reduction rate is only 26.21%, which is much smaller than Method 3. In a word, Method 3 is better than Method 4.

5.4 Combined methods

Then, what will happen if we combine methods of code mapping and code dividing? Let's have a try. Combining Method 3 to each of the code mapping methods, we get Method 5 and Method 6. Method 4 is worse than Method 3. We won't try to combine it to the code mapping methods.

Method 5 (Method 1 + Method 3): First, map the original character to its order number, and then divide it into two target jump codes. The corresponding formula of Method 5 is as follow:

$$\begin{cases} c1 & = (order(c) \gg 7) & + C \\ c2 & = (order(c) \,\&\, 7F) & + C \end{cases} \tag{5}$$

Method 6 (Method 2 + Method 3): First, map the original character to its frequency order number, and then divide it into two jump codes. The corresponding formula of Method 6 is as follow:

$$\begin{cases} c1 & = (freqorder(c) \gg 7) & + C \\ c2 & = (freqorder(c) \,\&\, 7F) & + C \end{cases} \tag{6}$$

Note that we don't shift by 8 bits any longer like in Method 3 and Method 4, because the total number of characters used in the dictionary is about 14 thousand, and so it needs only 14 valid bits to represent all the order numbers.

As shown in Table 5, Method 5 and Method 6 both need auxiliary space to store the mapping table like in Method 1 and Method 2. They both

	NC	AL	AS (bytes)	CR	SRR
Baseline	753412	1714339	0	43.95%	
Method 5	972703	1014204	131072	95.91%	39.88%
Method 6	925643	962857	131072	96.14%	42.88%

Table 5: Space usage of Method 5 and Method 6 compared with the baseline.

achieve a CR larger than 95% and reduce the space usage by a percentage near or even larger than 40%, which is similar to Method 3. However, Method 6 is slightly better than Method 5 from the aspect of space usage, just like Method 2 is slightly better than Method 1.

Now, we don't think there is still much room for improvement because the CR is close to 100% and neither combined method makes big improvement compared with Method 3.

6 Evaluation metric

If we evaluate several methods or systems from n aspects of resources consumption such as space usage and time cost, and then we denote the value on the ith aspect by V_{Ai} and the normalized weight of the ith aspect by w_i. We define the resource consumption ratio (RCR) of two methods A and B as follow:

$$RCR(A, B) = \prod_{i=1}^{n} \left(\frac{V_{Ai}}{V_{Bi}} \right)^{w_i} \tag{7}$$

RCR has the following properties:

- $RCR(A, A) = 1.0$, if a method A is compared with itself;
- $RCR(A, B) = 1.0$ means the two methods A and B are equally good or bad;
- $RCR(A, B) > 1.0$ means the method A is worse than the reference method B, because it consumes more resources.
- $RCR(A, B) < 1.0$ means the method A is better than the reference method B because it consumes fewer resources.

7 Experiment and Evaluation

In this section, We evaluate the six methods from the following aspects:

1. Total space usage (TSU), including the space for the double-array and the mapping table.
2. Construction time (CT), including the time spent on making the code mapping or the code dividing.

3. Retrieval time (RT) on searching all words in the dictionary.

7.1 Experiment

The dictionary used in this paper is the Modern Chinese Dictionary in Traditional Chinese.

Normally, a double-array allocates space many times to extend space to accommodate newly inserted nodes during the construction. As different methods have different space usage, they may need different times of space allocation, and thus need different time cost. We simply allocate a large enough space in advance for the double-array before the construction to eliminate the difference of time cost on space allocation.

It takes a short time to retrieve all words in the dictionary once. If we execute the experiment twice, the time costs will be very different from each other if it is interfered by some accidental factors. We do the retrieval 1000 times to alleviate the problem mostly and keep the time costs comparable.

The experiment is performed on a computer with an 8-core 2.80GHz Intel Core i7 CPU and 2.96GB memory. The experimental data is shown in Table 6. Note that SUR, CTR, RTR is the ratio of TSU, CT, RT in each method to that in the baseline respectively.

7.2 Evaluation

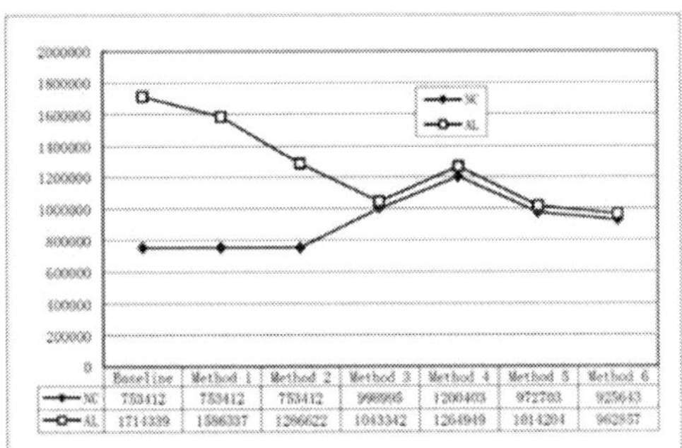

Figure 7: Node count and array length.

As we see from Figure 7 and Figure 8, Method 1 and Method 2 achieve space usage reduction of 6.51% and 23.99% respectively, but they take too much time on the construction. Method 3 achieves a space usage reduction of 39.14% while it takes very short time on the construction. It takes a little longer time on the retrieval than the baseline. Method 4 also takes very short time on the construction, but much more time on the retrieval and it only achieves a space usage reduction of 26.21%. Method 5 achieves a better space usage reduction, short time cost both on construction and retrieval than Method 3. Method 6 achieves the best space usage reduction by 42.88%, but it takes longer time cost on the construction and retrieval than Method 5. Method 3~6 have more nodes because they have divided original codes into two or more codes, but they makes the double-array more compact, so every one of them has a CR close to 97%. Method 6 takes more time on the construction than Method 5, which is similar to Method 2 and Method 1, because it has to spend time to sort the characters by frequency. All the methods take more retrieval time, but result from different reasons. Method 1 and Method 2 have to make the code mapping while Method 3~6 have to make the code dividing and visit more nodes while searching a key.

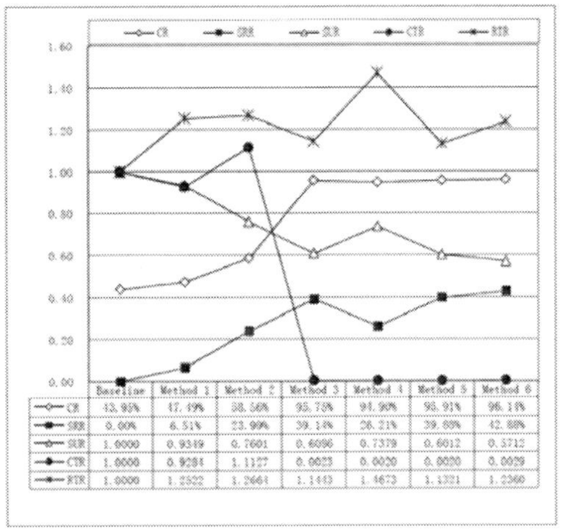

Figure 8: Comparison of the six methods.

Now, we evaluate the six methods with the metric proposed in the former section from three aspects: space usage, construction time, retrieval time. We assign the three aspects with weights (9/20, 1/10, 9/20) respectively. The construction is only performed once but the retrieval is performed many times for a double-array, so the construction time is assigned a smaller weight, and the space usage has an equal weight to retrieval time because we can't decide which is more important roughly without any application scenarios. We compare each method A with the baseline to calculate each RCR:

$$\begin{aligned} RCR(A) &= RCR(A, baseline) \\ &= SUR^{\frac{9}{20}} \times CTR^{\frac{1}{10}} \times RTR^{\frac{9}{20}} \end{aligned} \quad (8)$$

We calculate the RCR of each method with the

	NC	AL	CR	SRR	TSU(byte)	SUR	CT(ms)	CTR	RT(ms)	RTR	RCR
Baseline	753412	1714339	43.95%	0.00%	13714712	1.0000	504437	1.0000	23172	1.0000	1.0000
Method 1	753412	1586337	47.49%	6.51%	12821768	0.9349	468328	0.9284	29015	1.2522	1.0655
Method 2	753412	1286622	58.56%	23.99%	10424048	0.7601	561265	1.1127	29344	1.2664	0.9935
Method 3	998995	1043342	95.75%	39.14%	8346736	0.6086	1140	0.0023	26516	1.1443	0.4621
Method 4	1200403	1264949	94.90%	26.21%	10119592	0.7379	1015	0.0020	34000	1.4673	0.5570
Method 5	972703	1014204	95.91%	39.88%	8244704	0.6012	984	0.0020	26234	1.1321	0.4506
Method 6	925643	962857	96.14%	42.88%	7833928	0.5712	1484	0.0029	28641	1.2360	0.4773

Table 6: Comparison of the six methods and the baseline.

values collected from the experiment, and the results are shown in Figure 9.

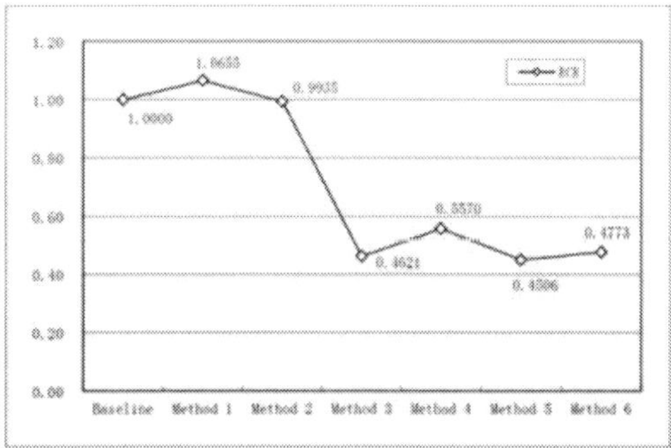

Figure 9: RCRs of the six methods.

As we see in Figure 9, most of the six methods are better than the baseline except Method 1, whose RCR is slightly larger than 1.0. Method 5 has the smallest RCR and it outperforms others.

8 Conclusion

We propose six methods to reduce the space usage of Chinese double-array. Method 1 and Method 2 achieve space usage reduction of 6.51% and 23.99% by code mapping into the order number or frequency order number respectively, but they take too much time on the construction. Method 3 achieves a space usage reduction of 39.14% by dividing each original jump code into two codes while it takes very short time on the construction. It takes a little longer time on the retrieval than the baseline. Method 4 divides the original jump code into three codes. It also takes very short time on the construction, but much more time on the retrieval and it only achieves a space usage reduction of 26.21%. Method 5 and Method 6 are the combinations of Method 3 with Method 1 and Method 2 respectively. Method 5 achieves a better space usage reduction, short time cost both on construction and retrieval than Method 3. Method 6 achieves the best space usage reduction by 42.88%, but it takes longer time cost on the construction and retrieval than Method 5.

Also, an approach is proposed to evaluate those methods by a metric called Resource Consumption Ratio (RCR) which compares the total resource consumption of two methods such as space usage and time cost. Under the proposed criteria, five of the six methods are better than the baseline, and the best one (Method 5) achieves a space usage reduction by 39.88% and takes only 0.20% time of the baseline on the construction, while it takes 13.21% more time on the retrieval. As preprocessing methods, these methods can be used to reduce more space by combining to other compression method which improves the double-array structure itself.

Acknowledgements

We would like to thank the anonymous reviewers for their critical and constructive comments and suggestions that helped us improve the quality of the paper. The research is partially supported by National Science and Technology Major Project (No.2010ZX01036-001-002, No.2010ZX01036-001-002), and CAS Action Plan for the Development of Western China (No.KGCX2-YW-512).

References

Alfred V. Aho, and Margaret J. Corasick. 1975. *Efficient string matching: an aid to bibliographic search*. Communications of the ACM, 18(6):333–340.

Alfred V. Aho, Monica S. Lam, Ravi Sethi, and Jeffrey D. Ullman. 2007. *Compilers principle tech-niques and tools (2nd Edition)*. Addison-Wesley.

Arne Andersson, and Stefan Nilsson. 1993. *Efficient implementation of suffix trees*. Software: Practice and Experience, 25(2):129–141.

Jun-ichi Aoe, Katsushi Morimoto, and Takashi Sato. 1992. *An efficient implementation of trie structures*. Software-Practice and Experience, 22(9):695–721.

Jun-ichi Aoe, Katsushi Morimoto, Masami Shishibori, and Ki-Hong Park. 1996. *A trie compaction algorithm for a large set of keys*. IEEE Transactions on Knowledge and Data Engineering, 8(3): 476–491.

Jun-ichi Aoe. 1989. *An efficient digital search algorithm by using a double-array structure.* IEEE Transactions on Software Engineering, 15(9): 1066–1077.

Nikolas Askitis, and Ranjan Sinha. 2007. *HAT-trie: A cache-conscious trie-based data structure for strings.* In Proceedings of the 30th Australasian computer science conference, Ballarat, Australia.

Ricardo A. Baeza-Yates, and Gaston H. Gonnet. 1996. *Fast text searching for regular expressions or automaton searching on tries.* Journal of the ACM, 43(6):915–936.

Jon L. Bentley, and Robert Sedgewick. 1997. *Fast algorithms for sorting and searching strings.* In Proceedings of the 8th annual ACM-SIAM sympo-sium on discrete algorithms.

Marshall D. Brain, and Alan L. Tharp. 1994. *Using tries to eliminate pattern collisions in perfect hashing.* IEEE Transactions on Knowledge and Data Engineering, 6(2):239-247.

O'Neil Delpratt, Naila Rahman, and Rajeev Raman. 2006. *Engineering the LOUDS succinct tree representation.* In fifth international workshop on experimental algorithms, WEA2006. LNCS 4007: 134–145.

Masaki Dono, Masako Fuketa, Yutaka Inada, Yo Murakami, and Jun-ichi Aoe. 2006. *A Compression Method Using Link-Trie Structure for Natural Language Dictionaries.* International Conference on Computing and Informatics. 1–4.

Tshering C. Dorji, El-sayed Atlam, Susumu Yata, Mahmoud Rokaya, Masao Fuketa, Kazuhiro Morita, and Jun-ichi Aoe. 2010. *New methods for compression of MP double array by compact management of suffixes.* Information Processing and Management, 46:502–513.

John A. Dundas. 1991. *Implementing dynamic minimal prefix tries.* Software-Practice and Experience, 21(10):1024-1040.

Philippe Flajolet, and Claude Puech. 1986. *Partial match retrieval of multidimensional data.* Journal of the ACM, 33(2):371–407.

Philippe Flajolet. 2006. *The ubiquitous digital tree. In Proceedings in lecture notes in computer science.* LNCS 3884:1–22. Berlin/Heidelberg: Springer.

Edward Fredkin. 1960. *Trie memory.* Communications of the ACM, 3(9):490–500.

Jing Fu, Olof Hagsand, and Gunnar Karlsson. 2007. *Improving and analyzing LC-Trie performance for IP-address lookup.* Journal of Networks, 2:18–27.

Steven Heinz, Justin Zobel, and Hugh E. Williams. 2002. *Burst tries: A fast, efficient data structure for string keys.* ACM Transactions on Information Systems, 20(2):192–223.

Lesk, M. E. (1975). *Lex - a lexical analyzer generator.* CSTR 39. NJ: Bell Lab, 1–13.

Jiangbo Li, Qiang Zhou, and Zushun Chen. 2006. *A Study on Fast Algorithm for Chinese Dictionary Lookup.* Journal of Chinese Information Processing, 20(5):31–40.

Gonzalo Navarro. 2004. *Indexing text using the Ziv-Lempel trie.* Journal of Discrete Algorithms, 2(1): 87–114.

Michael J. Nelson. 1997. *A prefix trie index for inverted files.* Information Processing and Manage-ment, 33(6):739–744.

Stefan Nilsson and Gunnar Karlsson. 1999. *IP-address lookup using LC-tries.* IEEE Journal on Selected Areas in Com-munication, 17(6):1083–1092.

Makoto Okada, Kazuaki Ando, Sangkon, Yoshitaka Hayashi, and Jun-ichi Aoe. 2001. *An efficient substring search method by using delayed keyword extraction.* Information Processing and Management, 37:741-761.

Masaki Oono, El-Sayed Atlam, Masao Fuketa, Kazuhiro Morita, and Jun-ichi Aoe. 2003. *A fast and compact elimination method of empty elements from a double-array structure.* Software-Practice and Experience, 33, 1229–1249.

Derek Pao and Yiu-Keung Li. 2003. *Enabling incremental updates to LC-trie for efficient management of IP forwarding tables.* Communications Letters, IEEE, 7(5), 245–247.

James L. Peterson. 1980. *Computer programs for spelling correction: An experiment in program design.* LNCS 96:1–129. Springer-Verlag.

Guy Shani, Christopher Meek, Tim Paek, Bo Thiesson, and Gina Venolia. 2009. *Searching large in-dexes on tiny devices: Optimizing binary search with character pinning.* In Proceedings of the 13th international conference on Intelligent user interfaces, 257–266.

Sili Wang, Huaping Zhang, and Bin Wang. 2006. *Research of Optimization on Double-Array Trie and its Application.* Journal of Chinese Informa-tion Processing. 20(5): 24–31.

Shikun Wang, Shaozi Li, and Xiao Ke. 2009. *Double-array Trie based on genetic algorithm and idea of Sherwood.* Computer Engineering and Applications, 45(29):128–130.

Susumu Yata, Masaki Oono, Kazuhiro Morita, Masao Fuketa, Toru Sumitomo, and Jun-ichi Aoe. 2007. *A compact static double-array keeping character codes Source.* Information Processing and Management, 43(1): 237–247.

Functional Elements and POS Categories

Qiuye Zhao **Mitch Marcus**
Dept. of Computer & Information Science
University of Pennsylvania
qiuye, mitch@cis.upenn.edu

Abstract

We propose a bootstrapping algorithm which successfully resolves two fundamental tasks: morphology acquisition and the acquisition of a subset of functional words. Given the outputs of these fundamental tasks, we build a nearly state-of-art morphology analyzer performing with a F1-score of 80.94%; also, we can improve the baseline model for acquiring functional words by an absolute error reduction of 26%. Furthermore, with these acquisition outputs, a minimally supervised tagging system proposed before can be turned into a totally unsupervised one, achieving a tagging accuracy of 85.26% for open-class words.

1 Introduction

Studies of child language acquisition have shown that functional elements as distinctive categories are available to the child from very early on. These include both functional words (closed class items) such as determiners (Valian et al., 2009), and functional bound morphemes such as verbal inflections (Yang, 2002). Motivated by such studies, we propose that functional categories, including both functional words and functional morphemes, should be identified first in the process of acquiring syntactic categories automatically from language input. Further motivation comes from the experimental results of the minimally supervised tagging system in (Zhao and Marcus, 2009)[1], which, given only seven functional features, including four contextual features, whether modal verbs or determiners are left or right neighbours, and three specific morphological features, whether *'-ing'*, *'-ed'*, or *'-s'* are observed as endings, performs clustering in order to generate the two fundamental open class categories, verbal vs. nominal. This work suggests that functional elements are highly useful in further classification of open class items.

This is quite different from most other POS induction systems in the Natural Language Processing (NLP) field for inducing Part-of-Speech (POS) tags, which, instead of generating clusters complying with the common understanding of 'syntactic' categories, such as distinct clusters of determiners, nouns or inflections of verbs, tend to output scattered clusters consisting words of interesting similarities on many different dimensions (Christodoulopoulos et al., 2010). This is because, in these clustering-based systems, a vector space over the words is spanned by lexical features and suffix/prefix features, so that the generated clusters mix semantic and syntactic similarities (Clark, 2000).

In this work, we explore an alternative 'top-down' view of deriving categories, as opposed to the 'bottom-up' view adopted by these earlier distributional clustering methods. Here, we report on experiments which acquire functional elements first and integrate the acquisition output into a full unsupervised POS tagging system later. Since we are not aware of previous work to acquire functional elements, we approach the problem by seeking answers for the following two questions: 1) What are the special properties of the distribution of functional elements that enables the child to distinguish them easily from other categories at a very early stage of acquisition? 2) What might the acquisition processes of the two forms of functional elements (bound vs. free) have in common, reflecting some deeper distributional property of functional elements in general?

[1]The tagging system in (Zhao and Marcus, 2009) was referred to as 'unsupervised' in their paper, because back then, a lexicon was a common input to so-called unsupervised POS tagging systems. We classify their system as minimally supervised here, so as to differentiate it from this work which requires only raw text as input.

We believe that answers to these questions begins to emerge from the success of a single bootstrapping algorithm proposed here to the acquisition of both bound and free functional elements, i.e. closed class words and bound morphemes. This bootstrapping algorithm explores a particular simple contextual property of functional elements, which we call the *diversity property*, and resolves both fundamental acquisition tasks without any input beyond raw written text:

1) **Bound morphemes** Separating functional elements in the form of bound morphemes from contentful elements. As for English, the two output sets are a list of productive endings such as *'-ed'*, and *'-s'*, and a list of base stems such as *'consist-'* and *'bootstrapp-'*.

2) **Free morphemes** Separating 'first-order' functional elements in form of free morphemes (words) from contentful elements. As for English, the two output sets are a list of modal verbs and determiners (in a general sense[2]), and a list of nominal elements as well as verbs in bare forms.

The bootstrapping algorithm we propose here operates by iteratively generating two complementary sets, (e.g. base stems and productive endings for the bound morpheme task); in these way, it reflects the intuition behind co-training (Abney, 2004), but in a greatly reduced form and requiring no seeds for initialization. For both tasks, the bootstrapping algorithm generates highly reliable outputs, with barely any errors and requires no task-specific parameter settings. For example, it discovers 26 modal verbs and determiners (in a general sense) from raw text of WSJ Treebank (Marcus et al., 1993) with only a single noisy term.

We validate these outputs on a range of useful applications. Given the two sets output by the bound morpheme task, we can straightforwardly build an unsupervised morphology analyzer which achieves an F1-score of 80.94 evaluated on the CELEX corpus, comparable to a state-of-art morph analyzer (Lignos, 2010) which achieves 82.21 F1 on the same task. Next, given this new morphology analyzer and the two output sets from the free morpheme task, we give a new very simple algorithm for acquiring the full set of functional/closed class words, improving on a reasonable baseline model for acquiring functional/closed-class words by an absolute error reduction of 26%, from 63% to 89% type accuracy as evaluated on the WSJ Treebank[3]. Finally, we plug this newly acquired closed-class lexicon into a minimally supervised tagging system, (Zhao and Marcus, 2009), which requires as input exactly such a lexicon. The resulting system, now completely unsupervised, achieves a tagging accuracy of 85.26% for tagging open-class words as evaluated on the whole WSJ Treebank. Although the evaluation is done over 6 open-class tags only, and thus is not directly comparable to related works, the tagging performance reported here is still satisfying given that recently reported unsupervised tagging accuracy vary among 50%-70% e.g. (Abend et al., 2010), (Reichart et al., 2010) and (Moon et al., 2010).

2 Acquiring Functional Elements

Functional elements are those elements that provide structural clues in expressions, which form a complementary set to the contentful elements that provide semantic content of the expressions. Two forms of elements in languages come into our attention, bound morphemes and free morphemes (words). As for English, functional elements of bound morphemes are inflectional endings or derivational endings/prefixes, for example, in a word *'runs'* the contentful part *'run-'* provides us with some contentful information, whereas, the functional part *'-s'* provide us with some grammatical specification which are specially important when the word is used in context. On the other hand, functional elements of free morphemes, generally refer to those closed-class words that don't fall into lexical categories, i.e. those words that are not nouns, verbs, adjectives or adverbs; however, the functional roles these closed-class words play in context are more complicated.

The algorithm described in section 2.2 solves two tasks on acquiring functional elements: 1) identifying productive endings/prefixes vs. base stems (the contentful parts of words), and 2) identifying determiners (possessive determiners and

[2]In this paper, we refer to determiners in a general sense which includes determiners, possessive determiners and demonstratives.

[3]Given the lack of previously reported results, the baseline model we compare against is to select the most frequent words in the corpus as closed-class items.

demonstratives as well) and modal verbs vs. nouns and verbs. Given these acquisition outputs, we can acquire a full set of closed-class words, falling in all functional categories, with a simple extra step. The subset of functional words that are acquirable by the bootstrapping algorithm is referred as 'first-order' functional words in this work, since they include determiners and modal verbs only which don't project to other functional words.

Before introducing the bootstrapping algorithm in section 2.2, we discuss the diversity property of functional elements first, in section 2.1, which is an important concept to be explored in the algorithm.

2.1 Diversity Property

Our algorithm is built upon a distributional property of functional elements well-known to linguists: they occur in diverse contexts. For example, determiner *'the'* in English is observed everywhere in text and inflectional ending *'-ed'* can be concatenated to most verbs to derive past forms. As discussed above, functional elements provide structural clues to compose expressions and are basically independent to the meanings conveyed by the expressions; therefore, they are not bound to co-occur with specific contentful elements and are natively expected to occur in diverse contexts.

In the NLP field, a more popular property known for distinguishing functional elements is that they occur more often. Although frequency can be used to approximate 'diversity', the high frequency of functional elements is only a reflection of their high degree of contextual diversity, which, following the definition, is more accurately approximated by the types of contexts that an element occurs in.

There are few previous works that quantitatively demonstrate that 'contextual' diversity is a better diversity measurement than frequency regarding experimental results. In this work, we are going to explicitly compare these two options for measuring diversity within the bootstrapping algorithm. As shown in all applications (section 3), measuring contextual diversity for diversity brought in a consistent improvement as compared to measuring frequency.

Proper Contexts

We haven't define in what occurrences two elements may form a contextual relationship, and let's consider the case for bound morphemes first. Given a type of word, e.g. *'laughing'*, several ways of dividing it can yield a pair of possible morphemes with either one being *as/in*-context of the other morpheme: for the division *'laugh-ing'*, *'laugh-'* can be considered *in*-context of *'-ing'* and *'-ing'* considered *as*-context of *'laugh-'* or vice verse; or for the division *'laughin-g'*, *'laughin-'* *in*-context of *'-g'* and *'-g'* *as*-context of *'laughin-'*, or vice verse.

For words, ideal scopes to define contextual relationships should be phrases/phases, from a linguistic point of view, such as N(ominal)P, V(erbal)P and so on. However, it is not easy to detect boundaries of phases in unannotated input; therefore, we only consider contextual relationships between two words in adjacency. For the sake of coherence, we consider the preceding word *as*-context of the following word and the following word *in*-context of the preceding one, however, it could also be vice verse, though with worse experimental results.

As one may have noticed, without any further constraints on the concept of contexts, the top 3 bound morphemes with the highest contextual diversity will be *'-d'*, *'-e'* and *'-t'*, which do not comply with our understanding of functional morphemes in English. In other words, for acquiring inflectional or derivational suffix/prefixes, we want to compute contextual diversity of bound morphemes according to properly justified contextual relations only, instead of from all arbitrary divisions of words. The most simple way of justifying one element as proper contexts for other elements is to check whether it can serve *as*-context of more than one type of element, by which criteria *'laughin-'* is not justified, since it cannot be concatenated by other suffixes than *'-g'* to form a legal word. It is first noticed in (Chan, 2008) that morphological transformations should be discovered with respect to 'base forms', i.e. properly justified contentful stems; and we generalize this idea for a better measurement of diversity to acquire both forms of functional elements in this work.

Suppose that we are given a set of properly justified contexts of bound morphemes including *'laugh-'* but not *'b-'*, the diversity measurement of *'-ing'* will increase by one given the existence of word *'laughing'* but not given word *'bing'*. For the case of words, if only nouns are justified to be proper contexts, then the top words of highest diversity should be determiners. More formally, given a set $\mathbb{B}$ of justified contexts, we can define two measurements of diversity for an element e, frequency or contextual diversity as discussed above:

$$tokenC(e, \mathbb{B}) = \sum_{e' \in \mathbb{B}} \text{\# occur. of } e' \textit{ in}\text{-context of } e$$

$$typeC(e, \mathbb{B}) = \sum_{e' \in \mathbb{B}} \text{\# occur. of } e' \textit{ in}\text{-context of } e > 0$$

2.2 The Bootstrapping Algorithm

The proposed bootstrapping algorithm in Algorithm 1 generates two complementary sets during the bootstrapping process, both of which justify proper contexts for each other. As the two sets updated during bootstrapping, the diversity measurement of the other set is expected to be more and more accurate. This strategy reflects the intuition behind co-training (Abney, 2004), but in a greatly reduced form and requiring no seeds for initialization.

Given a specific form of elements (bound or free morphemes), inputs to this algorithm are a dataset $\mathbb{S}$[4] containing all the elements of this form in some corpus and a choice of diversity measurement, $tokenC$ or $typeC$ as defined in section 2.1.

Assuming that functional elements can be distinguished by higher diversity degree, as discussed in section 2.1, we explicitly let a set $\mathbb{F}$ contain the most diverse elements as computed by the diversity measurement function with respect to its complementary set $\mathbb{B}$; and at each bootstrapping iteration, we increase the size of $\mathbb{F}$ by one.

On the other hand, set $\mathbb{B}$, which is generated to provide proper contexts for $\mathbb{F}$, contain those elements of a diversity degree greater than one with respect to $\mathbb{F}$, implementing our understanding of properly justified contexts in section 2.1. Since the order of diversity ranking of elements in $\mathbb{S}$ varies over iterations with respect to $\mathbb{B}$, which is also updated at each iteration according to current $\mathbb{F}$, an element classified into $\mathbb{F}$ at some iteration is not guaranteed to show up in $\mathbb{F}$ in the following iterations.

In addition to the update of $\mathbb{F}$ and $\mathbb{B}$, we also introduce a special 'filtering' step to prevent those elements that are ever seen *as/in*-context of elements in $\mathbb{F}$ from being classified into $\mathbb{F}$. This filtering idea is implemented through a set $\mathbb{R}$ containing elements to be excluded from $\mathbb{F}$, which is also updated at each iteration after the update of $\mathbb{F}$. This filtering step guarantees that there is no element in $\mathbb{F}$ ever occurring *as/in*-context of any other element in $\mathbb{F}$. We will explain more about the linguistic motivation behind this filtering step in section 4.

[4]For each element e in $\mathbb{S}$, the number of its occurrences *in/as*-context of other elements are also provided.

2.3 The Acquisition Output

We run the bootstrapping algorithm introduced in Section 2.2 for two acquisition tasks: acquiring functional morphemes and acquiring 'first-order' functional words. The outputs of both tasks, which are done separately, are depicted in Table 1 and 2 respectively. For each task, we experiment with two options of diversity measurement: $tokenC$ or $typeC$ as defined in section 2.1. If any element classified to be functional is of a diversity degree lower than a threshold, the bootstrapping process stops.

First of all, as clearly shown by the quality of acquisition outputs, this algorithm is sensitive to the choice of diversity measurement, and $typeC$, which measures the contextual diversity of an element in proper contexts, is always a better option compared to $tokenC$, which measures the frequency of an element in proper contexts. *tokenC* produces better outputs in the sense that fewer noisy elements are acquired and if acquired, they are acquired later in the bootstrapping process.

In both Table 1 and 2, functional elements are shown ordered by diversity in the second column, which order varies over the bootstrapping iterations, corresponding to the update of its complementary set, which is shown at the last column.

For the case of acquiring words, it is worth wondering about why, at the first few iterations, there were only determiners generated as functional, but at later iterations, modal verbs also show up. This fact seems to contradict our intuition that modal verbs are not of high diversity with respect to a complementary set containing nominal words only, which are generated according to determiners. However, we know that, at least in English, words are of ambiguous categories; therefore, those words of both nominal and verbal senses, such as *'consider'* and *'help'*, are classified to the complementary set by determiners according to their nominal sense, but their existence in the complementary set also enlarges the diversity of modal verbs due to their verbal sense.

While measuring the diversity by $typeC$, the

Algorithm 1 The bootstrapping algorithm for acquiring functional elements

Require: a data set $\mathbb{S}$ to be classified and a diversity measurement function C
  initialize set $\mathbb{F}$ and set $\mathbb{R}$ to be empty and initialize set $\mathbb{B}$ to be $\mathbb{S}$
  for k iterations **do**
    let $\mathbb{F}$ be the top k most diverse elements with respect to $C(e, \mathbb{B})$, for e in $\mathbb{S} - \mathbb{R}$
    let $\mathbb{B}$ be those elements with a diversity greater than one, i.e. $C(e, \mathbb{F}) > 0$, for e in $\mathbb{S}$
    let $\mathbb{R}$ be those elements ever *as/in*-context of any element in $\mathbb{F}$
  end for
  return $\mathbb{F}$ and $\mathbb{B}$

Measure the diversity by $typeC$		
kth iter.	the smaller set	the bigger set
5th	*the a its their his*	[2697] *protest, code, hats...*
10th	*the a its their his some this any no an*	[3203] *emerging, results, seemed...*
15th	*the a its their his some this an any no will these our another those*	[3525] *help, consider, follow...*
26th	*the a its their his some will an any would can could these those our another may her several* ***york*** *my might each whose your every*	[3653] *all, settlements, just, four, help, dollar, teaching, soon...*
Measure the diversity by $tokenC$		
16th	*the a its will an would their ... could may any* ***york*** *these* ***according***	[4228] *concept, consider, all...*

Table 1: The acquisition outputs at each iteration of the bootstrapping algorithm running for words.

Measure the diversity by $typeC$		
kth iter.	the smaller set	the bigger set
5th	*-\$, -s, -ing, -ed, -e*	[2616] *degree-, cook-, topp-, excit-...*
10th	*-\$, -s, -ing, -ed, -e, -er, -es, -ion, -ers, -ly*	[3343] *comply-, drink-, opt-, devot-, ...*
15th	*-\$, -s, -ing, -ed, -e, -er, -ly, -ion, -es, -ers, -al, -y, -or, -ive, -ity*	[3496] *poor-, recept-, arriv-, mot- ...*
26th	*-\$, -s, -ing, -ed, -e, -er, -ly, -ion, -es, -y, -ers, -al, -ies, -or, -ive, -ity, -ist, -man, -ic, -est, -on, -en, -ism, -ors, -ant, -ial*	[3772] *shell-, deliver-, comparabl-, juni-produc-, buri-, specifi-, impress-, good-...*
Measure the diversity by $tokenC$		
15th	*-\$, -s, -e, -ed,* ***-t****, -ing, -ion, -y, -er, -al,* ***-n****, -ly, -ic, -or, -th*	[9576] *diploma-, conduc-, begin-, leg-...*

Table 2: The acquisition outputs at each iteration of the bootstrapping algorithm running for morphemes.

notable noisy item for acquiring functional words is *'york'*, which is classified as functional because 1) we lowercase all texts and 2) in WSJ articles, there are a lot complex NPs composed of *'York'*, i.e *'York'* is seen in many occurrences followed by nominal elements that may have already been classified as contentful during the bootstrapping process. On the other hand, with the diversity measurement $tokenC$, *'York'* has showed up as noisy much earlier in the bootstrapping process, as well as other noisy items.

It is even clearer in table 2 that the contextual diversity is a better measurement to distinguish functional elements than frequency. While measuring the diversity by $tokenC$, there are two noisy items show up as early as 15th iteration, *'-t'* and *'-n'*, which are successfully excluded from the output with diversity measurement $typeC$. While measuring the diversity by $typeC$, a possibly noisy item is *'-ers'*, which can be decomposed into *'-er'* and *'-s'*.

3 Applications

As shown above, the proposed bootstrapping algorithm generates outputs of high accuracy for both acquisition tasks: acquiring productive endings and acquiring 'first-order' functional words. In addition to the functional elements, this algorithm also generates complementary sets of contentful elements, which are base stems of words when acquiring morphemes and nouns plus verbs when acquiring words. Given these acquisition outputs, we can immediately accomplish the following two tasks, using very straightforward strategies only: 1) building a morph analyzer (section 3.1) ; and 2) acquiring the full set of functional categories, not just the first-order ones (section 3.2). Finally, we can plug the acquired list of closed-class words into a minimally supervised tagging system, (Zhao and Marcus, 2009), which requires the input of such a lexicon only. The resulting tagging system is then totally unsupervised and performs with satisfying accuracy as a totally unsupervised POS tagger for open-class words (section 3.3). The bootstrapping algorithm runs over the WSJ Treebank, which contains 1173766 words, with raw text input only for both tasks. And all experiments described below are trained over the same corpus.

3.1 Morphological Analysis

Those syntactic related morphological features, such as *'ended with -ed'* or *'ended with -ing'* have already been proven useful in syntactic related tasks such as POS tagging, parsing and so on; therefore, accomplishing such a morph analysis in an unsupervised way is meaningful for related unsupervised works.

Given an acquired set $\mathbb{B}$ of base stems, e.g. $\mathbb{B}$ = { *'laugh-'*, *'analyz-'* and *'-define'*}, and a set $\mathbb{F}$ of functional morphemes , e.g. $\mathbb{F}$ = {*'-ed'*, *'-s'* and *'pre-'*}, we can divide a word w into morphemes *b-* and *-e* where $b + e == w$, if *b-* in $\mathbb{B}$ and *-e* in $\mathbb{F}$; or if vice verse, i.e. *b-* in $\mathbb{F}$ and *-e* in $\mathbb{B}$. If such a division $b+e$ can be successfully performed on the word w with *-e* in $\mathbb{F}$, we specify that w has a morph feature *'ended with -e'*. For instance, given the above examples of $\mathbb{B}$ and $\mathbb{F}$, *'laughed'* has an ending *'-ed'* but not ending *'-ing'*, and *'analyzed'* has an ending *'-ed'*, but *'red'* doesn't have such an ending *'-ed'* as its morph feature. Overall, given two lists of morphemes, we can build a morph analyzer implementing this constrained stemming strategy for detecting morph features of interest.

For evaluating the morph analyzer composed by our acquisition outputs from WSJ Treebank, we use the CELEX corpus (Baayen et al., 1996) providing gold annotations of 6 syntactic related morphological features: {*'-s'*, *'-es'*, *'-ed'*, *'-ing'*, *'-er'*, and *'-est'*}. Among the 20058 types of words seen in both WSJ and CELEX corpus, 8789 types are annotated with these features. The precision number reported in Table 3 is the percentage of correct predictions out of all predictions the analyzer makes about the 6 morph features; and the recall is calculated by the percentage of correctly-predicted featured words out of all types of words with these features (8789).

We report the performance of two morph analyzers: one is composed by the acquired outputs with the diversity measurement $tokenC$; and the other one acquired with $typeC$. We also compare our results against a state-of-art morphology analyzer, (Lignos, 2010), which is adapted for this experiment. As shown in Table 3, our general bootstrapping algorithm, which is designed for various applications, is able to generate useful outputs for building a morph analyzer that performs comparably well as the stat-of-art achievements.

Algorithm	Precision	Recall	F-score
bootstrap-$tokenC$	77.89	82.38	80.07
bootstrap-$typeC$	78.71	83.31	80.94
(Lignos, 2010)	80.16	84.37	82.21

Table 3: The performance of morph analyzers evaluated for syntactic related morphological features.

3.2 Acquiring Closed-class Words

The bootstrapping algorithm is not designed to generate closed-class words falling in all functional categories, instead, it acquires those 'first-order' functional words, including only determiners and modal verbs. Given this acquired subset of closed-class words and the morph analyzer built in section 3.1, it is only a step away from acquiring all closed-class words falling in various functional categories.

We are not aware of previous work that acquires closed-class words in an automatic process, and in the NLP field, they are often approximated by the most frequent words. In other words, as a baseline model, we can acquire closed-class words by selecting k top words of the highest diversity measured by $tokenC$. Given discussion of diversity measurement in section 2.1, we also experiment with another baseline model, which acquires closed-class words by selecting k top words of the highest diversity measured by $typeC$. As shown in Table 4, with a better approximation of diversity, the type accuracy of predicting closed-class words is improved by an absolute error reduction of 11%, from 63% to 74% (k=100).

Moreover, as discussed in section 2, we know that those 'first-order' functional words, which can be generated by the bootstrapping algorithm with high accuracy, don't project onto other functional words. Therefore, after running the bootstrapping algorithm for words, we have already obtained a list of words that can be used for filtering the output of the baseline models. More specifically, given a set of 'first-order' functional words, those words that occur relatively often *in-context* of them should not be output as closed-class words. For example, two common noisy

top k *words*	20	40	80	100
baseline-*tokenC*	90.00	80.00	68.75	63.00
baseline-*typeC*	100.0	90.00	76.25	74.00
bootstrap-*tokenC*	95.00	95.00	90.00	86.00
bootstrap-*typeC*	**100.0**	**97.50**	**93.75**	**89.00**

Table 4: The percentage of correctly predicted closed-class word types out of k predictions

items in the output of the baseline models, *'billion'* and *'say'*, can be successfully filtered by the output set shown in Table 1.

In addition, since we have already built an unsupervised morph analyzer as described in section 3.1, which is acquired by the same bootstrapping algorithm, we would like to make use of them as well, in a straightforward way: as long as a word can be analyzed by the acquired morph analyzer, it should not be output as closed-class items.

Models 'bootstrap-*tokenC*' and 'bootstrap-*typeC*' implement the above idea using diversity measurement *tokenC* and *typeC* respectively. For example, the model 'bootstrap-*typeC*' uses the diversity measurement *typeC* to both acquire the morph analyzer and to acquire the set of 'first-order' functional words, and it uses these acquisition outputs to filter the baseline model that uses *typeC* as diversity measurement as well. The gold lexicon we use to evaluate the acquired list contains 288 closed-class words as described in (Zhao and Marcus, 2009).

With the help of acquisition outputs by a single algorithm running for different tasks, we can significantly improve the baseline model for acquiring closed-class words. As shown in Table 4, the performance of the baseline models drops rapidly as the size k grows; however, by taking acquired categories as constraints, we achieve quite reliable models. For example, 'bootstrap-*typeC*' improves 'baseline-*tokenC*' by an absolute error reduction of 26% (k=100), from 63% to 89%. So as to show how the models perform as k keeps growing, we provide more results in Figure 1, which plots the percentage of correctly predicted closed-class word types out of k predictions.

3.3 Unsupervised POS Tagging

Finally, to demonstrate the value of such a highly pure list of closed-class words, which previously could not be acquired through unsupervised learning, we plug the acquired list into a previously existing minimally supervised tagging system, (Zhao

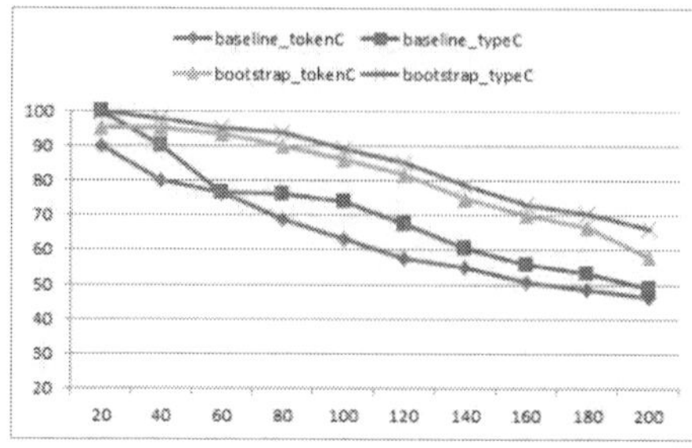

Figure 1: The percentage of correctly predicted closed-class word types out of k predictions

and Marcus, 2009), which only requires a closed-class lexicon for tagging all words. The resulting system now provides a totally unsupervised system for tagging open-class words, inducing both the categorical information itself and also the disambiguation rules for tagging open-class words.

Following (Zhao and Marcus, 2009), the six open-class POS categories to be predicted are verbs, nouns, past participles, present participles and numbers. The tagging predictions for open-class words (any word not in the closed-class list) are evaluated by the percentage of correct predictions on all tokens in the open-class set. Although all tagging experiments are done over the whole WSJ Treebank, the total number of tagging predictions may vary according to different input closed-class lists.

We experiment with four lists of closed-class words of the top 200 words acquired by the 'baseline-*typeC*', 'baseline-*tokenC*', 'bootstrap-*typeC*' and 'bootstrap-*tokenC*' respectively, as introduced in section 3.2. We evaluate against a gold-standard closed-class lexicon containing 288 words, also used for evaluation in section 3.2.

closed-class input	accuracy	totally tagged
baseline-*tokenC*	81.68	536535
baseline-*typeC*	75.51	554012
bootstrap-*tokenC*	77.30	627803
bootstrap-*typeC*	**85.26**	612997
gold lexicon	*91.03*	*611028*

Table 5: The percentage of correctly tagged tokens out of all predictions. The system tags open-class words only and distinguishes 6 POS categories.

As shown in Table 5, the tagging system using the closed-class set acquired by 'bootstrap-*typeC*' tags 612997 open-class tokens, which accounts for more than half of all the tokens in the WSJ Treebank, with an accuracy of 85.26%. In recent work on unsupervised tagging, tagging accuracys are reported in the range of 50-70%, e.g. (Abend et al., 2010), (Reichart et al., 2010), (Moon et al., 2010) and so on. Compared to these results, the tagging performance reported here, even though only on open-class words for six categories, is quite promising.

Because most previous work distinguishes between more categories than we do here, our results may be misleading, in that we appear to be reporting on a simpler task. However, these previous systems operate by clustering over a vector space of lexical features and suffix/prefix features, resulting in a large number of scattered clusters with similarities on different semantic and syntactic dimensions. As a result, it has proven difficult for them to use further agglomerative processing to induce simple distinct syntactic categories which map to POS tags naturally (Christodoulopoulos et al., 2010), and thus operating in a mode which achieves a higher tagging accuracy with coarser categories is not available to those systems at all. Therefore, achieving high accuracy with a smaller tag set is the harder, not easier, task for those systems.

4 Discussion

We propose a bootstrapping algorithm which successfully resolves two fundamental acquisition tasks: acquiring functional morphemes and acquiring 'first-order' functional words. We have shown that the outputs of these two fundamental acquisition tasks are very useful for more generalized tasks: they can be directly used to built a nearly state-of-art morph analyzer and they can be used to acquire a full set of closed-class words with high accuracy. Furthermore, the acquired list of closed-class words allows us to turn a minimally supervised tagging system into a totally unsupervised tagger for tagging open-class words. As a completely unsupervised tagger, the resulting system performs at a satisfying tagging accuracy above 85%.

The bootstrapping algorithm proposed here also gives us cause to think about the connection between functional categories in two forms: bound morphemes and words. As shown in this work, identically the same computational process that acquires functional morphemes also can be used to acquire the subset of functional words that includes modal verbs and determiners. All these elements share the property that, from the point of view of modern generative grammar, they only project locally, in other words, the elements that are acquired by this algorithm project to contentful elements *directly* most of the time but not through any other functional elements. Since all productive bound morphemes project mainly locally, they can all be acquired by the algorithm; in contrast, those functional words that project in larger scopes quite often, rather than in local contexts (i.e. not determiners and modal verbs), will not be acquired by this algorithm directly. This understanding of viewing local contexts as first-order functional projections motivates the filtering step in the bootstrapping algorithm. This overall understanding was motivated for us by the strict locality constraints assumed in phase theory (Chomsky, 2006).

References

Omri Abend, Roi Reichart, and Ari Rappoport. 2010. Improved unsupervised pos induction through prototype discovery. In *ACL*.

S. Abney. 2004. Understanding the yarowsky algorithm. *Computational Linguistics*, 30(3):365–395.

R.H. Baayen, R. Piepenbrock, and L. Gulikers. 1996. Celex2. Linguistic Data Consortium, Philadelphia.

E. Chan. 2008. *Structures and distributions in morphology learning*. Ph.D. thesis, University of Pennsylvania.

N. Chomsky. 2006. Approaching UG from below.

C. Christodoulopoulos, S. Goldwater, and M. Steedman. 2010. Two decades of unsupervised pos induction: How far have we come? In *EMNLP*.

A. Clark. 2000. Inducing syntactic categories by context distribution clustering. In *Proceedings of the Computational Natural Language Learning and the Second Learning Language in Logic Workshop (CoNLL-LLL)*.

C. Lignos. 2010. Learning from Unseen Data. In *Proceedings of Morpho Challenge 2010*, pages 35–38, Helsinki, Finland, September 2–3. Aalto School of Technology.

Mitch Marcus, Beatrice Santorini, and Mary Ann Marcinkiewicz. 1993. Building a large annotated corpus of english: The penn treebank. *Computational linguistics*, 19(2):313–330.

T. Moon, K.Erk, and J. Baldridge. 2010. Crouching dirichlet, hidden markov model: unsupervised pos tagging with context local tag generation. In *EMNLP*.

R. Reichart, R. Fattal, and A.Rappoport. 2010. Improved unsupervised pos induction using intrinsic clustering quality and a zipfian constraint. In *CoNLL*.

V. Valian, S. Solt, and J. Stewart. 2009. Abstract categories or limited scope formulae: The case of children's determiners. *Journal of Child Language*, 36:743–778.

C. Yang. 2002. *"Knowledge and Learning in Natural Language"*. Oxford University Press.

Q. Zhao and M. Marcus. 2009. A simple unsupervised learner for pos disambiguation rules given only a minimal lexicon. In *EMNLP*.

Joint Alignment and Artificial Data Generation: An Empirical Study of Pivot-based Machine Transliteration

Min Zhang[1] Xiangyu Duan[1] Ming Liu[1] Yunqing Xia[2] Haizhou Li[1]

[1]Institute for Infocomm Research, A-STAR, Singapore
{mzhang,xduan,mliu,hli}@i2r.a-star.edu.sg

[2]Dept. of Comp. Sci. & Tech., Tsinghua University, Beijing
yqxia@tsinghua.edu.cn

Abstract

In this paper, we first carry out an investigation on two existing pivot strategies for statistical machine transliteration, namely *system*-based and *model*-based strategies, to figure out the reason why the previous model-based strategy performs much worse than the system-based one. We then propose a joint alignment algorithm to optimize transliteration alignments jointly across source, pivot and target languages to improve the performance of the model-based strategy. In addition, we further propose a novel *synthetic data*-based strategy, which artificially generates source-target data using pivot language. Experimental results on benchmarking data show that the proposed joint alignment optimization algorithm significantly improves the accuracy of model-based strategy and the proposed synthetic data-based strategy is very effective for pivot-based machine transliteration.

1 Introduction

Machine transliteration refers to the phonetic translation of names across languages by computer. With the rapid growth of the Internet data and the dramatic changes in the user demographics especially among the non-English speaking parts of the world, machine transliteration is important in many cross-lingual NLP, MT and CLIR applications as their performances have been shown to positively correlate with the correct conversion of names between the languages in several studies (Demner-Fushman and Oard, 2002; Mandl and Womser-Hacker, 2005; Hermjakob *et al.*, 2008; Udupa *et al.*, 2009). However, the traditional source for name equivalence, the bilingual dictionaries — whether handcrafted or statistical built — offer only limited support because new names always emerge.

All of the above points to the critical need for high-performance machine transliteration technology. Much research effort has been made to address this issue in the research community (Knight and Graehl, 1998; Meng *et al.*, 2001; Al-Onaizan and Knight, 2002; Oh and Choi, 2002; Klementiev and Roth, 2006; Sproat, 2006; Zelenko and Aone, 2006; Li *et al.*, 2004, 2009a, 2009b; Sherif and Kondrak, 2007; Bertoldi *et al.*, 2008; Goldwasser and Roth, 2008). These previous work falls into three categories, i.e., grapheme-based, phoneme-based and hybrid methods (Li *et al.*, 2009a, 2009b). The report of the first machine transliteration shared task NEWS 2009 (Li *et al.*, 2009a, 2009b) provides common benchmarking data in diverse language pairs and systematically evaluate the state-of-the-art technologies using their provided data.

Although promising results have been reported, one of major issues is that the current transliteration methods rely heavily on significant amount of source-target parallel data to learn transliteration model. However, such corpora are not always available and the amounts of the currently available corpora, even for language pairs with English involved, are far from enough for training, letting alone many low-density language pairs. Indeed, transliteration corpora for most language pairs without English involved are unavailable and are usually rather expensive to manually construct (Khapra *et al.*, 2010; Zhang *et al.*, 2010). To date, only two previous works (Khapra *et al.*, 2010; Zhang *et al.*, 2010) touch this issue of transliterating names across low-density language pairs. Both of them resort to pivot language-based approaches to address this issue.

Khapra *et al.* (2010) proposes the system-based pivot strategy for machine transliteration, which learns a source-pivot model from source-pivot data and a pivot-target model from pivot-target data, respectively. In decoding, it first transliterates a source name to *N*-best pivot names and then transliterates each pivot name to target names which are finally re-ranked using the combined two individual transliteration scores. Zhang *et al.* (2010) verifies the system-based strategy together with joint source-channel model (Li *et al.*, 2004) on Chinese, English, Korean and Japanese data (Li *et al.*, 2009a, 2009b) and they further proposes a model-based strategy, which learns a direct source-target transliteration model from two independent[1] source-pivot and pivot-target name pair corpora, and does direct source-target decoding without relying on pivot languages. However, it was reported that the model-based strategy performed much worse than the system-based one (Zhang *et al.*, 2010).

This paper investigates the reason why previous model-based strategy performs worse than system-based one and then proposes a joint alignment algorithm to solve the alignment unit inconsistent issue, which is the main reason of leading to the worse performance of model-based strategy. The key point of the proposed joint alignment algorithm is to jointly optimize transliteration unit alignments among source, pivot and target languages. In addition, the paper further proposes a novel synthetic data-based strategy for pivot-based machine transliteration. It automatically constructs source-target data using source-pivot and pivot-target data, and then trains a direct source-target transliteration model using the synthetic data. We verify the proposed methods using the benchmarking data released at NEWS2009 (Li *et al.*, 2009a, 2009b). Experiential results show that our proposed joint alignment optimization algorithm is able to effectively solve the transliteration unit mismatching issue and the proposed synthetic data-based strategy is very effective, achieving the best-reported performance.

The rest of the paper is organized as follows. Section 2 introduces the direct transliteration model. Section 3 discusses our proposed joint alignment algorithm and synthetic data-based strategy. Experimental results are reported at section 4. Finally, we conclude the paper in section 5.

[1] Here "independent" means the source-pivot and pivot-target data are not from the same English name source.

2 The Transliteration Model: JSCM

To make our study language-independent, we select joint source-channel model (JSCM, also named as *n*-gram transliteration model) (Li *et al.*, 2004) under grapheme-based framework as our transliteration model due to its state-of-the-art performance and using orthographical information only (Li *et al.*, 2009a). In addition, unlike other feature-based methods, such as CRFs (Lafferty *et al.*, 2001), MaxEnt (Berger *et al.*, 1996) or SVM (Vapnik, 1995), the JSCM model directly computes model probabilities using maximum likelihood estimation (Dempster *et al.*, 1977). This property facilitates the implementation of the model-based strategy.

JSCM directly models how both source and target names can be generated simultaneously. Given a source name *S* and a target name *T*, it estimates the joint probability of *S* and *T* as follows:

$$\begin{aligned} P(S,T) &= P(s_1 \dots s_i \dots s_K, t_1 \dots t_i \dots t_K) \\ &= P(<s_1,t_1>, \dots, <s_i,t_i>, \\ &\quad \dots, <s_K,t_K>) \\ &= P(<s,t>_1, \dots, <s,t>_i, \\ &\quad \dots <s,t>_K) \\ &= \prod_{k=1}^{K} P\left(<s,t>_k \mid <s,t>_1^{k-1}\right) \\ &\approx \prod_{k=1}^{K} P\left(<s,t>_k \mid <s,t>_{k-n+1}^{k-1}\right) \quad (1) \end{aligned}$$

where s_i and t_i is an aligned transliteration unit[2] pair, and *n* is the *n*-gram order.

In our implementation, we compare different unsupervised transliteration alignment methods, including Giza++ (Och and Ney, 2003), JSCM-based EM algorithm (Li *et al.*, 2004), edit distance-based EM algorithm (Pervouchine *et al.*, 2009) and Oh et al.'s alignment tool (Oh *et al.*, 2009). Based on the aligned transliteration corpus, we learn the transliteration model using maximum likelihood estimation (Dempster *et al.*, 1977) and decode the transliteration result $T^* = \text{argmax}_T P(S,T)$ using stack decoder (Schwartz and Chow, 1990).

[2] Transliteration unit is language dependent. It can be a Chinese character, a sub-string of English words, a Korean Hangual or a Japanese Kanji or several Japanese Katakanas.

3 Joint Alignment and Synthetic Data-based Strategy

In this section, we elaborate our proposed joint alignment algorithm and synthetic data-based strategy for pivot-based machine transliteration.

3.1 System-based Strategy

Given a source name S, a target name T and let Z be the n-best transliterations of S in a pivot language $\acute{Z}$ [3], the system-based transliteration strategy under JSCM can be formulized as follows:

$$\begin{aligned} P(S,T) &= \sum_{Z} P(S,Z,T) \\ &= \sum_{Z} P(T|S,Z) * P(S,Z) \\ &\approx \textstyle\sum_{Z} P(T|Z) * P(S,Z) \\ &\approx \sum_{Z} \frac{P(S,Z) * P(T,Z)}{P(Z)} \end{aligned} \quad (2)$$

where $P(S,Z)$ and $P(T,Z)$ can be computed using JSCM as formalized at Eq. (1). Eq. (2) assumes that T is independent of S when given Z because the parallel name corpus between S and T is not available under the pivot transliteration framework. The n-best transliterations in pivot language are expected to be able to carry enough information of the source name S. Following the nature of JSCM, Eq. (2) directly models how the source name S and pivot name Z and how the pivot name Z and the target name T are generated simultaneously. Since Z is considered twice in $P(S,Z)$ and $P(T,Z)$, the duplicated impact of Z is removed by being divided by $P(Z)$.

3.2 Joint Alignment Algorithm for Model-based Strategy

Rather than combining the transitive transliteration results at system level, the model-based strategy aims to learn a direct model $P(S,T)$ by combining the two individual models of $P(S,Z)$ and $P(T,Z)$. Here we use bigram as an example to illustrate how to learn the JSCM transliteration model $P(S,T) = \prod_{k=1}^{K} P(< s,t >_k \mid <$ *s,t>k−1* using the model-based strategy.

$$P(< s,t >_k \mid < s,t >_{k-1}) = \frac{P(< s,t >_k, < s,t >_{k-1})}{P(< s,t >_{k-1})} \quad (3)$$

where,

$$\begin{aligned} &P(< s,t >_k, < s,t >_{k-1}) \\ &\quad = P(s_k, s_{k-1}, t_k, t_{k-1}) \\ &\quad = \sum_{z_k, z_{k-1}} P(s_k, s_{k-1}, t_k, t_{k-1}, z_k, z_{k-1}) \\ &\quad = \sum_{z_k, z_{k-1}} P(t_k, t_{k-1} | s_k, s_{k-1}, z_k, z_{k-1}) \\ &\qquad\qquad * P(s_k, s_{k-1}, z_k, z_{k-1}) \\ &\quad \approx \sum_{z_k, z_{k-1}} P(t_k, t_{k-1} | z_k, z_{k-1}) \\ &\quad * \qquad P(s_k, s_{k-1}, z_k, z_{k-1}) \\ &\quad \approx \sum_{z_k, z_{k-1}} P(t_k, t_{k-1}, z_k, z_{k-1}) \\ &\qquad\qquad * P(s_k, s_{k-1}, z_k, z_{k-1}) \\ &\qquad\qquad / P(z_k, z_{k-1}) \end{aligned} \quad (4)$$

$$P(< s,t >_{k-1}) = \sum_{<s,t>_k} P(< s,t >_k, < s,t >_{k-1}) \quad (5)$$

where $P(t_i, t_{i-1}, z_i, z_{i-1})$, $P(s_i, s_{i-1}, z_i, z_{i-1})$ and $P(z_i, z_{i-1})$ can be directly estimated at training corpus.

In summary, eq. (2) formalizes the system-based strategy while eq. (3) formalizes the model-based strategy, where we can find that eq. (2) involves the pivot language Z in modeling and decoding while eq. (3) does not (its model parameters are pre-computed using eq. (4) and (5) during training).

In previous work (Zhang *et al.*, 2010), the model-based strategy was reported to perform much worse than the system-based. We find that the main reason is due to the size inconsistence of transliteration unit of pivot language in the source-pivot and pivot-target alignments during training. As shown at eq. (4), the source-target model is calculated using the source-pivot el$P(s_k, s_{k-1}, z_k, z_{k-1})$and the pivot-target model $P(t_k, t_{k-1}, z_k, z_{k-1})$ directly. This requests that the pivot transliteration unit z_k, z_{k-1} must be consistent in the two individual modes. Thus, all the source-pivot and pivot-target model parameters $P(*_k, *_{k-1}, z_k, z_{k-1})$ are of no use if their involved pivot unit z_k, z_{k-1} can only be found at either source-pivot or pivot-target model. Unfortunately in the only previous work (Zhang *et al.*, 2010), the source-pivot model and pivot-target

[3] There can be multiple pivot languages used. However, same as Khapra *et al.* (2010) and Zhang *et al.* (2010), without loss of generality, we only use one pivot language to facilitate our discussion. It is straightforward to extend one pivot language to multiple ones by considering all the pivot transliterations in all pivot languages.

model are trained separately, i.e., their object function is to maximize $P(S,Z)$and $P(T,Z)$ independently. This results in serious pivot transliteration unit inconsistent issue for some language pairs. For example, in our experiment (Chinese→English→ Japanese) with English as pivot language, we find that the English transliteration unit size in Chinese→English model is much larger than that in English→Japanese model. This is because from phonetic viewpoint, in Chinese→English model, the English unit is at syllable level (corresponding one Chinese character) while in English→Japanese model, the English unit is at sub-syllable level (consonant or vowel or syllable, corresponding one Japanese Katakana). Following example excerpted from our training corpus illustrates the pivot transliteration unit mismatching issue, where the English word "Aachen" is segmented into "Aa" and "chen" in Chinese-English model while it is segmented into "A", "a", "che" and "n" in English-Japanese model. This trilingual pair is then of no use in model-based strategy.

To solve the mismatching issue, this paper proposes a joint alignment algorithm to jointly optimize transliteration unit alignments among source, pivot and target languages for model-based strategy. To facilitate discussion, we base on the task of using English as pivot language for Chinese-Japanese transliteration (see Table 1) to present our proposed algorithm. The core idea of this algorithm is to use Chinese-English alignments as a constraint to do English-Japanese alignment. The algorithm consists of the following 6 steps:

Algorithm 1. Joint Alignment

Inputs:

Chinese-English Name List (CE).
English-Japanese Name List (EJ).

Outputs:

More consistent CE and EJ alignments at Chinese syllable level and a direct Chinese-Japanese (CJ) JSCM.

1. Align the CE names at Chinese syllable level using the JSCM-based EM algorithm (Li *et al.*, 2004).
2. Train a transliteration unit-based English bi-gram LM with the transliteration unit-segmented (at step 1) English side names of CE using SRILM toolkits (Stolcke, 2002). Note that here the English transliteration units are corresponding to Chinese syllable level.
3. Align the Chinese-English-Japanese (CEJ) names that are the intersection of the entire CE and EJ names (with the same English names).
   a. CE part of CEJ has been aligned at Step 1.
   b. Align the CJ part of CEJ at Chinese syllable level using the JSCM-based EM algorithm (Li *et al.*, 2004).
   c. Construct the CEJ name alignments by

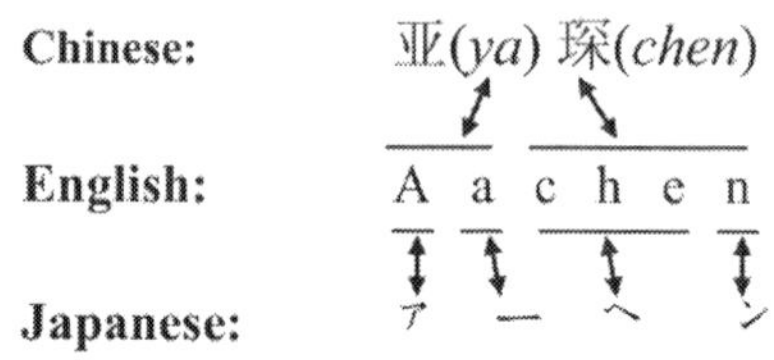

   merging the CE and CJ alignments.
4. Align EJ names at Chinese syllable level.
   a. The intersection part of EJ with CJ (*i*EJ) has already been aligned at Chinese syllable level at step 3.
   b. Align the remaining non-intersection part of EJ name pairs (*ni*EJ) using Algorithm 2 with the help of the aligned intersection part done at step 4.a and the transliteration unit-based English bi-gram LM learned at step 2.
   c. Merge the above two parts.
5. Train two individual JSCMs using the Chinese syllable level-aligned CE and EJ name corpus, respectively.
6. Train a direct CJ JSCM using the two individual JSCMs learned at step 5 by the model-based pivot strategy as formulated at eqs. (3), (4) and (5).

Algorithm 2. Constrained EM-based Alignment

Inputs:

1. Non-intersection part of EJ name pairs (*ni*EJ).
2. Intersection part of EJ name pairs (*i*EJ) aligned at Chinese syllable level and the initial JSCM (named as iJSCM) learned from this corpus (step 3.d of Algorithm 1).
3. The transliteration unit-based English bi-gram LM (named as eLM, step 2 of Algorithm 1).

Output:

English-Japanese name pairs aligned at Chinese syllable level.

1. Bootstrap initial alignment of the *ni*EJ name using the initial model iJSCM.

2. **Expectation**: re-train iJSCM using both the input *i*EJ name alignments and the updated *ni*EJ name alignments.
3. **Maximization**: Apply the re-trained iJSCM and the input eLM to obtain new alignments of the *ni*EJ names. Note that different from previous EM-based transliteration alignment algorithm (Li *et al.*, 2004) that only maximizes the JSCM probabilities, here we maximize two kinds of probabilities:

$$A^* = \underset{A}{\operatorname{argmax}} P(E,J,A) * P(E,A) \quad (6)$$

   where E refers to English and J refers to Japanese; A is an alignment which defining the transliteration unit segmentations of E and J, and their mappings; $P(E,J,A)$ is the JSCM probability of E and J under A; and $P(E,A)$ is the eLM transliteration unit bigram probability of E segmented by A.
4. Go to step 2 until the alignment converges.
5. Output the *ni*EJ name alignments.

The motivation of the joint alignment algorithm (Algorithm 1 and 2) is to address the English transliteration unit mismatching issue by aligning the EJ at Chinese syllable level with the help of CE alignment. While the mismatching issue in the intersection part of the data is easy to solve by step 3 of Algorithm 1, it is more complicated at the non-intersection part. As illustrated at step 3 of Algorithm 2, the core idea is to use English segmentation learned from CE alignment (step 2 of Algorithm 1) and already-aligned intersection part of EJ (*i*EJ, step 3 of Algorithm 1) to constrain the EM alignment process. Therefore, the English bigram LM and the aligned intersection part (*i*EJ) keep unchanged during all the EM iterations. But in E step (step 2 of Algorithm 2), the iJSCM model is updated at each iteration using the entire EJ data while in M step (step 3 of Algorithm 2), the alignments are decoded out using both the iJSCM and the English bi-gram LM. Indeed, in our implementation, we introduce more knowledge sources, including transliteration unit insertion penalty and Japanese LM, into the M step by simply considering these two features at eq. (6).

Given the jointly optimized CE and EJ aligned name corpus, we can easily learn a direct CJ model using the pivot-based strategy (steps 5 and 6 of Algorithm 1).

3.3 Synthetic Data-based Strategy

Different from previous two strategies, the synthetic data-based strategy automatically constructs source-target data using source-pivot and pivot-target data, and then trains a direct source-target transliteration model using the synthetic and any other available source-target data. The philosophy of this strategy is straightforward while the key is how to generate "good" data. Next, we also use Chinese-English-Japanese as example to elaborate this strategy.

Algorithm 3. Artificial Data Generation

Inputs:
Chinese-English Name List (CE).
English-Japanese Name List (EJ).

Outputs:
Synthetic Chinese-Japanese name pairs.

1. Directly output those CJ names (*i*CJ), which are the intersection of the entire CE and EJ names (with the same English names).
2. Transliterate those Chinese names which are not in *i*CJ to Japanese using either the system-based or model-based strategy. To maintain the transliteration quality, we consider both forward and backward transliteration probabilities as well as the information whether the original Chinese can be recovered from a transliterated Japanese name. The process is formalized as follows:

$$J^* = \underset{J}{\operatorname{argmax}} P(J|C) * P(\acute{C}|J) * I(\acute{C},C) * P(J) \quad (7)$$

   where $P(J|C)$ is the forward transliteration probability, $P(\acute{C}|J)$ is the backward transliteration probability, and $I(\acute{C},C)$ is a penalty function to penalize those cases where $\acute{C}$ is not equal to C, i.e., C fails to be covered from J. $P(J)$ is a Japanese Katakana language model.
3. Translate those Japanese names which are not in *i*CJ to Chinese in the similar way as step 2.

$$C^* = \underset{C}{\operatorname{argmax}} P(C|J) * P(\acute{J}|C) * I(\acute{J},J) * P(C) \quad (8)$$

   Note that the outputs of step 2 and 3 do not overlap with each other. $P(C)$ is a Chinese character-based language model.
4. Merge the results of step 1, 2 and 3. Given the merged data, we can easily train a direct Chinese-Japanese transliteration model.

The core idea of Algorithm 3 lies in eqs. (7) and (8). Among the three strategies (system-based, model-based and synthetic data-based), the first and the third ones are transliteration model independent while the second one is not.

3.4 Comparison with Previous Work

Almost all previous work on machine transliteration focuses on direct transliteration or transliteration system combination. Only two recent work (Khapra *et al.*, 2010; Zhang *et al.*, 2010) touches on the issue of pivot transliteration. Khapra *et al.* (2010) proposes the system-based strategy and does extensively empirical study together with CRF model on Indic/Slavic/Semetic languages and English. Zhang *et al.* (2010) proposes the model-based strategy, but reporting very bad performance. To address the low performance issue of the model-based strategy, this paper proposes the joint alignment algorithm to optimize the source-pivot-target alignment directly, resulting in significant performance improvement. Moreover, the paper proposes a new synthetic data-based strategy for pivot-based machine transliteration.

Machine translation carries out similar pivot-based translation studies. Bertoldi *et al.* (2008) studies two pivot approaches for phrase-based statistical machine translation. One is at system level and one is to re-construct source-target data and alignments through pivot data. Cohn and Lapata (2007) explores how to utilize multilingual parallel data (rather than pivot data) to improve translation performance. Wu and Wang (2007, 2009) study the model-level pivot approach and explore how to leverage on rule-based translation results in pivot language to improve translation performance. Utiyama and Isahara (2007) compare different pivot approaches for phrase-based statistical machine translation. All of the previous work on machine translation works on phrase-based statistical machine translation. Therefore, their translation model is to calculate phrase-based conditional probabilities at unigram level ($P(t_k|s_k)$) while our transliteration model is to calculate joint transliteration unit-based conditional probabilities at bigram level ($P(<s,t>_k \mid <s,t>_{k-1})$). This is the fundamental difference.

4 Experimental Results

4.1 Experimental Settings

Language Pair	Training	Test
Chinese-English (CE)	31,961	2,896
English-Japanese (EJ)	23,225	1,489
Chinese-English-Japanese (CEJ, the intersection part of CE and EJ)	10,071	1,030

Table 1. Statistics on the data set

We use the NEWS 2009 Chinese-English and English-Japanese benchmark data as our experimental data (Li *et al.*, 2009a). All of the names originate from Western names, i.e., no native Chinese and Japanese names are involved in this experiment. Considering the fact that those language pairs with English involved have the most training data, it is reasonable to select English as pivot language. Table 1 reports the statistics of all the experimental data. The Chinese-English-Japanese data is the intersection of the Chinese-English and English-Japanese data.

We compare different alignment algorithms on the DEV set (Li *et al.*, 2009a). Finally we use Pervouchine *et al.* (2009)'s alignment algorithm for Chinese-Japanese and Li *et al.* (2004)'s for Chinese-English and English-Japanese. Given the aligned corpora, we directly learn each individual JSCM model (i.e., *n*-gram transliteration model) using SRILM toolkits (Stolcke, 2002). We also use SRILM toolkits to do decoding. For the system-based strategy, we output top-10 pivot transliteration results. For the evaluation matrix, to save space, we only use top-1 accuracy (ACC) (Li *et al.*, 2009a) to measure transliteration performance since other five evaluation matrix used at Li *et al.* (2009a) are reported to have great correlation with ACC.

4.2 Experimental Results

4.2.1 Results of Direct Transliteration

Language Pair	ACC
English-Chinese	0.681049
English-Japanese	0.456755
Chinese-English	0.394490
Japanese-English	0.314970
Chinese-Japanese	0.288022
Japanese-Chinese	0.366559

Table 2. Performance of direct transliterations

Table 2 reports the performance of direct transliteration. The first two experiments (line 1-2) are part of the NEWS 2009 share tasks and the others are our additional experiments for our pivot studies. Comparison of the first two experimental results and the results reported at NEWS 2009 shows that we achieve comparable performance with their best-reported systems under the same conditions of using single system and orthographic features only. This indicates that our baseline represents the state-of-the-art performance. In

Methods	Chinese-English-Japanese	Japanese-English-Chinese
Baseline 1: Independent alignment of Chinese-English and English-Japanese (Zhang *et al.*, 2010)	0.065949 (5816/16989)	0.043011(5816/16989)
Baseline 2: Linguistically heuristic-based re-construction of Chinese-English and English-Japanese alignment (Zhang *et al.*, 2010)	0.282638 (26351/34812)	0.378299 (26351/34812)
Method 1: Joint alignment on intersection part of Chinese-English and English-Japanese data (Ours)	0.287360 (26432/34920)	0.378796 (26432/34920)
Method 2: Joint alignment on entire data set (Ours)	**0.325367 (37437/48590)**	**0.440782 (37437/48590)**

Table 4. Performance of model-based strategy (in ACC/# of unigram/# of bigram of the different transliteration models learned y the model-based strategy)

addition, we find that the backward transliteration (line 3-4) consistently performs worse than its corresponding forward transliteration (line 1-2). This observation is consistent with what reported at previous work (Li *et al.*, 2004; Zhang *et al.*, 2004). The main reason is because English has much more transliteration units than foreign C/J languages. This makes the transliteration from English to C/J a many-to-few mapping issue and backward transliteration a few-to-many mapping issue. Therefore backward transliteration has more ambiguities and thus is more difficult. Moreover, due to the less available training data for the language pairs without English involved (Chinese/Japanese), the lowest two experiments (line 5-6) performs worse than the case with English involved . This observation motivates us the study using pivot language for machine transliteration.

4.2.2 Results of System-based Strategy

Language Pair	ACC
Chinese-English-Japanese **(System)**	0.324361
Chinese-English **(Direct)**	0.394490
English-Japanese **(Direct)**	0.456755
Chinese-Japanese **(Direct)**	0.288022
Japanese-English-Chinese **(System)**	0.445748
Japanese-English **(Direct)**	0.314970
English-Chinese **(Direct)**	0.681049
Japanese-Chinese **(Direct)**	0.366559

Table 3. Performance of system-based strategy

Table 3 reports the experimental results of system-based strategy. It confirms the previous observations (Khapra *et al.*, 2010; Zhang *et al.*, 2010).

- The system-based pivot strategy is very effective, achieving significant performance improvement over direct transliteration.
- Different from other pipeline methodologies, system-based pivot strategy does not suffer from the error propagation issue. Its ACC is significantly better than the product of the ACCs of the two individual systems.

The main reasons of the good performance reported at the above observations are due to the following reasons:

- The pivot approach is able to use large amount of source-pivot and pivot-target data.
- The nature of transliteration is a phonetic translation process. Therefore a little bit variation in orthography may not hurt or even help to improve transliteration performance in some cases as long as the orthographical variations keep the phonetic equivalent information.
- The N-best accuracy of machine transliteration is very high (Li *et al.*, 2004; Zhang *et al.*, 2004). It means that in most cases the correct transliteration in pivot language can be found in the top-10 results and the other 9 results hold the similar pronunciations with the correct one, which can serve as alternative "quasi-correct" inputs to the

second stage transliterations and thus largely improve the overall accuracy.

4.2.3 Results of Model-based Strategy

Table 4 reports the performance of model-based strategy with different alignment refinements, where we can find:

- Baseline 1 clearly shows that the model-based strategy performs extremely worse than the other three settings if we align the Chinese-English and English-Japanese data independently. The major reason attributes to the size mismatching of the English transliteration units between the two data sets (syllable level *vs*. phoneme or syllable level).
- The other three experiments demonstrate the effectiveness of the alignment refinements. However Baseline 2 is more heuristic while ours are more mathematically principled.
- Method 1 performs comparably with Baseline 2 even utilizing fewer training data.
- Method 2 achieves the best performance. It convincingly shows the effectiveness of the proposed joint optimization algorithm.
- Among all the models, Method 2 has the largest amounts of model parameters (# of unigram and bigram). From modeling viewpoint, it indicates that this model is more powerful than others. This is due to the contribution of the more consistent English transliteration units.
- Comparing Tables 4 and Table 3, we can see that the model-based strategy performs as well as the system-based strategy. This clearly demonstrates the effectiveness of our proposed joint alignment algorithm.

4.2.4 Results of Synthetic Data-based Strategy

Language Pair	ACC
Japanese-Chinese (**Synthetic Data**)	0.465648
Japanese-Chinese (**System**)	0.445748
Japanese-Chinese (**Model**)	0.440782
Japanese-Chinese (**Direct**)	0.366559
Chinese-Japanese (**Synthetic Data**)	0.338930
Chinese-Japanese (**System**)	0.324361
Chinese-Japanese (**Model**)	0.325367
Chinese-Japanese (**Direct**)	0.288022

Table 5. Performance comparison of the three pivot strategies

Table 5 shows the advantage of synthetic data-based strategy over the other methods.

- The synthetic data-based strategy significantly outperforms the direct one. This clearly shows the effectiveness of the additional synthetic data.
- Using the same amount of data, the synthetic data-based strategy significantly outperforms the model-based one. This is not surprising since model-based strategy suffers from the transliteration unit mismatching issue and its performance is also compromised by the independent assumption of eq. (4) while the synthetic data-based directly learns the model from bilingual data without suffering from the above two issues.
- Using the same amount of data, the synthetic data-based strategy significantly outperforms the system-based one. This is because the synthetic data-based strategy directly learns a source-target transliteration model while system-based method utilizes two indirect models and has to bear with the independent assumption of eq. (2).
- It is worth noting the transliteration performance of the synthetic data-based strategy highly depends on the quality of the artificially generated data. Table 5 reports the performance using the default setting of eq. (7) and (8) at Algorithm 3. We expect that the synthetic data-based strategy has the potential to further improve its performance by simply introducing more features into eq. (7) and (8).

5 Conclusions

A big challenge to statistical-based machine transliteration is the lack of the training data, esp. to those low-density language pairs without English involved. To address the above issue, this paper propose a simple, but very effective solution, namely synthetic data-based strategy, to artificially generate direct source-target training data using pivot language. Experimental results on NEWS 2009 data shows that the proposed strategy is very useful, achieving the best-reported performance. The paper also proposes a joint alignment algorithm to jointly optimize the alignments between source, pivot and target data. Experimental results show that the joint alignment algorithm is able to largely boost the performance of model-based strategy.

The system-based and the proposed synthetic-based strategy are transliteration model-independent while model-based strategy is not. However, the three strategies and the proposed joint alignment algorithm are not limited to the machine transliteration task. They can be applied to those tasks which possess the similar "transitive" property as machine transliteration, such as paraphrasing, domain adaptation and some multilingual tasks.

References

Yaser Al-Onaizan and Kevin Knight. 2002. *Translating named entities using monolingual and bilingual resources*. ACL-02

Adam L. Berger, stephen A. Della Pietra and Vincent J. Della Pietra. 1996. *A Maximum Entropy Approach to Natural Language Processing*. Computational Linguistics. 22(1):39–71

N. Bertoldi, M. Barbaiant, M. Federico and R. Cattoni. 2008. *Phrase-based Statistical Machine Translation with Pivot Languages*. IWSLT-08

Trevor Cohn and Mirella Lapata. 2007. *Machine Translation by Triangulation: Making Effective Use of Multi-Parallel Corpora*. ACL-07

Andrew Finch and Eiichiro Sumita. 2008. *Phrase-based machine transliteration*. IJCNLP-08

Dan Goldwasser and Dan Roth. 2008. *Transliteration as constrained optimization*. EMNLP-08

D. Demner-Fushman and D. W. Oard. 2002. *The effect of bilingual term list size on dictionary-based cross-language information retrieval*. The 36th Hawaii Int'l. Conf. System Sciences

A.P. Dempster, N.M. Laird and D.B.Rubin, 1977. *Maximum likelihood from incomplete data via the EM algorithm*, J. Roy. Stat. Soc., Ser. B. Vol. 39

Ulf Hermjakob, Kevin Knight and Hal Daum'e. 2008. *Name translation in statistical machine translation: Learning when to transliterate*. ACL-08

John Lafferty, F. Pereira, Andrew McCallum. 2001. *Conditional random fields: Probabilistic models for segmenting and labeling sequence data*. ICML-01

Mitesh Khapra, Kumaran A and Pushpak Bhattacharyya. 2010. *Everybody loves a rich cousin: An empirical study of transliteration through bridge languages*. NAACL-HLT-10

A. Klementiev and Dan Roth. 2006. *Weakly supervised named entity transliteration and discovery from multilingual comparable corpora*. COLING-ACL-06

K. Knight and J. Graehl. 1998. *Machine Transliteration*, Computational Linguistics, Vol 24, No. 4

P. Koehn, F. J. Och and D. Marcu. 2003. *Statistical phrase-based translation*. HLT-NAACL-03

J. Lafferty, A. McCallum and F. Pereira. 2001. *Conditional random fields: Probabilistic models for segmenting and labeling sequence data*. ICML-01

Haizhou Li, A Kumaran, Vladimir Pervouchine and Min Zhang. 2009a. *Report of NEWS 2009 Machine Transliteration Shared Task*. IJCNLP-ACL-09 Workshop: NEWS-09

Haizhou Li, A Kumaran, Min Zhang and Vladimir Pervouchine. 2009b. *Whitepaper of NEWS 2009 Machine Transliteration Shared Task*. IJCNLP-ACL-09 Workshop: NEWS-09

H. Li, M. Zhang and J. Su. 2004. *A Joint Source-Channel Model for Machine Transliteration*. ACL-04

Thomas Mandl and Christa Womser-Hacker. 2004. *How do Named Entities Contribute to Retrieval Effectiveness?* CLEF-04

H. Meng, W. Lo, B. Chen and K. Tang. 2001. *Generate Phonetic Cognates to Handle Name Entities in English-Chinese cross-language spoken document retrieval*. ASRU-01

Jong-Hoon Oh and Key-Sun Choi. 2002. *An English-Korean Transliteration Model Using Pronunciation and Contextual Rules*. COLING-02

Jong-Hoon Oh, Kiyotaka Uchimoto, and Kentaro Torisawa. 2009. *Machine Transliteration with Target-Language Grapheme and Phoneme: Multi-Engine Transliteration Approach*. NEWS 2009

Franz Josef Och and Hermann Ney. 2003. *A Systematic Comparison of Various Statistical Alignment Models*. Computational Linguistics 29(1)

V. Pervouchine, H. Li and B. Lin. 2009. *Transliteration Alignment*. ACL-IJCNLP-09

R. Schwartz and Y. L. Chow. 1990. *The N-best algorithm: An efficient and exact procedure for finding the N most likely sentence hypothesis*, ICASSP-90

Tarek Sherif and Grzegorz Kondrak. 2007. *Substring-based transliteration*. ACL-07

Richard Sproat, Tao Tao and ChengXiang Zhai. 2006. *Named entity transliteration with comparable corpora*. COLING-ACL-06

Andreas Stolcke. 2002. *SRILM - an extensible language modeling toolkit*. ICSLP-02

R. Udupa, K. Saravanan, A. Bakalov and A. Bhole. 2009. *They are out there, if you know where to look: Mining transliterations of OOV query terms for cross-language information retrieval*. In LNCS: Advances in Information Retrieval, volume 5478, pages 437–448. Springer

Masao Utiyama and Hitoshi Isahara. 2007. *A Comparison of Pivot Methods for Phrase-based Statistical Machine Translation*. NAACL-HLT-07

Vladimir N. Vapnik. 1995. *The Nature of Statistical Learning Theory*. Springer

H. Wu and H. Wang. 2007. *Pivot Language Approach for Phrase-based SMT*. ACL-07

H. Wu and H. Wang. 2009. *Revisiting Pivot Language Approach for Machine Translation*. ACL-09

Dmitry Zelenko and Chinatsu Aone. 2006. *Discriminative methods for transliteration*. EMNLP-06

Min Zhang, Haizhou Li and Jian Su. 2004. *Direct Orthographical Mapping for machine transliteration*. COLING-04

Min Zhang, Xiangyu Duan, Vladimir Pervouchine and Haizhou Li. 2010. *Machine Transliteration: Leveraging on Third Languages*. COLING-10 (poster)

Incremental Joint POS Tagging and Dependency Parsing in Chinese

Jun Hatori[1] **Takuya Matsuzaki**[1] **Yusuke Miyao**[3] **Jun'ichi Tsujii**[4]
[1]University of Tokyo / 7-3-1 Hongo, Bunkyo, Tokyo, Japan
[2]National Institute of Informatics / 2-1-2 Hitotsubashi, Chiyoda, Tokyo, Japan
[3]Microsoft Research Asia / 5 Danling Street, Haidian District, Beijing, P.R. China
{hatori,matuzaki}@is.s.u-tokyo.ac.jp
yusuke@nii.ac.jp jtsujii@microsoft.com

Abstract

We address the problem of joint part-of-speech (POS) tagging and dependency parsing in Chinese. In Chinese, some POS tags are often hard to disambiguate without considering long-range syntactic information. Also, the traditional pipeline approach to POS tagging and dependency parsing may suffer from the problem of error propagation. In this paper, we propose the first incremental approach to the task of joint POS tagging and dependency parsing, which is built upon a shift-reduce parsing framework with dynamic programming. Although the incremental approach encounters difficulties with underspecified POS tags of look-ahead words, we overcome this issue by introducing so-called *delayed features*. Our joint approach achieved substantial improvements over the pipeline and baseline systems in both POS tagging and dependency parsing task, achieving the new state-of-the-art performance on this joint task.

1 Introduction

The tasks of part-of-speech (POS) tagging and dependency parsing have been widely investigated since the early stages of NLP research. Among mainstream approaches to dependency parsing, an incremental parsing framework is commonly used (e.g. Nivre (2008); Huang and Sagae (2010)), mainly because it achieves state-of-the-art accuracy while retaining linear-time computational complexity, and is also considered to reflect how humans process natural language sentences (Frazier and Rayner, 1982).

However, although some of the Chinese POS tags require long-range syntactic information in order to be disambiguated, to the extent of our knowledge, none of the previous approaches have addressed the joint modeling of these two tasks in an incremental framework. Also, since POS tagging is a preliminary step for dependency parsing, the traditional pipeline approach may suffer from the problem of error propagation.

In the example sentence in Figure 1, 的 has POS ambiguity between DEG (a genitive marker), which connect two noun phrases as "'s" in English, and DEC (a complementizer), which introduces a relative clause. Since both can take the form of NP-的-NP (NP: noun phrase), it is hard to distinguish these two tags only by considering local context. Based only on local context, a standard n-gram tagger is likely to assign the wrong tag DEG to 的, which inevitably makes the following parsing step fail to process the sentence correctly. However, knowing that the NP preceding 的 is the object of 沟通/VV (VV: verb), we can assume that 的 is a complementizer because 的/DEG is unlikely to follow a verb phrase.

In this paper, we propose the first incremental approach to the task of joint POS tagging and dependency parsing. Given a segmented sentence, our model simultaneously considers possible POS tags and dependency relations within the given beam, and outputs the best parse along with POS tags. However, the combined model raises two challenges: First, since the combined search space is huge, efficient decoding is difficult while the naïve use of beam is likely to degrade the search quality. Second, since the proposed model performs joint POS tagging and dependency parsing in a left-to-right manner, the model cannot exploit look-ahead POS tags to determine the next action.

To deal with the increased search space, we adopt a recently-proposed dynamic programming (DP) extension to shift-reduce parsing (Huang and Sagae, 2010), which enables the model to pack equivalent parser states, improving both speed and accuracy. Also, we overcome the lack of look-ahead POS information by introducing a concept of *delayed features*. The delayed features are those features that include underspecified POS tags, and shall be evaluated at the step when the look-ahead tags are determined. Based on experiments on the Chinese Penn Treebank (CTB) 5, we show that our joint models substantially improve over the

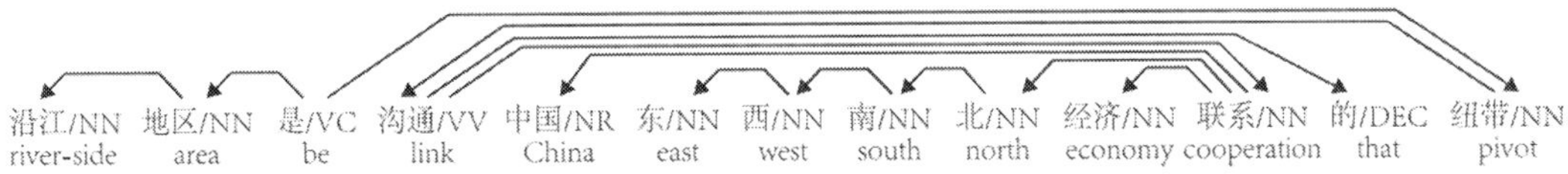

Figure 1: An example sentence from the Chinese Penn Treebank (CTB) 5.
(*"The river-side area is the pivot that links China's across-the-country economic cooperation."*)

w_j	t_{j-1}	$t_{j-1} \circ t_{j-2}$	w_{j+1} [1)]
$w_j \circ E(w_{j-1})$ [2)]	$w_j \circ B(w_{j+1})$ [2)]		
$E(w_{j-1}) \circ w_j \circ B(w_{j+1})$ [3)]			
$B(w_j)$	$E(w_j)$	$P(B(w_j))$	$P(E(w_j))$
$C_n(w_j)$	$(n \in \{2, \ldots, len(w_j) - 1\})$		
$B(w_j) \circ C_n(w_j)$	$(n \in \{2, \ldots, len(w_j)\})$		
$E(w_j) \circ C_n(w_j)$	$(n \in \{1, \ldots, len(w_j) - 1\})$		
$C_n(w_j)$	(*if* $C_n(w_j)$ *equals to* $C_{n+1}(w_j)$)		

1) if $len(w_{j+1}) < 3$; 2) if $len(w_j) < 3$; 3) if $len(w_j) = 1$.

Table 1: Feature templates for the baseline POS tagger, where t_i is the tag assigned to the i-th word w_i, $B(w)$ and $E(w)$ is the beginning and the ending character of word w, $C_n(w)$ is the n-th character of w, $P(c)$ is the set of tags associated with the single-character word c based on the dictionary.

pipeline and baseline systems in both POS tagging and dependency parsing accuracy. We also present some discussion on the results and error analysis. Although we specifically focus on Chinese in this work, our joint model is applicable to any languages for which a projective shift-reduce parser works well.

2 Baseline Models

First of all, we describe our baseline POS tagger and dependency parsers. These models will later be combined into pipelined models, which are then used as the baseline models in Section 4.

2.1 Baseline POS Tagger

We build a baseline POS tagger, which uses the same POS-tagging features as those used in the state-of-the-art joint word segmentation and POS tagging model for Chinese (Zhang and Clark, 2008a). The list of features are shown in Table 1. We train the model with the averaged perceptron (Collins, 2002), and the decoding is performed using the Viterbi algorithm with beam search.

Following Zhang and Clark (2008a), we use a tag dictionary and closed-set tags, which lead to improvement in both speed and accuracy. During training, the model stores all word–tag pairs into a tag dictionary, and for each word occurring more than N times in the training data, the decoder only assigns one of the tags that have been seen in the training data. For words that do not exist in the dictionary, the decoder still considers every possible tag. We also construct a dictionary for the closed-set tags (Xia, 2000), and allow the decoder to assign these tags only to the words listed in the dictionary.

2.2 Baseline Parsers

For the baseline parsers for experiments, we build two dependency parsers: a reimplementation of the parser by Huang and Sagae (2010) (hereinafter *Parser-HS*), which is a shift-reduce dependency parser enhanced with dynamic programming (DP) using graph-structured stack (GSS; Tomita (1991)), and our extension of Parser-HS by incorporating a richer set of features taken from Zhang and Nivre (2011) (hereinafter *Parser-ZN*), which is originally a non-DP arc-eager dependency parser and achieves the current state-of-the-art performance for Chinese dependency parsing. In this section, we briefly describe these models since the features and DP formalism serve as a basis for the joint models described in Section 3.

2.2.1 Shift-reduce parsing

Shift-reduce dependency parsing algorithms incrementally process an input sentence from left to right. In the framework known as "arc-standard" (Nivre, 2008), the parser performs one of the following three actions at each step:

- SHIFT (SH): move the first word in the input queue, q_0, onto the stack
- REDUCE-RIGHT (RR): combine the top two trees on the stack, (s_0, s_1), into a subtree $s_0^{\curvearrowright} s_1$
- REDUCE-LEFT (RL): combine the top two trees on the stack, (s_0, s_1), into a subtree $s_0^{\curvearrowleft} s_1$

where $S = (\ldots, s_1, s_0)$ is a stack of trees and $Q = (q_0, q_1, \ldots, q_{n-j-1}) = (w_j, w_{j+1}, \ldots, w_{n-1})$ is an input queue where j is the index of the first word in the queue Q and n is the number of words in the input sentence. Note that $s_0^{\curvearrowleft} s_1$ denotes a combined tree where s_1 is a child of s_0.

To deal with conflicts between more than one of these actions, each action is associated with a score, and the score of a parser state is the total score of the actions that have been applied. To train the model, we adopt the averaged perceptron algorithm (Collins, 2002) with early update (Collins and Roark, 2004), following Huang and Sagae (2010). With the early update, whenever the gold action sequence falls off from the beam, the parameters are immediately updated with the rest of the sentence neglected.

2.2.2 Merging equivalent states

Dynamic programming is enabled by merging *equivalent states*: if two states produce the same feature vector, they are merged into one state. Formally, a parser state (or configuration) ψ is described by $\langle \ell, i, j, S \rangle$, where ℓ is the current step, $[i \ldots j]$ is the span of the top tree s_0 in the stack $S = (s_{d-1}, \ldots, s_0)$, where d is the depth of the stack. The equivalence of two states $\psi : \langle \ell, i, j, S \rangle$ and $\psi' : \langle \ell', i', j', S' \rangle$ is then defined as

$$\psi \sim \psi' \text{ iff } j = j' \wedge \vec{f}(j, S) = \vec{f}(j', S'), \quad (1)$$

where $\vec{f}(j, S)$ is the feature vector of the state $\langle \ell, i, j, S \rangle$. In practice, just remembering a minimal set of features called *kernel features* $\tilde{\vec{f}}(j, S)$ suffices to evaluate the equivalence of states:

$$\tilde{\vec{f}}(j, S) = \tilde{\vec{f}}(j', S') \Rightarrow \langle \ell, i, j, S \rangle \sim \langle \ell', i', j', S' \rangle. \quad (2)$$

By merging equivalent states based on this condition, we only need to remember relevant information from the top d ($d = 3$ in our models) trees on the stack to evaluate the score of the next actions. However, since the stack shrinks when a REDUCE-LEFT/RIGHT action is applied, you often need to recover the last element of the stack from the history. Following Huang and Sagae (2010), we use a concept of *predictor states* $\Pi(\psi)$ to retain the links to multiple different histories.

(a)	$s_0.w$	$s_0.t$	$s_0.w \circ s_0.t$		
	$s_1.w$	$s_1.t$	$s_1.w \circ s_1.t$		
	$q_0.w$	$q_0.t$	$q_0.w \circ q_0.t$		
	$s_0.w \circ s_1.w$		$s_0.t \circ s_1.t$		
	$s_0.t \circ q_0.t$		$s_0.w \circ s_0.t \circ s_1.t$		
	$s_0.t \circ s_1.w \circ s_1.t$		$s_0.w \circ s_1.w \circ s_1.t$		
	$s_0.w \circ s_0.t \circ s_1.w$		$s_0.w \circ s_0.t \circ s_1.w \circ s_1.t$		
	$s_0.t \circ q_0.t \circ q_1.t$		$s_1.t \circ s_0.t \circ q_0.t$		
	$s_0.w \circ q_0.t \circ q_1.t$		$s_1.t \circ s_0.w \circ q_0.t$		
	$s_1.t \circ s_1.\text{rc}.t \circ s_0.t$		$s_1.t \circ s_1.\text{lc}.t \circ s_0.t$		
	$s_1.t \circ s_1.\text{rc}.t \circ s_0.w$		$s_1.t \circ s_1.\text{lc}.t \circ s_0.w$		
	$s_1.t \circ s_0.t \circ s_0.\text{rc}.t$		$s_1.t \circ s_0.w \circ s_0.\text{lc}.t$		
	$s_2.t \circ s_1.t \circ s_0.t$				
(b)	$s_0.w \circ d$	$s_0.t \circ d$	$s_1.w \circ d$	$s_1.w \circ d$	
	$s_0.w \circ s_0.v_l$		$s_0.t \circ s_0.v_l$		
	$s_1.w \circ s_1.v_r$		$s_1.t \circ s_1.v_r$		
	$s_1.w \circ s_1.v_l$		$s_1.t \circ s_1.v_l$		
	$s_0.\text{lc}.w$	$s_0.\text{lc}.t$	$s_1.\text{rc}.w$	$s_1.\text{rc}.t$	
	$s_1.\text{lc}.w$	$s_1.\text{lc}.t$	$s_0.\text{lc}_2.w$	$s_0.\text{lc}_2.t$	
	$s_1.\text{rc}_2.w$	$s_1.\text{rc}_2.t$	$s_1.\text{lc}_2.w$	$s_1.\text{lc}_2.t$	
	$s_0.t \circ s_0.\text{lc}.t \circ s_0.\text{lc}_2.t$		$s_1.t \circ s_1.\text{rc}.t \circ s_1.\text{rc}_2.t$		
	$s_1.t \circ s_1.\text{lc}.t \circ s_1.\text{lc}_2.t$				
(c)	j	$s_2.t$	$q_0.w$	$q_0.t$	$q_1.t$
	$s_1.w$	$s_1.t$	$s_1.\text{rc}.t$	$s_1.\text{lc}.t$	
	$s_0.w$	$s_0.t$	$s_0.\text{rc}.t$	$s_0.\text{lc}.t$	
(d)	d	$s_0.v_l$	$s_1.v_l$	$s_1.v_r$	
	$s_0.\text{lc}.w$	$s_1.\text{rc}.w$	$s_1.\text{lc}.w$		
	$s_0.\text{lc}_2.w$	$s_1.\text{rc}_2.w$	$s_1.\text{lc}_2.w$		
	$s_0.\text{lc}_2.t$	$s_1.\text{rc}_2.t$	$s_1.\text{lc}_2.t$		

Table 2: (a) Feature templates for Parser-HS; (b) Additional feature templates for Parser-ZN$^-$; (c) Kernel features for Parser-HS; (d) Additional kernel features for Parser-ZN$^-$.

2.2.3 Features

The feature templates used in the baseline parser Parser-HS are listed in Table 2 (a), where $s.w$ and $s.t$ are the form and tag of the root word of tree s, $s.\text{rc}$ and $s.\text{lc}$ are the right- and left-most children of s, and $\circ$ denotes conjunction of features. Note that these features can be constructed by only using 13 kernel features listed in Table 2 (c). The baseline parser Parser-ZN$^-$ additionally utilizes features in Table 2 (b), where d denotes the distance between the root nodes of s_0 and s_1, $s.v_r$ and $s.v_l$ are the numbers of the right and left modifiers of s, $s.\text{rc}_2$ and $s.\text{lc}_2$ are the second right- and left-most children of s. Note that some of the features described in Zhang and Nivre (2011), which are associated with dependency labels and head information of stack elements, are not included since our framework is based on unlabeled dependencies and the arc-standard strategy. The additional features for Parser-ZN$^-$ require the features in Table 2 (d) to be added into the set of kernel features.

2.2.4 Beam search with DP

In the shift-reduce parsing with dynamic programming, we cannot simply apply beam search as in a non-DP shift-reduce parsing, because each state does not have a unique score any more. To decide the ordering of states within the beam, the concept of *prefix score* and *inside score* (Stolcke, 1995) is adopted. The prefix score ξ is the total score of the best action sequence from the initial state to the current state, while the inside score η

is the score of the tree on the top of the stack. With these scores and a set of predictor states $\Pi(\psi)$ of state ψ, the full description of state ψ takes the form $\psi : \langle \ell, i, j, S; \xi, \eta, \Pi \rangle$. The calculation of the prefix and inside scores is described in Huang and Sagae (2010). By using these scores, the ordering of states is defined as

$$\langle \ell, \ldots; \xi, \eta, \_ \rangle \prec \langle \ell, \ldots; \xi', \eta', \_ \rangle$$
$$\textit{iff } \xi < \xi' \vee (\xi = \xi' \wedge \eta < \eta'),$$

where "_" denotes "match anything".

3 Joint POS Tagging and Parsing Model

In this section, we describe our models that jointly solve POS tagging and dependency parsing, which are based on the shift-reduce parsers described in Section 2.2. Corresponding to the two baseline parsers Parser-HS and Parser-ZN$^-$, we investigate two joint models: Joint-HS$^+$ and Joint-ZN$^-$. Although the latter uses a richer set of features, the formers can take more advantage of DP because a compact representation of features results in more frequent state packing.

3.1 POS Tagging with Modified Shift Action

Our joint parsers incorporate POS tagging during the course of shift-reduce parsing, by modifying the SHIFT action so that it assigns a tag to the word when it is shifted:

- SHIFT(t) (SH(t)): move the head of the queue, q_0, onto the stack, and assign tag t to it.

Along with REDUCE-LEFT/RIGHT actions, our joint model utilizes a total of $n+2$ actions, where n is the number of tags in the given dataset ($n = 33$ for the CTB-5 tag set (Xia, 2000)). A trace of an example joint parsing is illustrated in Figure 2.

3.2 Training and Decoding

We formulate the task of POS tagging and dependency parsing in a joint framework: given an input segmented sentence x, the model tries to find the best output y that satisfies:

$$\tilde{y} = \underset{y \in \mathcal{Y}(x)}{\operatorname{argmax}} \vec{w} \cdot \vec{\theta}(y),$$

where $\mathcal{Y}(x)$ is a set of possible outputs for x, $\vec{w}$ is the global feature vector, and $\vec{\theta}(y)$ is the feature vector of y. As in the baseline parsers, we train our models with the averaged perceptron; the beam search and early update strategy is almost the same except that the update is now caused by an error in POS tagging as well as by an error in dependency parsing. Similarly to the baseline tagger, we use the tag dictionary and closed-set tags to prune unlikely tags during decoding.

(a)	$q_0.t$ $q_0.w \circ q_0.t$		$s_0.t \circ q_0.t$	
	$s_0.t \circ q_0.t \circ q_1.t$		$s_1.t \circ s_0.t \circ q_0.t$	
	$s_0.w \circ q_0.t \circ q_1.t$		$s_1.t \circ s_0.w \circ q_0.t$	
(b)	$t \circ s_0.w$		$t \circ s_0.t$	
	$t \circ s_0.w \circ q_0.w$		$t \circ s_0.t \circ q_0.w$	
	$t \circ B(s_0.w) \circ q_0.w$		$t \circ E(s_0.w) \circ q_0.w$	
	$t \circ s_0.t \circ s_0.\mathrm{rc}.t$		$t \circ s_0.t \circ s_0.\mathrm{lc}.t$	
	$t \circ s_0.w \circ s_0.t \circ s_0.\mathrm{rc}.t$		$t \circ s_0.w \circ s_0.t \circ s_0.\mathrm{lc}.t$	
(c)	j	$s_2.t$ $q_0.w$	$q_{-1}.t$	$q_{-2}.t$
	$s_1.w$	$s_1.t$	$s_1.\mathrm{rc}.w$	$s_1.\mathrm{lc}.t$
	$s_0.w$	$s_0.t$	$s_0.\mathrm{rc}.w$	$s_0.\mathrm{lc}.t$

Table 3: (a) List of delayed features for the joint parsers. (b) Syntactic features for the joint parsers, where t is the POS tag to be assigned to q_0. (c) Kernel features for the joint parser Joint-HS$^+$.

3.3 Features

For the features of the models, we incorporate the union of the features in the baseline tagger and the baseline parsers; features from Parser-HS are used for Joint-HS, and features from Parser-ZN$^-$ for Joint-ZN$^-$. Furthermore, we additionally incorporate a set of *syntactic features* for POS tagging that capture dependencies between syntactic elements in the stack and the POS to be tagged (described in Section 3.3.1).

The features for the baseline tagger (shown in Table 1) and Parser-ZN$^-$ (shown in Table 2 (b)) can be used *in situ*, because they do not rely on look-ahead POS tags (i.e. POS tags of the words in the queue). However, it is not straightforward to incorporate the features for Parser-HS: in the joint framework, since the look-ahead POS tags are unavailable when the model tries to determine the next action, we cannot easily incorporate those features that include look-ahead POS (listed in Table 3 (a)). In order to deal with this issue, we introduce a concept of *delayed features*, which enables the model to incorporate the look-ahead information by delayed evaluation of feature scores (described in Section 3.3.2).

Note that the features from the baseline parsers are used for all actions (i.e. SHIFT(t) and REDUCE-LEFT/RIGHT) while the features from the tagger are only used for SHIFT(t) actions in the joint models. The addition of the tagging features requires a few new elements to be added into the set of kernel features; the new set of kernel features for Joint-HS$^+$ is shown in Table 3 (c).

step	action	stack S	queue Q	translation
0	-	ϕ	我/? 想/? 把/? ...	
1	SH(PN)	我/PN	想/? 把/? 这/? ...	我: "I"
2	SH(VV)	我/PN 想/VV	把/? 这/? 个/? ...	想: "want"
3	SH(BA)	我/PN 想/VV 把/BA	这/? 个/? 句子/? ...	把: *object marker*
4	SH(DT)	我/PN 想/VV 把/BA 这/DT	个/? 句子/? 翻译/? ...	这: "this"
5	SH(M)	我/PN 想/VV 把/BA 这/DT 个/M	句子/? 翻译/? 成/? ...	个: *quantifier*
6	RL	我/PN 想/VV 把/BA 这/DT⌒[个/M]	句子/? 翻译/? 成/? ...	
7	SH(NN)	我/PN 想/VV 把/BA 这/DT⌒[个/M] 句子/NN	翻译/? 成/? 英语/?	句子: "sentence"
8	RR	我/PN 想/VV 把/BA [这/DT⌒[...]]⌒句子/NN	翻译/? 成/? 英语/?	
9	RL	我/PN 想/VV 把/BA⌒[[...]⌒句子/NN]	翻译/? 成/? 英语/?	
10	SH(VV)	我/PN 想/VV 把/BA⌒[[...]⌒句子/NN] 翻译/VV	成/? 英语/?	翻译: "translate"

Figure 2: A trace of joint shift-reduce parsing for "我想把这个句子翻译成英语" ("*I want to translate this sentence into English.*"), where grandchildren of stack elements are omitted.

Specifically, $q_{-1}.t$ and $q_{-2}.t$ are added in order to accommodate some of the tagging features, while $q_0.t$ and $q_1.t$ are removed because the look-ahead POS tags are not available when the equivalence of the states are evaluated. Joint-ZN$^-$ additionally requires kernel features in Table 2 (d).

3.3.1 Syntactic Features

Since our joint framework performs tagging and parsing simultaneously, we can think of incorporating a combined feature of the next tag (to be assigned to q_0) with syntactic information from stack elements, which cannot be used in an n-gram POS tagger. Specifically, we propose to use the features shown in Table 3 (b). Intuitively, these features try to capture dependencies between the POS to be assigned and syntactic structure encoded in the trees being built in the stack. For example, at step 9 in Figure 2, the next word 翻译 can be either a noun or a verb. In determining the tag of this word to be VV, the existence of the preceding phrase "把/BA [...]" on the top of the stack plays an important role, because the phrase headed by 把 represents an object for the following verb; in contrast, in an n-gram POS tagger, capturing this information is not easy because 把/BA is located at a distance of four words. Note that the addition of those syntactic features does not require the addition of any elements to the set of kernel features.

3.3.2 Delayed Features

A challenge in the incremental joint approach is that since the shift-reduce model processes an input sentence in a left-to-right manner, it cannot exploit look-ahead POS tags, which a pipeline shift-reduce parser can consider, to determine the next action. In our experiment with Parser-HS, the ablation of the features including look-ahead POS results in 0.67% decrease in parsing performance on the development set, suggesting that the look-ahead POS information is indispensable to achieve the state-of-the-art performance. In order to relieve this problem, we introduce a concept of *delayed features*, which are a set of features that are evaluated later when certain information becomes available. In our model, the parser features that require look-ahead POS information are defined as the delayed features, and shall later be evaluated at the step when the look-ahead POS are determined.

Let us see an example in Figure 2. At step 2, a parser encounters a shift-reduce conflict: the next action can be any of REDUCE-LEFT/RIGHT and SHIFT(t). If this were a (non-joint) shift-reduce parser, the model can utilize the look-ahead POS information by features such as

$$(s_0.t = \text{VV}) \circ (s_1.t = \text{PN}) \circ (q_0.t = \text{BA}),$$

to determine the next action, because the POS of all words in the sentence are already given. However, in the joint parser, the POS of the first word in the queue, 把, remains undetermined until the word is shifted. To deal with this, we define a *delayed feature* that takes look-ahead POS tag(s) as argument(s), as in

$$(s_0.t = \text{VV}) \circ (s_1.t = \text{PN}) \circ (q_0.t = \lambda_1), \lambda_1 = w_2.t.$$

At step 3, after SHIFT(BA) is performed, the delayed features from the previous step becomes a non-delayed feature

$$(s_0.t = \text{VV}) \circ (s_1.t = \text{PN}) \circ (q_0.t = \text{BA}),$$

which can be evaluated in the same way as normal (non-delayed) features.

More formally, each state carries with it a set of delayed feature vectors $\langle \vec{d_1}, \vec{d_2} \rangle$, where $\vec{d_n}$ is the n-th order delayed feature vector, which has n arguments to be filled in[1]. At each step, a REDUCE-LEFT/RIGHT action a adds a set of delayed features to the delayed feature vectors of state ψ:

$$\langle \vec{d_1}, \vec{d_2} \rangle \leftarrow \langle \vec{d_1} + \vec{\Phi}_1(\psi, a), \vec{d_2} + \vec{\Phi}_2(\psi, a) \rangle,$$

where $\vec{\Phi}_1(\psi, a)$ and $\vec{\Phi}_2(\psi, a)$ are the first-/second-order delayed features generated by action a being applied to ψ. When a SHIFT(t) action is performed, the model fills in the argument in the delayed features with the newly-assigned tag t, as well as adding new delayed features it generates:

$$\langle \vec{d_1}, \vec{d_2} \rangle \leftarrow \langle \vec{\Phi}_1(\psi, \text{SH}(t)) + \mathcal{T}(t, \vec{d_2}), \vec{\Phi}_2(\psi, \text{SH}(t)) \rangle,$$

where $\mathcal{T}(t, \vec{d_2})$ is the resulting feature vector after tag t is filled in to the first argument of the features in $\vec{d_2}$. Note that action SH(t) also adds $\vec{d_0} = \mathcal{T}(t, \vec{d_1})$ to its (non-delayed) feature vector.

Note that the above formulation with the delayed features is equivalent to the model with full look-ahead features if the exact decoding is performed. Although the approximate search with beam takes the risk of the gold derivation falling off the beam before delayed features are evaluated, we show in Section 4 that the current solution works well in practice.

3.4 Deduction System with DP

With the delayed features, a parser state ψ takes the form of $\langle \ell, i, j, S, \vec{d_1}, \vec{d_2}; \xi, \eta, \Pi \rangle$. Now, if two equivalent states are still merged according to Eq. (1), one state might have multiple sets of delayed feature vectors depending on the previous action sequences. In order to make the joint model still tractable with the DP formalism, we modify the equivalence condition in Eq. (1): in addition to the condition in Eq. (1), two states now need to share the same delayed feature vectors in order for them to be merged:

$$j = j' \wedge \vec{f}(j, S) = \vec{f}(j', S') \wedge \vec{d_1} = \vec{d_1'} \wedge \vec{d_2} = \vec{d_2'}.$$

This guarantees that a parser state has only one unique set of delayed feature vectors.

We can prove by induction that the *correctness* (i.e. the optimality of the deductive system) is still assured (proof omitted due to limited space) even with the delayed features incorporated. However, because any number of REDUCE-LEFT/RIGHT actions can occur between two SHIFT actions, the delayed features might need to refer to unboundedly deep elements from stack trees; therefore, the *boundedness* (see Huang and Sagae (2010)) of the kernel features no longer holds and the worst-case polynomial complexity is not assured. Nonetheless, we show that our models work sufficiently well in practice, with the aid of beam search.

[1] In our joint models, the use of only the first- and second-order delayed vectors suffices, because the feature templates refer to the tags of the first two words in the queue at most.

4 Experiment

4.1 Experimental Settings

We evaluate the performance of our joint parsers and baseline models on the Chinese Penn Treebank (CTB) 5 dataset. We use the standard split of CTB-5 described in Duan et al. (2007) and the head-finding rules in Zhang and Clark (2008b).

We iteratively train each of the models and choose the best model, in terms of the tagging accuracy (for tagger) or word-level dependency accuracy (for parsers and joint parsers) on the development set, to use in the final evaluation. When building a tag dictionary, we discarded instances that appear less than three times (tuned on the development set) in the training data. An Intel Core-i7 950 3.2GHz machine is used for evaluation.

4.2 Baseline Performance

First of all, we evaluate the performance of our baseline tagger and parsers described in Section 2. Based on our preliminary experiments, we set the beam size to 16 for the baseline tagger and Parser-HS, and to 32 for Parser-ZN$^-$. Our baseline tagger achieved a tagging accuracy of 94.15% on the development set, and 93.82% on the test set. Since most recent works on Chinese POS tagging (e.g. Kruengkrai et al. (2009); Sun (2011)) are joint approaches integrating word segmentation, the only directly-comparable work we could find is Li et al. (2011), where they built a perceptron-based POS tagger with the same feature set as we used (Zhang and Clark, 2008a). They reported 93.51% accuracy on test set, which is slightly lower than ours.

The upper part of Table 7 shows the performance of our baseline parsers with a comparison to other state-of-the-art parsers, where (unlabeled) attachment accuracies of word, root, and complete match are shown (with punctuations excluded). Our reimplementation of Huang and Sagae (2010) has reproduced almost the same accuracy. Interestingly, Parser-ZN$^-$ also has comparable performance to that of Zhang and Nivre (2011) even though we could not use some of their features (as described in Section 3.3).

beam	Joint-HS$^+$			Joint-ZN$^-$		
	tag	dep	speed	tag	dep	speed
4	94.37	79.98	37.5	94.26	80.55	25.4
8	94.57	80.56	19.3	94.64	81.47	13.5
16	94.56	80.97	10.1	94.48	81.50	7.0
32	94.66	80.72	4.7	94.40	81.68	3.3
64	94.50	81.09	2.0	94.50	81.88	1.5
128	-	-	-	94.43	81.89	0.69

Table 4: Tagging and word-level dependency accuracies and parsing speed (in sentence/second) on the development set with respect to beam size.

Model	tag	word	non-root	root	compl.
Parser-HS	(100)	85.15	85.61	75.76	34.50
Parser-ZN$^-$		85.77	86.18	77.46	34.99
Pipeline-HS	94.15	78.10	78.49	70.03	26.77
Pipeline-ZN$^-$		78.67	78.92	73.32	27.90
Joint-HS$^+$	94.56*	80.97*	81.32	73.64	29.51
Joint-ZN$^-$	94.50*	81.88*	82.21	74.94	30.26

Table 5: Development result of the proposed models. Joint-HS$^+$/ZN$^-$ perform better than Pipeline-HS/ZN$^-$ in terms of both tagging and word-level dependency accuracies, with statistical significance of $p < 0.05$ (denoted by *) by MeNemar's test.

Model		default	wo/delay	wo/dp	wo/syn
Joint-HS$^+$	tag	94.56	±0.00	−0.06	+0.04
	dep	80.97	−0.26	−0.22	−0.60
Joint-ZN$^-$	tag	94.40	+0.10	+0.05	−0.07
	dep	81.68	−0.16	−0.01	−0.23

Table 6: Feature ablation results for the joint models on the development set.

Model	tag	word	root	compl.	speed
Huang+ '10		85.20	78.32	33.72	-
Zhang+ '11		86.0	-	36.9	-
Li-11-2nd	(100)	86.18	78.58	34.02	5.8
Parser-HS		85.12	78.30	32.77	32.7
Parser-ZN$^-$		85.96	80.87	35.03	9.0
Li-11(v2,3rd)	92.80	80.79	75.84	29.11	0.3
Li-11(v1,3rd)	92.89	80.69	75.90	29.06	0.5
Li-11(v1,2nd)	93.08	80.74	75.80	28.24	1.7
Pipeline-HS	93.82	77.13	72.59	25.13	32.7†
Pipeline-ZN$^-$		78.04	75.55	26.07	9.0†
Joint-HS$^+$	**94.01***	79.83*	73.86	27.85	9.5
Joint-ZN$^-$	93.94	**81.33***	**77.93**	**29.90**	1.5

Table 7: Final result of the proposed model and the baseline. * denotes the statistical significance over the corresponding pipeline model ($p < 0.05$). †Only the parsing speed is shown; the tagging speed was 210.6 sentence/sec.

4.3 Development Results

Table 4 shows the tagging and word-level dependency accuracies of the joint models with respect to the beam size, where "tag" and "dep" show the tagging and word-level dependency accuracies, and "speed" is the joint parsing speed (in sentence per second). Based on this experiment, we use the beam size of 16 for Joint-HS$^+$ and 64 for Joint-ZN$^-$ in the following experiments.[2] The best dependency accuracies are achieved after 36-th and 31-st iterations, respectively.

Table 5 shows the performance of the baseline and joint models on the development set, where "Pipeline-HS" and "Pipeline-ZN$^+$" are the pipeline combinations of the baseline tagger with Parser-HS and Parser-ZN$^+$, respectively. Joint-HS$^+$ and JointZN$^-$ have 0.35–0.41% (tagging) and 2.87–3.21% (word-level dependency) higher accuracies than the pipeline models.

Table 6 shows feature ablation results on the development set, where "wo/delay", "wo/dp", and "wo/syn" correspond to the models that do not use the delayed features, dynamic programming, and syntactic features, respectively. Overall, the tagging accuracies are only slightly affected by the ablation of these features (with differences no larger than 0.10%), while the parsing accuracies decreased in most settings. The ablation of the delayed features resulted in 0.26% and 0.16% decreases of word-level dependency accuracies for Joint-HS$^+$ and Joint-ZN$^-$, showing the effectiveness of these features. The contribution of the dynamic programming is clearly shown for Joint-HS$^+$ with 0.22% improvement in dependency accuracy, although no meaningful effect for Joint-ZN$^-$ is confirmed; this is probably because the use of richer features results in less frequent packing of states. Lastly, the ablation of the syntactic features results in as much as 0.60% and 0.23% decreases of dependency accuracies for Joint-HS$^+$ and Joint-ZN$^-$. As opposed to our first expectation, the syntactic features made little effect on the tagging accuracies; on the contrary, the result suggests that capturing the dependencies between the stack elements and the next word's tag is quite effective to improve parsing accuracy.

4.4 Final Results

Table 7 shows the final result of the proposed models compared to the baseline models. "Li-

[2]Due to limited time, the beam size of 32 is used for Joint-ZN$^-$ for the feature ablation experiment shown in Table 6.

error pattern	#↓	total	error pattern	#↑	total
NN → VV	61	169	VV → NN	29	128
DEC → DEG	35	65	NN → NR	16	64
DEG → DEC	19	72	JJ → NN	14	62
NN → JJ	11	59	VA → VV	8	12
P → CC	8	13	JJ → NR	6	2
P → VV	8	18	NR → JJ	6	4

Table 8: POS tagging error patterns that decrease (left side) and increase (right side) by joint decoding (on dev. set). The numbers of errors made by the baseline tagger ("total") and the increases and decreases by Joint-ZN$^+$ (#↓ and #↑) are shown.

11(...)" shows the graph-based models by Li et al. (2011), where v1/2 and 2nd/3rdcorrespond to their version 1/2 and second-/third-order models. The joint models Joint-HS$^+$ and Joint-ZN$^-$ achieve improvements of 0.19% and 0.12% in tagging accuracy over the baseline tagger, and 2.70% and 3.29% improvements in word-level dependency accuracy over the pipeline models, showing the effectiveness of the joint approach. Furthermore, the tagging and parsing accuracies of Joint-ZN$^-$ surpass the graph-based models by Li et al. (2011), achieving the new state-of-the-art performance on this joint task. Since our framework is at least comparable in speed to their models, these results suggest that our incremental framework is suitable to this joint task.

4.5 Discussion and Analysis

Table 8 shows the increase and decrease of error patterns of Joint-ZN$^-$ over the baseline tagger. Notably, the joint model has a clear advantage in the disambiguation of DEC and DEG and the discrimination of NN from VV. While these tags are those that critically influence the overall syntactic structure, the increased error patterns include those tags that are considered less important[3] in deciding the syntactic structure (e.g. NN/NR: general/proper nouns); this observation is largely similar to those reported by Li et al. (2011).

It is noteworthy that we obtained the first positive result that the joint decoding does improve POS tagging, while, in contrast, Li et al. (2011) have reported that the joint decoding has negative effect on the tagging accuracy: their third-order models have 0.6–0.7% lower tagging accuracies than their baseline tagger. When comparing our error patterns with those of their model, although the overall increase and decrease of the error patterns look largely similar, our model has a relatively smaller number of increased error patterns than the decreased ones. Therefore, by selectively improving syntactically-important tags, our joint model is considered to have improved the POS tagging accuracy over the baseline tagger.

[3]although VV → NN errors look like an exceptional case

5 Related Works

In recent years, joint segmentation and tagging have been widely investigated (e.g. Zhang and Clark (2010); Kruengkrai et al. (2009); Zhang and Clark (2008a); Jiang et al. (2008a); Jiang et al. (2008b)). Particularly, our framework of using a single perceptron to solve the joint problem is motivated by Zhang and Clark (2008a). Also, our joint parsing framework is an extension of Huang and Sagae (2010)'s framework, which is described in detail in Section 2.2. In constituency parsing, the parsing naturally involves the POS tagging since the non-terminal symbols are commonly associated with POS tags (e.g. Klein and Manning (2003)). Rush et al. (2010) proposed to use dual composition to combine a constituency parser and a trigram POS tagger, showing the effectiveness of taking advantage of these two systems.

In dependency parsing, Lee et al. (2011) recently proposed a discriminative graphical model that solves morphological disambiguation and dependency parsing jointly. However, their main focus was to capture interaction between morphology and syntax in morphologically-rich, highly-inflected languages (such as Latin and Ancient Greek), which are unlike Chinese. More recently, Li et al. (2011) proposed the first joint model for Chinese POS tagging and dependency parsing in a graph-based parsing framework, which is one of our baseline systems. On the other hand, our work is the first incremental approach to this joint task.

6 Conclusion

In this paper, we have presented the first joint approach that successfully solves POS tagging and dependency parsing on an incremental framework. The proposed joint models outperform the pipeline models in terms of both tagging and dependency parsing accuracies, and our best model achieved the new state-of-the-art performance on this joint task, while retaining competitive parsing speed. Although we mainly focused on Chinese in this work, our framework is generally applicable to other languages including English; for future work, we hope to further investigate the effectiveness of our joint approach in those languages.

References

Michael Collins and Brian Roark. 2004. Incremental parsing with the perceptron algorithm. In *Proceedings of ACL*.

Michael Collins. 2002. Discriminative training methods for hidden markov models: Theory and experiments with perceptron algorithms. In *Proceedings of EMNLP*.

Xiangyu Duan, Jun Zhao, and Bo Xu. 2007. Probabilistic parsing action models for multilingual dependency parsing. In *Proceedings of the CoNLL Shared Task Session of EMNLP-CoNLL 2007*.

Lyn Frazier and Keith Rayner. 1982. Making and correcting errors during sentence comprehension: Eye movements in the analysis of structurally ambiguous sentences. *Cognitive Psychology*, 14:178–210.

Liang Huang and Kenji Sagae. 2010. Dynamic programming for linear-time incremental parsing. In *Proceedings of ACL*.

Wenbin Jiang, Liang Huang, Qun Liu, and Yajuan Lu. 2008a. A cascaded linear model for joint Chinese word segmentation and part-of-speech tagging. In *Proceedings of ACL/HLT*.

Wenbin Jiang, Haitao Mi, and Qun Liu. 2008b. Word lattice reranking for Chinese word segmentation and part-of-speech tagging. In *Proceedings of COLING*.

Dan Klein and Christopher D. Manning. 2003. Accurate unlexicalized parsing. In *Proceedings of ACL*.

Canasai Kruengkrai, Kiyotaka Uchimoto, Jun'ichi Kazama, Yiou Wang, Kentaro Torisawa, and Hitoshi Isahara. 2009. An error-driven word-character hybrid model for joint Chinese word segmentation and POS tagging. In *ACL*, Proceedings of ACL.

John Lee, Jason Naradowsky, and David A. Smith. 2011. A discriminative model for joint morphological disambiguation and dependency parsing. In *Proceedings of ACL*.

Zhenghua Li, Min Zhang, Wanxiang Che, Ting Liu, Wenliang Chen, and Haizhou Haizhou. 2011. Joint models for Chinese POS tagging and dependency parsing. In *Proceedings of EMNLP*.

Joakim Nivre. 2008. Algorithms for deterministic incremental dependency parsing. *Comput. Linguist.*, 34:513–553.

Alexander M. Rush, David Sontag, Michael Collins, and Tommi Jaakkola. 2010. On dual decomposition and linear programming relaxations for natural language processing. In *Proceedings of EMNLP*.

Andreas Stolcke. 1995. An efficient probabilistic context-free parsing algorithm that computes prefix probabilities. *Computational Linguistics*, 21:165–201.

Weiwei Sun. 2011. A stacked sub-word model for joint chineseword segmentation and part-of-speech tagging. In *Proceedings of ACL*.

Masaru Tomita. 1991. *Generalized LR Parsing*. Kluwer Academic Publishers.

Fei Xia. 2000. The part-of-speech tagging guidelines for the penn chinese treebank (3.0). Technical Report IRCS-00-07, University of Pennsylvania Institute for Research in Cognitive Science Technical Report, October.

Yue Zhang and Stephen Clark. 2008a. Joint word segmentation and POS tagging using a single perceptron. In *Proceedings of ACL-08: HLT*.

Yue Zhang and Stephen Clark. 2008b. A tale of two parsers: investigating and combining graph-based and transition-based dependency parsing using beam-search. In *Proceedings of EMNLP*.

Yue Zhang and Stephen Clark. 2010. A fast decoder for joint word segmentation and POS-tagging using a single discriminative model. In *Proceedings of EMNLP*.

Yue Zhang and Joakim Nivre. 2011. Transition-based dependency parsing with rich non-local features. In *Proceedings of ACL-2011 (short papers)*.

Extending the adverbial coverage of a NLP oriented resource for French

Elsa Tolone
LIGM, Université Paris-Est, France
FaMAF, Universidad Nacional de Córdoba, Argentina
tolone@univ-paris-est.fr

Stavroula Voyatzi
LIGM, Université Paris-Est, France
voyatzi@univ-mlv.fr

Abstract

This paper presents work on extending the adverbial entries of *LGLex*, a NLP oriented syntactic resource for French. Adverbs were extracted from the Lexicon-Grammar tables of both simple adverbs ending in *–ment* '–ly' (Molinier and Levrier, 2000) and compound adverbs (Gross, 1986; 1990). This work relies on the exploitation of fine-grained linguistic information provided in existing resources. Various features are encoded in both LG tables and they haven't been exploited yet. They describe the relations of deleting, permuting, intensifying and paraphrasing that associate, on the one hand, the simple and compound adverbs and, on the other hand, different types of compound adverbs. The resulting syntactic resource is manually evaluated and freely available under the LGPL-LR license.

1 Introduction

Recognising adverbs such as *extrêmement* 'extremely' and *à long terme* 'in the long run' in texts is likely to be useful for information retrieval and extraction because of the information that some of these adverbials convey.

Adverbs, or more generally circumstantial complements, have often been overlooked in the compilation of lexical resources (Nølke, 1990: 3). Several reasons explain this lack of interest. Firstly, adverbials are usually felt as less useful than nouns for information retrieval and extraction. Secondly, compound adverbs in particular are difficult to distinguish from prepositional phrases assuming other syntactic functions, such as arguments or noun modifiers: the distinction is hardly correlated to any material markers in texts and lies in complex linguistic notions (Villavicencio, 2002; Merlo, 2003).

The availability of large-coverage lexicons providing lexical, syntactic and semantic information is essential in order to gain insight on the recognition of adverbs, including the dual problems of variability and ambiguity. In addition, it is likely to help solving prepositional phrase attachment during shallow or deep parsing (Agirre *et al.*, 2008).

In this paper, we present work on extending the adverbial entries of *LGLex*, a NLP oriented syntactic resource for French. These adverbs were extracted from the Lexicon-Grammar tables (hereafter LG tables) of both simple adverbs ending in *–ment* '–ly' (Molinier and Levrier, 2000) and compound adverbs (Gross, 1986; 1990).

The paper is organized as follows. In section 2, we provide an overview of the three resources used in our work. In section 3, we describe how we enhanced *LGLex* thanks to various features that are encoded in LG tables. In section 4, we present results and discuss the manual evaluation process. Finally, we conclude in section 5 by pointing out several possible extensions and issues for future research.

2 Resources

Lexicon-Grammar tables (hereafter LG tables) are currently one of the major sources of lexical syntactic information for the French language; several LG tables exist for other languages (see section 2.1). Their development was initiated as early as the 1970s by Maurice Gross, at the LADL (Gross, 1975; 1994), and then at the LIGM, University Paris-Est (Boons *et al.*, 1976; Guillet and Leclère, 1992).

Lexical information is represented in the form of tables. Each table puts together elements of a given lexical-grammatical category (for a given language) that share a certain number of defining features, which usually concern subcategorization information. These elements form a class. These tables are represented as matrices (see section 2.1.2): each row corresponds to a lexical item of the corresponding class; each column lists all features that may be valid or not for the different members of the class; at the intersection of a row and a column, the symbol + (resp. –) indicates that the feature corresponding to the column is valid (resp. not valid) for the lexical entry corresponding to the row.

The resources described in this paper correspond to the LG tables of both simple and compound adverbs, in which previously implicit features have been made explicit[1] for more convenient use in NLP. All tables are fully available[2] under a free license (LGPL-LR).

2.1 The LG tables of adverbs

LG tables of adverbs are available in several languages, notably in English (Gross, 1986), German (Seelbach, 1990), Spanish (Blanco and Català, 1998/1999), Italian (De Gioia, 2001), Portuguese (Baptista, 2003), Korean (Jung, 2005) and Modern Greek (Voyatzi, 2006).

In French, there are two resources of adverbs that follow different principles both in classification and in representation within the Lexicon-Grammar framework. That is, firstly, tables of simple adverbs ending in *–ment* '–ly' (Moliner, 1984; Molinier and Lévrier, 2000), which are mainly derived from adjectives and, secondly, tables of compound adverbs (Gross, 1986; 1990). In this section, we describe briefly the different classes, morphosyntactic structures and features provided in the tables of both types of adverbs.

2.1.1 The LG tables of simple adverbs

According to Molinier and Levrier (2000), adverbs ending in *–ment* '–ly' form a large class of French adverbs. Moreover, as opposed to other types of adverbs, they form a quite open class.

These adverbs constitute a morphologically homogeneous class, since most of them are created according to the pattern `adjective + -ment '-ly'`. In total, there are 3,203 simple adverbial entries which are represented in sixteen LG tables.

The first partition has been established between sentential adverbs and adverbs integrated into the sentence; that means attached to the predicate or any other component of the sentence.

Three major classes of sentential adverbs are worth mentioning: conjuncts, style disjuncts (or utterance-level adverbs) and attitude disjuncts (or statement adverbs). The latter are divided into four classes: evaluative adverbs, e.g. *curieusement* 'curiously', adverbs of habit, e.g. *habituellement* 'usually', modal adverbs, e.g. *certainement* 'certainly', and subject oriented attitude adverbs, e.g. *bêtement* 'foolishly'.

On the other hand, there are six major classes of adverbs integrated into the sentence:

(i) adverbs of subject oriented manner, e.g. *gentiment* 'kindly', *Max traite les gens gentiment = Max est gentil dans la (façon + manière) dont il traite les gens* 'Max treats people kindly = Max is kind in the way he treats people';

(ii) adverbs of verbal manner, e.g. *démocratiquement* 'democratically', *Ce parti est arrivé au pouvoir démocratiquement = C'est démocratiquement que ce parti est arrivé au pouvoir* 'This party came to power democratically = It is democratically that this party came to power';

(iii) adverbs of quantity (including intensifiers), e.g. *excessivement* 'excessively';

(iv) adverbs of time expressing time, e.g. *actuellement* 'actually', duration, e.g. *temporairement* 'temporarily' or frequency, e.g. *régulièrement* 'regularly';

(v) viewpoint adverbs, e.g. *linguistiquement = d'un point de vue linguistique* 'linguistically = from a linguistic point of view';

(vi) focus adverbs, e.g. *essentiellement* 'essentially'.

Features included in the LG tables can be organized into four main groups: distributional features (e.g. the possibility for an adverb to occur at the beginning of a negative clause), local syntactic features (e.g. the possibility for an adverb to have a function as an indefinite determiner), semantic features (e.g. knowing what type of interrogative adverb corresponds to an adverb allows it to be categorized semantically), and paraphrasing features (e.g. *Adv, Pindicatif = C'est Adj que Psubjonctif =: Bizarrement, Marie n'est pas venue à la soirée = C'est bizarre que Marie ne soit pas venue à la soirée* ' Oddly, Mary did not come to the party = It is odd that Mary did not come to the party').

2.1.2 The LG tables of compound adverbs

The scope of the LG tables of compound adverbs is delimited by the intersection of two criteria: (i) multiword expressions and (ii) adverbial func-

[1] In order to make previous implicit features explicit, a table of classes has been created (Tolone, 2009; 2011). Its role is to assign features when their value is constant over a class, e.g. class definition features. Each row stands for a class and each column stands for a feature. Each cell corresponds to the validity of a feature in a class. In particular, the table of French adverb classes is composed of 32 different classes and 163 features.

[2] http://infolingu.univ-mlv.fr/english > Language Resources > Lexicon-Grammar > Download.

tion. As Laporte and Voyatzi (2008) state "a phrase composed of several words is considered to be a multiword expression if some or all of its components are tied together, that is, if their combination does not obey productive rules of syntactic and semantic compositionality". This criterion ensures a complementarity between lexicon and grammar. In other words, it tends to ensure that any combination of linguistic elements which is correct in the language, but is not represented in common syntactic-semantic grammars, should be stored in lexicons.

In terms of the adverbial function, LG tables of compound adverbs deal only with circumstantial complements, namely, complements that modify the predicate or any other element of the sentence in which they occur. Sentential adverbs modify or enhance the entire sentence. They are identified through criteria (Gross, 1986; 1990) involving the fact that they are optional, they combine freely with a wide range of predicates and some of them typically answer questions such as *comment?* 'how?', *où?* 'where?', *quand?* 'when?', etc. The compound adverbs described in LG tables (Gross, 1986; 1990) take several morphosyntactic forms: unsuffixed adverbs, e.g. *demain*[3] 'tomorrow', suffixed adverbs, e.g. *nuitamment*[4] 'by night', prepositional phrases, e.g. *à la dernière minute* 'at the last minute', noun phrases, e.g. *le cas échéant* 'if necessary' or adverbial clauses, e.g. *jusqu'à ce que mort s'ensuive* 'until death comes'.

These compound adverbs are classified according to their internal morphosyntactic structure which is described at the elementary level of sequences of parts of speech. The classification is based mainly on the number, type and position of the fixed and variable lexical components of adverbs. These classificatory morphosyntactic structures have a three-fold aim: first, they are intended as an aid to organize the heterogeneous compound adverbs in an electronic lexicon; second, they are intended as an aid to identify the compound adverbs in a parser; finally, they have impact on the syntactic-semantic subcategorization of compound adverbs. For instance, most of the adverbial clauses represented in table PF are interpolated clauses, e.g. *si ma mémoire est bonne* 'if my memory serves me well".

Table 1 illustrates the sixteen formal classes, together with their defining internal morphosyntactic structure, an illustrative example[5] and the number of entries listed:

Identifier	Morphosyntactic structure	Example	Size
PADV	C	enfin	520
PC	Prép C	par exemple	664
PDETC	Prép Det C	de nos jours	848
PAC	Prép Det Adj C	à la dernière minute	776
PCA	Prép Det C Modif pré-adj Adj	à la nuit tombante	840
PCDC	Prép Det1 C1 de Det2 C2	dans la limite du possible	750
PCPC	Prép Det1 C1 Prép2 Det2 C2	à cent pour cent	287
PCONJ	Prép Det1 C1 Conj Prép2 Det2 C2	tôt ou tard	333
PCDN	Prép Det1 C1 de N2	à l'insu de N	555
PCPN	Prép Det1 C1 Prép2 N2	en comparaison avec N	151
PV	Prép V Prépv Detv Cv	à dire vrai	285
PF	ConjS (Det0 C0 + N0) V Prép1 (Det1 C1 + N1)	jusqu'à ce que mort s'ensuive	396
PECO	(Adj) comme Det C	(fidèle) comme un chien	305
PVCO	(V) comme Det C	(travailler) comme un chien	338
PPCO	comme Prép Det C	(disparaître) comme par enchantement	50
PJC	Conjc Det C1 Prép C2	mais aussi et surtout	185
		Total	7,283

Table 1. Morphosyntactic structures of French compound adverbs

Compound adverbs are represented in sixteen LG tables[6], one for each of the defining morphosyntactic structures[7]. Unlike simple adverbs, compound adverbs are represented in the tables within a structure of elementary sentence which is composed of a verbal predicate (intransitive in most cases) and its arguments. This representation takes into account the combination of the

[3] According to Gross (1990: 153), *demain* 'tomorrow' is a compound form from an etymological point of view: from the Latin expression *de mane* which means literally "in the morning". But, it is now regarded as a simple form since it is represented by a single word. These forms are derived from noun or prepositional noun phrases previously analyzed that were tied at various times.

[4] According to Gross (1986: 2), *nuitamment* 'by night' can also be considered as an idiomatic compound, though not constituted of words but of a word and a suffix. Lack of compositionality stems from the observation that *quotidiennement* 'daily', *mensuellement* 'monthly', etc. which are derived adverbs of the same formal type have a regular formation, in the sense that their interpretation is homogeneous. Thus, *nuitamment* 'by night' is an isolated case, as opposed to an open series of identical forms with a different interpretation.

[5] It is possible that one or more of the components defined in a morphosyntactic structure are absent. For instance, in the adverb *à cent pour cent* 'one hundred percent', which is assigned the structure PCPC, `Dét1` and `Dét2` are empty.

[6] The LG tables of adverbs described in this paper have been updated by the members of LIGM, so that previously implicit linguistic information becomes explicit and convenient for NLP applications. Tolone (2009; 2011) and Tolone *et al.* (2010) give a thorough account of this work.

[7] Symbols with obvious interpretation are used such as: `Prép` (preposition), `Det` (determiner), `Adj` (adjective), `Modif pré-adj` (pre-adjectival modifier), `N` (noun), `V` (verb), `Conj` (conjunction), and `C` (noun tied with the rest of the adverbial).

adverb with a structure of elementary sentence, and, thus provides precise information about various types of constraints occurring between compound adverbs and the predicate they modify. An example of time constraint is given below:

*Les tablettes (remplaceront + *ont remplacé + *remplacent) les PC dans un avenir proche*

'Ipads (will replace + *replaced + *replace) desktop PC in a near future'

The LG tables of French compound adverbs contain 7,283 entries. Table 2 displays a sample of the table PCA which is defined by the morphosyntactic structure `Preposition, Determiner, Constrained noun, Pre-adjectival Modificr, Adjective`:

N0 =: Nhum	N0 =: N-hum	Neg obl	Ppv	Prédicat type	<ENT>Prép	<ENT>Det	<ENT>C	<ENT>Modif pré-adj	<ENT>Adj	Prép Det C	Prép Det Modif pré-adj Adj C	Prép Modif pré-adj Adj C	Conjonction
-	+	-	:se	produire	dans	le	cas	<E>	contraire	-	-	-	+
-	+	-	:se	produire	<E>	le	cas	<E>	échéant	-	-	-	-
-	+	-	:se	produire	à	le	cas	<E>	où	-	-	-	-
-	+	-	:se	produire	dans	le	cas	qui	préoccupe ":Nhum'	-	-	-	-
-	+	-	:se	produire	dans	le	cas	<E>	présent	-	+	-	+
-	+	-	:se	produire	dans	un	cas	<E>	semblable	-	+	-	+

Table 2. Compound adverbs of table PCA

In this table, each row corresponds to a lexical item with adverbial function, and each column corresponds to:

- one of the components in the morphosyntactic structure of the items, i.e. features with identifiers `Prép, Det, C, Modif pré-adj,` and `Adj`;
- a syntactic feature holding binary values, for example: `Prép Det Modif pré-adj Adj C` describes the possible permutation (without loss of information) of the adjectival phrase represented in this table as `Modif pré-adj Adj`; moreover, `Neg obl` encodes the constraint that the adverbial occurs obligatorily in a negative clause;
- a semantic feature holding binary values, for instance, `Conjonction` points out whether the compound adverb has a connector function in discourse, i.e. it links the clause in which it occurs with the previous clause as, for example, *dans le cas contraire* 'otherwise';
- an item of information provided as an aid to help human readers find examples of sentences containing the compound adverb: features with identifiers `Ppv` and `Prédicat type` give an example of a verbal predicate that combines commonly with the adverb.

Unlike simple adverbs, the sixteen classes of compound adverbs, represented in sixteen LG tables, are both syntactically and semantically heterogeneous. For instance, the table PAC encodes adverbs that are defined by the morphosyntactic structure `Prép Det Adj C`, but belong to different syntactic and semantic classes of Molinier and Lévrier (2000): conjuncts, e.g. *dans un premier temps* 'initially', disjuncts, e.g. *à Posss0 humble avis* 'in Poss0 humble opinion', adverbs of time, e.g. *depuis cent sept ans* 'one hundred and seven years since', adverbs of verbal manner, e.g. *n'importe comment* 'no matter how', etc.

Despite their differences, both types of adverbs are often related by productive and regular relations such as, for example, paraphrasing relations allowing the creation of pairs of synonyms, as shown in Table 3:

Adverbs encoded in LG tables of simple adverbs	Adverbs encoded in LG tables of compound adverbs
pratiquement (ADVPS) 'practically'	*en pratique* (PC) 'in practice'
franchement (ADVPS) 'frankly'	*à franchement parler* (PV) 'frankly speaking'
sincèrement (ADVMS) 'sincerely'	*de (E+une) (manière+ façon) sincère* (PCA) 'in a sincere way'
politiquement (ADVMP) 'politically'	*du point de vue politique* (PCA) 'from a political point of view'

Table 3. Paraphrasing relations between simple and compound adverbs

2.2 The syntactic lexicon *LGLex*

The current version of the French LG tables has to consider the use of these lexical data in NLP tools (Tolone, 2009). Therefore, the tables have been converted into an interchange format, based on the same linguistic concepts as those handled in the tables. This conversion is based on *LGExtract*: a generic tool for generating a syntactic lexicon for NLP from the LG tables (Constant and Tolone, 2010). It relies, first, on a global table of classes in which we added the missing features and, second, on a single extraction script including all operations related to each feature to be performed for all tables.

Thanks to *LGExtract*, a French lexicon for NLP has been generated from all LG tables and for most lexical-grammatical categories: verbs, predicative nouns, idioms and adverbs. This syntactic lexicon is named *LGLex* (Constant and Tolone, 2010; Tolone, 2011) and it is freely available[8] under the LGPL-LR license in both plain text format and XML.

LGLex is currently composed of 13,867 verbal entries (from 67 tables), 12,696 nominal entries (from 78 tables), 39,628 idioms (from 69 tables) and 10,487 adverbial entries (from 32 tables) of which 3,203 are simple adverbs (from 16 tables) and 7,284 are compound adverbs (from 16 tables).

3 Extending the LGLex

Each entry of the lexicon includes three sections:

(i) section `Lexical information` identifies the lexical entry, for instance, the adverb *jusqu'à la fin des* (=de les) *temps* 'until the end of time' which is encoded in table PCDC, and also gives the category of each lexical component. We added the information of `paraphrases`, `other structures` and `other entries with intensification` (see section 3.2);

(ii) section `Arguments` gives information about the arguments of the predicate: for instance, the subject argument `N0`, assigned to the predicate that can be modified by the adverb *jusqu'à la fin des temps* 'until the end of time' is a non human noun phrase, represented by `N0 = N-hum`;

(iii) section `Constructions` enumerates the identifiers of all constructions of the lexical entry (e.g. `N0 V Adv W` or `Adv parlant, P`) and of all internal morphosyntactic structures, that is `Adv` for all simple adverbs or `Prép1 Det1 C1 Prép2 Det2 C2` for compound adverbs like *jusqu'à la fin des temps* 'until the end of time', but also `Prép1 Det1 C1` for its variant without prepositional noun phrase modifier, e.g. *jusqu'à la fin* 'until the end'.

So, we first extended *LGLex* with respect to adverbial entries by using various types of features that are encoded in the tables of both simple and compound adverbs. We added 11,328 entries (+108%), so the lexicon is now composed of 21,815 adverbial entries in total.

[8] http://infolingu.univ-mlv.fr/english > Language Resources > Lexicon-Grammar > Download.

3.1 Using the paraphrasing features

The viewpoint adverb *linguistiquement* 'linguistically' accepts the following paraphrasing constructions (Sekine, 2005) that are encoded in the table ADVMP by means of binary features:

linguistiquement 'linguistically'
= *(du+d'un+au) point de vue linguistique*
'from a linguistic point of view'
= *du point de vue de la linguistique*
'from the point of view of linguistics'
= *au niveau linguistique*
'at the linguistic level'
= *(au+sur le) plan linguistique*
'on the linguistic level'
= *en linguistique*
'in linguistics'
= *linguistiquement parlant*
'linguistically speaking'.

For this work, we first dealt with paraphrasing constructions that are described directly in the LG tables through explicit features, as it is shown in Table 4:

Paraphrasing features encoded in the LG tables	Lexical values of the paraphrasing features in the script
`Adj-ment = avec Adj-n`	`"avec @Adj-n@"`
`Adj-ment = (du+d'un) point de vue Adj`	`"d'un point de vue @Adj@", "du point de vue @Adj@"`
`Adj-ment = du point de vue de Ddef Ndomaine`	`"du point de vue de Ddef @Ndomaine@"`
`Adj-ment = au niveau Adj`	`"au niveau @Adj@"`
`Adj-ment = au point de vue Adj`	`"au point de vue @Adj@"`
`Adj-ment = au plan Adj`	`"au plan @Adj@"`
`Adj-ment = sur le plan Adj`	`"sur le plan @Adj@"`
`Adj-ment = de source Adj`	`"de source @Adj@"`
`Adj-ment = en Adj-n`	`"en @Adj-n@"`
`Adj-ment = en Ndomaine`	`"en @Ndomaine@"`
`Adj-ment = en termes Adj`	`"en termes @Adj@"`
`Adj-ment = en toute Adj-n`	`"en toute @Adj-n@"`

Table 4. Paraphrasing features encoded directly in LG tables

The notation @...@ specifies the lexical value of a lexical feature which is encoded systematically in a LG table. For instance, when @Adj@ refers to table ADVMP, it can take the following values: *linguistique* 'linguistic', *politique* 'political', *informatique* 'computational', etc .

Thanks to these features, we added to *LGLex* 2,084 adverbial entries (+20%).

However, a certain number of paraphrases are part of construction features, and thus need to be extracted from them. Construction features are encoded in LG tables by means of binary features, as it is shown in Table 5:

Construction features encoded in the LG tables	Lexical values of the paraphrasing features in the script
Adv parlant, P	"@<ENT>Adv@ parlant"
N0 V W C-a-ment	"@C-a-ment@"
N0 V W avec Adj-n	"avec @Adj-n@"
N0 V W de (E+une) (façon + manière) C-a	"de façon @C-a@", "de manière @C-a@", "d'une façon @C-a@", "d'une manière @C-a@"
N0 V W de (E+une) (façon + manière) Adj	"de façon @Adj@", "de manière @Adj@", "d'une façon @Adj@", "d'une manière @Adj@"
N0hum V W avec Adj-n	"avec @Adj-n@"
N0hum V W de (E+une) (façon + manière) Adj	"de façon @Adj@", "de manière @Adj@", "d'une façon @Adj@", "d'une manière @Adj@"
à Adv parler, P	"à @<ENT>Adv@ parler"

Table 5. Paraphrasing features embedded in construction features

Using this type of features, we enhanced *LGLex* with 7,125 adverbial entries (+68%). Using both types of paraphrasing features, the number of adverbial entries in *LGLex* raised from 10,487 to 19,695 (+88%).

3.2 Other structures

Within the other structures, we distinguish three types of features: deletion, permutation and transformation. They are all described in the following sections.

3.2.1 Using the deletion features

The adverb *jusqu'à la fin des* (=de les) *temps* 'until the end of time' is defined by the morphosyntactic structure Prép1 Det1 C1 Prép2 Det2 C2. It accepts also the substructure *jusqu'à la fin* 'until the end', which is obtained after deletion of the prepositional noun phrase modifier *des* (=de les) *temps* 'of time', and without loss of information. The new adverb has the structure Prép1 Det1 C1. Table 6 displays the deletion features present in LG tables of adverbs:

Deletion features encoded in the LG tables	Lexical value of the deletion features in script
ConjC Det1 C1 Prép2 C2 = Det1 C1 Prép2 C2	"@<ENT>Det1@ @<ENT>C1@ @<ENT>Prép2@ @<ENT>C2@"
Prép Det C	"@<ENT>Prép@ @<ENT>Det@ @<ENT>C@"
Prép1 Det1 C1	"@<ENT>Prép1@ @<ENT>Det1@ @<ENT>C1@"

Table 6. Deletion features encoded in LG tables

The notation @<ENT>...@ specifies the lexical value of an entry described in a LG table. In the case of compound adverbs, an entry is composed by two or more lexical components.

Thanks to the deletion features, we added to *LGLex* 1,519 adverbial entries (+14%).

3.2.2 Using the permutation features

The adverb *dans un avenir proche* 'in a near future', which is defined by the morphosyntactic structure Prép Det C Modif pré-adj Adj, can also take the form *dans un proche avenir* due to the permutation of the adjectival phrase *proche* 'near'. The new adverb has the structure Prép Det Modif pré-adj Adj C, as it is shown in the Table 7:

Permutation features encoded in the LG tables	Lexical value of the permutation features in the script
Prép Det Modif pré-adj Adj C	"@<ENT>Prép@ @<ENT>Det@ @<ENT>Modif@ @<ENT>pré-adj@ @<ENT>Adj@ @<ENT>C@"
Prép Modif pré-adj Adj C	"@<ENT>Prép@ @<ENT>Modif@ @<ENT>pré-adj@ @<ENT>Adj@ @<ENT>C@"

Table 7. Permutation features encoded in LG tables

Let us consider now the compound adverb *dans les délais les plus brefs* 'as soon as possible', which is defined by the morphosyntactic structure `Prép Det C Modif pré-adj Adj`. Although it accepts the permutation of the adjectival phrase *les plus brefs* 'the shortest', it produces an agrammatical entry **dans les les plus brefs délais*. This happens only when `Modif pré-adj` corresponds to a complex unit, that is, in our example, the superlative determiner *les plus* 'the most'. To remedy this situation, we added to table PCA a specific feature enabling both the deletion and permutation of certain components without loss of information, i.e. the feature `Prép Modif pré-adj Adj C`.

This kind of problem is rather widespread since multiword units raise specific difficulties as regards their representation[9] in an electronic resource. Semantically, by definition, compound adverbs cannot be decomposed into simple units. In other words, the resulting overall meaning of the compound adverb cannot usually be deduced from the sum of the meaning of its component elements. Consequently, the various lexical components of compound adverbs are sometimes represented in the tables in an ambiguous or even arbitrary way. This is due, of course, to their irregular syntax and internal word combination constraints.

By means of the permutation features, we enhanced *LGLex* with 103 adverbial entries (+1%).

3.2.3 Using transformational features

Finally, `other structures` can result from general transformations applied to the free prepositional noun phrase modifier *de N* 'of N', which is part of semi-fixed adverbial expressions. For instance, the adverb *pour le bénéfice* 'for the benefit', defined by the morphosyntactic structure `Prép1 Det1 C1 de N2`, can take the following two forms: *pour le bénéfice général* 'for the general benefit' and *pour son benefice* 'for his benefit'. Table 8 displays the transformational features that are encoded in the corresponding LG tables:

Transformation features encoded in the LG tables	Lexical value of the transformational features in the script
`Prép1 Det1 C1 de N2 = Prép1 Det1 C1 général`	`"@Prép1@ @Det1@ @C1@ général"`
`Prép1 Det1 C1 de N2 = Prép1 Poss2 C1`	`"@Prép1@ Poss2 @C1@"`

Table 8. Transformational features encoded in LG tables

Thanks to these features, we added to *LGLex* 288 adverbial entries (+3%).

Taking into account the three different types of features included in `other structures`, the number of adverbial entries in *LGLex* increased from 10,487 to 12,397 (+18%).

3.2.4 Using the intensifying features

The focus adverb *particulièrement* 'particularly' can be modified by two specific intensifiers conveying a greater emphasis to its meaning, and thus produce the two following entries: *tout particulièrement* 'quite particularly' and *plus particulièrement* 'more particularly'. Intensifying features are represented in LG tables as shown in Table 9:

Intensifying features encoded in the LG tables	Lexical value of the intensifying features in the script
`bien Adv`	`"bien @<ENT>Adv@"`
`fort Adv`	`"fort @<ENT>Adv@"`
`plus Adv`	`"plus @<ENT>Adv@"`
`tout Adv`	`"tout @<ENT>Adv@"`
`très Adv`	`"très @<ENT>Adv@"`
`(plus+moins) Adv`	`"plus @<ENT>Adv@", "moins @<ENT>Adv@"`

Table 9. Intensifying features encoded in LG tables

Thanks to these features, the number of adverbial entries in *LGLex* augmented from 10,487 to 10,697 (+2%).

4 Evaluation of the extended *LGLex*

The Table 10 shows the number of the initial adverbial entries in *LGLex* and the detail of the 11,328 new entries:

[9] According to Gross (1986: 1), the unit of representation in a linear lexicon is roughly the word, defined as a sequence of letters separated from neighboring sequences by boundary blanks or other kind of separators, e.g. apostrophe. As a consequence, multiword units cannot be put directly into a lexicon the way simple words are. An identification procedure is needed for their occurrences in texts, and this procedure will make use of the various simple lexical components included in the multiword unit (and described in the LG tables at the elementary level of sequences of parts-of-speech). Hence, the formal linguistic properties of multiword units will determine both the procedure of identification in texts and the type of storage they require.

Initial entries	10,487
Paraphrases	9,208
Other structures	1,910
Intensifying features	210
Final entries	21,815

Table 10. Number of entries in *LGLex*

The results are quite satisfactory as we obtain more than double, precisely 108% new entries in the lexicon, only by exploiting precise linguistic information of high coverage, which is freely available in existing resources.

We manually evaluated the new entries of the lexicon in order to detect errors.

Indeed, a manual validation was necessary when the generated entries corresponded to one single word. For example, the adverb *pourboire compris* 'tip included', which is defined by the morphosyntactic structure `Prép Det C Modif pré-adj Adj`, accepted the deletion of the participial phrase modifier *compris* 'included', but produced a non-adverbial entry **pourboire* 'tip'.

Then, we mention the problem of duplicates that may be produced once the generation of new adverbial entries completed. They concern a few pairs of tables, notably, the pairs PCDC and PCDN, PCA and PAC or PDETC. For example, *ces temps derniers* 'recently', defined by the morphosyntactic structure `Prép Det C Modif pré-adj Adj` and encoded in table PCA, can also take the form *ces derniers temps* due to the permutation of the adjective *derniers* 'recent'. This latter is already encoded in table PAC.

We can also evoke the case of the deleting relation that associates the adverbs of table PCDC with those of table PCDN. For example, *en l'état actuel des choses* 'in the current state of things' accepts also the substructure *en l'état actuel*[10] 'in the current state', which is obtained after deletion of the prepositional noun phrase modifier *des choses* 'of things', and without loss of information. The generated substructure is already an entry of table PCDN. In a similar manner, *en l'état actuel des connaissances* 'in the current state of knowledge' produces the same substructure. Moreover, the adverbs *dans l'état actuel des choses* 'in the current state of things' and *dans l'état actuel des connaissances* 'in the current state of knowledge', which are both encoded in table PCDC, accept the substructure *dans l'état actuel* 'in the current state'.

In fact, each substructure provides information about the corresponding entry, and the generated substructures can be filtered automatically to easily delete duplicates.

Last, errors in the new entries are sometimes due to the way initial adverbial entries are encoded in tables. Considering the adverb *à cette heure-ci* 'at the present time' represented in table PCA: the noun component *heure* 'time' is encoded together with the hyphen, and thus form an amalgam that is automatically reproduced in the substructure *à cette heure-* 'at this time'.

5 Conclusion and future work

At a time when the lack of large scale lexical syntactic resources for French impedes on NLP research, we showed the interest of using fine-grained linguistic information, which is provided in existing resources, in order to enrich or diversify their content. This work led to an increase of 108% of the adverbial entries in *LGLex*.

These encouraging results confirm it is worthwhile exploiting features such as paraphrases. Therefore, we plan to complete the LG tables in that direction, starting, for example, with the table of verbal manner adverbs:

Adj-ment = en tout Nabstrait =:
amicalement = en toute amitié
'friendly' 'in all friendship'

Adj-ment = par Nmoyen_communication =:
téléphoniquement = par téléphone
'by telephone' 'by telephone'

Furthermore, we plan to convert the new adverbial entries into the L*efff* format (Sagot, 2010), in order to integrate them into a parser, following similar work by Tolone and Sagot (2011) and Tolone (2011).

Besides, the new adverbial entries will be added to the French morphological lexicon DELA, which will enable us to evaluate their accuracy by means of both a corpus' annotation practice and a detailed comparison with related work by Laporte *et al.* (2008).

Finally, we can also consider enhancing the French Wordnet with respect to adverbial entries (Sagot *et al.*, 2009).

[10] Normally, in table PCDN, the fixed part of the semi-fixed adverbial expression comprises also the second preposition *de* 'of' which is constant for all entries of the table, and for that reason it is not encoded explicitly.

References

E. Agirre, T. Baldwin and D. Martinez. 2008. Improving parsing and PP attachment performance with sense information. In *Proceedings of ACL*, Columbus, Ohio.

J. Baptista. 2003. Some Families of Compound Temporal Adverbs in Portuguese. In *Proceedings of the Workshop on Finite-State Methods for Natural Language Processing*, Budapest, Hungaria.

X. Blanco and D. Català. 1998/1999. Quelques remarques sur un dictionnaire électronique d'adverbes composés en espagnol. *Lingvisticae Investigationes*, 22: 213-232.

J.-P. Boons, A. Guillet and C. Leclère. 1976. *La structure des phrases simples en français: Constructions intransitives*. Droz, Genève, Suisse.

M. Constant and E. Tolone. 2010. A generic tool to generate a lexicon for NLP from Lexicon-Grammar tables. *Lingue d'Europa e del Mediterraneo, Grammatica comparata*, 1: 79-93.

M. De Gioia. 2001. *Avverbi idiomatici dell'italiano. Analisi lessico-grammaticale, prefazione di Maurice Gross*. L'Harmattan, Torino.

M. Gross. 1975. *Méthodes en syntaxe : Régimes des constructions complétives*. Hermann, Paris, France.

M. Gross. 1986. Lexicon-Grammar. The representation of compound words. In *Proceedings of the Eleventh International Conference on Computational Linguistics*, Bonn, West Germany.

M. Gross. 1990. *Grammaire transformationnelle du français: 3. Syntaxe de l'adverbe*. ASSTRIL, Paris.

A. Guillet and C. Leclère. 1992. *La structure des phrases simples en français : les constructions transitives locatives*. Droz, Geneva, Switzerland.

J. E. Jung. 2005. *Grammaire des adverbes de durée et de date en coréen*. Thèse de doctorat en Informatique Linguistique. Université Paris-Est Marne-la-Vallée, France.

E. Laporte and S. Voyatzi. 2008. An electronic dictionary of French multiword adverbs. In *Proceedings of the the LREC workshop Towards a Shared Task on Multiword Expressions*. Marrakech, Morocco.

E. Laporte, T. Nakamura and S. Voyatzi. 2008. A French corpus annotated for multiword expressions with adverbial function. In *Proceedings of the LREC Second Linguistic Annotation workshop*. Marrakech, Morocco.

P. Merlo. 2003. Generalised PP-attachment Disambiguisation using Corpus-based Linguistic Dia- gnostics. In *Proceedings of the 10th Conference of the European Chapter of the Association for Computational Linguistics, EACL*. Budapest, Hungaria.

C. Moliner. 1984. *Etude syntaxique et sémantique des adverbes de manière en -ment*. Thèse de doctorat, Université de Toulouse – Le Mirail, France.

C. Molinier and F. Lévrier. 2000. *Grammaire des adverbes : description des formes en -ment*. Droz, Genève, Suisse.

H. Nølke. 1990. Classification des adverbes. *Langue française*, 88: 3-127.

B. Sagot, K. Fort and F. Venant. 2009. Extending the adverbial coverage of a French wordnet. In *Proceedings of the NODALIDA 2009 workshop on WordNets and other Lexical Semantic Resources*. Odense, Danemark.

B. Sagot. 2010. The Lefff, a freely available and large-coverage morphological and syntactic lexicon for French. In *Proceedings of the Seventh Language Resources and Evaluation Conference*. La Valette, Malte.

D. Seelbach. 1990. Zur Entwicklung von bilingualen Mehrwortlexica Französisch-Deutsch-Stützverbkon struktionen und adverbiale Ausdrücke. *Lexicon und Lexikographie*, 11: 179-207.

S. Sekine. 2005. Automatic Paraphrase Discovery based on Context and Keywords between NE Pairs. In *Proceedings of the Third International Workshop on Paraphrase*, Jeju Island, South Korea.

E. Tolone. 2009. Les tables du Lexique-Grammaire au format TAL. In *Proceedings of MajecSTIC 2009*, Avignon, France.

E. Tolone, S. Voyatzi and C. Leclère. 2010. Constructions définitoires des tables du Lexique-Grammaire. In *Proceedings of the Twenty Ninth International Conference on Lexis and Grammar*, Belgrade, Serbie.

E. Tolone and B. Sagot. To appear. Using Lexicon-Grammar tables for French verbs in a large-coverage parser. *Lecture Notes in Artificial Intelligence*. Springer Verlag.

E. Tolone. 2011. *Analyse syntaxique à l'aide des tables du Lexique-Grammaire du français*. Thèse de doctorat en Informatique Linguistique, Université Paris-Est, 340 pp.

A. Villavicencio. 2002. Learning to distinguish PP arguments from adjuncts. In *Proceedings of the 6th Conference on Natural Language Learning*, Taipei, Taiwan.

S. Voyatzi. 2006. *Description morphosyntaxique et sémantique des adverbes figés en vue d'un système d'analyse automatique des textes grecs*. Thèse de doctorat en Informatique Linguistique. Université Paris-Est, France, 406 pp.

Linguistic Phenomena, Analyses, and Representations: Understanding Conversion between Treebanks

Rajesh Bhatt
Univ. of Massachusetts
Amherst, MA 01003, USA
bhatt@linguist.umass.edu

Owen Rambow
CCLS, Columbia University
New York, NY 10115, USA
rambow@ccls.columbia.edu

Fei Xia
Univ. of Washington
Seattle, WA 98195, USA
fxia@uw.edu

Abstract

Treebanks are valuable resources for natural language processing (NLP). There is much work in NLP which converts treebanks from one representation (e.g., phrase structure) to another (e.g., dependency) before applying machine learning. This paper provides a framework in which to think about the question of when such a conversion is possible.

1 Introduction

There has been much interest in converting treebanks from one representation to another; for instance, from phrase structure to dependency structure (e.g., motivated by the recent surge in interest in dependency parsing), or from phrase structure to other grammatical frameworks such as LTAG, HPSG, CCG, or LFG. While there has been much work on converting between treebank representations (Collins et al., 1999; Xia and Palmer, 2001; Cahill et al., 2002; Nivre, 2003; Hockenmaier and Steedman, 2007), there has not been a general yet precise discussion of what conditions are necessary for such conversion to happen.

In this paper, we provide an analytical framework for determining how difficult it would be to convert representations under one set of annotation guidelines M_1 to representations under another set of guidelines M_2. We are only interested in cases where annotation guidelines are available for both levels of representation, since it is not clear how one would interpret an undocumented representation, and thus it would not be clear how to evaluate the conversion results. Given two sets of guidelines and a particular linguistic phenomenon, there are three possible scenarios: (1) the phenomenon is represented only on one side; (2) the phenomenon is represented on both sides with incompatible analyses; (3) the phenomenon is represented on both sides with compatible analyses. We give a formal definition of *compatibility* and a procedure for distinguishing these three scenarios. We also discuss how each scenario will affect automatic conversion. Using this framework, researchers can determine the difficulty of a conversion task between existing guidelines, or they can design guidelines for new treebanks so automatic conversion to other representations can be as smooth as possible.

Note that we are not addressing general questions such as "In general, is it easier to convert dependency to phrase structure or *vice versa*?" We believe that such general questions cannot be answered. One needs to examine what information is being represented before the issue of conversion can be addressed, i.e., we must first study the guidelines of the two levels of representation.

While we propose a general approach to analyzing syntactic representations, throughout the paper we will use examples based on converting dependency structures to phrase structures. Specifically, we will use as a source of examples the Hindi/Urdu Treebank (HUTB) (Palmer et al., 2009). The HUTB is unusual in that it contains a dependency structure (DS) annotation, a PropBank-style annotation (PB) (Kingsbury et al., 2002) for predicate-argument structure, and an independently motivated phrase-structure (PS) annotation which is automatically derived from DS plus PB. For lack of space, we will not discuss the PropBank layer in this paper and instead draw all examples from PS and DS.

The structure of the paper is as follows. Section 2 introduces some terminology which helps in our analysis. Section 3 discusses the notion of compatibility and syntactic consistency. Section 4 introduces a procedure for comparing two sets of annotation guidelines with respect to conversion. Section 5 discuss examples from the HUTB that fall into the two "harder" scenarios for conversion.

2 Important concepts in a treebank

This study focuses on the relation between DS and PS treebanks. To understand whether an automatic conversion between DS and PS is possible, it is important to distinguish a few concepts in a treebank. Following (Rambow, 2010), we distinguish three concepts: the linguistic phenomena (what he calls "content"), the representation type, and the linguistic theory (what he calls "syntactic theory"). We reinterpret these concepts and extend them, in terms of the HUTB.

2.1 Linguistic phenomena

The **linguistic phenomena** are what we want to represent about the words which make up our treebank: they are the reason for treebanking. If there were no interesting linguistic phenomena, there would be no reason to create treebanks. The task of treebanking consists of identifying which of the phenomena of interest appear in a given sequence of words (a data token) and then to choose the correct representation for these phenomena in the given data token. The types of linguistic phenomena range from general concepts such as recursive constituency (which words in this sentence form phrases?) to types of relations between words or between a word and a phrase (e.g., subjecthood, or temporal modification) to specific constructions (e.g., small clauses). Linguistic phenomena also include finer-grained distinctions within coarser categories (e.g., unergative/unaccusative as two classes of intransitive verbs). For all of these phenomena, while linguists may disagree about the proper representation or whether the phenomenon is present in a particular instance, they typically agree on the fact that the phenomenon exists in the language, or exists in some language.

Consider first the example of syntactic constituency. There is broad agreement among syntacticians that syntax groups words recursively into hierarchies; to our knowledge, no serious syntactic theory uses only flat representations (such as base phrases). Crucially, this is independent of whether the syntactician uses DS or PS: DS also assumes a recursive structure and represents constituency (in a DS, each subtree represents a constituent, headed by its root).[1] It is difficult to assume that a treebank (DS or PS) would not represent syntactic constituency – there would have to be an explicit disclaimer that what looks like constituents (in DS or PS) are in fact not linguistically meaningful units, and are just notationally expedient devices.

Now consider the example of an embedded small clauses, as in the English sentence *Atif considered Seema stupid*, or its Hindi counterpart in (1). This is a particular construction; it is characterized (in both English and Hindi) by the fact that the NP *Seema* is an argument of the predicate *stupid*, but its case and word order is that of an object of the main verb *considered*, not a subject (as can be seen if we replace it with a pronoun, *her*).

(1) Atif-ne Seema-ko bewakuuf samjhaa
Atif-Erg Seema-Acc stupid consider.Pfv
'Atif considered Seema stupid.'

2.2 Representation type

The **representation type** is the type of mathematical object that is used to represent syntactic facts. A DS is a tree in which all nodes are labeled with words or empty strings (e.g., empty categories). A PS is a tree in which all and only the leaf nodes are labeled with words or empty strings, and the internal nodes are labeled with nonterminal symbols (e.g., syntactic labels). In addition, each representation type can decide what more specific representation devices it will employ, such as labels on the arcs of a tree (e.g., dependency type in a DS), or the use of empty nodes, or coindexation between nodes (e.g., to mark syntactic movement).

2.3 Linguistic theory

A **formal linguistic description** explains how linguistic phenomena are represented in the chosen representation type; a formal description is thus tied to a particular representation type. It can be thought of as a mapping from linguistic phenomena to linguistic representations in the chosen representation type. It has two components: a theoretical framework, and linguistic analyses. If, in addition, the analyses provided by a formal description are such that they rule out certain strings in the language and make falsifiable predictions, then we call the formal linguistic description a **linguistic theory**. These notions of "formal linguistic description" and of "linguistic theory" should not be confused with a **theoretical framework**, such as

[1] Of course, PS allows for intermediate projections. These have two functions. First, they distinguish functionally distinct dependents, such as subject from object. Second, an intermediate projection may actually occur as an empirically identifiable constituent, as in VP fronting in English. In both cases, DS can use alternate representational devices. We leave a fuller discussion to future work.

Government and Binding (GB) or LFG. The goal of theoretical framework is not to provide a complete description of a single language, but rather to provide vocabulary and constraints in which linguistic theories can be formulated.

Once a linguistic theory has chosen a theoretical framework such as GB, the next step is to determine how to represent the linguistic phenomena in that framework. For instance, given the Hindi embedded small clause example in (1), there are many possible ways to represent the phenomenon in a PS-based linguistic theory (e.g., the ones in Figure (1a-c)) or in a DS-based linguistic theory (e.g., the ones in Figure (1d-f)). We call them different **analyses** of this phenomenon.

It is important to stress that elements of the representation on their own may have no meaning. For example, the trace **CASE** in (1c) is not meaningful in isolation. Instead, the trace and its coindexed partner, the NP *Seema ko*, along with their structural configuration, together signify the phenomenon (which we are calling embedded small clause) that was identified by the annotator as happening in this particular sentence. The annotator chose this way of representing the phenomenon for this data token because the annotation guidelines say to do so. But the annotation of course also manifests the particular analysis chosen (namely, the raising-to-object analysis of (1c) and (1f)). However, this analysis is *not* specific to this particular data token; rather, for all annotations that use the guidelines, it must be used whenever an embedded small clause is identified by the annotator. The annotator cannot identify an embedded small clause but suddenly change the analysis on his or her own. It is also impossible that annotation guidelines would identify a unified phenomenon and propose two analyses based on arbitrary conditions (say, the first letter of the head noun). Thus, annotators must learn how to represent each phenomenon, and then must decide which phenomena a specific data token exhibits.

2.4 Annotation guidelines

Every treebank requires annotation guidelines, which can be regarded as a formal linguistic description, typically a very detailed and explicit one with descriptions and examples. The guidelines are used to train annotators, for annotators as a reference, and for users of the treebank as a guide to its meaning. Some annotation guidelines may even be linguistic theories (if they can be used to make predictions about ungrammatical sentences in the language, for example), though this is not generally the case.

To create annotation guidelines, the guideline designers need to choose a theoretical framework and a set of linguistic phenomena to be captured. Next, they need to determine a linguistic analysis for each linguistic phenomenon, and demonstrate the analysis with descriptions and examples (e.g., sentences and the corresponding DS or PS trees).

Take the HUTB as an example. Because it contains both representation types, DS and PS, it has two sets of guidelines for syntactic annotation, one for each representation type. The DS annotation guidelines follow the Paninian grammatical model (Bharati et al., 1995; Begum et al., 2008). The PS guidelines are inspired by the Principles-and-Parameters methodology, as instantiated by the theoretical developments starting with Government and Binding Theory (Chomsky, 1981).

3 Compatibility and conversion

As mentioned in the previous section, annotation guidelines provide linguistic analyses for a set of linguistic phenomena, and they are tied to a representation type (DS or PS). Now given two sets of annotation guidelines (one for DS and the other for PS), the central question is whether automatic conversion between DS and PS is possible; that is, is it possible to write a conversion algorithm that takes as input a DS tree annotated according to the DS guidelines, and produces a PS tree that would be correct according to the PS guidelines, or vice versa? In the rest of the paper, we will focus on the DS-to-PS conversion.

The answer to the question depends on the guidelines. If the DS and PS guidelines cover the same set of linguistic phenomena (explicitly or implicitly) and they choose *compatible* analyses for the phenomena, automatic conversion is possible. If these conditions do not hold, automatic conversion would require additional information or mechanism, as explained in Section 5. In this section, we will provide a formal definition of *compatibility*.

3.1 Intuition about compatibility

To define compatibility between linguistic analyses, let us first look at an example. Figure 1 shows several analyses for small clause: three for PS and

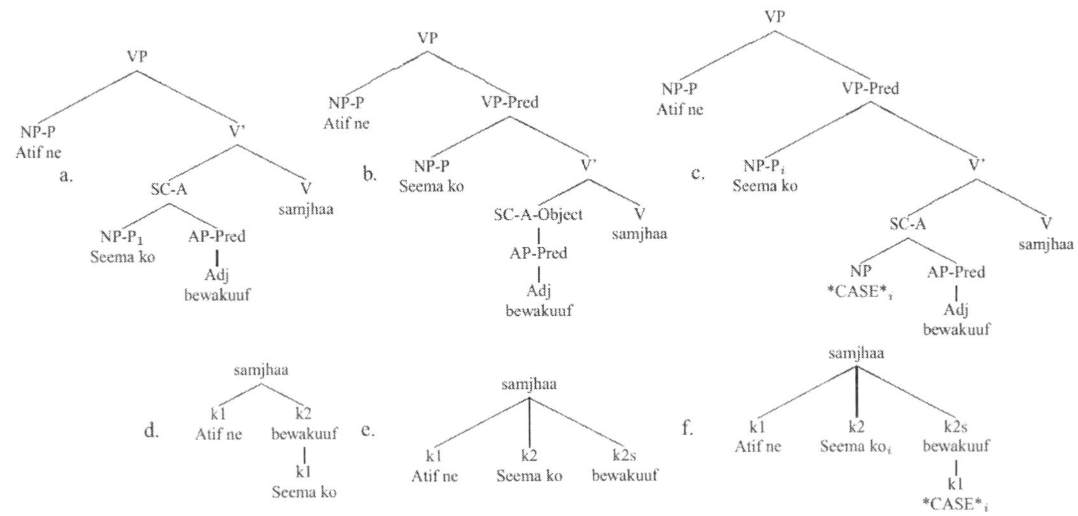

Figure 1: Possible analyses for the Hindi small clause example in Ex (1)

three for DS. It is clear that the analyses in (a) and (d) have something in common (the "exceptional case-marking" analysis), in which the semantic relationship between the adjectival predicated *bewakuuf ('stupid')* and *Seema ko* is seen as primary and the source of the object case marking *ko* on *Seema ko* is not represented explicitly. Similarly, (b) and (e) share an analysis, in which the presence of the object case marking *ko* is seen as primary, and predicate-argument relation between *Seema ko* and *bewakuuf ('stupid')* is deduced only from the label *SC-A-Object* in (b) or *k2s* in (e). Finally, the trees in (c) and (f) share an analysis (the "raising-to-object" analysis), in which a trace is used to indicate that the NP *Seema ko* participates in two relations.

Intuitively, analyses in (a) and (d) are compatible, so are the ones in (b) and (e), and the ones in (c) and (f). The next question is whether we can provide a formal definition of compatibility and write code that automatically checks whether the DS and PS analyses for a linguistic phenomenon is compatible. The answer is affirmative, as we can do that via the definition of *consistency* between (DS, PS) tree pairs, as is explained below.

3.2 Implicit vs. explicit information

Before we define *consistency*, there are two points that are worth mentioning. First, DS and PS, as two representation types, use different representation devices to describe syntactic structure: DS uses edges to represent the dependency or modifier-modifiee relation between words, whereas PS uses internal nodes to mark the spans and types of syntactic constituents. As a result, there are certain aspects of information that DS has to provide *explicitly* but PS does not need to (e.g., DS has to mark the direction of each edge, indicating which node is the head and which node is the dependent). The converse is also true (e.g., each internal node in a PS has to be labeled, indicating the syntactic category of the phrase).

Second, not explicitly providing certain information does not mean that the corresponding concept does not exist in the syntactic theory. For instance, PS does not need to mark the head of an internal node explicitly, but it does not mean that the syntactic theory chosen for PS does not have the concept of *headedness*.

3.3 Syntactic consistency

Our definition of consistency assumes that each phrase in a PS has a special word called *head word* which represents the main properties of the phrase, an assumption shared by all major contemporary syntactic frameworks. A pair (DS, PS) of DS and PS trees for the same sentence is called *consistent* if there is a way to assign a head word to each internal node in the PS so that all the words in the subtree rooted at that internal node are descendants of the head word in the DS. A formal definition is given later, but let us start with an example.

Figure 2 shows a simple PS with two internal nodes and three leaf nodes. Because the head words for the internal nodes are not marked in the PS, there are several possibilities in choosing the

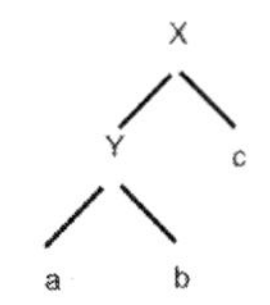

Figure 2: A simple PS: *a*, *b*, and *c* are leaf nodes, *X* and *Y* are internal nodes

head words for the internal nodes: the head word of the Y can be a or b, and the head word of X can be c or the head word of Y, resulting in four possible DSs, as shown in Figure 3. In contrast, no matter which head words we choose for the internal nodes in the PS, the resulting DSs will not be the ones in Figure 4. We call the DSs in Figure 3 *consistent* with the PS, and the DSs in Figure 4 *inconsistent* with the PS.

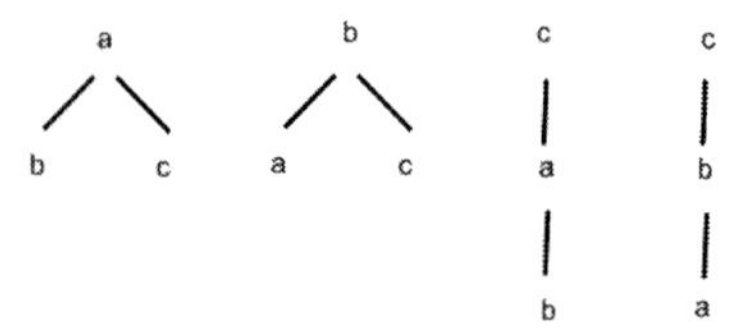

Figure 3: The DSs *consistent* with PS in Fig. 2

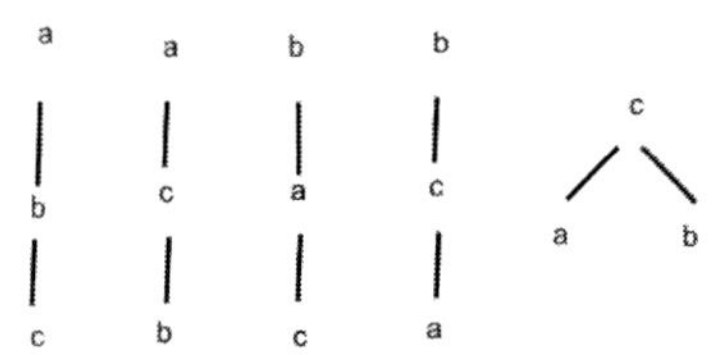

Figure 4: The DSs *inconsistent* with PS in Fig. 2

More formally, let us define two operations on a PS. Given a PS and an assignment of head words for the internal nodes in the PS, a *flatten* operation recursively merges each internal node X with its head child (a head child is a node which has the same head word as its parent). When two nodes, X and its head child h, are merged, the other children of X and the children of h (if any) become the children of the new merged node. Then, a *label replacement* operation replaces the label of each internal node with the node's head word. For instance, given the PS in Figure 2 and the assignment where a is the head word of Y and c is the head word of X, the tree after the flatten operation is in Figure 5(ii), and the tree after the label replacement operation is in Figure 5(iii). A PS and a DS are called *consistent* if and only if there exists an assignment of head words for the internal nodes in PS such that after the flatten operation and the label replacement operation, the new PS is identical to the DS.

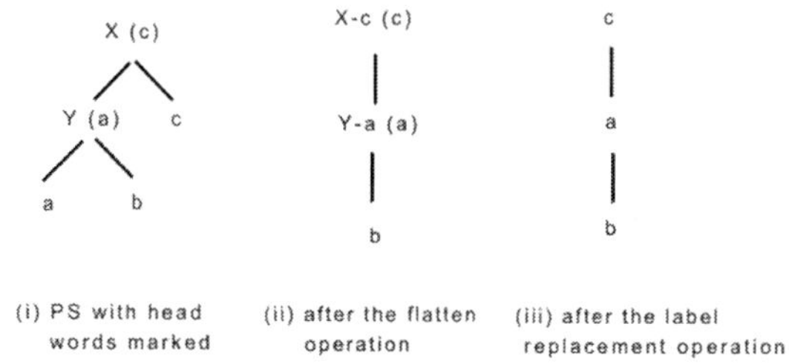

Figure 5: The resulting PS after the flatten and label replacement operations: *X(c)* in (i) means that c is the head word of X; *X-c* in (ii) means the nodes X and c are merged.

Given a (DS, PS) pair, one can use the following process to check whether the DS and the PS are consistent. For each edge, (*head*, *dep*), in the DS, find the nodes for *head* and *dep* in the PS and their closest common ancestor *ancest*; for each node on the path between *head* and *ancest* (including *ancest*), assign *head* as its head word; for each node on the path between *dep* and *ancest* (excluding *ancest*), assign *dep* as its head word. The DS and PS are consistent *iff* after all the edges in the DS have been used, each internal node in the PS is assigned exactly one head word.

Now we can define the notion of *compatible analyses*. Given a linguistic phenomenon, let D be the set of (DS, PS) pairs provided in the guidelines for that phenomenon. The analyses in the DS and PS guidelines are *compatible* if and only if every (DS, PS) pair in D is *consistent*.

3.4 Conversion between DS and PS

Given a DS, there are multiple PSs that are consistent with the DS. The reason that a DS-to-PS conversion algorithm could make the right selection is that the (DS,PS) pairs in the annotation guidelines indicate what a PS should look like for a given DS. For instance, Figure 6 shows some patterns in the (DS,PS) pairs: the first pattern says that when a noun depends on a verb with the type *SBJ* in a DS, the corresponding PS should include a *S* node which has two children, an *NP* node that dominates the noun and a *VP* node that dominates the verb. The meaning of the second pattern can be interpreted similarly. Xia et al. (2009) showed that such patterns can be learned from (DS, PS) pairs automatically and with these patterns their conversion algorithm produced good results when tested on the English Penn Treebank.

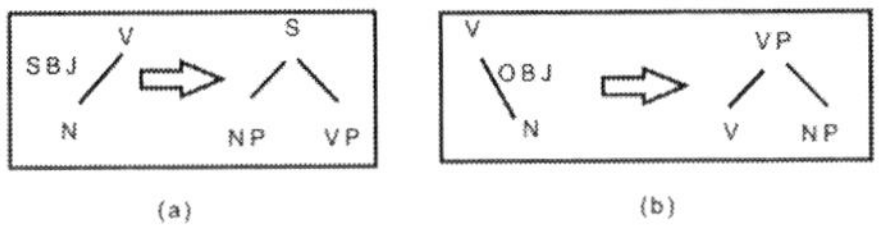

Figure 6: Two patterns that could help a DS-to-PS conversion to produce the correct PS tree as output

4 Analytic Framework for Comparing Treebank Guidelines

We now present our procedure for comparing two sets of treebank guidelines, with the goal of determining whether automatic conversion is possible. The devil is in the details. It is impossible to read the introduction to two sets of annotation guidelines and then to be able to say whether automatic conversion is possible. Instead, it is necessary to look at every single phenomenon: one phenomenon may be easy to convert, while another may be quite hard. We illustrate our procedure assuming we want to transform DS into PS.

For each linguistic phenomenon Φ, we ask two questions: (1) is Φ captured in both DS and PS guidelines? (2) if so, are the analyses in DS and PS guidelines compatible? The answers to the questions lead to three scenarios:

- **The phenomenon is represented by both sides and the analyses are compatible**: automatic conversion can be done using the procedure presented in Section 3, using knowledge which is general to Φ.
- **The phenomenon is represented by both sides but the analyses are incompatible**: automatic conversion is possible but it requires additional mechanisms (e.g., *DS+* as introduced in Section 5.1.2) to bridge the gap in analyses. The knowledge needed is general to Φ.
- **The phenomena is represented only on one side**: If it is represented in the DS only, the conversion algorithm can simply ignore it when creating PS. If it is represented on the PS side only, automatic conversion will require additional information which is not general to Φ, but which provides information specific to each **instance** of Φ (for example, a list of unaccusative verbs, as used in Section 5.2.1).

Of course, establishing the range of phenomena to be considered may not be entirely trivial. It includes not only the set of all constructions in a narrow sense, but also which constituents are represented, which empty arguments are included, what types of dependencies are represented, and so on. We discuss some examples in the following section.

5 Preliminary results in HUTB

As a case study, we compared the PS and DS guidelines of the HUTB with the process outlined in Section 4. The guidelines currently include 209 sentences where both DS and PS trees are provided. Each sentence has a sentence id, which indicates the linguistic phenomenon the sentence intends to represent. We ran the consistency check algorithm on the (DS, PS) pairs and found that 162 out of 209 pairs are consistent.

We then used the consistency results to group the corresponding phenomena into one of the three categories in Section 4. It turns out that most phenomena belong to the first category. For the other two categories, we present one example below and discuss how that will affect conversion.

5.1 Phenomena represented on both sides but differently

This category comprises several constructions in the HUTB: long scrambling and extraposition (which are non-projective), small clauses, local scrambling, and support verb constructions. We discuss small clauses in detail as a typical case.

5.1.1 Small clause

In HUTB, both the DS and the PS analysis represent the sharing aspect of small clauses, but they do so differently, which leads to incompatibility. In the PS analysis, as in Figure (1c), *Seema* is interpreted as the argument of the predicate *bewakuuf* ('stupid') and hence, given the theoretical assumptions adopted by the PS guidelines, it must combine with this predicate. But it gets case from the matrix predicate and hence also has a relationship with the matrix predicate. As a result, *Seema-ko* corresponds to two positions in the PS tree: a lower position (the empty category

CASE) as the subject of the lower predicate and a higher position as the object of the higher predicate. The two positions and the coindexation between them indicate the movement of *Seema-ko* from the lower position to the higher position to acquire case.

In contrast, the DS analysis, as shown in Figure (1e), does not represent the relationship between *Seema* and *bewakuuf ('stupid')* structurally: *Seema* is not a dependent on *bewakuuf*; Instead both *Seema* and *bewakuuf* are dependents of the matrix predicate *samjhaa ('consider')*. The relationship between *Seema* and *bewakuuf* is encoded into their dependency labels: *Seema* has the label *k2* and *bewakuuf* the label *k2s*. The (*k2, k2s*) pair indicates that semantically the *k2* node is dependent on the *k2s* node and the dependency relation between them is *k1*.

5.1.2 Handling incompatibility by introducing DS+

When a linguistic phenomenon (e.g., argument sharing in an embedded small clause) is represented in both DS and PS but in different ways, the automatic DS-to-PS conversion is still possible if we can automatically create a new DS, let us call it DS+, which is derived from the original DS but is consistent with the PS. That is, DS+ and PS represent that phenomenon in the same way. For instance, the DS in Figure (1e) is not consistent with the PS in Figure (1c), but the DS in Figure (1f) is because it encodes the sharing aspect of small clause as two coindexed nodes just like in the PS. Furthermore, from the meaning of the (*k2, k2s*) pair, it is easy to write an *ad-hoc* procedure that generates the DS in Figure (1f) from the DS in Figure (1e) automatically.

Therefore, the incompatibility due to representation difference can be handled by introducing a DS+, and the DS-to-PS conversion can be done in two steps: first, given a DS, DS+ is created automatically from the DS; second, a PS is generated from DS+ by applying a conversion algorithm. Determining the shape of DS+ and writing the DS-to-DS+ procedure require good understanding of the difference between the DS and PS analyses. But note that the DS-to-DS+ procedure is entirely independent of the data tokens we are trying to convert; we only need to understand the different representations for the type of phenomenon.

5.2 Phenomena represented only in one side

The DS and PS guidelines are formal linguistic descriptions, but they need not be a complete description of the language. The designers of the treebank may choose not to represent certain linguistic information for practical reasons. For example, the English Penn Treebank does not represent the syntactic structure of prenominal nominal and adjectival modifiers, even though it is generally assumed that such structure exists. Consequently, there could be certain phenomena that are represented in either the DS or PS analyses, but not in both. In the HUTB, one such case is the phenomenon of the unaccusativity/unergativity distinction.

5.2.1 Unaccusativity/unergativity

The unaccusativity/unergativity distinction refers to the fact that intransitive verbs cross-linguistically do not form a unified class - they break down into two classes: unaccusative verbs in which, roughly speaking, the sole argument is semantically a patient (e.g., *open, break*), and unergative verbs in which the sole argument is semantically an agent (e.g., *dance, laugh*). Two examples in Hindi are given in (2) and (3). This meaning difference correlates with a number of syntactic differences and many linguistic theories appeal to the unaccusative/unergative distinction to explain these differences. Other linguistic theories, however, do not make a distinction between these two classes.

(2) Unaccusatives:

darwaazaa khul rahaa hai
door.M open Prog.MSg be.Prs.Sg

'The door is opening.'

(3) Unergatives:

Ravi naac rahaa hai
Ravi.M dance Prog.MSg be.Prs.Sg

'Ravi is dancing.'

In the HUTB, the DS guidelines do not make the distinction and the sole argument of both unaccusative and unergative verbs is annotated as *k1*, as shown in Figure 7.

The PS guidelines assume that particular semantic relations (such as patient) are associated with designated structural configurations. Hence, the sole argument of an unaccusative verb needs to combine with the verb in the same position as canonical objects would (as a sister of V). But

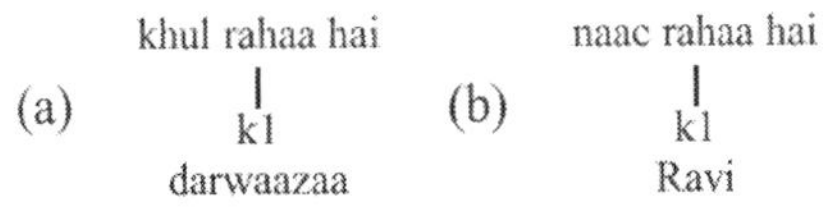

Figure 7: DS for the sentences in (2) and (3)

since the argument also functions as the subject, it must also occupy the position occupied by canonical subjects (sister of V'). This is accomplished in the PS by inserting a special trace in the object position (**CASE**), representing the fact that semantically, the constituent in subject position originates in the object position. The PS analysis follows the standard analysis of unaccusativity as articulated in (Burzio, 1986), and the tree for (2) is shown in Figure 8. In contrast, the sole argument of an unergative verb semantically behaves like an agent and functions as the subject, so it occupies the subject position, as in Figure 9, and there is no object position or the movement from the object position to the subject position. It is easy to show that the (DS, PS) tree pair for the unergative sentence (3) is consistent, whereas the pair for the unaccusative sentence (2) is not.

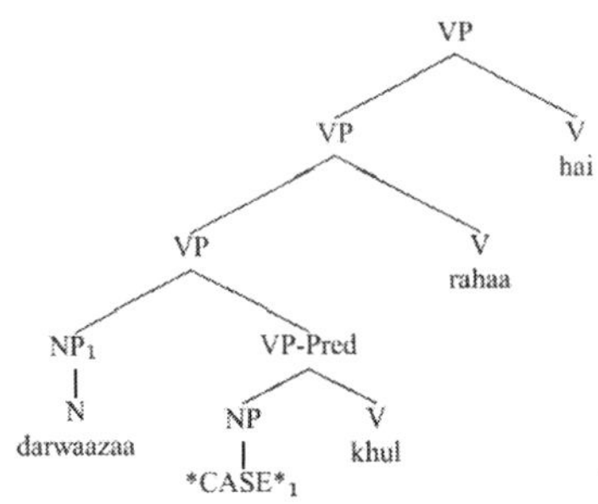

Figure 8: PS for the unaccusative in (2)

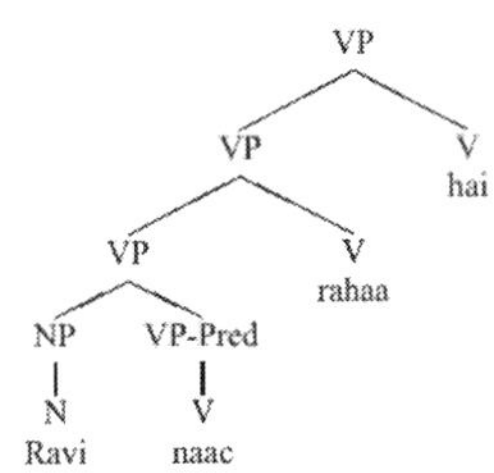

Figure 9: PS for the unergative in (3)

5.2.2 Handling incompatibility requires additional resource

How can we handle the problem that the DS and PS analyses for unergative verbs are compatible, while the ones for unaccusative verbs are not? While one could propose to create a DS+ for unaccusatives like what is done for small clauses, the problem is that this is a property of a data token, and not of the phenomenon of intransitive verbs. We cannot simply use knowledge about this type of phenomenon, since we need to know properties of the particular data token. Because the unaccusative/unergative distinction is not made in the DS, DS+ cannot be created automatically from DS without resorting to an additional resource that will explain the data token. In this case, a list of unergative and unaccusative verbs in Hindi can provide this information, since all instances of a particular intransitive verb are always either unergative or unaccusative. In other words, automatic DS-to-PS conversion is impossible unless an additional resource is provided that allows the conversion mechanism to make the unaccusative/unergative distinction. In the HUTB, the PropBank turns out to be such a resource as it makes the relevant distinction for independent reasons and this allows automatic conversion to proceed.

6 Conclusion

This paper has addressed the issue of when a treebank can be automatically converted to another. We have discussed several important concepts in a treebank and defined compatibility between analyses and consistency between syntactic structures (DS and PS). We have then provided a procedure for comparing treebanks guidelines with respect to conversion. Specifically, we have argued that the conversion from one treebank to another must be examined on a phenomenon-by-phenomenon basis, and that for each phenomenon, there are three scenarios that may arise: the two guidelines have compatible analyses; they have incompatible analyses; and one represents the phenomenon but the other does not. In the first case, automatic conversion is fairly direct; in the second case, we need to study the phenomenon and the analyses proposed for it and provide an intermediate representation to bring the gap; in the third case, we need additional information to achieve the conversion.

Acknowledgments This work is supported by NSF grants CNS-0751089, CNS-0751171, and CNS-0751213. We would like to thank the anonymous reviewers for helpful comments and our colleagues on the Hindi-Urdu Treebank Project for their support.

References

Rafiya Begum, Samar Husain, Arun Dhwaj, Dipti Misra Sharma, Lakshmi Bai, and Rajeev Sangal. 2008. Dependency annotation scheme for indian languages. In *Proceedings of The Third International Joint Conference on Natural Language Processing (IJCNLP)*, Hyderabad, India.

Akshar Bharati, Vineet Chaitanya, and Rajeev Sangal. 1995. *Natural Language Processing – A Paninian Perspective*. Prentice-Hall of India.

Luigi Burzio. 1986. *Italian syntax: a government-binding approach*. Studies in natural language and linguistic theory. Kluwer, Dordrecht.

Aoife Cahill, Mairead McCarthy, Josef van Genabith, and Andy Way. 2002. Automatic Annotation of the Penn-Treebank with LFG F-Structure Information. In *LREC 2002 Workshop on Linguistic Knowledge Acquisition and Representation - Bootstrapping Annotated Language Data*.

Noam Chomsky. 1981. *Lectures on Government and Binding*. Dordrecht: Foris.

Michael Collins, Jan Hajič, Lance Ramshaw, and Christoph Tillmann. 1999. A statistical parser for czech. In *Proceedings for the 37th Annual Meeting of the Association for Computational Linguistics (ACL-1999)*, pages 505–512. Association for Computational Linguistics.

Julia Hockenmaier and Mark Steedman. 2007. Ccgbank: A corpus of ccg derivations and dependency structures extracted from the penn treebank. *Computational Linguistics*, 33(3):355–396.

Paul Kingsbury, Martha Palmer, and Mitch Marcus. 2002. Adding semantic annotation to the Penn TreeBank. In *Proceedings of the Human Language Technology Conference (HLT-2002)*, San Diego, CA.

Joakim Nivre. 2003. Theory-supporting treebanks. In *In Proceedings of the TLT 2003 Workshop*.

Martha Palmer, Rajesh Bhatt, Bhuvana Narasimhan, Owen Rambow, Dipti Misra Sharma, and Fei Xia. 2009. Hindi Syntax: Annotating Dependency, Lexical Predicate-Argument Structure, and Phrase Structure. In *Proceedings of ICON-2009: 7th International Conference on Natural Language Processing*, Hyderabad.

Owen Rambow. 2010. The simple truth about dependency and phrase structure representations. In *Proceedings of NAACL-2010*.

Fei Xia and Martha Palmer. 2001. Converting Dependency Structures to Phrase Structures. In *Proc. of the Human Language Technology Conference (HLT-2001)*, San Diego, CA.

Fei Xia, Owen Rambow, Rajesh Bhatt, Martha Palmer, and Dipti Misra Sharma. 2009. Towards a multi-representational treebank. In *The 7th International Workshop on Treebanks and Linguistic Theories (TLT-7)*, Groningen, Netherlands.

*** Formatting Issue - Best Available Paper/Graphic ***

Automatic Transformation of the Thai Categorial Grammar Treebank to Dependency Trees

Christian Rishøj
CST
University of Copenhagen
crjensen@hum.ku.dk

Taneth Ruangrajitpakorn
HLT Lab
NECTEC
taneth.rua@nectec.or.th

Prachya Boonkwan
HLT Lab
NECTEC
prachya.boo@nectec.or.th

Thepchai Supnithi
HLT Lab
NECTEC
thepchai.sup@nectec.or.th

Abstract

A method for deriving an approximately labeled dependency treebank from the Thai Categorial Grammar Treebank has been implemented. The method involves a lexical dictionary for assigning dependency directions to the CG types associated with the grammatical entities in the CG bank, falling back on a generic mapping of CG types in case of unknown words. Currently, all but a handful of the trees in the Thai CG bank can unambiguously be transformed into directed dependency trees. Dependency labels can optionally be assigned with a learned classifier, which in a preliminary evaluation with a very small training set achieves 76.5% label accuracy. In the process, a number of annotation errors in the CG bank were identified and corrected. Although rather limited in its coverage, excluding e.g. long-distance dependencies, topicalisations and longer sentences, the resulting treebank is believed to be sound in terms of structural annotational consistency and a valuable complement to the scarce Thai language resources in existence.

1 Introduction

Syntactic resources play an essential role for the majority of NLP applications, but for the Thai language, openly available syntactic resources are few in number: So far, the only reported resources are the CG treebank [Ruangrajitpakorn et al., 2009] and the NAiST dependency bank [Wacharamanotham et al., 2007, Sudprasert, 2008]. Others are either unpublished or minuscule in size. Rather than relying exclusively on labor-intensive manual annotation for further expanding the resources, it would be economically sound to leverage existing efforts and transform an existing treebank in one formalism into another.

1.1 Categorial grammar

Categorial grammar (CG) is a lexicalised theory in natural language syntax motivated by the principle of constitutionality and organised according to the syntactic elements [Steedman, 2000, Ajdukiewicz, 1935], and forms the theoretical basis for the Thai CG treebank. The resource building effort has been very fruitful, but there remains phenomena of Thai language, including long-distance dependencies and topicalisation [Warotamasikkhadit, 1997], which are unhandled by the instantiation of CG currently in use.

Additionally, although the Thai language belongs to a fixed word order typology, Thai spoken language exhibits some flexibility in word order, due to the occasional preference of Thai language users for correspondence in rhyme. As an example, consider the following sentence[1]:

• •

• • • • • • • • • • • • • • • • • • • •

(**Lit**: England/NE invent/V "-ly"/ADVPFX heavy/ADJ vaccine/N protect/V virus/N avian_flu/NP)

"The British are strenuously developing an Avian Flu vaccine."

The adverbial compound formed by • • • • • • • • ("strenuously") conventionally occurs after the direct object, but is in this sentence, it is realised in the pre-direct object position[2] in order for the last syllable [nak^L] of • • • • • • • • to rhyme with the first syllable [wak^H] of • • • • ("vaccine"). To some degree, this phenomenon from spoken language shines through in written language, especially in the domains of news and recent politics, and is causing a challenge for the employment of CG grammar.

[1]The Thai adverbialising prefix • • • • can be likened to the English "-ly" suffix, which produces an adverbial form from an adjective. Artificial word boundaries are inserted for clarity.

[2]When language users exploit this flexibility in word order to produce aesthetically pleasing sound patterns, it results in a marked form, but the phenomenon is nonetheless productive, and encountered frequently enough to necessitate handling in NLP applications.

*** Formatting Issue - Best Available Paper/Graphic ***

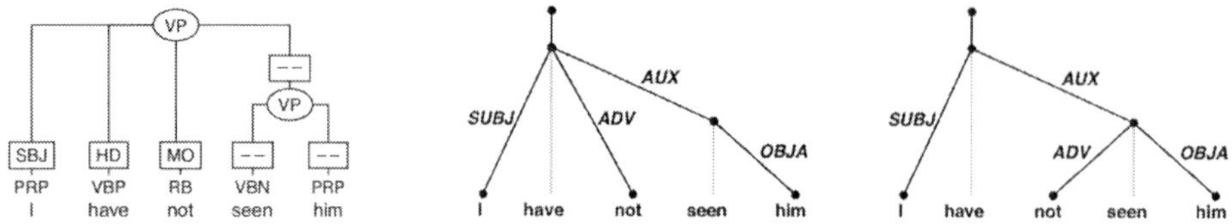

Figure 1: Example of ambiguity arising only in dependency representation [Daum et al., 2004]

1.2 Dependency representation

In recent years, dependency grammar has seen a dramatic increase in interest, likely due to a number of appealing properties of the representation. In comparison to phrase structure grammar, dependency structures provide a relatively direct encoding of predicate-argument structure, which is relevant to subsequent analyses [Nivre, 2005]. Dependency representation is arguably better suited for languages with flexible word order. Additionally, having no non-terminal nodes, dependency structures are often perceived as leaving room for less ambiguity as well as being more computationally manageable.

Certainly, dependency representation has drawbacks of its own in terms of ambiguity, some of which are specific to dependency representation. In particular, Figure 1 shows a construction with an unambiguous constituent structure, which in dependency space is ambiguous with respect to the attachment of the adverb [Daum et al., 2004].

Furthermore, dependency structure allows for a number of ways to represent coordinated phrases, some having the *coordinating conjunction as head* (CCH) of the coordinate structure, and a special dependency label *CJT* that does not describe the grammatical function of the conjuncts (Figure 2a). Another option is having the *coordinating conjunction as dependent* (CCD) of one of the conjuncts, thus allowing one conjunct to occur with a dependency label denoting its grammatical function (Figure 2b). McDonald and Nivre [2007] offer a thorough review of these and other candidate analyses in use. Unfortunately, none of the conceivable representations are unproblematic from a linguistic perspective [Daum et al., 2004], or offer the same transparency as the coordination rules of CCG do [Boonkwan, 2009].

Nonetheless, given the availability of generally applicable, trainable dependency parsers, and reports of beneficial applications of dependency analysis in tasks such as word-alignment [Ma et al., 2008] and reordering [Chang et al., 2009] for statistical machine translation, a dependency treebank of good quality is a highly desirable resource.

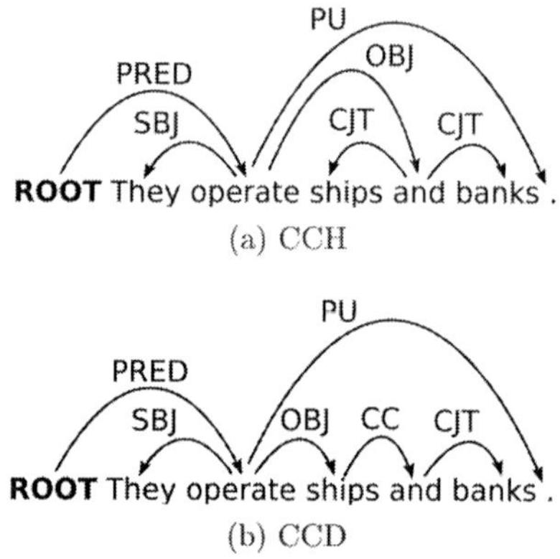

Figure 2: Two possible analyses of a coordination [Kübler et al., 2009]

1.3 Outline

The rest of the paper is organised as follows. In Section 2 we briefly review other works dealing with similar transformations, before presenting the approach taken in this work in Section 3. Section 4 describes the experimental setting and results. A discussion follows in Section 5, and conclusions in Section 6 .

2 Related work

In preparation for the CoNLL-X shared task on dependency parsing [Buchholz and Marsi, 2006], a number dependency trees were derived from a number of constituency-based phrase structure treebanks, most of which have grammatical function (e.g. "subject" and "object") as part of the annotation. The conversion process for such treebanks would involve a *head table* with rules of the form

- "the head child of a VP/clause is the child with the HD/predicator/hd/Head function" and
- "[the dependency label] for a token is the function of the biggest constituent of which this token is the lexical head".

The case of the Thai CG bank is different, as it does not directly contain any grammatical functions. On the other hand, identifying head tokens is relatively straight-forward when augmenting the CG annotation with dependency directions.

Chanev et al. [2006] faced a similar situation in their transformation of the BulTreeBank to dependency representation. Heads were first identified from explicitly stated rules in a head table. Lacking explicit grammatical functions in the source treebank, they explored a heuristic rule-based approach for the labeling with a *dependency table*, containing rules based on parent constituents. Although good results are achieved, they report of errors like mistaken subjects and objects.

3 Methodology

The situation with the Thai CG bank is a little different. Together with a set of combinatory grammar rules, the CG type tags and bracketing present in the treebank unambiguously specify the constituent structure of the treebank sentences. When the CG type tags are augmented with dependency directions, a dependency tree can be derived with relative ease from the CG-based constituents. Grammatical functions, however, are not immediately evident from the CG trees.

We first describe a relatively straight-forward method for deriving the dependency trees, and next consider the more daunting task of assigning functional labels to the dependency arcs. Figure 3 shows a schematical overview of the proposed method.

3.1 Terminology

For any given CG type t, we use the *arity* (admittedly a bit sloppily) to denote the ordered list of arguments expected by a type. The arity of the type `s\np/ws/np` is thus `/np`, `/ws` and `\np` — that is,

- a noun phrase from the right, followed by
- a subordinate clause beginning with the Thai word •• ("that", subordinate clause marker), and
- another noun phrase from the left.

Complementary, we define the *yield* of t as the set of possible CG types which may result from functional application of a CG rule. The transitive verb type `s\np/np`, for example, yields

- `s\np` and
- `s`

after receiving a `np` to the right, and another `np` to the left, respectively. This is simply the basic combinatory CCG rules:

$$X/Y \quad Y \quad \Rightarrow \quad X$$
$$Y \quad X\backslash Y \quad \Rightarrow \quad X$$

Algorithm 1 Pseudo-code for propagating dependency directions to non-terminal nodes.

```
def propagateDirections(node):
  for child in node.children:
    propagateDirections(child)
  if node.hasDependencyDirection:
    return
  for child in node.children:
    if child.yields(node.type):
      node.depDirs = child.depDirs
      break
```

3.2 Dependency directions

The first transformation step, which can be regarded as a preprocessing step before the actual transformation, involves a lexical dictionary for assigning dependency directions to the CG types associated with the grammatical entities in the CG bank, falling back on a generic CG to CDG mapping in case of unknown words.

Note that only terminal nodes will have assigned dependency directions assigned by this procedure. Dependency directions are propagated to non-terminal nodes in a bottom-up fashion by the procedure `propagateDirections` (Algorithm 1). In identifying which child to adopt dependency directions from, the parent node type is checked against the yield of each child node.

3.3 Head finding

Dependency arcs are assigned by a procedure that implements the CDG dependency derivation rules introduced by Boonkwan and Steedman [2011] (motivated by Collins, 1999). The idea is to trace the derivation implied by the CG rules, registering the dependency relations specified by the CDG-augmentation along the way.

The derivation rules handled are as follows. Let $c : d$ signify a CDG type c and a dependency structure d, and the notion $h(\mathrm{d}_1) \rightarrow h(\mathrm{d}_2)$ represent a dependency arc between the head of d_1 and the head of d_2 (with $h(\mathrm{d}_1)$ governing $h(\mathrm{d}_2)$) . Then the derivation rules are:

$$\mathrm{X}/\!<\!\mathrm{Y}{:}\mathrm{d}_1 \quad \mathrm{Y}{:}\mathrm{d}_2 \quad \Rightarrow \quad h(\mathrm{d}_1) \leftarrow h(\mathrm{d}_2)$$
$$\mathrm{X}/\!>\!\mathrm{Y}{:}\mathrm{d}_1 \quad \mathrm{Y}{:}\mathrm{d}_2 \quad \Rightarrow \quad h(\mathrm{d}_1) \rightarrow h(\mathrm{d}_2)$$
$$\mathrm{Y}{:}\mathrm{d}_1 \quad \mathrm{X}\backslash\!<\!\mathrm{Y}{:}\mathrm{d}_2 \quad \Rightarrow \quad h(\mathrm{d}_1) \leftarrow h(\mathrm{d}_2)$$
$$\mathrm{Y}{:}\mathrm{d}_1 \quad \mathrm{X}\backslash\!>\!\mathrm{Y}{:}\mathrm{d}_2 \quad \Rightarrow \quad h(\mathrm{d}_1) \rightarrow h(\mathrm{d}_2)$$

In a simple example, *Mary*[np] *drinks*[$\mathtt{s}\backslash<\mathtt{np}/>\mathtt{np}$] *fresh*[$\mathtt{np}/<\mathtt{np}$] *milk*[np], *fresh* would combine with *milk*, yielding an `np` and a dependency arc specifying *milk* as head of *fresh*.

In addition to the standard combinatory rules for forward and backward functional application above, the Thai CG bank makes use of a CCG-style *serialisation* rule to handle e.g. serial verb

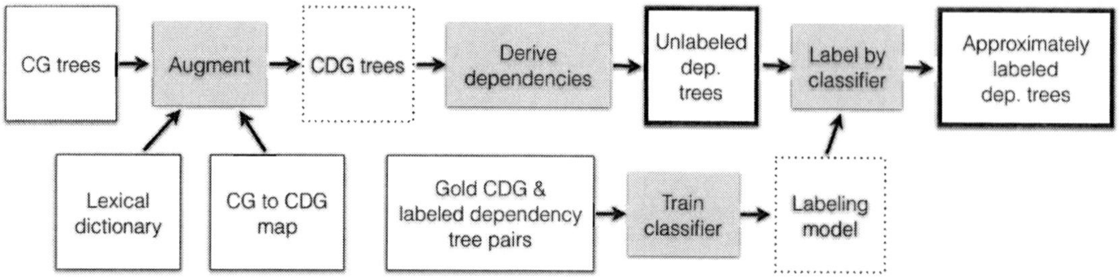

Figure 3: Transformation overview

constructions, which are used in Thai (and Chinese) to express serial or consecutive events. As Boonkwan [2009], we take the notion of a *serial verb construction* to mean a series of verbs or verb phrases without explicit connectives marked with (or understood to have) the same grammatical categories, and sharing at least one common argument, typically a subject.

As an example, the verbs •••• ("examine") and •• ("find") occur serially in the following sentence[3] from the CG bank, indicating a resultative course of events [Thepkanjana and Uehara, 2009]:

••••••••••••••••••••••••••••
•••••••

(**Lit**: scientist/N examine/V find/V virus/N corona/N in/PP civet/N)

"The scientist examined the civet and found coronavirus."

We introduce a generalised derivation rule for serial constructions which simply designates the head of the first dependency structure as governing the head of the following dependency structure:

$$\mathrm{X{:}d_1}\ \ \mathrm{X{:}d_2} \quad \Rightarrow \quad h(\mathrm{d_1}) \rightarrow h(\mathrm{d_2})$$

The rule is generalised in the sense that it handles *serial noun constructions* as well as serial verb constructions.

Further CCG-style combinatory rules, such as functional composition and type raising, are not currently in use in the Thai CG bank, and therefore not handled by the transformation.

An outline of the head finding procedure is given as Algorithm 2. Intuitively, the algorithm proceeds by, for each node in turn, beginning at the terminal nodes, identifying sibling nodes which satisfy the arity of the of the node CG type. For each sibling node satisfying an argument, the dependency derivation rule is applied and the sibling is removed.

[3]Artificial word boundaries inserted for clarity.

Algorithm 2 Pseudo-code for the head-finding procedure.

```
def assignHeads(node):
  for c in node.nonterminalChildren:
    assignHeads(c)
  for c in node.terminalChildren:
    assignHeads(c)
  for arg in node.type.arguments:
    if arg.side == 'right':
      sibl = node.rightSiblings.first
    else
      sibl = node.leftSiblings.last
    break unless arg.matches(sibl)
    if arg.side == 'right':
      if arg.dependencyDir == '>':
        registerHead(sibl, node)
      else: # <
        registerHead(node, sibl)
      node.rightSiblings.shift
    else: # left
      if arg.dependencyDir == '>':
        registerHead(node, sibl)
      else: # <
        registerHead(sibl, node)
      node.leftSiblings.pop
```

It is worth noting that while both terminal and non-terminal nodes are involved in this process, we are only interested in assigning dependency arcs to terminal nodes, as non-terminals are absent in the all-terminal dependency structure. This is ensured by an implementation detail of the procedure `registerHead` (omitted from Algorithm 2), in which non-terminal nodes act as proxies for their terminal heads.

3.4 Dependency labeling

Although the CDG-augmentation of the CG treebank implies a dependency structure for each sentence, there are no immediate clues available about the specific grammatical functions of dependency arcs. Obviously, there are some clear-cut cases: When a token with CDG type $((\mathtt{s}\backslash<\mathtt{np})\backslash>(\mathtt{s}\backslash<\mathtt{np}))\backslash<\mathtt{num}$ modifies a token with CDG type `num`, it must be an application of a *quantifier* (with dependency type "quan"), as exemplified in Figure 4.

Other cases are less obvious. Even when taking

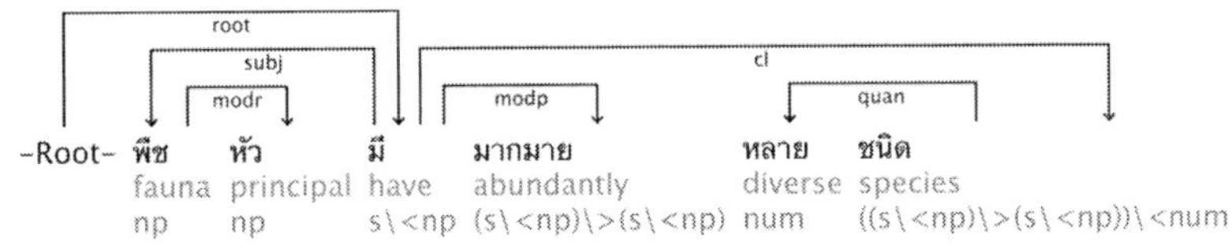

Figure 4: An unmistakable labeling case: Given the CDG types of •••• ("diverse") and ••• ("species"), the only dependency label supported by the examined data is "quan" (*quantifier*).

dependency direction and argument position into consideration, there are still cases with several possible dependency types, as shown in Figure 5.

While for many practical purposes an unlabeled dependency structure is sufficient, having proper dependency labels is nonetheless desirable. In lack of an exact transformation, the approach explored in this work relies instead on training a classifier to predict the correct dependency label given local features of the tokens involved, as they occur in the dependency structure derived from the CDG tree.

From a related work (manuscript in preparation), we have obtained a number of CDG trees from labeled dependency trees. Such pairs of *labeled* dependency trees and CDG trees can serve as training material for the label classifier.

We evaluate different feature sets for classification task. The basic feature set contains:

- CDG type of token and its head
- # of left siblings
- # of right siblings
- Dependency direction (L/R)
- Concatenations of token/head CDG and # of left siblings

Other feature sets extend the basic set including additional information:

+forms Token and head word form.

+POS(L) Part-of-speech tag for the token, as assigned by a learned part-of-speech tagger[4].

+POS(G) "Gold" part-of-speech tag as found in the labeled dependency tree.

4 Experiments

The Thai CG bank made available for this research contains 1,428 phrases with corresponding CG trees. Trees are mostly medium to low in token count, with 49 single-token trees, and the longest phrase having 9 tokens. Median phrase length is 3

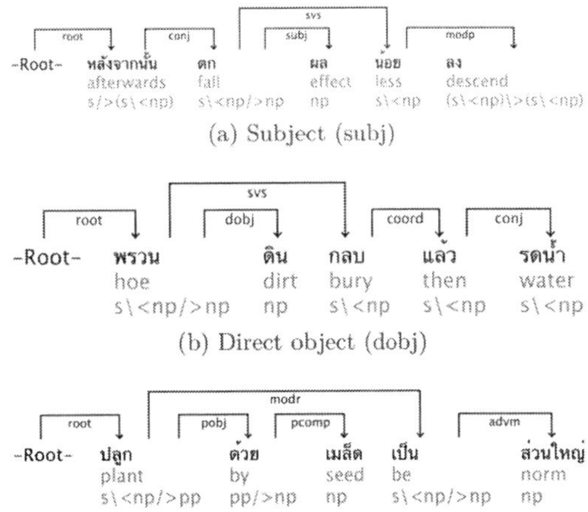

(a) Subject (subj)

(b) Direct object (dobj)

(c) adverbialiser (advm)

Figure 5: Different labeling of left-pointing dependency arcs with $\mathtt{s}\backslash < \mathtt{np}/ > \mathtt{np}$ as head CDG type and np as dependent CDG type. See Figure 6 for depency type abbreviations.

tokens. With a total token count of 5,143 tokens, the arithmetic mean length is 3.60.

As there is no explicit sentence boundary marker in Thai [Satayamas and Kawtrakul, 2004], it is often unclear what constitutes a sentence. Thus, rather than ordinary sentences, the treebank contains phrases of different types, reflecting the partitioning of token sequences made by the treebank annotators for the purpose of treebanking:

- 539 verb phrases or subject-omitted phrases (s\np),
- 363 sentences (s),
- 372 noun phrases (np) and
- 4 prepositional phrases (pp).

The lexical dictionary used contains possible CDG types for 38.250 word forms, with an average of 2 types listed per word form. For six of the word forms, the dictionary lists several possible dependency directions for a single CG type. These confusable CDG types and the dictionary entries they occur for are listed in Table 1.

An example sentence from the treebank affected by the ambiguous mapping of the adverb •••••

[4] SVMTool [Giménez and Marquez, 2004], trained on the Orchid corpus [Sornlertlamvanich et al., 1997].

Word form(s)	CG type	Possible CDG equivalents	Interpretation
••	$(s\backslash np)/(s\backslash np)$	$(s\backslash < np)/ > (s\backslash < np)$ $(s\backslash < np)/ < (s\backslash < np)$	Adverb "please" Auxiallary verb "should"
••••• ("at that time") •••••("at present") ••••• ("at that moment") •••••("this moment")	s/s	$s/ > s$ $s/ < s$	Conjunction Adverb of time
••	$np\backslash np/np$	$np\backslash > np/ > np$ $np\backslash < np/ > np$	Preposition "with" Conjunction "and"

Table 1: Entries in the lexical dictionary which are ambiguous with respect to dependency direction

("at present") is [5]:

••••••••••••••••••••

(**Lit:** this-moment/ADV she/PRON "-ing"/AUX busy/ADJ very/ADV)

"At this moment she is being very busy."

Examples of the latter two ambiguity classes of the lexical dictionary (Table 1) were not encountered in the treebank — i.e. the affected word forms do not occur with an ambiguous CG type. In dealing with these ambiguous entries in the lexical dictionary, we simply (and naively) choose the first mapping option.

The generic CG to CDG mapping, used in addition to the lexical dictionary as fallback for word forms not found in the lexical dictionary, also exhibits some degree of ambiguity. The seven CG types with multiple possible CDG equivalents are listed in Table 2.

In evaluating the classification-based approach to assigning dependency labels, a sample of 678 labeled dependency edges from the NAiST dependency treebank [Wacharamanotham et al., 2007] was used, along with corresponding CDG trees. The feature sets suggested in section 3.4 on page 4 were evaluated with four different classifiers[6] (see Table 3).

5 Discussion

Transforming CDG-augmented CG trees to unlabeled dependency trees was successful. In this work, the issue of ambiguous CDG types affects only a very small number of trees, but remains an issue to be aware of.

[5]The Thai auxillary verb •••• indicates the present participle, meaning "in the act of", similar to the English suffix, "-ing". Artificial word boundaries are inserted for clarity.

[6]Experiments with the learners were done using leave-one-out cross-validation, with the exception of LibSVM, which was run using the standard K-fold cross-validation of the easy.py script [Chang and Lin, 2001].

CG type	Possible CDG equivalents
$np\backslash np/np$	$np\backslash > np/ > np$ $np\backslash < np/ > np$
s/s	$s/ > s$ $s/ < s$
$s\backslash s$	$s\backslash > s$ $s\backslash < s$
$(s\backslash np)/(s\backslash np)$	$(s\backslash < np)/ > (s\backslash < np)$ $(s\backslash < np)/ < (s\backslash < np)$
$s/(s\backslash np)$	$s/ > (s\backslash < np)$ $s/ < (s\backslash < np)$
$s\backslash(s\backslash np)$	$s\backslash < (s\backslash < np)$ $s\backslash > (s\backslash < np)$
$s/(s\backslash np)/np$	$s/ > (s\backslash np)/ > np$ $s/ < (s\backslash np)/ > np$

Table 2: Cases of CD to CDG mappings which are ambigous with respect to dependency direction

For dependency labeling, only a small amount of training data (in the form of sentences with both CDG and labeled dependency analyses) was available for this prelimenary experiment. Using this, dependency labels were not reliably recoverable (76.5% label accuracy). However, it seems hopeful that better recovery of dependency labels can be obtained with this approach once more training material become available.

Head and dependent word forms, as well as part-of-speech tags, were beneficial as added features for the label classifier, resulting in a substantial reduction in error rate — from 0.357 to 0.235 ($\approx$ 34%).

On the other hand, rather than the approximated classfier-based approach to labeling, one could consider settling for an exact but partial labeling by only assigning those dependency labels which unambigously arise from tuples of head and dependent CDG types. However, the dependency labels obtainable with absolute certainty in this way are often of the less interesting kind — e.g. "conj" for a $s\backslash < np$ governed by a $s/ > (s\backslash < np)$ — while more useful labels remain ambiguous.

Classifier	Basic	+forms	+POS(L)	+POS(G)	+POS(L) & +forms	+POS(G) & +forms
Random Forest	61.9%	69.6%	66.1%	68.9%	72.9%	71.8%
LibSVM	64.3%	73.9%	66.1%	70.2%	74.5%	**76.5%**
Nearest Neighbors	60.5%	64.8%	62.4%	64.5%	70.5%	70.4%
Naive Bayes	60.6%	63.7%	61.7%	65.8%	63.7%	66.2%

Table 3: Accuracy of different classifiers and feature sets in recovering the correct dependency labels

Complements *subject* (subj) • *clausal subject* (csubj) • *direct object* (dobj) • *indirect object* (iobj) • *prepositional object* (pobj) • *prepositional complement* (pcomp) • *subject or object predicative* (pred) • *clausal predicative* (cpred) • *conjunction* (conj) • *subordinating conjunction* (sconj) • *nominaliser* (nom) • *adverbialiser* (advm)

Adjuncts *parenthetical modifier* (modp) • *restrictive modifier* (modr) • *tense modifier* (modt) • *mood modifier* (modm) • *aspect modifier* (moda) • *locative modifier* (modl) • *parenthetical apposition* (appa) • *restrictive apposition* (appr) • *relative clause modification* (rel) • *determiner* (det) • *quantifier* (quan) • *classifier* (cl) • *coordination* (coord) • *negation* (neg) • *punctuation* (punc) • *double preposition* (dprep) • *parallel serial verb* (svp) • *sequence serial verb* (svs)

Figure 6: Dependency types from the annotation guidelines [Sudprasert, 2008] for the NAiST dependency treebank.

6 Conclusion and future work

In the process, a considerable amount of syntactical and annotational errors in the Thai CG bank were identified and corrected. The authors are of the belief that this work has not only provided a means for continual expansion of resources for Thai natural language processing, but also helped improve the quality the existing CG resource.

As a related work (manuscript in preparation) progresses, more CDG trees for labeled NAiST dependency trees will become available. With this extra training material, the learned classifier used for labeling in this work should become more reliable. Further improvement might also be achievable from an expanded feature set, including for example the argument position (in addition to side) and one or two generations of grandparent nodes.

Further development of the Thai CDG formalism is also expected, in particular for the analysis of sentence-like noun phrases. This will likely need special handling in the dependency representation as well. Currently, the NAiST annotation guidelines do not specify a label for this phenomenon.

Acknowledgements

The authors wish to thank the NAiST unit of Kasetsart University and the HLT Lab of NECTEC for making their treebanks available for experiments.

References

K. Ajdukiewicz. Die syntaktische konnexität. *Studia Philosophica*, 1(1):27, 1935.

P. Boonkwan. A memory-based approach to the treatment of serial verb construction in combinatory categorial grammar. In *Proceedings of the 12th Conference of the European Chapter of the Association for Computational Linguistics: Student Research Workshop*, page 10–18, 2009.

P. Boonkwan and M. Steedman. Grammar induction from text using small syntactic prototypes. In *Proceedings of the 5th International Joint Conference on Natural Language Processing (to appear)*, Chiang Mai, 2011.

S. Buchholz and E. Marsi. CoNLL-X shared task on multilingual dependency parsing. In *Tenth Conference on Computational Natural Language Learning*, page 149, 2006.

A. Chanev, K. Simov, P. Osenova, and S. Marinov. Dependency conversion and parsing of the BulTreeBank. In *Proc. of the LREC-Workshop Merging and Layering Linguistic Information*, 2006.

C. Chang and C. Lin. LIBSVM: a library for support vector machines, 2001. URL `http://www.csie.ntu.edu.tw/cjlin/libsvm`.

P. C Chang, H. Tseng, D. Jurafsky, and C. D Manning. Discriminative reordering with chinese grammatical relations features. In *Proceedings of the Third Workshop on Syntax and Structure in Statistical Translation*, page 51–59, 2009.

M. Collins. *Head-driven statistical models for natural language parsing*. PhD thesis, University of Pennsylvania, 1999.

M. Daum, K. Foth, and W. Menzel. Automatic transformation of phrase treebanks to dependency trees. In *Proceedings of LREC*, 2004.

J. Giménez and L. Marquez. SVMTool: a general POS tagger generator based on support vector machines. In *In Proceedings of the 4th International Conference on Language Resources and Evaluation*, 2004.

S. Kübler, R. McDonald, and J. Nivre. Dependency parsing. *Synthesis Lectures on Human Language Technologies*, 2(1):1–127, 2009.

Y. Ma, S. Ozdowska, Y. Sun, and A. Way. Improving word alignment using syntactic dependencies. In *Proceedings of the ACL-08: HLT Second Workshop on Syntax and Structure in Statistical Translation (SSST-2)*, page 69–77, 2008.

R. McDonald and J. Nivre. Characterizing the errors of data-driven dependency parsing models. In *Proc. of the Joint Conf. on Empirical Methods in Natural Language Processing and Computational Natural Language Learning (EMNLP-CoNLL)*, 2007.

J. Nivre. Dependency grammar and dependency parsing. *MSI report*, 5133, 2005.

T. Ruangrajitpakorn, K. Trakultaweekoon, and T. Supnithi. A syntactic resource for thai: CG treebank. In *Proceedings of the 7th Workshop on Asian Language Resources*, page 96–101, 2009.

V. Satayamas and A. Kawtrakul. Wide-Coverage grammar extraction from thai treebank. In *Proceedings of Papillon 2004 Workshops on Multilingual Lexical Databases*, 2004.

V. Sornlertlamvanich, T. Charoenporn, and H. Isahara. ORCHID: thai part-of-speech tagged corpus. Technical Report TR-NECTEC-1997-001, 1997.

M. Steedman. *The syntactic process*, volume 131. MIT Press, 2000.

S. Sudprasert. Dependency annotation guideline for thai, version 1.4 (in thai). Technical report, 2008. URL `http://naist.cpe.ku.ac.th/tred/`.

K. Thepkanjana and S. Uehara. Resultative constructions with "implied-result" and "entailed-result" verbs in thai and english: a contrastive study. *Linguistics*, 47(3):589–618, 2009. ISSN 0024-3949. URL `http://www.thefreelibrary.com/-a0204693751`.

C. Wacharamanotham, M. Suktarachan, and A. Kawtrakul. The development of web-based annotation system for thai treebank. page 305, Thailand, 2007. URL `http://naist.cpe.ku.ac.th/tred/`.

U. Warotamasikkhadit. Fronting and backing topicalization in thai. *Mon-Khmer Studies*, 27: 303–6, 1997.

Parse Reranking Based on Higher-Order Lexical Dependencies

Zhiguo Wang and **Chengqing Zong**
National Laboratory of Pattern Recognition
Institute of Automation, Chinese Academy of Sciences, Beijing, China, 100190
{zgwang, cqzong}@nlpr.ia.ac.cn

Abstract

Existing work shows that lexical dependencies are helpful for constituent tree parsing. However, only first-order lexical dependencies have been employed and investigated in previous work. In this paper, we propose a method to employing higher-order[1] lexical dependencies for constituent tree evaluation. Our method is based on a parse reranking framework, which provides a constrained search space (via *N*-best lists or parse forests) and enables our parser to employ relatively complicated dependency features. We evaluate our models on the Penn Chinese Treebank. The highest F_1 score reaches 85.74%, thus outperforming all previously reported state-of-the-art systems. The dependency accuracy of constituent trees generated by our parser has been significantly improved as well.

1 Introduction

The most commonly used grammar for constituent structure parsing is probabilistic context-free grammar (PCFG). However, as demonstrated in Klein and Manning (2003a), PCFG estimated straightforwardly from Treebank does not perform well. The reason is that the basic PCFG has certain recognized drawbacks: its independence assumption is too strong, and it lacks of lexical conditioning (Jurafsky and Martin, 2008). To address these drawbacks, several variants of PCFG-based models have been proposed (Klein and Manning, 2003a; Matsuzaki et al., 2005; Petrov et al., 2006; Petrov and Klein, 2007). Lexicalized PCFG (LPCFG) (Collins, 1999; Charniak, 2000; Bikel, 2004) is a representative work that tries to ameliorate the deficiency of lexical conditioning. In LPCFG, non-terminals are annotated with lexical heads and the probabilities of CFG rules are estimated conditioned upon these lexical heads. Thus LPCFG becomes sensitive to lexical heads, and its performance is improved. However, the information provided by lexical heads is limited. To obtain higher parsing performance, we must seek additional information. We believe that dependency trees are good candidates because they encode grammatical relations between words and provide much more lexical conditioning than lexical heads for PCFG.

Dependency trees are usually factored into sets of lexical dependency parts for evaluation. The order of a lexical dependency part can be defined according to the number of dependency arcs it contains. For example, in Figure 1, *dependency* is first-order, *sibling* and *grandchild* are second-order and *grand-sibling* and *tri-sibling* are third-order. During the past few years, higher-order[1] lexical dependencies have been successfully used for dependency parsing (McDonald et al., 2005; McDonald and Pereira, 2006; Koo and Collins, 2010). But for constituent tree evaluation, only first-order (bigram) lexical dependencies have been used (Collins, 1996; Klein and Manning, 2003a; Collins and Koo, 2005). However, first-order lexical dependency parts are quite limited and thus lose much of the contextual information within the dependency tree. To improve parsing performance, we propose to evaluate constituent trees with higher-order lexical dependencies.

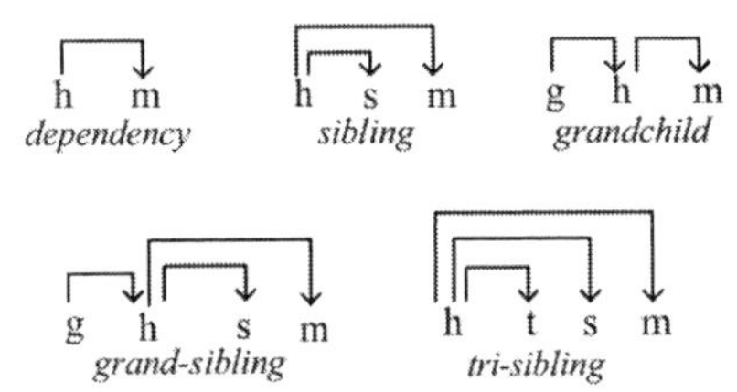

Figure 1. Lexical dependency types. The lower-case letters h, m, s, g are words in a sentence.

In this paper, we propose a method for evaluating constituent trees using higher-order lexical dependencies within a parse reranking framework. We evaluate our method on the Penn Chinese Treebank (CTB). The F_1 score reaches 85.74%, thus outperforming the best previously reported systems. Thanks to the lexical dependencies, the dependency accuracy of the generated constituent trees is improved as well. These experimental results show that higher-order lexi-

[1] Lexical dependency part which contains more than one dependency arcs is called higher-order, e.g., *sibling*, *grandchild* and *grand-sibling* in Figure 1.

cal dependencies are highly beneficial for constituent tree evaluation.

The remainder of this paper is organized as follows: Section 2 briefly reviews related work and proposes our ideas. Section 3 describes our parsing approach. Section 4 describes our parse reranking algorithms based on higher-order lexical dependencies. In Section 5, we describe our training algorithms. We discuss and analyze our experiments in Section 6. Finally, we conclude and mention future work in Section 7.

2 Related Work and Our Ideas

Over the past few years, two kinds of *parse reranking* methods have been proposed. The first is *N*-best reranking (Charniak and Johnson, 2005; Collins and Koo, 2005). In this method, an existing generative parser is used to enumerate *N*-best parse trees for an input sentence, and then a reranking model is used to rescore the *N*-best lists with the help of various sorts of features. However, the *N*-best reranking method suffers from the limited scope of the *N*-best list in that potentially good alternatives may have been ruled out. The second method, called the forest reranking model, was proposed by Huang (2008). In Huang's method, a forest, instead of an *N*-best list, is generated first. Then a beam search algorithm is used to generate *N*-best sub-trees for each node in bottom-up order and the best-first sub-tree of the root node is chosen as the final parse tree.

In recent years, there have been many attempts to use dependency trees for constituent parsing. All these approaches can be classified into three types. The first type is *dependency-driven* constituent parsing (Hall et al., 2007; Hall and Nivre, 2008). Given an input sentence, this approach first parses it into a labeled dependency tree (with complex arc labels, which makes it possible to recover the constituent tree) and then transforms the dependency tree into a constituent tree. The second approach is *dependency-constrained* constituent parsing (Xia and Palmer, 2001; Xia et al., 2008; Wang and Zhang, 2010; Wang and Zong, 2010). In this approach, dependency trees, once generated, are used to constrain the search space of a constituent parser. The third approach is *dependency-based* constituent parsing (Collins, 1996; Klein and Manning, 2003b). In this approach, the constituent tree is evaluated with the help of its corresponding lexical dependencies.

All three existing approaches have certain limitations. In the first approach, the dependency-driven constituent parser is not constrained by the Treebank grammar, so a constituent tree transformed from its corresponding dependency tree may contain context-free productions not seen in the Treebank grammar. Although this limitation may not affect the parsing F_1 score, it often has undesirable effects on applications. For the second approach, if the generated dependency tree includes some erroneous parts, the correct constituent tree may be pruned out directly, leaving no way to recover the correct tree again. The third approach parses sentences making use of first-order lexical dependencies only. As mentioned, first-order lexical dependencies are quite limited, and thus may lose much information about the grammatical relations between words. Consequently, the performance improvement of this approach is limited as well.

To overcome the drawbacks of the existing approaches, we propose to evaluate constituent trees using higher-order lexical dependencies within a parse reranking framework. Our approach has the following advantages: 1) It utilizes the higher-order lexical dependencies, which provide more contextual information within the dependency tree for constituent tree evaluation; 2) the parse reranking method provides high-quality candidates (*N*-best list or parse forest) which yields a small search space, enabling the use of relatively complicated features.

3 Our Approach

For a sentence x, we define constituent parsing as a search for the highest-scoring parse c^* of x:

$$c^* = \arg\max_{c \in GEN(x)} Score(x,c) \qquad (1)$$

Where, $GEN(x)$ is a set of candidate parsers for x, and $Score(x,c)$ evaluates the event that tree c is the parse of sentence x.

In order to evaluate c with higher-order lexical dependencies, we define:

$$Score(x,c) = \Phi(x,c)\cdot\overline{\alpha} = \sum_i \alpha_i \Phi_i(x,c) \quad (2)$$

Where, Φ maps each $(x,c) \in X \times C$ to lexical dependency feature vector $\Phi(x,y) \in \Re^d$, and $\overline{\alpha} \in \Re^d$ is the corresponding weight vector.

3.1 Representation of Constituent Tree with Labeled Dependency Tree

The discriminative parsing model in Eq. (1) takes lexical dependencies as features, so we must design a method of representing constituent trees

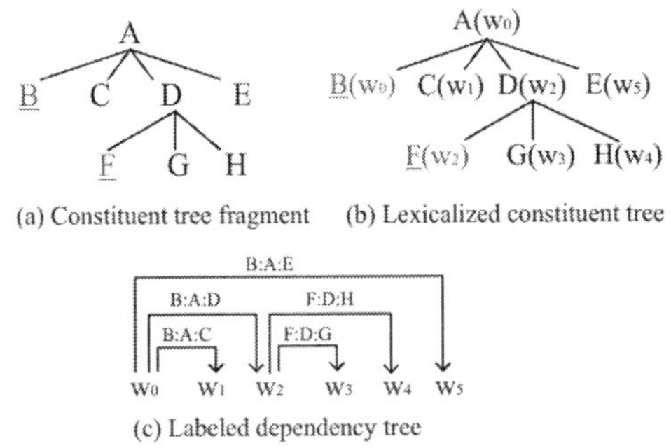

Figure 2. Representation of constituent tree with labeled dependency tree

with associated dependency trees. Our method includes the following two steps:

Step 1: ***Lexicalize the constituent tree***, i.e. annotate each node in the constituent tree with its head-word. First, find the head-child of each non-terminal node using a head percolation table (Yamada and Matsumoto, 2003). For example, in Figure 2(a), node B is identified as the head-child of rule A $\rightarrow$ B C D E. Then the head-words propagate up through the leaf nodes and each parent receives its head-word from its head-child. For example, in Figure 2(b), w_0 is propagated up from node B to A. According to this procedure, we can get the lexicalized constituent tree (shown in Figure 2(b)) for the constituent fragment shown in Figure 2(a).

Step 2: ***Transform the lexicalized tree into a labeled dependency tree***. First, let the head-word of each non-head-child depend on the head-word of the head-child for each rule. For example, in Figure 2(b) for rule A $\rightarrow$ B C D E, the head words of non-head-child (node C, D and E) which are w_1, w_2 and w_5 should depend on w_0 which is the head word of head-child (node B). In order to encoding the syntactic symbols in the constituent tree into dependency tree, we annotate each dependency arc with a label $N_h : P : N_m$, where N_h is the head-child's syntactic category, P is the parent's syntactic category and N_m is the non-head-child's syntactic category. For example, in Figure 2(c), the dependency arc between w_1 and w_0 is built through rule A $\rightarrow$ B C D E, where w_0 associates with B, w_1 associates with C and the parent node is A, so we can annotate the dependency arc with B:A:C. According to the procedure, the lexicalized tree in Figure 2(b) can be transformed into the labeled dependency tree shown in Figure 2(c).

3.2 Mapping Higher-Order Lexical Dependencies into Feature Vectors

To map lexical dependencies into feature vectors, we define certain feature templates, as shown in Table 1. We work with binary indicator features[2] for each lexical dependency. The feature vector $\Phi(x, C)$ of constituent tree C can be calculated through the dependency tree D transformed from C using the follow formula:

$$\Phi(x, C) = \sum_{d \in S(D)} \phi(d) \qquad (3)$$

In this formula $S(D)$ is a set of all the lexical dependencies extracted from D, and d is a lexical dependency in $S(D)$. The function ϕ is used to map each lexical dependency d into feature vector according to the templates in Table 1.

Algorithm 1: Constituent Tree Evaluating

```
function Eval(C)
  for P ∈ C in bottom up topological order do
    EvalSubTree (C_P)
return Score(C)

procedure EvalSubTree (C_P)
  ▷ Assume the constituent is P → N_1 ··· N_n
  Find the head-child N_h for P
  W_P ← W_{N_h}
  ▷ Building D_P
  for N_i ∈ {N_1,..., N_n} \ N_h do
      Link D_{N_h} and D_{N_i} with a dependency arc
      Annotate the arc with label N_h : P : N_i
  Make the root of D_{N_h} as D_P 's root
  Extract all lexical dependencies for P
        and map them into feature vector Φ(P)
  Score(C_P) = Φ(P)·ᾱ + Σ_{i=1}^{n} Score(C_{N_i})
```

4 Parse Reranking Algorithms

A critical problem when training the discriminative model in Eq. (1) is the extensive training time required, in which we must parse all the sentences in the training set repeatedly. In this paper, we adopt an approximate method: parse reranking. In parse reranking, $GEN(S)$ in Eq. (1) is an N-best list or a parse forest which provides a small and well-formed search space for constituent parsing. Given this small space, we can exploit higher-order lexical dependencies efficiently.

[2] Binary indicator features are defined as follows: if a certain feature is observed in an instance, the value of that feature is 1; otherwise, the value is 0.

h m *dependency*	**Basic Uni-gram Features** h , POS(h), N(h) h , POS(h) h , N(h) m , POS(m), N(m) m , POS(m) m , N(m) **Basic Bi-gram Features** P(m) , h , POS(h), N(h), m), POS(m), N(m) h , POS(h), N(h), m , POS(m), N(m) P(m) ,POS(h), N(h), POS(m), N(m) P(m) , h , N(h), m , N(m) P(m) ,h , POS(h), m , POS(m) P(m) ,h , m P(m) , POS(h),POS(m) P(m) , N(h), N(m) **Surrounding Word POS Features** P(m), N(h), POS(h), N(m), POS(m), POS(h)+1, POS(m)-1 P(m), N(h), POS(h), N(m), POS(m), POS(h)-1, POS(m)-1 P(m), N(h), POS(h), N(m), POS(m), POS(h)+1, POS(m)+1 P(m), N(h), POS(h), N(m), POS(m), POS(h)-1, POS(m)+1	h s m *sibling*	POS(h),N(h),POS(s),N(s),P(s),POS(m),N(m),P(m) POS(h),N(h),N(s),P(s),N(m),P(m) POS(h),N(h),POS(s),P(s),POS(m),P(m) POS(h),N(h),POS(s),N(s),POS(m),N(m) POS(h),POS(s),POS(m) N(h),N(s),N(m) N(h),P(s),P(m)
		g h m *grandchild*	POS(g),N(g),POS(h),N(h),P(h),POS(m),N(m),P(m) POS(g),N(g),N(h),P(h),N(m),P(m) POS(g),N(g),POS(h),P(h),POS(m),P(m) POS(g),N(g),POS(h),N(h),POS(m),N(m) POS(g),POS(h),POS(m) N(g),N(h),N(m) N(g),P(h),P(m)
		g h s m *grand-sibling*	POS(g),POS(h),POS(s),POS(m) N(g),N(h),N(s),N(m) N(g),P(h),P(s),P(m)
		h t s m *tri-sibling*	POS(h),POS(t),POS(s),POS(m) N(h),N(t),N(s),N(m) N(h),P(t),P(s),P(m)

Table 1. Feature templates of various lexical dependency types. The lowercase letters h, m, s, g are words in a sentence. POS(x) is x's POS tag. POS(x)+1 is the POS tag of the word to the right of x. POS(x)-1 is the POS tag of the word to the left of x. P(x), N(x) are syntactic categories of P and N_h (or N_m), which are annotated on dependency arcs (We ignore dependency arc labels in the table for simplicity. More details can be found in section 3.2).

4.1 *N*-best Reranking Based on Higher-Order Lexical Dependencies

The method of sub-section 3.1 determines that each constituent sub-tree must have a corresponding dependency sub-tree. Accordingly, we now describe an efficient algorithm for evaluating constituent trees with higher-order lexical dependencies. We define a quadruple $< C_N, D_N, score(C_N), W_N >$ for each non-terminal node N, in which C_N is the constituent sub-tree rooted at N; D_N is the dependency sub-tree transformed from C_N ; $score(C_N)$ is the score of C_N evaluated using Eq. (2); and W_N is the head-word of N in the tree.

Our algorithm (Algorithm 1) works bottom-up to fill $< C_N, D_N, score(C_N), W_N >$ for each node N. For a constituent P in the parse tree, we first find the head-child N_h for P (line 8), then propagate the head-word of N_h to P (line 9). To build D_P, we simply build dependency arcs for current constituent P ; then link D_{N_1}, …, D_{N_n} with these dependency arcs; and then let the root of D_{N_h} be D_P's root (line 11 to line 14). We extract all the lexical dependencies rooted at P's head-word W_P through D_P. For example, in Figure 2(b), all the lexical dependencies rooted at node A's head-word w_0 can be extracted from the dependency tree in Figure 2(c); and all the lexical dependencies have been shown in

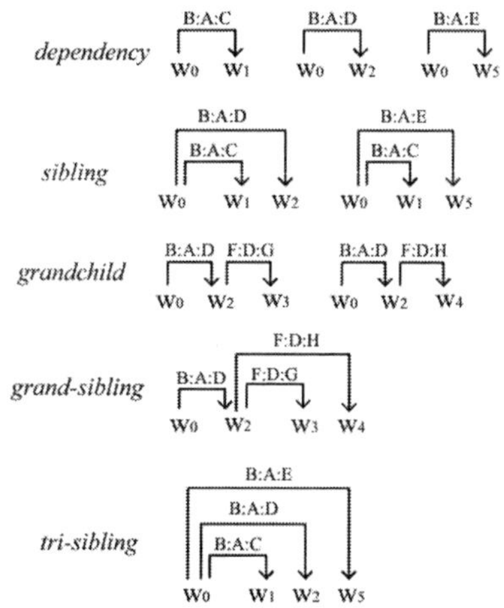

Figure 3. Lexical dependencies for w_0 in Figure 2(c).

Figure 3. Then we map the lexical dependencies into feature vectors and sum over them as the feature vector $\Phi(P)$ for P. Finally, we evaluate the score of C_P using formula (4) below:

$$Score(C_P) = \Phi(P) \cdot \vec{\alpha} + \sum_{i=1}^{n} Score(C_{N_i}) \quad (4)$$

4.2 Forest Reranking Based on Higher-Order Lexical Dependencies

As mentioned, *N*-best reranking suffers from the limited scope of *N*-best list. Forest reranking, by contrast, can rerank a packed forest of exponentially many parses, and thus provides a good way to overcome these limitations. Thus we also use the forest reranking method, based on higher-order lexical dependencies.

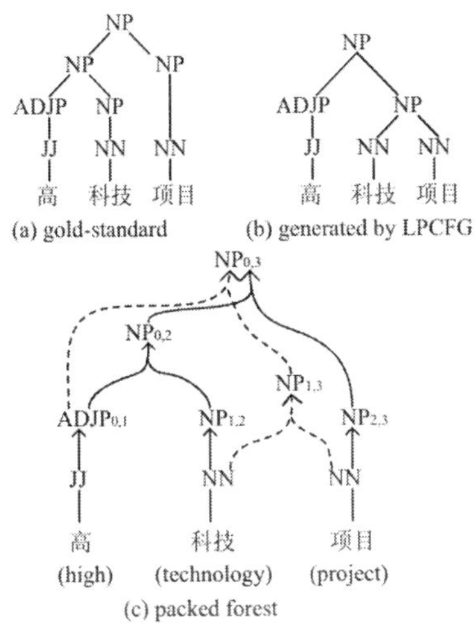

Figure 4. Constituent trees and forest

A forest is a compact representation of many parse trees. Figure 4(c) is a sample forest which is the compact representation of the constituent trees shown in Figures 4(a) and 4(b). To obtain forests, Huang (2008) tried to modify the Charniak parser to output forest directly. Inspired by parser combination methods (Sagae and Lavie, 2006; Fossum and Knight, 2009), we have designed a simple method of building forests starting from *N*-best lists. First, we convert each parse tree in an *N*-best list into context-free productions and label each constituent in each production with its span and syntactic category. Then these converted context-free productions are used to build the forest. For example, in Figure 4, given two candidates (Figure 4(a) and Figure 4(b)), we first convert them into context-free productions, e.g. $NP_{0,3} \rightarrow ADJP_{0,1}\ NP_{1,3}$, $NP_{0,3} \rightarrow NP_{0,2}\ NP_{2,3}$ and so on. Then we combine these productions into the forest shown in Figure 4(c). The recombined forest probably contains some parse trees that are not included in the *N*-best list, as will be shown in sub-section 6.1.

Our algorithm for forest reranking is similar to Algorithm 1. The only difference is that there may be more than one hyperedge for each node in a forest. So we make use of a beam search algorithm (Huang and Chiang, 2005) and store *N*-best sub-trees for each internal node. Finally, we choose the best-first sub-tree of the root node as the result.

5 Training Algorithm

The training task is to tune the parameter weights $\bar{\alpha}$ in Eq. (1) using the training examples as evidence. We employ the online-learning algorithm shown in Algorithm 2 because it has been proven

Algorithm 2:Generic online learning algorithm

1:**Input**: training data (x_t, c_t) for $t = 1 \ldots T$
2: $\bar{\alpha}^{(0)} \leftarrow 0$; $\mathbf{v} \leftarrow 0$; $i \leftarrow 0$ ▷ initial weights
3: **for** n in $1 \ldots N$ **do** ▷ N iterations
4: **for** t in $1 \ldots T$ **do** ▷ T training instances
5: $\bar{\alpha}^{(i+1)} \leftarrow$ update $\bar{\alpha}^{(i)}$ according to (x_t, c_t)
6: $\mathbf{v} \leftarrow \mathbf{v} + \bar{\alpha}^{(i+1)}$
7: $i \leftarrow i + 1$
8: $\bar{\alpha} \leftarrow \mathbf{v}/(N^*T)$ ▷ averaging weights
9: **return** $\bar{\alpha}$

to be effective and efficient in many studies (Collins, 2002; Collins and Roark, 2004; McDonald et al., 2005). For Algorithm 2, we define two parameter update strategies (line 5 in Algorithm 2) as follows.

The first strategy is *perceptron updating*. We first obtain the oracle tree c_t^+ that has the highest F_1 score according to the gold-standard tree c_t,

$$c_t^+ = \arg\max_{c \in GEN(x_t)} F_1(c, c_t) \quad (5)$$

Then we get the highest scoring tree $\hat{c}_t$ with current weights $\bar{\alpha}^{(i)}$,

$$\hat{c}_t = \arg\max_{c \in GEN(x_t)} \Phi(x_t, c) \cdot \bar{\alpha}^{(i)} \quad (6)$$

If $\hat{c}_t$ is not equal to c_t^+, the weights will be updated through

$$\bar{\alpha}^{(i+1)} \leftarrow \bar{\alpha}^{(i)} + \Phi(c_t^+) - \Phi(\hat{c}_t) \quad (7)$$

Otherwise, the current weights are kept.

Although the perceptron updating strategy works well, parameter updating must wait until the entire tree has been built. We believe that this strategy probably misses the best opportunity for parameter updating and introduces some noise into the updating procedure. So, inspired by Collins and Roark (2004), we propose an *early updating strategy* for forest reranking. The key idea is to insert the parameter updating procedure into the forest reranking procedure. We parse a forest bottom up with the current parameter $\bar{\alpha}^{(i)}$. When the best-first sub-tree $\hat{s}_N$ for internal node N is different from oracle sub-tree s_N^+, we stop the parsing procedure and update the parameters immediately using the following formula:

$$\bar{\alpha}^{(i+1)} \leftarrow \bar{\alpha}^{(i)} + \Phi(s_t^+) - \Phi(\hat{s}_t) .$$

Then we continue to parse the current forest with the newer parameters $\bar{\alpha}^{(i+1)}$. Unlike the perceptron updating strategy, this strategy updates parameters at the moment that an error sub-tree is built, and this is why we call it the *early updating* strategy.

6 Experiments and Analysis

We evaluate our method on the Penn Chinese Treebank Version 5.0 with the standard division: Art.301-325 as the development set, Art. 271-300 as the test set and others as the training set. All the F_1 scores are evaluated with EVALB[3].

6.1 To Obtain *N*-best Lists and Forests

We first employ existing parsers to generate *N*-best lists and then recombine the *N*-best lists into forests according to the method described in sub-section 4.2. We split the training set into 20 folds averagely and generate 50-best lists for one fold with both the Berkeley parser[4] and the Charniak parser[5] (trained on the remaining 19 folds) individually. The development set and the test set are parsed with models trained on the entire training set.

	Berkley(50)	Charniak(50)	Comb(100)
Nbest	89.13	89.20	**91.61**
Forest	90.22	90.38	**94.05**

Table 2. Oracle F_1 (%) of *N*-best lists and forests

The oracle F_1 scores of *N*-best lists and forests on test set are listed in Table 2, where 'Berkeley(50)' means the performance of 50-best lists from Berkeley parser; 'Charniak(50)' means the performance of 50-best list from Charniak parser; 'Comb(100)' means the performance of 100-best lists by combining the two 50-best lists; "Nbest" means the oracle F_1 of *N*-best lists; and "Forest" means the oracle F_1 of forests which are evaluated through the Forest Oracle Algorithm proposed in Huang (2008). In Table 2, we can see that the oracle F_1 scores of forests are much better than associated *N*-best lists. This result clearly demonstrates that the approach of obtaining forests by recombining *N*-best lists is effective.

6.2 Parameter Tuning on Development Set

We tuned some parameters manually for our models in the sub-section, including the number of iterations in the training algorithm, and the beam size *k* in the forest reranking algorithm. Models are trained with training set's 100-best lists and evaluated on development set's 100-best lists.

The F_1 score curves varying with iteration times are shown in Figure 5. Although there are some fluctuations, we can see that the F_1 score

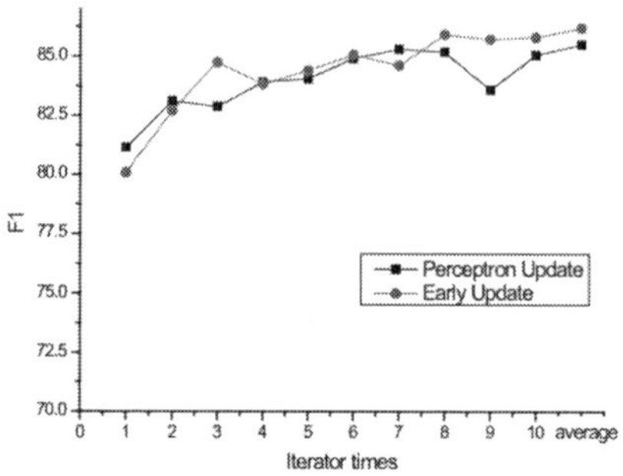

Figure 5. The F1 score curves on the development set varying with iteration times in Algorithm 2.

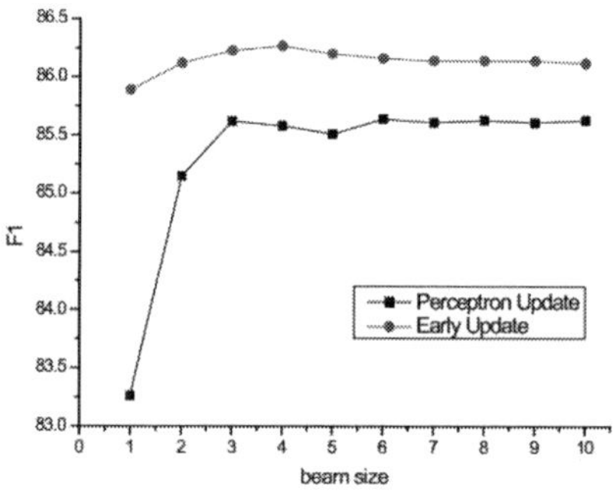

Figure 6. The F1 score curves on the development set varying with beam size in forest reranking.

tends to improve with the incremental iteration times, and that the average model yields additional improvement. To avoid the problem of overfitting to the training set, we fix the iteration times at 10 in the following experiments. Figure 6 shows F_1 score curves varying with beam size. We see that when the beam size exceeds 5, the performance fluctuates slightly, so we fix the beam size at 5 in our experiments. In Figure 6, we can also see that the model trained with the early updating strategy can obtain better performance than with the perceptron updating strategy.

6.3 Evaluation on Test Set

In this sub-section, we build three parsing systems using the methods described in the previous sections. For brevity, we annotate the *N*-best reranking system trained with the perceptron updating strategy as "NbestRerank"; the forest reranking system trained with the perceptron updating strategy as "ForestRerank"; and the forest reranking system trained with the early updating strategy as "EarlyUpdate". We also employ the Charniak parser (Charniak) and the Berkeley

[3] http://nlp.cs.nyu.edu/evalb/
[4] http://code.google.com/p/berkeleyparser/
[5] http://bllip.cs.brown.edu/download/reranking-parserAug06.tar.gz

	Berkeley	Charniak	Combine
Baseline	83.13	82.41	-----
NbestRerank	84.68	83.29	84.68
ForestRerank	84.31	83.11	85.72
EarlyUpdate	**85.06**	**83.32**	**85.74**

Table 3. F1 (%) scores on Test Set. The column headed by "Berkeley" is trained and tested with Berkley parser's 50-best list; the column headed by "Charniak" is trained and tested with Charniak parser's 50-best list; the column headed by "Combine" is trained and tested with 100-best list generated by Berkeley parser and Charniak parser.

Parsers	UA(%)
Charniak	82.31
Berkeley	84.05
NbestRerank	85.89
ForestRerank	85.69
EarlyUpdate	86.26
MST 1-ord (automatic POS)	79.62
MST 2-ord (automatic POS)	80.24
MST 1-ord (gold-standard POS)	85.23
MST 2-ord (gold-standard POS)	86.66

Table 4. Unlabeled dependency accuracy (UA). NbestRerank, ForestRerank and EarlyUpdate are trained and tested with combined 100-best lists

parser (Berkeley) as our baselines.

Using the parameter configuration tuned on development set, we have evaluated all the systems on test set. The F_1 scores are shown in Table 3.We can find that the F_1 scores are improved enormously when we make use of higher-order lexical dependencies. No matter which *N*-best list is used, EarlyUpdate system gets the highest F_1. However, the improved ranges vary with *N*-best list. The improvement is 1.93% for Berkeley parser's 50-best list, while it is 0.91% for Charniak parser's 50-best list. In our opinion, the reason is that Charniak parser has made use of head-word information during parsing, so it is less sensitive to lexical dependencies than Berkeley parser. When we use the combined 100-best lists for training and testing, all the three systems are improved. NbestRerank gets 1.55% improvements than Berkeley does, ForestRerank gets 1.04% improvements further than NbestRerank does, and EarlyUpdate makes the final performance up to 85.74%.

Intuitively, since they benefit from the higher-order lexical dependencies, the generated constituent trees should show better dependency accuracy as well. So we convert the generated constituent trees into dependency trees and calculate their unlabeled dependency accuracy (UA)[6].

[6] To compare with dependency parsing systems whose dependency arc labels are different from ours, we simply calculate the UAs.

	F_1(%)
Baseline	84.59
+*dependency* (first-order)	85.46
+*sibling* & *grandchild* (second-order)	86.20
+*grand-sibling* & *tri-sibling* (third-order)	86.37

Table 5. F_1 (%) score on development set of the EarlyUpdate system using different lexical dependency types.

To demonstrate the effectiveness of our systems, we also train a 1-order MSTPaser[7] (MST 1-ord) and a 2-order MSTParser (MST 2-ord), and then use them to parse the test set with gold-standard POS tags and automatically annotated POS tags (accuracy is 95.17%). All of the results are shown in Table 4. We see that the UAs of our systems are much better than those of Charniak and Berkeley. Although our systems employ no gold-standard POS tags during parsing, their UAs exceed those of MST 1-ord, which does employ such tags; and the UA of EarlyUpdate is even comparable with those of MST 2-ord, which also employs such tags.

The figures shown in Table 3 and Table 4 clearly reveal that our parsing approach obtains constituent trees with both better F_1 scores and better UAs.

6.4 Ablation studies

The experimental results above have shown that reranking parses based on higher-order lexical dependencies is effective. To verify the contributions of different lexical dependency types, we further evaluate the development set using the EarlyUpdate system trained with combined forests. First, we reranked forests with first-order (*dependency*) lexical dependencies. Then we added the second-order (*sibling* and *grandchild*) lexical dependencies into our system. Finally, we added the third-order (*grand-sibling* and *tri-sibling*) lexical dependencies. All of the parsing results are shown in Table 5. It is clear that all of the lexical dependency types are helpful for constituent tree evaluation.

6.5 Comparison with State-of-the-art Results

Table 6 compares our best results with that of state-of-the-art parsers. Compared to the

[7] http://sourceforge.net/projects/mstparser/

Individual System	
(Petrov and Klein, 2007)	83.32
(Huang and Harper, 2009)	84.15
***N*-best Reranking**	
Charniak & Johnson Reranker[8]	83.30
Our NbestRerank System	84.68
Parsers Combination	
(Zhang et al., 2009)	85.45
Using Extra Resource	
(Burkett and Klein, 2008)	84.24
(Huang and Harper, 2009)	85.18
(Niu et al., 2009)	85.20
Reranking with Lexical Dependencies	
Our EarlyUpdate System	**85.74**

Table 6. F1 (%) scores of state-of-the-art methods compared with ours on the Chinese Treebank.

"Charniak & Johnson Reranker" [8] which is a parse reranking system and exploits various sorts of features including 1-order lexical dependencies (Charniak and Johnson, 2005), our NbestRerank parser, which uses higher-order lexical dependency features, gets a higher F_1. Comparing with the parsers combination system (Zhang et al., 2009) which combines scores evaluated by Berkeley parser and Charniak parser to evaluate a parse tree, our EarlyUpdate system haven't used scores evaluated by first stage parsers and still gets a higher F1 score. Although our EarlyUpdate system uses no resources other than CTB, it still obtains better results than other parsers which have employed extra resources (Burkett and Klein, 2008; Huang and Harper, 2009; Niu et al., 2009). These comparisons allow us to confidently conclude that exploitation of higher-order lexical dependencies is highly beneficial for constituent parsing.

7 Conclusion and Future Work

We have presented a method for evaluating constituent trees using higher-order lexical dependencies. Within a parse reranking framework, our models rerank *N*-best lists and forests based on dependency features. Experimental results show that higher-order lexical dependencies can yield greater improvements in constituent parsing performance than commonly used first-order lexical dependencies. The best results of our models outperformed all previous results on the CTB, and the dependency accuracy of generated constituent trees is significantly improved as well. All of the results demonstrate that exploitation of higher-order lexical dependencies provides significant benefits for constituent tree evaluation.

Although all of our experiments were carried out only on the Chinese Treebank, our method is language independent. It can be adapted to any languages which can represent constituent trees with labeled dependency trees. We will apply our methods to other languages in the future.

Acknowledgments

The research work has been funded by the Natural Science Foundation of China under Grant No. 60975053 and 61003160, supported by the External Cooperation Program of the Chinese Academy of Sciences, and also partially supported by the China-Singapore Institute of Digital Media (CSIDM) project under grant No. CSIDM-200804 as well. Sincere thanks to Mark Seligman for his careful revision work.

References

Daniel M. Bikel, 2004. Intricacies of Collins' parsing model. Computational Linguistics, 30 (4). pages 479-511.

David Burkett and Dan Klein, 2008. Two languages are better than one (for syntactic parsing). In EMNLP 2008.

Eugene Charniak, 2000. A maximum-entropy-inspired parser. In NAACL 2000.

Eugene Charniak and Mark Johnson, 2005. Coarse-to-fine n-best parsing and MaxEnt discriminative reranking. In ACL 2005.

Michael Collins, 1999. Head-driven statistical models for natural language parsing. University of Pennsylvania.

Michael Collins, 2002. Discriminative training methods for hidden markov models: Theory and experiments with perceptron algorithms. In EMNLP 2002.

Michael John Collins, 1996. A new statistical parser based on bigram lexical dependencies. In ACL 1996, pages 184-191.

Michael Collins and Terry Koo, 2005. Discriminative reranking for natural language parsing. Computational Linguistics, 31 (1). pages 25-70.

Michael Collins and Brian Roark, 2004. Incremental parsing with the perceptron algorithm. In ACL 2004.

Victoria Fossum and Kevin Knight, 2009. Combining constituent parsers. In NAACL 2009, pages 253-256.

[8] The F1 score of Charniak & Johnson Reranker on CTB was reported in Niu et al. (2009).

Johan Hall and Joakim Nivre, 2008. A dependency-driven parser for German dependency and constituency representations. In PaGe-08, pages 47-54.

Johan Hall, Joakim Nivre and Jens Nilsson, 2007. A Hybrid Constituency-Dependency Parser for Swedish. In NODALIDA 2007, pages 284-287.

Liang Huang, 2008. Forest reranking: Discriminative parsing with non-local features. In ACL 2008.

Liang Huang and David Chiang, 2005. Better k-best parsing. In IWPT 2005.

Zhongqiang Huang and Mary Harper, 2009. Self-Training PCFG grammars with latent annotations across languages. In ACL 2009.

Daniel Jurafsky and James H. Martin, 2008. Speech and Language Processing: An introduction to natural language processing, computational linguistics, and speech recognition: Prentice Hall.

Dan Klein and Christopher D. Manning, 2003a. Accurate unlexicalized parsing. In ACL2003, pages 423-430.

Dan Klein and Christopher D. Manning, 2003b. Fast exact inference with a factored model for natural language parsing. In NIPS 2003.

Terry Koo and Michael Collins, 2010. Efficient Third-Order Dependency Parsers. In ACL 2010.

Takuya Matsuzaki, Yusuke Miyao and Jun'ichi Tsujii, 2005. Probabilistic CFG with latent annotations. In ACL 2005.

Ryan McDonald, Koby Crammer and Fernando Pereira, 2005. Online large-margin training of dependency parsers. In ACL 2005.

Ryan McDonald and Fernando Pereira, 2006. Online learning of approximate dependency parsing algorithms. In EACL 2006.

Zheng-Yu Niu, Haifeng Wang and Hua Wu, 2009. Exploiting heterogeneous treebanks for parsing. In ACL 2009.

Slav Petrov, Leon Barrett, Romain Thibaux and Dan Klein, 2006. Learning accurate, compact, and interpretable tree annotation. In ACL 2006.

Slav Petrov and Dan Klein, 2007. Improved inference for unlexicalized parsing. In ACL 2007.

Kenji Sagae and Alon Lavie, 2006. Parser combination by reparsing. In NAACL 2006, pages 129-132.

Rui Wang and Yi Zhang, 2010. Hybrid Constituent and Dependency Parsing with Tsinghua Chinese Treebank. In LREC 2010.

Zhiguo Wang and Chengqing Zong, 2010. Phrase Structure Parsing with Dependency Structure. In Coling 2010.

Fei Xia and Martha Palmer, 2001. Converting dependency structures to phrase structures. In The 1st Human Language Technology Conference (HLT-2001).

Fei Xia, Owen Rambow, Rajesh Bhatt, Martha Palmer and Dipti Misra Sharma, 2008. Towards a multi-representational treebank. Proc. of the 7th Int'lWorkshop on Treebanks and Linguistic Theories (TLT-7). pages.

Hiroyasu Yamada and Yuji Matsumoto, 2003. Statistical dependency analysis with support vector machines. In IWPT 2003.

Hui Zhang, Min Zhang, Chew Lim Tan and Haizhou Li, 2009. K-best combination of syntactic parsers. In EMNLP 2009.

Ying Zhang, Stephan Vogel and Alex Waibel, 2004. Interpreting BLEU/NIST scores: How much improvement do we need to have a better system. In LREC 2004.

Improving Part-of-speech Tagging for Context-free Parsing

Xiao Chen and Chunyu Kit
Department of Chinese, Translation and Linguistics
City University of Hong Kong
Tat Chee Avenue, Kowloon, Hong Kong SAR, P. R. China
{cxiao2,ctckit}@cityu.edu.hk

Abstract

In this paper, we propose a factored parsing model consisting of a lexical and a constituent model. The discriminative lexical model allows the parser to utilize rich contextual features beyond those encoded in the context-free grammar (CFG) in use. Experiment results reveal that our parser achieves statistically significant improvement in both parsing and tagging accuracy on both English and Chinese.

1 Introduction

Part-of-speech (POS) tagging, or tagging for short, is usually considered a front-end preparation for parsing. Folk wisdom holds that accurate tagging result is helpful to alleviate the syntactic ambiguity problem in parsing, motivating a huge amount of research on perfecting tagging techniques.

In the past two decades, most POS tagging systems were based on a sequential classification approach, decomposing a sequence labeling task into a series of classification subtasks. The state of the art of tagging was achieved by virtue of well-developed machine learning methods, e.g. the Maximum Entropy model as in Ratnaparkhi (1996) and the Support Vector Machine as in Gimenez and Marquez (2003). All these techniques boosted the performance of POS tagging significantly. The error rate of the best English POS tagger is less than 3% (Ratnaparkhi, 1996; Toutanova et al., 2003; Shen et al., 2007), very close to the inter-annotator discrepancy of the Penn Treebank (Marcus et al., 1993).

For a long time, however, parsing seems to have been evolving in parallel to tagging without much interaction with each other. Generative parsers (Collins, 1997; Charniak, 2000; Charniak and Johnson, 2005; Petrov and Klein, 2007), owing to their generative nature, all include a lexical probability model in the form $P(w|t)$. The information used to predict the POS tag of a word mainly comes from the word itself and/or the ancestors that derive this word in a tree. Local context, which is proved to be the most useful information source for tagging (Ratnaparkhi, 1996; Toutanova and Manning, 2000), is not efficiently utilized by these parsers. Another noticable fact is that these high-performance parsers cannot do a better job of POS tagging than most of the state-of-the-art taggers (see Section 4 for a comparison). This is quite against our intuition that a parser having access to syntactic and contextual information from all over an input sentence should outperform a tagger that is limited to utilizing only local context and sequential dependency. This is an observation in Charniak et al. (1996). But their explanation is that a parser is built to find phrase markers, not tags. Then an interesting question arises: if a parser cannot tag words better, how can we expect it to do better on phrases?

Driven by this question, our research is intended to explore an approach to integrating parsing with the strength of successful tagging, in the hope of improving both. Firstly, we factor the conventional PCFG-based parsing into a lexical and a constituent model. Then, two candidate lexical models are formulated to incorporate enriched contextual features and sequential dependency into the parsing, with an averaged perceptron algorithm for parameter estimation. Our experiments on English and Chinese treebanks show that this approach achieves a significant performance enhancement in both parsing and tagging over the baseline Berkeley parser.

2 A Factored Parsing Model

2.1 POS Tagging in Parsing

For PCFG-based parsing, the joint probability $\mathcal{P}(T, S)$ for a parse tree T of a sentence S is usually defined as the product of the probability of every CFG rule $\mathcal{R}$ involved in T:

$$\mathcal{P}(T, S) = \prod_{\mathcal{R} \in T} \mathcal{P}(\mathcal{R})^{|\mathcal{R}|} \quad (1)$$

where $|\mathcal{R}|$ is the number of occurrences of $\mathcal{R}$ in T. In a CFG, such as the one induced from the Penn Treebank, there are usually two types of grammar rules: *lexical rule*, e.g. `NN` $\rightarrow$ `consumer`, to indicate a possible POS-tag for a word, and *constituent rule*, e.g. `PP` $\rightarrow$ `IN NP`, to indicate the composition of a constituent.

Let r denote a lexical rule and R a constituent rule, the probability defined in (1) can be rewritten as

$$\mathcal{P}(T, S) = \prod_{R \in T} \mathcal{P}(R)^{|R|} \prod_{r \in T} \mathcal{P}(r)^{|r|} \quad (2)$$

Accordingly, the parsing model can be decomposed into two factors:

$$\mathcal{P}(T, S) = \mathcal{P}(\mathcal{C}, S)\mathcal{P}(\mathcal{L}, S) \quad (3)$$

where $\mathcal{P}(\mathcal{C}, S) = \prod_{R \in T} \mathcal{P}(R)^{|R|}$ is a constituent model and $\mathcal{P}(\mathcal{L}, S) = \prod_{r \in T} \mathcal{P}(r)^{|r|}$ a lexical model. The best parse is then selected by the joint inference with these two submodels. This factored-out lexical model provides the flexibility of integrating various well-developed POS tagging techniques into parsing, and it is also easier for optimization, in contrast to a complex joint model. It is reasonable that a better lexical model is expected to have better effects on parsing.

2.2 Product of Experts

The two separated models may score in different magnitudes, even if they are all properly normalized. Usually, when combining two heterogeneous models, a weighting scheme is needed to balance their unequal effect. For this, we introduce another parameter λ to our factorized parsing model as

$$\mathcal{P}(T, S) = \mathcal{P}(\mathcal{L}, S)^{\lambda}\mathcal{P}(\mathcal{C}, S) \quad (4)$$

This is known as a product-of-experts (Hinton, 2002; Cohen and Smith, 2007), where a combined distribution is defined by multiplying several component distributions and renormalizing them. The parameter λ can be tuned with the Gold Section Search algorithm (Press et al., 2007) on a development set, using the F-measure of PARSEVAL (Black et al., 1991) as objective function for training.

3 Lexical Model

3.1 Model I

Sequential dependency and local context have shown their strength in tagging disambiguation (Ratnaparkhi, 1996; Toutanova and Manning, 2000; Toutanova et al., 2003). However, in the high-performance PCFG-based parsers (Collins, 1997; Charniak, 2000; Petrov and Klein, 2007), none of these features can be used due to the generative nature of these parsing models.

To address this problem and incorporate the advantages of POS tagging technique into parsing, we propose a discriminative lexicon model following the global linear model (Collins, 2002). Let $\tau = \{t_0, t_1, t_2 ... t_n\}$ be a tag sequence for a sentence $S = \{w_0, w_1, w_2 ... w_n\}$, we define the score of a tagged sequence to be

$$\text{SCORE}(\tau, S) = \theta \cdot \mathbf{f}(\tau, S) = \sum_{i=1}^{n} \theta \cdot f(\tau_i, S) \quad (5)$$

where $\mathbf{f}(\tau, S)$ is a global feature vector and θ a vector of associated weights. A global feature is defined through a collection of local features $f(\tau_i, S)$. We train θ on a treebank using an averaged perceptron algorithm similar to the one presented in Collins and Duffy (2002) and Collins (2002). The number of iterations needed is optimized on the development set.

However, introducing sequential dependency into this lexical model would cause a severe efficiency problem with the joint inference for parsing. When the Viterbi algorithm is used to search for the best parse tree, its efficiency relies heavily on tree structure. The interdependency of adjacent POS tags actually changes the structure of the parse under operation. For example, to determine the best sub-tree for a non-terminal `XP` covering a span of words $[w_i ... w_j]$, we need to calculate the score for w_i's tag, which may largely depend on w_{i-1}'s tag. Unfortunately, such information is not available from the current word span under processing. The inference algorithm thus has to keep all possible sub-trees in memory, resulting in an intractable inference problem.

To deal with this joint inference problem, we approximate the lexical model in a unigram-factored form:

$$\mathcal{P}(\mathcal{L}, S) = \mathcal{P}(\mathcal{L}|S)\mathcal{P}(S) \propto \prod_{i \in [0,n]} \mathcal{P}(t_i|S) \quad (6)$$

where $\mathcal{P}(S)$ is the probability of a given input sentence, a constant that can be dropped if search only for the best parse, and t_i a candidate tag for w_i. The conditional distribution $\mathcal{P}(t_i|S)$ can be estimated by

$$\mathcal{P}(t_i|S) = \frac{\sum_{\tau \in \mathbb{T}(t_i)} \exp\left(\text{SCORE}(\tau, S)\right)}{\sum_{\tau' \in \mathbb{T}} \exp\left(\text{SCORE}(\tau', S)\right)} \quad (7)$$

where $\mathbb{T}$ is the set of all possible tag sequences for S, and $\mathbb{T}(t_i)$ a subset of $\mathbb{T}$, consisting of all tag sequences that contain t_i. The numerator is the sum of scores for all possible tag sequences with t_i for w_i. The denominator is the total score of all possible tag sequences of the input sentence. For efficient calculation, we also adopt variants of the forward and backward algorithm, which are similar to those for HMM (Baum and Eagon, 1967; Baum and Sell, 1968). Different from the conventional tagging systems, our lexical model does not generate the best tag sequence for the whole sentence, but a lattice of tags, on which the joint inference with the constituent model can be performed.

In our model, feature functions $f_m(\tau_i, S)$ are primarily binary, each of which maps the local context to 1 if its feature exists, or to 0 otherwise. The only exception is the first one. Using a similar design as in discriminative re-scoring parsing models (Collins, 2000; Charniak and Johnson, 2005; Huang, 2008), we have the first feature f_0 to be the logarithm of the probability of t_i being w_i's tag in S, as proposed in Petrov and Klein (2007), which is $f_0(\tau_i, S) = \log q(t_i, S)$.[1]

Beside $f_0(\tau_i, S)$, all other features are similar to those in the previous works (Ratnaparkhi, 1996; Toutanova et al., 2003; Shen et al., 2007), as listed in Table 1.

The signature features *prefix* and *suffix*, as used in Toutanova et al. (2003), each return a substring of certain length from the current word. In our experiments, this length ranges from 1 to 8. Since these prefix and suffix features are blindly extracted with templates that can be applied to any language, our lexical model is more language-independent than those using a predefined language-specific affix list.

For feature selection, we also follow other researchers' previous works to use a simply cut-off threshold. During the process to generate features for each word in the training treebank, a feature is not included in the final model if its count falls below a predefined threshold. We set the threshold to 2 for word and tag features, and to 35 for signature features.

Type	Feature Template	
Word	$[w_i]$ $(i = -2, -1, 0, 1, 2)$	$\&[t_0]$
	$[w_{i-2}, w_{i-1}]$ $(i = 0, 1, 2)$	$\&[t_0]$
	$[w_{-1}, w_1]$	$\&[t_0]$
	$[w_{i-2}, w_{i-1}, w_i]$ $(i = 0, 1, 2)$	$\&[t_0]$
Tag	$[t_i]$ $(i = -2, -1, 1, 2)$	$\&[t_0]$
	$[t_{i-2}, t_{i-1}]$ $(i = 0, 3)$	$\&[t_0]$
Signature	punctuator	$\&[t_0]$
	digit	$\&[t_0]$
	prefix	$\&[t_0]$
	suffix	$\&[t_0]$

Table 1: Feature templates of lexical model

3.2 Model II

The lexical model I enables the parsing to utilize a large variety of features other than those encoded in the CFG in use. However, the computation of forward/backward variables is expensive in both time and space. This inefficiency is practically more severe in training, which requires repetitive computation of these values for many times. Lexical model II is proposed as an aggressive approximation of model I, aimed at improving its efficiency at the least cost of performance.

The inefficiency of model I is primarily due to the complexity of the forward/backward procedure. For model II, we propose a lazy procedure as a simple approximation, which calculates the conditional probability $\mathcal{P}'(t_i|S)$ deterministically from left to right. As the procedure proceeds, all features that contain a preceding tag are instantiated with the best predicted tags for those previously processed words. For the features that contain a succeeding tag, we use the tag with the highest score by $f_0(\tau_i, S)$. This lazy procedure traces only one arbitrary best tag sequence. Its time complexity is linear in the length of input sentence.

Accordingly, for lexical model II, the distribu-

[1] In the lexical model, for $t_i = \mathcal{A}$ (a non-terminal symbol), the score $q(t_i, S)$ is calculated by:

$$q(t_i, S) = \frac{\sum_x O(\mathcal{A}_x, i, i+1)\mathcal{P}(\mathcal{A}_x \rightarrow w_i)}{I(ROOT, 0, |S|)} \quad (8)$$

where x is the latent variable (Petrov et al., 2006), and $I(\cdot)$ and $O(\cdot)$ are *inside* and *outside* scores. For more details of $q(t_i, S)$, please refer to Figure 3 in Petrov and Klein (2007).

tion $\mathcal{P}'(t_i|S)$ is estimated as

$$\mathcal{P}'(t_i|S) \propto \frac{\exp(\theta \cdot \mathbf{f}(\tau_i^*, S))}{\sum_{\substack{j\in[0,n-1],\\ t_j \in E(S)}} \exp(\theta \cdot \mathbf{f}(\tau_j^*, S))} \quad (9)$$

where τ_i^* is the arbitrary best tag sequence and $E(S)$ the collection of all possible POS tags for every word in S. The denominator is introduced for two reasons. Firstly, it is used to map the score of every t_i to the interval $[0, 1]$, so as to make the lexical model to have the similar magnitude as the constituent model. Secondly, we deliberately let it not to be a local normalizer. This allows some confident tags to vote stronger than others in the joint inference.

4 Experiments

We implement a parser for experiments with necessary support from the open source Berkeley parser. To evaluate the performance of this parsing model across languages, we conduct a number of experiments on both English and Chinese treebanks, using the WSJ section of Penn Treebank 3.0 (LDC99T42) and the Chinese Treebank 5.1 (LDC2005T01U01). Since both the constituent and lexical models use the PCFG-LA trained with the Berkeley parser,[2] we take it as the baseline for our evaluation. For comparison purpose, we use exactly the same splits of the treebanks as in Petrov and Klein (2007), as listed in Table 2.

	English	Chinese
Train.	Section 2-21	Art. 1-270,400-1151
Dev.	Section 22	Art. 301-325
Test.	Section 23	Art. 271-300

Table 2: Experiment Setup

As mentioned in Section 3, the parameter estimation for the lexical model requires reparsing the training treebank in use for calculating $q(t_i, S)$ with the PCFG-LA trained with the Berkeley parser. In order to obtain a representative set of training examples, the PCFG-LA is expected to create as much noise as it does in testing. For this, the training set for each language is divided into 20 folds as in Collins (2000) and Charniak and Johnson (2005). Each fold is reparsed with the PCFG-LA trained on the other 19 folds. The number of split-and-merger iterations is set to 6 for the training of all these grammars on the treebanks of both languages.

To examine how much the rich contextual features introduced into the lexical model improve parsing performance, the tagging accuracy of our parser is compared with the state-of-the-art taggers, e.g. the open source Stanford tagger. Although this tagger was developed several years ago, its performance on English is still in the lead according to Spoustová et al. (2009). We train and test this tagger on the same datasets as for parsing, using the default parameter settings for each language.

All parsing results are evaluated with the standard `evalb`. It is noteworthy that the tags are not counted as part of parsing output. The tagging accuracy has to be evaluated with our own program, for `evalb` eliminates some `DELETE LABEL`s when evaluating tagging.

4.1 Tagging Helps Parsing

Table 3 compares the performance of our parser and other baseline systems. When trained on the same data set, the Stanford tagger indeed outperforms the Berkeley parser and the re-scoring parser[3] on POS tagging for both languages. Then, we impose various tagging results into parsing to see how they affect parsing performance. Both the gold POS tags and the output of the Stanford tagger are submitted to the Berkeley parser, using the "`-goldPOS`" option. The results are presented in Table 3, denoted as *Berkeley+GoldTag* and *Berkeley+Stanford* respectively.[4] Surprisingly, however a significant loss of parsing performance is caused by imposing the better yet non-perfect tagging output of the Stanford tagger onto the Berkeley parser. We can see that better tagging does not necessarily improve parsing if the two separate systems work in the conventional "tag then parse" order.

The two lexical models are tested in the other experiments. We use all features as listed in Table

[2]The version released in September, 2009. The option "-Chinese" is not used for parsing Chinese, for it does not give the best parsing performance. All the PCFG-LA mentioned in this paper are trained with this version of the Berkeley parser with default settings.

[3]C&J Parser: the open source re-scoring parser of Charniak and Johnson (2005)

[4]Note that the tagging accuracy of *Berkeley+GoldTag* is not 100%. When some of the gold tags could cause parsing failure, the Berkeley parser will skip them and use its own tagging output.

	English			Chinese		
	Parsing	Tagging	Lex.	Parsing	Tagging	Lex.
	F1 (%)	Accuracy (%)		F1 (%)	Accuracy (%)	
Stanford	-	97.47	-	-	95.44	-
C&J Parser	91.40	94.50	-	-	-	-
Berkeley	89.87	97.30	-	83.22	95.33	-
Berkeley+Stanford	89.13	97.44	-	81.35	95.44	-
Berkeley+GoldTag	89.88	99.82	-	88.35	99.75	-
LM I Word	89.95	97.43	97.18	84.37	96.38	95.82
LM I Word+Tag	**90.02**	97.46	97.41	84.48	96.57	96.27
LM I Word+Tag+λ	89.99	97.52	97.41	**84.59**	96.64	96.27
LM I Word+Tag w/o f_0	89.98	97.51	97.18	84.09	95.95	94.48
LM II Word	89.92	97.41	97.28	84.18	96.09	95.79
LM II Word+Tag	90.01	97.49	97.39	84.27	96.34	96.04
LM II Word+Tag+λ	89.99	97.59	97.39	84.44	96.34	96.04

Table 3: Results on English and Chinese testing sets (all sentences).

1 for English. For Chinese, however, we select a smaller subset of it by removing word trigram templates and all tag templates that contain any tag to the right of the current word.[5] We find that using such tags as features cause a loss of performance, which is consistent with the default setting of the Stanford tagger for Chinese. Another difference in feature design for these two languages is the length of prefix and suffix. The max length of affix is set to 6 for English and 3 for Chinese. This is because the average word length is different in the two languages. And we use no specific Chinese characters for the feature templates of *punctuator* and *digit*, in order to maintain the language independency of our models as much as possible.

As presented in Table 3, our parser with both candidate lexical models performs significantly better than the baseline Berkeley parser.[6] For Chinese, the best labelled F-score 84.59% is 1.3% beyond the baseline 83.22%. For English, our best result 90.02% is even better than 89.88% using gold POS tags. It is evident that our enhanced lexical model can effectively help parsing. With its help, our parser also outperforms both the Berkeley parser and the Stanford tagger on tagging. The observation that the improvement on English looks not as much as that on Chinese could be explained by the fact that the tagging accuracy of English is very close to the inter-annotator discrepancy of the Penn Treebank, leaving a too tiny room for further improvement. According to Dalrymple (2006), parsing ambiguity in about 30% sentences cannot be reduced even by a perfect tagger, implying that improving tagging may only have a limited influence on parsing.

We also examine the effect of different feature set in both lexical models. With only word features, the parser already achieves some improvement on both parsing and tagging, in consistence with the findings in Toutanova et al. (2003). The surrounding words provide most information for the disambiguation for tagging. However, the weight parameter λ seems not as effective as expected for English. This might be caused by the overfitting when it is tuned it on the development set. We also try to remove the feature f_0 from the model (w/o f_0). Then, the performance is still higher than the baseline Berkeley parser, indicating that the effectiveness of our lexical model does not rely on this feature too much. More interestingly, the approximate deterministic lexical model II achieves a similar performance as the complex lexical model I. In practice, model II is a better choice with a lower computational complexity.

Before the joint inference with the constituent model, a lexical model calculates a score for every candidate tag of each word. A choice is to collect the tags with the highest scores as a baseline output of tagging. The tagging accuracy of a lexical model can be compared with this output, as shown in the last column "Lex." for each language in Table 3. Comparing this column with the tagging accuracy of our parser in the second column for each language, we can observe an increase by 0.1-0.3%, indicating that syntactic knowledge as used in our parser does help the disambiguation for tagging.

[5]Specifically, tag templates with $i > 0$ are removed for experiments on Chinese.

[6]All results are tested with Dan Bikel's Randomized Parsing Evaluation Comparator (http://www.cis.upenn.edu/~dbikel/download/compare.pl), resulting in $p < 0.05$.

System	F1 (%)
Berkeley	89.87
Charniak (2000)	89.70
Collins (2000)	89.70
Bod (2003)	90.70
Henderson (2004)	90.10
Charniak and Johnson (updated 2006)	91.40
Huang (2008)	91.69
Attia et al. (2010)	89.88
This work	90.02

Table 4: Comparison with other parsers on English testing set

System	F1 (%)
Berkeley	83.22
Burkett and Klein (2008)	84.24
This work	84.59

Table 5: Comparison with other parsers on Chinese testing set

4.2 Comparison with Previous Work

Table 4 and 5 compare the performance of our parser with other high-performance parsers. Those parsers using self-training or parser combination methods are not included in this comparison, because they use extra resources or more than one parsing model.

For English, our parser outperforms all generative parsers (Collins, 1997; Charniak, 2000). But there is still a gap to the discriminative re-scoring methods (Charniak and Johnson, 2005; Huang, 2008). Given that our parser only improves the lexical model, the re-scoring method using a variety of subtree features indeed has some advantages. For Chinese, our parser has achieved the best performance so far on this data set. It is even better than the one that employs additional knowledge from the Chinese-English Parallel Treebank (Burkett and Klein, 2008).

5 Analysis

The experiments reported in the previous section seems to give a positive answer to the question: whether tagging can help parsing. However, several other questions follow: How does tagging affect paring? Why can this independently optimized lexical model improve parsing? We will look into these issuess in this section.

5.1 Profiling the Improvement of Tagging

We firstly divide the word/tag pairs in the testing data into to two groups: known v.s. unknown, according to the definition in Jin and Chen (2009). The tagging performance of our parser and the two baseline systems are compared in Table 6.

	English		Chinese	
	Known	Unk.	Known	Unk.
Stanford	98.09	77.33	96.47	72.02
Berkeley	97.93	76.13	96.91	59.23
This work	98.09	80.04	97.59	73.81

Table 6: Tagging accuracy (%) for known and unknown word/tag pairs

It is evident that our parser outperforms the Berkeley parser on both groups. The contrast on unknown tags is more significant, especially for Chinese. Since our parser uses the same constituent model as the Berkeley parser, this difference has to be explained by a better lexical model. A similar case can also be observed when our parser is compared against the Stanford tagger. Since our lexical model uses a very similar feature set as the Stanford tagger, the difference in performance should be attributed to the constituent model, which provides more detailed contextual information from the whole sentence to facilitate guessing unknown POS tags.

5.2 Profiling the Improvement of Parsing

In order to profile the parsing errors that can be fixed by better tagging, we count the number of correct constituents in the output of our parser and the other systems for a comparison under a variety of partition schemes, as shown in Table 7 and 8. The span length of a constituent is the number of words in it. Usually, a longer span correlates with a higher position near the root in a parse tree.

Table 7 shows that correct constituents increase in number in almost all types. Without any feature designed for a specific POS tag (such as `IN`), our lexical model brings about a general improvement to the parsing of both languages. Interestingly, however, the comparison in Table 8 presents a different view. The improvement mainly takes place in the constituents of span length ≤ 4, especially those base-level ones of length 1, which are parents of tags, e.g. `NP` $\rightarrow$ `NNS` and `VP` $\rightarrow$ `VBG`. The recognition of these constituents is greatly influenced by a lexical model. This influence tapers off on higher constituents, for the constituent model becomes more dominant when working on larger subtrees. This is also observed on the Chinese side. But the Chinese treebank has many different characteristics from English. According to our

English				Chinese			
Label	Berk.	E-LMII	Diff.	Label	Berk.	C-LMI	Diff.
NP	17049	17077	28	VP	1593	1638	45
VP	7953	7964	11	NP	3049	3073	24
ADJP	612	619	7	ADVP	301	313	12
PP	4748	4754	6	IP	780	795	15
S	5103	5109	6	PP	294	301	7
SBAR	1511	1514	3	CP	172	178	6
PRT	131	133	2	QP	181	185	4

Table 7: Correct constituents by constituent label

English						Chinese				
Span	Gold	C&J.	Berk.	E-LMII	Diff.	Span	Gold	Berk.	C-LMI	Diff.
1	6543	6034	5995	6015	20	1	2951	2594	2645	51
2	7645	7186	7159	7173	14	2	1385	1210	1221	11
3	5633	5237	5181	5188	7	3	844	679	699	20
4	3509	3183	3172	3175	3	4	528	433	452	19
≥ 5	20852	18385	17947	17970	23	≥ 5	2819	2234	2257	23

Table 8: Correct constituents by span length

statistics, about 34% of the constituents in the Chinese testing data are base-level ones. This explains why the impact of tagging to parsing for Chinese is much stronger than that for English. Since there are other languages that share similar characteristics with Chinese, our method should be also helpful in parsing these languages.

Currently, tagging and parsing are treated equally in a unified framework of parsing. However, our experiments show that our independently defined and optimized lexical model performs better than the one integrated into the Berkeley parser, especially for the recognition of the base-level constituents mentioned above. This is mostly attributable to the nature of a generative parsing model, for its lexical model can only use the features encoded in the grammar in use, which is never enough for accurate parsing. In fact, the research on POS tagging and chunking shows that the most important information for disambiguation at this level comes from local context (Toutanova et al., 2003), especially the surrounding words. Our current work is an attempt to fill this gap between tagging and parsing, by the way of enabling a parser to use rich contextual features in its lexical model.

6 Related Work

Most successful parsing models are generative models. Therefore, a large portion of previous related work did not change the generative nature of the lexical models involved (Goldberg et al., 2009; Huang and Harper, 2009; Attia et al., 2010). The key idea of these approaches is basically to advance smoothing techniques for the distribution $\mathcal{P}(w|t)$. Goldberg et al. (2009) adopt a trigram HMM tagging model trained on unannotated data to help prediting tags of rare words, but only the emission probabilities are used in parsing. Huang and Harper (2009) propose a better way to smooth the lexical model in a PCFG-LA parser similar to the Berkeley parser. Some morphological features are also used to handle unknown words in Chinese. In their evaluation, however, they exclude all unary rules that cause one of the major difficulties in parsing this language, according to our experiments. Their experiment settings obstruct comparing their results with others'. Attia et al. (2010) head in the same direction extending this method to other languages. Their experiment results are compared with ours in Table 4. The comparison shows that our method is more sophisticated in utilizing the sequential dependency between tags.

A motivation of our current work is that a discriminative lexical model can incorporate rich contextual features. In this respect, Cohen and Smith (2007) combine the strengths of a generative parsing model and a discriminative segmentation-tagging model under the notion of product-of-experts. Here we apply a similar idea to combine parsing and tagging. The discriminative re-scoring method (Charniak and Johnson, 2005; Huang, 2008) is also very successful. It enables a parser to use a large variety of local and non-local features, so as to boost the performance. Interestingly, however, the comparison in Table 3 shows that the parser of Charniak and Johnson (2005) achieves the highest parsing performance with the lowest tagging accuracy. This parser seems to select the parse trees that contain correct constituents with relatively poor POS tags. This controversial result raises at least two questions: (a) Why correct constituent structures can be built on incorrect POS tags? (b) Does tagging have any effect on parsing? The first question points to the too strong generative capacity of the CFG in use. Note that without semantic and/or pragmatic knowledge as constraints, a CFG induced from a treebank usually can generate many possible but implausible structures for an input sentence. For the second question, the controversial result indeed gives us an impression that tagging has no effect on parsing, strongly against our intuition. Since tagging and parsing are unified into the same framework as a parser, it is reasonable to expect the correct tag sequence for a sentence to appear in the theoretically best parse tree. If a parser has to sacrifice tagging for parsing, it is suspectable that the re-scoring does not help the parser to reach its maximum capacity yet. Besides, the re-scoring method should have subsumed our current work. In fact, incorporating the sequential dependency between adjacent tags into the forest re-scoring model will also cause the efficiency problem in the inference as mentioned in Section 3. Given that no feature for tagging has been adopted in the forest re-scoring method so far, our current work is certainly a complement to this part.

The recent work of Rush et al. (2010) integrates parsing and tagging under the framework of dual-decomposition. This approach has the advantage to combine heterogeneous models, and solves the complex combinatory optimization problem via Lagrangian relaxation. However, it has a inevitable defect of inefficiency, since it requires to parse and tag the input sentence repetitively (usually 10 times for each sentence). Comparatively, our approach is more efficient. Note that lexical model II takes only a linear time in the length of input sentence. Without systematic comparison, however, it is difficult to tell which approach can provide a better performance. We will keep this for our future research.

7 Conclusion

In this work, we have proposed a parsing model which is factored into a lexical and a constituent model, in the hope of enabling the beneficial interaction between tagging and parsing. The relatively independent discriminative lexical model allows our parser to incorporate rich contextual features and even sequential dependency. Our experiments show that our lexical models can help parsing. With access to the syntactic knowledge from all over an input sentence, this parser outperforms the state-of-the-art POS tagging system in terms of tagging accuracy. Moreover, tagging should be an organic part of a parsing model to bring in a mutual positive effect for both parsing and tagging through joint inference. The conventional notion of tagging-parsing pipeline seems to leave no room for this possibility of enhancement.

Finally, individual words in an input sentence are found to be very useful in the disambiguation for POS tagging and even for recognizing base-level constituents. However, the structural parameterization of conventional parsing models cannot incorporate and utilize them effectively. Nevertheless, how to make use of all sorts of information available to enhance parsing is still a challenging research topic.

Acknowledgement

The research described in this paper was partially supported by the Research Grants Council (RGC) of HKSAR, China, through the GRF grant 9041597.

References

Mohammed Attia, Jennifer Foster, Deirdre Hogan, Joseph Le Roux, Lamia Tounsi, and Josef van Genabith. 2010. Handling unknown words in statistical latent-variable parsing models for Arabic, English and French. In *NAACL HLT 2010*, pages 67–75.

Leonard E. Baum and J. A. Eagon. 1967. An inequality with applications to statistical estimation for probabilistic functions of Markov processes and to a model for ecology. *Bull. Amer. Math. Soc.*, 73(3):360–363.

Leonard E. Baum and George R. Sell. 1968. Growth transformations for functions on manifolds. *Pacific J. Math.*, 27(2):211–227.

E. Black, S. Abney, D. Flickenger, R. Grishman, P. Harrison, D. Hindle, R. Ingria, F. Jelinek, J. Klavans, M. Liberman, M. Marcus, S. Roukos, B. Santorini, and T. Strzalkowski. 1991. A procedure for quantitatively comparing the syntactic coverage of English grammars. In *Proceedings of DARPA Speech and Natural Language Workshop*, pages 306–311.

Rens Bod. 2003. An efficient implementation of a new dop model. In *EACL 2003*, pages 19–26.

David Burkett and Dan Klein. 2008. Two languages are better than one (for syntactic parsing). In *EMNLP 2008*, pages 877–886.

Eugene Charniak and Mark Johnson. 2005. Coarse-to-fine n-best parsing and MaxEnt discriminative reranking. In *ACL 2005*, pages 173–180.

Eugene Charniak, Glenn Carroll, John Adcock, Anthony Cassandra, Yoshihiko Gotoh, Jeremy Katz, Michael Littman, and John McCann. 1996. Taggers for parsers. *Artif. Intell.*, 85:45–57.

Eugene Charniak. 2000. A maximum-entropy-inspired parser. In *NAACL 2000*, pages 132–139.

Shay B. Cohen and Noah A. Smith. 2007. Joint morphological and syntactic disambiguation. In *EMNLP-CoNLL 2007*, pages 208–217.

Michael Collins and Nigel Duffy. 2002. New ranking algorithms for parsing and tagging: kernels over discrete structures, and the voted perceptron. In *ACL 2002*, pages 263–270.

Michael Collins. 1997. Three generative, lexicalised models for statistical parsing. In *ACL 1997*, pages 16–23.

Michael Collins. 2000. Discriminative reranking for natural language parsing. In *ICML 2000*, pages 175–182.

Michael Collins. 2002. Discriminative training methods for hidden Markov models: Theory and experiments with perceptron algorithms. In *EMNLP 2002*, pages 1–8.

Mary Dalrymple. 2006. How much can part-of-speech tagging help parsing? *Nat. Lang. Eng.*, 12(4):373–389.

Jesus Gimenez and Lluis Marquez. 2003. Fast and accurate part-of-speech tagging: The SVM approach revisited. In *Proceedings of the Fourth RANLP*.

Yoav Goldberg, Reut Tsarfaty, Meni Adler, and Michael Elhadad. 2009. Enhancing unlexicalized parsing performance using a wide coverage lexicon, fuzzy tag-set mapping, and EM-HMM-based lexical probabilities. In *EACL 2009*, pages 327–335.

James Henderson. 2004. Discriminative training of a neural network statistical parser. In *ACL 2004*, pages 95–102.

Geoffrey E. Hinton. 2002. Training products of experts by minimizing contrastive divergence. *Neural Computation*, 14(8):1771–1800.

Zhongqiang Huang and Mary Harper. 2009. Self-training PCFG grammars with latent annotations across languages. In *EMNLP 2009*, pages 832–841.

Liang Huang. 2008. Forest reranking: Discriminative parsing with non-local features. In *ACL-HLT 2008*, pages 586–594.

Guangjin Jin and Xiao Chen. 2009. The fourth international chinese language processing bakeoff: Chinese word segmentation, named entity recognition and Chinese POS tagging. In *IJCNLP 2009*, pages 69–81.

Mitchell P. Marcus, Mary Ann Marcinkiewicz, and Beatrice Santorini. 1993. Building a large annotated corpus of English: the Penn Treebank. *Comput. Linguist.*, 19(2):313–330.

Slav Petrov and Dan Klein. 2007. Improved inference for unlexicalized parsing. In *HLT-NAACL 2007*, pages 404–411.

Slav Petrov, Leon Barrett, Romain Thibaux, and Dan Klein. 2006. Learning accurate, compact, and interpretable tree annotation. In *COLING-ACL 2006*, pages 433–440.

William Press, Saul Teukolsky, William Vetterling, and Brian Flannery. 2007. *Numerical Recipes: the art of scientific computing*. Cambridge University Press, 3rd edition.

Adwait Ratnaparkhi. 1996. A maximum entropy part-of-speech tagger. In *EMNLP 1996*, pages 133–142.

Alexander M Rush, David Sontag, Michael Collins, and Tommi Jaakkola. 2010. On dual decomposition and linear programming relaxations for natural language processing. In *EMNLP 2010*, pages 1–11.

Libin Shen, Giorgio Satta, and Aravind Joshi. 2007. Guided learning for bidirectional sequence classification. In *ACL 2007*, pages 760–767.

Drahomíra "johanka" Spoustová, Jan Hajič, Jan Raab, and Miroslav Spousta. 2009. Semi-supervised training for the averaged perceptron POS tagger. In *EACL 2009*, pages 763–771.

Kristina Toutanova and Christopher D. Manning. 2000. Enriching the knowledge sources used in a maximum entropy part-of-speech tagger. In *SIGDAT EMNLP 2000*, pages 63–70.

Kristina Toutanova, Dan Klein, Christopher D. Manning, and Yoram Singer. 2003. Feature-rich part-of-speech tagging with a cyclic dependency network. In *NAACL 2003*, pages 173–180.

Models Cascade for Tree-Structured Named Entity Detection

Marco Dinarelli
LIMSI-CNRS / Orsay Cedex, France
marcod@limsi.fr

Sophie Rosset
LIMSI-CNRS / Orsay Cedex, France
rosset@limsi.fr

Abstract

Named Entity Recognition (NER) is a well-known Natural Language Processing (NLP) task, used as a preliminary processing to provide a semantic level to more complex tasks. In this paper we describe a new set of named entities having a multilevel tree structure, where base entities are combined to define more complex ones. This definition makes the NER task more complex than previous tasks, even more due to the use of noisy data for the annotation: transcriptions of French broadcast data. We propose an original and effective system to tackle this new task, putting together the strengths of solutions for sequence labeling approaches and syntactic parsing via cascading of different models. Our system was evaluated in the 2011 Quaero named entity detection evaluation campaign and ranked first, with results far better than those of the other participating systems.

1 Introduction

Named Entity Detection is a well-known NLP task used to extract semantic information in other more complex tasks such as Relation Extraction (Doddington et al., 2004) or Question Answering (Voorhees, 2001). After its definition in MUC-6 (Grishman and Sundheim, 1996), the NER task evolved increasing its complexity. Current definitions provide a fine-grained semantic information level with a broad coverage (Sekine, 2004). This has increased the interests in developing named entity detection systems.

In this paper we describe a new set of named entities defined recently(Grouin et al., 2011). These named entities have a multilevel tree structure where components are combined to define more complex and general entity structures. This definition increases significantly the complexity of the NER task, even more due to the type of data used for the annotation: manual and automatic transcriptions of French broadcast data.

Given such a definition, it is not possible to tackle the task with traditional sequence labeling approaches. At the same time, solutions able to reconstruct tree structures from flat sequences, like syntactic parsing solutions, may have serious limitations, due to the noisy data used. In order to solve these problems, we studied and implemented a two-stage system that put together the strengths of the two approaches: i) a complex linear-chain Conditional Random Field (CRF) model, integrating a huge number of features, takes the noisy data as input and generates the corresponding sequence of components; ii) a syntactic parsing model based on Probabilistic Context Free Grammar (PCFG) reconstructs the tree-structured named entities.

We describe our solution showing that it is equivalent, in the processing steps, to a syntactic parsing analysis solution, and that it can better handle noisy data. Additionally, given the amount of data used and the relatively slow training time of CRF models when using large amount of data and features, we describe a procedure for incremental CRF model training that solves this particular efficiency problem. The system we propose ranked first at the 2011 Quaero NER evaluation campaign (Galibert et al., 2011), with results far better than those of the other participating systems, though results on automatic transcriptions are largely affected by ASR system errors.

The remainder of the paper is organized as follows: in the next section we describe the new set of named entities defined and the data used for annotation. In section 3 we describe the system we propose, and implemented for the 2011 Quaero Named Entity Recognition evaluation campaign. In section 4 we detail the experimental setup, and

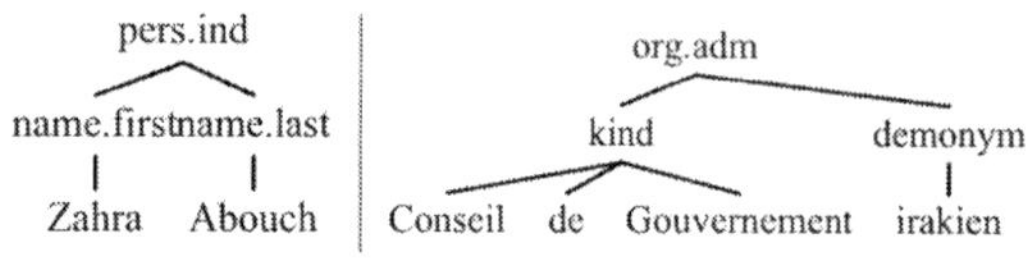

Figure 1: Examples of structured named entities defined within the Quaero project. Left: Iraqi Governing Council

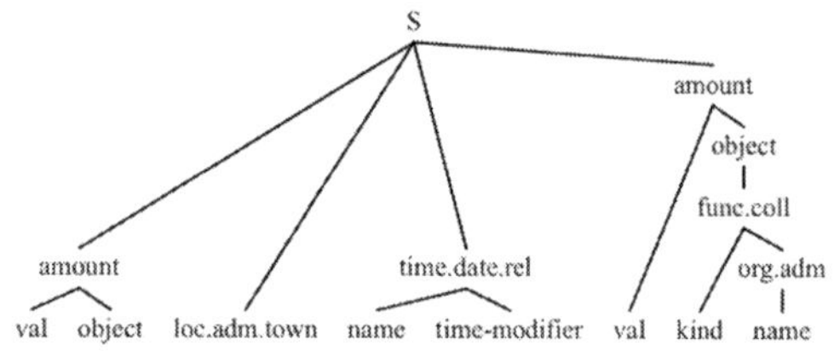

Figure 2: An example of named entity tree corresponding to entities of a whole sentence. Tree leaves, corresponding to sentence words have been removed to keep readability.

describe and comment the results. Finally in section 5 we draw our conclusions and propose some perspectives for future work.

2 Towards Tree Structured Named Entities

Named Entity Recognition was first defined as recognizing proper names (Coates-Stephens, 1992). Since MUC-6 (Grishman and Sundheim, 1996) named entities are proper names falling into three major classes: persons, locations and organizations. There are some propositions to sub-divide these entities into fine-grained classes. For example, politicians for the person class (Fleischman and Hovy, 2002) or cities for the location class (Fleischman, 2001). Some are sometimes added like product (Bick, 2004; Galliano et al., 2009).

Recently some extensions of named entity have been proposed. For example, (Sekine, 2004) defined a complete hierarchy of named entities containing about 200 types.

A well-known task of named entity detection is the one proposed for the CoNLL shared task 2003, described in (Tjong Kim Sang and De Meulder, 2003), where only four named entities were involved: *Person*, *Organization*, *Location* and *Other*. The latter was used for proper names belonging to any other entity different from the first three types.

After this task, named entity detection has been refined to include other entities, e.g. describing time expressions, events, quantity, currency etc. Current named entity detection tasks provide a fine-grained semantic representation level of the lexical surface form, sometimes comparable to other semantic representations like those used in Semantic Role Labeling (Carreras and Marquez, 2005) or Spoken Language Understanding (De Mori et al., 2008). The increasing complexity of named entities definition reflects the change of needs in computer science activities, that in turn is the consequence of the tremendous growth of the amount of information to deal with nowadays.

The set of named entities used in this work has been recently defined in (Grouin et al., 2011) and presents an important difference with respect to previous sets. Beyond the presence of subtypes, named entities have a tree structure. For example, the *Organization* type can be characterized by the subtypes *administrative* or *enterprise* giving the named entities *org.adm* and *org.ent* starting from the entity *org*. Each entity is composed of at least one component, which trigger in any case an entity type. The component allows to characterize more precisely the semantic content of the entity. For example the entity *pers*, used to describe persons, has, among others, the components *name.first*, for first name, and *name.last*, for last name. The presence of either *name.first* or *name.last* (or both) triggers the entity *pers*. The results of the composition is a tree-structured named entity. Two examples of structured named entities are shown in figure 1. In addition we report a named entity tree in figure 2, where words, corresponding to tree leaves, have been removed to keep readability, and it was generated starting from the sentence:

> **90 personnes** toujours présentes **à Atambua** c'est là qu'**hier matin** ont été tués **3 employés du haut commissariat des Nations unies** aux réfugiés, le **HCR**[1]

Here words realizing entities have been highlighted in bold. More details on the definition of this new set of named entities can be found in (Grouin et al., 2011), where also statistics on inter-annotators agreements are reported.
Given this structured named entities definition, the corresponding NER task is significantly more complex than previous equivalent tasks, where the entity structure was flat. Moreover, the complexity of the task is increased also by the type of data used for the annotation, that is manual and automatic transcriptions of French broadcast data. In

[1] 90 people still present in Atambua is where yesterday morning killed three employees of the United Nations High Commissioner for Refugees UNHCR.

Quaero	training		dev	
# sentences	43,251		112	
	words	entities	words	entities
# tokens	1,251,432	245,880	2,659	570
# vocabulary	39,631	134	891	30
# components	–	133662	–	971
# components dict.	–	28	–	18
# OOV rate [%]	–	–	17.15	0

Table 1: Statistics on the training and development sets of the Quaero corpus.

Quaero	test BN		test BC	
# sentences	1704		3933	
	words	entities	words	entities
# tokens	32945	2762	69414	2769
# vocabulary		28		28
# components	–	4128	–	4017
# components dict.	–	21	–	20
# OOV rate [%]	3.63	0	3.84	0

Table 2: Statistics on the test set of the Quaero corpus, divided in Broadcast News (BN) and Broadcast Conversations (BC)

particular the data have been collected not only from French radio channels, but also from a North-African French-speaking radio channel. This aspect introduces complexity due to different expressions used from French non-native speakers as well as to their particular accents and sometimes vocabulary.

The training data are the same used for the ESTER2 evaluation campaign (Galliano et al., 2009). The transcriptions have been re-annotated with the named entities described above.

The corpus will be referred in this work as `Quaero`. Description of training, development and test data are reported in table 1 and 2. In particular the test set is constituted by different kind of data: transcriptions of broadcast news, and broadcast conversations. the merge of the first two types. An interesting point in table 1 and 2 is the Out-of-Vocabulary (OOV) rate of dev and test sets.

3 Tree-Structured Named Entity Detection System

Given the definition of named entities described in previous section, we consider that, even if possible, the best solution cannot be a sequence labeling approach as largely used in standard named entity detection task (Tjong Kim Sang and De Meulder, 2003). In contrast, an approach coming from syntactic parsing would be possible. In that case syntactic parse trees could be replaced by named entity trees like the one shown in figure 2[2].

A first problem with this choice is constituted by the noisy data involved in our task. Indeed, our preliminary evaluations of a classic algorithm used successfully for syntactic parsing, resulted in quite poor results. Note also that most syntactic parsing solutions, are designed to perform parsing using Part-of-Speech (POS) tags, annotated upon words, as tree leaves, instead of words. This solution introduces a good generalization over surface forms, allowing algorithms to deal with relatively noisy data, although the same solutions proved to be much less effective on automatic transcriptions. Moreover, this solution is effective for syntactic parsing, since syntactic constituents are directly related to POS tags, but it would not be reasonable for named entity detection, since the generalization introduced by POS tags over lexical surface forms would make it impossible to discriminate between different entities. Indeed, most of the named entities syntactic heads are known to be nouns. Additionally, since our named entity detection task must be performed also on automatic transcriptions containing ASR mistakes, a solution designed for syntactic parsing and adapted to be applied directly on lexical surface forms would be not robust enough, due to OOV words and ASR mistakes that alter significantly the syntactic structure of the input sentence. Our idea is thus to split the annotation process in two phases:

1. In the first step we use a model robust to noisy input and Out-of-Vocabulary words in order to annotate entity components, i.e. components of named entities that can be annotated directly on words (tree leaves in figure 2).
2. In the second step we use a model for syntactic parsing in order to reconstruct the entire entity trees.

The first step is a sequence segmentation and labeling task, thus any model suitable for this kind of problems can be adopted. Given its characteristics and its success in sequence labeling tasks, we adopt CRF (Lafferty et al., 2001) for the first step. For the second step we adopt a Probabilistic Context-Free Grammar (Booth and Thomson, 1973; Krenn and Samuelsson, 1997). The next two subsections describe these two models.

3.1 Linear-Chain Conditional Random Fields

CRFs have been proposed for the first time for sequence segmentation and labeling tasks in (Lafferty et al., 2001). This model belongs to the family of exponential or log-linear models. Its main characteristics are the possibility to include a huge number of features, like the Maximum Entropy

[2]where words are not shown for readability reason

model, but computing global conditional probabilities normalized at sentence level, instead of position level. In particular this last point results very effective since it solves the label bias problem, as pointed out in (Lafferty et al., 2001).

Given a sequence of N words $W_1^N = w_1, ..., w_N$ and its corresponding sequence of named entities $E_1^N = e_1, ..., e_N$, CRF trains the conditional probabilities

$$P(E_1^N|W_1^N) = \frac{1}{Z} \prod_{n=1}^{N} \exp\left(\sum_{m=1}^{M} \lambda_m \cdot h_m(e_{n-1}, e_n, w_{n-2}^{n+2})\right) \quad (1)$$

where λ_m are the training parameters. $h_m(e_{n-1}, e_n, w_{n-2}^{n+2})$ are the feature functions capturing conditional dependencies of entities and words. Z is a probability normalization factor in order to model well defined probability distribution:

$$Z = \sum_{\tilde{e}_1^N} \prod_{n=1}^{N} H(\tilde{e}_{n-1}, \tilde{e}_n, w_{n-2}^{n+2}) \quad (2)$$

where $\tilde{e}_{n-1}$ and $\tilde{e}_n$ are the entities hypothesized for the previous and current words, $H(\tilde{e}_{n-1}, \tilde{e}_n, w_{n-2}^{n+2})$ is an abbreviation for $\sum_{m=1}^{M} \lambda_m \cdot h_m(e_{n-1}, e_n, w_{n-2}^{n+2})$.

Two particular effective implementations of CRFs have been recently proposed. One is described in (Hahn et al., 2009) and uses a margin based training criteria for probabilities estimation. The other is described in (Lavergne et al., 2010) and has been implemented in the software *wapiti*[3]. The latter solution in particular trains the model using two different regularization parameters at the same time: Gaussian prior, also known as *l2* regularization and used in many software to avoid over fitting; and Laplacian prior, also known as *l1* regularization (Riezler and Vasserman, 2010), which has the effect to filter out features with very low scores. These two regularization parameters are used together in the model implementing the so-called *elastic net* regularization (Zou and Hastie, 2005):

$$l(\lambda) + \rho_1 \|\lambda\|_1 + \frac{\rho_2}{2} \|\lambda\|_2^2 \quad (3)$$

λ is the set of parameters of the model introduced in equation 1, $l(\lambda)$ is the minus-logarithm of equation 1, used as loss function for training CRF. $\|\lambda\|_1$ and $\|\lambda\|_2$ are the *l1* and *l2* regularization, respectively, while ρ_1 and ρ_2 are two parameters that can be optimized as usual on development data or with cross validation.

[3]available at http://wapiti.limsi.fr

As explained in (Lavergne et al., 2010), using *l1* regularization is an effective way for feature selection in CRF at training time. Note that other approaches have been proposed for feature selection, e.g. in (McCallum, 2003). In this work we refer to the CRF implementation described in (Lavergne et al., 2010).

3.1.1 Incremental CRF Training

Despite the improvements on CRF implementations, this model remains hard to train on large amount of data when using a reasonable amount of features. Using the data described in section 2 and using features as word prefixes and suffixes, capitalization, punctuation and morpho-syntactic features, our CRF model creates more than 2 billions feature functions. Training such a model is infeasible on current machines.

Exploiting the characteristics of the CRF software *wapiti* and the definition of feature functions, we implemented a procedure for incremental training of CRF models that can be used with an arbitrary number of features. Feature functions $h_m(e_{n-1}, e_n, w_{n-2}^{n+2})$ used in our CRF models have the form:

$$h_{w,e}(e_i, w_i) = \delta(w_i^{'}, w_i) \cdot \delta(e_i^{'}, e_i) \quad (4)$$

where $\delta(.,.)$ is the Kronecker function. This particular function fires when the current word $w_i^{'}$ in the sequence matches w_i and the corresponding entity $e_i^{'}$ matches e_i. When using such simple features, there is usually no limitation on the amount of data that can be used for training. Indeed, more accurate models can be trained using complex features, using also words and entities at previous or next positions, i.e. adjacent tokens. For example:

$$\begin{aligned} h_{w,e}(e_i, w_i) \;=\; & \delta(w_{i-1}^{'}, w_{i-1}) \cdot \delta(w_i^{'}, w_i) \\ & \cdot\delta(e_{i-1}^{'}, e_{i-1}) \cdot \delta(e_i^{'}, e_i) \end{aligned} \quad (5)$$

This feature function fires if both words and entities at current and previous positions match. The higher accuracy reached with this type of features is paid at training time with the number of feature function generated in situations like the one reported above, and makes direct CRF model training unfeasible. The solution to this limitation is given observing that:

1. The software we use for CRF model training performs an effective feature selection thanks to *l1* regularization and can reload models for further refinements.

2. Feature functions like 5 fire if and only if both words and both entities at previous and current position matches.

The second point means that if a simple feature matching only the word (and/or entity) at current position is filtered away from *l1* regularization, it doesn't make sense to include in the training any complex feature function involving that word (and/or entity). In order to train our model using all the features, we proceed in three different steps:

1. we train a model with simple feature functions like 4
2. we search the model for simple feature functions corresponding to adjacent words (and/or entities), that in turn corresponds to complex features
3. we retrain the model where we added the complex features found at previous step

In the second step, the features kept in the model are some order of magnitude fewer in number than those generated including directly complex features in step 1, like it can be done with less data. As a consequence, the number of complex features is limited. Moreover, the fact that simple feature functions must correspond to adjacent words (and/or entities) is a further constraint for the number of added features. As we will see in section 4.1, training CRF model with this procedure provides the same prediction accuracy than what we could have training the model directly with all features.

3.2 Structured Named Entities Reconstruction

Models described in this section are well-known solutions for syntactic parsing. We report them to provide a self-contained and complet work, our main contribution in this respect is to have implemented and adapted algorithms to our task.

The model we use for entity tree reconstruction is PCFG (Booth and Thomson, 1973; Krenn and Samuelsson, 1997). There are more accurate models for the same purpose, e.g. the one used in (Charniak and Johnson, 2005). In practice, the first annotation step being carried out with CRF, which provide a high robustness on noisy data, there is no need for complex and expensive models. Moreover PCFG are quite accurate and very fast for parsing (Collins and Koo, 2005).

The input of the CRF model described in the previous section is a sentence like the one reported in section 2[4]. The output is the sequence of entities corresponding to the leaves of the tree in Figure 2, i.e. entity tree components. For example the chunk **Nations unies** (*United Nations*) is annotated by CRF as

org.adm-B{**Nations**} *org.adm-I*{**unies**}

where suffixes -B and -I (for Begin and Inside) are used to have a one-to-one correspondence between words and entities. This makes the NER task a sequence segmentation and labeling problem, without having to deal with alignment issues. From the annotation above it is immediate to reconstruct the annotation

org.adm{**Nations unies**}

Afterwards words are removed and only components are used as input of the PCFG model to reconstruct the entity tree. In our example, the input would then be:
val object name time-modifier val kind name.
PCFG production rules are extracted directly from the trees. For example from the tree in Figure 2 the following set of rules is extracted:

S ⇒ *amount loc.adm.town ... org.adm*
amount ⇒ *val object*
time.date.rel ⇒ *name time-modifier*
object ⇒ *func.coll*
func.coll ⇒ *kind org.adm*
org.adm ⇒ *name*

where the first production as been cut to keep readability and corresponds to the children of the tree root *S*. Once the rules have been generated from all trees in the training set, probabilities are estimated with simple maximum likelihood estimation as the probability of a production given the right-hand side (RHS) of the rule. The parsing algorithm using the PCFG generated from entity trees is the *Cocke-Younger-Kasami* (CYK) described in (Johnson, 1998). In order to use this algorithm production rules must be in Chomsky Normal Form (CNF), i.e. rules must have one of the two forms: i) $X_i \Rightarrow X_j X_k$; ii) $X_i \Rightarrow w$, where X are non-terminal symbols and w are terminal symbols. The corresponding probabilities are

$$p_{i \rightarrow j,k} = \frac{P(X_i \Rightarrow X_j, X_k)}{P(X_i)} \quad (6)$$

$$p_{i \rightarrow w} = \frac{P(X_i \Rightarrow w)}{P(X_i)} \quad (7)$$

[4] ***90 personnes*** *toujours présentes* ***à Atambua*** *c' est là qu'* ***hier matin*** *ont été tués* ***3 employés du haut commissariat des Nations unies*** *aux réfugiés ,* ***le HCR***

There are well-known algorithms to convert a grammar into CNF, e.g. (Krenn and Samuelsson, 1997). Probabilities are then re-estimated using the Expectation Maximization algorithm called *Inside-Outside* (Krenn and Samuelsson, 1997). The latter is equivalent to the *forward-backword* algorithm for HMM (Rabiner, 1989), where *Inside* and *Outside* variables are used instead of *Forward* and *Backward* variables.

Inside variables $I_i^w(s,t)$ store the probability $P(X_i \Rightarrow^* \mathbf{w}_{s,t} \mid X_i)$, that is the probability of producing the sub-sequence $\mathbf{w}_{s,t} = w_s, ..., w_t$ of the string $\mathbf{w}_{1,T} = w_1, ..., w_T$ from the non-terminal symbol X_i, given the non-terminal symbol X_i, in any number of steps ($\Rightarrow^*$ is the closure of the production symbol $\Rightarrow$). *Outside* variables $O_i^w(s,t)$ store the probability $P(S \Rightarrow^* \mathbf{w}_{0,s}, X_i, \mathbf{w}_{t,T} \mid S)$, that is the probability of producing the subsequence $w_0, ..., w_s, X_i, w_t, ..., w_T$ from the root symbol S, given the root symbol S.

Probability re-estimation consists in computing the quantities $P(X_i \Rightarrow X_j, X_k)$, $P(X_i \Rightarrow w)$ and $P(X_i)$ in terms of *Inside* and *Outside* variables. This give a new estimation of rules probabilities that is used to re-compute *Inside* and *Outside* variables. This procedure is repeated until a convergence criterion is met, e.g. the likelihood doesn't increase significantly.

Given the two annotation steps implemented with CRF and PCFG, our system is in principle equivalent to a single system for syntactic parsing performing a "one-shot" annotation. In particular, solutions like (Charniak and Johnson, 2005) and (Collins and Koo, 2005) use POS tags as tree leaves. This has a two-fold benefit: i) introduces a generalization level over surface forms; ii) provide to the parsing algorithm only the essential information, since POS tags are directly related to syntactic constituents and are sufficient to induce the syntactic structure of a sentence. In our system, the role played by POS tags in syntactic parsing is played by entity components, annotated by CRF.In contrast, for named entity annotation it is not true that components are sufficient to induce the entity tree. Nevertheless, as we will see in next section, this solution does not prevent having good results.

4 Experiments and Results

In this section we first describe the experimental setup, and then we discuss the results. As mentioned in section 3.1, the software used for CRF models is *wapiti*.[5] The procedure for incremental training of CRF models is realized with our own software. We didn't optimize parameters ρ_1 and ρ_2 of the elastic net (see section 3.1), default values lead in most cases to very accurate models. We used a wide set of features in CRF models, in a window of [-2,+2] around the target word:

- A set of standard features like word prefixes and suffixes of length from 1 to 5, plus some *Yes/No* features like *"Does the word start with capital letter ?" "Does the word contain non alphanumeric characters ?"*, etc.
- Morpho-syntactic features extracted from the output of the tool *tagger* (Allauzen and Bonneau-Maynard, 2008)
- Features extracted from the output of the tool *WMatch* (Galibert, 2009; Rosset et al., 2008).

The output provided by *WMatch* contains detailed motpho-syntactic information as well as semantic information at the same level of named entities. Concerning the PCFG model, for preliminary studies we used our own implementation, but for this work we used the much faster implementation described in (Johnson, 1998).[6]

Concerning data, for preliminary studies carried out to validate our incremental training procedure, we used the same data used in the ESTER2 named entity detection evaluation campaign, Thus our results can be directly compared with those reported in (Galliano et al., 2009).

The final results of the 2011 Quaero evaluation campaign are obtained on the data described in section 2. The test data contains transcriptions of both broadcast news and broadcast conversation data. Results are provided on both manual and automatic transcriptions. In the last case, three different ASR systems were used in order to study robustness of the named entity detection systems with respect to different ASR errors and accuracies. These systems are referred to as **ASR1**, **ASR2** and **ASR3** and have word error rates of:

- 16.32%, 18.77%, 24.06% on broadcast news
- 23.34%, 22.99%, 29.18% on broadcast conversations
- 20.96%, 21.56%, 27.44% on the whole test data

[5]available at `http://wapiti.limsi.fr`

[6]available at `http://web.science.mq.edu.au/~mjohnson/Software.htm`

CRF model training		Incremental procedure	
Model features	SER	**Model features**	SER
Words	27.4%	Words+MS+WM unigrams	24.6%
+ MS	26.3%	-	-
+ WM	22.8%	+ Observation bigrams	20.6%
+ MS + WM	20.0%	+ Label bigrams	20.0%

Table 3: Results of CRF models on ESTER2 task obtained with a "normal" training procedure and our incremental procedure. **MS** are morpho-syntactic features, **WM** are features extracted from *WMatch* output

Model	DEV	TEST
CRF (SER)	24.8%	26.7%
$CYK_{ref.}$ (NER)	6.8%	7.4%
CYK (SER)	30.9%	33.3%

Table 4: Results of preliminary experiments obtained with the CRF model and with PCFG separately

Additionally, since manual transcriptions were provided with punctuation, the **ASR1** output has been automatically annotated with punctuation to try to fit manual transcription conditions.

All results are reported in terms of Slot Error Rate (SER) (Makhoul et al., 1999), which has a similar definition of word error rate for ASR systems, with the difference that correct entity with wrong boundaries and wrong entity with correct boundaries are given half points.

4.1 Results

4.1.1 Evaluation of the incremental procedure

Our incremental procedure was evaluated and results are reported in table 3. We compare two models trained and tested on the ESTER2 data used for the evaluation described in (Galliano et al., 2009). The two models are based on the same features, described in previous section, but use them in two different ways: In the first model, trained with "traditional procedure", the three different type of features (words, features from *tagger* and features from *WMatch*) were integrated in three different steps, using each time unigrams and bigrams on observations and labels. The three steps are mandatory since the total amount of features would not fit into memory.
In the second model, we used directly all type of features, but generating at first only simple features. 3.1.1. In the two other training steps, we added compound features, i.e. bigrams of observations and labels, and we retrained at each step.
As we can see from results in table 3, the two models reach the same final accuracy (a SER of 20.0%), which proves that our incremental training procedure doesn't leave out meaningful features. Additionally, although we don't report training time, we can comment that CRF model training was roughly 10 times faster with our incremental procedure. This is normal since in the second and third steps only compound features corresponding to simple features kept by the first model are added, with the additional constraint that simple features must correspond to adjacent positions. As explained in sub-section 3.1.1, the simple features kept at the end of the training are some orders of magnitude fewer in number than the original features. This limits tremendously the number of compound features added in the other steps. Note also that the results shown in Table 3 are much better than those shown in (Galliano et al., 2009), compared with other solutions.

Average score	Feature type
0.114053	wrd-2
0.0988316	Pre4
0.0914648	Wrd-1
0.084988	wrd-1
0.083699	Suf4
0.0751365	Pre3
0.0745788	WMatch2-2
0.0483077	WMatch1-1
-	...
0.00889771	POS+agree-1
0.00810903	WMatch4-1
0.00789857	POS-2
-0.0022887	POS+type-1
-0.0262062	POS-1
-0.0294334	Suf1
-0.0337793	Pre1

Table 5: Ranks of average score given by the CRF model to feature types

4.1.2 Features relevance

In order to understand features relevance, we report in table 5 feature types ranked by the average score given by the CRF model. Each type correspond to features at any position with respect to the target word, with label unigrams and bigrams. Unigrams are distinguished from bigrams using suffixes *-1* and *-2* respectively. Feature types *wrd* are words converted to lower case, *Wrd* are words kept with original capitalization. Feature types *Pren* are word prefixes of length n, *Sufn* are word suffixes of length n. Features extracted from *WMatch* output are indexed starting from 1. As we can see from the table, morpho-syntactic features (those marked with *POS*) receive quite low scores, especially POS tags. This point validates our intuition about using POS tags for named entity detection, pointed out in section 3. Note that feature types correspond to different layers of information added upon surface level, from less, like prefixes, to more general, like *WMatch* semantic layer. Thus, although some features may have outlier scores, the average score is a good indicator of the relevance of each feature type.

4.1.3 Models for tree-structured named entities

In table 4 we report an evaluation of the two models composing our system. In the first row we report the SER of the CRF model used in the system, taking into account only components, i.e. base entities annotated directly on words. They can be compared for the test set (TEST) with the 20% SER of table 3. We go from a SER of 20% to 26.7%, but it is important to note that the ESTER2 evaluation campaign was performed using only 17 labels, while 26.7% is obtained using 196 entity components. We can thus be satisfied by that result. In order to evaluate the robustness of the CYK algorithm on our task, we computed the Node Error Rate (NER in table 4) on reference components ($CYK_{ref.}$). The CYK module is applied on the reference components instead of those output by the CRF model. The rate of wrong tree nodes with respect to the reference trees is then computed. The NER being under 10%, we can assume that the PCFG model is robust on unseen data. This also confirms the effectiveness of using components directly, instead of the lexical surface forms. Finally we report the results obtained combining the two approaches (CRF+CYK). Errors of the CYK algorithm are summed to errors of CRF, thus we go from a SER of 24.8% and 26.7% on DEV and TEST (row 1, table 4), to 30.9% and 33.3%.

4.1.4 Official results

We report results of the 2011 Quaero named entity detection evaluation campaign (Galibert et al., 2011) in table 6, where **BN** correspond to broadcast news, **BN** to broadcast conversations and **Mrg** to the merge of these two types. Our system is indicated as *CRF+CYK*. The other two participants, *P1* and *P2*, used a system based on CRF and deep syntactic analysis, respectively.[7]

Looking at results we can see that our system outperforms the others in all cases by several points. Nevertheless error rates are quite high, over 50% on ASR output. The complexity of the task must without a doubt be taken into account. It is indeed the first time that structured named entities are handled with an automatic detection. Also the type of data used for the task, i.e. transcriptions of French broadcast data, contributes to increase the task complexity. Despite these results, our approach seems promising since it worked far better than the others in all cases.

		Manual	ASR1	ASR1+	ASR2	ASR3
BN	**WER**		16.32%	16.32%	18.77%	24.06%
	P1	42.7%	55.3%	52.7%	58.5%	61.4%
	P2	39.1%	55.6%	54.5%	60.3%	61.8%
	CRF+CYK	29.7%	48.5%	53.8%	52.2%	53.5%
CN	**WER**		23.34%	23.34%	22.99%	29.18%
	P1	55.3%	87.9%	89.9%	78.3%	89.2%
	P2	43.0%	89.3%	83.3%	81.2%	84.1%
	CRF+CYK	37.0%	73.9%	79.0%	66.6%	73.0%
Mrg	**WER**		20.96%	20.96%	21.56%	27.44%
	P1	48.9%	71.4%	71.1%	68.3%	75.2%
	P2	41.0%	72.2%	68.7%	70.7%	72.9%
	CRF+CYK	33.3%	61.1%	66.3%	59.3%	63.2%

Table 6: SER results for the 2011 evaluation campaign on broadcast news (**BN**), broadcast conversation (**BC**) and their merge (**Mrg**) on both manual and automatic transcriptions

Oracles VS Evaluations	**DEV**	**TEST**
CRF+CYK (SER)	30.9%	33.3%
CRF+CYK (OER)	18.6%	21.1%

Table 7: Comparison of Oracle Error Rate (OER) and SER obtained in the evaluation for DEV and TEST sets

We report a comparison of results on manual transcriptions with Oracle Error Rates (OER), i.e. results of our system using the best annotation of CRF among the 10-best hypotheses. This comparison is reported in table 7, and shows that we have a large margin for improvements on our system.

5 Conclusions

In this paper we proposed a system for structured named entity detection. We describe the definition of these structured named entities. The proposed system is based on CRF and syntactic parsing approaches, which combines the effectiveness and robustness of the former with the capability of easily and quickly parsing trees of the latter. Additionally, we proposed an incremental training procedure for CRF model, which showed to be correct and effective and allows to train CRF models with huge number of features. The proposed system participated in the Quaero evaluation campaign and obtained the best results. Although results on ASR output are not satisfactory, taking all results into account the proposed approach seems promising and encourages further studies.

Acknowledgments

This work was partly realized as part of the Quaero Programme, funded by Oseo, French State agency for innovation

[7]There are not more details on the other participant's systems, since they have not been published yet

References

Erik F. Tjong Kim Sang and Fien De Meulder. 2003. Introduction to the conll-2003 shared task: language-independent named entity recognition. In *Proceedings of NLL at HLT-NAACL 2003 - Volume 4*, pages 142–147, Morristown, USA.

Ellen M. Voorhees. 2001. The trec question answering track. *Nat. Lang. Eng.*, 7:361–378, December.

X. Carreras and Lluis Marquez. 2005. Introduction to the conll-2005 shared task: Semantic role labeling.

R. De Mori, F. Bechet, D. Hakkani-Tur, M. McTear, G. Riccardi, and G. Tur. 2008. Spoken language understanding: A survey. *IEEE Signal Processing Magazine*, 25:50–58.

Sylvain Galliano, Guillaume Gravier, and Maura Chaubard. 2009. The ester 2 evaluation campaign for the rich transcription of french radio broadcasts. In *Proceedings of Interspeech*, Brighton, U.K.

Olivier Galibert, Sophie Rosset, Cyril Grouin, Pierre Zweigenbaum, Ludovic Quintard 2011. Structured and Extended Named Entity Evaluation in Automatic Speech Transcriptions In *Proceedings of IJCNLP*, Chang Mai, Thailand.

E. Charniak and M. Johnson. 2005. Coarse-to-fine n-best parsing and maxent discriminative reranking. In *Proceedings of ACL*, page 363370, Ann Arbor, MI.

Michael Collins and Terry Koo. 2005. Discriminative re-ranking for natural language parsing. *Computational Linguistic (CL)*, 31(1):25–70.

J. Lafferty, A. McCallum, and F. Pereira. 2001. Conditional random fields: Probabilistic models for segmenting and labeling sequence data. In *Proceedings of ICML*, pages 282–289, Williamstown, USA.

T.L. Booth and R.A. Thompson. 1973. Applying Probability Measures to Abstract Languages. In IEEE Transactions on Computers, 22:442–450.

Brigitte Krenn and Christer Samuelsson. 1997. The linguist's guide to statistics - don't panic.

Thomas Lavergne, Olivier Cappé, and François Yvon. 2010. Practical very large scale CRFs. In *Proceedings ACL*, pages 504–513.

Stefan Hahn, Patrick Lehnen, Georg Heigold, and Hermann Ney. 2009. Optimizing crfs for slu tasks in various languages using modified training criteria. In *Proceedings of Interspeech*, Brighton, U.K.

Stefan Riezler and Alexander Vasserman. 2010. Incremental feature selection and l1 regularization for relaxed maximum-entropy modeling.

Hui Zou and Trevor Hastie. 2005. Regularization and variable selection via the Elastic Net. *Journal of the Royal Statistical Society B*, 67:301–320.

Andrew McCallum. 2003. Efficiently inducing features of conditional random fields. In *19th Conference on Uncertainty in Artificial Intelligence*.

Lawrence R. Rabiner. 1989. A tutorial on hidden markov models and selected applications in speech recognition. *Proceedings of the IEEE*, 77(2):257–286.

Mark Johnson. 1998. Pcfg models of linguistic tree representations. *Computational Linguistics*, 24:613–632.

Olivier Galibert, Ludovic Quintard, Sophie Rosset, Pierre Zweigenbaum, Claire Ndellec, Sophie Aubin, Laurent Gillard, Jean-Pierre Raysz, Delphine Pois, Xavier Tannier, Louise Delger, and Dominique Laurent. 2010. Named and specific entity detection in varied data: The quro named entity baseline evaluation. In *Proceedings of LREC*, La Valletta, Malta.

Olivier Galibert. 2009. *Approches et méthodologies pour la réponse automatique à des questions adaptées un cadre interactif en domaine ouvert.* Ph.D. thesis, Universit Paris Sud, Orsay.

Sophie Rosset, Olivier Galibert, Fuillaume Bernard, Eric Bilinski, and Gilles Adda. 2008. The LIMSI participation to the QAst track. In Working Notes of CLEF 2008 Workshop.

G. Doddington, A. Mitchell, M. Przybocki, L. Ramshaw, S. Strassel, and R. Weischedel. 2004. The Automatic Content Extraction (ACE) Program–Tasks, Data, and Evaluation. *Proceedings of LREC 2004*, pages 837–840.

Sam Coates-Stephens. 1992. The analysis and acquisition of proper names for the understanding of free text. *Computers and the Humanities*, 26:441–456.

Ralph Grishman and Beth Sundheim. 1996. Message Understanding Conference - 6: A brief history. In *Proceedings of COLING*, pages 466–471, Copenhagen, Denmark.

Michael Fleischman and Eduard Hovy. 2002. Fine grained classification of named entities. In *Proceedings of COLING*, pages 1–7.

Michael Fleischman. 2001. Automated subcategorization of named entities. In *Proceedings of the ACL 2001 Student Research Workshop*, pages 25–30.

Eckhard Bick. 2004. A named entity recognizer for danish. In *LREC'04*, Lisbon, Portugal.

Satoshi Sekine. 2004. Definition, dictionaries and tagger of extended named entity hierarchy. In *LREC'04*, Lisbon, Portugal.

Alexandre Allauzen and Hélène Bonneau-Maynard. 2008. Training and evaluation of pos taggers on the french multitag corpus. In *Proceedings of LREC*, Marrakech, Morocco.

John Makhoul, Francis Kubala, Richard Schwartz, and Ralph Weischedel. 1999. Performance measures for information extraction. In *Proceedings of DARPA Broadcast News Workshop*, pages 249–252.

Cyril Grouin, Sophie Rosset, Pierre Zweigenbaum, Karen Fort, Olivier Galibert, Ludovic Quintard. 2011. Proposal for an Extension or Traditional Named Entities: From Guidelines to Evaluation, an Overview. In *Proceedings of the Linguistic Annotation Workshop (LAW)*.

Clausal parsing helps data-driven dependency parsing: Experiments with Hindi

Samar Husain*, Phani Gadde*, Joakim Nivre† and Rajeev Sangal*
* Language Technologies Research Centre, IIIT-Hyderabad, India.
† Department of Linguistics and Philology, Uppsala University, Sweden.
{samar, phani.gadde}@research.iiit.ac.in,
joakim.nivre@lingfil.uu.se, sangal@mail.iiit.ac.in

Abstract

This paper investigates clausal data-driven dependency parsing. We first motivate a clause as the minimal parsing unit by correlating inter- and intra-clausal relations with relation type, depth, arc length and non-projectivity. This insight leads to a two-stage formulation of parsing where intra-clausal relations are identified in the 1st stage and inter-clausal relations are identified in the 2nd stage. We compare two ways of implementing this idea, one based on hard constraints (similar to the one used in constraint-based parsing) and one based on soft constraints (using a kind of parser stacking). Our results show that the approach using hard constraints seems most promising and performs significantly better than single-stage parsing. Our best result gives significant increase in LAS and UAS, respectively, over the previous best result using single-stage parsing.

1 Introduction

There has been a recent surge in addressing parsing for morphologically rich free word order languages such as Czech, Turkish, Hindi, etc. These languages pose various challenges for the task of parsing mainly because the syntactic cues necessary to identify various relations are complex and distributed (Tsarfaty et al., 2010; Ambati et al., 2010; Nivre and McDonald, 2008; Tsarfaty and Sima'an, 2008; Seddah et al., 2009; Gadde et al., 2010; Husain et al., 2009; Eryigit et al., 2008). There has also been a lot of interest in building ensemble systems (Zeman and Zabokrtsky, 2005; Sagae and Lavie, 2006) and parser stacking (Nivre and McDonald, 2008; Martins et al., 2009) to improve the overall parsing accuracy by combining the strengths of multiple parsers.

In this paper, we formulate clausal parsing as a two-stage setup where intra-clausal relations are identified in the 1st stage and inter-clausal relations are identified in the 2nd stage. We attempt to find out whether this two-stage parsing approach that has earlier been successful in constraint-based systems for parsing Hindi (Bharati et al., 2009) can also benefit data-driven parsing approaches (Nivre et al., 2006), and compare two ways of implementing this idea, one based on hard constraints (similar to the one used in constraint-based parsing), and one based on soft constraints (using a kind of parser stacking; (Nivre and McDonald, 2008). We show that one of the ways in which clausal parsing helps is by better learning of features that leads to improved label accuracy for Hindi. In particular we show that ambiguous case markers (or suffixes) that appear with many relations can be disambiguated successfully. We also show that the setup reduces many of the traditional MaltParser (Nivre et al., 2006) errors (McDonald and Nivre, 2007). Our results show that the approach using hard constraints seems most promising and performs significantly better than single-stage parsing.

The paper is arranged as follows. In Section 2, we introduce the clause as a basic parsing unit. Section 3 gives a brief overview of two-stage parsing. In Section 4 we discuss data-driven parsing for Hindi and present two methods for implementing two-stage parsing within this framework. Section 5 explains the experimental setup, and Section 6 discusses the results. We conclude the paper in Section 7.

2 Clauses as minimal parsing units

We begin with the observation that certain dependency relations are more likely to occur between the elements inside a clause and a different set of relations are more likely in showing dependencies across clauses. We also note that the notion of clause can be correlated with short distance and long distance dependencies.

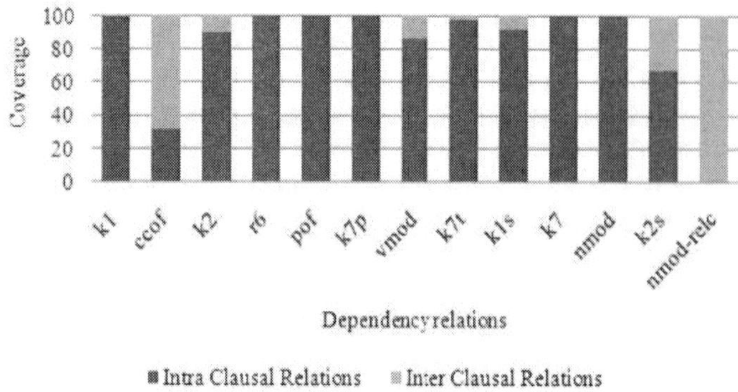

Fig 1. Dependency label distribution.

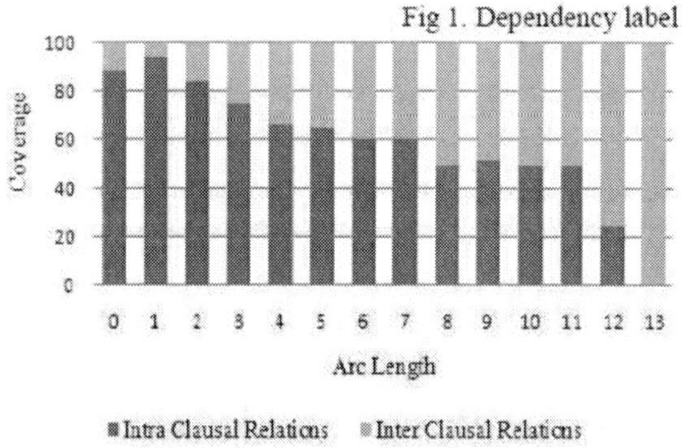

Fig 2. Arc length and relation type

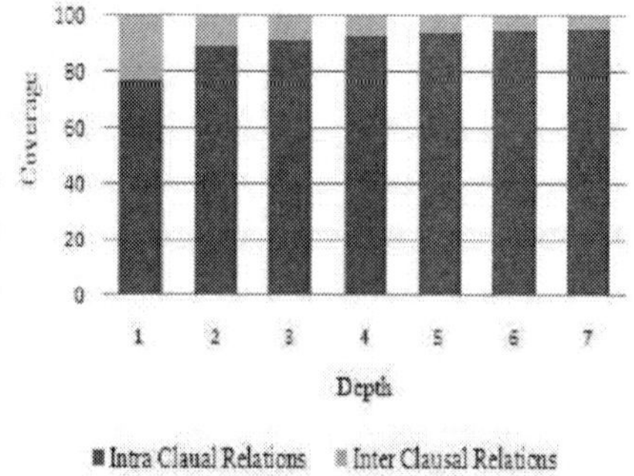

Fig 3. Depth and relation type

Figure 1 shows the distribution of dependency labels with respect to clause type (intra-clausal vs. inter-clausal) in the Hyderabad dependency treebank (Begum et al., 2008; Husain 2009). For ease of exposition, Figure 1 only shows the labels with considerable coverage, together amounting to 93% of all dependency label occurrences. We can see clearly that many labels like k1[1], r6, etc. are overwhelmingly intra-clausal relation, while others like nmod-relc, ccof, etc. have an inter-clausal bias.

Figure 2 shows that short-distance dependencies are mostly intra-clausal, whereas long-distance dependencies tend to be inter-clausal. It is clear from Figure 1 and 2 that there is a clear correlation between labels and relation type on one hand and arc length and relation type on the other. Further, there is a correlation between inter- vs. intra-clausal relations with respect to depth of relations as well. Figure 3 shows that low depth dependencies are both inter-clausal (in case of complex sentences involving coordination, relative clauses, embeddings, etc.) and intra-clausal (simple sentences). It also shows that the percentage of inter-clausal relations decrease with increase in depth.

Finally, there is a correlation between clause and non-projectivity: 70% of the non-projective relations are inter-clausal (Mannem et al., 2009).

Properties such as relation type, arc length, depth, and non-projectivity are known to have specific effect on errors in data-driven dependency parsing (McDonald and Nivre, 2007). Therefore, it is worth exploring the effect of clause (when treated as a minimal unit) on dependency parsing accuracy. For all the experiment described in this paper, the following definition of clause is used: '*A clause is a group of words containing a single finite verb and its dependents*'. More precisely, let T be the complete dependency tree of a sentence, and let G be a clausal subgraph of T. Then an arc $x \rightarrow y$ in G is a valid arc, if (a) x is a finite verb; (b) y is not a finite verb; (c) there is no z such that $y \rightarrow z$, where z is a finite verb and y is a conjunct.

[1] The dependency label *k1* can be roughly translated to 'agent', *r6* is a dependency label for genitive relation, *ccof* is a relation signifying conjunction and *nmod-relc* is used for relative clause modification. For the complete description of the tagset and the dependency scheme see (Begum et al., 2008).

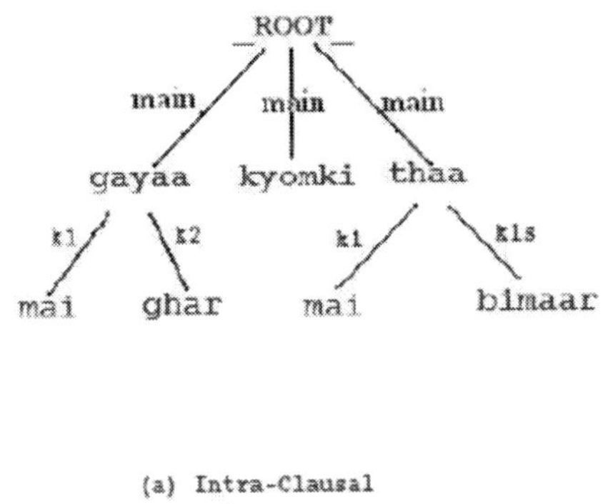

Fig. 4(a). 1st stage output

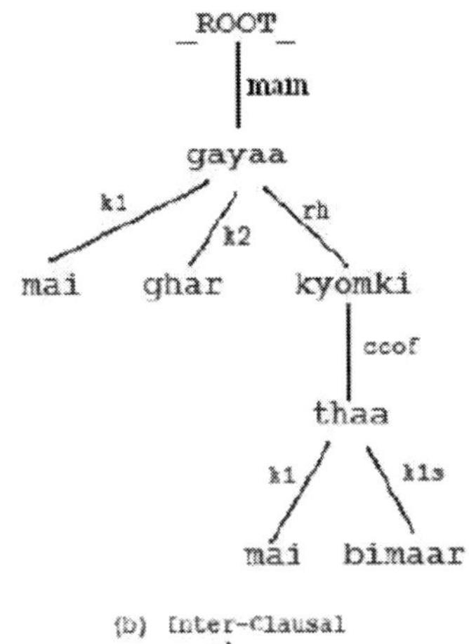

Fig. 4(b). 2nd stage output

3 Two-stage parsing

Two-stage parsing has been successfully used in a constraint based system for Hindi (Bharati et al., 2009, 2009b). This parser tries to analyze the given input sentence, which has already been POS tagged and chunked, in 2 stages; it first tries to extract intra-clausal dependency relations. In the 2nd stage it then tries to handle more complex relations such as those involved in constructions of coordination and subordination between clauses.

(1) *mai* *ghar* *gayaa* *kyomki* *mai*
'I' 'home' 'went' 'because' 'I'
*bi*maar *thaa*
'sick' 'was'
'I went home because I was sick'

The 1st stage output for sentence (1) is shown in Figure 4a. In Figure 4a, the parsed matrix clause subtree *mai ghar gayaa* and the subordinate clause are attached to _ROOT_. The subordinating conjunction *kyomki* is also seen attached to the _ROOT_. The dependency tree thus obtained in the 1st stage is partial, but linguistically sound. By introducing _ROOT_ we are able to attach all unprocessed nodes to it. _ROOT_ ensures that the output we get after each stage is a tree. Later in the 2nd stage the relationship between the two clauses are identified. The 2nd stage parse for the above sentence is shown in Figure 4b. The 2nd stage does not modify the parse sub-trees obtained from the 1st stage, it only establishes the relations between the clauses.

4 Two-stage data-driven parsing

Since the availability of the Hyderabad Dependency Treebank for Hindi (Begum et al., 2008) a considerable amount of work has gone into exploring various data-driven approaches for Hindi parsing (Bharati et al., 2008; Husain et al., 2009; Mannem et al., 2009b; Gadde et al., 2010). The ICON09 and ICON10 tools contests on Indian language parsing (Husain, 2009; Husain et al., 2010) have also showcased various parsing efforts and established the state-of-the-art for Hindi dependency parsing. During both these parsing contest MaltParser was used to achieve the best accuracy for Hindi.

Through the experiments described in this paper, we aim to investigate the following questions:

- What are the different ways in which one can treat clauses as minimal unit during the parsing process?
- Will this help improve parsing accuracy using MaltParser?

We now present two data-driven paradigms that incorporate the notion of clause in different ways. Both paradigms use two stages to parse a sentence, but the way the two stages interact is different.

4.1 2-stage parsing with hard constraints (2-Hard)

The basic idea behind this strategy is essentially the same as constraint-based two-stage parsing. The 2nd stage MaltParser takes as input partial 1st stage trees and establishes relationships between clauses (and conjunctions). The 1st stage predictions are mutually exclusive of the 2nd stage predictions and cannot be overridden in the 2nd stage. However, they can be used as features in the 2nd stage predictions.

We now define the input to the 2nd stage for 2-Hard more precisely, Let T be the complete tree that should be output by the 2nd stage parser and let G be the subgraph of T that is input to the second stage. Then G should satisfy the following constraint: if the arc $x \rightarrow y$ is in G, then, for every z such that $y \rightarrow z$ is in T, $y \rightarrow z$ is also in G. In other words, if an arc is included in the 1st stage partial parse, the complete subtree under the dependent must also be included. Unless this constraint is satisfied, there are trees that the second-stage parser cannot construct. This means that the 2nd stage MaltParser gets initialized with only those nodes that are attached to the _ROOT_ in the first stage parse (cf. Figure 4(a)). Figure 5 below shows the initial configuration of 2nd stage Malt for sentence 3, the input will be the 1st stage parse shown in Figure 4(a).

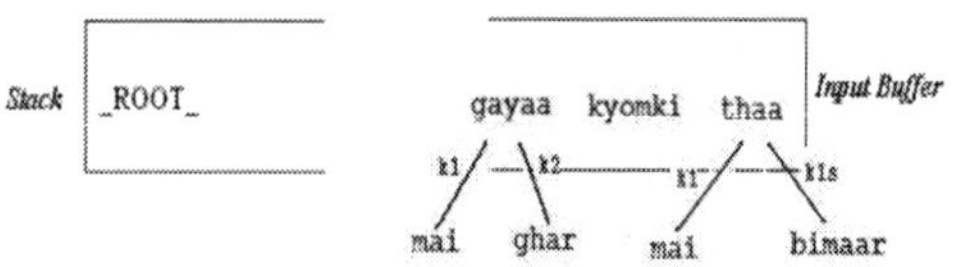

Fig 5. 2nd stage initialization using the 1st stage parse shown in Fig. 4(a)

The 1st stage and 2nd stage parser will cater to different types of constructions. Note that, given the above constraint on the 2nd stage input structures, a relative clause (though being subordinate clause) cannot be handled in the 2nd stage and will have to be handled in the 1st stage itself. We explain the handling of relative clause using sentence (2).

(2) *vaha vahaan waba puhuchaa*
'He' 'there' 'when-COREL' 'reached'
jaba sab jaa chuke the
'when-REL' 'everyone' 'go' 'had'
'He reached there when everyone had left'

Figure 6(a) shows the 1st stage output of a relative clause construction in a standard 2-stage setup. Both the relative clause and the matrix clause are seen attached to the _ROOT_, the analysis of these clauses is complete. In second stage the relation between these two clauses is established (Figure 6b). Recall that we initialize the 2nd stage of 2-Hard with the children of _ROOT_ which in this case is the finite verbs of the two clauses (Figure 6c). Now recall the constraint on the input of the 2nd stage in 2-Hard; given this constraint the 2nd stage can only establish a relation between the two verbs and not, as is correct, between the relative clause verb and a noun dependent on the matrix verb. The noun 'waba' is not present in the input buffer and can never be considered as a head of 'jaa'. Because of this reason, 2-Hard handles relative clauses through a separate classifier after the 1st stage. This parse is then fed into the 2nd stage. This system is discussed in the next section.

4.1.1 Handling relative clauses

We add the relative clause relations to the 1st stage parse, before they are fed into the 2nd stage. This task comprises of two sub-tasks, a) relative clause identification from the 1st stage output and b) identifying the head of the relative clause from the matrix clause.

Most of the time, relative clause sentences in Hindi contain relative pronouns such as *jo* 'who', *jaba* 'when', *jisa* 'which' in the relative clause, which modifies an element (sometimes identified as a co-relative pronoun) in the matrix clause. The matrix clause, on the other hand, contains co-relative pronouns like *waba* 'then'. This can be seen in the example sentence (2) in the previous section. However, both these elements can be dropped (though dropping relative pronouns is rare). This information is used in doing both the sub-tasks for the relative clause relation identification.

The identification of relative clauses is rule based and depends on the presence of an exhaustive list of relative and co-relative pronouns. Such a lexically driven approach is possible because of nature of relative clause constructions in Hindi. This system has an accuracy of 94%. The errors are mainly due to the dropping of the two type of cues discussed earlier.

Having identified the relative clause in a sentence, the remaining finite clauses are considered as possible matrix clauses. The nodes in each of these clauses are considered as possible heads for the relative clause. We use a maximum entropy (MaxEnt) based boolean classifier [2] to predict whether a node is a head or not. If more than one node is predicted as the head, we pick the node with the highest classifier confidence.

[2] http://homepages.inf.ed.ac.uk/lzhang10/maxent_toolkit.html

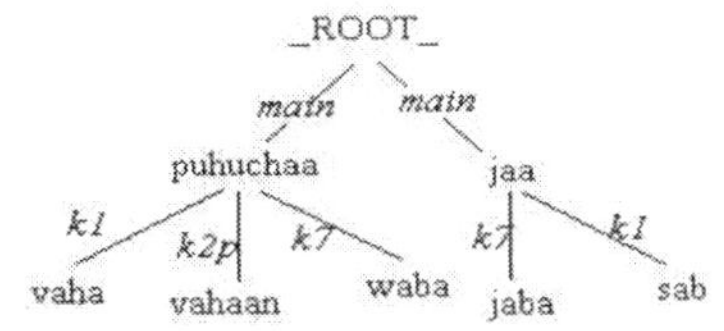

(a) 1st stage output for a relative clause construction in a standard 2 stage setup

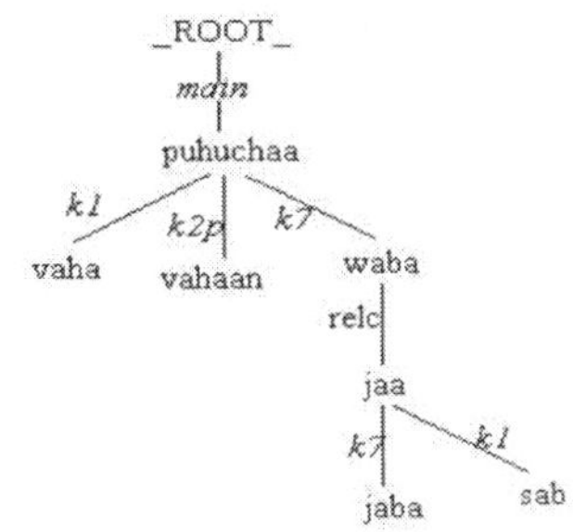

(b) 2nd stage output for a relative clause construction in a standard 2 stage setup

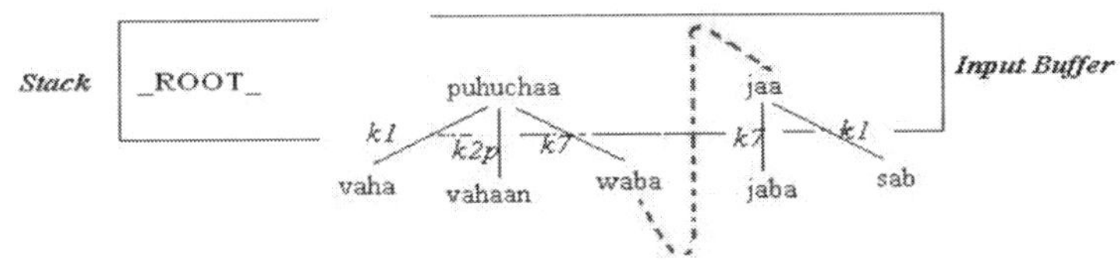

(c) 2-Hard cannot establish the correct attachment for 'relc' (relative clause) in 2nd stage because of input constraint.
2-Hard handles relative clause constructions in 1st stage itself.

Fig. 6

The Part-Of-Speech (POS) tag of a node, its direction and distance from the relative clause are some of the important features to identify the modified noun. Note that identification of the head noun in the absence of the co-relative pronoun can be very subjective. Table 1 shows the features that are used to train the classifier.

Feature	Description	Values
Lex	Lexical item	the lexical item
POS	POS tag	NN, RB etc..
Dir	Direction of node	-1, 1
Dist	Distance of node	4,8,12, 16, 20, 24
Cue	Relative pronoun	*jaba, jo etc..*

Table 1: Features used in maxent based node classification

Dir is given 1 if a node is to the left of the relative clause and -1 if it is on the right. The distance of the node from the relative clause, *Dist*, is actually the modulus of the distance as direction is already taken care of. Further, it is normalized to the above mentioned values to reduce the sparsity. *Cue* is given "None" if there is no relative pronoun (if it is dropped) modifying the node.

We note that when compared to Husain et al. (2009) (who also do 2 stage parsing and use clauses as hard constraint) our method differs in two significant ways. The first one is obvious; they don't handle constructions such as relative clauses etc in their setup. But more importantly, unlike Husain et al. (2009), the novel thing here is the combination of data-driven parsing and hard constraints, made possible by the new version of MaltParser that accepts partial dependency graphs as input (both during training and parsing) (cf. Figure 5).

4.2 2-stage parsing with soft constraints (2-Soft)

We can, instead of treating the output of the first-stage parser as hard constraints for the second-stage parser, treat them as soft constraints by simply defining features over the arcs produced in the first stage and making a complete parse in the second stage. Technically, this is the same technique that (Nivre and McDonald, 2008) used to integrate Malt and MST, called *guided parsing* or *parser stacking*. In this setup we 'guide' Malt with a 1st stage parse by Malt. The additional features added to the 2nd stage parser during 2-Soft parsing encode the decisions by the 1st stage parser concerning potential arcs and labels considered by the 2nd stage parser, in particular, arcs involving the word currently on top of the stack and the word currently at the head of the input buffer. For more details on the guide features for MaltParser, see (Nivre and McDonald, 2008). Note again that, unlike the standard two-stage setup the 1st stage relations can now be overridden during the 2nd stage (because we are guiding), and unlike the standard guided parsing setup a parser guides with only 1st stage relations.

Unlike the 2-stage parsing, guided parsing parses complete sentences twice. The results from one parser are used to extract features that guide the second parser. In 2-stage parsing, different components of a sentence are parsed in two stages. Interestingly, Gadde et al. (2010) have proposed an alternative way of incorporating clauses as soft constraint by using clause boundary and clausal head/non-head features during parsing. Of course, theirs is not a 2-stage setup.

5 Experimental setup

All the results are reported for Hindi. We use the Hindi data set that was released as part of ICON10 parsing contest (Husain et al., 2010). The training set had 2972 sentences, the development and test set had 543 and 321 sentences respectively. The parser models were trained using 5-fold cross validation; all the results are also reported for the cross-validation data. The setup used by (Ambati et al., 2010) for MaltParser[3] is used as our baseline.

Recall that the 1st stage and 2nd stage parser of 2-Hard will cater to different types of constructions. This is sometimes also reflected in the features that get selected for each stage when compared to the Baseline settings. One such case was the absence of morphological features of lexical items in the 2nd stage for 2-Hard. The morphological properties such as suffix, category, case, etc. are crucial in establishing relations between verbs and its arguments. This in 2-Hard will be handled in the 1st stage. The relations in the 2nd stage do not require such features. On the other hand, the POS category and the lexical item of the elements in Stack and Input buffer are more crucial for 2nd stage relations than for the 1st stage specific relations. This is reflected in the selection of 'lemma' of the word under consideration in 2nd stage and not in baseline.

Both 2-Soft and 2-Hard 1st stage parsers are trained on a modified treebank. The original trees are transformed into 1st stage trees. This is done by using the clause definition described in Section 2. For example, the 1st stage tree for sentence 3 is shown in Figure 4 (a). On the other hand, a normal single stage parser (our baseline parser) is trained on the full tree that looks like Figure 4 (b).

[3] MaltParser (version 1.3.1)

6 Results and discussion

Table 2 shows the performance of the different parsers with 5-fold cross-validation. In all tables statistical significance with respect to baseline is marked with *. Significance is calculated using McNemar's test ($p <= 0.05$). These tests were made with MaltEval (Nilsson and Nivre, 2008).

	LAS	UAS	LA
Baseline	75.02	88.82	77.80
2-Soft	75.24	88.92	78.00
2-Hard	**75.65***	**89.1***	**78.73***

Table 2: Overall parsing accuracy (5-fold cross-validation)

We see that both 2-Soft and 2-Hard outperform the Baseline result. However, only 2-Hard is statistically significant with that of Baseline for LAS, UAS as well as LS. 2-Soft, though giving a minimal improvement in the accuracies, is not statistically significant with the baseline. However, on analyzing the output parses of all the three setups, we found clear and similar improvement patterns (listed below) in case of both 2-Hard and 2-Soft. This led us to look at the sentences having at least two clauses, where the effect of the proposed approaches is more prominent. These constitute 50.4% of the total sentences in the data. Table 3 below shows the parsing accuracies of all the setups on these complex sentences.

	LAS	UAS	LA
Baseline	74.87	88.82	77.44
2-Soft	**75.25***	89.03	**77.78***
2-Hard	**75.83***	**89.36***	**78.85***

Table 3: Parsing accuracy on complex sentences (sentences having >1 finite clauses) (5-fold cross-validation)

Interestingly, the improvements in both 2-Soft and 2-Hard are better than those shown in Table 2. Also, 2-Soft is now statistically significant compared to the Baseline w.r.t. LAS and LS. Overall, both the approaches seem to perform better for labels over attachments. To analyze the results further, we breakdown the overall accuracy (shown in Table 2) into inter-clausal and intra-clausal accuracies. Table 4 below shows these results.

	LAS		UAS		LA	
	Intra	Inter	Intra	Inter	Intra	Inter
Baseline	72.18	85.43	89.05	87.98	75.26	87.13
2-Soft	**72.44**	85.54	**89.13**	88.16	**75.49**	87.17
2-Hard	72.36	**87.71**	88.87	**90.10**	75.47	**90.68**

Table 4: Overall accuracy for intra- and inter-clausal dependency relations

Table 4 shows some interesting facts. 2-Hard performs far better than Baseline and 2-Soft in case of inter-clausal relations, where as its effect is less for intra-clausal relations. 2-Soft, on the other hand, gives the best accuracies for intra-clausal relations over all the metrics. Note that the 2nd stage in 2-Soft approach has the flexibility to modify the dependencies given by the 1st stage parse. This could be the possible reason for 2-Soft performing better than 2-Hard for the intra-clausal relations, which are large in number as well as consisting of more deviant patterns compared to the inter-clausal relations.

These experiments show us that there is a clear pattern in cases where parsing benefits from 2-Soft and 2-Hard. These benefits are spread over both 1st stage and 2nd stage. These cases are:

1. Better identification of some relations with deviant/ambiguous postpositions in the 1st stage. For example, when 'se' appears for beneficiary/cause, instead of its default usage for instrument. Table 5 shows the label identification for some frequent postpositions.
2. Better handling of non-finite verbs in the 1st stage
3. Better handling of NULL nodes in the 2nd stage. Most NULL nodes are cases of ellipses where a syntactic heads such as finite verb or a conjunct is missing. Most of these cases fall into 2nd stage and are being better handled there.
4. Better handling of some 2nd stage specific constructions, e.g. clausal complements.

Closely related to the above four points is the performance of the clausal setups with respect to arc length, depth and non-projectivity. It is known that Malt suffers on the dependencies closer to the root (less depth) due to error-propagation. Also, Malt suffers at long distance dependencies because of local feature optimization (McDonald and Nivre, 2007). In other words, for Malt, depth and errors are negatively correlated while arc-distance and errors are positively correlated.

Figure 7 shows the LAS of relations at various arc-lengths for the Baseline and clausal setups. Figure 8 shows the performance of relations at different depths. The 2nd stage of 2-Hard considers the heads of the partial trees produced by the 1st stage as the nodes (minimal parsing unit), which reduces the arc-length of the inter-clausal dependencies. Hence, as the arc-length increases, the advantage of 2-Hard becomes more pronounced.

Postposition	Baseline	2-Hard/ 2-Soft
0		✓
meM		✓
para	✓	
GEN		✓
ko	✓	
se		✓

Table 5: Label identification comparison between Baseline and the clausal approaches for ambiguous postpositions. ✓ signifies better performance. 0 and GEN signify null postposition and genitive postpositions respectively

By distinguishing intra-clausal structures from inter-clausal structures, the 2-Hard setup is using shallower trees and is able to take better global decisions by using more contextual information. It is expected to reduce the error propagation for the low-depth dependency relations. This effect is clearly seen in Figure 8, where for less depth 2-Hard outperforms Baseline. Cases (3) and (4) above reflect this.

Cases (1) and (2) on the other hand show that the clausal setups also effects 1st stage performance by learning verbal arguments (both complements and adjuncts) better. It is known that MaltParser has a rich feature representation but with increase in sentence length its performance gets affected due error propagation. By treating a clause as a parsing unit we reduce this error propagation as the features are being exploited properly.

It was found that both the clausal setups did not help in reducing the non-projective relations. As all the setups use the Arc-Eager parsing algorithm, they fare equally badly in handling non-projectivity. There were some sentences where non-projectivity got removed in the 1st stage,

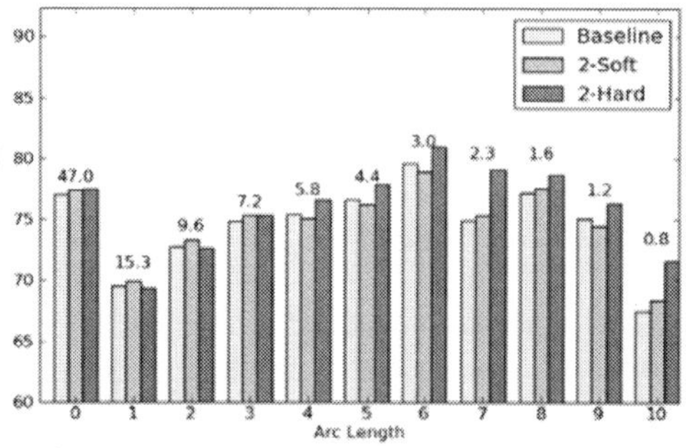

Fig. 7. LAS at arc-length (1-10) for Baseline, 2-Soft and 2-Hard. The numbers above the bars represent the % of relations at respective arc lengths.

however the non-projective arc reappeared in the 2nd stage, this happened in the case of paired connective constructions (cf., Mannem et al., 2009). We are yet to investigate if pseudo-projective parsing in the 2nd stage might prove beneficial in such cases.

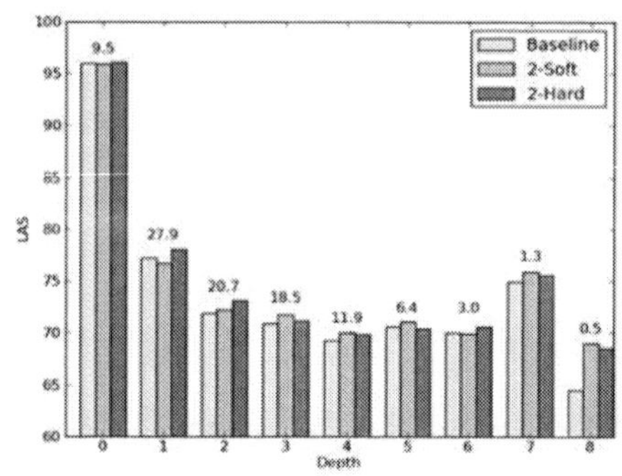

Fig. 8. LAS at depth (1-7) for Baseline, 2-Soft and 2-Hard. The numbers above the bars represent the % of relations at respective depths.

7 Conclusion

This paper investigated clausal data-driven dependency parsing. We implemented this idea using two methods, one based on hard constraints (similar to the one used in constraint-based parsing), and one based on soft constraints (using a kind of parser stacking). Our results showed that the approach using hard constraints seems most promising and performs significantly better than single-stage parsing. We showed that 2-Hard benefits from parsing shallower trees, and shorter arc lengths when compared to the Baseline. We also showed that by better learning of features many case markers that appear with more than one relation can be disambiguated successfully using both 2-Hard and 2-Soft. 2-Hard seems to perform better than 2-Soft in case of inter-clausal relations w.r.t. all the evaluation metrics, whereas 2-Soft is doing good in intra-clausal relations. This gives us a future direction to explore a combination of 2-Hard and 2-Soft for inter and intra-clausal relations respectively, to see if one can benefit from the other.

Since the improvement in LS and LAS in both 2-Hard and 2-Soft seems to be more than in the UAS, it would be interesting to see the effect of clausal parsing on label identification and attachments separately. To do this, we plan to explore sequential parsing by using different feature models for transitions and labels, as the current parsing schemes do both attachments and labels at the same time.

References

B.R. Ambati, S. Husain, J. Nivre, R. Sangal. 2010. On the Role of Morphosyntactic Features in Hindi Dependency Parsing. In *NAACL-HLT 2010 workshop on SPMRL*, Los Angeles, CA.

R. Begum, S. Husain, A. Dhwaj, D. Sharma, L. Bai, R. Sangal. 2008. Dependency annotation scheme for Indian languages. In *IJCNLP08.*

A. Bharati, S. Husain, D. Misra, R. Sangal 2009. Two stage constraint based hybrid approach to free word order language dependency parsing. In *the 11th IWPT09*. Paris.

A. Bharati, S. Husain, B. Ambati, S. Jain, D. Sharma, R. Sangal. 2008. Two semantic features make all the difference in parsing accuracy. In *ICON08.*

G. Eryigit, J. Nivre, K. Oflazer. 2008. Dependency Parsing of Turkish. *Computational Linguistics 34(3), 357-389.*

P. Gadde, K. Jindal, S. Husain, D. Sharma, R. Sangal. 2010. Improving Data Driven Dependency Parsing using Clausal Information. In *NAACL-HLT 2010*, Los Angeles, CA.

Y. Goldberg, M. Elhadad. 2009. Hebrew Dependency Parsing: Initial Results. In *the 11th IWPT09*. Paris.

J. Hall, J. Nilsson, J. Nivre, G. Eryigit, B. Megyesi, M. Nilsson M. Saers. 2007. Single Malt or Blended? A Study in Multilingual Parser Optimization. In *EMNLP-CoNLL shared task.*

S. Husain, P. Mannem, B. Ambati, P. Gadde. 2010. The ICON-2010 Tools Contest on Indian Language Dependency Parsing. 2010. In *ICON10 NLP Tools Contest on Indian Language Dependency Parsing*. Kharagpur, India.

S. Husain. 2009. Dependency Parsers for Indian Languages. *In Proceedings of ICON09 NLP Tools Contest: Indian Language Dependency Parsing. Hyderabad, India.*

S. Husain, P. Gadde, B. Ambati, D. Sharma, R. Sangal. 2009. A modular cascaded approach to complete parsing. In *the COLIPS International Conference on Asian Language Processing (IALP)* Singapore.

P. Mannem, H. Chaudhry, A. Bharati. 2009. Insights into non-projectivity in Hindi. In *ACL-IJCNLP Student Research Workshop*.

P. Mannem, A. Abhilash, A. Bharati. 2009b. LTAG-spinal Treebank and Parser for Hindi. In *ICON09*.

A. F. Martins, D. Das, N. A. Smith, E. P. Xing. 2009. Stacking dependency parsers. In *EMNLP*.

R. McDonald, F. Pereira, K. Ribarov, J. Hajic. 2005. Non-projective dependency parsing using spanning tree algorithms. In *HLT/EMNLP*.

R. McDonald, J. Nivre. 2007. Characterizing the Errors of Data-Driven Dependency Parsing Models. In *EMNLP/CONLL*.

J. Nilsson and J. Nivre. 2008. Malteval:An evaluation and visualization tool for dependency parsing. In *the Sixth LREC*, Marrakech, Morocco.

J. Nivre. 2009. Non-Projective Dependency Parsing in Expected Linear Time. In *ACL-IJCNLP*.

J. Nivre, R. McDonald. 2008. Integrating graph-based and transition-based dependency parsers. In *ACL-HLT*.

J. Nivre, J. Hall, J. Nilsson. 2006. MaltParser: A Data-Driven Parser-Generator for Dependency Parsing. In *LREC*.

J. Nivre. 2003. An efficient algorithm for projective dependency parsing. In *the 8th International Workshop on Parsing Technologies (IWPT)*.

D. Seddah, M. Candito, B. Crabbé. 2009. Cross parser evaluation : a French Treebanks study. In *the 11th IWPT09*. Paris.

K. Sagae, A. Lavie. 2006. Parser combination by reparsing. In *the human Language Technology Conference of the NAACL*.

R. Tsarfaty, K. Sima'an. 2008. Relational-Realizational Parsing. In *the 22nd COLING*. Manchester, UK.

R. Tsarfaty, D. Seddah, Y. Goldberg, S. Kuebler, Y. Versley, M. Candito, J. Foster, I. Rehbein, L, Tounsi. 2010. What, How and Wither. In *NAACL-HLT 2010 workshop on SPMRL*.

D. Zeman, Z. Zabokrtsky. 2005. Improving parsing accuracy by combining diverse dependency parsers. In t*he 9th IWPT*.

Word-reordering for Statistical Machine Translation Using Trigram Language Model

Jing He
IIS, Tsinghua University
Beijing, China
hejing2929@gmail.com

Hongyu Liang
IIIS, Tsinghua University
Beijing, China
sjqxzlhy@gmail.com

Abstract

In this paper we study the word-reordering problem in the decoding part of statistical machine translation, but independently from the target language generating process. In this model, a permuted sentence is given and the goal is to recover the correct order. We introduce a greedy algorithm called *Local-(k,l)-Step*, and show that it performs better than the DP-based algorithm. Our word-reordering algorithm can be used in the statistical machine translation process for improving the quality of the translation. Furthermore, motivated by the rank evaluation method, we introduce a novel way for evaluating the results of word-reordering by calculating the inversion pair cardinality.

1 Introduction

Statistical machine translation is a machine translation method based on statistical models, which is in contrast with rule-based machine translation as well as with example-based machine translation. The most commonly used model in statistical machine translation is the source-channel model built by Brown et. al. (1993). In their proposal of translation between English and French, English strings are generated according to some stochastic process and then transformed stochastically into French strings. Therefore, to translate French to English, it is needed to search for an English source string that is most likely according to the English language model (Ponte and Croft, 1998) and the channel model. This process of translation is called decoding. Usually, a decoding process in statistical machine translation is combined with two sub-processes (Chang and Toutanova, 2007; Koehn, Och and Marcu, 2003): generating the words or phrases of the target language, and deciding the correct order of the words or phrases to get a desired target language sentence. For some language pairs, such as English and Chinese, the word-reordering problem is really hard to solve, as the target word order differs a lot from the source word order and little information about the target word order is obtainable from the source sentence. This is because the grammars of English and Chinese differ from one another significantly.

Language model has been successfully applied in the word-reordering process of statistical machine translation. Generally speaking, a language model assigns a probability to a sequence of words according to some probability distribution. A sentence then gets a score under the language model by means of standard conditional probability. Knight (1999) studied this abstract problem and proved that the word-reordering (also called word-replacement) problem under bigram language model is **NP**-hard.

In this article, we study the word-reordering problem under trigram language model in the decoding part of statistical machine translation, but independently from the target language generating process. More precisely, suppose we want to translate a sentence from one language to another, and some methods have been applied to generate all the target words, whereas the words need reordering because two languages may have totally different grammars (like English and Chinese). Thus, our goal is to recover the correct, or reasonable, word order of the target sentence.

We reduce this problem to the traveling salesman problem (TSP) in 3-uniform hypergraphs. We show that by some modification, the dynamic-programming (DP) based algorithm for TSP (Held and Karp, 1962) can be used in solving this generalized problem. Nevertheless, the time complexity of this DP-based algorithm is exponential in the number of words in the sentence, and is thus unreasonable in practice. We design a class of greedy algorithms called **Local-(k, l)-Step**, parameterized by k and l. Roughly speaking, the **Local-(k, l)-Step** algorithm finds, in each step, k words which maximize the language model score, and then add the first l words to the partial sentence. For small k, say $k < 5$, this algorithm runs much faster then the DP-based algorithm.

We also propose a novel way to evaluate the results of word-reordering, motivated by the rank (ordering) evaluation measures in information retrieval. Standard retrieval evaluation measures, such as Mean Average Precision (MAP), are used for evaluating the results of retrieval systems. The reordering or ranking of items is an important task in many real-world applications, and it is needed to compare two different orderings of the same item list. One commonly-used measure is the Kendall's tau coefficient (Kendall, 1938) which uses the notion of *inversion pairs*.

Motivated by these existing methods, we design the following evaluation process for word-reordering: Given a sentence outputted by the algorithm, we regard it as a permutation of the correct sentence, and count the the number of inversion pairs in it, which can be seen as the distance between the result sentence and the correct one. The notion of inversion pairs is often used to measure the distance between permutations. Due to the special structure of our model, it is also a proper measurement of the quality of word-reordering results. Note that to calculate the number of inversion pairs, the correct sentence, or a "standard answer", should be given as well. This can be done by the following design of experiments: We choose 1500 English sentences from http://www.nlp.org.cn, and randomly permute each sentence. Then, the permuted sentences are given as the input to the word-reordering problem, while the original sentences are just "standard answers" which will be used in the evaluation.

We implement both the DP-based algorithm and the **Local-(k, l)-Step** algorithm, and evaluate their results according to their performance on the chosen sentences. From the comparison, it is shown that for well chosen parameters k and l, the **Local-(k, l)-Step** algorithm performs even better than the DP-based algorithm. This seems to contradict with the fact that the latter solves the problem exactly while the former only obtains an "approximate" solution. This, however, is not a real problem since the score under the language model is not always compatible with that under the evaluation using inversion pairs. In fact, neither of the two evaluation methods can accurately measure the "quality" or "correctness" of sentences, because the human language itself comprises many other perspectives that cannot be qualified or characterized exactly by current techniques. It is possible that a sentence that makes no sense obtains a higher language model score than that of a normal sentence in real world.

Finally let us mention that, although throughout the paper we talk about the word-based reordering model, our algorithms can be easily modified to be applicable in the re-ordering process of statistical machine translation whose working unit is phrase (Koehn, Och and Marcu, 2003).

This paper is organized as follows: Section 2 defines the word-reordering model rigorously, and introduces the dynamic programming algorithm and the greedy **Local-(k, l)-step** algorithm. In Section 3 we show the experimental results as well as the evaluation based on the inversion pair cardinality. The last section concludes the whole article with some remarks and future work.

2 The Word-reordering Model

In the word-reordering model, a disordered English sentence is given and the goal is to find the most reasonable order. For example, given the sentence "overrate to is importance their it easy", the best answer should be "It is easy to overrate their importance."

It is hard to establish a standard criterion for evaluating the "quality" of a sentence. In practice, language model is used as a statistical tool to help people find approximate solutions. For our purpose, we adopt the commonly-used trigram source model, given by $lm(w_0|w_1, w_2)$ for all possible English words w_0, w_1 and w_2. Given a disordered sentence, we want to rearrange its words in order to get a maximum score according to the trigram source model. This can be theoretically formalized as the following search problem.

Word-reordering Problem

Input:

1. A dictionary $D = \{d_i \mid 1 \leq i \leq m\}$;
2. A trigram source model $\{lm(w_i \mid w_j, w_k) : 1 \leq i, j, k \leq m\}$;
3. A set of words $S = \{s_1, s_2, \ldots, s_n\} \subseteq D$.

Output: A sentence $s_{i_1} s_{i_2} \ldots s_{i_n}$, where $(i_1, i_2, \ldots, i_n)$ is a permutation of $\{1, 2, \ldots, n\}$, such that $\prod_{j=3}^{n} lm(s_{i_j} \mid s_{i_{j-1}}, s_{i_{j-2}})$ is maximized.

A similar problem with bigram source model $\{lm(w_i|w_j)\}$ is proved to be NP-hard by Knight (1999) using a reduction from the famous HAMILTONIAN PATH problem. The NP-hardness of this problem with trigram source model can be proved analogously.

Despite the hardness result, we can still cope with many instances in practice, since a sentence is usually not so long. The trivial way is to enumerate all $n!$ permutations and find the one achieving maximum score, which takes $O(n \cdot n!)$ time. We will describe better ways for solving it.

2.1 Dynamic Programming

An instance of the TSP problem consists of a directed graph $G = (V, E)$ and a cost function $c : E \to \mathbf{R}$, and the goal is to find a path of minimum cost which visits each vertex in V exactly once (that is, a Hamiltonian path). Note that the word-reordering problem can be reduced to TRAVELING SALESMAN PROBLEM (TSP) with a slight modification that each edge in the graph is a triple instead of a pair (i.e., TSP in 3-uniform hypergraphs). The reduction is as follows: Construct a vertex v_i for each word $s_i \in S$, and then add an hyperedge (v_i, v_j, v_k) with cost $-\ln(lm(w_k|w_i, w_j))$ for every triple (v_i, v_j, v_k). Then, finding a sentence s with maximum score is equivalent to finding a minimum cost Hamiltonian path in this hypergraph, where the cost of a path is defined to be the sum of costs of all triples containing three consecutive nodes in the path. We can assume that the graph is complete (i.e., all possible edges (v_i, v_j, v_k) exist) by adding dummy edges with sufficiently large costs.

Held and Karp (1962) designed a dynamic-programming based (DP-based) algorithm for the original TSP which runs in time $O(2^n \cdot n^2)$, n being the number of vertices in the graph. Their algorithm runs iteratively on all subsets of vertices and finds a minimum cost tour in that subset, with the start and end points specified. We will describe a similar algorithm for solving TSP on 3-uniform hypergraphs, which can be directly applied to the word-reordering problem.

DP-based algorithm for TSP in 3-uniform hypergraphs (3-uni-DP)

Input: A 3-uniform hypergraph $G = (V, E)$; a cost function $c : E \to \mathbf{R}$.

Output: A minimum cost Hamiltonian path.

Algorithm:

- Return $fail$ if $|V| < 3$.
- For each triple (v_i, v_j, v_k) where all three vertices are pairwise distinct, let $C(\{v_i, v_j, v_k\}, v_i, v_j, v_k) = c(v_i, v_j, v_k)$.
- For $m = 4$ to $|V|$ do
  - For each tuple (V', v_1, v_2, v_3) where $\{v_1, v_2, v_3\} \subseteq V' \subset V$ and $|V'| = m$, compute: $C(V', v_1, v_2, v_3) = \min_{v_4 \in V'}\{C(V' \setminus \{v_3\}, v_1, v_4, v_2) + c(v_4, v_2, v_3)\}$
- Find the vertices v_1, v_2, v_3 for which $C(V, v_1, v_2, v_3)$ is minimized. Trace back to find the corresponding path.

The algorithm **3-uni-DP** runs in time $O(2^n \cdot n^4)$, where $n = |V|$. In each step it computes $C(V', v_1, v_2, v_3)$, which stands for the minimum cost Hamiltonian path in V' that starts with v_1 and ends at (v_2, v_3), by enumerating the third vertex on the path from end and concatenating the shorter path and the last edge. It is not hard to see that this algorithm correctly computes the minimum cost Hamiltonian path in 3-uniform hypergraphs.

2.2 Local-(k, l)-Step Algorithm

The DP-based algorithm **3-uni-DP** solves the word-reordering problem exactly but runs in exponential time, which is unaffordable for long sentences. An idea for reducing the running time is to consider the problem "locally". In each step, we look for a fixed number of unvisited points and try to minimize the cost of the "local path" in which these points are involved. More specifically, we seek for k unvisited points $v_2, v_3, \ldots, v_{k+1}$ minimizing $\sum_{i=0}^{k-1} c(v_i, v_{i+1}, v_{i+2})$, where v_0 and v_1 are the last two nodes in the current partial path. Then, we add the first l points to our partial path, for some $l \leq k$. We give a more formal description as follows.

Algorithm Local-(k, l)-Step

Input: A 3-uniform hypergraph $G = (V, E)$; a cost function $c : E \to \mathbf{R}$.
Output: A minimum cost Hamiltonian path.

Algorithm:

Do the following for all vertex pairs (v_0, v_1) to find the best solution:

- $V' \leftarrow V \setminus \{v_0, v_1\}$.
- $PartialPath \leftarrow (v_0, v_1)$.
- While $|V'| \geq k$ do
  - Find k distinct vertices $v_2, v_3, \ldots, v_{k+1}$ in V' which minimizes $\sum_{i=0}^{k-1} c(v_i, v_{i+1}, v_{i+2})$.
  - Add $(v_2, \ldots, v_{l+1})$ to the end of $PartialPath$.
  - $V' \leftarrow V' \setminus \{v_2, v_3, \ldots, v_{l+1}\}$.
- In case $V' \neq \emptyset$, perform an exhaustive search to find the best order to visit the remaining vertices in V', and add this to $PartialPath$.

Return the best $PartialPath$ (with the minimum cost) over all start pairs (v_0, v_1).

The algorithm **Local-**(k, l)**-Step** runs in time $O(n^2 \cdot n^k \cdot \frac{n}{l}) = O(n^{k+3}/l)$, where n is the number of vertices in the graph. This is efficient in practice if we choose a small k, say, $k < 5$. It should be noticed that this algorithm cannot be a constant-factor approximation algorithm for TSP, since for any constant k it runs in polynomial time, and thus cannot approximate TSP within any constant ratio unless **P** = **NP**. However, it may perform well on real-world instances of the word-reordering problem.

In fact we will show that, for some well chosen parameters k and l, the algorithm **Local-**(k, l)**-Step** performs even better than the algorithm **3-uni-DP**. This seems to contradict with the fact that the latter solves the problem optimally while the former only looks for a reasonable solution. However, this is not a problem because our word-reordering model itself cannot catch accurately the quality of a sentence. Thus, when evaluating the outcomes of our algorithms, it is more proper to use some other measurements, like the *inversion pair* which will be introduced later. The reason why this measurement cannot be adopted in the design of our algorithms is that it can only be calculated if a standard answer to the problem is given.

3 Experiments

3.1 The trigram language model training

In order to build a reasonable trigram language model for the experiment, we download the third version of the Europarl corpus (Koehn, 2005) which is extracted from the proceedings of the European Parliament. This data set is usually used as a base material in statistical machine translation contest or other research projects involving European languages, and the English part can be used for training a trigram English language model. There are about 0.307 million English sentences in the material. Thus, the trigram language model built by SRILM (Stolcke, 2002) can reflect the properties of the English language.

3.2 The reordering experiment

How to evaluate the results of our algorithms is a key problem in our research, as there is no standard for testing the accuracy of word-reordering. Usually, the reordering of words in sentences serves as a subprocess in statistical machine translation, especially in the decoding step. All the existing methods and standards are designed to test the accuracy of the translation results, but not the single process of word-reordering. Therefore, we designed an experiment model and a testing principle for our own purpose, shown as follows.

First, we choose 1500 English-Chinese sentence pairs (from http://www.nlp.org.cn) as the collection of standard answers. We then choose from them all sentences of length less than 10 as our data set. For every sentence in this data set, we generate a disordered sentence by performing a random permutation on the set of words in the original sentence. For example, if the original sentences is "sometimes you are overly frank", one possible disordered sentence could be "overly are sometimes frank you". The original sentence is used as a standard answer for later evaluation. We run the **Local-**(k, l)**-Step** algorithm on all the permuted sentences for all pair of parameters (k, l) such that $1 \leq l \leq k \leq 4$. We also run the **3-uni-DP** algorithm on these sentences for the sake of contrast.

There is another issue considering the start of a sentence. Since the language model includes the possibility of a word being the first word of a sentence, we may add a special "start symbol" to every disordered sentence and force it to be the first word in the output sentence. This is easy to implement in practice, and will make the result more reasonable. In all the experiments we adopt this setting.

Now comes the evaluation part. How to measure the quality of our results, or, the distances between the output sentences and the standard answers? It turns out that any method for determining the distance between permutations also works in our model. The concept of *inversion pairs* is usually used to measure the distance between two permutations, and is thus brought into our experiments. Let σ be a permutation of $\{1, 2, \ldots, n\}$. A pair of indices (i, j), where $1 \leq i < j \leq n$, is called an *inversion pair* of σ if $\sigma(i) > \sigma(j)$. The total number of inversion pairs of σ, also called *inversion pair cardinality* of σ, is a proper measurement of the distance between σ and the identity permutation $(1, 2, \ldots, n)$. Although distances between two arbitrary permutations can be similarly defined, this measurement already suffices for our purpose since we only need to calculate the distance between a permuted sentence and the standard answer.

Take again the sentence "sometimes you are overly frank" as an illustration. We mark this sentence as the identity permutation $(1, 2, 3, 4, 5)$. If the disordered sentence is "sometimes are you frank overly", it should be associated with the permutation $(1, 3, 2, 5, 4)$, and thus has 2 inversion pairs in total (3 comes before 2, and 5 appears before 4).

In this way we can calculate the number of inversion pairs to measure the degree of disordering. For every pair of parameters (k, l) used in the **Local-(k, l)-Step** algorithm, we count the number of output sentences which have smaller inversion pair cardinality than the corresponding randomly permuted sentences. Call this number $Better(k, l)$. We then choose the pair (k, l) which maximizes $Better(k, l)$, denoted by (k_0, l_0), and adopt it as the proper parameter for our algorithm. We also calculate $Better(DP)$, which is the number of sentences outputted by the **3-uni-DP** algorithm having smaller inversion pair cardinality than the corresponding disordered ones.

All the experiments are conducted repeatedly for 5 times, each time generating different randomly disordered sentences. The final result $Better(DP)$ and $Better(k, l)$ are the average of the results of 5 independent experiments. These results are shown in Tables 1 and 2.

	1	2	3	4	5	average
(1,1)	347	354	329	360	349	347.8
(2,1)	376	389	370	386	388	381.8
(2,2)	383	390	369	395	388	385
(3,1)	392	396	386	399	399	394.4
(3,2)	392	397	383	388	388	389.6
(3,3)	396	406	380	401	387	394
(4,1)	399	413	390	405	407	402.8
(4,2)	400	406	398	407	403	402.8
(4,3)	412	414	401	421	416	412.8
(4,4)	406	412	404	421	420	412.6
DP	362	370	364	372	353	364.2

Table 1: $Better(DP)$ and $Better(k, l)$ under all chosen parameters

	average number	percentage
$Better(k_0, l_0)$	412.8	62.55%
$Better(DP)$	364.2	55.18%
All sentences	660	100%

Table 2: The comparison between DP-based and greedy algorithms

3.3 Analysis

The experimental result shows that setting $(k, l) = (4, 3)$ gives the best outcome among all chosen parameters. Thus we let $k_0 = 4$ and $l_0 = 3$. It is a little surprising that $Better(DP)$ is less than $Better(k_0, l_0)$, which indicates that the exact algorithm performs worse than the "approximate" algorithm. As explained before, this is due to our lack of modeling the "quality" or "correctness" of sentences. It is possible that a sentence with high score under trigram language model makes little sense, and a normal sentence appearing in real word obtains a low score under this language model. The algorithm **Local-(k, l)-Step**, on the other hand, makes use of the locality of English sentences, and thus it should be expected to perform well.

4 Conclusions

In this paper, we study the word-reordering problem in the decoding process of statistical machine translation. We adopt the commonly-used trigram language model, and abstract the word-reordering problem as instances of Traveling Salesman Problem in 3-uniform hypergraphs. We show that Held and Karp's dynamic-programming based algorithm for solving TSP (in normal graphs) can be adapted to solve this problem. We also design a greedy algorithm called **Local-(k, l)-Step**, parameterized by k and l, which has a faster running time but gets a non-optimal solution, where by optimal we mean achieving maximum score under the trigram language model.

We implement both algorithms and conduct some experiments. To evaluate the results, we adopt the concept of inversion pairs to measure the distances between the standard answers and the sentences outputted by the algorithms. From the experimental results, we find that setting $k = 4$ and $l = 3$ makes the **Local-(k, l)-Step** algorithm perform best. Moreover, the result obtained by the greedy algorithm is even better than that of the dynamic-programming based algorithm. This is because we are not able to model the quality and correctness of sentences accurately, and thus a sentence with maximum score under trigram language model is not necessarily a best answer to the reordering problem.

Since we study the word-reordering problem independently from the target language generating process, one future direction for our research is to combine the two parts, namely, predicting the collection of words and deciding the correct order of the target sentences, together to design better decoding algorithms.

References

M. Kendall. A New Measure of Rank Correlation. *Biometrika*, 30(1–2): 81–89, 1938.

P. Brown, S. Della-Pietra, V. Della-Pietra, and R. Mercer. The mathematics of statistical machine translation: Parameter estimation. *Computational Linguistics*, 19(2): 263-311, 1993.

P. Chang and K. Toutanova. A Discriminative Syntactic Word Order Model for Machine Translation. In *Proceedings of the 45th Annual Meeting of the Association of Computational Linguistics*, pp. 9-16, Prague, Czech Republic, June 2007.

M. Held and R. M. Karp. A dynamic programming approach to sequencing problems. *Journal of Society for Industrial and Applied Mathematics*, 10(1):196–210.

K. Knight. Decoding Complexity in Word-Replacement Translation Models. *Computational Linguistics*, 25(4):607–615, 1999.

P. Koehn. Europarl: A Parallel Corpus for Statistical Machine Translation. MT Summit, 2005.

P. Koehn, F. J. Och, and D. Marcu. Statistical Phrases-Based Translation. HLT/NAACL, 2003.

J. M. Ponte and W. B. Croft. A Language Model Approach to Information retrieval. *Research and Development in Information Retrieval*, 275–281, 1998.

A. Stolcke. SRILM – An Extensible Language Modeling Toolkit. In *Proceedings of the International Conference on Spoken Language Processing*, vol. 2, pp. 901–904, Denver, 2002.

A. Aho and J. Ullman. *The Theory of Parsing, Translation and Compiling*, vol. 1. Prentice-Hall, Englewood Cliffs, NJ, 1972.

Extracting Hierarchical Rules from a Weighted Alignment Matrix

Zhaopeng Tu, Yang Liu, Qun Liu and **Shouxun Lin**
Key Lab. of Intelligent Info. Processing
Institute of Computing Technology
Chinese Academy of Sciences
P.O. Box 2704, Beijing 100190, China
{tuzhaopeng,yliu,liuqun,sxlin}@ict.ac.cn

Abstract

Word alignment is a fundamental step in machine translation. Current statistical machine translation systems suffer from a major drawback: they only extract rules from 1-best alignments, which adversely affects the rule sets quality due to alignment mistakes. To alleviate this problem, we extract hierarchical rules from *weighted alignment matrix* (Liu et al., 2009). Since the sub-phrase pairs would change the inside and outside areas in the weighted alignment matrix of the hierarchical rules, we propose a new algorithm to calculate the relative frequencies and lexical weights of hierarchical rules. To achieve a balance between rule table size and performance, we construct a scoring measure that incorporates both frequency and lexical weight to select the best target phrase for each source phrase. Experiments show that our approach improves BLEU score by ranging from 1.4 to 1.9 points over baseline for hierarchical phrase-based, and 1.4 to 1.5 points for tree-to-string model.

1 Introduction

Word alignment plays an important role in statistical machine translation (SMT). Most SMT systems, not only phrase-based models (Och and Ney, 2004; Koehn et al., 2003; Xiong et al., 2006), but also syntax-based models (Chiang, 2005; Liu et al., 2006; Galley et al., 2006; Huang et al., 2006; Shen et al., 2008), usually extract rules from word aligned corpora. However, these systems suffer from a major drawback: they only extract rules from 1-best alignments, which adversely affects the rule sets quality due to alignment mistakes.

Typically, syntax-based models are more sensitive to word alignments because they care about

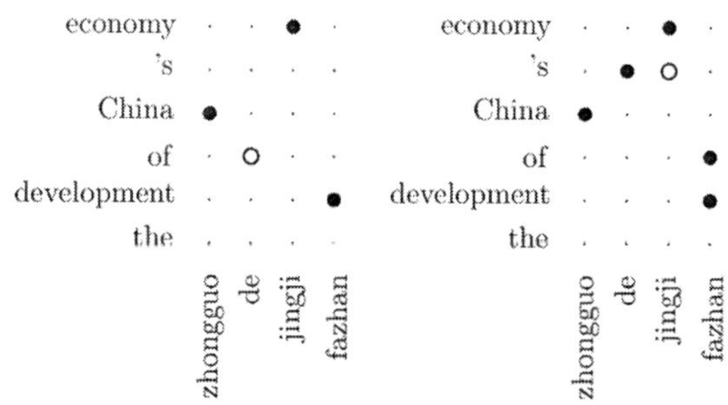

Figure 1: (a) One alignment of a sentence pair; (b) another alignment of the same sentence pair. Here coreless dots denote wrong links.

inside (i.e., subtracted phrases). Figure 1(a) shows an alignment of a sentence pair. Since there is a wrong link (*de*, *of*), we could not extract many useful hierarchical rules such as (*zhongguo* X_1 *jingji*, *China* X_1 *economy*).To alleviate this problem, a natural solution is to extract rules from n-best alignments (Venugopal et al., 2008).

However, using n-best alignments still face two major challenges. First, n-best alignments have to be processed individually although they share many links, see (*zhongguo*, *China*) and (*jingji*, *economy*) in Figure 1. Second, regardless of probabilities of links in each alignment, numerous wrong rule would be extracted from n-best alignments. For example, a wrong rule (X_1 *de jingji*, *of* X_1 *'s economy*) would be extracted from the alignment in Figure 1(a).

Since Liu et al. (2009) show that weighted alignment matrix provides an elegant solution to these two drawbacks, we apply it to the hierarchical phrase-based model (Chiang, 2005) and the tree-to-string model (Liu et al., 2006; Huang et al., 2006). While such an idea seems intuitive, it is non-trivial to extract hierarchical rules from weighted alignment matrices.

Our work faces two major challenges. The first is how to calculate the relative frequencies and lex-

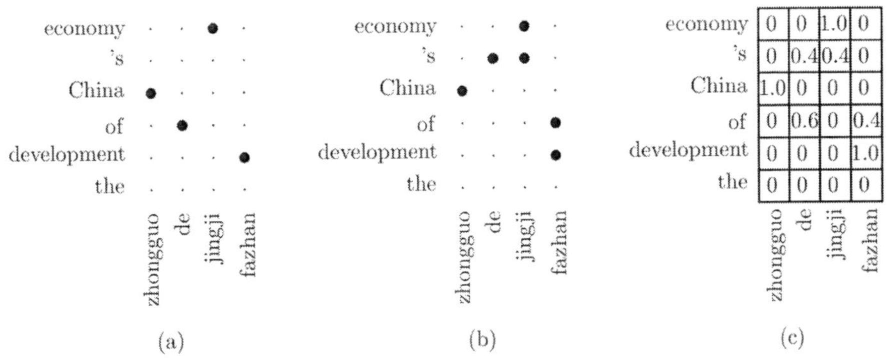

Figure 2: (a) One alignment of a sentence pair; (b) another alignment of the same sentence pair; (c) the resulting weighted alignment matrix that samples the two alignments, of which the initial probabilities are 0.6 and 0.4 respectively.

ical weights of the rules with non-terminals (NTs). The sub-phrase pairs that are replaced with NTs in a rule, would change the inside and outside areas in the weighted alignment matrix of the rule. In addition, the sub-phrase pairs have their own probabilities and we should incorporate them to better estimate the probabilities of the hierarchical rules. Therefore, the calculations of relative frequencies and lexical weights for hierarchical rules are more complicated.

Another challenge is how to achieve a balance between performance and rule table size. Note that given a source phrase, there would be plenty of "potential" candidate target phrases in weighted matrices (Liu et al., 2009). If we retain all of them, these phrase pairs would produce even more hierarchical rules. For computational tractability, we need to design a measure to score the phrase pairs and wipe out the low-quality ones.

We propose a new algorithm to calculate the relative frequencies of rules, and construct a measure that incorporates both frequency and lexical weight to score target phrases. Experiments (Section 4) show that our approach improves BLEU score by ranging from 1.4 to 1.9 points over baseline for hierarchical phrase-based, and 1.4 to 1.8 points for tree-to-string model.

2 Weighted Alignment Matrix

A weighted alignment matrix (Liu et al., 2009) m is a $J \times I$ matrix to encode the probabilities of n-best alignments of the same sentence pair. Each element in the matrix stores a link probability $p_m(j,i)$, which is estimated from an n-best list by calculating relative frequencies:

$$p_m(j,i) = \frac{\sum_{a \in \mathcal{N}} p(a) \times \delta(a,j,i)}{\sum_{a \in \mathcal{N}} p(a)} \quad (1)$$

where

$$\delta(a,j,i) = \begin{cases} 1 & (j,i) \in a \\ 0 & \text{otherwise} \end{cases} \quad (2)$$

Here $\mathcal{N}$ is an n-best list, $p(a)$ is the probability of an alignment a in the n-best list. The numbers in the cells in Figure 2(c) are the corresponding p_m.

Since $p_m(j,i)$ is the probability that f_j and e_i are aligned, the probability that the two words are not aligned is

$$\bar{p}_m(j,i) = 1.0 - p_m(j,i) \quad (3)$$

Figure 2 shows an example. The probability for the two words *zhongguo* and *China* being aligned is 1.0 and the probability that they are not aligned is 0.0. In another way, the two words are definitely aligned.

Given a phrase pair $(f_{j1}^{j2}, e_{i1}^{i2})$, Liu et al. (2009) calculate relative frequencies following Och and Ney (2004):

$$\phi(\tilde{e}|\tilde{f}) = \frac{count(f_{j1}^{j2}, e_{i1}^{i2})}{\sum_{e_{i'_1}^{i'_2}} count(f_{j1}^{j2}, e_{i'_1}^{i'_2})} \quad (4)$$

The key point to calculate the relative frequency of the phrase pair is to obtain its fractional count. Liu et al. (2009) use the product of inside and outside probabilities as the fractional count of a phrase pair. Liu et al. (2009) define that inside probability indicates the probability that at least

economy	0	0	1.0	0
's	0	0.4	0.4	0
China	1.0	0	0	0
of	0	0.6	0	0.4
development	0	0	0	1.0
the	0	0	0	0
	zhongguo	de	jingji	fazhan

Figure 3: A weighted alignment matrix of a phrase pair. The light shading area is the outside area of phrase pair, and the area inside the pane with bold lines is the inside area.

one word in source phrase is aligned to a word in target phrase, and outside probability indicates the chance that no words in one phrase are aligned to a word outside the other phrase. The fractional count is calculated:

$$count(f_{j_1}^{j_2}, e_{i_1}^{i_2}) = \alpha(f_{j_1}^{j_2}, e_{i_1}^{i_2}) \times \beta(f_{j_1}^{j_2}, e_{i_1}^{i_2}) \quad (5)$$

where $\alpha(\cdot)$ and $\beta(\cdot)$ denote the inside and outside probabilities respectively, which can be calculated as

$$\alpha(\cdot) = 1 - \prod_{(j,i)\in in(\cdot)} \bar{p}_m(j,i) \quad (6)$$

$$\beta(\cdot) = \prod_{(j,i)\in out(\cdot)} \bar{p}_m(j,i) \quad (7)$$

Here $in(\cdot)$ denotes the inside area, which includes elements that fall inside the phrase pair, while $out(\cdot)$ denotes the outside area including elements that fall outside the phrase pair while fall in the same row or the same column. Figure 3 shows an example. The light shading area is the outside area of phrase pair and the area inside the pane with bold lines is the inside area.

To calculate the lexical weights, Liu et al. (2009) adapt $p_m(j,i)$ as the fractional count $count(f_j, e_i)$. The fractional counts of NULL words can be calculated as:

$$count(f_j, e_0) = \prod_{i=1}^{I} \bar{p}_m(j,i)$$

For example, in Figure 2, $count(de,'s)$ is 0.4 and $count(de, NULL)$ is 0.24.

Then the lexical weight can be calculated as:

$$p_w(\tilde{e}|\tilde{f}, m) = \prod_{i=1}^{|\tilde{e}|} \left(\left(\frac{1}{\{j|p_m(j,i) > 0\}} \times \sum_{\forall j: p_m(j,i)>0} p(e_i|f_j) \times p_m(j,i) \right) + p(e_i|f_0) \times \prod_{j=1}^{|\tilde{f}|} \bar{p}_m(j,i) \right) \quad (8)$$

where

$$p(e_i|f_j) = \frac{count(f_j, e_i)}{\sum_{e_i'} count(f_j, e_i')} \quad (9)$$

We apply weighted alignment matrix to the hierarchical phrase-based model (Chiang, 2007) and the tree-to-string model (Liu et al., 2006; Huang et al., 2006).

3 Rule Extraction

In hierarchical rules, both source and target sides are strings with NTs. In tree-to-string rules, the source side is a tree with NTs, while the target side is a string with NTs. Since the tree structure of source side has no effect on the calculations of relative frequencies and lexical weights, we can represent both tree-to-string and hierarchical rules as below:

$$X \rightarrow \langle \gamma, \alpha, \sim \rangle$$

where X is a nonterminal, γ and α are source and target strings (consist of terminals and NTs), and $\sim$ represents word alignments between NTs in γ and α.

The bulk of syntax grammars consists of two parts: *phrase pairs* and *variable rules*. The difference between them is containing NTs or not. Since we can calculate relative frequencies and lexical weights of phrase pairs as in Liu et al. (2009), we only focus on the calculation of variable rules.

3.1 Extraction Algorithm

Following Chiang (2007) and Liu et al. (2006), our extraction algorithm involves two steps. First, we extract phrase pairs from weighted alignment matrices. Then, we obtain variable rules by replacing sub-phrase pairs with NTs.

Figure 4 shows the algorithm of extracting phrase pairs from a weighted matrix for the hierarchical phrase-based model. The input of the algorithm is a sentence pair (f_1^J, e_1^I) that are both

```
1: procedure PHRASEEXTRACTION(f_1^J, e_1^I, m, l)
2:     R ← ∅
3:     for j_1 ← 1 ... J do
4:         j_2 ← j_1
5:         while j_2 < J ∧ j_2 − j_1 < l do
6:             T ← {i | ∃j : j_1 ≤ j ≤ j_2 ∧ p_m(j, i) > 0}
7:             i_l ← MIN(T)
8:             i_u ← MAX(T)
9:             r ← NULL
10:            s(r) ← −1
11:            for n ← 1 ... l do
12:                for i_1 ← i_l − n + 1 ... i_u do
13:                    i_2 ← i_1 + n − 1
14:                    if s(f_{j1}^{j2}, e_{i1}^{i2}) > s(r) then
15:                        r ← (f_{j1}^{j2}, e_{i1}^{i2})
16:                        s(r) ← s(f_{j1}^{j2}, e_{i1}^{i2})
17:            R ← R ∪ {r}
18:            j_2 ← j_2 + 1
19:    return R
```

Figure 4: Algorithm of extracting phrase pairs from a sentence pair $\langle f_1^J, e_1^I \rangle$ annotated with a weighted alignment matrix m. We just retain the best target phrase for each source phrase. Here $s(\cdot)$ denotes the selection criteria in Section 3.2

target phrase	α	β	*count*
China 's economy	1.0	0.4	0.4
of China 's economy	1.0	0.6	0.6
China 's	1.0	0.0	0.0
of China 's	1.0	0.0	0.0

Table 1: Some candidate target phrases of the source phrase *zhongguo de jingji* in Figure 3 (suppose the structure of *zhongguo de jingji* is a complete sub-tree). Here α is inside probability, β is outside probability, and *count* is fractional count.

strings, a weighted alignment matrix m, and a phrase length limit l. Note that we just retain the target phrase of highest score for each source phrase (lines 13-16). We describe these in Section 3.2. After we extract phrase pairs, we can obtain variable rules by replacing sub-phrase pairs with NTs.

We can also extend this algorithm to tree-to-string model. The difference is that the source sentence should be a tree instead of a string and additional syntactic constraints operate.

3.2 Selection Criteria

(Liu et al., 2009) show that given a source phrase, there would be multiple "potential" candidate target phrases in weighted matrices. Table 1 lists some candidate target phrases of the source phrase *zhongguo de jingji* in Figure 3. If we retain all of them, it will lead to an exponentially increasing rule table. To achieve balance between rule table size and performance, we just select the best candidate target phrase.

An interesting finding is that a target phrase with the largest fractional count is not always the best one. For example in Table 1, the target phrase *of China 's economy* has a larger fractional count than *China 's economy*. However, we can see that (*zhongguo de jingji*, *China 's economy*) is better.

To alleviate this problem, we incorporate lexical weight to distinguish good target phrases from bad ones. While frequency indicates how often the source phrase and target phrase occur together, lexical weight models the correspondence between them. Therefore, we can construct a scoring measure that incorporates both frequency and lexical weight. The scoring equation below models this effect:

$$s(\tilde{f}, \tilde{e}) = \omega \cdot count(\tilde{f}, \tilde{e}) + (1 - \omega) \cdot p_w(\tilde{e}|\tilde{f}, m) \quad (10)$$

where ω is the interpolation weight, $count(\tilde{f}, \tilde{e})$ is calculated by Equation 5, and $p_w(\tilde{e}|\tilde{f}, m)$ by Equation 8. In practice, we set $\omega = 0.5$.[1] Suppose p_w(*China 's economy* | *zhongguo de jingji*) is 0.7 and p_w(*of China 's economy* | *zhongguo de jingji*) is 0.4, then we should choose the target phrase *China 's economy* although *of China 's economy* has a larger fractional count.

Note that we select the best target phrase for each source phrase for just one sentence. It means there could still be many target phrases for each source phrase during decoding.

3.3 Calculating Relative Frequencies

Figure 5 shows an example of the matrix of a hierarchical rule, which is generated from the phrase pair in Figure 3. Due to the existence of sub-phrase pairs, the inside and outside areas changes (see the difference between Figure 3 and Figure 5). Therefore, we can not simply calculate the outside probability of the hierarchical rule using the product of outside probabilities of phrase pair and sub-phrase pairs.

We follow Liu et al. (2009) to calculate relative frequencies using the product of inside and outside probabilities. We now extend the definitions of inside and outside probabilities to hierarchical rules that contain NTs.

[1] We tried a few other settings and found them to be less effective.

rule	α	β	$count$
X_1 *de jingji*, X_1 *'s economy*	1.0	0.4	0.4
zhongguo X_1, *China* X_1	1.0	0.4	0.4
zhongguo de X_1, *China 's* X_1	1.0	0.24	0.24
X_1 *de* X_2, X_1 *'s* X_2	1.0	0.24	0.24

Table 2: Some hierarchical rules generated from the phrase pair (*zhongguo de jingji, China's economy*) in Figure 3 (suppose the structure of *zhongguo de jingji* is a complete sub-tree). Here α is inside probability, β is outside probability, and $count$ is fractional count.

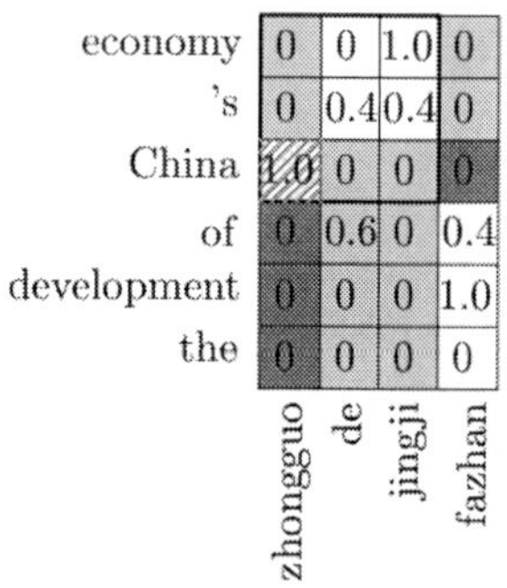

Figure 5: A weighted alignment matrix of a variable rule, which is obtained by replacing (*zhongguo,China*) with X in (*zhongguo de jingji,China 's economy*). The diagonal area is the inside area of the sub-phrase pair. The shading area is the outside area of the variable rule, and heavy shading area is the duplicate outside area. The no shading area inside the pane with bold lines is the inside area.

Given a variable rule (f', e'), which is generated from the phrase pair $(f_{j_1}^{j_2}, e_{i_1}^{i_2})$ by replacing sub-phrase pairs with X. We denote R as the variable rule, P as the phrase pair $(f_{j_1}^{j_2}, e_{i_1}^{i_2})$, and X_k as the kth sub-phrase pair that is replaced with X. Therefore, the inside probability of a variable rule is calculated as:

$$\alpha(R) = \prod_k \alpha(X_k) \quad (11)$$

We tried to follow the constraints of Chiang (2007): (1) unaligned words are not allowed at the edges of phrases; (2) a rule must have at least one pair of aligned words. This would take into account the terminals in the variable rule, but make the calculation more complicated (especially constraint (1)). However, it didn't work well. Therefore, we only constraint that the rule should respect the word alignment, which means one terminal in a phrase could not align to another word outside the phrase (using outside probability).

Accordingly, the outside probability is calculated as:

$$\beta(R) = \prod_{(j,i)\in out(R)} \bar{p}_m(j,i) \quad (12)$$

where

$$out(R) = out(P) \bigcup \Big(\bigcup_k out(X_k)\Big)$$

For example, the inside probability of (X_1 *de jingji*, X_1 *'s economy*) in Figure 5 is 1.0, and its outside probability is 0.4.

We also use Equation 5 to calculate the fractional counts of hierarchical rules. We follow Liu et al. (2009) to prune rule table using a threshold of frequency. Table 2 lists some hierarchical rules generated from the phrase pair (*zhongguo de jingji, China's economy*) in Figure 3. If the threshold is 0.2, we retain all the rules in Table 2.

3.4 Calculating Lexical Weights

We denote S_R as all words in source side of the inside area of variable rule R, and T_R as the words in target side. For the rule (X_1 *de jingji*, X_1 *'s economy*) in Figure 5, S_R is {*de, jingji*} and T_R is {*'s, economy*}. Then, we can calculate the lexical weight as:

$$p_w(\tilde{e}|\tilde{f},m) = \prod_{i\in T_R} \Bigg(\Big(\frac{1}{|\{j|p_m(j,i)>0\}|} \times \sum_{\forall j:p_m(j,i)>0} p(e_i|f_j)\times p_m(j,i)\Big) + p(e_i|f_0)\times \prod_{j\in S_R} \bar{p}_m(j,i)\Bigg) \quad (13)$$

Note that we only consider each word pair (f_j, e_i) in the inside area of the variable rule. For example, the lexical weight of (X_1 *de jingji*, X_1 *'s economy*) is

$$\Big(\frac{1}{2} \times \big(p('s|de) \times 0.4 + p('s|jingji) \times 0.4\big) + p('s|NULL) \times 0.36\Big) \times \Big(p(economy|jingji) \times 1.0\Big)$$

Here the probability that *economy* translates a source NULL token is 0.0.

4 Experiments

4.1 Data Preparation

Our experiments are on Chinese-English translation based on replications of hierarchical phrase-based system (Chiang, 2007) and tree-to-string system (Liu et al., 2006). We train a 4-gram language model on the Xinhua portion of GIGAWORD corpus using the SRI Language Modeling Toolkit (Stolcke, 2002) with modified Kneser-Ney smoothing (Kneser and Ney, 1995). We optimize feature weights using the minimum error rate training algorithm (Och and Ney, 2002) on the NIST 2002 test set. We evaluate the translation quality using case-insensitive BLEU metric (Papineni et al., 2002) on the NIST 2003/2004/2005 test sets.

To obtain weighted alignment matrices, we follow Venugopal et al. (2008) to produce n-best lists via GIZA++. We produce 20-best lists in two translation directions, then used "grow-diag-final-and" (Koehn et al., 2003) to all 20×20 bidirectional alignment pairs. We follow Liu et al. (2009) to use $p_{s2t} \times p_{t2s}$ as the probabilities of an alignment pair. Analogously, we abandon duplicate alignments that are produced from different alignment pairs. After these steps, there are 110 candidate alignments on average for each sentence pair. We obtained n-best lists by selecting the top n alignments from 110-best lists. We re-estimated the probability of each alignment in the n-best list using re-normalization (Venugopal et al., 2008). Finally, we construct weighted alignment matrices from these n-best alignments.

We will first report results trained on a small-scaled corpus, and then scale to a larger one. When extracting tree-to-string rules, we limit the maximal height of rules to 3. We use the pruning threshold: $t = 0.5$.

4.2 Results on Small Data

To test the effect of our approach, we firstly carried out experiments on FBIS corpus, which contains 230K sentence pairs. Table 3 shows the rule table size and translation quality. Using n-best alignments slightly improved the BLEU score, but at the cost of much slower extraction, since each of top-n alignments has to be processed individually although they share many align links. Matrix-based extraction, by contrast, is much faster due to packing and produces consistently better BLEU scores. The absolute improvements of ranging from +1.6 to +1.8 BLEU points and +1.4 to +1.8 BLEU points over 1-best alignments for hierarchical phrase-based and tree-to-string models respectively, are statistically significant at $p < 0.01$ by using *sign-test* (Collins et al., 2005).

Basically, in the matrix case of the hierarchical phrase-based model, we can use about twice as many rules as in the 1-best case, or 1.3 times of 10-best extraction. However, in tree-to-string scenario, matrix-based extraction produces less rules than k-best extraction. We contribute this to the extra complete sub-tree constraint.

4.3 Results on Large Data

We also conducted experiments on a larger training data, which contains 1.5M sentence pairs coming from LDC dataset.[2]

The ruletable size and BLEU score are shown in Table 4. An interesting finding is that BLEU scores decline when using k-best extraction in some cases. We conjecture that some low-quality rules that harm the performance of decoder, are extracted from k-best alignments. Using weighted matrices on larger corpus also achieved significant and consistent improvements over using 1-best and n-best lists. These results confirm that our approach is a promising direction for syntax-based machine translation.

4.4 Comparison of Parameter Estimation

In this section we investigated the question of how many rules are shared by n-best and matrix-based extractions on small data (FBIS corpus). Our motivation is that weighted alignment matrices have been reported to be beneficial for better estimation of rule translation probabilities and lexical weights

[2]The corpus includes LDC2002E18, LDC2003E07, LDC2003E14, Hansards portion of LDC2004T07, LDC2004T08 and LDC2005T06.

Rules from...	Extraction	Total Rules	NIST03		NIST04		NIST05	
			Rules	BLEU	Rules	BLEU	Rules	BLEU
hierarchical phrase-based model								
1-best	17	39.7M	2.5M	30.14	4.2M	33.82	3.0M	30.33
10-best	155	62.7M	4.2M	30.59	7.0M	34.30	5.0M	30.73
$m(10)$	89	86.7M	5.7M	**31.81**	9.5M	**35.67**	6.6M	**31.94**
tree-to-string model								
1-best	21	9.3M	532K	27.39	762K	30.30	614K	27.06
10-best	231	19.6M	890K	27.57	1.13M	30.65	1.02M	27.07
$m(10)$	44	9.2M	590K	**28.92**	836K	**31.77**	677K	**28.87**

Table 3: Results with different rule extraction methods on small data. Here 1-best, 10-best and $m(10)$ denote 1-best alignments, 10-best lists and weighted matrices estimated from 10-best lists respectively. The rules are filtered on the corresponding test set. "Extraction" denotes extraction time in millsecs per sentence pair. We evaluate the translation quality using 4-grams case-insensitive BLEU metric.

Rules from...	Total Rules	NIST03		NIST04		NIST05	
		Rules	BLEU	Rules	BLEU	Rules	BLEU
hierarchical phrase-based model							
1-best	204M	10.3M	33.40	16.1M	34.65	11.7M	32.88
10-best	288M	16.5M	33.18	25.2M	34.75	18.6M	32.47
$m(10)$	524M	26.1M	**35.10**	40.7M	**36.56**	29.5M	**34.31**
tree-to-string model							
1-best	30.7M	1.99M	30.76	2.68M	32.69	2.21M	30.36
10-best	71.4M	3.53M	31.54	4.63M	33.47	3.89M	31.09
$m(10)$	30.7M	2.24M	**32.23**	2.99M	**34.24**	2.48M	**31.88**

Table 4: Results with different rule extraction methods on large data. We use $m(10)$ for the weighted matrices estimated from 10-best lists.

(Liu et al., 2009). The experiments are tested on NIST 2005 dataset.

Table 5 gives some statistics. We use $m(10)$ for the weighted matrices estimated from 10-best lists. "All" denotes the full rule table, "Shared" denotes the intersection of two tables, and "Non-shared" denotes the complement. There were 18.8% of rules learned from weighted matrices included by both tables in hierarchical phrase-based case, while 36.5% for tree-to-string rules, indicating that complete sub-tree constraint played an important role in matrix-based tree-to-string rule extraction. Note that the probabilities of "Shared" rules are different for the two approaches. Liu et al. (2009) shows that using matrices outperformed using n-best lists even with the same rules. Our experiments confirmed these findings.

4.5 Best Rule or More Rules

Someone would argue that using more rules could improve the performance, especially for the tree-to-string model. Therefore, we carried out experiments on small data for tree-to-string model to investigate which one is better. Note that even though we retain the best target side for each source side for each sentence, there could still be many target sides for each source side when decoding.

Table 6 shows the results of different criterions. The first column "Criteria" indicates how many target phrases are preserved: the best one or all phrases that reach pruning threshold. We can see that "More Rules" could not outperform "Best Rule" even using almost 2.5 times rules. One possible reason is that it might introduce some low-quality target phrase such as *of China 's economy* in Table 1, which will generate more substandard variable rules.

5 Related Works

Recent works have shown that machine translation can benefit when offered more alternatives. Mi

Rules from...	Shared		Non-shared		All	
	Rules	BLEU	Rules	BLEU	Rules	BLEU
hierarchical phrase-based model						
10-best	1.56M	28.42	4.66M	18.60	6.22M	30.73
$m(10)$	1.56M	29.07	6.89M	22.90	8.45M	31.94
tree-to-string model						
10-best	311K	23.00	707K	10.94	1018K	27.07
$m(10)$	311K	23.55	366K	11.92	677K	28.87

Table 5: Comparison of rule tables learned from n-best lists and weighted matrices. The rules are filtered on both development and test sets. "All" denotes the full rule table, "Shared" denotes the intersection of two tables, and "Non-shared" denotes the complement. Note that the probabilities of "Shared" rules are different for the two approaches.

Criteria	Total Rules	NIST03		NIST04		NIST05	
		Rules	BLEU	Rules	BLEU	Rules	BLEU
Best Rule	9.2M	590K	28.92	836K	31.77	677K	28.87
More Rules	21.4M	1.54M	29.07	1.97M	31.66	1.72M	29.02

Table 6: Comparison of rule tables learned from weighted matrices using different criterions. "Best Rule" denotes the rule table using the criteria described in Section 3.2, "More Rules" denotes the rule table using the criteria that retains all candidate target phrases that reach pruning threshold.

and Huang (2008) and Tu et al. (2010) use forests instead of 1-best trees; Venugopal et al. (2003) and Deng et al. (2008) soft the alignment consistency constraint to extract more rules; Dyer et al. (2008) use word lattices instead of 1-best segmentations to generate more alignments for a sentence pair; Venugopal et al. (2008) use n-best alignments directly for rule extraction.

To generate larger rule sets, de Gispert et al. (2010) extract hierarchical rules from alignment posterior probabilities. They concern how to extract larger rule sets using simple yet powerful hierarchical grammar, while we focus on whether weighted alignment matrix could overcome the alignment errors for different translation models (e.g. phrase-based, hierarchical phrase-based and tree-based models). They use phrase posteriors as the fractional count, while we use the product of inside and outside probabilities. Besides, they filter rules after extracting all rules from corpus, while we prune rules when extracting.

6 Conclusion and Future Works

Liu et al. (2009) proposed a new structure named weighted alignment matrix that make a better use of noisy alignments. Since weighted matrices proves effective for phrase-based model, we apply it to syntax-based models, which are more sensitive to word alignments. Due to the difference in structure between phrases and hierarchical rule, we develop new algorithms to calculate relative frequencies and lexical weights of hierarchical rules. To achieve a balance between rule table size and performance, we develop a scoring measure that incorporates both frequency and lexical weight to select the best target phrase for each source phrase. Our experiments show that our approach improves BLEU score significantly, with reasonable extraction speed, indicating that weighted alignment matrix also works for syntax-based models.

Besides the hierarchical phrase-based model and tree-to-string model, our method is also applicable to other paradigms such as the string-to-tree models (Galley et al., 2006) and the string-to-dependency models (Shen et al., 2008). Another interesting direction is to use a simpler alignment model that can compute alignment point posteriors directly, such as word-based ITG model (Zhang and Gildea, 2005; Haghighi et al., 2009).

7 Acknowledgement

The authors were supported by National Natural Science Foundation of China Contract 60736014 and 60903138. We thank the anonymous reviewers for their insightful comments.

References

David Chiang. 2005. A hierarchical phrase-based model for statistical machine translation. In *Proceedings of the 43rd Annual Meeting on Association for Computational Linguistics*, pages 263–270. Association for Computational Linguistics.

David Chiang. 2007. Hierarchical phrase-based translation. *computational linguistics*, 33(2):201–228.

M. Collins, P. Koehn, and I. Kučerová. 2005. Clause restructuring for statistical machine translation. In *Proceedings of the 43rd Annual Meeting on Association for Computational Linguistics*, page 540. Association for Computational Linguistics.

Adrià de Gispert, Juan Pino, and William Byrne. 2010. Hierarchical phrase-based translation grammars extracted from alignment posterior probabilities. In *Proceedings of the 2010 Conference on Empirical Methods in Natural Language Processing*, pages 545–554, Cambridge, MA, October. Association for Computational Linguistics.

Yonggang Deng, Jia Xu, and Yuqing Gao. 2008. Phrase table training for precision and recall: what makes a good phrase and a good phrase pair? In *Proceedings of ACL-08: HLT*, pages 81–88, Columbus, Ohio, June. Association for Computational Linguistics.

Christopher Dyer, Smaranda Muresan, and Philip Resnik. 2008. Generalizing word lattice translation. In *Proceedings of ACL-08: HLT*, pages 1012–1020, Columbus, Ohio, June. Association for Computational Linguistics.

Michel Galley, Jonathan Graehl, Kevin Knight, Daniel Marcu, Steve DeNeefe, Wei Wang, and Ignacio Thayer. 2006. Scalable inference and training of context-rich syntactic translation models. In *Proceedings of the 21st International Conference on Computational Linguistics and 44th Annual Meeting of the Association for Computational Linguistics*, pages 961–968, Sydney, Australia, July. Association for Computational Linguistics.

Aria Haghighi, John Blitzer, John DeNero, and Dan Klein. 2009. Better word alignments with supervised itg models. In *Proceedings of the Joint Conference of the 47th Annual Meeting of the ACL and the 4th International Joint Conference on Natural Language Processing of the AFNLP*, pages 923–931, Suntec, Singapore, August. Association for Computational Linguistics.

Liang Huang, Kevin Knight, and Aravind Joshi. 2006. Statistical syntax-directed translation with extended domain of locality. In *Proceedings of AMTA*, pages 66–73. Citeseer.

Reinhard Kneser and Hermann Ney. 1995. Improved backing-off for m-gram language modeling. In *ICASSP IEEE INT CONF ACOUST SPEECH SIGNAL PROCESS PROC*, volume 1, pages 181–184.

Philipp Koehn, Franz Joseph Och, and Daniel Marcu. 2003. Statistical phrase-based translation. In *Proceedings of the 2003 Conference of the North American Chapter of the Association for Computational Linguistics on Human Language Technology-Volume 1*, pages 48–54. Association for Computational Linguistics.

Yang Liu, Qun Liu, and Shouxun Lin. 2006. Tree-to-string alignment template for statistical machine translation. In *Proceedings of the 21st International Conference on Computational Linguistics and 44th Annual Meeting of the Association for Computational Linguistics*, pages 609–616, Sydney, Australia, July. Association for Computational Linguistics.

Yang Liu, Tian Xia, Xinyan Xiao, and Qun Liu. 2009. Weighted alignment matrices for statistical machine translation. In *Proceedings of the 2009 Conference on Empirical Methods in Natural Language Processing*, pages 1017–1026, Singapore, August. Association for Computational Linguistics.

Haitao Mi and Liang Huang. 2008. Forest-based translation rule extraction. In *Proceedings of the 2008 Conference on Empirical Methods in Natural Language Processing*, pages 206–214, Honolulu, Hawaii, October. Association for Computational Linguistics.

Franz Josef Och and Hermann Ney. 2002. Discriminative training and maximum entropy models for statistical machine translation. In *Proceedings of 40th Annual Meeting of the Association for Computational Linguistics*, pages 295–302, Philadelphia, Pennsylvania, USA, July. Association for Computational Linguistics.

Franz J. Och and Hermann Ney. 2004. The alignment template approach to statistical machine translation. *Computational Linguistics*, 30(4):417–449.

Kishore Papineni, Salim Roukos, Todd Ward, and Wei-Jing Zhu. 2002. Bleu: a method for automatic evaluation of machine translation. In *Proceedings of 40th Annual Meeting of the Association for Computational Linguistics*, pages 311–318, Philadelphia, Pennsylvania, USA, July. Association for Computational Linguistics.

Libin Shen, Jinxi Xu, and Ralph Weischedel. 2008. A new string-to-dependency machine translation algorithm with a target dependency language model. In *Proceedings of ACL-08: HLT*, pages 577–585, Columbus, Ohio, June. Association for Computational Linguistics.

Andreas Stolcke. 2002. Srilm - an extensible language modeling toolkit. In *Proceedings of Seventh International Conference on Spoken Language Processing*, volume 3, pages 901–904. Citeseer.

Zhaopeng Tu, Yang Liu, Young-Sook Hwang, Qun Liu, and Shouxun Lin. 2010. Dependency forest for statistical machine translation. In *Proceedings of the 23rd International Conference on Computational Linguistics (Coling 2010)*, pages 1092–1100, Beijing, China, August. Coling 2010 Organizing Committee.

Ashish Venugopal, Stephan Vogel, and Alex Waibel. 2003. Effective phrase translation extraction from alignment models. In *Proceedings of ACL*.

Ashish Venugopal, Andreas Zollmann, Noah A. Smith, and Stephan Vogel. 2008. Wider pipelines: n-best alignments and parses in mt training. In *Proceedings of AMTA*, Honolulu, Hawaii.

Deyi Xiong, Qun Liu, and Shouxun Lin. 2006. Maximum entropy based phrase reordering model for statistical machine translation. In *Proceedings of the 21st International Conference on Computational Linguistics and 44th Annual Meeting of the Association for Computational Linguistics*, pages 521–528, Sydney, Australia, July. Association for Computational Linguistics.

Hao Zhang and Daniel Gildea. 2005. Stochastic lexicalized inversion transduction grammar for alignment. In *Proceedings of the 43rd Annual Meeting on Association for Computational Linguistics*, pages 475–482. Association for Computational Linguistics.

Integration of Reduplicated Multiword Expressions and Named Entities in a Phrase Based Statistical Machine Translation System

Thoudam Doren Singh[†]
Department of Computer Science and Engineering
Jadavpur University
Kolkata-700032, India
thoudam.doren@gmail.com

Sivaji Bandyopadhyay
Department of Computer Science and Engineering
Jadavpur University
Kolkata-700032, India
sivaji_cse_ju@yahoo.com

Abstract

The language specific Multiword expressions (MWEs) play important roles in many natural language processing (NLP) tasks. Integrating reduplicated multiword expressions (RMWEs) into the Phrase Based Statistical Machine Translation (PBSMT) to improve translation quality is reported in the present work between Manipuri, a highly agglutinative Tibeto-Burman language and English. In addition, Multiword Named Entities (MNEs) coupled with Transliterated non-named entities (non-NE) between Manipuri and English phrase based SMT system are also integrated. The tighter integration of RMWEs and NEs into the PBSMT is carried out after automatic extraction using SVM based machine learning technique followed by automatic bilingual RMWE and MNE extraction using GIZA++ alignment. Our experimental results show improvement in the PBSMT system BLEU and NIST scores over the baseline system. Subjective evaluation indicates the improvement in the adequacy.

1 Introduction

Multiword expressions (MWEs) are a key challenge for the development of large-scale, linguistically sound natural language processing technology (Sag et al, 2002). The various kinds of multiword expressions should be analyzed in distinct ways. An adequate comprehensive analysis of multiword expressions must employ both symbolic and statistical techniques. MWEs span a range of constructions, from completely frozen, semantically opaque idiomatic expressions, to frequent but morphologically productive and semantically compositional collocations. Various linguistic processes (orthographic, morphological, syntactic, semantic and cognitive) apply to MWEs in idiosyncratic ways. Notably, MWEs blur the distinction between the lexicon and the grammar, since they often have some properties of words and some properties of phrases. The MWE identification works concentrate on compound nouns, noun-verb combination, idioms and phrases for several languages such as Hindi and Hebrew but not much on RMWEs. The reason may be that the reduplicated words are either rare or easy to identify for these languages since only complete duplication and some amount of partial reduplication may be present in these languages.

On the other hand, reduplicated MWEs (RMWE) of several varieties are widely present in Manipuri[1]. In the present work, the identification of Manipuri Named Entities (NEs) and the identification and classification of RMWEs is carried out using the SVM based machine learning approach.

---

† Presently at Center for Development of Advanced Computing (CDAC), Mumbai, India

[1] Manipuri, locally known as Meiteilon or Meeteilon, is a less privileged, morphologically rich, highly agglutinative language spoken basically in the states of Manipur, Assam, Tripura and Mizoram in India and in the neighboring countries of Myanmar and Bangladesh approximately by three million speakers. Manipuri became the first Tibeto-Burman (TB) language to receive recognition in the year 1992 as a schedule VIII language of India.

Manipuri is very rich in RMWEs like other Tibeto-Burman languages. The work of (Singh, 2000) describes the linguistic rules for identifying reduplicated words. Manipuri is the direct descendant of the conglomeration of Tibeto-Burman dialects of seven different clans. This is reflected in the commonly found use of double synonyms in Manipuri, technically known as 'semantic reduplication'. The process of reduplication (Singh, 2000) is defined as: 'reduplication is that repetition, the result of which constitutes a unit word'. These single unit words are the MWEs. The RMWEs in Manipuri are classified as: (i) Complete RMWEs, (ii) Partial RMWEs, (iii) Echo RMWEs and (iv) Mimic RMWEs. Apart from these four types of RMWEs, there are also cases of (a) Double RMWEs and (b) Semantic RMWEs.

Complete RMWEs: In the complete RMWEs the single word or phrase is repeated once forming a single unit regardless of the phonological or morphological variations. Interestingly in Manipuri these complete reduplicated MWEs can occur as Noun, Adjective, Adverb, *Wh-* question type, Verbs, Command and Request.

মৰিক মৰিক ('*marik marik*') which means 'drop by drop'. [Noun]

অটেক অটেকপা ('*atek atek-pa*') which means 'fresh' [Adjective]

কৰি কৰি ('*kari kari*') means 'what/which'. [Wh-question]

Partial RMWEs: In case of partial reduplication the second word carries some part of the first word as an affix to the second word, either as a suffix or a prefix.

For example, চথোক চত্সিন ('chat-thok chat-sin') means 'to go to and fro'; শামী লানমী ('*saa-mi laan-mi*') means 'army'.

Mimic RMWEs: In the mimic reduplication the words are complete reduplications but the morphemes are onomatopoetic, usually emotional or natural sounds. For example, কৰক কৰক ('*krak krak*') means 'cracking sound of earth in drought'.

Echo RMWEs: The second word does not have a dictionary meaning and is basically an echo word of the first word. For example, থকসি থাসি ('*thak-si kha-si*') means 'good manner'.

Double RMWEs: Such type of reduplication generally consists of three words where the prefix or suffix of the first two words is reduplicated but in the third word the prefix or suffix is absent. An example of double prefix reduplication is ইমুন ইমুন মুনবা ('*i-mun i-mun mun-ba*') which means, 'completely ripe'.

Semantic RMWEs: Both the reduplication words have the same meaning that is shared by the MWE itself. Such types of MWEs are very special to the Manipuri language. For example, পামবা কৈ ('paamba kei') means 'tiger' and each of the component words means 'tiger'.

The performance of the SMT is heavily dependent on the quality of the Parallel Corpora and the alignment models used. Integrating MWEs into the Machine Translation (MT) systems in general and phrase based Statistical Machine Translation (PBSMT) system in particular is a critical problem. Thus, there is the need for identifying Manipuri RMWE and integrating into the PBSMT system. In the present work, we integrate Manipuri Named entities (both single word and multiword), RMWEs and non-NE transliterated entities into the existing phrase-based model.

2 Related Works

Koehn and Knight (2003) discussed empirical methods for compound splitting by learning rules from monolingual and parallel corpora. Lambert and Banchs (2005) proposed technique for extracting bilingual MWEs based on grouping as units before performing the statistical alignment. (Ren et al., 2009) presented the Log Likelihood Ratio based hierarchical reducing algorithm to automatically extract bilingual MWE and investigated the performance of three different strategies in applying bilingual MWEs for SMT system using Moses (Koehn et al., 2007). Carpuat and Diab (2010) explored static integration strategy that segments training and test sentences according to the MWE vocabulary, and dynamic integration strategy that adds a new MWE-based feature in SMT translation lexicon. Handling of named entities and compound verbs in PBSMT (Pal et al., 2010) has been reported in the English-Bengali task in the Indian language context. They established prior NE alignments in the parallel corpora by transliterating source NEs into the target language using modified joint source channel transliteration technique (Ekbal et al., 2006) which incorporates different contextual information into the model. In the process, the identified NEs and compound verbs are converted into a single token by replacing spaces between the constituent words by underscores.

3 Manipuri-English Parallel Corpora

The Manipuri-English Parallel corpus (Singh and Bandyopadhyay, 2010b) on News Domain is used for training and testing. The Manipuri news corpus is collected from the website http://www.thesangaiexpress.com/. On analyzing the corpus, the statistics shows that Named entities (both single word and multiword), RMWEs and non-NE transliterated entities are present in significant numbers.

The presence of NEs in the Manipuri News corpus is approximated at 11.39%. However, the presence of non-NE transliterated entities is lesser and estimated at 9.2%. The following example (a) demonstrates the usage of the transliterated non-NE in the Manipuri news.

The following translation examples demonstrate the usage of NEs, transliterated non-NEs and RMWEs in the Manipuri source sentences.

(a)

হায় পব্বার কম্মিটিগী ইন্সত্রক্সন মতুং ইন্না য়ুঠ এফিয়ার্স এণ্ড স্পোর্টসকি জোইন্ট সেক্রেটরিনা চহি অসিগী এপ্রিল ২৪ দা ডিপার্টমেন্টশিংদগী অহাঙবা পোষ্টশিং পীথত্লক্কবা থঙহনখ্রবনি

According to the instruction of the high power committee, the joint secretary of youth affairs and sports notified to submit the vacant posts in the departments on 24 April of this year.

Considering the above translation example (a) between Manipuri and English sentence, the Manipuri transliteration of the non-NE is shown in Table 1. This significant presence of these entities plays an important role in the news corpus. These are the examples of enrichment of Manipuri languages using Manipuri transliteration from English.

Manipuri Transliteration	**English Words**
ইন্সত্রক্সন	Instruction
জোইন্ট	Joint
সেক্রেটরি	Secretary
এপ্রিল	April
ডিপার্টমেন্ট	Department
পোষ্ট	Post
হায়	High
পব্বার	Power
কম্মিটি	Committee
য়ুঠ	Youth
এফিয়ার্স	Affairs
এণ্ড	And
স্পোর্টস	Sports

Table 1: Sample Manipuri Transliterated non-NE

(b)

মোনিকা ইম্ফালদা থোরক্লবা ফ্লাইটকি টিকেত্ তাল্লবদা ফংখিদবদগী থোরকপা ঙমখিদবনি

Monika could not come due to the unavailability of the flight ticket to Imphal.

From the example (b), the NEs are given in Table 2.

Manipuri Named Entities	**English Transliteration**
মোনিকা	Monika
ইম্ফাল	Imphal

Table 2: Sample Manipuri Named Entities

(c)

অশোক অপন , মীশি মীনা , অফা অপুন য়াওরক্লবদি মদুদা থোক্লকপা অফ ফত্ত পূন্নমকি দায়ত্ব পল্ফনা

পুগদবনি হায়নসু ঙসিগী মীফমনা মত অমত্তা ওইনা য়ানথি হায়রি

It is said that the meeting unanimously agreed that PULF should be held sole responsible of dire consequences in case of untoward incidents, killing and kidnapping.

From the translation example (c), the Manipuri RMWEs are given in Table 3.

Manipuri RMWE	English Meaning
অশোক অপন	untoward incidents
মীশি মীনা	killing
অফা অপুন	kidnapping
অফ ফত্ত	dire consequences

Table 3: Sample Manipuri RMWEs

4 NE Transliteration

A transliteration system takes as input a character string in the source language and generates a character string in the target language as output. The process can be conceptualized as two levels of decoding: segmentation of the source string into transliteration units; and relating the source language transliteration units to units in the target language, by resolving different combinations of alignments and unit mappings. The problem of machine transliteration has been studied extensively in the paradigm of the noisy channel model. Translation of named entities is a tricky task: it involves both translation and transliteration. For example, the organization name *Jadavpur viswavidyalaya* is translated to *Jadavpur University* in which *Jadavpur* is transliterated to *Jadavpur* and *viswavidyalaya* is translated to *University*.

A bilingual training set of Manipuri NEs and their respective English transliterations, has been created by collecting Manipuri person, location and organization names from Manipuri news corpus and then manually entering their English transliterations. This bilingual training set is automatically analyzed to acquire mapping knowledge in order to transliterate new Manipuri person, location and organization names to English. Transliteration units (TUs) are extracted from the Manipuri-English name pairs and Manipuri TUs are associated with their English counterparts. Some examples are given below:

(a) মনিপুর(*manipur*) → ম । নি । পু । র

manipur → ma | ni | pu | r

(b) রাজকুমার(*rajkumar*) → রা । জ । কু । মা । র

rajkumar → ra | j | ku | ma | r

(c) অভিনন্দন(*abhinandan*) → অ । ভি । ন । ন্দ । ন

abhinandan → a | bhi | na | nda | n

The TUs are the lexical units for machine transliteration. The Manipuri NE is divided into Transliteration Units (TU) with patterns C+M?, where C represents a consonant or a vowel or a conjunct and M represents the vowel modifier or matra. An English NE is divided into TUs with patterns C*V*, where C represents a consonant and V represents a vowel. The system automatically learns mappings from the bilingual training set of 20,000 NEs. Aligned TUs along with their contexts are automatically derived from this bilingual training set to generate the collocation statistics.Transliteration units (TUs) are extracted from the Manipuri and the corresponding English names, and Manipuri TUs are associated with their English counterparts along with the TUs in context. For *K* aligned TUs, the Manipuri-English transliteration model based on the Modified Joint Source Channel Model for transliteration (Ekbal et. al., 2006) is given by the following equations (1) and (2).

$$P(S,T) = \prod_{k=1}^{K} P(<s,t>_k \mid <s,t>_{k-1})\, s_{k+1} \quad (1)$$

$$S \rightarrow T(S) = \arg\max_T \{P(T) \times P(S,T)\} \quad (2)$$

A TU correspondence <s, t> is called a transliteration pair of the source language S and the target language T. In this model, the previous TUs in both the source and target sides are considered as context. This model is extended to Manipuri since the Bengali script is used in Manipuri also.

5 SVM based RMWEs identification and Bilingual RMWE Extraction

The Support Vector Machine (SVM) based machine learning approach (Vapnik, 1995) works on discriminative approach and makes use of both positive and negative examples to learn the distinction between the two classes. The SVMs are known to robustly handle large feature sets and to develop models that maximize their generalizability. Consider a set of training data for a two-class problem: $\{(x_1, y_1), ..., (x_N, y_N)\}$, where $x_i \varepsilon R^D$ is a feature vector of the ith sample in the training data and $y_i \varepsilon \{+1, -1\}$ is the class to which x_i belongs. The goal is to find a decision function that accurately predicts class y for an input vector x.

A non-linear SVM classifier gives a decision function f (x) = sign $(g(x))$ for an input vector where,

$$g(x) = \sum_{i=1}^{m} w_i K(x, z_i) + b \quad (3)$$

Here, $f(x) = +1$ means x is a member of a certain class and $f(x) = -1$ means x is not a member. The support vectors that are representatives of training examples are z_i and m is the number of support vectors. Therefore, the computational complexity of $g(x)$ is proportional to m. Support vectors and other constants are determined by solving a certain quadratic programming problem. $K(x, z_i)$ is a *kernel* that implicitly maps vectors into a higher dimensional space. Typical kernels use dot products: $K(x, z_i) = k(x.z)$. A polynomial kernel of degree d is given by $K(x, z_i) = (1+x)^d$. We can use various kernels and the design of an appropriate kernel for a particular application is an important research issue.

The MNE/RMWE tagging system includes two main phases: training and classification. The training process has been carried out by YamCha[2] toolkit, an SVM based tool for detecting classes in documents and formulating the MNE/RMWE tagging task as a sequence labeling problem. Here, both one vs rest and pairwise multi-class decision methods have been used. Different experiments with the various degrees of the polynomial kernel function have been carried out. In one vs rest strategy, K binary SVM classifiers may be created where each classifier is trained to distinguish one class from the remaining K-1 classes. In pairwise classification, we constructed K (K-1)/2 classifiers considering all pairs of classes, and the final decision is taken by their weighted voting. For classification, the TinySVM-0.07 [3] classifier has been used that seems to be one of the best optimized among publicly available SVM toolkits.

In the present work, the bilingual RMWEs are extracted automatically. The difficulty lies in how to integrate the bilingual MWEs into existing the SMT system to improve system performance. The RMWEs are identified from the Manipuri source side of the parallel corpora. The RMWEs are identified (Singh and Bandyopadhyay, 2010) using support vector machine (SVM) based machine learning technique. The various features used are context word, prefix, suffix, previous RMWE information, POS information, word length, digit and infrequent word features. The SVM based RMWE identification system shows recall, precision and F-Score of 94.62%, 93.53% and 94.07% respectively.

The target equivalents of the RMWEs are extracted by running the GIZA++ alignment tool followed be candidate translation extraction from the sentence pairs using the algorithm described in (Och, 2002). There are 25,921 RMWEs in the training corpus. Thus, an additional phrase table containing the automatically extracted RMWEs is constructed.

6 Bilingual NEs Extraction

Named Entities (NEs) are indentified using the SVM based Manipuri named entity recognition technique (Singh et al., 2010a) on news corpus. At present, 4649016 Manipuri wordforms has been collected from the website. The NE identification in Manipuri is difficult and challenging because (a) Manipuri is less privileged and resource constrained language, (b) unlike English, Manipuri lacks capitalization, (c) NEs can appear in the Manipuri dictionary as well and (d) Manipuri is highly agglutinative. The major NE tags are person name, location name, organization name and miscellaneous name. The identified Manipuri NEs are transliterated using the modified joint source channel techniques discussed in Section 4. There

[2]http://chasen-org/~taku/software/yamcha/

[3]http://cl.aist-nara.ac.jp/~taku-ku/software/TinySVM

are 529522 NEs identified and transliterated of which 284521 are multiword named entities (MNE). An additional phrase table of the bilingual NEs is constructed.

7 Transliterated non-NE list Preparation

Manipuri is influenced and enriched by the Indo-Aryan languages of Sanskrit origin and English. So the presence of transliterated English words in the Manipuri news corpus is significantly high and it is important to handle these words during the translation process at the appropriate step. So, a list of 2611 Manipuri words and their English transliterations is developed from the news corpus. The non-NE list consists of both single word as well as multiple words. An additional phrase table based on this non-NE transliteration list is built in order to integrate in the present system.

8 Integration of MWE

In the present task, we employed multiple phrase tables using the Moses decoder. One phrase table is trained from the parallel corpora and second one is built using the MWEs extracted using the techniques described in section 5 and 6. For simplicity, the probability 1 is assigned to all the four probabilities of the MWE phrase table. During the decoding process, the MWEs are searched in both the phrase tables.

One of the possible techniques of integrating MWE in the SMT system is by introducing a new feature in a phrase table that indicates the presence of MWE.

9 The SMT Systems

We developed the Manipuri-English SMT systems using the state-of-the-art Moses. The various features are combined in the log-linear model. The log linear model to obtain the best translation ê of the source sentence f is given by the equation below:

$$\hat{e} = \arg\max_{e} P(e|f)$$

$$= \arg\max_{e} \sum_{i=1}^{n} \lambda_i h_i(e, f) \qquad (4)$$

where, h_i and λ_i denote the ith feature function and weight respectively. The feature weight λ_i in the log linear model is determined by using the minimum error rate training method (Och, 2003). Intuitively, the $P(e|f)$ depend on *language model* — $P(e)$ and *translation model* — $P(f|e)$.

10 Experimental Setup

The first Manipuri-English SMT task is reported in (Singh and Bandyopadhyay, 2010c) on news domain using factored translation model demonstrating improvement not only in the BLEU and NIST scores but also improvement in the fluency and adequacy by subjective evaluation method. Earlier, an English-Manipuri SMT system using morpho-syntactic and semantic information is reported by (Singh and Bandyopadhyay, 2010d). In the present experimental setup, Moses decoder (Koehn et al., 2005) is used which can support multiple phrase tables. The target language model is developed using the SRILM (Stolcke, 2002) toolkit. The language model is the 4-gram model using Kneser-Ney smoothing (Kneser and Ney, 1995) of the target language news corpus collected from the www.thesangaiexpress.com. GIZA++ is used to build IBM Model 4. The minimum error rate training (Och, 2003) determine the feature weights on the development set.

Several experiments are conducted using the phrase tables built from the MWEs. There is also an experiment on the combination of all the phrase tables consisting of the baseline, RMWE, NEs and transliterated non-NEs.

11 Evaluation Results

The corpus statistics used in the experiment is given in the table below.

	Number of sentences	Number of words
Training	10350	296728
Development	600	16520
Test	500	15204

Table 4: Corpus Statistics

The automatic scoring metrics are useful for fast evaluation of higher number of test sentences. The automatic evaluation scores are carried out using the BLEU (Papineni, 2002) with brevity penalty and NIST (Doddington, 2002). The BLEU and NIST automatic scores of various models are given in the table below:

Model	BLEU	NIST
Baseline	**13.452**	**4.31**
Baseline + RMWE	13.829	4.43
Baseline +NE	13.901	4.47
Baseline + Transliterated non-NE	13.911	4.21
Baseline + RMWE + NE + Transliterated non-NE	**15.023**	**5.21**

Table 5: Automatic Scores of Manipuri-English SMT systems

Level	Interpretation
4	Flawless with no grammatical error
3	Good output with minor errors
2	Disfluent ungrammatical with correct phrase
1	Incomprehensible

Table 6: Fluency scale

Level	Interpretation
4	Full meaning is conveyed
3	Most of the meaning is conveyed
2	Poor meaning is conveyed
1	No meaning is conveyed

Table 7: Adequacy scale

Subjective evaluation is carried out on 100 test sentences using the fluency and adequacy scales given in the Tables 6 and 7. The subjective evaluation is carried out by two bilingual human judges. The evaluation indicates the improvement in adequacy but not much on fluency as shown in Table 8. The case markers and the inflectional suffixes are not taken care of with special treatment despite the agglutinative behavior of Manipuri language towards RMWEs, NEs and non-NEs; hence the fluency is not addressed significantly.

Statistical significant test is performed to judge if a change in score that comes from a change in the system reflects a change in the overall translation quality. It is found that the difference between the baseline and the (Baseline + RMWE + NE + Transliterated non-NE) model is significant producing statistically significant improvements as measured by the bootstrap resampling method (Koehn, 2004) on BLEU.

	Manipuri Sentence length	Fluency	Adequacy
Baseline	<=15 words	1.93	2.31
	>15 words	1.51	1.76
Baseline+ RMWE	<=15 words	1.92	2.85
	>15 words	1.62	2.07
Baseline + NE	<=15 words	2.06	2.82
	>15 words	1.75	2.10
Baseline + Transliterated non-NE	<=15 words	2.10	2.79
	>15 words	1.67	2.10
Baseline + RMWE + NE + Transliterated non-NE	<=15 words	2.11	3.11
	>15 words	1.72	2.78

Table 8: Subjective Evaluation Scores

12 Conclusion and Future Work

The present work reports the tight integration of the RMWE, named entities (both single word and multiword) and transliterated non-NE entities into the Manipuri-English SMT task. The presence of these entities in the Manipuri news corpus is significantly high and their special treatment in the machine translation is absolutely necessary. In order to identify the language specific multiword expressions, the SVM based machine learning technique is utilized. Since the translation output of the SMT system is further propagated from the quality of the automatic RMWE and MNE identification using SVM based machine learning technique and multiword extraction using GIZA++ alignment, it is very important that these steps are better addressed in an effective way with more training data in future. By integrating RMWEs, MNEs and non-NEs, the adequacy of the translation output is improved; however, there is no significant improvement in the fluency. The fluency can be better addressed by incorporating morphological information such as proper handling of the case markers of the MNEs. On the other hand, the BLEU and NIST scores are improved over the baseline from 13.452 and 4.31 to 15.023 and 5.21 respectively.

References

Carpuat, Marine, and Mona Diab. 2010. Task based Evaluation of Multiword Expressions: aPilot Study in Statistical Machine Translation. In Proceedings of Human Language Technology conference and the North American Chapter of the Association for Computational Linguistics conference (HLT-NAACL 2010), Pages 242-245, Los Angeles, CA.

Doddington, George. 2002. Automatic evaluation of machine translation quality using n-gram co-occurrence statistics. In Proceedings of the Second International Conference on Human Language Technology Research (HLT-2002), Pages 128-132, San Diego, CA.

Ekbal, Asif, Sudip Kumar Naskar, Bandyopadhyay, S. 2006. A Modified Joint Source-Channel Model for Transliteration, Proceedings of the COLING/ACL 2006 Main Conference Poster Sessions, Pages 191–198, Sydney.

Lambert, Patrik and Rafael Banchs. 2005. Data inferred multi-word expressions for statistical machine translation. In Proceedings of Machine Translation Summit X, Pages 396–403.

Koehn, Philipp and Knight, Kevin. 2003. Empirical Methods for Compound Splitting, Proceedings of the EACL 2003. Pages 187-194.

Koehn, Philipp. 2004. Statistical significance tests for machine translation evaluation. In EMNLP- 2004: Proceedings of the 2004 Conference on Empirical Methods in Natural Language Processing, 25-26 July 2004, Pages 388-395, Barcelona, Spain.

Koehn, Philipp, Hieu Hoang, Alexandra Birch, Chris Callison-Burch, Marcello Federico, Nicola Bertoldi, Brooke Cowan, Wade Shen, Christine Moran, Richard Zens, Chris Dyer, Ondřej Bojar, Alexandra Constantin, and Evan Herbst. 2007. Moses: open source toolkit for statistical machine translation. In Proceedings of the 45th Annual meeting of the Association for Computational Linguistics (ACL 2007): Proceedings of demo and poster sessions, Pages 177-180, Prague, Czech Republic.

Och, Franz J., 2002, Statistical Machine Translation: From Single-Word Models to Alignment Templates. Ph.D. Thesis, Computer Science Department, RWTH, Aachen, Germany.

Och, Franz J., 2003. Minimum error rate training in Statistical Machine Translation, Proceedings of ACL.

Och, Franz J. and H. Ney. 2003. A systematic comparison of various statistical alignment models. Computational Linguistics, 29(1):19–51.

Pal, Santanu, Sudip Kumar Naskar , Pavel Pecina, Sivaji Bandyopadhyay, Andy Way, 2010. Handling Named Entities and Compound Verbs in Phrase-Based Statistical Machine Translation, In Proceedings of the Multiword Expressions: From Theory to Applications (MWE 2010), Pages 46–54, Beijing.

Papineni, K.A., Roukos, S., Ward, T., and Zhu, W.J., 2002. BLEU: a Method for Automatic Evaluation of Machine Translation. *In Proceedings of the 40th Annual Meeting of the Association for Computational Linguistics* (ACL), Philadelphia,.

Ren, Zhixiang, Yajuan Lü, Jie Cao, Qun Liu, and Yun Huang. 2009. Improving statistical machine translation using domain bilingual multiword expressions. In Proceedings of the 2009 Workshop on Multiword Expressions, ACLIJCNLP 2009, Pages 47-54, Suntec, Singapore.

Sag, Ivan A., Timothy Baldwin, Francis Bond, Ann Copestake, and Dan Flickinger. 2002. Multiword expressions: A pain in the neck for NLP. In Proceedings of the 3th International Conference on Intelligent Text Processing and Computational Linguistics(CICLing-2002), Pages 1–15.

Singh, Thoudam Doren, Nongmeikapam Kishorjit, Asif Ekbal, Sivaji Bandyopadhyay, 2009. Named Entity Recognition for Manipuri using Support Vector Machine, In proceedings of 23rd Pacific Asia Conference on Language, Information and Computation (PACLIC 23), Pages 811-818, Hong Kong.

Singh, Thoudam Doren and Sivaji Bandyopadhyay, 2010a. Web Based Manipuri Corpus for Multiword NER and Reduplicated MWEs Identification using SVM, Proceedings of the 1st Workshop on South and Southeast Asian Natural Language Processing (WSSANLP), the 23rd International Conference on Computational Linguistics (COLING), Pages 35–42, Beijing.

Singh, Thoudam Doren and Sivaji Bandyopadhyay, 2010b. Semi Automatic Parallel Corpora Extraction from Comparable News Corpora, In the International Journal of POLIBITS, Issue 41 (January - June 2010), ISSN 1870-9044, Pages 11-17.

Singh, Thoudam Doren and Sivaji Bandyopadhyay, 2010c. Manipuri-English Bidirectional Statistical Machine Translation Systems using Morphology and Dependency Relations, *In Proceedings of Syntax and Structure in Statistical Translation* (SSST-4) *of 23rd International Conference on Computational Linguistics* (COLING), Pages 75-83, Beijing.

Singh, Thoudam Doren and Sivaji Bandyopadhyay, 2010d. Statistical Machine Translation of English-Manipuri using Morpho-Syntactic and Semantic Information, *In proceedings of Ninth Conference of the Association for Machine Translation in Americas* (AMTA 2010), Pages 333-340, Denver, Colorado, USA.

Singh, Ch. Yashawanta, 2000, Manipuri Grammar, *Rajesh Publications*, Pages 190-204, Delhi.

Vapnik, Vladimir N. 1995: The nature of Statistical learning theory. Springer

Regularizing Mono- and Bi-Word Models for Word Alignment

Thomas Schoenemann
Lund University, Sweden

Abstract

Conditional probabilistic models for word alignment are popular due to the elegant way of handling them in the training stage. However, they have weaknesses such as garbage collection and scale poorly beyond single word based models (DeNero et al., 2006): not all parameters should actually be used.

To alleviate the problem, in this paper we explore regularity terms that penalize the used parameters. They share the advantages of the standard training in that iterative schemes decompose over the sentence pairs. We explore the models IBM-1 and HMM, then generalize to models we term *Bi-word* models, where each target word can be aligned to up to *two* source words.

We give two optimization strategies for the arising tasks, using EM and projected gradient descent. While both are well-known, to our knowledge they have never been compared experimentally for the task of word alignment. As a side-effect, we show that, against common belief, for parametric HMMs the M-step is *not* solved by renormalizing expectations.

We demonstrate that the regularity terms improve on the f-measures of the standard HMMs and that they improve translation quality.

1 Introduction

State-of-the art approaches for word alignment are based on probabilistic models. They can be split into joint models (Melamed, 2000; Marcu and Wong, 2002) and conditional models (Brown et al., 1993; Vogel et al., 1996; Wang and Waibel, 1998; Toutanova et al., 2002; Sumita et al., 2004; Deng and Byrne, 2005; Fraser and Marcu, 2007a). While in early works the underlying basic entity was a single word, today's advanced approaches build on sequences of words, called *phrases*.

For joint models the advanced models are stand-alone approaches (Marcu and Wong, 2002). However, these models are computationally hard to handle, which frequently results in maximum approximations being made. This is different for the conditional models, which are easier to handle but where most approaches are based on initializing from single-word based models (Brown et al., 1993; Vogel et al., 1996; Al-Onaizan et al., 1999). However, the recent work of Mauser et al. (2009) deals with pairs of source words and is trained without considering single word based models.

In this paper we much generalize on this work, considering a class of models we term *Bi-word models*. We consider a variant of (Mauser et al., 2009) which we call Bi-1, then proceed to derive a Bi-HMM. Our main focus is however on regularizing such models. We first address known conditional models called *single-word based* models, focusing on a weakness known as *garbage collection*. We show that this weakness can be alleviated by adding an entry to every dictionary distribution as well as adding a regularity term (a weighted L_1 norm). Afterwards we generalize this idea to Bi-word models. The regularity term will now become crucial since the garbage problem is known to worsen for conditional models that generalize single-word based ones (DeNero et al., 2006).

We cast all this as compact objective functions subject to simplex constraints, and show two ways to optimize these: via EM and via projected gradient descent (Bertsekas, 1999, chap. 2.1). Since each iteration decomposes over the sentence pairs, the approach is efficient and scalable. In contrast to our recent work (Schoenemann, 2011) (where we used an L_0-norm) we do not use the maximum approximation and also address Bi-word models.

Related Work on Word Alignment For a systematic comparison of the most commonly used models see (Och and Ney, 2003). Apart from the classical approaches, a few other lines of work have been pursued. Indeed, for single word based models regularity terms have been considered before, in particular in our recent work on the L_0-norm (Schoenemann, 2011). Otherwise most of the work has focused on combining asymmetric conditional approaches. Zens et al. (2004) intertwine the training of both directions by exchanging information in-between the iterations. Liang et al. (2006) propose to include the products of the conditional marginals for each training direction into the objective function. Graça et al. (2010) postulate that the posterior marginals for both directions be equal. They also propose an asymmetric variant that favors 1-to-1 alignments. The idea of posterior regularization has further been pursued in the machine learning community (Mann and McCallum, 2007).

We further note the approaches (Matusov et al., 2004; Taskar et al., 2005; Lacoste-Julien et al., 2006) that focus on the computation of alignments given symmetrized cost. Some of them also include novel ways to train the models.

Finally, our EM-scheme bears resemblance to the works (Berg-Kirkpatrick et al., 2010; Ganchev et al., 2010), but we address substantially different models.

2 Mono-Word Models

In this section we review the employed single word based models. We call them *Mono-word models* as we find the term more handy, in particular when it comes to distinguishing them from the pair-based models in the next section.

All discussed models formalize the (conditional) probability that a given English sentence $\mathbf{e} = e_1^I$, consisting of I words, produces a foreign sentence $\mathbf{f} = f_1^J$ with J words. This probability is denoted $p(\mathbf{f}|\mathbf{e})$. We will refer to $\mathbf{e}$ as the source sentence and to $\mathbf{f}$ as the target sentence. The considered models are all based on hidden variables called *alignments*. For Mono-word models the assumption is that each target word is aligned to at most one source position. The aligned position of target word j is denoted $a_j \in \{0, \ldots, I\}$, where 0 indicates unaligned words. The alignment of the entire sentence pair is denoted $\mathbf{a} = a_1^J$ and the probability is modeled as

$$p(\mathbf{f}|\mathbf{e}) = \sum_{\mathbf{a}} p(\mathbf{f}, \mathbf{a}|\mathbf{e}) \ .$$

The models differ in how this new joint probability is modeled, but they all factor it as

$$p(\mathbf{f}, \mathbf{a} \,|\, \mathbf{e}) = \prod_j p(f_j \,|\, e_{a_j}) \cdot p(a_j \,|\, a_{j-1}, j, I) \ .$$

For the first term (dictionary probability) all models use the same non-parametric representation. For the second term (alignment probability) they differ. The IBM-1 simply sets $p(a_j|a_{j-1}, j, I) = 1/(I+1)$, resulting in a convex model. We also consider the non-convex HMM, which models $p(a_j|a_{j-1}, I)$, getting rid of the dependence on j. To avoid overfitting a parametric model is used, based on considering the difference $a_j - a_{j-1}$. Details are given in the next section.

3 Bi-Word Models

In this paper we consider a more general class of conditional models, which we call Bi-word models. Here we are much generalizing on the work of (Mauser et al., 2009).

Now each target word is allowed to align to up to *two* source words. The alignment of target word j is expressed as the tuple $(a_{j,1}, a_{j,2})$, where the allowed set of values is a subset of $\{0, \ldots, I\} \times \{0, \ldots, I\}$. The value $(0, 0)$ will denote unaligned words. In any other case we require that $a_{j,2} > a_{j,1}$. If $a_{j,1}$ is 0 the word is aligned only once. If $a_{j,1} > 0$ it is aligned twice. We further forbid the case where $a_{j,1} > 0$ and $a_{j,2} = I$ since at the sentence end the considered data usually contain a punctuation mark which aligns only once. Note that otherwise there are no restrictions, in particular we do not require that the two aligned words are at consecutive positions (although such knowledge could be enforced in our framework).

In the generative story of the models we first take a decision of whether the alignment of position j is a double alignment or not. We denote this by a binary variable $b_j \in \{0, 1\}$, where a value of 1 denotes a Bi-alignment. Obviously $b_j = 0$ implies $a_{j,1} = 0$. Afterwards we decide on the aligned positions and the identity of the target word:

$$p(\mathbf{f}, \mathbf{a}|\mathbf{e}) = \prod_j p(f_j \,|\, e_{a_{j,1}}, e_{a_{j,2}}) \cdot p(b_j) \cdot p(a_{j,1}, a_{j,2} \,|\, b_j, a_{j-1,1}, a_{j-1,2}, I) \ . \quad (1)$$

Note that compared to the Mono-word models we have now many more dictionary parameters, as well as much more probability mass to spread. Moreover, $e_{a_{j,1}}$ and $e_{a_{j,2}}$ can be the empty word $NULL$.

In this work we consider two models that generalize the IBM-1 and the HMM to the new set of alignments. We call them Bi-1 (a variant of Mauser et al.'s model) and Bi-HMM, and again they differ only in the alignment probabilities. The values $p(b_j=0)$ and $p(b_j=1)$ are chosen independently of j and fixed to 0.1 and 0.9 in this work.

The **Bi-1** is a convex model and treats non-Bi-alignments as $p(0, a_{j,2} \mid b_j = 0, I) = 1/(I+1)$, just like the IBM-1. For Bi-alignments it sets $p(a_{j,1}, a_{j,2} \mid b_j = 1, I) = 1/K$, where K is the number of possible Bi-alignments (and where $a_{j,1}, a_{j,2}$ is an allowed constellation). Note the (subtle) difference to the work of Mauser et al.: this work did not consider the variables b_j, so for long sentences the pairwise alignments become dominant. Further, for our models the word order matters, i.e. generally $p(f|e_1, e_2) \neq p(f|e_2, e_1)$.

The proposed **Bi-HMM** factors the alignment probability in a manner similar to the Mono-HMM. First of all, for a given alignment we introduce the notion of the *head* of target position j, denoted h_j. In case the position was aligned at least once, we define h_j as the smallest target position aligned to j, i.e. $h_j = a_{j,1}$ if $a_{j,1} \neq 0$ and $h_j = a_{j,2}$ else. In case of unaligned positions h_j is set to the head of the largest *aligned* previous target position. Hence we use a full first-order dependence, which in practice requires doubling the state space - see (Vogel et al., 1996). The alignment probabilities are now

$$p(0, a_{j,2} \mid h_{j-1}, b{=}0, I) \;=\; p_{inter}(a_{j,2} \mid h_{j-1}, I)$$

and for $a_{j,1} > 0$

$$p(a_{j,1}, a_{j,2}|h_{j-1}, b{=}1, I) = p_{inter}(a_{j,1} \mid h_{j-1}, I) \cdot p_{intra}(a_{j,2} \mid a_{j,1}) \,.$$

Note that both cases rely on the same probability model $p_{inter}(\cdot|\cdot)$. The second case has an additional distribution $p_{intra}(\cdot|\cdot)$. Both are modeled separately using a parametric distribution described below. Note that $p_{intra}(i|i') = 0$ if $i \leq i'$.

Superficially the Bi-HMM looks similar to (Deng and Byrne, 2005). However, this latter is actually a Mono-word model.

Parametric HMMs. It is well-known that HMMs for word alignment perform best using parametric alignment probabilities. For both the Mono-HMM and the Bi-HMM, we follow Vogel et al. (1996) and consider only the difference $i - i'$ to model $p_{inter}(i|i', I)$. Here, only differences between -5 and 5 are modeled by separate parameters $r_{-5}, \ldots, r_5$, all larger differences are captured by a single parameter r_L. To make this a probability distribution, the latter parameter is spread uniformly over all possible differences (with absolute larger than 5) in the respective context. Lastly, we introduce parameters p_0 and p_1 ($p_0{+}p_1 = 1$), where p_0 denotes the probability for unaligned words. The alignment probability is now

$$p_{inter}(i \mid i', I) = \begin{cases} p_0 & \text{if } i = 0 \\ p_1 \, \frac{r_{i-i'}}{\tau_{i',I}} & \text{if } i > 0,\ |i - i'| \leq 5 \\ \frac{p_1 \cdot r_L}{\tau_{i',I} \, |\{i'' : |i'' - i'| > 5\}|} & \text{else,} \end{cases}$$

with[1]

$$\tau_{i',I} = \sum_{1 \leq i \leq I : |i-i'| \leq 5} r_{i-i'} + r_L \quad . \qquad (2)$$

A special case arises for the initial alignment probabilities $p(h_1 = i|I)$. Rather than fixing them to $1/(2I)$ (including empty words), as is common, we model these parametrically (with renormalization, but without grouping).

In case of the Bi-HMM, there is further the probability $p_{intra}(\cdot|\cdot)$, which we also parameterize based on positive distances, grouping those larger than 5. In principle, each of the three arising distributions has its own parameter set. However, the initial probability and the inter-alignment model share the parameters p_0 and p_1.

4 Objective Functions

In word alignment one is given a large set of sentence pairs, not a single pair. We denote the sth pair by $\mathbf{f}^s, \mathbf{e}^s$. The standard approach to word alignment is maximum likelihood, i.e. minimizing

$$-\sum_s \log(p(\mathbf{f}^s \mid \mathbf{e}^s))$$

over the parameters of the model. Here, we are considering a conditional model, which can be any of the above mentioned.

[1] If differences of more than 5 are impossible, the term r_L is dropped from the equation.

Such models are known to have weaknesses called *garbage collection*. This refers to the phenomenon that rarely occurring source words tend to align to a significant portion of the target words in the respective sentences, since the probability mass of the frequent words is better used to explain the sentences without rare words. The effect is known to worsen when one moves beyond single word based models (DeNero et al., 2006).

It is known that joint models suffer less from this deficiency when dealing with the same set of possible alignments. However, joint models are usually hard to handle computationally, whereas the mentioned conditional models behave quite nicely. Hence, we use conditional models, but propose to alter the training criterion. We add a regularity term that penalizes the used probability mass in a (non-negative) weighted L_1 manner. We state this for Bi-word models, but note that the Mono-word models are included by fixing $e_1 = NULL$:

$$-\sum_{s} \log(p(\mathbf{f}^s \mid \mathbf{e}^s)) + \sum_{\mathbf{e_1},\mathbf{e_2},f} w^f_{e_1,e_2}\, p(f|e_1, e_2) \quad (3)$$

Here $w_{e_1,e_2} \geq 0$ are known weights (see below). For the new objective to make sense, we need to augment the parameter space: for every constellation e_1, e_2, we add a probability $p(NULL|e_1, e_2)$. In the standard ML-criterion this entry will always be set to 0. Not so with our new criterion: since we set the respective weighting factor $w^{NULL}_{e_1,e_2}$ to 0 it may be cheaper not to use the entire mass to explain the corpus.

Choice of Weights. When dealing with Mono-word models we only penalize rare words since they cause the garbage collection phenomenon. Let $N(e)$ be the number of times the source word e occurs in the corpus. If $N(e) \geq 6$ we set $w^*_{0,e}$ to 0, otherwise it is set to $\lambda[6 - N(e)]$, where λ is some weight. We found $\lambda = 2.5$ to work well.

For Bi-word models we presently set all Mono-word weights $w^*_{0,*}$ to 0. The Bi-word penalties are based on a value of $\lambda = 0.5$, but rare source word pairs pay a larger penalty (The equation is $\lambda \cdot \max\{1, 5 - N(e_1, e_2)\}$, where $N(e_1, e_2)$ is the number of times the pair e_1, e_2 occurred).

5 Optimization Strategies

We present two optimization schemes to handle the arising minimization problems: one is based on Expectation Maximization (EM), the other on projected gradient descent (PGD). To make the paper self-contained, we include a sketch of the relevant equations, noting that they are probably known in other contexts. We detail the scheme on the Bi-word models, the Mono-word models can be handled analogously.

Constraints First of all we note that we are dealing with a *constrained* optimization problem, since the objective (3) is minimized over the parameters of probability distributions. For the dictionary parameters we have positivity constraints and normalization constraints:

$$p(f|e_1, e_2) \geq 0 \quad \forall f, e_1, e_2 \ ,$$

$$\sum_f p(f|e_1, e_2) = 1 \quad \forall e_1, e_2 \ .$$

This is known as a *product of simplices*, a relatively easy constraint system. For the Bi-1 there are no more parameters to optimize.

For the Bi-HMM (and also the Mono-HMM) there are the parameters $r_{-5}, \ldots r_5$ and r_L of the inter-alignment model. Each one comes with a positivity constraint. Moreover, these parameters are determined only up to scale, so we introduce the simplex constraint that they sum to 1: $\sum_{k=-5}^{5} r_k + r_L = 1$. The same principle applies to the parameters of the initial probability and of $p_{intra}(\cdot|\cdot)$.

5.1 Projected Gradient Descent

We first present a solution based on *projected gradient descent* (PGD) (Bertsekas, 1999, chap. 2), which is applicable since our constraint set is convex. Even though EM is usually the better suited method, we recommend reading this section as some auxiliary problems of EM are optimized by a very similar method.

PGD is similar to unconstrained gradient descent: one iteratively computes the gradient of the objective and takes a step in this direction. In general one will leave the feasible region, so one takes the closest feasible point instead. This operation is called *projection*. In our case we use the method of (Michelot, 1986). Finally, this point can have a higher energy than the previous, but the direction between the two points is a *descent direction*. We do a backtracking line-search to find a step in this direction that gives a sufficient decrease in the objective value. For the convex Bi-1 model this will eventually reach the global optimum, for the Bi-HMM a local optimum (as is standard for HMMs).

Obviously, the gradient of the regularity term (w.r.t. the dictionary parameters) is the weight vector with entries $w^f_{e_1,e_2}$. Further, the gradient of the standard maximum likelihood term is additive over the sentences. Hence, in the following we only state the gradients of a single sentence pair, i.e. $\frac{\partial}{\partial\theta} - \log(p(\mathbf{f}^s|\mathbf{e}^s))$, where θ is either a dictionary or an alignment parameter.

All considered models are so-called *multinomial* distributions. As shown in the appendix, for such distributions the gradient w.r.t. the dictionary parameters is given by

$$\frac{\partial}{\partial p(f|e_1,e_2)} - \log(p(\mathbf{f}^s|\mathbf{e}^s)) = -\frac{\sum_{\mathbf{a}} k_{\mathbf{a}}(f,e_1,e_2)\, p(\mathbf{a}|\mathbf{f}^s,\mathbf{e}^s)}{p(f|e_1,e_2)} \tag{4}$$

where $k_{\mathbf{a}}(f,e_1,e_2)$ is the number of times f aligns to both e_1 and e_2 in the alignment $\mathbf{a}$ and for the considered sentence pair. Note that the numerator of the ratio is the *expectation* of f aligning to e_1 and e_2 in the given sentence pair. This expression is also a fundamental building block of standard EM. For the Mono-1 and Bi-1 this is simply a sum over the source positions j. For the Mono- and Bi-HMM it can be calculated by the forward-backward algorithm (Baum et al., 1970).

With a similar argument one can derive the partial derivatives of the alignment parameters. We exemplarily detail this for p_{inter}. Let θ denote any of the parameters $p_0, p_1, r_{-5}, \ldots, r_5$ and r_L. Then one can show that

$$\frac{\partial}{\partial\theta} - \log(p(\mathbf{f}^s|\mathbf{e}^s)) = -\sum_{i,i'} \frac{\sum_{\mathbf{a}} k_{\mathbf{a}}(i|i',I_s)\, p(\mathbf{a}|\mathbf{f}^s,\mathbf{e}^s)}{p(i|i',I_s)} \cdot \frac{\partial p(i|i',I_s)}{\partial\theta}, \tag{5}$$

where $k_{\mathbf{a}}(i|i')$ denotes the number of times a source word is aligned to position i when the head of the previous source word was i'.

It remains to derive the partial derivatives of $p(i|i',I_s)$ w.r.t. the alignment parameters. For p_0 and p_1 this is straightforward. For a regular count r_k with $|k| \leq 5$ we have

$$\frac{\partial}{\partial r_k} p(i|i',I) = \begin{cases} p_1 \frac{\tau_{i',I} - r_k}{\tau^2_{i',I}} & \text{if } k = i - i' \\ p_1 \frac{-r_{i-i'}}{\tau^2_{i',I}} & \text{if } |i-i'| \leq 5 \\ p_1 \frac{-r_L}{\tau^2_{i',I} \cdot n^L_{i',I}} & \text{else ,} \end{cases}$$

where $\tau_{i',I}$ is as in (2). The derivative w.r.t. r_L is

$$\frac{\partial}{\partial r_L} p(i|i',I) = \begin{cases} p_1 \frac{\tau_{i',I} - r_L}{\tau^2_{i',I} \cdot n^L_{i',I}} & \text{if } |i-i'| > 5 \\ p_1 \frac{-r_{i-i'}}{\tau^2_{i',I} \cdot n^L_{i',I}} & \text{else ,} \end{cases}$$

with $n^L_{i',I} = |\{i'' : 1 \leq i'' \leq I, |i'' - i'| > 5\}|$.

5.2 Expectation Maximization

A very commonly used method for word alignment is *expectation maximization* (Neal and Hinton, 1998). We give a modified version that handles our new objective function. Note that modifications of EM have been derived before, e.g. (Ganchev et al., 2010).

Traditionally, EM is used for standard maximum likelihood optimization. Denoting the parameters of the model as $\boldsymbol{\theta}$, the respective minimization problem would be

$$\min_{\boldsymbol{\theta}} \sum_{s=1}^{S} - \log(p(\mathbf{f}_s|\mathbf{e}_s,\boldsymbol{\theta})) \ .$$

The function to be minimized is called *negative log-likelihood*. It follows from (Neal and Hinton, 1998) that the function

$$F(\boldsymbol{\theta},\tilde{\boldsymbol{\theta}}) = \sum_{s=1}^{S} \sum_{\mathbf{a}_s} - p(\mathbf{a}_s|\mathbf{f}_s,\mathbf{e}_s,\tilde{\boldsymbol{\theta}}) \Big[\log(p(\mathbf{f}_s,\mathbf{a}_s|\mathbf{e}_s,\boldsymbol{\theta})) - \log(p(\mathbf{a}_s|\mathbf{f}_s,\mathbf{e}_s,\tilde{\boldsymbol{\theta}}))\Big]$$

is an upper bound on the negative log-likelihood function, independent of the choice of $\tilde{\boldsymbol{\theta}}$. In fact, $F(\boldsymbol{\theta},\boldsymbol{\theta})$ is exactly the negative log-likelihood for $\boldsymbol{\theta}$. As a consequence,

$$F(\boldsymbol{\theta},\tilde{\boldsymbol{\theta}}) + \sum_{\mathbf{e}_1,\mathbf{e}_2} \sum_{f} w^f_{e_1,e_2}\, p(f|e_1,e_2) \tag{6}$$

upper bounds our new objective (3) - note that all $p(f|e_1,e_2)$ are entries in the vector $\boldsymbol{\theta}$. As in standard EM, we now perform coordinate descent on this new function: we iteratively update $\tilde{\boldsymbol{\theta}}$ to the vector that minimizes the objective for fixed $\boldsymbol{\theta}$. The optimal value is given as the expectation of alignments given $\boldsymbol{\theta}$ (Neal and Hinton, 1998), which is why this term is generally called E-step. The respective calculations in our case are exactly as the ones performed in gradient descent.

The second step in each iteration is called M-step and consists of setting $\boldsymbol{\theta}$ to the optimal value for the given $\tilde{\boldsymbol{\theta}}$ and hence the given coefficients $p(\mathbf{a}_s \mid \mathbf{f}_s, \mathbf{e}_s, \tilde{\boldsymbol{\theta}})$. While for simple models there is often an analytic solution, in our case we are not aware of one for *any* of the parameters (except for special cases, e.g. when all $w^f_{e_1,e_2}$ are 0). Note, that this implies that the popular toolkit GIZA++ is not doing the M-step correctly: when applying the equations derived below, we verified that renormalizing expectations does *not* minimize the M-step energy. Moreover, with the common procedure the total energy usually only decreases in the first few iterations, after that it often increases.

The arising M-step decomposes into several independent optimization problems. In particular, there is a separate problem for each e_1, e_2 to update the respective dictionary distribution. The function to be minimized is

$$\sum_f \left[w^f_{e_1,e_2} p(f|e_1,e_2) - c^f_{e_1,e_2} \log(p(f|e_1,e_2))\right] ,$$

where the weights c_{f,e_1,e_2} are the expectations (under the previous $\boldsymbol{\theta}$) of f aligning to e_1 and e_2. We solve this via gradient descent with the gradient

$$\frac{\partial}{\partial p(f|e_1,e_2)} = \sum_f \left[w^f_{e_1,e_2} - \frac{c^f_{e_1,e_2}}{p(f|e_1,e_2)}\right] ,$$

In special cases more efficient schemes are applicable. In particular it is well-known that if $w^f_{e_1,e_2} = 0$ for all f the optimal solution is given by re-normalizing the coefficients $c^f_{e_1,e_2}$. If $w^f_{e_1,e_2}$ is constant for all $f \neq NULL$, then in principle one only has to determine the probability $p(NULL|e_1,e_2)$. The remaining mass can again be spread according to normalized coefficients.

For the alignment parameters, we again only discuss $p_{\text{inter}}(\cdot|\cdot)$, where the auxiliary energy is

$$\sum_I \sum_{i,i'=1}^{I} -c^I_{i,i'} \log(p(i|i',I)) ,$$

and the gradient for an alignment parameter θ

$$\frac{\partial}{\partial \theta} = \sum_{i,i'=1}^{I} -\frac{c^I_{i,i'}}{p(i|i',I)} \frac{\partial p(i|i',I)}{\partial \theta} .$$

The inner derivatives were given in section 5.1. The parameters p_0 and p_1 are very simple to derive.

6 Experiments

We report results on three different data sets, in both directions each. The first two are Europarl sets (in the original casing), where we consider English-German[2] and English-Spanish[3]. Further, we consider the well-known Canadian Hansards task (French-English, lowercased). In all cases we report weighted f-measures (Fraser and Marcu, 2007b) on the publicly available gold alignments. We use a weighting factor of $\alpha = 0.1$, which performed well in Fraser and Marcu's work.

	EP De-En	**EP** Es-En	**Hs.** Fr-En
#sentences (large task)	500K	500K	1M
#sentences (small task)	15K	15K	25K
sent. length	80	75	40

Table 1: Statistics of the considered tasks. Es = Spanish, De = German, Fr = French, En = English, Hs. = Canadian Hansards, EP = Europarl. "K" denotes a thousand, "M" a million.

For the Mono-word models we consider large scale tasks with at least 500000 sentence pairs. For the Bi-word models the demand on computational resources is much higher, so we use tasks with 15000 to 25000 sentence pairs. We also evaluate the Mono-word models here, showing that the regularity term becomes more important in the case of scarce training data.

The most important statistics of all tasks are listed in Table 1. The methods required no more than 4 GB memory on these tasks. The running times on the large scale tasks sometimes slightly exceeded a day. For the small scale tasks even the Bi-word models need less than 12 hours. Without regularity, EM is clearly faster. But with regularity terms, EM and PGD are roughly equal in speed. In general, PGD finds a slightly higher energy than EM.

6.1 Comparison of Models

In this paper we have introduced new objective functions and argued that they alleviate some of the deficiencies of standard maximum likelihood for conditional models. As a consequence, we are interested in comparing models and objective functions, and not so much in getting the last bit of practical performance (f-measure).

Hence, when comparing[4] to GIZA++ we turn

[2]Gold alignments available at `http://www.maths.lth.se/matematiklth/personal/tosch/download.html`.

[3]Gold alignments from (Lambert et al., 2005).

[4]It is common to run GIZA++ with smoothing and only 5 iterations. Indeed, this improves the f-measures. However,

	EUParl Es-En 500K		EUParl De-En 500K		CHans Fr-En 1M	
	Es|En	**En|Es**	**De|En**	**En|De**	**Fr|En**	**En|Fr**
IBM-1, EM, no reg.	64.0	64.6	68.5	71.5	82.7	83.3
IBM-1, EM, with reg.	64.5	64.9	68.6	72.0	83.1	83.5
IBM-1, PGD, no reg.	63.5	63.6	67.0	71.0	82.6	82.3
IBM-1, PGD, with reg.	63.8	64.1	66.9	71.8	83.3	81.8
HMM, EM (GIZA++)	75.0	74.2	72.5	75.3	91.4	90.8
HMM, EM (our), no reg.	77.4	76.1	73.2	77.8	89.6	90.3
HMM, EM (our), with reg.	77.7	76.3	73.1	78.2	90.3	90.6
HMM, PGD, no reg.	75.3	73.5	70.9	75.3	89.2	88.8
HMM, PGD, with reg.	74.9	73.8	72.2	75.7	89.3	88.7
IBM-4 (GIZA++)	79.6	80.0	76.8	80.5	92.3	93.2

Table 2: F-measures ($\times 100$) for the large-scale tasks.

off smoothing. Also, we run more iterations than usual: for all methods (GIZA++, EM, PGD) we run 30 iterations of IBM-1, followed by 50 for the HMM. Here we use the same regularity terms for both models. For reference, we also evaluate the IBM-4 as implemented in GIZA++ (starting from the 50 HMM iterations, then doing 5 iterations of IBM-3 and 5 iterations of IBM-4).

For the Bi-word models we initialize the non-convex Bi-HMM by running the Bi-1 first (with the same regularity term, if any). The number of iterations is the same as for the respective Mono-word models.

Large Scale Tasks. In Table 2 we show the resulting f-measures on the large scale tasks for all mentioned strategies, including GIZA++'s HMM and IBM-4. Often our HMM outperforms GIZA++ (without smoothing), which may be due to the more precise M-step. Moreover, the regularity terms usually improve the results, where the effect is generally stronger the higher inflected the source language is. Still, the IBM-4 performs best everywhere, so in future work we will transfer our new objective to this model.

Small Scale Tasks. The results for the small tasks are given in Table 3. Here it can be seen that adding the regularity to the Mono-word models greatly improves on the f-measures of the baseline HMM and sometimes gets close to the IBM-4. For the Bi-word models the regularity terms also help greatly, and in the majority of cases beat the baseline Mono-HMM (without regularity).

Like for the large scale tasks, EM performs better than PGD and the corrected M-steps often beat GIZA++.

with the new objective function we also get better results for less iterations. A systematic comparison of this is left for future work.

Method	BLEU	TER
our HMM, no reg.	27.94	56.98
our HMM, with reg.	28.33	56.20
GIZA++, HMM	28.04	56.83
GIZA++, IBM-4	28.71	56.15

Table 4: Evaluation of the translation quality for the large scale German $\rightarrow$ English task.

Method	BLEU	TER
our HMM, no reg.	21.50	63.44
our HMM, with reg.	21.77	62.97
GIZA++, HMM	21.90	63.34
GIZA++, IBM-4	22.24	62.81
Bi-HMM, no reg.	21.78	63.58
Bi-HMM, with reg.	21.70	63.38

Table 5: Evaluation of the translation quality for the small scale German $\rightarrow$ English task.

6.2 Effect on Phrase-based Translation

We give a first evaluation of the effect of our alignments on phrase-based translation, where we ran MOSES with a 5-gram language model. We randomly picked translation from German to English with 750 unseen development and 3000 unseen test sentences.

As shown in the tables 4 and 5 the regularity terms do improve translation for Mono-word models. The Bi-word models are presently not competetive. Here we are showing the BLEU accuracy measure and the Translation Edit Rate (TER).

7 Conclusion

This paper has introduced the idea of regularizing the mass of the probability parameters that is

	EUParl Es-En 15K		EUParl De-En 15K		CHans Fr-En 25K	
	Es|En	**En|Es**	**De|En**	**En|De**	**Fr|En**	**En|Fr**
IBM-1, EM, no reg.	54.5	56.0	59.0	63.6	77.1	79.2
IBM-1, EM, with reg.	56.0	57.2	60.4	64.5	78.7	79.5
IBM-1, PGD, no reg.	50.6	56.0	59.2	63.1	76.6	79.3
IBM-1, PGD, with reg.	55.8	56.9	60.0	63.5	78.0	79.4
HMM, EM, (GIZA++)	68.0	66.9	65.7	67.9	82.8	84.9
HMM, EM, (our), no reg.	69.3	68.9	65.0	70.2	80.9	86.9
HMM, EM, (our), with reg.	72.2	72.0	68.0	71.8	83.5	87.7
HMM, PGD, no reg.	68.0	68.9	57.9	68.7	79.3	85.6
HMM, PGD, with reg.	68.0	71.0	61.0	69.4	82.1	86.1
IBM-4 (GIZA++)	72.5	72.3	76.8	73.0	86.4	89.0
Bi-1, EM, no reg.	52.0	54.7	57.8	63.8	74.2	77.3
Bi-1, EM, with reg.	54.2	55.8	59.3	64.3	76.8	78.8
Bi-1, PGD, no reg.	52.8	55.2	58.0	64.0	75.0	77.8
Bi-1, PGD, with reg.	53.7	56.0	59.1	63.8	75.7	77.8
Bi-HMM, EM, no reg.	66.2	68.5	64.4	67.2	79.6	82.2
Bi-HMM, EM, with reg.	70.8	71.2	66.0	70.8	80.5	86.8
Bi-HMM, PGD, no reg.	68.4	68.2	71.5	68.0	78.2	84.3
Bi-HMM, PGD, with reg.	69.8	71.2	63.5	68.1	78.4	84.1

Table 3: Resulting F-measures ($\times 100$) for the small scale tasks.

used to explain the data. We have argued that these terms reduce overfitting and demonstrated experimentally that the introduced objectives improve the f-measures of the generated alignments. We often beat the baseline HMM, and transferring our objective to the IBM-4 would probably beat a baseline IBM-4.

Our comparison of projected gradient descent (PGD) and expectation maximization (EM) revealed that EM leads to better alignments, although PGD finds a comparable but slightly higher objective value. We also showed that parametric HMMs induce non-trivial M-steps.

In future work we want to address IBM-3 and IBM-4 and explore the effect on phrase-based translation in greater detail.

To facilitate further research in this area, the source code associated to this work is integrated into a tool called **RegAligner**, publicly available at the author's homepage and at `https://github.com/Thomas1205/RegAligner`.

Acknowledgments The author thanks Ben Taskar and João Graça for helpful discussions, as well as Alexander Engau and UC Denver for helping out with computational resources after the author had left Lund University. This work was in large part funded by the European Research Council (GlobalVision grant no. 209480).

Appendix

We now derive the partial derivative of the negative log-likelihood of a general (multinomial) probability w.r.t. a dictionary parameter $p(f|e_1, e_2)$. This derivation is probably not novel, but included here for completeness. The partial derivative is given by

$$\frac{\partial}{\partial p(f|e_1,e_2)} - \log(p(\mathbf{f}^s|\mathbf{e}^s)) =$$
$$-\frac{1}{p(\mathbf{f}^s|\mathbf{e}^s)} \cdot \left[\sum_{\mathbf{a}^s} \frac{\partial}{\partial p(f|e_1,e_2)} p(\mathbf{f}^s, \mathbf{a}^s|\mathbf{e}^s)\right] .$$

Now take a fixed $\mathbf{a}$, and denote $k_\mathbf{a} \in \mathbb{N}_0$ the number of times the factor $p(f|e_1, e_2)$ is used in its probability, i.e.

$$p(\mathbf{f}^s, \mathbf{a}|\mathbf{e}^s) = c_\mathbf{a} \cdot p(f|e_1, e_2)^{k_\mathbf{a}} \ ,$$

where $c_\mathbf{a}$ is constant w.r.t. $p(f|e_1, e_2)$. Clearly

$$\frac{\partial p(\mathbf{f}^s, \mathbf{a}|\mathbf{e}^s)}{\partial p(f|e_1,e_2)} = c_\mathbf{a} \cdot k_\mathbf{a} \cdot p(f|e_1,e_2)^{k_\mathbf{a}-1}$$
$$= k_\mathbf{a} \frac{p(\mathbf{f}^s, \mathbf{a}|\mathbf{e}^s)}{p(f|e_1,e_2)} .$$

This is how the claimed formula arises, i.e. the entire derivative is

$$-\frac{\sum_\mathbf{a} k_\mathbf{a}\, p(\mathbf{a}|\mathbf{f}^s, \mathbf{e}^s)}{p(f|e_1,e_2)} .$$

References

Y. Al-Onaizan, J. Curin, M. Jahr, K. Knight, J. Lafferty, I. D. Melamed, F. J. Och, D. Purdy, N. A. Smith, and D. Yarowsky. 1999. Statistical machine translation, Final report, JHU workshop. http://www.clsp.jhu.edu/ws99/.

L.E. Baum, T. Petrie, G. Soules, and N. Weiss. 1970. A maximization technique occuring in the statistical analysis of probabilistic functions of markov chains. *Annals of Mathematical Statistics*, 41(1):164–171.

T. Berg-Kirkpatrick, A. Bouchard-Côté, J. DeNero, and D. Klein. 2010. Painless unsupervised learning with features. In *Conference of the North American Chapter of the Association for Computational Linguistisc (NAACL)*, Los Angeles, California, June.

D.P. Bertsekas. 1999. *Nonlinear Programming, 2nd edition*. Athena Scientific.

P.F. Brown, S.A. Della Pietra, V.J. Della Pietra, and R.L. Mercer. 1993. The mathematics of statistical machine translation: Parameter estimation. *Computational Linguistics*, 19(2):263–311, June.

J. DeNero, D. Gillick, J. Zhang, and D. Klein. 2006. Why generative phrase models underperform surface heuristics. In *StatMT '06: Proceedings of the Workshop on Statistical Machine Translation*, pages 31–38, Morristown, NJ, USA, June.

Y. Deng and W. Byrne. 2005. HMM word and phrase alignment for statistical machine translation. In *HLT-EMNLP*, Vancouver, Canada, October.

A. Fraser and D. Marcu. 2007a. Getting the structure right for word alignment: LEAF. In *Conference on Empirical Methods in Natural Language Processing (EMNLP)*, Prague, Czech Republic, June.

A. Fraser and D. Marcu. 2007b. Measuring word alignment quality for statistical machine translation. *Computational Linguistics*, 33(3):293–303, September.

K. Ganchev, J. Graça, J. Gillenwater, and B. Taskar. 2010. Posterior regularization for structured latent variable models. *Journal of Machine Learning Research*, 11:2001–2049, July.

J. Graça, K. Ganchev, and B. Taskar. 2010. Learning tractable word alignment models with complex constraints. *Computational Linguistics*, 36, September.

S. Lacoste-Julien, B. Taskar, D. Klein, and M. Jordan. 2006. Word alignment via quadratic assignment. In *Human Language Technology Conference of the North American Chapter of the Association of Computational Linguistics*, New York, New York, June.

P. Lambert, A.D. Gispert, R. Banchs, and J.B. Marino. 2005. Guidelines for word alignment evaluation and manual alignment. *Language Resources and Evaluation*, 39(4):267–285.

P. Liang, B. Taskar, and D. Klein. 2006. Alignment by agreement. In *Human Language Technology Conference of the North American Chapter of the Association of Computational Linguistics*, New York, New York, June.

G.S. Mann and A. McCallum. 2007. Simple, robust, scalable semi-supervised learning via Expectation Regularization. In *International Conference on Machine Learning*, Corvallis, Oregon.

D. Marcu and W. Wong. 2002. A phrase-based, joint probability model for statistical machine translation. In *Conference on Empirical Methods in Natural Language Processing (EMNLP)*, Philadelphia, Pennsylvania, July.

E. Matusov, R. Zens, and H. Ney. 2004. Symmetric word alignments for statistical machine translation. In *International Conference on Computational Linguistics (COLING)*, Geneva, Switzerland, August.

A. Mauser, S. Hasan, and H. Ney. 2009. Extending statistical machine translation with discriminative and trigger-based lexicon models. In *Conference on Empirical Methods in Natural Language Processing (EMNLP)*, Singapore, August.

D. Melamed. 2000. Models of translational equivalence among words. *Computational Linguistics*, 26(2):221–249.

C. Michelot. 1986. A finite algorithm for finding the projection of a point onto the canonical simplex of $\mathbb{R}^n$. *Journal on Optimization Theory and Applications*, 50(1), July.

R.M. Neal and G.E. Hinton. 1998. A view of the EM algorithm that justifies incremental, sparse, and other variants. In M.I. Jordan, editor, *Learning in Graphical Models*. MIT press.

F.J. Och and H. Ney. 2003. A systematic comparison of various statistical alignment models. *Computational Linguistics*, 29(1):19–51.

T. Schoenemann. 2011. Probabilistic word alignment under the l_0-norm. In *Conference on Computational Natural Language Learning (CoNLL)*, Portland, Oregon, June.

E. Sumita, Y. Akiba, T. Doi, A. Finch, K. Imamura, H. Okuma, M. Paul, M. Shimohata, and T. Watanabe. 2004. EBMT, SMT, Hybrid and more: ATR spoken language translation system. In *International Workshop on Spoken Language Translation (IWSLT)*, Kyoto, Japan, September.

B. Taskar, S. Lacoste-Julien, and D. Klein. 2005. A discriminative matching approach to word alignment. In *Conference on Empirical Methods in Natural Language Processing (EMNLP)*, Vancouver, Canada, October.

K. Toutanova, H.T. Ilhan, and C.D. Manning. 2002. Extensions to HMM-based statistical word alignment models. In *Conference on Empirical Methods in Natural Language Processing (EMNLP)*, Philadelphia, Pennsylvania, July.

S. Vogel, H. Ney, and C. Tillmann. 1996. HMM-based word alignment in statistical translation. In *International Conference on Computational Linguistics (COLING)*, pages 836–841, Copenhagen, Denmark, August.

Y.-Y. Wang and A. Waibel. 1998. Modeling with structures in statistical machine translation. In *International Conference on Computational Linguistics (COLING)*, Montreal, Canada, August.

R. Zens, E. Matusov, and H. Ney. 2004. Improved word alignment using a symmetric lexicon model. In *International Conference on Computational Linguistics (COLING)*, Geneva, Switzerland, August.

Parametric Weighting of Parallel Data for Statistical Machine Translation

Kashif Shah, Loïc Barrault, Holger Schwenk
LIUM, University of Le Mans
Le Mans, France.
FirstName.LastName@lium.univ-lemans.fr

Abstract

During the last years there is increasing interest in methods that perform some kind of weighting of heterogeneous parallel training data when building a statistical machine translation system. It was for instance observed that training data that is close to the period of the test data is more valuable than older data (Hardt and Elming, 2010; Levenberg et al., 2010). In this paper we obtain such a weighting by resampling alignments using weights that decrease with the temporal distance of bitexts to the test set. By these means, we can use all the available bitexts and still put an emphasis on the most recent one. The main idea of our approach is to use a parametric form or meta-weights for the weighting of the different parts of the bitexts. This ensures that our approach has only few parameters to optimize. We report experimental results on the Europarl corpus, translating from French to English and further verified it on the official WMT'11 task, translating from English to French. Our method achieves improvements of about 0.6 points BLEU on the test set with respect to a system trained on data without any weighting.

1 Introduction

Statistical machine translation (SMT) systems are based on two types of resources: monolingual data to build a language model (LM) and bilingual data – also called bitexts – to train the translation model (TM). The parallel data often comes from different sources, *e.g.* Europarl, UN, in-domain data in limited amounts, data crawled from the Internet or even bitexts automatically extracted from comparable corpora. It seems obvious that the appropriateness and the usefulness of this parallel data for a particular translation task may vary quite a lot. Nevertheless, the standard procedure is to concatenate all available parallel data, to perform word alignment using GIZA++ (Och and Ney, 2000) and to extract and score the phrase pairs by simple relative frequency. Doing this, the parallel data is (wrongly) considered as one homogeneous pool of knowledge. We argue that the parallel data is quite inhomogeneous in many practical applications with respect to several factors:

- the data may come from different sources that are more or less relevant to the translation task (in-domain versus out-of-domain data).
- more generally, the topic or genre of the data may be more or less relevant.
- the data may be of different quality (carefully performed human translations versus automatically crawled and aligned data).
- the recency of the data with respect to the task may have an influence. This is of interest in the news domain where named entities, etc change over time.

There have been several attempts in the literature to address some of these problems. Matsoukas et al. (2009) proposed to weight each sentence in the training bitexts by optimizing a discriminative function on a tuning set. Sentence-level features are extracted to estimate the weights that are relevant to the given task. Foster et al. (2010) proposed an extended approach by an instant weighting scheme which learns weights on individual phrase pairs instead of sentences and incorporated the instance-weighting model into a linear combination of feature functions.

The technique presented in this paper is related to these previous works as it concerns the weighting of corpora or sentences. However, it does not

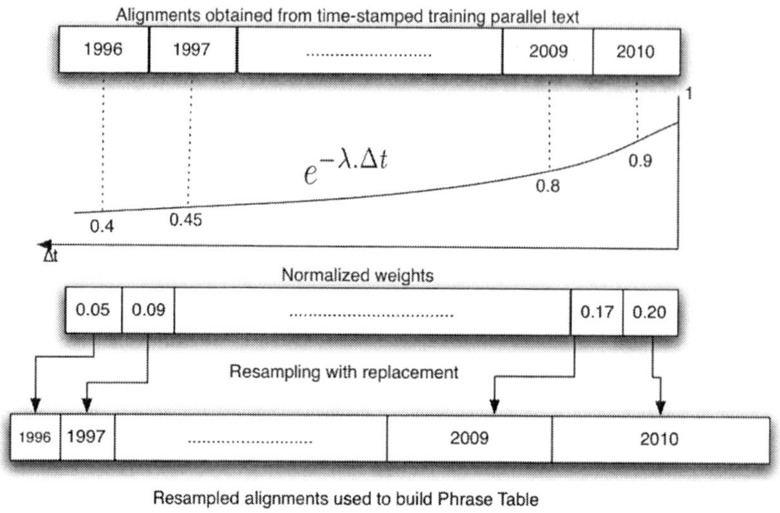

Figure 1: Overview of the weighting scheme. The alignments are weighted by an exponential decay function, parameterized by λ. Resampling with replacement is used to create a new corpus (parts with higher weight will appear more often). The phrase table is built from this corpus using the standard procedure.

require the calculation of additional sentence-level features.

In our previous work Shah et al. (2010) we proposed a technique to weight heterogeneous data by weighted resampling of the alignments. The weights were numerically optimized on development data.

Hardt and Elming (2010) has shown recency effect in terms of file-context and concluded that the data within the same file is of greater importance than the rest. Levenberg et al. (2010) proposed an incremental training procedure to deal with a continuous stream of parallel text. Word alignment was performed by the stepwise online EM algorithm and the phrase table was represented with suffix arrays. The authors showed that it is better to use parallel data close to the test data than all the available data.

The research presented in this paper is the extension of our previous work Shah et al. (2010) to weight corpora by resampling and is inspired by the work of Levenberg et al. (2010) to consider the recency of the training data. In fact, we could split the training data into several parts over time scale and use our previous resampling approach Shah et al. (2010) to automatically optimize the weights of each time period. However, this approach does not seem to scale very well when the number of individual corpora increases. Numerical optimization of more than ten corpus weights would probably need a large number of iterations, each one consisting in the creation of a complete phrase table and its evaluation on the development data.

The main idea of our work is to consider some kind of meta-weights for each part of the training data. Instead of numerically optimizing all the weights, these meta-weights only depend on few parameters that need to be optimized. Concretely, in this work we study the exponential decrease of the importance of parallel data in function of its temporal distance to the development and test data. The weighting of the parts is still done by resampling the alignments. However, our general approach is not limited to weighting the training data with respect to recency to the development and test data. Any other criterion could be used as long as it can be calculated by a parametric function, *i.e.* to measure the topic appropriateness.

2 Weighting Scheme

The main idea of our work is summarized in Figure 1. We consider that time information is available for the bitexts. If this is not the case, one can consider that the time advances sequentially with the lines in the file. First, the data is considered in parts according to the time information. In Figure 1, we group together all data within the same year, but any other granularity is possible (months, weeks, days, etc). Given the observation that more recent training data seems to be more important than older one, we apply an exponential decay function:

$$e^{-\lambda \cdot \Delta t} \quad (1)$$

where λ is the decay factor and Δt is the discretized time distance (0 for most recent part, 1 for the next one, etc.). Therefore, our weighting scheme has only one parameter to be optimized.

Following our previous work Shah et al. (2010), we resample the alignments in order to obtain a weighting of the bitexts according to their recency. The weight of each part of the bitexts is normalized (sum to one). The normalized weights represent the percentage of final aligned corpus that is originated from each part of the source corpus: word alignments corresponding to bitexts that are close to the test period will appear more often than the older ones in the final corpus.

In addition, we considered the quality of the alignments during resampling, as described in our previous work (Shah et al., 2010). Alignments produced by GIZA++ have alignment scores associated with each sentence pair in both direction, *i.e.* source to target and target to source. Alignment scores have a very large dynamic range and are concentrated around very low values, consequently the following logarithmic mapping is applied in order to flatten the distribution:

$$\log(\alpha \cdot \frac{(\sqrt[n_{trg}]{a_{src\_trg}} + \sqrt[n_{src}]{a_{trg\_src}})}{2}) \quad (2)$$

where a is the alignment score, n the size of a sentence and α a smoothing coefficient to optimize. We used these normalized alignment scores as confidence measurement for each sentence pair.

3 Description of the algorithm

The architecture is presented in Figure 2. The starting point is a parallel corpus. We performed word alignment in both directions using GIZA++. The corpus is then separated into several parts on the basis of a given time span. We performed experiments with different span sizes, namely year, month, week and day. The decaying function is scaled so that the range does not change when using different span sizes. A weighting coefficient obtained with the exponential decay function is then associated to each part.

[1]required_size depends upon the number of times we resample - see section 5.

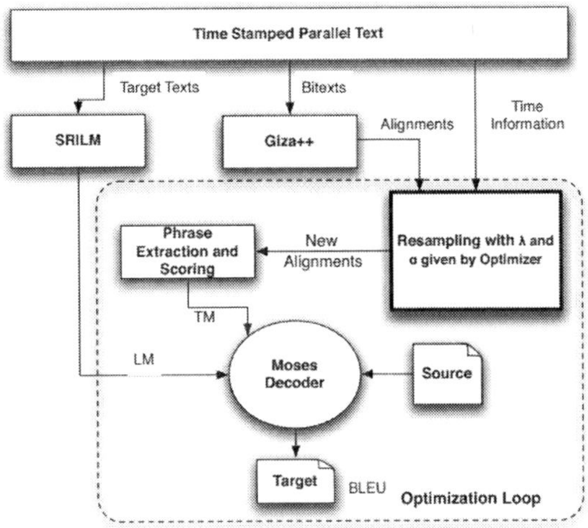

Figure 2: Architecture of SMT Weighting System.

Algorithm 1 Weighting with Exponential Decay function using resampling

```
Determine word to word alignment with GIZA++ on concatenated bitexts.
Initialize λ and α with equal weights.
while not Optimized do
  Compute time-spans weights by eq. 1
  Normalize weights
  for i = 0 to #time-span do
    proportion ← required_size[1] * weights[i]
    j = 0
    while j < proportion do
      Al ← Random alignment
      Al_score ← normalized score of Al
      Flatten Al_score with α
      Threshold ← rand[0, 1]
      if Al_score > Threshold then
        keep it
        j = j + 1
      end if
    end while
  end for
  Create new resampled alignment file.
  Extract phrases and build the phrase table.
  Decode
  Calculate the BLEU score on Dev
  Update λ and α
end while
```

Then, for each part, resampling with replacement is performed in order to select the required number of alignments and form the final corpus. The resampling is done as follows: for each alignment considered, a new random threshold is generated and compared to the alignment score. The alignment is kept only if its score is above the threshold. This ensures that all alignments have a chance to be selected, but this chance is proportional to its alignment score.

Note that some alignments may appear several times, but this is exactly what is expected as it will increase the probability of certain phrase pairs which are supposed to be more related to the test data (in terms of recency) and of better quality. The smoothing and decay factors, α and λ respectively, are optimized with a numerical optimizer called CONDOR (Berghen and Bersini, 2005). The procedure and steps involved in our weighting scheme are shown in algorithm 1.

4 Experimental evaluation

Our first experiments are based on the French-English portion of the freely available time-stamped Europarl data (Koehn, 2005) from April 1996 to December 2010. We have built several phrase-based systems using the Moses toolkit (Koehn et al., 2007), though our approach is equally applicable to any other approach based on alignments and could be used for any language pairs. In our system, fourteen feature functions are used. These feature functions include phrase and lexical translation probabilities in both directions, seven features for the lexicalized distortion model, a word and phrase penalty, and the target language model. The coefficients of these feature functions are optimized by minimum error training.

In the first experiments, the whole Europarl corpus was split into train, development and test as shown in Figure 3. The most recent 5K sentences are split into two sets of equal size, one for development and the other for testing. The remaining data was used as training bitexts to build the different systems.

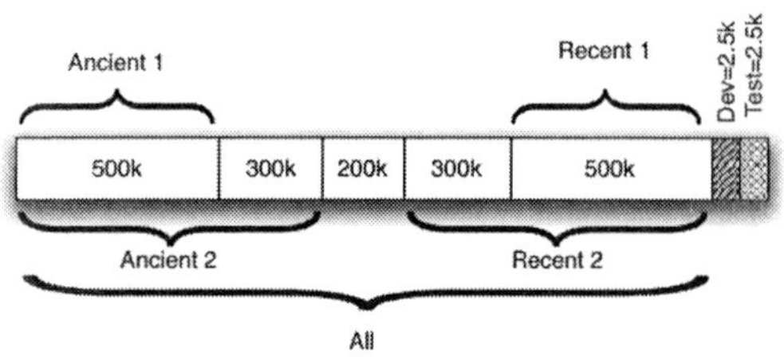

Figure 3: Data used to build the different systems (# sentences)

Since we want to focus on the impact of the weighting scheme of the bitexts, we used the same language model for all systems. It has been trained with the SRILM toolkit (Stolcke, 2002) on the target side of all the training data. In addition, the weights of the feature functions were tuned once for the system that uses all the training data and then kept constant for all the subsequent experiments, *i.e.* no tuning of the feature functions weights is done during the optimization of the weighting coefficients λ and α.

Table 1 presents the results of the systems trained on various parts of the available bitexts without using the proposed weighting scheme. The best performance is obtained when using all the data (55M words, BLEU=30.48), but almost the same BLEU score is obtained by using only the most recent part of the data (24M words, part *Recent 2*). However, if we use the same amount of data that is further away from the time period of the test data (25M words, part *Ancient 2*), we observe a significant loss in performance. These results are in agreement with the observations already described in (Levenberg et al., 2010). Using less data, but still close to the evaluation period (15M words, part *Recent 1*) results in a small loss in the BLEU score. The goal of the proposed weighting scheme is to be able to take advantage of all the data while giving more weight to recent data than to older one. By these means we are not obliged to disregard older parts of the data that may contain additional useful translations. If the weighting scheme does work correctly, we cannot perform worse than using all the data. Of course, we expect to achieve better results by finding the optimal weighting between recent and ancient data.

The amount of data per year in the Europarl data can vary substantially in function of time period since it depends on the frequency and length of the sessions of the European Parliament. As an example Figure 4 shows the histogram of the data per year.

One can ask which time granularity should be used to achieve best weights. Only one weight is given to each time span, consequently the span size will have an impact on the alignment selection process. Using smaller spans results in a more fine grained weighting scheme. We have tested different settings with different time spans to see whether the impact of weighting changes with the

Europarl	Ancient data		Recent data		
	Ancient 1	Ancient 2	Recent 1	Recent 2	All
# of sentences/words	500K/15M	800K/25M	500K/15M	800K/24M	1800K/55M
BLEU (on dev)	29.84	30.08	30.80	31.09	**31.34**
BLEU (on test)	29.30	29.43	30.32	30.44	**30.48**

Table 1: BLEU scores obtained with systems trained on data coming from different time spans.

Europarl	Weighting + alignment selection				Best+retune
Time span	Days	Weeks	Months	Years	Years
Optimized λ	0.0099	0.0109	0.0110	0.0130	0.0130
BLEU (on dev)	31.73	31.82	31.75	31.80	**31.92**
BLEU (on test)	30.94	30.97	30.92	**30.98**	**31.09**

Table 2: Results in BLEU score after weighting.

size of each span. The results are shown in Table 2.

It is observed that all four systems obtained very similar results, which indicates that the size of the spans is not very important. One surprising observation is that the optimized decay factor for all time span sizes are really close to each other. The reason to this could be the scaling of the exponential decaying function based on the time span size. In fact scaled values ensure that the oldest data point get roughly the same value independent of using years, months or days as time span. Looking at the optimized values of λ in Table 2, we can observe that the relative difference between recent and ancient data is rather small, *i.e.* the ancient data is still somehow important and cannot be neglected.

By using years as time span, we obtain an improvement of +0.50 BLEU score on the test set compared to using all data without weighting (30.48 $\rightarrow$ 30.98). It is clear that recency has a positive impact on system performance, however, weighting properly the different parts gives better performance than using the most recent or all available data.

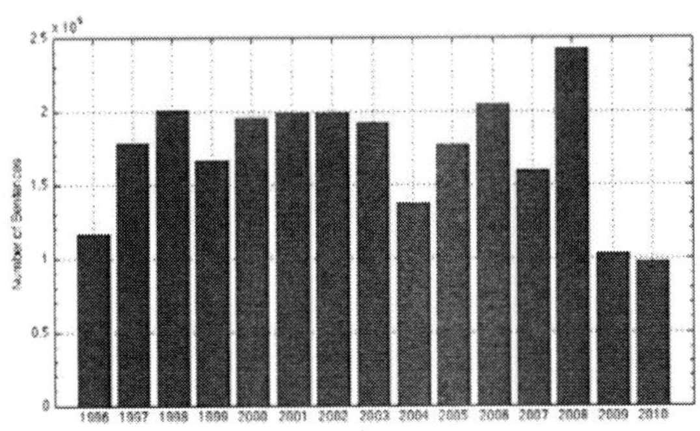

Figure 4: Amount of data available in the Europarl corpus for each year

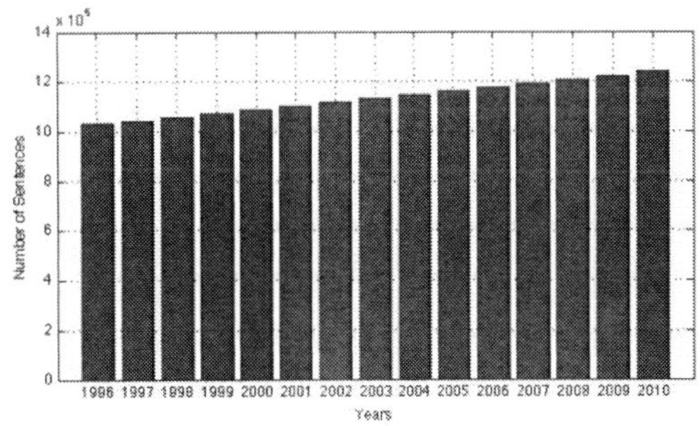

Figure 5: Distribution of data after weighting

Finally, the best system is retuned (feature functions weights) and an overall improvement of +0.61 in the BLEU score is observed on test set.

5 Discussion

The optimal decay factor of approximately 0.01 actually leads to an almost linear decrease over time. The difference in the quantity of data taken from most recent and least recent data is only 1.4% (which still represent 200k sentences). Therefore, one could think that the weighting does not favor recent data that much. This is not the case as we can see in Figure 5 where the distribution of data used to build the adapted model is presented.

Europarl	Resampling only	Weighting only	alignment selection only
BLEU (on dev)	31.36	31.69	31.45
BLEU (on test)	30.51	30.84	30.64

Table 3: Results in BLEU score with different settings.

Example 1	
A:	Mr Ribeiro e Castro, we **shall** see all this in the Conference of Presidents.
B:	Mr Ribeiro e Castro, we **will** see all this at the Conference of Presidents.
R:	Mr Ribeiro e Castro, we **will** look at all these questions in the Conference of Presidents' meeting.
Example 2	
A:	We **shall** most probably consider again lodge a complaint with the **Court of Justice of the European Communities**.
B:	We **will** most probably consider again to lodge a complaint to the **European Court of Justice**.
R:	Most probably we **will** again discuss renewed recourse to the **European Court of Justice**.
Example 3	
A:	no Member State has *not* led to **field trials** as regards the BST .
B:	no Member State has led to **tests on the ground** as regards BST .
R:	No Member State has yet carried out **field tests** with BST .

Table 4: Example translations produced by systems *All* (A) and *Best+retune* (B) versus reference (R)

When comparing to Figure 4, the overall proportion of data coming from recent years is clearly bigger when using our resampling approach. This leads to different word choices while decoding.

Note that resampling is performed several times to estimate and select the samples which better represent the target data set. The more often we resample, the closer we get to the true probability distribution. The *required-size* in algorithm 1 depends upon the number of times we resample. We resampled ten times in our experiments. It is also worth to note that, we keep the original training data along with resampled one. It ensures that no information is lost and the set of extracted phrase pairs remain the same - only the corresponding probability distributions in the phrase table are changed.

In order to get more insight in our method, we separately performed the different techniques:

- resampling the training data without weighting;
- resampling the training data using weighting only (with respect to recency);
- resampling the training data using alignment selection.

These results are summarized in Table 3.

Note that the first case does not correspond to duplicating the training data a certain amount of time (which would of course produce exactly the same phrase-table). Since we perform resampling with replacement, this procedure introduces some randomness which could be beneficial. According to our results, this is not the case: we obtained exactly the same BLEU scores on the dev and test data than with the standard training procedure. Weighting with respect to recency or alignment quality both slightly improve the BLEU, but not as much as both techniques together. The performance increase seems actually to be complementary.

Some comparative examples between the translations produced by systems *All* and *Best+retune* versus the reference translations are given in Table 4. It was noticed that a lot of occurrences of *"will"* in the reference are actually translated into *"shall"* with system *All* whereas the correct word choice is made by the system *Best+retune* as shown in Example 1. This could be explained by the fact that recently the word *"will"* is more frequently seen in the training corpus and adapting the model by weighting the most recent data pro-

WMT Task	Baseline	Receny weighting + alignment selection	Recency weighting + alignment selection + relative importance
BLEU (on dev)	26.08	26.51	**26.60**
BLEU (on test)	28.16	28.59	**28.69**

Table 5: Results in BLEU score after weighting on English to French WMT Task.

duced correct translation. Actually, it was found that the word *"will"* is 10% more frequent in recent data (*Recent 1*) than in ancient data (*Ancient 1*) while the word *"shall"* is 2% less frequent.

Another interesting example is Example 2, in which the correct name for the *European Court of Justice* is proposed by the adapted system unlike the system *All* which proposed *Court of Justice of the European Communities*. Actually, it appears that the *Court of Justice of the European Communities* is the former name of the *European Court of Justice* prior to December 2009. The use of recent data allows to correctly translate the named entities which can change over time. The correct translation proposed by System *Best+retune* could be observed in Example 3 because of alignment selection procedure.

In our experiments, we assume that the test data is in present time (the usual case in a news translation system), and consequently we decrease the weight of the bitexts towards the past. This principle could be of course adapted to other scenarios.

An alternative approach could be to directly use the time decay function as the count for each extracted phrase. However, resampling the alignments and changing the counts of extracted phrases is not exactly the same. Same phrase pairs could be extracted from different parallel sentences coming from different time spans. Furthermore, weighting the alignments with their scores has shown improvements in the BLEU score as presented in Table 3, but considering the alignment score at the phrase level is not straight forward.

6 Experiments on the WMT task

To further verify whether our results are robust beyond the narrow experimental conditions, we considered a task where the development and test data do not come from the same source than the bitexts. We took the official test sets of the 2011 WMT translation tasks as dev and test sets (Schwenk et al., 2011) *i.e* news-test09 and news-test10 respectively. We built English-French systems by using the Europarl and News-Commentary (NC) corpora, both contain news data over a long time period.

For this set-up, there are three coefficients to optimize: the decay factor for Europarl λ_1, the decay factor for the news-commentary texts λ_2 and a coefficient for the alignments α. The Europarl corpus was divided into time span according to years and *NC* corpus was assumed to be sorted over time since time-stamp information was not available for the *NC* corpus. Remaining settings are kept same as mentioned in previous experiments to build the system *Best+retune*. The results are shown in Table 5. Finally, we considered the relative importance of the Europarl and *NC* corpora. For this, a weight is attached to each corpus which represents the percentage of the final aligned corpus that comes from each source corpus. These weights are also optimized on the development data using the same technique as proposed in our previous work (Shah et al., 2010). Using all these methods, we have achieved an overall improvement of approximately +0.5 BLEU on the development and test data, as shown in Table 5.

7 Conclusion and future work

In this paper, a parametric weighting technique along with resampling is proposed to weight the training data of the translation model of an SMT system. By using a parametric weighting function we circumvented the difficult problem to numerically optimize a large number of parameters. Using this formalism, we were able to weight the parallel training data according to the recency with respect to the period of the test data. By these means, the system can still take advantage of all data, in contrast to methods which only use a part of the available bitexts. We evaluated our approach on the Europarl corpus, translating from French into English and further tested it on official English to French WMT Task. A reasonable improvement in

BLEU score on the test data was observed in comparison to using all the data or only the most recent one. We argue that weighting the training data with respect to its temporal closeness should be quite important for translating news material since word choice in this domain is rapidly changing.

An interesting continuation of this work is to consider other criteria for weighting the corpora than the temporal distance. It is clear that recency is a relevant information and this could be associated with other features, *e.g.* thematic or linguistic distance. Also, this work can be included into a stream-based framework where new data is incorporated in an existing system by exponential growth function and making use of online retraining procedure as discussed in (Levenberg et al., 2010).

Acknowledgments

This work has been partially funded by the European Commission under the project Euromatrix-Plus, the French government under the project Cosmat and by an Overseas scholarship of Higher Education Pakistan. We would like to thank the unknown reviewers for their valuable comments.

References

Frank Vanden Berghen and Hugues Bersini. 2005. CONDOR, a new parallel, constrained extension of Powell's UOBYQA algorithm: Experimental results and comparison with the DFO algorithm. *Journal of Computational and Applied Mathematics*, 181:157–175, September.

George Foster, Cyril Goutte, and Roland Kuhn. 2010. Discriminative instance weighting for domain adaptation in statistical machine translation. In *Proceedings of the 2010 Conference on Empirical Methods in Natural Language Processing*, EMNLP '10, pages 451–459, Stroudsburg, PA, USA. Association for Computational Linguistics.

Daniel Hardt and Jakob Elming. 2010. Incremental re-training for post-editing smt. In *The Ninth Conference of the Association for Machine Translation in the Americas 2010.*

Philipp Koehn, Hieu Hoang, Alexandra Birch, Chris Callison-Burch, Marcello Federico, Nicola Bertoldi, Brooke Cowan, Wade Shen, Christine Moran, Richard Zens, Chris Dyer, Ondřej Bojar, Alexandra Constantin, and Evan Herbst. 2007. Moses: open source toolkit for statistical machine translation. In *Proceedings of the 45th Annual Meeting of the ACL on Interactive Poster and Demonstration Sessions*, ACL '07, pages 177–180, Stroudsburg, PA, USA. Association for Computational Linguistics.

Philipp Koehn. 2005. Europarl: A Parallel Corpus for Statistical Machine Translation. In *Conference Proceedings: the tenth Machine Translation Summit*, pages 79–86, Phuket, Thailand. AAMT.

Abby Levenberg, Chris Callison-Burch, and Miles Osborne. 2010. Stream-based translation models for statistical machine translation. In *Human Language Technologies: The 2010 Annual Conference of the North American Chapter of the Association for Computational Linguistics*, HLT '10, pages 394–402, Stroudsburg, PA, USA. Association for Computational Linguistics.

Spyros Matsoukas, Antti-Veikko I. Rosti, and Bing Zhang. 2009. Discriminative corpus weight estimation for machine translation. In *Proceedings of the 2009 Conference on Empirical Methods in Natural Language Processing*, pages 708–717.

Franz Josef Och and Hermann Ney. 2000. Improved statistical alignment models. In *Proceedings of the 38th Annual Meeting on Association for Computational Linguistics*, ACL '00, pages 440–447, Stroudsburg, PA, USA. Association for Computational Linguistics.

Holger Schwenk, Patrik Lambert, Loïc Barrault, Christophe Servan, Sadaf Abdul-Rauf, Haithem Afli, and Kashif Shah. 2011. Lium's smt machine translation systems for wmt 2011. In *Proceedings of the Sixth Workshop on Statistical Machine Translation*, pages 464–469, Edinburgh, Scotland. Association for Computational Linguistics.

Kashif Shah, Loïc Barrault, and Holger Schwenk. 2010. Translation model adaptation by resampling. In *Proceedings of the Joint Fifth Workshop on Statistical Machine Translation and MetricsMATR*, WMT '10, pages 392–399,

Stroudsburg, PA, USA. Association for Computational Linguistics.

Andreas Stolcke. 2002. Srilm—an extensible language modeling toolkit. *In Proceesings of the 7th International Conference on Spoken Language Processing (ICSLP 2002*, pages 901–904.

An Effective and Robust Framework for Transliteration Exploration

Ea-Ee Jan, Niyu Ge
IBM T.J. Watson Research Center
Yorktown Height, NY 10598
{ejan,niyuge}@us.ibm.com

Shih-Hsiang Lin, Berlin Chen[#]
National Taiwan Normal University
Taipei, Taiwan
{shlin,berlin}@csie.ntnu.edu.tw

Abstract

Transliteration is the process of proper name translation based on pronunciation. It is an important process in many multilingual natural language tasks. A common and essential component of transliteration approaches is a verification mechanism that tests if the two names in different languages are translations of each other. Although many transliteration systems have verification as a component, verification as a stand-alone problem is relatively new. In this paper, we propose a simple, effective and robust training framework for the task of verification. We show the many applications of the verification techniques. Our proposed method can operate on both phonemic and orthographic inputs. Our best results show that a simple, straightforward orthographic representation is sufficient and no complex training method is needed. It is effective because it achieves remarkable accuracies. It is robust because it is language-independent. We show that on Chinese and Korean our technique achieves equal error rate well below 1% and around 1% for Japanese using 2009 and 2010 NEWS transliteration generation share task dataset. Our results also show that the orthographic system outperforms the phonemic system. This is especially encouraging because the orthographic inputs are easier to generate and secondly, one does not need to resort to more complex training algorithm to achieve excellent results. This approach is integrated for proper name based cross lingual information retrieval without translation.

This work was partially sponsored by "Aim for the Top University Plan" of National Taiwan Normal University and Ministry of Education, Taiwan.

1 Introduction

Proper name transliteration is important in many multilingual natural language processing tasks, such as Machine Translation (MT), Cross Lingual Information Retrieval (CLIR), multilingual spoken document retrieval and transliteration mining. The research community has investigated automatic proper name transliteration generation. The best performance with 10 references is approximately 70% for alphabet based edit distance error (Li et al., 2009). With one reference, the error rate can be as high as 50% (Meng et al., 2001; Virga and Khudanpur, 2003). If the error rate is measured using the whole proper name as a unit, the error rate will be even higher.

Alternatively, method for transliteration verification starts to draw attention in the research community. Given a pair of proper names in the source and target languages, the task is to decide whether they are transliterations of each other. This task is important for many applications. For example, in word alignment (Ittycheriah and Roukos, 2005), the unknown words are handled by computing a similarity score with the words in the target language. A similarity score derived from transliteration verification has been successfully applied to CLIR (Jan et. al., 2010). In their approach, CLIR can be achieved without translation of input proper name queries. More importantly, this technique is extremely useful in creating proper name pair training data (Kumaran et al., 2010). Given the vast amount of comparable data on the Internet, a technique that can reliably identify name pairs in different language is indispensable. (Kumaran et al., 2010) launched a new NEWS Transliteration Mining task. This task depends heavily on the accuracy of proper name verification techniques. In this paper, we propose a framework for the problem of transliteration verification. We show a highly accurate scoring mechanism that achieves very impressive results. This mechanism can be used as a tool for screening the transliteration parallel corpus, validating good data and filtering out bad data. In addition to the applications mentioned above, our method can also be used as an evaluation metric. The research community has been using methods such as word error rate, EER, precision and recall and its many variants as metrics to evaluate systems. However, due to homonyms and phone-set differences across multiple languages, word error rate is not always sufficient to distinguish transliteration accuracy. We envision our method as a novel and reliable metric in evaluating transliteration systems. Its simplicity, accuracy, and robustness will serve well as an automatic metric.

2 Background and Related Work

The problem of name transliteration was previously viewed as a translation problem. Virga and Khudanpur (2003) applied SMT models to translate English names into Chinese characters. Knight and Graehl (1997) proposed a generative transliteration model for Japanese and English using finite state transducers. Meng et al. (2001) developed an English-Chinese Named Entity transliteration technique using pronunciation lexicon and phonetic mapping rules. Li et al. (2004) proposed direct orthographic mapping with a joint source-channel model for proper name transliteration.

There have also been other approaches to transliteration. Al-Onaizan and Knight (2002) used verification as a stepping stone to transliteration. More recently, the JHU Workshop (2008) reported on the importance of the similarity scoring method and conducted a comparative study on the various scoring methods for name transliterations.

Data harvesting is another way of improving transliteration. Additional data source such as comparable corpora (Klementiev and Roth, 2006; Kuo et al., 2007; Sproat et al., 2006) and the web (Jiang et al., 2007) have also been explored to improve the performance. One of the vital building blocks in all of these approaches is a scoring component that tests how likely a given pair of names in source and target languages is transliteration of each other. This is a key component and is the aspect we focus on in this work. We propose a method for transliteration verification that achieves the best EER compared to other approaches on the same dataset.

Our work differentiates itself from the previous work in the following areas. We take the verification as a stand-alone problem the solution of which has a variety of NLP applications. We tackle the problem by using highly accurate and robust techniques. The verification task can be cast into an alignment problem. We use a generative model for alignment which renders similarity relationships between the source and target name pairs in phone sequences. In phoneme-based systems where phoneme generation might be ambiguous and error prone, we show a discriminative training method together with an HMM-based decoding strategy that works remarkably well within the framework. In orthographic systems where the input can be reliably generated, we show that the HMM-based strategy is sufficient. Section 3 presents our novel approach to verification. Section 4 and 5 show experiments and results. Section 6 and 7 demonstrate an application of our approach and future work.

3 A Highly Reliable Similarity Score

Transliteration between English and foreign language, especially Asian languages: e.g. Chinese, remains a big challenge. We investigate ways of using verification techniques for transliteration. To that end, we need a high quality verification mechanism. For a given proper name pair, one from source language and the other from target language, we want to verify with high precision if this pair refers to the same proper name. Our goal is to devise a scoring method that yields high accuracy with low computational complexity.

Intuitively, proper name transliteration "translates" a proper name based on pronunciation. For a pair of foreign name w_f, and English name w_e, the similarity can be defined as:

$$Sim(w_f, w_e) \cong Sim(ph_f, ph_e), \tag{1}$$

where ph_f and ph_e are the corresponding phonetic sequences for the English and foreign names, respectively. Eq. (1) can be formulated as

$$\begin{aligned} Sim(ph_f, ph_e) = {} & \lambda P(ph_f \mid \Lambda_{ph_e}) \\ & + (1-\lambda) P(ph_e \mid \Lambda_{ph_f}) \end{aligned} \tag{2}$$

where Λ_{ph_e} and Λ_{ph_f} are the English and foreign phonetic models, respectively. For simplification, it can be assumed that $\lambda = 0.5$ since the similarity function could be symmetric. Because the distributions of $P(ph_f \mid \Lambda_{ph_e})$ and $P(ph_e \mid \Lambda_{ph_f})$ are unknown, they need to be estimated through learning. Section 3.1 details the discriminative training process and section 3.2 presents an HMM-based decoding strategies to find the optimal alignment between ph_f *and* ph_e.

3.1 Model Estimation via SMT

One straightforward way to estimate the model parameters is to utilize the phrase tables produced by a phrase-based SMT framework. The phrase tables contain conditional probabilities of both *p(e|f)* and *p(f|e)*, which are the probabilities of English phrase given by foreign phrase and foreign phrase given by English phrase, respectively. When the phonetic sequences (either phonemic or orthographic) of English and foreign name pairs are the input into the SMT, the "phrase" table contains the phone set mappings between English and foreign phone sets together with their probabilities. We use these probabilities as the observation model in our HMM. We refer to this model as M_{SMT}.

3.2 Model Estimation via Discriminative Training

The discriminative training process involves finding an initial seed model and training in a decision-feedback learning framework.

One straightforward way to get an initial estimation for $P(ph_f \mid \Lambda_{ph_e})$ and $P(ph_e \mid \Lambda_{ph_f})$ is to utilize the phrase tables produced by the widely used phrase-based SMT system. The phrase tables contain both conditional probabilities of p(e|f) and p(f|e), which are the probabilities of English phrase given by foreign phrase and foreign phrase given by English phrase, respectively. When the phonetic sequences of English and foreign name pairs are fed into SMT, the "phrase" table contains the phone set mappings between English and foreign phone sets together with their probabilities. The phone set mapping is now data driven, and is free from the expensive and less flexible hand crafted linguistic phone set mapping rules. We refer to this model as M_{SMT}.

M_{SMT} is a straightforward and effective way to estimate the model parameters. Phoneme-based systems rely on the input texts being correctly converted to baseforms (phonemic sequences) representation. This process could be ambiguous, context-dependent, and error prone. In such systems, M_{SMT} serves as a good initial model. The model parameters can be further improved in a decision feed-back learning framework. The minimum classification error (MCE) training algorithm widely used in speech recognition can be applied here to improve the discrimination of the translation probability. We call this model M_{MCE}. Given a correct transliteration pair and other competitive transliteration hypotheses, we can define the transliteration error function as:

$$d_i(ph_f \mid \Lambda_{\mathbf{P}_e}) = -P(ph_f \mid \Lambda_{ph_e}) + \max_{f', f' \neq f} P(ph_{f'} \mid \Lambda_{ph_e}) \tag{3}$$

where $P(ph_f \mid \Lambda_{ph_e})$ is the alignment score obtained from the correct transliteration pair and $\max_{f', f' \neq f} P(ph_{f'} \mid \Lambda_{ph_e})$ is the highest competing score obtained from error transliteration pairs. The transliteration error function can be further transformed to a loss function ranging from 0 to 1 with the sigmoid operator:

$$l(d_i(ph_f \mid \Lambda_{ph_e})) = \frac{1}{1 + e^{(-\gamma d_i(ph_f \mid \Lambda_{ph_e}) + \theta)}} \tag{4}$$

where γ is used to control the slope of the function and θ is an offset factor. Above equation was then applied iteratively to update the translation probability:

$$p^{t+1}(ph_f \mid ph_e) = p^t(ph_f \mid ph_e) - \varepsilon \frac{\partial l(d_i(ph_f \mid \Lambda_{\mathbf{P}_e}))}{\partial p(ph_f \mid ph_e)} \tag{5}$$

3. 2 Decoding: Similarity Score Calculation

In order to calculate the similarity score for a given proper name pair (w_f, w_e), their respective phonetic sequence (ph_f, ph_e) is first determined. Then, for this task, we employ an HMM-based decoding strategy. The models $P(ph_f \mid \Lambda_{ph_e})$ and $P(ph_e \mid \Lambda_{ph_f})$ learned in section 3.1 are used as observation models. Two monotonic HMM models (one with ph_f as states and one with ph_e

as states) are then used to align the phonetic sequences according to Eq. (6) below:

$$P^*(ph_f \mid \Lambda_{ph_e}) = \arg\max_{S_e} P(ph_f, S_e \mid \Lambda_{ph_e}),$$
$$P^*(ph_e \mid \Lambda_{ph_f}) = \arg\max_{S_f} P(ph_e, S_f \mid \Lambda_{ph_f}) \quad (6)$$

where S_e is the English state sequence and S_f is the foreign state sequence.

The state transition probabilities are set to be uniform. We extend the traditional HMM to allow a broader range of phone mapping configurations. Specifically, the null transition (Bahl et al., 1982) is used to represent skipping a state without consuming any observations. This allows one to null mapping. The null state is introduced so it can emit those observations without any correspondence states. This allows null to one mapping. The combination of null transition and null state allow many to many and many to one configurations as well. The valid state transition is constrained to be from left to right with self loop, and with maximum jump of three states as well as a null state and a null transition.

Figure 1 depicts the actions of the HMM trellis at decode time. In Figure 1, the x-axis represents the observations (foreign language) and the y-axis represents the states (English). Take for example, the circle where dashed lines with arrows are emanating from. When this circle makes a horizontal move (from ph_{f2} to ph_{f3}), the single state ph_{e2} produces multiple observations. Null transition happens when the shaded circle makes a vertical move (from ph_{e2} to ph_{e3}) without consuming any observation.

4 Experiment setup for transliteration similarity

We evaluate the performance of our similarity scoring mechanism on 3 language pairs, Chinese-English (CE), Korean-English (KE), and Japanese-English (JE). Both Type I errors (false reject of the matched pairs) and Type II errors (false accept of the unmatched pairs) are evaluated. The Equal Error Rate (EER) is used as the evaluation metric.

For Chinese-English, a parallel corpus of proper name pairs is extracted from the *people* section of the multilingual Wikipedia. Among these, approximately 3,000 pairs are used for training and 300 pairs for testing. The 300 pairs are used as a matched condition test. A separate 1000 un-

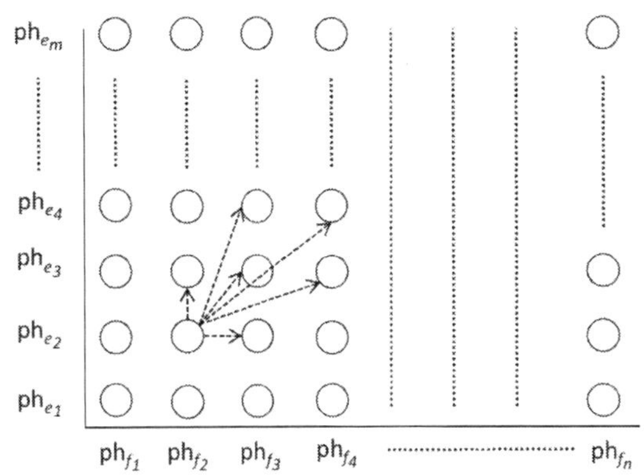

Figure 1 HMM Trellis

matched test pairs are created randomly from the 300 matched pairs.

We also use the 2009 and 2010 NEWS transliteration generation shared task data as our test data. Although test our objective is different from those in the shared task, we choose this data because it is publicly available and can be used in the future for fair comparisons. We did not use NEWS 2010 transliteration miming shared task dataset because it did not contain Korean or Japanese. For Chinese, the 2009 data consists of 30K training and 2896 testing proper name pairs. Three systems are developed using 30K, 3K and 1K pairs of training data for our experiments. The 2896 proper name test pairs are used as matched pairs. Three unmatched test set pairs of size 10k, 100k and 1M are randomly generated. A 9M (2985x2986) unmatched pairs are also generated as an extreme test condition.

The Korean-English data comes from the 2010 NEWS transliteration generation data. It consists of 4,785 training pairs and 1,082 test pairs. Two systems with 1K and 4K of training pairs are developed; three sets unmatched pairs of size 10K, 100K, and 1M are generated. The Katakana Japanese-English data is from the same set (2010 NEWS data). It is bigger than the Korean data with 28K training instances and 1941 test pairs. Three systems with 1K, 4K and 28K training pairs are developed; three sets of unmatched pairs of size 10K, 100K, and 1M are also generated.

Training on 1K data matches the 2010 NEWS transliteration miming shared task (Kumaran et al., 2010) seed condition. Training on 3K-4K data matches the Wikipedia condition. Training on 28k for Japanese-English and 30K on Chinese-English demonstrates the best performance we can achieve while using all of the available training corpus.

We experiment with both phonemic and orthographic representations of input texts. The phonemic approach seems more intuitive since the transliteration is a pronunciation based translation. The orthographic system is simple because it does not require additional baseform generation tools to convert proper name to phonemic sequences, and it does not need to address the multiple pronunciation issue. For Chinese, the orthographic form of a character is its Pinyin. Tones in Pinyin are removed. Korean characters are converted according to Romanization tables from the web[1] . Japanese characters are Romanized in the same way using a different table[2] . We add 11 additional rules to the Japanese conversion process to deal with short versions of a few vowels and consonants. These 11 characters are: ァ, ィ, ゥ, ェ, ォ, ャ, ュ, ョ, ヮ, ー, and ッ. In orthographic systems, the Pinyin (for Chinese), Romanized spellings (for Korean and Japanese), and word spellings (for English) are then segmented into space delimited alphabet streams. For example, the English word 'Clinton' is segmented into seven letters separated by space 'c l i n t o n'. In phoneme-based systems, diphthongs (such as 'oi', 'ae') and compound constants (such as 'sh') are treated as one unit. The English and Chinese baseforms are generated automatically from a speech recognition vendor toolkit. Multiple pronunciations for a given word are considered uniformly distributed. All possible combinations of pronunciation are created in both the training and the testing sets. All possible pronunciation combinations are used for training. The best score for all possible pronunciation combinations for a given proper pair is used for final score in testing.

In addition to the new approach described in section 3, we also build two phrase-based SMT systems, orthographic and phonemic based approach, for the Chinese-English Wikipedia datasets as a baseline. This SMT approach has been widely used and yields solid performance in shared task (Li et al, 2009, 2010). Equation (1) is reformulated as:

$$Sim(w_e, w_f) \cong Sim(tr(w_e), w_f) \approx BLEU(tr(w_e), w_f) \quad (7)$$

where tr(w_e) is the translation of w_e .

We chose BLEU (Papeneni et al., 2001) because it is more favorable to n-gram matches and is smoother than edit distance. We build a phonetic-based SMT and an alphabet orthographic-based SMT. In the former, the parallel data is converted to phonetic sequences using its own phone set. In

Model	EER
Orthographic edit distance	22%
Alphabet-based Orthographic SMT	6.47%
Phonetic SMT	7.10%
Our framework with M_{SMT}	3.73%
Our framework with M_{MCE}	3.33%

Table 1. CE Wikipedia Results with Baseline

Test	1K-Training			3K-Training		
	M_{SMT}	M_{MCE}	change	M_{SMT}	M_{MCE}	change
10K	1.37	1.27	7.06%	1.15	1.09	5.15%
100K	1.35	1.25	7.65%	1.17	1.11	5.52%
1M	1.39	1.26	9.09%	1.18	1.13	5.05%
9M	1.38	1.26	8.86%	1.18	1.12	5.23%
	30K-Training					
10k	1.07	1.02	4.63%			
100k	1.11	0.99	10.42%			
1M	1.17	1.00	14.47%			
9M	1.16	0.99	14.6%			

Table 2. CE 2009 NEWS Data

Test	1K-Training			4K-Training		
	M_{SMT}	M_{MCE}	Change	M_{SMT}	M_{MCE}	Change
10K	1.23	1.12	9.00%	1.12	0.99	10.79%
100K	1.21	1.16	4.03%	1.10	1.02	7.96%
1M	1.20	1.13	5.85%	1.09	1.00	8.67%

Table 3. KE 2010 NEWS Data

Test	1K-Training			4K-Training		
	M_{SMT}	M_{MCE}	change	M_{SMT}	M_{MCE}	change
10K	2.33	2.11	9.44%	2.09	2.02	3.35%
100K	2.40	2.19	8.75%	2.07	2.07	-
1M	2.40	2.19	8.75%	2.09	2.08	0.48%
	28K-Training					
10k	1.77	1.71	3.39%			
100k	1.76	1.70	3.41%			
1M	1.76	1.71	2.84%			

Table 4. JE 2010 NEWS Data

[1] The Korean Romanization table is from www.thelapan.com .
[2] The Japanese Romanization table is from http://www.omniglot.com/writing/japanese_katakana.htm

the orthographic SMT, the proper names are converted to their Pinyin in spelling form. The English proper names are put into spelling form as well. The standard SMT training recipe is then applied.

5 Results and discussions

The CE Wikipedia results are shown in Table 1. Our method with model M_{SMT} outperforms the traditional SMT methods and the orthographic edit distance approach. Our M_{MCE} further reduces the EER and achieves the best EER of 3.33%. This low EER shows that our verification approach is highly reliable.

Phoneme-based results on the NEWS data are shown in Tables 2, 3 and 4 for CE, KE, and JE respectively. Each table shows results of M_{SMT}, M_{MCE} and relative improvement (in that order) under different training and test conditions. From table 2, our approach yields less than 1.4% of EER using only 1K training pairs. Using 3K training data, the proposed method achieves ERR under 1.2%, which is comparable to the system using 30K training pairs. The MCE can further improve the performance relatively by 5-14%. In additions, the performance is very stable against to all different unmatched test conditions, especially at the 9M unmatched test pair condition.

The Japanese-English set performs worse than either Chinese or Korean. Upon inspection of the data, we find that the majority of the problems are due to incorrect baseforms representations. This, in turn, is because the Japanese data contains more non-English names. For example, in JE test set, there are 1941 matched pairs. For a 2% false reject rate, approximately 38 matched pairs are false rejected. Out of these false-reject entries, about a third is European names. Table 5 shows a few such examples. The bottom two entries in this table are actually incorrect transliteration pairs, which means they should be rejected but the system is penalized because the reference truth is not entirely clean. This is an example of using our method as a data screening tool to sift through the data and automatically pick out suspicious pairs. Because of our high accuracies, those questionable pairs can be either reliably excluded or down-weighted. They can also be given to annotators for further inspection. Instead of scanning through the entire dataset, human annotators can focus on just the disputable pairs that the system picks out. This annotation process is both efficient and cost-effective.

Japanese Katakana	**English**	**Romanized Japanese**
レ ー ブ	Low	r e_ b u
ビ ユ デ	Bade	b y u d e
ズ バ ー	Zwar	z u b a_
ム ジ エ ー ル	Mjor	m u j e_ r u
ベ ア	Beer	b e a
ベ ー ア	Bar	b e_ a
ミ ロ ス ラ フ	Cipar	m i r o s u r a f u
チ ヤ ー チ	Chruch	ch a_ ch i

Table 5. JE problematic pair examples

Test	**1K-Training**	**3K-Training**	**30K-Training**
10K	0.87	0.73	0.58
100K	0.88	0.74	0.55
1M	0.87	0.73	0.56
9M	0.87	0.73	0.56

Table 6. $\mathbf{M_{SMT}}$ on orthographic CE

Test	**1K-Training**	**4K-Training**
10K	0.81%	0.74%
100K	0.83%	0.78%
1M	0.83%	0.79%

Table 7. $\mathbf{M_{SMT}}$ on orthographic KE

Test	**1K-Training**	**4K-Training**	**28K-Training**
10K	1.52%	0.97%	0.96%
100K	1.53%	1.05%	1.05%
1M	1.55%	1.04%	1.04%

Table 8. $\mathbf{M_{SMT}}$ on orthographic JE

Orthographic results are shown in Tables 6, 7, and 8 for CE, KE, and JE respectively. It is evident from the tables that orthographic-based systems are significantly better than the phoneme-based systems without using the more complex model M_{MCE}. These results are very promising because first, orthographic representations do not need to deal with diphthongs and compound consonants. Every alphabet is a token by itself. In Table 5 for example, 'r e_ b u' in the first row will have '_' separated from 'e' in its orthographic form. Secondly, results in Tables 6, 7, and 8 are from systems using the straightforward SMT

Test	1K-Training		3K-Training	
	FR	FA	FR	FA
10K	0.79%	1.01%	0.76%	0.78%
100K		0.93%		0.73%
1M		0.56%		0.73%
9M		0.57%		0.73%
	30K-Training			
10K	0.59%	0.64%		
100K		0.55%		
1M		0.56%		
9M		0.57%		

Table 9. CE FR and FA rates

Test	1K-Training		4K-Training	
	FR	FA	FR	FA
10K	0.73%	1.07%	0.46%	1.13%
100K		1.04%		1.08%
1M		1.05%		1.09%

Table 10. KE FR and FA rates

Test	1K-Training		4K-Training	
	FR	FA	FR	FA
10K	1.80%	0.92%	1.13%	0.78%
100K		1.15%		1.01%
1M		1.16%		0.99%
	28K-Training			
10K	1.08%	0.73%		
100K		0.94%		
1M		0.93%		

Table 11. JE FR and FA rates

method without further discriminative training by *MCE*. This simplifies the overall system architecture and makes the system more efficient and effective.

One reason orthographic models perform better than phonemic models is that baseforms generation is ambiguous and error-prone. Our baseforms are statistically trained from a generic model. The conversion from input texts to their baseforms is a lossy process. The errors in Japanese show a clear example. When the names are non-English, the English baseforms all become incorrect which leads to verification errors. The orthographic representation alleviates this problem quite significantly and thus is able to improve the system. In addition to measuring ERR, we also measure False Rejection (FR) rate of the matched proper name pairs and False Acceptance (FA) rate of the unmatched pairs. Tables 9, 10, and 11 detail the results for all the language pairs under all testing and training conditions. For each language pair, under the same training condition, the FR rate is the same because given a fixed threshold, the number of matched pairs is the same.

FA and FR results in the above tables show that the system is very robust. Across all language pairs, FA and FR rates improve consistently as the training data size gets larger. The rates also remain stable across test data of different sizes.

6 Application

We incorporate the verification component into the retrieval model for CLIR. We use a language model (LM) based retrieval model. The query Q is treated as a sequence of words, $Q = w_1 w_2 \ldots w_N$. The query words are assumed to be independent of each other and conditionally independent given the document. The relevance score of a document to the query can be computed by Eq. (8):

$$P(Q|D) = \prod_{w_i \in Q} P(w_i|D)^{c(w_i,Q)}, \quad (8)$$

where $c(w_i, Q)$ is the number of times that each distinct word w_i occurs in Q and $P(w_i|D)$ is the probability of the word w_i generated by the document model. For CLIR, we rewrite (8) as:

$$P(Q_e \mid D_f) = \prod_{w_e \in Q_e} P(w_e \mid D_f)^{c(w_e,Q_e)}$$

$$\overset{rank}{=} \sum_{w_e \in Q_e} c(w_e, Q_e) \log\left(\sum_{w_f \in D_f} P(w_e \mid w_f) P(w_f \mid D_f) \right) \quad (9)$$

where the $P(w_e \mid w_f)$ is the probability of the English token given by foreign token. We propose to estimate this probability by a combination function of similarity function and translation table.

$$P(w_e \mid w_f) = \lambda \delta_0(w_e, w_f) + (1-\lambda)\delta_1(w_e, w_f), \quad (10)$$

where

$$\delta_0(w_e, w_f) = \frac{1}{1 + \exp(-\gamma \cdot sim(w_e, w_f) + \beta)},$$

$$\delta_1(w_e, w_f) = f(Tr(w_f \mid w_e))$$

$$f(Tr(w_f \mid w_e)) = \frac{1}{1 + \exp(-\gamma_1 \cdot sim(w_e, w_f) - \gamma_2 P(w_f \mid w_e) + \beta)}, \quad (11)$$

Where, $sim(w_e, w_f)$ is the similarity function discussed in previous section, $Tr(w_e | w_f)$ is translations from the SMT phrase table, and f is a function to validate the phrase table entries. f is a function that combines the scores of the valid entries in the phrase table, $p(w_f | w_e)$, and the similarity score, $\delta_0(w_e, w_f)$, with higher recall rate. Thus, the entries in the phrase table with high scores are the candidates. These candidates will be discarded only if they are incorrect in pronunciation. The λ is the weighted factor for transliteration similarity scores, which can be a function of the total similarity scores. In our experiments, it is estimated by:

$$\lambda = \frac{k}{\sum_{w_f \in V_f} \delta_0(w_e, w_f)}, \quad (13)$$

where v_f is the vocabulary and k is a constant.

We conduct experiments on the NTCIR-7 Information Retrieval for QA (IR4QA) task (Sakai et al. 2008). We select 10 proper name query topics as the query set. To test CLIR with multiple transliterations, we need a document collection with controlled multiple transliterations. We create a homogenous name list for those proper names used in the test query topics and uniformly place those names into the original document collections. Thus, each proper name in the query is replaced by 4-5 different names with similar pronunciation. The baseline (unigram document LM with Dirichlet smoothing) performance using the original queries against the synthetic document collection is 0.18 (in mAP). Without any given transliterations, the mAP of our method is 0.406, substantially better than 0.18 if one transliteration is given. This is shown in Table 12 where $\lambda = 1$ and # of known translations = 0. (λ is defined in Eq. (10)). In Table 12, $\lambda = 1$ implies all transliterations are ignored. We then test when two, or all transliterations are given without using the transliteration similarity by setting $\lambda = 0$. The results are 0.3819 and 0.7268, respectively. The mAP of 0.7268 is better than the mAP of 0.6911 from the ad-hoc baseline. It implies that the original document collections already have multiple transliterations. We further assume that all transliterations are known and one additional incorrect transliteration is provided. By disabling the filtering capability in Eq (11), (i.e. $f(Tr(w_f | w_e)$ =1, when $p(w_f | w_e)$ exists), the performance is degraded to 0.55. Table 12 shows that our approach is, in contrast, quite robust and maintains the performance of 0.65. This scenario with one incorrect transliteration can be very common because the entries in phrase table can be very noisy. We also evaluate the effect of name entities. If the entire document vocabulary is used to calculate similarity score, (cf. Eq (10)), the mAP=0.40, which means this task is very difficult and the name entities do not help significantly because too many name entities are extracted from the document collection. In fact, the name entities extraction may not be necessary while using our approach because the similarity score can be calculated based on the document vocabulary.

# of known Transliterations	λ =0	λ = variable	λ =1
0	0	0.4062	0.4062
1	0.1983	0.42	0.4062
2	0.3819	0.48	0.4062
All	0.7268	0.65	0.4062
All plus 1 wrong	0.55	0.65	0.4062

Table 12: mAP under various expanded transliterations for proper name queries

7 Conclusion and Future Work

In this paper, we propose a simple and effective transliteration verification framework. On the 2009 and 2010 NEWS transliteration generation shared task data, we achieve EER well below 1% for Chinese and Korean, and around 1% for Japanese. These promising results show that verification can not only provide an alternative approach to transliteration but also can be reliably used for exploring name pairs from comparable data. We show how the method is used in CLIR applications. It can also serve as a parallel corpus screening tool to indentify possible incorrect name pairs. In addition, it can be used for post processing of transliteration generation by filtering out incorrect top-n hypothesis to improve performance. Moreover, this approach can be turned into an automatic transliteration evaluation tool for such task as the NEWS shared task. In the future, we will explore each of these possibilities.

References

Yaser Al-Onaizan and Kevin Knight, 2002. Translating named entities using monolingual and bilingual resources. In Proc. of ACL-02. Pages: 400-408.

Lalit Bahl, Frederick Jelinek and Robert Mercer, A Maximum likelihood approach to continuous speech recognition. IEEE Transaction on attern Analysis and achine Intelligence, vol. PAMI-5, No.2, 1983, Pages 179-190.

Peter F. Brown, Stephan A. Della Pietra, and Robert L. Mercer, 1993. The mathematics of statistical machine translation: Parameter estimation. Computational Linguistics, 19(2):263–311.

Abraham Ittycheriah and Salim Roukos, 2005. A maximum entropy word aligner for Arabic English machine translation. In Proceedings of EMNLP, pages 96-103

JHU Workshop Report, Multilingual Spoken Term Detection: Finding and Testing New Pronunciations In the final report of JHU Workshop 2008

Ea-Ee Jan, Shih-Hsiang Lin and Berlin Chan, Transliteration Retrieval Model for Cross Lingual Information Retrieval, AIRS 2010, Springer Lecture Notess Computer Science 6458, page 183-192

Long Jiang, Ming Zhou, Lee-Feng Chien, and Cheng Niu, Named entity translation with web mining and transliteration, Proceedings of the 20th international joint conference on Artificial intelligence, p.1629-1634, January 06-12, 2007, Hyderabad, India

Alexandre Klementiev and Dan Roth 2006, Weakly supervised named entity transliteration and discovery from multilingual comparable corpora. In Proceedings of the ACL 2006, Pages. 817-824 (2006)

Kevin Knight and Jonathan Graehl, 1998. Machine transliteration. Computational Linguistics, 24(4), Pages. 599-612, 1998

Philipp Koehn, Franz Josef Och, and Daniel Marcu, 2003, "Statistical Phrase based Translation", in Proc. Of HLT/NAACL Pages. 48-54, 2003.

Kumaran A, Mitesh Khapra and Haizhou Li, Report of NEWS 2010 Trasliteration Mining Shared Task. In Proc of 2010 Names Entities Workshop, ACL 2010, pages 21-28

Jin-Shea Kuo, Haizhou Li, and Ying-Kuei Yang, 2007. A phonetic similarity model for automatic extraction of transliteration pairs. ACM Transactions on Asian Language Information Processing. 6(2) Article 6: 1-24

Haizhou Li, A Kumaran, Vladimir Pervouchine, and Min Zhang, 2009. Report on news 2009 machine transliteration shared task. In Proceedings of ACLIJCNLP 2009 Named Entities workshop. pages. 1-18, Singapore.

Haizhou Li, Kumaran A, Zhang M. and Pervouchine V. Report of NEWS 2010 Transliteration Generation Shared Task. In Proceedings of ACL2010 Nameed Entity Workshop, Pages 1-11

Haizhou Li, Min Zhang, and Jian Su. 2004. A joint source-channel model for machine transliteration. In Proceedings of ACL-04, pages 159–166, Barcelona, Spain, July.

Huma Lodhi, Craig Saunders, John Shawe-Taylor, Nello Cristianini, and Chris Watkins, 2002, Text Classification using String Kernels, Journal of Machine Learning Research 2 . pages 419-444

A Martin, G. Doddington, T. Kamm, M. Ordowski, and M. Przybocki, 1997, 'The DET Curve in Assessment of Detection Task Performance'. In: Proc. Eurospeech '97. Rhodes, Greece, Pages. 1895–1898.

Helen M. Meng, Wai-Kit Lo, Berlin Chen and Karen Tang. 2001. Generate Phonetic Cognates to Handle Name Entities in English-Chinese cross-language spoken document retrieval, Proceeding of ASRU 2001

Franz Josef Och, Hermann Ney, 2003, A Systematic Comparison of Various Statistical Alignment Models, Computational Linguistics, 29(1), 19-51 (2003).

Kishore A. Papeneni, Salim Roukos, Todd Ward, and Wei-Jing Zhu. 2001. Bleu: a method for automatic evaluation of machine translation, In Proceedings of the 40th Annual of the Association for Computational linguistics, pages 311–318, Philadelphia, USA.

Richard Sproat, Tao Tao, and ChengXiang Zhai, 2006 Named entity transliteration with comparable corpora. In Proceedings of the COLING/ACL 2006. Pages 73-80

Tetsuya Sakai, Noriko Kando, Chuan-Jie Lin, Teruko Mitamura, Hideki Shima, Donghong Ji, Kuang-Hua Chen, Eric Nyberg, 2008. Overview of the NTCIR-7 ACLIA IR4QA Task. In: NTCIR-7 Workshop Meeting, Pages. 77-114

Paola Virga and Sanjeev Khudanpur. 2003. Transliteration of proper names in cross-lingual information retrieval. In Proceedings of the ACL 2003 Workshop on Multilingual and Mixed-language Named Entity Recognition, pages 57–64, Sapporo, Japan.

An Evaluation of Alternative Strategies for Implementing Dialogue Policies Using Statistical Classification and Rules

David DeVault, Anton Leuski, and Kenji Sagae
USC Institute for Creative Technologies
12015 Waterfront Drive, Playa Vista, CA 90094
{devault,leuski,sagae}@ict.usc.edu

Abstract

We present and evaluate a set of architectures for conversational dialogue systems, exploring rule-based and statistical classification approaches. In a case study, we show that while a rule-based dialogue policy is capable of high performance if perfect natural language understanding is assumed, a direct classification approach that combines the dialogue policy with NLU has practical advantages.

1 Introduction

In this paper we present and evaluate a set of alternative dialogue system architectures that could be used to implement dialogue policies for conversational characters or virtual humans. The motivation for this work is to improve our understanding of the development costs and performance benefits associated with alternative system architectures for virtual human dialogue systems (Traum et al., 2005; Swartout et al., 2006; Kenny et al., 2009; Jan et al., 2009; Swartout et al., 2010).

We focus on the language processing steps used in a specific virtual human system described in Section 2. We analyze the relationship between Natural Language Understanding (NLU), which maps a user's natural language input to system-specific semantic representations, and Dialogue Management (DM), which executes a dialogue policy that dictates what the virtual human will say or do in response to the user's input.

Traditionally, designing a two step NLU+DM pipeline involves defining semantic representations for the dialogue domain and writing rules that constitute the dialogue policy. This modular design has the benefit of making the DM policy easy to express in explicit rules, but carries the development cost of requiring significant linguistic expertise. Additionally, as we illustrate in this paper, its performance can depend critically on the reliability of the NLU module.

As an alternative, we contrast this design with a direct classification approach that relies only on textual examples and effectively combines the dialogue policy with NLU. In our case study evaluation, we find that this approach offers superior performance, owing to the high frequency of NLU errors in the two step pipeline.

The research presented in this paper extends our previous work. As we summarize in Section 2, this paper relies on the same data set and evaluation metric as DeVault et al. (2011), which reports results for learned policies based on maximum entropy models. In this paper, we add a comparison to a hand-authored policy (Rules) and a new policy based on relevance models (RM). These new policies are described in Section 3. We conclude with some discussion of our new findings.

2 Research Setting and Data Set

We begin by summarizing our research setting, data set, and evaluation metric. We refer the reader to DeVault et al. (2011) for additional details.

We use an existing virtual human scenario designed for Tactical Questioning (TACQ) (Traum et al., 2008), where military personnel interview individuals for information of military value. TACQ characters are designed to be non-cooperative at times. They may answer some of the interviewer's questions, but either lie or refuse to answer others until certain conditions are met (Gandhe et al., 2009). The dialogue policy for a TACQ character is relatively simple in that the character is willing to answer most questions, but correctly implementing the policy requires that certain questions only be answered under certain conditions.

Our work builds on an existing TACQ scenario involving a virtual human called Amani (Gandhe et al., 2009). The user plays the role of a commander whose unit has been attacked by a sniper. The

Lieutenant: *(User Utterance)* *can you tell me what you know of the incident?* **NLU Speech Act:** `elicit-whq-tellmemoreabouttheincident` **Paraphrases:** - *what information do you have about the incident?* - *could you please tell me what you saw?* - *what can you tell me about the incident?* - *can you tell me about the incident?* - *please, tell me what you know about the incident* - *tell me what you saw, please*
Amani: *(System Response, as English text)* - *i saw the shooting. what do you want to know about it?* **Other appropriate speech acts, as English text:** - *i remember that the gun fire was coming from the window on the second floor of assad's shop.* - *what is it you want to know about the incident?*

Figure 1: A dialogue turn from the Amani dataset.

user interviews Amani, who was a witness to the incident and has information about the identity of the sniper. Amani is willing to tell the interviewer what she knows, but she will only reveal certain information in exchange for specific promises of safety, secrecy, and monetary compensation (Artstein et al., 2009). Figure 1 provides an excerpt of a user interaction with Amani.

Gandhe et al.'s TACQ system uses speech acts (SAs) to represent the meaning of user and system utterances. In this paper, user utterances are modeled using 46 distinct SA labels. For example, the label `elicit-whq-tellmemoreabouttheincident` is assigned to the user's utterance of *can you tell me what you know of the incident?* in Figure 1. The system also defines a different set of 96 unique SAs (responses) for the Amani character.

We perform our experiments and evaluation using an existing set of 19 annotated Amani dialogues (DeVault et al., 2011). The dialogues were collected through teletype-based role play. Each dialogue turn includes a single user utterance followed by the response chosen by a human role player in the role of Amani. There are a total of 296 turns, for an average of 15.6 turns/dialogue.

The task of Amani's dialogue manager (DM) is to select the most appropriate system SA to use in response to a user utterance. In the experiments reported here, the user's utterance may be provided to the DM either directly as text or using a SA label. We call the DM's decision process a *dialogue policy*. The system builders' intended policy for Amani is detailed in DeVault et al. (2011).

Because Amani has only a fixed set of system responses, the policy problem looks like a traditional classification task. However, there are two sources of uncertainty that complicate the task. Firstly, the mapping between the user's utterance and an appropriate system SA is often one-to-many. In our data set, 6 referees independently linked each user utterance to the best system SA response. In Figure 1, we provide an example in which three different system SAs were selected by the 6 referees. In other cases, up to 6 different system SAs were selected (DeVault et al., 2011). Our first experimental question is therefore: how well can a dialogue policy select an appropriate system SA, if it is provided with an accurate user SA? Would a statistical classification-based policy perform as well as a rule-based policy?

Secondly, the user SAs in the Amani dataset were assigned to the user's utterance by a computational linguist, and we may assume that these "gold" SAs accurately represent the user's intended meaning. In a run-time system, however, the SAs are identified by an automatic NLU module that is likely to introduce errors. It is not obvious *a priori* to what extent the dialogue policy will suffer due to these NLU errors, and our second experimental question is therefore: how well can a policy select an appropriate system SA, if provided with the NLU's hypothesized user SA?

In training the NLU module, as well as our dialogue policies, we can make use of an additional resource in the Amani data set, which is the availability of approximately 6 textual paraphrases for each utterance; see Figure 1 for an example.

As a final empirical question, we consider combining the NLU and DM in a design that classifies user utterances, together with shallow features of the dialogue history, directly into system responses. This approach is similar to the NLU module, but tries to determine system SAs instead of user SAs. This makes unnecessary the labor and knowledge intensive steps of developing the user SA set and annotating utterances with these SAs.

2.1 Evaluation Metric

We evaluate the dialogue policies learned in each of our experimental conditions through 19-fold cross-validation of our set of 19 dialogues. In each fold, we hold out one dialogue and use the remaining 18 dialogues as training data.

To measure the performance of the dialogue policy, we follow the approach of DeVault et al. (2011), which counts an automatically produced system SA as correct if that SA was chosen by at least one referee for that dialogue turn in the data set. We then count the proportion of the correct SAs among all the SAs produced across all 19 dialogues, and use this measure of *weak accuracy* to score competing dialogue policies.

We can use the weak accuracy of one referee, measured against all the others, to establish a performance ceiling for this metric. (We do not expect that an automatic system would outperform a human referee.) This score is .79; see DeVault et al. (2011) for discussion.

3 Experimental Setup

Our experimental setup evaluates three different dialogue policy models: a rule-based approach (Rules), discussed in Section 3.2; a statistical classification technique that uses maximum-entropy classification (MaxEnt), discussed in Section 3.3; and another statistical technique called relevance models (RM), discussed in Section 3.4.

For the Rules approach, the user's utterance is represented in SA form, and we evaluate the performance of the rules using both hand-annotated or "gold" SA (G-SA) as well as automatically assigned NLU SAs (NLU-SA), as described in Section 3.1. For the two statistical policy techniques, MaxEnt and RM, the user's utterance may be represented in SA form or in plain text form. In the latter case, the NLU and DM modules are effectively consolidated into a single classification step.

3.1 NLU

Our NLU module treats the problem of mapping an utterance text to a single SA label as a multi-class classification problem, which it solves using a maximum-entropy model (Berger et al., 1996). The utterance is represented using shallow features such as unigrams and the length of the user utterance (Sagae et al., 2009). Paraphrases of user utterances are included in the training set.

3.2 Rule-based Policy

We developed our rule-based policy (Rules) by manually writing the simple rules needed to implement Amani's dialogue policy. Given a user SA label A_t for turn t, the rules for determining Amani's response R_t take one of three forms:

$$\text{if } A_t = \text{SA}_i \text{ then } R_t = \text{SA}_j$$
$$\text{if } A_t = \text{SA}_i \wedge \exists k\ A_{t-k} = \text{SA}_l \text{ then } R_t = \text{SA}_j$$
$$\text{if } A_t = \text{SA}_i \wedge \neg\exists k\ A_{t-k} = \text{SA}_l \text{ then } R_t = \text{SA}_j$$

The first rule form specifies that a given user SA should always lead to a given system response. The second and third rule forms enable the system's response to depend on the user having previously performed (or not performed) a specific SA. For example, Amani will only tell the name of the shooter if the user has previously promised to protect her from danger. If such a promise has not yet been made, she will ask the user to protect her in exchange for the information.

Amani's set of 51 rules was developed in 115 minutes by a computational linguist and system developer. Given the existing set of SAs, the rules were very straightforward to develop.

3.3 MaxEnt Policy

Like the NLU, the MaxEnt policy is based on a multi-class maximum-entropy classifier. It uses text-based features including unigrams and the length of the current and previous user utterance, as well as the SA label for Amani's previous utterance. For experiments in which user utterances are represented as text, the MaxEnt policy is trained using all available paraphrases of user utterances. In experiments in which the user utterance is represented using SA labels rather than text, the paraphrase data is ignored, and the MaxEnt policy is trained using the user SA label in place of the text-based features. In all cases, the MaxEnt policy is trained using all the alternative acceptable Amani SA responses as examples of correct output.

3.4 Relevance Model Policy

The text classification task of assigning the system SAs using either the user SAs or the user text input can be viewed as a cross-language information retrieval (IR) task: we have a fixed collection of system SAs ("documents") and a user's input ("query"), and we need to find the best SA that matches the user's input. This is similar to the task of searching Chinese documents using an English query, where the training data that maps user inputs to the system SAs can be viewed as a "parallel corpus" (Lavrenko et al., 2002).

For our third approach we use the Relevance Model (RM) information retrieval technique first suggested by Lavrenko et al. (2002) and recently adapted to a question-answering task by Leuski et al. (2006). We have experimented with different feature sets and we found that (1) when the text data is not available, the combination of the current user SA and the last system SA is the most

	Policy models		
Utterance Features	Rules	MaxEnt	RM
G-SA	.79	.71	.73
NLU-SA	.58	.57	.60
NLU-SA+Text	-	-	.65
Text	-	.66	.71

Table 1: Weak accuracy results for alternative system architectures.

effective; (2) when both the utterance text and SA are available, the combination of the current user SA and unigram text features from all available paraphrases works the best; and (3) when only the text is available, the unigram word features work well by themselves. We should note that we found it is significantly better to train the model on "gold" SAs even when testing on NLU-SAs. We also observed that integrating the unigram features with the history information in the form of SAs or words from previous utterances tended to over-fit the model, resulting in degraded performance.

4 Results and Discussion

We present our results in Table 1. The highest performance is achieved when "gold" SAs (G-SA) are provided to Rules. Indeed, the weak accuracy of .79 is approximately at the ceiling level of performance observed when one human referee is scored against 5 other human referees. This suggests that, with human-level NLU performance, a hand-authored rule-based policy can effectively implement Amani's intended dialogue policy. However, the table also shows that when automatically-assigned NLU speech acts (NLU-SA) are provided as input to Rules, the performance drops significantly to .58. Note that Rules cannot interpret text representations of user utterances; SA labels are needed, which is a cost of using Rules.

For the MaxEnt policy, a score of .71 is achieved with "gold" SAs, and a lower .57 with run-time SAs. Note that .71 is an inferior performance to the .79 achieved with G-SA/Rules, indicating that MaxEnt does not learn a policy as effective as the hand-authored Rules, even if it is trained and evaluated on gold SA labels. As previously reported in DeVault et al. (2011), a performance of .66 is achieved with the MaxEnt policy when trained on text-based features. It is interesting to see here, however, that this .66 performance is significantly higher than the .58 that is achieved using Rules together with run-time SAs. In fact, the accuracy of the NLU-SA labels in this data set, with respect to the gold SAs, is 53%. Thus, while Rules can achieve very good performance with gold SAs, the high frequency of NLU errors causes a significant degradation in policy performance. Interestingly, the alternative Text/MaxEnt design that combines NLU and DM into a single step ends up performing significantly better (.66).

The RM performance shows a pattern broadly similar to MaxEnt; performance is highest (.73) with gold SAs, and when trained to classify directly from Text to system SAs, performance is significantly better (.71) than NLU-SA/Rules (.58). For RM, we additionally explored using both Text features as well as the NLU-SA label as input features, but observed performance degraded to .65 (presumably due to NLU errors). Our best overall performance not requiring gold SAs, .71, was achieved by Text/RM. Our intuition is that a couple of factors helped RM to outperform the MaxEnt approach: (1) MaxEnt treats word features as binary, while RM explicitly takes into account the word occurrence frequencies; (2) RM is better designed to handle multi-label classification, where a single input instance can be assigned to multiple classes.

5 Conclusion and Future Work

We have presented and evaluated a set of alternative dialogue system architectures in a case study domain. In this domain, we have shown that the theoretical performance that is achievable with a rule-based dialogue policy is high, but that two classification approaches that omit a separate NLU step and directly select system responses perform significantly better. In future work, we plan to address some of the remaining questions, including how these learned policies would perform in live dialogues, how these results would change if NLU performance could be improved, and to what extent this pattern of results would transfer to other domains with more complex NLU and policy requirements.

Acknowledgments

We thank our anonymous reviewers. The project or effort described here has been sponsored by the U.S. Army Research, Development, and Engineering Command (RDECOM). Statements and opinions expressed do not necessarily reflect the position or the policy of the United States Government, and no official endorsement should be inferred.

References

Ron Artstein, Sudeep Gandhe, Michael Rushforth, and David R. Traum. 2009. Viability of a simple dialogue act scheme for a tactical questioning dialogue system. In *DiaHolmia 2009: Proceedings of the 13th Workshop on the Semantics and Pragmatics of Dialogue*, page 43–50, Stockholm, Sweden, June.

Adam L. Berger, Stephen D. Della Pietra, and Vincent J. D. Della Pietra. 1996. A maximum entropy approach to natural language processing. *Computational Linguistics*, 22(1):39–71.

David DeVault, Anton Leuski, and Kenji Sagae. 2011. Toward learning and evaluation of dialogue policies with text examples. In *12th annual SIGdial Meeting on Discourse and Dialogue*.

Sudeep Gandhe, Nicolle Whitman, David R. Traum, and Ron Artstein. 2009. An integrated authoring tool for tactical questioning dialogue systems. In *6th Workshop on Knowledge and Reasoning in Practical Dialogue Systems*, Pasadena, California, July.

Dusan Jan, Antonio Roque, Anton Leuski, Jackie Morie, and David R. Traum. 2009. A virtual tour guide for virtual worlds. In Zsófia Ruttkay, Michael Kipp, Anton Nijholt, and Hannes Högni Vilhjálmsson, editors, *IVA*, volume 5773 of *Lecture Notes in Computer Science*, pages 372–378. Springer.

Patrick G. Kenny, Thomas D. Parsons, and Albert A. Rizzo. 2009. Human computer interaction in virtual standardized patient systems. In *Proceedings of the 13th International Conference on Human-Computer Interaction. Part IV*, pages 514–523, Berlin, Heidelberg. Springer-Verlag.

Victor Lavrenko, Martin Choquette, and W. Bruce Croft. 2002. Cross-lingual relevance models. In *Proceedings of the 25th annual international ACM SIGIR conference on Research and development in information retrieval*, pages 175–182, Tampere, Finland.

Anton Leuski, Ronakkumar Patel, David Traum, and Brandon Kennedy. 2006. Building effective question answering characters. In *Proceedings of the 7th SIGdial Workshop on Discourse and Dialogue*, Sydney, Australia, July.

Kenji Sagae, Gwen Christian, David DeVault, and David R. Traum. 2009. Towards natural language understanding of partial speech recognition results in dialogue systems. In Short Paper Proceedings of NAACL HLT.

W. Swartout, J. Gratch, R. W. Hill, E. Hovy, S. Marsella, J. Rickel, and D. Traum. 2006. Toward virtual humans. *AI Mag.*, 27(2):96–108.

William R. Swartout, David R. Traum, Ron Artstein, Dan Noren, Paul E. Debevec, Kerry Bronnenkant, Josh Williams, Anton Leuski, Shrikanth Narayanan, and Diane Piepol. 2010. Ada and grace: Toward realistic and engaging virtual museum guides. In Jan M. Allbeck, Norman I. Badler, Timothy W. Bickmore, Catherine Pelachaud, and Alla Safonova, editors, *IVA*, volume 6356 of *Lecture Notes in Computer Science*, pages 286–300. Springer.

David Traum, William Swartout, Jonathan Gratch, Stacy Marsella, Patrick Kenney, Eduard Hovy, Shri Narayanan, Ed Fast, Bilyana Martinovski, Rahul Bhagat, Susan Robinson, Andrew Marshall, Dagen Wang, Sudeep Gandhe, and Anton Leuski. 2005. Dealing with doctors: Virtual humans for non-team interaction training. In *Proceedings of ACL/ISCA 6th SIGdial Workshop on Discourse and Dialogue*, Lisbon, Portugal, September.

David R. Traum, Anton Leuski, Antonio Roque, Sudeep Gandhe, David DeVault, Jillian Gerten, Susan Robinson, and Bilyana Martinovski. 2008. Natural language dialogue architectures for tactical questioning characters. In *Army Science Conference*, Florida, 12/2008.

Reducing Asymmetry between language-pairs to Improve Alignment and Translation Quality

Rashmi Gangadharaiah
IBM Research, India
rashgang@in.ibm.com

Abstract

This paper presents a novel method to remove asymmetry between the source and the target languages thereby improving alignment and machine translation (MT) quality. Some words in the source language are redundant for MT tasks but necessary for the source sentence to be grammatical. This paper proposes a method to automatically detect such words. In addition, constraints under which these words should or should not be removed are extracted automatically from the target language. A lattice scheme is used for test sentences to provide alternate paths with and without removal of these words. Such a constraint-based removal technique gives a significant improvement ($p < 0.001$) of 5.29 BLEU points over the baseline Phrase-based MT system for the English-Hindi language-pair.

1 Introduction

Different languages express the same piece of information with different number of words. As a result, in many language-pairs, not all source words have correspondences in the target half of the sentence-pair. The aligner is expected to align these redundant source words to an empty word ("*NULL*") in the target sentence. However, in data-sparse conditions, this is not perfectly learnt.

The IBM models in *GIZA++* (Och and Ney, 2003) align each source word to exactly one target word and a target word can be aligned to multiple source words. Currently in most MT systems, this limitation in alignment is overcome by aligning the data bi-directionally (Koehn et al., 2003) and later combining the resulting alignments. Inspite of using information from bi-directional alignments, due to the noisy nature and limitations in the amount of parallel data available, low quality word-alignments are obtained. To illustrate this, consider the top ten maximum likelihood lexical translation-table entries for the English source words, "*the*" and "*india*" obtained after combining the bi-directional alignments with the English-Hindi language-pair in Figures 3A and 3B. For the sake of clarity, the actual English translations of the Hindi words (with case-markers transliterated) are displayed instead of the Hindi words themselves. As seen, the probability mass is used up by many other Hindi words that are not the right translations of the source words. Also, in Figure 3B, "*india*" has a higher probability of being aligned to "*NULL*" than to its actual translation. The most common errors in data that result in low quality alignments and translations are:

1) Property of a language-pair: Certain words are necessary to be present in a sentence for the sentence to be grammatical but unnecessary for MT. For example, *the* in *"the government was highly perturbed by his activities"* has no correspondence in Hindi. For MT, these words can hurt the performance of the aligner (illustrated in Figure 1) and translation quality (Section 4). This is true for many language-pairs including English to all Indian languages.

2) Noisy and Imperfect nature of the data: (a) Human translation errors: Humans cause typograpical errors (many times the same error is created consistently) during translation. Usually monolingual data is first collected from a source such as the world-wide-web and then given to human translators who are usually non-experts in MT and add redundant words or leave certain source words untranslated.

(b) Errors in automatic extraction: the world-wide-web is often used to obtain parallel data. Articles describing the same event in multiple languages are aligned at the sentence-level to create parallel corpora. Sentence-alignment is not

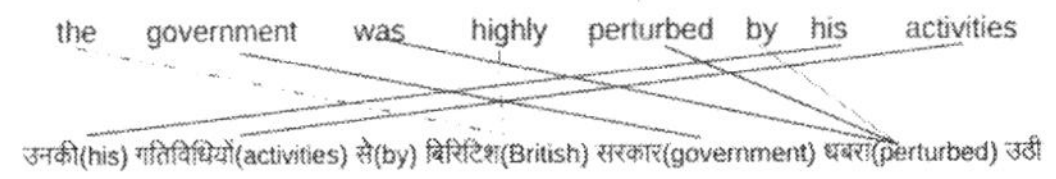

Figure 1: Alignment links provided by the aligner. Dotted lines indicate alignment errors. Correct translations of the Hindi words given in brackets.

perfect when the data used to train the sentence-aligner is limited. Also, not all words in a source sentence have actual correspondences in the target (and vice versa). Errors in word-alignments are seen when a word-aligner is forced to align words in this noisy corpus. For example, the Hindi sentence in Figure 1 has a word that corresponds to "*British*" which is absent in the English sentence.

2 Related Work

Lee (2004) induced only morphological symmetry by identifying morphemes to be merged or deleted from their stems in the morphologically rich source language. They implement the idea that if a morpheme in the source language is robustly translated into a distinct POS in the other language, the morpheme is likely to have an independent counterpart in the other language.

Since unaligned words cause ambiguity in phrase-pairs, Zhang et al. (2009) remove unaligned words before extracting phrase-pairs. Candidates for deletion are collected based on their POS tags and a simple threshold scheme on the probability of a word being aligned.

Lee et al. (2006) found many unaligned function words while translating from Korean to English and removed them using their POS information. In Li et al. (2008), source words that do not have an alignment are added to the phrase-table with ϵ as their translation. Only source context and POS features are used to determine if a word is spurious. For many language-pairs including languages considered in this paper, source context and POS tags of words do not always indicate their 'spuriousness'. Hence, we need other features.

All the above methods depend on a POS tagger to collect redundant source words which may not be available for rare and low density languages. Li et al. (2008) and Zhang et al. (2009) only modify the phrase-extractor or the phrase-pairs and do not concentrate on improving the word-alignments between the language-pair. As will be shown in this paper, the information that a source word is spurious can be valuable even for word-alignment which in turn improves translation quality.

Hong et al. (2008) insert pseudo words and reorder the source and the target sentences to have similar lengths. Pseudo words are generated with the help of dependency parsers. Chung and Gildea (2010) look at recovering dropped pronouns while translating from pro-drop languages like, Chinese and Korean to English.

In this paper, frequently occuring redundant source words caused due to the inherent nature of the language-pair or noise are automatically detected and removed to improve alignments of other words in the corpus and ultimately translation scores when data available is limited. The method does not make use of any rich knowledge sources. Features extracted from word-alignment models are used to score and rank words that form candidates for removal. Top ranking N Redundant source words satisfying target constraints are removed from the training corpus and the corpus is re-aligned. Redundancy is not removed in the target as it hinders the translation generation process and would require post-processing of the translations. During testing, a lattice scheme is used to provide alternate paths, both with and without removal of redundant words.

3 Method for detecting redundant words

Bi-directional word-alignments of the training data are first obtained using GIZA++ and later combined using *grow-diag-final-and* in Moses (Koehn et al., 2007). A maximum likelihood lexical translation table $p(w_i|w_j)$ is estimated between the source words (w_j) and target words (w_i) from the alignments. Features are extracted from the resultant lexical probabilities and linearly combined to obtain a score (eqn. 1). The weights can be tuned with the objective of improving the alignment (with hand alignments) or the translation quality on a tuning set. This can be done using a simple hill climbing procedure or any unconstrained optimization technique that does not require derivatives (Powell, 1964).

$$score = \sum_i \lambda_i f_i \quad where, \sum_i \lambda_i = 1 \qquad (1)$$

3.1 Features

Entropy: If the distribution of the lexical translation probabilities $(P(w_i|w_j))$ for a source word, w_j, (excluding its "*NULL*" probability) is close to

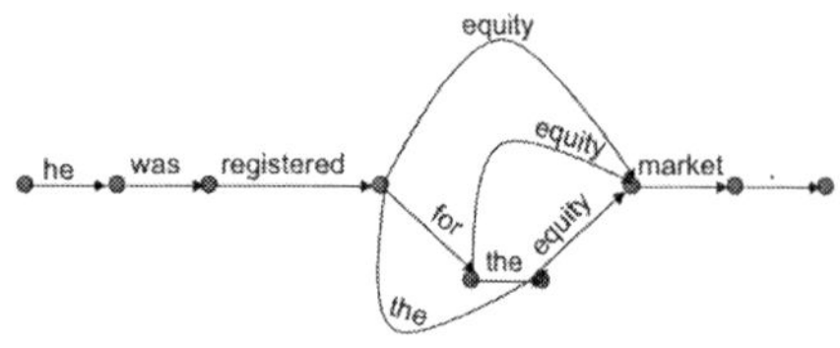

Figure 2: Test/input sentences as a lattice.

a		the		india	
एक	(one/a)	के	(of/CM)	भारत	(india)
की	(of/CM)	की	(of/CM)	इंडिया	(india)
में	(in/CM)	को	(to/CM)	भारतीय	(indian)
का	(of/CM)	का	(of/CM)	हिंदुस्तान	(india)
कुछ	(some/anything)	में	(in/CM)	देश	(country)
कोई	(someone)	ने	(CM)	निगम	(corporation)
किसी	(some)	यह	(this)	हिन्दुस्तानी	(indian)
यह	(this/it)	इस	(this)	अखिल	(all)
(		पर	(but)	आकाशवाणी	(air)
इस	(this)	इन	(these)		
		एक	(one/a)		

Table 1: Constraints for English source words, "*a*", "*the*" and "*india*".

a uniform distribution, the entropies seen will be higher than seen with a non-uniform distribution. For example, English words such as "*the*" do not have translations in Indian languages. A plot of the top ten lexical translation probabilities and corresponding lexical translations for "*the*" is given in Figure 3A. Since the "*NULL*" alignment probability is not considered in eqn. 2, the remaining lexical translation probabilities for a source word are re-normalized to sum to 1.

$$f_1(w_j) = \sum_i -p(w_i|w_j)logp(w_i|w_j) \quad (2)$$

Probability of corresponding to "*NULL*": A very high probability of being aligned to "*NULL*" ($f_2(w_j) = p(NULL|w_j)$) is a good indicator that w_j has no target correspondences.
Number of unique target words: The number of lexical translation probability entries for w_j,

$$f_3(w_j) = \frac{\#unique\ translations\ for\ w_j}{\#target\ words\ in\ the\ corpus} \quad (3)$$

Constraints for removal of source words: certain words like "*a*" or "*an*" in English do not always have translations in Hindi. When these words do have a translation, we do not want to remove them from the source sentence. Hence, constraints are extracted from the lexical translation table to determine when a word from a source sentence can be removed. Figure 3 shows the top ranking lexical translations for the source words, "*the*" and "*india*". Target words (w_i) for a given source word (w_j) with translation probability ($p(w_i|w_j)$) less than the thresholds in eqn. 4 are removed from the constraint list of w_j. The thresholds are determined from all the translation probabilities for a given source word (w_j). The ratio between the number of target words removed to the number of words the source word was originally aligned to is also considered as a feature ($f_4(w_j)$).

$$th_1(w_j){=}median[p(w_1|w_j), p(w_2|w_j)...]\&\&$$
$$th_2(w_j){=}0.7 * max[p(w_1|w_j), p(w_2|w_j)...] \quad (4)$$

Top ranking N redundant candidates are removed from the source half of the training corpus based on their target constraints. However, during testing, as the reference translations cannot be used, test sentences are converted into a lattice (Dyer et al., 2008) where two alternate paths are included, one with the redundant source word removed and another with the redundant source word as is. An example input lattice for the test sentence "*he was registered for the equity market .*" is given in Figure 2. The scores for taking each of the paths are computed as follows. For any redundant source word, the ratio between the number of times the source word was removed from the training corpus to the total number of times it appeared in the training corpus ($score_1$) is used to score the path that does not include the source word. ($score_2 = 1 - score_1$) is added to the alternate path. If a path contains multiple source words removed, the products of the probabilities ($score_1$) of the redundant source words is taken.

4 Preliminary Results and Analysis

The experiments in this paper are performed with the English-Hindi language-pair. We chose Hindi as it is one of the few Indian languages that have moderate amounts of data to perform translation tasks. However, the method adopted and the analysis done in this paper can be applied to all Indian languages. Indian languages not only suffer from data sparsity, many of these languages also do not have rich knowledge sources (like, POS taggers, parsers, etc.). The parallel corpus included the Darpa TIDES surprise language dataset in 2002 and internally collected parallel corpus from news articles. 200k sentence-pairs were used for training both the Baseline (no removal of redundant source words) and the system with removal of redundant source words using Moses. The basic parameters of Moses were tuned using MERT (Och,

f_1	f_2	f_3	f_4	*comb*
the	-	the	it	the
there	's	in	when	in
a	,	a	i	a
says	has	it	but	"
"	will	there	this	as
in	.	"	one	for
what	country	as	some	with
as	have	for	the	to
after	is	this	he	an
for	of	to	if	there

Table 2: Top ranking candidates for removal sorted with respect to each of the feature scores.

2003) on a development set of 500 sentences. The test set contained 4000 sentences. The test set was divided into 20 sub files to determine the statistical significance with the Wilcoxon signed-rank test (1945).

Features from Section 3.1 are normalized to fall within [0,1]. The weights are tuned using a simple grid-search that tried multiple combinations of weights, starting from 0 and keeping the sum of the weights equal to 1. The weights were incremented in steps of 0.2. The objective chosen was to improve the translation quality score (BLEU (Papineni et al., 2002)) on a small tune set of 200 sentence-pairs. For each set of parameters, the training corpus was modified by removing top ranking N redundant candidates based on target constraints and aligned, the tune set was also modified each time into a lattice and translated to compute the translation quality. As translation for every set of parameters with a large training set is computationally expensive, a small training corpus of size 15k sentence-pairs was chosen to tune the parameters. As alignment is also expensive, only four iterations of IBM Model 1 and two iterations of HMM alignments were performed. The lexical translation table obtained from the alignment of 15k sentence-pairs showed that 798 source words had more than two possible translations. The best N was found to be 42 which contained function words and content words.

Top ranking candidates based on each of the features, $f_1(w_j)$, $f_2(w_j)$, $f_3(w_j)$ and $f_4(w_j)$ along with their tuned combination (eqn. 1) are given in Table 2. Examples of target constraints extracted for the words, "*a*", "*the*" and "*india*", are given in Table 1. The target constraints of "*the*" mostly include case-markers. Blind removal of all instances of "*the*" in the training corpus resulted in a drop of 0.3 BLEU points over the constraint-based removal of "*the*". The reason is that, the case-markers in Hindi have no correspondences in English and require spurious words on the source for their generation. This suggests that redundancy has to be tackled both in the source and in the target to bring about balance in the number of words in the source and target sentences.

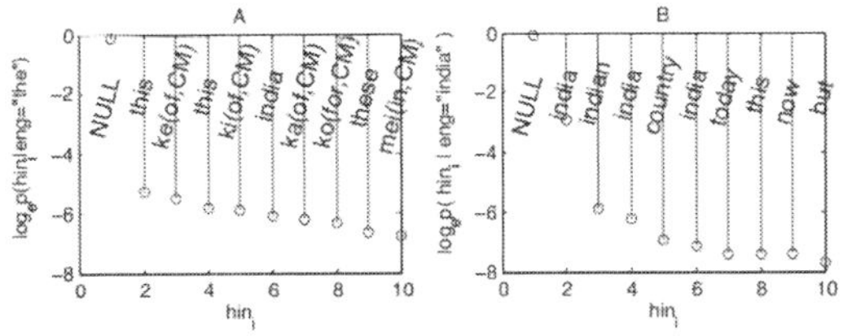

Figure 3: Lexical translation probabilities for source words, "*the*" and "*india*" obtained without removal of redundant source words from the training corpus. CM: case-markers in Hindi.

Score	Base	Rem
3-gram BLEU	12.09	18.57
4-gram BLEU	7.06	12.35
f-score (4k)	49.08	50.74

Table 3: Alignment scores (w.r.t 4k hand-aligned sentence-pairs), n-gram BLEU scores and modified precision scores (p_k) obtained with (Rem) and without (Base) removal of redundant words.

A small set of 4k sentence-pairs (from the 15k sentence-pairs) were hand-aligned to compute the f-score on the automatic alignments. While computing the alignment score, alignments of redundant source words were not considered in order to see the alignment improvements of other source words in the training corpus. Improvements in alignment and translation scores w.r.t the baseline are shown in Table 3. Statistically significant improvement ($p<0.001$) of 5.29 BLEU points in translation quality was seen on the test set with removal of redundant words.

5 Conclusion and Future Work

A novel approach to detect and remove redundancy was proposed which gave improvements in alignment as well as translation quality.

Future work will concentrate on removing redundancy even in the target before aligning the corpus and during testing, perform post-processing to insert target words in the translation. It would be interesting to see the performance of the method with other language-pairs.

References

Tagyoung Chung and Daniel Gildea 2010. Effects of empty categories on machine translation, *In Proceedings of the 2010 Conference on Empirical Methods in Natural Language Processing (EMNLP '10)*, pp. 636-645.

Christopher Dyer, Smaranda Muresan and Philip Resnik. 2008. Generalizing Word Lattice Translation, *In Proceedings of the 46th Annual Meeting of the Association for Computational Linguistics: Human Language Technologies (ACL-08: HLT)*, pp. 1012-1020.

Gumwon Hong, Seung-Wook Lee and Hae-Chang Rim. 2009. Bridging morpho-syntactic gap between source and target sentences for English-Korean statistical machine translation, *In Proceedings of the ACL-IJCNLP 2009 Conference Short Papers (ACLShort '09)*, pp. 233-236.

Philipp Koehn, Franz Josef Och and Daniel Marcu, 2003. Statistical phrase-based translation, *In Proceedings of the 2003 Conference of the North American Chapter of the Association for Computational Linguistics on Human Language Technology (HLT-NAACL '03) - Volume 1*, pp. 48-54.

Philipp Koehn, Hieu Hoang, Alexandra Birch, Chris Caliison-Burch, Marcello Federico, Nicola Bertoldi, Brooke Cowan, Wade Shen, Christine Moran, Richard Zens, Chris Dyer, Ondřej Bojar, Alexandra Constantin and Evan Herbst. 2007. Moses: Open Source Toolkit for Statistical Machine Translation, *In Proceedings of the 45th Annual Meeting of the ACL on Interactive Poster and Demonstration Sessions (ACL'07)*.

Jonghoon Lee, Donghyeon Lee and Gary Geunbae Lee. 2006. Improving Phrase-based Korean-English Statistical Machine Translation, *In Proceedings of the Ninth International Conference on Spoken Language Processing (Interspeech-ICSLP '06)*.

Young-Suk Lee. 2004. Morphological analysis for statistical machine translation, *In Proceedings of Human Language Technology conference-North American chapter of the Association for Computational Linguistics annual meeting (HLT-NAACL-Short '04)*, pp. 57-60.

Chi-Ho Li, Dongdong Zhang, Mu Li, Ming Zhou and Hailei Zhang. 2008. An empirical study in source word deletion for phrase-based statistical machine translation, *In Proceedings of the Third Workshop on Statistical Machine Translation (StatMT '08)*, pp. 1-8.

Franz Josef Och and Hermann Ney. 2003. A Systematic Comparison of Various Statistical Alignment Models, *Computational Linguistics*, volume 29, number 1, pp. 19-51.

Franz Josef Och. 2003. Minimum error rate training in statistical machine translation, *Proceedings of the 41st Annual Meeting on Association for Computational Linguistics (ACL '03)*, Volume 1, pp. 160-167.

Kishore Papineni, Salim Roukos, Todd Ward and Wei-Jing Zhu. 2002. BLEU: a method for automatic evaluation of machine translation, *In Proceedings of the 40th Annual Meeting on Association for Computational Linguistics (ACL '02)*, pp. 311-318.

Michael James David Powell. 1964. An efficient method for finding the minimum of a function of several variables without calculating derivatives, *Computer Journal*, pp. 155-162.

Frank Wilcoxon. 1945. Individual comparisons by ranking methods, *Biometrics*, 1 ,80-83. *tool:http://faculty.vassar.edu/lowry/wilcoxon.html*.

Yuqi Zhang, Evgeny Matusov and Hermann Ney. 2009. Are Unaligned Words Important for Machine Translation ?, *Proceedings of the 13th Annual Conference of the European Association for Machine Translation (EAMT '09)*, pp. 226-233.

Clause-Based Reordering Constraints to Improve Statistical Machine Translation

Ananthakrishnan Ramanathan[1], **Pushpak Bhattacharyya**[2], **Karthik Visweswariah**[1], **Kushal Ladha**[2] **and Ankur Gandhe**[1]

[1]IBM Research India
{aramana2,v-karthik,ankugand}@in.ibm.com

[2]Department of CSE, IIT Bombay
{pb,kush}@cse.iitb.ac.in

Abstract

We demonstrate that statistical machine translation (SMT) can be improved substantially by imposing clause-based reordering constraints during decoding. Our analysis of clause-wise translation of different types of clauses shows that it is beneficial to apply these constraints for finite clauses, but not for non-finite clauses. In our experiments in English-Hindi translation with an SMT system (DTM2), on a test corpus containing around 850 sentences with manually annotated clause boundaries, BLEU improves to 20.4 from the baseline score of 19.4. This statistically significant improvement is also confirmed by subjective (human) evaluation. We also report preliminary work on automatically identifying the kind of clause boundaries appropriate for enforcing reordering constraints.

1 Introduction

It has been recognized widely that reordering is the Achilles' heel of most SMT models (Birch et al., 2009; Hoang and Koehn, 2009), especially when applied to languages with large syntactic differences. In our experiments in English-Hindi SMT, we observe that it is quite frequent in multi-clause sentences for phrases to move out of their respective clauses due to incorrect reordering. While such mistakes can be avoided by restricting reordering over clause boundaries, this paper demonstrates that such a strategy works well only for finite clauses, and not for non-finite clauses.

Clause-wise or part-by-part translation has been a standard approach in traditional transfer-based systems. In Systran, as described by Hutchins and Somers (1992), conjunct and relative clauses were segmented in a preprocessing step. Similar methods were used in the the Stanford Machine Translation project (Wilks, 1973). Chandrasekar (1994) applies a sentence simplification method to machine translation, where sentences are split at conjunctions, relative pronouns, etc., before translation. Rao *et al.* (2000) describe a clause-wise translation strategy within an English-Hindi transfer-based MT system.

In the context of SMT, Koehn and Knight (2003) use a dedicated noun phrase (NP) translation subsystem to obtain significant improvements in German-English translation. Other similar work includes (Watanabe et al., 2003) for Japanese-English SMT and (Hewavitharana et al., 2007) for Arabic-English. Sudoh et al. (2010) propose methods to perform clause-level alignment of the parallel corpus, and to translate clauses (all clauses identified by a syntactic parser) as a unit to improve long-distance reordering in a specialized domain – English-Japanese translation of research paper abstracts in the medical domain.

While our approach draws from many of the above, it is novel in the following ways: (i) We provide an analysis of different clause types in translation – we show that only some kinds of clauses benefit from the use of reordering constraints, and (ii) We demonstrate significant improvements using this strategy for English-Hindi SMT in a general domain.

2 Problem Statement

We analyzed a set of 225 sentences translated through the baseline system. Of the 120 sentences in this set which had more than one clause, 45 sentences were found to have inter-clause reordering problems; that is, some words or phrases are wrongly placed in a clause where they do not belong. Such long-range reordering problems obviously have a serious detrimental effect on translation quality, and it is quite likely that even limiting the reordering problems to the respective clauses will aid comprehensibility.

3 Analysis of Clause Types in Translation

We will now look at how finite and non-finite clauses behave in translation. Finite clauses are basically tensed clauses, while non-finite clauses are untensed.

- **Finite clauses**: Finite clauses appear most commonly in conjunct or relative constructions. In such cases, each finite clause can be translated separately and glued together using the correct translation of the conjunction or the relative pronoun. While this strategy works very well for conjunct clauses, in relative clauses the resulting translation is sometimes not completely natural, but it is nevertheless always clearly understandable. Consider the following example:

  Input: The boy, who stays in Delhi, won the match.

  Using a clause-wise translation approach, this would be translated as,

  लडका, जो दिल्ली में रेहता है, मैच जीत गया।

  ladakaa, jo dillii men rehtaa hai, match jiita gayaa

  Gloss:boy, who Delhi in stays, match won

  However, a more natural translation would be using correlatives:

  जो लडका दिल्ली में रेहता है, वो मैच जीत गया।

  jo ladakaa dillii men rehtaa hai, vo match jiita gayaa

  Gloss:which boy Delhi in stays, he match won

  Certain kinds of nominal clauses also result in similar disfluencies. For example, in the sentence "The playground is where the statue is situated", putting a reordering constraint around the clause "where the statue is situated" results in an unnatural translation.

- **Non-finite clauses**: Compared to finite clauses, the translation of a non-finite clause is much more dependent on its role within the sentence. There are two main issues: (i) all or part of the non-finite clause could get reordered with the surrounding clause, or (ii) the overall meaning is conveyed by a phrase or group of words from the non-finite clause and a surrounding or neighbouring clause.

  Taking *to-infinitives* as the example category, consider the following constructions:

  a. *To-infinitive clause in raising constructions*: Here the embedded clause with the raised element is translated as a finite clause with *that* as a complementizer. For example,

  Input: John is certain to win,

  which is translated as "It is certain that John will win":

  यह तय है कि जॉन जीतेगा।

  yaha tay hai ki John jiitega

  Gloss:it certain is that John will-win

  It is the combination of "certain" (or similar word) and the to-infinitive that results in this translation.

  b. *To-infinitive with a copular verb*: In such cases, the infinitive is inflected with a कर (*kara*) ending to indicate sequentiality:

  Input: John was happy to see him

  जॉन उसे देखकर खुश हुआ।

  John use dekhakara khusha huaa

  Gloss:John him-to seen-having happy was/became

  Here, the non-finite clause "to see him", gets reordered into the main clause, something that will not be possible if reordering constraints are applied.

  Similarly, there are differences in the way other non-finite clauses (with -ed and -ing participles) are treated. The point being made here is that handling these differences is crucial to the correct meaning being conveyed. In other words, simply translating non-finite clauses separately with reordering constraints around them, will not lead to good translation, because the translation of these clauses is often dependent on the superordinate clause, and also there is reordering between these clauses and the superordinate clause.

	BLEU	Adequacy	Fluency
baseline	19.4	2.04	2.41
finite	20.4^{δ}	2.32^{δ}	2.67^{δ}
non-finite	19.6	2.17^{ψ}	2.5
finite + non-finite	19.8^{ψ}	2.17	2.51^{ψ}

Table 1: Manually identified clauses. δ: 99% statistical significance; ψ: 95% statistical significance

Method	ACI accuracy	BLEU	Adequacy	Fluency
parser	0.42	19.3	-	-
CRF – word and pos	0.69	19.8^{ψ}	2.27^{δ}	2.59^{δ}

Table 2: Automatically identified finite clauses

Based on the above analysis, we are encouraged to test the hypothesis that it is helpful to put reordering constraints around finite clauses, but not around non-finite clauses.

Finiteness is one broad dimension along which clauses may be categorized. Subordinate clauses can be further classified based on the position in which they occur in the sentence – that is, whether they occur in the complement position, the specifier position, or the adjunct position. We may also classify clauses based on whether they play an adjectival, nominal, or adverbial role in the sentence. The focus of the present work, however, is only on the finiteness aspect.

4 Experiments

In this section, we first describe briefly our baseline system and our approach to handling clauses within this system. We then summarize the datasets used and our evaluation methodology, before describing the results of various experiments.

4.1 Approach

The baseline system we use is *DTM2* (a direct translation model) (Ittycheriah and Roukos, 2007). The word-alignments were done using an HMM aligner. We used the best-performing parameter setting in the decoder [1].

A beam search decoder (Ittycheriah and Roukos, 2007) similar to other phrase-based decoders (Tillmann and Ney, 2003) is used for translation. The reordering restriction is applied by treating the relevant clause-boundaries as *barriers*, and putting a hard constraint on reordering across barriers – that is, during decoding, if a new hypothesis requires reordering over a barrier, the hypothesis is discarded.

We experiment with clause boundaries identified in three ways: (i) manually (section 4.3.1), (ii) automatically using a constituency parser (section 4.3.2), and (iii) automatically using a CRF-based clause-boundary classifer using part-of-speech and parser features (section 4.3.3).

4.2 Data and Evaluation

The system was trained on a parallel corpus with 289k sentences (combining the LDC English-Hindi parallel texts with internal datasets) consisting of various domains including news, and tested on 844 sentences. The language model was trained on around 1.5 million sentences.

Automatic evaluation was done using BLEU (Papineni et al., 2001) with a single reference translation per sentence. Statistical significance of the test results with BLEU was computed using paired bootstrap resampling (Koehn, 2004). Subjective evaluation was performed on hundred randomly selected multi-clause sentences, using a five-point scale.

4.3 Results

4.3.1 Manual annotation: finite vs. non-finite clauses

For this experiment, the sentences in the test sets were manually annotated with finite and non-finite clause boundaries. The results in table 1 indicate that reordering constraints around finite clauses work much better than around non-finite clauses.

[1] Specifically, the skip-length (distortion limit) was set to 8. Lower skip-lengths led to much poorer performance. For example, with a skip-length of 4, the BLEU score dropped by around 2 points compared to a skip-length of 8

	improved	degraded
finite (manual)	36	8
finite (auto)	35	17
non-finite (manual)	17	10
finite + non-finite (manual)	19	11

Table 3: Number of translations improved/degraded

4.3.2 Automatic clause identification using a parser

The goal of this experiment was to determine whether clauses obtained from a parser could be used for the purpose of imposing clause-based constraints. We performed the experiment by using a state-of-the-art maxent parser (Ratnaparkhi, 1999) to mark all clause boundaries (clause-level nodes based on the Penn Treebank II Style bracketing guidelines – S, S-BAR, SQ, SBARQ, and SINV). The results were negative (table 2 – row titled *parser*), indicating that straightforward use of a parser is not sufficient to help in identifying clauses suitable for reordering constraints. The column titled *ACI accuracy* has the F-measure for automatic clause-boundary identification measured over the entire test corpus.

4.3.3 Automatic clause identification using a CRF classifier

We annotated a set of 1500 English sentences with finite-clause boundaries, and used this to train a CRF-based clause-boundary classifier (Ram and Devi, 2008; Tjong et al., 2001). Unigram and bigram word features, unigram, bigram and trigram POS features, and the POS of the following verb group were used in the model (Kashioka et al., 2003) [2]. We see (table 2) that a reasonable gain is obtained using the classifier, though not nearly as much as with manual annotation.

5 Discussion

The subjective evaluation scores reveal that only a few translations degrade in quality when reordering constraints are used with finite clauses (largely due to fluency issues of the kind described in section 3). Table 3 shows the number of translations that improved (i.e., the average adequacy and fluency score increased) due to clause-based translation, and the number which degraded, among the hundred sentences taken up for subjective evaluation. The following is an illustration of the kind of improvements clause-based translation brings:

Input: America claims that Iran wants to continue its nuclear programme, and secretly builds atomic weapons.

Baseline translation: अमरीका का दावा है कि उसके परमाणु कार्यक्रम रहना चाहते हैं और् ईरान परमाणु हथियार निर्माण करता है।

amerika kaa daavaa hai ki usake paramaanu kaaryakrama rahanaa caahate hain aur iraana paramaanu hathiyaara nirmaana karataa hai

Gloss: America's claim is that their nuclear programme continue want and Iran nuclear weapons builds

Clause-based translation: अमरीका का दावा है कि ईरान अपने परमाणु कार्यक्रम को जारी रखना चाहता है और परमाणु हथियार निर्माण करता है।

amerika kaa daavaa hai ki iran apane paramaanu kaaryakrama ko jaarii rakhanaa caahataa hai aura paramaanu hathiyaara nirmaana kartaa hai

Gloss: America's claim is that Iran its nuclear programme to continue wants and nuclear weapons builds

6 Conclusion and Future Work

We have shown that the quality of English-Hindi statistical machine translation can be improved by performing clause-wise translation. An important finding in our work is that, in general, finite clauses are more directly suited for such translation compared to non-finite clauses.

Possible directions of future work include: (i) using clause-based constraints also in training, (ii) learning from word-alignments, the kinds of clauses that can benefit from reordering constraints, (iii) analyzing the impact of finer-grained clause types (as mentioned in section 3) on translation, (iv) comparing with other SMT models (Galley and Manning, 2010; Chiang, 2005), and (v) using soft constraints instead of hard constraints for reordering (Marton and Resnik, 2008).

[2] Adding clause-boundary information from the parser as features in the classifier resulted in a lower F-measure of 0.65

References

Adwait Ratnaparkhi, Learning to parse natural language with maximum entropy models, *Machine Learning*, 34(1-3), 1999.

Birch, A., Blunsom, P., and Osborne, M., A quantitative analysis of reordering phenomena, *Proceedings of the Fourth Workshop on Statistical Machine Translation*, 2009.

Chandrasekar, R., *A Hybrid Approach to Machine Translation using Man Machine Communication*, Ph.D. thesis, Tata Institute of Fundamental Research, Mumbai, 1994.

Chiang, D., A hierarchical phrase-based model for statistical machine translation, *Proceedings of ACL*, 2005.

Galley, M. and Manning, C., Accurate Non-Hierarchical Phrase-Based Translation, *Proceedings of HLT-NAACL*, 2010.

Hewavitharana, S., Lavie, A., and Vogel, S., Experiments with a noun-phrase driven statistical machine translation system, *Proceedings of the MT Summit XI*, 2007.

Hoang, H. and Koehn, P., Improving mid-range re-ordering using templates of factors, *Proceedings of EACL*, 2009.

Hutchins, J., and Somers, H., *An Introduction to Machine Translation*, pages 175–189, Academic Press, 1992.

Ittycheriah, A., and Roukos, S., Direct translation model 2, *Proceedings of NAACL-HLT*, 2007.

Kashioka, H., Maruyama, T., and Tanaka, H., Building a parallel corpus for monologue with clause alignment, *Proceedings of the MT Summit IX*, 2003.

Koehn, P., and Knight, K., Feature-rich statistical translation of noun phrases, *Proceedings of ACL*, 2003.

Koehn, P., Statistical significance tests for machine translation evaluation, *Proceedings of EMNLP*, 2004.

Marton, Y. and Resnik, P., Soft syntactic constraints for hierarchical phrase-based translation, *Proceedings of ACL-HLT*, 2008.

Papineni, K., Roukos, S., Ward, T., and Zhu, W., BLEU: a method for automatic evaluation of machine translation, *IBM Research Report*, Thomas J. Watson Research Center, 2001.

Ram, V., S. and Devi, S., L., Clause boundary identification using conditional random fields, *Proceedings of CICLing*, 2008.

Rao, D., Mohanraj, K., Hegde, J., Mehta, V., and Mahadane, P., A practical framework for syntactic transfer of compound-complex sentences for English-Hindi machine translation, *Proceedings of KBCS*, 2000.

Sudoh, K., Duh, K., Tsukada, H., Hirao, T., and Nagata, M., Divide and translate: improving long distance reordering in statistical machine translation, *Workshop on Statistical Machine Translation and Metrics*, 2010.

Tillmann, C. and Ney, H., Word reordering and a dynamic programming beam search algorithm for statistical machine translation *Computational Linguistics*, 29(1), 2003.

Tjong, E., F., Sang, K., and, Dejean, H., Introduction to the CoNLL-2001 shared task: clause identification *Proceedings of CoNLL*, 2001.

Watanabe, T., Sumita, E., and Okuno, H., Chunk-based statistical translation, *Proceedings of ACL*, 2003.

Wilks, Y., The Stanford Machine Translation project, *Natural Language Processing*, Algorithmics Press, pages 243-290, 1973.

Generalized Minimum Bayes Risk System Combination

Kevin Duh, Katsuhito Sudoh, Xianchao Wu, Hajime Tsukada, Masaaki Nagata
NTT Communication Science Laboratories
2-4 Hikari-dai, Seika-cho, Kyoto 619-0237, JAPAN
kevin.duh@lab.ntt.co.jp

Abstract

Minimum Bayes Risk (MBR) has been used as a decision rule for both single-system decoding and system combination in machine translation. For system combination, we argue that common MBR implementations are actually not correct, since probabilities in the hypothesis space cannot be reliably estimated. These implementations achieve the effect of consensus decoding (which may be beneficial in its own right), but does not reduce Bayes Risk in the true Bayesian sense.

We introduce *Generalized* MBR, which parameterizes the loss function in MBR and allows it to be optimized in the given hypothesis space of multiple systems. This extension better approximates the true Bayes Risk decision rule and empirically improves over MBR, even in cases where the combined systems are of mixed quality.

1 Introduction

Minimum Bayes Risk (MBR) is a theoretically-elegant decision rule that has been used for single-system decoding and system combination in machine translation (MT). MBR arose in Bayes decision theory (Duda et al., 2000) and has since been applied to speech recognition (Goel and Byrne, 2000) and machine translation (Kumar and Byrne, 2004). The idea is to choose hypotheses that minimize *Bayes Risk* as oppose to those that maximize posterior probability. This enables the use of task-specific loss functions (e.g BLEU).

However, the definition of Bayes Risk depends critically on the posterior probability of hypotheses. In single-system decoding, one could approximate this probability using model scores. However, for system combination, the various systems have incompatible scores. In practice, MT designers resort to uniform probability, but the result is that the chosen hypothesis no longer has anything to do with Bayes Risk. This hypothesis can be seen as a *consensus* of multiple hypotheses, and in practice the consensus translation is often good, but it cannot be accurately thought of as MBR.

Here, we propose a method that better achieves MBR in system combination settings. The insight is to generalize the loss function in the MBR equation and allow it to be parameterized. The parameters are then tuned on a small development data so that the loss function is converted to one that gives low Bayes Risk under the assumption of uniform posteriors. We will show that a small bitext is sufficient for tuning this generalized loss, and that it vastly outperforms the conventional MBR approach in system combination.

In the following, we first review MBR and explain the difficulty in applying it to system combination (Section 2). Then, we propose our Generalized MBR (Section 3) and evaluate it under the NTCIR Patent Translation tasks (Section 4). Finally, we conclude in Section 5.

2 The Difficulty with MBR

Consider the task of translation from a French sentence (f) to an English sentence (e). Our goal is to find a decision rule $\delta(f) \to e'$, which takes f as input and generates a e' as output, to minimize the expected loss (i.e. Bayes Risk) over the possible space of sentence pairs ($p(e, f)$):

$$E_{p(e,f)}[L(\delta(f)|e)] \quad (1)$$

Note that we write loss $L(\delta(f)|e)$ rather than the conventional $L(\delta(f), e)$ to emphasize that it is asymmetric. The loss allows us to incorporate task-specific knowledge. For example, with 1-BLEU as the loss function, we can quantify that the sentence with 2-word mismatch is preferable to one that has 3-word mismatch, even though both do not perfectly match the reference. The incorporation of the task-specific loss is why MBR is attractive in applications.

What decision rule minimizes the expected loss? By reorganizing Eq. 1 as follows:

$$\begin{aligned} E_{p(e,f)}[L(\delta(f)|e)] &= \sum_{e,f} L(\delta(f)|e)p(e,f) \\ &= \sum_{e,f} L(\delta(f)|e)p(e|f)p(f) \\ &= \sum_{f} \left[\sum_{e} L(\delta(f)|e)p(e|f) \right] p(f) \quad (2) \end{aligned}$$

we observe that expected loss can be minimized if the term in the bracket (known as the *conditional risk*) is minimized for each f:

$$\arg\min_{\delta(f)} \sum_{e} L(\delta(f)|e)p(e|f) \quad (3)$$

$$\approx \arg\min_{e' \in N(f)} \sum_{e \in N(f)} L(e'|e)p(e|f) \quad (4)$$

Eq. 3 is the Minimum Bayes Risk (MBR) decision rule. Eq. 4 is the N-best approximation commonly used in practice: $N(f)$ contains the set of hypotheses in the N-best list, and the argmin and sum is only performed within this finite set. There are two difficulties with Eq. 4:

1. The N-best approximation is much smaller than the *true* space of *all* English hypotheses in the argmin and sum of Eq. 3. The approximation in the argmin causes search errors, while the approximation in the sum introduces bias. This problem can be somewhat mitigated by increasing the N-best list size or extending this space using lattices and hypergraphs (Tromble et al., 2008; DeNero et al., 2009; Kumar et al., 2009). We do not address this issue here.

2. The posterior probability $p(e|f)$ in Eq.3 and Eq. 4 refers to the *true* posterior probability arising from $E_{p(e,f)}[\cdot]$ in the derivation of Eq. 2. In practice, this can only be estimated from the MT decoder's model scores:

$$p(e|f) \approx \frac{(\exp \sum_i \lambda_i h_i(e,f))^\alpha}{\sum_{e' \in N(f)} (\exp \sum_i \lambda_i h_i(e',f))^\alpha} \quad (5)$$

where $h_i(e,f)$ are features, λ_i are feature weights, and α is a scaling factor that determines the flatness of the posterior distribution (Ehling et al., 2007). It is important to emphasize that we are *assuming* that the decoder's score is an accurate surrogate for the true posterior distribution $p(e|f)$.

The second difficulty poses a particular problem for system combination. Although the assumption in Eq. 5 is reasonable for single-system MT, it becomes unclear how to compare the model scores $\sum_i \lambda_i h_i(e,f)$ in a multi-system setting. To illustrate, consider two MT systems, their 2-best lists, and corresponding model scores:

- System A: e_1, score=7; e_2, score=3;
- System B: e_3, score=90; e_4, score=10;

It is unclear what is the ranking of posterior probabilities in the space of these four hypotheses. The possibilities include:

- $p(e_1|f) > p(e_2|f) > p(e_3|f) > p(e_4|f)$,
- $p(e_3|f) > p(e_4|f) > p(e_1|f) > p(e_2|f)$,
- $p(e_1|f) > p(e_3|f) > p(e_2|f) > p(e_4|f), \ldots$

From the model scores, we can assume that $p(e_1|f) > p(e_2|f)$ and $p(e_3|f) > p(e_4|f)$ but we cannot say anything about how, e.g., $p(e_1|f)$ and $p(e_3|f)$ compare because the scores are not calibrated across systems. If we cannot even rank the posteriors, there is little hope of estimating its actual values.

Due to this difficulty, previous work in MBR system combination disregard the estimation and assume that $p(e|f)$ is an uniform distribution. The effect is *consensus decoding*, i.e. picking a sentence most similar to others in the N-best list. Consensus decoding may be beneficial in its own right, as shown by positive results in (de Gispert et al., 2009; Sim et al., 2007), but the consensus rule and the MBR rule are *different*.

In fact, the consensus rule may suffer if the N-best list contains many poor translations that are similar to each other. On the other hand, if these poor translations all have small posterior (which ought to be), it does not affect the MBR rule whatsoever. Unfortunately, the bottleneck is the difficulty in estimating the posteriors.

3 Generalized MBR

3.1 Theory

The idea of *Generalized* MBR (GMBR) is to parameterize the loss function in Eq. 4 and allow it to adapt to the hypothesis space of a set of given systems. Specifically, we write a loss function $L(e'|e;\boldsymbol{\theta})$, parameterized by $\boldsymbol{\theta}$, as a linear combination of sub-components:

$$L(e'|e;\theta) = \sum_{k=1}^{K} \theta_k L_k(e'|e) \quad (6)$$

The sub-components are related to the original loss function in some fashion. For example, suppose the desired loss function is 1-BLEU. Then the sub-components could be: $L_1(e'|e)$=1 - 1gramPrecision, $L_2(e'|e)$=1 - 2gramPrecision, $L_3(e'|e)$=1 - 3gramPrecision, $L_4(e'|e)$=1 - 4gramPrecision, $L_5(e'|e)$=brevaltyPenalty.

The GMBR rule is defined generically as:

$$\arg\min_{e' \in N(f)} \sum_{e \in N(f)} L(e'|e;\boldsymbol{\theta}) p(e|f) \quad (7)$$

And in the case of system combination, we will assume uniform $p(e|f)$ and re-write the GMBR decision rule as:

$$\arg\min_{e' \in N(f)} \sum_{e \in N(f)} L(e'|e;\boldsymbol{\theta}) \frac{1}{|N(f)|} \quad (8)$$

$$= \arg\min_{e' \in N(f)} \sum_{e \in N(f)} \sum_{k=1}^{K} \theta_k L_k(e'|e) \quad (9)$$

Our goal is to minimize the expected loss (Eq. 1) under the constraint of uniform $p(e|f)$. The central idea is this: we will tune $\theta_k, k = 1, \ldots, K$ so that the generalized loss in the uniform hypotheses space gives the same decision as the original loss in the true space $p(e|f)$.

This can be done if a small dev set is available: For any two hypotheses e_1, e_2, and a reference e_r (not in $N(f)$) we first compute the true loss: $L(e_1|e_r)$ and $L(e_2|e_r)$. If $L(e_1|e_r) < L(e_2|e_r)$, then we would want $\boldsymbol{\theta}$ such that:

$$\sum_{e \in N(f)} \sum_{k=1}^{K} \theta_k L_k(e_1|e) < \sum_{e \in N(f)} \sum_{k=1}^{K} \theta_k L_k(e_2|e) \quad (10)$$

so that GMBR would select the hypothesis achieving lower loss. Conversely, if e_2 is a better hypothesis, then we want the opposite relation: $\sum_e \sum_k \theta_k L_k(e_1|e) > \sum_e \sum_k \theta_k L_k(e_2|e)$. Thus, in light of the fact that posterior probabilities $p(e|f)$ are not reliable, we directly compute the true loss (using a development set) and ensure that our GMBR decision rule minimizes this loss.

The disadvantage of GMBR is, of course, that a development set is needed. Note, however, that MBR may also require tuning the global scaling factor (Eq. 5). Empirically, we observe that a small set (500 sentences) seems sufficient.

Algorithm 1 Tuning $\boldsymbol{\theta}$ for GMBR

Input: Development data $\mathcal{D}$, with $(e_r, f) \in \mathcal{D}$
Input: N-best list $N(f)\ \forall f \in \mathcal{D}$.
Input: Regularization hyperparameter c
Output: $\theta_k, k = 1, \ldots, K$ such that Eq. 9 minimizes $L()$ on $\mathcal{D}$.

1: $\mathcal{P} = \emptyset$
2: **for** $f \in \mathcal{D}$ **do**
3: Compute true loss $L(e|e_r)\ \forall e \in N(f)$
4: **for** All pair $e_i, e_j \in N(f)$ **do**
5: Add (e_i, e_j) to $\mathcal{P}$ if $L(e_i|e_r) < L(e_j|e_r)$
6: **end for**
7: **end for**
8: $\arg\min_{\boldsymbol{\theta}} ||\theta||^2 + c\sum_{ij} \xi_{ij}$
s.t. $\sum_k \theta_k C_k(e_j) - \sum_k \theta_k C_k(e_i) \geq 1 - \xi_{ij}$
$\forall (e_i, e_j) \in \mathcal{P}$

3.2 Implementation

We now describe how GMBR and the tuning procedure can be implemented in practice. First, note that we can reorganize the sums in the GMBR decision rule: $\sum_e \sum_k \theta_k L_k(e'|e) = \sum_k \theta_k \sum_e L_k(e'|e) = \sum_{k=1}^{K} \theta_k C_k(e')$, where $C_k(e') = \sum_e L_k(e'|e)$ represents the combined loss for e'. So we first compute $C_k(\cdot)$ for all hypotheses, for an $O(|N(f)|^2)$ run-time. To find the GMBR decision then requires a search $\arg\min_{e' \in N(f)} \sum_{k=1}^{K} \theta_k C_k(e')$. So in test, GMBR is on the same order as conventional MBR.

To tune $\boldsymbol{\theta}$, we first extract all pairs of hypotheses where a difference exists in the true loss, then optimize $\boldsymbol{\theta}$ in a formulation similar to RankSVM (Joachims, 2006). The pair-wise nature of Eq. 10 makes the problem amenable to solutions in "learning to rank" literature (He et al., 2008a). The pseudocode is shown in Algorithm 1. The RankSVM (line 8) tries to satisfy the relations (Eq. 10) in its constraints while allowing for some slack ξ, whose amount depends on hyperparameter c.

4 Experiments

We experiment with the NTCIR-9 (2011) English-to-Japanese Patent Translation task[1]. This includes 3 million sentences for training individual MT systems; the official dev set is split into 1000 sentences for MERT of individual systems, 500 for system combination optimization (MBR, GMBR), and 500 for final evaluation. We combine three systems:

- Phrase-based Moses with lexical reordering, distortion=6 (Koehn and others, 2007)
- Forest-to-string system (Mi et al., 2008)
- Weighted finite-state Transducer (WFST) (Zhou et al., 2006) with rule-based reordering as preprocessing (Isozaki et al., 2010b).

Each system generates a 100-best list, so our system combination task involves hypothesis selection out of 300 hypotheses. As evaluation measure, we focus on BLEU, Normalized Kendall's Tau (NKT), a metric that has been shown to correlate well with humans on this language pair (Isozaki et al., 2010a)[2], and a combination thereof. The loss function used for MBR is therefore the sum of BLEU and NKT. For GMBR, the sub-components of this loss function are derived from the n-gram precisions, brevity penalty, and Kendall's score. We also multiply the n-gram precisions with the Kendall score as additional loss sub-components. Finally we add identity features indicating which of the three systems the hypothesis comes from, for a total of $K = 14$ sub-components. The hyperparameter c in Algorithm 1 is chosen by 80/20% cross-validation from the set $\{0.001, 0.01, 0.1, 1, 10, 100\}$.

The test scores for MBR, GMBR, and the single systems are shown in Table 1. The single systems are anonymized by A, B, C and sorted by decreasing performance. The top1 indicates the first hypothesis in the 100-best list, while bottom1 indicates the 100st (last) hypothesis. Observations:

1. GMBR outperforms MBR on all metrics.
2. GMBR is able to improve upon the best single system (A), despite the fact that a poor system (C) is included. This implies that criteria like Eq. 10 is effective.
3. For MBR, the inclusion of C drastically degrades performance since it implements consensus decoding, not Bayes Risk.

We also summarize results for Chinese-English and Japanese-English tasks in NTCIR9. The system combination setting is similar (3-way combination of 100-best lists) but uses different MT systems. In Chinese-English, GMBR outperforms the best single system by 1 BLEU point (32.08 vs. 31.08); in Japanese-English, GMBR outperforms by 1.85 BLEU points (29.39 vs. 27.54).

We conclude that GMBR is a robust method for system combination. It consistently improves over the top system, even when the combinations are of varying quality (e.g., the range of BLEU score in the 300-best list can be more than 10 BLEU points between A-top1 and C-bottom1). This degrades MBR and consensus decoding, but does not impact GMBR because these poor translation would achieve high loss on the development set, and therefore θ will be optimized away from them.[3]

	BLEU	NKT	(BLEU+NKT)/2
GMBR	**36.65**	**77.50**	**57.08**
MBR	35.45	76.25	55.85
A top1	35.87	76.87	56.37
B top1	34.20	75.93	55.07
C top1	24.23	67.68	45.96
A bottom1	34.92	76.20	55.56
B bottom1	33.97	75.99	54.93
C bottom1	22.95	65.99	44.47
oracle	45.82	84.32	65.07

Table 1: Test results on English-Japanese.

5 Conclusions

We introduced *Generalized* MBR, which enables one to adapt the loss function of MBR to a given hypothesis space. By tuning this generalized loss under the constraint of uniform posteriors, we show that GMBR can consistently outperform MBR in system combination. Future work includes (1) combination with methods that can generate novel hypotheses (Rosti et al., 2007; He et al., 2008b; Matusov et al., 2006; Bangalore et al., 2001), and (2) comparison with recent work that attempts to directly estimate posteriors with mixture models (Duan et al., 2010).

[1] `http://ntcir.nii.ac.jp/PatentMT/`

[2] Code available at `http://www.kecl.ntt.co.jp/icl/lirg/ribes`

[3] It's worth noting that system identity features account for less than 30% of weights in all GMBR systems, implying that the flexibility of adjustable loss function is important and a straightforward weighted version of MBR is insufficient.

References

Srinivas Bangalore, German Bordel, and Giuseppe Riccardi. 2001. Computing consensus translation from multiple machine translation systems. In *ASRU*.

Adria de Gispert, Sami Virpioja, Mikko Kurimo, and Willliam Byrne. 2009. MBR combination of translation hypotheses from alternative morphological decompositions. In *NAACL*.

John DeNero, David Chang, and Kevin Knight. 2009. Fast consensus decoding over translation forests. In *ACL*.

Nan Duan, Mu Li, Dongdong Zhang, and Ming Zhou. 2010. Mixture model-based minimum bayes risk decoding using multiple machine translation systems. In *COLING*.

Richard Duda, Peter Hart, and David Stork. 2000. *Pattern Classification*. Wiley-Interscience, 2nd edition.

Nicola Ehling, Richard Zens, and Hermann Ney. 2007. Minimum bayes risk decoding for BLEU. In *ACL Demo and Poster session*.

Vaibhava Goel and William Byrne. 2000. Minimum bayes-risk automatic speech recognition. *Computer Speech and Language*, 14(2):115–135.

Chuan He, Cong Wang, Yi xin Zhong, and Rui fan Li. 2008a. A survey on learning to rank. In *International Conference on Machine Learning and Cybernetics*.

Xiaodong He, Mei Yang, Jianfeng Gao, Patrick Nguyen, and Robert Moore. 2008b. Indirect-HMM-based hypothesis alignment for combining outputs from machine translation systems. In *EMNLP*.

H. Isozaki, T. Hirao, K. Duh, K. Sudoh, and H. Tsukada. 2010a. Automatic evaluation of translation quality for distant language pairs. In *EMNLP*.

Hideki Isozaki, Hajime Tsukada, Katsuhito Sudoh, and Kevin Duh. 2010b. Head finalization: a simple reodering rule for SOV langauges. In *ACL Workshop on Statistical Machine Translation (WMT)*.

T. Joachims. 2006. Training linear SVMs in linear time. In *KDD*.

P. Koehn et al. 2007. Moses: open source toolkit for statistical machine translation. In *ACL*.

Shankar Kumar and William Byrne. 2004. Minimum bayes-risk decoding for statistical machine translation. In *HLT-NAACL*.

Shankar Kumar, Wolfgang Macherey, Chris Dyer, and Franz Och. 2009. Efficient minimum error rate training and minimum bayes risk decoding for translation hypergraphs and lattices. In *ACL*.

Evgeny Matusov, Nicola Ueffing, and Hermann Ney. 2006. Computing consensus translation from multiple machine translation systems using enhanced hypotheses alignment. In *EACL*.

Haitao Mi, Liang Huang, and Qun Liu. 2008. Forest-based translation. In *ACL*.

Antti-Veikko I. Rosti, Necip Fazil Ayan, Bing Xiang, Spyridon Matsoukas, Richard M. Schwartz, and Bonnie J. Dorr. 2007. Combining outputs from multiple machine translation systems. In *NAACL-HLT*.

Khe Chai Sim, William J. Byrne, Mark J.F. Gales, Hichem Sahbi, and Phil C. Woodland. 2007. Consensus network decoding for statistical machine translation system combination. In *ICASSP*.

Roy Tromble, Shankar Kumar, Franz Och, and Wolfgang Macherey. 2008. Lattice minimum bayes-risk decoding for statistical machine translation. In *EMNLP*.

Bowen Zhou, Stanley Chen, and Yuqing Gao. 2006. Folsom: A fast and memory-efficient phrase-based approach to statistical machine translation. In *IEEE Spoken Language Technology Workshop*.

Enhancing scarce-resource language translation through pivot combinations

Marta R. Costa-jussà
Barcelona Media Innovation Center
Av. Diagonal, 177
08018 Barcelona
marta.ruiz@barcelonamedia.org

Carlos Henríquez
TALP-UPC
Jordi Girona, s/n
08034 Barcelona
carlos.henriquez@upc.edu

Rafael E. Banchs
Institute for Infocomm Research
1 Fusionopolis Way 21-01
Singapore 138632
rembanchs@i2r.a-star.sg.edu

Abstract

Chinese and Spanish are the most spoken languages in the world. However, there is not much research done in machine translation for this language pair. We experiment with the parallel Chinese-Spanish corpus (United Nations) to explore alternatives of SMT strategies which consist on using a pivot language. Particularly, two well-known alternatives are shown for pivoting: the cascade system and the pseudo-corpus. As Pivot language we use English, Arabic and French. Results show that English is the best pivot language between Chinese and Spanish. As a new strategy, we propose to perform a combination of the pivot strategies which is capable to highly outperform the direct translation strategy.

1 Introduction

Although they are very distant languages, Chinese and Spanish are very close to each other in the ranking of the most spoken languages in the world[1]. Nevertheless, when interested in bilingual resources between these two languages they become far apart again. Similarly, the related amount of work we have found within the computational linguistic community, can be reduced to a very small set of references.The most popular research event recently performed was the 2008 IWSLT evaluation campaign [2]. This evaluation organized two Chinese-to-Spanish tracks. One of them was focused on direct translation and the other one on pivot translation through English. Best translation results were obtained by far in the pivot task. The best system in the pivot task (Wang et al., 2008) compared two different approaches: The first one, training two translation models on the Chinese-English corpus and English-Spanish corpus, and then building a pivot translation model for Chinese-Spanish translation using English as a pivot language as proposed in (Wu and Wang, 2007); the second one obtained better results and it was based on a cascade approach. The idea here is to translate from Chinese into English and then from English to Spanish, which means performing two translations. Besides the research mentioned above, which directly addressed the Chinese-Spanish language pair, we may also find in the literature another approach similar to Wu's (2007) authored by Cohn and Lapata (2007). Basically, they also used several intermediate pivot language to create source-to-target phrases that are lately interpolate with a direct system build with a source-to-target parallel corpus.

Apart from the BTEC[3] corpus available through the IWSLT[4] competition and *Holy Bible* datasets described in (Paul, 2008) and (Banchs and Li, 2008), respectively, there is a recent release of a six language parallel corpus (including both Chinese and Spanish) from United Nations (UN) for research purposes (Rafalovith and Dale, 2009). Using the recently released UN parallel corpus as a starting point, this work focuses on the problem of developing Chinese-Spanish phrase-based SMT technologies with a limited set of bilingual resources. We explore and evaluate different alternatives for the

[1] www.ethnologue.org/ethno_docs/distribution.asp?by=size
[2] http://mastarpj.nict.go.jp/IWSLT2008/
[3] Basic Traveller Expressions Corpus
[4] International Workshop on Spoken Language Translation

problem in hand by means of pivot-language strategies through the other languages available in the UN parallel corpus, such as Arabic, English and French. More specifically, strategies such as system cascading and pseudo-corpus generation are implemented and compared against a baseline system implementing a direct translation approach. We propose a system combination different from previous ones (Wu and Wang, 2009) and based on the Minimum Bayes Risk (MBR) (Kumar and Byrne, 2004) technique using both pivot strategies which is capable to highly outperform the direct system. To the best of our knowledge, this idea was not explored before and it is a way of increasing the quality of translation between languages with scarce bilingual resources. In addition, we are performing a combination of the same system but introducing new information through the pivot language.

The paper is structured as follows. Section 2 describes the main strategies for performing Chinese-to-Spanish translation which are tested in this work. Section 3 presents the evaluation framework. Then, section 4 reports the experiments (including the system combination) and the results. Finally, section 5 concludes and proposes new research directions.

2 Direct and pivot statistical machine translation approaches

There are several strategies that we can follow when translating a pair of languages in Statistical Machine Translation. The next three sub-sections present the details of the ones we are using in this work.

2.1 Direct system

Our direct system uses the phrase-based translation system (Koehn et al., 2003). This popular system implements a log-linear model in which a source language sentence $f^J = f_1, f_2, \ldots, f_J$ is translated into another language (target) sentence $e^I = e_1, e_2, \ldots, e_I$ by searching for the translation hypothesis $\hat{e}^I$ maximizing a log-linear combination of several feature models (Och, 2003).

The main system models are the translation model and the language model. The first one deals with the issue of which target language phrase f_j translates a source language phrase e_i and the latter model estimates the probability of translation hypothesis. Apart from these two models, there are other standard models such as the lexical models, the word bonus, and the reordering model.

For decoding, we used the MOSES toolkit (Koehn et al., 2007) with the option of Minimum Bayes Risk (MBR) (Kumar and Byrne, 2004) decoding. Therefore the 1best translation obtained is not the one with highest priority but the one that is most similar to the most likely translation. The option was activated with its default parameters so it considered the top 200 distinct hypothesis to compute the 1best.

2.2 Cascade System

This approach handles the source-pivot and the pivot-target system independently. They are both built and tuned to improve their local translation quality and then joined to translate from the source language to the target language in two steps: first, the 1best translation output from source to pivot is computed and, second, it is used to obtain the 1best target translation output as the final translation.

There is an alternative approach that considers the nbest list in each step instead of the 1best. For instance, it was used in (Khalilov et al., 2008) with their cascade approach in order to obtain the best Chinese-Spanish translation. We also implemented it but the results were similar that those using MBR decoding in each system and keeping the 1best translation. Therefore we maintained MBR decoding for the rest of the experiments, which is also easier to work with.

2.3 Pseudo-Corpus System

This approach translates the pivot section of the source-pivot parallel corpus to the target language using a pivot-target system built previously. Then, a source-target SMT system is built using the source side and the translated pivot side of the source-pivot corpus. The pseudo-corpus system is tuned using a direct source-target development corpus.

2.4 Pivot combination

Using the 1-best translation output from the different pivot strategies, we built an N-best list and computed the final translation using MBR. MBR has been used both during decoding (Kumar and Byrne, 2004; Ehling et al., 2007) and as a postprocess over an N-best list. The current version of the MOSES toolkit includes both MBR implementations. For the system combinations we used the second one.

The MBR algorithm implemented in MOSES uses $(1 - BLEU)\beta$ as the Loss Function. The value β weights the hypothesis proportionally to its translation score, but we considered all our hypothesis as equal so β was a constant and therefore could be discarded. At the end, MBR choose the hypotheses E' that fulfills:

$$E' = \arg\min_{\hat{E}'} \left(\sum_{E \neq \hat{E}'} 1 - BLEU(E, \hat{E}') \right) \quad (1)$$

It is important to mention that all N-best list must have at least 3 hypothesis per sentence. Having only two hypothesis would not work as expected because the Loss Function would always choose the longest one, which can be explained by the definition of BLEU:

$$BLEU(E, E') = \exp\left(\sum_{n=1}^{N} \log \frac{p_n(E, E')}{N} \right) * \gamma(E, E') \quad (2)$$

where $p_n(E, E')$ is the precision of n-grams in the hypothesis E' with reference E; and $\gamma(E, E')$ is a brevity penalty if the hypothesis E' is shorter than the reference E. Then $p_n(E, E') = p_n(E', E)$ and $\forall E, E' : length(E) > length(E') :$

$$1 - BLEU(E, E') \geq 1 - BLEU(E', E) \quad (3)$$

3 Evaluation Framework

This section introduces the details of the evaluation framework used. We report the UN corpus statistics, a description of how we built the systems and the evaluation details.

3.1 Corpus statistics

In this study we use the UN corpus taking advantage of the fact that (as far as we are concerned) it is the biggest parallel corpus freely-available in Chinese-Spanish and it contains the same sentences in six other languages, therefore we can experiment with different pivot languages.

When experimenting with different pivot languages, in order to make the systems as comparable as possible, we first did a sentence selection over the corpus so all systems were built exactly with the same training, tuning and testing sets. All corpora were tokenized, using the standard MOSES tokenizer for Spanish, English and French; ictclass (Zhang et al., 2003) for Chinese; and MADA+TOKAN (Habash and Rambow, 2005) for Arabic. The Spanish, English and French corpora were lowercased. If a sentence had more than 100 words in any language, it was deleted from all corpora. If a sentence pair had a word ratio bigger than three for any Chinese-Pivot or Pivot-Spanish parallel corpora, it was deleted from all corpora. For all languages, we identify all sentences that occur only once in the corpora. The tuning and testing sets where drawn from the available multilingual corpus by using a maximum perplexity and lowest out-of-vocabulary word criterion over the English part of the dataset. In order to do this, perplexity was computed on a sentence-by-sentence basis by using a leave-one-out strategy; then, we selected the two thousand sentences which had the highest perplexity and the lowest out-of-vocabulary words for constructing the tuning and testing sets. Table 1 shows the main statistics for all corpora.

	training		development		test	
	s	w	s	w	s	w
Zh	58.6k	1.6M	1k	30.9k	1k	32.6k
Es	58.6k	2.3M	1k	42.2k	1k	44.0k
En	58.6k	2.0M	1k	36.7k	1k	38.3k
Ar	58.6k	2.6M	1k	47.9k	1k	49.9k
Fr	58.6k	2.3M	1k	42.1k	1k	43.9k

Table 1: UN Corpus Statistics (s stands for number of sentences and w for number of words)

3.2 System details

Our systems were build using MOSES. For all systems, we used the default MOSES parameters, which includes the grow-final-diagonal alignment symmetrization, the lexicalized reordering, a 5-gram language model using Kneser-Ney smoothing and phrases up to length 10. The optimization was done using MERT (Och, 2003). The decoding was done using MBR.

4 Chinese-to-Spanish MT strategies

Given the different languages available in the UN corpora, we tested three different pivot languages. Additionally, we compared the cascade and the pseudo-corpus pivot strategies. Finally, we combined the system outputs.

4.1 Experimenting with different pivot languages

Using most of the languages available in the UN parallel corpora (English, Spanish, Chinese, Arabic and French) we built and compare several translation systems in order to study the impact of the different pivot languages when translating from Chinese to Spanish.

Specifically, we built seven Chinese-Spanish systems: the direct Chinese-Spanish system as a quality upper bound; three cascade approach and three pseudo-corpus, using English, Arabic and French as pivots.

Therefore, the first step was to build the different Chinese-Pivot and Pivot-Spanish systems. Table 2 shows the BLEU achieved with the intermediate systems trained with the UN Corpus. These systems are used in the next section when experimenting with different pivot languages.

	BLEU
Chinese-English	35.67
Chinese-Arabic	**46.11**
Chinese-French	28.31
English-Spanish	**51.64**
Arabic-Spanish	41.79
French-Spanish	46.42

Table 2: UN Pivot Systems

As we can see in Table 2 the best Chinese-Pivot system is the Chinese-Arabic system. As for the Pivot-Spanish system, the one that achieved the best BLEU score was the English-Spanish system.

Tables 3 shows the results for our Chinese-Spanish configurations with the UN corpus. We can see there that the best pivot system used the cascade approach with English as the pivot language.

The fact that the pseudo-corpus through English outperforms cascade through English is not statistically significant, with a 95% confidence (Koehn, 2004). These results, however, are coherent with previous works using the same language pair (Bertoldi et al., 2008; Henríquez Q. et al., 2010) that also reported the pseudo-corpus strategy was better than the cascade strategy.

Languages	System	BLEU
Chinese-Spanish	direct	**33.06**
Chinese-English-Spanish	cascade	**32.90**
Chinese-French-Spanish	cascade	30.37
Chinese-Arabic-Spanish	cascade	28.88
Chinese-English-Spanish	pseudo	**32.97**
Chinese-French-Spanish	pseudo	32.61
Chinese-Arabic-Spanish	pseudo	32.23

Table 3: UN pivot languages. Best results in bold.

In all cases English is statistically significant the best pivot language, with a 99% confidence, which is coherent with the Pivot-Spanish results in table 2. Further analysis is required in order to understand why the cascade through English is able to help so much in the Chinese-to-Spanish translation.

4.2 Pivot combination

Table 4 shows the results of the different output systems combined (from table 3) with the MBR technique. $En + Ar + Fr\ Cascade + Pseudo$ (which combines all system outputs from table 3 except the direct approach) is better than the Chinese-to-Spanish direct system and it is significant with a 99% of confidence. When adding the direct approach (dir) it increases the translation performance slightly and we obtain the best Chinese-to-Spanish translation.

	casc	pseudo	casc+pseudo
En+Ar+Fr	32.66	33.30*	**33.97***
dir+En+Ar+Fr	33.60*	33.77*	**34.09***

Table 4: Output system combination using MBR. * shows statistically significantly better results than the direct system (with a 99% of confidence). Best results in bold. Casc stands for cascade.

5 Conclusions

This work has presented experimental research for the Chinese-Spanish translation pair. The main conclusions derived from our study are:

- English is the best Pivot language for Chinese-to-Spanish compared to languages such as French or Arabic. The system built using English as Pivot was significantly better than the ones built with either French or Arabic, with a 99% confidence in both cases.

- There is not a significant difference among the best cascade and pseudo-corpus pivot approaches.

- The output combination using MBR is able to improve the direct system in 1 BLEU point in the best case. This improvement is significantly better with a 99% confidence.

6 Acknowledgment

The authors would like to thank Barcelona Media Innovation Center and Institute for Infocomm Research for its support and permission to publish this research. This work has been partially funded by the Spanish Department of Science and Innovation through the *Juan de la Cierva* fellowship program.

References

R. Banchs and H. Li. 2008. Exploring spanish morphology effects on chinese-spanish smt. In *MATMT 2008: Mixing Approaches to Machine Translation*, pages 49–53, Donostia-San Sebastian, Spain, February.

N. Bertoldi, R. Cattoni, M. Federico, and M. Barbaiani. 2008. FBK @ IWSLT-2008. In *Proc. of the International Workshop on Spoken Language Translation*, pages 34–38, Hawaii, USA.

T. Cohn and M. Lapata. 2007. Machine Translation by Triangulation: Making Effective Use of Multi-Parallel Corpora. In *Proc. of the ACL*.

N. Ehling, R. Zens, and H. Ney. 2007. Minimum bayes risk decoding for bleu. In *Proc. of the ACL*, pages 101–104, Prague, Czech Republic, June. Association for Computational Linguistics.

N. Habash and O. Rambow. 2005. Arabic tokenization, part-of-speech tagging and morphological disambiguation in one fell swoop. In *Proc. of the 43rd Annual Meeting of the Association for Computational Linguistics*, pages 573–580, Ann Arbor, MI, June.

C. A. Henríquez Q., R. E. Banchs, and J. B. Mariño. 2010. Learning reordering models for statistical machine translation with a pivot language. Internal Report TALP-UPC.

M. Khalilov, M. R. Costa-Jussà, C. A. Henríquez, J. A. R. Fonollosa, A. Hernández, J. B. Mariño, R. E. Banchs, B. Chen, M. Zhang, A. Aw, and H. Li. 2008. The TALP & I2R SMT Systems for IWSLT 2008. In *Proc. of the International Workshop on Spoken Language Translation*, pages 116–123, Hawaii, USA.

P. Koehn, F. J. Och, and D. Marcu. 2003. Statistical phrase-based translation. In *HLT-NAACL*, pages 48–54.

P. Koehn, H. Hoang, A. Birch, C. Callison-Burch, M. Federico, N. Bertoldi, B. Cowan, W. Shen, C. Moran, R. Zens, C. Dyer, O. Bojar, A. Constantin, and E. Herbst. 2007. Moses: Open source toolkit for statistical machine translation. In *Proc. of the ACL*, pages 177–180, Prague, Czech Republic.

P. Koehn. 2004. Statistical significance tests for machine translation evaluation. In *Proceedings of EMNLP*, volume 4, pages 388–395.

S. Kumar and W. Byrne. 2004. Minimum bayes-risk decoding for statistical machine translation. In *Proceedings of the Human Language Technology and North American Association for Computational Linguistics Conference (HLT/NAACL'04)*, pages 169–176, Boston, USA, May.

F.J. Och. 2003. Minimum error rate training in statistical machine translation. In *Proc. of the 41th Annual Meeting of the Association for Computational Linguistics*, pages 160–167.

M. Paul. 2008. Overview of the IWSLT 2008 Evaluation Campaign. In *Proc. of the International Workshop on Spoken Language Translation*, pages 1–17, Hawaii, USA.

A. Rafalovith and R. Dale. 2009. United nations general assembly resolutions: A six-language parallel corpus. In *Proc. of the MT Summit XII*, pages 292–299, Ottawa.

H. Wang, H. Wu, X. Hu, Z. Liu, J. Li, D. Ren, and ZhengyuNiu. 2008. The TCH Machine Translation System for IWSLT 2008. In *Proc. of the International Workshop on Spoken Language Translation*, pages 124–131, Hawaii, USA.

H. Wu and H. Wang. 2007. Pivot Language Approach for Phrase-Based Statistical Machine Translation. In *Proc. of the ACL*, pages 856–863, Prague.

H. Wu and H. Wang. 2009. Revisiting Pivot Language Approach for Machine Translation. . In *Proc. of the ACL-IJCNLP*, pages 154–162, Singapore.

H. Zhang, H. Yu, D. Xiong, and Q. Liu. 2003. HHMM-based chinese lexical analyzer ICTCLAS. In *Proc. of the 2nd SIGHAN Workshop on Chinese language processing*, pages 184–187, Sapporo, Japan, July.

A Baseline System for Chinese Near-Synonym Choice

Liang-Chih Yu[1], **Wei-Nan Chien**[1,2] **and Shih-Ting Chen**[1]
[1]Department of Information Management, Yuan Ze University, Taiwan, R.O.C.
[2]Information Technology Center, National Taiwan Normal University, Taiwan, R.O.C.
Contact: lcyu@saturn.yzu.edu.tw

Abstract

Near-synonym sets represent groups of words with similar meaning, which are useful knowledge resources for many natural language applications such as query expansion for information retrieval (IR) and computer-assisted language learning. However, near-synonyms are not necessarily interchangeable in contexts due to their specific usage and syntactic constraints. Previous studies have developed various methods for near-synonym choice in English sentences. To our best knowledge, there is no such evaluation on Chinese sentences. Therefore, this paper implements two baseline systems: *pointwise mutual information (PMI)* and a *5-gram language model* that are widely used in previous work for Chinese near-synonym choice evaluation. Experimental results show that the 5-gram language model achieves higher accuracy than PMI.

1 Introduction

Lexical semantics plays an important role in many natural language applications. For instance, knowing that the word "arm" has (at least) the senses *weapon* and *bodypart* enables systems to perform word sense disambiguation. Knowing in addition the near-synonyms of a word can further improve the applications' effectiveness. For instance, knowing that the weapon sense of "arm" corresponds to the weapon sense of "weapon" and of "arsenal" means that systems can in addition perform term expansion for information retrieval (Moldovan and Mihalcea, 2000; Bhogal et al., 2007), (near-)duplicate detection for summarization, alternative word selection for writing support systems (Inkpen and Hirst, 2006; Inkpen, 2007; Wu et al., 2010), as well as computer-assisted language learning (Cheng et al., 2004; Ouyang et al., 2009).

Recent studies have shown that near-synonyms are not necessarily interchangeable in practical use due to their specific usage and collocational constraints, as shown in the following examples.

(1) {strong, powerful} coffee (Pearce, 2001)

(2) ghastly {error, mistake} (Inkpen, 2007)

(3) {bridge, overpass, tunnel} under the bay (Yu et al., 2010)

Example (1) and (2) present an example of collocational constraints in given contexts. In (1), the word "strong" in the near-synonym set {strong, powerful} is more suitable than "powerful" to fit the given context "coffee", since "powerful coffee" is an anti-collocation. Similarly, in (2), "mistake" is more suitable than "error" because "ghastly mistake" is a collocation and "ghastly error" is an anti-collocation. In (3), the near-synonym set {bridge, overpass, tunnel} represents the meaning of a physical structure that connects separate places by traversing an obstacle. Suppose that the original word in the given context "under the bay" is "tunnel". It can be found that the word "tunnel" cannot be substituted by the other words in the same set because all the substitutions are semantically implausible. The above examples indicate that not all words in a near-synonym set can be substituted with each other even though they share the same or similar meaning. Actually, some near-synonyms may produce inadequate substitutions, which may reduce the applications' effectiveness.

In order to verify whether near-synonyms do match the given contexts, previous studies have formulated the problem of near-synonym choice

English Sentence: This will make the ____ message easier to interpret.
Original word: error
Near-synonym set: {error, mistake, oversight}
Chinese Sentence: 這 將 使 這 ____ 訊息 容易 解釋
Original word: 錯誤
Near-synonym set: {錯誤, 錯, 差錯, 失察, 過失}

Figure 1. Example of the near-synonym choice evaluation for English and Chinese sentences.

as the "fill-in-the-blank" (FITB) task, and evaluated on English sentences (Edmonds, 1997; Inkpen, 2007; Gardiner and Dras, 2007, Islam and Inkpen, 2010). Figure 1 illustrates an example of FITB task on English and Chinese sentences. Given a near-synonym set and a sentence with one of the near-synonyms in it, the near-synonym is removed from the sentence to form a lexical gap. The goal is to predict an answer (best near-synonym) that can fill the gap from the given near-synonym set (including the original word). An evaluation can then be performed to examine whether the involved systems can restore the original word by filling the gap with the best near-synonym. To our best knowledge, there is no such evaluation for Chinese sentences. Therefore, this paper follows the FITB procedure to build a baseline system for Chinese near-synonym choice evaluation. Applications can benefit from such evaluation to provide more effective services. For instance, a writing support system can assist users, especially Chinese as Second Language (CSL) learners, to select a best alternative near-synonym when they have a need to avoid repeating the same word in composing a text.

In the following sections, we first present some previous work on near-synonym choice. Section 3 describes the two baseline systems: pointwise mutual information (PMI) and a 5-gram language model for Chinese near-synonym choice evaluation. Section 4 first introduces the Chinese near-synonym sets and test sets used in experiments, and then shows the evaluation results of the two baseline systems. Conclusions are finally drawn in Section 5.

2 Related Work

In the field of lexical semantics, the contextual information is useful for representing the meaning of words, phrases, as well as sentences (Mitchell and Lapata, 2008; Erk and Pado, 2008; Thater et al., 2010; Ó Séaghdha and Korhonen, 2011; Grefenstette et al., 2011). Therefore, the co-occurrences between a target word (the gap) and its context words have been commonly used in statistical approaches to measuring the substitutability of words. Edmonds (1997) built a lexical co-occurrence network from 1989 Wall Street Journal to determine the near-synonym that is most typical or expected in a given context. Inkpen (2007) used the PMI formula to select the best near-synonym that can fill the gap in a given context. The PMI scores for each candidate near-synonym are computed using a larger web corpus, the Waterloo terabyte corpus, which can alleviate the data sparseness problem encountered in Edmonds' approach. Following Inkpen's approach, Gardiner and Dras (2007) also used the PMI formula with a different corpus (the Web 1T 5-gram corpus) to explore whether near-synonyms differ in attitude.

Islam and Inkpen (2010) also used the Web 1T 5-gram corpus to build a 5-gram language model for near-synonym choice. Yu *et al.* (2010) presented a method to compute the substitution scores for each near-synonym based on n-gram frequencies obtained by querying Google. The dataset used in their experiments are derived from the OntoNotes copus (Hovy et al., 2006; Pradhan et al., 2007; Yu et al., 2008), where each near-synonym set corresponds to a *sense pool* in OntoNotes.

Besides the PMI and n-gram-based methods, another direction is to identify the senses of a target word and its near-synonyms using word sense disambiguation (WSD), comparing whether they were of the same sense (McCarthy, 2002; Dagan et al., 2006). Dagan *et al.* (2006) described that the use of WSD is an indirect approach since it requires the intermediate sense identification step, and thus presented a sense matching technique to address the task directly.

3 Baseline Systems

The baseline systems used for Chinese near-synonym choice are the PMI-based method (Inkpen, 2007; Gardiner and Dras, 2007) and the 5-gram language model (Islam and Inkpen, 2010). We choose these two methods because they are commonly used in previous work.

3.1 PMI-based method

The mutual information can measure the co-occurrence strength between a near-synonym and the words in a given context. A higher mutual information score indicates that the near-synonym fits well in the given context, thus is more likely to be the correct answer. The pointwise mutual information (Church and Hanks, 1991) between two words x and y is defined as

$$PMI(x,y) = \log_2 \frac{P(x,y)}{P(x)P(y)}, \quad (1)$$

where $P(x,y) = C(x,y)/N$ denotes the probability that x and y co-occur; $C(x,y)$ is the number of times x and y co-occur in the corpus, and N is the total number of words in the corpus. Similarly, $P(x) = C(x)/N$, where $C(x)$ is the number of times x occurs in the corpus, and $P(y) = C(y)/N$, where $C(y)$ is the number of times y occurs in the corpus. Therefore, (1) can be re-written as

$$PMI(x,y) = \log_2 \frac{C(x,y) \cdot N}{C(x) \cdot C(y)}. \quad (2)$$

Inkpen (2007) computed the PMI scores for each near-synonym using the Waterloo terabyte corpus and a context window of size $2k$ (k=2). Given a sentence s with a gap, $s = \ldots w_1 \ldots w_k \_\_\_ w_{k+1} \ldots w_{2k} \ldots$, the PMI score for a near-synonym NS_j to fill the gap is defined as

$$PMI(NS_j, s) = \sum_{i=1}^{2k} PMI(NS_j, w_i). \quad (3)$$

The near-synonym with the highest score is considered as the answer. In this paper, we use the Chinese Web 5-gram corpus to compute PMI scores. The frequency counts $C(\cdot)$ are retrieved from this corpus in the same manner within the 5-gram boundary.

3.2 5-gram language model

The n-grams can capture contiguous word associations in given contexts. Given a sentence $s = \ldots w_{i-4} w_{i-3} w_{i-2} w_{i-1} w_i w_{i+1} w_{i-2} w_{i-3} w_{i+4} \ldots$, where w_i represents a near-synonym in a set. In computing the 5-gram scores for each near-synonym, Islam and Inkpen (2010) considers only the five product items $P(w_i | w_{i-4}^{i-1})$, $P(w_{i+1} | w_{i-3}^{i})$, $P(w_{i+2} | w_{i-2}^{i+1})$, $P(w_{i+3} | w_{i-1}^{i+2})$, and $P(w_{i+4} | w_{i}^{i+3})$. The other items are excluded because they do not contain the near-synonym and thus will have the same values. Accordingly, the 5-gram language model (n=5) with a smoothing method can be defined as

$$P(s) = \prod_{i=0}^{5} P(w_i | w_{i-n+1}^{i-1}) = \prod_{i=0}^{5} \frac{C(w_{i-n+1}^{i}) + (1+\alpha_n) M(w_{i-n+1}^{i-1}) P(w_i | w_{i-n+2}^{i-1})}{C(w_{i-n+1}^{i-1}) + \alpha_n M(w_{i-n+1}^{i-1})} \quad (4)$$

where $M(w_{i-n+1}^{i-1})$ denotes a missing count used in the smooth method, defined as

$$M(w_{i-n+1}^{i-1}) = C(w_{i-n+1}^{i-1}) - \sum_{w_i} C(w_{i-n+1}^{i}) \quad (5)$$

where $C(\cdot)$ denotes an n-gram frequency, which can be retrieved from the Chinese Web 5-gram corpus. Additionally, the 5-gram language model is implemented as a back-off model. That is, if the frequency of a higher-order n-gram is zero, then its lower-order n-grams will be considered. Conversely, if the frequency of a higher-order n-gram is not zero, then the lower-order n-grams will not be included in computation.

4 Experimental Results

4.1 Experiment setup

1) Chinese near-synonym sets: Since there is no standard dataset for Chinese near-synonym sets, we created seven Chinese near-synonym sets based on the seven English near-synonym sets used as the standard dataset in the previous studies (Edmonds, 1997; Inkpen, 2007; Gardiner and Dras, 2007, Islam and Inkpen, 2010). For each English near-synonym set, we first identified its corresponding senses (entries) in the Chinese WordNet (CWN) (Huang et al., 2008). Each corresponding Chinese near-synonym set

	Near-Synonym sets	Sinica Corpus		News Corpus		All	
		PMI	5GRAM	PMI	5GRAM	PMI	5GRAM
1	難懂的, 困難的, 艱難的, 艱苦的 (difficult, hard, tough)	67.14%	**70.32%**	71.51%	71.51%	68.83%	**70.78%**
2	錯誤, 錯, 差錯, 失察, 過失 (error, mistake, oversight)	**67.25%**	52.64%	**60.13%**	54.22%	**63.58%**	53.46%
3	任務, 工作, 義務 (job, task, duty)	65.08%	**76.43%**	67.62%	**70.91%**	66.54%	**73.26%**
4	責任, 職責, 職務, 約定 (responsibility, burden, obligation, commitment)	50.03%	**68.05%**	**56.79%**	56.67%	54.41%	**60.67%**
5	質料, 物質, 材料 (material, stuff, substance)	**72.98%**	59.84%	**75.90%**	65.32%	**74.09%**	61.92%
6	給, 給予, 給與, 供應, 供給 (give, provide, offer)	**69.39%**	65.89%	51.88%	**58.11%**	60.59%	**61.98%**
7	決定, 定奪, 終結, 確定 (settle, resolve)	61.43%	**71.97%**	60.59%	**72.35%**	60.85%	**72.23%**
	Average	65.20%	**70.05%***	61.38%	**66.62%***	62.99%	**68.07%***
	Number of test cases	26,504		36,427		62,931	

* Statistically significant ($p < 0.05$) using *Binomial Exact Text*

Table 1. Accuracy of PMI and 5GRAM on different test sets.

can then be created by selecting the Chinese translations of the identified entries in the Chinese WordNet. Table 1 shows the seven Chinese near-synonym sets.

2) Test set: The test sentences containing the near-synonyms were selected from two corpora: the Sinica Corpus and Chinese News Corpus, released by the Association for Computational Linguistics and Chinese Language Processing (ACLCLP). If a test sentence contained two (or more) near-synonyms, then this sentence was divided into two (or more) test examples. The near-synonyms were then removed from the test examples for FITB evaluation.

3) Implementation of baseline systems: The two baseline system, PMI and 5GRAM, were implemented using the (3) and (4), respectively. For PMI, the size of the context window k was set to 2. For 5GRAM, only the 5-gram with a near-synonym in the middle position of each test example was selected the s for testing.

4) Evaluation metric: The answers proposed by PMI and 5GRAM are the near-synonyms with the highest score. The correct answers are the near-synonyms originally in the gap of the test examples. The performance is measure by the accuracy, which is defined as the number of correct answers made by each baseline system, divided by the total number of test examples.

4.2 Evaluation results

Table 1 shows the evaluation results of Chinese near-synonym choice using PMI and 5GRAM. The results show that 5GRAM achieved better performance than PMI on both test corpora. In comparison with the results on the seven English near-synonym sets, previous studies reported that the accuracy of PMI and the 5-gram language model were 66.0 (Inkpen, 2007) and 69.9 (Islam and Inkpen, 2010), respectively, which was greater than 62.99 and 68.07 reported in Table 1. One possible reason is that the total number of near-synonyms in the seven Chinese near-synonyms sets is 28 and the average is 4 for each set, and that in the seven English near-synonyms sets is 21 and the average is 3 for each set. More near-synonyms in a set may decrease systems' ability to discriminate among near-synonyms.

5 Conclusion

This work has presented the use of the PMI and 5-gram language model for Chinese near-synonym choice. Additionally, this work has also created seven Chinese near-synonym sets based on the standard dataset of the seven English near-synonym sets. Experimental results show that the 5-gram language model that can capture contiguous word associations in given contexts achieved higher accuracy than PMI.

Acknowledgement

This work was supported by National Science Council, Taiwan, R.O.C (NSC99-2221-E-155-036-MY3 and NSC100-2632-S-155-001), and Aim for the Top University Plan, Ministry of Education, Taiwan, R.O.C. The authors would like to thank the anonymous reviewers and the area chairs for their constructive comments.

References

J. Bhogal, A. Macfarlane, and P. Smith. 2007. A Review of Ontology based Query Expansion. *Information Processing & Management*, 43(4):866-886.

C. C. Cheng. 2004. Word-Focused Extensive Reading with Guidance. In *Proc. of the 13th International Symposium on English Teaching*, pages 24-32.

K. Church and P. Hanks. 1991. Word Association Norms, Mutual Information and Lexicography. *Computational Linguistics*, 16(1):22-29.

I. Dagan, O. Glickman, A. Gliozzo, E. Marmorshtein, and C. Strapparava. 2006. Direct Word Sense Matching for Lexical Substitution. In *Proc. of COLING/ACL-06*, pages 449-456.

P. Edmonds. 1997. Choosing the Word Most Typical in Context Using a Lexical Co-occurrence Network. In *Proc. of ACL-97*, pages 507-509.

K. Erk and S. Pad´o. 2008. A Structured Vector Space Model for Word Meaning in Context. In *Proc. of EMNLP-08*, pages 897-906.

M. Gardiner and M. Dras. 2007. Exploring Approaches to Discriminating among Near-Synonyms, In *Proc. of the Australasian Technology Workshop*, pages 31-39.

E. Grefenstette, M. Sadrzadeh, S. Clark, B. Coecke, and S. Pulman. 2011. Concrete Sentence Spaces for Compositional Distributional Models of Meaning. In *Proc. of IWCS-11*, pages 125-134.

E. H. Hovy, M. Marcus, M. Palmer, L. Ramshaw, and R. Weischedel. 2006. OntoNotes: The 90% Solution. In *Proc. of HLT/NAACL-06*, pages 57–60.

C. R. Huang, S. K. Hsieh, J. F. Hong, Y. Z. Chen, I. L. Su, Y. X. Chen and S. W. Huang. 2008. Chinese Wordnet: Design, Implementation, and Application of an Infrastructure for Cross-lingual Knowledge Processing. In *Proc. of the 9th Chinese Lexical Semantics Workshop*.

D. Inkpen. 2007. A Statistical Model of Near-Synonym Choice. *ACM Trans. Speech and Language Processing*, 4(1):1-17.

D. Inkpen and G. Hirst. 2006. Building and Using a Lexical Knowledge-base of Near-Synonym Differences. *Computational Linguistics*, 32(2):1-39.

A. Islam and D. Inkpen. 2010. Near-Synonym Choice using a 5-gram Language Model. *Research in Computing Science: Special issue on Natural Language Processing and its Applications*, Alexander Gelbukh (ed.), 46: 41-52.

D. McCarthy. 2002. Lexical Substitution as a Task for WSD Evaluation. In *Proc. of the SIGLEX/SENSEVAL Workshop on Word Sense Disambiguation at ACL-02*, pages 109-115.

J. Mitchell and M. Lapata. 2008. Vector-based Models of Semantic Composition. In *Proc. of ACL-08*, pages 234-244.

D. Moldovan and R. Mihalcea. 2000. Using Wordnet and Lexical Operators to Improve Internet Searches. *IEEE Internet Computing*, 4(1):34-43.

D. Ó Séaghdha and A. Korhonen. 2011. Probabilistic Models of Similarity in Syntactic Context. In *Proc. of EMNLP-11*, pages 1047-1057.

S. Ouyang, H. H. Gao, and S. N. Koh. 2009. Developing a Computer-Facilitated Tool for Acquiring Near-Synonyms in Chinese and English. In *Proc. of IWCS-09*, pages 316-319.

D. Pearce. 2001. Synonymy in Collocation Extraction. In *Proc. of the Workshop on WordNet and Other Lexical Resources at NAACL-01*.

S. Pradhan, E. H. Hovy, M. Marcus, M. Palmer, L. Ramshaw, and R. Weischedel. 2007. OntoNotes: A Unified Relational Semantic Representation. In *Proc. of ICSC-07*, pages 517-524.

S. Thater, H. Fürstenau, and M. Pinkal. 2010. Contextualizing Semantic Representations Using Syntactically Enriched Vector Models. In *Proc. of ACL-10*, pages 948-957.

C. H. Wu, C. H. Liu, H. Matthew, and L. C. Yu. 2010. Sentence Correction Incorporating Relative Position and Parse Template Language Models. *IEEE Trans. Audio, Speech and Language Processing*, 18(6):1170-1181.

L. C. Yu, C. H. Wu, R. Y. Chang, C. H. Liu, and E. H. Hovy. 2010. Annotation and Verification of Sense Pools in OntoNotes. *Information Processing & Management*, 46(4):436-447.

L. C. Yu, C. H. Wu, E. H. Hovy. 2008. OntoNotes: Corpus Cleanup of Mistaken Agreement Using Word Sense Disambiguation. In *Proc. of COLING-08*, pages 1057-1064.

Cluster Labeling based on Concepts in a Machine-Readable Dictionary

Fumiyo Fukumoto
Interdisciplinary Graduate School of
Medicine and Engineering
Univ. of Yamanashi
fukumoto@yamanashi.ac.jp

Yoshimi Suzuki
Interdisciplinary Graduate School of
Medicine and Engineering
Univ. of Yamanashi
ysuzuki@yamanashi.ac.jp

Abstract

This paper addresses the issue of cluster labeling and presents a method for assigning labels by using concepts in a machine-readable dictionary. We assume that salient terms in the cluster content have the same hypernym because hypernymic semantic relation represents a generalization that goes from specific to generic. Our experimental results reveal that hypernymic semantic relations can be exploited to increase labeling accuracy, as the results of 0.441 F-score improves over the two baselines.

1 Introduction

With the exponential growth of information on the Internet, finding and organizing relevant materials on the Internet is becoming increasingly difficult. Internet directories such as Yahoo! and Google, which classify Web pages into pre-defined hierarchical categories, provide one solution to the problem. Categories in the hierarchical structures are carefully defined by human experts and documents are well-organized. However, manual category-tagging is extremely costly. Moreover, categories on some Internet is often insufficient in finding relevant documents for users. Because these categories tend to have some bias in both defining and classifying documents. Cluster labeling is one of the techniques to attack the problem.

Most of the work on cluster labeling identifies salient terms in the cluster content that characterize the cluster in contrast to other clusters. Salient terms are extracted by using statistical feature selection, *e.g.*, maximum sum of the individual term frequencies of documents assigned to a cluster (Cutting et al., 1992), an adapted versions of Information Gain (Geraci et al., 2007), χ^2 method (Popescul and Ungar, 2000), and the Jensen-Shannon Divergence (Camel et al., 2009). Other works based on salient terms are frequent phrases by (Osinski and Weiss, 2005), and integration of hierarchical information by (Muhr et al., 2010). However, the suggested terms, even when related to each other, tend to represent different aspects of the topic underlying the cluster, and it is often the case that a good label does not occur directly in the document. Carmel *et. al* addressed the issue and presented a method to use Wikipedia as an external knowledge. They showed the effectiveness of the method. However, Wikipedia is the free online encyclopedia, and everyone can access and edit the information. Therefore, it is often included noise information such as categories which do not characterize the cluster in the pages. Chin *et. al* presented a method to use WordNet (Chin et al., 2006). They used machine learning through extending the given term set with synonyms, hypernyms, hyponyms and so on. However, their method needs training data to determine the actual weights. Through supervised training in the labeling process the actual influence of synonyms, hypernyms, hyponyms information remains unclear.

This paper focuses on cluster labeling, and presents a method for assigning labels automatically by using concepts in a machine-readable dictionary. Similar to Chin *et. al* work, we focused on semantic relation in a dictionary, namely hypernymic semantic relation that represents a generalization, *i.e.*, goes from specific to generic (Fellbaum, 1998), and used it in the cluster labeling process. We assume that salient terms in the cluster content have the same hypernym in a hierarchical structure of a dictionary. The hypernym represents generic concepts of a set of documents, thus can be a label of a cluster.

2 Cluster Labeling

The procedure for cluster labeling consists of four steps: documents clustering, term weighting, hypernym extraction, and ranking labels.

2.1 Documents clustering

The first step is to classify documents into a set with semantically similar documents. In the document clustering, we do not know how many clusters there are in a given input documents. Moreover, the algorithm should allow each data point to belong to more than one cluster because of multi-label classification. We used a graph-based unsupervised clustering technique developed by (Reichardt and Bomholdt, 2006); we call this the RB algorithm. This algorithm detects the node configuration that minimizes the energy of the material. The energy function, called the Hamiltonian, for assignment of nodes into communities clusters together those that are linked, and keeps separate those that are not by rewarding internal edges between different clusters. Here, "community" or "cluster" have in common that they are groups of densely interconnected nodes that are only sparsely connected with the rest of the network. Only local information is used to update the nodes which makes parallelization of the algorithm straightforward and allows the application to very large networks. Moreover, comparing global and local minima of the energy function allows the detection of overlapping nodes. Reichardt et al. evaluated their method by applying several data including a large protein folding network, and reported that the algorithm successfully detected overlapping nodes (Reichardt and Bornholdt, 2004). We thus used the algorithm to cluster documents. Let d_i $(1 \leq i \leq n)$ be a document in the input, and σ_i be a label assigned to the cluster in which d_i is placed. The Hamiltonian H is defined as:

$$H(\{\sigma_i\}) = -\sum_{i<j}(A_{ij}(\theta) - \gamma p_{ij})\delta_{\sigma_i\sigma_j}. \quad (1)$$

δ denotes the Kronecker delta. The function $A_{ij}(\theta)$ refers to the adjacency matrix of the graph, which is defined as:

$$A_{ij}(\theta) = \begin{cases} 1 & \text{if } sim(d_i, d_j) > 0 \\ 0 & \text{otherwise.} \end{cases} \quad (2)$$

$sim(d_i, d_j)$ in Eq (2) refers to cosine similarity between d_i and d_j. The matrix p_{ij} in Eq. (1) denotes the probability that a link exists between d_i and d_j, and is defined as:

$$p_{ij} = \sum_{i<j} \frac{A_{ij}(\theta)}{N(N-1)/2}, \quad (3)$$

where N refers to the number of documents and $\frac{N(N-1)}{2}$ is the total number of document pairs. As the parameter γ in Eq. (1) increases, each document is distributed into larger number of clusters. Eq. (1) thus shows comparison of the actual values of internal or external edges with its respective expectation value under the assumption of equally probable links and given data sizes. The minima of the Hamiltonian H are obtained by simulated annealing (Kirkpatrick et al., 1983). We applied simulated annealing for T runs [1].

2.2 Term weighting

For the results of clustering, we extracted salient terms from each clusters obtained by the RB algorithm. We tested four metrics which are commonly used as feature selection, *i.e.*, TF∗IDF, mutual information, χ^2 statistics, and information gain. The terms we used are noun words in the documents. Each term is scored according to its contribution to the metrics between the cluster and other clusters. The top k scored terms are then selected as a candidate of the cluster salient terms.

2.3 Hypernym extraction

The third step is to extract hypernym for each term selected by term weighting method. We used Japanese word and concept dictionaries of EDR [2]. The word dictionary consists of 270,000 words. Each word has concept identifier as well as lexical and grammatical information. The concept identifier is to identify words and their concepts. The concept dictionary consists of 410,000 concepts. Each concept is linked to other concepts, and the link is a relation between concepts, namely super-sub relation. We used this super-sub relation as hypernymic semantic relation. Let $W = \{w_1, w_2, \cdots, w_n\}$ be a set of words in a cluster selected by feature selection. For each pair of words, w_i and w_j, we identified its hypernym c_k by using Eq. (4).

$$c_k = hy(w_i) \cap hy(w_j) \quad (4)$$

where $hy(w_i)$ and $hy(w_j)$ satisfy $min(dis(hy(w_i), w_i))$ and $min(dis(hy(w_j), w_j))$, respectively. In Eq. (4), $hy(x)$ refers to the hypernym of a word x. $min(dis(hy(w_i), w_i))$ shows the minimum distance between $hy(w_i)$ and w_i. We extracted hypernym by using Eq. (4), and regarded these as label candidates.

[1] We set T to 1,000 in the experiments

[2] http://www2.nict.go.jp/r/r312/EDR/index.html

Second level	Third level	Fourth level
sports	gymnastics	winter ski
music	opera	song
medicine	pharmacy	pharmaceuticals
education	school	teacher
architecture	house	flat
nature	environment	lebensraum
plants	botany	dicots
religion	religion in India	Buddhism
military	national defense	army
earth	geology	geomorphology
organism	anthropology	anthropologist
economy	labour	labour market
management	post	mail service
agriculture	animal care	poultry
animals	zoology	animal physiology
international law	UN	UNSC
finance	stock	bond

Table 1: Categories

2.4 Ranking Labels

The final step for cluster labeling is to rank label candidates according to their scores. The score of candidate c is obtained by using Eq. (5).

$$Score(c) = -\log \frac{freq\_p(c)}{N} \quad (5)$$

where $N = \frac{1}{freq\_p(w_i)+freq\_p(w_j)}$. w_i and w_j are words selected by feature selection. $freq\_p(x)$ is the number of senses that the word x has.

3 Experiments

3.1 Data

We used two types of test data: one is a collection that correct labels occur directly in the documents. Another is that a label does not appear in the documents. The data we used is RWCP corpus labeled with UDC codes selected from 1994 Mainichi newspaper (RWC, 1998). It consists of 27,755 documents organized into fine-grained categories, 9,951 categories with a seven-level hierarchy. We used categories/labels assigned to the second, third and fourth level of a hierarchy, each of which has more than five documents [3]. Each level consists of 17 categories shown in Table 1. For each category, we randomly selected five documents, and created each type of test data. We extracted the top 20 scored words by term weighting as a candidate of the cluster salient terms.

[3] We did not use categories assigned to the top level, as it was defined by only one label.

	RB						EM		
Level	γ	θ	C	Prec	Rec	F	Prec	Rec	F
2nd	.1	.8	12	.601	.673	.635	.583	.673	.625
3rd	.9	.9	9	.620	.703	.659	.500	.742	.598
4th	1.0	.2	9	.398	.647	.493	.333	.633	.437
Avg	–	–	10	.539	.674	.595	.472	.682	.553

Table 2: Clustering Results

3.2 Clustering accuracy

For each category, we randomly selected five documents and created a training data to estimate two parameters, γ and θ. We represented each document as a vector of noun word frequencies, and applied RB algorithm. For evaluation of document clustering, we used F-score, especially to capture how many documents does the algorithm actually detect more than just one category. Precision was defined by the percentage of documents appearing in the correct clusters compared to the number of documents appearing in any cluster, and recall was defined by the percentage of documents within the correct clusters compared to the total number of documents to be clustered. For comparison of clustering algorithm, we used the EM algorithm that is widely used as a soft clustering technique(Nock et al., 2009). We set the initial probabilities by using the result of k-means clustering, where k is set to the number of correct clusters,1 7. We used up to 30 iterations to learn the model probabilities. The results are shown in Table 2.

Table 2 shows average performance between two types of test data. γ and θ in Table 2 denote the values that maximized the F-score obtained by using the training data. "C" refers to the number of clusters obtained by RB. The overall results obtained by the RB algorithm were better to those obtained by the EM algorithm regardless of the level of a hierarchy.

3.3 Labeling accuracy

We tested two types of document collection. For evaluation of cluster labeling, we used 11-point average precision. For comparison of the method, we used two baselines: (i) a feature selection by TF$*$IDF, and (ii) the use of Wikipedia for labeling. The method using Wikipedia is based on (Camel et al., 2009) [4]. The difference is that we used RB for clustering, and TF$*$IDF to extract salient

[4] We used Wikipedia downloaded from http://download.wikimedia.org.jawiki.

Level	Labels are included						Labels are not included				
	EDR				TF∗IDF	Wiki	EDR				Wiki
	TF∗IDF	MI	χ^2	IG			TF∗IDF	MI	χ^2	IG	
Second	0.460	0.318	0.281	0.288	0.150	0.236	0.500	0.304	0.288	0.272	0.153
Third	0.533	0.276	0.281	0.396	0.220	0.187	0.523	0.340	0.334	0.343	0.140
Fourth	0.310	0.254	0.214	0.256	0.183	0.194	0.299	0.262	0.193	0.220	0.142
Average	**0.434**	0.283	0.259	0.284	**0.184**	**0.206**	**0.441**	0.302	0.272	0.278	**0.145**

Table 3: The results of cluster labeling

Second level	Third level	Fourth level
vertebrate, life-form	**contest, sport**	**ski, athlete**
music, opera	**music, opera**	**song, music**
sick, hypofunction	sick, food	sick, antibiotic
book, building	rule, human	guide, rule
cook, **building**	**building**, activity	**building**, activity
nature, natural phenomenon	think, information	study, phenomenon
plants,botany	**botany, tree**	animals and plants, animal
religion, human	**belief, statue**	life, plants
reader, staff	**military, military affairs**	**military, army**
earth, planet	**geology**, message	**geology**, loss
organism, life	**life anthropology**	human, animal
economy social economy	**labour, worker**	**labour market, market**
management, organization	money, market	information, service
agriculture, vegetables	food, cook	care vegetables
animals, mammals	zoo, plant	care, food
international law, law	**UN**, USA	**UNSC**, society
bank, money	**stock, share**	**bond**, market

Table 4: Lists of top 2 terms (The top 20 term weighting scored terms)

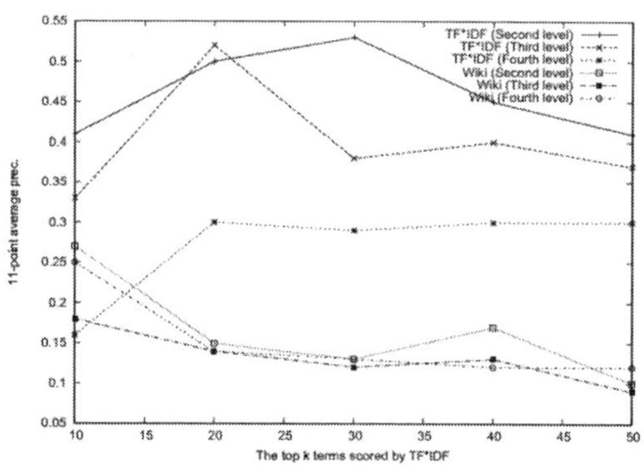

Figure 1: Performance against the top k terms

terms. The results are shown in Table 3. As can be seen clearly from Table 3, the results obtained by concepts based method were better than TF∗IDF and Wikipedia in both types of data. The results obtained by concepts based method show that there is no significant difference between two types of data, while the results by Wikipedia go down when we tested data that correct labels do not occur in the documents. This shows that the use of concepts in a dictionary improves overall performance. Table 4 shows a list of top 2 terms identified by concepts based method. Bold font terms are correctly identified by the method. Table 4 shows that more than half of the terms are correctly identified in the second and third level of a hierarchy.

We note that we set the number of scored terms to 20. To examine how the number of scored terms affects the overall performance, we performed an experiment by varying the values. Figure 1 shows performance plots against the top k terms scored by TF∗IDF. The best performance by both methods was around the top 20 terms scored by TF∗IDF term weighting method. The larger the number of scored terms becomes low precision. This is reasonable because a good label for a cluster generally consists of a few words.

4 Conclusions

We focused on cluster labeling, and presented a method for assigning labels by using concepts in a machine readable dictionary. Comparison with baselines showed improvements regardless of the level of a hierarchy. Future work will include: (i) incorporating hierarchical structure of documents, and (ii) applying the method to other data and thesaurus such as ODP dataset and WordNet.

Acknowledgement

The authors would like to thank the referees for their comments on the earlier version of this paper. This work was partially supported by the Telecommunications Advancement Foundation.

References

D. Camel, E. Yom-Tov, A. Darlow, and d. Pelleg. 2009. What Makes a Query Difficult? In *Proc. of the 32rd International ACM SIGIR Conference on Research and Development in Information Retrieval*, pages 139–146.

O. S. Chin, N. Kulathuramaiyer, and A. W. Yeo. 2006. Automatic Discovery of Concepts from Text. In *Proc. of the 2006 IEEE/WIC/ACM International Conference on Web Intelligence*, pages 1046–1049.

D. R. Cutting, J. O. Pedersen, D. Karger, and J. W. Tukey. 1992. Scatter/ gather: A Cluster-based Approach to Browsing Large Document Collections. In *Proc. of the 15th Annual International ACM SIGIR Conference on Research and Development in Information Retrieval*, pages 318–329.

C. Fellbaum. 1998. *An WordNet Electronic Lexical Database*. The MIT Press.

E. Gabrilovich and S. Markovitch. 2007. Computing Semantic Relatedness using Wikipedia-based Explicit Semantic Analysis. In *Proc. of the 20th International Joint Conference on Artificial Intelligence*, pages 1606–1611.

F. Geraci, M. Pellegrini, m. Maggini, and F. Sebastiani. 2007. Cluster Generation and Labeling for Web Snippets: A Fast, Accurate Hierarchical Solution. *Internet Mathematics*, 3(4):413–443.

S. Kirkpatrick, C. G. Jr., and M. Vecchi. 1983. Optimization by simulated annealing. *Science*, 220(4598):671–680.

M. Muhr, R. Kern, and M. Granitzer. 2010. Analysis of Structural Relationships for Hierarchical Cluster Labeling. In *Proc. of the 33rd International ACM SIGIR Conference on Research and Development in Information Retrieval*, pages 19–23.

R. Nock, P. Vaillant, C. Henry, and F. Nielsen. 2009. Soft Membershipfs for Spectral Clustering with Application to Premeable Language Distinction. *Pattern Recognition*, 42:43–53.

S. Osinski and D. Weiss. 2005. A Concept-Driven Algorithm for Clustering Search Results. *IEEE Intelligent Systems*, 20(3):48–54.

A. Popescul and L. H. Ungar. 2000. Automatic Labeling of Document Clusters.

J. Reichardt and S. Bomholdt. 2006. Statistical Mechanics of Community Detection. *PHYSICAL REVIEW E*, 74.

J. Reichardt and S. Bornholdt. 2004. Detecting Fuzzy Community Structure in Complex Networks with a Potts Model. *PHYSICAL REVIEW LETTERS*, 93(21).

RWC. 1998. *RWC Text Database*. In Real World Computing Partnership.

Z. S. Syed, T. Finin, and A. Joshi. 2008. Wikipedia as an Ontology for Describing Documents. In *Proc. of the International Conference on Weblogs and Social Media 2008*, pages 136–144.

Text Patterns and Compression Models for Semantic Class Learning

Chung-Yao Chuang
Institute of Information Science
Academia Sinica, Taiwan
cychuang@iis.sinica.edu.tw

Yi-Hsun Lee
Institute of Information Science
Academia Sinica, Taiwan
rog@iis.sinica.edu.tw

Wen-Lian Hsu
Institute of Information Science
Academia Sinica, Taiwan
hsu@iis.sinica.edu.tw

Abstract

This paper proposes a weakly-supervised approach for extracting instances of semantic classes. This method constructs simple wrappers automatically based on specified seed instances and uses a compression model to assess the contextual evidence of its extraction. By adopting this compression model, our approach can better avoid erroneous extractions in a noisy corpus such as the Web. The empirical results show that our system performs quite consistently even when operating on a noisy text with a lot of possibly irrelevant documents.

1 Introduction

Extracting instances of semantic classes is a fundamental task in natural language processing (NLP). Such a task aims to extract instances belonging to a specific category such as acquiring *Tom Hanks* and *Al Pacino* into a list containing other actors. This kind of information serves as building blocks for various NLP tasks. For example, major search engines such as Yahoo and Google gather large amount of such classes (Paşca, 2007; Chaudhuri et al., 2009) to better interpret queries and provide search suggestions. Other applications include ontology learning (Cimiano et al., 2004), co-reference resolution (McCarthy and Lehnert, 1995) and advertisement matching (Chang et al., 2009).

Most of the approaches for this task can be roughly classified into two categories: distributional and pattern-based. The distributional approaches use contextual similarity to model the instances of a given class. Following the distributional hypothesis (Harris, 1970), these methods take a small set of seed instances and generate new instances from noun phrases that are most similar to the seeds in terms of the distributions of surrounding words (Sarmento et al., 2007; Pantel et al., 2009).

The pattern-based approaches use text patterns to extract instances of a given semantic class (Riloff and Shepherd, 1997; Riloff and Jones, 1999; Banko et al., 2007; Paşca, 2007). The most representative study is the group of patterns proposed by Hearst (1992). For example, patterns like '*X such as Y*' and '*X including Y*' can be applied to extract instances from '*actors such as Tom Hanks*' and '*countries including Japan*'. In these approaches, semantic classes are specified by providing small sets of seed instances or seed patterns such as (Kozareva et al., 2008) which utilized a single hyponym pattern combined with graph structure to extract semantic lexicons from the Web. In addition to natural language patterns, Wang and Cohen (2007) demonstrated an approach that learns the pattern of specific meta-structure of the document (e.g., tags in HTML) automatically from seed instances.

In this paper, we propose a method similar to (Kozareva et al., 2008) and (Wang and Cohen, 2007) in that it also employs graph ranking algorithm to assess the reliability of the extracted candidates and uses the Web as the source of extraction. Different from them, the wrappers we induced from web pages are less specific and do not contain any structural cues such as HTML tags. In our approach, those wrappers serve primarily as a means to bracket candidate mentions. The main discriminative power resides in adopting a text compression model called Prediction by Partial Matching (PPM) (Cleary and Witten, 1984) to evaluate the contextual similarity between a mention and seed instances. The similarity is measured by compression ratio achieved when compressing the surrounding context of the mention using the PPM model loaded with context statistics of seed instances. In this work, we focused on assessing the effectiveness of such measurement and this effort can potentially be extended to systems that adopt more elaborated text patterns.

The rest of this paper is organized as follows. Section 2 briefly describe the PPM compression model. In section 3, we detail the idea of using compression ratio as similarity measure. Section 4 outlines our approach. Section 5 shows the results of experiments and section 6 concludes this paper.

2 Prediction by Partial Matching

In this work, we use the Prediction by Partial Matching (PPM) compression scheme (Cleary and Witten, 1984) which has become a benchmark in the lossless text compression. It generates "predictions" for each input token in turn. Each prediction takes the form of a probability distribution that is provided to an encoder, which is usually an arithmetic coder. However, the details of actual coding technique are of no relevance to this paper.

PPM can be seen as an n-gram approach that uses finite-context models of tokens, where the previous few tokens predict the upcoming one. The conditional probability distribution of tokens, conditioned on the preceding context, is maintained and updated as each token of input is processed. This distribution, along with the the preceding few input tokens, is used to predict each upcoming token. Exactly the same distributions are maintained by the decoder, which updates the appropriate distribution as each token is received.

Rather than using a fixed context length, the PPM chooses a maximum context length, say ℓ, and maintains statistics for this and all shorter contexts. To combine these statistics, for each upcoming token, the PPM starts with the order ℓ model. If that model contains a prediction for the token, the token is encoded according to the order ℓ model. Otherwise, both encoder and decoder *escape* down to order $\ell - 1$. There are two possible situations. If the order ℓ context has not been encountered before, then escaping to order $\ell - 1$ is inevitable, and both encoder and decoder can arrive at that fact without any communication. On the other hand, if the preceding ℓ tokens have been encountered in sequence before but not followed by the upcoming character, then only the encoder knows that an escape is necessary. In this case, it must signal the decoder by transmitting an *escape event*. Thus, space must be reserved for this event in every probability distribution that encoder and decoder maintain.

Once any necessary escape event has been transmitted and received, both encoder and decoder agree that the upcoming token will be coded by $\ell - 1$ order model. Of course, this may not be possible either, and further escapes may take place. Ultimately, the order 0 model may be reached; in this case, the token can be encoded if it has occurred before. Otherwise, there is one further escape, and both encoder and decoder will agree that the token itself will be literally transmitted.

There is one remaining question regarding this backoff strategy: how much space to preserve for the escape probability. In this work, we assign the escape probability in particular context as

$$\frac{\frac{1}{2}d}{n}$$

where n is the number of times that context has appeared and d is the number of different tokens that have directly followed it. And the probability of a token that has occurred c times in that context before is

$$\frac{c - \frac{1}{2}}{n}$$

This allocation strategy is called PPMD (Howard, 1993) and has shown great performance in text compression. Once the token has been processed, the model will be updated to include this context-to-token prediction.

Most of the discourses of PPM were on character-based compression, although the above backoff strategy can be equally applied to other class of symbols such as words. Previous experiments with a wide range of English text has shown that word-based models consistently outperform the character-based counterpart (Teahan and Cleary, 1997). In this work, we adopt the word-based model for our task. A more comprehensive description of the PPM algorithm can be found in (Bell et al., 1990).

3 Compression Ratio as Similarity

In this work, we use the compression ratio as a measure of similarity between the context of a mention and the contexts of seed instances. More specifically, this ratio is defined as

$$\frac{\lambda_M(\mathbf{x})}{\lambda_B(\mathbf{x})}$$

where $\mathbf{x}$ is the sequence of words surrounding the mention, $\lambda_B(\mathbf{x})$ is the code length of $\mathbf{x}$ encoded by a blank PPM, i.e., the PPM without any context statistics pre-loaded. And $\lambda_M(\mathbf{x})$ is the code length of $\mathbf{x}$ compressed by the model M which loaded with the context statistics of seed instances, i.e., the model that has run through the contexts collected from the vicinity of seed instances observed in the corpus.

The encoding of a token x_i in $\mathbf{x} = x_1x_2\cdots x_n$ is based on the probability predicted by the PPM, which conditioned on the preceding tokens $\mathbf{y_i} = \cdots x_{i-2}x_{i-1}$. Let p_M and p_B be the probabilities predicted by those two models, from an information theoretic perspective, the above ratio can be interpreted as follows,

$$\frac{\lambda_M(\mathbf{x})}{\lambda_B(\mathbf{x})} = \frac{\sum_{i=1}^{n} -log_2 p_M(x_i|\mathbf{y_i})}{\sum_{i=1}^{n} -log_2 p_B(x_i|\mathbf{y_i})} = \frac{-log_2 \prod_{i=1}^{n} p_M(x_i|\mathbf{y_i})}{-log_2 \prod_{i=1}^{n} p_B(x_i|\mathbf{y_i})}$$

which is the log-likelihood ratio. Intuitively, this ratio gives an estimate of how much better M predicts $\mathbf{x}$ compared to the prediction without any prior assumptions. And the more effective the prediction, the more similar $\mathbf{x}$ and the contexts of seed instances, which M was built upon.

Leveraging this concept, we can filter possibly irrelevant mentions by comparing the ratio to a threshold θ. More specifically, we test whether

$$\frac{\lambda_M(\mathbf{x})}{\lambda_B(\mathbf{x})} > \theta \qquad (1)$$

If this inequality holds, we skip the corresponding mention. In this work, we adopt $\theta = 0.3$, which empirically gives a good performance.

4 Proposed Approach

Our approach is outlined in Algorithm 1. The procedure starts at collecting the contexts of seed instances observed in the corpus and making wrappers based on these occurrences. In this work, a wrapper is constructed as a regular expression of two tokens[1] preceding and one or two tokens following a seed occurrence depending on what next to the occurrence is a punctuation or word. The collected contexts are then fed into a PPM. Utilizing this PPM, we filter the mentions according to Inequality 1. Following that, a graph G is build based on the wrappers and remaining mentions. In this graph, a vertex represents either a wrapper or a mention, and an edge denotes a captured-by or produced-by relationship. The vertices in G are then ranked by graph ranking algorithm. In this work, we adopt RageRank with Prior (White and Smyth, 2003). Finally, we obtain a list of mentions according to the vertices ranking in G.

[1]A token means a word or a punctuation.

Algorithm 1 The Proposed Approach

Input: A set of seed instances S and corpus C
Output: A ranked list of extracted instances

```
W = φ, T = φ
for each s in S do
    for each occurrence of s in C do
        Make a wrapper and add it into W.
        Collect the surrounding text into T.
    end for
end for
Build a PPM M based on T.
for each w in W do
    for each mention in C captured by w do
        x ← text surrounding this mention
        if λ_M(x)/λ_B(x) > θ then
            Skip this mention.
        end if
    end for
end for
Construct a wrapper-mention graph G.
Rank the vertices in G by graph random walk.
return ranked list of mentions.
```

5 Experiment Settings and Results

In this work, the experiments are designed to evaluate the effectiveness of the proposed filtering strategy in learning semantic classes. The proposed approach is compared with a baseline counterpart which runs *without* the filtering mechanism. A noted impediment (McIntosh and Curran, 2009) to a fair evaluation is that the same seeds used to initiate the algorithms can cause different algorithms to generate diverse lexicons which vary greatly in precision. This makes evaluation unreliable — seeds which perform well on one algorithm can perform poorly on another.

To conduct a fair comparison, we adopt a bagging approach which resembles to the one used by McIntosh and Curran (2009) to aggregate the results over 30 runs for each algorithm. In each run, our system uses three seeds randomly selected from a set of ten prepared instances. The resulting 30 lexicons are then merged by a weighted voting function which is based on two hypotheses of the ranked lexicons: firstly, the candidates ranked higher in lexicons are considered more reliable; secondly, this ranking evidence can be better supported if a run extracted more candidates. More specifically, for each run, the candidate extracted with the r-th rank is assigned with a score by

$$S_c(r) = \frac{m}{log(r)}$$

in which m is the number of candidates extracted in this run. This score is averaged over all lexicons in which the candidate is listed.

In this work, we evaluated the algorithms on nine semantic classes as listed in Table 1. In each run, the systems operate on 50 web pages retrieved from Google by submitting a query containing three seed instances. To further test the ability of the filtering mechanism, we also conducted experiments which added another 500 web pages gathered from `reddit.com`[2] into the original retrieval to simulate a noisy source.

It can be observed from the results that the proposed approach consistently outperforms the baseline system and maintains the precision better as the evaluation includes more instances. Moreover, the results of experiments that includes noise web pages further demonstrate the effectiveness of the filtering mechanism. In those experiments, the baseline system often exhibits a performance drop compared to the results obtained without the additional noise web pages. On the other hand, the proposed approach displays a consistent performance regardless whether there is additional noise or not. This shows that the filtering mechanism does help the overall performance and is better in preventing erroneous extractions.

Class	Method	Noise	Precision @ 25	50	75	100
Actor Actress	Baseline	no	0.76	0.84	0.87	0.84
		with	0.76	0.68	0.79	0.83
	Proposed	no	1.0	0.98	0.99	0.97
		with	1.0	0.98	0.99	0.97
Animal	Baseline	no	0.84	0.72	0.69	0.66
		with	0.68	0.42	0.36	0.27
	Proposed	no	0.88	0.86	0.77	0.77
		with	0.84	0.82	0.76	0.75
Kitchen Item	Baseline	no	0.76	0.68	0.56	0.48
		with	0.68	0.56	0.47	0.47
	Proposed	no	0.88	0.72	0.72	0.72
		with	0.88	0.76	0.68	0.70
Outdoor Activity	Baseline	no	0.92	0.70	0.56	0.47
		with	0.80	0.66	0.56	0.44
	Proposed	no	0.96	0.94	0.87	-
		with	0.96	0.96	0.87	-
Philosopher	Baseline	no	0.76	0.68	0.60	0.63
		with	0.60	0.42	0.41	0.42
	Proposed	no	1.0	0.94	0.91	0.86
		with	1.0	0.94	0.91	0.86
Portland Attraction	Baseline	no	0.76	0.58	0.55	0.54
		with	0.76	0.58	0.47	0.43
	Proposed	no	0.88	0.94	0.87	0.83
		with	0.88	0.94	0.87	0.83
Software Dev. Tool	Baseline	no	0.88	0.82	0.73	0.73
		with	0.84	0.74	0.71	0.69
	Proposed	no	0.88	0.84	0.84	0.82
		with	0.88	0.84	0.83	0.83
Shape	Baseline	no	0.84	0.6	0.51	0.4
		with	0.56	0.42	0.35	0.32
	Proposed	no	0.88	0.82	0.77	0.69
		with	0.88	0.84	0.79	0.69
Politician	Baseline	no	0.8	0.78	0.81	0.85
		with	0.72	0.72	0.69	0.74
	Proposed	no	0.96	0.96	0.92	0.84
		with	0.96	0.96	0.92	0.85

Table 1: Empirical results compared with the baseline system on the precision of the instances extracted. The experiments include settings with and without the addition of 500 noise web pages collected randomly from `reddit.com`.

6 Conclusion and Future Works

In this work, we have proposed a weakly-supervised approach for extracting instances of semantic classes. The proposed approach utilizes a compression model for filtering possibly irrelevant mentions, and uses a graph ranking algorithm for sorting the extraction.

This study focused primarily on assessing the effectiveness of using PPM model for evaluating the contextual evidence, and thus we use only very simple wrappers. Our approach can potentially be extended to adopt more elaborated patterns such as Kozareva et al. (2008) and Xu et al. (2007). In addition, as our future work, we plan to apply this method to other languages such as Japanese and Chinese.

Acknowledgments

This research was supported in part by the National Science Council under grant NSC99-3112-B-001-005, the Academia Sinica Investigator Award 95-02 and the research center for Humanities and Social Sciences under grant IIS-50-23.

[2] `www.reddit.com`, a social bookmark website. 500 URLs gathered in May, 25th, 2011.

References

Michele Banko, Michael J. Cafarella, Stephen Soderland, Matt Broadhead, and Oren Etzioni. 2007. Open information extraction from the web. In *Proceedings of the 20th International Joint Conference on Artifical Intelligence*, pages 2670–2676, San Francisco, CA, USA. Morgan Kaufmann Publishers Inc.

Timothy C. Bell, John G. Cleary, and Ian H. Witten. 1990. *Text compression*. Prentice-Hall, Inc., Upper Saddle River, NJ, USA.

William Chang, Patrick Pantel, Ana-Maria Popescu, and Evgeniy Gabrilovich. 2009. Towards intent-driven bidterm suggestion. In *Proceedings of the 18th International Conference on World Wide Web*, WWW '09, pages 1093–1094, New York, NY, USA. ACM.

Surajit Chaudhuri, Venkatesh Ganti, and Dong Xin. 2009. Exploiting web search to generate synonyms for entities. In *Proceedings of the 18th International Conference on World Wide Web*, WWW '09, pages 151–160, New York, NY, USA. ACM.

Philipp Cimiano, Aleksander Pivk, Lars S. Thieme, and Steffen Staab. 2004. Learning taxonomic relations from heterogeneous sources of evidence. In *Proceedings of the ECAI 2004 Ontology Learning and Population Workshop*.

John G. Cleary and Ian H. Witten. 1984. Data compression using adaptive coding and partial string matching. *IEEE Transactions on Communications*, 32:396–402.

Zelig Harris. 1970. Distributional structure. In *Papers in Structural and Transformational Linguistics*, pages 775–794. D. Reidel Publishing Company, Dordrecht, Holland.

Marti A. Hearst. 1992. Automatic acquisition of hyponyms from large text corpora. In *Proceedings of the 14th Conference on Computational Linguistics*, volume 2 of *COLING '92*, pages 539–545, Stroudsburg, PA, USA. Association for Computational Linguistics.

Paul Glor Howard. 1993. *The design and analysis of efficient lossless data compression systems*. Ph.D. thesis, Providence, RI, USA. UMI Order No. GAX94-06956.

Zornitsa Kozareva, Ellen Riloff, and Eduard Hovy. 2008. Semantic class learning from the web with hyponym pattern linkage graphs. In *Proceedings of the 46th Annual Meeting of the Association of Computational Linguistics: Human Language Technologies*, pages 1048–1056, Columbus, Ohio, June. Association for Computational Linguistics.

Joseph F McCarthy and Wendy G Lehnert. 1995. Using decision trees for coreference resolution. In *In Proceedings of the 14th International Joint Conference on Artificial Intelligence*, pages 1050–1055.

Tara McIntosh and James R. Curran. 2009. Reducing semantic drift with bagging and distributional similarity. In *Proceedings of the Joint conference of the 47th Annual Meeting of the Association for Computational Linguistics and the 4th International Joint Conference on Natural Language Processing*, volume 1 of *ACL-IJCNLP '09*, pages 396–404, Stroudsburg, PA, USA. Association for Computational Linguistics.

Marius Paşca. 2007. Weakly-supervised discovery of named entities using web search queries. In *Proceedings of the 16th ACM Conference on Information and Knowledge Management*, CIKM '07, pages 683–690, New York, NY, USA. ACM.

Patrick Pantel, Eric Crestan, Arkady Borkovsky, Ana-Maria Popescu, and Vishnu Vyas. 2009. Web-scale distributional similarity and entity set expansion. In *Proceedings of the 2009 Conference on Empirical Methods in Natural Language Processing*, volume 2 of *EMNLP '09*, pages 938–947, Stroudsburg, PA, USA. Association for Computational Linguistics.

Ellen Riloff and Rosie Jones. 1999. Learning dictionaries for information extraction by multi-level bootstrapping. In *Proceedings of National Conference on Artificial Intelligence*, AAAI-99, pages 474–479.

Ellen Riloff and Jessica Shepherd. 1997. A corpus-based approach for building semantic lexicons. In *Proceedings of the 2nd Conference on Empirical Methods in Natural Language Processing*, pages 117–124.

Luis Sarmento, Valentin Jijkuon, Maarten de Rijke, and Eugenio Oliveira. 2007. "more like these": growing entity classes from seeds. In *Proceedings of the 16th ACM Conference on Information and Knowledge Management*, CIKM '07, pages 959–962, New York, NY, USA. ACM.

W. J. Teahan and John G. Cleary. 1997. Models of english text. In *Proceedings of the Conference on Data Compression*, pages 12–21, Washington, DC, USA. IEEE Computer Society.

Richard C. Wang and William W. Cohen. 2007. Language-independent set expansion of named entities using the web. In *Proceedings of the 7th IEEE International Conference on Data Mining*, volume 0 of *ICDM '07*, pages 342–350, Washington, DC, USA. IEEE Computer Society.

Scott White and Padhraic Smyth. 2003. Algorithms for estimating relative importance in networks. In *Proceedings of the 9th ACM SIGKDD International Conference on Knowledge Discovery and Data Mining*, KDD '03, pages 266–275, New York, NY, USA. ACM.

Feiyu Xu, Hans Uszkoreit, and Hong Li. 2007. A seed-driven bottom-up machine learning framework for extracting relations of various complexity. In

Proceedings of the 45th Annual Meeting of the Association of Computational Linguistics, pages 584–591, Prague, Czech Republic, June. Association for Computational Linguistics.

Potts Model on the Case Fillers for Word Sense Disambiguation

Hiroya Takamura
Tokyo Institute of Technology
takamura@pi.titech.ac.jp

Manabu Okumura
Tokyo Institute of Technology
oku@pi.titech.ac.jp

Abstract

We propose a new method for word sense disambiguation for verbs. In our method, sense-dependent selectional preference of verbs is obtained through the probabilistic model on the lexical network. The mean-field approximation is employed to compute the state of the lexical network. The outcome of the computation is used as features for discriminative classifiers. The method is evaluated on the dataset of the Japanese word sense disambiguation.

1 Introduction

Polysemous words can be obstacles to many applications of natural language processing such as information retrieval, question answering, and machine translation. The task of distinguishing word senses given a token of a polysemous word and its context is often referred to as word sense disambiguation and has been studied by many researchers (Agirre and Edmonds, 2006). Among a number of word sense disambiguation tasks including noun sense disambiguation, adjective sense disambiguation, and named entity disambiguation, we focus on the verb sense disambiguation with the supervised setting, where we are supposed to construct a classifier given labeled training instances.

It is learned in the previous work that case fillers are often good clues for the verb sense disambiguation. Consider, for example, the following two sentences:

1. "He drove a car to the next town."
2. "He drove the dogs away."

The "drive" in Sentence 1 means "operate (a vehicle)", while "drive" in Sentence 2 means "urge (something to move)". Although there might be long contexts to these instances, looking at the case fillers "car" and "dog" alone would lead to the correct interpretations of the meanings. This kind of preference on nouns as case fillers is called $selectional\ preference$, which in this case depends on sense. It is sometimes impractical, however, to expect that the training dataset covers all the nouns as case fillers, if case fillers of the target verb are diverse. The purpose of this article is to propose a method for propagating the information on the case fillers in the training dataset to other nouns, so that the sense of polysemous words is correctly disambiguated. In our method, the information propagation is implemented as estimation of the state of the probabilisitc model on the lexical network. One advantage of our method is that we can overcome the difficulty caused by the noise contained in the lexical network.

2 Related Work

Recent work on general word sense disambiguation is summarized in the book edited by Agirre and Edmonds (2006). We focus on the work of the verb sense disambiguation.

The idea of using case frames for the verb sense disambiguation is not novel, and dates back to 90's. Fujii et al. (1998) proposed a method for the verb sense disambiguation, which is based on the k-nearest neighbors. In their method, each instance is represented as a case frame and the similarity of two instances is calculated as a weighted sum of the similarities of case fillers. Fujii et al. also proposed a framework of active learning.

To disambiguate verb senses, Chen and Palmer (2009) proposed to use linguistic and semantic features including the voice of the given sentence, the presence of a PP adjunct, and the named entity tags. Dligach and Palmer (2008) proposed to use co-occurrence with other verbs as features. Wagner et al. (2009) proposed to use verb clusters generated with statistics on verb subcategorization.

3 Potts Model

We introduce the probability model that we will use for our task. This model gives the probability distribution over a set of nodes associated with random variables, where some pairs of variables are dependent on each other. If the variables can have more than two values and there is no order relation between the values, the network comprised of such variables is called *Potts* model (Wu, 1982), which has been used in applications such as image restoration (Tanaka and Morita, 1996) and rumor transmission (Liu et al., 2001).

Suppose a network consisting of nodes and weighted edges is given. Let c denote the value of a node, and w_{ij} the weight between i and j. Energy function $H(\mathbf{c})$ is represented as

$$H(\mathbf{c}) = -\beta \sum_{ij} w_{ij}\delta(c_i, c_j) - \alpha \sum_{i \in L} \delta(c_i, a_i), \quad (1)$$

where β is a constant called *the inverse-temperature*, L is the index set for the observed variables, a_i is the value of an observed variable i, and α is a positive constant representing a weight on labeled data. δ returns 1 if two arguments are equal to each other, 0 otherwise. The state is penalized if c_i $(i \in L)$ is different from a_i. The probability distribution of the network is represented as $P(\mathbf{c}) = \exp\{-H(\mathbf{c})\}/Z$, where Z is a normalization factor.

Instead of minimizing $H(\mathbf{c})$, we attempt to minimize the free energy, which is defined to be the sum of $H(\mathbf{c})$ and the negative entropy. However, this minimization is computationally hard. We hence resort to the mean-field approximation method (Nishimori, 2001), in which $P(\mathbf{c})$ is replaced by factorized function $\rho(\mathbf{c}) = \prod_i \rho_i(c_i)$. The evergy function with the factorized probability function is called *variational free energy*:

$$\begin{aligned} F(\mathbf{c}) &= \sum_{\mathbf{c}} \rho(\mathbf{c}) H(\mathbf{c}) - \sum_{\mathbf{c}} -\rho(\mathbf{c}) \log \rho(\mathbf{c}) \\ &= -\alpha \sum_i \sum_{c_i} \rho_i(c_i)\delta(c_i, a_i) \\ &\quad -\beta \sum_{ij} \sum_{c_i, c_j} \rho_i(c_i)\rho_j(c_j) w_{ij}\delta(c_i, c_j) \\ &\quad -\sum_i \sum_{c_i} -\rho_i(c_i) \log \rho_i(c_i). \end{aligned} \quad (2)$$

By minimizing $F(\mathbf{c})$ under the condition that $\forall i, \sum_{c_i} \rho_i(c_i) = 1$, we obtain the following fixed point equation for $i \in L$:

$$\rho_i(c) = \frac{\exp(\alpha\delta(c, a_i) + \beta \sum_j w_{ij}\rho_j(c))}{\sum_n \exp(\alpha\delta(n, a_i) + \beta \sum_j w_{ij}\rho_j(n))}. \quad (3)$$

The fixed point equation for $i \notin L$ can be obtained by removing $\alpha\delta(c, a_i)$ from above. This fixed point equation is solved by an iterative computation. In the actual implementation, we represent ρ_i with a linear combination of the discrete Tchebycheff polynomials (Tanaka and Morita, 1996). Details on the Potts model and its computation can be found in the literature (Nishimori, 2001).

4 Proposed Method

4.1 Construction of Lexical Networks

We follow the work by Takamura et al. (2005) to construct a lexical network. We link two words if one word appears in the gloss of the other. Each link belongs to one of two groups: the same-orientation links SL and the different-orientation links DL. If a negation word appears in the gloss of an entry word, the words after the negation word are linked to the entry word with DL. Otherwise, those words are linked with SL. In case of Japanese, the auxiliaries "nai" and "nu" are regarded as negation words.

We next set weights $W = (w_{ij})$ to links :

$$w_{ij} = \begin{cases} \frac{1}{\sqrt{d(i)d(j)}} & (l_{ij} \in SL) \\ -\frac{1}{\sqrt{d(i)d(j)}} & (l_{ij} \in DL) \\ 0 & otherwise \end{cases}, \quad (4)$$

where l_{ij} denotes the link between word i and word j, and $d(i)$ denotes the degree of word i, which indicates the number of words linked with word i. We call this network *the gloss network (G)*. We construct another network, *the thesaurus network (T)*, by linking synonyms and hypernyms in a thesaurus. We also merge the two networks above to construct another network *the gloss-thesaurus network (GT)*.

4.2 Use of Potts Model

We estimate the tendency of each word to be the case filler for a verb sense. For example, "car" would have a high tendency to be the case filler for "drive" with the sense "operate (a vehicle)". Such tendency is measured as the probability $P_i(c)$ over senses c for noun n_i. We will use the Potts model for this purpose. Namely, the local approximate probability $\rho_i(c)$, equivalently the mariginal probability $\sum_{\boldsymbol{c}} \rho(\boldsymbol{c})$, is regarded as probability $P_i(c)$.

The values of each random variable are senses of the target verb. For each case and each verb, we estimate the probability of the sense assignments on the whole set of nodes by means of the mean-field approximation. The case fillers of the training instances are used as observed variables, with their index set being L in Equation (2). $P_i(c)$ is estimated for each case.

In our experiments on Japanese, surface cases are employed: wo (accusative), ga (nominative), ni (dative/locative), de (locative/instrumental), no (genitive/others), e (locative/illative), to (comitative), $kara$ (elative), $yori$ (comparative), $made$ (terminative). Although our model is also applicable to deep cases, we focus on surface cases since deep case recognition itself is a challenging task.

4.3 Estimation of β

In some pieces of previous work (Takamura et al., 2005; Takamura et al., 2007), it has been shown that the optimal β can be obtained by estimating the critical temperature, at which phase transition occurs from *paramagnetic phase* (variables are randomly oriented) to *ferromagnetic phase* (most of the variables have the same value). We follow these pieces of previous work.

In practice, when the maximum of the spatial averages of the approximated probabilities $\max_c \sum_i \rho_i(c)/N$ exceeds a threshold during increasing β, we consider that the phase transition has occurred. We select the value of β slightly before the phase transition.

4.4 Discriminative Training

Probability $\rho_i(c)$ is expected to be a strong clue for sense disambiguation. However, it is not clear how we can effectively use the probabilities of different cases c; $\rho_i(c)$ for some cases would be reliable, while some others less reliable. In addition, the word tokens that appear before and after the target word also give evidence for senses. We therefore use a discriminative approach to construct a classifier with those various clues as features. Support vector machines are employed in this work, although other classifiers are also applicable.

Note that even if a case filler in the test instance did not appear in the training data, the feature $\rho_i(c)$ corresponding to this case filler conveys the information on the selectional preference of the verb against the case filler.

5 Experiments

5.1 Experimental Settings

The proposed method for verb sense disambiguation is evaluated on the white paper part of BCCWJ corpus, the first balanced corpus of contemporary written Japanese (Maekawa, 2008), which was also used as a test set for SemEval-2 Japanese word sense disambiguation task (Okumura et al., 2010). The dataset used in this research was created by the preliminary annotation for SemEval-2. The senses are defined in the Iwanami Kokugo Jiten (Nishio et al., 1994), a Japanese dictionary. Among three levels of sense IDs defined in this dictionary, the middle-level sense was used in the empirical evaluation, which is the same level of senses used in the SemEval-2. From the dataset above, we selected most ambiguous 14 verbs whose empirical sense distributions (i.e., estimated with the maximum likelihood principle) have a high entropy and appear more than 100 times in the dataset. The statistics of this dataset is shown in the middle columns of Table 1. 5-fold cross-validation was employed for each verb.

TinySVM version 0.09[1] was used for SVM training and classification. The linear kernel was used as a kernel function of SVM. The soft-margin parameter C indicating the tradeoff between the model complexity and the training error was tuned to the best value among $0.01, 0.1, 1, 10$ for each method. The glosses of the Iwanami Kokugo Jiten Japanese dictionary are used to construct a lexical network G (gloss network). Japanese WordNet version 0.9 (Bond et al., 2009) was used to construct a lexical network T (thesaurus network). The numbers of nodes in G, T, and GT are respectively 35225, 66218, and 87038. Due to a large number of polysemous words in the thesaurus, many synsets of Japanese WordNet are connected.

Two baselines are evaluated on the test datasets. Baseline 1 is SVMs trained with basic features: the target verb itself and 3 words before and after the target verb. Baseline 2 is also SVMs trained with the basic features above and the case filler features: the nouns that appear as case fillers.

The proposed methods are SVMs trained with the basic features, the case filler features, and the lexical network features: the probability $\rho_i(c)$ introduced in Section 4 for each case and each sense c when w_i appears as a case filler.

[1] http://chasen.org/~taku/software/TinySVM/

Table 1: Classification accuracy on *hard* verbs (%)

target word	English translation	# of instances	# of senses	baselines 1	2	G	T	GT
ataru	hit, correspond	463	7	83.2	85.3	87.9	88.1	87.7
dasu	take out, cause	173	3	73.4	75.1	74.6	79.2	75.1
deru	go out, appear	189	3	86.2	86.8	89.4	87.8	87.8
kiku	listen, be effective	141	2	87.2	87.2	87.2	86.5	87.2
susumu	proceed, advance	931	2	81.8	83.1	84.2	83.5	84.4
average	–	379.4	3.4	82.0	83.5	84.7	84.6	84.8

Table 2: Average classification accuracy on *easy* verbs (%)

	# of instances	# of senses	baselines 1	2	G	T	GT
average on *easy* verbs	1216.9	3.0	94.6	94.8	95.0	95.1	95.0
total average	917.8	3.1	93.1	93.4	93.7	93.8	93.7

The classification accuracy, i.e., the number of correctly classified instances divided by the total number of instances, is employed as evaluation measure. Averages in this paper are micro averages. The methods are evaluated first for *hard* verbs, for which the classification accuracy of the baseline method is less than 90 %. There are 5 *hard* verbs; the other 9 verbs are *easy* verbs, for which the classification accuracy is already equal to or better than 90 %. Note that the proposed method aims at *hard* verbs as mentioned in Section 1, although we would like the proposed method not to degrade the classification performance for *easy* verbs.

5.2 Results

The classification result for *hard* verbs is shown in Table 1. Baseline 2 is better than baseline 1, meaning that the simple information on the word as a case filler improves the classification performance. The proposed methods on lexical networks G, T, and GT mostly outperformed baselines with a few exceptions. On average, the proposed method on GT increases the classification accuracy by 2.8 points compared with the baseline 1, 1.3 points compared with the baseline 2. This result shows that the information propagation on the lexical network offers useful clues for verb sense disambiguation. Table 2 shows that the proposed method is at least comparable to the baselines when it is applied to *easy* verbs. The accuracy for each *easy* verb was omitted from the table due to the space limitation, and only the average values are written in the table. These results also show that the difference of lexical networks does not have a significant effect on the average classification performance.

In order to gain more intuitive understanding on the method, we give an example of the computational result for case *wo* (accusative) of verb *dasu*. We used all of the 173 instances that are available. Nouns that have high probability $\rho_i(c)$ for $c = sense1$ (take out, let out, send, pay) are, for example, price, application, permission, demand, request, wish, command, permit, and certificate. Nouns that have high $\rho_i(c)$ for $c = sense2$ (show) are, for example, speed, advance, agility, effect, driving force, breakthrough, and activity.

6 Conclusion

We proposed a new method for word sense disambiguation for verbs. In our method, sense-dependent selectional preference of verbs was obtained through the probabilistic model on the lexical network. The mean-field approximation was employed to compute the state of the lexical network. The outcome of the computation was used as features for discriminative classifiers. The method is evaluated on the dataset of the Japanese word sense disambiguation.

Future work includes the use of words that are not on the lexical network, the incorporation of interactions between multiple cases, and theoretical study of the Potts model for lexical network.

References

Eneko Agirre and Philip Glenny Edmonds, editors. 2006. *Word Sense Disambiguation: Algorithms And Applications*. Springer-Verlag.

Francis Bond, Hitoshi Isahara, Sanae Fujita, Kiyotaka Uchimoto, Takayuki Kuribayashi, and Kyoko Kanzaki. 2009. Enhancing the japanese wordnet. In *Proceedings of the 7th Workshop on Asian Language Resources (in conjunction with ACL-IJCNLP 2009)*.

Jinying Chen and Martha S. Palmer. 2009. Improving English verb sense disambiguation performance with linguistically motivated features and clear sense distinction boundaries. *Language Resources and Evaluation*, 43:181–208.

Dmitriy Dligach and Martha Palmer. 2008. Novel semantic features for verb sense disambiguation. In *Proceedings of the 46th Annual Meeting of the Association for Computational Linguistics on Human Language Technologies: Short Papers*, HLT-Short '08, pages 29–32, Stroudsburg, PA, USA. Association for Computational Linguistics.

Atsushi Fujii, Kentaro Inui, Takenobu Tokunaga, and Hozumi Tanaka. 1998. Selective sampling for example-based word sense disambiguation. *Computational Linguistics*, 24(4):573–597.

Zhongzhu Liu, Jun Luo, and Chenggang Shao. 2001. Potts model for exaggeration of a simple rumor transmitted by recreant rumormongers. *Physical Review E*, 64:046134,1–046134,9.

Kikuo Maekawa. 2008. Balanced corpus of contemporary written japanese. In *Proceedings of the 6th Workshop on Asian Language Resources*, pages 101–102.

Hidetoshi Nishimori. 2001. *Statistical Physics of Spin Glasses and Information Processing*. Oxford University Press.

Minoru Nishio, Etsutaro Iwabuchi, and Shizuo Mizutani. 1994. *Iwanami Japanese Dictionary (5th edition)*. Iwanami-shoten.

Manabu Okumura, Kiyoaki Shirai, Kanako Komiya, and Hikaru Yokono. 2010. Semeval-2010 task: Japanese wsd. In *Proceedings of the 5th International Workshop on Evaluating Word Sense Disambiguation Systems*, pages 69–74.

Hiroya Takamura, Takashi Inui, and Manabu Okumura. 2005. Extracting semantic orientations of words using spin model. In *Proceedings of the 43rd Annual Meeting of the Association for Computational Linguistics (ACL'05)*, pages 133–140.

Hiroya Takamura, Takashi Inui, and Manabu Okumura. 2007. Extracting semantic orientations of phrases from dictionary. In *Proceedings of the Human Language Technologies: The Annual Conference of the North American Chapter of the Association for Computational Linguistics (NAACL-HLT2007)*, pages 292–299.

Kazuyuki Tanaka and Tohru Morita. 1996. Application of cluster variation method to image restoration problem. In J.L. Morán-López and J.M. Sanchez, editors, *Theory and Applications of the Cluster Variation and Path Probability Methods*, pages 353–373. Plenum Press, New York.

Wiebke Wagner, Helmut Schmid, and Sabine Schulte im Walde. 2009. Verb sense disambiguation using a predicate-argument-clustering model. In *Proceedings of the CogSci Workshop on Distributional Semantics beyond Concrete Concepts*.

Fa-Yueh Wu. 1982. The potts model. *Reviews of Modern Physics*, 54(1):235–268.

Improving Word Sense Induction by Exploiting Semantic Relevance

Zhenzhong Zhang
Institute of Software, Graduate University, Chinese Academy of Sciences, Beijing, China
Zhenzhong@nfs.iscas.ac.cn

Le Sun
Institute of Software, Chinese Academy of Sciences, Beijing, China
sunle@iscas.ac.cn

Abstract

Word Sense Induction (WSI) is the task of automatically inducing the different senses of a target word from unannotated text. Traditional approaches based on the vector space model (VSM) represent each context of a target word as a vector of selected features (e.g. the words occurring in the context). These approaches assume that the words occurring in the context are independent and do not exploit semantic relevance between words. In this paper we propose a WSI method which can exploit semantic relevance between words by incorporating a word graph into the framework of clustering of context vectors. The method is evaluated on the testing data of the Chinese Word Sense Induction task of the first CIPS-SIGHAN Joint Conference on Chinese Language Processing (CLP2010). Experimental results show that our method significantly outperforms the baseline methods.

1 Introduction

It has been shown that using word senses instead of surface word forms can improve performance on many natural language processing tasks such as machine translation (Vickrey et al., 2005) and information retrieval (Uzuner et al., 1999; Véronis, 2004). Historically, using word senses usually involved the use of manually compiled resources in which word senses were represented as a fixed list of definitions. However, there seem to be some disadvantages associated with such fixed list of senses paradigm. Firstly, since dictionaries usually contain general definitions, they can not reflect the exact contents of the contexts where target words appear (Véronis, 2004). Secondly, because the "fixed list of senses" paradigm makes the fixed granularity assumption of the senses distinction, it may not be suitable in different applications (Kilgarriff, 1997; Brody and Lapata, 2009).

To overcome these limitations, some techniques like WSI have been proposed for discovering words senses automatically from unannoteted corpuses. WSI algorithms are usually based on the Distributional Hypothesis which shows that words with similar meanings appear in similar contexts (Harris, 1954). This concept can be leveraged to induce different senses of a target word by clustering the contexts where the target word appears.

Much work in WSI is based on the vector space model, in which each context of a target word is represented by a vector of selected features (e.g. the words occurring in the context). These context vectors are clustered and the resulting clusters are taken to represent the induced senses. However, when constructing context vectors, the approaches based on VSM assume that the words occurring in the contexts are independent and do not exploit semantic relevance between words. This will cause the problem that two contexts using semantically related but distinct words will show no similarity. Figure 1 shows a simple example of three context vectors taken from three contexts of the target word *bank*, which appears with one sense i.e. *sloping land*. If we assume that context words are independent, the similarity between context 1 and context 3 will be zero, which means that the senses of the target word *bank* in the two contexts are different. But, in practice, *bank* appears with one sense in the two contexts. Some methods have been proposed to use information beyond that which is found in the immediately surrounding context. For example, in (Schütze, 1998), second order co-occurrence matrix was used to construct rich vectors of word contexts.

```
Context 1: river flood sandbag
Context 2: river water fish
Context 3: water lake bridge
```

Figure 1: Three context vectors for the target word *bank*.

In this paper, we propose a WSI method which can exploit semantic relevance between words by incorporating a word graph into the framework of clustering of context vectors. Firstly, we build a graph, where each vertex corresponds to a selected word and edges between vertices are weighted based on the semantic relevance between their associated words. Then we adapt the Personalized PageRank method (Agirre and Soroa, 2009) for incorporating semantic relevance between words into context vectors. The resulting vectors are clustered and each cluster represents an induced sense of the target word. Our method bears some similarity with some graph-based methods of WSI since they all need a graph of words. But in our method the graph is used to incorporate semantic relevance between words into context vectors while in graph-based approaches of WSI it is clustered to induce different senses of a target word. We use two vector-based approaches and one graph-based approach as baselines. Our evaluation under the framework of CLP2010 Chinese Word Sense Induction task shows that our approach significantly outperforms the baseline systems.

The structure of this paper is as follows: in Section 2, we will present our approach. In Section 3, we will introduce the experimental setup and show the experimental results. We will end with a conclusion and future work in Section 4.

2 Our Approach

In this section, we introduce how to build a word graph and how to use Personalized PageRank method to incorporate semantic relevance between words into context vectors. Then we describe how to cluster the resulting context vectors to induce senses of target words.

2.1 Building A Word Graph

In this section, we aim to build a graph where each vertex corresponds to a word and edges between vertices are weighted based on the semantic relevance between their associated words. Initially, we construct a word-by-context matrix P with the entry $P_{i,j}$ giving the weight of word i in context j. In this paper, we set

$$P_{i,j} = \frac{n_{i,j}}{\sum_i n_{i,j}} \times \log \frac{N}{n(i)} \quad (1)$$

where $n_{i,j}$ is the frequency of word i occurring in the context j, and $n(i)$ is the number of the contexts containing the word i and N is the total number of contexts. Just like contexts can be seen as bags of words, words can be viewed as bags of contexts. So a row of the matrix P can be seen as the context-vector for a word. We assume that two words that have more correlated context-vectors will have a greater semantic relevance. In this case, the semantic relevance of two words is evaluated through the inner product of vectors corresponding to the two words. Support that $M=PP^T$, then $M_{i,j}$ gives the semantic relevance between word i and j. Singular Value Decomposition (SVD) is used to reduce the dimensionality of matrix M. M is evaluated by the equation (2)

$$M \approx \sum_{i=1}^{K} \lambda_i x_i x_i^T \quad (2)$$

where x_i is the eigenvector of M, and λ_i is the corresponding eigenvalue and x_i^T denotes the transpose of x_i. K is the minimum k that satisfies $\sum_{i=1}^{k} \lambda_i \geq 0.85 \times \sum_{i=1}^{D} \lambda_i$, where D is the number of eigenvectors of M. Now we have built the graph, in which each vertex corresponds to a word and the weight of edge between vertex i and j is given by $M_{i,j}$ indicating the semantic relevance between the word i and j.

2.2 Incorporating semantic relevance between words into context vectors

Personalized PageRank algorithm is adapted from PageRank algorithm (Brin and Page, 1998). In the PageRank formulation ($\Pr = cM\Pr + (1-c)v$), the element values of the vector v are all $\frac{1}{N}$, where N is the total number of vertices in the graph. But in the Personalized PageRank, the vector v can be non-uniform and assign stronger probabilities to certain kinds of vertices.

We assume that the weight of a feature (word) in the context vector depends on not only its frequency in contexts but also the words that co-occur with it. This means, if two words i and j co-occur in a context and are semantic related, the weight of i (or j) should be strengthened by j (or i). We adapt Personalized PageRank algorithm for this process. The weight of the word i at t+1 step is defined as:

$$W(i)^{t+1} = (1-d)W(i)^0 + d\sum_{j\in In(i)} \frac{M_{j,i}}{\sum_{k\in In(j)} M_{j,k}} W(j)^t \quad (3)$$

where $M_{j,i}$ is the weight of the edge between vertices i and j, which is defined in Section 2.1. $W(j)^t$ is the weight of the word j at t step and $W(i)^0$ is the initial weight of the word i in the context. $In(i)$ stands for the set of vertices that connect to i. d is the damping factor and is usually set at 0.85.

The weight of each word is initialized based on its frequency and the Personalized PageRank algorithm iterates until convergence. After the running of the Personalized PageRank algorithm, each word gets a new weight. In this way, we incorporate semantic relevance between words into context vectors.

2.3 Inducing Word Senses

The k-means algorithm is used for clustering the resulting vectors produced in Section 2.2. The similarity between two objects is computed using cosine function. The number of clusters, k, is automatically determined using PK2 criterion function (Pedersen and Kulkarni, 2006). Each resulting cluster represents a kind of sense of the target word.

3 Experiments

3.1 Experimental Setup

Our experiments are based on the CLP2010 Chinese Word Sense Induction task testing dataset which contains 100 target words (22 target words are constituted by a single character and 78 target words are constituted by two or more characters) and total 5000 instances. The number of senses on average per word is 2.5. The original testing data contains the number of target word senses. But in practice, the number of target word senses is unknown and it need to be indentified automatically. So in the experiments we discover the number of target word senses automatically using the PK2 criterion.

Each instance of a target word is processed by segmenting Chinese word and removing stop-words and target words. The remaining words are used to build the word graphs and construct the vectors of contexts.

We use two vector-based approaches and one graph-based approach as baselines. The first one is a vector-based WSI approach, which represents the contexts of a target word using second order co-occurrence vectors (Schűtze, 1998). This approach constructs a word-by-word co-occurrence matrix by identifying bigrams whose number of occurrences is greater than a pre-specified threshold. A row in the matrix is the vector for a context word. Each context is represented by the centroid of all vectors of the words which make up the context. Then these context vectors are clustered to induce senses of target words. This approach has a good performance in public evaluation (e.g. Semeval-2007 task 02) (Agirre and Soroa, 2007).

The second one is also a vector-based WSI approach which represents the contexts of a target word using bag-of-words vectors and weights each feature (word) based on its TF and IDF. The two vector-based WSI approaches use k-means algorithm to cluster the context vectors of target words and the maximum number of k-means iterations is set to 100.

The third one is a graph-based WSI approach. We build a graph according to the approach described in (Agirre et al., 2006). Chinese Whispers algorithm (Biemann, 2006) is used to cluster the graph. The maximum number of Chinese Whispers iterations is set to 100. We also include the "one cluster per word" baseline (1c1w), where all instances of a target word are grouped into a single cluster. In SemEval-2010 task 14, none of the participating systems outperform this baseline in paired F-score (Artiles et al., 2009), which indicates that this baseline is quite strong.

According to (Pedersen, 2010), we employ paired F-score as evaluation measure. Let $C=\{C_j|j=1,2,...,n\}$ be a set of clusters generated by a WSI system and $S=\{G_i|i=1,2,...,m\}$ be the set of gold standard classes. For each cluster C_j, we generate $\binom{|C_j|}{2}$ instance pairs, in which $|C_j|$ is the total number of instances that belong to C_j. Similarly, we generate $\binom{|G_i|}{2}$ instance pairs for each gold standard class G_i. Let $F(C)$ is the set of instance pairs generated from any clusters in C and $F(S)$ is the set of instance pairs generated from any gold standard classes in S. Precision and recall are defined in Equation 4 and 5 respectively.

$$P = \frac{|F(C) \cap F(S)|}{|F(C)|} \quad (4)$$

$$R = \frac{|F(C) \cap F(S)|}{|F(S)|} \quad (5)$$

Then the paired F-score is defined in Equation 6.

$$Fs = \frac{2 \times P \times R}{P + R} \quad (6)$$

3.2 Experimental Results

Table 1 shows the results of experiments with 100 target words (total 5000 instances). Just like what have been shown in (Agirre and Soroa, 2007) and (Manandhar et al., 2010), the 1c1w baseline shows the best performance. However, it only discoveries one sense for each target word, which is the most frequent sense of the target word. In contrast, WSI_SR and WSI_SOV predict 2.1 and 2.4 senses on average per word respectively, which is more close to the actual number of senses (2.5).

System	Fs(%) (All)	Fs(%) (C)	Fs(%) (W)	#Cl
WSI_SR	58.5	42.78	62.82	2.1
WSI_SOV	56.37	42.46	60.28	2.4
WSI_BOW	51.24	40.68	54.25	3.7
WSI_CW	40.99	30.68	43.72	6.7
1c1w	60.6	44.5	65.14	1

Table 1: Evaluation of WSI systems. WSI_SR stands for our method which can exploit semantic relevance between words for WSI system, WSI_SOV for the WSI system based on second-order vectors, WSI_BOW for the WSI system based on bag-of-words vectors, WSI_CW for the graph-based WSI system which employs Chinese Whispers clustering algorithm. C stands for the target words which are constituted by one character while W stands for the target words which are constituted by two or more characters.

WSI_SR achieves 0.585 paired F-score, outperforming WSI_BOW with absolute improvements of 7.26%, which indicates that exploiting semantic relevance between words can improve the performance of WSI systems.

The performance of WSI_SR is well above that of WSI_SOV. This may be due to the fact that WSI_SOV only exploits semantic relevance between words occurring in the certain contexts while WSI_SR can exploit semantic relevance between words occurring in the all contexts. For example, in Figure 1, if we use the binary weighting scheme, WSI_SOV will set the weight for word *lake* and *bridge* to 0, which indicates that WSI_SOV cannot exploit the semantic relevance between the words occurring in context #1 and the two words. In contrast, WSI_SR sets the weight for word *lake* and *bridge* to 0.08, which shows that WSI_SR can exploit the semantic relevance between the words occurring in context #1 and them.

The system WSI_CW performs the worst. The possible reason is that the graph constructed from the testing dataset is made up of lots of unconnected subgraphs, which causes that the Chinese Whispers algorithm cannot cluster words correctly and induces too many senses. Compared to WSI_CW, WSI_SR incorporates the word graph into the framework of clustering of context vectors, which makes it avoid the drawback of WSI_CW.

A Chinese word can be constituted by a single character or multiple characters, which is different from English. Usually, the Chinese word containing only one character has more senses (e.g. Chinese word, "打" (beat), has twenty one senses in the testing dataset), which makes it more difficult to induce the senses of such words. In Table 1, we report the performance of systems on Chinese characters and Chinese words containing two or more characters. WSI_SR performs better than three baseline systems on Chinese words but has a similar performance with WSI_SOV on Chinese characters, which indicates that other information (e.g. syntactic information) should be exploited to improve the performance on Chinese characters.

4 Conclusions

In this paper, we present a WSI method, which can exploit semantic relevance between words by incorporating a word graph into the framework of clustering of context vectors. We build a word graph and use it to incorporate semantic relevance between words into context vectors. The resulting vectors are clustered to induce the senses of target words. Experimental results on the testing data of CLP2010 Chinese Word Sense Induction task demonstrate the effectiveness of our method.

Further work focuses on exploiting different kinds of information such as topic information and syntactic information to improve the performance of our method, especially for Chinese characters.

Acknowledgments

This work has been partially funded by National Natural Science Foundation of China under grant #60773027, #60736044 and #90920010 and by "863" Key Projects #2006AA010108. We would like to thank anonymous reviewers for their detailed comments.

References

Adam Kilgarriff, 1997. *I Don't Believe in Word Senses,* Computers and the Humanities 31(2): 91-113.

Chris Biemann, 2006. *Chinese whispers - an efficient graph clustering algorithm and its application to natural language processing problems*, In Proceedings of TextGraphs, pages 73–80, New York, USA.

David Vickrey, Luke Biewald, Marc Teyssley, and Daphne Koller. 2005. *Word-sense disambiguation for machine translation*. In Proceedings of the conference on Human Language Technology and Empirical Methods in Natural Language Processing, pages 771-778, Vancouver, British Columbia, Canada

Eneko Agirre, David Martínez, Oier López de Lacalle and Aitor Soroa. 2006. *Two graph-based algorithms for state-of-the-art WSD*. In Proceedings of the 2006 Conference on Empirical Methods in Natural Language Processing, pages 585–593, Sydney.

Eneko Agirre and Aitor Soroa. 2007. *Semeval-2007 task2: Evaluating word sense induction and discrimination systems*. In Proceedings of SemEval-2007. Association for Computational Llinguistics, pages 7-12, Prague.

Eneko Agirre and Aitor Soroa. 2009. *Personalizing PageRank for Word Sense Disambiguation*. In Proceedings of the 12th Conference of the European Chapter of the ACL, pages 33–41.

Hinrich Schütze. 1998. *Automatic Word Sense Discrimination*. Computational Linguistic, Vol. 24, No. 1, pages 97-123.

Javier Artiles, Enrique Amig´o, and Julio Gonzalo. 2009. *The role of named entities in web people search*. In Proceedings of EMNLP, pages 534–542, pages 534–542, Singapore, August.

Jean. Véronis. 2004. *Hyperlex: lexical cartography for information retrieval*. Computer Speech & Language, 18(3):223.252.

Ozlem Uzuner, Boris Katz, and Deniz Yuret. 1999. *Word sense disambiguation for information retrieval*. In Proceedings of the sixteenth national conference on Artificial intelligence and the eleventh Innovative applications of artificial intelligence conference innovative applications of artificial intelligence, page 985, Orlando, Florida, United States.

Samuel Brody and Mirella Lapata, 2009. *Bayesian word sense induction*. In Proceedings of the 12th Conference of the European Chapter of the Association for Computational Linguistics, pages 103-111, Athens, Greece.

Sergey Brin and Lawrence Page. 1998. *The anatomy of a large-scale hypertextual web search engine*. Computer Networks and ISDN Systems, 30(1-7).

Suresh Manandhar, Ioannis P. Klapaftis, Dmitriy Dligach and Sameer S. Pradhan. 2010. *SemEval-2010 task 14: Word sense induction & disambiguation*. In Proceedings of the 5th International Workshop on Semantic Evaluation, ACL 2010, pages 63–68, Uppsala, Sweden

Ted Pedersen and Anagha Kulkani, 2006. *Automatic cluster stopping with criterion functions and the gap statistic*. In Proceedings of the Human Language Technology Conference of the NAACL, Companion Volume, pages 276–279, New York City, USA.

Ted Pedersen. 2010. *Duluth-WSI: SenseClusters applied to the sense induction task of SemEval-2*. In Proceedings of the 5th International Workshop on Semantic Evaluation, ACL 2010, pages 363–366, Uppsala, Sweden.

Zellig Harris. 1954. *Distributional Structure*, pages 146-162.

Predicting Word Clipping with Latent Semantic Analysis

Julian Brooke **Tong Wang** **Graeme Hirst**
Department of Computer Science
University of Toronto
{jbrooke,tong,gh}@cs.toronto.edu

Abstract

In this paper, we compare a resource-driven approach with a task-specific classification model for a new near-synonym word choice sub-task, predicting whether a full or a clipped form of a word will be used (e.g. *doctor* or *doc*) in a given context. Our results indicate that the resource-driven approach, the use of a formality lexicon, can provide competitive performance, with the parameters of the task-specific model mirroring the parameters under which the lexicon was built.

1 Introduction

Lexical resources, though the focus of much work in computational linguistics, often compare poorly to direct statistical methods when applied to problems such as sentiment classification (Kennedy and Inkpen, 2006). Nevertheless, such resources offer advantages in terms of human interpretability and portability to many different tasks (Argamon et al., 2007). In this paper, we introduce a new sub-task of near-synonym word choice (Edmonds and Hirst, 2002), prediction of word clipping, in order to provide some new evidence that resource-driven approaches have general potential.

Clipping is a type of word formation where the beginning and/or the end of a longer word is omitted (Kreidler, 1979). This phenomenon is attested in various languages; well-known examples in English include words such as *hippo* (*hippopotamus*) and *blog* (*weblog*). Clipping and related kinds of word formation have received attention in computational linguistics with respect to the task of identifying source words from abbreviated forms, which has been studied, for instance, in the biomedical and text messaging domains (Okazaki and Ananiadou, 2006; Cook and Stevenson, 2009).

Compared to many near-synonyms, clipped forms have the important property that the differences between full and abbreviated forms are almost entirely connotational or stylistic, closely tied to the formality of the discourse.[1] This fact allows us to pursue two distinct though related approaches to this task, comparing a supervised model of word choice (Wang and Hirst, 2010) with a mostly unsupervised system that leverages an automatically-built lexicon of formality (Brooke et al., 2010). Our findings indicate that the lexicon-based method is highly competitive with the supervised, task-specific method. Both models approach the human performance evidenced in an independent crowdsourced annotation.

2 Methods

2.1 Latent Semantic Analysis

Both approaches that we are investigating make use of Latent Semantic Analysis (LSA) as a dimensionality-reduction technique (Landauer and Dumais, 1997).[2] In LSA, the first step is to create a matrix representing the association between words as determined by their co-occurrence in a corpus, and then apply singular value decomposition (SVD) to identify the first k most significant dimensions of variation. After this step, each word can be represented as a vector of length k, which can be compared or combined with the vectors of other words. The best k is usually determined empirically. For a more detailed introduction to this method, see also the discussion by Turney and Littman (2003).

[1] Shortened forms might also be preferred in cases where space is at a premium, e.g. newspaper headlines or tweets.

[2] Note that neither technique is feasible using the full co-occurrence vectors, which have several hundred thousand dimensions in both cases; in addition, previous work has shown that performance drops off with increased dimensionality.

2.2 Classifying Context Vectors

Our first method is the lexical choice model proposed by Wang and Hirst (2010). This approach performs SVD on a term–term co-occurrence matrix, which has been shown to outperform traditional LSA models that use term–document co-occurrence information. Specifically, a given word w is initially represented by a vector v of all its co-occurring words in a small collocation context (a 5-word window), i.e., $v = (v_1, \ldots, v_n)$, where n is the size of the vocabulary, and $v_i = 1$ if w co-occurs with the i-th word in lexicon, or $v_i = 0$ otherwise. The dimensionality of the original vector is then reduced by SVD.

A context, typically comprising a set of words within a small collocation context around the target word for prediction (though we test larger contexts here), is represented by a weighted centroid of the word vectors. Together with the candidate words for prediction, this context vector can then be used as a feature vector for supervised learning; we follow Wang and Hirst in using support vector machines (SVMs) as implemented in WEKA (Witten and Frank, 2005), training a separate classifier for each full/clipped word form pair. The prediction performance varies by k, which can be tested efficiently by simply truncating a single high-k vector to smaller dimensions. The optimal k value reported by Wang and Hirst testing on a standard set of seven near-synonyms was 415; they achieved an accuracy of 74.5%, an improvement over previous statistical approaches, e.g. Inkpen (2007).

2.3 Using Formality Lexicons

The competing method involves building lexicons of formality, using our method from Brooke et al. (2010), which is itself an adaption of an approach used for sentiment lexicon building (Turney and Littman, 2003). Though it relies on LSA, there are several key differences as compared to the context vector approach. First, the pre-LSA matrix is a binary word–document matrix, rather than word–word. For the LSA step, we showed that a very low k value (20) was appropriate choice for identifying variation in formality. After dimensionality reduction, each word vector is compared, using cosine similarity, to words from two sets of seed terms, each representing prototypical formal and informal words, which provides a formality score for each word in the range of -1 to 1. The derivation of the final formality score involves several normalization steps, and therefore a full discussion is precluded here for space reasons; for the details, please see Brooke et al. (2010). Our evaluation suggests that, given a large-enough blog corpus, this method almost perfectly distinguishes words of extreme formality, and is able to identify the more formal of two near-synonyms over 80% of the time, better than a word-length baseline.

Given a lexicon of formality scores, the preferred form for a context is identified by averaging the formality scores of the words in the context and comparing the average score to a cutoff value. Here, the context is generally understood to be the entire text, though we also test smaller contexts. We take the cutoff to be midpoints of the average scores for the contexts of known instances; although technically supervised, we have found that in practice just a few instances is enough to find a stable, high-performing cutoff. Note that the cutoff is analogous to the decision hyperplane of an SVM. In our case, building a lexical resource corresponds to additional task-independent reduction in the dimensionality of the space, greatly simplifying the decision.

3 Resources

Blog data is an ideal resource for this task, since it clearly contains a wide variety of language registers. For our exploration here, we used a collection of over 900,000 blogs (216 million tokens) originally crawled from the web in May 2008. We segmented the texts, filtered out short documents (less than 100 words), and then split the corpus into two halves, training and testing. For each of the two methods described in the previous section, we derived the corresponding LSA-reduced vectors for all lower-case words using the collocation information contained within the training portion.[3] The testing portion was used only as a source for test contexts.

We independently collected a set of common full/clipped word pairs from web resources such as Wikipedia, limiting ourselves to phonologically-realized clippings. This excludes orthographic shortenings like *thx* or *ppl* which cannot be pro-

[3]We used the same dataset for each method so that the difference in raw co-occurence information available to each method was not a confounding factor. However, we also tested the lexicon method using the full formality lexicon from Brooke et al. (2010), built on the larger ICWSM blog corpus; the difference in performance was negligible.

nounced. We also removed pairs where one of the words was quite rare (fewer than 150 tokens in the entire corpus) or where, based on examples pulled from the corpus, there was a common confounding homonym–for instance the word *prob*, which is a common clipped form of both *problem* and *probably*. However, we did keep words like *doc*, where the *doctor* sense was much more common than the *document* sense. After this filtering, 38 full/clipped word pairs remained in our set. For each pair, we automatically extracted a sample of usage contexts from texts in the corpus where only one of the two forms appears. For each word form in each of our training and testing corpora, we manually removed duplicate and near-duplicate contexts, non-English and unintelligible contexts, and any remaining instances of homonymy until we had 50 acceptable usage examples for each word form in each sub-corpus (100 for each of the word pairs), a total of 3800 contexts for each of training and testing.

One gold standard is provided by the original choice of the writer, but another possible comparison is with reference to an independent human annotation, as has been done for other near-synonym word choice test sets (Inkpen, 2007). For our annotation, we used the crowdsourcing website Crowdflower (www.crowdflower.com), which is built on top of the well-known Amazon Mechanical Turk (www.mturk.com), which has been used, for instance, to create emotion lexicons (Mohammad and Turney, 2010). In general terms, these crowdsourcing platforms provide access to a pool of online workers who do small tasks (HITs) for a few cents each. Crowdflower, in particular, offers a worker-filtering feature where gold standard HITs (75 clear instances taken from the training data) are interspersed within the test HITs, and workers are removed from the task if they fail to answer a certain percentage correct (90%). For each word form, we randomly selected 20 of 50 test contexts to be judged, or 1520 altogether. For each case, the workers were presented with the word pair and three sentences of context (additional context was provided if less than 40 tokens), and asked to guess which word the writer used. To get more information and allow participants to express a tentative opinion, we gave the workers five options for a word pair A/B: "Probably A/B", "Definitely A/B", and "I'm not sure"; for our purposes here, however, we will not distinguish between "Probably" and "Definitely". We queried for five different judgments per test case in our test corpus, and took the majority judgment as the standard, or "I'm not sure" if there was no majority judgment.

4 Evaluation

First, we compare our crowdsourced annotation to our writer's choice gold standard, which provides a useful baseline for the difficulty of the task. The agreement is surprisingly low; even if "I'm not sure" responses are discounted, agreement with the writer's choice gold standard is just 71.7% for the remaining datapoints. For certain words (such as *professor*, *doctor*), workers avoided the non-standard clipped forms almost entirely, though there were other pairs, like *photo/photograph*, where the clipped form dominated. Expected frequency, rather than document context, is clearly playing a role here.

Our main evaluation consists of comparing the predictions of our two methods to the original choice of the writer, as seen in our corpus. Accuracy is calculated as the number of predictions that agree with this standard across all the (3800) contexts in our test set. We first calibrated each model using the training set, and then prompted for predictions with various amount of context.[4] The 3-sentence context includes the sentences where the word appeared, and the sentences on either side. Other options we investigated were, for the vector classification, the option of using a single classifier for all pairs, or using a different k-value for each pair, and, for the lexicon-based prediction, the option of using a single cutoff for all pairs. The best k were determined by 10-fold cross-validation on the training set. The results are given in Table 1. Since our test sets are balanced, the random guessing performance is 50%.

A chi-square test indicates the difference between the best performing result for each method is not statistically significant. We see that both methods show an improvement with the addition of context beyond the sentence where the word appears, with full document context providing the best results; the improvement with full document context is statistically significant for the vector classification model ($p < 0.001$). Overall, the two methods make similar choices, with the agreement

[4]In all cases, other appearances of the word or an inflected form in the context were removed.

Table 1: Clipping prediction results, all pairs

Vector classification	
Options	**Accuracy**
Sentence context only (k=17)	62.9
3-sentence context (k=15)	64.6
Full document (FD) (k=16)	**67.9**
FD, single (generalized) classifier	66.8
FD, best k for each pair	65.9
Formality lexicon	
Options	**Accuracy**
Sentence context only	65.2
3-sentence context	65.5
Full document (FD)	**66.7**
FD, single (generalized) cutoff	65.1

Table 2: Clipping prediction results, by pair

	Accuracy	
Clipped pair	**VC model**	**FL model**
prof/professor	68	74
tourney/tournament	64	55
plane/airplane	61	42
doc/doctor	81	78
stats/statistics	74	75
meds/medication	82	82
fridge/refrigerator	65	63
app/application	66	62
mic/microphone	54	59
fam/family	84	85

of the predictions at 78.1% for the full document models. Another result that points to the similarity of the final models is that the best single k value is very close to the best k value for lexicon building from Brooke et al. (2010) The generalized clipping models (of both kinds) do worse than the pair-specific models, but the drop is fairly modest. An even more individualized vector classification model, in the form of individual k values for each pair, does not improve performance. If we instead take the worker judgements as a gold standard, the performance of our two models on that subset of the test data is worse than with a writer-based standard: 61.1% for the best lexicon-based model, and 63.6% for the best vector classification model.

Finally, we look at individual full/clipped word pairs. Table 2 contains the results for a sample of these pairs, using the best models from Table 1. Some word pairs (e.g. *mic/microphone*) were very difficult for the models, while others can usually be distinguished. The main difference between the two models is that there are certain pairs (e.g. *plane/airplane*) where the vector classification works much better, perhaps indicating that formality is not the most relevant kind of variation for these pairs.

5 Discussion

Our initial hypothesis was that the formality of the discourse plays a key role in determining whether a clipped form of a word will be used in place of a full form, and thus a lexicon of formality could be a useful tool for this kind of word choice. Our results mostly bear this out: although the vector classification model has a slight advantage, the lexicon-based method, which has the advantage of compactness, interpretability, and portability, does reasonably well. Tellingly, the best vector-based model is very similar to the lexicon in terms of its parameters, including a preference for the use of the entire document as context window and low LSA k, rather than the local context and high LSA k that was preferred for a previous near-synonym choice task (Wang and Hirst, 2010). In comparison to that task, clipping prediction is clearly more difficult, a fact that is confirmed by the results of our crowdsourced annotation.

The fact that the models do better on certain individual word pairs and more poorly on others indicates that the degree of formality difference between clipped and full forms is probably quite variable, and in some cases may be barely noticeable. Under those circumstances, the advantages of a vector classification model, which might base the classification on other kinds of relevant context (e.g. topic), are clear. We conclude by noting that for a highly specialized problem such as word clipping prediction, a single lexical resource can, it appears, complete with a task-based supervised approach, but even here we see signs that a single resource might be insufficient to cover all cases. For wider, more complex tasks, any particular resource may address only a limited part of the task space, and therefore a good deal of work may be required before a lexicon-based method can reasonably compete with a more straightforward statistical approach.

Acknowledgements

This work was supported by the Natural Sciences and Engineering Research Council of Canada.

References

Shlomo Argamon, Casey Whitelaw, Paul Chase, Sobhan Raj Hota, Navendu Garg, and Shlomo Levitan. 2007. Stylistic text classification using functional lexical features. *Journal of the American Society for Information Science and Technology*, 7:91–109.

Julian Brooke, Tong Wang, and Graeme Hirst. 2010. Automatic acquisition of lexical formality. In *Proceedings of the 23rd International Conference on Computational Linguistics (COLING '10)*, pages 90–98, Beijing.

Paul Cook and Suzanne Stevenson. 2009. An unsupervised model for text message normalization. In *Proceedings of the NAACL HLT 2009 Workshop on Computational Approaches to Linguistic Creativity*, pages 71–79, Boulder, Colorado.

Philip Edmonds and Graeme Hirst. 2002. Near-synonymy and lexical choice. *Computational Linguistics*, 28(2):105–144, June.

Diana Inkpen. 2007. A statistical model for near-synonym choice. *ACM Transactions on Speech and Language Processing*, 4(1):1–17.

Alistair Kennedy and Diana Inkpen. 2006. Sentiment classification of movie reviews using contextual valence shifters. *Computational Intelligence*, 22:110–1225.

Charles Kreidler. 1979. Creating new words by shortening. *Journal of English Linguistics*, 13:24–36.

Thomas K. Landauer and Susan Dumais. 1997. A solution to Plato's problem: The latent semantic analysis theory of the acquisition, induction, and representation of knowledge. *Psychological Review*, 104:211–240.

Saif Mohammad and Peter Turney. 2010. Emotions evoked by common words and phrases: Using Mechanical Turk to create an emotion lexicon. In *Proceedings of the NAACL HLT 2010 Workshop on Computational Approaches to Analysis and Generation of Emotion in Text*, pages 26–34, Los Angeles.

Naoaki Okazaki and Sophia Ananiadou. 2006. A term recognition approach to acronym recognition. In *Proceedings of the Joint Conference of the International Committee on Computational Linguistics and the Association for Computational Linguistics (COLING/ACL '06)*.

Peter Turney and Michael Littman. 2003. Measuring praise and criticism: Inference of semantic orientation from association. *ACM Transactions on Information Systems*, 21:315–346.

Tong Wang and Graeme Hirst. 2010. Near-synonym lexical choice in latent semantic space. In *Proceedings of the 23rd International Conference on Computational Linguistics (COLING '10)*, pages 1182–1190, Beijing.

Ian H. Witten and Eibe Frank. 2005. *Data Mining: Practical Machine Learning Tools and Techniques*. Morgan Kaufmann, San Francisco.

A Semantic Relatedness Measure Based on Combined Encyclopedic, Ontological and Collocational Knowledge

Yannis Haralambous
Institut Télécom – Télécom Bretagne
Département Informatique
UMR CNRS 3192 Lab-STICC
Technopôle Brest Iroise
CS 83818, 29238 Brest Cedex 3, France
yannis.haralambous@telecom-bretagne.eu

Vitaly Klyuev
University of Aizu
Aizu-Wakamatsu
Fukushima-ken 965-8580, Japan
vkluev@u-aizu.ac.jp

Abstract

We describe a new semantic relatedness measure combining the Wikipedia-based Explicit Semantic Analysis measure, the WordNet path measure and the mixed collocation index. Our measure achieves the currently highest results on the WS-353 test: a Spearman ρ coefficient of 0.79 (vs. 0.75 in (Gabrilovich and Markovitch, 2007)) when applying the measure directly, and a value of 0.87 (vs. 0.78 in (Agirre et al., 2009)) when using the prediction of a polynomial SVM classifier trained on our measure.

In the appendix we discuss the adaptation of ESA to 2011 Wikipedia data, as well as various unsuccessful attempts to enhance ESA by filtering at word, sentence, and section level.

1 Introduction

1.1 Semantic Relatedness and Corpora

Semantic relatedness describes the degree to which concepts are associated via any kind of semantic relationship (Scriver, 2006). Its evaluation is a fundamental NLP problem, with applications in word-sense disambiguation, text classification, information retrieval, automatic summarization and many other fields. In recent decades, a great variety of relatedness measures have been defined, based on corpora such as Wikipedia, Wiktionary, WordNet, etc.

Wikipedia is one of the most successful collaborative projects of all time. By a constantly growing number of additions, corrections and verifications, its contents grows in both quantity and quality, and is considered by many linguists as the corpus they had always dreamed of (Medelyan et al., 2008).

By measuring the normalized tfidf values of words in a page, we can consider the page to be a weighted vector in the space of words. Inverting the matrix of these vectors we obtain weighted vectors of words in the space of pages. As every page deals with a single topic, we consider these vectors as being concept vectors. The ESA (Explicit Semantic Analysis) measure between two words is obtained by taking the cosine of their concept vectors (Gabrilovich and Markovitch, 2007).

Unlike Wikipedia, WordNet (Miller, 1995), a semiformal lexical ontology (Huang et al., 2010), has a fine and carefully-crafted ontological structure: word senses are represented by sets of synonyms ("synsets"), and there is a graph structure on synsets based on hypernymic relations. Several WordNet-based semantic relatedness measures have been defined, based on distances in the hypernymic graph, and often combined with word distribution in sense-tagged corpora.

1.2 Evaluation of Results, WS-353 Test

(Finkelstein et al., 2001) introduce WS-353, a semantic relatedness test set consisting of 353 word pairs[1] and a gold standard defined as the mean value of evaluations by up to 17 human judges. Although this test suite contains some quite controversial word pairs,[2] it has been widely used in literature and has become the de facto standard for semantic relatedness measure evaluation.

Technically, the final result of the test is the Spearman ρ rank correlation coefficient (Spearman, 1904) between the relatedness ranking of pairs by human judges and that by the tested algorithm. So, in fact, it is not the value obtained for each pair that counts, but only the ranks.

1.3 Our Approach

By closely examining word pairs that failed to be ranked correctly by ESA, we came to the conclusion that the WS-353 word pairs belong (non-exclusively) to four classes, corresponding to different kinds of semantic relatedness and requiring different kinds of knowledge:

1. *encyclopedic*: see Section 2;
2. *ontological*: see Section 3;
3. *collocational*: see Section 4;
4. *pragmatic*: see Section 6.

In this paper, we define a new semantic relatedness measure by combining knowledge related to these four classes.

[1] Actually 352 pairs, since "money / cash" appears twice.

[2] For example: "Arafat / terror" (0.765), "Arafat / peace" (0.673), "Jerusalem / Israel" (0.846), "Jerusalem / Palestinian" (0.765), etc.

2 Encyclopedic Knowledge

This class contains pairs that are best sorted by ESA. We note that (Agirre et al., 2009) qualify ESA as a distributional approach. Indeed, technically two words are semantically related in ESA if they appear together frequently in Wikipedia pages. But since pages are descriptions of topics (= concepts), words are ESA-close when they appear frequently in common concept descriptions, and therefore in common semantic domains. Hence, ESA is semantically richer than a merely distributional approach.

ESA is the first and most important component of our combined relatedness measure. By adapting our implementation of the ESA algorithm to 2011 Wikipedia data (see App. A), we obtain a Spearman $\rho = 0.7394$. In the following sections we describe the components added to ESA in order to optimize its performance even further.

3 Ontological knowledge

To get a better insight into the shortcomings of ESA on WS-353, we calculate Spearman ρ for the WS-353 set minus a single pair, for every pair. In Fig. 1 one can see the top 40 "most problematic" pairs: those whose removal increases ρ the most. By taking a closer look at them we can get hints for further improvements of the measure.

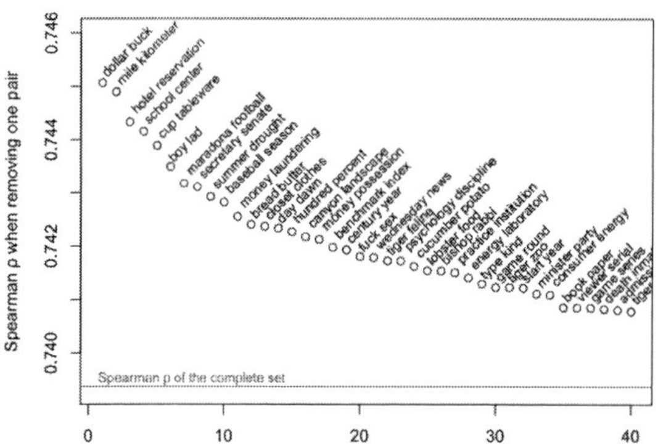

Figure 1: Spearman ρ when removing a single pair from WS-353.

First of all, we see pairs having a relation that is ontological in nature: "tiger / feline" (hyponym), "mile / kilometer" (coordinate terms, or "classmates" (Kuroda et al., 2010b)), "dollar / buck" (synonyms), etc. These relations are strong enough to justify the presence of the pairs in the test set, but do not necessarily imply high frequency of terms in common Wikipedia pages.

A good place for information of an ontological nature is WordNet. There have been several WordNet-based measures defined in the literature. When applying them[3] to the WS-353 test set we get the following ρ:

WNP (Path-based)	0.2873
WUP (Wu and Palmer, 1994)	0.1356
RES (Resnik, 1995)	0.2112
JCN (Jiang and Conrath, 1997)	**0.3172**
LCH (Leacock and Chodorow, 1998)	0.1437
HSO (Hirst and St-Onge, 1998)	0.1598
LIN (Lin, 1998)	0.1987
LESK (Banerjee and Pedersen, 2002)	0.1304

Despite the fact that JCN (which combines WordNet-graph calculations and word frequencies from a corpus[4]) rates best when used alone, the measure which we are going to use is WNP, which gives the best results when combined with ESA (see below). This measure is based exclusively on the shortest-path distance in WordNet and hence is purely ontological. For example, the WNP-measure of "wood / forest" is 1 (synonyms), "bird / cock" is 0.5 (hypernym), "century / year" is 0.33, "bishop / rabbi" is 0.25, etc.

We found that this measure provides bad results in its lower range (since the path length between distant nodes strongly depends on the density of WordNet for each knowledge domain). To understand the behavior of ESA and WNP measures in their low ranges, we progressively remove pairs from WS-353 *in order of increasing relatedness*.

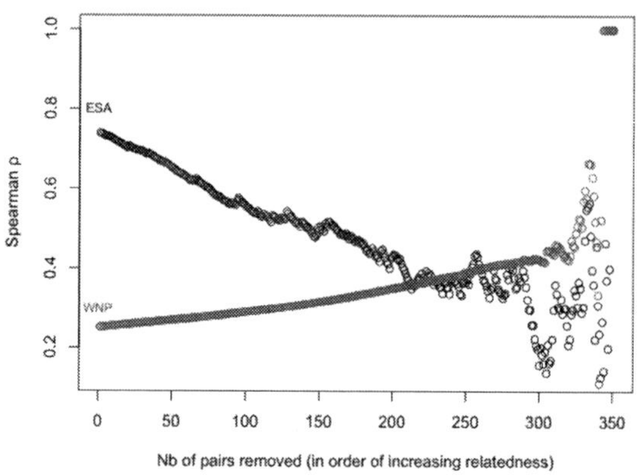

Figure 2: The effect on Spearman ρ of the progressive removal of pairs in order of increasing relatedness, for ESA and WNP measures.

As we can see in Fig. 2, removing pairs in the small-value range of the measure *strongly decreases* ESA (which, after half of the pairs are removed, becomes chaotic), while the same operation steadily *increases* WNP. In other words, small-value pairs are crucial positive contributors for ESA, but rather negative contributors for WNP. For this reason, we use only the upper range of WNP, and ignore its results for low-valued pairs. To achieve a smooth "fade-out" of WNP's lower range we multiply it by a sigmoid logistic function. We

[3]In fact, these measures apply to synsets rather than to words. To avoid going through a sense-disambiguation process, we take the optimistic approach of using for each pair of words, the pair of senses which are the most closely related. Hence, if $\hat{\mu}$ is a synset-measure, s, s' are synsets and w, w' words, we define the induced word-measure μ as $\mu(w, w') := \max_{s \ni w, s' \ni w'} \hat{\mu}(s, s')$.

[4]For the distributional part of Jiang & Conrath, Resnik and Lin, we use the Wikipedia 2011 corpus.

hence define a new measure

$$\mu_{\mathrm{EW}}(w_1, w_2) = \mu_{\mathrm{ESA}}(w_1, w_2) \cdot (1 + \lambda\sigma_{m,s}(\mu_{\mathrm{WNP}}(w_1, w_2))), \tag{1}$$

where λ weights WNP with respect to ESA, m is the sigmoid inflection point (= a soft boundary of WNP's lower range), s is the steepness of the sigmoid (small s makes the central part of the sigmoid closer to a vertical line), and "EW" stands for "ESA and WordNet."

Calculations give the following optimal result:

$\lambda = 4.665, m = 0.26, s = 0.05$	$\rho = \mathbf{0.7779}$

which surpasses the (Gabrilovich and Markovitch, 2007) ESA result of 0.75 by 5.2%. The parameter values have been obtained by gradient descent. In the next section we will further enhance this result by taking collocations into account.

4 Collocational Knowledge

Returning to Fig. 1, we see that many "problematic" pairs are in fact collocations: "baseball / season," "money / laundering", "hundred / percent," etc. We claim that the collocational nature of these word pairs has motivated their inclusion in WS-353. To show this, we calculated the collocation index (defined as $\frac{2\#(w_1 w_2)}{\#(w_1)+\#(w_2)}$) of all WS-353 pairs[5].

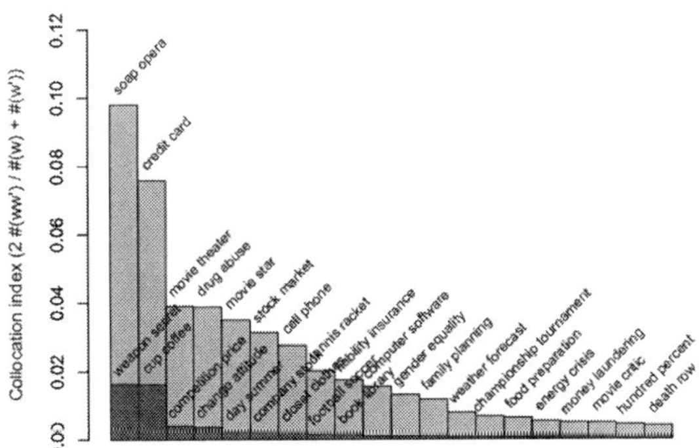

Figure 3: Top twenty direct (in gray) and inverse (in red) collocation indices for WS-353.

The primary goal of WS-353 is to evaluate relatedness measures, and these are symmetric by definition (we always have $\mu(w_1, w_2) = \mu(w_2, w_1)$). If the word pairs were chosen on strictly semantic criteria, and if collocations were purely accidental, then we would have a roughly equal number of pairs (w_1, w_2) where $w_1 w_2$ is a collocation and pairs where $w_2 w_1$ is a collocation.

Fig. 3 shows that this is not the case: for the word pairs concerned, WS-353 developers have almost systematically chosen to write the words in the order in which they form a collocation.

[5]We obtained WS-353 pair and word frequencies from the 53.45 billion-word GoogleBooks corpus (Michel et al., 2011). We considered only books published after 1970.

But neither ESA nor WNP recognize collocations: the former because of the bag-of-words principle underlying tfidf, and the latter only in the case where the collocational pair is a concept on its own. Indeed, most of the collocations in Fig. 3 are WordNet concepts (the exceptions being: "gender / equality," "food / preparation," "secret / weapon," "energy / crisis," etc.) but knowledge of that fact is not sufficient for ranking, since there is no mention in WordNet of the strength of the collocational relation.

We use the collocation index to further enhance our EW relatedness measure.

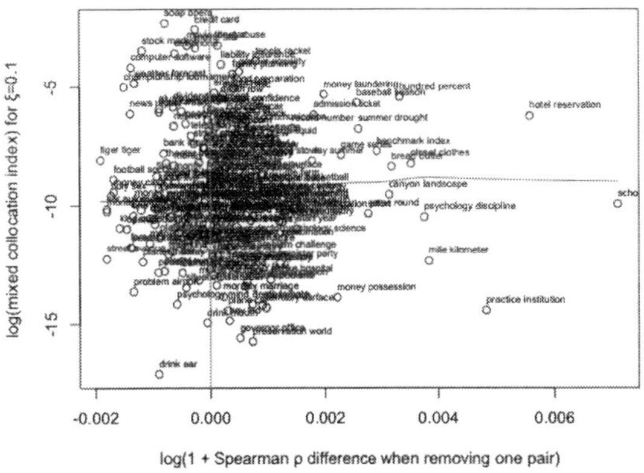

Figure 4: Collocation index vs. Spearman stability of EW. The red line is LOWESS polynomial regression (Cleveland, 1981).

Note that this index is *not* a measure (for example, the collocation index of "tiger / tiger" is not 1) and cannot be used directly as such.

How do collocational pairs contribute to the WS-353 Spearman ρ value? In Fig. 4 one can compare collocation index and Spearman stability (that is, the effect on ρ of the removal of a single word pair). Pairs located on the green vertical line are those whose removal does not affect Spearman ρ. Those on the right increase ρ when removed. We observe that most collocations are on the right; in other words, they are negative contributors. The most problematic ones are collocations which are not individual WordNet concepts (typical examples: "school / center," "hotel / reservation," "canyon / landscape," etc.).

On the other hand, on the left side we find collocations that contribute positively to ρ: in many cases these have a strong ontological relation ("tiger / tiger," "street / avenue," "football / soccer," etc.) which is probably the main reason for their positive contribution. The LOWESS polynomial regression line is quasi-horizontal, so we cannot infer whether or not collocation index is correlated with ρ.

An auxiliary question is whether collocation index values (at least in the high range) are correlated with the actual values of the WS-353 gold standard. Fig. 5 compares these two quantities. As we can see, LOWESS polynomial regression is almost steadily monotonically increasing, which shows that, although not a measure per se, (high-range) collocation index could be useful for relatedness measurement.

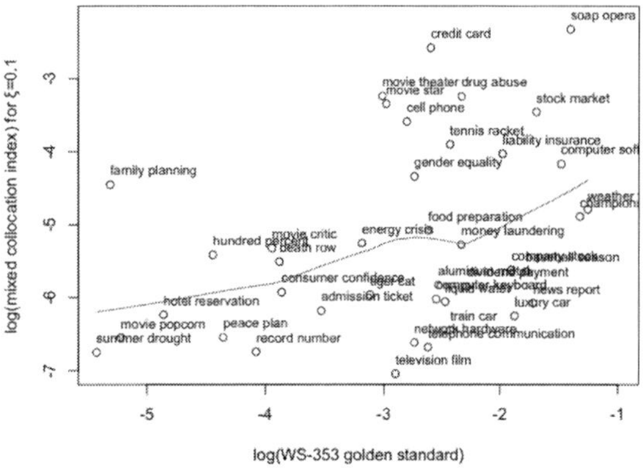

Figure 5: Collocation index vs. WS-353 gold standard. The red line is LOWESS polynomial regression.

We combine the previously defined EW measure with collocation index, by defining measure EWC (= "ESA + WordNet + collocations") as follows:

$$\begin{aligned}\mu_{\mathrm{EWC}}(w_1,w_2) = \mu_{\mathrm{ESA}}(w_1,w_2) \\ \cdot (1+\lambda\sigma_{m,s}(\mu_{\mathrm{WNP}}(w_1,w_2))) \\ \cdot (1+\lambda'\sigma_{m',s'}(C_\xi(w_1,w_2))),\end{aligned}$$

where λ, m, s are as in (1), λ', m' and s' are similar, and the *mixed collocation index* C_ξ is defined as follows:

$$C_\xi(w_1,w_2) = \frac{2\#(w_1w_2)}{\#(w_1)+\#(w_2)} + \xi\frac{2\#(w_2w_1)}{\#(w_1)+\#(w_2)}$$

where $\#(.)$ is the frequency in the corpus.

Calculations give the following optimal result:

$\lambda = 5.16, \mu = 0.25, \lambda' = 48.7,$ $\mu' = 0.19, s = s' = 0.05, \xi = 0.55$	$\rho = \mathbf{0.7874}$

which is 1.2% higher than EW and, to the best of our knowledge, currently the highest result for WS-353 by a direct measure (not using a support vector machine). The parameter values have been obtained by gradient descent.

We can interpret this result as follows: *the EWC measure works best when the lower fourth of WordNet measure and the lower fifth of collocation index values are ignored, and when inverse collocations count half as much as direct ones.*

5 Supervised Approach Using an SVM

(Agirre et al., 2009, p. 25) train an SVM on pairs of WS-353 pairs; this allows them to get an insight on performance increase obtained by combining various measures. By combining knowledge from a Web corpus and from WordNet, they obtain a highest value of Spearman $\rho = 0.78$. We calculated predictions of (4th degree polynomial) SVMs based on our EW and EWC measures, and obtained the following results, using 10-fold cross-validation:

Measure	Result
EW (ESA + WNP)	$\rho = 0.7996$
EWC (ESA + WNP + collocations)	$\rho = \mathbf{0.8654}$

We observe that even without collocations we already get a better value than (Agirre et al., 2009), and also that the collocation component increases this value significantly, hence validating our choice of using collocational knowledge to enhance semantic relatedness measurement.

6 Pragmatic Knowledge

This class contains pairs not captured by the previous methods. The typical example is "hotel / reservation": its ESA value is very low, there is no ontological relation, and the collocation index is quite low as well. To capture the relatedness of such a pair, we need specific knowledge domain ontologies, providing relations such as "A is part of a functional process of system B" (in this case: "a 'reservation' is part of the process of renting a room in a 'hotel' "). We leave this as an open task for future development.

7 Conclusion

By combining two pre-existing semantic relatedness measures and by adding a component based on frequency of collocations, we have obtained a new measure that surpasses the one given in (Agirre et al., 2009) by 11% (when comparing results obtained by SVMs). We conjecture that this measure can further be enhanced by using pragmatic knowledge taken, for example, from specialized domain ontologies.

Appendices

A Adapting ESA to 2011 Wikipedia

The original (and unreleased) C++ ESA implementation (Gabrilovich and Markovitch, 2007) is based on 2005 Wikipedia data (2.2 GB) and achieves a Spearman $\rho = 0.75$. A later implementation in Python and Java (Çallı, 2010), based on the same corpus, achieves $\rho = 0.74$. We implemented ESA in Perl and similarly obtained $\rho = 0.7404$ when based on 2005 data. The same algorithms applied to 2011 data (31 GB), produced a disappointing $\rho = 0.7047$. Indeed, between 2005 and 2011, Wikipedia has evolved as follows:

	2005	2011
#concepts	866,881	4,178,454
#terms/concept	96.1971	97.4243

where by "concepts" we mean Wikipedia pages in the main namespace, and by "terms," distinct stemmed words.

Following advice by Gabrilovich (personal communication), we increased the generality of concepts by filtering Wikipedia pages by two criteria: minimum number of terms, and minimum number of in- and outgoing links. The original values were: 100 terms and 5 links; by requiring a minimum of 200 terms and 14 links, we have attained the 2005 ρ value (more precisely: $\rho = \mathbf{0.7394}$). Fig. 6 displays ρ as a function of our two criteria.

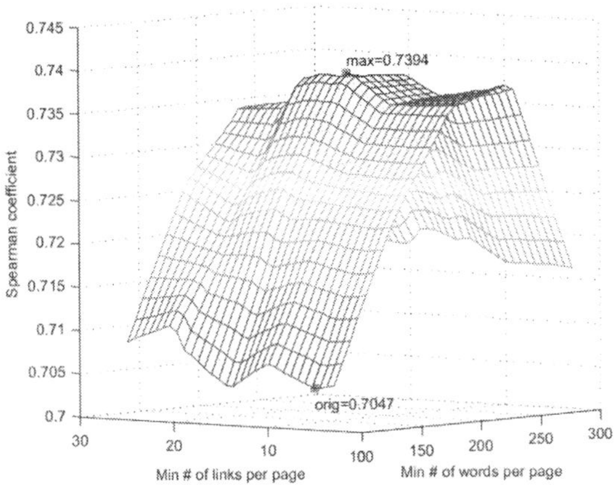

Figure 6: Adapting ESA to 2011 Wikipedia data by increasing the minimum number of distinct (stemmed) words and of in- and outgoing links per page.

In the following table, the column 2011 displays the results with original ESA setting, 2011* the ones with modified settings, $\overline{\text{df}}$ is mean document frequency of terms and term density is $\frac{\overline{\text{df}}}{\#\text{concepts}}$:

	2005	2011	2011*
#concepts	132,689	311,209	155,767
#terms/concept	165	279	414
#terms	187,971	503,368	408,299
$\overline{\text{df}}$	116.3307	173.7199	159.0395
term density	0.00088	0.00056	0.00102

As we see, terms are less densely distributed in the 2011 corpus, since the increase of their mean document frequency, though important, is overruled by an even more important increase in the number of concepts. By more efficiently pruning concepts and leaving $\overline{\text{df}}$ relatively stable, we manage to increase term density anew and hence, enhance performance.

B Experiments

(Giraud-Carrier and Dunham, 2010) emphasize the importance of sharing negative results. Responding to their call, here are some of our failed attempts at increasing ESA performance on the 2005 corpus. Note that the standard ESA value we challenge is $\rho = 0.7404$.

B.1 At the Word Level: Lemmatization and POS Filtering

ESA removes stop words and words with fewer than three letters before applying the Porter stemmer thrice. Instead of stemming, we lemmatized and then applied two strategies: keeping only nouns and proper names (Penn tags NN, NNP, and plurals), or also verbs and adjectives (tags starting with NN, NNP, VB, and JJ). Here are the results obtained:

Penn tags NN, NNS, NNP, NNPS	$\rho = 0.7194$
Penn tags NN*, NNP*, VB*, JJ*	$\rho = 0.7178$

The performance loss is due to lemmatization, proving once again that while Porter stemming may seem a brutal technique, it works better than anything else. Note that, surprisingly, when adding verbs and adjectives we get a (slightly) *smaller* ρ.

B.2 Filtering at the Sentence Level

We attempted to triple the weight of sentences containing either the page title, or one of the (non stop-)words of the page title, or one of the anchors pointing to the page. This operation affected 1,399,165 sentences. Here are the results obtained:

Tripling weight of selected sentences	$\rho = 0.7293$

B.3 Filtering at the Section Level

The idea is to avoid "historical sections" in pages describing current notions or objects. Historical sections are detected by a higher frequency of past-tense verbs, unless of course the whole page is of a historical nature, and hence using primarily the past tense. Let $\pi = \frac{\#\text{ past-tense verbs}}{\#\text{ verbs}}$ for each Wikipedia page. We pruned sections of $\pi \geq 0.8$ when the page had $\pi < 0.8$. We also pruned sections named "History," "External links," "References," "See also," "Further reading," and "Bibliography." This affected 111,028 sections out of 470,948. Here are the results obtained:

Pruning of "historical" and other sections	$\rho = 0.6608$

C Implementation Details

Implementation of ESA was done from scratch in Lex and Perl. To access WordNet v3, we used the Perl module `WordNet::Similarity` (Pedersen et al., 2004). SVM calculations as well as 2D figures were done in R, and the 3D figure in Matlab. For lemmatizing and POS-tagging, we used TreeTagger (Schmid, 1994). Our code is publicly available at `http://omega2.enstb.org/yannis/similarity.php`.

D Acknowledgments

We wish to thank Evgeniy Gabrilovich and Çağatay Çallı for their help in implementing ESA, and Sophia Ananiadou for her helpful advice.

References

Eneko Agirre, Enrique Alfonseca, Keith Hall, Jana Kravalova, Marius Paşca, and Aitor Soroa. 2009. A study on similarity and relatedness using distributional and WordNet-based approaches. In *Human Language Technologies: The 2009 Annual Conference of the North American Chapter of the ACL*, pages 19–27.

Eneko Agirre, Montse Cuadros, German Rigau, and Aitor Soroa. 2010. Exploring knowledge bases for similarity. In *Proceedings of IJCAI*, pages 373–377.

Satanjeev Banerjee and Ted Pedersen. 2002. An adapted Lesk algorithm for word sense disambiguation using WordNet. *Springer Lecture Notes in Computer Science*, 2276:136–145.

Alexander Budanitsky and Graeme Hirst. 2006. Evaluating WordNet-based measures of lexical semantic relatedness. *Comput. Linguist.*, 32:13–47, March.

Çağatay Çallı. 2010. Improving search result clustering by integrating semantic information from Wikipedia. Master's thesis, Middle East Technical University, Ankara.

W.S. Cleveland. 1981. LOWESS: A program for smoothing scatterplots by robust locally weighted regression. *The American Statistician*, 35:54.

Lev Finkelstein, Evgeniy Gabrilovich, Yossi Matias, Ehud Rivlin, Zach Solan, Gadi Wolfman, and Eytan Ruppin. 2001. Placing search in context: the concept revisited. In *Tenth International World Wide Web Conference (WWW10), Hong Kong*, pages 406–414.

Evgeniy Gabrilovich and Shaul Markovitch. 2007. Computing semantic relatedness using Wikipedia-based explicit semantic analysis. In *IJCAI'07: Proceedings of the 20th International Joint Conference on Artificial Intelligence*.

Evgeniy Gabrilovich and Shaul Markovitch. 2009. Wikipedia-based semantic interpretation for natural language processing. *Journal of Artificial Intelligence Research*, 34(1):443–498.

Christophe Giraud-Carrier and Margaret H. Dunham. 2010. On the importance of sharing negative results. *SIGKDD explorations*, 12(2):3–4.

Graeme Hirst and David St-Onge. 1998. Lexical chains as representations of context for the detection and correction of malapropisms. In Christiane Fellbaum, editor, *WordNet: An electronic lexical database*, pages 305–332. The MIT Press.

Cha-Ren Huang, Nicoletta Calzolari, Aldo Gangemi, Alessandro Lenci, Alessandro Oltramari, and Laurent Prévot, editors. 2010. *Ontology and the lexicon*. Studies in Natural Language Processing. Cambridge.

Jay J. Jiang and David W. Conrath. 1997. Semantic similarity based on corpus statistics and lexical taxonomy. In *Proceedings on International Conference on Research in Computational Linguistics, Taiwan 1997*.

Kow Kuroda, Francis Bond, and Kentaro Torisawa. 2010a. Why Wikipedia needs to make friends with WordNet. In *The 5th International Conference of the Global WordNet Association (GWC-2010)*.

Kow Kuroda, Jun'ichi Kazama, and Kentaro Torisawa. 2010b. A look inside the distributionally similar terms. In *Proceedings of the Second Workshop on NLP Challenges in the Information Explosion Era (NLPIX 2010)*, pages 40–49.

Claudia Leacock and Martin Chodorow. 1998. Combining local context and WordNet similarity for word sense identification. In Christiane Fellbaum, editor, *WordNet: An electronic lexical database*, pages 265–283. The MIT Press.

Dekang Lin. 1998. An information-theoretic definition of similarity. In *Proceedings of 15th International Conference On Machine Learning, Madison WI, 1998*.

Olena Medelyan, Catherine Legg, David Milne, and Ian H. Witten. 2008. Mining meaning from Wikipedia. Technical report, Department of Computer Science, University of Waikato, New Zealand.

Jean-Baptiste Michel, Yuan Kui Shen, Aviva Presser Aiden, Adrian Veres, Matthew K. Gray, The Google Books Team, Joseph P. Pickett, Dale Hoiberg, Dan Clancy, Peter Norvig, Jon Orwant, Steven Pinker, Martin A. Nowak, and Erez Lieberman Aiden. 2011. Quantitative analysis of culture using millions of digitized books. *Science*, 331(6014):176–182.

George A. Miller. 1995. WordNet: a lexical database for English. *Commun. ACM*, 38:39–41, November.

Ted Pedersen, Siddharth Patwardhan, and Jason Michelizzi. 2004. WordNet::Similarity - Measuring the relatedness of concepts. In *Proceedings of the Nineteenth National Conference on Artificial Intelligence (AAAI-04)*, pages 1024–1025.

Simone Paolo Ponzetto and Michael Strube. 2006. Exploiting semantic role labeling, WordNet and Wikipedia for coreference resolution. In *Proceedings of the Human Language Technology Conference of the North American Chapter of the ACL*, pages 192–199.

Simone Paolo Ponzetto and Michael Strube. 2007. Knowledge derived from Wikipedia for computing semantic relatedness. *Journal of Artificial Intelligence Research*, 30:181–212.

R Development Core Team, 2011. *R: A Language and Environment for Statistical Computing*. R Foundation for Statistical Computing, Vienna, Austria.

Kira Radinsky, Eugene Agichtein, Evgeniy Gabrilovich, and Shaul Markovitch. 2011. A word at a time: Computing word relatedness using temporal semantic analysis. In *WWW 2011*.

Daniel Ramage, Anna N. Rafferty, and Christopher D. Manning. 2009. Random walks for text semantic similarity. In *Proceedings of the 2009 Workshop on Graph-based Methods for Natural Language Processing*, TextGraphs-4, pages 23–31, Stroudsburg, PA, USA. ACL.

Philip Resnik. 1995. Using information content to evaluate semantic similarity in a taxonomy. In *Proceedings of the 14th International Joint Conference on Artificial Intelligence, Montréal*, pages 448–453.

Helmut Schmid. 1994. Probabilistic part-of-speech tagging using decision trees. In *Proceedings of International Conference on New Methods in Language Processing*, Manchester, UK.

Aaron D. Scriver. 2006. Semantic distance in WordNet: A simplified and improved measure of semantic relatedness. Master's thesis, University of Waterloo.

Charles Spearman. 1904. The proof and measurement of association between two things. *Amer. J. Psychol.*, 15:72–101.

Zhi-Biao Wu and Martha Palmer. 1994. Verb semantics and lexical selection. In *Proceedings of the 32nd Annual Meetings of the Association for Computational Linguistics*, pages 133–138.

Torsten Zesch, Iryna Gurevych, and Max Mühlhäuser. 2007. Analyzing and accessing Wikipedia as a lexical semantic resource. Preprint of the Technische Universität Darmstadt.

Torsten Zesch, Christof Müller, and Iryna Gurevych. 2008. Extracting lexical semantic knowledge from Wikipedia and Wiktionary. In *Proceedings of the 6th International Conference on Language Resources and Evaluation*.

Going Beyond Text: A Hybrid Image-Text Approach for Measuring Word Relatedness

Chee Wee Leong and Rada Mihalcea
Department of Computer Science and Engineering
University of North Texas
cheeweeleong@my.unt.edu, rada@cs.unt.edu

Abstract

Traditional approaches to semantic relatedness are often restricted to text-based methods, which typically disregard other multimodal knowledge sources. In this paper, we propose a novel image-based metric to estimate the relatedness of words, and demonstrate the promise of this method through comparative evaluations on three standard datasets. We also show that a hybrid image-text approach can lead to improvements in word relatedness, confirming the applicability of visual cues as a possible orthogonal information source.

1 Introduction

Measuring the semantic relatedness of words is an important task with applications in information extraction and retrieval, query reformulation, word sense disambiguation, plagiarism detection and textual entailment. Owing mainly to the nature of this task, research efforts in the past have typically centered around methodologies employing the use of knowledge-based or corpus-based textual resources, with only little (if any) work paying attention to evidence provided by other multimodal sources, such as visual cues presented by the images that are associated with a given word. While it can be shown that the human cognitive system is sensitive to visual information, and incorporating a dual linguistic-and-pictorial representation of information can actually enhance knowledge acquisition (Potter and Faulconer, 1975), the use of visual information to improve tasks in natural language processing has been largely unexplored.

In this paper, we hypothesize that the relatedness between the visual representations of a pair of words can be effectively used to gauge their similarity. We first discuss a technique widely used in computer vision termed as "bag of visual words" to show how distinctive features of an image can be harvested. We next introduce the main resource, ImageNet, used in our work to bridge the semantic gap between words and images. Finally, we show how a new relatedness metric based exclusively on visual information can be constructed for the semantic relatedness task. We evaluate this metric alongside existing corpus-based (Turney and Pantel, 2010) and knowledge-based metrics (Pedersen et al., 2004) either in a standalone or combined setting and present our findings.

2 Bag of Visual Words

Inspired by the bag-of-words approach employed in information retrieval, the "bag of visual codewords" is a similar technique used mainly for scene classification (Yang et al., 2007). Starting with an image collection, visual features are first extracted as data points from each image. By projecting data points from all the images into a common space and grouping them into a large number of clusters such that similar data points are assigned to the same cluster, we can treat each cluster as a "visual codeword" and express every image in the collection as a "bag of visual codewords." This representation enables the application of methods used in text retrieval to tasks in image processing and computer vision.

Typically, the type of visual features selected can be *global* – suitable for representing an entire image, or *local* – specific to a given region in the image, depending on task requirement. For a global representation, features are often described using a continuous feature space, such as a color histogram in three different color spaces (RGB, HSV and LAB), or textures using Gabor and Haar wavelets (Makadia et al., 2008). Likewise, local descriptors such as key points (Fei-Fei and Perona, 2005) can also adopt such a representation. Regardless of the features used, visual codeword generation involves the following three important phases.

1. Feature Detection: The image is divided into partitions of varying degrees of granularity from which features can be extracted and represented. We can employ normalized cuts to divide an image into irregular regions, or apply uniform seg-

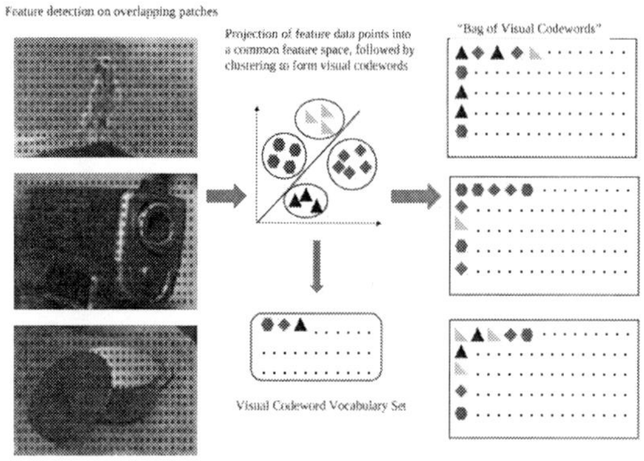

Figure 1: An illustration of the process of generating "Bag of Visual Codewords"

mentation to break it into smaller but fixed grids, or simply locate information-rich local patches on the image using interest point detectors.

2. Feature Description: A descriptor is selected to represent the features extracted from the image. Typically, feature descriptors are represented as numerical vectors, with each vector describing the feature extracted in each region. This way, an image is represented by a set of vectors from its constituent regions.

3. Visual Codeword Generation: Clustering methods are applied to group vectors into clusters, where the center of each cluster is defined as a visual codeword, and the entire set of clusters defines the visual vocabulary for that image collection. Each image region or patch abstracted in feature detection is now represented by the codeword mapped from its corresponding feature vector.

The process of visual codeword generation is illustrated in Figure 1. Fei-Fei and Perona (2005) have shown that, unlike most previous work on object or scene classification that focused on adopting global features, local regions are in fact extremely powerful cues. In our work, we use the Scale-Invariant Feature Transform (SIFT) introduced by Lowe (2004) to describe distinctive local features of an image in the feature description phase. SIFT descriptors are selected for their invariance to image scale, rotation, differences in 3D viewpoints, addition of noise, and change in illumination. They are also robust across affine distortions.

3 ImageNet

Given the maturity of techniques used to extract visual content from images, it is possible to study the synergistic relationships between semantic representations of words and images given the availability of a large lexical resource with associated relevant images. For such a resource, we turn to the ImageNet[1] database (Deng et al., 2009), which is a large-scale ontology of images developed for advancing content-based image search algorithms, and serving as a benchmarking standard for various image processing and computer vision tasks. ImageNet exploits the hierarchical structure of WordNet by attaching relevant images to each synonym set (known as "synset"), hence providing pictorial illustrations of the concept associated with the synset. On average, each synset contains 500-1000 images that are carefully audited through a stringent quality control mechanism. Compared to other image databases with keyword annotations, we believe that ImageNet is suitable for evaluating our hypothesis for two important reasons. First, by leveraging on reliable semantic annotations in WordNet (i.e., words in the synset), we can effectively circumvent the propagation of errors caused by unreliable annotations, and consequently hope to reach more conclusive results for this study. Second, unlike other image databases, ImageNet consists of millions of images, and it is a growing resource with more images added on a regular basis. This aligns with our long-term goal of extending our image-based similarity metric to cover more words in the lexicon. Figure 2 shows an example of a synset and the corresponding images in ImageNet.

Figure 2: A subset of images associated with a node in ImageNet. The WordNet synset illustrated here is {*Dog, domestic dog, Canis familiaris*}

4 Datasets

To evaluate the effectiveness of our image-based model for measuring word-to-word relatedness, we selected three datasets widely used in the past:

[1]http://image-net.org/. ImageNet currently hosts 12,184,113 images in 17624 synsets, each of which is classified under a high level category such as animal, fish, plant, structure etc

Rubenstein and Goodenough (RG65) consists of 65 word pairs ranging from synonymy pairs (e.g., car - automobile) to completely unrelated terms (e.g., noon - string). The 65 noun pairs were annotated by 51 human subjects. All the nouns pairs are non-technical words scored using a scale from 0 (not-related) to 4 (perfect synonymy).
Miller-Charles (MC30) is a subset of the Rubenstein and Goodenough dataset, consisting of 30 word pairs, whose relatedness was rated by 38 human subjects, using a scale from 0 to 4.
WordSimilarity-353 (WS353), also known as Finkelstein-353, consists of 353 word pairs annotated by 13 human experts, on a scale from 0 (unrelated) to 10 (very closely related). The dataset also includes proper names and technical terms, therefore posing an additional degree of difficulty for any relatedness metric.

5 Experiments

In our experiments, we seek answers to the following questions. First, what is the effectiveness of our image-based method in measuring word-to-word relatedness, as compared to existing text-based methods? Second, can our image-based method complement these text-based methods via a combination of their outputs ?

Note that as ImageNet is still a resource under development, not all word pairs in the datasets presented in section 4 are covered. To level the playing field, in our experiments we only select those pairs of words of which both words would appear as surface forms in the synsets of ImageNet with validated images. Moreover, due to coverage issues, an anomaly exists in situations such as $monk - slave$, where both words may appear in single-candidate synsets, i.e., {monk,monastic} and {slave ant} respectively, but are represented using fundamentally different images (person vs animal). To prevent this, we further constrain the selection of word pairs of which at least a pair of candidate synsets each representing a word in the pair belong to the same high level category. Note that both selection steps are performed automatically, and thus the identification of the word pairs that can be used in conjunction with the image-based approach can be effectively applied to any dataset, regardless of size. Our trimmed dataset consists of 10 word-pairs from the Miller-Charles dataset (**MC10**), 18 word-pairs from the Rubenstein-Goodenough dataset (**RG18**) and 56 word-pairs from the Word Similarity dataset (**WS56**).

For each word in a pair, we randomly select 50 images from the validated image pool of its associated synset[2], and extract all the visual codewords from all such images, using the technique explained in section 2. Each image is first preprocessed to have a maximum side length of 300 pixels. Next, SIFT gray-scale descriptors are obtained by densely sampling the image on 20x20 overlapping patches spaced 10 pixels apart using a publicly available image-processing toolkit.[3] K-means clustering is applied on a random subset of 10 million SIFT descriptors to derive a visual vocabulary of 1,000 codewords. Each descriptor is then quantized into a visual codeword by assigning it to the nearest cluster. As such, each image J can now be expressed as a vector $< tf_i.w_i >$, where i=1:1000 and tf_i is the frequency of occurrence of visual codeword w_i in image J. For each synset, we sum the vectors of all 50 images and normalize each w_i by its total frequency in the synset.
Image Metric: Given a word pair w_i and w_j, let $S_i = \{v_k^i\}$ and $S_j = \{v_m^j\}$ be their set of candidate visual vectors respectively. Then, computing the semantic relatedness of two words amounts to finding the maximum visual relatedness between all the possible pairings of synsets representing both words, using the cosine similarity between the visual vectors of the synsets, given below. The dimensionality of the vector, n, is set to 1000, which is the size of the visual codeword vocabulary.

$$Sim_{img}(w_i, w_j) =$$

$$\max_{v_k \in S_i, v_m \in S_j} \frac{\sum_{p=1}^{n} v_k^p v_m^p}{\sqrt{\sum_{p=1}^{n} (v_k^p)^2} \sqrt{\sum_{p=1}^{n} (v_m^p)^2}}$$

Text Metric: For a comparative study, we evaluate several knowledge-based methods, including Roget and WordNet Edges (Jarmasz, 2003), H&S (Hirst and St-Onge, 1998), L&C (Leacock and Chodorow, 1998), J&C (Jiang and Conrath, 1997), LIN (Lin, 1998), RES (Resnik, 1995), and two corpus-based methods Latent Semantic Analysis (LSA) (Landauer and Dumais, 1997) and Explicit Semantic Analysis (ESA) (Gabrilovich and Markovitch, 2007).
Combined Metric: In the combined setting, we attempt to integrate the output of our image-based metric with that of existing text-based metrics in a pairwise manner via two combination functions, which were previously noted for

[2]Note that a word may appear as surface forms across multiple synsets. In such cases, we randomly sample 50 images from each of the synsets

[3]http://www.image-net.org/challenges/LSVRC/2011

	Text-based measures								Image metric
	WNE	H&S	J&C	L&C	LIN	RES	LSA	ESA	
				MC10					
STANDALONE	0.846	0.883	0.685	0.846	0.685	0.328	0.867	0.515	0.851
SUM	**0.879**	**0.927**	**0.830**	**0.855**	0.806	0.842	0.915	**0.842**	
F1	0.855	0.855	0.806	**0.855**	**0.842**	**0.891**	**0.927**	0.782	
				RG18					
STANDALONE	0.867	0.775	0.828	0.867	0.820	0.580	0.546	0.611	0.820
SUM	0.887	**0.826**	**0.867**	0.887	0.863	**0.813**	**0.728**	**0.827**	
F1	**0.893**	0.796	0.833	**0.907**	**0.869**	0.793	0.607	0.627	
				WS56					
STANDALONE	**0.482**	0.453	0.454	0.515	0.496	0.469	0.520	0.453	0.404
SUM	0.457	0.474	0.471	0.507	**0.523**	0.524	0.538	0.440	
F1	0.453	**0.583**	**0.513**	**0.546**	0.520	**0.570**	**0.588**	**0.475**	

Table 1: Results obtained with individual knowledge-based and corpus-based text-based measures, with our image measure, and with two combination functions (SUM and F1). The bold correlation numbers represents the highest among all metrics per text-based measure per dataset.

their effectiveness in Information Retrieval systems (Fox and Shaw, 1994). Specifically, we combine the text-based and image-based metrics by summing their relatedness figures (SUM) and by calculating their F-measure (F1) defined as the harmonic mean of the two input metrics. Because the similarity scores are differently distributed across various methods, we apply a normalization step within each metric to assert the same lower and upper-bound prior to the combination: $Score_{norm} = (Score_{original} - Score_{min})/(Score_{max} - Score_{min})$.

For each dataset and metric, we obtain the Spearman rank correlation of the automatically generated similarity scores with the ground-truths by human subjects.

6 Discussion

The results in Table 1 show that our image-based method can be an effective metric on its own, scoring a competitive Spearman correlation of 0.851 on the MC10 dataset, and 0.820 on the RG18 dataset. Perhaps not surprisingly, these two datasets consists mainly of words such as car, $forest$, $bird$, $furnace$, which are *picturable*, concrete entities that possess distinctive and unambiguous visual representations. Its performance, however, degrades on the WS56 dataset with a somewhat low correlation rating of 0.404, possibly due to the presence of more broadly defined words lacking a visual identity (e.g., $equipment$ in the word pair $phone-equipment$),

Regardless of the performance of the individual image-based metric, the hybrid image-text approach improves over the standalone text-based metric in almost all cases, and this holds for both knowledge-based and corpus-based methods. These results are encouraging, as they suggest that image-based approaches can be effectively used to improve even basic tasks in natural language processing such as word relatedness.

While we are aware that the limited coverage of ImageNet restricts the applicability of this hybrid image-text method to word relatedness, the continued growth of this resource should provide alleviation. Future work will also consider a comparison of multi-way combinations between knowledge-based, corpus-based and image-based metrics for further advancement of the state-of-the-art.

7 Related Work

Recently, some attention has been given to modelling synergistic relationships between the semantics of words and images (Leong and Mihalcea, 2011; Bruni et al., 2011). The research that is most closely related to ours is the work of (Feng and Lapata, 2010), where it has been shown that it is possible to combine visual representations of word meanings into a joint bimodal representation constructed by using probabilistic generative latent topic models. Unlike our approach, however, (Feng and Lapata, 2010) relied on a news corpus where images and words in a document are assumed to be generated by a set of latent topics, rather than a lexical resource such as ImageNet. While they provided a proof-of-concept that using the visual modality leads to an improvement over their purely text-based model (an increase of Spearman correlation of 0.071 on a subset of WordSim353 dataset), no attempt has been made to evaluate the image-based models independently, or to combine image models with previously proposed knowledge-based and corpus-based measures of relatedness.

Acknowledgments

This material is based in part upon work supported by the National Science Foundation CAREER award #0747340. Any opinions, findings, and conclusions or recommendations expressed in this material are those of the authors and do not necessarily reflect the views of the National Science Foundation.

References

Elia Bruni, Giang Binh Tran, and Marco Baroni. 2011. Distributional semantics from text and images. *Proceedings of the EMNLP Geometrical Models for Natural Language Semantics Workshop*.

Jia Deng, Wei Dong, Richard Socher, Lia-Ji Li, Kai Li, and Li Fei-Fei. 2009. ImageNet: A Large-Scale Hierarchical Image Database. In *Proceedings of the IEEE Conference on Computer Vision and Pattern Recognition*.

Li Fei-Fei and Pietro Perona. 2005. A bayesian hierarchical model for learning natural scene categories. In *Proceedings of the IEEE Conference on Computer Vision and Pattern Recognition*.

Yansong Feng and Mirella Lapata. 2010. Visual information in semantic representation. In *Proceedings of the Annual Conference of the North American Chapter of the ACL*.

Edward A. Fox and Joseph A. Shaw. 1994. Combination of multiple searches. In *Proceedings of the 2nd Text REtrieval Conference (TREC-2)*.

Evgeniy Gabrilovich and Shaul Markovitch. 2007. Computing semantic relatedness using wikipedia-based explicit semantic analysis. In *International Joint Conferences on Artificial Intelligence*.

Graeme Hirst and David St-Onge. 1998. Lexical chains as representations of context for the detection and correction of malapropisms. In *WordNet: An Electronic Lexical Database*, pages 305–332. MIT Press.

Mario Jarmasz. 2003. Rogets thesaurus as a lexical resource for natural language processing. In *Ph.D. Dissertation*, Ottawa-Carleton Institute for Computer Science, School of Information Technology and Engineering, University of Ottawa.

Jay J. Jiang and David A. Conrath. 1997. Semantic similarity based on corpus statistics and lexical taxonom. In *Proceedings of International Conference Research on Computational Linguistics (ROCLING X)*.

Thomas Landauer and Susan Dumais. 1997. A solution to platos problem: The latent semantic analysis theory of acquisition. In *Psychological Review*, volume 104, pages 211–240.

Claudia Leacock and Martin Chodorow. 1998. Combining local context and wordnet similarity for word sense identification. In *The MIT Press*, pages 265–283.

Chee Wee Leong and Rada Mihalcea. 2011. Measuring the semantic relatedness between words and images. In *Proceedings of International Conference on Computational Semantics*.

Dekang Lin. 1998. An information-theoretic definition of similarity. In *Proceedings of the Fifteenth International Conference on Machine Learning*.

Ameesh Makadia, Vladimir Pavlovic, and Sanjiv Kumar. 2008. A new baseline for image annotation. In *Proceedings of European Conference on Computer Vision*.

Ted Pedersen, Siddharth Patwardhan, and Jason Michelizzi. 2004. Wordnet::similarity - measuring the relatedness of concepts. In *Proceedings of the Nineteenth National Conference on Artificial Intelligence*, pages 1024–1025.

Mary C. Potter and Babara A. Faulconer. 1975. Time to understand pictures and words. In *Nature*, volume 253, pages 437–438.

Philip Resnik. 1995. Using information content to evaluate semantic similarity in a taxonomy. In *Proceedings of the International Joint Conference on Artificial Intelligence*.

Peter D. Turney and Patrick Pantel. 2010. From frequency to meaning: Vector space models of semantics. In *Journal of Artificial Intelligence Research*, volume 37, pages 141–188.

Jun Yang, Yu-Gang Jiang, Alexander G. Hauptmann, and Chong-Wah Ngo. 2007. Evaluating bag-of-visual-words representations in scene classification. In *ACM Multimedia Information Retrieval Workshop*.

Domain Independent Model for Product Attribute Extraction from User Reviews using Wikipedia

Sudheer Kovelamudi[+] Sethu Ramalingam[*] Arpit Sood[+] Vasudeva Varma[+]

[+]International Institute of Information Technology, Hyderabad, India
sudheer.k@research.iiit.ac.in, arpit.soodug08@students.iiit.ac.in, vv@iiit.ac.in
[*]24/7 Customer Ilabs, India
sethu.s@247customer.com

Abstract

The world of E-commerce is expanding, posing a large arena of products, their descriptions, customer and professional reviews that are pertinent to them. Most of the product attribute extraction techniques in literature work on structured descriptions using several text analysis tools. However, attributes in these descriptions are limited compared to those in customer reviews of a product, where users discuss deeper and more specific attributes. In this paper, we propose a novel supervised domain independent model for product attribute extraction from user reviews. The user generated content contains unstructured and semi-structured text where conventional language grammar dependent tools like parts-of-speech taggers, named entity recognizers, parsers do not perform at expected levels. We used Wikipedia and Web to identify product attributes from customer reviews and achieved $F_1 score$ of 0.73.

1 Introduction

The online retail market is growing immense, offering millions of products for customers. The products are generally described in terms of a few set of attributes. Such product attributes are mined from the descriptions to represent the product in a structured manner.

Often descriptions deal with generic attributes. For example, specific attributes like power consumption, pulsator, load, spin-dry effectiveness, noise, water usage, water leakage, etc for a product like washing machine cannot be correctly found in descriptions. On the other hand, customers express their opinions in the form of reviews. The opinions expressed are in terms of attributes they like and dislike but not always in terms of those attributes that are provided by the retailer for that particular product. Hence mining the attributes about which the customers discuss can be really helpful for retailers as well as for other customers.

Mining product attributes from customer reviews can lead retailers to fetch and group other products that are having similar specific attributes and forecast more precisely. Hence many retailers are trying to enrich their product knowledge bases with these domain specific and product specific attributes. Attribute extraction from reviews is also useful in tasks like review summarization, product rating, sales agent assessment, opinion mining of reviews, product recommendation systems, customer relationship management, customer satisfaction analysis, customer profiling, etc.

On the customers' side, they are prone to seek the opinions of other customers who actually used the product or bought it from a retailer website. They ask for unbiased evaluation of a product by leveraging information from multiple reviews, although each individual review can be subjective in nature. Therefore a person is more interested to read a featured review than overall reviews like "the product is really great, awesome!" or "this is the greatest product I have ever seen!!!" or simply the product rating.

Consider an unstructured customer review on the product
LG Electronics Flatron L1920P monitor:

> Excellent *picture* quality.. videoz are in *HD*.. no complaintz from me. Never had any trouble with gamez.. Paid WAAAAY to much for it at the time th0.. it sellz now fer like a third the *price* I paid.. heheh.. oh well....the fact that I didn't wait a year er so to buy a bigger *model* for half the price.. most likely from a different *store*.. ..not namin any namez th0.. *cough*BBHOSEDMe*cough*

The italicized terms are some product attributes discussed in this review. Our aim is to extract such attributes automatically. The reviews act as good sources in supplying such product specific attributes.

Mining attributes from customer reviews is a challenging task as they mostly comprise of user generated content. The text in such user generated content is low in natural language grammar, structure, formality. It often hinders the performance of natural language processing tools like parts of speech tagging, parsing and named entity recognition.

By this motivation, we have designed a novel framework that can extract attributes of a product with out making use of any natural language tools but treating the text as 'Bag Of words' and using the knowledge of Wikipedia.

2 Related Work

A good amount of research had been put into product attribute extraction in recent years. But the focus was laid in extraction of attributes from product descriptions and a little was done in extracting the same or more specific attributes from user reviews. Much of the existing work focuses on whole review classification and overall opinion extraction.

Work related to word order occurrences where product attributes are believed to exist as noun phrases was already contributed (Justeson and Katz, 1995; Daille, 1996). But it (Hu and Liu, 2006; Hu and Liu, 2004; Liu et al., 2005) was shown that using noun phrases tend to produce too many non-terms (low precision), while using reoccurring phrases misses many low frequency terms, terms with variations, and terms with only one word. Their work presents the identification of product attributes with the help of Parts-Of-Speech(POS) tags and the occurrence of adjectives. But in most of the cases when free format reviews are considered, the POS taggers do not function at the expected level as grammar is not guaranteed in user generated text.

Efforts like training noun phrase recognizer model (Raju et al., 2009) to extract attributes from product descriptions worked well on structured text, but when tested did not work on unstructured text and long reviews.

The major extraction problem that has been studied extensively is the named entity extraction. We tried extracting product attributes from a set of reviews which consist of incomplete sentences and short phrases (using the technique given by (Liu et al., 2005)), but the results are not consistent. The reason we believe is that, in most of the cases product attribute terms do not have indicators (like beginning with capitalization of letters) as in the scenario of customer reviews which consequently result in named entity recognition failure.

3 Attribute extraction

For any given product, our approach to attribute extraction involves:

1. Collection of customer reviews of the given product.
2. Filter out stop words.
3. Compute features that we have defined, for the remaining words.
4. Identification of possible attribute words using classification model trained on these features.

Support vector machines (SVMs), are a set of related supervised learning methods for classification and regression analysis which are used to facilitate our model. The features on which our system has been trained are explained in the following sections.

3.1 Most Frequent Items-MFI

Words related to topics that are discussed more occur at high frequencies in any given text. In general people discuss about the attributes of a product in their reviews frequently. The 'Most Frequent Items' feature boosts the importance of attribute words by their frequency of occurrence in customer reviews.

The set of words $\{z_1, z_2, z_3, ...z_m\}$ used for this feature are obtained from customer reviews of a given product after stop word removal is done. For any word z_i the 'Most Frequent Items' feature is computed by

$$MFI(z_i) = \frac{Freq(z_i)}{\sum_{j=1}^{m} Freq(z_j)}$$

$Freq(z_i)$ gives total number of occurrences of z_i in reviews of a given product.

3.2 Context Relation using Wikipedia - CR

To understand a context or to identify a context, we need the set of keywords that portray the context. So, we assume that any context C can be expressed as $C = \{t_1, t_2, t_3, ...t_n\}$ where 't_i' are the related keywords dealt in C.

The product forms the context in customer reviews. People talk about the product and its attributes in their reviews. Its attributes and other highly related things belong to the set of keywords of the context.

The CR feature is about identifying the list of related keywords mentioned in customer reviews that can be found in Wikipedia. We start with identifying all words that have been discussed in reviews of a given product in Wikipedia and then proceed with calculating the most semantically related words among them.

When we make judgments about semantic relatedness between any two words, we draw huge amount of background knowledge about the concepts that these words represent. Hence, any trial to state the semantic relatedness between different words automatically also needs to do the same. One can use hand-crafted lexical structures like thesauri and taxonomies, or statistical analysis of large corpora to process the semantic decisions automatically (Milne, 2007). The limiting factors of such techniques when carried across domains are the background knowledge, precision, scalability and scope. With more than a 18 million articles and thousands of volunteers all over the world, Wikipedia which is a growing massive repository of knowledge, is the best alternative when targeted by such limitations.

We explore Wikipedia's link structure, category structure, article titles, and page types from the static and latest pages-articles xml dump[1] of Wikipedia. We only need Wikipedia's structure rather than it's full textual content. We have created SQL database, tables to store and access the page titles and articles fast, which has been suggested and explored already (Milne and Witten, 2009). We map a word in customer reviews to a Wikipedia article if the word is contained in that Wikipedia article title. We call such words as *Wikipedia words* and if cannot be mapped, we refer them as *Non-Wikipedia words* in later sections of this paper. A word can be mapped to all its homonyms in Wikipedia. For instance the word 'bank' can refer to 'river bank' or a 'savings bank' in Wikipedia. To disambiguate and identify the correct possible article mappings for a given word, we need to first disambiguate words which may possibly contain mappings in more than one domain. To address this, we used a method (Milne and Witten, 2009) where articles for unambiguous words are used to disambiguate the ambiguous words.

Computing semantic relatedness between two words that are mapped to Wikipedia, is equal to finding the semantic relatedness between articles in Wikipedia to which these words refer. And to do this, the best known way is to compute the relation from the links to these articles in Wikipedia (Medelyan et al., 2008; Milne, 2007).
The relation between two Wikipedia articles x and y is given by

$$Relation_{x,y} = 1 - \frac{max(log|A|, log|B|) - log|A \cap B|}{T - min(log|A|, log|B|)}$$

Here A and B are the set of articles which link to the articles x and y respectively, T is the total number of Wikipedia articles, $A \cap B$ is their overlap. Thus for every *Wikipedia word*, we find the semantic relatedness to all other such words. Context relatedness feature (CR) of a word is computed as the sum of its similarity

[1] `http://dumps.wikimedia.org/enwiki/`

scores with all other such words in the context which is then normalized by the total number of such words. Therefore for a Wikipedia words set $\{x_1, x_2, x_3, ...x_k\}$, semantic relatedness of x_i to the context is given by

$$CR_{x_i} = \frac{\sum_{\substack{j=1 \\ j \neq i}}^{K} Relation_{x_i,x_j}}{k}$$

The applicability of CR feature is justified in terms of high scalability and the ever growing knowledge of Wikipedia.

For *Non-Wikipedia words* $\{y_1, y_2, y_3, ...y_l\}$ in the product reviews, the CR feature is modified as the average of all CR feature values for *Wikipedia words*, from reviews of that particular product. Hence the CR value for any non-Wikipedia word y_i is uniformly given as

$$CR_{y_i} = \frac{\sum_{j=1}^{k} CR_{x_j}}{k}$$

where x_j is a Wikipedia word.

3.3 Role of surrounding window - SW

We have taken into account the surrounding text of 't' Wikipedia words to the left and right of a given Wikipedia word to examine its role in identifying an attribute. As some topics arise and eventually diminish in a small window of discussion, the situation motivates us to consider the relation with the surrounding text as a classification feature in identifying product attributes.

This feature can help in identifying sub-attributes (attributes of attributes). The sub-attributes may not seem related when overall context is considered, but they are relevant when limited contexts in which they occur are considered.

Suppose if there are p instances of Wikipedia word x_i in the reviews. The relation of x_i with the surrounding text is computed as

$$SW_{x_i} = \frac{\sum_{\substack{j=-t \\ j \neq i}}^{t} Relation_{x_i,x_j}}{(k)(N)(p)}$$

Where N is the total number of words in customer reviews of a given product. The window length t is arbitrarily taken as $\frac{N}{20}$. "-t" means t words to the left of x_i and vice-versa.

The SW feature for the non-Wikipedia words is uniformly given as average of all SW feature values of Wikipedia words from reviews.

$$SW_{y_i} = \frac{\sum_{j=1}^{k} SW_{x_j}}{k}$$

3.4 Web search engine reference-WR

As there are words that cannot be mapped to Wikipedia, we may loose a few trivial attributes in the candidate selection stage. To boost such words we use knowledge on the Web. The WR feature measures the association of a particular word from customer reviews of a product with that product on the Internet.

We have used Bing search API[2] to compute WR for a word. WR value for a word z_i is given by

$$WR_{z_i} = \frac{Res(z_i, P)}{S_N}$$

$Res(Z_i, P)$ is the number of instances where the word z_i and the product name P both occur within the text snippets given as search results by the search engine. This frequency is normalized by the total number of search results S_N that are taken into account.

4 Experiments and Evaluation

We have trained our system with the above features using SVM. We have evaluated our system against two popular datasets of reviews, the Reviews-9-products dataset (Ding et al., 2008) and the Customer Reviews dataset (Hu and Liu, 2004). These datasets have been used for the opinion mining tasks and referred by several other publications[3]. They were annotated manually in terms of product attributes. These annotations consists of trivial words, terminologies, and concepts. The datasets contain customer reviews of products from different domains of Amazon[4].

Experiments are carried out at two levels. First, crucial features are tested to know their respective performance, and then the complete combination of features is tested. To train our model we used $Reviews-9-products$ dataset and for testing $CustomerReviews$ dataset is used. Similarly we have also done testing on $Reviews-9-products$ dataset by generating the training data from $CustomerReviews$ dataset.

We have considered MFI feature as baseline for this approach. The reason is that MFI is intuitive due to the fact that people when discussing about a product mention the attributes a good number of times in their reviews.

$$Precision = \frac{No.\ of\ Attributes\ Identified\ correctly}{No.\ of\ words\ Identified\ as\ Attributes}$$

and the recall is given by

$$Recall = \frac{No.\ of\ Attributes\ Identified\ correctly}{No.\ of\ Attributes\ Actually\ Annotated}$$

4.1 Product attribute extraction using Wikipedia

When we have tested our Wikipedia based features CR, SW along with the baseline feature MFI, we encountered a low recall but a good average precision of approximately 88%. The reason behind this low recall is that trivial words and some verbs cannot be mapped to Wikipedia. For example, for the *DiaperChamp* product listed in Table 1 the annotated attributes like $bang-for-the-buck, deal, looking, filelimit, cost-effective, works, pull, assemble, costlier, clean, safer,$ $etc.$, cannot be correctly linked to the articles of

[2] `http://msdn.microsoft.com/en-us/library/dd251072.aspx`

[3] `http://www.cs.uic.edu/\~liub/FBS/sentiment-analysis.html`

[4] `http://www.amazon.com/`

Table 1: Performances of different combinations of features

Product Name	Annotated Attributes	CR,SW,MFI		CR,SW,MFI,WR	
		Candidates Selected	**Attributes Identified**	**Candidates Selected**	**Attributes Identified**
Diaper Champ	68	16	14	57	45
Canon G3	106	30	25	93	70
Hitachi router	82	14	11	79	66
Canon S100	99	26	23	91	73
Nokia 6600	147	48	44	112	85
MicroMP3	196	41	35	133	102
Nikon coolpix 4300	76	16	13	54	46
ipod	92	23	10	85	66
Creative Labs Nomad Jukebox Zen Xtra 40GB	186	47	43	157	122
norton	107	24	23	94	73
Linksys Router	85	24	18	79	52
Apex AD2600 Progressive-scan DVD player	115	24	19	90	79
Canon PowerShot SD500	70	13	12	63	52
Nokia 6610	111	35	31	92	74

Table 2: Overall scores

Feature combination	**Recall**	**Precision**	**F-score**
Baseline(MFI)	0.112	0.603	0.189
CR, SW, MFI	0.202	**0.878**	0.328
CR, SW, MFI, WR	**0.666**	0.802	**0.727**

Wikipedia. To rule out such discrepancies we can use an ontology like Wordnet. But it adds a lot of noise. The statistics of the identified attributes from both datasets are shown in Table 1 and their collective precision, recall and f-score values are given in Table 2.

4.2 Product attribute extraction using Wikipedia & Web

The web based feature WR when combined with other features increased recall of our system.

We can clearly see that the combination of all the four features which include Wikipedia based features and other frequency, web based features has performed the best in terms of f-score. The increase in recall is due to gain in knowledge using WR. The fall in precision can be explained by the boosting of insignificant words in search results.

In Table 1, the given products *Diaper Champ* and *ipod* belong to the most divergent domains. For *Diaper Champ* our model identified 45 out of 68 annotated attributes where as for *ipod*, it identified 66 out of 92 annotated attributes. Similarly for the product *Apex AD2600 Progressive-scan DVD player*, it identified 79 out of 115 attributes. This shows that the recall is approximately equal across the products which is an evidence that the model does not depend on the domain of a product.

5 Conclusion and Future Work

In this paper, we presented a domain independent approach for automatic discovery of product attributes from user reviews. Our work has highlighted the possibility of providing an incremental learning capability for an extraction system. The performance scores of our system show that it is a good design to apply Wikipedia to carve out product attributes from customer reviews. Our contribution is in leveraging information and in getting assistance from greater knowledge sources like Wikipedia and world wide web when doing tasks across domains while discarding all the help from language tools.

In this work we have trained and tested our system over products that belong to different domains but interestingly found it works uniform for all the products. In future we want to test our model extensively across domains and explore new methodologies for generic attribute extraction. We would like to extend the model for sentiment analysis on product attributes mined from reviews. Our future research work also include testing our system using other machine learning techniques (like CRF) and to consider more baselines for evaluation. As we did not make use of any natural language processing tools, this work can be extended to any other language with little changes in the preprocessing stage.

References

B. Daille. 1996. Study and implementation of combined techniques for automatic extraction of terminology. *The Balancing Act: Combining Symbolic and Statistical Approaches to Language*, 1:49–66.

Xiaowen Ding, Bing Liu, and Philip S. Yu. 2008. A holistic lexicon-based approach to opinion mining. In *Proceedings of the international conference on Web search and web data mining*, WSDM '08, pages 231–240, New York, NY, USA. ACM.

M. Hu and B. Liu. 2004. Mining and summarizing customer reviews. SIGKDD '04, pages 168–177, NY, USA. ACM.

M. Hu and B. Liu. 2006. Opinion extraction and summarization on the web. In *The National Conference On Artificial Intelligence*, volume 21, page 1621. Menlo Park, CA; Cambridge, MA; London; AAAI Press; MIT Press; 1999.

J.S. Justeson and S.M. Katz. 1995. Technical terminology: some linguistic properties and an algorithm for identification in text. *Natural language engineering*, 1(01):9–27.

B Liu, M Hu, and J Cheng. 2005. Opinion observer: analyzing and comparing opinions on the web. WWW '05, pages 342–351, New York, NY, USA. ACM.

O. Medelyan, I.H. Witten, and D. Milne. 2008. Topic indexing with Wikipedia. In *AAAI WikiAI workshop*.

D. Milne and I.H. Witten. 2009. An open-source toolkit for mining Wikipedia. In *Proc. New Zealand Computer Science Research Student Conf., NZCSRSC*, volume 9.

D. Milne. 2007. Computing semantic relatedness using wikipedia link structure. In *New Zealand Computer Science Research Student Conference*. Citeseer.

S. Raju, P. Pingali, and V. Varma. 2009. An unsupervised approach to product attribute extraction. *Advances in Information Retrieval*, pages 796–800.

Finding Problem Solving Threads in Online Forum

Zhonghua Qu and **Yang Liu**
The University of Texas at Dallas
{qzh, yangl}@hlt.utdallas.edu

Abstract

Online forum is an important source that people use to find answers to questions. Most search engines simply retrieve "relevant" threads, but those are not necessarily good threads in terms of providing quality answers. In this paper we propose a two-step approach to classify online forum threads according to their informativeness in terms of question answering. We use statistical models to first categorize posts inside a thread. Then, a variety of features including post level information and other meta-data information are used to classify the thread. We show promising results using the online support forum data we have collected.

1 Introduction

Online forums often contain useful information, such as answers to questions. When people use search engines to search the forum for answers, the returned threads can be of very low quality in terms of providing informative answers. Some threads are either long conversations without any final conclusive answers or contain answers that do not work. This is especially the case in technical forums. There has been some work on extracting information from online forums. For example, Cong et al. (Cong et al., 2008) used labeled sequential patterns to detect question sentences in online forums. Ding et al. (Ding et al., 2008) used Conditional Random Fields to extract context of questions for answer detection. Huang et al. (Huang et al., 2007) used SVM to automatically extract and rank title-reply pairs from online discussion forums for chatbot knowledge. These previous studies provide a relatively good foundation for answer finding and extraction. In online environments like mailing list or forums, question answering is carried out in conversations. In this paper we take advantage of the structure of conversation and language cues to answer a basic yet important question: Does the thread actually solve the problem?

We will make use of the conversation within the thread to determine how users think of the answers. To classify the usefulness of a thread, we propose a two-step approach using statistical models. First we classify the posts inside a thread into different categories (e.g., problem description, solution, feedback). Different models using both content and contextual information are evaluated. Then, we develop features generated from the post categories together with forum meta-data to classify a thread's usefulness. In our collection of forum threads, we show that our proposed methods achieve good results, significantly better than the rule-based baseline.

2 Data Collection and Annotation

We created our own data collection and annotation.[1] We crawled 20,000 threads from an active online forum (Oracle database support forum – general section). As an initial study, we selected 200 threads randomly and asked two annotators to label the threads and posts in them. The two annotators are computer science students with adequate knowledge to understand the content of those posts. For thread level annotation, we asked the annotators to label the thread based on whether they think it solves the problem and to what extent. We did not give annotators detailed instructions, but rather let them read the threads and make their own judgment. Each thread is given a score from 1 to 5, 1 being least helpful and 5 being most helpful. In the 200 threads we used, 50 have a usefulness score of 1, 19 with 2, 7 with 3, 61 with 4, and 83 with a score of 5. The distribution has a U

[1]Please contact the authors for data sharing.

shape – many threads are annotated as absolutely solved the problem (usefulness of 5), or absolutely not helpful at all (usefulness of 1). This also shows that the confidence of annotators is very high.

Another annotation we performed is for the posts inside each thread. We defined four classes for the posts based on their main purpose. The categories and brief explanation for them are shown in Table 1, along with the number of posts for each category. Note that sentences inside a post may have different purposes, however, we instructed the annotators to label it with its main purpose. The post classes are very imbalanced in the annotated corpus. The feedback classes account for only about 10% of all the posts, while the majority classes are problems and solutions.

Post category	Description	number
Problem	Ask a question or ask for answer clarification.	399
Solution	Give answers/clarifications to previous questions.	557
Good Feedback	State that the problem is solved.	78
Bad Feedback	State that the answer did not solve the problem.	18

Table 1: Annotated categories for posts inside threads.

Table 2 shows the Kappa statistics on thread and post annotation using 20 threads that we randomly selected and let both annotators label them. For the thread annotation agreement, we use binary labels – usefulness greater than 3 is considered as 1, and usefulness less than 3 is considered as 0. The Kappa scores are very reasonable, suggesting that humans do not have much trouble with this task definition.

Classes	Kappa Coefficient
Thread Usefulness	0.93
Post - Problem	0.86
Post - Solution	0.70
Post - Good Feedback	0.93

Table 2: Kappa statistics between two annotators for thread and post category annotation.

3 Approaches

For the ultimate goal of classifying how likely a thread provides a good solution (its usefulness), we propose to use a two-step approach. First we determine the categories for the posts, then we classify the threads using information from the first step along with other information.

3.1 Post Level Classification

We use the content of a post as well as its context for post classification. First we used Naive Bayes classifier with a bag-of-word model for post classification. Naive Bayes classifiers have been proved to be robust and perform well in document classification. After performing tokenization using space, we use the top 600 words from the training set as the dictionary.[2] Each post is thus represented by a feature vector of tokens that appear in the dictionary. We use binary features for these words. This has been shown to perform better than using word frequency information for many classification tasks. We use the implementation of multinomial Naive Bayes classifier provided by Weka (Hall et al., 2009).

We expect that posts in a thread, like turns in dialogs, are very dependent on the context. For example, a "problem description" post is more likely to be followed by "solution" posts than a "feedback" one. People are more likely to give "feedback" after some "answers" are provided rather after a "question" is asked. Hence we evaluate using an HMM for this post categorization task, in order to take advantage of context information. Figure 1 shows a first order HMM for this setup.

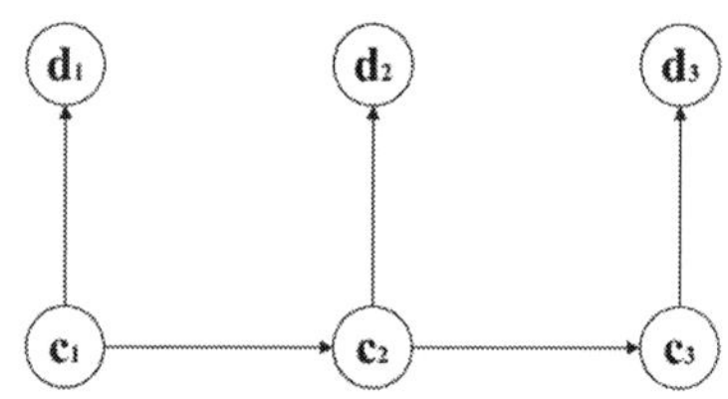

Figure 1: Illustration of HMM for post categorization. An observation d_i is a post, and c_i corresponds to its category.

The generative process is as follows. The category of current post is generated according to a multinomial distribution $P(c_i|c_{i-1})$ conditioned on its previous post category. Then, given the category of current post, words in the post are generated according to multinomial distribution $P(d_i|c_i)$ based on the post's category.

The problem can be formulated to find the most likely state sequence C (post categories) given all

[2]We varied the dictionary size, but observed performance degradation.

the words in all the posts D. The posterior probability of C given D is:

$$P(C|D) = P(c_1, .., c_n|d_1, .., d_n)$$
$$\propto P(d_1, .., d_n|c_1, .., c_n) \times P(c_1, .., c_n)$$
$$= \prod_{i=1}^{n} P(d_i|c_i) \times P(c_i|c_{i-1}) \quad (1)$$

The last equation is due to the first order HMM assumption where a post document is only dependent on its category (in a generative process), and a post category is only dependent on its previous category. For parameters in this HMM, the transition probabilities are estimated from the training set, similar to training a bigram language model (LM) for the post categories.

It is possible to use an n-gram language model to model the generation of text in posts given its category. However, since our data set is rather small, there is a data sparsity issue for these n-gram LMs. Hence, we only use a unigram-like model for a subset of the words (same as those in the Naive Bayes model), and each word is represented in binary form: whether or not it appeared.

In practice, when combining the state transition probabilities and emission probabilities, we use a weighting factor γ that is determined empirically. This is needed because the two scores are in different scales and contribute to the final hypothesis differently.

3.2 Thread Level Classification

The second step in our system is thread level classification, where the system determines whether a thread is useful or not. Using our annotated threads, we grouped them into binary classes: useful when the label is equal to or greater than 3; and not useful otherwise. We use a variety of features for thread level classification. Table 3 lists all the features we use for thread classification.

Since the post level classifier is optimized for the classification accuracy for that particular task, its hypotheses might not be optimal for subsequent thread classification. For example, if a post "looks" like both a "good feedback" and a "problem", we may prefer "good feedback" to "problem" since the former is more related to our final decision for the thread usefulness. To achieve this, we adjust the priors in the post classification process for different categories. We found that by increasing the prior for "good feedback" by 1.5 times, the final performance is improved – even though the classification precision decreases, the improved recall seems to be helping.

Name	Description
num_solution	The number of solution posts
feedback_p	Number of positive feedbacks
num_prob_sol	Times of back and forth between problem and solutions
author_post	Number of posts posted by author
author_postend	How far the author's last post is from the end
length	Length of a thread (measured using number of posts)

Table 3: Features used for thread level classification. 'Author' means the user who first posted the problem and started the thread.

We use a maximum entropy model for thread classification. This classifier is chosen because of its good performance in many language processing tasks, as well as our own preliminary experiments when comparing to other classifiers including decision trees and SVMs.

4 Experiments

4.1 Post Level Classification Results

We performed leave-one-out-cross-validation (using threads as the units) for post classification. Table 4 shows the results using different methods. We developed a rule-based baseline system for this task. Posts containing typical question words like "what","where" are classified as "problem" posts. Those containing cue words for positive feedbacks, like "thanks", "solved", and having length of less than 50 words are classified as "positive feedback" posts. The rest are classified as solutions.

The results shown in the table include the F_1 score for 3 individual post categories: problem (F-P), solution (F-S), and good feedback (F-F), as well as the micro averaged F_1 score. Here we ignored the classification results for "bad feedback" category since it is not very useful in later thread classification.

We can see that the basic Naive Bayes (NB) classifier can achieve reasonable performance already. It is significantly better than the baseline. This shows that lexicon features (bag-of-word model) are strong and reliable in classifying post type. We also tried using an SVM (with linear kernels) for post level classification, but its performance is worse than the Naive Bayes clas-

Method	F_{micro}	F_1-P	F_1-S	F_1-F
Baseline: rule	44.58	49.59	46.53	18.58
NB	77.57	76.81	85.52	28.57
HMM	83.17	83.21	87.75	36.04

Table 4: Post classification results using different methods. Results are the F-measures for problem, solution, and good feedback categories, and the overall performance.

sifier. After using context information through HMM, post level classification performance increased substantially. There is consistent improvement for all the categories. In particular, there is a relatively larger gain for the "feedback" class, which we expect may have a great impact on subsequent thread level classification. This performance gain using HMM demonstrates that contextual information is useful and HMM can well model such information (e.g., an 'answer' post is likely to follow a 'problem' one). We also increased HMM to higher order in order to model the transitions using more previous post categories, but found there is no additional improvement. In fact, it is slightly worse than using the first order HMM. This can be explained by either that the long distance relationship is not very crucial for this task, or more likely that we do not have a large training set to learn high order transition information reliably.

In general, we can see that the classifiers perform relatively well for the majority categories, such as problems and solutions. However, for minority classes, e.g., "feedback" (that is only 9.8% among all the posts), the classifiers are not able to learn well. We also observe that many "problem" types are classified as "solutions". This may be explained by two reasons. First, problem description posts use very similar vocabulary as solution posts. Second, there are more solution posts in the training data.

4.2 Thread Level Classification Results

For thread level classification, we use a binary setup, useful vs. not. We used leave-one-out-cross-validation for the 200 labeled threads. Inside each fold, first we use the training set to train the post level classifiers. Then we relabel all the posts in the training set as well as in the testing set with the classifier just trained to obtain the post category hypotheses. After the post level labeling, we extract features for thread classification as described in Section 3. We then train the maximum entropy classifier and test it for the final classification of threads. We use the precision, recall, and F_1 score as the evaluation metrics. Results are shown in Table 5. For a comparison, we also show the performance when using reference post labels for both training and test sets (last row). This is expected to give an upper bound performance regarding the use of post level information for thread classification.

Post Classifier	Precision	Recall	F_1
Baseline: rule	68.50	97.16	80.35
NB	78.21	86.52	82.15
HMM	79.14	91.32	84.97
Ref	84.62	93.62	88.89

Table 5: Thread level binary classification results using features extracted from output of different post level classifiers.

We can see from Table 5 that in general thread classification results depend heavily on the performance of post level classification. HMM achieves the best performance. Using reference post category shows the upper bound of how post level classification could affect thread level classification. We also evaluated using the reference post tags in training the thread classifier, and automatic tags for testing, but that did not perform as well as using automatically obtained tags for both training and testing, suggesting a matched training and testing condition is better. Overall we achieved very good performance – an F_1 score of about 85% using HMM for post categorization. This is a promising result given that we have a quite small data set for training.

5 Conclusion

In this paper, we described a two-step classification approach to determine whether a thread is helpful to users seeking solutions. We perform post level classification in the first step, then use the generated post tag information with other global features for thread level classification. We showed in the experiment that our approach worked well in a technical support online forum. For future work, we plan to use joint optimization for the two tasks. In addition, instead of using predefined categories for posts, we may derive post categories automatically from the corpus that suit better for the thread classification task.

References

Gao Cong, Long Wang, Chin-Yew Lin, Young-In Song, and Yueheng Sun. 2008. *Finding question-answer pairs from online forums*. In *SIGIR*, pages 467–474.

Shilin Ding, Gao Cong, Chin-Yew Lin, and Xiaoyan Zhu. 2008. *Using conditional random fields to extract contexts and answers of Questions from online forums*. In *ACL*.

Mark Hall, Eibe Frank, Geoffrey Holmes, Bernhard Pfahringer, Peter Reutemann, and Ian H. Witten. 2009. The weka data mining software: an update. *SIGKDD Explorations*, 11(1):10–18.

Jizhou Huang, Ming Zhou, and Dan Yang. 2007. *Extracting Chatbot Knowledge from Online Discussion Forums*. In *SIGIR*, pages 423–428.

Compiling Learner Corpus Data of Linguistic Output and Language Processing in Speaking, Listening, Writing, and Reading

Katsunori Kotani
Kansai Gaidai University / Osaka, Japan
kkotani@kansaigaidai.ac.jp

Takehiko Yoshimi
Ryukoku University / Shiga, Japan
yoshimi@rins.ryukoku.ac.jp

Hiroaki Nanjo
Ryukoku University / Shiga, Japan
nanjo@rins.ryukoku.ac.jp

Hitoshi Isahara
Toyohashi University of Technology / Aichi, Japan
isahara@tut.jp

Abstract

A learner's language data of speaking, writing, listening, and reading have been compiled for a learner corpus in this study. The language data consist of linguistic output and language processing. Linguistic output refers to data of pronunciation, sentences, listening comprehension rate, and reading comprehension rate. Language processing refers to processing time and learners' self-judgment of their difficulty of processing in speaking, listening, and reading and the fluency of their writing. This learner corpus will contribute to making the language learning process more clearly visible.

1 Introduction

Learner corpora have contributed to second language acquisition (SLA) research. For instance, SLA research using learner corpora examines learners' proficiency on the basis of what vocabularies/grammars learners actually use (Tono 2009, among others). Thus, most learner corpora are compiled of linguistic outputs that learners produce in speaking and/or writing.

In order to enhance SLA research, a learner corpus should be compiled of a learner's language data of the four modalities (speaking; listening; writing; reading). Language data of each modality are further classified into two types: linguistic output and language processing data. Language output data consist of linguistic objects that learners produce. Language processing data indicate how they produce linguistic outputs. Thus, we have eight types of language data that are useful for the SLA research on the development of learners' proficiency (Hinkel 2010, Segalowitz 2003). Among these eight types of language data, the previous studies (Granger et al. 2009, Izumi et al. 2004, Meurers et al. 2010, Wen et al. 2008) compiled the language output data of speaking, writing, and reading for constructing a learner corpus. See Section 2 for further detail. On the other hand, the other previous studies (Zechner & Bejar 2006, Arthur 1979, Hirai 1999, Kotani et al. 2010, Chang 2010) compiled the language processing data not for constructing a learner corpus but for examining learners' performance. See Section 3 for further detail. Thus, there is a shortage of language output data of listening, and furthermore we have to construct a learner corpus that integrates all these eight types of data. Hereafter, we refer to this corpus as I(ntegrated)-Learner Corpus. In order to construct I-Learner Corpus, we have compiled data of linguistic output and language processing of the four modalities when learners actually use the target language, which in this study is English.

2 Background

Written data are compiled in the International Corpus of Learner English (ICLE) (Granger et al. 2009). The written data are taken from essays written by learners of English as a foreign language (EFL). ICLE consists of learners' essays (approximately 500 words long) and learner information, but has no error tags.

Spoken data are compiled in the National Institute of Information and Communication Technology Japanese Learner English (NICT JLE) Corpus (Izumi et al. 2004). The spoken data are obtained by transcribing one-to-one interviews of EFL learners whose native language is Japanese. The NICT JLE Corpus includes error tags and reference data spoken by native speakers, but has no sound data for phonetic/phonological analyses.

Both spoken and written data are compiled in the Spoken and Written Corpus of Chinese

Learners (SWECCL) (Wen et al. 2008). The spoken data of SWECCL consist of both sound data and transcription data of retelling, monologues, and role plays. This corpus also includes three years' worth of longitudinal data.

Read data are compiled in the Task-based Corpus (Meurers et al. 2010). This corpus consists of written answers for text comprehension questions. Since written answers for text comprehension questions can demonstrate both learners' reading and writing proficiency, the Task-based Corpus is taken as a learner corpus that integrates written and read data.

3 Corpus design

Table 1 summarizes the design criteria of the I-Learner Corpus on attributes of learners and those of language. The criteria follow the attributes of a learner corpus (Granger 2007).

		Attributes
Age		18 years old and older
Sex		male, female
Mother tongue		Japanese
Level		beginner, intermediate, advanced
Learning context		EFL
Experience		36 months or more
Modality		spoken (S), written (W), listened (L), read (R)
Medium	**S, L, R**	news broadcast
	W	question answering, description
Genre		expository language use
Topic	**S, L, R**	general news topic/topic related to university life
	W	learning profiles, daily events
Technicality		general
Task setting		paid task, no dictionary

Table 1. Design criteria.

The target learners are EFL learners of university students whose native language is Japanese. In Japan, students study English at least three years in junior high school.

The modality of language data covers spoken, written, listened, and read data. Spoken, listened, and read data are taken from news broadcast. Written data are taken from question answering and picture description. The genre is expository contexts in daily-life language use. Though there are other contexts such as academic/professional contexts, these contexts contain more non-linguistic aspects. Thus, we chose daily-life contexts in order to minimize non-linguistic aspects such as background knowledge. Hence, the topics in news broad cast are general news topic and the ones related to university life. The topic of writing covers learners' learning profiles and daily events.

We basically use the compiling procedure stated in the previous studies reviewed in Section 2. Following the Task-based Corpus (Meurers et al. 2010), we compile read and listened data from answers to comprehension questions.

Although the comprehension-question-based procedure is suitable for compiling comprehension rate of a whole text or that of some part(s) of a text, it unfits for compiling comprehension rate at a sentence level. Of course, it is possible to compile comprehension rate at the sentence level by preparing comprehension questions for each sentence, but this is just not realistic. However, we have to compile read and listened data at the sentence level just like for spoken and written data.

Our solution of this problem is to compile language processing. It is reported that language performance can be evaluated on the basis of language processing: speaking performance (Zechner & Bejar 2006), writing performance (Arthur 1979), listening performance (Hirai 1999), and reading performance (Kotani et al. 2010, Chang 2010). An advantage of language processing is the possibility to measure at the sentence level. In addition, language processing (speaking speed) is compiled in native speaker corpora (Braun 2006, Gut 2009). Hence, we compile data of both language processing and linguistic output across the four modalities.

Language processing has two parts. One is the processing time how long a learner takes for linguistic output. The other is the judgment how difficult a learner judges processing in speaking, listening, and reading to be and how fluent a learner judges his or her writing to be. Table 2 lists the data to be stored in the I-Learner Corpus.

	Linguistic Output	Language Processing
Speaking	sound output	time, difficulty
Writing	sentence output	time, fluency
Listening	comprehension rate	difficulty
Reading	comprehension rate	time, difficulty

Table 2. Data specification.

Spoken data of the I-Learner Corpus consist of recordings of oral reading (linguistic output), and oral reading time and a learner's judgment of pronunciation difficulty on a five-point scale (1: Very Easy, 2: Easy, 3: Moderate, 4: Difficult, 5:

Very Difficult) (language processing). In addition to learners' data, we prepare reference sound data read by native speakers.

Written data of the I-Learner Corpus consist of sentences of question answering, sentences of picture description (linguistic output), writing time, and a learner's judgment of his or her fluency on a five-point scale (language processing).

Listened data of the I-Learner Corpus consist of comprehension rate (linguistic output) and a learner's judgment of listening difficulty (language processing).

Read data of the I-Learner Corpus consist of the comprehension rate (linguistic output), reading time, and a learner's judgment of reading difficulty on a five-point scale (language processing).

4 Data compiling

4.1 Procedures

Data compiling proceeded in the following order: listening task, reading task, speaking task, and writing task.

In the listening task, learners listened to four news articles that were read by native speakers of English sentence-by-sentence using a data collecting tool described in Section 4.4. Learners judged listening difficulty of a sentence after listening to it. When learners finished listening to an article, they answered five comprehension questions on the data collecting tool. Learners could listen to a sentence only once.

Listened data are often gathered in a situation where learners listen to sentences in an article from start to finish without a stop. However, learners in this study listened to a news article sentence-by-sentence in order to report their judgments for listening difficulty.

In the reading task, learners silently read four news articles sentence-by-sentence using the data collecting tool. Learners judged reading difficulty of a sentence after reading it. When learners finished reading an article, they answered five comprehension questions. Learners could not read a sentence again nor use a dictionary.

Read data are often taken in a situation where learners see a news article as a whole. However, learners in this study read a news article sentence-by-sentence so that processing time and their judgments of reading difficulty could be kept track of.

In the speaking task, learners read aloud four news articles sentence-by-sentence using the data collecting tool. Learners judged pronunciation difficulty of a sentence after reading it aloud. Learners had no comprehension questions in the speaking task, because the speaking task and the reading task used the same articles in order for learners to grasp the contents of the articles before reading aloud.

Spoken data are often taken from utterances in actual discourse (Izumi et al. 2004). However, we chose an oral reading task in which learners read the same sentences, because we can directly compare phonetic/phonological properties between learners.

The writing task had two sub-tasks. In the first, learners wrote answers for twenty questions on their profiles. In the second, learners wrote sentences describing four pictures of a series of events on the data collecting tool. Learners were instructed to write at least five sentences for a picture. In both tasks, learners judged the fluency of a sentence after writing it. Learners could not rewrite a sentence after moving on to another sentence nor use a dictionary.

Although written data are often taken from essays (Granger et al. 2009), we chose question answering and picture description in order to minimize the non-linguistic aspects. While essay writing depends on logical, analytical, and critical thinking, learners can answer profile questions and describe pictures without depending too much on non-linguistic skills as long as questions and pictures are simple enough.

4.2 Participants

Ninety EFL learners took part in the data compiling (48 Male, 42 Female: mean age 21.6 years old, ranging from 19–40 years old). They were university students in Tokyo, Japan. Their practical experience ranged 53 months to 216 months. The learners were paid for their participation.

The learners submitted scores of the Test of English for International Communication (TOEIC) taken within a year before the data started to be compiled. On the basis of the TOEIC scores, they were classified into three proficiency levels: beginner (N=30, TOEIC score range, 280-495), intermediate (N=30, TOEIC score range, 500-725), and advanced (N=30, TOEIC score range, 730-985) levels.

4.3 Materials

The following are questions for learner profiles in the writing task: "Which languages do you speak and read, and how well?" "What language did you learn?" (Ehrman 1996, Eignor et al.

1998). Pictures (Figure 3) described in the writing task were cited from Hughes (2003).

Figure 3. Pictures for description.

News articles used in the speaking, listening, and reading tasks were taken from Voice of America (VOA) (http://www.voanews.com). The length of articles was approximately 350 words (within plus/minus 5%). Each article had five comprehension questions that were made by the authors following question formats (Nation & Malarcher 2007).

These articles had two difficulty levels. Low-difficulty articles were taken from Special English program developed for learners of English, e.g., "Grading Grades." These articles are written in short, simple sentences that contain only one idea, and the sentences consist of a core vocabulary of 1500 words without idiomatic expressions. Low-difficulty articles were limited to the topic "studying in the U.S." High-difficulty articles were taken from VOA editorials that present differing points of view on a wide variety of issues, e.g., "Educating Marginalized Children."

4.4 Data compiling devices

The data collecting tool that learners used presents a sentence on a computer screen in the speaking and reading tasks. This tool keeps track of processing time for a sentence in the speaking, writing, and reading tasks. This tool provides comprehension questions and saves answers in the listening and reading tasks. In the writing task, this tool presents a question/a picture, and provides a blank space in which to write a sentence. The tool further keeps scores (1-5) of sentence difficulty/fluency judged by a learner in all the tasks.

In addition to this data collecting tool, the following devices were used. In the listening task, learners listened to audio files of news articles with headphones. In the speaking task, each learner reads aloud news articles in a recording booth. The recording booth is a sound-attenuated chamber (1700mm, 1900mm, 2100mm (approximately WDH)). A learner sat on a chair at a desk. The oral reading was recorded using a unidirectional electric-condenser microphone on a solid-state stereo. The sampling rate used was 44.1KHz, and quantization was set to 16 bits.

5 Application of the corpus

One application of the I-Learner Corpus is to use the corpus data as a language resource for examining learners' performances across multiple modalities, because the I-Learner Corpus includes linguistic output and language processing of the four modalities. This examination will reveal whether a learner's proficiencies in these modalities have developed equally. It will also enable us to examine how learners' proficiency develops from beginner to advanced levels, because the I-Learner corpus includes data of learners at these levels. These linguistic analyses constitute an important part of the I-Learner Corpus.

Another application is to use the corpus data as training data for a machine learning algorithm to construct an automatic evaluation method for learners' performances of the four modalities. When this automatic evaluation method and the data compiling devices are implemented in a computer-assisted language learning (CALL) system, the CALL system becomes able to compile learners' data. The CALL system can add new corpus, especially, longitudinal data if learners use the system for a certain period.

6 Conclusion

This paper described data compiling for constructing an I-Learner Corpus, a learner corpus that is compiled of data of linguistic output and of language processing of the four modalities. The I-Learner Corpus enables us to examine learners' performances in more detail and serves as a language resource for a learner model that predicts learners' performance.

A future work is to provide annotation data such as error information of pronunciation and written sentences. Another work is to enlarge corpus data by adding data of learners with different native languages.

Acknowledgments

This work was supported in part by Grant-in-Aid for Scientific Research (B) (22300299).

References

Arthur, Bradford R. 1979 Short-term changes in EFL composition skills. In Carlos A. Yorio, Kyle Perkins, and Jacquelyn Schachter, editors, *On TESOL '79: The Learner in Focus*. TESOL, Washington D.C., pages 330-342.

Braun, Sabine. 2006. ELISA: A pedagogically enriched corpus for language learning purposes. In Sabine Braun, Kurt Kohn, and Joybrato Mukherjee, editors, *Corpus Technology and Language Pedagogy: New Resources, New Tools, New Methods*. Peter Lang, Frankfurt, pages 25-47.

Chang, Anna C.-S. 2010. The effect of a timed reading activity on EFL learners: Speed, comprehension, and perceptions. *Reading in a Foreign Language*, 22(2): 284-303.

Ehrman, Madeline E. 1996. *Understanding Second Language Learning Difficulties*. SAGE Publications, London.

Eignor, Daniel, Carol Taylor, Irwin Kirsch, and Joan Jamieson. 1998. Development of a scale for assessing the level of computer familiarity of TOEFL examinees. Research Reports RR98-7, Educational Testing Service, Princeton, New Jersey.

Granger, Sylviane. 2007. The computer learner corpus: A versatile new source of data for SLA research. In Wolfgang Teubert and Ramesh Krishnamurthy, editors, *Corpus Linguistics: Critical Concepts in Linguistics*, volume 2. Routledge, London, pages 166-182.

Granger, Sylviane, Estelle Dagneaux, Fanny Meunier and Magali Paquot. 2009. *International Corpus of Learner English*, version 2. Presses Universitaires de Louvain, Louvain-la-Neuve, Belgium.

Gut, Ulrike. 2009. *Non-native Speech: A Corpus-based Analysis of Phonological and Phonetic Properties of L2 English and German*. Peter Lang, Frankfurt.

Hinkel, Eli. 2010. Integrating the four skills: Current and historical perspectives. In Robert B. Kaplan, editor, *Oxford Handbook in Applied Linguistics*, 2nd edition. Oxford University Press, New York, pages 110-126.

Hirai, Akiyo. 1999. The relationship between listening and reading rates of Japanese EFL learners. *The Modern Language Journal*, 83(3): 367-384.

Hughes, Arthur. 2003. *Testing for Language Teachers*, 2nd edition. Cambridge University Press, Cambridge, UK.

Izumi, Emi, Kiyotaka Uchimoto, and Hitoshi Isahara, editors. 2004. *Nihonjin 1200 nin no Eigo Spiking Koopasu* [A Speaking Corpus of 1200 Japanese Learners of English]. ALC Press, Tokyo, Japan.

Kotani, Katsunori, Takehiko Yoshimi, and Hitoshi Isahara. 2010. A prediction model of foreign language reading proficiency based on reading time and text complexity. *US-China Education Review*, 7(10): 1-9.

Meurers, Detmar, Niels Ott, and Ramon Ziai. 2010. Compiling a task-based corpus for the analysis of learner language in context. In Sam Featherston and Britta Stolterfoht, editors, *Proceedings of Linguistic Evidence 2010*, pages 214—217.

Nation, Paul and Casey Malarcher. 2007. *Reading for Speed and Fluency*. Compass Publishing, Seoul, Korea.

Segalowitz, Norman. 2003. Automaticity and second languages. In Catherine J. Doughty and Michael H. Long, editors, *The Handbook of Second Language Acquisition*. Blackwell, Oxford, pages 382-408.

Tono, Yukio. 2009. Integrating learner corpus analysis into a probabilistic model of second language acquisition. In Paul Baker, editor, *Contemporary Corpus Linguistics*. Continuum International Publishing Group, London, pages 184-203.

Wen, Qiufang, Maocheng Liang, and Xiaoqin Yan. 2008. *Spoken and Written Corpus of Chinese Learners (SWECCL)* 2.0. Foreign Language Teaching and Research Press, Beijing, China.

Zechner, Klaus and Isaac I. Bejar. 2006. Towards automatic scoring of non-native spontaneous speech. In Robert C. Moore, Jeff A. Bilmes, Jennifer Chu-Carroll, Mark Sanderson, editors, *Proceedings of the 2006 Human Language Technology Conference and the North Linguistics Annual Meeting (HLT/NAACL 2006)*, pages 216-223.

Mining the Sentiment Expectation of Nouns Using Bootstrapping Method

Miaomiao Wen
Language Technologies Institute
Carnegie Mellon University
mwen@andrew.cmu.edu

Yunfang Wu
Key Laboratory of Computational Linguistics (Peking University)
Ministry of Education, China
wuyf@pku.edu.cn

Abstract

We propose an unsupervised bootstrapping method to generate a new type of affect knowledge base: the sentiment expectation of nouns (e.g., "high salary" is desirable while "high price" is usually undesirable, because people have opposite sentiment expectation towards "salary" and "price"). A bootstrapping framework is designed to retrieve patterns that might be used to express complaints from the Web. The sentiment expectation of a noun could be automatically predicted with the output patterns. We evaluate the retrieved patterns and show that our method yields good results. Also, they are applied to improve both sentence and document level sentiment analysis results.

1 Introduction

In recent years, sentiment analysis has attracted considerable attention in the NLP community due to its wide applications. The task is mining positive and negative opinions from text and an in-depth review of its literature can be found in Pang and Lee (2008). Previous work on this problem falls into three groups: opinion mining of documents, sentiment classification of sentences and polarity prediction of words. Sentiment analysis both at document and sentence level rely heavily on word level.

The most frequently explored task at the word level is to determine the sentiment orientation (SO) of words or word senses in the lexicon. While adjectives and verbs are often considered, the sentiment classification of nouns still poses a challenge. This paper aims at identifying people's sentiment expectation towards a noun, even though the noun itself does not carry polarity. We propose three categories of sentiment expectation (SE) of nouns: positive expectation nouns (Pn), negative expectation nouns (Nn) and neutral. For example, "工资|salary" is a Pn, as "high salaries" is desirable for most people. Also, the noun "价格|price" describes an object that is generally neutral, but it is a Nn, as most people in most cases expect that the product prices become lower.

There are several significances lying in this study. First, the SE of noun reflects world knowledge about an object, which is not readily available in existing semantic resources. This knowledge is useful in determining the context dependent SO of adjectives or verbs. For example, "*high* salary" is desirable while "*high* price" is undesirable. Also, "*receive* money" will probably impart positive state onto its patient while "*receive* hepatitis" will impart negative state onto its patient. Second, our method requires very little human supervision.

We introduce an unsupervised bootstrapping approach. Our system is initialized with a very small seed set of nouns, and then iterates between (a) retrieving a set of *complaint patterns* (*CPs*) - lexico-syntactic patterns such as "<n> is a little a" [1] that tend to occur only in people's complaints - from search engine snippets and (b) using the acquired patterns to determine the SE of new nouns.

The rest of this paper is organized as follows: The related work is discussed in Section 2. In Sections 3,

[1] In this paper, <n> represents a noun and a represents an adj.

we present our bootstrapping method. In Section 4, we conduct evaluation experiments at both sentence and document level sentiment analysis. The paper is concluded in Section 5.

2 Related Work

Bootstrapping and pattern-based methods have been shown to be very effective in previous information extraction research (Riloff, 1996; Riloff and Jones, 1999; Ravichandran and Hovy, 2002; Thelen and Riloff, 2002; Riloff et al., 2003; Mooney and Bunescu, 2005; Wiebe and Mihalcea, 2006; Kozareva et al., 2008). These previous works derive patterns that reveal direct relationship between two words or the property of the word. Though similar in methodology, we focused on patterns that express an implicit relationship between the target noun and the opinion-bearing adjective.

There has been a large body of work on automatic SO prediction of words (Hatzivassiloglou and McKeown, 1997; Turney and Littman, 2003; Kim and Hovy, 2004; Esuli and Sebastiani, 2006), but unfortunately they did not consider the SE of nouns in their research and regarded most of the nouns as "neutral". Recently, some studies try to disambiguate the context dependent SO of adjectives (e.g. distinguish between "the battery life is very *long*" and "it takes a *long* time to focus") (Ding et al., 2008). They infer the context dependent SO by inferring with intra-sentence conjunction rule. Our task is more challenging as we have no global or domain information. Thus our method could be applied to isolated phrase or sentence and is domain independent. Wu and Wen (2010) present the first algorithm for retrieving SE of nouns automatically but the results critically depends on access to a high quality, carefully chosen collection of CPs.

3 Our Approach

Our main insight is to make use of CPs [2], which co-occur frequently with the target noun and the adjective that is opposite to the noun's SE. E.g. people might say "工资有点低| salary is a little low" but seldom say "工资有点高| salary is a little high". Utilizing this property, we try to (a) extract patterns like "$< n >$ is a little a" from snippets returned queries like "工资低|salary low";[3] (b) Use SVM to determine the SE of new nouns with page counts based features. E.g. "价格有点低| price is a little low" obtains 1080 hits while "价格有点高| price is a little high" obtains 19400 hits.

Input: Noun_Pool = $\{Pn, Nn\}$, A = $\{Pa, Na\}$;
Output: CP_Pool = {N CPs}; $i = 0$;
Bootstrapping
1. Candi_CP_Pool ← patterns extracted from snippets. For each pattern p,
$score(p) = TScore\ (p.CPFreq, p.WPFreq)$
2. CP_Pool = the N patterns with the highest score in Candi_CP_Pool. If CP_Pool remains unchanged for two succeeding loops or if $i > K$, stop bootstrapping.
3. Candi_Noun_Pool = Extract new nouns from snippets.
4. Train SVM with CP_Pool. Training set ← Noun_Pool, testing set ← Candi_Noun_Pool
For each noun n, the feature vector $F_i = TScore($ $\sum_{a \in Na} Hits(p_i(n,a)), \sum_{a \in Pa} Hits(p_i(n,a))), i = 1, ..., N$.
5. Add the nouns with the largest posterior probability and the smallest posterior probability to Pn and Nn respectively.
6. $i = i + 1$, Go to Step 1.

Table 1: The Whole Bootstrapping Process.

We use a bootstrapping method to automatically discover CPs and predict sentiment expectation of nouns (Table 1). In iteration phase 1, with a few seed nouns, the candidate CPs are retrieved from search engine snippets. We rank these CPs according to their ability to express SE. In iteration phase 2, we infer the sentiment expectation of a noun by mining the Web with CPs. The SVM is trained to classify positive expectation nouns and negative expectation nouns.

Initiation: The bootstrapping begins with a seed noun set Noun_Pool = $\{Pn, Nn\}$={{"工资|salary"}, {"价格|price"}}, and an adjective set A. A is grouped into two sets: positive-like adjectives (Pa) and negative-like adjectives (Na):

[2]Wish patterns (WP), which are usually used in people's praises and wishes, might also serve our purpose (Goldberg et. al., 2009). But using the Web as a corpus, we found that the CPs are much easier to be retrieved than WPs. Thus we will just focus on CPs in this paper and leave WPs for future work.

[3]We use Baidu as our search engine in this paper, `http://baidu.com.cn`

(1) Pa = {大|large, 多|many, 高|high, 厚|thick, 深|deep, 重|heavy}
(2) Na = {小|small, 少|few, 低|low, 薄|thin, 浅|shallow, 轻|light}

Phase 1. Extract CPs from Snippets: For each snippet returned by the query "$n\ a$" $\in Noun\_Pool : A$, extracts word n-grams after word segmentation. We select n-grams which contain exactly one <n> and one a. Counts the frequency of a pattern p appears as a CP (where $(<n>, a) \in (Pn, Na) or (Nn, Pa)$) and the frequency of p appears as a WP (where $(<n>, a) \in (Nn, Na) or (Pn, Pa)$). Finally, we adopt T-Score to measure the confidence with which we can assert whether this pattern is a CP (Step 1 in Table 1). The top ranking N patterns are selected as CPs experimentally.

Phase 2. Determine the SE of new nouns: We create a feature vector F using the harvested CPs for each noun. The two-class support vector machine (SVM) is trained to find the optimal combination of the page counts-based features (Step 4 in Table 1). We define the SE of a noun as the posterior probability (converted from SVM output with a sigmoid function (J. Platt., 2000)) that they belong to the positive expectation noun class. Then the nouns with the largest and smallest probability are added to the Noun_Pool.

4 Evaluation

4.1 Direct Evaluation

We examine the harvested CPs directly to determine whether they are actually CPs or not. Our evaluation metric is the precision of the output CPs at each bootstrapping iteration. We recruited two Chinese speakers to label them as "being CP", "not CP" or "hard to decide".

Figure 1 plots the number of correctly retrieved CPs in the output at each iteration. Clearly, we see general substantial improvement along with the bootstrapping process, although the increases level off in later iterations. As the number of the output CPs increases, there are more patterns that are labeled as "hard to decide", but some of these patterns could still serve our purpose. E.g., "因<n><a>|because <n>is <a>" and "我<n><a>|my <n>is <a>", as people often

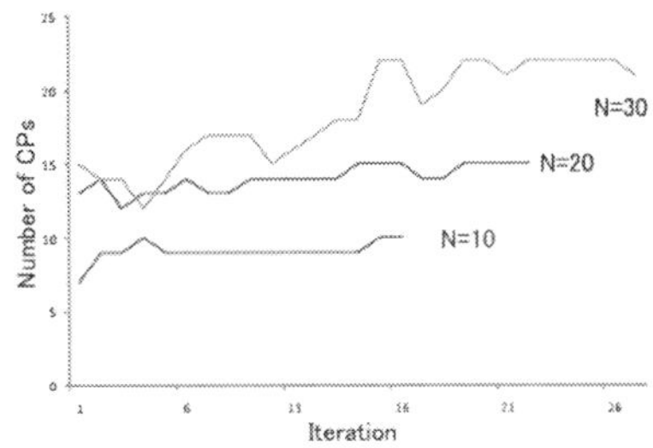

Figure 1: Number of CPs in results returned by the bootstrapping method at each iteration. N is the number of output patterns. Items labeled as "hard to decide" are not included.

post their problems and complaints on Web. These patterns may serve as possible indicators of the presence of a noun and the reversed expectation adjective, regardless of whether they are actually restricted in negative contexts.

The top ranked 10 CPs are of high quality. The manually chosen patterns in Wu and Wen (2010) have been successfully retrieved. This shows that our method yields good results. The 10 CPs and the nouns added in the bootstrapping process are listed below:

CPs: <n>有点a | <n> is a little a, <n>太a | <n> is too a, <n>是不是太a | isn' t <n> too a, <n>实在太a | <n> is really too a, 解决<n> a | solve a <n>, <n> a怎么办| <n> is a, what should I do, 嫌<n>a | hate a <n>, 因<n> a | because <n> is a, <n>过a |<n> is too a
Pn: 空间|room, 素质|quality，水平|level，效率|efficiency，内存|PC memory，收入|income，孩子|children，时间|time
Nn: 要求|requirement, 压力|pressure，成本|cost，风险|risk，问题|problem，花费|expense，代价|cost，房价|house price，损失|lost

4.2 Sentiment Analysis at Sentence Level

We apply the SE of nouns to predict the SO of sentiment ambiguous adjectives, which is SemEval-2010 Task 18 (Wu and Jin, 2010).

Data: We use the benchmark dataset of SemEval-2010 Task 18. The task consists of 14 sentiment ambiguous adjectives (SAA) (devided to Pa and Na sets same as in Section 3), which are all high-frequency words in Mandarin Chinese. Each of the 2917 sentences in the dataset contains a target noun and a SAA.

Methods: The SO of SAA can be determined by the target noun in noun-adjective phrases. If the SAA has the same polarity as the SE of noun, then the SAA has positive sentiment; if the SAA has the opposite polarity to the SE of noun, the SAA has negative sentiment.

Results: Compared with the other 16 systems that participated in Task 18, our system ranks fifth and is substantially better than baseline (Table 2). Note that all the top ranked 11 systems are supervised or incorporate manually built library. Our system also outperforms Wu and Wen (2010), indicating our bootstrapping method works better than the manually selected patterns.

	Micro Acc.	Macro Acc.
Our Method	77.63	79.52
Wu & Wen	75.83	71.67
Baseline	61.20	62.37

Table 2: The scores on SemEval-2010 Task 18.

4.3 Sentiment Analysis at Document Level

We also investigated the impact of recognizing SE of nouns and CPs on the sentiment classification of product reviews. SAAs are frequently used in product reviews and could be sentiment disambiguated by the SE of nouns. Also, CPs usually indicate the speaker is complaining and unsatisfied with the product (i.e. negative reviews). For example, "按键设计太紧密| keyboards are designed *too* close" and "价格偏贵| It is *a little* expensive".

Data: Following the work of Wan (2008) and Wan (2009), we selected the same dataset[4]. The dataset of Wan (2008) contains 886 Chinese product reviews. The dataset of Wan (2009) contains another 1000 unlabeled Chinese product reviews. We manually annotated these product reviews with positive or negative polarity labels. We use both these two datasets as our test set, which includes 1886 reviews. In order to examine the impact of recognizing SE of nouns, we extracted the files that contain the following strings, where the nouns are modified by SAAs in most cases:

(3) noun+adjective (adjective∈SAA)
noun+adverb+adjective
noun+adverb+adverb+adjective.

We obtained 449 files (SAA-set for short), up to 24% of the overall data.

Methods: The baseline method is the same algorithm with Wan (2008). The semantic orientation value for a review is computed by summing the polarity values of all words in the review, making use of both the word polarity defined in the positive and negative lexicons and the contextual valence shifters defined in the negation and intensifier lexicons. We also use the same parameter setting and the same sentiment lexicon [5].

Our method: (a) Add the disambiguation of SO of SAAs to the algorithm. When a word ∈ SAA, compute its SO with our method in Section 4.2, rather than using its prior polarity specified in the sentiment lexicon. (b) Use the CPs as indicators of negative comments. If any CP appears in a review, then it is judged as negative SO.

Results: Our method obviously outperforms the baseline by 12.16% in f-score and 17.02% in accuracy (on SAA-set, see Table 3). The improvement in recall is especially obvious. The results also indicate using more CPs could bring further improvement.

		Base line	SE N=10	SE N=20	SE N=30
Pos.	Pre.	65.69	81.93	83.44	85.28
	Rec.	76.40	74.16	76.40	75.96
	F	70.16	79.07	79.77	80.35
Neg.	Pre.	87.43	84.35	84.53	83.77
	Rec.	60.96	88.05	89.24	90.24
	F	71.83	86.16	86.82	86.89
Total	MacroF	70.98	82.46	83.14	83.49
	Acc.	66.90	83.46	83.92	84.15

Table 3: The sentiment classification results at document level. SE denotes our method. N is the number of CPs.

5 Conclusions

This paper presents an unsupervised bootstrapping method to retrieve the sentiment expectation of nouns from the Web. We utilize the predicted SE of nouns in determining the SO of sentiment ambiguous adjectives. For the sentiment analysis at sentence level, our method achieves promising result that is significantly better than baseline and comparable to the supervised methods. For the sentiment analysis at document level, our method also achieves obvious improvement in performance, which validates the effectiveness of our approach.

[4]Available here: http://sites.google.com/site/wanxiaojun1979/publicationlist-1

[5]Sentiment Hownet, a manually constructed Chinese opinion lexicon: http://www.keenage.com/html/c_index.html

References

Ding, X., Liu, B. and Yu, P. 2008. A holistic lexicon-based approach to opinion mining. *In Proceedings of WSDM'08.*

Esuli, A. and Sebastiani, F. 2006. SentiWordNet: a publicly available lexical resource for opinion mining. *In Proceedings of LREC'06.*

Goyal, A., Riloff, E., Daume III, H. 2010. Automatically Producing Plot Unit Representations for Narrative Text. *In Proceedings of EMNLP2010.*

Goldberg, A., Fillmore, N., Andrze-jewski, D., Xu, Z., Gibson, B., and Zhu, X.. 2009. May all your wishes come true: A study of wishes and how to recognize them. *In Proceedings of NAACL-HLT2009.*

Hatzivassiloglou, V. and McKeown, K. 1997. Predicting the semantic orientation of adjectives. *In Proceedings of ACL1997.*

J. Platt. 2000. Probabilistic outputs for support vector machines and comparison to regularized likelihood methods. *Advances in Large Margin Classifiers.*

Kozareva, Z., Riloff, E. and Hovy, E. 2008. Semantic Class Learning from the Web with Hyponym Pattern Linkage Graphs. *In Proceedings of ACL-HLT2008.*

Kim, S.and Hovy, E. 2004. Determining the sentiment of opinions. *In Proceedings of COLING2004.*

Pang, B. and Lee, L. 2008. Opinion mining and sentiment analysis *Foundations and Trends in Information Retrieval.*

Ravichandran, D and Hovy, E. 2002. Learning surface text patterns for a question answering system. *In Proceedings of ACL2002.*

Riloff, E. 1996. Automatically generating extraction patterns from untagged text. *In Proceedings of the 13th National Conference on Artificial Intelligence.*

Riloff, E., Wiebe, J., and Wilson, T.. 2003. Learning subjective nouns using extraction pattern bootstrapping. *In Proceedings of CoNLL2003.*

Riloff, Ellen and Jones, Rosie. 1999. Learning dictionaries for information extraction by multi-level bootstrapping. *In Proceedings of AAAI1999.*

Raymond J. Mooney and Razvan Bunescu. 2005. Mining knowledge from text using information extraction. *In ACM SIGKDD Exploration Newsletter, 7(1):3 - 10.*

Thelen, M. and Riloff, E. 2002. A Bootstrapping Method for Learning Semantic Lexicons Using Extraction Pattern Contexts. *In Proceedings of EMNLP2002.*

Turney, P. and Littman, M. 2003. Measuring praise and criticism: inference of semantic orientation from association. *In ACM transaction on information systems.*

Turney, P. D., and Pantel, P. 2010. From frequency to meaning: Vector space models of semantics. *In Journal of Artificial Intelligence Research.*

Wan, X. 2008. Using Bilingual Knowledge and Ensemble Techniques for Unsupervised Chinese Sentiment Analysis. *In Proceedings of EMNLP2008.*

Wan, X. 2009. Co-Training for Cross-Lingual Sentiment Classification. *In Proceedings of ACL-IJCNLP2009.*

Wiebe, J. and Mihalcea, R. 2006. Word Sense and Subjectivity. *In Proceedings of OLING-ACL2006.*

Wu, Y. and Jin, P. 2010. SemEval-2010 task 18: disambiguating sentiment ambiguous adjectives. *In Proceedings of SemEval 2010.*

Wu, Y and Wen, M. 2010. Disambiguating Dynamic Sentiment Ambiguous Adjectives. *In Proceedings of COLING2010.*

An Analysis of Questions in a Q&A Site Resubmitted Based on Indications of Unclear Points of Original Questions

Masahiro Kojima and **Yasuhiko Watanabe** and **Yoshihiro Okada**
Ryukoku University, Seta, Otsu, Shiga, 520-2194, Japan
t10m101@mail.ryukoku.ac.jp, {watanabe, okada}@rins.ryukoku.ac.jp

Abstract

In this study, we analyzed how answerers indicated unclear points in questions, and how questioners modified and resubmitted their questions based on indications of unclear points.

1 Introduction

In these days, many of us use question and answer (Q&A) sites where we share our problems and get solutions of them. For example, about 3.11 million questions were submitted to Yahoo! chiebukuro [1] from April/2004 to October/2005. Because of this large numbers of questions, questioners had better submit questions which give enough information to answerers. However, it is difficult to make good questions. For example, in Yahoo! chiebukuro, we often found unclear questions (e.g. Q1 in Figure 1) and their answers where answerers indicated unclear points of the questions (e.g. A1 in Figure 1).

(Q 1) I cannot access a web page which I could read yesterday. What should I do?

(A 1) Show URL.

In (A 1), the answerer pointed out that the questioner did not describe important information to answer the question: URL. Unclear questions may decrease chances of getting good answers. As a result, it is important to investigate supporting methods of making clear questions. One idea is to indicate unclear points of questions, as the questioner of (A 1) did. In order to obtain helpful knowledge and develop a help system for making clear questions, it is important to analyze

- how answerers indicated unclear points in questions, and
- how questioners modified and resubmitted their questions based on indications of unclear points in their original questions.

[1] Yahoo Answers in Japan. http://chiebukuro.yahoo.co.jp

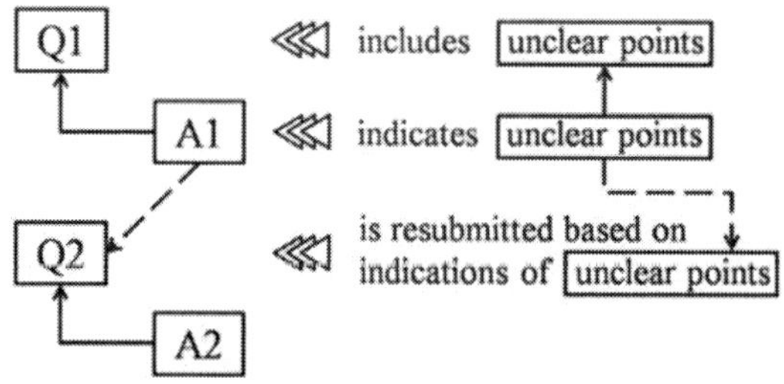

Figure 1: An example of a resubmitted question based on the indication of unclear points in the original question.

Our approach differs from previous analyses on Yahoo! Answers (Su et al., 2007) (Adamic et al., 2008). In this study, we used the data of Yahoo! chiebukuro for observation and examination. The data of Yahoo! chiebukuro was published by Yahoo! JAPAN via National Institute of Informatics in 2007 [2]. This data consists of about 3.11 million questions and 13.47 million answers which were posted on Yahoo! chiebukuro from April/2004 to October/2005.

2 Types of indication of unclear points in questions and modification of questions

2.1 Types of indication of unclear points in questions

We observed answers submitted to PC category of Yahoo! chiebukuro and found the following five types of indication of unclear points in questions (Table 1).

TYPE (A1-1) Answerers wanted detailed accounts of what questioners did.

(Q 2) I got a warning from Symantec. How do I extend the software license.

(A 2) Did you buy an extension key?

[2] http://research.nii.ac.jp/tdc/chiebukuro.html

Table 1: Types of indication of unclear points in questions

TYPE	indication of unclear points in questions
A1-1	detailed accounts of what questioners did
A1-2	detailed accounts of what happened
A1-3	detailed accounts of conditions
A1-4	information other than (A1-1), (A1-2), and (A1-3)
A1-5	unhelpful solution

TYPE (A1-2) Answerers wanted detailed accounts of what happened.

(Q 3) When I try to maximize my IE window, it is positioned about 2cm below from the top of the screen! What should I do?

(A 3) What's there? blank?

TYPE (A1-3) Answerers wanted detailed accounts of conditions. For example, the indication of (A 1) is classified into this type.

TYPE (A1-4) Answerers wanted detailed accounts of information which were not asked in answers of TYPE (A1-1), (A1-2), and (A1-3).

(Q 4) I don't know the connection type. What should I do?

(A 4) Which connection type do you want to know?

TYPE (A1-5) Answerers submitted solutions, however, they were not helpful to solve questioners' problems. In these cases, answerers did not indicate unclear points of questions. However, we think these unhelpful solutions are one type of indication of unclear points of questions. This is because these unhelpful solutions often made questioners aware of unclear points of their questions. For example, the answerer of (A 5) showed one solution with detailed instruction. The questioner of (Q 5) tried to solve his/her problem according to the instruction and found the solution was unhelpful.

(Q 5) Windows XP crashed. How do I boot my computer?

(A 5) Just put a recovery disc into CD/DVD drive. And restart your PC.

(Q 6) Windows XP crashed. I put a recovery disc into CD drive, but my PC didn't work. How do I boot my computer?

Table 2: Types of modification of questions based on indication of unclear points

TYPE	modification of questions
Q2-1	added explanation based on the indication
Q2-2	added explanation based on other information
Q2-3	described the solution was unhelpful
Q2-4	asked about unknowns in the indication
Q2-5	resubmitted in disregard of the indication

2.2 Types of modification of questions

We observed resubmitted questions in PC category of Yahoo! chiebukuro and found the following five types of modification of questions (Table 2).

TYPE (Q2-1) Questioners added explanations based on the indications of unclear points to their questions and resubmitted them. In this type, it is likely that answerers asked about what questioners knew or could find out easily.

(Q 7) How do I reset my iMac to default settings, except IE and Outlook settings.

(A 7) Show the versions of OS, IE, and Outlook Express.

(Q 8) How do I reset my iMac to default settings, except IE and Outlook settings. My mac OS is version 9 and both IE and Outlook are version 5.

TYPE (Q2-2) Questioners added explanations based on information other than the indications to their questions and resubmitted them. In this type, it is also likely that answerers asked about what questioners knew or could find out easily.

(Q 9) Can I boot my XP PC with Windows 98 HDD?

(A 9) Did you install 98 first? You cannot boot your PC by using Windows 98 if your primary OS is XP.

(Q 10) Can I boot my XP PC with Windows 98 HDD? I don't want to set up a dual boot system. I want to know my PC gets in trouble when I boot it with Win 98 HDD.

TYPE (Q2-3) In resubmitted questions, questioners described that solutions received from answerers were unhelpful to solve their questions. For example, in (Q 6), the questioner described the solution received from the answerer of (A 5) was unhelpful to solve his/her problem. In this type, it is likely that answerers showed one solution which questioners did not know.

TYPE (Q2-4) In resubmitted questions, questioners asked about unknown points in the indication received from answerers. For example, the questioner of (Q 11) received one solution and got the key to solve his/her problem: module deletion. However, he/she did not know it and submitted (Q 12) for requesting detailed information about it.

(Q 11) I removed all macros from my excel file. Then, whenever I open the file, excel asks me if I want to enable/disable macros. How do I stop it?

(A 11) Open visual basic editor and delete the module.

(Q 12) I removed all macros from my excel file. Then, whenever I open the file, excel asks me if I want to enable/disable macros. I want to stop it. The module should be deleted by using visual basic editor. But, how do I do it?

TYPE (Q2-5) Questioners resubmitted almost the same questions as they had. They did not mentioned any kinds of information received from answerers. For example, in (Q 14), the questioner did not mention any kinds of information described in (A 14) although he/she selected (A 14) as a best answer.

(Q 13) My optical mouse is faulty. The cursor sometimes freezes. Is it end of life?

(A 13) Look the back side and remove dust gathered around the red light.

(Q 14) My optical mouse is faulty. The cursor sometimes freezes. Is it end of life?

3 Extraction of original and resubmitted questions and their answers from Yahoo! chiebukuro

We intended to extract

- original questions which included unclear points (e.g. Q1 in Figure 1),
- answers which indicated unclear points in the original questions (e.g. A1 in Figure 1),
- resubmitted questions based on the indications of unclear points in the original questions (e.g. Q2 in Figure 1), and
- answers to the resubmitted questions

from PC category of Yahoo! chiebukuro in the next way.

step 1 extract an answer which indicated unclear points in a question (e.g. A1 in Figure 1). This kind of answer can be extracted by using a method based on machine learning techniques (Isogai et al., 2009).

step 2 extract the question which had the answer extracted in step 1 (e.g. Q1 in Figure 1). This question is regarded as an original question.

step 3 extract the first question submitted by the questioner after he/she received the answer extracted in step 1.

step 4 examine whether the questions extracted in step 1 and step 3 met one of the following conditions:

- they shared more than 10 content words when both of them consisted of more than 20 content words, or
- they shared more than 5 content words.

When one of the conditions was satisfied, the question extracted in step 3 is regarded as a resubmitted question (e.g. Q2 in Figure 1).

step 5 extract the answers to the resubmitted question extracted in step 4 (e.g. A2 in Figure 1).

4 Experimental results

We applied our method described in section 3 to 171848 questions and 474687 answers which were submitted to PC category of Yahoo! chiebukuro from April/2004 to October/2005, and extracted 4271 cases of questions and their answers. Among them, we selected 200 cases randomly and found 133 cases of them where

- an original question (e.g. Q1 in Figure 1),
- the answer which indicated unclear points in the original questions (e.g. A1 in Figure 1),
- the resubmitted questions based on the indication of unclear points in the original questions (e.g. Q2 in Figure 1), and
- the answers to the resubmitted questions (e.g. A2 in Figure 1)

were extracted adequately. We observed these 133 cases and show

Table 3: The results of the analyses: (1) how answerers indicated unclear points in original questions (A1-1, 2, 3, 4, and 5), (2) how questioners utilized indications in answers when they resubmitted their questions (Q2-1, 2, 3, 4, and 5). The numbers in parentheses are the numbers of best answers.

(a) 122 cases where questioners obtained good answers.

	A1-1	A1-2	A1-3	A1-4	A1-5	total
Q2-1	5 (5)	15 (14)	21 (16)	4 (4)	10 (10)	55 (49)
Q2-2	0 (0)	1 (1)	1 (1)	7 (6)	6 (4)	15 (12)
Q2-3	1 (1)	0 (0)	0 (0)	0 (0)	18 (14)	19 (15)
Q2-4	1 (1)	4 (3)	0 (0)	0 (0)	12 (10)	17 (14)
Q2-5	0 (0)	4 (4)	1 (1)	1 (1)	10 (8)	16 (14)
total	7 (7)	24 (22)	23 (18)	12 (11)	56 (46)	122 (104)

(b) 11 cases where questioners did not obtain good answers.

	A1-1	A1-2	A1-3	A1-4	A1-5	total
Q2-1	0 (0)	0 (0)	0 (0)	0 (0)	0 (0)	0 (0)
Q2-2	0 (0)	0 (0)	0 (0)	1 (1)	0 (0)	1 (1)
Q2-3	0 (0)	0 (0)	0 (0)	0 (0)	0 (0)	0 (0)
Q2-4	0 (0)	0 (0)	0 (0)	0 (0)	0 (0)	0 (0)
Q2-5	0 (0)	2 (1)	2 (1)	1 (1)	5 (4)	10 (7)
total	0 (0)	2 (1)	2 (1)	2 (2)	5 (4)	11 (8)

1. whether questioners obtained good solutions or useful clues by resubmitting their questions, especially, when they added explanations based on indications to their questions.
2. how answerers indicated unclear points in questions.
3. whether questioners gave good evaluations to answerers who indicated unclear points of their questions.
4. how questioners utilized indications of unclear points of their original questions when they resubmitted their questions.

Table 3 shows the results of these analyses.

First, we examined whether questioners obtained good solutions or useful clues by resubmitting their questions. As shown in Table 3, there were 26 cases where questioners resubmitted TYPE (Q2-5) questions (questions resubmitted in disregard of indications), and then, 16 of these 26 cases where questioners obtained good solutions or useful clues. On the other hand, there were 107 cases where questioners resubmitted TYPE (Q2-1), (Q2-2), (Q2-3), and (Q2-4) questions, in other words, they accepted indications from answerers and modified their questions. Then, there were 106 of these 107 cases where questioners obtained good solutions or useful clues. As a result, questioners can increase their chances to obtain good solutions or useful clues when they accepted indications from answerers and modified their questions.

Secondly, we examined how answerers indicated unclear points in questions. As shown in Table 3, TYPE (A1-5) answer (unhelpful solution) was the most common answer. As a result, questioners had chances to recognize unclear points in their questions even if they received unhelpful solutions.

Thirdly, we examined whether questioners gave good evaluations to answerers who indicated unclear points of their questions. As shown in Table 3, there were 112 cases (84%) where questioners gave good evaluations to answerers who indicated unclear points of their questions. On the other hand, in PC category of Yahoo! chiebukuro, 474687 answers were submitted and 171848 of them (36%) were received good evaluations. As a result, many questioners gave good evaluations to answerers who indicated unclear points of their questions.

Finally, we examined how questioners utilized indications of unclear points of their original questions when they resubmitted their questions. In this experiment, there were 107 cases where questioners resubmitted TYPE (Q2-1), (Q2-2), (Q2-3), and (Q2-4) questions, in other words, they accepted indications from answerers and modified their questions. Then, there were 17 of these 107 cases where questioners resubmitted TYPE (Q2-4) questions, in other words, they had unknown points in indications received from answerers and needed to ask about what they were. In other 90 cases, questioners resubmitted TYPE (Q2-1), (Q2-2), and (Q2-3) questions, in other words, they knew or could find out easily what answerers indicated. As a result, just to indicate unclear points in questions is useful to make good questions.

References

Adamic,L., Zhang,J., Bakshy,E., and Ackerman,M.: Knowledge Sharing and Yahoo Answers: Everyone Knows Something, WWW2008, (2008).

Isogai,N., Nishimura,R., Watanabe,Y., and Okada,Y.: Information Extraction for Supporting a Learner's Efforts to Recognize What the Learner did not Understand, CSEDU 2009, (2009).

Su,Q., Pavlov,D., Chow,J., and Baker,W.: Internet-scale collection of human-reviewed data, WWW2007, (2007).

Diversifying Information Needs in Results of Question Retrieval

Yaoyun Zhang, Xiaolong Wang, Xuan Wang, Ruifeng Xu, Jun Xu and Shixi Fan
Key Laboratory of Network-oriented Intelligent Computation
Harbin Institute of Technology, Shenzhen Graduate School, China
{xiaoni5122, xuruifeng.hitsz, hit.xujun}@gmail.com
{wangxl, wangxuan}@insun.hit.edu.cn

Abstract

Information need is an important factor in question retrieval. This paper proposes a method to diversify the results of question retrieval in term of types of information needs. *CogQTaxo*, a question hierarchy is leveraged to represent users' information needs cognitively from three linguistic levels. Based on a prediction model of question types, three factors, i.e., scores of IR model, question type similarity and question type novelty are linearly combined to re-rank the retrieved questions. Preliminary experimental results show that the proposed method enhances the question retrieval performance in information coverage and diversity.

1 Introduction

Most current question retrieval system attempts to fetch questions semantically similar to the query question (Jeon et al, 2005), together with the accepted answers from a large question-answer pair archive. Previous works focus on reducing the lexicon gap between the query question and retrieved questions (Cao et al, 2010) or recognize the single question type, i.e., the type of information needs(*infoNeeds*) in the query, and confine the types of retrieved questions to be the same as the query (Lytinen and Tomuro, 2002). Normally, the retrieved questions are ranked according to the semantic similarity to the query question.

However, Taylor (1962) argues that the user may fail to express his *infoNeeds* fully in the question. Besides, given different contextual situations, users may have different intentions, which lead to different *infoNeeds* for the same question (Small and Strzalkowski, 2008).

For an example question q_1, "which bank provides the best credit card?", if the user wants to confirm the bank he knows, the name of the bank is enough for an answer; while the user plans to open a credit card account, he may want to obtain detailed descriptions and comparisons between credit card services of different banks in addition to a single bank name. Furthermore, a play-it-safe user may expect the information source of the answer to be of authority or expertise, while a casual user may expect it to be commonsense that anyone can answer.

Considering these requirement, the following two questions q_2 and q_3 should be provided to the user under a certain context. Nevertheless, such *infoNeeds* are not given explicitly in the q_1.

q_2: Which bank should I choose for credit card, Citi Bank and Bank of America?

q_3: How to choose credit card?

As can be observed, the three questions have different types, which are *entity*, *alternative* and *method*, respectively (Diekema et al, 2003). Apparently, the single-dimensional question taxonomies employed at present are insufficient to model those aspects of users' *infoNeeds* (Pomerantz, 2005). Thus, more comprehensive question taxonomy is needed. The question retrieval results should also be diversified accordingly to fulfill these implicit and context-dependent *infoNeeds*, thus making the results more comprehensive for average users.

Present works (Clark et al, 2009; Santos et al, 2010) mainly target on search result diversification for short queries instead of questions. Their focus is to mine the different interpretations of ambiguous queries or navigations for a broad-sense query. Achananuparp et al. (2010) attempted to diversify the aspects of the answer to complex questions, while they also focus on the short information nuggets returned by search engines.

Based on our knowledge, no previous work has been done on the results diversification for question retrieval. In this paper, we utiliz *CogQTaxo*, a multi-dimensional question taxonomy to model both the explicit and implicit *infoNeeds* of questions. Based on this, we propose an algorithm to diversify the results of question retrieval in terms of *infoNeed* types. The comparative experimental results show that the proposed algorithm enhances the information coverage and diversity of retrieved questions.

2 *CogQTaxo* - Three Dimensional Question Taxonomy

CogQTaxo is proposed by Zhang et al (2010). It is a framework of three-dimensional question taxonomy by using different levels of linguistic analysis (syntactic, semantic and pragmatic) as the classification criteria.

Let T_i (i=1,2,3) denotes the *i*th dimension of *CogQTaxo*, then:

1. T_1 represents the surface information need (*surfaceIN*), which corresponds to the conventional definition of question types (*QuesTs)*. A question can has one definite type in *surfaceIN*; 14 types are defined for *surfaceIN*, namely *location, person, time, quantity, thing, alternative, definition, comparison, description, procedure, reason, yesNo, abstractEnity* and *other*.

2. T_2 represents implicit information needs (*implicitIN*). *QuesTs* in this dimension are the same as in *surfaceIN*. Nevertheless, it represents the *infoNeeds* which are not expressed explicitly in the question, yet are required to fill the user's information gap. A question has at least one type in *implicitIN*.

3. T_3 represents users' pragmatic expectations (*pragmaticE*) from the answer. Four binary-valued pragmatic aspects are currently considered: (1) *Specification*: whether the question contains detailed specific information as the context; (2) *Knowledge source*: whether the question requires commonsense or expertise to answer; (3) *Temporal constraint*: whether the answer is time sensitive, i.e., whether the answer should be constraint to a time-frame; (4)*Subjectivity Orientation*: whether the information in the expected answer is subjective-oriented or objective-oriented.

A prediction model is built by Zhang et al (2010) to recognize the types of a question in each dimension of *CogQTaxo*. In this study, *CogQTaxo* is employed to diversify the *infoNeeds* in the results of question retrieval.

3 Diversification Algorithm for Question Retrieval Result

According to the definition of *CogQTaxo*, the three dimensions have different functions in user *infoNeeds* fulfillment, in which *surfaceIN* is fundamental and indispensable from the answer. *implicitIN* provides supportive information and helps to make the answer coverage more comprehensive. Therefore, we use *surfaceIN* and *implicitIN* to diversify the types of *infoNeeds* in retrieval results. The predicted *QuesT* sets in these two dimensions are merged into an extended one, in which the *QuesT*s are equally weighted at present. Meanwhile, the third dimension in *CogQTaxo*, *pragmaticE*, adds pragmatic constraints to the former two.

As displayed in figure 1, our question diversification algorithm is given as follows:

For a input question *p*, the question retrieval system will:

Step 1: Question analysis: The content words (nouns, verbs and adjectives) are extracted from *p* as the question content. Types of *p* in line with *CogQTaxo* are recognized automatically by using the model proposed in (Zhang et al, 2010).

Step 2: Question retrieval: retrieve relevant questions with the information retrieval (IR) model by using question content as the query. The relevance score is denoted as *IRScore*, which is normalized by the highest score of retrieved questions for *p*.

Step 3: Question Reranking with *QuesT* Similarity: Similar to (Lytinen and N. Tomuro, 2002) and (Cao et al, 2010), this step considers the relevance of *QuesT* between *p* and *q* for result ranking. Nevertheless, the question taxonomy deployed here is multi-dimensional. For each question *q* in the retrieved question set, T_i*Score* is defined as the *QuesT* set distance between *p* and *q* in the *i*th dimension of *CogQTaxo*, i=1, 2, 3. It is calculated by MASI (Passonneau, 2006). Since we

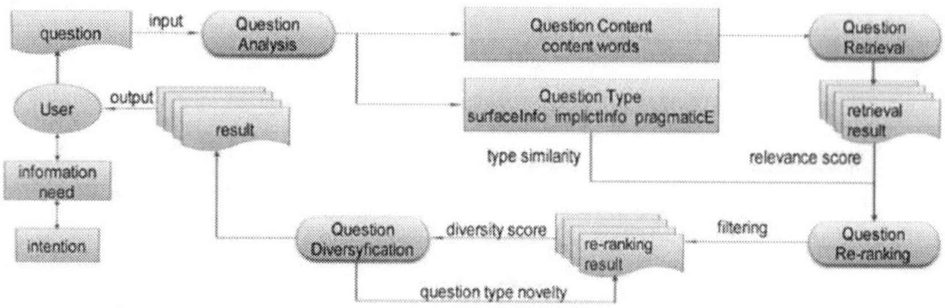

Figure 1 Diversification Procedure of Question Retrieval Results

merge T_1 with T_2, the retrieved results are re-ranked by *rerankScore*, which is defined as:

$$rerankScore = (1 - l_{1+2} - l_3) * IRScore + l_{1+2} * T_{1+2}Score + l_3 * T_3Score$$

where $l_{1+2}, l_3 \in [0,1], l_{1+2} + l_3 \in [0,1]$.

Result questions with the *rerankScore* lower than a threshold λ are filtered.

Step 4: Question *infoNeeds* diversification: This step employs a greedy algorithm to add one question with the largest *infoNeeds* novelty into the final returned question list in each iteration.

Suppose m questions are left in the result set after step 3, we denote *DiverseList* as the list of r questions re-ranked by diversity. For a question q in the m-r remaining result questions, its *QuesTs* novelty is defined as:

$$Novelty(T) = avg(\sum \frac{1}{e^{df_{type_j}+1}}),\ \exists type_j \in T^q_{1+2} \cap T^p_{1+2},$$

where df_{typej} is the frequency of $type_j \in T^q_{1+2} \cap T^p_{1+2}$ in *DiverseList*.

Then *diverseScore* is computed as follows:

$$diversScore = (1-w) * rerankScore + w * Novelty(T),\ 0 \le w \le 1.$$

The question with the highest *diversScore* value is added to *DiverseList*[1].

Repeat Step 4 until the *DiverseList* with top n ($m \ge n$) questions are returned to the user.

4 Experiment and Discussion

4.1 Dataset and Experimental Setup

Questions with accepted answers are collected from the Yahoo! Knowledge portal and Baidu Zhidao portal, respectively. After removing redundancy and invalid questions, more than 1,380,000 postings are obtained [2] postings are obtained. The title of the posting is used as the question, while the accepted response is regarded as the answer.

100 questions chosen randomly as the query questions, the other questions are indexed to build the question retrieval system. Only the content words of questions are indexed. In the experiment, we used three IR model, namely Okapi BM25 model, Vector space model and language model, respectively, in which BM25 outperforms. Therefore, only the performance achieved by BM25 is reported in the rest of this section.

Relevance set: The relevance set of the 100 query questions are built by judging the content relevance between the query and the results regardless of the *infoNeeds*. Poolings among the top 10 results by the evaluated methods are conducted. Finally, 2258 relevant questions are collected.

Information need annotation: Three annotators annotate the *QuesTs* of the 100 query questions individually, by following the same instruction as Zhang et al (2010). In this way, three different *infoNeeds* sets of the query questions are generated. The algorithm performance is evaluated on each *infoNeeds* set separately, while the average performance is reported.

Evaluation criteria: We use *MAP_IA*, *MRR_IA* and *P@K_IA* designed by Agrawal et al (2009) as the evaluation metrics. These metrics are originally defined as the weighted arithmetic mean of performance of each subtopic of a query. In this paper, we substitute the subtopics of a query into the potential types of a question. At present we consider all of *QuesTs* as equally weighted. For example, the formula of *MAP_IA* is as follows:

$$MAP\_IA = \frac{\sum_{QuesT_i \in T_1 \cup T_2} W_i MAP(QuesT_i)}{(|T_1| + |T_2|)}$$

Furthermore, the relevance judgment in those metrics between question p and q is not simply bi-

[1] The reported experimental results are derived by l_{1+2}=0.2, l_3 =0.2, w=0.4, λ=0.5, which are obtained in a pilot experiment using 20 randomly selected test queries.

[2] Data used in this paper can be downloaded from Http://qa.haitianyuan.com/cogQTaxo.html

Table 2 Question retrieval results are listed for the query "Which stock is good to buy?", using BM25 as the retrieval model.

Predicted question type : entity/ description procedure alternative	
BM25 model	BM25 model with question type diversity
Which stock is good to buy?	Which stock is good to buy?
Which stock is good recently?	Which stock is good recently?
Which stock should I buy recently?	What characteristics good stocks have?
Recommend some good stocks to me.	How to identify a good stock?
Is there any good stock to buy?	Which stocks should I buy; good recommendations will be highly rewarded.

Table 3 Information needs diversification performance of the evaluated methods.

	Retrive_M	*Pop_Div*	*SurfaceIN_M*	*implicitIN_M*	*PragmaticE_M*	*LinearC*	*Bow_Div*	*Predict_Div*
MRR_IA	0.343	0.526	0.375	0.371	0.347	0.390	**0.527**	**0.529**
MAP_IA	0.114	0.140	0.138	0.134	0.120	**0.149**	0.058	**0.164**
P_IA @1	0.181	0.211	0.239	0.237	0.213	**0.245**	0.245	**0.262**
P_IA@5	0.192	0.197	0.218	0.215	0.205	**0.230**	0.106	**0.244**

nary valued, as either relevant or not; it is replaced by the similarity between p and q in *pragmaticE*. As mentioned before, *pragmaticE* add pragmatic constraints to the other two dimensions of *infoNeeds*.

$$infoNeed\_relevance(q) = \begin{cases} T_3Score, & \text{if } relevance(q) = 1 \\ 0, & \text{if } relevance(q) = 0 \end{cases}$$

Evaluated question diversification methods: (1) ***Retrieve_M***: only using the IR model; (2) ***Pop_Div***: Instead of using the *QuesT* prediction model built by (Zhang et al, 2000), the *QuesT*s with the highest relative frequency (larger than 10%), i.e., the most popular *QuesT*s in the top 200 retrieved results by *Retrieve_M* are used as the potential type of *infoNeeds* of the query question; (3) ***SurfaceIN_M***, ***implicitIN_M***, ***PragmaticE_M***: using each of the three dimensions of *CogQTaxo* in the diversification algorithm, individually; (4) ***LinearC***: The first three steps of the diversification algorithm, i.e., without the diversification iteration step; (5) ***Bow_Div***: treating the question as bag-of-words, follows the same procedure without Step 3 in section 3, and only considers the novelty of content words in result questions in Step 4; (6) ***Predict_Div***: the complete proposed diversification algorithm.

4.2 Experimental Results

Table 2 illustrates the top 5 search results of query "Which stock is good to buy?" using *Retrive_M* and *Predict_Div*, respectively. As can be seen, the *infoNeeds* in questions retrieved by *Predict_Div* are more diverse than those retrieved by *Retrive_M.*

Table 3 lists the *infoNeeds* diversification performance achieved by each method, respectively. It is observed that *Predict_Div* outperforms. It is also shown that performance of *Bow_Div* is comparable with *Predict_Div* in *MRR_IA* and *P_IA @1*; however, it is even inferior to *Retrieve_M* in *MAP_IA* and *P_IA @5*. This indicates that the naïve bag-of-word baseline is unable to recall diverse *infoNeeds* of the query, and even deteriorates the performance. *Pop_Div* and *Predict_Div* are comparable in *MRR_IA*. However, in terms of other metrics, *LinearC* and *Predict_Div* are consistently at the top 2 ranks. The reason is that since the predicted types of a question are already diversified by *CogQTaxo*, incorporating it into question re-ranking already enables us to diversify the *infoNeeds* in the results implicitly. Therefore, the explicit diversification step enhances the performance further.

One deficit of the evaluation framework is that the *infoNeeds* of questions in the relevance set are predicted automatically instead of manually annotated; this may result in a bias towards our proposed algorithm. However, since the training set of the question classifier is manually annotated. Thus, it reflects the real user *infoNeeds* distribution. It is assumed that the automatic prediction can also reflect real user *infoNeeds* to some extent. More detailed analysis will be conducted later to examine this problem.

5 Conclusion

This paper proposes a method to diversify the results of question retrieval in term of types of information needs. Comparison results show that the proposed method improves the information need coverage and diversity in retrieved questions.

Acknowledgements

This work is supported in part by the National Natural Science Foundation of China (No. 61173075 and 60973076).

References

Anne R. Diekema, Ozgur Yilmazel, Jiangping Chen, Sarah Harwell, Lan He, Elizabeth D. Liddy. 2003. What do you mean? Finding answers to complex questions. *Proceedings of the AAAI Spring Symposium: New Directions in question Answering* .

Charles L. A. Clarke, Nick Craswell, Ian Soboroff. 2009. Overview of the trec 2009 web track. *Proceedings of the 18th Text Retrieval Conference.*

Elizabeth D. Liddy. 1998. Enhanced text retrieval using natural language processing. *Bulletin of the American Society for Information Science and Technology*, 24(4): 14–16.

Ingrid Zukerman and Eric Horvitz. 2001. Using Machine Learning Techniques to Interpret WH-questions. *Proceedings of the 39th Annual Meeting on Association for Computational Linguistics*, pp. 547–554.

Jeffrey Pomerantz. 2005. A Linguistic Analysis of Question Taxonomies. *Journal of the American Society for Information Science and Technology*, 56(7):715–728.

Jiwoon Jeon, W. Bruce Croft and Joon Ho Lee. 2005. Finding Similar Questions in Large Question and Answer Archives. *Proceedings of Conference on Information and Knowledge Management*, pp. 84–90.

John Burger, Claire Cardie, Vinay Chaudhri, Robert Gaizauskas, Sanda Harabagiu, David Israel, et al. 2001. Issues, Tasks and Program Structures to Roadmap Research in question & Answering (Q&A). *Technical Report, NIST.*

Lytinen and N. Tomuro. 2002. The use of question types to match questions in faqfinder. *AAAI Spring Symposium on Mining Answers from Texts and Knowledge Bases.*

Palakorn Achananuparp, Xiaohua Hu, Tingting He. 2010. Answer Diversification for Complex Question Answering on the Web. *Proceedings of the Pacific-Asia Conference on Knowledge Discovery and Data Mining*, pp.375-382

Passonneau, Rebecca J. 2006. Measuring agreement on set-valued items (MASI) for semantic and pragmatic annotation. *Proceedings of the International Conference on Language Resources and Evaluation*, pp.831–836.

Rakesh Agrawal, Sreenivas Gollapudi, Alan Halverson, and Samuel Ieong. 2009. Diversifying search results. *Proceedings of the Second ACM International Conference on Web Search and Data Mining*, pp.5-14.

Robert S. Taylor. 1962. The Process of Asking Questions. *American Documentation*, 13(4):391-396.

Rodrygo L. T. Santos, Craig Macdonald and Iadh Ounis. 2010. Exploiting Query Reformulations for Web Search Result Diversification. *Proceedings of International World Wide Web Conference*, pp.881-890.

Sharon Small, Tomek Strzalkowski. 2008. HITIQA: High-quality intelligence through interactive question answering. *Natural Language Engineering*, 15 (1): 31–54

Xin Cao, Gao Cong, Bin Cui, Christian S. Jensen. 2010. A Generalized Framework of Exploring Category Information for Question Retrieval in Community Question Answer Archives. *Proceedings of International World Wide Web Conference*, pp. 201-210.

Yaoyun Zhang, Xiaolong Wang, Xuan Wang, Shixi Fan. 2010. *CogQTaxo*: Modeling human cognitive process with a three-dimensional question taxonomy. *International Conference on Machine Learning and Cybernetics*, pp.3305 – 3310.

Beyond Normalization: Pragmatics of Word Form in Text Messages

Tyler Baldwin
Department of Computer
Sciencc and Engineering
Michigan State University
East Lansing, MI 48824
baldwi96@cse.msu.edu

Joyce Y. Chai
Department of Computer
Science and Engineering
Michigan State University
East Lansing, MI 48824
jchai@cse.msu.edu

Abstract

Non-standard spellings in text messages often convey extra pragmatic information not found in the standard word form. However, text message normalization systems that transform non-standard text message spellings to standard form tend to ignore this information. To address this problem, this paper examines the types of extra pragmatic information that are conveyed by non-standard word forms. Empirical analysis of our data shows that 40% of non-standard word forms contain emotional information not found in the standard form, and 38% contain additional emphasis. This extra information can be important to downstream applications such as text-to-speech synthesis. We further investigated the automatic detection of non-standard forms that display additional information. Our empirical results show that character level features can provide important cues for such detection.

1 Introduction

Text message conversations are often filled with non-standard word spellings. While some of these are unintentional misspellings, many of them are purposely produced. One commonly acknowledged reason that text message authors intentionally use non-standard word forms is to reduce the amount of time it takes to type the message, or the amount of space the message occupies.

This phenomenon has motivated the text message normalization task (Aw et al., 2006), which attempts to replace non-standard spelling and symbols by their standard forms. The normalization task is potentially critical for applications involving text messages, such as text-to-speech synthesis.

However, one important aspect that is overlooked when performing normalization is the use of non-standard word forms to express additional information such as emotion or emphasis. For instance, consider the following text message conversation:

A: They won the game!

B: Yesssss

The intent of the utterance by person B seems clear: he wishes to show that he is happy about the event described by person A. If the non-standard form *Yesssss* was normalized to the standard form *yes*, the intent conveyed by the utterance would be ambiguous; it could suggest that person B is happy about this turn of events, or he is indifferent, or he could simply be acknowledging that he already knows this fact. By using the non-standard form instead of the standard one, Person B communicated his excitement to A.

As shown in the above example, text message users often employ these non-standard forms to display extra pragmatic information that is not easily displayed otherwise. However, because normalization is only concerned about converting non-standard spellings to standard forms, it has the potential to remove this important pragmatic information.

To address this problem and to better understand some of the pragmatics of non-standard spellings in text messages, we conducted an initial investigation. In this study, we investigate the prevalence of non-standard spelling for the purpose of displaying information not captured in the standard word form. We also investigate the non-standard word form style associated with extra information and make a first attempt at identifying whether a non-standard form holds extra pragmatic information.

2 Related Work

There are two main areas of related work: text normalization and affective text classification. Because it may be unclear how non-standard forms should be read aloud, the field of text-to-speech synthesis has long been interested in text normalization. Sproat et. al. (2001) study several different corpora and identify several types of non-standard word, including several seen frequently in text message data, such as misspelling, abbreviation, and "funny spellings". More recent work (Zhu et al., 2007) has employed conditional random fields in an attempt to handle word normalization simultaneously with several related problems such as detecting sentence and paragraph boundaries.

Several different approaches have been proposed for normalization of text messages specifically, including those motivated by machine translation (Aw et al., 2006) and spell-checking (Choudhury et al., 2007). Most recently, Pennell and Liu (2010) use handcrafted rules as classification features to normalize SMS terms that contain character deletion, with a focus on normalization for text-to-speech systems. A few hybrid approaches (Kobus et al., 2008; Beaufort et al., 2010) and an unsupervised approach (Cook and Stevenson, 2009) have also been investigated. All of these methods assume that the normalized form is functionally equivalent to the non-standard form found in the text; none address the potential existence of extra information in the non-standard form.

Affective text classification attempts to identify the type or polarity of emotion that is expressed by the text, without the aid of extra linguistic cues such as gesture or prosody. Kao et. al. (2009) survey the field and divide approaches into 3 categories: 1) keyword based approaches (Bracewell, 2008), 2) learning-based approaches (Alm et al., 2005; Yang et al., 2007; Binali et al., 2010), and 3) hybrid approaches (Wu et al., 2006; Agarwal et al., 2009). Although there has been some recognition of the effect that non-standard word forms play in emotion detection (Zhang et al., 2006), the primary feature sources for emotion detection systems has been at the word and sentence level (Quan and Ren, 2010). To our knowledge, no previous work has focused on the role non-standard word form plays in conveying emotional and other pragmatic information in text messages.

Figure 1: Example dialogue from our corpus

3 Empirical Analysis

3.1 Data Set

In order to access whether non-standard word forms have additional pragmatic information, it is necessary to study these forms in their original dialogue context. Because no currently available text message dataset contains messages in context, we collected our own. The website "Damn You Autocorrect"[1] posts screenshots of short text message conversations that contain mistakes produced by automatic spelling correction systems. To create an initial dataset, 1190 text message conversations were transcribed. A sample dialogue is shown in Figure 1.

The speech bubbles originating from the left of the image in Figure 1 are produced by one participant, while those originating from the right are produced by the other. The dialogue shown contains several examples of non-standard spelling. The non-standard form *lookin* drops the letter *g* from the end of the morpheme *ing*, a technique commonly used in informal writing. Two other non-standard spellings, *hiii* and *goooooood* exemplify the use of letter repetition. This dialogue also includes the common texting slang term *lol*.

Since we are interested in studying the presence of extra information in non-standard word forms, we must first identify word forms that contain non-standard spelling. To create a set of non-standard word forms, we used the CMU pronouncing dictionary[2] as a vocabulary set and selected all tokens that were out of our vocabulary. Those tokens that were simply legitimate words in the lexicon, such as proper names or obscure terms not in our dictionary, were manually removed. This left us with a data set of 764 non-standard word tokens.

[1] www.damnyouautocorrect.com

[2] http://www.speech.cs.cmu.edu/cgi-bin/cmudict

3.2 Survey

To assess which word forms displayed extra pragmatic information, we created a short survey that asked users of Amazon Mechanical Turk[3] to determine whether this form contained information not present in the standard form. Survey participants were given the word in context and asked to answer the following four questions:

1. "What is the standard form of this word?"
2. "What type of emotion, if any, is provided by the spelling used that is not provided by the standard form?" (Choose from the following: none, fear, suprise, happiness, disgust, sadness, anger, other)
3. "What other information, if any, is provided by the spelling used that is not provided by the standard form?" (Choose from the following: friendliness/closeness, emphasis, other, none)
4. "Why do you think the writer chose to use the modified spelling instead of the standard form?" (Choose from the following: wanted to display extra information, wanted to save time or space, made an unintentional mistake, other)

Three separate annotators were asked to examine each word form. The observed agreement between any two annotators was around 80% for a given question. For our analysis, we consider a case in which 2 or more annotators agreed as the gold standard. Cases in which no annotators agreed were thrown out, judged separately for each question[4].

3.3 Analysis Results

Figure 2 shows the results of question 2. The emotions used include the six basic emotions (Ekman, 1993) often used in affective text literature. If several emotions were displayed, annotators were asked to pick the emotion that was displayed most strongly. As shown, 5 of the 6 emotions were present in our corpus, with only fear being absent. Although many forms did not contain extra emotion, a full 40% of them did. When additional emotional information was present, it was

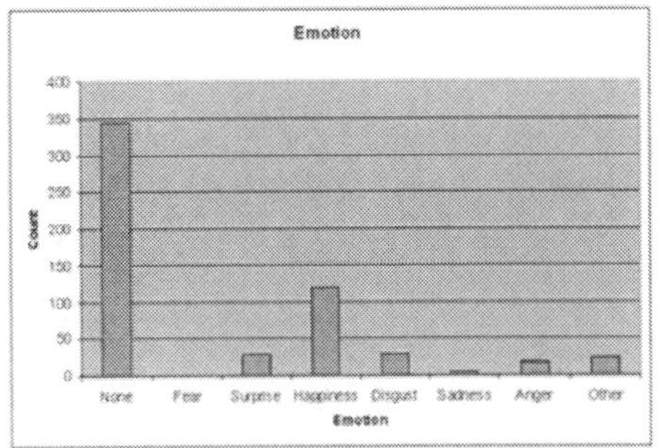

Figure 2: Distribution of forms containing emotion not present in normalized form

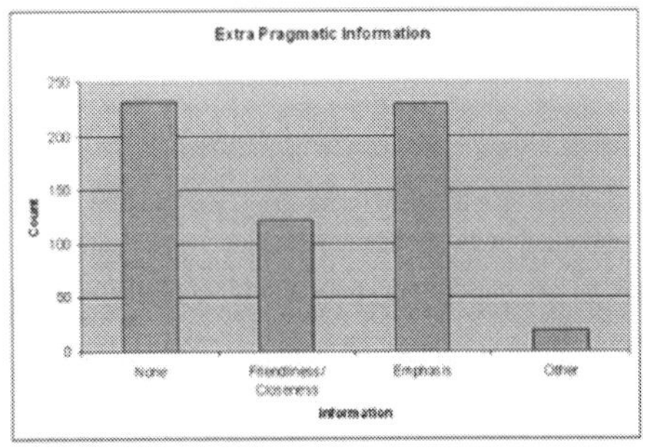

Figure 3: Distribution of forms containing additional information not present in normalized form

most commonly positive; happiness was by far the most common emotion displayed.

Figure 3 shows the results of question 3. Although it was again common for no extra information to be present, cases in which non-standard forms were used to emphasize a word were nearly as common, appearing in 38% of our instances. The use of non-standard forms to express emphasis appears to be widespread in text messaging data. This is an important finding, especially relevant to text-to-speech research. Additionally, Figure 3 suggests that another common usage of non-standard forms, found in 20% of our data, is to display a sense of kinship with the reader through subtle expressions of friendliness or closeness.

Results for question 4 are shown in Figure 4. Wanting to display extra information was perceived as a primary reason why text message authors chose a non-standard spelling. This seems to suggest that, in choosing non-standard word forms, expressiveness is a primary concern for text message writers.

Overall, the results in the figures suggest that the need for greater expressiveness is a paramount reason why text message writers choose non-

[3] mturk.amazon.com

[4] This accounts for the difference in total instances between Figures 2, 3, and 4

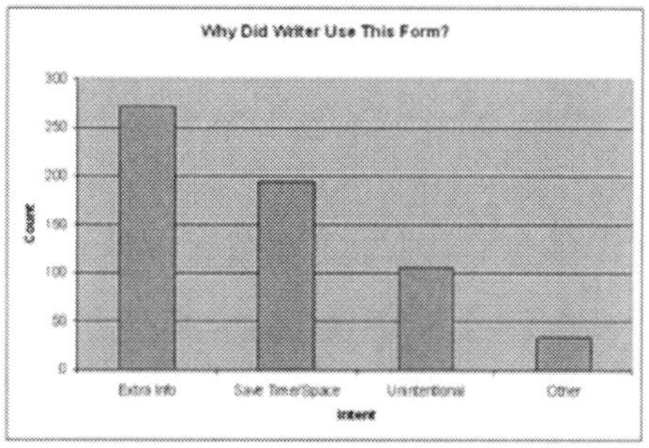

Figure 4: Perceived intent of text message author

standard spellings. It is thus relevant for text message normalization systems to consider the intent of the writer in producing a non-standard form, to ensure that the intended meaning is not lost. This leads to the question of whether an automated system can accurately recognize words that carry extra pragmatic information. In the next section, we take an initial look at this problem.

4 Automatic Identification of Words with Extra Information

We model the task of identifying whether a non-standard word form is intended to display extra information as a binary classification task. All instances that were marked by annotators as having some form of emotion or extra information were considered to be positive instances.

We drew features from three sources for our classification: character level features, punctuation features, and positional features. Because we are focused on classifying the emotional or pragmatic content of the word and not the utterance, we restrict our feature set to only features that pertain the to the word itself.

Character level features. Our feature set focused primarily on character level features. Several features focused on identifying the type of abbreviation used. Features indicating whether the word contained the same letter repeated more than twice, the maximum number of times a letter was repeated in the word, and whether deletion of repeated characters produced an in-vocabulary word were used to detect cases of word elongation. Edit distance from the closest word using only insertions was used as an indicator of word shortening and truncation. One additional feature recorded whether the non-standard form was longer than the normalized form. Features were also included to detect whether the non-standard form contained concatenated words or contained numbers or non-alphanumeric characters. Whether or not a word was written in all capital letters was also observed.

Punctuation features. Punctuation features capture some information beyond that of the word form. The punctuation features detected whether the word was followed by a comma, period, question mark, exclamation point, or emoticon.

Positional features. Positional features were the most discourse dependent features examined. These features indicated whether the word was the first, last, or only word in the current message.

Classification was performed using an SVM classifier. Ten-fold cross validation was performed. The results are shown in Table 1. A majority class baseline suggests that classification is not trivial; although many instances carry extra information, many do not. As shown, the use of character level feature alone achieves above baseline performance of 72.4% ($p < 0.01$). Adding additional features on top of this does not result in an increase in performance.

	Accuracy
Baseline	59.5%
Character Level Features Only	72.4%
Character Level + Punctuation	72.3%
All Features	72.4%

Table 1: Classification of word forms by the presence of added information

5 Conclusion

The analysis presented in this paper shows that non-standard word forms contain additional pragmatic information not present in the standard form. Some of the main functions of this extra information include the expression of emphasis, happiness, and friendliness. It is important that text message normalization systems recognize and address this fact, as it is relevant for downstream applications such as text-to-speech synthesis.

Additionally, this work introduced the problem of identifying whether a non-standard text messaging form was intended to display pragmatic information beyond that of the base form. Our initial investigation showed that above baseline performance could be achieved, but that the problem was non-trivial and required further study. Future work is needed to more robustly address this problem, as well as more closely examine the relationship between non-standard spellings and individual types of emotional and other pragmatic information.

References

Apoorv Agarwal, Fadi Biadsy, and Kathleen Mckeown. 2009. Contextual phrase-level polarity analysis using lexical affect scoring and syntactic N-grams. In *Proceedings of the 12th Conference of the European Chapter of the ACL (EACL 2009)*, pages 24–32, Athens, Greece, March. Association for Computational Linguistics.

Cecilia Ovesdotter Alm, Dan Roth, and Richard Sproat. 2005. Emotions from text: machine learning for text-based emotion prediction. In *Proceedings of the conference on Human Language Technology and Empirical Methods in Natural Language Processing*, HLT '05, pages 579–586, Stroudsburg, PA, USA. Association for Computational Linguistics.

AiTi Aw, Min Zhang, Juan Xiao, and Jian Su. 2006. A phrase-based statistical model for sms text normalization. In *Proceedings of the COLING/ACL on Main conference poster sessions*, pages 33–40, Morristown, NJ, USA. Association for Computational Linguistics.

Richard Beaufort, Sophie Roekhaut, Louise-Amélie Cougnon, and Cédrick Fairon. 2010. A hybrid rule/model-based finite-state framework for normalizing sms messages. In *Proceedings of the 48th Annual Meeting of the Association for Computational Linguistics*, pages 770–779, Uppsala, Sweden, July. Association for Computational Linguistics.

H. Binali, Chen Wu, and V. Potdar. 2010. Computational approaches for emotion detection in text. In *Digital Ecosystems and Technologies (DEST), 2010 4th IEEE International Conference on*, pages 172 – 177.

D.B. Bracewell. 2008. Semi-automatic creation of an emotion dictionary using wordnet and its evaluation. In *Cybernetics and Intelligent Systems, 2008 IEEE Conference on*, pages 1385 –1389.

Monojit Choudhury, Rahul Saraf, Vijit Jain, Animesh Mukherjee, Sudeshna Sarkar, and Anupam Basu. 2007. Investigation and modeling of the structure of texting language. *Int. J. Doc. Anal. Recognit.*, 10(3):157–174.

Paul Cook and Suzanne Stevenson. 2009. An unsupervised model for text message normalization. In *Proceedings of the Workshop on Computational Approaches to Linguistic Creativity*, pages 71–78, Boulder, Colorado, June. Association for Computational Linguistics.

Paul Ekman. 1993. Facial expression and emotion. *American Psychologist*, 48:384–392.

E.C.-C. Kao, Chun-Chieh Liu, Ting-Hao Yang, Chang-Tai Hsieh, and Von-Wun Soo. 2009. Towards text-based emotion detection a survey and possible improvements. In *Information Management and Engineering, 2009. ICIME '09. International Conference on*, pages 70 –74.

Catherine Kobus, François Yvon, and Géraldine Damnati. 2008. Normalizing SMS: are two metaphors better than one ? In *Proceedings of the 22nd International Conference on Computational Linguistics (Coling 2008)*, pages 441–448, Manchester, UK, August. Coling 2008 Organizing Committee.

D.L. Pennell and Yang Liu. 2010. Normalization of text messages for text-to-speech. In *Acoustics Speech and Signal Processing (ICASSP), 2010 IEEE International Conference on*, pages 4842 –4845.

Changqin Quan and Fuji Ren. 2010. An exploration of features for recognizing word emotion. In *Proceedings of the 23rd International Conference on Computational Linguistics (Coling 2010)*, pages 922–930, Beijing, China, August. Coling 2010 Organizing Committee.

Richard Sproat, Alan W. Black, Stanley F. Chen, Shankar Kumar, Mari Ostendorf, and Christopher Richards. 2001. Normalization of non-standard words. *Computer Speech and Language*, pages 287–333.

Chung-Hsien Wu, Ze-Jing Chuang, and Yu-Chung Lin. 2006. Emotion recognition from text using semantic labels and separable mixture models. 5:165–183, June.

Changhua Yang, Kevin Hsin-Yih Lin, and Hsin-Hsi Chen. 2007. Emotion classification using web blog corpora. In *Proceedings of the IEEE/WIC/ACM International Conference on Web Intelligence*, WI '07, pages 275–278, Washington, DC, USA. IEEE Computer Society.

Li Zhang, John A. Barnden, Robert J. Hendley, and Alan M. Wallington. 2006. Developments in affect detection in e-drama. In *Proceedings of the Eleventh Conference of the European Chapter of the Association for Computational Linguistics: Posters & Demonstrations*, EACL '06, pages 203–206, Stroudsburg, PA, USA. Association for Computational Linguistics.

Conghui Zhu, Jie Tang, Hang Li, Hwee Tou Ng, and Tiejun Zhao. 2007. A unified tagging approach to text normalization. In *Proceedings of the 45th Annual Meeting of the Association of Computational Linguistics*, pages 688–695, Prague, Czech Republic, June. Association for Computational Linguistics.

Chinese Discourse Relation Recognition

Hen-Hsen Huang
Department of Computer Science and Information Engineering,
National Taiwan University,
Taipei, Taiwan
hhhuang@nlg.csie.ntu.edu.tw

Hsin-Hsi Chen
Department of Computer Science and Information Engineering,
National Taiwan University,
Taipei, Taiwan
hhchen@csie.ntu.edu.tw

Abstract

The challenging issues of discourse relation recognition in Chinese are addressed. Due to the lack of Chinese discourse corpora, we construct a moderate corpus with human-annotated discourse relations. Based on the corpus, a statistical classifier is proposed, and various features are explored in the experiments. The experimental results show that our method achieves an accuracy of 88.28% and an F-Score of 63.69% in four-class classification and achieves an F-Score of 93.57% in the best case.

1 Introduction

A discourse relation is the way that two successive arguments logically connected. Recognizing discourse relations attracts much attetions in recent years due to many potential applications. In the annotation scheme of Penn Discourse Treebank 2.0 (PDTB-2.0), the first level of discourse relations includes four classes such as *Temporal*, *Contingency*, *Comparison*, and *Expansion* (Prasad et al., 2008).

The first challenge of discourse relation recognition is the lack of corpus. To construct a discourse corpus has several difficulties. First, the definition of discourse is unclear and varied over different areas. Thus, finding the clear boundary of a discourse argument is a vexing problem by itself. Second, the relationship between arguments is often difficult to decide and inherently subjective. Thus, the annotation and the evaluation are problematic and labor-intensive.

In recent years, the study of discourse relation recognition is growing in the English domain rapidly. One of the reasons is the availability of English corpora with discourse annotations. The two most popular discourse corpora are the Rhetorical Structure Theory Discourse Treebank (RSTDT) (Carlson et al., 2001) and PDTB-2.0. Both of them are based on the Wall Street Journal corpus with human-annotated discourse information. The PDTB-2.0 consists of 36,592 pairs of successive arguments and is tagged with three classes, including *Implicit*, *Explicit*, and *AltLex*, and with the relation types at three levels. Based on these corpora, a number of aspects on discourse relation are explored in these years.

Compared to the English corpora, there is still no Chinese discourse corpus worldwide available. For this reason, the dataset is the first challenge encountered in the study of Chinese discourse relation recognition. To address this issue in this work, we construct a moderate Chinese discourse corpus as a starting point. A supervised statistical classifier is trained and tested on this data set to deal with the problem. Various features are extracted from the corpus and evaluated in the experiments.

The rest of this paper is organized as follows. First, we review the related work in Section 2. In Section 3, the Chinese discourse relation problem is illustrated. Our corpus and the details on the annotation work are presented in Section 4. In Section 5, the method and the features are introduced. The experimental results are discussed in Section 6, and we conclude this paper in Section 7.

2 Related Work

Pitler and Nenkova (2009) reported an explicit discourse relation recognizer that achieves an accuracy of 94.15%. On the other hand, the implicit discourse relation recognition is much more challenging than the explicit one. The implicit discourse relation recognition is to predict the relation of two successive arguments without connectives. In the work of Marcu and Echihabi (2002), the dataset for implicit discourse relation detection is automatically derived from explicit samples by removing the connectives. Though this approach is efficient to obtain a large corpus, the pseudo implicit corpus does not exactly capture the property in the real world.

Based on PDTB, in which the argument pairs are distinguished between implicit and explicit, Pitler et al. (2009) and Lin et al. (2009) addressed the task of real implicit discourse relation recognition. In the work of Pitler et al., the implicit discourse relation detection achieves an average accuracy of 62.78% for four-class classification. In the work of Lin et al., the implicit discourse relations are classified into 11 types (selected from the second level tagging in PDTB), and their classifier achieves an accuracy of 40.2%.

From the other aspect, the semi-supervised approach is explored to deal with some relations that are rare in the corpus (Hernault et al., 2010).

3 The Discourse Relation in Chinese

In this work, we adopt the top level classes of PDTB to deal with the Chinese materials.

When two arguments are temporally related, they form a *Temporal* relation. There are two subtypes of Temporal relation, ordered in time (*Asynchronous,* as defined in PDTB-2.0 annotation manual[1]) and overlapped (*Synchronous*). For example, the events in the two arguments in (S1) occur sequentially in time. The event in the second argument happened after the event in the first argument.

(S1) 他首先證實傅爾和中谷義雄的理論。'He first confirmed the theory of Voll and Yoshio Nakatani.'

其次，他發現經絡不僅是電流的良導體，也是電磁波的良導體。'Second, he found that the meridian is not only a good conductor of current, but also a good conductor of electromagnetic waves.'

The *Contingency* relation talks about the situation that the event in one of the arguments casually affects the event in the other argument. In Chinese, the typical compound connective of Contingency is '因為…，所以…' ('Because…, …'). In sample (S2), the event '颱風來襲' is the cause, and the event '學生停課在家' is its result. Such a relation is defined in PDTB-2.0 as *Cause*, a subtype of Contingency. In sample (S3), the connective '因為…，所以…' is removed. Obviously, the relation between the two clauses is still Contingency. This situation is similar to the case of implicit relation in English.

(S2) 因為颱風來襲，所以學校停止上課。'Because of the typhoon struck, the school has broken up.'

(S3) 颱風來襲，學校停止上課。'The typhoon struck; the school has broken up.'

Condition is another typical subtype of Contingency. Condition relation between two arguments specifies the situation in which the event in one argument is conditioned on the event in the other argument.

Comparison is used to show the difference between two arguments. A subtype of Comparison is *Contrast,* where the two arguments share a common predicate or property, and their difference is highlighted.

Expansion, the most common relation, either expands the information for one argument in the other one or continues the narrative flow. In sample (S4), the second argument expands the information to the first argument.

(S4) 伏爾泰是啟蒙運動的領導者，一位偉大的思想家。'Voltaire is the leader of the Enlightenment, a great thinker.'

除此之外，他也是著作等身的作家。'In addition, he is also a prolific writer.'

Some words that are usually used as marks to indicate the discourse relations are given in Table 1 for reference.

Relations	Sample Marks
Temporal	同時 (at the same time) 之前 (before)
Contingency	因為 (because) 所以 (therefore) 如果 (if)
Comparison	然而 (however) 雖然 (although) 相反的 (in contrast)
Expansion	而且 (furthermore) 也 (also) 或者 (or) 例如 (for example) 除了 (in addition)

Table 1. Chinese Discourse Relations

[1] http://www.seas.upenn.edu/~pdtb/PDTBAPI/pdtb-annotation-manual.pdf

4 Dataset

To deal with the problem of Chinese discourse relation recognition, we firstly construct a corpus for training and testing. The corpus is based on Sinica Treebank 3.1. Total 81 articles are randomly selected from the Sino and Travel sets.

The first issue we encountered is how to segment an article into arguments. In other words, the issue concerns the determination of the argument boundaries. In PDTB, both the boundaries of arguments and the type of discourse relations are annotated by human. In this data set, an argument is not always a sentence. That is, it may be a clause. Sometimes it may be composed of a number of sentences. However, to annotate in such a way is costly and time-consuming. For convenience, we regard an argument as a sentence in this work. A sentence is defined to be a sequence of words ended by a full-stop, a question mark, or an exclamation mark.

In this way, each article is segmented into sentences and shown to three annotators. An annotator assigns one of four discourse relations to each pair of successive sentences. Under this scheme, the annotators regard a sentence as a discourse unit and determine how successive sentences relate to each other. Finally, the majority among the three labels are taken. In the case of ties, an additional annotator will be involved in the final labeling.

The shortage of this annotation scheme is that the samples of Contingency are very rare. In Chinese, the Contingency relation usually occurs inside a sentence. In sample (S3), the two arguments of Contingency, i.e., "因為颱風來襲" and "所以學校停止上課", are two clauses within a single sentence. For this reason, only 94 inter-sentence Contingency relations are tagged in our corpus.

The statistics of the corpus are shown in Table 2. Due to the genre of the Sino and the Travel is descriptive writings, the major relation among the corpus is Expansion.

5 Method

The multi-class support vector machine (SVM) is utilized as our classifier[2]. Due to the unbalance distribution among the four relations, we duplicate the samples of Temporal, Contingency, and Comparison in the training sets proportionally to derive balanced training data.

[2] http://svmlight.joachims.org/svm_multiclass.html

5.1 Features

Length (*Len*): This feature includes the word counts of the first argument, the second argument, the first clause in the first argument, the last clause in the first argument, the first clause in the second argument, and the last clause in the second argument.

***Punctuation* (*Pun*):** The punctuations which end the first and the second arguments are regarded as features. The possible punctuation is a full-stop, a question mark, or an exclamation mark.

***Connective* (*Connect*):** Similar to the connectives in English, some words are usually used as discourse relation marks in Chinese. We prepare a dictionary that contains 319 single words and 489 word pairs. The number of matching words (word-pairs) and their corresponding relation types are considered as features.

***Shared Word* (*SW*):** The number of words shared in the first and the second arguments is considered as a feature. Besides, the common hypernyms shared in both arguments are also counted.

***Word*:** The bags of words in the first argument, in the second argument, and in the first clause of the second argument are considered.

***Part-of-Speech* (*POS*):** The bags of POS in the first argument, in the second argument, and in the first clause of the second argument.

***Hypernym* (*Hyper*):** The bags of hypernym words in the first argument, in the second argument, and in the first clause of the second argument are considered.

***Collocated Word* (*CW*):** Collocated words are the frequent word pairs mined from the training set. The first word and the second word in the pair come from the first argument and the second argument, respectively.

***Number*:** The binary features capture if the dates, the times, the periods, and the numbers exist in the arguments.

6 Experiments

The experimental results for the four relation types are shown in Tables 3, 4, 5, and 6, respectively and the overall performance is given in Table 7. All the performances are evaluated by 5-fold cross-validation.

In general, no single feature is efficient for all the types. For Temporal relation, the feature *Number* contributes the highest recall to capture most candidates. The precision of using single feature only is no more than 25%.

Source	#Articles	#Sentence Pairs	Temporal (#, %)	Contingency (#, %)	Comparison (#, %)	Expansion (#, %)
Sino	27	1594	(104, 6.52)	(51, 3.20)	(156, 9.79)	(1283, 80.49)
Travel	54	1487	(63, 4.24)	(43, 2.89)	(51, 3.43)	(1330, 89.44)
Total	81	3081	(167, 5.42)	(94, 3.05)	(207, 6.72)	(2613, 84.81)

Table 2. Dataset Statistics

Comparatively, the model using all the features achieves a precision of 60.22%. In other words, these features are complementary for recognizing the Temporal relation. The performance is relatively poor for Contingency relation identification. As discussed in Section 4, our annotation does not capture the intra-sentence Contingency relation, thus the most representative examples of Contingency are lost.

The feature *Connect* achieves the highest recall of 70.53% for Comparison relation labeling. The feature *Word*, which achieves a recall of 70.05%, has the similar identification capability. With all the features, an F-Score of 61.24% is achieved.

Expansion is the largest class among the four types. The performance of this type is much better than that of the other three types. Our classifier achieves an F-Score of 93.57% for Expansion.

The performance in macro average is shown in Table 7. Overall, our classifier trained with all features achieves an F-Score of 63.69% and an accuracy of 88.28%.

7 Conclusion

In this work, we address the issue of discourse relation recognition in Chinese. A moderate corpus sampled from Sinica Treebank 3.1 is labeled with discourse relations. The top-level classes used in PDTB are adopted in the data annotation. The SVM classifier trained with various features recognizes the relations between successive arguments automatically. As a result, our classifier achieves an accuracy of 88.28% and an F-Score of 63.69%. In the best case, our classifier achieves an F-Score of 93.57% for the recognition of Expansion relation.

Features	Precision	Recall	F-Score
Len	7.36%	45.51%	12.68%
Pun	5.67%	10.18%	7.28%
Connect	10.07%	41.92%	16.24%
SW	7.54%	23.35%	11.40%
Word	25.23%	64.67%	36.30%
POS	12.76%	65.27%	21.35%
Hyper	13.48%	67.66%	22.49%
CW	25.18%	62.87%	35.96%
Number	7.73%	**73.65%**	13.99%
All	60.22%	67.07%	63.46%

Table 3. Performance of Temporal

The poor performance of the Contingency relation recognition is due to the lack of representative training samples. That needs further investigation.

Features	Precision	Recall	F-Score
Len	3.71%	17.02%	6.10%
Pun	3.07%	20.21%	5.34%
Connect	5.14%	64.89%	9.52%
SW	2.97%	26.60%	5.35%
Word	13.12%	22.34%	16.54%
POS	5.55%	34.04%	9.54%
Hyper	11.81%	37.20%	17.93%
CW	26.09%	44.68%	32.94%
Number	3.28%	15.96%	5.44%
All	50.00%	28.72%	36.49%

Table 4. Performance of Contingency

Features	Precision	Recall	F-score
Len	8.33%	21.74%	12.05%
Pun	6.22%	28.02%	10.18%
Connect	24.79%	**70.53%**	36.68%
SW	7.48%	18.36%	10.63%
Word	34.77%	**70.05%**	46.47%
POS	14.84%	47.83%	22.65%
Hyper	11.81%	37.20%	17.93%
CW	24.29%	62.32%	34.96%
Number	10.83%	24.64%	15.04%
All	60.66%	61.84%	61.24%

Table 5. Performance of Comparison

Features	Precision	Recall	F-score
Len	85.90%	35.44%	50.18%
Pun	84.32%	39.72%	54.01%
Connect	91.48%	21.35%	34.63%
SW	85.84%	39.92%	54.49%
Word	93.35%	**74.17%**	82.66%
POS	94.00%	35.36%	51.39%
Hyper	92.96%	30.81%	46.28%
CW	96.10%	72.52%	82.66%
Number	90.75%	19.52%	32.13%
All	93.27%	93.88%	93.57%

Table 6. Performance of Expansion

Features	Precison	Recall	F-Score	Accuracy
Len	26.33%	29.93%	20.25%	34.50%
Pun	24.82%	24.53%	19.20%	36.74%
Connect	32.87%	49.67%	24.27%	27.10%
SW	25.96%	27.06%	20.47%	37.16%
Word	41.62%	57.81%	45.49%	71.79%
POS	31.79%	45.62%	26.23%	37.78%
Hyper	30.84%	43.76%	23.93%	33.50%
CW	42.91%	60.60%	46.63%	70.46%
Number	28.15%	33.44%	16.65%	22.69%
All	66.04%	62.88%	63.69%	88.28%

Table 7. Overall Performance

References

L. Carlson, D. Marcu, and M. E. Okurowski. 2001. Building a Discourse-Tagged Corpus in the Framework of Rhetorical Structure Theory. In *Proceedings of Second SIGDIAL Workshop on Discourse and Dialogue-Volume 16,* pages 1-10.

Hugo Hernault, Danushka Bollegala, and Mitsuru Ishizuka. 2010. A Semi-Supervised Approach to Improve Classification of Infrequent Discourse Relations using Feature Vector Extension. In *Proceedings of the 2010 Conference on Empirical Methods in Natural Language Processing,* pages 399-409.

Ziheng Lin, Min-Yen Kan, and Hwee Tou Ng. 2009. Recognizing Implicit Discourse Relations in the Penn Discourse Treebank. In *Proceedings of the 2009 Conference on Empirical Methods in Natural Language Processing,* pages 343-351.

D. Marcu and A. Echihabi. 2002. An unsupervised Approach to Recognizing Discourse Relations. In *Proceedings of the 40th Annual Meeting on Association for Computational Linguistics (ACL 2002)*, pages 368–375, Morristown, NJ, USA.

Emily Pitler, Annie Louis, and Ani Nenkova. 2009. Automatic Sense Prediction for Implicit Discourse Relations in Text. In *Proceedings of the 47th annual Meeting of the ACL and the 4th IJCNLP of the AFNLP,* pages 683-691.

Emily Pitler and Ani Nenkova. 2009. Using Syntax to Disambiguate Explicit Discourse Connectives in Text. In *Proceedings of the 47th annual Meeting of the ACL and the 4th IJCNLP of the AFNLP*. Short Papers.

R. Prasad, N. Dinesh, A. Lee, E. Miltsakaki, L. Robaldo, A. Joshi, and B. Webber. 2008. The Penn Discourse TreeBank 2.0. In *Proceedings of LREC'08.*

Improving Chinese POS Tagging with Dependency Parsing

Zhenghua Li, Wanxiang Che, Ting Liu*
Research Center for Social Computing and Information Retrieval
MOE-Microsoft Key Laboratory of Natural Language Processing and Speech
School of Computer Science and Technology
Harbin Institute of Technology, China
{lzh,car,tliu}@ir.hit.edu.cn

Abstract

Recent research usually models POS tagging as a sequential labeling problem, in which only local context features can be used. Due to the lack of morphological inflections, many tagging ambiguities in Chinese are difficult to handle unless consulting larger contexts. In this paper, we try to improve Chinese POS tagging by using long-distance dependencies produced by a statistical dependency parser. Experimental results show that, despite error propagation, the syntactic features can significantly improve the tagging accuracy from 93.88% to 94.41% ($p < 10^{-5}$). Detailed analysis shows that these features are helpful for ambiguous pairs like {NN,VV} and {DEC,DEG}.[1]

1 Introduction

Part-of-speech (POS) tagging is a necessary and important step for many natural language tasks, for example, named entity recognition, parsing and sentence boundary detection. In the current literature, POS tagging is treated as a typical sequence labeling problem, to which many models have been successfully applied, such as maximum-entropy (Ratnaparkhi, 1996), conditional random fields (CRF) (Lafferty et al., 2001) and perceptron (Collins, 2002). To facilitate fast decoding, these models make the Markovian independence assumption that the current tag depends on one or two previous tags. In addition, they can merely consider local context features, e.g. two words in both sides of the focus word. This works quite well for English, because inflections are useful and strong clues for POS tags. However, due to the lack of morphological inflections, Chinese POS tagging has proven to be much more challenging than English. With a typical sequential labeling model such as Conditional Random Fields (CRF), the tagging accuracy is about 97% for English, while less than 94% for Chinese (Huang et al., 2009).

NN-VV ambiguities are one of the most notorious difficulties for Chinese POS tagging. Figure 1 gives two examples. We can see that the POS tagger can effortlessly assign the right tags to both "development" and "develop" in the English side. However, it is very difficult in the Chinese side since no word form inflection is available and the context features may be too sparse or uninformative. However, the introduction of long-distance dependencies can largely reduce this difficulty. In the upper example of Figure 1, the coordinate relation between "贸易/NN" and "发展" is a strong clue to "发展/NN". In the lower example of Figure 1, it is also easy to tag "发展" as "VV" if its coordination with "维护/VV" is known.

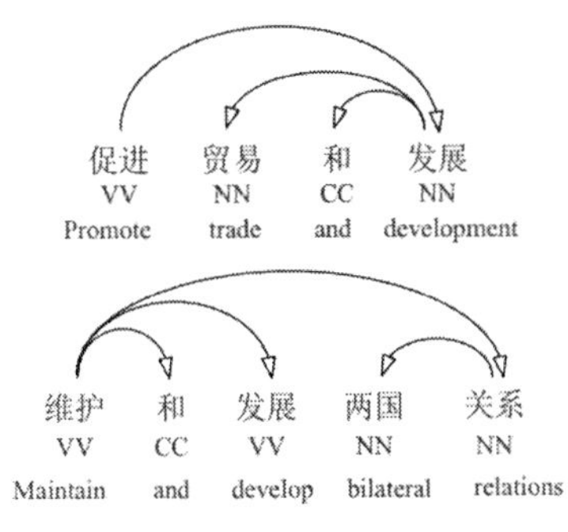

Figure 1: Examples of NN-VV ambiguities with dependency structures. The focus word is "发展".

As far as we know, there has been few research that tries to improve POS tagging with dependency

*Correspondence author: tliu@ir.hit.edu.cn

[1]DEG and DEC are the two POS tags for the frequently used auxiliary word "的" (dē, of) in Chinese. The associative "的" is tagged as DEG, such as "父亲/father 的 眼睛/eyes (eyes of the father)"; while the one in a relative clause is tagged as DEC, such as "他/he 取得/made 的 进步/progress (progress that he made)".

parsing . The reason for this may be three-fold. Firstly, POS tags are indispensable features for dependency parsing since pure lexical features lead to severe sparseness problem. Therefore, POS tagging is traditionally considered as a supporting task for dependency parsing. Secondly, Chinese dependency parsing performs not well. The accuracy is about 85% when gold-standard POS tags are given, and quickly drops to about 79% when using automatically assigned POS tags. Therefore, error propagation may be an obstacle to research on this idea. Thirdly, inefficiency of syntactic parsing may be another concern. However, we believe that this problem can be relieved in the case of dependency parsing, since efficient cubic-time or even linear-time parsing models have been proposed for dependency parsing (McDonald, 2006; Nivre and Hall, 2005).

In this paper, we propose several kinds of syntactic features based on the output of a statistical dependency parser. And we use these features to enhance a traditional POS tagging model so that long-distance information can be explored. Experimental results show that this effort is rewarding, and the tagging accuracy is significantly improved. Detailed error analysis confirms the usefulness of these syntactic features.

2 Baseline POS Taggers

Given an input sentence $\mathbf{x} = w_1...w_n$, we denote its *POS tag sequence* by $\mathbf{t} = t_1...t_n$, where $t_i \in \mathcal{T}$, $1 \leq i \leq n$, and $\mathcal{T}$ is the POS tag set. The goal of POS tagging is to find the highest-scoring sequence:

$$\hat{\mathbf{t}} = \arg\max_{\mathbf{t}} \mu(\mathbf{x}, \mathbf{t})$$

We implement two baseline taggers, i.e., a Perceptron-based tagger and a CRF-based tagger. As a linear model, Perceptron defines the score of a tag sequence to be

$$\mu(\mathbf{x}, \mathbf{t}) = \mathbf{w} \cdot \mathbf{f}(\mathbf{x}, \mathbf{t})$$

where $\mathbf{f}(\mathbf{x}, \mathbf{t})$ refers to the feature vector and $\mathbf{w}$ is the corresponding weight vector. We use standard *averaged perceptron* to learn the weight vector (Collins, 2002).

As a probabilistic model, CRF defines the probability of a sequence to be

$$\mu(\mathbf{x}, \mathbf{t}) = P(\mathbf{t}|\mathbf{x}) = \frac{e^{\mathbf{w} \cdot \mathbf{f}(\mathbf{x}, \mathbf{t})}}{\sum_{\mathbf{t}'} e^{\mathbf{w} \cdot \mathbf{f}(\mathbf{x}, \mathbf{t}')}}$$

We adopt the *exponentiated gradient* algorithm to learn the weight vector (Collins et al., 2008).

For POS tagging features $\mathbf{f}(\mathbf{x}, \mathbf{t})$, we follow the work of Zhang and Clark (2008a). Besides standard *POS unigram* ($\underline{w_i\ t_i}$), *bigram* ($\underline{t_{i-1}\ t_i}$) and *trigram* ($\underline{t_{i-2}\ t_{i-1}\ t_i}$) features, they explore many features composed of Chinese characters, such as $\underline{c_{i,0}\ t_i}$ and $\underline{c_{i,-1}\ t_i}$, where $c_{i,0}$ and $c_{i,-1}$ denote the start and end characters of w_i. These character-based features are very helpful for tagging accuracy. Due to space limitation, we refer to Zhang and Clark (2008a) for the complete feature description. In order to distinguish these features from our proposed syntactic features, we refer to them as the *basic features* and denote them as $\mathbf{f}_b(\mathbf{x}, \mathbf{t})$. Given $\mathbf{w}$, we adopt the Viterbi algorithm to get the optimal tagging sequence.

3 POS Tagging with Syntactic Features

The framework of our method is shown in Figure 2. Given an input sentence $\mathbf{x}$, we first use the CRF-based model to produce a tagging sequence $\mathbf{t}^C$. Then, based on $\mathbf{t}^C$, we use a statistical dependency parser to obtain the syntactic tree $\mathbf{d}^A$. Finally, both $\mathbf{t}^C$ and $\mathbf{d}^A$ are used as additional features in the enhanced Perceptron-based model. We use Perceptron to build our model because it is competitive to CRF in tagging accuracy but requires much less training time. During training phase, we adopt the 10-fold cross validation strategy to produce both $\mathbf{t}^C$ and $\mathbf{d}^A$ for the training set.

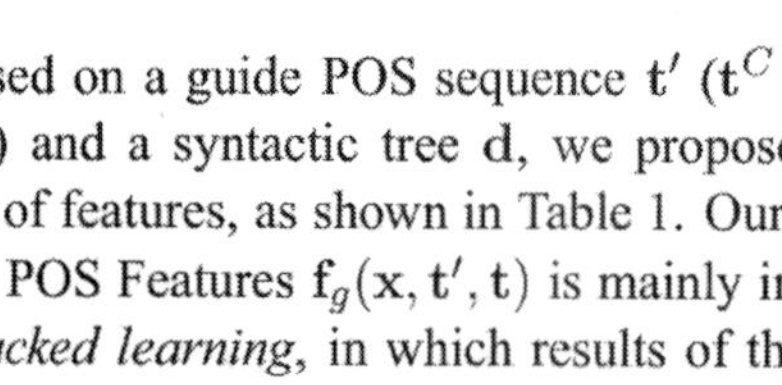

Figure 2: Framework of our method.

Based on a guide POS sequence $\mathbf{t}'$ ($\mathbf{t}^C$ in this paper) and a syntactic tree $\mathbf{d}$, we propose three kinds of features, as shown in Table 1. Our use of guide POS Features $\mathbf{f}_g(\mathbf{x}, \mathbf{t}', \mathbf{t})$ is mainly inspired by *stacked learning*, in which results of the first-level predicator are used to guide the second (Cohen and de Carvalho, 2005; Nivre and McDonald, 2008; Martins et al., 2008).

Syntactic features $\mathbf{f}_s(\mathbf{x}, \mathbf{d}, \mathbf{t})$ explore features related with the head and children of the focus word. Syntactic features with guide POS tags

Guide POS Features: $\mathbf{f}_g(\mathbf{x}, \mathbf{t}', \mathbf{t})$		Syntactic Features: $\mathbf{f}_s(\mathbf{x}, \mathbf{d}, \mathbf{t})$		Syntactic Features with Guide POS: $\mathbf{f}_{sg}(\mathbf{x}, \mathbf{t}', \mathbf{d}, \mathbf{t})$			
$t'_i\ t_i$	$t'_{i-1}\ t'_i\ t_i$	$\#lc(i)\ t_i$	$w_{h(i)}\ t_i$	$\#lc(i)\ t'_i\ t_i$	$\#rc(i)\ t'_i\ t_i$	$t'_{h(i)}\ t_i$	$t'_i\ d(i)\ t_i$
$t'_{i-1}\ t_i$	$t'_i\ t'_{i+1}\ t_i$	$w_{lc(i,k)}\ t_i$	$d(i)\ t_i$	$t'_{lc(i,k)}\ t'_i\ t_i$	$t'_{rc(i,k)}\ t'_i\ t_i$	$t'_{h(i)}\ t'_i\ t_i$	$t'_{h(i)}\ d(i)\ t_i$
$t'_{i+1}\ t_i$	$t'_{i-1}\ t'_{i+1}\ t_i$	$\#rc(i)\ t_i$	$w_{h(i)}\ d(i)\ t_i$	$t'_{lc(i,k)}\ t_i$	$t'_{rc(i,k)}\ t_i$	$t'_{h(i)}\ w_i\ t_i$	$t'_{h(i)}\ t'_i\ d(i)\ t_i$
$t'_i \sim \mathbf{f}_b(\mathbf{x})$	$t'_{i-1}\ t'_i\ t'_{i+1}\ t_i$	$w_{rc(i,k)}\ t_i$	$w_i\ d(i)\ t_i$				$t'_{h(i)}\ w_i\ d(i)\ t_i$

Table 1: Feature templates for our enhanced Perceptron-based tagger. $\mathbf{t}'$ denotes a guide POS sequence, which is $\mathbf{t}^C$ in this paper. $t'_i \sim \mathbf{f}_b(\mathbf{x})$ means that we concatenate t'_i and each feature in $\mathbf{f}_b(\mathbf{x}, \mathbf{t})$ to obtain a new one. $h(i)$ denotes the index of the head of i in the syntactic tree $\mathbf{d}$; while $d(i)$ means the distance and direction of the dependency $h(i) \rightarrow i$. $\#lc(i)$ means the number of left-side children of i, and $lc(i, k)$ is the index of the kth left child of i. Analogously, $\#rc(i)$ and $rc(i, k)$ considers right-side children of i.

$\mathbf{f}_{sg}(\mathbf{x}, \mathbf{t}', \mathbf{d}, \mathbf{t})$ further make use of the POS tags of the head and children of the focus word. The effectiveness of these features will be examined in the experiments.

4 Experiments and Analysis

The Penn Chinese Treebank 5.1 (CTB5) is used as the labeled data (Xue et al., 2005). We follow the setup of Duan et al. (2007) and split CTB5 into training (secs 001-815 and 1001-1136), development (secs 886-931 and 1148-1151), and test (secs 816-885 and 1137-1147) sets. Head-finding rules are used to turn the bracketed sentences into dependency structures (Zhang and Clark, 2008b).

We adopt the second-order graph-based model of McDonald and Pereira (2006) for our statistical dependency parser. Its time complexity for decoding is $O(n^3)$. On the test set, its parsing accuracy is 85.01% when using gold-standard POS tags, and is 78.82% when using automatic POS tags produced by the baseline CRF tagger.

4.1 Main Results

Table 2 gives the final results. The first row contains two baseline tagging models which only use the basic features $\mathbf{f}_b(\mathbf{x}, \mathbf{t})$. We can see that the Perceptron-based and CRF-based models achieve comparable accuracies.

From the results in the second row, we can find that using guide POS features only modestly (but significantly) improve the accuracy. This model can be regarded as the integrated model of both Perceptron-based and CRF-based models.

In the third row, we explore syntactic features based on gold-standard trees and aim to find out the usefulness of syntactic features without error propagation. Obviously, correct syntactic features can greatly help resolve tagging ambiguities. Using all the features leads to the best accuracy.

Method	Token	Known	Unknown
Perceptron with $\mathbf{f}_b(\mathbf{x}, \mathbf{t})$	93.82	94.65	81.32
CRF with $\mathbf{f}_b(\mathbf{x}, \mathbf{t})$	93.88	94.70	81.51
+$\mathbf{f}_g(\mathbf{t}^C)$	94.02	94.84	81.67
+$\mathbf{f}_s(\mathbf{d}^G)$	96.02	96.85	83.51
+$\mathbf{f}_s(\mathbf{d}^G)$+$\mathbf{f}_{sg}(\mathbf{t}^C, \mathbf{d}^G)$	96.19	96.99	84.27
+$\mathbf{f}_s(\mathbf{d}^G)$+$\mathbf{f}_{sg}(\mathbf{t}^C, \mathbf{d}^G)$+$\mathbf{f}_g(\mathbf{t}^C)$	**96.26**	**97.05**	**84.37**
+$\mathbf{f}_s(\mathbf{d}^A)$	94.06	94.91	81.44
+$\mathbf{f}_s(\mathbf{d}^A)$+$\mathbf{f}_{sg}(\mathbf{t}^C, \mathbf{d}^A)$	**94.41**	**95.26**	81.67
+$\mathbf{f}_s(\mathbf{d}^A)$+$\mathbf{f}_{sg}(\mathbf{t}^C, \mathbf{d}^A)$+$\mathbf{f}_g(\mathbf{t}^C)$	94.37	95.20	**81.95**

Table 2: Tagging accuracy on the test set (%). $\mathbf{t}^C$ denotes the tagging sequence of the baseline CRF model. $\mathbf{d}^G$ refers to the gold-standard tree; while $\mathbf{d}^A$ denotes the automatically parsed tree. Note that we omit $\mathbf{x}$ and $\mathbf{t}$ in $\mathbf{f}_{s/g/sg}(.)$ for brevity.

In the fourth row, we examine our method in the realistic scenario. The syntactic tree is automatically produced by the parser trained on the training set. The accuracy improvement is modest but significant when only adding pure syntactic features $\mathbf{f}_s(\mathbf{x}, \mathbf{d}^A, \mathbf{t})$ ($p < 0.01$).[2] Using syntactic features with guide POS tags, i.e., $\mathbf{f}_{sg}(\mathbf{x}, \mathbf{t}^C, \mathbf{d}^A, \mathbf{t})$, can boost the accuracy by a large margin. Compared with the baseline models, the improvement is significant ($p < 10^{-5}$). Then, adding guide POS features $\mathbf{f}_g(\mathbf{x}, \mathbf{t}^C, \mathbf{t})$ slightly decreases the accuracy, but somehow improves the accuracy of unknown words.

4.2 Error Analysis

To find out how the syntactic features help tagging, we conduct detailed error analysis through comparing the results of different models, as shown in Table 3. We choose the most frequent error pat-

[2]We adapt Dan Bikel's randomized parsing evaluation comparator to do significant test for POS tagging. http://www.cis.upenn.edu/~bikel/software.html

terns made by the baseline CRF-based model, and presents them in descending order of frequency.

error pattern	CRF	Gold Parse	Auto Parse
VV → NN	456	-197	-15
NN → VV	341	-180	-30
DEC → DEG	227	-222	-66
NR → NN	224	+1	-5
DEG → DEC	191	-187	-57
JJ → NN	135	+10	0
NN → NR	84	-3	0
NN → JJ	63	0	+1

Table 3: The number of error patterns made by different models. An error pattern "X → Y" means that the focus word, whose true tag is 'X', is assigned a tag 'Y'. "CRF" refers to the baseline CRF-based model. "Gold Parse" and "Auto Parse" are two perceptron-based models augmented with syntactic features, and correspond to the best models in the third and fourth rows of Table 2, respectively. The signed numbers in the last two columns present the change of error number.

From the column of "Gold Parse" we can see that using correct syntactic features can greatly reduce the errors for ambiguous pairs {NN, VV} and {DEC, DEG}. Especially, nearly all ambiguities of {DEC, DEG} are correctly resolved.However, syntactic features are not helpful for ambiguities like {NN,NR} and {NN,JJ}. One common characteristic of these two pairs are that the two POS tags play similar roles from syntactic view. In other words, their syntactic contexts are usually similar, which naturally explains why the gold-standard syntactic features fail to help. In contrast, "NN" and "VV" (or "DEC" and "DEG") usually have completely different syntactic structures. This demonstrates that our proposed syntactic features are very effective.

Using automatic syntactic features still help resolve {NN, VV} and {DEC, DEG}. However, the error reduction is much less than that of using correct parse trees, which is obviously due to error propagation. Likewise, the errors over {NN, NR} and {NN,JJ} are not influenced.

5 Related Work

Recently, extensive research on Chinese POS tagging has been done. Tseng et al. (2005) enhance the tagging accuracy of unknown words by using rich morphological features. Huang et al. (2009) improve a bigram HMM POS tagger by latent annotation and self-training. Several methods are proposed to handle joint word segmentation and POS tagging of Chinese (Jiang et al., 2008; Zhang and Clark, 2008a; Kruengkrai et al., 2009).

The most closely related work to our approach is the one of Huang et al. (2007), which also explores syntactic features to boost the tagging accuracy. In stead of directly using syntactic features in a discriminative POS tagger, they adopt the RankBoost-based algorithm to rerank the N-best output of a sophisticated HMM tagger (Collins and Koo, 2005). As a discriminative model, the reranker can make use of rich features including morphological features, word/tag n-grams and syntactic features. Another difference from our work is that their syntactic tree is produced by the constituent parser of Charniak (2000) which jointly solves POS tagging and parsing. In this way, they might obtain higher-quality syntactic features since error propagation can be alleviated to some extent. Their reranking approach lead to an improvement of about 1% in tagging accuracy over the HMM tagger. In this paper, we propose another way to incorporate long-distance information for POS tagging. In another perspective, our approach may be more promising in real applications, since dependency parsing is simpler and potentially more efficient than constituent parsing.

6 Conclusions

In this paper, we show that the accuracy of a discriminative sequential POS tagger can be substantially improved by exploring syntactic features. We also show that the syntactic features can help resolve ambiguities like {NN,VV} and {DEC,DEG}, which are difficult to handle when only local contexts are considered. In the future, we will investigate joint POS tagging and dependency parsing models to further improve tagging accuracy.

Acknowledgments

This work was supported by National Natural Science Foundation of China (NSFC) via grant 60803093, 61133012, the Natural Scientific Research Innovation Foundation in Harbin Institute of Technology (HIT.NSRIF.2009069) and the Fundamental Research Funds for the Central Universities (HIT.KLOF.2010064).

References

Eugene Charniak. 2000. A maximum-entropy-inspired parser. In *ANLP'00*, pages 132–139.

William W. Cohen and Vitor Rocha de Carvalho. 2005. Stacked sequential learning. In *IJCAI'05*, pages 671–676.

Michael J. Collins and Terry Koo. 2005. Discriminative reranking for natural language parsing. *Computational Linguistics*, pages 25–70.

Michael Collins, Amir Globerson, Terry Koo, Xavier Carreras, and Peter Bartlett. 2008. Exponentiated gradient algorithms for conditional random fields and max-margin markov networks. *JMLR*, 9:1775–1822.

Michael Collins. 2002. Discriminative training methods for hidden markov models: Theory and experiments with perceptron algorithms. In *Proceedings of EMNLP 2002*.

Xiangyu Duan, Jun Zhao, , and Bo Xu. 2007. Probabilistic models for action-based Chinese dependency parsing. In *Proceedings of ECML/ECPPKDD*.

Zhongqiang Huang, Mary Harper, and Wen Wang. 2007. Mandarin part-of-speech tagging and discriminative reranking. In *EMNLP-CoNLL07*, pages 1093–1102.

Zhongqiang Huang, Vladimir Eidelman, and Mary Harper. 2009. Improving a simple bigram hmm part-of-speech tagger by latent annotation and self-training. In *Proceedings of Human Language Technologies: The 2009 Annual Conference of the North American Chapter of the Association for Computational Linguistics, Companion Volume: Short Papers*, pages 213–216, Boulder, Colorado, June. Association for Computational Linguistics.

Wenbin Jiang, Liang Huang, Qun Liu, and Yajuan Lü. 2008. A cascaded linear model for joint chinese word segmentation and part-of-speech tagging. In *Proceedings of ACL-08: HLT*, pages 897–904.

Canasai Kruengkrai, Kiyotaka Uchimoto, Jun'ichi Kazama, Yiou Wang, Kentaro Torisawa, and Hitoshi Isahara. 2009. An error-driven word-character hybrid model for joint chinese word segmentation and pos tagging. In *Proceedings of the Joint Conference of the 47th Annual Meeting of the ACL and the 4th International Joint Conference on Natural Language Processing of the AFNLP*, pages 513–521.

John Lafferty, Andrew McCallum, and Fernando Pereira. 2001. Conditional random fields: Probabilistic models for segmenting and labeling sequence data. In *Proceedings of ICML 2001*, pages 282–289.

André F. T. Martins, Dipanjan Das, Noah A. Smith, and Eric P. Xing. 2008. Stacking dependency parsers. In *EMNLP'08*, pages 157–166.

Ryan McDonald and Fernando Pereira. 2006. Online learning of approximate dependency parsing algorithms. In *EACL06*.

Ryan McDonald. 2006. *Discriminative Training and Spanning Tree Algorithms for Dependency Parsing*. Ph.D. thesis, University of Pennsylvania.

Joakim Nivre and Johan Hall. 2005. Maltparser: A language-independent system for data-driven dependency parsing. In *In Proc. of the Fourth Workshop on Treebanks and Linguistic Theories*, pages 13–95.

Joakim Nivre and Ryan McDonald. 2008. Integrating graph-based and transition-based dependency parsers. In *Proceedings of ACL 2008*, pages 950–958.

Adwait Ratnaparkhi. 1996. A maximum entropy model for part-of-speech tagging. In *Proceedings of EMNLP 1996*.

Huihsin Tseng, Daniel Jurafsky, and Christopher Manning. 2005. Morphological features help pos tagging of unknown words across language varieties. In *SIGHAN Workshop on Chinese Language Processing*.

Nianwen Xue, Fei Xia, Fu-Dong Chiou, and Martha Palmer. 2005. The Penn Chinese Treebank: Phrase structure annotation of a large corpus. In *Natural Language Engineering*, volume 11, pages 207–238.

Yue Zhang and Stephen Clark. 2008a. Joint word segmentation and POS tagging using a single perceptron. In *ACL08*, pages 888–896.

Yue Zhang and Stephen Clark. 2008b. A tale of two parsers: Investigating and combining graph-based and transition-based dependency parsing. In *EMNLP08*, pages 562–571.

Exploring self training for Hindi dependency parsing

Rahul Goutam
Language Technologies Research Centre
IIIT-Hyderabad, India
rahul.goutam@research.iiit.ac.in

Bharat Ram Ambati
Language Technologies Research Centre
IIIT-Hyderabad, India
ambati@research.iiit.ac.in

Abstract

In this paper we explore the effect of self-training on Hindi dependency parsing. We consider a state-of-the-art Hindi dependency parser and apply self-training by using a large raw corpus. We consider two types of raw corpus, one from same domain as of training and testing data and the other from different domain. We also do an experiment, where we add small gold-standard data to the training set. Comparing these experiments, we show the impact of adding small, but gold-standard data to training data versus large, but automatically parsed data on Hindi parser.

1 Introduction

Parsing morphologically rich free-word-order languages like Czech, Hindi, Turkish, etc., is a challenging task. Unlike English, most of the parsers for such languages have adopted the dependency grammatical framework. It is well known that for these languages, dependency framework is better suited (Shieber, 1985; Mel'čuk, 1988, Bharati et al., 1995). Due to the availability of annotated corpora in recent years, data driven dependency parsing has achieved considerable success. In spite of availability of annotated treebanks, state-of-the-art parsers for these languages have not reached the performance obtained for English (Nivre et al., 2007a). Frequently stated reasons for low performance are small treebank size, complex linguistic phenomenon, long distance dependencies, and non-projective structures (Nivre et al., 2007a; Nivre et al., 2007b; Bharati et al., 2008).

In this paper, we try to address the problem of small treebank size. We have lots of un-annotated data. One way to increase treebanks' size is to manually annotate this data. But it is very time consuming task. Other way is to automatically parse this data and consider highly reliable parses. But, what criteria should be used for extracting reliable parses is a really challenging task. In this paper, we explore a bootstrapping technique called self training and see its impact on dependency parsing accuracy. We consider a state-of-the-art Hindi dependency parser and analyze its performance using self-training. We consider two types of raw corpus, one from the same domain as of training and testing data and the other from a different domain. We also show the impact of adding small, but gold-standard data to training data versus large, but automatically parsed data on Hindi dependency parsing.

The paper is arranged as follows. In section 2, we describe the related work in this field. In section 3, we present the current state-of-the-art of Hindi dependency parser. Section 3, talks about different experiments conducted and presents the results. We conclude with possible future work in section 4.

2 Related Work

In this section, we briefly describe major works on bootstrapping using statistical parsers.

Steedman et al. (2003) did experiments to show that raw data can be used to improve the performance of statistical parsers by bootstrapping. Although their main focus was on co-training between two statistical parsers, they have also performed self-training for each parser but the results are not that promising with self-training. They have also done cross-genre experiments to show that co-training is beneficial even when the seed set was from a different domain compared to the raw data.

Reichart and Rappoport (2007) also perform similar cross-genre experiments to improve the quality of their parser and to adapt the parser to a different domain. They have also reported significant reduction in annotation cost and amount of work because only small amount of manually annotated seed data was used.

McClosky et al. (2006) used a two phase parser-reranker system for self-training using readily available raw data. In their approach, instead of adding the raw data in steps, they have added the entire data in one go. They have reported significant improvement in accuracy over the previous state-of-the-art accuracy for Wall Street Journal parsing. They have also performed sentence length analysis to show that there is a general improvement in intermediate-length sentences, but no improvement at the extremes.

All the above mentioned works are on phrase structure parsing of English. There is an attempt at exploring usefulness of large raw corpus for dependency parsing by Chen et al. (2008). They could achieve considerable improvement over baseline for Chinese using only high confident edges instead of entire sentences. In our work the focus is dependency parsing of Hindi. We also explore how domain and quality of data affects the parser performance.

3 Hindi Dependency Parsing

In ICON 2009 and 2010, two tools contests were held that focused on Indian Language dependency parsing (Husain, 2009; Husain et al., 2010). In these contests, rule-based, constraint based, statistical and hybrid approaches were explored towards building dependency parsers for Hindi. In 2009 contest, given the gold standard chunk heads, the task was to find dependencies between them. But in 2010 contest, given words with gold features like part-of-speech (POS) and morph information, the task was to find word level dependency parse. Table 1, gives the basic statistics about the data.

Type	*Sentences*	*Words*	*Average Sentence Length*
Training	2,972	64632	22.69
Development	543	12617	23.28
Testing	320	6589	20.59

Table 1: Hindi ICON 2010 data statistics

3.1 Baseline (State-of-the-art) System

We consider the best system (Kosaraju et al., 2010) in ICON 2010 tools contest as the starting point. Kosaraju et al. (2010) used MaltParser (Nivre et al., 2007b) and achieved 94.5% Unlabeled Attachment Score (UAS) and 88.6% Labeled Attachment Score (LAS). They could achieve this using *liblinear* learner and *nivrestandard* parsing algorithm. But, as mentioned above, POS and other features used in this system were gold standard. The only available system which uses automatically extracted features and does complete word level parsing for Hindi is Ambati et al. (2010). Though both Ambati et al. (2010) and Kosaraju et al. (2010) used MaltParser, the data used is the subset of the one used by the latter and the parser settings were slightly different.

Taking training data and parser settings of Kosaraju et al. (2010) and automatic features similar to Ambati et al. (2010), we developed a parser and evaluated it on the ICON 2010 tools contest test data. We could achieve LAS of 77.9% and UAS of 86.5% on test set. This is the state-of-the-art system for Hindi dependency paring using automatic features. We consider this system as our baseline and try to explore self-training technique.

System	**UAS**	**LAS**	**LS**
1) Ambati et. al. (2010); automatic features	85.5%	75.4%	78.9%
2) Kosaraju et. al. (2010); gold features	94.5%	88.6%	90.0%
3) Kosaraju et. al. (2010) + automatic features	**86.5%**	**77.9%**	**81.7%**

Table 2: Comparison of different systems

4 Experiments and Analysis

We have modified the Malt parser used in baseline system so that it gives a confidence value for each arc-decision taken. We have taken the average confidence value for all the arcs in the sentence to be the confidence value of a sentence. This system was first trained on ICON 2010 tools contest training data for Hindi. The model generated was then used to parse the large raw corpus. The output sentences were then sorted in descending order based on their scores.

In the self-training experiments, in each iteration, we have added 1000 sentences from the sorted output generated above, to the training data and re-trained the parser. The resulting model was then used to parse the test data.

Hindi data released in ICON-2010 tools contest is a portion of large treebank (Bhatt et al., 2009), which is under development. This is a news corpus taken from well-known Hindi news daily. Self-training experiments were performed using two types of data: one from the same news domain (in-domain) and another from a different domain (out-of-domain).

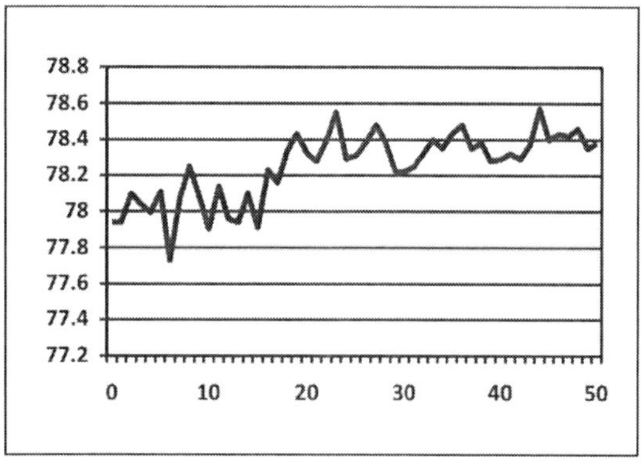

Figure 1a. Self training in-domain (LAS)

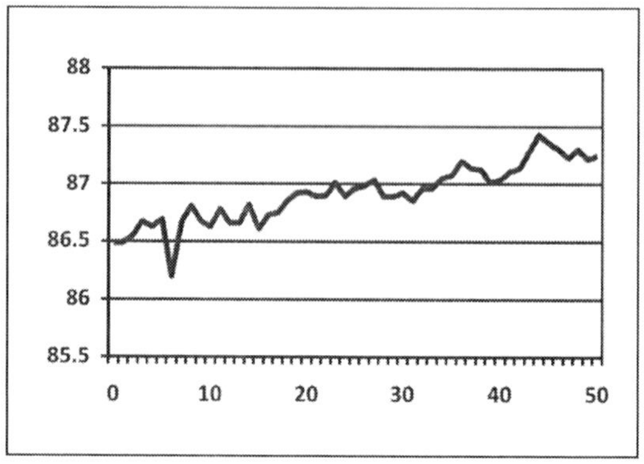

Figure 1b. Self training in-domain (UAS)

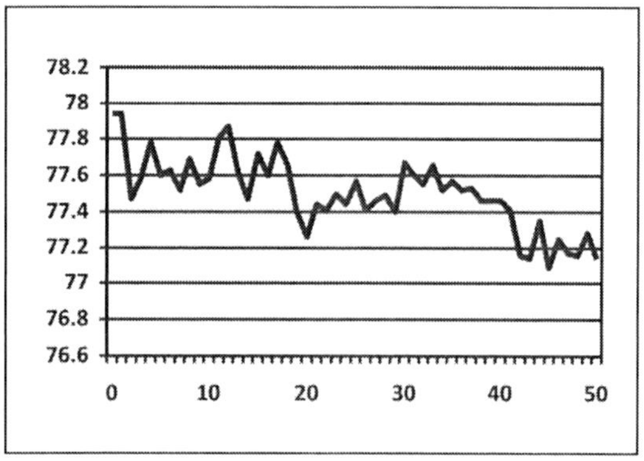

Figure 2a. Self training out-of-domain (LAS)

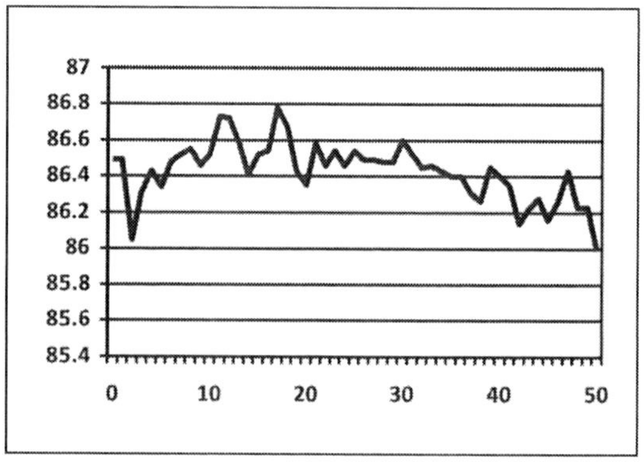

Figure 2b. Self training out-of-domain (UAS)

4.1 Self training: In-domain

We have taken raw news corpus of about 108,000 sentences. As a first step, we have cleaned the data. In this process, we removed the repeated sentences, and very large sentences (>100 words per sentence). Using the above mentioned approach of self-training, we added top 1000 sentences one by one to the training data. Performance of the resulting system on test data for the first 50 iterations is shown in Figures 1a and 1b. After 50 iterations, there was steady drop in the accuracy of the system. This could be because of less confidence values of the sentences after 50th iteration. As the confidence values are low, major arcs in these sentences might be wrong. As a result, these sentences were giving negative impact on the parser performance. There were slight fluctuations in the initial iteration and peeked at 23rd iteration. At this iteration, accuracy of 78.6% LAS and 86.9% UAS was achieved. With this data, we could achieve 0.7% and 0.4% improvement in LAS and UAS respectively over the baseline.

4.2 Self training: Out-of-domain

In this experiment, raw data of a domain different from the actual training, and testing data was used for self-training. For this purpose, we have taken raw non-news corpus of about 700,000 sentences. Major part of this data is from tourism domain. Similar to in-domain data, we first cleaned the data. Apart from repeated, and very large, there were a few non-Hindi sentences. We also removed them during the process of cleaning. Using the above mentioned approach of self-training (see section 4), we added top 1000 sentences one by one to the training data. Performance of the resulting system on test data for the first 50 iterations is shown in Figures 2a and 2b. After 50 iterations, there was sharp drop in the accuracy of the system. There isn't any improvement in LAS over the baseline. But in case of UAS after initial fluctuations, accuracy peeked at 17th iteration. At this iteration, accuracy of 77.8% LAS and 86.8% UAS was observed. We could achieve an improvement of 0.3% in UAS, but a decrement 0.1% in LAS.

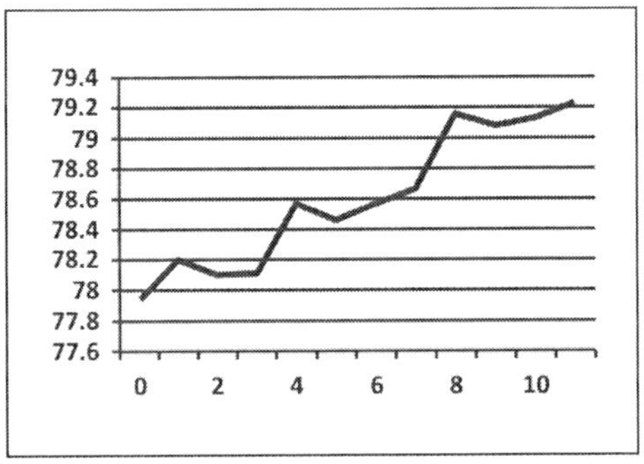

Figure 3a. Gold-standard data (LAS)

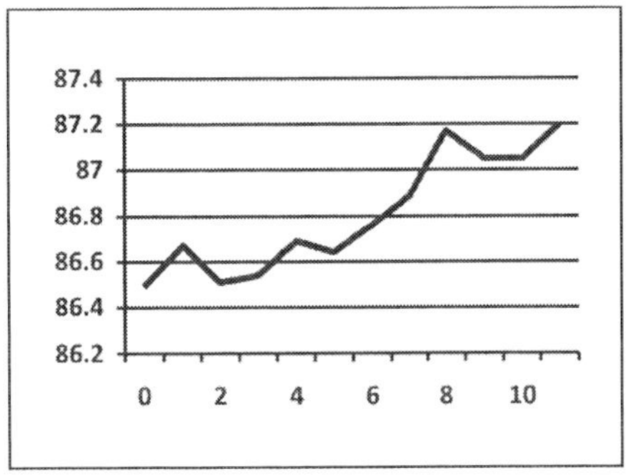

Figure 3b. Gold-standard data (UAS)

4.3 Gold-Standard Data

In the previous two experiments (sections 4.1 and 4.2), we have taken large amount of raw data from same and different domains and applied self-training technique. In both these experiments, impact of large automatically annotated data was observed. In this experiment, we shall observe the impact of small but, gold-standard data. We have taken the development data of ICON 2010 tools contest. We have divided the data into sets of 50 sentences and added one by one similar to above experiments. We could achieve the accuracy of 79.2% LAS and 87.2% UAS at the final iteration. With this gold standard data, we could achieve an improvement of 0.7% in UAS and 1.3% in LAS.

4.4 Analysis

Table 3, gives the summary comparing all the experiments performed. "*" mark in the table shows that, accuracy is statistically significant over the baseline. Significance is calculated using McNemar's test ($p <= 0.05$) made available with MaltEval (Nilsson and Nivre, 2008).

System	UAS	LAS	LS
1) Baseline System	86.5%	77.9%	81.7%
2) In-domain self-training	87.0%*	78.6%*	82.3%*
3) Out-of-domain self-training	86.8%	77.8%	81.6%
4) Gold-Standard Data	**87.2%***	**79.2%***	**82.9%***

Table 2. Summary of Experiments.

We could achieve significant improvement in the accuracy when the raw data is from the same domain. But, when the data is from different domain, we haven't seen any significant increase in the performance. This clearly shows the importance of domain of the training data. One can get better accuracies when training data is similar to testing data. As expected, adding gold-standard data outperformed both the self-training experiments. Our experiments show that gold-standard data is the best solution for improving the parser performance. When this is not possible, raw data from same domain seems to be a better option.

Interesting observation is that even when gold data is being added, there isn't steady increase. Slight drop was observed when some sentences are added. This clearly shows that nature of the sentences being added to training data is very important. Currently, criterion being used to extract reliable sentences from automatically parsed ones is average confidence score given by the parser. We are considering all the nodes in the sentences for calculating confidence score of sentence. It was shown by Ambati et al. (2010) that accuracy for intra-chunk dependencies is pretty high and that of inter-chunk dependencies is low. We can explore considering sentences with high confidence scores for inter-chunk nodes, rather than average score considering all the nodes. We can also explore considering only high confidence nodes rather than entire sentence, similar to works of Chen et al. (2008) and Mannem and Dara (2011).

5 Conclusions and Future Work

We explored the effect of self-training on Hindi dependency parsing. We showed the impact of adding small, but gold-standard data to training data versus large, but automatically parsed data on Hindi dependency parsing.

We are planning to explore the importance of co-training technique also using another parser like MSTParser, as the parser can learn new information in case of co-training. We did experiments on Hindi. There are several other languages like Telugu, Bangla etc. for which annotated data is less but large amount of raw corpus is available. We are also planning to explore the importance of self-training and co-training techniques for parsing these languages.

References

B. R. Ambati, M. Gupta, S. Husain and D. M. Sharma. 2010. A high recall error identification tool for Hindi treebank validation. In *Proceedings of The 7th International Conference on Language Resources and Evaluation (LREC), Valleta, Malta.*

A. Bharati, V. Chaitanya and R. Sangal. 1995. *Natural Language Processing: A Paninian Perspective,* Prentice-Hall of India, New Delhi.

A. Bharati, S. Husain, B. Ambati, S. Jain, D. Sharma, and R. Sangal. 2008. Two semantic features make all the difference in parsing accuracy. In *Proceedings of ICON-08.*

R. Bhatt, B. Narasimhan, M. Palmer, O. Rambow, D. M.Sharma and F.Xia. 2009. Multi-Representational and Multi-Layered Treebank for Hindi/Urdu. In *Proceedings of the Third Linguistic Annotation Workshop at 47th ACL and 4th IJCNLP.*

W. Chen, Y. Wu, and H. Isahara. 2008. Learning reliable information for dependency parsing adaptation. In *Proceedings of the 22nd International Conference on Computational Linguistics (COLING).*

S. Husain. 2009. Dependency Parsers for Indian Languages. In *Proceedings of ICON09 NLP Tools Contest: Indian Language Dependency Parsing.* Hyderabad, India.

S. Husain, P. Mannem, B. Ambati and P. Gadde. 2010. The ICON-2010 Tools Contest on Indian Language Dependency Parsing. In *Proceedings of ICON-2010 Tools Contest on Indian Language Dependency Parsing. Kharagpur, India.*

P. Kosaraju, S. R. Kesidi, V. B. R. Ainavolu and P. Kukkadapu. 2010. Experiments on Indian Language Dependency Parsing. In *Proceedings of the ICON10 NLP Tools Contest: Indian Language Dependency Parsing.*

P. Mannem and A. Dara. 2011. Partial Parsing from Bitext Projections. Accepted at *the 49th Annual Meeting of the Association of Computational Linguistics.*

D. McClosky, E. Charniak and M. Johnson. 2006. Effective Self-Training for Parsing. In *Proceedings of the main conference on Human Language Technology Conference of the North American Chapter of the Association of Computational Linguistics.*

R. McDonald, K. Lerman, and F. Pereira. 2006. Multilingual dependency analysis with a two-stage discriminative parser. In *Proceedings of the Tenth Conference on Computational Natural Language Learning (CoNLL-X)*, pp. 216–220.

I. A. Mel'čuk. 1988. *Dependency Syntax: Theory and Practice*, State University Press of New York.

J. Nilsson and J. Nivre. 2008. Malteval:An evaluation and visualization tool for dependency parsing. In *Proceedings of the Sixth LREC*, Marrakech, Morocco.

J. Nivre, J. Hall, S. Kubler, R. McDonald, J. Nilsson, S. Riedel and D. Yuret. 2007a. The CoNLL 2007 Shared Task on Dependency Parsing. In *Proceedings of EMNLP/CoNLL-2007.*

J. Nivre, J. Hall, J. Nilsson, A. Chanev, G. Eryigit, S. Kübler, S. Marinov and E Marsi. 2007b. *MaltParser: A language-independent system for data-driven dependency parsing. Natural Language Engineering*, 13(2), 95-135.

R. Reichart, and A. Rappoport. 2007. Self-Training for Enhancement and Domain Adaptation of Statistical Parsers Trained on Small Datasets. In *Proceedings of the 45th Annual Meeting of the Association of Computational Linguistics.*

S. M. Shieber. 1985. Evidence against the context-freeness of natural language. In *Linguistics and Philosophy*, p. 8, 334–343.

M. Steedman, M. Osborne, A. Sarkar, S. Clark, R. Hwa, J. Hockenmaier, P. Ruhlen, S. Baker and J. Crim. 2003. Bootstrapping Statistical Parsers from Small Datasets. In *Proceedings of the tenth conference on European chapter of the Association for Computational Linguistics – Volume 1.*

Reduction of Search Space to Annotate Monolingual Corpora

Prajol Shrestha **Christine Jacquin** **Beatrice Daille**
Laboratore d'Informatique de Nantes-Atlantique (LINA)
Université de Nantes
44322 Nantes Cedex 3, France
{prajol.shrestha;christine.jacquin;beatrice.daille}@univ-nantes.fr

Abstract

Monolingual corpora which are aligned with similar text segments (paragraphs, sentences, etc.) are used to build and test a wide range of natural language processing applications. The drawback wanting to use them is the lack of publicly available annotated corpora which obligates people to make one themselves. The annotation process is a time consuming and costly task. This paper describes a new corpus-based measure to significantly reduce the search space for a faster and easier manual annotation process for monolingual corpora. This measure can be used in making alignments on different types of text segments. The performance of this measure is evaluated on a manually annotated paragraph corpus, whose alignments are freely available, with promising results.

1 Introduction

In the field of Natural Language Processing (NLP), annotated monolingual corpora are used to build and test a wide range of applications such as information retrieval, summarization, plagiarism detection, dictionary building and so on. With a number of applications to be built, the field of NLP requires a wide range of monolingual corpus with different annotations on different level of text segments. Our focus is on the fast and easy way of aligning short text segments based on similarity. These annotations are usually done manually by annotators as done by Hatzivassiloglou et al. (1999) where a corpus with alignments between similar short texts are created by two or more annotators who look at each possible short text pair independently and analyse them to make a decision on whether each pair should be aligned as similar or not. Finally, the annotators discuss the disagreements between their annotations and come to an agreement with reasoning. A corpus containing n number of short texts will generate $\frac{n(n-1)}{2}$ number of short text pairs for comparing similarities which becomes a tedious and time consuming task even if a corpus contains a few hundred of short texts. For example, the corpus we use consists of 239 paragraphs, explained in section 3.1, generating a total of 28,441 text pairs to compare.

There are few publicly available annotated corpus, some are manually annotated like the TDT corpus[1] for topic detection and tracking and the METER corpus (Gaizauskas et al., 2001) for detection of text reuse and some are automatically annotated like the PAN-PC-10 (Barrón-Cedeño et al., 2010) for plagiarism detection and the MSRPC (Dolan and Brockett, 2005) for paraphrase detection. Annotating a corpus automatically is easier and faster than manual annotation but they have a major limitation which allows the corpus to include only a subset of the problem which prevents the corpus to represent many of the naturally occurring instances. This limitation in turn might cause some incompleteness issues on the applications built on it as mentioned by Barrón-Cedeño et al. (2010) and Dolan and Brockett (2005). To reduce this effect of coverage in a corpus, annotations on corpus are done manually.

We propose manual annotation to be done in two phases. At first, the number of pairs to compare are reduced and then manual annotation is done. We present a corpus-based measure to automatically reduce the search space for manual annotation making the annotation process faster and easier. We evaluate this measure using a manually annotated paragraph corpus[2], created by reducing the search space manually.

[1] http://projects.ldc.upenn.edu/TDT-Pilot/

[2] Alignments can be freely downloaded from : http://www.projet-depart.org/public/LINA-PAL-1.0.tar.gz

2 Search Space Reduction

In this section, we show how we reduce the search space manually to find similar short texts (e.g. thematic segments, paragraphs, sentences) and present a measure to automatize this manual process. Similarity is a vague concept and its definition depends on the application for which it is intended. The most general intuition of similarity is that, two short texts are similar if they have something in common (Lin, 1998). This intuition includes paraphrases, reused text, plagiarized text and so on as similar texts. Each application specifies what commonality is required to call it similar and we believe our reduction of search space will be useful for all the application based on this general intuition of similarity. This reduction of search space is the first phase towards manual annotation. This phase produces *candidate* similar pairs which is a subset of the total short text pairs within which all the actual similar pairs are present. The number of candidate similar pairs will be less than the total number of short text pairs which allows many annotators in the second phase to efficiently annotate the small set of text pairs manually in less human hours.

The manual reduction of search space is done by going through all the possible short text pairs and selecting the candidate similar pairs using a criteria which states that: each short text in a candidate similar pair consists at least one common entity (Shrestha, 2011a). This criteria for selection theoretically guarantees that all the actual similar pairs will be present in the candidate similar pairs because for two short texts to be similar they must have at least one entity in common. The entities that we use are noun, noun phrase, and transitive verb (Loberger and Shoup, 2009). Two entities are said to be common when they both have the same meaning or in other words share the same concept for example, the entities 'crashed', 'rammed into a wall', 'fatal impact' can all be mapped to the concept 'crashed' and the entities 'Prince Charles', 'heir to the British throne' can be mapped to the concept 'Prince Charles'. The context within the short text also helps to identify the concept that the entity represents.

The selection of candidate similar pairs is easier and faster because the analysis of the pairs is not required unlike when selecting actual similar pairs. This manual reduction is used while building the paragraph corpus for evaluation. As this phase is done manually, the annotator can remove a selected candidate similar pair if a decision of it not being useful can be taken easily and without any doubt to further reduce the search space.

2.1 Short text Vector Space Measure (SVSM)

We present a corpus-based measure called Short text Vector Space Measure (SVSM) (Shrestha, 2011b) based on Vector Space Model (VSM) (Salton et al., 1975) to reduce the search space. SVSM assigns a value to each text pair and text pairs having a value greater than a threshold is considered as candidate similar pairs. For simplicity reasons, we explain the method using sentences. For each sentence a sentence vector is created from term vectors. Given a corpus C of n sentences and m unique terms, the term vector, $\vec{t_j}$, for term t_j is a vector created with n number of possible dimensions where each dimension represents a unique sentence. The presence of the term in a sentence is indicated by its sentence id and the term's inverse document frequency, idf, here a document is a sentence, as shown below:

$$\vec{t_j} = [(S_1, idf_j), (S_5, idf_j), ..., (S_i, idf_j)]$$

where S_i is the sentence id where the term t_j is present, $i \in 1, .., n$ and idf_j is the idf value of term t_j. This term vector is a reduced vector space representation where sentences that do not contain the term is absent which saves space. The dimension of the matrix formed by term vectors can be further reduced using Latent Semantic Analysis (Deerwester et al., 1990) or Principle Component Analysis (Jolliffe, 1986) but are not used here. Once we have the term vectors we can create sentence vectors by adding the term vectors of the terms present in that sentence. For a sentence consisting of terms $t_1, t_2, .., t_k$, the dimension, d_i, of the sentence vector corresponding to the sentence S_i will be:

$$d_i = \Sigma_{j=1; t_j \in S_i}^{k} idf_j$$

where idf_j is the idf value of the term j and $i \in 1, .., n$. This term vector shows the different senses that the term may have. Here, the sense of the term means the idea with which it can be related to. Our assumption is that sentences are independent to each other making each sentence presenting a unique idea and therefore, each term present in a sentence is related to this idea. This assumption like the assumption of VSM (Wong et al., 1987) is unrealistic but the effect of this assumption can

-William and Harry, with their father Prince Charles and their grandmother Queen Elizabeth, are thought likely to remain in seclusion at Balmoral Castle in Scotland until Saturday's ceremony. -The royal family remained at Balmoral in Scotland Tuesday, with reports that Charles and his younger son Prince Harry went for a walk in the afternoon. It was not clear when they would return to London.
-Dodi Al Fayed's father, Harrods Department Store owner Mohammed Al Fayed, arrived here immediately after learning of his son's death. -Bernard Dartevelle, a lawyer for Mohamed Al Fayed, Dodi Fayed's wealthy businessman father and also the owner of the Hotel Ritz, said the revelation "changes absolutely nothing." He spoke of an "ambience of harassment" created around Diana and Fayed by the constant presence of paparazzi.

Table 1: Examples of similar and dissimilar paragraph pairs. The first block consists of a similar paragraph pair whereas the second block consists of a dissimilar paragraph pair.

be reduced using clustering techniques like hierarchical clustering (Han and Kamber, 2006) to group sentences that give the same idea or in other words similar sentences.

This method is similar to the method of Kaufmann (2000) using lexical cohesion but includes more information which are i) the importance of each term using its idf; ii) the co-occurrence of terms by adding up the idf value in term vectors while creating sentence vectors; and iii) the distribution of term along various sentences as the dimensions of the sentence vector is equal to the number of sentences present in the corpus. Using these sentence vectors we can now compute the similarity value between two sentences using the cosine similarity measure (Barron-Cedeno et al., 2009). In this method, other types of short text can be used in place of sentences.

3 Experiments and Results

3.1 Corpus

The corpus used for experiments was made from 12 articles on the same topic, the death of Diana, from the Linguistic Data Consortium's (LDC) North American News Text Corpus (LDC Catalog number: LDC95T21). The articles contain newswire text from three different news services which were published within two consecutive days. The articles contained 239 paragraphs, each of which contains more than 10 non stopwords, which produces 28,441 paragraph pairs for comparisons.

3.2 Manual Alignment

We have manually aligned 28,441 paragraph pairs from the corpus based on similarity. The alignment was done in two phases as explained in section 1. The first phase was performed by one annotator who selected 3,418 candidate similar paragraph pairs from a total of 28,441 paragraph pairs which took about 71 hours of work.

The second phase was done manually by two annotators who independently selected similar pairs from the candidate pairs. The similarity definition given to the annotators is an intuitive definition which states that two paragraphs are similar if one of the main information that the paragraph conveys is common. This definition is slightly different from the definition given by Shrestha (2011a) based on sub-topics. There exist few definitions on text similarity but they are all specific to the size of the text segment (Barzilay, 2003) or entities within the sentences (Hatzivassiloglou and Klavans, 2001) which make them unsuitable for a general text similarity definition. In Table 1, we present a positive and a negative example to further explain the definition. The first block presents a positive example whose main information in common is that the royal family will remain at Balmoral Castle. The paragraph pair in the second block is not similar even though the information about Dodi's father is a businessman is common because the main information conveyed by the paragraphs is different. We used kappa statistics (Carletta, 1996; Cohen, 1960) to evaluate the annotations made by the annotators in the second phase. Kappa statistics is defined as $k = \frac{P_A - P_E}{1 - P_E}$ where, in our case P_A=0.959, which is the probability of two annotators agreeing in practice and P_E=0.918, which is the expected probability of the two annotators agreeing, and k=0.5, indicating a moderate agreement (Artstein and Poesio, 2008). The error between the annotators is about 5% due to the intuitive definition of similarity. The annotators jointly resolved annotation disagreements between them by reasoning.

The second phase produced 144 similar paragraph pairs and took about 20 hours for both annotators. The total time that took to annotate the corpus manually was about 91 hours. If we had directly tried to find the actual similar paragraph

	CS		SVSM			Overlap	
T	Retri.	Rec.	Retri.	Rec.	T	Retri.	Rec.
0	**15415**	**100**	28406	100	0	**15415**	**100**
0.1	**957**	**72.92**	**17245**	**100**	1	**6618**	**96.53**
0.2	**169**	**36.11**	**7253**	**97.92**	2	**2991**	**87.5**
0.3	**51**	**17.36**	**3009**	**93.06**	3	**1434**	**77.78**
0.4	14	6.25	**1218**	**76.39**	4	735	63.89
0.5	4	2.08	412	53.47	5	398	50.69
0.6	2	1.39	134	27.78	6	197	32.64

Table 2: Rec. (Recall) and Retri. (Retrieved pairs) of methods CS, SVSM, and stem overlap according to T (Threshold).

pairs without phase one, with an assumption that the time taken per paragraph pair ($\approx$21 sec) is the same as in the second phase, it would take about 166 hours. The total time saved is 75 hours of work.

3.3 Automatic Selection of Candidate Pairs

The manual alignment method is still time consuming and difficult as manual effort has to be done. SVSM, presented in section 2.1, is used to reduce the search space for annotators. Its performance is compared with stem overlap (Overlap) and cosine similarity measure (CS) with TF*IDF as weights (Salton and McGill, 1983). For each method, stop-words were removed and the remaining words were stemmed using the snowball stemmer[3]. We decide a paragraph pair is a candidate similar pair if the value given by a method exceeds a threshold. Table 2 shows the performance based on recall compared to the manually selected actual similar pairs of section 3.2 and the number of retrieved paragraph pairs by each method on the total paragraph pairs at different thresholds.

If we look at the table, the best result with 100% Recall is given by CS and Overlap methods with 15,415 retrieved pairs but still this is a large number. Using automatic methods, we would like to optimize our threshold so that we can reduce the retrieved paragraph pairs as much as possible without losing much of the actual similar paragraph pairs. According to the optimization issue SVSM is the best among the three methods at threshold 0.3 with 3009 retrieved paragraph pairs almost equal to the manually selected candidate pairs and with a recall of 93.06%. Another property we would like in a method for automatic reduction of search space is the slow rate of decrease in recall making sure with a small variation of threshold the recall will not have a drastic change. The rate of decrease in recall is shown in Figure 1 where four highest varying recall are plotted for each method. These values are boldfaced in Table 2. From Figure 1 we can see that SVSM is the method that has the most gradual decrease in recall making it the most suitable method for automatic reduction of search space. CS on the other hand is the least suitable with a sharp decrease in recall showing that similarity measures based only on term overlap is not suitable to find similar short text as discussed by Abdalgader (2011). Using this method at the threshold 0.3 we can reduce the time for manual annotation to about 17.5 hours (3009x21) with a loss of about 10 similar paragraph pairs only.

[3]http://snowball.tartarus.org/

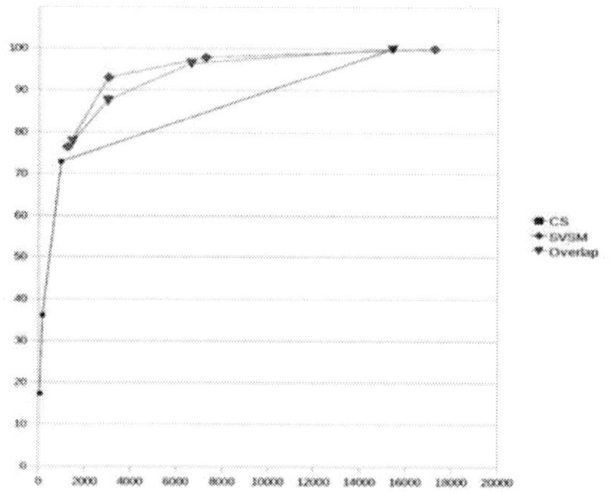

Figure 1: The rate of decrease in recall as the retrieved paragraph decreases.

4 Conclusion and Future Work

We present an automatic method using SVSM to reduce the total number of paragraph pairs from which actual similar paragraph pairs are manually selected. Using the manual method we reduced the 28,441 total paragraph comparisons to only 3,418 paragraph comparisons from which 144 paragraph pairs were aligned as similar. This shows that 99.5% of the effort in selecting the similar paragraph is wasted in terms of the difference between the end number of aligned paragraph pairs and the total initial pairs. Using the manual method we were able to save 75 hours of human work which can be further increased to 148.5 hours by using the automatic method in expense of few similar pairs. In future, the reliability of the threshold will be tested on other corpus and the present manually annotated corpus will be populated with more manually selected similar paragraph pairs using the automatic method.

Acknowledgements. This work is supported by the French Region Pays de Loire in the context of the DEPART project (http://www.projet-depart.org/).

References

Khaled Abdalgader and Andrew Skabar. 2011. Short-text similarity measurement using word sense disambiguation and synonym expansion. *AI 2010:Advances in Artificial Intelligence, Lecture Notes in Computer Science*, 6464:435–444.

Ron Artstein and Massimo Poesio. 2008. Inter-coder agreement for computational linguistics. *Computational Linguistics*, 34(4):555–596.

Alberto Barron-Cedeno, Andreas Eiselt, and Paolo Rosso. 2009. Monoligual text similarity measures: A comparison of models over wikipedia articles revisions. *Proceedings of ICON-2009: 7th International Conference on Natural Language Processing*.

Alberto Barrón-Cedeño, Martin Potthast, Paolo Rosso, Benno Stein, and Andreas Eiselt. 2010. Corpus and Evaluation Measures for Automatic Plagiarism Detection. *Proceedings of the Seventh conference on International Language Resources and Evaluation (LREC 10)*.

Regina Barzilay. 2003. Sentence alignment for monolingual comparable corpora. In *18th Conference of the 2003 conference on Empirical methods in natural language processing*, pages 25–32.

Jean Carletta. 1996. Assessing agreement on classification tasks: The kappa statistic. In *Computational Linguistics*, pages 249–254.

Jacob Cohen. 1960. A coefficient of agreement for nominal scales. In *Educational and Psyhological Measurement*, pages 37–46.

Scott Deerwester, Susan T. Dumais, George W. Furnas, Thomas K. Landauer, and Richard Harshman. 1990. Indexing by latent semantic analysis. *Journal of the American Society for Information Science*, 41(6):391–407.

William B. Dolan and Chris Brockett. 2005. Automatically constructing a corpus of sentential paraphrases. *3rd International Workshop on Paraphrasing (IWP2005)*.

Robert Gaizauskas, Jonathan Foster, Yorick Wilks, John Arundel, Paul Clough, and Scott Piao. 2001. The meter corpus: A corpus for analysing journalistic text reuse. pages 214–223.

Jiawei Han and Micheline Kamber. 2006. *Data Mining: Concepts and Techniques*. Number Edition, Second. Morgan Kaufmann.

Vasileios Hatzivassiloglou and Judith L. Klavans. 2001. Simfinder: A flexible clustering tool for summarization. In *Proceedings of NAACL Workshop of Automati Summarization*, pages 203–212.

Vasileios Hatzivassiloglou, Judith L. Klavans, and Eleazar Eskin. 1999. Detecting text similarity over short passages: Exploring linguistic feature combinations via machine learning. In *Proceedings of the 1999 joint sigdat conference on empirical methods in natural language processing and very large corpora*, pages 203–212.

I T Jolliffe. 1986. Principal component analysis. *Chemometrics and Intelligent Laboratory Systems*, 2(1-3):37–52.

Stefan Kaufmann. 2000. Second-order cohesion. *Computational Intelligence*, 16(4):511–524.

Dekang Lin. 1998. An information-theoretic definition of similarity. In *ICML*, pages 296–304.

Gordon Loberger and Kate Shoup. 2009. *Websters New World English Grammar Handbook*. Wiley, Hoboken.

Gerard Salton and Michael J. McGill. 1983. *Introduction to Modern Informational Retrieval*. McGraw-Hill.

Gerard Salton, Anita Wong, and C S Yang. 1975. A vector space model for automatic indexing. *Communications of the ACM*, 18(11):613–620.

Prajol Shrestha. 2011a. Alignment of monolingual corpus by reduction of the search space. In *Proceedings of the 18th Conference on the Traitement Automatique des Langues Naturelles*, volume 1, pages 543–551.

Prajol Shrestha. 2011b. Corpus-based methods for short text similarity. In *Proceedings of the 15th Rencontre des Etudiants Chercheurs en Informatique pour le Traitement automatique des Langues*, volume 2, pages 297–302.

S K M Wong, W Ziarko, V V Raghavan, and P C N Wong. 1987. On modeling of information retrieval concepts in vector spaces. *ACM Transactions on Database Systems TODS*, 12(2):299–321.

Toward a Parallel Corpus of Spoken Cantonese and Written Chinese

John Lee
The Halliday Centre for Intelligent Applications of Language Studies
Department of Chinese, Translation and Linguistics
City University of Hong Kong
jsylee@cityu.edu.hk

Abstract

We introduce a parallel corpus of spoken Cantonese and written Chinese. This sentence-aligned corpus consists of transcriptions of Cantonese spoken in television programs in Hong Kong, and their corresponding Chinese (Mandarin) subtitles. Preliminary evaluation shows that the corpus reflects known syntactic differences between Cantonese and Mandarin, facilitates quantitative analyses on these differences, and already reveals some phenomena not yet discussed in the literature.

1 Introduction

While standard Chinese, also known as Mandarin or Putonghua, is served by an ever-expanding set of linguistic resources[1], its various dialects have received relatively little attention. The use of these Chinese dialects, however, is as widespread as many other national languages. For example, Cantonese is spoken by more than 52 million people, mostly in southern China and overseas Chinese communities.

Although considered the "most widely known and influential variety of Chinese other than Mandarin" (Matthews & Yip, 1994), Cantonese currently has rather limited linguistic resources. This paucity may be due to its unofficial status, as opposed to Mandarin, which is the official language of China. Furthermore, as a primarily spoken language, it does not traditionally have any standard written form. This paper presents the first parallel corpus of transcribed Cantonese speech and its equivalent written Mandarin. The corpus is expected to be useful for language learners, linguists and developers of natural language processing applications.

The corpus provides students with authentic, parallel examples of sentences in both languages, which are not mutually intelligible. Native speakers of Cantonese must learn Mandarin for use in writing and official communication; conversely, many Mandarin speakers living in Hong Kong also want to learn Cantonese.

The corpus also serves as a repository for linguistic research. In particular, it facilitates research in comparative grammar, by lending statistical evidence, and potentially demonstrating exceptions or other differences yet unnoticed.

Finally, it can be exploited as training material for natural language processing systems, such as cross-lingual spoken document retrieval (Meng & Hui, 2001), and especially machine translation (MT) systems. For example, MT systems may be trained to automatically generate Chinese subtitles for Cantonese television programs, as has been done for Scandinavian languages (Volk et al., 2010).

2 Previous Work

Cantonese grammar has been well studied (Matthews & Yip, 1994; Cheung, 2007), and a few monolingual corpora for Cantonese have been compiled (Lee & Wong, 1998; Leung & Law, 2001; Wong, 2006). While the present corpus may also be used simply as Cantonese data, its primary contribution is as parallel data between Cantonese and Mandarin.

The main difference between Cantonese and Mandarin is in phonology and vocabulary; indeed, various bilingual dictionaries and lexical comparisons are already available (Zhang & Yang, 2008). In terms of syntax, although the "grammatical structure is similar in most major respects", the differences are not insignificant (Ouyang, 1993). So far, there have been few

[1] For example, (Chen et al., 1996), (Xue et al., 2005), and (Tsou & Kwong, 2006), among many others

studies on direct comparisons between the grammars of Cantonese and Mandarin (Ouyang 1993; Liang 1996), none of which was conducted on a large-scale, empirical methodology using naturally occurring Cantonese speech. This corpus is intended to lay the foundation for this direction of research.

3 Corpus

We motivate the design principles of the corpus (section 3.1), then describe how the corpus was constructed and processed (section 3.2).

3.1 Choice of material

The material of the corpus comes from television programs, including news and dramas, broadcast on a Cantonese channel in Hong Kong (see Table 1). All have Mandarin subtitles, which we aligned to the transcription of the Cantonese that was simultaneously spoken. The corpus contains 4,135 pairs of such "sentences", with a total of 36,775 characters in Mandarin, and 39,192 in Cantonese.

The choice of these sources of material follows considerations on two main issues: register variations, and speech and translation quality. Cantonese has a wide range of registers, from formal to colloquial. The formal register closely resembles Mandarin, and diverges significantly from the colloquial; this divergence is in fact a topic of active research in its own right. For any contrastive studies between Cantonese and Mandarin, a corpus balanced between formal and colloquial registers would be desirable. Thus, the TV drama provides the colloquial register; the news program contributes mostly to the formal register with the speeches of the anchor and reporters, but also some colloquial register with those of the spontaneous interviewees.

With the exception of these spontaneous interviews, all materials consist of pre-planned speech. They are thus largely free of false starts, sentence fragments, repairs, repetitions and other errors, which would have led to a considerable amount of spurious word alignments. This is an important advantage, as the parallel corpus will be used for word-level comparative studies.

The Mandarin subtitles, professionally translated, are in general of high quality. However, they are sometimes condensed, likely due to constraints posed by speech timing and screen size (Prokopidis, 2008).

3.2 Corpus construction

The Mandarin side of the corpus comes from subtitles, which consist of characters only; in contrast, the Cantonese side mixes orthographic transcriptions (characters) with a small number of phonetic transcriptions and English. Phonetic transcriptions, conforming to the Jyutping standard, are used when the Cantonese morpheme does not traditionally correspond to any standard Chinese characters. Code-mixing between English and Cantonese is not infrequent, and the English words are preserved in these cases.

Sentence-final particles in Cantonese, such as 啦 *la*, present a challenge for orthographic transcription. "Many of the particles differ only in tone and in nuance of meaning. Given that there is little uniformity of representation in relation to these particles", they are written as the same form in (Leung & Law, 2001). We also follow this practice.

The metadata records both the name and the category of the speaker. Speakers in the drama are always assigned as the "Character" category; those in the news are assigned one of four, namely "Anchor", "Reporter", "Live Reporter", or "Interviewee". "Anchor" and "Reporter" are considered to belong to the formal register, and all others, to the colloquial. Overall, about 60% of the corpus belongs to the colloquial.

Automatic word segmentation was performed on the Mandarin sentences (Chang et al., 2008). A subset of these words was then manually aligned to their Cantonese counterparts to facilitate a preliminary investigation, which will be reported in the next section.

TV Program	Size
六點半新聞報道 "TVB News at Six-Thirty" (2011)	*Time*: 5 episodes x 20 min *Length (chars)*: 19,069 Mandarin; 20,900 Cantonese
溏心風暴之家好月圓 "Moonlight Resonance" (2008)	*Time*: 2 episodes x 45 min *Length (chars)*: 17,706 Mandarin; 18,292 Cantonese

Table 1. The source material of the corpus comes from two TV programs, news (top) and drama (bottom).

4 Evaluation

The usefulness of the corpus may be gauged in two ways. First, it should reflect known differences between Mandarin and Cantonese (section

4.1), and those between formal and colloquial registers in Cantonese (section 4.2). Secondly, it should not only corroborate, but also contribute new information to previous studies. For this second goal, we give examples in three specific areas, namely the plural marker for personal nouns (section 4.3), agentless passives (section 4.4), and possessive constructions (section 4.5). In what follows, 'CL' refers to "classifier" and "PL" to "plural".

4.1 Coverage of Grammatical Differences

One of the most detailed comparative study between Mandarin and Cantonese to-date is (Ouyang, 1993), which lists 18 major differences. Table 2 lists some of these[2].

To investigate the degree to which the corpus exhibits known grammatical differences the two languages, we search for examples for each of the 18 differences in the corpus. Out of these 18 differences, 15 are found. The three differences for which no examples exist are the following. The first is concerned with word order involving the gender marker of animals. For example, The marker *gong* precedes the animal in Mandarin 公鷄 *gong ji* 'rooster', but its Cantonese equivalent *gung* follows the animal, as in 鷄公 *gai gung* 'rooster'. The second deals with word order in a negated resultative verb when the direct object is a personal pronoun. In Mandarin, the pronoun is always placed after the two-character verb, but in Cantonese it may be placed between as an infix. For example, 我 *ngo* 'I' is placed between the resultative verb 打贏 *daa-jeng* 'beat' in the sentence 你打我唔贏 'you did not beat me'. Finally, the third is the use of 過 *gwo* as a dative marker in Cantonese verbs of giving, e.g., 話過你知 'tell *gwo* you know' "tell you". This marker is normally omitted in contemporary Cantonese spoken in Hong Kong.

In summary, the corpus reflects well the known grammatical differences between the two languages as set out in (Ouyang, 1993). Two of the missing differences deal with rather specific constructions, and the third is no longer valid for the Hong Kong variety of the language.

Modal verbs: verbs such as 能 *neng* is used in Mandarin, vs. the 得 *dak* construction in Cantonese
能 忍耐 就真的 不是 人 了 忍 得 嗰個都 唔係 人 㗎喋 'can' 'tolerate' 'can' 'not' 'man' 'No man can tolerate [that]'
Plural marker of personal nouns: Suffix 們 *men* for Mandarin, prefix 啲 *di* for Cantonese
你要 照顧 弟妹 們 你要 睇住 啲 細 喋 'you should' 'take care' PL 'young' PL 'You should take care of your younger siblings'
Double objects: different word orders
那 你 給 我 一個地址 咁一係 你 俾 個地址 我 呀 'you' 'give' 'me' 'address' 'me' 'Please give me an address'
Predicative adjectives: the adjective may be placed in front of the topic in Cantonese
她 年紀 這麼大 演奏香蓮? 佢 咁大 年紀 演奏香蓮呀? 'she' 'so big' 'age' 'so big' 'She is so old, can she still play Chin Xianglian?'
Comparison of quantities: the adjective 多 *do* is placed after the verb in Cantonese
多 補 半天假 補 多 半日假 'more' 'compensate' 'more' 'half-day holiday' 'compensate for another half-day holiday'
Comparison of adjectives: different word orders
保管得 比 你的容貌 還 好 keep 得 好 過 你個樣喎 'keep' 'good' 'compare' 'your face' 'more' 'good' 'keep [one's face] in better conditions'
Use of Numerals: Certain numerals can be omitted in Cantonese in large numbers
我 出夠 一 萬 五 千 我 出夠 萬 五 'I' 'pay' 'one' '10000' '5' 'thousand' 'I pay 15000'

Table 2. Grammatical differences between Cantonese and Mandarin listed in (Ouyang, 1993). In the example sentences, Mandarin is placed on top and Cantonese at the bottom, with their words roughly aligned. A total of 18 differences are discussed in (Ouyang, 1993); please see footnote 2 for the rest.

[2] For lack of space, we describe here briefly the other differences, and refer the interested reader to (Ouyang, 1993). They include: the lack of distinction in Cantonese between inclusive and exclusive "we"; the use of the *dak* construction with 有 you 'have', and in the negated resultative verbs, both impossible in Mandarin; the use of 去 *heoi* 'go' in Cantonese without a preceding 到 *dou* 'arrive', as in Mandarin; the reduplication of verbs and adjectives in yes/no questions; and finally, the distinctive use of a number of particles in Cantonese, including the assertive particles 嚟㗎 *lai-gaa* in copular sentences; the delimitative particle 吓 *haa*, and the verbal particle 過 *gwo* for repetition.

4.2 Coverage of Register Differences

It has been observed that "almost any Mandarin grammatical pattern can be used in Cantonese and be understood, but such locutions are often not idiomatic" (Ramsey, 1987), and in general formal Cantonese is closer to Mandarin. These remarks are corroborated by our corpus. In the formal portion of the corpus, 30% of the Cantonese sentences are identical to the Mandarin; whereas in the colloquial portion, only 4% are.

Modality also highlights the differences in registers. To express modality, Mandarin typically uses modal verbs such as 可以 *ke-yi* or 能夠 *neng-gou* 'may'. While Cantonese has its equivalents *ho-ji* and *nang-gau*, in many contexts it is more idiomatic to employ syntactic constructions with 得 *dak* and 到 *dou*. The former indicates potential, and can mean possibility or permission; the latter is a verbal particle. Both can also be used in Mandarin, but much less frequently.

A comparison between the formal and colloquial registers again confirms their known differences (Matthews & Yip, 1994) and provides some quantitative evidence. In the colloquial register, there were 88 instances of *ke-yi* and *neng-gou* and their respective abbreviated forms; 27% of these instances were spoken in Cantonese with the *dak* or *dou* construction. In contrast, in the 23 instances of the same modal words in the formal register, neither *dak* nor *dou* appear.

4.3 Plural marker for personal nouns

Although not mentioned in the list of (Ouyang, 1993), it is well known that Mandarin uses the suffix 們 *men* to mark personal nouns as plural, while Cantonese has the analogous suffix 哋 *dei* for personal pronouns, and the classifier 啲 *di* for other nouns (Matthew & Yip, 1994). Our corpus shows, however, two additional details.

First, the Cantonese suffix may be omitted. For example, in the noun phrase 你兩個 *nei loeng go* 'you two CL', the suffix *dei* is expected to mark 'you' as plural but is missing. These omissions all occur in the colloquial register.

Second, besides *dei* and *di*, the classifier 班 *baan* 'group' can also serve as the plural marker. For example, 孩子們 *hai-zi-men* 'child PL' 'children' is equivalent to 班細路 *baan-sai-lou* 'group child' 'children'. These also were observed exclusively in the colloquial register. This classifier is also used for the vocative case. In Mandarin, *men* is used in vocative plural, but the Cantonese *di* itself will not do. Instead, both the plural 'you' and *baan* are prefixed before the personal noun, as in 你哋班師奶 *nei dei baan si naai* 'you PL group wife' 'O you wives'.

4.4 Agentless passive

Both Cantonese and Mandarin mark passives with the word 被 bei, followed by the agent. If the agent unknown, it can be simply dropped in Mandarin, but in Cantonese the "generic" agent 人 *jan* 'person' must still be supplied.

Of the 16 sentences with passives, 9 are agentless in Mandarin. As for their Cantonese counterparts, 7 conform to the normal practice using *jan*, but the other two are agentless. These latter may be considered a form of "Mandarinism", i.e., usage that is not ungrammatical, but atypical of Cantonese speech. As expected, one of these occurs in the formal portion of the corpus; the other, in the colloquial, turns out to be a read speech in the drama.

4.5 Possessive constructions

Mandarin uses the possessive marker 的 *de*, whose Cantonese counterpart is 嘅 *ge*. In Cantonese, the marker may be omitted when expressing kinship or a "close" and "inalienable" link (Matthews & Yip, 1994; Pacioni 1998), as in 佢哋老豆 *keoi-dei lou-dau* 'they father' 'their father', without *ge* in between 'they' and 'father'.

The corpus shows, on the one hand, that this phenomenon extends to other nouns such as 佢心願 *sam jyun* 'wish'. On the other hand, for some expressions of kinship, the marker is not simply omitted but replaced by a classifier, such as 我個仔 *ngo-go-zai* 'I CL son' 'my son'. The number of syllables may be a determining factor.

5 Conclusion

We have presented the first large-scale parallel corpus of transcribed spoken Cantonese and written Chinese. Have shown its coverage of grammatical differences between the two languages, and its potential in corroborating and adding to known issues, we plan to further exploit it for quantitative studies in comparative grammars.

Acknowledgments

The author gratefully thanks Man Chong Mak for transcribing the TV programs and performing initial analyses. This work was partially supported by a Small-Scale Research Grant from the Department of Chinese, Translation and Linguistics at City University of Hong Kong.

References

Pi-Chuan Chang, Michel Galley, and Chris Manning, 2008. Optimizing Chinese Word Segmentation for Machine Translation Performance. Proc. ACL 3rd Workshop on Statistical Machine Translation.

K.-J. Chen, C.-R. Huang, L.-P. Chang, and H.-L. Hsu, 1996. Sinica Corpus: Design Methodology for Balanced Corpora. Proc. 11th Pacific Asia Conference on Language, Information and Computation (PACLIC). Seoul, Korea.

Samuel Hung-nin Cheung, 2007. Cantonese as Spoken in Hong Kong 香港粵語語法的研究. The Chinese University of Hong Kong Press, Hong Kong.

T. H. T. Lee and C. Wong, 1998. CANCORP: The Hong Kong Cantonese Child Language Corpus. *Cahiers de Linguistique Asie Orientale* 27(2):211---228.

Man-Tak Leung and Sam-Po Law. 2001. HKCAC: The Hong Kong Cantonese Adult Language Corpus. International Journal of Corpus Linguistics 6(2):305---325.

Stephen Matthews and Virginia Yip, 1994. *Cantonese: A Comprehensive Grammar*. Routledge, London.

Helen M. Meng and Pui Yu Hui. 2001. Spoken Document Retrieval for the Languages of Hong Kong. Proc. International Symposium on Intelligent Multimedia, Video and Speech Processing. Hong Kong, China.

Jueya Ouyang 歐陽覺亞, 1993. 《普通話廣州話的比較與學習》。北京：中國社會科學出版社。

Patrizia Pacioni, 1998. Possessive Constructions, Classifiers and Specificity in Cantonese. *Studies in Cantonese Linguistics*, Stephen Matthew (ed.), Linguistic Society of Hong Kong.

Prokopis Prokopidis, Vassia Karra, Aggeliki Papagianopoulou, and Stelios Piperidis, 2008. Condensing Sentences for Subtitle Generation. *Proc. Linguistic Resources and Evaluation Conference (LREC).*

S. R. Ramsey, 1987. The Languages of China. Princeton University Press.

B. K. Tsou and O. Y. Kwong, 2006. Toward a Pan-Chinese Thesaurus. Proc. 5th International Conference on Language Resources and Evaluation (LREC). Genoa, Italy.

Martin Volk, Rico Sennrich, Christian Hardmeier, and Frida Tidström, 2010. Machine Translation of TV Subtitles for Large Scale Production. *Proc. 2nd Joint EM+/CNGL Workshop on Bringing MT to the User: Research on Integrating MT in the Translation Industry (JEC).* Denver, CO.

Ping-Wai Wong, 2006. The Specification of POS Tagging of the Hong Kong University Cantonese Corpus. International Journal of Technology and Human Interaction 2(1):21---38.

Nianwen Xue, Fei Xia, Fu-Dong Chiou, and Martha Palmer, 2005. The Penn Chinese TreeBank: Phrase structure annotation of a large corpus. *Natural Language Engineering* 11:207-238.

Yaling Liang 梁雅玲, 1996. 《普通話與廣州話常用句型對譯》。香港：香港文化出版社。

Bennan Zhang 張本楠, Ruowei Yang 楊若薇, 2008. 《同形異義：粵普詞語對比例釋》。香港：三聯書局。

Query Expansion for IR using Knowledge-Based Relatedness

Arantxa Otegi
IXA NLP Group
Univ. of the Basque Country
arantza.otegi@ehu.es

Xabier Arregi
IXA NLP Group
Univ. of the Basque Country
xabier.arregi@ehu.es

Eneko Agirre
IXA NLP Group
Univ. of the Basque Country
e.agirre@ehu.es

Abstract

The limitations of keyword-only approaches to information retrieval were recognized since the early days, specially in cases where different but closely-related words are used in the query and the relevant document. Query expansion techniques like pseudo-relevance feedback rely on the target document set in order to bridge the gap between those words, but they might suffer from topic drift. This paper explores the use of knowledge-based semantic relatedness in order to bridge the gap between query and documents. We performed query expansion, with positive effects over some language modeling baselines.

1 Introduction

The potential pitfalls of keyword retrieval have been noted since the earliest days of Information Retrieval (IR). Keyword retrieval proves ineffective when different but closely-related words are used in the query and the relevant document. The use of different words creates a lexical gap between the query and the document.

In order to bridge the gap, IR has resorted to distributional semantic models. Most research concentrated on Query Expansion (QE) methods, which typically analyze term co-occurrence statistics in the corpus and/or in the highest scored documents in order to select terms for expanding the query terms (Manning et al., 2009). The work presented here is complementary, in that we explore QE, but we use an approach based on semantic relatedness instead of distributional methods.

In a closely related work, (Agirre et al., 2010) proposed a WordNet-based document expansion method using random walks: given a document, a random walk algorithm over the WordNet graph, inspired in (Agirre et al., 2009b), ranks concepts closely related to the words in the document. Note that the method can return concepts which are not explicitly mentioned in the document. The highest ranking concepts were then selected to expand the document.

In this work, we explore an alternative method to exploit relatedness, query expansion, so we thus run the relatedness algorithm over the queries and we expand the queries. We adopt a language modeling framework to implement the query likelihood and pseudo-relevance feedback baselines, as well as our relatedness-based query expansion method.

In order to test the performance of our method we selected several datasets with different domains, topic typologies and document lengths. Given the relevance among the community using WordNet-related methods, we selected the Robust-WSD dataset from CLEF (Agirre et al., 2009a), which is a typical ad-hoc dataset on news. As we think that our method is specially relevant for short queries and/or short documents, we also selected the Yahoo! Answers dataset, which contains questions and answers as phrased by real users on diverse topics (Surdeanu et al., 2008), and ResPubliQA, a paragraph retrieval task on European Union laws organized at CLEF (Peñas et al., 2009).

The results show that our method provide improvements in all three datasets, when compared to the query likelihood baseline, and that they compare favorably to pseudo-relevance feedback in two datasets.

The paper is structured as follows. We first briefly introduce related work. We then mention the random walk model for query expansion. The design of the experiments is presented in Section 4. Section 5 shows our results, and, finally, Section 6 presents the conclusions.

2 Related Work

Query expansion methods analyze user query terms and incorporate related terms automatically (Voorhees, 1994). They are usually divided into local and global methods.

Local methods adjust a query relative to the documents that initially appear to match the query (Manning et al., 2009). Pseudo-relevance Feedback (PRF) is one of the most widely used expansion methods (Rocchio, 1971; Xu and Croft, 1996). This method assumes top-ranked documents to be relevant (and sometimes, also that low-ranked documents are irrelevant), and selects additional query terms from the top-ranked documents.

Global methods are techniques for expanding query terms without checking the results returned by the query. These methods analyze term co-occurrence statistics in the entire corpus or use external knowledge sources to select terms for expansion (Manning et al., 2009). For example, techniques using Word Sense Disambiguation (WSD) techniques and synonyms from WordNet have been used for query expansion with some success (Voorhees, 1994; Liu et al., 2005).

The query expansion method proposed in this paper is a global expansion technique based on WordNet, but in contrast to the previous work based on WordNet, it does not perform WSD and adds related words beyond synonyms.

(Agirre et al., 2010) is the work which is closest to ours. They use the same WordNet-based relatedness method in order to expand documents, following the BM25 probabilistic method for IR, obtaining some improvements, specially when parameters had not been optimized. In contrast to their work, we investigate methods to apply relatedness to query expansion, and we compare the results with pseudo-relevance feedback. Besides, we found that a language modeling (Ponte and Croft, 1998) approach to IR combined with inference networks (Turtle and Croft, 1991) offered more flexibility for query expansion.

Our work stems from the use of random walks over the WordNet graph to compute the relatedness between pairs of words (Hughes and Ramage, 2007). In this work a single word was input to the random walk algorithm, obtaining the probability distribution over all WordNet synsets. The similarity of two words was computed as the similarity of the distributions of each word. In later work, (Agirre et al., 2009b) tested different configurations of the graph, and obtained the best results for a WordNet-based system, comparable to the results of a distributional similarity method which used a crawl of the entire web. The same authors later released their UKB software, which is the one we use here.

3 Relatedness-based Query Expansion (RQE)

The key insight of our model is to expand the query with related words according to the background information in WordNet (Fellbaum, 1998), which provides generic information about general vocabulary terms.

In contrast with previous work using WordNet, we select those concepts that are most closely related to the query as a whole. To this end, we follow the approach in (Agirre et al., 2010), which, based on random walks over the graph representation of WordNet concepts and relations, obtains concepts related to the documents. We use the same settings and implementation for the graph algorithm, which is publicly available[1]. Details are omitted here due to lack of space, please refer to (Agirre et al., 2010).

In order to select the expansion terms, we choose the top N highest scoring concepts, and get all the words that lexicalize the given concept. We explored several values of N, and tune it in order to get the optimum value, as discussed in Section 4. For instance, given a query like "*What is the lowest speed in miles per hour which can be shown on a speedometer?*", our method suggests related terms like *vehicle*, *distance* and *mph*.

Our retrieval model runs queries which contain the original terms of the query and the expansion terms. Documents are ranked by their probability of generating the whole expanded query (Q_{RQE}), which is given by:

$$P_{RQE}(Q_{RQE} \mid \Theta_D) = P(Q \mid \Theta_D)^w P(Q' \mid \Theta_D)^{1-w} \quad (1)$$

where w is the weight given to the original query and Q' is the expansion of query Q.

The query likelihood probability is estimated following the multinomial distribution:

$$P(Q \mid \Theta_D) = \prod_{i=1}^{|Q|} P(q_i \mid \Theta_D)^{\frac{1}{|Q|}} \quad (2)$$

[1] http://ixa2.si.ehu.es/ukb/

where q_i is a query term of query Q and $|Q|$ is the length of Q. And following the Dirichlet smoothing (Zhai and Lafferty, 2001) we have

$$P(q_i \mid \Theta_D) = \frac{tf_{q_i D} + \mu \frac{tf_{q_i C}}{|C|}}{|D| + \mu} \tag{3}$$

where $tf_{q_i D}$ and $tf_{q_i C}$ are the frequency of the query term q_i in the document D and the entire collection, respectively, and μ is the smoothing free parameter.

The probability of generating the expansion terms is defined as

$$P(Q' \mid \Theta_D) = \prod_{q'_i}^{|Q'|} P(q'_i \mid \Theta_D)^{\frac{w_i}{W}} \tag{4}$$

where q'_i is a expansion term, $W = \sum_{i=1}^{|Q'|} w_i$ and w_i is the weight we give to a expansion term, which we can see as the relatedness between the original query Q and the expansion term, and is computed as

$$w_i = P(q' \mid Q) = \sum_{j=1}^{N} P(q' \mid c_j) P(c_j \mid Q) \tag{5}$$

where c is a concept returned by the expansion algorithm, N is the number of concepts we chose for the expansion, $P(q' \mid c_j)$ is estimated using the sense probabilities estimated from Semcor (i.e. how often the query term q' occurs with sense c_j), and $P(c_j \mid Q)$ is the similarity weight that the mentioned expansion algorithm assigned to c_j concept.

4 Experiments

In order to test the performance of our method we selected several datasets with different domains, topic typologies and document lengths. Table 1 shows some statistics for each.

The first is the English dataset of the **Robust-WSD** task at CLEF 2009 (Agirre et al., 2009a), a typical ad-hoc dataset on news. This dataset has been widely used among the community interested on WSD and WordNet-related methods. The documents in the Robust-WSD comprise news collections from LA Times 94 and Glasgow Herald 95.

The **Yahoo! Answers** corpus is a subset of a dump of the Yahoo! Answers web site, where people post questions and answers, all of which are public to any web user willing to browse them

	docs	length	q. train	q. test	length
Robust	166,754	532	150	160	8.6
Yahoo!	89,610	104	1,000	30,000	11.7
ResPubliQA	1,379,011	20	100	500	12.2

Table 1: Number of documents, average document length, number of queries for train and test in each collection, and average query length.

	QL	PRF				RQE		
	μ	μ	d	t	w	μ	N	w
Rob	1000	1000	10	50	0.3	2000	100	0.5
Yah	200	200	2	20	0.8	200	50	0.7
Res	100	100	10	30	0.8	100	125	0.7

Table 2: Optimal values in each dataset for free parameters.

(Surdeanu et al., 2008). The document set was created with the best answer of each question (only one for each question). We use the dataset as released by its authors[2].

The other collection is the English dataset of **ResPubliQA** exercise at the Multilingual Question Answering Track at CLEF 2009 (Peñas et al., 2009). The exercise is aimed at retrieving paragraphs that contain answers to a set of 500 natural language questions.

Our experiments were performed using the Indri search engine (Strohman et al., 2005), which is a part of the open-source Lemur toolkit[3].

To determine whether the query expansion model we developed is useful to improve retrieval performance, we set up a number of experiments in which we compared our expansion model with other retrieval approaches. We used two baseline retrieval approaches for comparison purposes. One of the baselines is the default query likelihood (**QL**) language modeling method implemented in the Indri search engine. The other one is pseudo-relevance feedback (**PRF**) using a modified version of Lavrenko's relevance model (Lavrenko and Croft, 2001), where the final query is a weighted combination of the original and expanded queries, analogous to Eq. 1. As in our own model presented in the previous section, we chose the Dirichlet smoothing method for the baselines. We consider **QL** and **PRF** to be strong, reasonable baselines.

All the methods have several free parameters. The PRF model has three: number of documents (d) and terms (t), and w (cf. Eq. 1). The RQE

[2]Check the features of the dataset at Yahoo! Webscope dataset: http://webscope.sandbox.yahoo.com/ ("ydata-yanswers-manner-questions-v1_0")

[3]http://www.lemurproject.org

		QL	PRF	Δ QL	RQE	Δ QL	Δ PRF
Rob	MAP	33.22	**36.69**	10.44% ***	33.67	1.36%	-8.22% ***
	GMAP	13.21	**14.38**	8.90% ***	14.34	8.59% **	-0.29%
	P@5	42.50	**43.63**	2.65%	42.25	-0.59%	-3.15%
	P@10	35.31	**37.38**	5.84% ***	35.81	1.42%	-4.18% *
Yah	MRR	26.36	26.40	0.15%	**27.22**	3.26% ***	3.11% ***
	P@5	6.67	6.63	-0.56% **	**6.88**	3.21% ***	3.79% ***
	P@10	3.95	3.96	0.25%	**4.10**	3.91% ***	3.65% ***
Res	MRR	48.77	46.33	-5.00% ***	**49.78**	2.07%	7.44% ***
	P@5	12.44	12.00	-3.54% *	**12.68**	1.93%	5.67% ***
	P@10	**6.80**	6.78	-0.29%	6.78	-0.29%	0.00%

Table 3: Results of all methods. Δ columns show relative improvement with respect to QL or PRF.

model has two parameters: w (cf. Eq.. 1) and N the number of concepts for the expansion (Eq. 5). In addition, all methods use Dirichlet smoothing, which has a smoothing parameter μ. We used the train part of each dataset to tune all these parameters via a simple grid-search. The μ parameter was tested on the [100,1200] range for ResPubliQA and Yahoo! and [100,2000] for Robust, with increments of 100. The w parameter ranged over [0,1] with 0.1 increments. The d parameter ranged over [2,50] and the t and N in the range [1,200] (we tested 10 different values in the respective ranges). The parameter settings that maximized mean average precision for each model and each collection are shown in Table 2.

5 Results

Our main results are shown in Table 3. The main evaluation measure for Robust is Mean Average Precision (MAP), as customary. In two of the datasets (Yahoo! and ResPubliQA), there is a single correct answer per topic, and therefore we use Mean Reciprocal Rank (MRR). We also report Mean Precision at ranks 5 and 10 (P@5 and P@10). GMAP is also included (we will introduce and mention it afterwards). Statistical significance was computed using Paired Randomization Test (Smucker et al., 2007). In the tables throughout the paper, we use * to indicate statistical significance at 90% confidence level, ** for 95% and *** for 99%.

QL and PRF. The first two columns in Table 3 shows the results for QL and PRF and the performance difference between them. The results for PRF are mixed. It is very effective in the Robust dataset, with dramatic improvements, specially in MAP. All differences are statistical significant, except for P@5. In Yahoo! the improvement is small in MRR and P@10, without statistical significance, but P@5 is lower. In ResPubliQA the results are bad, with statistical significant degradation in MRR.

RQE. Continuing rightwards with Table 3, the following columns show the results for RQE, together with its difference with respect to QL and PRF. Note that figures in bold mean the best performance for each metric. It can be seen that, although RQE is not effective for Robust, it is the best method for Yahoo! and ResPubliQA. Moreover, the improvements over QL, and also over PRF, for Yahoo! are all statistical significant.

PRF is known to perform well for some topics and datasets but not for others. Table 3 includes results for the geometrical mean, GMAP (Robertson, 2006), in the Robust dataset, as it is not relevant in the other datasets. GMAP tries to promote systems which are able to perform well for all topics, in contrast to systems that perform better in some but worse in others. The figures show that RQE approximate the performance of PRF, showing that it perform better for difficult topics.

Combining PRF and RQE. In a preliminary experiment, we added the expansion terms produced both by RQE and PRF, obtaining a **MAP of 37.67** in the Robust collection, the best result. We would like to explore the potential for combination further in the future.

6 Conclusions

Motivated by the recent success of knowledge-based methods in word similarity and relatedness tasks (Agirre et al., 2009b), we explored a generic method to improve IR results using WordNet-based query expansion, and compared it to baseline query likelihood and pseudo-relevance feedback methods.

Our results on a diverse range of ad-hoc datasets with different domains, topic typologies and document lengths show that our method improves over a query likelihood baseline in all three datasets, while Pseudo Relevance Feedback is beneficial in only two datasets. Our method compares favorably to PRF in two datasets, and, in a preliminary experiment, the combination of PRF and our method yielded the best results in the third dataset.

In the future, we would like to analyze the differences between PRF and our method, and explore further combinations. We would also like to use our method on domains where large lexical resources are available, such as UMLS (Humphreys et al., 1998) and linked data repositories

Acknowledgments

This work has been supported by KNOW2 (TIN2009-14715-C04-01). Arantxa Otegi's work is funded by a PhD grant from the Basque Government. Part of this work was done while Arantxa Otegi was visiting ILPS group of the University of Amsterdam.

References

E. Agirre, G. M. Di Nunzio, T. Mandl, and A. Otegi. 2009a. CLEF 2009 Ad Hoc Track Overview: Robust - WSD Task. In *Working Notes of the Cross-Lingual Evaluation Forum*.

E. Agirre, A. Soroa, E. Alfonseca, K. Hall, J. Kravalova, and M. Pasca. 2009b. A Study on Similarity and Relatedness Using Distributional and WordNet-based Approaches. In *Proc. of NAACL*, Boulder, USA.

E. Agirre, X. Arregi, and A. Otegi. 2010. Document expansion based on WordNet for robust IR. In *Proceedings of the 23rd International Conference on Computational Linguistics: Posters*, COLING '10, pages 9–17, Stroudsburg, PA, USA. Association for Computational Linguistics.

C. Fellbaum, editor. 1998. *WordNet: An Electronic Lexical Database and Some of its Applications*. MIT Press, Cambridge, Mass.

T. Hughes and D. Ramage. 2007. Lexical semantic relatedness with random graph walks. In *Proceedings of EMNLP-CoNLL-2007*, pages 581–589.

L. Humphreys, D. Lindberg, H. Schoolman, and G. Barnett. 1998. The Unified Medical Language System: An Informatics Research Collaboration. *Journal of the American Medical Informatics Association*, 1(5):1–11.

V. Lavrenko and W. B. Croft. 2001. Relevance based language models. In *Proceedings of the 24th annual international ACM SIGIR conference on Research and development in information retrieval*, SIGIR '01, pages 120–127, New York, NY, USA. ACM.

S. Liu, C. Yu, and W. Meng. 2005. Word sense disambiguation in queries. In *Proceedings of CIKM '05*, pages 525–532.

C. D. Manning, P. Raghavan, and H. Schütze. 2009. *An introduction to information retrieval*. Cambridge University Press, UK.

A. Peñas, P. Forner, R. Sutcliffe, A. Rodrigo, C. Forăscu, I. Alegria, D. Giampiccolo, N. Moreau, and P. Osenova. 2009. Overview of ResPubliQA 2009: Question Answering Evaluation over European Legislation. In *Working Notes of the Cross-Lingual Evaluation Forum*.

J. M. Ponte and W. B. Croft. 1998. A language modeling approach to information retrieval. In *Proceedings of the 21st annual international ACM SIGIR conference on Research and development in information retrieval*, SIGIR '98, pages 275–281, New York, NY, USA. ACM.

S. Robertson. 2006. On GMAP: and other transformations. In *Proceedings of the 15th ACM international conference on Information and knowledge management*, CIKM '06, pages 78–83, New York, NY, USA. ACM.

J. J. Rocchio. 1971. Relevance feedback in information retrieval. In G. Salton, editor, *The Smart retrieval system - experiments in automatic document processing*, pages 313–323. Englewood Cliffs, NJ: Prentice-Hall.

M. D. Smucker, J. Allan, and B. Carterette. 2007. A comparison of statistical significance tests for information retrieval evaluation. In *Proc. of CIKM 2007*, Lisboa, Portugal.

T. Strohman, D. Metzler, H. Turtle, and W. B. Croft. 2005. Indri: a language-model based search engine for complex queries. Technical report, in Proceedings of the International Conference on Intelligent Analysis.

M. Surdeanu, M. Ciaramita, and H. Zaragoza. 2008. Learning to Rank Answers on Large Online QA Collections. In *Proceedings of ACL 2008*.

H. Turtle and W. B. Croft. 1991. Evaluation of an inference network-based retrieval model. *ACM Trans. Inf. Syst.*, 9:187–222, July.

E. M. Voorhees. 1994. Query expansion using lexical-semantic relations. In *Proceedings of SIGIR '94*, page 69.

J. Xu and W. B. Croft. 1996. Query expansion using local and global document analysis. In *Proceedings of the 19th annual international ACM SIGIR conference on Research and development in information retrieval*, SIGIR '96, pages 4–11, New York, NY, USA. ACM.

C. Zhai and J. Lafferty. 2001. A study of smoothing methods for language models applied to Ad Hoc information retrieval. In *Proceedings of the 24th annual international ACM SIGIR conference on Research and development in information retrieval*, SIGIR '01, pages 334–342, New York, NY, USA. ACM.

Word Sense Disambiguation Corpora Acquisition via Confirmation Code

Wanxiang Che and Ting Liu*
Research Center for Social Computing and Information Retrieval
MOE-Microsoft Key Laboratory of Natural Language Processing and Speech
School of Computer Science and Technology
Harbin Institute of Technology, China
{car, tliu}@ir.hit.edu.cn

Abstract

Word Sense Disambiguation (WSD) is one of the fundamental natural language processing tasks. However, lack of training corpora is a bottleneck to construct a high accurate all-words WSD system. Annotating a large-scale corpus by experts costs enormous time and financial resources. Human Computation is a novel idea for integrating human resources behind the Web, which has been wasted, to solve practical problems that are difficult for computers. Based on human computation, we design a confirmation code system, which can not only distinguish between human beings and computers (the function of normal confirmation code system), but also annotate WSD corpora. The preliminary experimental result shows that the proposed method can annotate large-scale and high-quality WSD corpora within a short time. To the best of our knowledge, this is the first attempt to use confirmation code in natural language processing for corpora acquisition.

1 Introduction

It is a common phenomenon that a word has multiple senses in natural languages. The aim of word sense disambiguation (WSD) is to identify the correct senses of ambiguous words according to their surrounding contexts. WSD is a basic task of natural language processing. The state-of-the-art in WSD is dominated by supervised machine learning methods where a model is trained to recognize word senses in a given context based on various features. Although it is important to use powerful machine learning algorithms, latest studies have found that large-scale and high-quality corpora are more important for WSD (Agirre and Edmonds, 2006). Therefore, building such corpora is key challenge to be addressed.

Currently, corpora are created mainly through manual annotation by expert annotators. However, the cost of annotating a necessary size of corpora is prohibitive. Consequently, in the research field of WSD, some common ambiguous words are sampled and then annotated with a necessary amount of examples. The sampling method promotes the research in WSD algorithms. However, these algorithms are difficult to be used in practical applications due to lack of large-scale corpora in which all ambiguous words are annotated. For example, SemCor[1] corpus contains WSD annotation of about 250,000 words sampled from a subset of the Brown corpus. However, for most of the ambiguous words, the number of examples is still too small to train a high performance all-words WSD model. The best performance of Senseval-3 English all-words evaluation task (Snyder and Palmer, 2004) is only about 65%.

Semi-supervised methods have been applied to build large-scale corpora, such as bootstrapping (Yarowsky, 1995). However, the quality of corpora built with such methods is not high enough to train accurate WSD models. Therefore, the methods are not feasible to be used in practice.

Crowdsourcing is an "online, distributed problem-solving and production model. (Brabham, 2008)" A benefit of this distributed model is that a job can be shared amongst a wide variety of demographics, where such diversity would be difficult to obtain otherwise. Previous research has demonstrated the successful application of crowdsourcing in a variety of natural language processing areas including relevance evaluation (Alonso et al., 2008), machine

*Correspondence author: tliu@ir.hit.edu.cn

[1] http://www.cse.unt.edu/~rada/downloads.html#semcor

translation (Ambati et al., 2010), and language processing (Callison-Burch and Dredze, 2010). However, the submissions of crowdsourcing are always needed to review to separate the legitimate work from the rest. Additionally, the crowdworkers are always motivated by money. These increase the extra cost of time and finance.

Human Computation is a novel method for collecting corpora (von Ahn, 2007). In this method, a computer asks a person or a large group of people to solve a problem, and then collects, interprets, and integrates their solutions. The methods of human computation include interactive online games, confirmation code, and so on. For instance, reCAPTCHA (von Ahn et al., 2008) system is a kind of confirmation code, also called CAPTCHA (Completely Automated Public Turing test to tell Computers and Humans Apart). Confirmation code systems are widely used on the Web as security measures to prevent automatic programs from abusing online services by asking a question that computers cannot yet answer. In reCAPTCHA, to pass the confirmation stage, users must input the content of word images from scanned old books. Two scanned word images are shown to a user at the same time. The system knows the content of one word and does not know the other. If the user wants to pass the confirmation stage, he must input the correct content of the known word. Because the user does not know which word the system knows, he has to input the contents of both words. Thus, once the confirmation function is successfully achieved, the content of the unknown word can be obtained. Finally, reCAPTCHA helps to digitize plenty of old books that an optical character recognition (OCR) cannot decipher.

Different from crowdsourcing, human computation does not need to review the results again nor pay users. The method can take advantage of a larger range of people. However, human computation methods are rarely used in natural language processing tasks. The main reason is that natural language processing tasks are usually very complex. It is difficult to design an appropriate game and also be annotated by normal users. Seemakurty et al. (2010) designed a game which helps to collect WSD corpora. The game chooses two participants randomly and then shows a sentence to them. The two users are asked to input as many synonyms of the same ambiguous word in the sentence as possible within a limited period of game round time. Once there are identical input words by them, they are awarded scores and then a synonym of the ambiguous word is obtained. Based on these synonyms, the correct sense of the ambiguous word can be recognized. However, a big problem is how to attract a considerable number of users. In addition, it needs long time to collect these synonyms[2]. More seriously, the game can be cheated under some extreme circumstances, e.g., when all users just input the same words, or we use a robot to input all words in a dictionary quickly.

In this paper, we are inspired by the idea of reCAPTCHA system and propose a confirmation code based method to annotate WSD corpora with low cost. The method can help to collect large-scale and high-quality corpora within a short time. Preliminary experimental result shows that the method can achieve 80.65% accuracy on an annotated WSD corpus which is close to the inter-rater agreement of the corpus. It only needs about 8 to 10 seconds to annotate an example by a person.

2 System Description

A WSD confirmation code includes two questions. Each question consists of a sentence and a highlighted ambiguous word in the sentence. All senses of the ambiguous word are provided as optional answers. The system only knows the answer for one of the two questions, which is named as *known* question and the other is *unknown* question. A user needs to choose a word sense for each ambiguous word. The user can pass the confirmation stage if and only if his answer to the known question is correct. Like in reCAPTCHA, users do not know which one is known question. They must choose each word sense carefully in order to pass confirmation stage. Therefore, they provide the correct sense for the ambiguous word of unknown question. If WSD confirmation code system is widely used by lots of Web sites, we can easily collect large-scale corpora.

The data flow chart of the WSD confirmation code system is shown in Figure 1. ① two questions are randomly selected from known and unknown question databases respectively. ② the two questions are asked to a user and the user needs to answer them. ③ once the user's answer is correct,

[2] In their work, a game round is to be set 30 seconds, i.e. it needs 30 seconds to annotate the sense of an ambiguous word at least.

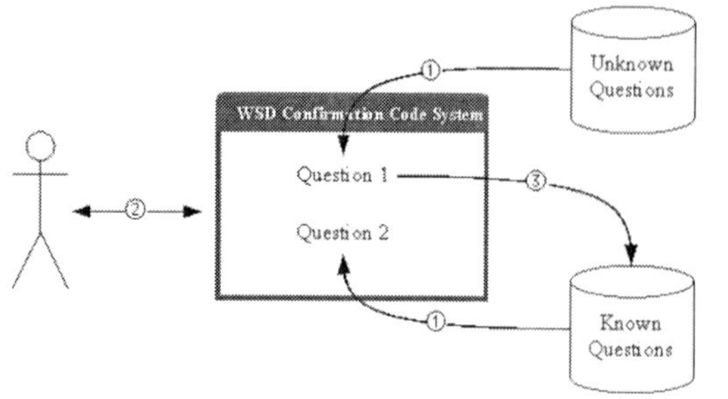

Figure 1: The data flow chart of WSD confirmation code system

i.e. it is equal to the answer of known question, he can pass the confirmation stage. Then we can know the answer of the unknown question, which becomes a new known question and can be added into the known question database. Otherwise, the confirmation stage cannot be passed and the user has to answer another pair of questions.

The known question is used to distinguish between human beings and computers, i.e. this is the function of commonly used confirmation code. Usually, it is either impossible or less possible for a computer to automatically choose correct answers. In order to further prevent automatic WSD programs from passing the confirmation stage, we convert original sentences into images with randomly distorted background and font. This method makes it impossible to recognize the contents of the original sentences and to do WSD automatically. If users correctly annotate the known word sense, the system can assume that they are human and gain confidence that they can also annotate the other word sense correctly.

Figure 2 shows an example of WSD confirmation code[3]. Sentences are in image forms and the target ambiguous words are highlighted with red font. The senses of these ambiguous words are shown in pull-down menus.

In order to improve the consistency of the final corpora, we allow each example to be annotated more than once. Then, a voting method can be used to determine the final word sense.

3 Experiment

3.1 Experimental Data

To evaluate the correctness of the corpus annotated by our WSD confirmation code method, we

[3]In this paper, we use Chinese as an example. However, the method is not restricted to specific language.

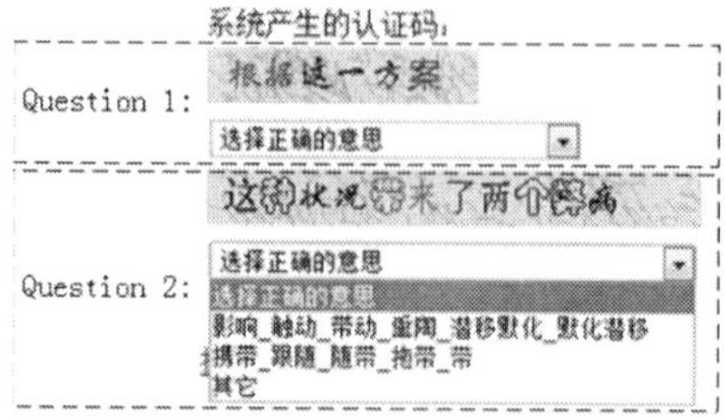

Figure 2: An example of WSD confirmation code system. Here, the two sentences are "根据这一方案 (according to the scheme)" and "这种状况带来了两个弊端 (this situation brings two drawbacks)" respectively. The two ambiguous words are "根据 (according to)" and "带来 (bring)". Here, "带来" has two senses: "影响 触动 · · · (influence)" and "携带 跟随 · · · (bring)". Because of the incompleteness of the thesaurus, there are some words whose senses cannot be found. Therefore, we add a "其它 (other)" option for every word since the current word sense does not belong to any of above options. The other Chinese sentences in the example instruct the users how to use the system. "系统产生的验证码" means "The confirmation codes provided by the system" and "选择正确的意思" means "Please choose the correct word sense".

built a trial system and took advantage of an annotated Chinese all-words WSD corpus consisting of about 10,000 sentences containing about 200,000 words sampled from Chinese news documents. In these words, there are about 78,800 ambiguous words and all of which have been annotated with their corresponding senses by human experts. Among them, we randomly set 5,000 words as unknown questions and remaining as known.

3.2 Thesaurus

We use WordMap (Che et al., 2010) as a thesaurus to represent word senses. There are more than 100,000 Chinese words in WordMap. Each word sense belongs to a tree node with five levels. There are 12 top level nodes, such as "entity" and "human beings". There are about 100 second, 15,000 third, and more fourth and fifth level nodes. Under the fifth level nodes, there are some synonyms which have the same word sense. For instance, the word "材料" has two senses which are represented by five level nodes as follows:

1. 物 (entity) → 统称 (common name) → 物资 (goods) → 物资 (goods) → 材料 (material)

# of times an example is annotated	# of annotated examples	# of correct annotated examples	Acc.
Random			41.01%
1	2,387	1,609	67.41%
≥2	336	271	80.65%

Table 1: Comparison of Experimental Results

2. 人 (human beings) → 才识 (ability) → 俊杰 (hero) → 人才 (talents) → 人才 (talents)

We can see that the two word senses belong to two top level nodes "物 (entity)" and "人 (human beings)" respectively. In each sense, the concept becomes more and more specific as the level increases.

However, the above sense representation method is not suitable to be shown as word sense options directly since it is too abstract to be understood by normal users. Therefore, we use synonyms of each word sense to represent the word sense. For instance, the synonyms of the two senses of the word "材料" are "材质 生料 质料 (materials)" and "人才 佳人 才子 奇才 天才 (talents)" respectively. Then we show these synonyms to the users for better understanding of the word sense.

3.3 Preliminary Results

We invited 20 volunteers to test the system. We collected 2,723 examples which passed the confirmation successfully. Table 1 shows the comparison of the experimental results.

From Table 1, we can see that when an example is annotated once, the accuracy (67.41%) is much higher than the random sense selection (41.01%)[4]. This tells us that the human efforts have a positive effect on the annotation. However, the accuracy is still not high enough and this can be attributed to volunteers' lack of experience in WSD. They maybe make mistakes. The accuracy, along with an increase of the annotation times, is improved. When an example is annotated more than once, the accuracy reaches 80.65% and is close to the inter-rater agreement (83.84%) of the original corpus.

On average, it needs about 8 to 10 seconds for a person to successfully input a WSD confirmation code. It is faster than common confirmation code systems (with six to eight randomly characters), which need 13.51 seconds on average (von Ahn et al., 2008). This is not surprising, because choosing an answer is faster than inputting some characters. So, in practice, the WSD confirmation code system can be adopted without reducing the quality of user experience.

[4]In WordMap, there are 2.44 senses for each ambiguous word on average. Therefore, the accuracy of random selection is 41.01%.

4 Conclusion and Future Work

To address the lack of WSD corpora, we propose a human computation based method. When users successfully input a confirmation code, they annotate a WSD example incidentally. The preliminary experiments show that the novel method can annotate large-scale and high-quality WSD corpora within a short time. As far as we know, there is no work done to annotate natural language processing corpora with confirmation code.

In the future, we plan to improve the annotation speed and reduce the complexity of confirmation process by showing two sentences with the same ambiguous words. Thus, users can easily compare the two sentences. More importantly, they only need to read the options once, which can save confirmation time further. We also can use unsupervised clustering method which determines senses that are very similar and displays only one of the alternatives. Secondly, we will apply this method to other languages. Our method is general enough and can be applied to any languages as long as the language has a thesaurus and some initial WSD corpora. Of course, a particular language WSD confirmation code system can only be used in Web sites of the same language because it is difficult for a normal user to perform WSD task on the foreign language that they are unfamiliar with. Thirdly, we can apply this method to other natural language processing tasks which need corpora acquisition such as co-reference resolution, named entity recognition, and parsing. Finally, we will use the corpora annotated by the confirmation code method to train a more effective WSD model.

Acknowledgement

This work was supported by National Natural Science Foundation of China (NSFC) via grant 60803093, 61133012, Natural Scientific Research Innovation Foundation in Harbin Institute of Technology (HIT.NSRIF.2009069), and Fundamental Research Funds for the Central Universities (HIT.KLOF.2010064).

References

Eneko Agirre and Philip Edmonds, editors. 2006. *Word Sense Disambiguation: Algorithms and Applications*, volume 33 of *Text, Speech and Language Technology*. Springer, 1 edition, July.

Omar Alonso, Daniel E. Rose, and Benjamin Stewart. 2008. Crowdsourcing for relevance evaluation. *SIGIR Forum*, 42:9–15, November.

Vamshi Ambati, Stephan Vogel, and Jaime Carbonell. 2010. Active learning and crowd-sourcing for machine translation. In *Proceedings of the Seventh conference on International Language Resources and Evaluation (LREC'10)*, Valletta, Malta, May. European Language Resources Association (ELRA).

D C Brabham. 2008. Crowdsourcing as a model for problem solving: An introduction and cases. *Convergence: The International Journal of Research into New Media Technologies*, 14(1):75–90.

Chris Callison-Burch and Mark Dredze. 2010. Creating speech and language data with amazon's mechanical turk. In *Workshop on Creating Speech and Language Data With Mechanical Turk at NAACL-HLT*.

Wanxiang Che, Zhenghua Li, and Ting Liu. 2010. Ltp: A chinese language technology platform. In *Coling 2010: Demonstrations*, pages 13–16, Beijing, China, August. Coling 2010 Organizing Committee.

Nitin Seemakurty, Jonathan Chu, Luis von Ahn, and Anthony Tomasic. 2010. Word sense disambiguation via human computation. In *Proceedings of the ACM SIGKDD Workshop on Human Computation*, HCOMP '10, pages 60–63. ACM.

Benjamin Snyder and Martha Palmer. 2004. The english all-words task. In Rada Mihalcea and Phil Edmonds, editors, *Senseval-3: Third International Workshop on the Evaluation of Systems for the Semantic Analysis of Text*, pages 41–43, Barcelona, Spain, July. Association for Computational Linguistics.

Luis von Ahn, Ben Maurer, Colin McMillen, David Abraham, and Manuel Blum. 2008. reCAPTCHA: Human-based character recognition via web security measures. *Science*, 321(5895):1465–1468.

Luis von Ahn. 2007. Human computation. In *Proceedings of the 4th international conference on Knowledge capture*, K-CAP '07, pages 5–6, New York, NY, USA. ACM.

David Yarowsky. 1995. Unsupervised word sense disambiguation rivaling supervised methods. In *Proceedings of the 33rd annual meeting on Association for Computational Linguistics*, ACL '95, pages 189–196, Stroudsburg, PA, USA. Association for Computational Linguistics.

Author Index

Association for Computational Linguistics
209 N. Eighth Street
Stroudsburg, Pennsylvania 18360

CURRAN ASSOCIATES INC
proceedings.com